ENCYCLOPEDIA OF
ARTIFICIAL INTELLIGENCE
SECOND EDITION

VOLUME 1

EDITORIAL BOARD

ENCYCLOPEDIA OF ARTIFICIAL INTELLIGENCE SECOND EDITION

VOLUME 1

Stuart C. Shapiro, *Editor-in-chief*

A Wiley-Interscience Publication

John Wiley & Sons, Inc.

New York / Chichester / Brisbane / Toronto / Singapore

Copyright © 1992 by John Wiley & Sons, Inc.

Library of Congress Cataloging in Publication Data:

Encyclopedia of artificial intelligence / Stuart C. Shapiro, editor-in
-chief. — 2nd ed.
    p.   cm.
    "A Wiley-Interscience publication."
    Includes bibliographical references and index.
    ISBN 0-471-50307-X (set). — ISBN 0-471-50305-3 (v. 1). — ISBN
0-471-50306-1 (v. 2)
    1. Artificial intelligence—Encyclopedias.   I. Shapiro, Stuart
Charles.
  Q335.E53 1992
  006.3'03—dc20   91-37272

Printed in the United States of America
10 9 8 7 6 5 4 3 2 1
Printed and bound by Courier Companies, Inc.

EDITORIAL STAFF

Editor-in-Chief: Stuart C. Shapiro
Managing Editor: Michalina Bickford

Assistant Managing Editor: Lee Wylegala
Associate Managing Editor: Linda Indig

CONTRIBUTORS

Phillip L. Ackerman, *University of Minnesota, Minneapolis, Minn.,* Intelligence, human

Sanjaya Addanki, *IBM Corporation, Yorktown Heights, N.Y.,* Connectionism

Richard M. Adler, *Symbiotics, Inc., Cambridge, Mass.,* Blackboard systems; Reasoning, causal

J. K. Aggarwal, *University of Texas, Austin, Tex.,* Sensors and sensor fusion

Gul Agha, *Now at the University of Illinois, Urbana, Ill.,* Actor formalisms

Ashok K. Agrawala, *University of Maryland, College Park, Md.,* Computer systems

P. E. Agre, *University of California, San Diego, Calif.,* Control structures

Narendra Ahuja, *University of Illinois, Urbana, Ill.,* Texture

Janice S. Aikins, *Aion Corporation, Palo Alto, Calif.,* Agenda-based systems

Selim G. Akl, *Ecole Normale Superieure de Lyon, Lyon, France,* Checkers-playing programs

Yiannis Aloimonos, *University of Maryland, College Park, Md.,* Visual recovery

Richard Alterman, *Brandeis University, Waltham, Mass.,* Adaptive planning; Analog semantic features; Sss; Text summarization

Sergio J. Alvarado, *University of California, Davis, Calif.,* Argument comprehension; OpEd; Scripts

S. Amarel, *Rutgers University, New Brunswick, N.J.,* Problem solving

Charles Ames, *Eggertsville, N.Y.,* Music, AI in

R. A. Amsler, *Bell Communications Research, Morristown, N.J.,* Literature, AI

D. Angluin, *Yale University, New Haven, Conn.,* Inductive inference

Michael A. Arbib, *University of Southern California, Los Angeles, Calif.,* Neural networks; Schema theory

K. S. Arora, *State University of New York, Buffalo, N.Y.,* Caduceus; Epistle; Eurisko; FOL; FRL; Merlin; Ms Malaprop; Noah; Parry; Phran and Phred; Rosie

J. F. Baldwin, *University of Bristol, Bristol, UK,* Fuzzy and probabilistic uncertainties

Bruce W. Ballard, *AT&T Bell Laboratories, Murray Hill, N.J.,* Computational linguistics

R. B. Banerji, *St. Joseph's University, Philadelphia, Pa.,* Game playing; Minimax procedure

Ray Bareiss, *Northwestern University, Evanston, Ill.,* Protos

Stephen T. Barnard, *SRI International, Menlo Park, Calif.,* Stereo vision

Gerhard Barth, *Deutsches Forschungszentrum für Künstliche Intelligenz GmbH, Kaiserslautern, Germany,* DFKI

John A. Bateman, *University of Southern California, Marina del Rey, Calif.,* Grammar, systemic

A. K. Bejczy, *Jet Propulsion Laboratory, Pasadena, Calif.,* Teleoperators

Paul Besl, *University of Michigan, Ann Arbor, Mich.,* Range data analysis

Wolfgang Bibel, *Technische Hochschule Darmstadt, Darmstadt, Germany,* Connection method; Intellectics

Alan W. Biermann, *Duke University, Durham, N.C.,* Automatic programming

Thomas O. Binford, *Stanford University, Stanford, Calif.,* Shape

Roberto Bisiani, *Carnegie Mellon University, Pittsburgh, Pa.,* Search, beam

Daniel G. Bobrow, *Xerox PARC, Palo Alto, Calif.,* Clos; Loops; Student

Bran Boguraev, *IBM T. J. Watson Research Center, Yorktown Heights, N.Y.,* Dictionary/lexicon

P. Bonissone, *General Electric, Schenectady, N.Y.,* Reasoning, plausible

Lawrence A. Bookman, *Brandeis University, Waltham, Mass.,* Analog semantic features

John H. Boose, *Boeing Computer Services, Seattle, Wash.,* Knowledge acquisition

Albert Boulanger, *Bolt, Beranek & Newman, Cambridge, Mass.,* Simulated annealing

E. J. Briscoe, *University of Cambridge, Cambridge, UK,* Speech understanding

C. Brown, *University of Rochester, Rochester, N.Y.,* Hough transforms

D. C. Brown, *Worcester Polytechnic Institute, Worcester, Mass.,* Design, AI in

Frank M. Brown, *University of Kansas, Lawrence, Kans.,* Z modal quantification logic

B. C. Bruce, *Bolt, Beranek & Newman, Cambridge, Mass.,* Discourse understanding; Grammar, case

Maurice Bruynooghe, *Katholieke Universiteit Leuven, Heverlee, Belgium,* Backtracking; Coroutines; Meta-interpretation

Bruce G. Buchanan, *University of Pittsburgh, Pittsburgh, Pa.,* Dendral

Bill P. Buckles, *Tulane University, New Orleans, La.,* Fuzzy databases

J. Buhmann, *University of Southern California, Los Angeles, Calif.,* Neural networks

Alan Bundy, *University of Edinburgh, Edinburgh, UK,* Incidence calculus

Hans-Jürgen Burckert, *Deutsches Forschungszentrum fur Kunstliche Intelligenz GmbH, Kaiserslautern, Germany,* Resolution, graph-based

Jaime G. Carbonell, *Carnegie Mellon University and Carnegie Group Inc., Pittsburgh, Pa.,* Natural language understanding

Gail Carpenter, *Boston University, Boston, Mass.,* Adaptive resonance theory

John Case, *University of Delaware, Newark, Del.,* Recursion; Turing machines

R. Chellappa, *University of Maryland, College Park, Md.,* Image models

William J. Clancey, *Institute for Research on Learning, Palo Alto, Calif.,* Guidon; Knowledge level

Harold Cohen, *University of California, La Jolla, Calif.,* Art, AI in

A. G. Cohn, *University of Leeds, Leeds, UK,* Logic, order-sorted

Gerard Comyn, *European Computer-Industry Research Centre GmbH, Munich, Germany,* ECRC

Daniel D. Corkill, *University of Massachusetts, Amherst, Mass.,* Distributed problem solving

D. A. Cruse, *University of Manchester, Manchester, England,* Presupposition

R. E. Cullingford, *Intelligent Business Systems, Milford, Conn.,* Sam; Scripts

George Curet, *LISP Machines Company, Cambridge, Mass.,* Lisp machines

M. R. Cutkosky, *Stanford University, Stanford, Calif.,* Robot hands and end-effectors

G. R. Dattatreya, *University of Maryland, College Park, Md.,* Pattern recognition

Ernest Davis, *Courant Institute of Mathematics, New York, N.Y.,* Reasoning, commonsense

Larry Davis, *University of Maryland, College Park, Md.,* ALV

Laura Davis, *Naval Research Laboratory, Washington, D.C.,* Military applications of AI

Martin Davis, *New York University, New York, N.Y.,* Church's thesis

Rina Dechter, *University of California, Irvine, Calif.,* Constraint networks

Johan de Kleer, *Xerox Palo Alto Research Center, Palo Alto, Calif.,* Physics, qualitative

Danny De Schreye, *Katholieke Universiteit Leuven, Leuven, Belgium,* Meta-interpretation

Keith J. Devlin, *Colby College, Waterville, Me.,* Situation theory and situation semantics

M. Dincbas, *Cosytec SA, Orsay, France,* Chip

Gavan Duffy, *University of Texas, Austin, Tex.,* Hermeneutics

Edmund H. Durfee, *University of Michigan, Ann Arbor, Mich.,* Distributed problem solving

Michael G. Dyer, *University of California, Los Angeles, Calif.,* Boris; Scripts

Mark Eckman, *New England Medical Center, Boston, Mass.,* Decision theory

Shimon Edelman, *Weizmann Institute of Science, Rehovot, Israel,* Visual perception

George W. Ernst, *Case-Western Reserve University, Cleveland, Ohio,* Means-ends analysis

L. M. Fagan, *Stanford University, Stanford, Calif.,* Oncocin

Dan Fass, *Simon Fraser University, Burnaby, British Columbia, Canada,* Lexical decomposition; Preference semantics

Jerome A. Feldman, *International Computer Science Institute, Berkeley, Calif.,* ICSI

Carl R. Feynman, *Thinking Machines Corporation, Cambridge, Mass.,* Connection machines

Richard Fikes, *Stanford University, Stanford, Calif.,* REF-ARF; Sniffer; Strips

Robert Filman, *Intellicorp, Inc., Mountain View, Calif.,* KEE

Martin A. Fischler, *SRI International, Menlo Park, Calif.,* Stereo vision

Jude Franklin, *Planning Research Corporation, McLean, Va.,* Military applications of AI

P. W. Frey, *Northwestern University, Evanston, Ill.,* Horizon effect

Bertram Fronhöfer, *Technical University of Munich, Munich, Germany,* LOPS; Planlog

R. Gabriel, *Lucid, Inc., Menlo Park, Calif.,* Lisp

Adam R. Galper, *Stanford University, Stanford, Calif.,* Medicine, AI in

Anne v.d.L. Gardner, *Stanford University, Stanford, Calif.,* Law, AI in

Gerald Gazdar, *University of Sussex, Brighton, UK,* Grammar, generalized phrase structure

Hector Geffner, *IBM T. J. Watson Research Center, Yorktown Heights, N.Y.,* Reasoning, default

Dan Geiger, *Technion IIT, Haifa, Israel,* Probabilistic networks

J. Geller, *New Jersey Institute of Technology, Newark, N.J.,* Eliza; Epam; Hacker; Logo; Microplanner; Scholar; Simula; Snobol-4

Ken Gilbert, *Digital Equipment Corp., Marlborough, Mass.,* OPS-5

Maria Gini, *University of Minnesota, Minneapolis, Minn.,* Problem reduction

Adele Goldberg, *ParcPlace Systems, Palo Alto, Calif.,* Smalltalk

John Grant, *University of Maryland, College Park, Md.,* Deductive database systems

R. Greenblatt, *LISP Machines Company, Cambridge, Mass.,* Lisp machines

W. E. L. Grimson, *Massachusetts Institute of Technology, Cambridge, Mass.,* Object recognition

Stephen Grossberg, *Boston University, Boston, Mass.,* Adaptive resonance theory

H. Hall, *University of Delaware, Newark, Del.,* Phenomenology

Kristian J. Hammond, *University of Chicago, Chicago, Ill.,* Chef

Robert Haralick, *University of Washington, Seattle, Wash.,* Segmentation

S. L. Hardt, *Bellcore, Murray Hill, N.J.,* Conceptual dependency; Physics, naive

Larry R. Harris, *AICorp, Inc., Waltham, Mass.,* Intellect; KBMS; Robot

P. E. Hart, *Syntelligence, Sunnyvale, Calif.,* Prospector

John R. Hayes, *Carnegie Mellon University, Pittsburgh, Pa.,* Creativity

Philip J. Hayes, *Carnegie Mellon University, Pittsburgh, Pa.,* Natural language understanding

F. Hayes-Roth, *Cimflex Teknowledge Corporation, Palo Alto, Calif.,* Expert systems; Rule-based systems

A. C. Hearn, *RAND, Santa Monica, Calif.,* Reduce

David Heckerman, *University of Southern California, Santa Monica, Calif.,* Certainty-factor model

A. J. Hendriks, *North American Philips Corp., Briarcliff Manor, N.Y.,* Planning, reactive

L. J. Henschen, *Northwestern University, Evanston, Ill.,* Inference

Carl Hewitt, *Massachusetts Institute of Technology, Cambridge, Mass.,* Actor formalisms

Ellen C. Hildreth, *Massachusetts Institute of Technology, Cambridge, Mass.,* Edge and local feature detection

J. C. Hill, *Dickinson College, Carlisle, Pa.,* Language acquisition

Donald Hindle, *AT&T Laboratories, Murray Hill, N.J.,* Deep structure

Thomas R. Hinrichs, *Georgia Institute of Technology, Atlanta, Ga.,* Julia

Geoffrey Hinton, *Carnegie Mellon University, Pittsburgh, Pa.,* Boltzmann machine

Jessica K. Hodgins, *Massachusetts Institute of Technology, Cambridge, Mass.,* Robots, legged

C. J. Hogger, *University of London, London, UK,* Logic programming

Bruce A. Hohne, *Rohm and Haas Company, Spring House, Pa.,* Chemistry, AI in

Steffen Hölldobler, *Technische Hochschule Darmstadt, Darmstadt, Germany,* Equality inferencing

Keith J. Holyoak, *University of California, Los Angeles, Calif.,* Cognitive psychology

Thomas S. Huang, *University of Illinois, Urbana, Ill.,* Visual motion analysis

Jonathan J. Hull, *State University of New York, Buffalo, N.Y.,* Character recognition

Roger Hurwitz, *Massachusetts Institute of Technology, Cambridge, Mass.,* Hermeneutics

Robert Ingria, *BBN Systems and Technologies Corporation, Cambridge, Mass.,* Dictionary/lexicon

Robert J. K. Jacob, *Naval Research Laboratory, Washington, D.C.,* Human-computer interaction

Ramesh Jain, *University of Michigan, Ann Arbor, Mich.,* Range data analysis

Philip N. Johnson-Laird, *Princeton University, Princeton, N.J.,* Mental models

Menachem Y. Jona, *Northwestern University, Evanston, Ill.,* Dynamic memory; Reasoning, case-based

Mark A. Jones, *AT&T Bell Laboratories, Murray Hill, N.J.,* Computational linguistics

Aravind K. Joshi, *University of Pennsylvania, Philadelphia, Pa.,* Grammar, phrase-structure

Janusz Kacprzyk, *Polish Academy of Sciences, Warsaw, Poland,* Fuzzy sets and fuzzy logic

L. N. Kanal, *University of Maryland, College Park, Md.,* Pattern recognition

R. L. Kashyap, *Purdue University, West Lafayette, Ind.,* Image models

Alex Kass, *Northwestern University, Evanston, Ill.,* Swale

David E. Kieras, *University of Michigan, Ann Arbor, Mich.,* Cognitive modeling

J. L. Klavans, *IBM T. J. Watson Research Center, Yorktown Heights, N.Y.,* Morphology

Kevin Knight, *Carnegie Mellon University, Pittsburgh, Pa.,* Unification

Janet L. Kolodner, *Georgia Institute of Technology, Atlanta, Ga.,* Cyrus; Mediator; Reasoning, case-based

Richard E. Korf, *University of California, Los Angeles, Calif.,* Heuristics; Search

Stephen M. Kosslyn, *Harvard University, Cambridge, Mass.,* Mental imagery representation

Phyllis Koton, *Mitre Corp., Bedford, Mass.,* Casey

Robert A. Kowalski, *University of London, London, UK,* Logic programming

Bryan Kramer, *University of Toronto, Toronto, Ontario, Canada,* Knowledge representation

M. Kreeger, *LISP Machines Company, Cambridge, Mass.,* LISP machines

H. Kučera, *Brown University, Providence, R.I.,* Brown corpus

C. Kulikowski, *Rutgers University, New Brunswick, N.J.,* Domain knowledge

Vipin Kumar, *University of Texas, Austin, Tex.,* Search, branch-and-bound; Search, depth-first

Richard Laing, *Logical Mechanisms, Eugene, Ore.,* Self-replication

John E. Laird, *University of Michigan, Ann Arbor, Mich.,* Soar

Pat Langley, *NASA Ames Research Center, Moffet Field, Calif.,* Learning, machine

Kai-Fu Lee, *Apple Computer, Inc., Cupertino, Calif.,* Sphinx

Michael Lebowitz, *Morgan Stanley and Company, New York, N.Y.,* Memory organization packets; Unimem

Pierre Lescanne, *Centre de Recherche en Informatique de Nancy, Vandoeuvre-les-Nancy, France,* Reve

Victor R. Lesser, *University of Massachusetts, Amherst, Mass.,* Distributed problem solving

R. Letz, *Technische Universität München, Munich, Germany,* Setheo

H. Lieberman, *Massachusetts Institute of Technology, Cambridge, Mass.,* Languages, object-oriented

G. Jack Lipovski, *University of Texas, Austin, Tex.,* Associative memory

Donald W. Loveland, *Duke University, Durham, N.C.,* Completeness

D. M. Lyons, *North American Philips Corp., Briarcliff Manor, N.Y.,* Planning, reactive

Alan K. Mackworth, *University of British Columbia, Vancouver, British Columbia, Canada,* Constraint satisfaction; Logic and depiction

Anthony S. Maida, *Southwestern Louisiana University, Lafayette, La.,* Frames

John C. Mallery, *Massachusetts Institute of Technology, Cambridge, Mass.,* Hermeneutics

T. Anthony Marsland, *University of Alberta, Edmonton, Alberta, Canada,* Computer chess and search

Chad J. Marsolek, *Harvard University, Cambridge, Mass.,* Mental imagery representation

João P. Martins, *Instituto Superior Técnico, Lisbon, Portugal,* Belief revision; Truth maintenance systems

John McCarthy, *Stanford University, Palo Alto, Calif.,* Advice taker

W. W. McCune, *Argonne National Laboratory, Argonne, Ill.,* Otter

D. McDermott, *Yale University, New Haven, Conn.,* Reasoning, spatial; Reasoning, temporal

John McDermott, *Digital Equipment Corp., Marlborough, Mass.,* OPS-5; XCON

David D. McDonald, *University of Massachusetts, Amherst, Mass.,* Natural language generation

M. Eugene Merchant, *Institute of Advanced Manufacturing Sciences, Inc., Cincinnati, Ohio,* Manufacturing, AI in

Ryszard S. Michalski, *University of Illinois, Urbana, Ill.,* Clustering; Concept learning

Donald Michie, *The Turing Institute, Glasgow, UK,* Freddy

Dale Miller, *University of Pennsylvania, Philadelphia, Pa.,* Logic, higher-order

Jack Minker, *University of Maryland, College Park, Md.,* Deductive database systems

Daniel A. Moon, *Symbolics, Burlington, Mass.,* Flavors

J. H. Moor, *Dartmouth College, Hanover, N.H.,* Turing test

Paul Morawski, *Naval Research Laboratory, Washington, D.C.,* Military applications of AI

E. Morgado, *Instituto Superior Técnico, Lisbon, Portugal,* Meta-knowledge, meta-rules, and meta-reasoning

Paul Morris, *Intellicorp, Inc., Mountain View, Calif.,* Kee

M. G. Moser, *Bolt, Beranek & Newman, Cambridge, Mass.,* Grammar, case

M. A. Musen, *Stanford University, Stanford, Calif.,* Opal; Protege

John Mylopoulos, *University of Toronto, Toronto, Ontario, Canada,* Knowledge representation

Makoto Nagao, *Kyoto University, Kyoto, Japan,* Machine translation

Nils J. Nilsson, *Stanford University, Menlo Park, Calif.,* Shakey the robot

D. Nitzan, *SRI International, Menlo Park, Calif.,* Robotics

Sam H. Noh, *University of Maryland, College Park, Md.,* Computer systems

Peter Norvig, *University of California, Berkeley, Calif.,* Story analysis

Carol L. Novak, *Carnegie Mellon University, Pittsburgh, Pa.,* Color vision

Vilem Novak, *Czechoslovak Academy of Sciences, Ostrava-Poruba, Czechoslovakia,* Fuzzy logic: applications to natural language

Donald Nute, *University of Georgia, Atlanta, Ga.,* Logic, conditional

J. T. Nutter, *Virginia Institute of Technology, Blacksburg, Va.,* Epistemology

Brian B. Oakley, *Logica Cambridge Ltd., London, UK,* Alvey

Andrew Ortony, *Northwestern University, Evanston, Ill.,* Emotion modeling

S. Papert, *Massachusetts Institute of Technology, Cambridge, Mass.,* Perceptrons

R. Parikh, *Brooklyn College, Brooklyn, N.Y.,* Logic, modal

Ramesh S. Patil, *Massachusetts Institute of Technology, Cambridge, Mass.,* Medicine, AI in

Stephen G. Pauker, *New England Medical Center, Boston, Mass.,* Decision theory

Azaria Paz, *Technion IIT, Haifa, Israel,* Graphoids

Judea Pearl, *University of California, Los Angeles, Calif.,* AND/OR graphs; Bayesian inference methods; Branching factor; Epsilon semantics; Game trees

D. Perlis, *University of Maryland, College Park, Md.,* Circumscription; Reasoning, nonmonotonic

S. Petrick, *University of Wyoming, Laramie, Wy.,* Parsing

Frederick E. Petry, *Tulane University, New Orleans, La.,* Fuzzy databases

Thomas H. Pierce, *Rohm and Haas Company, Spring House, Pa.,* Chemistry, AI in

L. Polanyi, *Rice University, Houston, Tex.,* Discourse understanding

Robin Popplestone, *University of Massachusetts, Amherst, Mass.,* Poplog; Pop-11

James Pustejovsky, *Brandeis University, Waltham, Mass.,* Dictionary/lexicon; Lexical decomposition; Lexical semantics

Zenon W. Pylyshyn, *University of Western Ontario, London, Ontario,* Cognitive science

Francis Quek, *University of Michigan, Ann Arbor, Mich.,* Range data analysis

Marc H. Raibert, *Massachusetts Institute of Technology, Cambridge, Mass.,* Robots, legged

W. J. Rapaport, *State University of New York, Buffalo, N.Y.,* Belief representation systems; Logic; Logic predicate; Logic, propositional

Bertram Raphael, *Compass Point Travel, Inc., Mountain View, Calif.,* A*Algorithm; Sir

James Reggia, *University of Maryland, College Park, Md.,* Abduction

Glen D. Rennels, *Massachusetts Institute of Technology, Cambridge, Mass.,* Medicine, AI in

Christopher K. Riesbeck, *Northwestern University, Evanston, Ill.,* Eli

H. Roediger III, *Rice University, Houston, Tex.,* Episodic memory

J. Rosenberg, *Kilchberg, Switzerland,* Baseball; Chess 4.5; Kaissa; Machack-6

Azriel Rosenfeld, *University of Maryland, College Park, Md.,* Image properties; Visual recovery

R. J. H. Scha, *Universiteit van Amsterdam, Amsterdam, Netherlands,* Discourse understanding

Roger C. Schank, *Northwestern University, Evanston, Ill.,* Dynamic memory

Jeffery C. Schlimmer, *Carnegie Mellon University, Pittsburgh, Pa.,* Learning, machine

J. Schneeberger, *Technische Hochschule Darmstadt, Darmstadt, Germany,* Kokon

Terrence J. Sejnowski, *University of California, San Diego, Calif.,* Nettalk

Oliver G. Selfridge, *GTE Laboratories, Waltham, Mass.,* Pandemonium

Glenn Shafer, *University of Kansas, Lawrence, Kan.,* Dempster-Shafer theory

Steven A. Shafer, *Carnegie Mellon University, Pittsburgh, Pa.,* Color vision

Stuart C. Shapiro, *State University of New York, Buffalo, N.Y.,* Artificial intelligence; Processing, bottom-up and top-down; Sneps

D. E. Shaw, *D. E. Shaw & Co, New York, N.Y.,* Non-von

Y. Shoham, *Yale University, New Haven, Conn.,* Reasoning, temporal

Edward H. Shortliffe, *Stanford University, Stanford, Calif.,* Medicine, AI in; Mycin; Oncocin

Randall Shumaker, *Naval Research Laboratory, Washington, D.C.,* Military applications of AI

J. H. Siekmann, *Universität Kaiserslautern, Kaiserslautern, Germany,* Hades; Mathematical knowledge representation; MKRP; Proof transformation

James Slagle, *University of Minnesota, Minneapolis, Minn.,* Alphabeta pruning; Problem reduction

S. L. Small, *University of Rochester, Rochester, N.Y.,* Parsing, word-expert

C. H. Smith, *University of Maryland, College Park, Md.,* Inductive inference

Stephen Smith, *Thinking Machines Corporation, Cambridge, Mass.,* Data parallelism

John F. Sowa, *IBM Systems Research, Thornwood, N.Y.,* Semantic networks

Karen Sparck Jones, *University of Cambridge, Cambridge, UK,* Information retrieval; Thesaurus

Sargur M. Srihari, *State University of New York, Buffalo, N.Y.,* Character recognition

D. Sriram, *Massachusetts Institute of Technology, Cambridge, Mass.,* Engineering, knowledge-based expert systems in

Craig Stanfill, *Thinking Machines Corporation, Cambridge, Mass.,* Reasoning, memory-based

R. E. Stepp, *University of Illinois, Urbana, Ill.,* Clustering

Mark E. Stickel, *SRI International, Menlo Park, Calif.,* PTTP; Resolution, theory

Salvatore J. Stolfo, *Columbia University, New York, N.Y.,* Dado

Herbert Stoyan, *University of Erlangen, Erlangen, Germany,* Programming styles

William Swartout, *University of Southern California, Marina del Rey, Calif.,* Explanation

Katia P. Sycara, *Carnegie Mellon University, Pittsburgh, Pa.,* Persuader

J. C. Syre, *Bull SA EDPS, Les Clayes sous Bois, France,* Parallel machine architecture, Pepsys

M. R. Taie, *AT&T Bell Labs, Murray Hill, N.J.,* AM; Emycin; Internist; Macsyma; Pam; Politics; Sophie

Akikazu Takeuchi, *SONY Computer Science Laboratory Inc., Tokyo, Japan,* Parallel logic programming languages

H. Tennant, *Texas Instruments, Inc., Dallas, Tex.,* Ellipsis

Robert H. Thibadeau, *Carnegie Mellon University, Pittsburgh, Pa.,* Inspection

Kenneth Thompson, *AT&T Bell Laboratories, Murray Hill, N.J.,* Belle

Charles E. Thorpe, *Carnegie Mellon University, Pittsburgh, Pa.,* Robots, mobile

D. S. Touretzky, *Carnegie Mellon University, Pittsburgh, Pa.,* Inheritance hierarchy

John K. Tsotsos, *University of Toronto, Toronto, Ontario, Canada,* Image understanding

Elise H. Turner, *University of New Hampshire, Durham, N.H.,* Judis

Roy M. Turner, *University of New Hampshire, Durham, N.H.,* Medic

E. Tzoukermann, *AT&T Bell Laboratories, Murray Hill, N.J.,* Morphology

Hans Uszkoreit, *University of Saarbrucken, Saarbrucken, Germany,* Stuf

Robert Van Gulick, *Syracuse University, Syracuse, N.Y.,* Philosophical questions

Pascal van Hentenryck, *Brown University, Providence, R.I.,* Constraint logic programming

Raf Venken, *Belgian Institute of Management, Everberg, Belgium,* Backtracking; Coroutines

S. Vere, *Lockheed AI Center, Palo Alto, Calif.,* Planning

R. Veroff, *University of New Mexico, Albuquerque, N. Mex.,* Resolution, binary

Heinz Von Foerster, *Pescadero, Calif.,* Cybernetics

Walther von Hahn, *University of Hamburg, Hamburg, Germany,* Ham-ans

Christoph Walther, *Technische Hochschule Darmstadt, Darmstadt, Germany,* Induction, mathematical

David Waltz, *Thinking Machines Corporation and Brandeis University, Cambridge, Mass.,* Planes

Mitchell Wand, *Northeastern University, Boston, Mass.,* Lambda calculus

Y. F. Wang, *University of California, Santa Barbara, Calif.,* Sensors and sensor fusion

M. Watkins, *Rice University, Houston, Tex.,* Episodic memory

Yorick Wilks, *New Mexico State University, Las Cruces, N. Mex.,* Preference semantics

T. Winograd, *Stanford University, Stanford, Calif.,* KRL; Shrdlu

W. A. Woods, *Harvard University, Cambridge, Mass.,* Grammar, augmented transition network; HWIM; Lunar

Beverly Park Woolf, *University of Massachusetts, Amherst, Mass.,* Education, AI in

Lawrence Wos, *Argonne National Laboratory, Argonne, Ill.,* Aura; Resolution, binary

A. Hanyong Yuhan, *AT&T Bell Laboratories, Murray Hill, N.J.,* Conniver; Frump; GPS; Harpy; Hearsay II; KL-One; Lifer; Planner; Saint; Slip

Lotfi A. Zadeh, *University of California, Berkeley, Calif.,* Fuzzy sets and fuzzy logic: an overview

Xiru Zhang, *Thinking Machines Corporation, Cambridge, Mass.,* Protein structure prediction

H.-J. Zimmermann, *Rheinisch-Westfälische Technische Hochschule, Aachen, Germany,* Fuzzy mathematical programming

Steven W. Zucker, *McGill University, Montreal, Quebec, Canada,* Early vision

EDITOR'S FOREWORD TO THE FIRST EDITION

The *Encyclopedia of Artificial Intelligence* defines the discipline of Artificial Intelligence (AI) by bringing together the core of knowledge from all its fields and related disciplines. The articles are written primarily for the professional from another discipline who is seeking an understanding of AI, and secondarily for the lay reader who wants an overview of the entire field or information on one specific aspect. The *Encyclopedia* clarifies and corrects misperceptions as well as provides a proper understanding of AI.

The object of research in AI is to discover how to program a computer to perform the remarkable functions that make up human intelligence. This work leads not only to increasingly useful computers, but also to an enhanced understanding of human cognitive processes, of what it is that we mean by "intelligence" and what the mechanisms are that are required to produce it. AI is surely one of the most exciting scientific and commercial enterprises of our century. Its limits are yet to be discovered.

The *Encyclopedia* has significant contributions to the AI literature, not only because it brings many disciplines into one comprehensive reference, but also because it contains many landmark articles, such as: Blackboard Systems; Computer Chess Methods; Cognitive Psychology; Grammar (Augmented Transition Network; Case; Definite-Clause; Generalized Phrase-Structure; Semantic;

and Transformational); Limits of AI; Lisp; Natural-Language (Generation; Interfaces; and Understanding); Path Planning and Obstacle Avoidance; Reasoning (Causal; Commonsense; Default; Nonmonotonic; Plausible; Resource-Limited; Spatial; and Temporal); Robotics; Search (Best-First; Bidirectional; Branch-and-Bound; and Depth-First); and Social Issues of AI. All of the material is specifically written for the *Encyclopedia*.

In addition, the *Encyclopedia* has separate articles on various game-playing programs, vision, speech understanding, image understanding, matching, multisensor integration, and parsing, as well as many short articles.

The articles and the authors invited to write them were chosen with the cooperation of an editorial advisory board of distinguished authorities. The author of each article is a recognized research expert on the topic. Each article has a bibliography and extensive cross-references to other articles. The reader may start with almost any article and be led by cross-references to almost every other article in the *Encyclopedia*. There are more than 450 tables and figures. Stressing readability, accuracy, and completeness of facts as well as overall usefulness of material, this great work brings you the result of years of labor and experience.

STUART C. SHAPIRO
State University of New York at Buffalo

PREFACE

It was in the fall of 1987, while I was on sabbatical getting refreshed from sixteen years of university teaching and from four years working on the first edition of this *Encyclopedia,* that Diane Cerra, of John Wiley & Sons, started talking me into editing a second edition. I eventually agreed, and we set about to create what you now have in your hands. Our goals were threefold: to reflect advances made in the field of Artificial Intelligence since the articles of the first edition had been written; to fill in areas of AI that were poorly represented in the first edition; and to answer some of the inevitable complaints that were made about the first edition. We asked Azriel Rosenfeld to join the Editorial Board to reorganize the vision and robotics articles, Judea Pearl to organize the probabilistic reasoning and heuristic search articles, and John Hopfield to organize the (new) neural networks articles. We asked Wolfgang Bibel, Makoto Nagao, and Luc Steeles to join the Editorial Board to help make sure that European and Japanese researchers and their work were adequately represented. First Edition Board members Saul Amarel, John McDermott, and David Waltz agreed to remain on the Board for the Second Edition.

Of the approximately 450 articles in the second edition, over 200, including about 65 system entries, are newly written, and almost all of the old articles have been re-vised and updated. Most of the old system entries have been rewritten by the researchers actually responsible for the systems, and all the new system entries were so written. Groups of articles that are totally new in the second edition include articles on neural networks, fuzzy sets and fuzzy logic, and significant large projects such as ALV and Alvey. I rewrote the ARTIFICIAL INTELLIGENCE article so that it serves, in part, to organize and point to many other articles. If you have no idea where to start looking in this *Encyclopedia,* that is a good place.

Responding to readers' requests, we included the full index in each volume.

I am grateful to all the authors and reviewers of the articles in this *Encyclopedia.* This is your work. I hope you are proud of the result. Much thanks to the members of the Editorial Board and to the folks at Wiley, especially Diane Cerra, Mickey Bickford, and Lee Wylegala who are the real workers who got the job done. Thanks also to Lynda Spahr, my secretary on this project. Last, but far from least, thanks to my wife Caren for all her support and patience.

STUART C. SHAPIRO
State University of New York at Buffalo

ABBREVIATIONS AND ACRONYMNS

AA	ACT assisters
AAAI	American Association for Artificial Intelligence
AAR	*Association for Automated Reasoning*
AC	applicability conditions
ACH	*Association for Computers and the Humanities*
Ack	acknowledge
ACL	*Association for Computational Linguistics*
ACM	*Association for Computing Machinery*
ACT	accumulation time; actions or abstract nouns; Adaptive Control of Thought
ADJ	adjective
AFCET	*Association Francaise pour la Cybernetique, Economique et Technique*
AFIPS	*American Federation of Information Processing Societies*
AGE	attempt to generalize
AGV	automatic guided vehicle
AI	artificial intelligence
AIM	artificial intelligence in medicine
AI/PL	AI Programming Language
AIRPLAN	planning military air-traffic movement
AISB	*Society for the Study of Artificial Intelligence and Simulation of Behavior*
AJCL	*American Journal of Computational Linguistics*
AKO	a kind of
ALCS	Analogue Concept Learning System
ALLC	*Association for Literary and Linguistic Computing*
ALPAC	*Automated Language Processing Advisory Committee*
ALU	arithmetic and logic unit
AM	Automated Mathematician
AML	a manufacturing language
AMRF	Automated Manufacturing Research Facility
AMS	*American Mathematical Society*
APIC	Automatic Programming Information Center
APL	a programming language
APSG	augmented phrase-structure grammar
AR	autoregressive
ARC	*Association pour la Recherche Cognitive*
ARMA	autoregressive/moving average
ARPA	Advanced Research Projects Agency, now called DARPA
ARPANET	ARPA's telecommunication network
ASCII	American Standard Code for Information Interchange
ASEE	*American Society for Engineering Education*
ATE	automatic test equipment
ATC	Air Traffic Control
AT/I	Advice Taker/Inquirer
ATN	augmented transition network
AU	argument unit
AUX	auxiliary
B&B	branch-and-bound
BC	behaviorally correct
BCD	binary coded decimal
BHFFA	bidirectional heuristic front-to-front algorithm
BIM	*Belgian Institute of Management*
BIP	Basic Instructional Program
BIT	built-in test
BNF	Backus Normal (Naur) Form
bpa	basic probability assignment
bps	bits per second
BRDF	bidirectional reflectance distribution function
BSC	Binary Synchronous Communication
BTN	Basic Transition Network
C	CONTACT; a popular programming language
ca	circa
CA	Concept Analyzer, *Chemical Abstracts*
CACM	*Communications of the Association for Computing Machinery*
CADAM	computer-augmented design and manufacturing
CAD/CAM	computer-aided design/computer-aided manufacturing
CAE	computer-assisted engineering
CAI	computer-assisted instruction
CAP	control agreement principle

CAR	contents of the address part of register number
CASNET	Causal Association Network
CASREP	Casualty Report
CAT	Computer Aided Tomography; category
CATV	Community Antenna television system
CC	conceptual cohesiveness
CCD	charge couple device
CCITT	*Consultive Committee International for Telepathy and Telegraphy*
CCTA	*Central Computer and Telecommunications Agency*
CD	conceptual dependency; collision detection
CDR	contents of the decrement part of register number
CD-ROM	Compact disk read-only memory
CF	certainty factor; context-free
CFG	context-free grammar
CFL	context-free language
CF-PSG	context-free phrase-structure grammar
CG	causal graph
CHI	computer-human interfaces
C³I	command, control, communications, and intelligence
CIE	*International Commission on Illumination*
CIM	computer-integrated manufacturing
CIRP	*College Internationale de Recherches pour la Production*
CK	control knowledge
CKY	Cocke, Kasami, and Younger
CL	computational linguistics
CLS	Concept Learning System
CM	Connection Machine
CMU	Carnegie Mellon University
CNC	Computer Numerical Controls
CNET	*Centre National d'Etudes des Telecommunications*
CNF	conjunctive normal form
Coax	coaxial cable
COLING	*International Conference on Computational Linguistics*
COMPCON	*Computer Society International Conference*
CPVR	*Computer Vision and Pattern Recognition*
CPU	central processing unit
CRC	cyclical redundancy check
CRIB	computer retrieval incidence bank
CRT	cathode-ray tube
CSCSI	*Canadian Society for Computational Studies of Intelligence*
CSG	context-sensitive grammar; constructive solid geometry
CSL	concept-learning program
CSMA	carrier sense-multiple access
CSP	Communicating Synthetic Processes; constraint-satisfaction problem
CSS	*Cognitive Science Society*
CTM	computational theory of mind
CWA	closed-world assumption
CWR	contents of the word in register number
DAG	directed acyclic graph
DARPA	*Defense Advanced Research Projects Agency* (DOD)
DBMS	database-management systems
DCE	data circuit-terminating equipment; data communication equipment
DCG	definite-clause grammar
DCL	Department of Computational Logic
DCS	Department of Computer Science
dcu	discourse constituent unit
DDL	data definition language
DDM	dynamic discourse model
DDP	distributed data processing
DET	determiner
DFA	deterministic finite state automaton
DFID	depth-first iterative-deepening
DH	direct header
DI/DO	digital input/output
DL	default logic
DLC	digital logic circuit; data link control
DLPA	decoupling, linearization, and poles assignment
DNF	disjunctive normal form
DO	derivation origin
DOD	*US Department of Defense*
DOF	degree of freedom
DOG	difference of Gaussians
DP	data processing; dynamic programming
DPS	Distributed Planning Systems
DRA	Data-Representation Advisor
DRS	Discourse Representation Structure
D-S	Dempster-Shafer
DSS	decision support system
DT	decision tree
DTC	Derivational Theory of Complexity
DTE	data terminal equipment
DU	Discourse Unit
DVA	dictionary Viterbi algorithm
DWIM	do what I mean
E....	episode
EBCDIC	extended binary-coded decimal interchange code
ECC	error-correcting code
EDC	error-detecting code
EDM	electron-density map
EDP	electronic data processing
EEG	electroencephalogram
eg	*exempli gratia,* for example
EGI	extended Gaussian image
EIU	Economist Intelligence Unit
EKG	electrocardiogram
EL	electronics laboratory
ELI	English-language interpreter
E-MOP	episodic memory-organization packet
EMYCIN	Empty MYCIN
EPAM	Elementary Perceiver and Memorizer
ER	entity-relationship
ES	expert system

EST	Extended Standard Theory; Expert System Technology
EX	explanatory
FAA	Federal Aviation Administration
FA/C	functionally accurate, cooperative
FALOSY	fault localization system
FCR	feature cooccurrence restriction
FDM	frequency division multiplexing
FEP	front-end processor; Finite Element Program
FEM	Finite Element Method
FES	Functional Electrical Stimulation
FFP	foot-feature principle
FFT	fast Fourier transform
FIS	fault–isolation system
FJCC	*Fall Joint Computer Conference*
FLPL	Fortran list-processing language
FMS	flexible manufacturing system
fopc	first-order predicate calculus
forcel	force element
FRL	frame representation language
FRUMP	Fast Reading, Understanding, and Memory Program
FSA	finite state automaton
FSD	functional sequence diagram; feature specification default
FUG	Functional Unification Grammar
g	gram
G	grammar; general
GB	general background
GBT	Government-Binding Theory
GC	generalized cone; generalized cylinder
GDN	goal-dependency network
GIMADS	Generic Integrated Maintenance Diagnostics
GKS	Graphics Kernel System
GPF	generalized potential field
GPRS	generalized production system
GPS	general problem solver; global positioning satellite
GPSG	generalized phrase-structure grammar
GPSS	general-purpose simulation system
GT	group technology
HAM	Human Associative Memory
HASP	high-altitude sounding projectile; Heuristic Adaptive Surveillance Project
HDLC	high-level data link control
HFC	head-feature convention
HG	Head Grammar
HT	Hough transform
HV	hidden variable
HWIM	Hear What I Mean
IATG	Intelligent Automatic Test Generation
IC	instantaneous configuration; integrated circuit
ICAI	intelligent computer-assisted instruction
ICI	intelligent communications interface
ICMC	*International Computer Music Conference*

ICOT	*Institute for New Generation Computing Technology*
ICPR	*International Conference on Pattern Recognition*
ICU	intensive care unit
ID	immediate dominance
IDA*	iterative-deepening A*
ie	*id est,* that is
IEEE	*Institute of Electrical and Electronics Engineers*
iff	if and only if
IFIP	*International Federation for Information Processing*
IGES	Intermediate Graphics-Exchange Standard
IH	instrumental header
IJCAI	*International Joint Conference on Artificial Intelligence*
IJCPR	*International Joint Conference on Pattern Recognition*
IKBM	Integrated Knowledge-Based Modeling System
IKBS	Integrated Knowledge-Based System
IMIS	integrated maintenance-information system
IMS	information-management system
INFL	inflection
INS	inertial navigation systems
I/O	input/output
IPP	Integrated Partial Parser
IQ	Intelligence Quotient
ir	infrared
IR	information retrieval; industrial robot
IRCC	instrumented remote center of compliance
IRE	*Institute of Radio Engineers* (later IEEE)
IRIA	*Institut de Recherche d'Informatique et d'Automatique*
ISA	indirect speech act
ISI	*Information Sciences Institute*
ISPEC	Information Specification
IU	image understanding
IUS	image-understanding system
IV	intransitive verb
JIRA	*Japanese Robotic Industries Association*
JPL	*Jet Propulsion Laboratory*
KB	knowledge base
KE	knowledge engineering
kHz	kilohertz
KNOBS	Knowledge-based System
KR	Knowledge Representation
KRL	Knowledge-representation Language
KS	knowledge source
KSL	Knowledge Science Laboratory
KSAR	knowledge-source activation record
KWIC	keyword in-context
KWOC	keyword out-of-context
L	language
LAS	Language-acquisition System

LCC	location-centered, cooperative (mode)
LDS	legal (product liability) decisions
LED	light-emitting diode
LF	logical form
LFG	Lexical-functional Grammar
L(G)	string language
LGN	lateral geniculate nucleus
LH	locale header
LHASA	Logic and Heuristics Applied to Synthetic Analysis
LHS	left-hand side (or system)
LIFO	last-in, first-out
LIL	Lexical Interaction Language
LIPS	Logical inferences per second
LISP	List-processing language
LP	linear precedence
LPC	linear predictive coding
LPE	large processing element
LR	long range
LSI	large-scale integration
LT	Logic Theory
LTM	long-term memory
m	meter
M....	Maincon
MA	moving average
MAP	Manufacturing Automation Protocol
MASES	Microcomputer Advice and Selection
MATADOR	Material Advice Organizer
MB	measure of belief
MBR	multiple belief reasoner
MD	measure of disbelief
MFP	morph-fitting program
MG	metamorphosis grammar
MGCI	most general common instance
MGU	most general unifier
MIFASS	Marine Integrated Fire and Air Support System
MIMD	multiple-instruction, multiple data
MIPS	million instructions per second
MME	man-machine environment
MMI	man-machine interaction
MMU	memory-management unit
MOP	Memory-organization packet
Mp	consistent modal operator
MP	*modus ponens*
MPP	message-processing program
MRP	material requirements planning
ms	mass spectr(al, um); millisecond (10^{-3} s)
MSG	modifier-structure grammar
MSIMD	multiple single instruction, multiple data
MT	machine translation
MTS	model theoretic semantics
μs	microsecond (10^{-6} s)
N	noun
na	not available
NACCC	*North American Computer Chess Championship*
NAFIPS	*North American Fuzzy Information Processing Society*

Nak	negative acknowledgement
Nand	not and
NASA	*National Aeronautics and Space Administration*
NBS	*National Bureau of Standards*
NC	numerically controlled
NFA	nondeterministic finite state automaton
NL	natural language
NLI	natural-language interface
NLMenu	menu-based natural-language understanding
NLP	natural-language processing
NLU	natural-language understanding
nm	nanometer (10^{-9} m)
NML	nonmonotonic logic
nmr	nuclear magnetic resonance
Nor	not or
NP	noun phrase; class of functions that are nondeterministically computable in a polynomial amount of time
NP-complete	any NP-hard problem that is also NP
NP-hard	if a quick polynomial time program exists, then everything in NP is computable in a polynomially bounded amount of time
NPR	proper noun
ns	nanosecond (10^{-9} s)
NSF	*National Science Foundation*
NT	narrower term
NTPM	normalized-texture-property map
NTSC	*National Television Film Council*
OCR	optical character recognition
ONR	*Office of Naval Research*
OpEd	opinions to/from the editor
OPM	operations per minute
OS	origin set
OSI	Open Systems Interconnection
OT	origin tag
OV	open variable
P	preposition; pressure
PA	Programmer's Apprentice; PP assisters
PABX	private automatic branch exchange
PAS	phase array system
PC	personal computer; printed circuit
PD	problem data domain
PDE	partial differential equations
PDN	public data network; public display network
PE	processing element
PF	phonetic form
PG	puzzle grammar
PH	precondition header
PIM	Parallel Inference Machine
PIP	Present Illness Program
Pixel	picture element
Pl	plausibility
PLA	programming logic array
PLNLP	Programming Language for Natural-Language Processing
PMPM	parallel-marker-propagation machine

PNF	Prenex Normal Form
POM	program operation mode
POP	end of phrase; ascent to the upper network
PP	prepositional phrase; Picture Producer
PREP	preposition
PRIP	*Conference on Pattern Recognition and Image Processing*
PRO	pronoun
PRR	problem reduction representation
PS	production system
PSG	phrase-structure grammar
PSI	Personal Sequential Inference
PSL	portable Standard Lisp
PSM	patient-specific model
PSN	procedural semantic network
Pt	proper analysis of a tree
PTIM	point in time
PUFP	Pulmonary Function Program
PUGG	Plot Unit Graph Generation
PVS	principal variation search
Q/A	question answering
QCPE	Quantum Chemistry Program Exchange
QO	Quasi-optimizer
qv	*quod vide*, which see (*a cross reference*)
RAM	random-access memory
RAND	research and development
RBS	rule-based system
RCC	remote center compliance device
R&D	research and development
REL	Rapidly Extensible Language
rf	radio frequency (noun)
r-f	radio-frequency (adj.)
RHS	right-hand side (or system)
RIA	*Robot Institute of America; Robotic Industries Association*
RISC	Reduced-Instruction-Set Computer
ROM	read-only memory
RPS	robot-programming system
RPV	remotely piloted vehicle
RS	restriction set
RT	related term
s	second
S	sentence; specific
SAINT	Symbolic Automatic Integration
SAM	Script-Applier Mechanism
SAT	symmetric axis transform
SC	situation calculus; schema of problem conditions
SCA	sensor-controlled automation
SCARA	selective compliance-assembly robot arm
SCI	Strategic Computing Initiative
SCS	*Society for Computer Simulation*
SD	structural description
SDL	Sense-discrimination Language
SECS	Simulation and Evaluation of Chemical Synthesis
SEG	Sequence of Events Generator
SIAP	Surveillance Integration Automation Project

SIGART	*Special Interest Group* (of the ACM) *on AI*
SIGMOD	*Special Interest Group* (of the ACM) *on Management of Data*
SIGPLAN	*Special Interest Group* (of the ACM) *on Programming Languages*
SIMD	single-instruction multiple data
SIMULA	Simulation Language
SIPE	System for Interactive Planning and Execution
SIR	Semantic Information Retrieval
SL	support list; Linear resolution with Selection function
SLS	smoothed local symmetries
SME	*Society of Manufacturing Engineers*
S-MOP	Simple Memory Organization Packet
SNA	Systems Network Architecture
SNePS	Semantic Network Processing System
SNF	Skolem Normal Form
SPD	spectral power distribution
SPE	small processing element
SPIE	*Society of Photo-Optical Instrumentation Engineers*
S-R	stimulus-response
SR	short range
SRI	Stanford Research Institute
SRL	Semantic Representation Language
STRIPS	System for Theorem Proving in Problem Solving
SUS	speech-understanding system
SWM	Shapiro, Wand, and Martins
SYNCHEM	Synthetic Chemistry System
SYNTHEX	System Synthesis Expert
t	tree
T	temperature
TAG	tree-adjoining grammar
TATR	Tactical Air Targeting
TAU	Thematic Abstraction Unit
TCP/IP	transmission control protocol/Internet protocol
TDIDT	top-down induction of decision trees
TELENET	a telecommunications network
TG	tree grammar; transformation grammar
TINLAP	*Workshop on Theoretical Issues in Natural-Language Processing*
TLC	Teachable Language Comprehender
TLU	threshold logic unit
TMS	truth-maintenance system
TPS	test program set
TQA	transformational question answering
TR	temporal reasoning
TV	transitive verb
UIMS	user-interface management system
ULSI	ultra-large-scale integration (see bottom of page)
UPI	*United Press International*
UR	unit resulting
USE	preferred term
USPS	*United States Postal Service*
uv	ultraviolet

V	verb; volume
VC	Virtual Copy
VDU	visual display unit
VLR	very long range
VLSI	very large-scale integration
VP	verb phrase
V/R	Valve Restriction
VT	verb transitive
WEP	word expert pars(ing, er)
wff	well-formed formula
wfp	well-formed proposition
WM	working memory
WORM	write once, read many times
WTA	Winner Take All
WYSIWYG	What You See Is What You Get

X	noun, verb, or prepositional phrase
XG	extraposition grammar

Fifth Generation Computers (see COMPUTER SYSTEMS; LOGIC PROGRAMMING)—the computer technology of the next decade

First	vacuum-tube-based
Second	transistor-based
Third	IC-based
Fourth	microprocessors (LIS and VLSI), up to two million transistors per chip
Fifth	new languages (logic-based), new architecture (eg, parallel processing), and ULSI hardware (2–64 million transistors per chip)

ENCYCLOPEDIA OF ARTIFICIAL INTELLIGENCE
SECOND EDITION

VOLUME 1

A

A* ALGORITHM

Problem-solving (qv) approaches usually are either purely formal (eg, dynamic programming), and therefore neglect available data that does not fit the chosen mathematical framework, or purely heuristic (eg, GPS) (see HEURISTICS), and therefore cannot be proven to be generally valid. People who use automated problem-solving techniques often have to modify results derived by formal methods, thereby losing precision, in order to take advantage of additional "informal" sources of knowledge. The A* Algorithm introduced in 1968 (Hart and co-workers, 1968) provides an innovative way to embed heuristic knowledge directly into a formal mathematical search process.

A* is a procedure for analyzing graphs, a type of formal model. However, in addition to processing information in the graph itself, A* prescribes how to use additional knowledge about the problem situation from which the graph was derived. As a result, A* often uses far less computational effort than traditional algorithms that achieve the same results.

THE CLASS OF PROBLEMS ADDRESSED

A* is an algorithm for finding a path in a graph (a network of nodes connected by arcs). Each node in the graph may have any number of successor nodes, indicated by directed arcs drawn from the node to its successors. Each arc has a number associated with it that represents the cost of traversing that arc.

A path is a sequence of connected nodes. A solution path is any path whose first node is a designated Start node and whose last node is one of a designated set of Goal nodes. The cost of a path is the sum of the costs of the arcs in the path. A preferred path is a path with the lowest possible cost of getting from its first to its last node.

Figure 1 shows a graph with many solution paths; for example,

$$(\text{Start, n2, n4, G1})$$

is a solution path whose cost is 24. For this graph the preferred solution path is

$$(\text{Start, n1, n3, G1})$$

whose cost is 9.

This kind of formal model may be used in a variety of situations. For example, the nodes of a graph may represent cities and the arcs railways; or the nodes may be positions in a game (see GAME TREES) and the arcs the legal moves; and so on. Many problems can be posed in the following general form: given a graph, find a preferred solution path—and do so with a minimum amount of computational effort.

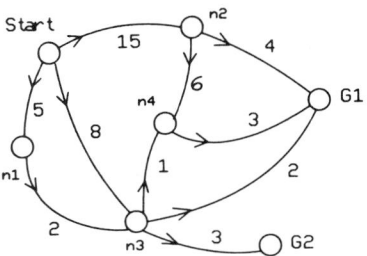

Figure 1. Graph example.

INTRODUCING ADDITIONAL KNOWLEDGE

In addition to the nodes, arcs, and costs that comprise a conventional graph, A* uses one more kind of data: a number $\hat{h}(n)$ associated with each node that is an estimate of a lower bound on the cost of getting from that node to a goal node. If the nodes represent cities and the arc costs are railroad miles, $\hat{h}(n)$ might be airline distance from city n to the goal city; if the nodes are puzzle positions, $\hat{h}(n)$ might be the minimum number of moves before the puzzle can possibly be solved—for example, $\hat{h}(\text{Start})$ for a tic-tac-toe game is 3. These estimates are usually based on logical or physical knowledge that is not otherwise represented in the graph.

THE A* ALGORITHM

The following is a simplified statement of the A* Algorithm. (See Hart and co-workers, 1968 for a more precise statement.)

1. Let $g(n)$ represent the cost of a preferred path from Start to node n, and set $g(\text{Start}) = 0$. Let OPEN be a list of nodes that initially contains only the Start node. Calculate the estimate $\hat{h}(\text{Start})$.
2. Select the node N on the list OPEN for which the quantity $[g(N) + \hat{h}(N)]$ is smallest. If N is a goal node, the path to N is a preferred solution path, and its cost is $g(N)$. If there are no OPEN nodes, there is no solution path in the graph.
3. Remove N from OPEN. Find all the successors of N, and add them to OPEN. For each successor S, let $g(S) = g(N) + (\text{cost on arc from } N \text{ to } S)$. Calculate $\hat{h}(S)$.
4. Go to step 2.

PROPERTIES OF A*

It can be shown that A* has the following properties:

1. Let $h(n)$ be the actual cost of a preferred path from n to a goal node. If $\hat{h}(n) \le h(n)$ for all n, then A* is

guaranteed to find a preferred solution path if one exists.

2. A* is the best possible algorithm in the sense that no other algorithm with access to the same amount of "additional knowledge" can do any less work than A* and still be sure of finding a preferred solution.

FINAL COMMENTS

Pearl (1984) has more precise (and complex) explanations of the properties of A* as well as extensions and refinements of this approach. An application of A* to critical path scheduling is discussed by Marcus (1984).

BIBLIOGRAPHY

P. E. Hart, N. J. Nilsson, and B. Raphael, "A Formal Basis for the Heuristic Determination of Minimum Cost Paths", *IEEE Trans. Syst. Sci. Cybern.* **SSC-4**(2), 100–107 (1968).

R. Marcus, "An Application of Artificial Intelligence to Operations Research", *Commun. ACM* **27**(10), 1044–1052 (1984).

J. Pearl, *Heuristics*, Addison-Wesley, Reading, Mass., 1984.

B. RAPHAEL
Compass Point Travel, Inc.

ABDUCTION

Abduction or abductive inference is generally taken to mean "inferring the best or most plausible explanation for a given set of facts." Abduction is frequently used in everyday common sense reasoning and in expert-level problem-solving and is sometimes confused with deductive inference. For example, "I deduced that the car's battery was dead because the engine would not start and the headlights did not come on." While this is certainly a plausible explanation for the facts at hand, one cannot *deduce* such a conclusion in this situation, because other explanations are possible, eg, that both headlights have burned out simultaneously and that the fuel line is blocked. It may seem that the former hypothesis or explanation is more plausible, consisting as it does of one fault (dead battery) rather than three (two headlights plus fuel line). Still, one cannot deduce this hypothesis with certainty in this situation. The most one can do is to consider a dead battery to be a plausible hypothesis among other possible hypotheses, to be subsequently tested and validated. As this example illustrates, abduction involves not only making hypotheses, but also discriminating among them based on their plausibility or probability.

Abduction, along with deduction and induction, is fundamental to reasoning and scientific inquiry. Deduction, induction, and abduction can be contrasted through simple but instructive syllogisms. With deductive reasoning, one is given a general rule, such as $(\forall x) [A(x) \rightarrow B(x)]$, and a specific case, $A(c)$, and deduces a specific result, which is $B(c)$ in this example. In contrast, with inductive reasoning

one is given a set of specific cases and results, $A(c_i)$ and $B(c_i)$, where $i = 1, 2, \ldots n$, from which a general rule such as $(\forall x) [A(x) \rightarrow B(x)]$, can be hypothesized. From this perspective, abductive reasoning differs in that it can be viewed as starting from a general rule and specific result, $(\forall x) [A(x) \rightarrow B(x)]$ and $B(c)$, and hypothesizing a specific case or antecedent, $A(c)$. However, there is much more to abduction than such a simple illustration would suggest. Abductive inference usually involves probabilistic causal relations, eg, $A(x)$ is likely to cause $B(x)$, rather than categorical implications like in the syllogism above. Further, there are generally multiple possible causes of any observation ($A_1(x), A_2(x), \ldots$ may each cause $B(x)$), and one must select from amongst these causes based on some criteria of plausibility.

Capturing general abductive inference abilities in artificial intelligence (AI) systems has proven to be a very difficult task. There have been many applications, most prominent of which has been diagnostic problem-solving (Allemang and co-workers, 1987; deKleer and Williams, 1986). Abductive diagnostic systems are told that various symptoms are present, and use their knowledge of causal relations between disorders (diagnoses) and symptoms to hypothesize the presence of one or more disorders. They test their working hypothesis(es) by seeking additional information until one or a few most plausible diagnoses are offered as the problem solution. Other applications exist in machine vision, natural language processing, legal reasoning, plan interpretation, scientific discovery, and learning. For example, natural language understanding models that abductively construct plausible interpretations of stories have been developed (Charniak and McDermott, 1985). These models involve motivational analysis, which is the recognition of the intention of others, and plan recognition.

Recently, several approaches have been explored in attempting to precisely characterize abductive inference in an application-independent fashion. These include parsimonious set covering (Allemang, 1987; Josephson and co-workers, 1987; Reggia and co-workers, 1985), probability theory (Pearl, 1988; Peng and Reggia, 1990), logic-based models (Levesque, 1989; Reiter, 1987), and heuristic principles (Thagard, 1989). Because of space limitations, we briefly introduce only the first two of these approaches here, and use general diagnostic problem-solving to illustrate the concepts involved.

With the simplest form of parsimonious set covering there is a set of disorders D and a set of manifestations, or symptoms, M. For each disorder d_i, there is a connection, or association, between d_i and each manifestation m_j that can be caused by d_i. A subset of M, denoted M^+, represents the set of all manifestations known to be present. A set of disorders D_l is called a cover of the given M^+ when the disorders in D_l can cause all of the manifestations in M^+. A set of disorders D_l is an explanatory hypothesis if: D_l is a cover of M^+, and D_l is parsimonious. A difficult issue in diagnostic reasoning theories in general, including parsimonious set covering models, has been precisely defining what is meant by the "best," most plausible, simplest, or most parsimonious explanation for a given set of facts.

An early criterion of plausibility is minimal cardinality: explanatory hypotheses with the fewest number of hypothesized components are preferable. In applying this criterion to specific diagnostic problems, however, it quickly becomes evident that minimal cardinality is an inadequate measure of plausibility. For example, in medical diagnosis, two common diseases may together be more plausible than a single rare disease in explaining a given set of symptoms (Reggia and co-workers, 1985). For this reason, parsimonious set covering models as well as other models of diagnostic inference have adopted a more relaxed criterion of plausibility which is referred to here as irredundancy. (Irredundancy is sometimes called "minimality", but we use the former term here to avoid any confusion with minimal cardinality.) A set of disorders D_l that covers (causes all of) the manifestations in M^+ is irredundant if it has no proper subsets which also cover M^+. Although this criteria does not directly favor the smallest set of propositions, irredundancy is preferable because it handles cases like the medical examples referenced above while still constraining the number of disorders in an hypothesis. However, irredundancy has the problem that in some applications it may identify many implausible hypotheses as well as the plausible ones, and may in some cases still fail to identify the most reasonable hypothesis.

Another approach to formalizing abductive reasoning is through probability theory (Pearl, 1988; Peng and Reggia, 1990). The parsimony criteria described above, while widely used in various models of abduction, are subjective and do not account for the possibility that some manifestations are more typical of a given disorder than others. Probability theory provides a means for determining the most probable explanatory hypothesis, which is then taken as the most plausible explanation.

Typically, with models of abductive reasoning based on probability theory, each disorder d_i is associated with its prior probability p_i. Each causal relation is associated with a number c_{ij}, the causal strength from d_i to m_j representing how frequently d_i causes m_j. The relative likelihood $L(D_l, M^+)$ of any potential explanatory hypothesis D_l given the presence of M^+ can be calculated using relevant p_i and c_{ij} values. $L(D_l, M^+)$ can be proven to differ from the posterior probability $P(D_l|M^+)$ by only a constant. Using the objective, albeit limited, measure $L(D_l, M^+)$, one can analyze the conditions under which various plausibility criteria such as minimal cardinality, irredundancy, and others would be guaranteed to identify the most probable hypothesis. Models of abductive inference based on probability theory have yielded substantial insights, but are limited to a certain extent from a practical viewpoint. This is because in many real-world problems the needed probabilities (p_i, c_{ij}) are not readily available.

BIBLIOGRAPHY

D. Allemang, M. Tanner, T. Bylander, and J. Josephson, "Computational Complexity of Hypothesis Assembly," *Proceedings of the Tenth International Conference on Artificial Intelligence,* 1987, pp. 1112–1117.

E. Charniak and D. McDermott, "Abduction, Uncertainty and Expert Systems," and "Language Comprehension," *Intro. Art. Intell.* **8** and **10** (1985).

J. deKleer and B. Williams, "Reasoning About Multiple Faults," *Proceedings of the Fifth National Conference on Artificial Intelligence,* AAAI, Philadelphia, 1986, pp. 132–139.

J. Josephson, B. Chandrasekran, J. Smith, and M. Tanner, "A Mechanism for Forming Composite Explanatory Hypothesis," *IEEE Trans. Sys. Man Cybern.* **17,** 445–454 (1987).

H. Levesque, "A Knowledge-Level Account of Abduction," *Proceedings of the Eleventh International Joint Conference on Artificial Intelligence,* 1989, pp. 1061–1067.

J. Pearl, *Probabilistic Reasoning in Intelligent Systems,* Morgan-Kaufmann, San Mateo, Calif., 1988.

Y. Peng and J. Reggia, *Abductive Inference Models for Diagnostic Problem Solving,* Springer-Verlag, New York, 1990.

J. Reggia, D. Nau, P. Wang, and Y. Peng, "A Formal Model of Diagnostic Inference," *Infor. Sci.* **37,** 227–285 (1985).

R. Reiter, "A Theory of Diagnosis from First Principles," *Artif. Intell.* **32,** 57–95 (1987).

P. Thagard, "Explanatory Coherence," *Behav. and Brain Sci.* **12,** 435–502 (1989).

JAMES A. REGGIA
University of Maryland

ACOUSTIC ANALYSIS. See SPEECH UNDERSTANDING.

ACTOR FORMALISMS

Actors provide a conceptual basis for the development and continued research of open systems—ie, open-ended, continuously evolving systems (Hewitt and de Jong, 1983; Hewitt and Lieberman, 1983). Dealing with issues surrounding open systems is important to progress in the fields of AI and database theory, which have so far been based on the closed-world assumption.

ACTORS: DEFINITION

The actor model is a paradigm of concurrent computation in open systems. Actors unify functional programming and object-oriented programming. An actor carries out its computation only in response to accepting a communication that can cause it to take the following primitive actions:

Send communications to other actors.

Create new actors.

Specify a replacement actor to process the next communication.

All actions specified by an actor's behavior are carried out concurrently. In particular, computation is speeded up to use available resources by pipelining the replacement process: the new actor may accept the next communication even as the actor it replaces is sending communications or creating other actors.

The Nature of Actor Communication

Actors use buffered, asynchronous communication. Each actor has a mail address that may be freely communicated to other actors resulting in a dynamic interconnection network topology on actors. To send an actor a communication, its address must be specified as the target of the communication. The mail system guarantees delivery of pending communications after a finite, but arbitrary delay. Control structures are viewed as patterns of message passing (Hewitt, 1977) using the dynamic creation of actors called customers (see CONTROL STRUCTURES). Customers provide a parallel analog to continuations.

Transactions

In transactional terms communications can be either requests or responses. Each request eventually results in a unique response and the pair is considered a transaction. A request may activate several requests, which has the result that transactions are often nested. Transactions provide a high-level view of events since one can view the transactions at successively finer levels of granularity. Important debugging tools for large actor systems have been based on an analysis of the transactional structure.

THEORETICAL ISSUES

The actor model incorporates the laws of parallel processing (Hewitt and Baker, 1977) and, in contrast to models such as Petri nets and data flow, accounts for the causal effects of a computation on the dynamic structure of the system (Clinger, 1981; Agha, 1987). The actor model also addresses problems of distributed computing (see DISTRIBUTED PROBLEM SOLVING), such as mutual exclusion, divergence, and deadlock (Agha, 1986).

Guarantee of Mail Delivery

The guarantee of mail delivery provides a form of fairness. An important consequence of the guarantee is that potentially infinite processes can nevertheless be made to halt. This can be useful for halting processes (for maintenance and upgrading) that may otherwise function for an arbitrarily long period of time. Examples of such processes include operating systems and servers (Agha, 1986).

Abstraction and Compositionality

An actor system is analyzed in terms of transitions between configurations from some viewpoint. In order to build large systems, one must be able to program and compose independent modules. Message passing is used to achieve the parallel composition of independent actor systems. Information hiding (abstraction) in independent modules is essential so that, upon composition, all internal actions in the systems composed need not be considered. Such abstraction is achieved by defining a set of receptionist actors (which can accept communications from outside the configuration). When actors in one system receive the mail addresses of the receptionists in another, the two systems are in effect composed (Agha, 1986).

IMPLEMENTATIONS AND APPLICATIONS

Actors are best suited to programming intelligent systems. The Apiary (Hewitt, 1980; Lieberman, 1983) has been developed by the Message-Passing Semantics Group at the Artificial Intelligence Laboratory at Massachusetts Institute of Technology. The Apiary network architecture supports dynamic resource management using such techniques as load balancing and real-time garbage collection (Lieberman and Hewitt, 1983).

Several high-level actor languages (Theriault, 1983) have also been developed to facilitate further research in human interaction with actor communities. Act3 (Hewitt and co-workers, 1984) is the latest of these, embodying basic control structures, resource management tools, and a description system (Hewitt and co-workers, 1980; Barber, 1982).

Probably all attempted axiomatizations of large real systems necessarily contain conflicting information and contradictory beliefs. It follows that in the context of real-world systems, logical proof is an inadequate tool for reasoning (qv); instead due process reasoning involving different sides of beliefs, goals, and hypothesis needs to be used. Actors serve as an ideal tool for modeling real systems since they do not impose a priori consistency requirements and can therefore accommodate distinct viewpoints (Hewitt, 1985).

BIBLIOGRAPHY

G. Agha, *Actors: A Model of Concurrent Computation in Distributed Systems*, M.I.T. Press, Cambridge, Mass., 1986.

G. Agha, *Actors: A Model of Concurrent Computation in Distributed Systems*, M.I.T. Press, Cambridge, Mass., 1987.

G. R. Barber, *Office Semantics*, Ph.D. dissertation, Massachusetts Institute of Technology, 1982.

W. D. Clinger, *Foundations of Actor Semantics*, AI-TR-633, MIT Artificial Intelligence Laboratory, May 1981.

C. E. Hewitt, "Viewing Control Structures as Patterns of Passing Messages," *Artif. Intell.* 8(3), 323–364 (June 1977).

C. Hewitt and H. Baker, "Laws for Communicating Parallel Processes," *1977 IFIP Congress Proceedings*, IFIP, Aug. 1977, pp. 987–992.

C. E. Hewitt, "The Apiary Network Architecture for Knowledgeable Systems," *Conference Record of the 1980 Lisp Conference*, Stanford University, Stanford, Calif., Aug. 1980, pp. 107–118.

C. Hewitt, G. Attardi, and M. Simi, "Knowledge Embedding with a Description System," *Proceedings of the First National Conference on Artificial Intelligence*, American Association for Artificial Intelligence, Stanford, Calif., 1980, pp. 157–164.

C. Hewitt and P. de Jong, "Analyzing the Roles of Descriptions and Actions in Open Systems," *Proceedings of the Third National Conference on Artificial Intelligence*, Washington, D.C., Aug. 1983, AAAI, pp. 162–167.

C. Hewitt and H. Lieberman, *Design Issues in Parallel Architectures for Artificial Intelligence*, A.I. Memo 750, MIT Artificial Intelligence Laboratory, 1983.

C. Hewitt, T. Reinhardt, G. Agha, and G. Attardi, "Linguistic Support of Receptionists for Shared Resources," *Proceedings of the NSF/SERC Seminar on Concurrency*, LNCS, Springer-Verlag, New York, 1984, pp. 330–359.

C. Hewitt, "The Challenge of Open Systems," *Byte* **10**(4), 223–242 (April 1985).

H. Lieberman and C. Hewitt, "A Real Time Garbage Collector Based on the Lifetimes of Objects," *CACM* **26**(6), 419–429 (June 1983).

H. Lieberman, "An Object-Oriented Simulator for the Apiary," *Proceedings of the Third AAAI Conference*, Washington, D.C., Aug. 1983, AAAI, pp. 241–246.

D. Theriault, *Issues in the Design and Implementation of Act2*, Technical Report 728, MIT Artificial Intelligence Laboratory, June 1983.

C. HEWITT
G. AGHA
Massachusetts Institute of
Technology

ADAPTIVE PLANNING

Since the mid 1980s, there has been a tremendous upheaval in research on planning. The change in framework can be characterized along three dimensions: from ahistoric to historic; from planning and acting independently of each other to various mixtures of planning and acting; from disembodied to embodied. A few of these approaches include: planning and acting (McDermott, 1978), reactive robot architectures (Brooks, 1985; Kaebling, 1987), case-based planning (Hammond, 1986; Kolodner and Simpson, 1989; Carbonell, 1983), plan elaboration (Georgeff and Lansky, 1987; Firby, 1987), plan refitting (Kambhampati and Hendler, 1989), plan repair (Wilkins, 1988; Hammond, 1986; Simmons, 1973), experimentation (Shrager, 1987), opportunistic action (Hammond, 1989; Birnbaum, 1986; Hayes-Roth and Hayes-Roth, 1979), marker passing (Hendler, 1986), situated activity theory (Agre and Chapman, 1987; Agre, 1987; Suchman, 1987), and universal plans (Schoppers, 1987). Although many of the newer positions existed in one form or another before the mid 80s, it was not until recently that they converged and resulted in some fundamental changes in the framework from which planning research is viewed.

All three of these dimensions come into play in the following example: a planner attempts to use the airphone for the first time. A historic planner attempts this task under the assumption that the planner has previously done similar sorts of tasks, for example, using a payphone. A planner that mixed planning and acting does not attempt to resolve the usage of the device until it has an opportunity to interact with it. An embodied planner deals with some of the variance in the situation of using an airphone as a result of some embodied skills, for example, the cluster of embodied skills involved in pulling the phone out of its seat in the wall unit.

Adaptive planning (Alterman, 1985, 1986, 1987, 1988) has been a part of this movement and has been responsive to all three themes, drawing heavily from the work of Wilensky (1983) on commonsense planning, Schank (1982) on the role of memory in understanding, and the early work of Simmons (1973) on semantic networks/memory.

An adaptive planner works in commonsense planning situations, which refers to the mundane day-to-day activities of human planners (Wilensky, 1983). A key feature of such domains is that it is less the case that the activities of the planner vary a great deal, and more the case that the circumstances under which the plans are applied vary. An adaptive planner has a memory of previous plans (routines) and retrieves a plan from that memory that seems to match the situation at hand. It then adapts that plan (improvises) during the period of engagement as a function of an interpretive process; it constructs a representation of the relationship between a prestored "routine + circumstance" concept and the current circumstances. Semantic memory is the storehouse of notions and practices shared in the culture, and an adaptive planner constructs its representation/understanding out of the vocabulary it provides.

The case of using the airphone for the first time is an example of an adaptive planning problem. Rather than planning from scratch, the planner retrieves from memory a related routine such as using a pay phone. Rather than adapting the plan before engagement, an adaptive planner adjusts the routine during an interaction with the airphone device. The adaptations occur as a function of an interpretive process. So, if the planner sees an iconograph of a credit card on the device, he/she interprets (understands) that to be an indicator of the method of payment. It then operationalizes the understanding, eventually converting a routine for using an ATM (Automatic Teller Machine) card into a procedure for payment at the airphone.

The earliest model of an adaptive planner was PLEXUS (Alterman, ibid). An example of a problem that PLEXUS worked on is the New York City subway problem. Suppose a planner is about to ride the NYC subway for the first time and attempts to treat a routine for riding BART, the Bay Area Rapid Transit system, as a basis for guiding the current activity. There are a number of differences between the BART plan and that which the planner must eventually devise for riding the NYC subway. In the BART case, a ticket is bought from a machine, and in the NYC subway, a token is bought from a teller. In the BART station, the ticket is returned after entering the station and is later used for exiting, and in the NYC subway, the token is not returned during entrance, nor is it needed for exiting.

FLOABN (For Lack Of A Better Name) (Alterman and Zito-Wolf, 1990) is an implementation in progress of an adaptive planner that reasons about the usage of mechanical and electronic devices. When action and interpretation break down, FLOABN reads instructions (Alterman and co-workers, in press). The current domain of FLOABN is to learn to use a series of telephone devices, gradually building up its memory of procedures after each encounter. The example of using the airphone for the first time is the type of problem that FLOABN works on. FLOABN includes a text inferencer, IIMP (Alterman and Carpenter, 1991) that reads instructions and makes sense of them. SCAVENGER (Zito-Wolf and Alterman, 1991) operationalizes the sense made of the instructions, modifying an existing routine in order to incorporate the change. FLOABN includes a blackbox model of a hand with embodied skills. The current implementation of the hand uses the RAP control structure described by Firby (1987).

THEMES

Constructing an Interpretation

The notion that understanding plays a role (or roles) in the planning process has been heard from several quarters. One view has it that in a community of agents, understanding is used to recognize the plans of other agents (eg, Cohen, Perrault, and Allen, 1981). A second view is that the planner must interpret the problem, eg, missionaries and cannibals, in order to set up a representation from which heuristic search can be applied (eg, VanLehn, 1989). Or sometimes this interpretation process can be used to assess the situation; this is especially true in domains of subjective interpretation (eg, Carbonell, 1978). A third view is that understanding and planning share knowledge: not only first order knowledge of plans and goals (eg, Schank and Abelson, 1977), but also second order knowledge about control knowledge for plan-based activities (eg, Wilensky, 1981). The work on adaptive planning (Alterman, 1986, 1988, 1990) draws on all three of these earlier themes, focusing on the constructive role of understanding; that is, planning and acting that directly result from understanding.

One reason for the significance of understanding in engagement-time planning derives from the fact that reality for a commonsense planner lacks objectivity. Traditional models of planning in the AI community are based on a viewpoint that objects and situations in the world can be individuated without any interpretation. In the Robby-the-Robot world, the planner not only is omniscient, in the sense that it has a model of the complete layout of all the rooms, but is also able to immediately apprehend each of the objects that it manipulates: this is a chair, those are bananas, that is a doorway, and so on. But in the world that people normally operate in, the apprehension of situations and objects in the world is an interpretive process. For the type of commonsense planning domains that people engage in on a daily basis, the world is underdetermined, and a central and constructive part of the planning process is to assign (determine) significance to (of) the relevant features of the situation.

A second reason is that for mundane day-to-day activities, it is more often the case the circumstances vary slightly than that the goals of the planner have changed.

Frequently, these changes are due to changes in practice (Lave, 1988). For example, this variance in practice might occur due to changes in economic conditions, the technological base, social institutions, individual circumstances, and social trends. In short, from the perspective of an individual agent, the world of engagement is slowly but constantly mutating, as are the required practices.

Nevertheless, there is constancy in the world, and it is due to the shared set of practices from which new practices are created (Minsky, 1975; Schank and Abelson, 1975; Rumelhart, 1980). This history of practices acts as a background from which new practices are created, that is, revised into being. For a rational agent operating in such a world, the ability to function effectively is in many cases due largely to the ability to construct an interpretation, or understanding, of this variance (novelty) in terms of shared concepts of culture, community, home, and workplace.

A key feature of adaptive planning is that it emphasizes the constructive role of understanding in planning. A simple kind of understanding is recognizing the features of the situation that allow one to make a cup of coffee in the morning. The constructive role of understanding is understanding that accounts for variance in circumstance in a manner that directly leads to action. In the case of the iconograph of a credit card printed on the airphone device, it is an understanding process that directly leads to action of using a credit card as the method of payment. Where previous views of understanding in planning have emphasized a supportive role (as in the case of plan recognition or framing and elaboration) or emphasized the necessity of the two processes sharing knowledge, adaptive planning excavates the occasions where planning and understanding coincide—that is, planning as understanding.

The Operational Level, Routines, and Situated Plans

Another critical part of adaptive planning is that an adaptive planner has a memory of prestored plans or routines (situated plans). Situated plans are cases (cf Kolodner and Simpson, 1989; Hammond, 1986; Rissland and Ashley, 1986) or customized routines or practices that are developed out of the planner's experiences. Examples of prestored plans are the plan to ride BART and the plan to use a payphone. PLEXUS differed from other early approaches to case-based planning in three ways: it worked primarily by constructing an interpretation, it performed adaptation during engagement (explained below), and it viewed adaptive planning as a shift in operational level.

Recall that an important characteristic of commonsense planning domains is the habitual nature of many of the planning situations: variance in circumstances, not in goals. It is because of the habitual nature of commonsense planning situations that an adaptive planner bases its activities on a memory of pre-existing plans. In adaptive planning, specific routines are foregrounded in order to take advantage of the mass of details associated with the more specific plan. In order to deal with the variance in circumstances, more general plan notions are included in the background, serving more to organize pre-stored plans into categories. Because an adaptive planner foregrounds pre-stored routines but has access to more abstract plan notions in the background, the difference between an adaptive planner and a refinement-based hierarchical planner (Sacerdoti, 1974) is sometimes referred to as a shift in operational level (Alterman, 1987). The operational level of an adaptive planner is more detailed (situated) than that of a hierarchical planner.

In adaptive planning, routines are referred to as *situated plans* to emphasize that they are coupled to particular contexts (environments). By nature, situated plans are not just a sequence of steps, but a sequence of steps coupled to a particular context. Situated plans tend to drift towards the agent's habitats. A planner does not have a routine for any fast food place, but it has a routine for the fast food place that the planner normally visits. A planner does not just have a recipe for cooking french toast, but it has a situated plan for cooking french toast given, for example, the layout of the planner's kitchen.

Background Knowledge

For an adaptive planner, memory consists not only of a set of routines (situated plans) but also of background knowledge. The background knowledge takes the form of a network, which encodes plans in terms of both its semantic and contingent properties. Background knowledge serves as a conceptual webbing that holds the various plans together. It also provides the language for constructing interpretations of the situation of engagement. By making the background knowledge associated with the pre-stored plan explicit, it becomes possible to re-use the pre-stored plan in a wide variety of situations. The background knowledge associated with a pre-stored plan is determined by the plan's position in a network. The network includes category, causal, role, and partonomic knowledge. The term partonomic structure refers to the part hierarchy (Tversky and Hemenway, 1984); cf meronymic hierarchy (Winston and co-workers, 1987).

The background knowledge provides two types of encodings of the situated plans. The first, semantic encoding, ties the structure of the plan to semantic memory. This encoding provides the framework for the planner understanding/interpretation processing of the plan. The semantic coding ties the plan into semantic memory in three ways: through the categoric structure of the plan and its steps, through the partonomic structure, and through role knowledge. The PAYPHONE-PLAN is in the category of PHONE-PLAN. A piece of partonomic structure associated with the PAYPHONE-PLAN is that its steps include LIFT-RECEIVER, LISTEN-FOR-DIAL-TONE, INSERT-COIN, and DIAL. Similarly, a part of the DIAL step (subplan) is DIAL-A-DIGIT. Role knowledge associated with the PAYPHONE-PLAN includes the receiver and the touch-tone pad.

The second type of encoding involves the contingency properties of the situation. Where the semantic coding can be viewed as largely decontextualized information, the contingent properties are highly contextualized. Two ex-amples of these contingency properties are causal, eg, reason, purpose, precondition, and step ordering information. For the PAYPHONE-PLAN, the purpose of INSERT-COIN is payment, the reason for INSERT-COIN is to enable successful DIALING, and a precondition of INSERT-COIN is that there exists a coin slot. A piece of ordering information associated with the PAYPHONE-PLAN is that before DIALING can be performed, LIFT-RECEIVER must be performed.

Adaptation During Engagement

An adaptive planner acts on retrieved situated plans, but delays refitting until during the period of engagement. By delaying refitting, the immediate circumstances can act both to trigger new matching activity between circumstance and memory and to provide valuable cues to aid that matching/interpretive process.

Consider the role of retrieval in adaptive planning. The scenario is that the planner has an initial reminding which it then proceeds to adapt during the period of engagement. Not only does the initial retrieval rest on the ability to have useful remindings, but so do the adaptations. For an adaptive planner, the adaptive remindings occur as a function of the interpretation it constructs of the ongoing situation. If one fragment of the pre-stored situated plan is at odds, it is replaced by another by constructing an interpretation of the immediate circumstances that leads to an alternate fragment of a situated plan.

One of the issues here is that there are potentially a great number of remindings that can occur. How is it that one is able to retrieve and adapt, fairly efficiently, a workable situated plan? Part of the answer to that question lies in the organization of memory (Kolodner, 1983; Schank, 1982). A second part of the answer lies in the situation of engagement (Alterman, 1988).

Kolodner's model (1983) is that memory is a lock-key system. The retriever steps through memory, one step at a time. Each step is allowed if the right key is available. These keys are features of the problem. Given the request, "When was the last time you visited an oil field?" one feature of the problem that can be used for retrieval is "oil field".

Given the situation of engagement, other features are available for adaptive purposes. Suppose that in one case the question is asked of Secretary Vance while he is walking in the rain, and in an alternate case, at a state department dinner. Suppose that the last time Secretary Vance visited an oil field, it was raining. If Secretary Vance is walking in the rain, his circumstances might provide a feature (a key) that aids in reminding. But no such feature exists in the second situation of engagement.

These types of situational cues are not working in a fashion that is merely incidental. For example, the first time one uses an airphone, the iconograph of a credit card depicted on the device acts as a situational cue that helps interpret the method of payment for airphones. For the BART-NYC-SUBWAY example, the perception of the exit turnstile acts as a cue to the way in which the planner exits the station without a ticket.

ISSUES AND TECHNIQUES: PLEXUS

Several critical features of, and constraints on, the constructive role of understanding in adaptive planning can be defined. The first feature is that understanding in artificial intelligence means constructing a representation. In the case of adaptive planning, this translates to a planner/understander that operates by constructing a representation of the current circumstances. In the case of the airphone, the planner/understander works to construct a representation of the airphone device and its usage. The second feature is that the representation/understanding is constructed out of the language and structure provided by semantic memory, the individual's storehouse of concepts and practices shared in his or her culture and community. Because of the representational aspect of understanding, adaptive planning is sometimes described as a matching process. The adaptive planner is matching concepts in semantic memory to the situation of engagement. The collection of concepts it pulls out of the background semantic knowledge that match the important features of the situation is the representation/understanding.

A third feature is that understanding establishes correspondence; this is the referential characteristic of the representation. Fourth, the representation/understanding constructed by the planner/understander must be coherent. Fifth, the understanding to be constructed must be related to the planner/understander's current goal. The representation/understanding the adaptive planner constructs is selecting some of the features of the situation and characterizes their internal consistency. Without the internal consistency, the situation, or part of the situation, fails to make sense. Without correspondence, the plan/interpretation lacks substantiation. Without the relation to goal, the plan/interpretation lacks relevance. These latter three features are all constraints that are active during the adaptation process.

PLEXUS (Alterman, 1986, 1988) reasoned about semantic memory from a given perspective (routine or situated plan). The correspondences for PLEXUS were between the elements of the situation and fragments of situated plans in memory. The restriction of correspondence was maintained from a tight interaction of current circumstances and memory from the perspective of a given situated plan.

In the direction of memory-to-world, the situated plan pre-selects elements of the situation. The situation of engagement potentially provides an infinite number of features from which to select. Memory serves the function of helping the agent to select the relevant feature of the situation. In the direction of world-to-memory the world helps to control retrieval in situated plan memory and explanation in semantic memory. There are several sorts of information to aid in the matching/interpretive process. The planner has access to various observable features in the situation and can copy the actions of other agents. In many cases, instructions are available in the situation of engagement.

Top-Level Control

PLEXUS used the partonomic structure of a plan concept to aid in determining the piece of the network which needs

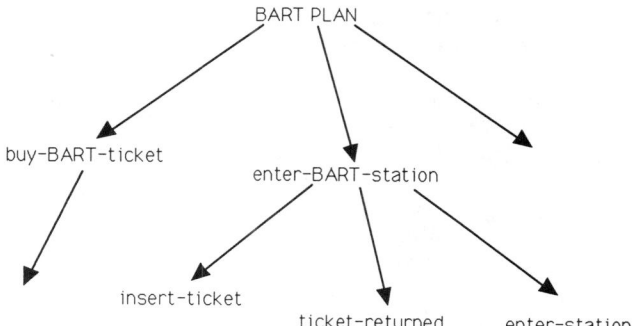

Figure 1. A portion of the partonomic structure of the BART Plan.

to be refitted in a given situation. The partonomic structure of a situated plan is essentially an AND-TREE of steps. Figure 1 shows a part of the AND-TREE for the BART plan. Given the situation-of-engagement, PLEXUS interpreted the circumstances from the perspective of the AND-TREE. It stepped through the situated plan in a recursive-descent left-to-right fashion.

Each node in the partonomic structure of a plan is visited twice. If a step is an action, the ongoing representation that is being constructed is checked both before and after the action is taken. If the step is a composite action, it is visited immediately before any of the component actions are taken, and immediately after all of them are taken. In all cases, if there is a discrepancy between the current representation of the situation and the world (immediate circumstances), adaptations are made.

If a step in a plan cannot be adjusted, then PLEXUS can recursively abandon the step of which the current plan/step/concept is a component. So if PLEXUS is unable to adapt the "buy BART ticket" step of the BART plan, it can abandon the BART plan as a basis of action and select an alternate plan out of the "intercity mass transit" category.

Core Matcher: Adapting the Representation

The top-level control localizes the piece of representation/plan that needs to be adjusted. The core matcher finds an alternate description of the situation from semantic memory that better matches the circumstances and results in a routine that will accomplish the agent's current goal(s).

PLEXUS adapts a step by staying within the categorization hierarchy related to the purpose of that step. (PLEXUS works from pre-existing categorization hierarchies. In Zito-Wolf and Alterman (1990), SCAVENGER, the adaptive planner for FLOABN, develops a mechanism that creates ad hoc categories (Barsalou, 1983) as a function of the situation of engagement.) A category of concepts can be modelled by a set of necessary and sufficient conditions for category membership (the classic view) (Smith and Medin, 1981); or by summary of the concept (the probabilistic view) (ibid); or by a cluster of generalizations (radial category structure) (Lakoff, 1987). Features associated with a given category/concept can be rated for typicality. Membership within a category is graded (prototype effects) (Rosch and Mervis, 1975; Rosch, 1978). A concept can be characterized by at least three levels of category structure: superordinate, ordinate, and subordinate. For example, at the superordinate level, there is the concept "furniture"; at the ordinate level is a concept such as "chair"; and at the subordinate, a "kitchen stool". More developed categories can have more than three levels of category structure. At the superordinate level a few abstract features of the category are captured. At the ordinate level, the greatest number of shared features exist. At the subordinate level, the members of the category are maximally differentiated. What counts for similarity and coherence within the category depends on an implicit background theory (Murphy and Medin, 1985). The relationships between features in the category can be represented using structured object representations (Cohen and Murphy, 1984; cf Bobrow and Winograd, 1977; Minsky, 1975).

PLEXUS assumes the same sort of principles of category structure at work for defining plan and action concepts. At the superordinate level, PLEXUS might have an abstract functional notion like "permitted entry"; at the ordinate level, "buying tickets"; and the subordinate level, a set of situated plans, eg "buying a BART ticket" or "buying a movie ticket". PLEXUS uses a semantic network to represent relations between both concepts and features of the concept. It reasons about the category as a whole from the perspective of a given subcategory [see Rosch (1981) on reference point reasoning; Lakoff (1987) on metonymic reasoning]. When the notion of "buying a BART ticket" breaks down at the NYC subway station because there is no ticket machine, PLEXUS attempts to find an alternate subcategory (reference point) in the category of "ticket buying" in order to continue action, eg "buy movie ticket". PLEXUS preferred working from reference points because they are customized and contextualized plan/representations; due to the habitual nature of commonsense planning situation, PLEXUS was biased towards the continuation and slow transformation of old routines/practices.

Extracting the Features in Common. Within a category, PLEXUS determines the features in common between the old plan step and the new situation by a process of abstraction within category structure. By staying within concept defining category hierarchies, PLEXUS attempts to mitigate the propagated effects of changes by maintaining its current sense of what is the appropriate interpretation of the agent's course of action. During abstraction, PLEXUS moved up the categorization hierarchy, removing the representational details from the step of the pre-stored plan that made it inappropriate in the current context. Effectively, the movement of abstraction is generating a representation of the generalization which holds between the pre-stored plan/concept and the new situation given that a difference has occurred. PLEXUS incrementally moves up the categorization hierarchy; at each level it looks for a specialization that results in a concept/routine that will describe, and work in, the current circumstances. If it fails to find such a routine it moves up the next level in the hierarchy.

A given plan/step/concept can be a member of more than one category. Consider the routine for "buying a

BART ticket": This routine could be a member of the category of plans for "buying tickets" or/and a member of the category of "transactions involving machines". A second in this latter category might be using an ATM machine. In general, PLEXUS uses two techniques for selecting a categorization hierarchy to ascend.

From Circumstance-to-Memory. If a plan is failing due to the existence of a particular feature of a plan, move to the point in the abstraction hierarchy from which that feature was inherited.

From Memory-to-Circumstance. Ascend the abstraction hierarchy that maintains the function (purpose relation) of the step in the plan that is being refitted.

The first technique applies in situations where there is a specific feature in the pre-stored plan that does not exist in the current situation. In the case of buying a ticket at the NYC subway, the missing feature is the "ticket machine" which rules out the category of "transaction involving machine". The first technique would also apply if the NYC subway station had a ticket machine, if it worked more like, for example, an Automatic Teller Machine. The second technique is used by PLEXUS as the default technique under circumstances where there is no readily identifiable feature which has to be removed.

Find a Situated Plan/Concept Within Category. PLEXUS moves from a more abstract plan notion/concept/representation toward more specific notion/representation/routines via the process of specialization. PLEXUS descends the classification hierarchy one step at a time. PLEXUS tests the applicability of a specialization by checking the before-appropriacy conditions; if one of these conditions fails, the movement is rejected. At each point in the hierarchy PLEXUS is faced with one of five options:

1. Is the plan sufficiently detailed to act on?
2. Is there a feature suggested by the type of situation difference which cross-indexes some subcategory of the current category of plan? (Δ circumstance and memory)
3. Is there an observable feature which cross-indexes some subcategory of the current category of plan? (From circumstance to memory or From memory to circumstance)
4. Is there an observable feature with an abstraction that cross-indexes a subcategory of the current category? (From circumstance to memory or From memory to circumstance)
5. Is there a salient subcategory? (From memory to circumstance)

PLEXUS stops descending the categorization hierarchy when it gets to a leaf node (option 1). If the node is not a leaf, it continues to descend (options 2–5). Sometimes the type of situation difference suggests cues for subcategory selections (option 2). Sometimes observable features act as cues for subcategory selection (options 3–4). Observable features can either be accidentally discovered, from circumstance to memory, or can be actively searched for, from memory to circumstance. For example, the ticket booth at the NYC subway station could have been accidentally discovered or the planner could have formed the expectation that such a place would exist. Observable features either directly cross-index some subcategory of plan (option 3), or have an abstraction which cross-indexes a subcategory of plan (option 4). Certain subcategories are salient regardless of context and can always be selected (option 5).

Hierarchical Planners. The usage of abstraction and specialization relates PLEXUS to a family of planners that are referred to as hierarchical planners (eg, Sacerdoti, 1974). A hierarchical planner forms an abstract plan which it then proceeds to refine in an attempt to plan for a given goal. A key issue for hierarchical planners is the ordering of (sub)goals. Unlike hierarchical planner PLEXUS begins with a detailed, or routine, plan. PLEXUS substitutes action and the immediate circumstances of action for critics of the structure of the plan. Rather than planning by reasoning about the internal structure, eg, the goal dependencies of the plan, PLEXUS primarily plans by attempting to locate a practice in semantic memory that makes sense of the situation to which it is engaged. For an adaptive planner, abstraction and specialization occur within concept-defining categorization hierarchies embedded within semantic memory; it is a semantic process. It is because abstraction and specialization are occurring as a semantic process that instruction usage becomes possible.

Consider what it would entail to convert the standard block-stacking problems into an adaptive planning problem. It would be necessary to represent the set of concepts and practices as in the Sussman Anomaly (1975) shared by the community of researchers working on such problems. The planner would need to assume that the solution to the problem is a minor variation of some problem/solution it already knows. Another working assumption would be that the problem creator intends to communicate to the problem-solver the significant concepts of the problem/solution. The task would have to be situated within the discourse of block stacking problems. Finally, in order to insure performance on the part of the planner, the laboratory setting would have to include various cues/clues/affordances and/or instructions to aid it in discovering a solution to the problem. One might exclaim that this reduces the problem in a manner that makes it uninteresting for a heuristic-search based planner, but in the world that most human planners confront on a daily basis, this is exactly the sort of conditions under which planning and acting occur.

Tactics Derived from the Types of Situation Difference

GPS (Newell & Simon, 1963) was based on a notion of difference between problem states. The basic idea of the means-end analysis was to select an operator that reduced the difference between two problem states in a search space. In the case of adaptive planning, there are differences, but not between problem states; rather there are differences between the pre-stored representation of the

situated plan/step/concept and the planner's current circumstances. This second sort of difference is referred to as a situation difference. In the case of PLEXUS, such differences focus the planner on features of its current circumstances and a set of tactical strategies for adjusting the match between the pre-stored representation of the situation of engagement, which is provided by the situated plan, and the actual situation of engagement. These tactics work to set up one or another probe into memory and can be roughly divided into two groups: those used before a step is performed and those used after the step is performed.

Before the Step is Performed. Before a step in a plan is acted on, the preconditions and goals of pre-stored plan/representation are matched against the situation of engagement. A failing precondition represents a feature that must be removed from the planner's representation of the situation of engagement. The to-be-deleted feature is a circumstance-to-memory cue.

Substitute a New Step. It might be the case that in the given circumstances, practice is such that this step in the plan is done in an alternate fashion, in which case the probe to memory is: Is there an alternate version of this step that does not require this feature?

Re-Order the Steps. Alternately, practices in the given circumstances are such that order of steps in the routine are different. To establish that such an interpretation is possible, PLEXUS checks: Are the conditions such that another step in the plan can be performed? If such an interpretation is possible, PLEXUS probes memory looking for an alternate interpretation of the (sub)plan in which the failing step is embedded which obeys the new ordering constraint provided by the circumstances. PLEXUS can use the new ordering constraint as an index for specialization purposes.

The problem of goal (step) ordering is one of the traditional problems of the artificial intelligence planning community. In one approach (linear assumption), the planner commits itself to any ordering of actions, and if difficulties arise due to subgoal interactions, it makes the appropriate changes (Sussman, 1975). A second approach (least commitment) (Sacerdoti, 1974) is to make a commitment to an ordering only when necessary. A third approach (opportunism) (Hayes-Roth and Hayes-Roth, 1979; Birnbaum, 1986; Hammond, 1989) is to perform a given step when convenient. Adaptive planning offers another approach to this problem: selecting an old ordering. The set of practices available to a commonsense planner, in effect, offers a short list of possible orderings. Encoded in each practice are sequencing considerations, many of which, unbeknownst to the reasoner, are dictated by causal factors and logical constraints. Thus, a good heuristic for domains of habitual activity is to select, or reselect, orderings from the short list.

Delete the Step. Alternately, it might be possible to interpret the practice of the current circumstances such that this step is not required at all. PLEXUS probes memory to see if there is an alternate interpretation of practice that does not require this step: Is there an interpretation of the (sub)plan this step is embedded in that can be made that deletes this step? The to-be-deleted step acts as a circumstance-to-memory cue. If it is unable to make such an interpretation, PLEXUS attempts to re-interpret the steps dependent on this step in a manner that makes the outcomes of this step unnecessary. This is treated as a case of failing outcome, which is discussed below.

Different Goals. Sometimes the observed feature of difference is internal as in the case where the planner's goals have changed. For this kind of situation difference, PLEXUS removes from the match those goals which are no longer operative and adds to the match those goals that are newly operative. In either case the different constellation of goals act as a circumstance-to-memory cue.

After the Step is Taken. After applying a plan (step), PLEXUS can discover that one of the expected outcomes of that plan was not achieved. PLEXUS determines if the failed outcome is needed. It uses the reason relation to determine the other steps of the plan which are effected by the failed outcome. For each of these effective steps it must use the core matching process to see if it can determine alternate interpretations of these steps in a manner consistent with failed outcomes. Here, the failed outcome feature is used as a circumstance-to-memory cue. During these probes to memory, PLEXUS is in projection mode (Wilensky, 1983), and it assumes, by default, that all of the conditions of the dependent steps are met except for the failed one. If the dependent steps can be re-interpreted, PLEXUS assumes that the failing outcome was not needed for the current practice. If the dependent steps cannot be re-interpreted, PLEXUS probes memory looking for an alternate version of the step with the failed outcome. In such a case the failed outcome is a circumstance-to-memory cue.

An example of the projection capacity occurs in the NYC subway station. At BART tickets are returned during entrance to be used later when it is time to exit the station. At the NYC subway station the token is not returned. PLEXUS assumes that the token is not available for exiting, the step dependent on the failed outcome. In PLEXUS' visual field is an exit turnstile that acts as a cue to forming an alternate interpretation of how exiting occurs. Thus PLEXUS is able to proceed.

FLOABN

Instructions

The prevalence of instructions is one piece of evidence that in many cases understanding occurs before action and is not merely imposed *post hoc*. In general, instructions can convey a variety of information to a planner, ranging from short fixes to a given plan (imagine encountering a detour sign on the road to the specification of an entirely new plan (eg, instructions for assembling a piece of furniture). Instances in which reading instructions aids the construction of a new plan include reading manuals,

learning a new game, and following instructions for the use of mechanical and electronic devices. In all of these cases, the instructions are not serving as a device to educate, but rather as additional features of the situation used by the agent to interpret the circumstances.

Instructions are difficult to understand in the abstract because they are schematic. Most instructions, written or verbal, omit an enormous amount of presumably shared detail, but since the planner shares general background and an understanding of the situation up to that point, it can fill them in itself. Outside of the context of use, the planner can grasp only the general sense of what the instructions mean and the operations they depict.

Adaptive planner affords an ideal environment for using instructions. FLOABN, as an adaptive planner, does not plan primarily from the instructions (although it might skim them first); it begins by engaging in the activity. When a situation arises to which it cannot adapt, FLOABN refers to the instructions. The situation of difficulty provides a context, a backdrop, against which the instructions can be made concrete. FLOABN initially makes sense of the instructions by establishing their coherence and relation to the ongoing activity. It then proceduralizes that interpretation, converting a known routine in a manner consistent with the instructions. Failures in interpretation can be further adapted as action proceeds. For further details on instruction usage see Alterman, Zito-Wolf, Carpenter (1991).

Learning

The stream of constructed representations and generalizations produced by an adaptive planner provides a basis for learning. As a learner, the bias of an adaptive planner is towards the continuation of old routine and their transformation slowly, but continuously, over time. Plan knowledge, its organization and semantics, is steadily and incrementally changing. Although at any given point in time the routines appear to be settled, the flux of experience and circumstance causes an adaptive planner to continually refine, and reinterpret, its knowledge. Learning consists of the accumulation of detailed experience that can be adapted to future situations.

SCAVENGER, the planner in FLOABN, combines an adaptive planner with a learner. Learning, planning, and action are integrated and distributed across many situations; every situation of engagement is an opportunity to learn. Two characteristics of the learning done by SCAVENGER are that it is *ad hoc* and it is fail-safe. Learning is *ad hoc* because because SCAVENGER does not set out to learn anything, yet it can learn any number of things either related or unrelated to the goal. The term fail-safe is used to suggest not infallibility, but rather that adaptation functions during execution, compensating for imperfections and omissions in learning, and insulating the learner from small variations across otherwise similar situations.

SCAVENGER actually does two kinds of learning. The bulk of learning done by SCAVENGER is the constant mutation of known routines/concepts/practices. In part these mutations are extending plans to cope with new contingencies that may arise and tease out descriptions of situations to which a given plan pertains. In part, the mutations result in the dynamic re-organization of memory through the accumulation of generalizations (See DYNAMIC MEMORY) (Schank, 1982; cf Kolodner, 1983a; Lebowitz, 1983). SCAVENGER also is capable of seeding memory by inventing synthetic concepts (Kant, 1965). For further details, see Zito-Wolf and Alterman (1990).

BIBLIOGRAPHY

P. E. Agre and D. Chapman, "Pengi: An Implementation of a Theory of Activity," *Proceedings of the Sixth National Conference on Artificial Intelligence*, AAAI, Menlo Park, Calif., 1987, pp. 268–272.

R. Alterman, "A Dictionary Based on Concept Coherence," *Artif. Intell.* **25**, 153–186 (1985).

R. Alterman, "Summarization in the Small," in Noel Sharkey, ed., *Advances in Cognitive Science*, Ellis Horwood, 1986, pp. 72–93.

R. Alterman, "The Operational Level of a Commonsense Planner," in *Proceedings of the Cognition Science Society*, 1987, pp. 623–631.

R. Alterman, "Adaptive Planning," *Cog. Sci.* **12**, 393–421 (1988).

R. Alterman and R. Zito-Wolf, "Planning and Understanding: Revisited," *Proceedings of 1990 AAAI Spring Symposium*, 1990.

R. Alterman, T. Carpenter, and R. Zito-Wolf, "An Architecture for Understanding in Planning, Action, and Learning," *SIGART J.*, in press.

L. W. Barsalou, "Ad Hoc Categories," *Mem. and Cognit.* 11(3), 211–227 (1983).

L. Birnbaum, "*Integrated Processes in Planning and Understanding*," Technical report CSD/RR 489, Yale University, 1986.

D. Bobrow and T. Winograd, *An Overview of KRL, A Knowledge Representation Language*, 1977.

R. A. Brooks, "*A Robust Layered Control System for a Mobile Robot*," Technical report AI Memo 864, MIT Artificial Intelligence Laboratory, 1985.

J. Carbonell, "Politics: Automated Ideological Reasoning," *Cog. Sci.* **1**, 27–51 (1978).

J. Carbonell, "Derivational Analogy and Its Role in Problem Solving," *Proceedings of the Third National Conference on Artificial Intelligence*, AAAI, Menlo Park, Calif., 1983.

B. Cohen and G. Murphy, "Models of Concepts," *Cog. Sci.* **8**, 27–58 (1984).

P. Cohen, C. Perrault, and J. Allen, "Beyond Question-Answering," Technical report 4644, Bolt Beranek and Newman, 1981.

R. J. Firby, "An Investigation Into Reactive Planning in Complex Domains," *Proceedings of the Sixth National Conference on Artificial Intelligence*, AAAI, Menlo Park, Calif., 1987, pp. 202–206.

M. P. Georgeff and A. K. Lansky, "Reactive Reasoning and Planning," *Proceedings of the Sixth National Conference on Artificial Intelligence*, AAAI, Menlo Park, Calif., 1987, pp. 677–682.

K. J. Hammond, "CHEF: A Model of Case-Based Planning," *Fifth National Conference on Artificial Intelligence*, 1986, pp. 267–271.

K. J. Hammond, "Opportunistic Memory," *Proceedings of the Eleventh International Joint Conferences on Artificial Intelligence*, Morgan-Kaufmann, San Mateo, Calif., 1989, pp. 504–510.

B. Hayes-Roth and F. Hayes-Roth, "A Cognitive Model of Planning," *Cog. Sci.* 275–310 (1979).

J. Hendler, *Integrating Marker-Passing and Problem-Solving: A Spreading Activation Approach to Improved Choice in Planning*. Ph.D. dissertation, Brown University, Providence, R.I., 1986.

L. P. Kaelbling, "An Architecture for Intelligent Reactive Systems," *Reasoning About Actions and Plans: Proceedings of the 1986 Conference*, Morgan-Kaufmann, Los Altos, Calif., 1987.

S. Kambhampati and J. A. Hendler, "Control of Refitting Furing Plan Reuse," *Proceedings of Eleventh International Joint Conferences on Artificial Intelligence*, Morgan-Kaufmann, San Mateo, Calif., 1989, pp. 943–948.

Emanuel Kant, *Critique of Pure Reason*, St. Martin's Press, New York, 1965. Trans. Norman Kemp Smith.

J. L. Kolodner, "Maintaining Organization in a Dynamic Long-term Memory," *Cog. Sci.* **7**, 243–280 (1983).

J. L. Kolodner, "Reconstructive Memory, a Computer Model," *Cog. Sci.* **7**, 281–328 (1983).

J. Kolodner, R. Simpson, and K. Sycara-Cyranski, "A Process Model of Case-based Reasoning in Problem Solving," *Proceedings of the Ninth International Joint Conferences on Artificial Intelligence*, Los Angeles, Morgan-Kaufmann, San Mateo, Calif., 1985, pp. 284–290.

J. L. Kolodner and R. L. Simpson, "The MEDIATOR: Analysis of an Early Case-Based Problem Solver," *Cog. Sci.* **13**, 507–549 (1989).

G. Lakoff, *Women, Fire, and Dangerous Things*, University of Chicago Press, 1987.

J. Lave, *Cognition and Practice*, Cambridge University Press, Cambridge, UK, 1975.

M. Lebowitz, "Generalization from Natural Language Text," *Cog. Sci.* **7**, 1–40 (1983).

D. McDermott, "Planning and Acting," *Cog. Sci.* **2**, 71–109 (1978).

M. Minsky, "A Framework for Representing Knowledge," in P. W. Winston, ed., *The Psychology of Computer Vision*, McGraw-Hill, New York, 1975, pp. 211–277.

D. J. Mostow, "Machine Transformation of Advice Into Heuristic Search Procedure," In R. Michalski, J. Carbonell, and T. Mitchell, eds., *Machine Learning, Volume 1*, Tioga Publishing Company, Palo Alto, Calif., 1983, pp. 367–403.

G. Murphy and D. Medin, "The Role of Theories in Conceptual Coherence," *Psychol. Rev.* **92**, 289–316 (1985).

A. Newell and H. A. Simon, "GPS: A Program That Simulates Human Thought," in E. A. Feigenbaum and J. Feldman, eds., *Computers and Thought*, McGraw-Hill, New York, 1963, pp. 279–293.

E. Rissland and K. Ashley, "Hypotheticals as Heuristic Device," *Proceedings of the Fifth National Conference on Artificial Intelligence*, AAAI, Menlo Park, Calif., 1986.

E. Rosch and C. B. Mervis, "Family Resemblances: Studies in the Internal Structure of Categories," *Cog. Psychol.* **7**, 573–605 (1975).

E. Rosch, "Principles of Categorization," *Cognition and Categorization*, Lawrence Erlbaum Associates, Hillsdale, N.J., 1978.

E. Rosch, "Prototype Classification and Logical Classification: The Two Systems," paper presented at a meeting of the Jean Piaget Society, Philadelphia, 1981.

D. E. Rumelhart, "Schemata: The Building Blocks of Cognition," in R. Sprio, B. Bruce, and W. Brewer, eds., *Theoretical Issues in Reading Comprehension*, Lawrence Erlbaum, Hillsdale, N.J., 1980.

E. Sacerdoti, "Planning in a Hierarchy of Abstraction Spaces," *Artif. Intell.* **5**, 115–135 (1974).

R. Schank, "The Structure of Episodes in Memory," in D. Bobrow and A. Collins, eds., *Representation and Understanding*, Academic Press, New York, 1975, pp. 237–272.

R. Schank and R. Abelson, *Scripts, Plans, Goals, and Understanding*, Lawrence Erlbaum Associates, Hillsdale, N.J., 1977.

R. Schank, *Dynamic Memory*. Cambridge University Press, 1982.

M. J. Schoppers, "Universal Plans for Reactive Robots in Unpredictable Environments," *Proceedings of the Sixth International Joint Conferences on Artificial Intelligence*, Morgan-Kaufmann, San Mateo, Calif., 1987, pp. 1039–1046.

J. Shrager, "Theory Change Via View Application in Instructionless Learning," *Mach. Learning* **2**, 247–276 (1987).

R. F. Simmons, "Semantic Networks: Their Computation and Use For Understanding English Sentences," R. C. Schank and K. M. Colby, eds., *Computer Models of Thought and Language*, W. H. Freeman and Company, San Francisco, Calif., 1973.

E. Smith and D. Medin, *Categories and Concepts*, Harvard University Press, Cambridge, Mass., 1981.

L. A. Suchman, *Plans and Situated Actions*, Cambridge University Press, 1987.

G. Sussman, *A Computational Model of Skill Acquisition*, Elsevier, New York, 1975.

B. Tversky and K. Hemenway, "Objects, Parts and Categories," *J. Exp. Psychol.: General* **113**, 170–193 (1984).

K. VanLehn, "Problem Solving and Cognitive Skill Acquisition," in M. Posner, ed., *Foundations of Cognitive Science*, Bradford Books, MIT Press, Cambridge, Mass., 1989, pp. 527–580.

R. Wilensky, "Meta-Planning: Representing and Using Knowledge About Planning in Problem Solving and Natural Language Understanding," *Cog. Sci.* **5**, 197–233 (1981).

R. Wilensky, *Planning and Understanding*, Addison-Wesley, 1983.

D. E. Wilkins, *Practical Planning: Extending the Classical AI Planning Paradigm*, Morgan-Kaufmann, San Mateo, Calif., 1988.

M. Winston, R. Chaffin, and D. Herrimann, "A Taxonomy of Part-whole Relations," *Cog. Sci.* **11**, 417–444 (1987).

R. Zito-Wolf and R. Alterman, "Ad Hoc Fail-Safe Plan Learning," *Proceedings of the 1990 Cognitive Science Conference*, 1990.

RICHARD ALTERMAN
Brandeis University

This work was supported in part by the Defense Advanced Research Projects Agency, administered by the U.S. Airforce Office of Scientific Research under contract #F49620-88-C-0058.

ADAPTIVE RESONANCE THEORY

Adaptive resonance theory (ART) was introduced in 1976 (Grossberg, 1976a, 1976b) in order to analyze how brain networks can learn sensory and cognitive recognition codes in a stable fashion in response to arbitrary sequences of input patterns presented under real-time con-

ditions. ART networks are at present the only computationally realized biological theory that analyze how fast, yet stable real-time learning of recognition codes can be accomplished in response to an arbitrary stream of input patterns. Such a general-purpose ability is needed by any autonomous agent in order to successfully learn about unexpected events in an unpredictable environment. One cannot restrict the agent's processing capability if one cannot predict the environment in which it must function. Other learning theories lack one or more of the essential properties needed for autonomous learning under real-time conditions (Table 1). Note that the term "real time" here refers to a neural network model that requires no external control of system dynamics. "Real time" can also be used more generally to describe any system that is able to process inputs as fast as they arrive.)

The ability of ART networks to carry out fast stable real-time learning is derived from their incorporation of architectural elements that have been derived from a behavioral and neural analysis of human and mammalian learning data (Grossberg, 1982, 1987, 1988) and a mathematical and computational analysis of how to design networks that rigorously implement these biological heuristics (Carpenter and Grossberg, 1987a, 1987b, 1988, 1990). Such an interdisciplinary analysis has required that ART architectures be simultaneously developed to realize both macroscopic design principles and microscopic mechanistic constraints. Correspondingly, the data explanations and predictions of the theory have ranged from microscopic neurobiological assertions about membrane and neurotransmitter dynamics to more macroscopic network assertions about resonance, attention, and learning, to still more macroscopic assertions about uncertainty principles and complementarity principles that bind together network subsystems into a total architectural design.

COMPARISON WITH ALTERNATIVE LEARNING SCHEMES

Many computational details have been worked out to make the ART process work well in an autonomous setting. Before outlining some of these details, this article will first describe how ART architectures differ from other popular neural network learning schemes, such as autoassociators, the Boltzmann machine, and backpropagation (Ackley and co-workers, 1985; Kohonen, 1984; Rumelhart and co-workers, 1986) in a number of basic ways, as schematized in Table 1.

The most robust differences are that an ART architecture is designed to learn quickly and stably in real time in response to a possibly nonstationary world with an unlimited number of inputs until it utilizes its full memory capacity. Many alternative learning schemes become unstable unless they learn slowly in a controlled stationary environment with a carefully selected total number of inputs and do not use their full memory capacity. For example, a learning system that is not self-stabilizing experiences a capacity catastrophe in response to an unlimited number of inputs: new learning washes away memories of prior learning if too many inputs perturb the system. To prevent this from happening, either the total number of

Table 1. A Comparison of ART Architecture and Other Popular Neural Network Learning Schemes

ART Architecture	Alternative Learning Properties
Real-time (on-line) learning	Laboratory-time (off-line) learning
Nonstationary world	Stationary world
Self-organizing (unsupervised)	Teacher supplies correct answer (supervised)
Memory self-stabilizes in response to arbitrarily many inputs	Capacity catastrophe in response to arbitrarily many inputs
Effective use of full memory capacity	Can use only partial memory capacity
Maintain plasticity in an unexpected world	Externally shut off plasticity to prevent capacity catastrophe
Learn internal top-down expectations	Externally impose costs
Active attentional focus regulates learning	Passive learning
Slow or fast learning	Slow learning or oscillation catastrophe
Learn in approximate-match phase	Learn in mismatch phase
Use self-regulating hypothesis testing to globally reorganize the energy landscape	Use noise to perturb system out of local minima in a fixed energy landscape
Fast adaptive search for best match	Search tree
Rapid direct access to codes of familiar events	Recognition time increases with code complexity
Variable error criterion (vigilance parameter) sets coarseness of recognition code in response to environmental feedback	Fixed-error criterion in response to environmental feedback
All properties scale to arbitrarily large system capacities	Key properties deteriorate as system capacity is increased

input patterns that perturbs the system needs to be restricted, or the learning process itself must be shut off before the capacity catastrophe occurs.

Shutting off the world is not possible in many applications. In particular, how does such a system subsequently allow a familiar input to be processed and recognized but block the processing of a novel input pattern before it can destabilize its prior learning? In the absence of a self-stabilization mechanism, an external teacher must act as the system's front end to independently recognize the inputs and make the decision. Shutting off learning at just the right time to prevent the occurrence of either a capacity catastrophe or a premature termination of learning would also require an external teacher. In either case the external teacher must be able to carry out the recognition tasks that the learning system was supposed to carry out. Hence, non-self-stabilizing learning systems are not capable of functioning autonomously in ill-controlled environments.

In learning systems wherein an external teacher is needed to supply the correct representation to be learned, the learning process is often driven by mismatch between desired and actual outputs. Such schemes must learn slowly, and in a stationary environment, or else risk unstable oscillations in response to the mismatches. They can also be destabilized if the external teaching signal is noisy, because such noise creates spurious mismatches. These learning models are also prone to getting trapped in local minima, or globally incorrect solutions. Models such as simulated annealing and the Boltzmann machine use internal system noise to escape local minima and to thereby approach a more global minimum. An externally controlled (temperature) parameter regulates this process as it is made to converge more slowly to a critical value. In ART, by contrast, approximate matches, rather than mismatches, drive the learning process. Learning in the approximate match mode enables rapid and stable learning to occur while buffering the system's memory against external noise. A hypothesis testing cycle replaces internal system noise as a scheme for discovering a globally correct solution, and does not utilize an externally controlled temperature parameter or teacher.

CONTROL OF DISTRIBUTED HYPOTHESIS TESTING

This article outlines neural network designs that control local cellular properties, such as transmitter dynamics, to achieve global network properties, such as resonance, attention, and learning. In particular, model mechanisms capable of implementing parallel search of compressed or distributed recognition codes in a neural network hierarchy are summarized. The search process is a form of hypothesis testing capable of discovering appropriate representations of a nonstationary input environment. The search process functions well with either fast or slow learning, and can robustly cope with sequences of asynchronous input patterns in real time. Such a search process emerges when computational properties of short-term memory (STM), medium-term memory (MTM), and long-term memory (LTM) are suitably organized. STM concerns cell activations, LTM concerns changes due to learning in adaptive weights, and MTM concerns the dynamics of chemical transmitters at the synapse, including the processes of release, inactivation, and modulation.

CONTROL OF RECOGNITION AND SEARCH

In terms of its functional properties, ART was derived from an analysis of the instabilities inherent in feed-forward adaptive coding structures (Grossberg, 1976a, 1976b). More recent work has led to the development of three classes of ART neural network architectures, specified as systems of differential equations. The first class, ART 1, self-organizes recognition categories for arbitrary sequences of binary input patterns (Carpenter and Grossberg, 1987a). A second class, ART 2, does the same for either binary or analog inputs (Carpenter and Grossberg, 1987b).

When MTM processes are embedded within an ART architecture, called ART 3, useful search properties emerge (Carpenter and Grossberg, 1990). A key part of the search process utilizes formal analogs of synergetic interactions between ions such as Na^+ and Ca^{2+}, regulated by specific and nonspecific signal pathways. These interactions control a nonlinear feedback process that enables the spatial pattern of presynaptic MTM transmitters to model the spatial pattern of postsynaptic STM activation that constitutes the recognition code. If activation of the recognition code leads to a predictive failure that causes a reset event, the postsynaptic STM activation pattern is restored to its equilibrium values, but the presynaptic MTM transmitter pattern remains unchanged. The hypothesis or recognition code that is next selected is thereby biased against those features that were most responsible for the predictive failure. When no reset event follows such a hypothesis, the network's STM patterns become resonant and generate a focus of attention that selectively drives learned changes in the LTM traces that support the resonance.

Both ART 1 and ART 2 use a maximally compressed, or choice, pattern recognition code. Such a code is a limiting case of the partially compressed recognition codes. Partially compressed recognition codes have been mathematically analyzed in models for competitive learning, also called self-organizing feature maps, which are incorporated into ART models as part of their bottom-up dynamics (Grossberg, 1978, 1982; Kohonen, 1984). Indeed, the coding instabilities of self-organizing feature maps, whether compressed or distributed, led to the introduction of ART in 1976. The basic equations and main computational properties of these models had by then been described by Grossberg (1972, 1976a, 1978a, 1978b) and Malsburg (1973; Willshaw and Malsburg, 1976) and were followed by applications and expositions of Kohonen (1984). The name "GKM model" may thus be used to summarize this historical development.

Maximally compressed, or winner-take-all, codes were used in ART 1 and ART 2 to enable a rigorous analysis to be made of how the bottom-up and top-down dynamics of ART systems can be joined together in a real-time self-organizing system capable of learning a stable pattern recognition code in response to an arbitrary sequence of input patterns. These results provide a computational foundation for designing ART systems capable of stably learning partially compressed recognition codes.

The main elements of a typical ART 1 module are illustrated in Figure 1. F_1 and F_2 are fields of network nodes. An input is initially represented as a pattern of activity across the nodes, or feature detectors, of field F_1. The pattern of activity across F_2 corresponds to the category rep-

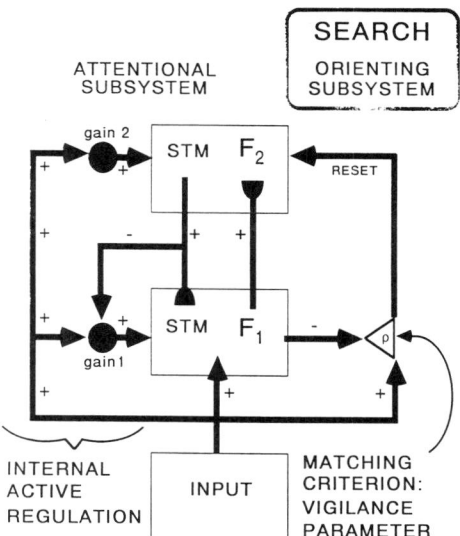

Figure 1. Typical ART 1 neural network module (Carpenter and Grossberg, 1978a).

resentation. The two fields, linked both bottom-up and top-down by adaptive filters, constitute the attentional subsystem. An auxiliary orienting subsystem becomes active during search.

AN ART SEARCH CYCLE

Figure 2 illustrates a typical ART search cycle. An input pattern I registers itself as a pattern X of activity across F_1 (Fig. 2a). The F_1 output signal vector S is then transmitted through the multiple converging and diverging pathways emanating from F_1. In these pathways, vector S is multiplied by the matrix z of adaptive weights, sending a net input signal vector $T = zS$ to F_2. The internal competitive dynamics of F_2 contrast-enhance T. The F_2 activity vector Y therefore registers a compressed representation of the filtered $F_1 \rightarrow F_2$ input and corresponds, in the winner-take-all case, to a category representation for the input active at F_1. These are the standard operations of GKM models. In ART, vector Y generates a signal vector U that is sent top-down through the second adaptive filter, giving rise to a net top-down signal vector V to F_1 (Fig. 2b). F_1 now receives two input vectors, I and V. An ART system is designed to carry out a matching process whereby the original activity pattern X due to input pattern I may be modified by the template pattern V that is associated with the current active category. If I and V are not sufficiently similar according to a matching criterion established by a dimensionless vigilance parameter ρ, a reset signal quickly and enduringly shuts off the active category representation (Fig. 2c), allowing a new category to become active. Search ensues (Fig. 2d) until either an adequate match is made or a new category is established. The search process is not, however, exhaustive. Only those representations that are sufficiently similar to the input pattern are searched before a new representation is selected.

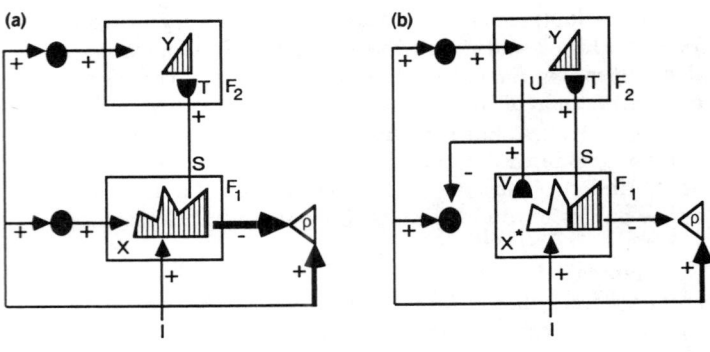

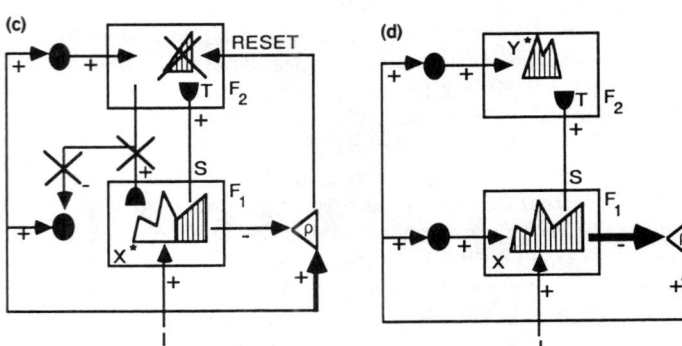

Figure 2. ART search cycle (Carpenter and Grossberg, 1987a).

ART RECOGNITION CATEGORIES

As a result of this search and learning cycle, ART systems establish recognition codes whose coarseness is scaled by the vigilance parameter. Figure 3 illustrates learning and categorization of 50 input patterns into 34 recognition categories at a higher level of vigilance. Learning stabilizes

after a single presentation of each input. Figure 4 shows categorization of the same inputs into 20 coarser recognition categories at a lower level of vigilance. The network contains another parameter, called the *quenching thresh-*

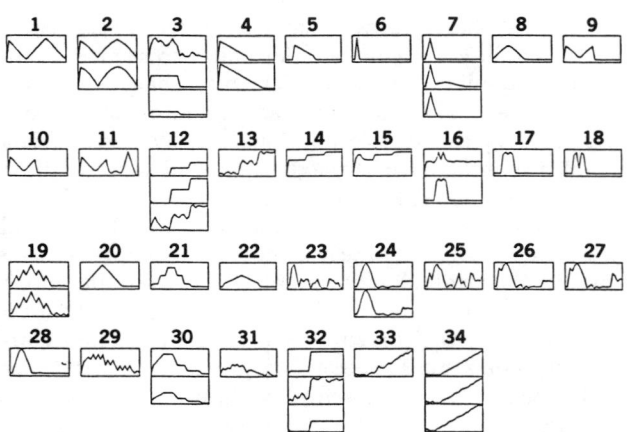

Figure 3. Category grouping of 50 analog input patterns into 34 recognition categories. Each input pattern I is depicted as a function of i ($i = 1 \ldots M$), with successive I_i values connected by straight lines. The category structure established on one complete presentation of the 50 inputs remains stable thereafter if the same inputs are presented again (Carpenter and Grossberg, 1987b).

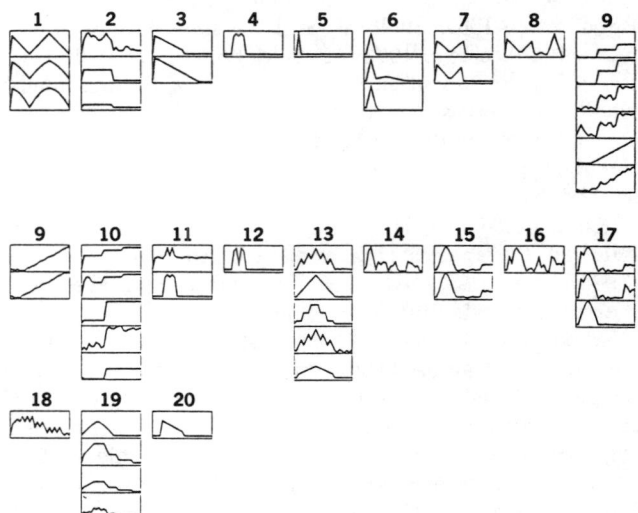

Figure 4. Lower vigilance implies coarser grouping. The same ART 2 system as used in Figure 3 has here grouped the same 50 inputs into 20 recognition categories. Note, for example, that categories 1 and 2 of Figure 3 are here joined in category 1; categories 14, 15, and 32 are here joined in category 10; and categories 19–22 are here joined in category 13 (Carpenter and Grossberg, 1987b).

old, that suppresses low amplitude activity before the contrast-enhanced and normalized activity pattern is classified. This operation helps to cope with background activity levels that carry no information. See, for example, the input exemplars that are classified together in Figure 4, categories 2, 9, and 17.

ART DESIGN PRINCIPLES

ART architectures are derived from analysis of design principles for neural networks that form stable recognition codes from arbitrary sequences of analog or binary input patterns. ART systems have been developed to satisfy the multiple design principles or processing constraints that give rise to the architectures' emergent properties. A number of variations on the ART architectures have been identified that are capable of satisfying these constraints. Indeed, the heart of the ART analysis consists of discovering how different combinations of network mechanisms work together to generate particular combinations of desirable emergent properties. That is why theoretical ablation experiments on ART architectures have proved to be so useful, since they reveal which emergent properties are spared and which are lost in reduced architectures. In each ART architecture, combinations of normalization, gain control, matching, and learning mechanisms are interwoven. The main ART design principles will now be described.

Stability–Plasticity Trade-off. An ART system needs to be able to learn a stable recognition code in response to an arbitrary sequence of analog or binary input patterns. Since the plasticity of an ART system is maintained for all time, and since input presentation times can be of arbitrary duration, STM processing is defined in such a way that a sustained new input pattern does not wash away previously learned information. Likewise, an input can be presented an arbitrary number of times in an arbitrary sequence. Removal, or ablation, of certain parts of an ART STM subsystem, such as its bottom-up self-organizing feature map, can lead to a type of instability in which a single input, embedded in a particular input sequence, can jump between categories indefinitely. The total architecture is designed so that this type of instability cannot occur.

Search–Direct-Access Trade-off. An ART system carries out a parallel search in order to regulate the selection of appropriate recognition codes during the learning process, yet automatically disengages the search process as an input pattern becomes familiar. Thereafter, the familiar input pattern directly accesses its recognition code no matter how complex the total learned recognition structure may have become, much as we can rapidly recognize our parents at different stages of our life even though we may continue to learn as we grow older.

Match–Reset Trade-off. An ART system needs to be able to resolve several potentially conflicting properties that can be formulated as variants of a design trade-off between the requirements of sensitive matching and for-

mation of new codes. The system should, on one hand, be able to recognize and react to arbitrarily small differences between an active F_1 STM pattern and the LTM pattern being read out from an established recognition code. In particular, if vigilance is high, the F_1 STM pattern established by a bottom-up input exemplar should be nearly identical to the learned top-down $F_2 \rightarrow F_1$ expectation pattern in order for the exemplar to be accepted as a member of an established category. On the other hand, when an uncommitted F_2 node becomes active for the first time, it should be able to remain active, without being reset, so that it can encode its first input exemplar, even though in this case there is no top-down/bottom-up pattern match whatsoever. A combination of an appropriately chosen ART reset rule and LTM initial values work together to satisfy both of these processing requirements. In fact, ART parameters can be chosen to satisfy the more general property that learning increases the system's sensitivity to mismatches between bottom-up and top-down patterns.

STM Invariance Under Read-Out of Matched LTM. Suppose that an active F_2 node has undergone no prior learning. On the node's first learning trial, its LTM traces will progressively learn the STM pattern that is generated at F_1. Such learning must not be allowed to cause a mismatch capable of resetting F_2, because the LTM traces have not previously learned any other pattern. This property is achieved by designing F_1 so that STM activity patterns are not changed at all by the read-out of these LTM traces as they learn their first pattern values. More generally, F_1 is designed so that read-out by F_2 of a previously learned LTM pattern that matches perfectly the STM pattern at F_1 does not change that STM pattern. Thus, in a perfect match situation, or in a situation where a new vector of LTM values learns a perfect match, the STM activity patterns are left invariant; hence, no reset occurs.

This invariance property enables F_1 to nonlinearly transform the input pattern in a manner that remains stable during learning. In particular, the input pattern may be contrast-enhanced while noise in the input is suppressed. If read-out of a top-down LTM pattern could change even the baseline of activation at the F_1 levels that execute this transformation, the degree of contrast enhancement and noise suppression could be altered, thereby generating a new STM pattern for learning by the top-down LTM traces. The STM invariance property prevents read-out of a perfectly matched LTM pattern from causing reset by preventing any change whatsoever from occurring in the STM patterning at the lower F_1 levels.

Coexistence of LTM Read-Out and STM Normalization. The STM invariance property leads to the use of an F_1 field consisting of multiple layers, in particular, three layers in ART 2 and ART 3. The top F_1 layer copes with the fact that the F_1 nodes at which top-down LTM readout occurs receive an additional input when both top-down and bottom-up signals are active as compared to when they are not. The top F_1 layer both reads out top-down LTM and normalizes the total STM pattern before this normalized STM pattern can interact with the middle F_1 layer at which top-down and bottom-up information is matched. In a similar fashion, the bottom F_1 layer enables an input pattern to be normalized before this normalized STM pattern can interact with the middle F_1 layer. Thus separate bottom and top F_1 layers provide enough degrees of computational freedom to compensate for fluctuations in total input levels. In the absence of such normalization, confusions between useful pattern differences and baseline fluctuations could easily upset the matching process and cause spurious reset events to occur, thereby destabilizing the network's search and learning processes.

No LTM Recoding by Superset Inputs. Although read-out of a top-down LTM pattern that perfectly matches the STM pattern at F_1's top layer never causes F_2 reset, even a very small mismatch in these patterns is sufficient to reset F_2 if the vigilance parameter is chosen sufficiently high. The middle F_1 layer plays a key role in controlling the attenuation of STM activity that causes such a reset event to occur. An important example of such a reset-inducing mismatch occurs when one or more, but not all, of the top-down LTM traces equal zero or very small values and the corresponding F_1 nodes have positive STM activities due to bottom-up activation. When this occurs, the STM activities of these F_1 nodes are suppressed. If the total STM suppression is sufficient to reset F_2, then the network searches for a better match. If the total STM suppression is not sufficient to reset F_2, then the top-down LTM traces of these nodes remain small during the ensuing learning trial, because they sample the small STM values that their own small LTM values have caused.

This property is a version of the 2/3 rule that has been used to prove stability of learning by an ART 1 architecture in response to an arbitrary sequence of binary input patterns. It also is necessary in order for ART to achieve stable learning in response to an arbitrary sequence of analog input patterns. In ART 1, this property was achieved by an intentional gain control channel. In the versions of ART 2 developed so far, it is realized as part of F_1's internal levels. These design variations are still a subject of ongoing research.

Stable Choice Until Reset. Match–reset trade-off also requires that only a reset event that is triggered by the orienting subsystem can cause a change in the chosen F_2 code. This property obtains at any degree of mismatch between a top-down $F_2 \rightarrow F_1$ LTM pattern and the circulating F_1 STM pattern. Thus all the network's real-time pattern processing operations, including top-down $F_2 \rightarrow F_1$ feedback, the fast nonlinear feedback dynamics within F_1, and the slow LTM changes during learning must be organized to maintain the original $F_1 \rightarrow F_2$ category choice, unless F_2 is actively reset by the orienting subsystem.

Contrast Enhancement, Noise Suppression, and Mismatch Attenuation by Nonlinear Signal Functions. A given class of analog signals may be embedded in variable levels of background noise. A combination of normalization and nonlinear feedback processes within F_1 determines a noise criterion that enables the system to separate signal from noise. In particular, these processes contrast-enhance the

F_1 STM pattern and suppress the activities that fall below the noise criterion. The degree of contrast enhancement and noise suppression is determined by the degree of nonlinearity in the feedback signal functions at F_1. The contrast-enhanced STM pattern is then read into LTM.

Rapid Self-Stabilization. A learning system that is unstable in general can be made more stable by making the learning rate so slow that LTM traces change little on a single input trial. In this case, many learning trials are needed to encode a fixed set of inputs. Learning in an ART system needs to be slow relative to the STM processing rate, but no restrictions are placed on absolute rates. Thus ART is capable of stable learning in the "fast learning" case, in which LTM traces change so quickly that they can approach new equilibrium values on every trial. Such fast learning can occur, for example, when we attend to an exciting movie. Self-stabilization is accelerated by the action of the orienting subsystem, but can also occur rapidly without it.

Normalization. Several different schemes may be used to normalize activation patterns across F_1. ART 2 and ART 3 use nonspecific inhibitory interneurons. Each such normalizer uses $O(M)$ connections, where M is the number of nodes to be normalized. Alternatively, a shunting on-center–off-surround network could be used as a normalizer, but such a network uses $O(M^2)$ connections.

Local Computations. ART system STM and LTM computations use only information available locally and in real time. There are no assumptions of weight transport, as in backpropagation, nor of an *a priori* input probability distribution, as in simulated annealing. Moreover, all ART 2 equations have a simple form. It is the architecture as a whole that endows the model with its desirable emergent computational properties.

ART 2: THREE-LAYER COMPETITIVE FIELDS

Figure 5 shows the principal elements of a typical ART 2 module. It shares many characteristics of the ART 1 module, having both an input representation field F_1 and a category representation field F_2, as well as attentional and orienting subsystems. Figure 5 also illustrates one of the main differences between the examples of ART 1 and ART 2 modules so far explicitly developed; namely, the ART 2 examples all have three processing layers within the F_1 field. These layers allow the ART 2 system to stably categorize sequences of analog input patterns that can, in general, be arbitrarily close to one another. Unlike models such as backpropagation, this category learning process is stable even in the fast learning situation, in which the LTM variables are allowed to go to equilibrium on each learning trial.

In Figure 5, one F_1 layer reads in the bottom-up input, one layer reads in the top-down filtered input from F_2, and a middle layer matches patterns from the top and bottom layers before sending a composite pattern back through the F_1 feedback loop. Both F_1 and F_2 are shunting competi-

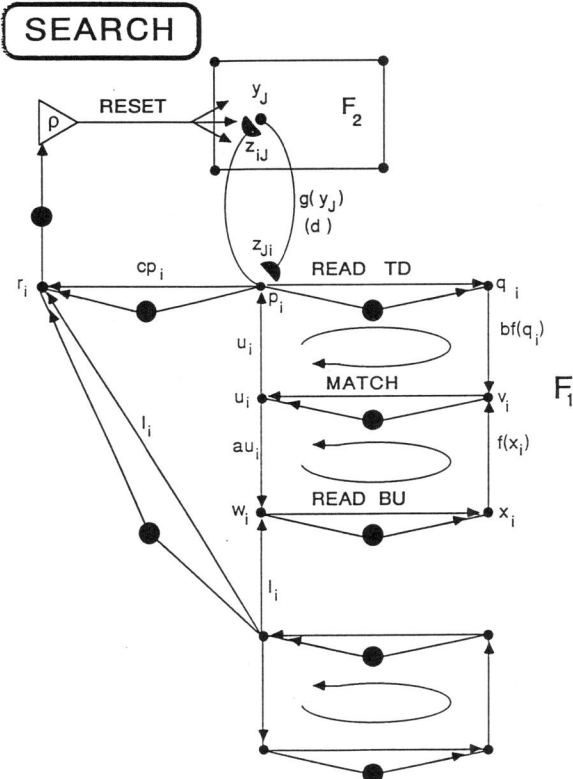

Figure 5. Typical ART 2 neural network module, with three-layer F_1 field (Carpenter and Grossberg, 1987b). Large filled circles are gain control nuclei that nonspecifically inhibit target nodes in proportion to the Euclidean norm of activity in their source fields.

tive networks that contrast-enhance and normalize their activation patterns.

ART HIERARCHIES

In many applications, ART modules are embedded in larger architectures that are hierarchically organized. When an ART module is embedded in a network hierarchy, it may no longer be possible to make a sharp distinction between the characteristics of the input representation field F_1 and the category representation field F_2. In order for them to serve both functions, the basic structures of all the network fields in a hierarchical ART system should be homologous. This constraint is satisfied if all fields of the hierarchy are endowed with the F_1 structure of an ART 2 module. Such a design is sufficient for the F_2 field as well as the F_1 field because the principal property required of a category representation field, namely, that input patterns be contrast-enhanced and normalized, is a property of the three-layer F_1 structure.

The problem of implementing hypothesis testing and parallel memory search among the distributed codes of a hierarchical ART system is now considered. Assume that a top-down–bottom-up mismatch has occurred somewhere in the system. How can a reset signal search the hierarchy

in such a way that an appropriate new category is selected? The search scheme for ART 1 and ART 2 modules incorporates an asymmetry in the design of levels F_1 and F_2 that is inappropriate for ART hierarchies having homologous fields. The ART 3 search mechanism described below eliminates that asymmetry.

A key observation is that a reset signal can act on an ART hierarchy *between* its fields F_1, F_2, F_3, . . . at the terminals, or synapses, that lie at the ends of adaptive filter pathways. Locating the site of action of the reset signal at the synapses allows each individual field to carry out its pattern processing function without introducing processing biases directly into a field's internal feedback loops.

HABITUATIVE CHEMICAL TRANSMITTERS IN ART SEARCH

In vivo, synapses contains mechanisms for regulating the production and release of chemical transmitters, whose binding at a postsynaptic cell membrane initiates excitation or inhibition of the cell. Remarkably, the computational requirements of the ART search process can be fulfilled by formal properties of such chemical transmitters, if these properties are appropriately embedded in the total

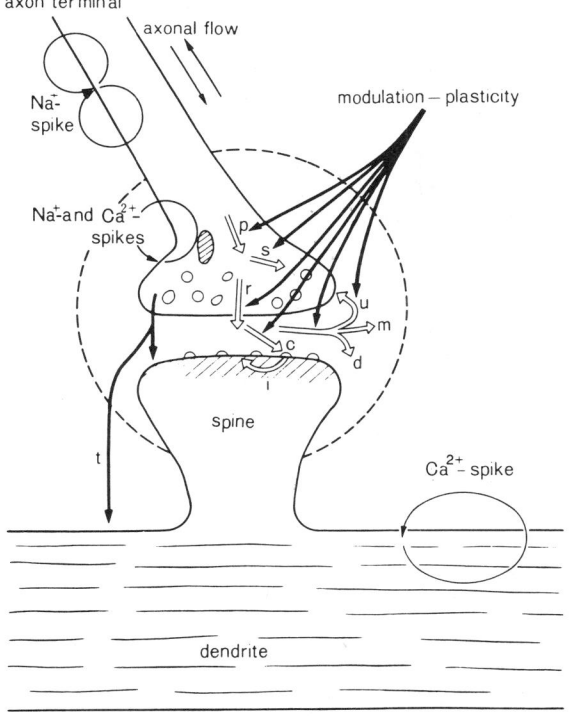

Figure 6. Schematic diagram showing electrical, ionic, and chemical events in a dendritic spine synapse. Open arrows indicate steps from production of neurotransmitter substance (p) to storage (s) or release (r) to reaction with subsynaptic receptors (c), leading to change of ionic permeability of subsynaptic membrane (i) or to removal to extracellular space (m), enzymatic destruction (d), or uptake by presynaptic terminal (u).t, action of trophic substance (Ito, 1984, p. 52; reprinted with permission).

architecture. The main properties used are illustrated in Figure 6, which is taken from Ito (1984). In particular, the ART 3 equations incorporate the dynamics of production and release of a chemical transmitter substance, the inactivation of a transmitter at postsynaptic binding sites, and the modulation of these processes via the nonspecific reset signal.

In such a system, after a reset event occurs, a presynaptic MTM bias is established that diminishes postsynaptic STM activation of those nodes that were most responsible for the predictive failure that led to the reset event. The transmitter signal pattern **T** originally sent to target nodes before the reset event is proportional to **zS**, as in ART 1 and ART 2. However, the transmitter signal pattern **T** = **uS** after the reset event is no longer proportional to **zS**. Instead, it is selectively biased against those features that were previously most active. The new signal

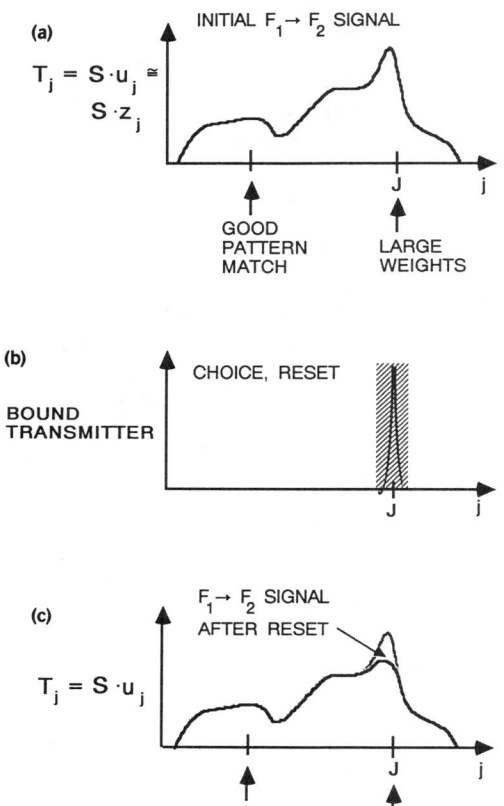

pattern will lead to selection of another contrast-enhanced representation, with more activation given to previously unattended features. This representation may or may not then be reset. This search process continues until an acceptable match is found, whence an attentive resonance is established and learning is triggered in those adaptive weights, or LTM traces, that abut resonant activations.

SUMMARY OF SYSTEM DYNAMICS

Figure 7 summarizes system dynamics of the ART model during a single input presentation. Initially the transmitted signal pattern **T** = **uS**, as well as the postsynaptic activity pattern, are proportional to the weighted signal pattern **zS** of the linear filter (Fig. 7a). The postsynaptic activity pattern **Y** is then contrast-enhanced, as a result of the internal competitive dynamics of the target field, and the amount of bound transmitter is greatly amplified in proportion to the level of postsynaptic activity (Fig. 7b). A subsequent reset signal inactivates a bound transmitter. Following the reset wave, the new signal **T** = **uS** is no longer proportional to **zS** but is instead biased against the previously active sites (Fig. 7c), thereby causing a shift in the focus of attention to a potentially more predictive pattern of features in short-term memory. A series of such reset events may ensue until an adequate match or a new category is found, thereby allowing the network to go into resonance and to maintain its attentional focus. New code learning can then occur on a time scale that is long-relative to that of the search process.

Taken together, these results about ART 1, ART 2, and ART 3 illustrate how functional analyses of cellular and network neurobiological processes and of behavioral processes of attention and learning can be joined in a multilevel interdisciplinary theory for enhancing our understanding of behavioral adaptation to a changing world.

Figure 7. Change of transmitter and STM patterns due to search. (*a*) Initially the signal pattern **T** = **uS** ≅ **zS** may deliver a greater input to nodes with larger adaptive weights than to nodes with adaptive weights that better match the input pattern. (*b*) Contrast enhancement and amplification select the preferred F_2 nodes, selectively depleting the transmitter in LTM traces abutting those nodes. (*c*) A reset event biases the transmitted signal pattern **T** against the previously preferred nodes, so that **u** ≠ **z** after reset. More than one reset event may be needed to accumulate sufficient bias to select a new representation capable of supporting resonant attention and learning.

BIBLIOGRAPHY

D. H. Ackley, G. E. Hinton, and T. J. Sejnowski, "A Learning Algorithm for Boltzmann Machines," *Cogn. Sci.* **9**, 147–169.

G. A. Carpenter and S. Grossberg, "A Massively Parallel Architecture for a Self-organizing Neural Pattern Recognition Machine," *Comput. Vision Graph. Image Proc.* **37**, 54–115 (1987a).

G. A. Carpenter and S. Grossberg, "ART 2: Self-Organization of Stable Category Recognition Codes for Analog Input Patterns," *Appl. Opt.* **26**, 4919–4930 (1987b).

G. A. Carpenter and S. Grossberg, "The ART of Adaptive Pattern Recognition by a Self-Organizing Neural Network," *Computer* [special issue on artificial neural systems] **21**, 77–88 (1988).

G. A. Carpenter and S. Grossberg, "ART 3: Hierarchical Search Using Chemical Transmitters in Self-organizing Pattern Recognition Architectures," *Neural Networks*, **3**, 129–152 (1990).

S. Grossberg, "Neural Expectation: Cerebellar and Retinal Analogs of Cells Fired by Learnable or Unlearned Pattern Classes," *Kybernetik* **10**, 49–57 (1972).

S. Grossberg, "Adaptive Pattern Classification and Universal Recoding. I: Parallel Development and Coding of Neural Feature Detectors," *Biol. Cybern.* **23**, 121–134 (1976a).

S. Grossberg, "Adaptive Pattern Classification and Universal Recoding. II: Feedback, Expectation, Olfaction, and Illusions," *Biol. Cybern.* **23,** 187–202 (1976b).

S. Grossberg, "A Theory of Visual Coding, Memory, and Development," in E. Leeuwenberg and H. Buffart, eds., *Formal Theories of Visual Perception,* John Wiley and Sons, Inc., New York, 1978a.

S. Grossberg, "A Theory of Human Memory: Self-organization and Performance of Sensory-Motor Codes, Maps, and Plans," in R. Rosen and F. Snell, eds., *Progress in Theoretical Biology,* Vol. 5, Academic Press, New York, pp. 233–374, 1978b.

S. Grossberg, *Studies of Mind and Brain: Neural Principles of Learning, Perception, Development, Cognition, and Motor Control,* Boston, Reidel Press, 1982.

S. Grossberg, ed., *The Adaptive Brain. I: Cognition, Learning, Reinforcement, and Rhythm,* Elsevier, North-Holland, Amsterdam, 1987.

S. Grossberg, ed., *Neural Networks and Natural Intelligence,* MIT Press, Cambridge, Mass., 1988.

M. Ito, *The Cerebellum and Neural Control,* Raven Press, New York, 1984.

E. R. Kandel and J. H. Schwartz, *Principles of Neural Science,* Elsevier, North-Holland, New York, 1981.

T. Kohonen, *Self-organization and Associative Memory,* Springer-Verlag, New York, 1984.

C. von der Malsburg, "Self-organization of Orientation Sensitive Cells in the Striate Cortex," *Kybernetik* **14,** 85–100 (1973).

D. E. Rumelhart, G. E. Hinton, and R. J. Williams, "Learning Internal Representations by Error Propagation," in D. E. Rumelhart and J. L. McClelland, eds., *Parallel Distributed Processing,* MIT Press, Cambridge, Mass., 1986.

D. J. Willshaw and C. von der Malsburg, "How Patterned Neural Connections Can Be Set up by Self-Organization," *Proc. Roy. Soc. London Ser. B* **194,** 431–445 (1976).

General References

S. Grossberg, "Classical and Instrumental Learning by Neural Networks," in R. Rosen and F. Snell, eds., *Progress in Theoretical Biology,* Academic Press, New York, 1974.

S. W. Kuffler, J. G. Nicholls, and A. R. Martin, *From Neuron to Brain,* 2nd ed., Sinauer Associates, Sunderland, Mass., 1984.

W. B. Levy, "Associative Changes at the Synapse: LTP in the Hippocampus," in W. B. Levy, J. Anderson, and S. Lehmkuhle, eds., *Synaptic Modifications, Neuron Selectivity, and Nervous System Organization,* Erlbaum Associates, Hillsdale, N.J., pp. 5–33, 1985.

GAIL A. CARPENTER
STEPHEN GROSSBERG
Boston University

The authors received partial support from British Petroleum (89-A-1204), DARPA (AFOSR 90-0083), and the National Science Foundation (NSF IRI-90-00530); and from the Air Force Office of Scientific Research (AFOSR 90-0128 and AFOSR 90-0175), the Army Research Office (ARO DAAL-03-88-K-0088), and the National Science Foundation (NSF IRI-87-16960), respectively. The authors wish to thank Cynthia E. Bradford, Carol Yanakakis Jefferson, and Diana Meyers for their valuable assistance in the preparation of the manuscript.

ADVICE TAKER

Program proposed by J. McCarthy intended to show common sense and improvable behavior by using declarative and imperative sentences as the representation, and immediate deduction as the reasoning mechanism (see J. McCarthy, "Programs with Common Sense," in *Mechanization of Thought Processes*, Her Majesty's Stationery Office, London, pp. 75–84, 1959; reprinted in J. McCarthy, *Formalizing Commonsense*, Ablex, 1989. The sentence representation suggested for the Advice Taker is the forerunner of the Situational Calculus (see J. McCarthy and P. J. Hayes, "Some Philosophical Problems from the Standpoint of Artificial Intelligence," *Mach. Intell.* **4,** 463–502 (1969)).

The Advice Taker had not been realized as of early 1990, and its goals could still be regarded as ambitious. The development of formalized nonmonotonic reasoning since the late 1970s makes them more feasible.

JOHN MCCARTHY
Stanford University

AGENDA-BASED SYSTEMS

An agenda, or job list, has become one of the most popular methods used in AI systems to express control of the inference process because it does so in explicit, modular steps. The agenda itself is a data structure whose entries are commonly called "tasks." Each task is some piece of work to be accomplished during the problem-solving (qv) process. The principal advantage of listing tasks explicitly on an agenda is that it allows the inference process to reason about the best sequence for pending tasks in order to choose more intelligently the next task to be attempted.

An agenda task entry may also include a source for the task (ie, where did it come from?), a reason for placing the task on the agenda (ie, why should the system execute this task?), and a priority for executing the task (ie, how important is it to execute this task now?). Tasks may be placed on an agenda as a side effect of executing other tasks or may be placed there directly by some other means, for example, the action of a production rule (see RULE-BASED SYSTEMS) might place new tasks on the agenda. Tasks are removed from agendas either according to some algorithm based on the task reasons or priorities, or the agenda can function simply as a stack, with the task that has been most recently placed on the agenda being the first one removed.

AI AGENDA SYSTEMS

One of the earliest AI systems to use an agenda was one of the DENDRAL (Lindsay and co-workers, 1980) programs used to elucidate molecular structures. DENDRAL's agenda is used by the "predictor" to keep track of information about fragment ions waiting to be processed by a set of rules. Initially, the agenda contains only chemical representations of unfragmented molecular ions. Rules are applied to simulate fragmentation of these ions, and representations of the resulting fragmented ions are then added to the agenda. The use of an agenda allows a breadth-first search behavior in which the primary ion fragmentations are analyzed first. A history of where each ion originated (how it came to be placed on the agenda) is saved and printed in a summary, but no interactive explanation is available (see CHEMISTRY, AI IN).

In AM (Lenat, 1976), a system for generating mathematical discoveries, an agenda was used principally to manage a huge task selection problem. The agenda permitted each of many plausible tasks to be evaluated prior to selection and execution of that task having the most significant potential. Tasks were selected on the basis of a computed priority. The reasons associated with tasks in AM's agenda were useful in computing scores in order to determine the top-priority task. Figure 1 shows a typical entry from AM's agenda.

The agenda used in the CENTAUR system (Aikins, 1980) for prototype-directed reasoning was designed to allow an easily accessible and explicit representation of control steps. Each control step in CENTAUR is placed on the agenda as a task so that the system can reason about all tasks remaining to be executed. Tasks are executed in a LIFO order and are removed only as a result of executing them. The sources and reasons of a task are defined for purposes of understanding system performance, and an interactive explanation (qv) facility is provided that prints a description of the task being executed and the reason for choosing that task upon user request. Figure 2 shows a sample task from CENTAUR's agenda.

The agendas in GUS (Bobrow and co-workers, 1977) and KRL (Bobrow and Winograd, 1977) are used as part of the central control process but not to explain reasoning, as is done in CENTAUR. In GUS the agenda is used to decide what should be done next. The system puts potential processes on the agenda and then operates in a cycle in which it examines this agenda, chooses the next job to be done, and then does it. In KRL the agenda is a priority-ordered list of queues, with all processes on a higher priority queue run before any process on a lower priority queue.

BENEFITS OF AGENDA SCHEME

As is illustrated in the systems just discussed, agendas may be used for many different reasons. One motivation for placing tasks on an agenda is that it allows a system to

Task: Fill-in generalizations of equality of lists.
Priority: 850
Reasons:
      400:    No known nontrivial generalizations of equality of lists.
      600:    Equality of lists rarely returns true on random examples.
      200:    Focus of attention: AM recently worked on the concept of equality of lists:

Figure 1. Sample AM agenda entry.

Task: Order the hypothesis list.
Source: Task adding new prototypes to the hypothesis list.
Reason: Because new prototypes have been added to the hypothesis list, it should be checked to see that it is ordered according to which prototype best fits the facts.

Figure 2. Sample CENTAUR agenda entry.

"look ahead" and see what tasks are remaining to be executed and to reason about those tasks. This feature is used in CENTAUR, for example, to help decide which production rules can be usefully applied to solve pending control tasks. Thus, the state of the agenda at any time shows exactly which tasks remain to be executed. A second advantage of having an agenda is that it provides a means for printing an ongoing record of the system's tasks and the reasons for considering them, which is done, for example, in both DENDRAL and CENTAUR. A third advantage of agendas is that they force key steps in the system's execution to be defined as single tasks, resulting in a highly modular, cleanly structured system. Isolating key steps in the execution of a system in turn makes it easier to explain what the system is doing at any time. This explanation feature is used extensively in CENTAUR, which must interact with medically expert users to solve actual human pathology problems, in which the consequences of mistakes are important.

RECOMMENDATIONS

Control in systems in which explanation, look-ahead, or any of the other features just described are not needed may be just as well represented implicitly within the inference engine. Using an agenda requires more memory (to represent the necessary data structures) and more processing time (to evaluate and choose tasks and to explain agenda activity and task choices to users). The choice of whether to use an agenda depends on the nature of the application and the requirements for explaining control processes to the user. For example, agendas are recommended for applications that have a large task selection problem as in AM or for those that perform a breadth-first exploration of the solution space as in DENDRAL. They are also recommended for systems like CENTAUR, which attempt to explain control steps to the user.

BIBLIOGRAPHY

J. S. Aikins, *Prototypes and Production Rules: A Knowledge Representation for Computer Consultations,* STAN-CS-80-814 (HPP-80-17), Stanford University, Stanford, Calif., Aug. 1980.

D. G. Bobrow and T. Winograd, "An Overview of KRL, a Knowledge Representation Language," *Cog. Sci.* 1(1), 3–46 (1977).

D. G. Bobrow, R. Kaplan, M. Kay, D. Norman, H. Thompson, and T. Winograd, "GUS, a Frame-Driven Dialog System," *Artif. Intell.* 8(2), 155–173 (1977).

D. B. Lenat, *AM: Artificial Intelligence Approach to Discovery in Mathematics as Heuristic Search,* STAN-CS-76-570 (AIM-286), Stanford University, Stanford, Calif., July 1976.

R. Lindsay, B. G. Buchanan, E. A. Feingenbaum, and J. Lederberg, *DENDRAL*, McGraw-Hill, New York, 1980.

J. S. AIKINS
Aion Corp.

ALPHA-BETA PRUNING

The alpha-beta procedure is an efficient procedure for searching for a good move in a two-person game like checkers or chess. From the search tree, the procedure prunes subtrees that, according to its computations, are irrelevant to choosing a good move (see GAME TREES). An algorithm for the alpha-beta procedure is given in Figure 1.

To understand the alpha-beta procedure it is necessary to understand the depth-first minimax procedure, which is a search procedure that combines an evaluation function, a depth-first generation procedure (see SEARCH, DEPTH-FIRST), and the minimax backing-up procedure to search for a good move in a two-person game like checkers or chess (see GAME PLAYING). The alpha-beta procedure is equivalent to the depth-first minimax procedure in the sense that each chooses the same move as the other, when given the same top position, termination criteria, and evaluation function.

Suppose that the game tree of Figure 2 had been given implicitly. A binary tree has been given for simplicity, but a tree of any branching factor applies here. The depth-first minimax procedure starts with position P and generates positions P1, P11, and P111 (see Fig. 3a). The depth-first minimax procedure then uses its evaluation function to evaluate position P111, which has a value of 4. It then generates P112 and gets the value 1. The better value of P111 and P112, namely 4, is backed up to P11. The procedure generates P12. It generates and evaluates P121 and likewise P122 (see Fig. 3b). To P12, it backs up the better value of P121 and P122, namely 8. It then backs up to P1 the better value for P11 and P12, namely 4. It generates P2 and P21. It generates and evaluates P211 and P212

```
function Alphabeta (p: position; α: integer; β: integer): integer;

    var m, i, t, d: integer;

begin

    determine the successor positions p₁,...,p_d of position p;

    if d = 0

        then Alphabeta := f(p)

        else begin

            m := α;

            for i := 1 to d do

                begin

                    t := −Alphabeta(p_i, −β, −m);

                    if t > m then m := t;

                    if m >= β then go to done

                end;

            done: Alphabeta := m

        end

end;
```

Figure 1. An algorithm for the alpha-beta procedure. The evaluation function is f.

(see Fig. 3c). It continues until it obtains the result shown in Figure 3d. It chooses to move to position P1, which has a higher value than that of position P2.

The alpha-beta procedure almost always chooses its move after it has generated only a small fraction of the tree that would be generated by the equivalent depth-first minimax procedure when choosing the identical move. Thus the alpha-beta procedure can save a great deal of time in the search. In the two simple examples given below, the alpha-beta procedure generates fewer moves than (and chooses the same move as) the equivalent depth-first

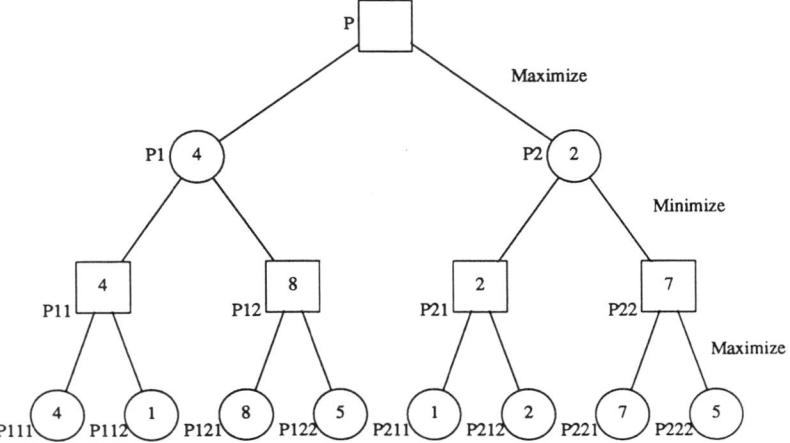

Figure 2. A game-tree with minimax backed-up values.

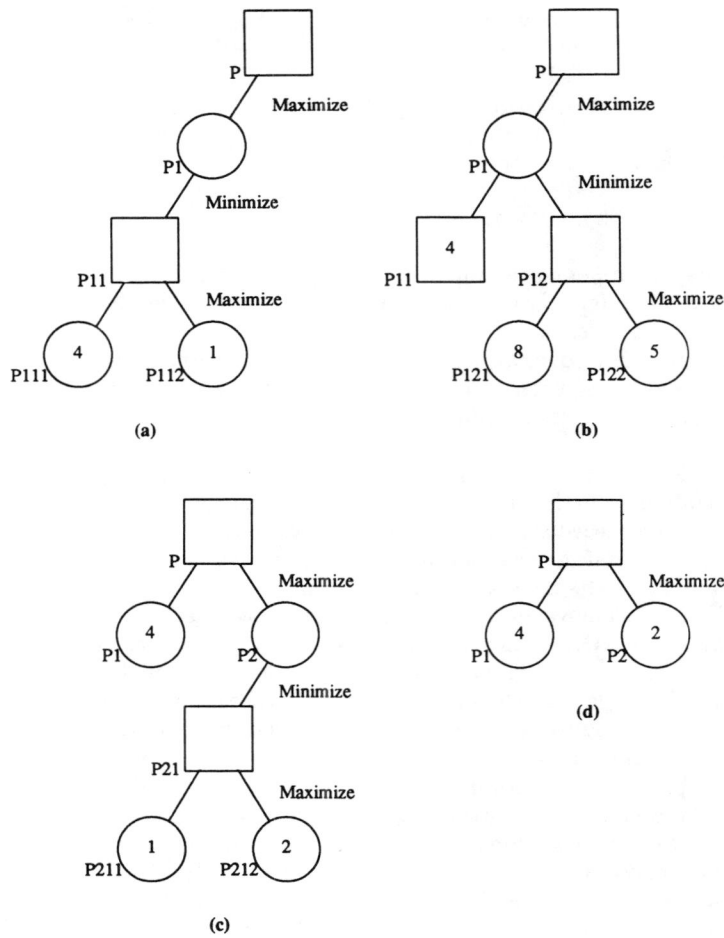

Figure 3. Depth-first minimax procedure.

(a)

(b)

(c)

(d)

minimax procedure. The alpha-beta procedure is used in the tree at levels deeper than 2 or 3. The reader is urged to think about such extensions. In Figure 4, the alpha-beta procedure has already obtained the (possibly backed-up) value v1 = 4. The alpha-beta procedure sets a parameter $\alpha = 4$ at P2, which is the least that Max (square, the maximizing player) can be held to; beta is the most that Min (circle, the minimizing player) can be held to. When the procedure finds that the (possibly backed-up) value of a max-position (Max's turn to move) does not exceed alpha, it makes an alpha cutoff; that is, the procedure does

not bother to generate more successors of the predecessor of the max-position, but generates the next successor of the predecessor of the predecessor of the max-position. Thus, after obtaining v21 = 2, the procedure finds an alpha cutoff; that is, the procedure does not bother to generate positions P22, P23, P24, . . . (and their successors), but generates next P3. Since the minimax backing-up pro-

Figure 4. The alpha-beta procedure finds an alpha cutoff.

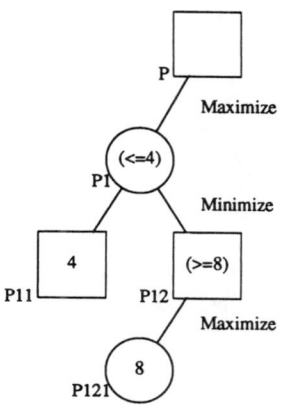

Figure 5. The alpha-beta procedure finds a beta cutoff.

cedure is being used and v21 = 2, the depth-first minimax procedure would obtain a backed-up value of v2 that did not exceed 2, which is worse than v1 = 4. Without generating any more positions below P2, the alpha-beta procedure "knows" that Max will not choose to move to P2. This shows that the further generation below P2 performed by the depth-first minimax procedure is a waste of time. Similarly, in Figure 5, after obtaining v11 = 4, the alpha-beta procedure sets the parameter β = 4 at P12. In general, when the procedure finds that the (possibly backed-up) value of a min-position is greater than or equal to beta, it makes a beta cutoff; it does not bother to generate more successors of the predecessor of the min-position, but generates the next successor of the predecessor of the predecessor of the min-position. Thus, after obtaining v121 = 8, the procedure makes a beta cutoff; that is, the procedure does not bother to generate P122, P123, P124, . . . but generates P13 next.

A uniform game tree of depth d and branching factor (qv) b contains b^d leaf nodes, all of which would be examined by the depth-first minimax procedure. The number of nodes that must be generated and evaluated in the best case performance of the alpha-beta procedure (when the best moves are searched first) is $2b^{d/2} - 1$, for d even, and $b^{(d+1)/2} + b^{(d-1)/2} - 1$, for d odd. In the worst case performance, alpha-beta examines all the leaf nodes.

For information on the historical development of the alpha-beta procedure, and an excellent analysis, see Knuth and Moore (1975). For a branching factor analysis, see Pearl (1982). For an evaluation of the overall effectiveness of the procedure, see Slagle and Dixon (1969). Kumar and co-workers (1988) show that the alpha-beta procedure (and the AO*, B*, and SSS* procedures) are special cases of a branch-and-bound procedure.

BIBLIOGRAPHY

C. Ferguson and R. E. Korf, "Distributed Tree Search and Its Application to Alpha-Beta Pruning," *Proceedings of the Seventh National Conference on Artificial Intelligence (AAAI-88)*, St. Paul, Minn., 1988.

D. E. Knuth and R. N. Moore, "An Analysis of Alpha-Beta Pruning," *Artif. Intell.* **6**, 293–326 (1975).

R. Korf, "Search: A Survey of Recent Results," in H. Shrobe, ed., *Exploring Artificial Intelligence*, Morgan-Kaufmann, San Mateo, Calif., 1988, pp. 197–237.

V. Kumar, D. Nau, and L. Kanal, "A General Branch-And-Bound Formulation for AND/OR Graph and Game Tree Search," in L. Kanal and V. Kumar, eds., *Search in Artificial Intelligence*, Springer-Verlag, New York, 1988, pp. 91–130.

J. Pearl, "The Solution for the Branching Factor of the Alpha-Beta Pruning Algorithm and Its Optimality," *CACM* **25**(8), 559–564 (1982).

J. Slagle and J. Dixon, "Experiments with Some Programs That Search Game Trees," *JACM* **16**(2), 189–207 (April 1969).

J. Slagle and J. Dixon, "Experiments with the *m & n* Tree-searching Program," *CACM* **13**(3), 147–154 (1970).

JAMES R. SLAGLE
University of Minnesota

ALV

The Autonomous Land Vehicle (ALV) was a computer-vision controlled robot vehicle developed by the Martin Marietta Corporation of Denver, Colorado under support of the Defense Advanced Research Projects Agency Strategic Computing Program during the period 1985–1989. The ALV was used by both Martin Marietta and university and industrial research groups as an experimental testbed for visual navigation. The vehicle was equipped with a color video camera mounted on a digitally controlled pan and tilt mechanism, a laser ranger that produced two frames of range information per second, and an inertial navigation system for measuring location and heading. The computer systems onboard included a VICOM image processing systems and various microprocessor systems for control and path planning. The ALV was able to navigate along open roads at speeds of up to 20 km/hour, and was also able to detect and avoid stationary obstacles on roads at much lower speeds. Some preliminary cross-country demonstrations were also performed at speeds of approximately 5 km/hour [see M. Turk, D. Morganthaler, K. Gremban, and M. Marra, "VITS—A Vision System for Autonomous Land Vehicle Navigation," *IEEE Transactions on Pattern Analysis and Machine Intelligence* **10**, 342–361 (1988)].

LARRY S. DAVIS
University of Maryland

ALVEY

Interest in artificial intelligence in the United Kingdom was stimulated by the work of Turing. His 1938 paper proposing a universal calculating machine, the Turing machine, led within a few years to the development of the Colossus machine for code-cracking work at Bletchley Park. At Bell Labs in 1943, remarks by Turing about the application of such a machine to handling predictions for stock and share purchases show that he was, even then, thinking about the application of such machines to inference computing, a branch of what we now know as artificial intelligence. With him at Bletchley Park worked a young assistant called Michie. Within a few years after the end of the war, a department of artificial intelligence was created at Edinburgh University, led by Michie. This department acted as the focal point for AI research in the UK, and over the years, many of Michie's students went on to populate other academic and industrial AI laboratories throughout the UK and the USA.

By 1970, the department at Edinburgh University had become quite large: so large that the research funding body, the Science Research Council, asked Professor Sir James Lighthill to investigate AI and the work at Edinburgh. The Lighthill report became infamous within the AI community of the UK because it was used as a reason for considerable cutbacks in funding, not only at Edinburgh but throughout the UK. So when in 1982 the Alvey Committee recommended a program of research in advanced information technology (IT), centered around AI, the community saw this as its salvation, manna from heaven after the hungry years of the 1970s.

The Alvey Committee had been established by the British government for two reasons. In the early 1980s, IT was seen as the key to a regrowth of industrial strength as the old smoke-stack industries declined, and so worthy of support and encouragement. Another reason, perhaps the key attraction, was the perceived Japanese threat. In the autumn of 1981, the Japanese announced their Fifth Generation Program. This ten-year cooperative program involves Japan's eight large *zaibatsus* and various state research establishments, and is centered around a new research establishment, ICOT (qv), staffed with secondees from the firms. Its work was based in AI, but actually centered around the development of an efficient parallel processor hardware and software system for handling logic languages. However, what may have been more of a spur to the British government was the knowledge that the Japanese were determined to become a major power in IT, which could only be at the expense of the IT industries of the West. The Alvey Committee consisted of individuals drawn from the major IT firms in the UK, including BT, GEC, Plessey, ICL, and Logica. It recommended a five-year cooperative program of research in the enabling technologies of IT. The government accepted most of the recommendations and agreed to fund the program on a 50/50 basis, sharing the cost with industry.

THE ALVEY PROGRAM

During the first five years (1983–1988) of the program, some 198 collaborative projects were carried out, involving firms and teams from virtually every university in the country and from the major government research laboratories. It is estimated that more than 2500 research workers took part in the program. Probably every significant AI team in the UK was involved in some projects, with the larger teams such as those of Edinburgh and Sussex University in many projects. The project teams were normally made up of four partner bodies, of which two or three would be from industry and one or two from the academic world. There were also 113 longer-term "uncle" projects, so called because the work of an academic team was monitored closely by an "uncle" from industry. The program was run by a directorate and staffed by secondees from industry, universities, and government departments.

The four main fields initially covered by the program were VLSI, software engineering, intelligent knowledge-based systems (KBS), and man–machine interface (MMI). A section on computer architecture was subsequently pulled together. This concentrated largely on parallel processors and system architectures for inference computing. The parts of the program that included large components normally classified as falling within AI comprised the KBS section, while much of the MMI section dealt with speech processing and natural language, and much of the computer architecture work. The importance of the other sections to AI is obvious. In the case of the human-computer interface work in the MMI section, it became increasingly apparent as the program progressed that KBS are often highly dependent on good human interfaces, so

that much of this work would first find its application in the AI field. Part of the software engineering program was concerned with logic and the development of logic languages of the GHC or Prolog type, with direct applicability in the AI field.

As it happens, the term Artificial Intelligence was not used in the program, because it has unfortunate implications in the UK. And no particular attempt was made to pull the AI components of the program together, perhaps because it was thought that the coherence of the parts with AI implications was not any greater than that of many other sections. An attempt to integrate the technologies was made by supporting four large demonstrator projects, each of which was originally intended to have AI or KBS elements in it. One of these demonstrators was concerned with the application of KBS to three different problems in the government department that administered social security. One of these was a forms helper designed to aid applicants in filling in a form; another was designed to aid the counter clerk with administering the massive number of social security regulations, and the third was designed to help the regulation planners see the implications of their work. In retrospect, it seems unfortunate that another potential demonstrator project, designed to test the feasibility of applying an expert system shell in several widely different fields, was not approved, since it would have served to illuminate the limitations and benefits of the shell approach to KBS design.

While the intellectual property developed on a project remained the property of the partners, steps were taken to encourage transfer between the workers in coherent parts of the program. Special Interest Clubs were established, for example, Novel Architectures for logic programming and for speech and image processing. Many of these clubs continued after the program was completed.

There were some 55 projects in the KBS section of the program, with a further 46 uncle projects. The high number of uncle projects in this part of the program reflects the relatively immature state of the art at that time. When the program started in 1983, there were very few AI-trained people in British industry, so many of these projects were designed to give firms experience in AI techniques and methods. Other projects were designed to develop tools and techniques. For example, a coherent set of tools was developed to aid natural language parsing and processing. Other club-type projects were designed to give firms some understanding of the field. There were eight of these awareness clubs, involving from 15 to 30 firms, working with some expert firms or university team to explore the building of some particular KBS application. Most of these clubs went on to develop commercial KBS systems in their fields of application.

AFTER ALVEY

It was hoped that there would be a follow-up program when the Alvey program came to an end in 1988. (Some of the individual projects ran on until 1990.) The Bide Committee recommended a continuation of the basic research work, with the introduction of an applications stream. But the government of the day no longer had the same enthusiasm for acting as a catalyst for such developments, so the recommendation for an application theme was not accepted. A smaller program, known as the IED program, did continue, but with conditions that rather reduced its attractiveness and so its potential for successful impact.

One factor influencing the future UK AI program was the rise of collaborative research programs under the control of the European Community Commission. With the continuing convergence of Europe in industrial affairs, it was appropriate that emphasis should shift away from national programs like Alvey to international programs like ESPRIT. In 1990, more support for the UK AI community came from the EEC programs than from the national IED program.

VALUE OF THE ALVEY PROGRAM

Programs of support for research and development without measures to ensure the health of the industry are not useless, but tend to be less useful. Because of the environment of high interest rates in the UK in the 1980s, much of the work of the Alvey program that required significant capital investment to reach commercial fruition did not achieve successful exploitation. On the other hand, a pattern of collaboration between firms, and between firms and universities, was created. Technology and techniques were transferred from the academic world into industry. People with experience in advanced methods were established in industry, and a widespread awareness of the potential of, for example, AI was achieved. In the long run, this is the most important legacy of the Alvey program. The AI community in the UK has come out of the closet of the academic world and into the marketplace.

BIBLIOGRAPHY

B. Oakley and K. Owen, *Alvey, Britain's Strategic Computing Initiative*, MIT Press, Cambridge, Mass., 1990.

Report of the Alvey Committee, *A Programme for Advanced Information Technology*, HMSO, London, UK, 1982.

B. OAKLEY
Logica Cambridge, Ltd.

AM

A knowledge-based system that conjectures interesting concepts in elementary mathematics, written in 1976 by D. Lenat at the Stanford Heuristic Programming Project. AM demonstrates that some aspects of creative research can be effectively modeled as heuristic search (see D. B. Lenat, "AM: Discovery in Mathematics as Heuristic Search," in R. Davis and D. B. Lenat, eds., *Knowledge-Based Systems in Artificial Intelligence*, McGraw-Hill, New York, 1980, pp. 3–228).

M. R. TAIE
AT&T Bell Labs

ANALOGIES. See LEARNING, MACHINE.

ANALOG SEMANTIC FEATURES

Features have been used in many contexts, eg, as a semantic theory of language (Katz and Fodor, 1963), as an encoding of the background frame of lexical entries (microfeatures$_1$) (Waltz and Pollack, 1985; Bookman, 1987; Sharkey, in press), as a set of defining characteristics of concepts (microfeatures$_2$) (Hendler, 1989), as evidence for psychological theories of categories (Smith and Medin, 1981), as part of a structured representation of concepts (aspects) (Weber, 1989), as a model of memory (Nairne, 1990), as an encoding of memory and context (analog semantic features) (Bookman, 1988; Bookman and Alterman, 1991), as representations of subsymbolic information (microfeatures$_3$) (Rumelhart and co-workers, 1986; Hinton and co-workers, 1986; McClelland and Kawamoto, 1986; Hinton, 1981). The term microfeature is used in several ways in the literature. The subscripts are meant to distinguish among usages of the term.

As evidenced above, features have a plethora of uses, although with some common threads. To get a handle on the similarities and distinctions, it is useful to begin with a dichotomy proposed by Smith and Medin (1981): if concepts are represented in terms of components, one choice is in terms of qualitative components, called features. An alternate choice is in terms of quantitative components called dimensions. For example, the concept of *automobiles* could be represented in terms of a few scaling dimensions, such as degree of luxury, with Hyundai near one end and Mercedes near the other. Alternatively, the automobile concept could be represented by a set of features: eg, for Hyundai these might include vehicle, transportation, and foreign.

Features can also be classified as structured, ie, there exists an expressed relationship between the features, or nonstructured, ie, a simple list of features describing the concepts. For example, the concept of *bachelorhood* could be described by using a simple list of features: single, male, etc (Katz and Fodor, 1963). In contrast, the *arch* concept (Winston, 1975) is an example of a structured object, consisting of the features (lintel and two posts) and the relationships between the features (eg, the lintel is supported by the two posts).

A further characteristic is that they can be either analog or binary. The analog property measures the feature's strength of association to the parent concept. In contrast the binary property only determines if the feature is present or absent. For example, if the feature is degree of luxury and the concept is Hyundai, its analog property might be -1.0 (indicating a strong negative association), whereas its binary property would be 0 (indicating that the feature does not apply).

Analog semantic features are derived from the notion of microfeatures (Waltz and Pollack, 1985), which have the following properties: they are analog, they have semantic content, and they are nonstructured. As originally conceived, they were used to partially define concepts and to associate a concept with others that share the microfeatures. The microfeatures functioned as a representation for global contextual influences of competing word senses during sentence processing. For example, given the sentence "John shot some bucks" and an appropriate microfeature encoding of its concepts, a priming of the concept *hunting* would yield the "fired at" sense of shot, whereas a priming of the concept *gamble* would result in the "wasted money" sense. In contrast, in the parallel distributed processing (PDP) use of microfeature (Hinton and co-workers, 1986; Hinton, 1981) each active feature has no semantic meaning in and of itself, but rather it is the feature's participation in an overall learned pattern of activity over a collection of units that determines its semantic content. The term analog semantic feature (ASF) was coined to avoid confusion with the PDP use of microfeature.

Recent work (Bookman, 1991) extends the Waltz and Pollack notion to encode the background frame (Fillmore, 1982) associated with concepts and their interrelationships. Fillmore defines the background frame as some body of understandings, some pattern of practices, or some history of social institutions against which a particular category is intelligible to the community (Fillmore, 1982). Suppose we are given the following vector of ASFs: necessity, health, alarm, restraint, confinement, subjection, obedience, and unpleasantness. This vector of AFSs can be then used to distinguish the background frame associated with the concepts *hospital* and *interrogation*. These concepts share the ASFs alarm, unpleasantness, obedience, subjection, and confinement, but can be discriminated based on their analog values by the ASFs unwillingness, necessity, health, and restraint. Furthermore, the analog property says to what degree these ASFs discriminate these concepts. In Bookman (ibid), the ASFs function as a representation of working memory from which fine-grain inferences are generated and new relationships are learned as the result of the processing of an input text. The ASFs are based on the category structure of *Roget's Thesaurus* and can be roughly described by eight classes: abstract relations, space, physics, matter, sensation, intellect, volition, and affections.

BIBLIOGRAPHY

L. A. Bookman, "A Microfeature Based Scheme for Modelling Semantics," in *Proceedings of the Tenth IJCAI*, Milan, Italy, Morgan-Kaufmann, San Mateo, Calif., 1987, pp. 611–614.

L. A. Bookman, "A Connectionist Scheme for Modelling Context," in D. Touretzky, G. Hinton, and T. Sejnowski, eds., *Proceedings of the 1988 Connectionist Models Summer School*, Morgan-Kaufmann, San Mateo, Calif., 1988, pp. 281–290.

L. A. Bookman, *Breaking the Knowledge Barrier: Experiments in Comprehension*, Ph.D. dissertation, Brandeis University, Waltham, Mass., 1991.

L. A. Bookman and R. Alterman, "Schema Recognition for Text Understanding: An Analog Semantic Feature Approach," in J. Barnden and J. Pollack, eds., *Advances in Connectionist and Neural Computation Theory, Vol. 1: High-Level Connectionist Models*, Ablex Publishing Corp., Norwood, N.J., 1991.

C. Fillmore, "Frame Semantics," in The Linguistic Society of Korea, ed., *Linguistics in the Morning Calm*, Hanshin Publishing Co., Seoul, Korea, 1982.

J. Hendler, "Marker-Passing Over Microfeatures: Towards a Hybrid Symbolic/Connectionist Model," *Cogn. Sci.* **13**, 79–106 (1989).

G. Hinton, "Implementing Semantic Networks in Parallel Hardware," in G. Hinton and J. Anderson, eds., *Parallel Models of Associative Memory*, Lawrence Earlbaum, Hillsdale, N.J., 1981, pp. 161–188.

G. Hinton, J. McClelland, and D. Rumelhart, "Distributed Representations," in J. McClelland and D. Rumelhart, eds., *Parallel Distributed Processing: Explorations in the Microstructures of Cognition*, Vol. 1, MIT Press, Cambridge, Mass., 1986, pp. 77–109.

J. Katz and J. Fodor, "The Structure of a Semantic Theory," *Language* **39**, 170–210 (1963).

J. McClelland and A. Kawamoto, "Mechanisms of Sentence Processing: Assigning Roles to Constituents," in J. McClelland and D. Rumelhart, eds., *Parallel Distributed Processing: Explorations in the Microstructures of Cognition*, Vol. 2, MIT Press, Cambridge, Mass., 1986.

J. Nairne, "A Feature Model of Immediate Memory," *Memory Cogn.* **18**(3), 251–269 (1990).

D. Rumelhart, P. Smolensky, J. McClelland, and G. Hinton, "Schemata and Sequential Thought Processes in PDP Models," in J. McClelland and D. Rumelhart, eds., *Parallel Distributed Processing: Explorations in the Microstructures of Cognition*, Vol. 2, MIT Press, Cambridge, Mass., 1986, pp. 7–57.

N. Sharkey, "A Connectionist Model of Text Comprehension," in D. Balota, G. Flores d'Arcais, and K. Rayner, eds., *Comprehension Processes in Reading*, Lawrence Earlbaum, Hillsdale, N.J., in press.

E. Smith and D. Medin, *Categories and Concepts*, Harvard University Press, Cambridge, Mass., 1981.

D. Waltz and J. Pollack, "Massively Parallel Parsing: A Strongly Interactive Model of Natural Language Interpretation," *Cogn. Sci.* **9**, 52–74 (1985).

S. Weber, *A Structured Connectionist Approach to Direct Inferences and Figurative Adjective-Noun Combinations*, Ph.D. dissertation, University of Rochester, Rochester, N.Y., 1989.

P. Winston, "Learning Structural Descriptions From Examples," in P. Winston, ed., *The Psychology of Computer Vision*, McGraw-Hill, New York, 1975.

LAWRENCE A. BOOKMAN
RICHARD ALTERMAN
Brandeis University

This work was supported in part by the Defense Advanced Research Projects Agency, administered by the U.S. Airforce Office of Scientific Research under contract #F49620-88-C-0058.

AND/OR GRAPHS

An AND/OR graph is an explicit representation of the relationship between all situations and options that may be encountered in the solution of decomposable problems (Nilsson, 1980), that is, those made up of independently soluble constituents (see Fig. 1). The nodes in an AND/OR graph represent subproblems to be solved or subgoals to

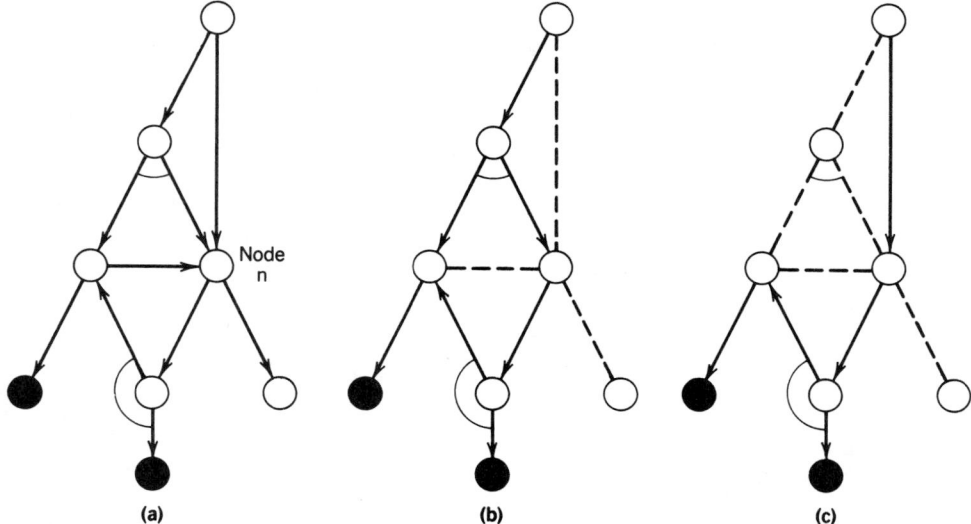

Figure 1. (*a*) AND/OR graph and (*b, c*) two of its solution graphs. Solved terminal nodes are shown as black dots.

be achieved, with the top node (n_0) representing the specification of the overall problem. The nodes are connected by two types of directed links: OR links that represent alternative options of handling the problem node from which they emanate and AND links that connect a parent problem node to the individual subproblems of which it is composed. All these subproblems must be solved before the parent problem is considered solved, thus, the AND links pointing toward these subproblems are normally shown connected by arcs, as in Figure 1. A terminal node (Fig. 1a: n_1, n_2, and n_3) (having no successors) in an AND/OR graph represents either a primitive problem, whose solution is readily available, or a subproblem that cannot be decomposed any further. The former is labeled solved, the latter unsolvable.

A complete solution is represented by an AND/OR subgraph, called a solution graph (see Fig. 1b, c), having the following properties: it contains the top node (n_0), all its terminal nodes are SOLVED, and if it contains an AND link L, it must also contain the entire group of AND links that are siblings of L (eg, see links L and L' in Fig. 1b).

APPLICATIONS

AND/OR graphs are typically used to represent the record of search (qv) in a problem-solving system that attempts to find a solution by a problem reduction (qv) method (Nilsson, 1971). Generally, AND/OR graphs are suited to problems in which the final solution is conveniently represented as a tree or a graph rather than an ordered sequence of actions (Pearl, 1984). Strategy-seeking tasks are typical examples of this class of problems, where the AND links represent changes in the problem situation caused by external, uncontrolled conditions, and the OR links represent alternative ways of reacting to such changes. In planning, the uncontrolled conditions could be the possible outcomes of an uncertain event or the results of a given test. In games those conditions are created by the legal moves available to the adversary. In program

synthesis they consist of the results of applying certain computations to unspecified data.

Another important class of problems suitable for AND/OR graph representations includes cases in which the solution required is an unordered set of actions. In symbolic integration (Moses, 1971), for example, certain legal transformations (eg, integration by parts, long division of polynomials) split the integrand into sums of expressions to be integrated separately in any order. The set of applicable transformations will be represented as OR links emanating from the node representing the integrand, and the AND links represent individual summands within the integrand, all of which must eventually be integrated.

The tasks of logical reasoning (see REASONING) and theorem proving (qv) also give rise to AND/OR structures (vanderBrug and Minker, 1975). One begins with a set of axioms and a set of inference rules that allows, in each step, deduction of a new statement from a subset of axioms and previously deduced statements. The new statement is added to the database, and the process continues until the desired conclusion (eg, the theorem) is derived. The solution object pursued by the search is a plan specifying in each step which of the inference rules is to be applied to which subset of statements in the database and what the deduced statement is. This plan, again, is best structured as an unordered tree because when a certain conclusion is derived from a given subset of statements, the internal order in which these statements were themselves derived is of no consequence as long as they reside in the database at the appropriate time. Thus, the solution structure is a tree, and hence, the appropriate search space would be an AND/OR graph (Chang and Slagle, 1971). Backward reasoning from a theorem to a set of axioms involves a search space of identical structure.

AND/OR graphs are also suitable for representing problems in which the solution sought is an ordered sequence of actions, as long as the search for some subsequences that make up the soluton can be conducted in any order. A classic example is the Tower-of-Hanoi puzzle (Pearl, 1984) where the three main subgoals, that is, clearing the largest disk, moving that disk to a given peg, and placing the other disks on top of the largest one, must be executed in a certain order, but the search for their solutions can be conducted in any order.

SEARCHING AND/OR GRAPHS

AND/OR graphs lend themselves to systematic search methods such as backtracking (qv), depth-first, breadth-first, and various forms of heuristic best-first algorithms (Nilsson, 1980; Pearl, 1984). The basic rationale behind heuristic search methods is that the examination of alternative solution candidates (OR links) should start with the candidate most likely to succeed, although the examination of subgoals within each candidate (AND links) should begin with the one most likely to fail. Heuristic estimates of these likelihoods are often used to guide the search so that a solution graph can be found after exploring only a small portion of the AND/OR graph that underlies a given problem. The algorithm AO*, for example, estimates the costs of the solution graphs rooted at the various candidate nodes and is guaranteed to find a cheapest solution if all cost estimates are optimistic (Bagchi and Mahanti, 1983). Game-playing (qv) strategies, on the other hand, are guided by estimating the strengths of positions a few moves ahead and normally employ backtracking (qv) search with irrevocable pruning (see ALPHA-BETA PRUNING) (Pearl, 1984).

BIBLIOGRAPHY

A. Bagchi and A. Mahanti, "Admissible Heuristic Search in AND/OR Graphs," *Theoretical Comp. Sci.* 24(2), 207–219 (1983).

C. L. Chang and J. R. Slagle, "An Admissible and Optimal Algorithm for Searching AND/OR Graphs," *Artif. Intell.* **2**, 117–128 (1971).

J. Moses, "Symbolic Integration: The Stormy Decade," *CACM* **14**(8), 548–560 (1971).

N. Nilsson, *Problem Solving Methods in Artificial Intelligence*, McGraw-Hill, New York, 1971.

N. Nilsson, *Principles of Artificial Intelligence*, Tioga, Palo Alto, Calif., 1980.

J. Pearl, *Heuristics: Intelligent Search Strategies for Computer Problem Solving*, Addison-Wesley, Reading, Mass., 1984.

G. J. vanderBrug and J. Minker, "State Space, Problem-Reduction, and Theorem-Proving—Some Relationships," *CACM* **18**(2), 107–115 (1975).

J. PEARL
UCLA

ARGUMENT COMPREHENSION

A central component of intelligence is the ability to understand and engage in arguments. This ability is essential to reading editorials in newspapers and magazines, to following political debates, and to comprehending religious, legal, and scientific reasoning. Humans also use this ability to express and defend their opinions when giving expert advice, when presenting court cases, and when discussing world affairs. As computer systems become more widely used to aid in complex decision-making and the generation of expert advice, it will become ever more important for such systems to exhibit skills similar to those which human beings use in debates, discussions, and editorials. Computers should be able not only to evaluate given situations and present their beliefs on possible courses of actions, but also to justify their beliefs, understand opposing beliefs, and argue persuasively for or against various positions. No individual should have to unquestioningly trust or follow the suggestions of any complex decision-making or advice-giving system which can propose a course of action, but which cannot understand or counter those objections that may be raised to its suggestions.

Designing computer systems capable of arguing also requires characterizing the interrelationships that exist between planning, reasoning, language comprehension, and language generation. People reason about whether or not a goal should be achieved, and use reasoning to justify beliefs about the efficacy, side-effects, and cost of selecting and executing various plans. That is, a reasoner can justify a belief that an act should or should not be performed on the basis that it will achieve or thwart a goal. At the same time, people possess planning information where the plans consist of information for selecting and applying various argument strategies. Modeling this argument process provides an ideal framework for exploring fundamental issues in knowledge representation (qv), knowledge organization, and knowledge application that must be addressed within any intelligent computer system.

A first step towards building computer systems capable of arguing is to address the problem of computer comprehension of arguments. This article describes a theory of the knowledge structures and processes involved in argument comprehension. The theory has been implemented in a prototype editorial comprehension and question answering system called OpEd (Opinions to/from the Editor) (Alvarado, 1990). OpEd (qv) is designed to take editorial text as input and answer subsequent questions about the beliefs or arguments of the editorial writer and of others whom the writer may criticize. The editorials read by OpEd are in the politico-economic domain and contain arguments for or against protectionist policies used to resolve conflicts in international trade.

BACKGROUND

The problem of modeling beliefs and argument knowledge has been addressed in a number of fields, including rhetoric, psychology, logic, and artificial intelligence (AI). In rhetoric, Toulmin (1958) has proposed a model for analyzing the structure of arguments. According to Toulmin, an argument is composed of six major elements: (1) a claim, or conclusion of the argument, (2) the grounds for believing the claim, (3) a warrant that justifies using the grounds as the basis for the claim, (4) the backing (eg, statistics) that supports the ground and/or the warrant,

(5) a modal qualifier (eg, "certainly") that indicates the degree of reliance on the claim, and (6) a rebuttal that indicates the circumstances on which the claim can be questioned. The central element of Toulmin's model is the warrant. Warrants may involve a general principle (eg, "all men are mortal"), a cause-effect relationship, a generalization, an analogy, a statement that associates the occurrence of two states or events, or a statement about the credibility of the source of a belief. As pointed out by Toulmin and co-workers (1979) and Rieke and Sillars (1984), Toulmin's model can be used to test the structure of arguments in disparate domains, including science, law, religion, politics, economics, and the arts.

In psycholinguistics, van Dijk and Kintsch (1983) have analyzed the structure of expository text in editorials by applying a general theory of discourse and scheme coherency, which includes coherency structures at the local (sentence), macrostructure, and schematic levels. Other researchers in psychology, such as McGuigan and Black (1986), have postulated a frame-based representation as the basis for simulating how humans create and evaluate arguments. Logicians, on the other hand, have a long history in examining the notions of knowledge and belief (Hintikka, 1962; Chellas, 1980), but their approach has been to establish axiomatic systems for deducing consistent beliefs, without regard as to how humans understand the beliefs of others and relate them to their own beliefs.

In AI, a number of researchers have concentrated on truth maintenance (qv) (Doyle, 1979; de Kleer, 1986) and evidential reasoning (Pearl, 1986; Dechter and Dechter, 1988). The goal of these systems is to maintain and/or propagate evidence for or against beliefs, once these beliefs and their relationships are already resident in a knowledge base. A major task of such systems is to maintain logical consistency among a set of beliefs by dynamically altering the truth value of tentative beliefs (ie, assumptions). AI research has also addressed the problem of modeling reasoning in the legal domain (see LAW, AI IN). This research effort has produced models for the analysis of the tax consequences of corporate transactions (McCarty and Sridharan, 1982), the generation of justifications based on hypotheticals and examples (Ashley, 1990; Rissland, 1985, 1986), and the analysis of the formation of contracts by offer and acceptance (Gardner, 1987; Goldman and co-workers, 1987). Other AI researchers, such as Cohen (1983, 1987) and Reichman (1983), have developed structural models of argument and discourse. According to Cohen's model, argument understanding requires building a tree where propositions are connected by a single evidence link, and the root of the tree contains the major claim made in the argument. Reichman's discourse grammar characterizes a conversation as a sequence of conversational moves, such as presenting a claim, supporting a claim, and challenging a claim.

The task of comprehension of natural language in arguments requires dynamically constructing a knowledge base of the beliefs and belief justifications of an arguer "on the fly" from textual input. The OpEd project (Alvarado, 1990; Alvarado and co-workers, 1985, 1986, 1990a, 1990b, 1990c) has been concerned with the domain knowledge,

conceptual representations, and natural language processing strategies involved in understanding arguments that arise in editorial text. In OpEd, argument comprehension is not considered as an isolated process but rather as an integral aspect of natural language understanding. OpEd involves the use of techniques for parsing input editorial text into a network of beliefs that represents the conceptual content of the editorial and maintains the context for subsequent question answering.

OpEd theory builds upon theories developed for computer comprehension of narrative text. Natural language processing (qv) (NLP) systems by Schank (1975), Cullingford (1978), DeJong (1979), Dyer (1983), Lebowitz (1980), and Wilensky (1983) can understand stories dealing with stereotypical and goal/plan situations. However, these systems lack explicit representations of beliefs, belief relationships, and argument structure. Understanding editorial text requires applying such abstract knowledge, in addition to those knowledge structures and processing strategies used for narrative comprehension. The philosophy behind OpEd's design has been to extend these previous theories of conceptual analysis of narrative text into the domain of editorial text.

ISSUES IN ARGUMENT COMPREHENSION

In some respects editorials are similar to argument dialogues. In both, argument participants present and justify their opinions. However, editorials lack the interactive elements of argument dialogues, due to the fact that editorial writers are the only active argument participants. As a result, editorials can be viewed as one-sided arguments where writers contrast their opinions against those of their implicit opponents (Bush, 1932; Stonecipher, 1979). That is, beliefs and arguments that happen to be in opposition to the editorial writer's own beliefs and arguments are explicitly mentioned only so that they may be refuted, thus indirectly increasing support for those beliefs held by the writer. By restricting OpEd's input to one-sided arguments in editorial text, it is possible to examine the process of argument comprehension without having to deal with the interactive processes and rhetorical structures that arise in argument dialogues.

In OpEd, understanding one-sided arguments in editorial text involves six major tasks: (1) applying domain-specific knowledge (ie, politico-economic knowledge), (2) recognizing beliefs and belief relationships, (3) following causal chains of reasoning about goals and plans, (4) applying abstract knowledge of argument structure, (5) mapping input text into conceptual structures which compose the internal representations of editorial arguments, and (6) indexing recognized concepts for later retrieval during question answering. Input editorial segments are in English and contain the essential wording, issues, and arguments of the original editorials. Here "essential" means that the original editorials have been edited to remove those parts which involve addressing issues that fall outside the scope of OpEd's process model (eg, references to specific historic events, extended metaphors, and handling sarcastic or humorous statements).

Below is an actual sample of OpEd's current input/output behavior. The input editorial is labeled ED-JOBS, and is a fragment of an editorial by Friedman (1982). ED-JOBS presents Friedman's arguments against the Reagan administration's policies on international trade. The editorial text and questions (labelled Q1–Q4) are read by OpEd, and the output generated by OpEd is shown as A1–A4.

ED-JOBS

Recent protectionist measures by the Reagan administration have disappointed us. Voluntary limits on Japanese automobiles and voluntary limits on steel by the Common Market are bad for the nation. They do not promote the long-run health of the industries affected. The problem of the automobile and steel industries is: in both industries, average wage rates are twice as high as the average. Far from saving jobs, the limitations on imports will cost jobs. If we import less, foreign countries will earn fewer dollars. They will have less to spend on American exports. The result will be fewer jobs in export industries.

Q1: What has disappointed Milton Friedman?

A1: Protectionist policies by the Reagan administration.

Q2: Who believes that the limitations on imports will save jobs?

A2: The Reagan administration.

Q3: What is the result of the limitations on imports?

A3: Milton Friedman believes that protectionist policies by the Reagan administration do not lead to the achievement of normal profits of the steel industry and the automobile industry.

The Reagan administration believes that protectionist policies by the Reagan administration lead to the achievement of normal profits of the steel industry and the automobile industry.

Milton Friedman believes that protectionist policies by the Reagan administration will thwart the preservation of jobs for U.S.

The Reagan administration believes that protectionist policies by the Reagan administration achieve the preservation of jobs for U.S.

Q4: Why does Milton Friedman believe that the limitations on imports will cost jobs?

A4: Milton Friedman believes that protectionist policies by the Reagan administration will thwart the preservation of jobs for U.S. because Milton Friedman believes that as a consequence of protectionist policies by the Reagan administration, U.S. imports fewer products; and if U.S. imports fewer products, then there is a decrease in profits of foreign countries; and if there is a decrease in profits of foreign countries, then foreign countries buy fewer American exports; and if foreign countries buy fewer American exports, then there is a decrease in profits of export industries; and if there is a decrease in profits of export industries, then there is a decrease in jobs in export industries; and a decrease in jobs in export industries thwarts the preservation of jobs for U.S.

Editorial comprehension requires the representation, organization, and application of both domain independent and domain specific knowledge. The major form of domain independent knowledge in OpEd is organized around abstract structures, called *argument units* (AUs). Each AU represents the point of an argument segment as a configuration of attack/support relationships among beliefs, where each belief refers to predications concerning plans and goals. Knowledge of AUs allows OpEd to recognize and interpret arguments in the politico-economic domain, as long as the system has sufficient planning skill and domain knowledge to build up instances of the particular goals, plans, and beliefs occurring within that domain. Several argument units may be instantiated within a given editorial. The AUs instantiated when reading ED-JOBS are:

AU-ACTUAL-CAUSE: Although opponent O believes that plan P should be used because P will achieve goal G, arguer A believes that P will not achieve G because G is being thwarted by state S1 AND P can not result in S2, the opposite of S1. Therefore, A believes that P should not be used.

AU-OPPOSITE-EFFECT: Although opponent O believes that plan P should be used because P will achieve goal G, arguer A believes that P will not achieve G because P will thwart G. Therefore, A believes that P should not be used.

AU-ACTUAL-CAUSE is instantiated to interpret Friedman as arguing against the Reagan administration's implicitly stated position that import quotas are needed to help domestic industries become profitable. Friedman argues that import quotas cannot achieve the goal of attaining profitability because that goal is being thwarted by the high salaries paid to U.S. workers, and because implementing import restrictions does not decrease the level of salaries in the industries being protected. AU-OPPO-SITE-EFFECT is instantiated to represent Friedman's argument that import restrictions should not be used because, contrary to the Reagan administration's beliefs, such restrictions will not achieve the goal of preserving U.S. jobs, but will thwart it.

In order to recognize argument units, OpEd must establish relationships of support between the editorial writer's beliefs and their justifications, and relationships of attack between the editorial writer's beliefs and the beliefs of his opponents. Recognizing these relationships is essential for comprehension because editorial arguments often include the arguments of opponents, along with arguments intended to refute them.

Domain specific knowledge is also required to identify and keep track of causal chains of reasoning that support beliefs in editorial text. These chains are sequences of cause-effect relationships and each chain shows: why plans should or should not be selected, implemented, or terminated; or why goals should or should not be pursued. Causal relationships within a chain often are not explicitly stated in editorial text, but left to be inferred by the reader. For example, Friedman's belief that "the limitations on imports will cost jobs" is supported by a reasoning chain that contains the following relationships:

1. Import restrictions by the U.S. result in a decrease in imports to the U.S.
2. The decrease in imports to the U.S. causes a decrease in foreign countries' export earnings.
3. The decrease in foreign countries' earnings causes a decrease in their spending on American exports.
4. The decrease in spending on American exports results in a decrease in earnings of American export industries.
5. The decrease in earnings of American export industries causes a decrease in the number of occupations in these industries.
6. The decrease in occupations thwarts the Reagan administration's goal of saving jobs.

In ED-JOBS, not all of these causal relations are explicitly stated. To follow Friedman's reasoning, OpEd must recognize explicit and implicit cause-effect relationships by applying knowledge about the economic quantities, goals, and plans associated with the activity of trade.

Finally, OpEd must contain knowledge of natural language in order to map words and phrases into their appropriate conceptual structures. In OpEd, editorial comprehension and question answering are performed using the techniques for conceptual parsing implemented in BORIS (qv) (Dyer, 1983), an in-depth understander of narrative text. OpEd reads input editorial text and questions in a left-to-right manner, one word or phrase at a time. As each word and/or phrase is read, OpEd's lexicon is accessed in order to identify the conceptualization underlying that word or phrase. Associated with entries in the lexicon are knowledge structures, and associated with those structures are processing strategies called *demons*. Demons are delayed procedures that implement test or action rules, where tests and actions may involve tasks such as disambiguating word senses, resolving pronoun and concept references, searching and retrieving information, matching and binding conceptualizations, and recognizing beliefs and argument structures. When a lexical item is recognized, an instance of the associated knowledge structure is placed in OpEd's working memory, and instances of the associated demons are placed in a demon agenda. Then, OpEd tests all demons in the agenda and executes those whose test portions are satisfied. After demons are executed, they are removed from the agenda. The result of executing demons is the construction of the editorial's *argument graph* (Flowers and co-workers, 1982), which represents explicitly belief content, relationships of support and attack among beliefs, and configurations of beliefs as AUs. The argument graph aids the understanding process by representing and maintaining the current context of the editorial. The argument graph also includes indexing structures and access links which provide access to the graph and are used by search and retrieval processes when answering questions about the editorial.

During question answering, OpEd uses search and re-

trieval strategies that have been developed as an extension to the question-categorization scheme proposed by Lehnert (1978) and the retrieval heuristics proposed by Dyer and Lehnert (1982). The process of selecting appropriate retrieval strategies depends on parsing and analyzing the conceptual content of each question into one of a number of conceptual question categories. Different question categories lead to different search and retrieval processes. These processes must select indexes according to the questions' input information. Once an index is selected, these processes must traverse access and memory links in order to locate an appropriate conceptualization which will be retrieved. For instance, consider another question that OpEd can answer after reading Ed-JOBS:

Q5: What does Milton Friedman believe?

A5: Milton Friedman believes that protectionist policies by the Reagan administration are bad because Milton Friedman believes that protectionist policies by the Reagan administration do not lead to the achievement of normal profits of the steel industry and the automobile industry. Milton Friedman believes that protectionist policies by the Reagan administration do not lead to the achievement of normal profits of the steel industry and the automobile industry because Milton Friedman believes that normal salary in the steel industry and the automobile industry higher than the norm thwarts the achievement of normal profits of the steel industry and the automobile industry. Milton Friedman believes that the Reagan administration is wrong because the Reagan administration believes that protectionist policies by the Reagan administration lead to the achievement of normal profits of the steel industry and the automobile industry.

Milton Friedman believes that protectionist policies by the Reagan administration are bad because Milton Friedman believes that protectionist policies by the Reagan administration will thwart the preservation of jobs for U.S. Milton Friedman believes that the Reagan administration is wrong because the Reagan administration believes that protectionist policies by the Reagan administration achieve the preservation of jobs for U.S.

To answer this question, OpEd must retrieve the instantiations of the argument units used in ED-JOBS, namely AU-ACTUAL-CAUSE and AU-OPPOSITE-EFFECT. Retrieving these instantiated AUs requires indices from argument participants to their professed beliefs, access links between beliefs and associated argument units, and retrieval functions that take argument participants as input and retrieve argument units. Once the answer is found, it must be converted from memory representation into adequate English. OpEd produces English sentences in a left-to-right manner by traversing instantiated knowledge structures and using generation patterns associated with each class of knowledge structure. OpEd's output is somewhat verbose, due to the fact that linguistic style in answer generation is not a major issue addressed in OpEd.

The memory structures retrieved during question answering are generated in English for the purpose of making them understandable to OpEd's users.

REPRESENTING POLITICO-ECONOMIC KNOWLEDGE

OpEd's model of politico-economic knowledge includes three major elements: (1) authority triangles (Schank and Carbonell, 1979), which represent conflicts involving domestic and foreign industries, (2) a trade graph (Riesbeck, 1984), which organizes cause-effect relationships among the economic quantities associated with economic actors, and (3) reasoning scripts (Dyer and co-workers, 1987; Flowers and Dyer, 1984, see SCRIPTS), which represent common chains of reasoning about the effects of protectionist plans.

Authority Triangles and Beliefs Associated With Situations of Protectionism

OpEd's representation of politico-economic conflicts is based on social acts, a representational system originally proposed by Schank (1978) and later expanded by Schank and Carbonell (1979) and Carbonell (1981). Seven basic social acts have been proposed by Schank and Carbonell: DISPUTE, PETITION, AUTHORIZE, ORDER, INVOKE, RESOLVE, and PRESSURE. Using these social acts, any conflict situation can be represented in terms of a configuration composed of two basic elements including a DISPUTE between two actors and a resolution method for settling the conflict. Such a configuration is termed authority triangle (Carbonell, 1981).

Authority triangles also provide a method for representing situations of protectionism, ie, conflicts between domestic and foreign industries that are resolved through the application of economic protection plans. Those conflicts arise when domestic industries experience decreases in sales due to increases in sales of imports by foreign industries. Such decreases in sales motivate goals to preserve domestic earnings, profitability, and jobs of workers. When these economic goals become active, domestic industries ask their government to implement trade policies that either decrease the amount of low priced imports (ie, an import quota) or increase their price (ie, an import tax). Those restrictions can be unilaterally imposed through legislation or be negotiated with foreign governments (Greenaway, 1983; Greenaway and Milner, 1979; Yoffie, 1983). In OpEd, two main situations of protectionism are distinguished:

IMPOSED-LIMIT triangle: Industry I1 from country C1 has a DISPUTE with industry I2 from country C2 over the sale price of product P2 by I2. To settle the conflict, I1 PETITIONs to government G1 of C1 for a limit (quota or tax) on P2 and G1 AUTHORIZEs such a limit.

NEGOTIATED-LIMIT triangle: Industry I1 from country C1 has a DISPUTE with industry I2 from country C2 over the sale price of product P2 by I2 in C1. To settle the conflict, I1 PETITIONs to government G1 of C1 for a limit (quota or tax) on P2. G1

RESOLVEs the conflict by INVOKing negotiations with government G2 of C2. The negotiations result in a quota that is AUTHORIZEd by G2.

For example, consider the following editorial segment (Morrow, 1983) read by OpEd:

ED-RESTRICTIONS
The American machine-tool industry is seeking protection from foreign competition. The industry has been hurt by cheaper machine tools from Japan. The toolmakers argue that restrictions on imports must be imposed so that the industry can survive. It is a wrongheaded argument. Restrictions on imports would mean that American manufacturers would have to make do with more expensive American machine tools. Inevitably, those American manufacturers would produce more expensive products. They would lose sales. Then those manufacturers would demand protection against foreign competition.

Here, the American machine-tool industry has a DISPUTE with the Japanese machine-tool industry over low-priced Japanese machine tools sold in the U.S. Due to this DISPUTE, the American manufacturers have PETITIONed for economic protection from the U.S. government. Furthermore, the American manufacturers believe that imports restrictions must be AUTHORIZEd (as opposed to negotiated) by the U.S. government. Thus, the conflict between the American and Japanese manufacturers and its proposed resolution can be represented in terms of the IMPOSED-LIMIT triangle. This representation is illustrated in Figure 1.

In contrast to ED-RESTRICTIONS, the conflict in international trade in ED-JOBS is an instance of the NEGOTIATED-LIMIT triangle. Consider this fragment of ED-JOBS:

> Recent protectionist measures by the Reagan administration . . . Voluntary limits on Japanese automobiles . . .

In ED-JOBS, the DISPUTE between the American automobile industry and the Japanese automobile industry has been RESOLVEd through the negotiations INVOKEd by the Reagan administration. Those negotiations resulted in a limit on Japanese cars AUTHORIZEd by the Japanese government. The conflict settled through the use of "voluntary limits" can be modeled as an instance of the NEGOTIATED-LIMIT triangle (Fig. 2).

Authority triangles can be integrated with the beliefs and goals of the actors involved in conflict situations. In the case of the IMPOSED-LIMIT triangle and NEGOTI-

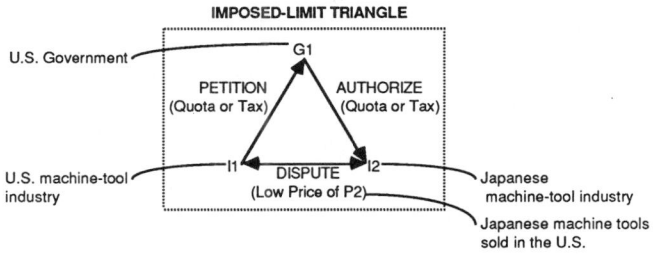

Figure 1. Representation of a trade conflict in ED-RESTRICTIONS.

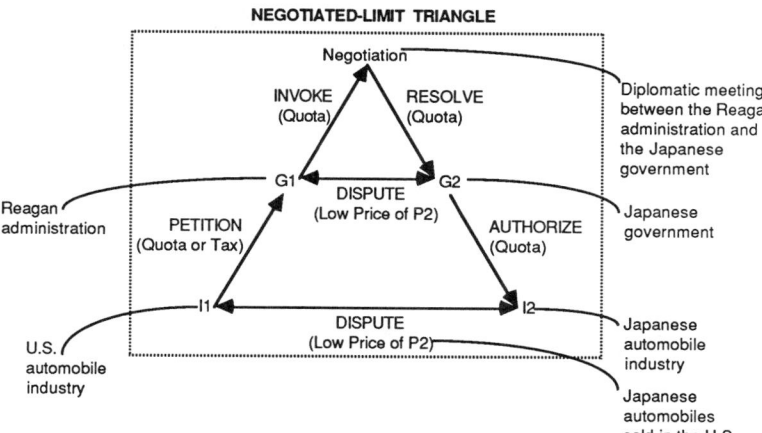

Figure 2. Representation of a trade conflict in ED-JOBS.

ATED-LIMIT triangle, knowledge of goals and beliefs is organized by the basic social acts that characterize the methods for settling conflicts in international trade. Two main rules encode such knowledge in OpEd's politico-economic model:

> *Economic-Protection Rule 1.* IF government G1 of country C1 has the active goals of preserving jobs in C1 and helping industry I1 from C1 preserve earnings and attain profitability, AND G1 believes those goals will be achieved by implementing economic protection P, THEN G1 will AUTHORIZE P or INVOKE negotiations to implement P.
>
> *Economic-Protection Rule 2.* IF industry I1 from country C1 has the active goals of preserving earnings and attaining profitability, AND I1 believes that those goals will be achieved by economic protection P from government G1 of C1 THEN I1 will PETITION G1 to implement P.

The above rules summarize the goals and beliefs of governments that impose or negotiate economic protec-

tion, and industries that PETITION for economic protection. These rules can be applied to represent relationships that are implicitly stated in editorial text. For example, the second rule can be used in ED-RESTRICTIONS to represent explicitly the connections among the American machine-tool industry's act of PETITIONing for "protection from foreign competition," its active preservation goal of not being hurt by cheaper imports, and its belief that "import restrictions must be imposed so that the industry can survive." The representation of those relationships is shown in Figure 3.

Trade Graph of Economic Quantities

As proposed by Riesbeck (1984), causal knowledge in the domain of economics can be modeled in terms of a network of economic quantities. Riesbeck's modeling approach has been adopted in OpEd to represent the causal relationships that characterize the activity of trade. The graph in Figure 4 organizes causal dependencies from the perspectives of producers and consumers. From a producer's point of view, trade can be characterized in terms of that producer's level of earnings, volume of sales, production costs,

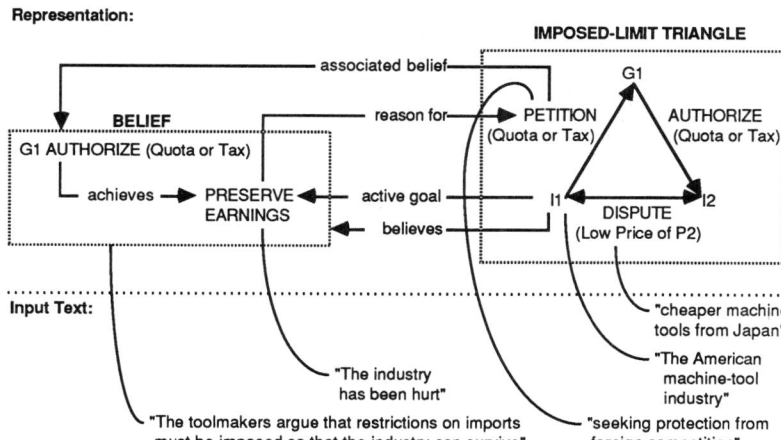

Figure 3. Goals and beliefs associated with a PETITION for economic protection.

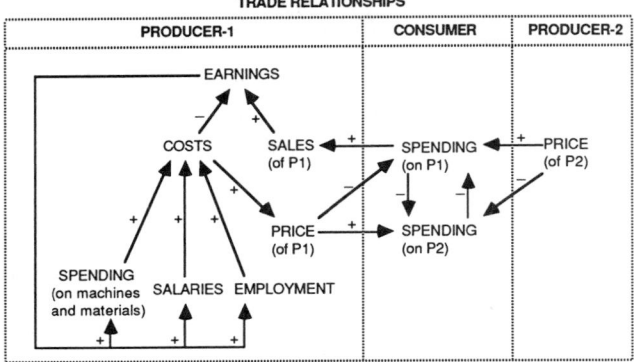

Figure 4. Graph of trade relationships.

and product prices. From a consumer's point of view, trade can be characterized in terms of product prices and level of consumer spending. The graph also shows that two economic quantities can be connected by a signed and directed link that indicates whether the quantities are directly proportional or inversely proportional to one another.

In OpEd, the graph of trade relationships provides the representational foundation for causal chains of reasoning associated with economic goals. For instance, the graph shows that the price of product P2 is connected to the earnings of PRODUCER-1 by a positive sequence of links involving consumer spending on P2, consumer spending on P1, and sales of P1. According to that sequence, when the price of P2 is low, the level of earnings of PRODUCER-1 is low. This causal relationship explains decreases in earnings experienced by producers whose prices are higher than their competitors' prices.

Modeling Reasoning About Protectionism With Reasoning Scripts

Some of the possible paths through the graph of trade relationships are more common than others and are organized in OpEd as prespecified reasoning chains called reasoning scripts (Dyer and co-workers, 1987; Flowers and

Dyer, 1984, see Scripts). Each of OpEd's reasoning scripts (prefixed by "$R-") holds a chain of cause-effect relationships involving economic quantities associated with the activity of international trade. Such a causal chain shows: (a) why economic goals become active as a result of changes in import prices and consumer spending; or (b) why economic-protection plans result in changes in the level of earnings and employment in domestic industries. For example, a side-effect of economic-protection plans is that they may not preserve (or increase) the number of jobs in an importing country, but rather decrease it. In politico-economic editorials, this side-effect is frequently brought up in arguments against the use of import restrictions, as in the following excerpt from ED-JOBS: *"Far from saving jobs, the limitations on imports [by the Reagan administration] will cost jobs. If we import less, foreign countries will earn fewer dollars. They will have less to spend on American exports. The result will be fewer jobs in export industries."* The above excerpt contains a reasoning chain on how import restrictions cause a decrease in U.S. exports and, consequently, a decrease in jobs in U.S. export industries. In OpEd, this chain is represented in terms of $R-ECON-PROTECTION→LOWER-EXPORT-JOBS. An instantiation of this reasoning script is shown in Figure 5. Figure 5 makes explicit the following relationships implicitly stated in ED-JOBS: the relationship between import restrictions and the level of U.S. spending on imports; the relationship between U.S. spending and the level of earnings by foreign countries; and the relationship between foreign earnings and the number of jobs in U.S. export industries. Thus, reasoning scripts provide a method for representing and dealing with missing steps in chains of reasoning in editorials.

BELIEFS AND BELIEF RELATIONSHIPS

Computer comprehension of editorial arguments in OpEd is based on the capability of modeling beliefs and their relationships. Abelson (1973, 1979) has pointed out that beliefs are not goals, plans, events, or states, but rather predications about these structures and their relation-

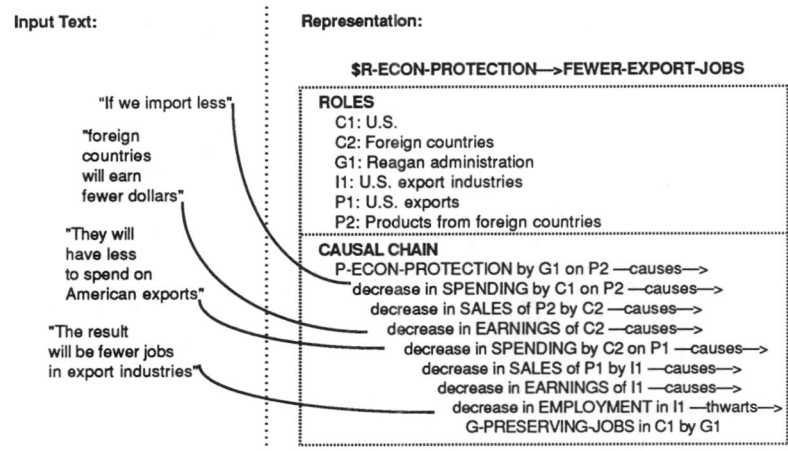

Figure 5. Instantiation of a causal reasoning chain in ED-JOBS.

ships. Three types of predications have been characterized in OpEd: (1) *evaluative beliefs,* which are judgments about the goodness or badness of domain-specific plans; (2) *causal beliefs,* which are expectations about the possible causes for the failure or achievement of domain-specific goals and the possible effects of implementing domain-specific plans; and (3) *beliefs about beliefs,* which are predications about evaluative and causal beliefs, eg, "belief B1 should not be held," "belief B1 does/does not provide evidence for belief B2," and "belief B1 contradicts belief B2." Other predications in this category, eg, "*X* believes that *Y* believes *Z*" are discussed elsewhere (Wilks and Bien, 1983).

Why is it necessary to distinguish among these types of beliefs? A basic problem in editorial comprehension is to build an internal conceptual model of editorial arguments. This model, known as an argument graph (Flowers and co-workers, 1982), represents explicitly whether beliefs in the editorial are involved in support relationships, because they provide evidence for one another, or attack relationships, because they contradict one another. The way in which a belief is supported or attacked in editorial arguments depends upon the nature of that belief. For instance, the evaluative belief that "a plan P should not be implemented" can be supported by the causal belief that "implementing P will either fail to achieve or thwart a goal G." Similarly, the evaluative belief that "a plan P should be implemented" can be supported by the causal belief that "implementing P will achieve a goal G." Editorial comprehension requires a taxonomy of the support and attack relationships that exist among different types of beliefs.

OpEd characterizes attack relationships in terms of contradictions involving planning situations that cannot occur at the same time, and opposite effects of a plan on goals that are interrelated. In contrast, the representation of support relationships captures the ways in which causal domain-knowledge, analogies, and examples can be used to justify why plans should or should not be implemented, and why plans achieve, fail to achieve, or thwart goals.

Belief Representation

Each belief in OpEd consists of three major components: the holder of the belief, the content of the belief, and links that indicate whether the belief attacks, supports, or is supported by other beliefs. The contents of beliefs involve a causal dependency between a plan and a goal, a chain of causal dependencies organized by a reasoning script, or an evaluative component. Causal dependencies include intentional relationships among goals, plans, events, and states, such as goal achievement, goal failure, goal motivation, goal suspension, plan intention, plan enablement, plan disablement, event realization, and forced events. These dependencies are represented by means of intentional links (I-links) (Dyer, 1983a), a representational system that encodes the motivations and intentions of narrative characters. Other nonintentional causal dependencies, such as those among states of economic quantities, are represented using a general causal link. The major causal dependencies used in OpEd are summarized in

Relationship Name	Representation
Goal Achievement	STATE —achieves—> GOAL
Goal Failure	STATE —thwarts—> GOAL
Goal Motivation	STATE —motivates—> GOAL
Goal Suspension	GOAL1 —suspends—> GOAL2
Plan Intention	GOAL —intends—> PLAN
Plan Enablement	STATE —enables—> PLAN
Plan Disablement	STATE —disables—> PLAN
Event Realization	PLAN —realizes—> EVENT
Forced Event	STATE —forces—> EVENT
Consequent State	EVENT —causes—> STATE
	STATE1 —causes—> STATE2

Figure 6. Causal dependencies in OpEd.

Figure 6, which indicates that goals are motivated by desires to attain, change, or maintain given states, and plans are intended to achieve active goals. Further interactions among plans and goals are mediated by chains of causal effects among events and states. For each I-link, there is a negative relation, such as STATE—not-achieves→GOAL. It is important to notice that the plan-goal relationship PLAN—thwarts→GOAL is not the same as the relationship PLAN—not-achieves→GOAL. Instead, the goal-thwarting relationship indicates one of the reasons why P can not achieve G. Similarly, the relationship PLAN—achieves→GOAL is not equal to the relationship PLAN—not-thwarts→GOAL, but rather a reason why P can not result in G's failure.

Plan-goal dependencies form the representational foundation underlying evaluative components of beliefs. Evaluative components are high level abstractions that categorize and organize concepts in terms of being "good" or "bad," or leading to "good" or "bad" (Abelson, 1979). In OpEd, evaluative components are used to represent the main positions that argument participants hold with respect to a given plan P, ie, whether they support or oppose the use of P. These plan evaluations are captured by the following constructs:

OUGHT-TO (P): A plan P should be executed IF the following situations can be expected: (1) P will achieve the goal G1 which has intended P; AND (2) P will not thwart a goal G2 which is more important than or as important as G1.

OUGHT-NOT-TO (P): A plan P should not be executed IF any of the following situations can be expected: (1) P will not achieve the goal G1 which has intended P; OR (2) P will thwart a goal G2 which is more important than or as important as G1.

For example, in the following excerpt from an editorial by the *Los Angeles Times* (Dec. 9, 1984):

ED-WRONG-POLICY
American negotiators are pursuing a protectionist course . . . in what seems a vain effort to protect U.S. steel makers . . . This is the wrong way to go . . .

the phrase "wrong way to go" indicates that the *L.A. Times* opposes restrictions on steel imports. This sentence is represented as an instantiation of OUGHT-NOT-TO.

OpEd's evaluative components categorize plans in terms of the possible positive or negative effects of implementing those plans. The notion of evaluative components in OpEd is similar in nature to the deontic notion of the "ought" of reasons (Harman, 1986), which characterizes judgments that use the term "ought" to indicate reasons for doing or not doing something.

Attack Relationships

Contents of beliefs serve as the basis for establishing whether those beliefs attack one another. In OpEd, an attack is modeled as a bidirectional relationship between two contradictory beliefs, ie, if belief B1 attacks belief B2, then belief B2 attacks belief B1. Two beliefs are considered contradictory if their contents involve either: (1) planning situations that cannot occur at the same time (ie, mutually-exclusive planning situations); or (2) opposite effects of a plan P on two interrelated goals.

Attacks Based on Mutually-Exclusive Planning Situations. An evaluative or causal belief B1 about a plan P can be contradicted by stating a belief B2 which negates the content of B1. This type of contradiction, termed *contradiction by negation* (Flowers, 1982), is the basis for three different attack structures developed within the framework of OpEd.

A-OBJECTIONABLE-PLAN: Although arguer A1 believes that plan P should be executed, arguer A2 believes that P should not be executed.

A-UNREALIZED-SUCCESS: Although arguer A1 believes that plan P achieves goal G, arguer A2 believes that P does not achieve G.

A-UNREALIZED-FAILURE: Although arguer A1 believes that plan P thwarts goal G, arguer A2 believes that P does not thwart G.

Both A-OBJECTIONABLE-PLAN and A-UNREALIZED-SUCCESS can be used to represent attacks on two beliefs associated with the execution of a plan P, namely: (1) the actor of P believes that P OUGHT-TO be implemented, and (2) the actor of P believes that P will achieve the goal G which has intended P. Frequently, these beliefs

are implicitly stated in editorial arguments. Consider again the text of ED-WRONG-POLICY, which expresses the *L.A. Times'* belief that import restrictions will not achieve the U.S. government's goals of helping steel makers preserve earnings and attain profitability. This belief attacks the implicitly stated belief by the U.S. government that import restrictions will achieve its goal of helping steel makers. Similarly, the L.A. *Times'* belief that import restrictions are "wrong" (ie, OUGHT-NOT-TO be executed) attacks the implicitly stated belief by the U.S. government that import restrictions OUGHT-TO be executed. These two attacks correspond to instances of A-UNREALIZED-SUCCESS and A-OBJECTIONABLE-PLAN, respectively.

A-UNREALIZED-FAILURE is used to represent attacks on a belief often professed by opponents of a plan P, ie, the belief that P thwarts the goal G which has intended P. For instance, consider the following excerpt from an editorial by Lee Iacocca (1986):

ED-TOUGH-POLICY
It's time to quiet down all . . . [free-trade purists] who keep telling us that getting tough on [international] trade will cost us jobs. It won't.

Here, Iacocca argues against the free-trader's belief that imposing restrictions on international trade thwarts the goal of preserving jobs. Since this goal is one of the goals that import restrictions are intended to achieve, then Iacocca's argument can be represented in terms of A-UN-REALIZED-FAILURE (Fig. 7).

Attacks Based on Opposite Effects on Interrelated Goals. Another way to contradict a belief about the effect a plan P has on a goal G1 is by stating that P has the opposite effect on G2, a goal more important than or equally important to G1. According to this type of contradiction by opposite effects, four attack relationships can be distinguished.

A-GREATER-SUCCESS: Although arguer A1 believes that plan P thwarts goal G1, arguer A2 believes that P achieves a more important goal G2.

A-GREATER-FAILURE: Although arguer A1 believes that plan P achieves goal G1, arguer A2 believes that P thwarts a more important goal G2.

A-EQUIVALENT-FAILURE: Although arguer A1 believes that plan P achieves goal G1, arguer A2

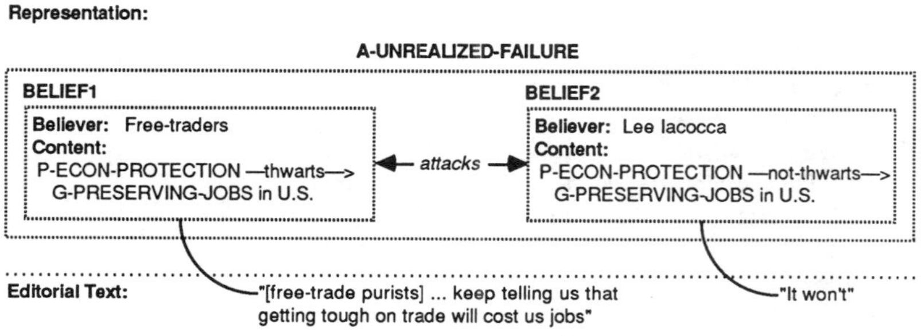

Figure 7. Attack relationship in ED-TOUGH-POLICY.

believes that P thwarts an equally important goal G2.

A-SPIRAL-FAILURE: Although arguer A2 believes that the instance P1 of plan P achieves goal G1, arguer A2 believes that P1 thwarts an equally important goal G2 AND G2's failure will require using P2, another instance of P.

These four attack relationships are used to represent arguments that contrast the negative and positive effects of a plan P in order to show that P should be favored or opposed. For example, A-GREATER-SUCCESS shows that the negative side-effects of a plan P are a small price to pay for P's positive effects. The other attack relationships involving opposite effects show that the negative side-effects of a plan P do not grant the implementation of P. For example, the following excerpt from an editorial by the L.A. *Times* (Oct. 4, 1985): *". . . legislation to limit textile and apparel imports . . . will do more harm than good . . ."* is an instance of A-GREATER-FAILURE. This instance contrasts the implicitly stated belief by legislators that import restrictions will lead to goal achievements, and the L.A. *Times'* belief that those restrictions cause major goal failures.

Support Relationships

Beliefs can also relate to one another via relationships of support. In OpEd, a support is a construct composed of three major elements: (1) a supported belief B, (2) a justification J that contains a single supporting belief or a conjunction of supporting beliefs, and (3) and a warrant W (Flowers and co-workers, 1982; Toulmin, 1958; Toulmin and co-workers, 1979) that grants the existence of the support relationship from J to B. Warrants are inference rules that establish why conclusions can be drawn from supporting evidences (ie, warrants are beliefs about beliefs).

Support structures are used in OpEd to represent instances of plan-based reasoning in editorial arguments, ie, the reasoning used by arguers to justify why plans should or should not be implemented or why plans will or will not cause goal achievements or failures. According to the nature of these reasoning instances, three basic types of sup-

port relationships in OpEd are characterized here: (1) refinements of plan evaluations, (2) refinements of plan-goal relationships, and (3) support based on analogies.

Supports Based on Refinements of Plan Evaluations. An evaluative belief about a plan P can be justified by refining that evaluation, ie, by stating the goal failures or achievements that result from implementing P. There are five support structures in OpEd that are refinements used to represent arguments in favor or against the use of a plan P. For example, S-REALIZED-SUCCESS embodies the following reasoning:

S-REALIZED-SUCCESS: Arguer A believes that plan P should be executed because A believes that P will achieve goal G which has intended P.

To illustrate this support structure, consider the following excerpt from an editorial by the *Los Angeles Times* (Feb. 16, 1984):

> ED-JOB-SAVING-QUOTAS
> The Japanese quotas were pushed hardest by the United Auto Workers union, which touted them . . . as a means of restoring American jobs . . .

In ED-JOB-SAVING-QUOTAS, the position of the U.A.W. is that restrictions on Japanese automobiles should be imposed, and import restrictions will achieve the goal of preserving jobs in the U.S. ED-JOB-SAVING-QUOTAS is represented in terms of S-REALIZED-SUCCESS (Fig. 8).

S-UNREALIZED-SUCCESS involves the use of a negative achievement relationship to justify the belief that a plan P should be opposed:

S-UNREALIZED-SUCCESS: Arguer A believes that plan P should not be executed because A believes that P will not achieve the goal G which has intended P.

This support structure is used in OpEd to represent the following fragment of Ed-JOBS: *"Recent protectionist measures by the Reagan administration have . . . disap-*

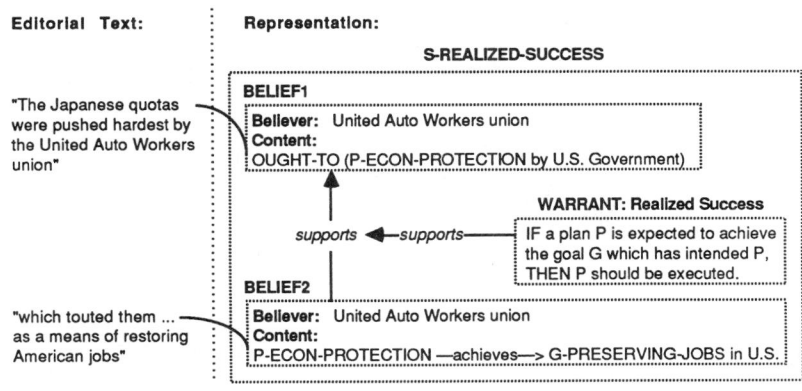

Figure 8. Support relationship in ED-JOB-SAVING-QUOTAS.

pointed . . . us . . . They do [not] . . . promote the long-run health of the industries affected . . ." In ED-JOBS, the affect description "disappointed" indicates that Friedman believes that import restrictions should not be implemented. This belief is justified by the negative achievement relationship stated in the latter sentence, where the phrase "long-run health" refers to the industries' goal of attaining profitability. Since this goal is one of the goals that import restrictions are intended to achieve, then Friedman's argument involves an instance of S-UNREALIZED-SUCCESS.

The remaining support structures involving refinements of plan evaluations are:

S-GREATER-FAILURE: Arguer A believes that plan P should not be executed because A believes that P will thwart a goal G2 more important than the goal G1 which has intended P.

S-EQUIVALENT-FAILURE: Arguer A believes that plan P should not be executed because A believes that P will thwart a goal G2 as important as the goal G1 which has intended P.

S-SPIRAL-FAILURE: Arguer A believes that the instance P1 of plan P should not be executed because A believes that P1 will thwart a goal G2 as important as the goal G1 (which has intended P) AND G2's failure will require using P2, another instance of P.

For example, the following excerpt from an editorial by Bresnahan (1984) is an instance of S-GREATER-FAILURE: *". . . I think the import quotas are terrible public policy . . . [P]rotecting domestic industries from foreign competition does more harm than good."*

Supports Based on Refinements of Plan-Goal Relationships. One of the ways to justify the belief that a plan P leads to a goal achievement or a goal failure is by providing a chain of causal effects that describes how those goal relationships may take place. At the abstract level, this reasoning strategy is captured by the following support structures:

S-POSSIBLE-SUCCESS: Arguer A believes that plan P will achieve goal G because A believes that P causes state S1 AND S1 causes . . . state Sn AND Sn achieves G.

S-POSSIBLE-FAILURE: Arguer A believes that plan P will thwart goal G because A believes that P causes state S1 AND S1 causes . . . state Sn AND Sn thwarts G.

At the level of domain-knowledge, the chains of causal effects organized by instances of the above support structures in editorials correspond to instances of reasoning scripts. For example, consider the following passage from Greenaway and Milner (1979, pp. 40–41):

ED-BENEFICIAL-TARIFF
Suppose . . . policy-makers impose a tariff on low price textiles from abroad . . . Because the post-tariff price of imports

is higher than their free-trade price, domestic textile producers . . . can now supply more of the (diminished) market. Thus, . . . domestic procedures . . . benefit from tariffs.

Here, the belief that tariffs achieve the goal of attaining profitability for domestic producers is supported by a causal chain on how tariffs switch domestic spending from imports to domestic products and, consequently, increase the level of earnings of domestic producers.

Instances of reasoning scripts can also be used to justify beliefs about the negative-spiral effects resulting from implementing a plan P. At the abstract level, those justifications are characterized by the following support structure:

S-POSSIBLE-SPIRAL-FAILURE: Arguer A believes that plan P1 (an instance of P) will thwart goal G AND G will intend plan P2 (another instance of P) because A believes that P1 causes state S1 AND S1 causes . . . state Sn AND Sn thwarts G AND G's failure requires using P2.

For example, consider the following paragraph which summarizes an argument presented in Cuddington and McKinnon (1979, pp. 4–6):

ED-COUNTERATTACK
Free-trade economists believe that import restrictions by the U.S. will cause foreign countries to retaliate. They argue that import quotas will cause trade losses for foreign countries. To recover from those losses, foreign countries will impose tariffs on products they import from the U.S.

The above argument involves the use of S-POSSIBLE-SPIRAL-FAILURE and the reasoning script $R-ECON-PROTECTION→ECON-RETALIATION to justify the belief that import restrictions lead to retaliations. These constructs are illustrated in Figure 9.

Supports Based on Analogies. Another strategy used to justify causal beliefs in editorial arguments is reasoning by analogy. For example, consider S-SIMILAR-SPIRAL-FAILURE. This structure embodies the following reasoning:

S-SIMILAR-SPIRAL-FAILURE: Arguer A believes that plan P1 (an instance of P) will thwart goal G1 AND G1's failure will require using P2 (another instance of P) because A believes that plan P3 (similar to P1) has thwarted goal G2 (similar to G1) in the past AND G2's failure has required using plan P4 (similar to P2).

S-SIMILAR-SPIRAL-FAILURE is used in the following segment from an editorial by Feldstein and Feldstein (1985):

ED-1930-RETALIATION
. . . [A] 20% tax on imports . . . could easily provoke retaliation by foreign governments . . . The last major trade war [was] precipitated by our 1930 Hawley-Smoot tariff . . .

Text:

"Free trade economists believe that import restrictions by the U.S. will cause foreign countries to retaliate"

"They argue that import quotas"

"will result in trade losses"

"To recover from those losses"

"foreign countries will impose tariffs"

Representation:

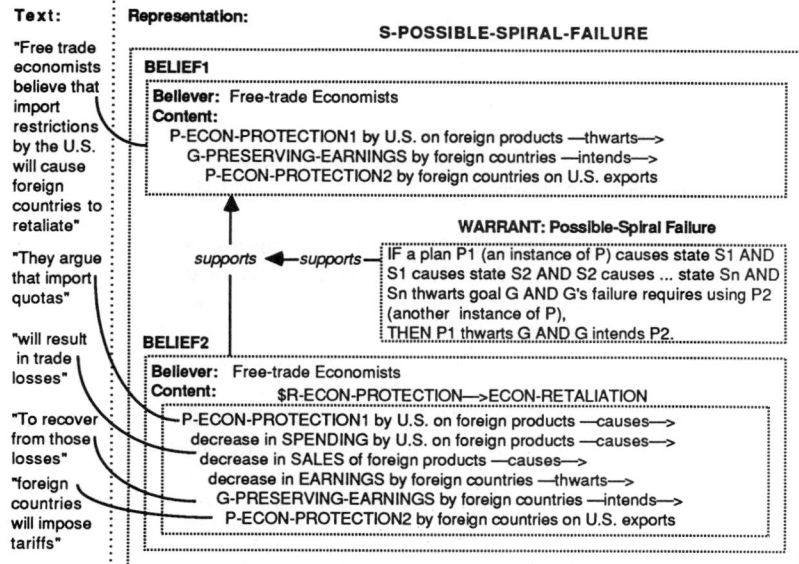

S-POSSIBLE-SPIRAL-FAILURE

BELIEF1

Believer: Free-trade Economists
Content:
    P-ECON-PROTECTION1 by U.S. on foreign products —thwarts—>
        G-PRESERVING-EARNINGS by foreign countries —intends—>
        P-ECON-PROTECTION2 by foreign countries on U.S. exports

WARRANT: Possible-Spiral Failure

supports ◀— *supports*

IF a plan P1 (an instance of P) causes state S1 AND
S1 causes state S2 AND S2 causes ... state Sn AND
Sn thwarts goal G AND G's failure requires using P2
(another instance of P),
THEN P1 thwarts G AND G intends P2.

BELIEF2

Believer: Free-trade Economists
Content: $R-ECON-PROTECTION—>ECON-RETALIATION
    P-ECON-PROTECTION1 by U.S. on foreign products —causes—>
    decrease in SPENDING by U.S. on foreign products —causes—>
    decrease in SALES of foreign products —causes—>
    decrease in EARNINGS by foreign countries —thwarts—>
    G-PRESERVING-EARNINGS by foreign countries —intends—>
    P-ECON-PROTECTION2 by foreign countries on U.S. exports

Figure 9. Supporting causal chain in ED-COUN-TERATTACK.

Here, Feldstein and Feldstein predict the outcome of the 20% tax on imports by using a historical precedent. Specifically, their argument contains the following relationships: (1) the proposed tax on imports will thwart the goal by foreign countries of preserving earnings, (2) this goal failure will cause foreign countries to impose import restrictions on U.S. products, (3) the proposed tax is similar to the Hawley-Smoot tariff which caused trade losses for foreign countries in the 1930s, and (4) those losses caused foreign countries to impose tariffs on U.S. products. Clearly, ED-1930-RETALIATION is an instance of S-SIMILAR-SPIRAL-FAILURE.

Reasoning by analogy also serves as the basis for showing why a plan P cannot achieve a goal G, or may achieve or thwart a goal G. For more discussion of belief support and attack relationships, see Alvarado (1990).

ARGUMENT UNITS

In addition to knowledge of belief content and belief relationships, OpEd must know how attack and support relationships are combined to argue against an opponent. This abstract knowledge of argument structure is fundamental to the comprehension process because one-sided arguments in editorials are not instances of single attack or support relationships, but rather configurations of such relationships. Those configurations allow editorial writers to show awareness of their opponents' beliefs, contradict their opponent's beliefs, and provide justifications for their own beliefs.

AUs provide a system for representing one-sided arguments about the use of plans. Such arguments are centered on two contradictory plan evaluations espoused by an arguer and the arguer's implicit opponent. Each AU is composed of six major elements: (1) opponent's plan evaluation, (2) arguer's attack on opponent's plan evaluation,

(3) arguer's justification for the attack on opponent's plan evaluation, (4) opponent's justification for his or her plan evaluation, (5) the arguer's attack on opponent's justification, and (6) arguer's justification for the attack on opponent's justification. According to the nature of the arguer's attacks and justification, four basic types of AUs have been characterized in OpEd: unrealized success, realized failure, realized success, and unrealized failure.

Argument Units Based on Unrealized Successes

In order to rebut the argument that "a plan P should be implemented because P will achieve goal G," an arguer may use the following strategy: show that P will not achieve G, and use that negative-achievement relationship as the reason to claim that P should not be implemented. In this argumentation strategy, showing that P will not achieve G involves using one of the following justifications:

- P thwarts G.
- G is being thwarted by state S1, and P can not cause S2 (the opposite of S1).
- G can only be achieved by plan P1.
- P1 (similar to P) has not achieved goal G1 (similar to G) in the past.
- P1 (prototypic instance of P) has not achieved G1 (prototypic instance of G) in the past.

Examples of three AUs, based on the fact that a plan will not achieve a goal, include AU-OPPOSITE-EFFECT, AU-ACTUAL-CAUSE, and AU-SIMILAR-UNREALIZED-SUCCESS.

AU-SIMILAR-UNREALIZED-SUCCESS characterizes arguments in which the effects of a plan P1 serve as the basis to justify why a similar plan P will not work:

AU-SIMILAR-UNREALIZED-SUCCESS: Although opponent O believes that plan P should be used because P will achieve goal G, arguer A believes that P will not achieve G because plan P1 (similar to P) has not achieved goal G1 (similar to G) in the past. Therefore, A believes that P should not be used.

For example, consider the following excerpt from an editorial by Thurow (1983):

ED-HARLEY-DAVIDSON

. . . [A] tariff on large motorcycles . . . will not give America a world-class motorcycle industry. And if a world-class . . . industry is not . . . [achieved], we should not have . . . [an] industrial policy . . . for motorcycles . . . Harley-Davidson [the only U.S. producer] argues that it needs time to become competitive . . . But . . . [t]he American steel industry has been protected since the late 1960s and is less competitive today than it was then . . .

Thurow's argument is an instance of AU-SIMILAR-UN-REALIZED-SUCCESS, as shown in Figure 10. Thurow's refutation to Harley-Davidson's argument is based on the historical precedent set by restrictions on steel imports. Specifically, Thurow's argument contains the following relationships: import restrictions have been used in the past to help the U.S. steel industry become competitive; those restrictions did not work for the steel industry; the proposed tariff on large motorcycles is similar to the import restrictions used to protect the steel industry; and the proposed tariff will also fail to help Harley-Davidson become competitive.

Argument Units Based on Realized Failures

Another way to rebut an opponent's argument for endorsing a plan P is by showing that P causes negative side-effects which cannot be outweighed by P's benefits. Three types of negative side-effects can be distinguished here: (1) P thwarts a goal G1 more important than the goal G which has intended P; (2) P thwarts a goal G1 equally important or equivalent to G which has intended P; and (3) P causes goal failures that require repeated applications of P. An example of an argument unit involving goal-failure rebuttals is AU-SPIRAL-EFFECT:

AU-SPIRAL-EFFECT: Although opponent O believes that P1 (an instance of plan P) should be used because P1 will achieve goal G, arguer A believes that P1 will thwart an equally important goal G1 which will intend P2 (another instance of P) because P1 causes state S1 AND S1 causes . . . state Sn AND Sn thwarts G1 AND G1's failure requires using P2. Therefore, A believes P1 should not be used.

To illustrate this AU, consider again Morrow's argument in ED-RESTRICTIONS. In this editorial, Morrow opposes the toolmakers position that import restrictions are needed to achieve the toolmakers' goal of preserving earnings. Morrow argues that:

1. Import restrictions will force U.S. manufacturers to buy expensive American machine tools.
2. U.S. manufacturers will experience an increase in their production costs.
3. U.S. manufacturers will have to raise their prices and, consequently, will lose sales to cheaper imports.
4. To recover from their losses, U.S. manufacturers will need help in the form of import restrictions.

Thus, Morrow establishes that the proposed import restrictions are a bad idea because they will trigger a protectionist spiral in the U.S. The representation of Morrow's argument is illustrated in Figure 11.

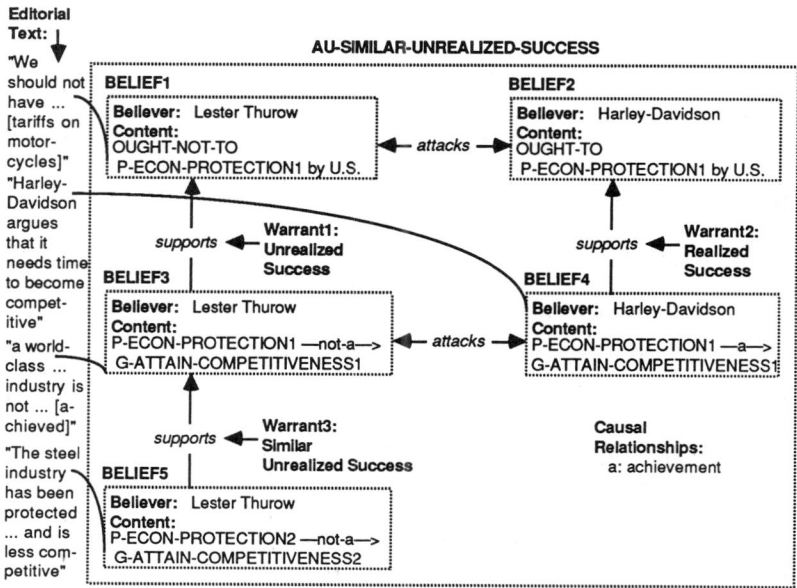

Figure 10. Instance of AU-SIMILAR-UNREAL-IZED-SUCCESS.

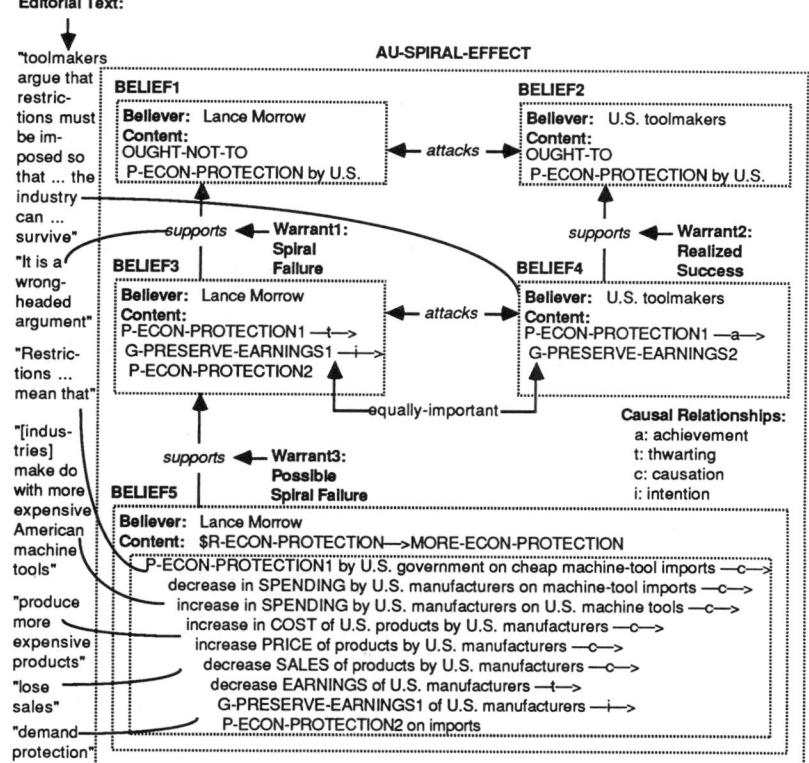

Editorial Text:

"toolmakers argue that restrictions must be imposed so that ... the industry can ... survive"

"It is a wrongheaded argument"

"Restrictions ... mean that"

"[industries] make do with more expensive American machine tools"

"produce more expensive products"

"lose sales"

"demand protection"

Figure 11. Instance of AU-SPIRAL-EFFECT.

Argument Units Based on Realized Successes

Editorials may also involve rebuttals to the argument that "plan P should not be used because P will not achieve the goal G which intended P." In those rebuttals, an editorial writer may use cause-effect chains, analogies, or examples in order to demonstrate that P will achieve G. For instance, consider Iacocca's (1986) response to the U.S. government's position on import restrictions:

ED-FORGOTTEN-JOBS

. . . A job is a . . . commitment . . . involving . . . the government . . . [T]hat's why Japanese trade policies . . . [k]eep unemployment rate so low that it's even tough to measure. But the people making our trade policies . . . seem to believe that [American] jobs can take care of themselves . . . It's time to . . . [start] getting touch on trade . . .

Iacocca's argument is an instance of AU-SIMILAR-SUCCESS:

AU-SIMILAR-SUCCESS: Although opponent O believes that plan P should not be used because P will not achieve goal G, arguer A believes that P will achieve G because plan P1 (similar to P) has achieved goal G1 (similar to G) in the past. Therefore, A believes that P should be used.

Iacocca uses the preceding structure to present a counter analogy to the U.S. policy maker's argument that impos-

ing import restrictions will not save U.S. jobs. Iacocca argues that import restrictions should be imposed because: Japan has imposed import restrictions in the past; those restrictions have saved Japanese jobs; and similar restrictions by the United States will also save U.S. jobs.

An arguer can also bring up the major goal achievements resulting from a plan P to rebut the argument that "P should not be used because P will lead to a goal failure." This argumentation strategy is the basis for AU-MAJOR-SUCCESS:

AU-MAJOR-SUCCESS: Although opponent O believes that plan P should not be used because P will thwart goal G2 more important than or equally important to G1 (one of the goals which has intended P), arguer A believes that P will achieve an even more important goal G because P causes state S1 AND S1 causes . . . state Sn and Sn achieves G. Therefore, A believes P should be used.

Argument Units Based on Unrealized Failures

Another way to defend the use of a plan P against the claim that "P leads to goal failures" involves two steps: (1) showing that P will not cause the alleged failures, and (2) stating that P should be used because it will achieve the goal G which has intended P. Showing that P does not lead to the failure of a goal G involves using one of the following justifications:

- P achieves G.
- G is being achieved by state S1, and P cannot cause S2 (the opposite of S1).
- G can only be thwarted by plan P1.
- P2 (similar to P) has not thwarted goal G2 (similar to G) in the past.
- P2 (prototypic instance of P) has not thwarted G2 (prototypic instance of G) in the past.

As an example of rebuttals involving unrealized-goal failures, consider a liberal argument in favor of wage controls appearing in Staebler and Ross (1965, pp. 132–133):

ED-GENERAL-MOTORS

. . . As for . . . [the conservative] charge that liberal [minimum-wage] legislation [to increase the living standard of U.S. workers] has been . . . to the [great] detriment of business, it just isn't true . . . [L]ook at the auto industry . . . Profits are at a record high and . . . there is no indication that . . . [legislation] ha[s] kept GM from growing spectacularly . . . Business performance and conditions have never been better. Liberals can be proud . . .

The preceding excerpt is an instance of AU-PROTOTYPI-CAL-UNREALIZED-FAILURE, which is illustrated in Figure 12 and embodies the following abstract argument:

AU-PROTOTYPICAL-UNREALIZED-FAILURE:
Although opponent O believes that plan P should not be used because P will thwart goal G more important than or equally important to G1 (the goal which has intended P), arguer A believes that P will not thwart G because P2 (a prototype of P) has not thwarted G2 (prototype of G) in the past. Therefore, A believes that P should be used because P will achieve G1.

In ED-GENERAL-MOTORS, the conservative position is that imposing wage controls is a bad idea because it thwarts businesses' goal of attaining profitability. To rebut this position, the liberal argues that: (1) wage controls help U.S. workers achieve the goal of attaining a higher standard of living, and (2) wage controls do not thwart businesses' goal of attaining profitability because that has not been the result in the prototypical case involving wage controls in General Motors. Thus, the liberal uses AU-PROTOTYPICAL-UNREALIZED-FAILURE to argue that wage controls should be continued.

Generality of Argument Units

The editorial segments considered so far correspond to instances of single AUs. In general, larger editorial excerpts (and editorials themselves) are composed of configurations of instantiated AUs. Consider again the complete text and representation of Friedman's arguments in ED-JOBS. As seen in Figure 13, ED-JOBS is composed of instances of AU-ACTUAL-CAUSE, AU-OPPOSITE-EFFECT, and S-POSSIBLE-FAILURE.

In addition to organizing patterns of belief relationships in argument graphs, AUs provide a general system for representing editorial arguments in any language or domain. AU theory also implies that the same abstract argument knowledge maybe used to represent editorials

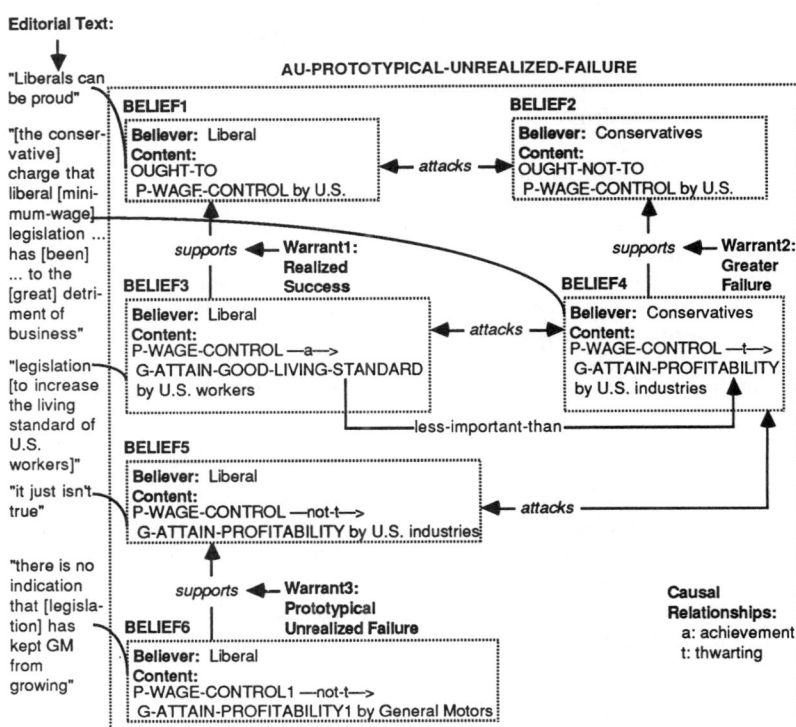

Figure 12. Instance of AU-PROTOTYPICAL-UN-REALIZED-FAILURE.

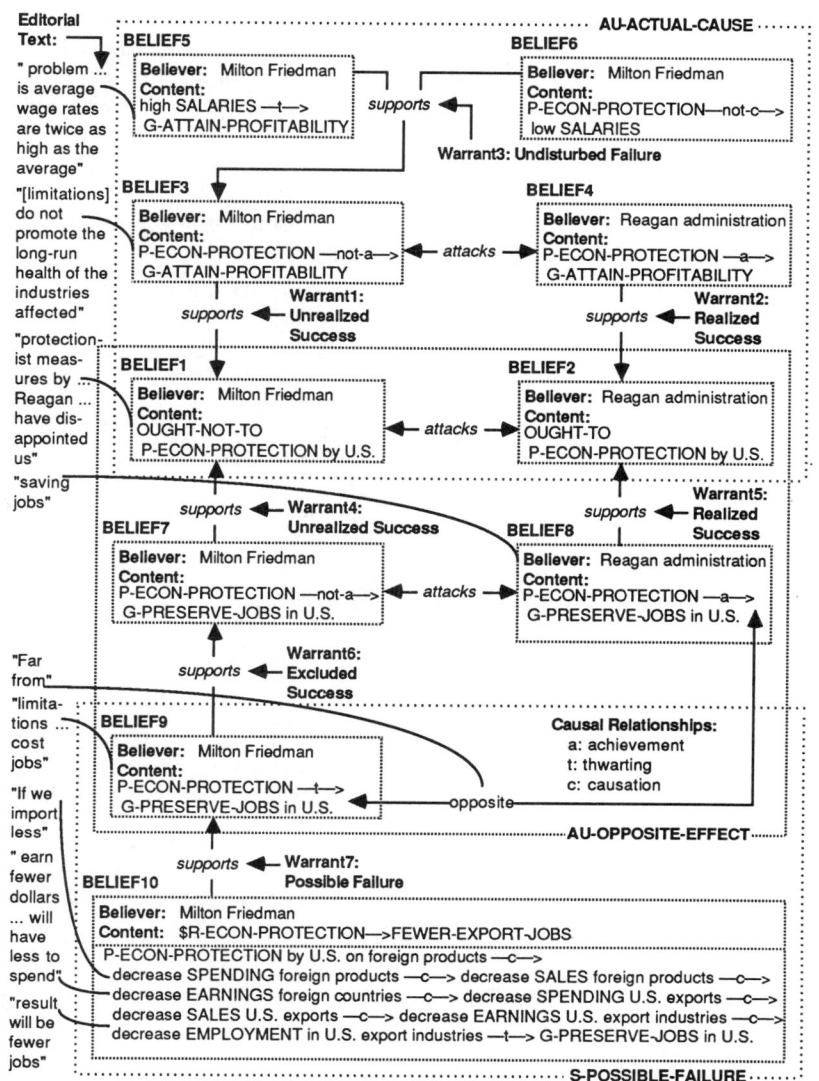

Figure 13. Argument graph of ED-JOBS.

in any domain. For example, consider an editorial segment (*L.A. Times,* Dec. 26, 1984) in the domain of arms control:

ED-STAR-WARS

. . . The case is growing against programs . . . which would turn outer space into a target range . . . President Reagan's "Star Wars" . . . is a shield . . . that would shoot down Soviet missiles . . . before they could reach a target . . . The . . . argument against "Star Wars" is that . . . [it] could be overwhelmed by what the Soviet Union does best—building more missiles than the shield . . . [is] designed to stop . . . "Star Wars" . . . works directly against Reagan's declared goal—an absolute reduction of nuclear warheads in the world. With "Star Wars," the incentive would be to build more, not to throw away any . . .

At an abstract level, the one-sided argument in ED-STAR-WARS is characterized by the combination of an AU and a support structure, namely:

AU-OPPOSITE-EFFECT: The editorial writer refutes the argument that a plan P (build Star Wars) should be implemented because P achieves the goal G (protect USA). The writer argues that P will not achieve G because P will thwart G.

S-POSSIBLE-FAILURE: The editorial writer argues that P will thwart G because P causes a state S1(increased Soviet missiles) which thwarts G.

Thus, AU theory provides a representational scheme able to support computer comprehension of arguments in multiple domains. See Alvarado (1990) for a detailed description of the taxonomy of argument units.

Finally, AU theory also provides an explanation of how humans organize and apply their own abstract knowledge of argumentation. Long and Alvarado (1991) have performed experiments to examine the psychological validity of the concept of AU. The experiments were designed to investigate whether AUs contribute to readers' ability to recognize similarities among editorial texts. Subjects were asked to read a number of short editorials. Included in the corpus of texts were editorials based on three different types of AUs. Subjects were asked to sort the texts into groups with similar argument strategies. The results indicated that subjects were able to recognize the similarity among editorials based on the same AUs, but could only do so after they were required to write a summary of each editorial before performing the sorting task. These data provide preliminary support for the psychological validity of AUs as knowledge structures that influence editorial text comprehension.

META-ARGUMENT UNITS

Meta-arguments (Alvarado, 1990; Alvarado and co-workers, 1990a, 1990b) are one-sided arguments involving attacks on warrants. Meta-arguments occur in editorial text whenever the editorial writer shows that his or her opponent cannot use a given belief B1 to justify another belief B2. These one-sided arguments are represented in terms of meta-Argument Units (meta-AUs). Each meta-AU is composed of three elements: (1) opponent's belief B1 and its justification J1 (2) arguer's belief B2 that opponent should not use J1 to support B1, and (3) arguer's justification J2 for B2. According to the nature of the arguer's justification, two types of meta-AUs can be distinguished including meta-AUs based on hypocritical behavior and meta-AUs based on unsound reasoning. The first type captures meta-arguments that appear in editorials dealing with the use of plans, such as editorials on how protection-

ism undermines a government's professed free-trade views. The second type characterizes meta-arguments that occur in discussions about the validity of an opponent's reasoning, such as discussions about what kind of support strategies are acceptable when justifying the existence of God.

Meta-Argument Units Based on Hypocritical Behavior

One way to disallow an opponent's argument A1 for opposing the use of a plan is by showing that A1 is inconsistent with the opponent's behavior. This argumentation strategy involves the theme of hypocrisy (Dyer, 1983) and is frequently used in editorials to argue that: (1) an opponent's professed opposition to using a plan P is inconsistent with that opponent's implementation of an instance of P; or (2) that an opponent's criticism of a plan P1 used by a third party is inconsistent with that opponent's use of a plan P2 that has the same negative side-effects of P1. That is, hypocrisy-based arguments specify argument errors that result from inconsistencies between actions and professed beliefs or from inconsistencies between actions and criticisms. For example, consider the following segment from an editorial by Thurow (1983):

ED-TARIFF-INCREASE
The Reagan administration argues that America does not need an industrial policy . . . to guarantee economic success under capitalism. Yet, the Reagan administration has just . . . increase[d] . . . tariffs on large motorcycles from 4.4 percent to 49.4 percent . . .

Thurow's argument in ED-TARIFF-INCREASE is an instance of the following meta-AU:

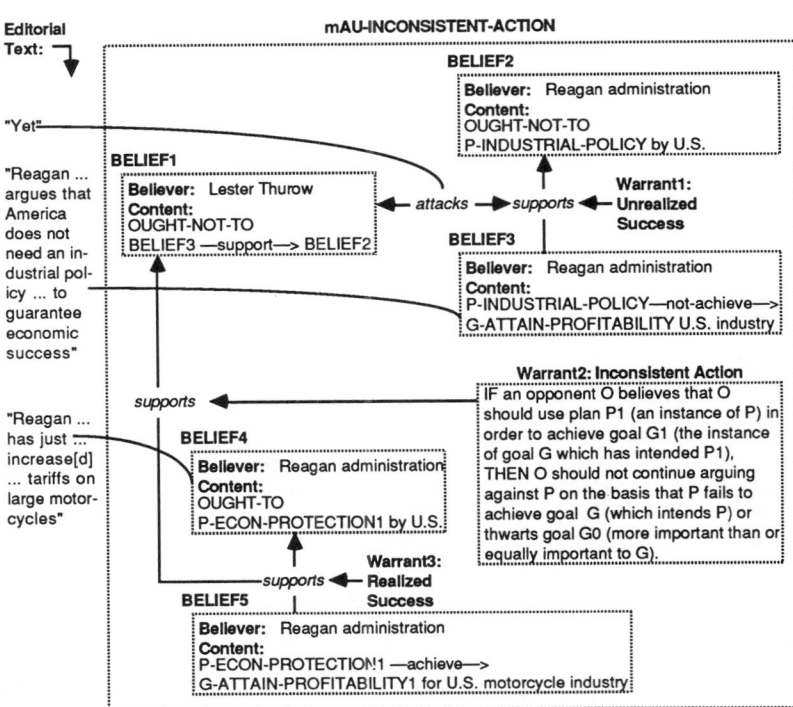

Figure 14. Instance of mAU-INCONSISTENT-ACTION.

mAU-INCONSISTENT-ACTION: Although opponent O has argued that plan P should not be used because P fails to achieve G (the goal which intends P) or thwarts G0 (a goal more important than or equally important to G), arguer A believes O should not continue arguing that way because O also believes O's plan P1 (an instance of P) should be used to achieve goal G1 (an instance of G).

Thurow uses mAU-INCONSISTENT-ACTION to attack the Reagan administration's professed position that the U.S. does not have to implement an industrial policy to help domestic industries become profitable. Thurow believes that the Reagan administration cannot use such an argument because: the administration has just imposed tariffs on motorcycles; tariffs are industrial policies to help domestic industries become profitable; and the tariffs on motorcycles are inconsistent with the administration's nonintervention argument. The representation of Thurow's argument is shown in Figure 14.

mAU-INCONSISTENT-ACTION organizes a configuration of supports and attacks in which an arguer's evaluation of his or her opponent's professed position is justified with the opponent's own beliefs about a plan he or she just implemented. Such plan-based beliefs are frequently unstated in editorials and are made explicit in meta-AU representations. For example, in ED-TARIFF-INCREASE, Thurow's attack on the Reagan administration's nonintervention position is justified by using the administration's implicitly stated belief that tariffs on motorcycles are needed to help the U.S. motorcycle industry attain profitability.

Meta-Argument Units Based on Unsound Reasoning

Another way to disallow an opponent's argument A1 is by showing that A1 contains reasoning errors. This strategy is the basis for meta-AUs involving attacks on the reasoning underlying an opponent's belief that a given explana-

tion is correct. According to the nature of the errors in the opponent's reasoning, four meta-AUs have been characterized: burden of proof, plausibility, tautology, and self-contradiction. For instance, mAU-BURDEN-OF-PROOF is used to refute the argument that an explanation E is correct if E cannot be disproved.

mAU-BURDEN-OF-PROOF: Although opponent O has argued that E is the correct explanation of situation S because E cannot be disproved, arguer A believes O should not argue that way because O has not proved E AND disproving E only causes an infinite disproof spiral.

For example, consider Johnson's (1981, pp. 11–14) reply to an argument about God's existence:

ED-UNIVERSE
. . . Many theists insist that it is the responsibility of the atheist to offer evidence justifying his lack of belief . . . [that] God . . . is necessary in order to explain the existence of [the universe] . . . The . . . point to notice is that . . . if one offers an explanation of something, one must be prepared to provide reasons for accepting the explanation . . . By . . . [this] token, it is incumbent upon the theist to provide reasons for his belief that God is the true explanation of the universe . . . The atheist, for his part, . . . need only demonstrate that the theist has failed to justify his position . . . The reason for this procedure is fairly straightforward: . . . The theist claims that the atheist must disprove God's existence. The atheist could reply that there is conclusive evidence to suggest that God does not exist and thus it is the theist who must disprove the existence of such evidence. The demand for disproof inevitably leads to an inconclusive farce . . .

Johnson does not argue against the belief that God is the explanation of the universe, but rather against the disproof-based strategy used to justify such a belief. Johnson argues that the theist should not use that strategy because: (1) the theist has not provided proof of the exis-

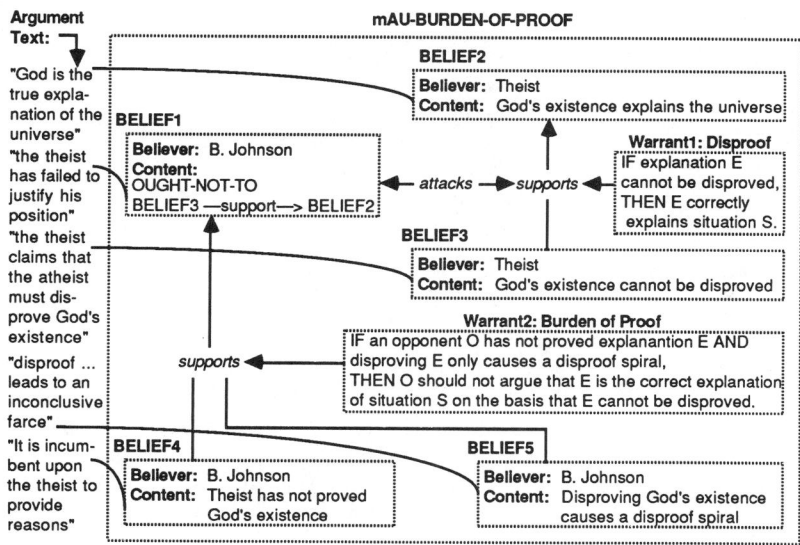

Figure 15. Instance of mAU-BURDEN-OF-PROOF.

tence of God; (2) the theist believes God's existence cannot be disproved; and (3) disproof only leads to attempts to disprove evidence for prior disproof and, consequently, does not validate the theist's claim that God is the explanation of the universe. Thus, Johnson believes that the theist can not argue by shifting burden of proof of God's existence. The representation of Johnson's argument is shown in Figure 15. (In Fig. 15, the conceptual contents of beliefs involving religions concepts are described in English. Modeling religions concepts currently falls outside OpEd's scope.)

RECOGNIZING ARGUMENT STRUCTURES AND INFERRING BELIEFS

Understanding an editorial can be viewed as a process that involves: (1) extracting the beliefs, belief relationships, and AUs underlying the editorial; and (2) integrating those structures into an argument graph. A fundamental problem that must be faced during this process is that the editorial may not contain explicit descriptions of all the beliefs held by the editorial writer and his or her implicit opponents. As a result, those beliefs must be inferred from the editorial text. OpEd applies strategies to infer: evaluative beliefs from descriptions of emotional reactions and explicit beliefs; causal beliefs from evaluative beliefs, reasoning scripts from causal beliefs; and AUs from various linguistic constructs and from beliefs involving plan failures. For example, consider a simplified, annotated trace of the major inferences OpEd makes when reading Friedman's argument in ED-JOBS.

"... *measures ... disappointed us*"
$\Longrightarrow$ NEGATIVE-AFFECT by Friedman
$=$infer$\Rightarrow$ B1: Friedman believes (Reagan administration OUGHT-NOT-TO execute measures)

In ED-JOBS, Friedman does not ever explicitly say that he is against the Reagan administration's plan of "protectionist measures." Friedman simply states that these measures have "disappointed" him. OpEd must actually infer that Friedman therefore does not believe in his plan.

"... *limits ... bad for the nation*"
$\Longrightarrow$ limits —thwart$\rightarrow$ GOAL U.S.
$=$infer$\Rightarrow$ B2: Friedman believes (limits —thwart$\rightarrow$ GOAL U.S.)
          B2 —supports$\rightarrow$ B1

The text does not explicitly state what the connection is between "limits" and "protectionist measures." The inference, that belief B2 supports B1, is made by examining the relationship between "limits on Japanese automobiles" and "protectionist measures" and recognizing that limitations on product imports is an instance of the general plan of protectionism.

"... *not promote health of industries ...*"
$\Longrightarrow$ limits —not-achieve$\rightarrow$ G-ATTAIN-PROFITABIL-ITY

$=$infer$\Rightarrow$ B3: Friedman believes (limits —not-achieve$\rightarrow$ G-ATTAIN-PROFITABILITY)
          B3 —supports$\rightarrow$ B1

"... *The problem ... is ... wage rates ...*"
$\Longrightarrow$ high wage-rates —thwart$\rightarrow$ G-ATTAIN-PROFITABILITY
$=$infer$\Rightarrow$ B4: Friedman believes (high wage-rates —thwart$\rightarrow$ G-ATTAIN-PROFITABILITY)
$=$activate$\Rightarrow$ AU-ACTUAL-CAUSE (Arguer: Friedman)
$=$infer$\Rightarrow$ B5: Reagan administration believes (limits —achieve$\rightarrow$ G-ATTAIN-PROFITABILITY)

As each belief content is constructed, the goal/plan relationships are compared against argument units that have similar I-links. Since wage-rates thwart the same goal that limits achieve, the argument unit AU-ACTUAL-CAUSE is recognized.

"... *Far from saving ... limitations cost ...*"
$\Longrightarrow$ OPPOSITE: Success (limits —achieve$\rightarrow$ G-PRE-SERVE-JOBS)
              Failure (limits —thwart$\rightarrow$ G-PRE-SERVE-JOBS)
$=$refine$\Rightarrow$ B2: Friedman believes (limits —thwart—G-PRESERVE-JOBS U.S.)
$=$activate$\Rightarrow$ AU-OPPOSITE-EFFECT (Arguer: Friedman)
$=$infer$\Rightarrow$ B6: Reagan administration believes (limits —achieve$\rightarrow$ G-PRESERVE-JOBS U.S.)

Here, the same plan both achieves and thwarts the same goal. This opposition is built by a demon attached to the pattern ⟨"far from" x, y⟩. This demon examines the conceptual structures bound to x and y. If they are conceptual opposites and believed by different individuals, then AU-OPPOSITE-EFFECT is instantiated.

"... *import less ... earn fewer dollars ... less to spend ... fewer jobs ...*"
$\Longrightarrow$ \$R-ECON-PROTECTION$\rightarrow$FEWER-EXPORT-JOBS
          decrease imports —cause$\rightarrow$
          decrease foreign-income —cause$\rightarrow$
          decrease export —cause$\rightarrow$
          decrease jobs
$=$infer$\Rightarrow$ B7: Friedman believes (\$R-ECON-PROTECTION$\rightarrow$FEWER-EXPORT-JOBS)
          B7 —supports$\rightarrow$ B2

During editorial comprehension, the occurrence of reasoning scripts is signaled by beliefs involving: (a) a goal-achievement or a goal-failure relationship between a plan P and a goal G; or (b) a negative-spiral failure caused by an instance of a plan P. In ED-JOBS, Friedman's belief B2 signals the occurrence of the reasoning script \$R-ECON-PROTECTION$\rightarrow$FEWER-EXPORT-JOBS, which provides OpEd with the context for understanding why import restrictions will cause a decrease in U.S. exports and, consequently, a decrease in U.S. jobs.

Once an editorial's argument graph and indexing structures have been built in memory, OpEd then answers belief-related questions concerning the conceptual content of the editorial. When a question word is encountered (eg, "what", "why", "how"), a question-answering demon is activated which then examines the conceptual content of the question. For example, if a demon attached to "why" encounters a belief of x (eg, "Why does the Reagan administration believe in limitations?"), then it will search the argument graph for this belief and return its supporting beliefs.

The theory of argument comprehension implemented in OpEd is not tailored to a particular editorial. For instance, OpEd is also able to read and answer questions about ED-RESTRICTIONS. Handling both ED-JOBS and ED-RESTRICTIONS did not require modifying OpEd's process model of argument comprehension, but rather augmenting its lexicon, its politico-economic knowledge, and its knowledge of argument units. In addition, the conceptual representations of several other editorials have been hand-coded in OpEd, to test its search, retrieval and question-answering capabilities. For these editorials, OpEd's search and retrieval processes did not need any modifications to retrieve answers to similar question types. For a more discussion of OpEd's knowledge structures and processing strategies see Alvarado (1990).

OTHER ARTIFICIAL INTELLIGENCE APPROACHES TO ARGUMENT COMPREHENSION

Cohen (1983) has postulated a structural model for argument understanding, in contrast to the conceptual model presented in OpEd. In Cohen's model, understanding an argument requires building a tree where argument propositions are connected by a single evidence link. The root of the tree contains the major claim made in an argument. Relations between propositions are determined by using: a proposition analyzer that produces a proposition from the input and integrates it into the tree built so far; a clue interpreter that analyzes the role of special linguistic connectives (eg, "as a result" and "similarly"); and an evidence oracle that accesses a knowledge base and model of the speaker in order to determine whether any evidence relation exists between two propositions. Unfortunately, Cohen's model has not been fully implemented (Cohen, 1987), so it is difficult to assess its potential. One limitation of the model stems from the fact that arguments do not conform to a simple tree structure, but rather consist of a complex directed graph. In addition, since Cohen's trees lack conceptual content, they cannot indicate how either explicit or implicit conceptualizations (contained in a given proposition) relate to, and/or provide evidence for, conceptualizations contained in other propositions. Moreover, by using an oracle, the model avoids having to deal with the critical problems of how lexical items are mapped from natural language to conceptual structures, how world knowledge is represented and applied during the comprehension process, and how argument strategies are represented and applied within a given domain.

In contrast to Cohen's strictly structural approach, OpEd analyzes editorial arguments by building a conceptual graph which captures interactions between goals, plans, events, emotional states, beliefs, and argument units. This conceptual graph results from recognizing and instantiating those knowledge structures along with causal relationships and belief relationships. In addition, OpEd's comprehension process also results in building indices that are subsequently used during question answering. All these knowledge structures and processes are missing in Cohen's model.

Another model for computer comprehension of arguments is the one developed by Roesner (1985). That model has been designed to understand newspaper text dealing with job market developments. Roesner's model assumes that it is possible to determine the propositions that compose a given text, and recognize the logical and causal dependencies that exist among those propositions. Those relationships are cued by surface structures (eg, "in spite of" proposition1, proposition2) in which two propositions are linked by a surface connective that may signal a cause-effect dependency, a refinement dependency, or a contradiction. Surface structures are mapped into argumentation schemata (or frames) whose slots take propositions as arguments. Roesner's model characterizes three types of argumentation schemata: (1) explanation schemata that deal with reasons for a given fact, (2) interpretation schemata that deal with the consequences of a given fact, and (3) rhetorical schemata that contrast contradictory interpretations of factual statements in order to favor one over the others.

In Roesner's model, understanding argumentation text in terms of schemata is viewed as the process of establishing constraint relationships between given propositions. This process is handled by an inference mechanism that has access to a network of domain-specific causal dependencies. Unfortunately, no theory of the content of argument schemata is provided in Roesner's model. That is, Roesner's model characterizes argument schemata as frames with slots, but it does not state what goal, plan, or belief relationships may be used to fill in those slots. In contrast to Roesner's argument schemata, OpEd represents abstract knowledge of argumentation in terms of argument units that organize goals, plans, beliefs, support relationships, and attack relationships. In OpEd, each AU can be cued by specific constructs that involve: (1) argument connectives (eg, "far from," "but," and "yet") that signal opposition and expectation failures; and (2) goal, plan, and belief relationships. In order to follow an argument, OpEd must recognize these linguistic constructs, access the specific conceptualizations they refer to, and map from these conceptualizations into their appropriate AUs. This process of recognizing AUs relies on expectations generated after an argument connective is found. These expectations involve specific information about the type of conceptualization that may follow and/or precede the argument connective.

A third computer model designed to address the problem of argument comprehension and generation is the

ABDUL/ILANA system (Birnbaum and co-workers, 1980; Flowers and co-workers, 1982; McGuire and co-workers, 1981). ABDUL/ILANA embodies a partial theory of the reasoning processes that an arguer may use when engaged in an adversary argument, ie, an argument in which the participants intend to remain adversaries and present their views for the judgment of an audience. The program models either side of an argument between an Arab (ABDUL) and an Israeli (ILANA) over who was responsible for the 1967 Arab-Israeli war. During the argument dialogue, ABDUL/ILANA constructs an argument graph that represents the entire history of the argument between the program and its opponent. That argument graph aids understanding because the role of every input utterance is determined by finding how that utterance can be integrated into the graph using support and attack links. Furthermore, the program uses the argument graph to determine how to respond to an opponent's statement according to three argument tactics: (1) attacking the given statement directly, (2) attacking the statement's supporting evidences, or (3) attacking the warrants connecting the given statement to its supporting evidences.

ABDUL/ILANA has also provided a model to investigate functional properties of commonly occurring substructures in the argument graph (Birnbaum, 1982; Flowers and co-workers, 1982). Those substructures, known as argument molecules, organize knowledge about the logical structure of arguments and provide expectations about which propositions are likely to be attacked or supported by the program's opponent, and which propositions should be attacked or supported by the program. Two argument molecules, contrastive-positions and stand-off, have been identified within the context of ABDUL/ILANA. The contrastive-positions molecule characterizes arguments centered on two mutually exclusive propositions that summarize the main positions of two arguers. In arguments that conform to this molecule, each arguer may try to offer additional support for his or her own position, or attack the position of his or her opponent by using an appropriate argument tactic. In contrast, the stand-off molecule characterizes arguments in which an arguer attacks his or her opponent's use of a warrant by showing that such a warrant can also be used to support a position that is unacceptable to the opponent. In arguments that conform to this molecule, each arguer may try to support his or her own position or attack directly the evidence supporting his or her opponent's position.

Argument molecules differ from OpEd's argument units in terms of the type of abstract argument knowledge they organize. That is, argument molecules contain functional knowledge on how to determine which beliefs should be attacked in an argument, while AUs contain declarative knowledge on how to represent those attacks in terms of goals, plans, beliefs, and belief relationships. However, functional and declarative knowledge are two sides of the same coin. That is, the contrastive-positions molecule provides the functional knowledge associated with the AUs that are used to refute an opponent's argument about a plan on the basis of goal achievements and goal failures. Similarly, the stand-off molecule organizes the functional knowledge associated with the meta-AUs

that are used to attack the underlying logic of an opponent's argument on the basis of that opponent's hypocritical behavior. Clearly, argument molecules and argument units provide two complementary methods for modeling argument comprehension and generation.

CONCLUSIONS

This article has presented a highly knowledge-based approach to argument comprehension which has been implemented in OpEd, a prototype editorial comprehension and question answering system in the politico-economic domain. The process of editorial comprehension is viewed as one of managing many different knowledge sources, including scripts, social acts, affects, causal chains of reasoning, economic entities, goals, plans, actions, characters, beliefs, and belief relationships. Argument Units (AUs) are postulated as central organizing constructs of language-free and domain-free knowledge of argumentation. Knowledge of AUs allows OpEd to recognize and interpret arguments in the politico-economic domain, as long as the system has sufficient planning skill and domain knowledge to build up instances of the particular goals, plans, and beliefs occurring within that domain. Modeling the knowledge of expert economists is beyond the scope of OpEd. Instead, OpEd is designed to model a portion of what an average, well-informed adult reader must know to understand editorials. The design of OpEd, even if limited in the number and type of editorials processed, yields much computational insight in the following areas: common sense knowledge and everyday human reasoning in politico-economic arguments; representation of beliefs and arguments; strategies for reasoning about plans and goals; interactions among different sources of knowledge; memory organization, indexing, and retrieval strategies involved in argument comprehension; processing strategies for retrieving answers to belief-related questions; and conceptual analysis of natural language use in editorial text.

The theory of argument comprehension implemented in OpEd provides a basis for understanding how computers may someday be able to engage in discussions about politics, economics, law, or religion. Although OpEd has provided an initial testbed for this theory, there are a number limitations to OpEd that indicate directions for future research. In particular, editorial comprehension in OpEd does not account for the processes responsible for: (1) establishing the intention of an editorial, ie, whether the editorial is intended to explain or persuade; (2) recognizing what it means to be persuaded by, in agreement with, or in disagreement with an argument; (3) reorganizing and updating beliefs once a persuasive argument has been recognized; and (4) recognizing whether an argument is sound or contains errors in reasoning. We must first model the process of parsing editorial text into conceptual representations before we can ever attempt to model such processes as persuasion, agreement, belief revision, and argument-error recognition.

The experience of designing and implementing OpEd has clearly shown that argument comprehension is a knowledge-intensive task. Given the complexity of the knowledge and processing needed in handling editorials, it is all the more important to design and build whole, functioning prototypes, so that both the strengths and weaknesses of the proposed theories can be tested and revealed. The major benefit derived from building OpEd has been to characterize a framework for making explicit the knowledge required for developing more sophisticated systems capable arguing. As such, OpEd can be viewed as one small step toward understanding the nature of argument comprehension and modeling the basic components of intelligence.

BIBLIOGRAPHY

R. P. Abelson, "The Structure of Belief Systems," in R. C. Schank and K. M. Colby, eds., *Computer Models of Thought and Language*, Freeman, San Francisco, 1973.

R. P. Abelson, "Differences Between Beliefs and Knowledge Systems," *Cogn. Sci.* **3**, 355–366 (1979).

S. J. Alvarado, *Understanding Editorial Text: A Computer Model of Argument Comprehension*, Kluwer Academic Publishers, Boston, Mass., 1990.

S. J. Alvarado, M. G. Dyer, and M. Flowers, "Memory Representation and Retrieval for Editorial Comprehension," *Proceedings of the Seventh Annual Conference of the Cognitive Science Society*, University of California, Irvine, 1985, pp. 228–235.

S. J. Alvarado, M. G. Dyer, and M. Flowers, "Editorial Comprehension in OpEd Through Argument Units," *Proceedings of the Fifth National Conference on Artificial Intelligence*, Philadelphia, Pa., AAAI, Menlo Park, Calif., 1986, pp. 250–256.

S. J. Alvarado, M. G. Dyer, and M. Flowers, "Natural Language Processing: Computer Comprehension of Editorial Text," in H. Adeli, ed., *Know. Eng.*, McGraw-Hill, New York, 1990a.

S. J. Alvarado, M. G. Dyer, and M. FLowers, "Argument Representation for Editorial Text," *Knowledge-Based Systems* **3**, 87–107 (1990b).

S. J. Alvarado, M. G. Dyer, and M. Flowers, "Argument Comprehension and Retrieval for Editorial Text," *Knowledge-Based Systems* **3**, 139–162 (1990c).

K. D. Ashley, *Modeling Legal Argument: Reasoning with Cases and Hypotheticals*, MIT Press, Cambridge, Mass., 1990.

L. Birnbaum, "Argument Molecules: A Functional Representation of Argument Structure," *Proceedings of the Second National Conference on Artificial Intelligence*, Pittsburgh, Pa., 1982, pp. 63–65.

L. Birnbaum, M. Flowers, and R. McGuire, "Towards an AI Model of Argumentation," *Proceedings of the First National Conference on Artificial Intelligence*, Stanford, Calif., 1980, pp. 313–315.

T. F. Bresnaham, "Quotas, Not Bonuses, Hurt Auto Industry," *Los Angeles Times*, part II, May 11, 1984, p. 7.

C. R. Bush, *Editorial Thinking and Writing*, D. Appleton, New York, 1932.

J. G. Carbonell, *Subjective Understanding: Computer Models of Belief Systems*, UMI Research Press, Ann Arbor, Mich., 1981.

B. F. Chellas, *Modal Logic*, Cambridge University Press, Cambridge, Mass., 1980.

R. Cohen, *A Computational Model for the Analysis of Arguments*, Ph.D. thesis, Research Report CSRG-151, Department of Computer Science, University of Toronto, Toronto, Canada, 1983.

R. Cohen, "Analyzing the Structure of Argumentative Discourse," *Comput. Ling.* **13**, 11–30 (1987).

J. T. Cuddington and R. I. McKinnon, "Free Trade Versus Protectionism: A Perspective," in Institute of Contemporary Studies, ed., *Tariffs, Quotas, and Trade: The Politics of Protectionism*, Institute of Contemporary Studies, San Francisco, 1979, pp. 4–6.

R. E. Cullingford, *Script Application: Computer Understanding of Newspaper Stories*, Ph.D. thesis, Research Report #116, Department of Computer Science, Yale University, New Haven, Conn., 1978.

R. Dechter and A. Dechter, "Belief Maintenance in Dynamic Constraint Networks," *Proceedings of the Seventh National Conference on Artificial Intelligence*, St. Paul, Minn., AAAI, Menlo Park, Calif., 1988.

J. de Kleer, "An Assumption-Based TMS," *Artif. Intell.* **28**, 127–162 (1986).

G. F. DeJong, II, *Skimming Stories in Real Time: An Experiment in Integrated Understanding*, Ph.D. thesis, Research Report #158, Department of Computer Science, Yale University, New Haven, Conn., 1979.

J. Doyle, "A Truth Maintenance System," *Artif. Intell.* **12**, 231–272 (1979).

M. G. Dyer, *In-Depth Understanding: A Computer Model of Integrated Processing for Narrative Comprehension*, MIT Press, Cambridge, Mass., 1983.

M. G. Dyer and W. G. Lehnert, "Question Answering for Narrative Memory," in J. F. Le Ny and W. Kintsch, eds., *Language and Comprehension*, North-Holland, Amsterdam, 1982.

M. Feldstein and K. Feldstein, "Judicious Steps at Home Can Lessen Trade Deficit," *Los Angeles Times*, part IV, Apr. 10, 1985, p. 5.

M. Flowers, "On Being Contradictory," *Proceedings of the Second National Conference on Artificial Intelligence*. Pittsburgh, Pa., AAAI, Menlo Park, Calif., 1982, pp. 63–65.

M. Flowers and M. G. Dyer, "Really Arguing with Your Computer in Natural Language," *Proceedings of the National Computer Conference*, Las Vegas, Nev., 1984, pp. 651–659.

M. Flowers, R. McGuire, and L. Birnbaum, "Adversary Arguments and the Logic of Personal Attacks," in W. G. Lehnert and M. G. Ringle, eds., *Strategies for Natural Language Processing*, Lawrence Erlbaum, Hillsdale, N.J., 1982.

M. Friedman, "Protection That Hurts," *Newsweek*, Nov. 15, 1982, p. 90.

A. vdL. Gardner, *An Artificial Intelligence Approach to Legal Reasoning*, MIT Press, Cambridge, Mass., 1987.

S. R. Goldman, M. G. Dyer, and M. Flowers, "Precedent-Based Legal Reasoning and Knowledge Acquisition in Contract Law: A Process Model," *Proceedings of the First International Conference on Artificial Intelligence and Law*, Boston, Mass., 1987, pp. 210–221.

D. Greenaway, *Trade Policy and the New Protectionism*, St. Martin Press, New York, 1983.

D. Greenaway and C. Milner, *Protectionism Again . . . ? Causes and Consequences of a Retreat from Freer Trade to Economic Nationalism*, Hobart Paper 84, The Institute of Economic Affairs, London, 1979, pp. 40–41.

G. Harman, *Change in View: Principles of Reasoning*, MIT Press, Cambridge, Mass., 1986.

J. Hintikka, *Knowledge and Belief*, Cornell University Press, Ithaca, N.Y., 1962.

L. A. Iacocca, "How Many Jobs Do We Save as Doormat of World Trade?" *Los Angeles Times*, part IV, Oct. 26, 1986, p. 5.

B. C. Johnson, *The Atheist Debater's Handbook,* Prometheus Books, Buffalo, N.Y., 1981, pp. 11–14.

M. Lebowitz, *Generalization and Memory in an Integrated Understanding System,* Ph.D. thesis, Research Report #186, Department of Computer Science, Yale University, New Haven, Conn., 1980.

W. G. Lehnert, *The Process of Question Answering: A Computer Simulation of Cognition,* Lawrence Erlbaum, Hillsdale, N.J., 1978.

D. Long and S. J. Alvarado, "The Psychological Validity of Argument Units," *Proceedings of the Symposium on Argumentation and Belief,* American Association for Artificial Intelligence, Stanford, Calif., 1991, pp. 133–144.

Los Angeles Time, "Car Quotas: Costly Folly," *Los Angeles Times,* part II, Feb. 16, 1984, p. 6.

Los Angeles Times, "No Walls or New Walls," *Los Angeles Times,* part V, Dec. 9, 1984, p. 4.

Los Angeles Times, "Weapons in Space," *Los Angeles Times,* part II, Dec. 26, 1984, p. 4.

Los Angeles Times, "The Wrong Solution," *Los Angeles Times,* part II, Oct. 4, 1985, p. 4.

L. T. McCarty and N. S. Sridharan, *A Computational Theory of Legal Argument,* Technical Report LRP-TR-13, Laboratory for Computer Science Research, Rutgers University, New Brunswick, N.J., 1982.

S. McGuigan and J. B. Black, "Creation and Comprehension of Arguments," in J. A. Galambos, R. P. Abelson, and J. B. Black, eds., *Knowledge Structures,* Lawrence Erlbaum, Hillsdale, N.J., 1986.

R. McGuire, L. Birnbaum, and M. Flowers, "Opportunistic Processing in Arguments," *Proceedings of the Seventh International Joint Conference on Artificial Intelligence,* Vancouver, Canada, Morgan-Kaufmann, San Mateo, Calif., 1981, pp. 58–60.

L. Morrow, "The Protectionist Temptation," *Time,* Jan. 10, 1983, p. 68.

J. Pearl, "Fusion, Propagation, and Structuring in Belief Networks," *Artif. Intell.* **29,** 241–288 (1986).

R. Reichman, *Getting Computers to Talk Like You and Me,* MIT Press, Cambridge, Mass., 1983.

R. D. Rieke and M. O. Sillars, *Argumentation and the Decision Making Process,* Scott, Foresman and Company, Glenview, Ill., 1984.

C. K. Riesbeck, "Knowledge Reorganization and Reasoning Style," *Int. J. Man-Machine Stud.* **20,** 45–61 (1984).

E. L. Rissland, "Argument Moves and Hypotheticals," in C. Walter, ed., *Computing Power and Legal Reasoning,* West Publishing Co., St. Paul, Minn., 1985.

E. L. Rissland, "Learning How to Argue: Using Hypotheticals," in J. L. Kolodner and C. K. Riesbeck, eds., *Experience, Memory, and Reasoning,* Lawrence Erlbaum, Hillsdale, N.J., 1986.

D. Roesner, "Schemata for Understanding of Argumentation in Newspaper Texts," in L. Steels and J. A. Campbell, eds., *Progress in Artificial Intelligence,* Ellis Horwood, Chichester, England, 1985.

R. C. Schank, *Conceptual Information Processing,* North-Holland, Amsterdam, 1975.

R. C. Schank, "What Makes Something "Ad Hoc."" *Proceedings of Theoretical Issues in Natural Language Processing-2,* University of Illinois, Urbana-Champaign, 1978, pp. 8–13.

R. C. Schank and R. P. Abelson, *Scripts, Plans, Goals, and Understanding,* Lawrence Erlbaum, Hillsdale, N.J., 1977.

R. C. Schank and J. G. Carbonell, "Re: The Gettysburg Address, Representing Social and Political Acts," in N. Findler, ed., *Associative Networks,* Academic Press, Inc., New York, 1979.

W. Schneider, "Free Trade: Fury Grows in Congress—President vs. Protectionism," *Los Angeles Times,* part IV, Sept. 22, 1985, pp. 1, 3.

N. Staebler and D. Ross, *How to Argue with a Conservative,* Grossman Publishers, New York, 1965.

H. W. Stonecipher, *Editorial and Persuasive Writing,* Hastings House, New York, 1979.

L. C. Thurow, "The Road to Lemon Socialism," *Newsweek,* Apr. 25, 1983, p. 63.

S. Toulmin, *The Uses of Argument,* Cambridge University Press, Cambridge, Mass., 1958.

S. Toulmin, R. D. Rieke, and A. Janik, *An Introduction to Reasoning,* Macmillan, New York, 1979.

T. A. van Dijk and W. Kintsch, *Strategies of Discourse Comprehension,* Academic Press, Inc., New York, 1983.

R. Wilensky, *Planning and Understanding,* Addison-Wesley Publishing Co., Inc., Reading, Mass., 1983.

Y. Wilks and J. Bien, "Beliefs, Points of View, and Multiple Environments," *Cog. Sci.* **7,** 95–119 (1983).

D. B. Yoffie, *Power and Protectionism,* Columbia University Press, New York, 1983.

Sergio J. Alvarado
University of California at
Davis

ART, AI IN

AARON is an "expert artist" program that has gone through a series of versions dating back to the mid 1970s, all of them autonomously capable of generating original works of art. A version featured in the U.S. Pavilion in the Tsukuba World Fair of 1985, for example, produced some 7000 unique drawings without human interaction. AARON is better regarded as an "expert's system," however, for while the conventional goal of expert systems is to encapsulate expert knowledge for the use of nonexperts, AARON has been designed to further its author's own expertise, and thus to function in a kind of dynamic symbiosis with him.

AARON is knowledge-based, and its development from version to version may be described in terms of the changing patterns of knowledge represented in the program. In all cases, that knowledge has fallen into two classes: on the one hand, knowledge of the outside world and of the behavior of some of the things in that world; on the other, knowledge pertaining to the building of a "visual" representation of the world and its objects. AARON has never been concerned with depicting the surfaces of objects, however. Its object-specific knowledge is embodied in a sparse "core" of lines which is then "fleshed out" into a drawing akin to the outline freehand drawings of human artists. In making these outline drawings, AARON's two classes of knowledge are, necessarily, closely interdependent.

AARON's development has consequently involved both increased world knowledge and increasingly sophisticated

(a)

(b)

(c)

Figure 1. AARON is a knowledge-based program designed to generate original artworks and to further the user's expertise. (**a**) "Meeting on Gauguin's Beach" (1988, oil on canvas, 90 in. × 68 in., collection of Gordon and Gwen Bell) and (**b**) "In Search of the Sources" (1988, oil on canvas, 77 in. × 54 in., collection of Pamela McCorduck and Joseph Traub) are paintings by AARON's author, Harold Cohen; (**c**) a drawing generated by AARON and colored by hand (1988, 8½ in. × 11 in., collection of Becky Cohen). Photographs by Becky Cohen. (See color plates.)

representational modalities. For example, AARON's ability to draw the human figure as a posturally coherent whole has always involved a hierarchy of world knowledge, declarative at the top, intensely procedural at the bottom. But the earlier versions had more knowledge of the appearances of figures than they had of the figure

itself. That is, although lacking fully three-dimensional knowledge, AARON nevertheless knew that the thigh of a seated figure facing forward should be foreshortened.

In more recent versions, AARON has a fully three-dimensional knowledge base of the figure, and poses it in an imagined three-space before drawing it. This has resulted in far greater postural diversity, precluding, in turn, any reliance on knowledge of appearances; nor is that knowledge needed in dealing with issues like foreshortening. However, the fleshing out process now has to deal with much more complex, and much less predictable, configurations of the parts of the figure. Its strategies in dealing with this added complexity have become more general than was previously the case, yet simultaneously more dependent on the program's knowledge of what it is drawing.

Earlier versions of the program are described in Cohen (1979); a more recent version in Cohen (1988).

BIBLIOGRAPHY

H. Cohen, "How to Make a Drawing," invited talk, Sixth IJCAI, Tokyo, 1979.

H. Cohen, "How to Draw Three People in a Botanical Garden," invited talk, Seventh National Conference on AI, Minneapolis, Minn., 1988.

HAROLD COHEN
University of California, San
Diego

ARTIFICIAL INTELLIGENCE

There have been many definitions of artificial intelligence (AI) offered over the years. Perhaps a good one is:

> Artificial Intelligence is a field of science and engineering concerned with the computational understanding of what is commonly called intelligent behavior, and with the creation of artifacts that exhibit such behavior.

This may be examined more closely by considering the field from the points of view of three goals that AI researchers have, which might be called *computational psychology, computational philosophy,* and *advanced computer science.*

Computational Psychology

The goal of computational psychology is to understand human intelligent behavior by creating computer programs that behave in the same way people do. For this goal, it is important that the algorithm expressed by the program be the same algorithm that people actually use, and that the data structures used by the program be the same data structures used by the human mind. The program should do quickly what people do quickly, should do more slowly what people have difficulty doing, and should even tend to make mistakes where people tend to make mistakes. If the program were put into the same experimental situations that human subjects are subjected to, the program's results should be within the range of human variability.

Computational Philosophy

The goal of computational philosophy is to form a computational understanding of human-level intelligent behavior, without being restricted to the algorithms and data structures that the human mind actually does (or conceivably might) use. By *computational understanding* is meant a model that is expressed as a procedure that is at least implementable (if not actually implemented) on a computer. By "human-level intelligent behavior" is meant behavior that, when engaged in by people is commonly taken as being part of human intelligent cognitive behavior. It is acceptable, though not required, if the implemented model perform some tasks better than any people would. Bearing in mind Church's Thesis (qv), this goal might be reworded as asking the question, is intelligence a computable function?

In the AI areas of vision and robotics, computational philosophy is replaced by computational natural philosophy (science). For example, computer vision researchers are interested in the computational optics question of how can the information contained in light waves reflected from an object be used to reconstruct the object. Notice that this is a different question from the computational psychology question of how the human visual system uses light waves falling on the retina to identify objects in the world.

Advanced Computer Science

The goal of advanced computer science is to push outwards the frontier of what we know how to program on computers, especially in the direction of tasks that, although we don't know how to program them, people can perform them. This goal led to one of the oldest definitions of AI: the attempt to program computers to do what until recently only people could do. Although this gets across the idea of pushing out the frontier, it is also perpetually self-defeating in that as soon as a task is conquered, it no longer falls within the domain of AI, AI is left only with its failures as its successes become other areas of computer science. The most famous example of this is the area of symbolic calculus. When Slagle wrote the SAINT (qv) program, it was the first program in history that could solve symbolic integration problems at the level of freshman calculus students, and was considered an AI project. Now that there are multiple systems on the market that can do much more than what SAINT did, these systems are not considered to be the results of AI research.

Heuristic Programming

Computational psychology, computational philosophy, and advanced computer science are subareas of AI divided by their goals. Any given AI researcher probably wanders among two or all three of these areas throughout his or her career, and may even have a mixture of these goals at the same time.

Another way of distinguishing AI as a field is by noting the AI researcher's interest in heuristics rather than in algorithms. Here I am taking a wide interpretation of a *heuristic* as any problem solving procedure that fails to be an algorithm, or that has not been shown to be an algorithm, for any reason. An interesting view of the tasks that AI researchers consider to be their own may be gained by considering those ways in which a procedure may fail to be an algorithm.

The common definition of an algorithm for a general problem P is: an unambiguous procedure that, for every particular instance of P, terminates and produces the correct answer. The most common reasons that a heuristic H fails to be an algorithm are: it doesn't terminate for some instances of P; it has not been proved correct for all instances of P because of some problem with H; or it has not been proved correct for all instances of P because P is not well-defined. Common examples of AI heuristic programs that don't terminate for all instances of the problem they have been designed for are search and theorem proving programs. Any search procedure will run forever if given an infinite search space that contains no solution state. Gödel's Incompleteness Theorem states that there are formal theories that contain true but unprovable propositions. In actual practice, AI programs for these problems stop after some prespecified time, space, or work bound has been reached. They can then only report that they were unable to find a solution—in any given case, a little more work might have produced an answer. An example of an AI heuristic that has not been proved correct is any static evaluation function used in a computer chess program. The static evaluation function returns an estimate of the value of some state of the board. To be correct, it would return $+\infty$ if the state were a sure win for the side to move, $-\infty$ if it were a sure win for the opponent, and 0 if it were a forced stalemate. Moreover, for any state it is theoretically possible to find the correct answer algorithmically by doing a full minimax search of the game tree rooted in the state being examined. However, such a full search is infeasable for almost all states because of the size of the game tree. Static evaluation functions are still useful, even without being proved correct. An example of an AI heuristic program that has not been proved correct because the problem for which it has been designed is not well-defined is any natural language understanding program or natural language interface. Since no one has any well-defined criteria for whether a person understands a given language, there cannot be any well-defined criteria for programs either.

EARLY HISTORY

Although the dream of creating intelligent artifacts has existed for many centuries, the field of artificial intelligence is considered to have had its birth at a conference held at Dartmouth College in the summer of 1956. The conference was organized by Minsky and McCarthy, and McCarthy coined the name "artificial intelligence" for the proposal to obtain funding for the conference. Among the attendees were Simon and Newell, who had already implemented the Logic Theorist program at the Rand Corp. These four people are considered the fathers of AI. Minsky and McCarthy founded the AI Laboratory at the Massachusetts Institute of Technology; Simon and Newell founded the AI laboratory at Carnegie Mellon University; and McCarthy later moved from M.I.T. to Stanford and founded the AI laboratory there. These three universities, along with Edinburgh University, whose Department of Machine Intelligence was founded by Michie, have remained the premier research universities in the field. The name artificial intelligence remained controversial for some years, even among people doing research in the area, but it eventually was accepted.

The first AI text was *Computers And Thought,* edited by Feigenbaum and Feldman and published by McGraw-Hill in 1963. *Computers and Thought* is a collection of 21 papers, some of them short versions of Ph.D. dissertations, by early AI researchers. Most of the papers in this collection are still considered classics of AI, but of particular note is a reprint of Turing's 1950 paper in which the Turing Test was introduced.

Regular AI conferences began in the mid to late 1960s. The Machine Intelligence Workshops series began in 1965 in Edinburgh. A conference at Case Western University in the Spring of 1968 drew many of the U.S. AI researchers of the time, and the first biennial International Joint Conference on Artificial Intelligence was held in Washington, D.C. in May, 1969. *Artificial Intelligence,* still the premier journal of AI research, began publishing in 1970. For a more complete history of AI, see McCorduck (1979). (see LITERATURE, AI).

NEIGHBORING DISCIPLINES

Artificial Intelligence is generally considered to be a subfield of computer science, though there are some computer scientists who have only recently and grudgingly accepted this view. There are several disciplines outside computer science, however, that strongly impact AI and which AI strongly impacts.

Cognitive psychology (qv) is the subfield of psychology that uses experimental methods to study human cognitive behavior. The goal of AI called computational psychology above is obviously closely related to cognitive psychology, differing mainly in the use of computational models rather than experiments on human subjects. However, most AI researchers pay some attention to the results of cognitive psychology, and cognitive psychologists tend to pay attention to AI as suggesting possible cognitive procedures that they might look for in humans.

Cognitive science (qv) is an interdisciplinary field that studies human cognitive behavior under the hypothesis that cognition is (or can usefully be modeled as) computation. AI and cognitive science overlap in that there are researchers in each field that would not consider themselves to be in the other. AI researchers whose primary goal is what was called advanced computer science above generally do not consider themselves to be doing cognitive science. Cognitive science contains not only AI researchers, but also cognitive psychologists, linguists, philosophers, anthropologists, and others, each using the methodology of his or her own discipline on a common problem—that of understanding human cognitive behavior.

Computational linguistics (qv) researchers use computers, or at least the computational paradigm, to study and/or to process human languages. Like cognitive science, computational linguistics overlaps AI. It includes those areas of AI called natural language understanding (qv), natural language generation (qv), speech understanding (qv), and machine translation (qv), but also non-AI areas such as the use of statistical methods to find index keywords useful for retrieving a document.

AI-COMPLETE TASKS

There are many subtopics in the field of AI, as one can see by contemplating the individual articles in this encyclopedia. These subtopics vary from the consideration of a very particular, technical problem, to broad areas of research. Several of these broad areas can be considered *AI-complete,* in the sense that solving the problem of the area is equivalent to solving the entire AI problem: producing a generally intelligent computer program. A researcher in one of these areas may see himself or herself as attacking the entire AI problem from a particular direction. These areas are also ways of organizing the articles of this encyclopedia. The following sections discuss some of the AI-complete areas covered by this encyclopedia, and point to some of the articles relevant to those areas. Not every article in the encyclopedia is included in the following lists.

Natural Language

The AI subarea of natural language is essentially the overlap of AI and computational linguistics (see above). The goal of the area is to form a computational understanding of how people learn and use their native languages, and to produce a computer program that can use a human language at the same level of competence as a native human speaker. Virtually all human knowledge has been (or could be) encoded in human languages (consider this encyclopedia and others, textbooks, etc). Moreover, research in natural language understanding has shown that encyclopedic knowledge is required to understand natural language. Therefore, a complete natural language using system will also be a complete intelligent system. The articles in this Encyclopedia relevant to natural language include: ARGUMENT COMPREHENSION; COMPUTATIONAL LINGUISTICS; CONVERSATIONAL IMPLICATURE; DEEP STRUCTURE; DICTIONARY/LEXICON; DISCOURSE UNDERSTANDING; ELLIPSIS; GRAMMAR, AUGMENTED TRANSITION NETWORK; GRAMMAR, CASE; GRAMMAR, GENERALIZED PHRASE STRUCTURE; GRAMMAR, PHRASE STRUCTURE; GRAMMAR, SEMANTIC; GRAMMAR, SYSTEMIC; HERMENEUTICS; LEXICAL DECOMPOSITION; MACHINE TRANSLATION; MORPHOLOGY; NATURAL LANGUAGE GENERATION; NATURAL LANGUAGE UNDERSTANDING; PARSING; PARSING, WORD EXPERT; PREFERENCE SEMANTICS; PRESUPPOSITION; QUESTION ANSWERING; SPEECH RECOGNITION; SPEECH SYNTHESIS; SPEECH UNDERSTANDING; STORY ANALYSIS; TEXT SUMMARIZATION; THESAURUS.

Problem Solving and Search

Problem solving is the area of AI that is concerned with finding or constructing the solution to a problem. That sounds like a very general area, and it is. The distinctive characteristic of the area is probably its approach of seeing tasks as problems to be solved, and of seeing problems as spaces of potential solutions that must be searched to find the true one, or the best one. Thus the AI area of search is very much connected to problem solving. Since any area investigated by AI researchers may be seen as consisting of problems to be solved, all of AI may be seen as involving problem solving and search. The articles in the encyclopedia that are most directly about problem solving and search include: A* ALGORITHM; AND/OR GRAPHS; BACKTRACKING; BRANCHING FACTOR; DISTRIBUTED PROBLEM SOLVING; HEURISTICS; MEANS-ENDS ANALYSIS; MINIMAX PROCEDURE; PROBLEM REDUCTION; PROBLEM SOLVING; SEARCH; SEARCH, BEAM; SEARCH, BEST-FIRST; SEARCH, BI-DIRECTIONAL; SEARCH, BRANCH-AND-BOUND; SEARCH, DEPTH-FIRST; SIMULATED ANNEALING.

Knowledge Representation and Reasoning

Knowledge representation is the area of AI concerned with the formal symbolic languages used to represent the knowledge (data) used by intelligent systems, and the data structures used to implement those formal languages. However, one cannot study static representation formalisms and know anything about how useful they are. Instead, one must study how they are helpful for their intended use. In most cases, the intended use is to use explicitly stored knowledge to produce additional explicit knowledge. This is what reasoning is. Together, knowledge representation and reasoning can be seen to be both necessary and sufficient for producing general intelligence—it is another AI-complete area. Although they are bound up with each other, knowledge representation and reasoning can be teased apart according to whether the particular study is more about the representation language–data structure, or about the active process of drawing conclusions.

The articles in this encyclopedia that are most concerned with knowledge representation include: BELIEF REPRESENTATION SYSTEMS; CONCEPTUAL DEPENDENCY; DYNAMIC MEMORY; EPISODIC MEMORY; FRAMES; KNOWLEDGE REPRESENTATION; LOGIC; LOGIC, CONDITIONAL; LOGIC, HIGHER ORDER; LOGIC, MODAL; LOGIC, ORDER-SORTED; LOGIC, PREDICATE; LOGIC, PROPOSITIONAL; MEMORY ORGANIZATION PACKETS; MENTAL MODELS; SEMANTIC NETWORKS.

The articles in this encyclopedia that are most concerned with reasoning include: ABDUCTION; BAYESIAN INFERENCE METHODS; CIRCUMSCRIPTION; DEMPSTER-SHAFER THEORY; EQUALITY INFERENCING; FUZZY SETS AND FUZZY LOGIC: AN OVERVIEW; META-KNOWLEDGE, META-RULES, AND META-REASONING; QUALITATIVE PHYSICS; REASONING, CASE-BASED; REASONING, CAUSAL; REASONING, COMMONSENSE; REASONING, DEFAULT; REASONING, MEMORY-BASED; REASONING, NONMONOTONIC; REASONING, PLAUSIBLE, REASONING, SPATIAL; REASONING, TEMPORAL; RESOLUTION; RESOLUTION, GRAPH-BASED; RESOLUTION, THEORY; THEOREM PROVING; TRUTH MAINTENANCE; UNIFICATION.

Learning

Learning is often cited as the criterial characteristic of intelligence, and it has always seemed like the easy way to producing intelligent systems: Why build an intelligent system when we could just build a learning system and send it to school? The articles in this encyclopedia that are most concerned with learning include: CONCEPT LEARNING; INDUCTIVE INFERENCE; LEARNING, MACHINE.

Vision

Vision, or image understanding, has to do with interpreting visual images that fall on the human retina or the camera lens. The actual scene being looked at could be 2-dimensional, such as a printed page of text, or 3-dimensional, such as the world about us. If we take "interpreting" broadly enough, it is clear that general intelligence may be needed to do the interpretation, and that correct interpretation implies general intelligence, so this is another AI-complete area. The articles in this encyclopedia that are most concerned with vision include: CHARACTER RECOGNITION; COLOR VISION; EARLY VISION; EDGE AND LOCAL FEATURE DETECTION; HOUGH TRANSFORMS; IMAGE MODELS; IMAGE PROPERTIES; IMAGE UNDERSTANDING; ISPECTION; OBJECT RECOGNITION; PATTERN RECOGNITION; RANGE DATA ANALYSIS; SCALE SPACE; SEGMENTATION; SENSORS AND SENSOR FUSION; SHAPE; STEREO VISION; VISUAL MOTION ANALYSIS; VISUAL PERCEPTION; VISUAL RECOVERY.

Robotics

The area of robotics is concerned with artifacts that can move about in the actual physical world, and/or that can manipulate other objects in the world. The articles in this encyclopedia that are most concerned with robotics include: PROTHESES; ROBOT CONTROL SYSTEMS; ROBOT HANDS AND END EFFECTORS; ROBOT MANIPULATORS; ROBOT PATH PLANNING AND OBSTACLE AVOIDANCE; ROBOTICS; ROBOTS, LEGGED; ROBOTS, MOBILE; TELEOPERATORS.

APPLICATIONS

Throughout its existence as a field, AI research has produced spin-offs into other areas of computer science. Lately, however, programming techniques developed by AI researchers have found application to many programming problems. This has largely come about through the subarea of AI known as expert systems. Whether or not any particular program is intelligent, or is an expert is largely irrelevant pragmatically. From the point of view of the field as a whole, probably the best thing about this development is that after many years of being criticized as following an impossible dream by inappropriate and inadequate means, AI has been recognized by the general public as having applications to everyday problems.

The articles in this encyclopedia that are most relevant to expert systems as a subarea of AI include: BLACKBOARD SYSTEMS; CERTAINTY FACTORS; EXPERT SYSTEMS; RULE-BASED SYSTEMS. The articles in this encyclopedia that discuss past, current, and potential applications of AI include: ART, AI IN; CHEMISTRY, AI IN; EDUCATION, AI IN; ENGINEERING, AI IN; LAW, AI IN; MANUFACTURING, AI IN; MEDICINE, AI IN; MILITARY APPLICATIONS OF AI; MUSIC, AI IN; PROGRAMMING ASSISTANTS.

BIBLIOGRAPHY

E. A. Feigenbaum and J. Feldman, *Computers and Thought,* McGraw-Hill Book Company, New York, 1963.

P. McCorduck, *Machines Who Think,* W. H. Freeman and Company, San Francisco, 1979.

A. M. Turing, "Computing Machinery and Intelligence," *Mind* **59,** 433–460 (October 1950).

STUART C. SHAPIRO
SUNY at Buffalo

ASSOCIATIVE MEMORY

Memory architectures can be classified as random, sequential, and associative (Hwang and Briggs, 1984). First introduced by Bush (1945), associative memories have found considerable use in hardware and have been discussed in innumerable papers. This section overviews the use of associative memories from controllers to database memories and concludes with their importance to AI systems.

An associative memory is composed of a memory that is a two-dimensional array of bits $\mathbf{M}[1, \ldots, i; 1, \ldots, j]$ of i rows and j columns and a search mechanism that can search this array and extract information from it. The array of bits can be considered a set of equal-length words $\mathbf{M}[n; 1, \ldots, j]$ for $n = 1, \ldots, i$. A comparand $\mathbf{C}[1, \ldots, j]$ and a mask $\mathbf{M}[1, \ldots, j]$ can be used to search $\mathbf{M}$ and set bits in a result register $\mathbf{R}[1, \ldots, i]$, see Figure 1. For each $n = 1, \ldots, i$, if for $m = 1, \ldots, j$, $\mathbf{H}[m] = 1$ or $(\mathbf{M}[n; m] = \mathbf{C}[m])$, one can say word $\mathbf{M}[n; 1, \ldots, j]$ matches $\mathbf{C}$ under $\mathbf{H}$, and $\mathbf{R}[n]$ of set to 1; otherwise $\mathbf{R}[n]$ is cleared. Matched words can be output to a bus $\mathbf{B}[1, \ldots, j]$; for $m = 1, \ldots, j$, $\mathbf{B}[m]$ is the OR of $\mathbf{M}[n; m]$ wherever $\mathbf{R}[n]$ is 1.

Consider this simple example of a telephone directory searched in an associative memory. Each word is (person's name, telephone number, address). Suppose one wants to know Mr. Smith's address or telephone number. The search and output operation would use $\mathbf{C}$ = (SMITH, xxx, xxx) and $\mathbf{H}$ = (00000, 111, 111). In the search operation the row having SMITH in the leftmost part will match, and the result bit for that row is set. In the output part that row is put on the bus $\mathbf{B}$, where the unknown parts can be obtained.

MEMORY MANAGEMENT AND HARDWARE CONTROL

The search and output operation is often combined in a single step in an associative memory, which is the MMU used in virtual memories (Hwang and Briggs, 1984). In such a system a processor (CPU) reads and writes data in RAM. The processor sends an address to RAM in order to read or write a word in it. This address is put into the MMU, as a comparand, like the name SMITH in the example above. The output on the bus, rather like the telephone number of the example, is the actual address that is

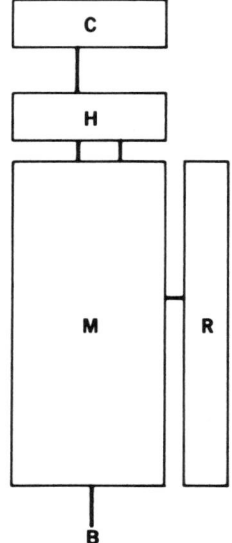

Figure 1. Basic associative memory.

sent to RAM. An MMU lets the address maintained and sent by the CPU (called the virtual address) be different from the real address used in RAM.

Another common application, where the associative memory is a read-only memory, is the PLA. Used in the control logic of a processor, microprogrammed commands are put in as comparands, and the outputs of the bus are sent to control registers, adders, and other parts of the hardware. The PLA lets the microprogram use commands that are efficiently encoded, which control a vast number of hardware units.

STARAN

The associative memory may be extended with a rewrite function so that each word appears to be a processor. Matched words may be partially rewritten using the comparand **C** and mask **H**. For each $n = 1, \ldots, i$, if $\mathbf{R}[n] = 1$, then for each $m = 1, \ldots, j$, if $\mathbf{H}[m] = 0$, $\mathbf{C}[m]$ is put into $\mathbf{M}[n; m]$. Searching and rewriting permit arithmetic and logical operations on all words simultaneously in a SIMD parallel computer such as STARAN (Batcher, 1974). A large number of programs have been written for STARAN, and highly parallel SIMD algorithms, such as those found in radar-signal processing, have been considerably faster in STARAN than in a conventional machine. But large database searches are not suited to STARAN because the time to load **M** dominates the time to search it; even if the search time were zero, STARAN is slowed to the speed of conventional machines by the time to load its memory.

SET SEARCH

A plethora of papers (Minker, 1971; Maryanski, 1980) have been written on the use of associative memories for searching databases. If the words are considered ordered

(whereas they are unordered in the examples above), sequential addressing (eg, the notion of next lower word) can be combined with associative addressing. After a search that sets the result bit in **R**, a "next search" can be made, where only words below a word where the **R** bit was set are searched to set the **R** bit at the end of the search. A string of characters can be searched, one character after another, forming the basis for text-oriented information retrieval. Partitioning the rows into contiguous blocks and using a delimiter to mark the beginning of each block, a "set search" can be made, where only words in a block, where the **R** bit was set in some word in the block, can be searched to set the **R** bit at the end of the search. This is the basis of most relational, hierarchical, and network database machines.

ASSOCIATIVE DISKS

Although it may become feasible to build large associative memories using integrated circuits for the memory, associatively addressed disk memories have been proposed for large databases (Bray and Freeman, 1979). As the data on a disk track pass over a read head, searching may be accomplished essentially as described above. Using additional techniques (eg, storing the data on a track in RAM called a disk cache), data can be modified and later written back on the track. If each disk head has these capabilities, a large amount of data can be associatively searched where it is stored rather than transported to and from a large mainframe computer.

OUTLOOK

Finally, the associative memory continues to find new applications as new problems are studied. Associative memory integrated circuits have been sold for over 15 years now, but they have not been widely used because they were considerably slower and smaller than RAMs. However, custom VLSI is becoming commercially accepted, and an associative memory can be integrated with other processor logic and memory in these custom chips with less relative cost than in current systems. Also, considerable work is in progress in the design of database processors. In these systems the disk is made associative, as discussed above. A group of researchers in Japan and in the Microelectronics and Computer Corporation in the United States are competing to make these database machines commercially useful. These advances should contribute to better AI systems. For instance, in PROLOG (see LOGIC PROGRAMMING) the database can be searched, the Horne clauses can be matched, variables can be instantiated, and control can be effected using associative memories from associative disks to associative VLSI memories and associative controllers (scoreboards and PLAs).

BIBLIOGRAPHY

K. E. Batcher, "STARAN Parallel Processor System Hardware," *Proceedings of AFIPS-NCC* **43**, 405–410 (1974).

O. H. Bray and H. A. Freeman, *Data Base Computers*, Lexington Books, Lexington, Mass., 1979.

V. Bush, "As We May Think," *Atl. Mo.* **176**(1), 101 (1945).

K. Hwang and F. Briggs, *Computer Architecture and Parallel Processing*, McGraw-Hill, New York, 1984, pp. 57–80.

F. Maryanski, "Backend Database Systems," *ACM Comput. Surv.,* **12**(1), 3–27 (March 1980).

J. Minker, "An Overview of Associative Memory or Content-Addressable Memory Systems and a KWIC Index to the Literature," *Comput. Rev.*, 453–504 (Oct. 1971).

G. J. LIPOVSKI
University of Texas

ASSOCIATIVE NETWORKS. See ASSOCIATIVE MEMORY; SEMANTIC NETWORKS.

AUGMENTED TRANSITION NETWORKS. See GRAMMAR, AUGMENTED TRANSITION NETWORK.

AURA

AURA, an automated reasoning program developed in 1978, was used to answer a previously open question in algebra (Winker, 1978). Written in IBM assembly language, AURA was designed and implemented by Overbeek with contributions from Smith, Winker, and Lusk. Although the use of AURA led to a number of useful results in mathematics and logic, its lack of portability proved to be a serious disadvantage. LMA, a collection of subroutines written in Pascal for the purpose of implementing automated reasoning programs tailored to the user's specification, was designed and implemented to address the concern of portability (see RESOLUTION, BINARY; B. Smith, *Reference Manual for the Environmental Theorem Prover, an Incarnation of AURA*, Technical Report ANL-88-2, Mathematics and Computer Science Division, Argonne National Laboratory, Argonne, Ill., 1988; S. Winker and L. Wos, "Automated Generation of Models and Counterexamples and Its Application to Open Questions in Ternary Boolean Algebra," *Proceedings of the Eighth International Symposium on Multiple-Valued Logic*, IEEE, Rosemont, Ill., 1978, pp. 251–256.

L. WOS
Argonne National Laboratory

AUTOMATIC PROGRAMMING

Computer programming is the process of constructing executable code from fragmentary information. This information may come in many forms including vague ideas of how the output should look, the nature of the expected input, the type of algorithm to be used, and possibly, examples of the target behavior. The result of the programming is a section of code which is capable of receiving inputs from the target domain and processing them to yield appropriate outputs.

When computer programming is done by a machine, the process is called automatic programming. Artificial intelligence researchers are interested in studying automatic programming for two reasons: First, it would be highly useful to have a powerful automatic programming system which could receive casual and imprecise specifications for a desired target program and then correctly generate that program (Fig. 1a). Second, automatic programming is widely believed to be a necessary component of any intelligent system and is therefore a topic for fundamental research in its own right. Thus a system might discover a successful way to achieve a given result and program itself to achieve that result. For example, a legged being might assemble code to enable itself to walk after a series of walking experiences (Fig. 1b).

A number of approaches to automatic programming have been developed over the years and the most important ones will be described here. The following sections, as illustrated in Figure 2, describe methodologies for synthesis from formal input-output specifications, from examples of the desired program behavior, from natural language dialogue, and from cooperative interaction between a human programmer and a mechanical programmer's assistant.

The methodologies based upon synthesis from formal specifications utilize predicate calculus notation and derive the target program in a sequence of logical steps. Because the resulting program is mathematically derived from its specification, its correctness with respect to the specification is assured. Thus the methodologies are very attractive and their development has implications for the foundations of computer science as well as artificial intelligence.

The synthesis-from-example methodologies involve generalization and learning behaviors. Since the examples do not completely specify the target program, the initially generated program may not achieve all of the desired behaviors. But the addition of appropriate examples can force the synthesizer to efficiently converge to a satisfactory program. The attractiveness of this approach comes partly from the ease with which a user can provide examples. These techniques are also important for artificial intelligence researchers to understand because they seem to be fundamental to certain kinds of intelligent behavior (see INDUCTIVE INFERENCE).

The third approach, program generation from natural language dialogue, involves translating informal descriptions into formal specifications which can be programmed using formal methods. This approach uses those technologies mentioned above as well as natural language processing, knowledge representation, and artificial intelligence systems design.

The final approach, program synthesis using an automated programmer's assistant, assumes that a human will be the primary programmer and that the proper role for a machine is to supplement his or her efforts. The human's role is to develop and refine a set of formal specifications and make some implementation decisions with the machine assisting by checking consistency, retrieving in-

Figure 1. Examples of automatic programming. (*a*) Generating the user's program. The computer automatically generates code from casual specifications. (*b*) Learning new behaviors. The intelligent being internally assembles code to enable itself to function in the world.

formation from libraries, and so forth. At some point in the specification process, the machine can take the primary role in selecting data structures and building the code and documentation for the software product.

The following sections thus describe these four approaches to automatic programming.

SYNTHESIS FROM INPUT-OUTPUT SPECIFICATIONS

Stating the Problem

The first approach to the study of automatic programming assumes that a specification of the input-output behavior is given and that the automatic system is to find a program to implement the specification. Very often the specification is written as:

$$\forall a(P(a) \Rightarrow \exists z R(a,z))$$

Here $P(a)$ is an input predicate that is true if and only if a is an acceptable input for the target program. $R(a,z)$ is an input-output relation that is true if and only if z is the desired output when the target program reads a as its input. The specification states that for all a such that the input requirement P is met, there is a z such that the input-output relation $R(a,z)$ holds. The program synthesis will proceed by proving this theorem. It turns out that in order to complete the proof, the theorem prover must constructively find the z that is asserted to exist and the method for finding z is the target program (see also THEOREM PROVING).

As an illustration, suppose it is desired to automatically generate a program to add up a list of numbers a to obtain their sum z. Then one should define the input predicate $P(a)$ to be true if and only if a is a list of numbers of length zero or more. Thus $P((4\ 2\ 9))$ is true and $P((A(B)))$ is false. The input-output relation $R(a,z)$ should be defined to be true if and only if z is the sum of the numbers in a. For example, $R((4\ 2\ 9),15)$ is true and $R((4\ 2\ 9),16)$ is false (z is zero if a has length zero). Then the proof of the specifying theorem,

$\forall a\ (P(a) \Rightarrow \exists z\ R(a,z))$

if a = NIL then 0
else car(a) + f(cdr(a))

(a) Synthesis from formal specifications.

Input: ((A.B).C)

Output: (C.(B.A))

f(x) = cond ((atom(x) x)
             (t cons(f$_2$(x), f$_3$(x)))
f$_2$(x) = f(cdr(x))
f$_3$(x) = f(car(x))

(b) Synthesis from examples.

User: Please write a program to
add up a set of numbers.
SYSTEM: WHAT WOULD YOU LIKE
TO CALL THE PROGRAM ?
etc.

PROGRAM SUM(INPUT,OUTPUT)
VAR X, ANS: INTEGER;
         -
         -
END.

(c) Synthesis from natural language
dialogue.

(Interactive human-machine generation of
formal specifications. Interactive creation
of code and documentation.)

Formal Specifications
Programming Product
Complete Documentation

(d) Synthesis through cooperative interaction
between human and mechanical assistant.

Figure 2. Four research areas in automatic programming.

$$\forall a(P(a) \Rightarrow \exists z R(a,z))$$

requires the system to find a way of constructing z for every acceptable a. This proof will thus yield the target program.

Of course, it is not possible to carry out the proof unless many facts are known about P and R. For example, one needs the fact that if a is the list of length zero, that is $a =$ NIL, Then $R(a,0)$ is true.

$$R(a,0) = \text{true if } a = \text{NIL}.$$

Also, let $car(a)$ be defined to be the first element of list a and let $cdr(a)$ be defined to be list a with its first element removed. The synthesis will use the fact that the sum of a is simply obtained by adding $car(a)$ to the sum of $cdr(a)$ if a is not NIL.

$$R(a,\ car(a) + z') = \text{true if } R(cdr(a),z') \text{ and not } (a = \text{NIL})$$

The program synthesis methodology uses these kinds of facts to prove the above theorem and generate the following program:

$$f(a) = \text{if } a = \text{NIL then } 0 \quad \text{else } car(a) + f(cdr(a))$$

The proof of the specifying theorem will involve manipulation of formulas of the form:

if $\forall x A_1(x)$ and $\forall x A_2(x)$ and $\cdots$ and $\forall_x A_n(x)$ then

$\exists x G_1(x)$ or $\exists x G_2(x)$ or $\cdots$ or $\exists x G_m(x)$

Following the methodology of Manna and Waldinger (1980), such formulas can be written into a tableau of columns labelled assertions, goals, and outputs as follows.

Assertions	Goals	Outputs
$A_1(x)$		
$A_2(x)$		
.		
.		
.		
$A_n(x)$		
	$G_1(x)$	
	$G_2(x)$	
	.	
	.	
	.	
	$G_m(x)$	

This notation enables one to write such formulas omitting quantifiers and connectives. If an entry $t_i(x)$ appears in the output column in the same row as some goal $G_i(x)$, that output $t_i(x)$ expresses the desired program output when $G_i(x)$ is true.

Using this tabular convention, the specifying theorem can be written as follows:

Assertions	Goals	Outputs
$P(a)$		
	$R(a, z)$	z

The Manna and Waldinger (1980) program synthesis procedure involves adding rows to this table such that the correctness of the above meaning formula is maintained. If a goal can be deduced which is always true and such that its corresponding output entry is in terms of the input and primitive functions, that output entry will be the target program:

Assertions	Goals	Outputs
	True	Target program

The Deductive Mechanism

Once the problem is stated and appropriately entered into the above table, methods are needed for deducing new entries in the table so that progress toward the target program can be made. Following the methodology of Manna and Waldinger (1980), two kinds of rules are introduced here, transformations which convert portions of an assertion or goal to a new form, and resolution rules which allow one to combine assertions and/or goals to obtain new assertions or goals.

Transformations have the form:

$$r \Rightarrow s \text{ if } Q$$

which means that r may be converted to s if Q is true.

In order to illustrate usage, suppose there is a goal G that contains a subexpression r. It can be written as $G[r]$. Then the transformation $r \Rightarrow s$ yields $G[s]$, and this substitution can be made if Q is true.

This gives a way to generate a new goal in the deductive table if $G[r]$ is an existing goal. The new goal is $G[s]$ and Q. It means that if $G[r]$ is a valid goal, then $G[s]$ is one also provided that Q is true. In terms of the deductive table, the transformation $r \Rightarrow s$ if Q enables one to begin with:

Assertions	Goals	Outputs
	$G[r]$	p

and deduce the new entry:

Assertions	Goals	Outputs
	$G[s]$ and Q	p

An example of a transformation is:

$$U(x,-x) \Rightarrow \text{true if } x < 0$$

and its usage can be shown on the following example goal and output:

Assertions	Goals	Outputs
	$U(b,y)$	y

The transformation can convert $U(x,-x)$ to true, but this expression does not occur in the given goal. However, one can make substitutions into the transformation and the goal and output so that the transformation is applicable; that is, unification is being used as described elsewhere in this volume. Specifically, one can substitute $x = b$ into the transformation to obtain:

$$U(b,-b) \Rightarrow \text{true} \quad \text{if } b < 0$$

and one can substitute $y = -b$ into the goal and output to obtain:

Assertions	Goals	Outputs
	$U(b,-b)$	$-b$

Now the transformation can be applied using the above rule to obtain a new row in the tableau.

Assertions	Goals	Outputs
	True and $b < 0$	$-b$

Another way to construct new entries in a deductive table is to resolve (see RESOLUTION) two goals to yield a new one. Suppose one has two goals F with associated output p_1 and G with associated output p_2. Further suppose that F and G both have the same predicate subexpression e so they will be written $F[e]$ and $G[e]$.

Assertions	Goals	Outputs
	$F[e]$	p_1
	$G[e]$	p_2

In the following, the notation $F[e \leftarrow \text{true}]$ stands for the goal F with subexpression e replaced by true. $G[e \leftarrow \text{false}]$ is similarly defined. Then the two goals $F[e]$ and $G[e]$ can be combined to obtain a new goal $F[e \leftarrow \text{true}]$ and $G[e \leftarrow \text{false}]$ with associated output if e then p_1 else p_2. The new row in the tableau is:

Assertions	Goals	Outputs
	$T[e \leftarrow \text{true}]$ and $G[e \leftarrow \text{false}]$	if e, then p_1 else p_2

An example of such a resolution occurs if one has these goals.

Assertions	Goals	Outputs
	$a < 0$	$-a$
	Not $(a < 0)$	a

Then resolution of these two goals where e is $a < 0$ yields the following new entry:

Assertions	Goals	Outputs
	True and not (false)	If $a < 0$, then $-a$, else a

Two kinds of deductive rules have been described here: transformations and goal-goal resolutions. Manna and Waldinger (1980) have given numerous other deductive rules but these examples illustrate the nature of the technique. Once the problem is properly represented and rules are available for deduction for new table entries, one can proceed to synthesize programs as shown in the next section.

Synthesizing Programs

The program synthesis procedure follows the problem solving paradigm so well known in the AI community. An initial state is given and transitions are available for moving from one state of the domain to another. The problem solving system attempts to find a sequence of applicable transitions that will transform the world from the initial state to an acceptable final state.

In the program synthesis domain, the initial state is the specification of the program input-output characteristics. The applicable transitions are the transformations, resolution schemes, and other available rules for deducing new forms from the original specification. An acceptable final state is one that gives a program in a machine executable language which meets the original specification. In terms of the deductive table, a final state has a goal which is true and an associated output in terms of the input and primitive machine operations.

One can illustrate the whole process by synthesizing a program to compute the absolute value function h:

$$h(x) = \begin{cases} x \text{ if not } (x < 0) \\ -x \text{ otherwise} \end{cases}$$

Then the input specification must require x to be a real number: $V(x)$ is true if and only if x is real. The input-output relation $U(x,z)$ will be true whenever z is the absolute value of x. This information must be available to the system in the form of transformations:

T1: $U(x,-x) \Rightarrow$ true if $x < 0$

T2: $U(x,x) \Rightarrow$ true if not $(x < 0)$

The synthesis proceeds by applying the available transfor-

mations and deductive rules until a program is synthesized.

Following the methodology described above, one begins with the original specification:

Assertions	Goals	Outputs
$V(b)$		
	$U(b,y)$	y

Applying T1 and T2 to the goal $U(b,y)$ obtains the following two goals:

Assertions	Goals	Outputs
	$b < 0$	$-b$
Not $(b < 0)$		b

Resolving these two goals results in the final program:

Assertions	Goals	Outputs
	True	If $b < 0$, then $-b$, else b

A more interesting example appears in Figure 3 where a program is generated to add a list of numbers. In this case, $P(a)$ is true if and only if a is a list of integers of length zero or more. $R(a,z)$ is true if and only if z is the sum of the numbers in a. If a has length zero, then $R(a,0)$ is true. Two transformations carry the critical information:

T3: $R(a,0) \Rightarrow$ true if $a =$ NIL

T4: $R(a,car(a) + z') \Rightarrow$ true if $R(cdr(a),z')$ and not $(a =$ NIL$)$

Step 5 is the inductive hypothesis for an inductive proof which introduces a looping behavior into the synthesis. It states that the synthesized program f works properly (ie, if

step	assertions	goals	outputs	remarks
(1)	P(a)			input spec.
(2)		R(a,z)	z	i-o relation
(3)		a = NIL	0	T3 on (2)
(4)		R(cdr(a),z') and not (a = NIL)	car(a) + z'	T4 on (2)
(5)	if v < a then if P(v) then R(v,f(v))			inductive hypothesis
(6)		not(.if cdr(a) < a then if P(cdr(a)) then false) and not (a = NIL)	car(a) + f(cdr(a))	resolving (4) and (5)
(7)		not (a = NIL)	car(a) + f(cdr(a)	simplifying (6)
(8)		true	if a = NIL then 0 else car(a) + f(cdr(a))	resolving (3) and (7)

Figure 3. Synthesizing the program to add a list of numbers.

$P(v)$ then $R(v,f(v))$) for all lists shorter than the input a (ie, $v < a$). The proof that f then also works on a completes the inductive argument and enables the introduction of recursion in the generated program. Step 6 is a goal-assertion resolution that functions similarly to the goal-goal resolution above. The final synthesized program is:

$$f(x) = \text{if } x = \text{NIL then } 0 \text{ else } car(x) + f(cdr(x)).$$

Manna and Waldinger (1987) show a detailed example of these mechanisms in the generation of binary search programs.

Searching for Loops

One of the central problems in program synthesis is the discovery of loops and information is often available to help find them. Bibel (1980) and Bibel and Hornig (1984), for example, suggest breaking the input into parts and attempting to discover the contribution of the parts to the output. If the synthesizer can find a way to do one part of the calculation on a pass through the body of the loop, then perhaps repeated passes will enable it to consume the rest of the input and complete the target output.

This strategy is easy to illustrate on the example of Figure 3, adding up a list of numbers. In this example, the input is a list of numbers, and Bibel and Hornig (1984) suggest that one should guess at a way to break this input into parts. If a method can be found to isolate the effects of the parts on the result of the computation, perhaps code can be found to process the parts individually and combine the results to yield the answer. An example is the method of splitting input a into $car(a)$ and $cdr(a)$. Observing the function definition for f, we see

$$f(a) = \sum_{i=1}^{length\ (a)} a[i]$$

and this can be separated to observe the effects of $car(a)$ (or $a[1]$) and $cdr(a)$ (or $a[2] \ldots , a[length(a)]$).

$$f(a) = a[1] + \sum_{i=2}^{length\ (a)} a[i]$$

But the last term of this expression is simply the function f applied to the rest of the list, $cdr(a)$:

$$f(a) = a[1] + f(cdr(a))$$

So the program for addition needs to only add its first entry to the result of applying itself to the rest of the list. Then if we include code to handle the trivial case, the program can be completed:

$$f(a) = \text{if length } (a) = 0 \text{ then } 0$$
$$\text{else } car(a) + f(cdr(a))$$

The reason to try to program such mechanisms is that they may automatically discover the strategy for making a loop work and eliminate the requirement that knowl-

edge of the type represented by T3 and T4 be explicitly coded in the system.

If the synthesizer had guessed another way to break up the input, another algorithm might result. Thus one could break a into $a[1], \ldots , a[length(a)/2]$ and $a[length(a)/2 + 1], \ldots , a[length(a)]$ and find an algorithm that recursively calls f on both the first and second halves of its input list until a trivial list of length 0 or 1 is found. Bibel and Hornig (1984) implemented this methodology in their LOPS system and demonstrated it on many examples. Their system included many features including methodologies for guiding the search to obtain a final program. One of its more novel mechanisms generated examples in the problem domain and generalized from them to produce hypothesized theorems to be used in the synthesis.

Other work using this insight is described by Smith (1987) on the automatic construction of divide and conquer algorithms. This work includes an interesting study of sorting methods and shows how a variety of algorithms result from different initial decompositions of the input.

Transformational Methodologies

A type of transformation different from the transformations discussed above has been investigated in the literature (Bauer and co-workers, 1989; Broy, 1983; Burstall and Darlington, 1977; Gerhart, 1976; Manna and Waldinger, 1979). In this methodology, the original specification of the program is transformed repeatedly until a final program is derived. Such transformations have the form shown in Figure 4. An initial specification gives the format of the schema to be modified. An applicability condition specifies all relationships that are prerequisite to the use of the transformation. A final specification gives the new format for the schema after the application of the transformation. Program synthesis involves the repeated application of such transformations, beginning with the initial specification, until the final program is created.

The approach assumes the existence of a library of such transformations and synthesis proceeds by automatically or manually selecting the sequence to be used. Some transformations may perform rather small changes to the existing form while others may create dramatic changes and enable great leaps toward the final product.

An example of a transformation for creating simple linearly recursive code from a specification appears in Figure 5. This transformation can solve many standard synthesis examples including the list summing problem mentioned above. For this example, one needs to discover the substitutions $C(x)$ is $length(x) = 0$, $T(x) = 0$, $H_1(x) = car(x)$, $H_2(x) = cdr(x)$, and $G(x,y) = x + y$. With these substitutions, the applicability conditions hold, and the final program can be created in a single step.

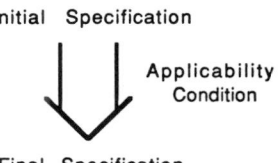

Initial Specification

Applicability Condition

Final Specification

Figure 4. The format for a program transformation.

f(x) = z where R(x,z)

C(x) ==> R(x,T(x))
¬C(x) and R(H₂(x),y) ==> R(x,G(H₁(x),y))
length(x) = 0 ==> C(x)
length(x) > 0 ==> length(H₂(x)) < length(x)

f(x) = if C(x) then T(x) else G(H₁(x), f(H₂(x)))

Figure 5. A program transformation to create a recursive program.

Historical Remarks

It was discovered in the late 1960s (Green, 1969; Waldinger and Lee, 1969) that the proof of a theorem with existential quantifiers will implicitly contain the sequence of operators required to find the objects asserted to exist. This sequence of operators can be considered to be a program for finding those objects and the discovery became the basis for much research in automatic programming. The task of theorists then became one of finding methods to extract the operators from the proofs and developing theorem proving strategies which would properly introduce the desired looping, branching, and subroutine constructions into the code. The methodology of Manna and Waldinger (1980, 1987) systematizes and generalizes on the techniques that had been developed earlier.

Simultaneously, other work in program synthesis has shown how program loops are formed as described above and has created the transformational synthesis methodology. The total of this literature has had a substantial effect on the theory of programming and on software engineering.

PROGRAM SYNTHESIS FROM EXAMPLES

This section will first give an algorithm for synthesizing flowcharts from traces and an example of its usage, the generation of a Turing machine program to sort A's and B's. Then it shows how this leads to a program synthesis methodology for LISP code. Also methods will be given for creating LISP programs from recurrence relations and for factoring behavior graphs to create real time programs. The last methodology shows how PROLOG programs can be created from example behaviors. The section concludes with some general observations regarding program synthesis from examples.

Constructing Flowcharts from Example Traces

Suppose a computer program has executed the following computation trace in completing a particular calculation.

Time	Condition	Instruction
1		I_1
2	a	I_2
3	b	I_2
4	c	I_2
5	b	I_2
6	b	I_3

That is, at the first instant of time, I_1 was executed. Then condition a was tested and found to be true and I_2 was executed. This proceeds until the final statement at time 6 when I_3 was executed. The instructions I_j may be any instructions such as READ(x) or $x = x + 1$ and the conditions a, b and c may be any predicates such as $x > 3$ or $x < y$. It is desired to find an algorithm capable of building a program that can do this trace.

One can, in fact, begin building the desired program by starting at the beginning of the trace and moving downward building the code to account for each step. From the first instruction (Time = 1), the beginning of the target program can be created (Fig. 6a). Next Condition a is observed and Instruction I_2 executed. I_2 is added to the flowchart (Fig. 6b). The trace indicates the next condition is b out of I_2 and this leads to another execution of I_2. Since an example of I_2 already exists, this transition is sent to it (Fig. 6c). Examining Condition c from this instruction to I_2 at Time 4, again this transition is sent to the existing version of I_2 (Fig. 6d). At Time 5, the trace indicates a b transition to I_2 and the existing program already has such a b transition to I_2. Whenever the current trace condition matches the condition on an outgoing transition of the active node of the program, one has what is called a forced move. If the current version of the program is correct, as it is here, that transition will properly predict the next instruction in the trace. At Time 6, however, a contradiction occurs: the move is forced and the program uses the b transition to predict the next instruction to be I_2, but, the trace indicates the next instruction should be I_3. Apparently an error has occurred in the synthesis.

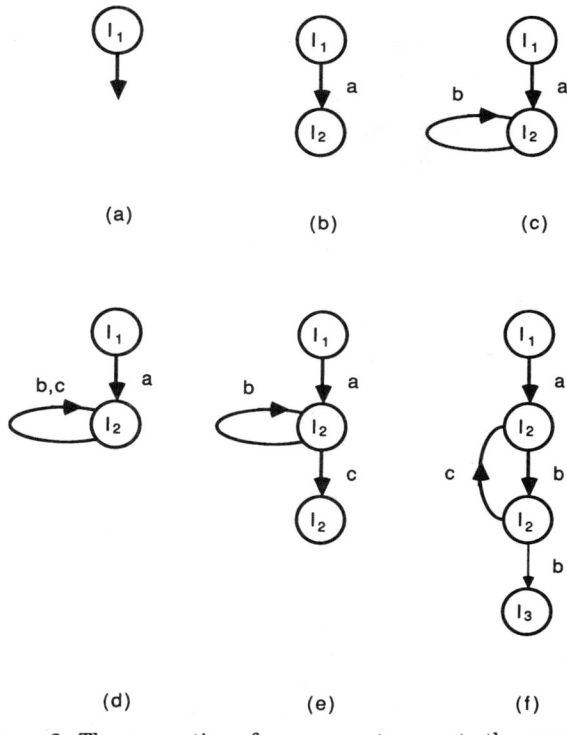

(a)   (b)   (c)

(d)   (e)   (f)

Figure 6. The generation of a program to execute the example trace.

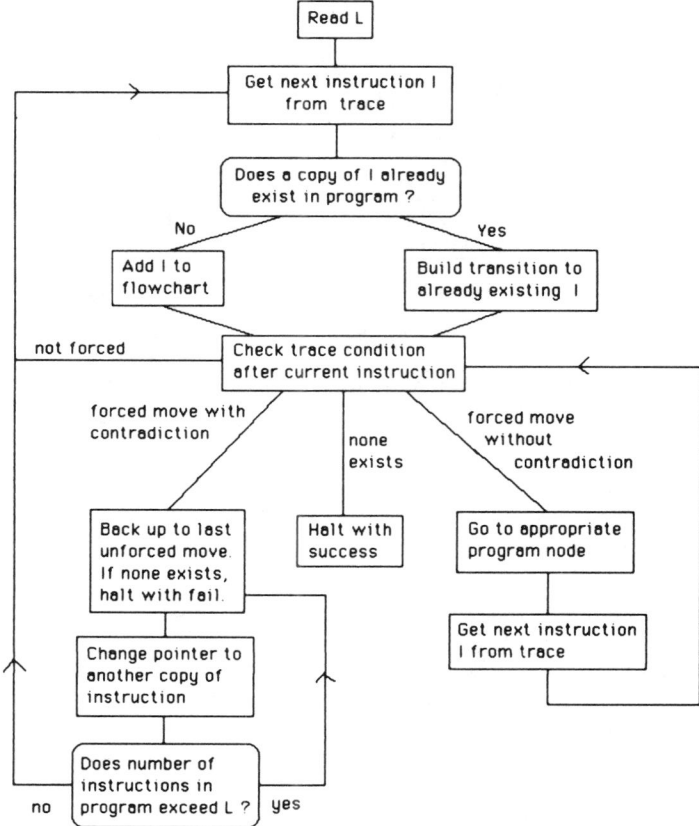

Figure 7. The algorithm for program creation from trace information.

At this point, the procedure backs up to the last unforced move and changes its decision. Returning to Time 4, the c transition will not be directed backward but instead to a new copy of I_2 (Fig. 6e). Moving forward again, a second contradiction will be found, another back up, and then the final flow chart of Figure 6f will be built.

A general algorithm for creating flowcharts from traces appears in Figure 7. This algorithm requires the user to specify a limit L on the number of nodes to appear in the target program and will always find a program of that size or less which can execute the trace. If none exists, backup will occur to the first instruction and above resulting in a termination with failure. The algorithm can then be restarted with a larger L. The following section shows some applications of the method.

The Trainable Turing Machine

An interesting application of this methodology is the trainable Turing machine as described by Biermann (1972) (Fig. 8). This system resembles the traditional model of a Turing machine with an infinite two-way tape and a tape-head that can move left or right reading and writing symbols. This machine differs from the traditional model in that it begins without any finite-state controller; it builds its own controller on the basis of examples.

Suppose, as an illustration, it is desired to train the machine to sort a string of A's and B's so that the A's all precede the B's. In order to train the machine to do this

calculation, one must put the machine in learn mode and physically force its read-write head through one or more sample computations. These examples will enable the machine to construct a general program, using the algorithm of the previous section, to sort any string of A's and B's. A simple example calculation appears in Figure 9.

The algorithm of Figure 9 starts the head at the left end of the nonblank symbols of the tape. It moves right in search of an A, and, on finding it, prints a B and moves left. When it finds the end of the string or another A, it moves right one step, prints the A, and moves right again looking for another A. It continues moving A's back toward the front until no more symbols, A's or B's, are found.

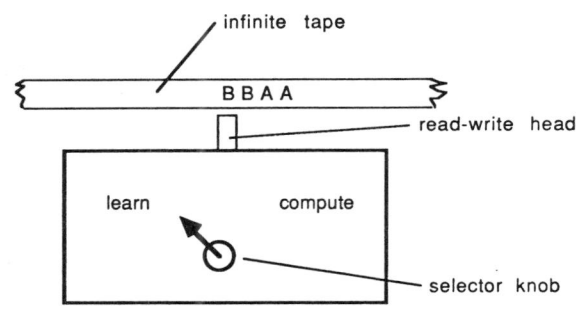

Figure 8. The trainable Turing machine.

Time	Current Tape	Condition	Instruction
1	BBAA		start
2	BBAA	B	BR
3	BBAA	B	BR
4	BBAA	A	BL
5	BBBA	B	BL
6	BBBA	B	BL
7	_BBBA	ø	øR
8	BBBA	B	AR
9	ABBA	B	BR
10	ABBA	B	BR
11	ABBA	A	BL
12	ABBB	B	BL
13	ABBB	B	BL
14	ABBB	A	AR
15	ABBB	B	AR
16	AABB	B	BR
17	AABB	B	BR
18	AABB_	ø	halt

Figure 9. The trace of a Turing machine computation to sort a string of A's and B's.

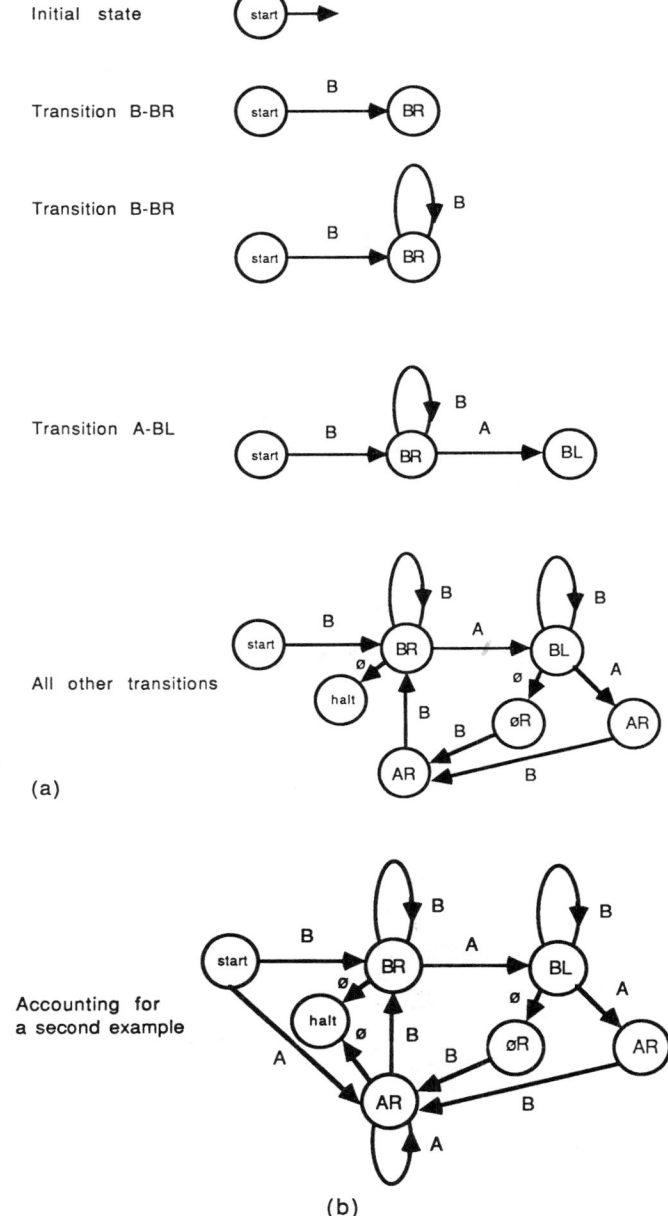

Figure 10. (a) Constructing the Turing machine controller to sort A's and B's; (b) completing the controller.

To the right of the tape configurations in Figure 9, the symbols being read are shown in the column labelled condition. These correspond to the conditions described in the algorithm synthesis method of the previous section. The instructions to the tape head give the symbol to be printed: A, B, or blank, and the direction of the next head move, left L or right R. The combination of these two columns is the needed information for the synthesizer of Figure 7. In fact, when it is executed, the controller of Figure 10a results. It is the proposed program for sorting any string of A's and B's into ascending order. This program has a small bug in that it will not sort a string that begins with an A. The omission can be removed if one more example is processed, the sorting of the list AA, and the result appears in Figure 10b. The machine can now be put into compute mode and used to sort any string of A's and B's.

The methodology is algorithmic and capable of creating any Turing machine. For example, Biermann, Baum, and Petry (1975) showed that it can create a universal Turing machine from a single example computation. The major problem with the approach is its high execution time. A variety of strategies were developed by Biermann, Baum, and Petry (1975) for speeding it up.

The algorithm for synthesis has had many other applications. Another example is the trainable desk calculator of Biermann and Krishnaswamy (1976) that enables a user to do hand calculations at a machine display with a light pen and which creates programs from the resulting traces. Using this system, many programs have been generated including various matrix manipulation routines, sorting programs, a finite state machine minimizer, and a compiler for a small ALGOL-like language. In a sequel to this work, Biermann (1978) showed that certain types of instructions for indexing can be omitted from such example traces while still allowing for correct program synthesis.

An application for this approach was also developed by Waterman and co-workers (1984) in the construction of a

programmer's helper called EP. This system observes the user in typical daily applications and builds programs to automatically mimic the user behaviors. Then when repetitive tasks occur, the user can release control to the machine which has built code to finish them automatically. Fink and Biermann (1986) used the idea to create a dialogue acquisition mechanism in a natural language processor.

Synthesis of LISP Code

A popular area for research in recent years (Smith, 1984) has centered around the creation of LISP programs from examples of their behaviors. Thus, one might be given the fact that the input $x = ((A \cdot B) \cdot C)$ is to yield output $z = (C \cdot (B \cdot A))$. The goal is to construct a LISP program that is capable of executing this and all similar examples.

The synthesis of the code begins with the discovery of the LISP operations required to yield the output from the input.

$$z = cons(cdr(x), cons(cdr(car(x)), car(car(x))))$$

Here $cons(u,v)$ is defined to be the dotted pair $(u \cdot v)$. $car(x)$ and $cdr(x)$ are defined to be the left and right sides of dotted pair x. Thus, if $x = (A.B)$ then $car(x) = A$, $cdr(x) = B$, and $cons(x,x) = ((A.B).(A.B))$. The breakdown of output z in terms of primitive functions is unique and easy to find. Furthermore, it corresponds to the trace of instructions employed in the previous examples. In fact, the concatenated operators can be broken apart into primitives in preparation for the program synthesis:

$$z = f_1(x)$$
$$f_1(x) = cons(f_2(x), f_3(x))$$
$$f_2(x) = f_4(cdr(x))$$
$$f_3(x) = f_5(car(x))$$
$$f_4(x) = x$$
$$f_5(x) = cons(f_6(x), f_7(x))$$
$$f_6(x) = f_8(cdr(x))$$
$$f_7(x) = f_9(car(x))$$
$$f_8(x) = x$$
$$f_9(x) = x$$

Here the flowchart construction methodology can again be applied; instead of merging separate instructions from the trace, however, different f_i's will be merged. Also, conditional tests need to be created during the synthesis procedure.

The process of merger is made possible by the existence of the cond operator in LISP which is written as follows:

$$cond((p_1 g_1)(p_2 g_2)(p_3 g_3) \ldots (p_n g_n))$$

The predicates $p_1, p_2, \ldots, p_n$ are evaluated sequentially and when the first p_j is found that evaluates to true, cond returns g_j as its value. LISP has some built-in predicates such as atom(x) which is defined to be true if and only if x is a LISP atom. Suppose x is a dotted pair of the atoms A and B (ie, $x = (A.B)$) then:

$$f(x) = cond((atom(x) \, car(x))$$
$$(atom(car(x)) \, cdr(x))$$
$$(T \, cons(x,x)))$$

will evaluate to B. That is, atom(x) is false, and atom $(car(x))$ is true, so $cdr(x)$ is returned as the result.

One can thus see how the cond operator can be used to merge functions from the above trace. Suppose, for example, it is desired to merge $f_1(x)$ and $f_4(x)$ and that a predicate generator has discovered that function f_4 should be selected if x is an atom. Then f_1 and f_4 can be merged to produce f.

$$f(x) = cond((atom(x) \, x)(T \, cons(f_2(x), f_3(x))))$$

In fact, the flow chart synthesis procedure with automatic predicate generation can merge f_1, f_4, f_5, f_8, and f_9 to produce f as shown. It will also merge f_6 into f_2 and f_7 into f_3 leaving them unchanged:

$$f_2(x) = f(cdr(x)) \qquad f_3(x) = f(car(x))$$

The combination of the three functions f, f_2, and f_3 comprise a program that will achieve the target behavior. In fact, it will reverse any LISP S-expression of any level of complexity. Thus a complete program for reversing LISP S-expressions has been synthesized from one example.

This function merging technique is capable of generating any member in the class of regular LISP programs (Biermann, 1978). These programs include most LISP functions that have only one parameter, no auxiliary variables, and use only the atom predicate. The process reliably generates programs from randomly selected examples and always converges to a correct regular program if one exists and if enough examples are given. Its main disadvantage is that it is a searching procedure which becomes very expensive to execute if the target program is large.

LISP Synthesis Using Recurrence Relations

Summers (1977) has developed a LISP synthesis methodology based upon the discovery of recurrence relations in a sequence of examples. This methodology has the advantage that it creates programs more quickly than the above method but it also requires more carefully constructed training examples. Suppose it is desired to create a program which will delete the negative numbers in a list. One might present the system with these examples:

Example	Input	Output
1	NIL	NIL
2	(2)	(2)
3	(−1,2)	(2)
4	(0,−1,2)	(0,2)
5	(1,0,−1,2)	(1,0,2)
6	(−2,1,0,−1,2)	(1,0,2)

The Summers method involves discovering relationships between the sequential examples and the construction of single loop recursive programs to implement them. One can begin by writing each output in terms of its corresponding input using LISP primitives:

Example	Input	Output
1	NIL	$f_1(x) = $ NIL
2	(2)	$f_2(x) = cons(car(x),$ NIL$)$
3	(−1,2)	$f_3(x) = cons(car(cdr(x)),$ NIL$)$
4	(0,−1,2)	$f_4(x) = cons(car(x),$ $cons(car(cdr(cdr(x))),$NIL$))$
5	(1,0,−1,2)	$f_5(x) = cons(car(x),$ $cons(car(cdr(x)),$ $cons(car(cdr(cdr(cdr(x)))),$ NIL$)))$
6	(−2,1,0,−1,2)	$f_6(x) = cons(car(cdr(x)),$ $cons(car(cdr(cdr(x)))$ $cons(car(cdr(cdr(cdr(cdr(x))))),$ NIL$)))$

Although this step was quite straightforward, the next one requires a key discovery. Specifically, if one studies each f_i in the above sequence, it can be seen that each can be rewritten in terms of the previous f_i in a very systematic way. In fact, the following pattern arises:

Example	Input	Output
1	NIL	$f_1(x) = $ NIL
2	(2)	$f_2(x) = cons(car(x), f_1(cdr(x)))$
3	(−1,2)	$f_3(x) = f_2(cdr(x))$
4	(0,−1,2)	$f_4(x) = cons(car(x), f_3(cdr(x)))$
5	(1,0,−1,2)	$f_5(x) = cons(car(x), f_4(cdr(x)))$
6	(−2,1,0,−1,2)	$f_6(x) = f_5(cdr(x))$

Examining this sequence, one can see two recurrence relations arising consistently:

$$f_i(x) = cons(car(x), f_{i-1}(cdr(x)))$$

and

$$f_i(x) = f_{i-1}(cdr(x)).$$

One can then run a test generation procedure on the inputs to determine when each recurrence relation is appropriate. In fact, it is easy to discover that if x is an atom, $f_i(x)$ is NIL, and if the first entry of x is negative then $f_i(x)$ takes the second recurrence form given above. Otherwise, $f_i(x)$ takes the first form given. The synthesized program is thus:

$$f(x) = cond((\text{atom } (x) \text{ NIL})$$
$$(neg(car(x)) \, f(cdr(x)))$$
$$(T \, cons(car(x), f(cdr(x))))))$$

Summers has given a basic synthesis theorem that specifies the nature of the required recurrence relations and a recursive program schema that will implement the observed recurrences. He also shows a fascinating strategy for introducing new auxiliary variables into the synthesized program if they are needed.

Synthesizing Programs Using Factorization of the Behavior Graph

Fahmy (1988) has given an algorithm for creating real time acceptors using a graph factorization technique. The procedure begins with a set of examples of the target behavior and assembles these into a behavior graph. Then the behavior graph is factored into two graphs, a finite-state controller and a data structure graph. The data structure may be any from a library of such structures and the factorization technique seeks one that will yield a successful decomposition.

Suppose, as an illustration, one would like to create an acceptor for strings of the form $a^n b^n$ where n could be any natural number. Specifically, it is desired that a small set of examples of the target behavior be input to the synthesis system and the system should print a program to recognize the whole set. This problem can be better understood if one writes down a few examples of the behavior and then creates the smallest possible flowchart that will accept them. If the examples are ab, $aabb$, $aaabbb$, and $aaaabbbb$, then the flowchart for the acceptor is shown in Figure 11. Clearly if a larger number of examples had been included, the graph would extend farther to the right. If the whole language were to be represented, the graph would extend infinitely far.

The next concept in this theory is of the data structure as a graph. Two examples appear in Figure 12. The first is a counter: it begins in the 0−state, moves right on each increment instruction, and moves left on each decrement. The second data structure is a stack: it starts in the empty state and each push of an a or b causes it to move to the appropriate lower state. A pop instruction causes it to move upward to a previous state.

The third idea in this theory is the concept of a program as a finite state controller. This idea is used in several of the approaches given above and is not new. Figure 13 shows two finite-state controllers that are capable of recognizing $a^n b^n$. One uses the counter data structure and the other uses the stack. A computation begins with the controller in its initial state. The input string is said to be accepted if the controller is in a final state when the last symbol has been processed. Otherwise the input is not accepted.

It is easy to see how these controllers work. At each instant of time, a symbol is read from the input, a condition is checked on data structure, and a transition in the controller is made. This transition results in an instruc-

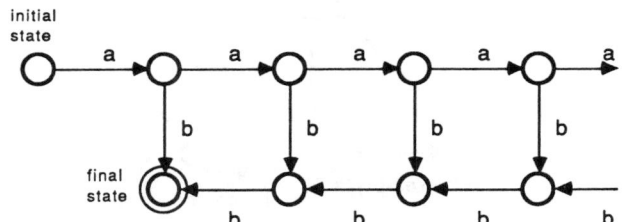

Figure 11. The behavior graph that accounts for the computations of $a^n b^n$.

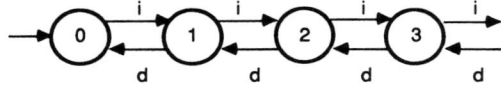

(a) Counter

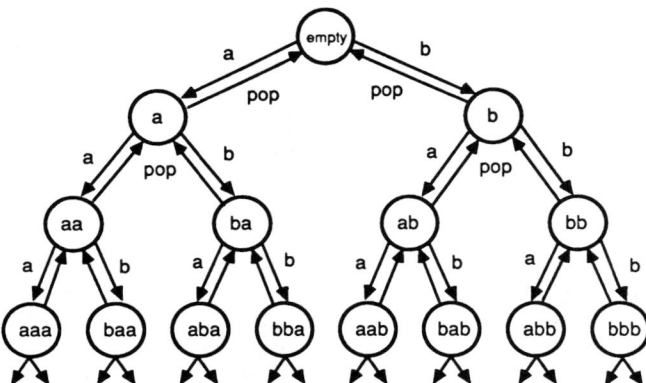

(b) Pushdown stack

Figure 12. Representing data structures with graphs.

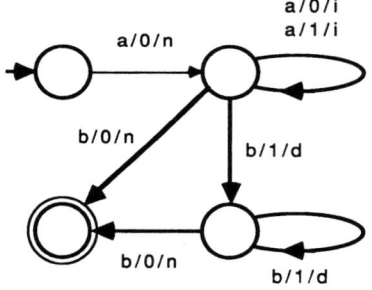

(a) Controller using a counter.

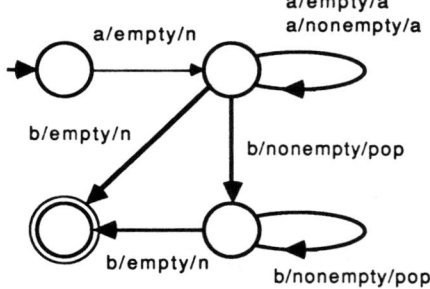

(b) Controller using a stack.

Figure 13. Two controllers for the computation of $a^n b^n$.

tion being sent to the data structure possibly changing its state. As an illustration, one can follow the acceptance of string $aabb$ by the first controller in Figure 13. The first a will be received with the controller in the initial state and the counter in state 0. The controller transition asserts that the move should be to the state on the right with no instruction n sent to the counter. Next a second a is read and the transition $a/0/i$ tells the controller to remain in that state and increment the counter to 1. Next a b will arrive moving the controller to another state and decrementing the counter to 0. Finally, the next b will move the controller to the final state. The string $aabb$ has been accepted.

The Fahmy (1988) theory of synthesis is based upon the discovery that the graph product of the control structure C and data structure D shown above is the behavior graph B: $B = C \times D$. This graph product is defined as follows: For each state c in C and each state d in D, create a state (c,d) in B. If c has transition $a/b/e$ to state c', and d in condition b has transition e to d', then state (c,d) in B should have transition a to state (c',d').

The synthesis procedure receives a set of strings of the target behavior, all of the strings of some length j or less. Then it builds the behavior graph B and attempts to find a data structure D such that the factorization $B = C \times D$ will hold. The factorization methodology is adapted from Hartmanis-Stearns (1966) machine decomposition theory. The procedure will create any real time acceptor if an appropriate data structure is available.

Synthesizing PROLOG Programs

Shapiro (1982) has developed a methodology for creating PROLOG logic programs from examples. The operation of his system will be illustrated here by showing how it creates the member function in PROLOG. Here member (X,Y) will be defined to be a predicate which is true if and only if X is a member of list Y. Following PROLOG notation, lists will be written with square brackets. Thus $[a,b,c]$ is the list containing entries a, b, and c and so member $(a,[a,b,c])$ and member $(b,[a,b,c])$ will be true while member $(d,[a,b,c])$ will be false.

PROLOG programs will be written here as sets of clauses of the form $p_1 \leftarrow p_2, p_3, \ldots, p_n$ where the p_i are predicates. The meaning of such a clause is that p_1 is true if $p_2, p_3, \ldots, p_{n-1}$, and p_n are true. A PROLOG program is executed by asserting such a p_1 and having the processor prove $p_2, p_3, \ldots, p_n$. Typically these latter proofs involve calls to other clauses in the program with very deep nestings possible.

The example to be studied here is the following program which has two clauses. The notation $[X|Y]$ stands for a list whose first element is X and whose other elements are contained in Y.

$$\{\text{member}(X,[X|Z]) \leftarrow \text{true},$$

$$\text{member}(X,[Y|Z]) \leftarrow \text{member}(X,Z)\}$$

The operation of this program can be understood by observing its action on some of the above example behaviors. Thus member $(a,[a,b,c])$ can be proved using the first clause with $X = a$ and $Z = [b,c]$. The case member $(b,[a,b,c])$ can be proved by invoking the second clause which asserts that member $(b,[a,b,c])$ if member $(b,[b,c])$ and then using the first clause to prove member $(b,[b,c])$. The concern here is to show how such a program can be generated automatically.

The synthesis methodology is shown in Figure 14. The user introduces facts in the form of ground instances of the predicates. Each such predicate must be accompanied by an indication of whether it is true or false. Thus the user might enter the facts "member $(a,[a,b])$ is true" and "member $(c,[a,b])$ is false". The system proposes various clauses which might be parts of the target program and stores them into the data structure called PROLOG program. Then the PROLOG interpreter executes the currently proposed program on the available facts and determines whether it produces the desired result in each case. That is, given the above two facts, the current program should evaluate to true for member $(a,[a,b])$ and false for member $(c,[a,b])$. If the current program is not able to prove a desired result as in member $(a,[a,b])$, it needs an additional clause and it calls for one. If the current program proves something which the facts indicate is wrong, the system finds the offending clause in the program and removes it.

The clause generator at the top of Figure 14 is basically enumerative in nature. However, Shapiro has designed it carefully to avoid any unnecessary enumeration. First the user must declare the predicate symbols to be used and then specify what predicates can appear on the right hand sides of clauses. The clause generator also omits the creation of many "refinements" of clauses that have been shown to be unsatisfactory. In the example of this section, the clause generator will produce the following series of proposed clauses:

$$\text{member }(X,Y) \leftarrow \text{true}$$
$$\text{member }(X,[X|Z]) \leftarrow \text{true}$$
$$\text{member }(X,[Y|Z]) \leftarrow \text{member }(X,Z)$$
$$\text{member }(X,Y) \leftarrow \text{member }(Y,X)$$

etc.

A dialog for doing this synthesis on the Shapiro system is as follows:

System: Declare the routine to be synthesized.
USER: member (,).
System: What routines does "member" call?
USER: member
System: The guessed program is { }, the empty program.
USER: member $(a,[a])$ is true.
System: The guessed program is incomplete. Member $(a,[a])$ is not covered. The revised program is (member $(X,Y) \leftarrow$ true}. (A call has been made to the clause generator.)
USER: member $(a,[b])$ is false.
System: The guessed program is incorrect. Member $(a,[b])$ is covered and it should not be. The revised program is { }. The guessed program is incomplete.

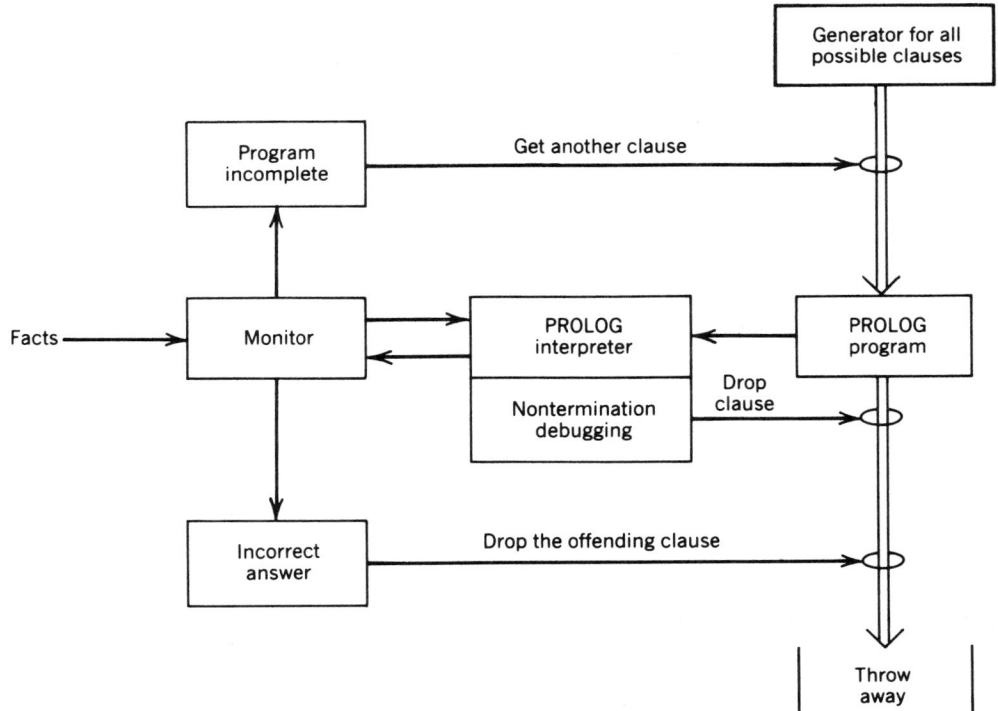

Figure 14. The Shapiro synthesis algorithm.

Member $(a,[a])$ is not covered. The revised program is {member $(X,[X|Z]) \leftarrow$ true}. (A second call to the clause generator has been made.)

USER: member $(a,[b,a])$ is true.

System: The guessed program is incomplete. Member $(a,[b,a])$ is not covered. The revised program is {member $(X,|X|Z) \leftarrow$ true, member $(X,[Y|Z]) \leftarrow$ member (X,Z)}. (A third call to the clause generator has been made.)

This example is somewhat contrived in order to show the mechanisms of the system in a short space. However, on more complicated examples, the system very efficiently uses the available facts to sort through the generated clauses until a solution is found.

The overall strategy is thus one of building approximations to the target program and then debugging them using facts provided by the user. Three kinds of errors may occur:

1. The program may compute a result which is undesired, an incorrect answer, as in the above dialog when the guessed program was able to prove member $(a,[b])$.
2. The program may be unable to compute a desired answer as was the case above when member (a,[a]) could not be proved.
3. The program may not terminate.

In the first type of error, the debugging mechanisms in the system simulate the incorrect computation and query the user and/or the data base of facts to check the correctness of every step in the computation. When a clause is found that computes an incorrect result from correct premises, that clause is discarded from the program. Thus in the above dialog, when the incorrect result member $(a,[b])$ was proven, the clause member $(X,Y) \leftarrow$ true was shown to be incorrect and was discarded. In the second type of error, a simulation of the failed computation is performed to find what predicate p_1 needed to be proven which was not proven. Then a call is made to the clause generator to find a new clause which will yield p_1 in the given computation. In the third type of error where nontermination occurs, the interpreter halts after a prespecified limit on the computation size has been exceeded. The processor than looks for an unending loop where the same computation state is reentered repeatedly, and it may also query the user concerning violations to a well founded ordering needed to insure termination. This debugging procedure leads to the discovery and removal of a clause in the program.

Shapiro tested this system in a variety of problem domains and compared it with various other program generation systems in the literature. For example, consider the problem solved by Biermann's LISP synthesizer (1978): Construct a program to find the first elements of lists in a list of atoms and lists. Thus the target program should be able to read input $[a,[b],c,[d],[e],f]$ and compute the result $[b,d,e]$. Shapiro's system needed 25 facts to solve this prob-

lem and generated the following code after 38 seconds of computation time.

$$\{\text{heads}([\ ],[\ ]) \leftarrow \text{true},$$

$$\text{heads}([[X|Y]|Z], [X|W]) \leftarrow \text{heads } (Z,W),$$

$$\text{heads}([X|Y],Z) \leftarrow \text{atom } (X), \text{heads } (Y,Z)\}$$

Biermann's system used only the single example given above and produced a correct regular LISP program after one half hour of computation.

Tinkham (1990) has developed a related methodology for PROLOG synthesis. It uses the insight that many target programs for synthesis resemble other well known programs, and synthesis need not begin with the empty program as does the Shapiro system. Tinkham uses a generalization technique to build a hierarchical tree of program schemas. At the bottom are a variety of well known programs organized in groups with similar structures. Above each group is a PROLOG schema which is a generalization of all of the members of its group. These schemas are organized into similarity groups that are generalized again by more abstract schemas higher in the tree. At the top of the tree is the most general schema from which all programs can be derived.

Synthesis proceeds by starting at the lowest level schema on the tree that is believed to be applicable to the task. If a schema can be chosen that is very near the target program, synthesis will be very fast. If the initial schema is very abstract and far from the target, synthesis may require substantially more time.

Theoretical Issues in Synthesis From Examples

A program synthesis system is called sound if whenever a program is generated from a set of examples, it can properly do all of those examples. The system is called complete for a class C of programs if it can generate all of the programs in the class. The properties of soundness and completeness are desirable for a program synthesis algorithm because they guarantee at least a minimal degree of behavioral acceptability for that algorithm.

An example of a synthesis method that is both sound and complete is the algorithm that simply enumerates all the members of a class C until a program is found that properly executes the given example behaviors. Two restrictions on the class C are needed before the algorithm will work: C must be enumerable, call its members P_1, P_2, P_3, etc., and it must be decidable for each behavior B and each program P_j in C whether P_j achieves B. The algorithm can be stated more precisely as shown below:

Algorithm

Input. A finite set S behaviors for the target program.

Output. A program P from class C with the property that P can execute each B in S.

1. $j \leftarrow 1$.
2. while there is B in S such that P_j cannot execute B, increment j.
3. *return with result P_j.*

This algorithm is sound by its very construction. One can show it is complete on C by considering its behavior in attempting to synthesize an arbitrary program in C. Suppose P_T is the first program in the enumeration P_1, P_2, P_3, . . . that is capable of executing all the behaviors of the target program. Then one can give the algorithm randomly selected behaviors of P_T and observe which P_j is generated. If P_j is not P_T, the user will detect the problem either by testing P_j or by studying its code. Then more examples can be given until the enumeration is forced to find P_T. There will always be examples to achieve this, because P_T is, by definition, the first program capable of all of the target behaviors. So the algorithm is complete. An interesting pragmatic discovery that has come out of this research is that very few examples are needed to achieve synthesis of most programs, even some very large ones.

Another important characteristic of the enumerative algorithm, as shown by Gold (1967), is that it is input optimal in the following sense: If another algorithm is proposed for generating programs in class C on the basis of behaviors, it will not be true that all programs in C will be generated from fewer behaviors than with the enumerative algorithm.

These results have practical significance because the flowchart synthesis algorithm of Figure 7 is functionally equivalent to the enumerative strategy if it is executed repeatedly for $L = 1, 2, 3, . . .$ until a program is synthesized. This means that the flowchart synthesis method is sound, complete, and input optimal on the class of all flowcharts. Furthermore, many of its variations have similar properties. For example, the function merging technique of LISP program synthesis is sound, complete, and input optimal on the class of regular LISP programs. Thus these methodologies are not heuristic in the sense that their abilities to converge to a solution are in any way unpredictable.

The Summers synthesis method is sound, and a variation of it has been proved to be complete over a class of programs defined by Smith (1977). The Shapiro methodology is sound and complete over the class of programs that can be constructed with rules from the rule generation routines.

Historical Remarks

One of the earliest papers on synthesis from examples was done by Amarel (1962). Later Solomonoff (1964) and Gold (1967) proposed the grammatical inference problem which resulted in a series of studies on the construction of grammars from their generated strings (Biermann and Feldman, 1982; Angluin, 1978; Blum and Blum, 1975; Feldman, Gips, Horning, and Reder, 1969). In the early 1970s, Biermann (1972, 1978) and Biermann and Krishnaswamy (1976) developed strategies for program synthesis from traces while a number of researchers were beginning to study synthesis procedures for LISP code (Biggerstaff, 1976; Hardy, 1975; Kodratoff and Jouannaud, 1984; Shaw, Swartout, and Green, 1975; Summers, 1977). Biermann and Smith (1979) developed a strategy for hierarchically decomposing examples and generating LISP code

using production rules. The synthesis from schemas technique of Tinkham used ideas from Dershowitz (1983).

PROGRAM SYNTHESIS THROUGH NATURAL LANGUAGE DIALOGUE

Although the techniques given above provide fundamental mechanisms for program synthesis, they need to be embedded in a larger system which can acquire the information for synthesis, provide the needed domain and programming knowledge, coordinate the various synthesis processes, and generate an acceptable output. Several of these large systems were constructed during the 1970s with very ambitious goals. The systems were to interview the user in natural language, acquire a model of the computational process to be undertaken, verify its correctness through further dialog, select data structures for efficient execution, and code the output in a traditional programming language. The goals of the research were twofold: To learn the nature of the problems associated with assembling a wide variety of technologies into a single automatic programming system, and to provide an environment within which these technologies could be further studied.

System Design

An example of this type of system is the PSI automatic programmer (Green, 1976) which is organized as shown in Figure 15. Here the first set of modules handle the acquisition phase of the synthesis when the user is being interviewed and a high level version of the program is being assembled. The lower portion of the figure shows the coding phase where efficiency decisions are made and code is generated.

The acquisition phase begins with a parser-interpreter which receives natural language input from the user and constructs a semantic net representation of what the user has said. The discourse module monitors the input, attempts to discover the user's intentions, and coordinates the various system functions to achieve the desired result. The explainer generates user friendly questions posed by the system or outputs a description of the program model. The domain expert builds fragmentary pieces of high level code for solving parts of the problem and passes them on to the model builder which assembles fragments into a high level version of the target program. The trace expert can interpret illustrative inputs from the user and usefully supplement other information sources. The coding phase of the processing can involve considerable revision to the program model received from the acquisition phase. The coder and efficiency expert work together to evaluate various alternative data structures for the target program, make choices on representation, and create the final code.

In the following sections, the flavor of each of these stages is illustrated by an example. However, the descriptions are necessarily approximate and oversimplified and the original sources should be consulted for more accurate and detailed information.

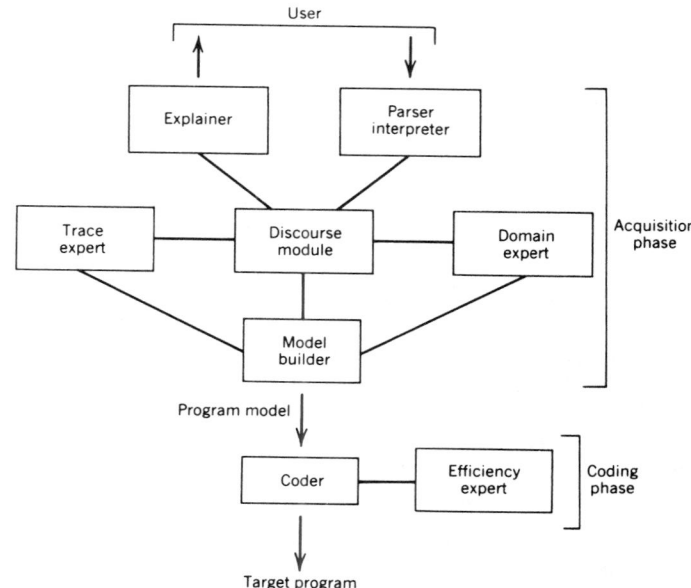

Figure 15. Functional diagram for the PSI system.

Example Dialog

The PSI system is designed to handle dialogs of the following kind where we are assuming the user wants a program to add a column of numbers.

USER: Please write a program to add up a set of numbers.

System: WHAT WOULD YOU LIKE TO CALL THE PROGRAM?

USER: Sum.

System: WHAT NUMBERS ARE TO BE ADDED UP?

USER: The program should read nonnegative integers from the user, sum them, and then print the answer.

System: WHEN SHOULD THE PROGRAM STOP READING?

USER: When a negative number is read.

System: IS THERE ANYTHING ELSE?

USER: The program should work as follows:

Output	READ:
Input	7
Output	READ:
Input	12
Output	READ:
Input	−1
Output	THE SUM IS 19.

System: Okay, how is this?

```
PROGRAM SUM (INPUT, OUTPUT);
VAR X, ANS: INTEGER;
BEGIN
ANS:=0;
WRITELN ('READ:');
READ (X);
```

```
WHILE X >= 0 DO
    BEGIN
    ANS: = ANS + X;
    WRITELN ('READ:');
    READ (X);
    END;
WRITELN ('THE SUM IS', ANS)
END.
```

The Functional Modules: Acquisition

The first module to process user inputs is the parser-interpreter (Ginsparg, 1978) which receives incoming sentences, parses them to identify their constituents, and then builds a meaning representation. The reader should consult portions of this volume on natural language processing to better understand the nature of this problem. The many issues concerning the analysis of complex sentences, construction of a meaning structure, resolution of pronominal and elliptical structures, handling of quantifiers and other problems are handled at this level. The output of this stage of processing is a semantic net that assembles as well as possible the individual parts of the dialogue into a cohesive unit. Figure 16 shows the nature of the meaning representation that would be constructed from the example dialogue. The individual sentences each contribute a few nodes and connections to the total network. As the information arrives, it is properly attached to the existing structure which gradually evolves toward a complete representation of the target program. It may not be possible for the parser-interpreter to complete the attachment of all parts of the description because domain or programming knowledge may be needed in places, but most of the primary connections can be made.

The discourse module (Steinberg, 1980) maintains a sense of progress in the dialogue by attempting to build a representation of the user's desires and initiating actions to satisfy them. It has communications with all acquisi-

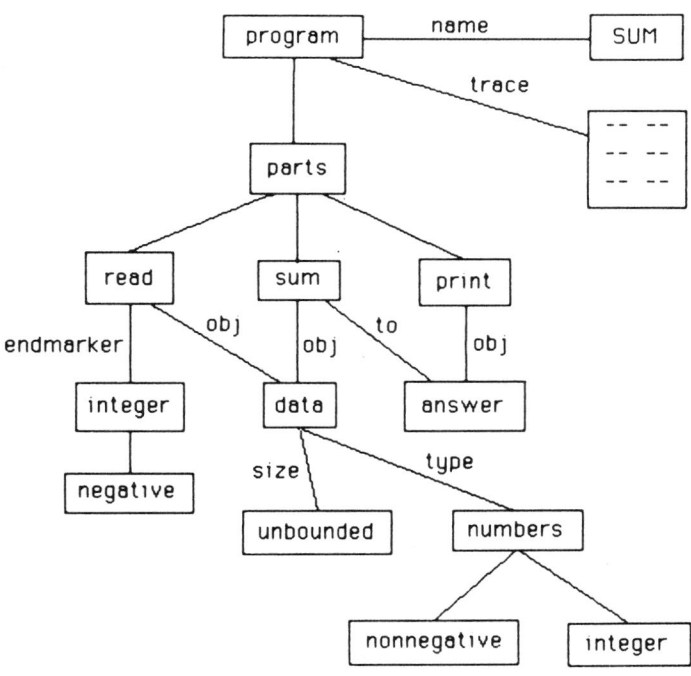

Figure 16. Representation of dialogue meaning structure.

tion modules and attempts to coordinate activities to achieve a cohesive interaction. The user may introduce concepts that need to be clarified and fit into the total theme. The system domain expert and model builder may recognize where information is needed to complete portions of the program description, and the discourse module must formulate queries to the user through the explainer (Gabriel, 1981) to obtain this information. Thus in the dialogue above, the system recognizes upon the mention of a program in the first sentence, that such a program should have a name, a body of code, and other related information. This causes it, for example, to formulate and return the next query. If the system finds all its internally generated questions answered, it may then pass control back to the user as is illustrated above in the last system query: "Is there anything else?" This is called a mixed initiative dialogue where one party introduces an issue that is resolved in subsequent interaction, then the other party mentions a point that requires discussion, and so forth.

The domain expert (Phillips, 1977) has the task of converting the semantic net class of information (Fig. 16) into code fragments written in a very high level language. Thus a generic input routine of the following form might be retrieved to handle the read function called for in Figure 16.

$$S \leftarrow 0$$
input (x)
while x is valid data
$\qquad S \leftarrow S \cup \{x\}$
$\qquad$ input x

And a generic collection routine might be instantiated to do the required summing operation.

ans $\leftarrow 0$
while more data
$\qquad$ retrieve y
$\qquad$ ans $\leftarrow$ ans $+ y$

Finally, high level codes would be produced for the print routine,

$$\text{output } (z)$$

and all of these code fragments would be transferred to the model builder for assembly of the high level program. Thus the domain expert instantiates somewhat vague information from the earlier stages in concrete though rather high level code. It fills in some information where domain knowledge is needed but certain connections between the fragments are still not made.

The trace expert (Phillips, 1977) is designed to receive example input-output pairs for the target program, traces of snapshots of the program's behavior, or high level traces expressed in natural language. This expert generates a sequence of state–characterizing schemata which are then used in the creation of code fragments for the model builder. In the example dialogue, two effects result from the given trace. First, it is noted that the user wants the target program to output a read prompt before each input so this code must be merged into the given code segment.

$$S \leftarrow 0$$
output ('READ:')
input (x)
while x is valid data
$\qquad S \leftarrow S \cup \{x\}$
$\qquad$ output ('READ:')
$\qquad$ input (x)

Second, the trace gives the system a way of checking its generated program for acceptability.

The model builder (McCune, 1977) receives fragments from the other processes and attempts to assemble a high level version of the target program. This assembly may involve very complex processing including the compilation of all the information units and control structures needed and their proper coordination. The model builder, besides receiving information, can return information to the earlier stages regarding the portion of the code currently being discussed and thus provide possible referents for unresolved incoming noun phrases. In the current example, the processor must collect the above three code segments and coordinate them by noting the set being read in the first segment is identical to that being added in the second. Also, the correct data object must be printed at the end.

```
*read*
        S ← 0
        output ('READ:')
        input (x)
        while x ≥ 0
                S ← S ∪ {x}
                output ('READ:')
                input (x)
*sum*
        ans ← 0
        while not empty S
                y ← remove from (S)
                ans ← ans + y
*print*
        output (ans)
```

The program model is then sent to the coding phase for the creation of efficient machine code.

The Functional Modules: Coding

The coding module (Barstow, 1979) contains a large amount of detailed programming knowledge in the form of production rules. These rules are capable of proposing wide variations in the form of the data structures and the code. At selected points in the generation process, possible alternatives are created and handed to the efficiency expert (Kant, 1977) for evaluation. The efficiency expert has tools similar to those of a human being for making choices: analysis of algorithms techniques, general knowledge, and simulation. The system uses probabilistic information about data and the costs of machine operations to compute space-time cost functions for various alternatives and passes results back to the coder. Thus through a process of generating alternatives, evaluation, and movement down the search tree, the production rule system refines the program model into machine executable form.

The general organization of the coding module follows the tradition of expert system technology. It receives the program model from the acquisition phase and has several hundred production rules for modifying this model and converting it one step at a time to concrete code.

```
Program model
        ⇓
Partially refined description
        ⇓
        .
        .
        .
        ⇓
Target program
```

Many possible rules may be applicable at a given stage in the development. For example, if a set of objects is represented in the program model, the coder must make a decision concerning how the set is to be represented in the target programming language. Production rules will be available to select specific representations such as arrays, linked lists, bit maps, and so forth. An agenda orders the tasks to be addressed in the coding process and guides the selection of the rule to be tried next. Evaluation of each new partially refined program description is done using heuristic methods and calls to the efficiency expert. The more attractive paths in the sequential search for an acceptable program are moved toward the top of the agenda for continued expansion and refinement.

The steps that the coding phase might follow in completing the example of this section will be described next. The production rules given here are not actually taken from the system but give a feeling for how it works.

The system might have a production rule for combining loops that scan the same set.

If two separate loops increment through the same set and their code segments have independent effects, then they can be combined into a single loop.

Following the style of the original author, the rules will be given here in English rather than in a detailed notational form. The result of this rule applied to the two loops in the program model for reading and summing would be the following:

```
S ← 0
output ('READ:')
input (x)
ans ← 0
while x ≥ 0
        S ← S ∪ {x}
        y ← remove from (S)
        ans ← ans + y
        output ('READ:')
        input (x)
print (ans)
```

At this point, the system could notice the redundancy of the S data structure and employ the following rule to delete it:

If a single data structure is loaded and then emptied without any intermediate references, it can be removed.

```
output ('READ:')
input (x)
ans ← 0
while x ≥ 0
            ans ← ans + x
            output ('READ:')
            input (x)
print (ans)
```

Finally, a long series of rules is needed to actually create the executable code. The initialization lines, declarations, and all other special syntax must be properly assembled to achieve the target code.

```
PROGRAM SUM (INPUT, OUTPUT);
VAR X, ANS: INTEGER;
BEGIN
ANS:=0;
WRITELN ('READ:');
READ (X);
WHILE X >= 0 DO
        BEGIN
        ANS: = ANS + X;
        WRITELN ('READ:')
        READ (X);
        END;
WRITELN ('THE SUM IS', ANS);
END.
```

The Implementation

The PSI system was completed in the mid 1970s and is capable of constructing programs of several types including some concept formation programs and some numerical programs. A number of example dialogues have been published (Green, 1976) including interactions of up to about fifty sentences which result in several dozen lines of LISP code.

Historical Remarks

Heidorn (1974) built the first and one of the most impressive natural language automatic programming systems, NLPQ, which was aimed at the solution of operations research queuing problems. The system translated incoming sentences into a semantic network problem representation which then could be translated back to the user in paraphrase for verification. Then the network was compiled into the GPSS simulation language and run on conventional software.

Simultaneously with the Green project (1976), a synthesizer called SAFE was built by Balzer and co-workers (1976, 1978) which emphasized the automatic acquisition of domain knowledge and the creation of software from informal specifications. Also Martin and co-workers (1974) built a system which placed heavy emphasis on high quality processing of natural language.

Biermann and Ballard (1980) constructed an interpreter for "natural language programs" which was robust enough to be used by college students in solving programming problems (Biermann and co-workers, 1983; Geist and co-workers, 1982).

PROGRAM CONSTRUCTION USING A MECHANIZED ASSISTANT

More recently researchers have been examining the role that artificial intelligence can play in industrial programming environments where large software systems are specified, coded, evaluated, and maintained. Here the whole life cycle of the software system is under consideration: The client and the professional systems analyst discuss informally a proposed software product. Then more formal specifications are derived, performance estimates are made, and a model of the system evolves. Many times specifications are modified or redefined as analysis proceeds. The next phase is the actual construction, documentation, and testing of the product. After release into the user environment, the system may be debugged and changed or improved on a regular basis over a period of years.

A developing idea in some current automatic programming projects (Rich and Shrobe, 1978; Balzer and co-workers, 1983) envisions a mechanized programmer's assistant that would intelligently support all of the above activities. It would provide a programming environment for the user capable of receiving many kinds of information from programmers including formal and informal specifications, possibly natural language assertions regarding goals, motivations, and justifications, and code segments. It would assist the programmer in debugging these inputs and properly fitting them into the context of the programming project. It would be knowledge based and thus capable of fully understanding all of the above inputs. It would provide library facilities for presenting the programmer with standardized program modules or with information concerning the current project. It would be able to generate code from specifications, program segments, and other information available from the programmer and other sources. It would be able to understand program documentation within the code and to generate documentation where necessary. Finally, it would maintain historical notes related to what was done, by whom, when, and most importantly why. All of these functions are envisioned as operating strictly in a supportive role for human programmers who are expected to carry on most high level tasks.

Thus, the concept of the automatic programmer's assistant places the human programmer in the primary position of specifying the program and guiding progress towards successful implementation and maintenance. The task of the assistant is to maximally utilize available technologies to automate as many lower level functions as possible.

This view emphasizes the decomposition of the programming task into two stages (Fig. 17), systems analysis and programming. The first stage involves the development of formal specifications and deals primarily with what performance is required; the latter includes the decomposition of the task into an appropriate hierarchy of subparts, the selection of data structures, and the coding and documentation of the product. The former is assumed to be the appropriate domain for considerable human involvement whereas the latter is expected to be more amenable to automation.

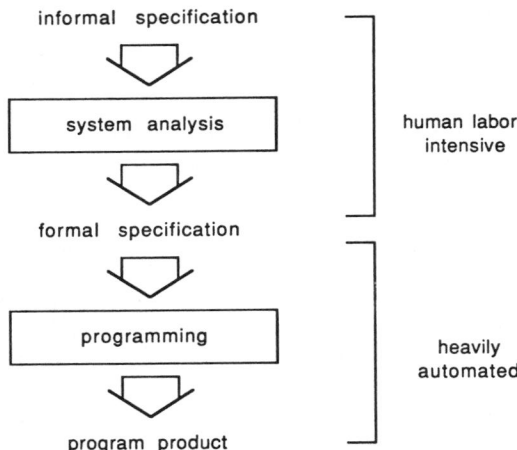

Figure 17. Stages in program construction.

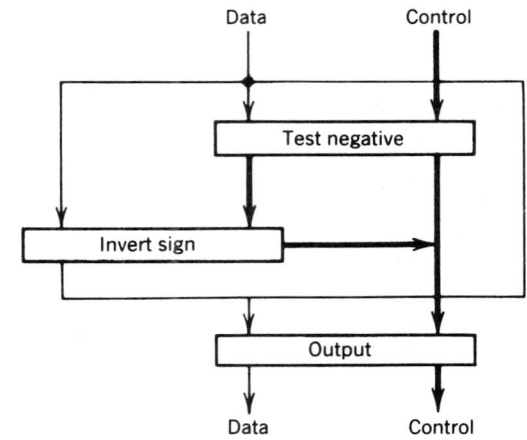

Figure 18. Example plan for computing absolute value showing both flow of data and flow of control.

All of this has implications for the program life cycle. The initial programming effort involves the human-machine team in developing the specification-system analysis followed by a largely automated generation of the programming product. Later stages in the program life cycle may involve revised specifications and improved approaches for doing the computation. These are implemented by replaying the complete construction process. Revisions are made to the informal specifications and these become reflected in the formal specifications. Then the automatic generation can be replayed possibly with revised decisions to account for the updated requirements.

The Programmer's Assistant

In order to begin implementing such an assistant, it is necessary to have appropriate languages to handle the many kinds of information that appear in this application. One approach is to introduce the concept of a wide-spectrum language that can be used at all levels of implementation from the specification of requirements to high-level coding of the actual target program. An example of such a language is REFINE (Smith and Westfold, 1987), which has as primitives sets, mappings, relations, predicates, enumerations, state transformation sequences, and other constructions.

Another approach (Rich and Waters, 1988) is based primarily on the concept of plans for programs that contain the essential data and control flow but exclude programming language details. An example of a plan appears in Figure 18, where the computation of absolute value is represented. The advantages of such plans are that because they locally contain essential information, they can be glued together arbitrarily without global repercussions. A complete plan will include both the graphical representation shown here and predicate calculus specifications on the plan behaviors. Commonly used plans, called cliches, can be stored in a library and can provide the building blocks for the assembly of large plans.

This approach uses code and plans as parallel representations for the program and allows the user to deal easily

with either one. If the user chooses to work in the plan domain, each action in creating or modifying a given plan results in appropriate updates in the code domain. The coder module translates the current version of the plan into code. If the user wishes to work with the code, the analyzer appropriately revises the associated plan.

The methodology utilizes plan transformations, called overlays, to do reasoning with plans. An example of an overlay appears in Figure 19 where the relationships between two plans are given as described in (Rich and Waters, 1988): the left side represents a plan for adding to an indexed sequence by incrementing an index and entering a data item; the right side represents a plan for pushing a data item on a stack. The overlay specifies the relation-

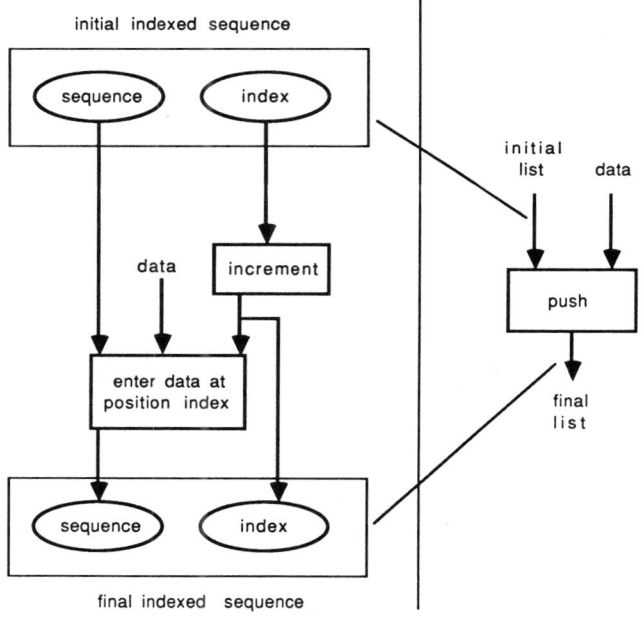

Adding to an indexed sequence.   Adding to a stack.

Figure 19. A plan transformation (or overlay).

ship between the two operations and allows a plan formulated in one paradigm to be revised to handle the other. The transformation can be used in either direction.

A knowledge-based editor KBEmacs has been developed (Waters, 1985) to create and manipulate plans and their associated code. It includes a layered reasoning system that works at the plan calculus level as well as at algebraic and predicate calculus levels. It has been demonstrated by creating a 54 line report generator program for a repair application in Ada from a five line specification as follows:

> Define a simple_report procedure UNIT_REPAIR_REPORT.
>
> Fill the enumerator with a chain_enumeration of UNITS and REPAIRS.
>
> Fill the main_file_key with a query_user_for_key of UNITS.
>
> Fill the title with ("Report of Repairs on Unit" & UNIT KEY).
>
> Remove the summary.

The system in this example contained an elaborate report cliche and substantial information related reporting the repair problem. The details of the generation appear in (Rich and Waters, 1988).

Automatically Generating Search Programs

Many of the ideas introduced here are illustrated in the KIDS system described by Smith (1990). This system utilizes algorithm theories which correspond to the plans of Rich and Waterman; they are stereotypic programming structures with associated input-output specifications. Included in the system is a reasoning mechanism that is used to instantiate such code structures with the appropriate details for the user's current problem. First, an inefficient prototype of the target program is created. Then it is refined repeatedly to improve its efficiency and quality until the final program is produced.

Although the approach is general, Smith has concentrated his efforts on the automatic creation of search programs (Smith, 1990) and divide-and-conquer programs (Smith, 1987). The approach will be illustrated here with the semi–automatic creation of a binary search routine. The synthesis will go through these steps:

1. Specification of the problem.
2. Selection of a theory from a library.
3. Specialization of the theory to the current problem.
4. Instantiation of the theory into a first draft program.
5. Refinement of the draft program.
6. Compilation into object code.

Suppose the problem is to create a program to search a sorted array for a given key and to return the index of the item when it is found. Step 1 of the process is to specify the problem in the KIDS language.

F_F: Ord Search
D_F: $\{\langle h, A, key\rangle \mid h \in \text{Nat} \wedge 1 \le h \wedge A \in map (\{1..h\}, \text{Nat}) \wedge \text{Ordered} (A) \wedge key \in \text{Nat}\}$
R_F: $\{index \mid index \in \text{Nat}\}$
O_F: $\lambda\langle h, A, key\rangle, index. A(index)=key \wedge index \in \{1..h\}$

Thus the program is to have name "OrdSearch" and it is to accept three inputs $h, A,$ and key as specified. A is a sorted array of size h and key is a natural number. The output as specified by R_F is to be a natural number and the relation O_F between the input $\langle h, A, key\rangle$ and output $index$ is that $A(index) = key$ where $index$ is in $\{1..h\}$. (The lambda notation λ specifies arguments followed by a period followed by the relationship.)

Step 2 is to select a theory for the computation and Smith has developed seven choices which cover most of the well known searching paradigms. For example, his system can semi–automatically create programs to solve k-queens, traveling salesman, 0–1 integer linear programming, propositional satisfiability, hamiltonian circuit, knapsack, topological sort, and long lists of other search programs. In the current example, a reasonable choice is to use the binary-split-of-integer-subrange theory as given here:

F_G: gs_binary_split_of_integer_subrange
D_G: $\{\langle m,n\rangle \mid m \in \text{integer} \wedge n \in \text{integer} \wedge m\le n\}$
R_G: $\{k \mid k \in \text{integer}\}$
O_G: $\lambda\langle m,n\rangle, k. k \in \{m..n\}$
$\hat{R}$: $\lambda\langle m,n\rangle. \{\langle i,j\rangle \mid i \in \text{integer} \wedge j \in \text{integer} \wedge m\le i\le j\le n\}$
Satisfies: $\lambda k, \langle i,j\rangle. i\le k\le j$
$\hat{f}_o$ $\lambda\langle m,n\rangle . \langle m,n\rangle$
Split: $\lambda\langle i,j\rangle, \langle i',j'\rangle. i<j \wedge (\langle i',j'\rangle=\langle i,(i+j) \text{ div } 2\rangle \vee \langle i',j'\rangle=\langle 1+ (i+j) \text{ div } 2,j\rangle)$
Extract: $\lambda k, \langle i,j\rangle. i=j \wedge k=i$

In words, this theory has the name gs_binary_split_of_integer_subrange and it receives a pair of integers $\langle m,n\rangle$ as input. The output is an integer k where k must be in the interval $\{m..n\}$ $\hat{R}$ specifies the set of objects to be searched, the set of intervals $\langle i,j\rangle$. An integer k will satisfy an interval $\langle i,j\rangle$ if $i\le k\le j$. The initial interval in the search $\hat{r}_o$ will be $\langle m,n\rangle$ which is the whole interval. The method of search will be to repeatedly split the current interval using the rule given: $\langle i,j\rangle$ is split into $\langle i,(i+j) \text{ div } 2\rangle$ and $\langle 1 + (i+j) \text{ div } 2, j\rangle$. A solution will be extracted when interval $\langle i,j\rangle$ is reached where $i=j$. The solution will be $k=i$. This theory of search is applicable to such problems as integer square root, maximum of a unimodal function, and binary search of a sorted array. The latter problem is the one being addressed here.

The third step of the process is largely done automatically. The theory given above is to be specialized to solve the specific problem at hand. The method is to prove the following theorem which has the side effect of producing a unifier θ. This unifier provides the substitution needed to produce the specialized theory.

$$\forall x \in D_F \; \exists y \in D_G \; \forall z \in R_F [O_F(x,z) \Rightarrow O_G(y,z)]$$

This theorem is instantiated in the current problem as follows:

$\forall x \in \{\langle h, A, key \rangle \mid$ (see D_F above)$\}$

$\exists y \in \{\langle m, n \rangle \mid$ (see D_G above)$\}$

$\forall z \in \{\langle index \mid$ (see R_F above)$\}$

[$\{index \mid index \in Nat\}$ is a subset of $\{k \mid k \in integer\}$ and

$(A(index) = key \land index \in \{l..h\}) \Rightarrow k \in \{m..n\}$]

The proof of this theorem yields the unifier θ: $n \leftarrow h$, $m \leftarrow 1$, $k \leftarrow index$. Making these substitutions into the general binary search theory yields a search theory for sorted linear arrays.

The fourth step of the procedure utilizes a synthesis theorem that gives a generalized program to compute the search. Smith has proved a number of such theorems and the one needed here says that the program to input x as specified in D_F and compute z meeting the requirement $O_F(x,z)$ is given here:

function $F(x : D_F) : \text{set } (R_F)$
                 returns $\{z \mid O_F(x, z)\}$
                 $= F\text{-}gs(x, \hat{r}_o(x))$

function $F\_gs\,(x : D_F, \hat{r} : \hat{R}) : \text{set } (R_F)$
                 returns $\{z \mid \text{Satisfies } (z, \hat{r}) \land O_F(x, z)\}$
                 $= \{z \mid \text{Extract } (z, \hat{r}) \land O_F(x, z)\} \cup$
                 $\{F\_gs(x, s) \mid \text{Split } (x, \hat{r}, s)\}$

Making the correct substitutions from above, the program becomes:

function

OrdSearch $(h:\text{Nat}, A:\text{map}(\{1..h\}, \text{Nat}), key:\text{Nat}): \text{set } (\text{Nat})$
returns $\{index \mid A(index) = key \land index \in \{1..h\}\}$
$= $OrdSearch$_gs (h, A, key, 1, h)$

function

OrdSearch$\_gs(h:\text{Nat}, A:\text{map}(\{1...h\}, \text{Nat}),$
         $key : \text{Nat}, i : \text{Nat}, j : \text{Nat}) : \text{set } (\text{Nat})$
returns $\{index \mid A(index) = key \land index \in \{i..j\}\}$
$= \{index \mid i = j \land index = i \land A(index) = key\}$
   $\cup \{index \mid i < j \land \langle i', j' \rangle = \langle i, (i+j) \text{ div } 2 \rangle \land$
         $index \in $OrdSearch$_gs(h, A, key, i', j')\}$
   $\cup \{index \mid i < j \land \langle i', j' \rangle = \langle 1 + (i+j) \text{ div } 2, j \rangle \land$
         $index \in $OrdSearch$_gs(h, A, key, i', j')\}$

This is a draft of the target program. It receives the specified input, executes the binary split strategy of search, and returns the correct answer. It has a shortcoming, however; it searches the complete list requiring an examination of every entry in A. There is a major improvement possible because A is sorted, and this leads to step 5 of the process, refinement of the program.

The primary efficiency improving technique for search programs is the deletion of fruitless subsearches. In most search problems, there are many subspaces that probably have no solutions, and tests must be inserted into the

program to prevent useless excursions. One such strategy is the derivation of a formula $\Phi(x, \hat{r})$ such that

$$\forall x \in D_F \; \forall \hat{r} \in \hat{R} \; \forall z \in R_F [\text{Satisfies}(z, \hat{r}) \land O(x, z) \Rightarrow \Phi(x, \hat{r})]$$

The formula $\Phi(x, \hat{r})$ provides a necessary condition for subspace $\hat{r}$ to contain a solution. If it fails to hold, the subspace can be discarded as a possible place for problem solutions.

In the current problem, the program OrdSearch_gs returns $\{index \mid A(index) = key \land index \in \{i, j\}\}$. An additional and previously unused fact in this problem is that A is sorted:

$$1 \le i \le j \le h \Rightarrow A(i) \le A(j)$$

These two facts combine to yield

$$A(i) \le A(index) \le A(j)$$
or $$A(i) \le key \le A(j)$$

The insertion of this guard into every entrance to a new subspace results in the pruning of a large fraction of the tree. It has changed the computation time from order n to order $log_2 n$.

function

OrdSearch $(h:\text{Nat}, A:\text{map}(\{1..h\}, \text{Nat}), key:\text{Nat}): \text{set}(\text{Nat})$
returns $\{index \mid A(index) = key \land index \in \{l..h\}\}$
$= $OrdSearch$_gs (h, A, key, 1, h)$

function

OrdSearch$\_gs(h:\text{Nat}, A:\text{map}(\{1..h\}, \text{Nat}), key:\text{Nat}, i:\text{Nat},$
       $:\text{Nat}): \text{set } (\text{Nat})$
returns $\{index \mid A(index) = key \land index \in \{i.j\}\}$
$= \{index \mid i = j \land index = i \land A(index) = key\}$
   $\cup \{index \mid i < j \land \langle i', j' \rangle = \langle i, (i+j) \text{div } 2 \rangle$
     $\land A(i') \le key \le A(j')$
     $\land index \in $OrdSearch$_gs (h, A, key, i', j')\}$
   $\cup \{index \mid i < j \land \langle i', j' \rangle = \langle 1 + (i+j) \text{div } 2, j \rangle$
     $\land A(i) \le key \le A(j')$
     $\land index \in $OrdSearch$_gs(h, A, key, i', j')\}$

The KIDS system is capable of finding many other optimizations in this program, with some interactions from the user. For example, one can simplify expressions and pull out common subexpressions. The derivation outlined here is given in substantially more detail in Smith (1987). One interesting speedup that can be made in some programs is called finite differencing. Sometimes an expression that is computed on each cycle through a loop can be eliminated by saving its results from the previous cycle. If the new value of the expression can be computed by updating its results from the previous cycle, a complete reevaluation of the expression is not necessary.

The product of this processing is a REFINE program (Smith and Westfold, 1987, Smith and co-workers, 1985) that is then compiled into LISP and is executable. Additional examples of the system's capabilities are described in Smith (1987). Many such derivations required about an hour or less of the user's time, and this may be faster than traditional methods of programming. An interesting derivation of a k-queens program appears in Smith (1990). The initial unoptimized global search program in this case required approximately one hour to enumerate the 92 solutions of the 8-queens problem. The optimized version could enumerate them in less than one second.

Other Work

Lubars and Harandi (1987) have built a knowledge-based system aimed at specification and design. Neighbors (1984) has defined two expert roles, the domain analyst and the domain designer, and attempted to code their knowledge so that new domains can be easily implemented from knowledge derived from earlier ones. Kelly and Nonnenmann (1987) have built a specification acquisition system for the creation of telephone switching software. McCartney (1987) has developed a synthesis system aimed at special problems in computational geometry. Kant (1985), Kant and Newell (1984), and Steier (1989) have studied humans in the process of algorithm design and attempted to emulate the process they observed on the Soar system. Bates and Constable (1985) have built a program development system that emphasizes logical specification of the target behavior and manipulation of the proof to derive a program. A survey of many of these projects appears in Lowry and Duran (1989).

CONCLUSION

Automatic programming is the process of mechanically assembling fragmentary information about target behaviors into machine executable code for achieving those behaviors. This article has described the four main approaches to the field followed by researchers in recent years. The field is still very much in its infancy but already many useful discoveries have been made. Because of its tremendous importance, it is clear automatic programming will be a research area central to artificial intelligence in the years to come.

Additional overviews of the subject are found in Balzer (1985), Barr and Feigenbaum (1982), Biermann (1976, 1985), Biermann and co-workers (1984), Goldberg (1986), Heidorn (1976), Partridge (1989), and Rich and Waters (1986).

BIBLIOGRAPHY

S. Amarel, "On the Automatic Formation of a Computer Program which Represents a Theory," in M. Yovits, G. T. Jacobi, and A. D. Goldstein, eds., *Self-Organizing Systems*, Spartan Books, 1962, pp. 107–175.

D. Angluin, "On the Complexity of Minimum Inference of Regular Sets," *Inf. Control* **39**, 337–350 (1978).

R. Balzer, "A 15–Year Perspective on Automatic Programming," *IEEE Trans. on Software Eng.* SE–11(11), 1257–1267 (1985).

R. Balzer, T. E. Cheatham, Jr., and C. Green, "Software Technology in the 1990s: Using a New Paradigm," *Computer* **16**, 39–45 (Nov. 1983).

R. M. Balzer, N. Goldman, and D. Wile, "Informality in Program Specifications," *IEEE Trans. on Software Eng.* SE–4, 94–103 (1978).

R. M. Balzer, N. Goldman, and D. Wile, "On the Transformational Implementation Approach to Programming," *Second International Conference on Software Engineering*, 1976, pp. 337–344.

A. Barr and E. A. Feigenbaum, *The Handbook of Artificial Intelligence*, William Kaufmann, Inc., 1982.

D. R. Barstow, *Knowledge-based Program Construction*, Elsevier North-Holland, 1979.

J. L. Bates and R. L. Constable, "Proofs as Programs," *ACM Trans. on Prog. Lang. Sys.* **7**(1), 113–136 (1985).

F. L. Bauer, B. Moller, H. Partsch, and P. Pepper, "Formal Program Construction by Transformations—Computer Aided, Intuition Guided Programming," *IEEE Trans. on Software Eng.* SE–15(2), 165–180 (1989).

W. Bibel, "Syntax-Directed, Semantics-Supported Program Synthesis," *Artif. Intell.* **14**(3), 243–261 (1980).

W. Bibel and K. M. Hornig, "LOPS—A System Based On A Strategical Approach to Program Synthesis," in A. Biermann, G. Guiho, and Y. Kodratoff, eds., *Automatic Program Construction Techniques*, Macmillan Publishing Co., 1984, pp. 69–90.

A. W. Biermann, "Approaches to Automatic Programming," in M. Rubinoff and M. C. Yovits, eds., *Advances in Computers*, Academic Press, 1976.

A. W. Biermann, "Automatic Insertion of Indexing Instructions in Program Synthesis," *Int. J. Comput. Inf. Sci.* **7**, 65–90 (1978).

A. W. Biermann, "Formal Methodologies in Automatic Programming: A Tutorial," *J. Symb. Comp.* **1** (1985).

A. W. Biermann, "On the Inference of Turing Machines from Sample Computations," *Artif. Intell.* **3**, 181–198 (1972).

A. W. Biermann, "The Inference of Regular LISP Programs from Examples," *IEEE Trans. on Systems, Man, and Cybernetics* SMC–8, 585–600 (1978).

A. W. Biermann and B. W. Ballard, "Towards Natural Language Programming," *Am. J. Computational Linguistics* **6**, 71–86 (1980).

A. W. Biermann and D. R. Smith, "A Production Rule Mechanism for Generating LISP Code," *IEEE Trans. on Systems, Man, and Cybernetics* SMC–9, 260–276 (1979).

A. W. Biermann and J. A. Feldman, "A Survey of Results in Grammatical Inference," in Y. H. Rao and G. W. Ernst, eds., *Context-Directed Pattern Recognition and Machine Intelligence Technologies for Information Processing*, IEEE Computer Society Press, 1982.

A. W. Biermann and R. Krishnaswamy, "Constructing Programs from Example Computations," *IEEE Trans. on Software Eng.* SE–2, 141–153 (1976).

A. W. Biermann, B. W. Ballard, and A. H. Sigmon, "An Experimental Study of Natural Language Programming," *Int. J. Man-Mach. Stud.* **18**, 71–87 (1983).

A. W. Biermann, I. R. Baum, and F. E. Petry, "Speeding Up the Synthesis of Programs from Traces," *IEEE Trans. Comput.* C–24 (1975).

A. W. Biermann, G. Guiho, and Y. Kodratoff, eds., *Automatic Program Construction Techniques*, Macmillan Publishing Co., 1984.

T. J. Biggerstaff, *C2: A Super Compiler Model of Automatic Programming*, Ph.D. dissertation, University of Washington, Seattle, Wash., 1976.

L. Blum and M. Blum, "Toward a Mathematical Theory of Inductive Inference," *Inf. Control* **28**, 125–155 (1975).

M. Broy, "Program Construction by Transformations: A Family Tree of Sorting Programs," in A. W. Biermann and G. Guiho, eds., *Computer Program Synthesis Methodologies*, D. Reidel Publishing Co., 1983, pp. 1–50.

R. M. Burstall and J. Darlington, "A Transformation System for Developing Recursive Programs," *JACM* **24**, 44–67 (1977).

N. Dershowitz, *The Evolution of Programs*, Birkhauser, Boston, 1983.

A. F. Fahmy, *Synthesis of Real Time Programs*, Doctoral dissertation, Dept. of Computer Science, Duke University, Durham, N.C., 1988.

J. A. Feldman, J. Gips, J. J. Horning, and S. Reder, *Grammatical Complexity and Inference*, Tech. Report CS–125, Computer Science Dept., Stanford University, 1969.

P. K. Fink and A. W. Biermann, "The Correction of Ill-Formed Input Using History Based Expectation with Application to Speech Understanding," *Computational Linguistics* **12**(1) (1986).

R. Gabriel, *An Organization for Programs in Fluid Dynamics*, Rep. No. STAN–CS–81–856, Computer Science Dept., Stanford University, 1981.

S. L. Gerhart, "Proof Theory of Partial Correctness Verification Systems," *SIAM J. Comp.* **5**, 355–377 (1976).

R. Geist, D. Kraines, and P. Fink, "Natural Language Computing in a Linear Algebra Course," *Proceedings of the National Educational Computing Conference*, 1982.

J. M. Ginsparg, *Natural Language Processing in an Automatic Programming Domain*, Rep. No. STAN–CS–78–671, Computer Science Dept., Stanford University, 1978.

E. M. Gold, "Language Identification in the Limit," *Inf. Control* **10**, 447–474 (1967).

A. T. Goldberg, "Knowledge-based Programming: A Survey of Program Design and Construction Techniques," *IEEE Trans. on Software Eng.* **SE–12**(7), 752–768 (1986).

C. Green, "The Design of the PSI Program Synthesis System," *Proceedings of the Second International Conference on Software Engineering*, San Francisco, 1976, pp. 4–18.

C. C. Green, "Application of Theorem Proving to Problem Solving," *Proceedings of the International Joint Conferences on Artificial Intelligence*, Washington, D.C., Morgan-Kaufmann, San Mateo, Calif., May 1969.

C. Green and S. Westfold, "Knowledge-based Programming Self-applied," *Mach. Intell.* **10**, Halsted Press, N.Y., 1981.

C. Green, J. Phillips, S. Westfold, T. Pressburger, B. Kedzierski, S. Angebrandt, B. Mont-Reynaud, and S. Tappel, *Research on Knowledge-based Programming and Algorithm Design— 1981*, Tech. Rep. KES.U.81.2, Kestrel Institute, Palo Alto, Calif., 1981.

S. Hardy, "Synthesis of LISP Functions from Examples," *Proceedings of the Fourth IJCAI*, 1975, Morgan-Kaufmann, San Mateo, Calif., 1975, pp. 240–245.

J. Hartmanis and R. E. Stearns, *Algebraic Structure Theory of Sequential Machines*, Prentice-Hall, 1966.

G. E. Heidorn, "Automatic Programming Through Natural Language Dialogue: A Survey," *IBM J. Res. Dev.*, 302–313 (1976).

G. E. Heidorn, "English as a Very High Level Language for Simulation Programming," *Proceedings of the Symposium on Very High Level Languages*, SIGPLAN notices **9**, 91–100 (1974).

E. Kant, "The Selection of Efficient Implementations for a High Level Language," *Proceedings of the Symposium on Artificial Intelligence and Programming Languages*, SIGART newsletter **64**, 140–146 (1977).

E. Kant, "Understanding and Automating Algorithm Design," *IEEE Trans. on Software Eng.* **SE–11**(11), 1361–1374 (1985).

E. Kant and A. Newell, "Problem Solving Techniques for the Design of Algorithms," *Inf. Processing and Management* **20**(1– 2), 97–118 (1984).

V. Kelly and U. Nonnemann, "Inferring Formal Software Specifications from Episode Descriptions," *Proceedings of the Sixth National Conference on Artificial Intelligence*, Seattle, AAAI, Menlo Park, Calif., 1987.

Y. Kodratoff and J. P. Jouannaud, "Synthesizing LISP Programs Working on the List Level of Embedding," in A. Biermann, G. Guiho, and Y. Kodratoff, eds., *Automatic Program Construction Techniques*, 1984, pp. 325–374.

M. R. Lowry and R. Duran, *Knowledge-based Software Engineering*, Tech. Rep. KES.U.89.4, Kestrel Institute, Palo Alto, Calif., 1989.

M. D. Lubars and M. T. Harandi, "Knowledge-based Software Design Using Design Schemas," *Ninth International Conference on Software Engineering*, IEEE Computer Society Press, 1987, pp. 253–262.

Z. Manna and R. Waldinger, "A Deductive Approach to Program Synthesis," *Trans. Prog. Lang. Sys.*, 1980.

Z. Manna and R. Waldinger, "Synthesis: Dreams=>Programs," *IEEE Trans. Software Eng.* **SE–5**, 294–328 (1979).

Z. Manna and R. Waldinger, "The Origin of a Binary-Search Paradigm," *Sci. Comput. Prog.* **9**, 37–83 (1987).

W. A. Martin, M. J. Ginzberg, R. Krumland, B. Mark, M. Morgenstern, B. Niamir, and A. Sunguroff, *Internal Memos*, Automatic Programming Group, Massachusetts Institute of Technology, Cambridge, 1974.

R. McCartney, "Synthesizing Algorithms with Performance Constraints," *Proceedings of the Sixth National Conference on Artificial Intelligence*, Seattle, AAAI, Menlo Park, Calif., 1987.

B. P. McCune, "The PSI Program Model Builder: Synthesis of Very High-level Programs," *Proceedings of the Symposium on Artificial Intelligence and Programming Languages*, SIGART newsletter **64**, 130–139 (1977).

J. Neighbors, "The DRACO Approach to Constructing Software from Reusable Components," *IEEE Trans. on Software Eng.* **SE–10**(5), 5–27 (1984).

H. Partach and R. Steinbruggen, *ACM Computing Surveys*, **15**(3), 199–236 (1983).

D. Partridge, ed., *Artificial Intelligence and Software Engineering*, Ablex Publishers, New York, 1989.

J. V. Phillips, "Program Reference from Traces Using Multiple Knowledge Sources," *Inter. Joint Conf. on Artif. Intell.* **5**, 812 (1977).

C. Rich and H. E. Shrobe, "Initial Report on a LISP Programmer's Apprentice," *IEEE Trans. on Software Eng.* **SE–4**, 456–467 (1978).

C. Rich and R. C. Waters, eds., *Readings in Artificial Intelligence and Software Engineering*, Morgan-Kaufmann, Los Altos, Calif., 1986.

C. Rich and R. C. Waters, "The Programmer's Apprentice," *IEEE Comput.* **21**(11), 10–25 (1988).

E. Y. Shapiro, *Algorithmic Program Debugging*, M.I.T. Press, Cambridge, Mass., 1982.

D. Shaw, W. Swartout, and C. Green, "Inferring LISP Programs from Examples," *Inter. Joint Conf. on Artif. Intell.* **4**, 260–267 (1975).

D. R. Smith, *A Class of Synthesizeable LISP Programs*, A. M. thesis, Duke University, 1977.

D. R. Smith, "Applications of a Strategy for Designing Divide-and-Conquer Algorithms," *Sci. Comp. Prog.* **8**, 213–229 (1987).

D. R. Smith, "KIDS: A Semi-Automatic Program Development System," *IEEE Trans. on Software Eng.* (Sept. 1990).

D. R. Smith, *Structure and Design of Global Search Algorithms*, Tech. Rep. KES.U.87.12, Kestral Institute, November 1987.

D. R. Smith, "The Synthesis of LISP Programs from Examples: A Survey," in A. Biermann, G. Guiho, and Y. Kodratoff, eds., *Automatic Program Construction Techniques*, Macmillan Publishers, 1984, pp. 307–324.

D. R. Smith and S. Westfold, "Application of REFINE to Knowledge-based Modeling," Application Note 1.3, Reasoning Systems, Inc., 1987.

D. R. Smith, G. B. Kotik, and S. J. Westfold, "Research on Knowledge-based Software Environments at Kestrel Institute," *IEEE Trans. on Software Eng.* **SE–11** (1985).

R. Solomonoff, "A Formal Theory of Inductive Inference," *Inf. Control* **1–22**, 224–254 (1964).

L. Steinberg, *A Dialogue Moderator for Program Specification Dialogues in the PSI System*, Doctoral dissertation, Computer Science Dept., Stanford University, 1980.

D. M. Steier, *Automating Algorithm Design Within a General Architecture for Intelligence*, Ph.D. dissertation, Carnegie-Mellon University, Pittsburgh, 1989.

P. D. Summers, "A Methodology for LISP Program Construction from Examples," *JACM* **24**, 161–175 (1977).

N. L. Tinkham, *Induction of Schemata for Program Synthesis*, Doctoral dissertation, Dept. of Computer Science, Duke University, Durham, N.C., 1990.

R. J. Waldinger and R. C. T. Lee, "PROW: A Step Toward Automatic Program Writing," *Proceedings of the International Joint Conferences on Artificial Intelligence*, Washington, D.C., Morgan-Kaufmann, San Mateo, Calif., May 1969.

D. A. Waterman, W. S. Faught, P. Klahr, S. J. Rosenschein, and R. Wesson, "Design Issues for Exemplary Programming," in A. Biermann, G. Guiho, and Y. Kodratoff, eds., *Automatic Program Construction Techniques*, Macmillan Publishing Co., 1984, pp. 433–461.

R. C. Waters, "The Programmer's Apprentice: A Session with KBEmacs," *IEEE Trans. on Software Eng.* **SE–11**(11), 1296–1320 (1985).

R. C. Waters, "The Programmer's Apprentice: Knowledge-based Program Editing," *IEEE Trans. on Software Eng.* **SE–8**(1), 1–12 (1982).

ALAN W. BIERMANN
Duke University

Preparation of this article was funded partially by Army Research Office Grant Number DAAG-29-84-K-0072 and the National Science Foundation Grant Number IRI 8803802).

B

BACKTRACKING

Almost all problems of search can be formulated as follows: given is a set of n variables $a_1, \ldots, a_n$, each associated with a domain D_i of possible values. Boolean constraints are associated with some subsets of these variables. The problem is to find a value for each variable without violating the constraints. In other words, to find a point in the product space $D_1 \times \cdots \times D_n$ that satisfies all constraints. A constraint is limiting the set of allowed values for the variables involved in it. So the set of solutions is a subset of the Cartesian product.

The most popular example of this problem is the n-queens problem. For $n = 8$, the formulation is: put eight queens on a chessboard so that no queen can attack another. Each variable a_i identifies a position on the board; the domains are identical and consist of the 64 possible positions (see COMPUTER CHESS AND SEARCH). A possible solution is shown in Figure 1.

For special product spaces there exist special techniques to solve such problems, for example, differential calculus, linear programming, and dynamic programming. However, backtracking constitutes a completely general and standard approach, which works by continually trying to extend a partial solution $(a_1, \ldots, a_k)$ with an a_{k+1} in a systematic way. The first general description was given in Walker (1960). Cohen (1979) has a long list of useful references.

The brute force approach to the problem considers all points in the solution space constituted by the Cartesian product of the variable domains $(D_1 \times \cdots \times D_n)$. The size of the search space is then $|D_1| \times \cdots \times |D_n|$ with $|D_i|$ the number of elements in the variable domain D_i. The basic idea of backtracking, however, is to construct the solution vector $(a_1, \ldots, a_n)$ a component at a time and to test whether a partial solution $(a_1, \ldots, a_k)$ still has a chance to satisfy the constraints in n components. The constraints restricted to the first k components are often called the modified constraints. A large part of the brute force search space can be eliminated ($|D_{k+1}| \times \cdots \times |D_n|$

points) when the test fails for a partial solution $(a_1, \ldots, a_k)$. In the case of the n-queens problem, the modified constraints consist of verifying whether the k queens already placed on the board do not attack each other. Thus, each time a queen is added, a test is done to see whether it attacks one of the already placed queens. In general, the modified constraints can be formalized as one or more predicates $P(x_1, \ldots, x_k)$. Sometimes it is possible to do better than simply restricting the original constraint to the k known components; however, to avoid a loss of solutions, the modified constraints $P(x_1, \ldots, x_k)$ must be implied by the original constraints.

The stronger the modified constraints are, the smaller the search space is. The best possible one is the constraint allowing only partial solutions $(a_1, \ldots, a_k)$, which can be extended to a solution $(a_1, \ldots, a_n)$. In general, finding such a strong modified constraint is not possible without first finding all solutions to the stated problem. The size of the backtrack search space consists of all considered partial solutions $(a_1, \ldots, a_k)$, $k \leq n$. This search space is potentially larger than the brute force search space; with sufficiently strong modified constraints, however, it will be smaller. The interested reader is referred to Cohen (1979) for a discussion of work on estimating the size of the backtrack search space.

Backtracking is a prototypical case of a tree-search algorithm. Such algorithms use simple decomposition steps to generate a tree of subproblems (each subproblem again generates a tree) of the original problem until a set of subproblems is obtained, each of which can be solved directly or can be shown to have no solution. It is worthwhile to note that tree search is not the only approach to solve such problems. A complementary approach is based on so-called relaxation (or network consistency or simplification) algorithms. Instead of decomposing the original problem, these algorithms simplify the problem either to a form that can be solved directly or to a form that is easier to solve. In the latter case, tree search must be applied to solve the simplified problem. In Nadel (1988) it is argued that a combination of relaxation and tree search gives the best results.

EFFECT OF PROBLEM FORMULATION ON SEARCH SPACE

A good problem formulation can have a dramatic effect on the size of the search space, whether a brute force approach or a backtracking approach is used. Consider the eight-queens problem. An extremely naive formulation associates 64 values with each domain: a search space of 64^8 points. By realizing that a solution can have two queens neither on the same row nor on the same column, the search space is reduced to the 8! permutations of the vector $(1, 2, \ldots, 8)$. The other extreme is to have a full knowledge of the problem: The size of the search space is equal to the number of solutions. Similarly, knowledge can be added to the modified constraints; for example, in

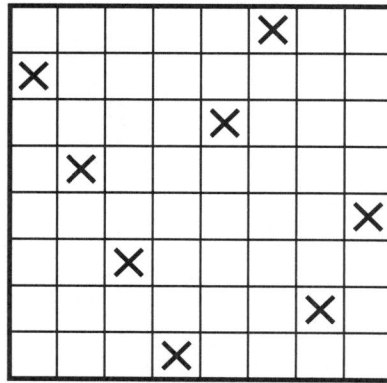

Figure 1. A solution for the 8-queens problem.

the four-queens problem no solution exists with a queen positioned in a corner. All partial solutions having a queen in a corner of the grid can be eliminated. The idea that a modification of the problem formulation can reduce the size of the search space underlies a number of optimization methods.

Another domain-dependent approach to reducing the search space is to exploit symmetry (Bitner and Reingold, 1975). In the queens problem, rotation and reflection of the board gives different states but preserves the existence of a solution: Only one of these equivalent states needs to be taken into account in the search process.

In Nadel (1988) it is shown that the n-queens problem can be formulated in nine different forms that are subsequently analyzed against a number of complexity criteria. It is clear that the number of variables needed to express the problem, the average size of the domains, the number of constraints to be checked, and the average satisfiability of the constraints are quantifiable characteristics of the problem formulation that can give guidance in selecting the best problem representation.

In general, the interpretation of these quantifiable characteristics is not trivial. For example, more constraints, all else being equal, might be good if these constraints are tight and thus contribute to better pruning of the search tree; loose constraints can have little effect on the pruning and yet require considerable constraint checking. Nevertheless, a full formal analysis taking these considerations into account constitutes a preliminary theoretical comparison allowing one to select the best representation before beginning problem solving *per se*.

ADVANTAGES AND DISADVANTAGES OF BACKTRACKING

The major advantage of backtracking is its universal applicability; the major disadvantage is its potential inefficiency. For example, in the configuration of the 8-queens problem of Figure 2, where four queens are already placed, one can verify that there is no solution possible for

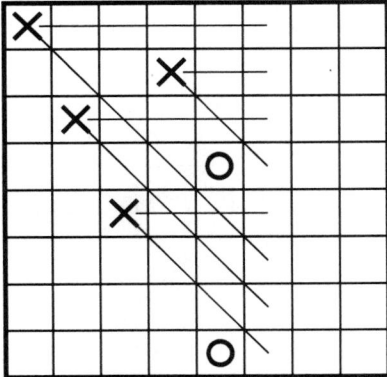

Figure 2. Thrashing: placing queen 5 in row 4 is followed by a failing attempt to place queen 6. The cause of the failure is not removed by placing queen 5 on another row, ie, row 8.

queen 6. Still, a naive backtracking algorithm would try queen 5 in all possible positions. Moreover, two attempts are made to place queen 6 (with queen 5 in row 4 and in row 8).

a-b-c Example

For a more general example, assume a_1 and a_2 range over the domain $\{a, b, c\}$, a_k ranges over $\{a, b\}$, and there is a set of variables $a_3, \ldots, a_{k-1}$. Some of the constraints are the conditions C_1, stating that the values of a_1 and a_2 have to be different, and C_2, that a_k has to be different from both a_1 and a_2. A backtrack search starts with $a_1 = a$ and, because of C_1, $a_2 = b$. Then a solution for $a_3, \ldots, a_{k-1}$ is searched for. Attempting to find a value for a_k fails because of C_2. At this point an exhaustive search over the subproblem $a_3, \ldots, a_{k-1}$ is started; for each solution another attempt to find a_k is made and fails. This behavior is known as thrashing. Several domain-independent approaches to remedy this behavior, sometimes occurring with this so-called naive (or chronological) backtracking, are known.

IMPROVEMENTS OVER CHRONOLOGICAL BACKTRACKING

Thrashing can be defined as the repeated exploration of subtrees of the search tree that differ only in nonessential features such as the subsequent assignment of values to variables that do not cause the failure of the subtree. Most techniques proposed to cure this phenomenon therefore provide the algorithms with a better memory.

Relaxation

Relaxation (or network consistency or simplification) algorithms analyze the constraints and derive stronger constraints. For example, adding a constraint disallowing queen 1 = 1, queen 2 = 3, queen 3 = 5, queen 4 = 2 will avoid the thrashing behavior illustrated in Figure 2. Similarly, for the a-b-c example, adding a constraint C_3 that excludes the combination $a_1 = a$ and $a_2 = b$ as well as $a_1 = b$ and $a_2 = a$ will avoid the thrashing over the set $a_3, \ldots, a_{k-1}$. Waltz's classic work (Waltz, 1975) on blocks world line labeling problems used a form of relaxation. The idea was further explored by Mackworth (1977), who introduced the notions of node consistency, arc consistency, and path consistency. This was further generalized into k-consistency by Freuder (1978), who also studied which level of consistency is required to make the problem directly solvable (Freuder, 1982). Although conceptually elegant, transforming the problem into an equivalent one with a high level of consistency is generally too expensive and relaxation has to be combined with tree-search algorithms as argued by Nadel (1988) (See CONSTRAINT SATISFACTION).

Reordering the Variables

Extending the partial solution in the order a_1, a_2, a_k, $a_3, \ldots$ solves the problem with the a-b-c example in a straightforward way. For large problems, selecting a dif-

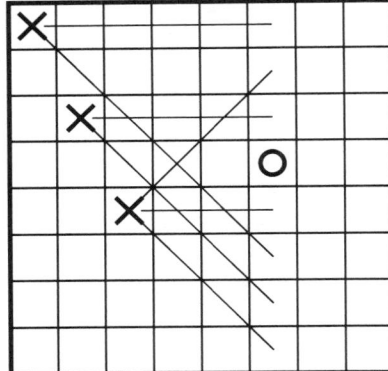

Figure 3. Dynamic reordering of variables: taking queen 6 as the next one to place instead of queen 4 results in a substantial reduction of the search space.

ferent ordering of variables to be instantiated can result in extremely large differences. Other factors being equal, it pays to preorder the variables in terms of increasing domain size; one thereby maximizes the average size of the subspace rejected by the constraint checking.

Actually, the ordering can be done dynamically and can be different in different branches of the search space. This reordering can be done at search time using a look ahead and selecting the variable with the smallest domain to be instantiated next. This gives the smallest branching factor in the search tree (Freuder, 1982, Purdom and co-workers, 1981). For example, in the 8-queens configuration pictured in Figure 3, queen 6 should be selected for instantiation next, since there is only one element in the domain left.

Intelligent Backtracking—Dependency-Directed Backtracking

In the a-b-c example above, the failure at a_k is essentially due to a_1 and a_2. An intelligent backtracking system avoids thrashing by detecting the real reason for failure and by backtracking directly to it. Moreover, if the search over $a_3, \ldots, a_{k-1}$ is independent of a_1 and a_2, this search can be saved and the components can be dynamically reordered (Bruynooghe, 1981). Whereas consistency methods elaborate constraints before a search is initiated, intelligent backtracking (or dependency-directed backtracking) elaborates constraints while searching.

Dependency-directed backtracking is a problem-solving (qv) technique for efficiently evading contradictions. It is invoked whenever the problem solver discovers that its current state is inconsistent. The goal is, in a single operation, to change the problem solver's current state to one that contains neither the contradiction just uncovered nor any contradiction encountered previously. This is achieved by consulting records of the inferences the problem solver has performed (called dependencies) and records of previous contradictions (called nogoods), which dependency-directed backtracking has constructed in response to previous contradictions.

Unlike chronological backtracking, which replaces the

most recent choice, dependency-directed backtracking replaces a choice that caused the contradiction. To be able to determine which choices underlie the contradiction requires that the problem solver store dependency records with every datum that it infers. When an inconsistency is encountered, these dependencies are consulted to determine which choices contribute to the inconsistency.

The following example and Figure 4 illustrate the basic principle of intelligent backtracking. As shown, this partial solution can not be extended with a queen in column 6 because of the following conflicts or nogoods:

$$\leftarrow x_1 = 1 \wedge x_6 = 1$$
$$\leftarrow x_3 = 5 \wedge x_6 = 2$$
$$\leftarrow x_2 = 3 \wedge x_6 = 3$$
$$\leftarrow x_4 = 2 \wedge x_6 = 4$$
$$\leftarrow x_3 = 5 \wedge x_6 = 5$$
$$\leftarrow x_1 = 1 \wedge x_6 = 6$$
$$\leftarrow x_2 = 3 \wedge x_6 = 7$$
$$\leftarrow x_3 = 5 \wedge x_6 = 8$$

On the other hand, x_6 must be assigned some value, ie,

$$x_6 = 1 \vee x_6 = 2 \vee x_6 = 3 \vee x_6 = 4 \vee x_6$$
$$= 5 \vee x_6 = 6 \vee x_6 = 7 \vee x_6 = 8 \leftarrow$$

Using hyperresolution (Robinson, 1965) one can infer

$$\leftarrow x_1 = 1 \wedge x_2 = 3 \wedge x_3 = 5 \wedge x_4 = 2$$

Or, the rejection of x_6 is due to the current values of the variables x_1–x_4, but independent of the actual value of x_5, and backtracking is done on x_4.

The previous example illustrates how the system backtracks to a partial solution that does not contain the contradiction just encountered. Pushing one step further, dependency-directed backtracking also tries to keep track of those contradictions that could possibly reappear later on in the search. The following example and Figure 5 illus-

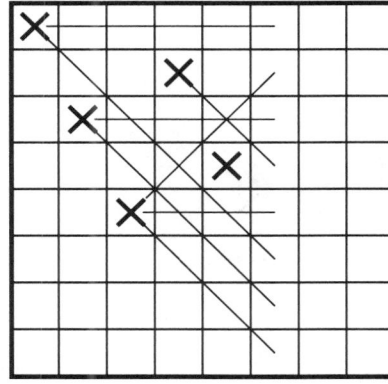

Figure 4. Intelligent backtracking: analyzing the failure to place queen 6 allows backtracking directly to queen 4.

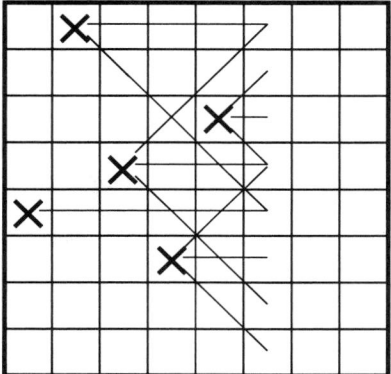

Figure 5. Dependency-directed backtracking keeps track of those contradictions that could reappear later.

trate this aspect. Trying to place queen 6 on the chessboard gives the following nogoods:

$$\leftarrow x_6 = 1 \wedge x_2 = 1 \qquad (1)$$

$$\leftarrow x_6 = 1 \wedge x_3 = 4 \qquad (2)$$

$$\leftarrow x_6 = 2 \wedge x_5 = 3 \qquad (3)$$

$$\leftarrow x_6 = 3 \wedge x_5 = 3 \qquad (4)$$

$$\leftarrow x_6 = 4 \wedge x_5 = 3 \qquad (5)$$

$$\leftarrow x_6 = 4 \wedge x_3 = 4 \qquad (6)$$

$$\leftarrow x_6 = 4 \wedge x_4 = 6 \qquad (7)$$

$$\leftarrow x_6 = 5 \wedge x_2 = 1 \qquad (8)$$

$$\leftarrow x_6 = 5 \wedge x_1 = 5 \qquad (9)$$

$$\leftarrow x_6 = 6 \wedge x_4 = 6 \qquad (10)$$

$$\leftarrow x_6 = 7 \wedge x_3 = 4 \qquad (11)$$

$$\leftarrow x_6 = 8 \wedge x_4 = 6 \qquad (12)$$

Again, x_6 should be assigned some value:

$$x_6 = 1 \vee x_6 = 2 \vee x_6 = 3 \vee x_6 = 4 \vee x_6 = 5 \vee$$

$$x_6 = 6 \vee x_6 = 7 \vee x_6 = 8 \leftarrow \qquad (13)$$

and applying hyperresolution on

$$(1) + (3) + (4) + (5) + (8) + (10) + (11) + (12) + (13)$$

yields

$$\leftarrow x_1 = 5 \wedge x_2 = 1 \wedge x_3 = 4 \wedge x_4 = 6 \wedge x_5 = 3 \quad (A)$$

Applying hyperresolution on

$$(2) + (3) + (4) + (5) + (8) + (10) + (11) + (12) + (13)$$

yields

$$\leftarrow x_2 = 1 \wedge x_3 = 4 \wedge x_4 = 6 \wedge x_5 = 3 \qquad (B)$$

Analyzing conflict A indicates that backtracking should occur on x_5, so $x_5 = 3$ is to be undone and backtracking can resume. However, it is useless to save this nogood, as it is clear from the example that this particular combination will not reappear later on in the search. Indeed, the variables x_1–x_5 all take part in the combination, and backtracking will never generate the same combination.

Analyzing conflict B results in the same observation that $x_5 = 3$ should be undone. However, in this case it is useful to store this particular nogood, as this combination can reappear later on in the search (eg, with $x_1 = 8$).

Practical applications of dependency-directed backtracking should also take into account the cost of duplicating work while rediscovering conflicts against the cost of storing all nogoods and checking whether each partial solution is not an extension of one of the stored nogoods (see also TRUTH MAINTENANCE). Note that intelligent backtracking can also be used in combination with the dynamic determination of the instantiation ordering of the variables.

HISTORICAL PERSPECTIVE ON INTELLIGENT AND DEPENDENCY-DIRECTED BACKTRACKING

The concept of dependency-directed backtracking was developed by Stallman and Sussman in their work on circuit analysis (Stallman and Sussman, 1977). Further research led to the development of truth maintenance systems (Doyle, 1979) as general problem-solving tools. Truth maintenance systems not only improve the backtracking behavior but also avoid expensive recomputations of intermediate results that are not affected by a failure but are lost because of the chronological nature of backtracking. More recently, a truth maintenance system has been proposed that achieves most of the goals of dependency-directed backtracking but without backtracking (De Kleer, 1986).

Independently of the work on truth maintenance systems, the ideas of Stallman and Sussman also triggered research in the area of logic programming (qv) and theorem proving (qv) under the heading of intelligent backtracking. In logic programming, intelligent backtracking was proposed as a way to enhance the search behavior of the PROLOG inference engine. The idea is to keep track of the purely syntactical dependencies between variables in a program, ie, to tag each binding of a variable with information about the computation step causing that binding. When a failure occurs, the tags of the conflicting bindings are used to determine the computation steps responsible for the failure. See Bruynooghe (1980) and Bruynooghe and Pereira (1984) for more details. The idea was also used to solve constraint satisfaction problems (Bruynooghe, 1981). A great deal of research has been done to devise methods that combine a maximum of "intelligence" with a minimum of overhead in the PROLOG engine. However, the overhead is still considered too large to apply the idea in general purpose PROLOG systems. Intelligent backtracking has also been used to control the backtracking in AND-parallel execution models of PROLOG. References to these applications in the implementation of

PROLOG can be found in Bruynooghe (1991). Independently of the work on logic programming, very similar ideas have also been developed for theorem provers. This work was initiated by Cox and Pietrzykowski (1981). For both logic programming and theorem proving, a concise argument based on hyperresolution (Robinson, 1965) can be used to show that the search remains complete (Bruynooghe, 1991).

BACKTRACKING IN PROGRAMMING LANGUAGES

Floyd (1967) was the first to propose a language construct facilitating the writing of backtrack programs and to point out the mechanical translation in constructs of conventional languages. A survey of useful primitive language constructs can be found in Cohen (1979). Backtracking plays a fundamental role in a number of AI programming languages, most notably PLANNER (Bobrow and Raphael, 1974) and PROLOG (Sterling and Shapiro, 1986). In these languages the basic operation consists of nondeterministically applying an operator on a state to derive a new state. Backtracking is used to explore all possibilities exhaustively. Programming consists of formulating the problem in such a way that the backtracking search performs an efficient computation (see also PROBLEM SOLVING). A recent development has integrated constraints in logic programming and uses these constraints to imporve on the chronological backtracking. Dincbas and co-workers (1988) give a survey of a particular system and references to several other ones.

BIBLIOGRAPHY

J. R. Bitner and E. M. Reingold, "Backtrack Program Techniques," *CACM* **18**(11), 651–656 (1975).

D. G. Bobrow and B. Raphael, "New Programming Languages for Artificial Intelligence Research," *Comput. Surv.* **6**(3), 155–174 (1974).

M. Bruynooghe, "Analysis of Dependencies to Improve the Behaviour of Logic Programs," *Proceedings of the Fifth Conference on Automated Deduction*, LNCS, Springer-Verlag, New York, 1980, pp. 293–305.

M. Bruynooghe, "Solving Combinatorial Problems by Intelligent Backtracking," *Inf. Proc. Let.* **12**(1), 36–39 (1981).

M. Bruynooghe, "Intelligent Backtracking Revisited," in J. L. Larrez, ed., *Computational Logic,* MIT Press, Cambridge, Mass., 1991.

M. Bruynooghe and L. M. Pereira, "Deduction Revision by Intelligent Backtracking," in J. A. Campbell, ed., *Implementations of PROLOG*, Ellis Horwood, London, 1984, pp. 194–215.

J. Cohen, "Non-Deterministic Algorithms," *Comput. Surv.* **11**(2), 79–94 (1979).

P. T. Cox and T. Pietrzykowski, "Deduction Plans: A Basis for Intelligent Backtracking," *IEEE Trans. Patt. Anal. Mach. Intell.* **PAMI-3**(1), pp. 52–65 (1981).

J. de Kleer, "An Assumption-Based TMS," *Artif. Intell.* **28**(2), 127–196 (1986).

M. Dincbas, P. Van Hentenryck, H. Simonis, A. Aggoun, T. Graf, and F. Berthier, "The Constraint Logic Programming Language CHIP," in *Proceedings of the International Conference on Fifth Generation Computer Systems*, North Holland, New York, 1988, pp. 693–702.

J. Doyle, "A Truth Maintenance System," *Artif. Intell.* **12**(3), 231–272 (1979).

R. W. Floyd, "Nondeterministic Algorithms," *JACM* **14**(4), 636–644 (1967).

E. C. Freuder, "Synthesizing Constraint Expressions," *CACM* **21**(11), 958–966 (1978).

E. C. Freuder, "A Sufficient Condition for Backtrackfree Search," *JACM* **29**(1), 24–32 (1982).

A. K. Mackworth, "Consistency in Network Relations," *Artif. Intell.* **8**, 99–118 (1977).

B. A. Nadel, "Tree Search and Arc Consistency in Constraint Satisfaction Algorithms," in L. Kanal and V. Kumar, eds., *Search in Artificial Intelligence*, Springer-Verlag, New York, 1988.

B. A. Nadel, "Representation Selection for Constraint Satisfaction Problems: A Case Study Using *n*-Queens," *IEEE Expert*, 1989.

P. W. Purdom, C. A. Brown, and E. L. Robertson, "Backtracking with Multilevel Dynamic Search Rearrangement," *Acta Inf.* **15**(2), 99–113 (1981).

J. A. Robinson, "Automated Deduction with Hyper-Resolution," *Int. J. Comput. Math.* **1**, 227–234 (1965).

R. M. Stallman and G. J. Sussman, "Forward Reasoning and Dependency-Directed Backtracking in a System for Computer-Aided Circuit Analysis," *Artif. Intell.* **9**(2), 135–196 (1977).

L. Sterling and E. Shapiro, *The Art of PROLOG*, MIT Press, Cambridge, Mass., 1986.

R. L. Walker, "An Enumerative Technique for a Class of Combinatorial Problems," *Combinatorial Analysis (Proceedings of Symposium in Applied Mathematics, Vol. X)*, Amer. Math. Soc., Providence, Rhode Island, 1960, pp. 91–94.

D. Waltz, "Understanding Line Drawings of Scenes with Shadows," in P. H. Winston, ed., *The Psychology of Computer Vision*, McGraw Hill, New York, 1975.

MAURICE BRUYNOOGHE
Katholieke Universiteit Leuven

RAF VENKEN
BIM

BASEBALL

Two distinct AI systems have chosen the name of Baseball. One, written in the early 1960s, is a program that answers questions posed in English about baseball scores. It syntactically parses the sentences into templates (or specification lists) for the processor to look up in a database (see B. F. Green, A. K. Wolf, C. Chomsky, and K. Laughery, "Baseball: An Automatic Question Answerer," in E. A. Feigenbaum and J. Feldman, eds., *Computers and Thought*, McGraw-Hill, New York, pp. 207–216, 1963).

The second system, written by Elliot Soloway, is a learning program that uses "snapshots" as its training instances. It uses domain knowledge (the rules of baseball), knowledge of physics, and the goals of the players to process these snapshots (see E. Soloway, "Learning = Interpretation + Generalization: A Case Study in Knowledge-Directed Learning," Report No. COINS-TR-78-12, Computer and Information Sciences Department, University of Massachusetts, Amherst, 1978; E. Soloway and E. M. Riseman, "Levels of Pattern Description in Learning," *Proceedings of the Fifth IJCAI*, Cambridge, Mass., 1977, pp. 801–811.

J. ROSENBERG
Kilchberg, Switzerland

BACKWARD CHAINING. See PROCESSING, BOTTOM-UP AND TOP-DOWN.

BAYESIAN INFERENCE METHODS

Bayesian methods provide a formalism for reasoning about partial beliefs under conditions of uncertainty. In this formalism propositions are quantified with numeric parameters signifying the degree of belief accorded them under some body of knowledge, and these parameters are combined and manipulated according to the rules of probability theory. For example, if A stands for the statement "Ted Kennedy will seek nomination in 1992," then $P(A|K)$ stands for a person's subjective belief in A given a body of knowledge K that may include that person's assumptions about American politics, specific proclamations made by Kennedy, an assessment of Kennedy's past and personality, and so on. The symbol K, indicating the source of the belief in A, is often suppressed from belief expressions, and one simply writes $P(A)$ or $P(\sim A)$. This is justified when K remains constant since the main purpose of the quantifier P is to summarize K without explicating its details. However, when this background information undergoes changes, one needs to identify specifically which assumptions account for one's beliefs, and an explicit mentioning of K or some of its elements is then required.

BASIC FORMULATION

In the Bayesian formalism, belief statements obey the three basic assumptions of probability theory:

$$0 \leq P(A) \leq 1 \qquad (1)$$

$$P(\text{sure proposition}) = 1 \qquad (2)$$

$$P(A \text{ or } B) = P(A) + P(B)$$
if A and B are incompatible $\qquad (3)$

Thus, a proposition and its negation must be assigned a total belief of unity,

$$P(\sim A) = 1 - P(A) \qquad (4)$$

to account for the fact that one of the two is certain to be true.

The heart of Bayesian techniques lies in the celebrated inversion formula:

$$P(H|e) = \frac{P(e|H)P(H)}{P(e)} \qquad (5)$$

stating that the belief one accords a hypothesis H on obtaining evidence e can be computed by multiplying one's prior belief $P(H)$ and the likelihood $P(e|H)$ that e will materialize assuming H is true. The denominator $P(e)$ of equation 5 hardly enters into consideration because it is merely a constant that can always be computed if one requires that $P(H|e)$ and $P(\sim H|e)$ sum to unity.

A formal mathematician might dismiss equation 5 as a straightforward identity stemming from the definition of conditional probabilities,

$$P(A|B) = \frac{P(A, B)}{P(B)} \qquad (6)$$

However, the Bayesian subjectivist does not regard equation 6 as a definition but, rather, as a faithful translation of the English expression "my degree of belief in A, given that I know B." Accordingly, equation 5 is treated as a normative rule for updating beliefs in response to evidence. The left side of equation 5 expresses a quantity $P(H|e)$ that people often find hard to assess in terms of more readily judged quantities, often available directly from the way experiential knowledge is encoded. For example, if a person at the next gambling table declares an outcome "12" and one wishes to know whether he was rolling a pair of dice or turning a roulette wheel, the quantities $P(12|\text{dice})$ and $P(12|\text{roulette})$ are readily known from the model of the gambling devices (giving 1/36 to the former and 1/38 for the latter). Similarly, one can judge the prior probabilities, $P(\text{dice})$ and $P(\text{roulette})$, by estimating the number of roulette wheels and dice-rolling tables at the gambling casino. However, issuing a direct judgment of $P(\text{dice}|12)$ is a much harder mental task, which could not be rendered reliably except by a specialist of such guesses trained at the very same casino.

COMBINING PROSPECTIVE AND RETROSPECTIVE SUPPORTS

The essence of the rule in equation 5 is conveniently portrayed using the odds and likelihood ratio parameters. Dividing equation 5 by the complementary form for $P(\sim H|e)$, one obtains

$$\frac{P(H|e)}{P(\sim H|e)} = \frac{P(e|H)}{P(e|\sim H)} \frac{P(H)}{P(\sim H)} \qquad (7)$$

Defining the prior odds on H to be

$$O(H) = \frac{P(H)}{P(\sim H)} = \frac{P(H)}{1 - P(H)} \qquad (8)$$

and the likelihood ratio as

$$L(e|H) = \frac{P(e|H)}{P(e|\sim H)} \qquad (9)$$

the posterior odds

$$O(H|e) = \frac{P(H|e)}{P(\sim H|e)} \qquad (10)$$

is given by the product

$$O(H|e) = L(e|H)O(H) \qquad (11)$$

Thus, Bayesian rule dictates that the overall strength of belief in a hypothesis H based on both one's previous knowledge K and a given evidence e should be the product of two factors: the prior odds $O(H)$ and the likelihood ratio $L(e|H)$. The former measures the causal or prospective support accorded to H by the background knowledge alone and the latter represents the diagnostic or retrospective support given to H by the evidence actually observed.

Strictly speaking, the likelihood ratio $L(e|H)$ may also depend on other propositions in the tacit knowledge base K. However, the power of Bayesian techniques comes primarily from the fact that in causal reasoning (qv) the relation $P(e|H)$ is fairly local; namely, given that H is true, the probability of e can be estimated fairly naturally and is not dependent on many other propositions in the database. For example, once it is established that a patient suffers from a given disease, it is fairly natural to estimate the probability that the patient will develop a certain symptom. This is what physicians learn in medical schools; a symptom is considered a stable characteristic of the disease and, therefore, should be fairly independent of other factors such as epidemic conditions, previous diseases, and the tests that help identify the disease. It is for this reason that the conditional probabilities $P(e|H)$ can meet the modularity requirements of rule-based expert systems (qv) in that it can serve to quantify confidence in rules such as "if H, then e" and retain its viability regardless of other rules or facts that may reside in the knowledge base at any given time.

Example 1. Imagine being awakened one night to the shrill sound of your burglar alarm system. What would be your degree of belief that a burglary attempt has taken place? For illustrative purposes, the following judgments are made: (a) There is a 95% chance that an attempted burglary will trigger the alarm system, P(alarm|burglary) = 0.95; (b) there is slight (0.01) chance that the alarm sound would be triggered by a mechanism other than an attempted burglary; thus, P(alarm|no burglary) = 0.01; (c) previous crime patterns indicate that there is a 1 in 10,000 chance that a given house will be burglarized on any given night; that is, P(burglary) = 10^{-4}.

Putting these assumptions together, using equation 5 or equation 11,

$$O(\text{burglary}|\text{alarm}) = L(\text{alarm}|\text{burglary})O(\text{burglary})$$

$$= \frac{0.95}{0.01}\frac{10^{-4}}{1-10^{-4}} = 0.0095$$

and so, from

$$P(A) = \frac{O(A)}{1+O(A)} \qquad (12)$$

one has

$$P(\text{burglary}|\text{alarm}) = \frac{0.0095}{1+0.0095} = 0.00941$$

Thus, the retrospective support imparted to the burglary hypothesis by the alarm evidence has increased its degree of belief from 1 in 10,000 to 94.1 in 10,000. Note that it was not necessary to estimate the absolute values of the probabilities P(alarm|burglary) and P(alarm|no burglary), only their ratio enters the calculation, and therefore, a direct estimate of this ratio could have been used instead.

POOLING OF EVIDENCE

Assume that the alarm system consists of not one but a collection of N burglary detection devices each sensitive to a different physical mechanism (eg, air turbulences, temperature variations, pressure, sound) and each producing a distinct sound.

Let H stand for the event that a burglary took place and let e^k stand for the evidence obtained from the kth detector, with e_1^k representing an activated detector and e_0^k representing a silent detector. The reliability (and sensitivity) of each detector is characterized by the probabilities $P(e_1^k|H)$ and $P(e_1^k|\sim H)$ or, more parsimoniously, by their ratio:

$$L(e^k|H) = \frac{P(e_1^k|H)}{P(e_1^k|\sim H)} \qquad (13)$$

If some detectors are triggered while others remain deactivated, there is conflicting evidence, and the combined belief in the hypothesis H would be computed by Eq. 11:

$$O(H|e^1, e^2, \ldots, e^N) = L(e^1, \ldots, e^N|H)O(H) \quad (14)$$

Strictly speaking, equation 14 requires an enormous database because one needs to specify the probabilities of activation for every subset of detectors conditioned on H and on $\sim H$. Fortunately, reasonable assumptions of independence can drastically cut this storage requirement. Assuming that the state of activation of each detector depends only on whether a burglary took place but is thereafter independent of the activation of other detectors, one can write

$$P(e^1, e^2, \ldots, e^N|H) = \prod_{k=1}^{N} P(e^k|H) \qquad (15)$$

and

$$P(e^1, e^2, \ldots, e^N|\sim H) = \prod_{k=1}^{N} P(e^k|\sim H) \qquad (16)$$

which lead to

$$O(H|e^1, \ldots, e^N) = O(H)\prod_{k=1}^{N} L(e^k|H) \qquad (17)$$

Thus, the individual characteristics of each detector are sufficient for determining the combined impact of any group of detectors.

MULTIHYPOTHESIS VARIABLES

The assumptions of conditional independence in equations 15 and 16 will be justified if the failure of a detector to react to an attempted burglary and the factors that may cause it to fire prematurely both depend solely on mechanisms intrinsic to the individual detection systems such as insufficient sensitivity or internal noise. However, if these can be caused by external circumstances affecting a selected group of sensors, such as a power failure or an earthquake, the two hypotheses H = burglary and $\sim H$ = no burglary may be too coarse to induce the sensors' independence, and additional refinement of the hypotheses' space may be necessary. This usually happens when the negation of a proposition entails several possible states of the world, each having its own distinct characteristics. For example, the state of no burglary entails the possibilities of an "ordinary peaceful night," or "night with an earthquake," or an "attempted entry by the neighbor's dog," and so on, each influencing the sensors present in a unique way. Equation 16 might hold with respect to each one of these conditions but not with respect to their aggregate, "no burglary." For this reason it is often necessary to refine the hypotheses' space beyond that of binary propositions and group them into multivalued variables, where each variable consists of a set of exhaustive and mutually exclusive hypotheses.

Example 2. One may choose to assign the variable name $H = \{H_1, H_2, H_3, H_4\}$ to the following set of conditions:

H_1 = no burglary, equipment malfunction ($\sim b, m$)

H_2 = attempted burglary, no malfunction ($b, \sim m$)

H_3 = attempted burglary combined with equipment malfunction (b, m)

H_4 = no burglary, no malfunction ($\sim b, \sim m$)

Each evidence variable e^k can also be multivalued (eg, e_1^k = no sound, e_2^k = low sound, e_3^k = high sound), in which case the causal link between H and e^k will be quantified by an $m \times n$ matrix where m and n are the number of values that H and e^k might take, respectively, and the (i, j)th entry of M^k stands for

$$M_{ij}^k = P(e_j^k | H_i) \quad (18)$$

For example, the matrix below could represent the various sensitivities of the kth detector to the four conditions in H:

	e_1^k (No Sound)	e_2^k (Low Sound)	e_3^k (High Sound)
H_1	0.5	0.4	0.1
H_2	0.06	0.5	0.44
H_3	0.5	0.1	0.4
H_4	1	0	0

Given a set of evidence readings $e^1, e^2, \ldots, e^k, \ldots, e^N$, the overall belief in the ith hypothesis is given by equation 5,

$$P(H_i | e^1, \ldots, e^N) = \alpha P(e^1, \ldots, e^N | H_i) P(H_i) \quad (19)$$

where $\alpha = [P(e^1, \ldots, e^N)]^{-1}$ is a normalizing constant to be computed by requiring that equation 19 sums to unity (over i). Assuming conditional independence with respect to each H_i, one obtains

$$P(H_i | e^1, \ldots, e^N) = \alpha P(H_i) \left[\prod_{k=1}^{N} P(e^k | H_i) \right] \quad (20)$$

Thus, one sees that the matrices $P(e^k | H_i)$ now play the role of the likelihood ratios in equation 17. If, for each detector reading e^k, the likelihood vector is defined as

$$\lambda^k = (\lambda_1^k, \lambda_2^k, \ldots, \lambda_m^k) \quad (21)$$
$$\lambda_i^k = P(e^k | H_i) \quad (22)$$

Equation 20 is computed by a simple vector product process. First, the individual likelihood vectors are multiplied together, term by term, to form an overall likelihood vector $\Lambda = \lambda^1 \cdots \lambda^N$, namely,

$$\Lambda_i = \prod_{k=1}^{N} P(e^k | H_i) \quad (23)$$

Then the overall belief vector $P(H_i | e^1, \ldots, e^N)$ is obtained by the product

$$P(H_i | e^1, \ldots, e^N) = \alpha P(H_i) \Lambda_i \quad (24)$$

reminiscent of equation 17.

Note that only the relative magnitude of the conditional probabilities in equation 22 need be estimated; their absolute magnitude does not affect the result because α is to be determined by the requirement $\Sigma_i P(H_i | e^1, \ldots, e^N) = 1$.

Example 3. Assume that the system contains two detectors having identical characteristics, given by the matrix above. Further, let the prior probabilities for the hypotheses in Example 2 be represented by the vector $P(H) = \{0.099, 0.009, 0.001, 0.891\}$ and assume that detector 1 was heard to issue a high sound while detector 2 remained silent. From equation 22 one has

$$\lambda^1 = (0.1, 0.44, 0.4, 0) \qquad \lambda^2 = (0.5, 0.06, 0.5, 1)$$
$$\Lambda = \lambda^1 \lambda^2 = (0.05, 0.0264, 0.2, 0)$$
$$P(H_i | e^1, e^2) = \alpha(4.95, 0.238, 0.20, 0)10^{-3}$$
$$= (0.919, 0.0439, 0.0375, 0)$$

Thus, the chance of attempted burglary (H_2 or H_3) is $0.0439 + 0.0375 = 8.14\%$.

The updating of belief need not wait, of course, until all the evidence is collected but can be carried out incrementally. For example, if one first observes e^1 = high sound, the belief in H calculates to

$$P(H_i|e^1) = \alpha(0.0099, 0.00396, 0.0004, 0)$$

$$= (0.694, 0.277, 0.028, 0)$$

This now serves as a prior belief with respect to the next datum, and after observing e^2 = no sound, it updates to

$$P(H_i|e^1, e^2) = \alpha'\lambda_i^2 P(H_i|e^1)$$

$$= \alpha'(0.347, 0.0166, 0.014, 0)$$

$$= (0.919, 0.0439, 0.0375, 0),$$

as before. Thus, the quiescent state of detector 2 lowers the chances of an attempted burglary from 30.5 to 8.14%.

UNCERTAIN EVIDENCE (CASCADED INFERENCE)

Although the relation $P(A|B)$ requires that the conditioning event B be known with certainty, Bayesian techniques can also handle uncertain evidence. To see how this is accomplished, consider a slight modification in the story of the alarm system.

Example 4. Mr. Holmes receives a telephone call from his neighbor Dr. Watson stating that he hears a burglar alarm sound from the direction of Mr. Holmes's house. Preparing to rush home, Mr. Holmes recalls that Dr. Watson is known to be a tasteless practical joker, and he decides to first call his other neighbor, Mrs. Gibbons, who, despite occasional drinking problems, is far more reliable.

Since the evidence variable S = sound is now uncertain, it cannot be used as evidence in equation 11 but, rather, equation 11 must be applied to the actual evidence at hand: W = (Dr. Watson's testimony)

$$O(H|W) = L(W|H)O(H) \qquad (25)$$

Unfortunately, the task of estimating $L(W|H)$ will not be as easy as that of estimating $L(S|H)$ because the former requires the mental tracing of a two-step process, as shown in Figure 1.

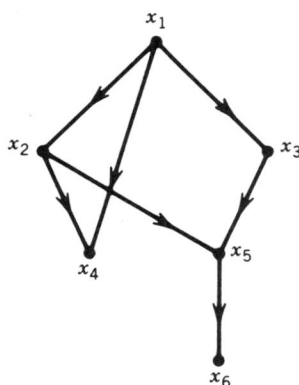

Figure 1. A diagram illustrating cascaded inference through an intermediate variable S.

Moreover, even if $L(W|H)$ could be obtained, one would not be able to combine it with other possible testimonies, say Mrs. Gibbons's (G), by a simple process of multiplication (equation 23) because those testimonies will no longer be conditionally independent with respect to H. What Mrs. Gibbons is about to say depends only on whether an alarm sound can be heard in the neighborhood, not on whether a burglary actually took place. Thus, it will be wrong to assume $P(G|\text{burglary}, W) = P(G|\text{burglary})$ because the joint event of a burglary together with Watson's testimony constitutes stronger evidence for the occurrence of the alarm sound than the burglary alone. Given the level of detail used in the story, it is more reasonable to assume that the testimonies W and G and the hypothesis H are independent of one another once one knows whether the alarm sound was actually triggered. In other words, each testimony depends directly on the alarm sound (S) and is only indirectly influenced by the possible occurrence of a burglary (H) or by the other testimony (see Fig. 1).

These considerations can be incorporated into Bayesian formalism using equation 3; equation 19 is simply conditioned and summed on all possible states of the intermediate variable S:

$$P(H_i|G, W) = \alpha P(G, W|H_i)P(H_i)$$

$$= \alpha P(H_i) \sum_j P(G, W|H_i, S_j)P(S_j|H_i) \qquad (26)$$

where $S_j(j = 1, 2)$ stands for the two possible activation states of S, namely, S_1 = alarm triggered and S_2 = alarm not triggered. Moreover, the conditional independence of G, W, and H_i with respect to the mediating variable S yields

$$P(G, W|H_i, S_j) = P(G|S_j)P(W|S_j) \qquad (27)$$

and equation 26 becomes

$$P(H_i|G, W) = \alpha P(H_i) \sum_j P(G|S_j)P(W|S_j)P(S_j|H_i) \qquad (28)$$

The computation in equation 28 can be interpreted as a three-state process: first, the local likelihood vectors $P(G|S_j)$ and $P(W|S_j)$ are multiplied together, componentwise, to obtain the likelihood vector $\Lambda_j(S) = P(e|S_j)$, where e stands for the total evidence collected, G and W. Second, the vector $P(e|S_i)$ is multiplied by the link matrix $M_{ij} = P(S_j|H_i)$ to form the likelihood vector of the top hypothesis $\Lambda_i(H) = P(e|H_i)$. Finally, using the product rule of equation 5 (see also equation 19 or 24), $\Lambda_i(H)$ is multiplied by the prior $P(H_i)$ to give the overall belief in H_i.

This process demonstrates the psychological and computational role of the mediating variable S. It permits one to use local chunks of information taken from diverse domains [eg, $P(H_i)$, $P(G|S_j)$, $P(W|S_j)$, and $P(S_j|H_i)$] and fit them together to form a global, cross-domain inference $P(H|e)$ in stages, using simple and local vector operations. This role suggests that conditional independence is not a grace of nature for which one must wait passively, but rather a psychological necessity that we satisfy actively by organizing our knowledge in a specific way, for example, by coining names to new, hypothetical variables that induce conditional independence. In medical diagnosis, for instance, when some symptoms directly influence one another, the medical profession invents a name for that interaction (eg, complication, pathological state) and treats it as a new auxiliary variable that induces conditional independence; knowing the state of the auxiliary variable renders the interacting symptoms independent of each other.

VIRTUAL (INTANGIBLE) EVIDENCE

Imagine the following development in the story of Mr. Holmes.

Example 5. When Mr. Holmes calls Mrs. Gibbons, he soon realizes that she is somewhat tipsy. Instead of answering his question directly, she goes on and on describing her latest operation and how terribly noisy and crime ridden the neighborhood has become. When he finally hangs up, all Mr. Holmes can make out of the conversation is that it is quite likely (say, 4:1) that Mrs. Gibbons did hear an alarm sound from her window.

The Holmes–Gibbons conversation is the kind of evidence that is hard to fit into any formalism. If one tries to estimate the probability $P(e|\text{alarm sound})$, one would get ridiculous numbers because it would entail anticipating, describing, and assigning probabilities to all possible courses Mrs. Gibbons's conversation might have taken under the circumstances.

These difficulties arise whenever the task of gathering evidence is delegated to autonomous interpreters who, for various reasons, cannot explicate their interpretive process in full detail but, nevertheless, often produce informative conclusions that summarize the evidence observed. In this case Mr. Holmes's conclusion is that, on the basis of his judgmental interpretation of Gibbons's testimony (alone!), the hypothesis alarm sound warrants a 4:1 greater support than its negation. The task is to integrate this probabilistic judgment into the body of hard evidence previously collected.

In Bayesian formalism the integration of virtual evidence proceeds as follows. Although the evidence e cannot be articulated in full detail, one interprets the probabilistic conclusion as conveying likelihood ratio information. In the story, for example, identifying e with G = Gibbons's testimony, Mr. Holmes's summary of attributing a 4:1 higher credibility to the alarm sound event can be interpreted as the statement $P(G|\text{alarm sound}):P(G|\text{no alarm sound}) = 4:1$. More generally, if the variable on which the tacit evidence e impinges most directly has several possible states $S_1, S_2, \ldots, S_i, \ldots$ the interpreter would be instructed to estimate the relative magnitudes of the terms $P(e|S_i)$ [eg, by eliciting estimates of the ratios $P(e|S_i):P(e|S_1)$], and since the absolute magnitudes do not affect the calculations, one can proceed to update beliefs as if this likelihood vector originated from an ordinary, propositional event e. For example, assuming that Mr. Watson's phone call already contributed a likelihood ratio of 9:1 in favor of the hypothesis alarm sound, the combined weight of Watson's and Gibbons's testimonies would yield a likelihood vector $\Lambda_i(S) = P(W, G|S_i) = (36, 1)$.

This vector can be integrated into the computation of equation 28, and using the numbers given in Example 1, one gets

$$\Lambda_i(H) = \sum_j \Lambda_j(S)P(S_j|H_i)$$

$$= \begin{pmatrix} 0.95 & 0.05 \\ 0.01 & 0.99 \end{pmatrix}\begin{pmatrix} 36 \\ 1 \end{pmatrix} = \begin{pmatrix} 34.25 \\ 1.35 \end{pmatrix} \quad (29)$$

$$P(H_i|G, W) = \alpha\Lambda_i(H)P(H_i)$$

$$= \alpha(34.25, 1.35)(10^{-4}, 1 - 10^{-4})$$

$$= (0.00253, 0.99747) \quad (30)$$

Note that it is important to verify that Mr. Holmes's summarization is indeed based only on Mrs. Gibbons's testimony and does not include prejudicial beliefs borrowed from previous evidence (eg, Watson's testimony or crime rate information); otherwise one is in danger of counting the same information twice. The likelihood ratio is, indeed, unaffected by such information. Bayesian practitioners claim that people are capable of retracing the origins of their beliefs and of answering hypothetical questions such as "What if you didn't receive Watson's call?" or "Estimate the increase in belief due to Gibbons's testimony alone."

An effective way of eliciting pure likelihood ratio estimates unaffected by previous information would be to first let one imagine that before obtaining the evidence, one is in the standard state of total ignorance and then estimates the final degree of belief given to a proposition as a result of observing the evidence. In this example, if prior to conversing with Mrs. Gibbons Mr. Holmes had a "neutral" belief in S, that is, $P(\text{alarm}) = P(\text{no alarm}) = 1/2$, the postconversation estimate $P(\text{alarm}|G) = 80\%$ would correspond to a likelihood ratio of 4:1 in favor of alarm.

PREDICTING FUTURE EVENTS

One of the attractive features of causal models in the Bayesian formulation is the ease they lend to the prediction of yet-unobserved events such as the possible denouements of social episodes, outcomes of a given test, or prognoses of a given disease. The need to facilitate such predictive tasks may, in fact, be the reason that human beings have adopted causal schema for encoding experiential knowledge.

Example 6. Immediately after his conversation with Mrs. Gibbons, as Mr. Holmes is preparing to leave his office, he recalls that his daughter is due to arrive home any minute and, if confronted by an alarm sound, would probably (0.7) phone him for instructions. Now he wonders whether he should not wait a few more minutes in case she calls.

To estimate the likelihood of the new target event: $D =$ daughter will call, one has to add a new causal link to the graph of Figure 1. Assuming that hearing an alarm sound is the only event that would induce his daughter to call, the new link should emanate from the variable S and be quantified by the following $P(D|S)$ matrix:

		D (will call)	$\sim D$ (will not call)
S	on	0.7	0.3
	off	0	1

Accordingly, $P(D|\text{all evidence})$ is given by

$$P(D|e) = \sum_j P(D|S_j, e)P(S_j|e)$$

$$= \sum_j P(D|S_j)P(S_j|e) \qquad (31)$$

which means that all the lengthy episodes with Dr. Watson and Mrs. Gibbons impart their influence on D only via the belief they induced on S, $P(S_j|e)$.

It is instructive to see now how $P(S_i|e)$ can be obtained from the previous calculation of $P(H_i|e)$. A natural temptation would be to use the updated belief $P(H_i|e)$ and the link matrix $P(S_j|H_i)$ and, through rote, write the conditioning equation

$$P(S_j|e) = \sum_i P(S_j|H_i)P(H_i|e) \qquad (32)$$

also known as Jeffrey's rule of updating (Jeffrey, 1965). This equation, however, is only valid in a very special set of circumstances. It will be wrong in the example because the changes in the belief of H actually originated from the corresponding changes in S; reflecting these back to S would amount to counting the same evidence twice. Formally, this objection is reflected by the inequality $P(S_j|H_i) \neq P(S_j|H_i, e)$, stating that the evidence obtained affects not only the belief in H and S but also the strength of the causal link between H and S. Fortunately, there is a simple way of incorporating these considerations in belief updating. The calculation of $P(S_j|e)$, for instance, can be performed as follows. Treating S as an intermediate hypothesis, equation 5 dictates

$$P(S_j|e) = \alpha P(e|S_j)P(S_j) \qquad (33)$$

The term $P(e|S_j)$ is the likelihood vector $\Lambda_j(S)$, which was calculated earlier to (36, 1), and the prior $P(S)$ is given by the matrix multiplication

$$P(S_j) = \sum_i P(S_j|H_i)P(H_i)$$

$$= (10^{-4}, 1 - 10^{-4})\begin{pmatrix} 0.95 & 0.01 \\ 0.01 & 0.99 \end{pmatrix}$$

$$= (0.0101, 0.9899) \qquad (34)$$

Thus, together, one has

$$P(S_j|e) = \alpha(36, 1)(0.0101, 0.9899)$$

$$= (0.2686, 0.7314) \qquad (35)$$

which gives the event S_1 = alarm-sound-on a credibility of 26.86% and predicts that the event D = daughter-will-call will occur with the probability of

$$P(D|e) = \sum_f P(D|S_i)P(S_j|e)$$

$$= (0.2686, 0.7314)\begin{pmatrix} 0.7 \\ 0 \end{pmatrix}$$

$$= 0.188 \qquad (36)$$

MULTIPLE CAUSES AND "EXPLAINING AWAY"

Tree structures like the one used in the preceding section require that only one variable be considered a cause of any other variable. This structure simplifies computations, but its representational power is limited because it forces one to group together all causal factors sharing a common consequence into a single node. By contrast, when people associate a given observation with multiple potential causes, they weigh one causal factor against another as independent variables, each pointing to a specialized area of knowledge. As an illustration, consider the following situation.

Example 7. As he is pondering this question, Mr. Holmes remembers having read in the instruction manual of his alarm system that the device is sensitive to earthquakes and can be triggered (0.2) by one accidentally. He realizes that if an earthquake had occurred, it would surely (0.99) be on the news. So, he turns on his radio and waits around for either an announcement or a call from his daughter.

Mr. Holmes perceives two episodes that may be potential causes for the alarm sound, an attempted burglary and an earthquake. Even though burglaries can safely be assumed independent of earthquakes, still a positive radio announcement would reduce the likelihood of a burglary, as it "explains away" the alarm sound. Moreover, the two causal events are perceived as individual variables (see Fig. 2); general knowledge about earthquakes rarely intersects knowledge about burglaries.

This interaction among multiple causes is a prevailing pattern of human reasoning. When a physician discovers evidence in favor of one disease, it reduces the credibility

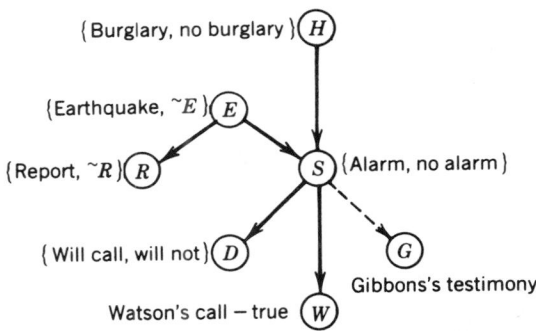

Figure 2. A diagram representing the causal dependencies among the variables in Examples 1–7.

of other diseases, although the patient may as well be suffering from two or more disorders simultaneously. A suspect who provides an alternative explanation for being present at the scene of the crime appears less likely to be guilty even though the explanation furnished does not preclude his committing the crime.

To model this sideways interaction a matrix M should be assessed giving the distribution of the consequence variable as a function of every possible combination of the causal variables. In the example one should specify $M = P(S|E, H)$, where E stands for the variable $E = \{$earthquake, no earthquake$\}$. Although this matrix is identical in form to the one described in Example 2, equation 18, where the two causal variables were combined into one compound variable $\{H_1, H_2, H_3, H_4\}$, treating E and H as two separate entities has an advantage in that it allows one to relate each of them to a separate set of evidence without consulting the other. For example, the relation between E and R (the radio announcement) can be quantified by the probabilities $P(R|E)$ without having to consider the irrelevant event of burglary, as would be required by compounding the pair (E, R) into one variable. Moreover, having received a confirmation of R, the beliefs of E and H can be updated in two separate steps, mediated by updating S, closely resembling the process used by people. An updating scheme for networks with multiple-parent nodes is described in Kim and Pearl (1983) and Pearl (1986).

If the number of causal factors k is large, estimating M may be troublesome because, in principle, it requires a table of size 2^k. In practice, however, people conceptualize causal relationships by creating hierarchies of small clusters of variables, and, moreover, the interactions among the factors in each cluster are normally perceived to fall into one of a few prestored, prototypical structures each requiring about k parameters. Common examples of such prototypical structures are noisy OR gates (ie, any one of the factors is likely to trigger the effect), noisy AND gates, and various enabling mechanisms (ie, factors identified as having no influence of their own except enabling other influences to become effective).

BAYESIAN NETWORKS

In the preceding discussion diagrams such as Figures 1 and 2 were used not merely for mnemonic or illustrative purposes. They in fact convey important conceptual information far more meaningful than the numeric estimates of the probabilities involved (see PROBABILISTIC NETWORKS). The formal properties of such diagrams, called Bayesian networks (Pearl, 1986), are discussed next.

Bayesian networks are directed acyclic graphs in which the nodes represent variables, the arcs signify the existence of direct causal influences between the linked variables, and the strengths of these influences are quantified by conditional probabilities (Fig. 3). Thus, if the graph contains the variables $x_1, \ldots, x_n$, and S_i is the set of parents for variable x_i, a complete and consistent quantification can be attained by specifying, for each node x_i, a subjective assessment $P'(x_i|S_i)$ of the likelihood that

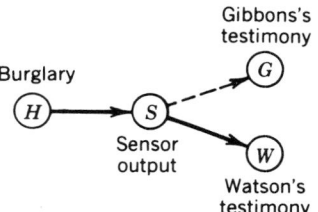

Figure 3. A typical Bayesian network with six variables.

x_i will attain a specific value given the possible states of S_i. The product of all these assessments,

$$P(x_1, \ldots, x_n) = \prod_i P'(x_i|S_i)$$

constitutes a joint-probability model that supports the assessed quantities. That is, if the conditional probabilities $P(x_i|S_i)$ dictated by $P(x_1, \ldots, x_n)$ are computed, the original assessments are recovered. Thus, for example, the distribution corresponding to the graph of Figure 3 can be written by inspection:

$$P(x_1, x_2, x_3, x_4, x_5, x_6)$$
$$= P(x_6|x_5)P(x_5|x_2, x_3)P(x_4|x_1, x_2)P(x_3|x_1)P(x_2|x_1)P(x_1)$$

An important feature of a Bayesian network is that it provides a clear graphic representation for the essential independence relationships embedded in the probability model (see GRAPHOIDS). The criterion for detecting these independencies is based on graph separation: Namely, if all paths between x_i and x_j are blocked by a subset S of variables, x_i is independent of x_j given the values of the variables in S. Thus, each variable x_i is independent of all its nondescendants, given the values of the variables in its parent set S_i. For this blocking criterion to hold in general, one must provide a special interpretation of separation for nodes that share common children. The pathway along arrows meeting head to head at node x_k is blocked by a set S if neither x_k nor any of its descendants is in S; otherwise, it is unblocked. In Figure 3, for example, x_2 and x_3 are independent given $S_1 = \{x_1\}$ or $S_2 = \{x_1, x_4\}$ because the two paths between x_2 and x_3 are blocked by either set. However, x_2 and x_3 may not be independent given $S_3 = \{x_1, x_6\}$ because x_6, as a descendant of x_5, unblocks the head-to-head connection at x_5, thus opening a pathway between x_2 and x_3.

BELIEF PROPAGATION IN BAYESIAN NETWORKS

Once a Bayesian network is constructed, it can be used to represent the generic causal knowledge of a given domain and can be consulted to reason about the interpretation of specific input data. The interpretation process involves instantiating a set of variables corresponding to the input data and calculating its impact on the probabilities of a set of variables designated as hypotheses. Alternatively, we may seek to identify the most likely interpretation of the data, that is, an assignment of values to the hypotheses set that obtains the highest posterior probability given the evidence (Pearl, 1987). Both tasks are NP-hard for general networks, and many algorithms have been developed for either calculating an approximate solution or exploiting the topological properties of networks that admit exact tractable solutions (see PROBABILISTIC NETWORKS). In general, assembling the most believable combination of hypotheses is no more complex than computing the degree of belief for any individual hypothesis.

Latter sections of this article discusses a distributed approach that was developed to mimic a human style of inferencing. One's limited short-term memory and narrow focus of attention combined with the resistance to shifting rapidly between alternative lines of reasoning seem to suggest that one's reasoning process is fairly local, progressing incrementally along prescribed pathways. Moreover, the speed and ease with which one performs some of the low-level interpretive functions, such as recognizing scenes, comprehending text, and even understanding stories, strongly suggest that these processes involve a significant amount of parallelism and that most of the processing is done at the knowledge level itself, not external to it.

A paradigm for modeling such an active knowledge base would be to view a Bayesian network not merely as a passive parsimonious code for storing factual knowledge but also as a computational architecture for reasoning about that knowledge. This means that the links in the network should be treated as the only pathways and activation centers that direct and propel the flow of data in the process of querying and updating beliefs. Accordingly, one can imagine that each node in the network is designated a separate processor that both maintains the parameters of belief for the host variable and manages the communication lines to and from the set of neighboring, logically related variables. The communication lines are assumed to be open at all times, that is, each processor may at any time interrogate the belief parameters associated with its neighbors and compare them to its own parameters. If the compared quantities satisfy some local constraints, no activity takes place. However, if any of these constraints is violated, the responsible node is activated to revise its violating parameter and set it straight. This, of course, will activate similar revisions at the neighboring processors and will set up a multidirectional propagation process, which will continue until equilibrium is reached.

The fact that evidential reasoning involves both top-down (predictive) and bottom-up (diagnostic) inferences (see PROCESSING, BOTTOM UP AND TOP DOWN) has caused apprehensions that, once the propagation process is allowed to run its course unsupervised, pathological cases of instability, deadlock, and circular reasoning will develop. Indeed, if a stronger belief in a given hypothesis means a greater expectation for the occurrence of its various manifestations and if, in turn, a greater certainty in the occurrence of these manifestations adds further credence to the hypothesis, how can one avoid infinite updating loops when the processors responsible for these propositions begin to communicate with one another?

It can be shown that singly connected Bayesian networks are supportive of self-activated, multidirectional propagation of evidence and guarantee rapid convergence to a globally coherent equilibrium Pearl (1986). This is made possible by characterizing the belief in each proposition as a vector of parameters similar to the likelihood vector of equation 20, with each component representing the degree of support that the host proposition obtains from one of its neighbors. Maintaining such a breakdown record of the origins of belief facilitates a distinction between causal and evidential support and serves to prevent the instabilities and circular reasoning discussed earlier. This distinction also permits the tracing of back evidence and assumptions for the purpose of either generating explanations or modifying the model.

As a computational architecture, singly connected Bayesian networks exhibit the following characteristics:

New information diffuses through the network in a single pass; that is, equilibrium is reached in time proportional to the diameter of the network.

The primitive processors are simple and repetitive, and they require no working memory except that used in matrix multiplication.

The local computations and the final belief distribution are entirely independent of the control mechanism that activates the individual operations. They can be activated by either data-driven or goal-driven (eg, requests for evidence) control strategies, by a clock, or at random.

This architecture lends itself naturally to hardware implementation capable of real-time interpretation of rapidly changing data. It also provides a reasonable model of cognitive processes involved in tasks such as plan recognition, reading comprehension, and associative retrieval where unsupervised parallelism is an uncontested mechanism, and where causal relationships constitute the main source of knowledge.

RATIONAL DECISIONS AND QUALITY GUARANTEES

In addition to belief updating, Bayesian methods also provide coherent prescriptions for choosing actions and meaningful guarantees of the quality of these choices. The prescription is based on the assumption that normative knowledge—that is, judgments about values, preferences, and desirability—represents an abstraction of actual human experience and that, like its factual knowledge counterpart, it can be encoded and manipulated to produce useful recommendations. Whereas judgments about the occurrence of events are quantified by probabilities, the desirability of action-consequences is quantified by utilities (also called payoffs, or values) (Raiffa, 1968).

Choosing an action amounts to selecting a set of variables in a Bayesian network and fixing their values unambiguously. Such a choice normally alters the probability distribution of another set of variables, judged to be consequences of the decision variables. If to each configuration of the consequence set C a utility measure $u(C)$ is assigned that represents its degree of desirability, the overall expected utility associated with action a is given by

$$U(a) = \sum_C u(C)P(C|a, e) \qquad (37)$$

where $P(C|a, e)$ is the probability distribution of the consequence set C conditioned on selecting action a given the evidence e.

Bayesian methodologies regard the expected utility $U(a)$ as a figure of merit of action a and treat it, therefore, as a prescription for choosing among alternatives. Thus, if one has the option of choosing either action a_1 or a_2, one can calculate both $U(a_1)$ and $U(a_2)$ and select that action that yields the highest value. Moreover, since the value of $U(a)$ depends on the evidence e observed up to the time of decision, the outcome of the maximum expected utility criterion will be an evidence-dependent plan (or decision rule) of the form: If e_1 is observed, choose a_1; if e_2 is observed, choose a_2, and so on (see DECISION THEORY).

The same criterion can also be used to rate the usefulness of various information sources and to decide which piece of evidence should be acquired first. The merit of querying variable x can be decided before actually observing its value, by the following consideration. If one queries x and finds the value v_x, the utility of action a will be

$$U(a|v_x) = \sum_c u(C|a, x = v_x)P(C|a, e, x = v_x) \qquad (38)$$

One is able, at this point, to choose the best action among all pending alternatives and attain the value

$$U(v_x) = \max_a U(a|v_x) \qquad (39)$$

However, since one is not sure of the actual outcome of querying x, one must average $U(v_x)$ over all possible values of v_x, weighed by their appropriate probabilities. Thus, the utility of querying x calculates to

$$U_x = \sum_{v_x} P(x = v_x|e)U(v_x) \qquad (40)$$

where e is the evidence available so far.

This criterion can be used to schedule many control functions in knowledge-based systems. For example, it can be used to decide what to ask the user next, what test to perform next, or which rule to invoke next. The expert system PROSPECTOR (qv) (Duda and co-workers, 1976) employed a scheduling procedure (called J^*) based on similar considerations (see RULE-BASED SYSTEMS). If the consequence set is well defined and not too large, this information-rating criterion can also be computed distributedly, concurrent with the propagation of evidence. Each variable x in the network stores an updated value of U_x, and as more evidence arrives, each variable updates its U_x parameter in accordance with those stored at its neighbors. At query time, attention will be focused on the observable node with the highest U_x value.

It is important to realize that the maximum expected utility rule was not chosen as a prescription for decisions for sheer mathematical convenience. Rather, it is founded on pervasive patterns of psychological attitudes toward risk, choice, preferences, and likelihoods. These attitudes are captured by what came to be known as the axioms of utility theory (von Neumann and Morgenstern, 1947). Unlike the case of repetitive long series of decisions (eg, gambling), where the expected value criterion is advocated on the basis of a long-run accumulation of payoffs, the expected utility criterion is applicable to single-decision situations. The summation operation in equation 37 originates not with additive accumulation of payoffs but, rather, with the additive axiom of probability theory (equation 3). An important feature of Bayesian decision methods is that choices can be justified in meaningful terms and the assumptions leading to these choices can readily be traced back and communicated for further elaboration.

BIBLIOGRAPHY

R. O. Duda, P. E. Hart, and N. J. Nilsson, "Subjective Bayesian Methods for Rule-based Inference Systems," *Proceedings of the 1976 National Computer Conference (AIFPS Conference Proceedings)* **45**, 1075–1082 (1976).

R. Jeffrey, *The Logic of Decisions*, McGraw-Hill, New York, Chapt. 11, 1965.

J. Kim and J. Pearl, "A Computational Model for Combined Causal and Diagnostic Reasoning in Inference Systems," *Proceedings of the Eighth International Joint Conference on Artificial Intelligence*, Karlsruhe, FRG, Morgan-Kaufmann, San Mateo, Calif., 1983, pp. 190–193.

J. Pearl, "Reverend Bayes on Inference Engines: A Distributed Hierarchical Approach," *Proceedings of the Second National Conference on Artificial Intelligence*, Pittsburgh, AAAI, Menlo Park, Calif., 1982, pp. 133–136.

J. Pearl, "Fusion, Propagation and Structuring in Belief Networks," *Artif. Intell.* **29**(3), 241–288 (Sept. 1986).

J. Pearl, "Distributed Revision of Composite Beliefs," *Artif. Intell.* **33**(2): 173–215 (1987).

H. Raiffa, *Decision Analysis: Introductory Lectures on Choices Under Uncertainty*, Addison-Wesley, Reading, Mass., 1968.

J. von Neumann and O. Morgenstern, *Theory of Games and Economic Behavior*, 2nd ed., Princeton University Press, Princeton, New Jersey, 1947.

General References

Bayesian Methodology

J. Pearl, *Probabilistic Reasoning in Intelligent Systems: Networks of Plausible Inference*, Morgan-Kaufmann Publishers, Palo Alto, Calif., 1988.

G. Shafer and J. Pearl, *Reading in Uncertain Reasoning*, Morgan-Kaufmann Publishers, San Mateo, Calif., 1990.

L. N. Kanal and A. Rosenfeld, series eds., *Uncertainty in Artificial Intelligence*, 1–5, Elsevier Science Publishers B.V., Amsterdam, The Netherlands, 1986–1990.

H. E. Kyburg and H. E. Smokler, *Studies in Subjective Probability*, Krieger, New York, 1980.

Bayesian Systems

B. Abramson and A. Finizza, "Using Belief Networks to Forecast Oil Prices," *Int. J. Forecasting*, in press.

S. Andreassen, M. Woldbye, B. Falck, and S. K. Andersen. "MUNIN: A Causal Probabilistic Network for Interpretation of Electromyographic Findings." *Proceedings of the Tenth International Joint Conference on Artificial Intelligence*, Milan,

Italy, Morgan-Kaufmann, San Mateo, Calif., 1987, pp. 366–372.

M. Ben-Bassat, R. W. Carlson, V. K. Puri, E. Lipnick, L. D. Portigal, and M. H. Weil, "Pattern-based Interactive Diagnosis of Multiple Disorders: The MEDAS System," *IEEE Trans. Pattern Anal. Mach. Intell.* **PAMI-2**, 148–160 (1980).

G. F. Cooper, *NESTOR: A Computer-based Medical Diagnostic Aid That Integrates Causal and Probabilistic Knowledge*, Report No. STAN-CS-84-1031, Stanford University, Stanford, Calif., November 1984.

R. P. Goldman, "A Probabilistic Approach to Language Understanding," Ph.D. dissertation, Brown University, Providence, Rhode Island, 1990.

D. Heckerman, E. Horvitz, and B. Nathwani, "Update on the Pathfinder Project." *Proceedings of the Thirteenth Symposium on Computer Applications in Medical Care*, Washington, D.C., IEEE Computer Society Press, Silver Spring, M.D., 1989, pp. 203–207.

J. Kim and J. Pearl, "*CONVINCE: A CONVersational INference Consolidation Engine*," *IEEE Trans. Systems Man Cybernetics,* **SMC-17**(2), 120–132 (1987).

D. J. Spiegelhalter and R. P. Knill-Jones, "Statistical and Knowledge-based Approaches to Clinical Decision-Support Systems, With an Application to Gastroenterology," *J. Roy Stat. Soc.* A(147), 35–77 (1984).

Quasi-Bayesian Systems

R. O. Duda, P. E. Hart, P. Barnett, J. Gaschnig, K. Konolige, R. Reboh, and J. Slocum, "Development of the PROSPECTOR Consultant System for Mineral Exploration, Final Report for SRI Projects 5821 and 6915," Artificial Intelligence Center, SRI International, Menlo Park, Calif., 1978.

C. Kulikowski and S. Weiss, "Representation of Expert Knowledge for Consultation: The CASNET and EXPERT Projects," in P. Szolovitz, ed., *Artificial Intelligence in Medicine*, Westview Press, Boulder, Colo., 1982, pp. 21–55.

R. A. Miller, H. E. Pople, and J. P. Myers, "INTERNIST-1, An Experimental Computer-based Diagnostic Consultant for General Internal Medicine," *N. Engl. J. Med.* **307**(8), 468–470 (1982).

J. R. Quinlan, "INFERNO: A Cautious Approach to Uncertain Inference," Rand Note N-1898-RC, September 1982.

E. H. Shortliffe, *Computer-Based Medical Consultation: MYCIN*, Elsevier, New York, 1976.

J. Pearl
UCLA

This work was supported in part by the National Science Foundation, Grant DSR 83-13875.

BEAM SEARCH. See Search, beam.

BELIEF REPRESENTATION SYSTEMS

A belief system may be understood as a set of beliefs together with a set of implicit or explicit procedures for acquiring new beliefs. The computational study of belief systems has focused on building computer sytems for representing or expressing beliefs or knowledge and for reasoning with or about beliefs or knowledge. Such a system is often expressed in terms of a formal theory of the syntax and semantics of belief and knowledge sentences.

Reasons for Studying Such Systems

There are several distinct, yet overlapping, motivations for studying such systems. As McCarthy and Hayes (1969), two of the earliest contributors to this field, have explained,

> A computer program capable of acting intelligently in the world must have a general representation of the world. . . . [This] requires commitments about what knowledge is and how it is obtained. . . . This requires formalizing concepts of causality, ability, and knowledge.

Thus, one motivation is as a problem in knowledge representation (see Knowledge representation). In the present context this might less confusingly be referred to as "information representation" since not only knowledge but also beliefs are represented. A second motivation is as a component of computational studies of action. Subcategories of the latter include planning systems (eg, Moore, 1977), systems for planning speech acts (eg, Cohen and Perrault, 1979), and systems for planning with multiple agents (eg, Appelt, 1980). These systems frequently involve representing and reasoning about other notions as well (such as can, want, etc).

A third motivation is the construction of AI systems that can interact with human users, other interacting AI systems, or even itself (eg, Konolige and Nilsson, 1980; McCarthy, 1977). Among the subcategories here are the study of user models for determining appropriate output (eg, Rich, 1979a,b) and the prediction of others' behavior and expectations on the basis of their beliefs (McCarthy, 1979). A fourth motivation is directly related to such interaction: the study of AI systems that can converse in natural language (eg, Wilks and Bien, 1979), either with users or with a "knowledge base" (eg, Levesque, 1984). A fifth motivation is the study of reasoning: how a particular individual reasons (Abelson and Reich, 1969), or how reasoning can be carried out with incomplete knowledge (eg, Halpern and McAllester, 1984), or in the face of resource limitations (eg, Konolige, 1983). Finally, there is the ever-present motivation of modeling a mind (eg, Abelson, 1973; Maida and Shapiro, 1982) or providing computational theories of human reasoning about beliefs (eg, Creary, 1979; Maida, 1983).

Types of Theories

There are four overlapping types of theories identifiable by research topics or by research methodologies. One is belief revision, which is concerned with the problem of revising a system's database in light of new, possibly conflicting information (cf Martins and Shapiro, 1988); such theories are dealt with in another entry. The other types of theory can be usefully categorized [by augmenting the scheme of McCarthy and Hayes (1969)] as (a) epistemological theories, concerned primarily with representational issues [eg, McCarthy (1979)]; (b) formal heuristic theories, concerned primarily with the logic of belief and knowledge, that is, with reasoning in terms of a formal representation [eg, Moore (1977)]; and (c) psychological heuristic theories, also concerned with reasoning but using techniques that make some explicit claim to psychological adequacy—such theories typically are not concerned with representational issues *per se* [eg, Colby and Smith (1969); Wilks and Bien (1983)].

PHILOSOPHICAL BACKGROUND

Much of the data, problems, and theories underlying AI research on formal belief systems has come from philosophy, in particular, epistemology, philosophy of language, and logic (especially modal and intensional logics).

Philosophical Issues

There are several philosophical issues—logical, semantic, and ontological—that have been faced by AI researchers working on belief systems.

1. The problem of the relationship between knowledge and belief. This problem, dating back to Plato's *Theaetetus*, is usually resolved by explicating knowledge as justified true belief (see Gettier, 1963 for the standard critique of this view and Fetzer, 1985 for a discussion in the context of AI).

2. The problem of the nature of the objects of belief, knowledge, and other intentional (ie, cognitive) attitudes: are such objects extensional (eg, sentences, physical objects in the external world) or intensional (ie, nonextensional; eg, propositions, concepts, mental entities)?

3. Problems of referential opacity: the failure of substitutability of co-referential terms and phrases in intentional contexts. This can best be illustrated as a problem in deduction. From

Susan believes that the Morning Star is a planet

and

The Morning Star is a planet if and only if the Evening Star is a planet,

it does not logically follow that

Susan believes that the Evening Star is a planet.

Nor from

Ruth believes that Venus is a planet

and

Venus = the Evening Star

does it logically follow that

Ruth believes that the Evening Star is a planet.

4. The problem of quantifying in (ie, into intentional contexts). From

Carol believes that the unicorn in my garden is white,

it does not logically follow that

There is a unicorn in my garden such that Carol believes that it is white.

5. Problems of logical form (or semantic interpretation, or "knowledge representation" in the sense of AI): how should the following kinds of sentences be understood, and what are their relationships with simpler cases of belief and knowledge?

Margot knows whether Ben's phone number is the same as Ariana's.
Mike knows who Sally is.
Jan believes that Stu believes that he is a philosopher.
Harriet and Frank mutually believe that the movie at Loew's starts at 9 p.m.

6. The problem of the distinction between *de re* and *de dicto* beliefs: When a belief is a cause of a person's actions, one is not only interested in what the person believes, but also in how the person believes it. That is, one is not only interested in a third-person characterization of the agent's beliefs, but also in the agent's *own* characterization of those beliefs. Suppose that Ralph sees the person whom he knows to be the janitor stealing some government documents, and suppose—unknown to Ralph—that the janitor has just won the lottery. Then Ralph believes *de dicto* that the janitor is a spy, and he believes *de re* that the lottery winner is a spy. That is, if asked, Ralph would assent to the proposition "The janitor is a spy"; but he merely believes of the man known to the hearer as the lottery winner that he is a spy—Ralph would not assent to "The lottery winner is a spy." Traditionally viewed, a belief *de dicto* is a referentially opaque context, whereas a belief *de re* is referentially transparent. Thus, the inference

Ralph believes [*de dicto*] that the janitor is a spy.
The janitor = the lottery winner.
_____
Ralph believes [*de dicto*] that the lottery winner is a spy.

is invalid. Moreover, its conclusion not only presents false information but it also represents a loss of information, namely, of the information about the propositional "content" of Ralph's belief. On the other hand,

Ralph believes [*de re*] of the janitor that he is a spy.
The janitor = the lottery winner.
_____
Ralph believes [*de re*] of the lottery winner that he is a spy.

is valid. But the conclusion conveys just as little information about Ralph's actual belief *de dicto* as does the first premise. An AI system that is capable of explaining or recommending behavior must be able to distinguish between these two kinds of belief reports by having two distinct means of representing them.

Epistemic Logic

Of central importance from the point of view of AI have been the logics of belief and knowledge proposed by Hintikka (1962). The propositional fragment of Hintikka's logic of knowledge (propositional epistemic logic) can be axiomatized as a notational variant of the modal logic **S4** (see LOGIC, MODAL), replacing the necessity operator by a family of proposition-forming operators $\mathbf{K}_a$, for each individual a ($\mathbf{K}_a p$ is to be read "a knows that p"). The axioms are

(A1) If p is a tautology, then $\vdash p$.

(A2) If $\vdash p$ and $\vdash (p \rightarrow q)$, then $\vdash q$.

(A3) If $\vdash p$, then $\vdash \mathbf{K}_a p$.

(A4) $\vdash (\mathbf{K}_a p \rightarrow p)$.

(A5) $\vdash (\mathbf{K}_a p \rightarrow \mathbf{K}_a \mathbf{K}_a p)$.

(A6) $\vdash ([\mathbf{K}_a p \wedge \mathbf{K}_a (p \rightarrow q)] \rightarrow \mathbf{K}_a q)$.

Roughly, (A3) says that a knows all theorems, (A4) says that what is known must be true (recall that knowledge is generally considered to be justified true belief), (A5) says that what is known is known to be known, and (A6) says that what is known to follow logically from what is known is itself known. A (propositional) logic of belief (a propositional doxastic logic) can be obtained by using operators $\mathbf{B}_a$ and deleting (A4); other epistemic and doxastic logics can be obtained by taking similar variants of other modal logics.

Possible-worlds semantics for epistemic and doxastic logics can be provided as in ordinary modal logics by interpreting the accessibility relation between possible worlds as a relation of epistemic or doxastic alternativeness. Thus, for example,

$\mathbf{K}_a p$ is true in possible world w if and only if p is true in possible world w' for all w' that are epistemic alternatives to w.

Intuitively, a knows that p if and only if p is compatible with everything that a knows [see Hintikka (1962, 1969) for details]. Various restrictions on the alternativeness (or accessibility) relation yield correspondingly different systems. Thus, **S4** can be characterized semantically by requiring the relation to be only reflexive and transitive. If symmetry is allowed, the semantics characterizes the stronger system $\mathbf{S5} = \mathbf{S4} + \vdash \neg \mathbf{K}_a p \rightarrow \mathbf{K}_a \neg \mathbf{K}_a p$. (Roughly, what is unknown is known to be unknown.)

Note that none of these systems is psychologically plausible. For example, no one knows or believes all tautologies or all logical consequences of one's knowledge or beliefs as suggested by (A6). Nor is it clear how to interpret (A5)—is the consequent to be read as "a knows that a knows that p" or as "a knows that he (or she) knows that p"?—nor whether it is plausible. Indeed, some philosophers feel that there are no axioms that characterize a psychologically plausible theory of belief. There is a large philosophical literature discussing these issues (eg, Castañeda, 1964, the special issues of *Noûs* 1 (1967), and *Syn-*

thèse 21 (1970)]. Other formalizations of epistemic logics that are of relevance to AI are to be found in Sato (1976) and McCarthy and co-workers (1978). Further discussion of the philosophical issues may be found in Linsky (1977), Edwards (1967), and through *The Philosopher's Index*. Interesting recent work on semantics of belief sentences dealing with linguistics and computational issues may be found in Moore and Hendrix (1982), Moravcsik (1973), and Partee (1967, 1973).

SURVEY OF THEORIES AND SYSTEMS

In this section the major published writings on belief systems are surveyed following the three-part categorization of types of theories and by lines within the types. The reader is reminded that the categorization is highly arbitrary and that virtually all of the research falls into more than one category.

Epistemological Theories

Early Work. One of the earliest works on AI belief systems, by McCarthy and Hayes (1969), begins by considering a system of interacting automata whose states at a given time are determined by their states at previous times and by incoming signals from the external world (including other automata). A person p is considered to be a subautomaton of such a system. Belief is represented by a predicate B, where $B_p(s, w)$ is true if p is to be regarded as believing proposition w when in state s. Four sufficient conditions for a "reasonable" theory of belief are given:

1. p's beliefs are consistent and correct.
2. New beliefs can arise from reasoning on the basis of other beliefs.
3. New beliefs can arise from observations.
4. If p believes that it ought to do something, then it does it.

However, criterion 1 is psychologically implausible and seems to better characterize knowledge; criterion 4 is similarly too strong. Knowledge is represented by a version of Hintikka's system (1962): The alternativeness relation, $shrug(p, s_1, s_2)$, is true if and only if: if p is in fact in situation s_2, then for all he knows he might be in situation s_1. (A "situation" is a complete, actual or hypothetical state of the universe.) $K_p q$ is true (presumably at s) if and only if $\forall t[shrug(p, t, s) \rightarrow q(t)]$, where $q(t)$ is a "fluent"—a Boolean-valued function of situations—that "translates" q, and where $shrug$ is reflexive and transitive. Although this paper is significant for its introduction of philosophical concepts into AI, it discusses only a minimal representation of knowledge and belief.

A more detailed representation is offered by McCarthy (1977, 1979) in which individual concepts—that is, intensional entities somewhat like Fregean senses—are admitted as entities on a par with extensional objects, to allow for first-order expression of modal notions without problems of referential opacity. Notationally, capitalized terms stand for concepts, lowercase terms for objects.

Thus, $know(p, X)$ is a Boolean-valued (extensional) function of a person p (an extensional entity) and a concept X (an intensional entity), meaning "p knows the value of X," defined as $true\ Know(P, X)$, where $true$ is a Boolean-valued function of propositions, and where $Know(P, X)$ is a proposition-valued (ie, concept-valued) function of a person = concept p and a concept X. Nested knowledge is handled by $Know$ rather than $know$; thus, "John knows whether Mary knows the value of X" is $Know$(John, $Know$(Mary, X)). The Hintikka-style knowledge ("knowledge-that") is represented by a function $K(P, Q)$, defined as $(Q\ And\ Know(P, Q))$; thus, "John knows that Mary knows the value of X" is K(John, $Know$(Mary, X)). A denotation function maps intensional concepts to extensional objects, and a denotation relation, $denotes$, is introduced for concepts that lack corresponding objects. An existence predicate can be defined in terms of the latter: $true\ Exists\ X$ if and only if $\exists x[denotes(X, x)]$. Belief is not treated in nearly as much detail. Functions $Believe$ and $believe$ are introduced, though so are functions $believespy$ and $notbelievespy$ (to handle a celebrated puzzle of referential opacity concerning spies; see Linsky, 1977), yet no axioms are provided to relate them to each other or to the ordinary belief functions. [A similar theory in the philosophical literature was described in Rapaport (1978).]

Creary (1979) extended McCarthy's theory to handle concepts of concepts. According to Creary, McCarthy's notation cannot represent three distinct readings of

Pat believes that Mike wants to meet Jim's wife

(generated by the de re/de dicto distinction) because it does not allow for the full hierarchy of Fregean senses (Frege, 1892). The three readings are

believes(pat, Wants{Mike, Meet${Mike$, Wife$ Jim$}})
believes (pat, Exist P$.Wants{Mike, Meet${Mike$, P$}} And Conceptof{P$, Wife Jim})
∃P$ P.believes(pat, Wants{Mike, Meet${Mike$, P$}}) ∧ conceptof(P$, P) ∧ conceptof(P, wife jim)

Here, if mike is the name of a person whose concept is: Mike, then Mike is the name of that concept and its concept is: Mike$, etc. It is not clear, however, that such a hierarchy is needed at all (cf Parsons, 1981) nor whether McCarthy's notation is indeed incapable of representing the ambiguity. Creary does, however, discuss reasoning about propositional attitudes of other agents by "simulating" them using "contexts"—temporary databases consisting of the agent's beliefs plus common beliefs and used only for reasoning, not for representation [thus escaping certain objections to "database approaches" raised by Moore (1977)]. Creary's system was subjected to criticism and refinement by Barnden (1983).

Barnden has revised and extended his own theory to solve a problem that he has identified as "incorrect imputation" (1986, 1989). For instance, the first reading above appears to "impute" to Pat a theory of concepts of concepts (ie, a theory of second-order concepts) that Pat might never have thought about. This seems, however, to be nothing more than the familiar de re/de dicto distinction.

Belief Spaces. The problems of nested beliefs and of the de re/de dicto distinction suggest that databases containing representations of beliefs should be partitioned into units (often called "contexts," "spaces," or "views") for each believer. One of the earliest discussions of these issues in a computational framework was by Moore (1973), who developed a LISP-like language, D-SCRIPT, that evaluates objects of belief in different environments (see also Bien, 1975). Another early use of such units was Hendrix's (1979) partitioning of semantic networks into "spaces" and "vistas": The former can be used to represent the propositions that a given agent believes; the latter are unions of such spaces. Similarly, Schneider (1980) introduced "contexts" to represent different views of a knowledge base, and Covington and Schubert (1980) used "subnets" to represent an individual's conception of the world. Filman and co-workers (1983) treat a context as a theory of some domain, such as an agent's beliefs, with the ability to reason with the agent's beliefs in the context and about them by treating the context as an object in a metacontext.

Fully Intensional Theories. The notions of intensional entities and belief spaces come together in the work of Shapiro and his associates. Maida and Shapiro (1982) go a step beyond the approach of McCarthy by dropping extensional entities altogether. Their representational scheme, SNePS (qv), uses a fully intensional semantic network in which all nodes represent distinct concepts, all represented concepts are represented by distinct nodes, and arcs represent binary relations between nodes but cannot be quantified over (they are "nonconceptual"). The entire network is considered to model the belief system of an intelligent agent: asserted propositional nodes represent the agent's beliefs, and "base" nodes represent individual concepts. [Similar philosophical theories are those of Meinong (1904) and Castañeda (1972); see Rapaport (1985).] Two versions of 'know' are treated (both via agent–verb–object case frames): know1 for "knows that" and know2 for "knows by acquaintance." There are corresponding versions of 'believe' (though it is not clear what believe2 is); the fundamental principle connecting knowledge and belief is that the system believes1 that an agent knows1 that p only if the system believes1 both that the agent believes1 that p and that the agent believes1 that p for the right reasons. Unlike other belief systems, their system can handle questions, as queries about truth values (which are represented by nodes). Thus, whereas most systems represent "John knows whether p" as "John knows that p or John knows that $\neg p$," Maida and Shapiro (1982) consider these to be merely logically equivalent but not intensionally identical; instead, they represent it as "John knows2 the truth value of p." Among the consequences of the fully intensional approach are (1) the ability to represent nested beliefs without a type hierarchy [see Maida (1983)], (2) the need for a mechanism of coreferentiality (actually, their "a EQUIV b" represents that the system believes that a and b are coreferential), (3) the dynamic introduction of new nodes, through user interaction, in the order they are needed (which sometimes requires node merging by means of EQUIV arcs), and (4) the treatment of all transitive verbs as referentially opaque unless there is an explicit rule to the contrary.

Rapaport (1986) [see also Rapaport and Shapiro (1984)] makes essential use of the notion of a "belief space" to represent the distinctions between *de re* and *de dicto* beliefs. In dynamically constructing the system's belief space, he follows the principle that if there is no prior knowledge of coreferentiality of concepts in the belief spaces of agents whose beliefs are being modeled by the system, then those concepts must be represented separately. This has the effect of reintroducing a kind of hierarchy [see the discussion of Creary (1979), above], but there is a mechanism for "merging" such entities later as new information warrants. Thus, the conjunctive *de dicto* proposition "John believes that Mary is rich and Mary believes that Lucy is rich" requires four individuals: the system's John, the system's John's Mary, the system's Mary, and the system's Mary's Lucy. But the *de re* proposition "John believes of Mary that she is not rich" only requires two: the system's John and the system's Mary. This technique is used to represent quasi-indicators (Castañeda, 1967; Sells, 1987): virtually all other systems fail to distinguish between "John believes that he* is rich" and "John believes that John is rich" [although Moore, 1980 and Smith (1986) briefly discuss this]; the starred, quasi-indexical occurrence of "he" is the *system's* way of depicting *John's* use of 'I' in John's statement, "I am rich." This is represented as a *de dicto* proposition requiring two individuals: the system's John and the system's John's representation of himself (which is distinct from the system's John's John). This theory has been extended by Wiebe (Wiebe and Rapaport, 1986).

Other Theories. Among other theories that may be classified as epistemological (though some have considerable overlap with formal heuristic theories) are the important early work of Konolige (1982), a series of papers by Kobsa (1984a–c) and Kobsa and Trost (1984), Xiwen and Weide (1983), and Soulhi (1984).

Konolige. Konolige (1982) is concerned with the other side of the coin of knowledge: ignorance. In order to prove ignorance based on knowledge limitations ["circumscriptive ignorance"; see McCarthy (1980)], he uses a representation scheme based on a logic called *KI*4, an extension of the work of Sato (1976). *KI*4 has two families of modal operators: knowledge operators, $[S]$, for each agent S, and (what might be called "context") operators, $[\alpha]$, for each proposition α; and it has an agent 0 ("fool"), where $[0]\alpha$ means "α is common knowledge." The axioms and rules of *KI*4 include analogs of (A1)–(A6)(system $K4$), plus:

(A7) $\vdash[0]\alpha \rightarrow [0][S]\alpha$

(A8) If $\alpha \vdash_{K4} \beta$, then $\vdash_{KI4} [\alpha]\beta$

(A9) If not-$(\alpha \vdash_{K4} \beta)$, then $\vdash_{KI4} \neg [\alpha]\beta$

Roughly, (A7) says that if α is common knowledge, then it is common knowledge that S knows it; (A8) says that if β follows from α in $K4$, then β is true in the context of α in *KI*4; and (A9) says that if β does not follow from α in $K4$,

then it is not true in the context of α in *KI*4. The context operator may be explained as follows: If $\alpha = [S]q$, then $[\alpha]$ identifies S's theory whose axiom is q. Thus, "all S knows about p is that q_1 or q_2" can be represented as: $[\alpha][S]p$, where $\alpha = [S]q_1 \lor [S]q_2$.

Kobsa and Trost. Kobsa and Trost (1984) use the KL-ONE knowledge representation system, augmented by their version of partitions: "contexts"—collections of "nexus" nodes linked to "concept" nodes, representing that the agent modeled by the context containing the nexus nodes believes propositions about the concepts. There is a system context and separate contexts for each agent whose beliefs are modeled, with explicit (co-referential-like) links between isomorphic structures in the different contexts (instead of structure sharing or pattern matching). Of particular interest is their use of "embedded" (ie, nested) beliefs to represent recursive beliefs (the special case of nesting where a lower level context models a higher level one, as in the system's beliefs about John's beliefs about the system's beliefs) and mutual beliefs (by linking the context for one agent embedded in the context for another with the embedding context).

Formal Heuristic Theories

Moore. One of the most influential of the formal theories (both epistemological and heuristic) has been that of Moore (1977, 1980, 1981). His was the first AI theory to offer both a representational scheme and a logic and to show how they can interact with other notions to reason about action. For his representation, Moore uses a first-order axiomatization of the possible-worlds semantics of Hintikka's **S4** [rather than the modal axiomatic version; it should be noted that Moore (1977) erroneously added the **S5** rule]. Specifically, he introduces a predicate $T(w, p)$ to represent that the object language formula p is true in possible world w, and the predicate $K(A, w1, w2)$ to represent that $w2$ is possible according to what A knows in $w1$. "A knows that p" is then represented by $Know(A, p)$, which satisfies the axiom: $T(w1, Know(a1, p1)) \equiv \forall w2(K(a1, w1, w2) \rightarrow T(w2, p1))$. Since Moore is concerned with using knowledge to reason about actions, he formulates a logic of actions, where complex actions are built out of sequences, conditionals (defined in terms of $Know$), and loops, and a logic for "can," understood as "knowing how to do." The criticisms one can offer of Moore's work are both two-sided: (*1*) its psychological inadequacy (primarily due to his reliance on Hintikka's system)—but, of course, this is shared by most other formal theories—and (*2*) its similarity to much work that had been going on in philosophy during the 1960s and 1970s, but here it must be noted that one advantage of (some) AI theories over (some) philosophical theories is the former's attention to detail, which can often indicate crucial gaps in the latter. (Moore's critique of the database approach is discussed below.) Moore's line of research has been extended, most recently, by Morgenstern (1986).

Konolige. Konolige and Nilsson (1980) consider, from a formal point of view, a planning system involving cooperating agents. Each agent is represented by a first-order language, a "simulation structure" (a partial model of the language), a set of facts (expressed in the language and including descriptions of other agents), a "goal structure" (consisting of goals and plans), a deduction system, and a planning system. An agent uses a formal metalanguage to describe the languages of other agents and can use its representation of other agents (or itself–but not quasi-indexically) to reason by simulation about their plans and facts in order to take them into account when making its own plans. Belief, rather than knowledge, is taken as the appropriate cognitive attitude, to allow for the possibility of error [not allowed by axiom (A4), above], and "agent A0 believes that agent A1 believes that agent A0 is holding object B" is represented by FACT(A1, 'HOLDING(A0, B)') appearing in A0's FACT-list. Although an analog of axiom (A5) is taken as an axiom here, the analog of (A6) is not, since (1) their system allows different agents to have different deduction systems and (2) the deductive capabilities of the agents are considered to be limited.

This theory was made more rigorous in Konolige (1983, 1984). Here, a planning system with multiple agents has a "belief subsystem" consisting of (1) a list of "base" sentences (about a situation) expressed in a formal language with a modal belief operator and a Tarski-like truth value semantics; (2) a set of deduction processes (or deduction rules) that are sound, effectively computable, have "bounded" input, and are, therefore, monotonic; and (3) a control strategy (for applying the rules to sentences). Belief derivation is "total"; that is, all queries are answered in a bounded amount of time. The system is deductively consistent (ie, a sentence and its negation are not simultaneously believed), but it is not logically consistent (ie, there might not be a possible world in which all beliefs are true). Thus, some measure of psychological plausibility is obtained. A system can be deductively though not logically consistent if there are resource limitations on deductions; that is, the deductive processes might be incomplete because of either weak rules or a control strategy that does not perform all deductions. Konolige uses the former (though his sample of a weak rule—*modus ponens* weakened by conjoining a "derivation depth" to each sentence—seems to require a nonstandard conjunction in order to prevent ordinary *modus ponens* from being derivable). The system satisfies two properties: *closure* (sentences derived in the system are closed under the deduction rules; ie, all deductions are made) and *recursion* (the belief operator $[S]$ is interpreted as another belief system). Thus, $[S]\alpha$ means that α is derivable in S's belief system. A "view" [similar to Hendrix's "vista" (1979)] is a belief system as "perceived through a chain of agents"; for example $\nu = $ *John, Sue* is John's perception of Sue's beliefs. To bound the recursive reasoning processes, the more deeply nested a system is, the weaker are its rules. Konolige presents a Gentzen-style propositional doxastic logic **B** consisting of: the axioms and rules of propositional logic; a set of rules for each view ν; and, for each ν, (1) a rule *Cut** (essentially *modus ponens*) that implements closure, (2) a rule B_5 that formalizes agent i's deductive system in view ν (roughly, the rule is that if a sentence δ from some set of sentences Δ can be inferred using the rules of

the view ν, i from a set of sentences Γ that are believed by S_i, then $[S_i]\Delta$ can be inferred using the rules of ν from $[S_i]\Gamma$), and (3) a rule B_c that says that anything can be derived from logically inconsistent beliefs. **B** is stronger than might be desired, since, if the ν rules are complete and recursion is unbounded, **B** is equivalent to **S5** $-$ (A4). Konolige points out, however, that it can be weakened to **S4** $-$ (A4).

Levesque. A very different approach was taken by Levesque in a series of papers (1981, 1984a,b) on knowledge bases. The problem he confronts is that of treating a knowledge base that is incomplete (ie, that lacks some information needed to answer queries) as an abstract data type. However, his use of epistemic logic is not as a representation device within the knowledge base but as a query language. He defines a first-order language $\mathcal{L}$ that has its singular terms partitioned by means of a relation v into equivalence classes of coreferential terms; the classes are referred to by numerical "parameters" (for the knowledge base to be able to answer wh-questions). $\mathcal{L}$ has a truth value semantics based on a set s of "primitive" (true) sentences, and $\mathcal{L}$ is said to describe a "world structure" $\langle s, v \rangle$. Levesque argues that although $\mathcal{L}$ may be sufficient to query the knowledge base about the world, it is not sufficient to query it about itself. For this, $\mathcal{L}$ is extended to a language $\mathcal{KL}$, containing a knowledge operator K and satisfying two principles: (1) "every logical consequence of what is known is also known," but not everything is known (ie, the knowledge base is "an incomplete picture of a" possible world); and (2) "a pure sentence (ie, one that is about only the knowledge base) is true exactly when it is known" (ie, the knowledge base is an accurate picture of itself). The operator K satisfies slightly modified axioms for $\mathcal{L}$ (which are like those for a typical first-order logic), plus:

$$\text{If } \vdash_{\mathcal{L}} \alpha, \text{ then } \vdash_{\mathcal{KL}} K\alpha.$$

$$\vdash_{\mathcal{KL}}((K\alpha \wedge K(\alpha \rightarrow \beta)) \rightarrow K\beta).$$

$$\vdash_{\mathcal{KL}}(\forall x K\alpha \rightarrow K\forall x\alpha).$$

$$\text{If } \alpha \text{ is pure, then } \vdash_{\mathcal{KL}}(\alpha \equiv K\alpha).$$

The first of these says, roughly, that if α is provable in $\mathcal{L}$, then "α is known" is provable in $\mathcal{KL}$; the second is similar to (A6); the third says, roughly, that if everything is such that α is known to hold of it, then it is known that everything is such that α holds of it; and the fourth says, roughly, that the K operator is redundant in pure sentences. Semantically, if k is a set of world structures (ie, those compatible with the knowledge base), then $K\alpha$ is true on s, v, k, if and only if α is true on all $\langle s', v' \rangle$ in k. It should be observed that K is more like a *belief* operator since $K\alpha \rightarrow \alpha$ is *not* a theorem, whereas $K(K\alpha \rightarrow \alpha)$ *is*. Two operations on an abstract data type KB can then be defined roughly as follows: (I) ASK: KB $\times \mathcal{KL} \rightarrow$ {yes, no, unknown}, where ASK = yes if $K\alpha$ is true in KB; ASK = no if $K\neg\alpha$ is true in KB; and ASK is unknown otherwise. (II) TELL: KB $\times \mathcal{KL} \rightarrow$ KB, where TELL = the intersection of KB with the set of all world structures on which the query is true. Although the query language is epistemic, Levesque proves a representation theorem stating that the knowledge in KB is representable using $\mathscr{L}$[essentially by trading in $\boldsymbol{K}\alpha$ for $\vdash_{\mathscr{L}}(k \rightarrow \alpha)$, where k may be thought of as the conjunction of sentences in KB].

In Levesque (1984b), principle 1 is weakened, for several psychologically interesting reasons: (a) it ignores resource limitations; (b) it requires belief of all valid sentences; (c) it ignores differences between logically equivalent, yet distinct, sentences; and (d) it requires belief of all sentences if inconsistent ones are believed. To achieve an interpretation sensitive to these, two belief operators are used: $B\alpha$ for "α is explicitly (or actively) believed" and $L\alpha$ for "α is implicit in what is believed." To distinguish (A) situations in which only α and $\alpha \rightarrow \beta$ are believed from (B) those in which they are believed together with β—without being forced to distinguish (C) situations in which only $\alpha \lor \beta$ is believed from (D) those in which only $\beta \lor \alpha$ is believed—Levesque uses "partial possible worlds," in which not all sentences get truth values. A formal logic is defined in which L is logically "omniscient" (much like Levesque's earlier $\boldsymbol{K}$), but B is not. More precisely: (i) $B\alpha \rightarrow L\alpha$ is valid, but its converse is not; (ii) B is not closed under $\rightarrow$; (iii) B need not apply to all valid sentences or to both of two logically equivalent ones; and (iv) B allows inconsistent beliefs. Of great philosophical interest is a theorem that $B\alpha \rightarrow B\beta$ if and only if α *entails* β, where *entails* comes from relevance logic (Anderson and Belnap, 1975). Levesque has summarized his most recent work (1986a,b).

Other Theories. Most of the recent research on formal heuristic theories has been collected in the proceedings of the Conferences on Theoretical Aspects of Reasoning about Knowledge (eg, Halpern, 1986a) (cf Rapaport, 1988). One application of Kripke-style possible-worlds semantics for propositional epistemic logic for m agents is in the analysis of distributed systems (Halpern, 1986b). The abstract notion of a possible world can be interpreted as a global state of a distributed system (ie, as a description of each processor's state), and the accessibility relation for agent i can be interpreted as the relation between two global states s and t such that processor i has the same state in s and t. Thus, processor i "knows" proposition ϕ if and only if ϕ is true in all global states consistent with i's current state, where ϕ expresses information about processors' states or the values of their variables, for example. (Computational interpretations such as this of the abstract paraphernalia of possible-worlds semantics for modal logics are among the clearest, most revealing, and least metaphysically suspect.)

Another major topic is the problem of "logical omniscience"—that all agents "know all valid formulas and all logical consequences of their knowledge" (Halpern, 1986b, p. 7). There are three approaches to the solution of this problem. First, there is Kurt Konolige's syntactic approach, which employs incomplete sets of deduction rules (1986). Second, there is Levesque's semantic approach, discussed above. Finally, there is the combined syntactic-semantic approach of Ronald Fagin and Halpern's "logic of general awareness", which "adds to each state [of a

Kripke structure] a set of formulas that the agent is 'aware' of at that state" (Halpern, 1986b, p. 8). On this view, implicit knowledge is the same as the standard epistemic-logic concept of knowledge, and an agent a explicitly knows ϕ if and only if a implicitly knows ϕ and ϕ is in a's awareness set. It is of some, perhaps sociological, interest that the most serious attention to the problem of logical omniscience has been paid, not by pure philosophers of mind or of language, but by computer scientists. [Cf also the work of Vardi (1986).]

Psychological Heuristic Theories

This category of research, which attempts to be more psychologically realistic than either of the preceding two, may be further subdivided along a spectrum ranging from the more formal to the more psychological.

More Formal than Psychological. There are two major, and related, topics investigated under this heading: speech act theory and mutual belief.

Speech Act Theory. Speech act theory, developed by the philosophers Austin, Grice, and Searle considers the basic unit of linguistic communication to be the rule-governed production of a token of a sentence (or word) in the performance of an illocutionary speech act (such as the act of making a statement or asking a question). According to Grice's version of this theory, meaning must be understood in terms of intending: a speaker S means something by his or her utterance U addressed to hearer H if and only if, roughly, S intended the utterance of U to produce a certain effect in H by means of the recognition of this intention (see references and further details in Searle, 1965).

Cohen and Perrault. Cohen and Perrault (1979) attempt to provide "a theory that formally models the possible intentions underlying speech acts . . . by treating intentions as plans" involving "the communication of beliefs." Plans are treated as prespecified sequences of "action" operators, which consist of preconditions, bodies, and effects and are evaluated relative to the planner's world model (including models of the planner's interlocutor's beliefs). When the action operator is a speech act, it takes beliefs and goals and returns plans for the appropriate speech act. Their criteria of adequacy for a theory of beliefs are that it must (*1*) distinguish agent AGT1's beliefs from AGT1's beliefs about AGT2's beliefs and (*2*) allow AGT1 to represent (a) that AGT2 knows whether P without AGT1 having to know which of P and ¬P AGT2 believes and (b) that AGT2 believes that Rab and that $\exists x \, Rax$ and that AGT2 knows what the x such that Rax is *without* AGT1 knowing what AGT2 thinks the x such that Rax is. Their logic of belief takes BELIEVE as a relation (though they call it a modal operator) between an agent and a proposition, satisfying the following axioms (for each agent a):

(B1)   If P is an axiom of first-order logic, then
        $\vdash$aBELIEVE(P)

(B2)   ⊢aBELIEVE(P) → aBELIEVE(aBELIEVE)(P))

(B3)   ⊢aBELIEVE(P) ∨ aBELIEVE(Q) → aBELIEVE(P ∨ Q)

(B4)   ⊢aBELIEVE(P & Q) → aBELIEVE(P) & aBELIEVE(Q)

(B5)   ⊢aBELIEVE(P) → ¬aBELIEVE(¬P)

(B6)   ⊢aBELIEVE(P → Q) → (aBELIEVE(P) → aBELIEVE(Q))

(B7)   ⊢∃x[aBELIEVE(P(x))] → aBELIEVE(∃xP(x))

(B8)   ⊢ All agents believe that all agents believe (B1)–(B7)

They admit that this is too strong to be psychologically plausible. Agents' wants are also represented but not axiomatized.

Cohen and Levesque. Cohen and Levesque (1980) claim that illocutionary act definitions can be derived from statements describing the recognition of shared plans and that this requires a definition of mutual beliefs. They offer perhaps the most honest, if not psychologically plausible, representation of belief:

(BEL x p) is true if and only if p follows from what x believes

(KNOW x p) is defined as (AND p(BEL x p)) and (KNOWIF x p) as (OR (KNOW x p)(KNOW x (NOT p))). The latter is used to define an if–then–else rule, along the lines of Moore (1977). Mutual belief (discussed in more detail below) is characterized by two axioms:

If ⊢p, then ⊢(MB x y p).

⊢(MB x y p) = (BEL x (AND p (MB y x p))).

A "plan" for an agent x to achieve goal q is defined as an action a and formulas $p_0, \ldots, p_k, q_0, \ldots, q_k = q$ such that (roughly) x believes that p_0 implies that the result of x doing a is q_0 and that p_i implies that x's making q_{i-1} true thereby makes q_i true (for $i = 1, \ldots, k$). Various illocutionary operators are characterized using notions such as these. This line of research has been extended by Cohen and Levesque (1990).

Allen and Perrault. This research program was continued by Allen and Perrault (1980) in order to model "helpful" linguistic behavior, that is, appropriate responses by a hearer (much in the manner of user modeling; see below). They offer a simple example (stated in the first person), which is presented here in more generality (in order to illustrate some of the complications that virtually all theories have ignored; compare the discussion of quasi-indicators, above): For S to inform H that he* (S) is tired, there must be two preconditions: that S believe that he* is tired and that he (S) intend that H believe that he* (S) is tired, and there should be the effect that H believe that S is tired. Their methodology is as follows: (*1*) There are

planning rules; for example, if an agent wants to achieve P and does not know whether P is true, then the agent may want to achieve "agent knows whether P is true." (*2*) Figuring out another agent's plans depends on the observer's knowledge of planning and his or her beliefs about the agent's goals. (*3*) There are inference rules for inferring actions; for example corresponding to the planning rule above, if S believes that A has a goal of knowing whether P is true, then S may believe that A has a goal of achieving P or S may believe that A has a goal of achieving $\neg P$. Their logic of belief and knowledge is based on Hintikka (1962). For instance, there is an axiom schema of the form (though in different notation) $(B_A(P \to Q) \wedge B_A P) \to B_A Q$, although their commentary suggests that such schemata are really of the form $B_S(B_A(P \to Q) \wedge B_A P) \to B_S B_A Q$. Knowledge is defined as true belief: $K_A P = (P \wedge B_A P)$, interpreted as $B_S K_A P$ if and only if $B_S(S$ and A agree that $P)$. Knowing-whether and knowing-who are defined as follows:

$$\text{KNOWIF}_A P = (P \wedge B_A P) \vee (\neg P \wedge B_A \neg P).$$

$$\text{KNOWREF}_A P = \exists y[y = \text{the } x \text{ such that } D(x)$$
$$\wedge B_A(y = \text{the } x \text{ such that } D(x))].$$

There are also numerous rules relating these forms of belief and knowledge to wants and actions.

Other theories include those of Allen, Sidner, and Israel. Allen (1984) continued this line of research, embedding it in a theory of action and time; here, BELIEVES(A, p, T_p, T_b) is taken to mean that A believes during time interval T_b that p holds during time interval T_p. Sidner and Israel (1981) and Sidner (1983) attack similar problems, treating the "intended meaning" of utterance U by speaker S for hearer H as a set of pairs of propositional attitudes (beliefs, wants, intentions, etc.) and propositional "contents" that are such that S wants H to hold the attitude toward the content by means of U.

Mutual Belief. The problems of mutual belief and mutual knowledge, notions generally accepted to be essential to research programs such as these, are most clearly stated by Clark and Marshall (1981). They raise a paradox of mutual knowledge: To answer a successful definite reference by speaker S to hearer H that term t refers to referent R, a doubly infinite sequence of conditions must be satisfied: $K_S(t \text{ is } R)$, $K_S K_H(t \text{ is } R)$, $K_S K_H K_S(t \text{ is } R)$, $\ldots$, and $K_H(t \text{ is } R), K_H K_S(t \text{ is } R), \ldots$. But each condition takes a finite amount of time to check, yet successful reference does not require an infinite time. Their solution is to replace the infinite sequences by mutual knowledge defined in terms of "copresence": S and H mutually know that t is R if and only if there is a state of affairs G such that S and H have reason to believe that G holds, G indicates to them that they have such reason, and G indicates to them that t is R. Typically, G will be either (*1*) community membership (ie, shared world knowledge), for example, when t is a proper name; (*2*) physical copresence (ie, a shared environment), for example, where t is an indexical; or (*3*) linguistic copresence (ie, a shared discourse), for example, where t is anaphoric (see Perrault and Cohen (1981) for a critique).

Mutual knowledge has been further investigated by Appelt (1980, 1982) and Nadathur and Joshi (1983). Appelt's planning system is an intellectual descendant of the work of Allen, Cohen, Perrault, and Moore. It reasons about A's and B's mutual knowledge by reasoning about the knowledge of a (virtual) agent—the "kernel"—whose knowledge is characterized by the union of sets of possible worlds that are consistent with A's and B's knowledge. Nadathur and Joshi replace Clark and Marshall's (1981) requirement of mutual knowledge for successful reference by a weaker criterion: if S knows or believes that H knows or believes that t is R, and if there is no reason to doubt that this is mutual knowledge, then S conjectures that it is mutual knowledge. This is made precise by using Konolige's $KI4$ to formulate a sufficient condition for S's using t to refer to R.

Other Theories. Other formal psychological heuristic work has been done by Taylor and Whitehill (1981) on deception and by Airenti and co-workers (1982) on the interaction of belief with conceptual and episodic knowledge.

More Psychological than Formal

Wilks and Colleagues. The various logics of nested beliefs in general and of mutual beliefs in particular each face the threat of infinite nestings or combinatorial explosions of nestings. Wilks and Bien (1979, 1983) have attempted to deal with this threat by using what might be called psychological heuristics. Their work is based on Bien's (1975) approach of treating natural-language utterances as programs to be run in "multiple environments" (one of the earliest forms of belief spaces): a global environment would represent a person P, and local environments would represent P's models of his or her interlocutors. The choice of which environment within which to evaluate a speaker's utterance U depends on P's attitude toward the discourse: if P believes the speaker, then U would be evaluated in P's environment, else in P's environments for the speaker and hearer. Wilks and Bien use this technique to provide an algorithm for constructing nested beliefs, given the psychological reality of processing limitations. They offer two general strategies for creating environments: (*1*) "Presentation" strategies determine how deeply nested an environment should be to represent information about someone. The "minimal" presentation strategy, for simple cases, constructs a level only for the subject of the information but none for the speaker; the "standard" presentation strategy constructs levels for both speaker and subject; and "reflexive" presentation strategies construct more complex nestings. (*2*) "Insertional" strategies determine where to store the speaker's information about the subject; for example, the "scatter gun" insertion strategy would be to store it in all relevant environments. A local environment is represented as a list of statements indexed by their behavior and nested within a relatively global environment: $A^{\{B\}}$ represents A's beliefs about B, $A^{\{B\{C\}\}}$ represents A's beliefs about B's beliefs about C. Suppose a *USER* informs the *SYSTEM* about person A. To interpret the *USER*'s utterance, a nested environment within which to run it is constructed, only temporarily, as follows: $SYSTEM^{\{A\}}$ and $SYSTEM^{\{USER\}}$ are constructed, and the former is "pushed down into" the latter to produce $SYSTEM^{\{USER\{A\}\}}$. Pushing is done according to several heuristics: (*1*) "Contradiction" heuristics: The $SYSTEM$'s beliefs about the $USER$'s beliefs about A are assumed to be the $SYSTEM$'s beliefs about A unless there is explicit evidence to the contrary. (*2*) Pragmatic inference rules change some of the $SYSTEM$'s beliefs about A into the $SYSTEM$'s beliefs about A's beliefs about A. (*3*) "Relevance" heuristics: Those of the $SYSTEM$'s beliefs about the $USER$'s beliefs that explicitly mention or describe A become part of the $SYSTEM$'s beliefs about A. (*4*) "Percolation" heuristics: Beliefs in $SYSTEM^{\{USER\{A\}\}}$ that are not contradicted remain in $SYSTEM^{\{A\}}$ when the temporary nested environment is no longer needed for evaluation purposes. Thus, percolation seems to be a form of learning by means of trustworthiness, though there is no memory of the source of the new beliefs in $SYSTEM^{\{A\}}$ after percolation has occurred; that is, the $SYSTEM$ changes its beliefs about A by merely contemplating its beliefs about the $USER$'s beliefs. Other difficulties concern "self-embedded" beliefs: In $SYSTEM^{\{SYSTEM\}}$, there are no beliefs that the $SYSTEM$ has about the $SYSTEM$ that are not its own beliefs, but surely a $SYSTEM$ might believe things that it does not believe that it believes; and there are potential problems about quasi-indicators when $SYSTEM^{\{A\}}$ is pushed into itself to produce $SYSTEM^{\{A\{A\}\}}$. Wilks has extended this line of research (Wilks, 1986; Wilks and co-workers, 1989).

Colby. Although the work of Wilks and Bien has a certain formality to it, they are not especially concerned with the explicit logic of a belief operator, an accessibility relation, or a formal logic. The lack of concern with such issues may be taken to be the mark of the more psychological approaches. The pioneers of this approach were Colby and Abelson and their co-workers.

Colby and Smith (1969) constructed an "artificial belief system," ABS_1. ABS_1 had three modes of operation: During "talktime" a user would input sentences, questions, or rules; these would be entered on lists for that user (perhaps like a belief space; but see below). If the input were a question, ABS_1 would either search the user's statement list for an answer (taking the most recent if there were more than one answer), or deduce an answer from the statement list by the rules, or else generate an answer from other users' lists. During "questiontime" ABS_1 would search the user's statement list for similarities and ask the user questions about possible rules; the user's replies would enable ABS_1 to formulate new rules. ABS_1 would also ask the user's help in categorizing concepts. During "thinktime" ABS_1 would infer new facts (assigned to a "self"-list) and compute "credibility" weightings for the facts, rules, and user.

It should be noted that beliefs in this system are merely statements on a user's list, which makes this approach seem very much like the database approach criticized by Moore (1977). Moore's objections are as follows: (*1*) If the system does not know which of two propositions p or q a user believes, then it must set up two databases for the user, one containing p and one containing q, leading to combinatorial explosion. (2) The system cannot represent that the user does not believe that *p*, since neither of the two database alternatives—omitting *p* or listing ¬*p*—is an adequate representation. Although these are serious problems, Colby and Smith's ABS_1 seems not to have them. First, ABS_1 only reasons about explicit beliefs; thus, it would never have to represent the problematic cases. Of course, a more psychologically adequate system would have to. Second, ABS_1 does not appear to reason about the fact that a user believes a statement but only about the statement and ABS_1's source for its believing the statement.

In Colby (1973) a belief is characterized as an individual's judgment of acceptance, rejection, or suspended judgment toward a conceptual structure consisting of concepts—representations of objects in space and time, together with their properties—and their interrelations. A statement to the effect that *A* believes that *p* is treated dispositionally (if not actually behavioristically) as equivalent to a series of conditionals asserting what *A* would say under certain circumstances. More precisely, "*U* Believe$_E$*C*, *t*" if and only if experimenter *E* takes the linguistic reaction (ie, judgment of credibility) of language user *U* to an assertion conceptualized as *C* as an indicator of *U*'s belief in *C* during time *T*. Thus, what is represented are the objects of a user's beliefs, not the fact that they are believed. Various psychologically interesting types of belief systems (here understood as sets of interacting beliefs)—neurotic, paranoid, and so on—can then be investigated by "simulating" them. The most famous such system is Colby's PARRY (1971, 1972), which has been the focus of much controversy [see Colby (1981) and Weizenbaum's (1974) critique].

Abelson. A similar research program has been conducted by Abelson (1973) and with his co-workers (Abelson and Reich, 1969). Underlying their work is a theory of "implicational molecules," that is, sets of sentences that "psychologically" (ie, pragmatically) imply each other; for example, a "purposive-action" molecule might consist of the sentence forms "person *A* does action *X*," "*X* causes outcome *Y*," and "*A* wants *Y*." The key to their use in a belief system is what Abelson and Reich consider a Gestalt-like tendency for a person who has such a molecule to infer any one of its members from the others. Thus, a computer simulation of a particular type of belief system can be constructed by identifying appropriate molecules, letting the system's beliefs be sentences connected in those molecules (together with other structures, such as Schank's "scripts") and then having the system understand or explicate input sentences in terms of its belief system. A model of a right-wing politician was constructed in this manner [see also the discussions of Colby's as well as Abelson's work in Boden (1977)].

User Models. An extended, database type of belief system is exemplified by user models such as those investigated by Rich (1979a,b). Here, instead of the system being a model of a mind, the system must construct a model of the user's mind, yet many of the techniques are similar in both cases. A user model consists of properties of the user ("facts") ranked in terms of importance and by degree of

certainty (or confidence) together with their justifications. The facts come from explicit user input and inferences based on these, on "stereotypes" (so that only minimal explicit user input is needed), and on the basis of the user's behavior (so that the model is not merely the user's self-model). The user model is built dynamically during interaction with the user. For further discussion, see Kobsa and Wahlster (1988).

DISCUSSION AND CONCLUSIONS

If there is any criticism to be leveled at the wide variety of current research, it is that the formal systems have not been sufficiently informed by psychology (and, hence, behave more like logicians than like ordinary people), and the psychological theories have not been flexible enough to handle some of the logical subtleties (which ordinary people, perhaps with some instruction, are certainly capable of). What is needed is a robust system whose input–output performance (if not the intervening algorithms) is psychologically plausible but whose underlying logic is competent, if needed, to handle the important (if often ignored) formal subtleties.

In spite of radically differing approaches and terminology, it seems clear that AI research into belief systems shares common issues and goals. This can be brought out by discussing Abelson's (1979) characterization of a belief system. For Abelson, a "system" is a "network of interrelated concepts and propositions" and rules, with procedures for accessing and manipulating them. Such a system is a "belief system" if:

1. The system's elements are not consensual.

This can be taken, perhaps, either as a rejection of $\mathbf{B}p \rightarrow p$ or as Wilks and Bien's heuristics. By contrast, a "knowledge system" *would* be consensual. Abelson urges that 1 be exploited by AI belief systems even though it makes them nongeneralizable.

2. The system is concerned with existence questions about certain conceptual objects.

The need to have a logic of the intensional objects of belief may be seen as a version of 2, even though 1 and 2 make it difficult to deal with beliefs that *are* held in common.

3. The system includes representations of "alternative worlds."

This desideratum may be taken as covering the notions of possible worlds and of nested and mutual beliefs.

4. The system relies on evaluative and affective components.
5. The system includes episodic material.

A "knowledge system" would rely more on general knowledge and principles. Clearly, though, a full system would need both.

6. The system's boundaries are vague.

7. The system's elements are held with different degrees of certitude.

Although these criteria are psychologically oriented, many of them are also applicable to formal approaches. In particular, 1–3 and 7 are relevant to logical issues; 4–7 are relevant to psychological issues.

Indeed, except for the choice of underlying logic, most of the systems discussed here seem compatible, their differences arising from differences in aim and focus. For instance, Abelson and Reich's implicational molecules could be among the ν rules in Konolige's system. Note that the rules do not have to be "logical" if they do not need to be consistent; moreover, as mentioned earlier, there might not be any (psychologically plausible) logic of belief. As a consequence, a psychologically plausible belief system, whether "formal" or not, must be able to deal with incompatible beliefs. This could be done by a belief revision mechanism or by representational or reasoning techniques that prevent the system from becoming "aware" of its inconsistencies (with, of course, occasional exceptions, as in real life). It is, thus, the general schemes for representation and reasoning that seem most important and upon which, as a foundation, specific psychological heuristics may be built.

In this way, too, it may be possible to overcome the computational complexity that is inevitably introduced when the underlying inference package is made to be as powerful as envisaged by, say, Konolige or when the underlying representational scheme is made to be as complete as proposed by, say, Shapiro and colleagues (Maida and Shapiro, 1982; Rapaport, 1985, 1986; Rapaport and Shapiro, 1984; Shapiro and Rapaport, 1987). A psychologically adequate "shell" that would be efficient at handling ordinary situations could be built on top of a logically adequate "core" that was capable of overriding the shell if necessary for correct interpretation.

The trade-offs between psychological and logical adequacy that have been made in most current systems can, in principle, be overcome. (They have, after all, been overcome in those humans who study the logic of belief yet have not been hindered from interacting in ordinary conversational situations.) Whether it is more feasible to make a formally adequate system psychologically adequate or to "teach" a psychologically adequate system to be logically subtle remains an interesting research issue.

BIBLIOGRAPHY

R. P. Abelson, "The Structure of Belief Systems," in R. C. Schank and K. M. Colby, eds., *Computer Models of Thought and Language*, W. H. Freeman, San Francisco, Calif., 1973, pp. 287–339.

R. P. Abelson, "Differences Between Belief and Knowledge Systems," *Cogn. Sci.* **3**, 355–366 (1979).

R. P. Abelson and C. M. Reich, "Implicational Molecules: A Method for Extracting Meaning from Input Sentences," *Proc. of the First IJCAI*, Washington, D.C., 1969, pp. 641–647.

G. Airenti, B. G. Bara, and M. Colombetti, "Knowledge and Belief as Logical Levels of Representation," *Proc. Cogn. Sci. Soc.* **4**, 212–214 (1982).

J. F. Allen, "Towards a General Theory of Action and Time," *Artif. Intell.* **23**, 123–154 (1984).

J. F. Allen and C. R. Perrault, "Analyzing Intention in Utterances," *Artif. Intell.* **15**, 143–178 (1980).

A. R. Anderson and N. D. Belnap, Jr., *Entailment: The Logic of Relevance and Necessity*, Princeton University Press, Princeton, N.J., 1975.

D. E. Appelt, "A Planner for Reasoning about Knowledge and Action," *Proceedings of the First National Conference on AI*, Stanford, Calif., 1980, pp. 131–133.

D. E. Appelt, "Planning Natural-Language Utterances," *Proceedings of the Second National Conference on AI*, Pittsburgh, Penn., 1982, pp. 59–62.

J. A. Barnden, "Intensions as Such: An Outline," *Proceedings of the Eighth IJCAI*, Karlsruhe, FRG, 1983, pp. 280–286.

J. A. Barnden, "Imputations and Explications: Representational Problems in Treatments of Propositional Attitudes," *Cogn. Sci.* **10**, 319–364 (1986).

J. A. Barnden, "Towards a Paradigm Shift in Belief Representation Methodology," *Journal of Experimental and Theoretical Artificial Intelligence* **2**, 133–161 (1989).

J. S. Bień, "Towards a Multiple Environments Model of Natural Language," *Proc. of the Fourth IJCAI*, Tbilisi, Georgia, 1975, pp. 379–382.

M. Boden, *Artificial Intelligence and Natural Man*, Basic Books, New York, 1977.

B. C. Bruce, *Belief Systems and Language Understanding*, BBN Report No. 2973, 1975.

H.-N. Castañeda, review of Hintikka, 1962, *J. Symbolic Logic* **29**, 132–134 (1964).

H.-N. Castañeda, "Indicators and Quasi-Indicators," *American Philosophical Quarterly* **4**, 85–100 (1967).

H.-N. Castañeda, "Thinking and the Structure of the World," *Philosophia* **4**, 3–40 (1974). Originally written in 1972; reprinted in 1975 in *Critica* **6**, 43–86 (1972).

H. H. Clark and C. R. Marshall, "Definite Reference and Mutual Knowledge," in A. Joshi, B. Webber, and I. Sag, eds., *Elements of Discourse Understanding*, Cambridge University Press, Cambridge, U.K., 1981, pp. 10–63.

P. R. Cohen and H. J. Levesque, "Speech Acts and the Recognition of Shared Plans," *CSCSI* **3**, 263–271, 1980.

P. R. Cohen and H. J. Levesque, "Intention is Choice with Commitment," *Artif. Intell.* **42**, 213–261 (1990).

P. R. Cohen and C. R. Perrault, "Elements of a Plan-based Theory of Speech Acts," *Cogn. Sci.* **3**, 177–212 (1979); reprinted in B. L. Webber and N. J. Nilsson, eds., *Readings in Artificial Intelligence*, Tioga, Palo Alto, Calif., 1981, pp. 478–495.

K. M. Colby, "Simulations of Belief Systems," in R. C. Schank and K. M. Colby, eds., *Computer Models of Thought and Language*, W. H. Freeman, San Francisco, Calif., 1973, pp. 251–286.

K. M. Colby, "Modeling a Paranoid Mind," *Behav. Brain Sci.* **4**, 515–560 (1981).

K. M. Colby, F. D. Hilf, S. Weber, and H. C. Kraemer, "Turing-like Indistinguishability Tests for the Validation of a Computer Simulation of Paranoid Processes," *Artif. Intell.* **3**, 199–221 (1972).

K. M. Colby and D. C. Smith, "Dialogues Between Humans and an Artificial Belief System," *Proceedings of the First IJCAI*, Washington, D.C., 1969, pp. 319–324.

K. M. Colby, S. Weber, and F. Dennis Hilf, "Artificial Paranoia," *Artif. Intell.* **2**, 1–25 (1971).

A. R. Covington and L. K. Schubert, "Organization of Modally

Embedded Propositions and of Dependent Concepts," *Proc. CSCSI*, **3**, 87–94 (1980).

L. G. Creary, "Propositional Attitudes: Fregean Representation and Simulative Reasoning," *Proceedings of the Sixth IJCAI*, Tokyo, 1979, pp. 176–181.

P. Edwards, ed., *Encyclopedia of Philosophy*, Macmillan and Free Press, New York, 1967.

J. H. Fetzer, "On Defining 'Knowledge'," *AI Mag.* **6**, 19 (Spring 1985).

R. E. Filman, J. Lamping, and F. S. Montalvo, "Meta-language and Meta-reasoning," *Proceedings of the Eighth IJCAI*, Karlsruhe, FRG, 1983, pp. 365–369.

G. Frege, "On Sense and Reference" (1892), translated by M. Black in P. Geach and M. Black, eds., *Translations from the Philosophical Writings of Gottlob Frege*, Basil Blackwell, Oxford, U.K., 1970, pp. 56–78.

E. L. Gettier, "Is Justified True Belief Knowledge?," *Analysis* **23**, 121–123 (1963); reprinted in A. P. Griffiths, ed., *Knowledge and Belief*, Oxford University Press, Oxford, 1967.

J. Y. Halpern, ed., *Theoretical Aspects of Reasoning About Knowledge: Proceedings of the 1986 Conference, Monterey, Calif.*, Morgan-Kaufmann, Los Altos, Calif., 1986a.

J. Y. Halpern, "Reasoning About Knowledge: An Overview," in J. Y. Halpern, ed., *Theoretical Aspects of Reasoning About Knowledge*, Morgan-Kaufmann, Los Altos, Calif., 1986b, pp. 1–17.

J. Y. Halpern and D. A. McAllester, "Likelihood, Probability, and Knowledge," IBM Research Report RJ 4313 (47141), 1984; shorter version in *Proceedings of the Fourth National Conference on AI*, Austin, Texas, 1984, pp. 137–141.

G. G. Hendrix, "Encoding Knowledge in Partitioned Networks," in N. V. Findler, ed., *Associative Networks*, Academic Press, New York, pp. 51–92, 1979.

J. Hintikka, *Knowledge and Belief: An Introduction to the Logic of the Two Notions*, Cornell University Press, Ithaca, N.Y., 1962.

J. Hintikka, "Semantics for Propositional Attitudes," in J. W. Davis and co-workers, eds., *Philosophical Logic*, D. Reidel, Dordrecht, 1969, pp. 21–45, reprinted in Linsky, 1977, pp. 145–167.

A. Kobsa, "VIE-DPM: A User Model in a Natural-Language Dialogue System," in *Proceedings of the 8th German Workshop on Artificial Intelligence*, Berlin, 1984a.

A. Kobsa, "Three Steps in Constructing Mutual Belief Models from User Assertions," in *Proceedings of the 6th European Conference on Artificial Intelligence*, Pisa, Italy, 1984b.

A. Kobsa, "Generating a User Model from Wh-Questions in the VIE-LANG System," in *Proceedings of GLDV Meeting on Trends in Linguistischer Datenverarbeitung*, 1984c.

A. Kobsa and H. Trost, "Representing belief models in semantic networks," *Cybern. Sys. Res.* **2**, 753–757 (1984).

A. Kobsa and W. Wahlster, eds., "User Modeling," special issue, *Computational Linguistics* 14(3), 1988.

K. Konolige, "Circumscriptive Ignorance," *Proceedings of the Second National Conference on AI*, Pittsburgh, Penn., 1982, pp. 202–204.

K. Konolige, "A Deductive Model of Belief," *Proceedings of the Eighth IJCAI*, Karlsruhe, FRG, 1983, pp. 377–381.

K. Konolige, *Belief and Incompleteness*, CSLI Report No. CSLI-84-4, Stanford University, 1984.

K. Konolige, "What Awareness Isn't: A Sentential View of Implicit and Explicit Belief," in J. Y. Halpern, ed., *Theoretical*

Aspects of Reasoning About Knowledge, Morgan-Kaufmann, San Mateo, Calif., 1986, pp. 241–250.

K. Konolige and N. J. Nilsson, "Multiple-Agent Planning Systems," *Proceedings of the First National Conference on AI*, Stanford, Calif., 1980, pp. 138–144.

H. J. Levesque, "The Interaction with Incomplete Knowledge Bases: A Formal Treatment," *Proceedings of the Seventh IJCAI*, Vancouver, Brit. Col., 1981, pp. 240–245.

H. J. Levesque, "Foundations of a Functional Approach to Knowledge Representation," *Artif. Intell.* **23**, 155–212 (1984a).

H. J. Levesque, "A Logic of Implicit and Explicit Belief," *Proceedings of the Fourth National Conference on AI*, Austin, TX, 1984b, pp. 198–202.

H. J. Levesque, "Making Believers Out of Computers," *Artif. Intell.* **30**, 81–108 (1986a).

H. J. Levesque, "Knowledge Representation and Reasoning," *Annual Review of Computer Science* **1**, 255–287 (1986b).

L. Linsky, ed., *Reference and Modality*, Oxford University Press, Oxford, 1977, corrected edition.

A. S. Maida and S. C. Shapiro, "Intensional Concepts in Propositional Semantic Networks," *Cogn. Sci.* **6**, 291–330 (1982).

A. S. Maida, "Knowing Intensional Individuals, and Reasoning about Knowing Intensional Individuals," *Proceedings of the Eighth IJCAI*, Karlsruhe, FRG, 1983, pp. 382–384.

J. Martins and S. Shapiro, "A Model for Belief Revision," *Artif. Intell.* **35**, 25–79 (1988).

J. McCarthy, "Epistemological Problems of Artificial Intelligence," *Proceedings of the Fifth IJCAI*, Cambridge, Mass., 1977, pp. 1038–1044.

J. McCarthy, M. Sato, T. Hayashi, and S. Igarashi, *On the Model Theory of Knowledge*, Stanford Artificial Intelligence Laboratory Memo AIM-312, Stanford University, 1978.

J. McCarthy, "First-order Theories of Individual Concepts and Propositions," in J. E. Hayes, D. Michie, and L. I. Mikulich, eds., *Machine Intelligence*, Vol. 9, Ellis Horwood, Chichester, UK, pp. 129–147, 1979.

J. McCarthy, "Circumscription—A Form of Non-monotonic Reasoning," *Artif. Intell.* **13**, 27–39 (1980).

J. McCarthy and P. J. Hayes, "Some Philosophical Problems from the Standpoint of Artificial Intelligence," in B. Meltzer and D. Michie, eds., *Machine Intelligence*, Vol. 4, Edinburgh University Press, Edinburgh, pp. 463–502, 1969, reprinted in B. L. Webber and N. J. Nilsson, eds., *Readings in Artificial Intelligence*, Tioga, Palo Alto, Calif., 1981, pp. 431–450.

A. Meinong, "Über Gegenstandstheorie" (1904), in R. Haller, ed., *Alexius Meinong Gesamtausgabe*, Vol. 2, Akademische Druck-u. Verlagsanstalt, Graz, 1971, pp. 481–535. English translation ("The Theory of Objects") by I. Levi and co-workers, in R. M. Chisholm, ed., *Realism and the Background of Phenomenology*, Free Press, New York, 1960, pp. 76–116.

J. Moravcsik, "Comments on Partee's paper," in K. J. J. Hintikka, J. M. E. Moravcsik, and P. Suppes, eds., *Approaches to Natural Language: Proceedings of the 1970 Stanford Workshop on Grammar and Semantics*, D. Reidel, Dordrecht, 1973, pp. 349–369.

R. C. Moore, "D-SCRIPT: A Computational Theory of Descriptions," *Proceedings of the Third IJCAI*, Stanford, Calif., 1973, pp. 223–229.

R. C. Moore, *Reasoning about Knowledge and Action*, Technical Note No. 191, SRI International, Menlo Park, Calif., 1980.

R. C. Moore, "Reasoning about Knowledge and Action," *Proceedings of the Fifth IJCAI*, Cambridge, Mass., 1977, pp. 223–227; reprinted in B. L. Webber and N. J. Nilsson, eds., *Readings in*

Artificial Intelligence, Tioga, Palo Alto, Calif., pp. 473–477, 1981.

R. C. Moore, "Problems in Logical Form," *Proc. ACL* **19**, 117–124 (1981).

R. C. Moore and G. G. Hendrix, "Computational models of belief and the semantics of belief sentences," in S. Peters and E. Saarinen, eds., *Processes, Beliefs, and Questions: Essays on Formal Semantics of Natural Language and Natural Language Processing*, D. Reidel, Dordrecht, pp. 107–127, 1982.

L. Morgenstern, "A First Order Theory of Planning," in J. Y. Halpern, ed., *Theoretical Aspects of Reasoning about Knowledge*, Morgan-Kaufmann, Los Altos, Calif., 1986, pp. 99–114.

G. Nadathur and A. K. Joshi, "Mutual Beliefs in Conversational Systems: Their Role in Referring Expressions," *Proceedings of the Eighth IJCAI*, Karlsruhe, FRG, 1983, pp. 603–605.

T. D. Parsons, "Frege's Hierarchies of Indirect Senses and the Paradox of Analysis," in P. A. French and co-workers, eds., *Midwest Studies in Philosophy* **6**, 3–57 (1981).

B. H. Partee, "The Semantics of Belief-Sentences," in K. J. J. Hintikka, J. M. E. Moravcsik, and P. Suppes, eds., *Approaches to Natural Language: Proceedings of the 1970 Stanford Workshop on Grammar and Semantics*, D. Reidel, Dordrecht, 1973, pp. 309–336.

B. H. Partee, "Belief-Sentences and the Limits of Semantics," in S. Peters and E. Saarinen, eds., *Processes, Beliefs, and Questions: Essays on Formal Semantics of Natural Language and Natural Language Processing*, D. Reidel, Dordrecht, 1982, pp. 87–106.

C. R. Perrault and P. R. Cohen, "It's for Your Own Good: A Note on Inaccurate Reference," in A. Joshi, B. Webber, and I. Sag, eds., *Elements of Discourse Understanding*, Cambridge University Press, Cambridge, U.K., 1981, pp. 217–230.

W. J. Rapaport, "Meinongian Theories and a Russellian Paradox," *Noûs* **12**, 153–180 (1978); errata, **13**, 125 (1979).

W. J. Rapaport, "Meinongian Semantics for Propositional Semantic Networks," *Proc. ACL* **23**, 43–48 (1985).

W. J. Rapaport, "Logical Foundations for Belief Representation," *Cogn. Sci.* **10**, 371–422 (1986).

W. J. Rapaport, Review of J. Y. Halpern, ed., *Theoretical Aspects of Reasoning about Knowledge*, in *J. Symbolic Logic* **53**, 660–670 (1988).

W. J. Rapaport and S. C. Shapiro, "Quasi-indexical Reference in Propositional Semantic Networks," *Proceedings of COLING-84*, 1984, pp. 65–70.

E. Rich, "Building and Exploiting User Models," *Proceedings of the Sixth IJCAI*, Tokyo, 1979a, pp. 720–722.

E. Rich, "User Modeling via Stereotypes," *Cog. Sci.* **3**, 329–354 (1979b).

M. Sato, *A Study of Kripke-Type Models for Some Modal Logics by Gentzen's Sequential Method*, Kyoto University Research Institute for Mathematical Sciences, Kyoto, 1976.

P. F. Schneider, "Contexts in PSN," *Proc. CSCSI*, **3**, 71–78 (1980).

J. R. Searle, "What is a Speech Act?," in M. Black, ed., *Philosophy in America*, Allen and Unwin, London, 1965, pp. 221–239; reprinted in J. R. Searle (ed.), *The Philosophy of Language*, Oxford University Press, Oxford, 1971, pp. 39–53.

P. Sells, "Aspects of Logophoricity," *Linguistic Inquiry* **18**, 445–479 (1987).

S. C. Shapiro and W. J. Rapaport, "SNePS Considered as a Fully Intensional Propositional Semantic Network," in N. Cercone and G. McCalla, eds., *The Knowledge Frontier: Essays in the Representation of Knowledge*, Springer-Verlag, New York, 1987, pp. 262–315.

C. L. Sidner, "What the Speaker Means: The Recognition of Speakers' Plans in Discourse," in N. Cercone, ed., *Computational Linguistics*, Pergamon Press, Oxford, 1983, pp. 71–82.

C. L. Sidner and D. J. Israel, "Recognizing Intended Meaning and Speaker's Plans," *Proceedings of the Seventh IJCAI*, Vancouver, Brit. Col., 1981, pp. 203–208.

B. C. Smith, "Varieties of Self-Reference," in J. Y. Halpern, ed., *Theoretical Aspects of Reasoning about Knowledge*, Morgan Kaufmann, Los Altos, Calif., 1986, pp. 19–43.

S. Soulhi, "Representing Knowledge about Knowledge and Mutual Knowledge," *Proceedings of COLING-84*, 1984, pp. 194–199.

G. B. Taylor and S. B. Whitehill, "A belief representation for understanding deception," *Proceedings of the Seventh IJCAI*, Vancouver, Brit. Col., 1981, pp. 388–393.

M. Y. Vardi, "On Epistemic Logic and Logical Omniscience," in J. Y. Halpern, ed., *Theoretical Aspects of Reasoning about Knowledge*, Morgan Kaufmann, Los Altos, Calif., 1986, pp. 293–305.

J. Weizenbaum, "Automating psychotherapy," *ACM Forum*, **17**, 543 (1974); reprinted with replies, *CACM* **26**, 28 (1983).

J. M. Wiebe and W. J. Rapaport, "Representing *De Re* and *De Dicto* Belief Reports in Discourse and Narrative," *Proc. IEEE* **74**, 1405–1413 (1986).

Y. Wilks, "Default Reasoning and Self-Knowledge," *Proc. IEEE* **74**, 1399–1404 (1986).

Y. Wilks and J. Bien, "Speech Acts and Multiple Environments," *Proceedings of the Sixth IJCAI*, Tokyo, 1979, pp. 968–970.

Y. Wilks and J. Bien, "Beliefs, Points of View, and Multiple Environments," *Cogn. Sci.* **7**, 95–116 (1983).

Y. Wilks, A. Ballim, and E. Dietrich, "Pronouns in Mind: Quasi-Indexicals and the 'Language of Thought'," *Computers and Artificial Intelligence* **8**, 493–503 (1989).

M. Xiwen and G. Weide, "W-JS: A Modal Logic of Knowledge," *Proceedings of the Eighth IJCAI*, Karlsruhe, FRG, 1983, pp. 398–401.

W. J. RAPAPORT
SUNY Buffalo

BELIEF REVISION

The ability to reason about and adapt to a changing environment is an important aspect of intelligent behavior. Most computer programs constructed by researchers in AI maintain a model of their environment (external and/or internal environment) that is updated to reflect the perceived changes in the environment. One reason for model updating is the detection of contradictory information about the environment. The conventional approach to handling contradictions consists of changing the most recent decision made (*chronological backtracking*) (see BACK-TRACKING). An alternative solution, *dependency-directed backtracking*, consists of changing not the last choice made, but an assumption that provoked the unexpected condition. This second approach generated a great deal of research in one area of AI, which became loosely called belief revision.

Belief revision is an area of AI research concerned with the issues of revising sets of beliefs when new information is found to contradict old information. Research topics in belief revision include the study of representation of beliefs, in particular how to represent the notion of belief dependency; the development of methods for selecting the subset of beliefs responsible for contradictions; and the development of techniques to remove some subset of beliefs from the original set of beliefs. The research on belief revision is related to the research on nonmonotonic logic, which aims at capturing parts of the logic of belief revision systems (see REASONING, NONMONOTONIC).

The field of belief revision is usually recognized to have been initiated by Doyle (1978, 1979), who, based on the work of Stallman and Sussman (1977), developed an early domain-independent belief-revision system, although a system which performs belief revision was developed at approximately the same time by London (1978). Following Doyle, several researchers pursued this topic, most of them building on the system of Doyle. Some of the important systems developed for belief revision are: TMS (Doyle, 1978); RUP (McAllester, 1980, 1985); MBR (Martins, 1983; Martins and Shapiro, 1983); and ATMS (de-Kleer, 1986a, 1986b). In the years since, some commercial systems that perform belief revision have become available, eg, DUCK from Smart Systems Technology, ART from Inference Corp. (1985); and LOOPS (qv) from Xerox.

ROOTS OF THE PROBLEM IN AI

Belief revision systems are AI programs that deal with contradictions. They work with a knowledge base, containing propositions about the state of the environment, performing reasoning from the propositions in the knowledge base, and "filtering" the propositions in the knowledge base so that only part of the knowledge base is perceived: the set of propositions which is under consideration. This set of propositions is usually called the set of believed propositions. When the belief revision system switches from one of these sets to another, we say that it changes its beliefs. Typically, belief revision systems explore alternatives, make choices, explore the consequences of the choices, and compare the results obtained when using different choices. If during this process a contradiction is detected, the belief revision system revises the knowledge base, "erasing" some propositions so that it gets rid of the contradiction. Belief revision systems have their roots both in the problems raised during search and in the frame problem of McCarthy and Hayes (1969).

The frame problem (McCarthy and Hayes, 1969; Hayes, 1973; Raphael, 1971) is the problem of deciding which conditions change and which conditions do not change when a system undergoes some modification. The basis of the problem is that although it is possible to specify the ways in which a system's environment might change, in terms of the effects of actions, it still remains to specify some way of deciding what stays unchanged in face of the actions.

Early systems approaching these problems [eg, STRIPS (qv) Fikes and Nilsson, 1971) and PLANNER (qv) (Hewitt, 1972; Sussman and co-workers, 1971)] basically worked in the same way: for each of the actions allowed,

there was a list of conditions which were deleted by the action and a list of conditions which were added by the action. When one action was executed, the conditions associated with these lists would be added to and deleted from the knowledge base. Insofar as the revision of the model of the environment is concerned, this approach presents two problems. First, the conditions to be added and deleted have to be carefully tailored as a set to avoid unintended infinite loops of adding and deleting information to the knowledge base; and second, if one proposition depends on another one that is deleted by some action, then the former may be kept in the knowledge base if it is not part of the set of propositions explicitly deleted by the action.

An alternative approach, *context-layered knowledge bases,* divides the knowledge base into smaller knowledge bases so that the consequences of the effect of an action can be grouped with a reference back to a causing action. Such an approach was taken by Fikes (1975), who stores situations of a model in a tree, the context tree, in which each node represents a situation. The root of the context tree represents the initial situation. Since most of the information in a given situation is the same as the information in the previous situation, as a matter of space efficiency, only the differences between the new situation and the old one are actually stored in the node of the context tree representing the new situation. Actions have the effect of creating a new situation in the context tree or returning to some previous situation. Fikes's approach presents the following drawbacks: the propositions about a given situation of the model are scattered along a path in the context tree, and there is no record of the sequence of actions performed. Similar approaches were taken in Fahlman (1974); Hayes (1975); McDermott and Sussman (1972); and Rulifson and co-workers (1972).

A new research direction was created by Stallman and Sussman (1977), who designed a system called EL in which dependencies of propositions are permanently recorded. EL maintains a complete record (trace) of its reasoning, using it both to decide which choices to make when something goes wrong and to explain its line of reasoning. Along with each derived proposition, EL stores the set of all propositions directly used in its derivation and the rule of inference used to derive it, ie, the dependency record of the proposition.

EL solves electric circuit problems. While searching for the values of the circuit parameters, EL may have to "guess" the operating range of some devices. Later, if an inconsistency is found, EL knows that somewhere along its way it guessed a wrong state for some device. The novelty of EL's approach to backtracking is that the assumption that is changed during backtracking does not necessarily correspond to the last choice made, but rather to the assumption that provoked the inconsistency (dependency-directed backtracking). When an inconsistency is detected, EL searches through the chain of dependency records of the inconsistent propositions until it finds all the assumptions upon which the inconsistent propositions depend. This set of assumptions is recorded as leading to a contradiction and is never tried again. Then heuristics are used to select one of them to rule out.

Stallman and Sussman's work (1977) had two major influences in AI: it opened a new perspective on the handling of alternatives (dependency-directed backtracking), and it triggered the research on belief revision systems.

EXPLICIT CONCERN ABOUT REVISING BELIEFS

Building upon Stallman and Sussman's work, Doyle (1978, 1979) designed the truth maintenance systems (qv) (TMSs), the first domain-independent belief revision systems. A TMS maintains a knowledge base of propositions, each of which is explicitly marked as believed or disbelieved. A TMS may be told that some propositions are contradictory, in which case it automatically revises its beliefs so that no inconsistent propositions are simultaneously believed.

TMSs are based on the definition of two kinds of objects: propositions and justifications. Justifications represent the reasons that a TMS believes or disbelieves a certain proposition. Attached to each proposition in the knowledge base is one or more justification(s) that support the TMS's belief or disbelief in the proposition. Although Doyle (1979, pp. 239–244) points out the usefulness of four types of justification, he implemented mainly one type, the SL (support list) justifications. This type of justification contains two lists of propositions, the *inlist* and the *outlist*. The proposition supported by an SL justification is believed if and only if every proposition in its inlist is believed and every proposition in its outlist is disbelieved. Whenever one proposition is derived, it is justified by an SL justification containing all the propositions directly used in its derivation and the rule of inference used to derive it.

Based on the SL-justifications, there are two distinct types of propositions in TMSs: premises are propositions whose current SL-justification has empty inlist and empty outlist (premises are always believed); and assumptions are propositions whose current SL-justification has nonempty outlist. Assumptions are propositions whose belief depends on the disbelief in other propositions. A TMS may be asked to add a new proposition to the knowledge base or to change (add or retract) a justification for a proposition. In either case, the TMS tries to find disbelieved propositions that will be believed by such addition or retraction, and believed propositions that will be disbelieved by the addition or retraction.

In addition, a TMS may be told that two believed propositions are contradictory. In this case the dependency-directed backtracking mechanism is invoked, which will search through the inlists of the propositions in the knowledge base, starting with the SL justifications of the contradictory propositions, until it finds all the assumptions considered by the contradictory propositions. One of those assumptions is selected as the culprit for the contradiction and is disbelieved. To disbelieve this assumption, the TMS believes in one of the propositions referenced in the outlist of the assumption and justifies this proposition with an SL justification whose inlist contains the proposition representing the contradiction. After selecting the culprit for the contradiction, it is necessary to disbelieve all

the propositions depending on it. This is done by following the chain of dependency records and disbelieving each proposition that has no SL justification other than the one that includes the selected culprit in its inlist. This disbelieving process is not as simple as it may seem, owing to the possibility of circular proofs. Suppose, following an example from Charniak and co-workers (1980, p. 197), that the knowledge base contains the following propositions:

$$(\forall x)[\text{Man}(x) \rightarrow \text{Person}(x)]$$

$$(\forall x)[\text{Person}(x) \rightarrow \text{Human}(x)]$$

$$(\forall x)[\text{Human}(x) \rightarrow \text{Person}(x)]$$

Adding Man(Fred) to the knowledge base will cause the derivation of Person(Fred), which in turn will cause the derivation of Human(Fred). The addition of Human(Fred) causes Person(Fred) to be rederived. Figure 1 represents the dependencies among the propositions in the knowledge base.

In Figure 1, the two directed arcs (labeled PR, for premises) pointing to a circle mean that the two propositions at the end of the arcs were combined to produce the proposition that is pointed by the arc leaving that circle (labeled C, for conclusion). The inlist of the SL justification of a proposition pointed by a conclusion arc contains the propositions at the end of the premises arcs leading to that proposition. If there exists a path of arcs from the proposition *A* to the proposition *B*, it means that *B* depends on *A*. In Figure 1, Human(Fred) depends on Person(Fred), which in turn depends on Human(Fred). This is called a circular proof. Suppose now that Man(Fred) is disbelieved. The dependency arcs leaving Man(Fred) lead to Person-(Fred). However, Person(Fred) has another justification and one is faced with the problem of whether to disbelieve

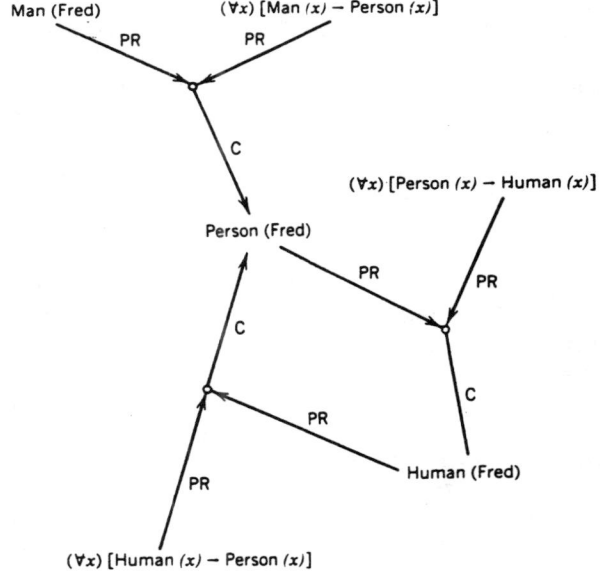

Figure 1. Knowledge base dependencies: PR = premise; C = conclusion.

Person(Fred) since, although one of its justifications is no longer valid, Person(Fred) may still be believed owing to the other justification. Handling circular proofs raises several problems. A discussion of possible solutions to these problems can be found in Doyle (1979) and Charniak and co-workers (1980).

Doyle's research triggered the development of several belief revision systems (McAllester, 1980; Goodwin, 1982; McDermott, 1982; Shrobe, 1979; Thompson, 1979). These systems share two characteristics: they are mainly concerned with implementation issues, paying no special attention to the logic underlying the system; and each proposition is justified by the propositions that directly originated it.

CONCERNS FOR FOUNDATIONS

The early 1980s saw the development of new research directions in belief revision systems, characterized by an explicit concern about the foundations of the systems independent of their implementations (Martins, 1983; Martins and Shapiro, 1983; Doyle, 1982; Goodwin, 1984) and the use of a new type of justification (Martins, 1983; Martins and Shapiro, 1983; deKleer, 1986a, 1986b, 1984). One such system, the multiple belief reasoner (MBR) system of Martins (1983, Martins and Shapiro, 1983), is described here. There are two distinct aspects to consider concerning MBR: the logic underlying the system, and the way the propositions in the knowledge base (generated according to the rules of inference of the logic) are interpreted by MBR.

Any logic underlying belief revision systems must keep track of and determine how to propagate propositional dependencies. The concern for this problem is shared, although for different reasons, with the relevance logicians, whose main goal is to avoid the paradoxes of implication. Relevance logicians developed logics that keep track of and propagate propositional dependencies. The logic underlying MBR, the SWM system, was influenced by the relevance logic of Shapiro and Wand (1976) and by the FR system of Anderson and Belnap (1975). The SWM system associates each proposition with one or more triples, its support, which justifies the existence of the proposition. Each triple contains the following information:

1. The *origin tag* (OT) tells how the proposition was obtained. Propositions can be hypotheses, normally derived propositions, or specially derived propositions (whose derivation sidesteps some of the relevance logic assumptions. This case is not discussed here; see Martins, 1983 for details.)

2. The *origin set* (OS) contains all the hypotheses that were really used in the derivation of the proposition.

3. The *restriction set* (RS) contains every set known to be inconsistent with the proposition's origin set. A set is known to be inconsistent with another if it is inconsistent and a contradiction was in fact derived from that union.

If the same proposition is derived in multiple ways, its support contains multiple triples. The OT and the OS re-

flect the way the proposition was derived. The RS, on the other hand, reflects the current knowledge about how the hypotheses underlying that proposition relate to the other propositions. Once a proposition is derived, its OT and OS remain constant, whereas its RS may change as contradictions are uncovered. The rules of inference of SWM use the RSs to prevent the derivation of propositions whose OSs would be known to be inconsistent.

MBR is a belief-revision system that works with a knowledge base containing propositions generated according to the rules of inference of SWM. In this knowledge base each proposition is associated with a support (in SWM's sense). MBR relies on the notions of context and belief space. A *context* is any set of hypotheses. A context determines a belief space, the set consisting of every proposition whose OS is a subset of the context which defines that belief space. At any moment there is one active context, the current context, and the knowledge base retrieval operations are defined such that they only retrieve the propositions in the belief space defined by the current context. Figure 2 shows MBR's knowledge base originated by the example of the last section. In Figure 2, a circle pointed to by an arc labeled DO (derivation origin) represents the support of the proposition at the end of the arc. Note that Person (Fred) has two supports. The arcs labeled OS leaving the support point to the hypotheses from which the proposition was derived. Since each proposition is directly connected with the hypotheses that underly it, there are no circular proofs.

When a contradiction is detected, the origin sets of the contradictory propositions are inspected, and their union becomes a set known to be inconsistent. Every proposition in the knowledge base whose origin set is not disjoint from this newly discovered inconsistent set has its restriction set updated in order to reflect the current knowledge about inconsistent sets in the knowledge base.

In MBR's implementation, there is a considerable amount of sharing between knowledge base structures, namely, origin sets and restriction sets, which is possible because SWM's formalism guarantees that two propositions with the same OS have the same RS as well.

JUSTIFICATION-BASED VS ASSUMPTION-BASED SYSTEMS

Any belief revision system must keep a record of where each proposition in the knowledge base came from. These records are inspected while searching for the culprit of a contradiction. There are two ways to record the origin of propositions, corresponding to justification-based and assumption-based systems (de Kleer, 1984). In justification-based systems, each proposition contains information about the propositions that directly originated it. This approach was used in Doyle (1978, 1979); McAllester (1980); Goodwin (1982); McDermott (1982); Shroge (1979); and Thompson (1979). In assumption-based systems, each proposition contains information about the hypotheses (nonderived propositions) that originated it. This approach was taken in Martins (1983); Martins and Shapiro (1983); de Kleer (1986a, 1986b, 1984).

Assumption-based systems present several advantages

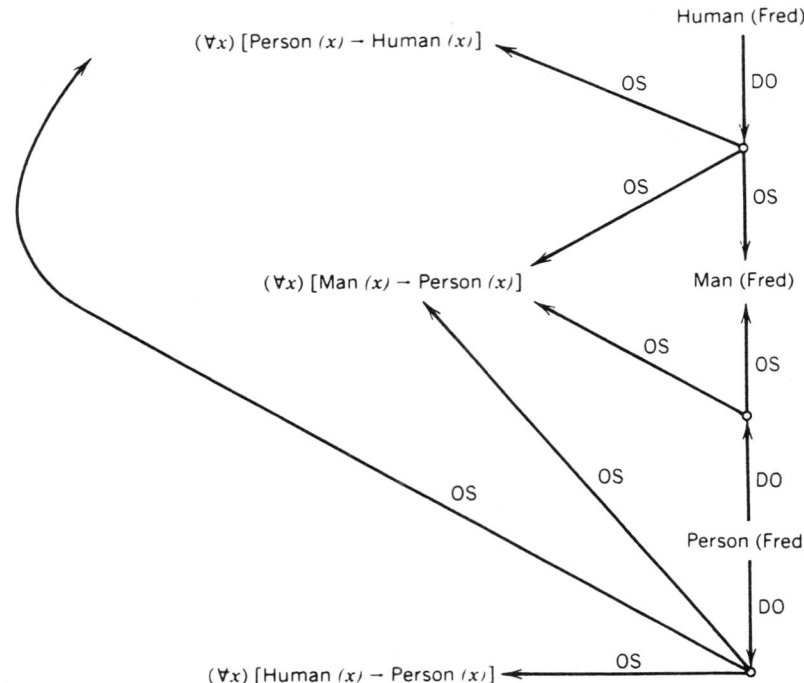

Figure 2. Knowledge base dependencies: DO = derivation origin; OS = origin set.

over justification-based systems. These advantages are exemplified by a comparison of the two systems discussed in this entry, TMS and MBR (see de Kleer, 1984) and are summarized as follows:

1. *Changing set of beliefs.* In TMS changing one set of beliefs into another can be accomplished only upon detection of a contradiction, in which case the dependency-directed backtracking goes through the entire knowledge base, marking and unmarking propositions. In MBR, changing sets of beliefs is done by changing the current context. Afterward the knowledge base retrieval operations will only consider the propositions in the new belief space. There is no marking or unmarking of any kind.

2. *Comparing sets of beliefs.* In TMS it is impossible to examine two sets of beliefs simultaneously. This may be important when one must weigh the outcome of several possible solutions. In MBR several sets of beliefs may coexist; thus, it is simple to compare two solutions.

3. *Backtracking.* TMS relies on the dependency-directed backtracking mechanism, which follows the dependency records, identifying all the assumptions leading to a given contradiction. In MBR there is no backtracking of any kind. Upon detection of a contradiction, all the assumptions underlying that contradiction are directly identifiable (they are the union of the origin sets of the contradictory propositions).

4. *Finding faulty assumptions.* In MBR, upon detection of a contradiction, the hypotheses underlying it are immediately identified, making it easy to compare sets of hypotheses underlying contradictions.

However, using only assumptions as support disables the explanation of the reasoning sequence followed by the

program. The system of de Kleer (1986a, 1986b, 1984) uses both assumptions and justifications, offering the advantages of both approaches.

APPLICATIONS

The capability of determining the source of information coupled with the possibility of changing beliefs are essential features of any intelligent system. In general, any system that has to choose among alternatives can use (and benefit from) the techniques developed by belief revision systems. However, there are some areas in which the techniques discussed in this entry are of paramount importance, some of which are listed below.

1. *Reasoning based on partial information, default assumptions, and potentially inconsistent data.* This kind of reasoning is likely to generate contradictions. Thus, it is of primary importance that the system be able to determine the causes of contradictions, remove them, and after doing so, be able to find every proposition in the knowledge base depending on the selected culprit (see REASONING, DEFAULT).

2. *Learning.* A potential source of learning (see LEARNING, MACHINE) consists of analyzing the mistakes so that the same mistake is not made twice. This calls for belief revision and assignment of credit to the source of the mistake.

3. *Replanning from failures.* In any planning (qv) system, there should be a component that analyzes sources of problems and prevents the generation of a plan that leads to trouble. Again, belief revision techniques can be used to detect the source of the problems and to prevent the generation of ill-formed plans.

4. *Reasoning about the beliefs of other agents.* Any program that reasons about the beliefs of other agents (see BELIEF REPRESENTATION SYSTEMS) should maintain a clear-cut distinction between its beliefs and the beliefs of the others. Belief revision techniques contribute to this application in their concerns with the changing of belief spaces. The program must be able to change belief spaces, must know which belief space is being considered, and must fail to consider the information from the other belief space(s).

5. *Systems for natural language understanding* (qv), in which one needs to consider several competing interpretations of a sentence, and *vision*, in which one needs to revise hypotheses about the contents of images.

6. *Qualitative reasoning,* a kind of reasoning that requires making choices among alternatives (see, eg, Williams, 1983).

7. *Systems that select between design alternatives,* which may have to change choices made.

8. *Diagnoses* (see MEDICINE, AI IN).

It should be kept in mind, however, that belief revision is only applicable in cases where credit for consequences of choices is assignable.

References to other work in the domain of belief revision (both in AI and in other disciplines) can be found in Doyle and London (1980), which presents an extensive reference list. de Kleer (1984) and de Kleer and Doyle (1982) present an excellent discussion of belief revision techniques and problems. Doyle (1979) and Martins (1983) give overviews of the field and discuss in detail the two systems presented here, TMS and MBR, respectively.

BIBLIOGRAPHY

A. Anderson and N. Belnap, *Entailment: The Logic of Relevance and Necessity,* Vol. 1, Princeton University Press, Princeton, N.J., 1975.

E. Charniak, C. Riesbeck, and D. McDermott, *Artificial Intelligence Programming,* Lawrence Erlbaum Associates, Hillsdale, N.J., 1980.

B. D. Clayton, "ART Programming Primer," Inference Corporation, April 1985.

J. de Kleer, "Choices Without Backtracking," *Proceedings of the Fourth National Conference on AI,* Austin, Texas, AAAI, Menlo Park, Calif., 1984.

J. de Kleer, "An Assumption-Based TMS," *Artif. Intell.* **28** (1986a).

J. de Kleer, "Problem Solving with the ATMS," *Artif. Intell.* **28** (1986b).

J. de Kleer and J. Doyle, "Dependencies and Assumptions," in *The Handbook of Artificial Intelligence,* Vol. 2, A. Barr and E. Feigenbaum, eds., William Kaufmann, Inc., Los Altos, Calif., 1982, pp. 72–76.

J. Doyle, "Truth Maintenance Systems for Problem Solving," Technical Report AI-TR-419, MIT AI Laboratory, Cambridge, Mass., 1978.

J. Doyle, "A Truth Maintenance System," *Aftif. Intell.* **12,** 231–272 (1979).

J. Doyle, "Some Theories of Reasoned Assumptions," Carnegie Mellon University, Pittsburgh, Penn., 1982.

J. Doyle and P. London, "A Selected Descriptor-Indexed Bibliography to the Literature on Belief Revision," *SIGART Newslett.* **71,** 7–23 (1980).

S. Fahlman, "A Planning System for Robot Construction Tasks," *Artif. Intell.* **5,** 1–49 (1974).

R. Fikes and N. Nilsson, "STRIPS: A New Approach to the Application of Theorem Proving to Problem Solving," *Artif. Intell.* **2,** 189–208 (1971).

R. Fikes, "Deductive Retrieval Mechanisms for State Description Models," *Proceedings of the Fourth IJCAI,* Tbilisi, USSR, 1975, pp. 99–106.

J. Goodwin, "An Improved Algorithm for Non-Monotonic Dependency Net Update," Technical Report LITH-MAT-R-82-23, Department of Computer and Information Science, Linköping University, Linköping, Sweden, 1982.

J. Goodwin, "WATSON: A Dependency Directed Inference System," *Proceedings of the Non-monotonic Reasoning Workshop,* AAAI, Menlo Park, Calif., pp. 103–114, 1984.

P. J. Hayes, "The Frame Problem and Related Problems in Artificial Intelligence," in B. Elithorn and B. Jones, eds., *Artificial and Human Thinking,* Jossey-Bass, San Francisco, Calif., pp. 45–59, 1973.

P. J. Hayes, "A Representation for Robot Plans, *Proceedings of the Fourth IJCAI,* Tbilisi, USSR, 1975, pp. 181–188.

C. Hewitt, *Description and Theoretical Analysis of PLANNER: A Language for Proving Theorems and Manipulating Models in a Robot,* Technical Report TR-258, MIT, Cambridge, MA, 1972.

P. London, *Dependency Networks as Representation for Modelling in General Problem Solvers,* Technical Report 698, Department of Computer Science, University of Maryland, College Park, 1978.

D. McAllester, *An Outlook on Truth Maintenance,* AI Memo 551, MIT AI Laboratory, Cambridge, Mass., 1980.

D. McAllester, "A Widely Used Truth Maintenance System," unpublished, MIT, Cambridge, Mass., 1985.

J. McCarthy and P. Hayes, "Some Philosophical Problems from the Standpoint of Artificial Intelligence," in B. Meltzer and D. Michie, eds., *Machine Intelligence,* Vol. 4, Edinburgh University Press, Edinburgh, U.K., pp. 463–502, 1969.

D. McDermott and G. Sussman, *The CONNIVER Reference Manual,* Technical Report Memo 259, MIT, Cambridge, Mass., 1972.

D. McDermott, *Contexts and Data Dependencies: A Synthesis,* Department of Computer Science, Yale University, New Haven, Conn., 1982.

J. Martins, *Reasoning in Multiple Belief Spaces,* Technical Report 203, Department of Computer Science, State University of New York at Buffalo, 1983.

J. Martins and S. C. Shapiro, "Reasoning in Multiple Belief Spaces," *Proceedings of the Eighth IJCAI,* Karlsruhe, FRG, 1983, pp. 370–373.

B. Raphael, "The Frame Problem in Problem Solving Systems," in N. Findler and B. Meltzer, eds., *Artificial Intelligence and Heuristic Programming,* Elsevier, New York, pp. 159–169, 1971.

J. Rulifson, J. Derksen, and R. Waldinger, *QA4: A Procedural Calculus for Intuitive Reasoning,* Technical Report Note 73, SRI International, Menlo Park, Calif., 1972.

S. C. Shapiro and M. Wand, *The Relevance of Relevance,* Technical Report 46, Computer Science Department, Indiana University, Bloomington, 1976.

H. Shrobe, "Dependency-Directed Reasoning in the Analysis of Programs Which Modify Complex Data Structures," *Proceedings of the Sixth IJCAI,* Tokyo, pp. 829–835, 1979.

R. M. Stallman and G. J. Sussman, "Forward Reasoning and Dependency-Directed Backtracking in a System for Computer-Aided Circuit Analysis," *Artif. Intell.* **9,** 135–196 (1977).

G. Sussman, T. Winograd, and E. Charniak, *MICRO-PLANNER Reference Manual,* Technical Report Memo 203, MIT, Cambridge, Mass., 1971.

A. Thompson, "Network Truth Maintenance for Deduction and Modeling," *Proceedings of the Sixth IJCAI,* Tokyo, 1979, pp. 877–879.

B. C. Williams, "Qualitative Analysis of MOS Circuits," Technical Report TR-567, MIT AI Lab, Cambridge, Mass., 1983.

J. MARTINS
Instituto Superior Tecnico,
Lisbon

BELLE

A chess-playing system (see COMPUTER CHESS AND SEARCH) developed at Bell Laboratories by Condon and Thompson, BELLE won the World Computer Chess Championship in 1983 and was rated at the master level. The system contains specialized hardware (see P. Frey, ed., *Chess Skill in Man and Machine,* Springer-Verlag, New York, 1980).

KENNETH THOMPSON
AT&T Bell Laboratories

BEST-FIRST SEARCH. See SEARCH, BEST-FIRST.

BIDIRECTIONAL SEARCH. See SEARCH, BIDIRECTIONAL.

BINARY RESOLUTION. See RESOLUTION, BINARY.

BIOLOGY, AI IN. See PROTEIN STRUCTURE PREDICTION.

BLACKBOARD SYSTEMS

Blackboard systems are domain-specific problem solving systems that exploit the blackboard architecture and exhibit a characteristically incremental and opportunistic problem solving style. The blackboard architecture was developed by Erman, Hayes-Roth, Lesser, and Reddy for the HEARSAY-II speech understanding system (Erman, 1980). Since then, it has been exploited in a wide range of knowledge-based systems and psychological simulations (eg, Hanson, 1978; Nagao, 1979; Rose, 1981; McClelland, 1981; Rumelhart, 1982). Four illustrative blackboard systems, HEARSAY-II, HASP, CRYSALIS, and OPM, and important architectural variations they introduce, are described below. Four blackboard system building environments, HEARSAY-III, AGE, BB1, and GBB, are reviewed. Current research directions in blackboard system architectures are also summarized.

THE BLACKBOARD ARCHITECTURE

Motivating Objectives

The blackboard architecture was designed to achieve several objectives that emerged in the HEARSAY-II speech-understanding project and reappear in a broad range of problem-solving domains:

1. *To reduce the combinatorics of search* (qv). Even with a restricted vocabulary and domain of discourse, the speech-understanding (qv) problem entailed a space of possible utterances too large for conventional search techniques.

2. *To incorporate diverse sorts of knowledge in a single problem-solving system.* The speech-understanding problem brought with it several sorts of knowledge (eg, about syntax, phonetics, word transition probabilities), but no method for integrating them in a single program.

3. *To compensate for unreliability in the available knowledge.* Much of the available speech-understanding knowledge was heuristics (qv).

4. *To compensate for uncertainty in the available data.* The acoustic signal for speech is inherently ambiguous, occurs against a noisy background, and incorporates idiosyncrasies in the speaker's articulation, diction, grammar, and conceptualization of utterances.

5. *To apply available knowledge intelligently in the absence of a known problem-solving algorithm.* Much of the available speech-understanding knowledge was simultaneously applicable, supporting multiple potential inferences from each intermediate problem-solving state but providing no known algorithm to guide the inference process.

6. *To support cooperative system development among multiple system builders.* Approximately seven individuals cooperated to design and implement HEARSAY-II.

7. *To support system experimentation, modification, and evolution.* Because HEARSAY-II was an experimental research effort, all aspects of the system evolved gradually over a period of several years.

Defining Features

The blackboard architecture has three defining features: a global database called the blackboard, independent knowledge sources that generate solution elements on the blackboard, and a scheduler to control knowledge source activity. These features are described directly below and illustrated with examples from HEARSAY-II, which is also discussed in more detail in a later section.

All solution elements generated during problem solving are recorded in a structured, global database called the blackboard. The blackboard structure organizes solution elements along two dimensions, solution intervals and levels of abstraction. Different solution intervals represent different regions of the solution on some problem-specific dimension, for example, different time intervals in the speech signal. Different levels of abstraction represent the solution in different amounts of detail, for example, the phrases, words, and syllables entailed in the speech signal. Solution elements at particular blackboard locations are linked to supporting elements in the same solution interval at lower levels. For example, the phrase "Are any by Feigenbaum and Feldman" in interval 1–225 in the speech signal might be supported by the word "Feigenbaum" in interval 70–150 and the syllable "Fa" in interval 70–95.

Solution elements are generated and recorded on the blackboard by independent processes called knowledge sources. Knowledge sources have a condition-action format. The condition describes situations in which the knowledge source can contribute to the problem-solving process. Ordinarily, it requires a particular configuration of solution elements on the blackboard. The action specifies the knowledge source's behavior. Ordinarily, it entails the creation or modification of solution elements on the blackboard. Only knowledge sources whose conditions are satisfied can perform their actions. For example, the knowledge source MOW's condition requires the appearance of new syllable hypotheses on the blackboard. MOW's action generates new word hypotheses encompassing sequential subsets of the syllables.

Knowledge sources may exploit both top-down and bottom-up inference methods (see PROCESSING, BOTTOM-UP AND TOP-DOWN). For example, MOW generates new word hypotheses bottom-up by integrating syllable hypotheses. The knowledge source PREDICT generates new word hypotheses top-down by extending phrase hypotheses. Knowledge sources are independent in that they do not invoke one another and ordinarily have no knowledge of each other's expertise, behavior, or existence. They are cooperative in that they contribute solution elements to a shared problem. They influence one another only indirectly, by anonymously responding to and modifying information recorded on the blackboard.

Although implementations vary, in most blackboard systems knowledge source activity is event-driven. Each change to the blackboard constitutes an event that in the presence of specific other information on the blackboard can trigger (satisfy the condition of) one or more knowledge sources. Each such triggering produces a unique knowledge source activation record (KSAR) representing a unique triggering of a particular knowledge source by a particular blackboard event. Because several KSARs may be triggered simultaneously and compete to execute their actions, a scheduler selects a single KSAR to execute its action on each problem-solving cycle. The scheduler may use a variety of criteria, such as the credibility of a KSAR's triggering information, the reliability of its knowledge source, or the importance of the solution element it would generate. When a KSAR is scheduled, its knowledge source action executes in the context of its triggering information, typically producing new blackboard events. These events may trigger knowledge sources, creating new KSARs to compete for scheduling priority with previously triggered, not yet executed KSARs (see AGENDA-BASED SYSTEMS).

Characteristic Behavior

Blackboard systems construct solutions incrementally. On each problem-solving cycle a single KSAR executes, generating or modifying a small number of solution elements in particular blackboard locations. Along the way, some elements are assembled into growing partial solutions; others may be abandoned. Eventually, a satisfactory configuration of solution elements is assembled into a complete solution, and the problem is solved.

Blackboard systems apply knowledge opportunistically. On each problem-solving cycle, the scheduler uses a set of heuristic criteria to select a KSAR to execute its action. Depending on the heuristics available to the scheduler, this may produce a more or less orderly approach to solving the problem. At one extreme, the scheduler may follow a rigorous procedure, scheduling a planned sequence of KSARs that monotonically assemble compatible solution elements. At the other extreme, it may apply many conflicting heuristics that are extremely sensitive to unanticipated problem-solving states, scheduling KSARs that assemble disparate, competing solution elements out of which a complete solution only gradually emerges.

The Blackboard Architecture's Approach to the Objectives

Each feature of the blackboard architecture is designed to address one or more of the seven objectives introduced above.

1. To reduce the combinatorics of search: first, the blackboard architecture integrates reasoning at multiple levels of abstraction. An application system can solve a simplified version of a problem and then use that solution to guide and limit exploration of a larger space of more detailed solutions (Newell and co-workers, 1959; Stefik and co-workers, 1982). Second, the blackboard architecture provides independent knowledge sources and opportunistic scheduling. As a consequence, an application system can generate and merge independent solution "islands," potentially reducing the search space dramatically (Minsky, 1961; Stefik and Conway, 1982).

2. To incorporate diverse sorts of knowledge in a single problem-solving system: the blackboard architecture permits different knowledge sources to embody qualitatively different sorts of expertise, applying idiosyncratic reasoning processes to idiosyncratic representations. It permits them to operate independently, contributing solution elements when and where they can. Thus, the blackboard architecture finesses the problem of integrating different sorts of knowledge per se. Instead, it integrates the results of applying different sorts of knowledge.

3. To compensate for unreliability in the available knowledge: the blackboard architecture permits multiple knowledge sources to operate redundantly upon the same subproblem. An application system can combine the implications of several unreliable, but redundant knowledge sources to converge upon the most credible solution elements.

4. To compensate for uncertainty in the available data: the blackboard architecture permits different knowledge sources to embody top-down and bottom-up inference methods. An application system can exploit top-down knowledge sources to prune solution elements generated by bottom-up knowledge sources operating upon uncertain data. Conversely, it can exploit bottom-up knowledge sources to prune solution elements generated top-down from uncertain expectations.

5. To apply available knowledge intelligently in the absence of a known problem-solving algorithm: the blackboard architecture provides an opportunistic scheduler that decides, on each problem-solving cycle, which potential action is most promising. The scheduler can integrate multiple, heuristic scheduling criteria. Its decisions depend on the available criteria and the current problem-solving situation.

6. To support cooperative system development among multiple system builders: the blackboard architecture permits functionally independent knowledge sources. Once a blackboard structure and representation of solution elements have been agreed upon, individual system builders can design and develop knowledge sources independently.

7. To support system modification and evolution: first, the blackboard architecture permits functionally independent knowledge sources, which can be added, removed, or modified individually. Second, the architecture makes a sharp distinction between domain knowledge and scheduling. Modifications to knowledge sources need not affect the scheduler. Conversely, experimentation with different scheduling heuristics need not affect any knowledge sources.

FOUR ILLUSTRATIVE BLACKBOARD SYSTEMS

This section describes four blackboard systems: HEARSAY-II, HASP, CRYSALIS, and OPM. These systems illustrate the range of problems attacked within the blackboard architecture and important variations on its major components.

HEARSAY-II. This system (Erman, 1980) interprets single spoken sentences, drawn from a one thousand word vocabulary, that request information from a database. As discussed above, it operates on an ambiguous signal in the presence of acoustic noise complicated by idiosyncrasies in the vocabulary, syntax, pronunciation, and conceptual style of individual speakers. Given training with a speaker's voice, HEARSAY-II interprets requests with 90% accuracy in a factor of ten of real time. HEARSAY-II begins with a parameterized representation of the speech signal and attempts to generate a coherent semantic interpretation of it. Between these two extremes, parameter and database interface, HEARSAY-II generates hypotheses at five additional levels of abstraction: segment, syllable, word, word sequence, and phrase. The blackboard's solution intervals represent different time intervals within the speech signal.

HEARSAY-II has twelve knowledge sources. Most knowledge sources operate bottom-up, inferring hypotheses at one level of abstraction from data or hypotheses at lower levels. For example, the knowledge source MOW hypothesizes all words that encompass sequential subsets of existing syllable hypotheses. A few knowledge sources operate top-down. For example, PREDICT hypothesizes all words that might syntactically precede or follow a given phrase hypothesis. Finally, some knowledge sources operate within a single level of the blackboard. For example, RPOL rates the credibility of each new or modified hypothesis at every level.

In HEARSAY-II, knowledge source conditions and actions are implemented as programs. Because they can be very large programs, both condition matching and action execution are scheduled. When a blackboard event occurs at a knowledge source's blackboard level of interest, it generates a "condition KSAR." When the condition KSAR is scheduled for execution, it runs the knowledge source's condition program. If the condition program concludes successfully, it generates an "action KSAR." When the action KSAR is scheduled for execution, it runs the knowledge source's action program and produces changes on the blackboard.

HEARSAY-II pursues a two-stage strategy. During phase 1, it schedules a sequence of KSARs that operate bottom-up until word-level hypotheses supported by the data are generated. During phase 2, it opportunistically schedules competing KSARs. However, HEARSAY-II's scheduler has no explicit representation of the two-phase strategy. It applies a uniform set of control heuristics throughout the problem-solving process. The two-phase strategy is implicit in the engineering of different knowledge sources.

During phase 1, three knowledge sources process the data bottom-up to the word level. SEG is triggered by input of data at the parameter level and hypothesizes all encompassing segments. POM is triggered by segment hypotheses and hypothesizes all encompassing syllables. MOW is triggered by the syllable hypotheses and hypothesizes all encompassing word hypotheses. Each of these knowledge sources is triggered exactly once during phase 1, produces the single KSAR available for scheduling on its problem-solving cycle, and generates all possible hypotheses at its target level. Thus, although the scheduler knows nothing about phase 1, it has no alternative but to schedule SEG, POM, and MOW in sequence.

During phase 2, multiple knowledge sources are triggered on each problem-solving cycle, accumulating in a growing list of pending KSARs. The scheduler assigns each KSAR a priority based on its required computing resources, the credibility of its triggering events, the reliability of its knowledge source, and its potential to extend high credibility partial solutions already on the blackboard. In general, on each problem-solving cycle, the scheduler selects the single, highest priority KSAR to execute its action. However, if several pending KSARs propose to extend existing hypotheses of equal credibility, the scheduler selects all of them, effecting a breadth-first interlude in an otherwise depth-first search. Processing halts when the system has pursued all credible partial hypotheses or when the system runs out of computing resources (time or space). In the former case, the system produces the most complete and credible solution. In the latter case, it may produce several equally complete and credible partial solutions.

As the first blackboard system, HEARSAY-II introduces the basic architectural features and the first specification of knowledge sources and scheduler. HEARSAY-II specifies an unstructured, procedural representation for knowledge source conditions and actions. Both condition and action procedures produce KSARs for scheduling. This specification allows individual system builders to tailor appropriate representations for different knowledge sources. It permits knowledge sources to examine all blackboard contents and perform any desired computations during both triggering and action execution. On the other hand, this specification entails computationally expensive methods for triggering and executing knowledge sources. HEARSAY-II defines a sophisticated scheduler that incorporates multiple criteria to make purely opportunistic scheduling decisions. It exhibits the power of a global control strategy and implements it in the engineering of individual knowledge sources. These specifications allow HEARSAY-II to make intelligent scheduling decisions in the absence of a known algorithm for speech understanding. However, the combination of an opportunistic scheduler and carefully engineered knowledge sources is an unprincipled approach to scheduling.

HASP. HASP (Nii, 1982) interprets sonar signals from a circumscribed area of the ocean in real time (see also MILITARY APPLICATIONS OF AI). Given the locations, ranges, and coded descriptions of the outputs of several hydrophone arrays, it detects, identifies, localizes, groups, and characterizes the movement of each ship or other vessel in the area. Some of these vessels are friendly or neutral, and others are wary and elusive. In addition, HASP must perform its interpretation against the background noise and distortions of the ocean environment. Finally, because the ocean scene is dynamic, with many ships coming and going and changing their behavior, HASP must "solve" the interpretation problem repeatedly. Its output is a series of reports presenting "snapshots" of the changing scene. These reports also contain explanations justifying their constituent hypotheses. HASP begins with a line representation of the sonar signal and attempts to characterize the situation it represents. Between these two extremes, Line and Situation Board, HASP generates hypotheses at three additional hypothesis levels: harmonics in the signal, sources such as engines or propellers, and vessels such as submarines or aircraft carriers. Its solution intervals categorically distinguish different ocean regions.

HASP has approximately forty knowledge sources. Most of them operate bottom-up, inferring hypotheses at one level of abstraction from data or hypotheses at lower levels. For example, the knowledge source CROSS.ARRAYRULES hypothesizes sources that encompass hypothesized harmonics. However, some knowledge sources operate top-down, confirming expectations implicit in hy-

potheses at higher levels of abstraction. For example, the knowledge source SOURCE.INCORPORATIONRULES hypothesizes sources that are implicit in vessel hypotheses. HASP uses a uniform condition-action syntax for all knowledge sources. Knowledge source conditions specify one or more predefined event labels representing classes of anticipated blackboard events. Actions are production systems whose rules generate, categorize, and label blackboard events. Rules categorize events as simple, clock, or expected events. Simple events add or modify hypotheses on the blackboard and can be processed by triggered knowledge sources at any time. Clock events also add or modify hypotheses, but they must be processed at particular times. Expected events describe expected blackboard modifications. Rules label events with the predefined labels used for triggering.

HASP's scheduler iterates a hierarchical procedure that sequentially selects all currently due clock events in LIFO order, sequentially selects all confirmed expected events in LIFO order, and selects the highest priority simple event by the LIFO rule. For each selected event, the scheduler executes a predetermined sequence of knowledge sources triggered by the event's label. HASP explains solution elements recorded on its blackboard by reviewing the sequence of knowledge source rules that produce them.

HASP introduces variations on both knowledge source specification and scheduling. HASP constrains the syntax of both condition and action components of knowledge sources. The restriction of conditions to event labels provides an efficient mechanism for triggering knowledge sources. However, it requires coordination of all knowledge sources to produce and respond to a manageably small set of event labels. The production system representation used for knowledge source actions is conceptually neat. HASP's hierarchical, event-based scheduling procedure is computationally efficient, but it severely limits flexibility in both the selection and sequencing of KSARs for execution.

CRYSALIS. This system (Terry 1983) determines the spatial locations of a protein's constituent atoms (see CHEMISTRY, AI IN). It uses two kinds of information, a complete description of the protein's amino acid sequence and its electron density map (EDM). An EDM is a function that gives the density of the protein's electron cloud, often represented as a three-dimensional contour map. Peaks, or local maxima, in the EDM correspond to atoms or groups of atoms, with peak height providing an approximate function of their atomic number. Stripping away low density peaks on the EDM reveals its skeleton, a graph structure approximating the connectivity among groups of atoms. Finally, identifiable segments of the skeleton represent meaningful components of the protein structure (eg, backbone or side chain). Using the amino acid sequence and these features of the EDM, CRYSALIS can solve a medium-sized protein in a day. Like human crystallographers, it locates about 75% of the nonhydrogen atoms in the protein with an accuracy of 8 nm.

CRYSALIS uses an expanded blackboard. As discussed

above, the EDM data themselves support hierarchical analysis independent of any efforts to interpret them. Accordingly, the CRYSALIS blackboard has two separate "panels," one for the EDM data and one for hypotheses. Each blackboard panel embodies different levels and solution intervals. The EDM panel has four levels: EDM points, peaks, nodes, and segments. Its solution intervals represent spatial location in the EDM. The hypothesis panel has three levels: atoms, superatoms (meaningful groups of atoms), and stereotypes (larger structures, like alpha-helices or beta-sheets). Its solution intervals represent different spatial locations in the protein. The blackboard permits interpanel links between related data and hypothesis elements as well as the conventional vertical links.

CRYSALIS's knowledge sources are structured like HASP's. They exploit predefined event labels and a production system representation for actions. However, CRYSALIS production rules are semantically more complex, referring to 250 LISP functions that define a crystallographic language for manipulating data and hypotheses.

CRYSALIS uses a knowledge-intensive scheduling procedure. The scheduler uses a domain-specific strategy in conjunction with global solution state to sequence domain-specific problem-solving tasks. It uses each task, in conjunction with local solution state, to select individual blackboard events. For each selected event, it executes a predetermined sequence of knowledge sources triggered by the selected event's label.

CRYSALIS introduces variations on blackboard specification and scheduling. The CRYSALIS blackboard specification introduces different panels to distinguish reasoning about data from reasoning about interpretations of the data. (HEARSAY-II and HASP effectively finessed this problem by operating upon hand-coded data.) CRYSALIS introduces a domain-specific scheduling procedure. By exploiting this knowledge, CRYSALIS further improves scheduling efficiency. Its knowledge-based scheduling procedure also provides a perspicuous framework for interpreting system behavior. Of course, this approach is possible only when an effective scheduling procedure is known.

OPM. OPM (Hayes-Roth, 1979a, 1979b) plans multiple-task sequences in a context of conflicting goals and constraints. Given a list of desirable tasks and a map of the region in which tasks can be performed, OPM plans: which tasks to perform; how much time to allocate for each task; an order for performing tasks; and the routes to travel between successive tasks. The problem is complicated by differences in task priorities and time requirements, constraints on when tasks can be performed, intertask dependencies, and limitations on the time available for performing tasks. OPM's blackboard is comprised of three coordinated panels, for plans, planning data, and planning heuristics. These panels all have four parallel levels of abstraction: outcomes (tasks) the plan should achieve; designs for the general spatial-temporal layout of the plan; procedures that sequence individual tasks; and operations that sequence task components. Solution intervals represent different plan execution time intervals. Each decision on the plan panel depends on a coordinated set of decisions on the other two panels. For example, Heuristic: Perform the closest task in the right direction next; Data: The closest task in the right direction is the newsstand; and Plan: Go to the newsstand next.

OPM has about fifty knowledge sources. Some operate bottom-up. For example, the knowledge source NOTICE-PATTERN detects spatial configurations of tasks at the design level from individual task locations at the procedure level on the data plane. Other knowledge sources operate top-down. For example, the knowledge source RE-FINE-DESIGN expands designs as sequences of procedures on the plan plane. OPM uses a two-part condition structure for knowledge sources. A condition's trigger is an event-based test of knowledge source relevance. Its precondition is a state-based test of the knowledge source's current applicability. Satisfaction of a knowledge source's trigger generates a KSAR, but a KSAR can be executed only at times when its precondition is true. Both triggers and preconditions may contain arbitrary LISP code as long as they can be evaluated true or false. As in HEARSAY-II, knowledge source actions are arbitrary programs that produce blackboard events.

OPM uses a uniform blackboard mechanism for reasoning about control. Control knowledge sources dynamically generate, modify, and execute a control plan out of modular control heuristics on the control blackboard. The control blackboard has different levels to represent control heuristics of varying scope. Its solution intervals represent different problem-solving time intervals. For example, at an intermediate point in the problem-solving process, OPM's control plan might contain this partial plan: *Solve problem P by generating an outcome level plan and successively refining it at lower levels of abstraction. Begin by generating an outcome level plan. Always prefer KSAR's with credible triggering information and reliable actions.* OPM's scheduler has no control knowledge of its own. Instead, it adapts its scheduling behavior to whatever heuristics are recorded on the control blackboard.

OPM introduces variations in blackboard structure, knowledge source specification, and scheduling. OPM uses separate blackboard panels to distinguish reasoning about problem data, planning heuristics, and the plan itself. It also provides a separate blackboard panel for reasoning about scheduling. Thus, OPM introduces explicit representation of all aspects of the problem-solving process. OPM introduces a two-part condition structure for knowledge sources that combines an efficient, event-based triggering mechanism with a precondition mechanism for restricting execution of triggered KSARs to appropriate contextual conditions. Finally, OPM introduces a simple scheduler that adapts to a dynamic control plan and a uniform blackboard mechanism for generating the control plan. This enables OPM to integrate opportunistic and strategic scheduling heuristics. Also, OPM need not commit to any particular combination of heuristics, but can dynamically adapt its control plan to unanticipated problem-solving situations. The control blackboard provides a perspicuous framework in which to interpret system behavior.

FOUR BLACKBOARD SYSTEM
BUILDING ENVIRONMENTS

This section describes four blackboard development environments: AGE, HEARSAY-III, BB1, and GBB. All four provide the basic architectural components: blackboard, knowledge sources, and scheduler. AGE is the most constrained of the four, and consequently provides the strongest guidance in system design. Hearsay-III and GBB are only weakly constrained, and allow considerable freedom in designing blackboard applications. BB1 and GBB adopt and elaborate selected features of the earlier AGE and Hearsay-III systems, and incorporate additional capabilities as well. Descriptions of other recent blackboard shells, such as Gest, Erasmus, and ATOME, are collected in Englemore (Englemore and Moran, 1988) and Jagannathan (Jagannathan and co-workers, 1989b).

AGE. AGE (Nii, 1979) permits a user to define a blackboard with any number of named levels and associated attributes. Any solution element created at a given level of the blackboard assumes the associated attributes. Although AGE does not explicitly distinguish multiple blackboard panels, it permits the system builder to distinguish panels implicitly in the behavior of specific knowledge sources.

Knowledge source conditions are lists of event labels that correspond to anticipated blackboard events. When an event with one of these labels is selected by the scheduler, as discussed below, the knowledge source is triggered. Knowledge source actions are local production systems. The left side of a rule specifies predicates that determine its applicability. The right side instantiates a template specifying a change to the blackboard and a label for that blackboard event. AGE provides a variety of blackboard access functions for use in the rules. The system builder can define parameters that determine: how many times individual rules can fire; how many rules can fire on each triggering of the knowledge source; and how predicates in the left sides of rules combine to invoke their right sides.

AGE's restrictions on knowledge source specification have advantages and disadvantages. First, the use of event labels permits an efficient table lookup method for knowledge source triggering. However, it also requires that the system builder anticipate all important blackboard events and the distinctive contexts in which they may occur. Knowledge sources that generate and respond to events must be coordinated to use the same labels. Second, AGE's production system representation for actions and its blackboard modification templates provides a neat, uniform syntax with detailed code hidden in referenced functions. They also provide a foundation for AGE's explanation capability, which reiterates the sequence of fired rules that produced a particular hypothesis, and for its elaborate interface for creating and editing knowledge sources. On the other hand, these restrictions sometimes hinder specification of complex knowledge source actions.

AGE's scheduler iterates the following procedure: (1) select a blackboard event according to a function specified by the system builder; (2) retrieve the list of knowledge sources triggered by the selected event; and (3) execute each triggered knowledge source's local production system. Efficiency is the primary advantage of this scheduler. However, it severely restricts system behavior and the system builder's control over system behavior. The system builder can supply only the event selection function. The scheduler always operates by first choosing an event and then executing a predetermined sequence of knowledge source triggered by the event's label. It cannot incorporate heuristics for selecting among or ordering knowledge sources.

HEARSAY-III. HEARSAY-III (Erman, 1981) is a general-purpose blackboard architecture. It is built upon the relational database system called AP3 (Goldman, 1982) and exploits AP3's capabilities for representing and searching directed graph structures, defining and preserving context, and triggering knowledge sources with a demon mechanism. HEARSAY-III partitions its blackboard into domain and scheduling blackboards. The system builder hierarchically decomposes each blackboard into any desired lower level panels as well as desired levels and attributes. Knowledge source conditions specify a triggering pattern and immediate code. The user must express a knowledge source's triggering pattern as a predicate on AP3 fact templates and any LISP predicates composed with AND and OR operators (see AND/OR GRAPHS). Whenever one of the constituent AP3 fact templates is modified, the entire pattern is evaluated. If it is evaluated as true, HEARSAY-III creates a KSAR that includes the knowledge source's name, the AP3 context in which the pattern matched, and the values of variables instantiated by the match. At the same time the knowledge source's immediate code, which may be any LISP code, is executed. It records potentially useful scheduling information in the KSAR and places the activation record at a particular level of the scheduling blackboard. Knowledge-source actions are arbitrary LISP programs.

The default scheduler simply selects any KSAR from the scheduling blackboard and executes its action program. However, the system builder can replace it with another scheduler tailored to the application. The scheduling blackboard provides an environment for explicit control reasoning through the activities of control knowledge sources. In illustrative HEARSAY-III systems, the control blackboard typically partitions pending KSARs into different priority levels. Control knowledge sources typically assign KSARs to particular levels, adjust KSAR priorities within a level, and generate lists of KSARs for sequential execution by the scheduler. However, HEARSAY-III does not place any constraints on the structure of the control blackboard or the activities of control knowledge sources. The system builder can use them in whatever manner appears useful.

HEARSAY-III is a weakly constrained blackboard environment in that it imposes almost no restrictions on specifying the defining features of the architecture: the scheduler, knowledge source conditions and actions can be arbitrary programs. HEARSAY-III's most important specification lies in its distinction between domain and control blackboards and its suggestion that control knowledge sources should record information on the control blackboard to influence the scheduler. However, HEARSAY-III leaves the productive use of this specification to the system builder. Thus, application builders have great freedom but little design guidance.

BB1. BB1 (Hayes-Roth, 1984) supports blackboard systems that explicitly and dynamically plan their own problem-solving behavior, explain their behavior in terms of an underlying control plan, and learn new control heuristics from experience. BB1 implements a blackboard control architecture (Hayes-Roth, 1985) which makes a sharp distinction between domain problems and the control problem: Which of its potential actions should a system execute on each problem-solving cycle? BB1 defines explicit domain and control blackboards to record solution elements for domain and control problems. The system builder defines the structure of the domain blackboard as named levels and attributes within levels. BB1 defines the control blackboard, whose levels distinguish the problem to be solved, sequential problem-solving strategies, local attentional foci, general scheduling policies, to-do sets of feasible actions, and chosen actions selected for execution. It also defines the attributes used to specify control decisions at each level. For example, a focus decision's goal attribute describes desirable actions, such as "generate solution elements at the outcome level." Its criterion describes the goal's expiration condition, such as "there is a complete and satisfactory solution at the outcome level." The control blackboard's solution intervals distinguish different problem-solving time intervals in terms of problem-solving cycles.

BB1 defines explicit domain and control knowledge sources. Domain knowledge sources operate primarily on the domain blackboard to solve the domain problem. They are domain specific and defined by the system builder. Control knowledge sources operate primarily on the control blackboard to solve the control problem. Some control knowledge sources are domain independent and provided by BB1. For example, the knowledge source implement strategy incrementally refines a strategy decision as a series of prescribed focus decisions. The system builder may define additional domain-specific control knowledge sources. All knowledge sources are data structures that can be interpreted or modified.

A knowledge source's condition comprises a trigger and a precondition. The trigger is a set of event-based predicates. When all of them are true in the context of a single blackboard event, the knowledge source is triggered and generates a representative KSAR. When running an application system, BB1 generates and uses a discrimination net of trigger predicates used in the system's knowledge sources. The precondition is a set of state-based predicates. When all of them are true, which may occur after an arbitrary delay, the triggered KSAR is executable. If the preconditions describe transient states, the KSAR may oscillate between triggered and executable states. This specification of knowledge source conditions provides an efficient event-based triggering mechanism with a state-based mechanism for restricting action execution to appropriate contexts.

A knowledge source's action is a local production system. The left sides of rules determine under what conditions they fire. The right sides instantiate blackboard modification templates. Control parameters determine how many times individual rules can fire, how many rules can fire on each triggering of the knowledge source, and how multiple left-side predicates are integrated to fire rules. In addition to its condition and action, each knowledge source has descriptive attributes that are potentially useful in scheduling. These include the blackboard panels and levels at which its triggering events and actions occur, its computational cost, its relative importance compared to other knowledge sources, and its reliability in producing correct results. BB1 provides a variety of functions for inspecting the blackboard, knowledge sources, and blackboard events for use in defining knowledge sources. It also provides a simple menu-driven facility for creating and editing knowledge sources.

BB1 defines a simple scheduler that adapts to foci and policies recorded on the control blackboard and schedules the execution of both domain and control knowledge sources. On each problem-solving cycle the scheduler rates executable KSARS against operative foci and policies. It applies a scheduling rule, which is also recorded on the control blackboard and modifiable by control knowledge sources, to the KSAR ratings to select one for execution.

BB1 provides a graphical run time interface with capabilities for: inspecting knowledge sources, blackboard contents, blackboard events, or pending KSARs; enumerating pending KSARs, recommending a KSAR for execution; explaining a recommendation; accepting a user's recommendation; executing a recommended KSAR; and running without user intervention until a specified condition occurs.

The specification of BB1's knowledge sources and control mechanism underlie its capabilities for control, explanation, and learning. BB1 provides a general blackboard mechanism for reasoning about control, incorporating any strategic or opportunistic scheduling heuristics specified by the user. Moreover, it can construct situation-specific control plans dynamically out of modular control heuristics, avoiding the need to enumerate important problem-solving contingencies or to predefine an effective control plan. BB1 explains its problem-solving actions by showing how they fit into the underlying control plan and by recursively explaining the control plan itself. BB1 learns new control heuristics when a domain expert overrides its scheduling recommendations. It identifies the critical features distinguishing the expert's preferred action from the scheduler's recommended action and generates a heuristic favoring actions with those features.

GBB. GBB (Corkill, 1986, 1987) is a generalized object-oriented shell for building high-performance blackboard applications. GBB features declarative languages for specifying: (1) application blackboard database architectures and database object structures; and (2) pattern objects for matching and retrieving blackboard objects. GBB database code generators compile developer specifications of these elements into an application-specific database kernel. Application knowledge sources and a control shell (eg, a scheduler) are then interfaced with this kernel to complete the blackboard system.

A GBB blackboard specification is comprised of a collection of structured spaces that are populated by objects called units. Spaces can have multiple dimensions (eg, time, position-*x*, position-*y*); each of which is either *ordered* with respect to a values range (such as the interval (0 . . . 256) or *enumerated* with respect to a set of labels or categories (eg, vehicle type-1, type-2 . . .). GBB's declarative blackboard specification language supports the definition of multiple replicated blackboards, each containing one or more multi-dimensional spaces, organized in hierarchical trees.

GBB units are either simple "scalar" objects, such as discrete lines or points, or complex composite objects comprised of multiple scalars, such as line pairs or vehicle track hypotheses. Declarative definitions for unit class objects specify: instance slots (eg, sensor-id, time-location-list); inter-unit links (eg, between hypotheses); and indexes (eg, line orientations, time-location-lists). Indexes determine how unit instances are mapped into a blackboard space (ie, positioned along its dimensions). Each one points to a slot and an indexing structure object that specifies how to extract index values from slot values, which may be complex structures. Index values for ordered dimensions determine the relative proximity or "closeness" of instance units within a space. For example, lines that are close together with respect to orientation index values are nearly parallel. Unit classes can also define demons for signalling events to the control shell (eg, creation or deletion of unit instances) and for triggering actions when instance slots or link values are modified.

GBB's second language defines pattern objects, which declaratively specify blackboard regions to search for retrieving database units. Pattern objects specify one or more index structures, simple or composite, or a concatenation of such structures. They also define criteria that specify how unit index values must match against pattern objects, including: matching relations such as overlap, inclusion, or exact; a lower bound on the number of elements that must match; and an upper bound on the allowable number of mismatches. GBB transparently handles concatenation of, and pattern matching across, heterogeneous index structures.

Application knowledge sources manipulate GBB blackboard databases through basic operations on unit instances, including creation/insertion (Make-Unit-Type), retrieval (Find-Units), deletion, merging, and modification. Developers supply application-specific arguments such as unit slot values, target blackboards and/or spaces for unit creation or retrieval, pattern objects to guide search, and so on. GBB incorporates rule- and frame-based representation languages for building knowledge sources. Procedural knowledge sources can be coded directly using Lisp and GBB's blackboard database operators. Like most blackboard systems, control in GBB is driven by events consisting of changes to the database. GBB provides predefined control shells for instantiating, scheduling, and executing knowledge sources. Custom shells can be developed or existing shells adapted, as necessary. GBB also provides development tools such as trace facilities and graphical interfaces.

Database storage and search functions are critical performance factors for blackboard systems. GBB provides several techniques for adjusting these functions for particular applications. First, the implementations for storing units in spaces can be tuned to optimize the retrieval of units with proximate index values. For example, units in an ordered dimension can be stored in array "buckets" according to range intervals. Second, the Find-Units operation allows users to tune retrieval behavior by specifying before and after search filters for eliminating unit candidates. Third, GBB analyzes the individual retrieval specifications within pattern objects and automatically generates procedures for efficient matching.

Whereas Hearsay-III and BB1 focus on generalizing control capabilities, GBB emphasizes development capabilities and performance. GBB's most noteworthy feature is its use of data abstraction to separate the specification of blackboard database organization and contents, insertion and search structures, and database implementations from one another and from application knowledge sources and control shells. GBB makes it possible to build blackboard systems that are both flexible (ie, database specifications and KSs are easily changed), and efficient (ie, application-specific bottlenecks can be alleviated by tuning implementations). Typically, these design attributes are antagonistic in generalized development tools.

CURRENT RESEARCH ISSUES

Three interrelated research issues dominate current studies of blackboard systems: control, performance, and distribution. Space limitations permit only a brief overview of recent literature on these topics. The primary research focus tends to be on blackboard schedulers, since effective control is crucial to the speed and accuracy with which blackboard systems solve problems. Generally, control decisions and their underlying reasoning are being made more explicit. For example, ATOME (Laasri, 1989) uses a hierarchy of rule-based strategy and task-level control knowledge sources to sharpen focus of attention, reducing scheduler overhead and improving efficiency. Explicit control reasoning also appears essential for automatic acquisition of more effective scheduling heuristics and for strategic explanation.

Performance issues are being addressed in a variety of ways. Several recent systems, such as HCVM (Fehling, 1989) and RT-1 (Dodhiawala, 1989) employ specialized control architectures to support real-time problem-solving. Major design features in these systems include: concurrent execution of knowledge sources; prioritized event channels; interruptible execution of low priority tasks; and adaptive scheduling based on explicitly parameterized control factors and current problem-solving status conditions. Second, as discussed above, GBB focuses on optimizing blackboard database operations. Third, data input and output (eg, to sensor channels and effectors) can be critical performance factors in blackboard systems. HCVM, RT-1, and BB1/CI (Hewett, 1989) employ specialized communications interfaces to address this issue. A fourth strategy is to modulate reasoning based on time constraints and acceptable tradeoffs between solution speed and accuracy (ie, completeness, precision, and certainty). Lesser (1988) investigates techniques for making approximations in data, knowledge, and search strategies that result in faster solutions. The DVMT activity planning loop is extended with rule-based heuristics for dynamically selecting and applying approximate reasoning methods. Fifth, blackboard systems appear to have great potential for exploiting parallel computing environments because of their modularity (Fennell and Lesser, 1977; Lesser and Erman, 1980). CAGE and POLIGON (Nii and co-workers, 1989) are the most detailed empirical investigations of concurrent blackboards to date. CAGE is based on a shared memory multiprocessor architecture, while POLIGON relies on purely local memory processors coupled by fast message-passing communication. CAGE provides a variety of options for performing blackboard processes in parallel rather than serially: triggering knowledge sources, executing KSARs; executing rules; and executing rule conditions and actions. POLIGON, which explored fine-grained, rule-level parallelism, eliminates the overhead from central scheduling, using daemons attached to blackboard data objects to control rule activations instead. Other investigations of concurrent architectures have employed existing shells including GBB (Corkill, 1989), Erasmus (Jagannathan, 1989a), Agora (Bisiani and Forin, 1989), and CAIBL (Buteau, 1990). Blackboard applications, like conventional programs, generally involve varying amounts of inherently serial processing: the degree of concurrency that is feasible is largely application-dependent. Moreover, to accommodate serial processing requirements, parallel blackboard systems must provide mechanisms for synchronizing processes and maintaining data consistency.

Finally, research is quite active on distributed blackboard architectures (see also DISTRIBUTED PROBLEM SOLVING). At least three broad motivations exist for distributed blackboard systems: (1) performance: exploiting multiprocessor hardware to execute processes for a single problem-solving system concurrently (discussed immediately above); (2) replication: using multiple, identical blackboards to address a single problem that can be partitioned into homogeneous but largely independent subproblems; and (3) integration and coordination: using blackboards as a uniform communication and control framework to couple heterogeneous applications that address distinct problems relating to a common domain.

The seminal research on replicated blackboards was the Distributed Vehicle Monitoring Testbed (Lesser and Corkill, 1983). DVMT interprets data from a spatially distributed network of sensors to identify vehicle positions, velocities, and clusters, similar to the HASP data fusion domain. The system employed a collection of Hearsay-III blackboards, one for each spatial sector within the sensor network. Each blackboard node was extended with communication knowledge sources (and hardware interfaces) for sending and receiving hypotheses and goals between nodes. The central research issue for such replicated blackboard systems is to coordinate autonomous nodes to converge to consistent global problem solutions using purely local (replicated) control structures. DVMT researchers have investigated a variety of models, most notably functionally accurate cooperative networks (Lesser and Corkill, 1981) and partial global plans (Durfee and Lesser, 1988). Other applications for replicated blackboards include distributed planning and control (eg, air traffic), document retrieval, concurrent engineering, and cooperative group work networks.

Recent research on heterogeneous distributed systems has led to hierarchical blackboard control architectures. In these systems, individual blackboards, called agents, address a complete distinct problem within a given domain, such as monitoring sensors, diagnosing problems, or planning problem resolution strategies. These application agents are internally complex and more or less functionally self-sufficient. They are weakly coupled in that they interact much less frequently and intensively than do subproblem-solving knowledge sources within a conventional blackboard system. Activities are coordinated across application agents by a higher level blackboard or control agent, which incorporates the customary task agenda, scheduler, and invocation mechanisms. This organization provides a uniform communication and control framework within and between agents. The Guardian/BB1 Control Agent (Hayes-Roth and co-workers, 1989) coordinates perception, action, and reasoning agents for monitoring and managing intensive care patients. OPERA's control agent (Adler, 1989) integrates and coordinates expert system blackboard Agents that isolate and manage faults within the main control subsystem for NASA's space shuttle launch processing system. SOCIAL (Adler, 1991) extends OPERA's control agent to supports multilevel hierarchies: high level control agents can manage lower level control agents as well as application agents. SOCIAL is constructed on top of MetaCourier, a modular tool for transparent interprocess communication across heterogeneous network systems (Symbiotics, 1989). All SOCIAL agents have independent communication capabilities, allowing knowledge sources and their blackboards to reside on different platforms. Other physically distributed systems, such as DVMT and CAIBL, implement communications via dedicated blackboard knowledge sources, which forces all application knowledge sources to be co-resident with their blackboard.

The blackboard architecture has been an extremely productive and influential problem-solving model in AI. The vigorous research and application efforts currently underway suggest that blackboard systems will continue to be play an important role in the future development of AI as well.

BIBLIOGRAPHY

R. M. Adler, "A Distributed Blackboard Architecture for Integrating Loosely-Coupled Knowledge-Based Systems," *Intell. Syst. Rev.* 1(4) (1989).

R. M. Adler, "A Hierarchical Distributed Control Model for Coordinating Intelligent Systems," *Proceedings, Goddard Confer-*

ence on Space Applications of AI, NASA Goddard Space Flight Center, Greenbelt, Md., May, 1991.

R. Bisiani and A. Forin, "Parallelization of Blackboard Architectures and the Agora System," in V. Jagannathan, R. Dodhiawala, and L. Baum, eds., *Blackboard Architectures and Applications,* Academic Press, San Diego, Calif., 1989.

A. Bond and L. Gasser, eds., *Readings in Distributed Artificial Intelligence,* Morgan-Kaufmann, San Mateo, Calif., 1988.

B. Buteau, "A Generic Framework for Distributed, Cooperating Blackboard Systems," *Proceedings ACM Computer Science Conference,* Washington, D.C., February, 1990.

D. D. Corkill, "Design Alternatives for Parallel and Distributed Blackboard Systems," in V. Jagannathan, R. Dodhiawala, and L. Baum, eds., *Blackboard Architectures and Applications,* Academic Press, San Diego, Calif., 1989.

D. D. Corkill, K. Q. Gallagher, and P. M. Johnson, "Achieving Flexibility, Efficiency, and Generality in Blackboard Architectures," *Proceedings of the Sixth National Conference on AI,* Seattle, Wash., 1987, AAAI, Menlo Park, Calif.

R. T. Dodhiawala, N. S. Sridharan, and C. Pickering, "A Real-Time Blackboard Architecture," in *Blackboard Architectures and Applications,* Jagannathan and co-workers, eds., Academic Press, Dan Diego, Calif., 1989.

E. H. Durfee and V. R. Lesser, "Using Partial Global Plans to Coordinate Distributed Problem Solvers," in L. Gasser and M. N. Huhns, eds., *Distributed Artificial Intelligence,* Vol. 2, Morgan-Kaufmann, San Mateo, Calif., 1989.

R. Englemore and T. Moran, eds., *Blackboard Systems,* Addison-Wesley, Reading, Mass., 1988. [An important collection of papers on blackboard architectures, shells, and current research directions.]

L. D. Erman, F. Hayes-Roth, V. R. Lesser, and D. R. Reddy, "The Hearsay-II speech-understanding system: Integrating knowledge to resolve uncertainty," *ACM Comput. Surv.* **12,** 213–253, 1980.

L. D. Erman, P. E. London, and S. F. Fickas, "The Design and an Example Use of Hearsay-III," *Proceedings of The Seventh International Joint Conference on Artificial Intelligence,* Vancouver, BC, 1981, pp. 409–415.

M. R. Fehling, A. M. Altman, and B. M. Wilber, "The Heuristic Control Virtual Machine: An Implementation of the Schemer Computational Model of Reflective, Real-Time Problem-Solving," in *Blackboard Architectures and Applications,* Jagannathan and co-workers, eds., Academic Press, San Diego, Calif., 1989.

R. Fennell and V. Lesser, "Parallelism in AI Problem-Solving: A Case Study of Hearsay-II," *IEEE Trans. Comput.* **C-26,** 98–111 (1977).

L. Gasser and M. N. Huhns, eds., *Distributed Artificial Intelligence,* Vol. 2, Morgan-Kaufmann, San Mateo, Calif., 1989.

N. M. Goldman, *AP3 Reference Manual,* Technical Report, Los Angeles, Calif., Information Sciences Institute, 1982.

A. Hanson and E. Riseman, "VISIONS: A Computer System for Interpreting Scenes," in A. Hanson and E. Riseman, eds., *Computer Vision Systems,* Academic Press, New York, 1978.

B. Hayes-Roth, *BB1: An Architecture for Blackboard Systems that Control, Explain, and Learn about Their Own Behavior,* Technical Report HPP-84-16, Stanford University, Stanford, Calif., 1984.

B. Hayes-Roth, "A Blackboard Architecture for Control," *Artif. Intell. J.* **26,** 251–321, 1985.

B. Hayes-Roth and F. Hayes-Roth, "A Cognitive Model of Planning," *Cogn. Sci.* **3,** 275–310, 1979a.

B. Hayes-Roth, F. Hayes-Roth, S. Rosenschein, and S. Cammarata, "Modeling Planning as an Incremental, Opportunistic Process," *Proceedings of the Sixth International Joint Conference on Artificial Intelligence,* Tokyo, Japan, 1979b, pp. 375–383.

B. Hayes-Roth, M. Hewett, R. Washington, R. Hewett, and A. Seiver, "Distributing Intelligence within an Individual," in L. Gasser and M. N. Huhns, eds., *Distributed Artif. Intell.,* Vol. 2, Morgan-Kaufmann, San Mateo, Calif., 1989.

M. Hewett and B. Hayes-Roth, "Real-Time I/O in Knowledge-Based Systems," in *Blackboard Architectures and Applications,* Jagannathan and co-workers, eds., Academic Press, San Diego, Calif., 1989.

E. Hudlicka, "Construction and Use of a Causal Model for Diagnosis," *International J. Intell. Syst.* **3,** 3, 315–349 (1988).

V. Jagannathan, "Realizing the Concurrent Blackboard Model," in V. Jagannathan, R. Dodhiawala, and L. Baum, eds., *Blackboard Architectures and Applications,* Academic Press, San Diego, Calif., 1989.

V. Jagannathan, R. Dodhiawala, and L. Baum, eds., *Blackboard Architectures and Applications,* Academic Press, San Diego, Calif., 1989. [An excellent collection of recent research in blackboard control, real-time designs, and applications.]

H. Laasri and B. Maitre, "Flexibility and Efficiency in Blackboard Systems: Studies and Achievements in ATOME," in V. Jagannathan, R. Dodhiawala, and L. Baum, eds., *Blackboard Architectures and Applications,* Academic Press, San Diego, Calif., 1989.

V. R. Lesser and D. Corkill, "Functionally Accurate Cooperative Distributed Systems," *IEEE Trans. Syst. Man Cybern.* **SMC-1,** 81–96 (1981).

V. R. Lesser and D. Corkill, "The Distributed Vehicle Monitoring Testbed: a Tool for Investigating Distributed Problem-solving Networks," *AI Mag.* 4(3), 15–33 (1983).

V. R. Lesser and L. R. Erman, "Distributed Interpretation: A Model and Experiment," *IEEE Trans. Comput.* **C-29,** 1144–1163 (1980).

J. L. McClelland and D. E. Rumelhart, "An Interactive Activation Model of Context Effects in Letter Perception: Part 1. An Account of Basic Findings," *Psychol. Rev.* **88,** 375–407 (1981).

M. Minsky, "Steps Toward Artificial Intelligence," in E. A. Feigenbaum and J. Feldman, eds., *Computers and Thought,* McGraw-Hill, New York, 1961, pp. 406–450.

M. Nagao, T. Matsuyama, and H. Mori, "Structured Analysis of Complex Photographs," *Proceedings of the Sixth IJCAI,* Tokyo, Japan, 1979, pp. 610–616.

A. Newell, J. C. Shaw, and H. A. Simon, "Report on a General Problem-Solving Program," *Proceedings of the International Conference on Information Processing,* UNESCO House, Paris, France, 1959.

H. P. Nii and N. Aiello, "AGE: A Knowledge-Based Program for Building Knowledge-Based Programs," *Proceedings of the Sixth IJCAI,* Tokyo, Japan, 1979.

H. P. Nii, N. Aiello, and J. Rice, "Experiments on Cage and Poligon: Measuring the Performance of Parallel Blackboard Systems," in L. Gasser and M. N. Huhns, eds., *Distributed Artificial Intelligence,* Vol. 2, Morgan-Kaufmann, San Mateo, Calif., 1989.

H. P. Nii, E. A. Feigenbaum, J. J. Anton, and A. J. Rockmore, "Signal-to Symbol Transformation: HASP/SIAP Case Study," *AI Mag.* **3,** 23–35 (1982).

M. Rose, *The Composition Process,* Ph.D. dissertation, University of California at Los Angeles, 1981.

D. E. Rumelhart and J. L. McClelland, "An Interactive Model of Context Effects in Letter Perception: Part 2. The Contextual Enhancement Effect and Some Tests and Extensions of the Model," *Psychol. Rev.* **89**, 60–94 (1982).

M. Stefik and co-workers, "The Organization of Expert Systems: A Prescriptive Tutorial," *Artif. Intell.* **18**, 135–173 (1982).

M. Stefik and L. Conway, "Towards the Principled Engineering of Knowledge," *AI Mag.* **3**, 4–16 (1982).

Symbiotics, Inc., *Object-Oriented Heterogeneous Distributed Computing with MetaCourier,* Technical Report, March 24, 1990.

A. Terry, *Hierarchical Control of Production Systems,* Ph.D. dissertation, University of California, Irvine, Calif., 1983.

R. ADLER
Symbiotics, Inc.

This article is an update of an original article which appeared in the first edition, authored by B. Hayes-Roth, Stanford University.

BOLTZMANN MACHINE

The Boltzmann machine (Ackley and co-workers, 1985) is a massively parallel architecture that uses simple *on–off* processing units and stores all its long-term knowledge in the strengths of the connections between processors. Its main difference from other connectionist architectures (Hinton and Anderson, 1981; Feldman and Ballard, 1982; Fahlman and co-workers, 1983) (see CONNECTIONISM; CONNECTION MACHINES) is that the units use a probabilistic decision rule to decide which of their two states to adopt at any moment. The network computes low-cost solutions to optimization problems by settling to thermal equilibrium with some of the units clamped into their *on* or *off* states to represent the current task. For a perceptual interpretation task the clamped units would represent the perceptual input; for a memory retrieval task they would represent a partial description of the item to be retrieved. At thermal equilibrium the units continue to change their states, but the relative probability of finding the network in any global configuration is stable and is related to the cost of that configuration by a Boltzmann distribution

$$\frac{P_\alpha}{P_\beta} = e^{-(E_\alpha - E_\beta)/T} \qquad (1)$$

where P_α is the probability of being in the αth global configuration and E_α is the cost of that configuration.

COOPERATIVE COMPUTATION OF BEST FITS BY ENERGY MINIMIZATION

Tasks like perceptual interpretation and content-addressable memory can be formulated as optimization problems in which there are massive numbers of plausible constraints, and low-cost solutions typically satisfy most but not all of the constraints (Ballard and co-workers, 1983; Rumelhart and McClelland, 1986). The Boltzmann machine allows the constraints to be implemented directly as interactions between units. If these interactions are symmetrical, it is possible to associate an energy E with each global configuration (Hopfield, 1982; Hummel and Zucker, 1983).

$$E = -\sum_{i<j} w_{ij}s_i s_j + \sum_i \theta_i s_i \qquad (2)$$

where w_{ij} is the weight of the connection from the jth to the ith unit, s_i is the state of the ith unit (0 or 1), and θ_i is a threshold.

Each unit can compute the difference in the global energy for its *off* and *on* states given the current states of all the other units. This energy gap is simply the sum of the weights on the connections coming from other *on* units. So to monotonically reduce the global energy, units should adopt their *on* state if and only if their energy gap is positive (Hopfield, 1982). Searches for minima of an energy function can be improved by adding thermal noise to the decision rule (Kirkpatrick and co-workers, 1983). The thermal noise allows the network to escape from local minima and to pass through higher energy configurations. By giving each of the very large number of higher energy configurations a small chance of being sampled, it effectively removes energy barriers between minima. In the Boltzmann machine the probabilistic decision rule used to simulate thermal noise is

$$p_k = \frac{1}{(1 + e^{-\Delta E_k/T})} \qquad (3)$$

where p_k is the probability that the kth unit adopts the *on* state, ΔE_k is its energy gap, and T is the temperature. If each unit is sampled with finite probability and if time delays are negligible, this decision rule will cause the whole network to approach thermal equilibrium. The fastest way to approach a low-temperature equilibrium (at which low-cost configurations are far more probable than high-cost ones) is to start with a high temperature and to gradually reduce it, a process called simulated annealing (qv) (Kirkpatrick and co-workers, 1983; Geman and Geman, 1984).

REPRESENTING PROBABILITIES

In a Boltzmann machine the probability that an atomic hypothesis is correct is represented by the probability of finding the corresponding unit in the *on* state. This allows the machine to correctly represent the probabilities of complex hypotheses that correspond to configurations of *on* and *off* states over many units. Systems that use real numbers to directly represent the probabilities of the atomic hypotheses (see REASONING, PLAUSIBLE) have great difficulty representing the higher order statistical structure correctly and so they cannot implement Bayesian inference (see BAYESIAN INFERENCE METHODS) unless exponentially many numbers are used or very strong independence assumptions are made (Hinton and Sejnowski, 1983). In a Boltzmann machine the weights implicitly encode the a priori probabilities of an exponential number of configurations.

LEARNING

There is a simple but powerful learning algorithm (Ackley and co-workers, 1985; Hinton and Sejnowski, 1983) that allows a Boltzmann machine to learn weights that constitute an internal, generative model of the structure of an environment in which it is placed. The environment clamps configurations of *on* and *off* states on a "visible" subset of the units. The learning algorithm modifies the weights so as to maximize the likelihood that the same probability distribution of configurations will occur over the visible units when the machine is run without environmental input. The learning works in two phases. In the positive phase the environment clamps the visible units, the network settles to thermal equilibrium at a finite temperature, and the weights between units are increased by an amount proportional to how often the units are both *on* together at equilibrium. In the negative phase the visible units are unclamped, the network settles to equilibrium, and the weights are decreased by an amount proportional to how often the two units are *on* together (Crick and Mitchison, 1983). The result of repeatedly applying this procedure is that the network turns its nonvisible units into feature detectors that allow it to represent the structure of its environment in the weights.

PROBLEMS

Several obstacles currently prevent Boltzmann machines from being of practical use. It can take a long time to reach thermal equilibrium (Geman and Geman, 1984) so if the weights are hand coded, care must be taken to avoid energy barriers that are too high for annealing searches to cross. If the weights are learned, equilibrium must be reached many times to know how to change the weights, and the weights must be changed many times to construct good models, so even very simple learning tasks require many hours of CPU time.

BIBLIOGRAPHY

D. H. Ackley, G. E. Hinton, and T. J. Sejnowski, "A Learning Algorithm for Boltzmann Machines," *Cog. Sci.* **9,** 147–169 (1985).

D. H. Ballard, G. E. Hinton, and T. J. Sejnowski, "Parallel Visual Computation," *Nature* **306,** 21–26 (1983).

F. Crick and G. Mitchison, "The Function of Dream Sleep," *Nature* **304,** 111–114 (1983).

S. E. Fahlman, G. E. Hinton, and T. J. Sejnowski, "Massively Parallel Architectures for A.I.: Netl, Thistle, and Boltzmann Machines," *Proceedings of the Third National Conference on AI,* Washington, D.C., 1983, pp. 109–113.

J. A. Feldman and D. H. Ballard, "Connectionist Models and Their Properties," *Cog. Sci.* **6,** 205–254 (1982).

S. Geman and D. Geman, "Stochastic Relaxation, Gibbs Distributions, and the Bayesian Restoration of Images," *IEEE Trans. Pattern Anal. Mach. Intell.* **PAMI-6,** 721–741 (1984).

G. E. Hinton and J. A. Anderson, eds., *Parallel Models of Associative Memory,* Erlbaum, Hillsdale, N.J., 1981.

G. E. Hinton and T. J. Sejnowski, "Optimal Perceptual Inference," *Proceedings of the IEEE Conference on Computer Vision and Pattern Recognition,* Washington, D.C., 1983, pp. 448–453.

J. J. Hopfield, "Neural Networks and Physical Systems with Emergent Collective Computational Abilities," *Proc. Nat. Acad. Sci. USA* **79,** 2554–2558 (1982).

R. A. Hummel and S. W. Zucker, "On the Foundations of Relaxation Labeling Processes," *IEEE Trans. Pattern Anal. Mach. Intell.* **PAMI-5,** 267–287 (1983).

S. Kirkpatrick, C. D. Gelatt, and M. P. Vecci, "Optimization by Simulated Annealing," *Science* **220,** 671–680 (1983).

D. E. Rumelhart and J. L. McClelland, eds., *Parallel Distributed Processing: Explorations in the Microstructures of Cognition, Vol. 1, Foundations,* MIT Press, Cambridge, Mass., 1986.

G. E. Hinton
Carnegie Mellon University

BORIS

An understanding program written by Michael Dyer at Yale in 1982, BORIS can read and then answer questions about several complex narrative texts. It uses the approach of integrating parsing and inferencing (see M. Dyer, *In-Depth Understanding,* MIT Press, Cambridge, Mass., 1983).

Michael Dyer
University of California, Los Angeles

BOTTOM-UP PROCESSING. See Processing, bottom-up and top-down.

BRANCH-AND-BOUND SEARCH. See Search, branch-and-bound.

BRANCHING FACTOR

A branching factor is a parameter that measures the effective complexity of a problem or a search (qv) algorithm, especially those characterized by an exponentially growing complexity. The term branching factor has evolved from the metaphor of a uniform tree where each internal node sprouts exactly b branches and the total number of nodes up to depth d is $(b^{d+1} - 1)/(b - 1)$. Thus, if an algorithm searches such a tree and generates every node up to depth d, the complexity of that algorithm will be roughly $[b/(b - 1)]b^d$, with b measuring the relative increase in complexity due to each additional level of search (see Problem solving).

This growth rate measurement can be extended to algorithms whose search spaces are nonuniform trees. If d stands for the maximal depth reached by an algorithm A, and N_A stands for the number of nodes generated during the search, then the effective branching factor, B_A, can be defined by

$$B_A = (N_A)^{1/d} \qquad (1)$$

Indeed, when applied to a uniform tree, this formula gives

$$B_A = \left(\frac{b}{b-1}\right)^{1/d} b \qquad (2)$$

which, for large d, reduces to

$$B_A = b \qquad (3)$$

In general, the complexity N_A may vary significantly from one problem instance to another and may be a complex function of d. Therefore, the definition of B_A is usually applied to the average number, I_A, of nodes generated by algorithm A and usually invokes the limit as $d \rightarrow \infty$:

$$B_A = \lim_{d \rightarrow \infty} [I_A(d)]^{1/d} \qquad (4)$$

This definition extracts the basis of the dominant exponential term in the expression of $I_A(d)$.

In summary, the branching factor measures the relative increase in average complexity due to extending the search depth by one extra level or, equivalently, it measures the average number of branches explored by an algorithm from a typical node of the search space (Knuth and Moore, 1975).

APPLICATIONS

The primary use of the branching factor has been in comparing the pruning power of various game-playing strategies (see GAME PLAYING; GAME TREES). Theoretical analysis of these strategies usually assumes uniform, b-ary game trees, searched to depth d, with random values assigned to nodes at the search frontier (Knuth and Moore, 1975). Based on this model, it can be shown (Pearl, 1982, 1984) that the branching factor of the alpha-beta pruning (qv) algorithm (as well as that of SCOUT and SSS*) is given by

$$B = \frac{\xi_b}{1 - \xi_b} \approx b^{3/4} \qquad (5)$$

where ξ_b is the unique positive root of the equation

$$x^b + x - 1 = 0 \qquad (6)$$

Moreover, this branching factor is the best achievable by any game-searching algorithm.

Roughly speaking, a fraction of only $B/b \approx b^{1/4}$ of the b legal moves available from each game position is explored by alpha-beta. Alternatively, for a given search time allotment, the alpha-beta pruning allows the search depth to be increased by a factor $\log b / \log B \approx 4/3$ over that of an exhaustive minimax search.

Under perfect ordering of successors, alpha-beta examines a total of $2b^{d/2} - 1$ game positions, thus,

$B = b$ for exhaustive search

$B \approx b^{3/4}$ for alpha-beta with random ordering

$B = b^{1/2}$ for alpha-beta with perfect ordering

It is important to mention that the branching factor only captures the asymptotic growth rate of a search strategy as the search depth increases indefinitely; it does not reflect the size of nonexponential factors in $I(d)$ regardless of how large they are. However, an exact evaluation of the average performances of three game-searching strategies shows that the ratio $I(d)/B^d$ is fairly small (Pearl, 1984); it remains below 5 over wide ranges of b and d ($b \leq 20$, $d \leq 20$).

BIBLIOGRAPHY

D. E. Knuth and R. E. Moore, "An Analysis of Alpha-Beta Pruning," *Artif. Intell.* **6**(4), 293–326 (1975).

J. Pearl, "The Solution for the Branching Factor of the Alpha-Beta Pruning Algorithm and Its Optimality," *CACM* **25**(8), 559–564 (1982).

J. Pearl, *Heuristics: Intelligent Search Strategies for Computer Problem Solving*, Addison-Wesley, Reading, Mass., 1984, Chapts. 8 and 9.

J. PEARL
UCLA

BROWN CORPUS

The Brown Corpus is the informal but widely used name for the Standard Corpus of Present-Day Edited American English, a language database of more than 1 million words of English prose texts, originally compiled and analyzed at Brown University in the 1960s. The corpus, which exists in several formats, has been a frequent source for research into various aspects of contemporary American English; it has also served as a model for other corpora, for example, British English (primarily the Lancaster-Oslo-Bergen Corpus named after the three European universities that participated in its compilation) and other texts, some still in progress. Several hundred copies of the various formats of the corpus have been made available to universities and other research institutions all over the world, and a large bibliography referencing the corpus data can be found in linguistic, psychological, and artificial intelligence literature. A partial bibliography of corpus-based studies was published recently (*ICAME News*, 1986).

THE HISTORY OF THE CORPUS

The impetus for the compilation of the Brown Corpus in the mid-1960s was the perceived need for a computerized and representative database of contemporary American English. Corpora of English and other languages had been assembled in the past, and some of them were even subjected to fairly detailed manual statistical analysis. However, the absence of a computer-processable database was believed to be a major obstacle to a more efficient study of language performance.

The various adjectives in the official title of the Standard Corpus of Present-Day Edited American English need to be interpreted with care. The designation of the corpus as "standard" was never intended to imply that the language data and grammatical structures represented in the database were to be taken as a prescriptive example of standard English. Rather, it was meant to indicate the hope (substantiated by further developments) that the Brown Corpus would form the design basis for other computer-based corpora, and that its data would serve as a source for comparison with other research results. The adjectives describing the corpus as containing "present-day edited American English" are of crucial significance. The term "edited" reflects the fact that the corpus is composed only of materials that appeared in print and thus had presumably gone through the hands of an editor. No unpublished letters, communications, or any records of spoken conversations have been included. Consequently, the corpus text is relatively easily segmentable into useful units such as sentences and paragraphs, and the number of spelling errors and ungrammatical constructions in the text is minimal. As the term "present-day" suggests, the corpus is a completely synchronic record of American English. Specifically, materials published in 1961 in the United States were the only admissible candidates for selecting the corpus samples; the decisive date was the year of publication, and it is possible that the actual authorship of some samples falls into previous years.

The decisions of the overall structure of the Brown Corpus were made by a small conference of linguists and English specialists that took place in 1963 (Kučera and Francis, 1967). Poetry was excluded entirely and so was drama, because it generally represents an artistic recreation of the spoken language and cannot be considered to be a representative subset of true spoken English. Consequently, the corpus consists of prose of two kinds: informative, such as newspaper reportage, editorials, essays, scientific and scholarly articles, etc, and imaginative, which is represented by various genres of fiction. The eligibility of samples that include dialogue (primarily, of course, those from imaginative prose) was governed by the percentage of dialogue text: selections were deemed eligible if they contained less than 50% dialogue.

One of the aims in assembling the corpus was that it be reasonably representative of present-day American English. This was sought to be accomplished by assembling the corpus from 500 different samples of approximately 2000 words each (hence the roughly 1 million words of the corpus text) taken from 15 different genres of writing. The nature of the genres and the numerical distribution of the 2000-word samples among them were decided by a consensus of the linguists attending the 1963 conference on the basis of an educated estimate of the amount of materials of various types published in a given year in the United States. The overall distribution thus favors informative prose, which is represented by 374 samples belonging to nine major genres, over imaginative prose, of which there

are 126 samples from six genres (Francis and Kučera, 1979).

Once the individual categories and numerical genre membership were established, the actual samples were selected by a variety of random procedures, including the use a random number generator, and were taken from publishing lists, library holdings, and similar sources. The proofread and reasonably error-free text of the corpus was first available in computer-processable form in 1964. A descriptive study and a series of statistical analyses of the texts have been published (Kučera and Francis, 1967).

GRAMMATICAL ANALYSIS OF THE CORPUS

The representative nature of the corpus and its clear division into samples of considerable variety were largely responsible for the continuing interest in the database. This interest then led the original compilers to undertake, during the 1970s, a grammatical analysis of the text in terms of a highly refined and expanded part-of-speech annotation system, consisting of 87 syntactically based tags. This annotation of the entire 1 million words, performed semi-automatically, became known as the Tagged Brown Corpus and has been available to interested scholars since 1979. A detailed description of the tagging system and its rationale, as well as new frequency lists based on the analysis of lexical items and their grammatical properties, have been published (Francis and Kučera, 1982). In essence, the tagging system employed not only all the conventional part-of-speech annotations and their subcategories (eg, nouns are tagged separately as common, proper, and adverbial) but also distinct tags for individual inflected categories, such as singular and plural nouns and past and participle forms of verbs. Some tags are syntactically motivated, for example, the positional constituents of the noun phrase (prequantifier, postdeterminer, qualifier, etc). Two results that this tagging system made possible were (1) the disambiguation of homographs (eg, words such as *chair* that can be either a noun or a verb are properly tagged depending on their function in the individual sentences) and (2) the provision of a statistical set of information about probabilities and transitional probabilities of grammatical categories that can significantly facilitate computer parsing of other English texts. The latest publications of the Brown Corpus frequency lists (Francis and Kučera, 1982) could thus present a so-called lemmatized frequency list (where inflected forms are grouped together under the basic entry of the word) as well as a study of sentence complexity based on the average number of predications in the various genres of the corpus.

The tagged corpus has become a useful source of numerous theoretical and practical research projects and has served, among other things, as an adjunct in the construction of English-language dictionaries (particularly the *American Heritage Dictionary*) as well as various spelling checkers and grammar correctors now available for word processors and personal computers. It is also being used as a source in several probabilistic parsing projects. Finally, the comparison of the Brown Corpus and Lancaster-Oslo-

Bergen Corpus of British English, modeled on the Brown project, has allowed for some interesting contrastive studies of these two forms of English usage (Hofland and Johansson, 1982; Johansson and Hofland, 1989).

BIBLIOGRAPHY

"Corpus Bibliography," *ICAME News* **10,** pp. 62–79, May 1986.

W. N. Francis and H. Kučera, *Manual of Information to Accompany a Standard Sample of Present-Day American English,* 3rd ed., Brown University, Providence, R.I., 1979.

W. N. Francis and H. Kučera, *Frequency Analysis of English Usage: Lexicon and Grammar,* Houghton Mifflin Co., Boston, 1982.

K. Hofland and S. Johansson, *Word Frequencies in British and American English,* The Norwegian Computing Centre for the Humanities, Bergen, Norway, 1982.

S. Johansson and K. Hofland, *Frequency Analysis of English Vocabulary and Grammar,* Vols. 1 and 2, Clarendon Press, Oxford, UK, 1989.

H. Kučera and W. N. Francis, *Computational Analysis of Present-Day American English,* Brown University Press, Providence, R.I., 1967.

H. Kučera
Brown University

C

CAD. See Design, AI in.

CADUCEUS

An expert system for medical diagnosis developed by Myers and Pople at the University of Pittsburgh and completed in 1985. This system is an enhancement of INTERNIST (qv) in that it incorporates causal relationships in its diagnosis (see P. Szolovits, ed., *Artificial Intelligence in Medicine*, Westview, Boulder, Colorado, 1982).

K. S. Arora
SUNY at Buffalo

CALCULUS, INCIDENCE. See Incidence calculus; Lambda calculus.

CASE-BASED REASONING. See Reasoning, case-based.

CASE GRAMMAR. See Grammar, case.

CASEY

A medical diagnosis program developed by Koton at MIT that combines empirical and analytical problem solving. CASEY uses case-based reasoning to diagnose patients similar to those it has seen before. It uses model-based reasoning to justify re-use of previous solutions and to solve unfamiliar problems. (See P. Koton, "Reasoning About Evidence in Causal Explanations," in *Proceedings of the Seventh National Conference on Artificial Intelligence*, 1988.)

Phyllis Koton
Mitre Corp.

CAUSAL REASONING. See Reasoning, causal.

CERTAINTY-FACTOR MODEL

The certainty-factor (CF) model is a method for managing uncertainty in rule-based systems. Shortliffe and Buchanan (1975) developed the CF model in the mid-1970s for MYCIN (qv), an expert system for the diagnosis and treatment of meningitis and infections of the blood. Since then the CF model has become the standard approach to uncertainty management in rule-based systems.

When the model was created, many artificial intelligence researchers expressed concern about using Bayesian (or subjective) probability to represent uncertainty. Of these researchers, most were concerned about the practical limitations of using probability theory. In particular, information science researchers were using the idiot-Bayes model to construct expert systems for medicine and other domains. This model included the assumptions that (1) faults or hypotheses were mutually exclusive and exhaustive and (2) pieces of evidence were conditionally independent, given each fault or hypothesis (see Bayesian inference methods). The assumptions were useful, because their adoption made the construction of expert systems practical. Unfortunately, however, the assumptions were often inaccurate in practice.

The CF model was created to avoid the unreasonable assumptions in the idiot-Bayes model. In this article, however, it will be seen that the CF model is no more useful than is the idiot-Bayes model. In fact, in certain circumstances, the CF model implicitly imposes assumptions of conditional independence that are stronger than those of the idiot-Bayes model. The flaws in the CF model will be traced to the fact that the model imposes the same sort of modularity on uncertain rules that are ascribed to logical rules, although uncertain reasoning is inherently less modular than is logical reasoning. In addition, the belief network, a graphical representation of beliefs in the probabilistic framework, will be examined. It will be noted that this representation overcomes the difficulties associated with the CF model.

MECHANICS OF THE MODEL

To understand how the CF model works, consider a simple example taken from Bayesian inference methods (qv):

> Mr. Holmes receives a telephone call from his neighbor Dr. Watson stating that he hears a burglar alarm sound from the direction of Mr. Holmes's house. Preparing to rush home, Mr. Holmes recalls that Dr. Watson is known to be a tasteless practical joker, and he decides to first call his other neighbor, Mrs. Gibbons, who, despite occasional drinking problems, is far more reliable.

A miniature rule-based system for Mr. Holmes's situation contains the following rules:

R_1: if WATSON'S CALL then ALARM, $CF_1 = 0.5$

R_2: if GIBBON'S CALL then ALARM, $CF_2 = 0.9$

R_3: if ALARM then BURGLARY, $CF_3 = 0.99$

In general, rule-based systems (qv) contain rules of the form "if e then h," where e denotes a piece of evidence for hypothesis h. Using the CF model, an expert represents uncertainty in a rule by attaching a single CF to each rule. A CF represents a person's (usually, the expert's) change in belief in the hypothesis given the evidence. In particular, a CF between 0 and 1 means that the person's belief in h given e increases, whereas a CF between -1 and 0 means that the person's belief decreases. Unlike a probability, a CF does not represent a person's absolute degree of belief in h given e. The nature of a CF in probabilistic terms will be discussed below.

Several implementations of the rule-based representation display a rule base in graphical form as an inference network. Figure 1 illustrates the inference network for Mr. Holmes's situation. Each arc in an inference network represents a rule; the number above the arc is the CF for the rule.

Using the CF model, the change in belief in any hypothesis in the network can be computed, given the observed evidence, by applying simple combination functions to the CFs that lie between the evidence and the hypothesis in question. For example, in Mr. Holmes's situation, the task is to compute the change in belief of BURGLARY, given WATSON'S CALL and GIBBON'S CALL. The CFs are combined in two steps. First, CF_1 and CF_2, the CFs for R_1 and R_2, are combined to give the CF for the rule R_4:

R_4: if WATSON'S CALL and GIBBON'S CALL
                    then ALARM, CF_4

CF_1 and CF_2 are combined using the function

$$CF_4 = \begin{cases} CF_1 + CF_2 - CF_1 CF_2 & CF_1, CF_2 \geq 0 \\ CF_1 + CF_2 + CF_1 CF_2 & CF_1, CF_2 < 0 \\ \dfrac{CF_1 + CF_2}{1 - \min(|CF_1|, |CF_2|)} & \text{otherwise} \end{cases} \quad (1)$$

In Mr. Holmes's case,

$$CF_4 = 0.5 + 0.9 - (0.5)(0.9) = 0.95$$

Equation 1 is called the parallel combination function. In general, this function is used to combine two rules that share the same hypothesis. Second, CF_3 and CF_4 are combined to give the CF for the rule R_5:

R_5: if WATSON'S CALL and GIBBON'S CALL
                    then BURGLARY, CF_5

$$CF_5 = \begin{cases} CF_3 CF_4 & CF_3 > 0 \\ 0 & CF_3 \leq 0 \end{cases} \quad (2)$$

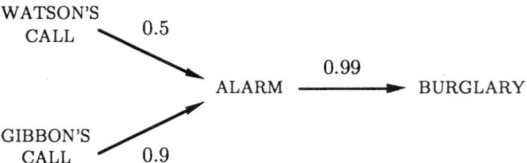

Figure 1. An inference network for Mr. Holmes's situation. Each arc represents a rule. For example, the arc from ALARM to BURGLARY represents the rule R_3 (if ALARM then BURGLARY). The number above the arc is the CF for the rule.

In Mr. Holmes's case,

$$CF_5 = (0.99)(0.95) = 0.94$$

Equation 2 is called the serial combination function. This function is used to combine two rules where the hypothesis in the first rule is the evidence in the second rule.

If all evidence and hypotheses in a rule base are simple propositions, it is necessary to use only the serial and parallel combination rules to combine CF. The CF model, however, can also accommodate rules that contain conjunctions and disjunctions of evidence. For example, suppose the following rule exists in an expert system for diagnosing chest pain:

R_6:   if   CHEST PAIN *and*
              SHORTNESS OF BREATH
        then   HEART ATTACK, $CF_6 = 0.9$

Furthermore, suppose there are rules that reflect indirect evidence for chest pain and shortness of breath:

R_7: if PATIENT GRIMACES
              then CHEST PAIN, $CF_7 = 0.7$

R_8: if PATIENT CLUTCHES THROAT
              then SHORTNESS OF BREATH, $CF_8 = 0.9$

CF_6, CF_7, and CF_8 can be combined to yield the CF for the rule R_9:

R_9:   if   PATIENT GRIMACES *and*
              PATIENT CLUTCHES THROAT
        then   HEART ATTACK, CF_9

The combination function is

$$CF_9 = CF_6 \min(CF_7, CF_8) = (0.9)(0.7) = 0.63 \quad (3)$$

That is, the serial combination of CF_6 and the minimum of CF_7 and CF_8 are computed. The minimum of CF_7 and CF_8 is used because R_6 contains the conjunction of CHEST PAIN and SHORTNESS OF BREATH. In general, the CF model prescribes that the minimum of CFs are used for evidence in a conjunction and the maximum of CF evidence in a disjunction.

There are many variations among the implementations of the CF model. For example, the original CF model used in MYCIN treats CFs less than 0.2 as though they were 0 in serial combination, to increase the efficiency of computation. Other variations exist.

AN IMPROVEMENT OVER IDIOT-BAYES?

In the simple case of Mr. Holmes, the CF model is an improvement over the idiot-Bayes model. In particular, WATSON'S CALL and GIBBON'S CALL are not conditionally independent, given BURGLARY, because even if Mr. Holmes knows that a burglary has occurred, receiving Watson's call increases Mr. Holmes belief that Mrs. Gibbons will report the alarm sound. The lack of conditional independence is due to the fact that the calls are triggered by the alarm sound, and not by the burglary. The CF model represents accurately this lack of independence through the presence of ALARM in the inference network.

Unfortunately, the CF model cannot represent most real-world problems in a way that is both accurate and efficient. In the next section, it will be seen that the assumptions of conditional independence associated with the parallel combination function are stronger (ie, are less likely to be accurate) than are those associated with the idiot-Bayes model.

THEORETICAL PROBLEMS WITH THE CF MODEL

Rules that represent logical relationships satisfy the principle of modularity. That is, given the logical rule "if e then h," and given that e is true, it can be asserted that h is true (1) no matter how it is established that e is true and (2) no matter what else is known to be true. These two points are called the principle of detachment and the principle of locality, respectively. For example, given the rule

R_{10}: if L_1 and L_2 are parallel lines
    then L_1 and L_2 do not intersect

It can be asserted that L_1 and L_2 do not intersect once it is known that L_1 and L_2 are parallel lines. This assertion depends on neither how it is known that L_1 and L_2 are parallel (the principle of detachment) nor what else is known (the principle of locality).

The CF model employs the same principles of detachment and locality to belief updating. For example, given the rule

R_3: if ALARM then BURGLARY, $CF_3 = 0.99$

and given that ALARM is known, the CF model allows Mr. Holmes's belief in BURGLARY to be updated by the amount corresponding to a CF of 0.99, no matter how Mr. Holmes established his belief in ALARM and no matter what other facts he knows.

Unfortunately, uncertain reasoning often violates the principles of detachment and locality. Use of the CF model, therefore, often leads to errors in reasoning. [Heckerman and Horvitz (1987, 1988) first noted the nonmodularity of uncertain reasoning, and the relationship of such nonmodularity to the limitations of the CF model. Pearl (1988) first decomposed the principle of modularity into the principles of detachment and locality.] In the remainder of this section, classes of such errors will be examined.

Multiple Causes of the Same Effect

Consider the simple embellishment to Mr. Holmes's problem given in Bayesian inference methods:

Mr. Holmes remembers having read in the instruction manual of his alarm system that the device is sensitive to earthquakes and can be triggered by one accidentally. He realizes that if an

earthquake had occurred, it would surely be on the news. So, he turns on his radio and waits around for a newscast.

Figure 2 illustrates a possible inference network for his situation. To the original inference network of Figure 1, the rules following rules have been added.

R_{11}: if RADIO NEWSCAST
    then EARTHQUAKE, $CF_{11} = 0.9998$

R_{12}: if EARTHQUAKE then ALARM, $CF_{12} = 0.95$

The inference network does not capture an important interaction among the propositions. In particular, the modular rule R_3 (if ALARM then BURGLARY) gives permission to increase Mr. Holmes's belief in BURGLARY, when his belief in ALARM increases, no matter how Mr. Holmes increases his belief for ALARM. This modular license to update belief, however, is not consistent with common sense. If Mr. Holmes hears the radio newscast, he increases his belief that an earthquake has occurred. Therefore, he decreases his belief that there has been a burglary, because the occurrence of an earthquake would account for the alarm sound. Overall, Mr. Holmes's belief in ALARM increases, but his belief in BURGLARY decreases.

When the evidence for ALARM came from WATSON'S CALL and GIBBON'S CALL, there was no problem propagating this increase in belief through R_3 to BURGLARY. In contrast, when the evidence for ALARM came from EARTHQUAKE, it was not possible to propagate this increase in belief through R_3. This difference illustrates a violation of the detachment principle in uncertain reasoning: the source of a belief update, in part, determines whether or not that update should be passed along to other propositions.

Pearl (1988) describes this phenomenon in detail. He divides uncertain inferences into two types: diagnostic and predictive. Henrion (1987) also makes this distinction. In a diagnostic inference, the belief in a cause is changed given an effect. All the rules in the inference network of Figure 2, except R_{12}, are of this form. In a predictive inference, the belief in an effect is changed given a cause. R_{12} is an example of such an inference. Pearl describes the interactions between the two types of

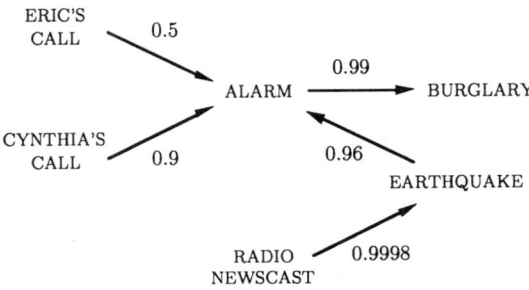

Figure 2. Another inference network for Mr. Holmes's situation. In addition to the interactions in Figure 1, RADIO NEWSCAST increases the chance of EARTHQUAKE, and EARTHQUAKE increases the chance of ALARM.

inferences. He notes that, if the belief in a proposition is increased by a diagnostic inference, then that increase can be passed through to another diagnostic inference, just what is expected for the chain of inferences from WATSON'S CALL and GIBBON'S CALL to BURGLARY. On the other hand, if the belief in a proposition is increased by a predictive inference, then that belief should not be passed through a diagnostic inference. Moreover, when the belief in one cause of an observed effect increases, the beliefs in other causes should decrease, just what is expected for the two causes of ALARM.

It might be tempting to repair the inference network in Figure 2, by adding the rule

R_{13}: if EARTHQUAKE then BURGLARY, $CF_{13} = -0.7$

Unfortunately, this addition leads to another problem. In particular, suppose that Mr. Holmes had never received the telephone calls. Then the radio newscast should not affect his belief in a burglary. The modular rule R_{13}, however, gives license to decrease Mr. Holmes's belief in BURGLARY, whether or not he receives the phone calls. This problem illustrates that uncertain reasoning also can violate the principle of locality: the validity of an inference may depend on the truth of other propositions.

To represent accurately the case of Mr. Holmes, a rule for every possible combination of observations must be included.

    if   WATSON'S CALL *and*
          GIBBON'S CALL *and*
          RADIO NEWSCAST
    then BURGLARY
    if   NOT WATSON'S CALL *and*
          GIBBON'S CALL *and*
          RADIO NEWSCAST
    then BURGLARY
          . . .

This representation is inefficient and difficult to modify; it needlessly clusters propositions that are only remotely related. Ideally, a representation that encodes only direct relationships among propositions and that infers indirect relationships is desired. The belief network, a representation with such a capability, will be examined below.

The same difficulties in representing Mr. Holmes's situation with the CF model are found whenever there are multiple causes of a common effect. For example, if a car will not start, initially it may be suspected that either the battery is dead or the gas tank is empty. Once it is found that the radio is dead, however, the belief that the tank is empty is decreased because now it is more likely that the battery is dead. Here, the relationship between CAR WILL NOT START and TANK EMPTY is influenced by RADIO DEAD, just as the relationship between ALARM and BURGLARY is influenced by RADIO NEWSCAST. In general, when one effect shares more than one cause, violations of the principles of detachment and locality are expected.

Figure 3. An inference network for the Chernobyl disaster (Henrion, 1986). When the CFs are combined as modular belief updates, the chance of THOUSANDS DEAD is overcounted.

Correlated Evidence

Figure 3 depicts an inference network for news reports about the Chernobyl disaster. On hearing radio, television, and newspaper reports that thousands of people have died of radioactive fallout, the belief that many people have died is increased substantially. When it is learned that each of these reports originated from the same source, however, the belief is decreased. The CF model, however, treats both situations identically.

In this example, another violation of the principle of detachment in uncertain reasoning is seen: the sources of a set of belief updates can strongly influence how those updates are combined. Because the CF model imposes the principle of detachment on the combination of belief updates, it overcounts evidence when the sources of that evidence are positively correlated, and it undercounts evidence when the sources of evidence are negatively correlated.

A Probabilistic Interpretation for Certainty Factors

Heckerman (1986) delineated precisely the limitations of the CF model. He proved that a probabilistic interpretation can be given to any scheme, including the CF model, that combines belief updates in a modular and consistent fashion. In particular, he showed that a belief update for hypothesis h, given evidence e, can be interpreted as a function of the likelihood ratio

$$\lambda = \frac{p(e \mid h, \xi)}{p(e \mid \text{NOT } h, \xi)} \qquad (4)$$

where $p(e \mid h, \xi)$ denotes the probability (ie, degree of belief) that e is true, given that h is true, and ξ denotes the background knowledge of the person to whom the belief belongs. Using Bayes's theorem it can be written as the ratio of the posterior odds to prior odds of the hypothesis:

$$\lambda = \frac{O(h \mid e, \xi)}{O(h \mid \xi)} = \frac{\dfrac{p(h \mid e, \xi)}{1 - p(h \mid e, \xi)}}{\dfrac{p(h \mid \xi)}{1 - p(h \mid \xi)}} \qquad (5)$$

Equation 5 shows more clearly that λ represents a change in belief in a hypothesis, given evidence. (See BAYESIAN INFERENCE METHODS for a detailed description of the likelihood ratio.)

For the CF model, Heckerman showed that, if the following identification is made

$$CF = \begin{cases} \dfrac{\lambda - 1}{\lambda} & \lambda \geq 1 \\ \lambda - 1 & \lambda < 1 \end{cases} \qquad (6)$$

then the parallel combination function (eq. 1) follows exactly from Bayes's theorem. In addition, with the identification in equation 6, the serial combination function (eq. 2) and the combination functions for disjunction and conjunction are close approximations to the rules of probability.

This probabilistic interpretation for CFs shows that each combination function imposes assumptions of conditional independence on the propositions involved in the combinations. For example, when the parallel combination function is used to combine CFs for the rules "if e_1 then h" and "if e_2 then h," it is assumed implicitly that e_1 and e_2 are conditionally independent, given h and NOT h. Similarly, when the serial combination function is used to combine CFs for the rules "if a then b" and "if b then c," it is assumed implicitly that a and c are conditionally independent, given b and NOT b.

With this understanding of the CF model, the problem with the representation of Mr. Holmes's situation can be precisely identified. There, serial combination is used to combine CFs for the sequence of propositions EARTHQUAKE, ALARM, and BURGLARY. In doing so, the inaccurate assumption (among others) is made that EARTHQUAKE and BURGLARY are conditionally independent, given ALARM. No matter how the arcs in the inference network of Figure 2 are manipulated, inaccurate assumptions of conditional independence are generated.

The assumptions of independence imposed by the CF model are not satisfied by most real-world domains. Moreover, the assumptions of the parallel-combination function are stronger than are those of the idiot-Bayes model. That is, when the idiot-Bayes model is used, it is assumed that evidence is conditionally independent given each hypothesis. When the parallel combination function is used, however, it is assumed that evidence is conditionally independent given each hypothesis and the negation of each hypothesis. Unless the space of hypotheses consists of a single proposition and the negation of that proposition, the parallel-combination assumptions are essentially impossible to satisfy, even when the idiot-Bayes assumptions are satisfied (Johnson, 1986).

For example, consider the task of identifying an unknown aircraft. Suppose that the aircraft could be any type of commercial or military airplane. Furthermore, suppose that there are clues to the identity of the aircraft such as the airspeed, the fuselage size, and the distribution of the plane's heat plume. It may be reasonable to assume that the clues are conditionally independent, given each possible aircraft type. Under this idiot-Bayes assumption, however, the clues cannot be conditionally independent, given each aircraft type and the negation of each aircraft type.

A Fundamental Difference

The problems with the CF model can be understood at a more intuitive level. Logical relationships represent what can be observed directly. In contrast, uncertain relationships encode invisible influences: exceptions to that which is visible. For example, a burglary will not always trigger an alarm, because there are hidden mechanisms that may inhibit the sounding of the alarm. These hidden mechanisms are summarized in a probability for ALARM given BURGLARY. In the process of summarization, information is lost. Therefore, when an attempt to combine uncertain information, unexpected (nonmodular) interactions may occur. It should not be expected that the CF model (or any modular belief updating scheme) will be able to handle such subtle interactions. Pearl (1988) discusses this point in detail.

A PRACTICAL PROBLEM WITH THE CF MODEL

In addition to the theoretical difficulties of updating beliefs within the CF model, the model contains a serious practical problem. Specifically, the CF model requires that rules are encoded in the direction in which they are used. That is, an inference network must trace a trail of rules from observation evidence to hypotheses. Unfortunately, the rules are not often used in the same direction in which experts can most accurately and most comfortably assess them. It has been shown (Tversky and Kahneman, 1982) that people are usually most comfortable when they assess predictive rules, that is, rules of the form

if CAUSE then EFFECT

For example, expert physicians prefer to assess the likelihood of a symptom, given a disease, rather than the likelihood (or belief update) of a disease, given a symptom (Tversky and Kahneman, 1982). Henrion (see Horvitz and co-workers, 1988) attributes this phenomenon to the nature of causality. In particular, he noted that a predictive probability (the likelihood of a symptom, given a disease) reflects a stable property of that disease. In contrast, a diagnostic probability (the likelihood of a disease, given a symptom) depends on the incidence rates of that disease and of other diseases that may cause the manifestation. Thus predictive probabilities are a more useful and parsimonious way to represent uncertain relationships, at least in medical domains.

Unfortunately for the CF model, effects are usually the observable pieces of evidence, and causes are the sought-after hypotheses. Thus experts are usually forced to construct rules of the form if EFFECT then CAUSE

Consequently, in using the CF model, experts are forced to provide judgments of uncertainty in a direction that makes them uncomfortable, thereby promoting errors in assessment.

BELIEF NETWORKS: A LANGUAGE OF DEPENDENCIES

The examples in this article illustrate the need for a language that helps to keep track of the sources of a belief and that makes it easy to represent or infer the propositions on which each belief is dependent. The belief network is such a language. In addition, it is a representation that allows an expert to represent knowledge in whichever direction is preferred. Other names for belief networks include probabilistic networks, causal networks, and Bayesian networks. Several researchers developed the representation independently (eg, Wright, 1921; Good, 1961; Rousseau, 1968). Howard and Matheson (1981) generalized the belief network to allow for the representation of decisions and the preferences of a decision maker (see PROBABILISTIC NETWORKS).

Figure 4 shows a belief network for Mr. Holmes's situation. The belief network is a directed acyclic graph. The nodes in the graph correspond to uncertain variables rele-

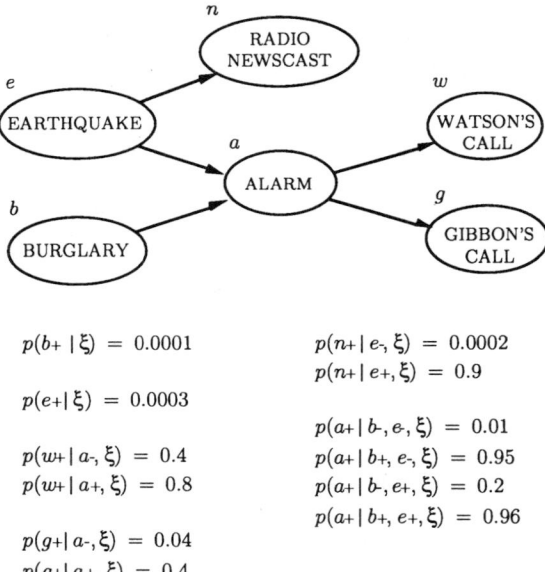

$$p(b_+ \mid \xi) = 0.0001$$

$$p(e_+ \mid \xi) = 0.0003$$

$$p(w_+ \mid a_-, \xi) = 0.4$$
$$p(w_+ \mid a_+, \xi) = 0.8$$

$$p(g_+ \mid a_-, \xi) = 0.04$$
$$p(g_+ \mid a_+, \xi) = 0.4$$

$$p(n_+ \mid e_-, \xi) = 0.0002$$
$$p(n_+ \mid e_+, \xi) = 0.9$$

$$p(a_+ \mid b_-, e_-, \xi) = 0.01$$
$$p(a_+ \mid b_+, e_-, \xi) = 0.95$$
$$p(a_+ \mid b_-, e_+, \xi) = 0.2$$
$$p(a_+ \mid b_+, e_+, \xi) = 0.96$$

Figure 4. A knowledge map for Mr. Holmes's situation. The nodes in the knowledge map represent the uncertain variables relevant to Mr. Holmes's situation. The arcs represent direct probabilistic dependencies among the variables, whereas the lack of arcs between nodes represents assertions of conditional independence. Each node in the knowledge map is associated with a set of probability distributions. These distributions appear below the graph. The variables in the probabilistic expressions correspond to the nodes that they label in the knowledge map. For example, $p(b_+ \mid \xi)$ denotes the probability that a burglary has occurred, given Mr. Holmes's background information, ξ. The figure does not display the probabilities that the events failed to occur. We can compute these probabilities by subtracting from 1.0 the probabilities shown.

vant to the problem. For Mr. Holmes, each uncertain variable represents a proposition and that proposition's negation. For example, node b in Figure 4 represents the propositions BURGLARY and NOT BURGLARY (denoted b_+ and b_-, respectively). In general, an uncertain variable can represent an arbitrary set of mutually exclusive and exhaustive propositions; each proposition is called an instance of the variable. In the remainder of the discussion, no distinction is made between the variable x and the node x that represents that variable.

Each variable in a belief network is associated with a set of probability distributions. (A probability distribution is an assignment of a probability to each instance of a variable.) In the Bayesian tradition, these distributions encode the knowledge provider's beliefs about the relationships among the variables. Mr. Holmes's probabilities appear below the belief network in Figure 4.

The arcs in the directed acyclic graph represent direct probabilistic dependencies among the uncertain variables. In particular, an arc from node x to node y reflects an assertion by the builder of that network that the probability distribution for y may depend on the instance of the variable x; it is said that x conditions y. Thus a node has a probability distribution for every instance of its conditioning nodes. (An instance of a set of nodes is an assignment of an instance to each node in that set.) For example, in Figure 4, ALARM is conditioned by both EARTHQUAKE and BURGLARY. Consequently, there are four probability distributions for ALARM, corresponding to the instances where both EARTHQUAKE and BURGLARY occur, BURGLARY occurs alone, EARTHQUAKE occurs alone, and neither EARTHQUAKE nor BURGLARY occurs. In contrast, RADIO NEWSCAST, WATSON'S CALL, and GIBBON'S CALL are each conditioned by only one node. Thus there are two probability distributions for each of these nodes. Finally, EARTHQUAKE and BURGLARY do not have any conditioning nodes, and hence each node has only one probability distribution.

The lack of arcs in a belief network reflects assertions of conditional independence. For example, there is no arc from BURGLARY to WATSON'S CALL in Figure 4. The lack of this arc encodes Mr. Holmes's belief that the probability of receiving Watson's telephone call from his neighbor does not depend on whether or not there was a burglary, provided Mr. Holmes knows whether or not the alarm sounded.

In probabilistic networks (qv), the exact semantics of missing arcs are described. Here, it is important to recognize that, given any belief network, the joint probability distribution for the variables in any belief network can be constructed from (1) the probability distributions associated with each node in the network and (2) the assertions of conditional independence reflected by the lack of some arcs in the network. The joint probability distribution for a set of variables is the collection of probabilities for each instance of that set. The distribution for Mr. Holmes's situation is

$$p(e, b, a, n, w, g \mid \xi)$$
$$= p(e \mid \xi)\, p(b \mid \xi)\, p(a \mid e, b, \xi)\, p(n \mid e, \xi)\, p(w \mid a, \xi)\, p(g \mid a, \xi)$$
$$\tag{7}$$

The probability distributions on the right-hand side of equation 7 are exactly those distributions associated with the nodes in the belief network.

Getting Answers from Belief Networks

Given a joint probability distribution over a set of variables, any conditional probability can be computed that involves those variables. In particular, the probability of any set of hypotheses, given any set of observations, can be computed. For example, Mr. Holmes undoubtedly wants to determine the probability of BURGLARY (b_+) given RADIO NEWSCAST (n_+) and WATSON'S CALL (w_+) and GIBBON'S CALL (g_+). Applying the rules of probability (see BAYESIAN INFERENCE METHODS) to the joint probability distribution for Mr. Holmes's situation, the following is obtained

$$p(b_+|n_+,w_+,g_+,\xi) = \frac{p(b_+,n_+,w_+,g_+|\xi)}{p(n_+,w_+,g_+|\xi)}$$
$$= \frac{\Sigma_{e_i,a_k}\, p(e_i,b_+,a_k,n_+,w_+,g_+|\xi)}{\Sigma_{e_i,b_j,a_k}\, p(e_i,b_j,a_k,n_+,w_+,g_+|\xi)}$$

where e_i, b_j, and a_k denote arbitrary instances of the variables e, b, and a, respectively.

In general, given a belief network, any set of probabilities can be calculated from the joint distribution implied by that network. Probabilities of interest can also be computed directly within a belief network. In doing so, it is possible to take advantage of the assertions of conditional independence reflected by the lack of arcs in the network: Fewer arcs lead to less computation (see PROBABILISTIC NETWORKS).

Belief Networks for Knowledge Acquisition

A belief network simplifies knowledge acquisition by exploiting a fundamental observation about the ability of people to assess probabilities. Namely, a belief network takes advantage of the fact that people can make assertions of conditional independence much more easily than they can assess numerical probabilities (Howard and Matheson, 1981; Pearl, 1986). In using a belief network, a person first builds the graph that reflects the assertions of conditional independence; only then are the probabilities underlying the graph assessed. Thus a belief network helps a person to decompose the construction of a joint probability distribution into the construction of a set of smaller probability distributions.

Advantages of the Belief Network over the CF Model

The example of Mr. Holmes illustrates the advantages of the belief network over the CF model. First, it is possible to avoid the practical problem of the CF model that was discussed earlier; namely, using a belief network, a knowledge provider can choose the order in which probability distributions are assessed. For example, in Figure 4, all arcs point from cause to effect, showing that Mr. Holmes prefers to assess the probability of observing an effect, given one or more causes. If, however, Mr. Holmes wanted to specify the probabilities of, say, EARTH-

QUAKE given RADIO NEWSCAST and of EARTHQUAKE given NOT RADIO NEWSCAST, he simply would reverse the arc from RADIO NEWSCAST to EARTHQUAKE in Figure 4. Regardless of the direction in which Mr. Holmes assesses the conditional distributions, any of the available belief network algorithms can be used to compute the conditional probabilities of interest, if the need arises (Schachter and Heckerman, 1987).

Second, using a belief network, the knowledge provider can control the assertions of conditional independence that are encoded in the representation. In contrast, the use of the combination functions in the CF model forces a person to adopt assertions of conditional independence that may be incorrect. For example, the inference network in Figure 2 dictates the erroneous assertion that EARTHQUAKE and BURGLARY are conditionally independent, given ALARM.

Third, and most important, a knowledge provider does not have to assess indirect independencies, using a belief network. Such independencies reveal themselves in the course of probabilistic computations within the network. In fact, it is not even necessary to perform numerical computations to derive such indirect independencies. An efficient algorithm exists that uses only the structure of the belief network to reveal these dependencies (Geiger and co-workers, 1990). Such computations can reveal, for example, that BURGLARY and RADIO NEWSCAST are normally independent, but become dependent, given WATSON'S CALL, GIBBON'S CALL, or both.

Thus the belief network helps to tame the inherently nonmodular properties of uncertain reasoning. Uncertain knowledge encoded in a belief network is not as modular as is knowledge about logical relationships. Nonetheless, representing uncertain knowledge in a belief network is a great improvement over encoding all relationships among a set of variables.

BIBLIOGRAPHY

D. Geiger, T. Verma, and J. Pearl, "Identifying Independence in Bayesian Networks," *Networks* **20**, 507–534 (1990).

I. Good, "A Causal Calculus (I)," *Brit. J. Philos. Sci.* **11**, 305–318 (1961).

D. Heckerman, "Probabilistic Interpretations for MYCIN's Certainty Factors," in L. Kanal and J. Lemmer, eds., *Uncertainty in Artificial Intelligence,* North-Holland, Amsterdam, 1986, pp. 167–196.

D. Heckerman and E. Horvitz, "On the Expressiveness of Rule-Based Systems for Reasoning under Uncertainty," in *Proceedings of the Sixth National Conference on Artificial Intelligence,* Seattle, Wash., Morgan-Kaufmann, San Mateo, Calif., 1987, pp. 121–126.

D. Heckerman and E. Horvitz, "The Myth of Modularity in Rule-Based Systems," in J. Lemmer and L. Kanal, eds., *Uncertainty in Artificial Intelligence,* Vol. 2, North-Holland, Amsterdam, The Netherlands, 1988, pp. 23–34.

M. Henrion, "Should We Use Probability in Uncertain Inference Systems?" in *Proceedings of the Cognitive Science Society Meeting,* Amherst, Penn., Carnegie Mellon, Pittsburgh, Penn., 1986.

M. Henrion, "Uncertainty in Artificial Intelligence: Is Probability Epistemologically and Heuristically Adequate?" in J. Mumpower, ed., *Expert Judgment and Expert Systems,* Springer-Verlag, New York, 1987, pp. 105–130.

E. Horvitz, J. Breese, and M. Henrion, "Decision Theory in Expert Systems and Artificial Intelligence," *Int. J. Approx. Reason.* **2,** 247–302 (1988).

R. Howard and J. Matheson, "Influence Diagrams," in R. Howard and J. Matheson, eds., *Readings on the Principles and Applications of Decision Analysis,* Vol. II, Strategic Decisions Group, Menlo Park, Calif., 1981, pp. 721–762.

R. Johnson, "Independence and Bayesian Updating Methods," in Kanal and Lemmer, eds., 1986, pp. 197–202.

J. Pearl, "Fusion, Propagation, and Structuring in Belief Networks," *Artif. Intell.* **29,** 241–288 (1986).

J. Pearl, *Probabilistic Reasoning in Intelligent Systems: Networks of Plausible Inference,* Morgan-Kaufmann, San Mateo, Calif., 1988.

W. Rousseau, *A Method for Computing Probabilities in Complex Situations,* Technical Report 6252-2, Center for Systems Research, Stanford University, Stanford, Calif., 1968.

R. Shachter and D. Heckerman, "Thinking Backward for Knowledge Acquisition," *AI Mag.* **8,** 55–63 (1987).

E. Shortliffe and B. Buchanan, "A Model of Inexact Reasoning in Medicine," *Math. Biosci.* **23,** 351–379 (1975).

A. Tversky and D. Kahneman, "Causal Schemata in Judgments under Uncertainty," in D. Kahneman, P. Slovic, and A. Tversky, eds., *Judgment under Uncertainty: Heuristics and Biases,* Cambridge University Press, New York, 1982.

S. Wright, "Correlation and Causation," *J. Agricult. Res.* **20,** 557–585 (1921).

DAVID HECKERMAN
University of Southern
California

This work was supported by the National Cancer Institute under Grant RO1CA51729-01A1.

CHARACTER RECOGNITION

Character recognition, also known as optical character recognition (OCR), is concerned with the automatic conversion of an image of a character, or of characters in running text, into the corresponding symbolic form. The long history of research in this area, some commercial successes, and the continuing need for implementations to handle less restricted forms of text, makes character recognition the most important application area, to date, in machine perception. The ability of humans to read printed text effortlessly is far from matched by today's machines which makes this an important research topic in artificial intelligence.

The processing steps involved in most OCR systems of today are indicated in Figure 1. The image scanning resolution is a function of point size of characters to be recognized (eg, for 8–point characters, 300 dots per inch (dpi) scanning is sufficient). Since text is printed as dark points on light backgrounds (or vice versa), the image is almost always mapped into a binary image, corresponding to the figure-ground dichotomy. Next the layout has to be analyzed, in a process referred to as document analysis, and the words segmented before attempting recognition.

Technical challenges in character recognition arise from three sources:

1. symbols: the set of idealized shapes that can occur, often in a hierarchy where simple symbols are assembled into more complex ones, at several levels of organization.
2. deformation: the range of shape variations that each symbol is allowed to undergo, including geometric transformations (translation, rotation, scaling, stretching, etc) and more complex or time-dependent distortions (eg, due to the biomechanics of handwriting).
3. imaging defects: imperfections in the image due to printing, optics, scanning, spatial quantization, binarization, etc.

Character recognition methods are sometimes specialized to handle subcategories such as digits only. Handwriting and machine print demand somewhat different approaches. Handwriting, particularly cursive script, consists of elongated strokes, whereas machine print consists of regularly spaced blobs. The shapes of characters in handwritten words are often influenced by the context in which they appear. Handwriting recognition has distinct technologies for the on-line and off-line cases; in the on-line case, an electronic surface is used for writing. On-line recognition is simpler than off-line recognition since the temporal data can be translated into stroke information.

The problem of character recognition is a special case of the general problem of reading. While characters occasionally appear in isolation, they usually appear with other characters. Characters group together to form words, words form sentences, sentences form paragraphs, paragraphs form text blocks, and text blocks together with illustrations form document pages, etc. Even though a deformed or degraded character in isolation may be unrecognizable, the context in which the character appears can make the recognition problem simple. The utilization of *a priori* knowledge about the domain of discourse as well as constraints imposed by the surrounding orthography is the main challenge in the development of robust methods. In this article, the discussion of automatic character recognition methods will be divided into two parts: isolated character recognition and word recognition, which includes character recognition in context. Isolated character recognition methods begin with the assumption that an object has been extracted from the surrounding background and it is necessary to assign it into one of a small set of pattern classes such as upper and lower case characters, digits, special symbols, etc. Word recognition involves assigning a compound object representing several characters into a word class. The performance of a given character recognition method is measured not only in terms of correct recognition rate but also in terms of having a low error rate, with the balance being rejected.

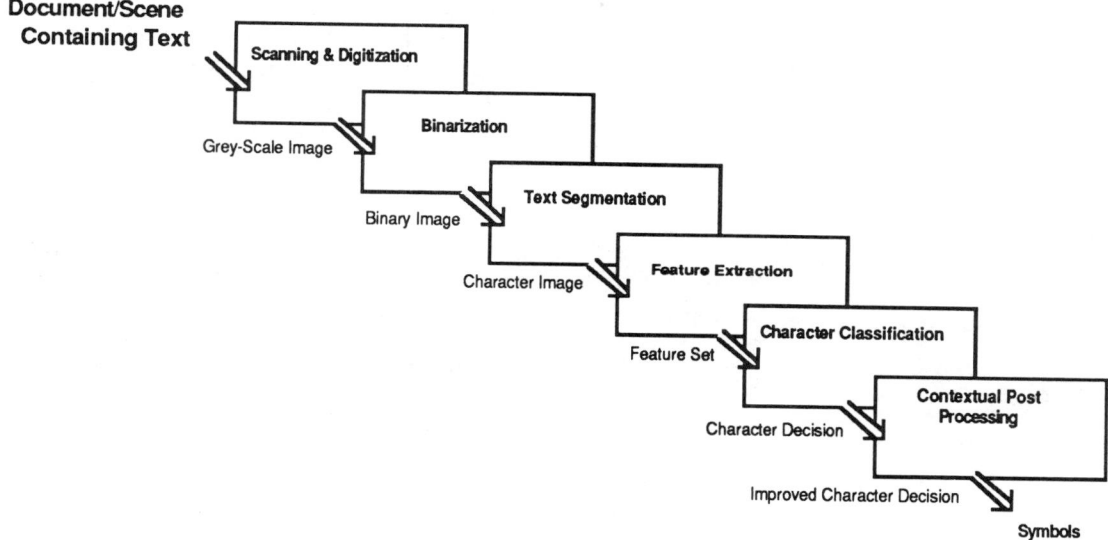

Figure 1. Typical character recognition process.

ISOLATED CHARACTER RECOGNITION

There are many techniques used to associate a symbolic identity with the image of a segmented, or isolated, character. The multitude of fonts in machine printing and the deformations encountered in handwriting make the problem of isolated character recognition a continuing challenge (Fig. 2). This section will describe several methods for the recognition of isolated characters, namely, template matching, discriminant function classifiers based on pixel arrays and structural feature vectors, rule-based analysis of contour feature strings, artificial neural networks, and combination classifiers.

Template Matching

In the process of template matching (qv), the observed pattern is directly compared to templates, or prototypes, representing each class. The classification is according to the best match, or minimum mismatch. Mathematically, the comparison is achieved with a distance measure. The distance between pattern x and the prototype of class C_i is computed by a function $d(x, C_i)$ and x is assigned to the class that minimizes this function. A metric that is useful for patterns having binary-valued features is the Hamming distance, which is the number of features, (typically pixel values) in which the observed pattern differs from the prototype of class C_i. A character recognition example using three prototypes and the Hamming distance is shown in Figure 3.

There are many variations of the template matching concept. Defining a similarity measure instead of a distance measure several different methods are obtained. For example, if n_{ij} is the number of pixels having values i and j in the template and pattern, then $n_{11}/(n_{11} + n_{01})$ is the ratio of the number of correct matches of 1's to the number of 1's in the unknown target pattern. Thus, the procedure ignores matches of 0's and does not penalize incorrect

matches. Several other similarity measures for binary matching are also appropriate for character template matching. Some of these weight individual matches and mismatches according to their statistical separability. Template matching is suitable for an application where a limited number of character types have to be recognized. When the number of prototypes is limited, it suffers from a lack of robustness because of a sensitivity to noise in the image and an inability to adapt to differences in character style. It is interesting that from an AI perspective, template matching has been ruled out as an explanation of human performance for similar reasons. However, when a large number of representative prototypes are available, template matching can yield surprisingly good results even with wide variability in patterns. For example, in the problem of handwritten digit recognition using several thousand training templates, correct recognition rates of over 90% have been reported. Such methods also suffer from having to perform a large number of computations, which may be a drawback on serial computers.

Discriminant Function Classifiers

These represent the character as a feature vector x, associate a function $f_i(x)$ with class C_i, and assign x to the class that has the maximum discriminant function value. Some discriminant functions are derived from a statistical (Bayesian) formulation of the problem. The parameters of the discriminant functions are typically estimated from a set of training samples. The polynomial method for character recognition has historically performed well enough to be incorporated into some commercial implementations for recognizing multi-font print. The binary character image is first mapped into a $n \times n$ binary array via character normalization. This image is then represented by a $n^2 = N$ element column vector $v = (v_1, v_2, \ldots, v_N)^t$. Using the components of v as linear terms and products of the components as polynomial terms, an M-element polynomial

(a)

(b)

(c)

feature vector x is constructed by a predefined mapping $\rho(v) = x$. Generally, the components of x are of degree two or less which results in a quadratic feature vector of the form,

$$x = (x_1, x_2, \ldots, x_M)^t = (1, v_1, v_2, \ldots, v_N,$$
$$v_1 * v_2, \ldots, v_{M-1} * v_M)^t.$$

Not all pixel pairs are typically used, and M tends to be far fewer than $1 + N*(N + 1)/2$. One successful implementation for recognizing handwritten digits utilizes $n = 16$, $N = 256$, and $M = 1240$, where the pairs are chosen to be within a small distance from each other (Fig. 4).

Given K classes to be discriminated, based on the polynomial feature vector x, a K-dimensional discriminant vector $d = (d_1, \ldots, d_K)$ is formed. Each of the K discriminant functions d_i is defined to be a linear expression in the components of x,

$$d_i = a_{i1} * x_1 + \cdots + a_{iM} * x_M, \quad i = 1, \ldots, K$$

and thus a quadratic polynomial expression in the components of v. The discriminant vector $d = (d_1 \, d_2 \ldots d_K)^t$ can therefore be written as $d = A^t * x$, where A is a $M \times K$ matrix, whose ith column, $i = 1, \ldots, K$, consists of the elements $a_{i1}, \ldots, a_{iM}$.

To obtain the coefficient matrix A, which gives the confidences to enable classification, the least mean square approach is chosen. Under the assumption that C training characters are available, a $C \times K$ objective matrix Y is defined as $Y = (y_1 \ldots y_K)^t$, where y_i is a binary vector indicating class membership of training character i. Similarly, let X be a $C \times M$ matrix such that row vector i equals $\rho(v)$, where v is the vector representation of the ith training image. The training proceeds by minimizing the mean–square deviation between the actual class membership matrix Y and the estimated class membership matrix given by XA. The minimization of $E\{|Y - XA|\}$ leads to the requirement that $E\{XX^t\} A = E\{XY^t\}$; it follows as a necessary condition for minimizing the norm. Consequently, the coefficient matrix A can be probabilistically approximated by $A = (XX^t)^{-1} XY^t$. After the coefficient matrix A is computed, the polynomial discriminant function can be evaluated for a test image, v. This evaluation consists of calculating the discriminant vector d and choosing the class corresponding to the largest component in this vector.

Structural Feature Vectors

Another approach is to extract structural features and represent them as a feature vector and use statistically determined discriminant functions. When asked to de-

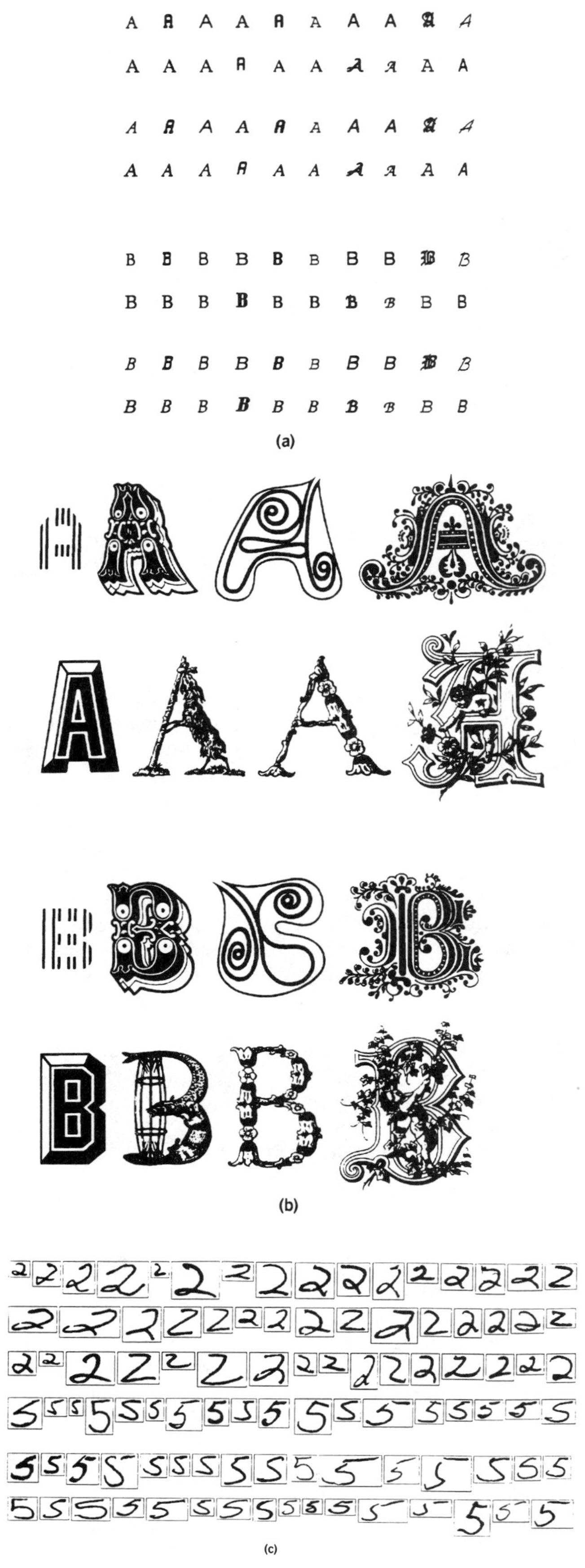

Figure 2. The presence of many different fonts and deformations in machine-printed and handwritten characters makes the character recognition task challenging: (a) examples of character shapes commonly used; (b) decorative fonts used in books [from Haab and Haettenschweiler, 1972]; and (c) handwritten numerals extracted from ZIP Codes on envelopes.

Templates

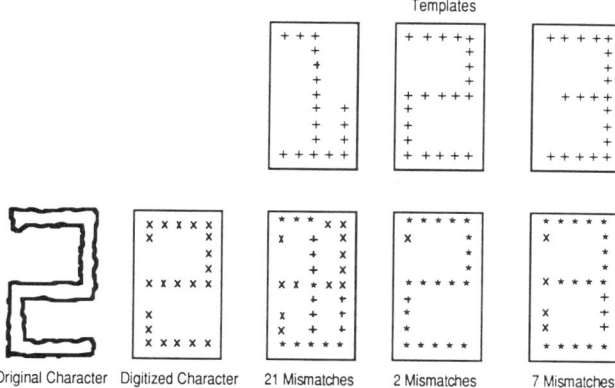

| Original Character | Digitized Character | 21 Mismatches | 2 Mismatches | 7 Mismatches |

Figure 3. Template matching using the Hamming distance. All points of the digitized character (ie, features) are compared with the corresponding points in each template. If the two are not the same (ie, both 0 or both 1), a mismatch, or distance 1, is counted. Here, the second template is selected as a result of minimum mismatch.

scribe an alphanumeric character, a person will most likely use a structural description. For example, an upper-case letter A has the following description: two straight lines meeting with a sharp point at the top, and a third line crossing the two at approximately their midpoint. The basis of any structural technique is the representation of the character icon, ie, figure, with a set of feature

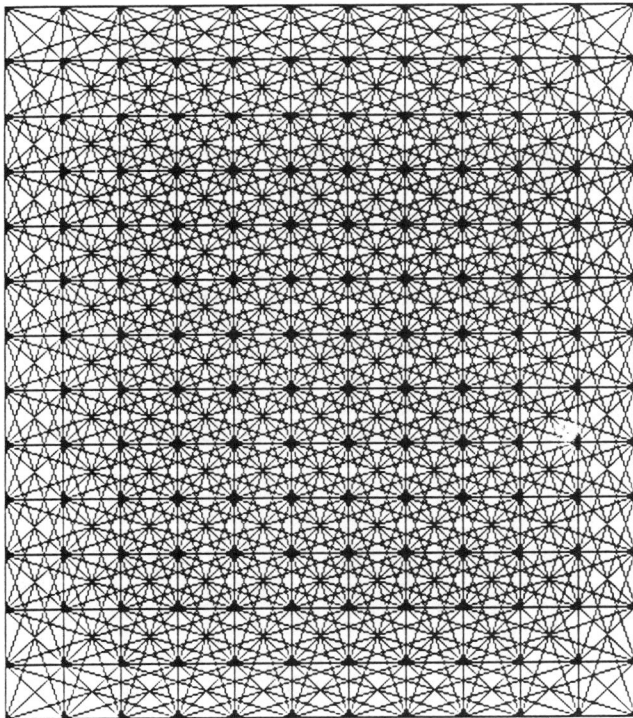

Figure 4. Pixel pairs used in polynomial discriminant classification. Each pair of pixels used in the feature vector v is indicated by a line segment in the 16×16 matrix.

primitives. These features must be able to describe each figure encountered as well as discriminate between them. The feature set can include descriptions for endpoints, line segments, arcs, curves, and crossings. The image could be normalized, smoothed, filtered, thinned, or any number of other operations applied to reduce noise and simplify feature extraction.

One such character recognition system consists of three stages: feature extraction, feature parameterization and statistical feature classification. The feature extractor looks for five types of features in a character: stroke, hole, concavity, cross point and end point (Fig. 5). The presence of these features can be detected by first determining a line adjacency graph (LAG). A LAG is obtained from a run-length representation of a binary image; its nodes correspond to runs of object pixels and its edges correspond to adjacent runs.

Feature parameterization is used to map the detected features into a binary feature vector. The parameter spaces may have different dimensions depending on the amount of information obtained from a feature. For example, the stroke parameter space is 4–D representing a 4–tuple $\langle x, y, r, \theta \rangle$ where $\langle x, y \rangle$ is the center of the stroke, r is the length, and θ is the angle formed with the positive x–axis. The cross point parameter space is two-dimensional, representing its location $\langle x, y \rangle$. Each dimension of a parameter space is divided into five equal-sized intervals; therefore, the stroke parameter space is partitioned into 625 hypercubes of equal size. By using a similar partition scheme, the cross point parameter space is partitioned into 25 squares. Each of these hypercubes and squares has a corresponding feature in the feature vector, ie, 625 features for strokes and 25 features for cross points. If the space of a hypercube has a stroke mapping, its corresponding feature in the vector will be set to one. This partition-

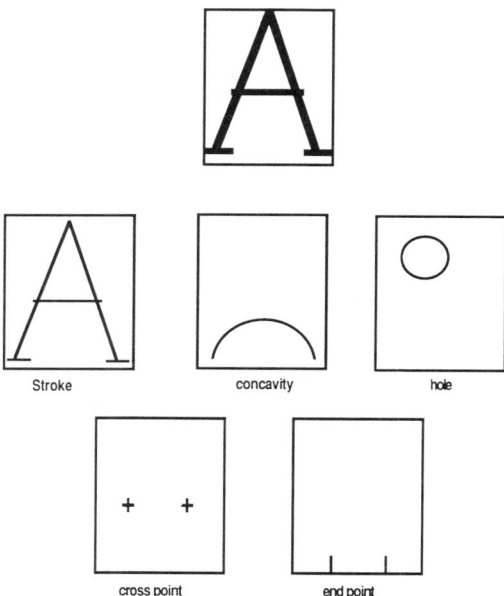

Figure 5. Structured features in characters. The five features are extracted using a line adjacency graph.

ing method is feasible based on the assumption that characters in the same class should have features which tend to map closely together in the parameter spaces.

Classification of the binary feature vector into character classes is done using a Bayes classifier which requires estimating the class-conditional statistical distributions of the binary feature vectors. Using the simplifying assumption that the feature vector elements are statistically independent, the method and its variations have been demonstrated to achieve very high recognition rates for multifont machine printed characters when the font mixture consists of those most often used in printed documents.

Stroke Analysis

A character represented by strokes can be assigned to a class by using one of several AI methodologies. Strokes are somewhat analogous to the strokes made by a person when a letter is drawn. Rule-based systems (qv) or semantic networks (qv) can be used not only to encode knowledge about strokes but also to direct the analysis. One such approach uses a network made up of many types of arcs and nodes, only a small portion of which is described here.

The subset arc *s* states that the node at its tail has the property at its head. Terminal nodes represent a primitive theoretic property about the image. A node with outgoing *s* and *p* arcs represents the largest subset of the set at the head of the *s* arc with the property at the head of the *p* arc. A node with more than one outgoing *s* arc represents the intersection of the sets at the heads of the *s* arcs. The example description of an upper-case 'F,' which consists of a long vertical stroke and two short horizontal strokes (Fig. 6) illustrates these concepts. Node 2 represents the

subset of all the input with a major vertical line on the left. Note that this includes many letters such as B, D, E, F, H, and so on. Nodes 4 and 5 represent the strokes near the top and middle of the major vertical line, and node 6 represents the concept that there is no other stroke near its bottom. Nodes 7 and 8 represent the concept that the horizontal line near the top of the major vertical line is on its top and to its right. Nodes 9 and 10 represent a similar concept for the horizontal line near the middle of the character. Finally, node 11 represents F as the intersection of the sets represented by nodes 6, 7, 8, 9, and 10.

This is not only a description of F but also a plan to follow for its recognition. The terminal node input reads a character image and begins recognition. The major vertical line is then tested for, and if it is located, additional tests are carried out to locate the appropriately oriented strokes near the top and middle of the image. If any of these tests fail, backtraining takes place and the presence of primitives from other characters is determined. For example, in the complete system, if the major vertical line cannot be located, a loop, such as occurs in an O, is tested for next. Advantages of this approach include its use of a more flexible control structure than most traditional methods. Disadvantages include its application to a limited alphabet of only 20 uppercase letters. Although many cases of distorted input were recognized correctly, the robustness of this technique remains unclear.

Contour Analysis

Another structural approach is to analyze the contour of a character. One such system for recognizing handwritten digits uses structural features based on the curvatures around the inner and outer contours of the figure. The primitive feature set consists of eight features: five concave features (three simple arc-like structures of varying curvature, and two endpoints), and three convex features of varying curvature. Associated with each feature is a direction quantized to eight compass points, and a location quantized to a 4×4 Cartesian grid with the origin in the upper left (Fig. 7).

The contour of the figure is first represented in the form of a chain-code; the chain-code is an eight direction code following the contour such that a change of one unit in the positive direction of the chain-code represents a 45–degree turn in the positive direction, likewise a negative change of one chain-code unit represents a negative 45–degree turn. The chain-code contour trace is converted to a curvature trace around the figure. The relative degree of curvature for each point along the original image is calculated. Local variations and noise are filtered by looking at the preceding and following points when calculating the curvature at the current point. Points along the image contour where the degree of curvature changes are the places where features are defined. A rule base is used to classify the extracted feature string. The rule base is designed as a decision tree, where each successive branch narrows down the possible candidates that can match the feature string. The rules are generalized to have a one-to-many relationship. Each class can be fully covered by only a few rules. In the complete system there are 130 rules for all ten classes of digits.

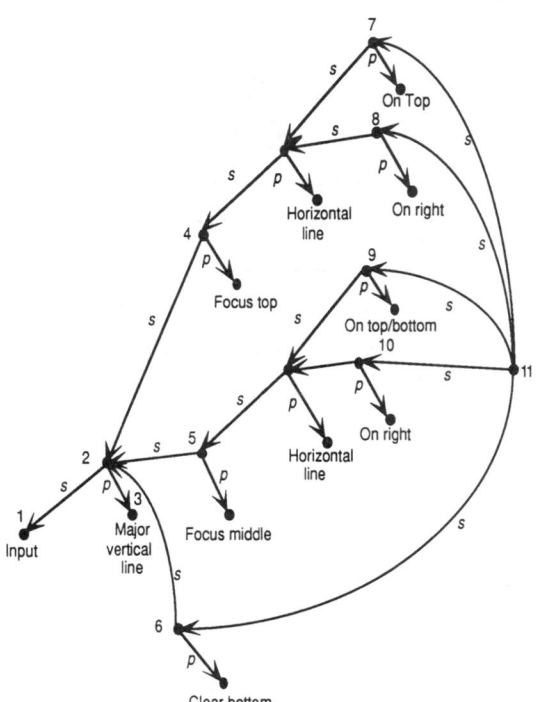

Figure 6. Representation of 'F' in a semantic network.

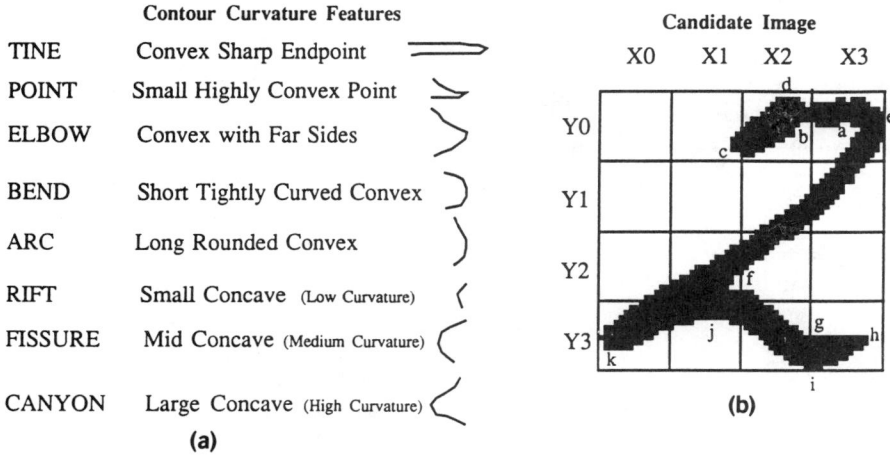

Contour Curvature Features

TINE	Convex Sharp Endpoint	
POINT	Small Highly Convex Point	
ELBOW	Convex with Far Sides	
BEND	Short Tightly Curved Convex	
ARC	Long Rounded Convex	
RIFT	Small Concave (Low Curvature)	
FISSURE	Mid Concave (Medium Curvature)	
CANYON	Large Concave (High Curvature)	

(a)

Candidate Image

X0   X1   X2   X3

(b)

Features Extracted

a = Canyon, West at (x3, y0)
b = Rift, South at (x2, y0)
c = Tine, West at (x1, y0)
d = Arc, North West at (x2, y0)
e = Bend, North East at (x3, y0)
f = Canyon, East at (x1, y2)
g = Rift, North at (x3, y3)
h = Tine, East at (x3, y3)
i = Arc, South at (x2, y3)
j = Fissure, South at (x1, y3)
k = Tine, South West at (x0, y3)

(c)

Symbolic Description of a '2'

1: Canyon @ x1x2x3y0y1 @ SE | S | SW | W
2: Tine @ x0x1x2y0y1 @ S | SW | W | NW
3: Elbow | Bend | Arc @ x2x3y0y1 @ N | NE | E
4: Fissure | Canyon @ x0x1x2x3y2y3 @ N | NE | E | SE
5: Tine @ x0x1x2x3y2y3 @ N | NE | E | SE | S
6: Tine @ x0x1x2x3y2y3 @ SW | W | NW

(d)

Feature - Rule Correspondence

Feature	Rule
a	1
c	2
e	3
f	4
h	5
k	6

(e)

Figure 7. Contour feature analysis: (*a*) contour features; (*b*) image in a 4×4 bounding box; (*c*) features extracted from (*b*); (*d*) rules in database that need to be satisfied for a digit 2; and (*e*) extracted features that match the six rules.

Phenomenological Attributes

One approach is to develop a character description scheme based on human experiments. The idea is that if features people use to recognize letters are properly described and used in a character recognition algorithm, the algorithm should perform as well as a human.

Three levels of human description are distinguished: functional, skeletal and physical. The abstract or functional level defines the essential meaning of letters in terms of a set of features or functional attributes. These are determined by a procedure that includes the presentation of ambiguous characters to human subjects and the use of their responses to determine the functional attribute at the pivot of the ambiguity. An intermediate skeletal level provides a description that distinguishes characters from everything else as well as from characters in other families of type fonts. This level of description is implemented as a set of graphs, one for each character in each font family. The lowest physical level in this hierarchy is where actual character images are placed.

This representational system can be used for recognition in several ways. Functional descriptions can be used directly if procedures are developed to detect the features they specify. This would be appropriate if it were known *a* *priori* that only character images (not graphics, halftones, etc) will be presented to a recognition system since functional descriptions can only distinguish one character from another. Otherwise, a skeletal representation would be a better choice since it can discriminate characters from everything else. This corresponds more closely to the way people read letters; however, its font-specific nature loses some robustness. The main advantage of this line of research is its acknowledgement of the complexity of the character recognition task and the necessity to incorporate knowledge about human character recognition in algorithms.

Neural Networks

Artificial neural networks provide an alternative methodology to the classification of patterns represented as feature vectors. The backpropagation model has been used most often in character recognition applications. Experiments with binary pixel arrays and feature vectors represented as binary feature vectors with a three-layer network have shown performance level comparable to first-order Bayesian linear discriminant functions for handwritten digits and characters.

Combination of Classifiers

It is found in character recognition practice that each of several approaches to character recognition perform well with different writing styles. For instance, a polynomial classifier, which is correlated with template matching, does well on broken characters that a structural approach fails on. On the other hand, the structural approach is tolerant to wide variations in strokes. Thus the approach of combining several different approaches with a decision tree can yield performance higher than using any individual approach.

WORD RECOGNITION

Several approaches to utilize context in recognizing characters are known. Contextual information is usually in the form of a lexicon of acceptable words, n-grams (legal letter combinations), or letter transition probabilities. Three distinct approaches to the use of context in character recognition can be identified. The first approach, referred to as *contextual postprocessing*, is a three-step approach. First, the word image is segmented into character images. Second, the segmented characters are recognized by using an isolated character recognition technique. Third, the resulting word is corrected, eg, by comparing to each word in a lexicon to determine a match. If none is found then a distance measure between the two words, eg, a Levenshtein metric, which measures the number of weighted editing operations, such as substitution, insertion and deletion, necessary to transform one word to the other, is used to find the closest word.

The second approach, referred to as *character recognition in context*, is a two-step approach, where contextual information is used in the process of recognizing individual characters. As with the previous approach, first the word image is segmented into character images. In the second step, features are extracted for each character image and the classification into a word is done by examining the entire (compound) feature set. A simplification of the second step is to weight the choices for a given character image by their frequencies of occurrence in the text and to eliminate the unlikely choices based on the neighboring character images and associated class decisions.

The third approach, *word-shape analysis*, is a one-step approach that bypasses segmentation. Features are extracted from the entire word and classification is attempted using a lexicon organized by word features. A simple set of features is used in a first level analysis to select a neighborhood of words and a more detailed analysis discriminates between a small subset of character classes. When the lexicon is small, there exists a strong top-down constraint on the word recognition problem. In such a case it is only necessary to compute those (bottom-up) features that discriminate between words. Thus the process becomes one of hypothesis-testing, or verification, instead of recognition.

Contextual Postprocessing

These techniques utilize knowledge at the word level to correct errors in character recognition. The methods use information about other characters that have been recognized in a word as well as knowledge about the text in which the word occurs to carry out this task. Typically, the knowledge about the text takes the form of a dictionary, a list of words that occur in the text. For example, a character recognition algorithm may not be able to reliably distinguish between a 'u' and a 'v' in the second position of $q*ote$. A contextual postprocessing technique would determine that 'u' is correct since it is very unlikely that *qvote* would be in an English language dictionary.

Methods of contextual postprocessing differ in their manner of representing the lexicon. Some methods use an approximation to a dictionary that often takes the form of probabilities of letter transitions. Other approaches use an exact representation such as a serial representation, a hash table, or a graph structure.

Binary n-Grams. The method of binary n-grams is one approach that uses an approximate representation. In this method a set of n-dimensional binary arrays represents a dictionary. Each of the dimensions can take on one of m values, where m is the number of letters in the alphabet, and the binary data in the matrix indicates whether the letter combination that specifies its location occurs in the dictionary. A 1 (logical true value) indicates the occurrence of the letter combination, and a 0 (logical false value) indicates its nonoccurrence. Typically, n values (position indices) are associated with each array. These tell the positions in which the letter combinations occur within each dictionary word. This method can be used to detect as well as correct errors in the output of a character recognition algorithm. Many error types can be handled by this approach; however, only the substitution of one character for another is described here since this is the most common error in character recognition. A word is considered correct only if the intersection of all its appropriate n-gram entries is nonzero. Otherwise, it must contain an error. The position of the error is determined by intersecting the sets of position indices that returned zero in the detection phase. If there is only a single position in this intersection, it contains the error. Vectors from all the arrays that involve that position, given that the other positions are correct, are then intersected. If there is only a single letter in that intersection, it can be substituted in the error position to produce a word that is acceptable to the n-gram arrays.

An example illustrates these points. Figure 8 shows a dictionary of the three-letter words {cat, cot, tot}. The three binary digram ($n = 2$) arrays for this dictionary are also shown.

If a character recognition technique outputs the string 'coo,' detection of the error would be done by

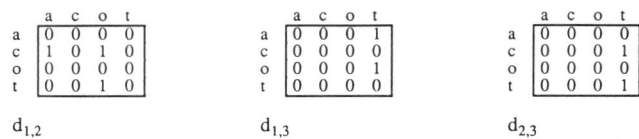

dictionary: {*cat, cot, tot*}:

	a	c	o	t
a	0	0	0	0
c	1	0	1	0
o	0	0	0	0
t	0	0	1	0

$d_{1,2}$

	a	c	o	t
a	0	0	0	1
c	0	0	0	0
o	0	0	0	1
t	0	0	0	0

$d_{1,3}$

	a	c	o	t
a	0	0	0	0
c	0	0	0	1
o	0	0	0	0
t	0	0	0	1

$d_{2,3}$

Figure 8. Example dictionary and its representation by binary digram arrays.

$$d_{1,2}(c, 0) \cap d_{1,3}(c, 0) \cap d_{2,3}(0, 0).$$

This would return 0 from both $d_{1,3}$ and $d_{2,3}$. Since the intersection of {1, 3} and {2, 3} yields {3}, correction is done by intersecting the vectors:

$$d_{1,3}(c, *) \cap d_{2,3}(0, *).$$

The resulting vector has only one nonzero element, corresponding to a '*t*.' Therefore, *coo* is corrected to *cot*. This short example illustrates several of the advantages and disadvantages of this method. The computations to locate and correct errors are relatively simple and involve only binary comparisons. Hence they can be economically implemented. However, the potential storage costs are also apparent by observation of the sparseness of the arrays. This is a major weakness of this method.

Character Recognition in Context

The problem of assigning a set of character images to a symbol string is addressed in the area of pattern recognition known as compound decision theory. The problem is formulated as follows:

The observed sequence of patterns, or vectors with feature elements, is

$$X = x_1, \ldots, x_m.$$

Each pattern x_i is to be assigned to one symbol, or character class, in the set

$$L = \{L_1, L_2, \ldots, L_r\}.$$

Since there are r possible choices for each pattern, there are r^m possible assignments for X. The goal is to choose that assignment

$$W_j = w_{j1}, \ldots, w_{jm}, \qquad w_{ij} \in L$$

which has the maximum probability over all possible assignments: $j = 1, \ldots, r^m$. Estimating all the joint prob-

abilities to perform the exact probability computation is impractical. One simplifying assumption is to assume that a character icon string arises from a Markov source. Assuming a first-order Markov source, the task of determining the joint probability of a given word reduces to a product involving first-order transitional probabilities between letters and the class-conditional, or confusion, probabilities associated with each pattern. The word with the highest probability is efficiently computed by a method known as the Viterbi algorithm; it involves $(m-1) \times r^2$ computations instead of r^m computations.

The Viterbi algorithm yields the most likely letter combination based on the probabilities assumed but can yield a string that is absent in the lexicon. The Dictionary Viterbi Algorithm (DVA) is a technique that brings in a dictionary to play a role in the search; it can be used for either contextual postprocessing or for character recognition in context. It uses an exact representation for a dictionary. A graph of letter alternatives (a *trellis*) produced by a segmentation of the word into characters is first set up. An example of such a graph in the contextual post-processing mode is shown in Figure 9. The string at the top of the graph is assumed to be input from a character recognition algorithm and {a, c, o, t} is the alphabet of the source text. Each node is labeled with a letter of the alphabet and has a cost associated with it that is the probability that the letter on the node is confused with the corresponding letter of the input word. Each arc in the graph also has a cost associated with it that is the probability that the letter at its head follows the letter at its tail in the source text. A path is traced through this graph in a left-to-right manner one column at a time. The costs of all the ways of reaching a node from nodes in the previous column are computed, and only the partial path with the best cost is retained. Each time the cost of an arc is evaluated, the presence in the dictionary of the substring composed of the letters on the path from the beginning of the graph to the node at the head of the arc is determined. If it does not occur in the dictionary, this partial path is discarded from future consideration. This evaluation process is performed once for every node in the graph of alternatives. The letters on the best path from the first node to the last node are output.

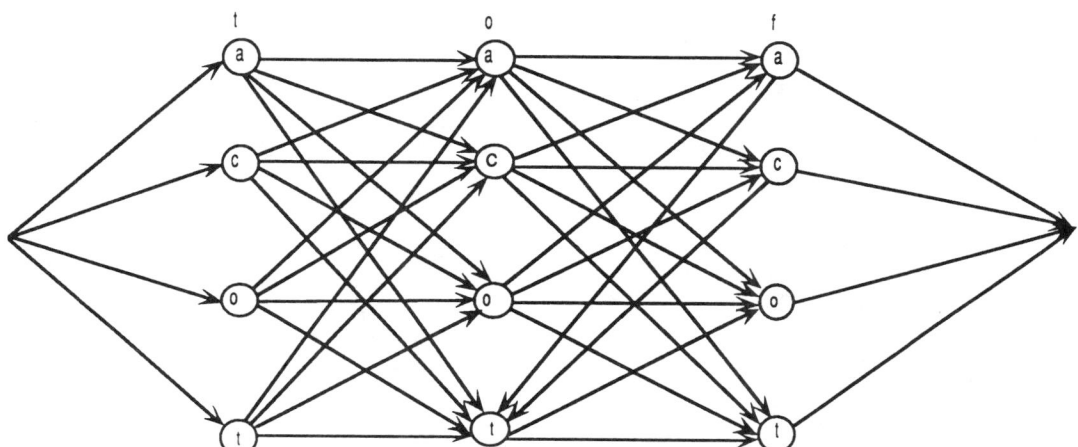

Figure 9. Example graph of alternatives for DVA.

The simultaneous searching of the graph of alternatives and the dictionary is done with a data structure for the dictionary known as a *trie*. An example for the dictionary {cat, cot, tot} is shown in Figure 10. If the graph of alternatives shown in the previous figure was evaluated with this trie, only the *c* and *t* nodes in the first column would be considered since these are the only two letters at the first level of the trie. At the next step only one path to each of the *a* and *o* nodes in the second column would be retained. These partial paths would most likely be *ca* and *to*. At the next step, only *cat* and *tot* would be considered because of the absence of any other paths in the trie. Most probably *tot* would be output because it is most like the input. The DVA, as other techniques that use an exact representation for a dictionary, is more accurate than methods that use an approximate representation. However, methods based on exact representations incur additional processing costs. The acceptability of these costs should be determined by the application and the need for improved performance.

Interactive Activation Model. A cognitive theory of how information in human memory could affect, top-down, the course of perceptual recognition is useful as a computational model of character recognition in context. This cognitive theory, known as the interactive activation model (IAM), posits three levels of representation arranged in a hierarchy: features, letters, and words. As illustrated in Figure 11, each level consists of a number of nodes at various states of activation for the entities relevant to that level. Each node is connected to a large number of other nodes from which it can receive either excitatory inputs (designated by an arrow at the end of the connection in Fig. 11), which raise its activation level, or inhibitory inputs (designated by a small disk in Fig. 11), which lower its activation level. Each node, in turn, transmits its activation as excitatory or inhibitory inputs to other nodes.

The presentation of a letter (actually, the letter's features) causes excitation of the nodes consistent with that letter's features and inhibition of the nodes for those features that are inconsistent with that letter. The nodes whose activity has been increased transmit their excitation by increasing the activation of letter nodes that contain those features. Similarly, the activation of the letter nodes results in excitation of word nodes that contain those letters and inhibition of word nodes that do not contain those letters. At all levels there is strong intralevel

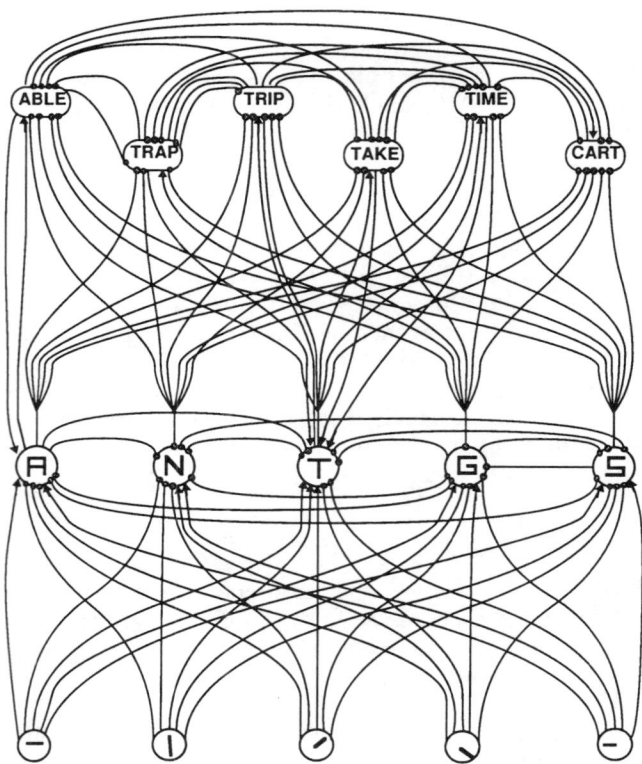

Figure 11. The three levels of the interactive activation model for the word superiority effect.

inhibition. Each node at a given level inhibits the other nodes at that level. There is also top-down excitation. Activity at the word level can excite or inhibit activity at the letter level.

We can now trace the time course of activation of a given node as a word, WORK for example, is presented. Assume that the subject successfully detected the first three letters, WOR, but detected only some of the features of the fourth letter, as indicated in Figure 12. Initially there is an increase in the activation level of those letters consistent with the features actually detected; we are only considering the letter nodes corresponding to the fourth position in the word. These would be R and K. These nodes transmit their excitation to the word level. Although WORK can benefit from activation of the K node, there is no word WORR to receive activation from R. As the activation of WORK increases, it starts to excite, top-down, the K node and inhibit the R node. R starts to weaken and the activation level of K grows until it clearly exceeds the activation level of R.

We can now see how IAM handles the major phenomenon of the word superiority effect as well as the advantage of a letter within a word over the letter itself. A nonword would not have a node at the word level. Consequently, there would be less chance for a letter in that string to benefit from top-down activation. It is possible, however, that words sharing letters with the nonword might generate, through their partial activation, some top-down facilitation from the word level.

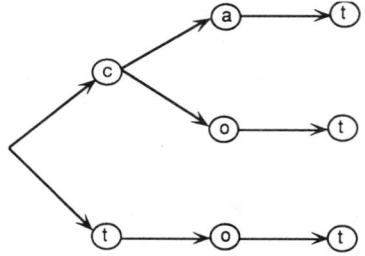

Figure 10. Trie representation for {cat, cot, tot}.

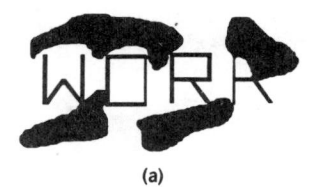

(a)

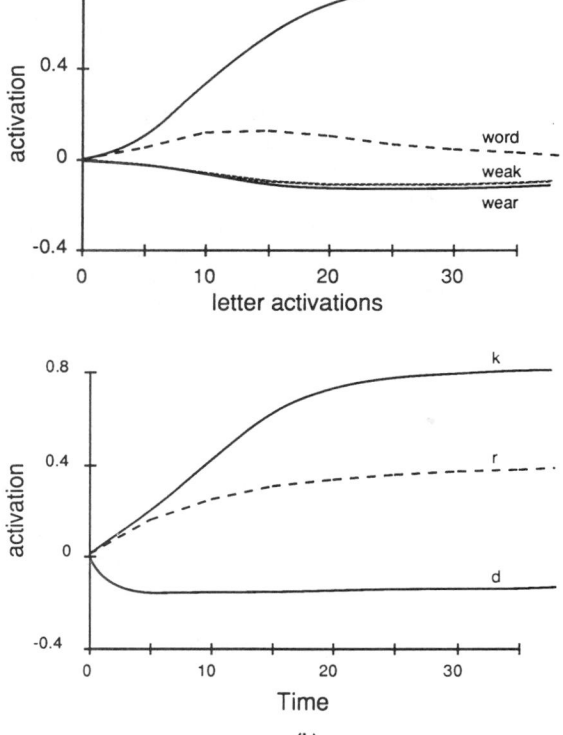

Figure 12. The interactive activation model's characterization of the activation of the letter 'K' in the fourth position, given that WORK was presented and that the features extracted were as shown in (a).

Word Shape Analysis

This is an approach for word recognition that is independent of character segmentation. This method is applicable to degraded images of machine-printed words where characters may be broken or touching. Word shape, such as the pattern of ascenders, descenders, and normal-height characters in a lower-case word, is a visual cue that has been known for many years to be useful for word recognition by humans. Several alternative representations for word shape have been explored, and a representation has been found that produces a small search space in a large dictionary. This representation is based on features that can be reliably extracted from word images and does not require the segmentation of words into characters. This avoids a pitfall of current reading algorithms and more closely reflects the way visual information is used in the early stages of word recognition by humans. The process re-

ceives an image of a word as input as well as a lexicon that is assumed to contain the word. A set of global and local shape features are extracted from the image, and registered with reference to a global coordinate frame. A set of highly specialized classifiers are used to match different subsets of the extracted shape features, and produce different rankings of the words in the input lexicon. A combination strategy is applied to produce a consensus ranking. The words with the highest ranks are output as a neighborhood containing the word in the image.

One such method utilizes 41 local feature sets. Some feature sets contain only one feature whereas others involve several. The specific feature sets were: stroke distribution (1), edges (9), end points of skeleton images (6), and letter shape features (19). The letter shape features include: vertical strokes, ascender, descender and short strokes; horizontal strokes, single horizontal strokes, two aligned horizontal strokes and two aligned vertical strokes; diagonal strokes, with positive and negative slopes; curves, left bent, right bent arcs; and topological features, holes, dots, bridges between strokes. An example involving computing six feature sets, that of end points, and the neighborhoods of words generated are shown in Figure 12. Six different classifiers (C14–C18) generate six different neighborhoods from a dictionary.

This method is an algorithmic model for a theory of human visual processing. The theory proposes that many features, extracted in parallel across an image, are selectively and dynamically combined to form higher level entities, which contribute to recognition of the object in the image. These events may be attended by cognitive processes. The method has been successfully applied to a da-

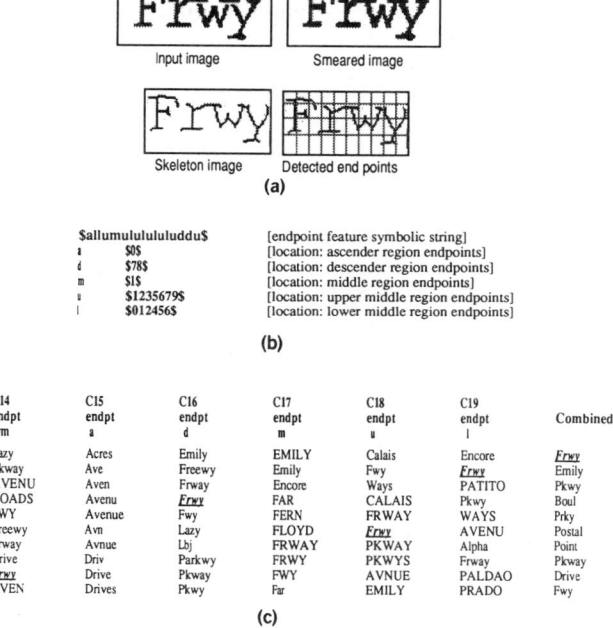

Figure 13. Word-shape feature computation: (a) word image with preprocessing operations; (b) six end-point feature strings; (c) neighborhood of words (top ten) generated by end-point classifiers, and neighborhood of words generated by overall classifier.

tabase of postal word images scanned on a postal OCR. The method has been proposed to be integrated with an OCR based word recognizer to achieve a robust word recognition system. The resulting system is to recognize words in various positions in an address block image so that contextual address information can be utilized to improve the currently achievable level of sort.

APPLICATIONS

Applications of automatic character recognition with economic importance include the reading of bank checks and forms, serial numbers (eg, of machine parts, automobiles), postal addresses on envelopes, and engineering drawings and maps, in addition to reading machines for the blind.

Small desktop character readers that can typically recognize up to six fonts and medium-sized character readers that can recognize a wide range of character fonts are now commercially available. The United States and other countries have installed large postal address-reading machines that must meet more stringent performance requirements than most other character readers. The performance of all these machines is controlled by many constraints. Deviations from these constraints can cause a large deterioration in performance. In most cases individual characters must not touch one another, and text must be clearly printed in dark ink on a lightly colored background. In some units the location of individual characters must fall within prespecified limits. Even the most versatile machines require that characters be unsmudged and that adjacent characters not touch one another. Furthermore, multifont capability is often achieved by requiring an operator to train the machine on new fonts. This constraint frequently causes the machine to misrecognize text printed in a font that it has not previously seen.

The mere presence of such constraints in even the most sophisticated reading machines illustrates that the ability to read text automatically with the same fluency as a human remains an unachieved goal. This is further evidenced by the performance of postal address-reading machines that have been the subject of much research and development and are designed to read relatively unconstrained text. These machines can correctly read over 90% of the addresses that appear on machine-printed first-class mail. However, they can only read about 34% of the addresses on mail from collection boxes. Overall, 62% of the addresses on mail processed by postal reading machines are correctly recognized. These percentages are based on mail samples that were readable by a human operator. This shows that even the most expensive commercial equipment is not nearly as fluent as a human reader. Obviously much work is needed if a program is to reach levels of human competence.

CONCLUSIONS

A high degree of success can be achieved in printed character recognition, particularly with high quality printed documents that do not use too many fonts. However, generalizations to handle a large number of fonts, decorative fonts, handwriting (hand-printing as well as cursive writing), and degraded text (such as that which is touching or has broken characters), continues to pose difficult problems.

BIBLIOGRAPHIC REMARKS

Character recognition is a topic that has been investigated for more than 30 years. An early influential paper was due to Bledsoe and Browning (1959). Functional components of optical scanners are discussed by Nagy (1983). The effect of sampling rate on character recognition is discussed by Pavlidis (1983). An overview of document analysis is given by Srihari and Zack (1986). The use of image defect models in algorithm development for character recognition was proposed by Baird (1990).

For an introduction to Bayes decision theory and binary feature vector classification, the reader is referred to the text by Duda and Hart (1973). A recent survey of binary template matching is given by Tubbs (1989). The polynomial discriminant method has been shown to be highly successful for postal address reading by Schurmann and co-workers (1978). The structural feature extraction method, due to Baird (1988) and Lee and co-workers (1990), are based on the line adjacency graph analysis of Pavlidis (1986). The contour-based method has its origins in the work of D'Amato and co-workers (1982). The semantic network approach to represent knowledge of character shapes was given by Krumme (1979). The use of multiple classifiers in character recognition is discussed by Hull and co-workers (1990) and Srihari and co-workers (1989).

There exists a large number of papers on neural network approaches to character recognition. An empirical evaluation of different neural network models for handwritten digit recognition was given by Pawlicki and co-workers (1988), and a performance comparison of back-propagation and first-order Bayesian methods were given by Lee and co-workers (1990). A high-performance neural network chip for handwritten digit recognition is described by Graf, Jackel, and Hubbard (1988).

The Viterbi algorithm (Viterbi, 1967) was adapted to text recognition by Neuhoff (1975) and later by Shinghal and Toussaint (1979a). The binary n-gram approach to lexical representation was explored by Hanson, Riseman, and Fisher (1976), which was experimentally compared to the Viterbi approach by Hull and Srihari (1982). Other representations of lexical knowledge include: serial representation (Shinghal and Toussaint, 1979b), a hash table (Doster, 1977) and a graph structure (Hull and co-workers, 1983). The contextual post-processing approach was rejected as a theory of human performance by Cattell (1886). The DVA was proposed by Srihari, Hull, and Choudhari (1983).

The recognition of off-line cursive handwritten words using probabilistic models and a trie were explored by Bozinovic and Srihari (1989). Some interesting similarities exist between the relaxation-based word recognition system of Hayes (1979) and the connectionist theory (interactive activation model) of word perception proposed by

McClelland and Rumelhart (1981). A preliminary study of word perception by humans was carried out by Brady (1981). The influence of syntax and semantics in reading handprinted FORTRAN coding sheets was explored by Brady and Wielinga (1978). The word shape approach, which has a cognitive basis (Haber and Haber, 1981), was developed by Hull (1988) and explored further in the context of reading postal address words by Ho, Hull, and Srihari (1990).

BIBLIOGRAPHY

H. S. Baird, "Feature Identification for Hybrid Structural/Statistical Pattern Classification," *Computer Vision, Graphics and Image Processing* **42**, 318–333 (1988).

H. S. Baird, "Document Image Defect Models," *Proceedings of the Workshop on Syntactic and Structural Pattern Recognition*, Murray Hill, N.J., 1990, pp. 38–46.

W. W. Bledsoe and I. Browning, "Pattern Recognition and Reading by Machine," *Proc. Eastern J. Comput. Conf.* **16**, 225–232 (1959).

R. Bozinovic and S. N. Srihari, "Off-line Cursive Script Word Recognition," *IEEE Trans. Patt. Anal. Mach. Intel.* **PAMI-11**, 68–83 (1989).

J. M. Brady and B. J. Wielinga, "Reading the Writing on the Wall," in A. R. Hanson and E. Riseman, eds., *Computer Vision Systems*, Academic Press, New York, 1978, pp. 283–299.

M. Brady, "Toward a Computational Theory of Early Visual Processing in Reading," *Visible Lang.* **XV**(2), 183–215 (Spring 1981).

J. K. Cattel, "The Time it Takes to See and Name Objects," *Mind* **11**, 63–65 (1886).

C. H. Cox, III, P. Coueignoux, B. Blesser, and M. Eden, "Skeletons: A Link Between Theoretical and Physical Letter Descriptions," *Patt. Recog.* **15**(1), 11–22 (1982).

D. D'Amato, L. Pintsov, H. Koay, D. Stone, J. Tan, K. Tuttle, and D. Buck, "High Speed Pattern Recognition System for Alphanumeric Handprinted Characters," *Proceedings of the IEEE-CS Conference on Pattern Recognition and Image Processing*, Las Vegas, Nev., July 1982, pp. 165–170.

W. Doster, "Contextual Postprocessing System for Coorporation With A Multiple-choice Character Recognition System," *IEEE Trans. Comput.* **C–26**(11) (November 1977).

R. O Duda and P. E. Hart, *Pattern Classification and Scene Analysis*, Wiley-Interscience, 1973.

H. P. Graf, L. D. Jackel, and W. E. Hubbard, "VLSI Implementation of a Neural Network Model," *IEEE Computer*, 41–49 (March 1988).

A. Haab and W. Haettenschweiler, *Lettera 4*, Hastings House Publisher, New York, 1972.

R. N. Haber and L. R. Haber, "Visual Components of the Reading Process," *Visible Lang.* **XV**(2), 147–181 (1981).

A. R. Hanson, E. Riseman, and E. G. Fisher, "Context in Word Recognition," *Patt. Recog.* **8**, 35–45 (1976).

K. C. Hayes, Jr., "Reading Handwritten Words Using Hierarchical Relaxation," Ph.D. dissertation, TR–783, University of Maryland, College Park, 1979.

T. K. Ho, J. J. Hull, and S. N. Srihari, "Combination of Structural Classifiers," *Proceedings of the Workshop on Syntactic and Structural Pattern Recognition*, Murray Hill, N.J., 1990, pp. 123–136.

J. J. Hull, "A Computational Theory of Visual Word Recognition," Ph.D. dissertation, SUNY at Buffalo, NY, 1988.

J. J. Hull and S. N. Srihari, "Experiments in Text Recognition With Binary n-Gram and Viterbi Algorithms," *IEEE Trans. Patt. Anal. Mach. Intell.* **PAMI-4**(5), 520–530 (September 1982).

J. J. Hull, S. N. Srihari, and R. Choudhari, "An Integrated Algorithm for Text Recognition: Comparison with a Cascaded Algorithm," *IEEE Trans. Patt. Anal. Mach. Intell.* **PAMI-5**(4), 384–395 (July 1983).

J. J. Hull, A. Commike, and T. K. Ho, "Multiple Algorithms for Handwritten Character Recognition," in C. Y. Suen, ed., *Frontiers in Handwriting Recognition*, Concordia University, Montreal, Canada, 1990.

D. W. Krumme, "Theory and Implementation of a Network Representation of Knowledge: Application to Character Recognition," Ph.D. dissertation, University of California, Berkeley, 1979.

D. S. Lee, S. W. Lam, and S. N. Srihari, "A Structural Approach to Recognize Hand-printed and Degraded Machine-printed Characters," *Proceedings of the Workshop on Syntactic and Structural Pattern Recognition*, Murray Hill, N.J., 1990, pp. 256–272.

D. S. Lee, S. N. Srihari, and R. Gaborski, "Bayesian and Neural Network Pattern Recognition: A Theoretical Connection and Empirical Comparison and Handwritten Digits," in I. Sethi and A. Jain, eds., *Artificial Neural Networks & Statistical Pattern Recognition*, in press.

J. L. McClelland and D. E. Rumelhart, "An Interactive Activation Model of Context Effects in Letter Perception: Part 1, An Account of Basic Findings," *Psychol. Rev.* **88**(5), 375–407 (September 1981).

G. Nagy, "Optical Scanning Digitizers," *IEEE Computer*, 13–24 (May 1983).

D. L. Neuhoff, "The Viterbi Algorithm as an Aid in Text Recognition," *IEEE Trans. Inform. Theory* **IT–21**, 222–228 (1975).

T. Pavlidis, "Effects of Distortions on the Recognition Rate of a Structural OCR System," *Proceedings of the IEEE-CS Conference on Computer Vision Pattern Recognition*, 1983, pp. 303–309.

T. Pavlidis, "A Vectorizer and Feature Extractor for Document Recognition," *Computer Vision, Graphics and Image Processing* **35**, 111–127 (1986).

T. F. Pawlicki, D. S. Lee, J. J. Hull, and S. N. Srihari, "Neural Network Models and Their Application to Handwritten Digit Recognition," *IEEE International Conference on Neural Networks*, San Diego, Calif., 1988, pp. 63–70.

J. Schurmann, "A Multifont Word Recognition System for Postal Address Reading," *IEEE Trans. Computers* **C-27**(8), 721–732 (April 1978).

R. J. Shillman, "Character Recognition Based on Phenomenological Attributes: Theory and Methods," Ph.D. dissertation, Massachusetts Institute of Technology, Cambridge, Mass., 1974.

R. Shinghal and G. T. Toussaint, "Experiments in Text Recognition with the Modified Viterbi Algorithm," *IEEE Trans. Patt. Anal. Mach. Intell.* **PAMI-1**(2), 184–192 (1979a).

R. Shinghal and G. T. Toussaint, "A Bottom-up and Top-down Approach to Using Context in Text Recognition," *Int. J. Man-Mach. Stud.* **11**, 201–212 (1979b).

S. N. Srihari and G. Zack, "Document Image Analysis," *Proceedings of the Sixth International Conference on Pattern Recognition*, Paris, 1986, pp. 434–436.

S. N. Srihari, J. J. Hull, and R. Choudhari, "Integrating Diverse Knowledge Sources in Text Recognition," *ACM Trans. Office Information Systems* 1(1), 68–87 (1983).

S. N. Srihari, E. Cohen, J. J. Hull, and L. Kuan, "A System to Locate and Recognize ZIP Codes in Handwritten Addresses," *Int. J. Res. Eng.* 1(1), 37–45 (1989).

J. D. Tubbs, "A Note on Binary Template Matching," *Patt. Recog.* 22(4), 359–364 (1989).

A. J. Viterbi, "Error Bounds for Convolutional Codes and an Asymptotically Optimum Decoding Algorithm," *IEEE Trans. on Inform. Theory* IT–13(2), 260–269 (April 1967).

Surveys and Tutorials

G. Nagy, Optical Character Recognition: Theory and Practice, in P. R. Krishnaiah and L. N. Kanal, eds., *Handbook of Statistics*, Vol. 2, pp. 621–649, 1982, is a survey of statistical feature analysis techniques for character recognition.

E. Reuhkala, "Recognition of Strings of Discrete Symbols with Special Application to Isolated Word Recognition," *Acta Polytech. Scand. Ma.* 38, 1–92 (1983) contains a brief survey of methods for contextual postprocessing and an exhaustive bibliography.

S. N. Srihari, *Computer Text Recognition and Error Correction*, IEEE Computer Society Press, Silver Spring, Md., 1984, is a tutorial on the reading of text by computer. Twenty basic papers and an extensive bibliography are given.

C. Y. Suen, M. Berthod, and S. Mori, "Automatic Recognition of Handprinted Characters—The State of the Art," *Proc. IEEE* 68(4), 469–487 (April 1980) is a survey of techniques developed for the recognition of isolated handprinted characters.

I. Taylor and M. M. Taylor, *The Psychology of Reading*, Academic Press, Orlando, FL, 1983, is an overview of research about human reading. Contains a comprehensive bibliography.

J. R. Ullmann, Advances in Character Recognition, in K. S. Fu, ed., *Applications of Pattern Recognition*, CRC Press, Boca Raton, Fla., pp. 197–236, 1982, is a general overview of character recognition techniques oriented toward practical applications. A comprehensive bibliography including many U.S. and U.K. patents is given.

SARGUR N. SRIHARI
JONATHAN J. HULL
SUNY, Buffalo

CHECKERS-PLAYING PROGRAMS

Programming computers to play games is one of the earliest areas of AI research (Jackson, 1974; Barr and Feigenbaum, 1981). As it did in the past, it continues today to attract workers for a number of reasons. The first and most obvious of these is that the ability to play complex games appears to be the province of the human intellect. It is therefore challenging to write programs that match or surpass the skills humans have in planning (qv), reasoning, and choosing among several options in order to reach their goal. Another motivation for this research is that the techniques developed while programming computers to play games may be used to solve other complex problems in real life, for which games serve as models. Finally, games provide researchers in AI in particular and

computer science in general with a medium for testing their theories on various topics ranging from knowledge representation (qv) and the process of learning (qv) to searching algorithms (see SEARCH) and parallel processing. The game of checkers was one of the first for which a program was written. This entry describes the early and important work of Samuel (1963, 1967) as well as more recent efforts by Griffith (1974) and Akl and Doran (1983) (see GAME PLAYING).

THE GAME OF CHECKERS

Checkers is an old board game believed to have originated in ancient Egypt (Ryan, 1978). It is played by two persons and involves no element of chance. The presence of clear rules and goals makes it a game of strategy. Also, the game is one of perfect information in the sense that at any given time both players have complete knowledge of all the previous moves and the current board situation. Finally, the outcome of a game is either a win for one of the two players and a loss for the other or a draw. Checkers is therefore a zero-sum game.

Like most other game-playing programs, all known programs for playing checkers search a game tree (qv), an example of which is shown in Figure 1. In such a tree nodes correspond to board positions and branches correspond to moves. The root node represents the board position from which the player whose turn it is to play is required to make a move. A node is at ply (or depth) k if it is at a distance of k branches from the root. A node at ply k, which has branches leaving it and entering nodes at ply $k + 1$, is called a nonterminal node; otherwise the node is terminal. A nonterminal node at ply k is connected by branches to its offspring at ply $k + 1$. Thus, the offspring of the root represent positions reached by moves from the initial board; offspring of these represent positions reached by the opponent's replies; offspring of these represent positions reached by replies to the replies, and so on. The number of branches leaving a nonterminal node is the

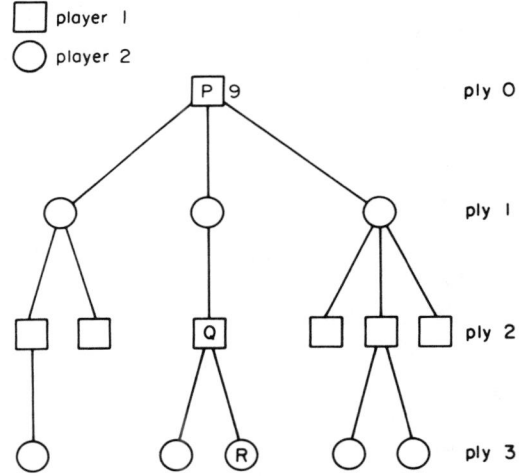

Figure 1. A game tree: *P*, *Q*, and *R* are board positions. Number 9 is the value of the alpha-beta search of position *P*.

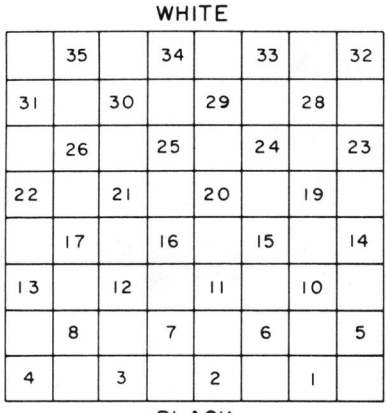

Figure 2. The standard 8 × 8 checkerboard.

fan-out of that node. The term branching factor (qv) is used to denote the average fan-out for a given tree over all nonterminal nodes.

A complete game tree represents all possible plays of the game. Each path from the root to a terminal node corresponds to a complete game with the terminal nodes representing a win, loss, or draw. It has been estimated that a complete game tree of checkers contains approximately 10^{40} nonterminal nodes (Samuel, 1963). Assuming that a program is capable of generating three billion (10^9) such nodes per second, it would still require in the vicinity of 10^{21} centuries in order to generate the whole tree. Instead, checkers-playing programs, like programs for playing most other similarly challenging games, search an incomplete tree. The depth of such a tree is limited and, in addition, it is often the case that not all paths are explored. In an incomplete tree terminal nodes are those appearing at some predefined ply k or less and do not necessarily represent positions for which the game ends. A static evaluation function is used to assign a value to each of the positions represented by terminal nodes. The alpha-beta algorithm (a refined version of minimax analysis) is then used to back up these values up the tree (see ALPHA-BETA PRUNING). When all the offspring of the root have been assigned backed-up values representing their "goodness," the program chooses the move that appears to be best (in light of this incomplete information). Once this move is made and the opponent has replied, the program generates and searches a new tree from the current position to determine its next move. Note that game trees are generated while they are searched. A so-called depth-first search (see SEARCH, DEPTH-FIRST) is usually followed. It starts by generating a complete path from the root to a terminal node; search then resumes from the latest nonterminal node on the path whose offspring have not all been generated or eliminated by the alpha-beta algorithm. Search continues until all nodes up to some depth k have been either generated or eliminated.

SAMUEL'S WORK

The best documented checkers-playing program was written by Samuel in the period 1947–1967. The program plays at a very high level. It can win against most players and loses only to the best. In 1962 it managed to win one game against a former champion of Connecticut and drew another with the world champion in 1965. The purpose of Samuel's work was to use the game of checkers to perform experiments in machine learning. The result was one of the earliest and most successful game-playing programs that could learn from its own mistakes to improve its play.

Representation

The program was written in assembly language for the IBM 700 series computers whose word length was 36 bits. A clever technique that saved both time and space was used to represent a board position and generate all possible next moves. Consider the standard 8 × 8 checkerboard shown in Figure 2, where black squares are numbered, and recall that checker pieces can be placed exclusively on

these squares. Thus, only four computer words, each with bits numbered 1–36, are needed to represent a given position. In the first word bit i is set to 1 if square i holds a black piece (man or king); otherwise, it is set to 0. In the second word bit i is set to 1 if square i holds a black king; otherwise, it is set to 0. The third and fourth words are defined similarly for the white pieces. Note that bits 9, 18, 27, and 36 correspond to squares not appearing on the board and are therefore unused in all four words.

To see how all the possible next moves can be generated quickly from a given position, assume that it is Black's turn to play. Ignoring kings and jumps for the moment, the rules of checkers specify that pieces are only allowed to move forward to a diagonally adjacent square. Hence a black piece on square i can go either to square $i + 4$ (by a right move) or to square $i + 5$ (by a left move) provided that such a numbered square appears on the board. For example, if there are four black men on squares 5, 13, 15, and 26, as shown in Figure 3, the squares reachable by these men are 10 and 17, 19 and 20, and 30 and 31, respectively. By shifting the contents of the word in Figure 3 four positions to the right, one obtains a representation of the squares potentially occupied by right moves, namely, 9, 17, 19, and 30, as shown in Figure 4 (square 9, of course, is not on the board). Similarly, by shifting five positions to the right, one obtains a representation of the squares potentially occupied by left moves, namely, 10, 18, 20, and 31, as shown in Figure 5 (square 18 is also not on the board). Now let EMPTY be a word such that bit i is set to 1 if square i in the current board position is unoccupied; otherwise, if square i is occupied by either a black or a white piece, bit i is set to 0 (note that bits 9, 18, 27, and 36 are also set to 0). By taking a bit-by-bit logical AND of the word in Figure 4 with EMPTY, it is possible to obtain simultaneously all right moves available to the four black men. Similarly, a logical AND of the word in Figure 5 with EMPTY yields all left moves. Backward king moves, jumps, and multiple jumps are handled by simple modifications to this approach. In terms of storage five words are needed to represent the moves: one word for each of the jump, forward right, forward left, backward right, and backward left moves. The various rules of checkers, such

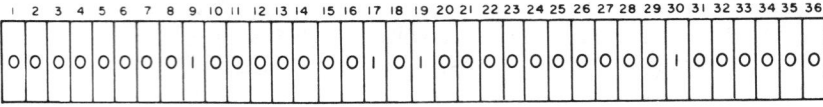

Figure 3. Four black men on squares 5, 13, 15, and 26.

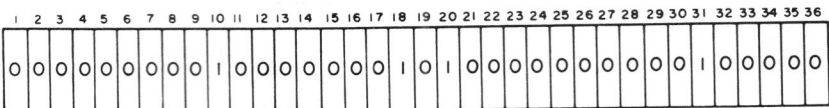

Figure 4. The word in Figure 3 is shifted four positions to the right to obtain all potential right moves.

Figure 5. The word in Figure 3 is shifted five positions to obtain all potential left moves.

as crowning, recognizing a win, loss or draw, and so on, are incorporated in the program within this representation in a straightforward way.

Search

The program uses the alpha-beta algorithm to search trees up to a maximum depth of 20 moves. Instead of holding the actual depth used while searching from a move to a constant, it is allowed to vary according to the position under consideration. Typically, the program begins by looking ahead three moves. Nodes at that level are evaluated directly if neither the last nor the next moves are jumps and no exchange offer is possible. If any of these conditions is satisfied for a given node, however, search proceeds from that node. For nodes at depth 4, search terminates if neither a jump nor an exchange are possible from that position. From ply 5 to ply 10, look-ahead is interrupted if no jump is possible. Search terminates for nodes at ply 11 or greater if one side is ahead by more than two kings.

In many situations during the search, the program needs to directly estimate the value of a node without having generated or examined its offspring. A static evaluation function, discussed in more detail below, is used for that purpose. It consists of a computational procedure that assigns a numerical value to the position the node represents based on various parameters such as the number and worth of the pieces the program has, the mobility of these pieces and their potential for capturing opponent pieces, their situation on the board, and so on. The primary application of a static evaluation function is in assigning scores to terminal nodes. It can also be used to enhance the alpha-beta algorithm through ordering and pruning of moves.

Fixed Ordering. When depth-first search coupled with the alpha-beta algorithm is used to generate and search a game tree, the order in which the offspring of a node are examined is of great importance. A perfect ordering of moves is defined as one in which, for any node in the tree, the first move generated is the best for the palyer whose turn it is. Then for a tree of depth D and branching factor B, the total number of terminal nodes generated by the alpha-beta algorithm is approximately $2B^{D/2}$ instead of the full B^D. This represents a significant savings in time due to the large number of nodes eliminated by the alpha-beta algorithm and that the program therefore need not examine. Consequently, for a constant number of terminal nodes, search depth can be almost doubled. Of course, there is no way of guaranteeing such ordering, and many heuristics (qv) exist that attempt to approximate it. One such heuristic used by Samuel's program is to perform a shallow look-ahead from a given node and use the static evaluation function to assign values to the resulting terminal nodes. These values are backed up by the alpha-beta algorithm to the offspring of the original node. The backed-up values are now used to order the offspring, and this order is to be respected in the search that follows. This method was called plausibility analysis by Samuel, and it ordered the available moves based on their promise.

Dynamic Ordering. Samuel also introduced a technique that allowed the program to revise the ordering of moves arrived at by the plausibility analysis. Suppose that the offspring of a node have been ordered as above; a search up to a limited depth is now started from the offspring ranked "best." At the end of this search the backed-up value is compared to that of the offspring ranked earlier as "second best." If the former is better, the search continues to a greater depth; otherwise, it is interrupted and a new limited search is started from the current best offspring. The method can be repeated as many times as needed and to any required depth.

Forward Pruning. Both fixed and dynamic ordering are simply time-saving heuristics and do not in any way affect the overall outcome of the search. Another way of reducing the number of nodes examined by the alpha-beta algorithm proceeds as follows. First, plausibility analysis is used to order all the legal moves from a node; then the best few of these are retained and the others discarded. The number of moves retained is inversely proportional to the depth at which they are generated. A variant of this method is used at a later stage when a node is chosen to begin a search. If the value assigned earlier to that node by plausibility analysis falls outside the range currently set by the alpha-beta algorithm, the node is discarded. Neither of these two forms of forward pruning is guaranteed not to discard a good move.

Learning

Two learning mechanisms were provided in the program to constantly better the quality of its play. The first was the ability to memorize moves (or rote learning), the second was a variable static evaluation function that could be improved through training (or learning by generalization) (see LEARNING, MACHINE).

Rote Learning. In rote learning, the program memorized boards and their evaluations that were encountered during the course of previous games. Assume that a good static evaluation function has already been constructed and that at some point during the game it is the program's turn to move from board position P. The program generates the game tree in Figure 1 and determines using its static evaluation function and alpha-beta search that the value of position P is 9, say. At this point the program makes the move suggested by the search and stores position P together with value 9. Now suppose that the situation depicted in Figure 6 were to arise in a later game. Rather than invoking the static evaluation function to assign a value to position P, the program could use the stored value of P. This would have two advantages. First, if the time required to retrieve the value of P from storage is much shorter than that required to compute the static evaluation function, time is saved that could be used to search deeper somewhere else in the tree. Second and more important, the value assigned to P in this manner was obtained by searching to depth 3 below P (Fig. 1) and is therefore more accurate than the static value that would otherwise be computed. The net effect therefore is an improvement of the look-ahead ability of the program.

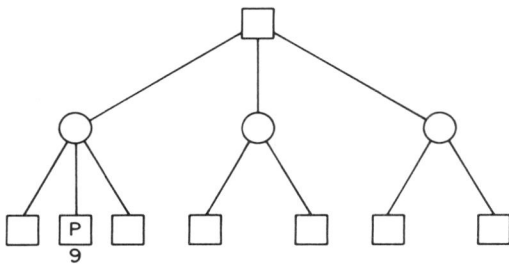

Figure 6. Example of rote learning. The stored value of 9 for position P was obtained by searching to depth 3 (Fig. 1); this stored value is more accurate and more quickly obtained than the value from the static evaluation function.

In addition to the board position and its value, the length of the path followed in the game tree to compute this value was also stored. Subsequently, when the program had to choose between two or more moves leading to positions with equal values, it favored the position whose value had been reached by the shortest search. A sense of direction was thus acquired by the program, which was able in this way to progress quickly toward its goal (eg, a win in the end game).

The board positions and their associated values were saved in a large file that was stored on magnetic tape due to central-memory limitations. The file was organized so as to achieve storage efficiency and fast retrieval. In order to use as little space as possible, all the positions were saved as though white is to move, various rotational symmetries were exploited, and least-used positions were deleted periodically. Quick access of stored values was made possible by indexing board positions according to some important characteristics (eg, number of pieces) and by keeping them on the tape in approximately the order in which they might occur in actual play. In order to study the effect of rote learning, the program was trained by playing against itself and against humans (including masters) and by following many book games between masters. It was noticed that rote learning is particularly useful in improving the program's play steadily during the opening and end games but not so much during the middle game, where the number of possible moves from a given position is fairly large by comparison. The program reached a better-than-average novice level, having stored over 53,000 positions. Samuel pointed out a limitation of rote learning if it were to be used alone. A program would need to accumulate an estimated number of about one million positions to play at the master level. He concluded that this would be too impractical, requiring an inordinate amount of playing time, not to speak of the storage and retrieval problems. Other learning processes are therefore needed.

Learning by Generalization. Samuel experimented with two static evaluation functions: a linear polynomial and a nonlinear signature table method. As with rote learning two training methods were used: in the first, the program played either against itself or against a human, and in the second it learned by following book moves.

The Linear Polynomial Approach. Here the static value assigned to a position is obtained from the polynomial $w_1p_1 + w_2p_2 + \cdots + w_np_n$, where the parameter p_i is a numerical measure of some feature of the board and w_i is a real-valued weight indicating the worth of p_i. The larger the value of the polynomial, the more attractive the position is to the player moving to it. Typical parameters used were ADV (advancement), EXCH (exchange), MOB (total mobility), and THRET (threat). THRET, for example, is defined as the number of squares to which the player whose turn it is can move a piece and in so doing threaten to capture an opponent piece on a subsequent move. Assume now that p_i corresponds to THRET for some i. If board position Q leads to board position R by a move as shown in Figure 1, the value of p_i is equal to the value of THRET for R minus the value of THRET for Q.

There are two decisions to be made when designing such an evaluation function: which parameters to use and what values the weights are to take. In this case the first of these decisions was made in part by Samuel himself. He initially selected a set of 38 board features. It was then left to the program to choose the 16 best of these as well as the values of the associated coefficients.

To begin, the program selected arbitrarily 16 parameters, $p_1, p_2, \ldots, p_{16}$. Two versions of the program were then created, call them X and Y, each with 16 arbitrary weights, $w_1, w_2, \ldots, w_{16}$. Version X played a sequence of games against Y. During any given game, X learned by generalizing on its experience and changed its coefficients correspondingly, while the coefficients for Y remained constant. At each move, X computed two evaluations for the current board position: the static value given by the polynomial and a backed-up value obtained by looking ahead a few ply in a game tree. On the assumption that the second value ought to be more accurate than the first, X adjusted its coefficients in order for the static value to better match the backed-up value. Whenever X won a game, its polynomial was used by Y in the next game. If X lost a sequence of games, it would change its coefficients at random in order to move away from the current local optimum. This technique is sometimes referred to as hill climbing or local neighborhood search.

Parameter selection proceeded in conjunction with the adjustment of coefficients. Starting with the 16 arbitrarily chosen parameters, the program keeps a count of the number of times each parameter is assigned the lowest coefficient. Following each move by X, this count is incremented until, for some parameter, it exceeds 32. This parameter is then removed from the polynomial and placed at the end of a queue formed by the currently unused parameters. The first element in that queue is now added to the polynomial. Similar approaches were used to select parameters and adjust weights in playing against humans. Samuel observed that the set of parameters and their weights reached a stable state after several games. Considerable, though slow, improvement in the quality of the program's play was obtained by this method, particularly during the middle game, where it attained a better-than-average level.

An alternative to actual play, book learning, proved to be a more efficient approach for adjusting the coefficients. Approximately 250,000 different board positions together with the move recommended by an expert for each of them were stored on tape. The program was then asked to produce, for each position, all possible next positions and the associated values of the 16 parameters. Then the coefficient w_i for every parameter p_i was obtained from $(L - H)/(L + H)$, where L is the overall number of positions for which the value of the parameter was lower than its value for the recommended position and H is the number of times it was higher.

The major drawback of the polynomial approach is its linear nature. Two techniques were used in one version of the program to overcome this weakness. One was to introduce new parameters that were logical combinations of earlier ones; the other was to divide the game into six phases, each employing an entirely different polynomial.

Signature Tables. A third method for obtaining a nonlinear function of the parameters was suggested by Griffith (1974) and used by Samuel very successfully in a later version of his checkers-playing program. Here each of the parameters measuring a board feature is restricted to take values from a small set of integers. Typically, the parameter GUARD is 0 if both or neither of the two players have complete control of their back rows, $+1$ if the player whose turn it is controls his back row while the opponent does not, and -1 if the latter condition is reversed. An n-dimensional table is then created (conceptually) with one dimension per parameter. Entries in this table represent static evaluations corresponding to various combinations of parameter values. Thus, if $n = 2$, for example, and the two parameters are GUARD and MOB, taking values from $\{-1, 0, 1\}$ and $\{-2, -1, 0, 1, 2\}$, respectively, then the signature table is as shown in Figure 7. If for the board under consideration MOB = 1 and GUARD = 0, this corresponds to cell $(1, 0)$ in the table. Since this is a desirable situation, a relatively high value is found in $(1, 0)$, and this signature is assigned to the position as its static evaluation. Signature tables therefore have potential to produce a fairly accurate estimate of the worth of a position, as they express the various dependencies among the parameters. Their major disadvantage, if implemented as described above, would be their inordinate storage space and learning time requirements for any nontrivial n.

Samuel dealt with these problems as follows. First, 18 of 24 chosen parameters were restricted to the values $\{-1, 0, 1\}$, and the remaining parameters took their values from $\{-2, -1, 0, 1, 2\}$. Next, a hierarchy of signature tables was constructed. In the first level of the hierarchy, the parameters were divided into six subsets, each containing one five-valued and three three-valued parameters. Six signature tables, one per subset, were constructed, with entries chosen from $\{-2, -1, 0, 1, 2\}$. For each three of these tables, there is one second-level table with entries from -7 to 7. The third level consists of just one table. When a position is to be evaluated, the parameters are measured and used to index the first-level tables. The program then moves up in the hierarchy, with values read from tables at one level giving access to tables at the next level. Finally, the entry obtained from the single

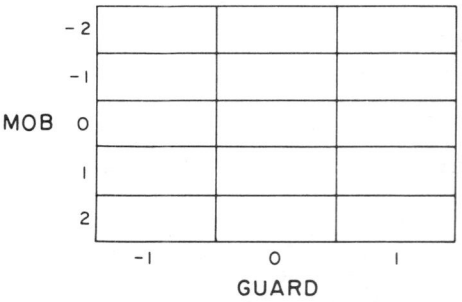

Figure 7. A signature table.

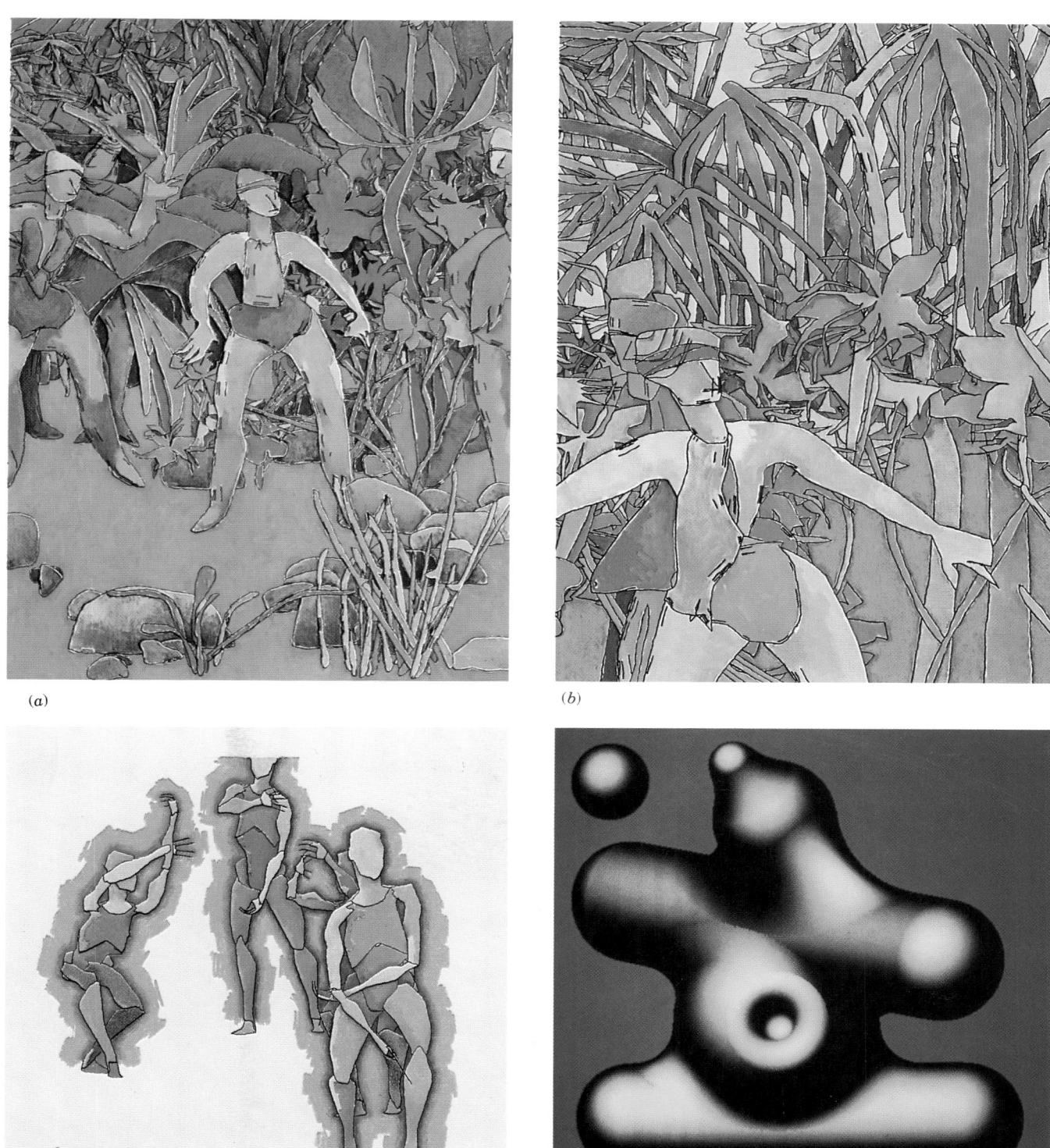

Art, AI in. AARON is a knowledge-based program designed to generate original artworks and to further the user's expertise. (*a*) "Meeting on Gauguin's Beach" (1988, oil on canvas, 90 in × 68 in, collection of Gordon and Gwen Bell) and (*b*) "In Search of the Sources" (1988, oil on canvas, 77 in × 54 in, collection of Pamela McCorduck and Joseph Traub) are oil paintings by AARON's author, Harold Cohen; (*c*) a drawing generated by AARON and colored by hand (1988, 8½ in × 11 in, collection of Becky Cohen). Photos by Becky Cohen. (*Below right*) **Visual recovery.** A shaded surface.

third-level table is the static evaluation of the board position under consideration.

As with the polynomial evaluation function, the game was divided into six phases with a different three-level signature table set for each phase, and the program was trained by following book moves. Two cumulative totals A (agree) and D (differ), initially set to zero, are associated with each cell in the hierarchy. As before, the program is made to follow book games. For any given position there is a number of next positions, one of which is recommended by the book. Each of these positions corresponds to one cell in each of the three levels of the signature table hierarchy. A 1 is added to the D totals of all such cells not representing the book move; for cells associated with the book move, however, the A count is incremented by the number of nonbook moves. Once in a while, the correlation coefficient $C = (A - D)/(A + D)$ would be computed for every cell as a measure of the goodness of the associated positions as book-recommended moves. The value obtained for C becomes the new cell entry after being adjusted to fall in the required range for every level in the hierarchy.

Book learning worked particularly well. After following 173,989 book moves, the program was tested on 895 new positions. It was able to predict the best move recommended by the book 38% of the time and the second best 26% of the time. This performance was attained using only the evaluation function. When it conducted a tree search in addition, the program's ability to follow book moves was increased substantially. The signature table method was distinctly superior to the polynomial evaluation function in improving the quality of the program's play.

Samuel's work was one of the first successful contributions to machine learning and game playing (Buchanan and co-workers, 1978; McCorduck, 1979; Samuel, 1983). No program before his had reached a championship level of play in a nontrivial game of strategy. Few other game-playing programs today exhibit a better performance. It remains therefore as one of the major achievements of AI research.

SIMPLE HEURISTICS AND THE PHASE TABLE METHOD

Additional experiments with various static evaluation functions were conducted by Griffith (1974). Using the book-learning approach, he showed that a very simple evaluator is better than the linear polynomial but not as good as signature tables in capturing checkers knowledge. This new method is based on four checkers-related heuristics: highest priority is given to moving a king, and next highest, to a move along the main diagonal and into the two central squares; third priority is given to all remaining moves, except those from specified squares in the first row and those leading to jumps, which are given lowest priority. Similarly, a second static evaluation function proposed by Griffith (1974) was found to be at least as good as signature tables and considerably simpler to implement. In this method, the game is divided into six consecutive phases, and for each phase, a table is created with 98 entries representing all legal moves in the game. When a

position is to be evaluated, its goodness is determined by the value in the appropriate table corresponding to the move that leads to it.

SEARCHING CHECKERS TREES IN PARALLEL

Besides being used as an experimental ground for research on learning, the game of checkers served to test the applicability of parallel processing ideas to AI. A parallel computer is one consisting of several processing units. A given computational task is subdivided into subtasks, each of which is assigned to a different processing unit. Such a computer is of particular use to a game-playing program, as the time required to search enormous trees could be significantly reduced through parallel processing. By speeding up the search, a program can examine deeper trees in a fixed amount of time and, as a consequence, improve the quality of its play. A number of experiments with parallel algorithms for searching game trees are described by Akl and Doran (1983). Two versions of a checkers-playing program are compared, each using a different parallel algorithm for tree search. The programs were tested on an experimental parallel computer. With the exception of the opening game, where all moves appear to be equally good, the results indicated that a parallel implementation of the alpha-beta algorithm was especially effective in reducing the running time as well as the total number of nodes examined and the total number of terminal nodes evaluated.

BIBLIOGRAPHY

S. G. Akl and R. J. Doran, "A Comparison of Parallel Implementations of the Alpha-Beta and Scout Tree Search Algorithms Using the Game of Checkers," in M. A. Bramer, ed., *Computer-Game Playing: Theory and Practice*, Ellis Horwood, Chichester, U.K., 1983, pp. 290–303.

A. Barr and E. A. Feigenbaum, *The Handbook of Artificial Intelligence*, Vol. 1, Kaufmann, Los Altos, Calif., 1981.

B. G. Buchanan, T. M. Mitchell, R. G. Smith, and C. R. Johnson, Jr., "Models of Learning Systems," in J. Belzer, A. G. Holzman and A. Kent, eds., *Encyclopedia of Computer Science and Technology*, Vol. 11, Marcel Dekker, New York, 1978, pp. 24–51.

A. K. Griffith, "A Comparison and Evaluation of Three Machine Learning Procedures as Applied to the Game of Checkers," *Artif. Intell.* **5**, 137–148 (1974).

P. C. Jackson, *Introduction to Artificial Intelligence*, Petrocelli, New York, 1974.

P. McCorduck, *Machines Who Think*, Freeman, San Francisco, 1979, pp. 148–153.

W. F. Ryan, *Play Winning Checkers*, Coles, Toronto, 1978.

A. L. Samuel, "Some Studies in Machine Learning Using the Game of Checkers," in E. A. Feigenbaum and J. Feldman, eds., *Computers and Thought*, McGraw-Hill, New York, 1963, pp. 71–105.

A. L. Samuel, "Some Studies in Machine Learning Using the Game of Checkers. II—Recent Progress," *IBM J. Res. Develop.* **11**(6), 601–617 (Nov. 1967).

A. L. Samuel, "AI, Where It Has Been and Where It Is Going," *Proceedings of the Eighth International Joint Conference on Artificial Intelligence*, Karlsruhe, FRG, 1983, Morgan-Kaufmann, San Mateo, Calif., pp. 1152–1157.

SELIM G. AKL
Queen's University

CHEF

CHEF was a case-based planner in the domain of Szechwan cooking. Its task was to build new recipes from existing plans, in response to the user's requests. Because it was a case-based system, CHEF constructed plans from an episodic memory of its own prior successes, failures, and repairs, rather than from a rule base describing the physics of its domain. CHEF was composed of six basic modules:

- A projector that predicted planning problems on the basis of the past failures.
- A retriever that selected plans from a dynamic memory on the basis of goals satisfied and problems avoided.
- A modifier that altered plans found by the retriever to achieve any unsatisfied goals from the input.
- An indexer that placed new plans back into memory, indexed by the goals that they satisfied and the problems that they avoided.
- A dependency-directed repairer that repaired faults uncovered during execution.
- An assigner that used the causal explanation built during repair to determine the features that would predict the repaired fault and then indexed them in the projector's memory for future anticipation.

KRISTIAN J. HAMMOND
University of Chicago

CHEMISTRY, AI IN

Chemistry was one of the first disciplines, aside from computer science, to actively engage in research on AI techniques. The first chemistry AI project was the DENDRAL (qv) project at Stanford University. This project began in 1964, involved more than 50 researchers, and produced more than 100 articles and two books. DENDRAL began with the goal of automatic interpretation of mass spectral data. However, during its 23-year history, it has also investigated other topics, including automated learning, computerized representation of chemical structures, applications of graph theory, exhaustive chemical structure generation, and proton ^{13}C NMR interpretation. A detailed account of the project can be found in Lindsay and co-workers (1980).

Defining which computer systems should be classified as AI systems has remained a problem throughout AI's history. In chemistry this problem is compounded because many AI applications rely heavily on numerical algorithms, and many applications that exhibit AI-like characteristics are completely numerical rather than symbolic in nature. Examples of the latter are pattern recognition (qv) techniques and learning machines. To avoid the difficult problem of defining AI exactly, this article is limited to work that uses expert systems (qv), symbolic manipulation, and natural language interpretation techniques (see NATURAL LANGUAGE UNDERSTANDING). Within these three areas, AI technologies have made many contributions to the practice of chemistry.

Work in applying AI technologies to chemistry has recently expanded beyond the traditional academic environment. Although academia continues to develop new techniques, industry has begun to apply older, more developed techniques to solve their problems. Vendors are using AI techniques to enhance existing products and develop new ones. Other industrial researchers are developing proprietary systems in an attempt to gain a competitive advantage.

Endeavors covered in this article can be divided into six general categories:

Natural and chemical language.
Chemical reaction synthesis.
Chemical structure elucidation.
Improving chemical instrumentation.
Symbolic algebraic manipulation.
Highly specific expert systems that do not fall into the above categories.
Probable directions for future applications.

NATURAL AND CHEMICAL LANGUAGE APPLICATIONS

Natural language applications may be divided into two classes: the language of chemical structures, substructures, and reactions; and the methods used to convert between that language and English sentences. Chemical structure language requires a method for representing molecules in the computer and a syntax for manipulating those representations (Wipke and co-workers, 1974; Whitlock, 1977). This language requirement was clearly defined by researchers who were storing chemical information in computer files. Wiswesser line notation (Wiswesser, 1954; Smith, 1968) and its derivatives were developed to define uniquely chemical structures as a string of characters. Each character represents a specific fragment of a molecule, allowing the computer to recognize a molecule.

An alternative approach uses graph theory, defining molecules as vertices and the connections between them (Bertz and co-workers, 1985). This approach creates a connection table, or matrix, whose rows and columns refer to atoms. The values stored in the matrix describe the type of connection between atoms. Syntax rules can be defined for manipulating these computer representations, allowing substructures of molecules to be defined and matched. Computer representations of molecules have led to chemical databases of molecular representations. Molecules may be graphically entered into a computer and the database searched for substructures. The popularity of these databases has created an entire industry to fill the demand (Gordon and Brockwell, 1983).

The second use of natural-language techniques is more familiar. Natural language systems attempt to understand English sentences that contain chemical information. These systems function as user-friendly interfaces to other chemical expert systems or as intelligent interfaces to chemical databases. Understanding English-phrased questions about databases is simpler than understanding problems relating to chemistry. Commercial natural language systems can perform some of these tasks in chemical applications, but several systems have been developed specifically for chemistry.

Chemical Abstracts Service is investigating automatic keyword indexing of papers based on a computer interpretation of the text (Moureau and co-workers, 1970; Cohen and co-workers, 1976; Baser and co-workers, 1978). Other work has focused on searching the chemical literature, based on an interpretation of the text (Smith and co-workers, 1985).

CHEMICAL REACTION SYNTHESIS

Chemical reaction synthesis is one of the oldest applications of AI in chemistry, begun in 1967 (Corey, 1967; Corey and Wipke, 1969). These programs attempt to design a sequence of chemical reactions that would result in a target molecule. Early work was based on a chemical synthetic tree. The target molecule was decomposed into its potential precursors using every possible single-step chemical synthesis. Each precursor was further decomposed into earlier antecedents, thus creating a synthetic tree. This decomposition led to an impossibly large number of potential synthetic paths. The deeper into a synthetic tree the procedure went, the more the number of potential paths multiplied. Initially, the selection of the best branch at each junction in the tree required the chemist's intervention in the program. This was necessary to limit the number of pathways and was accomplished by using interactive computer graphics to display the potential paths, and the best precursor was selected by the chemist (Corey and co-workers, 1985). The program, Simulation and Evaluation of Chemical Synthesis (SECS), improved the interactive graphics by enabling the chemist to select the reaction path and broadened the computer knowledge base by adding stereochemcial reactions and displays (Wipke and co-workers, 1974; Wipke and Dyott, 1974).

One technique, which eliminated the need for a chemist's intervention to find a synthetic route, incorporated synthetic rules and heuristic programming (Blower and Whitlock, 1976). The program uses only the molecular substructures of the target molecule that participate in the available synthetic methods. Heuristic rules determine the correct sequence of reactions required to protect any reactive functional groups on the target.

A second technique to eliminate a chemist's interven-

tion is based on the principle of minimum chemical distance (Jochum and co-workers, 1980). This technique allows the program to eliminate synthetic routes that are not likely to be useful. Future developments for this method include the potential of predicting chemical reactions that are not known today (Gasteiger and co-workers, 1985; Corey and co-workers, 1985).

Expert systems techniques have also been applied to this problem. These methods, before further evaluation, reduce chemical reactions to more general axioms. SYNLMA (Wang and co-workers, 1985) uses theorem-proving (qv) techniques to design organic synthesis. QED (Dolata, 1984) applies multivalue-logic predicate calculus with axioms to select a plan to choose among the possible precursors.

CHEMICAL STRUCTURE ELUCIDATION

Structure elucidation is a prime area for AI applications because it requires both scientific expertise and problem-solving capabilities. Information on molecular formula and structural fragments generally comes from spectral interpretation but can come from any source at the chemist's disposal. Internal consistency checks combine data from multiple sources to resolve conflicting information about the presence or absence of particular fragments. Enumeration programs connect the remaining fragments to obtain all chemically possible molecules. Those structures are ranked based on such properties as comparison of predicted and observed spectra and steric stresses. The chemist must then devise a way to distinguish between the remaining candidate structures.

Determination of Structural Fragments

There are three approaches to identifying compounds using spectroscopic data. The oldest method, library searching, compares the unknown spectrum with a collection of known spectra. This is straightforward, but it becomes impractical as the size of the reference libraries increases. In addition, library searching cannot identify compounds not in the library, such as newly synthesized compounds. The second approach, pattern recognition, compares the unknown spectrum with patterns that are characteristic of classes of compounds. This solves the two problems library searching presents but requires a substantial number of spectra for each class of compounds to be recognized. AI avoids these problems by interpreting spectra using the rules a spectroscopist would use. AI techniques have an advantage over spectroscopists because the computer system does not forget or confuse information. Unfortunately, AI systems do not have all the knowledge of the spectroscopist. AI structure elucidation systems are comparable in performance to a postgraduate spectroscopist (Hippe, 1985). Below, the approaches taken to interpret the various types of spectral data are described.

Infrared Spectroscopy. Spectroscopists have known for some time that certain functional groups and substitution patterns have characteristic absorptions in the IR. These patterns are documented in standard Colthup Charts.

Early work attempted to computerize these tables to automatically interpret IR spectra (Schrade and co-workers, 1980; Woodruff and Munk, 1977). These programs must be able to deal with the following problems: many functional groups absorb at each frequency, functional groups can cause more than one absorption, and the solvents used can shift or mask peaks. Recent work (Tomellini and co-workers, 1984a) focused on reducing the task of codifying the rules required to identify the functional groups of interest. This approach extracts rules automatically from the spectra of known compounds.

Mass Spectroscopy. The major work on mass spectroscope (ms) interpretation was done through the DENDRAL project. The first step in interpreting MS data was to determine, based on known mass–charge ratios, the probable molecular formula of an ion. The rules determining how a molecule will fragment were also codified. Using these rules, the mass spectrum of a candidate structure could be predicted. These spectra are compared to the unknown's mass spectrum to determine the likelihood that the candidate structure is the correct one. Later work from the DENDRAL project automatically determined molecular fragmentation rules using the mass spectra of known compounds. This work was called meta-DENDRAL (Buchanan and co-workers, 1981; Lindsay and co-workers, 1980).

A recent instrumental development is MS/MS which takes the MS of each peak in the original MS. Determination of the structure of each fragment from the original MS provides a unique way to preform internal consistency checking using the data from only one spectrometer (Cross and co-workers, 1985).

Nuclear Magnetic Resonance. Work in NMR has included both ^1H and ^{13}C analyses. Proton NMR is similar to IR in that functional groups tend to absorb in certain regions of the spectrum. The ranges of possible absorptions for each functional group makes ^1H NMR more suitable for eliminating functional groups determined from another source than for generating a list of fragments (Egli and co-workers, 1982). ^{13}C NMR, a more recent development, is very sensitive to the environment of the resonating carbon. This sensitivity causes every structurally unique carbon to resonate at a different frequency. The structural equivalence extends two or three bonds in all directions. Structurally equivalent carbons in different molecules absorb at similar frequencies. ^{13}C NMR is, therefore, good at generating a list of molecular fragments that are present. Work has been done to determine ^{13}C NMR interpretation rules (Mitchell and Schwenzer, 1978); however, the general method used is a library search. The library, in this case, is composed of molecular fragments and the characteristic absorption (Lindley and co-workers, 1982). Because the characteristic absorptions overlap, a list of possible functional groups is generated for each NMR peak.

X-Ray Powder Diffraction. Peak heights in x-ray powder diffraction are proportional to concentration; therefore, quantitative analysis is possible. Variations in rela-

tive peak heights from laboratory to laboratory and day to day preclude the use of simple least-squares fitting of reference spectra to the unknown. An expert system was developed to use the same knowledge that a mineralogist uses to solve this problem (Ennis, 1982; Dessy, 1984). This work was repeated using several different expert system development tools (EXPERT, UNITS, EMYCIN, OPS-5) and LISP. The study concluded that all the development tools and LISP had their shortcomings. The convenience of the expert system development tools can lead to restrictions that prevent the program from completely solving the problem. LISP, on the other hand, requires a great deal of programming effort. Fortunately, the knowledge base is generally easier to translate from one system to another than it is to extract from the expert.

Internal Consistency Checks

Internal consistency checks eliminate fragments that are inconsistent with the other fragments present. This elimination process helps to reduce the combinatorial explosion of possible structures. One of the most effective ways to provide this check is to combine information from different sources. As an example, one possible source of a ^{13}C NMR peak involves a carbonyl carbon, but there is no carbonyl absorption in the IR spectrum. These cross-checks can also come from different peaks in the same spectrum. Conversely, consistency checks can also increase the confidence in the presence of a fragment if more than one source of data suggests its presence.

Structure Enumeration

Once the various spectroscopic techniques have generated a list of molecular fragments, they must be connected to form possible structures for the unknown compound. The generation of possible structures must be exhaustive and nonredundant. Several problems arise during this procedure. The most serious problem is combinatorial explosion. Sometimes, there may be millions of possible structures. Enumeration programs must be able to eliminate chemically impossible structures and allow the chemist to eliminate other highly unlikely structures. Elimination is usually done at each step of a depth-first search to prune the search tree when possible. Another problem is that the list of fragments may not be complete or may contain ambiguities. The programs must handle multiple possible starting points and recognize when and where the assembled fragments begin to overlap. Additionally, the input fragments themselves may overlap one another (Carhart and co-workers, 1981). The enumeration program must also recognize the existence of stereoisomers and be able to distinguish between stereoisomers (Nourse and co-workers, 1979, 1980; Nourse, 1979).

Ranking of Candidate Structures

There are two methods of ranking candidate structures. The first method compares the unknown's spectrum with a predicted spectrum for the candidate structure. This is the approach taken by DENDRAL by using mass spectra. The second method, which is generally not as useful, discriminates against structures that are highly strained, such as three-membered rings. In the end, the chemist must devise physical tests to distinguish between remaining candidates.

Below is a comparison of packages developed to address various portions of the structure elucidation process.

DENDRAL. Uses MS data and ^{13}C NMR data. All other constraints on structures must be deduced by the chemist. It excels in the structure generation process, handling stereoisomers and overlapping substructures (*GENOA*, 1982; T. Monmaney, 1985). The candidate-testing procedure is built into the program (Lindsay and co-workers, 1980).

CHEMICS. Uses MS, ^{1}H and ^{13}C NMR, and IR data. It is a fully integrated package written in FORTRAN. It is limited to molecules containing only carbon, hydrogen, and oxygen. The structure generator cannot handle overlapping substructures (Fujiwara and co-workers, 1981; S. Saki and co-workers, 1978, 1981, 1982; Abe and co-workers, 1981).

CASE. Uses ^{13}C NMR and IR data. It is written in FORTRAN and cannot handle overlapping substructures (Munk and co-workers, 1982; Shelley and Munk, 1981; Trulson and Munk, 1983; Lipcus and Munk, 1985).

SEAC. Uses IR, ^{1}H NMR, and UV data. The structure generator cannot handle overlapping substructures (Debska and co-workers, 1981; Hippe, 1985; Sasaki and co-workers, 1978).

STREC. Uses MS, NMR, IR, and UV data. The program is written in FORTRAN and cannot handle overlapping substructures (Gribov and co-workers, 1977).

B. Curry. Uses MS, IR, and UV data. The package concentrates on the internal consistency check and conflict resolution (Curry and Michnowicz, 1985).

PAIRS. Is strictly an IR interpretation program, its strength being the ability to easily add new rules (Tomellini and co-workers, 1984a, 1984b; Dessy, 1984; Smith and Woodruff, 1984; Woodruff and Smith 1981a, 1981b).

EXMAT. Uses IR and MS data. Its strength is the ability to design the entire analysis and use other chemometric techniques to solve parts of the problem (Liebman and co-workers, 1985).

IMPROVING CHEMICAL INSTRUMENTATION

Infrared Spectroscopy. The IR interpretation program PAIRS has been incorporated into at least one vendor's Fourier transform IR spectrometer (Woodruff and co-workers, 1981). This gives the spectroscopic structural information for those spectra not found in the limited spectral library available on the spectrometer. The program is also being made available through QCPE (Woodruff and Smith, 1981b).

Mass Spectroscopy. One of the most complex mass spectrometers today is the triple quadrupole mass spectrome-

ter. The spectrometer is completely computerized with more than 30 controllable parameters. Tuning the spectrometer for an optimum signal requires a high level of operator expertise. The MS signal must be maximized, and the peak shape must be evaluated. An expert system was developed using the KEE (qv) expert system development facility to automatically tune the instrument (Wong and Lanning, 1984; Dessy, 1984). The expert system is capable of outperforming a simplex optimization but is not quite as good as a competent operator.

Chromatography. Expert Chromatography Assistance Team (ECAT) is an expert system designed to aid chemists in developing liquid chromatography methods (Dessy, 1984; Karnicky and co-workers, 1985). Liquid chromatography design involves analyzing, optimizing, and troubleshooting a particular separation. The expert system includes general chromatographic knowledge, specific literature references, an experiment designer, and chromatography data analysis.

Ultracentrifugation. Ultracentrifugation is a technique for separating biological samples by their density. Most researchers consider it simply a tool and are not interested in the intricacies of the separation process. The expert system SpinPro questions the user on their research goals and recommends the optimum set of operating conditions (Martz and co-workers, 1985). The operating parameters include rotor type, run speed, run time, gradient material, and gradient concentration. SpinPro also recommends the best set of conditions using only equipment available in the researcher's lab and details the results of those compromises. This expert system can be run on an IBM personal computer.

Process Control. The monitoring and control of chemical process systems is a new area for expert systems. Control systems are directly connected to instruments that monitor the temperatures, pressures, concentrations, and other variables of the process equipment. These measurements are used to predict the development of the chemical process and, if problems are discovered, modify the controlling instrumentation to correct the process. These control systems are specific to each process and require extensive measurements of the chemical system and knowledge of process behavior when the controlling instrumentation is varied (Moore and co-workers, 1985; Scarl and co-workers, 1985).

SYMBOLIC ALGEBRA APPLICATIONS

The fundamental theories in chemistry can be described by mathematical equations, which can be quite complex. Many chemical problems can be solved numerically using these equations (Borman, 1985). The solution of these equations has, however, been greatly simplified by the development of symbolic algebra packages (Ogilvie, 1982). These packages solve complex equations analytically instead of using numerical approximations.

As early as 1954 symbolic algebra techniques were applied to problems in quantum chemistry (Boys and co-workers, 1956). However, only recently have symbolic algebra programs become popular (Johnson, 1983). This delay was caused by the high cost of computers powerful enough to run the software and the availability of commercial packages with full user support. The applications of symbolic algebra have become so diverse that an entire symposium was devoted to the subject at the August 1984 American Chemical Society national meeting. Twenty-two papers were presented at the symposium (Pavelle, 1985).

There are five commercially available packages that perform algebraic, calculus, and differential manipulations. They are MACSYMA (1977, 1982) [available through Edunet and Arpanet]; REDUCE (Hearn, 1983); MAPLE (Geddes and co-workers); SMP (Cole and co-workers, 1981), written in C for speed of execution; and mu-Math (Johnson, 1983; Williams, 1985; D. Stoutemyer, 1985), a microcomputer version. A useful feature of several of these packages is their ability to translate their answers into FORTRAN code, which can be used by numerical programs.

OTHER EXPERT SYSTEMS

Computer-Aided Education. A chemical tutor called GEORGE (Cornelius and co-workers, 1985) is an expert system developed to understand dimensional analysis problems dealing with basic chemistry. The program knows how to manipulate the dimensions of physical properties (such as moles, density, concentration) and conversion factors to different units of measure. Using these, the program can solve a wide variety of problems. The unique feature of this program is that the student specifies the problem, and GEORGE explains the solution with text and diagrams.

Formulation of Agricultural Chemicals. Biologically active chemicals must be combined with various other chemicals to make a commercial product with the desired application characteristics. An expert system developed to assist in this process takes into account cost, marketing, legal, chemical, and end-use considerations in determining the best formulation (Hohne and Houghton, 1985). The program also uses several FORTRAN programs that calculate chemical parameters necessary to the decision-making process.

Analysis of Water Chemistry in Steam Power Plants. Corrosion because of improper water and steam chemistry is a major cause of downtime at steam power plants. This corrosion can cost a company approximately $1 million per day. An expert system has been developed that receives data from both the operator and remote chemical sensors, recommends corrective measures, if necessary, and reports the likely result if no action is taken (Bellows, 1984, 1985).

Experimental Design. Deciding what experiments are required to answer a particular question is a pervasive problem in chemistry. Several expert systems have been

developed to solve the following problems: determination of intracellular Mg^{2+} levels, deriving enzyme kinetic models to fit experimental data, design of experiments to determine safety and efficacy of drugs (Garfinkel and co-workers, 1985), determination of the number of analyses (including blanks) that must be done for environmental water analysis (Keith and Stuart, 1985), and design of molecular genetics cloning experiments (Friedland, 1981).

Macromolecular Structure Determination. One expert system allows the construction of molecules using heuristic rules. The system creates a three-dimensional protein based on the protein amino acid sequence (Cohen and co-workers, 1983). This system includes heuristic rules that determine when the protein sequence turns on itself and which sequences form alpha- and beta-sheets (Kuntz, 1985). Similarly, another program, Artificial Intelligence in Model Building (AIMB), has been written for creating three-dimensional molecular models. This program can construct the three-dimensional model of a molecule from a two-dimensional drawing faster than a chemist can using mechanical models (Wipke and Hahn, 1985).

FUTURE APPLICATIONS

Computer software is dramatically increasing its penetration into the chemist's laboratory. The volume and sophistication of software is exceeding the chemist's desire and ability to keep current. However, the integration of numerical software, graphical displays, and expert systems promises to revolutionize the practice of chemistry. Expert systems will build on the vast library of existing chemical software and make these technologies available to the practicing chemist (Banaras-Alcantara, 1985).

Integration of these techniques will lead to intelligent computer assistants for every chemist. There will be structure elucidation assistants for analytical chemists, process control assistants for chemical engineers (Brooks, 1986), experimental design assistants for organic chemists, and mathematical assistants for physical chemists. However, before these assistants can be built, each different rule-base must be further developed.

This collation and development of chemical relationships, expressible as heuristic rules, is under way today in both academia and industry. It is thought that the intelligent application of these rules through expert systems can reduce problems that lead to combinatorial explosions of possible solutions. Problem simplification of this type will be necessary before the huge amount of chemical information that exists today can be integrated into intelligent assistants.

BIBLIOGRAPHY

H. Abe, T. Yamasaki, I. Fujiwara, and S. Sasaki, "Computer Aided Structure Elucidation Methods," *Anal. Chim. Acta* **133**, 4999–5006 (1981).

ACS, *Artificial Intelligence Applications in Chemistry*, ACS Symposium Series 306, American Chemical Society, Washington, D.C., 1985.

R. Banares-Alcantara, A. W. Westerberg, and M. D. Rychener, "Development of an Expert System for Physical Property Predictions," *Comput. Chem. Eng.* **9**(2), 127–142 (1985).

K. H. Baser, S. M. Cohen, D. L. Dayton, and P. B. Watkins, "Online Indexing Experiment at Chemical Abstracts Service: Algorithmic Generation of Articulated Index Entries from Natural Language Phrases," *J. Chem. Inf. Comput. Sci.* **18**(1), 18–25 (1978).

J. C. Bellows, "An Artificial Intelligence Chemistry Diagnostic System," *Proceedings of the 45th International Water Conference,* Engineering Society of Western Pennsylvania, 1984, pp. 15–25.

J. C. Bellows, "Chemistry Diagnostic System for Steam Power Plants," in ACS, 1985.

S. H. Bertz, W. C. Herndon, and G. Dabbagh, "On the Similarity of Graphs and Molecules," in ACS, 1985.

P. E. Blower, Jr., and H. W. Whitlock, Jr., "An Application of Artificial Intelligence to Organic Synthesis," *J. Am. Chem. Soc.* **98**(6), 1499–1510 (1976).

S. A. Borman, "Scientific Software," *Anal. Chem.* **57**(9), 983A (1985).

S. F. Boys, B. G. Cook, C. M. Reeves, and I. Shavitt, *Nature* **178**, 1207–1209 (1956).

K. Brooks, *Chem. Week* 38–39 (Sept. 10, 1986).

B. G. Buchanan, D. H. Smith, W. C. White, R. J. Gritter, E. A. Feigenbaum, J. Lederberg, and C. Djerassi, "Applications of Artificial Intelligence for Chemical Inference, 22. Automatic Rule Formation in Mass Spectrometry by Means of the meta-DENDRAL Program," *J. Am. Chem. Soc.* **98**(20), 6168–6178 (1976).

R. E. Carhart, D. H. Smith, N. A. B. Gray, J. G. Nourse, and C. Djerassi, "GENOA: A Computer Program for Structure Elucidation Utilizing Overlapping and Alternative Substructures," *J. Org. Chem.* **46**, 1708–1718 (1981).

F. E. Cohen, R. M. Abarbanel, I. D. Kuntz, and R. J. Fletterick, "Secondary Structure Assignment for Alpha/Beta Proteins by a Combinatorial Approach," *Biochem.* **22**, 4894 (1983).

S. M. Cohen, D. L. Dayton, and R. Salvador, "Experimental Algorithmic Generation of Articulated Index Entries from Natural Language Phrases at Chemical Abstracts Service," *J. Chem. Inf. Comput. Sci.* **16**(2), 93–99 (1976).

C. A. Cole and co-workers, *SMP Handbook,* Caltech, Pasedena, Calif., 1981.

E. J. Corey, "General Methods for the Construction of Complex Molecules," *Pure Appl. Chem.* **14**, 19 (1967).

E. J. Corey, A. K. Long, and S. D. Rubenstein, *Science* **228**, 408 (1985).

E. J. Corey and W. T. Wipke, "Computer-Assisted Design of Complex Organic Synthesis," *Science* **166**, 178 (1969).

E. J. Corey, W. T. Wipke, and R. D. Cramer, III, "Computer-Assisted Synthetic Analysis," *J. Am. Chem. Soc.* **94**(2), 421 (1972).

R. Cornelius, D. Cabrol, and C. Cachet, "Applying the Techniques of Artificial Intelligence to Chemical Education," in ACS, 1985.

K. P. Cross, A. B. Giordani, H. R. Gregg, P. A. Hoffmann, C. F. Beckner, and C. G. Enke, "Automation of Structure Elucidation from Mass Spectrometry–Mass Spectrometry Data," in ACS, 1985.

B. Curry and J. A. Michnowicz, "An Expert System for Organic Structure Determination, " in ACS, 1985.

B. Debska, J. Duliban, B. Guzowska-Swider, and Z. Hippe, "Computer Aided Structural Analysis of Organic Compounds by an AI System," *Anal. Chim. Acta* **133**, 303–318 (1981).

R. E. Dessy, ed., "Expert Systems Part II," *Anal. Chem.* **56**(12), 1312A–1332A (1984).

D. P. Dolata, *QED Automated Inference in Planning Organic Synthesis*, Ph.D. dissertation, University of California, Santa Cruz, 1984.

H. Egli, D. H. Smith, and C. Djerassi, "Computer Assisted Structural Interpretation of Proton NMR Spectral Data," *Helv. Chim. Acta* **65**, 1898–1919 (1982).

S. P. Ennis, "Expert Systems, A User's Perspective of Some Current Tools," *Proceedings of the Second National Conference on Artificial Intelligence*, Pittsburgh, Penn., AAAI, Menlo Park, Calif., 1982, pp. 319–321.

P. Friedland, "MOLGEN—Applications of Symbolic Computation and Artificial Intelligence to Molecular Biology," in M. Keenberg, ed., *Proceedings of the Battelle Conference on Genetic Engineering*, Vol. 5, Battelle Seminar Studies Program, Seattle, Wash., 1981, pp. 171–182.

I. Fujiwara, T. Okuyama, T. Yamasaki, H. Abe, and S. Sasaki, "Computer-Aided Structure Elucidation of Organic Compounds with the CHEMICS System," *Anal. Chem. Acta* **133**, 527–533 (1981).

D. Garfinkel, L. Garfinkel, V. W. Soo, and C. A. Kulikowski, "Interpretation and Design of Chemically Based Experiments with Expert Systems," in ACS, 1985.

J. Gasteiger, M. G. Hutchings, P. Low, and H. Saller, "The Acquisition and Representation of Knowledge for Expert Systems in Organic Chemistry," in ACS, 1985.

K. O. Geddes, G. H. Gonnet, and B. W. Char, *MAPLE User's Manual*, 2nd ed., University of Waterloo, Waterloo, Ont., Canada.

GENOA, Molecular Design Ltd., Hayward, Calif., 1982.

J. E. Gordon and J. C. Brockwell, "Chemical Inference," *J. Chem. Inf. Comput. Sci.* **23**, 117 (1983).

L. A. Gribov, M. E. Elyashberg, and V. V. Serov, "Computer System for Structure Recognition of Polyatomic Molecules by IR, NMR, UV, and MS Methods," *Anal. Chim. Acta* **95**, 75–96 (1977).

A. C. Hearn, ed., *REDUCE User's Manual*, Version 3.0, Rand Publication CP78(4/83), The Rand Corp., Santa Monica, Calif., 1983.

Z. Hippe, "Problems in the Application of AI in Analytical Chemistry," *Anal. Chim. Acta* **150**, 11–21 (1983).

B. Hohne and R. Houghton, "An Expert System for the Formulation of Agricultural Chemicals," in ACS, 1985.

C. Jochum, J. Gastiger, and I. Ugi, "The Principle of Minimum Chemical Distance," *Angew. Chem. Int. Ed.* **19**, 495 (1980).

C. S. Johnson, "Computer Algebra in Chemistry," *J. Chem. Inf. Comput. Sci.* **23**, 151–157 (1983).

J. Karnicky, R. Bach, and S. Abbott, "An Expert System for High-Performance Liquid Chromatography Methods Development," in ACS, 1985.

H. L. Keith and J. D. Stuart, "A Rule Induction Program for Quality Assurance-Quality Control and Selection of Protective Materials," in ACS, 1985.

I. D. Kuntz, personal communication, 1985.

S. A. Liebman, P. J. Duff, M. A. Schroeder, R. A. Fifer, and A. M. Harper, "Concerted Organic Analysis of Materials and Expert System Development," in ACS, 1985.

M. R. Lindley, N. A. B. Gray, D. H. Smith, and C. Djerassi, "Applications of AI for Chemical Inference. 40. Computerized Approach to Verification of ^{13}C NMR Spectral Assignments," *J. Org. Chem.* **47**, 1027–1035 (1982).

R. K. Lindsay, B. G. Buchanan, E. A. Feigenbaum, and J. Lederberg, *Applications of Artificial Intelligence for Organic Chemistry: The DENDRAL Project*, McGraw-Hill Inc., New York, 1980.

A. H. Lipcus and M. E. Munk, "Combinatorial Problems in Computer Assisted Structural Interpretation of C-13 NMR Spectra," *J. Chem. Inf. Comput. Sci.* **25**, 34–45 (1985).

MACSYMA Primer, MIT Mathlab Group, Cambridge, Mass., 1982.

MACSYMA Reference Manual, MIT Mathlab Group, Cambridge, Mass., 1977.

P. R. Martz, M. Heffron, and O. M. Griffith, "An Expert System for Optimizing Ultracentrifugation Runs," in ACS, 1985.

T. M. Mitchell and G. M. Schwenzer, "Applications of Artificial Intelligence for Chemical Inference. 25. A Computer Program for Automated Empirical ^{13}C NMR Rule Formation," *Org. Magn. Reson.* **11**(8), 378–384 (1978).

T. Monmaney, *Smithsonian* **114** (July 1985).

R. L. Moore, C. G. Knickerbocker, and L. B. Hawkinson, "A Real-Time Expert System for Process Control," in ACS, 1985.

M. Moureau, A. Girard, and J. Delaunay, "Natural Language Bibliographic Searches. PRETEXT Program," *Rev. Inst. Fr. Petrole Ann. Combust. Liq.* **25**(10), 1117–1143 (1970).

M. E. Munk, C. A. Shelley, H. B. Woodruff, and M. O. Trulson, "Computer Assisted Structure Elucidation," *F.Z. Anal. Chem.* **313**, 473–479 (1982).

J. G. Nourse, "The Configuration Symmetry Group and Its Application to Stereoisomer Generation, Specification, and Enumeration," *J. Am. Chem. Soc.* **101**(5), 1210 (1979).

J. G. Nourse, R. E. Carhart, D. H. Smith, and C. Djerassi, "Exhaustive Generation of Stereoisomers for Structure Elucidation," *J. Am. Chem. Soc.* **101**, 1216–1223 (1979).

J. G. Nourse, D. H. Smith, R. E. Carhart, and C. Djerassi, "Computer Assisted Elucidation of Molecular Structure with Stereochemistry," *J. Am. Chem. Soc.* **102**, 6289–6295 (1980).

J. F. Ogilvie, "Applications of Computer Algebra in Physical Chemistry," *Comput. Chem.* **6**, 169–172 (1982).

R. Pavelle, ed., *Application of Computer Algebra*, Kluwer, Boston, Mass., 1985.

S. Sasaki and co-workers, "CHEMICS F: A Computer Program System for Structure of Organic Compounds," *J. Chem. Inf. Comp. Sci.* **18**(4), 211 (1978).

S. Sasaki, H. Abe, I. Fujiwara, and T. Yamasaki, "The Application of ^{13}C NMR in CHEMICS, the Computer Program System for Structure Elucidation," *Stud. Theor. Chem.* **16**, 186–204 (1981).

S. Sasaki, H. Abe, I. Fujiwara, T. Yamasaki, Z. Hippe, B. Debska, J. Duliban, and B. Guzowska-Swider, "Recent Problems of Application of Artificial Intelligence in Computer-Aided Elucidation of Chemical Structures," *Chem. Anal. (Warsaw)* **27**(3–4), 171–181 (1982).

E. A. Scarl, J. R. Jamieson, and C. I. DeLaune, "Process Monitoring and Fault Location at the Kennedy Space Center," *SIGART Newslett.* **93**, 38 (1985).

B. Schrade and co-workers, "Automatic Reduction and Evaluation of IR and Raman Spectra," *F.Z. Anal. Chem.* **303**, 337–348 (1980).

C. A. Shelley and M. E. Munk, "CASE, A Computer Model of the Structure Elucidation Process," *Anal. Chim. Acta* **133**, 507–516 (1981).

E. G. Smith, *The Wiswesser Line-Formula Chemical Notation*, McGraw-Hill Inc., New York, 1968.

G. M. Smith and H. B. Woodruff, "Development of a Computer Language and Compiler for Expressing the Rules of IR Spectral Interpretation," *J. Chem. Inf. Comp. Sci.* **24**, 33–39 (1984).

P. J. Smith, D. A. Krawczak, and S. Shute, "EP-X: A Knowledge-Based System to Aid in Bibliographic Searches of the Environmental Pollution Literature," paper presented at the American Chemical Society Meeting, Chicago, Sept. 1985.

D. Stoutemyer in G. Goos and J. Hartmanis, eds., *Eurocal '85*, Springer-Verlag, 1985.

S. A. Tomellini, R. A. Hartwick, J. M. Stevenson, and H. B. Woodruff, "Automated Rule Generation for PAIRS," *Anal. Chim. Acta* **162**, 227–240 (1984a).

S. A. Tomellini, J. M. Stevenson, and H. B. Woodruff, "Rules for Computerized Interpretation of Vapor Phase IR Spectra," *Anal. Chem.* **56**, 67–70 (1984b).

M. O. Trulson and M. E. Munk, "Table Driven Procedure for IR Spectrum Interpretation," *Anal. Chem.* **56**, 2137–2142 (1983).

T. Wang, L. Burnstein, S. Ehrlich, M. Evens, A. Gough, and P. Johnson, "Using a Theorem Prover in the Design of Organic Synthesis," in ACS, 1985.

H. W. Whitlock, "An Organic Chemist's View of Formal Language," in W. T. Wipke and J. Howe, eds., *Computer Assisted Organic Synthesis*, ACS Symposium Series 61, American Chemical Society, Washington, D.C., 1977.

G. Williams, "Mu Math 79 Symbolic Math System," *BYTE* **11**, 325–338 (1980).

T. Wipke and T. Dyott, "Simulation and Evaluation of Chemical Synthesis," *J. Am. Chem. Soc.* **96**(15), 4825 (1974).

W. Wipke and M. A. Hahn, "Analogy and Intelligence in Model Building," in ACS, 1985.

W. T. Wipke, S. R. Heller, R. J. Feldman, and E. Hyde, eds., *Computer Representation and Manipulation of Chemical Information*, Wiley, New York, 1974, pp. 147–174.

W. J. Wiswesser, *A Line-Formula Chemical Notation*, Thomas Y. Crowell, Co., New York, 1954.

C. Wong and S. Lanning, "AI in Chemical Analysis, *Energ. Technol. Rev.*, Lawrence Livermore National Laboratory, Berkeley, Calif., Feb. 1984.

H. B. Woodruff and co-workers, "Automated Interpretation of IR Spectra with an Instrument Based Minicomputer," *Anal. Chem.* **53**, 2367–2369 (1981).

H. B. Woodruff and M. E. Munk, "Computer-Assisted Interpretation of IR Spectra," *Anal. Chim. Acta* **95**, 13–23 (1977).

H. B. Woodruff and G. M. Smith, "Computer Program for the Analysis of IR Spectra," *Anal. Chem.* **52**, 2321–2327 (1980).

H. B. Woodruff and G. M. Smith, "Generating Rules for PAIRS— A Computerized IR Spectral Interpreter," *Anal. Chim. Acta* **133**, 545–553 (1981a).

H. B. Woodruff and G. M. Smith, "Program for the Analysis of IR Spectra (PAIRS) (QCPE 426)," *QCPE Bull.* **1**, 58 (1981b).

B. Hohne
T. Pierce
Rohm and Haas Co.

CHESS 4.5

Chess 4.5 is a chess program (see COMPUTER CHESS AND SEARCH) that uses a method called "iterative deepening" to determine its next move. It is a brute force method that does exhaustive search, first to the second level and then to the third level. It continues with this iteration until a fixed time limit is reached. The newer version is known as Chess 4.7 (see D. Slate and L. Atkin, "Chess 4.5: The Northwestern University Chess Program," in P. Frey, ed., *Chess Skill in Man and Machine*, Springer-Verlag, New York, pp. 82–118, 1977).

J. ROSENBERG
Kilchberg, Switzerland

CHESS PROGRAMS. See COMPUTER CHESS AND SEARCH.

CHIP

A constraint logic programming system developed at the European Computer Industry Research Centre (ECRC) in Munich, CHIP has been designed to tackle real world "constrained search problems." It extends usual PROLOG-like logic languages in two ways: by introducing three new computation domains besides the Herbrand universe (finite domains, Boolean algebra, and linear rational arithmetic); and by providing powerful control structures (coroutining, demons, forward checking). For each of the new computation domains, CHIP uses specialized constraint solving techniques: consistency checking for finite domains, equation solving in Boolean algebra for Booleans and a symbolic simplex-like algorithm for rationals. CHIP has been successfully applied to a large number of problems especially in the areas of planning, scheduling, circuit design, and decision making (see M. Dincbas and co-workers, "The Constraint Logic Programming Language CHIP," *Proceedings of the International Conference on Fifth Generation Computer Systems*, Tokyo, 1988, pp. 693–702).

M. DINCBAS
ECRC GMbH

CHURCH'S THESIS

Church's thesis is the assertion that any process that is effective or algorithmic in nature defines a mathematical function belonging to a specific well-defined class, known variously as the recursive, the λ-definable, or the Turing computable functions. These terms originated in the 1930s to designate what appeared superficially to be three quite different notions: Gödel's characterization of functions definable by means of recursive definitions of the most general kind (see RECURSION), Church's and Kleene's notion of functions definable using the λ-operation (subsequently incorporated by John McCarthy into the LISP programming language; see LISP), and Turing's notion of a function computable by an abstract computing device (see TURING MACHINES). However, it was very soon seen that the three notions define the very same class of functions. Church announced his proposal to identify the class of functions definable by means of an effective process with the class of recursive functions (Church, 1936) in April 1935 at a professional meeting, a year after he had first suggested it to his student Kleene. Quite independently, Turing developed his own equivalent version during the spring of 1935. Gödel, who had been skeptical of Church's arguments in favor of his thesis, was fully convinced by Turing's work.

Gödel had made use of a more restricted class of functions, later called primitive recursive, in his famous work on undecidability. The fact that there were functions like Ackermann's that were clearly definable by recursive means but were not primitive recursive led Gödel to attempt to characterize recursive definitions in general. Using a suggestion from Herbrand, Gödel was led to his class of general recursive functions. Gödel went so far as to suggest, in lectures at the Institute for Advanced Study in Princeton in 1934, that if this definition really included all possible recursive definitions, then all functions computable by "finite procedures" would be general recursive, but he was not yet prepared to assert that his definition was really so inclusive. Meanwhile, Church and his students developed the concept of λ-definability as part of an effort to salvage a theory of the λ-operator from an ambitious system of logic developed by Church that had been proved inconsistent by his students Kleene and Rosser. Turing developed his machines in connection with his work on Hilbert's *Entscheidungsproblem*, the problem of finding an algorithm for testing inferences in first-order logic for validity. Turing was able to show that no such algorithm could exist, a conclusion that Church also reached. Post, who had developed some of these ideas many years earlier, now proposed a formulation very similar to Turing's. Post's work was independent of Turing, but not of Church. When these various concepts were proved equivalent to one another, it was clear that something of great importance had been discovered. [For a discussion and analysis of this history as well as the importance of the work of Kleene and of Post, see Davis (1982), which also contains references to the original literature and to other historical accounts.]

CHURCH'S THESIS AND AI

Church's thesis had made it possible to prove the algorithmic unsolvability of important problems in mathematics, provided an important basic tool in mathematical logic, made available an array of models in theoretical computer science, and provided the basis for an entirely new branch of mathematics. However, quite apart from all this, Church's thesis provides a crucial philosophical foundation for the proposition that AI is possible and that digital computers provide an appropriate instrument for realizing it. Before World War II large-scale computing machines were conceived and built as engines of numerical calculation. After the pioneering work of Church, Gödel, Kleene, Post, and especially Turing, it became clear that the notion of computation includes far more than numerical calculation; indeed, it encompasses everything expressible as an effective process or (as Turing once put it) by a "rule of thumb." This insight is physically embodied in the von Neumann architecture for computers. Thus, the project of producing computer programs that successfully emulate human cognitive functions, which seems evidently preposterous so long as a computing machine is conceived of as merely a device for carrying out numerical calculations, comes into focus as an ultimate goal. Of course, this is precisely the goal of AI research. These same considerations lead to the proposal that computer programs provide an appropriate theoretical model for cognitive functions, which is the principal paradigm held forth by workers in cognitive science (Pylyshyn, 1984).

CHURCH'S THESIS AND MECHANISM

The belief that AI is possible, in principle, is closely associated with a mechanist view of the human mind. Such a view holds that the properties of "mind" are ultimately to be understood on the basis of the behavior of the brain (and other relevant organs) as a material object obeying the laws of nature. This is opposed to a mentalist position that mental states are irreducible and extramaterial. Church's thesis is related to these matters in several ways. Turing's version of Church's thesis (called Turing's thesis in Pylyshyn, 1984) identifies effectiveness with mechanical computability. Thus, Church's thesis implies (as emphasized in Webb, 1980) that mechanism is incapable of being refuted by effective means. That is, a mentalist who wishes to claim that some particular human mental activity is incapable of being duplicated on a purely mechanical basis had best be very sure that this activity is uneffective. On the other hand, evidence of the extensiveness of mechanical computability, for example, Turing's construction of a "universal" machine as well as the equivalence of the various precise explications of effectiveness, tends to refute a mentalist critique based on the alleged limitations of the purely mechanical. Even the main negative consequence of Church's thesis, the existence of algorithmically unsolvable problems, serves to help refute mentalism. The mentalist has traditionally ridiculed the claims of mechanists by contrasting the varied, unpredictable, and complex behavior of human beings with the rigid and simple behavior of clockwork automata. However, the fact that there are problems concerning Turing machines for which no effective solutions can exist shows that computing mechanisms as well as people can exhibit a behavioral repertoire of great complexity and unpredictability.

BIBLIOGRAPHY

A. Church, "An Unsolvable Problem of Elementary Number Theory," *Am. J. Math.* **58**, 345 (1936).

M. Davis, "Why Gödel Didn't Have Church's Thesis," *Inf. Contrl.* **54**, 3–24 (1982).

W. Pylyshyn, *Computation and Cognition: Toward a Foundation for Cognitive Science*, MIT Press, Cambridge, Mass., 1984.

J. C. Webb, *Mechanism, Mentalism, and Metamathematics*, D. Reidel, Dordrecht, The Netherlands, 1980.

General References

A. Church, *Calculi of Lambda Conversion*, Princeton University Press, Princeton, N.J., 1941.

M. Davis, *The Undecidable*, Raven Press, New York, 1965.

M. DAVIS
New York University

CIRCUMSCRIPTION

Circumscription is a technique devised by McCarthy (1980) for formalizing certain notions in commonsense reasoning, and specifically in nonmonotonic reasoning. Since then, circumscription has become one of the major tools in the formalist AI camp, spawning half a dozen or more variations and dozens of papers in the hands of a number of investigators. This article will attempt mainly to introduce the underlying concept of circumscription, and point the way to more advanced aspects.

McCarthy describes circumscription as a "rule of conjecture" about what objects have a given property P. A useful example exploited by McCarthy is the familiar "missionaries and cannibals" puzzle. Three missionaries and three cannibals must cross a river, using a boat that can hold only two persons; if the cannibals outnumber the missionaries on either bank of the river, the missionaries will be eaten. How can the crossing be arranged safely? There are numerous features of interest in the puzzle. The one of concern here is that it is, in fact, a puzzle, ie, the puzzler is expected to recognize certain implicit ground rules, such as that the boat does not have a leak or any other incapacity for transporting people. Moreover, there are no additional cannibals or missionaries lurking in the background, who may upset otherwise sound plans, even though it was not specifically stated that there are *only* three cannibals and three missionaries. It is as if there is an implicit assumption that if something is not mentioned in the puzzle then it is not to be considered, an idea sometimes referred to as a closed-world assumption. It corresponds to minimizing the number of objects having certain properties. In effect, one is considering conjectures that, for certain properties P, an object x does not have P unless it is required to do so. Moreover, this sort of minimizing assumption appears to be very useful even in nonpuzzle situations. Circumscription provides one way to make this rather vague idea precise.

THE FORMALISM OF CIRCUMSCRIPTION

Circumscription involves the use of an axiom schema in a first-order language, intended to express the idea that certain formulas (well-formed formulas, wffs) have the smallest possible extensions consistent with certain given axioms. To illustrate, if B is a belief system including world knowledge W and specific domain knowledge $A[P]$ concerning a predicate P, then it may be desired to consider that P is to be minimized, in the sense that as few entities x as possible have property P as is consistent with $A[P]$. The world knowledge W together with $A[P]$ and the circumscriptive schema are used to derive conclusions in standard first-order logic, which then may be added to B (consistently and appropriately, it is hoped). It is this notion of consistency with a part of the belief system itself that causes conceptual as well as computational problems in nonmonotonic reasoning, essentially problems of self-reference. McCarthy has found a very ingenious way of finessing such self-reference in the context of minimization, allowing a mechanical means of establishing the effect of consistency tests in certain cases.

As suggested above, given a predicate symbol P and a formula $A[P]$ containing P, the minimization of P by $A[P]$ can be thought of as saying that the P objects consist of certain ones as needed to satisfy $A[P]$ and no more, in the sense that any tentative set of P objects x (such as those given by a wff Zx such that $A[Z]$ holds) already includes all P objects. Circumscription expresses this by means of a schema or set of wffs, which is denoted here by $A[P]/P$, as follows:

$$A[P]/P = \{[A[Z] \ \& \ (x)(Z(x) \to P(x))] \to$$
$$(y)(P(y) \to Z(y)) | Z \text{ is a wff}\}$$

(Here $A[Z]$ results from $A[P]$ by replacing every occurrence of P by Z.) One can think of $A[Z]$ as a test, to see whether Z is a viable reading of what P means. If so, and if Z does not introduce any new objects beyond what P does [which can be thought of as the significance of $Z(x) \to P(x)$], then, if P is to be minimal, one insists on the conclusion that Z can be no smaller than $P: P(y) \to Z(y)$.

Example. A key example, a variation on one emphasized by McCarthy (1980), is the following: Let $A[P]$ be $a \neq b$ and $P(a) \lor P(b)$. Let $Z_1(x)$ be $x = a$ and $Z_2(x)$ be $x = b$. Then from $P(a) \lor P(b)$ one gets that either Z_1 or Z_2 will serve for circumscription. That is, either $P(a)$ holds, so that $Z_1(x) \to P(x)$ and hence circumscription using Z_1 for P yields $P(x) \to Z_1(x)$, or $P(b)$ holds so that $Z_2(x) \to P(x)$ and hence, using Z_2 for P, $P(x) \to Z_2(x)$. Thus either a is the only P object or b is; indeed, $\neg P(a) \lor \neg P(b)$ will then be provable from $A[P] = A[P]/P$. In fact, it then follows that there is a unique P object; this, however, should not cause concern, for the intention is to explore the consequences of conjecturing the stated minimization of P.

A Major Generalization

McCarthy (1986) decisively generalizes his original notion of (predicate) circumscription to allow specified predicates other than P to vary as well as P; this decisively extends the range of applicability of circumscription, as will be seen. In the new formulation, called formula circumscription, the schema is replaced by a single second-order formula, but comparison with predicate circumscription is easier when a schema or set $A[P_1, \ldots, P_n]/E$ is retained, in the following form:

$$\{A[Z_1, \ldots, Z_n] \ \& \ (x)(E[Z_1, \ldots, Z_n] \to E) \to$$
$$(x)(E \to E(Z_1, \ldots, Z_n)) | \text{wffs } Z_1, \ldots, Z_n\}$$

where $E = E[P_1, \ldots, P_n]$ is a formula in which $P_1, \ldots, P_n$ may appear and $E[Z_1, \ldots, Z_n]$ is obtained from E by substituting Z_i for each P_i. Here the intuitive idea is to minimize (the extension of) the formula E, by allowing variations in (the extensions of) $P_1, \ldots, P_n$. The new second-order version of circumscription is called formula circumscription; the weakened version retaining a schema but allowing variable predicates will be called variable circumscription.

As McCarthy has observed, it is the presence of the predicate variables $P_1, \ldots, P_n$ that gives variable circumscription its power, and not the fact that E may be a formula. Indeed, forming an extension-by-definitions of $A[P]$ by adding the new axiom $(x)(P_0x \leftrightarrow Ex)$, where P_0 is a new predicate letter, one can simply circumscribe P_0 with $P_0, \ldots, P_n$ as variables in the extension of $A[P]$. That is, one can just as well take E to be a single predicate letter P_0, since any formula that one may wish to minimize can be made equivalent to such a P_0 by means of an appropriate axiom included in $A[P]$ itself. In the sequel then, E is the predicate letter P_0, and P stands for $P_0, P_1, \ldots, P_n$; ie, E plays the role of P_0 above, unless context dictates otherwise. Then the schema $A[P]/P$ is as above except that the predicate variables $P_0, \ldots, P_n$ appear, rather than simply $P_1, \ldots, P_n$, and the wffs $Z_0, \ldots, Z_n$ as well, again where P_0 is $E[P_0, \ldots, P_n]$ and Z_0 substitutes for $E[Z_0, \ldots, Z_n]$. To be precise, $A[P]/P$ will be the set of wffs

$$\{[A[Z_0, \ldots, Z_n] \ \& \ (x)(Z_0x \to P_0x)] \to$$
$$(y)(P_0y \to Z_0y) | Z_0, \ldots, Z_n \text{ are wffs}\}$$

The theory obtained from $A[P]$ by adjoining the set $A[P]/P$ as new axioms will be abbreviated with the notation $A[P]^*$ whenever the P can be understood from context. That is, $A[P]^* = A[P] + A[P]/P$.

An example using variable circumscription is the following "life and death" problem: Let $A[D,L]$ be the axiom

$$(x)(Dx \leftrightarrow \neg Lx) \ \& \ La \ \& \ Db \ \& \ Kc \ \& \ (a \neq b \ \& \ a \neq c \ \& \ b \neq c)$$

which is intended to have the interpretation that dead things (D) are those that are not living (L), and a is living, b is dead, and c is a kangaroo (K). The circumscription of D then corresponds to the notion that as few things as possible are to be considered dead. However, using mere predicate circumscription, ie, $A[D]^*$ rather than $A[D,L]^*$, D could not be "squeezed" down by means of an appropriate Z predicate since L, being unchanged, would force D to be its unchanging complement. Thus $A[D]^*$ would not have either Dc and Lc as theorems. On the other hand, $A[D,L]^*$ does have $\neg Dc$, and hence Lc, as theorems. This can be seen by circumscribing with the two predicates $x = b$ (for Z_0) and $x \neq b$ (for Z_1).

Of course, formula circumscription can accomplish all that variable circumscription does, and even more, as will be shown later. Etherington, Mercer, and Reiter (1985) establish several theorems characterizing the above kind of limitation of predicate circumscription, thereby bolstering the significance of variable and formula circumscription.

THE THEORETICAL BASIS FOR CIRCUMSCRIPTION

Minimal Models

In addition to giving examples, it is desirable to show in precise terms in what sense the circumscriptive schema $A[P]/P$ does in fact minimize. For this purpose McCarthy (1980) proposed the concept of minimal model in the context of predicate circumscription. Etherington (1984) has redefined minimal model in a manner appropriate to McCarthy's new (formula) version of circumscription, which is presented here in slightly modified form as follows. Let M and N be models of $A[P] = A[P_0, P_1, \ldots, P_n]$ with the same domains and the same interpretations of all constant, function, and predicate symbols, except possibly P_0, $P_1, \ldots, P_n$. M is a proper P submodel of N if the extension of P_0 in M is a proper subset of that in N. Then N is a P-minimal model of $A[P_0, \ldots, P_n]$ if N is a model of $A[P_0, \ldots, P_n]$ and no model M of $A[P_0, \ldots, P_n]$ is a proper P-submodel of N. [By 'model' here is meant 'normal model,' ie, a model in which equality is interpreted as identity. This, incidentally, shows the pointlessness of choosing P_0 to be the equality predicate, for then two distinct elements necessarily cannot be identical and so all (normal) models are minimal for equality. Etherington, Mercer, and Reiter (1985) have studied this and related points.]

As an example, consider again McCarthy's axiom $A[P]$: $a \neq b$ & $Pa \lor Pb$. Here P_0 is just P. It is easily seen that the P-minimal models are precisely ones of the form $\{Pa, a = a, b = b, c_1 = c_1, c_2 = c_2, \ldots\}$ or $\{Pb, a = a, b = b, c_1 = c_1, c_2 = c_2, \ldots\}$ where the number of c_i's may be none or any other cardinality. In particular, $M_1 = \{Pa\}$ and $M_2 = \{Pb\}$ are two such models. But $\{Pa\,Pb\}$, although it is a model of $A[P]$, is not minimal.

The clearly desirable situation would be to have a definition of model appropriate to the proof theory of the circumscriptive schema; ie, affording a completeness result of the form B is a consequence of $A[P]$ by circumscription, ie, a theorem of $A[P]/P$, iff B holds in all P-minimal models of $A[P]$. That this does not hold in general, as will be discussed below, indicates that at present there are unclear areas in the foundational status of circumscription.

Soundness

First, however, a positive result is stated, variants of which have been given in Davis (1980) (for what is often called domain circumscription), in McCarthy (1980) (for predicate circumscription), in Minker and Perlis (1984) (for protected circumscription), and extended by Etherington (1984) to formula circumscription. See also Lu and Subrahmanian (in press).

Soundness Theorem. For any formula B,

$$A[P]^* \vdash B \text{ implies } A[P]\,|P = B$$

where P is a vector of predicate symbols $P_0, P_1, \ldots, P_n$ and the P-double-turnstile means that the consequent holds in any P-minimal model of the antecedent.

Again, the example above will illustrate this. Since $A[P]^* \vdash \neg Pa \lor \neg Pb$ as seen earlier, then it follows that $\neg Pa \lor \neg Pb$ holds in the models M_1 and M_2. Of course, one also sees directly that this is the case.

Negative Completeness Results

Unfortunately, in general, the converse, which would provide a full completeness theorem, does not hold, as shown by Davis (1980). Let $A[N]$ be Peano arithmetic [with the postulates $N(0)$, $(x)(N(x) \to N(x + 1))$, etc.] Then the N minimal models contain N extensions isomorphic to the natural numbers, so that the formulas B relativized to N that are true in these models are precisely those that are true in arithmetic. But no recursive first-order theory, including one of the form $A[N]^* = A[N] + A[N]/N$, has as its theorems precisely those sentences true of the natural numbers, nor even its N-relativized theorems. [Etherington, Mercer, and Reiter (1985) noticed that, for certain other arithmetical theories $A[P]$ considered in Davis (1980), $A[P]^*$ may be inconsistent even though $A[P]$ is consistent. Specifically, $A[P]$ may fail to have minimal models. They also showed that certain theories, namely the universal ones, do not suffer this drawback.]

Kueker (1984) has found the following simpler illustration: Let $I[P]$ be the theory $Pa, Px \leftrightarrow Psx, a \neq sx, sx = sy \to x = y$. Then models of $I[P]$ are of two types: those that satisfy the sentence $(x).Px \to [\neg(Ey)x = sy \to x = a]$ and those that do not. But any minimal model is isomorphic to the natural numbers N, and is of the former type. Kueker has shown that this sentence is not a theorem of $I[P]^* = I[P] + I[P]/P$. It is worth noting, however, that the full second-order formula version of circumscription does entail Kueker's sentence, showing it to be more powerful than variable circumscription. To see this, it is sufficient to use the second-order formula $(Q)[Qa$ & $(y)(Qy \to Qsy) . \to Qx]$ to replace P in the second-order circumscription axiom. (This trick will not work, of course, in Davis' example, since second-order arithmetic is as prey to undecidability problems as is first-order arithmetic.)

Positive Completeness Results

Nevertheless, certain partial converses do hold, which have rather broad application. First, some terminology based on Doyle (1984): $A[P]$ is disjunctively-P-defining if it has theorems of the form

$$(x)(P_i x \leftrightarrow W_{i_1} x) \lor \cdots \lor (x)(P_i x \leftrightarrow W_{i k_i} x)$$

for each $i = 0, \ldots, n$ where the W's do not involve $P_0, \ldots, P_n$.

Perlis and Minker (1986) exploit this concept in the following partial completeness result: If $A[P]^*$ is disjunctively-P-defining, then $A[P]^* \vdash B$ whenever $A[P]\,|P = B$. They also show that if $A[P]$ has only finite models, then $A[P]^* \vdash B$ whenever $A[P]\,|P = B$.

EFFICIENCY

As with many commonsense reasoning techniques, circumscription naturally presents itself as a candidate for a reasoning mechanism that could in principle be used in an intelligent robot, for instance, in conjunction with a theorem prover. However, the fact that a schema or infinite set of axioms is involved presents practical difficulties, especially in the necessary choice of which instance(s) of the schema to use. That is, efficiency questions arise.

In this regard, Lifschitz (1984) has shown the significance of a subclass of theories *vis à vis* circumscription: the separable theories. Separable theories $A[P]$ are those that are formed, using conjunctions and disjunctions, from formulas containing no positive occurrences of P_0 and formulas of the form

$$(x)(E(x) \rightarrow P_0(x))$$

where E is a predicate that does not contain P_0. (These appear related to the disjunctively-P-defining theories, and may afford fruitful terrain for further investigation.) Such theories turn out to afford expression by means of a single first-order wff replacing the second-order circumscription axiom. Also in this regard, Perlis (1987) has shown that a single first-order formula in the language of set theory not only can express full second-order circumscription but also allows for the expression of axioms determining what formulas (properties) are or are not to be circumscribed.

APPLICATIONS, VARIATIONS, AND RELATED WORK

McCarthy (1986) gives applications of circumscription to various problems in commonsense reasoning. Paramount among these is his use of a predicate "ab" for abnormal aspects of entities. He shows how to represent reasoning to the effect that, for example, typically, birds can fly. The idea is to minimize (as a conjectural assumption) the objects that are abnormal with respect to any given aspect, for instance, birds that are abnormal with respect to flying (such as penguins or ostriches). This allows the expression of default reasoning to be given a uniform treatment in which the predicate ab is circumscribed while other predicates as desired may be considered variable. For instance, letting ab(B, F, x) stand for "x is an abnormal bird with respect to flying," then, from the following axioms,

$$\text{Bird}(x) \ \& \ \neg\text{ab}(B, F, x) \ .\rightarrow \text{Flies}(x)$$

$$\text{Ostrich}(x) \rightarrow \text{ab}(B, F, x)$$

$$\text{Ostrich}(x) \rightarrow \text{Bird}(x)$$

$$\text{Bird(Tweety)}$$

one can prove by formula circumscription that Tweety can fly (and consequently that Tweety is not an ostrich). Here it is sufficient to use the null predicate (eg, $x \neq x$) for both ab(B, F, x) and Ostrich(x), and $x =$ Tweety for both Bird(x) and Flies(x).

Grosof (1984) presents a translation scheme from Reiter's (1980) default logic into circumscription, in an effort to unify and clarify these two approaches to nonmonotonic inference (see also Konolige, 1989). Reiter (1982) shows that, for certain special cases, circumscription achieves

the effect of another formalism known as predicate completion (Clark, 1978). Papalaskaris and Bundy (1984) have applied circumscriptive reasoning to issues in natural language processing. In particular, they examine contextual cues that provide guidelines for appropriate predicates to circumscribe in formulating answers to questions.

Since McCarthy's two seminal papers, several other versions of circumscription have been devised, usually with an eye to increased power vis à vis commonsense reasoning. Details will not be given here, but a few points will be mentioned. For more information see the book of Genesereth and Nilsson (1987). One important advance is the introduction by Lifschitz (1986) of pointwise circumscription, in which minimization can be carried out independently with respect to each domain element, rather than with respect to the whole domain at once. This has been shown to be decisively more powerful than earlier versions. Another development is the notion of autocircumscription (Perlis, 1988), in which minimization is ignored altogether but the viability or consistency-testing feature is brought to the fore. This has had application in problems involving reasoning about an agent's lack of knowledge (see also Kraus and Perlis, 1989 and Lifschitz, 1989).

BIBLIOGRAPHY

AAAI, Workshop on Nonmonotonic Reasoning, New Paltz, N.Y., Oct. 17–19, 1984, AAAI, Menlo Park, Calif., 1984.

K. Clark, "Negation as Failure," in H. Gallaire and J. Minker, eds., *Logic and Data Bases*, Plenum, New York, 1978.

M. Davis, "The Mathematics of Nonmonotonic Reasoning," *Artif. Intell.* **13**, 73–80 (1980).

J. Doyle, "Circumscription and Implicit Definability," in AAAI, 1984.

D. Etherington, Personal communication, Week on Logic and Artificial Intelligence, University of Maryland, Oct. 22–26, 1984.

D. Etherington, R. Mercer, and R. Reiter, "On the Adequacy of Predicate Circumscription for Closed-World Reasoning," *J. Comput. Intell.* **1**, 11–15 (1985).

M. Genesreth and N. Nilsson, *Logical Foundations of Artificial Intelligence*, Morgan-Kaufman, Los Altos, Calif., 1987.

B. Grosof, "Default Reasoning as Circumscription," in AAAI, 1984.

K. Konolige, "On the Relation Between Autoepistemic Logic and Circumscription," in *Proceedings of the Eleventh IJCAI*, 1989.

S. Kraus and D. Perlis, "Assessing Others' Knowledge and Ignorance," *ISMIS* (1989).

D. Kueker, "Another Failure of Completeness for Circumscription," Notes, Week on Logic and Artificial Intelligence, University of Maryland, Oct. 22–26, 1984.

V. Lifschitz, "Some Results on Circumscription," in AAAI, 1984.

V. Lifschitz, "Pointwise Circumscription: Preliminary Report," *Proceedings of the Fifth National Conference on AI*, 1986, AAAI, Menlo Park, Calif., 1986, pp. 406–410.

V. Lifschitz, "Between Circumscription and Autoepistemic Logic," *KR* (1989).

J. J. Lu and V. S. Subrahmanian, "Protected Completions of First Order General Logic Programs," *J. Automat. Res.*, in press.

J. McCarthy, "Circumscription—A Form of Non-Monotonic Reasoning," *Artif. Intell.* **13**, 27–39 (1980).

J. McCarthy, "Applications of Circumscription to Formalizing Common Sense Knowledge," *Artif. Intell.* **28**, 89–116 (1986).

J. Minker and D. Perlis, "Protected Circumscription," in AAAI, 1984.

M. A. Papalaskaris and A. Bundy, "Topics for Circumscription," in AAAI, 1984.

D. Perlis, "Circumscribing With Sets," *Artif. Intell.* **31**, 201–211 (1987).

D. Perlis, "Autocircumscription," *Artif. Intell.* **36**, 223–236 (1988).

D. Perlis and J. Minker, "Completeness Results for Circumscription," *Artif. Intell.* **28**, 29–42 (1986).

R. Reiter, "A Logic for Default Reasoning," *Artif. Intell.*, **13**, 81–132 (1980).

R. Reiter, "Circumscription Implies Predicate Completion (Sometimes)," *Proceedings of the Second National Conference on AI*, Pittsburgh, Penn., 1982.

D. PERLIS
University of Maryland

CLOS

CLOS is an integration of object-oriented programming into the Common Lisp system. Adopted as part of the national standard for Common Lisp, CLOS supports multiple inheritance class definition, generic functions, and method combination. Called in the same way as ordinary functions, generic functions select at run time the appropriate combined methods based on the classes and/or identities of one or more arguments for that call. All objects in Common Lisp are part of an integrated type/class structure defined in CLOS, and hence can be used for specification of domains for methods. The object system itself is represented as CLOS objects. By specializing these object classes and specified methods defined in the CLOS metaobject protocol, users can extend the operation of the object system itself (see D. Bobrow, L. DeMichiel, R. Gabriel, S. Keene, G. Kiczales, and D. Moon, "Common Lisp Object System Specification," *Lisp and Symbolic Computation*, Vol. 1, Kluwer, 1989, pp. 245–394).

DANIEL G. BOBROW
Xerox PARC

CLUSTERING

Clustering is usually viewed as a process of grouping physical or abstract objects into classes of similar objects. According to this view, in order to cluster objects, one needs to define a measure of similarity between the objects and then apply it to determine classes. Classes are defined as collections of objects whose intraclass similarity is high and interclass similarity is low. Because the notion of similarity between objects is fundamental to this view, clustering methods based on it can be called similarity-based methods. Many such methods have been developed in numerical taxonomy, a field developed by social and natural scientists, and in cluster analysis, a subfield of pattern recognition (qv). Various similarity measures and clustering algorithms utilizing them are presented in this article (see also CONCEPT LEARNING).

Another view recently developed in AI postulates that objects should be grouped together not just because they are similar according to a given measure, but because as a group they represent a certain conceptual class. This view, called conceptual clustering, states that clustering depends on the goals of classification and the concepts available to the clustering system for characterizing collections of entities. For example, if the goal is to partition a configuration of points into simple visual groupings, one may partition them into those that form a T-shape, an L-shape, and so on, even though the density distributions and distances between the points may suggest different groupings. A procedure that uses only similarities (or distances) between the points and is unaware of these simple shape types clearly can only accidentally create clusterings corresponding to these concepts. To create such clustering, these descriptive concepts must be known to the system. Another example of conceptual clustering is the grouping of visible stars into named constellations. Conceptual clustering is contrasted with the classical view in the next section and described in more detail in the section Conceptual Clustering.

Clustering is the basis for building hierarchical classification schemes. For example, by first partitioning the original set of entities and then repeatedly applying a clustering algorithm to the classes generated at the previous step, one can obtain a hierarchical classification of the entities (a divisive strategy). A classification schema is obtained by determining the general characteristics of the classes generated.

Building classification schemes and using them to classify objects is a widely practiced intellectual process in science as well as in ordinary life. Understanding this process and the mechanisms of clustering underlying it is therefore an important domain of research in AI and other areas. This process can be viewed as a cousin of the "divide and conquer" strategy widely used in problem solving (qv). It is also related to the task of decomposing any large-scale engineering system into smaller subsystems in order to simplify its design and implementation.

THE CLASSICAL VIEW VS THE CONCEPTUAL CLUSTERING VIEW

In the classic approach to clustering mentioned above, clusters are determined solely on the basis of a predefined measure of similarity. To define such a measure, a data analyst determines attributes that are perceived as relevant for characterizing objects under consideration. Vectors of values of these attributes for individual objects serve as descriptions of these objects. Considering attributes as dimensions of a multidimensional description space, each object description corresponds to a point in the space. The similarity between objects can thus be measured as a reciprocal function of the distance between the points in the description space.

Let V_A and V_B denote the attribute vectors representing objects A and B, respectively. The distance of object A to object B is defined as a numeric function of the attribute vectors of A and B and is written as $d(V_A, V_B)$. For example, assuming that vector descriptions of objects A and B are $V_A = (x_1(A), x_2(A), \ldots x_n(A))$ and $V_B = (x_1(B), x_2(B), \ldots, x_n(B))$, respectively, where $x_1, x_2, \ldots, x_n$ are selected object attributes, a simple measure of distance is:

$$d(V_A, V_B) = \sum_{i=1}^{n} |x_i(A) - x_i(B)|$$

Because distance is a function of only the attributes of two compared objects, the similarity-based clustering can be performed relatively easily and without a need for knowledge about its purpose. The similarity-based approach has produced a number of efficient clustering algorithms, which have been useful in many classification-building applications.

The classical approach suffers, however, from some significant limitations. The results of clustering are clusters plus information about numerical similarities between objects and object classes. No descriptions or explanations of the generated clusters are supplied. The problem of cluster interpretation is simply left to the data analyst. Data analysts, however, are typically interested not only in clusters but also in their explanation or characterization.

To overcome this, one may postscript the similarity-based clustering process with an intelligent interpretation that tries to learn the conceptual significance of each cluster through the use of AI techniques. Such a process, however, is not easy. In fact, it may be even more difficult than that of generating clusters themselves. This is because it requires inducing category descriptions from examples, which is a complex inferential task. Even if one ignores this difficulty, this process may not produce desired results. Clusters generated solely on the basis of some predefined numerical measure of similarity may in principle lack simple conceptual explanations.

One reason for this is that a similarity measure typically considers all attributes with equal importance and thus makes no distinction between those that are more relevant and those that are less relevant or irrelevant. Consequently, if there is coincidental agreement between the values of a sufficient number of irrelevant attributes, objects that are different in a conceptual sense may be classified as similar. Even if one assigns some *a priori* "weights" to attributes, this will not change the situation very much, because the classical approach has no mechanisms for selecting and evaluating attributes *in the process* of generating clusters. Neither is there any mechanism for automatically constructing new attributes that may be more adequate for clustering than those initially provided.

Another reason for the difficulty of the postclustering interpretation is that in order to generate clusters that correspond to simple concepts, one has to take into consideration concepts useful for characterizing clusters as a whole in the process of clustering and not after clustering.

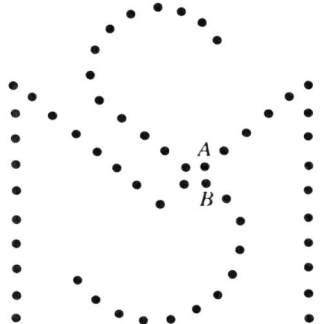

Figure 1. How would you cluster these points?

The following example illustrates this point. Consider the problem of clustering the points in Figure 1. Typically, a person looking at this figure would say that it is a letter S intersecting with a letter M. One should observe that points A and B, which are closer to each other than to any other points, are classified into conceptually different clusters. The reason seems to be that people are equipped with concepts such as letter shapes and straight lines to help them recognize certain concepts in the figure. Thus, clustering in this case is not based on local closeness of points but on global concepts characterizing collections of points together. A conceptual clustering program would solve this problem by matching the descriptions of the letter shapes (contained in its memory as background knowledge) against the given collection of points. The best match would be obtained for shapes "S" and "M."

One may add that, in general, classic techniques do not seem to be much concerned with the ways humans cluster objects. They do not take into consideration any gestalt concepts or linguistic constructs people use in describing object collections. Observations of how people cluster objects suggest that they search for one or more attributes (out of many potential attributes) that are most relevant to the goal of clustering and on that basis cluster the objects. Objects are put to the same cluster if they score similarly on these attributes. A description of the objects in the same cluster can therefore be expressed as a single statement or a conjunction of statements, each specifying one common property (attribute value) of the objects in the cluster. The above remark does not mean, however, that individual statements could not include a disjunction of values of the same attribute (the so-called internal disjunction). For example, a cluster may be characterized as "a set of large boxes, made of cardboard, and colored either blue or yellow." Different clusters are expected to have descriptions with different values of the relevant attributes.

Conceptual clustering has been introduced as a way to overcome the above-mentioned limitations of classic methods. Its basic premise is that objects should be arranged in classes that represent simple concepts and are useful from the viewpoint of the goal of clustering. Thus, objects in the same cluster do not necessarily have to be similar in some mathematically defined sense but must as a group represent the same concept. In order to cluster objects into conceptual categories, the notion of similarity must be replaced by a more general notion of conceptual cohesiveness (Michalski and Stepp, 1983b) (see also LEARNING, MACHINE).

The conceptual cohesiveness (CC) between two objects A and B depends on the attributes of these objects, the attributes of nearby objects, and the set of concepts available for describing object configurations. Thus, it is a function $CC(V_A, V_B, E, C)$, where V_A and V_B are vectors of attribute values for A and B, respectively, E denotes objects in the environment of A and B, and C is the set of available concepts. Thus, the conceptual cohesiveness is a four-argument function in contrast to a two-argument distance or similarity function.

In conceptual clustering there is a constant duality between category descriptions and cluster membership. Specifically, the result of conceptual clustering is not only a set of clusters (a classification of the initially given objects) but also a set of concepts characterizing the obtained clusters (a classification scheme).

One may say that from the viewpoint of AI, the similarity-based approach represents the so-called weak method, that is, a general method that uses little problem domain knowledge. Such a method can be called domain-general and knowledge-poor. In contrast, the conceptual clustering approach that is dependent on the background concepts and clustering goals can be called domain-generic and knowledge-modular. It requires an interchangeable module of knowledge defined for the problem at hand. A goal-dependency network (GDN) (Stepp and Michalski, 1986) may be used to indicate which attributes are relevant to which goals of classification. Various algorithms for classical methods and conceptual clustering methods are presented below.

A CLASSIFICATION OF CLUSTERING PROBLEMS

From the viewpoint of applications, it is useful to classify clustering problems on the basis of the dimensionality of objects to be clustered. Three classes of problems can be distinguished.

One-Dimensional Clustering (Quantization of Variables). For continuous variables or discrete variables with ranges of values that are significantly larger than necessary for a given problem, one wants to reduce the number of distinct values of variables by identifying equivalence classes of values. Clusters of values of individual variables are then treated as single units. For example, in image processing the scanners usually distinguish between a large number of gray levels, but only a few levels may be needed for solving a given problem (see IMAGE UNDERSTANDING). Rosenfeld (1979) has shown that clustering methods can be used for making such a reduction. Nubuyaki (1978) proposed a clustering algorithm for this purpose in which the clusters have minimal sums of squares of intracluster distances. Clustering techniques have also been used to analyze LANDSAT images (Swain, 1980).

Two-Dimensional Clustering (Segmentation). This type of clustering occurs most often in image processing (qv), where one searches for segments of an image in which all picture elements share some common properties. For example, they may have a similar gray level or similar texture. Coleman (1977) defined region segmentation (qv) as a problem of clustering (which he calls nonsupervised learning) and used the k-means algorithm of MacQueen (1967). Clustering has been used to analyze object shapes (Haralick and Shapiro, 1977).

Multidimensional Clustering. In multidimensional clustering objects are partitioned into clusters in a description space spanned by many attributes characterizing the objects. As mentioned earlier, the basis for clustering is typically a similarity measure. Traditional clustering techniques may assume different geometric distributions of the points in the space by the use of different normalization, transformation, and statistical treatments of the attributes. The next section gives more details on the similarity based methods. In conceptual clustering the concept of description space is also useful; however, here the space is not fixed but may change as new attributes are generated by background knowledge heuristics. In addition, the method is equipped with a set of concepts that can be used to characterize object configurations.

CLASSICAL METHODS OF CLUSTERING

The thrust of research in cluster analysis and numerical taxonomy has been toward determining various object similarity or proximity measures and developing clustering techniques utilizing them. A large number of such measures and corresponding clustering methods have been developed to date. Comprehensive surveys can be found in Sokal and Sneath (1963), Cormark (1971), Anderberg (1973), Gower (1967), and Diday and Simon (1976). A summary of various distance measures is described in Michalski and co-workers, 1981.

Clustering techniques can themselves be clustered in many interesting ways. One classification partitions the techniques on the basis of the type of control used in building the clusters. The categories of clustering techniques according to this classification are agglomerative, divisive, and direct.

Agglomerative Techniques

Agglomerative techniques are often used in numerical taxonomy. These techniques form clusters by progressive fusion, that is, by recursively joining separate entities and small groups together to form larger and larger groupings. Eventually a single universal group is formed and the process halts, leaving a record of the merges that took place. The history of merges is often displayed in the form of a dendrogram (see Fig. 2c) that shows, by the position of the horizontal location of the merge, the between-group similarities. As the groups encompass more and more entities, the between-group similarity scores decrease.

By adopting a threshold of minimum similarity, the agglomeration process can be halted before all entities are merged into a single group. Conversely, the complete dendrogram may be "cut" apart across some similarity boundary. This yields a number of clusters, each containing

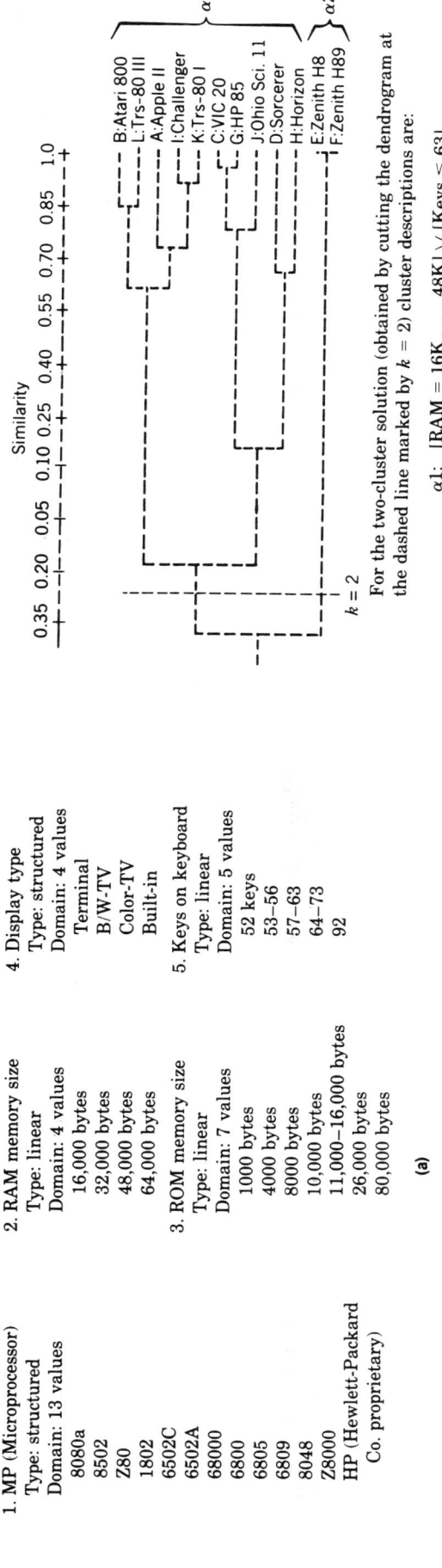
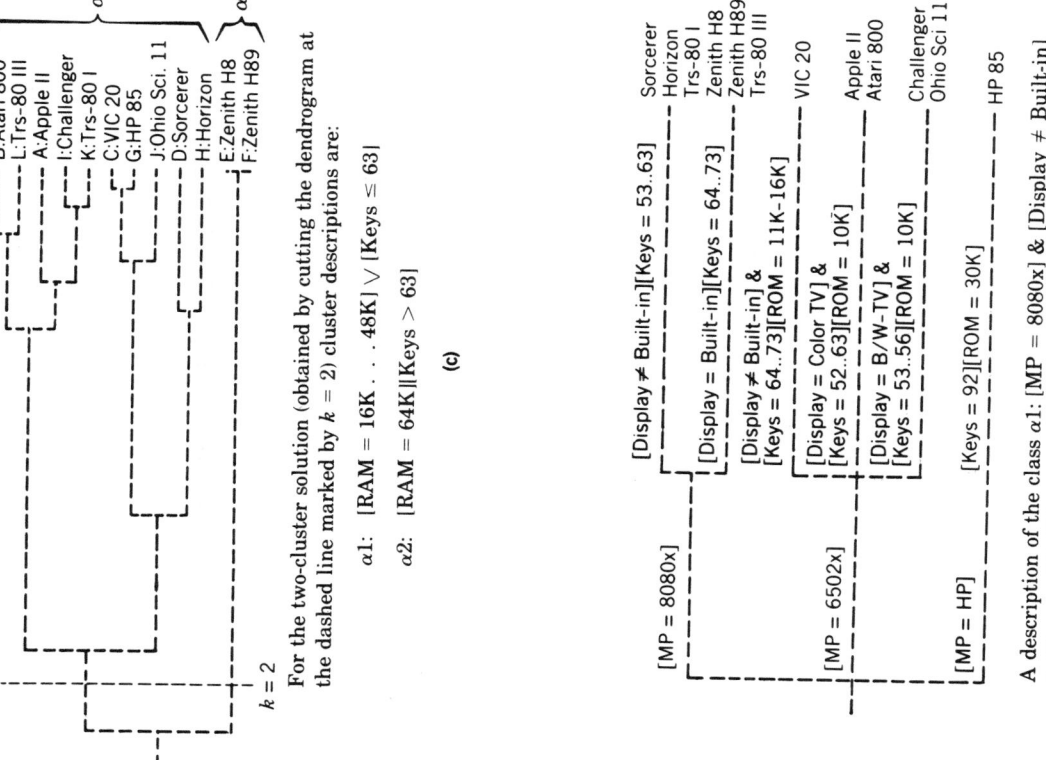
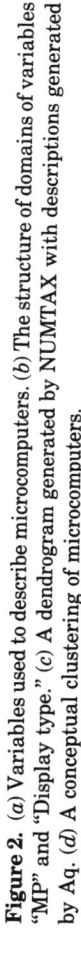

(a)

1. MP (Microprocessor)
Type: structured
Domain: 13 values
8080a
8502
Z80
1802
6502C
6502A
68000
6800
6805
6809
8048
Z8000
HP (Hewlett-Packard Co. proprietary)

2. RAM memory size
Type: linear
Domain: 4 values
16,000 bytes
32,000 bytes
48,000 bytes
64,000 bytes

3. ROM memory size
Type: linear
Domain: 7 values
1000 bytes
4000 bytes
8000 bytes
10,000 bytes
11,000–16,000 bytes
26,000 bytes
80,000 bytes

4. Display type
Type: structured
Domain: 4 values
Terminal
B/W-TV
Color-TV
Built-in

5. Keys on keyboard
Type: linear
Domain: 5 values
52 keys
53–56
57–63
64–73
92

(b)

MP
8080x (8080A Z80 8048) · 1802 68000 6805 6800 Z8000 HP · 6502x (6502 6502A 6502C)

The structured domain for the variable "MP."

Display type
External terminal · B/W TV · say TV (Color TV) · Built-in

The structured domain for the variable "display type."

(c)

Similarity
0.35 0.20 0.05 0.10 0.25 0.40 0.55 0.70 0.85 1.0

B:Atari 800
L:Trs-80 III
A:Apple II
I:Challenger
K:Trs-80 I
C:VIC 20
G:HP 85
J:Ohio Sci. 11
D:Sorcerer
H:Horizon
E:Zenith H8
F:Zenith H89

α1, α2

k = 2

For the two-cluster solution (obtained by cutting the dendrogram at the dashed line marked by $k = 2$) cluster descriptions are:

α1: |RAM = 16K . . . 48K| ∨ |Keys ≤ 63|

α2: |RAM = 64K||Keys > 63|

(d)

[MP = 8080x]

[Display ≠ Built-in][Keys = 53..63]   → Sorcerer, Horizon, Trs-80 I, Zenith H8
[Display = Built-in][Keys = 64..73]   → Zenith H89, Trs-80 III
[Display ≠ Built-in] & [Keys = 64..73][ROM = 11K-16K]

[MP = 6502x]

[Display = Color TV] & [Keys = 52..63][ROM = 10K]   → VIC 20, Apple II, Atari 800
[Display = B/W-TV] & [Keys = 53..56][ROM = 10K]   → Challenger, Ohio Sci 11

[MP = HP]

[Keys = 92][ROM = 30K]   → HP 85

A description of the class α1: [MP = 8080x] & [Display ≠ Built-in] & [Keys = 53..63]

Figure 2. (a) Variables used to describe microcomputers. (b) The structure of domains of variables "MP" and "Display type." (c) A dendrogram generated by NUMTAX with descriptions generated by Aq. (d) A conceptual clustering of microcomputers.

those entities that were merged at a similarity score above the given threshold.

During the agglomerative clustering process it is necessary to calculate the similarities between groups of entities. There are three standard ways to compute between-group similarities (measured as the reciprocal of distances). Suppose two groups are identified as X and Y. The single-linkage methods calculate between-group distance between one entity in group X and another entity in group Y. The complete-linkage methods use the maximum distance between one entity in group X and another entity in group Y. The average-linkage methods use the average of the distances between all possible pairs of entities with one taken from group X and the other from group Y.

Divisive Techniques

Divisive techniques form a classification by progressive subdivision, that is, by repeatedly breaking the initial set into smaller and smaller clusters until only single entities exist in each cluster. The result is a hierarchy of clusters. The divisive technique of Edwards and Cavalli-Sforza (1965) examines all $2^N - 1$ partitions of N objects and selects the one that gives the minimum intracluster sum of the squared interobject distances. The computational cost of the method limits its use to cases involving the clustering of only a few objects.

Direct Techniques

The direct techniques neither merge entities into clusters nor break large clusters into smaller ones. A direct technique is given the number (usually denoted k) of clusters to form and proceeds to find a partitioning of the entities into k clusters that optimizes some measure of the goodness of the clusters. Two early direct clustering techniques are k-means developed by MacQueen (1967) and the center adjustment method developed by Meisel (1972). A generalization of the k means and center adjustment techniques called the dynamic clustering method has been developed (Diday, 1978).

Another classification of clustering methods separates the monothetic techniques from the polythetic ones. A monothetic clustering algorithm divides the set of objects into clusters that differ in the value of one attribute. For example, such a technique might form one cluster in which attribute X_i has the value 1 and another cluster in which attribute X_i has the value 0. A polythetic clustering technique forms clusters in which the values of several attributes differ for different classes.

Traditional clustering relies on measures of similarity and the requisite need to "fold" the attribute values together to measure object-to-object similarities. When this occurs in a multidimensional space, the question of attribute weighting comes up, and there is much controversy over what weighting scheme is best for various purposes.

Weights on attributes have to be given a priori by the researcher. Problems with such an approach are that it is usually difficult to define such weights, and that some attributes may be dependent on other attributes. For example, attributes B and C may be important only if attribute A has the value 1. A similarity metric uses some static weights for attributes A, B, and C. The attributes B and C are weighted too high when attribute A takes the value 0 (since they should receive zero weight in that case), and they may be weighted too low when attribute A takes the value 1.

CONCEPTUAL CLUSTERING

As described above, conceptual clustering arranges objects into clusters corresponding to certain conceptual classes, for example, classes characterized by conjunctive concepts (ie, concepts defined by a simple conjunction of properties). The basic theory and an algorithm for conceptual clustering have been developed by Michalski (1980). Implementation and experimentation with the algorithm has been performed by Michalski and Stepp (1983a,b) and Stepp (1984) and has produced the programs CLUSTER/2 and CLUSTER/S. Other programs that work differently but provide conceptual clustering features include DISCON (Langley and Sage, 1984), RUMMAGE (Fisher, 1984), and GLAUBER (Langley and co-workers, 1986).

From the viewpoint of AI, clustering is a form of learning from observation (or learning without a teacher). It is a process that generates classes (conceptually defined categories) in order to partition a given set of observations. It differs from concept learning (qv) in that the latter creates descriptions of teacher-provided classes by generalizing from the examples of the classes.

Below, one method for conceptual clustering is briefly outlined. The method is based on the idea that conceptual clustering can be conducted by a series of conceptual discriminations similar to those used in learning concepts from examples. The method uses the extended predicate calculus proposed by Michalski (1980). Such a language is used to describe objects, classes of objects, and general and problem-specific background knowledge. The method employs a general-purpose criterion for measuring the quality of generated candidate classifications. Finding classifications that score high on the quality criterion is the most general goal of the method. Additional problem-specific goals may be supplied by the user or inferred by the system from a general goal-dependency network. Goal dependency is important to reduce the space of hypothetical classifications the method investigates.

Creating a classification is a difficult problem because there are usually many potential solutions with no clearly correct or incorrect answers. The decision about which classification to choose can be based on some perceived set of goals (Medin and co-workers, 1986), a goal-oriented, statistic-based utility function (Rendell, 1983), or some other measure of the quality of the classification.

One way to measure classification quality is to define various elementary, easy-to-measure criteria specifying desirable properties of a classification and to assemble them into one general criterion. Each elementary criterion measures a certain aspect of the generated classifications. Examples of elementary criteria are the relevance of descriptors used in the class descriptions to the general goal, the fit between the classification and the objects, the simplicity of the class descriptions, the number of attributes that singly discriminate among all classes, and the number of attributes necessary to classify the objects into the proposed classes.

Building a meaningful classification relies on finding good classifying attributes. The method presented below uses background knowledge in the search for such attributes. Background knowledge rules enable the system to perform a chain of inferences to derive values for new descriptors for inclusion in object descriptions. The new descriptors are tested by applying the classification quality criterion to the groupings formed by them.

Concept Formation by Repeated Discrimination

This section explains how a problem of concept formation (here, building a classification) can be solved via a sequence of controlled steps of concept acquisition (learning concepts from examples). Given a set of unclassified objects, k seed objects are selected randomly and treated as representatives of k hypothetical classes. The algorithm then generates descriptions of each seed that are maximally general, form a good match with a subset of the objects given, and do not cover any other seed. These descriptions are then used to determine the most representative object in each newly formed class (where the newly formed class is defined as the set of objects satisfying the generated class description). The k representative objects are then used as new seeds for the next iteration. The process stops either when consecutive iterations converge to some stable solution or when a specific number of iterations pass without improving the classification (from the viewpoint of the quality criterion).

This approach requires that the number of classes is specified in advance. Since the best number of classes to form is usually unknown, two techniques are used: varying the number of classes and composing the classes hierarchically.

For most purposes, it is desired that the classification formed be simple and easy to understand. With this in mind, the number of classes that stem from any node of the classification hierarchy can be assumed to be in some modest range such as from 2 to 7. With this small range, it is computationally feasible to repeat the whole clustering process for every number in the range. The solution that optimizes the score on the classification quality criterion (with appropriate adjustment for the effect of the number of classes on the score) indicates the best number of classes to form at this level of the hierarchy.

This method of repeated discrimination for performing clustering has been implemented in the program CLUSTER/2 for a subset of extended predicate calculus (see LOGIC, PREDICATE) involving only attributes (zero-argument functions). Besides its relative computational simplicity, this approach has other advantages stemming from use of quantifier-free descriptions (for both objects and classes). It should be noted that classifications normally have the property that they can unambiguously classify any object into its corresponding class. To have this property, the class descriptions must be mutually disjoint.

For conjunctive descriptions involving relations on attribute–value pairs, the disjointness property is easy to test and easy to maintain. For the more complex problems that require object representations involving quantified variables, predicates on these variables, and function–value relationships over quantified variables, the test for mutual disjointness of descriptions is much more complex. To cope with this difficulty, the problem of clustering of structured objects is decomposed into two steps. The first step finds an optimized characteristic description of the entire collection of objects and then uses it to generate a quantifier-free description of each object. The second step processes the quantifier-free object descriptions with the CLUSTER/2 algorithm to form optimized classifications. These two processes are combined in the program CLUSTER/S.

Example 1: Microcomputers. The problem is to develop a meaningful classification of popular microcomputers. Each microcomputer is described in terms of the variables shown in Figure 2a. Variables "MP" and "Display type" are structured, that is, their value set forms a hierarchy (Fig. 2b). Two programs were applied to solve this problem: NUMTAX, which implements several techniques of numerical taxonomy, and CLUSTER/2, which implements conjunctive conceptual clustering. A representative dendrogram produced by NUMTAX is shown in Figure 2c. The dashed lines indicate where the dendrogram is cut apart to form two clusters ($k = 2$). Accompanying the dendrogram is a logical description of the clusters. These descriptions were produced by an inductive learning program that accepts as input a collection of groups (clusters) of objects and generates the simplest discriminant description of each group. For example, the first cluster is described as

$$[RAM = 16K \ldots 48K] \lor [Keys \leq 63]$$

This description suggests that the cluster is composed of two kinds of computers, one that has [RAM = 16K . . . 64K] and the other that has [Keys $\leq$ 63]. The presence of disjunction raises the question of why these computers are in the same cluster.

The program CLUSTER/2 was given the same data and was told to use a classification quality criterion that maximizes the fit between the clustering and the objects in the cluster and then maximizes the simplicity of category descriptions. The clustering obtained is shown in Figure 2d. The first-level clustering is done on the basis of type of microprocessor.

Example 2: Trains. Consider a problem of classifying structured objects, for example, the problem of finding a classification of trains shown in Figure 3a. The trains are structured objects, each consisting of a sequence of cars of different shapes and sizes. The individual cars carry a variable number of items of different shapes.

Human classifications of the trains shown in Figure 3a have been investigated by Medin, Wattenmaker, and Michalski (1986). The ten trains were placed on separate index cards so they could be arranged into groups by the subjects in the experiment. The experiment was com-

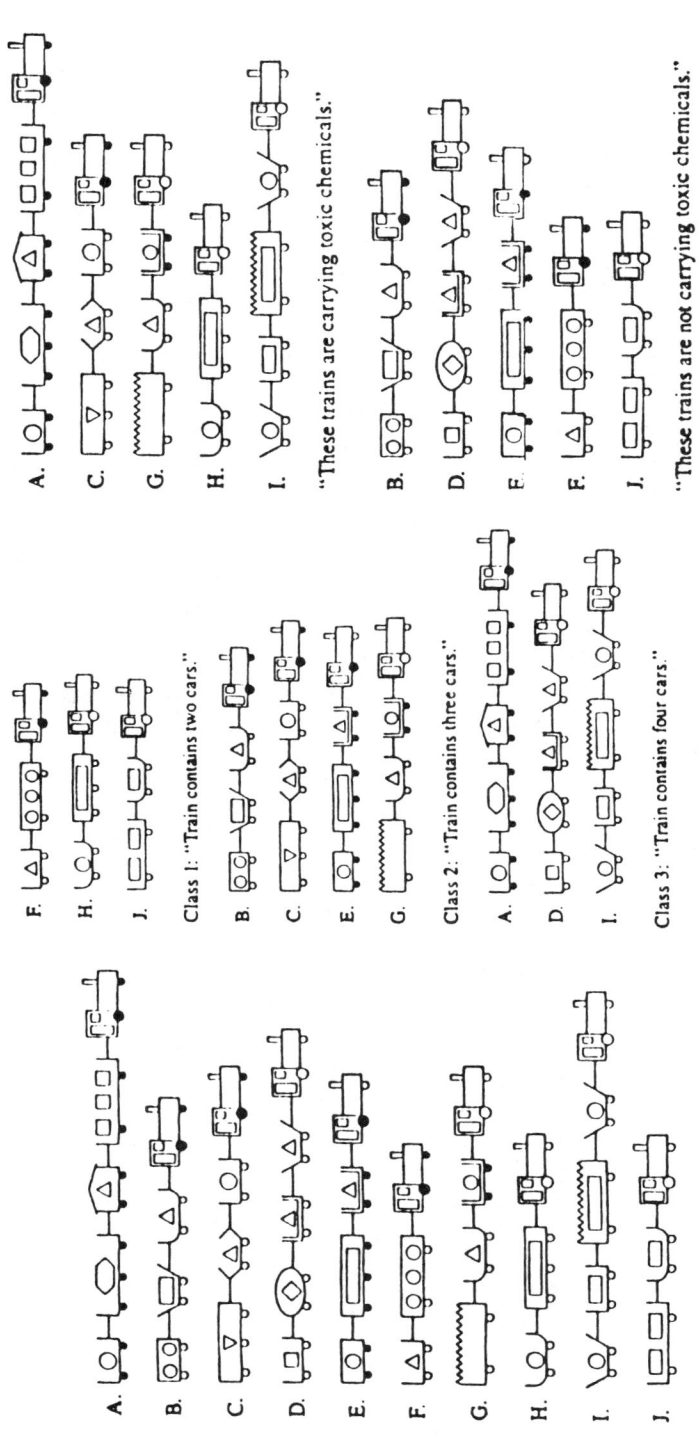

Figure 3. (a) Trains to be classified. (b) The most frequent human classification of trains.
(c) Conceptual clustering of trains carrying toxic chemicals.

174

pleted by 31 subjects who formed a total of 93 classifications of the trains. The most popular classification (17 repetitions) involved the number of cars in the trains. The three classes formed were "trains containing two cars," "trains containing three cars," and "trains containing four cars." This classification is shown in Figure 3b.

This problem is an example of a class of problems for which the implicit classification goal is to generate classes that are conceptually simple and based on easy-to-determine visual attributes. When people are asked to build such classifications, they typically form classes with disjoint descriptions, as in the above-mentioned study by Medin and co-workers. For this reason, methods that produce disjoint descriptions are of prime interest.

The problem of classifying trains represents a general category of classification problems in which one wants to organize and classify observations that require structural descriptions, for example, classifying physical or chemical structures, analyzing genetic sequences, building taxonomies of plants or animals, characterizing visual scenes, or splitting a sequence of temporal events into episodes with simple meanings.

One problem of concern here is to develop a general method that when applied to the collection of structured objects, such as trains, could potentially generate the conjunctive concepts occurring in human classifications or invent new concepts having similar appeal.

An extension of the trains problem illustrates the use of a goal-dependency network and problem-specific background knowledge. Suppose that the knowledge base includes an inference rule that can identify trains carrying toxic chemicals and that the general goal "survive" has a subordinate goal "monitor dangerous shipments." This background knowledge can be used to help build a classification.

In the illustrations of the trains a toxic chemical container is identified as a single sphere (circle) riding in an open-top car. A background-knowledge rule supplied to the program is

[contains(train,car)][car-shape(car) = opentop]
[cargo-shape(car) = circle][items-carried(car) = 1];
⇔ [has_toxic_chemicals(train)]

In this rule, equivalence is used to indicate that the negation of the condition part is sufficient to assert the negative of the consequence part. After this rule is applied, all trains will have descriptions containing either the toxic chemical predicate or its negation. The characteristic description generated by the program will now contain the additional predicate "has_toxic_chemicals(train)" (or its negation). By recognizing that this predicate is important to the goal "survival" through use of a GDN, the program produced the classification shown in Figure 3c.

Concept Formation by Finding Classifying Attributes

This section describes an alternative approach for building classifications. This approach searches for one or more classifying attributes whose value sets can be split into ranges that define individual clusters. The important aspect of this approach is that the classifying attributes can be derived through a goal-directed chain of inferences from the initial attributes. The classifying attributes sought are the ones that lead to classes of objects that are best according to the classification goal and the given classification quality criterion.

The promise of a descriptor to serve as a classifying attribute is determined by relating it to the goals or derived subgoals of the problem and by considering how many other descriptors it implies. For example, if the goal of the classification is "finding food," the attribute "edibility" might be a good classifying attribute.

The second way of determining the promise of an attribute can be illustrated by the problem of classifying birds. The question of whether "color" is a more important classifying attribute than "is-waterbird" is answered in favor of "is-waterbird" because the latter leads to more implied attributes than does the attribute "color" in a given GDN (ie, "is-waterbird" implies can swim, has webbed feet, eats fish, and so on) (Medin and co-workers, 1986).

Two fundamental processes operate alternately to generate the classification. The first process searches for the classifying attribute whose value set can be partitioned to form classes such that the produced classification scores best according to the classification quality criterion. The second process generates new descriptors by a chain of inferences using background knowledge rules. Descriptors that can be inferred are ordered by relevancy to the goals of the classification.

The search process can be performed in two ways. When the number of classes to form k is known in advance, the process searches for attributes having k or more different values in the descriptions of the objects to be classified. These values are called the observed values of the attribute. Attributes with the number of observed values smaller than k are not considered. For attributes with observed value sets larger than k, the choice of the mapping of value subsets to classes depends on the resulting quality criterion score for the classification produced and the type of the value set. When the number of classes to form is not known, the above technique is performed for several different values of k. The best number of classes, k, is indicated by the classification that best satisfies the quality criterion and goals.

The generate process constructs new attributes from combinations of existing attributes. Various heuristics of attribute construction are used to guide the process. For example, two attributes that have linearly ordered value sets can be combined using arithmetic operators. When the attributes have numeric values (as opposed to symbolic values such as small, medium, and large), a trend analysis can be used to suggest appropriate arithmetic operators, as in the BACON system by Langley and co-workers (1983). Predicates can be combined by logical operators to form new attributes through background knowledge rules. For example, a rule that says an animal is a reptile if it is cold-blooded and lays eggs can be written as

[cold-blooded(al)][offspring birth(al) = egg]
⇒ [animal-type(al) = reptile].

The application of this rule to the given animal descriptions yields the new attribute "animal-type" with the specified value "reptile." Using this rule and similar ones, one might classify some animals into reptiles, mammals, and birds even though the type of each animal is not stated in the original data.

SUMMARY

Clustering objects or abstract entities into meaningful categories is an important form of learning from observation. This article has described a classical, "similarity-based" approach and the more recent conceptual clustering approach to this problem. The fundamental notion is conceptual cohesiveness that groups together objects that correspond to certain concepts rather than objects that are similar according to a mathematical similarity function.

BIBLIOGRAPHY

M. R. Anderberg, *Cluster Analysis for Applications*, Academic Press, New York, 1973.

G. B. Coleman, "Scene Segmentation by Clustering," University of Southern California Image Processing Institute, Report USCIPI, 1977.

R. M. Cormark, "A Review of Classification," *J. Roy. Stat. Soc. A,* 134–321 (1971).

E. Diday, "Problems of Clustering and Recent Advances," *Eleventh Congress of Statistics*, Oslo, Norway, 1978.

E. Diday and J. C. Simon, "Clustering Analysis," *Communication and Cybernetics*, Springer-Verlag, New York, 1976.

A. W. F. Edwards and L. L. Cavalli-Sforza, "A Method for Cluster Analysis," *Biometrics* 21, 362–375 (1965).

D. Fisher, "A Hierarchical Conceptual Clustering Algorithm," Technical Report, Department of Information and Computer Science, University of California, Irvine, 1984.

D. Fisher and P. Langley, "Approaches to Conceptual Clustering," *Proceedings of the Ninth IJCAI*, Los Angeles, Morgan-Kaufmann, San Mateo, Calif., 1985, pp. 691–697.

J. C. Gower, "A Comparison of Some Methods of Cluster Analysis," *Biometrics* 23, 623–637 (1967).

R. M. Haralick and L. Shapiro, "Decomposition of Polygonal Shapes by Clustering," *Proceedings of the IEEE Conference on Pattern Recognition and Image Processing*, Troy, New York, 1977, p. 183.

P. Langley, G. L. Bradshaw, and H. A. Simon, "Rediscovering Chemistry with the BACON System," in R. S. Michalski, J. Carbonell, and T. M. Mitchell, eds., *Machine Learning: An Artificial Intelligence Approach*, Tioga, Palo Alto, California, 1983, pp. 307–329.

P. Langley and S. Sage, "Conceptual Clustering as Discrimination Learning," *Proceedings of the Fifth Biennial Conference of the Canadian Society for Computational Studies of Intelligence*, London, Ontario, 1984, pp. 95–98.

P. Langley, J. Zytkow, H. Simon, and G. Bradshaw, "The Search for Regularity: Four Aspects of Scientific Discovery," in R. S. Michalski, J. Carbonell, and T. M. Mitchell, eds., *Machine Learning: An Artificial Intelligence Approach*, Vol. 2, Morgan-Kaufmann Publishers, San Mateo, Calif., 1986, pp. 425–469.

J. MacQueen, "Some Methods for Classification Analysis of Multivariate Observations," *Proceedings of the Fifth Berkeley Symposium in Mathematics Statics and Probability*, 1967, p. 281.

D. L. Medin, W. S. Wattenmaker, and R. S. Michalski, "Constraints in Inductive Learning: An Experimental Study Comparing Human and Machine Performance," ISG Report 86-1, UIUCDS-F-86-952, University of Illinois, 1986.

W. Meisel, *Computer Oriented Approaches to Pattern Recognition*, Academic Press, New York, 1972.

R. S. Michalski, "Knowledge Acquisition Through Conceptual Clustering: A Theoretical Framework and an Algorithm for Partitioning Data into Conjunctive Concepts," *J. Pol. Anal. Inform. Sys.* 4, 219–244 (1980).

R. S. Michalski and R. E. Stepp, "Automated Construction of Classifications: Conceptual Clustering Versus Numerical Taxonomy," *IEEE Trans. Pattern Anal. Machine Intell.* 5(4), 396–410 (July 1983a).

R. S. Michalski and R. E. Stepp, "Learning From Observation: Conceptual Clustering," in R. S. Michalski, J. Carbonell, and T. M. Mitchell, eds., *Machine Learning: An Artificial Intelligence Approach*, Tioga, Palo Alto, Calif., 1983b, pp. 331–363.

R. S. Michalski, R. E. Stepp, and E. Diday, "A Recent Advance in Data Analysis: Clustering Objects into Classes Characterized by Conjunctive Concepts," in L. N. Kanal and A. Rosenfeld, eds., *Progress in Pattern Recognition*, Vol. 1, North-Holland, Amsterdam, 1981.

O. Nubuyaki, "Discriminant and Least Squares Threshold Selection," *Proceedings of the Fourth International Conference on Pattern Recognition*, Kyoto, Japan, 1978, p. 592.

L. A. Rendell, "Toward a Unified Approach for Conceptual Knowledge Acquisition," *AI Mag.* 4, 19–27 (Winter 1983).

A. Rosenfeld, "Some Recent Developments in Texture Analysis," *Proceedings of the Conference on Pattern Recognition and Image Processing*, Chicago, 1979.

R. R. Sokal and R. H. Sneath, *Principles of Numerical Taxonomy*, W. H. Freeman, San Francisco, 1963.

R. E. Stepp, "Conjunctive Conceptual Clustering: A Methodology and Experimentation," Ph.D. dissertation, Department of Computer Science, University of Illinois, Urbana, 1984.

R. E. Stepp and R. S. Michalski, "Conceptual Clustering: Inventing Goal-Oriented Classifications of Structured Objects," in R. S. Michalski, J. G. Carbonell, and T. M. Mitchell, eds., *Machine Learning: An Artificial Intelligence Approach*, Vol. 2, Morgan-Kaufmann Publishers, San Mateo, Calif., 1986, pp. 331–363.

P. H. Swain, "Image and Data Analysis in Remote Sensing," in R. M. Haralick and J. C. Simon, eds., *Issues in Digital Image Processing*, Sijthoff and Noordhoff, Amsterdam, 1980.

R. S. Michaliski
R. E. Stepp
University of Illinois

COGNITION. See Reasoning.

COGNITIVE MODELING

A cognitive simulation model is a computer simulation of mental or cognitive processes. Such a model is normally constructed by cognitive psychologists, who are members of the branch of experimental psychology that is concerned with the scientific and empirical study of human behavior, with an emphasis on understanding the internal mental mechanisms that underlie behavior (see COGNITIVE PSYCHOLOGY). The purposes of cognitive modeling are to express a theory of mental mechanisms in precise and rigorous terms, to demonstrate the sufficiency of a set of theoretical concepts, and to provide an explanation for observed human behavior.

Because cognitive models use many techniques and ideas from AI, they are similar to AI programs. But the goals of cognitive modeling and AI tend to differ substantially (Newell, 1970). Briefly put, the goal of AI is to build intelligent machines, whereas the goal of cognitive modeling is to build models of human mental mechanisms. These activities are similar, but they differ mainly in the criteria for success. The quality of a piece of AI work is measured in terms of how well the machine is able to perform the task. In a cognitive modeling effort, the question is not only whether the computer program is able to perform the task, but also the extent to which it behaves like a human performing the same task, and whether the mechanisms involved are plausible theoretical explanations for human mental processes. Notice that in AI terms, these mechanism may be inefficient or unnecessarily complex for the task.

This article touches on the contribution of cognitive modeling to AI. It is not a commonly accepted idea, but cognitive modeling work is relevant to AI in that some of the mechanisms in cognitive models are applicable to AI problems. This has often been true historically, and so we would expect to see it again in the future.

PURPOSES OF COGNITIVE MODELING

The rationale for cognitive modeling is best seen in terms of the history of theoretical development in cognitive psychology. Except for the temporary aberration of behaviorism, the goal of experimental psychology for more than a century of research has always been to construct an adequate theory of the mental processes that underlie behavior. An adequate theory of the human mind would explain the observed behavioral data in terms of plausible internal mechanisms. The traditional mode for describing such mechanisms has been in the form of verbal statements. As the ideas get more complex, such verbal theories become difficult to handle. Thus there is a need to express psychological theory precisely, to demonstrate that theoretical concepts are actually sufficient to explain the behavior, and to derive testable predictions about data in a rigorous fashion.

The idea of rigorous theoretical models in experimental psychology is a fairly old idea; an excellent early example is Hull's work conducted during the 1940s, which constructed one of the first large-scale mathematical theories of behavior. During the 1950s and 1960s, mathematical models of psychological processes were developed. These models represented perceptual and learning situations as stochastic processes, which were successful in accounting quantitatively for many details of human behavior. A

summary of these approaches has been published (Bower and Hilgard, 1981).

This combination of verbal and mathematical theory has produced what might be termed the standard theory of cognition, which is based on a decomposition of the human mind into major components. These consist of structures such as short-term and long-term memory and processes such as recognition, memory storage, and memory retrieval, which process and manipulate the information stored in the structures. This theory is the basic framework for most current cognitive models.

As interest in cognitive psychology moved from simple learning (see LEARNING, MACHINE) and perception (see EARLY VISION) to complex behavior such as reasoning (see LOGIC) and reading comprehension (see NATURAL LANGUAGE UNDERSTANDING), the mathematical models seemed to be inadequate, because they characterized behavior in terms of a small number of continuous mathematical variables. It seemed that complex qualitative, or symbolic, systems were needed instead, especially to represent knowledge (see KNOWLEDGE REPRESENTATION). In addition, many researchers came to believe that a psychological theory or model should describe the processes going on in the mind, rather than simply providing a characterization of the statistical properties of the behavior (Gregg and Simon, 1967). Thus computer programs, in which these complex entities can be represented directly, became the ideal mode for expressing theory (Kieras, 1981b).

Perhaps the most important event in symbolic cognitive modeling was the adoption of semantic networks (qv) from AI. For cognitive psychologists, the significance of the semantic network representation was that it provided a representation of knowledge in a form that tied into the classic concept of association very well (Anderson and Bower, 1973). Semantic networks were so appealing theoretically that AI quickly became of intense interest to cognitive psychologists, and cognitive simulation models were the best way to incorporate AI concepts into cognitive theory. Currently, there seems to be a consensus that cognitive simulation models best represent the core theoretical concepts in cognitive psychology. However, it is important to note that despite the recognized importance of cognitive simulation models and the AI concepts that underlie them, relatively few cognitive psychologists actually construct and make use of simulation models.

EVALUATION OF COGNITIVE MODELS

Theoretical Quality

Because cognitive psychology is an empirical science that is attempting to construct explanatory theory, the quality of a cognitive model depends both on its ability to mimic observed behavior and on the quality of the model as a piece of theory (Kieras, 1983, 1984). Most of the extant cognitive modeling work has been done with the primary theoretical goals of demonstrating that a theory is sufficient to produce the behavior and of stating the theory rigorously. Beyond these concerns, the architectural integrity of the model is critical. Does the model make a consistent use of a set of explicit theoretical mechanisms that comprise a cognitive architecture, or does it appear to contain ad hoc, arbitrary mechanisms? If the architecture has been maintained it will be relatively clear how the model works, but a theory is of little value if it cannot be understood by the scientists in the field. Thus there is a great premium on the model having a basically simple, and consistently maintained, architecture.

Empirical Quality

One criterion for empirical quality is apparent realism, which is the criterion that most AI projects attempt to meet. The system must be able to produce apparently realistic behavior. For example, most natural language processing systems are designed so that they appear to do the correct thing with the input. It is not necessary to evaluate such systems on a systematic scientific basis, because the established usage of language is adequate to characterize whether the model is reasonably correct. But more recently, simulation models have been used to account for experimental data in great detail. Thus, it is desirable for a model to go beyond the apparently realistic stage and account for data in a detailed way, preferably in a predictive, rather than an after-the-fact, manner. In many cases, the time characteristics of the model and of human behavior are compared; some measure of processing time or effort in the model should correspond to processing time on the part of humans.

The Nature of Behavioral Data

There are some characteristics of behavioral data that are probably not obvious to those not familiar with cognitive psychology. First, contrary to intuition, and perhaps common sense, introspection (self-observation of the thought processes) is neither a reliable nor a complete source of information about mental processes (Humphrey, 1963). The basic problems are that such observations are highly idiosyncratic and easily distorted by subjective bias on the part of the observer. More important, most of the major mental processes, especially those of interest to AI, go on below the level of conscious awareness. The popular think-out-loud protocol form of data is not strictly introspective data, but it suffers from related problems. Thus, modern cognitive psychology is based on behavioral, rather than introspective, data.

Second, behavior is highly variable and subject to the influence of many factors. This means that it is essential that behavioral data be obtained by the use of careful experimental methods and appropriate statistical analysis of the results. To outsiders, this meticulousness may be difficult to understand, but it is easy to collect data that are worthless and misleading because of improper attention to such considerations.

Third, human behavior is strongly determined by the task that the person is trying to do, meaning that the task should be carefully characterized, and inference from data to the internal processes must be qualified by the task. Thus the accuracy of a cognitive model is determined by how well it fits properly collected data on behavior in a suitable task, not by how well it agrees with the modeler's subjective impressions concerning mental processes.

Finally, and most important, it is necessary to constrain a person's behavior in order to study it conveniently. This means that much more is known about certain aspects of mental processes than others. For example, perceptual processes are perhaps the best understood, because the experimenter has great control over the stimulus and can require the subject to produce simple responses based only on observable properties on the stimulus. With more complex behavior, such as problem solving (qv), the behavior of a person becomes less determined by specific features of the stimulus, and more by the person's internal knowledge and processes, such as the subject's representation of the task. Normally, data from more complex tasks are much less reliable statistically and much harder to interpret. Thus perhaps the most interesting processes, such as reasoning and problem solving, are the hardest to work with in terms of data collection and the construction and evaluation of simulation models.

SURVEY OF COGNITIVE MODELS

The survey presented here is limited to those modeling efforts in which modeling human behavior was a direct goal, as opposed to pure AI projects. Note, however, that one survey (Bower and Hilgard, 1981) uses several AI projects directly as psychological models, because these are the most complete and explicit statements available of certain theoretical mechanisms. A brief description will be given of a variety of simulation models based on which of the processes were under investigation.

Basic Approaches

There are three basic approaches that have been used in cognitive models. In the first, a numeric simulation approach, representations of some sort are activated in specified ways over time, and the representations interact in terms of their activation. This is an old concept in psychology; precursors of it can be found in James (1890) and Hebb (1949), and it has great appeal because of its neurological flavor. This approach focuses mostly on the mathematical specifics of the time course of activation and how the representations interact. The currently popular form is connectionism (Rumelhart, 1989), but its scope and empirical adequacy are controversial (Pinker and Prince, 1988). Because connectionist models typically emphasize low level, rather than more obviously cognitive processing, they will not be further discussed here.

The second basic approach involves the manipulation of symbolic structures that represent knowledge, essentially the same approach as in current mainstream AI's use of symbol systems (Newell, Rosenbloom, and Laird, 1989). Many of the cognitive models that will be described here take this form. The third approach is a hybrid of the activation and symbolic approaches. That is, which knowledge structures are paid attention to and manipulated is determined by the amount of activation, which typically spreads from one piece of knowledge to another. Spreading activation has been used for more than 20 years (Quillian, 1968; Anderson, 1983). Such hybrid systems are often used because the activation mechanism provides an intuitive way for an otherwise purely symbolic system to be "sloppy," producing probabilistic behavior or responding to partially matching information.

Perception

Perceptual processes have usually been characterized as low level processes in which activation mechanisms are of primary importance. For example, one model recognizes four-letter words using a network of representations of letter features, letters, and words, which activate and inhibit each other (McClelland and Rumelhart, 1981; Rumelhart and McClelland, 1982). The network reaches a stable state in which the representation of the presented word is the most activated. Interestingly, there has not been much follow up of the classic blocks world work in AI (Winston, 1975), in which perception is seen as a matter of matching schemata for known objects against perceptual input. Although these concepts are central to current cognitive theory (Palmer, 1975; Bower and Hilgard, 1981) there has been little or no attempt to construct and evaluate simulation models of perceptual processes based on this concept. Perhaps the best stimulation of higher order perception is the model of chess expertise that learns to recognize patterns of pieces on the chessboard by building a discrimination net (Simon and Gilmartin, 1973).

Learning

Some of the earliest cognitive models dealt with learning processes. The first was the classic EPAM (qv) model (Simon and Feigenbaum, 1964), which constructed a discrimination network to perform simple learning. The presented stimulus was sorted by the net to find the response; if the response was incorrect, the net would be modified to produce a new path to the correct response. EPAM is an example of how a model of a psychological process contributed to the development of an important AI technique, the discrimination net. Hintzman (1968) later built a more elaborate version, SAL, in which additional mechanisms were added to account for a variety of experimentally observed phenomena of interference and forgetting in simple learning situations. This early work on learning was not followed up for quite a few years, because attention shifted to models of performance, rather than learning.

More recent work has focused on various learning processes. The LAS system (Anderson, 1975) learned the grammar for a language by constructing an augmented transition network (ATN) in response to pairs of semantic representations and input sentences. In the seminal ACT model (Anderson, 1976, 1983) a key architectural distinction is made between procedural knowledge, represented as production rules, and declarative knowledge, usually represented as propositions in a semantic network. The production rules examine and act on the semantic network. Only semantic representations that are active, as a result of spreading activation, can trigger the production rules.

Considerable attention is paid to the mechanisms by which new procedural knowledge, such as a skill, is learned; new production rules are acquired and refined through practice. This approach has been applied to the learning of geometry (Anderson, 1982) and learning programming in LISP (Anderson and co-workers, 1982). A similar, but greatly simplified analysis, has been applied to account for the learning of skills in interacting with equipment (Kieras, and Bovair, 1986; Bovair, Kieras, and Polson, 1990). Thus the representation of learning as the acquisition and refinement of production rules appears to be a powerful and comprehensive approach.

Memory Organization and Processes

Most simulation models of memory have dealt with long-term memory, which is the repository of general knowledge. This concern with knowledge representation makes long-term memory a fruitful area for application of AI concepts. An early paper (Frijda, 1972) presents the basic idea that knowledge can be represented in terms of labeled associations between concepts. This is perhaps the earliest paper to point out the extreme amount and complexity of human knowledge when expressed in these terms. It was suggested that the complexity of human thought, and its idiosyncrasies between individuals, could probably be accounted for in terms of the differences in knowledge rather than differences in basic cognitive processes that use the knowledge. This is the precursor of the current emphasis on knowledge-based systems in both AI and cognitive modeling. Other work (Quillian, 1968; Collins and Quillian, 1969, 1972) introduced the idea of semantic networks to cognitive psychology. This knowledge representation was widely accepted because it put the classic concept of association into a form adequate to represent knowledge. This work led to the idea of cognitive economy, in which inheritance relations are used to reduce the amount of stored information, and the basic mechanism of spreading activation is used to explain how knowledge can be retrieved in terms of its relevance to currently active knowledge (Anderson, 1983; Collins and Loftus, 1975).

Important early models of semantic memory were LNR (Rumelhart, Lindsey, and Norman, 1972) and Kintsch's (1974) model, both of which were based on case grammar representations (see GRAMMAR, CASE), and the influential HAM model (Anderson and Bower, 1973), which used a representation similar to predicate logic (see LOGIC, PREDICATE). The contrast between systems like LNR and HAM shows how different representation systems can be developed that are apparently adequate to represent human knowledge, but have substantial notational differences, and that cannot be distinguished from each other empirically, ie, the problem of nonidentifiability (Kieras, 1981b; Anderson, 1976). The case grammar form of representation has become popular both in cognitive modeling and AI. However, the HAM Model was probably more influential, simply because Anderson and Bower took more pains to bring their model into line with data on human performance. Also, Anderson's (1983) work has been more concerned with explicitly stated architectures for cognitive processes, which makes the theoretical status of the models more clear.

Language Comprehension

Similar to the large amount of work in AI on natural language processing, there has been considerable progress on cognitive models of how humans understand language, usually in the context of reading comprehension. A model was developed for how people acquire and recall information from text, which has become one of the most important theoretical representations of comprehension and memory processes (Kintsch and van Dijk, 1978). The model begins with a representation of the propositional content of the input text and selects which propositions are to be retained in the system's limited short-term memory as it goes from one sentence to the next, using simple heuristics that are based primarily on how the propositions are connected to each other. According to a basic principle of human learning, propositions that reside in short-term memory longer are more likely to be transferred to long-term memory and thus recalled better. This model can account for what is remembered from a text in a variety of reading and memory situations. Recent extensions have added activation mechanisms (Kintsch, 1988).

One model (Kieras, 1981a) used an ATN parser, in conjunction with a semantic network knowledge representation and spreading activation memory search mechanisms, and was able to account in considerable detail for the time required to read sentences in simple passages under different task conditions. In another model (Kieras, 1982) it was shown how certain higher level comprehension processes could be represented using production rules to perform inferences on a propositional representation of the text content. The model was able to recognize or extract generalizations from simple passages in a manner similar to human readers.

Perhaps the single most comprehensive simulation model of comprehension is that of Thibadeau, Just, and Carpenter (1982), again using a combination of production rules, propositional representation, and activation mechanisms. This model captures the highly parallel and interactive processing that apparently goes on in reading, all the way from syntactic analysis to the application of general knowledge. It was able to account for extremely detailed timing data from eye movement recordings of humans reading a technical passage.

Problem Solving and Reasoning

According to a classic paper (Newell, 1970), this area is the most important one for AI, but as pointed out, it is one of the most difficult topics in cognitive psychology. The best-known work in this field is the GPS model (Newell and Simon, 1972), which introduced the idea of means–end analysis. It was influential as a model for how humans solve problems as well as being one of the first representatives of what is now termed weak methods in problem solving. Another example of early work on problem solving (Simon and Kotovsky, 1963) was also one of the earliest cognitive simulation models. This was a model of how series completion problems, which often appear on IQ tests, could be solved by recognizing the patterns of repetition and succession. The model was able to account for which problems would be the easiest and most

difficult for people. Many of the processes involved in solving elementary proof problems in geometry were represented with a system involving both semantic structures and production rules, which would acquire and apply schemata representing proof approaches (Anderson, Greeno, Kline, and Neves, 1981). An influential model of planning was constructed that represented how people would select a route in an errand performing task, using a blackboard knowledge source architecture (Hayes-Roth and Hayes-Roth, 1979).

CONTRIBUTION TO AI

One way in which cognitive modeling work can contribute to AI is in the development of specific concepts and techniques. Several approaches, such as discrimination nets and rule-based systems (qv), apparently developed as cognitive models at the same time, if not before, their adoption as pure AI techniques. For example, the standard approach used in expert systems (qv) probably developed from the basic characterization of human expertise as the ability to recognize patterns, which could then be represented as a set of production rules. Tracing out the exact lines of descent of these ideas is beyond the scope of this article, but it certainly appears that historically, cognitive modeling efforts have made important contributions to AI.

One prime candidate for a new contribution is the general approach currently used in cognitive modeling. Because cognitive models are developed with a specific theoretical position in mind, they normally propose an explicit cognitive architecture. This consists of relatively small set of basic data types and processes, out of which are constructed all of the more complex knowledge representations and processes that the model uses to represent human mental mechanisms. Thus the overall goal of cognitive modeling is to arrive at a comprehensive architecture that is adequate for cognition, rather than simply constructing a multitude of unrelated special-purpose systems. Some of the specific cognitive architectures resulting from cognitive modeling might become directly applicable, but by adopting this architectural approach, as has been done in the SOAR (qv) project (Newell, Rosenbloom, and Laird, 1989), future work in AI could become more theoretically focused.

BIBLIOGRAPHY

J. R. Anderson, "Computer Simulation of a Language-Acquisition System," in R. L. Solso, ed., *Information Processing and Cognition: The Loyola Symposium,* Lawrence Erlbaum, Hillsdale, N.J., 1975, pp. 295–349.

J. R. Anderson, *Language, Memory, and Thought,* Lawrence Erlbaum, Hillsdale, N.J., 1976.

J. R. Anderson, "Acquisition of Proof Skills in Geometry," in J. G. Carbonell, R. Michalski, and T. Mitchell, eds., *Machine Learning, an Artificial Intelligence Approach,* Tioga, San Francisco, Calif., 1982, pp. 191–219.

J. R. Anderson, *The Architecture of Cognition,* Harvard University Press, Cambridge, Mass., 1983.

J. R. Anderson and G. H. Bower, *Human Associative Memory,* Winston, Washington, D.C., 1973.

J. R. Anderson, R. Farrell, and R. Sauers, *Learning to Plan in LISP,* Technical Report no. **ONR-82-2,** Carnegie-Mellon University, Pittsburgh, Pa., 1982.

J. R. Anderson, J. G. Greeno, P. J. Kline, and D. M. Neves, "Acquisition of Problem-Solving Skill," in J. R. Anderson, ed., *Cognitive Skills and Their Acquisition,* Lawrence Erlbaum, Hillsdale, N.J., 1981.

S. Bovair, D. E. Kieras, and P. G. Polson, "The Acquisition and Performance of Text Editing Skill: A Cognitive Complexity Analysis," *Human-Computer Interaction* **5,** 1–48 (1990).

G. H. Bower and E. R. Hilgard, *Theories of Learning,* 5th ed., Prentice-Hall, Inc., Englewood Cliffs, N.J., 1981. A. M. Collins and E. F. Lotfus, "A Spreading Activation Theory of Semantic Processing," *Psychol. Rev.* **82,** 407–428 (1975).

A. M. Collins and M. R. Quillian, "Retrieval Time from Semantic Memory," *J. Verb. Learn. Verb. Behav.* **8,** 240–247 (1969).

A. M. Collins and M. R. Quillian, "How to Make a Language User," in E. Tulving and W. Donaldson, eds., *Organization and Memory,* Academic Press, Inc., New York, 1972, pp. 309–351.

N. H. Frijda, "Simulation of Human Long-Term Memory," *Psychol. Bull.* **77,** 1–31 (1972).

L. W. Gregg and H. A. Simon, "Process Models and Stochastic Theories of Simple Concept Formation," *J. Math. Psychol.* **4,** 246–276 (1967).

B. Hayes-Roth and F. Hayes-Roth, "A Cognitive Model of Planning," *Cogn. Sci.* **3,** 275–310 (1979).

D. O. Hebb, *The Organization of Behavior,* Wiley, New York, 1949.

D. L. Hintzman, "Explorations with a Discrimination Net Model for Paired-Associate Learning," *J. Math. Psychol.* **5,** 123–162 (1968).

G. Humphrey, *Thinking: An Introduction to Its Experimental Psychology,* Wiley, New York, 1963.

W. James, *The Principles of Psychology,* Henry Holt & Co., New York, 1890.

D. E. Kieras, "Component Processes in the Comprehension of Simple Prose," *J. Verb. Learn. Verb. Behav.* **20,** 1–23 (1981a).

D. E. Kieras, "Knowledge Representations in Cognitive Psychology," in L. Cobb and R. M. Thrall, eds., *Mathematical Frontiers of the Social and Policy Sciences,* AAAS Selected Symposium **54,** Westview, Boulder, Colo., 1981b, pp. 5–36.

D. E. Kieras, "A Model of Reader Strategy for Abstracting Main Ideas from Simple Technical Prose," *Text* **2,** 47–82 (1982).

D. E. Kieras, "A Simulation Model for the Comprehension of Technical Prose," in G. H. Bower, ed., *The Psychology of Learning and Motivation,* Vol. 17, Academic Press, Inc., New York, 1983, pp. 39–80.

D. E. Kieras, "A Method for Comparing a Simulation Model to Reading Time Data," in D. Kieras, and M. Just, eds., *New Methods in Reading Comprehension Research,* Lawrence, Erlbaum, Hillsdale, N.J., 1984, pp. 299–325.

D. E. Kieras and S. Bovair, "The Acquisition of Procedures from Text: A Production-System Analysis of Transfer of Training," *J. Memory Lang.* **25,** 507–524 (1986).

W. Kintsch, *The Representation of Meaning in Memory,* Lawrence Erlbaum, Hillsdale, N.J., 1974.

W. Kintsch, "The Use of Knowledge in Discourse Processing: A Construction-Integration Model," *Psychol. Rev.* **95,** 163–182 (1988).

W. Kintsch and T. A. van Dijk, "Toward a Model of Discourse Comprehension and Production," *Psychol. Rev.* **85,** 363–394 (1978).

J. L. McClelland and D. E. Rumelhart, "An Interactive Model of Context Effects in Letter Perception: Part 1. An Account of Basic Findings," *Psychol. Rev.* **88,** 375–407 (1981).

A. Newell, "Remarks on the Relationship Between Artificial Intelligence and Cognitive Psychology," in R. Banerji and M. D. Mesarovic, eds., *Theoretical Approaches to Nonnumerical Problem Solving,* Springer-Verlag, New York, 1970, pp. 363–400.

A. Newell, P. S. Rosenbloom, and J. E. Laird, "Symbolic Architectures for Cognition," in M. Posner, eds., *Foundations of Cognitive Science,* MIT Press, Cambridge, Mass., 1989, pp. 93–132.

A. Newell and H. A. Simon, *Human Problem Solving,* Prentice-Hall, Inc., Englewood Cliffs, N.J., 1972.

S. E. Palmer, "Visual Perception and World Knowledge: Notes on a Model of Sensory-Cognitive Interaction," in D. A. Norman and D. E. Rumelhart, eds., *Explorations in Cognition,* W. H. Freeman, San Francisco, 1975, pp. 279–307.

S. Pinker, and A. Prince, "On Language and Connectionism: Analysis of a Parallel Distributed Processing Model of Language Acquisition," in S. Pinker and J. Mehler, eds., *Connections and Symbols,* MIT Press, Cambridge, Mass., 1988, pp. 73–194.

M. R. Quillian, "Semantic Memory," in M. Minsky, ed., *Semantic Information Processing,* MIT Press, Cambridge, Mass., 1968, pp. 227–270.

D. E. Rumelhart, "The Architecture of Mind: A Connectionist Approach," in M. Posner, ed., *Foundations of Cognitive Science,* MIT Press, Cambridge, Mass., 1989, pp. 133–160.

D. E. Rumelhart, P. H. Lindsay, and D. A. Norman, "A Process Model for Long-Term Memory," In E. Tulving and W. Donaldson, eds., *Organization and Memory,* Academic Press, Inc., New York, 1972, pp. 197–246.

D. E. Rumelhart and J. L. McClelland, "An Interactive Activation Model of Context Effects in Letter Perception: Part 2. The Contextual Enhancement Effect and Some Tests and Extensions of the Model," *Psychol. Rev.* **89,** pp. 60–94 (1982).

H. A. Simon and E. A. Feigenbaum, "An Information-Processing Theory of Some Effects of Similarity, Familiarization, and Meaningfulness in Verbal Learning," *J. Verb. Learn. Behav.* **3,** 385–396 (1964).

H. A. Simon and K. Gilmartin, "A Simulation of Memory for Chess Positions," *Cogn. Psychol.* **5,** 29–46 (1973).

H. A. Simon and K. Kotovsky, "Human Acquisition of Concepts for Sequential Patterns," *Psychol. Rev.* **70,** pp. 534–546 (1963).

R. Thibadeau, M. A. Just, and P. A. Carpenter, "A Model of the Time Course and Content of Reading," *Cogn. Sci.* **6,** pp. 157–203 (1982).

P. H. Winston, ed., *The Psychology of Computer Vision,* McGraw-Hill Book Co., Inc., New York, 1975.

DAVID E. KIERAS
University of Michigan

COGNITIVE PSYCHOLOGY

The term artificial intelligence evokes a contrast with the natural intelligence of higher organisms, most notably human beings. Some would argue that AI, as defined by successful AI programs, is likely to prove qualitatively different from the natural variety. Another view, however, is that AI should be directed toward imitation of the cognitive capabilities of humans. The latter view suggests that AI should be closely linked to cognitive psychology, the field that investigates how people acquire knowledge, remember it, and put it to use to make decisions and solve problems.

HISTORY AND SCOPE

Cognitive psychology, also sometimes called information-processing psychology, is currently the leading area of human experimental psychology. The origins of the field can be traced to nineteenth-century psychologists such as James (1950; originally published 1890) and the German Gestalt psychologists such as Duncker (1945) and Wertheimer (1959). For much of the twentieth century up until about 1960, however, American psychology was dominated by behaviorist theories that eschewed any reference to unobservable mental processes. The modern revival of cognitive psychology was fostered in part by developments in other disciplines, most notably linguistics and computer science. In linguistics the theory of generative grammar coupled with a scathing critique of behaviorist accounts of language use provided the impetus for cognitive approaches to language in the new field of psycholinguistics (Chomsky, 1957, 1959). In computer science the digital computer became a striking example of an information-processing system in which observable input–output relations clearly depended on complex but well-specified intervening computational steps, discrediting the behaviorist claim that only observable stimulus–response relations were respectable objects of scientific scrutiny. The use of the computer as a model for theories of human intelligence rose to prominence in a seminal monograph (Miller and co-workers, 1960) that set the stage for a book that gave the field of cognitive psychology its modern identity (Neisser, 1967). A landmark computational account of human problem solving (Newell and Simon, 1972) established a firm link between the view that AI should strive to imitate human cognition and the view that computer simulations afford testable theoretical models of cognitive processes. A thorough survey of the origins of cognitive psychology has been published (Lachman and co-workers, 1979) as well as a historical review (Newell and Simon, 1972). In recent years, work in cognitive psychology has become increasingly integrated with work in AI, neuropsychology, linguistics, and philosophy within the emerging field of cognitive science (qv). Theoretical work on parallel distributed processing and connectionism (qv) has had a major recent impact on cognitive psychology (Rumelhart and co-workers, 1986), and the rising field of cognitive neuroscience has intensified concern with the brain mechanisms underlying cognition (Kosslyn and Koeing, in press). Recent theoretical analyses of cognitive processes such as memory, learning, and reasoning have focused on their apparent adaptive significance (Anderson, 1990a).

Like any scientific discipline, the scope of cognitive psychology is delineated not only by its subject matter but also by the methods it employs. A variety of research methods are commonly used, including measurement of reaction time to perform simple tasks, patterns of eye movements, distributions of types of error, physiological recordings, and qualitative analyses of verbal protocols (Puff, 1982; Ericsson and Simon, 1984; Bower and Clapper, 1989). A major methodological approach has been to attempt to decompose cognitive processes into components and to estimate the temporal relations among them (Sternberg, 1966; Posner, 1982; McClelland, 1979; Meyer and co-workers, 1988).

COGNITIVE PSYCHOLOGY AND AI

Cognitive psychology and AI have been closely intertwined since the inception of each. AI has provided cognitive psychology with both a methodological tool and theoretical formalisms. Given the highly interactive nature of human cognition, computer simulation is often a useful tool for deriving predictions from a complex model. At the theoretical level, cognitive psychology has adapted numerous concepts that were developed in computer science in general and AI in particular, eg, content-addressable memory (see ASSOCIATIVE MEMORY), semantic networks (qv), and blackboard systems (qv).

Early work in cognitive psychology yielded theoretical concepts that anticipated some that are now being explored within AI. For example, the concept of a schema, a knowledge structure that actively generates expectations based on regularities abstracted from past experience, was introduced (Bartlett, 1932). Such AI concepts as frames (qv) and scripts (qv) are variants of the schema concept (Minsky, 1975; Schank and Abelson, 1977; Rumelhart, 1988). Work on mental maps and the representation of expectancies (Tolman, 1948) was a precursor to recent conceptions of mental models (Genter and Stevens, 1983). More generally, empirical and theoretical work in cognitive psychology has yielded a clearer understanding of some general principles of human information processing that can help direct development of AI systems modeled after human cognition. In particular, as is elaborated below, human intelligence appears to be based on multiple representational codes for knowledge (eg, visuospatial as well as linguistic), on a great deal of parallel processing of information, and on inference patterns that depend on similarity and associative links more than on strictly deductive logic. These properties of human information processing seem to be inextricably linked to powerful learning mechanisms, ranging from elementary detection of covariations among properties of the environment to exploitation of analogies between knowledge acquired in different domains (Holland and co-workers, 1986). These learning mechanisms allow humans to avoid the brittleness of typical AI expert systems (qv), which generally lack humanlike flexibility in adapting themselves to changes in their initial domain of application.

Theoretical approaches to cognition within cognitive psychology and AI are linked by two major types of formalism, production systems (see RULE-BASED SYSTEMS) and connectionist neural networks (see CONNECTIONISM). Systems based on production rules were first introduced into cognitive psychology as models of human problem solving (Newell and Simon, 1972); later developments extended versions of production systems, sometimes coupled with semantic networks, to serve as models of other cognitive processes (Anderson and Bower, 1973; Anderson, 1976, 1983; Thibadeau, 1982). Connectionist models (Rumelhart and co-workers, 1986; Hinton and Anderson, 1981; Seidenberg and McClelland, 1989) represent a current resurgence of interest in modeling cognitive processes at a relatively microscopic level of analysis analogous to neural units, as in some earlier psychological theories (Hebb, 1949).

MAJOR AREAS OF RESEARCH

The survey of active research areas in cognitive psychology presented below is of necessity selective and incomplete. In addition, much more could be said about the interconnections between the various areas of research. More extensive and integrative reviews can be found in recent textbooks (Glass and Holyoak, 1986; Anderson, 1990b).

Perception

The earliest stages in perception, such as extraction of information directly from the retinal image, are usually considered outside the scope of cognitive psychology (although early perception is an important topic in experimental psychology and is clearly relevant to AI). Cognitive work on perception is concerned with the construction of meaningful patterns from elementary components, with vision receiving by far the most attention. Since the classic research of Gestalt psychologists (Wertheimer, 1958), a basic concern has been with the principles that govern the construction of relatively constant interpretations of perceptual inputs despite wide variations in the input itself. For example, a square is perceived as such even though it may be tilted in various directions, partially occluded, or composed of broken rather than solid lines. An important theoretical position is that perception depends on the detection of invariant properties of the distal stimulus (ie, the object in the environment), which either remain constant or change systematically as the proximal stimulus (ie, the retinal image) undergoes a wide range of variations (Gibson, 1966).

Recent research has made considerable progress in addressing the long-standing basic issue of identifying the elementary features the human visual system detects and uses to construct visual patterns. A selective-attention task has been used to identify a level of visual processing in which the color, form, and location of an object appear to be represented as separate features not yet integrated into a unified representation of an object (Treisman and Gelade, 1980). These features are detected in parallel across the entire visual field so that time to detect a target embedded in an array is independent of the number of elements in the array, if and only if the target can be consistently discriminated from all distractors by considering a single feature (a phenomenon referred to as *pop-*

out). In contrast, discrimination must be based on a slower serial process when features must be combined to identify the target. Other work has used similar techniques to identify some of the elementary features that compose visual forms (Julesz, 1981; Pomerantz, 1981). Recent evidence suggests that under some conditions the visual system can process even conjunctions of features with some degree of parallelism (Treisman, 1988; Cave and Wolfe, 1990). A lucid introduction to the topic of perception has been provided (Rock, 1984).

Attention

The core issue in theories of attention concerns information reduction. Because humans are constantly faced with an immense amount of information as the result of both perception and memory retrieval and are limited in their capacity to process it, they must be selective in their analysis of inputs. The basic idea that humans can be viewed as limited-capacity information processing systems was first proposed by Broadbent (1958) and became a cornerstone of cognitive psychology.

This cornerstone, however, has been the focus of controversy since it was first erected. At issue is the degree and locus of parallelism in information processing. Broadbent proposed that inputs are filtered early in perceptual processing and that only a selected few are processed at higher levels (eg, at the level of meaning). Soon afterward, however, evidence accrued that people occasionally respond to the meaning of highly familiar inputs (ie, their names) even when the inputs are unattended, suggesting that unattended inputs are attenuated rather than filtered entirely (Treisman, 1960). These early-selection models, which emphasized limits on perceptual processing, were subsequently challenged by late-selection models (Deutsch and Deutsch, 1963), according to which all inputs are processed to the level of meaning, with selection occurring only among responses to the inputs.

Late-selection models imply a greater degree of parallel processing than do early-selection models. The concept of automaticity has been invoked to explain why humans can perform some tasks in parallel whereas other tasks demand serial processing (Shiffrin and Schneider, 1977; Posner and Snyder, 1975). The general notion is that particular types of experience result in a decrease in the capacity required to perform tasks so that multiple tasks can be performed concurrently without interference. Development of automaticity is sometimes theoretically associated with a reduction in control so that the person is unable to avoid making an overlearned automatic response to an input (eg, accessing the meaning of a familiar word). An important form of automatic responding is revealed by the tendency for processing of an input rapidly to prime related inputs (eg, words of similar meaning) so that subsequent processing of related inputs is facilitated (Meyer and Schvareveldt, 1971). Evidence has been provided of rapid automatic facilitation and slower conscious inhibition of the processing of inputs (Neely, 1977).

The relationship between selectivity and automaticity remains controversial. The various theoretical properties of automaticity do not always co-occur, and putative evidence for capacity-free processing beyond a stage of early perceptual selection has been challenged (Navon, 1984; Cheng, 1985). Neurophysiological evidence indicates that attention is not a unified mechanism, but rather a complex distributed system that performs selective modulation of information processing to provide coherent control of action (Roland and Friberg, 1985; Posner, 1988). Some aspects of attentional control have been modeled within parallel distributed systems (Schneider and Detweiler, 1987; Cohen and co-workers, 1990). A useful review and theoretical discussion has been published (Allport, 1990).

Memory

Research on memory is concerned with the processes by which information is stored, retained over some time interval, and subsequently retrieved. Memory is intimately related to perception and attention, because memory is often the incidental by-product of attentive perceptual processing. Learning roughly corresponds to the storage phase of memory; however, except for purely rote memory (if such a thing exists), learning typically implies some degree of generalization or integration of new information with old. A story, for example, is remembered as a hierarchical structure that reflects schematic knowledge about similar episodes (Kintsch and van Dijk, 1978; Rumelhart, 1977) (see Story analysis). Learning extends to the acquisition of knowledge more general than specific perceptual inputs, as when a child acquires a general notion of what *dog* means from experience with particular exemplars. Reviews of the extensive literature of human memory have been published (Anderson and Bower, 1973; Crowder, 1976; Baddeley, 1990).

Early theories of memory in cognitive psychology proposed a fundamental distinction between short-term and long-term memory stores (Waugh and Norman, 1965; Atkinson and Shiffrin, 1968). The short-term store was viewed as a bottleneck that limited the rate at which information can be transferred into permanent long-term storage. This view has since been modified as the result of various criticisms (Craik and Lockhart, 1972; Baddeley and Hitch, 1974). Data from both normal and amnesic subjects suggest that both short-term and long-term memory consist of multiple interacting subsystems (Baddeley, 1990; Schacter, 1990). Experience produces implicit effects on subsequent memory performance, such as various forms of priming; these implicit effects are sometimes dissociated from explicit, conscious retrieval (Schacter, 1987; Richardson-Klavehn and Bjork, 1988). The most important limit on the explicit retrievability of information is the time required to associate the input with other information in memory that will afford potential retrieval cues.

The existence of multiple subsystems implies that multiple traces of an experience are typically stored in memory. Connectionist models of memory further assume that memory representations are distributed, with a trace corresponding to a pattern of activity across neural units that tends to be reinstated upon representation of the same or a similar input (Anderson and co-workers, 1977; McClelland and Rumelhart, 1985). Similar assumptions are made by models based on vector representations (Murdoch, 1983; Gillund and Shiffrin, 1984; Hintzman, 1988). Although such models reproduce many important properties of human memory, such as content addressability and automatic generalization, they have serious limitations. Unlike humans, these models show massive interference effects when faced with a changing environment (McCloskey and Cohen, 1989; Ratcliff, 1990). More generally, theories of memory must accommodate evidence that memory retrieval sometimes resembles automatic activation of a trace by a retrieval cue and sometimes resembles a slow search process much like conscious problem solving.

Another controversial issue involves evidence suggesting that memory traces can be formed in qualitatively different codes. The focus of debate has centered on mental imagery, a memory code that preserves the spatial and visual properties of perceptual inputs. It has been demonstrated that when people are asked to judge whether two visual forms are the same despite a difference in orientation, the time to make the decision increases linearly with the difference in orientation, as if people mentally rotated one of the objects to place it into correspondence with the other (Shepard and Cooper, 1982). It has been proposed that images can be constructed in an inner space analogous to a display screen attached to a computer and that the results of spatial transformations can be read off of the imaginal representation (Kosslyn, 1980). The existence of perceptlike memory traces is supported by a large body of converging evidence from behavioral and neurophysiological studies (Farah, 1988).

Human memory stores not only representations of specific experiences but also representations of categories of experience, a distinction termed episodic versus semantic memory (Tulving, 1972). A great deal of research in cognitive psychology (Rosch, 1978), indicates that natural human categories tend to be organized around clear prototypical exemplars but have relatively ill-defined boundaries. Recent work on categorization has centered on the mechanisms by which categories are induced from experience with exemplars and the form in which categories are represented in memory (Medin and Smith, 1984) and on the roles of bottom-up, similarity-based generalization and of top-down, theory-driven generalization (Medin, 1989).

Thinking

Thinking involves the active transformation of existing knowledge to create new knowledge that can be used to achieve a goal (Holland and co-workers, 1986). The topic can be loosely divided into reasoning (drawing inferences from current knowledge or beliefs), decision making (the evaluation of alternatives and choice among them) (see Decision theory), and problem solving (qv) (methods for attempting to achieve goals). These topics are closely intertwined and reflect different emphases and experimental paradigms rather than strong conceptual distinctions.

Given the obvious power of human intellect, it is rather paradoxical that much of the work on thinking has served to reveal ways in which human reason seems to depart from the normative standards set forth by such disciplines as statistics and logic. Research indicates that intuitive decision making is often based on easily used but fallible heuristics (Kahneman and co-workers, 1982; Tversky and Kahneman, 1983; Nisbett and Ross, 1980). These heuristics are closely tied to basic memory processes, such as the ease of retrieving information from memory (the availability heuristic) and the similarity of an instance to a category prototype (the representativeness heuristic). A theoretical analysis of similarity judgments has been published (Tversky, 1977). Similarly, work on human deductive reasoning reveals major departures from the normative standards of formal logic (Johnson-Laird and Wason, 1978; Johnson-Laird, 1983).

Nonetheless, recent research indicates that human reasoning is far from capricious, and may in fact be highly adaptive (Anderson, 1990a; Cheng and Novick, 1990). Humans may base some inferences on an abstract natural logic (Braine and O'Brien, 1991), and everyday reasoning often seems to be based on rules induced and applied in the context of broad classes of pragmatically important tasks, such as understanding social regulations or causal relations among events (Cheng and Holyoak, 1985) (see REASONING, CAUSAL). The human inference engine appears to be very different in kind from the logic-based systems embodied in some AI reasoning programs. Recent cognitive models have applied some connectionist principles to high level reasoning tasks, such as analogical mapping and the evaluation of competing explanations (Holyoak and Thagard, 1989; Thagard, 1989). Human reasoning may in some respects be better than "normative" for the range of problems humans encounter most frequently in everyday life.

Human problem solving is also closely tied to basic properties of the memory system. A major area of current research involves the transition from novice- to expert-level problem-solving skills in domains such as physics (Chi and co-workers, 1981; Larkin and co-workers, 1980) (see PHYSICS, NAIVE). Expertise appears to reflect the reorganization of schemata representing categories of problems and the acquisition of specialized methods for dealing with the categories of problems encountered in the domain. The ability to generalize problem-solving methods so they can be applied to new problems with common goal structures (Singley and Anderson, 1989) and the ability to solve novel problems by analogy to known situations in other domains (Gentner and Gentner, 1983; Gick and Holyoak, 1983) distinguish human problem solving from the performance of typical AI expert systems. A recent survey of research and theory on expertise has been provided (Ericsson and Smith, 1991).

Language

The study of language (its acquisition, production, and comprehension) has been a distinct area within cognitive psychology, with a close relationship to work in developmental psychology on language acquisition. Psycholinguistics was initially devoted to tests of Chomsky's theory of transformational grammar as a performance model and

was heavily influenced by his nativist position regarding language acquisition (qv). Transformational grammar failed, however, as a performance model of actual language use (Fodor and co-workers, 1974). Explorations of the relationship between language and other cognitive processes, such as memory and learning, have led to greater integration of psycholinguistic theories with models of other aspects of cognition, as has been illustrated (Rumelhart and co-workers, 1986; Schank and Abelson, 1977; Rumelhart, 1980, 1977; Anderson and Bower, 1973; Anderson, 1976, 1983; Thibadeau and co-workers, 1982; Seidenberg and McClelland, 1989; Kintsch and van Dijk, 1978). Reviews of research in psycholinguistics (Clark and Clark, 1977; Carroll, 1986) and a discussion of language acquisition (Pinker, 1990) have been published.

Initial lexical access of word meanings (at least for familiar meanings) appears to be based on rapid parallel processes. At a global level language comprehension appears to reflect parallel analyses of speech sounds (see SPEECH UNDERSTANDING) or, in the case of reading, visual features of words (see CHARACTER RECOGNITION); syntactic and semantic constraints; and the pragmatic cues to meaning provided by conversational contexts, integrated to make serial decisions about the interpretation of the incoming speech stream (see DISCOURSE UNDERSTANDING). A model has been developed that integrates rule-based and connectionist processes to provide a broad description of the comprehension process (Kintsch, 1988).

FUTURE PROSPECTS

The links between the aims, methods, and theories in AI and cognitive psychology are likely to bring the two fields closer together over the next decade. It is increasingly the case that cognitive psychologists demand of their theories the kind of sufficiency test provided by computer simulation. To meet this standard, they will either adapt current AI concepts to build new theories of cognition or adapt theories of cognition to build new AI concepts. For their part AI researchers also have reason to remain aware of advances in cognitive psychology. Human beings, despite their cognitive shortcomings, remain by far the most general and flexible of all known intelligent systems. As long as this is so, a major strategy for AI will be the construction of programs that more closely imitate natural intelligence.

BIBLIOGRAPHY

A. Allport, "Visual Attention," in M. I. Posner, ed., *Foundations of Cognitive Science,* MIT Press, Cambridge, Mass., 1990.

J. R. Anderson, *Language, Memory, and Thought,* Lawrence Erlbaum, Hillsdale, N.J., 1976.

J. R. Anderson, *The Architecture of Cognition,* Harvard University Press, Cambridge, Mass., 1983.

J. R. Anderson, *The Adaptive Character of Thought,* Lawrence Erlbaum, Hillsdale, N.J., 1990a.

J. R. Anderson, *Cognitive Psychology and Its Implications,* 3rd ed., W. H. Freeman, San Francisco, Calif., 1990b.

J. R. Anderson and G. H. Bower, *Human Associative Memory,* Winston, Washington, D.C., 1973.

R. C. Atkinson and R. M. Shiffrin, "Human Memory: A Proposed System and Its Control Processes," in K. W. Spence and J. T. Spence, eds., *The Psychology of Learning and Motivation,* Vol. 2, Academic Press, Inc., New York, 1968.

J. A. Anderson, J. W. Silverstein, S. A. Ritz, and R. S. Jones, "Distinctive Features, Categorical Perception, and Probability Learning," *Psychol. Rev.* **84,** 413–451 (1977).

A. D. Baddeley, *Human Memory: Theory and Practice,* Allyn & Bacon, Boston, 1990.

A. D. Baddeley and G. Hitch, "Working Memory," in G. H. Bower, ed., *Recent Advances in Learning and Motivation,* Vol. 8, Academic Press, Inc., New York, 1974.

F. C. Bartlett, *Remembering,* Cambridge University Press, Cambridge, UK, 1932.

M. D. S. Braine and D. P. O'Brien, "A Theory of *if*: A Lexical Entry Reasoning Program, and Pragmatic Principles," *Psychol. Rev.* **98,** 182–203 (1991).

D. E. Broadbent, *Perception and Communication,* Pergamon Press, Oxford, UK, 1958.

G. H. Bower and J. P. Clapper, "Experimental Methods in Cognitive Science," in M. I. Posner, ed., *Foundations of Cognitive Science,* MIT Press, Cambridge, Mass., 1989.

D. W. Carroll, *The Psychology of Language,* Brooks/Cole, Pacific Grove, Calif., 1986.

K. R. Cave and J. M. Wolfe, "Modelling the Role of Parallel Processing in Visual Search," *Cogn. Psychol.* **22,** 225–271 (1990).

P. W. Cheng, "Restructuring Versus Automaticity: Alternative Accounts of Skill Acquisition," *Psychol. Rev.* **92,** 414–423 (1985).

P. W. Cheng and K. J. Holyoak, "Pragmatic Reasoning Schemas," *Cogn. Psychol.* **17,** 391–416 (1985).

P. W. Cheng and L. Novick, "A Probabilistic Contrast Model of Causal Induction," *J. Personality and Social Psychol.* **58,** 545–567 (1990).

M. T. H. Chi, P. J. Feltovich, and R. Glaser, "Categorization and Representation of Physics Problems by Experts and Novices," *Cogn. Sci.* **5,** 121–152 (1981).

N. Chomsky, *Syntactic Structures,* Mouton, The Hague, 1957.

N. Chomsky, "Review of B. F. Skinner's Verbal Behavior," *Language* **35,** 26–58 (1959).

H. H. Clark and E. V. Clark, *Psychology and Language,* Harcourt Brace Jovanovich, Orlando, Fla., 1977.

J. D. Cohen, K. Dunbar, and J. L. McClelland, "On the Control of Automatic Processes: A Parallel Distributed Processing Account of the Stroop Effect," *Psychol. Rev.* **97,** 332–361 (1990).

F. I. M. Craik and R. S. Lockhart, "Levels of Processing: A Framework for Memory Research," *J. Verbl. Learn. Verbl. Behav.* **11,** 671–684 (1972).

R. G. Crowder, *Principles of Learning and Memory,* Lawrence Erlbaum, Hillsdale, N.J., 1976.

J. A. Deutsch and D. Deutsch, "Attention: Some Theoretical Considerations," *Psychol. Rev.* **70,** 80–90 (1963).

K. Duncker, "On Problem Solving," *Psychol. Monographs* **58**(270) (1945).

A. K. Ericsson and H. A. Simon, *Protocol Analysis: Verbal Reports as Data,* MIT Press, Cambridge, Mass., 1984.

K. A. Ericsson and J. Smith, eds., *Toward a General Theory of Expertise: Prospects and Limits,* Cambridge University Press, Cambridge, UK, 1991.

M. J. Farah, "Is Visual Imagery Really Visual? Overlooked Evidence from Neuropsychology," *Psychol. Rev.* **95,** 307–317 (1988).

J. A. Fodor, T. G. Bever, and M. F. Garrett, *The Psychology of Language,* McGraw-Hill Book Co., Inc., New York, 1974.

D. Gentner and D. R. Gentner, "Flowing Waters or Teeming Crowds: Mental Models of Electricity," in D. Gentner and A. L. Stevens, eds., 1983.

D. Gentner and A. L. Stevens, eds., *Mental Models,* Lawrence Erlbaum, Hillsdale, N.J., 1983.

J. J. Gibson, *The Senses Considered as Perceptual Systems,* Houghton Mifflin, Boston, Mass., 1966.

M. L. Gick and K. J. Holyoak, "Schema Induction and Analogical Transfer," *Cogn. Psychol.* **15,** 1–38 (1983).

G. Gillund and R. M. Shiffrin, "A Retrieval Model for Both Recognition and Recall," *Psychol. Rev.* **91,** 1–67 (1984).

A. L. Glass and K. J. Holyoak, *Cognition,* 2nd ed., Random House, New York, 1986.

D. O. Hebb, *The Organization of Behavior,* John Wiley & Sons, Inc., New York, 1949.

G. E. Hinton and J. A. Anderson, *Parallel Models of Associative Memory,* Lawrence Erlbaum, Hillsdale, N.J., 1981.

D. L. Hintzman, "Judgments of Frequency and Recognition Memory in a Multiple-Trace Memory Model," *Psychol. Rev.* **95,** 528–551 (1988).

J. H. Holland, K. J. Holyoak, R. E. Nisbett, and P. R. Thagard, *Induction: Processes of Inference, Learning, and Discovery,* MIT Press, Cambridge, Mass., 1986.

K. J. Holyoak and P. Thagard, "Analogical Mapping by Constraint Satisfaction," *Cogn. Sci.* **13,** 295–355 (1989).

W. James, *The Principles of Psychology* [originally published 1890], Dover, New York, 1950.

P. N. Johnson-Laird, *Mental Models,* Harvard University Press, Cambridge, Mass., 1983.

P. N. Johnson-Laird and P. C. Wason, ed., *Thinking,* Cambridge University Press, Cambridge, UK, 1978.

B. Julesz, "Figure and Ground Perception in Briefly Presented Isodipole Textures," in M. Kubovy and J. R. Pomerantz, eds., *Perceptual Organization,* Lawrence Erlbaum, Hillsdale, N.J., 1981.

D. Kahneman, P. Slovic, and A. Tversky, eds., *Judgment under Uncertainty: Heuristics and Biases,* Cambridge University Press, Cambridge, UK, 1982.

W. Kintsch, "The Role of Knowledge in Discourse Comprehension: A Construction-Integration Model," *Psychol. Rev.* **95,** 163–182 (1988).

W. Kintsch and T. A. van Dijk, "Toward a Model of Text Comprehension and Production," *Psychol. Rev.* **85,** 363–394 (1978).

S. M. Kosslyn, *Image and Mind,* Harvard University Press, Cambridge, Mass., 1980.

S. M. Kosslyn and O. Koenig, *Wet Mind,* The Free Press, New York, in press.

J. L. Lachman, R. Lachman, and E. C. Butterfield, *Cognitive Psychology and Information Processing: An Introduction,* Lawrence Erlbaum, Hillsdale, N.J., 1979.

J. H. Larkin, J. McDermott, D. P. Simon, and H. A. Simon, "Expert and Novice Performance in Solving Physics Problems," *Science* **208,** 1335–1342 (1980).

J. L. McClelland, "On the Time Relations of Mental Processes: An Examination of Systems of Processes in Cascade," *Psychol. Rev.* **86,** 287–330 (1979).

J. L. McClelland and D. E. Rumelhart, "Distributed Memory and the Representation of General and Specific Information," *J. Exp. Psychol.* [*Gen.*] **114,** 159–188 (1985).

M. McCloskey and N. J. Cohen, "Catastrophic Interference in Connectionist Networks," in G. H. Bower, ed., *The Psychology of Learning and Motivation,* Vol. 24, pp. 109–165, Academic Press, San Diego, Calif., 1989.

D. L. Medin, "Concepts and Conceptual Structure," *Am. Psychol.* **44,** 1469–1481 (1989).

D. L. Medin and E. E. Smith, "Concepts and Concept Formation," *Ann. Rev. Psychol.* **35,** 113–138 (1984).

D. E. Meyer, D. E. Irwin, A. M. Osman, and J. Kounios, "The Dynamics of Cognition and Action: Mental Processes Inferred from Speed-Accuracy Decomposition," *Psychol. Rev.* **95,** 183–237 (1988).

D. E. Meyer and R. W. Schvaneveldt, "Facilitation in Recognizing Pairs of Words: Evidence of a Dependence Between Retrieval Operations," *J. Exp. Psychol.* **90,** 227–234 (1971).

G. A. Miller, E. Galanter, and K. H. Pribram, *Plans and the Structure of Behavior,* Holt, Rinehart and Winston, New York, 1960.

M. A. Minsky, "A Framework for Representing Knowledge," in P. H. Winston, ed., *The Psychology of Computer Vision,* Mc-Graw-Hill Book Co., Inc., New York, 1975.

B. B. Murdoch, Jr., "A Distributed Memory Model for Serial-Order Information," *Psychol. Rev.* **90,** 316–338 (1983).

D. Navon, "Resources—A Theoretical Soup Stone?" *Psychol. Rev.* **91,** 216–234 (1984).

J. H. Neely, "Semantic Priming and Retrieval from Lexical Memory: Role of Inhibitionless Spreading Activation and Limited Capacity Attention," *J. Exp. Psychol.* [*Gen.*] **106,** 226–254 (1977).

U. Neisser, *Cognitive Psychology,* Prentice-Hall, Inc., Englewood Cliffs, N.J., 1967.

A. Newell and H. A. Simon, *Human Problem Solving,* Prentice-Hall, Inc., Englewood Cliffs, N.J., 1972.

R. E. Nisbett and L. Ross, *Human Inference: Strategies and Shortcomings of Social Judgment,* Prentice-Hall, Englewood Cliffs, N.J., 1980.

S. Pinker, "Language Acquisition," in M. I. Posner, ed., *Foundations of Cognitive Science,* MIT Press, Cambridge, Mass., 1990.

J. R. Pomerantz, "Perceptual Organization in Information Processing" in M. Kubovy and J. R. Pomerantz, eds., *Perceptual Organization,* Lawrence Erlbaum, Hillsdale, N.J., 1981.

M. I. Posner, *Chronometric Explorations of Mind,* Lawrence Erlbaum, Hillsdale, N.J., 1982.

M. I. Posner, "Structures and Functions of Selective Attention," in T. Boll and B. K. Bryant, eds., *Clinical Neuropsychology and Brain Function,* American Psychological Association, Washington, D.C., 1988.

M. I. Posner and C. R. R. Snyder, "Attention and Cognitive Control," in R. Solso, ed., *Information Processing and Cognition: The Loyola Symposium,* Lawrence Erlbaum, Hillsdale, N.J., 1975.

C. R. Puff, ed., *Handbook of Research Methods in Human Memory and Cognition,* Academic Press, New York, 1982.

R. Ratcliff, "Connectionist Models of Recognition Memory: Constraints Imposed by Learning and Forgetting Functions," *Psychol. Rev.* **97,** 285–308 (1990).

A. Richardson-Klavehn and R. A. Bjork, "Measures of Memory," *Ann. Rev. Psychol.* **39,** 475–543 (1988).

P. E. Roland and L. Friberg, "Localization of Cortical Areas Activated by Thinking," *J. Neurophysiol.* **53,** 1219–1243 (1985).

I. Rock, *Perception,* W. H. Freeman, New York, 1984.

E. Rosch, "Principles of Categorization," in E. Rosch and B. B. Lloyd, eds., *Cognition and Categorization,* Lawrence Erlbaum, Hillsdale, N.J., 1978.

D. E. Rumelhart, "Understanding and Summarizing Brief Stories," in D. Laberge and S. J. Samuels, eds., *Basic Processes in Reading: Perception and Comprehension,* Lawrence Erlbaum, Hillsdale, N.J., 1977.

D. E. Rumelhart, "Schemata: The Building Blocks of Cognition," in R. Spiro, B. Bruce, and W. Brewer, eds., *Theoretical Issues in Reading Comprehension,* Lawrence Erlbaum, Hillsdale, N.J., 1980.

D. E. Rumelhart, J. L. McClelland, and the PDP Research Group, *Parallel Distributed Processing: Explorations in the Microstructure of Cognition,* MIT Press, Cambridge, Mass., 1986.

D. L. Schacter, "Implicit Memory: History and Current Status," *J. Exp. Psych.* [*Learn. Mem. Cogn.*] **13,** 501–518 (1987).

D. L. Schacter, "Memory," in M. I. Posner, ed., *Foundations of Cognitive Science,* MIT Press, Cambridge, Mass., 1990.

R. C. Schank and R. P. Abelson, *Scripts, Plans, Goals, and Understanding: An Inquiry into Human Knowledge Structures,* Lawrence Erlbaum, Hillsdale, N.J., 1977.

W. Schneider and M. Detweiler, "A Connectionist/Control Architecture for Working Memory," in G. H. Bower, ed., *The Psychology of Learning and Motivation,* Vol. 21, Academic Press, New York, 1987.

M. S. Seidenberg and J. L. McClelland, "A Distributed, Developmental Model of Word Recognition and Naming," *Psychol. Rev.* **96,** 523–568 (1989).

R. N. Shepard and L. A. Cooper, *Mental Images and Their Transformations,* MIT Press, Cambridge, Mass., 1982.

R. M. Shiffrin and W. Schneider, "Controlled and Automatic Human Information Processing. II. Perceptual Learning, Automatic Attending, and a General Theory," *Psychol. Rev.* **84,** 127–190 (1977).

M. K. Singley and J. R. Anderson, *The Transfer of Cognitive Skill,* Harvard University Press, Cambridge, Mass., 1989.

S. Sternberg, "High-Speed Scanning in Human Memory," *Science* **153,** 652–654 (1966).

P. Thagard, "Explanatory Coherence," *Behav. Brain Sci.* **12,** 435–467 (1989).

R. Thibadeau, M. A. Just, and P. A. Carpenter, "A Model of the Time Course of Reading," *Cogn. Sci.* **6,** 157–203 (1982).

E. C. Tolman, "Cognitive Maps in Rats and Men," *Psychol. Rev.* **55,** 189–208 (1948).

A. M. Treisman, "Contextual Cues in Selective Listening," *Q. J. Exp. Psychol.* **12,** 242–248 (1960).

A. M. Treisman, "Features and Objects: The Fourteenth Bartlett Memorial Lecture," *Q. J. Exp. Psychol.* **40A,** 201–237 (1988).

A. M. Treisman and G. Gelade, "A Feature-Integration Theory of Attention," *Cogn. Psychol.* **12,** 97–136 (1980).

E. Tulving, "Episodic and Semantic Memory," in E. Tulving, ed., *Organization of Memory,* Academic Press, New York, 1972.

A. Tversky, "Features of Similarity," *Psychol. Rev.* **84,** 327–352 (1977).

A. Tversky and D. Kahneman, "Extensional Versus Intuitive Judgment: The Conjunction Fallacy in Probability Judgment," *Psychol. Rev.* **90,** 293–315 (1983).

N. C. Waugh and D. A. Norman, "Primary Memory," *Psychol. Rev.* **72,** 89–104 (1965).

M. Wertheimer, "Principles of Perceptual Organization," in D. C. Beardsley and M. Wertheimer, eds., *Readings in Perception,* Van Nostrand, New York, 1958 [abridged translation].

M. Wertheimer, *Productive Thinking,* Harper & Row, New York, 1959.

K. HOLYOAK
UCLA

COGNITIVE SCIENCE

RELATION TO OTHER FIELDS

Cognitive science is an emerging field of study, boundaries of which are far from being well defined. A report prepared for the Alfred P. Sloan Foundation (a portion of which is reproduced as an appendix to Pylyshyn, 1983) defines it as "the study of the principles by which intelligent entities interact with their environments" and notes that "by its very nature this study transcends disciplinary boundaries." In particular, the distinctions among cognitive psychology (qv), AI, and cognitive science are extremely blurred in practice. This blurring is additionally exacerbated by the fact that research that clearly qualifies as cognitive science is being done in academic departments (as well as government and industrial research laboratories), the titles of which identify them with disciplines as diverse as psychology, computer science, linguistics, anthropology, philosophy, education, mathematics, engineering, physiology, and neuroscience. From an informal survey of cognitive science publications, it is shown that papers in cognitive science journals cited other papers in a very wide range of fields (Pylyshyn, 1983).

Cognitive science is also extremely closely related to AI. When the editors of the journal *Artificial Intelligence* decided to help their readership keep up with some of the literature in closely related disciplines by publishing regular "Correspondent's Reports" on work in these fields, they selected the areas of philosophy and logic, robotics, software engineering, natural language, cognitive psychology, and vision. Of these, all but perhaps software engineering and parts of robotics would be considered core areas of cognitive science research. Indeed, it has been argued (Newell, 1970, 1973; Pylyshyn, 1979, 1980) that AI and cognitive science may be nothing more than two paths to the same end: understanding the nature of intelligent action in whatever physical form it may occur. The difference between them, according to this view, consists mainly in research style: AI takes the high road of asking how instances of intelligence can be realized (ie, how they are possible) within the constraints of known computational mechanisms or how they might be attainable by the design of new mechanisms (ie, new computational architectures), whereas cognitive science places greater emphasis on the question of how instances of intelligence are in fact realized within one particular architecture, the one constituted by the human mind. Because of this difference in orientation, many experimentally oriented cognitive scientists tend to place a somewhat greater premium on empirical fit, on testing processes against psychological

data to determine not only whether the two are input–output equivalent but also whether they are strongly equivalent, that is, whether in both cases the behavior is produced by the same information-processing means. The notion of strong equivalence is central to much cognitive science, although it is not often discussed explicitly. According to one interpretation (Pylyshyn, 1984), two processes can be strongly equivalent only if they produce the same behavior using the same computational process (or algorithm) and the same symbolic representations, something that is possible only if the two systems have functionally identical computational architectures (ie, the same primitive operations, the same resource constraints, and the same symbolic notation).

Despite this difference in principle between cognitive science and AI, differences in practice are minimal. Indeed, it has even been argued (Pylyshyn, 1979) that a convergence of the two approaches may be inevitable inasmuch as both adhere to a notion of intelligence that is inherently anthropocentric or human relative, at least at the present time.

Of course, the two fields diverge considerably in their applied side. A great deal (though by no means all) of applied cognitive science deals with such problems as designing better human–machine interfaces (see HUMAN–COMPUTER INTERACTION), better pedagogical methods (see EDUCATION, AI IN) better communications techniques, better aids for the disabled (see PROSTHESES), or better methodologies for discovering such useful things as what experts know (see KNOWLEDGE ACQUISITION) or why children fail to read or do mathematics. What identifies these as cognitive science rather than simply applied psychology investigations is the fact that they take a fundamentally computational view of the nature of the cognitive process involved; they view cognitive process as consisting of the execution of symbol manipulation procedures. Although it is clear that the fruits of such pursuits are relevant to what people in AI do, the work itself frequently requires different skills and proceeds using different methodologies than are typically (though, again, not always) found in AI laboratories.

In contrast to this approach, applied AI places heavy emphasis on finding a practical match between available computational techniques and applications crying out for solution. As in all engineering or applied technology pursuits it must find suboptimal solutions to practical problems and proceed by incremental refinement. In terms of what has been referred to as the power generality trade-off (Ernst and Newell, 1969), applied AI must perforce settle for the power end of the dimension. But none of this need be true, and indeed generally is not true, of basic research in either AI or cognitive science, where the overlap is great enough that many are tempted to view AI as the more theoretical and more formal end of the spectrum of cognitive science research.

This still leaves the question: what is cognitive science? If it is simply the attempt to understand mental activity (or, as in the earlier quote from the Sloan report, to understand how intelligent entities interact with their environments), how is it different from psychology, especially from that branch of psychology that studies thinking, perception, memory, language, and so on, that is, cognitive psychology (qv)? Many people believe that cognitive science represents a new paradigm for understanding cognition, a paradigm that clearly owes much to developments in computer science. Yet a better characterization is desired, because if it is a new paradigm, it would be useful to know how it differs from other paradigms and on what assumptions it stands. It would be helpful to know this both in the abstract (ie, what are some distinguishing principles of cognitive science?) and in terms of concrete examples of how the new science is practiced and what it is seen as accomplishing, or at least trying to accomplish.

Many attempts at a statement of what cognitive science is have been made. One of the earliest was the unpublished report prepared by a committee (under the editorship of George Miller) for the Alfred P. Sloan Foundation from which the earlier quote was taken. This report characterizes what is special about cognitive science and what runs through all the diverse work that falls under its scope by defining its research objective as being "to discover the representational and computational capacities of the mind and their structural and functional representation in the brain." Although extremely general, this represents a fair statement. In addition to this early statement, the journal *Cognitive Science*, the official organ of the Cognitive Science Society, has published a number of articles that attempt to characterize the field, beginning with its initial editorial, and has included a number of papers first presented at the inaugural conference of the Cognitive Science Society in 1979 (these were published in several issues of the journal, beginning with volume 4, 1980). An attempt at a systematic argument that cognitive science is not just a marriage of convenience but a genuine field of study has been published (Pylyshyn, 1984).

This article provides examples of the kinds of problems that cognitive scientists are interested in pursuing and the approaches that they take, pointers to literature that gives further details of such examples, and a brief statement of why some people believe that cognitive science is not just a collection of research problems that in one way or another are concerned with reasoning but a genuine scientific domain or inquiry. It should be noted, however, that this review is not without personal bias. It is primarily an attempt to characterize cognitive science rather than to catalog its current research directions, which are likely to change radically in the next few years in any case. Moreover, this article presents a view of what is constitutive of cognitive science which the author believes to be correct and borne out by the classic work in the field (and which is defended at some length Pylyshyn, 1984), yet this view nonetheless flies in the face of claims being made by some people who are legitimate researchers in cognitive science. This view concerns the symbol-processing nature of cognition (what is referred to below as the representational metapostulate). Although this is not the proper forum for a debate on such issues, it is believed that the notion of symbolic representation is so very central to cognitive science and continues to be the central theoretical assumption underlying virtually all work in

the field that it is appropriate to lay it out explicitly, even in the sketchy form presented here.

SOME EXAMPLES OF COGNITIVE SCIENCE RESEARCH PROBLEMS

Language

The study of the human capacity for language is one of the oldest areas of research in cognitive science. It is also one that has changed dramatically in the past two decades, partly under the influence of formal linguistics and partly because of attempts to develop computer systems for understanding natural language (see NATURAL LANGUAGE UNDERSTANDING). It thus provides a prime example of cross-disciplinary cognitive science research, albeit one that continues to be steeped in controversy. In recent years this study has also encompassed work by philosophers, as researchers become more concerned with issues of semantics and pragmatics, with problems of meaning and discourse that had occupied philosophers long before these problems arose in AI. It also brought in the work of clinical neuroscience, which investigated the taxonomy of language deficits caused by trauma and disease.

This work has led to computational models of language performance. At the present time a number of alternative models of syntactic analysis (see PARSING) have been published and psycholinguistic research provides provocative evidence that parsing proceeds with only minimal input from the rest of the cognitive system, as is also the case, by the way, in most computational language understanding systems; a notable exception is the work of Schank and his colleagues (Schank and Abelson, 1977). Experimental studies have also shown clearly that the lexical lookup (see MORPHOLOGY) phase of grammatical analysis retrieves many homographs or homonyms of ambiguous words (Swinney, 1979; Seidenberg and Tanenhaus, 1985), thus empirically validating one computational proposal.

Vision

The idea, popular in the 1950s, that perception consists of hypothesis testing was challenged first by people working on computational vision (see EARLY VISION) (Zucker and co-workers, 1975; Marr, 1982), who argued that it would be highly wasteful to not extract as much information as possible from the initial image before bringing cognitive processes to bear. Some models (Marr, 1982) showed that a considerable amount of processing could be done in a data-driven manner (see PROCESSING, BOTTOM UP AND TOP DOWN). These ideas were then validated by psychophysical investigations as well as by findings from neuroscience [eg, concerning the existence of separate spatial frequency channels, motion detectors (see VISUAL MOTION ANALYSIS), sensitivity to maxima in intensity derivatives, etc]. Some of this cross-fertilization has been nicely illustrated (Brady, 1981). Although this work is described in some detail elsewhere in this encyclopedia, it is in fact an excellent example of cognitive science research that falls at the more computational end of the spectrum. The relevance of both the vision and the psycholinguistics work to the understanding of mind has been discussed in an insightful and provocative way (Fodor, 1983).

Expertise and Qualitative Reasoning

The study of expert systems (qv) (or, as it is sometimes called, knowledge engineering) both inspires and benefits from experimental investigations of how experts in such areas as physics, mathematics, electronics, medicine, or chess differ from their inexperienced counterparts. Findings concerning how experts structure their knowledge and how this structure differs from that of less experienced performers is an interesting chapter in recent cognitive science. These investigations also relate to studies in both psychology and AI of how people reason by building qualitative mental models (qv) (Hobbs and Moore, 1984; Gentner and Stevens, 1982; Johnson-Laird, 1983).

Models of Human Performance in Various Tasks

In this category is found computational models of human performance on arithmetic (Brown and Van Lehn, 1980), tasks involving interacting with text editors (Card and co-workers, 1983), typing and other skills (Cooper, 1983), and reasoning with spatial problems (Kosslyn, 1980). Closely related to this work is the general study of cognitive skill, its acquisition, and its nature (Anderson, 1982). Understanding cognitive skill requires distinguishing cognitive capacities from performance differences that arise from differences in knowledge or habit, a difference that parallels the distinction between functional architecture and computational procedures. The importance of this distinction to understanding the nature of cognitive processes (and of strong equivalence) has been discussed (Pylyshyn, 1984, 1981).

Learning

The area of learning was one of the most thoroughly investigated during the last half century of psychology, with very little progress on what people call learning in everyday life. The work was guided by preconceived ideas about the underlying mechanism (namely, association) rather than by a careful analysis of the types of learning and the types of mechanism capable of meeting the sufficiency condition that is central to cognitive science. More recent work on language learning by cognitive scientists has shown that the acquisition of syntax from the kind of evidence generally available to the child would not be possible without severe constraints on both the structure of the languages that can be learned and severe constraints on the mechanisms that could learn such languages. In particular, it is necessary that the range of grammars that the organism could consider as possible hypotheses must be extremely limited (Wexler and Cullicover, 1980). The same may also be true of concept acquisition (Demopoulos and Marras, 1985). More recent work on learning within AI has also provided new ways to look at some forms of learning in humans (Michalski and co-workers, 1986). (see also LEARNING, MACHINE).

CONCLUSION: SOME CHARACTERISTICS OF COGNITIVE SCIENCE

Cognitive science is not the only form in which the search for an understanding of mind is proceeding. What characterizes this particular class of approaches is an allegiance to the network of ideas that might roughly be summarized as follows (Pylyshyn, 1983).

1. The approach is formalist in spirit: that is, it attempts to formulate its theories in terms of symbolic mechanisms of the sort that have grown out of symbolic logic (qv), although the apparatus of formal logic itself very rarely appears in cognitive science theories.

2. The level of analysis, or the level at which the explanations or theories are cast, is functional and is described in terms of its information flow. What this means in particular is that this approach factors out questions such as how biological material carries out the function and how biochemical and biophysical laws operate to produce the required information-processing function. This factorization is analogous to the separation of electrical engineering considerations from programming considerations in computer science. This does not mean that questions of biological realization are treated as any less important, only that they represent a distinct and to a large extent independent area of study. According to this view, neuroscience contributes an understanding of how such computational processes as are uncovered by empirical observations of human capacities are realized by biological mechanisms.

Not everyone agrees that cognition can be studied independently of its neurophysiological instantiation. There is, for example, an approach, sometimes called connectionist (see CONNECTIONISM), which attempts to build models of cognition that are guided more closely by ideas from neuroscience than by symbol-processing ideas from current computer science. Some examples of such models have been published (Anderson and Hinton, 1981; *Cognitive Science* 9(1), 1985). Although this approach is extremely promising from the perspective of modeling the functional architecture of the mind, there is considerable doubt that it can displace rule-governed symbolic processes entirely, as some have claimed (Pylyshyn, 1984).

3. In addition to factoring apart questions of capacities from questions of biological realization, the approach is also characterized by the techniques it uses in formulating its theories and in exploring the entailments of its assumptions. The most widely used (although not universal) technique is that of computer implementation. Thus an important methodological goal of cognitive science is to specify symbol-processing mechanisms that can actually exhibit aspects of the behavior being modeled. Adherence to such a sufficiency criterion makes this approach in many respects like a design discipline rather than natural science, at least insofar as the latter typically attempts to uncover a small set of fundamental axioms or laws. Its concern with synthesis makes it one of the "sciences of the artificial," (Simon, 1969) along with AI.

4. The approach tends to emphasize a strategy some-times referred to as top-down analysis, in which a premium is given to the task of understanding how the general cognitive skill in question is possible (consonant with the constraint of mechanism) in contrast with the task of accounting for empirical particulars. This difference in style contrasts with the traditional approach in experimental psychology that emphasizes the observational fit of models. The contrast has been examined (Pylyshyn, 1979; Newell, 1970; Sloman, 1968).

5. This commitment to the informational level also places the enterprise in contrast to the phenomenological approach in which the existential notions of significance, meaningfulness, and experiential content are given a central role in the analysis and with behaviorism, which attempts to analyze behavior without appeal to internal representational states. These issues have been discussed (Pylyshyn, 1984; Cummins, 1983; Fodor, 1981; Haugeland, 1981; Dennett, 1979).

The above general characteristics of cognitive science are also shared to various degrees by other scientific disciplines. The formalist or symbolic mechanistic character 1 is deeply entrenched in contemporary linguistics (especially in generative grammar), decision theory, and even parts of anthropology (eg, Levi-Strauss). The functionalist perspective 2 is now quite general in psychology and philosophy of mind as well as in engineering, where it is referred to as the black-box approach. Both 1 and 2 are fundamental to computer science as well as to any science that concerns itself with notions such as the flow of information or the distribution of control. Such ideas have thus affected everything from engineering to management science and even political science (Deutsch, 1963). Criteria 3 and 4 are not quite so prevalent as the first two. For example, the desire to synthesize aspects of the phenomena being modeled as part of the attempt to understand it is not widespread in the social sciences outside of the areas of cognitive psychology and management science [especially the branch of the latter called industrial dynamics (Forrester, 1971)], nor is it yet very common in biology [see, however, Marr's critique (1975) of theories in neurophysiology that fail to characterize the constructive computational aspect of biological function]. Even modern linguistics, which is in many ways a prototypical cognitive science, places little emphasis on the human capacity to actually generate samples of performance. However, examples of the contrary trend are available (Marcus, 1979; Berwick and Weinberg, 1984).

The Representational Metapostulate

Although, as suggested earlier, there are a number of theoretical and methodological characteristics that pervade a variety of approaches to the understanding of intelligence and human cognition, there is one overriding theme that more than any other appears to characterize the field of cognitive science. There are a number of ways of expressing this theme, for example, as the attempt to view intelligent behavior as consisting of the processing of informa-tion or as the attempt to view intelligence as the outcome of rule-governed activity (see RULE-BASED SYSTEMS). These characterizations express the same underlying idea. Computation, information processing, and rule-governed behavior all depend on the existence of physically instantiated codes or symbols that refer to or represent things and properties extrinsic to the behaving system. In all these cases the behavior of the systems in question (be they minds, computers, or social systems) are explained not in terms of intrinsic properties of the system itself but in terms of rules and processes that operate on representations of extrinsic things. Cognition, in other words, is explained in terms of regularities holding over semantically interpreted symbolic representations, just as the behavior of a computer evaluating a mathematical function is explained in terms of its having representations of mathematical expressions (eg, numerals) and in terms of the mathematical properties of the numbers these expressions represent. This is also analogous to explaining economic activity not in terms of the categories of natural science (eg, speaking of the physicochemical properties of money and goods) but in terms of the conventional meaning or symbolic value of these objects (eg, that they are taken to represent such abstractions as legal tender). Although in both economics and cognitive science the meaning-bearing objects (or the instantiation of the symbols) are physical, it is only by referring to their symbolic or referential character that we can explain the observed regularities in the resulting behavior.

There has been some misunderstanding of the significance of the assumption that cognition is explained in terms of regularities. For example, some people have suggested that this is no different from any other science, because all scientific theories deal with representations (eg, mathematical symbols that designate certain objects or properties). Hence simulations involving such theories (eg, simulations of planetary motions) are sometimes thought to be no different in principle from simulations of cognition. But the difference in two types of simulation is in fact fundamental, because in the case of cognition, the claim is that the organism being modeled, not just the theorist, actually manipulates physical tokens of the symbols, a claim that clearly has no parallel in physics unless the physicist is being modeled!

This representation thesis, sometimes referred to in philosophy as the representational theory of mind (Fodor, 1981) and in cognitive science as the physical-symbol system hypothesis (Newell, 1980, 1982) is one of the cornerstones of the discipline of cognitive science and is one of the features that links it in a fundamental way to AI. The intellectual and philosophical underpinnings of these two fields are now so closely linked that the distinction between them remains mostly at the pragmatic level, resting on such things as how big a role actual computer programs play and how technical are the immediate applications of the research. Some people expect that as cognitive scientists become better trained in computer science, and as AI begins to tackle the harder problem of what makes general intelligence possible, the distinction between the fields will fade. Similarly, the philosophy of mind is being influenced more and more by developments in AI and might be expected to play a more central role in clarifying the difficult conceptual issues that face both empirical and theoretical studies of intelligence.

BIBLIOGRAPHY

J. R. Anderson, "Acquisition of Cognitive Skill," *Psychol. Rev.* **89**, 369–406 (1982).

J. A. Anderson and G. E. Hinton, "Models of Information Processing in the Brain," in G. E. Hinton and J. A. Anderson, eds., *Parallel Models of Associative Memory*, Lawrence Erlbaum, Hillsdale, N.J., 1981, pp. 9–48.

R. C. Berwick and A. S. Weinberg, *The Grammatical Basis of Linguistic Performance: Language Use and Acquisition*, MIT Press, Cambridge, Mass., 1984.

M. Brady, *Artif. Intell.* (Special vol.) **17**(1–3), (Aug. 1981).

J. S. Brown and K. Van Lehn, "Repair Theory: A Generative Theory of Bugs in Procedural Skills," *Cogn. Sci.* **4**, 379–426 (1980).

S. K. Card, T. P. Moran, and A. Newell, *The Psychology of Human-Computer Interactions*, Lawrence Erlbaum, Hillsdale, N.J., 1983.

W. E. Cooper, *Cognitive Aspects of Skilled Typewriting*, Springer-Verlag, New York, 1983.

R. Cummins, *The Nature of Psychological Explanation*, MIT Press, Bradford Books, Cambridge, Mass., 1983.

W. Demopoulos and A. Marras, *Language, Learning and Concept Acquisition: Foundational Issues*, Ablex, Norwood, N.J., 1985.

D. Dennett, *Brainstorms*, MIT Press, Bradford Books, Cambridge, Mass., 1979.

K. Deutsch, "The Nerves of Government," *Gen. Syst. Yearbk.* **21**, 125–176 (1963).

G. W. Ernst and A. Newell, *GPS: A Case Study in Generality and Problem Solving*, Academic Press, New York, 1969.

J. Fodor, *Representations*, MIT Press, a Bradford Book, Cambridge, Mass., 1981.

J. Fodor, *The Modularity of Mind: An Essay on Faculty Psychology*, MIT Press, a Bradford Book, Cambridge, Mass., 1983.

J. W. Forrester, *World Dynamics*, Wright-Allen, Cambridge, Mass., 1971.

D. Gentner and A. L. Stevens, *Mental Models*, Lawrence Erlbaum, Hillsdale, N.J., 1982.

J. Haugeland, *Mind Design*, MIT Press, Bradford Books, Cambridge, Mass., 1981.

J. R. Hobbs and R. C. Moore, *Formal Theories of the Commonsense World*, Ablex, Norwood, N.J., 1984.

P. N. Johnson-Laird, *Mental Models*, Harvard University Press, Cambridge, Mass., 1983.

S. M. Kosslyn, *Image and Mind*, Harvard University Press, Cambridge, Mass., 1980.

M. Marcus, *A Theory of Syntactic Recognition for Natural Language*, MIT Press, Cambridge, Mass., 1979.

D. Marr, "Approaches to Biological Information Processing," *Science* **190**, 875–876 (1975).

D. Marr, *Vision*, W. H. Freeman, San Francisco, 1982.

R. S. Michalski, J. G. Carbonel, and T. M. Mitchell, *Machine Learning: An Artificial Intelligence Approach*, Vol. 2, Tioga Press, Palo Alto, Calif., 1986.

A. Newell, "Remarks on the Relationship between Artificial Intelligence and Cognitive Psychology," in R. Banerji and M. D. Mesarovic, eds., *Theoretical Approaches to Non-Numerical Problem Solving*, Springer-Verlag, New York, 1970.

A. Newell, "Artificial Intelligence and the Concept of Mind," in R. C. Schank and K. Colby, eds., *Computer Models of Thought and Language*, W. H. Freeman, San Francisco, 1973.

A. Newell, "Physical Symbol Systems," *Cogn. Sci.* **4**, 135–183 (1980).

A. Newell, "The Knowledge Level," *Artif. Intell.* **18**, 87–127 (1982).

Z. Pylyshyn, "Validating Computational Models: A Critique of Anderson's Indeterminacy of Representation Claim," *Psychol. Rev.* **86**(4), 383–394 (1979).

Z. Pylyshyn, "Complexity and the Study of Human and Machine Intelligence," in J. Haugeland, ed., *Mind Design*, MIT Press, Cambridge, Mass., 1980.

Z. Pylyshyn, "The Imagery Debate: Analogue Media versus Tacit Knowledge," *Psychol. Rev.* **88**, 16–45 (1981).

Z. Pylyshyn, "Information Science: Its Roots and Relations as Viewed from the Perspective of Cognitive Science," in F. Machlup and U. Mansfield, eds., *The Study of Information: Interdisciplinary Messages*, Wiley, New York, 1983, pp. 63–80.

Z. Pylyshyn, *Computation and Cognition: Toward a Foundation for Cognitive Science*, MIT Press, Cambridge, Mass., 1984.

R. C. Schank and R. P. Abelson, *Scripts, Plans, Goals and Understanding*, Lawrence Erlbaum, Hillsdale, N.J., 1977.

M. S. Seidenberg and M. K. Tanenhaus, "Modularity and Lexical Access," in I. Gopnik and Myrna Gopnik, eds., *From Models to Modules: Studies in Cognitive Science*, Ablex, Norwood, N.J., 1985.

H. A. Simon, *The Sciences of the Artificial*, MIT Press, Cambridge, Mass., 1969.

A. Sloman, *The Computer Revolution in Philosophy: Philosophy, Science, and the Models of Mind*, Humanities Press, New York, 1968.

D. Swinney, "Lexical Access during Sentence Comprehension: (Re)consideration of Context Effects," *J. Verb. Learn. Berb. Behav.* **18**, 645–660 (1979).

K. Wexler and P. Cullicover, *Formal Principles of Language Acquisition*, MIT Press, Cambridge, Mass., 1980.

S. Zucker, A Rosenfeld, and L. Davis, "General Purpose Models: Expectations about the Unexpected," in *Proceedings of the Fourth IJCAI*, Tbilisi, USSR, Morgan-Kaufmann, San Mateo, Calif., 1975.

Z. W. PYLYSHYN
University of Western Ontario

COGNITIVE SIMULATION. See COGNITIVE MODELING.

COLOR VISION

Color enriches one's everyday visual experience. In comparison with a monochrome (black-and-white) image, a color picture seems to be alive with detail because of all the additional information in the image. In computer vision, researchers have attempted to harness this additional information. The simplest method for using color is by associating colors with objects, for example "trees are green" and "the sky is blue." If specific object colors are not known, an image can still be chopped into meaningful pieces by finding regions of uniform color. Analyzing color in terms of physical properties of objects and the physics underlying image formation has yielded significant advantages in understanding images. Research has also been conducted into modeling the processing of color information in the human visual system; the goal is to have computers that can mimic the color perception abilities that humans have.

COLOR AND COLOR IMAGING

Color arises from the spectral properties of light. Figure 1 shows the spectrum of electromagnetic energy. Wavelengths of energy are customarily denoted by λ, and the unit of measure is the nanometer (nm). Visible light lies within the range of approximately 380–760 nm, running the gamut from violet and blue at the low end of the visible spectrum, through green, yellow, and orange, to red at the high end.

The wavelengths just higher than the visible spectrum make up the near-infrared (near-IR) portion of the spectrum, which is also frequently used in computer vision. Visible light is normally a mixture of energy at many wavelengths and is characterized by the spectral power distribution (SPD), which tells how much energy is present at each wavelength. An SPD is usually denoted by $S(\lambda)$ (CIE, 1970). At each pixel (point) in an image the SPD of the incident light determines the pixel value.

Monochrome imaging is simpler than color imaging. An imaging sensor is sensitive to the different wavelengths of light to varying degrees, as expressed by the spectral responsivity $s(\lambda)$ of the sensor (Grum and Becherer, 1979). Typical spectral responsivities of the two principal types of sensors, vidicon tubes and silicon CCD chips, are shown in Figure 2. The output pixel value p at any point in the image is defined, for a calibrated camera, by

$$p = p_0 \int S(\lambda)s(\lambda)\, d\lambda$$

where p_0 is a scaling factor. Integration is performed over that portion of the spectrum for which $s(\lambda)$ is nonzero. For

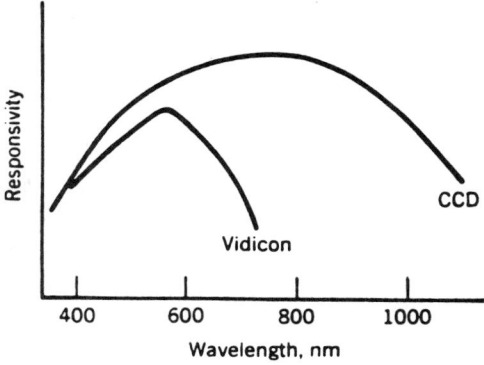

Figure 2. Spectral responsivities of vidicon tubes and CCD chips (Hamamatsu, 1983a, 1983b).

a vidicon, $s(\lambda)$ is approximately equal to $V(\lambda)$, the spectral luminous efficiency of the human eye, so a monochrome image from a vidicon is similar to the brightness seen by a person. However, CCD sensors are much more sensitive in the near-IR region of the spectrum; for this reason, CCD cameras are frequently fitted with IR cutoff filters or filters to match the responsivity to $V(\lambda)$.

Color imaging is more complex, requiring the assignment of a color to each SPD instead of a single number. However, the set of all perceivable colors, as determined by color-matching experiments, is only a three-dimensional space. Humans cannot distinguish all different SPDs from each other but only those SPDs that correspond to different colors in color space. Since this is a many-to-one correspondence, there can be many SPDs that have the same color; such SPDs are said to be metameric (Kuehni, 1983).

The axes of color space, called primary colors, can be chosen arbitrarily. A convenient set, universally used for color measurement, is the **X-Y-Z** set of colors adopted by the CIE (International Commission on Illumination). Each distinct point in **X-Y-Z** space corresponds to a unique color perception. A psychophysical color **C** is defined by

$$\mathbf{C} = \begin{bmatrix} \mathbf{X} \\ \mathbf{Y} \\ \mathbf{Z} \end{bmatrix} = \begin{bmatrix} \int s(\lambda)\bar{x}(\lambda)\, d(\lambda) \\ \int s(\lambda)\bar{y}(\lambda)\, d(\lambda) \\ \int s(\lambda)\bar{z}(\lambda)\, d(\lambda) \end{bmatrix}$$

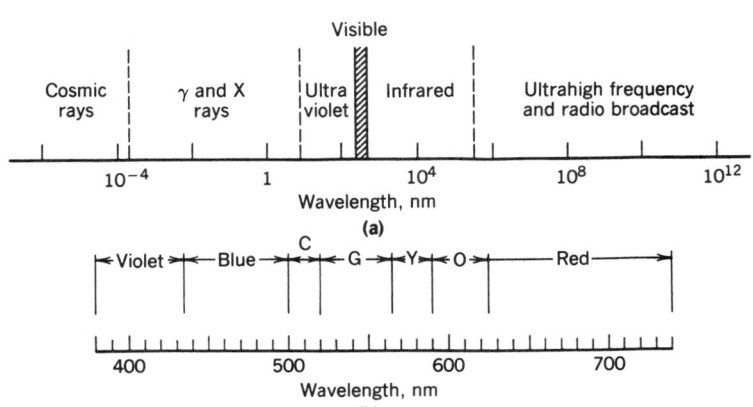

Figure 1. (a) Spectrum of electromagnetic radiation (Judd and Wyszecki, 1975); (b) magnification of visible portion of spectrum (Williamson and Cummins, 1983): C = cyan, G = green, Y = yellow, and O = orange.

The functions $\bar{x}(\lambda)$, $\bar{y}(\lambda)$, and $\bar{z}(\lambda)$ are CIE tristimulus values that define the primaries **X**, **Y**, and **Z** (Wyszecki and Stiles, 1982). Since $\bar{y}(\lambda) = V(\lambda)$, **Y** corresponds to luminance (brightness of color as seen by the human eye); the remaining coordinates **X** and **Z** determine chromaticity (the aspects of color independent of brightness).

Color imaging for computer vision follows the paradigm of color television, in which colors are measured using color filters. For any filter, the output pixel value p is determined by

$$p = p_0 \int S(\lambda)\tau(\lambda)s(\lambda)\, d\lambda$$

where $\tau(\lambda)$, the transmittance of the filter, is the fraction of light the filter allows to pass through at each wavelength. To yield color values that uniquely correspond to color perceptions, three filters that span the **X-Y-Z** space must be used. The filters used for color television are red, green, and blue to maximize the gamut of measurable color values. For a particular sensor $s(\lambda)$, the filter transmittances $\tau_r(\lambda)$, $\tau_g(\lambda)$, and $\tau_b(\lambda)$ of the red, green, and blue filters determine tristimulus values $\bar{r}(\lambda) = \tau_r(\lambda)s(\lambda)$, $\bar{g}(\lambda) = \tau_g(\lambda)s(\lambda)$, and $\bar{b}(\lambda) = \tau_b(\lambda)s(\lambda)$. For standard color television, these functions should obey (Wentworth, 1955)

$$\begin{bmatrix} \bar{r}(\lambda) \\ \bar{g}(\lambda) \\ \bar{b}(\lambda) \end{bmatrix} = \begin{bmatrix} 0.587 & -0.164 & -0.089 \\ -0.301 & 0.611 & -0.0087 \\ 0.0178 & -0.0362 & 0.274 \end{bmatrix} \begin{bmatrix} \bar{x}(\lambda) \\ \bar{y}(\lambda) \\ \bar{z}(\lambda) \end{bmatrix}$$

Color pixel values **P** are then determined by

$$\mathbf{P} = \begin{bmatrix} \mathbf{R} \\ \mathbf{G} \\ \mathbf{B} \end{bmatrix} = \begin{bmatrix} r_0 \int S(\lambda)\bar{r}(\lambda)\, d\lambda \\ g_0 \int S(\lambda)\bar{g}(\lambda)\, d\lambda \\ b_0 \int S(\lambda)\bar{b}(\lambda)\, d\lambda \end{bmatrix}$$

where r_0, g_0, and b_0 are scaling factors. "White" in a color TV image corresponds to CIE Standard Illuminant **C** (Hunt, 1967). A broadcast color camera contains three separate sensors, each with a color filter, and beam-splitting optics to direct the image simultaneously to all three sensors; for research in computer vision, a single monochrome camera is normally used with a filter wheel to rotate each filter in turn into position (Fig. 3). Three-color CCD sensor chips are also available, offering a cheaper and more compact method of obtaining color images. Unfortunately, the subdivision of the chip into areas with different filters means that the spatial resolution of resulting images is not as good as that obtained from monochrome cameras. In computer vision, most imaging systems do not behave in the ideal way described above. This is because several imaging factors are not controlled or accounted for; these include sensor spectral responsivity, gain within each color band, and nonlinear response to intensity (LeClerc, 1986; Klinker, 1988; Novak and co-workers, 1990). This results in a lack of correspondence between color computer images and National Television System Committee (NTSC) color TV standards. The usual color filters for computer vision are Kodak Wratten filters #25 (**R**), #58 (**G**), and #47b (**B**) (Levine, 1980; Ito, 1975). Infrared filters [$\tau(\lambda)$ highest in near IR] are also used in remote sensing. In this entry, *color* refers to colors measured in a computer vision system using these or similar filters.

COLOR SPACES AND TRANSFORMATIONS

In computer vision, color pixel values usually contain **R**, **G**, and **B** values each measured in 8 bits. The set of image colors is thus a cube called the color space (Fig. 4). Inten-

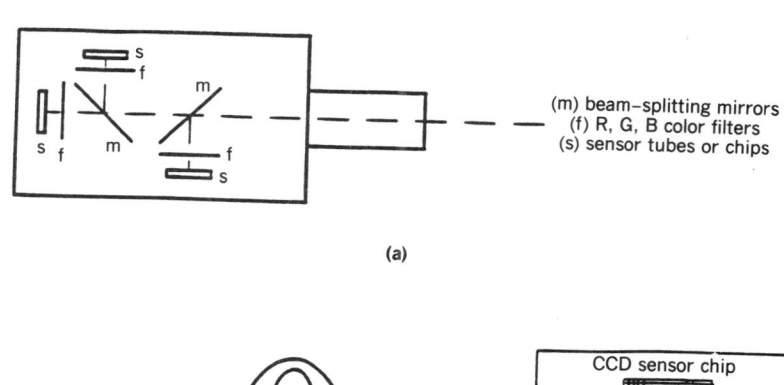

(m) beam–splitting mirrors
(f) R, G, B color filters
(s) sensor tubes or chips

(a)

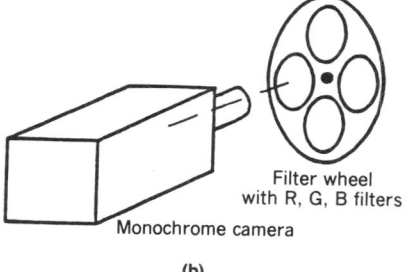

Filter wheel with R, G, B filters

Monochrome camera

(b)

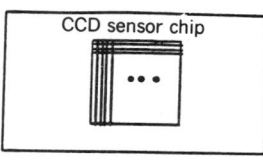

CCD sensor chip

Magnification of sensor area

(c)

Figure 3. Color camera arrangements. (*a*) Typical broadcast color television camera; (*b*) typical color computer vision camera; (*c*) single-chip color CCD sensor chip with **R**, **G**, or **B** filter on each pixel.

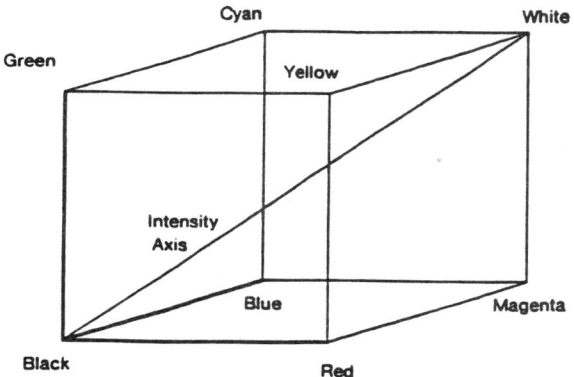

Figure 4. The **R-G-B** color space.

sity, measured by $\mathbf{I} = (\mathbf{R} + \mathbf{G} + \mathbf{B})/3$, is the main diagonal of this cube from black $(0, 0, 0)$ to white (max, max, max). Researchers in computer vision have frequently used **R-G-B** coordinates, but have also explored transformations to other coordinate systems that have useful properties. One such system is the CIE **X-Y-Z** system, a linear transform of **R-G-B** as defined above. The **X-Y-Z** system was proposed because of its use as an international standard. However, it is psychophysical rather than psychological and hence does not capture the subjective attributes of color perception in the way that humans talk about color. These are incorporated into systems such as the Munsell color order system (Judd and Wyszecki, 1975). The Munsell system defines three color attributes (value, hue, and chroma) that correspond roughly to the more familiar brightness, hue (color name, eg, blue, purple), and saturation (relative amount of pure hue as opposed to gray). In computer vision, normalized colors **r-g-b** are first defined by $\mathbf{r} = \mathbf{R}/\mathbf{I}$, $\mathbf{g} = \mathbf{G}/\mathbf{I}$, and $\mathbf{b} = \mathbf{B}/\mathbf{I}$; saturation **S** and hue **H** are then defined (Tenenbaum and co-workers, 1974) by

$$\mathbf{S} = 1 - 3 \min(\mathbf{r,g,b})$$

$$\mathbf{x} = \arccos \frac{2\mathbf{r} - \mathbf{g} - \mathbf{b}}{6^{1/2}[(\mathbf{r} - 1/3)^2 + (\mathbf{g} - 1/3)^2 + (\mathbf{b} - 1/3)^2]^{1/2}}$$

if $\mathbf{b} \le \mathbf{g}$, then $\mathbf{H} = \mathbf{x}$;   otherwise $\mathbf{H} = 2\pi - \mathbf{x}$

[See Kender (1977) for a fast algorithm to compute **H**.] In color space, **I** corresponds to distance along the intensity axis; on a plane of constant intensity, **S** and **H** form a polar coordinate system with **S** measuring distance from the center (gray) point and **H** measuring angle from pure red (Fig. 5). It is easily seen that the **H-S-I** system is analogous to the Munsell system for describing human color perceptions, but numerically the two are quite distinct.

Even the Munsell system, however, has drawbacks. Most work with color in computer vision has been based on the notion of color differences expressed as Euclidean distance in a color space, but Euclidean distance in Munsell coordinates does not correspond well to subjective perceived color difference magnitudes. Spaces with that property have been proposed, however, and are generically called uniform color spaces. The earliest, called **U-V-W**, has occasionally been proposed for computer vision; it has been replaced in the color science community by a newer system called CIELUV (Grum and Bartleson, 1980). The CIELUV system defines **L***, **u***, and **v*** for each color as follows (quantities denoted by subscript n refer to the incident illumination color):

$$\mathbf{L}^* = 116(\mathbf{Y}/\mathbf{Y}_n)^{1/3} - 16$$
$$\mathbf{u}^* = 13\mathbf{L}^*(\mathbf{u} - \mathbf{u}_n)$$
$$\mathbf{v}^* = 13\mathbf{L}^*(\mathbf{v} - \mathbf{v}_n)$$

where

$$\mathbf{u} = 4\mathbf{X}/(\mathbf{X} + 15\mathbf{Y} + 3\mathbf{Z})$$
$$\mathbf{v} = 9\mathbf{Y}/(\mathbf{X} + 15\mathbf{Y} + 3\mathbf{Z})$$

Color differences $\Delta\mathbf{E}$ are then expressed by

$$\Delta\mathbf{E} = \sqrt{(\Delta\mathbf{L}^*)^2 + (\Delta\mathbf{u}^*)^2 + (\Delta\mathbf{v}^*)^2}$$

However, it seems unlikely that even the use of CIELUV coordinates will solve the fundamental problems of color image segmentation and analysis. Other color spaces frequently used for computer vision include the NTSC television broadcasting encoding system **Y-I-Q** defined (De-Marsh, 1971; Levine, 1980) by

$$\begin{bmatrix} \mathbf{Y} \\ \mathbf{I} \\ \mathbf{Q} \end{bmatrix} = \begin{bmatrix} 0.299 & 0.587 & 0.114 \\ 0.596 & -0.274 & -0.322 \\ 0.211 & -0.523 & 0.312 \end{bmatrix} \begin{bmatrix} \mathbf{R} \\ \mathbf{G} \\ \mathbf{B} \end{bmatrix}$$

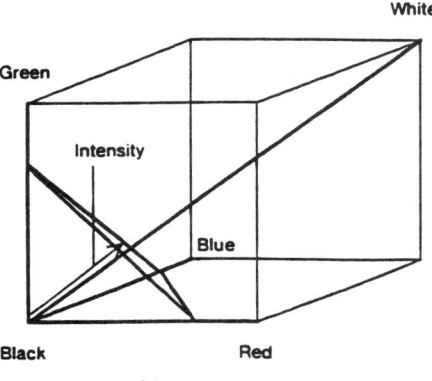

(a)

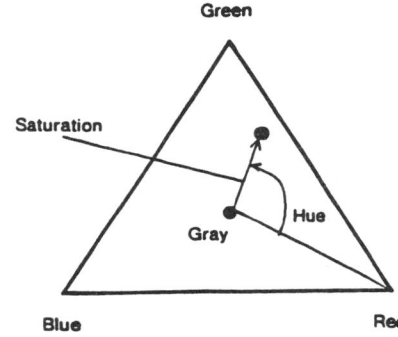

(b)

Figure 5. Hue, saturation, and intensity. (*a*) Color space; (*b*) a plane of constant intensity.

Y is the same as the CIE **Y** coordinate; **I** and **Q** measure chromaticity using parameters optimized for the acuity of the human eye. Other researchers have used opponent colors (black/white, blue/yellow, and red/green) or even normalized colors **r-g-b** themselves.

Kender has pointed out some serious problems in using certain features (Kender, 1977). All features defined by a division (including **H-S-I, r-g-b, U-V-W,** etc) contain singularities and tend to be unevenly distributed in an image because of the small integer nature of the values used in their computation. This creates problems for algorithms based on histograms, clustering, and edges. Kender recommends a small number of bits per output pixel value for such features, randomizing (adding a random real number from 0 to 1 to each pixel color coordinate), and avoiding these features entirely near their singularities (usually when **I** is low). It is better to use linear transformations of **R-G-B** instead, such as **Y-I-Q**; such linear transformations should themselves be scaled so the maximum value in each row of the transformation matrix is 1.0. Ohta derived statistics for over 100 image regions (using Ohlander's algorithm, described below) and statistically analyzed the color distributions (Ohta, Kanade, and Saki, 1980). He found that the feature that most frequently captured the greatest information was intensity, **I**. Ohta proposed the use of three features I1-I2-I3 that represent a simple linear transformation from **R-G-B** and capture the color information he observed very well: $I1 = (R + G + B)/3$; $I2 = R - B$; $I3 = (2G - R - B)/2$. Ohta found these features to perform at least as well as any other set of features (**X-Y-Z, R-G-B, Y-I-Q, U-V-W, I-r-g, H-S-I**) in his system. However, as he noted, "usefulness of a color feature is greatly influenced by the structure of the color scenes to be [analyzed]."

COLOR AS A STATISTICAL QUANTITY

Much research in color computer vision has been in the area of image segmentation, breaking an image into pieces that have uniform properties. In this work color is usually regarded as a random variable to be analyzed statistically but without regard for the specific physical processes that give rise to color and color variation. The earli-

est and most obvious technique is called spectral signature analysis, in which prior knowledge about characteristic object colors is used to classify pixels. Spectral signature analysis has been used extensively in remote sensing (satellite and aerial photograph interpretation) and biomedical image analysis; it has been applied occasionally in robotics research. For example, Noguchi classifies pixels in biomedical images of cells (Noguchi and co-workers, 1978). He measures the typical colors of background, cytoplasm, and nucleus in advance; then, for each image, each pixel is individually classified into one of these categories. Whichever category has a characteristic color closest to that pixel's color is assigned as the pixel label. The distance metric used in their work is Euclidean distance in **R-G-B** space, that is, $\Delta P = \sqrt{\Delta R^2 + \Delta G^2 + \Delta B^2}$. Frequently, nonstandard color filters or features are used that optimize discriminability for the specific task at hand (Akita and Kuga, 1979; Engvall and co-workers, 1981).

If specific object colors are not known in advance, clustering can be used instead. Haralick and many others have applied this standard pattern recognition technique to color image segmentation (qv) (Haralick and Kelly, 1969). A histogram is first created by the color values at all pixels; it tells, for each point in color space, how many pixels exhibit that color (Fig. 6). Typically, the colors tend to form clusters in the histogram, one for each object in the image. By manual or automatic analysis of the histogram, the shape of each cluster is found. Then each pixel in the image is assigned to the cluster that is closest to the pixel color in color space. Clustering differs from spectral signature analysis in that the clusters are found by analysis of the specific image under consideration rather than by prior consideration of the expected data. In some clustering systems, clusters are restricted to be rectangular boxes or ellipsoids (Ali and co-workers, 1979; Connah and Fishbourne, 1981; Sarabi and Aggarwal, 1981). Features that describe texture have been used along with color to create a "feature space" with additional dimensions (Coleman and Andrews, 1979). All clustering techniques suffer from the problem that adjacent clusters frequently overlap in color space, causing incorrect pixel labeling. In conjunction with clustering, a technique called relaxation is sometimes used to improve pixel labeling. In relaxation,

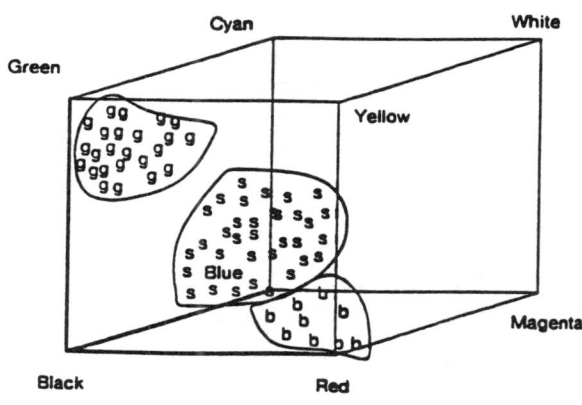

Figure 6. Clustering in color space. (*a*) Input image; (*b*) histogram in color space, wherein g, b, and s indicate pixels in grass, building, and sky; clusters are outlined.

pixel labels are assigned by an iterative method. Each pixel has a probability of belonging to each cluster, and in each iteration step those probabilities are modified. A probability is increased or decreased according to a weighted combination of two factors: the color resemblance of the pixel to the cluster center and the probabilities that the neighboring pixels belong to that same cluster (Rosenfeld, 1978; Nagin and co-workers, 1982).

Another segmentation technique is region splitting, in which the image is broken into successively smaller pieces until each piece has a uniform color (and presumably represents a single object or surface). Ohlander used color to perform this splitting operation (Ohlander and co-workers, 1978). His method begins by computing a variety of color features for each pixel (**H, S, I, Y, I,** and **Q**) before the actual segmentation begins. Then the splitting step is applied (the initial region is the entire image). In the splitting step a histogram is created for each color feature (**RGBHSIYIQ**) within the region. Each histogram is examined independently, and the feature whose histogram exhibits the most prominent peak is selected for use (Fig. 7). The image is then thresholded according to the boundaries of the peak to isolate the pixels that contribute to the selected peak. This splits the original region into smaller regions. The splitting step is then recursively applied to each region, stopping when a region has all flat histograms (ie, it has uniform color). Some of the general problems associated with histogram analysis in the algorithm are discussed in Shafer and Kanade (1982).

Region growing is a complementary segmentation technique in which small regions (initially, individual pixels) are merged together to form larger and larger regions according to color similarity. This method merges the pair of adjacent regions with the greatest similarity of colors, according to a statistical measure. It may take into account both the average color and color variance within each region. Merging continues until no two adjacent regions are sufficiently similar. Variations include simple color difference measures (Yachida and Tsuji, 1971; Bajcsy, 1973; Levine and Shaheen, 1979), the use of color features other than **R-G-B** (Yachida and Tsuji, 1971; Sloan, 1977; Nagao and co-workers, 1979), and the use of semantic information about object position and relations (Yakimovsky and Feldman, 1973; Tenenbaum and co-workers, 1974). Nagao determined the acceptable color difference limits by finding a valley in local color difference histograms (Nagao and co-workers, 1979).

Edge detection techniques have been adapted for color vision by extending algorithms originally designed for black-and-white (intensity) images to work on **R-G-B** images (Nevatia, 1977). Researchers in this area have observed that most color features detected by these color edge detectors are also detected by the black-and-white edge detectors. The color detectors offer a limited advantage, however, in that color features are more likely to be significant, since intensities often fluctuate because of lighting variations.

In summary, every major image segmentation method

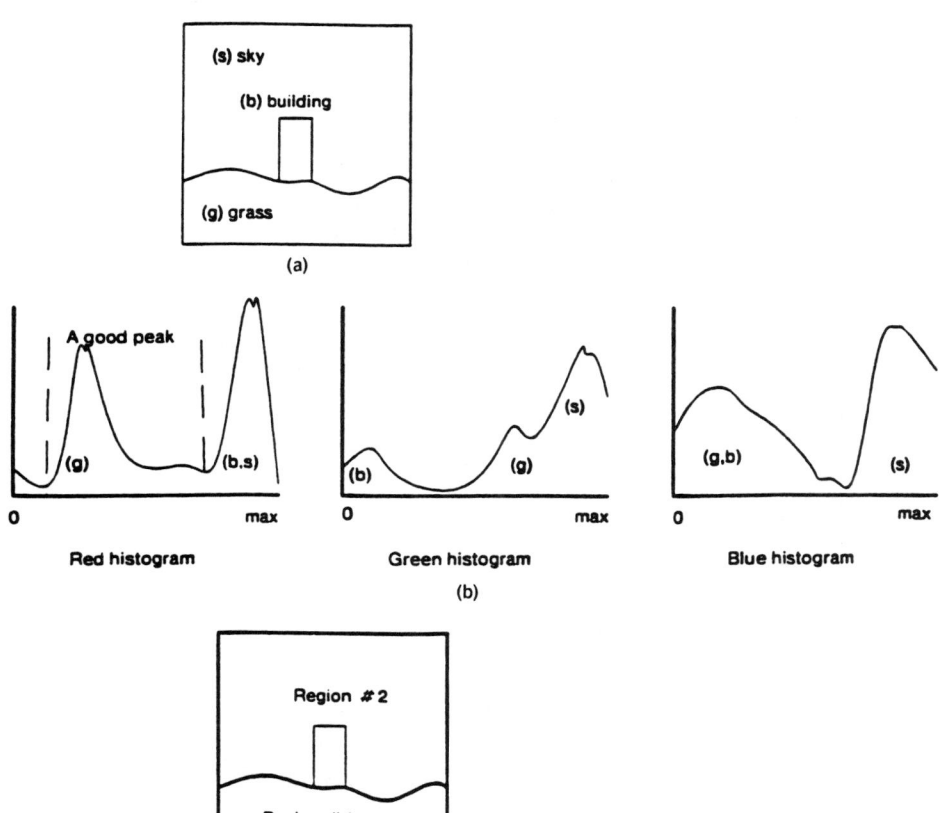

Figure 7. Region splitting by histogram analysis. (*a*) Input image; (*b*) red, green, and blue histograms, wherein g, b, and s indicate pixels of grass, building, and sky; (*c*) after thresholding. Region outlines are indicated by thick lines. Each region will now be split into smaller regions.

has been adapted for color, and some, like relaxation segmentation and region splitting, are almost always performed on color images. These color techniques have been used in robotics applications such as autonomous navigation (Crisman and Thorpe, 1988; Turk and co-workers, 1988).

COLOR AS A PHYSICAL QUANTITY

Most of the early work in color computer vision viewed color as a random variable to be used for image segmentation. Recently many researchers have tried using knowledge about how color is created to analyze a color picture and compute some important three-dimensional facts about the objects being viewed. The most basic avenue of research is this area has used heuristic rules, usually embedded in production systems, to label regions as shadows, highlights, and so on, using knowledge about color behavior. Nagao uses **IR/R**, the ratio of infrared to red at each pixel, to detect vegetation in aerial photographs (Nagao and co-workers, 1979). This is useful since chlorophyll typically has a high IR reflectance but low red reflectance. He also detects shadows by comparing **I** to a threshold; if the intensity is low, the region is assumed to be a shadow. Several others have detected shadows by adding the requirement that there be an adjacent region (presumably an illuminated part of the same surface) with higher intensity but similar chromaticity (hue and saturation) (Ali and co-workers, 1979; Schachter and co-workers, 1975). Ohlander (1975) similarly labeled a region as a highlight if there is an adjacent region with lower intensity and similar chromaticity. Sloan (1977), analyzing outdoor scenes, noted that distant objects appear somewhat bluish. All these heuristics are qualitative in nature and based on some simplifying assumptions about the images being viewed.

Quantitative analysis of color uses the equation which says that the SPD of light $S(\lambda)$ that is reflected by a point in the scene depends on the light illuminating the scene, $I(\lambda)$, and the reflectance of the surface at that point, $\rho(\lambda)$:

$$S(\lambda) = I(\lambda)\rho(\lambda)$$

The reflectance function $\rho(\lambda)$ may vary widely for different points on the same object because of changes in imaging geometry. In trying to analyze pictures, researchers have looked for models of ρ that contain structure, rather than try to treat it as an arbitrary function. One such model of object reflectance is based on the physical properties of reflection when light strikes an inhomogeneous surface. Inhomogeneous surfaces (including plastics, paints, ceramics, and paper) consist of a medium with particles of colorant suspended in it (Fig. 8). When light hits such a surface there is a change in index of refraction between the air and the medium, so some light is reflected at the interface. This reflection occurs in the "perfect specular direction," where angle of incidence equals angle of reflection, and forms the highlights seen on shiny materials. The light that penetrates through the interface is scattered and selectively absorbed by the colorant. The light that is re-emitted produces body reflection.

The dichromatic reflection model, proposed by Shafer, states that the reflectance ρ of an object may be divided into two components: an interface or highlight component ρ_i and a body or diffuse component ρ_b (Shafer, 1985). The theory further states that these two components may be further broken down into a geometric term m and a color term c:

$$\rho(\lambda) = \rho_i(\lambda) + \rho_b(\lambda) = m_i c_i(\lambda) + m_b c_b(\lambda)$$

The m terms are scale factors that depend on the viewing geometry. According to Fresnel's laws there is some interdependence between angle of reflection and wavelength; however, interface reflection is nearly constant over the visible portion of the spectrum, so this interdependence is usually ignored. The color term for interface reflection c_i is usually said to be constant over the spectrum, so that highlights are assumed to have the same color as the illumination.

Highlight color and object colors can be characterized by vectors in color space, and each pixel on a surface has a color that is a linear combination of these. The colors on a single surface thus form a parallelogram in color space and, by analyzing a histogram of such colors, the parallelogram can be found (Fig. 9). Then, by noting each pix-

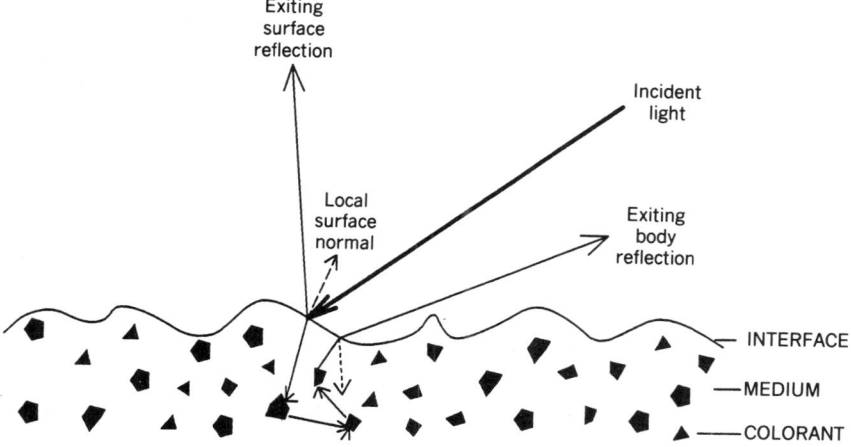

Figure 8. Reflection of light from an inhomogeneous material.

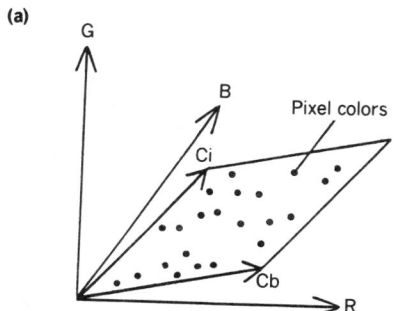

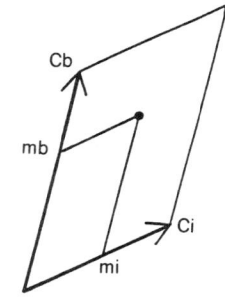

Figure 9. (*a*) Pixel values on a surface lie on a parallelogram in color space; (*b*) position within parallelogram determines reflection magnitudes.

el's color location within this parallelogram, the relative amounts of highlight and object color can be determined at that pixel. This method can then be used to determine the color of the illumination (Klinker and co-workers, 1988a), and to segment an image into regions of uniform color without being fooled by highlights (Klinker and co-workers, 1988b). Other methods of exploiting the dichromatic reflection model have included segmenting according to the normals of the planes defined by the two vectors (Brill, 1989), working in a two-dimensional chromaticity space (Lee, 1986), and finding the vector along which two planes intersect to determine illumination color (Klinker and co-workers, 1987; Tominaga and Wandell, 1989).

Healey has developed a unichromatic reflection model that applies to homogeneous materials such as metals (Healey, 1988). In metals there is no body reflection, and the interface reflection is colored by the surface material. Assuming that there is at least one inhomogeneous surface with highlights in the image, the color of the illumination may be found from the highlight. Metals can be distinguished from inhomogeneous materials, and the object colors of both types of materials can be found (Healey, 1989).

Rubin has presented a method for using color to distinguish material changes from artifacts such as shadows and highlights (Rubin and Richards, 1982). The spectral power distributions of nearby pixels may have a crossover point (wavelength at which the sign of the difference changes) only if the material being viewed at the two pixels is different. By looking for sign changes in the color components of adjacent pixels, material boundaries can be found. Gershon addressed the problem of situations where the ambient illumination color is significantly different from the direct illumination (Gershon, 1987), causing a violation of the crossover assumption.

Funt and Ho proposed a method for determining color based upon a model of lenses in the imaging system (Funt and Ho, 1988). The index of refraction for glass varies as a function of wavelength; this causes entering light to be spread out into its component wavelengths upon exiting, as seen with a prism. When this property is observed in lenses, it is known as chromatic aberration. A single image taken with a black-and-white camera will have some degree of blurring at the edges due to the chromatic aberration. This blurring can be examined to determine the SPD of the incoming illumination, effectively calculating color from a black-and-white image.

Researchers have recently begun to develop physical models further to analyze images containing inter- or mutual reflection. The usual model of illumination for color vision is that of a single point source or ambient illumination that is the same everywhere. There is no interaction between objects in the scene and illumination is usually assumed to be uniform or to vary slowly. However, objects that reflect light into the camera may equally reflect light onto each other, causing a local change in illumination that can cause unexpected color changes in the objects being viewed. New theories are being developed to deal with this difficult problem (Bajcsy and co-workers, 1989; Shafer and co-workers, 1990).

COLOR AS A PERCEPTUAL QUANTITY

Another view of color is to interpret it as a perceptual variable in human vision. Much of this work involves the explicit modeling of color processing within the human visual system in order to adapt it to machine vision. However, the exact mechanisms of human color perception remain unknown, so machine vision researchers concentrate on achieving the same effects. The actual methods used may be biologically plausible or may be suitable for machine computation only.

Researchers are currently studying the phenomenon of color constancy that allows humans to see object colors the same under widely varying illumination. In machine vision the problem is usually to take a picture of some scene under unknown illumination and to calculate automatically some transform that will determine what every object in the scene would look like under standard or known illumination. The solution may involve explicitly calculating the SPD of the illumination and/or the objects in the scene, which gives rise to physics-based methods based on principles similar to the methods described above.

It is not, in principle, possible to perform color constancy for all scenes. A picture consisting of an even orange color may equally well arise from an orange wall lit by white light or from a white wall lit by orange light. In order to perform color constancy, researchers need a reference property or assumption about scene characteristics. The methods of calculation used by researchers may be classified according to the assumptions made and the representation used to describe the SPDs.

One type of reference property is to assume that some kind of statistic holds true for the image. It may be assumed that the different colored objects in the scene are distributed in such a way that the average reflectance value is some known quantity. This quantity may be chosen arbitrarily [typically, that the average color of the scene is gray (D'Zmura and Lennie, 1986)] or may be based on an averaging of color data collected from a variety of materials that are considered likely to be in the scene (Gershon, 1987). The desired average is compared with the observed average of all areas in the picture; then the color bands are scaled to create a new picture with the desired property. Other researchers have looked for reference properties in an area of the scene rather than the whole scene. An object of known reflectance (typically a white test object) may be intentionally put in the scene, or it may be assumed that a white object is likely to occur in the scene naturally. A slight variation is to assume that the brightest object scene in each color band should average out to white (Land, 1977). The appearance of the object or objects yields scale factors to correct for colored incident light. Limitations of scaling methods of achieving color constancy are discussed in Worthey (1986). Hurlbert and Poggio use known correspondences between certain area of the scene under unknown illumination and the values they should have under standard illumination; an algorithm is then used to determine the best transformation that can then be applied to the rest of the scene (Hurlbert and Poggio, 1988).

Other researchers have appealed to the dichromatic reflection model and assumed that highlighted inhomogeneous objects are present in the scene. The highlight areas have the same color as the illumination, since the model assumes that the highlights are not colored by the objects. Once the highlights are found, the color of the illumination can be calculated and factored out of the scene (D'Zmura and Lennie, 1986; Healey and Binford, 1987; Tominaga and Wandell, 1989). Mathematical constraints can also be employed to limit the possible forms of illumination and surface reflectances. This may be done by using more sensors than degrees of freedom in the SPDs (Maloney and Wandell, 1986), by including spectral data in addition to or instead of **R-G-B** values (Ho and co-workers, 1988; Tominaga and Wandell, 1989), or by using qualitative knowledge about the nature of the SPDs (eg, real-world reflectances are never negative) (Tominaga and Wandell, 1990).

Another issue of research in color constancy is the method of representing the SPDs of the illumination and surface reflectances in the calculations. Researchers need to represent functions $S(\lambda)$ in a finite manner; such a finite representation must necessarily be inexact, since, in principle, SPDs may take any shape. They may be approximated by sampling at regular intervals with a spectroradiometer (eg, every 10 nm within the visible range); by sampling with broad-band physically realizable receptors such as $\bar{r}(\lambda)$, $\bar{g}(\lambda)$, and $\bar{b}(\lambda)$; by representation with a set of abstract basis functions such as Fourier functions (Wandell, 1987) or normalized Legendre polynomials (Healey and Binford, 1988); or by using a set of basis functions derived from a principal components analysis of spectral

data taken of natural and synthetic objects (Gershon, 1987). There is also some question of the number of basis functions needed to give an adequate representation of SPDs of real objects and illuminants (Maloney, 1986; Parkkinen and co-workers, 1989). Some researchers have argued that many SPDs corresponding to physically realizable objects are band-limited functions and thus a good fit may be achieved with even a small number of basis functions (Maloney, 1986).

Future work in this area may include more robust algorithms to work on a greater variety and number of materials and under more types of illumination, examination of the band limitation assumption and goodness-of-fit measures (Parkkinen and co-workers, 1989), and greater automation in selecting areas of scenes for analysis.

BIBLIOGRAPHY

K. Akita and H. Kuga, "Towards Understanding Color Ocular Fundus Images," in *Proceedings of the 6th IJCAI,* Tokyo, Morgan-Kaufmann, San Mateo, Calif., 1979, pp. 7–12.

M. Ali, W. N. Martin, and J. K. Aggarwal, "Color-Based Computer Analysis of Aerial Photographs," *Comput. Graph. Image Proc.* **9,** 282–293 (1979).

R. Bajcsy, "Computer Identification of Visual Surfaces," *Comput. Graph. Image Proc.* **2,** 118–130 (1973).

R. Bajcsy, S. W. Lee, and A. Leonardis, *Image Segmentation with Detection of Highlights and Inter-reflections Using Color,* MS-CIS 89-39, University of Pennsylvania, Philadelphia, June 1989.

C. J. Bartleson and F. Grum, *Optical Radiation Measurements,* Vol. 5, Academic Press, New York, 1984.

M. H. Brill, "Object-Based Segmentation and Color Recognition in Multispectral Images," *SPIE/SPSE* **1076,** 97–103 (Jan. 1989).

C. M. Brown, *Color Vision and Computer Vision,* Technical Report 108, University of Rochester Computer Science Dept., Rochester, N.Y., 1982.

International Commission on Illumination, *International Lighting Vocabulary,* CIE, Paris, 1970.

G. B. Coleman and H. C. Andrews, "Image Segmentation by Clustering," *Proc. IEEE* **67**(5), 773–785 (1979).

Committee on Colorimetry, *The Science of Color,* Optical Society of America, Washington, D.C., 1963.

D. M. Connah and C. A. Fishbourne, "The Use of Colour Information in Industrial Scene Analysis," in *Proceedings of the First International Conference on Robot Vision and Sensory Controls,* ICRVSC, Stratford-upon-Avon, UK, April 1981, pp. 340–347.

J. Crisman and C. Thorpe, "Color Vision for Road Following," *Proc. SPIE* **1007,** 175–184 (Nov. 1988).

L. E. Demarsh, "Color Reproduction in Color Television," in *Proceedings of the Inter-Society Color Council 1971 Conference on Optimum Reproduction of Color,* Inter-Society Color Council, Williamsburg, Va., 1971, pp. 69–97.

M. D'Zmura and P. Lennie, "Mechanisms of Color Constancy," *J. Opt. Soc. Am.* **3**(10), 1622–1672 (1986).

J. Engvall and co-workers, "Development of a Mathematical Model to Analyze Color and Density as Discriminant Features for Pulmonary Squamous Epithelial Cells," *Pattern Recognition* **13**(1), 37–47 (1981).

B. Funt and J. Ho, "Color from Black and White," in *International Conference on Computer Vision (ICCV)*, IEEE, New York, 1988, pp. 2–8.

R. Gershon, *Survey on Color: Aspects of Perception and Computation*, RCBV-TR 84-4, University of Toronto Computer Science Dept., Toronto, Canada, 1984.

R. Gershon, *The Use of Color in Computational Vision*, PhD dissertation, University of Toronto, Toronto, Canada, 1987.

F. Grum and C. J. Bartleson, eds., *Optical Radiation Measurements*, Vol. 2, Academic Press, New York, 1980.

F. Grum and R. J. Becherer, *Optical Radiation Measurements*, Vol. 1, Academic Press, New York, 1979.

Hamamatsu Corp., *Vidicons, Catalog SC-5-3*, Hamamatsu Corp., Middlesex, N.J., 1983a.

Hamamatsu Corp., *Silicon Photocells, Catalog SC-3-6*, Hamamatsu Corp., Middlesex, N.J., 1983b.

R. M. Haralick and G. L. Kelly, "Pattern Recognition with Measurement Space and Spatial Clustering for Multiple Images," *Proc. IEEE* **57**, 654–665 (April 1969).

G. Healey, "A Color Reflectance Model and Its Use for Segmentation," in *International Conference on Computer Vision (ICCV)*, IEEE, New York, 1988, pp. 460–466.

G. Healey, "Using Color for Geometry-Insensitive Segmentation," *J. Opt. Soc. Am. A* **6**(6), 920–937 (1989).

G. Healey and T. O. Binford, "The Role and Use of Color in a General Vision System," in *Proceedings of the ARPA Image Understanding Workshop*, DARPA, Arlington, Va., 1987, pp. 599–613.

G. Healey and T. O. Binford, "A Color Metric for Computer Vision," in *Proceedings of the International Conference on Computer Vision and Pattern Recognition*, IEEE, New York, 1988, pp. 10–17.

J. Ho, B. V. Funt, and M. S. Drew, *Disambiguation of Illumination and Surface Reflectance from Spectral Power Distribution of Color Signal: Theory and Applications*, CSS/LCCR 88-18, Simon Fraser University, Burnaby, B.C., Canada, 1988.

R. W. G. Hunt, *The Reproduction of Color*, Wiley, New York, 1967.

A. C. Hurlbert and T. A. Poggio, "Synthesizing a Color Algorithm from Examples," *Science* **236**, 482 (Jan. 1988).

T. Ito, "Color Picture Processing by Computer," in *Proceedings of the Fourth IJCAI*, Tbilisi, USSR, Morgan-Kaufmann, San Mateo, Calif., 1975, pp. 635–642.

D. B. Judd and G. Wyszecki, *Color in Business, Science and Industry*, Wiley, New York, 1975.

J. R. Kender, "Instabilities in Color Transformations," in *PRIP-77*, IEEE Computer Society, Troy, N.Y., June 1977, pp. 266–274.

G. J. Klinker, *A Physical Approach to Color Image Understanding*, PhD dissertation, Carnegie Mellon University, Pittsburgh, Pa., May 1988.

G. J. Klinker, S. A. Shafer, and T. Kanade, "Using a Color Reflection Model to Separate Highlights from Object Color," in *International Conference on Computer Vision (ICCV)*, IEEE, New York, June 1987, pp. 145–150.

G. J. Klinker, S. A. Shafer, and T. Kanade, "The Measurement of Highlights in Color Images," *Int. J. Comp. Vision* **2**(1), 7–32 (1988).

G. J. Klinker, S. A. Shafer, and T. Kanade, "Color Image Analysis with an Intrinsic Reflection Model," in *International Conference on Computer Vision (ICCV)*, IEEE, New York, 1988, pp. 292–296.

R. G. Kuehni, *Color: Essence and Logic*, Van Nostrand Reinhold Co., New York, 1983.

E. H. Land, "The Retinex Theory of Color Vision," *Sci. Am.* **237**(6), 108–128 (1977).

Y. LeClerc, "A Method for Spectral Linearization," private communication, 1986.

H. C. Lee, "Method for Computing the Scene-Illuminant Chromaticity from Specular Highlights," *J. Opt. Soc. Am. A* **3**(10), 1694–1699 (1986).

M. D. Levine, "Region Analysis Using a Pyramid Data Structure," *Structured Computer Vision*, Academic Press, New York, 1980, pp. 57–100.

M. D. Levine and S. I. Shaheen, "A Modular Computer Vision System for Picture Segmentation and Interpretation, Part I," in *PRIP-79*, IEEE Computer Society, Chicago, Ill., 1979, pp. 523–533.

L. T. Maloney, "Evaluation of Linear Models of Surface Spectral Reflectance with Small Numbers of Parameters," *J. Opt. Soc. Am.* **3**(10), 1673–1683 (1986).

L. T. Maloney and B. A. Wandell, "Color Consistency: A Method for Recovering Surface Spectral Reflectance," *J. Opt. Soc. Am. A* **3**(1), 29–33 (1986).

M. Nagao, T. Matsuyama, and Y. Ikeda, "Region Extraction and Shape Analysis in Aerial Photographs," *Comput. Graph. Image Proc.* **10**, 195–223 (1979).

P. A. Nagin, A. R. Hanson, and E. M. Riseman, "Studies in Global and Local Histogram-Guided Relaxation Algorithms," *IEEE Trans. PAMI* **PAMI-4**(3), 263–276 (1982).

A. Nazif, *A Survey of Color, Boundary Information, and Texture as Features for Low-Level Image Processing*, Technical Report 78-7R, McGill University Electrical Engineering Dept., Montreal, Canada, 1978.

R. Nevatia, "A Color Edge Detector and Its Use in Scene Segmentation," *IEEE Trans. Syst. Man Cybern.* **TSMC-7**(11), 820–826 (1977).

Y. Noguchi, Y. Tonjin, and T. Sugishita, "A Method for Segmenting a Clump of Cells into Cellular Characteristic Parts Using Multispectral Information," in *IJCPR-4*, Kyoto, 1978, pp. 872–874.

C. L. Novak, S. A. Shafer, and R. G. Willson, "Obtaining Accurate Color Images for Machine Vision Research," *Proc. SPIE* **1250**, 54–68 (1990).

R. Ohlander, *Analysis of Natural Scenes*, PhD dissertation, Computer Science Department, Carnegie Mellon University, Pittsburgh, Pa., 1975.

R. Ohlander, K. Price, and D. R. Reddy, "Picture Segmentation Using a Recursive Region Splitting Method," *Comput. Graph. Image Proc.* **8**, 313–333 (1978).

Y. Ohta, T. Kanade, and T. Sakai, "Color Information for Region Segmentation," *Comput. Graph. Image Proc.* **13**, 222–241 (1980).

J. P. S. Parkkinen, J. Hallikainen, and T. Jaaskelainen, "Characteristic Spectra of Munsell Colors," *J. Opt. Soc. Am. A* **6**(2), 318–322 (1989).

A. Rosenfeld, "Some Recent Results Using Relaxation-Like Processes," *Proceedings of the ARPA IU Workshop*, May 1978, pp. 100–101.

J. M. Rubin and W. A. Richards, "Color Vision and Image Intensities: When Are Changes Material?" *Biol. Cybern.* **45**, 215–226 (1982).

A. Sarabi and J. K. Aggarwal, "Segmentation of Chromatic Images," *Pattern Recognition* **13**(6), 417–427 (1981).

B. Schachter, L. S. Davis, and A. Rosenfeld, *Scene Segmentation by Cluster Detection in Color Space,* Technical Report 424, University of Maryland Computer Science Center, College Park, Md., 1975.

S. A. Shafer, "Optical Phenomena in Computer Vision," in *Proceedings CSCSI-84,* Canadian Society for Computational Studies of Intelligence, London, Ontario, May 1984.

S. A. Shafer, "Using Color to Separate Reflection Components," *Color Res. App.* **10**(4), 210–218 (1985).

S. A. Shafer and T. Kanade, "Recursive Region Segmentation by Analysis of Histograms," in *Proc. Intl. Conf. on Acoustics, Speech, and Signal Processing,* Paris, IEEE, May 1982, pp. 1166–1171.

S. A. Shafer, T. Kanade, G. J. Klinker, and C. L. Novak, "Physics-Based Models for Early Vision by Machine," *SPIE/SPSE* **1250,** 222–235 (1990).

K. Sloan, *World Model Driven Recognition of Natural Scenes,* PhD dissertation, University of Pennsylvania Moore School of Electrical Engineering, Philadelphia, June 1977.

D. Taenzer, *Physiology and Psychology of Color Vision—A Review,* AIM 369, MIT AI Lab, Cambridge, Mass., 1976.

J. M. Tenenbaum, T. D. Garvey, S. Weyl, and H. C. Wolf, *An Interactive Facility for Scene Analysis Research,* Technical Report TN 87, SRI International, Menlo Park, Calif., Jan. 1974.

S. Tominaga and B. A. Wandell, "Standard Surface-Reflectance Model and Illuminant Estimation," *J. Opt. Soc. Am. A* **6**(4), 576–584 (1989).

S. Tominaga and B. A. Wandell, "Component Estimation of Surface Spectral Reflectance," *J. Opt. Soc. Am. A* **7**(2), 312–317 (1990).

M. Turk, D. Morgenthaler, K. Gremban, and M. Marra, "VITS: A Vision System for Autonomous Land Vehicle Navigation," *IEEE Trans. Patt. Anal. Mach. Intell.* **PAMI-10**(3), 342–361 (1988).

B. A. Wandell, "The Synthesis and Analysis of Color Images," *IEEE Trans. Patt. Anal. Mach. Intell.* **PAMI-9**(1), 2–13 (1987).

J. Wentworth, *Color Television Engineering,* McGraw-Hill, New York, 1955.

S. J. Williamson and H. Z. Cummins, *Light and Color in Nature and Art,* Wiley, New York, 1983.

J. A. Worthey, "Heuristic Analysis of von Kries Color Constancy," *J. Opt. Soc. Am.* **3**(10), 1708–1712 (1986).

G. Wyszecki and W. S. Stiles, *Color Science: Concepts and Methods, Quantitative Data and Formulae,* Wiley, New York, 1982.

M. Yachida and S. Tsuji, "Application of Color Information to Visual Perception," *Pattern Recognition* **3,** 307–323 (1971).

Y. Yakimovsky and J. A. Feldman, "A Semantics-Based Decision Theory Region Analyzer," in *Proceedings of the Third IJCAI,* Stanford, Calif., Morgan-Kaufmann, San Mateo, Calif., 1973, pp. 580–588.

General References

The reader interested in color measurement is referred to Judd and Wyszecki (1975), a very readable discussion, and the more technical discussion of color standards in Grum and Bartleson (1980). Useful reference handbooks are Wyszecki and Stiles (1982), which contains many tables and formulas, and CIE (1970), which presents formal definitions of terms and units of measure. A discussion of the physiology of human color vision is found in Bartleson and Grum (1984); Committee on Colorimetry (1963) is older but also contains an excellent discussion of color perception. Surveys of color in computer vision are Taenzer

(1976), Nazif (1978), Brown (1982), Gershon (1984), and Shafer (1984); however, these tend to survey human color vision more deeply than computer color vision.

CAROL L. NOVAK
STEVEN A. SHAFER
Carnegie Mellon University

COMMONSENSE REASONING. See REASONING, COMMONSENSE.

COMPLETENESS

Completeness is a property of deductive systems, or theories, as are consistency and soundness; these terms inherit their meaning from logic (qv). Informally, a complete theory is one strong enough to allow proof of any statement that ideally one would want to prove, a consistent theory is a theory free of formal contradiction, and a sound theory is, in some sense, a "correct" theory, that is, only true statements are provable. Reference to completeness within AI has been primarily within the automated theorem-proving (qv) subarea. Although its exact importance for AI has been controversial, it is generally agreed that completeness is less important for an AI system than soundness and consistency (and even consistency may have to be given up in larger systems), but that completeness can be an important property when basic deductive systems are considered. The term completeness has also been used in the context of knowledge representations (qv) in AI to indicate that the notation can represent every entity within the intended domain.

PROOF PROCEDURES

To be precise, a first-order theory is complete if and only if (iff) for each closed formula *A* of the language of the theory either *A* or ~*A* is provable (Shoenfield, 1967). (A first-order theory is consistent iff for each formula *A* at most one of *A* and ~*A* is provable. A theory is sound iff its theorems are a subset of the intended set of theorems. This last definition involves interpretations of the theory; it is dependent on the notion of "intended" and so is less used in logic than the first two definitions.) Completeness is also defined for proof procedures and is the meaning usually intended in the automated theorem-proving field. A proof procedure for a logic (a theory) is complete iff it is capable of generating a proof for every valid (true) formula of the logic (theory). Implicit in this definition is the acknowledgment that normal forms for formulas may be used, and only the normal forms may be provable; indeed, one may view the logic as restricted to these normal forms whereupon the definition is literal. For refutation logics and their associated proof procedures, such as resolution (qv) and its various refutation procedures, the definition is the obvious variant: the refutation procedure is complete iff the procedure is capable of generating a refutation of every unsatisfiable formula (Chang and Lee, 1973; Loveland, 1978). (A refutation procedure is consistent iff for no formula A are both A and ~A refutable by the procedure. The refutation procedure is sound iff every formula refuted by the procedure is unsatisfiable.)

Concern with completeness entered the AI community via interest in automated theorem proving (ATP) in the late 1950s. Robinson (1960) was the first logician on record as proposing, in 1954, that a complete proof procedure be used for ATP, and Prawitz, Prawitz, and in 1957 Voghera (1960) implemented a proof procedure for the first-order predicate calculus closely related to Beth's (1951) semantic tableaux method. Several other logicians responded to the heuristic approach to proving propositional theorems taken by Newell, Shaw, and Simon (1957) by showing that complete proof procedures could perform as well as heuristic procedures (actually much better at that time) and could handle a much wider scope of problems. In particular, the procedure of Gilmore (1960) that used the so-called Herbrand theorem (better named the Skolem Herbrand Gödel theorem) was improved by Davis and Putnam (1960) and then J. A. Robinson (1965), who proposed the resolution procedure (see RESOLUTION). Each dramatically improved an aspect of the previous procedure while maintaining completeness, thus being able to claim that efficiency was not gained at the expense of generality (at least as a first-order approximation). (For a detailed view of this first period in ATP history see the opening articles in Siekmann and Wrightson, 1983.) However, the difficulties encountered in proving deeper theorems using resolution techniques, in spite of a sizable repertoire of resolution "strategies," led several AI researchers to alternative methods. In particular, both Nevins (1974) and Bledsoe (1971) developed incomplete theorem provers that proved some theorems not previously proved by resolution provers and illuminated techniques that promised further gains (Loveland, 1984). These provers and a general reaction to an apparent overemphasis on completeness moved the AI community to an "anticompleteness" attitude, which is gradually decreasing in intensity as researchers gain a feeling for contexts in which completeness makes sense. To oversimplify, completeness is useful when dealing with basic mechanisms for deduction since experience shows that otherwise some very simple deductions may be omitted. On the other hand, control structures (qv) are often designed with little regard for completeness because of the desire for anything that works well in reasonable domains; moreover, resource limitations (eg, time) in real life mean that completeness can never be fully exploited.

BIBLIOGRAPHY

E. W. Beth, "A Topological Proof of the Theorem of Löwenheim-Skolem-Gödel," *Kominkl. Nederl. Akademie van Wetenschappen,* Amsterdam, Proceedings, Series A, **54**(5); *Indagationes Math* 13(5), 436–444 (1951).

W. W. Bledsoe, "Splitting and Reduction Heuristics in Automatic Theorem Proving," *Artif. Intell.,* 55–77 (1971).

C. L. Chang and R. T. C. Lee, *Symbolic Logic and Mechanical Theorem Proving,* Academic Press, New York, 1973.

M. Davis and H. Putnam, "A Computing Procedure for Quantification Theory," *J. Assoc. Comput. Machin.* **7,** 201–215 (1960).

P. C. Gilmore, "A Proof Method for Quantification Theory: Its Justification and Realization," *IBM J. Res. Devel.,* 28–35 (Jan. 1960).

D. W. Loveland, *Automated Theorem Proving: A Logical Basis,* Fundamental Studies in Computer Science Series, North-Holland, Amsterdam, 1978.

D. W. Loveland, "Automated Theorem Proving: A Quarter-Century Review," *Automated Theorem Proving: After 25 Years,* Vol. 29, Contemporary Mathematics Series, American Mathematical Society, Providence, R.I., 1984.

A. J. Nevins, "A Human Oriented Logic for Automatic Theorem Proving," *J. Assoc. Comput. Machin.* **21,** 606–621 (1974).

A. Newell, J. C. Shaw, and H. Simon, "Empirical Explorations with the Logic Theory Machine," *Proceedings of the Western Joint Computer Conference,* 1957, pp. 218–239.

D. Prawitz, H. Prawitz, and N. Voghera, "A Mechanical Proof Procedure and its Implementation in an Electronic Computer," *J. Assoc. Comput. Machin.* **7,** 102–128 (1960).

A. Robinson, "Proving Theorems, as Done by Man, Machine and Logician," *Summaries of Talks Presented at the Summer Institute for Symbolic Logic, 1957,* 2nd ed., Institute for Defense Analysis, 1960.

J. A. Robinson, "A Machine Oriented Logic Based on the Resolution Principle," *J. Assoc. Comput. Machin.* **12,** 23–41 (1965).

J. Shoenfield, *Mathematical Logic,* Series in Logic, Addison-Wesley, Reading, Mass., 1967.

J. Siekmann and G. Wrightson, eds., *Automation of Reasoning,* Vol. 1, *Classical Papers of Computational Logic 1957–1966,* Symbolic Computation Series, Springer-Verlag, Berlin. 1983.

D. W. LOVELAND
Duke University

COMPUTATIONAL LINGUISTICS

Research in computational linguistics (CL) is concerned with the application of a computational paradigm to the scientific study of human language and the engineering of systems that process or analyze written or spoken language. The term *natural language processing* (NLP) is also frequently used, especially with regard to the engineering side of the discipline. As a historical note, the term computational linguistics included the study of formal languages and artificial computer languages (eg, ALGOL), as well as natural languages, until the middle 1960s, but this entry concerns CL as it is presently conceived.

Theoretical issues in CL concern syntax, semantics, discourse, language generation, language acquisition, and other areas, whereas areas for applied work in CL have included automatic programming, computer-aided instruction, database interface, machine translation, office automation, speech understanding, and other areas. Historically, much CL research has been done by researchers whose language interests overlap with interests in such related disciplines as AI, cognitive science, computer science and engineering, information science, linguistics, philosophy, psychology, and the speech sciences. The middle 1970s, however, witnessed an increase in hybrid efforts, so that present efforts in CL typically draw from and contribute to work in one or more of these cognate areas.

This entry serves primarily as an overview of the primary topics in CL. It begins with a historical introduction to the field, followed by brief remarks on some of the more important theoretical problems, and concludes with pointers to the literature. Since space has permitted only a general statement of the goals of a theory or implementation, with occasional examples of either I/O behavior or internal representation formalisms, conclusions cannot be drawn from this entry alone concerning the capabilities of the work to be described. More detailed information is available in the separate entries related to the topics considered here.

EARLY WORK (1950–1965)

Most CL work prior to 1960 concerned machine translation, as defined below, but the advent of transformational grammar and the emergence of paradigms for information retrieval also played an important role in the formation of a CL community. Following is a discussion of the essential work in these three areas.

Machine Translation

Many of the first attempts at using computers to process natural language concerned the problem of translating from one natural-language text into another. Although actual computer programs seeking to solve this task were not written until the early 1950s, the idea of mechanical translation can be traced to conversations as early as 1946 between Weaver and Booth. The initial impetus came in 1949, when Weaver wrote and privately circulated a paper titled "Translation" (1955). This paper, along with a detailed account of initial work in machine translation, can be found in Locke and Booth (1955).

Most early work on machine translation, also known as automatic translation, mechanical translation, or simply MT, was conducted in the United States and the USSR, where the political and military interests in natural-language translation were especially strong. There were also two British projects and some work done in Italy, Israel, and elsewhere. Typically, efforts at machine translation, which predated the important work in linguistics and computer science on syntax, grammars, and languages, were based on word-by-word translation schemes. In particular, no attempt was made to parse sentences (ie, determine their syntactic structure) and, at least as significantly, no attempt was made to actually understand the material to be translated. A characterization of the basic approach of word-for-word processing can be found in Oettinger (1960).

As an example of what had been achieved by about 1960, the first sentence of a 1956 Russian article yielded the output "'razviti' electronics (allowed permitted) (considerably significantly considerable significant important) to (perfect improve) (method way) 'fiz' (measurement metering sounding dimension) (speed velocity rate ratio) (light luminosity shine luminous)," where parentheses indicate uncertainty on the part of the system and where

razviti and *fiz* were unknown and thus untranslated (*fiz* derives from a proper name). From this output, a human posteditor produced "Development of electronics permitted considerably to improve method Fizeau of measurement of speed of light," which may be compared with the fully human translation, "The development of electronics has brought about a considerable improvement of Fizeau's method of measuring the velocity of light." This example is discussed in detail in Oettinger (1960).

Concerning the distinction between fully automated as opposed to machine-assisted human translation, even Bar-Hillel (1960), an outspoken detractor of much MT work, observed that "word-by-word Russian-to-English translation of scientific texts, if pushed to its limits, is known to enable an English reader who knows the respective field to understand, in general, at least the gist of the original text, though of course with an effort that is considerably larger than that required for reading a regular high quality translation." Nevertheless, researchers and government funding agencies continued to anticipate systems that would provide "fully automatic high-quality translation" (FAHQT). It was with respect to this more ambitious goal that the Automatic Language Processing Advisory Committee (ALPAC) was formed in April of 1964 "to advise the Department of Defense, the Central Intelligence Agency, and the National Science Foundation on research and development in the general field of mechanical translation of foreign languages." In essence, the committee found that "there has been no machine translation of general scientific text, and none is in immediate prospect" (National Research Council, 1966). They further observed that, in some cases, "the postedited translation took slightly longer to do and was more expensive than conventional human translation" and also noted that "unedited machine output from scientific text is decipherable for the most part, but it is sometimes misleading and sometimes wrong (as is postedited output to a lesser extent)."

Although the ALPAC committee had presumably intended its report to effect "useful changes in the support of research," their findings resulted in the virtual elimination of federal funding for work in MT. As a consequence, very little work was done, and few papers published, for roughly a decade. Since the middle 1970s, however, a number of projects have been spawned or reactivated. The entry on machine translation discusses more recent work in the area.

Transformational Grammar

In 1957 an event occurred that not only revolutionized the world of linguistics but left a lasting impression on philosophy, psychology, and other areas also. That event was the publication of a short monograph by Chomsky (1957) entitled *Syntactic Structures* that explored the implications of automata theory for natural language. In it, Chomsky first argued that the sentences of a natural language cannot be meaningfully generated by a finite-state machine or by any context-free grammar, or at least that "any grammar that can be constructed . . . will be extremely complex, ad hoc, and 'unrevealing'" (Chomsky,

1957, p. 34). He then proposed a theory of what he called *transformational grammar* (TG) and began to work out its details.

At the most abstract level, the theory of TG involves specifying a set of "kernel" sentences of a language; an assortment of "transformations," such as verb tensing and passive voice; and an ordering in which transformations are to be carried out. For example, to avoid producing a sentence such as "John are liked by the students," the passive transformation must apply to the kernel sentence "The students liked John" before the rule for subject–verb agreement. The entry on transformational grammar provides details of the theory.

With the publication of *Syntactic Structures*, Chomsky had argued for, if not established, the efficacy of a transformational component, but he recognized that TG would have to be "formulated properly in . . . terms that must be developed in a full-scale theory of transformations." As a suggestive first step, his appendix provided a sample grammar for a very small subset of English that included 12 content words and fairly elaborate auxiliary verb structures. The period from 1957 to 1965 was one of intense activity by Chomsky and several students, culminating in the publication of *Aspects of the Theory of Syntax* (Chomsky, 1965) and its far-reaching theory of *deep structure* (qv), which relates to an internal sentence-independent representation of (the meaning of) the sentence.

Although TG has had an uneven impact on CL, centered mostly around matters of syntax, its influence on early work in CL is evidenced through bibliographic references and, more substantively, by concepts and borrowed terminology that appeared in the CL literature of the 1960s. In the long term the hypothesis of TG most significant for work in CL is that an understanding of the syntax, or structure, of natural-language sentences can be arrived at on a solely grammatical basis, without considering the real-world properties (eg, meanings) of the terms being discussed. This notion, sometimes known as the "autonomy of syntax," continues to provide a useful, if regrettable, division in categorizing current work in CL, as the debate continues as to what interactions are desirable, or necessary, between the structural (syntactic) and interpretive (semantic, pragmatic) components of a theory or implementation.

Information Retrieval

It is fairly well known that the emergence of the modern digital computer occurred during the 1940s and that the problems first solved by these computers were numerical in nature and often military in origin. During the 1950s computers were increasingly called upon to provide access to large volumes of nonnumeric data for such purposes as database retrieval and on-line bibliographic search.

Most systems of the 1950s and early 1960s that provided for English "inputs" were directed toward bibliographic search and other library services, and these efforts coalesced into a field that became known as information retrieval (qv) (IR), which is "concerned with the structure, analysis, organization, storage, searching, and retrieval of information" and has grown to include procedures for "dictionary construction and dictionary look-up, statistical and syntactic language analysis methods, information search and matching procedures, automatic information dissemination systems, and methods for user interaction with the mechanized systems" (Salton, 1968). Although little association remained between CL and IR by the middle 1960s, early work in IR did overlap that being done by the early workers in CL (Becker and Hays, 1963; Hays, 1966; Salter, 1968; Sparck-Jones and Kay, 1973).

BROADENING INTERESTS (1960–1970)

In contrast to the 1950s, during which time CL researchers concentrated primarily on machine translation, the 1960s witnessed the application of CL techniques to database retrieval, problem solving, and other areas. For the most part, these early NL systems provided quite limited forms of interaction and were often based on techniques specifically tailored for a single domain of discourse. Nevertheless, the work represented interesting and important, if tenuous, first steps at seeking computational solutions to problems of human language processing. In addition, Raphael (1983) notes that these programs "contain the seeds, or at least surfaced the issues, that led to many of today's major computer science concepts: semantic net representations, data abstraction, pattern matching, object-oriented programming, syntax-driven natural language analysis, logic programming, and so on."

One important aspect of CL implementations of the 1960s, largely without counterpart in CL work of the 1950s, was that the "processing" to be done required programs to *understand* their inputs to some nontrivial degree. For example, although Bobrow recognized that "we are far from writing a program that can understand all, or even a very large segment, of English", he claimed that "a computer *understands* a subset of English if it accepts input sentences which are members of this subset and answers questions based on information contained in the input" (Bobrow, 1968, p. 146). This issue was not without controversy, however, as suggested by Giuliano (1965). His complaint was that an "arbitrary heuristic procedure . . . which is used in several computer programmed systems" does not "become a principle through its use." To this argument, Simmons (1965) responded that "theory often lags far behind model building and sometimes derives therefrom" and further maintained that the early systems represented "truly scientific approaches to the study of language" (Simmons, 1961, p. 70).

The following discussion seeks to convey a sense of the problems addressed by NL applications in the 1960s. They are grouped in terms of question-answering, problem-solving, consultation, and miscellaneous systems.

Question-Answering Systems

One of the first fully implemented data retrieval systems was BASEBALL (qv), "a computer program that answers questions posed in ordinary English about data in its store" (Green and co-workers, 1963). This system was designed to interact with a primitive database, stored as attribute-value pairs, that contained information about the month, day, place, teams, and scores for American League baseball games. An example input is "What teams won 10 games in July?"

Another early program was SAD SAM, designed to "parse sentences written in Basic English and make inferences about kinship relations" (Lindsay, 1963). This system comprised two modules, one for parsing (the syntactic appraiser and diagramer, SAD) and one for semantic analysis (the semantic analyzing machine, SAM). The basic operation of the semantics module involved searching a previously constructed parse tree for words denoting kinship relationships in order to construct a family tree, which was stored as a linked structure.

The SIR system had the goal of "developing a computer [program] . . . having certain cognitive abilities and exhibiting some humanlike conversational behavior" (Raphael, 1968). The system was similar to SAD SAM in allowing a user to input new information, then ask questions about it. However, SIR emphasized relations such as set-subset, part-whole, and ownership, as suggested by the following: "Every boy is a person. A finger is part of a hand. Each person has two hands. John is a boy. Every hand has 5 fingers. How many fingers does John have?"

The DEACON system (Craig and co-workers, 1966), which was designed to answer questions about a simulated Army environment, represents an important precursor of the database front-ends of the 1970s. Its internal ring-like data structures could be dynamically updated, thus enabling users to supply new information ("The 425th will leave Ft. Lewis at 21950!") as well as ask questions ("Is the 638th scheduled to arrive at Ft. Lewis before the 425th leaves Ft. Lewis?"). In reflecting upon their experiences with DEACON, the authors noted that "perhaps the most significant new feature needed is the ability to define vocabulary terms in English, using previously defined terms" (Craig and co-workers, 1966, p. 376). This realization led directly to the REL system and its successors.

The REL system (Rapidly Extensible Language) represented the logical continuation to the work with DEACON, and its primary goals were "to facilitate the implementation and subsequent user extension and modification of highly idiosyncratic language/database packages" (Thompson and co-workers, 1969). An example customization is

def:power coefficient:high speed memory size/add time

From a theoretical standpoint, REL was based on the notion that an English language subset could be treated as a formal language "when the subject matter which it talks about is limited to material whose interrelationships are specifiable in a limited number of precisely structured categories" (Thompson and co-workers, 1969, p. 404). The first sizable application of REL was to an anthropological database at Caltech of over 100,000 items. As indicated below, work on the REL project continued well into the 1970s, until the system, now quite advanced over its early prototypes, was renamed ASK.

Another early database interface, CONVERSE, was designed as an "on-line system for describing, updating,

and interrogating data bases of diverse content and structure through the use of ordinary English sentences" (Kellag, 1968). It was intended to strike "a reasonable compromise between the difficulties of allowing completely free use of ordinary English and the restrictions inherent in existing artificial languages for data base description and querying" (Kellog, 1968). An example input is "Which Pan Am flights that are economy class depart for O'Hare from the city of Los Angeles?" In addition to question-answering capabilities, the system included facilities for English-like data definitions and English-like means of populating the database.

Problem Solving

The STUDENT (qv) system was designed as "a computer program that could communicate with people in a natural language within some restricted problem domain" (Bobrow, 1968). It sought to solve high-school-level algebra word problems stated in what the author considered a "comfortable but restricted subset of English" by constructing an appropriate set of linear equations to be solved. As an example of STUDENT's capabilities, a sample problem is: "The price of a radio is $69.70. If this price is 15% less than the marked price, find the marked price." Having been given equations such as "distance equals speed times time" and by employing a number of clever pattern-matching techniques (eg, "years older than" is converted to "plus"), STUDENT could answer some very complex problems. Its designer suggested that the system "could be made to understand most of the algebra story problems that appear in first-year high-school textbooks" but noted that "the problems it cannot handle are those having excessive verbiage or implied information abut the world not expressible in a single sentence (Bobrow, 1968, p. 204).

In building upon Bobrow's work with STUDENT, Charniak (1969) set out to develop a program to solve calculus word problems. This led to the implementation of the CARPS system, which was restricted to freshman-level problems related to rates, as Bobrow had in fact suggested in his paper. An example input processed by CARPS follows:

Water is flowing into a conical filter at the rate of 15.0 cubic inches per second. If the radius of the base of the filter is 5.0 inches and the altitude is 10.0 inches, find the rate at which the water level is rising when the volume is 100.0 cubic inches. (Charniak, 1969, p. 305).

In reflecting on his work, Charniak noted that, despite its advances over STUDENT, "a very powerful calculus word problem solver will require a good deal of 'common sense' knowledge" (Charniak, 1969, p. 309). In advancing this claim, Charniak foreshadowed an interest on the part of the AI community in the 1970s in story understanding.

Consultation

One of the most widely publicized AI programs of the 1960s, the ELIZA (qv) system, was designed "for the study of natural language communication between man and machine" (Weizenbaum, 1966). In essence, ELIZA was intended "to respond roughly as would certain psychotherapists (Rogerians)" since "the psychiatric interview is one of the few examples of categorized dyadic natural language communication in which one of the participating pair is free to assume the poise of knowing almost nothing of the real world." An excerpt from a "typical" conversation with ELIZA follows (Weizenbaum, 1966).

"I need some help, that much seems certain."

WHAT WOULD IT MEAN TO YOU IF YOU GOT SOME HELP

"Perhaps I could learn to get along with my mother."

TELL ME MORE ABOUT YOUR FAMILY

"My mother takes care of me."

WHO ELSE IN YOUR FAMILY TAKES CARE OF YOU

"My father."

YOUR FATHER

As can be inferred after considering a dozen or so responses from the system, ELIZA sought to match its current input against one of a known set of patterns. It then selected one of possibly several transformations associated with that pattern. Actually, patterns were associated with a keyword, and the algorithm considered various priorities in choosing among candidate matches. The idea of maintaining a "script" of data separate from the algorithms of the program itself was not without precedent, but ELIZA carried this out more fully than had previous systems.

In addition to its technical contributions and the excitement it caused, the system convinced at least its designer that "the whole issue of the credibility (to humans) of machine output demands investigation" (Weizenbaum, 1966). This thought led Weizenbaum to his widely publicized social criticisms of AI research (1976). An interesting and also famous follow-up of ELIZA, in which the program played the role of the patient rather than the analyst, is reported in Colby and co-workers (1971).

Miscellaneous

Within the tradition of information retrieval established in the 1950s, but with greater attention to syntax and other linguistic issues, Protosynthex sought to accept natural English questions and search a large text to discover the most acceptable sentence, paragraph, or article as an answer (Simmons, 1965). The system was applied to portions of *Compton's Encyclopedia,* and an example of a question posed to the system is "What animals live longer than men?" The project continued for several years and evolved into "a general purpose language processor . . . based on a psychological model of cognitive structure that is grounded in linguistic and logical theory" (Simmons, 1970). A few systems were designed to produce English output, as described by Simmons (1965). One system, NAMER, was designed to generate natural-language sentences from line drawings displayed on a matrix (Simmons and Londe, 1964). It produced sentences such as, "The dog is beside and to the right of the boy." Another

system, the Picture Language Machine (Kirsch, 1964), would be given a picture and a sentence as input and, after translating both the picture and the English statement into a common intermediate logical language, would determine whether the statement about the picture was true. An example input is "All circles are black circles."

FORMALISM DEVELOPMENTS (1965–1970)

In addition to system-building activities, a number of formalisms were developed during the 1960s, especially in the latter half of the decade, relating to linguistic, psychological, and other aspects of natural languages. Based on experiences with previous attempts to construct natural-language-processing systems, and upon developments in linguistics and various areas of AI, these formalisms provided more sophisticated ways of representing the results of a partial or complete analysis of inputs to an NL system. A few of the more important of these formalisms are summarized here, namely, augmented transition networks, case grammar, conceptual dependency, procedural semantics, and semantic networks. Further details appear in the individual entries.

By extending the expressiveness of the transition network models described by Thorne and co-workers (1960) and Bobrow and Fraser (1969), which were themselves based on the basic finite-state machine model stemming from work in formal language theory, Woods (1970) developed an augmented transition network (ATN) model for the syntactic analysis of natural-language sentences. One of the primary advantages of the ATN model over its predecessors rested in its "hold-register" facility, which allowed information to be passed around in a parse tree under construction. This enabled the handling of deeply nested structures and other syntactic complexities. The hold-register facility derives, at least in spirit, from the desire to construct the deep structure corresponding to a sentence under analysis, a concept deriving from work in transformational grammar.

The theory of case grammar, as proposed by Fillmore (1968), expands on the view that "the sentence in its basic structure consists of a verb and one or more noun phrases, each associated with the verb in a particular case relationship." For instance, Fillmore observes that understanding the sentence "The hammer broke the window" involves recognizing that the noun *hammer* acts differently from *John* in "John broke the window." Specifically, it is an *instrument* ("the inanimate force or object causally involved in the action") rather than an *agent* ("instigator of the action identified by the verb"). Fillmore's original theory included these and six additional case roles. One important aspect of case grammar theory is its distinction between "surface" roles (eg, subject) and "deep" cases (eg, agent or instrument). Bruce (1975) provides a survey of ways in which the notion of case grammar was taken up by computationalists in the 1970s.

Having adopted a view that language-processing systems should not produce a syntactic analysis of an input divorced from its meaning, Schank proposed a conceptual dependency (CD) model of language and exhibited its operation in the context of an implemented parsing system

(1969). Deriving loosely from ideas to be found in Hays (1964), Kay (1967), and Lamb (1964), CD is based on a small number of "conceptual categories," including picture producers (PPs), PP assisters (PAs), actions or abstract nouns (ACTs), and ACT assisters (AAs). Developments in the original theory, including more sophisticated conceptual categories such as mental information transfer (MTRANS) and ingestion (INGEST), are outlined in Schank (1972). In addition to its central role in the development of the MARGIE system, discussed below, CD contributed to philosophical discussions concerning the role of "primitives" in theories of meaning.

In seeking to develop "a uniform framework for performing the semantic interpretation of English sentences," Woods (1968) devised a framework that he termed "procedural semantics" that acted as an intermediate representation between a language analyzer, eg, a question-answering system, and a back-end database retrieval component. In essence, the idea behind procedural semantics is to define, given a particular database, a collection of "semantic primitives" that comprise a set of predicates, functions, and commands. This strategy was first demonstrated in the context of a hypothetical question-answering system for an airlines reservation system and was used in building the LUNAR system, as described below.

Motivated by work in linguistics and psychology and attempting to formulate "a reasonable view of how semantic information is organized within a person's memory," Quillian (1968) proposed a memory model that has come to be known as a semantic network. Although precursors of semantic networks are to be found in the use of property lists by designers of early NL systems, Quillian provided a theoretical and more formal treatment. In essence, a semantic network consists of a set of "nodes," typically representing objects or concepts, and various "arcs" connecting them that are typically labeled to indicate a relation between nodes. Quillian's initial use of his network structures involved their role in making inferences and finding analogies. Semantic networks have been important not only because of the many systems that incorporate them, but also in their contribution to the development in the middle 1970s of various theories of knowledge representation. The evolution of semantic network structures, together with a discussion of applications based on them, is traced by Simmons (1973), Findler (1979), and Sowa (1984).

A TURNING POINT (ca 1970)

In the aftermath of disappointing results from work in machine translation in particular and the difficulty of constructing sophisticated natural language processing systems in general, two natural language projects in the early 1970s captured a degree of attention that served to boost the confidence of AI researchers regarding the prospects for broadly based, well grounded NL systems. These projects, which are discussed in turn, were the SHRDLU (qv) system of Winograd (1972) and the LUNAR (qv) system (Woods and co-workers, 1972; Woods, 1977).

SHRDLU

Winograd's SHRDLU system provided a natural-language interface to a simulated robot arm in a domain of blocks on a table. The system could handle imperatives such as "Pick up a big red block," questions such as "What does the box contain?" and declaratives such as "The blue pyramid is mine." Since SHRDLU maintained information about its actions, it could also be asked questions such as "Why did you pick up the green pyramid?" to which the system might respond, "To clean off the red cube."

The primary design principle of SHRDLU was that syntax, semantics, and reasoning about the blocks world should be combined in understanding natural-language input. The main coordinator of the system was a module (effectively a parser) consisting of a few large programs written in a special programming language called PROGRAMMAR, which was embedded in LISP. These programs corresponded to the basic structures of English (clauses, noun groups, prepositional groups, etc) and embodied a version of the systemic grammar theory of Halliday (1961). A semantics module that was similarly organized coordinated with the parser and made calls to a reasoning system programmed in MICROPLANNER (qv), a theorem-proving language. *Procedural representations for most of the knowledge in the system gave SHRDLU a considerable amount of flexibility to integrate semantic and pragmatic tests, to apply heuristic procedures for anaphora resolution, etc. The success of the procedural representations sparked the procedural–declarative controversy (Winograd, 1975), which led to the identification of important knowledge representation issues.

In the final analysis, many have agreed with Wilks (1977) that SHRDLU's power seems to derive in large measure from the constraints of its small, closed domain and that the techniques would fail to scale up to larger domains. Furthermore, the grammatical coverage of SHRDLU was spotty in the sense that "although a large number of syntactic constructions occur at least once in sample sentences appearing in the published dialog, our attempts to combine them into different sentences (involving no new words or concepts) produced few sentences that Winograd felt the system could successfully process" (Petrick, 1976). Nevertheless, SHRDLU was an impressive demonstration system that rekindled the hope of truly "natural" language-understanding systems and touched upon many still unsolved research topics.

LUNAR

The task of LUNAR, a system deriving from the work discussed above on procedural semantics, was to provide lunar geologists with a natural-language interface to the Apollo moon rock database. The system had three main components. The first phase formed a syntactic parse using an elaborate ATN grammar and a dictionary of 3500 words. The parser created a deep-structure representation, which was then passed to a rule-driven semantic interpreter. The antecedent of a semantic rule specified a tree fragment to be matched against the deep-structure representation plus semantic conditions on the matched nodes. The right side of a semantic rule was a procedural template for the final, retrieval component. For example, the sentence

What is the average concentration of aluminum in high alkali rocks?

was translated as

```
(FOR THE X13 /
  (SEQL (AVERAGE X14 /
    (SSUNION X15 / (SEQ TYPEAS):T;
    (DATALINE (WHQFILE X15) X15
    (NPR*X16 / (QUOTE OVERALL))
    (NPR*X17 / (QUOTE AL203)))):T))):T;
  (PRINTOUT X13)).
```

The database was a flat file containing 13,000 entries. Run time performance of the system was acceptable; the sentence above was parsed in just under 5 s. In an informal demonstration of the system at the Second Annual Lunar Science Conference held in Houston in January of 1971, 78% of the 111 requests were handled without error. After correcting minor dictionary coding errors, this rate was improved to 90%.

In discussing the coverage of the system, Woods considered the syntactic coverage to be "very competent" but noted that "if a [lunar geologist] really sat down to use the system to do some research he would quickly find himself wanting to say things which are beyond the ability of the current system" (Woods, 1977). In summary, the LUNAR system demonstrated that a sizable, important database problem could be handled using the techniques of ATNs and procedural semantics.

A VARIETY OF APPLICATION AREAS (1970–1984)

Following the technical advances of the 1960s and in the wake of the rather dramatic work of Winograd and Woods, the period from the early 1970s witnessed a variety of applied natural language projects. Application areas include database interface, computer-aided instruction, office automation, automatic programming (qv), and the processing of scientific text. These areas are discussed in turn.

Database Interface

Typical NL database interfaces operate by translating English or other natural-language inputs into a formal database query language to be run against an existing relational or other database management system. For a number of reasons, this formed the most frequent application area for applied NL work in the 1970s. First, the growing presence of database systems in business and industry resulted in a rapid increase in the number of potential computer users, many of whom preferred not to have to learn a "formal" computer language. Second, the idea of database query followed logically from the question-answering mode of many NL systems of the previous decade. Third, the NL system designer could, by starting with an existing set of data and by assuming an implemented

back-end retrieval module, avoid the need to address lowlevel representation issues.

An early attempt at providing natural-language access to a relational database is the RENDEZVOUS system, which emphasized human factors and concepts deriving from the database world, without less attention to techniques developed in AI and CL. The primary design goal of the system was "to accept queries stated in *any* English, grammatical or not, rejecting only those that are clearly outside the domain of discourse supported by the database at hand" (Codd and co-workers, 1974). To accomplish this, RENDEZVOUS temporarily ignored portions of the input it could not recognize and, to compensate, engaged the user in "clarification dialog" to refine its understanding. A representative initial input to RENDEZVOUS is "I want to find certain projects. Pipes were sent to them in Feb. 1975." To help ensure reliable processing, RENDEZVOUS provided a paraphrase of its current understanding of the user's request. In situations where a phrase was ambiguous to the system, a request for clarification was generated. Although RENDEZVOUS tended to overburden the prospective user with too many seemingly pointless questions (eg, it thought that "37" in "part 37" might be a quantity on order rather than a part number), it addressed human-factors issues that were taken up by PLANES (qv) and other systems.

A sharp contrast to the previous system in terms of linguistic sophistication is found in TQA, formerly REQUEST, whose syntactic processing is based on the principles of transformational grammar. This decision was made "in an attempt to deal with the complexity and diversity that are characteristic of even restricted subsets of natural language" (Plath, 1976). In essence, the parsing involves applying transformations in *reverse* to reconstruct the deep structure associated with a question to be answered. Details concerning this process, and further motivation for it, are given in Petrick (1973). Initial applications included Fortune 500 data and a database on White Plains land usage. During the latter field study, a set of operating statistics was collected (Damerau, 1981).

A system intermediate between the previous two in terms of linguistic sophistication is LADDER (Hendrix and co-workers, 1978), whose syntactic processing was based on a semantic grammar designed around the object types of the domain at hand, such as ship and port, rather than linguistically motivated lexical and syntactic categories, such as noun and verb. The system provided an ability "for naive users to input English statements at run time that extend and personalize the language accepted by the system" (Hendrix, 1977). The specific set of tools seeking to "facilitate the rapid construction of natural language interfaces" was called LIFER (qv). The system contained facilities for the user to add synonyms and define paraphrases; mechanisms to handle ellipsis (incomplete inputs) were also provided. For example, after asking "What is the salary of Johnson?" the user could type "position and date hired" and the system would answer the question "What are the position and date hired of Johnson?" The development of LADDER helped to reassure the CL community that "genuinely useful natural language interfaces can be created and that the creation process takes considerably less effort than might be expected" (Hendrix, 1977). Hershman and co-workers (1979) describe an experiment in which LADDER was used for a simulated Navy search-and-rescue operation.

Other interesting and important NL database systems were constructed, but space permits only brief descriptions. The TORUS system (Mylopoulos and co-workers, 1975) represented an early attempt at formulating an "integrated methodology" for designing NL database front ends. It employed a semantic network representation, and the prototype was developed around a database of graduate student files. As described in Thompson and Thompson (1975), work continued on the REL system mentioned earlier and eventually gave rise to the desk-top systems POL and ASK (Thompson and Thompson, 1981, 1983). In addition to manifesting refinements and extensions over earlier work, ASK was extended to allow for French as well as English inputs. Results of an experimental study with the REL-ASK family apepar in Thompson (1980). EUFID (Templeton, 1979; Templeton and Burger, 1983) was also designed to be database independent and, like LADDER, provided a "personal synonym" facility designed to be "forgiving of spelling and grammar errors" (Templeton, 1979).

Several systems seeking to address the issue of cooperative response were designed. For instance, the construction of CO-OP (Kaplan, 1978) was based on the belief that "NL systems must be designed to respond appropriately when they can detect a misconception on the part of the user." For example, the probable presumption of a user who asks, "how many students got a grade of F in CIS 500 in spring 1977?" is that the course was in fact given at the time in question. If this were not the case, CO-OP would so inform the user, rather than simply give the literal but misleading answer "nobody." The PLANES system (Waltz, 1978) was based on the notion that an effective NL system "must be able to help guide and train the user to frame requests in a form that the system can understand." According to the designers, the work derives in spirit from Codd's work (1974) with RENDEZVOUS. For instance, PLANES incorporated novel techniques of "concept case frames" for generating dialogue to flesh out an incomplete understanding of the user's request and "context registers" for handling pronouns and other anaphora. JETS, a successor to PLANES, responded to some "interesting questions about the conceptual completeness of question-answering systems" (Finin and co-workers, 1979) that arose during experiments with the earlier system (Tennant, 1979).

A number of high quality European systems were developed, each manifesting some interest in domain independence. The USL system (Lehman, 1978) was designed in Heidelberg as a domain-independent German language database front-end. It incorporated a revised version of a parser built by Kay (1977), and "the method of [semantic] interpretation used in the REL system . . . was taken as a point of departure" (Lehman, 1978, p. 560). Additional grammars were constructed to enable USL to answer questions posed in English, Dutch, and Spanish as well as German. A user study with the USL system was reported by Krause (1979). PHLIQA was built in Eindhoven to answer English questions about information stored in a CODASYL database (Bronnenberg and co-workers, 1978–1979). It operated on hypothetical data concerning computers installed at European establishments and was intentionally structured to include "some features that cause difficulties . . . and which are also found in 'real' databases" (ibid, p. 230). Attention was paid to isolating the parts of the system that depended on the chosen data base, and an effort was made "to derive the parts dependent on a data base in a systematic way from the structure of the data base and its subject domain" (ibid, 1978–1979, p. 230). HAM-ANS (qv) (Hoeppner and co-workers, 1983) was developed in Hamburg as "a robust and cooperative system" to enable natural-language access in German to database and other software services.

The ROBOT system (qv) (Harris, 1977a, 1978), rather than emphasizing linguistically complex (eg, deeply nested) English structures, represented a database front-end with concern for report generation facilities, as suggested by the representative input "Print a report of direct commission, net loss incurred, and change in INBR for region B, sorted by net loss." The system was interesting in its use of the database as a world model in which to carry out disambiguations, but its primary importance is that it led in the late 1970s to a product for mainframe database query, INTELLECT (qv) and the concomitant founding of Artificial Intelligence Corporation.

More recent systems for database and information retrieval, which represent an important direction but for which space does not exist and for which a historical perspective is not yet possible, are mentioned below in the section on current trends. Also, there has been a small amount of attention to providing natural language facilities for database *update*, as opposed to query. Examples of this work are found in Salveter (1982) and Davidson and Kaplan (1983).

Computer-Aided Instruction

The first attempt at incorporating AI and CL techniques into an integrated system for computer-aided instruction (CAI) was the SCHOLAR (qv) program (Carbonell, 1970). By representing the information to be learned in *semantic network* structures, this system was designed to be independent of the actual "lesson" at hand, which for the prototype consisted of information about South American geography. In particular, "no specific pieces of text, questions, with their predicted answers, errors, or anticipated branching form part of this data structure" (Carbonell, 1970). An example interaction with SCHOLAR follows.

THE LANGUAGE IN BRAZIL IS FRENCH. RIGHT OR WRONG?

"Wrong."

YOU ARE CORRECT. THE LANGUAGE IN BRAZIL IS PORTUGESE.

As incidated, the system included a nontrivial English-generation component. More significant, however, was the provision for "mixed-initiative" dialogues, where the user could ask questions of the system at any time rather than supply an answer for a pending question. For example, if the system had just asked "What is Brazil," the student might delay answering the question by asking the system to "Tell me something about Peru." In addition, the system allowed its user to switch to a question-answering mode, thus acting as a question answerer for the data at hand. Historically, however, SCHOLAR was most important by establishing the feasibility of mixed-initiative NL systems.

In continuing the work begun with the initial SCHOLAR prototype, Collins and co-workers (1976) extended the system's basic matching mechanisms to enable it to operate in situations in which requested information is missing. The resulting system would sometimes make inferences and sometimes inform the questioner that the requested information was not available. In the latter case, related or partial information might be given. As an example, the system would respond to the question "Is Bolivia a capital?" by answering "No, Bolivia is a country, not a capital." In formulating this response, SCHOLAR has used its knowledge that country and city are mutually exclusive object types and only a city can be a capital.

Another extension to the work of SCHOLAR is represented by the SOPHIE (qv) system, which sought to encourage "a wider range of student initiatives" by presenting "a 'reactive' environment in which the student learns by trying out his ideas rather than by instruction" (Brown and Burton, 1975). To explore this idea, SOPHIE was designed as an electronics lab troubleshooting system that would "mimic the roles of a human teacher" (Brown and Burton, 1975). To use the system, a student would receive a schematic diagram of a power supply and be told the control settings of a simulated faulty circuit. An example interaction follows.

"What is the output?"
THE OUTPUT VOLTAGE IS 11.7 VOLTS.
"What is it in a working circuit?"
IN A WORKING CIRCUIT THE OUTPUT VOLTAGE IS 19.9 VOLTS.
"What is the voltage between R8 and Q1?"
THE VOLTAGE AT N1 is 47.6 VOLTS.

When the student finally settled on a diagnosis of the problem and recommended a course of action, such as "replace Q6," SOPHIE would seize the initiative and begin asking questions of the student. In addition, SOPHIE could alter the parameters of its simulated circuit, thus providing "what-if" capabilities. Despite the fact that it was carefully designed for a troubleshooting application by the use of a "semantic" grammar and thus lacked the domain independence of SCHOLAR, SOPHIE contained a variety of non-NL capabilities that themselves proved to be interesting and important.

Subsequent to the efforts reported above, Weischedel and co-workers (1978) constructed a system to aid students in learning first-year German. The designers were interested, among other things, in enabling computers to deal with ungrammatical sentences, and in their chosen

setting, it was mandatory for the system to respond meaningfully to inputs that were linguistically flawed as well as those that were factually incorrect. An example of such a response follows (the system's question translates as "Where did Miss Moreau learn German?").

WO HAT FRÄULEIN MOREAU DEUTSCH GELERNT?
"Sie hat es gelernt in der Schule."
ERROR: PAST PARTICIPLE MUST BE AT END OF CLAUSE.
A CORRECT ANSWER WOULD HAVE BEEN:
SIE HAT DEUTSCH IN DER SCHULE GELERNT.

In addition to detecting incorrect grammar in the context of an otherwise acceptable response, the system was able to recognize when an input was incorrect or, more subtly, correct but not fully responsive to the question. As suggested above, the tutoring program dealt with reading comprehension, and the prototype was applied to several "lessons," each consisting of a paragraph. Concerning generality, the designers pointed out that "the texts that appear in foreign language textbooks very rapidly surpass the ability of artificial intelligence systems."

They also observed that "there does not seem to be any way to tune the system to particular types of errors," which means that an instructor would have to construct each lesson by hand, unlike for the semantic network approach adopted for SCHOLAR (which carefully avoided storing textual information). Perhaps the most significant outcome of the project was to demonstrate ways in which "ill-formedness" can extend to morphological, semantic, and pragmatic problems as well as syntactic ones.

The ILIAD system (Bates and Ingria, 1981) was conceived as a way of helping instruct people having a language-delaying handicap (eg, deafness) or who are learning English as a second language. It included a powerful English generator based on the transformational grammar model. (See also EDUCATION, AI IN.)

Office Automation

The SCHED system was based on techniques and formalisms developed for the automatic programming system NLPQ described below and represented an initial study of "the feasibility of developing systems which accomplish typical office tasks by means of human-like communication with the user" (Heidorn, 1978). Although the long-range goal of SCHED was to provide an on-line system to review and update one's own desk calendar and those of fellow office workers, the implemented system was restricted to information pertaining to a single user. An example input for SCHED is, "Schedule a meeting, Wed, my office, 2 to 2:30, with my manager and his manager, about 'a demo,'" to which the system would respond by stating in English its understanding of the input. Subject to user verification, the system would issue an appropriate command to a resident calendar management system. In situations where a user input failed to supply all necessary information, SCHED was able to ask for specific information, thus providing for mixed-initiative conversations reminiscent of the previously mentioned work in CAI.

The GUS system, similar in spirit to SCHED, though quite different in its methods, was "intended to engage a sympathetic and highly cooperative human in an English dialog, directed towards a specific goal within a very restricted domain of discourse" (Bobrow and co-workers, 1977).

In particular, GUS played the role of a travel agent able to assist a user in making a round trip from a city in California. Although its implementation was apparently less robust than SCHED, its designers suggested that "the system is interesting because of the phenomena of natural dialog that it attempts to model and because of its principles of program organization" (ibid).

The VIPS system, which seeks to "allow a user to display objects of interest on a computer terminal and manipulate them via typed or spoken English imperative sentences" (Biermann, Ballard and Sigmon, 1983), is unusual in that it incorporates a hardware voice recognizer into an NLP. Initial applications have been to the numerical domain of its predecessor (the automatic programming system NLC) and to text editing, where objects may be referenced either in English or by use of a touch-sensitive display screen.

ARGOT represents a long-term research project seeking to "partake in an extended English dialogue on some reasonably well-specified range of topics" (Allen, Frisch, and Litman, 1982). The initial task domain for ARGOT was that of a computer center operator.

The UC system is designed as "an intelligent natural language interface that allows naive users to communicate with the UNIX(TM) operating system in ordinary English" (Wilensky, 1982). It answers questions such as "How do I print the file fetch.1 on the line printer?"

Finally, some research has applied CL techniques to the analysis, as opposed to processing, of written texts. One such system is the Writer's Workbench (MacDonald and co-workers, 1982), which, upon scanning the draft of a document, flags words, phrases, and sentence types that have been felt to negatively affect the readability of the text. For example, the previous sentence could be improved by eliminating the passive voice ("have been felt") and unsplitting the infinitive ("to negatively affect"). Another system, CRITIQUE, formerly EPISTLE (qv) (Heidorn, 1982), similarly performs stylistic analyses but also diagnoses several classes of grammatical errors. For example,

Your statement of deficiencies *have* not been completed.

(should be *has*)

Automatic Programming

The term *automatic programming* (qv) refers to the effort to relieve a computer user from the details needed to get the machine to perform a desired task. In certain ways attempts at a natural-language solution to this problem are similar to the work on problem-solving systems (STU-

DENT and CARPS) described earlier, although no specific techniques from these systems appear to have been employed. A survey of early NL work in automatic programming appears in Heidorn (1976).

One early system, described by Gelb (1971), was designed to answer simple probability questions such as "What is the probability of getting two or more heads or exactly three tails when four coins are tossed once?"

Another early system is NLPQ (Heidorn, 1976) which produced simulation programs in GPSS for a class of queueing problems. An example of an initial specification of a user's problem follows: "When a vehicle arrives at a station, it leaves there immediately if the length of the line at a pump in the station is not less than 2. Seventy-five percent of the vehicles are cars and a fourth are trucks. There is just one pump. A simulation run time of 8 h is desired." At this point the system would take control and begin asking questions to clarify and extend what it had been told. For example, it would begin by asking "How often do the vehicles arrive at the station?" and the user might answer "The arrivals of vehicles are normally distributed with a mean of 8 minutes." Having acquired all requisite information, NLPQ would first produce an English statement of its understanding of the entire problem and then a complete program for the task.

As reported in Green (1977), the PSI system included modules for English input and output, along with many other components, in a large-scale automatic programming system. An excerpt from a session with the system follows.

"[The program] first inputs a concept. Then it repeatedly accepts an input scene from the user, classifies it based on whether or not it fits the concept, and outputs this classification to the user."
WHAT IS THE STRUCTURE OF THE CONCEPT?
"A concept is a collection of relations. Each relation is just a string."
WHAT IS THE EXIT TEST OF THE LOOP . . .

Due to the complexities involved in program synthesis, PSI was tested only on problems related to sorting, graph reachability, and determining prime number.

Unlike the preceding work, the NLC system (Biermann and Ballard, 1980) chose to regard an English input as a statement in a very-high-level program. The system acted as an interpreter, providing an interactive matrix-domain programming environment with visual feedback as each English command was processed. An example input follows.

"Subtract six from the next to last positive number in the row that was multiplied by 5."

In addition to simple imperatives, NLC provided for loops ("repeat"), conditionals ("if . . ."), and procedure definitions ("define a way to . . ."). An experiment study of programming with the system is described in Biermann and co-workers (1983), and an application of the system for college sophomore level linear algebra instruction is discussed in Geist and co-workers (1982).

Scientific Text Processing

Based on many years of work developing a comprehensive grammar for English (Sager, 1981), a group of researchers constructed a system intended "to allow the health care worker to create [a] medical report in the most natural way—in medical English, using whatever syntax is appropriate to the information (Hirschman and co-workers, 1976; Grishman and Hirschman, 1978). After gathering reports in English and converting them to a textual database form, the system could be interrogated as though it were a conventional database system, again using English for inputs. Some examples of the types of inputs gathered in a clinical setting are the following:

X rays taken 3-22-65 reveal no evidence of metastatic disease.

Chest X ray on 8-12-69 showed no metastatic disease.

3-2-65 chest film shows clouding along left thorax and pleural thickening.

and an example question is "Did every patient have a chest X ray in 1975?" A distinctive feature of the system is its method of creating so-called information format structures, which are similar to structured database records but capture the information initially supplied in textual form. Defining an information format for a particular application involves, first, isolating word classes by syntactic properties, eg, the verbs *reveal* and *show* are alike in taking *X ray* as a subject, although *X ray* and *film* are alike in taking *show* as a verb, and, second, defining the *columns* of the table from the word classes so that any input sentence will have a paraphrase like that shown above (Sager, 1978). The system, which is unusual in containing aspects of both database and information retrieval, was subsequently adapted to the domain of navy messages, as described in Marsh and Friedman (1985).

CURRENT TRENDS

Domain-Independent Implementations

Several domain-independent database systems have already been mentioned, but the intensity of effort at enhancing the transportability of systems for this and other applications areas should be noted. In particular, a number of projects are seeking either to allow users themselves to carry out a customization or to have the system adapt itself automatically to a user or a domain of discourse. Representative examples of this work include Haas and Hendrix (1980), Hendrix and Lewis (1981), Mark (1981), Thompson and Thompson (1980, 1981), Wilczynski (1981), Warren and Pereira (1982), Bates (1983), Ginsparg (1983), Grosz (1983), Ballard and co-workers (1984), and Grishman and co-workers (1984). Also, several papers deriving from a recent workshop on transportability (Ballard, 1985) have appeared, including Damerau (1985), Hafner and Godden (1985), Marsh and Friedman (1985), Slocum and Justus (1985), and Thompson and Thompson (1984).

The Reemergence of Machine Translation

As indicated earlier, the ALPAC report of 1966 nearly eliminated U.S. government funding of projects in machine translation (MT). Naturally, this caused a market decline in the amount of work being done in the area and in the number of papers published. Nevertheless, due in part to progress in AI and other areas of CL, a gradual resurgence of interest in MT occurred in the 1980s, and the field gives evidence of becoming well populated once again. A bibliography of about 450 publications since 1973 related to MT can be found in Slocum (1985) along with summary papers on several of the major full-scale translation systems in existence. Papers from a recent conference on MT (Nirenburg, 1987) are also available.

The Commercialization of NLP

As indicated above, Harris's database front-end, ROBOT, became the proprietary software of Artificial Intelligence Corporation in the late 1970s. Under the name INTELLECT, this system was for several years virtually the only natural language product on the market. In the early 1980s, however, several well-known NL researchers, including Hendrix and Schank, formed or became associated with start-up ventures. In recent years products from these and other companies have been appearing for database and other applications [eg, a developing expert system interface is discussed in Lehnert and Schwartz (1983)]. More recently researchers at Carnegie Mellon University and other academic institutions have formed companies; Texas Instruments has produced a menu-based natural-language-like interface; at least one project at BBN Laboratories is slated for commercial release; and other corporate flirtations are occurring. In addition to database query, machine translation systems are also being sold, and prospects exist for additional application areas. All of these activities, as well as an overview of ongoing research into the theoretical and applied side of CL, are reported in Johnson (1985).

THEORETICAL ISSUES

This article has thus far conducted a chronological review of projects within CL that relate more or less directly to specific applications. This section provides a brief overview of some of the major theoretical topics associated with CL. The discussion relates specific systems to the theoretical issues, but it primarily emphasizes theoretical techniques and formalisms that have contributed to the classification of research in CL. The topics are parsing and grammatical formalisms, semantics, discourse understanding, text generation, cognitive modeling, language acquisition, and speech understanding. Further information is available in separate articles.

Parsing and Grammatical Formalisms

Parsing (qv) issues have been of central interest in Cl since its inception, when CL included the study of formal languages and programming languages, as well as natural languages. As the term is used here, parsing refers to the process of assigning structural descriptions to an input string. Classically, parsers have used various forms of phrase structure grammars and have assigned phrase structure markers to produce derivation trees. Parsers with access to semantic and pragmatic knowledge, however, may build semantic descriptions directly without explicitly creating derivation trees.

Direction of Analysis. Parsing strategies are often classified as top-down (or goal-driven) if they begin with the start symbol and backward chain from the consequents of rules to their antecedents. Recursive-descent parsers, the PROLOG execution procedure for definite-clause grammars (DCGs) (Pereira and Warren, 1980), and the usual execution procedure for augmented transition network (ATN) grammars (Woods, 1970) all use top-down approaches (see PROCESSING, BOTTOM-UP AND TOP-DOWN). Bottom-up (or data-driven) techniques proceed in a forward direction from the terminal symbols (words) in the grammar toward the start symbol. Left-corner (including shift-reduce) parsers (Chester), word-based parsers (Riesbeck, 1975) and its descendants (Small, 1982), chart parsers (Earley, 1970; Kaplan, 1973; Kay, 1967; Ruzzo, 1980; Younger, 1967), and deterministic parsers (Marcus, 1980; Milne, 1986) are primarily bottom-up.

Parsers can also be classified according to how they analyze the input string: from left to right, from right to left, or from arbitrary positions in the middle outward. The left-to-right ordering is simple and natural and lends itself to easy bookkeeping. It is also of theoretical interest for parsers that attempt to model aspects of cognitive processes, such as attention focusing, that are dependent on temporal ordering. Middle-out, bottom-up parsers have been used particularly in speech systems (Woods, 1982; Erman and co-workers, 1980), where the parser can use its analysis in regions of greatest certainty to help in noisy or unintelligible regions, which would cause trouble for a rigid left-to-right parser.

Parsing techniques bear a close relationship to grammatical formalisms, although a particular grammar or class of grammars can sometimes be parsed in a variety of ways. ATN grammars, for example, have been parsed by both top-down/left–right and bottom-up/middle–out methods. Another technique for matching grammar and parser is to preprocess a grammar into an equivalent grammar suitable for a particular parsing method.

Search and Nondeterminism. Controlling the search effort for a parse and handling nondeterminism are major problems for parsers. Many actual parsers use a blend of top-down and bottom-up techniques. As a simple example of this, almost every recursive descent (top-down) parser uses some kind of (bottom-up) scanner to identify the tokens in the input. Part-of-speech classifications in a lexicon are a form of bottom-up information. Another method for improving top-down parsing techniques is the use of a precomputed left-branching reachability matrix that can be used to decide whether the next input symbol can appear in the leftmost branch of a derivation tree headed by a particular nonterminal. Word expert parsing (Small, 1982) uses an idiosyncratic combination of top-down expectations and bottom-up processing.

The three principal methods for dealing with nondeterminism are backtracking, parallelism, and transforming the grammar so that a deterministic algorithm (perhaps using bounded look-ahead) can efficiently parse it. Backtracking parsers pursue one alternative at a choice point and return to select another alternative on failure of the first one. Forcing failure after a successful parse can cause the backtracking parser to find additional parses. The standard execution procedure of PROLOG provides such a facility directly for logic grammars such as DCGs, which can be represented as PROLOG programs. Backtracking (qv) techniques are especially popular and natural for context-free grammar formalisms. Context-free grammars, which have a single consequent nonterminal, lend themselves to backward-chaining execution methods that work nicely in conjunction with backtracking.

Parallel parsing methods keep track of multiple derivations at each point in the processing. The derivations can be developed concurrently using sequential algorithms and machines or truly in parallel if multiple processing resources are available. Interest in parallel approaches has increased as parallel hardware is becoming available; it has also been buoyed by the resurgence of connectionist and neural network research (Cottrell, 1984; Jones and Driscoll, 1985; Waltz and Pollack, 1985). Chart parsing algorithms use a particularly efficient way of recording which derivations have already been found to cover substrings of the input string. By splitting the computation at choice points, backtracking methods can also be parallelized.

Another alternative, explored by Marcus (1980), is factoring the rules in such a way that limited look-ahead is sufficient to resolve most of the nondeterminism. Although not all of English, for example, can be treated deterministically in this manner, the parser interestingly fails on many of the same "garden path" sentences that cause people trouble. Cases of lexical and structural ambiguity that the parser cannot resolve are left for other modules.

Word-based parsing systems generally attempt to incorporate enough knowledge to determine a unique interpretation. When ambiguity cannot be resolved without look-ahead, two possibilities present themselves. One technique is to let a later constituent complete the interpretation; for example, verbs can be responsible for assigning the role of the subject noun phrase. Another solution is to spawn demons that check for the appearance of disambiguating items. For example, sense-specific demons might check for the presence of particular particles to detect multiword verbs.

Grammatical Formalisms. Many different grammatical formalisms have been used by natural-language-processing systems. One of the earliest systems, the Harvard Syntactic Analyzer (Kuno, 1965), recognized context-free grammars. Transformational grammar (TG) theories had a direct influence on the Mitre (Zwicky and co-workers, 1965) and Petrick (1965) parsers and an indirect influence on many others. The UCLA grammar combines TG with case grammar theory (Stockwell, Schacter, and Partee, 1973). In simplest terms, transformational grammars specify a set of (usually context-free) base phrase structure rules, a set of structure mapping rules, and various conditions, filters, or principles that generated structures must satisfy. Since TG is stated as a generative theory, parsers must try to guess which transformations must have been applied by effectively inverting the rules. This has proved to be quite difficult in practice.

One of the most comprehensive computer grammars of English has been developed at the Linguistic String Project (Sager, 1981). The grammar consists of a set of 180 BNF phrase structure rules, 180 restriction rules that check feature conditions, string-transformation rules, and ellipsis rules. Additional sub-language categorizations are added to the lexicon together with domain-specific restriction rules to increase parsing efficiency.

ATN grammars (Woods, 1970) have been very influential on computational approaches to language processing. They augment recursive transition-network grammars, which recognize context-free languages, with actions and tests that give them the recognition power of Turing machines. With suitable self-restraint, however, one can produce disciplined, well-structured grammars in many different grammar-writing styles. The LUNAR grammar (Woods, Kaplan, and Nash-Webber, 1972) was a quite detailed, large grammar. Other augmented phrase structure formalisms include the DIAMOND grammars at SRI [eg, DIAGRAM (Robinson, 1982)] and the APSG (augmented phrase structure grammar) formalism used in the CRITIQUE system developed at IBM (Heidorn, 1975). The systemic grammar theory of Halliday (1961) has been incorporated in many NLP systems, notably Winograd's SHRDLU system (qv) (Wingorad, 1972) and in the large NIGEL grammar (Mann and Mattheissen, 1985).

More recent work in linguistics has revived interest in nontransformational theories of phrase structure grammars, particularly context-free grammars. These theories hold that notational augmentations to phrase structure grammars can express such difficult, "transformational" phenomena as movement nontransformationally and, furthermore, in most cases, that there exist equivalent context-free grammars. From a parsing perspective it will be most useful if the augmentations can be processed on the fly with little overhead above that required for context-free parsing. The augmentations include metarules, complex features, and principles of feature instantiation (Kay, 1979). The major theoretical frameworks include generalized phrase structure grammar (GPSG) (Gazdar, 1982), tree adjoining grammar (TAG) (Joshi, 1984), head grammar (HG) (Proudian and Pollard, 1985), lexical functional grammar (LFG) (Bresnan and Kaplan, 1982), and functional unification grammar (FUG) (Kay, 1984).

Providing for Ungrammaticality. It has been observed that "while significant progress has been made in the processing of correct text, a practical system must be able to handle many forms of ill-formedness gracefully" (Allen, 1983). When the ill-formedness in question is syntactic in origin and when the expected deviations can be grouped into a manageable number of classes, it is possible to prepare for "errors" by explicitly including extra rules in the system grammar so that a predictably deviant input is in fact treated as though it were grammatical. Due to the possible ambiguities that this practice introduces and to

confront general situations where either the full range of errors cannot be predicted or the intended meaning cannot be recovered, more sophisticated mechanisms are called for.

Attacks on the problem of ungrammaticality are represented by work described by Weischedel and Black (1981), Hayes and Mouradian (1981), Kwasny and Sondheimer (1981), Jensen and co-workers (1983), Weischedel and Sondheimer (1983), Granger (1983), and Fink and Biermann (1986). It is also worth noting that, for some applications, grammatical errors are part of the problem being addressed rather than a regrettable accident. Examples include the German language CAI system and the text-critiquing systems mentioned earlier. In addition, most AI work in speech understanding is fundamentally concerned with the rampant and perhaps inherent uncertainties associated with speech recognition devices. These uncertainties actually make error conditions the rule rather than the exception.

Semantics

Semantics concerns the study of meaning. In the context of CL, this most often relates to problems of finding and representing the meaning of natural language expressions. The previous discussion has already touched on several approaches to semantics, including conceptual dependency, procedural semantics, and semantic networks (qv). Some others are preference semantics and other decompositional systems, Montague semantics, and situation semantics (qv).

Among the more significant questions to be asked of an approach to semantics, at least insofar as its relevance to CL is concerned, are what sorts of *noncompositionality* does the system involve and what role, if any, is played by *primitives*. In essence, the idea behind compositional semantics is to determine the meaning of an entire unit under analysis (phrase, sentence, text) in a systematic (ideally simple) way from the meanings of its parts. This approach has obvious advantages in terms of being tractable for incorporation into an automated scheme for language understanding. The idea behind primitives (in its strong sense) is to determine a finite set of terms that by themselves can express the meaning of any word and, by implication, the meaning of any utterance. Of the semantic schemes discussed earlier, conceptual dependency (qv) adheres to this goal, where procedural semantics does not. Many interesting debates on these and other issues of semantics have occurred, as discussed by Jackendoff (1983).

In building entire NL systems, many designers have attempted to separate syntax from semantics by performing syntactic analysis first and then converting the resulting structure (produced by the parser) to a meaning representation (see NATURAL LANGUAGE UNDERSTANDING). In other cases, however, the two processes have been much more tightly integrated. Whereas problems in CL related to syntax have largely involved issues also addressed by the field of conventional (as opposed to computational) linguistics, problems of semantics have typically concerned work in philosophy. In the context of AI, important work related to natural-language semantics is to be found in the area of knowledge representation (qv).

Discourse Understanding

Discourse understanding (qv) includes natural language processing phenomena that span individual sentences in multisentence texts or dialogue. The work in discourse understanding acknowledges that the syntactic and semantic representations of sentences in discourse contexts relate both explicitly (eg, by clue words such as *now, but, anyway*) and implicitly (eg, by world knowledge) to the representations of other sentences in the discourse.

As an example of how an amazing amount of complexity can enter into even simple interchanges, consider the following brief dialogue:

Q: Can you tell me where John is?
A: Oh, he was hungry for one of Joe's pizzas. He'll be back soon.

The petitioner's use of a yes–no question is an example of an *indirect speech act*. In an indirect speech act one illocutionary act is performed indirectly by way of performing another (Allen and Perrault, 1980; Cohen and Perrault, 1979; Searle, 1975).

The yes–no question is interpreted as a form of politeness instead of a more direct utterance such as "Where is John?" Grice (1975) noticed that conversational participants follow cooperative principles that he subcategorized as quantity (be informative), quality (be truthful), relation (be relevant), and manner (be brief). The response in the example above meets Gricean notions of appropriateness, but it, too, is indirect in communicating both where John is and why he is there. To infer John's location from his state of hunger and desire requires a plan and goal analysis from pragmatic (extralinguistic) knowledge. The final part of the answer responds to an inferred petitioner's goal of being copresent with John by suggesting that he will be back soon.

In cooperative conversations Grice noted that speakers caused listeners to make certain inferences, which he termed *conversational implicatures*. Hirschberg (1984) has studied a class of implicatures called *scalar implicatures*. In the sentence "some people left early," for example, the hearer may reasonably conclude that "not all people left early." A cooperative response occasionally requires that faulty presuppositions in the question be corrected. For a database query such as "How many juniors failed CS 200?" an answer of "none" is misleading if there were no juniors enrolled. The CO-OP system performed this type of presupposition checking (Kaplan, 1978). Another type of cooperative response involves informing the user of discontinuities (Siklossy, 1977). In a flight reservation database one might want to know of any flights leaving before noon. It might be helpful to suggest one at 12:05 P.M. or one the next or previous day if none are otherwise available.

A natural idea for discouse understanding was to extend some of the concepts of grammars and schemas from sentence parsing to discourse. Conversation-related work includes the Susie Software system (Brown, 1977; Tennant, 1981) and discourse ATN grammar (Reichman, 1984). In story understanding Rumelhart (1975) and Co-

reira (1980) developed the idea of story grammars. Many of the language-understanding systems of Schank and his students use knowledge structures [such as scripts, plans, memory organization packets (qv) (MOPs), and thematic abstraction units (TAUs)] to guide discourse-understanding processes. Dialog-games (Levin and Moore, 1977) were an attempt to use a goal-centered theory for dialogues. Litman and Allen (1987) also integrated work on planning and discourse.

Focus is an important technical notion in discourse work that relates to the shifts in attention during comprehension. Focus influences many aspects of language understanding, including choice of topic, syntactic ordering, and anaphoric reference. Grosz (1981) did pioneering work on *global focus*, ie, how attention shifts over a set of discourse utterances. *Immediate focus* represents how attention shifts over two consecutive sentences. Sidner (1981) used focus to disambiguate definite anaphora by tracking three things: the immediate focus of the sentence, a potential focus list created from discourse entities in the sentence, and the past immediate foci in a focus stack.

The resolution of anaphora is an important problem within discourse understanding. Early techniques principally used a simple history list of discourse entities combined with a heuristic method for selecting them (often a variation of the most recently encountered entity satisfying the reference). The simple techniques are inadequate, largely because they fail to account for focus effects and because discourse referents do not have to be explicitly mentioned (eg, the referent of *he* in the sentence "I got stopped yesterday for speeding, but he didn't give me a ticket"). Besides Sidner's technique described above, there are several other notable approaches (see Hirst for a more detailed account). Other methods include concept activatedness (Kantor, 1977), task-oriented dialogue techniques (Groz, 1981), logical representations (Webber, 1978), and discourse cohesion (Hobbs, 1979; Lockman, 1978).

Text Generation

Text generation is the process of translating internal representations into surface forms. The forms of internal representations have included deep structure, semantic networks, conceptual dependency graphs, and deduction trees. The *strategic* component of a generation system chooses what to say—the message to be conveyed including any propositional attitudes. The *tactical* component determines how to say it.

The earliest systems generated sentences at random to test grammars (Yngve, 1962; Friedman, 1969; Yngve, 1962). Later AI efforts used generation techniques as a part of paraphrase systems, which parsed input strings into meaning representations and then generated back out into surface representations. Klein (1965) used dependency grammars that generated a semantic dependency tree and a standard phrase structure derivation tree. Dependency trees from multiple sentences were related by nominal coreference links. A generation grammar matched portions of the dependency trees. Simmons and

Slocum (1972) produced sentences from a semantic network using an ATN modified for generation. Eventually, a parser was added to fully automate the paraphrase process (Simmons, 1973). Similarly, Heidorn (1977) reported an algorithm based on an augmented phrase structure grammar for producing English noun phrases to identify nodes in a semantic network. Goldman (1975) used a discrimination net for conceptual dependency graphs. The net tested the primitive action types and roles to select an appropriate surface verb. This generator was later used as a part of the MARGIE system (Schank, 1975).

The generation technique in SHRDLU (Winograd, 1972) is an example of the template-based approach that has predominated in generation techniques. The program used several types of patterned responses including completely canned phrases such as "ok," parameterized phrases such as "sorry, I don't know the word _____," and more complex parameterizations that involved the substitution of determiners, discourse phrases, and dictionary definitions. Small programs were responsible for formatting the descriptions of objects and events. For example, the definition for the event PUTON was

(APPEND (VBFIX (QUOTE PUT)) OBJ1
(QUOTE (ON)) OBJ2)

A heuristic pronominal substitution mechanism improved the quality of the responses, allowing for the generation of noun phrases as complex as "the large green one that supports the pyramid."

Although most generation systems of the 1970s used techniques similar to SHRDLU, two different, important generation programs appeared in 1974. Davey's PROTEUS program (Davey, 1979) described tic-tac-toe games. The program had a rich understanding of the tactics of the game and could provide natural summarizations at an appropriate, high level. An example is "I threatened you by taking the middle of the edge opposite that and adjacent to the one I had just taken but you blocked it and threatened me." The ERMA program (Clippinger, 1975) embodied a cognitive model of human generation that mimicked the real-time false starts and patching of utterances. The model was developed by studying transcripts of psychoanalysis sessions to determine a patient's reasoning patterns. As an example, the program generated "you know for some reason I just thought about the bill and payment" as a gentle way of beginning to argue that "you shouldn't give me a bill."

Interest in generation work has revived in the 1980s with a number of new research projects. Mann and co-workers (1982) provide a survey of text generation projects. Some of the major projects are as follows. The transformational grammar generation system of Bates and Ingria (1981), a very syntactically powerful generator, was used in a CAI application. McDonald's (1983) generator, MUMBLE, models spoken language and concentrates on the fluency and coverage of the tactical component. The KDS system (Mann and Moore, 1981) used a "fragment-and-compose" paradigm in which the knowledge structure is divided into small propositional units, which are then composed into large textual units. Mann and Mattheissen

(1985) used a systemic grammar (NIGEL) for the tactical component in a text generation system. In describing a system for generating stock market reports. Kukich (1983) proposed a "knowledge-intensive" approach to sentence generation; similarly specialized techniques form the basis of the generator for the previously mentioned UC project (Jacobs, 1985). The KAMP system (Appelt, 1985) views generation as a planning problem of proving what to say. In her TEXT system, McKeown (1985) adapted ideas of text schemas and focus from discourse-understanding research to the task of answer generation in a natural-language database system.

Cognitive Modeling

In the late 1960s at Stanford, Schank, while working on a parser for an automated psychiatrist project with Colby, developed a meaning representation known as conceptual dependency (qv) (CD). Having been exposed to machine translation as a graduate student, Schank was convinced that more of the underlying meaning of sentences needed to be represented. In particular, certain inferences were included in the CD graphs. The basic scheme was centered on approximately a dozen primitive action concepts. The translation of "X hit Y," for example, was approximately "X propelled some Z from X to Y which resulted in the state of Y and Z being in physical contact." The first fairly complete system, MARGIE, included a parser (conceptual analyzer), an inferencer, and a text generation system (Shank, 1975).

In an interesting early retrospective of the CD paradigm, Schank (1978) offered this perspective on the situation that he faced in the late 1960s:

Thus, my point was that Chomsky was wrong in claiming that we should not be attempting to build a point by point model of a speaker-hearer. Such a model was precisely what I felt should be tackled. Linguists viewed this as performance and thus uninteresting. I took my case to psychologists and found them equally uninterested. Psychologists interested in language were mostly psycholinguists, and psycholinguists for the most part bought the assumptions of transformational grammar (although it seemed very odd to me that given the competence/performance distinction, psychologists should be on the side of competence).

Schank's emphasis on semantic representations was supported by others [notably the work on preference semantics (qv) by Wilks (1975)] but has been slow to make a large impact on practical systems. Perhaps the slow acceptance was a result of methodology [the "free form speculation approach to theory building" (Schank, 1978)] of general attitudes inherited from linguistic theory, of the emphasis in CD systems on the I/O behavior of programs instead of formal computational models, and of the difficulty in discovering and representing conceptual knowledge structures.

One problem that plagued the inferencer in MARGIE was how to control the potential inferences that could be made. Later CD-based systems made inferences organized from knowledge sources such as scripts (qv) (Schank and

Abelson, 1977; Cullingford, 1978), plans and goals (Wilensky, 1983), beliefs (Carbonell, 1978), episodic memory (Kolodner, 1984), and thematic abstraction units (Dyer, 1983). Scripts provide prepackaged causal and temporal links for stereotypical situations. For less structured situations the links are created dynamically by a plan and goal analysis. Inferences are also affected by one's beliefs (eg, conservative/liberal political beliefs) and memory of past events. Although many of the ideas of schematic inference and planning are being incorporated in recent work, the difficulty of identifying and integrating a wide range of semantic and pragmatic representations remains a difficult problem for AI and CL.

Language Acquisition

Computational language acquisition (qv) research subdivides in much the same way that AI research generally does. Some researchers attempt to automate the acquisition of linguistic expertise by any efficacious method; other work is explicitly aimed at cognitive modeling and tries to be faithful to the psycholinguistic data on language acquisition. Most of the language-learning systems are concerned primarily with learning syntactic rules.

New computational approaches to language acquisition have generally followed developments in linguistics or natural language processing techniques. The ZBIE system (Siklossy, 1971) learned foreign language rules from input pairs consisting of a semantic representation and a surface string. For example, the representation (be (on table hat)) was paired with the sentence "The table is on the hat." To the extent that the appropriate syntactic structure of a sentence bears a particular relationship to the semantic structure, the semantic representation can guide in the induction of syntactic rules. Anderson's graph deformation condition (Anderson, 1977) is a statement of this principle, Klein's AUTOLING program (1973) derived a transformational grammar in cooperation with a linguist informant. The derived grammars contained context-free phrase structure rules and transformations. Harris (1971b) produced a language-learning system for a simulated robot. The system performed *lexicalization*, the process of mapping words to concepts, and the induction of a Chomsky normal-form grammar. Berwick (1980) investigated learning transformational grammar rules of the sort embodied in a Marcus parser.

Reeker (1971) explicitly modeled a child's acquisition of language with a problem-solving theory. The grammar was represented by context-free syntactic rules paired with a semantic representation modeled after conceptual dependency notation. The system received as input an "adult sentence" and its meaning. A heuristic reduction process formed a reduced sentence, which was then compared against a "child sentence" produced from the meaning by the child's current grammar. If a difference in the derived sentences was obtained, the grammar was adjusted. The AMBER system (Langley, 1982) similarly compares input sentences to internally generated sentences to identify discrepancies. The CHILD system (Selfridge, 1982) receives an adult sentence and a conceptual dependency representation of visual input. The model

builds lexical definitions similar to those of other word-based parsers.

The psychologist Anderson has made many contributions to language acquisition research. His LAS system (Anderson, 1977) accepted sentence–scene description pairs and learned an ATN grammar that was used for both recognition and generation. The scene descriptions were encoded in the HAM associative network representation (Anderson and Bower, 1973). Following this work, he developed a series of cognitive models and learning theories based on a hybrid architecture, called ACT (adaptive control of thought). An elaborate version of the model, ACT (Anderson, 1983), uses a production system to control spreading activation processes in a semantic network. Anderson has studied the learning of production rules for language generation, which is viewed as a problem-solving activity in ACT*.

Speech Understanding

The problem of understanding spoken natural language involves virtually all of the issues discussed above as well as others of its own (see SPEECH UNDERSTANDING).

FURTHER READING

In addition to the many references already cited and the discussions and references in related articles, Feigenbaum and Feldman (1963) and Minsky (1968) contain descriptions of, and Simmons (1965, 1970) discusses, early work in natural-language processing; Rustin (1973) and Zampolli (1975) consider the status of several question-answering systems of the early to middle 1970s; Kaplan (1982) contains brief summaries of several dozen projects underway in the early 1980s; and the brief articles in Johnson and Bachenko (1982) give prospects for work in several areas of CL. Tennant (1981) provides a fairly broad introduction to natural-language processing and contains technical details and historical remarks, as do the articles in Barr and Feigenbaum (1981) and Lehnert and Ringle (1982). Grishman (1986) provides a general introduction to technical problems in the field; matters of parsing and grammatical formalisms are discussed in King (1983), Winograd (1983), Sparck Jones and Wilks (1985), and Dowty and co-workers (1985); an interesting discussion of cognitive approaches to semantics is Jackendoff (1983); Brady and Berwick (1983) contains papers on discourse. Schank and Riesbeck (1981) and Simmons (1984) present the actual mechanisms by which specific processors have been constructed. Harris (1985) has written a recent textbook on natural language processing (see NATURAL LANGUAGE UNDERSTANDING).

Many articles have appeared in conference proceedings, including those of the annual meeting of the ACL, the biennial International Conference on Computational Linguistics (COLING), conferences sponsored by the American Association for Artificial Intelligence (AAAI), the biennial International Joint Conference on AI (IJCAI), a Conference on Applied Natural Language Processing, and two conferences on Theoretical Issues in Natural Language Processing. A primary journal is *Computa-*

tional Linguistics (formerly the *American Journal of Computational Linguistics*), and other important journals include *Artificial Intelligence*, the *Canadian Journal of Artificial Intelligence*, and *Cognitive Science*.

BIBLIOGRAPHY

J. Allen, ed., "Special Issue on Ill-formed Input," *Am. J. Computat. Ling.* 9(3-4), 123-196, 1983.

J. Allen, A. Frisch, and D. Litman, ARGOT: The Rochester Dialogue System, *Proceedings of the Second National Conference on Artificial Intelligence*, Pittsburgh, Penn., AAAI, Menlo Park, Calif., 1982, pp. 66-70.

J. Allen and C. Perrault, "Analyzing Intention in Utterances," *Artif. Intell.* 15(3), 143-178 (1980).

D. Appelt, *Planning English Sentences*, Cambridge University Press, New York, 1985.

J. Anderson, "Induction of Augmented Transition Networks," *Cog. Sci.* 1(2), 125-157 (April 1977).

J. Anderson, *The Architecture of Cognition*, Harvard University Press, Cambridge, Mass., 1983.

J. Anderson and G. Bower, *Human Associative Memory*, Winston and Sons, Washington, D.C., 1973.

B. Ballard, ed., "Special Issue on Transportable Natural Language Processing," *ACM Trans. Ofc. Inf. Sys.* 3(2), 104-230 (1985).

B. Ballard, J. Lusth, and N. Tinkham, "LDC-1: A Transportable, Knowledge-Based Natural Language Processor for Office Environments," *ACM Trans. Ofc. Inf. Sys.* 2(1), 1-25 (1984).

Y. Bar-Hillel, "The Present Status of Automatic Translation of Languages," in F. Alt, ed., *Advances in Computers*, Vol. 1, Academic Press, New York, 1960, pp. 102-103.

A. Barr and E. Feigenbaum, eds., *The Handbook of Artificial Intelligence*, Vol. 1, William Kaufmann, Los Altos, Calif., 1981.

M. Bates, "Information Retrieval Using a Transportable Natural Language" Interface, *Proceedings of the International ACM SIGIR Conference*, Bethesda, Md., 1983, pp. 81-86.

M. Bates and R. Ingria, "Controlled Transformational Sentence Generation," *Proceedings of the Nineteenth Annual Meeting of the ACL*, Stanford University, 1981, pp. 153-158.

J. Becker and R. Hayes, *Information Storage and Retrieval Tools, Elements, Theories*, Wiley, New York, 1963.

R. Berwick, Computational Analogues of Constraints on Grammars: A Model of Syntax Acquisition, *Proceedings of the Eighteenth Annual Meeting of the ACL*, Philadelphia, Pa., 1980, pp. 49-54.

A. Biermann and B. Ballard, "Toward Natural Language Computation," *Am. J. Computat. Ling.* 6(2), 71-86 (1980).

A. Biermann, B. Ballard, and A. Sigmon, "An Experimental Study of Natural Language Programming," *Int. J. Man-Mach. Stud.* 18(1), 71-87 (1983).

D. Bobrow, "Natural Language Input for a Computer Problem-Solving System," in M. Minsky, ed., *Semantic Information Processing*, MIT Press, Cambridge, Mass., 1968, pp. 133-215.

D. Bobrow and B. Fraser, "An Augmented State Transition Network Analysis Procedure," *Proceedings of the First International Joint Conferences on Artificial Intelligence*, Washington, D.C., Morgan-Kaufmann, San Mateo, Calif., 1969, pp. 557-567.

D. Bobrow, R. Kaplan, M. Kay, D. Norman, H. Thompson, and T. Winograd, "GUS: A Frame-Driven Dialog System," *Artif. Intell.* 8(2), 155-173 (1977).

M. Brady and R. Berwick, *Computational Models of Discourse*, MIT Press, Cambridge, Mass., 1983.

J. Bresnan and R. Kaplan, "Lexical-Functional Grammar: A Formal System for Grammatical Representation," in J. Bresnan, ed., *The Mental Representation of Grammatical Relations*, MIT Press, Cambridge, Mass., 1982.

W. Bronnenberg, S. Landsbergen, R. Scha, W. Shoenmakers, and E. van Utteren, "PHLIQA-1, A Question-Answering System for Data-Base Consultation in Natural English," *Philips Tech. Rev.* 38, 229-239, 269-284 (1978-1979).

G. Brown, *A Framework for Processing Dialog*, MIT Press, Cambridge, Mass., June 1977.

J. Brown and R. Burton, "Multiple Representations of Knowledge for Tutorial Reasoning," in D. Bobrow and A. Collins, eds., *Representation and Understanding*, Academic Press, New York, 1975, pp. 312-313.

B. Bruce, "Case Systems for Natural Language," *Artif. Intell.* 6, 327-360 (1975).

J. Carbonell, "AI in CAI: An Artificial Intelligence Approach to Computer-Assisted Instruction," *IEEE Trans. Man-Mach. Sys.* 11, 190-202 (1970).

J. Carbonell, "POLITICS: Automated Ideological Reasoning," *Cog. Sci.* 2, 27-51 (1978).

E. Charniak, "Computer Solution of Calculus Word Problems," *Proceedings of the First International Joint Conferences on Artificial Intelligence*, Washington, D.C., 1969, Morgan-Kaufmann, San Mateo, Calif., pp. 303-316.

D. Chester, "A Parsing Algorithm that Extends Phrases," *Am. J. Computat. Ling.* 6(2), 87-96 (1980).

N. Chomsky, *Syntactic Structures*, Mouton, The Hague, 1957.

N. Chomsky, *Aspects of the Theory of Syntax*, MIT Press, Cambridge, Mass., 1965.

J. Clippinger, "Speaking with Many Tongues: Some Problems in Modeling Speakers of Actual Discourse," *TINLAP* 1, 68-73 (1975).

K. Colby, S. Weber, and F. Hilf, "Artificial Paranoia," *Artif. Intell.* 2, 1-25 (1971).

P. Cohen and C. Perrault, "Elements of a Plan-Based Theory of Speech Acts," *Cog. Sci.* 3, 177-212 (1979).

A. Collins, E. Warnock, N. Aiello, and R. Miller, "Reasoning from Incomplete Knowledge," in D. Bobrow and A. Collins, eds., *Representation and Understanding*, Academic Press, New York, 1975, pp. 383-415.

E. Codd, R. Arnold, J. Cadiou, C. Chang, and N. Roussopoulos, "Seven Steps to RENDEZVOUS with the Casual User," in J. Kimbie and K. Koffeman, eds., *Data Base Management*, North-Holland, 1974, pp. 179-200.

A. Coreira, "Computing Story Trees," *Am. J. Computat. Ling.* 6(3-4), 135-149 (1980).

G. Cottrell, "A Model of Lexical Access of Ambiguous Words," *Proceedings of the Fourth National Conference on Artificial Intelligence*, Austin, Tex., AAAI, Menlo Park, Calif., Aug. 1984, pp. 61-67.

J. Craig, S. Berezner, C. Homer, and C. Longyear, "DEACON: Direct English Access and Control," *AFIPS Fall Joint Computer Conference*, 1966, p. 366.

R. Cullingford, *Script Application: Computer Understanding of Newspaper Stories, Research Report 116*, Yale University, Department of Computer Science, 1978.

F. Damerau, "Operating Statistics for the Transformational

Question Answering System," *Am. J. Computat. Ling.* **7**(1), 30–44 (1981).

F. Damerau, "Problems and Some Solutions in Customization of Natural Language Database Front Ends," *ACM Trans. Ofc. Inf. Sys.* **3**(2), 165–184 (1985).

A. Davey, *Discourse Production*, Edinburgh University Press, Edinburgh, 1979.

J. Davidson and S. Kaplan, "Natural Language Access to Data Bases: Interpreting Update Requests," *Am. J. Computat. Ling.* **9**(2), 57–68 (1983).

D. Dowty, L. Karttunen, and A. Zwicky, eds., *Natural Language Parsing*, Cambridge University Press, Cambridge, U.K., 1985.

M. Dyer, *In-Depth Understanding*, MIT Press, Cambridge, Mass., 1983.

J. Earley, "An Efficient Context-Free Parsing Algorithm," *CACM* **13**(2), 94–102 (Feb. 1970).

L. Erman, F. Hayes-Roth, V. Lesser, and D. Reddy, "The Hearsay-II Speech Understanding System," *Computing Surveys* **12**, 213–253 (1980).

E. Feigenbaum and J. Feldman, eds., *Computers and Thought*, McGraw-Hill, New York, 1963.

C. Fillmore, "The Case for Case," in E. Bach and R. Harms, eds., *Universals in Linguistic Theory*, Holt, Rinehart and Winston, New York, 1968, pp. 1–90.

N. Findler, ed., *Associative Networks: Representation and Use of Knowledge in Computers*, Academic Press, New York, 1979.

T. Finin, B. Goodman, and H. Tennant, "JETS: Achieving Completeness through Coverage and Closure," *Proceedings of the Sixth International Joint Conferences on Artificial Intelligence*, Tokyo, Japan, Morgan-Kaufmann, San Mateo, Calif., 1979, pp. 275–281.

P. Fink and A. Biermann, "Correction of Ill-Formed Input Using History-Based Expectation with Applications to Speech Understanding," *Computat. Ling.* **12**(1), 13–36 (1986).

J. Friedman, "Directed Random Generation of Sentences," *CACM* **12**(1), 40–46 (1969).

G. Gazdar, "Phrase Structure Grammar," in P. Jacobson and G. Pullum, eds., *The Nature of Syntactic Representation*, D. Reidel, Dordrecht, 1982, pp. 131–186.

R. Geist, D. Kraines, and P. Fink, "Natural Language Computation in a Linear Algebra Course," *Proceedings of the National Educational Computer Conference*, 1982, pp. 203–208.

J. P. Gelb, "Experience with a Natural Language Problem-Solving System," *Proceedings of the Second International Joint Conferences on Artificial Intelligence*, London, Morgan-Kaufmann, San Mateo, Calif., 1971, pp. 455–462.

J. Ginsparg, "A Robust Portable Natural Language Data Base Interface," *Proceedings of the Conference on Applied Natural Language Processing*, Santa Monica, Calif., 1983, pp. 25–30.

V. Giuliano, "Comments on the Article by Simmons," *CACM* **8**(1), 69 (1965).

N. Goldman, "Conceptual Generation," in R. Schank, *Conceptual Information Processing*, North-Holland, Amsterdam, 1975, pp. 289–371.

R. Granger, "The NOMAD system: Expectation-based Detection and Correction of Errors During Understanding of Syntactically and Semantically Ill-formed Text," *Am. J. Computat. Ling.* **9**(3–4), 188–196 (1983).

C. Green, "A Summary of the PSI Program Synthesis System," *Proceedings of the Fifth International Joint Conferences on Artificial Intelligence*, Cambridge, Mass., Morgan-Kaufmann, San Mateo, Calif., 1977, pp. 380–381.

B. Green, A. Wolf, C. Chomsky, and K. Laughery, "BASEBALL: An Automatic Question Answerer," in E. Feigenbaum and J. Feldman, *Computers and Thought*, McGraw-Hill, New York, 1963.

H. Grice, "Logic and Conversation," in P. Morgan and J. Cole, eds., *Syntax and Semantics*, Vol. 3, *Speech Acts*, Academic Press, New York, 1975, pp. 41–58.

B. Grosz, "Focusing and Description in Natural Language Dialogues," in *Elements of Discourse Understanding*, Cambridge University Press, 1981, pp. 84–105.

B. Grosz, "TEAM: A Transportable Natural Language Interface System," *Proceedings of the Conference on Applied Natural Language Processing*, Santa Monica, Calif., 1983, pp. 39–45.

R. Grishman, *An Introduction to Computational Linguistics*, Cambridge University Press, New York, 1986.

R. Grishman and L. Hirschman, "Question Answering from Natural Language Medical Data Bases," *Artif. Intell.* **7**, 25–43 (1978).

R. Grishman, N. Nhan, E. Marsh, and L. Hirschman, "Automated Determination of Sublanguage Syntactic Usage," *Proceedings of the International Conference on Computational Linguistics*, Stanford, July 1984, pp. 96–98.

N. Haas and G. Hendrix, "An Approach to Acquiring and Applying Knowledge," *Proceedings of the First National Conference on Artificial Intelligence*, Stanford University, Stanford, Calif., AAAI, Menlo Park, Calif., 1980, pp. 235–239.

C. Hafner and K. Godden, "Portability of Syntax and Semantics in DATALOG," *ACM Trans. Ofc. Inf. Sys.* **3**(2), 141–164 (1985).

M. Halliday, "Categories of the Theory of Grammar," *Word* **17**, 241–292 (1961).

L. Harris, "User-Oriented Data Base Query with the Robot Natural Language System," *Int. J. Man–Mach. Stud.* **9**, 697–713 (1977a).

L. Harris, "A System for Primitive Natural Language Acquisition," *Int. J. Man–Mach. Stud.* **9**, 153–206 (1977b).

L. Harris, "The ROBOT System: Natural Language Processing Applied to Data Base Query," *ACM Natl. Conf.* 165–172 (1978).

M. Harris, *Introduction to Natural Language Processing*, Reston Publ. Co., Reston, Va., 1985.

P. Hayes and G. Mouradian, "Flexible Parsing," *Am. J. Computat. Ling.* **7**(4), 232–242 (1981).

D. Hays, "Dependency Theory: A Formalism and Some Observations," *Language* **40**, 511–524 (1964).

D. Hays, ed., *Readings in Automatic Language Processing*, American Elsevier, New York, 1966.

G. Heidorn, "Natural Language Inputs to a Simulation Programming System," Ph.D. dissertation, Technical Report NPS-55HD72101A, Naval Postgraduate School, Monterey, Calif., 1972.

G. Heidorn, "Augmented Phrase Structure Grammars," in B. Webber and R. Schank, eds., *Theoretical Issues in Natural Language Processing*, Cambridge, Mass., 1975, pp. 1–5.

G. Heidorn, "Automatic Programming Through Natural Language Dialogue, A Survey," *IBM J. Res. Dev.* **20**(4), 302–313 (1976).

G. Heidorn, "Generating Noun Phrases to Identify Noun Phrases in a Semantic Network," *Proceedings of the Fifth International Joint Conferences on Artificial Intelligence*, Cambridge, Mass., Morgan-Kaufmann, San Mateo, Calif., 1977, p. 143.

G. Heidorn, "Natural Language Dialogue for Managing an On-line Calendar," *Proceedings of the Annual Meeting of the ACM*, Washington, D.C., 1978, pp. 45–52.

G. Heidorn, K. Jensen, L. Miller, R. Byrd and M. Chodorow, "The EPISTLE Text-Critiquing System," *IBM Sys. J.* **21**(3), 305–326 (1982).

G. Hendrix and W. Lewis, "Transportable Natural-Language Interfaces to Databases," *Proceedings of the Nineteenth Annual Meeting of the ACL*, Stanford University, 1981, pp. 159–165.

G. Hendrix, "Human Engineering for Applied Natural Language Processing," *Proceedings of the Fifth International Joint Conferences on Artificial Intelligence*, Cambridge, Mass., Morgan-Kaufmann, San Mateo, Calif., 1977, pp. 183–191.

G. Hendrix, E. Sacerdoti, D. Sagalowicz, and J. Slocum, "Developing a Natural Language Interface to Complex Data," *ACM Trans. Database Sys.* **3**(2), 105–147 (1978).

R. Hershman, R. Kelley, and H. Miller, *User Performance with a Natural Language Query System for Command Control*, Tech. Report TR 79–7, Navy Personnel Research and Development Center, San Diego, Calif., 1979.

J. Hirschberg, "Toward a Redefinition of Yes/No Questions," *Proceedings of Tenth International Conference on Computational Linguistics*, Stanford, Calif., 1984, pp. 48–51.

L. Hirschman, R. Grishman, and N. Sager, "From Text to Structured Information: Automatic Processing of Medical Reports," *Proceedings of the AFIPS National Computer Conference*, 1976, pp. 267–275.

G. Hirst, "Discourse-Oriented Anaphora Resolution in Natural Language Undertanding: A Review," *Am. J. Computat. Ling.* **7**(2), pp. 85–98.

J. Hobbs, "Coherence and Coreference," *Cog. Sci.* **3**(1), 67–90 (1979).

W. Hoeppner, T. Christaller, H. Marburger, K. Morik, B. Nebel, M. O'Leary, and W. Wahlster, "Beyond Domain-Independence," *Proceedings of the Eighth International Joint Conferences on Artificial Intelligence*, Karlsruhe, FRG, Morgan-Kaufmann, San Mateo, Calif., 1983, pp. 588–594.

R. Jackendoff, *Semantics and Cognition*, MIT Press, Cambridge, Mass., 1983.

P. Jacobs, "PHRED: a Generator for Natural Language Interfaces," *Computat. Ling.* **11**(4), 219–242 (1985).

K. Jensen, G. Heidorn, L. Miller, and Y. Ravin, "Parse Fitting and Prose Fixing: Getting a Hold on Ill-Formedness," *Am. J. Computat. Ling.* **9**(3–4), 147–160 (1983).

M. Jones and A. Driscoll, "Movement in Active Production Networks," *Proceedings of the Twenty-Third Annual Meeting of the Association for Computational Linguistics*, July 1985, pp. 161–166.

T. Johnson, *Natural Language Computing: the Commercial Applications*, Ovum, London, 1985.

C. Johnson and J. Bachenko, eds., "Applied Computational Linguistics in Perspective," *Am. J. Computat. Ling.* **8**(2), 55–84 (1982).

A. Joshi, "How Much Context-Sensitivity is Required to Provide Reasonable Structural Descriptions: Tree Adjoining Grammars," in D. Dowty, L. Karttunen, and A Zwicky, eds., *Natural Language Processing: Psycholinguistic, Computational and Theoretical Properties*, Cambridge University Press, New York, 1984.

R. Kantor, "The Management and Comprehension of Discourse Connection by Pronouns in English," Ph.D. dissertation, Ohio State University, 1977.

R. Kaplan, *A General Syntactic Processor*, Algorithmics, New York, 1973.

S. Kaplan, "Indirect Responses to Loaded Questions," *Theoretical Issues in Natural Language Processing*, Vol. 2, 1978, pp. 202–209.

S. Kaplan, ed., "Special Section on Natural Language Processing" *SIGART Newslett.* **79**, 42–108 (1982).

M. Kay, "Experiments with a Powerful Parser," *Proceedings of the Second International Conference on Computational Linguistics*, Grenoble, Aug. 1967.

M. Kay, "Functional Grammar," *Proceedings of the Fifth Annual Meeting of the Berkeley Linguistic Society*, 1979, pp. 142–158.

M. Kay, "Functional Unification Grammar: A Formalism for Machine Translation," *Proceedings of COLING 84*, Menlo Park, 1984, pp. 75–78.

C. Kellogg, "A Natural Language Compiler for On-line Data Management," *AFIPS Fall Joint Computer Conference*, 1968, pp. 473–492.

M. King, ed., *Parsing Natural Language*, Academic Press, London, 1983.

R. Kirsch, "Computer Interpretation of English text and Picture Patterns," *IEEE Trans. Electron. Comput.* **13**, 363–376 (1964).

S. Klein, "Automatic Paraphrasing in Essay Format," *Mechan. Transl.* **8**(3), 68–83 (1965).

S. Klein, *Automatic Inference of Semantic Deep Structure Rules in Generative Semantic Grammars*, Technical Report 180, Computer Science Department, University of Wisconsin, Madison, Wisc., May 1973.

J. Kolodner, *Retrieval and Organizational Strategies in Conceptual Memory: A Computer Model*, Lawrence Erlbaum, Hillsdale, N.J., 1984.

J. Krause, *Results of User Study with the User Specialty Language System and Consequences for the Architecture of Natural Language Interfaces*, Technical Report 79.04.003, IBM Heidleberg Scientific Center, 1979.

K. Kukich, "Design of a Knowledge-Based Report Generator," *Proceedings of the Twentieth Annual Meeting of the ACL*, Cambridge, Mass., 1983, pp. 145–150.

S. Kuno, "The Predictive Analyzer and a Path Elimination Technique," *CACM* **8**, 453–462 (1965).

S. Kwasny and N. Sondheimer, "Relaxation Techniques for Parsing Ill-Formed Input," *Am. J. Computat. Ling.* **7**(2), 99–108 (1981).

S. Lamb, "The Semantic Approach to Structural Semantics," *Am. Anthropol.* (1964).

P. Langley, "Language Acquisition through Error Recovery," *Cog. Brain Theor.* **5**, 211–255 (1982).

H. Lehmann, "Interpretation of Natural Language in an Information System," *IBM J. Res. Dev.* **22**(5), 560–571 (1978).

W. Lehnert and W. Ringle, eds., *Strategies for Natural Language Processing*, Lawrence Erlbaum, Hillsdale, N.J., 1982.

W. Lehnert and S. Schwartz, "EXPLORER: A Natural Language Processing System for Oil Exploration," *Proceedings of the Conference on Applied Natural Language Processing*, Santa Monica, Calif., 1983, pp. 69–72.

J. Levin and J. Moore, "Dialog-Games: Metacommunications Structures for Natural Language Interaction," *Cog. Sci.* **1**(4), 395–420 (1977).

R. Lindsay, "Inferential Memory as the Basis of Machines which Understand Natural Language," in E. Feigenbaum and J. Feldman, eds., *Computers and Thought*, McGraw-Hill, New York, 1963, p. 221.

D. Litman and J. Allen, "A Plan-Based Recognition Model for Subdialogues in Conversation," *Cog. Sci.* **11** (1987).

W. Locke and A. Booth, eds., *Machine Translation of Languages*, MIT Press, Cambridge, Mass., 1955.

A. Lockman, Contextual Reference Resolution, Ph.D. dissertation, Columbia University, New York, May 1978.

W. Mann, M. Bates, B. Grosz, D. McDonald, K. McKeown, and W. Swartout, "Text Generation: The State of the Art and Literature," *JACL* **8**, 2 (1982).

W. Mann and C. Mattheissen, "Nigel: a Systemic Grammar for Text Generation," in Freedle, ed., *Systemic Perspectives on Discourse: Selected Theoretical Papers of the Ninth International Systemic Workshop*, Ablex, Norwood, N.J., 1985.

W. Mann and J. Moore, "Computer Generation of Multiparagraph English Text," *Am. J. Computat. Ling.* **7**, 17–29 (1981).

M. Marcus, *A Theory of Syntactic Recognition for Natural Language*, MIT Press, Cambridge, Mass., 1980.

W. Mark, "Representation and Inference in the Consul System," *Proceedings of the Seventh International Joint Conferences on Artificial Intelligence*, Vancouver, BC, Morgan-Kaufmann, San Mateo, Calif., 1981, pp. 375–381.

E. Marsh and C. Friedman, "Transporting the Linguistic String Project System from a Medical to a Navy Domain," *ACM Trans. Ofc. Inform. Sys.* **3**(2), 121–140 (1985).

D. McDonald, "Natural Language-Generation as a Computational Problem: An Introduction," in M. Brady and R. Berwick, eds., *Computational Models of Discourse*, MIT Press, Cambridge, Mass., 1983, pp. 209–265.

N. MacDonald, L. Frase, P. Gingrich, and S. Keenan, "The Writer's Workbench: Computer Aids for Text Analysis," *IEEE Trans. Commun.* **30**, 105–110 (Jan. 1982).

K. McKeown, *Text Generation*, Cambridge University Press, New York, 1985.

R. Milne, "Resolving Lexical Ambiguity in a Deterministic Parser," *Computat. Ling.* **12**(1), 1–12 (1986).

M. Minsky, ed., *Semantic Information Processing*, MIT Press, Cambridge, Mass., 1968.

J. Mylopoulos, A. Borgida, P. Cohen, Roussopoulos, J. Tsotsos, and H. Wong, "TORUS: A Natural Language Understanding System for Data Management," *Proceedings of the Fourth IJCAI*, Tbilisi, USSR, Morgan-Kaufmann, San Mateo, Calif., 1975, pp. 414–421.

National Research Council, *Language and Machines: Computers in Translation and Linguistics*, Report by the Automated Language Processing Advisory Committee (ALPAC), National Academy of Sciences, Washington, D.C., 1966, p. 19.

S. Nirenburg, ed., *Machine Translation: Theoretical and Methodological Issues*, Cambridge University Press, New York, 1987.

A. Oettinger, *Automatic Language Translation*, Harvard University Press, Cambridge, Mass., 1960.

F. Pereira and D. H. D. Warren, "Definite Clause Grammars for Language Analysis: A Survey of the Formalism and a Comparison with Augmented Transition Networks," *Artif. Intell.* **13**, 231–278 (1980).

S. Petrick, *A Recognition Procedure for Transformational Grammars*, Ph.D. dissertation, MIT, Cambridge, Mass., 1965.

S. Petrick, "Transformational Analysis," in R. Rustin, ed., *Natural Language Processing*, Algorithmics, New York, 1973, pp. 27–41.

S. Petrick, "On Natural-Language Based Computer Systems," in A. Zampolli, ed., *Linguistic Structures Processing*, North-Holland, Amsterdam, 1975, pp. 313–340. Also appears in *IBM J. Res. Dev.* **20**(4), 314–325 (1976).

W. Plath, "REQUEST: A Natural Language Question-Answering System," *IBM J. Res. Dev.* **20**(4), 326–335 (1976).

E. Proudian and C. Pollard, "Parsing Head-Driven Phrase Structure Grammar," *Proceedings of the Twenty-Third Annual Meeting of the Association for Computational Linguistics*, July 1985, pp. 8–12.

M. Quillian, "Semantic Memory," in M. Minsky, ed., *Semantic Information Processing*, MIT Press, Cambridge, Mass., 1968, pp. 216–270.

B. Raphael, "SIR, a Computer Program for Semantic Information Retrieval," in M. Minsky, ed., *Semantic Information Processing*, MIT Press, Cambridge, Mass., 1968, p. 33.

B. Raphael, Hewlett-Packard, personal communication, July 1983.

L. Reeker, "A Problem Solving Theory of Syntax Acquisition," *J. Struct. Learn.* **2**, 1–10 (1971).

R. Reichman, "Extended Person-Machine Interface," *Artif. Intell.* **22**(2), 157–218 (March 1984).

C. Riesbeck, "Conceptual Analysis," in R. Schank, ed., *Conceptual Information Processing*, North-Holland, Amsterdam, 1975, pp. 83–156.

J. Robinson, "DIAGRAM: A Grammar for Dialogues," *CACM* **25**(1), 27–47 (Jan. 1982).

D. Rummelhart, "Notes on a Schema for Stories," in D. Bobrow and A. Collins, eds., *Representation and Understanding*, Academic, New York, 1975.

R. Rustin, ed., *Natural Language Processing*, Algorithmics, New York, 1973.

W. Ruzzo, S. Graham, and M. Harrison, "An Improved Context-Free Recognizer," *ACM Trans. Program. Lang. Sys.* **3**, 415–562 (July 1980).

N. Sager, "Natural Language Information Formatting: The Automatic Conversion of Texts to a Structured Data Base," in M. Yovits, ed., *Advances in Computers*, Vol. 17, Academic Press, New York, 1978, pp. 89–162.

N. Sager, *Natural Language Information Processing: A Computer Grammar of English and Its Applications*, Addison-Wesley, Reading, Mass., 1981.

G. Salton, *Automatic Information Organization and Retrieval*, McGraw-Hill, New York, 1968.

S. Salveter, "Natural Language Database Updates," *Proceedings of the Nineteenth Annual Meeting of the ACL*, University of Toronto, 1982, pp. 67–73.

R. Schank, "Conceptual Dependency: A Theory of Natural Language Understanding," *Cog. Psychol.* **3**, 552–631 (1972).

R. Schank, *Conceptual Information Processing*, with contributions from N. Goldman, C. Rieger, and C. Riesbeck, Vol. 3 of *Fundamental Studies in Computer Science*, North-Holland, Amsterdam, 1975.

R. Schank, *Inference in the Conceptual Dependency Paradigm: A Personal History*, Yale University, Department of Computer Science, Research Report 141, Sept. 1978.

R. Schank and R. Abelson, *Scripts, Plans, Goals, and Understanding*, Lawrence Erlbaum, Hillsdale, N.J., 1977.

R. Schank and C. Riesbeck, *Inside Computer Understanding*, Lawrence Erlbaum, Hillsdale, N.J., 1981.

R. Schank and L. Tesler, "A Conceptual Parser for Natural Language," *International Joint Conferences on Artificial Intelligence*, Morgan-Kaufmann, San Mateo, Calif., 1969, pp. 569–578.

J. Searle, "Indirect Speech Acts," in P. Morgan and J. Cole, eds., *Syntax and Semantics*, Vol. 3, *Speech Acts*, Academic Press, New York, 1975, pp. 59–82.

M. Selfridge, "Inference and Learning in a Computer Model of the Development of Language Comprehension in a Young Child," in W. Lehnert and M. Ringle, eds., *Strategies for Natural Language Processing*, Lawrence Erlbaum, Hillsdale, N.J., 1982, pp. 299–326.

C. Sidner, "Focusing for Interpretation of Pronouns," *Am. J. Computat. Ling.* **7**(4), 217–231 (1981).

L. Siklossy, "A Language-Learning Heuristic Program," *Cog. Psychol.* **2**, 479–495 (1971).

L. Siklossy, *Question-Asking Question-Answering*, Department of Computer Science Report TR–71, University of Texas, Austin, Tex., 1977.

R. Simmons, "Answering English Questions by Computer: A survey," *CACM* **8**(1), 53 (1965).

R. Simmons, "Natural Language Question Answering Systems: 1969," *CACM* **13**(1), 15–30 (1970).

R. Simmons, "Semantic Networks: Their Computation and Use for Understanding English Sentences," in R. Schank and K. Colby, eds., *Computer Models of Thought and Language*, W. H. Freeman, San Francisco, Calif., 1973, pp. 63–113.

R. Simmons, *Computations from the English*, Prentice-Hall, Englewood Cliffs, N.J., 1984.

R. Simmons and D. Londe, *NAMER: A Pattern Recognition System for Generating Sentences about Relationships between Line Drawings*, Report TM–1798, System Development Corp., Santa Monica, Calif., 1964.

R. Simmons and J. Slocum, "Generating English Discourse from Semantic Networks," *CACM* **15**(10), 891–905 (1972).

J. Slocum, ed., "Special Issues on Machine Translation," *Computat. Ling.* **11**(2–4) (1985).

J. Slocum and C. Justus, "Transportability to Other Languages," *ACM Trans. Ofc. Inf. Sys.* **3**(2), 204–230 (1985).

S. Small, "Parsing and Comprehending with Word Experts (A theory and Its Realization)," in W. Lehnert and M. Ringle, eds., *Strategies for Natural Language Processing*, Lawrence Erlbaum, Hillsdale, N.J., 1982.

J. Sowa, *Conceptual Structures: Information Processing in Mind and Machine*, Addison-Wesley, Reading, Mass., 1984.

K. Sparck-Jones and M. Kay, *Linguistics and Information Science*, Academic Press, London, 1973.

K. Sparck-Jones and Y. Wilks, *Automatic Natural Language Parsing*, Ellis Horwood, Chichester, UK, 1985.

R. Stockwell, P. Schachter, and B. Partee, *The Major Syntactic Structures of English*, Holt, Rinehart and Winston, New York, 1973.

M. Templeton, "EUFID: A Friendly and Flexible Frontend for Data Management Systems," *Proceedings of the Seventeenth Annual Meeting of the ACL*, 1979, pp. 91–93.

M. Templeton and J. Burger, "Problems in Natural-Language Interface to DBMS with Examples from EUFID," *Conference on Applied Natural Language Processing*, Santa Monica, Calif., 1983, pp. 3–16.

H. Tennant, "Experience with the Evaluation of Natural Language Question Answerers," *Proceedings of the Sixth International Joint Conferences on Artificial Intelligence*, Tokyo, Japan, Morgan-Kaufmann, San Mateo, Calif., 1979, pp. 874–876.

H. Tennant, *Natural Language Processing*, Petrocelli, New York, 1981.

B. Thompson, "Linguistic Analysis of Natural Language Communication with Computers," *Proceedings of the Eighth International Conference on Computational Linguistics*, Tokyo, 1980, pp. 190–201.

F. Thompson, P. Lockemann, B. Dostert, and R. Deverill, "REL: A Rapidly Extensible Language System," *ACM National Conference*, 1969, p. 400.

F. Thompson and B. Thompson, "Practical Natural Language Processing: The REL System as Prototype," in M. Rubinoff and M. Yovits, eds., *Advances in Computers*, Vol. 3., Academic Press, New York, 1975, pp. 109–168.

F. Thompson and B. Thompson, "Shifting to a Higher Gear in a Natural Language System," *National Computer Conference*, 1981, pp. 657–662.

B. Thompson and F. Thompson, "Introducing ASK, a Simple Knowledgeable System," *Conference on Applied Natural Language Processing*, Santa Monica, Calif., 1983, pp. 17–24.

B. Thompson and F. Thompson, "ASK is transportable in Half a Dozen Ways," *ACM Trans. Ofc. Inf. Sys.* **3**(2), 185–203 (1985).

J. Thorne, P. Bratley, and H. Dewar, "The Syntactic Analysis of English by Machine," in D. Mitchie, ed., *Machine Intelligence*, Vol. 3, American Elsevier, New York, 1968, pp. 281–299.

D. Waltz, "An English Language Question Answering System for a Large Relational Database," *CACM* **21**(7), 526–539 (1978).

D. Waltz and J. Pollack, "Massively Parallel Parsing," *Cog. Sci.* **9**(1), 51–74 (1985).

D. Warren and F. Pereira, "An Efficient Easily Adaptable System for Interpreting Natural Language Queries," *Am. J. Computat. Ling.* **8**(3–4), 110–122 (1982).

W. Weaver, W. Locke and A. Booth, eds., in *Machine Translation of Languages*, MIT Press, Cambridge, Mass., 1955, pp. 15–23.

B. Webber, *A Formal Approach to Discourse Anaphora*, Garland, New York, 1978.

R. Weischedel and J. Black, "Responding Intelligently to Unparasable Inputs," *Am. J. Computat. Ling.* **6**(2), 97–109 (1980).

R. Weischedel and N. Sondheimer, "Meta-Rules as a Basis for Processing Ill-Formed Output," *Am. J. Computat. Ling.* **9**(3–4), 161–177 (1983).

R. Weischedel, W. Voge, and M. James, "An Artificial Intelligence Approach to Language Instruction," *Artif. Intell.* **10**, 225–240 (1978).

J. Weizenbaum, "ELIZA: A Computer Program for the Study of Natural Language Communication Between Man and Machine," *CACM* **9**(1), 36–45 (1966).

J. Weizenbaum, *Computer Power and Human Reason*, W. H. Freeman, San Francisco, Calif., 1976.

D. Wilczynski, "Knowledge Acquisition in the Consul System," *Proceedings of the Seventh International Joint Conferences on Artificial Intelligence*, Vancouver, BC, Morgan-Kaufmann, San Mateo, Calif., 1981, pp. 135–140.

R. Wilensky, "Talking to UNIX in English: An Overview of UC," *Proceedings of the Second National Conference on Artificial Intelligence*, Pittsburgh, Penn., AAAI, Menlo Park, Calif., 1982, pp. 103–105.

R. Wilensky, *Planning and Understanding*, Addison-Wesley, Reading, Mass., 1983.

Y. Wilks, "A Preferential, Pattern-Seeking Semantics for Natural Language Inference," *Artif. Intell.* **6**, 53–74 (1975).

Y. Wilks, "Natural Language Understanding Programs Within the AI Paradigm: A Survey and Some Comparisons," in A. Zampolli, ed., *Linguistic Structures Processing*, North-Holland, Amsterdam, 1977, pp. 341–398.

T. Winograd, *Understanding Natural Language*, Academic Press, New York, 1972.

T. Winograd, "Frame Representations and the Declarative-Procedural Controversy," in D. Bobrow and A. Collins, eds., *Repre-*

sentation and Understanding, Academic Press, New York, 1975, pp. 185–210.

T. Winograd, *Language as a Cognitive Process*, Vol. 1, *Syntax*, Addison-Wesley, Reading, Mass., 1983.

W. Woods, "Procedural Semantics for a Question-Answering System," *AFIPS 1968 Fall Joint Computer Conference*, pp. 457–471.

W. Woods, "Transition Network Grammars for Natural Language Analysis," *CACM* **13**, 591–606 (Oct. 1970).

W. Woods, "Lunar Rocks in English: Explorations in Natural Language Question Answering," in A. Zampolli, ed., *Linguistic Structures Processing*, North-Holland, Amsterdam, 1977, pp. 521–569.

W. Woods, "Optimal Search Strategies for Speech Understanding Control," *Artif. Intell.* **18**, 295–326 (1982).

W. Woods, R. Kaplan, and B. Nash-Webber, *The Lunar Sciences Natural Language Information System: Final Report*, Report 2378, Bolt Beranek and Newman, Cambridge, Mass., 1972.

V. Yngve, "Random Generation of English Sentences," *Proceedings of the International Conference on Machine Translation of Languages and Applied Language Analysis*, National Physical Laboratory, Symposium No. 13, Her Majesty's Stationery Office, London, 1962, pp. 66–80.

D. Younger, "Recognition and Parsing of Context-Free Languages in Time n^3," *Inf. Ctr.* **10**, 129–208 (1967).

A. Zampolli, ed., *Linguistic Structures Processing*, North-Holland, Amsterdam, 1975.

A. Zwicky, J. Friedman, B. Hall, and D. Walker, "The MITRE Syntactic Analysis Procedure for Transformational Grammars," *IFIPS Proceedings Fall Joint Computer Conference*, Spartan, Washington, D.C., 1965, pp. 317–326.

B. BALLARD
M. JONES
AT&T Bell Laboratories

COMPUTER-AIDED DESIGN. See DESIGN, AI IN.

COMPUTER-AIDED INSTRUCTION. See EDUCATION, AI IN.

COMPUTER CHESS AND SEARCH

HISTORICAL PERSPECTIVE

Of the early chess-playing machines the most famous was exhibited by Baron von Kempelen of Vienna in 1769. As is well-known, von Kempelen's machine and the others were conjurer's tricks and grand hoaxes. In contrast, around 1890 a Spanish engineer, Torres y Quevedo, designed a true mechanical player for KR vs K (king and rook against king) endgames (Bell, 1978). A later version of that machine was displayed at the Paris Exhibition of 1914 and now resides in a museum at Madrid's Polytechnic University. Despite the success of this electro-mechanical device, further advances on chess automata did not come until the 1940s. During that decade there was a sudden spurt of activity as several leading engineers and mathematicians, intrigued by the power of computers, be-

gan to express their ideas about computer chess. Some, like Nemes (1951) and Zuse (1945) tried a hardware approach, but their computer-chess works did not find wide acceptance. Others, like Turing, found success with a more philosophical tone, stressing the importance of the stored program concept (Turing and co-workers, 1953). Today, best recognized are de Groot's 1946 doctoral dissertation (de Groot, 1965) and the much referenced paper on algorithms for playing chess by Shannon (1950), whose inspirational work provided a basis for most early chess programs. Despite the passage of time, Shannon's paper is still worthy of study.

Landmarks in Chess Program Development

The first computer-chess model in the 1950s was a hand simulation. Programs for subsets of chess followed, and the first full working program was reported in 1958. Most of the landmark papers reporting these results have now been collected together (Levy, 1988). By the mid-1960s there was an international computer-computer match, later reported by Mittman (1977), between a program backed by McCarthy of Stanford (developed by Kotok and a group of students from MIT) and one from the Institute for Theoretical and Experimental Physics (ITEP) in Moscow. The ITEP group's program won the match, and the scientists involved went on to develop Kaissa (qv), which became the first World Computer Chess Champion in 1974 (Hayes and Levy, 1976). For descriptions of Kaissa and other chess programs not discussed here, see Hayes and Levy (1976); Welsh and Baczynskyj (1985); Marsland and Schaeffer (1990). Meanwhile there emerged from MIT another program, Mac Hack Six (Greenblatt, Eastlake, and Crocker, 1967), which boosted interest in artificial intelligence. Firstly, Mac Hack was demonstrably superior not only to all previous chess programs, but also to most casual chess players. Secondly, it contained more sophisticated move-ordering and position-evaluation methods. Finally, the program incorporated a memory table to keep track of the values of chess positions that were seen more than once. In the late 1960s, spurred by the early promise of Mac Hack, several people began developing chess programs and writing proposals. Most substantial of the proposals was the twenty-nine point plan by Good (1968). By and large experimenters did not make effective use of these works; at least nobody claimed a program based on those designs, partly because it was not clear how some of the ideas could be addressed and partly because some points were too naive. Even so, by 1970 there was enough progress that Newborn was able to convert a suggestion for a public demonstration of chess-playing computers into a competition that attracted eight participants. Due mainly to Newborn's careful planning and organization, this event continues today under the title "The North American Computer Chess Championship," with the sponsorship of the ACM.

In a similar vein, under the auspices of the International Computer Chess Association, a worldwide computer-chess competition has evolved. Initial sponsors were the IFIP triennial conference at Stockholm in 1974 and Toronto in 1977, and later independent backers such as the Linz (Austria) Chamber of Commerce for 1980, ACM New York for 1983, the city of Cologne in Germany for 1986, and AGT/CIPS for 1989 in Edmonton, Canada. In the first World Championship for computers, Kaissa won all its games, including a defeat of the Chaos program that had beaten the favorite, Chess 4.0. An exhibition match between the new champion, Kaissa, and the eventual second place finisher, Chess 4.0 the 1973 North American Champion, was drawn (Mittman, 1977). Kaissa was at its peak, backed by a team of outstanding experts on tree-searching methods (Adelson-Velsky, Arlazarov, and Donskoy, 1988). In the second Championship at Toronto in 1977, Chess 4.6 finished first with Duchess and Kaissa tied for second place. Meanwhile both Chess 4.6 and Kaissa had acquired faster computers, a Cyber 176 and an IBM 370/165 respectively. The exhibition match between Chess 4.6 and Kaissa was won by the former, indicating that in the interim it had undergone far more development and testing, as the appendix to Frey's book shows (Frey, 1983). The Third World Championship at Linz in 1980 finished with a tie between Belle and Chaos. Belle represented the first of a new generation of hardware assists for chess, specifically support for position maintenance and evaluation, while Chaos was one of the few remaining selective search programs. In the playoff, Belle won convincingly, providing perhaps the best evidence yet that a deeper search more than compensates for an apparent lack of knowledge. Even today, this counter-intuitive idea does not find ready acceptance in the artificial intelligence community.

At the Fourth World Championship in New York in 1983, yet another new winner emerged, Cray Blitz (Hyatt, Gower, and Nelson, 1990). More than any other, that program drew on the power of a fast computer, here a Cray XMP. Originally Blitz was a selective search program, in the sense that is used a local evaluation function to discard some moves from every position, but often the time saved was not worth the attendant risks. The availability of a faster computer made it possible for Cray Blitz to switch to a purely algorithmic approach and yet retain much of the expensive chess knowledge. Although a main-frame program won the 1983 event, small machines made their mark and were seen to have a great future. For instance, Bebe, with special-purpose hardware, finished second (Scherzer, Scherzer, and Tjaden, 1990), and even experimental versions of commercial products did well. The Fifth World Championship in Cologne in 1986 was especially exciting. At that time Hitech, with the latest VLSI technology for move generation, seemed all powerful (Berliner and Ebeling, 1989), but faltered in a better position against Cray Blitz allowing a four-way tie for first place. As a consequence, had an unknown microprocessor system, Rebel, capitalized on its advantages in the final round game, it would have been the first micro-system to win an open championship. Finally came the most recent event of this type, the Sixth World Championship in Edmonton in 1989. The Carnegie Mellon favorite Deep Thought won convincingly, even though the program exhibited several programming errors. Still luck favors the strong, as the full report of the largest and strongest computer chess event ever held shows (Schaeffer, 1990). Al-though Deep Thought dominated the world championship, at the Twentieth North American Tournament that followed a bare six months later, it lost a game against Mephisto, and so only tied for first place with its deadly rival and stable-mate Hitech. All these programs were relying on advanced hardware technologies. Deep Thought was being likened to "Belle on a chip," showing how much more accessible increased speed through special integrated circuits had become.

From the foregoing, one might reasonably assume that most computer chess programs have been developed in the USA, and yet for the past two decades, participants from Canada have also been active and successful. Two programs, Ostrich and Wita, were at the inauguration of computer-chess tournaments at New York in 1970, and their authors went on to produce and instigate fundamental research in practical aspects of game-tree search (Campbell and Marsland, 1983; Newborn, 1988; Marsland, Reinefeld, and Schaeffer, 1987). Before its retirement, Ostrich (McGill University) participated in more championships than any other program. Its contemporary, renamed Awit (University of Alberta), had a checkered career as a Shannon type-B (selective search) program, finally achieving its best result with a second place tie at New York in 1983. Other active programs have included Ribbit (University of Waterloo), which tied for second at Stockholm in 1974, L'Excentrique, and Brute Force. By 1986 the strongest Canadian program was Phoenix (University of Alberta), a multiprocessor-based system using workstations (Schaeffer, 1989b). It tied for first place with three others at Cologne.

While the biggest and highest performing computers were being used in North America, European developers concentrated on microcomputer systems. Especially noteworthy are the Hegener & Glaser products based on the Mephisto program developed by Lang of England, and the Rebel program by Schröder from the Netherlands.

Implications

All this leads to the common question: When will a computer be the unassailed expert on chess? This issue was discussed at length during a panel discussion at the ACM 1984 National Conference in San Francisco. At that time it was too early to give a definitive answer, since even the experts could not agree. Their responses covered the whole range of possible answers with different degrees of optimism. Newborn enthusiastically supported "in five years," while Scherzer and Hyatt held to "about the end of the century." Thompson was more cautious with his "eventually, it is inevitable," but most pessimistic was Marsland who said "never, or not until the limits on human skill are known." Even so, there was a sense that production of an artificial Grandmaster was possible, and that a realistic challenge would occur during the first quarter of the 21st century. As added motivation, Edward Fredkin (MIT professor and well-known inventor) created a special incentive prize for computer chess. The trustee for the Fredkin Prize is Carnegie Mellon University, and the fund is administered by Berliner. Much like the Kremer prize for man-powered flight, awards are offered in three categories. The smallest prize of $5000 was presented to Thompson and Condon, when their Belle (qv) program earned a US Master rating in 1983. The second prize of $10,000 for the first program to achieve a USCF 2500 rating (players who attain this rating may reasonably aspire to becoming Grandmasters) was awarded to Deep Thought in August 1989 (Hsu, Anantharaman, Campbell, and Nowatzyk, 1990), but the $100,000 for attaining world-champion status remains unclaimed. To sustain interest in this activity, Fredkin funds are available each year for a prize match between the currently best computer and a comparably rated human.

One might well ask whether such a problem is worth all this effort, but when one considers some of the emerging uses of computers in important decision-making processes, the answer must be positive. If computers cannot even solve a decision-making problem in an area of perfect knowledge (like chess), then how can we be sure that computers make better decisions than humans in other complex domains, especially domains where the rules are ill-defined, or those exhibiting high levels of uncertainty? Unlike some problems, for chess there are well established standards against which to measure performance, not only through the Elo rating scale but also using standard tests (Kopec and Bratko, 1982) and relative performance measures (Thompson, 1982). The ACM-sponsored competitions have provided twenty years of continuing experimental data about the effective speed of computers and their operating system support. They have also afforded a public testing ground for new algorithms and data structures for speeding the traversal of search trees. These tests have provided growing proof of the increased understanding about how to program computers for chess, and how to encode the wealth of expert knowledge needed.

Another potentially valuable aspect of computer chess is its usefulness in demonstrating the power of man-machine cooperation. One would hope, for instance, that a computer could be a useful adjunct to the decision-making process, providing perhaps a steadying influence, and protecting against errors introduced by impulsive short-cuts of the kind people might try in a careless or angry moment. In this and other respects it is easy to understand Michie's support for the view that computer chess is the "*Drosophila melanogaster* (fruit fly) of machine intelligence" (Michie, 1980).

What then has been the effect of computer chess on artificial intelligence (AI)? First, each doubter who dared assert the superiority of human thought processes over mechanical algorithms for chess has been discredited. All that remains is to remove the mysticism of the world's greatest chess players. Exactly why seemingly mechanical means have worked, when almost every method proposed by reputable AI experts failed, remains a mystery for some. Clearly hard work, direct application of simple ideas and substantial public testing played a major role, as did improvements in hardware/software support systems. More than anything, this failure of traditional AI techniques for selection in decision-making, leads to the unnatural notion that many intellectual and creative activities can be reduced to fundamental computations. Ultimately this means that computers will make major con-

tributions to music and writing; indeed some will argue that they have already done so. Thus one effect of computer chess has been to force an initially reluctant acceptance of "brute-force" methods as an essential component in "intelligent systems," and to encourage growing use of search in problem-solving and planning applications. Several articles discussing these issues appear in a recent edited volume (Marsland and Schaeffer, 1990).

SEARCHING FOR CHESS

Since most chess programs work by examining large game trees, a depth-first search is commonly used. That is, the first branch to an immediate successor of the current node is recursively expanded until a leaf node (a node without successors) is reached. The remaining branches are then considered in turn as the search process backs up to the root. In practice, since leaf nodes are rarely encountered, search proceeds until some limiting depth (the horizon or frontier) is reached. Each frontier node is treated as if it were terminal and its value fed back. Since computer chess is well defined, and absolute measures of performance exist, it is a useful test vehicle for measuring efficiency of new search algorithms. In the simplest case, the best algorithm is the one that visits fewest nodes when determining the expected value of a tree. For a two-person game-tree, this value, which is a least upper bound on the merit (or score) for the side to move, can be found through a minimax search. In chess, this so called minimax value is a combination of both "MaterialBalance" (ie, the difference in value of the pieces held by each side) and "StrategicBalance" (eg, a composite measure of such things as mobility, square control, pawn formation structure, and king safety) components. Normally, an evaluation procedure computes these components in such a way that the MaterialBalance dominates all positional factors.

Minimax Search

For chess, the nodes in a two-person game-tree represent positions and the branches correspond to moves. The aim of the search is to find a path from the root to the highest valued *leaf node* that can be reached, under the assumption of best play by both sides. This is normally done by a depth-first search (see SEARCH, DEPTH-FIRST). To represent a level in the tree (that is, a move by one side) the term *ply* was introduced by Samuel in his major paper on machine learning (1959). How that word was chosen is not clear, perhaps as a contraction of "play" or maybe by association with forests, as in layers of plywood. In either case, it was certainly appropriate and it has been universally accepted.

In general, a true minimax search of a game tree will be expensive since every leaf node must be visited. For a uniform tree with exactly W moves at each node, there are W^D nodes at the layer of the tree that is D ply from the root. Nodes at this deepest layer will be referred to as terminal nodes, and will serve as leaf nodes in our discussion. Some games, like Fox and Geese, produce narrow trees (fewer than 10 branches per node) that can often be expanded to true leaf nodes and solved exhaustively. In contrast, chess produces bushy trees with an average branching factor, W, of about 35 moves (de Groot, 1965). Because of the size of the game tree, it is not possible to search until a mate or stalemate position (a true leaf node) is reached, so some maximum depth of search (ie, a horizon) is specified. Even so, an exhaustive search of all chess game trees involving more than a few moves for each side is impossible. Fortunately the work can be reduced, since the search of some nodes is unnecessary.

The Alpha-Beta (α-β) Algorithm

As the search of the game tree proceeds, the value of the best terminal node found so far changes. It has been known since 1958 that pruning was possible in a minimax search (Newell, Shaw, and Simon, 1958), but according to Knuth and Moore (1975) the ideas go back further, to McCarthy and his group at MIT. The first thorough treatment of the topic appears to be Brudno's paper (1963). The α-β algorithm employs lower (α) and upper (β) bounds on the expected value of the tree. These bounds may be used to prove that certain moves cannot affect the outcome of the search, and hence that they can be pruned or cut off. As part of the early descriptions about how subtrees were pruned, a distinction between deep and shallow cut-offs was made. Early versions of the α-β algorithm used only a single bound (α), and repeatedly reset the β bound to infinity, so that deep cut-offs were not achieved. To correct this flaw, Knuth and Moore (1975) introduced a recursive algorithm called F2 to prove properties about pruning in search. They also employed a *negamax* framework whose primary advantage is that by always passing back the negative of the subtree value, only maximizing operations are needed. Figure 1 uses a Pascal-like pseudo code to present our α-β function, AB, in the same negamax framework. Here a *return* statement is the convention for exit-

ing the function and returning the best subtree value or merit. Omitted are details of the game-specific functions *make* and *undo* (to update the game board), *generate* (to find moves), and *evaluate* (to assess terminal nodes). In the pseudo code of Figure 1, the $\max(\alpha, \text{merit})$ operation represents Fishburn's *fail-soft* condition (Fishburn, 1984), and ensures that the best available value is returned (rather than an α-β bound), even if the value lies outside the α-β window. This idea is usefully employed in some of the newer refinements to the α-β algorithm.

Although tree-searching topics involving pruning appear routinely in standard artificial intelligence texts, game-playing programs remain the major application for the α-β algorithm (for example, see ALPHA-BETA PRUNING). A typical discussion about game-tree search is based on alternate use of minimizing and maximizing operations. In practice, the negamax approach is preferred, since the programming is simpler. Figure 2 contains a small 3-ply tree in which a Dewey-decimal notation is used to label the nodes, so that the node name identifies the path from the root node. Thus, in Figure 2, p.2.1.2 is the root of a hidden subtree whose value is shown as 7. Also shown at each node of Figure 2 is the initial alpha-beta window that is employed by the negamax search. Note that successors to node p.1.2 are searched with an initial window of (α,5). Since the value of node p.1.2.1 is 6, which is greater than 5, a cut-off is said to occur, and node p.1.2.2 is not visited by the α-β algorithm.

Minimal Game Tree

If the best move is examined first at every node, the minimax value is obtained from a traversal of the minimal game tree. This minimal tree is of theoretical importance since its size is a lower bound on the search. For uniform trees of width W branches per node and a search depth of

```
FUNCTION AB (p : position; α, β, depth : integer) : integer;
                    { p is pointer to the current node    }
                    { α and β are window bounds           }
                    { depth is the remaining search length }
                    { the value of the subtree is returned }
   VAR merit, j, value : integer;
       moves : ARRAY [1..MAXWIDTH] OF position;
                                    { Note: depth must be positive }
BEGIN
   IF depth ≡ 0 THEN              { frontier node, maximum depth? }
      Return(Evaluate(p));

   moves := Generate(p);          { point to successor positions }
   IF empty(moves) THEN               { leaf, no moves?          }
      Return(Evaluate(p));
                                  { find merit of best variation }
   merit := -∞;
   FOR j := 1 TO sizeof(moves) DO BEGIN
      Make(moves[j]);                       { make current move }
      value := -AB (moves[j], -β, -max(α,merit), depth-1);
      IF (value > merit) THEN            { note new best merit   }
         merit := value;
      Undo(moves[j]);                        { retract current move }
      IF (merit ≥ β) THEN
         GOTO done;                                { a cut-off }
   END ;
done:
   Return(merit);
END ;
```

Figure 1. Depth-limited fail-soft alpha-beta function.

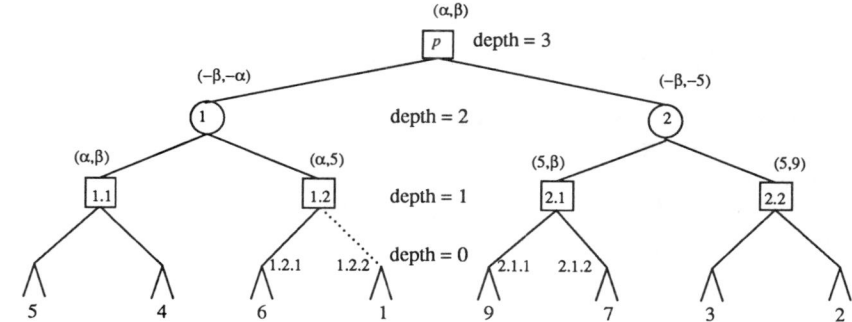

Figure 2. The effects of alpha-beta pruning under negamax search.

D ply, Knuth and Moore provide the most elegant proof that there are

$$W^{\left\lceil \frac{D}{2} \right\rceil} + W^{\left\lfloor \frac{D}{2} \right\rfloor} - 1$$

terminal nodes in the minimal game tree (Knuth and Moore, 1975), where $\lceil x \rceil$ is the smallest integer $\geq x$, and $\lfloor x \rfloor$ is the largest integer $\leq x$. Since such a terminal node rarely has no successors (ie, is not a leaf) it is often referred to as a horizon node, with D the distance from the root to the horizon (Berliner, 1973).

Aspiration Search

An α-β search can be carried out with the initial bounds covering a narrow range, one that spans the expected value of the tree. In chess these bounds might be (MaterialBalance-Pawn, MaterialBalance+Pawn). If the minimax value falls within this range, no additional work is necessary and the search usually completes in measurably less time. This aspiration search method, analyzed by Brudno (1963), referred to by Berliner (1973), and experimented with by Gillogly (1978), has been popular, though it has its problems (Kaindl, 1990). A disadvantage is that sometimes the initial bounds do not enclose the minimax value, in which case the search must be repeated with corrected bounds, as the outline of Figure 3 shows. Typically these failures occur only when material is being won or lost, in which case the increased cost of a more thorough search is acceptable. Because these re-searches use a semi-infinite window, from time to time people experiment with a *sliding window* of (V, V+PieceValue), in-

```
{     Assume V = estimated value of position p, and    }
{          e = expected error limit                    }
{      depth = current distance to the frontier        }
{          p = position being searched                 }
   α := V - e;                        { lower bound }
   β := V + e;                        { upper bound }

   V := AB (p, α, β, depth);
   IF (V ≥ β) THEN                    { failing high }
      V := AB (p, V, +∞, depth)
   ELSE
   IF (V ≤ α) THEN                    { failing low }
      V := AB (p, -∞, V, depth);

{     A successful search has now been completed       }
{     V now holds the current merit value of the tree  }
```

Figure 3. Narrow window aspiration search.

stead of (V, +∞). This method is often effective, but can lead to excessive re-searching when mate or large material gain/loss is in the offing. After 1974, iterated aspiration search came into general use, as follows:

> Before each iteration starts, α and β are not set to $-\infty$ and $+\infty$ as one might expect, but to a window only a few pawns wide, centered roughly on the final score [merit] from the previous iteration (or previous move in the case of the first iteration). This setting of 'high hopes' increases the number of α-β cutoffs. (Slate and Atkin, 1977).

Even so, although aspiration searching is still popular and has much to commend it, minimal window search seems to be more efficient and requires no assumptions about the choice of aspiration window (Marsland, 1983).

Quiescence Search

Even the earliest papers on computer chess recognized the importance of evaluating only positions which are *relatively quiescent* (Shannon, 1950) or *dead* (Turing and co-workers, 1953). These are positions that can be assessed accurately without further search. Typically they have no moves, such as checks, promotions or complex captures, whose outcome is unpredictable. Not all the moves at horizon nodes are quiescent (ie, lead immediately to dead positions), so some must be searched further. To limit the size of this so called quiescence search, only dynamic moves are selected for consideration. These might be as few as the moves that are part of a single complex capture, but can expand to include all capturing moves and all responses to check (Gillogly, 1972). Ideally, passed pawn moves (especially those close to promotion) and selected checks should be included (Slate and Atkin, 1977; Hyatt, Gower, and Nelson, 1985), but these are often only examined in computationally simple endgames. The goal is always to clarify the node so that a more accurate position evaluation is made. Despite the obvious benefits of these ideas, the ideal form of the quiescence search remains unclear, although some theories for controlling the search depth and limiting the participation of moves are emerging. Present quiescent search methods are attractive; they are simple, but from a chess standpoint leave much to be desired, especially when it comes to handling forking moves and mate threats. Even though the current approaches are reasonably effective, a more sophisticated method is needed for extending the search, or for identifying relevant moves to participate in the selective quiescence search (Kaindl, 1982). A first step in this direction is the notion of a singular extension (Anantharaman, Campbell, and Hsu, 1988). On the other hand, some commercial chess programs have managed well without quiescence search, using direct computation to evaluate the exchange of material. Another favored technique for assessing dynamic positions is use of the null move (Beal, 1989), which assumes that there is nothing worse than not making a move.

Horizon Effect

An unresolved defect of chess programs is the insertion of delaying moves that cause any inevitable loss of material to occur beyond the program's horizon (maximum search depth), so that the loss is hidden (Berliner, 1973). The *horizon effect* is said to occur when the delaying moves unnecessarily weaken the position or give up additional material to postpone the eventual loss. The effect is less apparent in programs with more knowledgeable quiescence searches (Kaindl, 1982), but all programs exhibit this phenomenon. There are many illustrations of the difficulty; the example in Figure 4, which is based on a study by Kaindl, is clear. Here a program with a simple quiescence search involving only captures would assume that any blocking move saves the queen. Even an 8-ply search (. . . , Pb2; Bxb2, Pc3; Bxc3, Pd4, Bxd4, Pe5; Bxe5) might not show the inevitable, believing that the queen has been saved at the expense of four pawns. Thus programs with a poor or inadequate quiescence search suffer more from the horizon effect. The best way to provide automatic extension of nonquiescent positions is still an open question, despite proposals such as bandwidth heuristic search (Harris, 1974).

ALPHA-BETA ENHANCEMENTS

Although the α-β algorithm is extremely efficient in comparison to a pure minimax search, it is improved dramatically both in the general case, and for chess in particular, by heuristic move-ordering mechanisms. When the heuristically superior moves are tried first there is always a statistical improvement in the pruning efficiency. Another important mechanism is the use of an iteratively deepening search, it too has the effect of dynamically reordering the move list at the root position, with the idea of reducing the search to that of the minimal game tree. Iteratively deepening searches are made more effective by the use of transposition tables to store results of searches from earlier iterations and use them to guide the current search more quickly to its best result. Finally, the α-β implementation itself has a more efficient implementation, based on the notion of a minimal (null) window search to prove more quickly the inferiority of competing variations.

Minimal Window Search

Theoretical advances, such as SCOUT (Pearl, 1980) and the comparable minimal window search techniques (Fishburn, 1984; Marsland, 1983; Campbell and Marsland, 1983) came in the late 1970s. The basic idea behind these methods is that it is cheaper to prove a subtree inferior, than to determine its exact value. Even though it has been shown that for bushy trees minimal window techniques provide a significant advantage (Marsland, 1983), for random game trees it is known that even these refinements are asymptotically equivalent to the simpler α-β algorithm. Bushy trees are typical for chess and so many contemporary chess programs use minimal window techniques through the Principal Variation Search (PVS) algorithm (Marsland and Campbell, 1982). In Figure 5, a Pascal-like pseudo code is used to describe PVS in a negamax framework. The chess-specific functions *make* and *undo* have been omitted for clarity. Also, the original version of PVS has been improved by using Reinefeld's depth=2 idea, which shows that re-searches need only be performed when the remaining depth of search is greater than 2. This point, and the general advantages of PVS, is illustrated by Figure 6, which shows the traversal of the same tree presented in Figure 2. Note that using narrow windows to prove the inferiority of the subtrees leads to the pruning of an additional frontier node (the node p.2.1.2). This is typical of the savings that are possible, although there is a risk that some subtrees will have to be re-searched.

Forward Pruning

To reduce the size of the tree that should be traversed and to provide a weak form of selective search, techniques that discard some branches have been tried. For example, tapered N-best search (Greenblatt, Eastlake, and Crocker, 1967) considers only the N-best moves at each node, where N usually decreases with increasing depth of the node from the root of the tree. As noted by Slate and Atkin, "The major design problem in selective search is the possi-

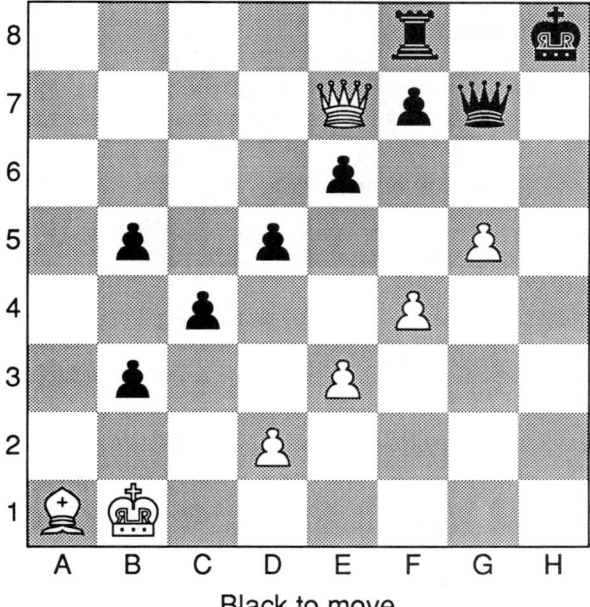

Black to move

Figure 4. The horizon effect.

```
                         FUNCTION PVS (p : position; α, β, depth : integer) : integer;
                                                    { p is pointer to the current node     }
                                                    { α and β are window bounds            }
                                                    { depth is the remaining search length }
                                                    { the value of the subtree is returned }
                         VAR merit, j, value : integer;
                             moves : ARRAY [1..MAXWIDTH] OF position;
                                                            { Note: depth must be positive }
                         BEGIN
                             IF depth ≡ 0 THEN                      { frontier node, maximum depth? }
                                Return(Evaluate(p));

                             moves := Generate(p);              { point to successor positions }
                             IF empty(moves) THEN                       { leaf, no moves? }
                                Return(Evaluate(p));
                                                                  { principal variation? }
                             merit := -PVS (moves[1], -β, -α, depth-1);
                             FOR j := 2 TO sizeof(moves) DO BEGIN
                                IF (merit ≥ β) THEN
                                    GOTO done;                                { cut off }
                                α := max(merit, α);                     { fail-soft condition }
                                                        { zero-width minimal-window search }
                                value := -PVS (moves[j], -α-1, -α, depth-1);
                                IF (value > merit) THEN         { re-search, if 'fail-high' }
                                    IF (α < value) AND (value < β) AND (depth > 2) THEN
                                        merit := -PVS (moves[j], -β, -value, depth-1)
                                    ELSE merit := value;
                             END ;
                         done:
                             Return(merit);
                         END ;
```

Figure 5. Minimal window principal variation search.

bility that the lookahead process will exclude a key move at a low level [closer to the root] in the game tree." Good examples supporting this point are found elsewhere (Frey, 1983), yet selective search methods remain an important tool for limiting search (see also SEARCH, BEAM). Other methods, such as marginal forward pruning and the gamma algorithm, omit moves whose immediate value is worse than the current best of the values from nodes already searched, since the expectation is that the opponent's move is only going to make things worse. Generally speaking these forward pruning methods are not reliable and should be avoided. They have no theoretical basis, although it may be possible to develop statistically sound methods which use the probability that the remaining moves are inferior to the best found so far.

One version of marginal forward pruning, referred to as razoring (Birmingham and Kent, 1977), is applied near horizon nodes. The expectation in all forward pruning is that the side to move can always improve the current value, so it may be futile to continue. Unfortunately, there are cases when the assumption is untrue, for instance in zugzwang positions. As Birmingham and Kent

(1977) point out, "the program defines zugzwang precisely as a state in which every move available to one player creates a position having a lower value to him (in its own evaluation terms) than the present bound for the position." Marginal pruning may also break down when the side to move has more than one piece *en prise* (eg, is forked), and so the decision to stop the search must be applied cautiously. On the other hand, use of the null move heuristic (Beal, 1989; Goetsch and Campbell, 1990) may be valuable here.

Despite these disadvantages, there are sound forward pruning methods and there is every incentive to develop more, since this is one way to reduce the size of the tree traversed, perhaps to less than the minimal game tree. A good prospect to through the development of programs that can deduce which branches can be neglected, by reasoning about the tree they traverse (Horacek, 1983).

Move Ordering Mechanisms

For efficiency (traversal of a smaller portion of the tree) the moves at each node should be ordered so that the more

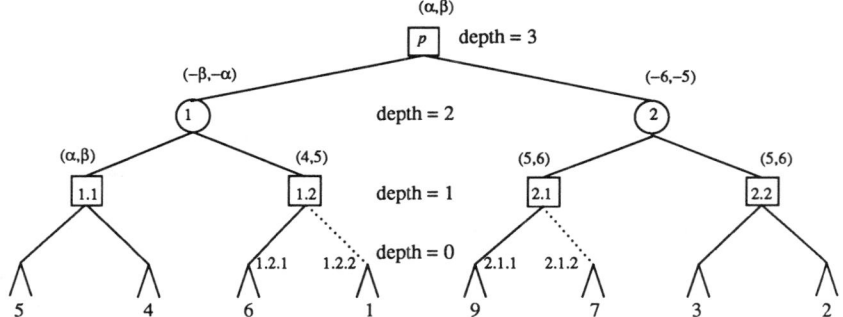

Figure 6. The effects of PVS pruning (negamax framework).

plausible ones are searched soonest. Various ordering schemes may be used. For example, "since the refutation of a bad move is often a capture, all captures are considered first in the tree, starting with the highest valued piece captured" (Gillogly, 1972). Special techniques are used at interior nodes for dynamically re-ordering moves during a search. In the simplest case, at every level in the tree a record is kept of the moves that have been assessed as being best, or good enough to refute a line of play and so cause a cut-off. As Gillogly (1972) puts it: "If a move is a refutation for one line, it may also refute another line, so it should be considered first if it appears in the legal move list." Referred to as the killer heuristic, a typical implementation maintains only the two most frequently occurring killers at each level (Slate and Atkin, 1977).

Later a more powerful and more general scheme for reordering moves at an interior node was introduced. For every legal move seen in the search tree, Schaeffer's history heuristic maintains a record of the move's success as a refutation, regardless of the line of play (Schaeffer, 1989a). At any point, the best refutation move is the one that either yields the highest merit or causes a cut-off. Many implementations are possible, but a pair of tables (each of 64×64 entries) is enough to keep a frequency count of how often a particular move (defined as a from-to square combination) is best for each side. Thus at each new interior node, the available moves are re-ordered so that the ones that have been most successful elsewhere are tried first. An important property of this so called history table is the ability to share information about the effectiveness of moves throughout the tree, rather than only at nodes at the same search level. The idea is that if a move is frequently good enough to cause a cut-off, it will probably be effective whenever it can be played.

Progressive and Iterative Deepening

The term progressive deepening was used by de Groot (1965) to encompass the notion of selectively extending the main continuation of interest. This type of selective expansion is not performed by programs employing the α-β algorithm, except in the sense of increasing the search depth by one for each checking move on the current continuation (path from root to horizon), or by performing a quiescence search from horizon nodes until dead positions are reached.

In the early 1970s several people tried a variety of ways to control the exponential growth of the tree search. A simple fixed depth search is inflexible, especially if it must be completed within a specified time. This difficulty was noted by Scott (1969) who reported on the effective use of an iterated search. Gillogly, author of the Tech chess program, coined the term iterative deepening to distinguish a full-width search to increasing depths from the progressively more focused search described by de Groot. About the same time Slate and Atkin (1977) sought a better time control mechanism, and introduced an improved iterated search for carrying out a progressively deeper and deeper analysis. For example, an iterated series of 1-ply, 2-ply, 3-ply . . . searches is carried out, with each new search first retracing the best path from the previous iteration and then extending the search by one ply. Early experimenters with this scheme were surprised to find that the iterated search often required less time than an equivalent direct search. It is not immediately obvious why iterative deepening is effective; as indeed it is not, unless the search is guided by the entries in a memory table (such as a transposition or refutation table) which holds the best moves from subtrees traversed during the previous iteration. All the early experimental evidence suggests that the overhead cost of the preliminary $D - 1$ iterations is usually recovered through a reduced cost for the D-ply search. Later the efficiency of iterative deepening was quantified to assess various refinements, especially memory table assists (Marsland, 1983). Now the terms progressive and iterative deepening are often used synonymously.

One important aspect of these searches is the role played by re-sorting root node moves between iterations. Because there is only one root node, an extensive positional analysis of the moves can be done. Even ranking them according to consistency with continuing themes or a long range plan is possible. However, in chess programs which rate terminal positions primarily on material balance, many of the moves (subtrees) return with equal merits. Thus at least a stable sort should be used to preserve an initial order of preferences. Even so, that may not be enough. In the early iterations moves are not assessed accurately. Some initially good moves may return with a poor expected merit for one or two iterations. Later the merit may improve, but the move could remain at the bottom of a list of all moves of equal merit, not near the top as the initial ranking recommended. Should this move ultimately prove to be best, then far too many moves may precede it at the discovery iteration, and disposing of those moves may be inordinately expensive. Experience with our test program, Parabelle (Marsland and Popowich, 1985), has shown that among moves of apparently equal merit the partial ordering should be based on the order provided by an extensive pre-analysis at the root node, and not on the vagaries of a sorting algorithm.

Transposition and Refutation Tables

The results (merit, best move, status) of the searches of nodes (subtrees) in the tree can be held in a large direct access table (Greenblatt, Eastlake, and Crocker 1967; Slate and Atkin, 1977). Re-visits of positions that have been seen before are common, especially if a minimal window search is used. When a position is reached again, the corresponding table entry serves three purposes. First, it may be possible to use the merit value in the table to narrow the (α-β) window bounds. Secondly, the best move that was found before can be tried immediately. It had probably caused a cut-off and may do so again, thus eliminating the need to generate the remaining moves. Here the table entry is being used as a move re-ordering mechanism. Finally, the primary purpose of the table is to enable recognition of move transpositions that have lead to a position (subtree) that has already been completely examined. In such a case there is no need to search again. This use of a transposition table is an example of exact forward pruning. Many programs also store their opening book in a way that is compatible with access to the transposition table. In this way they are protected against the myriad of small variations in move order that are common in the opening.

By far the most popular table-access method is the one proposed by Zobrist (1970). He observed that a chess position constitutes placement of up to 12 different piece types $\{K,Q,R,B,N,P,-K . . . -P\}$ onto a 64-square board. Thus a set of 12×64 unique integers (plus a few more for *en passant* and castling privileges), $\{R_i\}$, may be used to represent all the possible piece/square combinations. For best results, these integers should be at least 32 bits long, and be randomly independent of each other. An index of the position may be produced by doing an exclusive-or on selected integers as follows:

$$P_j = R_a \ xor \ R_b \ xor \cdot \cdot \cdot xor \ R_x$$

where the R_a etc are integers associated with the piece placements. Movement of a "man" from the piece-square associated with R_f to the piece-square associated with R_t yields a new index

$$P_k = (P_j \ xor \ R_f) \ xor \ R_t$$

By using this index as a hash key to the transposition table, direct and rapid access is possible. For further speed and simplicity, and unlike a normal hash table, only a single probe is made. More elaborate schemes have been tried, and can be effective if the cost of the increased complexity of managing the table does not undermine the benefits from improved table usage. Table 1 shows the usual fields for each entry in the hash table. *Flag* specifies whether the entry corresponds to a position that has been fully searched, or whether *Merit* can only be used to adjust the α-β bounds. *Height* ensures that the value of a fully evaluated position is not used if the subtree length is less than the current search depth, instead *Move* is played.

Correctly embedding transposition table code into the α-β algorithm needs care and attention to details. It can be especially awkward to install in the more efficient Principal Variation Search algorithm. To simplify matters, consider a revised version of Figure 5 in which the line

value := $-$PVS (moves[j], $-\alpha-1$, $-\alpha$, depth-1)

is replaced by

value := $-$MWS (moves[j], $-\alpha$, depth-1)

Table 1. Typical Transposition Table Entry

Lock	To ensure the table entry corresponds to the tree position.
Move	Preferred move in the position, determined from a previous search.
Merit	Value of subtree, computed previously.
Flag	Is the merit an upper bound, a lower bound or an exact value?
Height	Length of subtree upon which merit is based.

Basically the minimal window search portion is being split into its own procedure (this formulation also has some advantages for parallel implementations). Figure 7 contains pseudo code for MWS and shows not only the usage of the entries *Move, Merit, Flag,* and *Height* from Table 1, but does so in the negamax framework of the null window search portion of PVS. Of course the transposition access methods must also be put into PVS. It is here, for example, that *store* sets *Flag* to its EXACT value. Note too, in Figure 7, the introduction of the CUTOFF function to ensure that the LBOUND marker is stored in the transposition table when a cutoff occurs, while UBOUND is used when all the successors are examined. The contents of functions *retrieve* and *store*, which access and update the transposition table, are not shown here.

Transposition tables have found many applications in chess programs, not only to help detect replicated positions, but also to assess king safety and pawn formations (Nelson, 1985). Further these tables have been used to support a form of rote learning first explored by Samuel (1959) for checkers. Two major examples of improving performance in chess programs through learning are the works of Slate (1987) and Scherzer, Scherzer, and Tjaden (1990).

A transposition table also identifies the preferred move sequences used to guide the next iteration of a progressive deepening search. Only the move is important in this phase, since the subtree length is usually less than the remaining search depth. Transposition tables are particularly beneficial to methods like PVS, since the initial minimal window search loads the table with useful lines that will be used if a re-search is needed. On the other hand, for deeper searches, entries are commonly lost as the table is overwritten, even though the table may contain more than a million entries (Nelson, 1985). Under these conditions a small fixed size transposition table may be overused (overloaded) until it is ineffective as a means of storing the continuations. To overcome this fault, a special table for holding these main continuations (the refutation lines) is also used. The table has W entries containing the D elements of each continuation. For shallow searches ($D < 6$) a refutation table guides a progressive deepening search just as well as a transposition table. Thus a refutation table is the preferred choice of commercial systems or users of memory limited processors. A small triangular workspace ($D \times D/2$ entries) is needed to hold the current continuation as it is generated, and these entries in the workspace can also be used as a source of killer moves. A good alternative description of refutation and transposition techniques appears in the recent book by Levy and Newborn (1990).

Combined Enhancements

The various terms and techniques described have evolved over the years, with the superiority of one method over another often depending on which elements are combined. Iterative deepening versions of aspiration and PVS, along with transposition, refutation and history memory tables are all useful refinements to the α-β algorithm. Their relative performance is adequately characterized by Figure 8.

```
FUNCTION MWS (p : position; β, depth : integer) : integer;
   VAR value, Height, Merit : integer;
       Move, TableMove, BestMove : 1..MAXWIDTH;
       Flag : (VALID, LBOUND, UBOUND);
       moves : ARRAY [1..MAXWIDTH] OF position;
BEGIN
   Retrieve(p, Height, Merit, Flag, TableMove);
               { if no table move then                            }
               {    TableMove = 0, Merit = -∞ and Height < 0       }
   IF (Height ≥ depth) THEN BEGIN                  {Node seen before}
      IF (Flag ≡ VALID) OR (Flag ≡ LBOUND AND Merit ≥ β)
                         OR (Flag ≡ UBOUND AND Merit < β) THEN
         Return(Merit);
   END;
   IF (Height > 0) THEN BEGIN               {Save a move Generation?}
      Merit := -MWS (moves[TableMove], -β+1, depth-1);
      if (Merit ≥ β) THEN
         Return(CUTOFF(p, Merit, depth, Height, TableMove));
   END;

   IF (depth ≡ 0) THEN
      Return(Evaluate(p));                            {Frontier node}

   moves := Generate(p);
   IF empty(moves) THEN
      Return(Evaluate(p));                                {Leaf node}
   BestMove := TableMove;
   FOR Move := 1 TO sizeof(moves) DO
   IF Move ≠ TableMove THEN BEGIN
      IF (Merit ≥ β) THEN
         Return(CUTOFF(p, Merit, depth, Height, BestMove));
      value := -MWS (moves[Move], -β+1, depth-1);
      IF (value > Merit) THEN BEGIN
         Merit := value;
         BestMove := Move;
      END;
   END;

   IF (Height ≤ depth) THEN
      Store(p, depth, Merit, UBOUND, BestMove);
   Return(Merit);                               {full-width node}
END;

FUNCTION CUTOFF (p: position; Merit, depth, Height : integer;
               Move : 1..MAXWIDTH) : integer;
BEGIN
   IF (Height ≤ depth) THEN
      Store(p, depth, Merit, LBOUND, Move);
   return(Merit);                               {pruned node}
END;
```

Figure 7. Minimal window search with transposition table.

That graph was made from data gathered by a chess program's simple evaluation function, when analyzing the standard Bratko-Kopec positions (Kopec and Bratko, 1982). Other programs may achieve slightly different results, reflecting differences in the evaluation function, but the relative performance of the methods should not be affected. Normally, the basis of such a comparison is the number of frontier nodes (also called horizon nodes, bottom positions or terminal nodes) visited. Evaluation of these nodes is usually more expensive than the predecessors, since a quiescence search is carried out there. However, these horizon nodes are of two types, ALL nodes, where every move is generated and evaluated, and CUT nodes from which only as many moves as necessary to cause a cut-off are assessed (Marsland and Popowich, 1985). For the minimal game tree these nodes can be counted, but there is no simple formula for the general α-β search case. Thus the basis of comparison for Figure 8 is the amount of CPU time required for each algorithm,

rather than the leaf node count. Although a somewhat different graph is produced as a consequence, the relative performance of the methods does not change. The CPU comparison assesses the various enhancements more usefully, and also makes them look even better than on a node count basis. Analysis of the Bratko-Kopec positions requires the search of trees whose nodes have an average width (branching factor) of $W = 34$ branches. Thus it is possible to use the formula for horizon node count in a uniform minimal game tree to provide a lower bound on the search size, as drawn in Figure 8. Since search was not possible for this case, the trace represents the percentage of performance relative to direct α-β, but on a node count basis. Even so, the trace is a good estimate of the lower bound on the time required.

Figure 8 shows the effect of various performance enhancing mechanisms. At interior nodes, if the transposition (+trans) and/or refutation (+ref) table options are enabled, any valid table move is tried first. By this means,

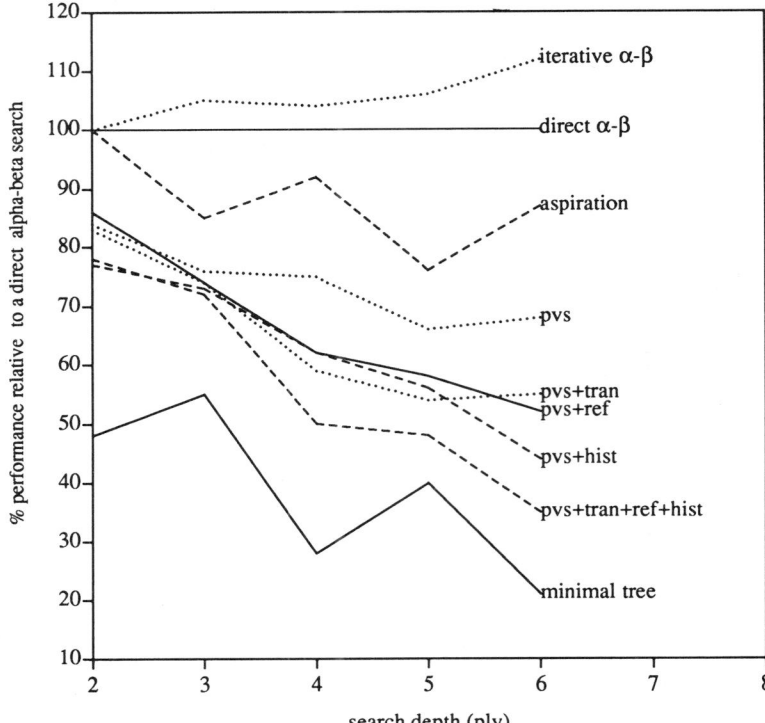

Figure 8. Time comparison of alpha-beta enhancements.

should a cut-off occur, the need for a move generation is eliminated. Otherwise the initial ordering simply places safe captures ahead of other moves. When the history table (+hist) is enabled, the move list is further re-ordered to ensure that the most frequently effective moves from elsewhere in the tree are tried soonest. For the results presented in Figure 8, transposition, refutation, and heuristic tables were in effect only for the traces whose label is extended with +trans, +ref and/or +hist respectively. Also, the transposition table was fixed at eight thousand entries, so the effects of table overloading may be seen when the search depth reaches 6-ply. Figure 8 shows that:

1. Pure iterative deepening costs little over a direct search, and so can be effectively used as a time control mechanism. In the graph presented an average overhead of only 5% is shown, even though memory assists like transposition, refutation, or history tables were not used.

2. When iterative deepening is used, PVS is superior to aspiration search (with a ± pawn window).

3. A refutation table is a space efficient alternative to a transposition table for guiding the early iterations.

4. Odd-ply α-β searches are more efficient than even-ply ones.

5. Transposition table size must increase with depth of search, or else too many entries will be overlaid before they can be used. The individual contributions of the transposition table, through move re-order-

ing, bounds narrowing, and forward pruning, are not brought out in this study.

Transposition and/or refutation tables combine effectively with the history heuristic, achieving search results close to the minimal game tree for odd-ply search depths. It is these combinations that have the most dramatic effect on iterative deepening's efficiency.

Overview

A model chess program has three phases to its search. Typically, from the root node an exhaustive examination of layers of moves occurs, and this is followed by a phase of selective searches up to a limiting depth (the horizon). This limiting depth is not necessarily a constant, since responses to check are not usually counted in the path length. The reason is clear, there are only a few responses to checking moves and so their cost is negligible. Programs that have no selective search component might be termed *brute force*, while those lacking an initial exhaustive phase are often selective only in the sense that they use some form of marginal forward pruning. An evaluation function is applied at the frontier nodes to assess the material balance and the structural properties of the position (eg, relative placement of pawns). To aid in this assessment a third phase is used, a variable depth quiescence search of those moves that are not dead (ie, cannot be accurately assessed). It is the quality of this quiescence search which controls the severity of the horizon effect exhibited by all chess programs. Since the evaluation function is expensive, the best pruning must be used. All major programs use the ubiquitous α-β algorithm, in its aspiration or principal variation search form, along with iterative deepening.

Dynamic move re-ordering mechanisms like the killer heuristic, refutation tables, transposition tables, and the history heuristic significantly improve these methods. Forward pruning methods are also sometimes effective. The transposition table is especially important because it improves the handling of endgames where the potential for a draw by repetition is high. Like the history heuristic, it is also a powerful predictor of cut-off moves, thus saving a move generation. The properties of these methods has been encapsulated in Figure 8, which shows their performance relative to a direct α-β search.

THE ANATOMY OF CHESS PROGRAMS

A typical chess program contains the following three distinct elements: Board description and move generation, tree searching/pruning, and position evaluation. Many people have based their first chess program on Frey and Atkin's (1979) instructive Pascal-based model. Even so, the most efficient way of representing all the tables and data structures necessary to describe a chess board is not yet known, although good proposals exist in readily available books (Frey, 1983; Welsh and Baczynskyj, 1985). Sometimes the *generate* function produces all the feasible moves at once from these tables. This has the advantage that the moves may be sorted to improve the probability of a cut-off. In small memory computers, on the other hand, the moves are produced one at a time. This saves space and perhaps time whenever an early cut-off occurs. Since only limited sorting is possible (captures might be generated first) the searching efficiency is generally lower, however.

In the area of searching/pruning methods, variations on the depth-limited α-β algorithm remain the preferred choice. All chess programs fit the following general model. A full width exhaustive (all moves are considered) search is done at the first few ply from the root node. At depths beyond this exhaustive layer some form of selective search is used. Typically, unlikely or unpromising moves are simply dropped from the move list. More sophisticated programs do an extensive analysis to select those moves that are to be discarded at an interior node. Even so, this type of forward pruning is known to be error prone and dangerous; it is attractive because of the big reduction in tree size that ensues. Finally, the *evaluate* function is invoked at the horizon nodes to assess the moves. Many of these are captures or other forcing moves which are not dead, and so a limited quiescence search is carried out to resolve the unknown potential of the move. The evaluation process is the most important part of a chess program, because it estimates the value of the subtrees that extend beyond the horizon. Although in the simplest case *evaluate* simply counts the material balance, for superior play it is also necessary to measure many positional factors, such as pawn structures. These aspects are still not formalized, but adequate descriptions by computer chess practitioners are available in books (Slate and Atkin, 1977; Ebeling, 1987; Hyatt, Gower, and Nelson, 1990).

Hardware Assists

Computer chess has consistently been in the forefront of the application of high technology. With Cheops (Moussouris, Holloway, and Greenblatt, 1979), the 1970s saw the introduction of special purpose hardware for chess. Later networks of computers were tried; in 1983 (New York), Ostrich used an eight processor Data General system (Newborn, 1985) and Cray Blitz a dual processor Cray X-MP (Hyatt, Gower, and Nelson, 1985). Some programs used special purpose hardware [see for example Belle (Condon and Thompson, 1982), Bebe (Scherzer, Scherzer, and Tjaden, 1990), Advance 3.0, and BCP (Welsh and Baczynskyj, 1985)], and there were several experimental commercial systems employing high performance VLSI chips. The trend towards the use of custom chips will continue, as evidenced by the success of the latest master-calibre chess program, Hitech from Carnegie Mellon University, based on a new circuit design for generating moves. Most recently Deep Thought, which has been likened to Belle on a chip, often runs as a multiprocessor system (Hsu and co-workers, 1990; Hsu, 1990). The advantages and difficulties of parallel systems have been described by Hyatt, Suter, and Nelson (1989) and Schaeffer (1989b). Although mainframes continue to be faster, the programs on smaller more special purpose computers are advancing more rapidly. It is only a matter of time before massive parallelism is applied to computer chess, as Stiller's endgame studies show (Stiller, 1989). The problem is a natural demonstration piece for the power of distributed computation, since it is processor intensive and the work can be partitioned in many ways. Not only can the game trees be split into similar subtrees, but parallel computation of such components as move generation, position evaluation, and quiescence search is possible.

Improvements in hardware speed have been an important contributor to computer chess performance. These improvements will continue, not only through faster special purpose processors, but also by using many processing elements.

Software Advances

Many observers attributed the advances in computer chess through the 1970s to better hardware, particularly faster processors. Much evidence supports that point of view, but major improvements also stemmed from a better understanding of quiescence and the horizon effect, and a better encoding of chess knowledge. The benefits of aspiration search, iterative deepening, especially when used with a refutation table, the killer heuristic and transposition tables were also appreciated, and by 1980 all were in general use. One other advance was the simple expedient of "thinking on the opponent's time" (Gillogly, 1972), which involved selecting a response for the opponent, usually the move predicted by the computer, and searching the predicted position for the next reply. Nothing is lost by this tactic, and when a successful prediction is made the time saved may be accumulated until it is necessary or possible to do a deeper search. Anticipating the opponent's response has been embraced by all microprocessor based systems, since it increases their effective speed.

Not all advances work out in practice. For example, in a test with Kaissa, the method of analogies "reduced the search by a factor of 4 while the time for studying one position was increased by a factor of 1.5" (Adelson-Velsky, Arlazarov, and Donskoy, 1979). Thus a dramatic reduction in the positions evaluated occurred, but the total execution time went up and so the method was not effective. This sophisticated technique has not been tried in other competitive chess programs. The essence of the idea is that captures in chess are often invariant with respect to several minor moves. That is to say, some minor moves have no influence on the outcome of a specific capture. Thus the true results of a capture need be computed only once, and stored for immediate use in the evaluation of other positions that contain this identical capture. Unfortunately, the relation (sphere of influence) between a move and those pieces involved in a capture is complex, and it can be as much work to determine this relationship as it would be to simply re-evaluate the exchange. However, the method is elegant and appealing on many grounds and should be a fruitful area for further research, as a promising variant restricted to pawn moves illustrates (Horacek, 1983).

Perhaps the most important improvements in software have come from the new ideas in selective and quiescent search. Great emphasis has been placed on self-limiting variable depth search (Kaindl, 1982) and on the method of singular extensions (Anantharaman, Campbell, and Hsu, 1988) to guide the quiescent down appropriately forcing lines. Also the widely mentioned idea of a null-move search, based on the assumption that nothing is worse than no move, has led Beal (1989) to formulate a theory of first-order and higher order null-move searches. These ideas tie in with McAllister's (1988) proposed use of "conspiracy numbers," although they have not yet been applied in a major way to chess. Some of these methods are still somewhat special purpose, but they all point to the existence of a theory for controlled search for games.

Endgame Play

During the 1970s there developed a better understanding of the power of pawns in chess, and a general improvement in endgame play. Even so, endgames remained a weak feature of computer chess. Almost every game illustrated some deficiency, through inexact play or conceptual blunders. More commonly, however, the programs were seen to wallow and move pieces aimlessly around the board. A good illustration of such difficulties is a position from a 1979 game between Duchess and Chaos, which was analyzed extensively in an appendix to an important reference (Frey, 1983). After more than ten hours of play the position in Figure 9 was reached, and since neither side was making progress the game was adjudicated after white's 111th move of Bc6–d5. White had just completed a sequence of 21 reversible moves with only the bishop, and black had responded correctly by simply moving the king to and fro. Duchess had only the most rudimentary plan for winning endgames. Specifically, it knew about avoiding a 50-move rule draw. Had the game continued, then within the next 29 moves it would either play an irrevers-

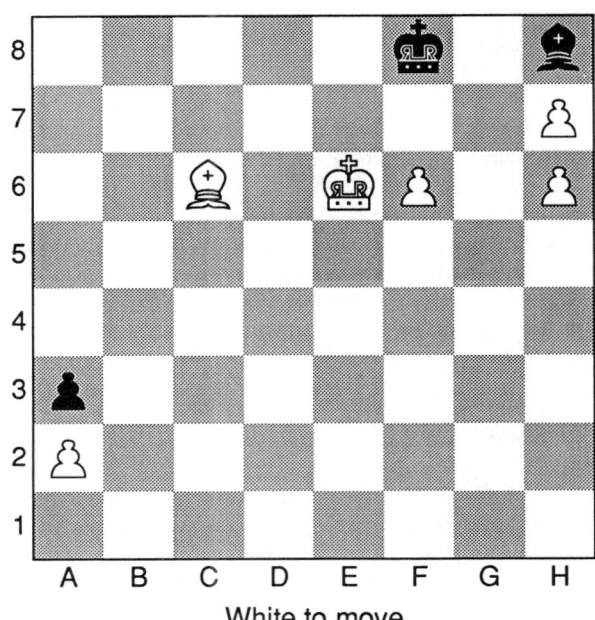

White to move

Figure 9. Lack of an endgame plan.

ible move like Pf6–f7, or give up the pawn on f6. Another 50-move cycle would then ensue and perhaps eventually the possibility of winning the pawn on a3 might be found. Even today it is doubtful if many programs can do any better. There is simply nothing much to be learned through search. What is needed here is some higher notion involving goal seeking plans. All the time a solution which avoids a draw must be sought. This latter aspect is important since in many variations black can simply offer the following sacrifice: bishop takes pawn on f6, because if the white king recaptures a stalemate results.

Sometimes, however, chess programs are supreme. At Toronto in 1977 in particular, Belle demonstrated a new strategy for defending the lost ending KQ vs KR against chess masters. While the ending still favors the side with the queen, precise play is required to win within 50 moves, as several chess masters were embarrassed to discover (Kopec, 1990). In speed chess even Belle often dominated the masters, and the newer machines like Deep Thought and Hitech are truly formidable. Increasingly, chess programs are teaching even experts new tricks and insights. Long ago Ströhlein built a database to find optimal solutions to several simple three and four piece endgames (kings plus one or two pieces). Using a Telefunken TR4 (48-bit word, 8 μsec. operations) he obtained the results summarized in Table 2 (Ströhlein, 1970). When one considers that it took more than 29 hours to solve the KQ vs KR endgame, one realizes what a major undertaking it was in 1969. In the next decade, many others built databases of the simplest endings. Their approach (Bramer and Clark, 1979; Bratko and Michie, 1980) was to develop optimal sequences backward from all possible winning positions, building all paths to mate (ie, reducing to a known subproblem). These works have recently been reviewed and put into perspective (van den

Table 2. Maximum Moves to Mate or Win an Endgame

Ströhlein (1970)		Thompson (1986)			
Pieces	Moves to Mate	Pieces	Moves to Win	Pieces	Moves to Mate
KQ vs K	10	KBB vs KN	66	KRR vs KR	31
KR vs K	16	KQ vs KNN	63	KRQ vs KR	35
KR vs KB	18	KQ vs KNB	42	KQN vs KQ	41
KR vs KN	27	KQ vs KBB	71	KQB vs KQ	33
KQ vs KR	31	KRN vs KR	33	KQR vs KQ	67
		KRB vs KR	59	KQQ vs KQ	30

Herik and Herschberg, 1985), but the other main results summarized in Table 2 were obtained by Thompson (1986).

In the five-piece endgames not all the positions are necessarily won, but of those that are, the maximum moves to mate or capture of a black piece is now known. These results were obtained in 1985/86 using a Sequent Balance 8000 computer, on which a "typical pure-piece endgame would be solved in two or three weeks of real time" (Thompson, 1986). Although the recent work by Stiller (1989) is interesting, the major contribution by Belle and Ken Thompson was the building of databases to solve five-piece endgames, specifically, KQ# vs KQ (where # Q, R, B or N) and KR# vs KR. Furthermore Thompson discovered that in general KBB vs KN is won (not drawn) and less than 67 moves are needed to mate or safely capture the knight, raising questions about revisions to the 50-move rule. Also completed was a major study of the complex KQP vs KQ ending. Again, often more than 50 maneuvers are required before a pawn can advance (Thompson, 1986). Although hard to top, in 1988 Lewis Stiller used a Connection Machine 2 to confirm these results and develop new ones, solving nearly all the five-piece endgames in the process (Stiller, 1989). He also exhaustively studied many of the four-piece plus pawn endgames, but had no means of storing the results to produce databases. For more complex endings involving several pawns, some exciting new ideas are those on chunking. Based on these ideas, it is claimed that the "world's foremost expert" has been generated for endings where each side has a king and three pawns (Berliner and Campbell, 1984).

Memory Tables

Others have pointed out (Slate and Atkin, 1977; Nelson, 1985) that a hash table can also be used to store information about pawn formations. Since there are usually far more moves by pieces than by pawns, the value of the base pawn formation for a position must be re-computed several times. It is a simple matter to build a hash key based on the location of pawns alone, and so store the values of pawn formations in a hash table for immediate retrieval. A 98–99% success rate was reported (Hyatt, Gower, and Nelson, 1985) for a pawn hash table, since otherwise 10–20% of the search time was taken up with evaluation of pawn structures. King safety can also be handled similarly (Nelson, 1985), because the king has few moves and for long periods is not under attack.

Transposition and other memory tables come into their own in endgames, since there are fewer pieces and more reversible moves. Search time reduction by a factor of five is common, and in certain types of king and pawn endings, it is claimed that experiments with Cray Blitz and Belle have produced trees of more than 30-ply, representing speedups of well over a hundredfold. Even in complex middle games, however, significant performance improvement is observed. Thus, use of a transposition table provides an exact form of forward pruning and as such reduces the size of the search space, in endgames often to less than the minimal game tree. The power of forward pruning is well illustrated by the position in Figure 10, which was apparently first solved by Chess 4.9 (Frey and Atkin, 1979) and then by Belle. The only complete computer analysis of this position was provided later. As Hyatt, Gower, and Nelson (1985) put it, a solution is possible because "the search tree is quite narrow due to the locked pawns." Here Cray Blitz is able to find the correct move of Ka1-b1 at the 18th iteration. The complete line of the best continuation was found at the 33rd iteration, after examining four million nodes in about 65 sec of real time. This was possible because the transposition table had become

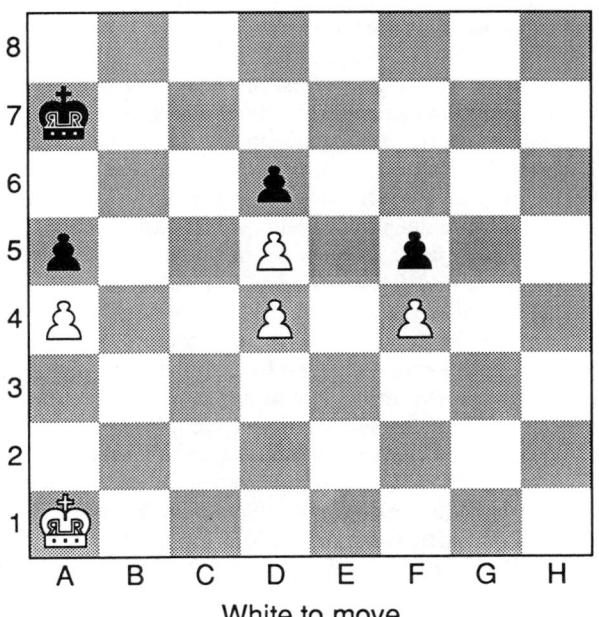

Figure 10. Transposition table necessity.

loaded with the results of draws by repetition, and so the normal exponential growth of the tree was inhibited. Also, at every iteration, the transposition table was loaded with losing defences corresponding to lengthy searches. Thus the current iteration often yielded results equivalent to a much longer $2(D - 1)$ ply search. Thompson refers to this phenomenon as "seeing over the horizon."

Selective Search

Many software advances came from a better understanding of how the various components in evaluation and search interact. The first step was a move away from selective search, by providing a clear separation between the algorithmic component (search) and the heuristic component (chess position evaluation). The essence of the selective approach is to narrow the width of search by forward pruning. Some selection processes removed implausible moves only, thus abbreviating the width of search in a variable way not necessarily dependent on node level in the tree. This technique was only slightly more successful than other forms of forward pruning, and required more computation. Even so, it too could not retain sacrificial moves. So the death knell of selective search was its inability to predict the future with a static evaluation function. It was particularly susceptible to the decoy sacrifice and subsequent entrapment of a piece. Interior node evaluation functions that attempted to deal with these problems became too expensive. Even so, in the eyes of some, selective methods remain as a future prospect since

> Selective search will always loom as a potentially faster road to high level play. That road, however, requires an intellectual break-through rather than a simple application of known techniques (Condon and Thompson, 1983).

The reason for this belief is that chess game trees grow exponentially with depth of search. Ultimately it will become impossible to obtain the necessary computing power to search deeper within normal time constraints. For this reason most chess programs already incorporate some form of selective search, often as forward pruning. These methods are quite *ad hoc* since they have a weak theoretical base.

Although nearly all chess programs have some form of selective search deep in the tree, even if it is no more than discarding unlikely moves, so far only two major programs (Awit and Chaos) had noted successes while not considering all the moves at the root node. Despite their past occasional good results, these programs no longer compete in the race for Grand Master status. Nevertheless, although the main advantage of a program that is exhaustive to some chosen search depth is its tactical strength, it has been shown that the selective approach can also be effective in handling tactics. In particular, Wilkin's Paradise program demonstrated superior performance in "tactically sharp middle game positions" on a standard suite of tests (Wilkins, 1983). Paradise was designed to illustrate that a selective search program can also find the best continuation when there is material to be gained, though searching but a fraction of the game

tree viewed by such programs as Chess 4.4 and Tech. Furthermore it can do so with greater success than either program or a typical A-class player. However, a nine to one time advantage was necessary, to allow adequate time for the interpretation of the MacLisp program. Paradise's approach is to use an extensive static analysis to produce a small set of plausible winning plans. Once a plan is selected "it is used until it is exhausted or until the program determines that it is not working." In addition, Paradise can "detect when a plan has been tried earlier along the line of play and avoid searching again if nothing has changed" (Wilkins, 1983). This is the essence of the method of analogies too. As Wilkins says, the "goal is to build an expert knowledge base and to reason with it to discover plans and verify them within a small tree." Although Paradise was successful in this regard, part of its strength lay in its quiescence search, which was seen to be "inexpensive compared to regular search," despite the fact that this search "investigates not only captures but forks, pins, multimove mating sequences, and other threats" (Wilkins, 1983). The efficiency of the program lies in its powerful evaluation, so that usually "only one move is investigated at each node, except when a defensive move fails." Pitrat also wrote extensively on the subject of finding plans that win material (1977), but neither his ideas nor those in Paradise were incorporated into the competitive chess programs of the 1980s.

Search and Knowledge Errors

The following game was the climax of the Fifteenth ACM NACCC, in which all the important programs of the day participated. Had Nuchess won its final match against Cray Blitz there would have been a 5-way tie between these two programs and Bebe, Chaos, and Fidelity X. Such a result almost came to pass, but suddenly Nuchess "snatched defeat from the jaws of victory," as chess computers were prone to do. Complete details about the game are not important, but the position shown in Figure 11 was reached. Here, with Rf6xg6, Nuchess wins another pawn, but in so doing enters a forced sequence that leaves Cray Blitz with an unstoppable pawn on a7, as follows:

> 45. Rf6xg6 ? Rg8xg6+
>
> 46. Kg5xg6   Nc8xd6
>
> 47. Pc5xd6

Many explanations can be given for this error, but all have to do with a lack of knowledge about the value of pawns. Perhaps black's passed pawn was ignored because it was still on its home square, or perhaps Nuchess simply miscalculated and "forgot" that such pawns may initially advance two rows. Another possibility is that white became lost in some deep searches in which its own pawn promotes. Even a good quiescence search might not recognize the danger of a passed pawn, especially one so far from its destination. In either case, this example illustrates the need for knowledge of a type that cannot be obtained easily through search, and yet humans recognize at a glance (de Groot, 1965). The game continued 47. . . . .

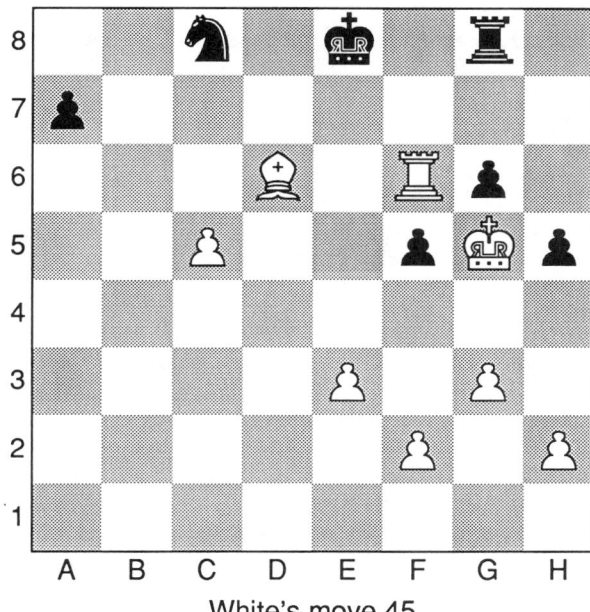

White's move 45

Figure 11. A costly miscalculation.

Pa5 and white was neither able to prevent promotion nor advance its own pawn.

There are many opportunities for contradictory knowledge interactions in chess programs. Sometimes chess folklore provides ground rules that must be applied selectively. Such advice as "a knight on the rim is dim" is usually appropriate, but in special cases placing a knight on the edge of the board is sound, especially if it forms part of an attacking theme and is unassailable. Not enough work has been done to assess the utility of such knowledge and to measure its importance. Schaeffer's interesting doctoral thesis (1986) addresses this issue; this thesis could also have some impact on the way expert systems are tested and built, since it demonstrates that there is a correct order to the acquisition of knowledge, if the newer knowledge is to build effectively on the old (Schaeffer and Marsland, 1985).

AREAS OF FUTURE PROGRESS

Although most chess programs are now using all the available refinements and tables to reduce the game tree traversal time, only in the ending is it possible to search consistently less than the minimal game tree. Selective search and forward pruning methods are the only real hope for reducing further the magnitude of the search. Before this is possible, it is necessary for the programs to reason about the trees they see and deduce which branches can be ignored. Typically these will be branches that create permanent weaknesses or are inconsistent with the current themes. The difficulty will be to do this without losing sight of tactical factors.

Improved performance will also come about by using faster computers, and through the construction of multiprocessor systems. Perhaps the earliest multiprocessor

chess program was Ostrich (Newborn, 1985). Other experimental systems followed including Parabelle (Marsland and Popowich, 1985) and ParaPhoenix. None of these early systems, nor the strongest multiprocessor program Cray Blitz (Hyatt, Gower, and Nelson, 1990), consistently achieved more than a 5-fold speed-up, even when eight processors were used. There is no apparent theoretical limit to the parallelism. Although the practical restrictions are great, some new ideas on partitioning the work and better scheduling methods have begun to yield improved performance (Hyatt, Suter, and Nelson, 1989; Schaeffer, 1989b).

Another major area of research is the derivation of strategies from databases of chess endgames. It is now easy to build expert system databases for the classical endgames involving four or five pieces. At present these databases can only supply the optimal move in any position (although a short principal continuation can be provided by way of expert advise). What is needed now is a program to deduce from these databases optimally correct strategies for playing the endgame. Here the database could either serve as a teacher of a deductive inference program, or as a tester of plans and hypotheses for a general learning program. Perhaps a good test of these methods would be the production of a program that derives strategies for the well-defined KBB vs KN endgame. A solution to this problem would provide a great advance to the whole of artificial intelligence.

BIBLIOGRAPHY

G. M. Adelson-Velsky, V. L. Arlazarov, and M. V. Donskoy, "Algorithms of Adaptive Search," in J. Hayes, D. Michie, and L. Michulich, eds., *Machine Intelligence 9*, Ellis Horwood, Chichester, U.K., 1979, pp. 373–384.

G. M. Adelson-Velsky, V. L. Arlazarov, and M. V. Donskoy, *Algorithms for Games*, Springer-Verlag, New York, 1988. Translation of Russian original (1978).

T. Anantharaman, M. Campbell, and F. Hsu, "Singular Extensions: Adding Selectivity to Brute-Force Searching," *Int. Computer Chess Assoc. J.* **11**(4), 135–143 (1988). Also in *Artif. Intell.* **43**(1), 99–110 (1990).

D. Beal, "Experiments with the Null Move," in D. Beal, ed., *Advances in Computer Chess 5*, Elsevier, 1989, pp. 65–79. Revised as "A Generalized Quiescence Search Algorithm," *Artif. Intell.* **43**(1), 85–98 (1990).

A. G. Bell, *The Machine Plays Chess?*, Pergamon Press, Oxford, 1978.

H. J. Berliner, "Some Necessary Conditions for a Master Chess Program," *Proceedings of the Third International Joint Conferences on Artificial Intelligence*, Stanford, AAAI, Menlo Park, Calif., 1973, pp. 77–85.

H. Berliner and M. Campbell, "Using Chunking to Solve Chess Pawn Endgames," *Artif. Intell.* **23**(1), 97–120 (1984).

H. J. Berliner and C. Ebeling, "Pattern Knowledge and Search: The SUPREM Architecture," *Artif. Intell.* **38**(2), 161–198 (1989). A revised version appears as "Hitech" in *Computers, Chess, and Cognition*, 1990.

J. A. Birmingham and P. Kent, "Tree-Searching and Tree-Pruning Techniques," in M. Clarke, ed., *Advances in Computer Chess 1*, Edinburgh University Press, Edinburgh, 1977, pp. 89–107.

M. A. Bramer and M. R. B. Clarke, "A Model for the Representation of Pattern-Knowledge for the Endgame in Chess," *Int. J. Man-Mach. Stud.* **11**, 635–649 (1979).

I. Bratko and D. Michie, "A Representation for Pattern-Knowledge in Chess Endgames," in M. Clarke, ed., *Advances in Computer Chess 2*, Edinburgh University Press, Edinburgh, 1980, pp. 31–56.

A. L. Brudno, "Bounds and Valuations for Abridging the Search of Estimates," *Probl. Cybern.* **10**, 225–241 (1963). Translation of Russian original in *Probl. Kibern.* **10**, 141–150 (May 1963).

M. S. Campbell and T. A. Marsland, "A Comparison of Minimax Tree Search Algorithms," *Artif. Intell.* **20**(4), 347–367 (1983).

J. H. Condon and K. Thompson, "Belle Chess Hardware," in M. Clarke, ed., *Advances in Computer Chess 3*, Pergamon Press, Oxford, 1982, pp. 45–54.

J. H. Condon and K. Thompson, "Belle," in P. Frey, ed., *Chess Skill in Man and Machine*, Springer-Verlag, 2nd Edition 1983, pp. 201–210.

C. Ebeling, *All the Right Moves: A VLSI Architecture for Chess*, MIT Press, 1987. See also Ph.D. dissertation, Carnegie Mellon University, Pittsburgh, Penn., 1986, pp. 145.

J. P. Fishburn, *Analysis of Speedup in Distributed Algorithms*, UMI Research Press, Ann Arbor, Mich., 1984. Also Comp. Sci. Tech. Rep. 431, University of Wisconsin, Madison, May 1981, pp. 118.

P. W. Frey, ed., *Chess Skill in Man and Machine*, Springer-Verlag, New York, 2nd ed., 1983.

P. W. Frey and L. R. Atkin, "Creating a Chess Player," in B. L. Liffick, ed., *The BYTE Book of Pascal*, BYTE/McGraw-Hill, Peterborough NH, 2nd Edition 1979, pp. 107–155. Also in D. Levy, ed., *Computer Games 1*, Springer-Verlag, 1988, pp. 226–324.

J. J. Gillogly, "The Technology Chess Program," *Artif. Intell.* **3**(1–4), 145–163 (1972). Also in D. Levy, ed., *Computer Chess Compendium*, Springer-Verlag, 1988, pp. 67–79.

J. J. Gillogly, *Performance Analysis of the Technology Chess Program*, Technical Report CMU-189, Computer Science, Carnegie-Mellon University, Pittsburgh, March 1978.

G. Goetsch and M. S. Campbell, "Experiments With the Null-Move Heuristic," in T. A. Marsland and J. Schaeffer, eds., *Computers, Chess, and Cognition*, Springer-Verlag, New York, 1990, pp. 159–168.

I. J. Good, "A Five-Year Plan for Automatic Chess," in E. Dale and D. Michie, eds., *Machine Intelligence 2*, Elsevier, New York, 1968, pp. 89–118.

R. D. Greenblatt, D. E. Eastlake, and S. D. Crocker, "The Greenblatt Chess Program," *Fall Joint Computing Conference Proceedings 31*, San Francisco, 1967, ACM, New York, 1967, pp. 801–810. Also in D. Levy, ed., *Computer Chess Compendium*, Springer-Verlag, 1988, pp. 56–66.

A. D. de Groot, *Thought and Choice in Chess*, Mouton, The Hague, 1965. Also 2nd ed., 1978.

L. R. Harris, "Heuristic Search Under Conditions of Error," *Artif. Intell.* **5**(3), 217–234 (1974).

J. E. Hayes and D. N. L. Levy, *The World Computer Chess Championship*, Edinburgh University Press, Edinburgh, 1976.

H. J. van den Herik and I. S. Herschberg, "The Construction of an Omniscient Endgame Database," *Int. Computer Chess Assoc. J.* **8**(2), 66–87 (1985).

H. Horacek, "Knowledge-based Move Selection and Evaluation to Guide the Search in Chess Pawn Endings," *Int. Computer Chess Assoc. J.* **6**(3), 20–37 (1983).

F-h. Hsu, *Large-Scale Parallelization of Alpha-Beta Search: An Algorithmic and Architectural Study With Computer Chess*, CMU-CS-90-108, Ph.D. dissertation, Carnegie Mellon University, Pittsburgh, Feb. 1990.

F-h. Hsu, T. S. Anantharaman, M. S. Campbell, and A. Nowatzyk, "Deep Thought," in T. A. Marsland and J. Schaeffer, eds., *Computers, Chess, and Cognition*, Springer-Verlag, New York, 1990, pp. 55–78.

R. M. Hyatt, A. E. Gower, and H. L. Nelson, "Cray Blitz," in D. Beal, ed., *Advances in Computer Chess 4*, Pergamon Press, Oxford, 1985, pp. 8–18.

R. M. Hyatt, A. E. Gower, and H. L. Nelson, "Cray Blitz," in T. A. Marsland and J. Schaeffer, eds., *Computers, Chess, and Cognition*, Springer-Verlag, New York, 1990, pp. 111–130.

R. M. Hyatt, B. W. Suter, and H. L. Nelson, "A Parallel Alpha/Beta Tree Searching Algorithm," *Parallel Comput.* **10**(3), 299–308 (1989).

H. Kaindl, "Dynamic Control of the Quiescence Search in Computer Chess," in R. Trappl, ed., *Cybernetics and Systems Research*, North-Holland, Amsterdam, 1982, pp. 973–977.

H. Kaindl, "Tree Searching Algorithms," in T. A. Marsland and J. Schaeffer, eds., *Computers, Chess, and Cognition*, Springer-Verlag, New York, 1990, pp. 133–158.

D. E. Knuth and R. W. Moore, "An Analysis of Alpha-Beta Pruning," *Artif. Intell.* **6**(4), 293–326 (1975).

D. Kopec, "Advances in Man-Machine Play," in T. A. Marsland and J. Schaeffer, eds., *Computers, Chess, and Cognition*, Springer-Verlag, New York, 1990, pp. 9–32.

D. Kopec and I. Bratko, "The Bratko-Kopec Experiment: A Comparison of Human and Computer Performance in Chess," in M. Clarke, ed., *Advances in Computer Chess 3*, Pergamon Press, Oxford, 1982, pp. 57–72.

D. N. L. Levy, *Computer Chess Compendium*, Springer-Verlag, New York, 1988.

D. N. Levy and M. M. Newborn, *How Computers Play Chess*, W. H. Freeman & Co., New York, 1990.

T. A. Marsland, "Relative Efficiency of Alpha-Beta Implementations," *Proceedings of the Eighth International Joint Conferences on Artificial Intelligence*, Karlsruhe, Germany, Morgan-Kaufmann, San Mateo, Calif., Aug. 1983, pp. 763–766.

T. A. Marsland and M. Campbell, "Parallel Search of Strongly Ordered Game Trees," *Comput. Surv.* **14**(4), 533–551 (1982).

T. A. Marsland and F. Popowich, "Parallel Game-Tree Search," *IEEE Trans. Patt. Anal. Mach. Intell.* **PAMI–7**(4), 442–452 (July 1985).

T. A. Marsland and J. Schaeffer, *Computers, Chess, and Cognition*, Springer-Verlag, New York, 1990.

T. A. Marsland, A. Reinefeld, and J. Schaeffer, "Low Overhead Alternatives to SSS*," *Artif. Intell.* **31**(2), 185–199 (1987).

D. Michie, "Chess with Computers," *Interdiscip. Sci. Rev.* **5**(3), 215–227 (1980).

B. Mittman, "A Brief History of Computer Chess Tournaments: 1970–1975," in P. Frey, ed., *Chess Skill in Man and Machine*, Springer-Verlag, 1977, pp. 1–33.

J. Moussouris, J. Holloway, and R. Greenblatt, "CHEOPS: A Chess-oriented Processing System," in J. Hayes, D. Michie, and L. Michulich, eds., *Machine Intelligence 9*, Ellis Horwood, Chichester, 1979, pp. 351–360.

H. L. Nelson, "Hash Tables in Cray Blitz," *Int. Computer Chess Assoc. J.* **8**(1), 3–13 (1985).

T. Nemes, "The Chess-Playing Machine," *Acta Technica*, Hungarian Academy of Sciences, Budapest, 1951, pp. 215–239.

M. Newborn, "A Parallel Search Chess Program," *Proceedings of the ACM Annual Conference,* Denver, 1985, ACM, New York, pp. 272–277. Also Tech. Rep. SOCS 82.3, Computer Science, McGill University, Montreal, Canada, 1982, pp. 20.

M. M. Newborn, "Unsynchronized Iteratively Deepening Parallel Alpha-Beta Search," *IEEE Trans. Patt. Anal. Mach. Intell.* **PAMI–10**(5), 687–694 (1988).

A. Newell, J. C. Shaw, and H. A. Simon, "Chess Playing Programs and the Problem of Complexity," *IBM J. Res. Dev.* 4(2), 320–335 (1958). Also in E. Feigenbaum and J. Feldman, eds., *Computers and Thought,* 1963, pp. 39–70.

J. Pearl, "Asymptotic Properties of Minimax Trees and Game Searching Procedures," *Artif. Intell.* **14**(2), 113–138 (1980).

J. Pitrat, "A Chess Combination Program which Uses Plans," *Artif. Intell.* **8**(3), 275–321 (1977).

A. L. Samuel, "Some Studies in Machine Learning Using the Game of Checkers," *IBM J. Res. Dev.* **3**, 210–229 (1959). Also in D. Levy, ed., *Computer Games 1*, Springer-Verlag, 1988, pp. 335–365.

J. Schaeffer, *Experiments in Search and Knowledge*, Ph.D. dissertation, University of Waterloo, Waterloo, Canada, 1986.

J. Schaeffer, "Distributed Game-Tree Search," *J. Parallel Distributed Comput.* **6**(2), 90–114 (1989).

J. Schaeffer, "The History Heuristic and Alpha-Beta Search Enhancements in Practice," *IEEE Trans. Patt. Anal. Mach. Intell.* **PAMI–11**(11), 1203–1212 (1989).

J. Schaeffer, "1989 World Computer Chess Championship," in T. A. Marsland and J. Schaeffer, eds., *Computers, Chess, and Cognition*, Springer-Verlag, New York, 1990, pp. 33–46.

J. Schaeffer and T. A. Marsland, "The Utility of Expert Knowledge," *Proceedings of the Ninth International Joint Conferences on Artificial Intelligence*, Los Angeles, Morgan-Kaufmann, San Mateo, Calif., 1985, pp. 585–587.

T. Scherzer, L. Scherzer, and D. Tjaden, "Learning in Bebe," in T. A. Marsland and J. Schaeffer, eds., *Computers, Chess, and Cognition*, Springer-Verlag, New York, 1990, pp. 197–216.

J. J. Scott, "A Chess-Playing Program," in B. Meltzer and D. Michie, eds., *Machine Intelligence 4*, Edinburgh University Press, 1969, pp. 255–265.

C. E. Shannon, "Programming a Computer for Playing Chess," *Philos. Mag.* **41**(7), 256–275 (1950). Also in D. Levy, ed., *Computer Chess Compendium*, Springer-Verlag, 1988, pp. 2–13.

D. Slate, "A Chess Program that Uses its Transposition Table to Learn from Experience," *Int. Computer Chess Assoc. J.* **10**(2), 59–71 (1987).

D. J. Slate and L. R. Atkin, "CHESS 4.5—The Northwestern University Chess Program," in P. Frey, ed., *Chess Skill in Man and Machine*, Springer-Verlag, 1977, pp. 82–118.

L. Stiller, "Parallel Analysis of Certain Endgames," *Int. Computer Chess Assoc. J.* **12**(2), 55–64 (1989).

T. Ströhlein, *Untersuchungen Über Kombinatorische Spiele*, Doctoral dissertation, Technische Hochschüle München, Munich, 1970.

K. Thompson, "Computer Chess Strength," in M. Clarke, ed., *Advances in Computer Chess 3*, Pergamon Press, Oxford, 1982, pp. 55–56.

K. Thompson, "Retrograde Analysis of Certain Endgames," *Int. Computer Chess Assoc. J.* **9**(3), 131–139 (1986).

A. M. Turing, C. Strachey, M. A. Bates, and B. V. Bowden, "Digital Computers Applied to Games," in B. V. Bowden, ed., *Faster Than Thought*, Pitman, 1953, pp. 286–310.

D. E. Welsh and B. Baczynskyj, *Computer Chess II*, W. C. Brown Co., Dubuque, Iowa, 1985.

David Wilkins, "Using Chess Knowledge to Reduce Speed," in P. Frey, ed., *Chess Skill in Man and Machine*, Springer-Verlag, 2nd ed., 1983, pp. 211–242.

A. L. Zobrist, *A New Hashing Method with Applications for Game Playing*, Tech. Rep. 88, Computer Sciences Dept., University of Wisconsin, Madison, April, 1970. Also in *Int. Computer Chess Assoc. J.* **13**(2), 169–173 (1990).

K. Zuse, "Chess Programs," in *The Plankalkül*, Report No. 106, Gesellschaft für Mathematik und Datenverarbeitung, Bonn, 1976, pp. 201–244. Translation of German original, 1945. Also as Report No. 175, Oldenbourg Verlag, Munich, 1989.

T. A. MARSLAND
University of Alberta

COMPUTER-INTEGRATED MANUFACTURING. See MANUFACTURING, AI IN.

COMPUTER SYSTEMS

In order to consider computer systems designed specifically for AI applications, an understanding of computer systems in general would be appropriate. Computer systems can be defined as an integrated functioning of computer components as a single entity. These computer components can be divided into software components and hardware components (Table 1). Examples of software components are the operating system, the various compilers, the editor, and the application programs. Hardware component examples are the memory such as the main memory and mass storage, the CPU, and the I/O processors.

A majority of the computer systems manufactured and distributed today are general purpose; that is, the use of the systems ranges anywhere from business database applications to number-crunching mathematical applications. These general-purpose computer systems are based on the von Neumann architecture, whose basic components are the memory and the processor. In this architecture the task to be executed is given as a sequential set of instructions that reside in the memory. The processor fetches one instruction at a time from the memory, decodes the instruction to check what operation must be executed, and fetches the data [source operand(s)] with which the operation takes place. On the operand fetch, the operation is executed and the result is stored in the destination operand location. Not only are the execution of instructions sequential, but each fetch of the instruction, fetch of the data operand, the actual execution, and the storing of the result operand are also done in strict sequential order. For example, let the instruction fetched from memory be $A = B + C$. The processor determines that the operation is an ADD, and the source operands B and C are fetched. The addition operation is executed on the two source operands, and the result is stored in the destination operand A. Computer systems based on the traditional von Neumann architecture may be used for AI programs, but they may suffer from various inefficiencies during execution. These inefficiencies and the reasons for

Table 1. Components of a Computer System

Hardware Component	Software Component
Main memory	Operating system
Mass storage	Compilers
I/O processors	Interpreters
CPU	Assembler
Bus network	Editor
	Application programs

Table 2. Characteristics of AI Applications and Examples

Characteristic	Examples
Representation of knowledge	Semantic networks, predicate calculus
Use of complex data structures	Graph, list, tree
Dynamic type checking	Symbolic and numeric data
Potential for parallelism	Search

the advent of computer systems targeted for AI applications are discussed later in this article.

Artificial intelligence applications differ from conventional programs in that AI programs need to represent the information, or knowledge (Abbott, 1987; McCalla and Cercone, 1983; McCarthy, 1987), of a given domain, and, given this knowledge, need operators to manipulate or deduce information from it. For AI programs to solve problems, they need to know about objects represented in the domain, their properties, and their interrelationships. This information is termed *knowledge* (see KNOWLEDGE REPRESENTATION). Semantic nets and predicate calculus (Charniak and McDermott, 1985) are examples of methods used in representing knowledge. The knowledge representation and the operations performed to extract information from this knowledge, such as unification and property inheritance (Charniak and McDermott, 1985), preclude AI applications from conventional applications.

Based on the difference between conventional applications and AI applications, one can justify the emergence of computer systems directed primarily for AI applications (Hwang and co-workers, 1987; Rice, 1989; Wah, 1987). First, general-purpose computer systems are optimized for arithmetic operations, not for the vast data manipulation that is necessary in AI applications. Complex data structures such as graphs, lists, and trees are used extensively in AI applications, instead of the usual simple linear structure used in conventional applications. The second characteristic of AI applications is that the contents of the data structure are often symbolic rather than numeric. The contents of the symbolic data structure can only be determined during the execution phase. This requires dynamic type checking, which incurs run-time overhead since general-purpose computer systems do not implement this operation in hardware.

Finally, another weakness of the von Neumann architecture for AI applications is the lack of simultaneity. In von Neumann architectures only one instruction can be executing at any time. Many AI applications have a potential for parallelism. The inference of knowledge from a given representation may be performed in many directions simultaneously, reducing the time it takes to reach a conclusion. Consider, for example, the search through a state space represented as a tree, where each node in the tree represents a certain state. Searching through each of the states can be expedited tremendously if every level of the tree could be searched in parallel instead of guessing which branch should be searched next. The advent of parallel computing systems such as the Connection Machine (qv) was initiated with this view in mind. The characteristics of AI applications independent of the computer system are summarized in Table 2.

The different characteristics of AI applications as compared with conventional business or numeric computations does not prohibit these applications from being executed in general-purpose systems. However, efficient execution has to be compromised in order to execute AI applications on general computer systems. Representing complex data structures with linear memory incurs the use of much more extra memory for information purposes along with the data itself. Although complex data structure manipulation such as pattern matching and searching, which comprise the majority of AI application operations, can be carried out on a conventional system, this results in a slow execution of the application. In the case of dynamic type checking, the information type must be kept along with each datum, again incurring more memory usage. Also, at each execution of an instruction, the type of the data must be checked, adding to the execution time overhead. Another price to pay is that the system programs such as the compiler or interpreter have to become more complex to accommodate this mode of operation. Clearly, a computer system with one processor can perform only one operation at a time and have no parallelism.

ISSUES IN COMPUTER SYSTEMS FOR AI APPLICATIONS

The obstacles that prevent efficient execution of AI applications on conventional computer systems also justify the need for systems that are specifically suited for AI applications. The key issues involved in the design of computer systems for AI applications are summarized in Table 3.

A conventional computer system is composed of two components: the data and the control. AI-based systems,

Table 3. Issues Related to Computer Systems for AI Applications

Issue	Example
Representation of knowledge	Hardware support for knowledge representation
Knowledge base	Hardware support for operations on knowledge
Control	Hardware support for parallelism
Human–computer interface	Real-time interface with the computer system
Other	Storage management and instruction set

on the other hand, generally have one other component in the form of a knowledge base (Nau, 1983), that is, the set of operators that reason on the given knowledge. The data are represented in the form of knowledge, and the control strategy decides which operator of the knowledge base to invoke. Since AI applications rely heavily on these components, hardware support provided for such operations can have a major performance impact. Thus, hardware support for representation and manipulation of knowledge need to be considered. In terms of control, parallel invocation of operations on knowledge could be supported.

One other component that is helpful in both the general-purpose system and systems designed for AI applications, but more so in the latter, is the human interface. The underlying complex data structure used in AI applications should be presented to the user in an easily comprehensible manner rather than in a verbose form that would generally be difficult to understand. In this regard, the complex operations that are provided in the computer systems for AI applications should also be manageable by the user without much difficulty. That is, the system should be usable without a great deal of technical understanding or training. Human interface with computer systems is becoming an important problem, especially as real-time AI applications become more prevalent (Laffey and co-workers, 1988). Thus a graphic and easy-to-use interface for users has to be supported, but to minimize the effect on the performance of the system due to this interface, separate hardware may have to be used to provide this functionality.

Other issues generally involved in conventional computer systems are memory management and the instruction set.

Memory Management

Memory management in conventional systems is based on the locality principle; that is, the memory to be referenced next will, with high probability, be close to the currently referenced memory location. For example, when an instruction is accessed to be executed, it is generally conceived that the next instruction to be executed will be the next one in the memory. This behavior results in strong locality in memory references. Unfortunately, memory references in AI applications are rarely sequential. A good example is a list that is the underlying data structure in AI languages such as LISP. The use of pointers in list accesses tend to show nonsequential behavior in memory reference, resulting in poor reference locality.

Another memory management issue is garbage collection. As data objects are assigned to memory locations, there comes a time when the data stored in the location is not needed and the location can be freed or reclaimed. This reclaiming process is called garbage collection. Garbage collection is an essential feature that should be supported for the efficient use of memory. Unfortunately, this process imposes a heavy burden on the processor.

Instruction Set

The advent of reduced instruction set computer (RISC) architecture (Lee, 1989; Patterson, 1985) has stirred up an argument on the set of instructions that should be provided by a computer system. While conventional systems based on complex instruction set computer (CISC) architecture provide a wide choice of instructions, RISC architecture advocates have suggested that only simple instructions that are used most heavily should be provided to the user through an efficient implementation. Since operations in AI applications concentrate on data structure manipulation such as pattern matching and searching, it would be efficient to provide such operations in hardware. Simulations of these instructions by conventional instructions, which are optimized for numeric operations, would only incur performance degradations.

SYSTEM EXAMPLES

Recent technological developments have provided a means of experimenting with new architectures and structures for computer systems. The effect of these developments may be seen in the multitudes of new and innovative computer systems that are available. Many of these systems have been designed for AI applications.

Table 4 lists some of the systems developed specifically for AI applications (Benker and co-workers, 1989; Hillis, 1985; Holmer and co-workers, 1990; Hwang and co-workers, 1987; Moon, 1987; Murakami and co-workers, 1983; Wah, 1987). Although some of the machines are commercially available, many are still research architectures. In the following we discuss three examples of such systems, presenting the aspects of system design most relevant to AI applications. The first system is the commercially available Symbolics Machine. Another, the Connection Machine Supercomputer, is also available commercially and is a high-performance engine. The third machine is a group of research machines based on the logic programming language PROLOG. The PROLOG machines have been a research interest in the computer systems field, and some features of these systems are discussed.

Symbolics Machine

The Symbolics Machine is a LISP machine produced by Symbolics, Inc. and is intended to support LISP programming and efficient execution of LISP programs. The Symbolics family of machines originated in 1974 from the MIT Laboratory LISP Machine Project (Ditzel and co-workers, 1987; Graham, 1988; Moon, 1987).

The Symbolics Machine is presented to the user as a dedicated single-user machine. It may share resources such as files and printers with other Symbolics or non-Symbolics machines through a local area network. A conventional external view is presented to the user through text and objects that are controlled by the use of a mouse and keyboard.

Because it is a machine optimized for LISP, the Symbolics Machine does not support, in hardware, the representation of knowledge or any knowledge base. Rather, it emphasizes the management of storage, which is essential for an effective execution of LISP, and hardware support of dynamic data type checking. In the following, we elaborate on these two issues as well as the interface and the

Table 4. Examples of Computer Systems for AI Categorized as Language-Based and Representation-Based Systems

Name	Source
Language-Based Systems	
Berkeley Abstract Machine (BAM)	UC Berkeley
EM3	Electrotechnical Lab
Fujitsu Alpha	Fujitsu Laboratories Ltd.
Integrated Prolog Processor (IPP)	Hitachi Research Lab
Knowledge Crunching Machine (KCM)	ECRC, Germany
LAMBDA family	LISP Machines, Inc.
Parallel Inference Machine (PIM)	University of Tokyo
Parallel Unification Machine (PLUM)	University of Michigan
Programmed Logic Machine (PLM)	UC Berkeley
Symbolics 3600 series	Symbolics, Inc.
Tamura Machine	Kobe University
Tektronix 4400 series	Tektronix
Texas Instruments Explorer	Texas Instruments
Xerox 1100 series	Xerox
Representation-Based Systems	
Butterfly	BBN
Connection Machine	Thinking Machines Corp.
DADO2	Columbia University
Happy Machine	Carnegie Mellon University
*i*Warp	Carnegie Mellon University
McMob	University of Maryland
Non-Von	Columbia University
PIPE	National Institute of Standards and Technology
Pyramid	University of Washington, Seattle
ZMob	University of Maryland

instruction set issues. These issues are summarized in Table 5.

The Symbolics Machine does not provide the user with any form of parallelism. The user can only perceive the machine as a single machine dedicated for just one user. The system, though, does provide faster execution through low-level parallelism that is transparent to the user.

A memory word in the earlier versions of Symbolics architecture was 36 bits long (Fig. 1), instead of the conventional 16 or 32 bits. Recent architectures have ex-

tended the word length to 40 bits (Graham, 1988) of which 32 bits compose the data word as in conventional systems and the additional 8 bits hold information that is needed during execution. Since operations are done on symbolic data, information on the type of data must be kept along with the data itself. Six bits of the additional 8 bits are used for this purpose. Hardware is provided such that the type checking of data can be accomplished in parallel with computations and memory accesses. This means that the dynamic data typing is accommodated without any time penalty. This modification of hardware provides faster ex-

Table 5. AI Issues Pertaining to the Symbolics Machine

Issue	
Representation of knowledge	Hardware support for LISP list, but no direct support to knowledge representation.
Knowledge base	No explicit support.
Control	No explicit support for parallel computation, but data type checking is done in parallel with computation and memory access, limiting the overhead associated with dynamic type checking.
Human–computer interface	High-resolution graphics monitor along with easy-to-use window and menu system is provided. Software tools such as debuggers are also available.
Others	*Storage management.* Explicit hardware support is provided for garbage collection. Extra bits are used for compact use of memory.
	Instruction set. Generic instructions are provided, along with direct LISP instruction support.

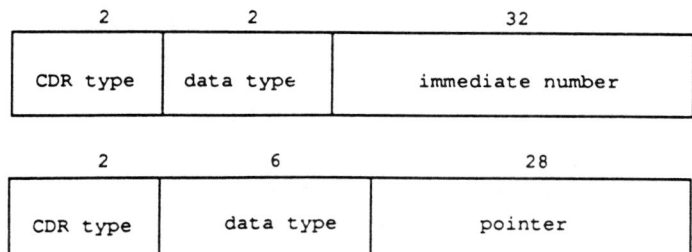

Figure 1. Two formats of the Symbolics 3600 memory word.

ecution as compared to the conventional system, which would have to execute the type checking explicitly.

The Symbolics Machine provides as its environment a high-resolution color or monochrome graphics monitor. It also provides windows and pop-up menus as a user interface. In order to reduce the load on the main processor, the Symbolics Machine provides a separate processor for the graphics console. Another noticeable feature of the Symbolics Machine is the software environment it provides. Programming tools such as debuggers, trace facilities, and intelligent editors are some of the facilities available on this system (Ditzel and co-workers, 1987).

Memory management in list processing plays a vital role in providing good performance to the system. A heap of memory locations used for storing data objects is available in list processing. When a new data item is created, a memory location from the heap is assigned the value of the new data and is appropriately inserted in the list of objects. The objects are connected by pointers that appropriately designate the next object in the list. In conventional systems, one memory word would be used for the data value and another memory word for designating the next data item. In the Symbolics Machines, a method is provided to avoid, in most cases, the extra memory word used for the pointer. Of the 8 extra bits provided for each word, 2 bits are used to represent whether the next memory word is a pointer to the next word or the next word itself. Thus, by assigning the objects to consecutive memory locations when possible, the extra pointer can be avoided (Fig. 2).

Garbage collection is another essential feature of list manipulation. There are two ways of providing this process. The first is collecting garbage when the system runs out of memory locations. Since the garbage collection process incurs large time overhead, this approach may result in long wait times for interactive users. In the second method, garbage collection proceeds concurrently with the processing; that is, the garbage collection process is interleaved with other programs the user may invoke. Overall, the second method evenly disperses the total time used for garbage collection in the first method, providing the user with a consistent response from the system.

The Symbolics Machine, being a dedicated, single-user, interactive system, uses the second method for garbage collection. Clearly, this system provides the user with a consistent response, but in addition, the system executes more efficiently overall. By garbage collecting regularly, the chance of being able to allocate the next memory location to the next data object in the list is greater.

Like most machines, the Symbolics Machine implements the machine instructions in hardware or in microcode. In this machine, the instruction set includes many LISP functions. Examples of such instructions are eq, not, fixp, floatp, symbolp, logand, car, cons, member, and aref. Another feature of the Symbolics Machine is that the instructions are generic. That is, the instructions are not type-specific. For example, an add instruction on a conventional machine would require checking the data type, to see whether the data are valid or if they are integer or floating-point data. Appropriate action, such as conver-

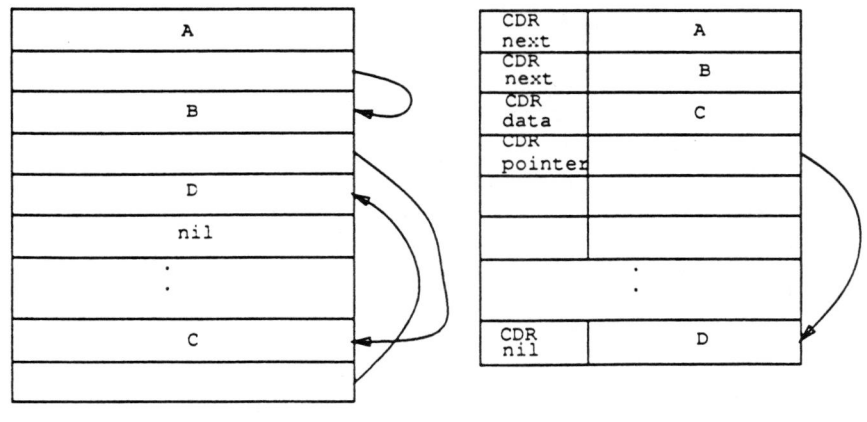

Figure 2. (a) Normal list representation using extra words as pointers. (b) Compact list representation of the Symbolics system, which uses sequential memory locations and two extra bits (the CDR field) to designate whether the next word is data or pointer.

sion from one type to another, must take place in some situations, and a type-specific add (integer add or floating-point add) instruction is invoked. In the Symbolics Machine, since the data are tagged with the type, only one add instruction is needed. All other complications are taken care of transparently. Also, unlike most machines, the Symbolics Machine does not have indexed and indirect addressing modes. This keeps the instruction formats simple so as to provide other instructions that are more useful to LISP.

Connection Machine

The Connection Machine originated in the MIT AI Laboratory in 1981 (Hillis, 1985; Thinking Machine Systems, 1989). The idea was first proposed by Mark Hillis in a Ph.D. dissertation and later became the foundation for the Thinking Machines Inc. version of the Connection Machine. Many of the original ideas have been modified, and, currently, the CM-2 is commercially available.

The Connection Machine is an architecture that may be configured to reflect the representation of knowledge in a given domain. Thousands of processors interconnected in an arbitrary manner are representative of a semantic network, where the link connecting two processors may represent the relationship between two objects, each object illustrated by a processor. The Connection Machine has precisely this configuration. This machine is unique in that it is configured to have a very large number of processors. It may be composed of 8192 to 65,536 processors in increments of 8192 processors. Sixteen processors are grouped within a single processor chip (Fig. 3a). The processor chips are connected in a hypercube topology (Saad and Schultz, 1988). Thus, for example, a system with 65,536 processors will have 4096 chips interconnected in a 12-dimensional hypercube. The hypercube has a unique topological feature that allows a processor in an n-dimensional hypercube to communicate with any other processor in n steps. This means that for our example, in a system with 65,536 processors, it takes only 12 steps for any two processors to communicate. The Connection Machine uses a single instruction multiple data (SIMD) paradigm of computation; that is, the same computation is executed in parallel on all or some of the processors, depending on the state of the flags.

Let us now take a closer look at how this system actually operates. The processors are organized in 8192 or 16,384 processor sections. A system may have as many as four sections. A processor also has 64K or 256K bits of bit-addressable local memory. Each of the sections may be treated as a parallel processing unit in itself or may be configured together to perform as a single processing unit. The sections have a sequencer whose task is to decode commands from the front-end and broadcast them to the data processors that then execute synchronously. The sequencers are connected to the front-end by a crossbar switch called the *nexus* (see Fig. 3b).

The front-end plays an essential part in the execution of programs. Computation in the Connection Machine can be divided into serial and parallel computations. The serial part of the computation is done at the front-end computer, which may be a Symbolics Machine, SUN-3, or a VAX. The parallel computation is done on the Connection Machine processors in SIMD mode.

Originally, only CM LISP, an extension of LISP, was considered for support on this system. Currently, however, *LISP, a new extension of LISP; C*, a parallel version of C; and CM FORTRAN are being supported as high-level languages. A low-level, effective assembly language named Paris is also supported (Thinking Machine Systems, 1989).

As for the interface to the system, the Connection Machine provides a high-resolution graphics monitor and frame buffer that contains a large video memory, which holds the actual raster image data. A pixel of the image may represent one processor in the system and reflect the activity of the processor, providing a visual effect of the processing to the user. The Connection Machine also provides various graphic software tools for displaying images, zooming, monitoring, and diagnostics. Table 6 summarizes the AI issues pertaining to the Connection Machine.

PROLOG Machines

The third example is a class of systems that are based on the logic programming language PROLOG (Clocksin and Mellish, 1984) (see PROLOG). PROLOG machines (Benker and co-workers, 1989; Holmer and co-workers, 1990; Hwang and co-workers, 1987; Morioka and co-workers,

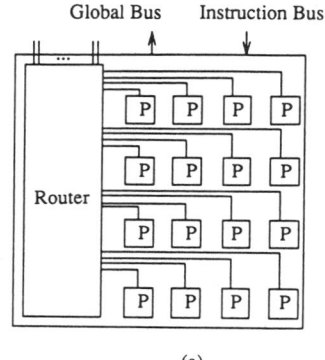

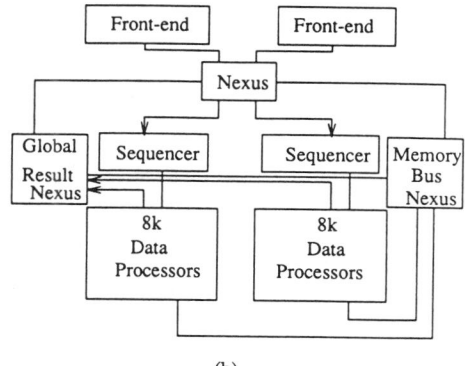

Figure 3. (a) Overview of CM-2 processor chip. (b) A simplified architectural overview of CM-2.

(a)

(b)

Table 6. AI Issues Pertaining to the Connection Machine

Issue	
Representation of knowledge	Hardware interconnection may be configured to match the application data structure. Knowledge representation such as semantic networks may be well suited for this machine.
Knowledge base	No explicit support.
Control	The Connection Machine is a SIMD architecture system capable of having more than 65-thousand processors. These processors may be executed simultaneously, providing enormous computing power.
Human–computer interface	High-resolution graphics monitor is provided. A frame buffer may be used to monitor the activities of each of the processors in the system. Since the Connection Machine is connected to a front-end, the services of the front-end may be used.
Storage management	The memory is bit-accessible, and there is no memory management.

Table 7. Approaches of Three PROLOG Machines to the AI Issues (see Table 8)

Berkeley Abstract Machine (BAM)

The goal of this machine is to design a general-purpose architecture with minimal extensions for high-performance Prolog execution, without compromising the execution of general-purpose applications. Instead of using special hardware such as stack registers to expedite memory transfer needed for faster backtracking, it uses double-word-sized buses. Separate buses are provided for instructions and data. These choices are consistent with its goal to provide efficient execution of general and Prolog applications. This machine provides three types of instructions: general purpose, Prolog inspired general purpose, and Prolog specific. Instructions for tagged data and unification are noteworthy.

Knowledge-Crunching Machine (KCM)

KCM is a single user, single-task high-performance back-end processor, that, together with a desktop workstation, can provide a powerful and user-friendly Prolog environment. Separate instruction and data paths along with separate instruction and dta cache is provided for faster memory access. Also, to improve the locality of stacks, which are essential for effective Prolog execution, two separate stacks are provided for environments and choice points. To expedite backtracking and minimize the transfer of data, the creation of a choice point is delayed so that in case of shallow backtracking the creation of the choice point can be completely avoided. Instructions for Prolog operations such as unification and backtracking are hardware or firmware supported.

Parallel Inference Machine (PIM)

This machine provides faster execution through parallelism. The machine is organized in two levels. Level-2 is comprised of 64 Level-1 modules that are all computed through a network. Each Level-1 module has 16 inference units (IU) that can operate in parallel. Parallel execution of the AND operation, which is parallel checking of the AND conditions, is implemented through a pipeline operation. Parallel OR operations and parallel unification are also provided by enabling several inference units (IU) simultaneously. Other operations for Prolog operations such as NOT and GUARD are also provided.

1989; Tanaka, 1986) are unique because most of the machines are still at a research state and these systems, unlike the Symbolics Machine or the Connection Machine, directly support knowledge-base operations such as unification and resolution.

When designing a PROLOG machine, a wide variety of choices are possible in approaching each of the AI issues. Many of the possibilities are still being researched and implemented, and no consensus has been reached on any of them. On the control issue, parallel OR-AND operations are considered. The parallel AND operation can be exploited when several goals of a clause are executed in parallel, whereas the parallel OR operation may be used in cases where multiple clauses are considered. Other forms of parallelism such as parallel unification may be possible. Because PROLOG incurs frequent backtracking, an efficient technique for memory management is crucial to efficient execution. The saving and restoring of processor environments is necessary for backtracking. This means that the organization of the system should be such that this functionality can be achieved with little overhead. Instructions pertaining to PROLOG execution are selected and implemented in hardware. Table 7 lists three systems, describing the approaches taken for some of the relevant issues, while Table 8 summarizes the general issues related to PROLOG machines.

SUMMARY

Recent developments in technology have made experimentation in new computer systems possible. Computer systems suited for AI applications in particular have been an active participant in this trend. Still, many of the systems are in their preliminary stages, and a consensus on how these systems should be designed and implemented has not been reached. Based on this premise, a unified discussion of the computer systems applicable for AI has been presented based on the issues relevant to AI application in general. Of the many possible examples, three systems were discussed in detail. The Symbolics machine, the Connection Machine, and the PROLOG machines were

Table 8. AI Issues Pertaining to Prolog Machines

Issue	
Representation of knowledge	Knowledge based on logic such as those of relational database or hypothesis of theorems would be suitable for these systems.
Knowledge base	Depending on the machine, hardware implementation of operations such as unification and resolution can be supported.
Control	The various systems currently under research provide diverse means of supporting parallelism. Parallel OR operation or parallel AND operations, and parallel execution of unification are examples of such possibilities.
Human–computer interface	The main objective is, like other systems, providing the user with a natural means of interaction, such as speech or images.
Others	*Storage management.* Memory reference pattern for Prolog is quite different from conventional systems. The extensive use of backtracking demands a change to accommodate this characteristic. An example of this change is the provision of hardware stacks.
	Instruction set. Each system has made decisions on which instructions to provide in hardware. Thus, this will vary from system to system.

chosen because each is representative of an aspect of AI application.

As for the future development of computer systems for AI applications, no single trend seems to exist. However, a digression from the traditional von Neumann architecture seems inevitable.

BIBLIOGRAPHY

R. J. Abbott, "Knowledge Abstraction," *CACM* **8**, 664–671 (Aug. 1987).

H. Benker, J. M. Beacco, S. Bescos, M. Dorochevsky, T. Jeffre, A. Pohlmann, J. Noye, B. Poterie, A. Sexton, J. C. Syre, O. Thibault, and G. Watzlawik, "KCM: A Knowledge Crunching Machine," *Proceedings of the Sixteenth International Symposium on Computer Architecture*, 1989, pp. 186–194.

E. Charniak and D. McDermott, *Introduction to Artificial Intelligence*, Addison-Wesley, Reading, Mass., 1985.

W. F. Clocksin and C. S. Mellish, *Programming in Prolog*, 2nd ed., Springer-Verlag, Berlin, 1984.

C. L. Ditzel, D. Schuler, and V. Thomas, "A LISP Machine Profile: Symbolics 3650." *AI Expert* **1**, 69–73 (Jan. 1987).

P. Graham, "Anatomy of a LISP machine," *AI Expert* **12**, 26–32 (Dec. 1988).

W. D. Hillis, *The Connection Machine*, MIT Press, Cambridge, Mass., 1985.

B. K. Holmer, B. Sano, M. Carlton, P. Van Roy, R. Haygood, W. R. Bush, and A. M. Despain. "Fast PROLOG with an Extended General Purpose Architecture." *Proceedings of the Seventeenth International Symposium on Computer Architecture*, 1990, 282–291.

K. Hwang, J. Ghosh, and R. Chowkwanyun, "Computer Architecture for Artificial Intelligence Processing," *Computer* 19–27 (Jan. 1987).

T. J. Laffey, P. A. Cox, J. L. Schmidt, S. M. Kao, and J. Y. Read, "Real-Time Knowledge-Based Systems," *AI Mag.* **1**, 27–45 (1988).

R. Lee, "Precision Architecture," *Computer* 78–91 (Jan. 1980).

G. McCalla and N. Cercone, "Guest Editors Introduction: Approaches to Knowledge Representation," *Computer* 12–18 (Oct. 1983).

J. McCarthy, "Generality in Artificial Intelligence," *CACM* **12**, 1030–1035 (Dec. 1987).

D. Moon, "Symbolics Architecture," *Computer* 43–52 (Jan. 1987).

M. Morioka, S. Yamaguchi, and T. Bandoh, "Evaluation of Memory System for Integrated Prolog Processor IPP," *Proceedings of the Sixteenth International Symposium on Computer Architecture*, 1989, pp. 203–210.

K. Murakami, T. Kakuta, R. Onai, and N. Ito, "Research on Parallel Machine Architecture for Fifth-Generation Computer Systems," *Computer* 76–92 (June 1983).

D. Nau, "Expert Computer Systems," *Computer* 63–85 (Feb. 1983).

D. A. Patterson, "Reduced Instruction Set Computers," *CACM* **1**, 8–21 (Jan. 1985).

J. Rice, "The Advanced Architectures Project," *AI Mag.* 26–39 (1989).

Y. Saad and M. H. Schultz, "Topological Properties of Hypercubes," *IEEE Trans. Comp.* **7**, 867–872 (July 1988).

H. Tanaka, "A Parallel Inference Machine," *Computer* 48–54 (May 1986).

Thinking Machines Systems, *The Connection Machine System: Release Notes*, version 5.1 ed., Thinking Machines Corp., Cambridge, Mass., June 1989.

B. W. Wah, "New Computers for Artificial Intelligence Processing," *Computer* 10–15 (Jan. 1987).

Ashok K. Agrawala
Sam H. Noh
University of Maryland

CONCEPT LEARNING

Among the fundamental characteristics of intelligent behavior are the abilities to pursue goals and to plan future actions. To exhibit these characteristics, an intelligent system—human or machine—must be able to classify some objects, behaviors, or events as equivalent for achieving given goals and some others as differing. For example, to satisfy hunger, an animal must be able to classify some objects as edible despite the great variety of their forms and the changes they undergo in the environment. Thus, an intelligent system must be able to form concepts, that is, classes of entities united by some principle. Such a principle might be a common use or goal, the same role in a structure forming a theory about something, or just similar perceptual characteristics. In order to use the concepts, the system must also develop efficient methods for recognizing concept membership of any given entity. The question, then, is of how concepts and concept recognition methods are learned.

The study and computer modeling of processes by which an intelligent system acquires, refines, and differentiates concepts is the subject matter of concept learning. Concept learning is a subdomain of machine learning. Research in this area originated with studies of concept development in humans (see Bruner and co-workers, 1956; Hoveland, 1952; Hunt and co-workers, 1966). It subsequently continued in the context of both AI efforts to build machines with concept-learning capabilities and cognitive science (qv) studies to construct computational models of learning. Selected publications covering this development are included in the bibliography.

At present, concept learning is one of the central research topics in machine learning, a subarea of AI concerned with the development of computational theories of learning and the building of learning machines (see LEARNING, MACHINE). In research on concept learning, the term "concept" is usually viewed in a narrower sense than that outlined above, namely, as an equivalence class of entities, such that it can be comprehensibly described by no more than a small set of statements. This description must be sufficient for distinguishing this concept from other concepts. Individual entities in the class are called instances of the concept.

The assumption that a concept is an equivalence class implies that its every instance is equally representative of the concept and that the concept description has precise boundaries, that is, it either matches or does not match any given entity. (This notion is more general than the classical definition, which postulates that a concept is characterized by singly necessary and jointly sufficient conditions and thus excludes a disjunctive description.) Such an idealization greatly facilitates research on concept learning, as it defines the learning task simply as the acquisition of a formal structure describing an equivalence class. It is, however, only a very rough approximation that ignores many important aspects of the human notion of a concept (Murphy and Medin, 1985). At the conclusion of this article, the weaknesses of this definition are briefly addressed and ideas are pointed out that attempt to capture the notion of a concept more adequately.

Within research on concept learning two major orientations can be distinguished: cognitive modeling (qv) and the engineering approach. They parallel the orientations of efforts in cognitive science and AI, respectively. Cognitive modeling strives to develop computational theories of concept learning in humans or animals. It blends original cognitive psychology techniques with efforts to develop well-defined computational methods and computer programs embodying those methods. In contrast, the engineering approach attempts to explore and experiment with all possible learning mechanisms, irrespective of their occurrence in living organisms.

CLASSIFICATION BY TYPE OF INFERENCE

In any learning process the student applies the knowledge possessed to information obtained from a source, for example, a teacher, in order to derive new useful knowledge. This new knowledge is then stored for subsequent use. Learning a new concept can proceed in a number of ways, reflecting the type of inference the student performs on the information supplied. For example, one may learn the concept of a butterfly by being given a description of it, by generalizing examples of specific butterflies, by constructing this concept in the process of observing and analyzing different types of insects, or by yet another way. The type of inference performed by the student on the information supplied defines the strategy of concept learning and constitutes a useful criterion for classifying learning processes.

Several basic concept-learning strategies have been identified in the course of machine-learning research. These are presented below in the order of increasing complexity of inference as performed by the learner. In some general sense, this order reflects the increasing difficulty for the student to learn the concept and the decreasing difficulty for the instructor to teach the concept. In any practical act of learning, more than one strategy is often simultaneously employed. It should also be noted that this classification of strategies applies not only to learning of concepts but also to any act of acquiring knowledge.

Direct Implanting of Knowledge

This strategy is an extreme case in which the learner does not have to perform any inference on the information provided. The knowledge supplied by the source is directly accepted by the learner. This strategy, also called *rote learning,* includes learning by direct memorization of given concept descriptions and learning by being programmed or constructed. For example, this strategy is employed when a specific algorithm for recognizing a concept is programmed into a computer or a database of facts about the concept is built. In Samuel's CHECKERS program (1959) rote learning was employed to save the results of previous game tree searches in order to deepen and speed up subsequent searches.

Learning by Instruction (or Learning by Being Told)

Here the learner acquires concepts from a teacher or other organized source, such as a publication or textbook, but does not directly copy into memory the information supplied. The learning process may involve selecting the most relevant facts and/or transforming the source information to more useful forms. The system NANOKLAUS (Hass and Hendrix, 1983), which builds a hierarchical knowledge base by conversing with a user, is an example of machine learning employing this strategy.

Learning by Deduction

The learner acquires a concept by deducing it from the knowledge given and/or possessed. In other words, this strategy includes any process in which knowledge learned is a result of a truth-preserving transformation of the knowledge given, including performing computation. A very simple example of this strategy is determining that the factorial of 6 is 720 by executing an already known algorithm and having this fact for future use. This technique is called *memo functions* (Michie, 1968). A form of learning by deduction is explanation-based learning, which transforms an abstract, not directly usable concept definition to an operational definition using a concept example for guidance (Mitchell and co-workers, 1986). In general, deductive learning is performing a sequence of deductions or computations on the information given and/or stored in background knowledge and memorizing the result.

More advanced deductive learning is exemplified by analytic or explanation-based learning methods (see, eg, Mitchell and co-workers, 1986). These methods start with the abstract concept definition and domain knowledge and by deduction derive an operational concept definition. A concept example is used to guide the deductive process. For instance, knowing that a cup is an open, stable, and liftable vessel, an explanation-based method can produce an operational description of a cup. Such a description characterizes the cup in terms of lower level, more measurable features, such as the presence of concavity, a handle, and a flat bottom. Current research attempts to combine such analytical learning with inductive learning in order to learn concepts when the domain knowledge is incomplete, intractable, or inconsistent.

Learning by Analogy

The learner acquires a new concept by modifying the definition of a known similar concept. That is, rather than formulating a rule for a new concept from scratch, the student adapts an existing rule by modifying it appropriately to serve the new role. For example, if one knows the concept of an orange, learning the concept of a tangerine can be accomplished easily by just noting the similarities and distinctions between the two. Another example is learning about electric circuits by drawing analogies from pipes conducting water.

Learning by analogy can be viewed as inductive and deductive learning combined and for this reason is placed between the two. Through inductive inference (see below) one determines general characteristics or transformations unifying concepts being compared. Then, by deductive inference, one derives from these characteristics features expected of the concept being learned. Winston (1979) de-

scribes a method for learning concepts by analogy based on matching semantic networks. Learning by analogy plays an important role in problem solving (see Carbonell, 1983).

Learning by Induction

In this strategy the learner acquires a concept by drawing inductive inferences from supplied facts or observations. Depending on what is provided and what is known to a learner, two different forms of this strategy can be distinguished: learning from examples and learning from observation and discovery.

Learning from Examples. The learner induces a concept description by generalizing from teacher- or environment-provided examples and (optionally) counterexamples of the concept. It is assumed that the concept already exists; it is known to the teacher or there is some effective procedure for testing the concept membership. The task for the learner is to determine a general concept description by analyzing individual concept examples.

An example of this strategy takes place when a senior doctor examines medical records and makes interviews with patients in the presence of one or more interns, noting that "this is a patient with hepatitis"; "this is another patient with hepatitis, but notice that . . .", and so on. The latter part of this entry briefly discusses a few methods for learning from examples.

Learning by Observation and Discovery. In this strategy the learner analyzes given and/or observed entities and determines that some subsets of these entities can be grouped usefully into certain classes (ie, concepts). Because there is no teacher who knows the concepts beforehand, this strategy is also called unsupervised learning. Once a concept is formed, it is given a name. Concepts so created can then be used as terms in subsequent learning of other concepts.

An important form of this strategy is clustering (ie, partitioning a collection of objects into classes) and the related process of constructing classifications. Classifications are typically organized into hierarchies of concepts. Such hierarchies exhibit an important property of inheritance. If an object is recognized as a member of some class, the properties associated specifically with this class, as well as with classes at the higher level of hierarchy, are (tentatively) assigned to the given object. For example, if one learns that Freddy is an elephant, then, without seeing Freddy, one will typically assume that Freddy has four legs, a trunk, and all the distinguishing properties of elephants, vertebrates, and generally, animals. Hierarchical classifications vary in height: some may be tall, such as the classification of living organisms, and some flatter, such as the social hierarchy. The topics of clustering (in particular, conceptual clustering) and classification construction are treated in a separate article in the encyclopedia (see CLUSTERING).

Another form of learning by observation and discovery is descriptive generalization. This form is concerned with discovering regularities and formulating new concepts and rules characterizing collections of any entities (objects, events, processes, etc). It produces statements such as "Most people are honest," "Whenever there are independent events, the normal distribution should hold," or "John is in the habit of amblin' down to the soda fountain every day about now."

Examples of research on this topic are two programs by Lenat (1976, 1983): AM (qv), which searches for and develops new "interesting" concepts after being given a set of heuristic rules and initial concepts in elementary mathematics and set theory, and EURISKO (qv), which formulates new heuristics. Another example is the BACON system (see, eg, Langley and Bradshaw, 1983), which synthesizes mathematical expressions representing chemical or physical laws on the basis of given empirical data.

In the AI literature the term concept learning is frequently used in a narrower sense than it is here, namely, to mean solely learning concepts from examples. One reason for this is historical, as this strategy was studied first, and most is known about it. It subsequently served as the springboard for studies of other strategies, but it continues to be the area most intensively investigated. Learning from examples and learning from observation and discovery (ie, inductive learning in general) are fundamental forms of concept learning. When acquiring any abstract concept, examples are typically needed to achieve a deeper understanding of the concept; and initial learning of any concepts and natural laws is typically achieved by generalizing from sensory observations. For these reasons, the remainder of this article concentrates on inductive learning. For coverage of other strategies, consult the references, in particular, Dietterich and Michalski, 1983. The nature of inductive inference, which is the core of inductive learning processes, will now be explored in more detail.

INDUCTIVE INFERENCE

Inductive inference (qv) is the primary vehicle for creating new knowledge and predicting future events. It is usually characterized as reasoning from specific to general, from particular to universal, or from part to whole. Such a characterization is simple but not too informative. It does not identify all the components playing a role in the inductive process, nor does it explain how this inference is possible. To understand inductive inference more precisely, its major components are distinguished, and the properties of its conclusions are specified.

Given:

Premise Statements
Facts, specific observations, intermediate generalizations that provide information about some objects, phenomena, processes, and so on.

Tentative Inductive Assertion
An a priori hypothesis held about the objects in the premise statements (in some acts of inductive inference there may not be any tentative hypothesis; if there is such a hypothesis, the inductive process may be simplified, as it may involve merely a modification of the tentative hypothesis rather than the creation of a new hypothesis from scratch.

Background Knowledge
Contains general and domain-specific concepts for interpreting the premises and inference rules relevant to the task of inference. It includes previously learned concepts, domain constraints, causality relations, assumptions about the premise statements and candidate hypotheses, goals for inference, and methods for evaluating the candidate hypotheses from these goals' viewpoints (specifically, the preference criterion or bias).

Determine:

Inductive Assertion
A hypothesis that strongly or weakly implies the premise statements in the context of background knowledge and is most preferable among all other such hypotheses.

A hypothesis strongly implies premise statements in the context of background knowledge if by using background knowledge (and standard rules of inference), the premise statements can be shown to be a logical consequence of the hypothesis. In other words, the assertion

Hypothesis & background knowledge
$$\Rightarrow \text{premise statements}$$

is valid, that is, true under all interpretations (the symbol $\Rightarrow$ denotes implication). A hypothesis that satisfies this condition is called a strong candidate hypothesis. In contrast, a weak hypothesis is one that only weakly implies premise statements, that is, these statements are a plausible, but not certain, consequence of the hypothesis. The following two-part example illustrates both types of hypotheses.

Example: Part 1

Premise Statements
Socrates was Greek. Aristotle was Greek. Plato was Greek.

Background Knowledge
Socrates, Aristotle, and Plato were philosophers. They lived in antiquity.
Philosophers are people. Greeks are people.

Preference Criterion. Prefer the hypothesis that is short and useful for deciding the nationality of philosophers.

Candidate Hypotheses (a selection).
1. Philosophers who lived in antiquity were Greek.
2. All philosophers are Greek.
3. All people are Greek.

Preferred Hypothesis

2. All philosophers are Greek. (It is shorter than 1 and more specific than 3; it allows one, unlike 1, to determine the nationality of all philosophers.)

It can be seen that the original premise statements are a logical consequence of the generated hypothesis and background knowledge. The fact that the generated hypothesis is too general is a result of the poverty of the background knowledge and/or the premise assertions.

Example: Part 2

Suppose that the stock of facts has been enlarged with statements such as "Spencer was British" and "Hume was British" and that the background knowledge includes also the statement "Hume and Spencer were philosophers."

In this case, a strong candidate hypothesis would be "All philosophers were Greek except Spencer and Hume, who were British." A weak hypothesis would be "Most (or some) philosophers were Greek." Given a fact that Plato was a philosopher, the new hypothesis, in contrast to the old one, does not allow one to conclude strongly that he was Greek. It allows one only to say that it is likely (or that it is possible) that he was Greek. However, unlike the first hypothesis, it will also not conclude strongly that philosopher Russell was Greek!

This example illustrates important properties of inductive inference. One is that it may not be truth preserving; that is, its conclusions may be incorrect though the premise statements are correct. Going back to the first hypothesis, though Socrates, Aristotle, and Plato were Greek, it certainly does not follow that all philosophers were Greek. This quality of nontruth preservation contrasts inductive inference with truth-preserving deductive inference. Figure 1 illustrates the relationship between deductive and inductive inference.

Inductive inference that produces strong hypotheses is falsity preserving. This means that if the original premise statements are false, the derived hypothesis will be false also. For example, if it were not true that Socrates was Greek, then clearly the first hypothesis, "All philosophers were Greek," could not be true either. Hypotheses gener-

ated by inductive inference have unknown truth status. They must be tested and verified before they become rules or accepted theories (see the section on hypothesis verification).

The premise statements, background knowledge, and derived hypotheses need to be expressed in some language. In human inference it is the language of the mind, a "mentalese," that at the surface level takes the form of natural language augmented with special representations of sensory stimuli, such as drawings, pictures, sounds, or gestures. In machine inference it is a formal language, such as propositional logic, predicate calculus, or other logic-style formalisms, or a knowledge representation system, such as semantic networks, mathematical expressions, frames, scripts, or conceptual structures (Sowa, 1984). Sometimes expressing the premise statements is easier in one language and expressing hypotheses is easier in another language.

In concept learning from examples (concept acquisition) the main concern is with a special case of inductive inference, called inductive generalization. Here both the premise statements and the hypothesis are either interpretable as descriptions of sets (in this case there is instance-to-class generalization) or as descriptions of components of some object or process (in the latter case there is part-to-whole generalization).

In instance-to-class generalization, properties known to hold for a set of objects are assigned to a larger set of objects. This form can be seen in Example 1, in which a property (the nationality) assigned by premise statements to a few individuals was assigned to all individuals in some class (all philosophers). In part-to-whole generalization the premise statements describe parts of some object, and the goal is to hypothesize a description of the whole object. For example, the following is a part-to-whole generalization.

Premise

His hands and his legs are strong.

Background Knowledge

Hands and legs are parts of a body.

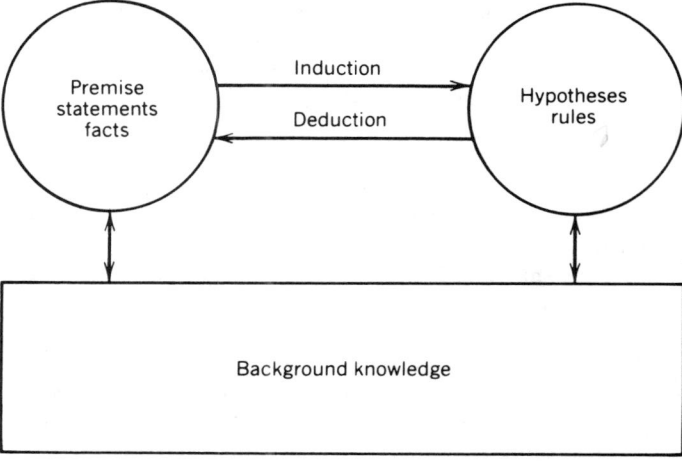

Figure 1. Relation between deduction and induction.

Hypothesis

His whole body is strong.

An important form of part-to-whole generalization is sequence or process prediction (Simon and Lea, 1974; Peirce, 1957).

Inductive inference was defined as a process of generating descriptions that imply original facts in the context of background knowledge. Such a general definition includes inductive generalization and abduction as special cases. The term *abduction* was coined by the American logician Peirce (1957). In abduction (qv), the generated descriptions are specific assertions implying the facts (in the context of background knowledge) rather than generalizations of them. For example, given a premise assertion, "These roses are purple," and background knowledge "All roses in Adam's garden are purple," an abductive assertion would be "Perhaps these roses are from Adam's garden."

A description that implies some facts can be viewed as an explanation of these facts. The most interesting form of an explanation is when it provides a causal, goal-oriented characterization of the facts. To derive such an explanation, background knowledge must contain, along with other inference rules, causal inference rules as well as a specification of the goal(s) of inference. Generating causal explanations can thus be viewed as a form of inductive inference.

INDUCTIVE INFERENCE BY RULE

One of the important results of research on inductive inference is the development of the concept of an inductive inference rule. An inductive inference rule performs some elementary act of inductive inference. It takes one or more assertions and generates an assertion that tautologically implies them. The concept of an inductive inference rule permits one to view inductive inference, at least conceptually, as a rule-guided process that starts with initial premises and background knowledge and ends with an inductive assertion (Michalski, 1983). Here are a few examples of such rules.

Dropping Conditions

Removing a conjunctively linked condition from a statement; for example, replacing the statement "A nation is strong if it has a strong economy and high determination" by "A nation is strong if it has high determination."

Turning Constants into Variables

An example would be to generalize the statement "This apple tastes good" into "All apples taste good."

Adding Options

Generalizing a statement by adding a disjunctively linked condition; for example, generalizing the statement "Peace will be preserved if all nations have peaceful intentions" into "Peace will be preserved if all nations have peaceful intentions or if nonaggressive nations are much stronger than aggressive ones."

Climbing Generalization Tree

Replacing a less general term by a more general term in a statement; for example, generalizing the statement "I like oranges" into "I like citrus fruits."

A systematic presentation of inductive rules can be found in Michalski (1983).

INSTANCE SPACE VERSUS DESCRIPTION SPACE

Earlier, two forms of inductive learning had been distinguished: learning from examples and learning by observation. Learning a concept from examples is a process of constructing a representation of a designated class of entities by observing only selected members of that class and optionally nonmembers (counterexamples). Learning from observations involves creating concepts as useful classes for characterizing observations or any given facts. Both processes depend on the learner's background knowledge, in particular, on the type of description language the learner uses for characterizing examples and learned concepts.

In this context it is instructive to distinguish between an instance space and a description space. The *instance space* consists of all possible examples and counterexamples of concepts to be learned. Actually observed positive and negative examples constitute subsets of such an instance space. The *description space* is the set of all descriptions of instances or classes of instances that are possible using the description language specified by the learner's background knowledge. Learning a concept involves an interaction between the two spaces. Such an interaction may involve reformulation or transformation of initial assertions as well as experimentation and active selection of training examples (Fig. 2).

Consider a simple case where examples of a concept (positive examples) and counterexamples (negative examples) are represented by attribute vectors, that is, by lists of values of certain attributes. Considering attributes as dimensions spanning a multidimensional space, each example maps to a point in this space. Points that do not correspond to any observed example represent potential examples. Such a space is called a feature space or an event space and can be viewed as a geometric model of an instance space.

One may ask where the attributes come from. In simple methods the attributes are defined by the teacher. Such methods are called selective because the learned concept does not include any new attributes but only those defined by a teacher. In more sophisticated methods the system is provided with some initial attributes plus various rules of inference, heuristics, or procedures that a learner uses for generating new attributes. The latter methods are called constructive (Michalski, 1983; Rendell, 1985).

Different subsets of the instance space correspond to different concepts. Descriptions of those concepts are elements of the description space. For simplicity, assume

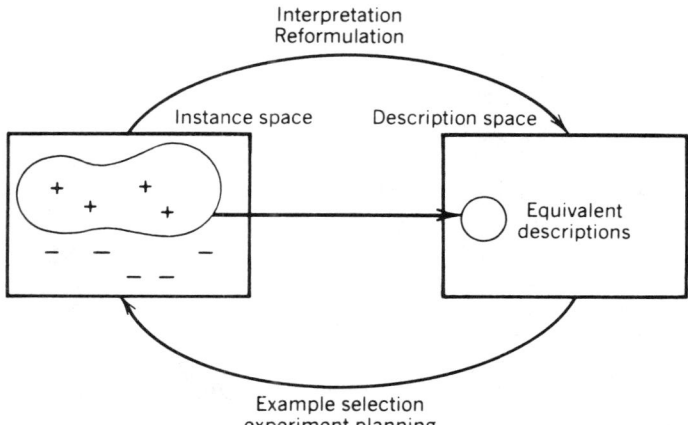

Figure 2. Interaction between instance space and description space.

that the description space is the set of all logical expressions involving attributes used in characterizing examples. Depending on the constraints imposed on these expressions, all (or only some) subsets of the instance space can be represented by an expression in this language. Usually, any concept corresponds to a subset of (logically equivalent) descriptions in the description space.

A concept is consistent with regard to the examples if it covers some or all positive examples and none of the negative examples. A concept description is complete with regard to the examples if it covers all positive examples. A description of a concept that is both complete and consistent with regard to all examples is a candidate hypothesis. The requirement for completeness and consistency follows from the assumption that the hypothesis should imply the initial examples (see Michalski, 1983). The set of all candidate hypotheses is called the candidate hypothesis space or the version space. The candidate hypothesis space can be partially ordered by the relation of generality that reflects the set inclusion relation between the corresponding concepts. The most general hypothesis describes the concept that is the complement of the union of negative examples; and the most specific hypothesis describes the concept that is the union of all positive examples.

Because the candidate hypothesis space is usually quite large, a preference criterion is used to decide which candidate hypothesis to choose. Such a criterion may favor, for example, hypotheses that are short, hypotheses that require the least effort to measure the attributes involved, or generally, hypotheses that best reflect the goal of learning.

If the concept representation language is incomplete, for example, and allows one to express only conjunctive hypotheses, and if a sufficient number of positive and negative examples is supplied, the resulting version space may contain only one candidate hypothesis. In such a case the preference criterion is not needed (Mitchell, 1977).

In summary, learning a concept can be described as a heuristic search through the description space for a most preferred hypothesis among all those that are consistent and complete with regard to the training examples.

SELECTED METHODS OF INDUCTIVE LEARNING

An important characteristic of learning methods is the way in which descriptions in the description space are generated and/or searched in relation to the examples or facts in the instance space. Three types of methods can be distinguished: data driven, model driven, and mixed. A data-driven method starts with selecting one or more examples, formulates a hypothesis explaining them, and then generalizes (and occasionally specializes) the hypothesis to explain further examples. A model-driven method starts with some very general hypotheses and then specializes (and occasionally generalizes) them to fit all the examples. Roughly speaking, data-driven methods proceed from specific to general, and model-driven methods proceed from general to specific. A mixed method has elements of both. It uses an example(s) to jump to one or more general hypotheses, tests the hypotheses, and then modifies them to fit other examples. Data-driven methods tend to be more efficient, and model-driven methods tend to be more tolerant of errors in data (Dietterich and Michalski, 1986). Below are examples of the three types of methods.

Data-Driven Methods

Winston's Blocks World: Learning by Incremental Generalization and Modification. Winston's program (1975) is an excellent representative of a data-driven method of concept learning. It learns structural descriptions of concepts in a blocks world (eg, the concept of an arch) from representative examples and counterexamples provided by a teacher. The program represents examples and concepts in the form of a semantic network. At each step of learning it maintains only one working hypothesis. In searching for the final hypothesis, it uses a simple form of best-first search method. The basic algorithm can be described as follows:

1. Take first positive example of the concept and assume that it is a concept description.
2. If the next example is positive and does not satisfy the current concept description, generalize the description so that it includes the example.

3. If the next example is negative but satisfies the current description, specialize the description so that it excludes the example.

4. Repeat steps 2 and 3 until the process converges on a stable concept description.

The generalization step (step 2) applies such operators as dropping conditions, turning constants to variables, or climbing a generalization tree. When confronted with multiple choice in generalizing, the program chooses the least drastic change to the current concept description. For example, it will replace a less general term by a more general term rather than drop a term. The specialization step (step 3) adds more conditions and introduces exceptions or the must-not conditions to the currently held hypothesis. There are usually many ways to specialize a hypothesis so that it does not cover a given negative example (as many as there are differences between the example and the hypothesis). For that reason the program favors the near misses, that is, negative examples that differ from the hypothesis in only a few or, in the best case, in only one aspect.

Other examples of data-driven methods are the candidate elimination algorithm (Mitchell, 1977; Mitchell and co-workers, 1983) for learning from examples and the method for learning from observation embodied in the BACON system (Langley and Bradshaw, 1983). The latter method discovers equations characterizing empirical laws.

Model-Driven Methods

Learning by Incremental Specialization and Modification: The Meta-DENDRAL Program. This program implements a model-driven method for discovering rules characterizing the operation of a mass spectrometer (Buchanan and Feigenbaum, 1978). These so-called cleavage rules predict which bonds in a molecular structure of a chemical compound will likely break when bombarded by electrons in the mass spectrometer. To avoid undue technical details of the specific domain, the rule-learning process is presented at a level of abstraction.

This process consists of two phases. First, the rule generation phase conducts a general-to-specific search of the space of possible cleavage rules (subprogram RULEGEN). Next, the rule modification phase makes the rules so obtained more precise and less redundant by performing local hill-climbing searches (subprogram RULEMOD). Training examples can be viewed as attribute vector descriptions of the environment of individual bonds in a molecule. Among the attributes are the type of atoms on both sides of the bond, the number of hydrogen and nonhydrogen atoms bound to each atom, and the number of unsaturated valence electrons of the atom. With each example is associated a decision as to whether the corresponding bond will break in the mass spectrometer. An important feature of this application is a large-sized, error-laden set of input examples.

The rule generation phase starts with the most general rule, stating that every bond will break. Abstracting from the specific domain-dependent notation, such a rule can be written:

If a bond is any bond, then it will break.

The next step specializes the left side of the parent rule by making a change to atoms at a specified distance from the bond. A change may involve changing properties of an atom or adding a new atom. New rules so obtained are then tested to see if they perform better in predicting the breaks in the given set of examples. This two-step process of rule specialization and testing repeats until a local optimum of performance is achieved. The resulting rules can be characterized as:

If a bond environment has properties so and so, then it will break.

Meta-DENDRAL was an important learning system that worked well in a real-world domain with noisy data. In addition to the process of rule development, outlined above, it also performed a sophisticated transformation of the initial data (the input spectrum) to usable training instances (the bond environment descriptions). In all aspects of its operation the program relied on a large amount of domain-specific knowledge.

Another example of a model-driven method is the concept-learning program, CSL (Hunt and co-workers, 1966), and its modified version, ID3 (Quinlan, 1983). The program starts by attempting to find the best one-attribute rule characterizing given examples. If this is not possible, it builds a decision tree of such rules that classifies all input examples. In such a tree nodes correspond to attributes, emanating branches to the attribute values, and leaves to classes.

Mixed Methods

Learning by Rapid Generalization and Stepwise Specialization: AQ11. Inductive concept learning can be viewed as a generate-and-test process. The generate part creates or modifies hypotheses and the test part tests how well the hypotheses fit the data. In data-driven methods the generate part is sophisticated and the test part is simple, whereas in model-driven methods the opposite holds. A mixed method, implemented in the program AQ11, attempts to more equally emphasize the generate and test parts.

AQ11 is a multipurpose learning program that formulates general rules describing various classes of examples (Michalski and Larson, 1978). Input to the program consists of attribute value vector descriptions of examples from different classes. It also includes background knowledge about the application domain and a hypothesis preference criterion. The output can be viewed as rules,

Condition ⇒ class

where *condition* may be a conjunction, or a disjunction of conjunctions, such that it describes all entities assigned to *class.* A simplified version of the algorithm, called AQ, which underlies the nonincremental learning part of the program is as follows:

1. Select at random one positive example (called the seed).

2. Comparing the seed with the first negative example, generate all maximally general hypotheses that cover the seed and exclude the negative example.

3. Specialize the hypotheses to exclude all negative examples. This is done by considering one negative example at a time and adding, whenever necessary, additional constraints to the hypotheses. After each step of specialization the newly generated hypotheses are ranked according to how well they classify remaining examples and according to other aspects defined in the preference criterion: only the most promising hypotheses are kept. The set of hypotheses obtained at the end of the specialization process is called a *star*.

4. Select from the star the best-ranked hypothesis. If this hypothesis covers all positive examples, exit (a solution has been found). Otherwise, find positive examples that remain uncovered.

5. Repeat steps 1–4 for the remainder set. Continue until all positive examples are covered. The disjunction of hypotheses selected at the end of each cycle is a consistent and complete description of all the positive examples and maximizes the preference criterion.

Thus, the program builds a disjunctive description of a concept when a conjunctive description is not possible. The individual conjuncts in such a disjunction may significantly differ as to the size of coverage of the training examples. This allows for an interesting interpretation: the conjunct that covers most of the events could be viewed as a characterization of the typical, or ideal, members and those with light coverage as a characterization of exceptional cases.

The incremental part of the program performs operations of modifying generated descriptions to fit new examples. The background knowledge of the program contains information about the properties of the attributes used to describe examples and various domain constraints. The program has been applied to various problems in medicine, agriculture, chess, and other areas. A more advanced version of the program, INDUCE (Michalski, 1983), is capable of learning not only attribute-based but also structure-based concept descriptions. These descriptions characterize concepts as structures of components bound by various relationships, and are expressed in an extended predicate calculus. The program has the ability to utilize general and domain-specific knowledge to generate new attributes.

VALIDATING LEARNED CONCEPTS

Although inductive inference represents the basic method for acquiring knowledge about the world and is one of the most common forms of inference, it suffers from a fundamental weakness. Except for special cases, results of this inference are inherently insusceptible to complete validation. This is because an inductively acquired hypothesis may have an infinite number of consequences, but only a finite number of tests can be performed. This property of inductive inference was observed early on by the Scottish philosopher Hume and subsequently analyzed by twentieth-century thinkers such as Popper (1979). Consequently, one typically assumes that concept descriptions learned inductively have only a tentative status. When new examples become available, these descriptions are tested on them and, if necessary, appropriately modified. A standard method for testing inductively acquired descriptions (rules) is to apply them to testing examples and compute a confusion matrix. Such a matrix records the number of correct and incorrect classifications of the testing examples by the rules.

EXTENDED NOTIONS OF A CONCEPT

The basic ideas and a few selected methods of concept learning have been described here. These methods were based on the notion that concepts are classes of entities describable by a logic-style description. This means that concept descriptions have sharp boundaries and all members are equal representatives of a concept. As pointed out above, this simplification, though useful for research, misses some important aspects of the human notion of a concept.

Human concepts, except for special cases occurring predominantly in science (concepts such as a triangle, a prime number, a vertebrate), are structures with flexible and/or imprecise boundaries. They allow a varying degree of match between them and observed instances and have context-dependent meaning. Flexible boundaries make it possible to "fit" the meaning of a concept to changing situations and to avoid precision when not needed or not possible. The varying degree of match reflects the varying representativeness of a concept by different instances. Instances of a concept are rarely homogeneous. Among instances of a concept, people usually distinguish a typical instance, a nontypical instance, or, generally, they rank instances according to their typicality. By the use of context, the meaning of almost any concept can be expanded in a multitude of directions that cannot be predicted in advance. An imaginative discussion of this property is by Hofstadter (1985), who shows how a seemingly well-defined concept, such as "First Lady," can express a great variety of meanings depending on the context in which it is applied.

Despite various efforts, the issue of how to represent concepts in such a rich and context-dependent sense remains open. This issue is, of course, crucial for concept learning because to learn concepts, the learner must be able to represent them. In view of this, a brief review of basic approaches to concept representation may be useful for understanding the current research limitations and directions in concept learning.

Smith and Medin (1981) distinguish between three approaches: the classic view, the probabilistic view, and the examplar view. The classic view assumes that concepts are representable by features that are singly necessary and jointly sufficient to define a concept. This view is a special case of the one assumed in this article, as it does not allow disjunctive concept descriptions.

The probabilistic view represents concepts as weighted, additive combinations of features. Using the aforementioned notion of a feature space, this means that concepts should correspond to linearly separable subareas in such a space. Experiments indicate, however, that this may be too limiting a view (Smith and Medin, 1981). The exemplary view represents concepts by one or more typical exemplars rather than by generalized descriptions.

The notion of typicality can be captured by a measure, called family resemblance. This measure represents the sum of frequencies with which different features occur in different subsets of a superordinate concept, such as furniture or vehicle. The individual subsets are represented by typical members. Nontypical members are viewed as corruptions of the typical, differing from them in various small aspects, as children differ from their parents (see Wittgenstein, 1921; Rosch and Mervis, 1975).

Another approach uses the notion of a fuzzy set as a formal model of a concept (Zadeh, 1976). Members of such a set are characterized by a gradual numeric set membership function rather than by the in–out function seen in the classic notion of a set. This set membership function is defined by people describing the concept and thus is subjective. This approach allows one to express the varying degree of membership of entities in a concept but does not have mechanisms for expressing the context dependence of the concept meaning (see FUZZY SETS AND FUZZY LOGIC).

Elements of these approaches have been unified in a more recent idea, which postulates that the concept is characterized by a well-defined description, but the use of this description is flexible (Michalski and Chilausky, 1980). If an entity does not satisfy the description precisely, a consonance degree is computed that specifies the degree to which the description is satisfied. Thus, objects precisely satisfying the formal description can be considered as typical concept members and those that satisfy approximately as less typical, with the degree of membership defined by the consonance degree. In the case of disjunctive descriptions the component (conjunction) that explains most of the examples can be viewed as representing the ideal form of a concept. Other components then represent exceptional cases. The method of computing consonance degree can be shared by many concepts; therefore, there is no need for storing a set membership function with each concept, as in the case of fuzzy sets. The dependencies among the attributes characterizing a concept and its relationship to other concepts can be expressed in the same logic-based formalism. Thus, in such a flexible logic approach the total meaning of a concept is distributed between its formal description and the function evaluating the degree of consonance. The description gives the basic meaning to a concept, and the evaluation function allows for its flexibility. Major questions, then, are how to properly distribute the concept meaning between these two components and how to express context-dependent meaning.

An adequate concept representation should include not only a description that permits one to recognize the given concept among other concepts or to evaluate the typicality of its members, but also a number of other components. It should specify the constraints and correlations among the defining or characteristic attributes, the relationship of the concept to other concepts, its typical and nontypical examples, the dependence of meaning on different contexts, the purpose and use of the concept, and its position and role in knowledge structures and theories in which it is embedded. Many of these components are present in the representation described in Lenat and co-workers, 1986. Murphy and Medin (1985) argue that the role a concept plays in a theory that uses it provides a basis for conceptual coherence, that is, for explaining why certain classes of entities constitute a meaningful concept and some others do not. Further progress on concept learning is predicated on progress in concept representation.

CONCLUSION

Concept learning has been presented as a process of constructing a concept representation on the basis of information provided by an external source, a teacher, or an environment. The type of transformation performed by the learner defines the learning strategy. The main emphasis of this article was on inductive learning, which is divided into learning from examples and learning from observation and discovery. Principles that underly inductive inference were described, and several methods were presented for concept learning from examples.

A number of topics in concept learning have not been covered. Among these are methods for creating new concepts, noninductive learning strategies, techniques for evaluating learned concept descriptions, and learning from noisy or incompletely defined examples. The general references include papers on these topics.

BIBLIOGRAPHY

S. Amarel, "On the Automatic Formation of a Computer Program Which Represents a Theory," in M. Yovits, G. Jacobi, and G. Goldstein, eds., *Self-Organizing Systems*, Spartan Books, Washington, D.C., 1962, pp. 107–175.

J. R. Anderson, "A Theory of Language Acquisition Based on General Learning Principles," *Proceedings of the Seventh International Joint Conference on Artificial Intelligence*, Vancouver, Canada, August 1981, pp. 97–103.

R. B. Banerji, "Computer Programs for the Generation of New Concepts from Old Ones," in K. Steinbuch and S. Wagner, eds., *Neue Ergebnisse der Kybernetik*, Oldenberg-Verlag, Munich, 1964, p. 336.

N. Bongard, *Pattern Recognition*, Spartan Books, New York, 1970 (translation from a Russian original, 1966).

J. S. Bruner, J. J. Goodnow, and G. A. Austin, *A Study of Thinking*, Wiley, New York, 1956.

B. G. Buchanan and E. A. Feigenbaum, "DENDRAL and Meta-DENDRAL: Their Applications Dimension," *Artif. Intell.* **11**, 5–24 (1978).

B. G. Buchanan, E. A. Feigenbaum, and J. Lederberg, "A Heuristic Programming Study of Theory Formation in Sciences," *Proceedings of the Second International Joint Conference on Artificial Intelligence*, London, 1971, pp. 40–48.

J. G. Carbonell, "Learning by Analogy: Formulating and Generalizing Plans from Past Experience," in R. S. Michalski, J. G. Carbonell, and T. M. Mitchell, eds., *Machine Learning: An Artificial Intelligence Approach*, Tioga, Palo Alto, Calif., 1983, pp. 137–161.

T. G. Dietterich and R. S. Michalski, "A Comparative Review of Selected Methods for Learning from Examples," in R. S. Michalski, J. G. Carbonell, and T. M. Mitchell, eds., *Machine Learning: An Artificial Intelligence Approach*, Tioga, Palo Alto, Calif., 1983, pp. 41–81.

T. Dietterich and R. S. Michalski, "Learning to Predict Sequences," in R. S. Michalski, J. G. Carbonell, and T. M. Mitchell, eds., *Machine Learning: An Artificial Intelligence Approach*, Vol. 2, Morgan-Kaufman, Los Altos, Calif., 1986, pp. 63–106.

N. Hass and G. G. Hendrix, "Learning by Being Told: Acquiring Knowledge for Information Management," in R. S. Michalski, J. G. Carbonell, and T. M. Mitchell, eds., *Machine Learning: An Artificial Intelligence Approach*, Tioga, Palo Alto, Calif., 1983, pp. 305–427.

D. F. Hofstadter, *Metamagical Themas: Questing for the Essence of Mind and Pattern*, Basic Books, New York, 1985, Chapter 24.

C. I. Hoveland, "A 'Communication Analysis' of Concept Learning," *Psychol. Rev.* **59**(6), 461–472, 1952.

E. B. Hunt, J. Marin, and P. J. Stone, *Experiments in Induction*, Academic Press, New York, 1966.

M. Kochen, "Experimental Study of 'Hypothesis Formation' by Computer," in C. Cherry, ed., *Information Theory: Fourth London Symposium*, Butterworth, London and Washington, D.C., 1961.

P. Langley, "BACON: A Production System that Discovers Empirical Laws," *Proceedings of the Fifth International Joint Conference on Artificial Intelligence*, Cambridge, Mass., 1977, pp. 344–346.

P. Langley and G. L. Bradshaw, "Rediscovering Chemistry with the Bacon System," in R. S. Michalski, J. G. Carbonell, T. M. Mitchell, eds., *Machine Learning: An Artificial Intelligence Approach*, Tioga, Palo Alto, Calif., 1983, pp. 307–329.

D. B. Lenat, *AM: An Artificial Intelligence Approach to Discovery in Mathematics as Heuristic Search*, Ph.D. dissertation, Stanford University, Stanford, Calif., 1976.

D. B. Lenat, "The Role of Heuristics in Learning by Discovery: Three Case Studies," in R. S. Michalski, J. G. Carbonell, T. M. Mitchell, eds., *Machine Learning: An Artificial Intelligence Approach*, Tioga, Palo Alto, Calif., 1983, pp. 243–306.

D. Lenat, M. Prakash, and M. Shepherd, "CYC: Using Common Sense Knowledge to Overcome Brittleness and Knowledge Acquisition Bottlenecks," *AI Mag.* **6**(4), 65–85 (1986).

R. S. Michalski, "A Variable-Valued Logic System as Applied to Picture Description and Recognition," in F. Nake, A. Rosenfeld, eds., *Graphic Languages*, North-Holland, Amsterdam, 1972, pp. 20–47.

R. S. Michalski, "Theory and Methodology of Inductive Learning," in R. S. Michalski, J. G. Carbonell, and T. M. Mitchell, eds., *Machine Learning: An Artificial Intelligence Approach*, Tioga, Palo Alto, Calif., 1983, pp. 83–134.

R. S. Michalski and R. L. Chilausky, "Learning by Being Told and Learning From Examples: An Experimental Comparison of the Two Methods of Knowledge Acquisition in the Context of Developing an Expert System for Soybean Disease Diagnosis," *Pol. Anal. Inform. Sys.* **4**(2), 125–161 (June 1980).

R. S. Michalski and J. B. Larson, "Selection of Most Representative Training Examples and Incremental Generation of VL1 Hypotheses: The Underlying Methodology and a Description of Programs ESEL and AQ11," Report 867, Department of Computer Science, University of Illinois, Urbana, 1978.

R. S. Michalski and R. E. Stepp, "Learning from Observation: Conceptual Clustering," in R. S. Michalski, J. G. Carbonell, and T. M. Mitchell, eds., *Machine Learning: An Artificial Intelligence Approach*, Tioga, Palo Alto, Calif., 1983, pp. 331–364.

D. Michie, "Memo Functions and Machine Learning," *Nature* **218**(5136), 19–22 (1968).

M. Minsky and S. Papert, *Perceptrons*, MIT Press, Cambridge, Mass., 1969.

T. M. Mitchell, "Version Spaces: A Candidate Elimination Approach to Rule Learning," *Proceedings of the Fifth International Joint Conference on Artificial Intelligence*, Cambridge, Mass., August 1977, pp. 305–310.

T. M. Mitchell, R. M. Keller, and S. T. Kedar-Cabelli, "Explanation-Based Generalization: A Unifying View," *Machine Learning* **1**(1), 47–80 (1986).

T. M. Mitchell, P. E. Utgoff, and R. Banerji, "Learning by Experimentation: Acquiring and Refining Problem-Solving Heuristics," in R. S. Michalski, J. G. Carbonell, and T. M. Mitchell (eds.), *Machine Learning: An Artificial Intelligence Approach*, Tioga, Palo Alto, Calif., 1983, pp. 163–190.

G. L. Murphy and D. L. Medin, "The Role of Theories in Conceptual Coherence," *Psychol. Rev.* **92**(3), 289–316 (1985).

A. Newell, J. C. Shaw, and H. A. Simon, "A Variety of Intelligent Learning in the General Problem Solver," Technical Report, Rand Corporation, Santa Monica, Calif., 1959.

C. S. Peirce, *Essays in the Philosophy of Science*, The Liberal Arts Press, New York, 1957.

K. R. Popper, *Objective Knowledge: An Evolutionary Approach*, Clarendon Press, Oxford, UK, 1979.

J. R. Quinlan, "Learning Efficient Classification Procedures and Their Application to Chess End Games," in R. S. Michalski, J. G. Carbonell, and T. M. Mitchell, eds., *Machine Learning: An Artificial Intelligence Approach*, Tioga, Palo Alto, Calif., 1983, pp. 463–482.

L. A. Rendell, "Substantial Constructive Induction: Feature Formation in Search," *Proceedings of the Ninth IJCAI*, Los Angeles, Calif., August 1985, pp. 650–658.

E. Rosch and C. B. Mervis, "Family Resemblances: Studies in the Internal Structure of Categories," *Cog. Psychol.* **7**(4), 573–605 (1975).

A. L. Samuel, "Some Studies in Machine Learning Using the Game of Checkers," *IBM J. Res. Dev.* **3**, 210–229 (1959), reprinted in E. A. Feigenbaum and J. Feldman, eds., *Computers and Thought*, McGraw-Hill, New York, 1963, pp. 71–105.

R. C. Schank, Looking at Learning, *Proceedings of the European Conference on Artificial Intelligence*, Orsay, France, July 1982, pp. 11–18.

H. A. Simon and G. Lea, "Problem Solving and Rule Induction: A Unified View," L. W. Gregg, ed., in *Knowledge and Cognition*, Lawrence Erlbaum, Potomac, Md., 1974, pp. 105–127.

E. E. Smith and D. L. Medin, *Categories and Concepts*, Harvard University Press, Cambridge, Mass., 1981.

J. F. Sowa, *Conceptual Structures: Information Processing in Mind and Machine*, Addison-Wesley, Reading, Mass., 1984.

S. Watanabe, *Pattern Recognition as an Inductive Process, Methodologies of Pattern Recognition*, Academic Press, New York, 1968.

P. H. Winston, "Learning Structural Descriptions from Examples," Ph.D. dissertation, Report No. TR-231, AI Laboratory, MIT, Cambridge, Mass., 1970, reprinted in P. H. Winston, ed., *The Psychology of Computer Vision*, McGraw-Hill, New York, 1975, Chapt. 5.

P. H. Winston, "Learning and Reasoning by Analogy," *CACM* **23**(12), 689–703 (1979).

L. Wittgenstein, *Tractatus Logico-Philosophicus*, Routledge & Kegan Paul, London, 1921.

L. A. Zadeh, "A Fuzzy-Algorithmic Approach to the Definition of Complex or Imprecise Concepts," *Int. J. Man-Machine Stud.* **8**(3), 249–291 (1976).

General References

T. G. Dietterich, B. London, K. Clarkson, and G. Dromey, "Learning and Inductive Inference," in P. R. Cohen and E. A. Feigenbaum, eds., *Handbook of Artificial Intelligence*, Vol. 3, W. Kaufmann, Los Altos, Calif., 1982, pp. 325–511.

J. McCarthy, "Programs with Common Sense," *Proceedings of the Symposium on the Mechanization of Thought Processes*, Vol. 1, National Physical Laboratory, 1958.

N. Zagoruiko in J. C. Simon, ed., *Empirical Prediction Algorithms, Computer Oriented Learning Processes*, Noordhoff, Leiden, The Netherlands, 1976.

R. S. MICHALSKI
University of Illinois

This work was supported in part by the NSF under grant No. DCR 84-06801, by the ONR under grant No. N00014-82-K-0186, and by DARPA under grant No. N00014-K-85-0878.

CONCEPTUAL DEPENDENCY

Conceptual dependency (CD) is a theory of natural language and of natural language processing (see NATURAL LANGUAGE GENERATION; NATURAL LANGUAGE UNDERSTANDING). It has been developed by Schank with the motivation to enhance one's ability to construct computer programs that can understand language well enough to summarize it, translate it into another language, and answer questions about it. At the heart of the theory lies the conjecture that language is a medium whose purpose is communication. Therefore, the central issue dealt with by the theory is that of the kinds of things that can be communicated, ie, the meaning content of the communication.

What inferences are made?
When are these inferences made?
Where do they come from?

For example, most people would agree that the sentence "John sold his old car" contains a reference to money even though the word "money" is not mentioned in the sentence. Furthermore, most people would agree that as a

consequence of John's action, he no longer owns that car. Any computer program that understands this sentence must answer no to the question "Does John own the car?" and yes to the question "Did John receive money?"

How could a program know that? To model language understanding on a computer, one needs a strong theory of human inference that operates on the level of conceptual manipulations. Furthermore, in order for a theory of language to have relevance in the field of AI, it must provide a representation of meaning as well as the means to map into and out of that representation (see KNOWLEDGE REPRESENTATION).

Conceptual dependency theory is a theory of the representation of meaning. It is a representation of everyday concepts and events in a way that reflects natural thinking and communication about those concepts and events. At the time of its development, the approach taken by Schank was not considered unusual within the AI framework. Since AI is largely an experimental field, the theory and its computer implementations were viewed as investigation into the dynamics of natural language understanding. However, in the field of linguistics thoughts about the nature and the purpose of language were oriented in a direction opposite to that reflected by Schank's theory, and the latter was considered radical.

CONCEPTUAL STRUCTURES

Conceptual dependency theory views understanding of natural language as a process of mapping linear strings of words into well-formed conceptual structures. A conceptual structure is defined as a network of concepts, where certain classes of concepts can be related in specific ways to other classes of concepts (see also SEMANTIC NETWORKS). The basic axiom of the theory is:

For any two sentences that are identical in meaning, regardless of language, there should be only one representation.

A corollary that derives from it is:

Any information in the sentence that is implicit must be made explicit in the representation of the meaning of that sentence.

The rules by which classes of objects combine may be viewed as conceptual syntax rules. It is important to note that these rules underly the language, but they are independent of it. They are rules of thought as opposed to rules of a language. The initial framework consists of the following rules (Schank, 1972):

The meaning of a linguistic proposition is called a conceptualization or CD form.
A conceptualization can be active or stative.
An active conceptualization consists of the following slots: actor; action; object; and direction, source (from) destination (to) (instrument).
A stative conceptualization consists of the following slots: object, state, and value.

Each CD has associated semantic constraints on the kinds of entities that can fill its slots. These semantic constraints reflect different levels of specificity. For example, some rules may be applied to any object that plays the actor role in any action. On the other hand, other rules will be very specific to a particular action and its slot values.

CONCEPTUAL DEPENDENCY RULES

The CD rules prefer combinations of concepts that go along with experience over those that violate experience. Of course, it is possible for the CD rules to be idiosyncratic, but most people share enough of them to be able to communicate. What is usually referred to as semantics in linguistics is the set of operations at the conceptual level. When the word "semantics" is used in the context of the CD theory, it means the experiential laws that allow for concept combinations. The vocabulary that expresses conceptual rules makes use of the following conceptual categories of objects.

PPs: Picture Producers or Conceptual Nominals. Only physical objects are PPs. PPs may serve in various roles in the conceptualization. PPs that are animate or have animate properties (such as machines) or that are natural forces (wind, gravity) may be actors. Any PP may serve in the role of an object. A PP in the role of source or destination refers to the location of that PP. Animate PPs may also serve as recipients.

ACTs: Actions. Actions can be done by an actor to an object. The major primitive ACTs will be given below.

LOCs: Locations. Every physical ACT has a location that modifies the place of occurrence of the conceptualization that included it. Locations are considered to be coordinates in space. LOCs can modify conceptualizations as well as serve as sources and destinations.

Ts: Times. Most conceptualizations have a time. The time is considered to be a point or a segment on a time line. This point or segment may be measured on some absolute scale (e.g., 2 p.m. on April 1, 1983) or relative (after last Christmas).

AAs: Action Aiders. Action aiders are modifications of features of an ACT. For example, PROPEL has a speed factor, which is an AA. Very few AAs have been developed.

PAs: Picture Aides, or Attributes of an Object. Every physical object can be defined by a set of attribute states with specific values. A PA is an attribute characteristic such as color or size, plus a value for that characteristic, for example, blue or 5 ft (1.5 m).

As part of the CD theory, Schank specified different ways in which these conceptual categories can combine. These rules may be viewed as formulating partial semantics of the knowledge representation since they specify some of the meaning incorporated in a given dependency between concepts. Six such rules follow. A more complete list and a detailed discussion of this important issue is given in Schank (1972, 1973).

Rule 1. Certain PPs Can ACT. For example, the sentence "Kevin walked" may be represented using the primitive act PTRANS (see below) as

Actor	Kevin
Action	PTRANS
Object	Kevin
Direction	from: unknown
	to: unknown

The graphic notation is

$$\text{Kevin} \Leftrightarrow \text{PTRANS} \xleftarrow{\;o\;} \text{Kevin} \leftarrow \begin{array}{l} \rightarrow ? \\ \\ < ? \end{array}$$

Here there is a mutual dependency link between the PP and the ACT. It is represented graphically by the double arrow. Exactly which PP can do what ACT is to be determined in each case by the semantic nature of the two objects.

Rule 2. PPs and Some Conceptualizations Can Be Described By an Attribute. For example, the sentence "Nancy is heavy" may be represented using the following stative conceptualization:

Object	Nancy
State	WEIGHT
Value	above average

Graphically,

$$\text{Nancy} \Leftrightarrow \text{WEIGHT(above average)}$$

This dependency between the object and the state is represented graphically by the triple arrow.

Rule 3. ACTs Have Objects. For example, the sentence "Perry kicked the cat" may be represented using the primitive act PROPEL (see below) as

Actor	Perry
Action	PROPEL
Object	cat
Direction	from: unknown
	to: unknown

Graphically,

$$\text{Perry} \Leftrightarrow \text{PROPEL} \xleftarrow{\;o\;} \text{cat} \leftarrow \begin{array}{l} \rightarrow ? \\ \\ < ? \end{array}$$

The dependency between the act and the object is represented by $\overset{O}{\leftarrow}$.

Rule 4. ACTs Have Direction. For example, the sentence "Bill fell from the ladder" may be represented using the primitive act PTRANS (see below) as

Actor	Bill
Action	PTRANS
Object	Bill
Direction	from: ladder
	to: ground

Graphically,

$$\text{Bill} \Leftrightarrow \text{PTRANS} \overset{O}{\leftarrow} \text{Bill} \leftarrow \begin{cases} \rightarrow \text{ground} \\ < \text{ladder} \end{cases}$$

The dependency between the act and the direction is represented graphically by $\leftarrow\square$.

Rule 5. ACTs Have Recipients. For example, the sentence "John donated blood to the Red Cross" may be represented using the primitive act ATRANS (see below) as

Actor	John
Action	ATRANS
Object	blood
Direction	from: John
	to: Red Cross

Graphically,

$$\text{John} \Leftrightarrow \text{ATRANS} \overset{O}{\leftarrow} \text{blood} \leftarrow \begin{cases} \rightarrow \text{Red Cross} \\ < \text{John} \end{cases}$$

The dependency between the act and the direction is represented graphically by $\leftarrow$.

Rule 6. ACTs Can Have Instrumental ACTs. For example, "John hit Bill with his hand" would be

Actor	John
Action	PROPEL
Object	Bill
Instrument	Actor: John
	Action: MOVE
	Object: hand
	Direction from: John
	to: Bill

Graphically,

$$\begin{array}{c} \text{John} \Leftrightarrow \text{PROPEL} \overset{O}{\leftarrow} \text{Bill} \\ \uparrow I \\ \text{John} \Leftrightarrow \text{MOVE} \leftarrow \text{hard} \\ \wedge\downarrow \\ \text{Bill} \end{array}$$

THE NEED FOR CONCEPTUAL PRIMITIVES

The requirement that sentences that have the same meaning be represented in the same way cannot be satisfied without some set of primitive ACTs. The ACTs presented here are not category names for verbs. Rather they can be considered to be elements of those verbs. An analogous situation is the formation of compounds from the basic elements in chemistry.

As is demonstrated below, the use of such primitives severely reduces the inference problem in AI since the inference rules need only be written once for any ACT rather than many times for each verb that references that ACT. For example, in a situation that involves the transfer of information, one rule may state that "if you MTRANS something to your long-term memory, then it is present there (ie, you know it)." This rule is true whether the MTRANSing was expressed using the verbs "see," "learn," "hear," "inform," or "remember." This is because the inference comes from the ACT rather than the verb.

The need to introduce a vocabulary of primitives into the knowledge representation scheme originates from the need to write general rules in the most succinct way. For example, when two sentences describe the same event and have the same overall meaning but a different form, the CD representation has to be identical. To illustrate this point, consider the following example (Schank and Riesbeck, 1981):

1. John gave Mary a book.
2. Mary took a book from John.
3. Mary received a book from John.
4. John sold Mary a book.
5. Mary bought a book from John.
6. Mary traded a cigar to John for a book.

Undoubtedly, these six sentences have common meaning elements. To uncover this fact, the following presents a stepwise analysis of the conceptual structures underlying the first two. As was mentioned earlier, in a CD representation an event is always described by a combination of actors, actions, objects, and directions. Thus, to represent the event "John gave Mary a book," one starts with:

Actor	unknown
Action	unknown
Object	unknown
Direction	unknown

Not all of the fillers for the slots are given in the sentence. What one is told though is that the actor is John and the object is book. For the moment one assumes that the action is give, whose direction is the animate object Mary. This produces:

Actor	John
Action	give
Object	book
Direction	Mary

Consider now the analysis of the sentence "Mary took a book from John." The actor here is Mary, the object is again a book, and the direction would seem to be John. But at this point it seems that there is something missing in this single-valued description of direction since there is a difference between "from" and "toward" that this representation does not capture. The problem is that directions must have at least two parts in order to be specified. If the direction is from John, it has to be to somebody else. Likewise, in the earlier sentence, just because there was only "to Mary" does not mean that there is no "from" part to be provided by the remainder of the text or to be figured out from previous knowledge. Therefore, the analysis must be revised as follows:

Actor	John	Actor	Mary
Action	give	Action	take
Object	book	Object	book
Direction	to: Mary	Direction	to: unknown
	from: unknown		from: John

At this stage of the analysis the meaning representation of the two sentences does not look very much alike. This is because the meanings of "give" and "take" have not yet been dealt with. To consider what their meanings might be, one can attempt to fill the empty slots in the direction roles.

Actor	John	Actor	Mary
Action	give	Action	take
Object	book	Object	book
Direction	to: Mary	Direction	to: Mary
	from: John		from: John

The two sentences have different actors, but they involve an event whose overall consequence is the same. The effect of the event is the transfer of possession of the book from John to Mary. The only difference between them is the focus on the actor of the event. In CD, transfer of possession is called ATRANS, and the representation for the two sentences now looks as follows:

Actor	John	Actor	Mary
Action	ATRANS	Action	ATRANS
Object	book	Object	book
Direction	to: Mary	Direction	to: Mary
	from: John		from: John

It is important to notice that the words "give" and "take" are not lost during the analysis but can be recovered from the direction information in the ATRANS conceptualization. The natural language generator that can do that is mentioned below. What are the benefits of this analysis?

Economy

Every time the system sees ATRANS, it can make the appropriate inferences by applying the inference rules attached to this primitive action. Consider a case where the inferences were attached to the verbs themselves. For ex-

ample, "give" would have attached to it the inference "if you give somebody something, then they have it," and "take" would have attached to it the inference "if somebody takes something, then they have it." This situation would involve tremendous duplication for every verb that inferred transfer of possession. This loss of economy would be considerable as it applies not only to "give" and "take" but to hundreds of other verbs that involve transfer of possession as well.

Similarity in Meaning

The representation captures the similarity in meaning between the two sentences. The perspective is slightly different in each case since the actors in the events are different, but the overall meaning is very close and the meaning representation reflects this fact.

To consider a further ATRANS example, examine next the sentence "Mary bought a book from John."

Actor	John	Actor	Mary
Action	ATRANS	Action	ATRANS
Object	book	Object	money
Direction	to: Mary	Direction	to: Mary
	from: John		from: John

The $\Leftarrow$ is a notation for causal. Thus, $A \Leftarrow B$ means A caused B. The double causal above indicates that the two events caused each other. What is the analysis of "John sold a book to Mary?" It seems obvious that the meaning is very close. [Context may introduce deviations in the meanings, but these are dealt with using higher-level memory structures, such as scripts and plans (Schank and Abelson, 1977; Schank, 1982).]

The sentence "Mary traded a cigar to John for a book" has a similar representation except that cigar replaces money in the object slot of the structure on the right.

THE PRIMITIVE ACTs

The following is a list of the most important primitive ACTs and examples of their use.

ATRANS is the transfer of an abstract relationship, such as possession, ownership, or control. For example, one sense of the verb "give" is to ATRANS something to someone else; one sense of the verb "take" is to ATRANS something to oneself. The verb "buy" is made up of two conceptualizations that cause each other: one is an ATRANS of money and the other is an ATRANS of an object being bought.

PTRANS is the transfer of the physical location of an object. For example, the action "go" is to PTRANS oneself to a place; the action "put" is to PTRANS an object to a place. In certain cases certain words only imply PTRANS during the analysis. For example, the verb "throw" means PROPEL (see below) and the PTRANS caused by it has to be inferred. Since most things that are PROPELed are also PTRANSed, the inference mechanism will have to decide in each case of PROPEL if PTRANS is true too.

PROPEL is the application of a physical force to an object. PROPEL is used whenever any force is applied regardless of whether a movement (PTRANS) took place. For example, the verbs "push," "pull," "throw," "shove," and "kick" have PROPEL as part of them. The sentence "John pushed the table to the wall" is a PROPEL that causes a PTRANS. The sentence "John threw the ball" is a PROPEL that involves a simultaneous ending of a GRASP act. Often words that do not necessarily mean PROPEL can imply PROPEL. For example, "break," which means to do something that causes a specific kind of physical state change, often implies that PROPEL caused the state change.

MOVE is the movement of a body part of an animal by that animal. MOVE is nearly always the ACT in the instrumental conceptualization for other ACTs. For example, in order to "throw," it is necessary to MOVE one's arm; in order to "kick," it is instrumental to MOVE one's foot; in order to "hand something," it is instrumental to MOVE one's hand. Noninstrumental uses of MOVE are verbs such as "raise your hand" and "scratch."

GRASP is the grasping of an object by an actor. For example, the verbs "hold," "grab," "let go," and "throw" involve GRASP or the ending of GRASP.

INGEST is the taking of an object by an animal to the inside of that animal. Most commonly, the objects of INGEST are food, liquid, and gas. Thus, the verbs "eat," "drink," "smoke," and "breathe" are common examples of INGEST.

EXPEL is the expulsion of an object from the body of an animal into the physical world. Whatever is EXPELed is very likely to have been previously INGESTed. Words for excretion and secretion as described by EXPEL. The verbs "sweat," "spit," and "cry" are common examples of EXPEL.

MTRANS is the transfer of mental information between animals or within an animal. For the purposes of the analysis here, memory is partitioned into three locations: the CP (conscious processor), where things are thought of; the LTM (long-term memory), where things are stored; and IM (intermediate memory), where the current context is stored. The various sense organs can also serve as sources in an MTRANS. Thus, the verb "tell" means MTRANS between people, the verb "see" means MTRANS from eye to CP, the verb "remember" means MTRANS from LTM to CP, the verb "forget" means the inability to MTRANS from LTM to CP, and the verb "learn" means the MTRANSing of new information to LTM.

MBUILD is the construction by an animal of new information from old information. The verbs "decide," "conclude," "imagine," and "consider" are common examples of MBUILD.

SPEAK is the action of producing sounds. Many objects can SPEAK. In the case of humans SPEAKing is usually instrumental for MTRANSing. The verbs "say," "sing," "purr," and "scream" are common examples involving SPEAK.

ATTEND is the action of attending or focusing a sense organ toward a stimulus. For example, the verb "listen" means ATTEND ear, and the verb "see" means ATTEND eye. ATTEND is almost always referred to as the instrument of MTRANS. Thus, for example, in CD "see" is treated as MTRANS to CP from eye by the instrument of ATTEND eye to object.

STATIVE CD FORMS

Stative conceptualizations that are attribute value statements use a large number of scales. These scales often run from −10 to 10 and can also be used to indicate changes in states. Some of the scales that are used are shown below.

> Health (−10 = dead, −3 = under the weather, −d = (negative increment) got sick, 10 = perfect health)
>
> Anticipate (−10 = terrified, −2 = nervous, +5 hoping)
>
> Anger (goes from −10 to 0)
>
> Mental state (−5 = depressed, +2 = happy, +9 = ecstatic)
>
> Physical state (−10 = end of existence, −5 = damaged, +10 = complete)
>
> Awareness (−10 = dead, −7 = unconscious, −2 = asleep, +5 = alert)

CD-BASED COMPUTER UNDERSTANDING

The development of the theory of CD went hand in hand with the development of the computer programs that implemented it. As is often the case in AI research, the computer program served as an experimental device that tested the theory and suggested modifications.

The first step in the evolution of the computer implementation of the CD theory was the MARGIE system (Schank, 1975). It had three distinct pieces: a parser that mapped sentences into CD forms, a memory mechanism that generated and stored inferences about the meanings generated by the parser, and a generator that translated the conceptual meanings back into natural language.

The following is an example of MARGIE input and output (Schank and Riesbeck, 1981):

Input:	John gave Mary an aspirin.
Output 1:	John believed that Mary wants an aspirin.
Output 2:	Mary is sick.
Output 3:	Mary wants to feel better.
Output 4:	Mary will ingest the aspirin.

Schank and his co-workers recognized at the time that the above division into modules was somewhat unrealistic since the three modules must share data and processes with one another. However, their intention was to test how CD could function as a meaning representation language, and the above modular design was sufficient for that purpose. MARGIE was the first computer program that made inferences from input sentences in the context of an overall theory of the inference process. (A full discussion of the MARGIE system and its modules is given in Schank, 1975).

To get the flavor of the computer programs that implement the CD theory, consider some examples of procedures that handle some of the conceptual information processing involved in using the primitive ACT ATRANS.

The code for these procedures, which is written in the programming language LISP (qv), is taken from the programs features in Schank and Riesbeck (1981).

Making Inferences

The primitive ACTs may be represented in the program as a data structure. For example, the following LISP function, when called with its four arguments, will build a conceptual structure for ATRANS.

```
(DE ATRANS(ACTOR OBJECT TO FROM)
 (LIST 'ATRANS(LIST 'ACTOR ACTOR)
  (LIST 'OBJECT OBJECT)
  (LIST 'TO TO)
  (LIST 'FROM FROM]
```

Organized around each primitive ACT, there should be inference-generating procedures. For example, to compute the consequences of an ATRANS, one may have the following:

```
(DE ATRANS-CONSEQS()
 (NOTICE $(ACTOR)*CD*)
 (NOTICE $(ACTOR) (ADD-CONSEQ (HAS $(TO)
                                  $(OBJECT))))
 (ADD-CONSEQ (IS-AT $(OBJECT) $(TO)))
 ((COND ($(FROM)
   (NOTICE $(ACTOR) (ADD-CONSEQ (NEGATE (HAS
                              $(FROM) $(OBJECT]
```

In this code, the dollar sign indicates a function that can fetch the filler of the slot (role) that follows it. The function ATRANS-CONSEQS essentially says the following about the consequences of an ATRANS: the actor of an ATRANS knows it happened; the actor knows that there is a resulting change of possession due to the ATRANS; the object that was ATRANSed changed location; and the filler of the FROM slot knows he no longer has the object. This list of consequences is obviously not complete, but it should serve as an illustration for the types of knowledge organized around the primitive actions.

Language Generation

In English, ATRANS may be expressed as "take" if the filler for the actor slot equals the filler of the TO slot or as "give" otherwise. This can be handled by the following simple procedure.

```
(DSP ATRANS
 (COND ((EQUAL $(ACTOR) $(TO))
   (SAY-SUBJ-VERB '(ACTOR) 'TAKE)
   (SAY-FILLER '(OBJECT))
   (SAY-PREP 'FROM '(FROM)))
  (T (SAY-SUBJ-VERB '(ACTOR) 'GIVE)
   (SAY-FILLER '(TO))
   (SAY-FILLER '(OBJECT)]
```

The function DSP attaches the procedure under the name of the ACT so that it can be evaluated by the generator when the ACT is to be expressed. It should be noticed that the information contained in this word definition comes from both conceptual as well as language-specific sources.

Parsing

The conceptual parser, like the generator, uses information from many different sources. Conceptual parsers use expectation to guide their processing. Since the knowledge representation contains semantic constraints around the primitive acts and their role filler, the parser uses this knowledge for effective focusing of attention and context-dependent disambiguation.

As an example of a lexical entry that can be used by a conceptual parser, consider the lexical definition of the verb "take." In this definition the verb "take" means that someone ATRANSed something to the subject. "Take" looks for a noun phrase to fill the object slot.

```
(DEF-WORD TAKE
 ((ASSIGN *PART-OF-SPEECH* 'VERB
   *CD-FORM*(ATRANS
         ?GET-VAR3
         ?GET-VAR2
         ?GET-VAR1
         ?GET-VAR3)
   GET-VAR1 *SUBJECT*
   GET-VAR2 NIL
   GET-VAR3 NIL)
 (NEXT-PACKET
   ((TEST (EQUAL *PART-OF-SPEECH* 'NOUN-PHRASE))
   (ASSIGN GET-VAR2 *CD-FORM*]
```

The function DEF-WORD stores a definition of a word under a word. The definition consists of a list of requests that represent different expectations. Further definitions of the concepts as well as implementation details of the parser are shown in Schank and Riesbeck (1981).

In both the parser and the generator the language-specific parts can be changed independently of the parts that contain the knowledge sources. This fact considerably facilitates the task of multilingual parsing and generation.

CONCLUDING REMARKS

The theory of CD and its various computer implementations have had an impact on the way natural language processing is perceived. It brought forward the notion of language-independent conceptual primitives. It provided a content-based knowledge organization scheme that facilitated expectation-based language processing. As any AI theory should, CD theory suggests extensions. Higher level memory structures, such as scripts (qv) and memory organization packets (qv), were later introduced into the theory of language processing. These processing structures are essential for effective understanding and learning in situations that involve complicated but commonly occurring sequences of CDs (Schank and Riesbeck, 1981; Schank, 1982). In retrospect, the theory of CD can be viewed as a part of a common-sense theory of language processing.

BIBLIOGRAPHY

R. C. Schank, "Conceptual Dependency: A Theory of Natural Language Understanding," *Cogn. Psychol.* **3**(4), 552–631 (1972).

R. C. Schank, "Identification of Conceptualizations Underlying Natural Language," in R. C. Schank and K. M. Colby, eds., *Computer Models of Thought and Language*, W.H. Freeman, San Francisco, 1973.

R. C. Schank, *Conceptual Information Processing*, Elsevier, New York, 1975.

R. C. Schank, *Dynamic Memory: A Theory of Learning in Computers and People*, Cambridge University Press, Cambridge, UK, 1982.

R. C. Schank and R. P. Abelson, *Scripts Plans Goals and Understanding*, Lawrence Erlbaum, Hillsdale, N.J., 1977.

R. C. Schank and C. K. Riesbeck, *Inside Computer Understanding*, Lawrence Erlbaum, Hillsdale, N.J., 1981.

General References

R. C. Schank and P. G. Childus, *The Cognitive Computer*, Addison-Wesley, Reading, Mass., 1984.

S. L. HARDT
Bellcore

CONNECTION MACHINES

Connection machines are a class of parallel computers designed for symbolic computation, especially AI. Many current AI programs run so slowly on conventional serial machines that they are impractical for everyday use and difficult to put to the test. Connection machines promise to increase the speed of these programs and to make possible the development of the even more complex, and hence slower, programs that will be written in the future.

In typical current machines, the CPU and the memory are separate. Data are stored in the memory, and all computation is performed in the CPU. Since the CPU can only do one thing at a time, the time to process a certain amount of data increases almost linearly with the amount of data. AI programs often have very large databases that take a long time to manipulate. The guiding idea behind the development of connection machines is that every piece of data should be able to do its own computation. The processing power is more uniformly distributed throughout the memory so that larger databases can have more computation devoted to them.

HARDWARE

Connection machines are composed of a very large number (50,000–1,000,000) of small processors connected by a high-speed communication network. Each processor stores a very small piece of data, such as might be stored in a few words on a conventional machine. The communication network, or "router," permits any processor to send a message to any other processor, with a delay of only a few dozen machine cycles. Each processor is too small to fetch its own instruction stream. Instead, all processors receive the same instruction stream, which is generated by a conventional serial machine, called the "host machine." The programmer does not always want all proces-

sors to do the same thing. To allow different processors to perform different actions, processors may selectively ignore the instruction stream. Each processor contains a hardware flag, which, when set, causes the processor to ignore the instruction stream. It is also possible for the host machine to issue unconditional instructions that are not blocked out by this flag.

The host machine provides a front end for the connection machine. It provides features that are not practically performed directly on the connection machine. These include programmer support such as text editors, operating systems, compilers, and network and terminal interfaces. Any task that cannot be done in parallel is faster on the host machine than on the connection machine. The connection machine can be thought of as a "symbolic manipulation accelerator" for the host machine, analogous to a floating-point accelerator. A single connection machine processor contains an ALU whose data paths are 1 bit wide. A 1-bit-wide ALU is capable of performing any computation that can be done by wider ALUs, albeit more slowly. Arithmetic operations that can be performed in a single clock cycle on conventional processors take time proportional to the length of the arguments on a connection machine. For example, to add two 16-bit numbers in every processor of a connection machine would require 16 clock cycles. For this reason, connection machines are not particularly distinguished as "number crunchers."

SOFTWARE

Symbolic data structures are formed out of objects connected by pointers. To manipulate these structures in parallel requires not only the ability to manipulate the data stored in each individual object simultaneously, as can be done on conventional array processor systems, but also the ability to perform operations on data spread out over several objects connected by pointers. In connection machines the router serves as a communication path between processors. Each object is stored in a single processor. If an object has a pointer to another object, this means it knows the address of the other object and can thus send messages to it. By using object-oriented programming methods, the activities of multiple objects can be coordinated to produce the desired computation. If different programs are to be run by different types of data objects, the instructions can be sent out for the various programs, but every processor is told to block out any program that does not apply to the data object stored in it. If the user is writing in a high level language, this method of instruction delivery is hidden, and it appears that different types of processors run different programs.

Algorithms that benefit from running on connection machines are those that require large numbers of similar operations on large symbolic database. Many AI tasks are of this type. Examples include sorting, unification, production systems, and retrieval from semantic networks. The early stages of vision, such as feature extraction and line detection, can be computed very quickly on connection machines by dedicating one processor to each pixel in the image. Connection machines include special hardware for fast communication between adjacent processors representing pixels in order to further accelerate vision computations.

Connection machines have been under development at the MIT Artificial Intelligence Laboratory. The Connection Machine Supercomputer is a commercial product of Thinking Machines Corporation.

BIBLIOGRAPHY

General References

A. Bawden, *What a Parallel Programming Language Has To Let You Say*, Memo No. 796, MIT AI Laboratory, Cambridge, Mass., 1984.

W. D. Hillis, "The Connection Machine: A Computer Architecture on Cellular Automata," *Physica* **10D,** 213–228 (1984).

W. D. Hillis, *The Connection Machine*, MIT Press, Cambridge, Mass., 1985.

C. Feynman
Thinking Machines Corp.

CONNECTION METHOD

Predicate logic is a formal language for specifying and representing problems in a precise way. Solutions for problems in this setting may be obtained by applying proof procedures to such formal specifications. Because of the existence of these procedures, logic may also be used as a programming and problem solving language. Such proof procedures are therefore of a very general nature and have many applications in artificial intelligence. They are the subject of research in the special area of automated deduction (or automated theorem proving).

For the development of a proof procedure, four different tasks must be accomplished. First, it must be decided exactly which logic is considered adequate for the problems in mind. For the following discussion, assume this to be first-order logic. Second, the details of the language of the logic, ie, of first-order logic, have to be agreed upon. Third, a calculus is needed that is complete and consistent (or rather, these properties are usually presumed of the calculus). Finally, a strategy must be provided that determines the sequence of rule applications for a given problem description (or formula).

The resolution principle provides the basis for a number of such calculi. While many proof procedures in use are based on these resolution calculi, there are many other calculi available for the same purpose. Different calculi may vary in their computational properties when used in the form of a proof procedure. For instance, some are provably not competitive with resolution calculi and thus play little role in this context. The connection method provides the basis for a family of calculi that are competitive in this respect. They even offer advantages not present in resolution calculi.

The connection method has its roots in Gentzen's calculi (Gentzen, 1935). In a sense it may in fact be regarded as a concentrated version of those formalisms designed for the purposes of automated deduction, in which as much redundancy as possible is eliminated. These roots may be traced in papers by Bibel (1974) and Bibel and Schreiber (1975), while a comprehensive treatment may be found in Bibel (1987). The method has been developed independently by Andrews (1976, 1989), with different terminology [see Bibel (1983) for the detailed correspondences and differences].

The connection method can handle arbitrary formulas of first-order predicate logic directly. They need not to be in clausal form as in resolution. However, using the computationally fast transformation given by Eder (1985) (or Bibel and Eder, 1991), any formula of first-order predicate logic can be transformed to a formula in clausal form without any resulting disadvantages (which is not true for the standard method of transformation). Therefore, attention may be restricted to the clausal form versions of the connection method.

The connection method is usually presented as an affirmative method for proving the validity of a formula in disjunctive normal form, whereas resolution is a refutational method for proving the unsatisfiability of a formula in conjunctive normal form. This difference is, however, an absolutely negligible one, since both methods could as well be presented in either way with no difference whatsoever in the computational consequences.

Consider a simple example, namely the formula

$$Ls \leftarrow \forall x (Mx \rightarrow Lx) \land Ms$$

which may be read as "Socrates is mortal since all humans are mortal and Socrates is a human." Transforming this into affirmative (or positive) clausal form, ie, the set-theoretic version of disjunctive normal form, yields the clauses

$$\{Ls\}, \quad \{Mx, \neg Lx\}, \quad \{\neg Ms\}$$

For the purposes of presentation, a two-dimensional display of these clauses is used:

$$\begin{array}{cc} \neg Lx & \neg Ms \\ Ls & Mx \end{array}$$

Here the clauses are represented in the form of a matrix whose columns represent the clauses (or disjuncts). In other words, conjunction is represented by a vertical listing, disjunction by a horizontal one.

A path through such a matrix is a set of literals (literal occurrences, to be precise), one taken from each clause. There are exactly two paths in the example, namely $\{Ls, \neg Lx, \neg Ms\}$ and $\{Ls, Mx, \neg Ms\}$. A connection in a matrix is an unordered pair of literals (ie, literal occurrences) with the same predicate symbol, but different signs. There are two connections in the example, namely $\{Ls, \neg Lx\}$ and $\{Mx, \neg Ms\}$. A connection is called complementary if both literals are identical except for the negation sign. In the example this is only the case after substituting the variable x by the constant s. A mating is a set of connections (such as the two connections in the example). A mating is said to span a matrix (or is called spanning) if each path contains a connection from the mating (which is the case for these two connections). A mating is called complementary if each of its connections is complementary.

If, for a given matrix M, there exists a mating C that spans M, and a substitution σ such that $C\sigma$ is complementary, then M is a valid formula. As just noted, the premise of this theorem is true for this example; hence its validity may be concluded.

The following example demonstrates an additional feature not present in the previous one.

$$\begin{array}{ccc} & \neg Pfx & \neg Pa \\ Pffa & Px & \end{array}$$

Here the three connections of the matrix are illustrated with connecting lines as is usually done. While this mating spans the matrix, there is no substitution that makes it complementary. Yet the formula is valid. The point is that one needs to account for the possibility of considering multiple instances of clauses and to specify the connections in the instances in which the literal occurrence is contained. In the present case one needs two instances of the middle clause, the left connection enters the first instance, the right connection leaves the second instance, and the vertical connection connects the bottom literal of the first instance with the top literal of the second. For illustration one may depict this in the following way as an expanded (or amplified) matrix.

$$\begin{array}{ccc} \neg Pfx_1 & \neg Pfx_2 & \neg Pa \\ Pffa & Px_1 & Px_2 \end{array}$$

There is no need to explicitly represent multiple copies separately, since obviously the only additional information is the index in association with the connection. Therefore, the following picture suggests a way of representing exactly the same information.

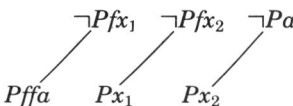

The notion of a path through an indexed matrix derives in a natural way from that of path through the same matrix in its expanded form. Since matrices are just representations of formulas, all notions discussed so far apply to formulas as well. With all these preliminaries, the fundamental theorem on which the connection method is based may now be stated.

Theorem. A formula F is valid iff there exists an indexed form of F, a mating C that spans it, and a substitution σ such that $C\sigma$ is complementary.

On the basis of this characterization, it is now obvious that the present example as well is valid. Take two indexes for the second clause and the mating as in the picture, along with the substitution that makes it complementary. This

mating spans the indexed matrix. For instance, take $\{Pffa, (Px)_1, (\neg Pfx)_2, \neg Pa\}$ out of the four possible paths to see that it contains the connection $\{(Px)_1, (\neg Pfx)_2\}$; similarly for the other three.

While this theorem characterizes the connection method as a framework, it leaves ample room for deriving specific connection calculi from it. Model elimination (Loveland, 1969) historically may be regarded as the first detailed "connection calculus" (although it was, of course, developed from a rather different perspective). To illustrate how this particular calculus would be applied in searching for a proof, consider again the present example.

Select any clause, say the goal clause $Pffa$ (and any literal or subgoal in it, but there is no choice here). Next select a connection containing this subgoal, namely $\{Pffa, (\neg Pfx)_1\}$, and a substitution σ that unifies the connected literals ($\sigma = \{x_1\backslash ffa\}$ in the present case). At this point it is verified that all those paths through the matrix that contain this connection are in fact complementary, so that only the remaining ones have yet to be tested. These include all paths that contain the previous subgoal $Pffa$ and the remainder of the clause connected with it, here the literal $(Px)_1\sigma$. From there, iterate what has just been done for the previous subgoal, and so forth. Briefly, this next iteration might attempt a connection with the rightmost clause, which fails since the terms do not unify. Alternatively, only a second instance of the middle clause may be taken into consideration, from which point the proof is completed in a straightforward way.

There are many ways to improve this particular calculus in terms of its computational properties, just as there are many alternative ways of calculi other than those of the model elimination type. Bibel (1987, see Chapt. 4) presents some of these. They include a particularly interesting one introduced by Prawitz (1970), called matrix reduction. It has been generalized in two different directions by Bibel (1979) and by Murray and Rosenthal (1987). To some extent Maslov's inverse method (Maslov, 1968) also falls into the present category.

While the connection method may use Skolem functions, as do most other methods, it also offers an alternative that dispenses with them and instead uses a relation among the terms originally present in the formula [see Section IV.8 in Bibel (1987) for the details]. In this alternative, the close relationship with Gentzen's calculi is reflected, as the relation has its origin in the proof tree relation of those calculi. Because of this intimate relationship any (partial or complete) connection proof may easily be transformed into the natural deduction proof it represents (Bibel, 1987; Miller, 1987), a feature particularly attractive for a comfortable man–machine interface.

In contrast to resolution, the connection method is an in-place method that characterizes proofs in terms of the given formula (rather than in terms of constructs such as resolvents that derive from the formula), a feature that offers great advantages for the development of strategies. On the other hand, it has been shown that the connection method computationally is at least as good as resolution. Namely, Eder (1989, 1991) has presented a calculus, called the connection structure calculus, that provably may simulate any resolution proof in a linear way.

Connection calculi have been developed for logics other than first-order logic, especially for higher order logic (Andrews, 1989) as well as for modal and intuitionistic logics (Wallen, 1990).

BIBLIOGRAPHY

P. B. Andrews, "Refutations by Matings," *IEEE Trans. Comput.* **C-25,** 193–214 (1976).

P. B. Andrews, "On Connections and Higher-Order Logic," *J. Automat. Reas.* **5,** 257–291 (1989).

W. Bibel and E. Eder, "Methods and Calculi for Automated Deduction," in D. M. Gabbay, C. J. Hogger, and J. A. Robinson, eds., *Handbook of Logic in Artificial Intelligence and Logic Programming,* Oxford University Press, Oxford, 1991, Chapt. 3.

W. Bibel, "An Approach to a Systematic Theorem Proving Procedure in First-Order Logic," *Computing* **12,** 43–55 (1974). [First presented to the GI Annual Conference in 1971.]

W. Bibel, "Tautology Testing with a Generalized Matrix Reduction Method," *Theoret. Comput. Sci.* **8,** 31–44 (1979).

W. Bibel, "Matings in Matrices," *CACM* **26,** 844–852 (1983).

W. Bibel, *Automated Theorem Proving,* 2nd ed., Vieweg Verlag, Braunschweig, Germany, 1987.

W. Bibel and J. Schreiber, "Proof Search in a Gentzen-Like System of First-Order Logic," in *Proceedings of the International Computing Symposium,* North-Holland, Amsterdam, 1975, pp. 205–212.

E. Eder, "An Implementation of a Theorem Prover Based on the Connection Method," in W. Bibel and B. Petkoff, eds., *Artificial Intelligence,* North-Holland, Amsterdam, 1985, pp. 121–128.

E. Eder, "A Comparison of the Resolution Calculus and the Connection Method," in E. Börger, H. Kleine Büning, and M. M. Richter, eds., *Second Workshop on Computer Science Logic,* 1988, Springer, Berlin, 1989, pp. 80–98.

E. Eder, *Relative Complexities of First Order Calculi,* Vieweg, Braunschweig, 1991.

G. Gentzen, "Untersuchungen Über das Logische Schließen," *Math. Z.* **39,** 176–210; 405–431 (1935). English translation in Szabo (1969).

D. W. Loveland, "A Simplified Format for the Model Elimination Theorem-Proving Procedure," *J. ACM* **16**(3), 349–363 (1969).

S. J. Maslov, "The Inverse Method for Establishing Deducibility for Logical Calculi," *Proc. Steklov Inst. Math.* **98,** 26–87 (1968).

D. A. Miller, "A Compact Representation of Proofs," *Studia Logica* **46,** 345–368 (1987).

N. V. Murray and E. Rosenthal, "Inference with Path Resolution and Semantic Graphs," *J. ACM* **34,** 225–254 (1987).

D. Prawitz, "A Proof Procedure with Matrix Reduction," in M. Laudet and co-workers, eds., *Symposium on Automatic Demonstration* (*Lecture Notes in Mathematics, 125*), Springer, Berlin, 1970, pp. 207–214.

M. E. Szabo, ed., *The Collected Papers of Gerhard Gentzen,* North-Holland, Amsterdam, 1969.

L. A. Wallen, *Automated Deduction in Non-Classical Logics,* MIT Press, Cambridge, Mass., 1990.

W. Bibel
Technical University of
Darmstadt

CONNECTIONISM

Connectionism is a highly parallel computational paradigm that appears to promise efficient support of intelligent activities such as vision (Brown, 1984; Ballard, 1984; Sabbah, 1985), knowledge representation (qv) (Quillian, 1968; Collins and Loftus, 1975; Fahlman, 1979; Hinton, 1981; Shastri and Feldman, 1985), natural language understanding (qv) (Cottrell and Small, 1983; Waltz and Pollack, 1985; McClelland and Rumelhart, 1981), learning (see LEARNING, MACHINE) (Hinton, Sejnowski, and Ackley, 1985; Feldman, 1982; Rumelhart and Zipser, 1985), and motor control (Rumelhart and Norman, 1981; Ballard, 1984; Addanki, 1983). Connectionism suggests that pieces of information be represented by very simple computing elements that communicate by exchanging simple messages. Complex computations are carried out by virtue of massively parallel interconnection networks of these elements. The approach is markedly different from the standard (von Neumann) model of computing, in which information is represented as passive patterns, and complexity of computations is dependent on the complexity of the processors (programs) that use this information.

MOTIVATIONS

Connectionism was born out of the difficulties in programming von Neumann computers to perform intelligent tasks and the recognition that the computational paradigm underlying the brain appears to be quite different from that of traditional computers. Intelligent activities require the integration and resolution of large numbers of interacting constraints and pieces of knowledge. For example, visual recognition consists of mapping the many bits of information (intensities at points, line segments, color patches, etc) in the image into an internal model of the object. The integration of these pieces of knowledge is subject to a great many interacting constraints imposed by world knowledge. The difficulty in visual recognition lies in quickly reducing the combinatorial number of possible interpretations to that one that "best" fits the input and constraints. Another example of complexity of intelligent behavior is the task of understanding the spoken sentences "I saw the Grand Canyon flying to New York" or "The cotton clothing is made of is grown in Mississippi." Understanding these sentences requires the interaction of many levels of knowledge, from low level knowledge that helps parse streams of morphemes into words, all the way to higher levels of knowledge that tell you that the Grand Canyon does not fly and that clothing is not grown.

To better understand the weakness of the von Neumann model for programming such tasks, consider the simple, low level vision problem of finding edges in an image. A reasonable image size is 1k × 1K, and edge-finding in such an image typically takes on the order of 10^7 machine cycles. On a state-of-the-art computer, this operation takes 500 ms. The human brain, on the other hand, carries out the entire recognition task in about 200 ms. The difference is really startling when one finds that the switching time of a gate in a computer is on the order of 10 ns, and the switching time of a neuron is on the order of 1 ms; a neuron is 10^5 times slower! Hence the belief that the success of the brain at complex tasks must hinge on its architecture. The brain, it appears, functions in a highly parallel, distributed manner. The computing elements in the brain, the neurons, are relatively simple (although this is a matter of some dispute), and the complexity of behavior appears to arise from massively parallel neuronal interconnection schemes. Connectionism as a field is an attempt to formalize such a computational paradigm and to examine how it furthers our understanding of intelligent systems. It is important to note, however, that the brain is far more complex than the connectionist paradigm, and it would be an overstatement to emphasize the analogy between the brain and the connectionist models as they exist today.

BASIC MODEL

The basic computing elements in connectionism are called units. A single unit (or perhaps a small group of units) represents a piece of knowledge (eg, a symbol, a feature, or a concept). Units maintain an internal potential or activation level. The potential is restricted to a small finite subset of the real line [eg, $(-1, 1)$]. Units are connected to other units in that they send and receive messages from other units. These messages are usually restricted to a small subset of the integers [eg, $(-10, 10)$] and are simple functions of the potential. A single cycle of a unit consists of accepting input messages, updating the potential based on a simple function of the inputs, and generating output messages. By "simple" it is meant that the complexity of computation is strictly limited; multiplication and thresholding are about the most complex operations allowed, and the number of operations is on the order of the number of input lines to the unit. It is important to note that the update computation usually integrates the input over many cycles.

For example, consider a fragment of a network that recognizes the written words BIT and TAB (Fig. 1). The lower layer of the network contains three sets of units. Units in the first set represent possible letters in the first position of the input, units in the second set represent possible letters in the second position of the input, and so on. By "represent" it is meant that the potential of a unit specifies the confidence that the letter represented by the unit occurred in that position in the input. For example, high potential for the B unit in the first set signifies high confidence that the first letter is a B. These units generate their outputs by suitably scaling and truncating their potentials. The higher layer consists of two units, one each for the words BIT and TAB. The potentials of the word

units specify the confidence that the input is that word. The word units update their potentials in direct proportion to their inputs. The connections in Figure 1, as specified by the arrows, are from the lower to the higher level. The operation of the network is as follows: if the net is presented with BIT as the input, the B, I, and T units in the first, second, and third position sets slowly integrate the input and increase in potential. This increase is reflected in an increase in the output messages of these units. The higher level units are continuously integrating their inputs, and hence the BIT unit increases its potential. The TAB unit, not getting any input, will remain at low potential. Eventually the BIT unit will saturate (reach maximum potential), and the input is then said to be recognized. This particular scenario is really quite simplistic; noise in the input will easily cause both units to saturate, but as shown below, connectionism has more machinery that helps build realistic networks.

Units are formally defined in terms of a 7-tuple, $(q, i, v, p, f, g, h,)$ (eg, Feldman and Ballard, 1982):

q, a small (<10) set of states

i, a small (~ 10) set of input tokens (usually the numbers 0, 1, . . . , 10)

v, a small set of outputs similar to the inputs

p, a small subset of the real line (eg, $[0, 1]$) that constitutes the internal potential of the unit

$f: q \times i \times p \Rightarrow p$, a next potential function

$g: q \times i \times p \Rightarrow q$, a next state function

$h: q \times i \times p \Rightarrow v$, a next output function

The function f usually adds a fraction of the normalized sum of the inputs to its current potential; g is typically based on potential; and h is a simple real-to-integer conversion of the potential. Note that even though p theoretically has infinite points, once implemented on a digital machine a unit becomes a finite-state automaton.

A link is defined by a triple, (S, D, W) (eg, Feldman and Ballard, 1982):

S, the source of the connection

D, the destination unit of the connection

W, a number from a small subset of the real line, called the weight of the link. Typically weights are both negative and positive; negative weights are termed inhibitory and positive weights, excitatory.

A link works by taking the output of the source unit, multiplying it by the weight, and delivering it as input to the destination unit. Quite often, the weight of a link is associated with the input site, reducing a link to a pair (S, D).

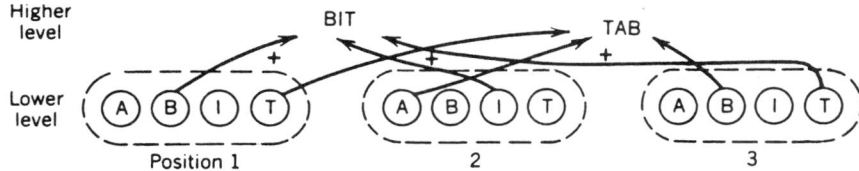

Figure 1. A simple network to recognize the words BIT and TAB.

A connectionist network is said to have a completed a computation when it has formed a stable coalition (Feldman and Ballard, 1982). When a correctly set-up network is given an input, the units spend a certain amount of time exchanging messages and updating their potentials. Eventually the network settles into a stable state. In this state the only units that have high potential are those that constitute the object that has been identified. All of the other units are at a low potential. The units that are active form a mutual support group and keep each other active. Such a mutual support group is termed a *stable coalition.*

The framework of connectionism as described above is sparse, leaving many details to the individual researcher. However, a core set of issues must be considered in the development of any connectionist system: representation of knowledge, choice of the three functions of the units, construction of the network, and the behavior prediction of the network. The first of these issues (representation) divides current connectionist research into two distinct approaches. The *localist* approach advocates the *unit-value principle,* which suggests that every concept or hypothesis be represented by a unique unit (Feldman and Ballard, 1982). The *distributionist* approach suggests that concepts and hypotheses are represented by patterns of activations over large numbers of units (see Hinton, Sejnowski, and Ackley, 1985). The architectures and behaviors of localist and distributionist networks differ enough that it is useful to divide further details of connectionist nets into these two categories.

LOCALIST CONNECTIONISM

Localism requires that each concept or hypothesis about the world be represented by one unit (as in Fig. 1). Links represent one of two relationships between hypotheses or concepts: support (excitatory) or opposition (inhibitory); this is akin to the logical A ⇒ B and A ⇒ NOT B. Localist nets tend to form hierarchical layers of units. This reflects the hierarchical nature of most problem spaces, the efficiency of hierarchical computations, and the ease with which IS.A and PART.OF relationships can be wired up using the one-unit one-concept approach and excitatory links. Building localist networks has a strong empirical component to it. This is primarily because formally deriving connectionist structures for a given task is difficult (with some exceptions, eg, Shastri and Feldman, 1985). However, there exist powerful heuristics and techniques for building localist networks.

Lateral Inhibition and Positive Feedback

With noisy input, all the letter units in Figure 1 will have some potential, and the whole network will eventually saturate at the peak potential. Lateral inhibition is a powerful technique to overcome such saturation effects (Feldman and Ballard, 1982) and is based on the idea that units that represent competing hypotheses should compete directly with each other. In the example, the individual letter units in each position set are competing hypotheses; each position in the input can have only one letter. Lateral inhibition sets up the competition among the units of a position set by allowing them to mutually inhibit each other. Lateral inhibition consists of setting up a complete graph of links between the units of a position set such that the weight of every link of the graph is −1 (see Fig. 2). This mutually inhibitory network is called a *winner-take-all* (WTA) net because it can be shown that it allows only one unit to reach peak potential; this unit is the one with the highest integral of input over an initial portion of the network's operation. WTAs sharpen the competition among the units of a class and significantly lower the overall level of activation in the network. The ideas underlying lateral inhibition can be extended to interactions between position sets. For example, given that the vocabulary does not consist of all possible combinations of the letters, the existence of certain letters in one position inhibits/supports the existence of other letters in different positions of the input. These interset links also increase the speed of decision making and help alleviate saturation effects.

Consider a recognition task in which a particular feature of the input is obscured by noise and a spurious feature is present nearby. With the usual bottom-up excitation and lateral inhibition, the spurious feature will quickly rise to peak confidence and the actual feature will be suppressed (see PROCESSING, BOTTOM-UP AND TOP-DOWN). The networks described thus far will not recover from this state. In conjunction with modified potential and output functions, positive feedback can help circumvent such states. In positive feedback, also called top-down excitation, links run from high to low level units, thus allowing high level knowledge (perhaps from context information) to guide the behavior of lower units (Sabbah, 1985; McClelland and Rumelhart, 1981; Ballard, 1984). Units are defined to include a second state that is entered when the potential reaches the peak value. The potential function (f) of the first state is modified to include a spontaneous decay component. In the second state f is set to nothing but decay. The output function of the second state is modi-

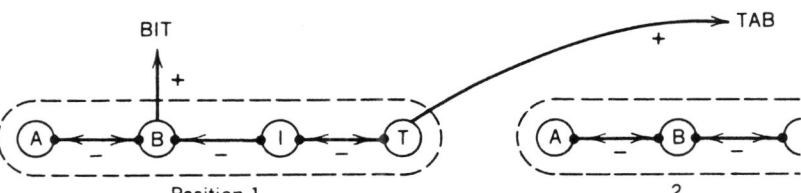

Figure 2. Lateral inhibition in the example of Figure 1.

Position 1

fied to clamp the output to zero. Hence, in the manner of the refractory period of neurons, units accept no input and generate no output in the second state. A unit in the second state will therefore take no part in the computation and will decay in its potential until it falls back into the first state. With these modifications a correct stable coalition will gently oscillate between the two states. In the noisy case it can be shown that if a spurious concept goes high, it enters the refractory state. During this time it can no longer inhibit the correct concept. Further, positive feedback can help raise the potential of the correct concept to a level where it is competitive with the spurious concept. Figure 3 shows the earlier example, complete with positive feedback, as it might look in a fully implemented connectionist net.

Cross-Talk, Binding, and Learning

Representing two new concepts at the same time, for example, red ball and green stick, leads to difficulties in localist nets. Given that the concepts red, green, ball, and stick exist in the system, the first problem is actually linking red to ball and green to stick and is called the *binding problem.* The second, called the *cross-talk problem,* is preventing the linking of red to stick and green to ball.

Cross-talk is usually prevented by detecting spatial or temporal order in the input (Sabbah, 1985). A possible mechanism for binding consists of forming dynamic links between concepts via a multilayered network in which each unit in a layer is connected to a fixed number of units in the next layer, and so on. If the last layer wraps around to the first, any unit in the first layer can set up a link with any other unit in that layer, even if the units have limited fan-out. Unfortunately, once a link has been set up, the units in that link can no longer participate in other links, and the efficacy of the scheme drops very quickly (Feldman, 1982).

Learning in connectionist nets is based on changing the weights on links. There is a long history of research into learning networks based on the Hebbian notion that the link between two units should be strengthened if the two units are active together (Hebb, 1949). However, making arbitrary connections is limited by the fan-out of the units, although the dynamic link approach can be used to extend the fan-out of units (Feldman, 1982). Another approach is to ensure that the network has many "free" units that are randomly connected to concept units. These free units are recruited in order to form a new combination out of existing concepts (Feldman, 1982). Unfortunately, none of these schemes have proved to be practically useful.

Predictability and Convergence

The previous discussion refers to networks "completing" their computations. It is actually a difficult matter to decide when a network has generated its answer because units continue to compute and communicate in the final state. A closely related issue is that of proving from the network structure that the net will actually converge to the desired answer in any situation. In practice, the final state of the system is obvious in its relative stability; building networks to perform given tasks is not a black art. Most localist systems are empirical in nature, and arguments about their predictability are rooted in the experimental verifications of the behaviors of the systems and their substructures (eg, Ballard, 1984; Sabbah, 1985). Formal proofs of behavior have yet to be developed for localist nets, though they will certainly prove useful as systems get larger. However, it must be pointed out that the units and networks of connectionism are nonlinear elements, and it is well known that convergence proofs for nonlinear systems are almost nonexistent. The directions toward a theory of convergence lie in the analysis of f (and perhaps g). The key appears to be to consider inputs to a unit to be pieces of evidence that must be integrated to make a decision. Unfortunately, existing theories of evidence (eg, Shafer, 1976) have not been helpful in analyzing localist nets. Shastri and Feldman (1985) have developed a theory of evidential reasoning that appears to be successful for a limited class of networks used in knowledge representation.

DISTRIBUTED CONNECTIONISM

The distributed approach to connectionism is based on representing concepts as patterns over large numbers of units (eg, Hinton, Sejnowski, and Ackley, 1985). Each unit is said to represent a *microfeature,* a part of a concept that is too small to have a name. Concepts that are similar share microfeatures (units), and therefore similar concepts have similar patterns. The sharing of units also results in efficiency of representation. (In the limit, N concepts require N binary units in a localist representation but only $\log_2 N$ units in a distributed representation.) Representing concepts as patterns over large numbers of microfeatures also increases the reliability of the network. The net can now suffer limited local damage without impairing performance significantly. The links represent *microrelations* (inferences, constraints), parts of a regular inference that are too small to be individually named. Though the actual update functions used by the units are different, the mechanisms of computation (ie, the units exchange activations and update potentials) are

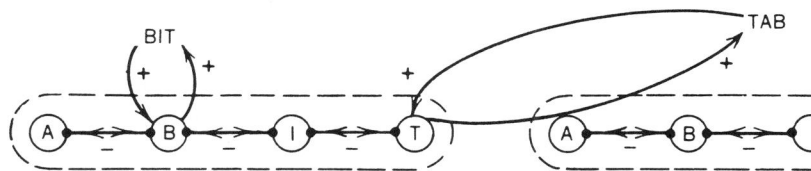

Figure 3. Network with positive-feedback links added.

much the same for distributed and localist networks. As in the localist approach, a distributed network finally settles on a stable coalition of active units, a pattern that least violates the microconstraints imposed by the links. The answer is the entire pattern of activation, instead of one high level unit as in localist nets.

Representing concepts as patterns over shared microfeatures admits a first-order solution to the problem of generalizing concepts. Activating or changing a concept in a computation consists of changing the pattern of activity and weights over the constituent units and links. Since these units and links are shared by similar concepts, the change is transferred to them. If the concepts were entirely unrelated, such transferrence would be interference, but because in reality the concepts are interrelated, the effect is a form of generalization.

The IS.A structure is relatively easy to implement in distributed networks. A pattern that represents a concept can be thought of as consisting of many subpatterns, each subpattern naming and providing the distinguishing information for its class in the hierarchy. For example, one subpattern distinguishes the concept within its immediate peer group, as in SPRINGER and ENGLISH among SPANIELS. Another distinguishes SPANIELS within DOGS and so on. The shared microfeatures, eg, the subpattern SPRINGER is shared with the concept SPANIEL, also give rise to inheritance via the transferrence mechanism described above. Unfortunately, once the pattern–subpattern relationship is used to represent IS.A information, it becomes very difficult to represent the PART.OF structure within distributed nets. Additionally, concepts are represented by entire patterns of activation, and it becomes difficult to represent concept and subconcept at the same time. A possible approach to representing PART.OF structure is to recognize that the subconcepts that compose a concept are actually role–filler pairs and to allow the subpatterns to represent such pairs. The representation now becomes significantly more complex than before, and the cross-talk problem restricts the network to activating only one concept at a time.

Construction of Networks

Hand-wiring a distributed network to perform a given task is practically impossible for obvious reasons: given that units and links have no immediately accessible semantics, there is no basis for choosing patterns of activation or interconnection. It is therefore clear that a successful distributed approach must be based on networks learning the appropriate representations. The approach must include a formal framework from which it must be possible to derive the learning rules and the proofs of convergence of the system once it has learned. An approach that has had some success in this is based on statistical mechanics (Hinton, Sejnowski, and Ackley, 1985). Consider a network built of units that have only two states, [0, 1], with the links still representing microinferences. If the structure of the links is such (eg, completely symmetrical connections) that each unit can decide if the global sum of constraint violations (or relation matches) is changed by switching state, and if such updates are car-

ried out asynchronously, it can be shown that the system will converge to a network optimum. Unfortunately, the optimum may be local in the space of network patterns. Overcoming local minima is made possible by introducing noise in the form of a global parameter called *temperature*. Each unit now switches to a better state with a probability dependent on the goodness of the state and the temperature:

$$p(\text{switch}) = \frac{1}{1 + e^{\Delta E/T}}$$

where E is the goodness of state and T the temperature. When T is high, units flip even if doing so takes the state away from an optimum point. When T is low, units flip only toward an optimum. The activation or confidence of a microfeature is now represented by the probability that its state is 1. The claim is that for any given probability p, there exists a temperature trajectory in time from high T to low T such that "cooling" the system thus will result in a probability p of the system being in its globally optimum state. The behavior of such a system is akin to many systems analyzed in statistical mechanics, and the cooling referred to above is exactly the process of annealing for atomic systems. It is also possible to derive a weight change algorithm, which offers one form of learning in such networks, from the physics of such systems (Hinton, Sejnowski, and Ackley, 1985). Unfortunately, although the approach is very elegant and offers the first formal convergence and learning theories in connectionism, in practice it has proved difficult and time consuming to get a system to learn even simple patterns.

APPLICATIONS AND SUMMARY

The ideas of connectionism date back to the work of McCulloch and Pitts (1943) and the perceptrons (qv) of Rosenblatt (1962). These early computational models of neural networks, (qv) used computing elements that were simple threshold logic units (TLUs). TLUs are devices that have binary output that goes high if the weighted sum of the inputs exceeds a threshold. Rosenblatt's work consisted primarily of showing that systems composed of multiple layers of such TLUs exhibited learning behavior in pattern association tasks. Unfortunately, the behavior of these networks did not scale to interesting tasks, and Minsky and Papert (1969) later showed that this was because the TLUs were too simple. Note that the elements of modern connectionism are more complex; they are multistate, continuous potential machines.

Around the same time, Quillian (1968) proposed using marker propagation between nodes of a semantic network to carry out associative matches. The computation was a simple digital version of connectionism, with the drawback that the network was quickly flooded with markers. A similar idea reappeared later in the form of NETL, a system developed by Fahlman (1979) that also used marker passing to carry out limited inference in a semantic network. Collins and Loftus (1975) attempted to overcome the problem of marker saturation by using analog messages and computations. They used decay in the activation to control saturation and, although the approach worked, it was fragile in that the behavior was very sensitive to the setting of the decay parameter. More recently Feldman and Shastri (1985) invoked much of modern connectionism, developed a theory of entropy, and proposed an inference mechanism that not only controls saturation but also attempts to provide a framework for evidential reasoning.

Vision was the arena in which modern connectionism made its initial appearance. Low level vision computations appear to be particularly well suited to connectionist computations because they require the integration of large numbers of simple, interacting pieces of knowledge. Ballard (1984) shows how different formulations of connectionist nets can be used for low level computations such as shape from shading, computing optical flow, and so on (see SHAPE; VISUAL MOTION ANALYSIS). It is possible to argue that connectionism is well suited to the entire vision enterprise. Viewed in one way, there is not much difference between the kinds of computations performed at the low, mid, and high levels of vision. Sabbah (1985) describes a system in which the basic connectionist paradigm is used for all levels of the vision task, from line finding to object recognition (qv). Although the system appears to show that connectionist vision is viable, full generality of connectionism for all of vision has yet to be demonstrated. Feldman (1985) attacks the interaction and representation issues for the highest levels of knowledge in vision. He attempts to provide a framework for representing knowledge of both individual objects and their spatial relationships in specific situations. The proposal has to be fully worked out but is the first approach to integrating a computational model of low and midlevel vision with the higher levels of knowledge that a system must possess.

Natural language is much like vision, in that early stages of processing appear to require much interaction between many pieces of different kinds of knowledge. Cottrell and Small (1983) propose a connectionist scheme for the disambiguation of word senses in a sentence. Waltz and Pollack (1985) also describe a connectionist architecture for parsing sentences. Early experiments show that the approaches do produce appropriate behavior (eg, handling garden-path sentences), but current implementations are quite small.

Connectionism has also provided a computational framework for the study of both high and low level motor control (Ballard, 1984). Rumelhart and Norman (1981) developed a connectionist system that simulated the interactions of high-level movement commands for finger placement in typing. Their model replicated many of the common error patterns found in skilled typists. Addanki (1983) complete the circle by showing that modern connectionism is a viable computational paradigm for the study of neural motor control circuits. The study shows how connectionist models can account for some of the nonlinearities and anomalies inherent in the oculomotor systems of the higher primates.

In summary, it can be said that connectionism offers a computational paradigm that appears to be well-suited for the synthesis of intelligent systems (Feldman, 1985; Feldman and Ballard, 1985). Although they are still in the early stages of development, formal theories of convergence, learning, and computation are immature, and the many systems that do exist today attack only a small portion of their domains. The wide range of applicability and the feasibility of overcoming the combinatorial nature of AI problems make connectionism very attractive. The simplicity of computing elements permits implementing connectionist nets in the technologies of tomorrow, and though it may be argued that connectionist nets do rely on massive amounts of communication (expensive in architectures), the expense may be outweighed by the gains in controlling combinatorial growth. It seems clear that connectionism holds much promise for future research in AI, and that this promise will be fulfilled as the properties of connectionist nets are better understood.

BIBLIOGRAPHY

S. Addanki, *Applications of Connectionist Techniques to Simulations of Motor Control Systems,* Ph.D. dissertation, University of Rochester, Rochester, N.Y., 1983.

D. H. Ballard, "Parameter Nets: Towards a Theory of Low-Level Vision," *Artif. Intell.* **22,** 235–267 (1984).

D. H. Ballard, "Task Frames in Robot Manipulation," *Proceedings of the Fourth National Conference on AI,* Austin, Texas, 1984, pp. 16–22.

C. M. Brown, "Computer Vision and Natural Constraints," *Science* **224**(4655), 1299–1305 (1984).

A. M. Collins and E. F. Loftus, "A Spreading Activation Theory of Semantic Processing," *Psychol. Rev.* **82,** 407–428 (1975).

G. W. Cottrell and S. L. Small, "A Connectionist Scheme for Modeling Word Sense Disambiguation," *Cog. Brain Theory* **6,** 89–120 (1983).

S. E. Fahlman, *NETL: A System for Representing and Using Real World Knowledge,* MIT Press, Cambridge, Mass., 1979.

J. A. Feldman, "Dynamic Connections in Neural Networks," *Biol. Cyber.* **46,** 27–39 (1982).

J. A. Feldman, "Four Frame Suffice: A Provisional Model of Vision and Space," *Behav. Brain Sci.* **8,** 265–289 (1985).

J. A. Feldman, ed., Special issue on connectionist models and their applications, *Cogn. Sci.* **9**(1) (1985).

J. A. Feldman and D. H. Ballard, "Connectionist Models and Their Properties," *Cogn. Sci.* **6,** 205–254 (1982).

J. A. Feldman, D. H. Ballard, C. M. Brown, and G. S. Dell, *Rochester Connectionist Papers: 1979–1985,* Technical Report 172, Computer Science Department, University of Rochester, Rochester, N.Y., 1985.

D. O. Hebb, *"The Organization of Behavior,"* Wiley, New York, 1949.

G. E. Hinton, "Implementing Semantic Networks in Parallel Hardware," in G. E. Hinton and J. A. Andersen, eds., *Parallel Models of Associative Memory,* Erlbaum, Hillsdale, N.J., 1981.

G. E. Hinton, T. Sejnowski, and D. Ackley, "Boltzmann Machines: Constraint Satisfaction Machines That Learn," *Cogn. Sci.* **9,** 147–169 (1985).

J. C. McClelland and D. E. Rumelhart, "An Interactive Model of Context Effects in Letter Perception. Part I: Basic Findings," *Psychol. Rev.* **88,** 375–407 (1981).

W. S. McCulloch and W. Pitts, "A Logical Calculus of the Ideas

Immanent in Neural Nets," *Bull. Math. Biophys.* **5,** 115–137 (1943).

M. Minsky and S. Papert, *Perceptrons,* MIT Press, Cambridge, Mass., 1969.

R. M. Quillian, "Semantic Memory," in M. Minsky, ed., *Semantic Information Processing,* MIT Press, Cambridge, Mass., pp. 227–270, 1968.

F. Rosenblatt, *Principles of Neurodynamics,* Spartan, New York, 1962.

D. E. Rumelhart and D. A. Norman, *Simulating a Skilled Typist: A Study of Skilled Cognitive-Motor Performance,* Technical Report 8102, Institute for Cognitive Science, University of California, San Diego, 1981.

D. E. Rumelhart and D. Zipser, "Feature Discovery by Competitive Learning," *Cogn. Sci.* **9,** 75–112 (1985).

D. Sabbah, "Computing with Connections in Visual Recognition of Origami Objects," *Cogn. Sci.* **9,** 25–50 (1985).

L. Shastri and J. A. Feldman, "Evidential Reasoning in Semantic Networks: A Formal Theory," *Proceedings of the Ninth IJCAI,* Los Angeles, Calif., 1985, pp. 465–474.

D. L. Waltz and J. B. Pollack, "Massively Parallel Parsing: A Strongly Interactive Model of Natural Language Interpretation," *Cogn. Sci.* **9,** 51–74 (1985).

General References

G. S. Dell, *A Spreading Activation Theory of Retrieval in Sentence Production,* Technical Report 21, Department of Psychology, University of Rochester, Rochester, N.Y., 1984.

M. Fanty, *A Connectionist Simulator for the Butterfly,* Technical Report 164, Computer Science Department, University of Rochester, Rochester, N.Y., 1986.

W. Kornfeld, *Using Parallel Processing for Problem Solving,* AI Memo 561, MIT AI Labs., Cambridge, Mass., 1979.

G. Shafer, *A Mathematical Theory of Evidence,* Princeton University Press, Princeton, N.J., 1976.

S. L. Small, L. Shastri, M. L. Brucks, S. G. Kaufman, G. W. Cottrell, and S. Addanki, *ISCON: A Network Construction Aid and Simulator for Connectionist Models,* Technical Report 109, Computer Science Department, University of Rochester, Rochester, N.Y., 1983.

S. Addanki
IBM

CONNIVER

CONNIVER is a model and language for general problem solving (qv) developed by Sussman and McDermott at the MIT AI Lab as a means of overcoming PLANNER's backtracking problem by introducing multiprocessing control in which a process with a certain data environment stays around to be resumed later as long as it is directed by some external program (see also CYBERNETICS). See G. Sussman and D. V. McDermott, "Why Conniving Is Better than Planning," MIT AI Lab Memo No. 2554, 1972; G. Sussman and D. V. McDermott, "From PLANNER to CONNIVER—A Genetic Approach," in *Proceedings of the Fall Joint Computer Conference,* Anaheim, Calif., Dec. 1972, AFIPS Press, Reston, Va., pp. 1171–1179.

A. Hanyong Yuhan
AT&T Bell Laboratories

CONSTRAINT LOGIC PROGRAMMING

Constraint logic programming (CLP) is a generalization of logic programming (LP) where unification, the basic operation of LP, is replaced by the more general concept of constraint solving over a computation domain. CLP defines a class of languages parameterized by the computation domain. Defining a CLP language amounts to choosing a computation domain, selecting a set of allowed constraints, and designing a constraint solver for the constraints. CLP combines the advantages of LP (declarative semantics, nondeterminism, and partial answer) with the efficiency of special-purpose constraint-solving algorithms. As a consequence, it reduces the programming effort for numerous applications, yet preserves most of the efficiency of specialized tools. Especially attractive is the combination of nondeterminism and constraint solving for combinatorial problems.

The term CLP was coined (Jaffar and Lassez, 1987) to characterize an increasing number of systems, the most well-known being PROLOG III (Colmerauer, 1987), CLP($\mathscr{R}$) (Jaffar and Michaylov, 1987), Trilogy (Voda, 1988), and CHIP (Dincbas and co-workers, 1988; Van Hentenryck, 1989).

SYNTAX

A CLP program is defined by a collection of clauses

$$H \leftarrow C_1 \wedge \ldots \wedge C_n \Diamond B_1 \wedge \ldots \wedge B_m$$

where H, B_1, $\ldots$, B_m are atoms and $C_1 \ldots$, C_n are constraints. A CLP query is a clause without head:

$$\leftarrow C_1 \wedge \ldots \wedge C_n \Diamond B_1 \wedge \ldots \wedge B_m$$

From a syntactical point of view, LP is a particular CLP language where the only constraints are equations on first-order terms.

DECLARATIVE SEMANTICS

The declarative semantics of LP is given in terms of logical consequences. An answer in a LP language for a query G and a program P is a substitution θ such that $\forall G\theta$ is logically implied by the program, denoted

$$P \models \forall G\theta$$

where $\forall F$ represents the universal closure of F. Hence a substitution can be seen as a finite representation of a potentially infinite set of solutions as any ground instance of $G\theta$ is logically implied by the program.

An answer in a CLP language for a query G and a program P is a conjunction of constraints $C_1 \wedge \ldots \wedge C_n$ such that

$$P, D \models \forall(C_1 \wedge \ldots \wedge C_n \Rightarrow G)$$

where D is the theory axiomatizing the computation domain. Once again the conjunction of constraints can be seen as a finite representation of a potentially infinite set of solutions as any valuation for the variables in G that satisfy $C_1 \wedge \ldots \wedge C_n$ in D is a solution.

Once again LP is a special case of CLP, as a substitution is a particular representation for a conjunction of equations. Particular care is devoted in CLP to present the conjunction of constraints in a way that makes one or all solutions apparent. It is, however, difficult to formalize this concept independently from the constraint-solver.

OPERATIONAL SEMANTICS

The operational semantics of LP is a top-down search procedure of an SLD tree where each node is labeled with a conjunction of atoms. The transition between nodes, denoted $\rightarrow$, is given by the rule

$$\frac{\begin{array}{l} H \leftarrow B_1, \ldots, B_m \in P \\ H\theta = A\theta \end{array}}{A \wedge G \mapsto B_1\theta \wedge \ldots \wedge B_m\theta \wedge G\theta}$$

where the clause has been renamed properly not to share any variable with the goal. Note that the order in a conjunction is irrelevant so that any atom can be selected by the above rule. The success set of the program is given by the set of nodes labeled with an empty goal, the result of a node being the projection of the accumulated substitutions on the query variables.

The operational semantics of CLP is a generalization where the nodes are labeled with configurations $\langle G, \sigma \rangle$ where G and σ are, respectively, conjunctions of atoms and constraints. The transition relation between nodes is now defined by the rule

$$\frac{\begin{array}{l} H \leftarrow C_1, \ldots, C_n \diamond B_1, \ldots, B_m \in P \\ D \models (\exists)\, (\sigma \wedge C_1 \wedge \ldots \wedge C_n \wedge H = A) \end{array}}{\langle A \wedge G, \sigma \rangle \mapsto \langle B_1 \wedge \ldots \wedge B_m \wedge G, \sigma \wedge C_1 \wedge}$$

$$\ldots \wedge C_n \wedge H = A \rangle$$

where $(\exists)F$ denotes the existential closure of F. Note that a CLP language generally represents the conjunction of constraints in some normal form to improve efficiency and incrementality. This normal form may or may not be connected with the output form.

The success set of the program is given by the set of nodes labeled with configurations whose goal part is empty, the result of a node being the constraint part. It appears clearly here that CLP is a generalization of LP where unification has been replaced by constraint solving. Various equivalence results have been studied (Jaffar and Lassez, 1987) between the declarative, operational, and fixpoint semantics; the key result was that the main properties of LP carry over to CLP, provided that the computation domain and its associated constraint solver satisfy some natural properties.

COMPUTATION DOMAINS

Various computation domains have been investigated in recent years, but only some of them will be mentioned here. Linear rational (resp. real) arithmetics (CHIP, CLP($\mathscr{R}$), PROLOG III) consider linear equations, inequalities, and disequations ($\neq$) over rational (resp. real) numbers. These systems are based on a simplex algorithm generalized to account for incrementality and disequations.

Boolean algebra (CHIP, PROLOG III) considers equations over Boolean terms. The constraint solver is based on Boolean unification (CHIP) or on a combination of SL resolution and saturation (PROLOG III). Finite domains (CHIP) consider equations, inequalities, and disequations over natural numbers as well as some symbolic constraints provided that the variables range over finite sets of values. The constraint solver is based on consistency techniques (Mackworth, 1977). Presburger arithmetics (Trilogy) consider linear equations, inequalities, and disequations over integers. Many other domains exist, including concepts such as strings, lists (PROLOG III), intervals (BNR-PROLOG), and various forms of terms (LOGIN).

EXTENSIONS

CLP is an active research area, and many extensions to the scheme have been proposed, including concurrent constraint programming (Saraswat and Rinard, 1990) and constraint hierarchies (Borning and co-workers, 1989).

BIBLIOGRAPHY

A. Borning and co-workers, "Constraint Hierarchies and Logic Programming," in *Proceedings of the Sixth International Conference on Logic Programming*, Lisbon, June 1989, MIT Press, Cambridge, Mass., 1989.

A. Colmerauer, "Opening the Prolog-III Universe," *BYTE* **12**(9) (Aug. 1987).

M. Dincbas and co-workers, "The Constraint Logic Programming Language CHIP," in *Proceedings of the International Conference on Fifth-Generation Computing Systems*, Tokyo, Dec. 1988.

J. Jaffar and J. Lassez, "Constraint Logic Programming," in *POPL-87*, Munich, Jan. 1987.

J. Jaffar and S. Michaylov, "Methodology and Implementation of a CLP System," in *Proceedings of the Fourth International Conference on Logic Programming*, Melbourne, Australia, May 1987.

A. K. Mackworth, "Consistency in Networks of Relations," *Artif. Intell.* **8**(1), 99–118 (1977).

V. Saraswat and M. Rinard, "Concurrent Constraint Programming," in *POPL-90*, San Francisco, Calif., Jan. 1990.

P. Van Hentenryck, *Constraint Satisfaction in Logic Programming*, MIT Press, Cambridge, Mass., 1989.

P. Voda, *The Constraint Language Trilogy: Semantics and Computations*, Technical Report, Complete Logic Systems, North Vancouver, B.C., Canada, 1988.

PASCAL VAN HENTENRYCK
Brown University

CONSTRAINT NETWORKS

Constraint-based reasoning is a paradigm for formulating knowledge as a set of constraints without specifying the method by which these constraints are to be satisfied. A variety of techniques have been developed for finding partial or complete solutions for different kinds of constraint expressions. These have been successfully applied to diverse tasks such as design, diagnosis, truth maintenance, scheduling, spatiotemporal reasoning, logic programming (qv), and user interface. Constraint networks are graphical representations used to guide strategies for solving constraint satisfaction problems (CSPs).

Basic Definitions

A constraint network (CN) consists of a finite set of variables, $X = \{X_1, \ldots, X_n\}$, each associated with a domain of discrete values, $D_1, \ldots, D_n$ and a set of constraints, $\{C_1, \ldots, C_t\}$. Each of the constraints is expressed as a relation, defined on some subset of variables, whose tuples are all the simultaneous value assignments to the members of this variable subset that, as far as this constraint alone is concerned, are legal. (This does not mean that the actual representation of any constraint is necessarily in the form of its defining relation, but that the relation can, in principle, be generated using the constraint's specification without the need to consult other constraints in the network.) Formally, a constraint C_i has two parts: (1) the subset of variables $S_i = \{X_{i_1}, \ldots, X_{i_{j(i)}}\}$, on which it is defined, called a *constraint subset*, and (2) a relation rel_i defined over S_i: $rel_i \subseteq D_{i_1} \times \cdots \times D_{i_{j(i)}}$. Because many properties of a CN depend on the structure of the constraint subsets, the scheme of a CN is defined as the set of subsets on which constraints are defined, namely, scheme (CN) = $\{S_1, S_2, \ldots, S_t\}$, $S_i \subseteq X$. The projection of a relation ρ on a subset of variables $U = U_1, \ldots, U_l$ is given by $\Pi_U (\rho) = \{x_u = (x_{u_1}, \ldots, x_{u_l}) \mid \exists \bar{x} \in \rho, \bar{x} \text{ is an extension of } x_u\}$.

An assignment of a unique domain value to each member of some subset of variables is called an *instantiation*. An instantiation is said to satisfy a given constraint C_i if the partial assignment specified by the instantiation does not violate C_i (ie, it belongs to the projection of rel_i on the common variables). An instantiation is said to be legal or locally consistent if it satisfies all the (relevant) constraints of the network.

A legal instantiation of all the variables of a constraint network is called a solution of the network, and the set of all solutions is a relation, ρ, defined on the set of all variables. This relation is said to be represented by the constraint network. Formally,

$$\rho = \{(X_1 = x_1, \ldots, X_n = x_n) \mid \forall \, S_i \in scheme, \ \Pi_{S_i} \rho \subseteq rel_i\} \quad (1)$$

Example 1. Figure 1a presents a simplified version of a crossword puzzle (see CONSTRAINT SATISFACTION). The variables are X_1 (1, horizontal), X_2 (2, vertical), X_3 (3, vertical), X_4 (4, horizontal), and X_5 (5, horizontal). The scheme of this problem is $\{X_1X_2, X_1X_3, X_4X_2, X_4X_3, X_5X_2\}$. The domains and some constraints are specified in Figure 1b. A tuple in the relation associated with this puzzle is the solution: (X_1 = sheet, X_2 = earn, X_3 = ten, X_4 = aron, X_5 = no).

Typical tasks defined in connection with constraint networks are to determine whether a solution exists, to find one or all of the solutions, to determine whether an instantiation of some subset of the variables is a partial solution (ie, is part of a global solution), etc. These tasks are collectively called constraint satisfaction problems.

Techniques used in processing constraint networks can be classified into three categories. The first category consists of search techniques for systematic exploration of the space of all solutions. The most common algorithm in this class is *backtracking* (qv), which traverses the search space in a depth-first fashion. The second category is *consistency algorithms* for transforming a CN into more explicit representation. These are used primarily in a preprocessing phase, to improve the performance of the subsequent backtracking search, but can be incorporated into the search procedure itself. Third are the *structure-driven algorithms*, which exploit the topological features of the network to guide the search. Structure-driven algorithms can support both the consistency algorithms as well as the backtracking search.

This survey concentrates on techniques of the third kind, namely, structure-based algorithms. These together with backtracking and consistency algorithms (see CONSTRAINT SATISFACTION) give a complete picture of the available techniques. A brief summary of backtracking and consistency enforcing procedures is presented next.

BACKTRACKING AND CONSISTENCY-ENFORCING STRATEGIES

The standard solution procedure for solving constraint-satisfaction problems is backtracking search. The algorithm typically considers the variables in some order and, starting with the first, assigns a provisional value to each

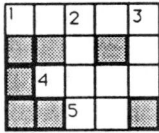

D_1 = (hoses, laser, sheet, snail, steer)

D_2 = D_4 = (hike, aron, keet, earn, same)

D_3 = (run, sun, let, yes, eat, ten)

D_5 = (no, be, us, it)

C_{12} = ((hoses,same), (laser,same), (sheet,earn), (snail,aron), (steer,earn))

Figure 1. A crossword puzzle and its CN representation.

(a)   (b)

successive variable in turn as long as the assigned values are consistent with those assigned in the past. When, in the process, a variable is encountered such that none of its domain values is consistent with previous assignments (a situation referred to as a dead-end), backtracking takes place. That is, the value assigned to the immediately preceding variable is replaced, and the search continues in a systematic way until either a solution is found or until it may be concluded that no such solution exists.

Improving backtracking efficiency amounts to reducing the size of its expanded search space. This depends on the way the constraints are represented (ie, on the extent of their explicitness), the order of variables instantiation, and, when one solution suffices, on the order in which values are assigned to each variable.

Using these factors to improve the performance of backtracking algorithms, researchers have developed procedures of two types: those that are employed in advance of performing the search, and those that are used dynamically during search. The former include a variety of *consistency-enforcing algorithms* (Montanari, 1974; Mackworth, 1977; Freuder, 1978). These transform a given constraint network into an equivalent, yet more explicit, network by deducing new constraints to be added on to the network.

Intuitively, a consistency-enforcing algorithm will make any partial solution of a small subnetwork extensible to some surrounding network. For example, the most basic consistency algorithm, called arc-consistency or 2-consistency (also known as constraint propagation and constraint relaxation), ensures that any legal value in the domain of a single variable has a legal match in any other selected variable. Path-consistency (or 3-consistency) algorithms ensure that any consistent solution to a two-variable subnetwork is extensible to any third variable, and, in general, i-consistency algorithms guarantee that any locally consistent instantiation of $i - 1$ variables is extensible to any ith variable.

Deciding the level of consistency that should be enforced on the network is not a clear-cut choice. Generally speaking, backtracking will benefit from representations that are as explicit as possible, having higher consistency level. However, the complexity of enforcing i-consistency is exponential in i. As a result, there is a trade-off between the effort spent on preprocessing and that spent on search (backtracking). Experimental analyses of this trade-off have been published (Dechter and Meiri, 1989; Dechter, 1990; Haralick and Elliott, 1980).

Variable orderings' decisions have also received much consideration, and several heuristics have been proposed (Freuder, 1982; Dechter and Pearl, 1989), all following the intuition that tightly constrained variables should come first. Strategies for dynamically improving the pruning power of backtracking can be conveniently classified as *look-ahead schemes* and *look-back schemes*. Look-ahead schemes are invoked whenever the algorithm is preparing to assign a value to the next variable. Some of the functions that such schemes perform are:

1. Calculate and record the way in which the current instantiations restrict future variables. This process has been referred to as constraint propagation. Examples include Waltz's (1975) algorithm and forward checking (Haralick and Elliott, 1980).

2. Decide which variable to instantiate next (when the order is not predetermined). Generally, it is advantageous to first instantiate variables that maximally constrain the rest of the search space. Therefore, the variable participating in the highest number of constraints is usually selected (Freuder, 1982; Purdom, 1983; Stone and Stone, 1986).

3. Decide which value to assign to the next variable (when there is more than one candidate). Generally, for finding one solution, an attempt is made to assign a value that maximizes the number of options available for future assignments (Haralick and Elliott, 1980; Dechter and Pearl, 1987).

Look-back schemes are invoked when the algorithm encounters a dead end and prepares for the backtracking step. These schemes perform two functions:

1. Decide how far to backtrack. By analyzing the reasons for the dead end, it is often possible to go back directly to the source of failure instead of to the immediate predecessor in the ordering. This idea is often referred to as *backjumping* (Gaschnig, 1979).

2. Record the reasons for the dead end in the form of new constraints so that the same conflicts will not arise again in a later search. Terms used to describe this idea are constraint recording and no-good constraints. Dependency-directed backtracking incorporates both backjumping and no-goods recording (Stallman and Sussman, 1977). Constraint recording can also be viewed as a form of explanation-based learning (EBL).

GRAPH-BASED ALGORITHMS

Graphical Representations

Graphical properties of CN were initially investigated through the class of binary constraint networks (Freuder, 1982). A *binary constraint network* is one in which every constraint subset involves at most two variables. In this case the network can be associated with a constraint graph, where each node represents a variable, and the arcs connect nodes whose variables are explicitly constrained; namely, they are members of the network's scheme. Figure 2 shows the constraint graph associated with the crossword puzzle in Figure 1.

A graphical representation of higher order networks can be provided by *hypergraphs,* where again, nodes represent the variables, and hyperarcs (drawn as regions) group those variables that belong to the same constraint. Two variations of this representation that can be used to facilitate structure-driven algorithms are primal-constraint graph and dual-constraint graph. A primal-constraint graph (a generalization of the binary constraint graph) represents variables by nodes and associates an arc with any two nodes residing in the same constraint. A dual-constraint graph represents each constraint subset

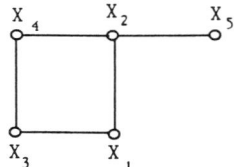

Figure 2. A constraint graph of the crossword puzzle.

by a node (also called a c-variable) and associates a labeled arc with any two nodes whose constraint subsets share variables. The arcs are labeled by the shared variables.

For example, Figure 3 depicts the primal, the dual, and the hypergraph representations of a CN with variables A, B, C, D, E, F and constraints on the subsets (ABC), (AEF), (CDE) and (ACE). The constraints themselves are symbolically given by the inequalities: $A + B \leq C$, $A + E \leq F$, $C + D \leq E$, $A + C \leq E$, where the domains of each variable are the integers $[2, 3, 4, 5, 6]$.

The dual constraint graph can be viewed as a transformation of a nonbinary network into a special type of binary network: the domain of the c-variables ranges over all possible value combinations permitted by the corresponding constraints, and any two adjacent c-variables must obey the restriction that their shared variables should have the same values (ie, the c-variables are bounded by equality constraints). For instance, the domain of the c-variable ABC is {224, 225, 226, 235, 236, 325, 326, 246, 426, 336} and the binary constraint between ABC and CDE is given by the relation: $rel_{ABC,CDE}$ = {(224, 415),(224, 426)}. Viewed in this way, any network can be solved by binary networks techniques.

Solving Tree Networks

Almost all the known structure-based techniques rely on the observation that binary constraint networks whose constraint graph is a tree can be solved in linear time (Freuder, 1982; Mackworth and Freuder, 1984; Dechter and Pearl, 1987). The solution of tree-structured networks are discussed, and later it is shown how they can be used to facilitate the solution of general CN.

Given a tree network over n variables (Fig. 4a), the first step of the tree-algorithm is to generate a rooted-directed tree. Each node in this tree (excluding the root) has one parent node directed toward it and may have several child nodes, directed away from it. Nodes with no children are called leaves. An ordering, $d = X_1, X_2, \ldots, X_n$, is then enforced such that a parent always precedes its

children. In the second step, the algorithm processes each arc (and its associated constraint) from leaves to root, in an orderly layered fashion. For each directed arc from X_i to X_j it removes a value from the domain of X_i if it has no consistent match in the domain of X_j. Finally, after the root is processed, a backtracking algorithm is used to find a solution along the ordering d.

It can be shown that the algorithm is linear in the number of variables. In particular, backtracking, which in general is an exponential procedure, is guaranteed to find a solution without facing any dead ends. The tree algorithm is sketched by the following procedures:

Tree-Algorithm (T)

1. begin
2.   generate a rooted tree ordering, $d = X_1, \ldots, X_n$.
3.   for i=n to 1 by -1 do
4.   revise$(X_{p(i)},X_i)$; $X_{p(i)}$ denotes the parent of X_i.
5.   if the domain of $X_{p(i)}$ is empty, stop (no solution exists).
6.   end
7.   use backtracking to instantiate variables along d.
8. end.

The revise procedure (Mackworth, 1977) is defined by:

Revise (X_j,X_i)

1. begin
2.   for each $v \in D_j$ do
3.   if there is no $u \in D_i$ s.t. $(X_j =v,X_i=u)$ is consistent,
4.   delete v from D_j.
5.   end.
6. end.

The complexity of the tree-consistency algorithm is bounded by $O(nk^2)$ steps where k bounds the domain size, because an ordering (step 2) can be produced in linear time, whereas the revise procedure, which is bounded by k^2 steps, is executed at most n times (loop 3–6). The tree algorithm is an instance of a general class of ordered algorithms, to be discussed next.

Directional and Adaptive Consistency

In general, a problem is considered easy when it admits a solution in polynomial time. In the context of constraint

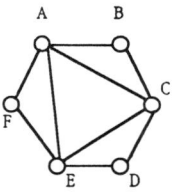

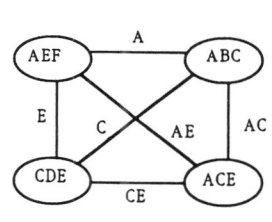

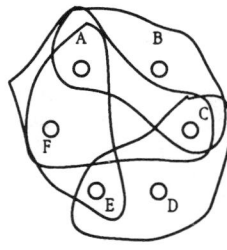

Figure 3. Primal and dual constraint graphs of a CSP.   **(a)**   **(b)**   **(c)**

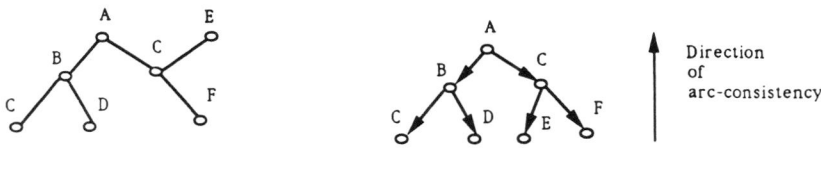

Figure 4. A tree network.

networks, a problem is easy if an algorithm like backtracking can solve it in a backtrack-free manner, ie, without dead ends, thus producing a solution in time linear in the number of variables and constraints. This concept has prompted a theoretical investigation (Freuder, 1982, 1985; Dechter and Pearl, 1987, 1989) into the level of local consistency that suffices for ensuring a backtrack-free search. The theory had identified topological features that determine this level of consistency, and has yielded tractable algorithms for transforming some networks into backtrack-free representations. The following paragraphs present a summary of this theory.

The theory is centered on a graphical parameter called width, and the definitions are relative to the primal constraint graph. An ordered (primal) constraint graph is defined as one in which the nodes are linearly ordered to reflect the sequence of variable assignments executed by backtracking algorithm. The width of a node is the number of arcs that connect that node to previous ones, the width of an ordering is the maximum width of all nodes, and the width of a graph is the minimum width of all orderings of that graph.

Figure 5 presents three possible orderings of the constraint graph of Figure 2. The width of node X_2 in the first ordering (from the left) is three, whereas in the second ordering it is two. It can be shown that no ordering can achieve width lower than two, hence the width of this constraint graph is two. [The graph has cycle, and it is known that only trees are width-one graphs (Freuder, 1982).]

The width of a graph can be determined by a greedy algorithm. The algorithm selects a node having the least number of neighbors and puts it last in the ordering. This node is then removed (together with its adjacent edges), and the algorithm proceeds recursively on the remaining graph. The ordering of Figure 5c, for instance, could have been generated by this procedure.

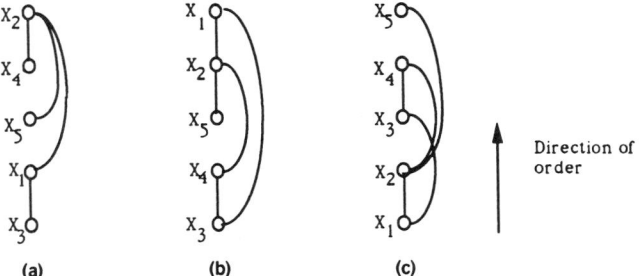

Figure 5. Three orderings of a constraint graph, representing widths of three, two, and two, respectively.

The connection between width and local consistency requires further elaboration. A constraint network is said to be *i*-consistent if for any set of $i - 1$ variables along with values for each that satisfy all the constraints among them, there exists a value for any *i*th variable, such that the *i* values together satisfy all the constraints among the *i* variables. Strong *i*-consistency holds when the problem is *j*-consistent for every $j \le i$. Given an ordering *d*, directional *i*-consistency along *d* (or *d-i*-consistency) requires that any consistent instantiation of $i - 1$ variables can be consistently extended only by variables that succeed all of them in the ordering *d*. Strong *d-i*-consistency is defined accordingly. The general relationship between the width of a network and the amount of local consistency required for tractability is summarized in the following theorem:

Theorem. An ordered constraint graph is backtrack-free if the level of directional strong consistency along this order is greater than the width of the ordered graph.

In particular, if the graph has width-one (ie, it is a tree), a directional two-consistency is sufficient. If it is width-two, strong directional three-consistency would suffice. The intuition behind this theorem rests on the fact that when backtrack works along a given ordering, it tests for consistency only among past and current variables, considering the relevant local constraints. If these constraints already ensure that a locally consistent partial solution will remain consistent relative to future variables, dead end will not occur. This required level of local consistency is related to the number of constraints future variables have with current variables. That is, when a future variable is constrained with many past variables (ie, when it has a high width), the required level of local consistency among past variables is higher.

Because most problem instances will not satisfy the desired relationship between the width and the consistency level, it is possible to try to push one of these two factors until the relationship holds. One possibility is to increase the level of directional consistency until it matches the width of the problem. Specifically, if a width-$i - 1$ problem is not *i*-consistent, algorithms enforcing directional *i*-consistency can be applied to it.

Consider, first, the case of width − 1. According to the theorem, if a tree is ordered along a width-one ordering and then enforced with directional two-consistency (ie, arc consistency), the result is a backtrack-free problem. Indeed, the tree algorithm presented earlier does exactly that: the rooted-tree ordering is a width-one ordering (each node has only one adjacent predecessor) and its internal loop (steps 3–6) enforces directional arc consistency along this ordering.

This seems to lead to a general scheme: given a constraint network, find its width w and enforce directional (strong) $(w + 1)$ consistency along the appropriate ordering, followed by a backtrack-free instantiation of the variables. Unfortunately, enforcing directional i-consistency $(i > 2)$ often requires the addition of new constraints, and these constraints are reflected by additional arcs in the constraint graph, which may cause the width to increase. The resulting problem will be directional-consistent, but its width may now be greater than w, thus backtrack-free search is no longer guaranteed. The next algorithm (Dechter and Pearl, 1987; Seidel, 1981) overcomes this difficulty.

Given an ordering d, algorithm adaptive consistency establishes directional i-consistency recursively, when i changes from node to node to match its width at the time of processing. This is accomplished by processing nodes in decreasing order, so that by the time a node is processed its final width is determined and the required level of consistency can be achieved. Let *parents(X)* denote the set of predecessors connected to X, when it is called for processing.

Adaptive Consistency $(X_1, \ldots, X_n)$

begin

1. for i=n to 1 by -1 do
2.   Compute parents(X_i)
3.   connect all elements in parents(X_i) (if they are not yet connected)
4.   perform consistency$(X_i,$ parents$(X_i))$
5. endfor

End

The procedure consistency(V, set) generates and records tuples of those variables in the set that are consistent both internally and with at least one value of V. The procedure may impose new constraints over clusters of variables as well as tighten existing constraints. When adaptive consistency terminates, backtracking can solve the problem in the order prescribed without any dead ends. It is important to realize that the topology of the resulting graph, called an *induced graph,* can be found prior to executing the procedure by recursively (in a decreasing order) connecting any two parents sharing a common successor.

Consider the ordering X_1, X_2, X_3, X_4, X_5 shown in Figure 5c. Adaptive consistency proceeds from X_5 to X_1 and imposes constraints on the parents of each processed variable. X_5 is chosen first and because it has only one parent, X_2, the algorithm merely tightens the domain of X_2, if necessary [which amounts to enforcing arc consistency on (X_2, X_5)]. X_4 is selected next and, having width two, the algorithm enforces a three-consistency on its parents $[X_3, X_2]$. This operation may require that a constraint between X_2 and X_3 be added, and in that case an arc (X_2, X_3) is added to the constraint graph. When the algorithm reaches node X_3, its width is two and, therefore a three-consistency is enforced on X_3's parents $[X_2, X_1]$. The arc

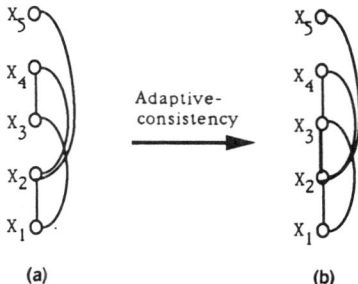

Figure 6. A constraint graph (a) before and (b) after adaptive consistency.

(X_1, X_2) already exists so this operation may merely tighten the corresponding constraint. The resulting graph is given in Figure 6b.

Let $w(d)$ be the width of the ordering d and let $w^*(d)$ be the width of the induced graph. The complexity of solving a problem using the adaptive consistency preprocessing phase and then backtracking (freely) along the order d is dominated by the former. The worst-case complexity of the *consistency(V, parents (V))* step, is exponential in the cardinality of V and its parent set, because it actually solves a network of constraints having that many variables. Because the maximal size of the parent set is equal to the width of the induced graph, solving the constraint network along the ordering d is bounded by $O(n \cdot \exp(w^*(d) + 1))$. Notice that had adaptive consistency been applied on the ordering in Figure 6b, the resulting induced width would have been three.

w^*-Tractability

It seems that w^*, the minimum induced width, can be used to identify classes of easy problems. Namely, if the primal graph of a constraint network has $w^* \leq r$ then the problem can be solved in $O(\exp(r))$ steps. However, finding the smallest induced width of a graph and its corresponding ordering is an NP-complete problem (Arnborg, 1985). Nevertheless, deciding whether the w^* of a problem is less than or equal to r is polynomial in r. In particular, deciding if a problem instance has small induced width, say $w^* = 1$, $w^* = 2$, or $w^* = 3$, can be efficiently determined. In trees, the width is equal to the induced width ($= 1$); hence any minimal width ordering is also an optimal induced-width ordering, and it can be found in linear time. A linear time algorithm recognizing problems having $w^* > 2$ is also available (Arnborg, 1985; Bertele and Brioschi, 1972). The algorithm selects as last a node having a smallest degree, eliminates it, connects its neighbors in the residual graph (if they were not previously connected), and continues recursively. If the result is an ordering having $w^* > 2$ it can be concluded that the graph, too, has $w^* > 2$. Otherwise, the network has induced width equals two (also called a regular width-two network).

In spite of the nice structure and complexity guarantees that are provided by adaptive consistency, experimental results have shown that unless w^* is very low (namely, one or two) the algorithm is too expensive on the average. Its cost stems from the determination to ensure an absolutely backtrack-free search, often investing a disproportional amount of computation trying to eliminate just a few remaining dead ends. Simple backtracking, which can potentially encounter all such dead ends, would often be more efficient. This suggests that a less vigorous consistency enforcing algorithm can be appropriate, striking a compromise between preprocessing and search. Indeed, bounded directional *i*-consistency algorithms (Dechter and Pearl, 1987) fulfill such a compromise by enforcing a limited directional consistency and eliminating as many dead ends as possible within some predetermined computational bounds. Instead of recording one constraint on all the parents of a node, these procedures record a set of smaller constraints on size-*i* subsets of the parents. It was shown that on classes of artificially generated CN, directional two-consistency eliminates a large subset of the dead ends, whereas directional three-consistency eliminates almost all (Dechter and Meiri, 1989).

Acyclic Networks and Tree-Clustering

Although w^* provides a measure of tractability, some problems admit easy solution, independently of their width. This happens when the induced width of an ordering is identical to its width (namely, no arcs are added by adaptive consistency), and when constraint recording consumes only a linear amount of computation (in the problem input). *Acyclic constraint networks* (ACNs) or acyclic CSPs have these two properties, and were first characterized and evaluated in the relational database literature (Beeri and co-workers, 1983). These can be viewed as trees in the dual-graph representation. Clearly, if the dual graph of a nonbinary CN is a tree, the tree algorithm would apply. But even when the dual graph is not a tree, some of its arcs may be redundant, and their removal might result in a tree structure. An arc in the dual graph can be deleted if its variables are shared by every arc along an alternative path between the two end points. The subgraph resulting from removal of redundant arcs is called a *join graph*.

For instance, the arc between (*AEF*) and (*ABC*) in Figure 7a can be eliminated because the variable *A* is common along the cycle (*AEF*)–*A*–(*ABC*)–*AC*–(*ACE*)–*AE*–(*AEF*), and so a consistent assignment to *A* is ensured by the remaining arcs. By a similar argument it is possible to remove the arcs labeled *C* and *E*, thus turning the join graph into a tree, called a *join tree* (Fig. 7b). In general, finding whether such a transformation exists is a tractable problem (Maier, 1983).

Constraint networks that can be represented by a join tree are called acyclic networks and can be solved efficiently as follows. If there are *p* constraints in the join tree (ie, *p* c-variables), each allowing at most *l* tuples, then a straightforward application of the algorithm developed for a tree of singletons (using $O(nk^2)$ steps) would yield a solution in $O(pl^2)$ steps. A further refinement based on indexing can reduce the complexity to $O(p \cdot l \cdot \log l)$ steps (Dechter and Pearl, 1989).

A generalization of acyclic networks called webs (Dalkey, 1991) permits backtrack-free solutions for a larger class of network topologies. This requires, however, that the constraints possess special properties, typical of causal mechanisms (Dechter and Pearl, 1991). Web structures are conveniently represented by a form of directed constraint networks (or causal networks) which indicate the ordering along which solutions can be obtained backtrack-free.

Recognizing Acyclic Networks. Several efficient procedures for identifying an *ACN* and finding a representative join tree have been described (Maier, 1983). One scheme that proved particularly useful is based on the observation that a CN is acyclic if and only if its primal graph is both chordal and conformal (Beeri and co-workers, 1983). A graph is *chordal* if every cycle of a length of at least four has a chord, ie, an edge joining two nonconsecutive vertices along the cycle. A graph is *conformal* if each of its maximal cliques (ie, subsets of nodes that are completely connected) corresponds to a constraint in the original CN. The chordality of a graph can be identified via an ordering called the maximal cardinality ordering, (*m*-ordering); it always assigns the next number to the node having the largest set of already numbered neighbors (breaking ties arbitrarily). For instance, the ordering in Figure 5c is an *m*-ordering, whereas in Figures 5a and 5b it is not.

It can be shown (Tarjan and Yannakakis, 1984) that in an *m*-ordered chordal graph, the parents of each node must be completely connected. If, in addition, the maximal cliques coincide with the constraint subsets of the original CN, both conditions for acyclicity would be satisfied. Because for chordal graphs each node and its parent set constitutes a clique, the maximal cliques can be identified in linear time, and then a join tree can be constructed by connecting each maximal clique to an ancestor clique with which it shares the largest set of variables.

As noted, acyclic networks have a chordal primal graph, thus their width and induced width are identical along an *m*-ordering. Hence, if applied to such ordered CNs, adaptive consistency will add no arcs to the graph. Also, because all tuples on each parent set are already locally consistent, the amount of constraint recording is bounded by $O(l \cdot \log l)$, resulting in an overall complexity bound of $O(n \cdot l \cdot \log l)$ steps.

Tree Clustering. The above recognition process suggests a scheme for combining subsets of constraints into higher level constraints until a join tree emerges (when the network is not acyclic to begin with). Such a tree-clustering scheme is based on a triangulation algorithm (Tarjan and Yannakakis, 1984) that transforms any graph into a

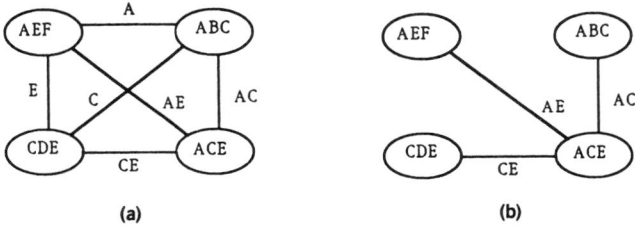

(a)   (b)

Figure 7. A dual-constraint graph and its join tree.

chordal graph by filling in edges (recursively) in a reverse order of the m-ordering, connecting any two nonadjacent nodes that are connected via nodes higher up in the ordering. The maximal cliques of the resulting chordal graph are the clusters necessary for forming an *ACN*. These clusters represent subproblems that must be independently solved, an operation that is exponential in the clique's size.

It can be shown that the maximal clique size, generated that way, equals $w^* + 1$; thus the whole transformation (into a join tree) is, once again, exponential in w^*. Although tree clustering differs conceptually from adaptive consistency, it effectively results in the same behavior and same performance. When applied on the same ordered constraint graph both, algorithms produce the same induced graph. In other words, adaptive consistency can be viewed as an effective scheme for assembling *ACNs*. It seems desirable to use adaptive consistency when one-time solutions are required, and to use tree-clustering when the network is used as a knowledge base subjected to repeated queries. Note that although tree clustering can be applied in any ordering, the m-ordering produces close to optimal induced width (for chordal graphs it is indeed optimal.)

A subclass of *ACNs* for which all maximal cliques have the same size is often characterized by a special class of chordal graphs called k-trees. A k-tree is a chordal graph whose maximal clues are of size $k + 1$, and it can be defined recursively as follows. (1) A complete graph with k vertices is a k-tree. (2) A k-tree with r vertices can be extended to $r + 1$ vertices by connecting the new vertex to the vertices in any clique of size k. In particular, one-trees are ordinary trees.

The addition of each vertex (step 2) generates a new clique of size $k + 1$, and by associating each new clique with one parent clique that shares k vertices with it, a join tree is obtained. The example of an acyclic CN given in Figure 7 is indeed a two-tree because its primal graph could be constructed in the order A, B, C, E, D, F. k-trees were investigated extensively in the graph theoretical literature. In particular, it was shown that a graph can be embedded in a k-tree if and only if it has an induced width $w^* = k$. Detailed discussions of the properties of k-trees are available (Arnborg, 1985; Freuder, 1990; Rossi and Montanari, 1989).

Decomposition into Nonseparable Components

Another approach that exploits the structure of the constraint graph involves the notion of nonseparable components (Freuder, 1985; Dechter and Pearl, 1987). Similar to tree clustering, the idea is to identify subsets of variables that, when grouped together, transform the problem into a tree; the nonseparable components of a graph have this property (Even, 1979).

A connected graph, $G = (V, E)$ (V, a set of nodes, E, a set of edges), is said to have a *separation node* v if there exists nodes a and b such that all paths connecting a and b pass through v. A graph that has a separation node is called separable, and one that has none is called *nonseparable*. A subgraph with no separation nodes is called a

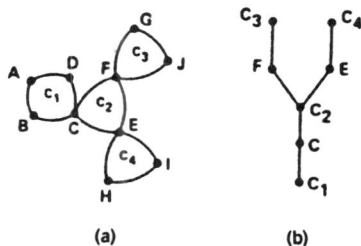

Figure 8. A graph and its decomposition into nonseparable components.

nonseparable component. An $O\,(|E|)$ algorithm exists for finding all the nonseparable components and the separation nodes; it is based on a depth-first search traversal of the graph, called a DFS ordering (Even, 1979).

Let G be a graph and super-G the tree whose nodes represents the components $C_1, C_2, \ldots, C_r$ and the separating nodes $V_1, V_2, \ldots, V_t$ (Fig. 8b). Figure 8 shows a graph G, its components, and its separating vertices. Once the components are recognized, each represents a subproblem that, when solved, defines the domains of a new compound variable. The tree algorithm can then be applied to the resulting problem, treating each component as a compound variable.

The complexity of this approach is $O\,(nk^r)$, where r is the size of the largest component. Therefore, in cases where the constraint network has a decomposition into small clusters of nonseparable components, the resulting performance is improved. In comparing the nonseperable component method with either tree clustering or adaptive consistency, it is immediately realized that it does not improve the worst-case complexity, namely, $w^* \le r$ and, frequently, $w^* < r$. Nevertheless, this scheme is the most natural extension of trees and can also be extended to the dual-graph representation.

The Cycle Cutset Scheme

The decomposition method presented in this section is based on identifying a *cycle cutset*, that is, a set of nodes that, once removed, would render the constraint graph cycle-free. The method uses trees in a different way then previous schemes, exploiting the fact that variable instantiation changes the effective connectivity of the constraint graph. In Figure 9, for example, instantiating X_2 to some value, say *hike*, renders the choices of X_1 and X_5 independent as if the pathway $X_1 - X_2 - X_5$ were blocked at X_2. Similarly, this instantiation blocks the pathway $X_1 - X_2 - X_4$, leaving only one path between any two variables. The effective constraint graph for the rest of the variables is shown in Figure 9b, where the instantiated variable X_2 is duplicated for each of its neighbors.

When the group of instantiated variables constitutes a cycle cutset, the remaining network is cycle free and can be solved by the tree algorithm. In the example above, X_2 cuts the single cycle $X_1 - X_2 - X_3 - X_4$ and renders the graph in Figure 9b cycle free. In most practical cases it would take more than a single variable to cut all the cycles in the graph. Thus a general way of solving a problem

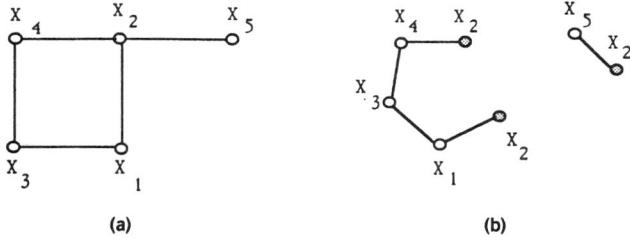

Figure 9. An instantiated variable cuts its own cycles.

of which the constraint graph contains cycles is to find a consistent instantiation of the variables in a cycle cutset and solve the remaining problem by the tree algorithm. If a solution to the restricted problem is found, then a solution to the entire problem is at hand. If not, another instantiation of the cycle cutset variables should be considered until a solution is found. Thus if the task is to solve the crossword puzzle (Fig. 1), first $X_2 = hike$ must be assumed, and the remaining tree problem is solved. If no solution is found, it is assumed that $X_2 = keel$ and another attempt is made, until a solution is found.

The complexity of the cycle cutset scheme is bounded by $O(\exp(c))$ steps, where c is the size of the cycle cutset, because the utmost number of times the tree algorithm is invoked equals the number of partial solutions to the cutset variables. Because finding a minimal-size cycle cutset is NP hard, it will be more practical to incorporate this scheme within a general problem solver such as backtracking. Because backtracking works by progressively instantiating sets of variables, all that is necessary is to keep track of the connectivity status of the constraint graph. As soon as the set of instantiated variables constitutes a cycle cutset, the search algorithm is switched to the tree algorithm on the remaining problem, ie, either finding a consistent extension for the remaining variables (thus finding a solution to the entire problem), or concluding that no such extension exists (in which case backtracking takes place and another instantiation is tried) (Dechter, 1990).

Graph-Based Schemes for Improving Backtracking

Two ideas for improving the look-back phases of backtracking have received wide attention (Gaschnig, 1979; Stallman and Sussman, 1977; Doyle, 1979; Dechter, 1990). These have often been referred to as *backjumping* and constraint recording in the constraint literature, but are more commonly recognized under the umbrella name dependency-directed backtracking in the truth-maintenance (qv) literature. Backjumping suggests jumping back several levels in the search tree to a variable that may have relevance to the current dead end, whereas constraint recording suggests storing the reasons for the dead end in the form of new constraints, so the same conflict will not arise again later in the search (ie, recording nogoods).

In this section, graph-based variants of both backjumping and constraint recording are presented. Exploiting the structure of the problem often simplifies the implementa-

tion of these schemes and enables an assessment of the complexity, using network parameters.

Backjumping. The idea of going back several levels (in a dead-end situation) rather than retreating to the chronologically most recent decision was exploited independently in Gaschnig (1979), where the term backjumping was introduced, and in Stallman and Sussman (1977). The idea has since been used in truth-maintenance systems (Doyle, 1979) and in intelligent backtracking in PROLOG (Bruynooghe and Pereira, 1984). Gaschnig's algorithm uses a marking technique where each variable maintains a pointer to the highest ancestor found incompatible with any of its values. In case of a dead end, the algorithm can safely jump directly to the ancestor pointed to by the dead end variable. Although this scheme retains only one bit of information with each variable, it requires an additional computation with each consistency check.

Graph-based backjumping (Dechter, 1990) extracts knowledge about dependencies from the constraint graph alone. Whenever a deadend occurs at a particular variable X, the algorithm backs up to the most recent variable connected to X in the graph. Consider, for instance, the ordered constraint graph in Figure 5a. If the search is performed in the order X_1, X_2, X_3, X_4, X_5 and a dead end occurs at X_5, the algorithm will jump back to variable X_2 because X_5 is not connected to either X_3 or X_4. If the variable to which the algorithm retreats has no more values, it should back up to the most recent parent of both the original variable and the new dead-end variable, and so on.

Whereas the implementation of this backjumping scheme would, in general, require a careful maintenance of each variable's parents set (Dechter, 1990), some orderings facilitate an especially simple implementation. If a depth-first search is used on the constraint graph (to generate a DFS tree) and then backjumping is conducted in an in-order traversal of the DFS tree (Even, 1979), finding the jump-back destination amounts to following a very simple rule: if a dead end occurred at variable X, go back to the parent of X in the DFS tree. Consider, once again, the example in Figure 2. A DFS tree of this graph is given in Figure 10b, and an in-order traversal of this tree is (X_1, X_2, X_5, X_4, X_3). If a dead end occurs at node X_4, the algorithm retreats to its parent X_2. When backjumping is performed on a DFS ordering of the variables, its complexity can be bounded by $O(\exp(m))$ steps, m being the depth of the DFS tree. However, like many other parameters encountered, finding a minimal-depth DFS tree is NP-hard.

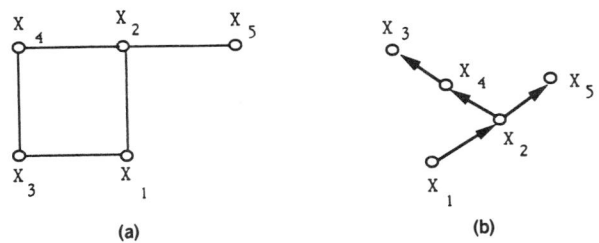

Figure 10. A DFS tree and its ordering.

Constraint-Recording or Dependency-Directed Backtracking. An opportunity to learn or deduce a new constraint is presented whenever backtracking encounters a dead end, ie, when the current instantiation $s = (X_1 = x_1, \ldots, X_{i-1} = x_{i-1})$ cannot be extended by any value of the next variable X_i. In such a case s is in conflict with X_i, or s is a *conflict set*. Had the problem included an explicit constraint prohibiting the instantiation s, the current dead end would have been avoided. However, there is no point recording such a constraint at this stage, because under the backtracking control strategy it will not recur. If, on the other hand, the set s contains one or more subsets that are also in conflict with X_i, then recording this information in the form of new explicit constraints might prove useful in the future because future states may contain these subsets. The constraint graph provides an easy way for identifying subsets of s that are in conflict; by removing from s all assignments of variables that are not connected to X_i, a subset is obtained that is still in conflict with X_i, because all the removed assignments are irrelevant to this dead end.

The procedure of graph-based dependency-directed backtracking [sometimes called graph-based constraint recording (Dechter, 1990)] implements this idea by recording these conflict sets as a new constraint on each dead end. Specifically, if the subsets $s' = (X_{i1} = x_{i1}, \ldots, X_{it} = x_{it}$ is the assignments in s connected to X_i, the procedure records a constraint on variables $X_{i1}, \ldots, X_{it}$ which disallows the tuple s'. For instance, suppose that backtracking solves the crossword puzzle using the ordering $(X_1, X_2, X_5, X_4, X_3)$ and is currently at state $(X_1 = snail, X_2 = aron, X_5 = no, X_4 = dock)$. This state cannot be extended by any value of X_4. Obviously, the tuple $(X_1 = snail, X_2 = aron, X_5 = no, X_4 = dock)$ is a conflict set; however, both the instantiations $X_2 = aron$ and $X_5 = no$ are irrelevant to this conflict, because there is no explicit constraint between X_3 and X_2 or between X_3 and X_5. Therefore, the tuple $(X_4 = down, X_1 = snail)$ will be disallowed by recording a new constraint on X_1 and X_4.

Dependency-directed backtracking can be performed on any variable ordering. Its worst-case complexity is $O(\exp(w^*))$ steps, thus providing yet another scheme whose performance is governed by the induced width.

CONCLUSION

Throughout this article several techniques were presented that exploit the structure of the given network. Four graph parameters stood out in the analysis: the induced width w^* (appearing in adaptive consistency, tree clustering, and constraint recording in dependency-directed backtracking), the cycle-cutset size c (appearing in the cycle-cutset method), the depth of a DFS-tree m (in backjumping), and the size of largest nonseparable component r (appearing in the tree-component scheme). It is clear that for any problem structure, the relationship $m \geq r \geq w^*$ holds, and it can also be shown that $w^* \leq c + 1$ (Bertele and Brioschi, 1972). Another parameter mentioned in the literature, bandwidth (Zabih, 1990) is also dominated by w^*. It can be concluded, therefore, that w^* provides the most informative graph parameter, and it can be regarded as an intrinsic measure of the worst-case complexity of any constraint network.

BIBLIOGRAPHY

S. Arnborg, "Efficient Algorithms for Combinatorial Problems on Graphs with Bounded Decomposability—A Survey," *BIT* **25**, 2–23 (1985).

C. Beeri, R. Fagin, D. Maier, and M. Yannakakis, "On the Desirability of Acyclic Database Schemes," *J. ACM* **30**(3), 479–513 (July 1983).

U. Bertele and F. Brioschi, *Nonserial Dynamic Programming*, Academic Press, Inc., New York, 1972.

M. Bruynooghe and L. M. Pereira, "Deduction Revision by Intelligent Backtracking," in J. A. Campbell, ed., *Implementation of Prolog*, Harwood Academic Publishers, New York, 1984, pp. 194–215.

N. C. Dalkey, *Modeling Probability Distributions with WEB Structures*, Technical Report R-164, University of California, Los Angeles, 1991.

R. Dechter, "Enhancement Schemes for Constraint Processing: Backjumping, Learning, and Cutset Decomposition," *Artif. Intell.* **41**(3), 273–312 (Jan. 1990).

R. Dechter, and I. Meiri, "Experimental Evaluation of Preprocessing Techniques in Constraint Satisfaction," in *Proceedings of the Eleventh IJCAI*, Detroit, Mich., Morgan-Kaufmann, San Mateo, Calif., 1989.

R. Dechter, and J. Pearl, "Network-Based Heuristics for Constraint-Satisfaction Problems," *Artif. Intell.* **34**(1), 1–38 (Dec. 1987).

R. Dechter and J. Pearl, "Tree Clustering for Constraint Networks," *Artif. Intell.* 353–366 (1989).

R. Dechter and J. Pearl, "Directed Constraint Networks: A Relational Framework for Causal Modeling," *Proceedings of the Twelfth IJCAI*, Sydney, Australia, Morgan-Kaufmann, San Mateo, Calif., 1991.

J. Doyle, "A Truth Maintenance System," *Artif. Intell.* **12**, 231–272 (1979).

S. Even, *Graph Algorithms*, Computer Science Press, Rockville, Md., 1979.

E. C. Freuder, "Synthesizing Constraint Expression," *CACM* **21**(11), 958–965 (1978).

E. C. Freuder, "A Sufficient Condition for Backtrack-Free Search," *J. ACM* **29**(1), 24–32 (Jan. 1982).

E. C. Freuder, "A Sufficient Condition for Backtrack-Bounded Search," *J. ACM*, **32**(4), 755–761 (Oct. 1985).

E. C. Freuder, "Complexity of k-Structured Constraint Satisfaction Problems," in *Proceedings of the Ninth National Conference on Artificial Intelligence*, Boston, Mass., AAAI, Menlo Park, Calif., 1990, pp. 4–9.

J. Gaschnig, *Performance Measurement and Analysis of Certain Search Algorithms*, Technical Report CMU-CS-79-124, Carnegie Mellon University, Pittsburgh, Pa., 1979.

R. M. Haralick and G. L. Elliott, "Increasing Tree-Search Efficiency for Constraint Satisfaction Problems," *Artif. Intell.* **14**, 263–313 (1980).

A. K. Mackworth "Consistency in Networks of Relations," *Artif. Intell.* **8**(1), 99–118 (1977).

A. K. Mackworth and E. C. Freuder, "The Complexity of Some Polynomial Network Consistency Algorithms for Constraint Satisfaction Problems," *Artif. Intell.* **25**(1) (1984).

D. Maier, *The Theory of Relational Databases,* Computer Science Press, Rockville, Md., 1983.

U. Montanari, "Networks of Constraints: Fundamental Properties and Applications to Picture Processing," *Inform. Sci.* **7,** 95–132 (1974).

P. Purdom, "Search Rearrangement Backtracking and Polynomial Average Time," *Artif. Intell.* **21,** 117–133 (1983).

F. Rossi and U. Montanari, "Exact Solution in Linear Time of Networks of Constraints Using Perfect Relaxation," in *Proceedings First International Principles of Knowledge Representation and Reasoning,* Toronto, Ont., Canada, May, 1989, pp. 394–399.

R. Seidel, "A New Method for Solving Constraint-Satisfaction Problems," in *Proceedings of the Seventh IJCAI,* Vancouver, B.C., Canada, Morgan-Kaufmann, San Mateo, Calif., 1981, pp. 338–342.

R. M. Stallman and G. J. Sussman, "Forward Reasoning and Dependency-Directed Backtracking in a System for Computer-Aided Circuit Analysis," *Artif. Intell.* **9**(2), 135–196 (Oct. 1977).

H. S. Stone and J. M. Stone, *Efficient Search Techniques—An Empirical Study of the N-Queens Problem,* Technical Report RC 12057 (#54343), IBM T. J. Watson Research Center, Yorktown Heights, N.Y., 1986.

R. E. Tarjan and M. Yannakakis, "Simple Linear-Time Algorithms to Test Chordality of Graphs, Test Acyclicity of Hypergraphs and Selectively Reduce Acyclic Hypergraphs," *SIAM J. Comput.* **13**(3), 566–579 (Aug. 1984).

D. Waltz, "Understanding Line Drawings of Scenes with Shadows," in P. H. Winston, ed., *The Psychology of Computer Vision,* McGraw-Hill Book Co., Inc., New York, 1975.

R. Zabih, "Some Applications of Graph Bandwidth to Constraint Satisfaction Problems," in *Proceedings of the Ninth National Conference on AI,* Boston, 1990, AAAI, Menlo Park, Calif., 1990, pp. 46–50.

RINA DECHTER
University of California at
Irvine

CONSTRAINT SATISFACTION

Constraint satisfaction is an umbrella term for a variety of techniques of AI and related disciplines. In this entry attention is focused on the main approaches, such as backtracking, constraint propagation, and cooperative algorithms, with some consideration given to the motivations and techniques underlying other constraint-based systems.

The first class of constraint satisfaction problems considered is those in which one has a set of variables, each to be instantiated in an associated domain and a set of Boolean constraints limiting the set of allowed values for specified subsets of the variables. This general formulation has a wide variety of incarnations in various applications: it is a general search (qv) problem. One standard approach involves backtracking (qv); various forms of "intelligent" backtracking are surveyed. A complementary approach based on the class of consistency algorithms has some nice properties that are described and illustrated.

The second class of problems considered is the numerical optimization problems that arise when one is designing a system to maximize the extent to which the solutions it provides satisfy a large number of local constraints. Algorithms for their solution are based on generalizations of the consistency algorithms for applications primarily in computational vision. These algorithms, which have a high degree of potential parallelism, are variously known as cooperative or probabilistic relaxation algorithms.

One can call these two problem classes Boolean constraint satisfaction problems and constraint optimization problems, respectively. As with all dichotomies, this one is not absolute. Some approaches lie between these two poles; others combine them. There are, in fact, many other dimensions along which one could categorize the area, but this is the best first cut.

BOOLEAN CONSTRAINT SATISFACTION PROBLEMS

A Boolean constraint satisfaction problem (CSP) is characterized as follows: given is a set V of n variables $\{v_1, v_2, \ldots, v_n\}$, associated with each variable v_i is a domain D_i of possible values. On some specified subsets of those variables, there are constraint relations, given that there are subsets of the Cartesian product of the domains of the variables involved. The set of solutions is the largest subset of the Cartesian product of all the given variable domains such that each n-tuple in that set satisfies all the given constraint relations. One may be required to find the entire set of solutions or one member of the set or simply to report if the set of solutions has any members—the decision problem. If the set of solutions is empty, the CSP is unsatisfiable.

A surprisingly large number of seemingly different applications can be formalized in this way. Some of them are enumerated below. Of particular theoretical interest is the map-coloring problem. Consider, for example, the problem of deciding if three colors suffice to color a given planar map such that each region is a different color from each of its neighbors. This is formulated as a Boolean CSP by creating a variable for each region to be colored, associating with each variable the domain {red, green, blue}, and requiring for each pair of adjacent regions that they have different colors. Since the map-coloring problem is known to be NP-complete and is therefore believed inherently to require exponential time to solve, one does not expect to find an efficient polynomial time algorithm to determine if a general CSP is satisfiable.

Various restrictions on the general definition of a CSP are possible. For example, the domains may be required to have a finite number of discrete values. If this is the case, the constraining relations may be specified extensionally as the set of all p-tuples that satisfy the constraint. One may further require that all the relations be unary or binary, that is, that they only constrain individual variables or pairs of variables. These restrictions apply to the map-coloring example above. However, they are not necessary for some of the techniques reported here to be applicable. For example, suppose one were planning the layout of furniture in an office. The position of each item of furniture would be a variable, with an associated domain that would contain an infinite number of pairs (or triples, if rotations are allowed) of real values. Those domains would have to be described intensionally by, for example, describing the boundaries of the connected subspaces permitted for that item. The constraints, such as "The wastebasket must be within three feet of the chair. The door must be unobstructed," must also be specified intensionally using, perhaps, algebraic inequalities on the values of the constrained variables. Moreover, one might have p-ary relations such as "The desk must be between the chair and the door."

Crossword puzzles are used here as a tutorial example of the concepts of constraint satisfaction. Consider the puzzle in Figure 1. To simplify the presentation, assume that one is required to find in the given word list the eight words that correspond to 1 across, 2 down, and so on, with duplicates allowed. The reader should try to solve this simple CSP now, introspecting on the methods used as one goes through the process of looking for a solution.

In general, one may represent the satisfiability decision problem for CSP as equivalent to determining the truth of a well-formed formula in first-order predicate logic (qv):

$$\exists x_1 \exists x_2 \cdots \exists x_n (x_1 \in D_1) \wedge (x_2 \in D_2) \wedge \cdots \wedge (x_n \in D_n)$$
$$\wedge P_1(x_1) \wedge P_2(x_2) \wedge \cdots \wedge P_n(x_n) \wedge P_{12}(x_1, x_2)$$
$$\wedge P_{13}(x_1, x_3) \wedge \cdots \wedge P_{n-1,n}(x_{n-1}, x_n) \quad (1)$$

Here P_{ij} is included in the formula only if $i < j$, since it is assumed that $P_{ji}(x_j, x_i) = P_{ij}(x_i, x_j)$. Initially here, only constraints representable as unary and binary predicates are considered. For the crossword puzzle the unary constraints $\{P_i\}$ specify the word length. P_1 requires that the word starting at 1 across have five letters. the binary constraints arise when a word across intersects a word down. For example P_{12} requires that the third letter of word 1 across be the same as the first letter of word 2 down. In general, but not for this example, p-ary predicates ($1 \le p \le n$) are required.

For binary predicates another convenient problem representation is a network consisting of a graph with a ver-

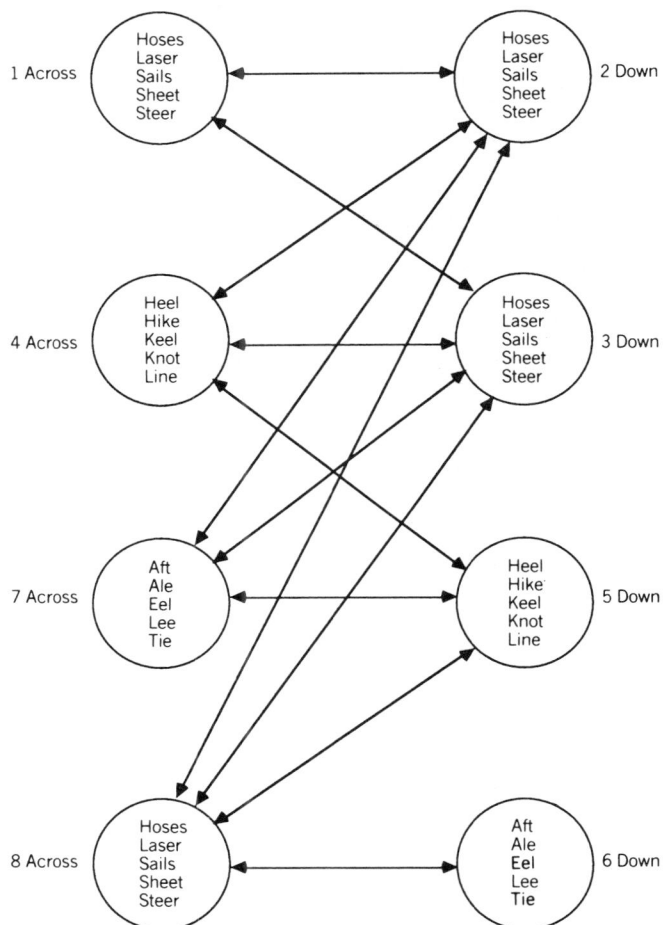

Figure 2. The crossword puzzle constraint network.

tex for each variable with its associated domain attached and an edge between the vertices corresponding to each pair of directly constrained variables. In the crossword puzzle constraint network shown in Figure 2, the initial domain of words for a variable is shown inside the vertex for that variable.

Note that only words satisfying the unary word length constraint are shown. In general, for p-ary constraints ($p > 2$), a hypergraph representation with a hyperedge for each constraint connecting the p vertices involved is required.

BACKTRACKING AND CONSISTENCY ALGORITHMS FOR CONSTRAINT SATISFACTION PROBLEMS

Generate and Test

Assuming finite discrete domains, there is an algorithm to solve any CSP. The assignment space $D = D_1 \times D_2 \times \cdots \times D_n$ is finite, and so one may evaluate the body of formula 1 on each element of D and stop if it evaluates to true. This generate-and-test algorithm is correct but slow. In the crossword puzzle the number of different assignments to be tested is 5^8 or 390,625.

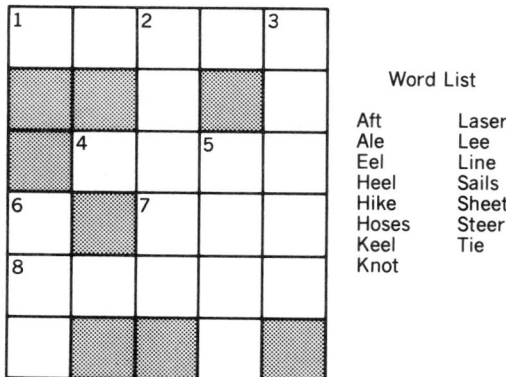

Figure 1. A constraint satifaction problem. Solve the crossword.

Backtracking Algorithms. Backtracking algorithms systematically explore D by sequentially instantiating the variables in some order. As soon as any predicate has all its variables instantiated, its truth value is determined. Since the body of formula 1 is a conjunction, if that predicate is false, that partial assignment cannot be part of any total valid assignment. Backtracking then fails back to the last variable with unassigned values remaining in its domain (if any) and instantiates it to its next value. The efficiency gain from backtracking arises from the fact that a potentially very large subspace of D, namely, the product space of the currently unassigned variable domains, is eliminated by a single predicate failure.

The reader is invited to solve the crossword puzzle by backtracking, instantiating the words in the order 1–8. Start with word 1 across as "hoses"; try word 2 down as "hoses," P_{12} is not satisfied, so all potential solutions with these two choices for 1 and 2 are illegal. Next try word 2 as "laser"; and so on.

The efficiency of backtracking has been investigated (Bitner and Reingold, 1975; Knuth, 1975; Gaschnig, 1979; Haralick and Elliot, 1980). Good analytical results are hard to come by, but see Haralick and Elliot (1980); Freuder (1982); Nudel (1982); and Purdom and Brown (1982). Other factors being equal, it pays to preorder the variables in terms of increasing domain size; one thereby maximizes the average size of the subspace rejected by the failure of a predicate. This principle has been extended to dynamic reordering (Bitner and Reingold, 1975; Purdom and co-workers, 1981) involving one or two more levels of look-ahead search to find the variable with the smallest domain of acceptable values to instantiate next. Regardless of the order of the instantiation, one almost always observes thrashing behavior in backtrack search (Bobrow and Raphael, 1974). *Thrashing* can be defined here as the repeated exploration of subtrees of the backtrack search tree that differ only in inessential features, such as the assignments to variables irrelevant to the failure of the subtrees (Sussman and McDermott, 1972; Mackworth, 1977). This ubiquitous phenomenon is indeed observed, in abundance, as one develops the search tree for the crossword puzzle. Many of the techniques reported in this section and the next are designed to reduce or eliminate thrashing essentially by providing the algorithms with better memories.

One form of so-called intelligent backtracking uses varying degrees of look-ahead to delete unacceptable values from the domains of all the uninstantiated variables (Haralick and Shapiro, 1979; Haralick and Elliot, 1980). Another form of intelligent backtracking identifies the latest instantiated variable causing the failure and fails back to it, possibly across many intervening levels (Sussman and McDermott, 1972; Gaschnig, 1979; Bruynooghen, 1981). Gaschnig's (1977) backmarking algorithm is another potential improvement on backtracking that looks backward to remember value combinations that guarantee failure or success so that they are not retried elsewhere in the tree.

Similar techniques are exploited in dependency-directed backtracking (Stallman and Sussman, 1977) and truth or belief maintenance systems (de Kleer, 1984) (see BACKTRACKING; TRUTH MAINTENANCE SYSTEMS). Those systems generally abandon the chronological stack-based control discipline of pure backtracking, allowing choices to be undone independent of the order in which they are made. The AI programming languages Micro-Planner and PROLOG are based on automatic backtrack control structures. The possibility of providing some of the techniques surveyed in this entry as general AI tools should not be overlooked (Sussman and McDermott, 1972; Mackworth, 1977; de Kleer, 1984).

Consistency Algorithms. Another family of algorithms complementary to the class of backtracking has been characterized as the class of consistency algorithms (Mackworth, 1977). By analyzing the various causes of thrashing behavior in backtracking, various authors have described algorithms that eliminate those causes (Ullman, 1966; Montanari, 1974; Waltz, 1975; Mackworth, 1977; Freuder, 1978; Mohr and Henderson, 1986). They are most easily described in the network method of CSPs given earlier. For binary constraints each edge in the graph between vertices i and j is replaced by arc (i, j) and arc (j, i).

Node i, composed of vertex i and the associated domain of variable v_i, is node consistent iff

$$\forall x(x \in D_i) \supset P_i(x) \qquad (2)$$

Each node can trivially be made consistent by performing the domain restriction operation:

$$D_i \leftarrow D_i \cap \{x \mid P_i(x)\} \qquad (3)$$

In the crossword puzzle this corresponds to the obvious strategy of deleting from each variable's domain any word of the wrong length (and, in a real crossword puzzle, any word that does not fit the clue).

Similarly, arc (i, j) is arc consistent iff

$$\forall x(x \in D_i) \supset \exists y(y \in D_j) \wedge P_{ij}(x, y) \qquad (4)$$

that is, if for every element in D_i there is at least one element in D_j such that the pair of elements satisfy the constraining predicate. Arc (i, j) can be made arc consistent by removing from D_i all elements that have no corresponding element in D_j with the following arc consistency domain restriction operation:

$$D_i \leftarrow D_i \cap \{x \mid \exists y(y \in D_j) \wedge P_{ij}(x, y)\} \qquad (5)$$

In the language of relational database theory this operation is known as a *semijoin* (Maier, 1983). A network is node and arc consistent iff all its nodes and arcs are consistent. A given network for a CSP can be made node consistent in a single pass over the nodes. However, a single pass of the arc consistency operation over the arcs will not guarantee that the network is arc consistent. One must either repeat that pass until there is no reduction in any domain in a complete pass or use a more selective constraint propagation technique that examines each of the arcs, keeping track of the arcs that may have become inconsistent as a result of deletions from the domain at their destination node (Waltz, 1975; Mackworth, 1977). The first approach is a symbolic relaxation algorithm and suggests parallel implementation techniques (Rosenfeld and co-workers, 1976). The second is usually more efficient on a single processor. The Waltz (1975) filtering algorithm uses the second approach. The arc consistency algorithm requires time linear in the number of constraints to make the network arc consistent (Mackworth and Freuder, 1984).

The best framework for understanding these algorithms is to see them as removing local inconsistencies from the network which can never be part of any global solution. When those inconsistencies are removed, they may cause inconsistencies in neighboring arcs that were previously consistent. Those inconsistencies are in turn removed so the algorithm eventually arrives, monotonically, at a fixed-point consistent network and halts. An inconsistent network has the same set of solutions as the consistent network that results from applying a consistency algorithm to it, but if one subsequently applies, say, a backtrack search to the consistent network, the resultant thrashing behavior can be no worse and may be much better.

The result of applying algorithm AC-3, a serial arc consistency algorithm (Mackworth, 1977), to the crossword puzzle constraint graph is shown in Figure 3.

The arcs to be initially examined are put on a queue in the order 12, 21, 13, 31, 42, 24, 43, . . . , 86, 68, and the deleted words are numbered. When words are deleted from a domain at a node, all the arcs into that node not currently waiting on the queue (except the reverse of the arc causing the deletion) are added to the end of the queue. In Figure 3, the numbers following the deleted words give the order in which they are deleted. Since each domain is eventually reduced to a singleton set of one element, there is a unique solution to the puzzle, shown in Figure 4.

A generalization of this technique is to path consistency (Montanari, 1974; Mackworth, 1977). A path of length 2 from node i through node m to node j is consistent iff

$$\forall x \forall z P_{ij}(x, z) \supset \exists y (y \in D_m) \land P_{im}(x, y) \land P_{mj}(y, z) \quad (6)$$

A path is made consistent by deleting entries in the relation matrix representing P_{ij} if it is not. Analogous relaxation and propagation techniques apply. If all paths of length 2 are consistent, then all paths are consistent (Montanari, 1974). In general, path consistency uses the operation of relational composition. If the relations are represented as matrices, then binary matrix multiplication implements that operation but other approaches are possible. In Allen (1983), for example, a finite number of possible relations between temporal intervals is specified and their composition table made explicit.

A further generalization to p-ary relations is the concept of k-consistency ($1 \leq p, k \leq n$) (Freuder, 1978). A network is k-consistent iff, given any instantiation of any $k - 1$ variables satisfying all the direct constraints among those variables, it is possible to find an instantiation of

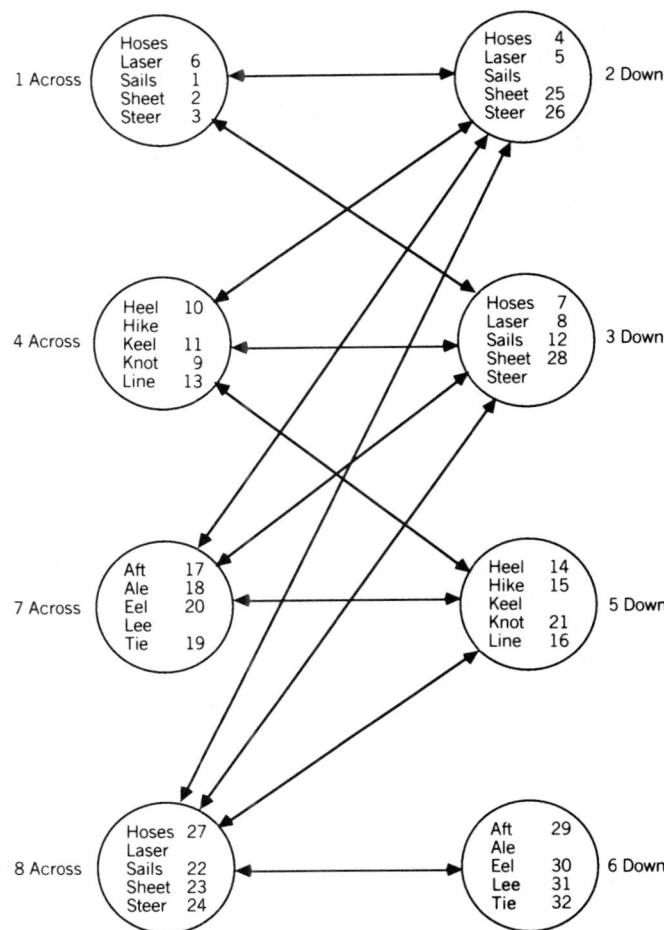

Figure 3. The arc consistent constraint network.

any kth variable such that the k values taken together satisfy all the constraints among the k variables. Node, arc, and path consistency correspond to k-consistency for $k = 1$, 2, and 3, respectively. A network is strongly k-consistent iff it is j-consistent for all $j \leq k$. Another generalization to p-ary relations (Mackworth, 1977) involves only arc consistency techniques.

Even if a network is strongly k-consistent for $k < n$, there is no guarantee that a solution exists unless each domain is reduced to a singleton. One approach to finding complete solutions is to achieve strong n-consistency

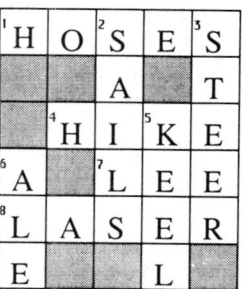

Figure 4. The crossword puzzle solution.

(Freuder, 1978), but that approach can be very inefficient as Freuder's algorithm for k-consistency is $O(n^k)$ (Seidel, 1983). A second approach is to acheive only strong arc consistency. If any node still has more than one element in its domain, choose the smallest such domain and recursively apply strong arc consistency to each half of it. Only the arcs coming into that node can initially be inconsistent in the two subproblems generated. A third and related approach is to instantiate the variable with the smallest domain that has more than one value in it and repeat arc consistency recursively, backtracking on failure; again, initially only the arcs coming into that node can be inconsistent. Or, fourth, one can simply backtrack on the consistent network using any of the backtracking algorithms shown above. This is the sense in which backtracking and consistency algorithms are complementary. Backtracking is a depth-first instantiation technique whereas consistency is an elimination approach ruling out all solutions containing local inconsistencies in a progressively wider context. Other names for the class of consistency algorithms include discrete relaxation, constraint propagation, domain elimination, range restriction, filtering, and full forward look-ahead algorithms, but these terms do not properly cover the range of consistency techniques described here.

Applications

As surveyed in Mackworth (1977) and Freuder (1980), various combinations of backtracking and consistency techniques have been applied to finite assignment space puzzles such as cryptarithmetic problems, Instant Insanity, magic and Latin squares, and the n-queens problem (not to mention crossword puzzles). Other applications reported include map coloring, Boolean satisfiability, graph and subgraph homomorphism and isomorphism, database retrieval for conjunctive queries, theorem proving (qv), temporal reasoning (Allen, 1983; Dechter and co-workers, 1989; Feldman and Golumbic, 1989; van Beek, 1989), and spatial layout tasks. The first application in computational vision was to edge labeling (Waltz, 1975), but there have been many others reported, including sketch map interpretation (Mackworth, 1977) and consistency for schema-based systems (Havens and Mackworth, 1983). In Woodham (1977) arc consistency is used on a vision problem in which the domains are not discrete. In that application the domains correspond to a range of allowable surface orientations at various locations in an image of a smooth surface. In general, the only requirement for using consistency is that one be able to carry out restriction operations typified by eq. 5 on the descriptions of the domains and relations, which may be intensional rather than extensional.

Various experimental and theoretical results on the running time of these algorithms have been reported (Waltz, 1975; Gaschnig, 1979; McGregor, 1979; Haralick and Elliot, 1980; Seidel, 1981, 1983; Mackworth and Freuder, 1984; Dechter and Meiri, 1989), but these results must be interpreted with care since the authors are not always discussing the same algorithms, different measures of time are used, some results are task specific, and

some authors analyze the decision problem and others analyze the problem of synthesizing the global n-ary relation, reporting all solutions. More work needs to be done, but at this point the situation is that arc consistency techniques can markedly improve the overall efficiency of backtracking algorithms, as can the various intelligent backtracking enhancements. The general lesson is that by doing a limited amount of local computation at each level using, say, linear, quadratic, or cubic time, one can optimize backtracking search sufficiently to effect an overall substantial improvement in performance on some difficult problems; however, there is still no adequate theory of how the nature of the task constraints affects the performance of these techniques.

Some aspects of such a theory are, however, emerging. In particular, the topology of the constraint graph itself is a crucial factor. If it is a tree, then the CSP can be solved in linear time (Freuder, 1982; Mackworth and Freuder, 1984). Other topological properties of the graph may also be exploited (Dechter and Pearl, 1987, 1989; Rossi and Montanari, 1989). Such a theory must also relate CSP consistency approaches to integer linear programming (Rivin and Zabih, 1989), ATMS formulations (de Kleer, 1989), database and graph-theoretic techniques (Dechter and co-workers, 1990), theorem proving (Bibel, 1988), dynamic programming (Seidel, 1981) and propositional satisfiability (Zabih and McAllester, 1988; Reiter and Mackworth, 1989).

The consistency algorithms are serial polynomial approximation algorithms for CSPs. Aspects of parallel complexity have been investigated. Kasif (1986) shows that arc consistency is log-space complete for P, the class of problems solvable on a single Turing machine in polynomial time. The implication of this is that it is unlikely that arc consistency can be solved in (worst-case) polylogarithmic time with a polynomial number of processors. This might be interpreted as saying that the problem of arc consistency is "inherently" sequential. Further results are presented on Kasif (1989). However, Gu and co-workers (1987) present a parallel architecture and the design for the AC Chip (Swain and Cooper, 1988) embodies a highly parallel algorithm for arc consistency implemented directly in VLSI.

Generalizations of the basic Boolean CSP have been considered. If there is no solution to a CSP, one may want to relax the constraints sufficiently to obtain a solution (Descotte and Latombe, 1985; Hertzberg and co-workers, 1988; Freuder, 1989; Freeman-Benson and co-workers, 1990). On the other hand, if there are a large number of possible solutions to the CSP one may wish to define a preference relation or metric on the solution space and find the most preferred solution(s) (Dechter and co-workers, 1990).

RELAXATION ALGORITHMS FOR CONSTRAINT OPTIMIZATION PROBLEMS

The restrictions on the Boolean CSP paradigm can be relaxed in several other ways. In computational vision and other AI domains one is often not just satisfying a set of

Boolean constraints but rather optimizing the degree to which a solution satisfies a variety of conflicting continuous constraints. Several generalizations of the consistency techniques have been invented to cope with that problem. In a paper by Zucker and co-workers (1977), the labels in the discrete domains have associated weights in the unit interval [0, 1], and the relation matrices are allowed to have entries from [−1, 1]. These entries measure the extent to which two values from related domains are compatible. The algorithm looks at each variable domain in parallel, adjusting the weight of each label based on an updating rule that adjusts the weight's previous value using the strength of the connection from this variable to each of its neighboring variables, the compatibility coefficient between this label and each of its neighbor's labels, and the previous weight of that neighboring label. This process iterates until a fixed point is reached when no significant change occurs in any weight or until some other stopping criterion applies. The details of the various updating and stopping rules used by these so-called *relaxation-labeling algorithms* can be found in the surveys by Davis and Rosenfeld (1981) and Ballard and Brown (1982), where applications and other variations on this formulation are also given. An interpretation of the weights as probabilities and the compatibilities as Bayesian conditional probabilities was suggested, hence the term "probabilistic relaxation algorithms." The term relaxation was suggested by the loose analogy with the numerical methods used to solve, say, the heat equation for a steel plate. However, the probabilistic interpretation has several problems of semantics and convergence, and other interpretations are now preferred. For example, this class of algorithms can be seen as finding the optimal solution to a linear programming problem as surveyed by Ballard and Brown (1982).

Algorithms in this generic class are often termed *cooperative algorithms* (Julesz, 1971; Marr, 1982). Here the sense is that compatible values in neighboring domains can cooperatively reinforce each other by increasing each other's weight. Simultaneously, incompatible values compete, trying to suppress each other. Each value in a domain is competing with each of the other values in that domain. This general class of algorithms is attractive because they are highly parallel, requiring only local neighborhood communication between uniform processors that need only simple arithmetic operations and limited memory. These features suggest various implementations for low-level perception (such as stereo vision) in artificial and biological systems, which are being explored (Julesz, 1971; Zucker and co-workers, 1977; Barrow and Tenenbaum, 1978; Ikechuchi and Horn, 1981; Marr, 1982; Zucker, 1983; Hinton and co-workers, 1984).

The semantics of these algorithms—the specification of what is being computed—has been clarified (Ullman, 1979; Hummel and Zucker, 1983). The best formal analysis and design of these algorithms is based on the concept of minimization of a figure of merit (or "energy") of the system under study. If that surface is everywhere a downward convex function of the configuration variables of the system, there is a unique global minimum, and steepest descent techniques will find it. If that requirement is not met, techniques such as simulated annealing (qv) based on the Metropolis algorithm and Boltzmann distributions are useful (Kirkpatrick and co-workers, 1983; Hinton and co-workers, 1984) (see BOLTZMANN MACHINES).

In Ikeuchi and Horn (1981) an iterative shape-from-shading algorithm is proposed in which a specific figure of merit is minimized. The algorithm is given an image of a smooth surface for which the dependence of the gray value on surface orientation is known. Since surface orientation at a point has two degrees of freedom, that single constraint is not sufficient. Accordingly, the additional regularizing requirement that the surface be as smooth as possible is introduced. The figure of merit is a weighted sum of measures of the extent to which these two constraints are violated. The requirement that it be minimized translates analytically to a very large, sparse set of equations on the values of surface orientation at each pixel in the image. That set of equations is solved by standard numerical iterative relaxation techniques using gradient descent, yielding a simple updating rule for approximations to the surface orientation values. Note, here, however, that the domains no longer consist of a discrete set of possible values with associated weights but simply the best current approximation to the value.

OTHER CONSTRAINT-BASED SYSTEMS AND LANGUAGES

The constraint satisfaction approach has considerable attraction both in AI and in other areas of computer science. In graphics and simulation, constraint propagation is the mechanism underlying two pioneering systems: Sutherland's (1965) Sketchpad and Borning's (1979) ThingLab. Stefik's (1981) Molgen system propagates constraints arising at different levels of planning abstraction to generate plans for gene-splicing experiments. Various systems have been implemented for domains such as circuit analysis (Stallman and Sussman, 1977; Kelly and Steinberg, 1982), job shop scheduling (Fox and co-workers, 1982), and mechanical design (Mittal and co-workers, 1986). Other applications in computational vision have been described (Brooks, 1981; Marr, 1982; Mackworth, 1983). Constraint propagation and data flow as the design principles for new computational architectures have also been discussed (Abelson and Sussman, 1985). Part of the appeal of logic programming (qv) (Kowalski, 1974) is that attention is focused more on the constraints of the problem and less on the way they are used. There is, for example, less of a distinction between input and output variables in a relational language like PROLOG than in a functional language like LISP. Personal computer spreadsheet systems, based on Visicalc and its descendants, already embody some of these constraint-based ideas. There the variables take only numeric values, and the constraints are simple algebraic formulas, but some of the latest systems allow relaxation for the solution of mutually dependent constraint sets.

A variety of systems that provide constraint-based tools in a programming environment have been proposed and implemented. REF-ARF (qv) (Fikes, 1970), Steele's (1980) constraint language, Bertrand (Leler, 1988), CON-

SAT (Güsgen, 1989), Platypus (Havens and Rehfuss, 1989), and ThingLab II (Maloney and co-workers, 1989; Freeman-Benson and co-workers, 1990), for example, cover a wide spectrum of classes of constraints, constraint-solving algorithms, and user tools.

A language class of particular interest is the set of constraint logic programming (qv) (CLP) languages. These generalize the use of unification in conventional logic programming to constraint solving over various domains. For example, CLP(D) is a scheme for a family of CLP languages parameterized by D, the domain for the constraints (Jaffar and Lassez, 1987). CHIP (van Hentenryck, 1989), CLP(R) (Jaffar and Michaylov, 1987), Prolog III and Trilogy (Voda, 1988) are implemented CLP languages that allow various domains for their constraints. CHIP (qv) augments the PROLOG interpreter with arc consistency and other constraint satisfaction algorithms.

Concurrent logic programming (Foster and Taylor, 1990), another generalization of logic programming, has led to the development of the cc family of concurrent constraint programming languages (Saraswat, 1989). Saraswat advocates the use of constraints for communication and control in concurrent programming languages. The model provides a global constraint store, but this request blocks if the constraint or its negation is not yet entailed. An agent may *Tell* a constraint to the store if the constraint is consistent with the constraints already placed. An agent may also *Ask* if a constraint is entailed by the constraints in the store, but this request blocks if the constraint or its negation is not yet entailed. This protocol provides concurrency control among the agents. Approaches such as this carry the promise of making accessible constraint-based computation systems that are both simple and powerful.

CONCLUSIONS

The definition of the word constraint varies enormously. It has been taken to mean a relation over a Cartesian product of sets, a Boolean predicate, a fuzzy relation, a continuous figure of merit analogous to energy, an algebraic equation, an inequality, a Horn clause in PROLOG, and various other arbitrarily complex symbolic relationships. Nevertheless, underlying this variety, a common constraint satisfaction paradigm is emerging. Much of one's knowledge of the world is best expressed in terms of what is allowed or, conversely, what is not allowed. On the other hand, most current artificial computational systems insist on a particular direction of use of that knowledge. This forces the designer or user to overspecify control information, leading to undesirable representational redundancy, a rigid input–output dichotomy, and conceptual mismatch at the human–computer interface. The constraint satisfaction paradigm allows the system designer to concentrate on what, not how. In computational vision, for example, it is crucial to determine precisely how an image constrains the equivalence class of scenes that could produce it and to identify other constraints that will further constrain the scene. The constraints implicit in

other knowledge and data sources can be analyzed and represented. These constraints may be uniformly introduced and used in various directions depending on the current availability to the system of specific data and knowledge.

BIBLIOGRAPHY

H. Abelson and G. J. Sussman, *Structure and Interpretation of Computer Programs*, MIT Press, Cambridge, Mass., 1985.

J. F. Allen, "Maintaining Knowledge about Temporal Intervals," *CACM* **26**, 832–843 (1983).

D. H. Ballard and C. M. Brown, *Computer Vision*, Prentice-Hall, Englewood Cliffs, N.J., 1982.

H. G. Barrow and J. M. Tenenbaum, "Recovering Intrinsic Scene Characteristics from Images," in E. M. Riseman and A. R. Hanson, eds., *Computer Vision Systems*, Academic Press, New York, 1978, pp. 3–26.

W. Bibel, "Constraint Satisfaction From a Deductive Viewpoint," *Artif. Intell.* **36**, 401–413 (1988).

J. R. Bitner and E. M. Reingold, "Backtrack Programming Techniques," *CACM* **18**(11), 651–656 (1975).

D. G. Bobrow and B. Raphael, "New Programming Languages for AI Research," *Comput. Surv.* **6**, 153–174 (1974).

A. Borning, *ThingLab: A Constraint-Oriented Simulation Laboratory*, Report No. CS-79-746, Computer Science Dept., Stanford University, Stanford, Calif., 1979.

R. A. Brooks, "Symbolic Reasoning among 3-D Models and 2-D Images," *Artif. Intell.* **17**(1, 3), 285–348 (1981).

M. Bruynooghe, "Solving Combinatorial Search Problems by Intelligent Backtracking," *Inform. Process. Lett.* **12**(1), 36–39 (1981).

L. S. Davis and A. Rosenfeld, "Cooperating Processes for Low-Level Vision: A Survey," *Artif. Intell.* **17**, 245–263 (1981).

R. Dechter and I. Meiri, "Experimental Evaluation of Preprocessing Techniques in Constraint Satisfaction Problems," *Proceedings of the Eleventh IJCAI*, Detroit, Mich., 1989, pp. 271–277.

R. Dechter and J. Pearl, "Network-Based Heuristics for Constraint-Satisfaction Problems," *Artif. Intell.* **34**(1), 1–38 (1987).

R. Dechter and J. Pearl, "Tree Clustering for Constraint Networks," *Artif. Intell.* **38**, 353–366 (1989).

R. Dechter, I. Meiri, and J. Pearl, *Temporal Constraint Networks*, Tech. Rep. R-113-L, Computer Science Dept., UCLA, Los Angeles, Calif., Oct. 1989.

R. Dechter, A. Dechter, and J. Pearl, "Optimization in Constraint Networks," in R. M. Oliver and J. Q. Smith, eds., *Influence Diagrams, Belief Nets and Decision Analysis*, Wiley, New York, 1990.

J. de Kleer, "Choices without Backtracking," *Proceedings of the Fourth National Conference on Artificial Intelligence*, Austin, Tex., 1984, pp. 79–85.

J. de Kleer, "A Comparison of ATMS and CSP Techniques," *Proceedings of the Eleventh IJCAI*, Detroit, Mich., 1989, pp. 290–296.

Y. Descotte and J. C. Latombe, "Making Compromises Among Antagonist Constraints in a Planner," *Artif. Intell.* **27**, 183–217 (1985).

R. Feldman and M. C. Golumbic, "Constraint Satisfiability Algorithms for Interactive Student Scheduling," *Proceedings of the Eleventh IJCAI*, Detroit, Mich., 1989, pp. 1010–1016.

R. E. Fikes, "REF-ARF: A System for Solving Problems Stated as Procedures," *Artif. Intell.* **1**, 27–120 (1970).

I. Foster and S. Taylor, *Strand: New Concepts in Parallel Programming*, Prentice-Hall, Englewood Cliffs, N.J., 1990.

M. S. Fox, B. Allen, and G. Strohm, "Job-Shop Scheduling: An Investigation in Constraint-Directed Reasoning," *Proceedings of the Second National Conference on Artificial Intelligence*, Pittsburgh, Penn., 1982, pp. 155–158.

B. N. Freeman-Benson, J. Maloney, and A. Borning, "An Incremental Constraint Solver," *CACM* **33**(1), 54–63 (1990).

E. C. Freuder, "Synthesizing Constraint Expressions," *CACM* **21**, 958–966 (1978).

E. C. Freuder, "A Sufficient Condition for Backtrack-Free Search," *J. ACM* **19**, 24–32 (1982).

E. C. Freuder, "Partial Constraint Satisfaction," *Proceedings of the Eleventh IJCAI*, Detroit, Mich., 1989, pp. 278–283.

J. A. Gaschnig, "A General Backtrack Algorithm That Eliminates Most Redundant Tests," *Proceedings of the Fifth IJCAI*, Cambridge, Mass., Aug. 1977, p. 457.

J. Gaschnig, Performance Measurement and Analysis of Certain Search Algorithms, Ph.D. dissertation, CMU-CS-79-124, Dept. of Computer Science, Carnegie Mellon University, Pittsburgh, Penn., 1979.

J. Gu, W. Wang, and T. C. Henderson, "A Parallel Architecture for Discrete Relaxation Algorithm," *IEEE Trans. Patt. Anal. Mach. Intell.*, **PAMI-9**, 816–831, 1987.

H. W. Güsgen, *CONSAT: A System for Constraint Satisfaction*, Pitman Publishing, London, 1989.

R. M. Haralick and G. L. Elliott, "Increasing Tree Search Efficiency for Constraint Satisfaction Problems," *Artif. Intell.* **14**, 263–313 (1980).

R. M. Haralick and L. Shapiro, "The Consistent-Labeling Problem: Part 1," *IEEE Trans. Patt. Anal. Mach. Intell.* **PAMI-1**, 173–184 (1979).

W. S. Havens and A. K. Mackworth, "Representing Knowledge of the Visual World," *IEEE Trans. Comput.* **C-16**(10), 90–96 (1983).

W. S. Havens and P. S. Rehfuss, "Platypus: A Constraint-Based Reasoning System," *Proceedings of the Eleventh IJCAI*, Detroit, Mich., 1989, pp. 48–53.

J. Hertzberg, H. W. Güsgen, A. Voss, M. Fidelak, and H. Voss, "Relaxing Constraint Networks to Resolve Inconsistencies," in W. Hoeppner, ed., *Kuenstliche Intelligenz—GWAI-88*, Springer, Berlin, 1988, pp. 61–65.

G. W. Hinton, T. J. Sejnowski, and D. H. Ackley, *Boltzmann Machines: Constraint Satisfaction Networks That Learn*, Technical Report CMU-CS-84-119, Dept. of Computer Science, Carnegie Mellon University, Pittsburgh, Penn., 1984.

R. A. Hummel and S. W. Zucker, "On the Foundations of Relaxation Labeling Processes," *IEEE Trans. Patt. Anal. Mach. Intell.* **PAMI-5**(3), 267–287 (1983).

K. Ikeuchi and B. K. P. Horn, "Numerical Shape from Shading and Occluding Boundaries," *Artif. Intell.* **17**, 141–184 (1981).

J. Jaffar and J.-L. Lassez, "Constraint Logic Programming," *Proceedings of the Fourteenth ACM Principles of Programming Languages Conference*, Munich, 1987, pp. 111–119.

J. Jaffar and S. Michaylov, "Methodology and Implementation of a CLP System" in *Proceedings of the Fourth International Conference on Logic Programming*, Melbourne, 1987, pp. 196–218.

B. Julesz, *Foundations of Cyclopean Perception*, University of Chicago Press, Chicago, 1971.

S. Kasif, "On the Parallel Complexity of Some Constraint Satisfaction Problems," *Proceedings of the Fifth National Conference on AI*, 1986, pp. 349–353.

S. Kasif, "Parallel Solutions to Constraint Satisfaction Problems," *Proceedings of the First International Conference on Principles of Knowledge Representation and Reasoning*, Toronto, 1989, pp. 180–188.

V. E. Kelly and L. I. Steinberg, "The Critter System: Analyzing Digital Circuits by Propagating Behaviors and Specifications," *Proceedings of the Second National Conference on Artificial Intelligence*, Pittsburgh, Penn., 1982, pp. 284–289.

S. Kirkpatrick, C. D. Gelatt, Jr., and M. P. Vecchi, "Optimization by Simulated Annealing," *Science* **220**, 671–680 (1983).

D. E. Knuth, "Estimating the Efficiency of Backtrack Programs," *Math. Comput.* **29**, 121–136 (1975).

R. Kowalski, *Predicate Logic as a Programming Language*, IFIP 74, North-Holland, Amsterdam, 1974, pp. 569–574.

W. Leler, *Constraint Programming Languages: Their Specification and Generation*. Addison-Wesley, Reading, Mass., 1988.

A. K. Mackworth, "Consistency in Networks of Relations," *Artif. Intell.* **8**(1), 99–118 (1977).

A. K. Mackworth, "On Reading Sketch Maps," *Proceedings of the Fifth IJCAI*, Cambridge, Mass., 1977, pp. 598–606.

A. K. Mackworth, "On Seeing Things, Again," *Proceedings of the Eighth IJCAI*, Karlsruhe, FRG, 1983, pp. 1187–1191.

A. K. Mackworth and E. C. Freuder, "The Complexity of Some Polynomial Network Consistency Algorithms for Constraint Satisfaction Problems," *Artif. Intell.* **25**(1), 65–74 (1984).

D. Maier, *The Theory of Relational Databases*, Computer Science Press, Rockville, Md., 1983.

J. Maloney, A. Borning, and B. Freeman-Benson, "Constraint Technology for User-Interface Construction in ThingLab II," *Proceedings of the ACM Conference on Object-Oriented Programming Systems, Languages, and Applications*, New Orleans, 1989, pp. 381–388.

D. Marr, *Vision*, W. H. Freeman, San Francisco, 1982.

J. J. McGregor, "Relational Consistency Algorithms and Their Application in Finding Subgraph and Graph Isomorphisms," *Inform. Sci.* **19**, 229–250 (1979).

S. Mittal, C. L. Dym, and M. Morjaria, "PRIDE: An Expert System for the Design of Paper Handling Systems" *IEEE Comput.* 102–114 (July 1986).

R. Mohr and T. C. Henderson, "Arc and Path Consistency Revisited," *Artif. Intell.* **28**(2), 225–233 (1986).

U. Montanari, "Networks of Constraints: Fundamental Properties and Applications to Picture Processing," *Inform. Sci.* **7**, 95–132 (1974).

B. Nudel, "Consistent-Labeling Problems and Their Algorithms," *Proceedings of the Second National Conference on Artificial Intelligence*, Pittsburgh, Penn., 1982, pp. 128–132.

P. Purdom, C. Brown, and E. Robertson, "Multi-Level Dynamic Search Rearrangements," *Acta Inform.* **15**, 99–114 (1981).

P. W. Purdom, Jr., and C. A. Brown, "Evaluating Search Methods Analytically," *Proceedings of the Second National Conference on Artificial Intelligence*, Pittsburgh, Penn., 1982, pp. 124–127.

R. Reiter and A. Mackworth, "A Logical Framework for Depiction and Image Interpretation," *Artif. Intell.* **41**, 125–155 (1989).

I. Rivin and R. Zabih, "An Algebraic Approach to Constraint Satisfaction Problems," *Proceedings of the Eleventh IJCAI*, Detroit, 1989, pp. 284–289.

A. Rosenfeld, R. A. Hummel, and S. W. Zucker, "Scene Labeling by Relaxation Operations," *IEEE Trans. Syst. Man Cybern.* **SMC-6**, 420–433 (1976).

F. Rossi and U. Montanari, "Exact Solution in Linear Time of Networks of Constraints Using Perfect Relaxation," *Proceedings First Int. Conf. on Principles of Knowledge Representation*, Toronto, 1989, pp. 394–399.

V. A. Saraswat, *Concurrent Constraint Programming Languages*, Ph.D. dissertation, Carnegie Mellon University, Pittsburgh, Penn., Jan 1989.

R. Seidel, "A New Method for Solving Constraint Satisfaction Problems," *Proceedings of the Seventh IJCAI*, Vancouver, B.C., Canada, 1981, pp. 338–342.

R. Seidel, *On the Complexity of Achieving k-Consistency, Tech. Report 83-4*, University of British Columbia, Dept. of Computer Science, Vancouver, B.C., Canada, 1983.

R. M. Stallman and G. J. Sussman, "Forward Reasoning and Dependency-Directed Backtracking in a System for Computer-Aided Circuit Analysis," *Artif. Intell.* 9(2), 135–196 (1977).

G. L. Steele, *The Definition and Implementation of a Computer Programming Language Based on Constraints*, Technical Report AI-TR 595, MIT, Cambridge, Mass., 1980.

M. Stefik, "Planning with Constraints," *Artif. Intell.* **16**, 111–140 (1981).

G. I. Sussman and D. V. McDermott, "Why Conniving is Better than Planning," *Artificial Intelligence Memo No. 255A*, MIT, Cambridge, Mass., 1972.

I. E. Sutherland, *Sketchpad: A Man-Machine Graphical Communication System*, MIT Lincoln Laboratory Technical Report 296, Cambridge, Mass., 1965.

M. J. Swain and P. R. Cooper, "Parallel Hardware for Constraint Satisfaction," *Proceedings of the Seventh National Conference on AI*, St. Paul, Minn., 1988, pp. 682–686.

J. R. Ullman, "Associating Parts of Patterns," *Inform. Contrl.* **9**(6), 583–601 (1966).

S. Ullman, "Relaxation and Constrained Optimization by Local Processes," *Comput. Graph. Image Proc.* **10**, 115–125 (1979).

P. van Beek, "Approximation Algorithms for Temporal Reasoning" *Proceedings of the Eleventh IJCAI*, Detroit, 1989, pp. 1291–1296.

P. van Hentenryck, *Constraint Satisfaction in Logic Programming*, MIT Press, Cambridge, Mass., 1989.

P. Voda, *The Constraint Language Trilogy: Semantics and Computations*, Technical Report, Complete Logic Systems, North Vancouver, B.C., Canada, 1988.

D. Waltz, "Understanding Line Drawings of Scenes with Shadows," in P. H. Winston, ed., *The Psychology of Computer Vision*, McGraw-Hill, New York, 1975, pp. 19–91.

R. J. Woodham, "A Cooperative Algorithm for Determining Surface Orientation From a Single View," *Proceedings of the Fifth IJCAI*, Cambridge, Mass., 1977, pp. 635–641.

R. Zabih and D. McAllester, "A Rearrangement Search Strategy for Determining Propositional Satisfiability," *Proceedings of the Seventh National Conference on AI*, St. Paul, Minn., 1988, pp. 155–160.

S. W. Zucker, "Cooperative Grouping and Early Orientation Selection," in O. J. Braddick and A. C. Sleigh, eds., *Physical and Biological Processing of Images*, Springer-Verlag, Berlin, 1983, pp. 326–334.

S. W. Zucker, R. A. Hummel, and A. Rosenfeld, "An Application of Relaxation Labeling to Line and Curve Enhancement," *IEEE Trans. Comput.* **C-26**, 394–403, 922–929 (1977).

ALAN K. MACKWORTH
University of British Columbia

CONTROL STRUCTURES

It is necessary to distinguish control structures from algorithms and from virtual machines. Control concerns what happens in a computational process. The word *control* has two different meanings. On the one hand, there is the problem of ensuring that a process does as little work as necessary. Thus, the term *search control* is applied to a search that explores a minimum of wrong paths. This is more properly a matter for the study of algorithms. On the other hand, there is the problem of specifying clearly what should happen in a computational process. The notion of a control structure concerns this problem of specification. It is a more general notion than that of an algorithm, although no precise line can be drawn.

The notion of a control structure must also be distinguished from the notion of a virtual machine. For simplicity, this article assumes that a virtual machine is defined by a programming language, which might be a machine language. A virtual machine provides the programmer with a collection of primitive operations (no matter if they have a direct physical embodiment in the architecture of a real machine). More important, though, a virtual machine provides an ontology of objects and processes, on top of which programmers can build their own abstractions. The notion of control originated in the days when computers all had simple von Neumann architectures and a programmer needed no more sophisticated a metaphor for control than simply running a finger through the code. The conclusion of this article suggests that the notion of control can become inappropriate on a virtual machine that departs substantially from this model.

Finally, it is necessary to distinguish between a particular control structure and a whole philosophy and style of programming. For example, object-oriented programming is a style that requires a particular control structure, the familiar type-dispatching procedure call. [With a sufficiently rigid model of types, the outcome of this dispatch can be determined at compile time (Liskov and co-workers, 1981). Thus, a control structure can be entirely a fiction of the virtual machine.] This distinction is particularly important for the history of AI because of the frequency with which subtle and profound philosophies of programming are melted down to catalogs of control and data structures. A control structure must be analyzed in the context of a coherent philosophy of programming.

A control structure is a technique, especially one set down as a linguistic construct, that an algorithm can use in determining what happens when on some virtual machine. This article does not exhaustively treat all the different control structures, because many of them are treated in their own articles in this encyclopedia. Instead, this article outlines current issues and describes the history of AI researchers' attitudes toward process organization in general. (For discussion of particular control structures, see AGENDA-BASED SYSTEMS; BACKTRACKING; BLACKBOARD SYSTEMS; COROUTINES; DISTRIBUTED PROBLEM SOLVING; LANGUAGES, OBJECT-ORIENTED; LOGIC PROGRAMMING; MEANS-ENDS ANALYSIS; META-KNOWLEDGE, META-RULES, AND META-REASONING; PARSING, WORD-EXPERT; PROCESSING, BOTTOM-UP AND TOP-DOWN; and RULE-BASED SYSTEMS. For discussion of languages, systems and machines for which control structures are a central issue, see CONNECTION MACHINES; CONNIVER; EURISKO; HEARSAY-II; LISP; LISP MACHINES; LOOPS; MERLIN; OPS-5; PLANNER; POPLOG; SIMULA; and SMALLTALK. For discussion of search techniques, see A* ALGORITHM; ALPHA-BETA PRUNING; SEARCH; SEARCH, BEAM; SEARCH, BEST-FIRST; SEARCH, BIDIRECTIONAL; SEARCH; BRANCH-AND-BOUND; and SEARCH, DEPTH-FIRST.)

History

The history of research into control structures is the history of the proposition that issues of control can usefully be pursued separately from issues of representation. The 1960s saw the development of good ways of implementing and using the basic techniques of serial machine programming: data abstraction, interaction and recursion, the procedure call, lexical scope, dynamic storage management, and the many varieties of search.

During the 1970s, AI researchers explored a variety of nonstandard virtual machines and control structures, including production system architectures, semantic networks and network-based constraint propagation, chronological and dependency-directed backtracking, declarative programming, and a large collection of LISP-embedded languages incorporating these and other ideas. In the search for methods of general value, control search was generally pursued with little regard for the peculiarities of individual domains.

The 1980s have brought an increasing awareness of the value of clearly separating control issues from representation issues, with control generally taking a back seat to representation. Research has increasingly concentrated on the details of particular problems and particular domains, especially in the areas of vision, language comprehension, and motor control. At the same time interest has grown in programming languages, such as PROLOG, that provide a generic control strategy and are intended to allow the programmer to write down not algorithms but knowledge. This emphasis on knowledge over control has continued into the 1990s. The sections that follow relate issues of control to issues of programming language design, representation design, and computer architecture.

CONTROL STRUCTURES AND PROGRAMMING LANGUAGE DESIGN

Research into novel control structures has often produced novel programming languages that presuppose them. Evaluating such languages is a subtle matter (Bobrow and Raphael, 1974).

A programming language defines a virtual machine. Ordinarily this virtual machine will have a simple correspondence to the physical machine on which the language is implemented. This simple correspondence is not simply a lack of imagination. The wisdom of an efficiency decision is determined by the physical machine; a good compiler can compensate for many differences between the virtual and physical machine, but any gross divergences will require the efficiency-minded programmer to outsmart the language. Consequently, the purpose of most program-

ming language constructs is, one might say, to provide abbreviated ways of invoking common conventions in machine language programming. AI language research has a built-in tension: new languages often appeal to as yet unrealized computer architectures, but users of these languages are stuck with traditional von Neumann machines.

This section concentrates on control structures in languages intended for traditional von Neumann machines. There are, roughly, two purposes that linguistic support for a control structure can serve: it can support a philosophy of program modularity, or it can permit some generalization of the serial nature of the language's semantics.

Philosophies of Modularity

Traditional languages like ALGOL and the early versions of LISP had a philosophy of modularity based on data abstraction and the procedure call. There was only a simple theory of data types, and individual procedures tended to be quite large. Over time programmers have learned to impose fine modularities on their programs, so that a LISP procedure of over 30 lines is now generally considered bad form. There have been about three responses to this trend: an increasing emphasis on efficient procedure call implementations, increasingly sophisticated theories of data types, and attempts to institutionalize fine-modularity programming in the form of productive systems.

The development of the SCHEME language (Abelson and Sussman, 1985; Steele and Sussman, 1978) is representative of the emphasis on efficient procedure call implementations. SCHEME is a variant of LISP, employing lexical scope and a heap-allocated stack. It has been demonstrated that these features permit a programming style based on intensive use of procedure calls and procedural data objects (Sussman and Steele, 1976; Steele, 1976). Other dialects of LISP based on dynamic scope are often difficult to optimize fully, and sequentially allocated stacks make it difficult to efficiently endow procedural objects with their proper semantics; this is called the funarg problem (Moses, 1970).

The most widespread philosophy of program organization in the AI community is object-oriented programming (Goldberg and Robinson, 1983; Symbolics, 1983). Bits of code (methods) are individuated by both the operation to be performed and the type of the object it is to be performed on. Types can be built up in a tree (as in SMALLTALK) or a general partial order (as in FLAVORS), with an assortment of conventions governing the combination of the different methods under the same operation in a given type. Much effort has gone into finding efficient implementations of the resulting generalized procedure call (called message passing). It is important to separate the program-organizing role of object-oriented programming from the highly parallel connotations of the vocabulary of objects and messages. The latter aspect of object-oriented programming is central to the actor formalism (Hewitt, 1977) but is not an element of everyday programming with SMALLTALK and FLAVORS (qv).

Production systems began as a model of the human mind (Newell and Simon, 1972; Davis and King, 1975).

Since their inception, they have been used both for psychological modeling (Rosenbloom, 1983) and for system building (Newell, 1973; Forgy, 1981, 1982). Production systems support a style of programming based on large numbers of small modules, each called a rule or production, arranged around a central database or blackboard. At the top level a production system is a loop, on each cycle selecting a production to run and then running it. The process of selecting a production to run has two steps. Each production has associated with it some indication, often called a trigger or left side, of when it is appropriate for that bit of code to be run. This trigger generally takes the form of a symbolic expression with some unfilled slots signified by variables. On the first step of production selection every production whose trigger matches an entry in the database becomes a candidate for execution. The second step, called conflict resolution, somehow selects one of the candidates. The virtual machine of a production system is parallel in the sense that all triggers are matched against the database in parallel. Production systems are also serial in the sense that only one production is run at a time. [Recent work relaxes this constraint, as well as the requirement of a fixed conflict resolution scheme (Laird and co-workers, 1984).]

With their fine modularity, production systems do not encourage intermediate levels of organization. Even the somewhat more structured "heterarchical" architectures, such as that of HEARSAY-II (Erman and Lesser, 1975; Erman and co-workers, 1980), were to be criticized as unprincipled by competence-oriented AI researchers. For a thorough treatment of heterarchical systems, see Waterman and Hayes-Roth (1978). The claim that large production systems actually support an effective fine modularity, in the sense that changes to a system can be localized to one or a few productions, is also open to question (Bachant and McDermott, 1984). Production systems have nonetheless proven a valuable vehicle for applications involving small rule sets; these questions only apply to large systems (Brownstone and co-workers, 1985).

Generalizations of Serial Virtual Machines

It is a simple matter to add a new iteration construct to an ALGOL-like language. But giving a language a new construct that generalizes its virtual machine will have pervasive effects in the language's implementation. It is useful to classify extensions to serial languages in terms of the additional work required of the implementation.

In FORTRAN, the compiler assigns every variable in every procedure to a fixed machine address. Once a language supports recursive procedure calls, a frame must be allocated to store the values of formal parameters and local variables for every procedure call. Such a scheme requires the architecture to efficiently implement a stack.

Most modern languages provide some dynamic storage allocation features, but it is in LISP that the matter has been most thoroughly pursued. But storage management is a module in the run time system; the implementation of arithmetic and the procedure call are independent of its sophistication. However, intermittent garbage collection can ruin the real-time properties of a system. LISP programming relies heavily on efficient dynamic storage allocation. This reliance is especially heavy in an implementation that allocates procedure call frames from the heap rather than on the stack. Efficiency considerations have led most LISP implementations to stack-allocate frames even though this scheme precludes making general use of procedures as data objects. SCHEME (Steele and Sussman, 1985) is an exception, and INTERLISP's spaghetti stacks (Xerox, 1983) are an attempt at a compromise.

Some languages [eg, SAIL (Feldman and co-workers, 1972)] support coroutining, a generalization of a serial virtual machine in which a number of processes sharing the same memory move through the same program. The single physical processor plays the part of the different virtual processors at different times. The compiler must keep track of what information must be saved and restored at various specific points in the program (say, at the calls to the intercoroutine communication constructs) when it is time for the physical processor to play a different virtual processor. It is common for an operating system to allow the processor to change virtual identities among various processes at arbitrary intervals at any place in the code outside of declared critical sections. This ability generally requires the compiled code to confine its local state to the registers.

Matters become more complicated if a language incorporates backtracking into its semantics, as did PLANNER (qv) (Hewitt, 1971). Bookkeeping is required if any information-losing operation is to be undone by backtracking. (For example, an assignment forgets the old value of the assigned variable and a branch forgets where it came from.) The POP-2 language's state-saving features are used in implementing not only chronological backtracking but also coroutining (Burstall and co-workers, 1971). This bookkeeping can grow immense if backtracking can always potentially reach arbitrarily far back. It has been pointed out that Planner had no way of indicating satisfaction for all time with the result of some calculation (Sussman and McDermott, 1972). In addition, PLANNER's chronological backtracking typically reversed far too many calculations; dependency-directed backtracking (Stallman and Sussman, 1977) is an attempt to automate a more accurate pinpointing of the choices that actually led to the difficulty that provoked backtracking.

The record for the most profound generalization of an underlying virtual machine is held by 3-LISP (Smith, 1982), which provides facilities for arbitrary run time modification of the underlying virtual machine. This ability is made possible by the existence of a simple metacircular 3-LISP interpreter, meaning, an interpreter for 3-LISP written in 3-LISP. The virtual machine of 3-LISP is an infinitely deep tower of 3-LISP interpreters, each one running the one above it. A user's program can *reflect*, that is, it can ask the interpreter running it to apply an arbitrary procedure to its own internal state. Reflection allows many common control structures, like nondeterministic choice and LISP's catch-and-throw operations, to be implemented as user code. The implementation involves no infinite towers, of course, but rather a scheme for running only as many levels of interpretation above the hardware as necessary (des Rivieres and Smith, 1984).

[A reconstruction of reflection that does not require the infinite-tower semantics can be found in Friedman and Wand (1984).] Needless to say, heavy use of reflection makes a 3-LISP program hard to compile efficiently.

The utility of being able to modify or advise the virtual machine running one's program has long been understood, although only recently has technology for doing so been developed (Genesereth, 1983; Lenat, 1983; Laird and co-workers, 1984). Research must now seek to reconcile semantic flexibility with efficient compilation. One promising approach views compilation as a process of specializing an interpreter to run a particular program, treating the program as a constant to be folded into the interpreter (Jones and co-workers, 1985; Ershov, 1982).

Making a control structure implicit in the semantics of a language raises it to the status of a virtual machine. The difference is that it is no longer optional: if your language incorporates chronological backtracking or backchaining search, for example, so will your program. Users of such languages often find themselves fighting the language to prevent activity that they know to be useless or destructive. Certainly this was the case with PLANNER, and it is often observed with PROLOG. CONNIVER (qv) went to the opposite extreme, giving the user's program access to its own run time internals (McDermott and Sussman, 1974). This insight of CONNIVER lives on in its essentials in SCHEME, which unlike CONNIVER can be efficiently compiled.

CONTROL STRUCTURES AND REPRESENTATION DESIGN

It has long been understood that giving a program more knowledge can simplify its reasoning tasks. For example, Waltz's scene-labeling program (Waltz, 1975) was able to rule out most interpretations of a line drawing when given information about edges and vertices. When given additional information about shadows, it could rule out all but the correct interpretation, using only a simple local-based constraint propagation algorithm. The developers of DENDRAL (qv) had a similar experience (Buchanan and co-workers, 1969; Carhart and co-workers, 1975). Rule sets were added for interpreting a variety of tests, each of which constrains the identity of an unknown chemical compound. As new information was added, the number of possible identifications that could typically be ruled out without search dropped from many millions to only a few. These programs did entirely without complex control schemes. This experience suggested to many that complex control schemes are unnecessary in general, given sufficient study of a program's domain. Although this is certainly an open question, it is generally considered bad engineering to use complex control structures to compensate for inadequate domain representations.

Much has come to be understood about the relationship between the knowledge a system possesses and the mechanism by which the system deploys this acknowledge. Attitudes toward the distinction are influenced by historical happenstance; the tendency to employ the distinction in order to ignore half of it is still widespread. These issues have been explored primarily in vision and linguistics, but they apply broadly.

Competence and Performance

The distinction between competence and performance was once poorly understood. Its principal origin is in Chomsky's (1965) distinction between competence and performance in linguistics (see the various articles in this encyclopedia on the theories of grammar). Chomsky makes the working assumption (roughly) that there is a mental module responsible for the generation of parse trees from sentences of natural language and vice versa. (Actually, a distinction should be made between the strong claim that there is a physical module in the brain and the weaker claim that there is a module in the competence, meaning that whatever mechanism performs the relevant computations employs no nongrammatical knowledge in performing them.) It is conceivable that one parses sentences by referring to explicit representations of grammatical competence, and at one time it was difficult for linguists and nonlinguists alike to conceptualize an alternative (Berwick and Weinberg, 1984; Stabler, 1984). This view is now widely considered naive.

Computational theory has considerably clarified these issues. Central to this development was the school of vision research founded by Marr (1982). Marr's importance was arguably less in specific theories than in his influential insistence on a clear distinction between computational theory, an algorithm instantiating that theory, and an implementation of that algorithm.

Two approaches to vision research (likewise other perceptual skills) can be characterized as top-down and bottom-up (see PROCESSING, BOTTOM-UP AND TOP-DOWN). Top-down research points to ambiguous percepts and insists on control schemes that can apply general cognition to perceptual interpretation. Bottom-up research prefers to consider unambiguous percepts and postulates self-sufficient [encapsulated (Fodor, 1983)] modules subserving perceptual interpretation. As a matter of engineering, there is a trade-off: modular perceptual interpretation gains efficiency at the price of the occasional illusion. The existence and experimental robustness [cognitive impenetrability (Pylyshyn, 1980)] of perceptual illusions is evidence for the modular view of human perceptual psychology.

Trend toward Priority of Competence Research

History has left the terms top-down and bottom-up with some unnecessary associations. Top-down research has emphasized general-purpose control schemes without paying extensive attention to the percepts themselves or the processes that generate them. Bottom-up research has emphasized that deep understanding of a problem can often eliminate search and the need for complex control schemes in solving it. (This observation is also at the base of the philosophy of most present-day expert systems.) Logically, however, sophisticated representations and sophisticated control are compatible.

The movement toward competence-oriented AI research emphasizes an ambiguity in the term representation. Much theory of representation attempted to design formalisms, called semantic networks, that allowed the meanings of arbitrary English declarative sentences to be captured (Schank, 1975, 1973, 1980; Schank and Rieger, 1974; Woods, 1975; Brachman, 1979; Brachman and Schmolze, 1985; Bobrow and Winogard, 1976). On this view, a representation may make ontological assumptions (eg, that there exist individuals and concepts and relationships of instantiation and subsumption among them) but no empirical assumptions. An alternative view of representation is that a good representation exploits knowledge about the world to simplify descriptions of it. If it is assumed that all physical surfaces are flat, for example, the visual world could be represented by using lists of corners of planar surface elements. For many researchers first-order logic serves as a general representation, and different ontologies are formulated for each domain (Hayes, 1979a, 1979b). Future research must lay out the middle ground between the top-down and bottom-up stereotypes.

The Procedural–Declarative Controversy

These distinctions clarify the issues in the procedural–declarative controversy (Winograd, 1975; Johnson-Laird, 1977; Fodor, 1978). At issue is whether the knowledge underlying human skills is best phrased in terms of propositions about the world or in terms of procedures for manipulating the world. Perhaps the most cogently argued position on the matter is that of Hayes (1977), for whom the question is one of apples and oranges, or, roughly, competence and performance. Hayes insists, furthermore, that the proper medium of expression for competence theories (the competence–performance and top-down–bottom-up distinctions) is formal logic, specifically some slight extension of first-order predicate calculus (FOPC). Hayes points out that many semantic network formalisms are simply improved syntaxes for FOPC.

It is controversial whether competence theories are best expressed in FOPC or in higher order or modal logics (eg, deontic, temporal, or default logics). The question is beyond the scope of this article except for one detail. Just as it was once routine to assume that a parser had to explicitly represent the transformations of its grammar, so it was once routine to assume that mechanized reasoning with a FOPC theory must employ a general theorem prover. This is a possible view, of course, and certainly at least occasionally correct. But it is much less plausible when the logic is very much more general than FOPC, for the proof theories of such logics are often computationally intractable. Instead, in designing a mechanism that deploys a competence theory in carrying out some task, a control scheme must be designed that has the effect of formal reasoning without the expense of fully general inference.

Logic Programming

This is the proper context for discussion of logic programming languages such as PROLOG (Kowalski, 1974; Clocksin and Mellish, 1984). Logic programming (qv) gives linguistic recognition to the distinction between competence and performance: the programmer writes domain competence in the form of a collection of logical expressions. Some mechanism then resolves queries by somehow traversing the space of logical inferences from the user's premises to some conclusion that answers the query. This mechanism could take any number of forms. At one extreme this mechanism could be a general-purpose theorem prover of exceptional sophistication. This approach would be inefficient for systems of any size. At another extreme, the programmer could additionally provide the query mechanism with extensive advice about how to search the inference space defined by the program. This advice would preferably be considered theorem-proving competence itself expressed in logical expressions. Although this is a common idea (eg, Hayes, 1977), MRS (Genesereth, 1983; Smith, 1985) is the only practical system that works on this principle.

All practical PROLOGs adopt some variant of a compromise position: code is limited to Horn-clause form, and the mechanism is simple back-chaining search through inference space. Textual ordering of expressions determines which branches in the space are to be pursued first, and a construct (called Cut) is provided to block search in unpromising directions. An important argument for a fixed control structure is compilation: PROLOG can be efficiently compiled (Warren, 1983), but it is quite possible that systems (like 3-LISP and MRS) that take broad classes of advice about control cannot, in general, be efficiently compiled. It is often argued that these amendments to PROLOG ruin the ideal of logic programming. A common response is that there is nothing wrong if real PROLOG corresponds as little to the ideal of logic programming as real LISP corresponds to "pure LISP." There is a deeper point, however. Until machines become infinite, efficiency-minded programmers will write logic programs with rough ideas about paths through inference space already in mind. This is not in itself bad unless there is a difference between the most elegant or parsimonious formulation of the competence and the formulation that leads a particular proof mechanism to operate efficiently. More experience is required on this point.

CONTROL STRUCTURES AND COMPUTER ARCHITECTURE

Computer architectures have long been designed to improve the efficiency of particular ways of using them. This trend is accelerating as architectures continue to differentiate as to size and intended application. For 40 years, though, almost all architectures have been based on serial virtual machines (even when, as is common in large mainframes, there are several processors present). Recalling the distinctions elaborated in the introduction, architectural adaptations can be divided into two classes: specializations to the traditional serial architecture that accelerate particular styles of programming and nonserial architectures that directly support nonserial virtual machines.

Adaptation of Serial Machines to Symbolic Computation

Most specialized architectures have been concerned with numerical computations, for example, pipelining of operations over large arrays. Because AI is primarily concerned with symbolic programming, these architectures are of no interest here. Architectures did not make many allowances for symbolic programming until the LISP, SMALLTALK, and PROLOG machines of the past ten years. One arguable exception, the hardware support for block-structured programming languages in the Burroughs machines of the 1960s (Siewiorek and co-workers, 1982; Organick, 1973), was far ahead of its time.

How does a serial architecture support a philosophy of programming? There are two broad answers that are relevant to AI practice, the first typified by the DEC PDP-10 (Bell and co-workers, 1978) and the second typified by the IBM 801 (Radin, 1983).

According to the PDP-10 philosophy, the most important adaptation an architecture makes to a style of programming is in its choice of instruction set. By providing a clean, orthogonal instruction set, the architecture encourages compiled languages over hand coding. Single instructions are provided for each of the language's basic operations. The PDP-10's instruction set, though quite conventional, was nonetheless designed with symbolic computation in mind. The word size (36 bits) was exactly twice the size of an address, allowing a cons node to be cleanly implemented in a word. Thus, its half-word instructions implement LISP's CAR and CDR. Furthermore, it has a single-instruction stack, push, and pop operations. The PDP-10's repertoire of specialized instructions forced later PDP-10 models, like most architectures of that era, to be microcoded.

The IBM 801 reverses most of these positions. The 801 group observed that compiler technology improved greatly in the 1970s. Hand coding is much less necessary than before, and optimizers can reason well about unconventional instructions and large register sets. To take advantage of these advances, they designed their compiler (for a variant of PL/1) alongside the architecture. Freed from having to second-guess the compiler, they could implement a much smaller and less conventional instruction set without microcoding. The result is both improved language support and decreased cycle time. These ideas have taken on great commercial significance through the spread of reduced instruction set (RISC) architectures.

The modern history of specialized symbolic architectures begins with the MIT CONS machine (Bawden and co-workers, 1977), a conventional tagged architecture heavily adapted to LISP, and its successor, the CADR machine. The CADR design has given rise to three lines of development, at Symbolics, at Lisp Machines Inc., and at Texas Instruments. Perhaps the critical feature of all these machines is their hardware support for run-time type checking and fast procedure calls. (Run-time type checking is necessary because LISP is not type safe.) The Symbolics 3600 has hardware support for garbage collection and is optimized for message passing, which has become central to LISP systems programming (Symbolics, 1983). A line of INTERLISP workstations developed at

Xerox (1983) is descended from the Alto, a remarkable early workstation introduced in 1973. Their architectures, however, are not specialized for LISP. All the LISP machines are designed from philosophies of program development and user interface. For example, the Symbolics 3600's designers counted fast incremental compilation among their original design goals, and the Xerox workstations are heavily optimized for fast redisplay of windows on their bitmap displays.

Japanese researchers are developing workstations based on PROLOG. The first such machine, called PSI, is a conventional microprogrammed architecture that implements a version of the Warren instruction set (Taki and co-workers, 1984). It speeds unification the same way the LISP machines speed list processing, using tagged data, a cache, and fast memory at the top of the stack. A more recent design, called PIM-R, is more ambitious (Onai and co-workers, 1985). The various branches of the program's space of inferences are assigned to different "inference modules." The machine promises to deliver as much parallelism as is inherent in the program, but the usefulness of the machine depends on finding natural PROLOG coding styles that allow for large amounts of parallelism. [See Singh and Genesereth (1985) on the inference distribution problem and Shapiro (1983) on a Concurrent PROLOG].

All architectures are informed by the statistical properties of the way a style of programming uses a machine. This principle has begun to be applied to AI architectures in a number of ways.

1. In SMALLTALK it happens that on almost all occasions that message M is sent to object O, O is of the same type as the last object that was sent message M. (There may be M methods for each of several types, and locating the right method requires some sort of table lookup on every call.) One SMALLTALK implementation (Deutsch and Schiffman, 1984) takes advantage of this observation by caching the method corresponding to the most recent use of each message name; the SMALLTALK chip (Ungar and co-workers, 1984) performs this caching in hardware.

2. The SCHEME chip (Batali and co-workers, 1982) has special support for heap-consed stacks (which, as mentioned above, are required for efficient support of SCHEME's general use of procedures). There is a separate stack for each register that must be pushed, and the top element of each stack is stored in an adjacent register, thus saving the call to cons that would ordinarily be required to push it. Because the depth of each stack fluctuates greatly (rather than tending to grow and shrink monotonically over long periods), much dynamic storage management is saved.

3. On the Symbolics 3600, recently created cons nodes are stored in a special page of memory that keeps track of pointers to nodes within the page from outside the page. When this page fills up, nodes that are still pointed to are allocated words of ordinary memory. It has long been observed that most cons nodes allocated by most LISP programs become garbage almost immediately (Clark and Green, 1977; Liberman and Hewitt, 1983). By never actually allocating these short-lived nodes, the 3600's ephem-

eral garbage collection" scheme can delay the headaches associated with ordinary garbage collection in large virtual address spaces (Moon, 1984). The future of commercial architectures that are optimized for symbolic programming is, however, currently unclear.

Novel Architectures for Symbolic Computation

Much current research is concerned with architectures comprising large numbers of small processors. Designing such a machine is easy; designing one that can be programmed is not. Decomposing a problem into natural pieces is much easier on a serial machine than on a parallel machine because there is no requirement that the pieces make themselves useful simultaneously. Discussion of control structures on massively parallel machines requires new metaphors. On a serial machine one thinks of a program as having spatial extent; the program is a map over which a locus of control passes. On a massively parallel machine the metaphor of spatial extent passes from the program to the process, which might be thought of as spread out over the machine. A programmer tries to decompose a problem into pieces that can be implemented in parallel. Such a decomposition exists when the problem has a structure that can be mirrored in the structure of a process. There may be many problems with no such structure.

Consequently, one principled approach to designing massively parallel machinery is to isolate a class of useful processes with a common structure and design a machine with that structure. One such structure is simple two-dimensionality, a trait shared by many problems, most notably in graphics and image processing. Two-dimensional machines are especially convenient to build because they are easily embedded in a three-dimensional physical space. There are several machines with two-dimensional connection topologies, including the NASA MPP (Batcher, 1980), the CMU WARP systolic array machine (Arnould and co-workers, 1985), and the Connection Machine Supercomputer (CM) (which also has a more general message-routing network) (Hillis, 1985). These architectures are designed to move information from a processor to its immediate neighbors. These machines have very simple organizations, but they can be difficult to program even on the simplest two-dimensional problems when the problem is not an even multiple of the machine size or when edge effects become clumsy. The NON-VON (qv) machines (Shaw, 1982, 1984) are specialized to tree-structured processes, particularly for applications involving large databases.

Other massively parallel machines can be classified according to the topology of the network by which the processors exchange information. Among machines whose processors are standard commercial microprocessors, the BBN Butterfly uses a crossbar circuit of the same name (BBN, 1985) and the Caltech Cosmic Cube is arranged in a four-dimensional hypertorus (Seitz, 1985). An alternative is represented by the CM, which consists of 64,000 very small processors. In addition to their two-dimensional connectivity, the CM's processors can communicate through a router whose topology (on the Thinking Machines Corp. prototype) is a Boolean hypercube. The CM (like the MPP) is a single-instruction, multiple-data (SIMD) machine, meaning that the processors do not have their own instruction fetch-and-decode circuits but instead share a common instruction bus. SIMD operation increases the total computational power of the machine at the price of restricting it to quite homogenous computations. Many AI applications have a homogenous process structure, especially graph-based operations like semantic network lookup (Fahlman, 1979) and electric circuit simulation.

Research on massively parallel architectures currently suffers from a severe shortage of understood programming techniques. It is inordinately difficult to find sensible decompositions of real problems into massively parallel forms. Often these decompositions are in fact brute force solutions of questionable advantage over their more sophisticated serial competitors. Especially sophisticated serial machines may be the most appropriate for these problems.

CONCLUSION

The first research into sophisticated control structures was largely motivated by the extraordinary flexibility of human thought. Computers were too rigid in their operation then, and they still are. There is now a widespread bias against sophisticated control structures that originates in a concern for good representations and principled engineering. The previous section has suggested that the problem lies in the very notion of control. If so, an alternative might be found in more general ideas about the overall structure of highly parallel processes. These ideas will ultimately be reflected in programming languages, representations, and architectures. Programming languages, in particular, have become very good at hiding details of an architecture from the programmer. But hiding the basic nature of an architecture behind a traditional virtual machine makes it impossible to design a process structure that fits comfortably into the structure of the real machine.

BIBLIOGRAPHY

H. Abelson and G. J. Sussman, *Structure and Interpretation of Computer Programs,* MIT Press, Cambridge, Mass., 1985.

E. Arnould, H. T. Kung, O. Menzilcioglu, and K. Sarocky, "A Systolic Array Computer," in *Proceedings of the International Conference on Acoustics, Speech, and Signal Processing,* IEEE, New York, 1985.

J. Bachant and J. McDermott, "R1 Revisited: Four Years in the Trenches," *AI Mag.* **5,** 21–32 (Fall 1984).

J. Batali, E. Goodhue, C. Hanson, H. Shrobe, R. M. Stallman, and G. J. Sussman, "The Scheme-81 Architecture: System and Chip," in *Proceedings of the 1982 MIT Conference on Advanced Research in VLSI,* Cambridge, Mass., 1982, pp. 69–77.

K. E. Batcher, "Design of a Massively Parallel Processor," *IEEE Trans. Comput.* **C-29**(9), 836–840 (1980).

A. Bawden, R. Greemblatt, J. Holloway, T. Knight, D. Moon, and D. Weinreb, *LISP Machine Progress Report,* Memo AIM-444, MIT AI Laboratory, Cambridge, Mass., Aug. 1977.

BBN, *Development of a Butterfly Multiprocessor Test Bed,* Report 5872, Quarterly Technical Report No. 1, Bolt, Beranek and Newman, Cambridge, Mass., 1985.

C. G. Bell, J. C. Mudge, J. E. McNamara, *Computer Engineering: A DEC View of Hardware Systems Design,* Digital Equipment Corp., Bedford, Mass., 1978.

R. C. Berwick and A. S. Weinberg, *The Grammatical Basis of Linguistic Performance: Language Use and Acquisition,* MIT Press, Cambridge, Mass., 1984.

D. G. Bobrow and B. Raphael, "New Programming Languages for AI Research," *ACM Comput. Surv.* **6,** 155–174 (Sept. 1974).

D. G. Bobrow and T. Winograd, *An Overview of KRL: A Knowledge Representation Language,* Xerox PARC Report CSL-76-4, Palo Alto, Calif., July 1976.

R. J. Brachman, "On the Epistemological Status of Semantic Networks," in N. V. Findler, ed., *Associative Networks: Representation and Use of Knowledge by Computers,* Academic Press, New York, 1979, pp. 3–50.

R. J. Brachman and J. G. Schmolze, "An Overview of the KL-ONE Knowledge Representation System," *Cogn. Sci.* **9,** 171–216 (1985).

L. Brownston, R. Farrell, E. Kant, and N. Martin, *Programming Expert Systems in OPS5: An Introduction to Rule-Based Programming,* Addison-Wesley, Reading, Mass., 1985.

B. Buchanan, G. Sutherland, and E. A. Feigenbaum, "Heuristic DENDRAL: A Program for Generating Explanatory Hypotheses in Organic Chemistry," *Machine Intelligence,* Vol. 4, Elsevier, New York, 1969, pp. 209–254.

R. M. Burstall, J. S. Collins, and R. J. Popplestone, *Programming in POP-2,* Edinburgh University Press, Edinburgh, UK, 1971.

R. E. Carhart, R. Smith, H. Brown, and A. Djerassi, "Applications of Artificial Intelligence for Chemical Inferences XVII: An Approach to Computer-Assisted Elucidation of Molecular Structure," *J. Am. Chem. Soc.* **97,** 5755 (1975).

N. Chomsky, *Aspects of the Theory of Syntax,* MIT Press, Cambridge, Mass., 1965.

D. W. Clark and C. C. Green, "An Empirical Study of List Structure in LISP," *CACM* **20,** 78–87 (Feb. 1977).

W. F. Clocksin and C. S. Mellish, *Programming in Prolog,* 2nd ed., Springer-Verlag, New York, 1984.

R. Davis and J. King, *An Overview of Production Systems,* Memo AIM-271, Stanford AI Laboratory, Stanford, Calif., 1975.

J. des Rivieres and B. C. Smith, *The Implementation of Procedurally Reflective Languages,* Report CSLI-84-9, Stanford Center for the Study of Language and Information, Stanford, Calif., 1984.

L. P. Deutsch and A. M. Schiffman, "Efficient Implementation of the Smalltalk-80 System," in *Proceedings of the Eleventh ACM SIGACT-SIGPLAN Symposium on the Principles of Programming Languages,* Salt Lake City, Utah, Jan. 1984.

L. D. Erman, F. Hayes-Roth, V. R. Lesser, and D. R. Reddy, "The Hearsay-II Speech-Understanding System: Integrating Knowledge to Resolve Uncertainty," *Comput. Surv.* **12,** 213–253 (June 1980).

L. D. Erman and V. R. Lesser, "A Multi-level Organization for Problem Solving Using Many, Diverse, Cooperating Sources of Knowledge, in *Proceedings of the Fourth IJCAI,* Tbilisi, USSR, Morgan-Kaufmann, San Mateo, Calif., 1975, pp. 483–490.

A. Ershov, "Mixed Computation: Potential Applications and Problems for Study," *Theor. Comput. Sci.* **18,** 41–67 (1982).

S. Fahlman, *NETL: A System for Representing and Using Real-World Knowledge,* MIT Press, Cambridge, Mass., 1979.

J. Feldman and co-workers, "Recent Developments in SAIL: An Algol-Based Language for Artificial Intelligence," in *Proceedings of the FJCC,* AFIPS Press, Reston, Virginia, 1972.

J. Fodor, "Tom Swift and His Procedural Grandmother," *Cognition* **6,** 229–247 (Sept. 1978) [this is a reply to Johnson-Laird (1977)].

J. A. Fodor, *The Modularity of Mind,* MIT Press, Cambridge, Mass., 1983.

C. L. Forgy, *OPS5 User's Manual,* Technical Report CMU-CS-81-135, Carnegie Mellon University, Pittsburgh, Penn., 1981.

C. L. Forgy, "Rete: A Fast Algorithm for the Many Pattern/Many Object Pattern Match Problem," *Artif. Intell.* **19,** 17–37 (1982).

D. P. Friedman and M. Wand, "Reification: Reflection Without Metaphysics," in *1984 ACM Symposium on Lisp and Functional Programming,* Austin, Tex., Aug. 1984, pp. 348–355.

M. R. Genesereth, "An Overview of Metal-Level Architecture," in *Proceedings of the Third National Conference on Artificial Intelligence,* Washington, D.C., AAAI, Menlo Park, Calif., 1983, pp. 119–123.

A. Goldberg and D. Robson, *Smalltalk-80: The Language and Its Implementation,* Addison-Wesley, Reading, Mass., 1983.

P. J. Hayes, "In Defense of Logic," in *Proceedings of the Fifth IJCAI,* Cambridge, Mass., Morgan-Kaufmann, San Mateo, Calif., 1977, pp. 559–565.

P. J. Hayes, "The Naive Physics Manifesto," in D. Michie, ed., *Expert Systems in the Micro-electronic Age,* Edinburgh University Press, Edinburgh, UK, 1979a, pp. 242–270.

P. J. Hayes, *Naive Physics I: Ontology for Liquids,* Memo, Centre pour les Etudes Semantiques et Cognitives, Geneva, 1979b.

C. Hewitt, "Procedural Embedding of Knowledge in Planner," in *Proceedings of the Second IJCAI,* London, Morgan-Kaufmann, San Mateo, Calif., 1971, pp. 167–182.

C. Hewitt, "Viewing Control Structures as Patterns of Passing Messages," *Artif. Intell.* **8,** 323–364 (June 1977).

W. D. Hilis, *The Connection Machine,* MIT Press, Cambridge, Mass., 1985.

P. N. Johnson-Laird, "Procedural Semantics," *Cognition* **5,** 189–214 (Sept. 1977) [reply is in Fodor (1978)].

N. D. Jones, S. Sestoft, and H. Sondergaard, "An Experiment in Partial Evaluation: The Generation of a Compiler Generator," in G. Goos and J. Hartmanis, eds., *Rewriting Techniques and Applications, Lecture Notes in Computer Science 202,* Springer-Verlag, New York, 1985, pp. 124–140.

R. A Kowalski, "Predicate Logic as a Programming Language," *Proceedings of the IFIP,* North-Holland, Amsterdam, 1974.

J. E. Laird, P. Rosenbloom, and A. Newell, "Towards Chunking as a General Learning Mechanism," in *Proceedings of the Fourth National Conference on Artificial Intelligence,* Austin, Tex., AAAI, Menlo Park, Calif., 1984, pp. 188–197.

D. B. Lenat, "EURISKO: A Program that Learns New Heuristics and Domain Concepts," *Artif. Intell.* **21,** 61–98 (1983).

H. Lieberman and C. Hewitt, "A Real-Time Garbage Collector Based on the Lifetimes of Objects," *CACM* **26,** 419–429 (June 1983).

B. Liskov, R. Atkinson, T. Bloom, E. Moss, J. C. Shaffert, R. Sheifler, and A. Snyder, *CLU Reference Manual, Lecture Notes in Computer Science 114,* Springer-Verlag, New York, 1981.

D. McDermott and G. J. Sussman, *The Conniver Reference Manual,* Memo AIM-259A, MIT AI Laboratory, Cambridge, Mass., 1974.

D. Marr, *Vision,* W. H. Freeman, San Francisco, 1982.

D. A. Moon, "Garbage Collection in a Large Lisp System," in *ACM Lisp and Functional Programming Conference,* Austin, Tex., Aug. 1984, pp. 235–246.

J. Moses, *The Function of Function in Lisp, or, Why the Funarg Problem Should Be Called the Environment Problem,* Memo AI-199, MIT Project MAC, Cambridge, Mass., June 1970.

A. Newell, "Production Systems: Models of Control Structures," in W. G. Chase, ed., *Visual Information Processing,* Academic Press, New York, 1973.

A. Newell and H. A. Simon, *Human Problem Solving,* Prentice-Hall, Englewood Cliffs, N.J., 1972.

R. Onai, M. Aso, H. Shimizu, K. Masuda, and A. Matsumoto, "Architecture of a Reduction-Based Parallel Inference Machine: PIM-R," *New Generat. Comput.* **3,** 197–228 (1985).

E. Organick, *Computer System Organization: The B5700/B6700 Series,* Academic Press, Inc., New York, 1973.

Z. W. Pylyshyn, "Computation and Cognition: Issues in the Foundation of Cognitive Science," *Brain Behav. Sci. 3,* 111–169 (1980).

G. Radin, "The 801 Minicomputer," *IBM J. Res. Dev.* **27,** 237–246 (May 1983).

P. S. Rosenbloom, *The Chunking of Goal Hierarchies: A Model of Practice and Stimulus-Response Compatibility,* Ph.D. dissertation, Carnegie Mellon University, Pittsburgh, Penn., 1983.

R. C. Schank, "Identification of Conceptalizations Underlying Natural Language," in R. C. Schank and K. M. Colby, eds., *Computer Models of Thought and Language,* W. H. Freeman, San Francisco, 1973, pp. 187–247.

R. C. Schank, *Conceptual Information Processing,* North-Holland Publishing, New York, 1975.

R. C. Schank, "Language and Memory," *Cogn. Sci.* **4,** 243–284 (July–Sept. 1980).

R. C. Schank and C. J. Rieger III, "Inference and the Computer Understanding of Natural Language," *Artif. Intell.* **5,** 393–412 (Winter 1974).

C. L. Seitz, "The Cosmic Cube," *CACM* **28,** 22–32 (Jan. 1985).

E. Shapiro, *A Subset of Concurrent Prolog and Its Implementation,* Report TR-003, ICOT, Tokyo, 1983.

D. E. Shaw, *The NON-VON Supercomputer,* Technical Report, Department of Computer Science, Columbia University, New York, Aug. 1982.

D. E. Shaw, "SIMD and MSIMD Variants of the NON-VON Supercomputer," in *Proceedings of the Computer Society International Conference,* Spring 1984, San Francisco, Feb. 1984.

D. P. Siewiorek, C. G. Bell, and A. Newell, *Computer Structures: Principles and Examples,* McGraw-Hill, New York, 1982.

V. Singh and M. R. Genesereth, "A Variable Supply Model for Distributing Deductions," in *Proceedings of the Ninth ICJAI,* Los Angeles, Calif., Morgan-Kaufmann, San Mateo, Calif., 1985, pp. 39–45.

B. C. Smith, *Reflection and Semantics in a Procedural Language,* Report TR-272, MIT Laboratory for Computer Science, Cambridge, Mass., 1982.

D. E. Smith, *Inference Control,* Ph.D. dissertation, Stanford University, Stanford, Calif., 1985.

E. P. Stabler, "Berwick and Weinberg on Linguistics and Computational Psychology," *Cognition* **12,** 155–179 (1984).

R. M. Stallman and G. J. Sussman, "Forward Reasoning and Dependency-Directed Backtracking in a System for Computer-Aided Circuit Analysis," *Artif. Intell.* **9,** 135–196 (Oct. 1977).

G. L. Steele, *Lambda: The Ultimate Declarative,* Memo 379, MIT AI Laboratory, Cambridge, Mass., Nov. 1976.

G. L. Steele and G. J. Sussman, *The Revised Report on Scheme: A Dialect of Lisp,* Memo 452, MIT AI Laboratory, Cambridge, Mass., Jan. 1978.

G. J. Sussman and D. McDermott, "From Planner to Conniver: A Genetic Approach," in *Proceedings of the FJCC,* Vol. 41, AFIPS Press, Reston, Va., 1972, pp. 1171–1179.

G. J. Sussman and G. L. Steele, *Lambda: The Ultimate Imperative,* Memo 353, MIT AI Laboratory, Cambridge, Mass., Mar. 1976.

Symbolics, *3600 Technical Summary,* Symbolics, Cambridge, Mass., 1983.

K. Taki and co-workers, "Hardware Design and Implementation of the Personal Sequential Inference Machine (PSI), "*Proceedings of the International Conference on Fifth Generation Computer Systems,* ICOT, Tokyo, Japan, 1984, pp. 398–409.

D. Ungar, R. Blau, P. Foley, D. Samples, and D. Patterson, "Architecture of SOAR: Smalltalk on a RISC," *Eleventh Symposium on Computer Architecture,* Ann Arbor, Mich., June 1984, pp. 188–197.

D. Waltz, "Understanding Line Drawings of Scenes with Shadows," in P. H. Winston, ed., *The Psychology of Computer Vision,* MIT Press, Cambridge, Mass., 1975, pp. 19–91.

D. Warren, *An Abstract Prolog Instruction Set,* Technical Note 309, AI Center, SRI International, Menlo Park, Calif., 1983.

D. A. Waterman and F. Hayes-Roth, eds., *Pattern-Directed Inference Systems,* Academic Press, New York, 1978.

T. Winograd, "Frame Representations and the Declarative/Procedural Controversy," in D. G. Bobrow and A. Collins, eds., *Representation and Understanding,* Academic Press, New York, 1975, pp. 185–208.

W. A. Woods, "What's In a Link?: Foundations for Semantic Networks," in D. G. Bobrow and A. Collins, eds., *Representation and Understanding,* Academic Press, New York, 1975, pp. 35–82.

Xerox, *Interlisp Reference Manual,* Xerox Corp., Palo Alto, Calif., Oct. 1983.

P. AGRE
University of California,
San Diego

COROUTINES

The word coroutine is attributed to Conway (1963), who describes coroutines as a set of autonomous programs communicating with adjacent modules as if they were input and output routines. Coroutines (sometimes called mutual subroutines) can be considered as subroutines at the same level. Each of them acts as the main program, although there is no main program. The best known example of coroutines is the interaction between a parser (see PARSING) and a lexical analyzer (see MORPHOLOGY). The parser calls the lexical analyzer each time it needs a token; the lexical analyzer calls the parser to dispose of tokens extracted from the input sequence.

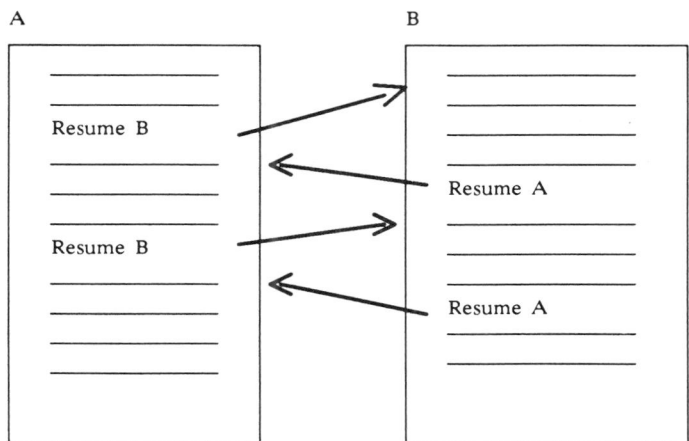

Figure 1. Control flow through coroutines.

Figure 1 illustrates a typical control flow through co-routines. However, a number of differing views on corou-tining have emerged and have been implemented in ex-perimental or practical programming languages. They illustrate relationships with backtracking (qv), multipass algorithms, network processes, lazy evaluation, concur-rent programming languages (see LOGIC PROGRAMMING), and object-oriented programming languages (see LANGUAGES, OBJECT-ORIENTED). Applications of coroutining can be found in the domains of business data processing, text process-ing, simulation, operating systems, and AI.

CONCEPTS

Coroutines: Explicit vs Implicit Sequencing

In the simplest and most conservative view of coroutining, the sequencing is explicitly controlled by the programmer (Marlin, 1980). It has the following characteristics: the control is explicitly passed from one coroutine to another, the execution of a coroutine is resumed from the point of deliberate suspension of control (resume), only one corou-tine is executing at any given time, and the values of the local data of a coroutine persist between successive reacti-vations (own variables).

Consider the two coroutines A and B (Fig. 1) that coop-erate in such a way that A sends items to B; B runs until it needs an item from A. At this point the control is passed to A, while B suspends. After supplying the item B asked for, A suspends and B resumes and continues from the point where it suspended, and so on.

Coroutining is appropriate whenever the algorithm to be implemented can be divided into two or more conceptu-ally distinct subalgorithms that must be executed alter-natively, and where it is difficult to impose a hierarchy between the different subalgorithms. The technique of coroutining can be used to split up the different concepts related to an algorithm in different modules. This modu-larity and the locality of data can facilitate the verifica-tion and the debugging of programs. Communication be-tween coroutines is possible either via global data, accessible to both, or by also passing data when control is passed.

A more liberal (and not generally accepted) view con-siders coroutines as a means of simulating parallelism on a single-processor machine. This generalization of corou-tining has been used primarily in AI domains to express an implicit sequencing of conceptually parallel programs. One good example of this approach is the principle of lazy evaluation in LISP (qv) (Friedman and Wise, 1976; Hen-derson and Morris, 1976). The LISP evaluation system consists of coroutines, each of which evaluates part of the program. They are synchronized by the mutual need for data, that is, the call by need. This is further generalized in the logic programming paradigm: control knowledge is added to the program to enable the system to decide which of its coroutines must be executed (Clark and McCabe, 1979; Gallaire and Lasserre, 1982). These concepts have finally led to the definition of concurrent logic program-ming languages (Clark and Gregory, 1984; Shapiro, 1983). This implicit sequencing of conceptually parallel programs is a language feature in which the flow of con-trol is not explicitly specified by the programmer but is dynamically determined by data dependencies.

Relation with Procedures

Procedures can be considered a special kind of coroutine with restrictions on their behavior: on completion of their tasks, procedures always return control to their caller. Procedures usually start with a fresh set of local data, and execution starts at the first statement. When calling an-other procedure, execution is suspended and later re-sumed with the same local data when the called procedure returns control. The difference between coroutines and procedures is characterized by the difference in control flow. With procedures, the caller decides on the return address, the instruction immediately following the call; this address is saved and always used to resume execution when the callee finishes. With coroutines, the callee de-cides on the control flow (eventually it calls another corou-tine); the caller saves the return address, that is, the ad-dress where it resumes execution when, at a later stage, it regains control either from the callee or from another co-routine. This address is called the *reactivation point* of the coroutine.

Reactivation Point

Some definitions of coroutining imply a fixed reactivation point: each time the coroutine is passed control, it resumes execution starting from a fixed instruction (like a called procedure). Other (more conventional) definitions have a dynamic reactivation point; execution is resumed at the point where control left on invoking another coroutine (coroutines that behave as read or write modules). A dynamic reactivation point asks for a different implementation than a static reactivation point. Indeed, not only must the values of the local variables be retained between the different reactivations of the coroutines, but also the address where execution of the coroutine must be resumed when it regains control.

Symmetric vs Semisymmetric

In symmetric coroutining, each coroutine acts as a main program; it can pass control to any other coroutine. The routine in control takes over the role of main program and thus has complete freedom to pass control to any existing coroutine without being tied to the caller. In semisymmetric coroutining a monitor module controls the flow through the coroutines. On return of a coroutine, control is returned to the monitor module, which decides to pass it eventually to another coroutine. However, each coroutine can be a monitor for some other coroutines, thus establishing a hierarchy.

Multipass Algorithms and Pipelines

Many multipass algorithms lend themselves naturally to coroutining. In a classic approach the first pass of a multipass algorithm is applied to the input of the algorithm, the results are saved in an intermediate storage and supplied to the next pass, and so on. In a coroutining approach the different passes are interconnected as coroutines, the first pass executes until it has a token available to transmit to the next pass, execution is suspended, and control is passed to the next coroutine, which implements the next pass in the algorithm. This routine, on terminating its execution in turn calls the next pass, and so on. On delivery of the final result, the last pass gives control back to the first pass, which resumes execution. This mechanism continues until the input sequence is completely processed. Note that not all multipass algorithms can be implemented in this way. Algorithms that need input tokens that appear after the actual processed input token in order to produce single-output tokens obviously do not lend themselves for coroutining, for example, if one step is a compiler for a language that allows forward references.

This coroutining of multipass algorithms has given rise to the concept of *pipelining*. In this approach the different passes of the algorithm are implemented as separate processes interconnected via FIFO queues. The first pass of the algorithm produces subsequent tokens that are put on the output queue to the next pass; the execution is not interrupted; the next pass consumes tokens from its input queue, processes them, puts result tokens on its output queue, and so on until the last pass, which produces the final results. The processes run in parallel, and the control

is not passed explicitly; but processes are triggered by tokens arriving on their input queues. This data-driven process (see PROCESSING, BOTTOM-UP AND TOP-DOWN) needs some synchronization mechanisms to prevent a process from reading an empty queue or pushing an item into a full buffer, and to wake up processes waiting for input. This kind of parallelism has been generalized in different implementations of concurrent programming languages and object-oriented languages. Because of the strong relationship with coroutining, this particular kind of parallelism is much easier to program than the more general mechanisms of concurrent processes proposed and implemented elsewhere. In this special case the synchronization between processes is handled by the system and is invisible to the user insofar as the processes do not access some common data. In the latter case the user must synchronize the processes using the primitives offered by the programming language. The pipes of the operating system Unix are a well-known example of pipelines between processes.

IMPLEMENTATION OF COROUTINING

Semantic Differences

The different implementations of coroutining in different programming languages attribute a different semantic meaning to the concepts of coroutines. Some definitions of coroutines separate the creation, referencing, and execution of coroutines in explicit steps, whereas other definitions only provide one mechanism that groups the three conceptual steps. Some implementations suspend automatically the execution of the coroutine that passes the control to another coroutine, whereas others provide an explicit suspend command and thus allow parallel execution of coroutines until all but one are explicitly suspended. Coroutines never terminate in some implementations; others, where coroutines can terminate, have different specifications for the target of the control when a coroutine ceases to exist: to the main program, to the creator of the coroutine, or to the activator of the coroutine. Some language definitions consider coroutines as distinct from procedures and require them to be declared as such. Others treat procedures as having the potential to become an instance of a coroutine when referenced properly during run time without any explicit declaration.

The Spaghetti Stack

When implementing a coroutining mechanism, the problem arises that some information concerning the suspended coroutine must be retained between the subsequent invocations of the coroutine: the values of the local data structures and the address of the reactivation point. The lifetime of this information is not tied to the control flow through the different coroutines. The information must remain available during the whole lifetime of the coroutine. This retentive control can be implemented with a heap: activation records are allocated in a storage pool and contain the local data of the coroutine, including sufficient space for temporaries, and the return address. This is a very simple scheme but has the drawback that there is wasted space due to the preallocation of storage for temporaries, the fragmentation of the storage, and the overhead of maintaining a free space list; these disadvantages also occur whenever a program does not need the retentive control. Another well-known implementation of retentive control is called the spaghetti stack. It was proposed by Bobrow and Wegbreit (1973) and can also support other control structures where the lifetime of frames is not associated with the nesting of control, eg, backtracking and multitasking. The spaghetti stack is a generalized stack where gaps can exist between different stack frames. The main advantage of this spaghetti stack lies in its ability to operate as a normal stack whenever retentive control is not needed so that no overhead is paid for programs not using coroutining.

The spaghetti stack stores activation records that include the storage for local data structures, the necessary control and access links, and sometimes storage space for temporaries. When control leaves a module, the activation record is reclaimed only if the module cannot be reactivated in the future. Frames retained on the stack can block the growth of temporary storage (which is a substack) of the activation frame of the routine where the control resides. In this case the complete activation record has to be copied to another part of the stack, leaving a gap that can be used for the substack of the temporaries of the frame immediately below it. This scheme is rather complex, and there is an overhead due to multiple reference counts and copying. Because the original technique was also designed to cover backtracking and dynamic scoping, apart from coroutines, it is sometimes too general. Different techniques have since been implemented that have different advantages and disadvantages, among others the Berry heap, which includes two heaps and one stack, and the stack heap, which has one stack and one heap (Berry and co-workers, 1975). A comparative study and an in-depth analysis of different techniques is given in Pauli and Soffa (1980).

Depending on the definition of coroutines used to define the programming language, the implementation may provide mechanisms for parallel execution of coroutines. One problem related to parallel execution of modules is the synchronization between different processes executing concurrently. There are two main techniques to synchronize processes: the first is based on shared variables and the second on message passing.

Relation to Backtracking

One of the methods to exhaustively search a problem space is backtracking (qv). It is a strategy that explores all possible paths of the search space in a depth-first way (see SEARCH, DEPTH-FIRST). Whenever a path is a dead end, the algorithm goes back to the latest-encountered choice point and explores another possible path. This process is continued until a solution for the problem is found or the search space is exhausted. To implement this search technique, a special kind of retentive control is needed; each choice point has to be retained on the run-time structures to facilitate the backtracking. Moreover, these choice points

are stored in a stackwise manner; the most recent choice point is retrieved first. When all related paths are explored, the system backtracks to the previous choice point, and so on. The spaghetti stack could be used to implement this retentive control, although this mechanism is too general for the restricted retentive control needed by backtracking. A normal stack that stores activation records for the currently executing procedure is sufficient; activation frames from modules that express a choice point are retained on the stack. These frames contain return addresses and local values needed for resuming execution on backtracking. On backtracking the frame on top of the stack is revisited. When all choices are exhausted, the frame is popped from the stack and the previous stack frame is considered.

A backtracking search can also be expressed with coroutines. Consider, for example, an algorithm consisting of two parts A and B to find a solution to a given problem. Suppose A has n and B has m possible solutions. The backtracking search consists of combining the n solutions of A with the m solutions of B. All combinations of a solution of A and B that are compatible are solutions to the overall problem. The coroutining approach consists of writing the algorithm to find all solutions of A. After each solution, control is passed to coroutine B, which checks the consistency with all solutions to B. Then A regains control to find the next solution, and so on until the search space is exhausted or until one solution to the global problem is found.

APPLICATIONS OF COROUTINES

Pauli and Soffa (1980) surveyed current literature to get a representative sample of coroutine usage. Examples were selected from various application fields, a brief description was given, and the characteristics of the algorithms using coroutining were analyzed. Some typical application domains for coroutining are summarized below. Some short descriptions of general-purpose languages that include features for coroutining such as COROUTINE PASCAL, an extension to FORTRAN, CLU, EXTENDED ALGOL, and so on can be found in Marlin (1980).

Compilers

Compilers are usually multipass algorithms that often, as already stated, lend themselves to coroutining. In the parsing step of a compiler, coroutines can be used in yet another way. Usually, part of the specification consists of the grammar of the language to be parsed. When using a top-down parsing strategy, mechanisms must be provided to cope with the eventual alternatives in the grammar rules. Backtracking is an appropriate technique in such a case, although coroutines can be used too. A coroutine containing the appropriate strategy is defined for each alternative in the grammar. This top-down parsing technique can be extended to include nonforgetful backtracking (Lindstrom, 1976).

Receiver–Sender Communication

Receiver–sender communication problems are a typical application for coroutining. A sender coroutine retrieves information until a buffer is full or a meaningful token has been produced. Then a receiver coroutine is activated that processes the input data and, on completion, reactivates the sender. Sometimes the sender transforms the input sequence before putting it in the buffer. The same applies to the receiver. An example can be found in Brinch Hansen (1973).

Operating Systems

A process scheduler of a multitasking operating system can be seen as semisymmetric coroutining. Its purpose is to assign scarce, nonsharable resources such as processor time to competing processes that must run on a single-processor machine. The scheduler acts as the monitor module, passing control of a limited amount of resources to the different processes. Upon exhaustion of the resources, control returns to the scheduler, which decides on the next process to become active depending on eventual dynamic priorities, waiting time, and so on. On the other hand, system services like input–output operations are typical examples of symmetrical coroutines. The user considers these services subprocedures to the program. However, for the operating system, the reverse is true. Although on the same level, they act as mutual input and output routines; they retain values for their local variables and thus obey the definition of coroutines. Examples of this view of operating systems can be found in Shapiro (1983). A description of BLISS, a systems-programming language including facilities for coroutining, can be found in Wulf and co-workers (1971).

Simulation

Simulation of systems involving different objects in interaction with each other, be it mechanical, software, economical, or other real-time systems, requires, on a sequential machine, a simulation of the parallel processes going on in the real system. This can be expressed with coroutines. Depending on the application, the external influences are represented by random generators or by sequences of typical examples of external impacts on the system. The different objects in the system are implemented by coroutines, and the interactions between the objects and the external world are coded as mutual invocations (Birtwistle and co-workers, 1974). The best known language for simulation that includes coroutine features is SIMULA (qv). A short description of the concepts of this language and some further references can be found in Marlin (1980).

ARTIFICIAL INTELLIGENCE

Lazy Evaluation

The concepts of lazy evaluation were initially investigated in the context of a purely applicative language, that is, a language without assignment. The intuitive idea behind this nonstandard method of evaluation is to perform an evaluation step only when it is absolutely necessary and never to perform any evaluation twice. The concept of lazy evaluation is a generalization of the call-by-need mechanism of Wadsworth (1971) and the delay rule of Vuillemin (1974), in the sense that list structures are evaluated incrementally; that is, an element of a list in the context of a functional language like LISP is not evaluated until and unless it is selected and examined by some later operation. This method allows a significantly different style of programming; for the comparison of two lists, a lazy evaluation system evaluates pairs of elements of the two lists, compares them, and proceeds to the next elements. When an inequality is encountered, the lists are different and the tails of the two lists are not constructed. A conventional evaluation would compute the two lists before starting to compare them. Lazy evaluation allows the efficient processing of huge and even infinite structures. It combines the advantages of call by value and call by name. The expressions are evaluated only when referenced, whereas the evaluation is done only once or even not at all. The expressions are treated symbolically (by name) as long as they are not referenced. When needed, the expressions are evaluated. In the case of structures or lists, this evaluation is only partial, and the unevaluated parts are kept in symbolic form.

The relation with coroutines is best exemplified by considering a producer–consumer problem. In the normal evaluation mode of a LISP-like language, the producer would generate its output first, possibly a huge list of elements. Then this list is fed as input to the consumer, which is evaluated next. Applying lazy evaluation, the first element of the output list would only be produced on demand of the consumer (call by need). At this point control passes to the evaluation of the producer, which supplies the first element. The consumer resumes and processes this first element and eventually proceeds to reference the second; this triggers the evaluation of the producer to deliver the second element; and so on. This is indeed a kind of coroutining behavior. The evaluation mechanism is changed from a recursive procedural approach to a coroutining approach. In the conventional approach the evaluator is called recursively to evaluate subexpressions; these are evaluated completely before control returns. The lazy evaluation system acts as a coroutine for each subexpression and delivers results incrementally on subsequent invocations. More details about lazy evaluation in functional languages and some useful references are given in Friedman and Wise (1976) and Henderson and Morris (1976).

The same result can be achieved in the logic programming (qv) paradigm. In Clark's IC-PROLOG (Clark and McCabe, 1979) PROLOG has been extended with mechanisms to describe a different order of evaluation than the standard, strictly left-to-right one. The concepts of a lazy producer and an eager consumer are defined for respective input or output variables of the calls in a PROLOG program. These language features allow a lazy evaluation of programs in much the same sense as LISP-like lazy evaluation, but also an eager evaluation (which starts execution with the producer, whereas lazy evaluation starts with the consumer, but further contains essentially the same data transmissions and requests), and a mixed-mode evaluation. Besides the work on lazy evaluation, the paper of Kahn and McQueen (1977) served as an important source for the ideas developed in IC-PROLOG. The language described in that paper provides concise and flexible means for creating complex networks of parallel processes that may evolve during execution. Channels, which are built as FIFO queues, interconnect and buffer the communication between the processes, which thus behave as coroutines in the pipelining approach.

Concurrent Languages

Generalizations of coroutining have been included in AI languages to be able to describe the execution of conceptually concurrent processes on sequential machines. Logic programming has been an important subject for this research because the language is inherently heavily oriented toward parallel execution due to the logic-based formalism and semantics, which allow both or- and and-parallelism. The most popular concurrent logic programming languages are CONCURRENT PROLOG (Shapiro, 1983) and PARLOG (Clark and Gregory, 1984). Both build on the coroutining approach of IC-PROLOG. Each call in the program creates a new instantiation of a coroutine; the variables shared between calls denote a pipelining communication channel between the concurrent running processes similar to the pipelines between the different passes of a multipass algorithm as described before. The scheduling of the processes is implicitly data driven. The definition of a concurrent logic programming language handles concurrency by the and-parallelism, indeterminacy by the or-parallelism, and communication and synchronization by the shared variables. Moreover, guarded clauses and read-only variables are added to the languages, which serve as a modification of the cut operation and the standard unification of sequential PROLOG, respectively. These features allow a better control of the execution of the program.

Object-Oriented Programming

The building blocks of object-oriented languages are objects that are grouped in hierarchical classes. Objects can have properties, and these are objects themselves and can be shared between different objects. The user interacts with the objects by sending messages, and the objects respond by changing their internal state and by sending messages to other objects. An object can be thought of as a process with an internal state. It becomes active when it receives a message (compare with pipeline coroutining); the internal state (ie, the coroutine's own variables) can only be changed by the object on receipt of a message, which specifies the operation to be done; the object can send messages to other objects (invoke other coroutines); and any number of instances can be generated from a definition of an object (multiple instantiations of the same coroutine).

Although there exist some purely object-oriented programming languages, of which SMALLTALK (qv) (Goldberg and co-workers, 1983) is the best known, some argue that object-oriented programming is more a question of style than of language, for example, Concurrent PROLOG can be used in an object-oriented style (Shapiro and Takeuchi, 1983). Others have added an object-oriented layer (Weinbreb and Moon, 1981; Zaniolo, 1984) to existing languages such as PROLOG and LISP.

BIBLIOGRAPHY

D. Berry, L. Chirica, J. Johnston, D. Martin, and A. Sorkin, "Time Required for Reference Count Management in Retention Block-structured Languages, Part 1." *Int. J. Comp. Inf. Sci.* **7**(11), 91–119 (1975).

G. Birtwistle, O.-J. Dahl, B. Myhrhaug, and K. Nyggard, *Simula Begin*, Wiley, New York, 1974.

D. G. Bobrow and B. Wegbreit. "A Model and Stack Implementation of Multiple Environments," *CACM* **16**(10), 153–174 (1973).

P. Brinch Hansen, "The Programming Language CONCURRENT PASCAL," *IEEE Trans. Softwr. Eng.* **SE-1**(2), 591–603 (1973).

K. Clark and S. Gregory, "Notes on Systems Programming in PARLOG," in *Proceedings of the International Conference on Fifth Generation Computer Systems*, 1984, pp. 299–306.

K. L. Clark and F. G. McCabe, "The Control Facilities of IC-PROLOG," in D. Michie, ed., *Expert System in the Micro-Electronic Age*, University of Edinburgh, Edinburgh, UK, 1979, pp. 122–152.

M. E. Conway, "Design of a Separable Transition-Diagram Compiler," *CACM* **6**(7), 396–408 (1963).

D. P. Friedman and D. E. Wise, "Cons Should Not Evaluate Its Arguments," in Michaelson and Milner, eds., *Automata, Languages and Programming*, Edinburgh University Press, Edinburgh, UK, 1976, pp. 257–284.

H. Gallaire and C. Lasserre, "Metalevel Control for Logic Programs," in K. L. Clark and S.-A. Tarnlund, eds., *Logic Programming*, APIC Studies in Data Processing, Vol. 16, Academic Press, London, 1982, pp. 173–188.

A. Goldberg, D. Robson, and D. Ingalls, *SMALLTALK-80: The Language and Its Implementation*, Addison-Wesley, Reading, Mass., 1983.

P. Henderson and J. H. Morris, "A Lazy Evaluator," in *Conference Record of the Third ACM Symposium on Principles of Programming Languages*, 1976, pp. 95–103.

G. Kahn and D. B. McQueen, "Coroutines and Networks of Parallel Processing," *Proc. IFIP* **77**, 993–998 (1977).

G. Lindstrom, *Non-forgetful Backtracking: An Advanced Coroutine Application*, Technical Report **76-13,** Department of Computer Science, University of Pittsburgh, Pittsburgh, Penn., 1976.

C. E. Marlin, *Coroutines, A Programming Methodology, a Language Design and an Implementation*, Springer-Verlag, New York, 1980.

W. Pauli and M. L. Soffa, "Coroutine Behaviour and Implementation," *Softwr. Pract. Exper.* **10**, 189–204 (1980).

E. Shapiro, *A Subset of CONCURRENT PROLOG and Its Interpreter*, Technical Report, Weizmann Institute of Science, Rehovat, Israel, 1983.

E. Shapiro and A. Takeuchi, "Object Oriented Programming in CONCURRENT PROLOG," *New Gen. Comput.* **1**, 25–48 (1983).

J. Vuillemin, "Correct and Optimal Implementations of Recursion in a Simple Programming Language," *J. Comput. Sys. Sci.* **9**(3), 332–354 (1974).

C. Wadsworth, *Semantics and Pragmatics of the Lambda-Calculus*, Ph.D. dissertation, Oxford University, Oxford, UK, 1971.

D. Weinreb and D. Moon, *LISP Machine Manual*, Symbolics Inc., Cambridge, Mass., 1981.

W. Wulf, D. C. Russell, and A. N. Habermann, "BLISS: A Language for Systems Programming," *CACM* **14**(12), 780–790 (1971).

C. Zaniolo, "Object-Oriented Programming in PROLOG," in *Proceedings of the International Symposium on Logic Programming*, Atlantic City, 1984, pp. 265–270.

M. Bruynooghe
Catholic University Leuven

R. Venken
BIM

CREATIVITY

A creative act may be defined as one that is viewed as both valuable and novel and one that, in addition, reflects well on the cognitive abilities of the actor (whether human, animal, or machine). There are a number of conflicting views as to the nature of creative acts. Currently, the most attractive view is that championed by Simon and co-workers (1962, 1966). According to this view, creative acts are problem-solving acts of a special sort. First, they are problem-solving acts that meet criteria such as those above; that is, they are seen as novel and valuable, and they reflect credit on the cognitive abilities of the problem solver. Second, they often, though not always, involve ill-defined problems, that is, problems that cannot be solved unless the problem solver makes decisions or adds information of his or her own. Ill-defined problems occur frequently, for example, in architecture where the client typically specifies a few of the properties of a building to be designed but the architect must supply many more before the design problem can be solved. For a more complete discussion of ill-defined problems see Hayes (1978, 1980); Reitman (1965); and Simon (1973). Simon and co-workers interpret problem solving broadly, so that it includes not only the sciences but the arts and humanities as well.

A corollary of the Simon view is that there is no special creative mental process to be found in creative acts, that is, no process that is not also found in more mundane problem-solving acts. This view is consistent with observations of Patrick on poets (1935) and on painters (1937) (see also ART, AI IN) and of Reitman (1965) and of Simon and Sumner (1968) on musical composition (see also MUSIC, AI IN). These authors examined creative performances carefully and failed to find any process that was not also a part of everyday problem solving (qv). Some have claimed that creative acts are in principle unanalyzable. The philosopher of science Popper holds such a view about invention of scientific theories. In *The Logic of Scientific Discovery* (1959) Popper says:

The initial stage, the act of conceiving or inventing a theory, seems to me neither to call for logical analysis nor to be susceptible of it. . . . My view of the matter, for what it is worth, is that there is no such thing as a logical method of having new ideas, or a logical reconstruction of this process. My view may be expressed by saying that every discovery contains "an irrational element," or "a creative intuition," in Bergson's sense.

In their book, *Scientific Discovery: An Account of the Creative Processes,* Langley, Simon, Bradshaw, and Zytkow (1986) present a position directly challenging Popper's view. These authors argue that it is indeed possible to account for scientific discovery in terms of well-specified heuristics procedures, and that vague terms such as "inspiration" or "creative intuition" are unnecessary. In particular, they hold that discoveries are achieved when the scientist applies sensible heuristic procedures in drawing inferences from data. They argue quite convincingly for the adequacy of this view by incorporating such heuristics (qv) in computer programs, for example, BACON (Simon and co-workers, 1981), and by showing that these programs can induce well-known scientific laws, such as Kepler's laws of planetary motion, from data. Lenat had demonstrated earlier (1976) that a well-specified set of heuristics, incorporated in his program AM, could make interesting discoveries in mathematics. For example, AM discovered de Morgan's laws, the unique factorization of numbers into primes, and Goldbach's conjecture.

An early but still quite influential attempt to characterize creative processes is that of Wallas (1926). Wallas analyzed the testimony of creative individuals (notably that of the mathematician Poincaré) and proposed that the creative process could be described as a sequence of four stages:

Preparation
A stage in which the creator works intensively, acquiring information and attempting to understand the problem.

Incubation
A stage in which the creator is not attending to the problem but during which progress toward solution occurs nonetheless.

Illumination
A stage in which important insights about the problem occur to the creator suddenly and unexpectedly.

Verification
The final stage in which the creator works out the implications of the insights gained during illumination.

Of these four stages, the first is the least controversial. Most commentators agree that creative acts involve a great deal of work. Pasteur's famous statement, "chance favors only the prepared mind," (Vallery-Radot, 1923) represents these views well. Work by Hayes (1985) has extended the notion of preparation to make it a necessary stage not just in individual creative acts but also in the careers of creative individuals. Hayes studied 76 outstanding composers (including Mozart and Mendelssohn) and 131 famous painters. He found that the careers of these individuals typically included a six- to ten-year period of preparation before they began to produce world-class work. Among the composers, only three composed outstanding works earlier than the tenth year of their careers, and these three were produced in years eight and nine. These results parallel the observations of Simon and Chase (1973) on chess masters (see also COMPUTER CHESS AND SEARCH). Together, the results suggest strongly that creators have to acquire very large amounts of knowledge before important creative activity can occur.

Wallas's second stage, incubation, is considerably more controversial than the first. Cook (1934, 1937) and Ericksen (1942) doubted that incubation occurred because many attempts to demonstrate it experimentally had failed. More recently, though, Fulgosi and Guilford (1968), Murray and Denny (1968), and Silviera (1972) have succeeded in demonstrating the phenomenon experimentally. They have shown that subjects who are interrupted for a period of time late in the course of solving a problem solve it in less total time on the problem than subjects who are not interrupted.

Although the controversy over the existence of incubation appears to have been resolved, the nature of the processes underlying incubation remain controversial. One possible view is that humans have two processors, each of which is capable of solving problems, the familiar conscious one and another unconscious one that can carry out the problem-solving work when the conscious processor is distracted. This dual-processor position is generally not supported by other observations of cognitive processes in problem solving. Most work is consistent with the view that human problem solving is accomplished with a single serial processor. As an alternative to the dual-processor view, Simon (1966) has proposed that the progress that results from incubation can be attributed to forgetting. He holds that during the interruption period inefficient plans are forgotten. When problem solving is resumed, new, more effective plans—plans based on knowledge of the problem gained during the earlier solution attempts—are formed and lead to faster solution.

The following additional alternative is plausible but not inconsistent with Simon's proposal: in the course of problem solving, the solver may establish a number of search goals—goals to find facts, or relations, and/or operators that might be useful in solving the problem. In effect, the solver sets up "watchers" for relevant information. If these watchers continue to be active during the interruption period, they could discover information that is useful for solution and would speed solution of the "unattended" problem.

Wallas (1926) suggested that his four stages are characteristic of creative acts generally. However, a reanalysis of his data (Hayes, 1978) reveals many instances in which creative acts proceeded from beginning to end without any pause that would allow for incubation, without any evidence of illumination, and thus without any opportunity for verification. It appears, then, that although some creative acts do exhibit Wallas's four stages, many, and perhaps most, do not.

It is often assumed that creativity is closely related to IQ. Indeed, both Roe (1953), studying eminent physicists, biologists, and social scientists; and McKinnon (1968), studying distinguished research scientists, mathematicians, and architects, found that the creative individuals they studied had IQs ranging from 120 to 177, well above the general average. However, these higher than average IQs cannot be taken as an explanation of the observed creativity and indeed may be unrelated to it.

Several studies indicate that highly creative individuals in a field do not have higher IQs than matched individuals in their field who are not judged to be creative. Harmon (1963) rated 504 physical and biological scientists for research productivity and found no relation between creativity and either IQ or school grades. Bloom (1963) studied two samples of chemists and mathematicians. One sample consisted of individuals judged outstandingly productive by colleagues. The other consisted of scientists who were matched in age, education, and experience to the first sample but were not judged outstandingly productive. Although the first group outpublished the second at a rate of 8:1, there was no difference between them in IQ. In a similar study, McKinnon (1968) compared scientists, mathematicians, and architects who had made distinguished contributions to their fields with matched groups who had not made distinguished contributions. There was no difference between the two groups in either IQ or school grades.

It may appear puzzling that creative scientists and architects have higher than average IQs when IQ does not predict which of two professionals will be the more productive. One explanation for this paradox may be that, in many fields, obtaining the opportunity to display creativity depends on getting through college or graduate school. Since school performance is well predicted by IQ, it may be that one's opportunity to be, say, a biologist depends on IQ because of the degree requirement. Once one is certified as a biologist, whether one will be creative is unrelated to IQ or school grades.

As IQ and school grades do not predict creativity, neither do pencil-and-paper 'creativity' tests. The Westinghouse Science Talent Search is the only organization that has demonstrated the ability to predict creativity. The Westinghouse Science Talent Search has selected 40 high school students each year since 1942 on the basis of projects rather than written tests. In the group of 1520 students selected between 1942 and 1979, there are 5 Nobel prize winners, 5 winners of MacArthur Fellowships, and 2 winners of the Fields Medal in Mathematics. It is interesting to ask if the success of the Westinghouse Science Talent Search in identifying creative individuals depends on its use of performance measures (eg, projects) rather than pencil-and-paper tests.

BIBLIOGRAPHY

B. S. Bloom, "Report on Creativity Research by the Examiner's Office of the University of Chicago," in C. W. Taylor and F.

Barron, eds., *Scientific Creativity: Its Recognition and Development*, Wiley, New York, 1963.

T. W. Cook, "Massed and Distributed Practice in Puzzle Solving," *Psychol. Rev.* **41**, 330–335 (1934).

T. W. Cook, "Distribution of Practice and Size of Maze Pattern," *Br. J. Psychol.* **27**, 303–312 (1937).

S. C. Ericksen, "Variability of Attack in Massed and Spaced Practice," *J. Exper. Psychol.* **31**, 339–345 (1942).

A. Fulgosi and J. P. Guilford, "Short Term Incubation in Divergent Production," *Am. J. Psychol.* **7**, 1016–1023 (1968).

L. R. Harmon, "The Development of a Criterion of Scientific Competence," in C. W. Taylor and F. Barron, eds., *Scientific Creativity: Its Recognition and Development*, Wiley, New York, 1963, pp. 44–52.

J. R. Hayes, *Cognitive Psychology: Thinking and Creating*, Dorsey Press, Homewood, Ill., 1978.

J. R. Hayes, *The Complete Problem Solver*, Franklin Institute, Philadelphia, 1980.

J. R. Hayes, "Three Problems in Teaching Problem Solving Skills," in S. Chipman, J. Segal, and R. Glaser, eds., *Thinking and Learning Skills*, Vol. 2: *Research and Open Questions*, Erlbaum, Hillsdale, N.J., 1985, pp. 391–406.

P. W. Langley, H. A. Simon, G. L. Bradshaw, and J. M. Zytkow, *Scientific Discovery: An Account of the Creative Process*, MIT Press, Cambridge, Mass., 1986.

D. Lenat, *AM: An Artificial Intelligence Approach to Discovery in Mathematics as Heuristic Search*, SAIL AIM-286, Artificial Intelligence Laboratory, Stanford University, Stanford, Calif., July 1976.

D. W. McKinnon, "Selecting Students with Creative Potential," in P. Heist, ed., *The Creative College Student: An Unmet Challenge*, Jossey-Bass, San Francisco, 1968, pp. 104–116.

H. G. Murray and J. P. Denny, "Interaction of Ability Level and Interpolated Activity (Opportunity for Incubation) in Human Problem Solving," *Psychol. Rep.* **24**, 271–276 (1968).

A. Newell, J. C. Shaw, and H. A. Simon, "The Process of Creative Thinking," in H. Gruber, G. Terrell, and M. Wertheimer, eds., *Contemporary Approaches to Creative Thinking*, Atherton, New York, 1962, pp. 63–119.

C. Patrick, "Creative Thought in Poets," *Arch. Psychol.* **26**, 1–74 (1935).

C. Patrick, "Creative Thought in Artists," *J. Psychol.* **4**, 35–73 (1937).

K. R. Popper, *The Logic of Scientific Discovery*, Hutchinson, London, pp. 31–32, 1959.

W. R. Reitman, *Cognition and Thought*, Wiley, New York, 1965.

A. Roe, *The Making of a Scientist*, Dodd Mead, New York, 1953.

J. M. Silviera, "Incubation: The Effects of Interruption Timing and Length on Problem Solution and Quality of Problem Processing," Ph.D. dissertation, University of Oregon, 1971; *Diss. Ab. Int.* **32**, 5500B (1972).

H. A. Simon, "Scientific Discovery and the Psychology of Problem Solving," in R. G. Colodny, ed., *Mind and Cosmos: Essays in Contemporary Science and Philosophy*, Vol. 3, University of Pittsburgh Press, Pittsburgh, Penn., 1966, pp. 22–40.

H. A. Simon and R. K. Sumner, "Pattern in Music," in B. Kleinmuntz, ed., *Formal Representation of Human Judgment*, Wiley, New York, pp. 219–250, 1968.

H. A. Simon, "The Structure of Ill-Structured Problems," *Artif. Intell.* **4**, 181–201 (1973).

H. A. Simon and W. Chase, "Skill in Chess," *Am. Sci.* **61**, 394–403 (1973).

H. A. Simon, P. W. Langley, and G. L. Bradshaw, *Synthese* **47** (1) (1981).

R. Vallery-Radot, *The Life of Pasteur*, Doubleday Page, Garden City, New York, 1923, p. 79.

G. Wallas, *The Art of Thought*, Harcourt Brace, New York, 1926.

JOHN R. HAYES
Carnegie Mellon University

CYBERNETICS

The phrase "control and communication in the animal and the machine" can serve as a definition of cybernetics. Although this term was used by Ampére about 150 years ago (Zeleny, 1979) and its concepts were used by Heron of Alexandria more than 1500 years ago (Mayr, 1969), it was the mathematician Wiener who, in 1948, with the publication of *Cybernetics*, gave name and meaning to this notion in the modern context. The name cybernetics is derived from the Greek word for steersman, κυβερνήτης, which in Latin became *gubernator*, governor in English. The concept associated with this term was to characterize a mode of behavior that is fundamentally distinct from the customary perception of the operations of machines with their one-to-one correspondence of cause–effect, stimulus–response, input–output, and so on. The distinction arises from the presence of sensors whose report on the state of the effectors of the system acts on the operation of that system. Specifically, if this is an inhibitory action that reduces the discrepancy between the reported state of the effectors and an internal state of the system, the system displays goal-oriented behavior (Conant, 1981); that is, if perturbed by any outside means, it will return to some representation of this internal state, the goal. Although this scheme does not specify the physical nature of the states alluded to, nor of the signals reporting about these states—whether they are electric currents, mechanical or chemical agents, abstract symbols, or whatever—the biological flavor of the language used is apparent. This is no accident; in the formative years of this concept the close cooperation of Wiener with the neurophysiologist Rosenblueth created a physiological context. Moreover, this cooperation stimulated the philosophical inclination of these two men, and together with Bigelow they set the stage for still ongoing epistemological inquiries with the publication of "Behavior, Purpose and Teleology" (Rosenblueth and co-workers, 1943).

Another fruitful *ménage à trois* of philosophy, physiology, and mathematics was the collaboration of McCulloch, philosopher, logician, neurophysiologist, or "experimental epistemologist," as he liked to call himself, and a brilliant young mathematician, Pitts, who published together two papers of profound influence on this emerging mode of thinking. The titles of these papers almost give away their content: "A Logical Calculus of the Ideas Immanent in Nervous Activity" (McCulloch and Pitts, 1943) and "How We Know Universals: The Perception of Auditory and Visual Forms" (Pitts and McCulloch, 1947). Then von Neumann's fascination with seeing a parallelism of the logical organization of computations in nervous tissue and in constructed artifacts (von Neumann, 1958) brought him close to McCulloch (von Neumann, 1951) and the people around him.

The underlying logic of these various concepts was the topic for ten seminal conferences between 1946 and 1953, bringing together mathematicians, biologists, anthropologists, neurophysiologists, logicians, and so on, who saw the significance of the notions that were spelled out in the title of the earlier conferences, "Circular Causal and Feedback Mechanisms in Biological and Social Systems." After Wiener's book *Cybernetics* appeared in 1948, "Cybernetics" became the main title of these conferences (von Foerster and co-workers, 1950–1955). Their participants became the catalysts for the dissemination of cybernetic concepts into everyday vernacular (eg, feedback) and for epistemological inquiries regarding mentality, and, of course, mentality in machines (MacKay, 1952). Should one name one central concept, a first principle of cybernetics, it would be circularity—circularity as it appears in the circular flow of signals in organizationally closed systems; or in circular causality, that is, in processes in which ultimately a state reproduces itself; or in systems with reflexive logic eg, self-reference (qv), self-organization, the psychological self, and so on. Today, recursiveness may be substituted for circularity, and the theory of recursive functions (see Recursion), calculi of self-reference (Varela, 1975; Kauffman, 1987), and autology (Löfgren), that is, the logic of concepts that can be applied to themselves, may be taken as appropriate formalisms.

MECHANISMS

Consider again a system with a functional organization whose operation diminishes the discrepancy between a specific state and a perturbation. The system's tendency to approach this specific state, the goal, the end, in Greek τέλος (hence teleology), may be interpreted as the system having a purpose (Pask, 1969). The purpose of invoking the autological notion of purpose is to emphasize the irrelevance of the trajectories traced by such a system en route from an arbitrary initial state to its goal. In synthesized systems, in machines, whose internal workings are known, this irrelevance has no significance. This irrelevance becomes highly significant, however, when the analytic problem, the machine identification problem, cannot be solved, because, for instance, it is transcomputational (Bremmermann, 1974) in the sense that with known algorithms the number of elementary computations exceeds the age of the universe expressed in nanoseconds. Hence, the notion of purpose can become effective when dealing with living organisms whose goals may be known but whose behavioral trajectories are indeterminable. Aristotle juxtaposed the *efficient cause,* ie, when "because" is used to explain the flow of events, with the *final cause,* ie, when "in order to" is used to justify forthcoming action. In the early, enthusiastic stages of cybernetics, language appropriate for living things such as memory, information, intelligence, mind, and ethics were sometimes used in talking about synthesized behavior, thus creating the im-

pression that by analogy of name one could hope for analogy of structure and function. Traces of this are still found today in such terms as "computer memory," "processing of information," and "artificial intelligence." The fascination with bio-mimesis, that is, immitating life, keeps the present-day followers of Aristotle searching for a synthesis of aspects of mentation by using the powers of large mainframe computers. On the other hand, the analytic problem "what is mind?" and "whence ideas?" in the Platonic sense keeps cyberneticians searching for principles of computation and logic underlying sensorimotor competence, thought, and language.

Although in the early phases of this search the notion of purpose appeared in many studies of these processes, it is significant that a completely purpose-free language can be developed for the same type of systems by paying attention to the recursive nature of the processes involved. Of interest are circumstances in which the dynamics of a system transforms certain states into these very states, where the domain of states may be numeric values, arrangements (arrays, vectors, configurations, etc), functions (polynomials, algebraic functions, etc), functionals, dynamic behaviors, and so on, as attested by the proliferation of books and papers addressing these fascinating developments. Depending on domain and context, these states are in theoretical studies referred to as fixed points, limit cycles, eigenbehaviors, eigenoperators, and so on, and lately also as *attractors,* a terminology reintroducing teleology in modern dress (Abraham and Shaw, 1985; Peitgen and Richter, 1986; Ashby, 1956; Koslow and co-workers, 1987; Grebogin and co-workers, 1987). Pragmatically, they correspond to the computation of invariants; they may be object constancy (Von Foerster, 1984b), perceptual universals, cognitive invariants, identifications, namings, and so on. However, the student of recursively operating systems should be prepared for the interesting cases in which dynamic stability is not attained: the systems develop chaotic behavior (Grebogin and co-workers, 1987).

EPISTEMOLOGY

While circularity, the central theme of cybernetics, could be seen as implicit in earlier philosophical positions (see, eg, Phenomenology; Epistemology), its fecundity became apparent when the concept was made explicit. Two comments, taken from McCulloch's vast literary output (1989) illustrate the two major epistemological branches that grew over the years and are popularly referred to as first-order and second-order cybernetics.

The case for first-order cybernetics has been made by the body of work of early cyberneticians including Wiener and Bigelow, and most clearly, for our purpose, by McCulloch's invention of heterarchy, postulating closure of the operations of the nervous system (McCulloch, 1945; Maturana, 1970). In contrast to *hierarchy* (from Greek: holiness is ruling), which defines the sacerdotal structure of the church in which the many ends are ordered by the right of each to inhibit all inferiors and thereby stipulates a *summum bonum* (a supreme good), *heterarchy* (the other one is ruling) identifies the structure of a nervous net that would allow the computation of the observed *value anomaly* in which A is preferred to B, B to C, but C to A. The topology of this net is that of the surface of the torus, circular in both the x and the y directions.

Another case of a net with circular organization that cannot be mapped onto a plane is *autopoiesis*. According to Maturana and Varela (1980), an autopoietic system consists of interactive components whose interactions produce these very same components. Autopoiesis is thus a special case of self-organizing systems, whose organization is its own *eigenorganization*. As these authors demonstrated, autopoiesis fulfills the necessary and sufficient condition for the organization of living organisms, that is, for the definition of life. Moreover, the notion of autopoiesis allows the phenomenon of language to emerge as a consequence, as the *eigenbehavior,* of the recursive interactions of two organisms, each in need of the other for the realization of its own autopoiesis (Maturana, 1978).

The most exhaustive treatment of this symmetry of dialogical partners has been developed in great depth by Pask in his theory of conversation (1980), which, in distinction to the theory of communication, rests on the autological nature of language as the conversational medium. Because language can speak of itself having language, syntax, word, and so forth in its vocabulary, in conversations speakers can speak of themselves, thus preserving their autonomy in a social context by uttering, for example, the first person singular pronoun in the nominative case, "I", thus generating the shortest self-referential loop (Von Foerster, 1984c).

It is precisely at this point that the perspectives of second-order cybernetics can be seen (Von Foerster, 1979). Let it be illustrated with another comment by McCulloch (1989, p. 651):

Let us compell our physicist to account for himself as a part of the physical world. In all fairness, he must stick to his own rules and show in terms of mass, energy, space, and time how it comes about that he creates theoretical physics.

Second-order cybernetics invites you to leave Helmholtz's *locus observandi* and to step into the dynamic circularity of human give-and-take by becoming part and partner of the universe of discourse and the discourse on the universe.

With the removal of the logical and semantic difficulties associated with the inclusion of the speaker into his speech and the observer into his observation, etc (see Spencer Brown, 1969)—difficulties that still plagued Russell and many of his predecessors—an epistemology built on responsiveness and responsibility in interpersonal relationships gives solid ground for theoretical developments of language and action where ethics is implicit (Von Foerster, 1984a). These developments are apparent in psychiatry, particularly in family therapy, which requires the inclusion of the therapist in a group of conversing individuals who are seeking the therapist's help (Griffith and co-workers, 1990; Telfener, 1990), or in social theories, which account for the theoretician being a member of the society of which he writes the theory (Lumann,

1984). The fathers and mothers who initiated this mode of thinking and, lacking a good term, outrageously called it "circular causal and feedback mechanisms in biological and social systems" might find it amusing that almost half a century later, there is serious concern with circular causal and feedback mechanisms in biological and social systems.

BIBLIOGRAPHY

R. H. Abraham and C. D. Shaw, *Dynamics—The Geometry of Behavior*, Santa Cruz, Calif., 1985.

W. R. Ashby, *An Introduction to Cybernetics*, Chapman & Hall, London, 1956.

H. J. Bremmermann, "Algorithms, Complexity, Transcomputability, and the Analysis of Systems," in W. D. Keidel, W. Haendler, and M. Spreng, eds., *Cybernetics and Bionics*, R. Oldenbourg, Munich, 1974, 250–263.

R. Conant, ed., *Mechanisms of Intelligence: Ross Ashby's Writings on Cybernetics*, Intersystems Publications, Seaside, UK, 1981.

C. Grebogin, E. Ott, and J. A. Yorke, "Chaos, Strange Attractors, and Fractal Basin Boundaries in Nonlinear Dynamics," *Science* **238**, 632–638 (1987).

J. L. Griffith, M. E. Griffith, and L. S. Slovik, "Mind-Body Problems in Family Therapy: Contrasting First- and Second-Order Cybernetics Approaches," *Family Process* **29**(1), 13–28 (1990).

L. H. Kauffman, "Self-Reference and Recursive Form," *J. Soc. Biol. Struct.* **10**, 53–72 (1987).

S. H. Koslow, A. J. Mandell, and M. F. Schlesinger, eds., *Perspectives in Biological Dynamics and Theoretical Medicine*, Ann. N.Y. Acad. Sci., Vol. 504, 1987.

L. Löfgren, "Autology for Second Order Cybernetics," in *Fundamentals of Cybernetics, Proceedings of the Tenth International Congress on Cybernetics*, Namur, Belgium, 1983, Association Internationale de Cybernetique, pp. 17–23.

N. Lumann, *Soziale Systeme: Grundriss Einer Allgemeinen Theorie*, Suhrkamp, Frankfurt, Germany, 1984.

D. M. MacKay, "Mentality in Machines," in *Proceedings of the Aristotelian Society*, Supplement 1952, pp. 61–86, 1952.

H. R. Maturana, "The Neurophysiology of Cognition" in P. L. Garvin, ed., *Cognition: A Multiple View*, Spartan Books, New York, 1970, pp. 3–23.

H. R. Maturana, "Biology of Language: The Epistemology of Reality," in G. A. Miller and E. Lenneberg, eds., *Psychology and Biology of Language and Thought*, Academic Press, New York, 1978, pp. 28–64.

H. R. Maturana and F. J. Varela, "Autopoiesis: The Organization of the Living," in *Autopoiesis and Cognition, The Realization of the Living*, D. Reidel, Dordrecht, Netherlands, 1980, pp. 73–141.

O. Mayr, *The Origins of Feedback Control*, MIT Press, Cambridge, Mass., 1969.

W. S. McCulloch, "A Heterarchy of Values Determined by the Topology of Nervous Nets," *Bull. Math. Biophys.* **7**, 89–93 (1945).

W. S. McCulloch, *Collected Works of Warren S. McCulloch*, Rook McCulloch, ed., Intersystems Publications, Salinas, Calif., 1989.

W. S. McCulloch and W. H. Pitts, "A Logical Calculus of the Ideas Immanent in Nervous Activity," *Bull. Math. Biophys.* **5**, 115–133 (1943).

G. Pask, "The Meaning of Cybernetics in the Behavioral Sciences (The Cybernetics of Behavior and Cognition: Extending the Meaning of "Goal")," in J. Rose, ed., *Progress of Cybernetics*, Vol. 1, Gordon and Breach, New York, 1969, pp. 15–44.

G. Pask "The Limits of Togetherness," in S. H. Levington, ed., *Information Processing 80,* IFIP, North-Holland, Amsterdam 1980, pp. 999–1012.

H. O. Peitgen and P. H. Richter, *The Beauty of Fractals*, Springer, New York, 1986.

W. Pitts and W. S. McCulloch, "How We Know Universals: The Perception of Auditory and Visual Forms," *Bull. Math. Biophys.* **9,** 127–147 (1947).

A. Rosenblueth, N. Wiener, and J. Bigelow, "Behavior, Purpose and Teleology," *Philos. Sci.* **10,** 18–24 (1943).

G. Spencer Brown, *Laws of Form*, George Allen and Unwin, London, 1969.

U. Telfener, "Some Thoughts on the Evolution of the Milan Approach," in J. Hargens, ed., *Systemic Therapy: A European Perspective*, Borgmann, Dortmund, Germany, 1990, pp. 62–71.

F. J. Varela, "A Calculus for Self-Reference," *Int. J. Gen. Syst.* **2,** 5–24 (1975).

H. Von Foerster, "Cybernetics of Cybernetics," in K. Krippendorff, ed., *Communication and Control in Society*, Gordon and Breach, New York, 1979, pp. 5–8.

H. Von Foerster, "Implicit Ethics," in A. Pedretti, ed., *Of/Of Book-Conference*, Princelet Edition, London, 1984a, pp. 17–20.

H. Von Foerster, "Objects: Tokens for (Eigen-) Behavior," in F. J. Varela, ed., *Observing Systems*, Intersystems Publications, Salinas, Calif., 1984b, 273–286.

H. Von Foerster, "Notes on an Epistemology of Living Things," in F. J. Varela, ed., *Observing Systems*, Intersystems Publications, Salinas, Calif., 1984c.

H. Von Foerster and co-workers, *Cybernetics: Circular Causal and Feedback Mechanisms in Biological and Social Systems*, Proceedings of the Sixth, Seventh, Eighth, Ninth, and Tenth Conferences on Cybernetics: Circular Causal and Feedback Mechanisms in Biological and Social Systems, 5 vols., The Josiah Macy, Jr. Foundation, New York, 1950–1955.

J. von Neumann, "The General and Logical Theory of Automata," in L. A. Jeffress, ed., *Cerebral Mechanisms in Behavior*, The Hixon Symposium, Wiley, New York, 1951, pp. 1–41.

J. von Neumann, *The Computer and the Brain*, Yale University Press, New Haven, Conn., 1958.

N. Wiener, *Cybernetics: Or Control and Communication in the Animal and the Machine*, Wiley, New York, 1948.

M. Zeleny, "Cybernetics and General Systems: A Unitary Science?" *Kybernetes* 8(1), 17–23 (1979).

HEINZ VON FOERSTER
University of Illinois

CYRUS

Cyrus kept track of the day-to-day events in Cyrus Vance's life while he was Secretary of State of the United States. It was built as both a model of human long-term memory and as a prototype for an intelligent fact retrieval system. Cyrus was the first implementation of Schank's dynamic memory and MOPs scheme. It organized events in redundant discrimination nets called E-MOPs. In order to constrain the redundancy of the discriminations, each node in the memory kept track of similarities between events organized below it. These similarities also served as generalized information available to guide inference procedures. In addition to storing events, Cyrus retrieved facts from its memory based on English-language queries. This often required elaborative inferences necessary to bridge the gap between the concepts in a question and those used as indexes in the system. Cyrus was the forerunner of case-based reasoning systems. The principles of its memory organization and indexing scheme continue to be adhered to in those systems. [See J. L. Kolodner, *Retrieval and Organizational Strategies in Conceptual Memory: A Computer Model*, Lawrence Erlbaum Associates, Hillsdale, N.J., 1984; J. L. Kolodner, "Reconstructive Memory: A Computer Model, *Cogn. Sci.* **7**(4), 281–328 (1983); J. L. Kolodner, "Maintaining Organization in a Conceptual Memory for Events," *Cogn. Sci.* **7**(4), 243–280 (1983); see also REASONING, CASE-BASED.]

JANET L. KOLODNER
Georgia Institute of Technology

D

DADO

A considerable amount of interest has been generated recently in specialized machine architectures designed for the very rapid execution of AI software (see PARALLEL MACHINE ARCHITECTURE). The Japanese fifth-generation machine project, for example, promises to deliver a device capable of computing solutions of PROLOG programs at execution rates on the order of many thousands of logical inferences per second. Such a device will require high-speed hardware executing a large number of primitive symbol manipulation tasks many times faster than today's fastest computers. This rather ambitious goal has led some researchers to suspect that a fundamentally different computer organization is necessary to achieve this performance. Thus, parallel processing has assumed an important position in current AI research. This article outlines the development of a specific parallel machine architecture called DADO, the class of problems it is well-suited to solving, and a specific load balancing technique designed to optimize its performance. DADO is a binary tree-structured multiprocessor architecture incorporating a large number of processing elements (PEs). Each PE consists of a fully programmable microcomputer with a modest amount of local memory. For example, the 1023 PE DADO2 (Stalfo and Miranker, 1986), completed in December 1985, consists of Intel 8751 microcomputers with 64k RAM at each PE, in the aggregate delivering over 570 MIPS. The most recent coarser-grain prototype, DADO4, completed in December 1989, is designed with 15 DSP32C chips delivering in the aggregate approximately 300 Mflops on a two-board system. Each DADO4 PE has a full megabyte of storage.

CLASS OF PROBLEMS

In earlier work, one approach to parallelizing the match task of rule-based programs on the DADO2 parallel computer was invented and implemented. This approach may be viewed as a *data parallel* activity. This work has been previously reported in Stolfo (1987), where it is carefully compared to a similar yet different approach proposed by Bentley and Kung. Bentley and Kung (1979) proposed a systolic parallel machine, based on a "dual tree" interconnection, to execute a stream of dictionary-type queries rapidly. (This machine was never realized.) For this article, a class of searching problems that generalizes those investigated by Bentley and Kung is outlined briefly and the method by which they are parallelized on the DADO parallel computer is described. The match task of AI rule-based programs are a specific example of this class.

A *decomposable searching problem* is a searching problem in which a query asking the relationship of a new object x to a set of objects F can be written as:

$$\text{Query } (x, \text{F}) = \text{Bq}(x, f)$$
$$f \text{ in F}$$

where B is the repeated application of a commutative, associative binary operator b that has an identity and q is a "primitive query" applied between the new object x and each element f of F. Hence, membership is a decomposable searching problem when cast as

$$\text{Member } (x, \text{F}) = \text{OR equal } (x, f).$$
$$f \text{ in F}$$

The *nearest neighbor problem*, which determines for an arbitrary point x in the plane its nearest neighbor in a set F of N points, can be cast as

$$NN(x, \text{F}) = \text{MIN distance}(x, f).$$
$$f \text{ in F}$$

Decomposable searching problems are well suited to direct parallel execution. The key idea about these kinds of problems is decomposability. To answer a query about F, one can combine the answers of the query applied to arbitrary subsets of F. The idea is simply to partition the set F into a number of subsets equal to N, the number of available PE's. (For pedagogical reasons, in what follows, assume a single set element f is stored at a PE.) Apply the query q in parallel at each PE between the unknown x that is communicated to all the PEs and the locally stored set element f. Finally, combine the answers in parallel by log N repetitions of b. This last step proceeds by applying $N/2$ b-computations simultaneously between "adjacent" pairs of PEs. The $N/2$ resultant values are processed again in the same fashion. Hence $N/4$ b-computations are applied in parallel, producing $N/8$ results. After log N steps, the final single result is computed.

The approach invented (and implemented on the DADO2 machine) is quite different from Bentley and Kung's approach to solving decomposable searching problems as well as variations that are called *almost* decomposable searching problems. (Almost decomposable searching problems exhibit phenomena that cause systolic pipe flushing, which is problematic for Bentley and Kung's idealized machine.) In a nutshell, queries are rapidly broadcast to all the PEs in the parallel processor. Primitive queries are executed in parallel by all PEs, and in several important cases, the combined result of applying operator b is obtained very quickly with parallel hardware support by a primitive operation called min-resolve. (In the case of DADO2, this step takes one instruction cycle for up to 8000 PEs.) This mode of operation is called Broadcast/Match/Resolve/Report.

Earlier reports (eg, Stolfo, 1984) detail a number of parallel algorithms to accelerate the execution of characteristically different production system (PS) programs. The simplest of these algorithms, called the *Full Distribution Algorithm*, is based on allocating each rule in the production memory (PM), as well as the working memory (WM) elements relevant to its left-hand side, to a single PE of a large-scale, fine-grain multiprocessor, such as the DADO2 machine. In essence, the original PS is coverted into a large number of "one-rule" PSs, each processed concurrently. In this form, rule-level parallelism can be cast as an almost decomposable searching problem as:

$$\text{Query}(\text{WM}_i, \text{PM}) = \underset{r \text{ in PM}}{\text{Max match}}(r, \text{WM}_i)$$

where "match" is the primitive operation of matching a single rule and WM_i is the WM on the ith cycle of execution of the PS program.

For some PS programs, however, the potential speed-up of the match phase using the Full Distribution Algorithm is not nearly as great as might be expected. Some rules may not need to be matched on each cycle and, as well, some rules may require more processing time than others. Both problems lead to inefficient use of the available PEs. In the first case the problem can be ameliorated simply by allocating multiple rules to each PE, taking care to allocate rules to separate PEs that may be matched concurrently (this is the approach taken with the DADO4). In the second case, load balancing is required. A rather simple scheme called *copy and constrain* that attempts to ameliorate the second problem has been proposed. The essence of the approach is to replicate anomalous rules that require more processing time than the others and to introduce constraints within the copies which restrict them to match smaller, disjoint portions of the set of potentially relevant WM elements.

The scheme is best introduced by means of a simple example. Consider the stylized rule

$$P_I = (C_1 C_2 \ldots C_n \rightarrow A_I \ldots A_m),$$

where $C_i (i = 1, \ldots, n)$ are condition elements, and A_i are actions of the rule P_I. If one interprets WM_I (the set of working memory elements relevant to P_I's left-hand side) as a relation, or set of tuples, then each condition element, C_i, may be viewed as a *relation selection*. The set of instantiations (matches) of P_I is the equijoin of the relations R_i selected by the condition elements C_i. The local memory requirements and execution time to match P_I are thus bounded by (and indeed may achieve) the size of the full Cartesian product of the individual relations R_i.

Suppose for concreteness that C_2 of this stylized rule is a relational selection of a large number of physical objects, represented by the OPS5-style pattern:

(PHYSICAL-OBJECT ^Name $\langle x \rangle$ ^Color $\langle y \rangle$ ^Shape $\langle z \rangle$)

and that the domain of the Color attribute of the relation WM_1 is {RED, GREEN}, that is, that physical objects are either RED or GREEN. To speed up the match of rule P_I, split the set of working memory elements associated with P_I and set two PEs to the concurrent tasks of matching

constrained versions of P_I. Thus two new condition elements are constructed:

$C_2' = $ (PHYSICAL-OBJECT ^Name $\langle x \rangle$
                          ^Color RED ^Shape $\langle z \rangle$)

$C_2'' = $ (PHYSICAL-OBJECT ^Name $\langle x \rangle$
                          ^Color GREEN ^Shape $\langle z \rangle$)

as well as two new rules:

$$P_I' = (C_1 C_2' \ldots C_n \rightarrow A_I \ldots A_m)$$
$$P_I'' = (C_1 C_2'' \ldots C_n \rightarrow A_I \ldots A_m)$$

and two new working memories:

$\text{WM}_I' = \{w \text{ in } \text{WM}_I : \text{Color}(w) = \text{RED if } w \text{ is a} \\ \text{PHYSICAL-OBJECT}\}$

$\text{WM}_I'' = \{w \text{ in } \text{WM}_I : \text{Color}(w) = \text{GREEN if } w \text{ is a} \\ \text{PHYSICAL-OBJECT}\}$

and assign them to distinct PEs, PE_I' and PE_I''. P_I' and P_I'' may clearly be matched in parallel, and the set of instantiations of P_I is exactly the disjoint union of the instantiations of P_I' and P_I''.

In the best case, half the tuples selected by the original condition C_2 of rule P_I reside in each of PE_I' and PE_I'', and the processing time required to match P_I decreases by half, since the two new rules can be matched in parallel. Local processing requirements and storage of WM elements for each rule decrease significantly as well. In the worst case, of course, all the tuples selected by C_2 of rule P_I reside in one of the two PEs, and PE_I'', and partitioning buys nothing. If more PEs are available, the scheme can be applied repeatedly, producing many copies of rules, each constrained to match a smaller range of distinct WM elements. Thus, with many PEs available, it should be possible to reduce the inter-PE variation in processing times, balancing the execution load over the entire system and increasing overall performance (see Pasik, 1989; Stolfo, 1987 for example performance runs demonstrating this approach).

If a small finite domain of attribute values is not known a priori (as in the above example with RED and GREEN objects), two variations on the technique are possible. The first is hash partitioning, whereby an easily computable function is used to partition the domain of the attribute artificially. The second variation of the basic technique applies when the domain is a totally ordered set: one can simply split it into disjoint subranges and assign each to a separate PE together with constrained versions of the original rule P_I.

The scheme outlined can be implemented by a simple preprocessor supplied with information on how to partition the domains of working memory attributes. These programs, or hints, can take the form of explicit values or ranges provided by the programs (derived from knowledge of the problem or from previous executions of the production system program), or can include hashing functions.

The preprocessor's role is simply to generate new productions incorporating the value, hashing function, or subrange tests, one for each value, function value, or subrange supplied.

It is interesting to note that the work on the parallel execution of PS programs is one example of an almost decomposable searching problem efficiently executed on the DADO machine. Another important example that is proposed is structural pattern recognition problems such as those in speech recognition applications. The DADO4 has been constructed to support this numerically intensive application (Stolfo and co-workers, 1989) in addition to the symbolic AI applications.

BIBLIOGRAPHY

J. Bentley and H. T. Kung, *A Tree Machine for Searching Problems*, Technical Report, Carnegie Mellon University, Computer Science Department, Pittsburgh, Pa., Sept. 1979.

A. Pasik, *A Methodology for Programming Production Systems and its Implications on Parallelism,* Ph.D. dissertation, Technical Report, Department of Computer Science, Columbia University, New York, 1989.

S. J. Stolfo, "Five Parallel Algorithms for Production System Execution on the DADO Machine," in *Proceedings of the Fourth National Conference on Artificial Intelligence*, Austin, Texas, AAAI, Menlo Park, Calif., 1984.

S. J. Stolfo, "Initial Performance of the DADO2 Prototype," *IEEE Computer* (Special Issue on AI Machines) **20**, 75–83 (Jan. 1987).

S. J. Stolfo, Z. Galil, K. McKeown, and R. Mills, "Speech Recognition in Parallel," in *Proceedings of the DARPA Speech and Natural Language Workshop*, Oct. 1989, pp. 353–373.

S. J. Stolfo and D. Miranker "The DADO Production System Machine," *J. Parallel Distrib. Syst.* (Aug. 1986).

SALVATORE J. STOLFO
Columbia University

DATABASES. See DEDUCTIVE DATABASE SYSTEMS; FUZZY DATABASES.

DATA-DRIVEN PROCESSING. See PROCESSING, BOTTOM-UP AND TOP-DOWN.

DATA PARALLELISM

Nature has a wealth of examples of massive parallelism, from the hundreds of paramecia independently functioning in a drop of water to the millions of neurons simultaneously firing and repolarizing in the human brain. Because many of today's most computationally expensive tasks involve simulating such natural processes it is not surprising that today's computers have also begun to exploit parallelism. To see how this is accomplished consider that computation can be broken down into two elements: control (the computer program) and data. In such a model there are two ways to achieve parallelism, either by si-multaneously performing different operations on the same data, or by simultaneously performing the same operation on different pieces of data. The first approach, which seeks to subdivide and overlap the processing, is called *control parallelism*. The second approach, which seeks to subdivide and concurrently operate on the data, is called data parallelism.

Data parallelism is thus a quality that can be displayed by computer hardware, computer software, or computer applications. In the case of computer hardware, data parallelism is generally manifest by large numbers of processing elements each with fast access to local memory and slower access to the local memories of other processing units. Examples include the MPP, the DAP, and the Connection Machine (qv) systems. Computer languages that exhibit data parallelism generally allow for data structures that can easily be subdivided into smaller structurally similar pieces that can be processed independently (eg, arrays). Examples of such languages include *LISP, C*, and FORTRAN 90 with its parallel array extensions. Data parallel applications are also generally noted as having large quantities of data where the data can be subdivided into pieces that can be processed relatively independently. An example application is the optimization of a population of simulated organisms in the study of genetic algorithms or artificial life. The above definitions and examples are, of course, simplifications. It is certainly possible to construct a two-processor data parallel computer or a two-data-element data parallel application. The fact that the definition of data parallelism allows for such small numbers of processing units and yet most data parallel computers consist of from hundreds to tens of thousands of processing units points out that the driving force behind data parallelism is the enormous computational size of the applications themselves.

DATA PARALLELISM IN CONTRAST TO CONTROL PARALLELISM

Despite the early recognition of data parallel problems, the earliest form of parallelism in both computer hardware and software was control parallelism. Generally control parallelism implies indivisible data and a long processing stage that can be subdivided and overlapped. An analogy may make the data–control parallelism distinction clear. Consider that a computer, its program, and its initial data are much like an automobile manufacturing plant. Raw materials for the cars enter one end of the plant and are processed as they move along the length of the plant. Finally, new cars emerge from the other end (Fig. 1). In this scenario, control parallelism is analogous to the breaking up of the manufacturing process such that certain pieces of it are performed in parallel (Fig. 2). For instance, one person could be manufacturing the windshield at the same time another person could be manufacturing the wheels. Because there is now overlap between sections of the plant, the total processing time is decreased.

Data parallelism takes a different approach. Here, the realization is that the raw materials (the data) can be subdivided, and the processing of the raw materials for

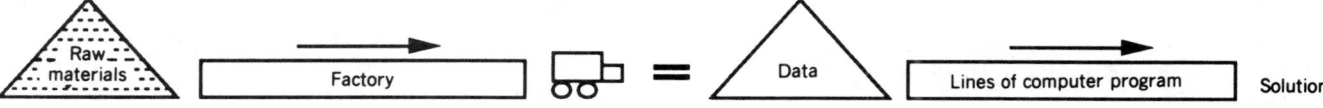

Figure 1. Serial processing.

each car can be performed somewhat independently (Fig. 3). In this case any number of cars can now be produced in the same amount of time that it took to produce one car. This analogy shows the benefits of data parallel computing and can also easily incorporate other forms of parallel computation such as pipelining. Note also that it is easy to conceive of applications that could benefit from combinations of control and data parallelism (Fig. 4). There are, however, subtleties to this analogy that do not hold in the case of the computer. (For example, the data parallel analogy assumes no communication among processing units.) In general, though, the conclusions that can be drawn from the analogy are valid: if it is necessary to produce lots of cars (data), then data parallelism is probably a good way to go. If there is only one car to build but a long processing stage that is easily subdivided, then the control parallel model is the correct model. It is also clear that no matter how long the processing stage is, if there are enough cars (data), there will always be a benefit from data parallelism. This has been nicely stated by Hillis and Steele (1986):

> We are beginning to suspect that this is an appropriate style wherever the amount of data to be operated upon is very large. Perhaps, in retrospect, this is a trivial observation in the sense that, if the number of lines of code is fixed and the amount of data is allowed to grow arbitrarily, then the ratio of code to data will necessarily approach zero. The parallelism to be gained by concurrently operating on multiple data elements will therefore be greater than the parallelism to be gained by concurrently executing lines of code.

DATA PARALLELISM IN COMPUTER HARDWARE

Data parallel computer hardware is generally characterized by large numbers of processing units with associated memory. Distinctions can be drawn between processors that can operate completely independently from one another (the MIMD parallel model) and those where processors either perform or abstain from the same operation at

each execution cycle (the SIMD parallel model) (Flynn, 1972). There are also differences in the way that interprocessor communication is affected; hypercube and simple two-dimensional grid patterns are common examples. These differences are, however, independent of the data parallel model. In general a data parallel computer can be recognized by the replication of many nonspecialized processing units and their local memory. This replication of identical processing units also holds an advantage for the manufacturing and maintenance of these machines and enables the hardware to scale nicely with the size of the problem.

DATA PARALLELISM IN COMPUTER SOFTWARE

Data parallel programming differs from sequential programming in that functions are generally applied to all the data at once. Consider the example where the elements of two one-dimensional arrays A and B are added together and the result placed in the elements of a third array C. In the serial machine model, this could be accomplished by acting on each individual element in a do loop:

```
do [i,0,10000]
    C[i] = A[i] + B[i]
```

In a data parallel programming model each element of each array could be stored in a processing unit and the addition could be accomplished in a single step by viewing the two arrays, rather than their elements, as the primary data objects:

$$C = A + B$$

DATA PARALLELISM IN COMPUTER APPLICATIONS

Many of the promising areas of research in artificial intelligence involve learning systems based on large quanti-

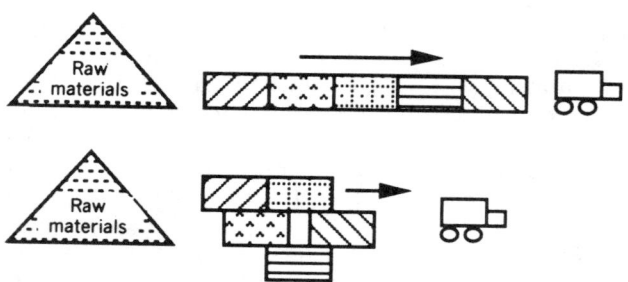

Figure 2. Control parallel processing.

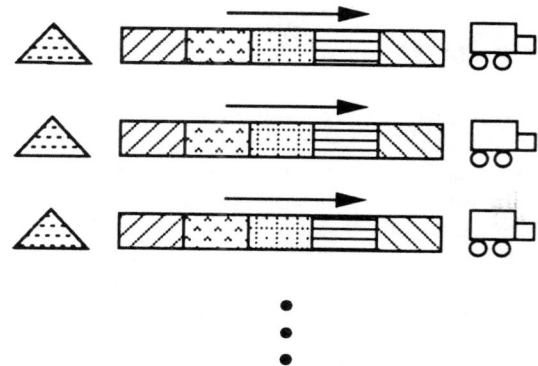

F.gure 3. Data parallel processing.

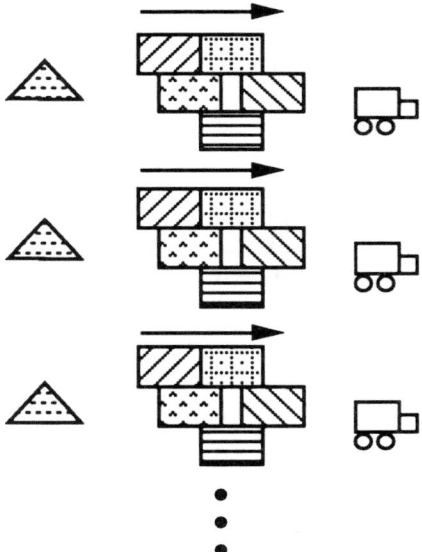

Figure 4. Hybrid data and control parallel processing.

ties of training data. Examples range in size from the two megabytes of data used in handwritten character recognition by neural networks, to the gigabytes and terabytes of data involved in intelligent text-based systems. Soon even petabytes of information will be available (Waltz, 1990) and will be found in useful and important problems. Data parallel approaches have been taken in systems that learn to pronounce English text (Stanfill and Waltz, 1986) or to control robot arms (Atkeson and Reinkensmeyer, 1989), by using a method called memory-based reasoning where each memory or example is stored in each processor. Neural networks have also been implemented in a data parallel manner where the training examples are stored on each processing unit and the connection weights are updated in parallel based on all examples simultaneously (Singer, 1990).

BIBLIOGRAPHY

C. G. Atkeson and D. J. Reinkensmeyer, *Using Associative Content-Addressable Memories to Control Robots*, AI Memo 1124, MIT AI Laboratory, Cambridge, Mass., 1989.

A. Singer, "Implementations of Artificial Neural Networks on the Connection Machine," *Parallel Computing* **14**, 305–315 (1990).

C. Stanfill and D. Waltz, "Toward Memory-Based Reasoning," *CACM* **29**(12), 1213 (1986).

D. Waltz, "Massively Parallel AI," *Proceedings of the Ninth National Conference on Artificial Intelligence*, Boston, Mass., 1990, AAAI, Menlo Park, Calif., 1990.

General References

P. J. Denning and W. F. Tichy, "Highly Parallel Computation," *Science* **250**, 1217–1222 (Nov. 30, 1990).

M. J. Flynn, *IEEE Trans. Comput.* **C-21**, 948 (1972).

D. Hillis, *The Connection Machine*, MIT Press, Cambridge, Mass., 1985.

D. Hillis and G. Steele, "Data Parallel Algorithms," *CACM* **29**(12), 1170 (1986).

Stephen J. Smith
Thinking Machines Corp.

DECISION AIDS. See Military applications.

DECISION THEORY

Decision theory provides a formal, prescriptive framework for making logical choices in the face of uncertainty. Although its origins can be traced back to the eighteenth century in the writings of Bernoulli, its axioms were not developed until the mid-twentieth century, by von Neumann, Borel, Morgenstern, Luce, Raiffa, and Savage. Continued research has focused around three main streams:

Descriptive (the use of decision theory to describe behavior).

Normative (the use of the axiomatic theory to select actions).

Prescriptive (the use of axiomatic systems or corrective techniques to improve decision making).

Conflict continues to be provoked by discrepancies between observed, potentially erroneous, human behavior, and what would be predicted if decision makers were acting on the basis of a consistent set of axioms. Diverse data about the world are often combined using Bayes' rule as a mechanism of inference (see Bayesian inference methods); hence, the field is sometimes called Bayesian decision theory. These techniques have been applied to such diverse fields as business, engineering design, medicine, military strategy, public health, public policy, and resource management. A variety of expert computer programs have used this basically probabilistic mechanism of reasoning, but relatively few programs have successfully combined it with categorical approaches employing frame or rule-based inference (see Frames; Rule-based systems).

FORMAL DECISION ANALYSIS

Formal decision analysis involves seven basic steps.

Step 1. The decision maker must structure the problem at hand, generating a list of possible actions, events, and attributes/states of the world to consider. Although decision analysis provides methods to manipulate this list, its generation is largely a creative process. A convenient representation for this structure is a decision tree. An alternative representation that makes explicit the conditional dependencies between events is the influence diagram. However, the present discussion will focus on the decision tree representation. Three types of data elements or nodes appear in such trees: *decision nodes*, which correspond to actions over which the decision maker has control; *chance nodes*, which correspond to events that can be described in terms of probabilities that are beyond control or states of the world that are unknown to the decision maker; and *terminal nodes*, or outcomes states, which provide summary descriptions of the present and future world (prognosis), beyond the time horizon of the decision tree but conditioned on each path through the tree.

Step 2. Once a decision problem has been structured, probabilities (either point estimates or distributions) are associated with the branches of each chance node. Because objective data are fundamentally descriptive of past events and the decision model uses its probabilities to predict future events, objective data can only serve as anchor points for the required subjective estimates. For example, the probability of disease in a given patient must be modified to reflect the other diagnostic information already obtained, and prognostic data must reflect the presence of other diseases (comorbidities).

Step 3. The next step in the decision analysis is to assign a consistent set of cardinal values to each of the outcome states. Frequently, outcomes are described in terms of multiple attributes that are condensed into a single scale, but alternative techniques allow analysis with disaggregated attributes (eg, cost-effectiveness analysis). The outcomes scales can reflect objective measures (eg, survival) or can reflect the preferences of the decision maker, the client, or the patient. If the outcome metric is preferential, a variety of techniques can be used to assess the attitudes of the decision maker, but all depend on the principle of substitution, whereby a decision model with many outcomes is reduced to a preferentially equivalent model with only two outcomes. The purpose of such a reduction is obvious—the decision rule can then become "choose the strategy with the highest chance of producing the better outcome." The most theoretically straightforward assessment technique is the lottery or standard gamble. The decision maker puts the outcomes in an ordinal scale and creates a standard two-state lottery with probability p of getting the best outcome and probability $1 - p$ of getting the worst. Each intermediate outcome is then considered, and the decision maker decides the value of p for which that intermediate outcome is preferentially equivalent to the standard gamble. The utility of the intermediate outcome is then proportional to the indifference value of p. Utilities can reflect not only preference for outcome (value) but usually also reflect the attitude of the decision maker toward risk and even regret about poor outcomes.

Step 4. Once probability and utility values have been assigned, the decision tree is evaluated by calculating the expectation of the utility at each chance node and by applying the maximization operator at each decision node. Evaluation begins at the distal end of the tree and proceeds backwards, averaging out and folding back until the

root node is reached. The branch of that node with the highest expected utility corresponds to the optimal course of action.

Step 5. Perhaps the most important step of decision analysis is to perform sensitivity analyses by varying the assumptions of the model in a systematic fashion to explore what the optimal choice would be under different conditions and to determine whether the best choice is robust or sensitive to reasonable variations. Such sensitivity analyses are often performed on computer systems and are expressed using a variety of standard graphical formats.

Step 6. Debugging the decision model occurs at all of the preceding steps in the process; however, it is not until dynamic sensitivity analyses are run that many of the errors become apparent. By pushing parameters to their limits, inconsistencies in the underlying model that would not have been appreciated in a static fold-back at the baseline values become manifest. Iteration is an important part of this process. As errors are discovered, they are corrected, and steps 4–7 are repeated. Refinements in our understanding of the basic issues may occur as a result of interactions with other decision makers using the model as a focal point for discussion. This may necessitate a return to Step 1. Additionally, new data may become available as we continue to refine our model, requiring a return to Steps 2 or 3. Many cycles of model debugging and refinement may transpire before the analysis is complete.

Step 7. The final step is to interpret the meaning and significance of the myriad results obtained through both the baseline foldback and the sensitivity analyses. In some cases the major significance of an analysis will be an increased understanding of the dynamics that drive the decision.

A MEDICAL PROBLEM

As an example, consider a simple, generic medical problem, represented as a simple tree in Figure 1. This corresponds to the problem of choosing among treating (action 1), performing a diagnostic test to gather additional information (action 2), and withholding treatment (action 3) with respect to a patient who may or may not have a given disease, where the test is imperfect and the treatment is associated with both risk and benefit. Decision nodes are represented as squares, chance nodes are circles, and terminal nodes are rectangles. If treatment is given or summarily withheld, prognosis is determined by the probability of the disease. If the test is performed, it may provide either correct or incorrect results, but those results will determine whether treatment is given. The probability of a positive test result in the presence of disease is called the sensitivity of the test; the probability of a negative test result in the absence of disease is called the specificity. The selection of the optimal action among these three depends on five factors:

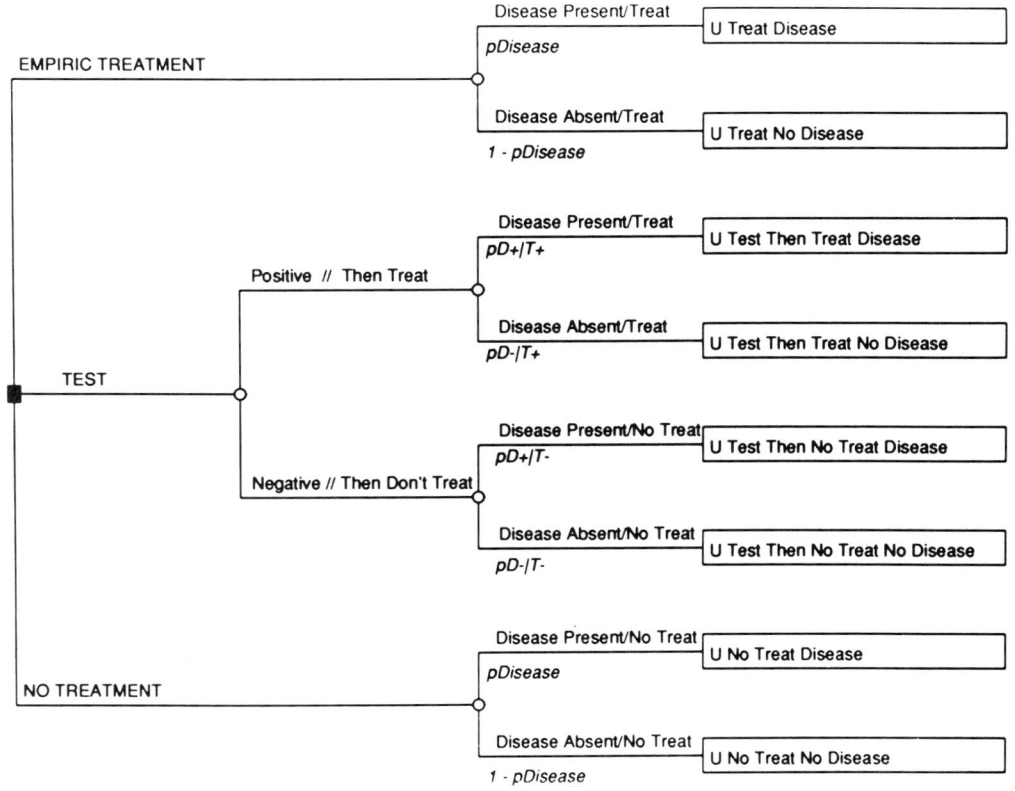

Figure 1. Simple tree illustrating the decision process used in the case of a generic medical problem. ■ = Decision node; ○ = Chance node; □ = Terminal node.

The probability of disease (*pDisease*).

The sensitivity of the test.

The specificity of the test.

The benefit of treating patients with disease ($U_{treat\ disease} - U_{no\ treat\ disease}$).

The risk of treating patients without disease ($U_{no\ treat\ no\ disease} - U_{treat\ no\ disease}$).

The expected utility of empiric treatment equals *pDisease* $\times$ $U_{treat\ disease}$ + (1 − *pDisease*) $\times$ $U_{treat\ no\ disease}$. Although sensitivity analyses may be performed on any parameter or combination of parameters, the softest datum is usually the probability of disease. Thus, it can be useful to divide the domain of *pDisease* into three regions (see Figure 2): if *pDisease* is high, treatment is best; if *pDisease* is low, withholding treatment is best, and if *pDisease* is intermediate, testing is the optimal action. The values of *pDisease* that delineate the transitions from treating to testing and from testing to withholding treatment are called thresholds. These values can be found by a variety of techniques. Simple algebraic solutions to this generic tree are available and have been applied to a broad variety of medical problems.

ALTERNATIVE MODELING TECHNIQUES

A number of other modeling techniques build on the basic structure of the decision tree, including Markov transition

state models and Monte Carlo simulations. Transition state models describe situations in which a limited set of events may occur repetitively over time. Health outcomes are represented by states, with transitions between states occurring instantaneously with every tick of the clock. In simple Markov chains, the transition probabilities remain constant from cycle to cycle, making these models amenable to matrix algebraic solutions. Such models provide es-

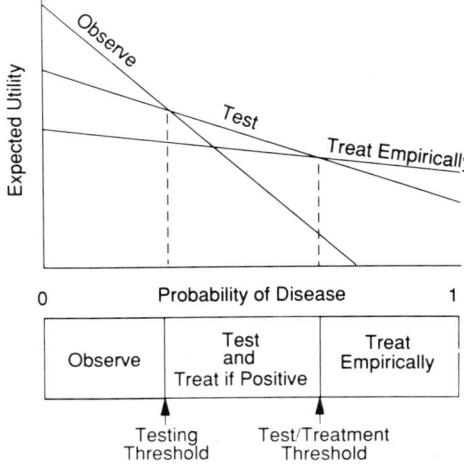

Figure 2. Thresholds of *pDisease* and optimal actions necessary for each.

timates of both expected utility and variance. General Markov processes, in which transition probabilities vary as a function of the cycle number (eg, time) are often solved by cohort simulation techniques. Similarly, Monte Carlo simulations consider the uncertainty inherent in all of the parameters of a decision model by using distributions instead of point estimates for probabilities and utilities. The outcome of each simulation run is decided by the random variation of each parameter, weighted by its probability and utility distributions. Monte Carlo simulations can estimate not only expected utility and variance, but also how often each strategy is best. New approaches even introduce limited memory into a semi-Markov process and Monte Carlo simulation.

BIBLIOGRAPHY

General References

T. Bayes, "An Essay Towards Solving a Problem in the Doctrine of Chances," *Philos. Trans. Roy. Soc. London* **53**, 370–375 (1763).

R. L. Keeney and H. Raiffa, *Decisions with Multiple Objectives: Preference and Value Tradeoffs*, Wiley, New York, 1976.

R. D. Luce and H. Raiffa, *Games and Decisions*, Wiley, New York, 1957.

S. G. Pauker and J. P. Kassirer, "The Threshold Approach to Clinical Decision Making," *N. Engl. J. Med.* **302**, 1109–1117 (1980).

S. G. Pauker and J. P. Kassirer, "Medical Progress: Decision Analysis," *N. Engl. J. Med.* **316**, 250–258 (1987).

H. Raiffa and R. Schlaifer, *Applied Statistical Decision Theory*, MIT Press, Cambridge, Mass., 1968.

L. J. Savage, *The Foundations of Statistics*, Wiley, New York, 1964.

F. A. Sonnenberg and S. G. Pauker, "Decision-Maker 6.0: Update of a Microcomputer System for Decision Analysis," *Proceedings of the Fifth World Congress on Medical Informatics*, 1986.

H. C. Sox, M. A. Blatt, M. C. Higgins, and K. I. Marton, *Medical Decision Making*, Butterworths, Boston, 1988.

P. Szolovits and S. G. Pauker, "Categorical and Probabilistic Reasoning in Medical Diagnosis," *Artif. Intell.* **11**, 115–144 (1978).

V. von Neumann and J. O. Morgenstern, *Theory of Games and Economic Behavior*, Princeton University Press, Princeton, N.J., 1944.

M. C. Weinstein, H. V. Fineberg, B. J. McNeil, and co-workers, *Clinical Decision Analysis*, Saunders, Philadelphia, 1980.

STEPHEN G. PAUKER
MARK H. ECKMAN
New England Medical Center

DEDUCTION. See LOGIC.

DEDUCTIVE DATABASE SYSTEMS

HISTORY AND PURPOSE

A historical account of deductive databases can be found in Minker (1988a). The history, which is presented from a personal point of view, is divided into three parts, each covering about a decade. The time period 1957–1968 is called "Beginning Experiences in Deduction." During this time period, active research on precursors to deductive databases was conducted at several locations, including the Rand Corp., MIT, and Stanford. At the Rand Corp. a relational data file (RDF) system with an inferential capability was implemented, and some important theoretical issues were raised. Green and Raphael at the Stanford Research Institute were the first to recognize by 1968 the connection of the resolution principle, discovered in 1963 by Robinson for theorem proving, to the problem of deduction for databases. Their system showed the viability of implementing deductive databases in a uniform manner.

The time period 1969–1978 is called "The Formative Years." In the early 1970s the concept of logic programming was proposed and then implemented in the language PROLOG. By 1977 there were enough researchers applying logic to databases with significant results that a Workshop on Logic and Databases was held in Toulouse. The resulting book of papers (Gallaire and Minker, 1978) established deductive databases as an important subject. The time period 1979–1987 is called "Theoretical Foundations." Reiter (1984) reinterpreted the conventional model-theoretic perspective on databases in purely proof-theoretic terms. The basic axioms he defined will be given in another section. The general foundations for logic programming with definite (Horn) clauses were also developed. The efficient implementation of recursion became an important topic. A survey paper (Gallaire and co-workers, 1984) made the literature on deductive databases more accessible and better known. The handling of negation was clarified, particularly with the definition of stratification. Toward the end of this period the Workshop on the Foundations of Deductive Databases and Logic Programming in Washington brought together some of the leading researchers in this field. The resulting book of papers (Minker, 1988b) provided the state-of-the-art and directions for future research.

The subject of deductive databases represents a convergence of work in databases and AI. Standard relational database systems are used successfully in business, government, and industry. But these systems have little or no reasoning capabilities. AI researchers have developed logical reasoning systems (see LOGIC) and logic programming (qv), but these systems typically deal with relatively small amounts of data. Deductive database systems provide the merging of the capabilities of database systems, including the efficient handling of large amounts of data, concurrency, security, and recovery, with logic-based reasoning systems in terms of deductive rules. Because present deductive database systems are mainly research prototypes, this article emphasizes the theoretical framework common to such systems. Additional examples and results about various types of deductive database theories are found elsewhere (Grant and Minker, 1989).

CONCEPTS FROM LOGIC AND LATTICE THEORY

The standard formalization of deductive databases is within first-order logic. Some important concepts of logic are given in this subsection. For additional background on first-order logic see Enderton (1972) and Mendelson (1987); for additional material on resolution theorem-proving see Chang and Lee (1973) and Loveland (1978); for logic in AI see Genesereth and Nilsson (1987); for a theoretical study of logic programming see Lloyd (1987); for practical aspects of logic programming see Clocksin and Mellish (1987) and Sterling and Shapiro (1986). The syntax of first-order logic is given through first-order languages, which contain infinitely many variables; logical symbols (connectives and quantifiers); punctuation symbols (comma and parentheses); constant symbols; function symbols; and predicate symbols. A first-order language for deductive databases is characterized by its constant, predicate, and function symbols. A term is a constant symbol or a variable or an n-ary function symbol followed by n terms in parentheses and separated by commas. An atom is an m-ary predicate symbol followed by m terms in parentheses and separated by commas. Usually, deductive databases are function-free to avoid infinite domains. The formulas, including sentences, of the language are defined in the standard way. The semantics of first-order logic is defined by an interpretation that assigns a meaning to each nonlogical symbol. An interpretation I is a model for a set of sentences S if every element of S is true in I. S $\models$ w (w is a logical consequence of S) if w is true in all models of S.

An inference system (proof theory) for first-order logic consists of a set of axiom schemas and rules of inference that provide proofs of formulas. S $\vdash$ w if there is a proof of w from S. An inference system is complete in case S $\vdash$ w iff S $\models$ w. Resolution is a complete inference system that yields S $\vdash$ w by deriving the empty clause from the clausal forms of S and $\neg$w. A clause is written in the form

$$\neg A_1 \vee \ldots \vee \neg A_n \vee B_1 \vee \ldots \vee B_m$$

where the A_i and B_j are atoms and all variables are universally quantified. An equivalent formulation,

$$B_1, \ldots, B_m \leftarrow A_1, \ldots, A_n$$

is the one used in deductive databases. Such a clause can be interpreted in two ways: (1) if $A_1, \ldots, A_n$ are all true, then at least one of $B_1, \ldots, B_m$ is true; (2) to solve for $B_1 \vee \ldots \vee B_m$, solve all of $A_1, \ldots, A_n$. The atoms $A_1, \ldots, A_n$ form the body of the clause; $B_1, \ldots, B_m$ form the head. The empty clause, $\leftarrow$, represents a contradiction. A clause of the form $\leftarrow A_1, \ldots, A_n$ is a query clause. Later, in dealing with stratified databases we will allow any literal (atomic formula or negation of atomic formula) in the body of a clause. For a query $Q(x_1, \ldots, x_m)$ (with free variables $x_1, \ldots, x_m$), a (definite) answer has the form $\langle a_1, \ldots, a_m \rangle$ such that DB $\vdash Q(a_1, \ldots, a_m)$, (meaning the substitution of a_i for x_i, $1 \leq i \leq m$, in Q), where DB is the set of database clauses. One must be careful about the queries that should be allowed for the answers to be enumerated. For example, the query $\leftarrow$ x > 10 has as its answers an infinite set: the set of all numbers bigger than 10. A query is safe if the answer is finite. Various sufficient conditions are known that guarantee safety.

The Herbrand universe for a language L is the set of constant symbols in L (assuming that there are no function symbols). A Herbrand interpretation is one whose domain is the Herbrand universe. A Herbrand interpretation that is a model for a theory is called a Herbrand model. Because of the assumption of the basic axioms in the next subsection, all models are Herbrand models modulo renaming the elements of the domain. The Herbrand base, HB, is the set of all ground atomic formulas (of L). HB contains all possible facts about the database.

A lattice is a set with a partial ordering ($\leq$) relation. For a lattice L and a set $X \subseteq L$, $a \in L$ is called an upper bound of X of $x \leq a$ for all $x \in X$. A least upper bound of X, $lub(X)$, is unique, if it exists. The notions of lower bound and greatest lower bound are defined in a similar but opposite manner. A lattice L is complete if lub(X) and glb(X) exist for every subset X of L. A mapping T: L $\rightarrow$ L is monotonic if $a \leq b$ implies $T(a) \leq T(b)$ for all $a,b \in L$, and continuous if $T(lub(X)) = lub(T(X))$ for every directed set (ie, which contains an upper bound for every finite subset) X of L. An element $a \in L$ is a fixpoint of T if $T(a) = a$. The least fixpoint of T, if it exists, is written as lfp(T).

Powers of a monotonic mapping T are defined as follows:

$T \uparrow 0 = \varnothing$ (The 0th power of T is the empty set)

$T \uparrow i + 1 = T(T \uparrow i)$ (The next power of T is obtained by applying T to the previous power)

$T \uparrow \omega = lub \{T \uparrow i | i < \omega\}$ (The ωth power of T is obtained by taking the lub of all finite powers)

The following results will be applied about lattices:

1. If T is monotonic, then lfp(T) exists
2. If T is continuous, then lfp(T) = T $\uparrow \omega$

THE BASIC AXIOMS

A deductive database may be defined as a triple DB = $\langle C,P,I \rangle$, where C is the set of constants (constant and predicate symbols) that defines a first-order language L, P is a finite set of axioms and may contain metarules (rules not expressible in L), and I is a set of sentences in L expressing integrity constraints. For the use of integrity constraints in deductive databases see Grant and Minker (1990). There is a basic set of axioms that is assumed to be in P for all deductive databases: the domain closure axiom, the unique name axioms, and the equality axioms. These axioms assure, respectively, that the database is finite and all constants can be named, that different constant symbols stand for different objects, and that equality stands for the identity relation. (In the case of function symbols in the language, there is an expanded set of basic axioms assuring that different terms stand for different objects and equality stands for the identity relation.)

The domain closure axiom has the form

$$\forall x (x = c_1 \lor \ldots \lor x = c_n)$$

where $c_1, \ldots, c_n$ are all the constant symbols in C.

The unique name axioms are

$$\neg c_1 = c_2, \neg c_1 = c_3, \ldots, \neg c_{n-1} = c_n$$

where, again, $c_1, \ldots, c_n$ are the constant symbols in C.

The equality axioms are

$$\forall x (x = x), \qquad \forall x \forall y (x = y \to y = x),$$

$$\forall x \forall y \forall z (x = y \, \& \, y = z \to x = z),$$

$$\forall x_1 \ldots \forall y_n (R(x_1, \ldots, x_n) \, \& \, x_1 = y_1 \, \& \ldots \& \, x_n = y_n \to$$

$$R(y_1, \ldots, y_n))$$

for all predicate symbols R. As explained in Gallaire and co-workers (1984), it is usually not necessary to include these axioms in an operational definition of a deductive database. We will not mention these basic axioms in later sections and will use P to stand for the rest of the axioms (of a particular deductive database).

DEFINITE DATABASES

In a definite database, P consists of formulas of the form $B \leftarrow A_1, \ldots, A_n$, where $B, A_1, \ldots, A_n$, are atoms (n may be 0). The ground atomic formulas represent database facts: this is called the extensional database. The other formulas represent database rules: this is called the intensional database. The intensional database constitutes the deductive part of the database and distinguishes definite databases from relational databases. The terminology *DATALOG* program is often used for a definite database where the language has no function symbols. A typical example of a definite database involves family relationships. The predicate Parent is given in the form of ground atoms, such as Parent(bob,susan) $\leftarrow$. Rules are used to define concepts such as Grandparent and Ancestor as follows:

$$\text{Grandparent}(x,y) \leftarrow \text{Parent}(x,z), \text{Parent}(z,y)$$

$$\text{Ancestor}(x,y) \leftarrow \text{Parent}(x,y)$$

$$\text{Ancestor}(x,y) \leftarrow \text{Parent}(x,z), \text{Ancestor}(z,y)$$

In words, a grandparent is a parent of a parent; an ancestor is either a parent or an ancestor of a parent. The definition for Ancestor is recursive because Ancestor is defined partially in terms of itself.

Examples of queries are

Q1. $\leftarrow$ Grandparent(jim,x),Parent(x,y)
   Who are the grandparents of Jim and their parents?
Q2. $\leftarrow$ Ancestor(joe,x)
   Who are Joe's ancestors?

Q3. $\leftarrow$ Parent(jim,x),$\neg$Parent(susan,x)
   Who are parents of Jim and not parents of Susan?

Semantics

Semantics deals with meaning. When we are given a database P we would like to determine formally the meaning of P. This would allow us to make sure that the answers obtained for a query are correct. In this subsection the three major semantics for positive formulas are presented: declarative, fixpoint, and procedural.

Declarative semantics for definite databases was introduced in van Emden and Kowalski (1976). It is based on the concept of Herbrand models. For a definite database the Herbrand base is always a Herbrand model because it satisfies the axioms of P, including the fundamental axioms. For example, given the Parent, Grandparent, and Ancestor predicates of the previous section and the appropriate constant symbols for a language, the Herbrand base would indicate that everyone is a parent, grandparent, and ancestor of everyone. So although the Herbrand base is a model, it is usually not the intended model: it is too big. In fact, the intended model should be the smallest model. A major theorem of van Emden and Kowalski states that the intersection of every (nonempty) set of Herbrand models for a definite database is a Herbrand model. So the intended model, M_P, is that intersection. In fact, the minimal model contains exactly the atoms logically implied by P. Hence $\langle a_1, \ldots, a_m \rangle$ is an answer to a query $Q(x_1, \ldots, x_m)$ if $Q(a_1, \ldots, a_m)$ is true in M_P.

Fixpoint semantics involves building the intended Herbrand model step by step using Herbrand interpretations. Fixpoint semantics for definite databases was also introduced by van Emden and Kowalski. The empty set is the starting point. Then, at each step, the rules of P are used to add new atoms to the existing Herbrand interpretation. For example, if $A_1, \ldots, A_n$ are in a Herbrand interpretation of P and $A \leftarrow A_1, \ldots, A_n$ is a clause in P, then A should be added to the Herbrand interpretation at that step. A fixpoint is reached when there are no additions. The smallest fixpoint is the intended Herbrand model. Consider 2^{HB}, the set of all Herbrand interpretations. As a power set, 2^{HB} is a complete lattice with $\text{lub}(X) = \cup S_i \{S_i \in X\}$ and $\text{glb}(X) = \cap S_i \{S_i \in X\}$. The top element is HB and the bottom element is $\varnothing$ (the empty set). The mapping $T_P: 2^{HB} \to 2^{HB}$ is defined on a Herbrand interpretation I by

$$T_P(I) = \{A \in HB_C \, | \, A \leftarrow A_1, \ldots, A_n \text{ is a ground}$$

$$\text{instance of a clause in P and } \{A_1, \ldots, A_n\} \subseteq I\}$$

$T_P(I)$ contains all immediate consequences of the rules of P applied to I. Because T_P is monotonic, powers of T_P may be defined as explained earlier. Also, for definite databases, T_P is continuous. Hence $\text{lfp}(T_P) = T_P \uparrow \omega$. Fixpoint semantics picks $\text{lfp}(T_P)$ as the meaning of P. Also, $\text{lfp}(T_P) = M_P$ (the intersection of all Herbrand models); hence declarative semantics and fixpoint semantics coincide.

Procedural semantics refers to a computation method, usually involving resolution, for obtaining the meaning of a deductive database. For definite databases, SLD-resolution is used as procedural semantics. In an SLD-refutation, a definite database P and a query clause of the form $\leftarrow B_1, \ldots, B_m$ are given. An SLD-derivation starts with the query clause as the top clause. The resolution is linear using the clauses of P with each clause in P given new variables not previously used in the derivation. The essence of the process involves the selection of an atom, B_i, in the present query and the selection of a clause in P whose head can unify with B_i by a substitution; the new query is obtained by replacing B_i with the body of the clause after applying the substitution required for unification. An SLD-refutation is an SLD-derivation that ends with the empty clause. The success set of P, $Succ(P)$, is defined as the set of all $A \in HB$ such that $P \cup \{\neg A\}$ has an SLD-refutation.

The major result due to van Emden and Kowalski is that $M_P = Succ(P)$. Thus the three different semantics produce equivalent results for definite databases. In answering queries, the equivalence of the declarative and fixpoint semantics assures identical answers by logical implication. For procedural semantics, SLD-resolution is used to obtain answers. Consider the query Q1. An answer is obtained by finding an SLD-refutation starting with Q1 as the top clause and using the clauses of P. The substitutions for x and y provide an answer. It is necessary to take care of the case where an SLD-refutation does not bind some query variables. For example, if P contains $R(x) \leftarrow$, then the SLD-refutation for the query $\leftarrow R(x)$ does not yield a constant substitution for x. This is taken to mean that all the constants are solutions. With this proviso, for a definite database the declarative, fixpoint, and procedural semantics provide identical answers to queries.

Negation

Negation has been problematic for databases in general because the volume of negative data is usually much greater than the volume of positive data. Because the storage of negative data might overwhelm a database system, databases typically only store positive data, and negation is implicitly defined. But there must still be a method to answer queries involving negation, such as Q3, even though the database does not specify the individuals who are not parents of susan. The three main methods for dealing with implicit negation in definite databases are the Closed World Assumption, the Completed Database, and Negation as Finite Failure.

The Closed World Assumption (CWA) was proposed in Reiter (1978): it is a metarule used in addition to the axioms of the database. Given a database P, the CWA infers a negated ground atom, $\neg A$, from P if it is not the case that $P \models A$. Intuitively, any positive ground atom not implied by P is taken to be false. The CWA formalizes the assumption that all positive information is known and specified. It is a powerful metarule as it determines a unique Herbrand model for definite databases, the minimal model discussed in the previous subsection.

The Completed Database (CDB) approach to the handling of negation was introduced in Clark (1978). According to the CDB, the facts and rules of P provide only the if parts of the definitions of predicates explicitly. But the

meaning of these definitions includes implicitly the only if parts as well. Recall, for example, the definition of the Grandparent predicate:

$$\text{Grandparent}(x,y) \leftarrow \text{Parent}(x,z), \text{Parent}(z,y).$$

This definition means that y is a grandparent of x if for some z, y is a parent of z, and z is a parent of x. The definition does not exclude the case where y is a grandparent of x for another reason. What is really meant, however, is that y is a grandparent of x only if there is a z such that y is a parent of z and z is a parent of x, that is,

$$\text{Grandparent}(x,y) \rightarrow \exists z(\text{Parent}(x,z),\text{Parent}(z,y)).$$

The grandparent predicate is defined by a single clause. For a predicate R defined by several clauses, what is meant is that R holds if and only if the conditions of R's definition are satisfied. Formally, the CDB is defined as follows.

Each definite clause of the form

$$R(t_1, \ldots, t_n) \leftarrow A_1, \ldots, A_m$$

containing the variables $y_1, \ldots, y_p$, is rewritten as

$$R(x_1, \ldots, x_n) \leftarrow (\exists y_1) \ldots (\exists y_p)(x_1 = t_1 \& \ldots \& x_n$$
$$= t_n \& A_1 \& \ldots \& A_m)$$

where $x_1, \ldots, x_n$ are new variables. For each R, call the right-hand sides of the definitions of R: $E_1, \ldots, E_r$. Then the completed database contains, in addition to P, for each R the formula

$$R(x_1, \ldots, x_n) \rightarrow E_1 \vee \ldots \vee E_r$$

(In the special case where there are no definitions for R, the CDB yields $\neg R(x_1, \ldots, x_n)$.) A negative query is answered in the CDB by invoking a theorem prover.

Both the CWA and CDB approaches are computationally complex. A more manageable approach, called Negation as Finite Failure (NFF), was also introduced in Clark (1978). The NFF is a metarule according to which for a ground atom A, $\neg A$ is proved if A fails finitely, that is, if every attempt to prove A fails in a finite number of steps. The addition of NFF to SLD-resolution, explained earlier, is called SLDNF-resolution. Using this method, $\leftarrow \neg A$ is solved by attempting to solve for $\leftarrow A$. If the latter succeeds, then the former is said to fail; if the latter fails the former is said to succeed. NFF can be applied to solve Q3 if Parent(jim,x) is solved first and so x is bound by the time $\neg$Parent(susan,x) is solved. In case a nonground negative atom must be solved, NFF is not applied and the query is said to *flounder*. Clark proved that NFF is sound in the sense that if $\neg A$ is proved using NFF then CDB $\models \neg A$. However, NFF is not complete because of floundering queries. NFF is complete for ground negated atoms, that is, if CDB $\models \neg A$ then $\neg A$ is proved by NFF from P. See also Shepherdson (1988) for a thorough study of negation in logic programming. More recently, constructive negation was introduced (Chan, 1988) to deal with floundering queries as SLD-CNF resolution. A nonground negative literal is solved by solving the corresponding positive atom, writing the answer as a disjunction, and taking the negation of all answers, using inequalities, as the answer to the query.

Implementation

This subsection deals with the major issues concerning the implementation of query processing for definite databases. Some information about specific systems is given in the next section as most implementations deal with stratification described below. If the database contains only an extensional component, then it is a relational database. Query processing for relational databases is not discussed here. So assume that there is an intensional component. The simplest case is where the database is hierarchic. For a hierarchic database, each predicate symbol may be given a level, a nonnegative integer, so that for every rule the level of each predicate symbol in the body is less than the level of the predicate symbol being defined in the head. Essentially, a hierarchic database does not allow recursive definitions. For instance, in the example with Ancestor, such a level mapping is impossible. A hierarchic database also disallows mutual recursion, where, for example P_1 is defined in terms of P_2, P_2 is defined in terms of P_3, . . . , P_n is defined in terms of P_1. Suppose now that in the family relationship, the predicates are Parent (extensional) and Grandparent and Greatgrandparent defined intensionally as follows:

Grandparent(x,y) ← Parent(x,z),Parent(z,y)

Greatgrandparent(u,v) ← Parent(u,w),Grandparent(w,v)

In this case a level mapping would be level(Parent) = 0, level(Grandparent) = 1, level(Greatgrandparent) = 2.

Two major approaches for answering queries in a hierarchic database are the interpretive method and the compiled approach (Gallaire and co-workers, 1984). Consider a query such as

←Greatgrandparent(jim,x).

The interpretive method works with a theorem prover and interleaves it with the search of the extensional database. For this query, it would use the definition of Greatgrandparent to obtain

← Parent(jim,z),Grandparent(z,x),

breaking the problem into two subproblems, and then continue with the solution, all this being done at execution time. The compiled approach compiles all the rules so that the body contains extensional predicates only. The rule for Greatgrandparent is transformed to

Greatgrandparent(u,v) ←

    Parent(u,w),Parent(w,z),Parent(z,v)

and the query becomes

← Parent(jim,w),Parent(w,z),Parent(z,x)

in one step, so the problem is reduced to a relational database search.

Many different approaches have been proposed for dealing with the difficulties introduced by recursion in query processing. It is useful to distinguish between bottom-up, also called forward chaining, and top-down, also called backward chaining, methods. A bottom-up method starts with existing facts and uses the rules to obtain new facts until the query is generated. A top-down approach starts with the query and uses the rules to verify premises of rules in order to make the query true. In general, bottom-up methods may be wasteful in generating many facts not related to the query, but they can be applied naturally in a set-oriented manner. Top-down methods avoid the generation of unrelated facts, but tend to work naturally one tuple at a time. Survey articles and books provide the details of these approaches and include examples (see Bancilhon and Ramakrishnan, 1986; Ceri and co-workers, 1990; Ullman, 1989).

Naive evaluation is a fundamental bottom-up technique. This is essentially the fixpoint semantics discussed in an earlier subsection using the T_P operator. When lfp(T_P) is reached, the answer is found as the tuples of constants that make the query true. One reason for inefficiency in the naive evaluation is that tuples may be computed many times during the iteration. Seminaive evaluation eliminates some of this redundancy by applying the T_P operator at the i+1st step, not to all of $T_P \uparrow$ i but only to a portion of $T_P \uparrow$ i. In the case of linear recursion where no rule contains more than one predicate in its body that is mutually recursive with the predicate in the head, it is possible to replace $T_P \uparrow$ i by $T_P \uparrow$ i $- T_P \uparrow$ (i $- 1$). In the case of nonlinear recursion finding the proper portion of $T_P \uparrow$ i to consider is more difficult. Both the naive and seminaive evaluation methods generate many facts not related to the query. So several rewriting methods have been proposed to eliminate useless derivations by using knowledge about some of the constants in the query, for example. The method of magic sets uses the query to transform the program into a larger program containing an additional predicate called Magic, as well as some of the old rules, some new rules, and some modifications of the old rules. After the transformation, the seminaive evaluation can be used on the new program to evaluate the query. In a certain way the magic sets simulate the top-down method in a bottom-up framework. Magic sets and other bottom-up techniques usually work with adorned predicates: an adornment gives a binding pattern, a sequence of b's and f's to a predicate. For Query 2 the adorned goal is *ancestor^{bf}*, indicating that the first argument (joe) is bound (b) and the second argument (x) if free (f).

Procedural semantics, as in SLD-resolution presented in an earlier subsection, is a fundamental top-down technique. Its inefficiency is due to its tuple at a time approach. The Prolog evaluation technique is based on SLD-resolution, but it may get into an infinite loop because of its depth-first approach. The Query/Subquery (QSQ) method is a more efficient top-down technique. The atoms in the body of a rule defining a predicate in the query form the subqueries in this approach. Two sets are maintained: (1) a set of answer tuples containing answers to the query and some subqueries, and (2) a set of current subqueries. The process generates both new answers and new subqueries as it proceeds. The advantage of the QSQ method is that although top-down, it is set-oriented and complete because of its breadth-first nature.

STRATIFIED DATABASES

Definition

A normal database consists of clauses of the form $B \leftarrow L_1, \ldots, L_n$, where each L_i, $1 \le i \le n$ is a literal and B is an atom. So the difference between a normal database and a definite database is that for a definite database the body must contain atoms only, but in a normal database the body may also contain negated atoms. The semantics of a normal database is not always clear. For example, if P contains the two clauses

$$\text{Female(pat)} \leftarrow \neg\text{Male(pat)}$$

$$\text{Male(pat)} \leftarrow \neg\text{Female(pat)}$$

the combination of recursion via negation makes the meaning of P unclear. But if we remove the second clause, for instance, then the meaning is that if Male(pat) is not true in the database, then Female(pat) is true. Stratification was introduced in several papers (Apt and co-workers, 1988; Chandra and Harel, 1987; Naqvi, 1986; Van Gelder, 1988) to provide a clear semantics for normal databases. Each predicate symbol R is given a level (or rank) r(R), which is a positive integer. The level of a literal is the level of the corresponding predicate symbol. A normal database, P, is stratified if there is a stratification (level mapping for all predicate symbols) such that for every clause in P of the form

$$B \leftarrow L_1, \ldots, L_n$$

for all i, $1 \le i \le n$, if L_i is an atom, then $r(L_i) \le r(B)$, and if L_i is a negated atom, then $r(L_i) < r(B)$. The set of clauses of P are placed into strata P_i with each P_i containing the definitions of predicates of level i. Essentially, a stratified database cannot have recursion via negation. In particular, the example P given above with the predicates Male and Female is not stratified. A stratified database may have many different level mappings, but the results about stratified databases hold for any choice of r. It is convenient to assume that the levels are 1, . . . , n. Now consider an example with predicates Edge, Path, and Acyclicpath. The predicate Edge is given in the form of ground atoms such as Edge(a,b) ←. The rules are

$$\text{Path(x,y)} \leftarrow \text{Edge(x,y)}$$

$$\text{Path(x,y)} \leftarrow \text{Edge(x,z),Path(z,y)}$$

$$\text{Acyclicpath(x,y)} \leftarrow \text{Path(x,y),}\neg\text{Path(y,x)}$$

This database is not definite because of the negated atom in the definition of Acyclicpath. It is stratified with the levels: r(Path) = 1, r(Edge) = 1, r(Acyclicpath) = 2. An example query might be

$$\text{Q4.} \leftarrow \text{Acyclicpath(a,y)}$$

To which nodes is there an acyclic path from a?

Semantics

For definite databases positive semantics was considered first followed by negation. But for stratified databases negation is not treated separately because negation is already built into the database definition. Thus the declarative, fixpoint, and procedural semantics all must involve negation.

Declarative semantics for stratified databases is defined in terms of Herbrand models using a level-by-level process. A model M is supported if every atom $A \in M$ is the conclusion of a ground instance of a clause in P whose body is true in M (or empty). For example, in the earlier example where the predicates are Female and Male with the single clause Female(pat) ← ¬Male(pat), the minimal model {Female(pat)} is supported, but the minimal model {Male(pat)} is not. Intuitively, the supported minimal model appears better than the nonsupported minimal model because there is no way to prove Male(pat), so we may assume Male(pat) to be false, and that makes Female(pat) true. The definition of the minimal supported model is given by levels as follows (assuming the strata $P_1, \ldots, P_n$):

$$M_i = \cap \{M: M \text{ is a supported model of } \cup \{P_j | 1 \le j \le i\} \text{ and}$$

coincides with M_{i-1} on predicates of level $\le i - 1\}$.

When i = 1, the second part of the definition involving M_{i-1} is omitted.

Assuming levels 1, . . . , n, M_n is taken as the minimal supported model. In the case of an example with the Edge, Path, and Acyclicpath predicates given earlier, at the first level a minimal model is constructed for Edge and Path only. At the second level, using the model for Edge and Path, a minimal model is constructed for Acyclicpath.

The problem with defining fixpoint semantics for stratified databases is that the T_P operator is not necessarily monotonic. Consider again the example with the single clause Female(pat) ← ¬Male(pat). If $I_1 = \varnothing$, then $T_P(I_1) = \{\text{Female(pat)}\}$ and if $I_2 = \{\text{Male(pat)}\}$, then $T_P(I_2) = \varnothing$. Here I_1 is a subset of I_2, but $T_P(I_1)$ is not a subset of $T_P(I_2)$. To get around this problem cumulative powers of T are defined as follows:

$$T \uparrow 0 \, (I) = I$$

$$T \uparrow (i + 1) \, (I) = T(T \uparrow i \, (I)) \cup T \uparrow i \, (I)$$

$$T \uparrow \omega \, (I) = \cup \{T \uparrow i \, (I) \mid i < \omega\}$$

The definition of fixpoint semantics proceeds through the

levels 1, . . . , n via the strata P_1, . . . , P_n of the program P:

$$M_i = T_{P_i} \uparrow \omega (M_{i-1})$$

$$\text{where } M_0 = \varnothing.$$

The major result (Apt and co-workers, 1988) is that for every stratified program P, the declarative semantics, M_n, and the fixpoint semantics, M_n, are identical.

A procedural semantics for stratified databases called SLS-resolution has been defined (Przymusinski, 1988). SLS-resolution is a generalization of SLDNF-resolution, where an infinite branch of a solution tree is said to fail. Determining when there is an infinite branch in a proof tree is a computationally difficult problem. The equivalence of the declarative, fixpoint, and procedural semantics is shown by the following result. For a stratified database P, M_n (declarative) = M_n (fixpoint) = Succ(P). Also, the declarative, fixpoint, and procedural semantics provide identical answers to nonfloundering queries.

Implementation

Several different implementations of stratified databases exist. Typically, query processing is done on a level-by-level basis as in the fixpoint construction using some technique discussed for definite database implementation within a level. For example, in computing the answer to Q4, the query

$$\leftarrow \text{Path(a,y)}, \neg \text{Path(y,a)}$$

must be solved. This subsection contains brief discussions of two research prototypes.

The LDL system was a project at the Microelectronics and Computer Technology Corp. (MCC). LDL refers both to the language and the system; a detailed exposition of the language is available (Naqvi and Tsur, 1989). LDL allows the representation of constructs in addition to recursion and stratified negation. Function symbols are used for the representation of complex objects. For example, an atom such as

car(vehicle(1989,ford,taurus),owner(susan,smith)) ←

represents a complex object car with the two components vehicle and owner, where vehicle has three components and owner has two. Recursion is allowed within complex objects. Another extension involves the use of sets. Sets may be constructed by enumeration or grouping. Several built-in predicates, such as member, are included in the language to facilitate the use of sets. Consequently, the semantics of LDL is more complicated than the one that has been presented for stratified databases; it includes a generalized Herbrand universe for sets and complex objects. The implementation within a level of stratification uses several rewriting techniques including magic sets.

The NAIL! system was implemented at Stanford University. Function symbols and sets are allowed here also in addition to recursion and stratified negation. The strategy-selection component chooses an evaluation strategy for an adorned goal. The construction of the strategy is made by the use of capture rules: Each capture rule corresponds to an evaluation technique, such as magic sets. The strategy is stored in a strategy database that is used in future evaluations of the same adorned goal. An important achievement of NAIL! is an extensible architecture that allows the use of a wide range of strategies for query evaluation.

ALTERNATIVE DATABASES

Normal Databases

For definite databases the CWA approach for handling negation was presented in an earlier section. A problem with the CWA is that all atoms must be either true or false; there is no way of handling exceptional data. In a protected database it is possible to protect atoms not known to be true from being falsified by the CWA. For each predicate R, an extra predicate ER, the protected version of R, is added. Thus EParent(joe,susan) ← means that Parent(joe,susan) is not to be assumed false. Minker and Perlis (1985) contains many results about protected databases, including implementation techniques.

The well-founded approach, introduced in Van Gelder and co-workers (1988) and further investigated in Przymusinski (1989), generalizes the semantics of stratified databases to permit a semantics to be defined for all normal databases. A key concept is the use of a three-valued logic with the truth values true, undefined, and false. For declarative semantics the notion of minimal model is defined in such a way that the true atoms are minimized and the false atoms are maximized. Every theory has a minimal model in this approach. If the theory is stratified, this model is two-valued and coincides with the minimal model discussed in the previous section for stratified databases. However, many nonstratified normal databases also possess a well-founded 2-valued minimal model. For fixpoint semantics two operators are used: one to derive new true facts and the other to derive new false facts. For procedural semantics an extended SLS-resolution is defined. The declarative, fixpoint, and procedural semantics are equivalent for normal databases and provide identical answers to non-floundering queries. Recently (Baral and co-workers, 1990a), the well-founded approach has been generalized in a way that allows more intuitively true atoms to be proved true.

Object-oriented databases have become important in recent years. Although there is not yet complete agreement about what constitutes an object-oriented database, the following features are considered important (Atkinson and co-workers, 1990): complex objects, object identity, encapsulation, types or classes, inheritance, overriding combined with late binding, extensibility, and computational completeness. Several researchers have attempted to combine deductive and object-oriented databases. One approach defines a new language supporting object identity and inheritance as an extension of the language LDL (Zaniolo, 1990), discussed in the previous section. Another develops a formal framework consisting of a structural object model and various higher-order concepts (Beeri,

1990). O-logic is described in Maier (1986) and an extension (F-logic) in Kifer and Lausen (1989). An alternate approach uses database logic (Grant and Sellis, 1990).

Disjunctive Databases

True disjunctive information is not expressible in a definite or stratified database. Suppose for example that the database contains two relations, Clerk and Secretary, and it is known that Pat is either a clerk or a secretary. In a stratified database it is possible to write the clause

$$\text{Secretary (pat)} \leftarrow \neg\text{Clerk(pat)}$$

but this rule is not symmetric. Its consequence is the conclusion that Pat is a secretary if Pat is not a clerk. We would really like to write

$$\text{Secretary(pat),Clerk(pat)} \leftarrow ,$$

that is, a true disjunctive formula. This is allowed in a disjunctive database, where clauses have the form $B_1, \ldots, B_m \leftarrow A_1, \ldots, A_n$ and all $A_i, B_j, 1 \leq i \leq n, 1 \leq j \leq m$ are atoms. In a disjunctive database answers may be disjunctive also. For example, if the database contains the disjunctive clause

$$\text{Age(joe,32),Age(joe,33)} \leftarrow$$

expressing the disjunctive fact that Joe's age is 32 or Joe's age is 33, the query

$$\leftarrow \text{Age(joe,x)}$$

asking for Joe's age has the answer $32 \lor 33$, that is, 32 or 33.

Declarative semantics for disjunctive databases involves Herbrand models. Usually a disjunctive database does not have a smallest Herbrand model; it has minimal Herbrand models. A positive clause is logically implied by a database if and only if that clause is true in every minimal model of the database (Minker, 1982). A fixpoint semantics for disjunctive databases was defined (Minker and Rajasekar, 1990) by using the extended Herbrand Base (EHB), which consists of disjunctions of atoms in the Herbrand Base. The operator is defined on subsets of the EHB. SLI-resolution (Minker and Zanon, 1982) provides the procedural semantics for disjunctive databases. For positive clauses the declarative, fixpoint, and procedural semantics are equivalent and provide identical answers to positive queries. The three approaches to negation presented for definite databases can be generalized to disjunctive databases as the Generalized Closed World Assumption (Minker, 1982), a generalized version of the Completed Database (Lobo and co-workers, 1988), and SLINF-resolution (Minker and Rajasekar, 1990). Several algorithms have been proposed for implementing disjunctive databases (Grant and Minker, 1986; Yahya and Henschen, 1985; Bossu and Siegel, 1985; Demolombe, 1989; Liu and Sunderraman, 1990). Stratified databases have been extended to stratified disjunctive databases (Rajasekar and Minker, 1990), and the Generalized Well-Founded Approach has also been extended to normal disjunctive databases (Baral and co-workers, 1990b, 1990c). A monograph is in preparation on disjunctive logic programming (Lobo and co-workers, 1991).

BIBLIOGRAPHY

K. R. Apt, H. A. Blair, and A. Walker, "Towards a Theory of Declarative Knowledge," in J. Minker, ed., (1988b), pp. 89–148.

M. Atkinson, F. Bancilhon, D. DeWitt, K. Dittrich, D. Maier, and S. Zdonik, "The Object-Oriented Database System Manifesto," in W. Kim, J. M. Nicolas, and S. Nishio, eds., *Deductive and Object-Oriented Databases*, Elsevier Science Publishers, New York, 1990.

F. Bancilhon and R. Ramakrishnan, "An Amateur's Introduction to Recursive Query Processing Strategies," *Proceedings of ACM SIGMOD Conference*, 1986, pp. 16–52.

C. Baral, J. Lobo, and J. Minker, "Generalized Well-Founded Semantics for Logic Programs," *Proceedings of the Tenth Conference on Automated Deduction*, 1990a.

C. Baral, J. Lobo, and J. Minker, "Generalized Disjunctive Well-Founded Semantics for Logic Programs: Declarative Semantics," *Proceedings of the Fifth International Symposium on Methodologies for Intelligent Systems*, 1990b.

C. Baral, J. Lobo, and J. Minker, "Generalized Disjunctive Well-Founded Semantics for Logic Programs: Procedural Semantics," *Proceedings of the Fifth International Symposium on Methodologies for Intelligent Systems*, 1990c.

C. Beeri, "Formal Models for Object Oriented Databases," W. Kim, J. M. Nicolas, S. Nishio, eds., *Deductive and Object-Oriented Databases*, Elsevier Science Publishers, New York, 1990.

G. Bossu and P. Siegel, "Saturation, Non-Monotonic Reasoning and the Closed-World Assumption," *Artif. Intell.* **25**, 13–63 (1985).

S. Ceri, G. Gottlob, and L. Tanca, *Logic Programming and Databases*, Springer-Verlag, New York, 1990.

C. Chan, "Constructive Negation Based on the Completed Database" in R. A. Kowalski and K. A. Bowen, eds., *Logic Programming: Proceedings of the Fifth International Conference and Symposium*, The MIT Press, Cambridge, Mass., 1988, pp. 111–125.

A. Chandra and D. Harel, "Horn Clause Queries and Generalizations," *J. Log. Prog.* **2,** 1–15 (1985).

C. L. Chang and R. T. C. Lee, *Symbolic Logic and Mechanical Theorem Proving*, Academic Press, New York, 1973.

K. L. Clark, "Negation as Failure" in Gallaire and Minker (1978), 293–322.

W. F. Clocksin and C. S. Mellish, *Programming in Prolog*, 3rd ed., Springer-Verlag, New York, 1987.

R. Demolombe, "An Efficient Strategy for Non-Horn Deductive Databases," *Proceedings of IFIP*, 1989.

H. B. Enderton, *A Mathematical Introduction to Logic*, Academic Press, New York, 1972.

H. Gallaire and J. Minker, eds., *Logic and Databases*, Plenum, New York, 1978.

H. Gallaire, J. Minker, and J. Nicolas, "Logic and Databases: A Deductive Approach," *ACM Comput. Surv.* **16,** 153–185 (1984).

M. R. Genesereth and N. J. Nilsson, *Logical Foundations of Artificial Intelligence*, Morgan-Kaufmann Publishers, San Mateo, Calif., 1987.

J. Grant and J. Minker, "Answering Queries in Indefinite Databases and the Null Value Problem" P. Kanellakis, ed., in *Advances in Computing Theory*, Vol. 3, *The Theory of Databases*, JAI Press, Greenwich, Conn., 1986, pp. 247–267.

J. Grant and J. Minker, "Deductive Database Theories," *Know. Eng. Rev.* **4**, 267–304 (1989).

J. Grant and J. Minker, "Integrity Constraints in Knowledge-Based Systems," in H. Adeli, ed., *Knowledge Engineering*, Vol. 2, *Applications*, McGraw-Hill, New York, 1990, pp. 1–25.

J. Grant and T. K. Sellis, "Extended Database Logic: Complex Objects and Deduction," *Inf. Sci.* **52**, 85–110 (1990).

M. Kifer and G. Lausen, "F-Logic: A Higher-Order Language for Reasoning About Objects, Inheritance, and Scheme," *Proceedings of ACM SIGMOD Conference*, 1989, pp. 134–146.

K. C. Liu and R. Sunderraman, "Indefinite and Maybe Information in Relational Databases," *ACM Trans. on Database Sys.* **15**, 1–39 (1990).

J. W. Lloyd, *Foundations of Logic Programming*, 2nd extended ed., Springer-Verlag, New York, 1987.

J. Lobo, J. Minker, and A. Rajasekar, "Weak Completion Theory for Non-Horn Programs" in R. A. Kowalski and K. A. Bowen, eds., *Logic Programming: Proceedings of the Fifth International Conference and Symposium*, The MIT Press, Cambridge, Mass., 1988, pp. 828–842.

J. Lobo, J. Minker, and A. Rajasekar, *Foundations of Disjunctive Logic Programming*, MIT Press, Cambridge, Mass., 1991.

D. Loveland, *Automated Theorem Proving: A Logical Basis*, Elsevier North-Holland, Amsterdam, 1978.

D. Maier, "A Logic for Objects" in J. Minker, ed., *Proceedings of the Workshop on Foundations of Deductive Databases and Logic Programming*, Washington, D.C., 1986, pp. 6–26.

E. Mendelson, *Introduction to Mathematical Logic*, 3rd ed., Wadsworth, Belmont, Calif., 1987.

J. Minker, "On Indefinite Databases and the Closed World Assumption" in *Proceedings of the Sixth Conference on Automated Deduction*, Springer-Verlag Lecture Notes in Computer Science No. 138, Springer-Verlag, New York, 1982, pp. 292–308.

J. Minker, "Perspectives in Deductive Databases," *J. Log. Prog.* **5**, 33–60 (1988a).

J. Minker, ed., *Foundations of Deductive Databases and Logic Programming*, Morgan-Kaufmann Publishers, San Mateo, Calif., 1988b.

J. Minker and D. Perlis, "Computing Protected Circumscription," *J. Log. Prog.* **4**, 235–249 (1985).

J. Minker and A. Rajasekar, "A Fixpoint Semantics for Disjunctive Logic Programs," *J. Log. Prog.* (1990).

J. Minker and G. Zanon, "An Extension to Linear Resolution with Selection Function," *Inf. Proc. Lett.* **14**, 191–194 (1982).

S. A. Naqvi, "A Logic for Negation in Database Systems" in J. Minker, ed., *Proceedings of the Workshop on Foundations of Deductive Databases and Logic Programming*, Washington, D.C., 1986, pp. 378–387.

S. Naqvi and S. Tsur, *A Logical Language for Data and Knowledge Bases*, Computer Science Press, Rockville, Maryland, 1989.

T. C. Przymusinski, "On the Declarative Semantics of Deductive Databases and Logic Programs" in Minker, 1988b, pp. 193–216.

T. C. Przymusinski, "Every Logic Program Has a Natural Stratification and an Iterated Least Fixed Point Model," *Proceedings of the ACM PODS Conference*, 1989, pp. 11–21.

A. Rajasekar and J. Minker, "On Stratified Disjunctive Programs," *Ann. Math. Artif. Intell.* (1990).

R. Reiter, "On Closed World Databases" in Gallaire and Minker, 1978, pp. 149–178.

R. Reiter, "Towards a Logical Reconstruction of Relational Database Theory," in M. L. Brodie, J. Mylopoulos, and J. W. Schmidt, eds., *On Conceptual Modelling*, Springer-Verlag, New York, 1984, pp. 191–233.

J. C. Shepherdson, "Negation in Logic Programming" in Minker, 1988b, pp. 19–88.

L. Sterling and E. Shapiro, *The Art of Prolog: Advanced Programming Techniques*, The MIT Press, Cambridge, Mass., 1986.

J. D. Ullman, *Principles of Database and Knowledge-Base Systems*, Vols. 1 and 2, Computer Science Press, Rockville, Maryland, 1989.

M. H. van Emden and R. Kowalski, "The Semantics of Predicate Logic as a Programming Language," *J. ACM* **23**, 733–742 (1976).

A. Van Gelder, "Negation as Failure Using Tight Derivations for General Logic Programs" in Minker, 1988b, pp. 149–176.

A. Van Gelder, K. A. Ross, and J. S. Schlipf, "Unfounded Sets and Well-Founded Semantics for General Logic Programs," *Proceedings of ACM PODS Conference*, 1988, pp. 221–230.

A. Yahya and L. J. Henschen, "Deduction in Non-Horn Databases," *J. Autom. Reas.* **1**, 141–160 (1985).

C. Zaniolo, "Object Identity and Inheritance in Deductive Databases—An Evolutionary Approach," in W. Kim, J. M. Nicolas, and S. Nishio, eds., *Deductive and Object-Oriented Databases* Elsevier Science Publishers, New York, 1990.

JOHN GRANT
Towson State University

JACK MINKER
University of Maryland

DEEP STRUCTURE

Deep structure is central to the description of natural language syntax within the framework of transformational grammar (Chomsky, 1965, 1981). It plays two key roles: to relate the words of a sentence to the meaning and to help express generalizations about grammatical structure.

The motivation for deep structure is the fact that the surface order of words in a sentence is only a partial indication of its relation to other sentences: Pairs of sentences that look alike are sometimes unrelated, and pairs of sentences that look different can be closely related. An example is a pair of active and passive sentences, such as 1 and 2 below, that are different in form but are quite similar in meaning.

1. John saw Mary.
2. Mary was seen by John.

In these two sentences the predicate-argument relations expressed are the same: there is an act of seeing described.

John did the seeing, and Mary was the person seen. Yet, the order of words and the grammatical structure of the two sentences are different. John is the subject of the first sentence; Mary is the subject of the second. The structural difference between the two sentences is best expressed in terms of tree diagrams (Figs. 1 and 2).

This relationship between the active and passive versions of the same sentence does not depend on the particular words; it is not a fact about *John* or *Mary* or *see*. Rather there is a general, systematic relation between active and passive sentences: namely, the subject of a passive sentence plays the same role as the object of an active sentence. In transformational grammar these facts are described by saying that each sentence is associated with two distinct syntactic structures. One is the surface structure description shown in Figures 1 and 2 and the other a deep structure, which is related to the surface structure by a set of transformations, or tree-to-tree mappings. In the active–passive example both sentences have the same deep structure, a structure similar to the surface structure of the active form: the passive and active sentences have the same deep subject and object. A passive transformation maps the deep structure onto the surface structure by moving the deep subject into a *by* phrase and moving the deep object into subject position. In the "standard theory" of transformational grammar (Chomsky, 1965) the syntactic component consists of a context-free base, which generates deep structures, and a set of transformations that map these transformations onto the surface (see Winograd, 1983, Chapt. 4, for an introduction).

More recent versions of transformational grammar (Chomsky, 1981), where the power and variety of transformations has been severely limited, would assign to active and passive sentences deep structures differing in certain aspects. In particular, the sites from and to which objects are moved are noted in the structure. Nevertheless, the deep subject and deep object would still be the same for active and passive sentences. In addition to the active–passive relationship, transformations of similar deep structures can relate questions to statements, and various subordinate clauses where arguments are missing on the surface to a deep structure where the arguments are present.

NATURAL LANGUAGE PROCESSING

The notion of deep structure has been used in natural language processing systems in three ways.

1. A parser may attempt to directly implement a transformational grammar, analyzing a sentence by

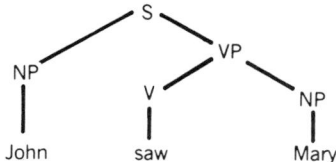

Figure 1. Phrase structure tree for active sentence.

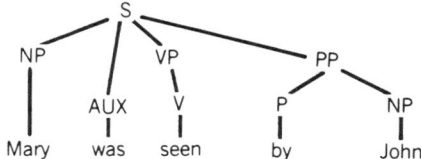

Figure 2. Phrase structure tree for passive sentence.

in effect running transformations in reverse (Petrick, 1973).

2. A parser may produce a deep structure representation (eg, as input to the semantics) without directly implementing transformations. For example, the LUNAR understanding system used an augmented-transition network to build a deep-structure representation that the semantic component then interpreted (Woods, Kaplan, and Nash-Webber, 1972; see GRAMMAR, AUGMENTED TRANSITION NETWORK).

3. The ideas of transformations and deep structure may be assumed in a parser that produces a phrase structure description annotated with indications of where elements must have been in the deep structure. The PARSIFAL parser (Marcus, 1980) follows this approach.

This last approach is closest to current transformational grammar known as Government-Binding Theory (Chomsky, 1981) where the input to semantics is through a kind of annotated surface structure, which includes indications of the transformations that have applied and therefore what the deep structure would be.

MEANING

Deep structure is where predicate-argument relationships are expressed. The idea that deep structure can be extended to capture all aspects of meaning was pursued in the 1970s under the label *generative semantics*, but it is now considered unsuccessful. As an example of the problems in treating deep structure as the sole input to semantics, note that in sentences 1 and 2, the paraphrase relation holds if John and Mary are simply people; but if Mary is a doctor, and *see* is being used in the sense of "consulted with," then "John saw a doctor" is not equivalent to "A doctor was seen by John." Similar inexact paraphrases can be easily found, for example, when quantifiers (*each, all, a,* etc) (see LOGIC, PREDICATE) are introduced in the noun phrases. Such problems make the notion that deep structure expresses all aspects of meaning difficult to hold.

The regularities of language expressed by deep structure can be expressed in other ways. For example, case frames (see GRAMMAR, CASE) are expressions of the meaning of predicates and arguments; they need not be seen as deep structures. Thus, the key claim of deep structure is not simply that there are relationships not evident on the surface but also that these are to be expressed in the same terms as the surface description (ie, as phrase structure trees).

The term "deep structure" is sometimes used metaphorically, not related to any theory of transformational grammar, to describe systematic structures that are not directly obvious and that relate more closely to meaning.

BIBLIOGRAPHY

N. Chomsky, *Aspects of the Theory of Syntax*, MIT Press, Cambridge, Mass., 1965.

N. Chomsky, *Lectures on Government and Binding*, Foris Publications, Dordrecht, The Netherlands, 1981.

M. Marcus, *A Theory of Recognition for Natural Language*, MIT Press, Cambridge, Mass., 1980.

S. R. Petrick, "Transformational Analysis," in R. Rustin, ed., *Natural Language Processing*, Algorithmics, New York, 1973, pp. 27–41.

T. Winograd, *Language as a Cognitive Process*, Addison-Wesley, Reading, Mass., 1983.

W. A. Woods, R. M. Kaplan, and B. Nash-Webber, *The Lunar Sciences Natural Language Information System: Final Report*, BBN Report No. 2378, Bolt, Beranek and Newman, Cambridge, Mass., 1972.

D. Hindle
AT&T Bell Laboratories

DEFAULT LOGIC. See Reasoning, default.

DEMPSTER-SHAFER THEORY

The Dempster-Shafer theory, also known as the theory of belief functions, is a generalization of the Bayesian theory of subjective probability. Whereas the Bayesian theory requires probabilities for each question of interest, belief functions allow us to base degrees of belief for one question on probabilities for a related question. These degrees of belief may or may not have the mathematical properties of probabilities; how much they differ from probabilities will depend on how closely the two questions are related.

The Dempster-Shafer theory owes its name to work by A. P. Dempster (1968) and Glenn Shafer (1976), but the kind of reasoning the theory uses can be found as far back as the seventeenth century. The theory came to the attention to AI researchers in the early 1980s, when they were trying to adapt probability theory to expert systems. Dempster-Shafer degrees of belief resemble the certainty factors in MYCIN (qv), and this resemblance suggested that they might combine the rigor of probability theory with the flexibility of rule-based systems (qv). Subsequent work has made clear that the management of uncertainty inherently requires more structure than is available in simple rule-based systems, but the Dempster-Shafer theory remains attractive because of its relative flexibility.

The Dempster-Shafer theory is based on two ideas: the idea of obtaining degrees of belief for one question from subjective probabilities for a related question, and Dempster's rule for combining such degrees of belief when they are based on independent items of evidence.

To illustrate the idea of obtaining degrees of belief for one question from subjective probabilities for another, suppose I have subjective probabilities for the reliability of my friend Betty. My probability that she is reliable is 0.9, and my probability that she is unreliable is 0.1. Suppose she tells me a limb fell on my car. This statement, which must be true if she is reliable, is not necessarily false if she is unreliable. So her testimony alone justifies a 0.9 degree of belief that a limb fell on my car, but only a zero degree of belief (not a 0.1 degree of belief) that no limb fell on my car. This zero does not mean that I am sure that no limb fell on my car, as a zero probability would; it merely means that Betty's testimony gives me no reason to believe that no limb fell on my car. The 0.9 and the zero together constitute a belief function.

To illustrate Dempster's rule for combining degrees of belief, suppose I also have a 0.9 subjective probability for the reliability of Sally, and suppose she too testifies, independently of Betty, that a limb fell on my car. The event that Betty is reliable is independent of the event that Sally is reliable, and we may multiply the probabilities of these events; the probability that both are reliable is $0.9 \times 0.9 = 0.81$, the probability that neither is reliable is $0.1 \times 0.1 = 0.01$, and the probability that at least one is reliable is $1 - 0.01 = 0.99$. Because they both said that a limb fell on my car, at least one of them being reliable implies that a limb did fall on my car, and hence I may assign this event a degree of belief of 0.99.

Suppose, on the other hand, that Betty and Sally contradict each other. Betty says that a limb fell on my car, and Sally says no limb fell on my car. In this case, they cannot both be right and hence cannot both be reliable; only one is reliable, or neither is reliable. The prior probabilities that only Betty is reliable, only Sally is reliable, and that neither is reliable are 0.09, 0.09, and 0.01, respectively, and the posterior probabilities (given that not both are reliable) are 9/19, 9/19, and 1/19, respectively. Hence we have a 9/19 degree of belief that a limb did fall on my car (because Betty is reliable) and a 9/19 degree of belief that no limb fell on my car (because Sally is reliable).

In summary, we obtain degrees of belief for one question (Did a limb fall on my car?) from probabilities for another question (Is the witness reliable?). Dempster's rule begins with the assumption that the questions for which we have probabilities are independent with respect to our subjective probability judgments, but this independence is only a priori; it disappears when conflict is discerned between the different items of evidence.

Implementing the Dempster-Shafer theory in a specific problem generally involves solving two related problems. First, we must sort the uncertainties in the problem into a priori independent items of evidence. Second, we must carry out Dempster's rule computationally. These two problems and their solutions are closely related. Sorting the uncertainties into independent items leads to a structure involving items of evidence that bear on different but related questions, and this structure can be used to make computations feasible. Suppose, for example, that Betty and Sally testify independently that they heard a burglar enter my house. They might both have mistaken the noise of a dog for that of a burglar, and because of this common uncertainty, I cannot combine degrees of belief based on their evidence directly by Dempster's rule. But if I consider explicitly the possibility of a dog's presence, then I can identify three independent items of evidence: my other evidence for or against the presence of a dog, my evidence for Betty's reliability, and my evidence for Sally's reliability. I can combine these items of evidence by Dempster's rule, and the computations are facilitated by the structure that relates the different questions involved.

For more information, see Shafer (1990) and the articles on the belief functions in Shafer and Pearl (1990).

BIBLIOGRAPHY

A. P. Dempster, "A Generalization of Bayesian Inference," *J. Roy. Stat. Soc. Ser. B* **30,** 205–247 (1968).

G. Shafer, *A Mathematical Theory of Evidence*, Princeton University Press, Princeton, N.J., 1976.

G. Shafer, "Perspectives on the Theory and Practice of Belief Functions," *Int. J. Approx. Reas.* **3,** 1–40 (1990).

G. Shafer and J. Pearl, eds., *Readings in Uncertain Reasoning*, Morgan-Kaufmann Publishers, San Mateo, Calif., 1990.

GLENN SHAFER
University of Kansas

DENDRAL

DENDRAL is the first knowledge-based system applied to science and is sometimes called the first expert system. It was designed and developed at Stanford by Lederberg, Feigenbaum, Buchanan, and a team of collaborators including chemists Djerassi, Smith, Carhart, Gray, and Nourse. It used a substantial body of explicit knowledge about organic chemistry (and the analytic technique of mass spectrometry). It is the first knowledge-based system to represent much of its knowledge in production rules.

In 1964 Lederberg designed the "dendritic algorithm" (from which the whole package gets its name), which is a graph-theoretic notational algorithm for naming chemical structures uniquely. The naming algorithm was then mapped into a generating algorithm. This generator, named CONGEN and later GENOA, became the "legal move generator" of the DENDRAL system. It was capable of exhaustively and nonredundantly enumerating all chemical structures with a specified atomic composition.

The number of chemical graphs that can be generated from fixed numbers of chemical atoms is exponential and too large for a generate-and-test program. For example there are about 10,000 graphical descriptions of possible chemical structures (obeying valence constraints only) with the empirical formula $C_6H_{13}NO_2$ (which is the composition of the amino acid leucine) and over 11 million with empirical formula $C_{20}H_{42}O$.

When used to assist in the interpretation of analytic data on unknown chemical compounds, the generator was constrained by a planning program. The DENDRAL planner used production rules encoding knowledge of analytic techniques (eg, mass spectrometry or NMR) to infer from the data some of the probable and improbable structural features of the compound. The results of the planner were represented as incomplete chemical graphs that must be (or probably are) present (GOODLIST) or must not be (or probably are not) present (BADLIST) in any complete structure that accounts for the data.

Because the generator might well produce many structures that are consistent with the planner's inferences, a testing program was added at the end. This module predicted additional data which could then be used to confirm or disconfirm each structure, and to rank the confirmed ones.

DENDRAL's method was known as Plan-Generate-Test. DENDRAL's overall paradigm for hypothesis formation is called the exclusion paradigm because large parts of the search space are excluded for explicit reasons and the remaining hypotheses are all and only those that are consistent with the constraints inferred from the input data (or added manually).

DENDRAL's performance on many different kinds of problems demonstrated the power of symbolic computation and heuristic inference in assisting chemists with important, difficult problems. Its success can be largely attributed to having (1) a canonical representation of the "answers" (chemical structures); (2) a systematic generator of the search space; (3) a program that inferred plausible constraints for the generator from the input data; and (4) a strong enough theory of the analytic instruments to make testable predictions. (See B. G. Buchanan and E. A. Feigenbaum, "DENDRAL and Meta-DENDRAL: Their Applications Dimension," *Artif. Intell.* **11,** 5–24 (1978); R. K. Lindsay, B. G. Buchanan, E. A. Feigenbaum, and J. Lederberg, "*Applications of Artificial Intelligence for Organic Chemistry: The DENDRAL Project,*" McGraw-Hill, New York, 1980.

BRUCE G. BUCHANAN
University of Pittsburgh

DESIGN

There are many activities that are referred to as design. It is normally considered to be "synthesis;" however, a large design task can involve much "analysis" too. Design is an intelligent human activity requiring many skills and much knowledge. Design problems can be solved by individuals or by teams. They may take minutes or years.

Design occurs in a wide variety of domains, ranging from the design of a nuclear power plant to that of a mounting bracket, and from a computer to a ship. In this article most references will be made to mechanical design, in order to provide focus. Given this enormous variety of problems and domains, it is important to try to define what is meant by design.

The general design process is often characterized as mapping needs to function to structure. It is carried out using many different types of reasoning and many different sources of knowledge. In general, design is the process of specifying a description of an artifact that satisfies a collection of constraints. These constraints may arise from a variety of sources. The constraints may be imposed by the problem, the designer, the manufacturer, the user, or by natural laws. They reflect the desired function of the artifact, the available resources (eg, money), the physical limitations of the materials (eg, strength), the demands on the artifact from the environment in which it will be used (eg, maintainability), the manufacturing processes required, general design criteria (eg, simplicity), and the design process itself (Mitchell and Mostow, 1987).

The term *constraint* usually means something that is either satisfied or not. For the definition above the meaning needs to be extended to include softer restrictions, such as preferences. In addition, there are usually special objectives to be met, such as minimizing cost, weight, or area. These act throughout the design process and can be used for evaluation of the design. Not all of these varied requirements need be specified initially. It is a characteristic of many design problems that new constraints emerge as decisions are made.

REASONS FOR STUDY

Because design is an ill-structured activity requiring intelligence, it is a suitable topic of study for AI. Simon (1969) even goes far as to say that "the proper study of mankind is the science of design."

A fundamental hypothesis shared by most design researchers in AI is that there are core reasoning mechanisms and types of knowledge that are common across domains (Maher and Gero, 1990). That is, although design problems in different domains require different domain knowledge (qv), there are underlying similarities in the form of that knowledge and in the way it is used. Of course, different domains and different design problems will require a different mix; eg, designing a mechanism might require a lot of spatial reasoning in three dimensions, whereas designing a circuit would require very little.

Investigating that fundamental hypothesis will result in a better understanding of what design actually is. This should allow useful intelligent computer-aided design (IntCAD) systems to be built, to do or to support design activity. Systems can range from autonomous design tools, that when given requirements will produce designs, to design aids that interact with human designers. Systems have been built for many different domains, such as

VLSI, graphical interfaces, electronic circuits, protein purification processes, elevators, computers, air cylinders, aluminum alloys, construction sites, molecular genetics experiments, copier paper paths, and high-rise buildings (Tong and Sriram, 1991a, 1991b; Sriram and Tong, 1991) (see also ENGINEERING, KNOWLEDGE-BASED EXPERT SYSTEMS IN; HUMAN-COMPUTER INTERFACE).

HISTORY

Computers have contributed to design for quite a while by providing analysis tools (eg, the finite element method), databases (eg, of drawings and components), and computer-aided drafting–drawing tools. The latter is what is naturally thought of when CAD is mentioned, as such tools have been under development since the early 1960s. Their progress runs parallel to that of computer graphics (Foley and co-workers, 1990).

Two-dimensional drafting tools, and three-dimensional display of objects as "wire-frames," were followed by *raster displays*. The capability to display a shaded image, along with developments in geometric modelling (Mantyla, 1988; see also SHAPE) allowed designers to consider objects on the screen as real. They were able to concentrate on decisions about objects rather than about drawings. This is much closer to computer-aided *design,* as opposed to computer-aided *drafting*.

Since its inception, CAD has gradually been concerned with representing increasing amounts about the objects being manipulated. Geometric information has moved from 2-D to 3-D, and from planar to curved surfaces. Information about surface finish and color has been added. Geometric and topological models specify the structural relationships between components. Descriptions of form features can be included. Application-specific information, such as material properties or manufacturing requirements, is also useful. Thus CAD representations have gradually been moving closer to being a knowledge representation (qv), to include all aspects of knowledge about the designed object. Suitable additions would be precise part-whole relations (Winston and co-workers, 1987), and the representation of function (Sembugamoorthy and Chandrasekaran, 1986). Researchers are concerned with what needs to be represented to support IntCAD systems (Arbab, 1990).

An additional type of information that has been added to CAD systems is the constraint. Constraints restrict the possible values of parameters. In 2-D a constraint might be added to require that two lines be maintained at a certain angle. In 3-D, two solids could be constrained to always touch. When constraints are used, a single change can propagate through constraints to produce new values for many other parameters, effectively generating a whole new design. Thus constraint satisfaction (qv) provides a *parametric design* capability, ie, the system "designs" values for some parameters. Companies such as Cognition and ICAD were able to base commercial products on this idea. With these developments, CAD has gradually turned from being mainly concerned with object representation towards consideration of the design process, ie, design process knowledge as opposed to design object knowledge.

Because most designers can be considered experts, systems that design can be considered expert systems (qv). Until quite recently, much of the expert systems research was concerned with *diagnosis,* and tools and techniques with which to build diagnostic systems. Now, design has become an important area to study, with a burgeoning literature (Gero, 1985; Mostow, 1985; Hong, 1986; Gero, 1987; Rychener, 1988; Brown and Chandrasekaran, 1989; Finger and Dixon, 1989a, 1989b; Coyne and co-workers, 1990; Maher and Gero, 1990; Dym and Levitt, 1991; Green, 1991; Sriram and Tong, 1991; Tong and Sriram, 1991a, 1991b). Other material can be found in the bibliography.

Expert systems technology has allowed for many new and practical applications. For example, in addition to systems that produce designs, systems can be built to check design decisions for conformance with standards or with company guidelines. Systems can be used to extract features, to select materials, to discover design flaws and suggest corrections, and to evaluate the manufacturability or constructability of the design.

ROLES FOR KNOWLEDGE-BASED REASONING IN DESIGN

These applications hint at the many roles that knowledge-based techniques and systems can play during design. Some of them are presented below. Each provides a particular function and can be implemented in different ways using AI techniques.

Abstraction can be used to discover the general design of which the current design is an example. This might lead to a better understanding of which design plans or analysis methods to use.

Acquisition can request and integrate new design knowledge (see KNOWLEDGE ACQUISITION).

Analysis, which is often numerical, is needed to understand the properties (such as strength) of the design or of subcomponents.

Association allows related concepts to be discovered and supports analogical reasoning.

Basic synthesis produces values for attributes, such as color or length, by calculation or decision.

Classification can be used to categorize the requirements or the current state of the design in order to decide what sort of method or analysis might be used.

Criticism compares a portion of the design against a standard, or some preferences, and points out the ways in which it is lacking. When design requirements are used this can be called "verification."

Decomposition divides a design problem into smaller, more manageable subproblems.

Estimation can be used to produce design values that are roughly correct, in order to discover more about the design problem.

Evaluation uses the results of analysis, or some aspects of the design, to provide an estimate of quality or the degree to which it meets some design goals (eg, low cost).

Execution follows the instructions given in a design plan.

Extraction can be used to find features of the design that can be used for analysis or evaluation.

Generation of acceptable candidate values that can be used for the design might be done by constraint satisfaction.

Guidance provides the designer with a methodology to be followed and can enforce it.

Learning can improve the resulting designs, or can improve the design process, making it more efficient (such as in knowledge compilation) or more knowledgeable (see LEARNING, MACHINE).

Memory allows a design history to be maintained that captures the intent or rationale of the designer. It can be used to remember successful methods or designs as cases for case-based reasoning (see REASONING, CASE-BASED).

Negotiation provides a way for a team of experts, or expert systems, to arrive at a design which is acceptable to all parties.

Note making occurs when a designer makes a mental note at some early stage of the design to do or check something later during the design process (Adelson and Soloway, 1985). It might correspond to forming a new constraint.

Notification is used to communicate the consequences of a design decision in order to affect other portions of the design (such as in constraint propagation).

Optimization, usually numeric, can produce the best values for design attributes, relative to some criteria that can be evaluated.

Patching can be used to modify an existing design after flaws have been found in it.

Planning (qv) the design process, in order to design subcomponents in an appropriate order, for example, is a vital part of design in general.

Prediction is often needed to determine the consequences of a design decision. It might be done by qualitative reasoning or some other form of knowledge-based simulation.

Presentation of information about the current state of the design, or about standards, for example, is important for assisting the human designer.

Recomposition takes finished designs for subcomponents and composes them into a component design.

Refinement occurs when a description (eg, of a function) is mapped to a less abstract description (eg, of a class of mechanisms).

Retraction allows previous design decisions to be discarded. This could be done using some form of backtracking (qv).

Reuse, by analogy, or its weaker cousin case-based reasoning, can save effort by reusing past methods or designs.

Simplification of the problem can be carried out by ignoring details, for example, by ignoring or "relaxing" less important constraints, or by noticing regularities. It may also be done by combining constraints [as in constraint subsumption (Tong, 1987)].

Suggestions, generated after criticism, can provide information to guide the patching, or any other redesign activity.

Selection is a major component of configuration. It can also be used to pick an appropriate plan or analysis method.

APPROACHES TO DESIGN STUDY

The IntCAD research community now consists of CAD researchers, who use AI techniques to expand the capabilities of CAD systems; AI researchers, who study design knowledge and reasoning; engineers, who are eager to use smarter tools; and cognitive scientists, who study how designers think. Consequently, the literature on AI in design is quite widespread.

Finger and Dixon (1989a, 1989b), from a mechanical engineering point of view, describe design research as falling into several categories, including descriptive models, languages, representations, environments, and computer-based models. Descriptive models of the design process are concerned with the "processes, strategies, and problem solving methods designers use." These efforts include collecting protocols from designers, building cognitive models that could mimic the human designer, and collecting and analyzing design cases. Such studies have revealed, for example, the importance of drawing in design and the many roles, such as memory aid, that it plays (Ullman and co-workers, 1989). Languages and representations research includes the representation of form, function and behavior, and features. Work on environments attempts to build systems that aid the designer during the design process by providing an integrated set of tools. Computer-based models research is concerned with how the computer can design or assist with designing. AI-based design research is mostly associated with the languages, representations, and computer-based models categories.

TYPES OF DESIGN

In literature concerning design problem-solving, many terms for types of design are found, including preliminary, conceptual, functional, innovative, creative, routine, embodiment, parametric, detailed, redesign, nonroutine, and configuration. However, there seems to be a general acceptance of the rough classification of design into *routine, innovative,* and *creative,* where each class has less known in advance by the designer. In routine design both the knowledge sources and the problem-solving strategies are known in advance. In innovative design, only the knowledge sources are known in advance, while in creative design neither is known.

For routine design, everything about the design process, including the knowledge needed, must be known in advance. This does not mean that either the specific design solution or the pattern of use of the knowledge (ie, the design trace) are completely known in advance. The underlying thesis is that design tasks become routine because of learning brought about by repetition of similar problem solving. That is, routineness is a direct reflection of experience. Routine designs are done more efficiently, and possibly with better results. In fact, this three-class model is much too simple. The level of experience with a certain type of design can be reflected by a position on a routine–nonroutine axis, with "very experienced" at one end, and "very inexperienced" at the other (see Brown in Waldron and Waldron, 1991). An orthogonal conceptual–parametric axis can be used to show the abstractness of the decisions being made. Types of design are points in the space defined by the axes.

Conceptual design means that the kind of things being decided at that point in the design are abstract (ie, conceptual), for example, that the design requirements can be satisfied by an object providing a particular function. *Parametric* design means that the things being decided are values for a prespecified set of attributes.

Another way of classifying design problems is to divide them into those that have subtask ordering decided a priori, those that know the dependencies in advance but order them during the design, and those for which the dependencies between subtasks are both discovered and ordered during the design (Balkany and co-workers, 1990). Routine problems would be expected to belong to the first type, and very nonroutine problems to belong to the third.

In Dixon's taxonomy of design problems (Dixon and co-workers, 1988), the levels are *functional, phenomenological, embodiment, attribute,* and *parametric,* depending on whether function, physical principles, general class of solution, type of object, or parameter values are decided at that level. Clearly, these levels correspond to portions of the conceptual–parametric axis.

In general, design activity can start at any level of abstraction and finish at any more specific level. Usually, the larger the gap between the level of the specification and the desired level for the design, the harder the design process is. Dixon states that conceptual design is often used to describe moving from the function level to the embodiment level. He considers *preliminary* design to be an extension of conceptual design to another level of specificity, ie, to artifact type. Parametric design goes from the artifact type level to the artifact instance level. As we move along the conceptual–parametric axis, less structure needs to be decided during the design process.

In *configuration,* which is a restricted form of design,

the components of the designed object can only come from a predefined set (Mittal and Frayman, 1989). They are selected and arranged together to satisfy some requirements. Each component describes the connections that it allows. It is usually not possible or practical to predetermine all possible configurations (Barker and O'Connor, 1989). Often, artifacts are configured according to a known functional architecture, and certain components can be predetermined as "key." These assumptions help to prune the search for a configuration. Depending on the complexity of the problem, the components may or may not need to have values provided for parameters. For example, a layout (or floor-planning) problem may just be concerned with spatial arrangement, but a resistor may need to be given a resistance value. Note that no new components are used, and a component's connectivity is not changed.

Rough design is an attempt to learn something additional about the design problem by deciding some aspects of the design and then evaluating that partial design. In a more routine design situation, "those values on which much of the rest of the design depends" are known by the designer and can be decided and checked first (Brown and Chandrasekaran, 1989). Other senses of "rough" rather than incomplete are abstract and approximate. Interval arithmetic may be able to contribute to approximate design (Navinchandra and Rinderle, 1989). Abstract designs are hard to evaluate. However, Tong (1987) suggests that information about "potential bottlenecks with respect to some resource" (such as the number of components needed) might be gathered by the formation and execution of abstract design plans.

Redesign problems are concerned with changing prior design decisions. This includes modifying an existing design in response to changing requirements, and making changes to decisions already made, during the design process, as a result of failing constraints (Daube and Hayes-Roth, 1989; Goel and Chandrasekaran, 1989; Brown, 1985; Steinberg and Mitchell, 1985). This can involve using suggestions about suitable changes that are either prestored or generated by analyzing the situation. A record of the reasons for the prior design decisions (ie, a design history) is also useful. A particular form of parametric redesign is *iterative redesign,* where an initial heuristically generated design is modified one parameter value at a time (Orelup and co-workers, 1988; Ramachandran and co-workers, 1988). After each modification an evaluation step leads to a suggestion about which parameter to change next and in which direction. This *hill-climbing* approach can be controlled by meta-knowledge (qv) to try to ensure that it keeps improving its solution and approaches a global optimum.

CHARACTERIZING THE DESIGN PROCESS

One goal of AI research in design is to try to characterize the design process in enough detail that systems can be built more easily, that design knowledge can be acquired more easily, and that design tools can be matched to de-

sign problems. At some level of abstraction the description above of the possible roles for knowledge-based reasoning in design could be used to provide a vocabulary with which to describe design activity. The challenge is to fully describe each function, to characterize the knowledge each uses, to describe their inputs and outputs, to list their alternative implementations (using AI methods), and to discover distinctive patterns of use.

Many people would agree that the general flow of design can be characterized by something like *requirements formulation + synthesis + analysis + evaluation.* There are many similar models in the design literature. Unfortunately, this characterization is too abstract and does little to help us build computer models. For example, analysis could be done by many methods, such as quantitative simulation or qualitative simulation. Tong (1987) provides an analysis based on characterizing certain kinds of design as *incremental refinement,* where specifications can be converted to implementations (ie, a design) directly, via multiple refinements, possibly using abstraction levels and decomposition, with details being provided by constrained inference, and corrections being provided by debugging.

Chandrasekaran (see Maher and Gero, 1990) attempts to characterize a large family of design tasks as *propose + critique + modify.* Each subtask can be carried out by different methods. For the purpose subtask he discusses decomposition and solution composition, for recursively reducing the problem, and case retrieval and constraint satisfaction for solving the problems or subproblems.

In a similar proposal, McDermott (see Marcus, 1988) argues that there are a set of methods "where each method defines the roles that the task-specific knowledge it requires must play and the forms in which that knowledge can be represented." His *propose + revise* method first extends the design, then identifies constraint violations, suggests potential fixes, selects the least costly fix to try, tries the fix, identifies resulting constraint violations (if there are any it loops to select another fix) and, if there are none, tidies up and loops to extend the design again until it is completed. This is a method to achieve constraint satisfaction. He also suggests an *extrapolate-from-a-similar-case* method.

Balkany, Birmingham, and Tommelein (1991) make a knowledge-level analysis and comparison of several design systems; that is, they attempt to isolate the behavior of each system from techniques used to implement that behavior. The systems are AIR–CYL (Brown and Chandrasekaran, 1989), M1 (Birmingham and co-workers, 1989), PRIDE (see Mittal and Araya in Tong and Sriram, 1991a), VT (see Marcus and co-workers, in Tong and Sriram, 1991a), and SightPlan (Tommelein and co-workers, 1991). For each system, they characterize its action in terms of sequences of *mechanisms,* such as extend-design, find-constraints, test-constraints, suggest-fixes, select-fix, modify-design, find-constraint, test-constraints, propagate-changes, and test-if-done. This sequence, from the VT system, corresponds to McDermott's propose + revise method.

USING AI TECHNIQUES

This section discusses how some AI techniques might be used to implement functions that play roles in the building of design systems. Only some of the AI in design research will be referred to; more information is available in other articles in this encyclopedia.

Knowledge Representation

In design many types of knowledge can be used, not all of which can be alluded to here (see KNOWLEDGE REPRESENTATION). Knowledge about things, design requirements, and processes are all useful. Knowledge about both the object being designed (eg, it is 3.45 cm long) and general object knowledge (eg, all #26 flanges have a 3:2 height-to-length ratio) needs to be represented. Frame representations are popular (see FRAMES). The basic knowledge about components concerns geometry and topology. Taxonomies of components and part-subpart descriptions need to be represented. Attributes such as color, hardness, material, and surface finish need to be stored. Properties of material must be available. Features can relate to form and function (Dixon and co-workers, 1989). Descriptions of function and behavior (Sembugamoorthy and Chandrasekaran, 1986; Ulrich and Seering, 1989) are useful during conceptual design, for criticism (Lai and Wilson, 1987), and for reasoning about mechanisms (Pu and Badler, 1988). Functional hierarchies are useful for reducing search during configuration (Mittal and Frayman, 1989; Birmingham, 1989).

Knowledge about the capabilities of processes is important if the design system needs to select an appropriate method. This can be as simple as picking a prestored plan, or as sophisticated as reasoning about which design method is most likely to produce the desired result. Other knowledge can be about which decision should take priority (Stefik, 1980), how to decompose a problem, or what tradeoffs might be made between conflicting goals (Tong, 1987).

Constraint Satisfaction

Constraints can be used to maintain consistency, prune search, and record interactions between subproblems. They can express many things, including design heuristics, basic equations, material compatibility, and physical limits on components due to strength or manufacturing. Many constraints refer to parameters with numerical values (eg, $L < 12$), but reference to symbols is possible (eg, M = one-of{Brass Steel Wood}). Adding constraints to the design as a result of making decisions is called *constraint formulation*. The creation of new constraints from old is called *constraint subsumption*. Decisions can be communicated by *constraint propagation,* or by propagating acceptable values. Propagation enables a least commitment strategy. There are several approaches to constraint satisfaction, ie, finding values that satisfy a set of constraints. Many problems can be solved using these methods (Stefik, 1980; see Steinberg in Tong and Sriram, 1991a; Bowen and O'Grady in Gero, 1990a). In some de-

sign problems, variables and constraints emerge during the design (Mittal and Falkenhainer, 1990). The use of constraints to handle large design problems has been criticized as being too computationally expensive, and not a good model of human problem-solving.

Search

In general, design cannot be completely modeled by a standard heuristic search (see SEARCH), because evaluation functions are not always available, and because, at best, several search spaces are required, such as possible plans, possible configurations, and possible combinations of parameter values. In addition, not all problems have fully specified requirements that can act as goals or goal recognizers for a search. However, despite the often exploratory nature of conceptual design, much of design can be described as search. The maintenance of consistency during the search for a design can be handled using truth maintenance (qv) methods. These are especially useful in situations where assumptions are made during the design. Chronological or dependency-directed backtracking (qv) can also be used. Dependencies between design decisions can be explicitly recorded and used for backtracking, but they can also serve as a form of design history, for possible subsequent redesign or case-based reasoning. They can also serve as the basis for a truth maintenance system (TMS).

Learning

Some researchers, especially those interested in automatic generation of design tools, have used a learning mechanism with a simple search to learn problem decompositions, or with *generate and test* to improve the generator by moving knowledge from the test back into the generator (Tong, 1990). These are examples of knowledge compilation systems, which learn in order to increase efficiency (Keller, 1991; Brown, 1991a). Other work on learning in design includes the learning apprentice, LEAP, which learns design "refinement rules" by generalizing the user's input (Tong, 1990); the Designer-Soar system that learns to design algorithms (Steier and Newell, 1988); and Bridger, which learns to classify designs for reuse (Reich, 1991). (See LEARNING, MACHINE.)

Case-based Reasoning and Analogy

The use of previous designs or design plans can reduce search. Mostow (1990) discusses the replaying of design plans, and compares some systems, including BOGART and ARGO (Mostow and co-workers, and Huhns and Acosta in Sriram and Tong, 1991), according to how cases are represented, stored, retrieved, and adapted. Case-based design is also discussed by Sycara and co-workers, and by Goel (in Sriram and Tong, 1991). An engineering view of design history keeping can be found in Chen and co-workers (1990). Gero (in Maher and Gero, 1990) proposes that design cases and all other design knowledge be organized into schema for efficient access during design.

Qualitative Reasoning

During the design process, qualitative reasoning techniques can be used to reason about space, flows (such as heat, fluid, or force), and, more generally, behavior. Required motions can determine shape (Joskowicz and Addanki, 1988), shape can be used to derive behavior (Joskowicz in Weld and de Kleer, 1990), and objects can be checked for fit (Carney and Brown, 1989) (see REASONING, SPATIAL). Innovative design is possible by mapping a network of qualitative interactions between quantities onto physical structure (Williams, 1990). In order to organize and move easily from one model of an object to another (eg, from a heat flow model to a kinematic model) the use of a metamodel (Tomiyama and co-workers, 1989) and a graph of models have been proposed (Addanki and co-workers in Weld and de Kleer, 1990).

Blackboards

Blackboard-based architectures are useful for the integration of many sources of knowledge, such as in building design (Sriram and co-workers, in Tong and Sriram, 1991b; Schmitt in Yoshikawa and Holden, 1990; see BLACKBOARD SYSTEMS).

SAMPLE SYSTEMS

Most of the well-analyzed systems are for routine tasks. Besides systems already mentioned, XCON (qv) (Barker and O'Connor, 1989) and VEXED (Steinberg in Tong, 1990) deserve study. Some systems have been generalized to provide expert system shells. These include DSPL from AIR–CYL, EDESYN from HI-RISE (Maher, 1988), and EVEXED from VEXED. Other systems for less routine design include, MOLGEN (Stefik, 1980), DONTE (Tong, 1990), DESIGNER (Kant, 1985), EDISON (Dyer and co-workers, 1986), and AM (qv) (Lenat and Brown, 1983).

RESEARCH

In such a complex and poorly understood area as design, there are many research issues. In addition to basic work on representing features, function, and other aspects of design objects, it will be necessary to devise ways to integrate these types of knowledge so that reasoning processes can use them fully. Languages are needed with which to express an expert's knowledge of design. Both learning (including knowledge compilation) and knowledge acquisition (Marcus, 1988) for design systems are vital. The use of neural networks (qv) needs to be studied for functions such as case classification or selection. More work is needed in creative design. This requires doing much more reasoning (qv) at design time and, consequently, representing and reasoning about goals, dealing with alternative designs, reasoning about resources, analogy, problem decomposition, evaluation of partial designs, dynamic constraint satisfaction, functional reasoning, using multiple models, combining quantitative and qualitative reasoning, model-based reasoning, and reasoning about failure, all become major issues. Large design problems will require cooperative, and perhaps distributed, design problem-solvers, as well as negotiation (Sycara, 1991). Papers presenting overviews of the work at Carnegie Mellon University, Rutgers University, the University of Sydney, Worcester Polytechnic Institute, the University of Illinois, Edinburgh University, North Carolina State University, and Wayne State University can be found in Gero (1989, 1990a). Other major centers include the University of Tokyo, the University of Massachusetts, MIT, the University of Michigan, and the Engineering Design Research Centers in the UK.

BIBLIOGRAPHY

B. Adelson and E. Soloway, "The Role of Domain Experience in Software Design," *Trans. Software Eng.* SE-11(11), 1351–1360 (1985).

V. Akman, P. J. W. ten Hagen, and P. J. Veerkamp, eds., *Intelligent CAD Systems II: Implementational Issues,* Springer-Verlag, New York, 1989.

F. Arbab, "Features and Geometric Reasoning," in H. Yoshikawa and T. Holden, eds., *Intelligent CAD II,* North-Holland, Amsterdam, 1990, pp. 45–65.

A. Balkany, W. P. Birmingham, and I. D. Tommelein, "A Knowledge-Level Analysis of Several Design Tools," *Artificial Intelligence in Design '91, Proceedings of the First International Conference on Artificial Intelligence in Design,* Edinburgh, UK, Butterworth-Heinemann Publishers, UK, 1991.

V. E. Barker and D. E. O'Connor, "Expert Systems for Configuration at Digital: XCON and Beyond," *CACM* 32(3), 298–318 (Mar. 1989).

W. P. Birmingham, A. P. Gupta, and D. P. Siewiorek, "The MICON System for Computer Design," *IEEE Micro* 9(5), 61–67 (Oct. 1989).

D. C. Brown, "Failure Handling in a Design Expert System," in J. S. Gero, ed., *Computer-Aided Design Journal,* Special ed., Butterworths, UK, Nov. 1985.

D. C. Brown, "Compilation: The Hidden Dimension of Design Systems," in H. Yoshikawa and F. Arbab, eds., *Intelligent CAD III,* North-Holland, Amsterdam, 1991a.

D. C. Brown and B. Chandrasekaran, *Design Problem Solving: Knowledge Structures and Control Strategies,* Research Notes in Artificial Intelligence series, Morgan-Kaufmann, San Mateo, Calif., 1989.

D. C. Brown, M. Waldron, and H. Yoshikawa, eds., *Intelligent Computer-Aided Design,* North-Holland, Amsterdam, 1992.

G. R. Bruns and S. L. Gerhart, *Theories of Design: An Introduction to the Literature,* Technical Report STP-068-86, Microelectronics and Computer Technology Corp. (MCC), Austin, Tex., 1986.

S. P. Carney and D. C. Brown, "A Continued Investigation Into Qualitative Reasoning about Shape and Fit," *AI EDAM J.* 3(2), 85–110 (Nov. 1989).

A. Chen, B. McGinnis, and D. G. Ullman, "Design History Knowledge Representation and its Basic Computer Implementation," in J. Rinderle, ed., *Proceedings of the Second ASME International Conference on Design Theory and Methodology,* DE-Vol. 27, Chicago, American Society of Mechanical Engineers, New York, 1990, pp. 175–184.

R. D. Coyne, M. A. Rosenman, A. D. Radford, M. Balachandran, and J. S. Gero, *Knowledge-Based Design Systems,* Addison-Wesley, Reading, Mass., 1990.

F. Daube and B. Hayes-Roth, "A Case-Based Mechanical Redesign System," *Proceedings of the Eleventh IJCAI,* Vol. 2, Morgan-Kaufmann, San Mateo, Calif., 1989, pp. 1402–1407.

J. R. Dixon, J. J. Cunningham, and M. K. Simmons, "Research in Designing with Features," in H. Yoshikawa and D. Gossart, eds., *Intelligent CAD I,* North-Holland, Amsterdam, 1989, pp. 137–148.

J. R. Dixon, M. R. Duffey, R. K. Irani, K. L. Meunier, and M. F. Orelup, "A Proposed Taxonomy of Mechanical Design Problems," *Proceedings of the ASME Computers in Engineering Conference,* Vol. I, San Francisco, Calif., ASME, New York, 1988, pp. 41–46.

M. G. Dyer, M. Flowers, and J. Hodges, "EDISON: An Engineering Design Invention System Operating Naively," *AI in Eng.* 1(1), 36–44 (1986).

C. L. Dym and R. E. Levitt, *Knowledge-Based Systems in Engineering,* McGraw-Hill, New York, 1991.

S. Finger and J. R. Dixon, "A Review of Research in Mechanical Engineering Design, Part I: Descriptive, Prescriptive, and Computer-Based Models of Design," *Res. Eng. Des.* 1, 51–67 (1989a).

S. Finger and J. R. Dixon, "A Review of Research in Mechanical Engineering Design, Part II: Representations, Analysis, and Design for the Life Cycle," *Res. Eng. Des.* 1, 121–137 (1989b).

S. Finger, S. L. Newson, and W. R. Spillers, eds., *Design Theory '88,* Springer-Verlag, New York, 1989.

J. D. Foley, A. van Dam, S. K. Feiner, and J. F. Hughes, *Computer Graphics: Principles and Practice,* 2nd ed., Addison-Wesley, Reading, Mass., 1990.

J. S. Gero, ed., *Knowledge Engineering in Computer-Aided Design,* North-Holland, Amsterdam, 1985.

J. S. Gero, ed., *Expert Systems in Computer-Aided Design,* North-Holland, Amsterdam, 1987.

J. S. Gero, ed., "Artificial Intelligence in Design," *Proceedings of the Fourth International Conference on Applications of AI in Engineering,* Cambridge, UK, Computational Mechanics Publications and Springer-Verlag, New York, 1989.

J. S. Gero, ed., "Applications of AI in Engineering V, Vol. 1: Design," *Proceedings of the Fifth International Conference on Applications of AI in Engineering,* Boston, Mass., Computational Mechanics Publications and Springer-Verlag, New York, 1990a.

J. S. Gero and M. L. Maher, eds., "Modelling Creativity and Knowledge-Based Design," *Proceedings of the Workshop on Modeling Creativity and Knowledge-Based Creative Design, 1989,* Lawrence Erlbaum and Associates, Hillsdale, N.J., 1991.

A. Goel and B. Chandrasekaran, "Functional Representation of Designs and Redesign Problem Solving," *Proceedings of the Eleventh IJCAI,* Vol. 2, Detroit, Mich., Morgan-Kaufmann, San Mateo, Calif., 1989, pp. 1388–1394.

V. Goel and P. Pirolli, "Motivating the Notion of Generic Design within Information-Processing Theory: The Design Problem Space," *AI Mag.* 10(1), 19–36 (Spring 1989).

M. Green, ed., *Knowledge Aided Design,* Academic Press, New York, 1991.

S. J. Hong, ed., *IEEE Computer,* Special issue 19(7) (1986).

M. N. Huhns and R. Acosta, "Argo: a System for Design by Analogy," *IEEE Expert* 3(3), 53–68 (Fall 1988).

L. Joskowicz and S. Addanki, "From Kinematics to Shape: An Approach to Innovative Design," *Proceedings of the Seventh National Conference on Artificial Intelligence,* Vol. I, St. Paul, Minn., AAAI, Menlo Park, Calif., 1988, pp. 347–352.

E. Kant, "Understanding and Automating Algorithm Design," *Trans. Software Eng.* SE-11(11), 1361–1374 (Nov. 1985).

R. M. Keller, "Applying Knowledge Compilation Techniques to Model-Based Reasoning," in A. K. Goel, ed., *IEEE Expert,* Special issue 6(2), 82–87 (Apr. 1991).

K. Lai and W. R. D. Wilson, "FDL—A Language for Function Description and Rationalization in Mechanical Design," *Proceedings of the International Computers in Engineering Conference,* Vol. I, American Society of Mechanical Engineers, New York, 1987, pp. 87–94.

D. B. Lenat and J. S. Brown, "Why AM and Eurisko Appear to Work," *Proceedings of the Third National Conference on Artificial Intelligence,* Washington, D.C., AAAI, Menlo Park, Calif., 1983, pp. 236–240.

M. L. Maher, "HI-RISE: An Expert System for Preliminary Structural Design," in M. D. Rychener, ed., *Expert Systems for Engineering Design,* Academic Press, New York, 1988, pp. 37–52.

M. L. Maher and J. S. Gero, eds., *AI Magazine,* Special issue 11(4) (Winter 1990).

M. Mantyla, *An Introduction to Solid Modelling,* Computer Science Press, Rockville, Md., 1988.

S. Marcus, ed., *Automating Knowledge Acquisition for Expert Systems,* Kluwer Academic Publishers, Boston, Mass., 1988.

S. Marcus, J. Stout, and J. McDermott, "VT: An Expert Elevator Designer," *AI Mag.* 9(1), 95–112 (1988).

T. Mitchell and J. Mostow, "Artificial Intelligence and Design," Tutorial TP2, *Proceedings of the Sixth National Conference on Artificial Intelligence,* Seattle, Wash., AAAI, Menlo Park, Calif., 1987.

S. Mittal and B. Falkenhainer, "Dynamic Constraint Satisfaction Problems," *Proceedings of the Eighth National Conference on Artificial Intelligence,* Vol. 1, AAAI, Menlo Park, Calif., and MIT Press, Cambridge, Mass., 1990, pp. 25–32.

S. Mittal and F. Frayman, "Towards a Generic Model of Configuration Tasks," *Proceedings of the Eleventh IJCAI,* Vol. 2, Detroit, Mich., Morgan-Kaufmann, San Mateo, Calif., 1989, pp. 1395–1401.

J. Mostow, "Towards Better Models of the Design Process," *AI Mag.* 6(1), 44–57 (1985).

J. Mostow, "Design by Derivational Analogy: Issues in the Automated Replay of Design Plans," in J. Carbonell, ed., *Machine Learning: Paradigms and Methods,* MIT Press, Cambridge, Mass., and Elsevier, New York, 1990, pp. 119–184.

D. Navinchandra and J. Rinderle, "Interval Methods for Concurrent Evaluation of Design Constraints," *Proceedings of the ASME Annual Conference,* Symposium on Concurrent Product and Process Design, 1989.

M. F. Orelup, J. R. Dixon, P. R. Cohen, and M. K. Simmons, "Dominic II: Meta-Level Control in Iterative Redesign," *Proceedings of the Seventh National Conference on Artificial Intelligence,* Vol. 1, St. Paul, Minn., AAAI, Menlo Park, Calif., 1988, pp. 25–30.

P. Pu and N. I. Badler, "Design Knowledge Capturing for Device Behavior Reasoning," in J. S. Gero, ed., *Artificial Intelligence in Engineering: Design,* Elsevier, New York, 1988, pp. 37–56.

N. Ramachandran, A. Shah, and N. A. Langrana, "Expert System Approach in Design of Mechanical Components," *Proceedings of the ASME International Computers in Engineering Conference,* San Francisco, Calif., 1988, pp. 1–10.

Y. Reich, "Design Knowledge Acquisition: Task Analysis and a Partial Implementation," in *Knowledge Acquisition: An Inter-*

national Journal of Knowledge Acquisition for Knowledge-Based Systems, 1991.

M. D. Rychener, ed., *Expert Systems for Engineering Design,* Academic Press, New York, 1988.

V. Sembugamoorthy and B. Chandrasekaran, "Functional Representation of Devices and Compilation of Diagnostic Problem Solving Systems," in J. Kolodner and C. Riesbeck, eds., *Experience, Memory and Reasoning,* Lawrence Erlbaum, Hillsdale, N.J., 1986, pp. 47–73.

H. A. Simon, *The Sciences of the Artificial,* MIT Press, Cambridge, Mass., 1969.

D. Sriram and C. Tong, eds., *Artificial Intelligence in Engineering Design: Models of Innovative Design: Reasoning about Physical Systems; Reasoning about Geometry,* Vol. 2, Academic Press, New York, 1991.

M. Stefik, "Planning with Constraints (MOLGEN: Part 1 and Part 2)," *Artif. Intell.* **16**(2), 111–169 (1980).

D. Steier and A. Newell, "Integrating Multiple Sources of Knowledge into Designer-Soar, an Automatic Algorithm Designer," *Proceedings of the Seventh National Conference on Artificial Intelligence,* Vol. I, St. Paul, Minn., AAAI, Menlo Park, Calif., 1988, pp. 9–13.

L. I. Steinberg and T. M. Mitchell, "The Redesign System: a Knowledge-Based Approach to VLSI CAD," *IEEE Design & Test,* 45–54 (Feb. 1985).

K. Sycara, "Negotiation in Design," in D. Sriram, R. Logcher, and S. Fukuda, eds., *Computer Aided Cooperative Product Development,* Lecture Notes Series, Springer-Verlag, New York, 1991.

P. J. W. ten Hagen and T. Tomiyama, eds., *Intelligent CAD Systems I: Theoretical and Methodological Aspects,* Springer-Verlag, New York, 1987.

T. Tomiyama, T. Kiriyama, H. Takeda, and D. Xue, "Metamodel: A Key to Intelligent CAD Systems," *Res. Eng. Des.* **1**(1), 19–34 (1989).

I. D. Tommelein, R. E. Levitt, B. Hayes-Roth, and T. Confrey, "SightPlan Experiments: Alternative Strategies for Site Layout Design," *J. Comput. Civil Eng.* **5**(1), 42–63 (Jan. 1991).

C. Tong, "Toward an Engineering Science of Knowledge-Based Design," *Artif. Intell. Eng.* **2**(3), 133–166 (1987).

C. Tong, "Knowledge-Based Design as an Engineering Science: the Rutgers AI/Design Project," in J. S. Gero, ed., *Applications of AI in Engineering V,* Vol. 1: *Design, Proceedings of the Fifth International Conference on Applications of Artificial Intelligence in Engineering,* Boston, Mass., Computational Mechanics Publications and Springer-Verlag, New York, 1990, pp. 297–319.

C. Tong and D. Sriram, eds., *Artificial Intelligence in Engineering Design,* Vol. 1: *Representation: Structure, Function and Constraints; Routine Design,* Academic Press, New York, 1991a.

C. Tong and D. Sriram, eds., *Artificial Intelligence in Engineering Design,* Vol. 3: *Knowledge Acquisition, Commercial Systems; Integrated Environments,* Academic Press, New York, 1991b.

D. G. Ullman, S. Wood, and D. Craig, "The Importance of Drawings in the Mechanical Design Process," *Comput. Graph.* **14**(2), 263–274 (1990).

K. T. Ulrich and W. P. Seering, "Synthesis of Schematic Descriptions in Mechanical Design," in *Res. Eng. Des.* **1**(1), 3 (1989).

M. Waldron and K. Waldron, eds., *Mechanical Design: Theory and Methodology,* Springer-Verlag, New York, 1991.

D. S. Weld and J. de Kleer, eds., *Qualitative Reasoning About Physical Systems,* Morgan-Kaufmann, San Mateo, Calif., 1990.

B. Williams, "Interaction-Based Invention: Designing Novel Devices from First Principles," AAAI Press, Menlo Park, Calif., and MIT Press, Cambridge, Mass., 1990, pp. 349–356.

M. E. Winston, R. Chaffin, and D. Herrmann, "A Taxonomy of Part–Whole Relations," *Cogn. Sci.* **2**, 417–444 (1987).

H. Yoshikawa and F. Arbab, eds., *Intelligent CAD III,* North-Holland, Amsterdam, 1991.

H. Yoshikawa and D. Gossard, eds., *Intelligent CAD I,* North-Holland, Amsterdam, 1989.

H. Yoshikawa and T. Holden, eds., *Intelligent CAD II,* North-Holland, Amsterdam, 1990.

General References

International Conference on AI in Design.

International Conference on AI in Engineering, Computational Mechanics Institute.

International Computers in Engineering Conference, ASME.

International Conference on Design Theory & Methodology, ASME.

NSF Design & Manufacturing Systems Conference.

IFIP WG 5.2 Working Conferences, North-Holland.

AI EDAM, Academic Press.

AI in Engineering, Computational Mechanics Institute.

Research in Engineering Design, Springer International.

D. C. BROWN
Worcester Polytechnic Institute

DETERMINISTIC PROGRAMS. See LOGIC; REASONING, PLAUSIBLE.

DFKI

The German Research Center for Artificial Intelligence Inc. (Deutsches Forschungszentrum für Künstliche Intelligenz GmbH) (DFKI) is a nonprofit organization with sites at Kaiserslautern and Saarbrücken. Its charter is to bridge the gap between academic and industrial research efforts in artificial intelligence and related fields and to serve as a national focal point for research in AI.

The DFKI was founded in 1988 as the result of a federal government initiative to comply with the demands and necessities of an increasingly innovative and expanding information technology market. The future economic prospects of AI especially influenced the decision to create a research facility dedicated solely to a combination of application-oriented and basic research in AI.

The structure of DFKI allows domestic computer companies as well as subsidiaries of international companies that conduct ongoing domestic AI research to become shareholders. The shareholder companies include ADV/Orga, AEG, IBM, Insiders, Fraunhofer Gesellschaft, GMD, Krupp-Atlas, Mannesmann-Kienzle, Nixdorf, Philips, and Siemens. The core is a contract research organization which aims to be economically independent by the mid-1990s. Currently, the project mix is based on grants provided by the German Ministry for Research and Technology, by the shareholder companies, and by other industrial firms.

Being located on the campuses of the universities of Kaiserslautern and Saarbrücken, the DFKI has close connections to the university computer science faculties and AI research groups. DFKI employees teach courses and supervise theses; university faculty members collaborate in DFKI projects and conduct research at the DFKI during leaves of absence from their universities.

The DFKI conducts basic application-oriented research in artificial intelligence and related subfields of computer science. The overall goal is to construct systems utilizing both technical knowledge and common sense. The following areas are currently being investigated by more than 100 researchers at the DFKI:

Intelligent engineering systems.
Intelligent communication networks.
Intelligent user interfaces.
Intelligent cooperative systems.

Major projects in these areas are described below.

Acquisition, Representation, and Compilation of Technical Knowledge (ARC-TEC)

Principal solutions to the AI problems of acquisition, representation, and compilation of knowledge for technical expert systems are the focus of the ARC-TEC project. This requires the development of a collection of knowledge processing software tools that interact seamlessly with each other. Working in an application domain within mechanical engineering, the goal is to show that the sample knowledge bases and expert systems are applicable in task categories as different as process planning and diagnosis. The technical knowledge will be comprised of elementary data, procedures, and textbook knowledge, as well as generally reasonable behavior descriptions. The idea of computer-integrated manufacturing (CIM) will be broadened and deepened by proceeding from a standard data model to a comprehensive knowledge model. This can be regarded as a symbiosis of CIM and AI, taking the integration aspect from CIM and the intelligence aspect from AI.

Dialogue System for Autonomous Cooperating Agents (DISCO)

Natural language is an indispensable medium for communication between humans and their autonomous machine partners (agents). The focus of the dialogue system for autonomous cooperating agents (DISCO) project is the basic research required to develop a system that will endow machine partners with the ability to communicate in natural language. In particular, the system should allow discourse with several such agents in a single conversation, adjusting to human and machine partners. At the same time, the project will be the central DFKI research project in the area of natural language, because the design, implementation, refinement, and maintenance of the most important program components and linguistic

knowledge bases needed in every natural language system will be conducted in this project.

Plan-Based Help Systems (PHI)

Intelligent help systems assist humans using computer systems. To achieve efficient support, it is important that help systems rely on plans. Through plan recognition it is possible to identify the user's plans and goals. Given a present goal, a plan generation component could be able to generate a plan helpful to the user. The recognized plans and goals and the generated plans serve as a basis for the production of the help information. In this process, domain-specific knowledge as well as knowledge from the user model are to be considered. The plan-monitoring component analyzes why a user altered a proposed plan. The plan-based help system (PHI) project focuses on the cross-fertilization between plan recognition and plan generation. To achieve that goal a logic-oriented approach will be pursued. Suitable logical formalisms for planning will be examined and will form the basis for an implementation.

Autonomous Cooperating Agents: Logical Foundations of Knowledge Representation and Processing (AKA-WINO)

The main approach used in this project (German acronym: AKA-WINO) is a combination of knowledge structures with efficient and logic-based inference formalisms. Here two principal approaches are pursued: extension of a logic programming language with knowledge structures and combination of KL-ONE-like knowledge structures and inference mechanisms. The project addresses enhancements of a logic programming language with special data structures for knowledge representation as well as integration of a special theorem prover into a knowledge representation language. In addition, the project explores an extension of inference components with nonclassic calculi supporting knowledge representation. Formalisms for time, space, action, and meta-knowledge will be considered to extend hierarchical and taxonomical knowledge structures with these features.

Knowledge-Based Information Presentation (WIP)

Intelligent user interfaces will be components of future computer systems. They will be able to adequately display represented knowledge in a flexible manner in various situations. This research project is intended to develop the fundamentals of a knowledge-based information presentation (German acronym: WIP) tool that selects information to be presented based on contextual information, makes decisions regarding the presentation, and creates different presentations. It will generate texts and natural language elements of graphics in several individual languages. To accomplish these tasks, not only the representation of domain-specific expert knowledge will be necessary but also commonsense knowledge.

GERHARD BARTH
DFKI

DICTIONARY/LEXICON

Natural language processing systems need access to knowledge about words. The lexicon of an NLP system must provide a systematic and efficient way of encoding this information about the words in a language. In this article the requirements of the lexicon are outlined from two different perspectives: information required for parsing and knowledge needed for semantic analysis. Finally, the problem of how to acquire lexical knowledge for NLP systems, ie, the problem of lexical acquisition, is examined.

Although there is little agreement on the exact nature of what should go into a lexicon, there are some important common assumptions held by researchers in computational and theoretical linguistics on the form of a lexical entry. It is generally assumed that there are three necessary components for the structure of a lexical item. These are:

1. Syntactic information, eg, what part of speech the word is.
2. Semantic information, ie, what the word translates to in the system.
3. Orthographic and morphological information, ie, how the word is spelled and what forms it appears in.

In addition, natural language systems for speech recognition (eg, Woods and co-workers, 1974; Bates, 1975) or speech synthesis may contain phonetic information.

Perhaps the easiest way to get a handle on the structure of a lexical item is to consider the matter from the standpoint of a parser. A parser is presented with one or more utterances; each utterance, in turn, is made up of sequences of characters delimited by whitespace (ignoring punctuation for the moment). Let us call such strings of characters *orthographic words* or, simply, *words*. It is the task of the parser, ultimately, to associate each word with at least one syntactic analysis and, ultimately, in a full understanding system, at least one semantic analysis. In the case of inflected categories, such as nouns and verbs, morphological analysis may be necessary prior to syntactic analysis. In the simplest model, there would be a one-to-one correlation between a word and its morphological, syntactic, and semantic analyses. This model is illustrated in Figure 1. However, this is not always the case. The one-to-one correlation breaks down in the following ways:

1. A word may be associated with more than one syntactic analysis. There are two cases of this:
   a. A word may be associated with more than one categorial analysis. For example, the ortho-graphic word *ships* may be either a noun or a verb. This is illustrated in Figure 2. (The various terms used in Figures 2–5 are meant to be suggestive of the distinctions under consideration and not to be interpreted as having any theoretical status).
   b. A word may be associated with more than one subcategorial analysis. For example, the orthographic word *went* may be either an intransitive verb that occurs with an optional directional phrase, as in "John went to the store," or it may be a verb that occurs with an adjective phrase, "John went crazy." This is illustrated in Figure 3.
2. A single syntactic analysis may be associated with more than one word. For example, *John McCarthy* is a single proper name consisting of two orthographic words. This is illustrated in Figure 4.
3. A single syntactic analysis may be associated with more than one semantic analysis. For example, *mouse* as a singular noun may refer either to a type of rodent or to a pointing device (Fig. 5). If this distinction is not treated as purely semantic, but as syntactic (because it has syntactic ramifications, eg, types of permissible modifier or position of occurrence) this distinction may be assimilated to class 2.

Mediating among all these different levels of analysis is the lexicon. The lexicon typically contains yet another unit of analysis: the *lexical entry*. As mentioned above, this is a unit that contains information about orthography (ie, the word or words that make up a given entry), morphology (ie, the words or entries that are related to the current entry), syntax (ie, category and subcategory information for the entry), and semantics (ie, the interpretation of the entry).

Because the terms (orthographic) word and lexical entry have been introduced, it is time to define one last term: *word sense*. As used here, a word sense represents a single syntactic or semantic analysis. An orthographic word will have more than one sense if it is associated with more than one syntactic or semantic analysis. For example, in the examples given above, *ships, went,* and *mouse* would all have more than one word sense. Many linguists make the distinction between lexical item and word sense (see, eg, Lyons, 1977).

Although lexicons differ with respect to the information they store, perhaps the greatest difference among lexicons stems from the relations that they impose between words, lexical entries, and word senses. It should be pointed out that what constitutes a word sense (ie, a "single syntactic or semantic analysis") is not given *a priori* and that systems that do distinguish word senses may differ as to how they assign word sense, just as human

word → [morphological analysis] → [syntactic analysis] → [semantic analysis]

Figure 1. One-to-one relation between a word and its analyses.

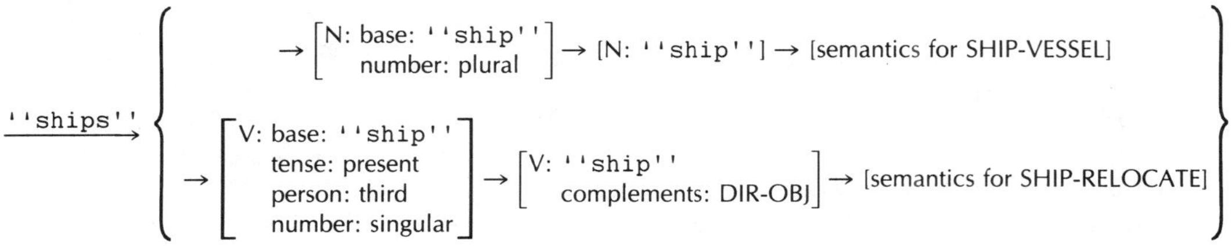

$$\text{''ships''} \longrightarrow \left\{ \begin{array}{l} \rightarrow \begin{bmatrix} \text{N: base: ''ship''} \\ \text{number: plural} \end{bmatrix} \rightarrow \text{[N: ''ship'']} \rightarrow \text{[semantics for SHIP-VESSEL]} \\[3em] \rightarrow \begin{bmatrix} \text{V: base: ''ship''} \\ \text{tense: present} \\ \text{person: third} \\ \text{number: singular} \end{bmatrix} \rightarrow \begin{bmatrix} \text{V: ''ship''} \\ \text{complements: DIR-OBJ} \end{bmatrix} \rightarrow \text{[semantics for SHIP-RELOCATE]} \end{array} \right\}$$

Figure 2. One-to-many relation between a word and its category analyses.

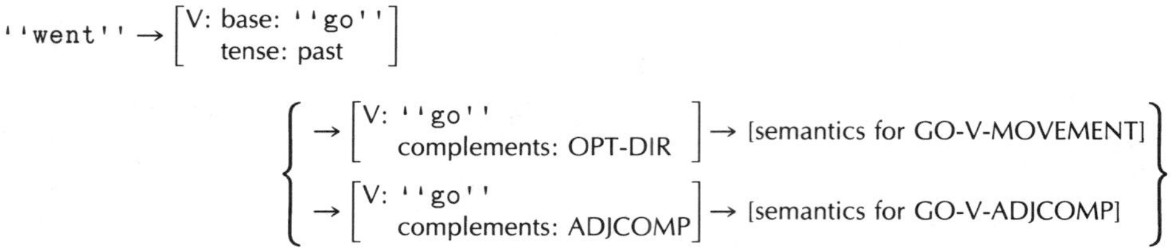

$$\text{''went''} \rightarrow \begin{bmatrix} \text{V: base: ''go''} \\ \text{tense: past} \end{bmatrix}$$

Figure 3. One-to-many relation between a word and its subcategory analyses.

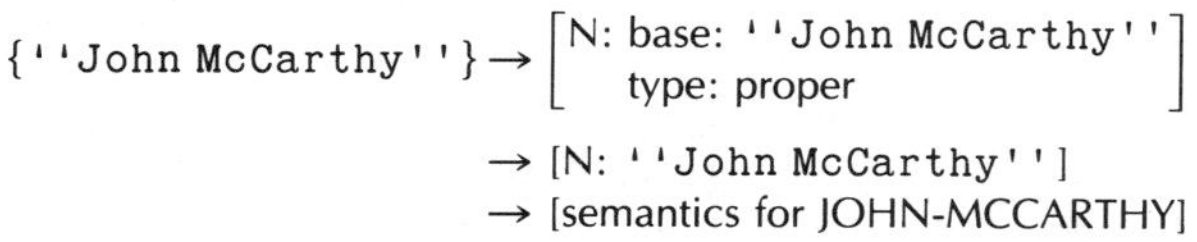

$$\left\{ \begin{array}{l} \rightarrow \begin{bmatrix} \text{V: ''go''} \\ \text{complements: OPT-DIR} \end{bmatrix} \rightarrow \text{[semantics for GO-V-MOVEMENT]} \\[2em] \rightarrow \begin{bmatrix} \text{V: ''go''} \\ \text{complements: ADJCOMP} \end{bmatrix} \rightarrow \text{[semantics for GO-V-ADJCOMP]} \end{array} \right\}$$

$$\{\text{''John McCarthy''}\} \rightarrow \begin{bmatrix} \text{N: base: ''John McCarthy''} \\ \text{type: proper} \end{bmatrix}$$
$$\rightarrow \text{[N: ''John McCarthy'']}$$
$$\rightarrow \text{[semantics for JOHN-MCCARTHY]}$$

Figure 4. Many-to-one relation between a word and its syntactic analyses.

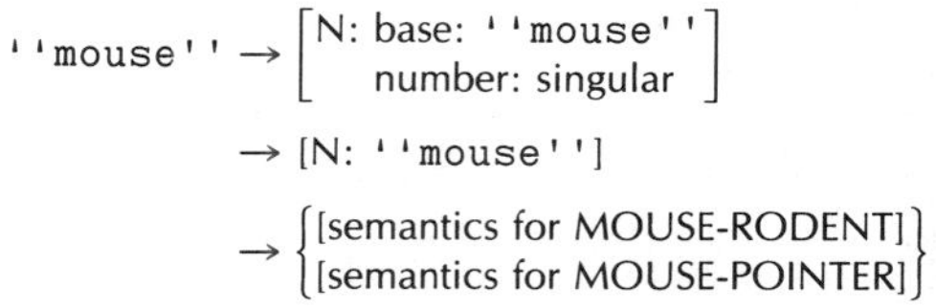

$$\text{''mouse''} \rightarrow \begin{bmatrix} \text{N: base: ''mouse''} \\ \text{number: singular} \end{bmatrix}$$
$$\rightarrow \text{[N: ''mouse'']}$$
$$\rightarrow \left\{ \begin{array}{l} \text{[semantics for MOUSE-RODENT]} \\ \text{[semantics for MOUSE-POINTER]} \end{array} \right\}$$

Figure 5. One-to-many relation between a word and its semantic analyses.

dictionaries will differ in how senses are carved up. The next section will introduce the actual information that is stored in parsing lexicons, and show how the decisions made about the relation between words, word senses, and lexical entries affect the form in which this information is stored.

PARSING LEXICONS

In this section, the types of information that have been stored in the lexicons for the major parsing and language understanding systems in the field will be reviewed. Because this discussion will be at a fairly abstract level, only the general types of information stored and the possible storage schemes are considered here. For a complete list and evaluation of these systems, see Ingria (in press).

The information stored in the lexicons of natural language understanding (qv) systems can be divided into two general sorts. The first, *processing information,* is information actually used by the system in its operation; syntactic category and subcategory information, and semantic information are of this type. The second is *mainte-*

nance information, information used by system maintainers to facilitate their efforts; information such as example sentences, comments, and edit information is of this type. This sort of information is not used by the system itself at all. The discussion that follows is concerned solely with the two subclasses of processing information: intra-entry information and inter-entry/word information.

Intra-Entry Information

The information that falls into this category may be broadly termed distributional information. It is information that determines the various contexts in which the word or words associated with a lexical entry may appear. Both syntactic and semantic information is in this class.

Syntactic. Syntactic information may be divided into the following subcategories.

Category Information. Category information includes traditional categories such as noun, verb, adjective, adverb, and preposition. Although most systems agree on these major categories, there are often great differences in the ways they classify minor categories, such as conjunctions, quantifier elements, determiners, etc. Some systems, such as DELPHI (Boisen and co-workers, 1989a, 1989b; Stallard, 1989; Bobrow and co-workers; 1990) do not even include these elements in the lexicon but place them directly in the grammar.

Subcategory Information. Subcategory information divides syntactic categories into subclasses. Following Chomsky (1965) this sort of information may be separated into two types: contextual and inherent.

Contextual Features. These are features that may be defined in terms of the contexts in which a given lexical entry may occur (hence, the name). There are two sorts of contextual information:

1. *Subcategorization Information.* This is information that specifies the complement structures with which a lexical item may occur; for example, a transitive verb is one that occurs with an object noun phrase.
2. *Selection Information.* This is information that specifies the nature of items that can appear in the complement or subject positions associated with the lexical item; for example, *frighten* is a transitive verb and restricts its direct object to be animate. In some dialects of English, the verb *demand*, when it takes a clausal complement, requires that the main verb of the complement clause appear in the "subjunctive," or unmarked, form: "I demand that John be/*is punished."

Typically, systems that include contextual information as part of the syntactic specification of a lexical entry include subcategorization information rather than selectional information. [LSP is an exception (Sager, 1981).] This is because many systems regard selectional information as semantic in nature and tend to handle it in the semantic specification of the entry, if anywhere. Those types of selectional information that seem more syntactic may be included as part of the syntactic specification of a lexical entry. For example, although many systems would treat the restriction of a direct object to animate noun phrases as semantic, they might include information about the type of a complement clause in the syntax.

Inherent Features. These are features of lexical entries that cannot, or cannot easily, be reduced to a contextual definition. They include such features as count/non-count, abstract, animate, human, etc. As was the case with selectional information, most inherent features are treated as semantic, rather than syntactic, except for those that have some direct syntactic reflex. For example, features such as animate or human might be handled in the semantics, whereas features such as abstract or non-count might be handled in the syntax, because they determine whether the lexical entry can occur with an article. [CRITIQUE is an exception (Heidorn and co-workers, 1982).]

Semantics. The information that is stored under the label *semantics* ranges from pointers to semantic rules or concepts in a semantic network to information that might be treated as syntactic. It has already been noted that some types of selectional information and inherent features are often treated as semantic. Some systems, particularly those that are more semantically oriented, treat subcategorization as semantic. Other information such as Case or tense, which might be classified as syntactic (or morphosyntactic), is treated as semantic in some systems. Moreover, in the popular unification and complex feature based grammar formalisms (Shieber and co-workers, 1983; Pereira and Shieber, 1987) the distinction between syntactic and semantic features may be formally blurred, because both syntactic and semantic items of information appear as features together in a single complex feature structure of some sort. For example, DELPHI (Bobrow and co-workers, 1991) handles subcategorization via a set (or "map") of "mapping units," which combine information about semantic interpretation and syntactic realization for every complement, optional or obligatory, that a verb may take. This is discussed in more detail below. A more detailed description of the semantic information associated with a lexical entry is also found below.

Inter-Word/Entry Information

The information that falls into this category relates a lexical entry to other lexical entries or to other words. The principle type of information of this sort is morphological, but there are others, as well.

Morphology. This is information that relates a lexical entry to orthographic words or lexical entries that are formed from the lexical entry (or, perhaps more properly, from the base form of its associated orthographic word). There are two types of morphological information.

Inflectional. Inflectional information determines the actual surface (orthographic) realization of a word in an inflectable category such as noun or verb. This is the information that determines, for example, that the past tense of *see* is *saw*, while that of *help* is *helped*. Parsing systems represent this information in diverse ways. A sample of the range of variations found in different systems is presented below.

Derivational. Derivational information relates a lexical entry to lexical entries that are built off of it. This is the type of information that relates *destroy* and *destruction, bad* and *badly*, etc. Most parsing systems do not contain this sort of information, although a few do. Systems that do handle derivational morphology typically do so by using a morphological analyzer as well as a lexicon (see MORPHOLOGY). For example, the large lexicon constructed by Russell and co-workers (1986), the system described by Cercone (1977), and CRITIQUE (Heidorn and co-workers, 1982) all provide facilities for recognizing derived forms not stored in the lexicon.

Word Sense. The notion of word sense was introduced above. Here, the general issue of how word senses are correlated with lexical entries is raised. There are three types of word sense distinction that are relevant:

1. *Multiple Category Analyses.* This occurs when one orthographic word is associated with more than one category; the case of *ships* as a noun vs *ships* as a verb (Fig. 2) is an example.
2. *Multiple Subcategory Analyses.* This occurs when one orthographic word is associated with more than one subcategory; the case of *went* as a motion verb ("go to Florida") vs *went* as a verb of mental state change ("go crazy") (Fig. 3) is an example.
3. *Multiple Semantic Analyses.* This occurs when one orthographic word is associated with more than one semantic interpretation; the case of *mouse* as an animal vs *mouse* as a pointing device (Fig. 5) is an example.

Systems differ in regard to which, if any, of these differences in word sense are expressed by having different lexical entries. Some systems are arranged in terms of words; that is, any word, no matter how many category, subcategory, or semantic analyses it may have, constitutes a single entry. Other systems distinguish word senses by having a separate entry for each word sense but differ as to where they draw the line. Some systems have separate entries for each categorial analysis, but do not distinguish subcategorial or semantic analyses. Others have separate entries for each syntactic (categorial or subcategorial) analysis but not for different semantic analyses. Finally, some systems do not correlate word senses with separate entries, but do associate them with subentries. This can be useful in the case of irregularly inflected words with multiples senses, because the subentry mechanism allows the irregularities to be stated once. Systems with separate entries must either have a way of sharing this information among the entries or must duplicate the information by restating the information in each entry. Details of systems that utilize these options will be presented below.

Systems that do distinguish word senses may use different criteria to distinguish what constitutes different word senses. For example, words like *eat* and *drink,* which are transitive, can omit their (direct object) complements relatively freely. Should this variation in overtly occurring complements be treated as a difference in subcategorization and, hence, in word sense or should each of these verbs be treated as having a single subcategorization frame with an optional complement and, hence, a single word sense? [See Fillmore (1982), and Bobrow and co-workers (1991) for more detail.] Again, consider perception verbs such as *see* and *hear.* Such verbs, seemingly without exception, take the same set of subcategorization frames: a finite complement with *that* ("see/hear that John is leaving"), a noun phrase + participle complement ("see/hear John leaving"), a noun phrase + bare verb complement ("see/hear John leave"). Should each subcategorization frame be treated as a separate word sense or should the entire set of subcategorization frames be treated as

one word sense? Different linguistic theories and language analysis systems answer these questions differently.

Abbreviations/Acronyms. In written language, it is common to replace one expression with a shorter one which is either a truncated version of the expression (an abbreviation) or a combination of the initial letters of each word of the expression (an acronym). Some examples from recent natural language research domains are

> *helo* for *helicopter*
> *casrep* for *casualty report*
> *DFW* for *Dallas-Fort Worth*
> *MUC* for *Message Understanding Conference*

Some natural processing systems provide facilities for specifying such replacements.

Synonyms. Because many natural language systems are used to retrieve information from data bases or other knowledge stores, they often provide a facility for defining multiple ways of saying the same thing. For example, in an administrative data base, it might be useful to define the following expressions as synonyms:

Department 45 = The AI Department

In spoken language systems, in which individual speakers may have different spoken equivalents for the same natural language expression, this facility can be most useful. For example, speech corpora collected in the Air Traffic Information System (ATIS) (Hemphill and co-workers, 1990) domain showed the following variants:

Text Form	Spoken Equivalent
SFO	S F O
SFO	San Francisco oh
RTN MAX	R T N max
RTN MAX	Return max
VU/1	V u slash one
VU/1	V u one

In some systems, the mechanism that is used to define synonyms is the same as that used to define abbreviations or acronyms.

Collocations (Multiword Lexical Entries). Frequently, a lexical entry is made up of more than one orthographic word. There are two subcases of collocation.

1. *The words make up a single (nonphrasal) constituent.* This occurs in the case of proper names (*John McCarthy, Long Island*) and multiword grammatical formatives (*in addition to, in back of, such that*). In this case, there is a single, nonphrasal category associated with the entire expression—an X^0 category, in the terminology of the *X*-bar theory of phrase structure (see Jackendoff, 1977, for discussion).

2. *The words make up more than one (nonphrasal) category.* This happens in the case of lexical items that must co-occur with a particular word, rather than an entire category. Examples include so-called "verb particle" combinations, such as *blow up* and *write down,* and verbs that select a prepositional phrase headed by a particular preposition, such as *look for* and *wait for.* Note that, in the verb + particle case, material may intervene between the verb and the particle ("blow the building up"). In both cases, inflectional material appears on the first word of the expression (*blew up, looked for*).

Many systems provide mechanisms for expressing this information in the lexicon, although the facilities are often different for the information of types 1 and 2.

Idioms. Idioms might be considered a special case of multi-constituent collocation. Idioms are distinguished from collocation by a number of criteria:

1. *Noncompositional Semantics.* Typically, the interpretation of an idiom is not derivable from its component parts: "kick the bucket," "the cat's got *X*'s tongue."

2. *Fixedness.* Often an idiom, unlike a collocation, is a fixed expression, specifying an entire complement structure, rather than some subpart. Contrast "kick the bucket" (idiom) with "look for NP" (collocation). This is not universally true of idioms, because some do allow non-fixed elements to appear as part of the complement structure: "the cat's got NP's tongue," "take advantages of NP." Note, however, that even in these cases, much more of the complement structure is specified than in the case of collocation. Also, lexical items, and not merely grammatical formatives (such as determiners), are specified in these examples.

3. *Violation of Grammatical Constraints.* The idiom "take advantage of" presents a good example of this. First, it violates the normal subcategorization frame of *take,* which does not permit *of* as the preposition following the object NP: "John took books from/to/*of Bill." Second, *advantage* appears without a determiner in this idiom, though it normally requires one: "I can see *(the) advantage in that."

Few language analysis systems handle idioms, so there are only a few lexicons that contain this information; those that do, such as BUP (Matsumoto and co-workers, 1983, 1985) and HAM-RPM (Hahn and co-workers, 1980), use the same mechanism to handle idioms and collocations. The treatment of collocations and idioms in various systems is surveyed below.

SEMANTICS FOR A LEXICAL ENTRY

In this section the semantic content of lexical entries is briefly described. As will become clear in the presentation, the style as well as content of semantic information for a lexical item varies from system to system, depending on the demands of the system. The section will be organized by lexical categories rather than particular approaches for

two reasons. First, the majority of work has been on the representation of verbal semantics. Second, computational implementations of lexicons tend to make use of similar data structures for encoding lexical information. (See LEXICAL SEMANTICS; LEXICAL DECOMPOSITION).

One of the most common representational devices for encoding semantic information is the *attribute-value structure.* A semantic feature is encoded as an attribute with an associated value (Kay, 1979).

$$\begin{bmatrix} [\text{Arg1} \quad \text{Val1}] \\ [\text{Arg2} \quad \text{Val2}] \\ \cdots \quad \cdots \\ [\text{Argn} \quad \text{Valn}] \end{bmatrix}$$

As with syntactic information, the semantic information is then manipulated by a unification algorithm (Shieber, 1986). Theoretical and computational linguistic approaches that make use of this representation include lexical-functional grammar (LFG) (Kaplan and Bresnan, 1982), generalized phrase structure grammar (GPSG) (Gazdar and co-workers, 1985), HPSG (Pollard and Sag, 1987), tree-adjoining grammar (TAG) (Schabes and co-workers, 1988), and others (Moore, 1989; Bobrow and co-workers, 1990).

Verbal Semantics

As mentioned above, most of the research on the semantics of lexical items has focused on verbs. The main problem with representing verbal semantics is to capture the arity information and assign the correct semantic function to each argument. To illustrate this problem, simple transitive verbs, such as *love* are considered. For most lexicons, the semantics of such relations includes associating the argument and function name by means of attribute−value structure.

Within LFG the lexicon plays a prominent role in determining the sentential semantics. There are essentially three components to LFG: the lexicon, the syntactic or constituent structure (c-structure), and functional structure (f-structure). Lexical and syntactic information are expressed as equational constraints, which are mapped into a set of equations called the f-structure.

An LFG-inspired representation for the verb *love* in the sentence "John loves Mary" might be as follows:

$$(\uparrow \text{Pred}) = \text{love} [(\uparrow \text{Subj}) (\uparrow \text{Obj})]$$

$$(\uparrow \text{Tense}) = \text{present}$$

This representation indicates only the arity of the verb. If we want to represent the names of case roles (or thematic relations), this can be encoded directly as a set of equational constraints as well.

$$((\uparrow \text{Subj}) \text{ Theta}) = \text{Agent}$$

$$((\uparrow \text{Obj}) \text{ Theta}) = \text{Theme}$$

The feature structure associated with the entire sentence would now take on the following form:

$$\begin{bmatrix} \text{Subj} & \begin{bmatrix} \text{Pred} & \text{John} \\ \text{Num} & \text{SG} \\ \text{Theta} & \text{Agent} \end{bmatrix} \\ \text{Obj} & \begin{bmatrix} \text{Pred} & \text{Mary} \\ \text{Num} & \text{SG} \\ \text{Theta} & \text{Theme} \end{bmatrix} \\ \text{Tense} & \text{Present} \\ \text{Pred love} & < (\uparrow \text{Subj})(\uparrow \text{Obj}) > \end{bmatrix}$$

A slightly different structure for verb representations is assumed by Bouma and co-workers (1988), utilizing graph notation.

$$\begin{bmatrix} \text{syn} : \ldots \\ \text{sem} : [\text{lambda} : \langle 1 \rangle \ \langle 2 \rangle \\ \qquad \text{formula} : [\text{pred} : \text{loves} \\ \qquad\qquad \text{arg1} : \langle 2 \rangle \\ \qquad\qquad \text{arg2} : \langle 1 \rangle]] \end{bmatrix}$$

Here the relational structure of the verb is explicitly represented. This structure is first applied to the proper noun translation of *Mary*, the direct object, and then to the subject *John*, to obtain the propositional structure associated with the sentence.

Influential in many of the approaches to semantic interpretation has been Montague Grammar (MG) (qv). Some systems have made direct use of MG-style semantics (cf Scha and Stallard, 1988), categorial syntax, and typed logic. Returning to the example above, the lexical entry for *love* specifies that it is of type $\langle e, \langle e,t \rangle \rangle$, meaning that it is a relation between individuals (eg, a transitive verb), $\lambda y \lambda x [love(x,y)]$. [This is the lower type for the verb. For a discussion of how type raising is handled, see Gamut (1991).] A computational version of this information would take the following form, which is modeled on the lexical entries in the earliest version of the DELPHI lexicon (Boisen and co-workers, 1989a).

```
[LOVE-V
    Spelling:            love
    Category:            V
    Subcat-Features:     ((transitive (realnp  :real) :passive))
    Semantics:           (fun (person person) tv)]
```

The semantic information in this entry specifies that *love* is a relation from a tuple of persons and persons to truth values, the functional equivalent of the type $\langle e, \langle e,t \rangle \rangle$.

There are many classes of verbs that pose difficulties for lexical representation because of their semantic properties. For example, verbs such as *persuade* and *promise* have superficial similarities but differ both syntactically and semantically.

1. Mary *persuaded* John to leave the party.
2. Mary *promised* John to leave the party.

In sentence 1, it is John who will leave, whereas in sentence 2, it is Mary. Such distinctions may be captured in the lexical representation of the verb to derive the correct interpretation of the sentence. [For details on lexical approaches to this phenomenon, see Kaplan and Bresnan (1982) and Gazdar (1985).] Other treatments of verbal semantics include case grammars, as well as decompositional predicates (see GRAMMAR, CASE; LEXICAL DECOMPOSITION; LEXICAL SEMANTICS).

Nominal Semantics

Much less work has been done on the semantics of nominal expressions within computational lexicons. Conventionally, however, a distinction is made between three types:

1. Proper names: *Mary, Brandeis, Boston.*
2. Common nouns: *woman, university, city.*
3. Pronouns: *she, it, himself.*

Common nouns are represented as properties (ie, sets of individuals), proper names are taken as sets of properties, and pronouns are taken as variables denoting sets of properties. Thus the semantics for nouns such as *Mary, woman,* and *she* in an LFG-inspired lexicon would be:

$$(\uparrow \ \text{Pred}) = \text{Mary}$$

$$(\uparrow \ \text{Pred}) = \text{woman}$$

$$(\uparrow \ \text{Pred}) = \text{PRO}$$

The semantics of the lexical entry may look deceptively simple because the structures point to a domain model that distinguishes, for example, what logical type the lexical item is, and what kind of arguments the word takes, if any. For example, within an MG-inspired approach, the difference in meaning between these nouns is made explicit in their logical type and translation.

$$\text{Type(Mary)} = \langle\langle e,t \rangle, t \rangle : \lambda P[P(m)]$$

$$\text{Type(woman)} = \langle e,t \rangle : \lambda x[\text{woman}(x)]$$

$$\text{Type(she)} = \langle\langle e,t \rangle, t \rangle : \lambda P[P(x)]$$

Although most systems assume the basic distinction given above, there are many nouns that do not lend themselves to standard semantic analysis. One such class is the *relational nouns.* These include nouns such as *sister, father,* etc, which seem to require more than simply a set of individuals as a denotation. Rather, they are relational and implicitly refer to a relation between two individuals. For example, *John's sisters* refers to the set of individuals who stand in the "sister-relation" to John, and not simply the set of individuals who are sisters (de Bruin and Scha, 1988). Thus *sister* might take on the following form: $\lambda x \lambda y [female(y) \land sister\text{-}of(y,x)]$. Thus the translation of *sister* is a set of ordered pairs such that the first element is the sister of the second.

There are of course many other issues to address when discussing the semantics of lexical entries. Topics that have not been covered include the interpretation of quantifiers, eg, *every, some, most.* Perhaps the most useful characterization of such determiner-like elements is the notion of *generalized quantifier* (see LEXICAL SEMANTICS) (Gamut, 1991; Barwise and Cooper, 1981). Other categories not examined include adjectives. There are many puzzles associated with the representation of adjectives. For example, the interpretation of phrases such as "a large butterfly" versus "a large elephant," and "a long record" versus "a long stick," Such issues have been addressed elsewhere (eg, Bierwisch, 1967; Bierwisch and Lang, 1987; Pustejovsky,1991).

ORGANIZATION OF THE LEXICON

Structure of a Lexical Entry

Cutting across the issues of how a lexicon relates lexical entries with words and word senses and the types of information stored is the general question of the storage strategy employed. There are several issues here. The first is whether the lexicon is a separate knowledge base in itself. Some systems require a separate lexicon as a repository for the types of information discussed earlier. Other systems treat such lexical information essentially as a type of annotation on phrase structure rules. In such systems, there is no need for a separate lexicon, because "lexical insertion rules" are really nothing more than another type of phrase structure rule. However, in practice, there may actually be such a separate lexicon. This is determined by the treatment of the next issue.

The second question is: Does the lexical information used by the system come from the permanent lexicon or from a virtual lexicon? There are three related issues here:

1. Does the grammar require all forms of a lexical entry to be available? Many of the unification-based grammar formalisms, such as PATR (Shieber and co-workers, 1983) and definite clause grammar (DCG) (Pereira and Warren, 1980), do, in fact, make this requirement. Other systems store all the inflected forms of a lexical entry because of efficiency considerations.

2. If it does, are all entries actually stored or are they generated on demand? Church (1980) introduced the notion of a *virtual lexicon,* as distinct from a permanent lexicon. While the grammar used in a particular system may require that all the inflected forms of a lexical entry be available on demand, this does not mean that they actually need to be stored in the permanent lexicon (the lexicon that physically resides on disk or whatever storage medium is used). All that is required is that they be available when needed. A virtual lexicon is a mechanism for doing just this; it stores the minimal amount of information required in the permanent lexicon and provides a mechanism, such as a morphological analysis program, for generating other entries when they are needed by the grammar.

3. If all entries are stored, are they entered by hand or automatically generated? Some systems, in order to improve efficiency, store all the inflected forms of a lexical entry in the permanent lexicon rather than generating them on demand. Nevertheless, they do not require that all inflected forms be entered by hand. Typically, only the base forms of regularly inflected words are entered by hand, with the other forms generated automatically and stored in the permanent lexicon. Such systems effectively incur the expense of morphological analysis only once, when the permanent lexicon is compiled, as it were, from the information entered by the system maintainers.

Relation of Categories and Subcategories. One area in which lexicons differ is in the treatment of category and subcategory information. Lexicons may actually distinguish categories from subcategories by classifying lexical entries by syntactic category and then adding features that specify the subcategory or subcategories that the lexical entry belongs to. On the other hand, some systems use a category system where a single specification simultaneously specifies the category and subcategory of the lexical entry. This is the difference between having a category of verb with a specification of intransitive (in effect, a complex symbol) as opposed to having a single category of intransitive-verb (a non-complex symbol).

Category and Subcategory Information Combined. A few lexicons combine category and subcategory information into a single specification. The number of lexical classes in such lexicons is usually quite large, equal to the number of subcategories of each syntactic category in an equivalently fine-grain system that does not combine this information. The Harvard Multi-path English Analyzer (Kuno and Oettinger, 1963a, 1963b, 1963c) used such a system; there were 133 syntactic word classes. For example, there were 10 verb subclasses: 3 intransitive subclasses and 7 transitive subclasses. Moreover, morphological information was also combined with the category and subcategory information into one specification. For example, VT1P indicates a *p*lural inflected *v*erb belonging to *t*ransitive class *1*; IT1 indicates an *i*nfinitive member of the same class, etc.

Categories with Subcategory Features. Most systems do not use a lexical specification system that combines category and subcategory information into a single class. Rather, they use a system in which a lexical entry is cross-classified with respect to category and subcategory. Systems may do this in several ways. Some distinguish different syntactic categories and use a feature system of some sort to distinguish subcategories of each syntactic category. The LUNAR (qv) (Woods, 1973) and IRUS (Ayuso and co-workers, 1987) dictionary used such a system; some example lexical entries from IRUS are presented in Figure 6. The feature TRANS indicates that the verb ACCOMPANY is transitive.

Note that the IRUS dictionary formally distinguished category and subcategory information as data structures: categories have a value (the inflectional paradigm that the lexical entry falls into in its use in that category) whereas features, which represent subcategory information, do not. It is possible to encode this information uniformly, with category, subcategory, and inflectional paradigm information all represented as features. The JANUS Master Lexicon (Cumming, 1986) uses this ap-

[ACCOMPANY   FEATURES   (PASSIVE TRANS)
               V   ES-ED]
[BOOK   N   -S]

Figure 6. Separate category and subcategory information, from the IRUS lexicon.

proach. An alternative approach to using features for the specification of the entire complement structure associated with a lexical entry is to specify the number of complement "slots" that the lexical entry can take and specify the types of syntactic elements that may fill each slot. The current lexicon of the DELPHI system (Bobrow and coworkers, 1991) uses this approach. A much-simplified example of such a subcategorization specification is given in Figure 7. Each of the units that appear in this *map,* as it is called, specifies four pieces of information: a grammatical relation, a syntactic element that bears this grammatical relation, the semantic type requirement on the element, and the (named) argument position of the semantic translation of the verb that the element will bear in semantic representation. In this example, the predicate FLY1 has three argument slots to be filled: FLYER, FROM-AIR-PORT, and TO-AIRPORT. One advantage of this approach is that it allows multiple syntactic realizations of the same semantic role to be specified in a single lexical entry, while still allowing only one filler for that role at run time. For instance, in this example, the FROM-AIR-PORT argument may be filled either by a noun phrase or by a prepositional phrase headed by the preposition *from* or *out of.* General semantic consistency principles allow a single argument position to be filled only once. Thus the example allows sentences such as "What flights fly from

Boston to Dallas?" or "What flights fly Boston to Dallas?" but not "*What flights fly Boston from New York to Dallas?" Other advantages of this approach include the ability to specify optionality of arguments and defaults for optional arguments.

Abbreviation Conventions. Lexicons for systems such as the Harvard Multi-path English Analyzer, LUNAR, and IRUS use a class or feature notation to express category and subcategory information. However, there are various systems that make use of unification formalisms and that use phrase-structure information more directly in their lexical entries. The example in Figure 7 shows this to some extent. The specifications for syntactic pattern, type requirement, and role set used actual fragments of the complex category structures introducing the syntactic complement elements. A lexical entry specifying the entire complex feature structure associated with a lexical can become quite large and confusing. Figure 8 contains entries for the verb *seem* in its use as an extraposition verb ("It seems that John is here") and as a Raising verb ("John seems to be here") in the PATR-II lexicon. The examples presented here are in a slightly older version of the PATR-II formalism. [See Shieber (1986) for a more recent version of the system.] The older version is presented here because it provides an example of the use of templates and lexical rules to create compact lexical entries.

The syncat specification is a list representation of the complement structure of the lexical entry. Because this is the uniform representation of complement structures in PATR-II, it is possible, using list manipulation mechanisms such as first, rest, and tail, coupled with unification, to identify parts of the complement structure of a

```
(FLY1
  (GRAMMAR-RELATION SUBJECT
   SYNTACTIC-PATTERN (NP :NOM-SEM)
   TYPE-REQUIREMENT (HAS-SORT :NOM-SEM
                              (THINGS (INANIMATES (NON-VALUES (FLIGHT)))))
   ROLE-SET (SET FLYER :NOM-SEM))
  (GRAMMAR-RELATION OTHER-NP
   SYNTACTIC-PATTERN (NP :NOM-SEM)
   TYPE-REQUIREMENT (HAS-SORT :NOM-SEM
                              (THINGS
                                (INANIMATES
                                  (NON-VALUES (LOCATIONS (AIRPORT))))))
   ROLE-SET (SET FROM-AIRPORT :NOM-SEM))
  (GRAMMAR-RELATION PP-COMP
   SYNTACTIC-PATTERN (PP (PP-SEM (:OR (FROMPREP) (OUTOFPREP)) :NOM-SEM))
   TYPE-REQUIREMENT (HAS-SORT :NOM-SEM
                              (THINGS
                                (INANIMATES
                                  (NON-VALUES (LOCATIONS (AIRPORT))))))
   ROLE-SET (SET FROM-AIRPORT :NOM-SEM))
  (GRAMMAR-RELATION PP-COMP
   SYNTACTIC-PATTERN (PP (PP-SEM (:OR (INTOPREP) (TOPREP)) :NOM-SEM))
   TYPE-REQUIREMENT (HAS-SORT :NOM-SEM
                              (THINGS
                                (INANIMATES
                                  (NON-VALUES (LOCATIONS (AIRPORT))))))
   ROLE-SET (SET TO-AIRPORT :NOM-SEM)))
```

Figure 7. Subcategorization in DELPHI.

DICTIONARY/LEXICON   349

```
seem₁: <cat> = v
        <head aux> = false
        <head trans pred> = <sense>
        <syncat first cat> = np
        <syncat tail> = <syncat rest rest>
        <heat trans argl> = <syncat rest first head trans>
        <syncat first lex> = it
        <syncat rest first cat> = sbar
        <head agr per> = p3.

seem₂: <cat> = v
        <head aux> = false
        <head trans pred> = <sense>
        <syncat first cat> = np
        <syncat rest first cat> = vp
        <syncat rest first head form> = infinitival
        <syncat rest rest> = <syncat tail>
        <head trans argl> = <syncat rest first head trans>
        <syncat rest first syncat first> = <syncat first>.
```

Figure 8. Unabbreviated lexical entries for PATR-II.

```
Let TakesIntransSbar be
        <syncat first cat> = sbar
        <syncat tail> = <syncat rest>

Let Monadic be
        <head trans argl> = <syncat first head trans>

Let TakesInf be
        <syncat first cat> = np
        <syncat rest first cat> = vp
        <syncat first head form> = infinitival
        <syncat rest rest> = <syncat tail>

Let RaisingtoS be
        <head trans argl> = <syncat rest first heat trans>
        <syncat rest first syncat first> = <syncat first>

Define Extrapos as
        <out cat> = <in cat>
        <out head> = <in head>
        <out head aux> = false
        <out head agr per> = p3
        <out syncat first cat> = np
        <out syncat first lex> = it
        <out syncat rest> = <in syncat rest>
        <out syncat tail> = <in syncat tail rest>
        <in syncat tail first> = <in syncat first>

seem    V - TakesIntransSbar Monadic Extrapos
        - TakesInf RaisingtoS;
```

Figure 9. PATR-II abbreviatory conventions and a compact lexical entry.

lexical item with those of its complement. For example, the specification ⟨syncat rest first syncat first⟩ = ⟨syncat first⟩ in the definition of seem₂ specifies that the first element of the subcategorization frame of *seem*, ie, its subject, must unify with the subject of its complement; this is how the raising aspect of this use of *seem* is encoded. This is a very powerful mechanism allowing information that might otherwise be encoded in phrase structure rules to be encoded in the lexicon (for details, see Shieber and co-workers, 1983; Shieber, 1986).

Despite their power, such entires have the disadvantage that they are difficult to interpret at a glance; all the necessary information is there, but it needs to be decoded. It is also possible to make mistakes in creating such entries. Unification-based grammars such as PATR-II often provide facilities that allow full lexical specifications to be abbreviated and the abbreviations to be used in place of the full specification. PATR-II, for example, provides two such mechanisms: *templates* and *lexical rules*. Templates, which begin with Let, are a simple abbreviatory convention. Once a template has been defined, its name can be used instead of the full specification. Lexical rules, which begin with Define, specify how a new lexical entry, with a different but related subcategorization frame, can be created from the current entry. The Extrapos lexical rule, for example, will take a lexical entry and create a related entry with *it* in the subject position and the old subject "extraposed" to the end of the sentence; this relates the uses of *surprise* in "That John did that surprised me" and "It surprised me that John did that." Figure 9 gives examples of the lexical rule and templates necessary to give an abbreviated definition of the two senses of *seem*. The next section discusses the issue of whether the lexical entries created by lexical rules are stored in the permanent lexicon or generated on demand in a virtual lexicon.

Morphology. Several issues arise in considering how morphological information is handled in a lexicon. There is the general question of whether all inflected forms are stored in the lexicon (such a lexicon might be called a *full entry lexicon* and the relation of the permanent and virtual lexicons, discussed above. There is also the question of how morphology is related to category (and subcategory) information. Just as some lexicons combine category and subcategory information into a set of composite features, some lexicons combine category and morphological information. For example, the Harvard Multi-path English Analyzer includes morphological information as part of a wordclass. The LSP (Sager, 1981) lexicon also combines some morphological information, in the case of verbs, into a single class with category information. Thus verbs are divided into the subclasses: TV, tensed verb; V, tenseless verb or infinitive; VING, present participle; and VEN, past participle.

All Forms Entered Directly. The Harvard Multi-path English Analyzer used a lexicon where all the inflected forms of a word were entered directly (Fig. 10). Note that the word classes of the Harvard Multi-path English Analyzer not only combine categorial and subcategorial information but also include morphological information, as well. For example VT1 indicates an inflected verb form of the first transitive verb subclass, IT1, the corresponding infinitive form, GT1, the corresponding gerund, and RT1, the corresponding present participle. Inflected forms contain a suffix, indicating the grammatical number: S, singular; P, plural; and C, singular/plural.

REQUIRE	VT1P	IT1	VT6P1	IT6 1
REQUIRED	VT1C	PT1	VT6C1	PT6 1
REQUIRES	VT1S	VT6S1		
REQUIRING	RT1	GT1S	RT6	GT6S

Figure 10. Entries from a full-entry lexicon, from the Harvard Multi-path English Analyzer.

All Forms Present in Lexicon but Machine Generated. As mentioned above, certain grammar formalisms require that the grammar have access to a lexical entry (or the equivalent phrase structure rule) for every inflected form. Some grammatical theories also argue in favor of a full entry lexicon. However, it is clearly time-consuming and repetitious to enter every inflected form of a regular word by hand. Therefore, even though the permanent lexicon associated with such formalisms and theories is usually a full entry lexicon, it is often compiled automatically from a specification of root forms.

The lexicon for Wehrli's (1984, 1985) GBPF parser uses such a compilation technique, generating all the inflected forms of a word based on directions specified by the user; Wehrli (1985) argued for the structure of his lexicon on both theoretical and efficiency grounds. The PLIDIS (Berry-Rogghe and Wulz, 1978; Berry-Rogghe and co-workers, 1980) system for analyzing German also uses a full entry lexicon, although the primary motivation for this decision was one of efficiency. In earlier versions of the system, there was a morphological analysis procedure. However, this process was found to be too slow. Later versions of the system incorporated a full entry lexicon, which is compiled from user specifications. In effect, PLI-DIS runs the former morphological analysis procedure "in reverse" to produce a fully specified lexicon. The first implementation of the RITA system (Ershov and co-workers, 1975) also used a full entry lexicon.

All Forms Present in Virtual Lexicon. Many systems that require a lexical entry or rule for each inflected form, utilize the strategy of a virtual lexicon, which was introduced above. For example, PATR-II (Shieber and co-workers, 1983; Shieber, 1986) and DELPHI (Bolsen and co-workers, 1989a) in effect utilize a virtual lexicon scheme, with the required lexical entries being produced on demand by a morphological analysis procedure. Because the form that entries take in the permanent lexicon associated with such a virtual lexicon depends on the decision about how morphological information is to be represented, the forms of the morphological information for such systems is discussed in the next section.

Specifying Inflectional Paradigm and Irregularity. Systems that do not have a full entry permanent lexicon face the question of how morphological information is to be represented. Irregular forms must always be present somewhere in the lexicon; it is regularities that pose a question for such systems. Does a regular entry contain a specification of the inflectional paradigm that it belongs to? Or does the system contain a morphological analysis procedure so that only the roots of regularly inflected

forms need to be entered? This section explores some of the answers that various lexicons have given to these questions.

One method, which is quite common, is to specify inflectional paradigms for inflected categories by the use of morphological features. IRUS (Ayuso and co-workers, 1987) and the JANUS Master Lexicon (Cumming, 1986), among others, use this mechanism. For example, the definition of *book* in IRUS (Fig. 6) has the morphological feature −S, indicating that its plural is formed by adding -s. The verb *accompany,* in the same example, has the morphological features ES−ED, indicating that its third person singular present is formed by adding -es and its past is formed by adding -ed. The change of *y* to *i* in such forms is treated as regular by IRUS and so is not specified in the lexical entry.

Some systems do not place paradigm information in the lexicon at all but rely on a morphological analyzer to determine the inflected forms of regularly inflected words. Such systems typically include only the base form in the lexicon, along with irregularly inflected forms. There are several different variations of this approach. In DIA-GRAM (Robinson, 1982), regularly inflected forms are entered in the lexicon with no paradigm information. The base of an irregularly inflected form is entered in the lexicon and, in the case of irregular verbs, may include an indication of the ending of the past participle form; the associated irregularly inflected forms are stored as separate lexical entries (Fig. 11).

The PATR-II lexicon uses a somewhat different scheme. Again, regularly inflected forms are stored in the lexicon with no paradigm information. However, the inflected forms of irregular words are not stored as separate entries, but rather are included as part of the lexical entry of the base form (Fig. 12).

The DELPHI lexicon (Boisen and co-workers, 1989a) uses a variation of this scheme, along with some innovations. Lexical entries have both a name and a spelling, ie, the overtly occurring base form. Names and spellings are kept distinct to allow for separate entries for different categorial analyses of a word, for example, the use of *ship* as a noun and a verb. Regularly inflected forms have no paradigm information. Inflectional information that is dif-

Words for N		Irregular Forms in N	
(APPRENTICE	(TYPE COUNT)	(FEET	(FOOT -S))
	(GENDER M F))		
(FISH	(TYPE MASS))		
(FOOT	(TYPE COUNT))		
(THING	(TYPE COUNT))		
(WATER	(TYPE MASS))		

Words for V		Irregular Forms in V	
(GO	(PPL EN))	(BOUGHT	(BUY ED))
(TRY	(INFOBJ T))	(BROKE	(BREAK ED))
(WANT	(DIROBJ T)	(GAVE	(GIVE ED))
	(INFOBJ T))	(GONE	(GO EN))
		(WENT	(GO ED))

Figure 11. Regular and irregular forms in DIAGRAM (Robinson, 1982).

ficult or impossible to predict on the basis of orthography (such as the doubling of a final consonant in inflected verb forms, or the use of -es as the plural ending of a noun) is indicated. Lexical entries with irregularly inflected forms contain information about those forms. Finally, the completely irregular lexical entries, *be*, *do*, and *have*, contain no morphological information whatsoever, but are handled specially by the morphological analyzer (Fig. 13). Note that the contents of the Rules field are not stored in the permanent lexicon, but are generated from the rest of the information in the lexical entry at load time. These rule skeleta, in which morphological features such as agreement (:AGR), number (:N), and mood (:MOOD) are left variables, are modified at run time, when the morphological analyzer creates (more) fully specified versions of these rules for use by the parser. Each rule schema also has a name, which is expanded further at run time, so that each inflected form of each sense of a spelling has a unique name. This is useful in collecting statistics about the distribution of word forms and senses, to tune the behavior of the parser (Bobrow, 1991).

Sharing Information Among Lexical Entries for Irregular Forms. Lexicons that contain separate lexical entries for the inflected forms of an irregularly inflected word face

ask	V TakeSfor Dyadic,
give	V (Past gave) (PastPrt given) TakesNPNP Triadic,
persuade	V TakesNPInf Triadic ObjectControl,
promise	V TakesNPInf Triadic SubjectControl NoPass,
believe	V - TakesSthat Dyadic - TakesNPInf RaisingtoO,

Figure 12. Regular and irregular forms in PATR-II (Shieber, 1986).

the question of where and how many times the information that is common to all the entries, such as subcategorization information, is to be stored. Does each entry contain this information or is it stated only once and shared among related entries? Full entry lexicons also face the same question. Typically, lexicons provide a way so that this information is stated only once.

Lexical entries for irregularly inflected forms in the IRUS dictionary indicate the word on which the form is based. This allows subcategorization information to be

```
[ARRIVE-V
    Spelling:            arrive
    Category:            V
    Rules:               (((V (|arrive|) (NO-CONTRACT) (T246) :AGR :MOOD) -ARRIVE-V))
    Subcat-Features:     ((T246))]

[BE
    Spelling:            nil
    Category:            V
    Rules:               (((V :ANY (NO-CONTRACT) (BE-MAP) :AGR :MOOD) -BE))
    Subcat-Features:     ((BE-MAP))]

[CLASS-N
    Spelling:            class
    Category:            N
    Morph-Features:      (ES T)
    Rules:               (((N (INTRANSNOUN) (AGR (3RD) :N)
                             (REALNP (NONUNITNP (-PRO (MISCNP))))
                             (+DET) (COUNT-N (BASIC-COUNT)) (-CONJ)
                             (NOM (NO-PARS)
                               (GENSET
                                 (THINGS
                                   (INANIMATES (NON-VALUES (CLASS-OF-SERVICE)))))
                               (THINGS
                                 (INANIMATES (NON-VALUES (CLASS-OF-SERVICE))))))
                          -CLASS-N-INTRANSNOUN-REALNP-MISCNP-+DET-COUNT-N-CLASS-OF-SERVICE)
    Subcat-Features:     ((INTRANSNOUN CLASS-OF-SERVICE))

[FLY-V
    Spelling:            fly
    Category:            V
    Morph-Features:      (PAST |flew|
                          EDPARTICIPLE |flown|
                          ES T)
    Rules:               (((V (|fly|) (NO-CONTRACT) (T256) :AGR :MOOD) -FLY-V))
    Subcat-Features:     ((T256))]
```

Figure 13. Regular and irregular forms in DELPHI.

```
[GO          FEATURES (ADJCOMP INTRANS PREDADJ)
             ADJ NOINFLECTIONS
             SEMANTICS (MOVEMENT * UPGRADE *)
             V (GO (PNCODE X3Sg)
                   (TNS PRESENT)
                   (UNTENSED))]
[GOES        V (GO (TNS PRESENT)
                   (PNCODE 3SG))]
[GOING       V (GO (PRESPART))]
[GONE        V (GO (PASTPART))]
[WENT        V (GO (TNS PAST))]
```

Figure 14. Sharing information among lexical entries for irregular forms, from the IRUS lexicon.

stated only once, in the lexical entry of the base form (Fig. 14). The DIAGRAM (Robinson, 1982) system also uses this device (Fig. 11).

The LSP (Sager, 1981) lexicon, which is a full entry lexicon, provides a mechanism for sharing information among the inflected forms of a word. Related lexical entries are arranged contiguously in a file; an up arrow (↑) in a lexical entry indicates that it has the same feature specification as the preceding entry. Thus common information does not need to be restated. On the other hand, information that is peculiar to a particular inflected form can be specified for that entry alone, in addition to the shared information. See Figure 15, particularly the entry for REQUIRED, for an example of the use of this mechanism. The GBPF lexicon (Wehrli, 1985) is structured in a network-like fashion to state information common to various word forms only once.

Global Structure

Most of the current work on the semantic component of computational lexicons seeks to extract and formalize the formation in certain fragments of dictionary definitions. Typically, the target lexical entries encode, in a variety of ways, notions like category (type) information, selectional restrictions, number, type and case roles of arguments, and so forth. While the utility of this kind of information

for NLP is beyond doubt, the emphasis on the individual entry misses out on the issue of global lexicon organization. This is not to dismiss ongoing work that does focus precisely on this issue; for instance the attempts to relate grammatical nature with diathesis (Levin, in press).

Theories of Lexical Inheritance. One obvious way to think about the organization of lexical knowledge is with the use of inheritance mechanisms (see INHERITANCE HIERARCHY). In fact, Flickinger and co-workers (1985) Calder and te Lindert (1987), and Daelemans (1987) suggest ways of providing shared data structures for syntactic and morphological knowledge. Recently, Evans and Gazdar (1990) have provided a formal characterization of how to perform inferences in a language for multiple and default inheritance of linguistic knowledge. The language they developed, DATR, uses value-terminated attribute tree to encode lexical information, just as PATR (Shieber, 1986) does. There are two kinds of expressions, *definitional*, using == , and *extensional*, using = .

$$N: \quad P \langle \rangle == L$$
$$N: \quad P \langle \rangle = L$$

The definitional sentences are used for defining the network itself, while extensional sentences define the values at the individual nodes. For example, the lexical entry for a verb such as *drink* within a network of lexical relations would be as follows (cf Gazdar and Evans, 1989):

```
Drink1:   ⟨ ⟩ == VERB
          ⟨syn args⟩ == NPCOMP
          ⟨mor root⟩ == drink
          ⟨mor past⟩ == drank
          ⟨mor past participle⟩ == drunk.
```

This entry states that the word *drink* is a verb that takes an NP object, and has a root form, past form, and past participle form, as specified by the sentence. Now consider the definition for a verb in DATR, in a somewhat abbreviated form.

```
(VTVPL)    require      .12 = OBJLIST:
                        .3, VSENT3, VSENT3.
                        .3 = NSTGO, VINGSTG, C1SHOULD, NTOVO, PHTHATSVO: .15.
                        .15 = PVAL:
                                ("OF").

(TVSI)     requires     ↑ .
(ING)      requiring    ↑ .
(TVVEN)    required     ↑ .
                        .14 = OBJLIST:
                        .3, VSENT2, VSENT3, POBJLIST: .4.
                        .4 = TOVO, PN: .15, NULLOBJ.


Canonical forms used in sample entries:
(VTVPL)    =            V: .12,
                        TV: .12, PLURAL
(TVSI)     =            TV: .12, SINGULAR.
(ING)      =            VING: .12.
(TVVEN)    =            TV: .12,
                        VEN: .14.
```

Figure 15. Sharing information among entries in a full-entry lexicon, from LSP (Sager, 1981).

VERB: ⟨syn aux⟩ == no
       ⟨syn cat⟩ == V
       ⟨mor form⟩ == MOR:⟨form⟩
       ⟨mor past⟩ == (' '⟨mor root⟩' ' ed)
       ⟨mor pres participle⟩ == (' '⟨mor root⟩' ' ing)
       ⟨mor pres tense sing three⟩ == (' '⟨mor root⟩' ' s)
```

What this states are the default inflectional forms for a verb. Now notice that from this node definition together with the definition of *drink* above, it can be inferred that the present participle and third person present singular forms for *drink* are *drinking* and *drinks,* respectively. The past form attribute from the verb node, however, is default information that is overridden by a local value specification, and the form remains *drank* rather than *drinked* (see Evans and Gazdar, 1990). (See INHERITANCE HIERARCHY for discussion of similar techniques for general knowledge representation.)

Along a similar line, Pustejovsky and Boguraev (in press) describe a theory of shared semantic information based on typed inheritance principles. Pustejovsky (1991) proposes several distinct levels of semantic description for a lexical item. In particular, a set of semantic roles called the *qualia structure* are relevant to just this issue. These roles specify the purpose (telic), origin (agentive), basic form (formal), and constitution (const). On this view, a lexical item inherits information according to the qualia structure it carries. In this way, the different senses for words can be rooted into suitable, but orthogonal lattices. To illustrate this point, consider the two is_a relations below and the differences in what relations the objects enter into.

|         | novel is_a book | dictionary is_a book |
|---------|-----------------|----------------------|
| read    | ok              | no                   |
| buy     | ok              | ok                   |
| consult | no              | ok                   |
| begin   | ok/(?)          | no                   |

This table illustrates a serious problem with most current inheritance systems for lexical knowledge. Namely, although it might seem reasonable to think of both novels and dictionaries as "books," they behave very differently in terms of how they are selected by different relations. This suggests that a single lattice for inheritance is inadequate for capturing the different dimensions of meaning for lexical items. Lexical inheritance theory, on the other hand, posits a separate lattice per role in the qualia structure. Briefly, inheritance through qualia amounts to the following relations for this example:

```
book is_formal phys-object,
book is_telic literature,
book is_agent literature,
dictionary is_formal book,
dictionary is_telic reference,
dictionary is_agent compiled-material,
novel is_agent literature,
novel is_telic book.
```

With the qualia roles differentiating the lattic structures, giving a *typed inheritance,* the unwanted inferences listed above can be excluded (Pustejovsky and Boguraev, in press).

Researchers working with machine-readable dictionaries have also been concerned with the global organization of lexical information. In particular, Byrd (1989) and Calzolari (1984) propose structures for how to achieve the most efficient and consistent structuring of knowledge for dictionaries.

The Mental Lexicon. Miller and co-workers (1990) have developed a lexical knowledge base, called WordNet, where the fundamental relation is that of synonymy. WordNet currently contains over 64,000 different lexical entries, which are organized into about 39,000 sets of synonyms. In WordNet, the lexicon is divided into four categories: nouns, verbs, modifiers, and function words. The function words are actually not represented explicitly, leaving three classes of words: nouns, verbs, and adjectives.

From the view of lexical organization principles, WordNet is interesting in the way that it structures these three categories. Nouns are organized into topical hierarchies, while verbs are organized by means of various entailment relations. Adjectives on the other hand, are structured as *n*-dimensional hyperspaces.

The relation between nouns is the conventional hyponymy relation, which is equivalent to the ISA relation of knowledge representation languages (see INHERITANCE HIERARCHY). Rather than assuming a single hierarchical structure with *entity* as the top-most element, for example, WordNet partitions the nouns into a set of semantic primes, each a generic concept that forms a separate hierarchy. These actually correspond to distinct semantic fields. For example, some of these fields are listed below:

{act, action, activity}	{natural object}
{animal, fauna}	{natural phenomenon}
{artifact}	{person}
{attribute}	{plant, flora}
{cognition, knowledge}	{process}
{food}	{state, condition}

Nouns are further distinguished by features that characterize them uniquely, for example a noun concept's function or attributes.

The organization of adjectives in WordNet follows a different set of principles. Adjectives divide into two classes: *ascriptive* and *nonascriptive.* The former involves a typically bipolar attribute predicates of the noun it modifies. For example, the adjective *heavy* in "the package is heavy" ascribes a value of the attribute of weight to the noun *package.* The antonym of this adjective, *light,* refers to the same attribute, ie, weight. Thus the class of ascriptive adjectives is organized along different principles.

Nonascriptive adjectives include those words that do not directly predicate the noun, but pertain to it in some unspecified way. For example, a *musical instrument* is an instrument used for music, not one that is musical.

Finally, verbs in WordNet are structured according to
```

a set of lexical entailment relations (see SEMANTIC NET-WORKS). For example, the verb *snore* lexically entails *sleep* because "He is snoring" entails "He is sleeping." This organization is similar to theories in formal semantics that adopt meaning postulates as the formal device relating lexical items.

Word Senses

Different parsing (qv) systems treat the relation between word senses and lexical entries in the following ways:

> *Word senses are conflated;* there are two cases of this:
>> *All uses are conflated;* all the category and subcategory analyses of a word are contained in a single lexical entry.
>> *Subcategory uses are conflated;* there are separate lexical entries for different categorial uses of a word, but the lexical entry for a single categorial use includes all subcategorial uses.
> *Word senses are distinguished;* there are two cases of this:
>> *There are separate lexical entries for each sense.*
>> *There are subentries for each sense within a single lexical entry.*

Word Senses Conflated. Many parsing systems, particularly some of the older ones, conflate all uses of a word into a single lexical item. See, for example, the definition of *go* in IRUS (Fig. 14). Other systems that similarly conflated senses include the Harvard Multi-path English Analyzer, LUNAR, and SPARSER (Bates, 1975). DIAGRAM, on the other hand, keeps categorial uses distinct, but to conflate subcategorial uses; see the definition of *want* in Figure 11 and of *find* and *look* in Figure 16b.

Word Senses Distinguished. The JANUS Master Lexicon has separate lexical entries for different categorial or subcategorial analyses of a word. For example, *have* has three separate lexical entries: for its use as an auxiliary, as a "causative" verb, and as a simple transitive verb. Unfortunately, certain information is duplicated in each of these entries, such as the irregularly inflected forms that are derived from it.

Lexicons that use subentries can eliminate this sort of duplication. For example, DELPHI has separate entries for different categorial uses of a word. Within the entry for a particular categorial use, there is a list of subcategorization frames. When the parser actually uses the lexicon, a separate virtual rule is created for each subcategorization; each of these entries will also include any other material that was in the entry that they were derived from. In effect, then, each subcategorization frame corresponds to a subentry (see Figure 17). PATR-II and VIE-LANG (Buchberger and co-workers, 1982; Steinacker and Buchberger, 1983) also use subentries (see Figures 9 and 12 for examples in PATR-II).

Collocations and Idioms

Although idioms and collocations were distinguished above, they will be treated together here because so few

```
EATS
    TV: .12, N: .11.
.12 = SINGULAR, NOTNOBJ: .1, NOTNSUBJ: .2, OBJLIST: .3.
.1 = NTIME1, NTIME2, NSENT1, NSENT2, NSENT3, NHUMAN.
.2 = NTIME1, NTIME2, NSENT1, NSENT2, NSENT3.
.3 = DP2: .6, DP3: .6, DP4: .6, PN: .5, NSTGO, NULLOBJ
.5 = PVAL: ('THROUGH', 'INTO').
.6 = DPVAL: ('UP', 'AWAY').
.11 = PLURAL, NONHUMAN
```

(a)

```
Words for V
(BREAK    (DIROBJ T)
          (PARTICLE UP OUT OFF)
          (PPL EN))
(BUY      (DIROBJ T)
          (INDIROBJ T)
          (DIRECTION FOR FROM BY))
(FIND     (ADJOBJ T)
          (DIROBJ T)
          (INDIROBJ T)
          (INFOBJ T)
          (INCGCOMP T)
          (SOBJ T)
          (DIRECTION FOR BY)
          (PARTICLE OUT))
(GIVE     (LIKE BUY)
          (DIRECTION TO BY)
          (PARTICLE UP)
          (PPL EN))
(LOOK     (DIROBJ T)
          (INSEPARABLE INTO)
          (ADJOBJ T)
          (PARTICLE UP))
```

(b)

Figure 16. Collocations contained in another lexical entry: (*a*) from LSP (Grishman, 1973); (*b*) from DIAGRAM (Robinson, 1982).

systems include idioms. Moreover, the few that do, handle collocations and idioms with the same mechanism.

There are several ways of treating collocations:

1. The collocation is entered directly in the lexicon, as a single lexical entry; this technique is most frequently used with collocations that make up a single, nonphrasal constituent (Fig. 18).

2. There is no separate lexical entry for the collocation; the elements making it up are entered as part of the lexical entry of the first word of the collocation. This technique is most frequently used with expressions involving a verb and a particle or a verb and a selected preposition (Fig. 16).

3. There is a separate lexical entry for the collocation, but there is a pointer to the collocation from the first word of the collocation; the IRUS dictionary uses this technique for most collocations, including the verb particle construction (Fig. 19).

4. The system uses a special mechanism to handle collocations, for example, BUP (Matsumoto and co-workers, 1985) provides quite sophisticated mecha-

```
[B-N
    Spelling:            b
    Category:            N
    Lex-Features:        (DETFLAG :DET)
    Rules:               (((N (INTRANSNOUN) (AGR (3RD) :N)
                           (REALNP (NONUNITNP (-PRO (MISCNP))))
                          :DET (COUNT-N (BASIC-COUNT)) (-CONJ)
                          (NOM (NO-PARS)
                            (INVERSE-VAL* (IDENTIFIER-OF) (STRING* (|b|))
                             (GENSET
                               (THINGS
                                 (INANIMATES (NON-VALUES (CLASS-OF-SERVICE))))))
                             (THINGS
                               (INANIMATES (NON-VALUES (CLASS-OF-SERVICE)))))))
                          -B-N-INTRANSNOUN-REALNP-MISCNP-DET-COUNT-N-INVERSE-VAL*-CLA
                          ((N (INRANSNOUN) (AGR (3RD) :N)
                           (REALNP (NONUNITNP (-PRO (MISCNP))))
                          :DET (COUNT-N (BASIC-COUNT), (-CONJ)
                          (NOM (NO-PARS)
                            (INVERSE-VAL* (MEAL-CODE-OF) (STRING* (|b|))
                             (GENSET
                               (THINGS
                                 (INANIMATES (NON-VALUES (MEAL))))))
                             (THINGS
                               (INANIMATES (NON-VALUES (MEAL)))))))
                          -B-N-INTRANSNOUN-REALNP-MISCNP-DET-COUNT-N-INVERSE-VAL*-MEA
    Subcat-Features:     ((INTRANSNOUN (INVERSE-VAL IDENTIFIER-OF "B" CLASS-OF-SERVICE
                          (INTRANSNOUN (INVERSE-VAL MEAL-CODE-OF "B" MEAL)))]
```

Figure 17. Subentries in DELPHI.

nisms for dealing with collocations (Fig. 20); the collocations that BUP handles represent quite a range and include

• Fixed expressions such as *as well.*
• Expressions where one of the elements is inflectable, such as *computer system.*
• Expressions where one of the elements is not fixed, but can be drawn from a restricted class of items, such as *by* in its use with a reflexive pronoun, such as *by myself, by yourself,* etc.
• Expressions where one of the elements is separable from the first member of the collocation, such as *look up.*
• Expressions that are composed of discontinuous constituents, such as *not only . . . but also . . .*

Two alternate definitions of this expression are given: the first allows the material following *not only* and *but also* to be of the same category, but does

```
NEW YORK CITY        NOUS

          (a)

Words in NP
  ((NEW YORK)  (NBR SG)
   (TYPE COUNT)
   (PROPN T))

          (b)
```

Figure 18. Collocations entered directly in the lexicon: (*a*) from the Harvard Multi-Path English Analyzer (Kuno and Oettinger, 1963c); (*b*) from DIAGRAM (Robinson, 1982).

not specify what the category must be; the second definition restricts the conjoined material to be either a noun phrase, adjective phrase, or prepositional phrase.

These definitions are not contained in the main BUP lexicon but in a separate idiom dictionary.

LEXICAL KNOWLEDGE ACQUISITION

One of the significant bottlenecks in NLP technology comes from having to populate a computational lexicon with entries for tens, and even hundreds, of thousands of words. A great number of language processing systems are strikingly limited in their range of application. This lack of versatility is to a large extent due to the typically small number of lexical entries available to them (it is still the case that average size of prototype lexicons does not significantly exceed hundreds or a few thousand entries (Ritchie, 1987). A further problem concerns the fragility of most experimental systems in the face of serious attempts to scale up laboratory prototypes or application programs carefully tuned for particular domains, because so much of the information contained in lexical entries is specific to the particular system in its current state. For this reason, the problem of knowledge acquisition for large lexicons will be examined. Several approaches to this problem will be discussed, falling in the general categories of manual crafting of (lexical) knowledge bases and automatic acquisition from on-line textual resources.

There are, essentially, two types of text resource used for lexical data acquisition: machine-readable dictionaries (MRDs) and text corpora. Dictionaries are, by definition,

```
[AS
        BINDER   *
              COMMENTS
              submarine tender — donb, 4/10/86
        COMP   *
        MULTIPLES
              (AS AGAINST) => (AS¯AGAINST)
              (AS FAR AS) => (AS¯FAR¯AS)
              (AS FOR) => (AS¯FOR)
              (AS FROM) => (AS¯FROM)
              (AS IF) => (AS¯IF)
              (AS IN) => (AS¯IN)
              (AS LONG AS) => (AS¯LONG¯AS)
              (AS MANY AS) => (AS¯MANY¯AS)
              (AS OF) => (AS¯OF)
              (AS OPPOSED TO) => (AS¯OPPOSED¯TO)
              (AS REGARDS) => (AS¯REGARDS)
              (AS RELATED TO) => (AS¯RELATED¯TO)
              (AS THOUGH) => (AS¯THOUGH)
              (AS TO) => (AS¯TO)
              (AS WELL AS) => (AS¯WELL¯AS)
        N    −S
        NPR   *
        PREP   *
        SEMANTICS (CONVENTIONAL.SURFACE.SHIP *)]
[AS¯WELL¯AS
        CONJ   (OR)]


[LOOK
        FEATURES (COPULA INTRANS)
        IMMOVABLEPARTICLES ((INTO LOOK\INTO))
        PARTICLES ((UP LOOK\UP))
        V S-ED]
[LOOK\INTO
        FEATURES (INDOBJFOR TRANS)
        V NOINFLECTIONS]
[LOOK\UP
        FEATURES (INDOBJFOR INTRANS TRANS)
        V NOINFLECTIONS]
```

Figure 19. Collocations dependent on other lexical entries (from the IRUS dictionary).

```
idiom(as,postmod,_,[Syn,Sem,[postmod,'as well']]) -->
      [well].
idiom(computer,n,_,[Syn,Sem,[n,[n,computer],Tree]]) -->
      word(system,_,n,[Syn1,Sem1,Tree]).
idiom(by,adv,_,[Syn,Sem,[adv,[prep,by],Tree]]) -->
      goal(pron,[Syn1,Sem1,Tree]),
      { type_of(Sny1,reflexive) }.
idiom(look,v,Arg1,Arg) -->
   ( goal(np,Arg2) ; [ ] ),[up],
      { look_up(Arg1,Arg2,Arg) }.
idiom(not,Goal,_,[Syn,Sem,[Goal,[not,not],[only,only],Tree1,
         [but,but],[also,also],Tree2]]) -->
      [only],
      goal(Goal,[Syn1,Sem1,Tree1]),[but,also],
      goal(Goal,[Syn2,Sem2,Tree2]).
idiom(not,Goal,_,[Syn,Sem,[Goal,[not,not],[only,only],Tree1,
         [but,but],[also,also],Tree2]]) -->
      [only],{ member(Goal,[np,adjp,pp]) },
      goal(Goal,[Syn1,Sem1,Tree1]),[but,also],
      goal(Goal,[Syn2,Sem2,Tree2]).
```

Figure 20. Collocations in BUP (Matsumoto and co-workers, 1985).

repositories of lexical information pertaining to a large number of words; most, if not all of this could be used for natural language processing. Text corpora reflect language as it is used and as it evolves; by studying regularities of use and patterns of behavior of words, which only emerge from analysis of very large samples of text and/or speech, it is possible to induce (among other things) lexical properties and thus populate a computational lexicon.

While certainly representative of lexical behavior of words, both dictionaries and corpora have their drawbacks. At best, a computational lexicon derived from MRD sources would tend to be incomplete, both with respect to coverage (words) and content (lexical properties). At worst, such a lexicon would leave a lot to be desired as far as consistency and organization of data are concerned. The question of organizing the lexical knowledge extracted from a text resource is equally pressing in the case of using text corpora; furthermore, until issues such as what constitutes the right kind of corpus given certain lexical properties, how to balance it, and how to abstract the information acquired through "learning" from the learning mechanism itself are resolved, the transition from corpus to lexicon will remain in need of streamlining.

For reasons like these, at least, there is a view in the field that time and effort notwithstanding, a substantial fragment of lexical knowledge can only be, and therefore should be, crafted by hand. This applies not only to building application- and domain-specific lexicons, but to general-purpose lexical knowledge and databases.

Manual Acquisition

The most labor intensive method of populating a lexicon with syntactic, morphological, and semantic information is manual entry. However, this method is probably still the most frequently used, for a number of reasons. First, the start-up costs are low. No corpora or existing dictionaries or lexicons need to be obtained and no automatic analysis programs need to be written. At the minimum, all that is needed is a text editor. Second, as was already noted, the lexicons of most natural language systems, excluding machine translation (qv), are typically small, on the order of tens of words. Even when domains [such as the Resource Management database query task (Price and co-workers, 1988) and the ATIS air travel task (Hemphill and co-workers, 1990)] have had significantly larger vocabularies (approximately 1,000 words), typically the vocabulary has remained at a fixed size over a long period, rather than requiring continual massive increases in size.

While vocabulary size may not have been an incentive to produce acquisition tools, grammar and lexicon complexity often have been. As the number and complexity of lexical features increases, it becomes correspondingly more difficult to use completely manual techniques. Acquisition programs are necessary to ensure the well-formedness of lexical entries. The widespread availability of workstations with window displays and mouse input has allowed very sophisticated acquisition tools to be constructed. One such program is LapItUp (Cumming and Albano, 1986) (for Lexical Aquisition Program Involving

Timely User Prompts), the acquisition tool for the JANUS Master Lexicon (Cumming, 1986). LapItUp makes crucial use of the fact that lexical features in the Master Lexicon are arranged in a tree structure. This hierarchical structure is easy to interpret as a decision tree, with the selection of some features permitting new choices and disallowing others. For example, in a verb definition, if the transitive subcategorization feature is chosen, then intransitive is no longer allowed, and the possibility of passivization and the presence of an indirect object become new choices. LapItUp maintains a structured history of the features chosen and allows the user to retreat to an earlier decision point at any time and chose a different path through the space of possible choices.

Even though the features in LapItUp have some semantic as well as syntactic import, the program essentially remains a tool for entering syntactic information into the JANUS Master Lexicon. Various other systems have used similar syntactic acquisition tools. Often, they supplement the syntactic acquisition tool with a corresponding semantic acquisition tool. For example, IRUS used IRACQ (Ayuso and co-workers, 1987) (for IRule—Interpretation Rule—ACQuisition). IRACQ was a tool that allowed a user to create logical expressions linking a word and its argument positions to concepts from an existing model of the task domain via a natural language expression, such as a noun phrase or sentence. For example, given that the user has specified that the verb *send* is to be linked to the domain model concept *deployment,* inputting the sentence "An admiral sent Enterprise to the Indian Ocean" will lead to the production of the IRule in Figure 21.

Not all of this would be generated directly from the natural language expression. When the system is uncertain of how far to generalize the semantic type of an argument it queries the user, presenting a menu of choices generated automatically from the taxonomic structure of the domain model. Also, the system queries the user for the possible semantic relations for the object of a prepositional complement, again automatically generating a menu of possibilities from the domain model. However, the overall structure of the IRule, in particular, the linking of constituents filling particular grammatical roles to particular semantic roles, is done automatically by IRACQ. KNACQ (for KNowledge ACQuisition) (Weischedel and co-workers, 1989) is a somewhat more flexible tool that grew out of IRACQ.

```
((IRule DEPLOYMENT.4
  clause subject (is-a COMMANDING.OFFICER)
      head * object (is-a UNIT)
        pp ((pp head to pobj (is-a REGION)))))
  ==>
  (bind ((commanding.officer.1 (optional subject))
        (unit.1 object)
        (region.1 (optional (pp 1 pobj))))
  (predicate '(destination.of *v* region.1))
  (predicate '(object.of *v* unit.1))
  (predicate '(agent *v* commanding.officer.1))
  (class 'DEPLOYMENT)))
```

Figure 21. A sample interpretation rule.

There are also other lexical acquisition tools that handle both syntactic and semantic information. TEAM (Grosz, 1982, 1983; Grosz and co-workers, 1985) had a highly sophisticated acquisition component that not only acquired syntactic and semantic information but also linked lexical entries to the underlying data base application. BBN's (1989) Parlance uses a similar tool, the Learner (Bates, 1989), for roughly equivalent purposes. One interesting aspect of the Learner, which places it somewhere between purely manual and entirely automatic means of acquisition, is that the Learner acquires the natural language names for tables, fields, and fillers directly from the database itself. In an interesting experiment, lexical and domain model knowledge acquired via the Learner for Parlance, an ATN-based system, were translated into forms usable by DELPHI, a unification-based system (Ingria and Ramshaw, 1989). Results were encouraging for nouns, adjectives, and prepositions, although semantic entries for verbs were essentially untranslatable and needed to be entered into DELPHI by hand. Still, this experiment indicates that it may be possible to acquire significant amounts of lexical syntactic and semantic information for one system and reuse it in the lexicon of a radically different system.

In addition to system- and domain-specific tools, there are projects totally devoted to knowledge acquisition for natural language processing. One project worth mentioning is the CYC project (Lenat and Guha, 1990) under way at MCC. CYC has the goal of capturing all human commonsense knowledge in a very large knowledge base. The CYC approach is to manually enter all knowledge relevant to making commonsense inferences. Thus the task for language analysis and, in particular, for lexicon design, is to hand-code all syntactic, morphological, semantic, and pragmatic information associated with a word. The representation language used for encoding knowledge in CYC is CYCL. Associated with every element in the ontology is a lexical item or perhaps a phrase. The set of these associations can essentially be seen as the lexicon within the CYC system.

Another example of a large effort to manually enter lexical knowledge into a knowledge base is the ONTOS project at CMU's Center for Machine Translation (CMT) (Nirenburg, 1989; Nirenburg and Levin, 1989). This effort is aimed at providing the concept lexicon for a language independent conceptual representation between languages for translation purposes. ONTOS provides an interactive environment for acquiring knowledge associated with the words in a language. This information is embedded within a frame network representation of objects, events, and situations.

The methodological point assumed by ONTOS is that the information needed for robust machine translation (or for that matter, analysis or generation in isolation) is not to be found in any systematic form in dictionaries or corpora alone. Thus we should concentrate on tools for entering knowledge about words and their meanings as well as for updating the knowledge through interactive systems.

It is perhaps worth noting that the lexicons associated with the CMT analysis and generation systems are among the largest and broadest available in NLP systems. This is due in part to the facility with which data may be entered by the human knowledge engineer.

Machine-Readable Dictionaries

Computational lexicons are unlike human dictionaries in many respects; it is certainly the case that a computer cannot just make a reference to a dictionary even if it is available on-line, because the form and content of lexical entries designed for people are substantially different from those required by computers. Still, dictionaries are the largest available repositories of organized knowledge about words, and it is only natural for computational linguists to turn to them in the hope that this knowledge can be extracted, formalized, and made available to NLP systems.

The appeal of using on-line dictionaries in the construction of formal computational lexicons is intuitively obvious: dictionaries contain information about words, and lexicons need such information. If automated procedures could be developed for extracting and formalizing lexical data, on a large scale, from existing on-line resources, NLP systems would have ways of capitalizing on much of the lexicographic effort embodied in the production of reference materials for human consumption.

Not surprisingly, then, one approach to scaling up the lexical components of natural language systems prototypes to enable them to handle realistic texts has been to turn to existing machine-readable forms of published dictionaries. On the assumption that they not only represent (trivially) a convenient source of words, but also contain (in a less obvious, and more interesting way) a significant amount of lexical data, recent research efforts have shown that automated procedures can be developed for extracting and formalizing explicitly available, as well as implicitly encoded, information (phonological, syntactic, and semantic) from machine-readable dictionaries.

Such work reflects a change in view: whereas early efforts for utilizing dictionary data were aimed primarily at what had been explicitly stated in the entries (as in Walker and co-workers, in press), comparatively recent developments have focused on carrying out much more detailed analysis of the sources, with a view of uncovering information that turns out to be systematically, albeit implicitly, represented by dictionary entry content, dictionary structure, and lexicographic conventions (as in Boguraev and Briscoe, 1989). More specific examples here would be:

- From simple word-list construction to part-of-speech and subcategorization extraction (Heidron and co-workers, 1982) to acquiring information about control and logical type of predicates (Boguraev and Briscoe, 1987).
- From deriving pronunciations (Streeter, 1978) to acquiring information about stress assignment (Church, 1985) to gaining insights into the phonetic structure of English and, in particular, what implications it might have for different methods of lexical access (Shipman and Zue, 1982) to developing better models of speech recognizer front ends (Carter, 1989).

- From constructing simple taxonomies for verbs and nouns (Amsler, 1981) to fleshing out semantic networks (Alshawi, 1989; Calzolari, 1988; Fox and co-workers, 1988) to building semantically sound lexical hierarchies (Copestake, 1990).
- From acquiring semantic features (eg, selectional restrictions) for lexical disambiguation (Byrd and co-workers, 1987) to using a dictionary as an on-line aid for lexical and structural disambiguation (Braden-Harder and Zadrozany, in press; Ravin, 1988) to deriving empirical evidence for the existence of semantically coherent word-sense clusters (Wilks and co-workers, in press).
- From "sprouting" networks of lexical relations between words (Chodrow and co-workers, 1988) to refining such networks to reflect word-sense distinctions (Guthrie and co-workers, 1990; Copestake, 1990) to populating richer lexical structures that introduce an additional dimension to the notion of lexical relation and promote more flexible interpretation of the notion of word sense (Boguraev, 1991; Levin, 1991).

To a large extent such approaches to the acquisition problem are motivated by the desire to make maximal use of the information in dictionaries; they are also, however, necessary to overcome some major disadvantages to the use of MRDs in natural language processing. First, because these are produced with the human user in mind, there is a strong assumption about the nature of the understanding and interpretation available to make use of a dictionary entry; second, due to the very nature of the process of (human) lexicography, present-day dictionaries are far from complete, consistent, and coherent, certainly with respect to virtually any of the numerous kinds of lexical data they choose to represent and encode. An important question then becomes: where is the line between useful and relevant data to be extracted from existing machine-readable sources, and the inconsistencies, misrepresentations, omissions, and so forth inherent in such sources and detrimental to the enterprise of deriving computational lexicons by (semi)automatic means?

Issues like these are at the core of computational analysis of language on the basis of information available in dictionaries. More specifically, they highlight questions pertaining to the infrastructure for any research effort of which the ultimate goal is to develop a general purpose computational lexicon and instantiate this, at least in part, with derived lexical data. For instance:

- How to make dictionary sources available to extraction procedures in a way that allows flexible access to an arbitrary depth of detail of (source) lexical description.
- How to make such procedures attuned to lexical demands of NLP systems and keep them open as language processing frameworks become better understood and more elaborate.
- How to satisfy these demands by suitably constrained search through on-line MRD sources.
- How the relationship between natural language pro-

cessing, formal syntax, and lexical semantic theories is reflected in the kind of information sought in dictionaries for incorporation into a computational lexicon.

A number of arguments have been put forward in support of a claim that, in effect, a dictionary is only as good as its worst (or least experienced) lexicographer and/or user, and by that token, it is not much good for developing systematic procedures for extraction of lexical data. For instance, in reference to recent work with MRDs in the field of computational linguistics, Atkins (1991) not only summarizes the process of building a large-scale lexicon as "trawling" a machine-readable dictionary in search for lexical facts, but points out an imbalance between the kinds of syntactic and semantic information that can be identified by minutely examining existing dictionaries: "the useful semantic information which may be extracted at present is more restricted in scope, and virtually limited to the construction of semantic taxonomies."

Although Atkins's assessment of the state of the field is essentially correct, this can be ascribed to the predominant paradigm of lexicon development on the basis of dictionary analysis. More specifically, several factors are instrumental to the relative inadequacy of the semantic information derived from dictionaries.

Formal Syntax vs Formal (Lexical) Semantics. From the perspective of building formal systems capable of processing natural language texts, there is (currently) a much better understanding of the nature of the syntactic information required for implementing such systems than of its semantic counterpart. In other words, the state of the art of (applied) computational linguistics is such that syntactic analysers are much better understood than semantic interpreters; consequently, there is a fairly concrete notion of what would constitute necessary, useful, and formalizable syntactic information of a general linguistic nature. Therefore, given the well-defined lexical requirements at the syntactic level, there is that much more leverage in searching for (and finding) specific data to populate a lexicon at the syntactic level (see, eg, Boguraev and Briscoe, 1987, Boguraev and co-workers, 1990).

Local vs Distributed Lexical Knowledge. Most of the investigations aimed at recovery of lexical data from dictionaries fall in the category of localist approaches. The notion has been that if the goal is to construct an entry for a given word, then all the relevant information concerning its lexical properties is to be found, locally, in the source dictionary entry for that word. This observation explains why extracting simple semantic features and constructing taxonomic networks on the basis of the genus-differentiae model of dictionary definitions (eg, Amsler, 1981; Byrd and co-workers, 1987; Calzolari, 1984; Alshawi, 1989) is essentially the extent to which identification of semantic information has been developed. It also underlies the pessimism concerning the useful semantic information extractable from a dictionary (Atkins, 1991). Most dictionary entries are, indeed, impoverished when viewed in isolation; therefore, the lexical structures derived from

them would be similarly under-representative. On the other hand, it turns out that a wide range of structural patterns in a dictionary, implemented by the mechanism of lexicographic convention, have a (not immediately obvious, yet fairly deep) interpretation in terms of lexical properties and values: there is lexical content to dictionary structure, and this fact alone makes it possible to enhance existing frameworks for exploiting lexical knowledge encoded configurationally and distributed across entire MRD sources.

Data Models for Lexical Acquisition. It is important to take into account the relationship between the expressive power of on-line dictionary models and the scope of lexical information available via the access methods such models support. A common characteristic of a number of efforts at lexical data extraction has been mounting a dictionary on-line only partially (ie, leaving out certain fields and segments of entries) and/or ignoring components of an entry whose function is perceived to be primarily of typographical or aesthetic nature (for instance, typesetter control codes are often used only as delimiters). Because typography in the printed source can distinguish qualitatively different kinds of information, such efforts suffer limitations on the kinds of lexical relationships that can be observed and recovered from the dictionary. In principle, computational dictionary analysis should be concerned not only with developing techniques and methods for extraction of lexical data but also with building tools for making lexical resources available to such techniques and methods. Until recently, however, the on-line dictionary model tended to fall short of being an adequate representation of lexical information on a large scale [see Boguraev and co-workers (1990) for a discussion of this issue].

Lexicon Construction Paradigms. A more realistic view concerning the nature of lexical data extractable from dictionaries is currently emerging. Hoping to derive, by fully automatic means, a computational lexicon from one, or several, dictionary sources is overly optimistic, and provably unrealistic. On the other hand, discarding the potential utility of such sources on the grounds that they have not yielded enough consistent and comprehensive information is unduly pessimistic. Between these two extremes there is an opinion that the potential of on-line dictionaries is in using them to facilitate and assist in the construction of large-scale lexicons (eg, Levin, 1991). The image is not that of "cranking the handle" and getting a lexicon overnight, but that of carefully designing a lexicon and then, for each aspect of lexical data deemed to be relevant for (semantic) processing of language, using the dictionary sources, in their entirety, to find instances of, and evidence for, such data. Such a paradigm relies on directed search for a number of specific lexical properties and requires a much stronger notion of a theory of lexical semantics than assumed in computational linguistics to date. Dictionary sources are far from being the only type of text resource from which knowledge about words can be extracted; corpora, citations, transcribed speech, and others are equally representative, if not better, repositories of such knowledge.

It is the interplay of lexical needs of current language processing frameworks and contemporary lexical semantic theories that very much influences the direction of computational dictionary analysis research for lexical acquisition. Given the increasingly more prominent place the lexicon is assigned, in linguistic theories, in language processing technology, and in domain description, it is no accident, nor is it mere rhetoric, that the term *lexical knowledge base* has become a widely accepted one. Researchers use it to refer to a large-scale repository of lexical information, which incorporates more than just static descriptions of words, eg, by means of clusters of properties and associated values. A lexical knowledge base would state

- Constraints on word behavior.
- Dependence of word interpretation on context.
- Distribution of linguistic generalizations (Byrd, 1989; Boguraev and Levin, 1990).

It is essentially a dynamic object, as it incorporates, in addition to its information types, the ability to perform inference over them and thus induce word meaning in context. This is the sense of computational lexicon, the population of which is giving new meaning to lexical acquisition from MRDs.

Recent research critically examines the notion of building a lexicon on the basis of existing dictionaries. A common feature is a certain amount of scepticism toward attempts to fully instantiate such a lexicon by automatic means. However, there is a shared attitude that, although there are many ways in which dictionaries fail as sources for a computational lexicon (infelicity, inconsistency, incompleteness, to name a few), there are also ways to maximize the value of the information found in them. The particular strategies developed (eg, Boguraev, 1991) follow from a mix of:

- Critical assessment of the nature of facts in dictionaries and the ways they are presented.
- Analysis of the lexical requirements of natural language processing frameworks, especially as such frameworks evolve toward generality and domain independence.
- Elaboration of the intersection between available and required data, which might take the form of, eg, a generic lexical template.
- Linguistically motivated justification for the utility of such templates, both as a holding device for data extracted from dictionaries, and as an underlying knowledge structure for NLP.
- Proposals for instantiating lexical templates: these are based on borrowing methods from lexicography and corpus studies, as well as applying special-purpose computational tools for dictionary analysis.

Overall, there is far more in a dictionary than meets the eye; however, this wealth of information typically cannot be observed or extracted without reference to a formal linguistic theory with very precise lexical requirements, and without a set of tools capable of making explicit the highly compacted and codified information typical of dictionary sources.

Text Corpora

One of the arguments brought against using dictionaries for lexical knowledge acquisition is that they are static objects, representing, at best, a frozen snapshot of language. Given that language is a dynamic and rapidly evolving object, there is a sense in which, by the time a dictionary makes it through the compilation and publication process, it has grown out of date. To a certain extent, this argument is used to motivate more recent efforts for manual crafting of lexicons. More important, however, it brings in focus the value of text corpora as alternative (or complementary) source of lexical information. Opinions in the field differ on whether to use, exclusively, one type of resource, or to complement sources and merge information acquired from either type.

This is a comparatively recent development, brought on by several factors. The field has its own canonical corpora, which have been in existence for many years: the Brown corpus (Francis and Kučera, 1982), the Lancaster-Oslo-Bergen (LOB) corpus (Garside and co-workers, 1987), and the London-Lund corpus (Svartvik and Quirk, 1980) are perhaps the best known examples for this category. They suffer from the same drawback as dictionaries, namely, they have been in existence for so long, that a whole fragment of language, as it has evolved over the last 20-odd years, is not reflected in them at all. However, recent technological developments in gathering, publishing, and distributing information have made it possible to have, more or less as a side product, immediate access to very large volumes of text as it is being created. Through services such as news wires, transcripts, electronic publishing, and so forth, text is available on a scale unmatched by any static language sample. Furthermore, developments in computer technology make it possible to handle such sizable samples without running into operational difficulties due to the limited processing power of earlier generation computers.

The combination of size of corpora (as word count climbs up into tens and hundreds of million, the value of a corpus as comprehensive and representative sample of language increases), their dynamic nature, wider availability [the ACL/Data Collection Initiative is just one channel through which large text samples are made generally available (Liberman, 1989)], and the ability to process them computationally accounts for a noticeable revival of empiricism. From the perspective of (applied) computational linguistics, this has taken the shape of making prominent a long and established tradition of quantificational analysis of language; a representative example is a line of work that uses corpora as the basis from which to induce stochastic models of language (eg, Garside and co-workers, 1987).

Clearly, the term *language model*, while typically associated with notions like probabilistic part-of-speech taggers (Garside and co-workers, 1987; Church, 1988; DeRose, 1988) and parsers (eg, Atwell, 1987; Ejerhed, 1988), has a substantial lexical component to it. A tagger assigns syntactic categories to lexical items; thus the output of such a program can be used to annotate a word list with part-of-speech labels. Similarly, the very existence of a parse tree would enable further enhancement of items in a word list by adding, eg, subcategorization information. It is just a matter of emphasis whether essentially the same operational mechanisms are applied for language analysis per se, or for language processing with a view of further integration of (aspects of) the output into a permanent lexical structure. In this vein, more recent, and explicitly of lexical acquisition nature, work includes, for instance, frequency based elicitation of word distribution patterns, concordance-driven definition of context and word behavior, extracting and representing word collocations, acquisition of lexical semantics of verbs from sentence frames, and even derivation of transfer lexicons for machine translation (van Berkel and De Smedt, 1988; Slator, in press; Smadja, in press; Webster and Marcus, 1989; Brown and co-workers, 1990).

The final, and a particularly strong, argument for using text corpora rather than machine-readable dictionaries for lexical knowledge acquisition comes from a relatively recent trend in (human) lexicography that interleaves several basic principles in applied linguistics and dictionary compilation. Because language is a constantly changing dynamic system, no existing, and by that token already out of date, reference materials (including other dictionary sources) should be used in the process of compiling a new dictionary. Rather, the analysis of words, from decisions concerning the make-up of the word list to the specific content of individual entries, should be carried out entirely on the basis of studies of a large representative corpus, both of spoken and written text. This is not just a matter of keeping up with language as it evolves: lexicographers "have learned what happens when [they] sit and intuit how words are used—[they] are likely to get it wrong" (Fox, 1987).

This is, in a nutshell, the difference in method between armchair lexicography and corpus lexicography: rigorous applications of a set of principles for measuring hard evidence of lexical behavior of words is, arguably, going to result in a representative, coherent, and consistent (altogether a more faithful) object than the dictionaries produced by conventional means or the lexicons crafted on the basis of (computational) linguists' intuition [Atkins (1987) argues this point in detail. The COBUILD dictionary (Sinclair, 1987a) stands as an example of the corpus-based methodology for dictionary construction. Sinclair (1987b) addresses the issues behind the principles, the motivations, and the realization of this methodology; incidentally, it is a particularly good text to read in the context of the issues discussed here, as it makes clear the richness of lexical information available in (and distributed over) millions of words of language samples. It also brings home the point that careful inspection of a dictionary entry (or a set of related entries) is likely to reveal considerably more in terms of lexical properties of the word (or class of words) than is apparently visible.]

From such a perspective, there are obvious questions: Why use existing dictionaries for lexical acquisition,

when even the lexicographers who created them agree that they are inadequate? Why wait for better dictionaries, when the source they will eventually be created from can (now) be tapped directly? A strong relation is being forged between computational methods for quantificational analysis of language and corpus lexicography (Church, 1990; Church and co-workers, in press; Justeson and Katz, in press), and this is certain to influence lexical knowledge acquisition.

There is no clear answer to these questions. If anything, the field has tended to associate lexicon construction on the basis of MRD sources with the AI-influenced tradition of using semantic networks, knowledge representation mechanisms, and inference techniques to address questions of lexical representation and organization. Likewise, the contrastive association has been that of corpus analysis with probabilistically based approaches to language processing, which require (seemingly) different lexicon models. This is, in fact, a very interesting issue, relevant to the whole practice of computational linguistics, and concerns the potential conflict between the two paradigms in NLP.

On the one hand, there is the traditional approach that aims to model the human cognitive mechanism and is implemented via a (complex) set of symbol manipulating inference procedures that make use of an extensive body of world, in addition to linguistic, knowledge. On the other hand, a paradigm based entirely on quantificational analysis of language relies heavily on the gathering and use of probabilistic measures for word collocations.

Although many would agree that the two approaches are complementary (Garside and co-workers, 1987, Introduction), there are equally (not to say fanatically) devoted proponents of the view that computational linguistics should be practiced on the basis of a mix between probabilistic and self-organizing connectionist methods. [For an argument supporting this view, see, in particular, Sampson (in Garside and co-workers, 1987, 1990). Complementary reading is Taylor and co-workers (1989) and Briscoe (1990).] An especially important reference is Hindle (1989), who argues for a synergy between the two extremes. He proposes a framework for using large corpora of naturally occurring text together with rule-based systems, in an attempt to build more effective linguistic processors:

It is important to emphasize that the question whether we can acquire linguistic information from text is independent of whether the model is probabilistic, categorical, or some combination of the two. The issue is not . . . symbolic versus probabilistic rules, but rather whether we can acquire the necessary linguistic information instead of building systems completely by hand.

More recent work supports this view. Wilks and co-workers (in press) have applied statistical measures to a dictionary, treating it as a (highly representative) text sample. Boguraev (1991) instantiated aspects of the lexical semantics of nominals and verbs on the basis of fine-grained analysis of dictionary sources and argued for the need to complement the extraction results with corpus-derived data. Hindle (1989) acquired semantic data of similar nature, on the basis of studying distributional patterns over syntactic structures associated with the sentences in a large text corpus. Anick and Pustejovsky (1990) argued for the value of a theory of lexical semantics as a constraining agent for purely statistical collocational analysis, aimed at populating lexical semantic templates. Warwick-Armstrong (in press) contains additional material concerning computational linguistics using large text corpora. Boguraev and Pustejovsky (in press) discussed in detail general questions of lexical acquisition (and representation) from on-line text resources.

BIBLIOGRAPHY

H. Alshawi, "Analyzing the Dictionary Definitions," in Boguraev and Briscoe, 1989, pp. 153–170.

R. Amsler, "A Taxonomy for English Verbs and Nouns," in *Proceedings of the Nineteenth Annual Meeting of the ACL*, Stanford, Calif., 1981, pp. 133–138.

P. Anick and J. Pustejovsky, "An Application of Lexical Semantics to Knowledge Acquisition from Corpora," in *Proceedings of COLING-13*, Helsinki, Finland, 1990, pp. 7–12.

B. Atkins, "Semantic ID Tags: Corpus Evidence for Dictionary Senses," in *Proceedings of the Third Annual Conference of the University of Waterloo Centre for the New Oxford English Dictionary*, Waterloo, Ont., 1987, pp. 17–36.

B. Atkins, "Building a Lexicon: The Contribution of Lexicography," in Boguraev, 1991.

E. Atwell, "Constituent-Likelihood Grammar," in Garside, Leech, and Sampson, 1987, pp. 57–65.

D. M. Ayuso, V. Shaked, and R. M. Weischedel, "An Environment for Acquiring Semantic Information," *Twenty-Fifth Annual Meeting of the Association for Computational Linguistics: Proceedings of the Conference*, Association for Computational Linguistics, Morristown, N.J., 1987, pp. 32–40.

J. Barwise and R. Cooper, "Generalized Quantifiers and Natural Language," *Ling. Philos.* **4**, 159–219 (1981).

M. Bates, *Syntactic Analysis in a Speech Understanding System*, BBN Report No. 3116, Bolt Beranek and Newman Inc., Boston, 1975.

M. Bates, "Rapid Porting of the Parlance Natural Language Interface," in *Speech and Natural Language: Proceedings of a Workshop Held at Philadelphia, Pennsylvania, February 21–23, 1989*, Morgan-Kaufmann, San Mateo, Calif., 1989, pp. 83–88.

BBN Parlance Learner Manual, BBN Systems and Technologies Corp., Cambridge, Mass., 1989.

G. L. Berry-Rogghe and H. Wulz, "An Overview of PLIDIS, A Problem Solving Information System With German as Query Language," in L. Bolc, ed., *Natural Language Communication with Computers*, Springer-Verlag, New York, 1978, pp. 87–132.

G. L. Berry-Rogghe, M. Kolvenbach, and H.-D. Lutz, "Interacting with PLIDIS, A Deductive Question Answering System for German," in L. Bolc, ed., *Natural Language Question Answering Systems*, Carl Hanser Verlag, Munich, 1980, pp. 137–216.

M. Bierwisch, "Some Semantic Universals of German Adjectivals," *Found. Lang.* **3**, 1–36 (1967).

M. Bierwisch and E. Lang, eds., *Dimensional Adjectives: Grammatical Structure and Conceptual Interpretation*, Springer-Verlag, New York, 1987.

R. Bobrow, "Statistical Agenda Parsing," in *Speech and Natural Language: Proceedings of a Workshop*, Pacific Grove, Calif., Morgan-Kaufmann, San Mateo, Calif., 1991.

R. Bobrow, R. Ingria, and D. Stallard, "Syntactic and Semantic Knowledge in the DELPHI Unification Grammar," in *Speech and Natural Language: Proceedings of a Workshop*, Hidden Valley, Pa., Morgan-Kaufmann, San Mateo, Calif., 1990, pp. 230–240.

R. Bobrow, R. Ingria, and D. Stallard, "The Mapping Unit Approach to Subcategorization," in *Speech and Natural Language: Proceedings of a Workshop*, Pacific Grove, Calif., Morgan-Kaufmann, San Mateo, Calif., 1991.

B. Boguraev, ed., Special issue on computational lexicons, *Int. J. Lexicog.* **4**(3) (1991).

B. Boguraev and E. Briscoe, "Large Lexicons for Natural Language Processing: Exploiting the Grammar Coding System of LDOCE," *Computat. Ling.* **13**(3–4), 203–218 (1987).

B. Boguraev and E. Briscoe, eds., *Computational Lexicography for Natural Language Processing*, Longman, London, 1989.

B. Boguraev, E. Briscoe, J. Carroll, and A. Copestake, "Database Models for Computational Lexicography," in *Proceedings of International Euralex-VOX Congress*, Malaga, Spain, 1990.

B. Boguraev and B. Levin, "Models for Lexical Knowledge Bases," in *Proceedings of the Sixth Annual Conference of the University of Waterloo Centre for the New Oxford English Dictionary and Text Research*, Waterloo, Ont., Canada, 1990, pp. 65–78.

B. Boguraev and J. Pustejovsky, *Lexical Knowledge: Acquisition and Representation*, MIT Press, Cambridge, Mass., in press.

S. Boisen, Y. Chow, A. Haas, R. Ingria, S. Roucos, R. Scha, D. Stallard, and M. Vilain, *Integration of Speech and Natural Language: Final Report*, Report No. 6991, BBN Systems and Technologies Corp., Cambridge, Mass., 1989a.

S. Boisen, Y.-L. Chow, A. Haas, R. Ingria, S. Roukos, and D. Stallard, "The BBN Spoken Language System," *Speech and Natural Language: Proceedings of a Workshop*, Philadelphia, Morgan-Kaufmann, San Mateo, Calif., 1989b, pp. 106–111.

G. Bouma, E. König, and H. Uszkoreit, "A Flexible Graph Unification Formalism and Its Application to NLP," *IBM J. Res. Dev.* **32**(2), 170–184 (1988).

L. Braden-Harder and W. Zadrozny, "Lexicons for Broad Coverage Semantics," in U. Zernik, ed., *Lexical Acquisition: Using On-Line Resources to Build a Lexicon*, Lawrence Erlbaum, Hillsdale, N.J., in press.

E. Briscoe, "English Noun Phrases Are Regular: A Reply to Professor Sampson," in J. Aarts and W. Meijs, eds., *Theory and Practice in Corpus Linguistics*, Rodopi, Amsterdam, 1990.

P. Brown and co-workers, "A Statistical Approach to Machine Translation," *Computat. Ling.* **16**(2), 79–85 (1990).

J. de Bruin and R. Scha, "The Interpretation of Relational Nouns," in the *Twenty-Seventh Annual Meeting of the Association for Computational Linguistics: Proceedings of the Conference*, Association for Computational Linguistics, Morristown, N.J., 1988, pp. 25–32.

E. Buchberger, I. Steinacker, R. Trappl, H. Trost, and E. Leinfellner, "VIE-LANG: A German Language Understanding System," in *Cybernetics and Systems Research*, North-Holland, Amsterdam, 1982, pp. 869–874.

R. Byrd, "Discovering Relationships Among Word Senses," *Proceedings of the Third Annual Conference of the University of Waterloo Centre for the New Oxford English Dictionary*, Oxford, UK, 1989, pp. 67–80.

R. Byrd, N. Calzolari, M. Chodorow, J. Klavans, M. Neff, and O.

Rizk, "Tools and Methods for Computational Lexicology," *Computat. Ling.* **13**(3–4), 219–240 (1987).

J. Calder and E. te Lindert, "The Protolexicon: Towards a High-Level Language for Lexical Description," in E. Klein and J. van Bentham, eds., *Categories, Polymorphism and Unification,* Centre for Cognitive Science, University of Edinburgh, Edinburgh, UK, 1987, pp. 355–370.

N. Calzolari, "Detecting Patterns in a Lexical Database," *Proceedings of COLING-10,* Stanford, Calif., 1984, pp. 170–173.

N. Calzolari, "The Dictionary and the Thesaurus Can Be Combined," in M. Evens, ed., *Relational Models of the Lexicon: Representing Knowledge in Semantic Networks,* Cambridge University Press, Cambridge, UK, 1988, pp. 75–96.

D. Carter, "LDOCE and Speech Recognition," in B. Boguraev and E. Briscoe, 1989, pp. 135–152.

N. Cercone, "Morphological Analysis and Lexicon Design for Natural-Language Processing," *Computers and the Humanities* **11**(4), 235–258 (1977).

M. Chodorow, Y. Ravin, and H. Sachar, "A Tool for Investigating the Synonymy Relation in a Sense Disambiguated Thesaurus," *Proceedings of the Second Conference on Applied Natural Language Processing,* Austin, Tex., 1988, pp. 144–151.

N. Chomsky, *Aspects of the Theory of Syntax,* MIT Press, Cambridge, Mass., 1965.

K. Church, *On Memory Limitations in Natural Language Processing,* Massachusetts Institute of Technology, Laboratory for Computer Science, Report MIT-LCS-TR-245, Cambridge, Mass., 1980.

K. Church, "Stress Assignment in Letter-to-Sound Rules for Speech Synthesis," in the *Twenty-Third Annual Meeting of the Association for Computational Linguistics: Proceedings of the Conference,* Association for Computational Linguistics, Morristown, N.J., 1985, pp. 246–254.

K. Church, "A Stochastic Parts Program and Noun Phrase Parser for Unrestricted Text," in the *Proceedings of the Second Conference on Applied Natural Language Processing,* Austin, Tex., 1988, pp. 136–143.

K. Church, W. Gale, P. Hanks, and D. Hindle, "Using Statistics in Lexical Analysis," in U. Zernick, ed., *Lexical Acquisition: Using On-Line Resources to Build a Lexicon,* Lawrence Erlbaum, Hillsdale, N.J., in press.

K. Church and P. Hanks, "Word Association Norms, Mutual Information and Lexicography," *Computat. Ling.* **16**(1), 22–29 (1990).

A. Copestake, "An Approach to Building the Hierarchical Element of a Lexical Knowledge Base from a Machine-Readable Dictionary," *Proceedings of a Workshop on Inheritance in Natural Language Processing,* Tilburg, The Netherlands, 1990, pp. 19–29.

S. Cumming, *Design of a Master Lexicon,* ISI Research Report, ISI/RR-85-163, ISI, Marina del Rey, Calif., 1986.

S. Cumming and R. Albano, *A Guide to Lexical Acquisition in the JANUS System,* ISI Research Report, ISI/RR-85-162, ISI, Marina del Rey, Calif., 1986.

W. M. P. Daelemans, "A Tool for the Automatic Creation, Extension, and Updating of Lexical Knowledge Bases," in *Proceedings of the Third European ACL,* 1987, pp. 70–74.

S. DeRose, "Grammatical Category Disambiguation by Statistical Optimization," *Computat. Ling.* **14**(1), 31–39 (1988).

E. I. Ejerhed, "Finding Clauses in Unrestricted Text by Finitary and Stochastic Methods," in *Second Conference on Applied Natural Language Processing: Proceedings of the Conference,* Association for Computational Linguistics, Morristown, N.J., 1988, pp. 219–227.

A. P. Ershov, I. A. Mel'cuk, and A. S. Nariniany, "RITA—An Experimental Man-Computer System on a Natural Language Basis," in *Advance Papers of the Fourth IJCAI,* Tbilisi, USSR, Morgan-Kaufmann, San Mateo, Calif., 1975, pp. 387–390.

R. Evans and G. Gazdar, *The DATR Papers,* Cognitive Science Research Paper No. CSRP-139, University of Sussex School of Cognitive Sciences, Brighton, UK, 1990.

M. Evens, ed., *Relational Models of the Lexicon,* Cambridge University Press, Cambridge, UK, 1988.

C. Fillmore, "Pragmatically Controlled Zero Anaphora," *BLS* **12,** 95–107 (1982).

D. Flickinger, C. Pollard, and T. Wasow, "Structure Sharing in Lexical Representation," in the *Twenty-Third Annual Meeting of the Association for Computational Linguistics: Proceedings of the Conference,* Association for Computational Linguistics, Morristown, N.J., 1985, pp. 262–267.

E. Fox, T. Nutter, T. Ahlswede, M. Evens, and J. Markowitz, "Building a Large Thesaurus for Information Retrieval," *Second Conference on Applied Natural Language Processing: Proceedings of the Conference,* Association for Computational Linguistics, Morristown, N.J., pp. 101–108.

G. Fox, "The Case for Examples," in Sinclair, 1987b, pp. 137–149.

W. Francis and H. Kučera, *Frequency Analysis of English Usage: Lexicon and Grammar,* Houghton-Mifflin, Boston, Mass., 1982.

L. Gamut, *Logic, Language and Meaning,* University of Chicago Press, Chicago, 1991.

R. Garside, G. Leech, and G. Sampson, eds., *The Computational Analysis of English: A Corpus-Based Approach,* Longman, Harlow, UK, 1987.

G. Gazdar and E. Evans, "Inference in DATR," in *Proceedings of the Fourth Conference of the European Chapter of the Association for Computational Linguistics,* 1989, pp. 66–71.

G. Gazdar, E. Klein, G. Pullum, and I. Sag, *Generalized Phrase Structure Grammar,* Basil Blackwell Publisher Ltd, Oxford, UK, 1985.

R. Grishman, "Implementation of the String Parser of English," in R. Rustin, ed., *Natural Language Processing,* Algorithmics Press, Inc., New York, 1973, pp. 89–109.

B. J. Grosz, "Transportable Natural-Language Interfaces: Problems and Techniques," in *Twentieth Annual Meeting of the Association for Computational Linguistics: Proceedings of the Conference,* Association for Computational Linguistics, Morristown, N.J., 1982, pp. 46–50.

B. J. Grosz, "TEAM, a Transportable Natural Language Interface System," *Conference on Applied Natural Language Processing: Proceedings of the Conference,* Association for Computational Linguistics, Morristown, N.J., 1983, pp. 39–45.

B. J. Grosz, D. E. Appelt, P. Martin, and F. Pereira, *TEAM: An Experiment in the Design of Transportable Natural-Language Interfaces,* SRI International Report 356, Menlo Park, Calif., 1985.

L. Guthrie, B. Slator, Y. Wilks, and R. Bruce, "Is There Contents in Empty Heads?" in *Proceedings of COLING-13,* Helsinki, Finland, 1990, pp. 138–143.

W. v. Hahn, W. Hoeppner, A. Jameson, and W. Wahlster, "The Anatomy of the Natural Language System HAM-RPM," in L. Bloc, ed., *Natural Language Based Computer Systems,* Carl Hanser Verlag, Munchen, 1980, pp. 119–253.

G. E. Heidorn, K. Jensen, L. A. Miller, R. J. Byrd, and M. S.

Chodorow, "The EPISTLE Text-Critiquing System," *IBM Sys. J.* **21**(3), 305–326 (1982).

C. T. Hemphill, J. J. Godfrey, and G. R. Doddington, "The ATIS Spoken Language Systems Pilot Corpus," in *Speech and Natural Language: Proceedings of a Workshop*, Hidden Valley, Pa., 1990, Morgan-Kaufmann, San Mateo, Calif., 1990, pp. 96–101.

D. Hindle, "Noun Classification from Predicate-Argument Structures," in *Proceedings of the Twenty-Eighth Annual Meeting of the ACL*, Vancouver, B.C., 1989, pp. 268–275.

R. J. P. Ingria, "Lexical Information for Parsing Systems: Points of Convergence and Divergence," in Walker and co-workers, in press.

R. J. P. Ingria and L. Ramshaw, "Porting to New Domains Using the Learner," in *Speech and Natural Language: Proceedings of a Workshop Held at Cape Cod, Massachusetts, October 15–18, 1989*, Morgan-Kaufmann, San Mateo, Calif., 1989, pp. 241–244.

R. Jackendoff, $\overline{X}$ *Syntax: A Study of Phrase Structure*, MIT Press, Cambridge, Mass., 1977.

J. Justeson and S. Katz, "Co-occurrences of Antonymous Adjectives and Their Contexts," *Computat. Ling.* **17**(1), in press.

R. Kaplan and J. Bresnan, "Lexical-Functional Grammar: A Formal System for Grammatical Representation," in J. Bresnan, ed., *The Mental Representation of Grammatical Relations*, MIT Press, Cambridge, Mass., 1982, pp. 173–281.

M. Kay, "Functional Grammar," in *Proceedings of the Fifth Annual Meeting of the Berkeley Linguistics Society*, Berkeley Linguistics Society, Berkeley, Calif., 1979.

S. Kuno and A. G. Oettinger, *Mathematical Linguistics and Automatic Translation to the National Science Foundation*, Report No. NSF-8, The Computation Laboratory, Harvard University, Cambridge, Mass., 1963a.

S. Kuno and A. G. Oettinger, *Volume I Mathematical Linguistics and Automatic Translation to the National Science Foundation*, Report No. NSF-9, The Computation Laboratory, Harvard University, Cambridge, Mass., 1963b.

S. Kuno and A. G. Oettinger, *Volume II Mathematical Linguistics and Automatic Translation to the National Science Foundation*, Report No. NSF-9, The Computation Laboratory, Harvard University, Cambridge, Mass., 1963c.

D. Lenat and R. Guha, *Building Large Knowledge-Based Systems*, Addison-Wesley, Reading, Mass., 1990.

B. Levin, "Building a Lexicon: The Contribution of Linguistics," in Boguraev 1991.

B. Levin, *Towards a Lexical Organization of English Verbs*, University of Chicago Press, Chicago, in press.

M. Liberman, "Text on Tap: the ACL/DCI," in *Speech and Natural Language: Proceedings of a Workshop Held at Cape Cod, Massachusetts, October 15–18, 1989*, Morgan-Kaufmann, San Mateo, Calif., pp. 173–188.

M. Liberman and D. Walker, "ACL Data Collection Initiative: First Release," in *FINITE STRING NEWSLETT.*, *Computat. Ling.* **15**(4), 46–47 (1989).

J. Lyons, *Semantics*, Cambridge University Press, Cambridge, UK, 1977.

Y. Matsumoto, K. Masaki, and H. Tanaka, "Facilities of the BUP Parsing System," in V. Dahl and P. Saint-Dizier, eds., *Natural Language Understanding and Logic Programming*, North-Holland, Amsterdam, 1985, pp. 97–106.

Y. Matsumoto, H. Tanaka, H. Hirakawa, H. Miyoshi, and H. Yasukawa, "BUP: A Bottom-Up Parser Embedded in Prolog," *New Generation Comput.* **1**(2), 145–158 (1983).

G. Miller, ed., Special issue on WORDNET, *Int. J. Lexicog.* **3**(4) (1990).

R. C. Moore, "Unification-Based Semantic Interpretation," in *Twenty-Seventh Annual Meeting of the Association for Computational Linguistics: Proceedings of the Conference*, Association for Computational Linguistics, Morristown, N.J., 1989, pp. 33–41.

S. Nirenburg, "Knowledge-Based Machine Translation," in *Machine Translation*, a special issue on knowledge-based MT **4**(1) (1989).

S. Nirenburg and L. Levin, "Knowledge Representation and Support," in *Machine Translation*, Special issue on knowledge-based MT **4**(1) (1989).

F. C. N. Pereira and S. M. Shieber, *Prolog and Natural-Language Analysis*, Center for the Study of Language and Information, Stanford, Calif., 1987.

F. C. N. Pereira and D. H. D. Warren, "Definite Clause Grammars for Language Analysis—A Survey of the Formalism and a Comparison with Augmented Transition Networks," *Artif. Intell.* **13**, 231–278 (1980).

C. Pollard and I. Sag, *Information-Based Syntax and Semantics*, CSLI Lecture Notes No. 13, Center for the Study of Language and Information, Stanford, Calif., 1987.

P. Price, W. M. Fisher, J. Bernstein, and D. S. Pallett, "The DARPA 1000-Word Resource Management Database for Continuous Speech Recognition," *IEEE International Conference Acoustics, Speech, and Signal Processing*, New York, 1988, pp. 651–654.

J. Pustejovsky, "The Generative Lexicon," *Computat. Ling.* **17**(3) (1991).

J. Pustejovsky and B. Boguraev, *Lexical Knowledge Representation and Natural Language Processing*, Technical Paper, IBM T. J. Watson Research Center, Yorktown Heights, N.Y., in press.

Y. Ravin, "Disambiguating and Interpreting Verb Definitions," in *Proceedings of the Twenty-Eighth Annual Meeting of the ACL*, Pittsburgh, Pa., 1988, pp. 260–267.

G. Ritchie, "The Lexicon," in P. Whitelock and co-workers, eds., *Linguistic Theory and Computer Applications*, Academic Press, Inc., New York, 1987, pp. 225–256.

J. J. Robinson, "DIAGRAM: A Grammar for Dialogues," *CACM* **25**(1), 27–47 (Jan. 1982).

G. J. Russell, S. G. Pulman, G. D. Ritchie, and A. W. Black, "A Dictionary and Morphological Analyser for English," in *Eleventh International Conference on Computational Linguistics: COLING '86*, University of Bonn, 1986, pp. 277–279.

N. Sager, *Natural Language Information Processing*, Addison-Wesley Publishing Co., Inc., Reading, Mass., 1981.

G. Sampson, "Probabilistic Models of Analysis," in Garside, Leech, and Sampson, 1987, pp. 16–30.

G. Sampson, "Evidence Against the Grammatical/Ungrammatical Distinction," in J. Aarts and W. Meijs, eds., *Corpus Linguistics and Beyond*, Rodopi, Amsterdam, 1990.

R. Scha and D. Stallard, "Multi-Level Plurals and Distributivity," in *Twenty-Seventh Annual Meeting of the Association for Computational Linguistics: Proceedings of the Conference*, Association for Computational Linguistics, Morristown, N.J., 1988, pp. 17–24.

Y. Schabes, A. Abeille, and A. K. Joshi, "Parsing Strategies with 'Lexicalized' Grammars: Application to Tree Adjoining Grammars," in *COLING Budapest: Proceedings of the Twelfth International Conference on Computational Linguistics*, Association for Computational Linguistics, Morristown, N.J., 1988, pp. 578–583.

S. M. Shieber, *An Introduction to Unification-Based Approaches to Grammar,* Center for the Study of Language and Information, Stanford, Calif., 1986.

S. Shieber, H. Uszkoreit, F. Pereira, J. Robinson, and M. Tyson, "The Formalism and Implementation of PATR-II," in B. J. Grosz and M. E. Stickel, eds., *Research on Interactive Acquisition and Use of Knowledge: Final Report SRI Project 1894,* SRI International, Menlo Park, Calif., 1983, pp. 39–79.

D. Shipman and V. Zue, "Properties of Large Lexicons: Implications for Advanced Isolated Word Recognition Systems," in *Proceedings of the IEEE International Conference on Acoustics, Speech and Signal Processing,* Paris, France, 1982, pp. 546–549.

J. Sinclair, ed., *The Collins COBUILD English Language Dictionary,* Collins, London, 1987a.

J. Sinclair, ed., *Looking Up: An Account of the COBUILD Project in Lexical Computing,* Collins ELT, London, 1987b.

B. Slator, "Using Context for Sense Preference," in U. Zernik, ed., *Lexical Acquisition: Using On-Line Resources to Build a Lexicon,* Lawrence Erlbaum, Hillsdale, N.J., in press.

F. Smadja, "Macrocoding the Lexicon with Co-occurrence Knowledge," in U. Zernik, ed., *Lexical Acquisition: Using On-Line Resources to Build a Lexicon,* Lawrence Erlbaum, Hillsdale, N.J., in press.

D. Stallard, "Unification-Based Semantic Interpretation in the BBN Spoken Language System," in *Speech and Natural Language: Proceedings of a Workshop Held at Cape Cod, Massachusetts, October 15–18, 1989,* Morgan-Kaufmann, San Mateo, Calif., 1989, pp. 39–46.

I. Steinacker and E. Buchberger, "Relating Syntax and Semantics: The Syntactico-Semantic Lexicon of the System VIE-LANG," in *Proceedings of the First Conference of the European Chapter of the Association for Computational Linguistics,* Pisa, Italy, 1983, pp. 96–100.

L. Streeter, "The Acoustic Determination of Phrase Boundary Perception," *J. Acoust. Soc. Am.* 64(6), 15–82 (1978).

J. Svartvik and R. Quirk, *A Corpus of English Conversation,* Lund Studies in English 56, GWK Gleerup, Lund, 1980.

L. Taylor, C. Grover, and E. Briscoe, "The Syntactic Regularity of English Noun Phrases," in *Proceedings of the Fourth Conference of the European Chapter of the ACL,* Manchester, UK, 1989, pp. 256–263.

B. van Berkel and K. DeSmedt, "Triphone Analysis: A Combined Method for the Correction of Orthographical and Typographical Errors," in *Proceedings of the Second Conference on Applied Natural Language Processing,* Austin, Tex., 1988, pp. 77–83.

D. Walker, A. Zampolli, and N. Calzolari, eds., *Automating the Lexicon: Research and Practice in a Multilingual Environment,* Oxford University Press, Oxford, UK, in press.

S. Warwick-Armstrong, ed., Special issue on computational linguistics using large corpora, *Comput. Ling.* 18 (in press).

M. Webster and M. Marcus, "Automatic Acquisition of the Lexical Semantics of Verbs from Sentence Frames," in *Proceedings of the Twenty-Seventh Annual Meeting of the ACL,* Vancouver, B.C., Canada, 1989, pp. 177–184.

E. Wehrli, *A Government-Binding Parser for French,* Working Paper No. 48, Institut pour les Études Semantiques et Cognitives, Universite de Geneve, Geneva, Switzerland, 1984.

E. Wehrli, "Design and Implementation of a Lexical Data Base," in *Proceedings of the Second Conference of the European Chapter of the Association for Computational Linguistics,* Geneva, Switzerland, 1985, pp. 146–153.

R. M. Weischedel, R. Bobrow, D. Ayuso, and L. Ramshaw, "Probability in the JANUS Natural Language Interface," in *Speech and Natural Language: Proceedings of a Workshop Held at Philadelphia, Pennsylvania, February 21–23, 1989,* Morgan-Kaufmann, San Mateo, Calif., 1989, pp. 112–117.

Y. Wilks, D. Fass, C.-M. Guo, J. McDonald, T. Plate, and B. Slator, "Providing Machine Tractable Dictionary Tools," in J. Pustejovsky, ed., *Semantics and the Lexicon,* Kluwer, Dordrecht, in press.

W. A. Woods, "Progress in Natural Language Understanding: An Application to Lunar Geology," in *AFIPS Conference Proceedings,* Vol. 42, 1973, pp. 441–450.

W. A. Woods, R. M. Kaplan, and B. Nash-Webber, *The Lunar Sciences Natural Language System: Final Report,* BBN Report No. 2378, Bolt Beranek and Newman Inc., Cambridge, Mass., 1972.

W. A. Woods and co-workers, *Natural Language Communication with Computers, Final Report, Vol. 1, Speech and Understanding Research at BBN,* BBN Report 2976, Bolt Beranek and Newman, Inc., Cambridge, Mass., 1974.

ROBERT INGRIA
BBN Systems and Technologies Corp.

BRAN BOGURAEV
IBM T. J. Watson Research Center

JAMES PUSTEJOVSKY
Brandeis University

DISCOURSE UNDERSTANDING

The term discourse understanding refers to all processes of natural language understanding (qv) that attempt to understand a text or dialogue. For such processes, the sentences of natural language are elements whose significance resides in the contribution they make to the development of a larger whole, rather than being independent, isolated units of meaning. To understand discourse, it is necessary to track the structure of an unfolding text or dialogue, and interpret every new utterance with respect to the proper context—taking into account the real-world setting of the utterance as well as the linguistic context built up by the utterances preceding it (see also SPEECH UNDERSTANDING). The problems of discourse understanding are thus closely related to those dealt with in the linguistic discipline of pragmatics, which studies the context dependence of utterance meanings.

Research on natural language understanding systems has often focused on the problem of analyzing the structure and meaning of isolated sentences. To deal with discourse instead, a system must have all the capabilities necessary for sentence understanding as well as be able to apply rules of discourse structure that specify how sentences may be combined to form texts or dialogues.

Even with such discourse-level extensions, however, a purely linguistic approach can only construct the meaning of a text insofar as it follows from the meaning of its constituent utterances and the explicitly stated relations between them. In AI the tendency is to take a broader perspective, which emphasizes the role of world knowledge in discourse understanding. By taking into account commonsense knowledge about the world, a system may derive semantic relations between constituents of the text that are not stated explicitly but that may be plausibly assumed. By invoking scripts (qv) and frames (qv), a system may analyze a text against the background of default assumptions about normal situations and normal courses of events, thereby filling in information left implicit in the text, and also noticing when something deviates from the usual pattern and is, therefore, worthy of special attention. In this way, a more complete understanding of the intended meaning of the text may be created.

A discourse understanding system worthy of that name should not only deal correctly with what is true or false in the world according to its input text, but should, at the same time, be able to distinguish between more and less important information, between what is crucial and what is mere background. With this capacity, a system would be able to generate adequate summaries of its input texts. A further level of understanding would involve the ability to infer what the point of a story or description is, to discover the more abstract, culturally relevant message that is instantiated by the text.

Much of the AI research on discourse understanding is oriented toward the development of systems to exhibit reasonable and cooperative behavior in a goal-directed interaction with a human-dialogue partner. Such systems would do more than understand the literal meanings of the utterances of their interlocutor; they would have to be able to assess, to some extent, the intentions and purposes behind these utterances. Methods to achieve this are usually based on the theory of speech acts (qv): the system recognizes the goals that are conventionally associated with various types of utterance, such as assertions, questions, commands, and requests. Understanding an utterance at a deeper level is then viewed as establishing what goal the speaker wanted to achieve by performing the speech act and what role the speech act plays in achieving that goal. Often the goal can be seen as a subgoal that plays a role in achieving a higher level goal, and so on. By invoking plausible hypotheses about the goals the speaker may have, and about the methods employed to achieve them, a system may infer the intention behind a speech act.

Empirical studies of human discourse usually deal with real-time oral communication or with written texts. Discourse understanding computer programs, however, will usually employ a video display terminal to communicate with their users in real time. They will thus use a new natural language interaction mode that did not exist before. It is, therefore, of some interest to study how the properties of discourse depend on the interaction mode, ie, on the amount of shared environment between the participants and on the sensory modality of the communication medium.

Each of the main topics mentioned above are discussed below in some detail: the structure of discourse, the semantics of discourse, speech acts and pragmatics, and different I/O modalities.

THE STRUCTURE OF DISCOURSE

Introduction

To understand a text or dialogue, one must understand the relations between its parts. Clearly, these parts are not just the individual sentences; sentences are joined together to form larger units, which in their turn may be the building blocks of yet larger units. It is important to discern these units correctly, because a discourse may assert specific semantic relations between the meanings of its constituent units: the content of one discourse segment may, for instance, present a more detailed version, a justification, or a series of consequences of an adjacent discourse segment. The structure of a discourse also affects the interpretation of the individual sentences: it defines the semantic contexts that must be invoked in order to determine the interpretation of a pronoun, a definite description, or, in fact, any descriptive term.

The formal description of the structure of spontaneous spoken discourse is even more complex than the formal description of the structure of written text. Everyday spoken discourse is characterized by interruptions, resumptions, backtracking, and jumping ahead. Somehow, despite the apparent disfluency of everyday discourse, speakers and hearers manage to follow what is going on and to produce responses that are situationally appropriate and demonstrate an understanding of all of the underspecified items of meaning that are found in sentences.

Faced with the transcripts of a natural interaction, it is surprisingly difficult to identify the descriptions, explanations, stories, plans, or other structural units that may have been there when the interaction was happening. With the move to the analysis phase, structural units become lost in all the talk.

The problem of locating a coherent discourse semantic unit in natural talk is illustrated by the following example from a corpus of spatial planning dialogues. There are five people involved: two primary speakers, A and B, who are jointly playing a game that involves a journey in Europe; C and D who are researchers; and E who is a secretary who came by.

A: We are in Spain, OK. So, let's go to France next. I love France anyway. We had a great time there last year. And then Italy; did I tell you about the little restaurant we went to in Florence?

B: Yeah. I think you did. It was better than the place in Rome we ate at before we took the plane. But, anyway, no. Let's go to Belgium next. Then—

C: Could you move closer to the camera, please.

D: You're out of range.

A: OK, yeah. But not if we have to go through Antwerp.

B: Then Holland.

A: When do we do Italy then? We can't miss it?

B: On the way back to—

E: Sorry. I was looking for Dave.

C: He's not here. We're running an experiment, I'll talk

to you later. You are still out of camera range, by the way.

A: Good.

B: Anyway. I saw the tulips last year. What about Italy?

A: On the way back to Spain. You taking a vacation this year? Or loafing at work as usual?

B: Haven't decided, you?

A: Might go to Spain again. Then Germany's next, right?

Competent language users would intuitively segment this discourse into sections in which A and B are planning (actually developing their plan) and other sections where they are commenting on places they have been, making small talk, or conversing with the researchers. In one exchange, neither A nor B are talking at all, but are listening in while C exchanges some quick words with the secretary who is looking for someone who is not there. In order to make it somewhat easier to find the planning, the text may be arranged graphically as an outline, showing the planning talk in leftmost position and moving farther to the right to represent the embedded or secondary status of the comments and other interruptions to the development of the plan. It should be noted that when other types of talk are completed, A and B return to developing the plan, which remains their central concern throughout this excerpt

A: We are in Spain, OK.
So, let's go to France next.
I love France anyway.
We had a great time there last year.
And then Italy;
Did I tell you about the little restaurant we went to in Florence?

B: Yeah.
I think you did.
It was better than the place in Rome we ate at before we took the plane.
(But, anyway, no.)
Let's go to Belgium next.
Then—

C: Could you move closer to the camera, please.

D: You're out of range.

A: OK, yeah.
But not if we have to go through Antwerp

B: Then Holland.

A: When do we do Italy then?
We can't miss it?

B: On the way back to—

E: Sorry.
I was looking for Dave.

C: He's not here.
We're running an experiment
I'll talk to you later.
You are still out of camera range, by the way.

B: (Anyway.)
I saw the tulips last year.
What about Italy?

A: On the way back to Spain.
You taking a vacation this year?
Or loafing at work as usual?

B: Haven't decided, you?

A: Might go to Spain again.
Then Germany's next, right?

Once the correct structural relations between the sentences in the discourse are established, it is possible to determine the semantic interpretation of the individual sentences, and of the discourse segments built up out of these sentences. Methods for determining discourse structure and for building up semantic representations are discussed in more detail below.

Many important phenomena that demonstrate the influence of discourse structure on semantic interpretation are illustrated by the example discourse above:

Appropriate material must be available to resolve ellipsis. ("Did I tell you about the little restaurant we went to in Florence?" "Yeah. I think you did ϕ.")

Appropriate candidate referents must be available to resolve anaphora. ("Did I tell you about the little restaurant we went to in Florence?" "Yeah. I think you did. It was better than the place in Rome we ate at before we took the plane.")

Temporal reference points must be maintained and, if necessary, updated (to understand when events are asserted to take place).

Spatial reference points must be maintained and, if necessary, updated (to understand the speaker's orientation in conceptual space).

The identity of the speaker and hearer must be available (to recover the intended referents of *I* and *you*).

The specific world in which events are asserted to take place must be known. In the example it is necessary to distinguish between the game world and the real world: A is planning to vacation in Spain this year in the real world and had a great time in France last year in the real world. In the game world, A and B are in Spain and planning a trip from Spain to France, Belgium etc.

In addition, it must be pointed out that correctly interpreting this discourse involves understanding the form and function of a number of linguistic and rhetorical structures, including

Narrative syntax mechanisms, encoding update of temporal and spatial reference points.

Sentential syntax and semantics.

Question–answer sequences.

Discourse operators such as *OK, yes, no, well,* and *anyway*, which do not add independent information but that either (1) affirm or deny information available elsewhere or (2) indicate a digression or a return to another topic.

Joking conventions (such as insulting a hard worker by accusing him of loafing on the job).

Discourse embedding and return conventions.

Recent Directions in Modeling Discourse Structure

Recent advances in understanding the structure of natural language discourse make it possible to segment complex talk and recover the integrity of discourse units despite the complexity of the actual talk in which they occur. An important research focus in the late 1980s has been to capture the semantic, or coherence relations among the clauses and text segments that function together to communicate a set of mutually interconnected ideas (Halliday and Hasan, 1977; Hobbs, 1979, 1985; Mann and Thompson, 1983; Polanyi, 1985a). A second research focus has been to understand the structural relations obtaining even in discourses that are not coherent but that are characterized by interruptions, resumptions, hesitations, and other complex phenomena arising from the social and processing constraints on actual talk (Reichman, 1981; Polanyi and Scha, 1984; Grosz and Sidner, 1986; Hinrichs and Polanyi, 1986).

Some discussions of coherence relations in discourse are reviewed below. The following sections discuss some frameworks that attempt to characterize the structure of discourse, accounting for coherence and also allowing for digressions and interruptions.

Discourse Coherence. It has been observed many times that not every sequence of sentences makes up a text. In a well-formed text, the sentences are perceived as working together to build up a unified whole, by expressing propositions that are related to each other in a limited number of specific ways.

A number of coherence relations that may obtain among the constituents of a well-formed text have been identified, for instance, by Hobbs (1979, 1985). He describes how a semantic structure for a whole discourse may be built up recursively by recognizing coherence relations obtaining between adjacent segments of a text. He addresses himself initially to why it is that discourses are coherent at all; what are the sources of discourse coherence? Not surprisingly, the ultimate sources of discourse coherence lies in the coherence of the world or object described. A text can be found to be coherent if it talks about a set of objects or states or events that are known to be coherent. Thus even a gasped out, jumbled narrative of a disaster may appear coherent and be understandable when one brings to the text the belief that the disaster formed a coherent set of events, related causally to one another and affecting in various ways the people, objects, and situations described. Discourse coherence in the usual, more narrow sense of the word refers to conventional semantic relation obtaining between adjacent discourse segments. For instance, a sequence of two sentences, two stories, or, generally speaking, two discourse constituents are found to be coherently related to one another if one gives more detail about the other, offers an

explanation, or otherwise gives more information about the proposition expressed by the other.

Hobbs provides a method for allowing the coherence relations in a discourse to emerge. He suggests segmenting the discourse in an intuitive way and then labeling the various naturally occurring segments with the coherence relation(s) that tie them to immediately preceding constituents. There are two types of relation: coordination and subordination relations. Coordinate coherence relations include parallel constructions and elaborations in which a common proposition is discovered as the assertion of the composite segment. Subordination relations obtain when one constituent provides background or explanatory information with respect to another. Hobbs's ideas of coherence make it possible to see how even the subsequent moves in a conversation, which may appear incoherent to an outside observer, may be appropriate conversational moves for the participants, entirely coherent and describable with the relations that he has outlined (Hobbs and Evans, 1980; Hobbs and Agar, 1985).

Mann and Thompson's (1983) work on rhetorical relations focuses exclusively on the relations that obtain within a coherent text. They assign a phrase-structure analysis to texts in which two subsequent constituents can be related through each of a number of specific relations. Their inventory of coherence relations is more detailed than that provided by Hobbs. It lists solutionhood, evidence, justification, motivation, reason, sequence, enablement, elaboration, restatement, condition, circumstance, cause, concession, background, and thesis–antithesis.

Discourse Structure and Pronoun Resolution. In early work on the structure of task oriented dialogues, Grosz (1974) provided an important demonstration of the hierarchical structure of natural texts. In the analysis of talk between an apprentice and an expert repairing an air compressor, she showed that the discourse could be represented as a tree or outline in which the relationships among the clauses could be chunked in a way that replicated the goal/subgoal structure of the original task. Perhaps not surprisingly, in taking apart one part of the compressor, the talk would focus on that operation; when the apprentice had finished dealing with that aspect of the job, and moved on to the next subtask, the talk would move along, reflecting in its structure what was going on in the joint endeavor. What was surprising, and most significant, however, was that the choice of possible referents for pronouns in the text reflected the structure of the task as well. In discussing a part of the object involved in the task at hand, it was possible to refer to it with a pronoun; similarly the entire higher level unit could be referred to with a pronoun, and even the compressor as a whole. It was not possible to use a pronoun to refer to the objects and subtasks involved in a part of the task that had already been completed. In the tree of the discourse task/subtask elements one was blocked from referring to a task element in a branch to the left of the branch currently being developed. Grosz's discovery, therefore, was that discourse has a structure in which the placement and semantic relations obtaining among the clauses making up the discourse plays a decisive role in the interpretation of given elements in that discourse.

Sidner (1983) has shown that a structurally analogous account of anaphora resolution also applies at a linguistic level of discourse structure that is independent of task structure. In her model the candidates for anaphoric reference are stored in a stack. An incoming discourse constituent that is treated as subordinated *PUSHes* new focused elements onto this stack, while the resumption of a suspended discourse constituent *POPs* the intervening focus elements off the stack.

The following sections present brief overviews of three frameworks that build on this seminal work and that try to provide more comprehensive accounts of the issues involved in understanding both coherent and interrupted discourse: contest space theory (Reichman, 1981), discourse structures theory (Grosz and Sidner, 1986), and dynamic discourse model (Polanyi, 1985a; Polanyi and Scha, 1984; Hinrichs and Polanyi, 1986).

Context Space Theory. Context space theory deals with the structure of conversation (Reichman, 1981). It associates with each topic of discussion a context space, a schematic structure with a number of slots. These slots hold the following information:

A propositional representation of the set of functionally related utterances said to lie in this context space.

The communicative function served by the utterances in this context space.

A marker reflecting the foreground–background status of this context space at any given point in the conversation.

Focus level assignments to the discourse elements in this context space.

Links to preceding context spaces in relation to which this context space was developed.

Specification of the relations involved.

The utterances that constitute the discourse are analyzed as conversational moves that affect the content of the various context spaces. Reichman has paid special attention to the conversational structures involved in arguments. Among the conversational moves she identifies, for instance, are assertion of a claim, explanation, illustration, support, challenge, interruption, and further development.

An important and influential part of Reichman's theory is her treatment of clue words: devices that speakers use to indicate when their discourse shifts from one structural level to another. Clue words are commonly divided into PUSH-markers and POP-markers. PUSH-markers are linguistic signals that indicate the initiation of a new embedded discourse constituent. Examples are *like, by the way,* and *for instance.* POP-markers have the complementary function. They close off the currently active embedded unit and signal a return to a higher level of structure. Examples are *Well, so, anyway,* and *OK.*

An extensive study of clue words in spoken French has been presented (Guelich, 1970) as well as one for English

(Schiffrin, 1982). The use of *OK* in service encounters has been discussed (Merritt, 1978). Cohen (1984) studied clue words from a computational perspective. She drew two important conclusions:

Clue words decrease the amount of processing needed to understand coherent discourse.

Clue words allow the understanding of discourse that would otherwise be incomprehensible.

Although Reichman's work provided much important insight into the functioning of discourse, her context space formalism fails to distinguish between those cases in which a previous topic can be returned to by use of a simple POP and those cases in which such a simple purely structural return is not possible and the topic must be reintroduced in order to continue talking about it. Reichman's context spaces are never closed off and inaccessible because people can always say anything they wish and continuing to talk about a matter dropped earlier always remains possible. Discourse structural relations, in her account, are thus finally obscured by discourse semantic relations obtaining among the topics of talk in the various units.

The work of both Grosz and Sidner (1986) and Polanyi and Scha (Polanyi, 1985a; Polanyi and Scha, 1984; Hinrichs and Polanyi, 1986) incorporates elements of Reichman's work, particularly her treatment of clue words and separates structural and semantic relations between clauses. This separation allows for a treatment of interruptions and resumptions that is based on structural properties of the discourse rather than being dependent on semantic relationships among topics of talk. These two frameworks generalize on Grosz's early work by providing an account of discourse structure that is not task dependent.

The Discourse Structures Theory

In the view of Grosz and Sidner (1986) the structure of a discourse results from three interacting components: a linguistic structure, an intentional structure, and an attentional state. These three components deal with different aspects of the utterances in a discourse. Grosz and Sidner have particularly focused on the intentional and the attentional aspects of discourse.

The intentional structure is a hierarchical structure that describes relations between the purpose of the discourse and the purpose of discourse segments. These purposes (such as "intend that a particular agent perform a particular task" or "intend that particular agent believe a particular fact") are linked by relations of dominance (between a goal and a subgoal) or ordering (between two goals that must be achieved in a specific order).

The attentional state is an abstraction of the participants' focus of attention as their discourse unfolds. The attentional state is a property of discourse, not of discourse participants. It is inherently dynamic, recording the object, properties, and relations that are salient at each point in the discourse. The attentional state is represented by a stack of focus spaces. Changes in attentional state are modeled by a set of transition rules that specify the conditions for adding and deleting spaces.

A focus space is associated with each discourse segment; this space contains those entities that are salient, either because they have been mentioned explicitly in the segment or because they became salient in the process of producing or comprehending the utterances in the segment, as in Grosz's original work on focusing (Cullingford, 1981). The focus space also includes the discourse segment purpose; this reflects the fact that the discourse participants are focused not only on what they are talking about but also on why they are talking about it.

Discourse structures theory provides a unified account of both the intentional and attentional dimensions of discourse understanding and makes explicit important links between the two. The dynamic discourse model, on the other hand, is more limited in its scope. It provides an account of the discourse segmentation process on an utterance by utterance basis and is thus a more developed theory of the strictly linguistic aspects of the discourse understanding process.

The Dynamic Discourse Model. The dynamic discourse model (DDM) (Polanyi, 1985a; Polanyi and Scha, 1984; Hinrichs and Polanyi, 1986) is a formal theory of discourse syntactic and semantic structure that account for how a semantic and pragmatic interpretation of a discourse may be incrementally built up from its constituent clauses.

The DDM is presented as a discourse parser. The parser segments the discourse into linguistically and socially relevant units on a clause by clause basis by proceeding through the discourse, examining the syntactic encoding form of each clause, its propositional content, and its situation of utterance.

The model consists of a set of recursive rules of discourse formation, which specifies how units may be built up of smaller units, and a set of semantic interpretation rules, which assigns a semantic and pragmatic interpretation to each clause, to each discourse unit, and to the discourse as a whole.

Each discourse is viewed as composed of discourse units that can be of many different types: jokes, stories, plans, question–answer sequences, lists, narratives (temporally ordered lists), and speech events (socially situated occasions of talk such as doctor—patient interactions and everyday conversations) (see "Speech Events," below). In the DDM every discourse unit type is associated with its own grammar that specifies its characteristic constituent structure and is interpreted according to specific rules of semantic interpretation.

The basic unit of discourse formation is the discourse constituent unit (DCU). For the purpose of joining with other clauses to create a complex discourse, each clause is considered an elementary DCU. DCUs are of three types: list structures (including narratives, which are sequentially ordered lists of events); expansion structures, in which one unit gives more detail of some sort about some aspect of a preceding unit, and binary structures such as *if/then, and, or,* and *but,* relations in which there is a logical connective connecting the constituents.

Discourse units (DUs) such as stories, descriptions, arguments, and plans are composed of DCUs that encode the propositions, which taken together and properly interpreted communicate elaborate semantic structures.

DCUs and DUs in their turn are the means of realization of the information exchange that is so basic in speech events, which are constituents of interactions.

The DDM provides an account of the coherence relations in texts by means of an explicit mechanism for computing the semantic congruence and structural appropriateness of strings of clauses (Polanyi, 1985a; Hinrichs and Polanyi, 1986). Simultaneously, it provides an account of the complexities of interrupted or highly attenuated discourse by providing a uniform treatment of all phenomena that can interrupt the completion of an ongoing DU: elaborations on a point just made, digressions to discuss something else, interruptions of one speech event by another or one ongoing interaction by another. All of these phenomena are treated as subordinated or embedded relative to activities that continue the development of an ongoing unit, whether it be a list of some sort, a story, or a speech event or interaction.

The structure that results from the recursive embedding and sequencing of discourse units with respect to one another has the form of a tree. This discourse history parse tree contains, at any moment in the discourse, a record of which units of what types have been completed, and which, having been interrupted before completion, remain to be completed.

To determine at which level of the discourse parse tree an incoming clause is to be added as a subordinated or coordinated constituent, a logical expression representing the meaning of the clause is constructed (note that this expression may still contain semantically undetermined, anaphoric elements.) On the basis of this expression, it can be computed whether the preconditions for attachment at any given level are fulfilled. Attachment at the lowest level is tried first: the system investigates the plausibility of a meaningful subordination or coordination relation between the incoming clause and the previous clause; then, relations at successively higher levels in the tree are considered. If no meaningful relation can be established at any level, the incoming clause is attached at the lowest level as a semantically unrelated interruption. If PUSH- or POP-markers occur, the discourse–parsing process takes them into account in the appropriate way.

Interruptions are accommodated in the tree as discourse embeddings in a way not dissimilar to their treatment in the discourse structures theory. However, in order to accommodate the fact that what may be an interruption to one participant, or from the point of view of one interaction, may be the ongoing discourse from another perspective; each participant in a discourse is associated with a unique discourse parse tree representing the individual's incremental analysis of the discourse. The degree to which participants' trees are identical determines their ability to understand each other's references to underdetermined elements in the discourse such as pronominals, deictics, or definite noun phrases.

The structural aspects of the DDM just discussed are related to the enterprise of developing an adequate discourse semantics, one that would allow the meaning of a discourse to be built up on a left to right basis along with the structural analysis of the discourse. Developing such a compositional semantics for discourse presupposes adequate ways of representing the semantics of both sentences and discourse, as well as effective ways of dealing with the context dependence of utterance meanings.

THE MEANINGS OF THE TEXT

Truth Conditions for Sentence and Text

Semantic studies in philosophic logic have focused on one important aspect of the meaning of indicative sentences: the truth conditions of the sentence, ie, a characterization of what must be the case in the world for the sentence to be seen as true rather than false. The truth conditions of a sentence can be mathematically described as a function from states of affairs to truth values. Logical languages, such as first-order predicate calculus or intensional logic, provide formulas for expressing such functions. (In an extensional logic, states of affairs are represented by models of the logical language; in an intensional logic, they are represented by elementary entities called possible worlds.)

This logical perspective on sentence meaning has had considerable influence in linguistics and AI. Many theories and systems account for the way in which the truth conditions of a sentence depend on its surface form, by providing a definition or procedure that translates a sentence into a formula of a logical language. The same paradigm can be applied to texts consisting of more than one sentence, because a report or description may also be said to be understood (though in a limited sense) by someone who knows what state of affairs in the world would make it true.

Carrying over the logical perspective on meaning from the sentence level to the text level raises the question how to build up a logical representation for the truth conditions of a text out of the logical representation of the truth conditions of its constituent utterances. To do this, a text-understanding program must be able to recognize the structure of a text, and to apply semantic operations that build meanings at the levels above the sentence. It must also deal correctly with the sentence-level text constituents; instead of analyzing the meaning of isolated, independent sentences, it must determine the meaning of particular utterances of sentences, taking into account the context that has been set up by the previous discourse.

Processing an individual utterance in a discourse thus entails three distinct operations:

Determining the utterance meaning in the applicable context.

Integrating the utterance meaning with the meaning of the text as processed so far.

Updating the context setting that will be used to interpret the next utterance.

The context-dependence of utterance interpretation is shown by several difficult phenomena. For instance, tem-poral, locative, or conditional interpretive frameworks may be introduced in the first sentence of a discourse segment and have scope over all other constituents of that segment. The reference time in a narrative moves on as the narrative proceeds (Polanyi and Scha, 1984; Kamp, 1979; Hinrichs, 1986). Anaphoric expressions may refer from a subordinate constituent to entities introduced by its superordinate constituent, or from a constituent of a coordinate paragraph to certain entities introduced by an earlier constituent of that same paragraph.

Consequences for Logical Formalisms

Context-Dependence. The context-dependence of utterance meanings in discourse can be dealt with by translating a sentence not directly into a proposition, but into a function from contexts to propositions, where by context is meant a data structure that contains all the relevant information that may influence sentence interpretation: speaker, addressee, speech time, speech location, reference time, candidates for anaphoric reference, topic, etc. Formally, contexts are very similar to indices as employed in Montague's (1968) systems (Bennett, 1978). The meaning of a particular utterance of a sentence is then constructed by evaluating the sentence meaning with respect to the proper context.

In processing an utterance, a discourse-understanding system must, therefore, determine what its proper context is and also how this utterance may create a new context, or modify existing ones, for the interpretation of subsequent utterances. Polanyi and Scha (1984) propose to use Woods's (1970) augmented transition network formalism to formulate a recursive definition of discourse constituent structure that is coupled with semantic rules that build up meaning representations for discourse constituent units; the register mechanism of the ATN is used to keep track of the correct contexts in this process (see GRAMMAR, AUG-MENTED-TRANSITION-NETWORK).

Discourse Anaphora

Beyond adopting a Montague-style context mechanism, some other departures from standard logical practice may be necessary to build up meaning representations for texts from meaning representations for sentences. Observations on anaphoric reference in discourse have motivated some proposals for significant innovations in representational formalisms, especially concerning the representation of the denotation of indefinite noun phrases. Several authors including Karttunen (1976) have argued that indefinite noun phrases should be translated into "indefinite entities" of some sort, as opposed to existential quantifiers. For instance,

John loves a woman.

would not be represented as

Ex: Woman (x) *and* Love (J, x)

but rather as

Woman (*u*) *and* Love (*J, u*)

where *u* is a Skolem-constant, a constant whose denotation is undetermined, therefore behaving, for all practical purposes, like a variable that is implicitly existentially quantified. Leaving the existential quantifier implicit has an advantage when dealing with discourse anaphora.

John loves a woman. Her name is Mary.

This sentence can be treated simply by conjoining the formula for "Her name is Mary" with the one for "John loves a woman," while resolving the pronoun *her* to corefer with the constant for *a woman*:

(Woman (*u*) *and* Love (*J, u*)) *and* name (*u*) = "Mary"

This procedure does not work if indefinite noun phrases are represented by existential quantifiers:

(Ex: Woman (*x*) *and* Love (*J, x*)) *and* name (*x*) = "Mary"

is infelicitous because a variable is used outside the scope of its defining occurrence.

The perspective just sketched has been pushed furthest in a formalism devised by Kamp (1979). The formulas used in this formalism are called discourse representation structures (DRS). They serve the role of logical formulas, representing the meaning of the text so far, as well as the role of contexts which set up the right reference times and anaphoric reference candidates for the interpretation of next utterances.

DRS differ from ordinary logical formulas in the way variables are used (see SEMANTIC NETWORKS). A DRS is defined to be true if it is embeddable in a model that corresponds to the actual world. Embeddability of DRS is recursively defined on the structure of the formulas.

An alternative approach to the problem of discourse anaphora is described by Webber (1982), where the representation of sentence meanings is separated from the representation of evoked entities.

Background Knowledge and Plausible Inferences

Understanding a text involves much more than understanding the literal meanings of its constituent utterances and their explicitly stated relations. The message of a text is rarely completely explicit: the author relies on the fact that the hearer–reader will integrate the meanings of the utterances with an independently given set of background assumptions about the domain and about the author. All implications that follow in a simple and direct way from the combination of the explicit utterances and the presupposed background knowledge are considered to be implicit in the text.

For a system to be capable of discourse understanding in this more extended sense, its mechanisms must be augmented with a representation of the required background knowledge, and with a system that performs inferences on the basis of explicit text meanings and background knowledge, generating representations of information that was implicit in the text. Different kinds of background information play a role. Ideally, a discourse understanding system should have a rather rich, encyclopedic knowledge base, or at least, a knowledge base comparable to the user's for the pertinent domain; and it should have particularly good coverage in knowledge that people consider common sense. How to model commonsense domains has, therefore, become a research area in itself (Charniak, 1977; Hobbs and Moore, 1985) (see REASONING, COMMON-SENSE).

An important set of background assumptions that has received a lot of attention concerns the characters in stories: unless told otherwise, story recipients must assume the characters to be normal, rational, purposeful people, and they must bring these assumptions to bear on the text to make sense of it. Various systems have been built that embody some knowledge of this sort and bring it to bear on the discourse understanding process.

SAM (qv) (Cullingford, 1981, 1978; Schank and Abelson, 1977), for instance, is a system for understanding narratives that is based on the notion of scripts (qv). A script is a knowledge structure that represents a stereotypical sequence of events, such as taking a bus, going to a movie theater, or going to a restaurant for dinner. SAM's representation of a script consists of a set of simple actions described as conceptual dependency structures, together with the causal connections between those actions. The actions in a script are further organized into a sequence of scenes, which in the case of the restaurant script includes entering the restaurant, ordering food, eating, paying, and leaving. Each script also has a set of roles and props characterizing the people and objects that are expected to appear in the sequence of events.

In processing a narrative about eating in a restaurant, SAM first must recognize that the restaurant script is the relevant context for interpreting the narrative. Once the script is chosen, SAM will try to interpret each new sentence as part of that script. It does this by matching the conceptual representation of the new sentence against the actions represented in the script. When it finds a match, it incorporates the sentence meaning into its representation of the narrative. It also fills in the script actions preceding the one matched. By this process, SAM infers actions that are implicit in the narrative it is reading. Thus when it reads the narrative:

John went to the Fisherman's Grotto for dinner. He ordered lobster. The bill was outrageous.

it includes in its representation that John actually ate his lobster, that he received a large bill, and that he paid it.

A later system, FRUMP (qv) (DeJong, 1979a, 1979b), pushes the idea of expectation-driven understanding a little further and dispenses with script-independent meaning representations altogether; it parses its input text directly into script slots, and anything that does not fit is ignored. (FRUMP is presented as a model of human text skimming.) IPP (Sidner and Israel, 1981; Levin and Moore, 1977) in its turn modifies the FRUMP approach by mixing script-based text skimming with a somewhat more careful semantic analysis of selected parts of the text. Its meaning representations contain not only scripts with filled-in slots, but also representations of unexpected events.

In a realistic application of the script approach, the scripts to be invoked must be selected from thousands of candidates; SAM chose from only three or four candidates. Furthermore, it will be necessary to drop SAM's assumption that each script contains one event that is always explicitly mentioned in the text in order to invoke the script. The task of finding which of the many candidate scripts matches the input sequence best, thus presents computational problems which deserve further study.

The idea of a script is usually associated with the description of predefined sequences of events that constitute the building blocks of everyday life. Almost by definition, scripts are not sufficient to understand interesting stories. Real stories tend to involve somewhat more complex plots, arising from conflicts between the perceptions, ideas and goals of the different characters. A program that interprets its input reports in terms of the goals and subgoals of the protagonist, is PAM (qv) (plan applier mechanism), designed by Wilensky (1981).

Later work derives plot structure from interacting plans, that is, plans involving two or more participants in cooperative or competitive interaction. Such plans differ from single-participant plans in several ways (Bruce, 1986); the most significant being that they are produced, interpreted, and executed in a belief context, ie, what participants believe about the interaction is significant, rather than any putative objective account of the events.

Thus, for example, in order for a system to make sense of a children's story such as "Hansel and Gretel," it must monitor the evolution of the children's, the parents', and the witch's beliefs about events as well as the events themselves (Bruce and Newman, 1978). When the parents tell the children that the family is going to "fetch wood," the system must note that the actions the parents subsequently take are designed to be interpretable by the children as simple wood fetching, but are simultaneously effecting the abandonment of Hansel and Gretel. Moreover, it must be able to compute embedded beliefs, eg, the parents do not know that Hansel has overheard their plan and hence that he believes that they intend him to believe the actions contribute to wood fetching, but in fact are intended to lead to his and Gretel's death. Central to this belief monitoring is the computation of mutual belief (Cohen, 1984; Bruce and Newman, 1978; Allen, 1979), ie, those beliefs fully shared and known to be shared among the participants (see BELIEF REPRESENTATION SYSTEMS).

Mechanisms for interacting plans calculations have been outlined in some detail (Bruce and Newman, 1978), but not fully implemented in any current systems. Analyses in terms of interacting plans have proved useful in studies of conversations (Bruce, 1986), classroom interactions, skits (Newman and Bruce, 1986), and written stories (Bruce and Newman, 1978; Bruce, 1980a, 1980b).

Summarizing Stories

Understanding a story as a communicative object requires more than dealing with its explicit content and the associated plausible inferences. When someone tells a story, not all the information reported is equally important. Truly understanding the story would mean, among other things, being able to see the distinctions between more important and less important information. Evidence of this kind of understanding would be a system's capability to generate adequate summaries of input texts.

Many approaches to the story summarization problem have been proposed. Four of them are discussed below; they are based, respectively, on surface text phenomena, on plot structure, on affective dynamics, and on the author–reader relationship.

The first approach implements the ideas formulated by Polanyi concerning the way in which human storytellers encode their information. She maintains that people explicitly mark the relative salience of different pieces of information in a text; they make sure that an important piece of information stands out against the surrounding information. They do this by means of various evaluative devices: metacomments, explicit markers, repetition, and the use of encoding forms that deviate from the local norm in the text (long vs short sentences; direct discourse vs narrated events; colloquial vs formal register, etc) (Polanyi, 1985b).

Based on these ideas, a system was developed that simply counts the number of evaluative devices used to highlight each proposition in a story and then puts the most highly evaluated states and the most highly evaluated events together in a summary of the input story. The system thus manages to construct a reasonable summary on the basis of the surface appearance of the story, without understanding it in any sense; it shows that it is necessary to be careful in ascribing understanding capabilities to a system that performs a specific task.

The relevant work on plot structure originates with Propp (1968) and Rumelhart (1975). Lehnert and co-workers developed a summarization algorithm based on the causal relations between the events and states reported in a story (Lehnert, 1981, 1983; Lehnert and co-workers, 1981; Lehnert and Loiselle, 1985). By inspecting the network of causal connections, it concludes that certain events play a crucial role in the development of the narrative, by moving the plot from one place to an essentially different place.

Closely related to Lehnert's work is Dyer's (1981, 1983) system, called BORIS (qv), which attempts in-depth understanding of narratives. Such understanding should include being able to summarize the point or moral that the author intended the narrative to represent. This work moves beyond earlier work on plan-based understanding, such as Wilensky's (1981) by abstracting the communicative intent.

BORIS embodies thematic patterns, called thematic abstraction units (TAU). For example, TAU-DIRE-STRAITS encodes the pattern: x has a crisis goal; x cannot resolve the crisis alone; x seeks a friend y to help out. TAU arise from errors in planning or plan execution. They refer to a plan used, its intended effect, why it failed and what can be done about the failure. As such, they allow BORIS to organize the narratives at an intentional level, which leads naturally to an appropriate summarization or even drawing of a moral.

A contrasting approach is that of Brewer and Lichtenstein (1981, 1982). They argue that stories are a subclass of narratives purpose of which is to entertain. Thus plan-based analyses ultimately miss the point of a story if they are not augmented by an affective component, one that shows how structural elements of the text influence the reader. For example, suspense is created when the author reveals that a negative outcome is in store for a central character and that the character is unaware of his or her fate. Thus relations among the author's, the reader's, and the characters' belief states become essential to understanding, or being affected by, the story.

In the line of the Brewer and Lichtenstein approach, Bruce (1980b) outlines a central model of the author–reader relationship. The model makes explicit not only the author and the reader as participants in the communicative act, but also a constellation of other implied participants. For instance, in an ironic text, the author establishes an apparent speaker whose beliefs and intentions conflict in some respects with the author's.

It is noteworthy that to date attempts such as those of Brewer and Lichtenstein, and Bruce have been purely theoretical; no working system addresses the interactions of author's and reader's goals at that level.

PLAN RECOGNITION

The Pragmatic Perspective on Discourse

Language, especially written language, is often viewed as a code for packaging and transmitting information from one individual to another. Under this view, a linguistic message is fully represented by the words and sentences it comprises; texts are thus objects that can be studied in isolation. By taking such a stance, it is natural, for instance, to regard words as referring back to other words. Concepts like coherence, relevance, and topic are then regarded as properties of texts, leading researchers to confine their search for these properties to words and sentences.

A contrasting view, proposed by Strawson (1950), Austin (1962), Searle (1969), and others is that speakers or writers use words to do things, for instance to refer to things, or to get a hearer or reader to believe or do something. They are produced by a person, who is attempting to use them to produce certain effects on an audience (perhaps an imagined audience). According to this view, utterances are tools used in social interaction and should be studied in that light. Morgan and Sellner (1980) suggest that properties like coherence, relevance, and text structure are likely to be obtained from a theory of plans and goals appropriately extended to linguistic actions. Properties such as *relevance* would be epiphenomenal by-products of the appropriate structuring of actions.

Pragmatics is the study of communication as it is situated relative to a particular set of communication demands, speakers, hearers, times, places, joint surroundings, linguistic conventions, and cultural practices. Including language in a theory of action, this suggests that pragmatics is just the application to verbal problems of general abilities for interpreting the everyday world (Morgan, 1978). People tend to interpret the behavior of other humans in terms of the situation and the actor's intention and beliefs. Much of what has been discussed under the rubric pragmatics is most reasonably seen as the interpretation of linguistic behavior in similar terms.

The pragmatic perspective on language has three important implications for discourse understanding research. The first is that the meaning of a linguistic message is only partly represented by its content; its meaning for a hearer also depends on the hearer's construal of the purpose that the speaker had for producing it. The second is that the attribution of intentions to a speaker must be an integral component of the listener's comprehension process. The third is that a theory of language comprehension should determine the extent to which the same strategies people use to arrive at satisfactory explanations of the physical behavior of others can be employed in their comprehension of speech acts.

The way the meaning of a message is shaped by its producer's goals and beliefs is most obvious in a case such as propaganda, but it is no less critical for apparently straightforward utterances. For example, a colleague at the office might say, "I brought two egg salad sandwiches today." Although the referential meaning of this statement might be simple to compute, its full meaning depends on whether the speaker's intention was, for example, to offer one of the sandwiches, to decline a luncheon invitation, or to explain why the office smelled bad. Whatever the speaker's goals, the meaning conveyed by the statement depends on the hearer's correctly inferring what they are (Adams and Bruce, 1982).

Thus understanding discourse requires inferring the intentions and beliefs that led the speaker to produce the observed behavior. But as Grice (1957) points out, simply recognizing an actor's plan, as an unseen observer might do (Wilensky, 1981; Schmidt and co-workers, 1979), is insufficient as a basis for communication. Instead, hearers should attribute to speakers intentions that the speakers intend for them to infer. To ensure successful communication, speakers attempt to maximize the likelihood that hearers will make the inferences they were supposed to make by relying on what Lewis (1969) terms conventions. Conventions are solutions to coordination problems (where any participant's actions depend on the actions of others) and themselves rely on mutual knowledge held among the parties involved. Mutual knowledge (Schiffer, 1972) occurs when two people know that a proposition P holds, that the other person knows as well that P holds, that the second knows that the first knows that P holds, and so on. In ordinary conversation, participants make assumptions about mutual knowledge, signal their assumptions through the pragmatic presuppositions (Stalnaker, 1974) of their utterances, and negotiate misunderstanding of the developing mutual knowledge.

Speech Acts

From a pragmatic perspective, the goal of discourse understanding should not be to merely assess the truth conditions of one's interlocutor's utterances. Instead, the concern should be with the goal that is being pursued through these utterances, and with the way in which every utterance contributes to that goal. From this perspective, every language utterance is viewed as a social act: it changes, be it perhaps on a small scale, the social relation between the speaker and his interlocutor. A simple assertion puts the speaker under the obligation to defend it if challenged. A question creates for the interlocutor the obligation to answer it, or to be prepared to justify his lack of an inclination to do so. And vows, promises, and threats clearly extend beyond the microsociology of the interactional situation, creating commitments in the social world at large. The social acts performed by means of linguistic utterances are called speech acts (qv) (Searle, 1969).

The speech acts types that play a role in current experimental dialogue systems are as follows:

Requests, typically formulated as questions of the form "Could you do X?"

Commands, directly expressed as imperative sentences ("Do X"). (Notice that for most programs, which slavishly try to satisfy every whim of their human dialogue partner, there is no distinction between a request and a command. The program takes no responsibility for its actions.)

Assertions, directly expressed as indicative sentences. (Assertions are usually interpreted as commands to store or evaluate the asserted information.)

Questions, directly expressed as interrogative sentences. (A question is usually interpreted as a command to provide the answer.)

Plan Recognition

If a system analyzes its input utterances as speech acts and has at its disposal a repertoire of plausible goals that its dialogue partner may pursue, it may be able to understand the purpose behind its input utterances by using a method that is reminiscent of the way in which a system such as PAM (Wilensky, 1981) understands reports about goal-oriented behavior: it tries to guess the more encompassing goal that the speaker may be trying to accomplish by executing a plan that has the surface speech act as one of its constituent actions.

A system that tries to derive the deeper intentions behind surface speech acts in exactly this way was developed by Allen (1979). His system exploits knowledge about what constitutes a rational plan, as well as beliefs about what goals the speaker is likely to have.

Allen specifies the plan inference process as a set of inference rules and a control strategy. Rules are all of the form "If agent S believes agent A has a goal X, then agent S may infer that agent A has a goal Y." Examples of such rules are

If S believes A has a goal of executing action ACT, and ACT has an effect E, then S may believe that A has a goal of achieving E.

If S believes A has a goal of knowing whether a proposition P is true, then S may believe that A has a goal of achieving P.

Of course, given the conditions in the second rule, S might alternatively infer that A has a goal of achieving not P; this is treated as a separate rule. Which of these rules applies in a given setting is determined by control heuristics (qv), as follows.

The plan-inference process can be viewed as a search through a set of partial plans. Each partial plan consists of two parts: one part is constructed using the plan inference rules from the observed action and the other is constructed using the plan construction rules on an expected goal. When mutually exclusive rules can be applied to one of these partial plans, the plan is copied and one rule is applied in each copy. Each of these partial plans is then rated as to how probable it is to be the correct plan. The highest rated partial plan is always selected for further expansion using the inference rules. The rating is determined using a set of heuristics that fall into two classes: those that evaluate how well-formed the plan is in the given context and those that evaluate how well the plan fits the expectations. An example of a heuristic is

Decrease the rating of a partial plan if it contains a goal that is already true in the present context.

Allen argues that whenever the intended plan can be derived from mutual knowledge, ie, from knowledge which is knowingly shared between speaker and hearer, the hearer is assumed to perceive the intended plan, and is expected to react to that plan, rather than to the surface speech act. The paradigm examples of such situations are known as indirect speech acts (Perrault and Allen, 1980); sentences such as

Can you pass the salt?

or

Is the salt near you?

uttered at the dinner table where the simple answer yes, without an accompanying action would be experienced as a joke or an insult.

The idea also applies, however, to cases that are normally not classified as indirect speech acts. For instance, when at the information counter of a train station someone asks

Does the 4:20 train go to Toronto?

the answer no is less helpful than the answer

No, but the 5:10 train does.

which responds to the speaker's perceived goal of going to Toronto.

Allen's plan-recognition paradigm has been developed in work by Sidner (1983, 1985) and Sidner and Israel (1981). Pollack (1986) has refined it to deal with situations where speaker and hearer have conflicting ideas about how certain goals may be achieved. Litman (1986) and Litman and Allen (1984) have introduced metaplans that allow for clarification subdialogues and plan corrections; they also integrate an awareness of the surface structure of discourse, as discussed above, into to the plan-recognition process.

Speech Events

An unframed interaction between "uninterpreted" people is a rare event. People use a refined system of subcategorization to classify the social situations they engage in. These subcategories, called speech event types (Hymes, 1967, 1972) often assign a specific purpose to the interaction, specify roles for the participants, constrain discourse topics and conversational registers, and, in many cases, specify a conventional sequence of component activities.

An awareness of what kind of speech event one is engaged in, thus helps the plan-recognition process: the overall goals of the interaction, and often the steps to achieve them, are shared knowledge among the participants.

The most precisely circumscribed kinds of speech events are formal rituals. Speech event types characterized by grammars that are less explicit and less detailed include service encounters (Merritt, 1978), doctor–patient interactions (Byrne and Long, 1976), and casual conversations. Schegloff (1973) has shown that the process of terminating a telephone conversation is a jointly constructed ending sequence unit with a predictable course of development.

The structure of talk that is exchanged in order to perform a task may follow the structure of some goal–subgoal analysis of this task (Allen, 1979). In speech event types that involve a more or less fixed goal, this often leads to a fixed grammar of subsequent steps taken to attain it. For instance, as described by Polanyi and Scha (1984) transcripts of the activities in Dutch butcher shops consistently display the following sequential structure in the interaction between the butcher and a customer:

1. It is established that it is this customer's turn.
2. The first desired item is ordered, and the order is dealt with, . . . , the nth desired item is ordered and the order is dealt with.
3. It is established that the sequence of orders is finished.
4. The bill is processed.
5. The interaction is concluded.

Each of these steps is filled in a large variety of ways: either of the parties may take the initiative at each step, question–answer sequences about the available meat, the right way to prepare it, or the exact wishes of the customer may all be embedded in the stage 2 steps, and clarification dialogues of various sorts may occur.

An important speech event type with characteristics slightly different from the types mentioned so far, is the casual conversation. In a casual conversation, all participants have the same role: to be equals; no purposes are preestablished; and the range of possible topics is open-ended, although conventionally constrained.

Dialogue Systems

Many dialogue systems have been designed to partake in specific types of speech events, in which the computer system and its human interlocutor each play a well-defined role. The assumption that every dialogue must fall within the patterns allowed by the speech event type makes it possible to resolve ambiguities in its input (anaphora, ellipsis) and to react to the intentions behind it, also when these are not explicitly stated. Most systems of this sort play the role of the professional in a consultation interaction of some sort, eg,

A system that teaches an assembly task (Grosz, 1974).

An information system at a train station (Allen, 1979).

A travel budget manager (Bruce, 1975).

Such speech event types involve the participants cooperating toward a common goal. In doing this, they decompose the common task into subtasks, and, eventually, into elementary subtasks that can be executed by one or both of the participants without requiring further dialogue. For instance, as discussed above in "Recent Directions in Modeling Discourse Structure," Grosz's (1974) original investigation of dialogues between a human instructor and an apprentice who was being told how to repair an air compressor, showed that the structure of such dialogues corresponds closely to the structure of the task.

It should be noticed, however, that the description of the task structure does not predict one fixed tree structure (Grosz, 1974). A task may involve subtasks that must all be done, but can be done in any order. It is not difficult to imagine further complexities: alternatives, preconditions, etc. When a task does specify one fixed sequence of subtasks, the task structure degenerates into a script (see "Background Knowledge and Plausible Inferences" above).

MODES OF NATURAL LANGUAGE

It is usual to think of language in two forms: oral and written. Thus AI research on discourse understanding is conveniently divided between research on understanding text and research on participating in interactive dialogues, which, although most often written rather than spoken, are thought of as analogous to oral conversations. That this division is inadequate and at times misleading, is shown by Rubin (1980) who postulates eight dimensions of variation among "language experiences."

The eight dimensions—(1) oral vs written modality, (2) interactiveness, (3) spatial commonality, (4) temporal commonality, (5) possibility of paralinguistic communication, (6) concreteness of referents, (7) audience specificity, and (8) separability of participants—define a range of communication modalities out of which AI research has focused on only a few, albeit significant ones.

From the perspective of this dimensional analysis, the research directed at the implementation of interactive computer programs that display reasonable behavior in conducting a dialogue with a person amounts to the development of a new mode of natural language, rather than the analysis of an existing one: real-time alphanumeric interaction, usually without shared awareness of physical context.

Most AI research [notable exceptions being speech understanding (qv) work and some efforts at modeling real conversations (Reichman, 1981; Hinrichs and Polanyi, 1986; Hobbs and Evans, 1980; Hobbs and Agar, 1985; Levin and Moore, 1977)] has focused on written language, and is thus clustered on one pole of Rubin's first dimension. What distinguishes the AI dialogue work from the AI text work then is that the former is interactive, and usually implies spatial and temporal commonality. On the other hand, neither of the two modes of language use includes paralinguistic communication, such as gestures, facial expressions, or body position cues. In some of the dialogue work, but not the text work, there are concrete referents, in the sense that objects are perceptually present to the user and the machine. The same holds for audience specificity; some of the dialogue work assumes fairly detailed speaker models of the hearer. Neither of the modalities typically allows separability of participants. Indeed, most of the communication is one to one.

Other AI research has focused on text understanding, usually assuming a nonspecific audience. (In contrast, note the many existing forms of text understanding, such as dealing with letters, memos, persuasive essays, etc, that do assume specific audience beliefs and plans).

Some studies (Cohen, 1984; Cohen and co-workers, 1982; Tierney and co-workers, 1983) have been devoted to the linguistic consequences of the use of different communication media. Cohen (1984), for example, used a plan-based model of communication to analyze dialogues in five modalities: face-to-face, telephone, linked CRT, (noninteractive) audiotape, and (noninteractive) written text. He found that speakers in the face-to-face situation, for example, attempted to achieve more detailed goals in giving instructions than did users of keyboards. More specifically, requests that the hearer identify the referent of a noun-phrase–dominated spoken instruction giving discourse, but were rare in the keyboard dialogues.

These studies suggest that it is important to understand the constraints of the communication system as well as the texts per se when an AI system is being designed. Moreover, they imply a need for caution in interpreting results of AI research. Any form of language use is valid to examine and can be illuminating in a general way, but specifics of language processing must be interpreted in light of the communication modality in which they arise.

BIBLIOGRAPHY

M. J. Adams and B. C. Bruce, "Background Knowledge and Reading Comprehension," in J. Langer and M. T. Smith-Burke, eds., *Reader Meets Author/Bridging the Gap: A Psycholinguistic and Sociolinguistic Perspective*, International Reading Association, Newark, Del., 1982, pp. 2–25.

J. L. Austin, *How to Do Things with Words*, Oxford University Press, Oxford, UK, 1962.

J. F. Allen, *A Plan-Based Approach to Speech Act Recognition*, Technical Report **131**, Department of Computer Science, University of Toronto, Toronto, Canada, Jan. 1979.

M. Bennett, "Demonstratives and Indexicals in Montague Grammar," *Synthese* **39**, 1–80 (1978).

W. F. Brewer and E. H. Lichtenstein, "Event Schemas, Story Schemas, and Story Grammars," in J. D. Long and A. D. Baddeley, eds., *Attention and Performance IX*, Lawrence Erlbaum, Hillsdale, N.J., 1981, pp. 363–379.

W. F. Brewer and E. H. Lichtenstein, "Stories Are to Entertain: A Structural-Affect Theory of Stories," *J. Pragmatics* **6**, 473–486 (1982).

B. C. Bruce, "Discourse Models and Language Comprehension," *AJCL* **35**, 19–35 (1975).

B. C. Bruce, "Analysis of Interacting Plans as a Guide to the Understanding of Story Structure," *Poetics* **9**, 295–311 (1980a).

B. C. Bruce, "Plans and Social Actions," in R. Spiro, B. C. Bruce, and W. Brewer, eds., *Theoretical Issues in Reading Comprehension*, Lawrence Erlbaum, Hillsdale, N.J., 1980b, pp. 367–384.

B. C. Bruce, "Robot Plans and Human Plans: Implications for Models of Communication," in I. Gopnick and M. Gopnick, eds., *From Models to Modules: Studies in Cognitive Sciences from the McGill Workshops*, Ablex, Norwood, N.J., 1986, pp. 97–114.

B. C. Bruce and D. Newman, "Interacting Plans," *Cogn. Sci.* **2**, 195–233 (1978).

P. S. Byrne and B. E. L. Long, *Doctors Talking to Patients*, Her Majesty's Stationery Office, London, 1976.

E. Charniak, "A Framed PAINTING: The Representation of a Commonsense Knowledge Fragment," *Cogn. Sci.* **1**(4), 355–394 (1977).

P. R. Cohen, "The Pragmatics of Referring and the Modality of Communication," *Comput. Ling.* **10**, 97–146 (1984).

P. R. Cohen, S. Fertig, and K. Starr, "Dependencies of Discourse Structure on the Modality of Communication: Telephone vs. Teletype," in *Proceedings of the Twentieth Annual Meeting of the Association of Computational Linguistics*, June 1982, pp. 28–35.

R. E. Cullingford, "Script Application: Computer Understanding of Newspaper Stories," Ph.D. dissertation, Yale University, New Haven, Conn., 1978.

R. E. Cullingford, "SAM," in R. C. Schank and C. K. Riesbeck, eds., *Inside Computer Understanding: Five Programs Plus Miniatures*, Lawrence Erlbaum, Hillsdale, N.J., 1981, pp. 75–119.

G. F. DeJong, "Prediction and Substantiation: A New Approach to Natural Language Processing," *Cogn. Sci.* **3**, 251–273 (1979a).

G. F. DeJong, "Skimming Stories in Real Time: An Experiment in Integrated Understanding," Ph.D. dissertation, Yale University, New Haven, Conn., 1979b.

M. G. Dyer, "The Role of TAUs in Narratives," in *Proceedings of the Third Annual Conference of the Cognitive Science Society*, Cognitive Science Society, Berkeley, Calif., 1981, pp. 225–227.

M. G. Dyer, *In-Depth Understanding: A Computer Model of Integrated Processing and Memory for Narrative Comprehension*, MIT Press, Cambridge, Mass., 1983.

H. P. Grice, "Meaning," *Philos. Rev.* **66**, 377–388, 1957.

B. Grosz, "The Structure of Task Oriented Dialogs," in *IEEE Symposium on Speech Recognition: Contributed Papers*, IEEE, Pittsburgh, Pa., 1974, pp. 250–253.

B. J. Grosz and C. L. Sidner, "Attention, Intentions, and the Structure of Discourse," *Comput. Ling.* **12**(3), 175–204 (1986).

E. Guelich, *Makrosyntax der Gliederungssignale im Gesprochenen Franzoesisch*, Wilhelm Fink Verlag, Munich, 1970.

M. Halliday and R. Hasan, *Cohesion in English*, Longman's, London, 1977.

E. Hinrichs, "Temporal Anaphora in Discourse of English," *Ling. Philos.* **9**(1), 63–82 (1986).

E. Hinrichs and L. Polanyi, "Pointing the Way: A Unified Account of Referential Gesture in Interactive Discourse," in *Papers from the Parasession on Pragmatics and Grammatical Theory*, Chicago Linguistics Society, Chicago, 1986, pp. 298–314.

J. R. Hobbs, "Coherence and Co-References," *Cogn. Sci.* **3**(1), 67–82 (1979).

J. R. Hobbs, *On the Coherence and Structure of Discourse*, Technical Report No. CSLI-85-37, Center for the Study of Language and Information, Stanford, Calif., Oct. 1985.

J. R. Hobbs and M. H. Agar, "The Coherence of Incoherent Discourse," *Lang. Social Psychol.* **4**(3–4), 213–231 (1985).

J. R. Hobbs and D. Evans, "Conversation as Planned Behavior," *Cogn. Sci.* **4**(4), 349–377 (1980).

J. R. Hobbs and R. C. Moore, *Formal Theories of the Commonsense World*, Ablex, Norwood, N.J., 1985.

D. Hymes, "Models of the Interaction of Language and Social Setting," *J. Social Issues* **23**(2), 8–28 (1967).

D. Hymes, "Models of the Interaction of Language and Social Life," in J. Gumperz and D. Hymes, eds., *Directions in Sociolinguistics*, Holt, Rinehart and Winston, New York, 1972, pp. 35–71.

H. Kamp, "Events, Instants and Temporal Reference," in U. Egli and A. van Stechow, eds., *Semantics from a Multiple Point of View*, de Gruyter, Berlin, 1979, pp. 376–471.

L. Karttunen, "Discourse Referents," in J. McCawley, ed., *Syntax and Semantics*, Vol. 7, Academic Press, Inc., New York, 1976.

W. G. Lehnert, "Plot Units and Narrative Summarization," *Cogn. Sci.* **5**(4), 293–331 (1981).

W. G. Lehnert, "An In-Depth Understander of Narratives," *Artif. Intell.* **20**(1), 15–62 (1983).

W. G. Lehnert, J. B. Black, and B. J. Reiser, "Summarizing Narratives," in *Proceedings of the Seventh IJCAI*, Vancouver, B.C., Canada, Morgan-Kaufmann, San Mateo, Calif., 1981, pp. 184–189.

W. Lehnert and C. Loiselle, "Plot Unit Recognition for Narratives," in G. Tonfoni, ed., *Artificial Intelligence and Text-Understanding: Plot Units and Summarization Procedures*, Ed. Zara, Parma, Italy, 1985, pp. 9–47.

J. A. Levin and J. A. Moore, "Dialogue Games: Metacommunication Structures for Natural Language Interaction," *Cogn. Sci.* **1**(4), 395–420 (1977).

D. K. Lewis, *Convention: A Philosophical Study*, Harvard University Press, Cambridge, Mass., 1969.

D. J. Litman, "Linguistic Coherence: A Plan-Based Alternative," in *Proceedings of the Twenty-Fourth Annual Meeting of the Association for Computational Linguistics*, New York, 1986, pp. 215–223.

D. J. Litman and J. F. Allen, *A Plan Recognition Model for Subdialogues in Conversations*, Technical Report TR 141, University of Rochester, Nov. 1984.

W. C. Mann and S. A. Thompson, *Relational Propositions in Discourse*, Technical Report RR-83-115, Information Sciences Institute, Marina del Rey, Calif., Nov. 1983.

M. Merritt, *On the Use of O.K. in Service Encounters*, Texas Working Papers in Sociolinguistics **42**, Southwest Educational Development Laboratory, Austin, Tex., 1978.

R. Montague, "Pragmatics," in R. Klibansky, ed., *Contemporary Philosophy: A Survey*, La Nuova Italia Editrice, Florence, Italy, 1968, pp. 102–122.

J. L. Morgan, "Two Types of Convention in Indirect Speech Acts," in P. Cole, ed., *Syntax and Semantics, Volume 9: Pragmatics*, Academic Press, Inc., New York, 1978, pp. 261–280.

J. L. Morgan and M. Sellner, "Discourse and Linguistic Theory," in R. J. Spiro, B. C. Bruce, and W. F. Brewer, eds., *Theoretical Issues in Reading Comprehension*, Lawrence Erlbaum, Hillsdale, N.J., 1980, pp. 165–200.

D. Newman and B. C. Bruce, "Interpretation and Manipulation in Human Plans," *Discourse Processes* **9**, 167–195 (1986).

C. R. Perrault and J. F. Allen, "A Plan-Based Analysis of Indirect Speech Acts," *Am. J. Comput. Ling.* **6**(3), 167–182 (1980).

L. Polanyi, "A Theory of Discourse Structure and Discourse Coherence," in *Proceedings of the Twenty-First Regional Meeting of the Chicago Linguistic Society*, Chicago Linguistic Society, University of Chicago, Apr. 1985a, pp. 306–322.

L. Polanyi, *Telling the American Story*, Ablex Publishing, Norwood, N.J., 1985b.

L. Polanyi and R. Scha, "A Syntactic Approach to Discourse Semantics," in *Proceedings of the International Conference on Computational Linguistics*, Stanford University, Stanford, Calif., 1984, pp. 413–419.

M. E. Pollack, "A Model of Plan Inference That Distinguishes between the Beliefs of Actors and Observers," in *Proceedings of the Twenty-Fourth Annual Meeting of the Association for Computational Linguistics*, New York, 1986, pp. 207–214.

B. Propp, *Morphology of the Folktale*, University of Texas Press, Austin, 1968.

R. Reichman, *Plain-Speaking: A Theory and Grammar of Spontaneous Discourse*, Ph.D. dissertation, Harvard University, Cambridge, Mass., 1981.

A. D. Rubin, "A Theoretical Taxonomy of the Differences Between Oral and Written Language," in R. J. Spiro, B. C. Bruce, and W. F. Brewer, eds., *Theoretical Issues in Reading Comprehension*, Lawrence Erlbaum, Hillsdale, N.J., 1980, pp. 411–438.

D. E. Rumelhart, "Notes on a Schema for Stories," in D. G. Bobrow and A. Collins, ed., *Representation and Understanding*, Academic Press, Inc., New York, 1975, pp. 211–236.

R. C. Schank and R. Abelson, *Scripts, Plans, Goals, and Understanding*, Lawrence Erlbaum, Hillsdale, N.J., 1977.

E. Schelgloff and H. Sacks, "Opening Up Closings," *Semiotica* **VIII**(4), 289–327 (1973).

S. Schiffer, *Meaning*, Oxford University Press, Oxford, UK, 1972.

D. Schiffrin, *Discourse Markers: Semantic Resource for the Construction of Conversation*, Ph.D. dissertation, University of Pennsylvania, Philadelphia, 1982.

D. F. Schmidt, N. S. Sridharan, and J. L. Goodson, "The Plan Recognition Problem: An Intersection of Artificial Intelligence and Psychology," *Artif. Intell.* **10**, 45–83 (1979).

J. R. Searle, *Speech Acts: An Essay in the Philosophy of Language*, Cambridge University Press, Cambridge, UK, 1969.

C. L. Sidner, "What the Speaker Means: The Recognition of Speakers' Plans in Discourse," *Int. J. Comput. Math.* **9**(1), 71–82 (1983).

C. L. Sidner, "Plan Parsing for Intended Response Recognition in Discourse," *Comput. Intell.* **1**(1), 1–10 (Feb. 1985).

C. L. Sidner and D. J. Israel, "Recognizing Intended Meaning and Speaker's Plans," in *Proceedings of the Seventh IJCAI*, Vancouver, B.C., Canada, Morgan-Kaufmann, San Mateo, Calif., 1981, pp. 203–208.

R. C. Stalnaker, "Pragmatic Presuppositions," in M. K. Munitz and P. K. Unger, eds., *Semantics and Philosophy*, New York University Press, New York, 1974, pp. 197–213.

P. F. Strawson, "On Referring," *Mind* **59**, 320–344 (1950).

R. J. Tierney, J. LaZansky, T. Raphael, and P. R. Cohen, "Author's Intentions and Readers' Interpretations," in R. J. Tierney, P. Anders, and J. N. Mitchell, eds., *Understanding Readers' Understandings*, Lawrence Erlbaum, Hillsdale, N.J., 1983.

B. L. Webber, "So What Can We Talk About Now?," in M. Brady, ed., *Computational Approaches to Discourse*, MIT Press, Cambridge, Mass., 1982.

R. Wilensky, "PAM," in R. C. Schank and C. K. Riesbeck, eds., *Inside Computer Understanding: Five Programs Plus Miniatures*, Lawrence Erlbaum, Hillsdale, N.J., 1981, pp. 136–179.

W. A. Woods, "Transition Network Grammars for Natural Language Analysis," *CACM* **13**(10), 591–606 (Oct. 1970).

R. J. H. Scha
B. C. Bruce
L. Polanyi
BBN Laboratories Inc.

This research was partially supported by the National Institute of Education under Contract No. 400-81-0030, and by the Advanced Research Projects Agency of the Department of Defense under Contract No. N0014-85-C-0079.

DISTRIBUTED PROBLEM SOLVING

Any intelligent system, artificial or not, is bounded (March and Simon, 1958; Simon, 1957, 1969). It has bounds on its reasoning rate, for example, as well as on the size of its memory, the knowledge it has available to apply to a problem, the completeness of its model of the world, and so on. An important response taken by natural systems to their individual limitations is to band together to achieve their goals collectively. It is this metaphor that is at the heart of distributed problem solving. In particular, distributed problem solving typically patterns itself after human collaboration, involving limited communication and substantial individual intellect.

Distributed problem solving thus studies how a loosely coupled network of problem-solving nodes (processing elements) can solve problems that are beyond the capabilities of the nodes individually. Each node is a sophisticated system that can modify its behavior as circumstances change and plan its own communication and cooperation strategies with other nodes (see PROBLEM SOLVING). Although distributed problem solving borrows ideas from numerous fields, including distributed processing, AI, and the social sciences, it differs significantly from each of those in the problems being attacked and the methods used to solve them.

Distributed problem-solving networks differ from dis-

tributed-processing systems in both the style of distribution and the type of problems addressed. These differences are most apparent when the interactions among nodes in each of the networks are studied. A distributed-processing system typically has multiple, disparate tasks executing concurrently in the network. Shared access to physical or informational resources is the main reason for interaction among tasks. The goal is to preserve the illusion that each task is executing alone on a dedicated system by having the network operating system hide the resource-sharing interactions and conflicts among tasks in the network. In contrast, the problem-solving procedures in distributed problem-solving networks are explicitly aware of the distribution of the network components and can make informed interaction decisions based on that information. This difference in emphasis is, in part, due to the characteristics of the applications being tackled by conventional distributed-processing methodologies. Traditional distributed-processing applications use task decompositions in which a node rarely needs the assistance of another node in carrying out its problem-solving function. Thus most of the research as well as the paradigms of distributed processing do not directly address the issues of cooperative interactions of tasks to solve a single problem. As discussed below, highly cooperative task interaction is a requirement for many problems that seem naturally suited to a distributed network.

Distributed problem solving in turn differs from much of the work in AI because of its emphasis on interaction, as opposed to AI's focus on autonomy. That is, traditional research in AI concentrates on building systems that need no help in solving complex problems. From this view, the answer to system brittleness (where the system abjectly fails when given problems beyond its expertise) is to provide the system with more and more knowledge. In contrast, distributed problem solving considers purely autonomous systems to be too limited by definition and unable to reap the benefits of pooling their knowledge and expertise. From the view of distributed problem solving, the answer to system brittleness is to allow a system to flexibly determine what help it currently needs and to coordinate with other systems to receive that help. Thus a distributed problem-solving node is semiautonomous: it is capable of independently acting in diverse ways, but it can cooperate to solve problems that are beyond its abilities. To appeal to a familiar analogy in human interaction, a physician is able to perform many intelligent tasks alone, but when faced with a particularly complicated case will consult with other physicians who have complementary expertise and experience.

Note that this perspective of distributed problem solving as occurring between individually sophisticated nodes sets distributed problem solving apart from approaches such as the Actor framework (Hewitt, 1977), Hearsay-II (Erman, 1980), the ETHER language (Kornfeld, 1979), the BEINGS system (Lenat, 1988), CAOS (Schoen, 1986), Poligon (Rice, 1986), and Connectionism (McClelland and co-workers, 1987). These latter systems compartmentalize very small pieces of knowledge into separate processing units, and those processing units are connected together in predefined ways. Through the tightly coupled interactions between the units, sophisticated behavior emerges from the actions of simplistic entities despite the fact that the entities each have little or no knowledge of the problem-solving task as a whole or of general techniques for communication and cooperation. As a result, one of these entities cannot function outside of the context of the other entities and the hardwired communication and cooperation protocols. In contrast, each node in a distributed problem-solving network possesses sufficient overall problem-solving knowledge to apply and communicate about its own local solutions to problems without assistance from other nodes. Communication and cooperation are knowledge-based activities in their own right, and a distributed problem-solving node applies its knowledge about how to interact with others to develop a strategy for communication and cooperation that is specifically suited to its current situation.

Finally, although, distributed problem solving borrows many ideas and insights from the social sciences, it is different in a crucial way: distributed problem solving studies how artifacts that people build can work together, rather than how naturally occurring systems cooperate. Because distributed problem-solving researchers build the cooperating artifacts, those artifacts can be designed to behave in well-understood ways. Thus although distributed problem solving researchers have considered issues in having artifacts exhibit less than fully cooperative behavior (such as lying or distracting each other), they do not face the same complexities as social scientists. On the other hand, whereas social scientists have goals of describing how existing intelligent systems already interact, distributed problem-solving researchers must go further by developing prescriptive theories and mechanisms for instilling cooperative behavior in their artificial systems.

WHY DISTRIBUTED PROBLEM SOLVING?

Given that AI is still grappling with fundamental issues about how to do problem solving, an important question is whether it is even necessary to worry about distributed problem solving yet. After all, is it not important to learn to walk before attempting to run?

In fact, it is unclear whether building a collection of semiautonomous problem solvers is truly more difficult than building a single autonomous problem solver. First of all, the principles of modular design and implementation dictate that structuring a complex problem into relatively self-contained pieces leads to systems that are easier to build, debug, and maintain and that are more resilient to software and hardware errors than a single, monolithic system. Second, many types of problem involve inherently distributed information or functionality, and distributed problem solving is the natural approach for those problems. Third, hardware technology is now at the point where many people have ready access to local area networks of tens or hundreds of computers. A distributed problem-solving network on this hardware platform could harness the combined computational power of the network and focus it on solving a single problem.

A fourth reason why distributed problem solving is an important research area is that a proliferation of stand-alone expert systems have been developed. However, combining the expertise of these separate systems requires one or more people to coordinate the flow of information between systems, often transforming the output of one system into a form that another system can use. Distributed problem-solving research includes efforts directed toward retroactively modifying existing knowledge-based systems to exploit potential synergies between them. Fifth, developing an understanding of cooperation and coordination is important in its own right, and distributed problem solving can help validate theories in sociology, management, and organizational theory through the use of computer models that embody theories, much like AI systems are used to validate theories in linguistics, psychology, and philosophy. A final reason for studying distributed problem solving is that, before an artificially intelligent system can truly be integrated into society, it must be flexible in how it can cooperate so that it will be accepted by people. Although achieving this goal remains distant, distributed problem solving is an important field contributing toward it.

USES OF DISTRIBUTED PROBLEM SOLVING

Like other areas of AI, distributed problem solving realizes theoretical advances in applications. Five general application areas that seem well suited to distributed problem-solving technology include the following.

Distributed Interpretation. Distributed interpretation applications require the integration and analysis of distributed data to generate a (potentially distributed) semantic model of the data. Application domains include distributed sensor networks (Lesser and Erman, 1980; Lesser and Corkill, 1983; Mason and co-workers, 1988; Wesson and co-workers, 1981) and communication network fault diagnosis (Conry and co-workers, 1991).

Distributed Planning and Control. Distributed planning (qv) and control applications involve developing and coordinating the actions of distributed effector nodes to perform desired tasks. Application domains include distributed air-traffic control (Finder and Lo, 1986; Thorndyke and co-workers, 1981), cooperating robots (Durfee and Montgomery, 1990), remotely piloted vehicles (Steeb and co-workers, 1986), distributed process control in manufacturing (Smith and Hynynen, 1987; Van Dyke Parunak and co-workers, 1985; Van Dyke Parunak, 1987), and resource allocation–control in a long-haul communication network (Adler and co-workers, 1989; Conry and co-workers, 1985; Goyal and Worrest, 1988). Distributed planning and control applications often involve distributed interpretation to determine appropriate node actions.

Cooperating Expert Systems. One means of scaling expert-system technology to more complex and encompassing problem domains is to develop cooperative interaction mechanisms that allow multiple expert systems to work together to solve a common problem. Illustrative situations include controlling an autonomous vehicle that uses separate expert systems for system status, mission planning, navigation, situation assessment, and piloting (Arkin and co-workers, 1987; Smith and Broadwell) or negotiation among expert systems that are designing an object (Lander and co-workers, 1991; Werkman, 1990).

Computer-Supported Human Cooperation. Computer technology promises to provide people with more and better information for making decisions. However, unless computers also assist people by filtering the information and focusing attention on relevant information, the amount of information can become overwhelming (Chang, 1987; Huhns and co-workers, 1987; Malone, 1988). By building AI systems with coordination knowledge, some of the burden can be removed from people. Domains where this is important include intelligent command and control systems and multiuser project coordination (Croft and Lefkowitz, 1988; Klein, 1991; Mazer, 1987; Nirenburg and Lesser, 1988; Pan and Tenenbaum, 1991; Sathi and co-workers, 1986).

Cognitive Models of Cooperation. Although the designers of distributed problem solving approaches have consistently used insights about human cooperation to build similar capabilities into their systems, little research to date has worked in the opposite direction. But AI methods have in the past served to implement and validate theoretical models of human intelligence, and distributed problem solving provides a similar methodological framework for testing theories about human cooperation and coordination (Sycara, 1988).

Initial work in distributed problem solving mostly focused on three application domains: distributed sensor networks, distributed air-traffic control, and distributed robot systems (see ROBOTICS). All of these applications need to solve in some form the tasks of distributed interpretation and distributed planning or control. Planning in this context refers not only to determining what actions to take (such as changing the course of an airplane) but also to deciding how to use the resources of the network to effectively carry out the interpretation and planning task. This latter form of planning encompasses the classic focus-of-attention problem in AI.

In addition to the commonality in terms of the generic tasks being solved, these application domains are characterized by a natural spatial distribution of sensors and effectors and by the fact that the subproblems of both the local interpretation of sensory data and the planning of effector actions are interdependent in time and space. For example, in a distributed sensor network that is tracking vehicle movements, a vehicle detected in one part of the sensed area implies that a vehicle of similar type and velocity will be sensed a short time later in an adjacent area. Likewise, a plan for guiding an airplane must be coordinated with the plans of other nearby airplanes in order to avoid collision. Interdependence also arises from redundancy in sensory data. Often different nodes sense the same event because of overlaps in the range of sensors and the use of different types of sensor that sense the same

event in different ways. Exploiting these redundant and alternative views and the interdependencies among subproblems require nodes to cooperate in order to interpret and plan effectively. This cooperation leads to viewing the network problem solving (qv) in terms of a single problem rather than a set of independent subproblems.

THE KEY ISSUES

The development of a distributed problem-solving architecture that can exploit the characteristics of these applications to limit internode communication, to achieve real-time response, and to provide high reliability represents a difficult task. Nodes must cooperate to exploit and coordinate their answers to interdependent subproblems but must do so with limited interprocessor communication. This requires the development of new paradigms that permit the distributed system to deal effectively with environmental uncertainty (not having an accurate view of the number and location of processors, effectors, sensors, and communication channels), data uncertainty (not having complete and consistent local data at a node), and control uncertainty (not having a completely accurate model of activities at other nodes). The development of these paradigms requires research on the three interacting issues discussed below.

Problem Decomposition

How a problem to be solved is distributed among a network of problem solvers depends on how the distributed network is viewed. From a reductionist perspective, a distributed network is viewed as a single system that is decomposed over a number of nodes. From a constructionist perspective, however, a distributed network is a society of nodes, where each node is a distinct system. Although both perspectives view the same reality, the reductionist viewpoint tends to encourage a search for ways of pulling apart existing centralized systems. The constructionist viewpoint tends to encourage a search for ways of organizing individually complete systems into a society of cooperating nodes. From both perspectives, there are several dimensions for task decomposition.

Functional vs Spatial. In a functional decomposition, each node is a specialist at solving some part(s) of the problem, so a problem to be solved is routed to the appropriate specialist as its abilities are needed. In a spatial decomposition, each node possesses all of the problem-solving abilities and is given a limited, nearby portion of the overall problem to solve. (Each node specializes in knowing what is happening in its own spatial neighborhood.) The problem could also be decomposed along a mixture of these lines, or along other lines leading to decompositions based on product lines or time (Malone and Smith, 1984; Durfee and Montgomery, 1990).

Hierarchical vs Lateral. The node-interaction structure is another important dimension of task decomposition. Hierarchical structures work well when control or results need to be concentrated at certain points in the network, but they are sensitive to the loss of a high level node in the hierarchy. Lateral (also called heterarchical) structures can be more robust to the loss of nodes but can exhibit increased communication and control problems. A particular problem might be best decomposed into a combination of hierarchical and lateral substructures.

Redundant vs Disjoint Activities. Redundant activities consume network resources, and efficiency considerations suggest that duplication of effort should be minimized. However, without some degree of redundancy, the network is susceptible to severely degraded performance when a crucial activity, located at only one node, is lost due to node failure. A preferable approach is to have crucial activities be at least potentially performable at multiple sites as insurance against unforeseen node failures.

Dealing with Incomplete and Inconsistent Information

In many applications, communication delays make it impractical for the network to be structured such that each node has all the relevant information it needs for its local computations and control decisions. Another way of viewing this problem is that the spatial decomposition of information among nodes is ill-suited to a functionally distributed solution. Each node might possess the information necessary to perform a portion of each function, but there is insufficient information to perform any function completely. Thus a second issue in distributed problem solving is designing a network so that the nodes can tolerate having possibly incomplete, inconsistent, and out-of-date data and control information.

Obtaining Global Coherence with Decentralized Control

Another issue in distributed problem solving is developing network-coordination policies that provide sufficient global coherence for effective cooperation. Coherent network problem solving requires the achievement of the following conditions.

Coverage. Any necessary portion of the overall problem must be included in the activities of at least one node.

Connectivity. Nodes must interact in a manner that permits the covering activities to be developed and integrated into an overall solution.

Capability. Coverage and connectivity must be achievable within the communication and computation resource limitations of the network.

Achieving coherence is difficult because the use of a global controller node is not an option for two reasons. First, because internode communication is limited, each node (including the controller) can have only a restricted view of network problem-solving activities. A global controller node would thus be a severe communication and computational bottleneck. Second, network reliability demands that the network's performance degrades gracefully if a portion of the network fails, but if the controller node were to fail, the resulting network collapse would not

be graceful. In the absence of a global controller node, each node must be able to direct its own activities in concert with other nodes based on potentially incomplete, inaccurate, inconsistent, and out-of-date information.

THE KEY IDEAS

Important approaches to distributed problem solving can be classified into the categories of negotiation, functionally accurate cooperation, organizational structuring, multiagent planning, sophisticated local control, and foundations for reasoning about belief and concurrency. In the following discussion, some of the ideas that have emerged from these different directions are highlighted.

Negotiation

An ongoing objective in distributed problem-solving research is to capitalize on insights about how humans coordinate their activities through negotiation. As the first distributed problem-solving approach to emphasize negotiation, the *contract-net protocol* (Smith, 1980) has remained highly influential in the field because it incorporates two very powerful ideas. The first idea is the use of negotiation between willing entities as a means of obtaining coherent behavior. Negotiation involves a multidimensional exchange of information by each member from its own perspective, and final agreement by mutual selection. Negotiation differs from voting in that dissident members are free to exit the negotiation rather than being bound by the decision of the majority.

The second idea is the use of contracts as a mechanism for establishing control relationships between nodes in the distributed problem-solving network. That is, the objective of negotiation is to let nodes agree to a contract, in which one node (a manager) has contracted another (the contractor) to perform a task for it. Contracts are elaborated in a top-down manner; at each stage a manager decomposes its tasks into subtasks and contracts out any tasks for which it needs help. It negotiates with potential contractors by announcing a task, collecting bids, and awarding the task to the node(s) whose bid(s) it considered best. Because potential contractors only bid on tasks they desire, a contract represents a manager and a contractor mutually selecting each other. After it is awarded a task, a contractor can further decompose the task and contract out subtasks, and this elaboration process continues until a node can complete a contract without assistance. The result of the iterative contracting process is a network of manager-contractor control relationships distributed throughout the network.

The contract-net protocol defines common message formats (task announcements, bids, task awards) and communication conventions (for example, nodes respond to task announcements with bids). As a general framework for contracting, it gives nodes a language for exchanging information they need for making decisions about how to work together. However, it does not provide the (typically application-dependent) knowledge that nodes need for deciding on how to use the language effectively, including knowledge about decomposing tasks appropriately for contracting, announcing the relevant aspects of subtasks, deciding on whether and how to bid on a subtask, and evaluating disparate bids. Because it views distributed problem solving in terms of three phases (problem decomposing and allocating, local subproblem solving, and subproblem solution collecting and integrating) the contract-net protocol is particularly suited for applications in which large tasks arrive at individual nodes and the objective of distributed problem solving is to match pieces of the large task to nodes that are capable of accomplishing them. This type of distributed problem solving is termed task-sharing (Smith and Davis, 1981).

Multistage negotiation (Conry and co-workers, 1988) extends the contract-net protocol to allow iterative negotiation between nodes. The main idea is that nodes can make and share tentative decisions about how they will apply their resources, and by iterating through this process they can converge on a mutually agreeable assignment of resources. Negotiation thus leads to distributed constraint satisfaction (Conry and co-workers, 1991; Sycara and co-workers, 1991; Yokoo and co-workers, 1990). Other extensions to contracting have allowed more flexible decisions about task decompositions by allowing contractors to make counterproposals instead of simply bidding on initial proposals (Durfee and Lesser, 1989). Negotiation has also been employed in the Rand work on air-traffic control (Cammarata and co-workers, 1983; Steeb and co-workers, 1986), in which a group of planes must negotiate to decide which of them is best suited to coordinate their actions. An important contribution of this work was in identifying criteria for assigning these responsibilities, and particularly in recognizing that criteria change depending on whether the planes have a lot of time to coordinate (where choosing the plane that knew the most about the other planes' flight plans was best) or they have little time to coordinate (where choosing the plane that had the most room to maneuver was best). Other work in negotiation has contributed ideas from cognitive modeling, including case-based techniques (Sycara, 1987, 1988, 1989) and human–computer interaction (Klein, 1991), and has introduced a variety of negotiation techniques for reaching compromises (Lander and co-workers, 1991; Sathi and co-workers, 1986; Werkman, 1990).

Functionally Accurate Cooperation

Lesser and Corkill (1981; Lesser, 1991) have approached distributed problem solving by developing nodes that are able to cooperate among themselves so that the network as a whole can function effectively even though the nodes have inconsistent and incomplete views of the information used in their computations. They call this type of distributed problem solving *functionally accurate, cooperative* (FA/C). The main idea behind the FA/C approach is that the distributed network is structured so that each node can perform useful processing with incomplete input data, while simultaneously exchanging partial, tentative, high level results of its processing with other nodes to construct a complete solution cooperatively. The intent is that the amount of communication required to exchange these

results is much less than the amount of communicated raw data and results that would be required by a conventional distributed-processing approach. In addition, the synchronization required among nodes can also be reduced, resulting in increased node parallelism and network robustness.

In contrast to the task-sharing perspective employed in approaches such as the contract-net, FA/C problem solving can be characterized as a result-sharing approach. It is particularly well suited to applications where a large problem to solve is inherently distributed among the nodes, such as in a distributed sensor network. Unlike a contracting approach where the managers know exactly where subproblems are being solved, nodes working on an inherently distributed problem might not know which other nodes are solving related subproblems. As a consequence, the nodes must share tentative results to identify nodes with whom they should cooperate and to converge on overall solutions. Similar ideas are manifested in the work of Hewitt (1986) on *open systems*, which emphasizes the need for agents in a large computing network to be able to cope with conflicting, inconsistent, and partial information and to be highly reliable so that the operation of the system is continuous. Open systems represents an important conceptual framework for structuring large and complex networks of heterogeneous components for which distributed AI will play a major role (Gasser, 1991; Hewitt and Inman, 1991).

Organizational Structuring

Network coordination is difficult in a cooperative distributed problem-solving network because limited internode communication restricts each node's view of network problem-solving activity. Furthermore, it is important that network coordination policies do not consume more processing and communication resources than benefits derived from the increased problem-solving coherence. Corkill and Lesser (1983) suggested that even in networks composed of a modest number of nodes, a complete analysis to determine the detailed activities at each node is impractical; the computation and communication costs of determining the optimal set and allocation of activities far outweigh the improvement in problem-solving performance. Instead they argued that coordination in distributed problem-solving networks must sacrifice some potential improvement for a less complex coordination problem.

To balance the effort spent on problem solving and on coordination, distributed problem solving research has drawn on ideas from organization theory (Galbraith, 1973, 1977; March and Simon, 1958; Simon, 1957, 1969; Maines, 1984; Shauss, 1978). The work of Corkill and Lesser, for example, introduced an approach to coordinating nodes through the use of organizational structures, which specify a general set of long-term node responsibilities and interaction patterns. Their framework thus incorporates two important ideas. One idea is to limit the effort nodes' need to coordinate their actions by giving them each knowledge about every node's long-term organizational roles. By making its roles broad enough, a node has sufficient flexibility to respond to the demands of a dynamic situation even if its roles change infrequently. This flexibility in turn leads to the second idea behind organizational structuring, which is that a node needs enough local intelligence to continuously elaborate suitable local activities while working within the organizational guidelines. The organizational structuring approach thus provides a control framework that reduces the amount of control uncertainty present in a node (due to incomplete or errorful local-control information) and increases the likelihood that the nodes will be coherent in their behaviors by providing a general and global strategy for network problem solving. The approach was extensively evaluated in Lesser and Corkill (1983), in which nodes simulate the tracking of vehicles moving through a large geographic area.

Organizational structuring requires expertise in selecting an organization that is appropriate for the particular distributed problem-solving situation (Corkill, 1983; Durfee and Montgomery, 1991; Fox, 1981; Gasser, 1986; Hewitt, 1986; Kornfeld and Hewitt, 1981). Malone and Smith (1984) have analyzed generic organizational classes mathematically to determine their performance strengths and weaknesses with respect to processing, communication, coherence, and flexibility. Their analyses have shown that different organizational classes are appropriate given different problem situations and performance requirements. Gasser and co-workers (1989) have taken a more fluid view of organizations, in which organizations arise based on "the settled and unsettled problems about belief and action through which agents view other agents," rather than through some imposed structure. Their research (Ishida and co-workers, 1990) has concentrated on developing techniques by which agents can change how they are organized to meet their objectives in their current environment.

Kornfeld and Hewitt (1981) have proposed that distributed problem solving can be organized analogously to the structure of scientific research. In their *scientific community metaphor* for problem solving, nodes would posit either questions (goals) or answers (results) into a mutually accessible archive. The presence of this information allows a node to draw on work already performed by other nodes. They also propose using the economics of funding as the basis for controlling activity in the network. Although the metaphor is an interesting way of viewing distributed problem-solving networks, there remains significant research on effectively implementing the archival and funding mechanism in a distributed environment.

Multiagent Planning

More traditional AI research has led to viewing the problem of coordinating multiple nodes as a planning problem. This is a powerful idea for applications in which imperfect coordination could be extremely costly. In contrast with the pairwise coordination of contracting, the error-tolerating coordination of FA/C, or the ballpark coordination of organizational structuring, multiagent planning emphasizes certain avoidance of inconsistent and conflicting situations, which is critical in applications such as air-traffic control. By forming a multiagent plan, the nodes determine all of their actions and interactions beforehand, leaving nothing to chance. Because it requires that nodes share and process substantial amounts of information, multiagent planning generally involves more computation and communication than other approaches.

One technique for multiagent planning is to allow the separate agents to form their individual plans and then to send these plans to a central coordinator who analyzes them and finds potential plan conflicts (Georgeff, 1983). The idea behind this approach is that the central coordinator can identify critical regions of plans around which nodes should synchronize and can insert plan steps for sending and waiting for synchronization messages to ensure proper synchronization. A disadvantage of this technique is that having the agents first form their plans as if they were acting alone and then coordinating these plans can miss opportunities for cooperation that would have been possible had the nodes built their individual plans concurrently with reasoning about what other nodes are doing.

A second technique for multiagent planning is to forego the use of a central coordinator, and instead allow nodes to model each other's plans (Corkill, 1979; Georgeff, 1984; Konolige, 1983). For example, Corkill's (1979) distributed hierarchical planner based on NOAH allowed nodes to represent each other using MODEL nodes and to synchronize their plans through the use of distributed critics. As another example, Rosenschein and Genesereth (1987) have studied how logic-based agents with a common goal but different local information can exchange propositions to converge on identical plans. Von Martial has studied multiagent planning techniques that stress synergy rather than conflict avoidance (Von Martial, 1990). In his work, agents compare plans to discover opportunities to do favors for each other.

Sophisticated Local Control

The idea of sophisticated local control evolved from experiences with the different approaches discussed previously. The motivation is that, although it is important to provide frameworks such as negotiation protocols and organizational structures through which nodes can potentially coordinate their activities, a node still needs substantial sophistication to be able to use these frameworks appropriately. In other words, just because agents (including people) share a language and a known social structure does not mean that they will necessarily work together as an effective team. This is because agents should not simply treat coordination as an interface problem. Sophisticated local control views reasoning about coordination as an integral part of a node's local reasoning activities, where coordination considerations permeate all levels of a node's decision making.

By concentrating on sophisticated local control, the *partial global planning* approach to coordinating nodes (Durfee and Lesser, 1987, 1991; Durfee, 1988) was able to draw together many of the important ideas from negotiation, functionally accurate cooperation, organizational structuring, and multiagent planning. In partial global planning, a node represents its anticipated future problem-solving activities as a problem-solving plan. Because effective cooperation requires that nodes working on related subproblems coordinate their plans, the nodes transmit their plans to other nodes based on their meta-level organization, which identifies the long-term coordination responsibilities of the nodes (in the same way that an organizational structure specifies the long-term problem-solving responsibilities of the nodes). At any given time, a node uses whatever information it has available to represent and reason about how the actions and interactions for groups of nodes should affect its local activities. These representations are called partial global plans because they specify how different parts of the network plan to achieve more global goals. Nodes independently and asynchronously form, revise, and use partial global plans. Although communication delays and domain dynamics might mean that cooperating nodes never converge on identical partial global plans, the approach allows them to coordinate satisfactorily while still maintaining enough local autonomy to respond to important local changes in their information (Durfee and Lesser, 1988).

Partial global planning has contributed several ideas to distributed problem-solving research. One idea is that, in partial global planning, the question nodes face about how to coordinate their problem solving is itself a problem that nodes need to solve asynchronously and in parallel with solving the application domain problem. A second idea is that effective network problem solving in dynamic application domains requires that nodes balance predictability with responsiveness. For example, in the vehicle monitoring domain, as simulated in Lesser and Corkill (1983), a node should be able to consider how unilaterally changing its plans in reaction to a new event (such as seeing an unexpected vehicle) will disrupt group problem solving and whether the gains of reacting are likely to outweigh the costs of disruption. An upshot of this is that, when coordinating their activities, nodes should not always spend the time needed to optimize coordination, because a coordinated plan might become obsolete quickly. Finally, a third idea is that communicating plans not only facilitates result-sharing (by identifying which nodes are forming relevant results), but also allows task sharing. For example, partial global planning views a contract as a shared plan between two nodes and provides mechanisms for proposing (and counterproposing) such plans. Thus partial global planning provides a unifying perspective that brings together task passing and result sharing, organizational structuring and multiagent planning. Recent extensions to the partial global planning ideas have identified generic relationships between the goals of nodes (Decker and Lesser, 1988) and have recognized the need for a richer representation of node behaviors (Durfee and Montgomery, 1990, 1991). Other work in sophisticated local control has examined how complex multiagent protocols naturally follow from giving an agent the capability for evidential reasoning about uncertainty (Carver and co-workers, 1991).

FOUNDATIONS FOR REASONING ABOUT BELIEFS AND CONCURRENCY

Researchers are following a number of different approaches to extending formalisms for use in a distributed problem-solving environment. Konolige (1982, 1983) has developed the deductive model in which an agent's beliefs are described as a set of sentences in formal language together with a deductive process for deriving the consequences of those beliefs. This approach can account for the effect of resource limitations on the derivation of the consequences of beliefs. Appelt (1982) has used a possible world formalism to represent and reason about belief. A formal theory for reasoning about an agent's intentions as combinations of what it has chosen and how it is committed to its choice has been developed (Cohen and Levesque, 1987; Levesque and co-workers, 1990). Werner (1989) has also been developing a theory of communication, intention, and social structures. Rosenschein (1983) has worked on a more general theory of multiagent planning that allows for the existence of other agents and their mental states as part of the environment within which plans can be constructed. Distributed truth maintenance systems (Bridgeland and Huhns, 1990; Mason and Johnson, 1989) have also been concerned with beliefs in multiagent systems and how distributed systems with local and shared beliefs can resolve important inconsistencies among their beliefs. Additional work by Halpern and Moses (1984) is relevant to those topics (see BELIEF REPRESENTATION SYSTEMS; REASONING, PLAUSIBLE). Finally, Conry and co-workers (1990) have been investigating cooperation among theorem-proving systems (MacIntosh and co-workers, 1990).

The work on multiagent planning is closely associated with that of dialogue comprehension in natural language processing (Cohen, 1978; Allen, 1979; Cohen and Levesque, 1990). In both research topics it is necessary to reason about multiple agents with distinct and possibly contradictory mental states; mental states include not only facts or knowledge but also beliefs and goals. The reasoning required in both domains is necessary for interpreting an agent's communication (this includes understanding what the communication implies about the agent's mental state), for altering another agent's mental state through appropriate communication, and for taking into account the potential actions of other agents that might influence how it can achieve its goals. Through dialogue, the agents can converge on shared plans (Grosz and Sidner, 1985, 1988).

Another research approach toward developing a formal theory for understanding the nature of cooperation, competition, and communication among multiple agents has incorporated ideas from economics and game theory into distributed problem solving (Rosenschein and Genesereth, 1985; Zlotkin and Rosenschein, 1989, 1990, 1991). The main idea behind this line of research is that agents can be viewed as rational, utility-maximizing entities who will negotiate to make deals that increase their individual expected utilities in both cooperative and noncooperative domains. This work has introduced *unified negotiation protocol* through which such agents converge on joint plans, called semicooperative deals, that increase all of their expected utilities despite the fact that each has a chance of not achieving its goals.

CONCLUSION

Distributed problem solving and the larger field of distributed AI (Bond and Gasser, 1988; Gasser and Huhns, 1989; Huhns, 1987), which includes studying systems composed of agents that might be competing or coexisting intelligently, is still undergoing evolution. It holds much promise for exploiting the technology available today, including large computer networks and multiple stand-alone expert systems, and for shedding light on how to design complex AI systems. As Nilsson (1980) has noted the challenges posed by distributed AI will contribute to (and may even be a prerequisite for) progress in ordinary AI. While none of the approaches developed to date represents a general answer to all the coordination needs in every distributed problem-solving network, this discussion has illustrated the richness of the ideas that have been developed so far.

BIBLIOGRAPHY

M. R. Adler, A. B. Davis, R. Weihmayer, and R. Worrest, "Conflict-Resolution Strategies for Nonhierarchical Distributed Agents," in Gasser and Huhns, 1989.

J. F. Allen, *A Plan-Based Approach to Speech Act Recognition,* Ph.D. dissertation, University of Toronto, 1979.

D. E. Appelt, *Planning Natural Language Utterances to Satisfy Multiple Goals,* Technical Note 259, SRI International, Menlo Park, Calif., 1982.

R. C. Arkin, E. M. Riseman, and A. R. Hanson, "ArRA: An Architecture for Vision-Based Robot Navigation," in *Proceedings of the DARPA Image Understanding Workshop,* Los Angeles, 1987, pp. 17–431.

A. H. Bond and L. Gasser, *Readings in Distributed Artificial Intelligence,* Morgan-Kaufmann, San Mateo, Calif., 1988.

D. M. Bridgeland and M. N. Huhns, "Distributed Truth Maintenance," in *Proceedings of the Ninth National Conference on Artificial Intelligence,* Boston, Mass., AAAI, Menlo Park, Calif., 1990, pp. 72–77.

S. Cammarata, D. McArthur, and R. Steeb, "Strategies of Cooperation in Distributed Problem Solving," in *Proceedings of the Eighth IJCAI,* Karlsruhe, FRG, Morgan-Kaufmann, San Mateo, Calif., 1983, pp. 767–770.

N. Carver, Z. Cretanovic, and V. Lesser, "Sophisticated Cooperation in FA/C Distributed Problem Solving Systems," in *Proceedings of the National Conference on Artificial Intelligence,* July 1991.

E. Chang, "Participant Systems," in Huhns, 1987, pp. 311–339.

P. R. Cohen, *On Knowing What to Say: Planning Speech Acts,* Ph.D. dissertation, University of Toronto, 1978.

P. R. Cohen and H. J. Levesque, "Intention = Choice + Commitment," in *Proceedings of the Sixth National Conference on Artificial Intelligence,* Seattle, Wash., AAAI, Menlo Park, Calif., 1987, pp. 410–415.

P. R. Cohen and H. J. Levesque, "Rational Interaction as the Basis for Communication," in P. R. Cohen, J. Morgan, and M. E. Pollack, eds., *Intentions in Communication,* MIT Press, Cambridge, Mass., 1990.

S. E. Conry, K. Kuwabara, V. R. Lesser, and R. A. Meyer, "Multistage Negotiation for Distributed Constraint Satisfaction," *IEEE Trans. Sys. Man Cybernet.,* 1991.

S. E. Conry, D. J. MacIntosh, and R. A. Meyer, "DARES: A Distributed Automated Reasoning System," in *Proceedings of the Ninth National Conference on Artificial Intelligence,* Boston, Mass., AAAI, Menlo Park, Calif., 1990, pp. 78–85.

S. E. Conry, R. A. Meyer, and V. R. Lesser, "Multistage Negotiation in Distributed Planning," in A. H. Bond and L. Gasser, eds., *Readings in Distributed Artificial Intelligence,* Morgan-Kaufman, San Mateo, Calif., 1988, pp. 367–384.

S. Conry, R. Meyer, and J. Searlemen, "A Shared Knowledge Base for Independent Problem Solving Agents," in *Proceedings of the IEEE Expert Systems in Government Symposium,* McLean, Va., Oct. 1985.

D. D. Corkill, "Hierarchical Planning in a Distributed Environment," in *Proceedings of the Sixth IJCAI,* Cambridge, Mass., Morgan-Kaufmann, San Mateo, Calif., 1979, pp. 168–175.

D. D. Corkill, *A Framework for Organizational Self-Design in Distributed Problem Solving Networks,* Ph.D. dissertation, University of Massachusetts, Amherst, 1983.

D. D. Corkill and V. R. Lesser, "The Use of Meta-Level Control for Coordination in a Distributed Problem Solving Network," in *Proceedings of the Eighth IJCAI,* Karlsruhe, FRG, Morgan-Kaufmann, San Mateo, Calif., 1983, pp. 748–756.

W. B. Croft and L. S. Lefkowitz, "Knowledge-Based Support of Cooperative Activities," in *Proceedings of the Twenty-first Annual Hawaii International Conference on System Sciences,* Vol. 3, IEEE Computer Society Press, Washington, D.C., 1988, pp. 312–318.

K. Decker and V. Lesser, "Extending the Partial Global Planning Framework for Cooperative Distributed Problem Solving Control," in *Proceedings of the 1990 DARPA Workshop on Innovative Approaches to Planning, Scheduling, and Control,* Nov. 1990, pp. 396–407.

E. H. Durfee, *Coordination of Distributed Problem Solvers,* Kluwer Academic Publishers, Boston, Mass., 1988.

E. H. Durfee and V. R. Lesser, "Using Partial Global Plans to Coordinate Distributed Problem Solvers," in *Proceedings of the Tenth IJCAI,* Milan, Italy, Morgan-Kaufmann, San Mateo, Calif., 1987, pp. 875–883.

E. H. Durfee and V. R. Lesser, "Predictability Versus Responsiveness: Coordinating Problem Solvers in Dynamic Domains," in *Proceedings of the Seventh National Conference on Artificial Intelligence,* St. Paul, Minn., 1988, pp. 66–71.

E. H. Durfee and V. R. Lesser, "Negotiating Task Decomposition and Allocation Using Partial Global Planning," in L. Gasser and M. N. Huhns, 1989, pp. 229–243.

E. H. Durfee and V. R. Lesser, "Partial Global Planning: A Coordination Framework for Distributed Hypothesis Formation," *IEEE Trans. Sys. Man Cybernet.* **21**(5), (Sept. 1991).

E. H. Durfee and T. A. Montgomery, "A Hierarchical Protocol for Coordinating Multiagent Behaviors," in *Proceedings of the Ninth National Conference on Artificial Intelligence,* 1990, pp. 86–93.

E. H. Durfee and T. A. Montgomery, "Coordination as Distributed Search in a Hierarchical Behavior Space," *IEEE Trans. Sys. Man Cybernet.,* 1991.

L. D. Erman, F. Hayes-Roth, V. R. Lesser, and D. R. Reddy, "The Hearsay-II Speech-Understanding System: Integrating

Knowledge to Resolve Uncertainty," *Comput. Surv.* **12**(2), 213–253 (June 1980).

N. V. Findler and R. Lo, "An Examination of Distributed Planning in the World of Air Traffic Control," *J. Parallel Distributed Comput.* **3**, 411–431 (1986).

M. S. Fox, "An Organizational View of Distributed Systems," *IEEE Trans. Sys. Man Cybernet.* **11**(1), 70–80 (Jan. 1981).

J. Galbraith, *Designing Complex Organizations,* Addison-Wesley Publishing Co., Inc., Reading, Mass., 1973.

J. R. Galbraith, *Organization Design,* Addison-Wesley Publishing Co., Inc., Reading, Mass., 1977.

L. Gasser, "The Integration of Computing and Routine Work," *ACM Trans. Office Inf. Sys.* **4**(3), 205–225 (July 1986).

L. Gasser, "Social Conception of Knowledge and Action: DAI Foundations and Open Systems Semantics," *Artif. Intell.* **48** (1991).

L. Gasser and M. N. Huhns, eds., *Distributed Artificial Intelligence,* Vol. 2, Research Notes in Artificial Intelligence, Pitman, London, 1989.

L. Gasser, N. Rouquette, R. W. Hill, and J. Lieb, "Representing and Using Organizational Knowledge in DAI Systems," in Gasser and Huhns, 1989, pp. 55–78.

M. Georgeff, "Communication and Interaction in Multi-Agent Planning," in *Proceedings of the Third National Conference on Artificial Intelligence,* Washington, D.C., Morgan-Kaufmann, San Mateo, Calif., 1983, pp. 125–129.

M. Georgeff, "A Theory of Action for Multiagent Planning," in *Proceedings of the Fourth National Conference on Artificial Intelligence,* Austin, Tex., San Mateo, Calif., 1984, pp. 121–125.

S. Goyal and R. Worrest, "Expert System Applications to Network Management," in J. Leibowitz, ed., *Expert System Applications to Telecommunications,* Vol. 1, John Wiley & Sons, Inc., New York, 1988, pp. 3–44.

B. J. Grosz and C. L. Sidner, "Discourse structure and the proper Treatment of Interruptions," in *Proceedings of the Ninth IJCAI,* Los Angeles, Morgan-Kaufmann, San Mateo, Calif., 1985, pp. 832–839.

B. J. Grosz and C. Sidner, "Plans for Discourse," in P. R. Cohen, J. Morgan, and M. E. Pollack, eds., *Intentions in Communication,* MIT Press, Cambridge, Mass., 1990.

J. Y. Halpern and Y. Moses, "Knowledge and Common Knowledge in a Distributed Environment," in *Third ACM Conference on Principles of Distributed Computing,* 1984.

C. Hewitt, "Viewing Control Structures as Patterns of Passing Messages," *Artif. Intell.* **8**(3), 323–364 (Fall 1977).

C. Hewitt, "Offices Are Open Systems," *ACM Trans. Office Inf. Sys.* **4**(3), 271–287 (July 1986).

C. Hewitt and J. Inman, "DAI Betwixt and Between: From 'Intelligent Agents' to Open Systems Science," *IEEE Trans. Sys. Man. Cybernet.,* 1991.

M. Huhns, ed., *Distributed Artificial Intelligence,* Morgan-Kaufmann, San Mateo, Calif., 1987.

M. N. Huhns and D. M. Bridgeland, "Multiagent Truth Maintenance," *IEEE Trans. Sys. Man Cybernet.,* 1991.

M. N. Huhns, U. Mukhopadhyay, L. M. Stephens, and R. D. Bonnell, "DAI for Document Retrieval: The MINDS Project," in M. Huhns, 1987, pp. 249–284.

T. Ishida, M. Yokoo, and L. Gasser, "An Organizational Approach to Adaptive Production Systems," in *Proceedings of the Ninth National Conference on Artificial Intelligence,* 1990, pp. 52–58.

M. Klein, "Supporting Conflict Resolution in Cooperative Design Systems," *IEEE Trans. Sys. Man. Cybernet.,* 1991.

K. Konolige, "Circumscriptive Ignorance," in *Proceedings of the Second National Conference on Artificial Intelligence,* Pittsburgh, Pa., AAAI, Menlo Park, Calif., 1982, pp. 202–204.

K. Konolige, "A Deductive Model of Belief," in *Proceedings of the Eighth IJCAI,* 1983, pp. 377–381.

W. A. Kornfeld, "ETHER: A Parallel Problem Solving System," in *Proceedings of the Sixth IJCAI,* 1979, pp. 490–492.

W. A. Kornfeld and C. E. Hewitt, "The Scientific Community Metaphor," *IEEE Trans. Sys. Man Cybernet.* **11**(1), 24–33 (Jan. 1981).

S. E. Lander, V. R. Lesser, and M. E. Connell, "Knowledge-Based Conflict Resolution for Cooperation Among Expert Agents," in D. Sriram, R. Logher, and S. Fukuda, eds., *Computer-Aided Cooperative Product Development,* Springer-Verlag, New York, 1991.

D. B. Lenat, "Beings: Knowledge as Interacting Experts," in *Proceedings of the Fourth IJCAI,* Tbilisi, Ga., Morgan-Kaufmann, San Mateo, Calif., 1975.

V. R. Lesser, "A Retrospective View of FA/C Distributed Problem Solving," *IEEE Trans. Sys. Man Cybernet.,* 1991.

V. R. Lesser and D. D. Corkill, "Functionally Accurate, Cooperative Distributed Systems," *IEEE Trans. Sys. Man Cybernet.* **11**(1), 81–96 (Jan. 1981).

V. R. Lesser and D. D. Corkill, "The Distributed Vehicle Monitoring Testbed: A Tool for Investigating Distributed Problem Solving Networks," *AI Mag.* **4**(3), 15–33 (Fall 1983).

V. R. Lesser and L. D. Erman, "Distributed Interpretation: A Model and Experiment," *IEEE Trans. Comput.* **29**(12), 1144–1163 (Dec. 1980).

H. J. Levesque, P. R. Cohen, and J. H. T. Nunes, "On Acting Together," in *Proceedings of the Ninth National Conference on Artificial Intelligence,* 1990, pp. 94–99.

J. L. McClelland, D. E. Rumelhart, and the PDP Research Group, *Parallel Distributed Processing: Explorations in the Microstructure of Cognition,* 2 vols., MIT Press, Cambridge, Mass., 1987.

D. J. MacIntosh, S. E. Conry, and R. A. Meyer, "Distributed Automated Reasoning: Issues in Coordination, Cooperation, and Performance," *IEEE Trans. Sys. Man Cybernet.* 1991.

D. Maines, *Urban Life,* Special issue on negotiated order theory (1984).

T. W. Malone, "What is Coordination Theory?" in *Proceedings of the National Science Foundation Coordination Theory Workshop,* Feb. 1988.

T. W. Malone and S. A. Smith, *Tradeoffs in Designing Organizations: Implications for New Forms of Human Organizations and Computer Systems,* Working Paper **CISR WP 112** (Sloan WP **1541-84**), Center for Information Systems Research, MIT, Cambridge, Mass., Mar. 1984.

J. G. March and H. A. Simon, *Organizations,* Wiley, New York, 1958.

C. L. Mason and R. R. Johnson, "DATMS: A Framework for Distributed Assumption Based Reasoning," in Gasser and Huhns, 1989, pp. 293–317.

C. Mason, R. Johnson, R. Searfus, D. Lager, and T. Canales, "A Seismic Event Analyzer for Nuclear Test Ban Treaty Verification," in *Proceedings of the Third International Conference on Applications of Artificial Intelligence in Engineering,* 1988.

M. S. Mazer, "Exploring the Use of Distributed Problem-Solving in Office Support Systems," in *Proceedings of the IEEE Com-*

puter Society Symposium on Office Automation, 1987, pp. 217–225.

N. J. Nilsson, "Two Heads Are Better Than One," *SIGART Newslett.* **73,** 43 (Oct. 1980).

S. Nirenburg and V. Lesser, "Providing Intelligent Assistance in Distributed Office Environments," in Bond and Gasser, 1988, pp. 590–598.

J. Y-C Pan and J. M. Tenenbaum, "An Intelligent Agent Framework for Enterprise Integration," *IEEE Trans. Sys. Man Cybernet.,* 1991.

J. P. Rice, *Poligon: A System for Parallel Problem Solving,* Technical Report KSL-86-19, Knowledge Systems Laboratory, Stanford University, Palo Alto, Calif., Apr. 1986.

J. S. Rosenschein and M. R. Genesereth, "Deals Among Rational Agents," in *Proceedings of the Ninth IJCAI,* 1985, pp. 91–99.

J. S. Rosenschein and M. R. Genesereth, "Communication and Cooperation Among Logic-Based Agents," in *Proceedings of the Sixth Phoenix Conference on Computers and Communications,* Scottsdale, Ariz., 1987, pp. 594–600.

S. Rosenschein, "Reasoning About Distributed Action," *SIGART Newslett.,* no. 84, 7 (1983).

A. Sathi, T. E. Morton, and S. F. Roth, "Callisto: An Intelligent Project Management System," *AI Mag.* **7**(5), 34–52 (1986).

E. Schoen, *The CAOS System,* Technical Report STAN-CS-86-1125, Computer Science Department, Stanford University, Stanford, Calif., Mar. 1986.

H. A. Simon, *Models of Man,* Wiley, New York, 1957.

H. A. Simon, *The Sciences of the Artificial,* MIT Press, Cambridge, Mass., 1969.

D. Smith and M. Broadwell, "Plan Coordination in Support of Expert Systems," in *Proceedings of the DARPA Image Understanding Workshop,* Los Angeles, 1987.

R. G. Smith, "The Contract Net Protocol: High-Level Communication and Control in a Distributed Problem Solver," *IEEE Trans. Comput.* **29**(12), 1104–1113 (Dec. 1980).

R. G. Smith and R. Davis, "Frameworks for Cooperation in Distributed Problem Solving," *IEEE Trans. Sys. Man Cybernet.* **11**(1), 61–70 (Jan. 1981).

S. F. Smith and J. E. Hynynen, "Integrated Decentralization of Production Management: An Approach for Factory Scheduling," in Liu, Requicha, and Chandrasekar, eds., *Intelligent and Integrated Manufacturing Analysis and Synthesis,* The American Society of Mechanical Engineers, New York, 1987, pp. 427–439.

R. Steeb, S. Cammarata, S. Narain, J. Rothenburg, and W. Giarla, *Cooperative Intelligence for Remotely Piloted Vehicle Fleet Control,* Technical Report R-3408-ARPA, Rand Corp., Santa Monica, Calif., Oct. 1986.

A. Strauss, *Negotiations: Varieties, Processes, Contexts, and Social Order,* Jossey Bass, San Francisco, 1978.

K. Sycara, "Planning for Negotiation: A Case-Based Approach," in *Proceedings of the DARPA Image Understanding Workshop,* Los Angeles, 1987, pp. 11.1–11.10.

K. Sycara, "Resolving Goal Conflicts via Negotiation," in *Proceedings of the Seventh National Conference on Artificial Intelligence,* 1988, pp. 245–250.

K. Sycara, S. Roth, N. Sadeh, and M. Fox, "Distributed Constrained Heuristic Search," *IEEE Trans. Sys. Man Cybernet.,* 1991

K. P. Sycara, "Multiagent Compromise via Negotiation," in Gasser and Huhns, 1989.

P. W. Thorndyke, D. McArthur, and S. Cammarata, "Autopilot: A Distributed Planner for Air Fleet Control," in *Proceedings of the Seventh IJCAI,* Vancouver, B.C., Morgan-Kaufmann, San Mateo, Calif., 1981, pp. 171–177.

H. Van Dyke Parunak, "Manufacturing Experience with the Contract Net," in Huhns, 1987, pp. 285–310.

H. Van Dyke Parunak, B. W. Irish, J. Kindrick, and P. W. Lozo, "Fractal Actors for Distributed Manufacturing Control," in *Proceedings of the Second IEEE Conference on AI Applications,* Dec. 1985, pp. 653–660.

F. von Martial, "Coordination of Plans in Multiagent Worlds by Taking Advantage of the Favor Relation," in *Proceedings of the 1990 Distributed AI Workshop,* Oct. 1990.

K. J. Werkman, *Multiagent Cooperative Problem Solving Through Negotiation and Perspective Sharing,* Ph.D. dissertation, Lehigh University, Bethlehem, Pa., 1990.

E. Werner, "Cooperating Agents: A Unified Theory of Communication and Social Structure," in Gasser and Huhns, 1989.

R. Wesson, F. Hayes-Roth, J. W. Burge, C. Statz, and C. A. Sunshine, "Network Structures for Distributed Situation Assessment," *IEEE Trans. Sys. Man Cybernet.* **11**(1), 5–23 (Jan. 1981).

M. Yokoo, T. Ishida, and K. Kuwabara, "Distributed Constraint Satisfaction for DAI Problems," in *Proceedings of the 1990 Distributed AI Workshop,* Bandara, Tex., Oct. 1990.

G. Zlotkin and J. S. Rosenschein, "Negotiation and Task Sharing Among Autonomous Agents in Cooperative Domains," in *Proceedings of the Eleventh IJCAI,* Detroit, Mich., Morgan-Kaufmann, San Mateo, Calif., 1989.

G. Zlotkin and J. S. Rosenschein, "Negotiation and Conflict Resolution in Noncooperative Domains," in *Proceedings of the Ninth National Conference on Artificial Intelligence,* 1990, pp. 100–105.

G. Zlotkin and J. S. Rosenschein, "Cooperation and Conflict Resolution Via Negotiation Among Autonomous Agents in Non-Cooperative Domains," *IEEE Trans. Sys. Man Cybernet.,* 1991.

EDMUND H. DURFEE
University of Michigan

VICTOR R. LESSER
DANIEL D. CORKILL
University of Massachusetts

DOMAIN KNOWLEDGE

Domain knowledge is the collection of problem-specific facts, goals, and procedures that a knowledge-based system needs in order to solve problems. Domain knowledge also includes the concepts, attributes, and relations that make up these facts, goals, and procedures. It contrasts with domain-independent knowledge, such as general heuristics (qv) and strategies of problem solving, and theories that cover many different domains and types of problems. Both kinds of knowledge can include declarative and procedural components. In an expert system, the knowledge base usually contains the domain knowledge, whereas the inference engine is domain independent.

For example, in a system that diagnoses computer malfunctions, the domain knowledge would at the very least include typical breakdown patterns, underlying causes, and the relations between the two, in other words, the empirical expertise needed to track down a malfunction. More detailed domain knowledge would include descriptions of the structure and function of the particular machine being analyzed together with procedures for interpreting or understanding these descriptions. Domain-independent knowledge would consist of the general diagnostic heuristics and reasoning strategies for identifying the causes of malfunctions in any kind of computer or even machine.

The boundary between domain knowledge and domain-independent knowledge depends on the goals defined for the knowledge-based system rather than on any inherent properties of the knowledge itself. In an expert system for diagnosing problems in any kind of personal computer, the domain knowledge would have to cover enough specifics for all machines falling into this very broad category. It is more effective to design knowledge bases for smaller and more circumscribed problems, such as the diagnosis of malfunctions in one specific computer model or at most a single family of personal computers that share the same architecture and operating system and hence similar modes of malfunction.

Domain knowledge was distinctively used as a term only after AI systems moved away from general problem-solving paradigms, such as heuristic search, and started to develop methods of symbolic reasoning that relied heavily on specific, qualitative knowledge of a problem or class of problems. An early example is the MACSYMA (qv) (Moses, 1975) system for symbolic integration, which has extensive domain knowledge of calculus, the rules of integration, and procedures for simplifying formulas. Another is heuristic DENDRAL (Buchanan and Feigenbaum, 1978), where domain knowledge of molecular structures, the process of mass spectrometry, and the heuristics used by chemists in interpreting mass spectra is used to elucidate the structure of a molecule. These and other early knowledge-based systems solved very specialized kinds of problems, and they did not result in any generalized representations for domain knowledge that could be shared by a wide variety of problems in different domains.

Research on natural language understanding (qv) and problem solving (qv) gave rise to useful general representations of domain knowledge, semantic networks (qv) and production systems (see RULE-BASED SYSTEMS), respectively. The former were particularly good for representing concepts and their relations in a declarative fashion, whereas the latter served to express the facts needed to solve a problem in terms of modular, easy to manipulate chunks of knowledge. Other representations, such as frames (see FRAMES), were developed to describe more complex, structured relations among concepts, objects, and events in a domain.

CONSULTATION PROGRAMS

It was research on expert reasoning in consultation programs such as MYCIN (qv) (Shortliffe, 1976), CASNET (Weiss and co-workers, 1978), INTERNIST (qv) (Pople, 1982), PIP (Pauker and co-workers, 1976) and PROSPECTOR (qv) (Duda and co-workers, 1979) that led to the clear division between domain knowledge and domain-independent reasoning procedures. In trying to represent human expertise in ways that could be practically reproduced on the computer, their developers naturally tended to ab-

stract those methods and heuristics of symbolic reasoning that were shared by a broad class of real-life problems. They used various declarative representations for domain knowledge (such as special types of semantic nets for encoding causal and hierarchical relations, frames for grouping these relations, and production rules for representing the rules of expertise). General strategies of symbolic reasoning (whether goal-driven, event-driven, or hypothesis-driven) were found to be applicable for wide varieties of diagnostic, therapy selection, and advice-giving interpretation problems, giving rise to the notion that the knowledge base could contain the domain-specific knowledge, whereas a separate inference engine could serve to capture the domain-independent strategies. At about the same time, research on speech understanding (qv) [the HEARSAY (qv) system (Erman and co-workers, 1980)] showed that domain knowledge is often naturally grouped according to distinct sources or levels of understanding, such as those referring to the signal, syntax, semantics, and pragmatics involved in recognizing a segment of speech. This gave rise to the notion of grouping knowledge in terms of different knowledge sources (which can contain groups of rules and networks of relations among concepts used by these rules). They communicate through a blackboard, which serves as the short-term memory for storing partial interpretations.

FIRST-GENERATION EXPERT SYSTEMS

From the experience with the first generation of expert systems rule-based representations of domain knowledge proved to be the most versatile and effective way of directly encoding expertise for problem solving. Rules can capture inferences about hypotheses from patterns of evidence, relations among goals and subgoals, or inferences about hypotheses (see Table 1). In some situations it is valuable to build a discrimination net among hypotheses to explicitly map out the flow of reasoning (as in PROSPECTOR), but it is more usual to let the inference engine select the production rules according to its strategies. Several general schemes for representing rule-based knowledge were developed as the result of experience with the first generation of expert systems: EMYCIN (qv) (Van Melle, 1979), EXPERT (Weiss and Kulikowski, 1979), KAS (Reboh, 1980), and ROSIE (qv) (Fain and co-workers, 1982). Other general schemes implemented the blackboard type of representation: HEARSAY-III (Erman and co-workers, 1981) and AGE (Nii and Aiello, 1979). They all provide the user with a way of encoding domain knowledge in the form of rules that are then interpreted by an inference engine with a fixed, though general repertoire of reasoning strategies. These systems can be viewed as knowledge engineering toolkits.

LANGUAGES AND ENVIRONMENTS

A different approach was taken by developers of rule-based languages such as OPS (Forgy and McDermott, 1977) and RLL (Greiner and Lenat, 1980), which permit the user to specify reasoning strategies as part of the domain knowledge. The control of reasoning in these lan-

Table 1. Examples Contrasting Different Degrees of Domain Dependency in Knowledge Within a Rule-Based System

1. Example of domain knowledge for thyroid disease diagnosis:
   a. Define primitive reasoning components: rapid heart beat is a symptom; fast finger tremor is a symptom.
   b. Define diagnostic statements: hyperthyroidism is a diagnosis; hypothyroidism is a diagnosis.
   c. Define reasoning rules relating them:
      If rapid heart beat is observed in a patient, suspect the possibility of hyperthyroidism with a confidence of 0.5.
      If both rapid heart beat and fine finger tremor are observed in a patient, suspect the possibility of hypothyroidism with a confidence of 0.7 and proceed to ask for laboratory tests.

   This information is only valid for problems involving thyroid disease.

2. Example of a diagnostic heuristic (only partially domain dependent):

   If no diagnosis has been assigned a level of confidence sufficient for treatment to be prescribed, and no life-threatening situation is present, continue accumulating data befor reaching a diagnosis.

   This heuristic is reasonable for any medical domain, but might not be applicable for problems of diagnosis machine failure.

3. Example of a completely domain-independent rule:

   If two diagnostic rules confirm the same conclusion with different degrees of confidence, a conservative strategy is to ascribe to the diagnosis the lower degree of confidence.

   This heuristic is applicable to any inference problem of the diagnostic type regardless of domain.

guages is very general (the recognize-act cycle in OPS is a simple loop in which rules with satisfied antecedents are detected, certain criteria are used to select one of them, and the actions specified in its consequent are executed). The user here has the burden of specifying the structure of goals and methods requir to solve a problem rather than being able to choose from a more fixed representation. This is necessary if the class of problems being solved does not fit one of the more traditional categories, such as diagnostic classification or advice giving, for which the expert systems representations were mostly devised. A related approach is to use logic programming (qv) languages such as PROLOG (Colmeraurer and co-workers, 1983) to represent domain knowledge in the form of clauses and rules for expert reasoning. The inference engine then consists of a domain-independent theorem prover specialized to certain kinds of clauses and inference procedures for efficiency. It has the advantage of making reasoning models more easy to check for logical consistency but at the cost of restrictions on the class of inference procedures. This method has been adopted by the Japanese Fifth Generation Computer Project to develop specialized hardware that will carry out symbolic reasoning tasks very rapidly. In PROLOG, as in OPS and other language systems, domain-specific reasoning strategies must be implemented by the user.

For more advanced knowledge-based expert systems the representational power of rules can be usefully augmented by introducing ways of explicitly describing the objects and predicates that enter into the antecedents and consequents of a rule. There are also situations where procedures are a more natural representation than rules, and it is important to provide the means of integrating the two. Graphical display of knowledge structures is also essential in managing large and complex knowledge bases. Several object-oriented languages (qv) and environments (see PROGRAMMING ENVIRONMENTS) that incorporate these features have been developed to facilitate the building of knowledge bases [eg, LOOPS (qv) (Stefik and co-workers, 1983) and STROBE (Smith, 1983)]. These are primarily toolkits for representing and manipulating knowledge. Special expert system building packages are sometimes built using many of the same components [eg, the KEE system (Kehler and Clemenson, 1984)]. Alternatively, a first-order resolution theorem prover can be used for reasoning with a frame-based description language, as in KRYPTON (Brachman and co-workers, 1985). This approach combines logical clarity with descriptive power, allowing a more precise definition of the semantics of the knowledge, so that the user can know what questions the system is capable of answering. All these hybrid reasoning systems add an extra degree of flexibility and complexity in helping structure domain knowledge since they usually come with built-in mechanisms for the inheritance of properties for hierarchically related objects as well as facilities for defining classes of objects and the reasoning elements that relate them. In so doing, it often happens that domain knowledge is strongly intertwined with domain-independent reasoning methods and heuristics since there is no clear boundary between them. Only as experience accumulates with large numbers of complex knowledge bases will the generality of certain heuristics and reasoning schemas be recognized and the types of specific domain-dependent knowledge more clearly defined.

BIBLIOGRAPHY

R. J. Brachman, V. P. Gilbert, and H. J. Levesque, "An Essential Hybrid Reasoning System: Knowledge and Symbol Level Accounts of KRYPTON," in *Proceedings of the Ninth IJCAI*, Los Angeles, Calif., Morgan-Kaufmann, San Mateo, Calif., 1985, pp. 533–539.

B. G. Buchanan and E. A. Feigenbaum, "DENDRAL and Meta-DENDRAL: Their Applications Dimension," *J. Artif. Intell.* **11**, 5–24 (1978).

A. Colmeraurer, H. Kanoui, and M. Van Caneghem, "Prolog, Theoretical Principles and Current Trends," *Technology and Science of Informatics*, **2**(4) (1983).

R. Duda, J. Gaschnig, and P. E. Hart, "Model Design in the PROSPECTOR Consultant System for Mineral Exploration," in D. Michie, ed., *Expert Systems in the Micro-Electronic Age*, Edinburgh University Press, Edinburgh, UK, 1979, pp. 153–167.

L. D. Erman, F. Hayes-Roth, and D. R. Reddy, "The HEARSAY-II Speech Understanding System: Integrating Knowledge to Resolve Uncertainty," *Comput. Surv.* **2**(12), 213–253 (1980).

L. D. Erman, P. E. London, and S. F. Fickas, "The Design and an Example Use of HEARSAY-III," in *Proceedings of the Seventh IJCAI*, Vancouver, B.C., Morgan-Kaufmann, San Mateo, Calif., 1981, pp. 409–415.

J. Fain, F. Hayes-Roth, H. Sowirzal, and D. Waterman, *Programming in ROSIE: An Introduction by Means of Examples*, RAND Technical Report N-1647-ARPA, Rand Corp., Santa Monica, Calif., 1982.

C. Forgy and J. McDermott, "OPS: A Domain-Independent Production System Language," in *Proceedings of the Fifth IJCAI*, Cambridge, Mass., Morgan-Kaufmann, San Mateo, Calif., 1977, pp. 933–939.

R. Greiner and D. Lenat, "A Representation Language Language," in *Proceedings of the First National Conference on Artificial Intelligence*, Stanford, Calif., AAAI, Menlo Park, Calif., 1980, pp. 165–169.

T. P. Kehler and G. D. Clemenson, "KEE: The Knowledge Engineering Environment for Industry," *Syst. Softw.* **34**, 212–224 (1984).

J. Moses, *A MACSYMA Primer*, Mathlab Memo, No. 2, Computer Science Laboratory, MIT, Cambridge, Mass., 1975.

H. P. Nii and N. Aiello, "AGE(Attempt to Generalize): A Knowledge-Based Program for Building Knowledge-Based Programs," in *Proceedings of the Sixth IJCAI*, Tokyo, Japan, Morgan-Kaufmann, San Mateo, Calif., 1979, pp. 645–655.

S. G. Pauker, G. A. Gorry, J. P. Kaissirer, and W. B. Schwartz, "Towards the Simulation of Clinical Cognition: Taking a Present Illness by Computer," *Am. J. Med.* **60**, 981–996 (1976).

H. Pople, "Heuristic Methods for Imposing Structure on Ill-Structured Problems: The Structuring of Medical Diagnostics," in P. Szolovits, ed., *Artificial Intelligence in Medicine*, Boulder, Colo., 1982, pp. 119–190.

R. Reboh, *Knowledge Engineering Techniques and Tools in the PROSPECTOR Environment*, SRI Technical Note No. **243**, SRI, Menlo Park, Calif., 1980.

E. H. Shortliffe, *Computer-Based Medical Consultations: MY-CIN*, Elsevier, New York, 1976.

R. G. Smith, Strobe: "Support for Structured Object Knowledge Representation," in *Proceedings of the Eighth IJCAI*, Karlsruhe, FRG, Morgan-Kaufmann, San Mateo, Calif., 1983, pp. 855–858.

M. J. Stefik, D. G. Bobrow, S. Mittal, and L. Conway, "Knowledge Programming in LOOPS," *AI Mag.* 4(3), 41–54 (1983).

W. Van Melle, "A Domain-Independent Production-Rule System for Consultation Programs," in *Proceedings of the Sixth IJCAI*, 1979, pp. 923–925.

S. M. Weiss and C. A. Kulikowski, "EXPERT: A System for Developing Consultation Models," in *Proceedings of the Sixth IJCAI*, 1979, pp. 942–950.

S. M. Weiss, C. A. Kulikowski, S. Amarel, and A. Safir, "A Model-Based Method for Computer-Aided Medical Decision-Making," *J. Artif. Intell.* **11**, 145–172 (1978).

C. KULIKOWSKI
Rutgers University

DYNAMIC MEMORY

Dynamic memory is the name of a theory of episodic memory (qv) organization proposed by Schank (1982). The basic idea of the theory of dynamic memory is that memory representations are dynamic, that is, they are constantly changing as a result of processing new inputs and making generalizations. The theory details how episodes are indexed and stored in memory, how they are analyzed at several levels of generality, and how they can be retrieved and used to understand new episodes.

DEVELOPMENT OF THE THEORY

The theory of dynamic memory developed in response to limitations of the script-based theory of memory, an earlier theory proposed by Schank and Abelson (1975). Although it was useful in early research on understanding stereotypical stories, the notion of scripts (qv) proved to be too limiting; they were too large and inflexible to be used in understanding new stories that did not conform to known stereotypes. In addition, systems that used scripts as their primary knowledge structure did not learn or generalize in any real sense. That is, they would process a story the same way the second time as it was done the first time. This is a serious limitation since it is so clearly at odds with the way people do it. People immediately recognize when they are hearing a story they have already heard; script-based programs like FRUMP (qv), SAM (qv), PAM (qv), and POLITICS (qv) did not.

In addition to the problems discovered while building computer models using scripts, psychological experiments on human memory also began to cast some doubts on the adequacy of existing models of memory. In an experiment conducted by Bower, Black, and Turner (1979), subjects confused events from stories even though the stories should have been activating different scripts. For example, when told stories about visits to doctors' and dentists' offices, subjects would mistakenly recall events that had taken place in the doctor's waiting room as having occurred in the dentist's waiting room and vice versa. This was a serious problem for a script-based theory of memory since information about stereotypical event sequences, like visits to doctors' and dentists' offices, were supposed to be stored in separate scripts. If this were the case, the subjects should not have confused the events like they did. This, in conjunction with the problems from the computer implementations, led to the desire for a theory that was flexible enough to overcome the limitations inherent in scripts.

OVERVIEW OF THE THEORY

The theory of dynamic memory was created to overcome the limitations of a static, script-based model of memory. The three main questions addressed by the theory are:

1. What high level structures are likely to be used in memory?
2. How does the information in these structures get used in processing new inputs and recalling old ones?
3. How do experiences that have been processed change the organization of memory?

In order to account for the kind of errors people make when understanding stories, it became clear that memory had to be reconstructive. That is, information about an episode appeared to be broken up into smaller, sharable pieces and stored in a distributed fashion throughout memory. When recalling an episode, the various pieces had to be collected and reconstructed. These pieces of memory are called scenes. Examples of scenes from the doctor's office example include WAITING ROOM, INNER-OFFICE, and PAY. Scenes may have particular scripts attached to them. In our example, the WAITING ROOM scene might point to the script $DOCTOR JONES' WAITING ROOM. Thus, in this conception of memory, scenes are general structures that describe how and where a particular set of actions take place, while scripts provide specific predictions about how the scene is instantiated in various familiar contexts. A script is bounded by the scene containing it; it does not cross scene boundaries.

Organizing scenes into larger sequences are structures called *memory organization packets* (qv), or MOPs. MOPs connect scenes together and help in processing by providing expectations about what might happen next. An example of a MOP that would be active in our doctor's office example is M-PROFESSIONAL OFFICE VISIT (the M- prefix indicates a MOP just as the $ symbol was used to indicate a script). This MOP would be used to provide the sequence of scenes relevant to a doctor's (or other professional's) office. Because scenes can be shared, several MOPs may contain the same scene. This sharing of scenes between MOPs helps explain subjects' confusion in the experiment described above.

So far, we have seen that scenes (that may have scripts attached to them) organize memories and that MOPs organize scenes into larger sequences. One level above MOPs are structures called *meta-MOPs*. Meta-MOPs organize MOPs in much the same way as MOPs organize scenes. Meta-MOPs point to the MOPs that are likely to be relevant when understanding a story. For example, when processing a story about a vacation, the meta-MOP mM-TRIP (mM is the prefix used to name meta-MOPs) points to various MOPs like M-AIRPLANE, M-RENT-A-CAR, and M-HOTEL that might be useful in understanding the story.

In order to account for people's ability to use more general, domain-independent, cross-contextual information, the theory introduces a structure called a *thematic organization point* or TOP. TOPs organize information about types of goals that people have and the kinds of planning that go into trying to achieve these goals under the various conditions in which the goal is typically pursued. An example of the use of a TOP is how people are reminded of *Romeo and Juliet* when seeing *West Side Story*. The TOP active in understanding both of these stories is one called *mutual goal; outside opposition* (MG; OO). In this example, both sets of lovers have a mutual goal (in this case, to be together in a love relationship) and they face the opposition and interference of outside agents (their families or gangs). TOPs explain how people are reminded of one situation by another even when the two events are quite different on the surface. This mechanism also helps explain

how people can come up with creative, cross-contextual solutions to new problems.

The basic processing mechanism posited by the theory is based on *expectation-failures*. That is, when an individual's expectations about the way things will happen turns out to be wrong, they tend to get reminded about situations in which something similar went awry. From this observation, the theory asserts that memory reorganization is triggered by expectation-failures. If nothing unexpected happens, there is little reason to update memory, but when something unexpected does happen, it is imperative that the unexpected event be explained and memory altered so that the correct expectations can be generated in the future.

The organization of a dynamic memory allows this to happen. Each episode in which something unexpected happened contains pointers to other episodes with similar expectation-failures. This turns out to be quite useful, for along with the expectation-failures for an episode are stored explanations of what went wrong. In order to explain a new expectation-failure, a person is reminded of old episodes with similar expectation-failures and can use the old explanations stored with those episodes to formulate an explanation for the current situation. The newly constructed explanation is then stored along with the episode that contained the expectation-failure. In this way, memory gets altered, and learning occurs, on the basis of expectation-failure and explanation. Further work on this process of reusing old explanations has also been done by Schank (1986).

DYNAMIC MEMORY RESEARCH

The first computer implementations to use the ideas of dynamic memory were CYRUS (qv) (Kolodner, 1984), IPP (Lebowitz, 1983), and MOPTRANS (Lytinen, 1984). Since dynamic memory was an important precursor to the theory of case-based reasoning (CBR), several CBR problem-solving systems also used MOPs (see REASONING, CASE-BASED). These include MEDIATOR (qv) (Kolodner, Simpson, and Sycara-Cyronski, 1985; Simpson, 1985), JUDGE (Bain, 1985, 1986), and CHEF (qv) (Hammond, 1986). These and other systems using MOPs are described in greater detail in (Kolodner, 1986; Riesbeck, Schank, 1989).

In addition to testing the theory of dynamic memory using computers, researchers in psychology have also been testing the theory's ability to account for data on human memory. A series of experiments on story comprehension has yielded evidence that people indeed make use of MOP- and TOP-like structures (Seifert, McKoon, Abelson, and Ratcliff, 1986; McKoon, Ratcliff, and Seifert, in press; Seifert, 1988), providing a converging line of support for the dynamic memory theory.

BIBLIOGRAPHY

W. M. Bain, "Assignment of Responsibility in Ethical Judgments," in J. L. Kolodner and C. K. Riesbeck, eds., *Memory,*

Experience, and Reasoning, Lawrence Erlbaum, Hillsdale, N.J., 1985, pp. 127–138.

W. M. Bain, *Case-Based Reasoning: A Computer Model of Subjective Assessment,* Ph.D. dissertation, Yale University, New Haven, Conn., 1986.

G. H. Bower, J. B. Black, and T. J. Turner, "Scripts in Text Comprehension and Memory," *Cogn. Psychol.* **11,** 177–220 (1979).

K. J. Hammond, *Case-Based Planning: An Integrated Theory of Planning, Learning, and Memory,* Ph.D. dissertation, Yale University, New Haven, Conn., 1986.

J. L. Kolodner, *Retrieval and Organizational Strategies in Conceptual Memory: A Cognitive Model,* Lawrence Erlbaum, Hillsdale, N.J., 1984.

J. L. Kolodner, *Experience, Memory, and Reasoning,* Lawrence Erlbaum, Hillsdale, N.J., 1986.

J. L. Kolodner, R. L. Simpson, and K. Sycara-Cyranski, "A Process Model of Case-Based Reasoning in Problem Solving," *Proceedings of the Ninth International Joint Conference on Artificial Intelligence,* Los Angeles, 1985, pp. 284–290.

M. Lebowitz, "Generalization From Natural Language Text," *Cogn. Sci.* **7,** 1–40 (1983).

S. L. Lytinen, "Frame Selection In Parsing," *Proceedings of the Fourth National Conference on Artificial Intelligence,* AAAI. Austin, Tex., Aug. 1984.

G. McKoon, R. Ratcliff, and C. M. Seifert, "Making the Connection: Generalized Knowledge Structures in Story Understanding," *J. Memory and Language* (in press).

C. K. Riesbeck and R. C. Schank, *Inside Case-Based Reasoning,* Lawrence Erlbaum, Hillsdale, N.J., 1989.

R. C. Schank and R. P. Abelson, *Scripts, Plans, Goals, and Understanding,* Lawrence Erlbaum, Hillsdale, N.J., 1975.

R. C. Schank, *Dynamic Memory,* Cambridge University Press, Cambridge, UK, 1982.

R. C. Schank, *Explanation Patterns: Understanding Mechanically and Creatively,* Lawrence Erlbaum, Hillsdale, N.J., 1986.

C. M. Seifert, "Goals in Reminding," *Proceedings of the 1988 Workshop on Case-Based Reasoning,* Morgan-Kaufmann, 1988, pp. 357–369.

C. M. Seifert, G. McKoon, R. P. Abelson, and R. Ratcliff, "Memory Connections Between Thematically Similar Episodes," *J. Experimental Psychology: Learning, Memory, and Cognition* **12,** 220–231 (1986).

R. L. Simpson, *A Computer Model of Case-Based Reasoning in Problem Solving: An Investigation in the Domain of Dispute Mediation,* Ph.D. dissertation, Georgia Institute of Technology, Atlanta, Ga., 1985.

ROGER C. SCHANK
MENACHEM Y. JONA
Northwestern University

This work was supported in part by the Defense Advanced Research Projects Agency, monitored by the Air Force Office of Scientific Research under contract F49620-88-C-0058. The Institute for the Learning Sciences was established in 1989 with the support of Andersen Consulting, part of The Arthur Andersen Worldwide Organization.

E

EARLY VISION

The study of biological perception has had an enormous influence on the development of computational vision. Unfortunately, the most common observation about biological—in particular, human—vision is its immediacy: simply open your eyes and a percept of the world appears. This apparently effortless speed implies to many that vision is relatively simple, and that general purpose vision systems should not be too difficult to construct. However, this effortless speed results not from the simplicity of vision, but rather from the immense amount of specialized wetware, the biological equivalent of hardware, dedicated to it. In humans, the visual system occupies a major portion of the cortex. Vision is, in fact, immensely complex, and it has turned out to be immensely difficult to construct successful vision systems. Endless applications in areas as diverse as robotics, biomedicine, and remote sensing all support this conclusion.

Two basic problems confront designers of complex vision systems: what are the fundamental pieces, or the individual tasks comprising vision, and how should they be solved. The problems are clearly related; the designer has either a problem for which a solution can be foreseen, or a solution "in search of a problem." Although much of the insight into how to decompose vision has come from mathematics, physics, and computer science/engineering, perhaps the most powerful influence to date has been from the study of biological vision systems. A historical survey of the modern development of computational vision will help to illustrate how diverse the influences on computational vision have been, and to argue that such diversity is necessary.

Over 100 years ago, two themes emerged from the different views of vision held by the two great vision scientists, von Helmholtz (1821–1894) and Mach (1838–1916). In Helmholtz, there is a clear separation between low-level and high-level processing, or what is now sometimes called *early* and *later processing;* in Mach, there is a separation between the analysis of a task and the mechanism proposed to accomplish it. Early processing is not meant to imply a temporal dimension; rather, the term "early" denotes processing from the retina back into the cortex, while "later" denotes the latter stages of cortical processing. These two themes were present in the first attempt at a complete computer vision system (Roberts, 1965) and they persist to the present. In Roberts' system there was a clear separation between low-level processing, or the extraction of a cartoon-like line drawing out of an image, and high-level processing, or the recognition of objects. The mechanisms applied at these levels depended on the tasks; the low-level mechanism being one of so called edge detection, and the higher-level object matching into a database. Modern computational theories, such as the one proposed by Marr (1976), postulate more elaborate interfaces, such as primal sketches. Although this thread is common, the main evolution of computational vision has

been an appreciation of the immense complexity involved in both of these stages, with one paradigm after another attempting to grapple with it. Different paradigms have arisen for low- and high-level processing, and some have even emerged for intermediate stages between them. Strong forms of so-called inverse optics, pieced together with little or no interaction, have now given way to an increased appreciation of abstract structure. That is, it has now become clear that it is essentially impossible to exactly invert the scene projection process; rather, the search is on for discovering which aspects of the structure of the world can and should be recovered.

The detailed evolution of the field can be thought of in terms of two pendula, one representing the tension between low-level and high-level vision, and the other between the formulation of the task and the techniques chosen to solve it. This is very much a personal view, as is the choice of examples used here to illustrate how these pendula swing back and forth in time. Interestingly, early on in the development of the field, they were assumed to be rather separate from one another, but as the field began to mature their interrelationships became more clear as well. The tension between low- and high-level vision developed into a concern for the type of knowledge to be applied, the specifics of which are clearly related to both task formulation and technique employed.

The vision problem can be summarized as follows. Three-dimensional physical structure in the scene projects into two-dimensional structure in the image. This process must be inverted; that is, somehow, physical structures must be inferred from image structures. For each class of related physical and image structures a micro-inverse problem can be formulated, and many such problems exist. Early (low-level) vision consists in those problems for which the solution is driven by general-purpose assumptions and special-purpose hardware, while later (high-level) vision consists in those problems for which the solution is driven by special-purpose assumptions and general-purpose hardware. Or stated differently, in early vision, if something is understood about structure (of the world), then something can be inferred about function in the visual system; while in later vision it appears that function must be understood before structure.

The focus of this article is on the evolution of ideas rather than on algorithms, and shall concentrate more on the classical foundations of the field than on current approaches. Several other articles in this encyclopedia (see, eg, EDGE AND LOCAL FEATURE DETECTION; SCALE SPACE; SEGMENTATION; VISUAL PERCEPTION; VISUAL RECOVERY) address these different aspects of vision in detail, and pointers to them are indicated whenever possible. Many book-length treatments of computational vision (Ballard and Brown, 1982; Duda and Hart, 1973; Levine, 1985; Pavlidis, 1977, 1982; Nevatia, 1982; Rosenfeld and Kak, 1982), image processing (Pratt, 1978; Gonzalez and Wintz, 1977), and visual perception (Cornsweet, 1970; Gregory, 1970; Haber and Herschenson, 1973; Kaufman, 1974; Rock, 1984; Uttal, 1981) are available, and should be consulted along with this article. It is also worthwhile to consult the annual list of publications in computer vision and image processing compiled every year by Rosenfeld and published in the journal *Computer Vision, Graphics, and Image Processing*.

THE FIRST PARADIGM: SEGMENTATION IN LOW-LEVEL AND HIGH-LEVEL VISION

Helmholtz: Physiological Optics and Unconscious Inference

In his *Treatise on Physiological Optics* (1962), Helmholtz sketched a theory of vision in which the eye acted as a transducer of light into the nervous system, which then performed "unconscious inferences" in order to compose internal versions of percepts. That is, he asserted that there was a low-level component to vision, dominated by physics and physical models, and a high-level component in which the inferences took place. Unfortunately, the only language that he had for talking about inferences was the rather loose one of what he took to be "conscious inferences," or the logic of premises and conclusions. High-level vision is, he therefore asserted, the same sort of activity as is normally involved in cognition and thinking, although we are unaware of it.

Although Helmholtz was rather vague about unconscious inferences, his studies of early vision are still remarkably fresh and insightful. To illustrate, consider his study of the transduction properties of the eye. Perhaps inspired by his work in physics, he countered a rather widespread belief that the eye was a perfect optical instrument by actually measuring its optical properties. He observed, as is commonly known today, that the eye is far from perfect (Fry, 1955). It exhibits the many different forms of aberration and distortion to which all physically-realized systems are susceptible.

The result of such optical imperfections in the eye is that images do not fall on the retina in perfect focus, but are blurred, regardless of how well the lens is functioning. Helmholtz looked for perceptual consequences of such blurring, and found many, one of which he believed to be the Mueller-Lyer illusion (Fig. 1). On a figure such as the Mueller-Lyer, the areas between the lines forming the acute angles will be blurred more than the areas within the obtuse ones, thereby stretching the lines into the acute angles more than the obtuse ones. Such a distortion is precisely in the direction of the illusion, and was, for Helmholtz, its causal explanation.

Such is visual theorizing of the best sort. A task is posed (what are the optical properties of the eye?) and solved in a theoretical fashion that is consistent with empirical data (the spherical aberration was actually measured). Finally, the theory was applied to explain observed phenomena (such as the Mueller-Lyer illusion).

Helmholtz was correct in observing that the eye is an imperfect optical instrument, but he was mostly wrong in

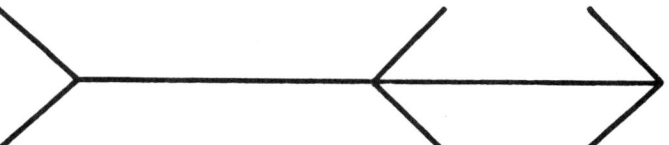

Figure 1. The Mueller-Lyer illusion. Although the arrow heads delimit two line segments of equal length, the one enclosed in the convex region appears shorter than the one in the concave region. Helmholtz believed that this is because our visual systems somehow "fill in" the convex portion more than the concave portion, thereby affecting our length judgments. Gregory (1970), on the other hand, believed that interpretations of these line segments as projections of three-dimensional structures lies at the foundation of the illusion. Whatever the mechanism responsible, however, such illusions indicate that our perception of structure in the world is not veridical, but rather depends on contextual influences from many possible sources.

that his explanation of the Mueller-Lyer illusion cannot account for the entire effect. This has been determined only recently using an elaborate optical technique to project a highly focused image onto the retina (Coren, Ward, Porac, and Fraser, 1978). Such techniques indicate that optical blurring can account for at most 15% of the illusory effect. Nevertheless, considerations of the physics inherent in the imaging process will emerge in different ways as a major theme in computational vision.

Roberts' System: Segmentation and Matching

Inherent in Helmholtz's theory is a distinction between the types of processing that take place early on and then later in the visual process. Such a distinction lies at the basis of modern computational theories as well, beginning with the first real attempt to design a full system. In a seminal thesis, Roberts (1965) described what is probably the first computer vision system. Although it is not clear that he was directly influenced by Helmholtz, he too decomposed processing into a low-level stage, in which a line drawing was abstracted out of an image, and a high-level stage, in which the line drawing was matched against a universe of prototypes. Thus the physically motivated processing was concentrated on the extraction of the line drawing, and unconscious inferences were used to match it into a database of objects.

In order to effect this matching, it was necessary for Roberts to restrict the possible universe of objects that his system could encounter. He worked in a mini-world of polyhedral objects composed entirely of blocks, the so called *blocks world*, a class of assumptions that influenced computational vision for more than a decade. Even though the universe of objects was simple, however, it did not follow that the matching would be trivial; in the process various transformation parameters such as complex object decomposition, depth, and rotation had to be computed.

The early portion of Roberts' system was concerned with the problem of edge detection, or the identification of those positions in images that indicate interesting physical events. The locus of these positions then comprised a line drawing. The motivation behind line drawings can be seen intuitively in cartoons, or drawings which are, in some sense, equivalent to full images. That is, both convey sufficient information to satisfy our high-level, inferential processes. More specifically, the line drawing was taken to represent a *segmentation* (qv) of the image into meaningful pieces, each of which was taken to be the projection of a meaningful portion of a physical object. The outlines of these pieces then comprised the line drawing.

Roberts' approach to edge detection was based on the observation that distinct physical events (say, the sides of a cube) give rise to distinct image events or intensities, and the image locations at which these events meet have special significance: they are the edges of the cube. Thus if the points of intensity change could be located and joined, the result would be a perfect line drawing of a projected cube.

To locate the edges of the cube, observe further that intensity changes rapidly there. Calculus tells us that, for smooth functions, rapid changes in the value of the function at a point are accompanied by large values in the derivative of the function at that point. Hence Roberts derived a discrete approximation to a gradient operator elegantly simple in computational form. His plan was to convolve this operator against the image, and then to select the strongest of these convolution values by thresholding. Finally, a linking process would select high gradient "edge" points to be fit by straight lines. Note how a distinct higher level constraint enters Roberts' formulation at this point: the straight sides of his scene polyhedra project into straight edges in the image. Helmholtz made similar observations about straight and converging lines. More will be said about the influence of such high-level or domain-specific knowledge on early processing later in the article.

There is much more to low-level, early processing than was thought at that time. Roberts was never actually able to get a perfect line drawing from this early processor, and there is a basic sense in which the perfect line drawing is still elusive. This is a fascinating story in itself, since what began as the pursuit of the perfect line drawing has evolved into the full study of early vision.

Similarities vs Differences

Before beginning the discussion of edge detection, we will raise a tangential point. Segmentation can be approached in two different ways; either by searching for differences, or points along segmentation boundaries, or by searching for similarities, or points within segmentation regions. Edge detection is the approach for determining which points are different, and it is the approach adopted by Roberts. Region growing is another approach to segmentation designed for determining which points are the same (Rosenfeld and Kak, 1982). The rationale for region growing was that, since differentiation emphasizes noise, segmentations might be found more reliably by smoothing within regions rather than differentiating between them.

However, it should be stressed that the duality of edge detection and region growing does not imply that one or the other is unnecessary. Rather, they are complementary and almost always work together. Consider Roberts' system again; note that after edge detection (differentiation) similar points (ie, the locations at which the differential convolution survived thresholding) are linked into lines; this linking process is a kind of one-dimensional region growing process. That is, points are defined to be similar if they are associated with a common straight line segment in the least-mean-square sense. Thus, following linking, it is as if all of the boundary points had been smoothed into a bounding contour, since their (prethresholding) individual differences are now gone. The key information provided by the discontinuity measurement, the edge operator, has now been summarized into a more global, abstract form. This complementarity emerges again and again throughout the evolution of early vision; eventually it will emerge as grouping. The edge detection route, however, was by far the most prominent of the two (see also EDGE AND LOCAL FEATURE DETECTION).

Laplacians, Mach, and Edges

The modern study of edges has its roots in the studies of Mach. To contrast him with his contemporary Helmholtz, Mach was interested in image sharpening rather than blurring, and in explanations couched in terms of neural networks rather than in physiological optics. The phenomenon of sharpening is known as *Mach bands,* or the addition of subjective bright and dark lines (bands) on either side of an intensity change (Fig. 2). Such bands indicate that the "eye" that is, the visual system, is sensitive not only to image intensities, but also to their first and second derivatives.

Mach bands give a clear indication that the subjective impression of brightness and of contrast is highly dependent on spatial context. That is, impressions of brightness and of contrast are not isomorphic with the intensity of light impinging on the retina, but rather are derived, or computed, from it.

How can these computations be understood? Mach believed that psychophysical laws, such as the ones underlying brightness and contrast phenomena, had their proper explanation in terms of properties of neural networks, not in terms of pure physics or purely psychical events. The particulars of Mach's explanation were posed mathematically in terms of "a reciprocal interaction of neighboring areas of the retina" (Ratliff, 1965; p. 267). He formulated mathematical relationships involving the Laplacian operator, a symmetric second differential of the image intensities. He cited (then) current neuro-anatomical data by Ritter that postulated a regular arrangement of cells on the retina, and characterized the function of these cells mathematically. He postulated that the result of the neural interactions between these cells was a "sensation surface" on which the brightness effects were present. Thus Mach, in discussing such surfaces, was talking directly about representations (read: re-presentations); he was concerned with possible constraints from the wetware.

Lateral Inhibition: From Operators to Cooperative Computation. While Mach was able to infer the nature of processing taking place immediately after the retina, it was not until a revolutionary innovation in neurophysiology,

Figure 2. An illustration of Mach bands. The image consists of a sequence of rectangular regions of constant intensity; the "edges" between regions are therefore perfect "step edges." However, the intensity does not appear constant to a viewer. On either side of each edge are two Mach bands, a darker one (on the dark side of the edge), and a lighter one on the other side. Again, these bands indicate that what one sees is not "what's out there," but rather is a context-dependent computation driven by it together with additional constraints.

the development of microelectrodes for single cell recording, that his inferences could be verified experimentally. This was first done in the eye of the horseshoe crab *limulus*, and has led to much more accurate mathematical models. Such models are said to exhibit lateral inhibition, or a regular structure in which the response at a particular retina point is derived from excitatory contributions at that point together with inhibitory interactions from neighboring points (Ratliff, 1965; Cornsweet, 1970) (Fig. 2). Notice, in particular, the regular neural architecture for implementing lateral inhibition, in which the same local structure is repeated across the spatial array. Viewed spatially, the lateral inhibitory structure looks circularly symmetric, with an excitatory central area enclosed within a negative, or inhibitory, surround. Or, in other words, the response at a retinal point is a function of the context around that point.

An essential aspect of this context is the presence of intensity changes in the visual array. As already said in the discussion of Roberts' system, such changes are important becasue they often indicate the presence of physical object contours. In fact, the functional significance of Mach bands has often been attributed to their edge-enhancement effect: if one is to navigate through the physical world on the basis of sensory information, one certainly needs to locate object contours.

Lateral excitatory and inhibitory networks are without doubt one of the most ubiquitous mechanisms in biological vision systems. Lateral inhibitory networks play a clear role in regulating the dynamic range of the eye (Werblin, 1972) and otherwise performing a sort of local sharpening, or maximal selection, at the neural level (Cornsweet, 1970). More generally they have led to a view of the kind of computatonal architecture that should be employed in early vision, an architecture consisting of regularly interconnected networks of rather simple processors. Before

developing these networks, we shall stay with the local view of lateral-inhibitory-based edge operators.

Discontinuity and Edge Detection

The classical approach to edge detection is differentiation. This is typically accomplished in two stages: (1) the convolution of an operator against the image and, (2) some process for interpretation of the operator's responses. Stated in more general terms, the stages consist of (1) a measurement process followed by (2) a detection process. It was already noted that there is a basic sense in which the two are complementary: if edge detection is a differential process then interpretation must be an integrative one. To begin, note that there are two convergent approaches to the design of measurement operators, either as numerical approximations to derivatives of different order, or as inferences about how primates might do it.

Edge Detection as Differentiation. If the surfaces of physical objects project different image intensities, then it would seem that the locations of the physical object "edges" could be inferred from the places where intensity changes rapidly. These rapid intensity changes can be detected, under the assumption that the world projects smooth image intensity functions to which differential calculus applies, by locating those positions at which the first derivative (spatial gradient) is high; or where the second derivative crosses zero. (We shall question this assumption, and the approach that it implies, later in this article.) However, there are important numerical issues to be confronted as well, so that the estimates of the derivatives are as accurate as they can be. Tradeoffs between these two issues, differentiation and numerical stability, are classical. They led to better approximations to the gradient than the Roberts operator (see the Sobel operator in Duda and Hart, 1973; as well as Kirsch (1971); the numerical issues are discussed in Hildebrandt (1956) and implications for edge detection are in many textbooks (Ballard and Brown, 1982; Levine, 1985; Rosenfeld and Kak, 1982). Before proceeding it should be noted that, in spite of the predominant identification of edge detection with differentiation, other approaches emerged. Chief among these were (1) a formulation of edge detection as hypothesis testing, so that both the differences in edge profiles and their inherent noisy variation could be taken into account (Herskovitz and Binford, 1970; Horn, 1973; Pavlidis, 1977); and (2) an observation that fitting "surfaces" to intensity distributions was a more numerically stable way of finding step discontinuities (Prewitt, 1970; Haralick, 1984; Heuckel, 1971). They still did not work sufficiently well (Fig. 3). The next subsection presents the evidence for the second major influence: early primate vision.

The Shape of Visual Receptive Fields. A virtual revolution in our understanding of early visual physiology took place from single cell recordings in cat and monkey visual systems. The receptive field of a cell indicates how arrangements of light stimuli will effect its activity; in effect, the receptive field characterizes aspects of what the

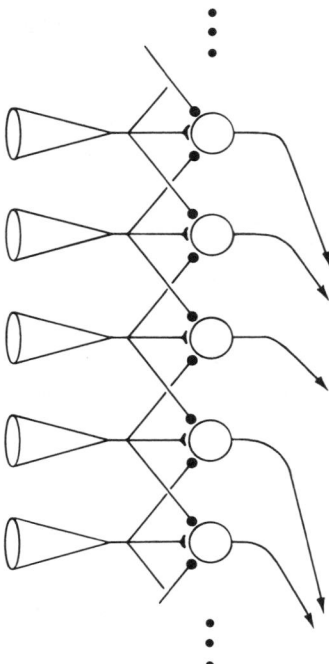

Figure 3. An example of the computational structure of lateral inhibition. In this diagram, the cones represent light receptors, and the large circles represent "summation" devices. Note how the level of activity in each receptor contributes positively to the result (excites the summation device), while the level of activity in neighboring receptors inhibit it (filled circles). In general, the architecture is one of arrays of units with near-neighbor interactions, both excitatory and inhibitory, with the local computation a simple one.

neuron is doing (Barlow, 1972). Hubel and Wiesel (1977, for a review) discovered a striking arrangement in receptive field structure. Their discovery can be appreciated as follows. Suppose an electrode is indicating the level of activity (firing rate) of a neuron in the visual system. If a spot of light is shone somewhere on the retina, then processing may percolate back to influence the firing of that cell. This will be true for some locations in the retinal array, and it may be either excitatory, leading to an increase in the firing rate, or inhibitory, leading to a decrease (below some "resting" or spontaneous level). The shapes of these receptive fields in retinal ganglion cells resemble a circular surround organization that has been modeled as a difference of two Gaussians (Rodieck, 1965; Enroth-Cugell and Robson, 1966) (Fig. 5). They come in two flavors: excitatory center with inhibitory surround, and inhibitory center with excitatory surround.

In the cortex, however, the structure of receptive fields changes dramatically. Here they exhibit the additional property of being orientation selective. That is, individual cells respond better to lines and intensity edges than to isolated points, and their response varies as a function of the orientation of the lines and points. The receptive fields are elongated (Fig. 6). The temptation to identify them with operators for edge and line detection is overwhelming, and this is normally done. However, at this point identification had been almost purely local, with little consideration of the network interaction necessarily tak-

ing place between these local pieces. The only interactions considered were those required for constructing hierarchies of cells as building blocks to more complex functionality.

Edge Detection and Scale. Visual receptive fields span a range of sizes, a point that is loosely consistent with quite a bit of psychophysics regarding threshold perception. Consider, for example, a display consisting of a sinusoidal grating. The minimal contrast necessary to see the grating is a function of its spatial frequency (Cornsweet, 1970). Wilson and Bergen (1979) have empirically determined that these psychophysical data are consistent with four separate channels of processing. Although these channels have not yet been related quantitatively back to the physiology, they seem to indicate, at least abstractly, a number of parallel functional streams. This point has always been puzzling to computational modelers. If the receptive fields of these cells participate in edge detection, why the variability in scale? What role does scale play in edge detection? Several suggestions have emerged. First, given the noise problems inherent in early vision, from quantization, occlusion, and receptor processes, some sort of averaging would seem necessary to reduce it. For example, if one wished to measure a local feature reliably, say an edge configuration, then increasing the size of the operators could lead to increased performance, or equivalent detectability with decreasing signal-to-noise ratio (Laughlin, Srinivasan, and Dubs, 1982). However, there must be more to it than this, because larger operators will cover more of the image; hence they may cover more structure than, say, one edge.

In addition to numerical issues, observe that structure in the world arises at different scales as well. Observe, in particular, that certain physical events are highly localized in space (say, the locus of points along which the faces of a cube meet), while others are much less localized; they span more space (say, the locus of points defining an animal's limb). These observations indicate the scale at which different physical events are taking place. Land (1977) observed, for example, that changes in physical objects are usually highly localized (say, at the occluding edge between them), while changes in lighting are typically much more diffuse. The scale of intensity events thus purportedly "decomposes" lighting from reflectance. Witkin (1986) has suggested a *scale space* (qv) for studying events at these different scales. Could it be that the variation in receptive field size is tuned to events of different "scales" in the world?

The Elusive Edge Operator. Marr and Hildreth (1980) tried to link the above notion of scale with specific ideas for edge detection. Selecting from the above facts, they observed that (1) the circular surround operators could be approximated mathematically as $\nabla^2 G$, the Laplacian of a Gaussian; that (2) since the Laplacian is a second derivative operator (recall Mach) step changes in intensity can be localized by its zero-crossings; and (3) that the different sizes of operators would be sensitive to events (ie, "edges") at different spatial scales (see EDGE AND LOCAL FEATURE DETECTION).

Such is a wonderful confluence of events. The problem

(a)

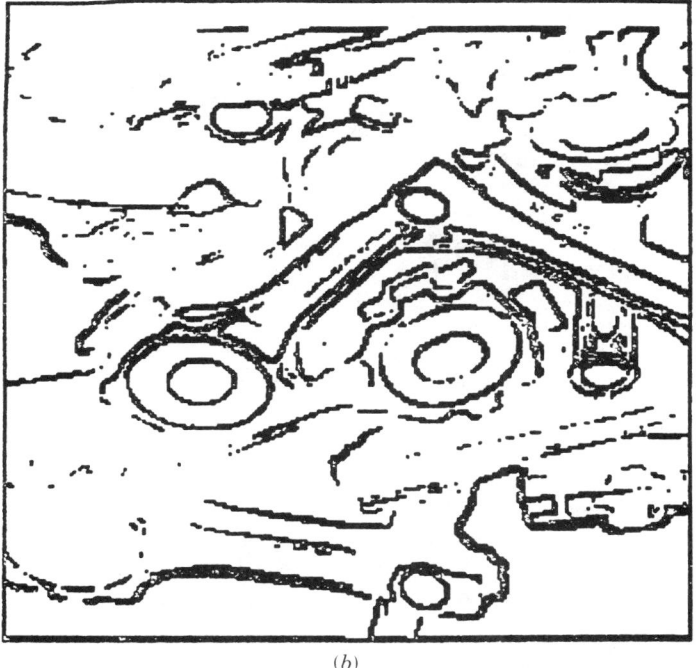

(b)

Figure 4. An illustration of the Sobel edge detector. (a) An original image of automotive parts, (256 by 256) pixel resolution. For display, this image has been quantized to six grey levels. (b) A binary image indicating the positions at which the maximal Sobel responses were located. Thresholds were specified by a locally adaptive algorithm. Note that although some of the prominent edges have been found, it is certainly not the case that all have been found. Problems clearly arise in image areas that do not contain step-like edge changes.

of edge detection, with which researchers in computational vision have been preoccupied for two decades, could now be solved in a way that is consistent with psychophysical and neurophysiological data and, moreover, provides a functional explanation for it. Unfortunately, however, the scheme cannot work in general for two reasons. First, implicit in it, and in the design of most other edge operators, is an assumption that the intensity structure is a step function across the edge, and that the curvature of the edge is zero; ie, that the edge is straight. It can be shown that these are precisely the conditions under which this operator works successfully, but that few edges in

natural scenes are of this form (Fig. 7). Rather, there is a plethora of different physical configurations that can give rise to edges, and these must be taken into account (see Leclerc and Zucker, 1986, and the section below on "From Structure into Function."). Moreover, consequent psychophysical predictions from the Marr/Hildreth operator have not been supported (Watt and Morgan, 1983). The perfect edge operator remains elusive.

Image Representation and Communication. If the circular surround receptive fields, especially those in the retina and the LGN, are not involved in edge detection, what

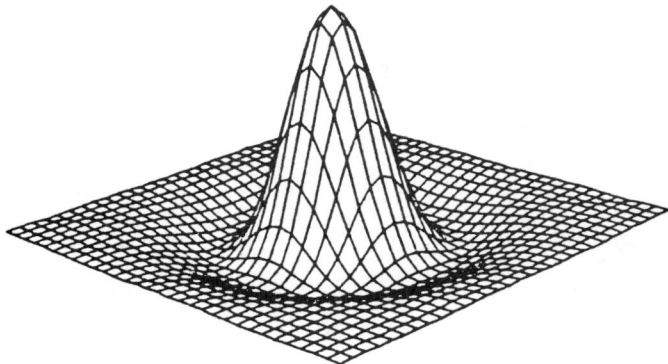

Figure 5. An illustration of Marr/Hildreth Laplacian of a Gaussian edge operator. The illustration also approximates the difference-of-Gaussian receptive fields typical of those found in primate retina.

other function might they be accomplishing? Since the retina is "an outgrowth of the brain," the problem of communicating image information from the retina to the cortex stably and reliably arises. Laughlan and co-workers (1982) have shown that linear predictive coding theory leads to a model that fits these receptive fields strikingly well, at least for certain animals, and considerations of numerical stability lead to the separation of opposite contrast data (Zucker and Hummel, 1986). It thus would seem that edge detection is likely to begin in the cortex, which opens up the door for much more complex processing. The classical idea of a single edge detection operator seems unlikely, it remains necessary to discover the mappings between physical scene structure and images, and between image structure and visual function.

Naive Physiology: Hierarchies of Feature Detectors

Although lurking in the background, the influence of (then) current notions in physiology on computer vision has always been quite strong. The basic model was feature detection, a two-stage procedure in which operators were first convolved against the image, and then the best match (ie, the strongest convolution) was selected by a process of thresholding. The operators were somehow matched to the image projections of certain stimuli in the world, following the ideas presented in the classic paper by Lettvin,

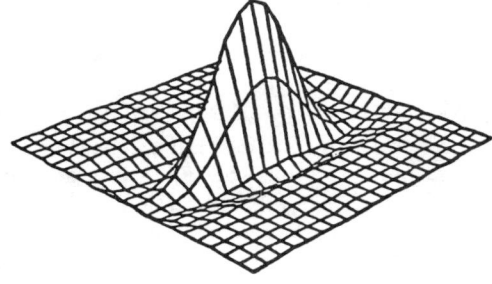

Figure 6. One type of simple cell receptive field of the sort that could be found in early primate visual cortex. Note that it resembles the circular-surround retinal receptive field in Figure 5, although now it is elongated. Such elongation illustrates an orientation preference. In computer vision such operators are known as "line detectors."

Maturana, McCullough, and Pitts (1959), in which circular-surround receptive fields most sensitive to movement of spots of a particular size and velocity were interpreted as bug detectors. In addition to this general perspective, the model of physiology that was most strongly influencing researchers in computer vision was the hierarchical one put forth by Hubel and Wiesel beginning in 1962 (Hubel and Wiesel, 1977) in which visual neurons exhibited three types of receptive field structures: simple, complex, and hypercomplex. Simple cells were defined as those in which the sub-domains were linear and separable (hence, simple to characterize); complex cells as those in which the sub-domains were non-linear and overlapping (and hence complex to characterize); and hypercomplex cells, which were the most difficult of all to capture. Hubel and Wiesel further hypothesized a hierarchical relationship between cells: retinal ganglion cells fed into the lateral geniculate nucleus (LGN), maintaining the circular-surround receptive fields discussed above. These LGN cells are then combined into elongated simple cells, which are then combined successively into complex and hypercomplex cells. It was loosely asserted that simple cells are involved in edge and curve detection, and hypercomplex cells in detection of higher-order properties such as corners or endpoints, although even at that point in time, problems were surfacing. How, for example, could such cells detect dashed curves in noise (Barlow, Narasimhan, and Rosenfeld, 1972)? More precisely, the receptive fields were modeled as operators, and the question became: How could operator convolutions followed by thresholding detect dashed curves in noise? No clear function was proposed for complex cells, and the wonderful simplicity of hierarchical arrangements of feature detectors will give way to more realistic computations. There's more to bug detection in the frog than circular-surround receptive fields, and there's more to edge detection in humans than individual simple cells.

Knowledge in the Edge Detection Process

As the measurements of image intensity changes evolved (recall the "edge detection" operators), so have the processes for interpreting, or selecting a "truest" one from among them. Such selection is necessary because the value of the convolution will be non-zero almost everywhere due to microstructure and noise. Somehow the significant responses must be separated from the insignificant ones.

Thresholding, Local Maxima Selection, and Hough Transforms. In the simplest case, normal thresholding suffices: simply select the strongest (highest value) convolutions; all others are discounted. The idea behind thresholding is that true edges will project to real intensity differences and hence will lead to high convolution values. This holds for nonoriented edge operators when the decision is, essentially, whether a particular image location is part of an edge or not. The case of oriented operators is just slightly more complicated, since not only the presence of edges must be separated from their absence (the noise responses must be eliminated), but the correct orientation of the edge must be chosen as well. Postulating the orientation at a point to be the same as the orientation of the operator

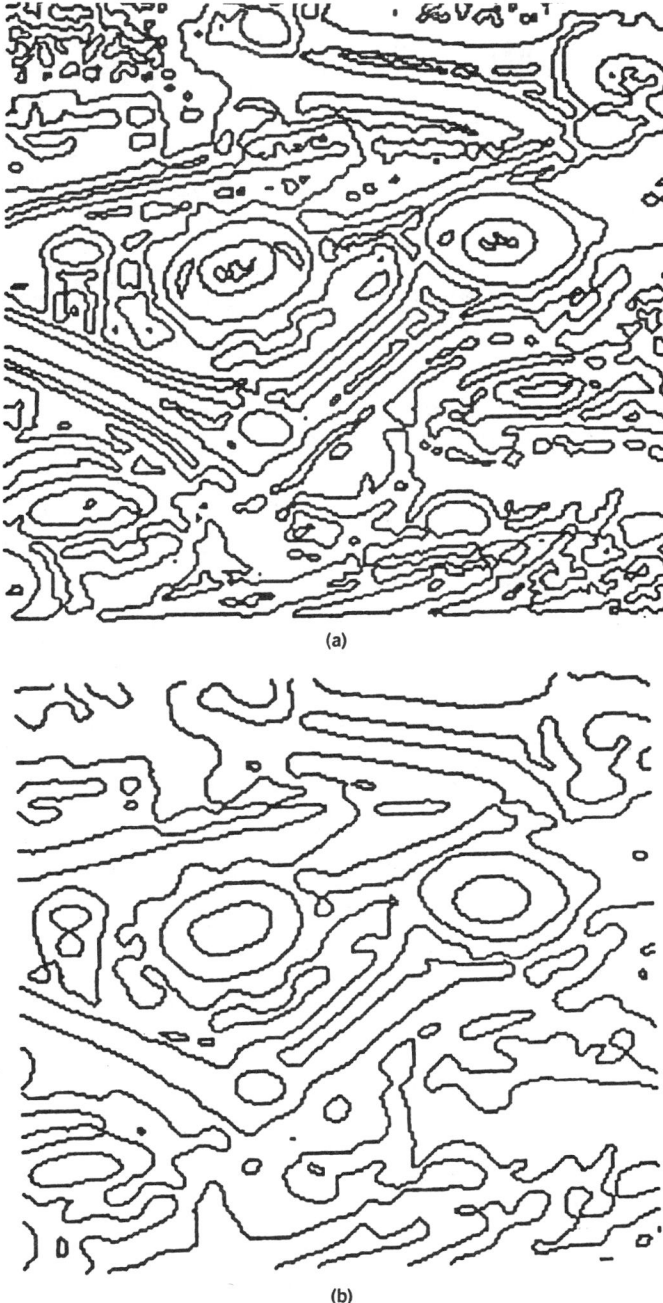

(a)

(b)

Figure 7. The edge locations (zero crossings) obtained with the operator in Figure 5 on the image in Figure 4a. Compare with Figure 4b. Note that the zero crossings form closed contours, although these sometimes have little connection with the physical objects comprising the scene. Two size operators are shown, in order to illustrate that the problem is not simply one of "scale." Neither one is completely satisfactory for locating edges.

mask with the highest convolution value is, in a sense, the best match, and thresholding is one way to select it.

Thresholding can therefore be interpreted as a selection based on maxima in some first-order statistic, and the idea has evolved to include statistics of more general or less local features. Perhaps the first example in computer vision is the Hough transform (qv) (Duda and Hart, 1973), in which long straight lines are found by histogramming local estimates of their orientation and intercept. The Hough transform has been generalized and applied by Ballard (1984) and Davis (1982).

Thresholding can also be viewed as a mapping that takes an image (in which entries are the value of a particular convolution at a point) into another, binary image (in which the locations with values that survived threshold-

ing have value 1, and all others have value 0). The recovery of more global structures thus requires further processing, say tracking along the 1s to find lines and contours.

Vision as Controlled Hallucination. While the above arguments may seem persuasive at first, thresholding's only virtue is its simplicity; it rarely works in practice. How can threshold values be selected? More than two decades of research have shown that, for any but the simplest of images and tasks, the knowledge required cannot be represented as threshold values (Rosenfeld and Kak, 1982). More sophisticated processing techniques must be employed, and a basic question arises regarding how to structure them. Two schools of thought have been prominent.

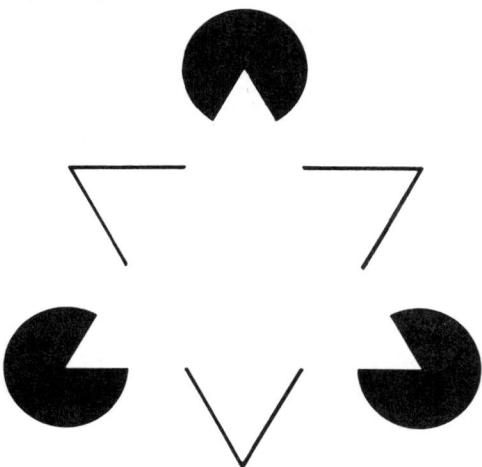

Figure 8. A Kanisza subjective edge. Note how the apparent (bright) triangle is indicated by the missing corners in the dark circles and by the line terminations. Edges seem to be present even with no intensity changes.

Originally, it was believed that edge descriptions could somehow be extracted directly out of arbitrary images. This led to elaborate thresholding algorithms, thinning algorithms, etc (Rosenfeld and Kak, 1982; Duda and Hart, 1973). But it is not at all clear that these mechanisms are sufficiently powerful to utilize the knowledge required for edge detection. That it is very difficult to evaluate the results of apparent failures in larger contexts led to the consideration of drastically different techniques. The suggestion that vision is, to a real extent, a process of "controlled hallucination" (Clowes, 1971) emerged, the thrust of which implied that hypotheses about (or knowledge of) the object being imaged should directly influence the edge extraction process. That is, knowledge from the highest, most abstract levels should influence the earliest, most primitive ones eg, (Minsky and Papert, 1969). The key to this change in view is the observation that not only are intensity edges difficult to locate; many of the edges that define objects have *no* image intensity counterparts. It is possible to see edges where there is no change in intensity (Kanisza, 1979) (Fig. 8).

Top-Down vs Bottom-Up. The question of which knowledge should be applied in the edge detection process is a special case of a more general one: should image analysis be top-down or should it be bottom-up? Should it be data-driven or hypothesis-driven? Different schools emerged, with Rosenfeld and the image processing community being associated with the bottom-up idea and much of the more traditional AI community associated with top-down (see PROCESSING, BOTTOM-UP AND TOP-DOWN). Perhaps the most prominent attempt at top-down edge detection was that of Shirai (1975), in which a knowledge-based edge detector was designed to work only for images of cubes.

The Flow of Control in Knowledge-Based Edge Finding. Shirai's system worked as follows. Standard image differential techniques were used to locate a prominent intensity change. Because the universe of possible objects was limited, as in Roberts case, to the blocks world, it could

then be assumed that such a prominent edge point would be part of the bounding contour around the cube. After finding the orientation and length of this edge, it was then possible to hypothesize a putative cube model with certain size, etc, parameters instantiated to particular values. This model could then be used to predict the location of other putative edges, which could then be verified by looking at the image intensities in detail.

The Complexity of Edge Detection. The use of knowledge all the way down to the lowest levels of the edge finding process thus becomes quite complex, necessitating elaborate mechanisms for its control. While this can lead to very high performance levels in restricted universes (such as the blocks micro-world), it also leads to brittle, highly specialized systems with little generality. Extending them to slightly larger domains became arbitrarily difficult. In terms of object models, there is a formidable gap between the blocks world and the real world. This forced another look at complexity tradeoffs and the flow of processing in vision systems. In retrospect it seems that too much was hoped for, with regard to the performance of local edge operators, a lesson that has still not clearly penetrated computational vision.

The Introduction of Surface Constraints. Intermediate between knowledge about the exact object and about its edges is knowledge about how they fit together. In the blocks world, knowledge about edges is intimately linked to knowledge about surfaces, and other researchers began to introduce surface intersection constraints directly into their programs as well. Mackworth (1973) for example, used the idea of gradient space (Horn, 1977; Shafer, 1985; Woodham, 1981), a representation of object surface normal properties (not image intensity gradients) to determine which edge segments could physically belong together for polyhedral objects. That is, gradient space makes explicit relations between the coordinates of polyhedral surface gradients and lines in an orthographically-projected image (Falk, 1972; Turner, 1974). Another intermediate step involved shape estimation; (Davis, 1979; Freeman, 1974).

The Rigidity of Early Systems

The problem with these early systems was rigidity; the knowledge on which they were based, eg, the Shirai constraints or the gradient-space constraints, were "hardwired" into the programs. They could work only for the idealized object classes within which the constraints held. Generalization was difficult, if not impossible. Historically it was time to back off from the detailed problems and to have a broader look, which is exactly what happened. The network parallelism that was so obvious in early visual physiology began to play a much more prominent role. It suggests, in particular, a framework, a point of view toward vision, of how to derive and use general purpose constraints from abstract assumptions about images and the world, assumptions that are far more realistic than those within the blocks world. The importance of intermediate-levels of knowledge, such as that first suggested by gradient space will increase greatly, but its form will be drastically different so that its use can become much more fluid and adaptable. For in-depth discussion of the use of high-level knowledge in vision systems, see Tsotsos (1984).

Constraints and Assumptions. There is often a minor point of confusion in the study of vision between the terms constraint and assumption. Assumptions made about the universe (eg, that it consists of flat surfaces) allow the derivation of constraints in algorithms (eg, the equations for fitting planes rather than for fitting fifth-order polynomials). Clearly, the assumption of the blocks world leads to many such constraints, some of which have been described.

ORGANIZATION AND COMPLEXITY

Two observations speak against the top down, rigid analysis of images, and they are both related to complexity in a particular way (Zucker, Davis, and Rosenfeld, 1975). First, if we only see what we expect to see, how can our visual systems be responsive to unexpected events in the world? In the limit, we would not even need to open our eyes! Second, on the basis of what trigger features, or database keys, are models selected? Somehow they must be derived from the image, and if the keys are just intensities then there is an immense complexity barrier to be overcome: there are an infinite number of different scenes that could project into any particular image. How can the correct one be selected in a reasonable amount of time?

The antidote to complexity is organization, and the answer to the complexity dilemma is classical. To illustrate, consider the Dewey decimal system. If the books in a library were organized randomly, and there were n of them, then it would take on average $n/2$ examinations to find any particular one. But if the books were organized, say according to hierarchical categories as in the Dewey decimal system, then the savings in search time would be enormous. Under certain schemes search time can be shown to grow with $\log (n)$ which, for large n is much slower than $n/2$. Analalogously, one needs to organize the knowledge in vision systems. The issue is not whether knowledge should be used, but how, what kind, and when it should be used. Intermediate, abstract (with respect to the models) knowledge must somehow be incorporated that captures the regularities of objects in the world. Of course, the earlier observation that physical edges project into image intensity changes is one kind of knowledge, but this must be further generalized. For a recent attempt to develop such a "computational-level" analysis of vision, see Tsotsos (1988).

Abstraction and General Purpose Models

Another demonstration can be invoked in support of intermediate levels of organization. Suppose you were looking at a totally unfamiliar scene, say one from a scanning electron microscope or from an ultrasound scanner. While it is unlikely that one would be able to recognize the object, the scene can even be chosen so that it does not contain any real objects, but it could still be described. The description will be in general terms, perhaps involving geometric forms, apparent contours or corners, and will be of the sort that can be derived from any image. Such intermediate descriptions, and the knowledge incorporated into making, and interpreting them, are what should be sought. What is needed are not assumptions about the entire universe of objects; as in the blocks world, by the time these assumptions give rise to useful constraints they are *too* constraining. Rather, more abstract assumptions are needed about the intermediate kinds of structure that can arise in a wide class of natural scenes. These assumptions and the constraints they give rise to will provide the backbone for early processing.

The Ubiquity of Uncertainty

While the metaphor of libraries is instructive regarding the role of organization, it is misleading in its directness. A better example would be a library in which the titles of some of the books were partly obscured. The reason for this was illustrated by the elusive edge operator. The term operator as it is usually used in computational vision denotes, in mathematical terms, a linear operator with local spatial support. While the design of nonlinear operators was also attempted (Rosenfeld, 1970), their success was little better. It is impossible, in general, to design an operator that responds if and only if a particular feature is present. Rather, they respond partly whether or not a feature is present. The mathematical problem here is related to noninvertibility of operators and L_2 matching theory. Somehow these responses must be interpreted, and it is in these interpretation processes that the general purpose constraints are embodied. It has been discovered that much of this interpretation can be carried out in mechanisms suitable for parallel implementation, thereby dealing with spatial complexity in a distributed fashion. Before doing so, however, it is essential to stress the change in viewpoint from segmentation to description.

From Segmentation to Description

The corners and occluding boundaries that arise in the blocks world are only a small subset of the diversity of physical events of interest in the natural world. Some of these are primitive events, like the change in orientation at the corner of a cube, and others are compound, like the texture of a forest. Thus it becomes essential to bring out the many levels of structure if there is to be any hope of eventually agglomerating them; and the more explicit they are, the easier, in a computational sense, they will be to use. Borrowing insights from another area that was attempting to grapple with complexity, structured programming, Marr (1976) proposed three principles to underlie the development of vision systems. The first of these was a principle of least commitment, or the postponing of limiting decisions as long as possible. This is another way to pose the blocks world criticism. The second principle was one of explicit naming, in which the distinct entities of importance to vision are named so that their description is easily referenced. It, too, deals with complexity. Finally, there is the principle of modularity, the reasons for which were discussed above in the context of organization. In early vision, modularity is realized most often by decomposing operations in space as well as into levels.

The Rise of Parallelism

In the discussion of lateral inhibition, it was pointed out that there were two ways to proceed. The first was toward local (differential or edge) operators, the one chosen. The second direction, or the observation that much of the wetware in early vision appears parallel in structure can now be explored. To understand the advantages of parallel computational machinery, it is helpful to compare it with sequential machinery.

Suppose one wanted to perform a convolution of a particular operator, say, an edge detection operator, against an image. To obtain numbers, suppose further that it takes η operations to evaluate the convolution at each location. Specifically, suppose the operator consists of a mask whose spatial support is $(n \times n)$ or n^2 locations. Then, by the convolution formula, there are $\eta = n^2$ (multiplications at each point) $+ n^2$ (additions) to add them up. Then, for a (100×100) image it would take $10^4 \eta$ operations to perform the entire convolution of the operator against the image. For biological "machinery" this is quite a long time. But rather than spend this amount of time performing all of the individual convolutions one after another, biology seems to have evolved a faster solution: perform all of them in parallel. This trades the cost in time for one in space (special purpose hardware) but provides the answer in the time required for only η operations. In almost all situations this is very fast indeed.

Researchers in computational vision were anxious to understand and, if possible, to capitalize on the parallelism constraint. There were two problems to face: (1) what classes of algorithms could be decomposed into parallel ones; and (2) how could knowledge be imbedded (represented) within them? It is rather straightfoward to show that parallel convolution machines can be built: take a large number of processors or units, and arrange them so that the units are connected to their neighbors. Then weight the interaction connections with the coefficients that define the convolution operator, and simply have the units perform the required multiplications and additions. Hierarchies or layered collections of such units could then be conceived, with interconnections between units established both across and between layers. This is the standard view of parallelism, and commercial hardware to accomplish such convolutions is now widely available (Tanimoto and Uhr, 1983).

Neural Modeling. The promise of parallel networks is much more than just measurements and convolutions. An abstract characterization of neurons into binary $\{0,1\}$ units led McCullough and Pitts (1943) to discover relationships between neural networks and a particular logical calculus. Other early researchers attempted to introduce some of the uncertainty apparent in neurons (McCarthy and Shannon, 1956) and to deal with fault tolerance (Winograd and Cowan, 1963; Arbib, 1972). Perceptrons, or linear threshold devices were introduced in the 1950s as devices actually capable of substantial pattern recognition, and Hebb (1949) suggested, in an exciting book, how neural assemblies could underlie much of behavior and learning. Unfortunately, most of these earlier claims about perceptrons were based on technical notions that have turned out to be inadequate (Minsky and Papert, 1969), and, while much of the earlier enthusiasm remains, new conceptual approaches became mandatory.

Cooperative Processes and Energy Minimization. Another conceptual approach to parallel processing emerged from two sources, one in psychology and the other in AI. The psychological contribution will be considered first.

Stereopsis is the process by which information about the depth of objects in the three-dimensional scene is extracted from relationships between the two retinal images. By trigonometry, a point in depth will project to different positions on each retina, and this difference in retinal disparity is proportional to depth. Thus depth information could be inferred if retinal disparities could be computed, but this requires the establishment of correspondence relations between structures in one image and those in the other that derive from the same physical event.

Two insights into what parallel processing could do were provided by two seemingly different approaches to the stereo correspondence problem. The first of these was obtained by Julesz, who envisioned the entities in each eye as different kinds of abstract "magnetic dipoles." This then implied that the dipoles could cooperate with one another as they relaxed into an equilibrium configuration. This is, of course, analogous to the Ising model of ferromagnetism (Ising, 1925), in which the local interaction terms are given by the equations of magnetism restricted to nearest neighbors. Such magnetic interaction terms model an abstract "affinity" or "compatibility" between local pieces of the retinal image.

The second approach is based on another metaphor from physics. Consider a mountain of sand and a billard ball, and think of the mountain as representing an "energy landscape." If the ball were rolled down the mountain, then intuitively it would seek a minimal energy position (Luenberger, 1969). The Gestalt psychologists observed early on that such notions could be applied to model vision, but we shall concentrate for now on the way that Sperling (1970) applied minimization to the stereo problem. He derived his energy landscape from considerations about similarity between retinal images. Correspondence can then be viewed as a process of finding the disparity matches, or corresopndences, between images that maximizes a measure of their total similarity.

Since stereo correspondence can be formulated in both ways, it is reasonable to conclude that they are two ways of expressing the same thing. While it may not be clear what the exact relationship between Julesz's and Sperling's approaches is without writing the equations in full, we can see that Julesz's approach concentrated on local interactions while Sperling's approach concentrated on their global "sum." Sperling also reduces his model to an interactive network. This paper is especially interesting to read for the early view of connectionism that it proposes, but an essential ingredient was still missing: how could optimization problems of the sort that Sperling was interested in be solved by the kind of local interactions that Julesz was interested in? The search for the answer sends us back to the emergence of parallelism within computer vision. Fischler and Elschlager (1973) indicated that the direction should be toward abstract structural matching.

Constraint Satisfaction and Discrete Relaxation Labeling. To return to computational vision, the pendulum is allowed to swing from technique back to task. An observation made by Waltz (1975) about using knowledge in vision systems, builds on the work of Guzman (1969), Clowes (1971), and Huffman (1971). Waltz and the others were interested in the high-level side of a vision system designed to function in the blocks world, or in aspects of what might be thought of loosely as the high-level side of Roberts' system. They were concerned, in particular, with what is called line labeling, or assigning semantically meaningful labels to the lines in a line drawing. Consider, for a moment, how such lines could arise physically. The outside edge of a cube occludes the background, while the edges between visible faces represent surface orientation changes. It would seem, then, that at least in the blocks world, it is possible to enumerate all of the ways in which physical edges (or their line representation) could arise. Waltz's task was to assign such representations to the lines in a line drawing so that these could then be synthesized into objects and their interrelationships. The synthesis was to be accomplished by search: try all combinations, say in a depth-first manner, until a match is found. Unfortunately, the simplicity of the search is overwhelmed by the combinatorics.

Necessity therefore motivated Waltz to shift his attention from the global task (which was now precisely formulated) to its local constituents. Waltz observed in particular that much of the search was unnecessary; it went into examining combinations that were in principle impossible. In fact, many of these impossible combinations could be detected locally, and then pruned, before the full graph was searched. All that was needed were rules, say about how lines could combine at junctions, to detect many physically impossible situations. Thus, in order to complete his search, Waltz implemented a sequential process that wandered around the graph of combinatorial possibilities deleting impossible ones. The efficiency was thereby improved to the point that the global searches could be completed after all locally impossible combinations were removed.

The next step was to show that the sequential elimination of labels could be done in parallel (Rosenfeld, Hummel, and Zucker, 1976). This step involved a shift in concentration from the task, labeling line drawings, to the technique. It yielded an algorithm in which, intuitively speaking, each label looked around at all of its neighbors and determined whether it was compatible with each of them; ie, whether there was at least one interpretation of possibly many that could be associated with each line meeting at a junction such that the pair formed a local combination that was realizable in a physical object. If not, then the inconsistent label was discarded. Of course, this inconsistent label may have been the only one supporting another label on one of its neighboring lines, so that the check for local consistency had to be iterated. In

this way information about inconsistencies propagates throughout the entire graph. Such a process was first known as discrete relaxation, and has now developed into the study of constraint satisfaction (qv).

Continuous Relaxation Labeling. The above algorithms are symbolic, in the sense that they deal with explicit symbols for example, an occluding edge associated with explicit image structures, say, a line. The image structures are easily abstracted to a graph, and the problem then becomes one of labeling a graph; or, more precisely, selection from among a set of labels (symbols) associated with nodes in the graph of a particular subset of labels that is consistent according to relations defined over pairs (or triples, etc) of labels associated with neighboring nodes. The selection need not be done solely on the basis of discrete relations, however; and the labels need not simply be an unordered set. Rather, continuous measures can be distributed over the label sets at each node, and the label-to-label relationships can be continuous rather than all-or-none functions. This essentially establishes a connection back to the previous subsection on optimization, and replaces the idea of discrete updating with a continuous, analog type of process. That is, the selection can now be done by maximizing a global criterion function of appropriate form, or by solving a variational problem with a particular structure (Hummel and Zucker, 1983). Such processes have been called relaxation labeling processes, in analogy with relaxation techniques for solving systems of differential equations, and their analysis and application in early vision has been widespread (Ballard, Hinton, and Sejnowski, 1983; Davis and Rosenfeld, 1981; Faugeras and Berthod, 1981).

Tasks, Tools, and Techniques

At this point in the discussion it is worthwhile to clarify a distinction that is often confused in computational vision: that between tasks, for example, determining what is an edge, and techniques, how can edges be detected. Marr (1982) put it slightly differently: he claimed that one needed to make a distinction between the problem and the algorithm for solving the problem. He further distinguished between the algorithm and the implementation of the algorithm. The discussion in the preceding subsections evolved into one of tools and techniques, and can be summarized by general queries of the form: what class of computations can be implemented on parallel, distributed hardware? Such investigations should lead to algorithms and their analyses. Two distinct kinds of analysis are, in fact, necessary. The first kind relates classes of algorithms to abstract characterizations of techniques; for example, there are many algorithms for solving linear programming problems, or for solving optimization problems. The second kind of analysis relates to properties of a particular algorithm, or class of algorithms: will they converge; are they sequential or parallel; are they numerically stable, etc. Although Gestalt psychologists are again mentioned later in this article, it is worth noting at this point in the development that it can be devastating to jump to conclusions regarding how minimization can be implemented.

The Gestalt psychologists took the electro-magnetic metaphor quite literally, and, when electrical potentials were discovered in the brain they assumed that their metaphor had been substantiated biologically. They thus took it quite literally for many aspects of brain and behavioural function, and the movement suffered substantially as a result (Kohler, 1969).

Although Marr advocated treating problem, algorithm, and implementation separately, there are clearly important relationships between them. The study of tasks interfaces with the study of algorithms through the abstract characterization of what they can do. For example, if edge detection could be formulated cleanly as an optimization problem, then appropriate optimization algorithms could be chosen. However, if it could not be formulated cleanly and if it does not work, then it is impossible to uniquely ascribe blame to either the task specification or to the technique proposed to solve it. Often both are at fault.

In general, it has been the case that there is a sort of pendulum of activity swinging between a concentration on tasks and on tools and techniques. Of course, to actually accomplish anything one must pay attention to both issues: what is the task and what techniques can be applied to solve it, and it is just this duality that keeps the pendulum swinging. Whenever a particular approach fails, either the formulation or the fabrication (the task or the technique) must be blamed, so the researcher then swings over to the other side. Of course, leaving out highly engineered situations, it is almost always the case that both the task and the technique have been inadequately formulated, which is why the pendulum keeps swinging! Therefore the pendulum now swings back to the task side.

Vision as "Inverse Optics"

Perhaps because they were physicists, both Mach and Helmholtz considered how images were formed, fields known today as photometry, optics, and physiological optics. This perspective has had an immense influence on shaping the second major paradigm for computational vision, or what might be viewed as second generation, or second paradigm, vision systems. The first generation, of course, is typified by Roberts system. The following will illustrate the particular, backwards, or inverse, way in which photometry entered, and then proceed to develop the second paradigm (see Shafer, 1985).

Shading from Shape (and Light Source). Light is emitted from a source, reflects off the surfaces of objects, and, if it is not obscured or absorbed by some intermediate object, is captured by the photoreceptors in our eyes. The standard formulation for matte reflection without highlights is well known to physicists, and Mach used it in his research in the latter part of the 19th century. The image intensity I (at each image point) is given by:

$$I = \rho(\mathbf{N} \cdot \mathbf{L})$$

where $\mathbf{N}$ is the normal vector to the surface at the point, $\mathbf{L}$ is the light source vector, and ρ is a scalar coefficient of surface reflectance. I is a function of two variables (say, x

and y retinotopic or image coordinates), while $\mathbf{N}$ and $\mathbf{L}$ are vectors in three-space. Clearly, if the scene is known (or, more particularly for this special case, $\mathbf{N}$, $\mathbf{L}$, and ρ), the image can be calculated. In words, the shading in the image of an object will vary in an appropriate way with the object, the viewing conditions, and the lighting conditions. But vision is concerned with running the above calculations backwards.

Shape from Shading. The inversion of the image formation process is under-determined. There are always essentially an infinite number of scenes that could have given rise to a particular image. Somehow three-dimensional variables must be inferred from two-dimensional ones. Many different sources of constraint are possible, but those that lead to an estimate of where the light source is with respect to the surface, where the surface is and how it is oriented with respect to the viewer, and what the surface's reflectance properties are, would seem to be among the most useful. Recently, Horn (1975), Woodham (1981), Pentland (1984), and others (Horn and Brooks, 1989) have tried to recover information about surface shape from changes in illumination, or shading, developing an activity initiated by Mach. Recently, in fact, an entire industry of approaches known as "shape-from-X," where X can be texture, contour, or motion (Kender, 1980; Witkin, 1981; Blostein and Ahuja, 1989), has emerged.

Beck (1972), among others, has studied such phenomena psychophysically. Since image formation is a complex of processes, it follows that segmentation is not just a matter of image differences, but can also be a matter of inferred physical object differences. Waltz's research was an important case in point (Mackworth, 1973; Malik, 1987). The next decade of computational vision research was, to a large extent, an attempt to verify this observation, to calculate and to make explicit these intermediate inferences from images back into the scene domain.

THE SECOND PARADIGM: FROM SEGMENTATION TO SURFACES

Image differences can arise from differences in lighting (as in cast shadows), differences in surface orientation (as at the corner of a cube), in surface composition (as when one object obscures another), and so on. The next major focus of computational vision research was onto exploring these differences both individually and together. While edge detection seems impossible solely on the basis of image intensities, each of the above individual properties, if it could be computed, could then be differentiated. The result would be a description not only of where intensities changed, but also of which estimated scene properties were changing as well.

The key difference between this second paradigm and the first one is how the line is drawn between low- and high-level vision. In the first paradigm, the goal of low-level processing was a segmentation, or the recovery of a line drawing of intensity outlines. Somehow these outlines are to be matched against a database of prototypical object outlines. Such matching is impossible for natural objects, however, since intensity discontinuities do not always correspond with object structure. For example, intraobject texture differences may obscure interobject edge differences. In the second paradigm, the attempt was to recover a richer, more abstract intermediate description, namely, surfaces, by attempting to invert the photometric equations. The difference between the paradigms is that now, in the second paradigm, *segmentation is to be carried out with respect to accurately inferred object properties, not only with respect to image intensity properties.* Then the matching can be guided by (abstract) object as well as a priori properties. This general purpose, intermediate level of description will incorporate information from many different sources, including stereo, motion, shape-from-shading, as well as many different kinds of constraints such as object smoothness. Data from range sensors also made the third dimension considerably more important for applications (Besl, 1988; Jain and Jain, 1989).

The influence from psychology is again clear here. Gibson (1950), who, like Helmholtz, had very limited ideas about the need for computation early on in the visual process, nevertheless had a clear idea of the importance of inferring abstract "surface" properties from images. To this end he and his students studied motion, texture, stereopsis, and shading, or many of the modes through which information about surfaces could be obtained. To be more precise, the statement here is not that earlier researchers, including Helmholtz, for example, were unaware of these sources of information, but rather that Gibson illustrates the enthusiastic revival of interest in them. Each of these appeared to be such a rich source of information to him that one could almost understand why he thought the visual system could resonate to them. It is striking, in fact, to compare illustrations from his highly influential 1950 book, and Marr's (1982) much more recent attempt to lay out a computational viewpoint. They are remarkably similar! Curiously, the enthusiasm surrounding Gibsonian resonances continues to the present (Ullman, 1980).

How, then, is it possible to structure the surface finding processes, ie, those processes that actually perform the inference of surfaces? The influence from physiology is again strong, as are inputs from mathematics and computation. In particular, physiologists began to question the idea of information processing taking place strictly hierarchically, replacing it with the view that there is a functional specification within the prestriate cortex, with different areas carrying out different functions (Zeki, 1978; van Essan and Maunsell, 1983).

Interacting Modules for Surface Interpolation

Two approaches emerged within this second paradigm almost simultaneously, one based on a working assumption of independence and the other on one of dependence.

Primal Sketches

The first of the frameworks around which second paradigm computational vision developed was the primal sketch idea of Marr (1976). The primal sketch is an explicit representation of the "important information about the two-dimensional image, primarily the intensity changes there and their geometrical organization" (Marr, 1982, p. 37). The primal sketch is therefore a data structure, and with development it actually evolved into several data structures: the raw primal sketch, which held the results of "edge detection;" the full primal sketch, in which geometric relationships were first made explicit; and the 2½-D sketch, in which certain depth properties were first computed. Model descriptions were then inferred from these data.

Marr took the principle of modularity very seriously, and proposed a research program in which each of these different stages, or the processing that actually comprised them, could be studied independently. Separate projects in stereo, motion, and edge detection were therefore begun. While modularity or independence is arguably just a first approximation, the competing framework stressed interrelationships.

It is interesting to examine the progress from Roberts' line drawings to Marr's primal sketch. Primal sketches are simply an elaboration of the data structure interfaces common to all computer vision systems. The question was, and is, precisely where they should be placed within the system (Aloimonos and Shulman, 1989).

Intrinsic Images

The other dominant framework for second paradigm vision was founded on the idea that since the surface/light source/viewer arrangements were all intrinsically coded within images, the role of early vision was to explicate them. Hence Barrow and Tenenbaum (1978) (Fig. 9) proposed the idea of intrinsic images, or a collection of arrays aligned in retinotopic (image) coordinates. Each array made one of the local intrinsic properties explicit, including image intensity, surface normal, distance (or disparity), and lighting. Since none of these intrinsic images could be computed by itself, functions were further defined between them which embodied, say, the photometric relationships that must hold between them. Each image further made discontinuities explicit, so that this information could be propagated between images as well.

Slicing Up The World For Constraints

The approaches to vision so far have indicated several different ways in which assumptions about the world can be obtained. First, it is possible to have a complete but artificial world. This is the case for the blocks world, from which one can conclude that although some quantitative analyses thereby become possible (for example, Horn's image intensity calculations), the results do not extend to more general universes. A second way to slice up the world is by introducing intermediate constraints that hold for some aspects of the general world. Examples of this are smoothness of surfaces (Grimson, 1983; Terzopoulos, 1984), the continuity of edges (Koenderinck and van Doorn, 1980, 1982), and the rigidity of objects (Johanssen, 1950; Wallach and O'Connell, 1953; Ullman, 1979). But beware when selecting assumptions that they do not conflict with the quantitative requirement above: there is

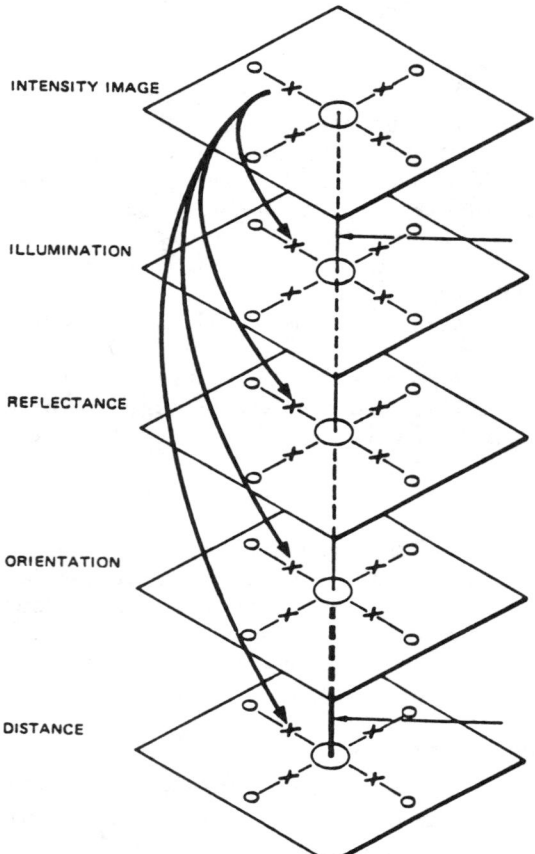

Figure 9. A typical second paradigm computational model, in this case Barrow and Tenenbaum's (1978) Intrinsic Images. The planes are intended to represent various intrinsic features, such as surface reflectance, arranged retinotopically, and the arrows indicate quantitative constraints between them (equations connecting them). But such purely quantitative, global models now appear to suffer from intractable stability and conditioning problems.

almost a sensitivity principle operating here, in which the consequences of violating an assumption should vary in proportion to the universe over which it holds. Stereo algorithms provide an exemplar domain in which constraints and algorithms interact (Bolles, Baker, and Marimont, 1987; Pradzny, 1985; Yeshurun and Schwartz, 1989; Baker and Bolles, 1989).

The Symbolic Side of Early Vision

In addition to making intrinsic properties explicit, the above framework began to confront the symbolic content of early vision as well. Implicit in the previous generation was an assumption that each stage was interpreted, in the logical sense of the term, by a subsequent one. Now researchers began to worry about the semantics of these symbols; ie, about what they meant (Fodor, 1984; Dennett, 1978). Early vision was shown to involve inferences about "what's out there." Such concerns developed from the concern in high-level vision with symbols, and ap-

peared explicitly in mechanisms such as relaxation labeling. This, in fact, is an essential difference between relaxation labeling as it emerged in the mid-1970s, and neural modeling, which is much older; in relaxation labeling the labels are treated in part like symbols. The importance of meaningful symbols, and the inferential processes that manipulated them, increased from this time on in all of vision.

The Realization of the Second Paradigm

The realization of the second paradigm has been attempted for the past decade, and hence much of the research is covered in detail elsewhere in this encyclopedia (see in particular COLOR VISION; VISUAL MOTION ANALYSIS; SCALE SPACE; TEMPLATE MATCHING; EDGE AND LOCAL FEATURE DETECTION; SHAPE; STEREO VISION; TEXTURE).

Organization of Primate Visual Systems

Decomposition of function arose in physiology as well as in computer vision. One certainly has the feeling that such anatomically apparent modularity lies behind the strong form of modularity advocated by Marr (1982). Consider the macroscopic organization of the primate visual system. The first level of organization is rather coarse, and can be characterized in terms of anatomically distinct areas to which the visual input is mapped. Recognizing that perhaps a few new visual areas will still be discovered, there are something in the range of 15–20 that have been at least partly characterized (van Essen and Maunsell, 1980). It is tempting to relate a visual function to each of these areas, say with one solving stereo, another solving edge detection, and so on. It is also the case that different neural layers within each of these anatomical areas may be involved in different functions, which adds up to another factor of three or four. However, this is dangerous since each visual area may well be involved in more than one function. Recall, for example, that simple cells are both orientation and velocity tuned. Computationally there are links between motion and specularities (Zisserman, Giblin, and Blake, 1989). An even more telling example has been found by Regan and Cynader (1981) in cells whose receptive fields are both motion and disparity sensitive. Receptive fields exist whose stimulus dependencies involve both velocity and disparity simultaneously; they cannot be decomposed. Even keeping such compositions in mind, however, a first-order estimate of functional complexity is possible. The number of distinct visual areas is significantly larger than two (for separating low- and high-level vision) and less than, say, 100, even taking the different layers into account.

The detailed organization of each of these visual areas exhibits structure of its own. The simple, complex, and hypercomplex cells of Hubel and Wiesel are found in the first few cortical visual areas. Fascinatingly, at least in the first of these visual areas (V1 in primates, area 17 in cats) these cells are not arranged randomly but rather form striking columnar patterns according to a number of criteria. First, there are ocular dominance columns in which cells take their dominant input from the left or the right visual field. Then there are orientation columns in which cells have a preferred orientation that changes sequentially along tangential (electrode) penetration. Finally, the receptive fields vary in size over several orders of magnitude, with some less than 10' (minutes of visual angle) and others more than 10°. In general, complex cells have larger receptive fields than simple cells. It would definitely seem that this organization provides strong support for parallel processing across spatial (and other) dimensions, although the mapping from anatomical area to visual function is still very obscure.

Parallel Functional Streams. Although we have concentrated on a few of the properties of cortical receptive fields, the story is undoubtedly more complex than this. Returning to the retina, the original view that ganglion cells only exhibit spatial circular-surround receptive fields has been replaced with a more modern one in which their temporal characteritics matter as well. It should be pointed out that even in the classical view there is evidence of two parallel processing streams with respect to contrast: one which is ON center/OFF surround, and the other which is OFF center/ON surround. It is now widely believed that there are many different classes of retinal ganglion cells, X and Y being among the most prominent. X cells are roughly linear in their response, and have relatively slow connections back to cortex. Y cells, on the other hand, are nonlinear in their response, have fast connections, and have receptive fields roughly twice the size of X cells. Both scale in size with retinal eccentricity. There is a third class of so-called W cells that is beyond the scope of this paper.

Although functional ideas regarding the X and Y systems are still hypothetical, it is held that the X system appears to be more concerned with spatial vision, while the Y system may be involved in motion (Orban, 1984). However, the significant point for us is that the X and Y pathways proceed in separate, parallel channels from the retina through the LGN to the cortex. There is even evidence that they give rise to separate populations of simple and complex cells as well. Thus, in addition to the hierarchical, layered organization, visual processing would appear to be accomplishing several functions in parallel as well. Furthermore, physiological evidence points to separate enervation to (at least some) simple and complex cells, which brings the strict hierarchy into question. And more recently the processing of color has been relegated to a partially separate system (Zeki and Shipp, 1985); other evidence regarding the functional streams and areas is in Blasdel and Salama (1986); and Livingstone and Hubel (1984). The feeding forward and the feeding back of visual information does not follow the simple branches of a tree, but rather flows around a graph. Complexity rises again.

What kinds of functions could the neurons along all of these parallel, layered pathways be computing? While the separation of color and luminance information makes evolutionary sense, and the separation of contrast makes mathematical sense, how can other visual functions be decomposed into parallel streams? It is fascinating that this is precisely the question that began to dominate researchers in computational vision, for different reasons, during this second paradigm. Decomposition and organization are the only ways to deal with complexity.

Summary of the Second Paradigm

In summary of this section, the second major paradigm in computational vision, it is interesting to stress that the partition of early and later processing, which began with Helmholtz and Roberts, has continued. The primal sketch and intrinsic images are far more complex interfaces than Roberts' line drawing, but nevertheless serve the same putative function. They certainly contain much more information, which underlines the complexity of early vision, a point which has emerged many times during this chapter. But the metaphor of photometry on which this style of analysis is based has become questionable. Just how far quantitative methods can be pushed remains an open question. The missing ingredient is qualitative structure.

GENERAL PURPOSE MODELS REVISITED

While the modular view has many attractions (recall the argument regarding the Dewey decimal system), the formulation it assumed within the second paradigm has serious problems. A decade of concentrated effort has not led to generally functional systems; rather, there have been only local successes, or successes only under many explicit and highly restrictive assumptions. The situation is reminiscent of the blocks world experience, in which knowledge of, or assumptions about, the physical situation were so restrictive as to be suffocating.

The problem with second-paradigm vision systems can be seen from the discussion of "inverse optics;" for the program to succeed, all of the details of surface normals, surface reflectance functions, spatial arrangements, etc, need to be recovered exactly. There is no place for approximation, noise, or uncertainty. But approximation, noise, and uncertainty are present in any real physical vision system. The strong form of the second paradigm cannot succeed.

The examples from perception presented earlier in the article also argue strongly against the second paradigm. The Mueller-Lyer illusion (Fig. 1) and Mach bands (Fig. 2) indicated that what is seen is not exactly what is there; rather, it is the result of a context-dependent computation. And the subjective Kanizsa edge (Fig. 7) suggests that the computation involves a form of inference.

If the exact structure of the scene cannot be recovered everywhere, which parts can be? Which aspects of structure are necessary (sufficient?) for visual inferences? Thus the question of what kinds of knowledge are employed, and to what ends, rises again. There are two major issues in particular: (1) whether the knowledge is truly quantitative; and (2) how to slice up the world so that appropriate general assumptions can be made.

Qualitative vs Quantitative Knowledge

The fact that image intensity formation is a complex process led to an early observation that intensity profiles are not always shaped like a step function, but also arise as roofs or slopes (Herschovitz and Binford, 1970). The structure of these intensity functions carries important information about the physical scene that gave rise to it (Horn, 1977), an observation that was instrumental, in large part, for the concentrated effort on "inverse optics." Much of this research was quantitative in motivation, if not in fact, with the goal precisely formulating the systems of differential equations and solving them exactly. Unfortunately, as Mach indicated, this is impossible in general, and those restrictive situations in which it is may not be all that relevant to the solution of the general vision problem. While photometers must be quantitative in their interpretation of, say, shading profiles on the moon as seen through telescopes, they are functioning as physicists and their goal is to recover the surface topography of the moon as accurately as possible from that source of information. It would appear that vision systems cannot accomplish this in general for all scenes.

Qualitative Shape from Shading. Because of its central position, the methodological presupposition within the second paradigm that our visual systems function as inverse photometers must be questioned. The evidence, in fact, is against it from a biological perspective. For example, if computer graphics techniques were used to render images of cylinders with different cross-sectional profiles, ranging, say, from circular to triangular, then one would expect the percept of the figure to change as well. This does not happen, however (Barrow and Tenenbaum, 1981); rather, a range of different surface shapes are all perceived as roughly circular. The impression is that shading cues are more qualitative than quantitative. Cavanagh (1986), in a recent psychophysical study, has shown that depth cues such as occlusion and shading interact only in certain ways, depending on whether they derive from color, motion, stereo, etc. The next example raises another kind of problem with strict quantitative constraints in early vision.

The Rigidity of the Rigidity Assumption in Structure-from-Motion. Humans have the remarkable ability to see structure from moving dot patterns (Johanssen, 1950; Wallach and O'Connell, 1953). There is, of course, much more to motion than shall be considered in this article (see Anadan, 1989; Heegar, 1988; Fleet and Jepson, 1989).

Imagine, for example, a clear cylinder covered with tiny specks of dust. Statically, the dust pattern would appear to just be random dots arranged on a plane. If the cylinder were rotated, however, its full three-dimensional structure would be apparent. Ullman (1979) has referred to this ability as inferring structure-from-motion, and a good deal of research, both computational and psychophysical, has been focused on it (Hoffman and Flinchbaugh, 1982; Cutting, 1981; Johanssen, 1950; Wallach and O'Connell, 1953). In particular, the apparent perceptual preference to see rigid configurations has inspired researchers to build the rigidity constraint directly into the computation, leading to models in which systems of algebraic equations need to be solved exactly.

However, the computations arising from such formulations are difficult, if not impossible, to realize biologically or perceptually, because of a numerical problem called ill conditioning. A system of equations is ill-conditioned if a small change in input (independent variable) leads to an arbitrary change in output (dependent variable). Such small changes in input arise from errors in measurement or lack of high numerical precision, and hence such quantitatively sensitive algorithms seem ideally unsuited for real vision. Visual systems must be designed to function in the presence of noise and uncertainty. Global rigidity assumptions are too rigid; they fracture under the slightest pressure from uncertainty.

General Algorithms and General Position

The above point about rigidity can be made in different terms by the notion of general position. Imagine viewing a line drawing of cube. From all positions except one this line drawing will be topologically similar; there is one, however, at which it looks different: when the corner nearest the viewer and the corner farthest from the viewer align along the viewing axis. In this singular configuration that line drawing no longer looks three-dimensional; rather it looks like a flat triangulated hexagon (Fig. 10). Note, however, that such singular configurations are destroyed if one moves ever so slightly off the axis connecting the two corners. In all but this one configuration the cube is viewed from a general position. By definition, then, a general positional view of an object is one in which the image does not change qualitatively. Other examples of singular arrangements could be obtained if one were to view scenes from singular viewpoints; recall the Ames room demonstrations (Ittleson, 1960). They did not look the same from any other viewpoint. Vision algorithms must be general in precisely this sense: the rigidity assumption is analogous to a singular view.

FROM STRUCTURE INTO FUNCTION

Early on in this article, two pendula were described, one of which indicated the tension between low- and high-level knowledge, and the other that between task and technique. Although the field has become much more experienced, the pendula still remain. Ten years ago, there was great concern about whether processing was top-down or bottom-up; now it is what kinds of knowledge must be applied, what are legitimate assumptions to make and what constraints do they imply. However, the assump-

 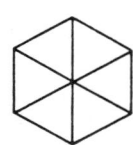

Figure 10. Two line drawings of cubes. The one on the left illustrates a cube from an arbitrary viewpoint; although the details change, the topological features remain the same. On the right is an illustration from a singular viewpoint, in which the three-dimensionality may or may not be present. Any slight change in viewpoint destroys the triangulated hexagon, and results in a drawing like the one on the left.

tions and constraints are usually ones of principle; eg, the assumption of rigidity in motion (Wallach and O'Connell, 1953; Ullman, 1979). How should they be discretized in practice? The need for modularity has arisen within both tensions: The question has become which structures in the scene project into which structures in the image (informational modularity), and how might these be recovered reliably and consistently (processing modularity)? Spatial parallelism is clearly indicated in the early stages; how high it goes is still an open question (Feldman and Ballard, 1982; Ullman, 1985).

The idea here is more than that certain scene structures are preserved under projection. Helmholtz and Gibson were both aware of this. The classic examples from Helmholtz concern how straight lines in space project into straight lines in the image; Gibson, of course, discovered texture gradients and optical flow. The idea rather is that vision consists of a fabric of inferences, some or many of which are inter-related. Not all of the scene information is recoverable directly; rather, only some kinds of structure in the scene domain give rise to image structures from which the "projection" transformation can be "inverted." It is this network of local (in every sense of the term) inferences on which the global scene recovery is anchored. Somehow the global structure must be interpolated from the local anchors. It is the discovery of such structures that provides the keys into visual function.

On the Mechanisms For Early Inferences

Three major lessons have been learned about how to approach early vision: (1) the mechanisms for structuring the early inferences must incorporate assumptions that hold abstractly over significant sub-classes of real-world structure; (2) they must be as insensitive to noise and uncertainty as possible; and (3) they must be utilizable within distributed "hardware" [either networks of neurons or VLSI circuits (Mead, 1989)] to deal with the complexity of size. Such inferences can be carried out by distributed optimization, relaxation, or related "neural networklike" machinery (Eckmiller and Malsberg, 1988). The constraints are more satisfiable when posed within minimization or hypothesis testing frameworks than as rigid systems of equations (Brady and Yuille, 1983; Horn and Shunk, 1981; Ikeuchi and Horn, 1981; Zucker, 1985). Since constraints on these inferences exist from many different sources, the mechanisms within which they are utilized must permit their interaction as well. Massively parallel processing is now feasible, and the design of computer vision algorithms for such processors is involving increasingly more effort (Margalit, 1989; Hillis, 1985; Geman and Geman, 1984).

The Local Structure of Intensity Discontinuities

Both issues—how qualitative and how encompassing assumptions are—emerge in the search for the elusive edge detection process (recall the above section on The Elusive Edge Operator). This example concentrates on the first lesson listed above: that there should be a significant but "local" problem; ie, a significant amount of knowledge about the local structure of images that provides a solid foundation for inferring a local piece of the scene that gave rise to it. Since the range of physical events is large that can project into what are called edges in the image, it follows that the description of the edge must be rich enough to support decisions about the physical cause. Edge events can arise from surface reflectance changes, surface orientation changes, occlusions, and lighting changes taken individually or in combination. Simple image differentials are unlikely to work, since they only localize changes in intensity (eg, Canny, 1984). More complex processing is needed for determining not only the locations of the image intensity discontinuities, but also the shape of the intensity function in a local neighborhood around it.

The importance of the local structure of image intensities in the neighborhood of an edge has been realized since the blocks world. Binford and Horn (Horn, 1973) matched intensity profiles along an edge, however their matching relied heavily on assumptions about the blocks world (eg, planarity of surfaces). More recently Quam (1978) used the intensity structure across linear features to track roads, and Witkin (1982) correlated intensity structure across putative edges to verify their presence. Most importantly, however, Witkin tried to use these across-edge correlations to infer something about the physical event that gave rise to the edge, observing that when objects stand in an occlusion relationship, the pattern of intensities on either side of the occlusion should be similar, but not necessarily across the occlusion. Such information clearly supports the mapping from the image back to the scene under certain circumstances.

One can go further. Not only should intensity structures be similar on either side of an edge, but their detailed structure can be used to support inferences about the edge (Leclerc and Zucker, 1986). To illustrate, recall the above discussion of shape-from-shading. Consider a matte surface smoothly varying in orientation. By the image irradiance equation, it follows that the projected intensity function will be smooth as well. Now, suppose that a shadow were cast on the surface. This would add a step to the log intensity distribution, resulting in an image structure in which the slope of the intensity function would be the same, and almost certainly not flat, on either side of the discontinuity. Therefore, to locate this type of edge, and to distinguish it from others, it is necessary to describe both the intensity function and its slope on either side of a discontinuity. Other schemes that simply locate discontinuities at the cost of irretrievably modifying the local intensities cannot support inferences back to the world.

Leclerc and Zucker (1986) have developed a nonlinear scheme for accomplishing this estimation of local intensity structure concurrently with detection of discontinuities. It involves spatial interactions between convolutions of similar sizes as well as level or scale interactions between different sizes. Such intra- and interscale interactions are necessary because of the tradeoff between neighborhood size and noise immunity: the larger the neighborhood, the better the performance at detecting and describing an edge. The performance will degrade if more local edge events are smoothed over in the process, and the network interactions are necessary to guarantee that this does not take place. For a reformulation in terms of minimal length encoding strategies, see Leclerc (1989).

Edge detection is therefore not just a matter of finding the right edge operator, but rather requires understanding the interactions between measurements as well. This leads to inferences. For edges we stressed the structure across it; the local structure of intensities in the neighborhood of discontinuities, now we shall concentrate on a different aspect of the structure; that along curves rather than across edges. This will force us into differential geometry.

Analysis of Orientation: Curve and Flow Recovery

As another example, consider the (related) problem of curve detection. Curves are an important subclass of structure in the world because they satisfy the above criteria: they occur in almost all images (as occluding contours; surface creases; hair and other surface coverings, etc); and they provide information on which subsequent surface inferences can be based (Stevens, 1981; Zucker, 1985). How can they be recovered, or inferred, from images? Early approaches to curve detection were barely distinguishable from early edge detection. Simple cell operators were convolved against images and maximal values selected by thresholding. This is because they respond maximally when centered exactly on a line and oriented similarly to it; hence they have been called *line detectors*. Unfortunately, they run into the same problems as edge detectors.

Lines vs Tangents. What relationship do so-called line detectors have to the actual detection of a curve? A logical place to start is by asking what a curve really is. Mathematically, a curve is a function that maps an interval of the line $\mathscr{R}^1$ into an embedding space (say, the plane $\mathscr{R}^2$ or space $\mathscr{R}^3$). What is given in an image is not a curve, but rather a discrete sampling of the trace of a curve, or a set of points through which it passes. Curve detection is the process of inferring a curve from its trace subject to additional constraints.

It is important to view curves abstractly and mathematically rather than pragmatically as image structures because this view suggests that the intermediate structures should be abstract as well. In this case, lines are not what need to be detected, but rather tangents to curves. Curvature can then also be shown to play a role, since curvature can be viewed as a relationship between tangents (Zucker, 1985; Parent and Zucker, 1989). Furthermore, since the tangent is the first derivative of the curve with respect to arc length, the global curve can be recovered from such local representations by a process of integration. Tangent fields are an arrangement of discretized and quantized tangents in retinotopic coordinates. Taken straightforwardly, the integration would require boundary conditions and global information (ie, the exact length of the curve, or where it starts and where it ends), but such global information is clearly not available to the integration process, unless it is accomplished interactively (Kass, Witkin, and Terzopoulis, 1988). Thus, new parallel

techniques are required that do not require global boundary conditions and may involve potential distributions (Zucker, Dobbins, and Iverson, 1989). The result is a two-stage algorithm, with reliable local information computed in the first stage, and global information in the second (Fig. 11). The connection to biological processing streams is also intriguing. Moreover, this abstract perspective suggests a connection with surface descriptions as well (Sander and Zucker, in press).

Viewing curves abstractly also raises additional possibilities for interpreting scale as well. Recall the traditional view that larger operators detect larger events (cf above section on Edge Detection and Scale). However, since curvature is a relationship over neighboring tangents along a curve, it suggests that perhaps the role of the larger operators is related to these higher-order properties (Zucker, 1985). One should certainly expect this to be the case mathematically, and computationally it works as well (Parent and Zucker, 1989). Indications are that the biological equivalent to curvature measurements are embodied in the hypercomplex cells (see the section above on Naive Physiology) or, more precisely, in their "end-stopping" property (Dobbins, Cynader, and Zucker, 1987). This is a case in which the explanation of biological data together with basic mathematics has yielded a successful computational vision algorithm (Zucker, 1985; Brady and Asada, 1984).

Parallel Surface Contours. Consider a surface covered in parallel pinstripes. These will project into parallel curves in the image. Stevens (1981) studied the inverse situation, or the inference of a surface from a collection of parallel curves. Such displays give strong impressions of surfaces when viewed (Fig. 12).

Flow Patterns. It is rarely the case that the surfaces of objects in natural scenes are covered with regularly arranged contours. The more natural case is that the curves are arranged so densely that they cover the surface in a physical sense, often winding in and out of occlusion relationships. This is the case for hair and fur patterns consisting of only roughly parallel arrangements of curves (hairs). In the case of motion, such flow patterns arise in waterfalls, or when the projected image of a complex physical arrangement changes rapidly as when one runs through a forest. Note that these are different from the pinstripe patterns discussed above, in that pinstrips almost never touch and are continued for a long distance, while hairs almost always touch and are rarely visible for long distances. Somehow the surface covering (the hair pattern) must be recovered from the (relatively) sparse information available in the image as highlights.

The issue here is another abstract mathematical one, and the way in which it connects image events (patterns of intensities) to events in the world (patterns of hairs). Topologically, curves are one-dimensional constructs; surface coverings are, like surfaces, two-dimensional constructs. One should therefore expect the recovery of surface-covering descriptions to require processing in addition to that required for curve inferencing. In particular, the recovery of orientation information for flow pat-

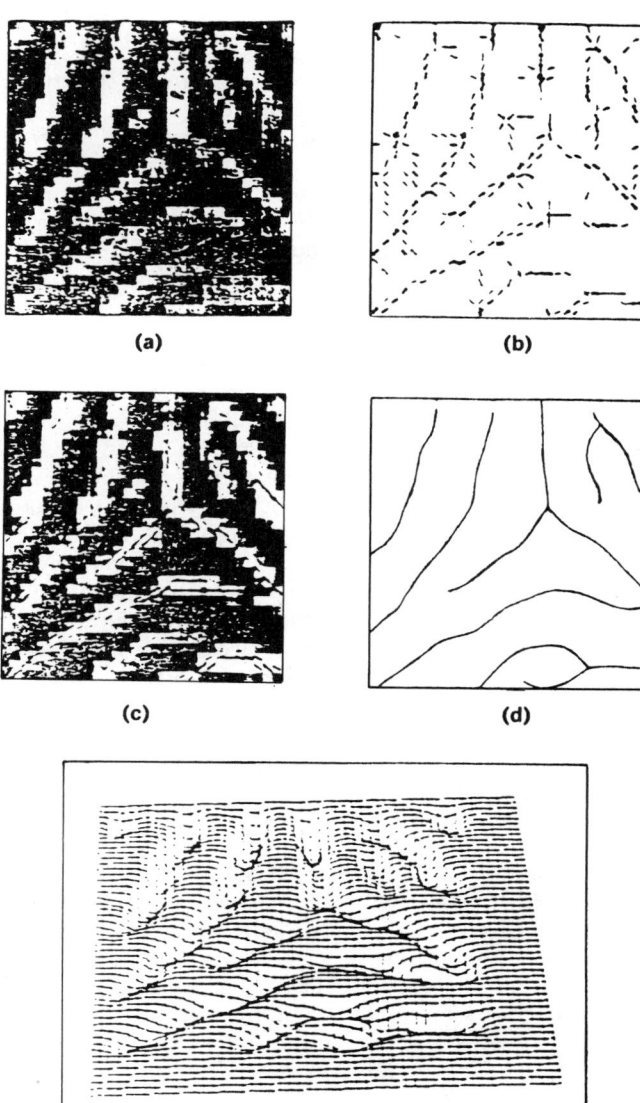

Figure 12. An illustration of how parallel surface contours (pinstripes) provide a strong cue for surface orientation.

terns involves a direct form of interpolation, or the spreading of curve information, to "fill in" the areas between "highlights" of projected image structure (Fig. 13). The result is a tangent field, or description of the orientation information, over an entire two-dimensional area.

Texture

Although we have concentrated on regularities in image structure that are connected to orientation, there are other regularities. Such arrangements are called textures (Gibson, 1950), and their structural geometric regularities have been modeled by Zucker (1976). Beck (1982) has shown that most of the perceptually relevant structure of (static) textures is contained in intensity, orientation, and color distributions, and Haralick (1978) has reviewed the different approaches to computing texture descriptions.

Figure 11. An illustration of the two stages in curve detection. (*a*) A small subsection of a fingerprint image is shown; note the smooth curves and discontinuities around the "Y" in the center. (*b*) Graphical illustration of the initial information, or those orientation/curvature hypotheses resulting from convolutions above the noise level. Note the presence of many artifactual responses, typical of virtually all local operators. (*c*) The discrete tangent field resulting from a relaxation labeling process using co-circularity compatabilities after two iterations; most of the inappropriate initial responses have been eliminated, and multiple values in the same spacial location indicate discontinuities. (*d*) Computation of a global covering of the curves from the potential distribution [shown in (*e*)] computed from the tangent field entries. Observe how the construction of the potential distribution accomplishes the transition from the local information in (*b*) and (*c*) to global information in (*e*). After Zucker and co-workers (1989).

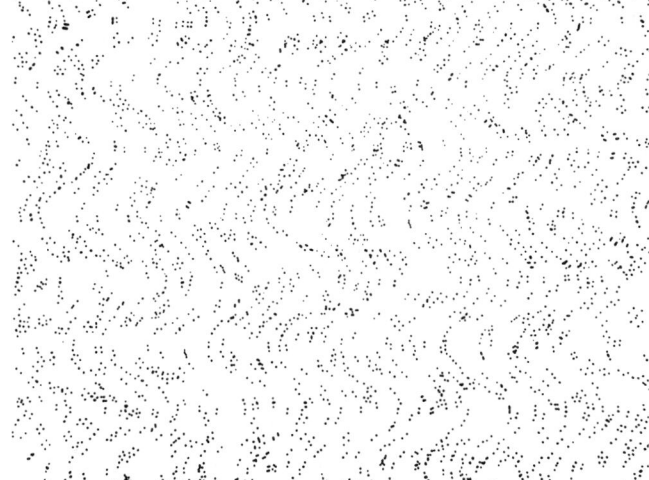

Figure 13. A flow pattern covering a surface with the same kind of undulations as the one in Figure 11. Now, however, the covering is more like a hair or flow pattern. Local indication of orientation is provided by pairs of random dots; global two-dimensional organization is inferred by our visual systems. Note that, unlike Figure 11, there are no long contours, and that they are not evenly spaced but rather appear to cover the surface densely.

If textures are that class of image structures that indicates regularity, at least in some sense, the other end of the extreme are those image structures that indicate (and arise from) chaos; consider, eg, clouds, trees covered with leaves, and the surf. Pentland (1984) has studied how such fractals can arise in images, and how their structure can be inferred (See also Dubuc and co-workers, 1989; Peleg and co-workers, 1984).

Surfaces

Once information about surface coverings, contours, and edges is available, the question arises regarding how to infer surfaces, or other abstract structures, from this. Many other examples of such inferences abound; recall the discussion of shape-from-X methods above. To illustrate the technique, recall the observation of Helmholtz that straight lines in space project to straight lines in images. Now, if it were known that the lines in space were regularly arranged, say as a square grid or as, in the case of contours, circles, then their projection onto a surface would give rise to a regular geometric distortion; the square grid would go into a trapezoidal one, and the circles would go into ellipses. Hence, given these figures, the projection equation could be inverted for them (Kanade, 1981; Kender, 1980). Again note that this is not a case of doing inverse optics in general (cf the section on Tasks, Tools and Techniques above), but rather doing it for a local problem (a specific grid). Such ideas underlie much of the three-dimensional vision in robotics, in which structured light arrays are projected onto objects using either patterned sources or lasers (Dodd and Rossol, 1979).

Kass and Witkin (1985) present a more radical attempt at structural inference; they would like to characterize the process by which objects are formed as for example the flow of tree bark around a knot. No matter what scheme is chosen, however, it must be stressed that multiple surface representations, such as those which can arise in transparency (Kanizsa, 1979), must be handled.

Corners and Parts. At a level of abstraction up from curves and edges, even sparsely supported, are structures that are derivable from them, say their discontinuities, inflexions, and extrema. For a discussion of how to detect corners, see Brady and Asada, 1984; Davis, 1979; Lee, 1990; for a novel approach to representing corners as multiple values at a position, see Zucker, Dobbins, and Iverson (1989). In a collection of parallel contours, for example, corners that align along smooth contours provide a curve inferencing problem one level higher (than the curve inferencing), and similarly these corner-contours could be grouped. The study of such grouping processes is related to the way in which complex objects are decomposed into parts, an area currently under investigation (Ferrie, Lagarde, and Whaite, 1989; Biederman, 1985; Solina and Bajcsy, 1990; Koenderinck and van Doorn, 1982; Hoffman and Richards, 1986; Pentland, 1990; Koenderink, 1989). Intersections between objects almost always map to singularities in the bounding contour.

Figure/Ground and Structural Grouping

The Gestalt psychologists emphasized the role of structure and organization in early vision nearly 65 years ago (eg, Koffka, 1935). They identified a phenomenological level of processing in which figure was separated from ground according to a number of principles, including proximity, good continuation, common fate, etc. But their proposals have defied quantification so far (Uttal, 1981). Perhaps the reason is because of the complexity issues that we have been discussing. There are, for example, many different ways in which curves can arise in the physical world, as is the case for edges, and their subsequent uses are likely different. Bounding contours arise from inferences that link discontinuities with similar local intensity structures, while surface contours may have similar intensities along them. As seen above, curves such as surface contours could be detected, but this required an assumption that the given trace of the curve was dense enough to properly stimulate the initial convolutions. Curves that are sparse with respect to this metric will certainly require different techniques. Kalman filtering is one possibility (Szeliski, 1989), as are scale similarities (Lowe, 1989), Bayes theory (Cernuschi-Frias, Cooper, Hung, and Belhumeur, 1989; Matthies, Kanade, and Szeliski, 1989; Geman and Geman, 1984) and techniques from computational geometry (Ahuja, 1982).

Grouping is a term usually taken to denote the agglomeration of local structures into more global, and perhaps more abstract, wholes. The standard example is Wertheimer's (1938) observation that collections of points are not seen as points, but rather as figures. As discussed earlier, the Gestalt psychologists believed that the (physical) minimization of real quantities was the mechanism by which this grouping was accomplished, in much the same way that soap bubbles minimize surface area. Although we now know that minimization can be accomplished by more computational methods (see, eg, the section on relaxation methods), the original idea that grouping could be accomplished by a single mechanism is still with us (eg, Marr, 1982). Given the arguments about the diversity of inference mechanisms for curves and edges, however, this seems unlikely, in much the same way that a single-edge mechanism now seems unlikely. Rather, one might guess that there are a diversity of grouping processes, each tailored to different (classes of) function (Zucker, 1985). Curve and edge processes were discussed above; a few other examples follow. This argument has now been generalized (Witkin and Tenenbaum, 1983; Lowe and Binford, 1982; Lowe, 1984). It holds that, in general, structure is unlikely to arise randomly in images; rather the structure of the world is such that, should events somehow line up then a common cause should be attributed to them. General purpose models capture this common cause at early, but still abstract, levels. For applications, see Mohan and Nevatia (1989) and Richards (1988).

Active Vision, or, Where To Look Next

One of the most immediate observations about biological perceivers is that people move around; if part of an object is hidden from sight, then one can alter the viewing position to see it better (Gibson, 1950). As the marriage between computer vision and robotics matures, active sensing systems will become much more commonplace (Bajcsy, 1986). This has several advantages: (1) problems that are ill-posed from a single viewpoint may become well posed with more than one view (Aloimonos, Weiss, and Bandyopadhyay, 1988); and (2) a representation of mathematical uncertainties within inferred representations of the world can suggest where to "look" next (Ferrie and coworkers, 1989). Thus the questions facing vision researchers will involve more of "what needs to be computed about the environment" rather than "what can be precisely computed about the environment."

The Differential Equation Metaphor

The way in which, say, occluding contours and hair patterns relate to the physical world leads to another difference between them, a difference that can be generalized to include many other classes of structural information. Occluding contours arise when surfaces intersect projectively; they give rise to intersurface constraints. Hair patterns, on the other hand, provide information about the particular surface on which they lie; they give rise to intrasurface constraints. This difference is fundamental to the processes that must put various sources of information together. Again we are lead to the metaphor provided by differential equations, in which the solution is governed by two distinct classes of constraints: the differential operator, which constrains how the solution varies over its domain, and the boundary condition, which constrains the domain and the value at the edges of this domain. Note that for two-dimensional differential equations, such as Laplace's equation, the differential operator is an infinitesimal function of two variables, while the boundary condition is given by, say, the values along a one-dimensional contour. Infinitesimally such differential operators represent the kind of constraint available from flow patterns; while the boundary conditions resemble one-dimensional contours. In terms of our previous examples, the Laplacian corresponds to the orientation information provided by an infinitesimal "piece" of a waterfall, while the boundary condition corresponds to its bounding contour.

The above example is, of course, metaphorical. The intent is not to say that intrasurface constraints are Laplacians. Rather, it is the abstract mathematical form that concerns us, and it is not limited to waterfalls. Other sources of static intrasurface constraint come from monocular shape cues such as shape-from-shading (Horn, 1970; Pentland, 1982), from binocular stereo disparities (Mayhew and Frisby, 1981; Julesz, 1971; Terzopoulos, 1984), and so on as we have discussed. Intrasurface cues only hold for particular surfaces; they take abrupt jumps as the projected image from one surface undergoes a transition into that from another. Similar arguments hold for the transitions in lighting which we also discussed, say from an illuminated area to one in a cast shadow (Leclerc and Zucker, 1986). Topologically all of these transitions are one-dimensional contour boundary conditions that constrain the area over which the other, two-dimensional intrasurface constraints can be integrated.

Free Boundary Value Problems. Clearly there are many sources of both inter- and intrasurface constraint, including motion, stereo, shading, texture, color, and their differences. It has already been argued that their inference will involve interpolation; and that "edges" provide the boundary conditions for limiting them. How can these different sources of information be put together? Clearly situations will arise in which the intrasurface information will be ambiguous, as will the intersurface information, and both inferences must occur simultaneously so that they can mutually constrain one another. Intuitively the situation is like computing the shape of a soap bubble over a flexible ring; clearly, the final shape will depend both on the ring and on the soap. Such problems are called free boundary value problems, and they arise in many areas of mathematical physics (Kindelehrer and Stampacchia, 1980).

An early attempt to implement these ideas in a simplified vision context involved dot clusters, in which the problem was to label the dots defining the edge of clusters simultaneously with labeling the dots interior to the clusters (Zucker and Hummel, 1979). Separate processes for intracluster and intercluster (edge) labeling were specified, as were their interactions. Briefly, one might speculate that, in the vision context, the intracluster processes would be integrative, region-growing-type algorithms over intensity (concretely) or shape and reflectance (abstractly) constraints; the intercluster processes would delimit the various type of edges between them. More recent attempts at integrating information from different sources in vision systems are discussed by Terzopoulos (1986). Much remains to be done along these lines.

Generalization of the Framework

The framework provided by inter- and intrasurface information, or, in different terms, by differential equations, holds not only for the features described here, but for abstractions over them. Contours arising from abrupt changes in, say, a flow or hair pattern could provide the boundary constraint to a higher level process. This could correspond to a physical situation in which the underlying surface changed orientation abruptly, but the surface markings smoothed it over somewhat. Thus issues of how to differentiate flows become as important as the flows themselves.

HIGH-LEVEL VISION

In the introduction to this article low-level and high-level vision were differentiated by asserting that low-level vision was the study of general constraints on special purpose hardware while high-level vision was special constraints on general purpose hardware. In the evolution of this article many different low-level constraints were uncovered with nontrivial roots in higher level vision. The earliest work on computational grouping may be Guzman's (1969) "matched T's" for joining pieces of contour occluded by a common block together. As these different constraints were refined and "moved down" in visual systems, the need emerged for intermediate level structures to support them. Perhaps the earliest tenable idea in this direction is Binford's (1971) notion of a generalized cylinder. More specialized constraints are bound to emerge here, in the sense that they are more global. Rather than searching for local structures that can be inverted, here we are searching for a vocabulary of intermediate objects; a kind of modeling language for prototypes. A recent contribution in this direction is a proposal by Pentland (1986) for "superquadrics," an extension of quadric surfaces done for solid modeling in computer graphics (Barr, 1984). But it is not yet clear how these superquadric constructs relate to more traditional graphics modeling primitives (Foley and van Dam, 1982). For important recent work, see Koenderink (1990) and Kimia and co-workers (1990).

The requirements for intermediate structures are influenced both by what is coming from "below" and what remains to follow from "above." Lowe (1984) makes the point that the result of grouping operations should provide indexes into model databases, and attention (Triesman, 1985) may well provide a connection in the opposite direction. Robotics imposes its own special constraints (eg, Faugeras, 1985).

High level vision has a very different structure than what we have been describing throughout most of this article. Although constraints still play a fundamental role (Brooks, 1981), now they relate properties of objects (in object databases) to image structure. "Analog" continuous methods, of the sort that have been described throughout this article get replaced by more symbolic programming tools (Garvey, 1976; Hanson and Riseman, 1978; Levine, 1985; Nagao and Matsuyama, 1980; Tsotsos and co-workers, 1980); for a review, see Binford (1982). It is these symbolic tools that provide the general "inference engine" for interpreting the specific, high level constraints. And these high level constraints are more symbolic than those in early vision; see, the complex frames and other data structures described in the references above. The mixture of the two can often provide nice solutions to constrained engineering problems; (eg, Ferrie, Levine, and Zucker, 1982) (see IMAGE UNDERSTANDING).

CONCLUSIONS

Light reflected from physical objects gives rise to images. Vision is the inverse of this process: the recovery of descriptions of objects in the world from images of them. It is clearly an underconstrained problem: somehow a description of three-dimensional scenes must be recovered from two-dimensional images. Yet it is possible, as the human visual system demonstrates. But where does the trick lie? How is the structure of the world reflected in the structure of our visual systems? Which aspects of the structure of the world are important; how are they—and how should they be—organized? Is it in the gross organization, or in the details of neural interconnections? How can the processing be described so that it could be understood and tested? How do our internal percepts relate back to the world? And how can principles be uncovered that allow observations about biological perception to be related to machine perception? These are the kinds of questions that computational vision research would like to be able to answer.

As shown, there are many ways to approach these questions. Psychology, physiology, anatomy, evolutionary biology, mathematics, computer science, engineering, physics, philosophy, and psychoanalysis all have something to contribute. The diversity of these fields gives some indication of the diversity of constraints that are active in vision, and our goal in this paper has been to try to illustrate how they can work together. Theoretical ideas from many different levels lead to constraints that percolate via reductionism and constructivism to other levels.

Investigations of the problems of vision rarely yield complete theories. Rather, their contribution results in the formulation of constraints for shaping any theory. Such constraints stand whether or not the parent theoretical framework changes. The evolution of our understanding of these constraints has been the principal theme running through this article and what is taken to be progress in understanding vision.

BIBLIOGRAPHY

N. Ahuja, "Dot Pattern Processing Using Voroni Neighborhoods," *IEEE Trans. Patt. Anal. Mach. Intell.* **PAMI-4,** 336–343 (1982).

J. Aloimonos and D. Shulman, *Integration of Visual Modules— An Extension of the Marr Paradigm,* Academic Press, Boston, 1989.

J. Aloimonos, I. Weiss, and A. Bandyopadhyay, "Active Vision," *Int. J. Comput. Vision* **4,** 333–356 (1988).

P. Anadan, "A Computational Framework and an Algorithm for the Measurement of Visual Motion," *Int. J. Comput. Vision* **2,** 283–310 (1989).

M. Arbib, *The Metaphorical Brain,* Wiley, New York, 1972.

R. Bajcsy, "Active Perception vs. Passive Navigation," *Proceedings of the Workshop on Active Vision,* University of Michigan, Ann Arbor, 1986.

H. H. Baker and R. Bolles, "Generalizing Epipolar-plane Image Analysis on the Spatiotemporal Surface," *Int. J. Comput. Vision* **3,** 33–49 (1989).

D. Ballard, "Parameter Networks," *Artif. Intell.* **22,** 235–267 (1984).

D. Ballard and C. Brown, *Computer Vision,* Prentice-Hall, Englewood Cliffs, N.J., 1982.

D. Ballard, G. Hinton, and T. Sejnowski, "Parallel Visual Computation," *Nature* **306,** 21–26 (1983).

H. Barlow, "Single Units and Sensation: A Neural Doctrine for Perception," *Perception* **1,** 371–394 (1972).

H. Barlow, R. Narasimhan, and A. Rosenfeld, "Visual Pattern Recognition in Machines and Animals," *Science* **177,** 567–575 (1972).

A. Barr, "Global and Local Deformation of Solid Primitives," *Comput. Graphics* **18,** 21–30 (1984).

H. Barrow and J. M. Tenenbaum, "Recovering Intrinsic Scene Characteristics from Images," in A. Hanson and E. Riseman, eds., *Computer Vision Systems*, Academic Press, New York, 1978.

H. Barrow and J. M. Tenenbaum, "Computational Vision," *Proc. IEEE* **69**, 572–595 (1981).

J. Beck, *Surface Color Perception*, Cornell University Press, Ithaca, New York, 1972.

J. Beck, "Texture Segregation," in J. Beck, ed., *Organization and Representation in Perception*, Erlbaum, Hillsdale, N.J., 1982.

J. Beck, B. Hope, and A. Rosenfeld, eds., *Human and Machine Vision*, Academic Press, New York, 1983.

P. Besl, *Surfaces in Range Image Understanding*, Springer, Berlin, 1988.

I. Biederman, "Human Image Understanding: Recent Research and Theory," *Comput. Vision, Graphics, and Image Proc.* **32**, 29–73 (1985).

T. Binford, "Visual Perception by Computer," *IEEE Conf. Systems and Control*, Miami, 1971.

T. Binford, "Inferring Surfaces from Images," *Artif. Intell.*, 1981.

T. Binford, "Survey of Model Based Image Analysis Systems," *Int. J. Robotics Res.* **1**, 18–64 (1982).

G. Blasdel, and G. Salama, "Voltage-Sensitive Dyes Reveal a Modular Organization in Monkey Striate Cortex," *Nature* **321**, 579–585 (1986).

D. Blostein and N. Ahuja, "Shape from Texture: Integrating Texture Element Extraction and Surface Estimation," *IEEE Trans. PAMI* **PAMI-11**, 1233–1251 (1989).

R. Bolles, H. Baker, and D. Marimont, "Epipolar-plane Image Analysis: An Approach to Determining Structure from Motion," *Int. J. Comput. Vision* **1**, 7–56 (1987).

O. Braddick, and A. Sleigh, eds., *Physical and Biological Processing of Images*, Springer, New York, 1983.

M. Brady and A. Yuille, "An Extremum Principle for Shape from Contour," *Proceedings of the Eighth IJCAI*, Morgan-Kaufmann, San Mateo, Calif., 1983.

M. Brady and Asada, "Smoothed Local Symmetries and their Implementation," *Int. J. Robotics Res.* **3**, 36–61 (1984).

R. Brooks, "Symbolic Reasoning Among 3-D Models and 2-D Images," *Artif. Intell.* **17**, 285–348 (1981).

J. Canny, "Finding Edges and Lines in Images," AI TR 720, MIT, Cambridge, Mass., 1984.

P. Cavanagh, "Reconstructing the Third Dimension: Interactions Between Color, Texture, Motion, Binocular Disparity, and Shape," *Comput. Vision, Graphics, and Image Proc.*, 1986.

B. Cernuschi-Frias, D. Cooper, Y. Hung, and P. Belhumeur, "Toward a Model-Based Bayesian Theory for Estimating and Recognizing Parameterized 3-D Objects Using Two or More Images Taken from Different Positions," *IEEE Trans. Patt. Anal. Mach. Intell.* **PAMI-11**, 1028–1053 (1989).

M. B. Clowes, "On Seeing Things," *Artif. Intell.* **2**, 79–116 (1971).

S. Coren, L. Ward, C. Porac, and R. Fraser, "The Effect of Optical Blur of Visual-Geometric Illusions," *Bull. Psychon. Soc.* **11**(6), 390–392 (1978).

T. Cornsweet, *Visual Perception*, Academic Press, New York, 1970.

J. Cutting, "Coding Theory Adapted to Gait Perception," *J. Exp. Psychol.: Hum. Perc. Perf.* **7**, 71–87 (1981).

L. Davis, "Shape Matching Using Relaxation Techniques," *IEEE Trans. Patt. Anal. Mach. Intell.* **PAMI-1**, 60–72 (1979).

L. Davis, "Hierarchical Generalized Hough Transform and Line-segment Based Generalized Hough Transforms," *Pattern Recognition* **15**, 277–285 (1982).

L. Davis and A. Rosenfeld, "Cooperating Processes for Low-level Vision: A Survey," *Artif. Intell.* **17**, 245–264 (1981).

D. Dennett, *Brainstorms*, Bradford Books/MIT Press, Cambridge, Mass., 1978.

A. Dobbins, S. W. Zucker, and M. Cynader, "Endstopped Neurons in the Visual Cortex as a Substrate for Calculating Curvature," *Nature* **329**(6138), 438–441 (1987).

G. Dodd and L. Rossol, *Computer Vision and Sensor-Based Robots*, Plenum, New York, 1979.

B. Dubuc, S. W. Zucker, C. Tricot, J. Quiniou, and D. Wehbi, "Evaluating the Fractal Dimension of Surfaces," *Proc. R. Soc. London*, Ser. A **425**, 113–127 (1989).

R. Duda and P. Hart, *Pattern Classification and Scene Analysis*, Wiley, New York, 1973.

R. Eckmiller and C. v.d. Malsberg, eds., *Neural Computers*, Springer, Berlin, 1988.

C. Enroth-Cugell and J. Robson, "The Contrast Sensitivity of Retinal Ganglion Cells of the Cat," *J. Physiol. London* **187**, 517–552 (1966).

G. Falk, "Interpretation of Important Line Data as a Three-dimensional Scene," *Artif. Intell.* **3**, 77–100 (1972).

O. Faugeras, "Steps Toward a Flexible 3-D Vision System for Robotics," in H. Hanufusa and H. Inoue, eds., *Robotics Research: The Second International Symposium*, MIT Press, Cambridge, Mass., 1985.

O. Faugeras, and M. Berthod, "Improving Consistency and Reducing Ambiguity in Stochastic Labeling: An Optimization Approach," *IEEE Trans. Patt. Anal. Mach. Intell.* **PAMI-3**, 245 (1981).

J. Feldman, and D. Ballard, "Connectionist Models and Their Properties," *Cogn. Sci.* **6**, 205–254 (1982).

F. Ferrie, M. D. Levine, and S. W. Zucker, "Cell Tracking: A Modeling and Minimization Approach," *IEEE Trans. Patt. Anal. Mach. Intell.* **PAMI-4**, 277–291 (1982).

F. Ferrie, J. Lagarde, and P. Whaite, "Darboux Frames, Snakes, and Superquadrics: Geometry from the Bottom Up," *Proceedings of the IEEE Workshop on Interpreting 3-D Scenes*, Austin, Tex., 1989.

M. Fischler, and R. Elschlager, "The Representation and Matching of Pictorial Structures," *IEEE Trans. Computers* **22**, 67–92 (1973).

M. Fischler, and R. Bolles, "Perceptual Organization and Curve Partitioning," *IEEE Trans. Patt. Anal. Mach. Intell.* **PAMI-8**, 100–105 (1986).

D. Fleet and A. Jepson, "Hierarchical Construction of Orientation and Velocity Filters," *IEEE Trans. Patt. Anal. Mach. Intell.* **PAMI-11**, 315–324 (1989).

J. Fodor, *The Modularity of Mind*, MIT Press, Cambridge, Mass., 1984.

J. Foley, and A. van Dam, *Fundamentals of Interactive Computer Graphics*, Addison Wesley, New York, 1982.

H. Freeman, "Computer Processing of Line Drawing Images," *Comput. Surv.* **5**, 57–97 (1974).

G. Fry, *Blur of the Retinal Image*, Ohio State University Press, Columbus, 1955.

T. Garvey, "Perceptual Strategies for Purposive Vision," *Tech. Note 117*, SRI International, Menlo Park, Calif., 1976.

S. Geman, and D. Geman, "Stochastic Relaxation, Gibbs Distributions, and the Bayesian Restoration of Images," *IEEE Trans. Patt. Anal. Mach. Intell.* **PAMI-6**, 721–741 (1984).

J. J. Gibson, *The Perception of the Visible World*, Houghton-Mifflin, Boston, 1950.

R. Gonzalez, and P. Wintz, *Digital Image Processing*, Addison-Wesley, Reading, Mass., 1977.

R. Gregory, *The Intelligent Eye*, McGraw-Hill, New York, 1970.

W. E. L. Grimson, *From Images to Surfaces*, MIT Press, Cambridge, Mass., 1983.

A. Guzman, "Decomposition of a Visual Scene into Three-dimensional Bodies," in A. Grasselli, ed., *Automatic Interpretation and Classification of Images*, Academic Press, New York, 1969.

R. Haber, and M. Herschenson, *The Psychology of Visual Perception*, Holt, Rhinehart, and Winston, New York, 1973.

A. Hanson, and E. Riseman, *Computer Vision Systems*, Academic Press, New York, 1978.

R. Haralick, "Statistical and Structural Approaches to Texture," *Proceedings of the Fourth International Joint Conference on Pattern Recognition*, Kyoto, 1978.

R. Haralick, "The Facet Model of Edge Detection," *Comp. Vision, Graphics, and Image Proc.*, 1984.

D. Hebb, *The Organization of Behavior*, Wiley, New York, 1949.

D. Heegar, "Optical Flow Using Spatiotemporal Filters," *Int. J. Computer Vision* **1**, 279–302 (1988).

H. von Helmholtz, *Treatise on Physiological Optics*, J. P. C. Southall, ed., Dover (reprint), 1962.

A. Herskovitz and T. Binford, "On Boundary Detection," AI Memo 183, MIT, Cambridge, Mass., 1970.

M. Heuckel, "An Operator Which Locates Edges in Digital Pictures," *JACM* **18**, 113–125 (1971).

A. Hildebrandt, *Introduction to Numerical Analysis*, Wiley, New York, 1956.

D. Hillis, *The Connection Machine*, MIT Press, Cambridge, Mass., 1985.

D. Hoffman and B. Flinchbaugh, "The Interpretation of Biological Motion," *Biol. Cybernetics* **42**, 195–204 (1982).

D. Hoffman and W. Richards, "Parts of Recognition," in A. Pentland, ed., *From Pixels to Predicates*, Ablex, Norwood, N.J., 1986.

B. Horn, "The Binford-Horn Line Finder," AI Memo 285, MIT, 1973.

B. Horn, "Obtaining Shape from Shading Information," in P. Winston, ed., *The Psychology of Computer Vision*, McGraw-Hill, New York, 1975.

B. Horn, "Understanding Image Intensities," *Artif. Intell.* **8**, 201–231 (1977).

B. Horn and B. Schunk, "Determining Optical Flow," *Artif. Intell.* **17**, 185–204 (1981).

B. Horn and M. J. Brooks, *Shape from Shading*, MIT Press, Cambridge, Mass., 1989.

D. Hubel and T. Wiesel, "Functional Architecture of Macaque Monkey Visual Cortex," *Proc. R. Soc. London*, Ser. B **198**, 1–59 (1977).

D. Huffman, "Impossible Objects as Nonsense Sentences," in Meltzer and Michie, eds., *Machine Intelligence 6*, Edinburgh, UK, 1971.

R. A. Hummel and S. W. Zucker, "On the Foundations of Relaxation Labeling Processes," *IEEE Trans. Patt. Anal. Mach. Intell.* **PAMI-5**, 267–287 (1983).

K. Ikeuchi and B. Horn, "Numerical Shape from Shading and Occluding Boundaries," *Artif. Intell.* **17**, 141–184 (1981).

E. Ising, "Contribution to the Theory of Ferromagnetism," *Z. Phys.* **31**, 253–258 (1925).

W. Ittleson, *Visual Space Perception*, Springer, New York, 1960.

A. Jain and R. Jain, *Range Image Understanding*, Springer, Berlin, 1989.

G. Johanssen, *Configurations in Event Perception*, Almquist and Wiksells, Uppsala, Sweden, 1950.

B. Julesz, *Foundations of Cyclopean Perception*, University of Chicago Press, 1971.

T. Kanade, "Recovery of the Three-Dimensional Shape of an Object from a Single View," *Artif. Intell.* **17**, 409–460 (1981).

G. Kanisza, *Organization in Vision*, Praeger, New York, 1979.

M. Kass and A. Witkin, "Analyzing Oriented Patterns," *Proceedings of the Ninth IJCAI*, Los Angeles, Morgan-Kaufmann, San Mateo, Calif., 1985.

M. Kass, A. Witkin, and D. Terzopoulos, "Snakes: Active Contour Models," *Int. J. Comput. Vision* **1**, 321–332 (1988).

L. Kaufman, *Sight and Mind*, Oxford University Press, New York, 1974.

J. Kender, "Shape from Texture," Technical Report, Computer Science Dept., Carnegie Mellon University, Pittsburgh, Pa., 1980.

B. Kimia, A. Tannenbaum, and S. W. Zucker, "Toward a Computational Theory of Shape: An Overview," in *Proceedings of the First European Conference on Computer Vision*, Antibes, France, 1990, O. Faugeras, ed., Lecture Notes in Computer Science, 427, Springer-Verlag, New York.

D. Kinderlehrer and G. Stampacchia, *An Introduction to Variational Inequalities and their Applications*, Academic Press, New York, 1980.

R. Kirsch, "Computer Determination of the Constituent Structure of Biological Images," *Comput. Biomed. Res.* **4**, 315–328 (1971).

J. J. Koenderink, *Solid Shape*, MIT Press, Cambridge, Mass., 1989.

J. J. Koenderinck and A. van Doorn, "Photometric Invariants Related to Solid Shape," *Op. Acta* **27**, 981–996 (1980).

J. J. Koenderinck and A. van Doorn, "The Shape of Smooth Objects and the Way Contours End," *Perception* **11**, 129–137 (1982).

K. Koffka, *Gestalt Psychology*, Harcourt, Brace and World, New York, 1935.

W. Kohler, *The Task of Gestalt Psychology*, Princeton University Press, Princeton, N.J., 1969.

E. H. Land, "The Retinex Theory of Color Vision," *Sci. Am.*, 108–128 (1977).

Y. Leclerc, "Constructing Simple, Stable Descriptions for Image Partitioning," *Int. J. Comput. Vision* **3**, 73–102 (1989).

Y. Leclerc and S. W. Zucker, "The Local Structure of Intensity Changes in Images," *IEEE Trans. Patt. Anal. Mach. Intell.*, 1986.

D. Lee, "Coping with Discontinuities in Computer Vision: Their Detection, Classification, and Measurement," *IEEE Trans. Patt. Anal. Mach. Intell.* **PAMI-12**, 321–344 (1990).

J. Lettvin, H. Maturana, W. McCulloch, and W. Pitts, "What the Frog's Eye Tells the Frog's Brain," *Proc. IRE* **47**, 1940–1951 (1959).

M. Levine, *Vision in Man and Machine*, Prentice Hall, 1985.

M. Levine and S. Shaheen, "A Modular Computer Vision System," *IEEE Trans. Patt. Anal. Mach. Intell.* **PAMI-3**, 540–556 (1981).

M. Livingstone, and D. Hubel, "Anatomy and Physiology of a Color System in Primate Visual Cortex," *J. Neurosci.* **4**, 309–356 (1984).

D. Lowe, "Perceptual Organization and Visual Recognition," Ph.D. dissertation, Stanford University, Stanford, Calif., 1984.

D. Lowe, "Organization of Smooth Curves at Multiple Scales," *Int. J. Comput. Vision* **3**, 119–130 (1989).

D. Lowe and T. Binford, "Segregation and Aggregation: An Approach to Figure/Ground Phenomena," *Proceedings of the DARPA Image Understanding Workshop*, 1982, pp. 168–178.

D. Luenberger, *Optimization by Vector Space Methods*, Wiley, New York, 1969.

A. K. Mackworth, "Interpreting Pictures of Polyhedral Scenes," *Artif. Intell.* **4**, 121–137 (1973).

J. Malik, "Interpreting Line Drawings of Curved Objects," *Int. J. Comput. Vision* **1**, 73–103 (1987).

A. Margalit, "A Parallel Algorithm to Generate a Markov Random Field Image on a SIMD Hypercube Machine," *Pattern Recognition Letters* **9**, 263–278 (1989).

D. Marr, "Early Processing of Visual Information," *Proc. R. Soc. London*, Ser. B **275**, 483–534 (1976).

D. Marr, *Vision*, Freeman, 1982.

D. Marr and E. Hildreth, "Theory of Edge Detection," *Proc. R. Soc. London*, Ser. B **207**, 187–217 (1980).

L. Matthies, T. Kanade, and R. Szeliski, "Kalman Filter-Based Algorithms for Estimating Depth from Image Sequences," *Int. J. Comput. Vision* **3**, 181–208 (1989).

J. Mayhew and J. Frisby, "Psychophysical and Computational Studies Towards a Theory of Human Stereopsis," *Artif. Intell.* **17**, 349–385 (1981).

J. McCarthy and C. Shannon, *Automata Studies*, Princeton University Press, Princeton, N.J., 1956.

W. McCulloch and W. Pitts, "A Logical Calculus of the Ideas Immanent in Nervous Activity," *Bull. Math. Biophys.* **5**, 115–133 (1943).

C. Mead, *Analog VLSI and Neural Systems*, Addison-Wesley, New York, 1989.

M. Minsky and S. Papert, *Perceptrons*, MIT Press, Cambridge, 1969.

R. Mohan and R. Nevatia, "Using Perceptual Organization to Extract 3-D Structures," *IEEE Trans. Patt. Anal. Mach. Intell.* **PAMI-11**, 1121–1139 (1989).

R. Navatia, *Machine Perception*, Prentice-Hall, 1982.

G. Orban, *Neuronal Operations in the Visual Cortex*, Springer, New York, 1984.

P. Parent and S. W. Zucker, "Trace Inference, Curvature Consistency, and Curve Detection," *IEEE Trans. Patt. Anal. Mach. Intell.* **PAMI-11**, 823–839 (1989).

T. Pavlidis, *Structural Pattern Recognition*, Springer, New York, 1977.

T. Pavlidis, *Algorithms for Graphics and Image Processing*, Computer Science Press, Rockville, Md., 1982.

S. Peleg, J. Naor, R. Hartley, and D. Avnir, "Multiple Resolution Texture Analysis and Classification," *IEEE Trans. Patt. Anal. Mach. Intell.* **PAMI-6**, 518–534 (1984).

A. Pentland, "Fractal Based Descriptions of Natural Scenes," *IEEE Trans. Patt. Anal. Mach. Intell.* **PAMI-6**, 661–675 (1984).

A. Pentland, "Local Shading Analysis," *IEEE Trans. Patt. Anal. Mach. Intell.* **PAMI-6**, 170–187 (1984).

A. Pentland, "Perceptual Organization and the Representation of Natural Form," *Artif. Intell.* **28**, 293–331 (1986).

A. Pentland, "Automatic Extraction of Deformable Part Models," *Int. J. Comput. Vision* **4**, 107–126 (1990).

S. Pradzny, "Detection of Binocular Disparities," *Biol. Cybernetics* **52**, 93–99 (1985).

W. Pratt, *Digital Image Processing*, Wiley-Interscience, New York, 1978.

J. M. S. Prewitt, "Object Enhancement and Abstraction," in A. Rosenfeld and J. Prewitt, eds., *Picture Processing and Psychopictorics*, Academic Press, New York, 1970.

L. Quam, "Road Tracking and Anomaly Detection," *Proceedings of the DARPA Image Understanding Workshop*, 1978, pp. 51–55.

F. Ratliff, *Mach Bands: Quantitative Studies on Neural Networks in the Retina*, Holden Day, San Francisco, 1965.

M. Regan and M. Cynader, "Motion-in-depth Neurons: Effects and Speed and Disparity," *Invest. Ophthalmol. and Visual Sci.* **20**, 148 (1981).

W. A. Richards, ed., *Natural Computation*, MIT Press, Cambridge, Mass., 1988.

L. Roberts, "Machine Perception of 3-dimensional Solids," in J. Tippett, ed., *Optical and Electro-Optical Information Processing*, MIT Press, Cambridge, Mass., 1965.

I. Rock, *The Logic of Perception*, MIT Press, Cambridge, Mass., 1984.

R. Rodieck, "Quantitative Analysis of Cat Retinal Ganglion Cell Response to Visual Stimuli," *Vis. Res.* **5**, 583–601 (1965).

A. Rosenfeld, "A Nonlinear Edge Detection Technique," *Proc. IEEE* **58**, 814–816 (1970).

A. Rosenfeld and A. Kak, *Digital Picture Processing*, Academic Press, New York, 1982.

A. Rosenfeld, R. Hummel, and S. W. Zucker, "Scene Labelling by Relaxation Operations," *IEEE Trans. Sys. Man Cybern.* **SMC-6**, 420–433 (1976).

P. Sander, and S. W. Zucker, "Inferring Differential Structure from 3-D Images: Smooth Cross Sections of the Fibre Bundles," *IEEE Trans. Patt. Anal. Mach. Intell.* **PAMI-9**, 833–854 (1990).

S. Shafer, *Shadows and Silhouettes in Computer Vision*, Kluwer Academic Publishers, Boston, 1985.

Y. Shirai, "Analyzing Intensity Arrays Using Knowledge About Scenes," in P. Winston, ed., *The Psychology of Computer Vision*, McGraw-Hill, New York, 1975.

F. Solina and R. Bajcsy, "Recovery of Parametric Models from Range Images: The Case for Superquadrics with Global Deformations," *IEEE Trans. Patt. Anal. Mach. Intell.* **PAMI-12**, 131–147 (1990).

G. Sperling, "Binocular Vision: A Physical and a Neural Theory," *Amer. J. Psychiatry* **83**, 461–534 (1970).

M. Srinivasan, S. Laughlin, and A. Dubs, "Predictive Coding: A Fresh View of Inhibition in the Retina," *Proc. R. Soc. London*, Ser. B, 427–459 (1982).

K. Stevens, "The Visual Interpretation of Surface Contours," *Artif. Intell.* **17**, 47–74 (1981).

R. Szeliski, *Bayesian Modeling of Uncertainty in Low-Level Vision*, Kluwer, Boston, 1989.

S. Tanimoto and L. Uhr, *Structured Computer Vision*, Academic Press, New York, 1983.

D. Terzopoulos, "Multilevel Computational Processes for Visible Surface Reconstruction," Ph.D. dissertation, MIT, Cambridge, Mass., 1984.

D. Terzopoulos, "Integrating Visual Information from Multiple Sources," in A. Pentland, ed., *From Pixels to Predicates*, Ablex, Norwood, N.J., 1986.

A. Triesman, "Preattentive Processing in Vision," *Comp. Vision, Graphics and Image Proc.*, 1–22 (1985).

J. Tsotsos, "Knowledge of the Visual Process: Content, Form and Use," *Pattern Recognition*, 1984.

J. Tsotsos, "A 'Complexity-Level' Analysis of Intermediate Vision," *Int. J. Comput. Vision* 1, 303–320 (1988).

J. Tsotsos, J. Mylopolous, D. Covvey, and S. W. Zucker, "A Framework for Visual Motion Understanding," *IEEE Trans. Patt. Anal. Mach. Intell.* PAMI–2, 563–573 (1980).

S. Ullman, *The Interpretation of Visual Motion*, MIT Press, Cambridge, Mass., 1979.

S. Ullman, "Against Direct Perception," *Behavioral and Brain Sciences* 3, 373–415 (1980).

S. Ullman, "Visual Routines," *Cognition* (1985).

W. Uttal, *A Taxonomy of Visual Processes*, Lawrence Erlbaum Associates, Hillsdale, N.J., 1981.

D. van Essen and J. Maunsell, "Two-Dimensional Maps of the Cerebral Cortex," *J. Comp. Neurology* 191, 255–281 (1980).

D. van Essen and J. Maunsell, "Hierarchical Organization and Functional Streams in the Visual Cortex," *Trends Neurosci.* 6, 370–375 (1983).

H. Wallach and D. O'Connell, "The Kinetic Depth Effect," *J. Exp. Psychol.* 45, 205–217 (1953).

D. Waltz, "Understanding Line Drawings of Scenes with Shadows," in P. Winston, ed., *The Psychology of Computer Vision*, McGraw-Hill, New York, 1975.

R. Watt and M. Morgan, "Mechanisms Responsible for the Assessment of Visual Location: Theory and Evidence," *Vision Res.* 23, 97–109 (1983).

F. S. Werblin, "Functional Organization of a Vertebrate Retina: Sharpening Up in Space and Intensity," *Ann. N.Y. Acad. Sci.* 193 (1972).

M. Wertheimer, "Laws of Organization in Perceptual Forms," *Psych. Forsch.* 4, 301–350 (1923); trans. in W. Ellis, *A Source Book of Gestalt Psychology*, Routledge and Kegan Paul, London, 1938, pp. 71–88.

H. Wilson and J. Bergen, "A Four Mechanism Model for Threshold Spatial Vision," *Vision Res.* 19, 19–32 (1979).

S. Winograd and J. Cowan, *Reliable Computation in the Presence of Noise*, MIT Press, Cambridge, 1963.

A. Witkin, "Recovering Surface Shape and Orientation from Texture," *Artif. Intell.* 17, 17–47 (1981).

A. Witkin, "Intensity Based Edge Classification," *Proceedings of the Second National Conference on Artificial Intelligence*, Pittsburgh, AAAI, Menlo Park, Calif., 1982, pp. 36–41.

A. Witkin, "Scale Space Filtering," in A. Pentland, ed., *From Pixels to Predicates*, Ablex, Norwood, N.J., 1986.

A. Witkin and J. M. Tenenbaum, "On the Role of Structure in Vision," in J. Beck, B. Hope, and A. Rosenfeld, eds., *Human and Machine Vision*, Academic Press, New York, 1983.

R. Woodham, "Analyzing Images of Curved Surfaces," *Artif. Intell.* 17, 17–45 (1981).

Y. Yeshurun and E. Schwartz, "Cepstral Filtering on a Columnar Image Architecture: A Fast Algorithm for Binocular Stereo Segmentation," *IEEE Trans. Patt. Anal. Mach. Intell.* PAMI–11, 759–767 (1989).

S. Zeki, "Uniformity and Diversity of Structure and Function in Rhesus Monkey Prestriate Visual Cortex," *J. Physiol. (London)* 277, 273–290 (1978).

S. Zeki and S. Shipp, "Segregation of Pathways Leading from Area V2 to Areas V4 and V5 of Macaque Monkey Cortex," *Nature* 315, 322–324 (1985).

A. Zisserman, P. Giblin, and A. Blake, "The Information Available to a Moving Observer from Specularities," *Image and Vision Computing* 7, 38–42 (1989).

S. W. Zucker, "On the Structure of Texture," *Perception* 5, 419–436 (1976).

S. W. Zucker, "Early Orientation Selection: Tangent Fields and the Dimensionality of their Support," *Comput. Vision Graphics and Image Proc.* 32, 74–103 (1985).

S. W. Zucker, A. Dobbins, and L. Iverson, "Two Stages of Curve Detection Suggest Two Styles of Visual Computation," *Neural Computation* 1, 68–81 (1989).

S. W. Zucker and R. A. Hummel, "Toward a Low-level Description of Dot Clusters: Labelling Edge, Interior, and Noise Points," *Comput. Graphics and Image Proc.* 9, 213–233 (1979).

S. W. Zucker and R. A. Hummel, "Receptive Fields and the Representation of Visual Information," *Human Neurobiology*, 1986.

S. W. Zucker, A. Rosenfeld, and L. Davis, "General Purpose Models: Expectations About the Unexpected," *Proceedings of the Fourth IJCAI*, Tblisi, U.S.S.R., Morgan-Kaufmann, San Mateo, Calif., 1975.

STEVEN W. ZUCKER
McGill University

The author thanks the Natural Sciences and Engineering Research Council (Canada), grant A4470, for support, and A. Dobbins, P. Parent, P. Sander, and J. Tsotsos for comments on the manuscript.

ECRC

The European Computer-Industry Research Centre (ECRC) was established in Munich in January 1984 by BULL, International Computers Ltd. (ICL), and Siemens. The activities of the center are intended to enhance the competitiveness of European information technology and thus to complement the work of national and international bodies. This article describes ECRC's activities, goals, policies, and strategies. It should be regarded as an overview of the peculiarities of the center, not as a detailed program of its technical activities.

TECHNICAL PROGRAM

The aim of ECRC is to develop fundamental know-how in the field of computer-assisted decision-making (CADM), which relies on specific techniques (such as optimization, operations research techniques, and databases) and on the wider field of artificial intelligence. ECRC's program deals with the major bottlenecks of CADM systems. The proposed solutions are integrated into prototypes and applications illustrating the relevance of the tools and ideas. The research program can be outlined as follows.

1. Logic programming (LP) and problem solving can be regarded as the kernel of ECRC's activities to date. LP is a good basis for the knowledge representation and inferencing capabilities needed for future knowledge-based management systems (KBMS). Among the most interesting

results in this area are a PROLOG compiler (SEPIA), a PROLOG debugger, and the CHIP language (Constraint Handling in PROLOG), which have been turned into products by the ECRC shareholders. Object-oriented programming and concurrency are other interesting paradigms. Linear logic is a support for them, and a language called Linear Objects is being developed.

2. Knowledge bases will lie at the heart of most software systems, to which they will bring power and flexibility. Deductive databases can be regarded as a first step toward future KBMSs, because they provide the user with deductive capabilities and offer a sound semantic basis for further extensions. A persistent PROLOG accessing large databases (MegaLog) is being transferred to the mother companies. A longer-term project is the ECRC Knowledge System (EKS), which integrates objects and deductive capabilities and offers several deduction engines. A first prototype called EKS/V1 has already been presented at several conferences. ECRC also participates in an ESPRIT Basic Research Action (COMPULOG) aimed at developing the foundations for an integrated, logic-based software environment for developing knowledge-rich applications.

3. Architectural issues are being addressed, with the aim of providing speed and an environment that makes these systems efficient. Symbolic computing architectures adapted to the execution of these systems have been developed since the foundation of ECRC; one of the results is the Knowledge Crunching Machine (KCM). ECRC is currently involved in the European Declarative System (EDS) project. Its contribution consists of defining and implementing a parallel PROLOG (called ElipSys) that integrates constraints and knowledge-base manipulation.

4. Interaction with the complex systems that assist the decision-making process is another area of research. This interaction involves such issues as the presentation of the knowledge used by a KBMS and the exploration of an application by its users. Building interactive systems and developing graphic interfaces tailored to specific applications are among ECRC's main objectives. One of the results in this domain is the TUBE software, which simplifies the task of interface production, following the paradigm of graphic direct manipulation. TUBE automates the most tedious parts of the interface construction: the management of the screen and the specification (coding) of the dialogue aspect of the interface.

STRUCTURE AND POLICIES

ECRC is supported as a common resource by the major European computer manufacturers BULL, ICL, and Siemens. It is owned equally by all three, and they also share its costs equally. In this regard, ECRC differs from MCC, for example. ECRC is an independent company operating under German law. The creation of ECRC reflects current thinking in European industry, with its aim toward consolidating Europe's presence in the electronic data processing market through scientific cooperation, standardization, implementation of technical standards, and so forth.

Structurally, ECRC is comprised of management; a shareholders' council, which approves programs and budgets and monitors their execution; and a scientific committee, which advises the shareholders' council on future research directions.

Research is carried out on behalf of the three shareholder companies, which use the results freely. Rights to the research results are shared among all three companies, who have free license to all patented results of ECRC. ECRC also produces a number of academic papers which are accepted by international conferences, and its researchers are frequently invited to give talks and participate in scientific committees. At the same time, ECRC is an industrial center: its results are applied to the core technologies of the shareholder companies, and the potential of the results is evaluated according to market orientations and future trends. The balance between the academic quality of the results and the industrial motivation may be regarded as one of most remarkable aspects of ECRC.

Personnel. ECRC has 80 employees, 56 of which are full-time researchers. In addition, there are several Ph.D. students, a technical support group, and a small administrative team. Nineteen nationalities are represented at ECRC. More than 50% of the researchers hold doctorates. Thirty percent of the researchers are on leave from the mother companies; the others were hired directly. Informal collaborations with universities, research centers, and the research teams of the shareholders are vital to maintaining the level of researchers hired.

Transfer of Results. The importance of the complexity of the transfer activities cannot be explained in a couple of lines. Each company has its own transfer policy (staff transfer, liaison officers, common projects, seminars, short-period exchanges) and its own way of utilizing the results (taking them as such, commercializing them, rewriting the code). The task of ECRC is to help the shareholder companies in this crucial activity, the success of which is vital to motivate the mother companies and researchers who are interested in products developed from their ideas.

CONCLUSION

Six years after its establishment, ECRC is an undeniable success, owing to the initiative and support of the shareholders and to Dr. Hervé Gallaire, who led the center during its first five years. The results can be measured by ECRC's academic impact and by the number of industrial products and transfers. Despite current financial difficulties among computer manufacturers, this investment is to be regarded as vital to European information technology in the long run.

GÉRARD COMYN
ECRC GmbH

EDGE AND LOCAL FEATURE DETECTION

For both biological systems and machines, vision begins with a large array of measurements of the amount of light reflected from surfaces in the environment. The goal of vision is to recover physical properties of objects in the scene, such as the location of object boundaries and the structure, color, and texture of object surfaces, from the two-dimensional image that is projected onto the eye or camera. The first clues about the physical properties of the scene are provided by the changes of intensity in the image. For example, in Figure 1 the boundaries of the sculpture, the markings and bright highlights on its surface, and the shadows that the trees cast on the snow all give rise to spatial changes in light intensity. The geometric structure, sharpness, and contrast of these intensity changes convey information about the physical edges in the scene. The importance of intensity changes and edges in early visual processing has led to extensive research on their detection, description, and use, both in computer and biological vision systems.

The process of edge detection can be divided into two stages: first, intensity changes in the image are detected and described; second, physical properties of edges in the scene are inferred from this image description. This article concentrates on the first stage, about which more is known at this time. It briefly describes areas of vision research that address the second stage. Some of these areas are discussed further in other articles of this encyclopedia (see, eg, Color vision; Early vision; Stereo vision; Texture; Visual motion analysis). This article mainly reviews some of the theory that underlies the detection of edges and the methods used to carry out this analysis. There is also some reference to studies of early visual processing in biological systems.

Figure 1. A natural image, exhibiting intensity changes due to many physical factors.

THE DETECTION OF INTENSITY CHANGES

Many methods for detecting intensity changes incorporate three basic operations. First, the image intensities are either smoothed or approximated locally by a smooth analytic function. Second, the smoothed intensities are differentiated, using either a first- or second-derivative operation. Third, simple features in the result of this differentiation stage, such as peaks (positive and negative extrema) or zero crossings (transitions between positive and negative values), are detected and described. For some applications of edge detection, extended segments of edges, lines, or curves, as well as local features such as corners, are also detected and described. This section first describes briefly the role of these operations in the analysis of intensity changes and then presents in more detail some of the methods used to carry out these operations.

The smoothing operation serves two purposes. First, it reduces the effect of noise on the detection of intensity changes. Second, it sets the resolution or scale at which intensity changes are detected. The sampling and transduction of light by the eye or camera introduces spurious changes of light intensity that do not correspond to significant physical changes in the scene. Smoothing of the intensities can remove these minor fluctuations due to noise. Figure 2a shows a one-dimensional intensity profile that is shown smoothed by a small amount in Figure 2b. Small variations of intensity, due in part to noise in the digitizing camera, do not appear in the smoothed intensities. Approximation of the intensity function by a smooth analytic function can serve the same purpose as a smoothing operation.

Significant changes in the image can also occur at multiple resolutions. Consider, for example, a leopard's coat. At a fine resolution, rapid fluctuations of intensity may delineate the individual hairs of the coat, whereas at a coarser resolution, the intensiy changes may delineate only the leopard's spots. Changes at different resolutions can often be detected by smoothing the image intensities by different amounts. Figure 2c illustrates a more extensive smoothing of the intensity profile of Figure 2a, which preserves only the gross changes of intensity.

The differentiation operation accentuates intensity changes and transforms the image into a representation from which properties of these changes can be extracted more easily. A significant intensity change gives rise to a peak in the first derivative or a zero crossing in the second derivative of the smoothed intensities, as illustrated in Figures 2d and e, respectively. These peaks, or zero crossings, can be detected straightforwardly, and properties such as the position, sharpness, and height of the peaks capture the location, sharpness, and contrast of the inten-

Figure 2. Detecting intensity changes. (*a*) One-dimensional intensity profile; the intensities along a horizontal scan line in an image are represented as a graph. (*b*) The result of smoothing the profile in (*a*). (*c*) The result of additional smoothing of (*a*). (*d*, *e*) The first and second derivatives, respectively, of the smoothed profile shown in (*c*). The vertical dashed lines indicate the peaks in the first derivative and zero crossings in the second derivative that correspond to two significant intensity changes.

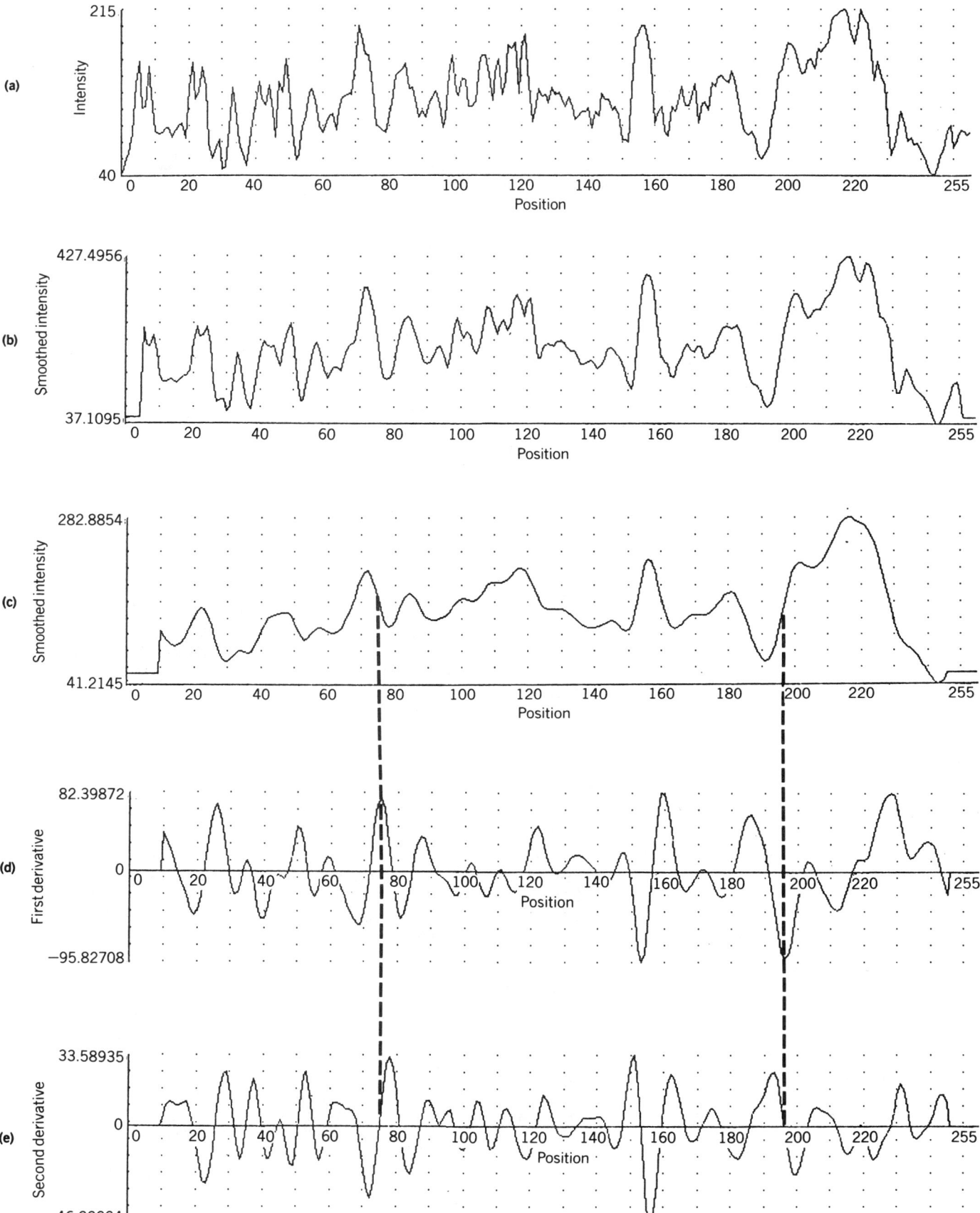

sity changes in the image. The detection and description of these features in the smoothed and differentiated image provides a compact representation that captures meaningful information in the image. Marr (1982) called this representation the primal sketch of the image. Later processes, such as binocular stereo, motion measurement, and texture analysis, whose goal is to recover the physical properties of the scene, may then operate directly on this description of image features.

One-Dimensional Detection of Intensity Changes

The theory that underlies the detection of intensity changes in two-dimensional images is based heavily on the analysis of one-dimensional signals. This section discusses three topics that have been addressed in this analysis: the design of optimal operators for performing smoothing and differentiation, the information content of the description of signal features such as zero crossings, and the relationship between features that are detected at multiple spatial resolutions. Studies of these issues have used a variety of theoretical approaches that appear to yield similar conclusions.

Some of the early methods for detecting intensity changes incorporated only limited smoothing of the intensities and performed the differentiation by taking first or second differences between neighboring image elements (eg, Rosenfeld and Thurston, 1971; Davis, 1975; Persoon, 1976; Rosenfeld and Kak, 1976; Brooks, 1978; Pratt, 1978). In one dimension this is equivalent to performing a convolution of the intensity profile with operators of the type shown on the left in Figures 3b and c. Additional smoothing can be performed by increasing the spatial extent of these operators.

The operators in Figures 3b and c contain steplike changes. Other studies have used Gaussian smoothing of the image intensities (eg, Macleod, 1972; Marr and Poggio, 1979; Marr and Hildreth, 1980; Hildreth, 1983; Horn, 1985). Combined with the first and second derivative operations, Gaussian smoothing yields convolution operators of the type shown in Figures 3d and e. Several arguments have been put forth in support of the use of Gaussian smoothing. Marr and Hildreth (1980) argued informally that the smoothing function should have both limited support in space and limited bandwidth in frequency. In general terms, a limited support in space is important because the physical edges to be detected are spatially localized. A limited bandwidth in frequency provides a means of restricting the range of scales over which intensity changes are detected, which can be important in applications of edge detection. The Gaussian function minimizes the product of bandwidths in space and frequency. The use of smoothing functions that do not have limited bandwidths in space and frequency can sometimes yield worse performance, reflected in greater sensitivity to noise, the false detection of edges that do not exist in the scene, or a poor ability to localize the position of edges (Marr and Hildreth, 1980; Canny, 1986).

An optimal frequency domain filter for detecting intensity changes was derived using the criteria that the filter yields maximum energy in the vicinity of an edge in the image, has limited frequency bandwidth, yields a small output when the input is constant or slowly varying, and is an even function in space (Shanmugam and co-workers, 1979). For the special case of detecting step changes of intensity, the optimal frequency domain filter corresponds to a spatial operator that is approximately the second derivative of a Gaussian (for a given bandwidth) shown in Figure 3e.

A later study (Canny, 1986) used the following criteria to derive an optimal operator: good detection ability, that is, there should be low probabilities of failing to detect real edges and falsely detecting edges that do not exist; good localization ability, that is, the position of the detected edge should be as close as possible to the true position of the edge; and uniqueness of detection, that is, a given edge should be detected only once. The first two criteria are related by an uncertainty principle; as detection ability increases, localization ability decreases, and vice versa. The analysis also assumed that extrema in the output of the operator indicate the presence of an edge. For the particular case in which a step intensity change is detected in the presence of noise, the operator that optimally satisfies these criteria is a linear combination of four exponentials, which can be approximated closely by the first derivative of a Gaussian shown in Figure 3d.

An optimal smoothing operator was derived using the tools of regularization theory from mathematical physics (Poggio and co-workers, 1988; Torre and Poggio, 1986). The investigators began with the observation that numeric differentiation of the image is a mathematically ill-posed problem (Hadamard, 1923) because its solution does not depend continuously on the input intensities (this is equivalent to saying that the solution is not robust against noise). The smoothing operation serves to regularize the image, making the differentiation operation mathematically well posed. In the case where the image intensities are assumed to contain noise, the following method was used to regularize the image. First, let $I(x)$ denote the continuous intensity function, which is sampled at a set of discrete locations x_k, $1 < k < N$, and let $S(x)$ denote the smoothed intensity function to be computed. It was assumed that $S(x)$ should both fit the sampled intensities as closely as possible and be as smooth as possible. Using the tools of regularization theory, this was formulated as the computation of the function $S(x)$ that minimizes the following expression:

$$\sum_{n=1}^{n} [I(x_k) - S(x_k)]^2 + \lambda \int [S''(x)]^2 \, dx$$

Figure 3. Smoothing and differentiation. (a) A one-dimensional intensity profile. (b) A first difference operator is shown in heavy lines on the left, and the result of its convolution with the profile in (a) is shown on the right. (c) A second difference operator is shown in heavy lines on the left, and its convolution with (a) on the right. (d) The first derivative of a Gaussian (left) and its convolution with (a) (right). (e) The second derivative of a Gaussian (left) and its convolution with (a) (right). [Note that in (b)–(e) the position of the filtered intensity profile is shifted relative to the position of the original intensity profile shown in (a).]

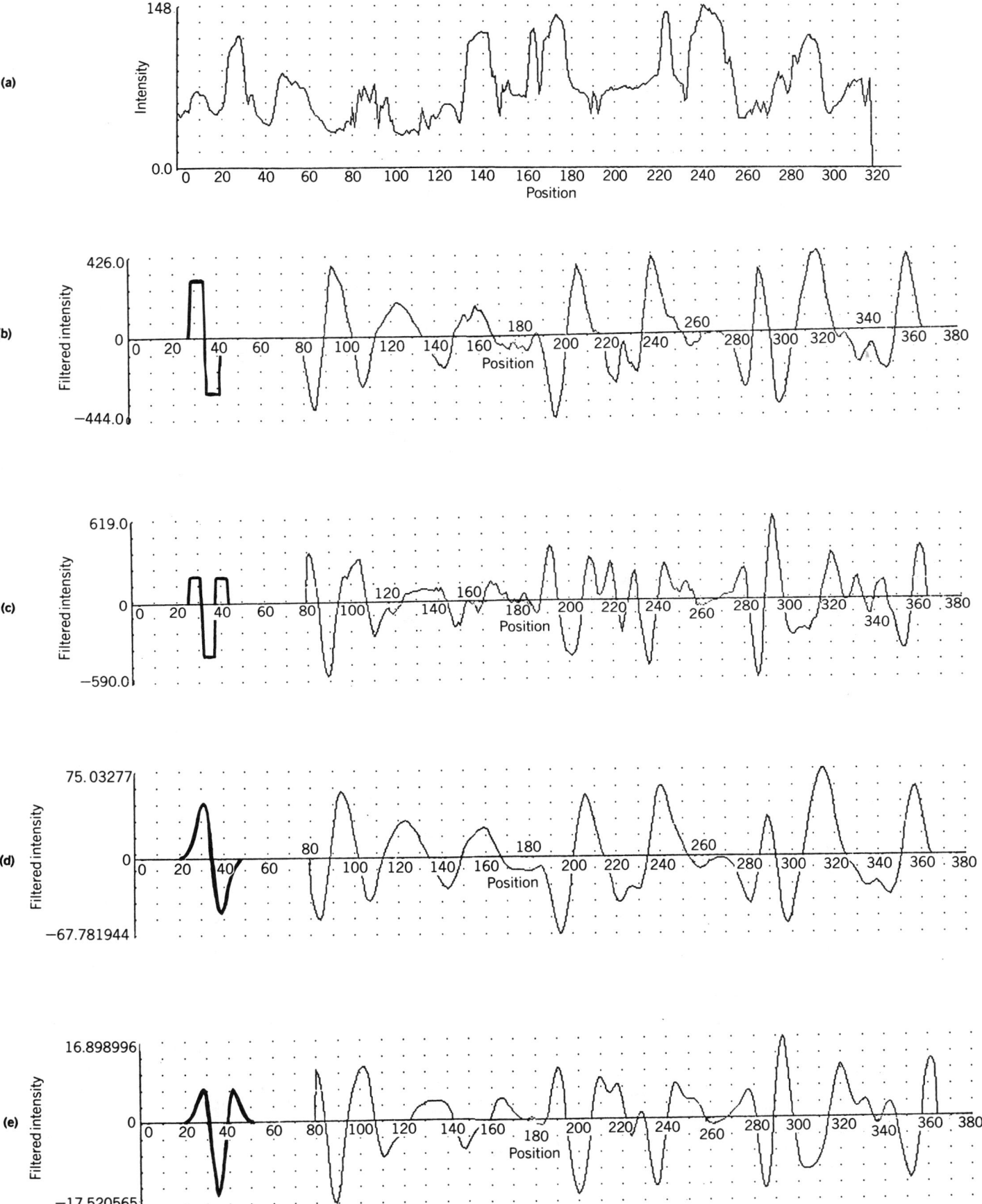

The first term measures how well $S(x)$ fits the sampled intensities, and the second term measures the smoothness of $S(x)$. The constant λ controls the trade-off between these two measures. The solution to this minimization problem is equivalent to the convolution of the image intensities with a cubic spline that is very similar to the Gaussian (Poggio and co-workers, 1988).

Another approach to the smoothing stage is to find an analytic function that best models or approximates the local intensity pattern. An early representative of this approach is the Hueckel operator (Hueckel, 1973; also see Rosenfeld and Kak, 1976; Pratt, 1978). Surface-fitting methods have used a variety of basis functions to perform the approximation, including planar functions (Haralick, 1980), quadratic functions (Prewitt, 1970), and the discrete Chebyshev polynomials Haralick (1983, 1984). A method has been recently proposed that uses a variety of directional surfaces (ie, surfaces that are constant in one direction) to approximate the two-dimensional intensity function, whose one-dimensional cross section can be linear, quadratic, cubic, or the function tanh (Nalwa and Binford, 1986). These investigators suggest that such flexibility in the approximation function allows greater precision at describing a variety of intensity variations, including those with step, ramp, and roof-shaped profiles. In these approximation methods a differentiation operation is often performed analytically on the polynomial approximation of the intensity function. The method of approximation used by Haralick (1983, 1984) is roughly equivalent to smoothing the image by convolution with spatial operators such as those derived by Canny (1986) and Poggio and co-workers (1988). A rigorous comparison between the performance of surface-fitting versus direct smoothing methods has not yet been made.

A second issue that bears on the choice of operator for the smoothing and differentiation stages is the information content of the subsequent description of image features. That is, to what extent does a representation of only the significant changes of intensity capture all the important information in an image? This question led to a number of theoretical studies of the reconstruction of a signal from features such as its zero crossings. Although the goal of vision is not to reconstruct the visual image, these results are important because they suggest that an image can be transformed into a compact representation of its features with little loss of information.

Several studies have addressed the information content of the representation of the zero crossings (or, more generally, the level crossings) of an image that is convolved with the second derivative of a Gaussian over a continuous range of scales. (The level crossings of a signal are the points at which a value v is crossed by the signal, where v may be nonzero.) Before stating the results of these studies, the scale space representation of zero crossings (Witkin, 1983), illustrated in Figure 4, is introduced (see also SCALE SPACE). First, let the one-dimensional Gaussian function be defined as follows (where σ is the standard deviation of the Gaussian):

$$G(x) = \frac{1}{\sigma} \exp^{\frac{-x^2}{2\sigma^2}}$$

The second derivative of the Gaussian function is then given by the expression:

$$G'' = \frac{d^2 G(x)}{dx^2} = \frac{1}{\sigma^3} \left(\frac{x^2}{\sigma^2} - 1 \right) \exp^{\frac{-x^2}{2\sigma^2}}$$

Suppose that a one-dimensional signal $I(x)$ is convolved with G'' for a continuous range of standard deviations σ and the positions of the zero crossings are marked for each size or scale. Figure 4 shows an intensity profile (Fig. 4a) that is convolved with a G'' function with large σ (Fig. 4b). The positions of the zero crossings are marked with heavy dots. In the scale space representation of Figure 4c the vertical dimension represents the value of σ and the horizontal dimension represents position in the signal. For each value of σ the position of the zero crossings of $I(x) * G''$ are plotted as points along a horizontal line in this diagram. For example, points along the dashed line at $\sigma = \sigma_l$ indicate the positions of the zero crossings of the signal in Figure 4b. The scale space representation of zero crossings illustrates the behavior of these features across scales. For small σ the zero crossings capture all the changes in the original intensity function. At coarser scales (larger σ) they capture only the gross changes of intensity.

The scale space representation is visually suggestive of a fingerprint. In fact, in much the same way that a fingerprint uniquely identifies a person, the scale space representation uniquely identifies an image. For almost all one-dimensional signals, the scale space map of the zero crossings of the signal convolved with G'' over a continuum of scales determines the signal uniquely, up to a multiplicative constant and an additional harmonic function (Yuille and Poggio, 1986). The proof provides a method for reconstructing a signal $I(x)$ from knowledge of how the zero crossings of $I(x) * G''$ change across scales. The use of Gaussian smoothing is critical to the completeness of the subsequent feature representation, but the basic theorem applies to zero crossings and level crossings of the result of applying any linear differential operator to the Gaussian-filtered signal. Other results regarding the completeness of the zero-crossing representation can be found in Hummel (1986).

Careful observation of the contours in the scale space representation of Figure 4c reveals that the contours either begin at the smallest scale and continue as a single, isolated contour through larger scales (Fig. 4d, A) or they form closed, inverted bowl-like shapes (Fig. 4d, B). Additional zero crossings are never created as scale increases; that is, there are no contours in the scale space represen-

Figure 4. The scale space representation. (a) An extended one-dimensional intensity profile. (b) The result of convolving the profile in (a) with a $G''(x)$ operator with large σ. The zero crossings are marked with heavy dots. (c) The scale space representation of the positions of the zero crossings over a continuous range of scales (sizes of σ). The zero crossings of (b) are plotted along the dashed horizontal line at $\sigma = \sigma_l$. (d) Contours of the type labeled A and B are commonly found in the scale space representation, whereas those of the type labeled C and D are never found.

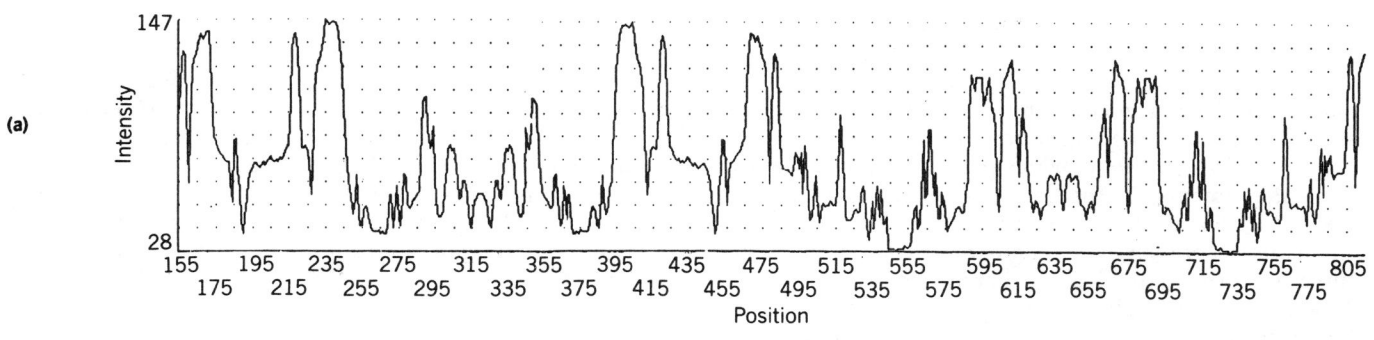

(a)

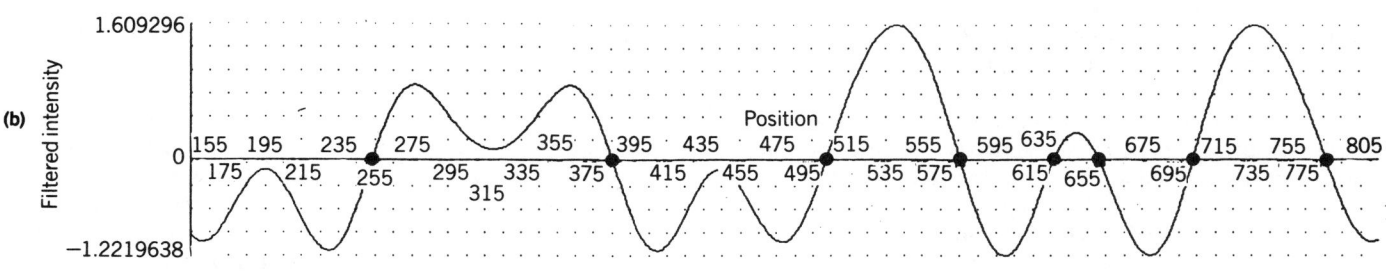

(b)

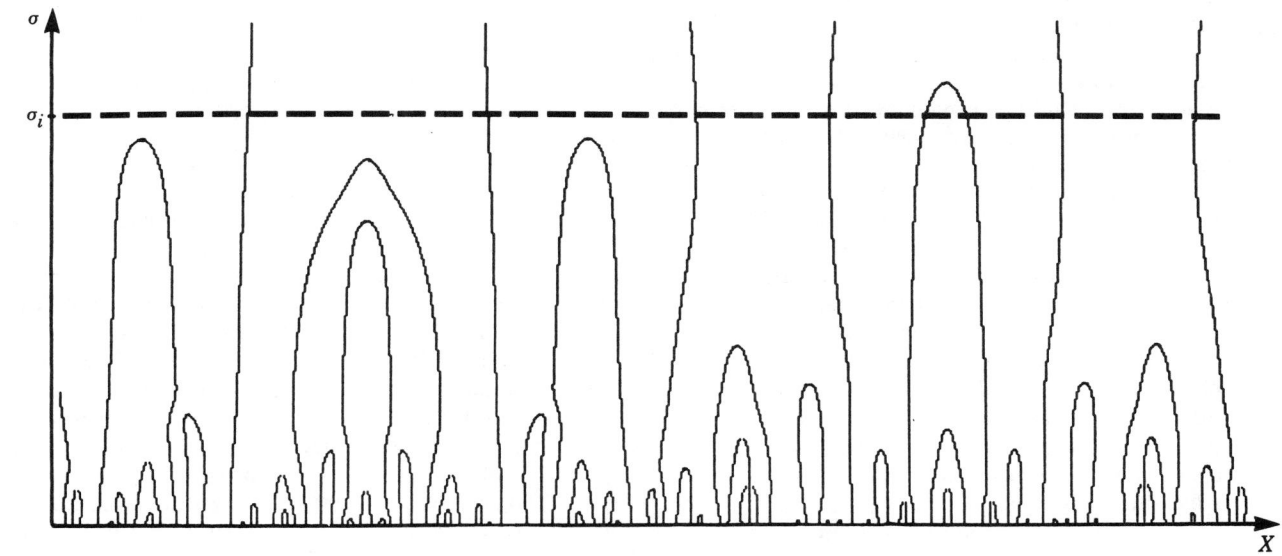

(c)

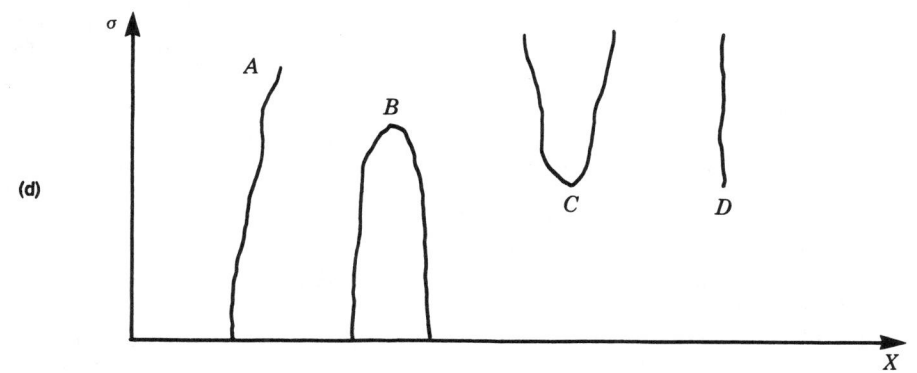

(d)

tation of the type shown in Fig. 4d (C and D). This observation has been supported by a number of theoretical studies (Babaud and co-workers, 1986; Koenderink, 1984; Yuille and Poggio, 1986), which have also shown that the Gaussian function is the only smoothing function that yields this behavior of subsequent features across scale (there are other approaches, however, that yield edge features with this behavior, eg, Perona and Malik, 1990). This observation applies to zero crossings and level crossings of the result of applying any linear differential operator to the Gaussian-smoothed signal. This behavior of features across scale has been exploited in the qualitative analysis of one-dimensional signals (eg, Witkin, 1983) (see also SCALE SPACE).

Many theoretical studies of the initial smoothing and differentiation operations implicitly assume that local edges are associated with an isolated step-change of intensity. Chen and Medioni (1989) present a one-dimensional scheme that is based on the detection of zero crossings in an intensity profile that is convolved with the second derivative of a Gaussian, which explicitly takes into account the interaction between nearby intensity changes. Such interactions can yield displacement of a zero crossing away from the true location of an edge in the original intensity distribution. An iterative scheme is devised to correct for the effects of this interaction, which attempts to minimize the difference between the convolution results that would be predicted from a hypothesized set of step changes of intensity (derived from the zero crossings) and the actual convoluton profile. Such a scheme yields improvement in the interpretation of the zero-crossing representation, but there may still be "spurious" zero crossings in the final result that do not correspond to an actual intensity edge in the image. Clark (1989) discusses methods for removing spurious zero crossings that are based on a theoretical analysis of the statistical distribution of real and spurious zero crossings, and the strength of zero crossings, both across scale and relative to other nearby intensity variations. Lu and Jain (1989) also present a reasoning system for interpreting the scale-space map of zero crossings in terms of real intensity edges in the image.

To summarize, the analysis of one-dimensional signals has been important for developing a solid theoretical foundation on which to base methods for detecting intensity changes in an image. Several theoretical studies attempted to derive an optimal operator for detecting intensity changes using a variety of criteria for evaluating the performance of the operator. These operators essentially perform a smoothing and differentiation of the image intensities. Furthermore, several one-dimensional analyses point to operators whose spatial shape is roughly the first or second derivative of a Gaussian function. (It should be noted again that some edge detection methods that compute an analytic approximation of the intensity function may be equivalent to those performing a direct smoothing operation with a Gaussian function.) Mathematical studies also addressed the information content of representations of image features and the behavior of these features across multiple scales. A number of these latter studies also stressed the importance of Gaussian smoothing. In-

terestingly, the initial filters in the human visual system appear to perform a spatial convolution of the image with a function that is closely approximated by the second derivative of a Gaussian. The retinal image is processed through a number of such filters that differ in the amount of spatial and temporal smoothing that is performed (eg, Wilson and Bergen, 1979; for review, see Boff and co-workers, 1986).

Two-Dimensional Detection of Intensity Changes

The problems addressed in the one-dimensional analysis of intensity signals also arise for the detection of intensity changes in two-dimensional images, although their solution is more complex. The design of optimal operators for performing smoothing and differentiation, for example, is complicated by a larger selection of possible derivative operations that can be performed in two dimensions. Many of the mathematical results regarding the information content of image features and behavior of features across scale have been extended to two dimensions, but the algorithms for extracting and describing these features in the image are also more complex than their one-dimensional counterparts. In addition, the analysis of extended edges, lines, or curves, as well as local features such as corners, arises in the two-dimensional analysis of intensity changes. This section reviews some of the techniques used to detect and describe two-dimensional image features.

Early work on edge detection primarily used directional first- and second-derivative operators for performing the two-dimensional differentiation (Prewitt, 1970; Rosenfeld and Thurston, 1971; Macleod, 1972; Davis, 1975; Persoon, 1976; Rosenfeld and Kak, 1976; Brooks, 1978; Pratt, 1978; Marr and Poggio, 1979; Haralick, 1980; Nevatia and Babu, 1980; Binford, 1981, 1982). A change of intensity that is extended along some orientation in the image gives rise to a peak in the first derivative of intensity taken in the direction perpendicular to the orientation of the intensity change, or a zero crossing in the second directional derivative. The simplest directional operators are formed by extending one-dimensional cross sections such as those shown in Figure 3 along some two-dimensional direction in the image. Directional operators have differed in the shape of their cross sections both perpendicular to and along their primary orientations. Macleod (1972) and Marr and Poggio (1979), for example, used directional derivatives that embodied Gaussian smoothing.

In principle, the computation of the derivatives in two directions, such as the horizontal and vertical directions, is sufficient to detect intensity changes at all orientations in the image. Several algorithms, however, use directional operators at a large number of discrete orientations (eg, Persoon, 1976; Pratt, 1978; Nevatia and Babu, 1980). A given intensity change is detected by a number of directional operators in this case, and the output of the directional operator that yields the largest response is typically used to describe the local intensity change (eg, Nevatia and Babu, 1980; Canny, 1986). An example of the results of Canny's algorithm is shown in Figure 5. The contours of

Figure 5. Canny's edge detection algorithm. (*a*) A natural image. (*b*) The positions of the intensity changes detected by Canny's algorithm. (Courtesy of J. F. Canny.)

Figure 5b represent only the positions of the significant intensity changes in Figure 5a.

Other related differential operators that are used in two dimensions are the first and second derivatives in the direction of the gradient of intensity (Haralick, 1984; Canny, 1986; Torre and Poggio, 1986). The intensity gradient, defined as follows:

$$\nabla I = \left(\frac{\partial I}{\partial x}, \frac{\partial I}{\partial y} \right)$$

is a vector that indicates the direction and magnitude of steepest increase in the two-dimensional intensity function. Let **n** denote the unit vector in the direction of the gradient. The differential operators $\partial/\partial \mathbf{n}$ and $\partial^2/\partial \mathbf{n}^2$ are nondirectional operators in the sense that their value does not change when the image is rotated. They are also nonlinear operators and, unlike the linear differential operators, cannot be combined with the smoothing function in a single filtering step. Methods such as those of Nevatia and Babu (1980) and Canny (1986) essentially use the directional derivative along the gradient for extracting features.

A second nondirectional operator that is used for detecting intensity changes is the Laplacian operator ∇^2 (Rosenfeld and Kak, 1976; Modestino and Fries, 1977; Shanmugam and co-workers, 1979; Marr and Hildreth, 1980; Hildreth, 1983; Horn, 1985):

$$\nabla^2 I = \frac{\partial^2 I}{\partial x^2} + \frac{\partial^2 I}{\partial y^2}$$

Combined with a two-dimensional Gaussian smoothing function,

$$G(r) = \frac{1}{\sigma^2} \exp^{\frac{-r^2}{2\sigma^2}}$$

the Laplacian yields the function $\nabla^2 G$ given by the expression:

$$\nabla^2 G = \frac{1}{\sigma^2} \left(\frac{r^2}{\sigma^2} - 2 \right) \exp^{\frac{-r^2}{2\sigma^2}}$$

where r denotes the distance from the center of the operator and σ is the standard deviation of the two-dimensional Gaussian. The $\nabla^2 G$ function is shaped something like a Mexican hat in two dimensions. Figure 6 shows an example of the convolution of an image (Fig. 6a) with a $\nabla^2 G$ operator (Fig. 6b). The Laplacian is a nondirectional second-derivative operation; the elements in the output of the Laplacian that correspond to the location of intensity changes in the image are therefore the zero crossings. The zero-crossing contours derived from Figure 6b are shown in Figure 6c. In this case the zero-crossing contours were located by detecting the transitions between positive and negative values in the filtered image by scanning in the horizontal and vertical directions. A single convolution of the image with the nondirectional $\nabla^2 G$ operator allows the detection of intensity changes at all orientations at a given scale. The two-dimensional orientation of a local portion of the zero-crossing contour can be computed from the gradient of the filtered image (Hildreth, 1983).

It is not yet clear whether directional or nondirectional operators are most appropriate for detecting intensity changes. Both have advantages and disadvantages. The use of the Laplacian is simpler and requires less computation than either directional derivatives or derivatives in the direction of the gradient. The directional operators, however, yield somewhat better localization of the position of intensity changes (Haralick, 1984; Canny, 1986), particularly in areas where the orientation of an edge is changing rapidly in the image (Berzins, 1984; Heurtas and Medioni, 1985). Features such as the zero-crossing contours, when derived with nondirectional operators,

Figure 6. Detecting intensity changes with the $\nabla^2 G$ operator. (a) A natural image. (b) The result of convolving the image with a $\nabla^2 G$ operator. The most positive values are shown in white and the most negative values in black. (c) The zero crossings of the convolution output shown in (b).

generally form smooth, closed contours, whereas features obtained with directional operators generally do not have such special geometric properties (Torre and Poggio, 1986). If the intensity function along the orientation of an intensity change varies at most linearly, the zero crossings of the Laplacian exactly coincide with the zero crossings of a directional operator taken in the direction perpendicular to the orientation of the intensity change (Marr and Hildreth, 1980). Torre and Poggio (1986) characterized more formally the relationship between the zeros of the Laplacian and those of the second derivative in the direction of the gradient in terms of the geometry of the two-dimensional intensity surface. Note that only the linear differential operators can be combined directly with the smoothing operation to yield a single filtering step. When performed separately, the smoothing operation can be achieved by approximating the two-dimensional intensity surface with a smooth analytic function, as noted earlier (Prewitt, 1970; Hueckel, 1973; Rosenfeld and Kak, 1976; Pratt, 1978; Haralick, 1980, 1983, 1984; Nalwa and Binford, 1986). With regard to the use of the directional versus nondirectional derivative operators, physiological studies reveal that the retina analyzes the visual image through a circularly symmetric filter whose spatial shape is given by the difference of two Gaussian functions (eg, Rodieck and Stone, 1965; DeMonasterio, 1978; for review, see Geiger, 1987; Kandel and Schwartz, 1985), which is closely approximated by the $\nabla^2 G$ function.

Mathematical results regarding the information content and behavior across scales of image features have some bearing on the choice of differential operators. For example, Yuille and Poggio (1986) showed that in two dimensions the combination of Gaussian smoothing with any linear differential operator yields zero crossings or level crossings that behave well with increasing scale in that no features are created as the size of the Gaussian is increased. In the case of the second derivative along the gradient, Yuille and Poggio proved that there is no smoothing function that avoids the creation of zero crossings with increasing scale. The completeness of the scale space representation of zero crossings or level crossings in two dimensions also required the use of linear differential operators.

The analysis of intensity changes across multiple scales is a difficult problem that has not yet found a satisfactory solution. There is a clear need to detect intensity changes as multiple resolutions (eg, Rosenfeld and Thurston, 1971). Important physical changes in the scene take place at different scales. Spatial filters that allow the description of fine detail generally miss coarser structures in the image, and those that allow the extraction of coarser features generally smooth out important detail. At all resolutions, some of the detected features may not correspond to real physical changes in the scene. For example, at the finest resolutions some of the detected intensity changes may be the consequence of noise in the sensing process. At coarser resolutions spurious image features may arise as a consequence of smoothing together nearby intensity changes (see, eg, Chen and Medioni, 1989; Clark, 1989; Lu and Jain, 1989). The problems of sorting out the relevant changes at each resolution and combining them into a representation that can be used effectively by later processes are difficult and unsolved problems. Some of the research that has attempted to address these problems is mentioned below. Note that some multiresolution methods for later processing tasks such as binocular stereo and motion analysis use the representations of intensity edges obtained at multiple spatial resolutions independently, and therefore do not require that these representations by combined explicitly (see STEREO VISION).

The combination of zero-crossing descriptions that arise from convolving an image with $\nabla^2 G$ operators of different size has been explored (Marr and Hildreth, 1980). An example of these descriptions is illustrated in Figure 7. The zero crossings from the smaller $\nabla^2 G$ operator primarily detect the bumpy texture on the surface of the leaf, whereas the zero-crossing contours from the larger operator also outline some of the highlights on the leaf surface that are due to changing illumination (the arrows point to one example). Marr and Hildreth suggested the use of spatial coincidence of zero crossings across scale as a means of indicating the presence of a real edge in the scene. Strong edges such as object boundaries often give rise to sharp intensity changes in the image that are detected across a range of scales in roughly the same location in the image. In the one-dimensional scale space rep-

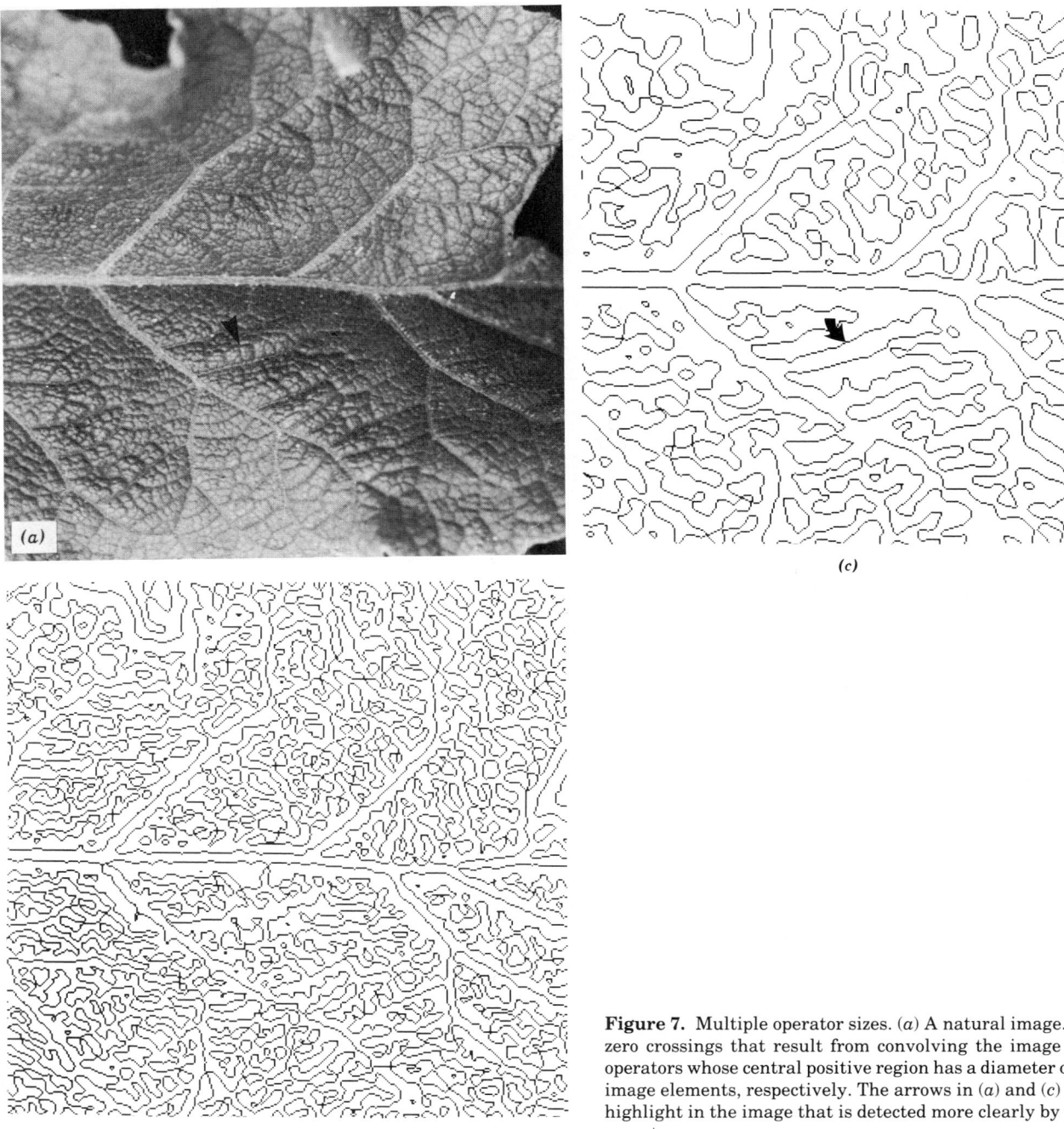

Figure 7. Multiple operator sizes. (*a*) A natural image. (*b, c*) The zero crossings that result from convolving the image with $\nabla^2 G$ operators whose central positive region has a diameter of 6 and 12 image elements, respectively. The arrows in (*a*) and (*c*) indicate a highlight in the image that is detected more clearly by the larger operator.

resentation these edges give rise to roughly vertical lines. (The scale space representation can be extended to two dimensions, in which the positions of the zero crossings on the x–y plane are represented across multiple operator sizes.) The existence of contours in the scale space representation that are roughly vertical and extend across a range of scales could be used to infer the presence of a significant physical change at the corresponding location in the scene.

A method was developed for constructing qualitative descriptions of one-dimensional signals that uses the scale space representation (Witkin, 1983). The method em-

bodies two basic assumptions: the identity assumption, that zero crossings detected at different scales, which lie on a common contour in the scale space description, arise from a single physical event; and the localization assumption, that the true location of a physical event that gives rise to a contour in the scale space description is the contour's position as σ tends to zero. Coarser scales were used to identify important events in the signal and finer scales were used to localize their position. Events that persisted over large changes in scale also had special significance. Witkins' method, called scale space filtering, begins with the scale space description and collapses it into a discrete tree structure that represents the qualitative behavior of the signal. Some of the heuristics embodied in this analysis may be useful for analyzing two-dimensional images. (See SCALE SPACE for further discussion of multiresolution methods based on the use of the scale space representation.)

Canny (1986) used a different approach to combining descriptions of intensity changes across multiple scales. Features were first detected at a set of discrete scales. The finest scale description was then used to predict the results of the next larger scale, assuming that the filter used to derive the larger scale description performs additional smoothing of the image. In a particular area of the image, if there was a substantial difference between the actual description at the larger scale and that predicted by the smaller scale, it was assumed that there is an important change taking place at the larger scale that is not detected at the finer scale. In this case features detected at the larger scale were then added to the final feature representation. Empirically, Canny found that most features were detected at the finest scale, and relatively few were added from coarser scales.

For some applications of edge detection, it is useful to detect local features such as corners, whose position can be localized in two dimensions (see, eg, STEREO VISION; TEXTURE; VISUAL MOTION ANALYSIS; OBJECT RECOGNITION). This need has stimulated the design of algorithms specialized to detect gray-level corners (Pratt, 1978; Rosenfeld and Kak, 1982). These algorithms typically use two basic approaches. Some are template-based in that they detect image locations at which the local intensity function has a high correlation with an ideal corner-shaped intensity pattern. Others are gradient-based in that they look for locations at which there is a significant change in the direction of the local intensity gradient. Discussion of some recent schemes can be found, for example, in Noble (1988), Rangarajan and co-workers (1989), and Singh and Shneier (1990). Corner points can also be detected after the local extraction of edge contours and used to segment and describe extended contours for the purpose of tasks such as recognition, as in the curvature primal sketch suggested by Asada and Brady (1986). (For an analysis of curve segmentation techniques, see also Fischler and Bolles, 1986.)

A further issue that has been addressed in recent studies is the extraction of salient image contours that are more likely to correspond to important scene features such as object boundaries. Ullman and Sha'ashua (1988) developed an iterative scheme that uses simple measures of properties such as contour curvature to extract salient contours from an edge map. The scheme is implemented on a uniform network of locally connected processing elements. It has been applied to zero-crossing maps derived from complex natural images and successfully extracts extended contours that human observers consider salient. Connelly and Rosenfeld (1990) present an algorithm that examines the behavior of image features across scale (using the pyramid representation discussed in SCALE SPACE) to extract such salient contours in an image. A general approach to the analysis of local orientation for tasks such as curve extraction can be found in Zucker (1985).

To summarize, there has been considerable progress on the detection and description of intensity changes in two-dimensional images, but there still exists many open questions. A large body of theoretical and empirical work has addressed the question of what operators are most appropriate for performing the smoothing and differentiation stages. Emerging from this work is a better understanding of the advantages and disadvantages of various operators and the relationship between alternative approaches. It is unlikely that a single method will be most appropriate for all tasks. The choice of operators depends in part on the application, the nature of the later processes that use the description of image features, and the available computational resources. Some interesting work has begun to address the problem of detecting and integrating intensity changes across multiple scales, but a satisfactory solution to this problem still eludes vision researchers. A problem that was not discussed here is the computation of properties such as contrast and sharpness of intensity changes. There has been some work on this problem, but it has not yet received a rigorous analytic treatment.

RECOVERING PROPERTIES OF THE PHYSICAL WORLD

In the opening paragraph it was noted that the goal of vision is to recover the physical properties of objects in the scene, such as the location of object boundaries and the structure, color, and texture of object surfaces, from the two-dimensional image that is projected onto the eye or camera. The detection of intensity changes in the image represents only a first, meager step toward achieving this goal. This section briefly mentions some of the areas of vision that address the recovery of physical properties of edges in the scene.

The property of edges that is perhaps most important and most studied is their three-dimensional structure. The structure of edges is conveyed through many sources. For example, the relative locations of corresponding edges in the left and right stereo views conveys information about the location of edges in three-dimensional space (see STEREO VISION). The relative movement between edges in the image can be used to assess their relative position in space (see VISUAL MOTION ANALYSIS). Three-dimensional structure can also be inferred from the shape of the two-dimensional projection of edge contours, the way in which edges intersect in the image, and variations in surface texture (see TEXTURE). These latter cues are essential in the interpretation of three-dimensional structure from a single, static photograph. Many algorithms that analyze these sources are feature-based in that the initial inferences regarding three-dimensional structure are made at the locations of features such as significant intensity changes in the image. Discussion of some of these processes for recovering three-dimensional structure can be found, for example in Rosenfeld and Kak (1976), Pratt (1978), Marr and Poggio (1980), Binford (1981, 1982), Brady (1981), Ballard and Brown (1982), Marr (1982), Koenderink (1984), and Horn (1985).

Another important property of edges is the type of

physical change from which they arise. For example, edges may be the consequence of object boundaries, changes in surface orientation, shadows, highlights or light sources, surface markings, changes in surface reflectance or material composition, and so on. Ultimately, it is necessary to determine the physical source of each edge in the scene. The recovery of these physical properties of edges is likely to be a main focus of future research on edge detection.

BIBLIOGRAPHY

H. Asada and M. Brady, "The Curvature Primal Sketch," *IEEE Trans. Patt. Anal. Mach. Intell.* **PAMI–8,** 2–14 (1986).

J. Babaud, A. P. Witkin, M. Baudin, and R. O. Duda, "Uniqueness of the Gaussian Kernel for Scale-Space Filtering," *IEEE Trans. Patt. Anal. Mach. Intell.* **PAMI–8,** 26–33 (1986).

D. H. Ballard and C. M. Brown, *Computer Vision*, Prentice-Hall, Englewood Cliffs, New Jersey, 1982.

V. Berzins, "Accuracy of Laplacian Edge Detectors," *Comput. Graph. Image Proc.* **27,** 195–210 (1984).

T. O. Binford, "Inferring Surfaces from Images," *Artif. Intell.* **17,** 205–244 (1981).

T. O. Binford, "Survey of Model-Based Image Analysis Systems," *Int. J. Robot. Res.* **1,** 18–64 (1982).

K. R. Boff, L. Kaufman, and J. P. Thomas, eds., *Handbook of Perception and Human Performance,* Vol. 1, *Sensory Processes and Perception*, Wiley, New York, 1986.

M. Brady, ed., *Computer Vision*, North-Holland Co., Amsterdam, 1981.

M. J. Brooks, "Rationalizing Edge Detectors," *Comput. Graph. Image Proc.* **8,** 277–285 (1978).

J. F. Canny, "A Computational Approach to Edge Detection," *IEEE Trans. Patt. Anal. Mach. Intell.* **PAMI–8,** 679–698 (1986).

J. S. Chen and G. Medioni, "Detection, Localization, and Estimation of Edges," *IEEE Trans. Patt. Anal. Mach. Intell.* **PAMI–11,** 191–198 (1989).

J. J. Clark, "Authenticating Edges Produced by Zero-Crossing Algorithms," *IEEE Trans. Patt. Anal. Mach. Intell.* **PAMI–11,** 43–57 (1989).

S. Connelly and A. Rosenfeld, "A Pyramid Algorithm for Fast Curve Extraction," *Comput. Vis. Graph. Image Proc.* **49,** 332–345 (1990).

L. Davis, "A Survey of Edge Detection Techniques," *Comput. Graph. Image Proc.* **4,** 248–270 (1975).

F. M. DeMonasterio, "Properties of Concentrically Organized X and Y Ganglion Cells of the Macaque Retina," *J. Neurophysiol.* **41,** 1394–1417 (1978).

M. A. Fischler and R. C. Bolles, "Perceptual Organization and Curve Partitioning," *IEEE Trans. Pattern Anal. Mach. Intell.* **PAMI–8,** 100–105 (1986).

S. R. Geiger, ed., *Handbook of Physiology*, American Physiological Society, Bethesda, Md., 1987.

J. Hadamard, *Lectures on the Cauchy Problem in Linear Partial Differential Equations*, Yale University Press, New Haven, Conn., 1923.

R. M. Haralick, "Edge and Region Analysis for Digital Image Data," *Comput. Graph. Image Proc.* **12,** 60–73 (1980).

R. M. Haralick, "Digital Step Edges from Zero Crossings of Second Directional Derivatives," *IEEE Trans. Patt. Anal. Mach. Intell.* **PAMI–6,** 58–68 (1984).

R. M. Haralick, L. T. Watson, and T. J. Laffey, "The Topographical Primal Sketch," *Int. J. Robot. Res.* **2,** 50–72 (1983).

A. Heurtas and G. Medioni, "Edge Detection With Subpixel Precision," *Proceedings of the IEEE Workshop of Computer Vision: Representation and Control*, IEEE Computer Society Press, Bellaire, Mich., October 1985.

E. C. Hildreth, "The Detection of Intensity Changes by Computer and Biological Vision Systems," *Comput. Vis. Graph. Image Proc.* **22,** 1–27 (1983).

B. K. P. Horn, *Robot Vision*, MIT Press, Cambridge, Mass., 1985.

M. H. Hueckel, "A Local Visual Operator Which Recognizes Edges and Lines," *J. Assoc. Comput. Mach.* **20,** 634–647 (1973).

R. A. Hummel, "Representations Based on Zero-Crossings in Scale-Space," *Proc. IEEE Comp. Vision Patt. Recog.*, Miami Beach, Fla., 204–209 (1986).

E. R. Kandel and J. H. Schwartz, eds., *Principles of Neural Science*, Elsevier, New York, 1985.

J. J. Koenderink, "The Structure of Images," *Biol. Cybern.* **50,** 363–370 (1984).

Y. Lu and R. C. Jain, "Behavior of Edges in Scale Space," *IEEE Trans. Patt. Anal. Mach. Intell.* **PAMI–11,** 337–356 (1989).

I. D. G. Macleod, "Comments on Techniques for Edge Detection," *Proc. IEEE* **60,** 344 (1972).

D. Marr, *Vision*, W. H. Freeman, San Francisco, 1982.

D. Marr and E. C. Hildreth, "Theory of Edge Detection," *Proc. Roy. Soc. Lond. B* **207,** 187–217 (1980).

D. Marr and T. Poggio, "A Theory of Human Stereo Vision," *Proc. Roy. Soc. Lond. B* **204,** 301–328 (1979).

J. W. Modestino and R. W. Fries, "Edge Detection in Noisy Images Using Recursive Digital Filtering," *Comput. Graph. Image Proc.* **6,** 409–433 (1977).

V. S. Nalwa and T. O. Binford, "On Detecting Edges," *IEEE Trans. Patt. Anal. Mach. Intell.* **PAMI–8,** 699–714 (1986).

R. Nevatia and R. Babu, "Linear Feature Extraction and Description," *Comput. Graph. Image Proc.* **13,** 257–269 (1980).

J. A. Noble, "Finding Corners," *Image Vis. Comput.* **6,** 121–128 (1988).

P. Perona and J. Malik, "Scale-Space and Edge Detection Using Anisotropic Diffusion," *IEEE Trans. Patt. Anal. Mach. Intell.* **PAMI–12,** 629–639 (1990).

E. Persoon, "A New Edge Detection Algorithm and Its Applications," *Comput. Graph. Image Proc.* **5,** 425–446 (1976).

T. Poggio, H. Voorhees, and A. Yuille, "A Regularized Solution to Edge Detection," *J. Complexity* **4,** 106–123 (1988).

W. Pratt, *Digital Image Processing*, Wiley, New York, 1978.

J. M. S. Prewitt, "Object Enhancement and Extraction" in B. Lipkin and A. Rosenfeld, eds., *Picture Processing and Psychophysics*, Academic Press, New York, 1970, 75–149.

K. Rangarajan, M. Shah, and D. Van Brackle, "Optimal Corner Detector," *Comput. Vis. Graph. Image Proc.* **48,** 230–245 (1989).

R. W. Rodieck and J. Stone, "Analysis of Receptive Fields of Cat Retinal Ganglion Cells," *J. Neurophysiol.* **28,** 833–849 (1965).

A. Rosenfeld and A. Kak, *Digital Picture Processing*, Academic Press, New York, 1976.

A. Rosenfeld and M. Thurston, "Edge and Curve Detection for Visual Scene Analysis," *IEEE Trans. Comput.* **C-20,** 562–569 (1971).

S. A. Shafer, *Shadows and Silhouettes in Computer Vision*, Kluwer Academic Pub., Boston, Mass., 1985.

K. S. Shanmugam, F. M. Dickey, and J. A. Green, "An Optimal Frequency Domain Filter for Edge Detection in Digital Pictures," *IEEE Trans. Patt. Anal. Mach. Intell.* **PAMI-1**, 37–49 (1979).

A. Singh and M. Shneier, "Grey Level Corner Detection: A Generalization and a Robust Real Time Implementation," *Comput. Vis. Graph. Image Proc.* **51**, 54–69 (1990).

V. Torre and T. Poggio, "On Edge Detection," *IEEE Trans. Patt. Anal. Mach. Intell.* **PAMI-8**, 147–163 (1986).

S. Ullman and A. Sha'ashua, "Structural Saliency: The Detection of Globally Salient Structures Using a Locally Connected Network," *MIT Artificial Intelligence Laboratory Memo* 1061 (1988).

A. L. Yuille and T. Poggio, "Fingerprints Theorems for Zero-Crossings," *Proceedings of the Fourth National Conference on Artificial Intelligence*, Austin, Tex., AAAI, Menlo Park, Calif., 1984.

A. L. Yuille and T. Poggio, "Scaling Theorems for Zero-Crossings," *IEEE Trans. Patt. Anal. Mach. Intell.* **PAMI-8**, 15–25 (1986).

H. R. Wilson and J. R. Bergen, "A Four Mechanism Model for Threshold Spatial Vision," *Vis. Res.* **19**, 19–32 (1979).

A. P. Witkin, "Scale Space Filtering" in *Proceedings of the Eighth International Joint Conferences on Artificial Intelligence*, Karlsruhe, Germany, 1983, 1019–1022.

S. W. Zucker, "Early Orientation Selection: Tangent Fields and the Dimensionality of Their Support," *Comput. Vision Graph. Image Proc.* **32**, 74–103 (1985).

ELLEN C. HILDRETH
MIT Artificial Intelligence
Laboratory

The author is supported by the Artificial Intelligence Laboratory and the Center for Biological Information Processing at the Massachusetts Institute of Technology. Support for the Artificial Intelligence Laboratory's research is provided in part by the Advanced Research Projects Agency of the Department of Defense under Office of Naval Research contract N00014-85-K-0124. The Center's support is provided in part by the Office of Naval Research, Cognitive and Neural Sciences Division, the National Science Foundation, and the McDonnell Foundation.

EDUCATION, AI IN

The field of AI in education is concerned with development of artificial intelligence techniques for the study of human teaching and for the engineering of systems that facilitate human learning. The field addresses questions that are long term in nature: how can systems facilitate learning and enable the measurement of learning progress (Lesgold, 1988)? The term intelligent tutoring system (ITS) is frequently used in regard to the engineering side of the discipline. Computational methods are used in support of AI activities such as planning, control, knowledge representation and acquisition, explanation, cognitive modeling, and dialogue management. Computational models are used to explore and evaluate alternative theories about learning. Research is motivated by the promise of building powerful teaching systems with greater knowledge about a domain, increased ability to make inferences about student behavior, and increased reasoning ability about topic selection and response generation. This article reviews the current state of the field and discusses the history of the field. It addresses basic approaches to building teaching systems, recent developments in the field, and open research issues.

Three research goals have become apparent. The first is to use AI and cognitive science techniques to model experts who problem solve in a domain, as well as tutors teaching and students learning in that domain. Computational models facilitate a degree of explicitness about learning theories and teaching strategies that is difficult to attain in classrooms. Such models encourage comparison of the results of using a teaching system with data from classroom-style teaching and aid in refining and evaluating a learning or problem-solving hypothesis.

The second research goal involves explaining learning and teaching as parts of the human information-processing system. Because all intelligent beings learn, differences in learning rates might be due to a level of prior knowledge or to the quality of teaching. Teaching efforts are often critical to learning, as when a learner makes errors or has deep misconceptions. Modeling human teaching efforts should help to understand learning characteristics such as student motivation and performance.

The third research goal is to demonstrate completeness and reliability in the engineering side of the discipline and to show that intelligent instructional systems can be used effectively in training and classroom situations. Sometimes this goal is expressed in terms of providing each student with a computer-based tutor that has some of the qualities of a master teacher, such as scope and depth of subject matter, excellent knowledge of teaching, powerful communication skills, and the ability to inspire and motivate the student to learn. Clearly, researchers have a long way to go to achieve this goal, and yet some progress can be shown. Subject matter expertise has been realized to a limited extent. Less progress has been made in modeling tutoring expertise and student knowledge. Even less progress has been made in simulating powerful communication skills. Human communicators use many verbal and nonverbal skills to convey information, including speech, informal sketches, and gestures. Computers are poor at verbal communication. On the other hand, they can be much better than (unaided) humans at visual or graphic communication of ideas and time-related processes. Many systems exploit this ability including STEAMER (Hollan and co-workers, 1984) and IMTS (Towne and co-workers, 1990). To increase the communication bandwidth for teaching systems, it may be more cost-effective to exploit their inherent nonverbal communication strengths rather than to improve their poor verbal skills. The least amount of progress has been made in the affective area, for example, the crucial aspect of student motivation has yet to be seriously confronted. Several intelligent instructional systems have been used generally by many students and some systems result in significant learning gains. However, many others provide only limited coverage of a domain and have, by and large, demonstrated only simple knowledge engineering capabilities.

Research activities in this field are important to education, not only because such systems might someday become routine in classrooms but also because such systems might support students in activities not available in traditional classrooms, such as extensive one-on-one collaboration with a tutor and freedom to explore hypothetical worlds, to make conjectures, and to test hypotheses.

Intelligent instructional systems are distinquished from earlier computer-based training (CBT) systems, including computer aided instruction (CAI), simulations, and microworlds, in that they dynamically reason about and customize their response to the individual student. Traditional CAI systems are scriptlike: all machine responses, text or graphics, are organized into screens, and encoded branching instructions define both the topic and response to be presented. Every machine response, as well as every path of instruction for a typical student, is predefined by the author. Simulations and microworlds of this type lack student monitoring capability and show few positive learning effects (Alperson and O'Neil, 1990).

Conversely, intelligent instructional systems define a variety of knowledge types and then define pedagogical knowledge about how to teach that knowledge; the latter might contain rules of inferencing for reasoning about a variety of possible ways to teach the given content knowledge. The system reasons about its stored knowledge and then dynamically generates its own path through the knowledge in response to student behavior.

Current systems vary in the type of knowledge they teach. Some teach concepts, eg, velocity and acceleration, as well as processes within whole systems, eg, an emergency shut-down procedure in a boiler system (Woolf and co-workers, 1986) or a hydraulic process involved in folding a helicopter's blades (Towne and co-workers, 1990). Other systems teach meta-cognition, or the knowledge needed to reason about learning (Richer and Clancey, 1985), and how to debug solutions (McArthur and co-workers, 1987). Some teach formal logic and formal knowledge, eg, ALGEBRALAND (Foss, 1987) and the Geometry Tutor (Anderson and co-workers, 1985).

THEORETICAL BASIS

Researchers in this field ask under what conditions a computer system might effectively teach and if such a system might teach in the same way as does a talented teacher. Definitions of teaching are typically grounded in computational models of the human participants, including the domain expert, teacher, and student. In addition, the definition frequently includes a model of effective communication. Typically, these four models work together to generate a system's intelligence. A model of the expert typically represents topics, concepts, definitions, or processes within the domain. A model of the teacher might include methods for providing remediation for errors as well as a selection of examples, analogies, and strategies for responding to idiosyncratic student behavior, and knowledge about when to interrupt. A model of the student or cognitive processes might represent general factors necessary for a person to learn in that domain, such as considerations about motivation. A general and ab-

stract student model might be dynamically updated to include more specific attributes such as whether a particular student needs more challenges or more remedial advice. A communication model might include dialogue and teaching principles in the domain couched within principles of good interface design. Building an intelligent instructional system entails building each of these models using a variety of AI technologies, including knowledge representation, control, and knowledge acquisition. These technologies are discussed below.

Knowledge Representation. In constructing intelligent tutors, two aspects of knowledge representation (qv) are important. First, what knowledge do teachers and trainers use to understand the domain, diagnose student behavior, and select new strategic approaches? Second, what are good representational schemes for encoding domain knowledge (qv)? Knowledge representation refers to how knowledge is used to model the domain, human thinking, learning processes, and teaching strategies. Knowledge bases might store concepts, activities, relations between topics, and other quantities needed to make expert decisions. They might also store a variety of lessons, topics, presentations, and response selections.

Control. Separation of the knowledge base (data structure) from the instructional strategies control (algorithms or heuristics) is critical to expanding the power of these systems and to enabling the author to work with each component separately. This separation enables designers to experiment by adding new control schemes, such as Socratic teaching, while keeping the knowledge base fixed. Control refers to passage of an interpreter through knowledge bases and its selection of appropriate pieces of knowledge for making a diagnosis, a prediction, or an evaluation. Control structures (qv) might be defined separately for selection of lesson, topic, presentation, and response.

Knowledge Acquisition. Knowledge acquisition (qv) is a difficult problem for any AI system. It requires facilitating incremental additions to an existing knowledge base. Frequently this means building an interface that enables a domain expert to easily add new instantiations of a chosen data structure (eg, a new frame or a new production rule) without requiring work in the implementation language. Knowledge acquisition requires and supports the identification and encoding of expertise. In constructing an intelligent tutor, knowledge acquisition should enable the expert to input questions, examples, analogies, and explanations; it should elicit not only tutoring primitives, such as topics and prerequisite knowledge, but also the reasoning the expert uses to know how and when to present each primitive. Tutoring knowledge might be described both in terms of content (ie, topics, questions, and examples) and context (ie, active tutoring strategies and current dialogue interventions).

Reasoning about Expert Knowledge

Building a domain or expert model requires, to some extent, specification of the relative difficulty of topics; identification of the strategies and tactics used for tailoring instruction to an individual student; and a corpus of analogies, examples, and error diagnosis techniques for teaching in the domain. Without the aid of shells, eg, expert systems shells and authoring systems, which currently do not exist, this task is difficult. Even with such software tools, each new domain requires identifications of curriculum topics and prerequisite topics, causal and temporal relations between topics, and the relative difficulty of learning each topic.

Choice of representations is also a large issue. Two roles might be played by the chosen representation: in those systems that focus on teaching problem-solving knowledge, the representation might first be used to solve the given problem and, second, used to communicate about the solution with the student. The first role suggests that the representation should be powerful enough for problem solving (eg, predicate calculus or rule-based language), and the second suggests that the language should be useful for explanations and should possibly contain a subset of terms a person might use to think about problems (eg, spatial or temporal relations between topics). Few languages are powerful enough to include both features.

Reasoning about Teaching Knowledge

Several styles of pedagogy or teaching knowledge have been explored in the process of developing customized responses to student behavior. Initially many systems were despotic in nature; incorrect student actions were quickly identified, based on reference to an error knowledge base, and quickly remediated. However, immediate help has several disadvantages: it may compete for short-term memory with newly learned material, and students might also become dependent on it (Schooler and Anderson, 1990). Researchers have moved away from building purportedly omniscient tutors and now focus on building empathetic environments that allow for independent exploratory behavior and also elicit information about student goals and plans. Such systems require less knowledge about the domain and can coach rather than tutor. These systems still reason about several forms of behavior before taking action using reasoning based on knowledge about how people solve problems or make inferences in the domain. Theoretical focus has shifted from exclusive diagnosis and remediation to identifying and supporting student management of their own cognitive processes.

Mixed-initiative dialogue refers to human–computer communication in which a student can control the conversation or ask questions as desired. Such control is now assumed in responsive instructional systems. Error diagnosis refers to the system's ability to diagnose mistakes, plausible misconceptions, overgeneralizations, and missing information. A diagnostic tutor compares student behavior with that of an expert before reasoning about how to elicit better learning performance.

Tutoring style might vary across domain types. Thus it could include explanation, guided discovery learning, coaching, coaxing, and critiquing. Although no one style is preferred over others, different domains will be better addressed with different primary styles. For example, didactic explanation is good for communicating a body of declarative knowledge shared by some community (eg, biologists). Students must learn the community's terminology and are not expected to rediscover all the principles in a field. On the other hand, more active discovery learning helps students own knowledge and is a better interaction style if students are expected to generate and test their own hypotheses, eg, while troubleshooting a circuit.

Tutoring style might also vary within a tutorial domain. For example, a human teacher might support guided discovery learning at first and yet change the strategy to opportunistic one-on-one tutoring once the student requests a specific activity or shows the need for remediation. How and why human teachers change teaching style is an open research question. Machine teaching style can range from natural language discourse to menu selection, although the importance of natural language has diminished considerably in recent years now that structured command languages or menu selection structures appear to be as effective for communication as state-of-the-art spoken or written languages.

Reasoning about Student Knowledge

Building an intelligent instructional system requires identifying presumed student knowledge within the domain as well as making inferences about the grasp of meta-cognitive skills. Frequently, a system will use a student model to represent how the student has organized and incorporated new knowledge. The student model should dynamically indicate a system's changing views of the student's strengths and weaknesses as well as aspects of the currently (mis)understood knowledge.

Reasoning about Communication

Building a variety of intelligent tutors has uncovered some design considerations about the model of communication between machine and student (Burton, 1988). For instance, extensive research is required to uncover the cognitive nature of the task. (See Anderson (1981) for research leading up to the Geometry Tutor and Woolf and co-workers (1986) for research leading to building a boiler tutor.) Another design consideration results from the need to isolate key tools required for attaining expertise in the domain. For example, the economics tutor used specific tools for selecting parameters during experimentation and scientific inquiry (Bonar and co-workers, 1986), and the Geometry Tutor, further discussed in the next section, used visualization tools to foster both forward and backward reasoning in the development of geometry proofs (Anderson and co-workers, 1985). The resulting tools were valuable motivational devices for learning even without help from an on-line tutor. A third consideration is the need to attain high fidelity to the modeled world (Hollan and co-workers, 1984). Fidelity is measured by how closely the simulated environment matches the real world, and high fidelity means the situation is almost indistinguishable from the actual environment. High conceptual fidelity, which is possibly the most powerful attribute of a communication interface, means that the simulation reflects more a mental model used by an expert than an exact physical model.

EXAMPLE SYSTEMS

Several intelligent instructional systems are discussed in this section along with the theoretical issues that they address. Collections of original papers and discussions of individual projects have been published (Sleeman and Brown, 1982; Wenger, 1987). Conventional computer programs for teaching have been around for decades. However, the field of AI in education is said to have begun with Carbonell's (1970) program.

Early Works (1970–1982)

During the first phase of AI in education, research was limited to building illustrations that showed ideas at work on toy domains. Carbonell's (1970) program SCHOLAR taught high-school geometry and differed substantially from other teaching systems of its day in that it separated knowledge about how to teach from the content or subject matter of teaching. Carbonell represented objects and concepts in grade-school geometry as nodes in a semantic network, suggesting that this was a feasible model of the way people store and access information. SCHOLAR held mixed-initiative dialogues (ie, interactions initiated by either the student or the system) by traversing the network and asking or answering questions about the stored information. SCHOLAR reasoned about student answers; responded opportunistically and, for the first time, was able to parse student questions.

Early research issues focused primarily on knowledge representation and grain size. Typically, ATNs (see GRAMMAR, AUGMENTED TRANSITION NETWORK), semantic networks (qv), and rule-based systems (qv) were used. SOPHIE (qv), a sophisticated instructional environment for electronic troubleshooting, reasoned about a trainee's solution for debugging an electronic circuit and decided whether a student's actions were appropriate given previous information about the circuit's behavior (Burton and Brown, 1982). The system used a simulated electrical circuit to test student hypotheses, typically conjectures about the cause of a malfunction, and refused to carry out probes that were irrelevant based on existing information. SOPHIE was a landmark effort in the development of domain representations. It innovated the use of semantic grammars to parse student input and used multiple representations to help explain results to the student (Brown and Bell, 1982). Syntactically meaningful categories, such as resistors, transistors, and measurements, were associated with grammar rules to parse the student's input. It answered hypothetical questions about circuit values, generated explanations about possible faults in the circuit, and used rules to solve electrical problems.

Early systems also focused on grain size or the way the world is divided up by the knowledge representation scheme. Grain size is often measured along an epistemological continuum beginning with bits and pieces and ending with chunked elements. At the bits-and-pieces extreme, distinct and unconnected elements are used to represent elements in the subject area, as in WHY (Stevens and co-workers, 1982), whereas at the chunked extreme, relations and morphisms between elements indicate temporal, logical, or pedagogic connections between the elements. GUIDON (qv) (Clancey, 1982) used a chunked representation to express connectedness and logical precedence of elements used to reason about medical diagnosis.

GUIDON (Clancey, 1979) is a tutor for medical students directed at teaching the process of diagnosis of infectious diseases. An early bits-and-pieces approach failed and a later implementation, based on chunked knowledge, succeeded. MYCIN (qv), a large medical expert system used to diagnose and prescribe remedies for infectious disease, was the basis for the original GUIDON. MYCIN has thousands of small rules for diagnosing diseases and was adequate for a performance system; it worked to achieve a diagnosis. However, it did not work as the basis for a learning—teaching system because students need to know the underlying deep and causal knowledge (from which the bits-and-pieces rules are compiled). Deeper causal knowledge is an example of the chunked elements mentioned above. MYCIN's rules were stripped of causal reasoning and cross-links needed by a student to cluster and learn the same rules. GUIDON was originally implemented by reversing the rules of MYCIN. Such a method was not effective because medical diagnosis is not taught cookbook style and medical practitioners do not use perfect recall on a huge number of medical facts and rules (Clancey and Letsinger, 1981). To teach from such rules, GUIDON had to decompile and cross-index the stripped-down rules to provide students with the needed generalizations and references between the rules.

GUIDON did not communicate rules *per se;* rather, it presented explicit reasoning strategies described in terms of managing the student's set of hypotheses during problem solving. Thus a student might be asked to justify why an active hypothesis was pursued or might be told to continue a specific line of reasoning. The shift in GUIDON's knowledge base was prompted by epistemological considerations, or the need to separate strategic tutoring knowledge from facts and rules. The strategic knowledge was expressed in terms of tasks that manipulated the space of hypotheses.

Broadening Interests (1982–1985)

During the next phase of AI in education, knowledge bases were broadened in scope, allowing systems to be applied to real problems. Gradually ideas about tutoring were shown to be powerful enough to handle practical teaching problems, for example, tutors in Pascal programming (Johnson and Soloway, 1984). Researchers began building systems in part as experiments to answer truly difficult questions about cognitive processes and learning, for example, the LISP and geometry tutor (Anderson and Reiser, 1986; Anderson and co-workers, 1985).

PROUST was designed to aid students in understanding nonsyntactic bugs in their programs (Johnson and Soloway, 1984). It modeled the presumed intentions of the programmer and tried to match an agenda of goals and

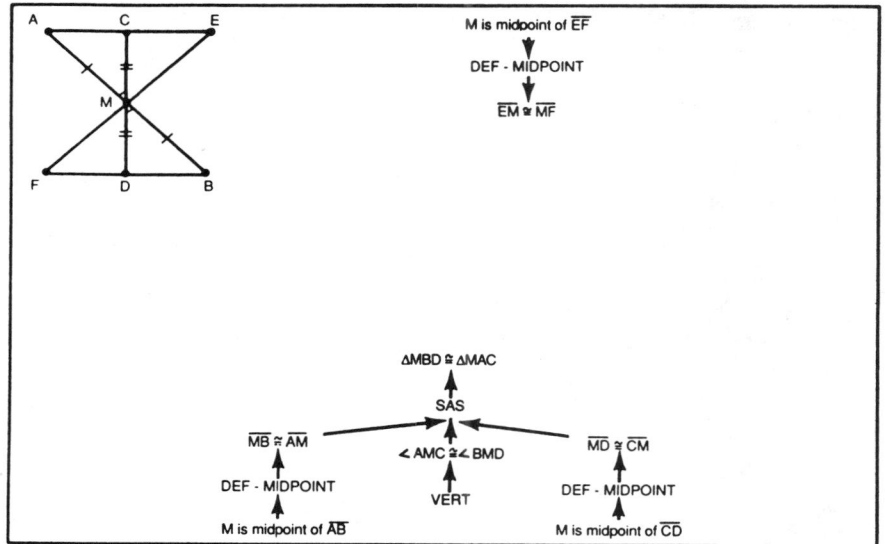

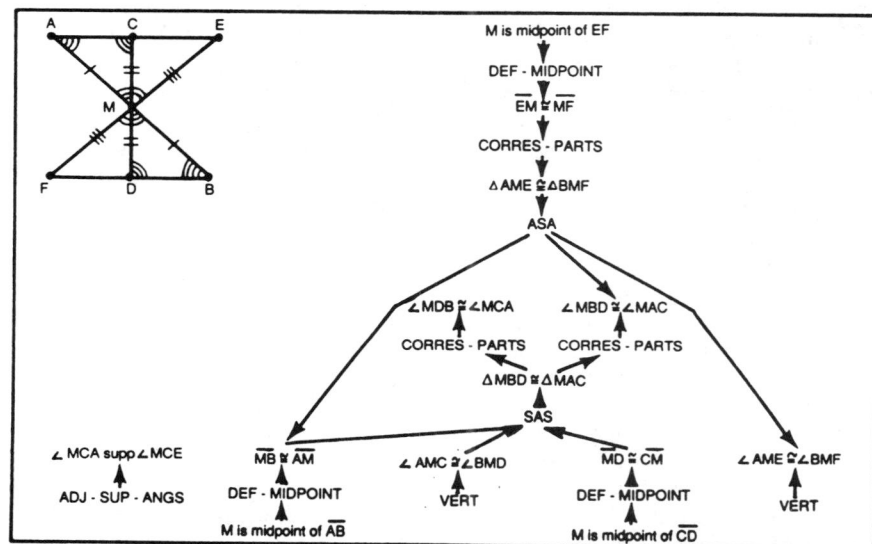

Figure 1. Geometry Tutor (Anderson and co-workers, 1985). Courtesy of IJCAI.

plans and then code which the student intended to use with the actual code produced. PROUST successfully discovered 81% of the bugs in 206 student programs. However, some students found PROUST's explanations difficult to use, suggesting the need for improved tutoring discourse.

Adaptive control of thought (ACT) theory, a well-specified cognitive model of learning, was used to develop geometry and LISP tutors (Anderson and Reiser, 1986; Anderson and co-workers, 1985). These tutors demonstrated that research in cognitive psychology can produce useful insights for building tutoring systems. The theory states, in part, that cognitive functions can be represented as sets of production rules. In this context the system used model tracing to clarify student misconceptions and to redirect the problem-solving effort by setting new goals. It provided immediate feedback on errors and intervened as soon as a meaningful error was detected. However, recent

work suggests that immediate feedback competes for working memory resources (Schooler and Anderson 1990). Moreover, delayed feedback appears to foster the development of secondary skills such as error detection and self-correction, skills necessary for successful performance once feedback has been withdrawn. Thus Anderson was led to refine his cognitive model and to modify his tutoring systems. This hypothesize–test–evaluate cycle enabled him to demonstrate improvement both in the cognitive theory and the building of intelligent tutors.

Several tutors built at this time also illustrated the importance of the communication model. The Geometry Tutor (Anderson and co-workers, 1985) made explicit use of several learning characteristics in geometry (Fig. 1) and enabled students to visualize features of problem solving that are typically left implicit in textbooks, including graphic effects on a geometric figure; the tree-structured nature of geometric proof; and movement between two possible problem-solving strategies, forward and backward reasoning. Geometric reasoning is often not a simple linear logical chain, but rather a bushy tree, including many possible, and frequently not optimal, logical paths. By using the interface to click on relevant proof elements, students may work from the goal backward or from the premises forward. These alternative paths are clearly articulated in the Geometry Tutor's communication model.

A Variety of Application Areas (1985–1991)

The next phase of tutor development indicated a clear emergence of new architectures and positive training results, leading to the belief that some progress has been made. Interest focused on communication and representation issues and on knowledge of the student. Systems were placed in elementary and high schools, universities, industrial sites, and military training sites.

Several systems focused on developing sophisticated interfaces that allowed a student to generate and test hypotheses. For instance, the Smithtown Economics Tutor (Shute and Bonar, 1986; Bonar and co-workers, 1986) provided students with scientific inquiry tools that enabled them to collect, organize, and reason about data in the domain of economics. These tools, for example, allowed students to explicitly state laws such as that of supply and demand. After setting population and income values, the price of tea and coffee, and the number of outlets or changes in the product quantity, the student made predictions about changes in economic variables such as supply and demand. Smithtown was implemented using a bite-size tutoring architecture (Bonar and co-workers, 1986), which organized the system around issues, called bites. Each bite was a miniature system containing some domain knowledge, curriculum knowledge, and indications about the student's mastery of the bite. Thus the old functional components, such as diagnostic or expert modules, were still present, but distributed across the representation of the curriculum.

During this time, several intelligent tutors were developed to teach algebra, in part by displaying a student's solution on the trace window (McArthur and co-workers, 1987; Foss, 1987; McArthur and Stasz, 1990). In the algebra tutor shown in Figure 2 (McArthur and Stasz, 1990), the system acted as a partner and encouraged the student to think about problem solutions at a high level, eg, using operators such as "collect the variables," "simplify the expression," and "multiply both sides by?" The system could invoke different tutoring styles and perform simple lesson planning or task sequencing. Students could easily change their own operations. This system provided a view of algebra that was intuitive, motivational, and helpful to the student. The tree representation of algebra solutions augmented a student's own abilities in the domain.

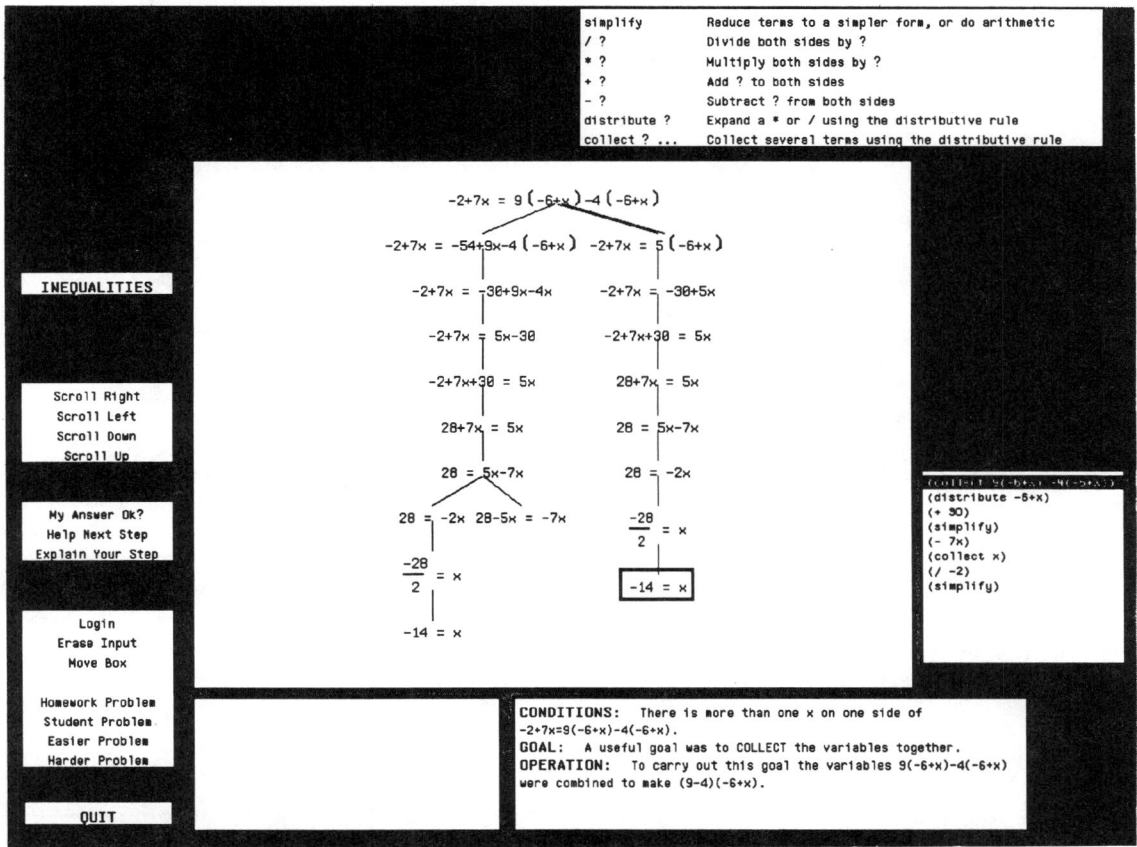

Figure 2. Algebra tutor interface (McArthur and Stasz, 1990).

STEAMER also provided a sophisticated interface (Hollan and co-workers, 1984) and supported students' development of an accurate mental model of a steam propulsion plant and related engineering principles (Fig. 3). STEAMER provided movable and sensitive icons, which students could insert into a simulation of the working steam propulsion plant. In this way, students could measure the effect of their actions and, for instance, see the change in water pressure after adding a pump or a toggle switch. Various screen indicators were linked to an underlying quantitative model and updated as the simulation proceeded. The view presented by STEAMER was meant to reflect more a mental model (as used by an expert) than an exact physical model of the steam propulsion plant.

An electronics troubleshooting program (White and Frederikson, 1986) also focused on supporting development of students' mental models. Like STEAMER, it contained an interactive graphic simulation that represented internal knowledge about an electronic circuit, in this case as a progression of increasingly complex qualitative models presented to students as they moved on to more complex topics. The authors recognized that true expertise does not consist of a simple progression of increasingly complex models, rather it requires sets of complementary models that vary along a set of dimensions, such as type, order, and degree (of sophistication).

The Intelligent Maintenance Tutoring System (IMTS) and its successor RAPIDS, provide a set of tools for constructing simulation-based tutoring environments (Towne and co-workers, 1990). Object and scene editors, such as that shown in Figure 4, allow an author to use graphics of generic objects, including switches, pumps, motors, lamps, and toggle switches to capture both the appearance and the behavior of the objects used in problem-solving environments. Authors enter rules to express the relationship between input and output values of an object and indicate the appearance (eg, light on, switch up) that objects should display under different conditions. Numerous simulations have been built using these systems; the largest contains more than 300 objects and represents the electrical, hydraulic, and mechanical process of the folding of a helicopter's blades. This system was used to train students to troubleshoot components of the blades; it determined which problem the student should solve next, kept track of how much time was taken to solve each problem, and maintained a model of the student's presumed learning.

Another simulation-based tutor is currently in use in more than 100 industrial sites in the United States. The Recovery Boiler Tutor (RBT) was built for a type of boiler found in paper mills throughout the United States (Woolf and co-workers, 1986). It provided multiple explanations and tutoring facilities geared to the individual user, an operator in a control room. The tutor was based on a mathematically accurate formulation of the boiler and provided an interactive simulation complete with help, hints, explanations, and tutoring (Fig. 5). A user initiated any of 20 training situations or emergencies, or asked that an emergency or inefficient situation be chosen by the system. Once a situation had been initiated, the operator was encouraged to adjust meters and perform any of 40 actions on the simulated boiler to solve the emergency. The system identified optimal, less than optimal, and clearly irrelevant actions.

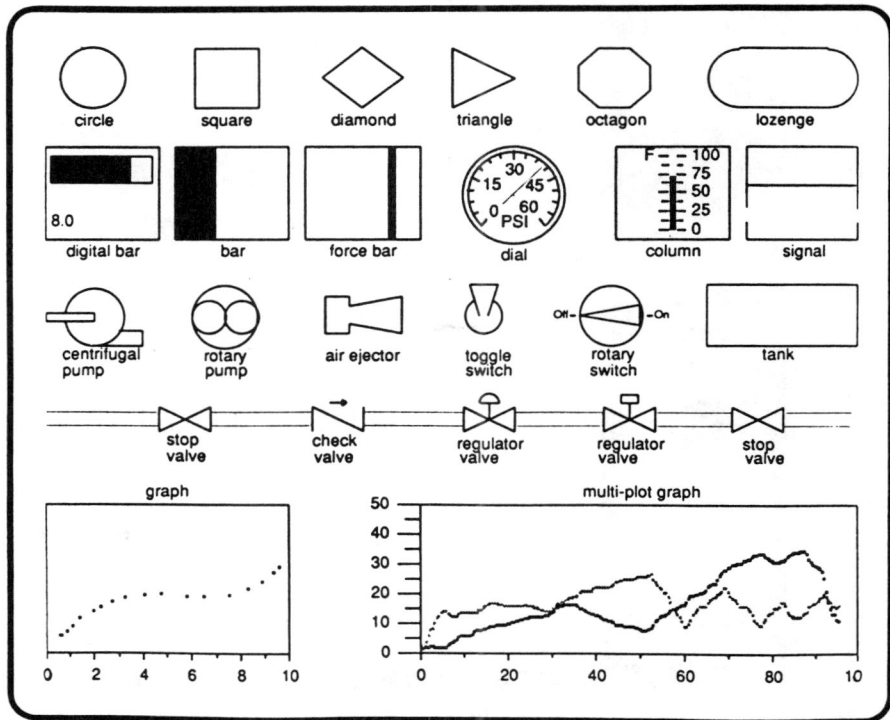

Figure 3. STEAMER icons (Hollan and co-workers, 1984). Courtesy of the American Association for Artificial Intelligence.

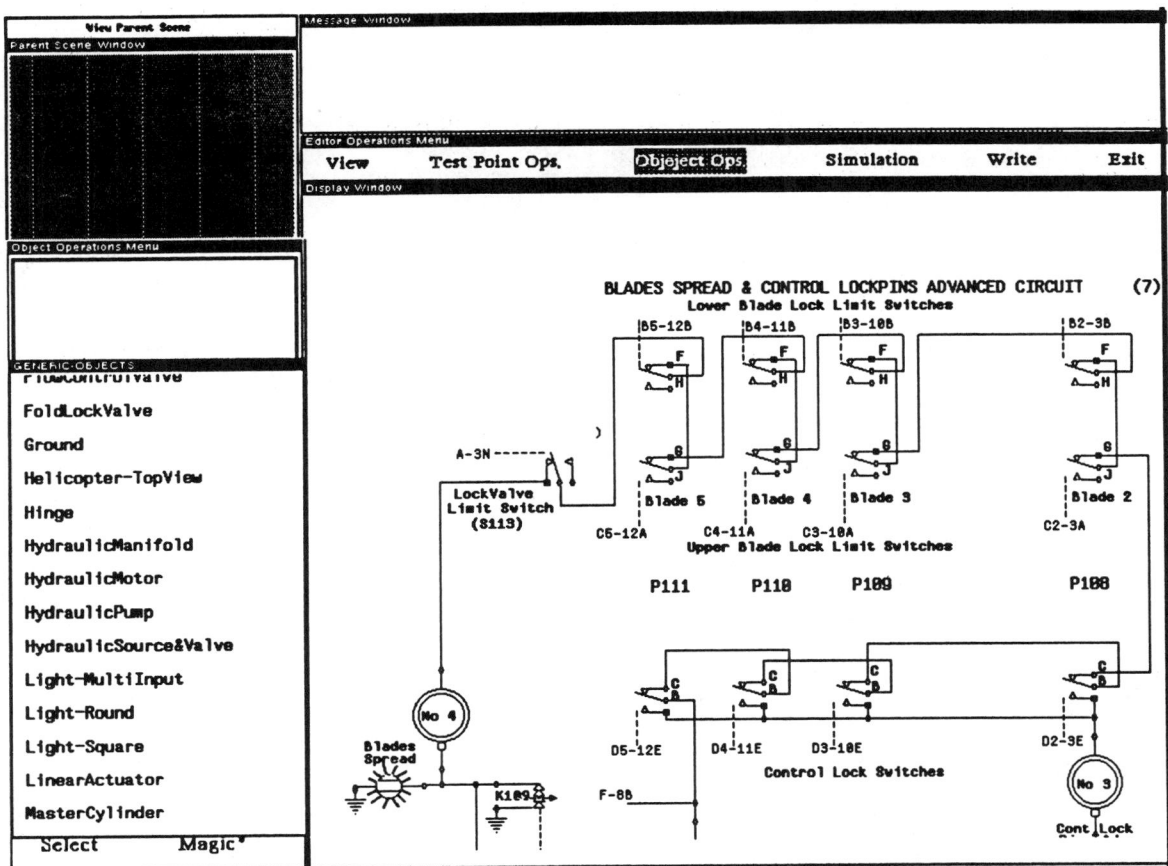

Figure 4. Using IMTS to edit simulation scenes (Towne and Munro, 1989). Courtesy of Allen Munro/IOS.

Evaluation

Until rather recently, intelligent instructional systems, like other AI systems, tended to be too computationally complex and memory intensive to be evaluated properly. Having been built on high performance, even special-purpose LISP machines, they were not available to traditional training and teaching sites. Now that personal computers with LISP environments have continued to improve in their price–performance ratios, instructional systems can be tested in traditional centers and evaluated by testing the goodness of the teaching result compared with standard lecture-style teaching. Formal evaluations of performance have resulted in several systems achieving the two-sigma effect (Bloom, 1984), which is the same

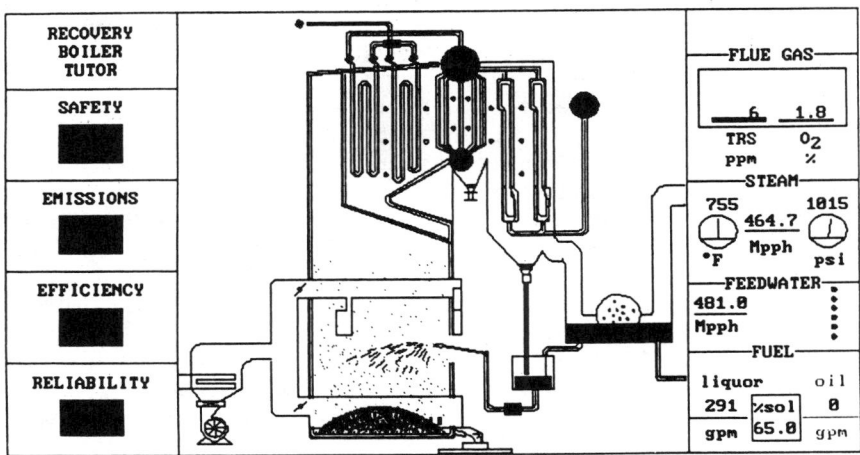

Figure 5. Sectional view of the recovery boiler (Woolf and co-workers, 1986). Courtesy of Ablex Publishing Corp.

improvement in learning that results from one-on-one human tutoring compared to classroom teaching. Several success stories indicate that tutors are effectively reducing by one-third to one-half the time required for learning (Shute, 1990).

In one special case, students working with an Air Force electronics troubleshooting tutor for only 20 hours gained proficiency equivalent to that of trainees with 40 months (almost four years) of on-the-job experience (Lesgold and co-workers, 1990). In another example, students using the LISP tutor at Carnegie-Mellon University (Anderson and co-workers, 1985; Anderson and Reiser, 1986) completed programming exercises in 30% less time than those receiving traditional classroom instruction and scored 43% higher on the final exam. In a third study, students using Smithtown learned general scientific inquiry skills and principles of basic economics in one-half the time required by students in a classroom setting (Shute and co-workers, 1989).

Although limited but encouraging results have been shown, the fact remains that classroom tests do not provide a measure of success for these systems, because often the material presented is not the same as that taught in a traditional classroom, and a system's content cannot easily be integrated into a traditional curriculum. For instance, both the Geometry and Algebra Tutors discussed earlier automate much of the symbol manipulation (eg, addition and multiplication) in the domain and provide an environment for students to learn problem solving. The systems have, in part, redefined the curriculum content to focus on problem solving, and this makes evaluation of learning outcomes difficult because the original classroom focused on symbol manipulation.

Several aspects of evaluation remain major research issues. For example, if a system succeeds, which models should be assigned the credit and how might the various models be fine-tuned to improve the next generation of systems? Portability between domains has been shown in only a few systems (Bonar and co-workers, 1986; Anderson, 1990); most systems are less effective when rebuilt in another domain, and generalizability has yet to be demonstrated.

RESEARCH ISSUES

Current research issues focus on traditional AI themes, ie, knowledge representation and acquisition, control, planning and plan recognition, natural language generation and recognition, explanation, dialogue processing, and architectures. Ideally, cognitive and pedagogical theories should form the basis of design for new systems to test new AI technology, and when built, new systems should be used to test the theory. The crucial activity is iteration based on improved performance, which allows results from one iteration to inform and constrain development of the next: working tutors should foster refinement and evaluation of AI and cognitive theories and vice versa. There is nothing so practical as a good theory. However, too little theory currently guides development of new systems.

Cognitive Modeling

Cognitive modeling (qv) is one research area that can make rich contributions to progress in this field. It should be applied at three stages of design within knowledge-based instructional systems: (1) development of pedagogical and subject matter theories, (2) design of instruction, and (3) delivery of instruction (Woolf and co-workers, 1991). Of these phases, the design of instruction is the one that seems to have achieved the most direct benefit from cognitive modeling thus far, including substantial benefits from modeling subject matter experts. For instance, Anderson and co-workers (1990) attributed much of the success of their tutors to the cognitive task analysis of experts in LISP, geometry, and algebra.

Work on modeling good teachers and tutors has only just begun [with the exception of a few early classics, such as the work of Stevens and Collins on Socratic tutoring (1977)]. Of the three phases of pedagogical work, the actual delivery of instruction is the area where cognitive modeling has thus far found the least fruitful application, mostly due to a historical accident. Working with classroom teachers and trainers seems to be a neglected activity during research and development of these systems.

Communication Modeling

Developing systems that are sensitive to student idiosyncrasies and able to customize their responses to teaching context is still a much-sought goal. Achieving flexible mixed dialogue between human and machine, whether text-based or visually based, is not yet possible. On the other hand, human–human dialogue succeeds despite ambiguity and digressions because both participants model the dialogue, the subject matter, and the other speaker; both actively work toward success of the dialogue. This suggests that continuing efforts be made to enhance the machine's ability to do its part to model the user and dialogue context. Techniques such as plan recognition and learning in active systems still play only a small role in current technology. Building responsive intelligent interfaces requires building mechanisms to support cooperative dialogue and a deeper understanding of domain perspectives from the viewpoint of the learner.

Research issues in communication models include identifying new representations and control mechanisms. Thus knowledge of didactic explanation might be represented and organized along with the basic domain knowledge. Indexing mechanisms for accessing different perspectives of a topic should be designed using abstractions appropriate for the content selection task.

Choosing and organizing domain knowledge for the communication effort provides the next set of research issues. Control should account for the tutor's ability to switch strategies dynamically according to multiple constraints and in a manner that is sensitive to features that human tutors use in tutorial interactions. Further work is required here to characterize relevance for selecting knowledge for didactic explanation, especially when multiple perspectives of the topic are available.

Other research issues center on development of an adequate model of the student and the pedagogical context, and then recognizing how a system might stimulate the student's own abilities and creativity. A separate issue concerns how relevant knowledge should be presented once it has been selected. Presentations, whether explanations or examples, should be delivered in a manner that helps the student understand new material and integrate it into an existing conceptual framework, or into one that has been built up during the preceding dialogue. In summary, despite much work attempting to do so, human–machine communication is not yet sensitive to dialogue context and to what is known or knowable about the student's knowledge state.

DESIGN AND IMPLEMENTATION ISSUES

Although some success has been seen, one might ask why more systems have not been deployed. The answer is that deep design and implementation issues remain, beginning with the lack of AI development tools, eg, shells and frameworks, similar to those used to build expert systems. Tools would facilitate large-scale development; a simple tool, such as a simulation tied to an expert system or to a lock-step tutor, might be a practical way for designers to get started on a path of incremental design through feedback from the expert and student. A teacher should interact with a variety of tools, in much the same way that a conductor orchestrates a suite of instruments. Another reason for slow development is the need to reduce cognitive task analysis to engineering practice. An excessive amount of time is still required to analyze each task to the depth required for building these systems. In addition, more information is needed about student motivation and cognitive development, specifically which activities engage particular students and how novice behavior is distinquished from expert behavior (Larkin and co-workers, 1980; Chi and co-workers, 1981).

The use of new knowledge representations should result in greater expressive power than that offered by first-generation expert system tools. For instance, qualitative simulations might be used to represent domain knowledge (Forbus, 1986; de Kleer and Brown, 1986), as when programming is seen as a space of problem-solving plans selected and executed by a student (Johnson and Soloway, 1984). Qualitative physics might be used to reason about stored stereotypical plans to explain a complex physical device; these plans might then be selected and reformulated for presentation to the student.

Social issues provide the final set of barriers to producing generalizable and pervasive systems. As a result of educational changes mandated by the industrial revolution, traditional didactic, classroom-based teaching has become a strong cultural fixture in many parts of the world. Current classroom environments have grown progressively lecture based. Although one-on-one tutoring is in fact very old (Plato, 1922), its reintroduction through this technology represents a radical change for modern educators and is strongly resisted. Intelligent instructional systems present a new tradition of one-on-one tutoring that is largely inquiry driven in nature. Because educational change works very slowly, new systems will require curricula and infrastructure changes before they can be established within education and industry.

DISCUSSION

Although much success has been evidenced, clearly much remains to be done to support the effective use of AI technology in education. Current research has succeeded in exploring a large number of domains and has explored some nontraditional pedagogical strategies, such as partnering, mentoring, and scaffolding. However, many of the rich and detailed tutoring methods used by talented teachers still elude researchers, and the next generation of systems will require development of accessible shells and testbeds to facilitate further experimentation and development. For some modeling tasks, notably those representing students and tutors, work is far from complete and issues have only just been identified.

Several predictions can be made about future development of intelligent teaching systems based on near-term goals and long-term opportunities. As the computer price–performance ratio continues to improve, a wide expansion of tutoring systems will continue to be seen in new teaching and training arenas. New initiatives incorporated within these systems, such as qualitative reasoning, machine learning, case-based reasoning, general-purpose architectures (eg, blackboards), hypertext (Yankelovich and co-workers, 1985), and multimedia (eg, AI systems that include videodisk, speech, or film) will further enhance the effectiveness of these systems. Such technologies should facilitate the study of human learning and teaching as well as accelerate the emergence of new systems and the willingness of new authors to develop them.

BIBLIOGRAPHY

J. Alperson and D. O'Neil, "The Boxscore; Tutorials 2, Simulations 0," *Academ. Comput.* **18**, 46–49 (Feb. 1990).

J. Anderson, "Tuning of Search of the Problem Space for Geometry Proofs," in *Proceedings of the Seventh IJCAI*, Vancouver, B.C., Morgan-Kaufmann, San Mateo, Calif., 1981.

J. Anderson, "Analysis of Student Performance with the LISP Tutor," in N. Frederickson and co-workers, eds., *Diagnostic Monitoring of Skill and Knowledge Acquisition*, Lawrence Erlbaum, Hillsdale, N.J., 1990.

J. Anderson and B. Reiser, "The LISP Tutor," *Byte* **10**, 159–175 (1986).

J. Anderson, C. F. Boyle, A. T. Corbett, and M. W. Lewis, "Cognitive Modeling and Intelligent Tutoring," *Artif. Intell.* **42**, 7–50 (1990).

J. Anderson, C. Boyle and G. Yost, "The Geometry Tutor," in *Proceedings of the Ninth IJCAI*, Los Angeles, Morgan-Kaufmann, San Mateo, Calif., 1985.

B. S. Bloom, "The 2-Sigma Problem: The Search for Methods of Group Instruction as Effective as One-to-One Tutoring," *Educ. Res.* **13**, 4–16 (1984).

J. Bonar, R. Cunningham, and J. Schultz, "An Object-Oriented Architecture for Intelligent Tutoring," in *Proceedings of the ACM Conference on Object-Oriented Programming Systems, Language and Applications*, ACM, New York, 1986.

J. S. Brown and A. Bell, "SOPHIE: A Sophisticated Instructional Environment for Teaching Electronic Troubleshooting (An Example of A.I. in C.A.I.)," in Sleeman and Brown, 1982.

R. Burton, "The Environment Module of Intelligent Tutoring Systems," in M. Polson and J. J. Richardson, eds., *Foundations of Intelligent Tutoring Systems,* Lawrence Erlbaum, Hillsdale, N.J., 1988.

R. Burton and J. S. Brown, "An Investigation of Computer Coaching for Informal Learning Activities" in Sleeman and Brown, 1982.

J. R. Carbonell, *Mixed-Initiative Man-Computer Instructional Dialogs,* Technical Report 1971, Bolt Beranek and Newman, Cambridge, Mass., June 1970.

M. Chi, P. Feltovich, and R. Glaser, "Categorization and Representation of Physics Problems by Experts and Novices," *Cogn. Sci.* **5,** 121–152 (1981).

W. Clancey, "Case Management for Rule-Based Tutorials," in *Proceedings of the Sixth IJCAI,* Tokyo, Morgan-Kaufmann, San Mateo, Calif., 1979.

W. Clancey, "Tutoring Rules for Guiding a Case Method Dialog," in Sleeman and Brown, 1982.

W. Clancey and R. Letsinger, "Neomycin: Reconfiguring a Rule-based Expert System for Application to Teaching," in *Proceedings of the Seventh IJCAI,* Vancouver, B.C., Morgan-Kaufmann, San Mateo, Calif., 1981, pp. 829–835.

J. de Kleer and J. S. Brown, "A Physics Based on Confluence," in D. C. Bobrow, ed., *Qualitative Reasoning about Physical Systems,* MIT Press, Cambridge, Mass., 1986.

K. Forbus, "Qualitative Process Theory," in D. C. Bobrow, ed., *Qualitative Reasoning about Physical Systems,* MIT Press, Cambridge, Mass., 1986.

C. L. Foss, *Learning from Errors in ALGEBRALAND,* Technical Report IRL-87-0003, Institute for Research on Learning, Palo Alto, Calif., 1987.

J. Hollan, E. Hutchins, and L. Weitzman, "STEAMER: An Interactive Inspectable Simulation-Based Training System," *AI Mag.* **5**(2), 15–27 (Summer 1984).

L. Johnson and E. M. Soloway, "Intention-Based Diagnosis of Programming Errors," in *Proceedings of the Fourth National Conference on Artificial Intelligence,* Austin, Tex., AAAI, Menlo Park, Calif., 1984, pp. 369–380.

J. Larkin, J. McDermott, D. Simon, and H. Simon, "Expert and Novice Performance in Solving Physics Problems," *Science* **208,** 1335–1342 (1980).

A. Lesgold, "Toward a Theory of Curriculum for Use in Designing Instructional Systems," in H. Mandl and A. Lesgold, eds., *Learning Issues for Intelligent Tutoring Systems,* Springer-Verlag, New York, 1988.

A. Lesgold, S. P. Laijoie, M. Bunzo, and G. Eggan, "A Coached Practice Environment for an Electronics Troubleshooting Job," in J. Larkin, R. Chabay, and C. Shefic, eds., *Computer Assisted Instruction and Intelligent Tutoring Systems: Establishing Communication and Collaboration,* Lawrence Erlbaum, Hillsdale, N.J., 1990.

D. McArthur and C. Stasz, *An Intelligent Tutor for Basic Algebra,* R-3811-NSF, RAND Corp., Santa Monica, Calif., 1990.

D. McArthur, C. Stasz, and J. Y. Hotta, "Learning Problem-Solving Skills in Algebra," *J. Educ. Technol. Sys.* **15**(3), 303–325 (1987).

Plato, *Laches, Protagora, Meno, and Euthydemus,* W. R. M. Lamb, trans., Harvard Press, Cambridge, Mass., 1922.

M. Richer and W. J. Clancey, "GUIDON-WATCH: A Graphic Interface for Viewing a Knowledge-Based System," *IEEE Comput. Graphics Applicat.* **5,** 51–64 (1985).

L. Schooler and J. Anderson, "The Disruptive Potential of Immediate Feedback," in *Proceedings of the Twelfth Annual Conference of the Cognitive Science Society,* Lawrence Erlbaum, Hillsdale, N.J., 1990.

V. Shute, "Rose Garden Promises of Intelligent Tutoring Systems: Blossom or Thorn?" paper presented at the *Space Operations, Applications and Research (SOAR) Symposium,* 1990.

V. Shute and J. Bonar, "Intelligent Tutoring Systems for Scientific Inquiry," in *Proceedings of the Cognitive Science Society,* Lawrence Erlbaum, Hillsdale, N.J., 1986.

V. J. Shute, R. Glaser, and K. Raghavan, "Inference and Discovery in an Exploratory Laboratory," in P. L. Ackerman, R. J. Sternberg, and R. Glaser, eds., *Learning and Individual Differences,* W. H. Freeman, New York, 1989, pp. 279–326.

D. Sleeman and J. S. Brown, eds., *Intelligent Tutoring Systems,* Academic Press, Inc., New York, 1982.

A. Stevens and A. Collins, "The Goal Structure of a Socratic Tutor," in *Proceedings of the Association for Computing Machinery Annual Conference,* 1977.

A. Stevens, A. Collins, and S. Goldin, "Misconceptions in Students' Understanding," in Sleeman and Brown, 1982, pp. 13–24.

D. Towne and A. Munro, "Artificial Intelligence in Training Diagnostic Skills" in D. Bierman, J. Breuker, and J. Sandberg, eds., *Proceedings of the Fourth International Conference on Artificial Instruction and Education,* IOS, Amsterdam, 1989.

D. Towne, A. Munro, Q. Pizzini, D. Surmon, L. Coller, and J. Wogulis, "Model-Building Tools for Simulation-Based Training," *Interactive Learning Environments* **1,** 33–50 (1990).

E. Wenger, *Artificial Intelligence and Tutoring Systems: Computational and Cognitive Approaches to the Communication of Knowledge,* Morgan-Kaufmann, San Mateo, Calif., 1987.

B. White and J. Frederiksen, "Intelligent Tutoring Systems Based upon Qualitative Model Evolutions," in *Proceedings of the Fifth National Conference on Artificial Intelligence,* Philadelphia, Pa., AAAI, Menlo Park, Calif., 1986.

B. Woolf, D. Blegen, J. Jansen, and A. Verloop, "Teaching a Complex Industrial Process," in *Proceedings of the Fifth National Conference on Artificial Intelligence,* Philadelphia, Pa., AAAI, Menlo Park, Calif., 1986.

B. Woolf, E. Soloway, W. J. Clancey, K. VanLehn and D. Suthers, "Knowledge-Based Environments for Teaching and Learning," *AI Mag.* **11**(5), 74–77 (1991).

N. Yankelovich, M. Meyrowitz, and A. vanDam, "Reading and Writing the Electronic Book," *IEEE Comput.* **20**(9), 15–30 (1985).

BEVERLY PARK WOOLF
University of Massachusetts

ELI

A natural language understanding system, developed at Yale in 1975 by Riesbeck for the SAM (qv) project, that translates English sentences into conceptual dependency (qv) representations, using primarily semantic rather than syntactic information. ELI predicts likely conceptual combinations in order to resolve ambiguities as in "John paid the check with a check." (See C. K. Riesbeck and R. C. Schank, "Comprehension by Computer: Expectation-Based Analysis of Sentences in Context," in W. J. M. Levelt and G. B. Flores d'Arcais, eds., *Studies in the Per-*

ception of Language, Wiley, Chichester, U.K., 1976; R. C. Schank and R. Abelson, *Scripts, Plans, Goals, and Understanding*, Lawrence Erlbaum, Hillsdale, N.J., 1977.)

CHRISTOPHER K. RIESBECK
Northwestern University

ELIZA

A program that mimics a "Rogerian" psychotherapist, uses almost no memory and no "understanding" of inputs, and creates answers by combining phrases that are stored under certain keywords with transformations of input sentences [see J. Weizenbaum, "ELIZA—A Computer Program for the Study of Natural Language Communication between Man and Machine," *CACM* 9(1), 36–45 (Jan. 1966)]. Information about the domain of discourse is isolated in a "script." By supplying new scripts (qv), an improved version of ELIZA has been adapted successfully to other domains [see J. Weizenbaum "Contextual Understanding by Computers," *CACM* 10(8), 474–480 (Aug. 1967); S. C. Shapiro and S. C. Kwasny, "Interactive Consulting via Natural Language," *CACM* 18(8), 459–462 (Aug. 1975)].

J. GELLER
New Jersey Institute of
Technology

ELLIPSIS

ELLIPSIS AND SUBSTITUTION

Ellipsis is leaving something unsaid, which will, nevertheless, be understood by the listener. It relies on the intelligence of the listener to fill in what is missing, thus allowing more information to be conveyed in fewer symbols. As such, ellipsis is a form of anaphora. Ellipsis differs from other forms of anaphora in that the primary clues as to what is missing through ellipsis are to be found in the structure of the sentence.

1. Balser was looking for one big mean black bear.
2. He found two.

In the second sentence *two* is understood as *two big mean black bears*. Part of the noun phrase has been omitted, which the listener is expected to fill in. The elliptical construction is not only briefer but it focuses attention on the difference between the two noun phrases: only the contrast is explicitly mentioned.

Ellipsis is a special case of substitution. In both cases a phrase is replaced by a substitute. A phrase may be replaced by a substitute word such as *one*. This is often called one-anaphora. In the case of ellipsis the phrase is replaced by nothing at all.

3. Balser was expecting to find a fluffy baby bear.
4. He found a nasty full-grown one.

In the fourth sentence *one* substitutes for the omitted *bear,* drawing a contrast between a fluffy baby bear and a nasty full-grown bear. In the fourth sentence *bear* is being repeated (through substitution), whereas *a fluffy baby* is replaced by *a nasty full grown*.

Ellipsis is often revealed as an incomplete structure. For example, in sentence two the head of the noun phrase has been omitted, leaving an incomplete noun phrase structure. In sentence four the same thing has happened, but the substitute word *one* has been inserted. In sentence six below,

5. Balser crawled into the cave and what do you suppose he found?
6. Two cuddly baby bears.

the fragment *two cuddly baby bears* is a structurally complete noun phrase, but the sentence structure to which it attaches has been left unsaid ("He found two cuddly baby bears"). Both of these forms of structural ellipsis can be found together as in sentence eight.

7. How many baby bears did Balser find in the cave?
8. Two.

Two is a fragment of a noun phrase ("two baby bears"), which is assumed to be attached to a sentence ("Balser found two baby bears").

UNDERSTANDING SENTENCES CONTAINING ELLIPSIS

The fragments omitted through ellipsis and substitution can usually be recovered by an analysis of meaning constraints, an analysis of sentence structure of previous sentences to locate the most probable candidate phrases, and an analysis of structure to identify what is being repeated and what is being replaced. A nonsense example helps illustrate the process.

9. Are there three brown gleeps with four glumps?
10. No, seven.

When an elliptical phrase is found, such as *seven* in sentence ten, the context must be examined to determine "seven what?"—the unknown has the meaning constraint that it is countable. Sentence nine has two countable candidates: gleeps and glumps. Most readers will choose "seven brown gleeps with four glumps" over "three brown gleeps with seven glumps" because the structure of sentence nine puts greater emphasis on gleeps (it is said to be in sharper focus). Having identified the candidate phrase as "three brown gleeps with four glumps," the structure of the original phrase and the elliptical phrase are compared to determine how much of the original phrase was intended to be carried into the elliptical phrase. Did the speaker intend seven brown gleeps with four glumps or seven gleeps (possibly some other color) with four glumps or seven gleeps (with unknown numbers of glumps). Because the contrast is on the number of gleeps, it is assumed that all the attributes that follow the number should be assumed to be the same. Hence, the expanded phrase is "seven brown gleeps with four glumps."

CONTRIBUTIONS OF ELLIPSIS TO CONTEXT

One of the effects of ellipsis is to bind sentences together into a context. When one sentence relies on those around it and on the situation described by the context, it is clearer that the sentences contribute to a coherent whole.

Other forms of anaphora, such as repeated reference (eg, pronouns and definite noun phrases), have a similar effect of binding sentences together into a coherent context. Repeated reference differs from ellipsis, however, in that the purpose of repeated reference is to refer again to a concept that already exists in the context. The purpose of ellipsis is to provide emphasis and contrast between one concept and another.

BIBLIOGRAPHY

General References

M. A. K. Halladay and R. Hasan, *Cohesion in English*, Longman, London, 1976.
G. Hirst, *Anaphora in Natural Language Understanding/A Survey*, Springer-Verlag, New York, 1981.
H. Tennant, *Natural Language Processing/An Introduction to an Emerging Technology*, Petrocelli Books, Princeton, N.J., 1980.
B. L. Webber, *A Formal Approach to Discourse Anaphora*, a part of the series *Outstanding Dissertations in Linguistics*, Garland Publishing, New York, 1979.

H. Tennant
Texas Instruments

EMOTION MODELING

It is probably as futile to ask whether machines can have emotions as it is to ask whether they can think or be conscious; these are philosophical rather than scientific questions. Consequently, for most AI researchers the goal of emotion modeling is not to produce in machines emotions as feelings but to model emotions from a functional point of view; that is, to model them as reactions to interpretations of perceived situations. This task is usually motivated by one or more of three considerations. The first of these is the theory-testing consideration: emotion modeling is a powerful way of testing theories about emotions. The second is a naive psychology consideration: beliefs (even erroneous ones) about the antecedents and consequences of emotions are frequently used in trying to understand, explain, and predict the behavior of others. Finally, there is a process-control consideration: emotions play an important role in the control of cognition, attention, and action.

THEORY TESTING

The first serious attempt to model emotion in computer programs was undertaken by Colby and co-workers in the 1960s and culminated a landmark paper (Colby and co-workers, 1971; Colby, 1981). Colby had two goals: to test a psychological theory of paranoia by modeling excessive fear and anger and to examine paranoia from the point of view of a structured belief system. Central to this enterprise was the view that because of the complexity and dynamic nature of higher mental processes a theory of such processes is best represented as a computer program. The program is then regarded as the theory, or at least, as an embodiment of it, and the theory can be tested by, for example, comparing its behavior with the behavior of people given similar inputs.

Colby's program PARRY accepted English-like input and responded as a patient in a psychiatric interview by attempting to construe inputs as directly or indirectly indicative of malevolence. If malevolence was detected, one or more of three affective responses, fear, anger, or mistrust, were triggered, depending on the nature of the construed malevolence. Physical malevolence induced fear and psychological malevolence anger, and the induction of either also induced mistrust. The linguistic output was designed to offset the construed malevolence either through counterattack or withdrawal. In all cases, the nature of the construals and the responses were determined by the constantly updated values of a number of key variables, including those for fear, anger, and mistrust.

Another example of the theory-testing approach is Pfeifer's system FEELER, which was motivated by a number of psychological questions, including What is an emotion? What is the relation between cognition, evaluation (of the current environment relative to goals), and the physiological–arousal aspect of emotions? What are the relationships between the emotions? What causes emotions to arise? What are the cognitive effects of emotions? What is the relationship between emotions and goal-directed activity? And, finally, how are the components of emotions represented? Pfeifer started from the general position that there are three kinds of emotions: those that depend on discrepancies between planned and actual states (interruption), those that depend on completed plans, and those that depend on other factors, such as memory (Pfeifer and Nicholas, 1985). He considered interruptions to be the psychological events that cause physiological changes, an account advocated most strongly in psychology by Mandler (1964). Pfeifer identified surprise and goal importance as the primary determinants of the extent to which interruptions cause an increase in arousal.

FEELER is implemented as a production system in which the quality of the emotion is determined by which rules fire and the intensity of the emotion is a function of the immediately prior level of arousal and the degree to which the specific emotion in question can have its intensity influenced by that arousal level. FEELER simulates attempts to execute plans that get interrupted. For example, FEELER might have the goal of attending a meeting in another city. Included in the input might be a specification of a goal-blocking event (a plan interruption), for example, the taxi to the airport getting a flat tire, causing the traveler to miss the flight. The output would be a description of the emotional, cognitive, and behavioral consequences of the interruption. In addition, the long-term memory of the system would be changed by adding a connection from a node for the generated emotion(s), say anger, to a representation of the unexpected undesirable event. An interesting aspect of FEELER is the way in which it deals with the time course of an emotion, an issue that few emotion theorists have addressed. As well as incorporating a built-in decay function for each emotion, FEELER also allows emotions to be sustained through either additional production rules of the form "if emotion X then emotion Y," or through the activation of emotions in memory as a result of inferences.

NAIVE PSYCHOLOGY

To understand and reason about a world populated with agents who have emotions, and to understand natural language that describes the activities of such agents, it is necessary to build knowledge representations that capture a naive psychology (see PHYSICS, NAIVE; REASONING, COMMONSENSE). Emotion modeling work that has been motivated by this representation issue has generally focused on the domain of natural language understanding (qv), especially story understanding. In stories things happen to characters that cause them to have emotions and these in turn can influence what the characters do. The emotional reactions of the characters are sometimes explicitly stated and sometimes only implicit. In either case, the comprehender needs an implicit theory of emotions, part of a theory of naive psychology. For example, if it is learned that John was furious at Mary, this emotional information would allow the anticipation or comprehension of certain likely subsequent actions, such as John's failure to return a telephone message left by Mary. Dyer (1983) approached these issues by working backward from explicitly stated emotions to make inferences about the characters, their goals, their interrelationships, and likely subsequent actions. Central to his enterprise was the notion that emotional reactions on the part of a character in a story convey information about that character's goals and perceptions of the events that occur, and the intensity of such reactions indicates how important the goal was to the character. Thus, for example, it is not plausible that a character would be furious over an event that was truly only of minimal importance to him, or that he would be only mildly irritated when high level goals were thwarted. To make appropriate inferences about such relationships requires that an implicit theory about emotions and how they are embedded in motivational and social life be made explicit. For example, consider the following passage from a story used by Dyer: "as Richard was driving to the restaurant, he barely avoided hitting an old man on the street. He felt extremely upset by the incident, and had three drinks at the restaurant." To understand this passage requires the application of knowledge about the motivational aspects of emotions. People prefer not to be extremely upset, and when they find themselves in such a state, they are likely to try to do something to get out of it, such as sitting down to rest, going off by themselves, or having a drink. Dyer incorporated these ideas in BORIS, a program developed to read

and answer questions about narratives. To use affective information, emotions are laid out for BORIS with respect to six basic components, indicating in each case whether the emotional state mentioned is positive or negative, which character is feeling the emotion, and the relevant goal situation. In some cases additional information is added, such as toward which character the emotion is directed (for example, in the case of anger or guilt), the intensity of the emotion (less than or greater than normal), and whether the event giving rise to the emotion was expected or not. More elaborate proposals for representing knowledge about a wide range of emotions have subsequently been made by Ortony and co-workers (1988) and Roseman (1984).

PROCESS CONTROL

Speculations about the function of emotions both from a psychological perspective and an AI perspective have led many researchers to conclude that emotions play a crucial role in the control of attention and behavior in an unpredictable and constantly changing world. Much of the thinking along these lines has been theoretical in nature and is exemplified in a seminal paper by Simon (1967), many of the ideas of which have been further developed and elaborated by Sloman and Croucher (1981). In essence, the view is that intelligent agents are usually pursuing multiple goals simultaneously, with other goals that are not being actively pursued lying dormant but capable of becoming active when the organism notices an aspect of the environment that, perhaps unexpectedly, affords the opportunity to achieve them (Birnbaum and Collins, 1984). According to this view, as in the case of FEELER, emotions arise when some ongoing process is interrupted (Mandler, 1964) to attend to some other aspect of the internal or external environment.

In spite of the obvious intuitive appeal of these ideas, they have not yet been exploited in AI programs in any significant way. However, the in principle practicality of this approach has been demonstrated in a system developed by Frijda and Swagerman (1987). Their system ACRES allows the user to engage in a (somewhat stilted) conversation on the topic of emotions (although neither the topic nor the quality of the natural language interface are crucial). What matters to ACRES is that the user does not violate any of its concerns, of which there are four, each of different importance. ACRES is set up in such a way that it (1) likes errorless input and dislikes errors (ie, typing mistakes and other unrecognizable character strings), (2) it likes the user to respond quickly and dislikes delays in input, (3) it likes varied inputs and dislikes repetitions, and (4) it does not want the user to issue the kill command (which disables the program). It evaluates user inputs in terms of their relevance to these concerns and then chooses some course of action that it deems appropriate to the situation. These actions are designed either to influence the user's behavior through commands, requests, or appeals or to constrain what the user can do by ignoring or delaying responses to user initiatives or by disabling certain user options. The particular action that ACRES takes is determined by constantly changing the control precedence accorded to currently active goals and plans as a function of the importance of the concerns that are implicated. Thus ACRES, although rudimentary, does demonstrate the feasibility of having (simple) emotional states arise from the satisfaction of and threats to important concerns and of having such states influence attention and action.

BIBLIOGRAPHY

L. Birnbaum and G. Collins, "Opportunistic Planning and Freudian Slips," *Proceedings of the Sixth Annual Conference of the Cognitive Science Society*, Boulder, Colo., 1984, pp. 124–127.

K. M. Colby, "Modeling a Paranoid Mind," *Behav. Brain Sci.* **4**, 515–560 (1981).

K. M. Colby, S. Weber, and F. D. Hilf, "Artificial Paranoia," *Artif. Intell.* **2**, 1–25 (1971).

M. G. Dyer, *In Depth Understanding*, MIT Press, Cambridge, Mass., 1983.

N. H. Frijda and J. Swagerman, "Can Computers Feel? Theory and Design of an Emotional System," *Cognition & Emotion* **1**, 235–257 (1987).

G. Mandler, "The Interruption of Behavior," in D. Levine, ed., *Nebraska Symposium on Motivation*, Nebraska University Press, Lincoln, 1964, pp. 163–219.

A. Ortony, G. L. Clore, and A. Collins, *The Cognitive Structure of Emotions*, Cambridge University Press, New York, 1988.

R. Pfeifer and D. W. Nicholas, "Toward Computational Models of Emotion," in L. Steels and J. A. Campbell, eds., *Progress in Artificial Intelligence*, Ellis Horwood, Chichester, UK, 1985, pp. 184–192.

I. Roseman, "Cognitive Determinants of Emotions: A Structural Theory," in P. Shaver, ed., *Review of Personality and Social Psychology: Vol. 5. Emotions, Relationships, and Health*, Sage, Beverly Hills, 1984, pp. 11–36.

H. A. Simon, "Motivational and Emotional Controls of Cognition," *Psych. Rev.* **74**, 29–39 (1967).

A. Sloman and M. Croucher, "Why Robots Will Have Emotions," *Proceedings of the Seventh IJCAI*, Vancouver, B.C., Morgan-Kaufmann, San Mateo, Calif., 1981, pp. 197–202.

ANDREW ORTONY
Northwestern University

EMYCIN

A nonspecific system for constructing rule-based expert consultation programs, EMYCIN was written in 1979 by van Melle at the Stanford Heuristic Programming Project. EMYCIN is abstracted from the domain-independent part of MYCIN (qv) and has been used to build several other expert systems in different problem domains (see W. J. van Melle, *System Aids in Constructing Consultation Programs*, UMI Research Press, Ann Arbor, Mich., 1980).

M. R. TAIE
AT&T Bell Laboratories

END EFFECTORS. See ROBOT HANDS AND END EFFECTORS.

ENGINEERING AUTOMATION. See COMPUTER SYSTEMS; DESIGN, AI IN.

ENGINEERING, KNOWLEDGE-BASED EXPERT SYSTEMS IN

Advances in computer hardware and software engineering methodologies in the 1960s and 1970s led to an increased use of computers by engineers. This use has been limited almost exclusively to algorithmic solutions such as finite-element methods and circuit simulators. However, many engineering problems are not amenable to purely algorithmic solutions: "The engineering method is the use of heuristics to cause the best change in a poorly understood situation within the available resources" (Koen, 1985). To deal with these ill-structured problems, an engineer relies on judgment and experience. Because knowledge-based expert systems (KBESs) provide a programming methodology for solving such ill-structured engineering problems, they are of increasing interest to the engineering community; KBESs also provide a flexible software development methodology, by separating the knowledge base from the control strategy.

RANGE OF APPLICATIONS

Engineering a product involves several stages (Fig. 1). The first stage involves a market survey for potential products. This is followed by the conceptualization stage, when a product is conceived either as a result of a need or a potential profit motive (determined at the market survey stage). In the research and development stage, the information needed for the design of the product is developed. Design involves configuring the product based on several constraints. The manufacturing process yields the actual product. The product is then tested for quality in the testing stage and marketed in the marketing stage. The maintenance of the product is a service provided by most organizations. The above process is iterative, for example, several problems may arise while manufacturing and the product may have to be redesigned.

The kinds of problems that are encountered in the above engineering cycle can be laid out along the derivation–formation spectrum (Amarel, 1978). How a KBES should be constructed to best address one of these problems depends on where the problem lies on the spectrum. In derivation problems, the problem conditions are posed

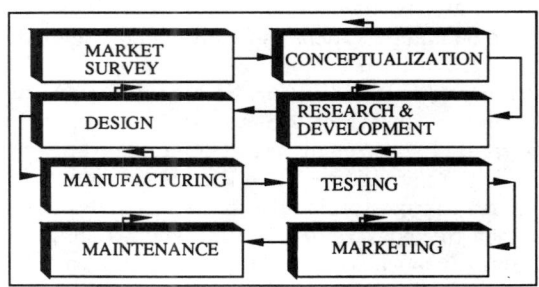

Figure 1. Engineering a product. Bent arrows indicate that the process is iterative.

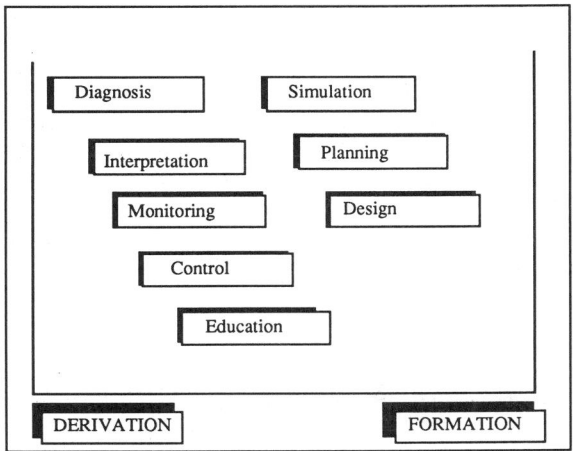

Figure 2. The derivation–formation spectrum of problem types.

as parts of a solution description; the possible outcomes exist in the knowledge base of a KBES. Essentially, the solution to these problems involves the identification of the solution path. In formation (or synthesis) problems, problem conditions are given in the form of properties that a solution must satisfy as a whole; an exact solution does not (normally) exist in the knowledge base, but the inference mechanism can generate the solution by utilizing knowledge in the knowledge base. Most real-life problems fall between these two categories.

Engineers normally encounter the following types of problem at the derivation end of the spectrum (Hayes-Roth and co-workers, 1983) (Fig. 2):

1. *Diagnosis.* The problem areas or faults are identified based on potentially noisy data; the diagnostician must be able to relate the symptoms to the appropriate fault(s). The task may involve reasoning based on incomplete and inexact data, faulty sensors, and causal interpretation of the system. Diagnosis is usually followed by repair, where a set of actions to rectify the faults in a system is determined.

2. *Interpretation.* The given data are analyzed to determine their meaning. The data are often either unreliable or erroneous or extraneous; hence, the system should be able to eliminate candidates based on incomplete information.

3. *Monitoring.* Signals are continuously interpreted and alarms set whenever required.

4. *Control.* Signals or data are interpreted and the system is regulated, based on derivations from expected response.

5. *Education.* The student's response to various problems is used to identify deficiencies in problem-solving knowledge. Based on these shortcomings, appropriate actions are recommended.

6. *Simulation.* A model of the system is created and the outputs for a set of inputs are observed.

Problems encountered at the formation end of the spectrum are

1. *Planning.* A program of actions is set up to achieve certain goals. The course of actions should be set up such that excessive resources are not expended and constraints are not violated.

2. *Design.* Systems or objects that satisfy particular requirements are configured. This type of problem involves satisfying constraints from a variety of sources; large design problems are usually solved by dividing the problems into a number of subtasks and the designer must be able to handle the interactions between those subtasks properly.

PROBLEM-SOLVING TECHNIQUES

The problem-solving techniques needed for engineering should deal with (1) goals and data, (2) multiple levels of abstraction, (3) assumptions and justifications, (4) inexactness of knowledge and data, (5) time, (6) multiple levels of abstraction and multiple knowledge sources (KSs), (7) spatial reasoning (see REASONING, SPATIAL), (8) qualitative reasoning, and (9) case-based reasoning (qv). Some of these techniques are discussed below.

Goals and Data

Forward chaining, backward chaining, theorem proving (qv), and GPS (qv) strategies deal with data and goals. Forward chaining works from data to goals, whereas backward chaining works from goals to data. Theorem proving involves two principles: unification and resolution by refutation principles. The unification principle is used to match variables in predicate formulas. Resolution by refutation tries to prove that a hypothesis is true by first negating the hypothesis and then showing that the negation of this hypothesis cannot be true. General problem solver (GPS) is a combination of the means–ends analysis and the operator subgoaling problem-solving tactics. In means–ends analysis the difference between the current state and the goal state is determined. This difference is used to find an operator most relevant to reducing the difference. In operator subgoaling, if the operator is not directly applicable to the current situation then the problem state is changed by setting up subgoals (or goals) so that the operator can be applied.

Multiple Levels of Abstraction

Hierarchical refinement involves solving problems at various levels of abstraction. The implementation of the hierarchical refinement strategy is known as hierarchical planning for planning problems and top-down refinement for design problems. The generate-and-test strategy involves generation and testing of all solutions. Heuristic-increment-generate-test reduces the combinatorial explosion by early pruning of inconsistent solution paths. In chronological backtracking, if no solution is found along the current solution path then the system backtracks to other nodes at the same level as the starting node that failed.

Assumptions and Contradictions

Backtracking (qv) without considering the reasons for failure may lead to combinatorial explosions. In dependency-directed backtracking a record of all deduced facts, their antecedent facts along with their support justifications and the relevant rules are maintained; these records are known as dependency records. When the problem solver comes to a dead end, it retrieves the antecedents of the contradiction. Those facts that give rise to the contradiction are removed from further consideration. The DDB technique was used to develop the truth maintenance system (TMS). TMS can be used by other reasoning programs to maintain consistency of statements generated by the reasoning programs.

Interactions between various nodes (spaces) in a solution tree can be handled by the constraint handling technique(s). Constraint posting, which is one of the several variations of the constraint handling techniques, involves a three-step process: constraint formulation, constraint propagation (qv), and constraint satisfaction (qv).

Inexact Knowledge and Data

Uncertainty in engineering problem solving stems from the following sources: (1) the data are erroneous, (2) the knowledge is not exact, and (3) an appropriate model is not used. The Dempster-Shafer theory of evidence, Bayesian, and certainty approaches are useful when the engineering hypotheses are conditionally independent. However, for some problems this criterion may not be true and the fuzzy approach seems appropriate. The above techniques use numerical confidence intervals. One problem with approach is the difficulty of assigning numerical values for uncertainty. Furthermore, the same expert may have different confidence factors for the same rule at different times. The use of reasoned assumptions, developed by Doyle (1983), and the method of endorsements, developed by Cohen and Grinsberg (1983), seem appropriate in such situations.

Time

Reasoning in real time involves three main issues: (1) performing a task within a specified time (time-constrained reasoning), (2) focusing on the right aspects of the problem (focus of attention), and (3) dealing with temporal constraints (temporal reasoning) (see REASONING, TEMPORAL). Problem-solving methods used for time-constrained reasoning are priority scheduling, progressing deepening, variable precision logic, real-time A*, and decision analytic techniques. The blackboard model of resource allocation is one method for dealing with the focus of attention problem. Allen's interval reasoning mechanisms address some issues involved with temporal constraints. A detailed survey of these problem-solving techniques has been published (Laffey, 1988).

Multiple Abstraction Levels and Multiple KSs

The blackboard model of problem solving can be used to deal with multiple levels of problem decomposition and multiple knowledge sources. It uses two basic strategies: (1) divide and conquer and (2) opportunistic problem solving. The divide-and-conquer strategy is realized by decomposing the working memory (or the context), which is

called a blackboard, into several levels depicting the problem-solution decomposition, whereas opportunistic problem solving is achieved by focusing on the parts of the problem that seem promising.

From the derivation–formation spectrum point of view, forward chaining and backward chaining are useful for the derivation-type problems and the hierarchical refinement and the consistency maintenance techniques (TMS and constraint handling) are essential for formation-type problems.

TOOLS

The spectrum of programming languages spans from assembly language, where the programmer has to specify *how* to perform a certain task in detail, to shells, where the programmer specifies *what* to do (Fig. 3). Current AI programming languages can be grouped into the following categories.

1. *General Purpose Programming Languages.* AI projects are usually implemented in high level languages. These high level languages need some novel features, such as facilities for experimentation with large chunks of knowledge, tentative modifications, planning, and reasoning strategies. In addition, these languages need powerful abstraction mechanisms with which other higher level constructs can be built so as to make programming flexible and easy. Current expert system frameworks have been built using a number of languages, of which LISP (qv) and PROLOG (PROLOG can also be classified under the next category) seem popular among AI researchers. Bobrow (1974) discussed some of the languages used in AI research.

2. *Single-Knowledge Representation Languages.* Knowledge representation languages are programming languages developed specifically for AI. These languages are not restricted to implementing any particular problem type, but facilitate the implementation of a wide range of problems. Depending on the kind of representational formalisms used, these languages can be classified into rule-based, frame-based, network-based, and logic-based. In rule-based languages, knowledge is encoded in the form of if–then rules. A frame-based representation allows a more structured data representation, where the basic data element is the frame. A frame has a name and a number of attributes (slots). When these frames are linked through some relations then a combination of frame and network based systems is achieved. Logic-based systems are founded on the theory of first-order predicate calculus. Some knowledge representation-based languages are OPS5 (qv) (Rule-based), Smalltalk-80 and C++ (object oriented), and PROLOG (logic based).

3. *Hybrid Languages.* Hybrid (integrated) languages combine different programming paradigms in one framework. In addition, some of these tools provide a rich user interface. Due to the flexibility offered, these languages are memory intensive and some of them require up to 16 megabytes of core memory on most engineering workstations, such as SUN. Examples of public domain tools are

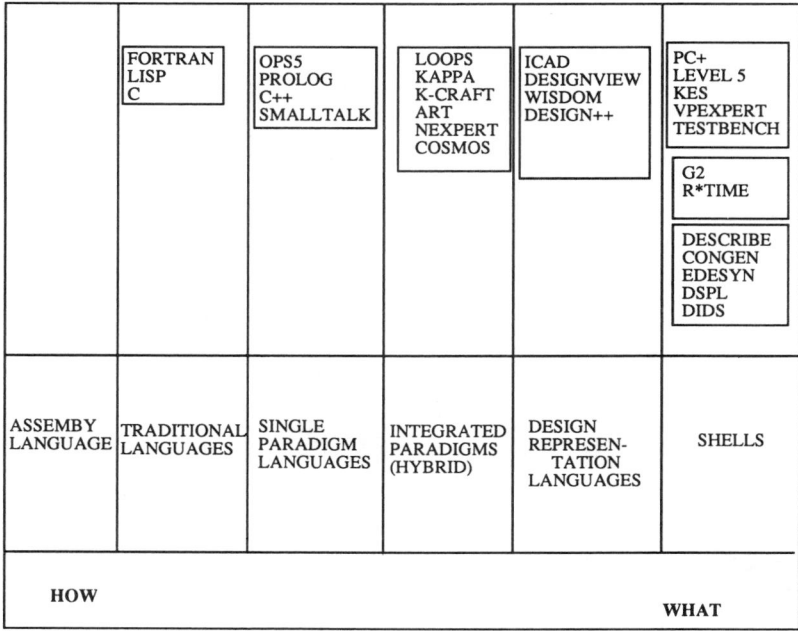

Figure 3. Tool spectrum.

COSMOS (implemented in C++ and available from MIT) and Parmenedis–Frulekit (implemented in Common LISP and available from CMU). Examples of some commercial tools are ART, KnowledgeCraft, KEE, KAPPA, and NEXPERT.

4. *Domain-Independent Expert System Frameworks (Shells).* A domain-independent expert system framework (also called a shell) provides the system builder with an inference mechanism with specific problem-solving techniques, from which a number of applications can be built by adding domain-specific knowledge. Such systems also provide knowledge acquisition and explanation modules to simplify the construction of the expert systems. Normally these frameworks are an outcome of domain-specific KBESs. Hence, their control strategies are restricted to those provided in the original system. However, in the recent past the distinction between shells and hybrid languages has become blurred, because many shells are offering multiple programming paradigms. Systems under this category for derivation-type problems include Personal Consultant Plus, RuleMaster, LEVEL-5, VP-EXPERT, and KES. Shells geared toward real-time control applications are G2 and R*TIME. Except for a few design representation languages (such as ICAD, DE-SIGN++, and CONCEPT MODELER), commercial tools that implement problem-solving techniques for formation-type problems are yet to be seen in the market. However, several shells are available from academia. Examples of these are EDESYN (CMU), CONGEN (MIT), EVEXED (Rutgers), DSPL (WPI), and DIDS (University of Michigan).

Figure 4 shoes the derivation–formation spectrum, the how–what tool spectrum, and the problem-solving strategies in three-dimensional space. The black circle depicts how an application maps into various planes in this space.

APPLICATIONS

Representative KBES are reviewed according to their location in the derivation–formation spectrum. An annotated bibliography for several hundred KBES is available (Sriram, in press).

Diagnosis–Classification

GTE's Central Office Maintenance Printout Analysis and Suggestion System (COMPASS) is a KBES that aids in the maintenance of a telephone-switching system. It analyzes maintenance printouts of telephone company central office switching equipment and suggests maintenance actions to be performed. The results from several field trails indicate that COMPASS performs well in identifying system faults and in suggesting corresponding actions. COMPASS is implemented in KEE on a LISP machine.

Kajima Corporation in Japan hs developed a tunnel entrance diagnosis KBES, which takes as input the following information: (1) recorded disasters; (2) weather; (3) topography of the site; (4) geological classification and structure; (5) plant growth and ground water conditions; (6) main features of the tunnel; and (7) measured data for site foundations and predicts the most likely problems that can occur at tunnel entrance sections. The system is implemented in the ES/KERNEL/W tool and has excellent user interfaces. In addition, the KBES is also well integrated into Kajima's information network.

Monitoring and Control

PROP monitors cycle water pollution of a thermal power plant in Italy. It was implemented in FranzLISP on a Sun workstation and utilizes a combination of production rules and event graphs (or causal graphs) for the diagnosis and

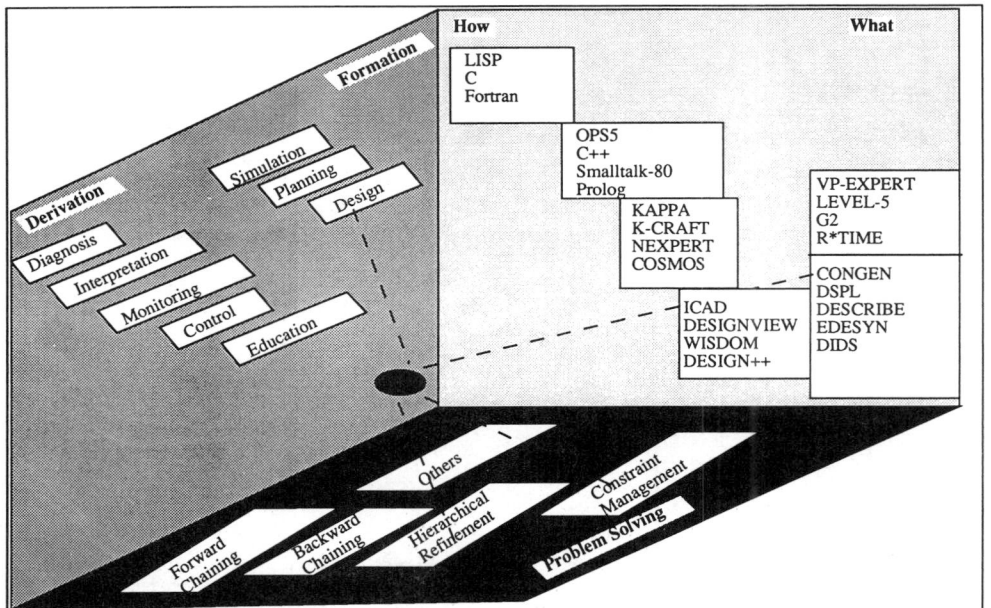

Figure 4. Three-dimensional space for problems, tools, and problem-solving techniques.

the monitoring of the thermal plant. Fuzzy ATO Controller, which is a fuzzy logic-based automatic train operation system, is being used to control trains at the Sendai Municipal Subway System in Japan.

The MIP Expert System was developed by the IIC (Knowledge Engineering Institute at Madrid), a customer partnership between IBM, the Autonomous University of Madrid, and several prominent Spanish companies. MIP, implemented on an IBM-PC running OS/2 using the TIERS expert system building tool, has been designed to monitor a petrochemical plant in real time, giving advice and warnings related to the stability and optimization of the process. MIPS consists of several knowledge-based and numerical simulation programs, which are controlled by an object-oriented blackboard. The system has been in continuous use since March 1991 in a plant of INH-Repsol, a partner in the IIC and the biggest Spanish Oil and Gas company.

EPAK, developed using Gensym's G2, provides supervisory control in a paper mill run by Norke Skog AS of Norway. The system assesses paper quality, recommends control actions, and utilizes simulation to predict effects of recommended actions. EPAK incorporates three types of knowledge: assessment knowledge, which classifies the paper quality as high, low, or OK; correction knowledge, which recommends the control actions; and process knowledge, which predicts the impact of manipulated variable changes on the product quality.

Education

THEVENIN is an intelligent computer aided instruction tool for teaching Thevenin equivalents, a bottleneck in electrical engineering education. The tutor system, based on the blackboard architecture, is robust in that many components of the present system can be used in other subjects in electrical engineering or even in disciplines other than electrical engineering. For example, circuit analysis can be used for any other electrical engineering subject; the mathematical part, the framework for tutoring style, and the problem generation and student modeling can be used in computer based tutors in a variety of domains. The current version with an average response time of about 15 seconds is currently being tested for acceptability.

Planning

Ship Planning System (SPS) schedules contain ship discharging and loading operations at the Singapore Port, which is one of the busiest ports in the world. SPS uses hierarchical refinement and constraint propagation problem solving strategies to generate the schedules (or plans). SPS also comes with a nice user interface. SPS is implemented in Flavors, an object-oriented extension to LISP, and Objective C. SPS was put into operation in early 1989. The system reduces the time for container loading and unloading operations by nearly 50%.

SCHEPLAN, currently in use at Nippon Kokan Co., Ltd. (Japan), schedules the various tasks involved in steel making. The problem involves the satisfaction of constraints from several sources, eg, idle time requirements for machines, conflicts among products, etc. SCHEPLAN generates several candidate schedules using hierarchical decomposition and merging of subtasks. The user modifies and evaluates these schedules through interactive refinement. POPSYS, which is an extended PROLOG, was utilized in the implementation of SCHEPLAN.

Design

R1, now called XCON (qv) is one of the few KBES being used in the industry. It is developed in OPS5 and configures the VAX line of computers for DEC. The knowledge base consists of the component information (ie, the voltage, frequency, and support devices for each component) and heuristic constraint knowledge (which is used to assemble components into partial configurations and those partial configurations into functionally acceptable systems). There are approximately 5000 components in the knowledge base and about 800 constraint rules. As an example of the constraint rule, consider the placement of a UNIBUS module. A backplane is needed to place the module. Backplanes come in two sizes: four slots and nine slots. Depending on the size of the module, the four-slot or nine-slot backplane may be chosen. However, choosing either one of these may depend on the size of the box that the backplane will be placed in. Other constraints may be posed by the placement of the modules. R1 does not use any basic search strategy in its configuration task. It uses a recognition-based control, which involves recognizing or expecting possible alternatives based on the current state (of the context). R1 (XCON) is very successful at the task of computer configuration. However, it presumes that the components for the configuration task are available. This task is performed by XSEL, which assists sales personnel in selecting the appropriate hardware and software components.

Alloy design is characterized by creativity, intuition, and conceptual reasoning. ALADIN is a knowledge-based system, developed as a cooperative venture between Carnegie Mellon University and ALCOA, U.S.A., that aids in designing aluminum alloys for aerospace applications. The system can be operated in several modes. As a decision-support system, it accepts alloy property targets as input and suggests alloying additives, processing methods, or microstructural features to meet the targets. As a design assistant, it can evaluate designs supplied by a metallurgist, or provide information that is useful for design from a knowledge bank. As a knowledge bank, it provides information to supplement the usual sources such as books, journals, databases, and specialized consultants. The domain of ALADIN requires expertise to be developed in the areas of alloy properties, chemical compositions, metallurgical microstructure, and thermomechanical (fabrication) processes. ALADIN works by taking in a description of the properties of a desired alloy and then searching to construct plausible candidate alloys to meet those properties. The output is a ranked list of candidates, along with predictions of their properties. Alloy candidates are specified by giving their chemical composition and the sequence of processes (including temperatures, timings, and other parameters) to be performed during their fabrication. ALADIN also produces a description of the expected microstructure of each alloy, which can be of use in analyzing an alloy, but does not have a direct impact on how the alloy is specified or produced.

CONCLUSION

KBES provide solutions to the ill-structured problems encountered by engineers. This approach allows the engineer to solve problems previously regarded as intractable.

KBES also facilitate the retention of in-house expertise. Although, these systems offer solutions to a wide range of engineering (and other) problems, it is important to study the feasibility of these systems before embarking into a major developmental effort. So far these systems have been successful in derivation-type problems and considerable research is being undertaken to solve formation-type problems. Furthermore, a close coupling of databases and algorithmic programs to knowledge bases is essential for many engineering problems. The importance of integrating KBES with conventional programming techniques is reflected in the following remarks (Sacerdoti, 1989).

> When the Pharoah's fishermen along the Nile River hauled their nets onto land and sweated under the noonday sun, they wanted the sun to hurry along its course. Though they probably weren't aware of it, the best scientific minds of the time were agreeing with the farmers' view of the world, one that put the earth in the center of the universe, with the sun, planets, and stars revolving around it.
>
> Thousands of years later, when North Sea fishermen hauled their nets onto land, they, too, wished for the sun to hurry. But the scientific view had changed: Nicholaus Copernicus' theory that the sun is the center of the universe, though not wholly correct, radically changed the way both scientists and fishermen saw themselves in the universe. No longer was earth center of all things.
>
> In a similar way, early developers of artificial intelligence (AI) systems and tools worked, for very good reasons, as though AI were at the center of the computing universe. Today, whether we work together over our nets by LAN or C, we benefit from a different perspective—that AI technology is only a fraction of an AI system, and that at the center of any solution is a large body of conventional programming.

There are a number of implications for KBES in education. As a part of hypermedia applications, these systems can be used as training aids, thus reducing the cost of many training programs. This would also help students organize and formalize their thought processes.

BIBLIOGRAPHY

S. Amarel, "Basic Themes and Problems in Current AI Research," in V. B. Ceilsielske, ed., *Proceedings of the Fourth Annual AIM Workshop*, Rutgers, N.J., 1978, pp. 38–46.

D. Bobrow, "New Programming Languages for AI Research," *Comput. Surv.* **6**(3), 153–174 (1974).

P. Cohen and M. R. Grinberg, "A Theory of Heuristic Reasoning About Uncertainty," *AI Mag.* **4**(2), 17–24 (Summer 1983).

J. Doyle, "Methodological Simplicity in Expert System Construction: The Case of Judgements and Reasoned Assumptions," *AI Mag.* **4**(2), 39–43 (Summer 1983).

F. Hayes-Roth, D. Waterman, and D. Lenat, eds., *Building Expert Systems*, Addison-Wesley Publishing Co., Inc., Reading, Mass., 1983.

B. V. Koen, "Toward a Definition of the Engineering Method," *The Bent*, 28–33 (Spring 1985).

T. J. Laffey, P. A. Cox, J. Schmidt, S. M. Kao, and J. Y. Read, "Real-Time Knowledge-Based Systems," *AI Mag.*, 27–45 (Spring 1988).

E. Sacerdoti, "The Copernician View of Artificial Intelligence," *SUN Technol.*, 46–53 (Winter 1989).

D. Sriram, *Computer-Aided Engineering: The Knowledge Frontier,* in press.

General References

R. Coyne, M. Rosenman, A. Radford, M. Balachandran, and J. Gero, *Knowledge-Based Design Systems,* Addison-Wesley Publishing Co., Inc., Reading, Mass., 1990.

C. Dym and R. Levitt, *Knowledge-Based Expert Systems for Engineering,* McGraw-Hill Book Company, Inc., New York, 1991.

M. Rychener, *Expert Systems for Engineering Design,* Academic Press, Inc., Orlando, Fla., 1988.

C. Tong and D. Sriram, *Artificial Intelligence in Engineering Design,* Academic Press, Orlando, Fla., 1991.

D. SRIRAM
MIT

EPAM

A program that simulates human learning of nonsense syllables by building a discrimination net (see LANGUAGE ACQUISITION), EPAM shows effects also observable with human subjects, namely oscillation, retroactive inhibition, and forgetting without information loss [see E. A. Feigenbaum, "The Simulation of Verbal Learning Behavior," in E. A. Feigenbaum and J. Feldmann, eds., *Computers and Thought,* McGraw-Hill, New York, pp. 297–309, 1963; E. A. Feigenbaum and H. A. Simon, "EPAM-Like Models of Recognition and Learning," *Cogn. Sci.* **8**(4), 305–336 (1984)].

J. GELLER
New Jersey Institute of
Technology

EPISODIC MEMORY

Memory is a mental phenomenon, but it is usually conceptualized from what is, broadly speaking, an artificial intelligence perspective. Thus the objective of virtually all contemporary memory theorizing is to devise a system, or model, that will simulate selected aspects of memory-based behavior. The model may take the form of a computer program that can actually produce simulations, but more often it is merely a schematic or verbal description of some critical component of the system.

Episodic memory is usually contrasted with knowledge, or semantic memory. The distinction, which was brought to the fore by Tulving (1972, 1983), takes a variety of forms but is perhaps most readily appreciated in a phenomenological way: episodic memory refers to the recollection of a particular event and is characterized by a definite awareness that the event was personally experienced, whereas an item of knowledge is usually more abstract in the sense that it is brought to mind with no recollection of the event or events from which it was derived.

Most theorists are uncomfortable about such a key distinction being made in phenomenological terms, and

somewhat less subjective criteria have been proposed. According to some of the more prominent of these, episodic memory (1) is of an event rather than a fact, (2) is temporary rather than permanent, (3) is related to other contents of mind in a temporal rather than a conceptual way, (4) has a veracity that is arbitrated by the rememberer rather than by experts, and (5) originates from a particular occasion rather than from many different occasions.

Such criteria are not entirely satisfactory. As an example, the occasion of hearing the news of President Kennedy's assassination might seem to constitute an excellent example of episodic memory, and yet it could be argued that it violates each of these criteria, in that it may (1) serve as a source of knowledge adequate for responding to factual questions, (2) endure until the rememberer dies, (3) be brought to mind in association with conceptually related events, (4) be shown to be at variance with objective evidence, and (5) be thoroughly fused with memory for the many occasions on which the incident has been thought about or pictures or replays of it seen. Conversely, knowledge of the assassination of President Lincoln is unlikely to be regarded as the product of episodic memory, and yet it (1) is about a particular event, (2) may have lost much of its detail during the time immediately following its acquisition, (3) may be organized in a way that reflects its temporal relation to other historic events, (4) could appropriately be judged for veracity by the knower (as when the knower happens to be an authority on the subject), and (5) could conceivably be entirely attributable to a single occasion even though the occasion as such may be beyond recollection. At a more general level, disentangling episodic memory and semantic memory is complicated by the need that each has of the other: knowledge, or at least the bulk of it, has its origin in events, and events require knowledge to be understood.

The strong interrelation of episodic memory and semantic memory and the lack of clear objective criteria for distinguishing between them have led some to conclude that the distinction is not of fundamental significance (McKoon and co-workers, 1986; Neely, 1989). But, regardless of its theoretical status, the distinction remains useful as a descriptive device, and for present purposes episodic memory will be used in reference to those experimental procedures in which, loosely speaking, subjects respond on the basis of their memory for specific events rather than of their general knowledge.

It is perhaps worth noting that the definition of an event is necessarily arbitrary. A vacation in Europe, an excursion to Paris during the vacation, a visit to the opera during the excursion, a particular aria in the opera, or a particular note in the aria could each be considered an event. In most episodic memory experiments events are typically defined as presentations of specific items, such as numbers, words, pairs of words, sentences, or pictures. Memory for these item presentations is usually referred to simply as memory for items. The conditions of item presentation, the number of items presented, and the study-to-test delay vary according to the purpose of the experiment. Most memory tests are of one of three forms: unaided recall, aided recall, or recognition. In an unaided recall test the set of to-be-recalled events is specified, albeit usually implicitly, and the subjects report as many events as they can. This test usually requires either serial recall, in which case the items have to be reported in their exact order of presentation, or free recall, in which case the items can be reported in any order. In an aided recall test, subjects are given hints, or cues, to facilitate recall. More often than not a separate cue is presented for each item, although sometimes more than one cue is presented for each item or one cue serves for more than one item. A cue may take many forms: for the word *eagle,* it may be a fragment of the word (eg, −*ag−e*), a context item (eg, *emerald* if the presentation item had been the word pair *emerald-eagle*), or something that had not formed part of the study list (eg, "a kind of bird" or "rhymes with beagle"). In a recognition test the to-be-remembered items are intermixed with new items, referred to as lures or distractors, and the subjects' task is to decide whether each item occurred in the study list. The proportion of items given a positive response is sometimes left up to the subjects and is sometimes specified by the experimenter. In addition, the subjects may be required to rate the confidence they have in each decision. A comprehensive account of these and other procedures for studying memory can be found in Puff (1982).

In discussing the issues and findings of episodic memory research, it is useful to distinguish between primary and secondary memory. The distinction was originally formulated by James (1890) in phenomenological terms. Specifically, primary memory refers to the remembering of events that have never left consciousness and that, therefore, belong to the psychological present. Secondary memory, or memory proper, refers to memory for events that, although represented in consciousness immediately after their presentation and again on recollection, are not continuously maintained in consciousness between these times; they belong to the psychological past. In more contemporary usage, primary and secondary memory are generally thought of in a more conceptual way: they are often cast as separate memory stores or systems. In any case, primary memory refers to events that have occurred most recently, and secondary memory to events from further back in time.

PRIMARY MEMORY

Most of what has been learned about primary memory concerns its qualitative nature and its capacity, and these topics form the basis of the present discussion. The dominant form of inquiry has been objective experimentation, but introspection, however informal, has also played an essential role.

Nature of Primary Memory

Objective experimentation and introspection both show that primary memory takes on the character of the perceptual-motor world. It assumes an auditory, visual, or some other sensory quality or, as when a manual task is mentally rehearsed, a proprioceptive quality. Depending on whether it preserves the sensory quality of the event

that gave rise to it, primary memory might be said to be direct or indirect.

A strong argument for direct auditory primary memory, or echoic memory, is given by the very fact of speech perception. Of its nature, speech is spread out over time and, in order to be understood, information occurring at any one instant must be integrated with a precise record of information that occurred immediately beforehand. Introspection confirms the existence of such a record. At each successive instant that speech is being heard, memory for the immediately preceding few words has a freshness far more original than does memory for earlier words. Not only is it plain exactly what these words were but it is almost as though they could still be heard, with such details as tone of voice, intonation, and accent clearly preserved. Memory of this sort is difficult if not impossible to sustain through further speech; subsequent words are apt to take their place in echoic memory whether or not the rememberer wishes it.

Much of the experimental research on echoic memory has involved the serial recall of spoken lists of about eight digits or words. Serial position functions, obtained by determining the probability of recall for each within-list position, show that level of recall increases sharply over the last two or three positions (Murdock, 1968). The echoic nature of this recency effect, as it is called, is indicated by its virtual absence when the items are presented visually (Conrad and Hull, 1968) or when they are acoustically similar to one another (Crowder, 1971). The vulnerability of echoic memory to the effects of additional auditory information is illustrated by a sharp reduction in the recency effect when the list items are followed by an additional, nominally irrelevant item (Morton and co-workers, 1971).

Direct visual primary memory, known as iconic memory, has a fidelity even more striking than that of echoic memory. Indeed, it is of such a quality as to create the illusion that the information is still present. The illusion occurs in watching a film, for it is through iconic memory that a picture shown in one frame continues to be seen during the time required to replace the frame by the next one, with the result that the film is seen not as a flickering sequence of still pictures but in the same smooth way that the real world is seen. The useful life of iconic memory depends on the prevailing conditions, although it is typically no more than a fraction of a second (Sperling, 1960; Haber and Standing, 1970).

An example of indirect primary memory can be found in the verbatim retention of material just read. The material was perceived visually, but introspection reveals its conscious representation to be more auditory or articulatory in nature, a sort of silent speech. Experimental confirmation of this impression comes from a study by Conrad (1964) in which subjects were given serial recall tests on short sequences of letters. To avoid extraneous difficulties, Conrad was interested in only those sequences in which subjects erred on just one letter. He found that the incorrect letter was often acoustically similar to the letter that should have been reported. Given that acoustically similar letters do not tend to be visually similar, the implication is that the visually presented letters were coded in a speechlike form. Not only can information be recoded for representation in conscious mind, but it can be rehearsed and otherwise manipulated in the service of a mental task. Such willful processing of information is commonly said to constitute working memory (Baddeley, 1986).

Capacity of Primary Memory

How much information can be retained in conscious mind at any one instant? What, in other words, is the capacity of primary memory? This question raises a number of unresolved issues, not the least of which is the appropriate unit of measurement. It is perhaps to minimize this particular difficulty that the question of capacity has been raised almost exclusively with respect to verbal material, because this can be broken into discrete units in a relatively objective fashion. The relevant research falls into two categories: one concerned with memory span, the other with the recency effect.

Memory span refers to the number of items for which there is an even chance of perfect reproduction after a single presentation. Roughly speaking, this turns out to be seven items. This fact suggests a model whereby primary memory is likened to a store containing seven distinct locations. Such a model may be adequate for some purposes, but it does not account for the modest variations in memory span that do occur between types of items or conditions of presentation. Thus memory span is about an item greater for letters than for words and about an item less for letters than for digits (Crannell and Parrish, 1957) and about half an item greater with auditory than with visual presentation (Drewnowski and Murdock, 1980). According to one theory, memory span corresponds, not to a fixed number of items, but rather to the number of items that can be recited within a fixed time, estimated to be between 1.5 and 2.0 s (Baddeley and co-workers, 1975; Schweikert and Boruff, 1986). This theory accounts for several puzzling findings, including the relative spans for letters, words, and digits (letters can be recited more quickly than words but not as quickly as digits), although it leaves other findings unaccounted for (Brooks and Watkins, 1990).

Apart from these empirical puzzles, there are reasons to doubt that memory span is, even in principle, a valid measure of primary memory capacity. For instance, memory span has been shown to be greater for words that have a high frequency of everyday occurrence than for words that occur less often, and because this variable is generally assumed to affect secondary memory but not primary memory, the implication is that memory span may include one or two items from secondary memory. Also, even if memory span were entirely the product of primary memory, it may reflect more its upper limit than the capacity typically used in attending to a continuous stream of information.

This latter possibility suggests that the capacity of primary memory might be more appropriately ascertained by using a list length substantially in excess of memory span and focusing on recall of the last few items. A great many studies of this sort have been conducted, most of them using lists of 12–20 randomly selected words and a

free recall test. Serial position functions reveal a recency effect spanning the last six or seven positions (Murdock, 1962), and this is generally attributed to primary memory. Of particular interest are findings that list length, the rate at which the words are presented, the concreteness of the words (or rather of their referents), the frequency of the words in everyday usage, and many other variables have an appreciable effect on recall of prerecency items but little if any effect on the recall of recency items (Glanzer, 1972). Although there has been much discussion of precisely how the capacity of primary memory should be estimated from the serial position function, the area under the recency part of the function (ie, the sum of the recall probabilities for the last few positions) can be taken as a first approximation, and this turns out to be about 3.5 items. Note that this is substantially less than the estimate given by memory span.

One or two variables have been shown to distinguish between prerecency and recency portions of the serial position function in just the opposite way—that is, they affect recency positions but not prerecency positions. Specifically, the recency effect is reduced slightly if the items are presented visually rather than auditorily (Murdock and Walker, 1969), and is largely eliminated if subjects engage in a verbal task (such as simple arithmetic or copying down several other words) between presentation and recall (Glanzer and Cunitz, 1966). Neither of these exceptions seriously undermines a primary memory interpretation of the recency effect. Thus it is not unreasonable to suppose that primary memory could be of slightly greater capacity when of a direct echoic form than when of an indirect phonological form and that an interpolated verbal task diverts conscious mind from the recency items. More serious are findings of a recency effect when subjects are distracted after the presentation of each individual item (Tzeng, 1973), simultaneous recency effects for more than one set of items (Watkins and Peynircioglu, 1983), and substantial recency effects over intervals spanning several weeks (Baddeley and co-workers, 1977). Plainly, recency effects can arise for reasons other than retention in primary memory. The implications for the measurement of primary memory capacity remain a matter of debate.

SECONDARY MEMORY

The dominant sense of the term memory, which James called secondary memory, refers to the remembering of events that have passed from current awareness. It is discussed in two parts, the first dealing with the events as experienced and the second with their recollection.

Events as Experienced

Events vary in how long they are remembered; some are remembered only fleetingly, others for most of a lifetime. Yet, as obvious as this is, very little effort has been made to identify and systematize the variables that control memory persistence. For present purposes, these variables are organized into seven factors: duration, meaningfulness, vividness, distinctiveness, organization, emotionality, and primacy and recency. These factors are not independent of one another, but often covary: emotional events may be meaningful, distinctive, and vivid; more time may permit a more meaningful interpretation or a better organization; and so on. Also, the effect of a given variable will depend on the particular individual, because one and the same event may be experienced and remembered quite differently depending on the remember's knowledge, interests, intentions, and the like.

Duration. The effect of event duration on memory has been shown by presenting lists of words or other items at different speeds: slower presentation rates result in better recall, if other factors are held constant (Murdock, 1960). Of course, the nominal time for which an item is presented is not necessarily the same as the functional time for which it is studied. An item may be thought about, or covertly rehearsed, while later ones are being presented. Some researchers have even claimed that the functional, or effective, study time is the primary determiner of memory (Rundus, 1971).

Meaningfulness. The importance of meaningfulness can be readily appreciated by considering the ease of remembering verbal messages presented in the native language relative to messages presented in an unfamiliar language. Similarly, expert radiographers remember x-rays revealing a pathological state better than novices do (Myles-Worsley and co-workers, 1988). Compelling experimental evidence for meaningfulness comes from studies showing that a clarifying sentence or picture can sharply enhance memory for an otherwise cryptic passage (Bransford and Johnson, 1972). Closely related to the issue of meaningfulness is the concept of depth of processing (Craik and Lockhart, 1972), which has given rise to numerous experiments wherein the type of attention given to events is systematically varied. Typically, subjects are given a series of randomly selected words and engaged in a task designed to draw attention either to the meaning of the words or to some nonsemantic characteristic. Semantic tasks, such as rating the pleasantness of the words (or, strictly, their referents) produce higher levels of recall and recognition than do nonsemantic tasks, such as deciding whether the words contain a designated letter (Hyde and Jenkins, 1973).

Vividness. Graphic events are more memorable than dull or vague events. For example, memorable talks tend to be lively and rife with concrete examples, whereas forgettable talks are usually neither. Experimental confirmation of the effects of vividness comes from the finding that concrete objects are better remembered than are pictures of the objects, which in turn are better remembered than the words naming the objects (Bevan and Steger, 1971). Also, if subjects are given words and told to form mental images of their referents, they will recall them better than if they had been instructed simply to remember them (Paivio, 1986). Most memory improvement techniques prescribe mental imagery to make abstract material more concrete. It is often suggested that the images be unusual or bizarre, but the evidence on this advice is mixed. Bizarre images are probably effective if they are used sparingly for items of particular difficulty against a background of common images (Einstein and co-workers, 1989), in which case the key factor would be distinctiveness.

Distinctiveness. A day at a cricket match is more memorable if it is the only day ever spent at a cricket match than if it is one of many. Experimentally, this point is illustrated by the Von Restorff (1933) effect, which refers to the comparatively high level of recall of an item that stands out in some way from among others with which it occurred. For example, the word *Aristotle* will have a much higher probability of recall if presented in an otherwise uniform list of vegetable names than if presented in a list of famous philosophers. More generally, the probability of recollecting an event falls off in a steady and systematic fashion with the number of similar events with which it occurred. This principle is illustrated by the finding that the probability of recalling the presentation of a given item in a study list declines as the length of the list increases (Murdock, 1960). It is also amply illustrated in a vast body of research conducted under the heading of interference theory. This research has involved a variety of experimental paradigms, although perhaps none more significant than the paired-associate procedure. In this procedure, subjects are presented with lists of paired items, in which the items are typically nonsense syllables, words, numbers, or geometric shapes. Thus a list might begin, "XUF-83, HIG-44, VEQ-90. . . ." Most interference studies involve the presentation of two such lists, and the finding of essential concern here is that, for either list, recall of a given second term in response to a first term (eg, 83 in response to XUF) is less likely if the first term had been used with another response term (XUF-26) in the other list (McGeogh, 1942). The impairment in recall of the first of two such related pairs is generally characterized as the product of retroactive interference and that in the recall of the second pair as the product of proactive interference.

Organization. The potential effects of organization are such that one prominent theorist has claimed that to organize is to remember (Mandler, 1967). In one experimental demonstration of the power of organization, subjects were presented with a set of 112 words displayed in treelike configurations in which the words were placed either at random or in a manner designed to bring out their relation [eg, *platinum, silver,* and *gold* were nested under *rare,* which (along with *common* and *alloys*) was nested under *metals,* which (along with *stones*) was nested under *minerals*]. After three successive presentations subjects in the random condition failed to recall an average of 59 words, whereas those in the organized condition missed none at all (Bower and co-workers, 1969).

Like imagery, organization plays a key role in most mnemonic systems. It is also used spontaneously by people unschooled in such systems. Experiments have shown that when required to master a list of words randomly selected from a homogeneous set, subjects impose their own idiosyncratic, or subjective, organization. In these experiments, the words were presented repeatedly, each time in a new random order, and a free recall test was given after each presentation. Consistent with the theory that the learning of such lists is fundamentally a matter of developing an organization, a steady improvement in recall across successive tests was paralleled by a steady increase in the consistency in the order in which the words were recalled (Tulving, 1962).

Effects of organization are also powerfully revealed in memory for prose. Simple sentences are better remembered than syntactically complex sentences, and stories organized according to a canonical story grammar (or schema or script) are better remembered than poorly organized stories (Bower and co-workers, 1979).

Emotionality. Experimental research on emotionality has been limited for practical and ethical reasons, but there is no doubt that this factor can exert a powerful impact on memory. Seeing a loved one in physical distress, being acutely embarrassed, or receiving praise from someone of high authority is likely to be long remembered. Most older Americans can remember with unusual clarity their first learning of the death of John F. Kennedy in 1963; other may have similar experiences for the explosion of the space shuttle *Challenger* or for the death of someone close (Brown and Kulik, 1977).

Primacy and Recency. Within a set of related events, the most recent are generally the most likely to be recollected, even when they cannot be attributed to primary memory. This point may be appreciated by trying to recall, for example, movies that have been seen or books that have been read. In some cases, there is also an enhanced likelihood of recollecting the first one or two of a set of events; people may, for example, recall their first dates. These primacy and recency effects have been demonstrated both within and beyond the laboratory. One proposal is that they are the consequence of a distinctiveness that accrues to the endpoints of a series (Murdock, 1962), and are thus an expression of the distinctiveness principle.

Recollection. A traditional conception of recollection is the strength/threshold theory, according to which each past experience is characterized by a memory strength and is remembered whenever this strength exceeds a threshold set by the prevailing conditions. Thus an experimenter might demonstrate that an item from a previously presented list may not be produced in a free recall test but may nevertheless be identified in a recognition test. The memory strength for this item would be said to exceed the recognition threshold but to fall short of the recall threshold. Strength/threshold theory not only accounts for the varying effectiveness of different types of test, but it can be reconciled with forgetting over time simply by assuming that memory strength declines with the passage of time.

Despite its intuitive plausibility, the strength/threshold theory is not without difficulty. Most important, its account of the differential effectiveness of different types of memory test founders on findings of various interactions between study and test manipulations. For example,

words presented in a list organized by meaningful categories (eg, first several fruits, then several articles of furniture, etc) are better recalled than a list of the same words arranged at random, but this effect appears not to occur in recognition (Bruce and Fagan, 1970). Even more problematic, some variables have opposite effects on recall and recognition (Tulving, 1976). For example, when high and low frequency words are mixed within the same list, free recall tests show a higher level of performance for high than for low frequency words whereas recognition tests sometimes show the opposite (Balota and Neely, 1980). Such interactions cannot be accounted for by the threshold model, for the results of different tests lead to conflicting conclusions about how the variables affect memory strength.

More sophisticated than strength/threshold theory is generate–recognize theory. Central to this theory is the idea that recollection consists of two distinct stages: a generate stage, in which representations of potential target items within some permanent knowledge system are found, or generated, and a recognize stage, in which each of these candidate items is subjected to a recognition test. In most theories, neither stage is conscious; only those items that are generated and given a positive recognition decision are made available to introspection. Like the strength/threshold theory, the generate–recognize model readily accounts for the effect that type of test has on performance: the recognition test provides a copy of the target item, which ensures the item's generation; the free recall test provides minimal guidance for the generation stage; and aided recall tests provide some guidance, although not enough to guarantee generation. Thus the effect of type of memory test is localized at the generation stage. The generate–recognize model also provides a plausible explanation of interactions between type of test and experimental conditions. The effect of using semantically structured lists, for example, would be to facilitate the generation process, so that the effect is shown in recall but not in recognition. The model can even account for findings of free recall and recognition being affected in opposite ways. For the effects of word frequency, for example, low frequency words are more likely to pass the recognition stage (perhaps because their presentations were comparatively distinctive events), but this advantage is not sufficient to offset the disadvantage that these words suffer at the generation stage.

Despite these accomplishments, the generate–recognize model does not adequately account for all of the evidence. In particular, it fails to account for evidence that recognition performance varies according to the context in which the recognition test item is presented (Thomson, 1972). According to the model, recognition performance should depend only on the decision of whether the permanent representation of the item is appropriately tagged and not on its context. The model is also undermined by findings that a word studied in the presence of a context word but not identified in a subsequent recognition task may be recalled when the context word is re-presented as a cue (Tulving and Thomson, 1973). The failure in recognition indicates that the word's permanent representation was not in a state that would support a positive recognition decision, whereas the success in aided recall indicates that it was.

In light of such difficulties, some theorists have abandoned the generate–recognize model and embraced instead the ideas of encoding specificity and transfer appropriate processing (Tulving, 1976; Morris and co-workers, 1977), whereby an experience is recollected or in one way or another subsequently manifested in behavior whenever cognitive processing matches sufficiently closely the processing that occurred at the time of the experience. No crucial distinction is drawn between recall and recognition. A recognition test is usually more successful than a recall test because the re-presentation of a central component of that experience as a test item (or copy cue) is likely to induce processing similar to the processing that defined the target experience. That a context word may under some conditions be more effective than the copy cue means merely that it is more successful in recreating the processing of the target event.

These ideas have considerable generality. For example, they provide a plausible account of why information learned under the influence of alcohol is often better remembered in the same inebriated state than in a sober state (Eich, 1980). The transfer appropriate processing ideas have also been applied to prose learning and education (McDaniel and Einstein, 1989). One problem is that the notions of specific encoding and test appropriateness are fuzzy and apt to lead to circular reasoning.

Part of the difficulty in formulating an adequate account of event recollection is that, at least for events involving complex material, such as lectures or conversations, recollection is likely to take the form of a summary rather than an unabridged verbatim reproduction. Moreover, it is likely to be expressed largely in the rememberer's own words. The implication is that such recollection is substantially a matter of reconstruction, of using knowledge of the world [perhaps conceptualized as schemata or scripts (qv) (Bower and co-workers, 1979)] to piece together an account faithful to the gist, or perhaps just to the tenor (Neisser, 1981), rather than to the details of the episode.

BIBLIOGRAPHY

A. D. Baddeley, *Working Memory,* Clarendon, Oxford, UK, 1986.

A. D. Baddeley and G. Hitch in S. Dornic, ed., *Attention and Performance,* Vol. 6, Lawrence Erlbaum, Hillsdale, N.J., 1977, pp. 647–667.

A. D. Baddeley, N. Thompson, and M. Buchanan, "Word Length and the Structure of Short-Term Memory," *J. Verb. Learn. Verb. Behav.* **14,** 575–589 (1975).

D. A. Balota and J. H. Neely, "Test Expectancy and Word-Frequency Effects in Recall and Recognition," *J. Exp. Psychol. Hum. Learn. Mem.* **6,** 576–587 (1980).

W. Bevan and J. A. Steger, "Free Recall and Abstractness of Stimuli," *Science* **172,** 597–599 (1971).

G. H. Bower, J. B. Black, and T. J. Turner, "Scripts in Memory for Text," *Cogn. Psychol.* **11,** 177–220 (1979).

G. H. Bower, M. C. Clark, A. M. Lesgold, and D. Winzenz, "Hierarchical Retrieval Schemes in Recall of Categorized Word Lists," *J. Verb. Learn. Verb. Behav.* **8,** 323–343 (1969).

J. D. Bransford and M. K. Johnson, "Contextual Prerequisites for Understanding: Some Investigations of Comprehension and Recall," *J. Verb. Learn. Verb. Behav.* **11,** 717–726 (1972).

J. O. Brooks and M. J. Watkins, "Further Evidence of the Intricacy of Memory Span," *J. Exper. Psychol. Learn. Mem. Cogn.* **16,** 1134–1141 (1990).

R. Brown, and J. Kulik, "Flashbulb Memories," *Cognition* **5,** 73–99 (1977).

D. Bruce and R. L. Fagan, "More on the Recognition and Free Recall of Organized Lists," *J. Exp. Psychol.* **85,** 153–154 (1970).

R. Conrad, "Acoustic Confusions in Immediate Memory," *Br. J. Psychol.* **55,** 75–84 (1964).

R. Conrad and A. J. Hull, "Input Modality and the Serial Position Curve in Short-Term Memory," *Psychonom. Sci.* **10,** 135–136 (1968).

F. I. M. Craik and R. S. Lockhart, "Levels of Processing: A Framework for Memory Research," *J. Verb. Learn. Behav.* **11,** 671–684 (1972).

C. W. Crannell and J. M. Parrish, "A Comparison of Immediate Memory Span for Digits, Letters, and Words," *J. Psychol.* **44,** 319–327 (1957).

R. G. Crowder, "The Sound of Vowels and Consonants in Immediate Memory," *J. Verb. Learn. Verb. Behav.* **10,** 587–596 (1971).

A. Drewnowski and B. B. Murdock, Jr., "The Role of Auditory Features in Memory Span for Words," *J. Exp. Psychol. Hum. Learn. Mem.* **6,** 319–332 (1980).

J. E. Eich, "The Cue Dependent Nature of State Dependent Retrieval," *Mem. Cogn.* **8,** 157–173 (1980).

G. O. Einstein, M. A. McDaniel, and S. Lackey, "Bizarre Imagery, Interference, and Distinctiveness," *J. Exp. Psychol. Learn. Mem. Cogn.* **15,** 137–146 (1989).

M. Glanzer in G. H. Bower, ed., *The Psychology of Learning and Motivation: Advances in Research and Theory,* Vol. 5, Academic Press, Inc. New York, 1972, pp. 129–193.

M. Glanzer and A. R. Cunitz, "Two Storage Mechanisms in Free Recall," *J. Verb. Learn. Verb. Behav.* **5,** 351–360 (1966).

R. N. Haber and L. G. Standing, "Direct Estimates of the Apparent Duration of a Flash," *Can. J. Psychol.* **24,** 216–229 (1970).

T. S. Hyde and J. J. Jenkins, "Recall for Words as a Function of Semantic, Graphic, and Syntactic Orienting Tasks," *J. Verb. Learn. Verb. Behav.* **12,** 471–480 (1973).

W. James, *The Principles of Psychology,* Holt, New York, 1890.

M. A. McDaniel and G. O. Einstein, "Material Appropriate Processing: A Contextualistic Approach to Reading and Studying Strategies," *Educ. Psychol. Rev.* **1,** 113–145 (1989).

J. A. McGeogh, *The Psychology of Human Learning,* Longmans, New York, 1942.

G. McKoon, R. Ratcliff and G. S. Dell, "A Critical Evaluation of the Semantic/Episodic Distinction," *J. Exp. Psychol. Learn. Mem. Cogn.* **12,** 295–306 (1986).

G. Mandler in K. W. Spence and J. T. Spence, eds., *The Psychology of Learning and Motivation.,* Vol. 1, Academic Press, Inc., New York, 1967, pp. 327–372.

C. D. Morris, J. D. Bransford, and J. J. Franks, "Levels of Processing Versus Transfer Appropriate Processing," *J. Verb. Learn. Verb. Behav.* **16,** 519–534 (1977).

J. Morton, R. G. Crowder, and H. A. Prussin, "Experiments with the Stimulus Suffix Effect," *J. Exp. Psychol. Monogr. Suppl.* **91,** 169–190 (1971).

B. B. Murdock, Jr., "The Immediate Retention of Unrelated Words," *J. Exp. Psychol.* **60**, 222–234 (1960).

B. B. Murdock, Jr., "The Serial Position Effect of Free Recall," *J. Exp. Psychol.* **64**, 482–488 (1962).

B. B. Murdock, Jr., "Serial Order Effects in Short-Term Memory," *J. Exp. Psychol. Monogr. Suppl.* **76**, 1–15 (1968).

B. B. Murdock, Jr., and K. D. Walker, "Modality Effects in Free Recall," *J. Verb. Learn. Verb. Behav.* **8**, 665–676 (1969).

M. Myles-Worsley, W. A. Johnston, and M. A. Simons, "The Influence of Expertise on X-Ray Image Processing," *J. Exp. Psychol. Learn. Mem. Cogn.* **14**, 553–557 (1988).

J. H. Neely in H. L. Roediger III and F. I. M. Craik, *Varieties of Memory and Consciousness: Essays in Honour of Endel Tulving,* Lawrence Erlbaum, N.J., 1989, pp. 229–270.

U. Neisser, "John Dean's Memory: A Case Study," *Cognition* **9**, 1–22 (1981).

A. Paivio, *Mental Representations, A Dual Coding Approach,* Oxford University Press, Oxford, UK, 1986.

C. R. Puff, ed., *Handbook of Research Methods in Human Memory and Cognition,* Academic Press, Inc., New York, 1982.

D. Rundus, "Analysis of Rehearsal Processes in Free Recall," *J. Exp. Psychol.* **89**, 63–77 (1971).

R. Schweikert and B. Boruff, "Short-Term Memory Capacity: Magic Number or Magic Spell?" *J. Exp. Psychol. Learn. Mem. Cogn.* **12**, 419–425 (1986).

G. Sperling, "The Information Available in Brief Visual Presentations," *Psychol. Monogr.* **74**(11), 498 (1960).

D. M. Thomson, "Context Effects in Recognition Memory," *J. Verb. Learn. Verb. Behav.* **11**, 497–511 (1972).

E. Tulving, "Subjective Organization in Free Recall of 'Unrelated' Words," *Psychol. Rev.* **69**, 344–354 (1962).

E. Tulving in E. Tulving and W. Donaldson, eds., *Organization of Memory,* Academic Press, Inc., New York, 1972.

E. Tulving in J. Brown, ed., *Recall and Recognition,* John Wiley & Sons, Inc., New York, 1976, pp. 37–73.

E. Tulving, *Elements of Episodic Memory,* Clarendon, Oxford, UK, 1983.

E. Tulving and D. M. Thomson, "Encoding Specificity and Retrieval Processes in Episodic Memory," *Psychol. Rev.* **80**, 352–373 (1973).

O. J. L. Tzeng, "Positive Recency Effect in a Delayed Free Recall," *J. Verb. Learn. Verb. Behav.* **12**, 436–439 (1973).

H. Von Restorff, "Analyse von Vorgangen im Spurenfeld. I. Uber die Wirkung von Bereichsbildungen im Spurenfeld," *Psychol. Forsch.* **18**, 299–342 (1933).

M. J. Watkins and Z. Peynircioglu, "Three Recency Effects at the Same Time," *J. Verb. Learn. Verb. Behav.* **22**, 375–384 (1983).

M. WATKINS
H. ROEDIGER III
Rice University

EPISTEMOLOGY

Epistemology is the field of philosophy that deals with the nature and sources of knowledge. Key concepts include belief, perception, representation, justification, description, and evaluation. Epistemologists investigate bases on which beliefs can be singled out as knowledge. This involves two tasks. First, beliefs must be characterized, usually by being built out of more basic components related to the nature of minds and their interaction with the world. From these components, subjects form representations of states of affairs, which are candidates for beliefs (see KNOWLEDGE REPRESENTATION). Characterizing beliefs is a largely descriptive task. Whatever arguments may be brought to bear, the idea is to describe beliefs, their sources, and their components accurately and usefully. Second, beliefs that qualify as knowledge must be distinguished from those that do not. Deciding which beliefs qualify as knowledge is an evaluative task. At any given time, epistemic approaches tend to divide into those that focus on the first task, and hence have a descriptive flavor, and those that focus on the second, and so have a more evaluative bias.

Epistemology has traditionally drawn insights from philosophy of mind, philosophy of science, philosophy of mathematics, and such outside fields as logic (qv), psychology (see COGNITIVE PSYCHOLOGY), mathematics, and the physical sciences. Some of these contributions have taken the form of raising questions about the limits of knowledge: for instance, mathematical knowledge is particularly problematic because the nature of mathematical objects seems to eliminate perception as a source of knowledge. In other cases, a particular discipline is treated as a paradigm of knowledge: in continental Europe, unlike the United States and the United Kingdom, epistemology today means the theory of scientific knowledge.

CENTRAL PROBLEMS

The traditional view equates knowledge with justified true belief (see BELIEF REPRESENTATION SYSTEMS). This view has been claimed to originate with Plato and has dominated epistemology since the Enlightenment. Viewing knowledge as belief ties it to subjects (most obviously, but not necessarily, people). Viewing knowledge as true belief ties it also to the world, since a belief that did not accurately reflect the actual state of affairs would not be true. Justification lies between the knowing subjects and the world, providing the grounds on which the particular believer can be claimed to know. Understanding the nature and bases of knowledge therefore involves investigating the ways in which minds and the rest of the world interact.

Sources of Knowledge

From ancient times, philosophers have investigated what sources of knowledge, if any, have authority. Such a source must reside either in the knowing subject (usually reason) or in something that links the subject to the world (usually sense perception). Since classical times, the authority of perception has been disputed on grounds ranging from hallucinations and dreams to modern claims that belief conditions perception. Yet if perception is rejected, what does reason have to work with? Many philosophers have been extremely hesitant to allow pure reason unaided by perception as a possible source of knowledge.

Although epistemologists and psychologists are both

concerned with sources of knowledge, they are concerned with them in entirely different senses. Psychology studies (among other things) the ways in which individuals come to believe things, the kinds of evidence people find persuasive, what affects responses to proposals, and the like. The question for epistemology is the question of what grounds form an adequate basis for the claim to knowledge, independent of whether those grounds historically contributed to belief or even whether people would actually find them convincing. Psychologists study human response and behavior; epistemologists examine what can in principle serve as grounds of knowledge for any knowing subject.

Justification

Justification traditionally involves a demonstration of truth, usually by appeal to logic. But logic can only show that an argument's conclusion is true provided that its premises are true. Either the premises need to be justified in turn or they do not. In the first case, it seems that the argument must either become circular or go into an infinite regress. In the second case, how can the conclusion be justified if its premises are not?

One way out of this dilemma is to identify a class of *basic beliefs* and argue that by their nature they require no external justification. Most frequently, basic beliefs are taken as absolute and certain, though it would be possible to hold this kind of view and also to hold that basic beliefs can be mistaken. Basic beliefs then provide a justificational foundation for other beliefs. This approach has come to be called *foundationalism*. Another way out justifies individual facts on the basis of their role within a larger system of beliefs. This view, called *coherentism*, is spelled out in Lehrer's *Knowledge* (1974).

Both coherentists and foundationalists have problems with views of justification that rest on formal logical demonstration or otherwise require that justification guarantee truth. In actual situations in which people claim knowledge, the kinds of justification presented are frequently less certain and more sophisticated than logical inference (qv) from accepted facts. Even in science, which has always seemed to provide a particularly clean example of knowledge, justifications often extrapolate beyond what logical inference justifies, involve probabilistic judgments, or follow other patterns of reasoning that differ from those of formal logic (see REASONING, COMMONSENSE; REASONING, DEFAULT; REASONING, PLAUSIBLE). Also, scientific knowledge is notoriously open to change. Given these difficulties, what kinds of justification warrant belief?

Certainty

Depending on the way in which a particular view of knowledge is spelled out, knowledge may be possible without certainty. But the search for certainty has preoccupied philosophers for centuries and recurs persistently in the claim that nothing can be called knowledge that could possibly be wrong. Hence many epistemic theories have involved a search for a basis that not only allows for justified true belief but also identifies a class of basic beliefs as both true and justified with no room for doubt. Hence, in this version of foundationalism, basic beliefs provide a

sort of safety net against the skeptical claim that people cannot properly be said to know anything at all. The search for epistemic certainty need not be tied to foundationalism; Wittgenstein's *Uber Gewissheit* (1969) can be viewed as an attempt to argue for certainty without basic beliefs.

Representation

Beliefs are in people's heads; the objects of those beliefs in general are not. Hence the relationship between beliefs and their objects matters greatly for epistemologists. What kinds of things are representations? How are they derived, and what links them to the things they represent? What relationships hold between the complex representations that constitute beliefs and the states of affairs they apply to? In twentieth-century philosophy, Quine focused attention on this class of issues in his classic *World and Object* (1960). In recent decades the question of representation has become especially central, inspiring works by thinkers as diverse as Searle (1980, 1983) and Fodor (1975, 1983). Artificial intelligence, computational models, cognitive psychology, and the interdisciplinary efforts in cognitive science (qv) are influencing new philosophical works, originally centered in philosophy of mind and language but increasingly involved in epistemology, which center on representation as the link between the mental and material level.

HISTORY

The Classical Period

Concerns with the nature and sources of knowledge were clearly established in ancient Greece by the time of Plato and the sophists (fourth and third centuries B.C.). The view that knowledge is justified true belief is traditionally attributed to Plato. In the *Meno*, an early dialogue, he distinguishes between true belief and knowledge, claiming that knowledge requires grounding as well as truth. In the famous parable of the cave in Book V of *The Republic*, Plato makes a three-way distinction between ignorance, belief, and knowledge, with knowledge requiring correct understanding of the Forms. It should be noted here that for Plato the proper object of knowledge lay in the eternal relations among universals, not in matters of material fact. The *Theaetetus* provides the longest discourse on knowledge and again stresses the need for a *logos* grounding true belief before it can properly be called knowledge. *Logos* is the root word underlying the word "logic," but Plato seems to have meant the term more in its sense of order and law, hence requiring a grounding for knowledge that was solid but, for Plato, still less than clearly understood.

For Aristotle, too, knowledge meant knowledge of universals. In his *Prior Analytics*, Aristotle limited his logical language to propositions of the forms "A is predicated of all of B," "A is predicated of part of B," "A is not predicated of all of B," and "A is predicated of none of B" (in modern terms, "All B's are A's," "Some B's are A's," "Some B's are not A's," and "No B's are A's"). He justified this restriction on the ground that he was providing the means of deriving knowledge, and all true knowledge is knowledge of relations among Forms. Hence despite the usual contrasts between Aristotle and Plato, in this regard their views largely coincide. Aristotle's contribution lies in his formulation of the first formal system of proof (ie, the development of logic).

The Enlightenment

Seventeenth-century epistemologists reinterpreted classical thought in light of the emergence of science. This epistemic development expressed itself in two trends: rationalism and empiricism. Descartes (1596–1650) was one of the earliest major proponents of rationalism. A mathematician as well as a philosopher, Descartes set himself the goal of adapting to epistemology the rigorous system of proof used in geometry. First, basic principles must be identified whose truth is immediate and unchallengeable. From these principles all else must be proven by principles of logic. This reliance on infallible first principles, which Descartes called clear and distinct ideas, forms one of the strongest characteristics of Cartesian thought. That these principles are clear and distinct *ideas* is important. The rationalist view holds that certainty is to be sought in the conceptual realm, not in the material. Descartes made a sharp distinction between mind and matter. This clearly defined gap brought the relationship between concepts and their objects into sharp relief. Beliefs consisted of combinations of ideas, independent mental entities that might or might not reflect any independent object of importance. Given this view, the need to link at least some representations to their objects arose. Descartes filled in this link with his famous principle of *cogito ergo sum* ("I think, therefore I am"), arguing that the very presence of doubts as to the existence of anything proved that at least one thing exists, namely the doubter. From this principle, based on orderly introspection and controlled argument, Descartes attempted to derive the rest of his metaphysics.

Leibniz (1646–1716) also took rational principles as the basis of his epistemology. His primary contribution to epistemology lies in the extent to which he held that justification could be reduced to logic, which for Leibniz largely replaced introspection. His view recognized two classes of truths: those of reason and those of fact. Truths of reason, he claimed, were based solely on logic, in that their subjects strictly contained their predicates: given a complete, correct definition of the subject of a truth of reason, the truth in question could be reduced to the form "*A* is *A*" by use of logic alone. Truths of fact could not be so treated, but, he held, they could be derived jointly from the complete definitions of the terms involved and the assumption that God chose to create the best of all possible worlds.

In England empiricism arose in reaction to the rationalist tradition. Whereas rationalist views seek their basic truths in human understanding and hold that knowledge arises either out of pure understanding or out of mind acting on sensory information, empiricism in its purest form denies the role of purely mental constructs and holds that all knowledge is ultimately based in sense experience. Early empiricist views appear in the works of Bacon (ca 1215–1292) and Locke (1632–1704), but the primary expositors of the school are Berkeley (1685–1753) and Hume (1711–1776). Because sensory information is unreliable, empiricist views tend toward skepticism. Berkeley attempted to form an empiricist epistemology that avoided skepticism. He began by accepting a dualist approach concerning mind and matter. On this view, only sensations are directly experienced; any link with an external reality is assumed, not perceived. But sense perception forms the only basis for knowledge: reason can elaborate on perception but cannot arrive at any knowledge that is not both constituted of sensory-derived parts and based on sense experience. By holding experience apart from any external reality and denying that perception is representative, Berkeley endorsed an idealist view under which all knowledge relates only to perception (mental constituents). In this way Berkeley claimed that he had avoided skepticism, since skepticism concerning perceptions themselves was clearly wrong, whereas the question of whether they faithfully captured the reality they were supposed to represent no longer arose.

Hume found this move unconvincing since it defined away all knowledge of interest. Under his view, all knowledge has its basis ultimately in sense experience or (in the case of mathematical and logical knowledge) necessary relations among ideas. In the first case, that of knowledge based on sense experience, Hume held that certainty was impossible in the sense that there is no way to show that such knowledge in fact reflects any real, external world. In the case of relations among ideas, he held that ideas again are based on specific sense impressions and that they are never universal except in the manner of their representation. Hence the truths of logic and mathematics can be viewed as artifacts of a manner of thinking about them. This view is a precursor of twentieth-century logical positivism, especially as espoused by Ayer in *Language, Truth and Logic* (1946).

Kant

Kant's (1724–1804) epistemology represents a direct reaction against Humean skepticism and empiricism. With the empiricists, Kant held that all knowledge arises out of sense experience. That is, without input from the senses, no knowledge whatever would be possible. However, he argued in the *Critique of Pure Reason*, it does not follow that sense experience provides the sole basis for knowledge. Kant held that there are principles about things (as opposed to tautologies) that are not based on experience, and that for knowledge to be possible at all, these principles governing reality must be applied to sense experience to structure it for human conception. These synthetic a priori principles he called necessary preconditions for the possibility of knowledge.

In presenting his analysis, Kant provided a new perspective on subjectivity. Heretofore, philosophers had divided reality into the objective and the subjective. Objective reality always included material reality; for some philosophers it also included objective, universal principles (for instance, Platonic Forms). Truths about objective reality were viewed as independent of facts about the knowers. Subjective reality was individual and internal, constituted by the internal states of a particular subject (person). That is, although one particular person's actual emotions are real, they belong to that person only. By definition, no one else can have those particular feelings, although others might have feelings like them in interesting ways. Another way to put this is that subjectivity was viewed as radically individual and relative. Kant held that subjective but universal principles could be discovered, which belong absolutely to any subjectivity whatsoever, and that these principles were united in a real, abstract universal, which he called transcendental subjectivity. To answer his fundamental question of how knowledge is possible, Kant examined the structure of transcendental subjectivity for structuring principles which themselves transcend experience and which, when applied to experience, yield knowledge. These principles include space, time, and the 12 principles in the table of categories: the categories of quantity (unity, plurality, totality), of quality (reality, negation, limitation), of relation (substance and accident, cause and effect, agent–patient reciprocity), and of modality (possibility/impossibility, existence/nonexistence, necessity/contingency).

As he had divided subjectivity into individual and transcendental subjectivity, Kant also divided the objective realm into phenomena and noumena. The noumenal level of things-in-themselves provides the grounding for knowledge but cannot itself be the subject of knowledge. Things-in-themselves constitute naked reality, unstructured by the principles of transcendental subjectivity. Phenomenal reality is objective reality as structured by the categories and intersubjectively available. Only phenomena can be objects of knowledge; but knowledge of phenomena becomes on this view reasonably straightforward.

The Twentieth Century

The early twentieth century saw the introduction and spread of two new approaches to epistemic thought. In Europe, philosophers influenced by resurgences of rationalism but repelled by the excesses of nineteenth-century romanticism began trying to develop systematic approaches to rationalist views. This trend started in the late nineteenth century with Frege and was taken up by Brentano and his follower Meinong. Another follower of Brentano, Husserl (1859–1938), provided probably the most powerful impetus in this direction. Although his primary concerns lay more in metaphysics and philosophy of mind than in epistemology proper, he took a view under which hypotheses about the nature of mind functioned also as an epistemic foundation. That is, his view of the mind provided units of conception that could serve also as the fundamental structuring units of knowledge. Husserl's technique consisted of an orderly, disciplined introspection of mental contents. This set of techniques formed the basis for phenomenology (qv). Like Descartes, Husserl based knowledge and certainty fundamentally on internal experience. However, he investigated the structure of mental components, abstracting from (in his terms, bracketing off) their actual referents, contexts, and individual-

ity. In this manner he aimed at discovering the fundamental elements of knowledge and reasoning. These elements were understood as real (no less, and perhaps more, real than tables and chairs) and as transcendentally subjective. On principles of transcendental subjectivity, Husserl based his analysis of knowledge not only of principles of reason but also of objective material reality.

In England and the United States focus also rested on founding knowledge on something fundamentally internal, accessible, and basic to understanding. The empiricist bias already present in the Anglo-American tradition guided this investigation in a direction different from that taken by Husserl, to concentrate instead on sense data as absolute units of knowledge. The sense data view seems to have been introduced by G. E. Moore and is closely associated with Moore, H. P. Grice, H. H. Price, and C. D. Broad. Like Berkeley, these philosophers recognized sense data as ultimately mental rather than material, so that this view shares the problem, so prevalent in epistemic theories, that it never seems quite to get to the world. However, they treated sense data as incorrigible: although a person could be mistaken about the interpretation of a sense datum, they claimed that it was impossible to be mistaken about having the datum itself. This form of certainty harkens back both to Descartes's cogito and to Berkeley's empiricism. Grice went further, arguing that sense data are also at some level incorrigible links to the external world because perception is linked causally to the object perceived. The sense data view formed a foundation from which complex knowledge could be built on the basis of epistemic simples—sense data—and according to which a causal theory of perception could provide the required link between reality and knowing subjects. In this manner it was believed that an epistemic theory could be developed that drew its elements from introspection but that nonetheless was rooted more in objective material reality than in any form of subjectivity.

These two traditions dominated epistemic thought in the early decades of the century. Then, shortly after World War II, a new trend arose. Up to this point epistemologists had concentrated primarily on characterizing the sources from which knowledge arose and the elements of which it was made. In the second half of the century English-speaking philosophers turned instead to analyzing the concept of knowledge itself. Instead of discussing where knowledge comes from, how it is possible, or what it is made of, philosophers began to ask what it means to have knowledge. Once again this trend split into two enterprises. In England a school of thought called ordinary language philosophy was approaching philosophical concepts by looking at how terms related to them are used in ordinary nonphilosophical discourse. This approach arose in the 1930s and was particularly popular in ethics, philosophy of language, and metaphysics. In the late 1940s philosophers like Wittgenstein, Gilbert Ryle, and J. L. Austin began applying it to epistemology, looking at nonphilosophical contexts in which it would or would not be considered correct to say that someone knows something. In the United States the analysis of the concept of knowledge took more the form of analyzing conditions for knowledge. At about this time it became common to divide the definition of knowledge as justified true belief into three explicit clauses. Disregarding minor variations, the following definition became standard:

> *X* knows that *P*, just in case
> (1) *X* beliefs that *P*; and
> (2) *X* has an appropriate justification for *P*; and
> (3) *P* is true.

Initially, this definition would be accompanied by examples showing the necessity of each clause. However, especially since the 1960s, the literature has teemed with challenges to the definition, in the form of exceptions and counterexamples, for which one or more of the clauses fails but that nonetheless would be called knowledge—or for which all three clauses hold but that seem nonetheless not to be cases of knowledge. The classic example of the latter is Gettier's "Is Justified True Belief Knowledge?" (1963).

The move to analysis focused attention on justification. Prior to this century it was generally held that scientific knowledge provides the best paradigm for knowledge in that scientific knowledge is particularly clearly stated, well-organized, and well-justified. It was also believed that the essence of scientific justification lay in proofs by the means of mathematics or logic. But new developments in physics undermined the view that science applies principles of logic to observations of phenomena. There had always been difficulty with the status of scientific laws based on the problem of induction (see INDUCTIVE INFERENCE): from finitely many observations it is impossible to derive claims that both cover an infinite number of cases and can be assured to preserve truth. But at least prior to the turn of the century, the idea of an experiment as a pure observation made sense. By the middle of the century it had become clear that a substantial burden of theory underlay the design of scientific experiments so that rather than deriving (justifying) theories logically from observations, scientists in fact derived the circumstances for observation from their theories. Philosophy of science became deeply concerned with the relationship between theory and observation and with the pattern of growth of scientific knowledge, and this concern spilled over into epistemology.

At the same time, new developments in logic began to raise questions about the force of logical arguments, even where available. The *intuitionists*, led by L. E. J. Brouwer and Arend Heyting, developed a system of logic that made sense, had an intuitive appeal, and outlawed inferences possible under the classical logic used by mathematicians. This achievement indicated that what had previously been viewed as principles of logic can successfully be denied without leading to nonsense. In doing so, the intuitionists showed that even proofs of logic involve inescapable metaphysical presuppositions about the nature of knowledge and truth. In addition, logic turned out to be less powerful than people had thought. It had generally been believed that any problem that could be given a mathematically precise statement could also be solved by applying logic. David Hilbert's program, a proposal based on that assumption, was widely viewed as a comprehen-

sive statement of the challenge before mathematics. In 1931 Gödel (1967) proved that the assumption was false by showing that there are statements in the formal language of natural number arithmetic that are logical consequences of the usual axioms of arithmetic but cannot be proved in the first-order theory (unless that theory is inconsistent). This is the famous incompleteness theorem (see COMPLETENESS). If Gödel was right, formal logical techniques did not even suffice for answering all arithmetic questions.

Taken together with the growing recognition that justification in the sciences did not follow axiomatic paradigms and dealt more with degrees than with absolutes, Gödel's theorem provided the first major attack on logic as a foundation for epistemic justification since Descartes adopted his quasimathematical approach. This challenge had profound consequences. As soon as epistemologists stopped taking logic for granted, the question of justification loomed. In the sciences, justification was becoming increasingly a matter measured in degrees rather than absolutes: it seemed reasonable to view justification in general that way as well. But if all justification is a matter of degree, at what point do we say that *X* has sufficient justification to qualify as knowing *P*? Worse yet, if something must be true to be known, and if justification never sufficed to establish anything as more than probable, how could *X* ever know that *X* knew *P*, even supposing *X* did in fact know *P*?

Taken to their natural limit, these concerns lead once again to skepticism. More recently another counterskeptical trend has arisen, this time in the form of what might be called a new epistemic naturalism, associated in the 1970s with Armstrong (1973) and in the 1980s with Dretske (1981). This view once again rests on a view of the mind, which takes it not as a single, undifferentiated black box, but as crucially layered and segmented. Different segments of the mind deliver knowledge of different kinds and at different levels. One of the central theses holds that if all these levels were as error-prone as seems to be suggested by views that hold that belief conditions perception, people would never survive. On this view, although at the top level one may frequently be confused or mistaken about perceptions, there are levels at which perception is not relative to beliefs or other higher mental states. That is, although some levels of perception and knowledge are prone to mistakes, there are also levels advanced enough to be called knowledge and to serve as epistemic bases for knowledge to which higher level mental states do not penetrate. This theory of impenetrable layers of the mind gives an answer to skeptics that is designed to provide both knowledge and, in some limited cases, certainty.

AI AND EPISTEMOLOGY

By its nature, AI both raises questions for philosophy and deals with areas traditionally philosophical in nature. It should not be surprising, then, that the relationship between the fields has proven reciprocal, each contributing to the other's development. In 1981 Newell reported on a survey that found that AI researchers consider philosophy more immediately relevant to their work than they do psychology (1981). From the other side, interest in issues arising from computational models has manifested itself clearly in works by Searle, Dretzke, and many others. Because AI research involves so many different kinds of philosophical problems, it is often hard to isolate the interaction with epistemology from interactions with philosophy of mind, philosophy of language, logic, and metaphysics in general. This section provides a brief glance at the most clearly epistemic interactions between philosophy and AI research.

McCarthy and Hayes (1969) pointed to the need to increase epistemological awareness in the AI community, especially when researchers claim that their systems not only provide adequate output but also capture some essential feature of human understanding. One issue underlying many disputes both within AI and between AI and philosophy is the question of whether AI research produces simulations of intelligent behavior, models of intelligence, or actual synthetic intelligence. The differences between these three, roughly speaking, is as follows. A simulation of intelligent behavior involves producing behavior that might be produced through the use of intelligence; such simulations can be fully successful, regardless of the means involved in producing the results, providing only that the actual system output simulates intelligent behavior to some reasonable degree. A model of intelligence must produce appropriate output; but, in addition, it must do so by embodying processes and information representations that mirror intelligent processes and knowledge. A synthetic intelligence is a full-fledged knowing subject, different from natural ones (people) primarily in its history, not in its status. Among other things, McCarthy and Hayes argued that AI research that wanted to produce either of the latter two kinds of system must involve itself in epistemic issues in order to show that its goals had been met.

The concern with epistemology within the AI community has grown partly because of the increasingly central role of knowledge representation (qv) in AI research. In recent years it has become more and more apparent that appropriate representations are critical to many AI tasks, including natural language processing (see NATURAL LANGUAGE GENERATION; NATURAL LANGUAGE UNDERSTANDING), learning, and planning. Developing knowledge representation systems involves embracing some theory of what constitutes knowledge and beliefs. The concern with representation in AI thus leads naturally to examining work on the parallel epistemic issue. In addition, once knowledge representation schemes have been developed, questions still remain on how to interpret the material they model. Brachman's article on epistemology and semantic networks (1979) presents a good example of the kinds of alternatives available and why they are important.

Interest in knowledge representation has led to concern with the relationship between acquaintance (*know-of*) and propositional content (*know-that*). This relationship is crucial for epistemic theories and provides an area of direct contribution from epistemology to AI and related work, and vice versa. In this century, strong links have formed between philosophy of language and epistemology, especially in the realm of semantics (see SEMANTIC NETWORKS). Beginning from such semantically motivated views, AI approaches to knowledge representation have resulted in highly articulated representational techniques, making clearer than before how internal contents can be structured to reflect meanings. Fodor (1983), Pylyshyn (1984), and others have been building on insights from these and other sources, trying to arrive at theories of meaning that will form bases of knowledge. Although less articulated than the neonaturalist school, these views also respond in new ways to the skepticism arising from the recent trend to analysis of knowledge, this time with an approach that, although drawing insights from empirical disciplines, is rationalist in flavor. Their models are in turn available to AI research in developing and arguing for knowledge representation schemes.

In addition to know-of and know-that, AI research must deal with *know-how*: competence. At a very high level the AI community has been involved in disputes over procedural versus declarative representations of information. To some extent, these disputes have their basis in issues such as efficiency; but there are also epistemic questions involved. Attempts simultaneously to represent competence and propositional knowledge have raised for AI questions of how these two kinds of knowledge are related. These are traditional philosophical questions, and some insight into them can be gained by studying the philosophical literature.

In the other direction, AI research has brought the distinction between competence and propositional knowledge into focus for philosophers and has shown how deep the distinction runs, in that representational techniques provide solid, natural support for propositional knowledge and belief support competence (as opposed to knowledge about competence) at best awkwardly, and vice versa. Traditional epistemology by and large neglects competence, except for reasoning ability and perception. Philosophers have worried about perception for centuries; however, most of that concern has centered on establishing a link between external phenomena and the data that get in. Now AI is raising new questions about perceptual competence that have philosophical implications.

Research into vision (see VISUAL PERCEPTION) and speech understanding (qv) has demonstrated dramatically that internalizing pixel maps of images or oscilloscope curves of sounds barely touches the requirements for acquaintance. Going from digital representations of images to recognition of the objects in them turns out to be a huge step, even for simple, unmoving images from highly restricted angles of very simple objects from small, predetermined sets. No one has the slightest idea how to get the most powerful machines made to process stereo images (see STEREO VISION) in real time under circumstances remotely like those under which human vision works. The classic exposition of a theory of vision from an AI perspective can be found in the pioneering work of Marr (1978).

Speech recognition (qv) is similarly complicated; for a discussion of the problems involved, see the 1980 report on the Department of Defense speech understanding project (Newell and co-workers, 1973). It seems clear that the structuring capacities needed to go from naked inputs to percepts far exceed those Kant described, in complexity if not in power.

Knowledge representation (qv) and natural-language understanding (qv) have together opened the question of how the information stored in symbols in a computer can be said to have meaning (represent knowledge) because those symbols seem to have no connection with anything outside the computer. This is a version of the problem of reference for language in general. Insofar as knowledge is related to language and meaning, it is a new version of a familiar epistemic problem: how does the knowledge that is in one's head relate to the reality that lies outside it? Pursuing this issue with regard to computer understanding has led AI researchers to related philosophical literature.

The attempt to develop systems that can understand natural language texts has also reopened for computer scientists the traditional philosophical problems of referential opacity and related limitations on consequence. For instance, systems that attempt to understand written stories must realize that "John knows that Jane's beagle has fleas" and "Jane's beagle is Fido" can both be true without it being true that "John knows that Fido has fleas." In fact, "John says that Jane's beagle has fleas" can be true even when Jane has no dog at all, let alone a beagle. But "Jane's beagle has fleas" cannot be true unless Jane has a beagle; and "Jane's beagle has fleas" and "Jane's beagle is Fido" certainly together imply that Fido has fleas. Distinguishing contexts in which such inferences are justified from those in which they are not has been a problem for epistemology for some time; with advances in AI research, it has also become a practical problem for AI researchers (see BELIEF REPRESENTATION SYSTEMS).

Artificial intelligence research has concentrated attention on areas of justification hitherto little understood. More and more, it is becoming clear that intelligence involves not only the ability to reason according to logic in situations of (at least assumed) certainty but also the ability to extend judgments reasonably, though in the technical sense unsoundly, into areas where information is known to be incomplete. These investigations into modes of reasoning that deal in degrees or that, in effect, jump to their conclusions instead of drawing them can be viewed from an epistemic point of view as attempts to formulate techniques of justification short of logic (see REASONING, DEFAULT; REASONING, PLAUSIBLE). As such, they contribute to the epistemological literature. In the other direction, the attempt to get systems to reason in contexts of uncertainty has focused attention on the traditional distinctions between knowledge and belief, and has led AI researchers both into the traditional epistemic literature on grounds for rational belief and into a specialized formal literature on alternative logics, which, although it is not strictly speaking a branch of epistemology, contains substantial epistemic content. A striking example of this literature is Hintikka's work on knowledge and belief (1962).

In addition to these interchanges, epistemologists are beginning to borrow from work in AI and cognitive science (qv) which has developed models of the mind for which the notion of level is central. These models go beyond accepting a mental–physical distinction to provide explanatory power for epistemic views like those of Armstrong (1973) and Dretske (1969, 1981).

The relationship between AI and epistemology is more complex than these remarks would indicate, though. When AI researchers discuss knowledge, it is frequently unclear whether they mean knowledge in a sense an epistemologist would accept or whether they mean what philosophers would call *reasonable belief*. Some researchers have explicitly retreated to discussion of belief as opposed to knowledge or truth; Doyle (1979) now refers to *belief maintenance* instead of truth maintenance (qv), for instance, and Martins (1983; Shapiro, 1983) has developed a belief revision (qv) system that draws heavily on technical results in epistemology and logic. However, even with that proviso, there remain substantial areas of overlap.

So the current status of epistemology again has two apparent thrusts, both influenced by research in AI and computational paradigms. Because of the interchange of concepts in recent years, both have much to offer AI researchers, even above the traditional distinctions and analyses that have been helpful to date, in terms of presenting groundworks on which to build representation systems and from which to argue that what is represented genuinely mirrors important aspects of knowledge and belief. The first, a naturalistic view, rests on a multilayered analysis of mind to provide an antiskeptical empiricism. The second trend also draws from analyses of mind influenced by cognitive psychology and derives its thrust from an emphasis on representation as the semantic link between knowledge and reality. It remains to be seen whether this will develop into a rationalist counterpart of the new empiricism.

BIBLIOGRAPHY

D. M. Armstrong, *Belief Truth and Knowledge,* Cambridge University Press, Cambridge, UK, 1973. [Early presentation of the new naturalism.]

A. J. Ayer, *Language, Truth and Logic,* Dover Publications, Inc., N.Y., 1946.

R. J. Brachman, "On the Epistemological Status of Semantic Networks," in N. V. Findler ed., *Associative Networks,* Academic Press, New York, 1979.

J. Doyle, "A Truth Maintenance System," *Artif. Intell.* **12,** 231–272 (1979).

F. I. Dretske, *Seeing and Knowing,* University of Chicago Press, Chicago, 1969. [Dretske's basic presentation of his naturalist view.]

F. I. Dretske, *Knowledge and the Flow of Information,* MIT Press, Cambridge, Mass., 1981. [Dretske's developed view.]

J. A. Fodor, *The Language of Thought,* Harvard University Press, Cambridge, Mass., 1975.

J. A. Fodor, *The Modularity of Mind,* MIT Press, Cambridge, Mass., 1983.

E. Gettier, "Is Justified True Belief Knowledge?" *Analysis* **23,** 121–123 (1963). [The classic list of counterexamples to the view of knowledge as justified true belief.]

K. Gödel, "Some Metamathematical Results on Completeness and Consistency; On Formally Undecidable Propositions of

Principia Mathematica and Related Systems I;" "On Completeness and Consistency," in J. Van Heijenoort, ed., *From Frege to Gödel, A Source Book in Mathematical Logic 1879–1931,* Harvard University Press, Cambridge, Mass., 1967, pp. 592–617.

J. Hintikka, *Knowledge and Belief: An Introduction to the Logic of the Two Notions,* Cornell University Press, Ithaca, N.Y., 1962.

K. Lehrer, *Knowledge,* Oxford University Press, Oxford, 1974. [An analysis-of-knowledge style attack on foundationalism and presentation of the coherentist position.]

J. P. Martins, *Reasoning in Multiple Belief Spaces,* Ph.D. dissertation, Technical Report 203, State University of New York at Buffalo, 1983.

J. P. Martins and S. C. Shapiro, "Reasoning in Multiple Belief Spaces," *Proceedings of the Eighth IJCAI,* Karlsruhe, FRG, 1983, pp. 370–373.

D. Marr, "Representing Visual Information," in A. R. Hanson and E. M. Riseman, ed., *Computer Vision Systems,* Academic Press, New York, 1978, pp. 61–80. [Pioneering work in vision, which makes clear the gap between pixel maps and perception with recognition.]

A. Newell, J. Barnett, J. Forgie, C. Green, D. H. Klatt, J. C. R. Licklider, J. Munson, D. R. Reddy, and W. A. Woods, *Speech Understanding Systems: Final Report of a Study Group,* North-Holland, Amsterdam, 1973. [Demonstrates the gap between sound wave reception and hearing with recognition.]

A. Newell, "The Knowledge Level," *AI Mag.* **2,** 1–20 (1981).

Z. W. Pylyshyn, *Computation and Cognition,* MIT Press, Cambridge, Mass., 1984.

W. V. O. Quine, *Word and Object,* MIT Press, Cambridge, Mass., 1960.

J. R. Searle, "Minds, Brains, and Programs," *Behav. Brain Scie.* **3,** 415–457 (1980). [Focuses on the centrality of semantics and reference.]

J. R. Searle, *Intentionality,* Cambridge University Press, Cambridge, UK, 1983. [On semantics and referentiality.]

L. Wittgenstein, *On Certainty (Über Gewissheit),* D. Paul and G. E. M. Anscombe, trans., G. E. M. Anscombe and G. H. Von Wright, eds., Basil Blackwell, Oxford, 1969.

General References

Surveys and Collections in Philosophy

H. L. Dreyfus, ed., *Husserl Intentionality and Cognitive Science,* MIT Press, Cambridge, Mass., 1982.

P. Edwards, ed., *The Encyclopedia of Philosophy,* Macmillan, New York, 1967. [Includes surveys of knowledge and belief, the history of epistemology, perception, sense (sense data), logic, philosophy of mind, philosophy of language, and most major philosophical thinkers.]

A. P. Griffiths, ed., *Knowledge and Belief,* Oxford University Press, Oxford, 1967. [Ordinary language tradition; once again, the editor's introduction provides a survey.]

G. S. Pappas and M. Swain, eds., *Essays on Knowledge and Justification,* Cornell University Press, Ithaca, New York, 1978. [Articles in the Anglo-American tradition of analysis of knowledge; the editor's introduction provides a survey.]

R. K. Shope, *The Analysis of Knowing,* Princeton University Press, Princeton, N.J., 1982.

R. J. Swartz, ed., *Perceiving, Sensing, and Knowing,* Doubleday Anchor, Garden City, N.Y., 1967. [Sense data approach.]

The Behavioral and Brain Sciences, Vol. 6, No. 1, March 1983. [Includes a precis by Dretske of his 1981 book, commentary by more than 20 researchers, and a response by Dretske.]

Primary Sources from Philosophy

These are original philosophical works, which supplement the collections above. Well-known works from before the twentieth century are given without reference to edition since many appear in multiple editions, and virtually all should be available from any reasonable academic library. Entries follow rough chronological order. The reader is warned that philosophical works of previous centuries make difficult reading for nonphilosophers.

Plato, *Meno, Theaetetus, Republic.* [Usually found in the collected dialogues.]

Aristotle, *Prior Analytics, Metaphysics.* [Frequently found in anthologies.]

R. Descartes, *Meditations, Discourse on Method.*

G. W. Leibniz. [Many of Leibniz's works take the form of letters and the like. A useful collection, with individual writings grouped by topic, is *Leibniz Selections,* P. P. Wiener, ed., Charles Scribners' Sons, New York, 1951. A more recent edition is *New Essays of Human Understanding,* P. Remnant and J. Bennett, trans. and ed., Cambridge University Press, New York, 1981. A more complete collection is the two-volume edition, *Leibniz. Philosophical Papers and Letters,* L. E. Loemker, trans., University of Chicago Press, Chicago, 1956.]

J. Locke, *An Essay Concerning Human Understanding.*

G. Berkeley, *New Theory of Vision, Principles of Human Knowledge, Three Dialogues Between Hylas and Philonous.*

D. Hume, *Enquiry Concerning Human Understanding.*

I. Kant, *Prolegomena to Any Future Metaphysics; Critique of Pure Reason.*

E. Husserl, *Logical Investigations,* J. N. Findlay, trans., Routledge and Kegan Paul, London, 1970; *Formal and Transcendental Logic,* D. Cairns, trans., Martinus Nijhoff. The Hague, 1969.

S. P. Stich, *From Folk Psychology to Cognitive Science: The Case Against Belief,* MIT Press, Cambridge, Mass., 1983.

Sources from Artificial Intelligence

These are original research works in artificial intelligence. Some of these works were deliberately directed at epistemological issues; others are on topics that have substantial epistemological interest. Many of these works are primary research reports, but most should be relatively accessible to outside readers.

J. F. Allen, "Towards a General Theory of Action and Time," *Artif. Intell.* **23,** 123–154 (1984). [Development of models to reflect knowledge involving time.]

M. Georgeff, "A Theory of Action for MultiAgent Planning," *Proceedings of the Fourth National Conference on Artificial Intelligence,* Austin, Tex., 1984, pp. 121–125. [Process model for knowledge about action.]

H. J. Levesque, "Foundation of a Functional Approach to Knowledge Representation," *Artif. Intell.* **23,** 155–212 (1984).

H. J. Levesque, "A Logic of Implicit and Explicit Belief," *Proceedings of the Fourth National Conference on Artificial Intelligence,* Austin, Tex., 1984, pp. 198–202.

A. Maida and S. C. Shapiro, "Intensional Concepts in Propositional Semantic Networks," *Cogn. Sci.* **6,** 291–330 (1982).

J. McCarthy, "Programs with Common Sense," in M. Minsky, ed., *Semantic Information Processing,* MIT Press, Cambridge, Mass., 1968.

J. McCarthy and P. Hayes, "Some Philosophical Problems from the Standpoint of Artificial Intelligence," in B. Meltzer and D. Michie, eds., *Machine Intelligence,* Vol. 4, Edinburgh University Press, Edinburgh, pp. 463–502, 1969. [Reprinted in Webber and Nilsson (see below).]

J. McCarthy, "Epistemological Problems of Artificial Intelligence," *Proceedings of the Fifth IJCAI,* 1977, pp. 1038–1044. [Reprinted in Webber and Nilsson (see below).]

J. McCarthy, "First Order Theories of Individual Concepts and Propositions," in J. E. Hayes, D. Michie, and L. I. Mikulich, eds., *Machine Intelligence,* Vol. 9, pp. 129–147, Ellis Horwood, London.

W. J. Rapaport, "Quasi-Indexical Reference in Propositional Semantic Networks," in *Proceedings of COLING-84,* Association for Computational Linguistics, 1984, pp. 65–70. [An AI representation of knowledge-related concepts based on philosophical works.]

B. L. Webber and N. J. Nilsson eds., *Readings in Artificial Intelligence,* Tioga, Palo Alto, Calif., 1981. [This collection contains many basic articles from across the AI spectrum. The last section contains several articles explicitly related to epistemology, including the 1969 McCarthy and Hayes paper.]

R. W. Weyrauch, "Prolegomena to a Theory of Mechanized Formal Reasoning," *Artif. Intell.* **13,** 133–170 (1980). [Reprinted in Webber and Nilsson (see above).]

W. A. Woods, "Procedural Semantics as a Theory of Meaning," in A. Joshi, B. Webber, and I. Sag, eds., *Elements of Discourse Understanding,* Cambridge University Press, Cambridge, UK, pp. 300–334, 1981.

Proceedings of the Eight International Joint Conference on Artificial Intelligence, Karlsruhe, FRG, 1983. This conference is so rich a source that it almost deserves a section to itself. Relevant articles include the following:

J. A. Barnden, "Intensions as Such: An Outline," pp. 280–286.

J. Doyle, "The Ins and Outs of Reason Maintenance," pp. 349–351.

J. W. Hearne, "Simulating Non-Deductive Reasoning," pp. 362–364.

J. P. Martins and S. C. Shapiro, "Reasoning in Multiple Belief Spaces," pp. 370–373.

M. Nilsson, "A Logical Model of Knowledge," pp. 374–376.

A. Sloman, D. McDermott, and W. A. Woods, Panel Discussion: "Under What Conditions Can A Machine Attribute Meaning to Symbols?" pp. 44–48.

J. T. NUTTER
Virginia Tech

EPISTLE

A text-critiquing system that checks spelling, grammar, and style in business correspondence, EPISTLE implements grammar checks, which constitute the central part of the system, using an augmented phrase structure grammar (qv). Style checks are currently limited to overly complex sentences. It was written by G. Heidorn, K. Jensen, L. Miller, R. Byrd, and M. Chodorow at IBM around 1981 [see G. Heidorn and co-workers, "The EPISTLE Text-Critiquing System," *IBM Sys. J.* **21**(3), 305–326 (1982)].

K. S. ARORA
SUNY at Buffalo

EPSILON-SEMANTICS

INFINITESIMAL PROBABILITIES

Epsilon-semantics (ε-semantics, for short) is a formal framework for belief revision in which belief statements are interpreted as statements of high probability, infinitesimally close to one, and where belief revision takes place by conditioning current beliefs on newly available evidence. The conditionalization of extreme probabilities yields nonnumeric belief revision, as if propositions were assigned qualitative truth values from the set {TRUE, BELIEVED, POSSIBLE, DISBELIEVED, FALSE}. The basic idea of ε-semantics can be traced back to the conditional logic (qv) of Adams (1966, 1975) and the ordinal condition functions (OCF) of Spohn (1988). Potential applications in nonmonotonic logic and default reasoning (qv) were noted in McCarthy (1986) and Pearl (1988) and further developed by Lehmann (1989), Geffner (1989), Pearl (1990) and Goldszmidt and co-workers (1990).

A simple way of viewing ε-semantics is to consider an ordinary probability function P defined over a set W of possible worlds (or states of the world), and to imagine that the probability $P(w)$ assigned to each world w is a polynomial function of some small positive parameter ε, for example, $\alpha, \beta\varepsilon, \gamma\varepsilon^2, \ldots$, etc. Accordingly, the probabilities assigned to any subset A of W, as well as all conditional probabilities $P(A|B)$, will be rational functions of ε. Now define the ranking function $\kappa(A|B)$ [which Spohn (1988) called non-probabilistic Ordinal Conditional Function (OCF)] as the power of the most significant term in the expansion of $P(A|B)$ into a power series of ε,

$$\kappa(A|B) = \text{lowest } n \text{ such that } \lim_{\varepsilon \to 0} P(A|B)/\varepsilon^n \text{ is nonzero} \tag{1}$$

In other words, $\kappa(A|B) = n$ iff $P(A|B)$ is of the same order of magnitude as ε^n, or equivalently, $\kappa(A|B)$ is of the same order-of-magnitude as $[P(A|B)]^{-1}$.

If we think of n for which $P(w) = \alpha\varepsilon^n$ as measuring the degree to which the world w is disbelieved (or the degree of surprise were we to observe w), then $\kappa(A|B)$ can be thought of as the degree of disbelief (or surprise) in A, given that B is true. Parameterizing a probability measure by ε, and extracting the lowest exponent of ε as the measure of (dis)belief, is a way of capturing the process by which people abstract qualitative beliefs from numeric probabilities and accept them as tentative truths, until rejected by future evidence. For other formalizations of belief acceptance see Kyburg (1961) and Pearl (1987b).

It is easy to verify (see Spohn, 1988) that κ satisfies the following properties:

1. $\kappa(A) = \min \{\kappa(w)|w \in A\}$
2. $\kappa(A) = 0$ or $\kappa(\neg A) = 0$, or both
3. $\kappa(A \cup B) = \min\{\kappa(A), \kappa(B)\}$
4. $\kappa(A \cap B) = \kappa(A|B) + \kappa(B)$ $\qquad$ (2)

These reflect (on a logarithmic scale) the usual properties of probability functions, with *min* replacing addition, and addition replacing multiplication:

1. $P(A) = \sum\limits_{w \in A} P(w)$

2. $P(A) + P(\neg A) = 1$

3. $P(A \cup B) = P(A) + P(B) - P(A \cap B)$

4. $P(A \cap B) = P(A|B)P(B)$ (3)

The result is a probabilistically sound calculus, employing integer addition, for manipulating order-of-magnitudes of disbeliefs. For example, if we make the following correspondence between linguistic quantifiers and ε^n:

$P(A) = \varepsilon^0$	A is believable	$\kappa(A) = 0$
$P(A) = \varepsilon^1$	A is unlikely	$\kappa(A) = 1$
$P(A) = \varepsilon^2$	A is very unlikely	$\kappa(A) = 2$
$P(A) = \varepsilon^3$	A is extremely unlikely	$\kappa(A) = 3$
–	——	–

then the infinitesimal approximation yields a nonmonotonic logic to reason about likelihood. It takes sentences in the form of quantified conditional sentences; for example, "Birds are likely to fly," (written $\kappa(\neg f|b) = 1$), "Penguins are most likely birds," (written $\kappa(\neg b|p) = 2$), "Penguins are extremely unlikely to fly," (written $\kappa(f|p) = 3$), and returns quantified conclusions in the form of "If x is a penguin-bird then x is extremely unlikely to fly" (written $\kappa(f|p \wedge b) = 3$).

The basic κ ranking system, as described in Spohn (1988), requires the specification of a complete probability model before reasoning can commence. In other words, the knowledge base must be sufficiently rich to define the κ associated with every world w. In practice, such specification might require knowledge that is not readily available in common discourse. For example, we might be given the information that birds fly (written $\kappa(\neg f|b) = 1$) and no information at all about properties of nonbirds, thus leaving $\kappa(f \wedge \neg b)$ unspecified. Hence, inferential machinery is required for drawing conclusions from partially specified models, such as those associating a κ with isolated default statements. Such machinery is provided by the conditional logic of Adams (1975), which forms the basis of ε-semantics.

Adams's logic can be regarded as a bivalued infinitesimal analysis, with input sentences specifying κ values of only 0 and 1, corresponding to "likely" and "unlikely" associations. However, instead of insisting on a complete specification of $\kappa(w)$, the logic admits fragmentary sets of conditional sentences, treats them as constraints over the distribution of $\kappa(w)$, and infers only such statements that are compelled to acquire high likelihood in every distribution $\kappa(w)$ satisfying these constraints. A multivalued extension of Adams's logic, accepting sentences with varying degrees of likelihood, is described in Goldenszmidt and Pearl (1991).

ε-SEMANTICS

Two Levels of Knowledge

Epsilon-semantics, like epistemic probabilities and many conditional logics, distinguishes between two types of sentences, those that convey knowledge about necessary truths and the general tendency of things to happen (eg, "Birds fly," "Birds are animals") and those that describe findings or observations specific to a given object or a situation (eg, "Tim is a bird," "All blocks on this table are green"). The first set of sentences, denoted K (for knowledge), corresponds to nomic (or lawlike) assertions and may include both defeasible (defaults) and strict sentences (denoted Δ and S, respectively). The second set of sentences, denoted E (for evidence), corresponds to incidental or transitory findings. This useful distinction is reflected in natural language by the selective usage of the word "If," especially in counterfactual forms. For example, it is legitimate to say "If I were a bird I would fly" but not "If this block were on this table it would be green." Accordingly, the sentence "Birds fly" will reside in K, whereas "All blocks on this table are green" will reside in E. Another distinguishing characteristic is that sentences in E accept the preemption "happen to," such as "Tim happened to be a bird." In contrast, those in K accept the preemption "always" or "almost always."

For simplicity of exposition, we first consider default theories in the form $T = \langle E, \Delta \rangle$, void of strict conditionals. The evidence sentences (E) will assign properties to specific individuals; for example, $p(a)$ asserts that individual a has the property p. The default statements (Δ) are of the type "p's are typically q's," written $p(x) \rightarrow q(x)$ or simply $p \rightarrow q$, which is short for saying "any individual x having property p typically has property q." The properties $p, q, r \ldots$ can be compound Boolean formulas of some atomic predicates $p_1, p_2, \ldots p_n$, with x as their only free variable. However, no ground defaults [eg, $p(a) \rightarrow q(a)$] are allowed in E and no compound defaults [eg, $p \rightarrow (q \rightarrow r)$] are allowed in Δ. The default statement $d' : p \rightarrow \neg q$ will be called the denial of $d : p \rightarrow q$.

Basic Definitions

Let L be the language of propositional formulas, and let a truth-valuation for L be a function t that maps the sentences in L to the set $\{1,0\}$, (1 for *TRUE* and 0 for *FALSE*,) such that t respects the usual Boolean connectives. To define a probability assignment over the sentences in L, we regard each truth valuation t as a world w and define $P(w)$ such that $\Sigma_w P(w) = 1$. This assigns a probability measure to each sentence l of L via $P(l) = \Sigma_w P(w) w(l)$.

Epsilon-semantics interprets Δ as a set of restrictions on P, in the form of extreme conditional probabilities, infinitesimally removed from either 0 or 1. For example, the sentence $Bird(x) \rightarrow Fly(x)$ is interpreted as $P(Fly(x)|Bird(x)) \geq 1 - \varepsilon$, where epsilon is understood to stand for an infinitesimal quantity that can be made arbitrarily small, short of actually being zero. Accordingly, ε-semantics qualifies a propositional formula r as a plausible conclusion of $T = \langle E, \Delta \rangle$, written $E \vdash_\Delta r$, whenever the restrictions of Δ force P to satisfy $\lim_{\varepsilon \to 0} P(r|E) = 1$.

It is convenient to characterize the set of conclusions sanctioned by this semantics in terms of the set of facts–conclusion pairs that are entailed by a given Δ. Adams (1975) named this relation p-entailment. However, the name ε-entailment better serves to distinguish this from other forms of probabilistic entailment (see the next section on Consistency and Ambiguity). ε-entailment is formally defined as follows.

Definition. Let $\mathcal{P}_{\Delta,\varepsilon}$ stand for the set of distributions licensed by Δ for any given ε; that is,

$$\mathcal{P}_{\Delta,\varepsilon} = \{P : P(v|u) \geq 1 - \varepsilon \text{ and } P(u) > 0,$$

$$\text{whenever } u \to v \in \Delta\} \quad (4)$$

A conditional statement $d : p \to q$ is said to be ε-entailed by Δ, if every distribution $P \in \mathcal{P}_{\Delta,\varepsilon}$ satisfies $P(q|p) = 1 - O(\varepsilon)$, [ie, for every $\delta > 0$ there exists a $\varepsilon > 0$ such that every $P \in \mathcal{P}_{\Delta,\varepsilon}$ would satisfy $P(q|p) \geq 1 - \delta$].

Axiomatic Characterization

The conditional logic developed by Adams (1975) faithfully represents this semantics by qualitative inference rules, thus facilitating the derivation of new sound sentences by direct symbolic manipulations on Δ. The essence of Adams' logic is summarized in the following inference rules, restated for default theories in Geffner (1988) (see also Lehmann and Magidor, 1988; Geffner and Pearl, 1990).

Inference Rules. Let $T = \langle E, \Delta \rangle$ be a default theory where E is a set of ground proposition formulas and Δ is a set of default rules. r is a plausible conclusion of F in the context of Δ, written $F \vdash_\Delta r$, iff r is derivable from F using the following rules of inference.

Rule 1
(Conditionals) $(p \to q) \in \Delta \Rightarrow p \vdash_\Delta q$

Rule 2
(Deduction) $p \vdash q \Rightarrow p \vdash_\Delta q$

Rule 3
(Cumulativity) $p \vdash_\Delta q, p \vdash_\Delta r \Rightarrow (p \wedge q) \vdash_\Delta r$

Rule 4
(Contraction) $p \vdash_\Delta q, (p \wedge q) \vdash_\Delta r \Rightarrow p \vdash_\Delta r$

Rule 5
(Disjunction) $p \vdash_\Delta r, q \vdash_\Delta r \Rightarrow (p \vee q) \vdash_\Delta r$ (5)

Rule 1 permits us to conclude the consequent of a default when its antecedent is all that has been learned, and this permission is granted regardless of other information that Δ may contain. Rule 2 states that theorems that logically follow from a set of formulas can be concluded in any theory containing those formulas. Rule 3, called triangularity in Pearl (1988) and cautious monotony in Lehmann and Magidor (1988), permits the attachment of any established conclusion (q) to the current set of findings (p),

without affecting the status of any other derived conclusion (r). Rule 4 says that any conclusion (r) that follows from an evidence set (p) augmented by a derived conclusion (q) also follows from the original evidence set alone. Finally, rule 5 says that a conclusion that follows from two findings also follows from their disjunction.

Some Meta-Theorems

T-1
(Logical Closure) $p \vdash_\Delta q, p \wedge q \supset r \Rightarrow p \vdash_\Delta r$

T-2
(Equivalent Contexts) $p \equiv q, p \vdash_\Delta r \Rightarrow q \vdash_\Delta r$

T-3
(Exceptions) $p \wedge q \vdash_\Delta r, p \vdash_\Delta \neg r \Rightarrow p \vdash_\Delta \neg q$

T-4
(Right Conjunction) $p \vdash_\Delta r, p \vdash_\Delta q \Rightarrow p \vdash_\Delta q \wedge r$

Some Nontheorems

(Irrelevance) $p \vdash_\Delta r \Rightarrow p \wedge q \vdash_\Delta r$
(Transitivity) $p \vdash_\Delta q, q \vdash_\Delta r \Rightarrow p \vdash_\Delta r$
(Left Conjunction) $p \vdash_\Delta r, q \vdash_\Delta r \Rightarrow p \wedge q \vdash_\Delta r$
(Contraposition) $p \vdash_\Delta r \Rightarrow \neg r \vdash_\Delta \neg p$
(Rational Monotony)

$$p \vdash_\Delta r, \text{ NOT } (p \vdash_\Delta \neg q) \Rightarrow p \wedge q \vdash_\Delta r \quad (6)$$

This last property, similar to CV of conditional logic (qv), has one of its antecedents negated; hence, its consequences cannot be derived from Δ using the five rules of ε-semantics. It is, nevertheless, a desirable feature of a consequence relation and can be restored within ε-semantics if we restrict $\mathcal{P}_{\Delta,\varepsilon}$ to probability functions that are analytic in ε.

Epsilon-semantics does not sanction transitivity, left conjunction, and contraposition as absolute inference rules, because there are contexts in which these rules fail. For instance, transitivity fails in the penguin example—all penguins are birds, birds typically fly, yet penguins do not. Left conjunction fails when p and q create a new condition unshared by either p or q. For example, if you marry Ann (p) you will be happy (r), if you marry Nancy (q) you will be happy as well (r), but if you marry both ($p \wedge q$), you will be miserable ($\neg r$). Contraposition fails in situations where $\neg p$ is incompatible with $\neg r$. For example, let $p \to r$ stand for $Birds \to Fly$. Now imagine a world in which the only nonflying objects are a few sick birds. Clearly, $Bird \to Fly$ holds, yet if we observe a nonflying object we can safely conclude that it is a bird, hence $\neg r \to p$, defying contraposition.

Semimonotonicity. The consequence relation defined by ε-semantics is monotonic relative to the addition of default rules, that is,

$$\text{if } p \vdash_\Delta r \quad \text{and} \quad \Delta \subseteq \Delta', \quad \text{then } p \vdash_{\Delta'} r \quad (7)$$

This follows directly from the fact that $\mathscr{P}_{\Delta',\varepsilon} \subseteq \mathscr{P}_{\Delta,\varepsilon}$ because each default statement imposes a new constraint on $\mathscr{P}_{\Delta,\varepsilon}$. Thus, ε-entailment is nonmonotonic relative to the addition of new findings (in E) and monotonic relative to the addition of new defaults (in Δ). Full nonmonotonicity will be exhibited in the section on Recent Extensions, where stronger forms of entailment are considered.

The cautious, semimonotonic character of ε-semantics, and especially its failure to accommodate arguments based on irrelevance, (eg, to conclude a red bird flies from "birds fly"), clearly shows the ε-semantics is not complete for default reasoning. Nevertheless, the set of conclusions that are derived by this semantics constitutes a core of plausible conclusions that should clearly be accommodated by every system of default reasoning (qv). Interestingly, it is this very core that dispositional approaches to default reasoning (eg, Reiter, 1987) find hardest to accommodate.

Consistency and Ambiguity

An important and unique feature of ε-semantics is its ability to distinguish theories portraying inconsistencies (eg, $\langle p \to q, p \to \neg q \rangle$) from those conveying ambiguity (eg, $\langle p \wedge q, p \to r, q \to \neg r \rangle$) and those conveying exceptions (eg, $\langle p \to q, p \wedge r \to \neg q \rangle$).

Definition. Δ is said to be ε-consistent if $\mathscr{P}_{\Delta,\varepsilon}$ is nonempty for every $\varepsilon > 0$, else, Δ is ε-inconsistent. A default statement $d: p \to q$ is said to be ambiguous, given Δ, if both $\{p \to q\} \cup \Delta$ and $\{p \to \neg q\} \cup \Delta$ are ε-consistent.

Consistency-Entailment Symmetry. ε-entailment and ε-consistency are connected by a symmetrical relation, reminiscent of that in classic logic (Adams, 1975). If Δ is ε-consistent, then a statement $d: p \to q$ is ε-entailed by Δ iff its denial $d': p \to \neg q$ is ε-inconsistent with Δ.

In addition to Rules 1–5, the logic also possesses a systematic procedure for testing ε-consistency (hence, ε-entailment), involving a moderate number of propositional satisfiability tests. The test is based on the notion of toleration.

Definition (Toleration). Given a truth-valuation t, a default statement $p \to q$ is said to be verified under t if t assigns the value 1 to both p and q. $p \to q$ is said to be falsified under t if p is assigned a 1 and q is assigned a 0. A default statement $d: p \to q$ is said to be tolerated by a set Δ' of such statements if there is a t that verifies d and does not falsify any statement in Δ'.

It can be shown (Adams, 1975) that a finite set Δ of default statements is ε-consistent iff in every nonempty subset Δ' of Δ there exists at least one statement that is tolerated by Δ'. This leads to a simple procedure of testing the consistency of defeasible databases (Goldszmidt and Pearl, 1989a).

Consistency Testing Procedure

1. Mark every default statement that is tolerated by Δ.
2. Remove every marked statement from Δ.

3. Repeat the process on the remaining set of statements, until there are no more default statements left.
4. If this process leads to an empty set, then Δ is ε-consistent, else it is ε-inconsistent.

This procedure requires $\frac{|\Delta|^2}{2}$ propositional satisfiability tests. Hence, if the material counterpart of $p \supset q$ of each statement $p \to q$ in Δ is a Horn expression, then consistency (hence entailment) can be tested in time quadratic with the number of literals in Δ. When Δ can be represented as a default network [ie, a set of default statements $p \to q$ where both p and q are atomic propositions (or negation thereof)], consistency can be established by a simple graphic criterion (Pearl, 1987a) generalizing that of Touretzky (1986).

Network Consistency. Δ is consistent iff every pair of conflicting arcs $p_1 \to q$ and $p_2 \to \neg q$

1. p_1 and p_2 are distinct, and
2. There is no cycle of positive arcs that embraces both p_1 and p_2.

These tests are valid only when K consists of purely defeasible conditionals. For mixtures $K = \Delta \cup S$ of defeasible and nondefeasible statements, consistency and entailment require a slightly modified procedure (Goldszmidt and Pearl 1989a): After removing all defeasible sentences (testing for toleration by $\Delta \cup S$), each sentence in S should be tolerated by S. This procedure attributes a special meaning to strict conditional statement $s: a \to b$, different than the material implication $a \supset b$. For example, conforming to common usage of conditionals, it will proclaim $S = \{a \Rightarrow b, a \Rightarrow \neg b\}$ as inconsistent and will entail $a \Rightarrow b$ from $\neg b \Rightarrow \neg a$ but not from $\neg a$.

Illustrations

To illustrate the syntactical and graphical derivations facilitated by ε-semantics, consider the celebrated Penguin triangle of Figure 1. T comprises the sentences:

$$E = \{Penguin(Tweety), Bird(Tweety)\} \quad (8)$$

$$\Delta = \{Penguin \to \neg fly, Bird \to Fly, Penguin \to Bird\} \quad (9)$$

Although Δ does not specify explicitly whether penguin-birds fly, the desired conclusion is derived in three steps, using Rule 1 and 3.

1. $Penguin(Tweety) \vdash_\Delta \neg Fly(Tweety)$ (from Rule 1)
2. $Penguin(Tweety) \vdash_\Delta Bird(Tweety)$ (from Rule 1)
3. $Penguin(Tweety), Bird(Tweety) \vdash_\Delta \neg Fly(Tweety)$
   (Applying Rule 3 to lines 1, 2)

Note that preference toward subclass specificity is maintained despite the defeasible nature of the rule $Penguin \to Bird$, which admits exceptional penguins in the form of nonbirds.

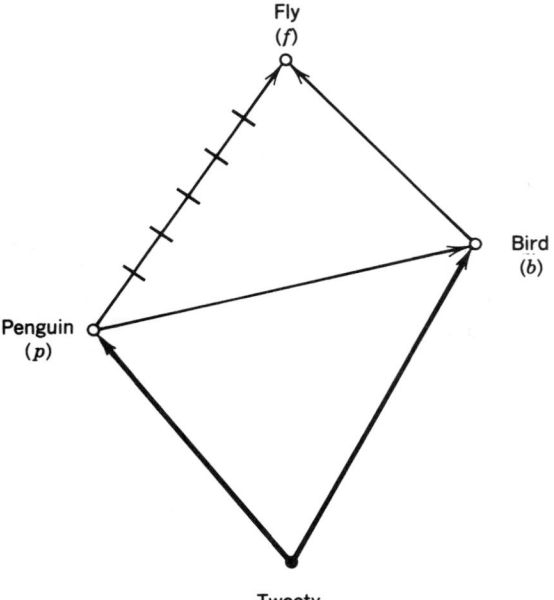

Figure 1. A network representing the knowledge base of eqs. 8 and 9. Heavy arcs represent evidence about individuals, thin arcs represent default statements, and slashed arcs represent default denials. The arc between Penguin and Bird imposes specificity preference, yielding the conclusion "Tweety does not fly."

The conclusion $p \wedge b \to \neg f$ can also be established by showing that its denial, $p \wedge b \to f$, is ε-inconsistent with

$$\Delta = \{p \to \neg f, b \to f, p \to b\} \qquad (10)$$

Indeed, no truth-valuation of $\{p, b, f\}$ can verify any sentence in

$$\Delta' = \{p \to \neg f, p \to b, p \wedge b \to f\} \qquad (11)$$

without falsifying at least one other sentence.

Applying theorem T-3 to the network of Figure 1 yields another plausible conclusion, $Bird \to \neg Penguin$, stating that when one talks about birds one does not have penguins in mind; that is, penguins are an exceptional kind of birds. It is a valid conclusion of Δ because every P in $\mathscr{P}_{\Delta,\varepsilon}$ must yield $P(p|b) = O(\varepsilon)$. Of course, if the statement $Bird \to Penguin$ is artificially added to Δ, inconsistency results; as ε diminishes below a certain level (1/3 in our case), $\mathscr{P}_{\Delta,\varepsilon}$ becomes empty. This can be predicted from purely topological considerations by testing whether the denial of the conclusion renders the network inconsistent. Adding the arc $Bird \to Penguin$ would create a cycle of positive arcs embracing "Bird" and "Penguin," and these sprout two conflicting arcs toward "Fly," which establishes inconsistency. Hence, the network of Figure 1 ε-entails $Bird \to \neg Penguin$. By the same graphic method one can show that the network also ε-entails the natural conclusion, $Fly \to \neg Penguin$. This contraposition of $Penguin \to \neg Fly$ is sanctioned only because the existence of flying nonpenguins (ie, normal birds) is guaranteed by the other rules in Δ.

RECENT EXTENSIONS

Summarizing the preceding discussion, ε-semantics yields a system of defeasible inference with the following features:

1. The system provides a formal distinction between exceptions, ambiguities, and inconsistencies and effective procedures for testing and maintaining consistency.
2. Multiple extensions do not arise, and preferences among arguments (eg, toward higher specificity) are respected by natural deduction.
3. There is no need to specify abnormality relations in advance [as in circumscription (qv)]; such relations (eg, that penguins are abnormal birds) are automatically inferred from the knowledge base.

However, default reasoning requires two facilities: one that forces conclusions to be retractable in the light of new refuting evidence; the second, which protects conclusions from retraction in the light of new but irrelevant evidence. Epsilon-semantics excels at the first requirement but fails at the second. For instance, in the example of Figure 1, if we are told that Tweety is also a blue penguin, the system would retract all previous conclusions (as ambiguous), even though there is no rule that in any way connects color to flying. [The opposite is true in default logic (Reiter, 1987) and circumscription (McCarthy, 1986)—they excel on the second requirement but do not retract conclusions refuted by more specific information, unless exceptions are enumerated in advance.]

The reason for this conservative behavior lies in the insistence that any issued conclusion attains high probability in *all* probability models licensed by Δ and one such model reflects a world in which blue penguins do fly. In order to respect the communication convention that, unless stated explicitly, properties are presumed to be irrelevant to each other, additional restrictions must be imposed on the family of probability models relative to which a given conclusion is checked for soundness. The restricted probabilities should embody only dependencies that are implied by Δ, but no others. Several such extensions to ε-semantics are described next.

System Z

One way of suppressing irrelevant properties is to restrict our attention to the "most normal" or "least surprising" probability models that comply with the constraints in Δ. This can be most conveniently done within the infinitesimal analysis of Spohn (see the first section), where the ranking function $\kappa(w)$ represents the degree of surprise associated with world w. The "least surprising" probability corresponds to assigning each world w the lowest possible ranking $\kappa(w)$ permitted by the constraints in Δ. To ratify a sentence $p \to q$ within this paradigm, we must first find this minimal ranking function κ and, then, test whether $\kappa(q|p) < \kappa(\neg q|p)$ holds in this ranking.

Translating the constraints of equation 4 to the language of infinitesimals, yields

$$\kappa(v \wedge u) < \kappa(\neg v \wedge u) \qquad \text{if } u \to u \in \Delta \qquad (12a)$$

where κ of a formula f is given by

$$\kappa(f) = \min_{w} \{\kappa(w): w \models f\} \qquad (12b)$$

Remarkably, if Δ is ε-consistent, such constraints admit a unique minimal κ distribution that was named **Z-ranking** in Pearl (1990). Moreover, finding this minimal distribution for a given world w requires no more computation than testing for ε-consistency according to the procedure given in the section on Consistency and Ambiguity. We first identify all default statements in Δ that are tolerated by Δ, assign to them a Z-rank of 0, and remove them from Δ. Next we assign a Z-rank of 1 to every default statement that is tolerated by the remaining set, and so on. Continuing in this way, we form an ordered partition of $\Delta = (\Delta_0, \Delta_1, \Delta_2, \ldots, \Delta_K)$, where Δ_i consists of all statements tolerated by $\Delta - \Delta_0 - \Delta_1 - \cdots \Delta_{i-1}$. This partition uncovers a natural priority among the default rules in Δ and represents the relative cost associated with violating any of these defaults, with preference given to the more specific classes.

Once we establish the Z-ranking on defaults, the minimal ranking on worlds is given by

$$\mathbf{Z}(w) = \min \{n: w \models (v \supset u), \quad \mathbf{Z}(v \to u) \geq n\} \quad (13)$$

In other words, $\mathbf{Z}(w)$ is equal to 1 plus the rank of the highest-ranked default statement falsified in w.

Given $Z(w)$, we can now define a useful extension of ε-entailment, which was called 1-entailment in Pearl (1990).

Definition (1-Entailment). A formula g is said to be 1-entailed by f, in the context Δ (written $f \vdash_1 g$), if g holds in all minimal-**Z** worlds satisfying f. In other words,

$$f \vdash_1 g \qquad \text{iff } \mathbf{Z}(f \wedge g) < \mathbf{Z}(f \wedge \neg g) \qquad (14)$$

Note that ε-entailment is clearly a subset of 1-entailment because, using the language of Z-ranking, it corresponds to $f \vdash_\Delta g$ iff $\mathbf{Z}(f \wedge g) = \infty$.

Lehmann (1989) has extended ε-entailment by closing it under the rational monotony rule of equation 6, thus obtaining a new consequence relation that he called rational closure. Goldszmidt and Pearl (1989b) have shown that 1-entailment and rational closure are identical whenever Δ is ε-consistent. Thus, the procedure for testing ε-consistency also provides a $O(|\Delta^2|)$ procedure for testing entailment in rational closure.

Illustrations

Figure 2 represents a knowledge base formed by adding three rules to that of Figure 1.

1. "Penguins live in the Antarctic" $p \to a$
2. "Birds have wings" $b \to w$
3. "Animals that fly are mobile" $f \to m$ (15)

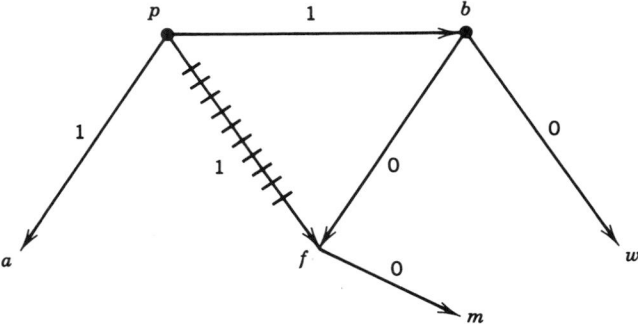

Figure 2. A knowledge base containing the defaults of eqs. 10 and 15, together with their Z-labels, yielding the consequences shown in eq. 16.

The numerical labels on the arcs stand for the Z-ranking of the corresponding rules.

The following are examples of plausible consequences that can be drawn from Δ by the various systems discussed in this section (ME will be discussed in the next section).

ε-entailed	1-entailed	ME-entailed
$b \wedge p \vdash_\Delta \neg f$	$\neg b \vdash_1 \neg p$	$p \vdash_{ME} w$
$f \vdash_\Delta \neg p$	$\neg f \vdash_1 \neg b$	$p \wedge \neg a \vdash_{ME} \neg f$
$b \vdash_\Delta \neg p$	$\neg f \vdash_1 m$	$p \wedge \neg a \vdash_{ME} w$
$p \wedge a \vdash_\Delta b$	$\neg m \vdash_1 \neg b$	
	$p \wedge \neg w \vdash_1 b$	(16)

1-Entailment sanctions many plausible inference patterns that are not ε-entailed, among them chaining, contraposition, and discounting irrelevant features. For example, from the knowledge base of Figure 2 we can now conclude that birds are mobile, $b \vdash_1 m$ and that immobile objects are nonbirds, $\neg m \vdash_1 \neg b$, and that green birds still fly. On the other hand, 1-entailment does not permit us to conclude that penguins who do not live in the Antarctic still do not fly, $p \wedge \neg a \to \neg f$. In general, from $\Delta = \{a \to b, c \to d\}$ we cannot conclude $a \wedge \neg b \wedge c \to d$.

This inability to sanction property inheritance from classes to exceptional subclasses represents the main weakness of 1-entailment. For example, given the knowledge base of Figure 2, 1-entailment will not sanction the conclusion that penguins have wings ($p \to w$) by virtue of being birds (albeit exceptional birds). The reason is that according to the Z-ranking procedure all statements conditioned on p should obtain a rank of 1, and this amounts to proclaiming penguins an exceptional type of birds in *all* respects, barred from inheriting *any* birdlike properties (eg, laying eggs, having beaks). To sanction property inheritance across exceptional classes, a more refined ordering is required that also takes into account the number of defaults falsified in a given world, not merely their rank orders. One such refinement is provided by the maximum-entropy approach (Goldszmidt and co-workers, 1990), where each world is ranked by the sum of weights on the defaults falsified by that world. Another refinement is provided by Geffner's conditional entailment (Geffner, 1989), where the priority of defaults induces a partial order on worlds. These two refinements are summarized next.

The Maximum Entropy Approach

The maximum entropy (ME) approach attempts to capture the convention that, unless mentioned explicitly, properties are presumed to be independent of one another; such presumptions are normally embedded in probability distributions that attain the maximum entropy subject to a set of constraints (Jaynes, 1979). Given a set Δ of default rules and a family of probability distributions that are admissible relative to the constraints conveyed by Δ (ie, $P(\beta_r \to \alpha_r) \geq 1 - \varepsilon, \forall\, r \in \Delta$), we single out a distinguished distribution $P^*_{\varepsilon,\Delta}$ having the greatest entropy $- \Sigma_w P(w)\log(w)$ and define entailment relative to this distribution by

$$f \vdash_{ME} g \quad \text{iff} \quad P^*_{\varepsilon,\Delta}(g|f) \underset{\varepsilon \to 0}{\to} 1 \quad (17)$$

An infinitesimal analysis of the ME approach also yields a ranking function κ on worlds, where $\kappa(w)$ corresponds to the lowest exponent of ε in the expansion of $P^*_{\varepsilon,\Delta}(w)$ into a power series in ε. It can be shown that this ranking function can be encoded parsimoniously by assigning an integer weight κ_r to each default rule $r \in \Delta$ and letting $\kappa(w)$ be the sum of the weights associated with the rules falsified by w. The weight κ_r, in turn, reflects the cost we must add to each world w that falsifies rule r, so that the resulting ranking function would satisfy the constraints conveyed by Δ, namely,

$$\min \{\kappa(w): w \models \alpha_r \wedge \beta_r\} < \min \{\kappa(w): w \models \alpha_r \wedge \neg\beta_r\},$$
$$r: \alpha_r \to \beta_r \in \Delta \quad (18)$$

These considerations lead to a set of $|\Delta|$ nonlinear equations for the weights κ_r, which, under certain conditions, can be solved by iterative methods. Once the rule weights are established, ME-entailment is determined by the criterion of equation 15, translated to

$$f \vdash_{ME} g \quad \text{iff} \quad \min \{\kappa(w): w \models f \wedge g\}$$
$$< \min \{\kappa(w): w \models f \wedge \neg g\} \quad (19)$$

where

$$\kappa(w) = \sum_{r:\, w \models \alpha_r \wedge \neg\beta_r} \kappa_r$$

We see that ME-entailment requires minimization over worlds, a task that is *NP*-hard even for Horn expressions (Ben-Eliyahu, 1990). In practice, however, this minimization is accomplished quite effectively in network-type databases, yielding a reasonable set of inference patterns. For example, in the database of Figure 2, ME-entailment will sanction the desired consequence $p \vdash w$, $p \wedge \neg a \vdash \neg f$, and $p \wedge \neg a \vdash w$, and, moreover, unlike 1-entailment, it will conclude $c \wedge p \vdash_1 \neg f$ from $\Delta \cup \{c \to f\}$, where c is an irrelevant property.

An interesting feature of the ME approach is its sensitivity to the format in which the rules are expressed. This is illustrated in the following example. From $\Delta = \{$Swedes are blond, Swedes are well-mannered$\}$, ME will conclude that dark-haired Swedes are still well-mannered, while no such conclusion will be drawn from $\Delta = \{$Swedes are blond and well-mannered$\}$. This sensitivity might sometimes be useful for distinguishing fine nuances in natural discourse, indicating, for example, that behavior and hair color are two independent qualities. It stands at variance with most approaches to default reasoning, where $a \to b \wedge c$ is treated as a shorthand notation of $a \to b$ and $a \to c$.

The ME approach fails to respond to causal information (see Pearl, 1988, pp. 463, 519 and Hunter, 1989). This prevents it from properly handling tasks such as the Yale shooting problem (Hanks and McDermott, 1986), where rules of causal character should be given priority over other rules. This weakness may perhaps be overcome by introducing causal operators into the ME formulation, similar to the way causal operators are incorporated within other formalisms of nonmonotonic reasoning (eg, Shoham, 1986; Geffner, 1989).

Conditional Entailment

Conditional entailment (Geffner, 1989) overcomes the weaknesses of 1-entailment by introducing two refinements. First, rather than letting rule priorities dictate a ranking function on worlds, a partial order on worlds is induced instead. To determine the preference between two worlds, w and w', we examine the highest priority default rules that distinguish between the two, that is, that are falsified by one and not by the other. If all such rules remain unfalsified in one of the two worlds, then this world is the preferred one. Formally, if $\Delta[w]$ and $\Delta[w']$ stand for the set of rules falsified by w and w', respectively, then w is preferred to w' (written $w < w'$) iff $\Delta[w'] \neq \Delta[w']$ and for every rule r in $\Delta[w] - \Delta[w']$ there exists a rule r' in $\Delta[w'] - \Delta[w]$ such that r' has a higher priority than r (written $r < r'$). Using this criterion, a world w will always be preferred to w' if it falsifies a proper subset of the rules falsified by w'. Lacking this feature in the Z-ordering has prevented 1-entailment from concluding $p \vdash w$ in the example of Figure 2.

The second refinement introduced by Geffner is allowing the rule-priority relation, $<$, to become a partial order as well. This partial order is determined by the following interpretation of the rule $\alpha \to \beta$; if α is all that we know, then, regardless of other rules that Δ may contain, we are authorized to assert β [see Rule 1 (Conditionals) in (5)]. This means that $r: \alpha \to \beta$ should get a higher priority than any argument (a chain of rules) leading from α to $\neg\beta$ and, more generally, if a set of rules $\Delta' \subset \Delta$ does not tolerate r, then at least one rule in Δ' ought to have a lower priority than r. In Figure 2, for example, the rule $r_3: p \to \neg f$ is not tolerated by the set $\{r_1: p \to b, r_2: b \to f\}$, hence, we must have $r_1 < r_3$ or $r_2 < r_3$. Similarly, the rule $r_1: p \to b$ is not tolerated by $\{r_2, r_3\}$, hence, we also have $r_2 < r_1$ or $r_3 < r_1$. From the asymmetry and transitivity of $<$, these two conditions yield $r_2 < r_3$ and $r_2 < r_1$. It is clear, then, that this priority on rules will induce the preference $w < w'$, whenever w validates $p \wedge b \wedge \neg f$ and w' validates $p \wedge b \wedge f$; the former falsifies r_2, while the latter falsifies the higher priority rule r_3. In general, we say that a proposition g *is conditionally entailed* by f (in the context of Δ) if g holds in all the preferred worlds of f induced by every priority ordering admissible with Δ.

Conditional entailment bridges the gap between the conditional and dispositional approaches to default reasoning. It rectifies the shortcomings of 1-entailment and ME-entailment, while respecting the basic core of plausibility norms derived from ε-semantics. However, having been based on model minimization as well as on enumeration of subsets of rules, its computational complexity might be overbearing. A proof theory for conditional entailment and its unification with causal theories can be found in Geffner (1989).

BIBLIOGRAPHY

E. Adams, "Probability and the Logic of Conditionals" in J. Hintikka and P. Suppes, eds., *Aspects of Inductive Logic,* North Holland, Amsterdam, 1966.

E. Adams, *The Logic of Conditionals.* D. Reidel, Dordrecht, Netherlands, 1975.

R. Ben-Eliyahu, "Minimizing Horn-Clause Violations is NP-hard," UCLA Cognitive Systems Laboratory, Computer Science Department, Technical Report (R-158), Los Angeles, 1990.

J. P. DelGrande, "An Approach to Default Reasoning Based on First-order Conditional Logic; Revised Report." *Artif. Intell.* **36**, 63–90 (1988).

H. Geffner, "On the Logic of Defaults," *Proceedings of the National Conference on Artificial Intelligence,* St. Paul, Minn., 1988, pp. 449–454.

H. Geffner, "Default Reasoning: Causal and Conditional Theories." PhD dissertation. UCLA, Computer Science Department, Los Angeles, 1989.

H. Geffner and J. Pearl, "A Framework for Reasoning with Defaults" in H. Kyburg, R. Loui, and G. Carlson, eds., *Knowledge Representation and Defeasible Inference,* Kluwer Academic Publishers, Boston, 1990, 69–87.

M. Goldszmidt and J. Pearl, "On the Consistency of Defeasible Databases," *Proceedings, Fifth Workshop on Uncertainty in AI,* Windsor, Canada, 1989a, 134–141; also, *Uncertainty in AI-5,* North Holland, 1990, 87–97.

M. Goldszmidt and J. Pearl, "On the Relation Between Rational Closure and System-Z," in *Third International Workshop on Nonmonotonic Reasoning,* 1990, pp. 130–140.

M. Goldszmidt, P. Morris, and J. Pearl, "A Maximum Entropy Approach to Nonmonotonic Reasoning," *Proceedings of the Ninth National Conference on Artificial Intelligence,* Boston, Mass., 1990, 646–652.

M. Goldszmidt and J. Pearl, "System-Z$^+$: A Formalism for Reasoning with Variable-Strength Defaults," *Proceedings of the Tenth National Conference on Artificial Intelligence,* Anaheim, Calif., 1991.

S. Hanks and D. V. McDermott, "Default Reasoning, Nonmonotonic Logics, and the Frame Problem," *Proceedings of the Fifth National Conference on Artificial Intelligence,* Philadelphia, 1986, pp. 328–333.

D. Hunter, "Causality and Maximum Entropy Updating," *Int. J. Approx. Reas.* **3**(1), 87–114 (1989).

E. T. Jaynes, "Where Do We Stand on Maximum Entropy?" in R. D. Levine and M. Tribus, eds., *The Maximum Entropy Formalism,* MIT Press, Cambridge, Mass., 1979.

H. E. Kyburg, *Probability and the Logic of Rational Belief.* Wesleyan University Press, Middletown, Conn., 1961.

D. Lehmann, "What Does a Conditional Knowledge Base Entail?" *Proceedings of the First International Conference on Principals of Knowledge: Representation and Reasoning,* Toronto, Morgan-Kaufmann Publishers, San Mateo, Calif., 1989, 212–222.

D. Lehmann and M. Magidor, "Rational Logics and Their Models: A Study in Cumulative Logics," Department of Computer Science, Hebrew University, Jerusalem, Israel, Technical Report TR-88-16, 1988.

J. McCarthy, "Circumscription—A Form of Non-monotonic Reasoning," *Artif. Intell.* **13**(1), 27–70 (1980).

J. McCarthy, "Applications of Circumscription to Formalizing Common-sense Knowledge," *Artif. Intell.* **28**(1), 89–116 (1986).

J. Pearl, *Deciding Consistency in Inheritance Networks,* UCLA Cognitive Systems Laboratory, Technical Report 870053 (R-96), 1987.

J. Pearl, "Distributed Revision of Composite Beliefs," *Artif. Intell.* **33**(2), 173–215 (1987).

J. Pearl, *Probabilistic Reasoning in Intelligent Systems: Networks of Plausible Inference,* Morgan-Kaufmann Publishers, San Mateo, Calif., 1988.

J. Pearl, "System Z: A Natural Ordering of Defaults with Tractable Applications to Nonmonotonic Reasoning, *Proceedings: Theoretical Aspects of Reasoning about Knowledge* (TARK-III), Asilomar, Calif., March 1990, Morgan-Kaufmann Publishers, San Mateo, Calif., 1990, 121–135.

R. Reiter, "A Logic for Default Reasoning," *Artif. Intell.* **13**, 81–132 (1980).

R. Reiter, "Nonmonotonic Reasoning," *Ann. Rev. Comput. Sci.* 2, 147–186 (1987).

Y. Shoham, "Chronological Ignorance: Time, Nonmonotonicity, Necessity, and Causal Theories," *Proceedings of the Fifth National Conference on Artificial Intelligence,* Philadelphia, 1986, pp. 389–393.

W. Spohn, "Ordinal Conditional Functions: A Dynamic Theory of Epistemic States" in W. L. Harper and B. Skyrms, eds. *Causation in Decision, Belief Change, and Statistics,* Vol. 2, Reidel, Dordrecht, Netherlands, 1988, pp. 105–134.

D. Touretzky, *The Mathematics of Inheritance Systems.* Morgan-Kaufmann Publishers, Los Altos, Calif., 1986.

JUDEA PEARL
University of California,
Los Angeles

This work was supported in part by National Science Foundation Grant IRI-8821444 and Naval Research Laboratory Grant N00014-87-K-2029. An earlier version of this paper was presented at the First International Conference on Principles of Knowledge Representation and Reasoning (KR '89), Toronto, May 1989.

EQUALITY INFERENCING

Equalities arise naturally in many areas of computer science, mathematical logic, and artificial intelligence. For example, if the domain of discourse contains an associative structure, then this fact can easily be specified in a first-order language (see THEOREM PROVING) by a binary function symbol ∘ and the axiom

$$\forall x, y, z: x \circ (y \circ z) \doteq (x \circ y) \circ z$$

However, the equality relation has many special properties. It is reflexive, symmetric, transitive, and allows the substitution of equals for equals. These properties can be expressed by the axioms of equality:

$$\forall x: x \doteq x \qquad \text{(reflexivity)}$$

$$\forall x, y: x \doteq y \Rightarrow y \doteq x \qquad \text{(symmetry)}$$

$$\forall x, y, z: x \doteq y \wedge y \doteq z \Rightarrow x \doteq z \qquad \text{(transitivity)}$$

$$\forall x, y, z: x \doteq y \Rightarrow x \circ z \doteq y \circ z \qquad \text{(substitutivity)}$$

$$\forall x, y, z: x \doteq y \Rightarrow z \circ x \doteq z \circ y \qquad \text{(substitutivity)}$$

and must be taken into account by any system that reasons about equality. Suppose it is necessary to prove that the associativity of ∘ entails the existence of an x such that the structures $c \circ x$ and $x \circ c$ are equal, where c denotes a constant. One way to show the existence of such an x is to explicitly compute the appropriate substitutions for it. Unfortunately, there are an infinite number of different substitutions that solve this problem. By the axiom of reflexivity it is found that the substitution $\{x/c\}$ is a solution to the problem. But $\{x/c \circ c\}$ is also a solution, which can be verified by applying the axiom of associativity. In fact, any substitution of the form $\{x/c \circ \ldots \circ c\}$ is an independent solution.

The main problem in equality inferencing is often called the E-unification problem and can be stated as follows. Given a set E of equational axioms (also called equational theory) and a set $S = \{s_i \doteq t_i \mid 1 \leq i \leq n\}$ of equations. Does there exist a substitution σ for the variables occurring in S such that each $\sigma s_i \doteq \sigma t_i$, $1 \leq i \leq n$, is a logical consequence of E and the axioms of equality? The E-unification problem is only semidecidable, and hence, the task is to develop E-unification algorithms which enumerate the set of solutions. However, such a set Σ of solutions should be as small as possible and complete, ie, for each solution θ there should be a solution σ in Σ such that σ is equal to θ under E or can be instantiated to a substitution that is equal to θ under E. Unfortunately, minimal complete sets of solutions do not always exist (Fages and Huet, 1986).

One possibility to compute a complete set of solutions for a given E-unification problem is to add to the equational theory E its axioms of equality and apply resolution (qv). However, such an E-unification algorithm would compute many irrelevant and redundant solutions because the resolution rule provides not enough control to guide the application of the equational axioms.

To overcome these problems unification algorithms for special theories such as associativity or commutativity were developed. The equational axioms are built into the deductive machinery. Such a special E-unification algorithm accepts a set S of equations as input and computes a complete set of solutions for S under E. Specialized unification algorithms offer good solutions for the E-unifica-

tion problems they were designed for and there is an ongoing interest in combining several special unification algorithms to obtain a good unification algorithm for larger equational theories.

The alternative is to develop universal E-unification algorithms. Such an algorithm accepts not only a set S of equations but also a certain equational theory E as input and computes the solutions for S under E. Typically, a universal unification algorithm does not explicitly apply (part of) the axioms of equality. They are built into the unification algorithm. A complete treatment has been published (Siekmann, 1989).

The most prominent universal unification algorithm uses an inference rule called paramodulation (Chang and Lee, 1973). Paramodulation is based on the fundamental property of equality that equals can be replaced by equals. Formally, let $A|r|$ be an equation with subterm r and let $A|r \leftarrow t|$ denote the replacement of one occurrence of r in A by the term t. $\sigma(A|r \leftarrow t|)$ is the paramodulant of $A|r|$ and $s \doteq t$ if and only if r and s are unifiable with most general unifier σ (see UNIFICATION). To solve a set S of equations under E, paramodulation is applied to the equations in S and E until all equations in S are simultaneously unifiable. As an example consider the equational theory E with axioms

$$a \doteq b \qquad (ab)$$

$$f(c(a), c(b)) \doteq g(c(a), c(b)) \quad (fg)$$

and the set

$$S = \{f(x, x) \doteq g(x, x)\}$$

Applying paramodulation successively to the first and second occurrence of a in (fg) using (ab) yields

$$f(c(b), c(b)) \doteq g(c(b), c(b)) \quad (fg')$$

Finally, by applying paramodulation to $f(x, x)$ in S using (fg') and the substitution $\{x/c(b)\}$ the following is obtained.

$$S' = \{g(c(b), c(b)) \doteq g(c(b), c(b))\}$$

The equation in S' is trivially unifiable and, hence, the substitution $\{x/c(b)\}$ is a solution for S under E. It should be observed that this result cannot be obtained if paramodulation is only applied to the equations in S.

Nevertheless, paramodulation has been shown to be complete under various restrictions. The goal of these restrictions is generally to reduce the number of candidate terms in a formula to which paramodulation can be applied. Narrowing is paramodulation, where the term r replaced by paramodulation is always a nonvariable term. Lazy paramodulation or lazy narrowing does not immediately unify the terms r and s if r and s are of the form $f(r_1, \ldots, r_n)$ and $f(s_1, \ldots, s_n)$, respectively. Rather the equations $\{r_i \doteq s_i \mid 1 \leq i \leq n\}$ are added to S. Lazy paramodulation has the advantage that under certain conditions it must be applied only to the outermost terms of an equation. Moreover, it suffices to apply lazy paramodulation only to equations in S (Gallier and Snyder, 1989). Furthermore, it can be shown that several other techniques for solving E-unification problems, such as resolution by unification and equality (RUE-resolution), equality graphs, and flattening, are just variations of lazy paramodulation (Hölldobler, 1989).

Special forms of paramodulation were developed that are complete for restricted classes of equational theories. If the equational theory is a canonical term rewriting system, then narrowing is complete even if applied only to equations in S. Rewriting is paramodulation, where the substitution σ used in the paramodulation step does not bind a variable in $A|r|$ (see REWRITING). Demodulation is a special form of rewriting, where the term σt, which replaces r, has strictly fewer symbols than r (Wos and coworkers, 1967). Often rewriting as well as demodulation can be applied as a simplification rule in paramodulation derivations.

If an equational theory E can be split into the theories E_1 and E_2 such that there exists a special E_1-unification algorithm, then this algorithm can be combined with paramodulation by restricting paramodulation to equations in S and E_2 and unifying the terms r and s under E_1.

All these techniques can be extended to conditional equational theories. Moreover, they can be combined with any technique, such as resolution (qv) or the connection method (qv), to prove theorems involving general atoms (see THEORY RESOLUTION).

BIBLIOGRAPHY

L. Chang and R. C. T. Lee, *Symbolic Logic and Mechanical Theorem Proving,* Academic Press, Inc., New York, 1973.

F. Fages and G. Huet, "Complete Sets of Unifiers and Matchers in Equational Theories," *J. Theor. Comput. Sci.* **43,** 189–200 (1986).

J. H. Gallier and W. Snyder, "Complete Sets of Transformations for General E-Unification," *J. Theor. Comput. Sci.* **67,** 203–260 (1989).

S. Hölldobler, *Foundations of Equational Logic Programming,* Vol. 353 of *Lecture Notes in Computer Science,* Springer-Verlag, New York, 1989.

J. H. Siekmann, "Unification Theory," *J. Symbolic Comput.* **7,** 207–274 (1989).

L. Wos, G. A. Robinson, D. Carson, and L. Shalla, "The Concept of Demodulation in Theorem Proving," *JACM* **14,** 698–709 (1967).

STEFFEN HÖLLDOBLER
Technische Hochschule
Darmstadt

EURISKO

A learning program that uses heuristics (qv) to develop new heuristics, EURISKO was developed in 1981 by Douglas Lenat at Stanford University. This program, along with AM (qv), presents the strategy called learning by discovery (see R. Michalski, J. Carbonell, and T. Mitch-

ell, eds., *Machine Learning,* Vol. 1, Tioga, Palo Alto, Calif., 1983).

K. S. ARORA
SUNY at Buffalo

EXPERT SYSTEMS

Knowledge-based expert systems, or knowledge systems for short, employ human knowledge to solve problems that ordinarily require human intelligence (Hayes-Roth and co-workers, 1983). Knowledge systems represent and apply knowledge electronically. These capabilities ultimately will make knowledge systems vastly more powerful than the earlier technologies for storing and transmitting knowledge, books and conventional programs. Both of these technologies suffer from fundamental limitations. Although today books store the largest volume of knowledge, they merely retain symbols in a passive form. Before the knowledge stored in books can be applied, a human must retrieve it, interpret it, and decide how to exploit it for problem solving (qv).

Although most computers today perform tasks according to the decision-making logic of conventional programs, these programs do not readily accommodate significant amounts of knowledge. Programs consist of two distinct parts, algorithms and data. Algorithms determine how to solve specific kinds of problems, and data characterize parameters in the particular problem at hand. Human knowledge does not fit this model, however. Because much human knowledge consists of elementary fragments of know-how, applying a significant amount of knowledge requires new ways to organize decision-making fragments into competent wholes.

Knowledge systems collect these fragments in a knowledge base and then access the knowledge base to reason about each specific problem. As a consequence, knowledge systems differ from conventional programs in the way they're organized, the way they incorporate knowledge, the way they execute, and the impression they create through their interactions. Knowledge systems simulate expert human performance, and they present a human-like facade to the user.

Some current knowledge engineering applications are medical diagnosis, equipment repair, computer configuration, chemical data interpretation and structure elucidation, speech and image understanding, financial decision making, signal interpretation, mineral exploration, military intelligence and planning, advising about computer system use, and VLSI design.

In all of these areas, system developers have worked to combine the general techniques of knowledge engineering (KE) with specialized know-how in particular domains of application. In nearly every case the demand for a KE approach arose from the limitations perceived in the alternative technologies available. The developers wanted to incorporate a large amount of fragmentary, judgmental, and heuristic knowledge; they wanted to solve problems automatically that required the machine to follow whatever lines of reasoning seemed most appropriate to the data at hand; they wanted the systems to accommodate new knowledge as it evolved; and they wanted the systems to use their knowledge to give meaningful explanations of their behaviors when requested.

This article presents a tutorial overview of the field of knowledge engineering. It describes the major developments that have led up to the current great interest in expert systems and then presents a brief discussion of the principal scientific and engineering issues in the field. The subsequent sections describe the process of building expert systems and the role of tools in that work, how expert systems perform human–computer interface functions, and the frontiers of research and development.

A BRIEF HISTORY OF KNOWLEDGE ENGINEERING

Throughout the last two decades, AI researchers have been learning to appreciate the great value of domain-specific knowledge (see DOMAIN KNOWLEDGE) as a basis for solving significant problems. Most of the world's challenging mental problems do not yield to general problem-solving (qv) strategies even when augmented with general efficiency heuristics (qv). To solve problems in areas of human expertise such as engineering, medicine, or programming, machine problem solvers need to know what human problem solvers know about that subject. Although computers have many advantages over humans, including speed and consistency, these cannot compensate for ignorance. In a nutshell, AI researchers learned that high IQ does not make a person expert, specialized know-how does. To make a fast and consistent symbol processor perform as well as a human expert, someone must provide it specialized know-how comparable to what a human expert possesses. This need gives rise to knowledge engineering.

Early KE applications arose in universities and emphasized matching the performance of human experts. DENDRAL (qv) (Lindsay and co-workers, 1980) and MACSYMA (qv) (Martin and Fateman, 1971) achieved expert performance first. DENDRAL identifies the chemical molecular structure of a material from its mass spectrographic and nuclear magnetic resonance (nmr) data. MACSYMA manipulates and simplifies complex mathematical expressions.

Beginning in the 1970s, AI researchers initiated several KE applications. By the end of the decade several projects had accomplished significant results:

MYCIN (qv) incorporated about 400 heuristic rules written in an English-like if–then formalism to diagnose and treat infectious blood diseases, but its major impact on the field arose from its ability to explain lucidly any conclusion or question it generated (Shortliffe, 1976).

HEARSAY-II (qv) employed multiple, independent, co-operating expert systems that communicated through a global database called a blackboard to understand connected speech in a 1000-word vocabulary (Erman and co-workers, 1980).

R1 (qv) incorporated about 1000 if–then rules needed to configure orders for Digital Equipment's VAX computers and eliminated the need for DEC to hire and train many new people to perform a task that had proved difficult and that had resisted solution by conventional computer techniques (McDermott, 1980).

INTERNIST (qv) contained nearly 100,000 judgments about relationships among diseases and symptoms in internal medicine and began to approach a breadth of knowledge and problem-solving performance beyond that of most specialists in internal medicine (Pople and co-workers, 1975).

TECHNIQUES USED IN KNOWLEDGE SYSTEMS

Figure 1 illustrates the primary building blocks of a knowledge system. The base level consists of those techniques that underlie nearly all applications. These include symbolic programming, propositional calculus (see LOGIC, PROPOSITIONAL), search (qv), and heuristics.

At the second level of techniques Figure 1 shows the most frequently used forms of knowledge representation (qv): constraints (see CONSTRAINT SATISFACTION), assertions, rules (see RULE-BASED SYSTEMS), and certain factors (see REASONING, PLAUSIBLE). Examples of constraints include "Two distinct physical objects cannot occupy the same space at the same time" and "Every beneficiary designated in the life insurance policy must have a financial interest in the health of the insured party." A knowledge system incorporates constraints to express restrictions on allowable states, values, or conclusions. In fact, some knowledge systems derive their value primarily through an ability to recognize and satisfy complex symbolic constraints sets. In this way KE extends the class of constraint satisfaction problems amenable to computation. Previously, computer systems focused primarily on linear constraints, whereas knowledge systems address arbitrary symbolic constraints such as requirements on spatial, temporal, or logical relationships.

Assertional databases provide means for storing and retrieving propositions. An assertion corresponds to a true proposition, a fact. Examples of assertions include "The King of Sweden visited my company to explore possible relationships with West Coast high-technology companies." "Morgan is a dog," and "Morgan is my dog's name." Many simple forms of assertions lend themselves to relational database implementations, but more complicated patterns do not. In general, most knowledge systems today incorporate their own specialized assertional database subsystems.

Rules represent declarative or imperative knowledge of particular forms. To illustrate an imperative rule, consider: "If you observe a patient with fever and a runny nose, you should suspect that the patient has the flu." This rule tells a knowledge system how to behave. A related declarative rule would tell the system what it could believe but would leave how unspecified: "If a patient has the flu, the patient tends to exhibit fever and a runny nose." Most knowledge systems use one or both of these

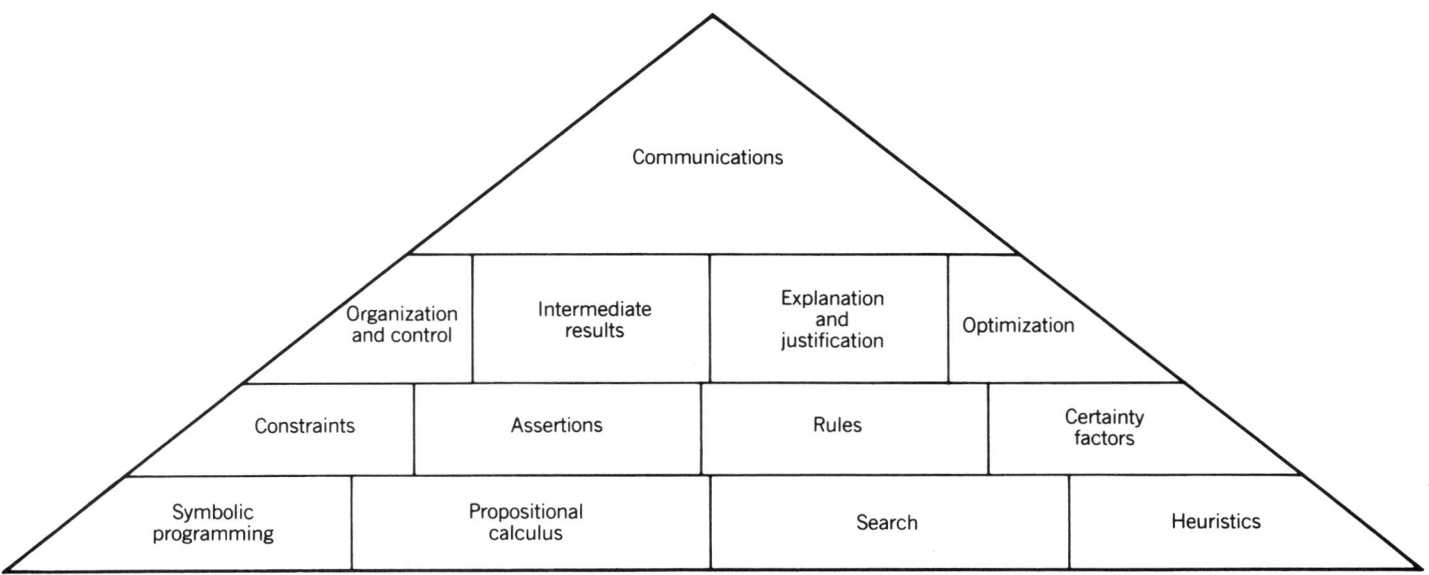

Figure 1. Building blocks of a knowledge system.

rule forms. Declarative rules, in general, describe the way things work in the world. On the other hand, imperative rules prescribe heuristic methods the knowledge system should employ in its own operations.

Certainty factors designate the level of confidence or validity a knowledge system should associate with its data, rules, or conclusions. These certainty factors may reflect any of a variety of different schemes for dealing with error and uncertainty. Some systems employ Bayesian conditional probabilities to estimate certainties (see BAYESIAN INFERENCE METHODS). Others use completely subjective systems, for example, where 1.0 implies certainty, −1.0 implies certainty of the proposition's negation, and 0.0 indicates either no opinion or no evidence. Many people devote considerable effort to the task of improving the certainty factor technology. To a large extent this may prove fruitless. First, knowledge systems must estimate the strength of their conclusions precisely because no valid and formal alternatives exist. The subjective quality of the decision process cannot be eliminated by any amount of formalization. Second, many alternative certainty factor schemes work equivalently well. Knowledge systems do well because they can mimic human performance. Humans could not solve problems well if they needed to calculate complex mathematical formulas to determine their own certainty factors. Rather, humans perform well because their knowledge *generally works well enough*. It is efficient, robust, and good enough to solve important problems. Knowledge systems simply exploit that power of the human's knowledge.

At the third level of techniques, Figure 1 shows organization and control (see CONTROL STRUCTURES), intermediate results, explanation (qv) and justification, and optimization. A knowledge system organizes and controls its activity according to the architectural design principles it embodies. For example, a diagnostic expert system might reason backward (see PROCESSING, BOTTOM UP AND TOP DOWN)

from all potential diseases it knows, searching for sufficient confirming evidence. It might consider first the disease thought most likely *a priori*. Then it might ask for evidence according to the most likely and characteristic syndromes. Only when it encountered overwhelming amounts of disconfirming data might it begin to consider the next possible disease. An expert system that operated in this manner would exhibit a depth-first, backward-chaining control scheme. Each distinct control scheme may require a corresponding organization of the knowledge base and appropriately tailored inferential mechanisms that search it and apply knowledge. Thus control and organization are closely linked.

Intermediate results arise in all systems. Because knowledge systems can face difficult performance requirements, they often must make effective use of intermediate results. In a backward-chaining system, for example, several possible alternatives under consideration all may require a common bit of evidence. Collecting this evidence may require extensive amounts of computation and inference. Once the knowledge system evaluates that evidence, it has an incentive to save that result so it may reuse it later. In every organization and control scheme, comparable issues of temporary storage and reuse arise. Most knowledge systems today employ specialized and *ad hoc* methods to accomplish these functions.

Because knowledge systems generally can explain and justify their results, they have captured the interest of a wide variety of potential users. Users (consumers) in many application areas must trust the recommendations of a knowledge system. By offering to explain how they reached their conclusions, these systems convey to the user an impression of reasonability. To construct an explanation (qv), these systems transform the expert heuristic rules and assertions into lines of reasoning. A line of reasoning shows how a starting set of assumptions and a collection of heuristic rules produce a particular conclusion. Consumers generally find these explanations as plausible as the rules themselves. The other people who interact with the knowledge system also exploit their explanation capabilities. Knowledge base maintainers, who may include experts and technicians, continually revalidate their knowledge systems by assessing their performance on test cases. They must validate that the system both reaches the right decisions and that it does so for the right reasons.

Optimization techniques play an important role in knowledge systems. Knowledge systems, like other computer applications, must perform their tasks as quickly as needed. Many knowledge system applications today interact with users so often that they generally are waiting for input. In these cases, knowledge engineers pay considerable attention to ensuring that the dialogue itself seems expert in terms of which queries, in which order, the knowledge system generates. This requires effective ways to optimize the structure of the dialogue itself. New tools for building knowledge systems provide improved methods for specifying such imperative knowledge clearly and separating it effectively from descriptive knowledge about the problem domain. The most important area of optimization in complex task domains, however, concerns the knowledge system's problem-solving performance: Does it generate and test candidate solutions in an efficient order, does it avoid redundant computation, does it compile the symbolic rules effectively, does it retrieve assertions efficiently, and does it transform the knowledge base into more appropriate organizations for specialized tasks that can exploit more efficient algorithms? In some applications, optimization of a knowledge system has reduced run times to as little as one-thousandth of 1% of initial completion times.

The capstone of knowledge system techniques is their communication capabilities. Knowledge systems communicate with knowledge engineers, experts, consumers, databases, and other computer systems. Just as humans access and interact with these various sources, a knowledge system must speak to each in its own appropriate language. Knowledge systems communicate with knowledge engineers through structure editors that allow them to access and modify components of the knowledge base easily. Knowledge systems communicate with experts through sample dialogues with explanations that elucidate their lines of reasoning and highlight for the expert where to make knowledge base changes. For consumers, knowledge systems may exploit natural language processes to generate questions and answers or to interpret user responses. Some knowledge systems today use videodisks to retrieve pictures and replay instructional sequences for consumers. Beyond their interactions with people, knowledge systems also interact with other computer systems. Knowledge systems often need to formulate and execute conventional data-processing applications as a subtask. In this way several knowledge systems have evolved almost like the new brain of higher animals that sits piggy-back atop powerful, preexisting, lower level "old brains." These piggy-back knowledge systems incorporate the scarce expert know-how needed to make effective use of the powerful, but often exceedingly com-

plex, computer programs employed today in fields such as structural engineering and seismic analysis. Quite commonly, knowledge systems incorporate means to access and retrieve information from on-line databases. In this way knowledge systems can apply their knowledge automatically and directly to the vast stores of data that now commonly reside on-line. Frequently, a knowledge system may serve the primary goal of weaving diverse sources of knowledge that reside in different databases, reflect different formats and coding practices, and require heuristic means to produce a meaningful, integrated interpretation. These needs arise most often in complex organizations, the order entry and manufacturing systems of large corporations, or the intelligence and analysis functions of defense departments.

Figure 2 illustrates the major components of a contemporary knowledge system and places the system in its environmental context. The figure depicts the knowledge system as a computer application with distinctive development and operational environments. The people who participate during knowledge system development and extension use the tools shown in Figure 2, tools for knowledge acquisition, knowledge base maintenance, validation, and interface design. Using these tools, the knowledge engineers construct knowledge systems that incorporate the three key components shown in Figure 2: a knowledge base, an inference engine, and a user interface. To do this, the knowledge engineer selects a tool for building the knowledge system whose built-in features fit the problem-solving knowledge in this domain. That tool generally will also embody an approach to organization and control that constitutes the specific problem-solving paradigm the knowledge system will adopt. Once a knowledge system completes development, it enters operation. In that environment it ordinarily accesses databases, connects to various communication networks, transfers to or integrates with existing installed equipment, and may receive data directly from sensor systems.

Later in this article an illustrative knowledge system called the Drilling Advisor is described in some detail. At this point, that knowledge system is used to illustrate more concretely these major components and environmental systems.

The Drilling Advisor addresses problems of sticking and dragging that can occur during the process of drilling for oil. In a nutshell, a drill string may encounter tremendous sticking forces arising from friction between geological strata and the drilling pipe, stabilizers, and bit. In operation, the knowledge system must access an on-line database of drilling operation reports that describe key parameters. It must communicate with regional or central operating management to receive knowledge base updates and to transmit its own reports. It must operate in harsh on-rig environments, and this means it must run on and integrate with special hardened equipment. It can also exploit direct access to sensors that generate drilling data, such as depth of the bit and pressure of the drilling mud.

The Drilling Advisor itself incorporates the knowledge representation and problem-solving paradigm of Teknowledge's S.1 expert system tool. The knowledge base for sticking includes approximately 300 heuristic rules and

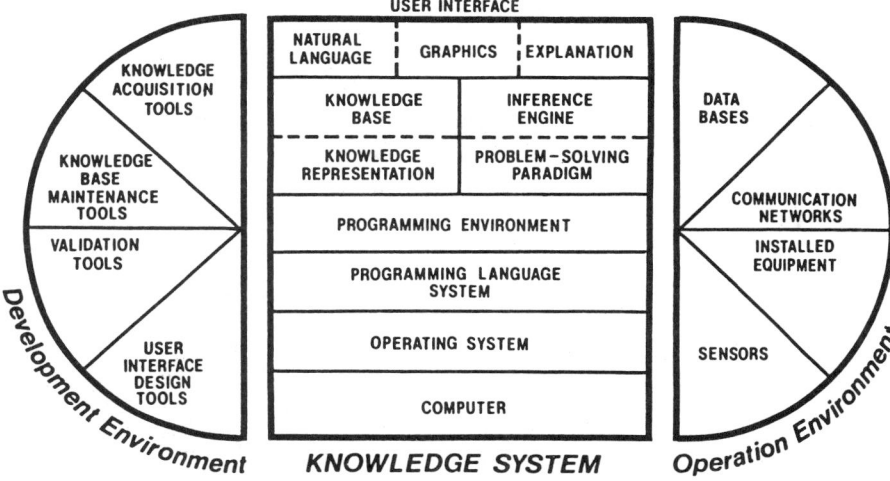

Figure 2. Technology applied: a knowledge system and its environmental context.

descriptions of approximately 50 key drilling parameters. The inference engine conducts a dialogue with the user, who is a drilling supervisor, in English or French. The dialogue mimics in its content and sequencing the manner of questioning and analysis of the human expert who served as the model. The pursuit of each hypothesis follows a depth-first, back-chaining approach starting with the most likely sticking problem and proceeding to collect necessary supportive evidence. Each hypothesis, datum, and heuristic rule may reflect uncertainty. The knowledge system combines these uncertain quantities to determine a certainty factor (CF) between -1 and 1 for each potential diagnosis. For all diagnoses with CFs exceeding 0.2, the Drilling Advisor formulates a treatment plan to cure the current problem and minimize the likelihood of problem recurrence.

The Drilling Advisor was developed in a programming environment composed of S.1 and LISP (qv), and it uses LISP as its underlying programming system. It can also conduct consultations using a C implementation of S.1 operating on any standard UNIX-based system.

The development environment consists of tools provided by S.1. That system provides special tools to help the knowledge engineer and expert acquire the expert's knowledge. These include both English language and abbreviated notations for rule display and entry, knowledge base browsing, structure editors, case libraries, and automated testing facilities. During the course of the system development, the expert became proficient in using the development tools so late stages of knowledge acquisition and knowledge base maintenance could be directed. Each time the expert or knowledge base maintainer modifies a rule, the S.1 system automatically validates that the knowledge system still performs its test cases correctly. Finally, the knowledge system conducts its interaction with the drilling supervisor in natural language by automatically translating, collecting, and formatting appropriate fragments of text associated with the knowledge base elements that participate in a line of reasoning. The interface tools make it possible for the knowledge system to produce a sophisticated and intelligible dialogue using only the short, descriptive phrases associated with each

drilling parameter that the expert provided. The Drilling Advisor also displays graphically several key factors, including the plausible sticking problems, the rock formations, and the drill bit and stabilizers constituting the "bottom hole assembly." Finally, using standard tools in the S.1 package, the Drilling Advisor displays dynamically its alternative lines of reasoning, its intermediate conclusions, and the heuristic rules momentarily under consideration.

FUNDAMENTALS OF KNOWLEDGE ENGINEERING

Knowledge engineering, as most engineering fields do, combines theory and practice. This section discusses the fundamentals of the engineering discipline as it exists today. The discussion makes three main points. First, because knowledge systems solve problems that ordinarily require human intelligence, they exhibit properties common to most intelligent problem-solving systems, whether natural or artificial. Second, to determine the best organization and design for any particular knowledge system, the type and complexity of the problem and the power and form of the heuristic knowledge available for solving it must be considered. Although KE has existed for only a short time, it makes some useful prescriptions for the best way to organize a knowledge system in various situations. Third, knowledge contains a capacity for intelligent action but does not typically carry with it a means for tapping and realizing that potential. Thus in building practical knowledge systems today, knowledge engineers always engineer knowledge; that is, they convert knowledge to applicable forms. These three facts convey in a simple manner the essential ideas that motivate the more detailed discussions that follow.

Basic Ideas

Table 1 makes five basic points, which are explained below. Knowledge in this context means those kinds of data that can improve the efficiency or effectiveness of a problem solver. Three major types of knowledge fit this description: facts express valid propositions, beliefs express

Table 1. The Basic Ideas of Intelligent Problem Solving

1. Knowledge = facts + beliefs + heuristics
2. Success = finding a good enough answer with the resources available
3. Search efficiency directly affects success
4. Aids to efficiency
   (a) Applicable, correct, and discriminating knowledge
   (b) Rapid elimination of blind alleys
   (c) Elimination of redundant computation
   (d) Increased speed of computer operation
   (e) Multiple, cooperative sources of knowledge
   (f) Reasoning at varying levels of abstraction
5. Sources of increased problem difficulty
   (a) Erroneous data or knowledge
   (b) Dynamically changing data
   (c) The number of possibilities to evaluate
   (d) Complex procedures for ruling out possibilities

plausible propositions, and heuristics express rules of good judgment in situations where valid algorithms generally do not exist. Experts differ from others in the quality and quantity of knowledge they possess. Experts know more, and what they know makes them more efficient and effective.

In contrast to conventional data-processing applications, most knowledge systems work in situations that do not admit optimal or correct solutions. Most human professionals perform tasks that require skilled, assertive, and informed judgment, and these requirements arise from the complexity, ambiguity, or uncertainty of the available data and problem-solving methods. In such cases the problem solver must balance the quality of the answer it produces against the effort it expends. An expert finds the best compromise, usually by seeing a way to find an acceptable answer with a reasonable expenditure of resources.

Given such a pragmatic orientation to performance, intelligent problem solvers benefit directly from improved efficiency. In particular, improvements in speed or selectivity can produce an acceptable solution more affordably, enabling the problem solver to find better solutions in the time available or take on and solve additional problems.

How then does an intelligent problem solver improve its efficiency? Table 1 lists the six most common ways. (1) It possesses knowledge that applies often, avoids errors, and makes useful distinctions to exploit significant differences among diverse types of situations. (2) It quickly eliminates paths of investigation that ultimately will prove useless. It prunes these blind alleys early by advancing in time those decisions that can remove fruitless classes of possibilities from further consideration. (3) It eliminates redundancy by computing things once and then reusing the results later if needed. (4) It accelerates its computations, which in the case of knowledge systems means that it increases the quality of its compilation and employs faster hardware. (5) It takes advantage of diverse bodies of knowledge that can contribute to the problem at hand. Specifically, it uses independent bodies of expertise to reduce ambiguities and eliminate sources of noise. Or it exploits knowledge bases from complementary disciplines to find a solution using whichever tech-

niques or heuristics work best on the given problem. (6) Last, it analyzes a problem in different ways, ranging from the high level and abstract to the low level and specific. Most complex problems require the problem solver to jump around in levels of abstraction, and they can reward an insightful observation at any level by obviating enormous amounts of additional analysis at the other levels. Examples of such insights at various levels include recognizing that the current problem has the same form as one previously solved; detecting that one of the problem requirements rules out all but two candidates; or noting that a figure incorporates orthogonal, horizontal, and vertical line segments, suggesting that it depicts a man-made object.

The difficulty of problem-solving tasks increases in four ways. (1) The problem solver may not possess accurate data sources or knowledge that performs without errors. These shortcomings cause it to explore many false paths. (2) When the data change dynamically, the problem solver must accelerate its reasoning, base some decisions on its expectations for the future, and revise its decisions when current data disconfirm erroneous prior assumptions. (3) Of course, the more possibilities it must consider, the harder the task. However, it is difficult in many applications to quantify the size of the search space and to find alternative formulations of the search space that simplify the problem as much as possible. (4) A problem solver that must use complex and time-consuming methods to eliminate alternatives from consideration works less efficiently than one possessing equally effective but simpler, cheaper measures.

Knowledge System Organization and Design

Unlike data-processing applications, current knowledge systems do not fit specific models, such as the typical update-master-file or input-process-put forms so common in commercial data processing. Moreover, the KE field does not yet have common schemes for characterizing its designs and systems. However, experienced knowledge engineers do adhere to some general principles when designing knowledge systems. These principles determine high level architectural properties of knowledge systems that permit them to perform their tasks effectively. To determine an appropriate knowledge system design, these principles ask questions about the kind of problem-solving complexity the task involves and the kind of heuristic problem-solving knowledge available. Figure 3 graphically shows many of the best understood design principles. The basic factors in this diagram are explained next and a detailed explanation is given in Hayes-Roth and co-workers (1983).

Figure 3 divides all knowledge system application problems into two categories characterized by small and large search spaces. It then elaborates each of these two basic categories by citing additional attributes that also may characterize the problem. For example, in the small-space problems it distinguishes three possibly overlapping subcategories based on the kinds of data the knowledge system must possess. When these data seem reliable and unchanging and the system knowledge performs reliably,

Problem characteristics

Design description

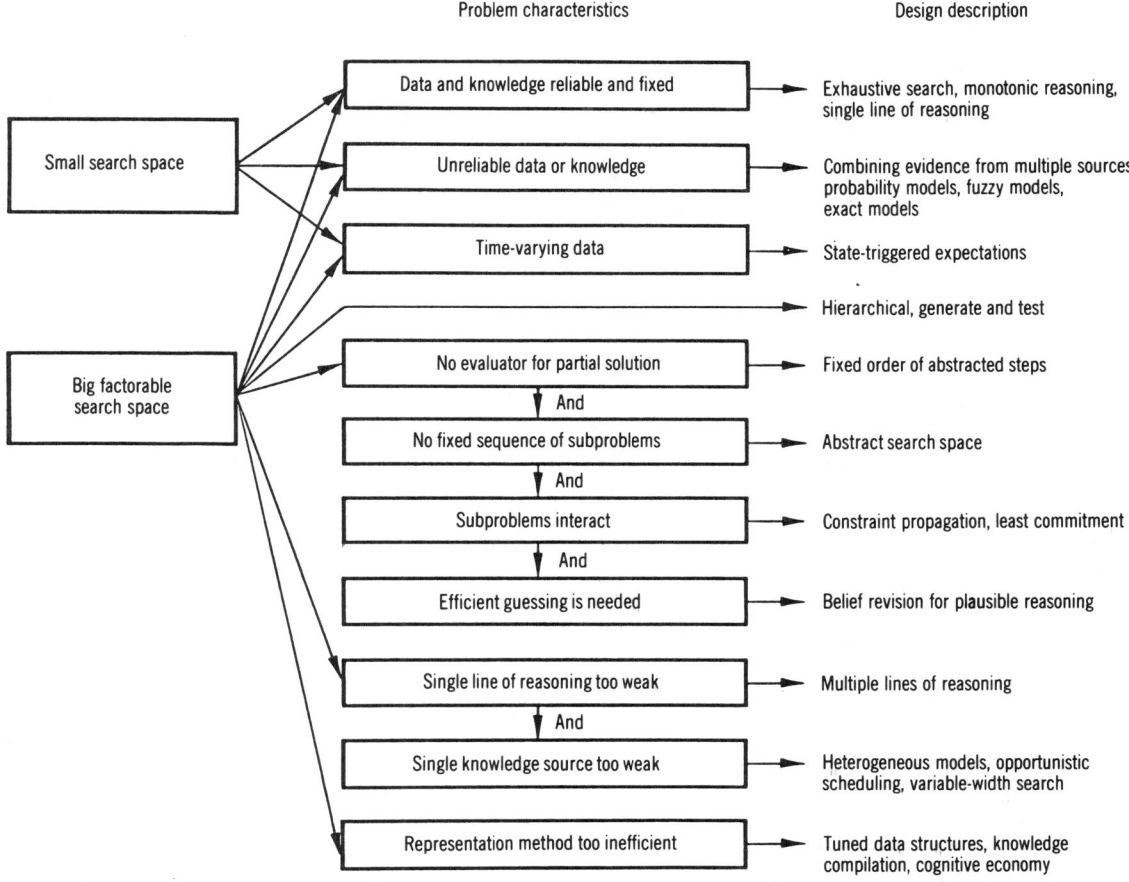

Figure 3. Knowledge-system application problems.

the figure prescribes the most typical knowledge system architecture: exhaustive search that pursues one line of reasoning at a time, such as depth-first backward-chaining. Furthermore, the prescribed system can reason monotonically: it need not initially formulate guesses that it later might need to retract. At the other extreme the figure addresses complex problems, such as those with large factorable search spaces (the search space can be broken into smaller subspaces corresponding to independent subproblems) in which pursuing one line of reasoning does not perform consistently well, no single body of knowledge provides enough power to solve all the problems the knowledge system faces, and the initial form of knowledge representation proves too inefficient to achieve the needed level of performance. In these cases the design principles prescribe several remedies, respectively. First, the knowledge system must explore and develop several promising lines of reasoning at once until it obtains more certainty about the actual solution. Second, it should incorporate several independent subsystems, each of which should contribute to decision making on an opportunistic basis. That is, the top-level knowledge system should maintain an agenda of pending subsystem actions and schedule for execution first those pending actions that promise to contribute most to the developing solution. This means the knowledge system will pursue a variable number of simultaneous, competing alternative solution paths, where

the actual number at any point reflects the momentary lack of certainty regarding the best path. Last, knowledge systems can exploit several advanced techniques for improving efficiency. Generally, these require making some kind of transformation to the initial knowledge representation and inference engine. These may include adopting data structures more attuned to the types of inference the knowledge system performs; compiling the knowledge into a new structure, such as a network or tree, that facilitates rapid search; or using dynamic techniques to cache intermediate results and perhaps compile incrementally more efficient methods for frequently repeated inferences that initially require complex chains of computation.

In short, today's design principles provide high level guidance to the knowledge system designer. Like architectural principles in housing and commercial construction, these principles suggest the broad outlines of a construction task without specifying the details. Knowledge systems built in a manner consistent with the principles in Figure 3 will prove similarly well adapted to their environments but will vary considerably in their fine structure.

Engineered Knowledge

One aspect of KE seems both obvious and subtle. What seems obvious is that knowledge engineers extract knowledge from experts and integrate it in an overall knowledge system architecture. Hence, they are engineers who construct systems out of elementary knowledge components. What is subtle is that the way a knowledge system uses knowledge to solve problems directly affects how the knowledge engineer extracts, represents, and integrates it. Knowledge does not come off the shelf, prepackaged, ready for use. On the contrary, *knowledge* is the word used to describe a variety of fragmentary bits of understanding that enable people and machines to perform otherwise demanding tasks reasonably well. As an example, an understanding of the way technology transfer generally occurs enables a technical manager to reason in many different ways for different purposes: if setting up a technology transfer program, the manager needs to shape and apply the knowledge in a manner different from what would be required if the manager were asked to review someone else's program, estimate a budget for it, forecast its likely results, or analyze its similarity to previously successful and unsuccessful programs. In short, people seem to possess a general understanding of the way things work. Today, a knowledge engineer building a knowledge system assesses what the knowledge system needs to do, evaluates the various ways it can do that, and formulates a version of an expert's know-how that allows the knowledge system to meet its goals.

In summary, knowledge systems today can incorporate significant quantities, of human knowledge to solve problems electronically that ordinarily require human intelligence. To do this, the knowledge systems adopt a general organization construct with high level design prescriptions and then fit the problem-solving knowledge into that framework. To make an expert's knowledge fit, the knowledge engineer molds the knowledge to produce the necessary performance. In this way knowledge engineers today genuinely *engineer* knowledge. The actual work of building a knowledge system is described below.

CONSTRUCTING KNOWLEDGE SYSTEMS

To build a knowledge system today, a knowledge engineer performs four types of function. Figure 4 defines these as knowledge-processing tasks informally referred to as min-

ing, molding, assembling, and refining. These terms arise in mining rare metals and seem an apt way to describe the processes involved in extracting knowledge and manufacturing knowledge systems. Knowledge, like a rare metal, lies dormant and impure, beneath the surfacer of consciousness. Once extracted, impure, beneath the surface of consciousness. Once extracted, an element of knowledge must undergo several transformations before it can add value. These four basic processing tasks are discussed here and, in particular, the iterative and incremental role of knowledge acquisition (qv) in the evolutionary development process is emphasized.

Figure 4 also provides the technical terms for each of the four primary construction activities and identifies the key products of each phase. Knowledge acquisition involves eliciting from experts or books the basic concepts of the problem domain, that is, the terms used to describe problem situations and problem-solving heuristics. From this starting point the knowledge acquisition process continues until it elicits enough problem-solving knowledge to enable the knowledge system to achieve expert performance. Heuristic rules constitute the key product of this activity.

Knowledge system design produces a framework or architecture for the knowledge system, as discussed above. In addition, the knowledge system designer selects an appropriate scheme for representing the problem-solving knowledge. Representation options include formal logic, semantic networks (qv), hierarchical frames (see FRAMES), active objects, rules, and procedures. Each of these alternative schemes has supported at least one previous knowledge system development effort. Any representation must accommodate the available knowledge and facilitate the search and inference required to solve the problems of interest.

Once a knowledge engineer has selected the framework and knowledge representation, knowledge programming begins. In this activity knowledge engineers transform human know-how into a knowledge base that will fuel an inference engine. Generally, people developing knowledge systems today adopt an existing knowledge engineering tool that incorporates a predefined inference engine, so knowledge programming need only produce a knowledge base.

Knowledge-processing tasks	Engineering activities	Engineering products
Mining	Knowledge acquisition	Concepts and rules
Molding	Knowledge system design	Framework and knowledge representation
Assembling	Knowledge programming	Knowledge base and inference engine
Refining	Knowledge refinement	Revised concepts and rules

Figure 4. Knowledge-processing tasks and KE activities used in constructing various types of knowledge system (engineering product).

The process of refining knowledge continues until the knowledge system achieves an adequate level of performance. Generally, a knowledge system performs poorly at the start. In transforming an inexact understanding of an expert's behavior into heuristic rules, both the expert and knowledge engineer err. They misunderstand abstract concepts, incorrectly express rules of thumb, and neglect many details needed to ensure the validity of knowledge base rules. These errors do not reflect poorly on their professionalism. On the contrary, no error-free approach exists. Experts do their tasks well because they use lots of knowledge, not because they think about or verbalize it. In fact, KE provides for most knowledge-intensive activities the first practical means for codifying and validating knowledge. Before the development of KE, experts generally could not express their know-how in any effective way, and they could not assess much of it empirically. Knowledge systems make it possible to test directly how well knowledge works. As a direct result, they also highlight the weaknesses and deficiencies. By focusing attention on these shortcomings, an expert often can improve a knowledge base rapidly. This leads to the common development pattern of an incremental, evolutionary development with performance that first approaches human levels and then generally exceeds them.

Figure 5 illustrates one key aspect of knowledge acquisition, the transfer of an expert's understanding to a knowledge engineer's knowledge system. This transfer involves two-way communication. At first, the knowledge engineer interrogates the expert to request insight into how the expert solves particular problems and how the expert thinks about the objects and relations of interest. In Figure 5 these components of understanding are labeled *World* and *Task* knowledge. The expert reveals some of this knowledge through the problem-solving task descriptions given to the knowledge engineer.

The knowledge engineer listens to the experts description to hear the problem-solving elements. Unlike a systems analyst, who formulates an algorithm to solve a client's problem, the knowledge engineer simply wants to capture the existing problem-solving method. To do this, the knowledge engineer will ordinarily adopt a KE tool and then try to fit the fragments of expertise into the structure the tool provides. This requires the knowledge engineer to create a description of the way the expert thinks about and solves problems in that domain. This description models the expertise of the expert. Once implemented as a knowledge system, this model generates problem-solving behaviors that the expert can critique and improve. Often this improves the expert's self-understanding.

Figure 6 depicts the iterative, evolutionary process of knowledge system development. This figure highlights the ways testing a knowledge system feeds back to earlier stages of construction. As this figure indicates, testing can indicate shortcomings in all earlier stages. Thus as development progresses there are usually changes in requirements, concepts, organizing structures, and rules.

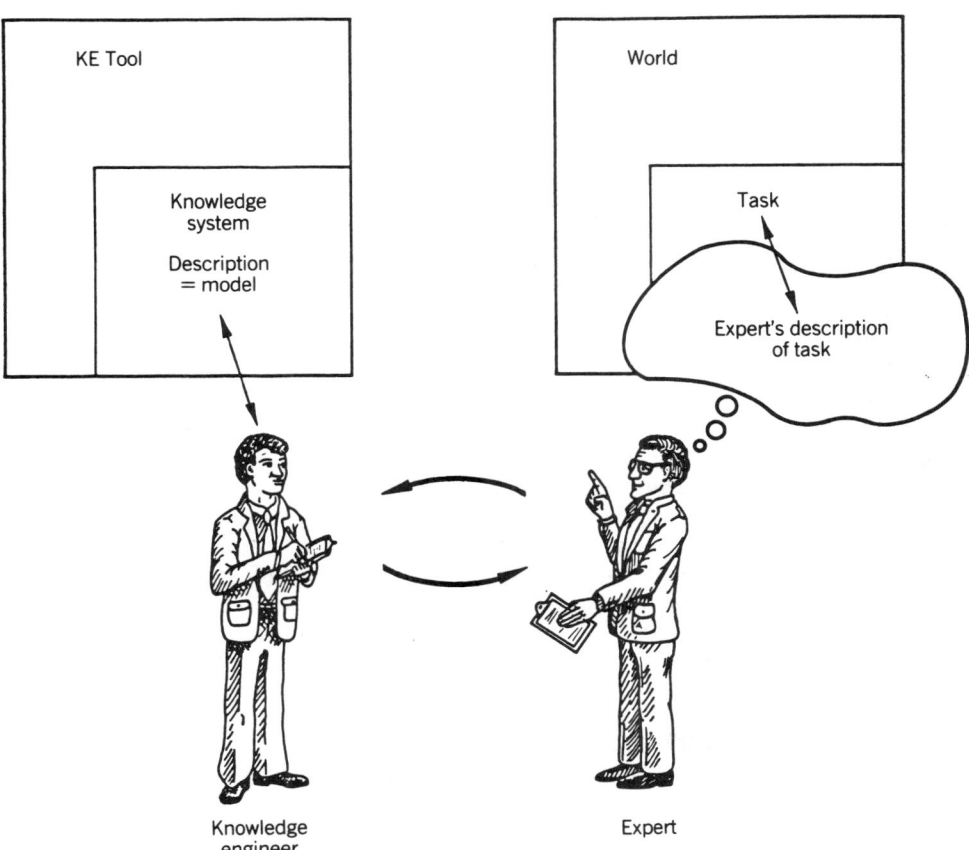

Figure 5. Transfer of an expert's understanding to knowledge engineer's system.

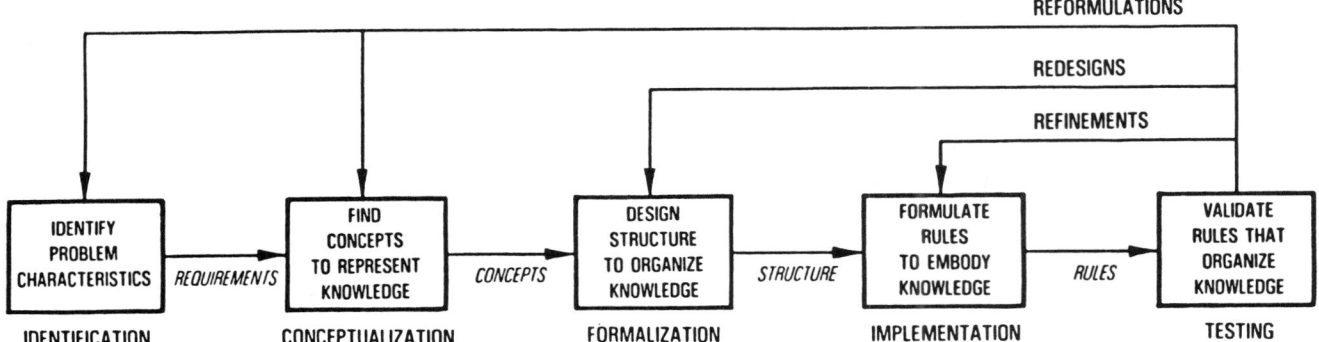

Figure 6. Evolutionary process of knowledge system development.

TOOLS FOR BUILDING KNOWLEDGE SYSTEMS

Many software aids exist to simplify the KE task. In fact, as discussed above, most knowledge engineers build knowledge systems by adopting an existing tool and then constructing a problem-specific knowledge base. A KE tool offers aids for knowledge acquisition, knowledge base maintenance, validation, and user interface design, as discussed previously (Fig. 2). Such software sits atop the programming environments (qv), programming languages, and operating systems of its host computer systems. Over the last 20 years, these tools have evolved, bottom up, from low level languages to high level KE aids.

What is a KE tool? It is more than software, or put another way, the KE tool software reflects a general KE viewpoint and a specific methodology for building knowledge systems. The tool reflects a high level problem-solving paradigm. It may, for example, build in an assumption that solutions to diagnostic problems ought to reason from design documents and causal models. Or, conversely, it might reflect a preference for building diagnostic experts by capturing an expert's empirical symptom–problem associations. In short, a paradigm constitutes a high level strategy for using knowledge to solve a class of problems. Today, different knowledge engineers are investigating diverse paradigms that vary along several dimensions: whether to use empirical associations or reason via first principles from underlying causal models, whether to formulate knowledge in terms of formal logic or in terms of more informal heuristics, whether to aggregate knowledge into relatively large functional units or disaggregate it so it fits a small-grain-size format, and so on.

Each paradigm suggests some additional design properties for the knowledge system architecture, and a KE tool generally builds these properties directly into its knowledge base structure and inference engine. A tool such as S.1, for example, built expert systems only with rule-based, backward-chaining, monotonic, and singular line of reasoning architectures. Does this sound restrictive? On the one hand, these design constraints surely restrict what a knowledge engineer can do and what the consumer knowledge systems can do. On the other hand, a tool like S.1 exploits its knowledge system design constraints to improve the quality and power of the assistance it gives. Because it knows the form of knowledge in the knowledge base, the detailed operation of the inference engine, and the organization and control of problem solving, the KE tool can simplify the development tasks considerably.

A KE tool offers a particular way to represent knowledge and, therefore, generally works well only for representing certain kinds of knowledge. Some tools emphasize heuristic rules, others emphasize categorical taxonomies, and still others address simulation and modeling. Paired with each kind of knowledge representation, KE tools generally provide one way to apply that knowledge. A tool that builds a backward-chaining knowledge system generally does not have the capability to build a forward-chaining system. A tool that helps reason with empirical cause–effect associations generally does not have capabilities to apply systematic search techniques to underlying causal models and so forth. However, several tools aim to provide a mixture of representations and inference techniques and may one day lead to more comprehensive KE frameworks. Examples of these include Xerox's LOOPS, Stanfords's MRS, MCC's CYC, and Inference's ART.

Tools generally provide some knowledge-programming language facilities and knowledge-processing utilities. S.1 provides abbreviated forms for experts to express domain rules and allows the expert to browse the knowledge base for rules with arbitrary characteristics, such as rules that determine the value for the shear stress in a structural engineering knowledge system. ROSIE (qv), another research tool, provides a general-purpose symbolic programming language and assertional database within the context of a standard sequential, modular programming system (Hayes-Roth and co-workers, 1981). It does not provide any particular problem-solving architecture, however. As a final example the research tool RLL (Greiner and Lenat, 1980) provides only a hierarchical knowledge base organization and a general agenda-based control scheme, leaving the knowledge engineer to implement all domain knowledge and problem-solving heuristics directly in LISP. The low level symbolic programming languages themselves, notably LISP and PROLOG, provide even less structure. Although they do not restrict the knowledge engineer in any way, they do not provide any specific assistance in knowledge acquisition, knowledge representation, or knowledge system evaluation.

In short, KE tools today span a wide range of software aids that reflect various assumptions about what kinds of knowledge systems to build and how to build them. Some tools, however, have evolved from dozens of related applications covering tens of person-years of development. These are discussed below in somewhat greater detail.

Some Relatively Mature Knowledge Engineering Tool Classes

Throughout the history of AI many researchers have focused their efforts on developing tools to aid the construction of problem-solving systems. Generally, tools developed in advance of applications have not correctly anticipated needed capabilities. This lack of foresight reflects primarily the general naïveté of researchers in a new and uncharted territory.

Several families of applications have given rise to useful paradigms, architectures, and related tools. Four of these families revolve around the MYCIN, HEARSAY-II, R1, and MOLGEN (qv) knowledge systems. These are illustrated in Table 2 and described briefly in turn.

The MYCIN family originated with a rule-based expert system for the diagnosis and treatment of infectious blood diseases. The general methodology employed by MYCIN gave rise to a research tool called EMYCIN (qv) and a related system called TEIRESIAS that could assist the knowledge acquisition process in EMYCIN. Figure 7 illustrates the history of EMYCIN and its descendants. PUFF, an expert system for interpreting respirometer data and diagnosing pulmonary disease, was the first actual application built using EMYCIN. S.1 combined many of the best features of EMYCIN and TEIRESIAS and has supported numerous commercial knowledge system developments. Two of these, called WAVES and Drilling Advisor, illustrate the breadth of systems that can be built using this tool. WAVES is an expert system that assesses a data analysis problem for a geophysicist and prescribes the

Table 2. Families of Systems and Tools

Family	Systems	Tools
MYCIN	MYCIN	EMYCIN
	PUFF	TEIRESIAS
	WAVES and Drilling Advisor	S.1
	Charlie and Mix	M.1
HEARSAY-II	HEARSAY-II	HEARSAY-III
	HASP/SIAP	AGE
	ACRONYM	
	PROTEAN and GUARDIAN	BB1
R1	R1 (XCON)	OPS5
	XSEL	OPS7
	AIRPLAN	OPS83
MOLGEN	MOLGEN	UNITS
	Various	KEE
		NEXPERT

best way to process the data using selected modules from a million-line FORTRAN analysis package. Drilling Advisor, on the other hand, determines the most likely cause for a stuck oil-drilling operation and prescribes expert curative and preventative treatments accordingly. In 1988, the S.1 tool was superseded by a next-generation product called Copernicus. Two other applications in this family are noteworthy because they reflect the great economic benefits companies began to derive from expert systems in the late 1980s: Charlie and Mix. Charlie collects physical vibratio data from rotating equipment and diagnoses all types of mechanical problem. It is used routinely throughout General Motors' manufacturing plants. Mix uses expert rules to blend ingredients into finished products that satisfy customer requirements and production constraints in ways that greatly reduce costs over alternative methods. The company using Mix is confidential. Both Charlie and Mix were built using Teknowledge's M.1 tool, providing back-chaining, PROLOG-style search, and certainty factors, and are implemented in C, operating on a personal computer.

The second family with an extensive range of applica-

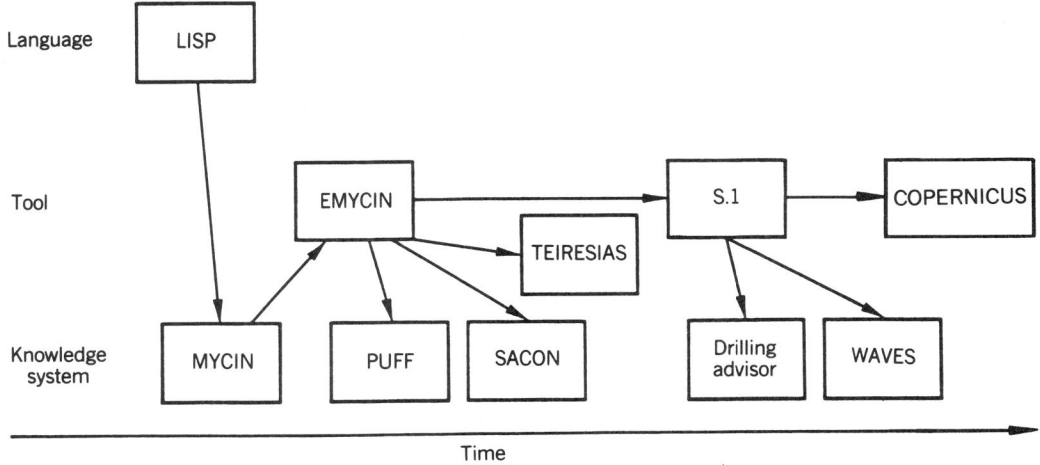

Figure 7. Schematic history of EMYCIN.

tions revolves about HEARSAY-II, one of the first 1000-word connected-speech-understanding systems (Erman and co-workers, 1980). HEARSAY-II embodies its own general paradigm in a characteristic architecture. HEARSAY-II embodies the cooperating experts paradigm. This paradigm views complex knowledge systems as collections of cooperating expert subsystems. In addition, part of the HEARSAY-II paradigm concerns how cooperating systems should interact. In particular, it proposes that they should exchange ideas via a global database called a blackboard (see BLACKBOARD SYSTEMS). Each independent source of knowledge should read that state of problem solving on the blackboard and contribute its own ideas by augmenting or modifying decisions on the blackboard. Although HEARSAY-II itself solved a problem of understanding connected speech, many other applications and some tools have embraced its paradigm. The HASP and SIAP applications used the HEARSAY-II approach to interpret sonar signals (Nii and co-workers, 1982), and the ACRONYM system exploited it to interpret photo images (Brooks and co-workers, 1979). Other applications of this general architecture have addressed problems in learning, planning, design, and information fusion. At the present time, PROTEAN, a major research project at Stanford, aims to develop a means for identifying the three-dimensional shape of proteins using an enhanced blackboard-based system called BB1 (Hayes-Roth, 1985) (see BLACKBOARD SYSTEMS).

Three general research tools have emerged thus far to support blackboard applications of this sort, HEARSAY-III (Erman and co-workers, 1981), AGE (Nii and Aiello, 1979), and BB1 (Hayes-Roth, 1985). HEARSAY-III provides a general representation for intermediate results, for independent sources of knowledge, and for flexible control but assumes the knowledge engineer will determine the appropriate problem-solving strategy and inference techniques. It also assumes the knowledge engineer will program knowledge directly in LISP. AGE, on the other hand, emphasizes modular and customized control algorithms to facilitate experimentation. It also provides a particular representation for intermediate results and asks the knowledge engineer to use LISP to represent knowledge. Where HEARSAY-III expects relatively large modules of knowledge, AGE expects fine-grain rules. BB1 provides both a flexible framework for building systems with cooperating knowledge specialists and a similar flexible and blackboard-based mechanism for implementing expert heuristics for making resource allocation and focus of attention control decisions. Many people believe that the blackboard architecture will become increasingly important as KE takes on more difficult and important tasks.

The third family of knowledge systems revolves around R1, which was renamed to XCON, a system to configure parts of a VAX computer (McDermott, 1980). R1 solved a problem that proved intractable to conventional data-processing methods because it required thousands of heuristic rules to capture the full variety of engineering components and relations. The tool used to implement R1 is called OPS (Forgy, 1979). (see A* ALGORITHM). This tool reflects the paradigm known as a pure production system.

The underlying philosophy of the pure production system holds that truly intelligent behavior, such as that of humans, consists entirely of many fine-grain, independent condition–action rules called productions. OPS makes it easy for a knowledge engineer to write such productions. OPS also includes an excellent compiler that eliminates many redundant computations and accelerates the selection of the first matching rule on each cycle of computation. OPS provides a simple but uniform representation method for describing problem-solving state data and for specifying rule conditions that match these state data. To program the action components of rules, OPS expects the knowledge engineer simply to alter the intermediate state data by changing property values or to write specialized LISP code.

OPS has been applied to a variety of applications. Two examples include XSEL, a program that DEC sales personnel can use to help a customer order and plan the layout for a VAX computer, and AIRPLAN, a knowledge system to plan and schedule flight training on board a U.S. Navy carrier. All applications of OPS exploit its capability to perform general computations specified in relatively independent rules. Each rule provides for a data-driven action. This gives OPS applications the flavor of interrupt-driven, or data flow, computations. Unlike many other KE tools, however, OPS provides little structure for representing facts, relationships, and uncertain knowledge, and it does not contain a general architecture for problem solving. Instead, it provides a novel scheme for pattern-directed inference that makes some symbolic programming tasks simple.

The MOLGEN family began with an effort at Stanford University to provide a mechanism for storing and managing large amounts of knowledge about molecular genetics. At first, the exact applications for the knowledge were unclear, and a primarily declarative knowledge representation was developed along the lines of earlier frame-representation systems. The representation developed for MOLGEN was call UNITS (Stefik, 1979), and it provided slots for object values and methods for determining these values or performing other actions as required. Over time, UNITS was adopted commercially by IntelliCorp and modified as its KEE product. KEE and a related product called NEXPERT Object, by Neuron Data, now offer object-oriented development environments to support this kind of knowledge representation. These tools have been used for a variety of applications.

Current Status of Tools

Tools will play a major role in the industrialization of KE. Their power derives from the paradigms, architectures, representations, inference engines, utilities, and programming systems they embody. Good tools will offer all of these kinds of aids to the knowledge engineer. As a consequence, good tools will require considerable work to develop. They approach in complexity and value the CAD, CAM, and CAE tools used in design, manufacturing, and engineering (see also DESIGN, AI IN; MANUFACTURING, AI IN).

Different KE tools will be desired, however, for different kinds of applications with different design requirements using different kinds of knowledge and specialized kinds of inference. Ultimately, KE tools will diversify in ways akin to electronic instruments. Because knowledge comes in different formats for different uses, tools appropriate to those uses will vary in form, purpose, and architecture.

KE is a very young field. Today's best tools have derived from many years' experience applying the same general kind of research tools repeatedly to a wide variety of applications. Out of that experience comes valid and useful criteria for tool designs. In the next few years many new kinds of applications will arise, and development of corresponding tools will lag those applications by several years.

BIBLIOGRAPHY

R. Brooks, R. Greiner, and T. Binford, "The ACRONYM Model-based Vision System," *Proceedings of the Sixth IJCAI,* Tokyo, Morgan-Kaufmann, San Mateo, Calif., 1979, pp. 105–113.

L. D. Erman, F. Hayes-Roth, V. Lesser, and D. Reddy, "HEARSAY-II Speech-Understanding System: Integrating Knowledge to Resolve Uncertainty," *Comp. Surv.* **12**(2), 213–253 (1980).

L. D. Erman, P. E. London, and S. F. Fickas, "The Design and an Example Use of HEARSAY-III," *Proceedings of the Seventh IJCAI,* Vancouver, B.C., Canada, Morgan-Kaufmann, San Mateo, Calif., 1981, pp. 409–415.

C. L. Forgy, *The OPS4 Users Manual Technical Report,* Technical Report CMU-CS-79-132, Computer Science Department, Carnegie Mellon University, 1979.

R. Greiner and D. Lenat, "A Representation Language Language," in *Proceedings of the First National Conference on Artificial Intelligence,* Stanford, Calif., AAAI, Menlo Park, Calif., 1980, pp. 165–169.

B. Hayes-Roth, "A Blackboard Architecture for Control," *J. Artif. Intell.* **26,** 251–321 (1985).

F. Hayes-Roth, D. Gorlin, S. Rosenchein, H. Sowizral, and D. Waterman, *Rationale and Motivation for ROSIE,* Technical Report N-1648-ARPA, The Rand Corp., 1981.

F. Hayes-Roth, D. A. Waterman, and D. B. Lenat, *Building Expert Systems,* Addison-Wesley Publishing Co., Inc., Reading, Mass., 1983.

R. K. Lindsay, B. G. Buchanan, E. A. Feigenbaum, and J. Lederberg, *Applications of Artificial Intelligence for Organic Chemistry: The DENDRAL Project,* McGraw-Hill Inc., New York, 1980.

J. McDermott, "R1: An Expert in the Computer Systems Domain," in *Proceedings of the First National Conference on Artificial Intelligence,* Stanford, Calif., pp. 269–271.

W. A. Martin and R. J. Fateman. "The MACSYMA System," in *Proceedings of the Second Symposium on Symbolic and Algebraic Manipulation,* 1971, pp. 59–75.

H. P. Nii and N. Aiello, "AGE: A Knowledge-based Program for Building Knowledge-based Programs," in *Proceedings of the Sxith IJCAI,* Tokyo, 1979, pp. 645–655.

H. P. Nii, E. A. Feigenbaum, J. J. Anton, and A. J. Rockmore, "Signal-to-Symbol Transformation: HASP/SIAP Case Study," *AI Magazine* 3(2), 1982.

H. E. Pople, J. D. Myers, and R. A. Miller, "DIALOG INTERNIST: A Model of Diagnostic Logic for Internal Medicine," *Proceedings of the Fourth IJCAI,* Tbilisi, USSR, Morgan-Kaufmann, San Mateo, Calif., 1975, pp. 849–855.

E. H. Shortliffe, *Computer-Based Medical Consultation: MYCIN,* Elsevier Science Publishing Co., Inc., New York, 1976.

M. J. Stefik, in *Proceedings of the Sixth IJCAI,* Tokyo, 1979.

General References

S. Brownstone, R. Farrell, E. Knat, and N. Morten, *Programming Expert Systems in OPS5: An Introduction to Rule-Based Programming,* Addison-Wesley Publishing Co., Inc., Reading, Mass., 1985.

B. G. Buchanan and E. H. Shortliffe, *Rule-Based Expert Systems,* Addison-Wesley Publishing Co., Inc., Reading, Mass., 1984.

R. Engelmore and T. Morgan, eds., *Blackboard Systems,* Addison-Wesley Publishing Co., Inc., Reading, Mass., 1988.

M. Richer, ed., *AI Tools and Techniques,* Ablex, Norwood, N.J., 1989.

F. Rose, *Into the Heart of the Mind,* Harper & Row, New York, 1984.

S. Shamoan. "The Expert that Thinks Like an Underwriter," *Management Technol.,* 54–59 (Feb. 1985).

D. Stamps, "Expert Systems," *PW/Software Publishing and Selling* **36** (Sept. 1984).

M. M. Waldrop, "The Intelligence of Organizations," *Science* **225,** 1136–1137 (1984).

D. A. Waterman, *A Guide to Expert Systems,* Addison-Wesley Publishing Co., Inc., Reading, Mass., 1986.

F. HAYES-ROTH
Cimflex Teknowledge
Corporation

The author gratefully acknowledges Addison-Wesley and IEEE *Computer* for granting permission to reprint figures. Drilling Advisor represents the work of numerous technical personnel at Elf-Acquitaine and Teknowledge, chief among these Cliff Hollander and Jacques-Marie Corteille.

EXPLANATION

Trust in a computer system comes not only from the quality of its results but also from the assurance that the system's reasoning is sound and appropriate to the task at hand. Explanation is the problem of producing machine-generated descriptions of the operation of a computer system: what it does, how it works, and why its actions are appropriate. In addition to the problem of actually producing explanations, the area of explanation research also includes the problem of designing computer systems so that they can be explained. Because providing explanations is so much a part of being a consultant (human or machine), explanatory capabilities are crucial to the ultimate acceptance of expert systems (Buchanan and Shortliffe, 1984). For that reason, most of the work on explanation has taken place in the context of expert systems, although other areas, such as software development, have been addressed (Swartout, 1983a, 1983b).

In addition to increasing users' confidence in a system

and allowing them to assess its applicability to a problem, an explanation facility can also be useful to system developers as a debugging tool. Machine-generated explanations often make errors apparent that are easily overlooked in more formal program code. The errors are revealed partly because the explanations provide a different viewpoint on the system, emphasizing aspects of the system obscured in the formal representation. An explanatory facility can also serve as an important component of a tutoring system (Clancey, 1979) (see EDUCATION, AI IN).

EARLY APPROACHES TO EXPLANATION

The simplest (and most primitive) way to provide explanations is to anticipate in advance all the questions that might be asked and store the answers as text. When a question arises during system execution, the explanation facility finds and displays the corresponding answer. This very simple approach (sometimes called the canned text approach) is frequently used to provide limited on-line documentation for text editors and operating systems. This approach is practical for small, slowly changing systems. However, several problems limit its applicability to larger, rapidly changing systems. The fact that the program code and the text strings that explain it can be changed independently makes it difficult to ensure that the text strings describe what the code actually does. Another problem is that all questions and answers must be anticipated in advance. For large systems this may be a nearly impossible task. Finally, the responses are inflexible. Because there is no model or internal representation of what is actually being said, it is difficult to customize the system's responses to particular situations or avoid repeating information that has already been presented.

These limitations are slightly ameliorated by allowing the text strings to contain blanks that are filled in, depending on the context in which the explanation occurs. However, this fill-in-the-blank approach still does not solve the problems, because the meaning of the response and the interrelationships among parts of the response remain implicit.

Another approach is to produce explanations by paraphrasing system code and, possibly, traces of its execution into natural language. This technique has been successfully used to describe how a system works and how it handles particular cases (Buchanan and Shortliffe, 1984; Winograd, 1971; Swartout, 1977). See Figure 1 for an example of an explanation produced by MYCIN (Buchanan and Shortliffe, 1984). Because explanations are produced by directly translating the code, they remain consistent with the system's behavior even if it is rapidly evolving. However, although this approach can describe what actions a system performs, it cannot describe the rationale behind those actions, that is, why those actions are appropriate.

The problem is that justifying a system's actions requires knowledge of the design decisions behind the system. These decisions do not have to be represented explicitly for the system to perform correctly. Just as it is possible to follow a recipe and bake a cake without ever

RULE009

PREMISE: ($AND (SAME CNTXT GRAM GRAMNEG)
(SAME CNTXT MORPH COCCUS))
ACTION: (CONCLUDE CNTXT IDENTITY NEISSERIA TALLY 800)

IF: 1)The gram stain of the organism is gramneg, and
2) The morphology of the organism is coccus
THEN: There is strongly suggestive evidence (.8) that the
identity of the organism is Neisseria

Figure 1. An explanation of a MYCIN rule.

knowing why the baking powder is there, so too an expert system can delivery impressive performance without any representation of the reasoning underlying its rules or methods. However, the absence of this knowledge makes it difficult to add explanation facilities to existing systems.

CAPTURING KNOWLEDGE FOR EXPLANATION

To capture the missing knowledge needed for explanation, new expert systems architectures have been developed. In NEOMYCIN (Clancey, 1981) descriptive facts of the domain (such as disease typologies and relations between diseases and symptoms) are explicitly represented and separated from metarules (see METAKNOWLEDGE, METARULES, AND METAREASONING) that represent the diagnostic strategies the system employs. These metarules capture the purpose behind the system's actions and can be used to explain the general diagnostic strategy the system is following. In related work, generic task theory (Chandrasekaran, 1986) has sought to identify general problem-solving strategies that are employed by broad classes of expert systems. It has been shown that a representation of the mapping between these general strategies and the particulars an actual expert system can provide an explanation facility with the knowledge it needs to produce better explanations (Tanner, 1989). The XPLAIN framework (Swartout, 1983b) and its successor, the Explainable Expert Systems (EES) framework (Neches and co-workers, 1985) also separate problem solving and descriptive knowledge. In addition, they use a program writer to compile an efficiently executable expert system from the problem solving and descriptive knowledge. As the program writer creates the expert system, the decisions it makes are recorded in a development history that provides explanation routines with the rationale behind the system. Related work has been published (Chandrasekaran and co-workers, 1986).

Recently, it has been argued that better explanations can be produced by using two completely separate knowledge bases (Wick and Thompson, 1989). One knowledge base is used to solve the problem, while the other is used to produce an explanation that justifies the solution. This approach is controversial, because it raises the question of whether or not the system's explanations can be trusted. Nevertheless, it is consistent with the observation that people often explain a solution to a problem using different knowledge than was used to solve the problem. This technique could be useful in domains where a system's problem-solving techniques are not likely to be understood by users.

EXPLANATION GENERATION

While most of the early work on explanation focused on the problem of representing sufficient knowledge to make explanations possible, more recently, researchers have begun to focus on the problem of explanation generation. As has been pointed out above, the explanations that early systems offered were limited because much of the knowledge needed for explanation was missing. In addition, there were also limitations that stemmed from the relatively simple natural language generation techniques that these systems used to produce explanations, such as templates (Buchanan and Shortliffe, 1984). These generation techniques could explain something in only one way. If a user failed to understand an explanation the system could not offer an alternative explanation. Because these techniques did not reason about the explanations they were producing they performed poorly in selecting what information to include in an explanation and what to leave out. This was not a big problem when knowledge bases were relatively simple, but it became a problem as knowledge bases were developed that contained more support knowledge for explanation. Perhaps most importantly, early generation techniques failed to recognize that explanation requires a dialogue between the system and user: the system should be prepared to answer questions within the dialogue context and be able to offer follow-up explanations that clarify or elaborate on explanations it has already given (Pollack and co-workers, 1982).

The first issue in producing explanations is recognizing and understanding the user's need for information. In most systems users usually indicate that they do not understand something by asking a question. This is a severe limitation because users must recognize that an explanation is needed. Some recent work has addressed the problem of inferring the need for explanation based on a user's actions (Shrager and Finin, 1982). Another style of interaction has been presented that creates an expert system for drug therapy that does not offer advice directly but instead provides a detailed critique of therapy plans that a user provides (Miller and Black, 1982). The system offers explanations on its own initiative when it discovers significant differences between its recommendations and the user's.

Once the need for information is identified, the next issue is to create a response that will provide it, taking into account what the user already knows and selecting a presentation style that is appropriate. Explanation facilities are beginning to emerge that use text-planning techniques (see NATURAL LANGUAGE GENERATION) to produce explanations (McKeown and Swartout, 1987; Moore and Paris, 1989). Given a discourse goal that represents the information that should be conveyed to the user, these systems use a set of explanation strategies to plan explic-itly an explanation for the user. Because more than one explanation strategy may exist for a given discourse goal, these systems can offer alternative explanations when an explanation is not understood. It is possible to record the processing that the text planner goes through in producing a text plan and thereby capture the *design* of the explanation (Moore and Swartout, 1989). This record provides the explanation facility with the information that it needs to support dialogue, such as what the explanation is intended to convey, what strategies were used to convey it, what alternative strategies exist, and what assumptions may have been made about the user's knowledge.

Figure 2 illustrates some of the advantages of text planning for explanation. The figure shows a dialogue between a user and a style critic for LISP programs developed within the EES framework. This program was designed to examine a user's program and suggest various ways that it could be improved to enhance its readability or maintainability. There are several things to notice about this dialogue. First, the user's *why* in line 6 is ambiguous. It could mean "Why are you trying to enhance the maintainability of the program?" (which is the interpretation that early systems such as MYCIN made) or it could mean "Why is setq-to-setf a transformation that enhances maintainability?" Because the system explicitly planned the response in line 5, it knows what it said and can thus make use of a local focus heuristic that states that interpretations that involve staying on the current topic are to be preferred over those that switch to a new topic. In this case, the current topic is the last line of line

SYSTEM (1) What characteristics of the program would you like to enhance?
USER (2) Maintainability.

.
.
.

SYSTEM (3) You should replace (**setq x 1**) with (**setf x 1**).
USER (4) Why?
SYSTEM (5) I'm trying to enhance the maintainability of the program by applying transformations that enhance maintainability. **Setq-to-setf** is a transformation that enhances maintainability.
USER (6) Why?
SYSTEM (7) Transformations that enhance maintainability are defined as transformations whose right-hand-side use is more general than its left-hand-side use. **Setf** can be used to assign a value to any generalized variable. **Setq** can only be used to assign a value to a simple variable.
USER (8) What is a generalized variable?
SYSTEM (9) Simple variables are storage locations named by symbols. This concept can be generalized to a storage location that can be named by any accessor function. These storage locations are called generalized variables.
USER (10) Huh?
SYSTEM (11) For example, the *car* and *cdr* of a cons are generalized variables, named by the accessor functions **car** and **cdr**. Other examples are an element of an array or a component of a structure.

Figure 2. Explanation dialogue (Moore and Swartout, 1989).

5, so the system interprets the question as asking why setq-to-setf enhances maintainability. Lines 8 to 11 illustrate another advantage of the text planning approach. In line 9 the system produces an explanation that the user fails to understand. Because the system knows what it was trying to explain, how it was trying to explain it, and what alternative strategies were available, it can produce a clarifying explanation in line 11.

OTHER BENEFITS

Although explanation facilities were originally developed to make systems more acceptable to users, they have provided additional benefits. Capturing the knowledge required to provide justifications forced the development of systems to be more explicit and principled. Separation of different kinds of knowledge such as problem solving and descriptive domain knowledge was originally necessary so that they would not be confounded in explanations, but this separation makes systems more modular and hence easier to maintain. Taking explanation concerns into account while a system is being built can have benefits that go beyond explanation, and result in a system that is easier to maintain and extend. Thus providing for explanation should not be regarded as something that is "added on" to an existing system, but instead, providing for explanation concerns should be treated as an intrinsic part of the system building process.

BIBLIOGRAPHY

B. G. Buchanan and E. H. Shortliffe, *Rule-Based Expert Systems, the MYCIN Experiments of the Stanford Heuristic Programming Project,* Addison-Wesley Publishing Co., Inc., Reading, Mass., 1984.

B. Chandrasekaran, "Generic Tasks in Knowledge-Based Reasoning," *IEEE Expert* 1(3), 23–30 (1986).

B. Chandrasekaran, J. Josephson, and A. Kekuneke, "Functional Representation as a Basis for Explanation Generation," in *Proceedings of the IEEE International Conference on Systems, Man and Cybernetics,* 1986, pp. 726–731.

W. Clancey, *Transfer of Rule-Based Expertise Through a Tutorial Dialogue,* Technical Report STAN-CS-769, Stanford University, Stanford, Calif., 1979.

W. Clancey, "Neomycin: Reconfiguring a Rule-Based Expert System for Application to Teaching," in *Proceedings of the Seventh IJCAI,* Vancouver, B.C., Canada, Morgan-Kaufmann, San Mateo, Calif., 1981.

K. McKeown and W. Swartout, "Language Generation and Explanation," *Ann. Rev. Comput. Sci.* **2** (1987).

P. Miller and H. Black, "Medical Plan-Analysis by Computer: Critiquing the Pharmacologic Management of Essential Hypertension," *Comput. Biomed. Res.* **17,** 38–54 (1982).

J. D. Moore and C. L. Paris, "Planning Text for Advisory Dialogues," in *Proceedings of the Twenty-Seventh Annual Meeting of the Association for Computational Linguistics,* Vancouver, B.C., Canada, June 1989.

J. D. Moore and W. R. Swartout, "A Reactive Approach to Explanation," in *Proceedings of the Eleventh IJCAI,* Detroit, Mich., Morgan-Kaufmann, San Mateo, Calif., 1989.

R. Neches, W. R. Swartout, and J. D. Moore, "Enhanced Maintenance and Explanation of Expert Systems Through Explicit Models of Their Development," *IEEE Trans. Softw. Eng.* **SE-11**(11), 1337–1351 (1985).

M. E. Pollack, J. Hirschberg, and B. L. Webber, "User Participation in the Reasoning Processes of Expert Systems," in *Proceedings of the Second National Conference on Artificial Intelligence,* Pittsburgh, Pa., AAAI, Menlo Park, Calif., 1982.

J. Shrager and T. Finin, "An Expert System That Volunteers Advice," in *Proceedings of the Second National Conference on Artificial Intelligence,* Pittsburgh, Pa., AAAI, Menlo Park, Calif., 1982.

W. Swartout, "A Digitalis Therapy Advisor With Explanations," in *Proceedings of the Fifth IJCAI,* Cambridge, Mass., Morgan-Kaufmann, San Mateo, Calif., 1977, pp. 819–825.

W. Swartout, "Gist English Generator," in *Proceedings of the Second National Conference on Artificial Intelligence,* Pittsburgh, Pa., AAAI, Menlo Park, Calif., 1982.

W. Swartout, "The Gist Behavior Explainer," in *Proceedings of the Third National Conference on Artificial Intelligence,* Washington, D.C., AAAI, Menlo Park, Calif., 1983a.

W. Swartout, "XPLAIN: A System for Creating and Explaining Expert Consulting Systems," *Artif. Intell.* **21**(3), 285–325 (Sept. 1983b).

M. Tanner, *Explaining Knowledge Systems: Justifying Diagnostic Conclusions,* Ph.D. dissertation, Ohio State University, Columbus, 1989.

M. R. Wick and W. B. Thompson, "Reconstructive Explanation: Explanation as Complex Problem Solving," in *Proceedings of the Eleventh International Joint Conference on Artificial Intelligence,* Detroit, Mich., Morgan Kaufmann, San Mateo, Calif., 1989, pp. 135–140.

T. Winograd, *A Computer Program for Understanding Natural Language,* Technical Report TR-17, MIT Artificial Intelligence Laboratory, Cambridge, Mass., 1971.

William Swartout
University of Southern
California

FIFTH-GENERATION COMPUTING. See COMPUTER SYSTEMS; LOGIC PROGRAMMING.

FILE-MAINTENANCE SYSTEMS. See PROGRAMMING ENVIRONMENTS.

FINDSPACE PROBLEM. See ROBOT CONTROL SYSTEMS.

FLAVORS

Flavors is an object-oriented programming facility for LISP (qv) developed at the M.I.T. LISP Machine (qv) project in 1979. Addition of Smalltalk-like message-passing facilities to LISP was investigated in the late 1970s. The original motivation of Flavors was to add multiple inheritance to this framework in a coherent way. By analogy to curry powder and to ice-cream toppings, a flavor is a mixture of several other flavors. Each component flavor can contribute behavior in response to a message, in the form of a method. When several methods exist, they are organized by a declarative "method combination" scheme that allows the programmer to think about each method separately and ignore the details of interactions between methods. Earlier languages required methods to contain explicit code to control interactions with related methods. The message-passing orientation of Flavors was later dropped in favor of the generic function concept, which better fits the LISP language.

The key concerns of Flavors were to encourage modularity so programs can be constructed out of existing parts, to provide tools for developing large programs incrementally, and to provide run-time efficiency close to non-object-oriented implementations. Flavors served as the basis for many object-oriented programs and for the Symbolics operating system throughout the 1980s. Along with Common LOOPS (qv), Flavors evolved into the CLOS (qv) standard for Common LISP Object-Oriented Programming. (See H. I. Cannon, "Flavors: A Non-Hierarchical Approach to Object-Oriented Programming," Symbolics, Inc., 1982; D A. Moon, "Object-Oriented Programming With Flavors," *First Annual Conference on Object-Oriented Programming Systems, Languages, and Applications*, ACM, 1986.)

DANIEL A. MOON
Symbolics

FOL

Primarily a proof checker for proofs stated in first-order logic (qv), FOL was developed by Weyhrauch and Filman around 1975 at Stanford University. FOL also provides a sophisticated, interactive environment for using logic to study epistemological problems (see R. Weyhrauch, *Prolegomena to a Theory of Mechanized Formal Reasoning,* Report No. STAN-CS-78-687, Computer Science Department, Stanford University, Stanford, Calif., 1979).

K. S. ARORA
SUNY at Buffalo

FORWARD CHAINING. See PROCESSING, BOTTOM-UP AND TOP-DOWN.

FRAMES

Frame theory is a paradigm for representing commonsense knowledge so that the knowledge is usable by a computer. This article reviews the history and motivation of frame theory, its use in AI, the structure of frame-based AI languages that were motivated in part by frame theory, and recent developments in frame theory.

BEGINNINGS

Frame theory emerged in AI primarily as the result of a technical report by Minsky (1974), which was subsequently published in full (Winston, 1975) and in abridged form (Haugeland, 1981; Brachman and Levesque, 1985). Minsky's "frames paper," as it became known, represented an effort to construct a framework or paradigm to account for the effectiveness of commonsense thought in real-world tasks. In part, Minsky wanted to construct a database containing the encyclopedic amounts of knowledge needed in a commonsense reasoning system, but more important, he wanted to create an enormously descriptive database that encoded knowledge in a structured, yet flexible manner. The structure provided by the knowledge base would allow a computer system to impose coherence on its experience (input information), and the flexibility would allow the system to access appropriate information in novel situations whose occurrence could not be anticipated in advance.

Briefly, Minsky envisioned a scheme where knowledge was encoded in packets, called frames (based on the metaphor of a single frame in a film), and frames were embedded in a retrieval network, called a frame system, so that if one frame was accessed, indexes to other potentially relevant frames would become available. A frame would be activated whenever a new situation was encountered; the tricky part would be to get the appropriate frame to be activated in the appropriate situation, and this would be the responsibility of the frame system (this term has since been changed to frame array). Part of the motivation of the use of frames at all, rather than being restricted to the use of more elemental propositions, was that a frame would be a large enough unit of knowledge to impose structure in a new situation, yet would be modular enough to be used as an element in a flexible database. Although Minsky's frames paper served as a rallying point in AI, setting off a flurry of research, aspects of the frame notion, namely that modules of knowledge impose coherence on experience, is traceable back to the schema notion of Bartlett (1961). In linguistics, Fillmore (1968) used the term case frame; this theorizing evolved into a blend of prototype theory and frame theory (Fillmore, 1975). In sociology, Goffman (1974) "borrowed the term [frame] from Gregory Bateson to refer to analytical frameworks within which human experience can be made intelligible" (Fillmore, 1975). Minsky noted that his frame is in the tradition of Kuhn's paradigm, used in the history of science, and is related to ideas in AI (Abelson, 1973; Minsky and Papert, 1972; Newell and Simon, 1972; Norman, 1973; Schank, 1973). Extensive work on what might be called frame-theoretic knowledge structures has been conducted (Schank and Abelson, 1977; Schank, 1979, 1981, 1982).

TERMINOLOGY

The term frame theory, as introduced above, is ambiguous in whether it denotes the theoretical developments deriving from the frames paper or whether it simply denotes the higher level knowledge structures such as scripts, based on the metaphor of a script for a play (Schank and Abelson, 1977), β-structures (Moore and Newell, 1973), or the schema notion (Bartlett, 1961). (To make matters worse, there is also the so-called frame problem, which has nothing directly to do with frame theory or knowledge structures.) The term frame was most popular in the mid- to late 1970s. In a recent AI textbook (Charniak and McDermott, 1985), in which one of the authors is a well-known frame theorist, the term *frame theory* does not appear in the index, nor are frame languages or frame systems covered. Instead, the issues of frame theory are subsumed under the topics of memory organization and abductive inference. In other AI textbooks framelike concepts are included under schemas and prototypes (Sowa, 1984), representation of commonsense knowledge (Winston, 1984), frames and scripts (Barr and Felgenbaum, 1981), structured object representations and units (Nilsson, 1980), and structured representations (Luger and Stubblefield, 1989).

Because the general use of higher level knowledge structure was fashionable at the time, and because the influences between research groups are difficult to untangle, this article will often use the word *frame* to generically mean "knowledge structure" or "higher level knowledge structure" when that seems appropriate. There are also frame languages, which were at least in part developed to implement frame-based AI programs and this article will be concerned with those as well. Often implementations of frame languages are called frame systems, but this usage is different than Minsky's (1974) use of the term. For Minsky, a frame system was the retrieval net-

work in which the frames were embedded. Minsky (1986) has abandoned the term frame system and replaced it with the term frame array.

THE PURPOSE OF FRAME THEORY

One of the best ways to communicate the intent and spirit of frame theory is to use a well-known example, consisting of an imaginary anecdote describing the correspondences and interactions between a person's expectations, perceptions, and sense experience as the person opens a door and enters a room. This example was elaborated with more detail, from which much of this discussion is drawn (Kuipers, 1975). Suppose a man is about to open a door to enter an unfamiliar room in a house. In the house, prior to opening the door, he has expectations or predictions about what will be visible on the other side of the door. For instance, if he were to see a landscape or seashore after opening the door, he would first have difficulty recognizing it; he would, after recognizing it, be quite surprised; and, finally, he would be somewhat disoriented because he could not interpret the input information and would be at a loss to choose a set of predictions about what might happen next. This, so the analysis goes, is because a room frame has been activated as a function of his opening the door, and the frame plays a major role in controlling his interpretation of perceptual input. The room frame even comes with certain default predictions: a room is expected to have a certain kind of shape; one would experience surprise upon entering a cylindrical room or a geodesic dome. If a bed is seen upon entering the room, then the room frame becomes specialized to a bedroom frame. In other words, the most specific frame available would be accessed. It is possible to use the information of being in a room to facilitate the recognition of furniture. This is often called top-down processing, or in the context of frame theory, frame-driven recognition. However, if a floating fire hydrant was seen (Biederman, 1981, it would be difficult to recognize, it would be surprising to identify it, and it would probably be disorientating, because the input information is apparently inconsistent with the predictions of the currently active frame. Indeed, psychologists (eg, Biederman) have demonstrated experimentally that drawings of objects are easier to identify (as indicated by reaction time and error rate) in their usual context than in an anomalous context.

From this example, it can be seen that a frame, as originally envisioned, was a module of knowledge that became active in a presumably appropriate situation and served to offer interpretation of, and new predictions for, that situation. Minsky made suggestions about the nature of a data structure that could do this sort of thing. He proposed a frame array (originally called a frame system) that consisted of a collection of related frames, many of which shared the same subcomponents (he referred to them as terminals) linked by a retrieval network. Thus when walking through a house, the course of expectations would be controlled by access processes operating on the retrieval network in the frame system. In the above case the relevant frame system would be that for a house, and the door and room frames would be subsystems in this system. Given that certain frames were active, adding the information to the database that the door was opened, would serve as an access trigger from the currently active door frame to a room frame. Furthermore, the door frame and the room frame would share whatever substructure was common between them. Minsky called this the sharing of terminals and considered it an important feature of frame systems because it meant a great savings on recomputing information. Although here the door frame and room frame are treated as being autonomous, they too would be embedded in frame systems. For instance, the room frame system would contain frames describing the appearance of the room at different view points and they would be linked by movements of the viewer.

In terms of the anecdotal example, descriptions were used that had the character of a folk psychology; these folk psychology descriptions are characterized below in the context of frame systems and higher level knowledge structures. Some of these are recognition of a situation as being of a certain category (such as realizing that you are in a room), interpretation of the situation in terms of that category (such as realizing that the room is in a house), prediction of what else is to arise in the situation (such as expecting to see a piece of furniture), surprise at failed predictions (such as identifying a fire hydrant after having construed a living room), disorientation when a category cannot be found to interpret the situation (as realizing it is not a living room, but having no alternative hypotheses), and possible reinterpretation of the situation. As mentioned in the beginning of this article, the goal of frame theory is to account for the effectiveness of commonsense thought in the performance of real-world tasks. These phenomena, which are familiar to those who do commonsense thought, may seem mundane. Recounting them may seem trivial. However, it was a basic tenet of frame theory that an attempt to mimic these phenomena in a computer system could lead to the development of a more intelligent computer system. This can be taken as the intent of frame theory.

FRAME LANGUAGES

Minsky introduced terminology and sketches for what he thought a frame language might look like. This terminology included terms such as frames, slots, terminals, and default assignments. The frames paper thus played a role in spawning, or influencing, two lines of research. One line was focused on the high level goals of frame theory, as stated above, and the other line was concerned with developing frame languages along the lines of Minsky's suggestions. Many of the same researchers were working on both lines of research simultaneously. It must also be observed that many of the researchers working in what this article treats as frame theory did so for their own independent reasons and did not necessarily conceptualize in terms of frames or frame languages. More will be said about frame languages at the end of this article.

FRAME THEORY AND FOLK PSYCHOLOGY

Although the examples in the frames paper were divided between perception and language, and Minsky viewed both problems as roughly being of the same nature, there have been many more frame-based applications to language than to visual perception, but see, for instance, Walker and co-workers (1988) and Weymouth and co-workers (1983). In particular, much frame-theoretic research has been done in the context of natural language and story understanding (Charniak, 1981b). This section sketches how folk psychology descriptions of thought can be characterized in terms of frame theory.

Recognition, Interpretation, and Prediction

As a simple illustration of recognition, interpretation, and prediction, consider the two stories below, taken from Schank and Abelson (1977). At the global level the first story is considerably different than the second.

Story A
1. John went to a restaurant.
2. He asked the waitress for a hamburger.
3. He paid the tip and left.

Story B
1. John went to a park.
2. He asked the midget for a mouse.
3. He picked up the box and left.

Although corresponding sentences in these stories are comparable in syntactic structure and type of semantic information conveyed in the literal meaning, comprehension for the sequences as a whole differs radically. Story A successfully accesses some kind of higher level knowledge structure (eg, the restaurant dining frame, or the restaurant dining script), and story B fails to access a comparable structure. If A did not access such a knowledge structure, comprehension would be reduced to the level of B and could be characterized as disorientation. This contrast provides a striking example of the immediate payoff of invoking higher level knowledge structures.

Story A activates more than just a restaurant frame. Each sentence activates at least one frame in its own right. Sentence one activates a frame for physical transfer (arrival), sentence two activates a frame for mental transfer (a request), and sentence three activates frames for abstract transfer (payment) and physical transfer (departure). Schank (1973, 1975a) used the terms ptrans, mtrans, and atrans to describe physical transfer, mental transfer, and abstract transfer, respectively. Minsky (1986) considers Schank's cross-realm notions of transfer important because they allow the application of the same kind of reasoning procedures, that of mental chaining, to the varied realms of physical movement, mental communication, and abstract forms of transfer such as possession and ownership. Because of this, Minsky has proposed a specific kind of frame called a trans-frame. A frame con-

Table 1. Trans-Frames for Story A

	Trans-frame #1		Trans-frame #2
Actor	John	Actor	John
Object	John	Object	Request
Origin	John's house	Origin	John's mind
Destination	Restaurant	Destination	Waitress's mind
Action	Ptrans	Action	Mtrans
Difference	John's location changes	Difference	Request is in waitress's mind
	Trans-frame: #3		Trans-frame #4
Actor	John	Actor	John
Object	Money	Object	John
Origin	John's pocket	Origin	Restaurant
Destination	Waitress's possession	Destination	John's house
Action	Atrans	Action	Ptrans
Difference	Waitress has more money	Difference	John's location changes

sists of a list of slots and terminals. A trans-frame has, among others, the slots actor, object, origin, destination, action, and difference. Trans-frames for story A are shown in Table 1. The italicized words represent terminals. Trans-frame 1 represents sentence one, trans-frame 2 represents sentence two, and trans-frames 3 and 4 represent sentence three. How is the information in a trans-frame determined? To over simplify, for sentence one, it is known that the action is a ptrans because the verb of the sentence is *went*. The subject of the sentence is *John*. This reveals that the actor is John. For the verb *went*, the object is the same as the actor, so it is known that the object is John. The destination is the restaurant because it is stated in the verb complement. It is known that the origin is John's house and the difference is a change of location. These are the defaults of the trans-frame for *went*. Similar analyses apply to the other trans-frames.

Story B has similar trans-frames. However, story B lacks a higher level frame to organize these frames. This would be some kind of event-sequencing frame or a script. For story A the restaurant script is a major component of Minsky's frame array. The frame array organizes the trans-frames into a coherent story. Notice that the actor is the same in all of the trans-frames of Table 1. This is the simplest case of the sharing of terminals. The same slots in different frames use the same terminals. Other terminals are shared in a weaker fashion where the same terminals appear in different slots for different frames.

Historically, Charniak (1972) represents the earliest attempt to consider methods for the processing of stories like A, which are about stereotyped situations such as restaurant dining or a child's birthday party. Charniak's work influenced Minsky's proposals. Minsky (1974) argued for the need for rich default structures for this kind of story. The use of a script for such stories has been specifically proposed (Schank, 1975b; Schank and Abelson, 1977) and that proposal was implemented in a program called SAM, a program that summarizes and answers questions about such stories (Cullingford, 1978; Schank and Reisbeck, 1981). A script is a kind of frame that is specialized toward describing stereotyped event sequences. For example, with respect to story A, SAM can answer the following questions, whose answers are not

explicitly stated in the story, by accessing a record of the predicted event sequence for restaurant dining.

Did John sit down in the restaurant?
Did John eat the hamburger?

In terms of the folk psychology processes mentioned previously, the SAM program must recognize the situation being described as that of restaurant dining and then predict the likely event sequence. In story A, recognition was trivial, and prediction was easy, once recognition was achieved. Recognition involved accessing the correct higher level structure, the structure encoded the predictions, and interpretation involved a simple manipulation of that structure (called script application) to retrieve the predictions. In the general case, recognition is not trivial and misrecognition is unavoidable.

Misrecognition, Interpretation, and Reinterpretation

There are story understanding programs that can recover from misrecognition, however. This has been shown with a story segment given by Collins and co-workers (1980), which has been used as challenge cases for testing story understanding programs (Charniak, 1978; O'Rorke, 1983).

Story C
1. He plunked down $5 at the window.
2. She tried to give him $2.50, but he wouldn't take it.
3. So when they got inside, she bought him a large bag of popcorn.

For most people this story invokes a cycle of repeated incorrect or incomplete recognition and reinterpretation. Many people, on reading the first sentence, invoke a bet-at-horse-race frame. After reading sentence two they interpret it as an attempt to return change. Finally, sentence three triggers a recovery from the misrecognition as a betting scenario to recognition as a movie scenario embedded within a dating scenario. In addition, the slot assignment for the pronoun *she* in sentences two and three must be changed from cashier to dating partner.

Systems that can recover from simple misrecognitions have been implemented (Norvig, 1983; O'Rorke, 1983). An example that one program uses is given below (O'Rorke, 1983).

1. John put two quarters in the slot.
2. Then he started his first game.

In this implementation, the initial sentence signals both the vending machine and video game frames, and the system initially elaborates both frames while noticing that they are incompatible because the coin insertion event cannot be assigned to a video game slot and a vending machine slot simultaneously (a consequence of interpretation); at this point the system arbitrarily chooses the vending machine frame while preserving both elaborations. The second sentence describes an event that is recognized as part of the rejected video game frame, thus triggering dependency directed backtracking (Doyle, 1979). The vending machine frame is rejected and the video game frame is selected, because it is the only frame compatible with all of the given information. This can be viewed as surprise leading to reinterpretation.

Frame-Driven Recognition

Minsky (1986) has suggested that there are frames for noun structures and verb structures. This means that the problem of disambiguating ambiguous words can be treated as frame recognition. Consider the sentences below, which contain ambiguous words (Charniak and McDermott, 1985).

The programmer was near the terminal.
The plane was near the terminal.

The word *terminal* in each of these sentences is ambiguous. It could mean computer terminal or airline terminal. It is plausible that this word is disambiguated using a frame that was recognized earlier in the sentence (Charniak, 1984; Cullingford, 1978; Granger, 1977; Hayes, 1977). Subjectively, people are often aware of only noticing the correct sense of the word without realizing that there are alternatives. One way of approaching this is to store a lexicon (word dictionary) with each frame. When that frame is activated, then the associated lexicon is searched for word meanings prior to searching the global lexicon. In terms of frame theory, there is recognition of a frame controlling interpretation processes that, in turn, control recognition of subsequent input. This scheme uses frame activation to control search order.

A striking application of frame-driven recognition appears the FRUMP program (DeJong, 1979; Schank and Abelson, 1977; Winston, 1984) for summarizing newspaper stories about certain classes of events, such as terrorism and earthquake disasters. This program keeps a tabulation of the things that are supposed to be described in each kind of story, and this tabulation drives the program's recognition process for described events.

In the 1970s and early 1980s practitioners of frame theory operated within the framework of symbolic computing. Minsky's (1986) later proposal embeds frame theory within his society of mind theory, and his theory is essentially connectionist, that is, the theory is based on metaphorical neural structures. In Minsky's revised theory, frames have activation levels and they have neural connections to other frames. These connections can vary in strength, and frames themselves are constructed from more primitive neural components.

When one frame has a high connection strength to a second frame, and the first frame is active, then the activation is likely to propogate and cause the second frame to become active. This allows the search-order theory to be implemented by a mechanism that propogates activation levels, rather than by associating a lexicon with each frame. Instead, strong connections are built from frames to their associated word senses. Thus a computer programming frame would have strong connections to the computer terminal sense for the word *terminal*. Similarly, the airplane frame would have strong connections to the airline terminal sense for the word *terminal*.

FRAME MANIPULATION AND MEMORY ORGANIZATION

So far little detail has been provided about the specifics of frame representations and the specifics of algorithms to manipulate the representations. At the level of analysis that has been operating, these specifics are less important than other factors. The principal factor controlling the performance of a program in a commonsense domain is the knowledge that it embodies (Newell, 1982). Thus it is important for a program to, say, determine that John is likely to eat at a restaurant after being told that John walked into a restaurant. The particulars of how this knowledge is embodied is less important. Similarly, it is important to somehow associate appropriate word senses with a frame. Whether this is done by table lookup or by manipulating connection strengths is less important.

However, if a frame-based computer program is desired, then issues of frame manipulation and memory organization must be addressed. When treating such issues, several questions come to mind. How are frames recognized, invoked, or accessed? How large are frames? How are frames used? Where do frames come from? A set of text comprehension principles for the domain of plan-based stories along with a collection of frame manipulation primitives has been proposed (Wilensky, 1983). Some of these frame manipulation primitives are shown in Table 2. They are used in service of the higher level and more important text comprehension principles. The text comprehension principles are shown in Table 3.

In Table 2 frame recognition is decomposed into two components: frame invocation and frame determination. Frame determination represents the latter stage of frame recognition. With story A, determining the lower level ptrans frame for sentence one and the higher level restaurant dining frame, also from sentence one, are examples of frame invocation (and determination). Frame elaboration involves both filling in slots with values that were explicitly mentioned in the story and with supplying defaults for values that were not explicitly mentioned. Determin-

Table 2. Some Frame Manipulation Primitives[a]

Invocation	Initially considering a frame
Determination	Deciding if enough evidence exists to infer an invoked frame
Elaboration	Filling in a slot of a determined frame
Termination	Inferring that a determined frame is no longer relevant

[a] Wilensky (1983).

ing that John is both the agent and the object of trans-frame #1 in Table 1 are examples of elaboration. Determining that John's house is the origin (by default) is also an example of elaboration. Once a frame is activated, it cannot persist forever. Frame termination is concerned with determining that a frame is no longer relevant. Lower level trans-frames usually terminate at the end of a sentence. This is the case with sentence one of story A. Higher level frames, such as the restaurant dining frame, terminate when there is a change of topic or when the topic has a resolution. In story A, the resolution is that John paid the tip and left. A change of topic could have been signaled by the phrase *by the way*.

Wilensky's text comprehension principles, shown in Table 3, attempt to identify exactly what it means for a person or computer to have comprehended text and, as such, they tell us what to use the frame manipulation primitives for. For instance, the rejection of the vending machine frame in favor of the video game frame in O'Rorke's program can be viewed as being consistent with the principles of coherence and exhaustion. This is because the vending machine frame cannot coherently explain all of the input, but the video game frame can. The text comprehension principles can be implemented either by Wilensky's frame manipulation primitives, O'Rorke's method, or by some other method. The operation of Cullingford's program is similarly consistent with the principle of coherence. Ideally, the mechanics of this process would be described in terms of the frame manipulation primitives. Notice that all of the principles in Table 3 are concerned with frame recognition (determination). This testifies to the overwhelming importance of accessing the right knowledge structure, indicating the importance of recognition, and suggesting that it is the structure of the frame array that is crucial to frame theory, rather than the structure of a frame.

Table 3. Some Text Comprehension Principles

Coherence	Determination frames that provide a coherent construal of the input
Concretion	Determine as specific a frame as possible the input
Exhaustion	Determine enough frames to account for all of the input
Parsimony	Determine frames that maximize connections between inputs

[a] Wilensky (1983).

Recognition, Matching, and Indexing

There has been much discussion in the literature of the processes involving frame recognition and the access of higher level knowledge structures (Fahlman, 1974; Kuipers, 1975; Minsky, 1974; Charniak, 1978; Schank and Abelson, 1977; Schank, 1979, 1981; Kolodner, 1983, 1984). As was alluded to in the context of Wilensky's text comprehension principles, frame recognition is of fundamental importance. Despite the fact that humans seem to recognize frames effortlessly, for computer programs it has been quite difficult in the general case. In fact, questions of frame recognition are still difficult and open questions in AI. Consider the following sentence (Charniak, 1978)

The man sawed the woman in half.

For most people this suggests the magic act frame, but how? The answer does not lie in the nature of the representation for the sentence. Rather, the world happens to be organized so that there is only one situation where this event occurs, and one's memory systems are able to detect this regularity. The indexing scheme controlling frame recognition thus is not a function of the represented information, the literal meaning of the sentence, but rather a function of the system's history of experience. Focusing on the problem of frame recognition leads to consideration of basic issues in memory organization. In particular, Schank has been concerned with the folk psychology phenomenon of reminding as a clue to the structure of memory access.

Examples of memory access by the use of abstract indexes has been recorded (Schank, 1979). For instance, being reminded of waiting for an hour in line to buy $1 of gas; this is called the gas line frame. The gas line frame was remembered after being told about someone who waited for 20 min in a line to buy one postage stamp (the postal line frame). The postal line frame lead to access of the gas line frame, presumably on the basis of the index "waiting in a long line to do just a little bit when it would be better to do more" (the inefficient queuing frame). This is a situation where it seems that any frame can potentially be used as an index to any other frame. In this case, it seems that inefficient queuing was initially an abstraction from the gas line frame, at the time of hearing about the gas line incident. This abstraction, a frame in its own right, then served as an index to subsequent access of the postal line frame. The inefficient queuing frame was subsequently reabstracted from the postal line frame, causing the reminding experience. This scenario is shown in Figure 1.

Why inefficient queuing was abstracted, rather than something else, is still open to debate. One possibility is that the human memory system keeps summary statistics, such as the mean and standard deviation, on slot values for frame instances. Whenever a new situation is encountered whose frame instance contains extreme values on more than one feature (eg, waiting in a line for a remarkably long time and obtaining a remarkably small amount of resource), the system constructs a new frame

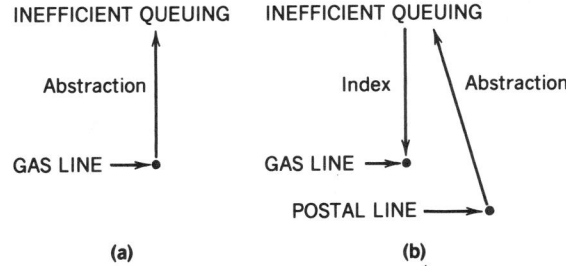

Figure 1. (*a*) An abstraction created from an experienced instance of the gas line frame; the abstraction becomes an index to that instance. (*b*) The same abstraction being recreated from a description of an instance of the postal line frame; this serves as an access route to the previously indexed gas line instance.

(eg, inefficient queuing) to represent that kind of situation. This theory can also be used to explain why the magic act sentence can serve as an index to the magic act frame. When hearing the sentence for the first time, a frame may initially be accessed for sawing things. However, the slot value for the object of the sawing action is a remarkably unusual value. This should trigger a process to construct a new frame for sawing a person. The frame should be indexed under the context in which it was created, namely, that of a magic act.

The size of a frame is more closely related to memory organization than is first suspected. This is because, in humans, the size of a frame is not strictly determined by its semantic content. One clue as to what these other factors might be comes from Schank's (1979) analysis of an earlier experiment (Bower and co-workers, 1979) in which it was demonstrated that there are memory confusions between the waiting room scenes of stories describing doctor's office visits and dentist's office visits. In other words, a doctor's office visit frame is composed of subframes, one of which is the health care waiting room frame. What is the moral? The size of a frame is not dependent on the semantic content of the represented frame (such as doctor's office visit), but depends on whether components of the descriptive information in the frame (such as the waiting room component) is useful elsewhere in the memory. It appears that when some set of knowledge becomes useful in more than one situation, the memory system detects this, then modularizes that component into a frame in its own right, and then restructures the original frame to use this new frame as a subcomponent. How the system detects when such modularization should take place and how the system actually does such restructuring are, again, open questions of memory organization and machine learning. A theory of frame access or memory organization has been constructed on the basis of these considerations (Schank, 1979, 1981, 1982; DeJong, 1979; Kolodner, 1983a, 1983b, 1984; Lebowitz, 1983).

FRAME THEORY AND CONCEPT HIERARCHIES

Although Minsky (1974) did not emphasize the use of concept hierarchies in his frames paper (Quillian (1968) and Collins and Quillian (1969) were two of the earliest to advocate concept hierarchies), the fact that he was concerned with sharing terminals across frames so that partial results would not have to be recomputed made the use of various generalization hierarchies implicit in his proposal. In fact Minsky (1986) discusses hierarchies and their acquisition in detail. Historically, it is safe to say that a frame language that does not have facilities for some kind of concept hierarchy is not a frame language. Concept hierarchies will be examined from a number of perspectives. It is via concept hierarchies that the transition from frame theory to frame languages is made.

The Initial Categories

It has been suggested that categories in humans exist at three levels of generality: basic, subordinate, and superordinate (Rosch, 1975). In the domain of furniture, the concept of a chair would be an example of a basic category, whereas the concept of furniture would be an example of a superordinate category. The concept of a lawn chair would be an example of a subordinate category. Knowledge representation language (KRL) was influenced by this taxonomy and included the three kinds of categories as distinct data types (Bobrow and Winograd, 1977). In humans, the basic categories are perceptually based and tend to be learned earlier than the other categories; the other categories emerge from the basic categories. Superordinate categories initially emerge from the basic categories by generalization operations; similarly, the subordinate categories emerge from the basic categories by discrimination or specialization operations. Minsky (1986) uses the term uniframing for generalization and the term accumulating for discimination or specialization. Once formed, the categories have an internal structure that maximizes the similarity among members within a category and the differences between members across categories. This structure forms a kind of feature space. Instances of a category can be located near the center of this space or near the periphery. In this way, a category has more structure than a set. Membership in a category can be a matter of degree, whereas membership in a set is all or none.

The notion of prototype can be defined in terms of feature space structure. According to prototype theory, instances of a category that are near the center of the feature space can be viewed as prototypes of that category. For example, a robin is considered a good example of a bird whereas a penguin is not. Therefore, a robin should occur near the center of the feature space for the bird category and a robin should be a good prototype for the category. Furthermore, a robin is more strongly a member of the bird category than a penguin is. If a category were simply a set, this would not happen. Some of these ideas have found their way into some frame languages, for example, NETL (Fahlman, 1979) and KRL (Bobrow and Winograd, 1977) via the construct of a typical member. In such languages, for the bird frame, there would be an associated description of the typical member. In addition, there may be a description of a few typical instances, such as a robin or an eagle. Minsky intended that default values in frames be used to represent what is typical.

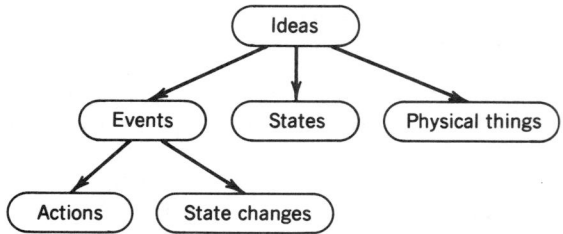

Figure 2. An example of the top of a concept hierarchy.

An Epistemological Viewpoint

Figure 2 shows the top of a concept hierarchy constructed on purely epistemic grounds in which an underlying premise is that all of the concepts that the system uses can be placed in the hierarchy. At the top of the hierarchy, there is the category "all conceivable ideas." The first level divides the universe of ideas into objects, states, and events. Events are divided into actions and state changes. This taxonomy is by no means accepted fact; it is only a first approximation that gets the general picture right. In terms of acquisition, new concepts are created by specializing, or discriminating, already existing concepts in the system. This differs from Rosch's framework where the earliest concepts in the system are the basic concepts and later concepts are the superordinate and subordinate concepts. In practice, frame languages adhere to the epistemological viewpoint, that is, they require the programmer to hand code a concept hierarchy starting from the top.

Figure 3 shows a concept hierarchy at the intermediate level. This hierarchy models the trans-frames used earlier to represent story A. In this figure, a transfer is a kind of action. Abstract transfer (atrans), physical transfer (ptrans), and mental transfer (mtrans) are each a distinct kind of transfer. There were four verbs used in the story: *ask* (request), *go, leave,* and *pay*. These verbs correspond to specialized forms of abstract transfer, physical transfer, or mental transfer. This is shown in Figure 3 where *pay* is one particular kind of abstract transfer; *go* and *leave* are closely related, but distinct, forms of physical transfer; and *request* is a particular kind of mental transfer.

Although the concept hierarchy appears as a tree, this is not necessarily the case. It could be a lattice. Sometimes these lattices are called tangled hierarchies. It is also the case that, that when comprehending text or interacting with the world, it may be necessary to introduce new entries into the concept hierarchy dynamically. Consider story D:

Story D

1. John was on an archaeological dig.
2. He unearthed a cup.
3a. He wondered if it could still hold fluids (instance cup-1 drinking tool).
3b. He wondered how valuable it was (instance cup-1 artifact).

Sentence one activates the archaeological dig frame and sentence two activates the drinking tool frame. Either sentence three-a or three-b could be the last sentence of this story. In the case of three-b the reader is led to view the cup as an archaeological artifact, which may not have been the conclusion before reading the story. For instance, the cup might be assigned to the found artifact slot of the archaeological dig frame. If the reader, or John, ever abstracts a category for cups found on digs, the new category will have two superordinates.

Slots and Property Inheritance

Users of frame languages model concepts with frames. Features of concepts correspond to slots in frames. With this structure, default reasoning can be implemented by property inheritance mechanisms. In frame systems, slots have default values and slots can propogate down the hierarchy. This propogation is called inheritance. For instance, in a frame database there might be a frame representing the concept of action. The action frame would be a specialization of the concept of event, which would be represented by an event frame. The action frame would have a slot for the actor of an action. Then if the concept of walking is included, indicating that it is a specialization of the action frame, then the walking frame will inherit the actor slot of the action frame. The walking frame will also inherit any slots that the event frame happens to have (Table 4). In Table 4 upper case identifiers indicate either frame names or slot names. Slots can only take values of a certain type and defaults may be specified. The action frame states that an action is an event. This frame has one slot called ACTOR. The actor slot can only be filled by a person. This is signaled by the expression *a PERSON*. A trans-frame (TRANS) is also defined in Table 4. A trans-frame is an action and has the slots OBJECT, ORIGIN, and DESTINATION. Each of these slots have a type specifier of ANYTHING. This places no constraint on the slot's value because a thing can be anything. The actor slot is not explicitly defined for a trans-frame. This is because the trans-frame inherits the actor slot from the action frame. Another frame defined in Table 4 is physical transfer (PTRANS). In this frame, the slots for OBJECT, ORIGIN, and DESTINATION are redefined to accept more specific values. These more local specifications take precedence over those in TRANS. In general, the most

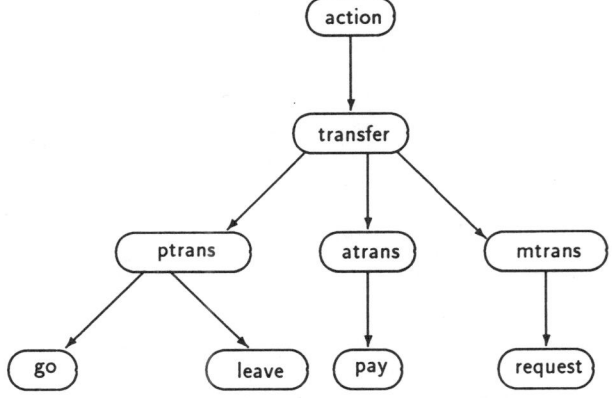

Figure 3. A hierarchy at the intermediate level.

Table 4. A Few Simple Frame Definitions

Frame	Is a	Slots
ACTION	EVENT	ACTOR (a PERSON)
TRANS	ACTION	OBJECT (a ANYTHING)
		ORIGIN (a ANYTHING)
		DESTINATION (a ANYTHING)
PTRANS	TRANS	OBJECT (a PHYSICAL THING)
		ORIGIN (a PLACE)
		DESTINATION (a PLACE)
GO	PTRANS	OBJECT (ACTOR)
		ORIGIN (house of ACTOR)

Table 5. Some Linguistic Cases

Proposed Case	Example of Use
Agent	JOHN broke a window.
Instrument	John broke a window with A HAMMER.
Source	John went FROM NEW YORK to San Francisco.
Destination	John went HOME.
Raw material	John made a bird OUT OF PLASTIC.

locally defined slot is the one that is used. Finally, there is a frame for the word *go*. This frame is a PTRANS. It does not define any new slots. However, it does specify default values. In particular, it says that the value of the OBJECT is the same as the value of the ACTOR slot. It also says that the value of the ORIGIN slot is the house of the actor.

Frame languages usually have facilities for various kinds of procedural attachment. For instance, there are procedures associated with a slot that become activated when the slot changes value (these are called if-added demons) or if the value of a slot must be determined (these are called if-needed demons).

The semantics of a concept hierarchy has been expressed as that of making a virtual copy of a description that is located higher in the hierarchy available to concepts lower in the hierarchy (Fahlman, 1979). If it is learned that Clyde is an elephant, it is desirable to have an elephant description immediately available. Assuming that stored with the elephant frame, there is an elephant description, this description should be available to help reason about Clyde; whether the description is really copied, or whether it is only a virtual copy implemented by property inheritance is immaterial.

In a tangled hierarchy, there would be multiple inheritance. That is, a frame with more than one superordinate would inherit slots from each of the superordinates. If both superordinates have some of the same slots, then there must be some kind of precedence scheme that determines which superordinate the slot is inherited from.

Cases, Slots, and Predicability

A number of researchers have suggested (Winston, 1984; Fillmore, 1977; Charniak, 1981a) that the cases of linguistic case grammar (Fillmore, 1968) and the slots of frame theory are one and the same. This has been termed the case-slot identity theory. Linguists have posited some small number of semantic cases, somewhere between 8 and 20, but have never been able to agree on the exact number. A partial list of cases is shown in Table 5 (Winston, 1984). Some of the cases, such as agent, are clearly indisputable as being general enough to classify as a linguistic case, but others such as source are arguable, and something like raw material is doubtful. According to the case-slot identity theory, the cases of linguistics correspond to the slots of frame languages. The more distinctive cases correspond to slots that go with concepts at the top of the concept hierarchy, whereas the more debatable cases, correspond to slots that go with fairly specialized concepts. This seems to explain why linguists have had such trouble deciding on exactly how many cases there really are.

A related line of reasoning comes from ontological hierarchies (Sommers, 1971; Keil, 1979). These are constructed in accordance with a notion of predicability. For instance, Sommers (1971) and Keil (1979) argue that both *man* and *flea* could have the property, or predicate, *is alive,* but only *man* could have the predicate *is honest.* In frame theory, it might be said that an animal frame has a binary-valued slot *is alive,* the main frame has a binary-valued slot *is honest,* and the flea frame would not have this slot or any way to inherit it. In short, there are largely unexplored connections between slots in frame theory and related constructs in linguistics (Fillmore, 1968; Lakeoff, 1987), philosophy (Sommers, 1971), and psychology (Keil, 1979).

ORGANIZATIONAL FEATURES IN FRAME LANGUAGES

As mentioned earlier, Minsky's frames paper is associated with two related traditions of research: higher level knowledge structures and frame languages. Most of this article has so far emphasized higher level knowledge structures and data structures and organizational features commonly found in frame languages are discussed.

Among the earliest frame languages were frame representation language (FRL) (Goldstein and Roberts, 1977; Roberts and Goldstein, 1977) and knowledge representation language (KRL) (Bobrow and Winograd, 1977). In FRL, as in subsequent frame languages, the primary data structure is a frame (or unit or something equivalent). Instances of this type are approximately record structures, in which the field names are called slots, the values are called terminals, and often the slots have default values. Furthermore, the frame definitions are embedded in a concept hierarchy, in which various kinds of inheritance are allowed, such as the inheritance of slots. In short, frames in a frame language will generally take the form of something like record structures with typed fields containing default values, and the record structures are embedded in a concept hierarchy, as described earlier.

One difficulty that has troubled many knowledge representation languages, including the early frame languages, was an explicit semantics was lacking. This made it difficult to compare the expressive abilities of different frame languages.

There are two ways to approach this comparison problem. One way is to specify a procedure to translate the features of a frame language into a standardized computer language such as PROLOG or the common LISP object system. This gives the language an operational semantics. Another way is to specify a method to translate the features of a frame language into a logic such as predicate calculus or a default logic. This gives the language a formal semantics. The first method, from an implementational standpoint is productive. Once the translation procedure is specified, then a method for implementing the frame language has also been specified. However, from a theoretical standpoint, this kind of operational semantics is unsatisfying. Issues of representation should be treated at a more abstract level. It should not be necessary to know a particular computer language to understand what a frame language is capable of expressing. Unfortunately, translating frame languages into logic is not a panacea either. The main reason for this is that there is really only one standard logic. This is predicate calculus. Unfortunately, predicate calculus cannot represent the default features of frame languages. This is because default reasoning is nonmonotonic and predicate calculus is monotonic.

Monotonicity means the following. In logic a database is viewed as a set of axioms. If there is a set of axioms Γ and a theorem τ can be proven from Γ, then if more axioms (more facts) are added to Γ to produce a larger database Γ' then it is still possible to prove theorem τ from the larger set of axioms Γ'. A logic that obeys this property is called monotonic because the number of theorems that are provable never decreases as the size of the database (axioms) grows.

Because frame languages allow defaults, they are nonmonotonic. To see this, recall from story A that it was concluded that John came to the restaurant from his house. That John came from his house was a default assumption. If the second sentence of the story stated that John had a hard day at work, then this new information would probably cause the retraction of the assumption that John came from his house. That is, the learning of new information caused the retraction of old information. This is nonmonotonicity. Because defaults are nonmonotonic and predicate calculus is monotonic, predicate calculus cannot represent defaults and, therefore, cannot fully represent frame languages. Unfortunately, nonmonotonic logics are in their infancy and are not yet standardized. Therefore, there is still difficulty in achieving the goal of formally comparing the expressive ability of various frame languages.

Slots in Frames and Functions in Predicate Calculus

Despite the discussion above, some features of frame languages can be translated into predicate calculus (Charniak, 1981b; Charniak and McDermott, 1985; Reimer and Hahn, 1983; Rich, 1982). If an instance of a frame corresponds to an object in some domain, then the frame corresponds to a predicate and its slots correspond to term-creating functions; both the predicate and functions take the instance as argument. Consider a frame for family as shown below. It contains three slots for mother, father, and child.

```
Frame   FAMILY
Is a    SOCIAL STRUCTURE
Slots   (MOTHER (a PERSON))
        (FATHER (a PERSON))
        (CHILD (a PERSON))
```

If the identifier $FAMILY-21$, is taken to denote a particular instance of the family frame, then this can be asserted by using the expression

$$Family(FAMILY-21)$$

In terms of predicate calculus, the symbol $Family$, corresponding to the frame that is named $FAMILY$ is a one-place predicate symbol. The symbol $FAMILY-21$, denoting the frame instance, is a constant symbol. The entire expression is a propositional sentence. It says that $FAMILY-21$ is a family. The family frame is a subconcept of the social structure frame. This can be represented in predicate calculus by the expression below.

$$\forall \times FAMILY(x) \Leftrightarrow Social\text{-}structure(x)$$

Slots in frames correspond to function symbols in predicate calculus. The slot names can be used to generate function terms to create representations of the mother, father, and child of the particular family denoted by $FAMILY-21$. In addition, equality assertions can be used to assert that various individuals fill the slots. This is shown below.

$$Mother(FAMILY-21) = CAROL$$
$$Father(FAMILY-21) = HENRY$$
$$Child(FAMILY-21) = JOHNNY$$

Each of these expressions is a propositional sentence. $FAMILY-21$ is still a constant symbol. However, the symbols $Mother$, $Father$, and $Child$, corresponding to slot names, are function symbols in predicate calculus. The expression $Mother(FAMILY-21)$ is a function term in predicate calculus.

Each of the slots have the type specifier $a\ person$. The follower predicate calculus expressions attempt to represent that the slot values for the family frame each must be a person.

$$\forall \times Family(x) \Leftrightarrow Person(Mother(x))$$
$$\forall \times Family(x) \Leftrightarrow Person(Father(x))$$
$$\forall \times Family(x) \Leftrightarrow Person(Child(x))$$

The first of these expressions says that if something is a family, then the mother of the family is a person. The other two expressions say analogous things. Although this is a simple example, more must be done to fully translate the family frame into logic. For instance, in place of the equality statement above, a frame language is likely to use the assignment operator, thus treating $CAROL$ as the value of the function term *Mother(FAMILY–21)*. Also, the semantic content of spot-specific heuristics must be translated into inference rules with special control information. For instance, if a slot has an associated if-added demon then the demon must be translated into a forward-chaining inference rule; if a slot has an associated if-needed demon, then it must be translated into a backward-chaining inference rule. This requires translation into a logic programming language, rather than into pure logic.

Further complications stem from the fact that frames are usually embedded in a concept hierarchy so that slots are inherited. Slots may also have multiple values and so cannot be straightforwardly treated as functions. Finally, slots may have default values, which require extensions of ordinary monotonic logic.

Formalizing Property Inheritance

Considerable work has been done on formalizing property inheritance in frame languages. Some of the earliest work was done by Etherington and Reiter (1983). Using default logic, they formalized property inheritance for NETL (Fahlman, 1979).

To see how default logic can be applied to formalizing property inheritance, consider a two-level concept hierarchy consisting of birds and penguins. Suppose that typically birds can fly and that penguins do not fly. The first statement that typically birds can fly is encoded as a default statement. The default is (intuitively) written as

$$\forall \times Bird(x) \land C(Flies(x)) \Leftrightarrow Flies(x)$$

This expression says that if something is a bird and it can be consistently assumed that it can fly (indicated by the C operator), then it can be concluded that it can fly. This expression is not first-order predicate calculus because it uses the C operator (mnemonic for consistently). The second statement, that penguins do not fly, is encoded as an ordinary first-order statement. This is written as

$$\forall \times Penguin(x) \Leftrightarrow \neg Flies(x)$$

If it is learned that Tweety is a bird, this logic allows us to infer that Tweety can fly. If it is later learned that Tweety is a penguin, the logic will no longer allow us to infer that Tweety can fly.

Difficulties arise when defaults conflict. For instance, what if a new species of flying penguin is discovered? Then the fact that penguins cannot fly can no longer be represented by a universally quantified first-order statement. It must be changed to a default statement. When it is changed to a default statement, then there will be two default statements that offer conflicting conclusions. Which has priority? In terms of computer implementation, this is a fairly easy question to answer. The default that occupies the more specific position in the hierarchy has priority. For reasons beyond the scope of this article, however, this heuristic is difficult to formalize. Etherington and Reiter (1983) handled the problem by treating exceptions explicitly. Unfortunately, it is impossible to anticipate all exceptions in advance. Touretzky

(1986) developed a heuristic called the inferential distance ordering, which allowed conflicts to be resolved without knowing exceptions in advance.

Determining Concept Subsumption

Concept subsumption refers to the location of a concept in a concept hierarchy, with respect to its subconcepts and superconcepts. If concepts were sets, then subsumption would correspond to set containment. However, because concepts, whatever they are, have more structure than sets, the term subsumption is used. In graphical representations of concept hierarchies, the closest subsumption relationships are represented by the links connecting the concepts. Often it is desirable to insert a new concept description into the concept hierarchy so that the subsumption relationships between the new concept and the already existing concepts in the hierarchy are correct (Schmolze and Lipkis, 1983). To give an example, suppose that there is a concept hierarchy containing the concept of killing and the concept of strangling. If it is wished to insert the concept of murdering into the hierarchy, then it should be placed between the concepts of killing and strangling. This is because killing subsumes murdering, but murdering subsumes strangling.

Frame languages often have elaborate sets of primitives for defining concepts. This in itself is a desirable feature. In principle, a language that is capable of describing any concept that the human mind is capable of representing is wanted. Unfortunately, there is a trade-off between the expressiveness of a language and the complexity of computing inferences in that language. This is well known in logic and it has recently been shown to occur in frame languages. It has been shown that a seemingly unimportant choice in the expressiveness of primitives in a frame language can make dramatic differences in the time complexity of a subsumption algorithm (Brachman and Levesque, 1984; Levesque and Brachman, 1985). In particular, it appears that when a language reaches a certain threshold of expressiveness, determining subsumption relations for expressions in that language becomes co-NP-complete. To give an example, the family frame that was described earlier encodes the concept of "a social structure with a mother, who is a person; a father, who is a person; and a child, who is a person." Type specifiers were used to indicate that each of the slot values were people. These type specifiers, depending on the exact expressive power of the language, can lead to subsumption complexity. Consequently, languages that are concerned with efficiency, such as object-oriented languages, do not include these representational features in their set of primitives.

Other Frame Languages

Frame systems are sometimes adapted to creating rich descriptions or definitions (eg, KL-ONE), rather than for encoding assertions. Given this, a hybrid language called KRYPTON has been developed that consists of a frame component to provide terms and predicates and a predicate calculus component to make assertions involving the terms and predicates (Brachman and Levesque, 1982; Brachman and co-workers, 1983). A similar partitioning is used by the frame-based AI language FRAIL (Charniak, 1983). In this language, a frame can have a set of predicate calculus facts associated with it and the facts make reference to the slots in the frame. When the frame becomes active, the facts become available to the inference engine. Similar ideas have been explored (Rich, 1982; Allen and Wright, 1983).

There are framelike languages that are in part inspired by the principles of uniformity, coherence, and expressiveness. The principle of uniformity embodies the maxim that all concepts are made of the same stuff, and hence a knowledge representation language should use exactly one datum type to represent concepts. The principle of coherence is based on the intuition that related concepts in the mind are well knit and not fragmented. The principle of expressiveness embodies the intuition that any concept conceivable by the human mind should also be representable in a knowledge representation language. Although these principles are well known and commonly receive lip service, it appears that the present-day limiting factors in the construction of intelligent systems involves putting massive quantities of information in the system (surface representation), but the quality of representation of the represented information (deep representation) is a minor factor. In other words, highly expressive, coherent, and uniform knowledge representation languages are not yet cost effective, although, theoretically they are more justified.

One of the earliest frame languages to take these principles seriously was OWL (Szolovits and co-workers, 1977; Martin, 1979a, 1979b, 1981). More recently, the languages KODIAK (Wilensky, 1984) and UniFrame (Maida, 1984) have appeared, which have been concerned with the epistemological issues of uniformity. These languages take as their starting point that there should be exactly one datum type in a frame-based memory, a concept, and not two (frames and slots), and that the representation of concepts in memory should be well knit.

Object-Oriented Languages

Parallel to the development of frame languages has been the development of object-oriented programming languages, such as SMALLTALK (Goldberg and Robson, 1983), LISP Machine Flavors (Weinreb and Moon, 1981), and the common LISP object system (CLOS) (Keene, 1989; Steele, 1990). It is often asked how frame languages differ from object-oriented programming languages. They are quite similar, differing primarily in emphasis. An object-oriented programming language is viewed as a practical programming language able to compete with standard programming languages, whereas a frame language tends to be either a research tool or a language to be used in the construction of AI databases.

An object-oriented programming languages uses hierarchies of classes of objects that have associated slots for state variables and methods (procedures for manipulating the state variables and objects). The methods and slots are inherited down the class hierarchy. The user can declare some object to be an instance of some class. The effect is

```
(defclass action (event)

  ((actor :initarg actor-of-action)))


(defun make-action (&key (actor '(make-person)))

  (make-instance 'action

    :actor-of-action actor))
```
Figure 4. The action frame represented in CLOS.

that the object acquires its own set of state variables and has access to the methods associated with its class.

To facilitate comparisons between frame languages and object-oriented languages, Figure 4 shows the result of translating the action frame in Table 4 into CLOS. In CLOS, the command defclass defines a class. A CLOS class is similar to a frame. The command defun defines a LISP function. A function is the analogue of a procedure or subroutine in a conventional programming language. The action frame cannot be directly translated into a CLOS class. This is because the action frame uses primitives that are not directly available in CLOS. However, part of the frame can be translated into a CLOS class. Much of the remaining untranslated information can be implemented by using a LISP function to augment the class definition.

The defclass expression in Figure 4 defines the class of action. This expression states that an action is an event and that an action has one actor slot. The defclass expression does not say that the value of the actor slot must be a person. This is done instead by the *make-action* function, where the default value of an action is an instance of the person class. Such instances are created by the function called (*make person*).

If the expression (*make-action*) is evaluated, it will create and return an instance of an action. The actor slot of the instance will be initialized to and anonymous instance of the person class. Alternatively, if the expression (*make-action :actor 'Henry*) is evaluated, it will create an instance of the action class where the actor slot of the instance is initialized to *Henry*. The default to the action slot is encoded in the function definition, rather than in the class definition. This is because CLOS does not allow the user to, in a direct fashion, supply the default. By encoding the defaults in the function definition, they will be invoked with the class instance is created. However, they will not be taken into account when determining class subsumption relationships. Therefore, Figure 4 is not a complete translation of the action frame shown in Table 4.

As was said earlier, slot restrictions can be the source of computational overhead in frame systems. CLOS is intended to be a practical programming language and, therefore, must take the efficiency–expressiveness trade-off seriously. Therefore, it is not surprising that CLOS does not allow slot restrictions.

SUMMARY

Frame theory is a paradigm that inspired an era of research on intelligent systems and a host of frame languages. The research issues have evolved, with little of the specific of Minsky's original suggestions surviving, in part because Minsky's suggestions where for the most part thought-provoking lines of argument rather than specific proposals. What used to be called frame theory is probably most actively developed by Schank's associates, under the name of memory organization. Frame languages have evolved into hybrid systems, consisting of a predicate calculus component and a frame component. The frame component is used to define predicates and terms for use by the predicate calculus component. What is persistently useful in frame languages will probably find its way into conventional programming languages via the route of object-oriented programming languages.

BIBLIOGRAPHY

R. P. Abelson, "The Structure of Belief Systems," in R. C. Schank and K. M. Colby, eds., *Computer Models of Thought and Language,* W. H. Freeman, San Francisco, 1973, pp. 287–340.

B. P. Allen and J. M. Wright, "Integrating Logic Programs and Schemata," *Proceedings of the Eighth IJCAI,* Karlsruhe, FRG, Morgan-Kaufmann, San Mateo, Calif., 1983, pp. 340–342.

A. Barr and E. Feigenbaum, *Handbook of Artificial Intelligence,* Vol. I, Kaufman, Los Altos, Calif., 1981.

F. C. Bartlett, *Remembering: A Study in Experimental and Social Psychology,* rev. ed., Cambridge University Press, Cambridge, UK, 1961.

I. Biederman, "On the Semantics of a Glance at a Scene," in M. Kubovy and J. R. Pomerantz, eds., *Perceptual Organization,* Erlbaum, Hillsdale, New Jersey, 1981.

D. Bobrow, and T. Winograd, "An Overview of KRL, a Knowledge Representation Language," *Cogn. Sci.* 1(1), 3–46 (1977).

G. Bower, J. Black, and T. Turner, "Scripts in Text Comprehension and Memory," *Cognitive Psychology* 11, 177–220 (1979).

R. Brachman and H. Levesque, "Competence in Knowledge Representation," *Proceedings of the Second National Conference on Artificial Intelligence,* Pittsburgh, Pa., AAAI, Menlo Park, Calif., 1982.

R. Brachman and H. Levesque, "The Tractability of Subsumption in Frame-based Description Languages," *Proceedings of the Fourth National Conference on Artificial Intelligence,* Austin, Tex., AAAI, Menlo Park, Calif., 1984.

R. Brachman and H. Levesque, *Readings in Knowledge Representation,* Kaufman, Los Altos, Calif., 1985.

R. Brachman, R. Fikes, and H. Levesque, "KRYPTON: Integrating Terminology and Assertion," *Proceedings of the Third National Conference on Artificial Intelligence,* Washington, D.C., AAAI, Menlo Park, Calif., 1983.

E. Charniak, *Towards a Model of Children's Story Comprehension,* Ph.D. dissertation, MIT, Cambridge, Mass., 1972.

E. Charniak, "With Spoon in Hand, This Must Be the Eating Frame," in D. Waltz, ed., *Theoretical Issues in Natural Language Processing,* Vol. 2, distributed by the Association for Computational Linguistics, 1978, pp. 187–193.

E. Charniak, "The Case-Slot Identity Theory," *Cogn. Sci.* 5, 285–292 (1981a).

E. Charniak, "A Common Representation for Problem Solving and Language Comprehension Information," *Artif. Intell.* 16, 225–255 (1981b).

E. Charniak, *The Frail/Nasl Reference Manual,* Technical Report CS-83-06, Department of Computer Science, Brown University, Providence, Rhode Island, 1983.

E. Charniak, "Cognitive Science is Methodologically Fine," in P. Polson and W. Kintsch, eds., *Methods and Tactics in Cognitive Science,* Erlbaum, Hillsdale, N.J., 1984, pp. 263–276.

E. Charniak and D. McDermott, *Introduction to Artificial Intelligence,* Addison-Wesley, Reading, Mass., 1985.

A. Collins, J. Brown, and K. Larkin, "Inference in Text Understanding," in R. Spiro, B. Bruce, and W. Brewer, eds., *Theoretical Issues in Reading Comprehension,* Erlbaum, Hillsdale, N.J., 1980.

A. Collins, and M. Quillian, "Retrieval Time from Semantic Memory," *J. Verbal Learning Verbal Behav.* 8, 240–247 (1969).

R. Cullingford, *Script Application: Computer Understanding of Newspaper Stories,* Report 116, Yale University Department of Computer Science, Yale University, New Haven, Conn., 1978.

G. DeJong, "A New Approach to Natural Language Processing," *Cogn. Sci.* 3(3), 251–273 (1979).

J. Doyle, "A Truth Maintenance System," *Artif. Intell.* 12, 231–272 (1979).

D. Etherington and R. Reiter, "On Inheritance Hierarchies With Exceptions," *Proceedings of the Third National Conference on Artificial Intelligence,* Washington, D.C., AAAI, Menlo Park, Calif., 1983, pp. 104–108.

S. Fahlman, *A Hypothesis-Driven Frame System for Recognition Problems,* Working Paper 57, MIT AI Lab, Cambridge, Mass., 1974.

S. Fahlman, *NETL: A System for Representing and Using Real-World Knowledge,* MIT Press, Cambridge, Mass., 1979.

C. Fillmore, "The Case for Case," in E. Bach and R. Harms, eds., *Universals in Linguistic Theory,* Holt, Rinehart, and Winston, New York, 1968.

C. Fillmore, "An Alternative to Checklist Theories of Meaning," in Coger, ed., *Proceedings of the First Annual Meeting of the Berkeley Linguistics Society,* Institute of Human Learning, Berkeley, Calif., 1975.

C. Fillmore, "The Case for Case Reopened," in P. Cole and M. Sadock, eds., *Syntax and Semantics 8: Grammatical Relations,* Academic Press, Inc., Orlando, Fla., 1977, pp. 159–181.

E. Goffman, *Frame Analysis,* Harper & Row, New York, 1974.

A. Goldberg and D. Robson, *Smalltalk-80: The Language and its Implementation,* Addison-Wesley Publishing Co., Inc., Reading, Mass., 1983.

I. Goldstein and B. Roberts, "NUDGE: A Knowledge-based Scheduling Program," *Proceedings of the Fifth IJCAI,* Cambridge, Mass., Morgan-Kaufmann, San Mateo, Calif., 1977, pp. 257–263.

R. Granger, "FOUL-UP: A Program That Figures Out Meanings of Words From Context," in *Proceedings of the Fifth IJCAI,* Morgan-Kaufmann, San Mateo, Calif., 1977, pp. 172–178.

J. Haugeland, ed., *Mind Design,* MIT Press, Cambridge, Mass., 1981.

P. Hayes, "In Defense of Logic," in *Proceedings of the Fifth IJCAI,* Morgan-Kaufmann, San Mateo, Calif., 1977, pp. 559–565.

S. Keene, *Object-Oriented Programming in Common Lisp: A Programmer's Guide to CLOS,* Addison-Wesley, Reading, Mass., 1989.

F. Keil, *Semantic and Conceptual Development: An Ontological Perspective,* Harvard, Cambridge, Mass., 1979.

J. Kolodner, "Maintaining Organization in a Dynamic Long-Term Memory," *Cogn. Sci.* **7**(4), 243–280 (1983a).

J. Kolodner, "Reconstructive Memory: A Computer Model," *Cogn. Sci.* **7**, 281–328 (1983b).

J. Kolodner, *Conceptual Memory: A Computational Model,* Erlbaum, Hillsdale, N.J., 1984.

B. Kuipers, "A Frame for Frames," in D. Bobrow and A. Collins, eds., *Representation and Understanding,* Academic Press, Inc., Orlando, Fla., 1975, pp. 151–184.

G. Lakoff, *Women, Fire, and Dangerous Things: What Concepts Reveal about the Mind,* University of Chicago Press, Chicago, 1987.

H. Levesque and R. Brachman, "A Fundamental Tradeoff in Knowledge Representation and Reasoning," in Brachman and Levesque, 1985, pp. 41–70.

G. Luger and W. Stubblefield, *Artificial Intelligence and the Design of Expert Systems,* Benjamin/Cummings, Redwood City, Calif., 1989.

A. Maida, "Processing Entailments and Accessing Facts in a Uniform Frame System," in *Proceedings of the Fourth National Conference on Artificial Inteligence,* AAAI, Menlo Park, Calif., 1984, pp. 233–236.

W. Martin, "Descriptions and the Specialization of Concepts," in P. Winston, eds., *Artificial Intelligence: An MIT Perspective,* MIT Press, Cambridge, Mass., 1979a.

W. Martin, *Roles, Co-Descriptors, and the Formal Representation of Quantified English Expressions,* TM-**139**, MIT Laboratory for Computer Science, Cambridge, Mass., 1979b.

W. Martin, "Roles, Co-Descriptors, and the Formal Representation of Quantified English Expressions (abridged)," *Am. J. Comp. Ling.* **7**, 137–147 (1981).

M. Minsky, *A Framework for Representing Knowledge,* Artificial Intelligence Memo 306, MIT AI Lab, Cambridge, Mass., 1974.

M. Minsky, *The Society of Mind,* Simon & Schuster, New York, 1986.

M. Minsky and S. Papert, *Progress Report on Artificial Intelligence,* MIT AI Lab Memo 252, Cambridge, Mass., 1972.

J. Moore and A. Newell, "How Can Merlin Understand?", in R. L. Gregg, ed., *Knowledge and Cognition,* Erlbaum, Hillsdale, N.J., 1973, pp. 201–252.

A. Newell, "The Knowledge Level," *Artif. Intell.* **18**, 87–127 (1982).

A. Newell, and H. Simon, *Human Problem Solving,* Prentice-Hall, Englewood Cliffs, N.J., 1972.

N. J. Nilsson, *Principles of Artificial Intelligence,* Tioga, Palo Alto, Calif., 1980.

D. Norman, "Memory, Knowledge, and the Answering of Questions," in R. L. Solso, ed., *Contemporary Issues in Cognitive Psychology: The Loyola Symposium,* W. H. Freeman, San Francisco, 1973.

P. Norvig, "Frame Activated Inferences in a Story Understanding Program," in *Proceedings of the Eighth IJCAI,* Karlsruhe, FRG, Morgan-Kaufmann, San Mateo, Calif., 1983, pp. 624–626.

P. O'Rorke, "Reasons for Beliefs in Understanding: Applications of Non-monotonic Dependencies to Story Processing," in *Proceedings of the Third National Conference on Artificial Intelligence,* AAAI, Menlo Park, Calif., 1983, pp. 306–309.

M. R. Quillian, "Semantic Memory," in M. Minsky, ed., *Semantic Information Processing,* MIT Press, Cambridge, Mass., 1968.

U. Reimer and U. Hahn, "A Formal Approach to the Semantics of a Frame Data Model," in *Proceedings of the Eighth IJCAI,* Karlsruhe, FRG, Morgan-Kaufmann, San Mateo, Calif., 1983, pp. 337–339.

C. Rich, "Knowledge Representation Languages and Predicate Calculus: How To Have Your Cake and Eat it Too," in *Proceedings of the Second National Conference on Artificial Intelligence,* Pittsburgh, Pa., AAAI, Menlo Park, Calif., 1982, pp. 193–196.

R. Roberts and I. Goldstein, *The FRL Manual,* MIT-AI-LAB memo 409, Cambridge, Mass., 1977.

E. Rosch, "Cognitive Representations of Semantic Categories," *J. Exper. Psychol.* **104**, 192–233 (1975).

R. Schank, "Identification of Conceptualizations Underlying Natural Language," in R. C. Schank and K. M. Colby, eds., *Computer Models of Thought and Language,* W. H. Freeman, San Francisco, 1973.

R. Schank, *Conceptual Information Processing,* North-Holland, Amsterdam, 1975a.

R. Schank, "Using Knowledge to Understand," in R. Schank and B. Nash-Webber, eds., *Theoretical Issues in Natural Language Processing,* Vol. 1, Association for Computational Linguistics, 1975b.

R. Schank, *Reminding and Memory Organization: An Introduction to MOPs,* Department of Computer Science, Research Report 170, Yale University, New Haven, Conn., 1979.

R. Schank and R. P. Abelson, *Scripts, Plans, Goals, and Understanding,* Erlbaum, Hillsdale, N.J., 1977.

R. Schank, "Failure-Driven Memory," *Cognitive and Brain Sci.* **4**, 41–60 (1981).

R. Schank, *Dynamic Memory: A Theory of Reminding and Learning in Computers and People,* Cambridge University Press, New York, 1982.

R. Schank and C. Reisbeck, *Inside Computer Understanding,* Erlbaum, Hillsdale, N.J., 1981.

J. Schmolze and T. Lipkis, "Classification in the KL-one Knowledge Representation System," in *Proceedings at the Eighth IJCAI,* Karlsruhe, FRG, Morgan-Kaufmann, San Mateo, Calif., 1983, pp. 330–332.

F. Sommers, "Structural Ontology," *Philosophia* **1**, 21–42 (1971).

J. Sowa, *Conceptual Structures: Information Processing in Mind and Machine,* Addison-Wesley, Reading, Mass., 1984.

G. Steele, *Common Lisp: The Language,* 2nd ed., Digital Press, Bedford, Mass., 1990.

P. Szolovits, L. Hawkinson, and W. Martin, *An Overview of OWL, a Language for Knowledge Representation,* MIT/LCS/TM-86, MIT Laboratory for Computer Science, Cambridge, Mass., 1977.

D. Touretzky, *The Mathematics of Inheritance Systems,* Kaufman, Los Altos, Calif., 1986.

E. Walker, M. Herman, and T. Kanade, "A Framework for Representing and Reasoning about Three-Dimensional Objects for Vision," *AI Magazine* **9**(2), 47–58 (1988).

D. Weinreb and D. Moon, *The Lisp Machine Manual,* MIT Press, Cambridge, Mass., 1981.

T. Weymouth, J. Griffith, A. Hanson, and E. Reisman, "Rule-based Strategies for Image Interpretation," in *Proceedings of the Third National Conference on Artificial Intelligence,* Washington, D.C., AAAI, Menlo Park, Calif., 1983, pp. 429–432.

R. Wilensky, *Planning and Understanding: A Computational Approach to Human Reasoning,* Addison-Wesley Publishing Co., Inc., Reading, Mass., 1983.

R. Wilensky, "KODIAK: A Knowledge Representation Language," *Proceedings of the Sixth Annual Conference of the*

Cognitive Science Society, Boulder, Colo., June 1984, pp. 344–352.

P. Winston, *The Psychology of Computer Vision*, McGraw-Hill Inc., New York, 1975.

P. H. Winston, *Artificial Intelligence*, 2nd ed., Addison-Wesley, Reading, Mass., 1984.

ANTHONY S. MAIDA
Pennsylvania State University

FREDDY

One of the early landmarks in the experimental study of machine intelligence was FREDDY, the Edinburgh University computer-controlled robot, completed and demonstrated in 1973. Following R. L. Gregory's move to Edinburgh with H. C. Longuet-Higgins, work began in 1968 towards the broad goal of a cognitive machine able to explore and manipulate a simple task environment. Under the direction of Michie, who had recently formed the University's Experimental Programming Unit, a mixed team of psychologists, engineers, and computer scientists carried the project through FREDDY-1 (1970) which studied visual recognition *via* computer control of a TV-eye-view to its culmination in FREDDY-2 which combined vision and tactile and proprioceptive feedback with horizontal movement of the work-table together with directed prehension. The resultant integrated problem solver formed and updated abstract models of its workplace and contents, manipulating a simple vice to make assemblies such as a toy car and toy ship. It separated parts from a heap, recognizing them with an overhead camera, then put them together by feel.

FREDDY-2 could be instructed to perform a new task with different parts by spending an hour or two showing it the parts and a day programming the manipulations. A hierarchical description of parts, views, outlines, etc, was used by the robot's planning program to construct its "mental models." Team members H. G. Barrow, A. P. Ambler, and R. M. Burstall developed an advanced structure-matching algorithm for use in recognition. Innovative mechanical design was introduced by S. H. Salter of Gregory's Bionics Research Laboratory (eg, use of pantographic manipulator linkages, and the "move the table, not the robot" principle). J. A. M. Howe of Bionics managed the project and subsequently led the world's first academic department of Artificial Intelligence.

The project's chief points of significance were:

1. It represented a break from the older design tradition of robot engineering, replacing reliance on pre-programmed predictability with a new principle of perceptual feedback and trainability;
2. By expressing the principle in R. M. Burstall and R. J. Popplestone's AI programming language POP-2 (see POPLOG), a versatility and resourcefulness of robot behavior was attained which, nearly 20 years later, has yet to be matched.

DONALD MICHIE
The Turing Institute

FRL

A frame-oriented representation language developed around 1977 by Roberts and Goldstein at MIT. FRL stresses demons, stereotypes, and instantiation aids, in contrast to other frame-representation languages. The language designers used an earlier version, FRL-O, to implement NUDGE, a system used to understand incomplete and possibly inconsistent management-scheduling requests (see R. B. Roberts and I. Goldstein, *The FRL Primer*, Report AIM-408, AI Lab, MIT, Cambridge, Mass., 1977).

K. S. ARORA
SUNY at Buffalo

FRUMP

A script-driven newspaper skimming and summarizing program, fast reading and understanding memory program (FRUMP) was written by DeJong at the Yale AI Project. Once a script is decided, it skims the news story looking for the expected words to fill the holes in the script. (See G. DeJong, *Skimming Stories in Real Time*, Ph.D. dissertation, Yale University, New Haven, Conn., 1979; G. DeJong, "An Overview of the FRUMP System," in W. G. Lehnert and M. H. Ringle, eds., *Strategies for Natural Language Processing*, Lawrence Erlbaum, Hillsdale, N.J., 1982, pp. 149–176.)

A. HANYONG YUHAN
SUNY at Buffalo

FUZZY SETS AND FUZZY LOGIC: AN OVERVIEW

The last decade has witnessed a rapid growth in the literature of fuzzy sets and fuzzy logic as well as a proliferation of applications ranging from automatic train control and tunnel-digging machinery to washing machines. There were and still are skeptics who maintain that anything that can be done with fuzzy logic and fuzzy set theory can be done equally well with classic logic and probability theory. Such views are likely to become muted with the passage of time and a better understanding of the basic ideas underlying the theories of fuzzy sets and fuzzy logic.

It is important to note that the term fuzzy logic is used in two distinct senses. In its narrower sense, fuzzy logic is a branch of fuzzy set theory, which deals (as logical systems do) with the representation and inference from knowledge; however, in the case of fuzzy logic, knowledge is assumed to be imprecise or uncertain. In this sense, such branches of fuzzy set theory as fuzzy mathematical programming, pattern recognition, decision analysis, fuzzy arithmetic, fuzzy topology, etc are not parts of fuzzy logic. In recent years, however, it has become increasingly common to employ the term fuzzy logic in a much broader sense; that is, in a sense that is coexistive with fuzzy set theory. Such an interpretation of fuzzy logic makes it redundant to speak of fuzzy set theory and fuzzy logic. Unfortunately, it also generates some confusion, because it may not be clear from the context whether the term fuzzy logic is used in a narrow or broad sense. In what follows, it will be used in the latter sense.

Most of the applications of fuzzy logic fall into two categories. In the first category are the applications in which a fuzzy rule-based system is employed to replace a skilled human operator. Prominent examples of such systems are the subway system in the city of Sendai, Japan; autofocusing systems in cameras; washing machines; automobile transmissions; rice cookers; and vacuum cleaners. In the second category are the applications that aim at replacing a human expert. Such applications are exemplified by medical diagnosis systems, securities funds and portfolio selection systems, traffic control systems, and expert systems with deductive capabilities. For obvious reasons, applications in the second category require a much higher degree of sophistication and are much harder to analyze and implement. There are many problems that remain to be addressed, and there is an especially pressing need for a better understanding of how to deal with knowledge-based systems in which knowledge is both uncertain and imprecise.

Viewed in this perspective, the articles on fuzzy sets and fuzzy logic in this volume fill this need with impressive success. The authors are among the leading contributors in their fields, and the issues that they address are central to the application of fuzzy logic to expert systems, natural language processing, optimization, decision analysis, and related areas. Their authoritative expositions provide a detailed and up-to-date view of the basic ideas underlying fuzzy logic and the way in which it is applied in the conception and design of intelligent systems. Such systems, based on fuzzy logic, may bring artificial intelligence much closer to reality than what was achievable in the past through the use of traditional methods based on classic logic and probability theory.

The following articles concerning fuzzy sets and fuzzy logic are included in this volume:

FUZZY DATABASES

FUZZY LOGIC: APPLICATIONS TO NATURAL LANGUAGE

FUZZY MATHEMATICAL PROGRAMMING

FUZZY AND PROBABILISTIC UNCERTAINTIES

FUZZY SETS AND FUZZY LOGIC

LOTFI A. ZADEH
University of California,
Berkeley

FUZZY DATABASES

Since the start of widespread use of databases in the 1960s there have been continuing efforts to adapt them to new environments and new problems. A first step was to embed the database into a total management–decision-making environment which included reporting and analysis procedures in addition to data and querying facilities. Many recent efforts have been devoted to the expansion of the domain that can be represented and effectively queried. In this, there is a trade-off between the complexity of the query mechanisms and the data domains represented.

The spread of information systems can be viewed as ranging from the highly structured conventional database and the less structured document retrieval system to more complex structures such as object-oriented databases. Representations of vagueness, uncertainty, and incompleteness have been considered in these various contexts. For instance, there are statistical databases which differ primarily in the area of query mechanisms, not data representation. Another innovation, still actively under investigation, is the null value. Databases and retrieval systems, which utilize fuzzy set concepts, are the most recent innovations within the areas covered by the information systems spectrum.

Here, the generalization of databases and retrieval systems using fuzzy set mechanisms are discussed. In the data models section, representation issues within the data model are addressed, generally in the context of their degree of departure from the homogeneity principle of ordinary databases. In the retrieval techniques section, the impact on query and retrieval is discussed. For databases, most researchers have approached the problem bottom-up from the relational algebra viewpoint. Others have adopted the goal-driven perspective of knowledge bases. Only occasionally have nonrelational database models been considered for possible incorporation of imprecise data representations. In addition to the relational model, the DBTG network model is discussed here and an approach to the inclusion of fuzzy set concepts in object-oriented databases is described.

DATA MODELS

Over the last decade, the relational database model (Codd, 1970) has been adopted in form (if not always in spirit) by researchers intent upon extending the range of information that databases can represent. This pattern is evident in the area of fuzzy database models. The conceptual (or user level) view of a relational database is simple. It consists of one or more two-dimensional tables called relations. The relation columns are called attributes; thus each row (called a tuple) is a sequence of attribute values. In third normal forms (abbreviated as 3NF), a subset of the attribute values in a tuple is called the key and the remaining attribute values are directly dependent upon (ie, determined by) the key.

Figure 1 illustrates an ordinary relational database having two relations. The key for relation ASSEMBLY-PARTS consists of domains ASSEMBLY and PART-NO. The key for relation SUPPLIERS consists of the domain SUPPLIER.

The distinguishing characteristic of an ordinary relational database (or ordinary databases of other forms) is the uniformity or homogeneity of the represented data. For the domain of each attribute, there is a prescribed set of values from which domain values may be selected. Fur-

Relation: ASSEMBLY-PARTS

ASSEMBLY	PART-NO	WEIGHT	COST	SUPPLIER
Box	#25	33 g	$1.26	Apex
Gauge	#13	14 g	4.17	Apex
Box	#82	126 g	8.14	Tenex
Port	#25	80 g	0.97	Haas

Relation: SUPPLIERS

SUPPLIER	CITY	PHONE
Apex	New York	212-837-4600
Tenex	Chicago	317-422-5911
Haas	Miami	305-918-7255

Figure 1. An ordinary relational database.

ther, each element of the domain set is of the same structure, eg, integers, real numbers, or character strings. Relations for which the domain sets are not homogeneous are "unrepresentable" within the ordinary database context. As an example of this, consider a relation consisting of a borrower and a borrowed item (Maier, 1983). The borrowed item may range from a book (represented by author and title) to an automobile (represented by model, year of production, and serial number).

Ordinary databases, therefore, can be characterized as largely organized around homogeneous data sets. Information retrieval systems, on the other hand, are largely organized around nonhomogeneous data sets. An information system may then be characterized as to the extent or degree to which it exhibits the following characteristics:

1. Heterogeneous data representation.
2. Weakly typed data domains.
3. Semantic knowledge required during query interpretation.

A more generalized system that has all of these characteristics strongly is more likely to have a direct representation for a larger class of information at the cost of more complex processing. Various fuzzy database formulations emulate ordinary database characteristics, or to some degree, the generalized characteristics.

Null and Range Values

The earliest extensions of the relational data model that incorporated nonhomogeneous domain sets did not utilize fuzzy set theory. Rather, they were attempts to represent null values and intervals. An ANSI report (ANSI/X3/SPARC, 1975), for instance, notes more than a dozen types of null. At one end of the spectrum, null means completely unknown. For example, a null value in the current salary of an employee could mean the actual value is any one of the permissible values for the salary domain set.

Without resorting to fuzzy measures, a user can specify some information about a value that further restricts it For example, a subset or range of values of the domain set

may be described within which the actual attribute value must lie. The user or the system (using functional dependencies) may specify subsets or subranges within which the actual value must not lie. Yet another option is to label null values in a manner that requires distinct nulls in different portions of the database to have a particular actual value relationship (usually equality) if they have the same label. The semantics of the null value range from "unknown" (eg, the current salary of an employee) to "not applicable" (eg, subassembly number of a part that is not a subassembly) to "does not exist" (eg, middle name of a person). These last two meanings, however, are not related to uncertainty.

Such relatively minor extensions have had many ramifications within the theory (Lipski, 1979, 1981; Codd, 1979; Grant, 1977), some of which have yet to be fully resolved. For example, if two domain values have the same representation, they are considered to be the same value in ordinary databases. This is clearly not a correct assumption for the null value when it means "unknown". One must take into account the semantics of null when encountered during query interpretation. Another problem is the occurrence of null as a key value. What does it mean for the remaining domain values to be dependent on null?

Uniform Data Models for Representation of Imprecision

The simplest form for a fuzzy database is the attachment of a membership value (numeric or linguistic) to each tuple. This permits maintenance of homogeneous data domains and strongly typed data sets. However, the semantic content of the fuzzy membership domain is used during query processing. Figure 2 clearly illustrates two distinct semantics for the membership domain. In the first relation, ATHLETE, the membership value, denotes the degree to which the tuple belongs within the relation (Giardina, 1979). In the relation COURSE-CONTENT, the membership value denotes the strength of the dependency between the key COURSE, and the attribute CONTENT (Baldwin, 1983).

Relation: ATHLETE

NAME	SPORT	FUZ-MEM
Tim	Baseball	0.0
Mary	Soccer	1.0
Scott	Ping-Pong	0.5
Sam	Auto-Racing	0.3
Kim	Basketball	1.0

Relation: COURSE-CONTENT

COURSE	CONTENT	FUZ-MEM
Chemistry	Science	1.0
Statistics	Analysis	0.8
Databases	Design	0.6
Thermodynamics	Analysis	0.7

Figure 2. Relations with fuzzy membership domains.

Some formulations (Anvari and Rose, 1987; Buckles and Petry, 1982) maintain homogeneity of data domains and also import little semantics in the query interpretation process. That is, little knowledge beyond symbol manipulation is required to implement the mechanics of querying. The major characteristic of these two data models is the existence of fuzzy measures that, within each domain set, describe for each pair of values the degree of similarity or distinguishability. Figure 3 illustrates the major components of this model in the context of the original formulation.

In this model, domain values are elements of the power set of strongly typed domain base sets. The degree to which the domain base set values may be interchanged is described in a similarity relation for which there is an instance in the preceeding figure. Fuzziness is inherent in two respects:

1. The domain base sets may consist of linguistic values or fuzzy numbers (but not both simultaneously).
2. The domain values themselves are (ordinary) sets whose cardinality increases with the degree of fuzziness.

Although such set-valued domains are not strictly relational (in first normal form), the development of nonfirst normal form models and nested relational models support this approach (Schek and Scholl, 1986; Roth and co-workers, 1987).

A keystone concept of the fuzzy databases utilizing similarities is the replacement of equivalence or identity relationships among domain values with a measure of "nearness." The relationship employed for discrete, finite domain sets in the similarity model cannot be directly extended to continuous sets because there is not a transitivity property that effects partitioning of the domain set in a manner that guarantees uniqueness of relation representation. However, "nearness" relationships called α-similar and α-proximate have been defined for fuzzy numbers (Buckles and Petry, 1984). q_i and q_j are α-similar, written $q_i S_\alpha q_j$, if given $\beta \varepsilon [0,1]$, $x \varepsilon (q_i \cup q_j)_\alpha$, $y \varepsilon (q_i \cup$

$q_j)_\alpha$, and $z = \beta x + (1 - \beta)y$ then $z \varepsilon (q_i \cup q_j)_\alpha$, where $\cup$ means fuzzy set union. $(q_i \cup q_j)_\alpha$ is the α-level set obtained from the fuzzy set $(q_i \cup q_j)$. q_i and q_j are α-proximate (with respect to set P), written $q_i S^+_x q_j$, if there exists zero or more fuzzy numbers, $q_h, q_k, \ldots q_p \varepsilon P$, such that $q_i S_\alpha q_h S_\alpha q_k S_\alpha \ldots S_\alpha q_p S_\alpha q_j$. This latter relationship is used in place of similarity for continuous domains.

This fuzzy relational form is particularly adaptable to the representation of information entities as they are simultaneously viewed from several perspectives. This form also has the advantage of assuring that a given informational unit exists at only one place in the database and that each algebraic operation is well defined. These characteristics are important when considering database updating and querying.

The desirable properties of a relational model are maintained in the fuzzy database using similarity relations for scalar and fuzzy number domains. The partitioning property was based on the transitivity of the similarity relation, but it was found (Shenoi and Melton, 1989) that proximity relations (without the transitivity property) were sufficient. Proximity relations are usually easier to elicit for many applications; however, some desirable query properties are not maintained.

Heterogeneous Data Models for Representation of Uncertainty

To more directly represent uncertainty within the domain values themselves requires departure from homogeneity of representation. Possibility theory (Zadeh, 1978) is frequently the medium employed in this context. This approach allows a straightforward unification of the cases:

1. The true value is within a known interval or one of a discrete set of values (ie, all are equally possible).
2. The domain attribute itself is not applicable (ie, all values are impossible).
3. Some information is known of the value, but it nevertheless remains ambiguous (ie, there is a possibilistic function whose range is [0,1]).

Figure 4 illustrates these three cases. For example, Tom has no wife; it is equally possible that Mary is 25 or 26: $(\Pi_{age(MARY)}(25) = \Pi_{age(MARY)}(26) = 1.0)$; and Mary may be paid any amount between \$1500 and \$2000.

$$\Pi_{salary(MARY)}(X) = \begin{cases} 1.0 & 1500 \leq x \leq 2000 \\ 0.0 & x < 1500 \text{ or } x > 2000 \end{cases}$$

The last tuple in the figure illustrates how possibility distributions are sometimes depicted directly in the relation. In that tuple,

$$\Pi_{age(KAY)}(X) = \begin{cases} 1.0 & x = 50 \\ 0.8 & x = 51 \\ 0.0 & \text{otherwise} \end{cases}$$

If the emphasis is on querying (rather than representation of data), the information may be represented in ordi-

Relation: FUEL-COST

TYPE	COST
Coal	moderate
Fuel-oil	{high, extreme}
Nat-gas	{moderate, high}
Wood	{low, medium}

Similarities

Extreme	1.0	0.81	0.81	0.75	0.25
High	0.81	1.0	0.90	0.75	0.25
Moderate	0.81	0.90	1.0	0.75	0.25
Medium	0.75	0.75	0.75	1.0	0.25
Low	0.25	0.25	0.25	0.25	1.0

Figure 3. Relation with domain similarity conditions.

Relation: EMPLOYEE

NAME	AGE	SALARY	SPOUSE
Tom	36	2000	null
Mary	{25, 26}	1500–2000	Vic
Sam	young	1600	Marge
Kim	30	1900	null
Kay	1.0/50,0.8/51	2100	Mark

(a)

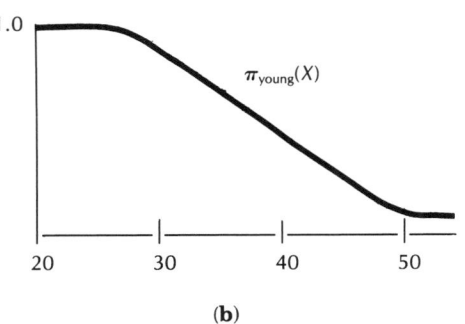

$\pi_{young}(X)$

(b)

Figure 4. (*a*) Relation with (*b*) possibilistic domain values.

nary homogeneous form while a separate binary relation contains the conversion of numeric values to fuzzy linguistic terms (Baldwin, 1983). Figure 5 illustrates this for the linguistic value "tall." The relation TALL has the additional special property of implicitly representing tuples through the process of interpolating between those present. Proportionality terms (eg, most, few, about half) are represented in relations similar to TALL.

A specialized representation for domain sets consisting of a single element has also been used (Zemankova, 1985). The attribute value represented is the (fuzzy) degree to which that element applies to tuple's key value. An example of this approach is shown in Figure 6.

An additional nonhomogeneous representation has been proposed (Montgomery and Ruspini, 1981; Ruspini,

Relation: PERSON

NAME	HEIGHT	WEIGHT
Jim	6–1	190
John	5–9	195
Kim	5–5	140
Irene	5–6	130
Pat	5–3	125
Tom	5–10	200

Relation: TALL

HEIGHT	FUZ-MEM
5–9	0
5–10	0.6
5–11	0.8
6–0	1
7–0	1

Figure 5. Relation with linguistic domain interpretation.

Relation: INTELLIGENCE

PERSON	SMART
Fred	0.98
Bill	0.99
Marsha	0.76
Mark	0.60

Figure 6. Relation with single-valued domain.

1982) in which domain sets are organized as a lattice and domain values are represented as one or more lattice points qualified by a possibility value. The power set of a base domain has been a frequently used lattice structure.

Many fuzzy database designs employ a tuple membership value, but it is not always clarified as to which of the two semantics given here is intended. Some designs (Umano, 1983; Prade and Testamale, 1984; Zemankova, 1985) utilize directly possibility distributions, but other designs (Ruspini, 1982; Baldwin, 1983) less directly employ possibilistic distributions as domain values because of the goal-directed nature of the query systems used.

Information Storage and Retrieval Models

The structure of an information system to be used for information storage and retrieval has a somewhat specialized homogeneous organization. The data is of a fixed type: documents (actually descriptions of documents) and indexing terms. Each document has a set of terms associated with it that is specified by some process, eg, author key words, indexing by specialists. Since an indexing term can, of course, refer to many documents, there exists a many-to-many relationship between terms and documents. However, since what is to be retrieved is the relevant document(s) associated to the terms, this relationship is somewhat simplified. Because of the subjective nature of the indexing process for linguistic terms, the inexactness or imprecision on the association of terms and documents can be formulated as a membership function indicating to what degree a document deals with, or is related to, the concept represented by the term (Kraft and Buell, 1983).

While the data model for information retrieval systems could be viewed conceptually as relational in form, it is not of particular advantage to do so. Assuming the retrieval objects are documents, the simplest schema is a file format (possibly an inverted file) where each record contains the title of the document, authors of the document, an abstract of the document, and keywords. Attached to each keyword is an optional membership value which indicates the degree to which the word describes the contents of the document. For flexibility, there may be a separate list of synonyms together with their pairwise degree of similarity.

RETRIEVAL TECHNIQUES

There are two aspects to retrieval languages which will be considered in this section: the syntactic form of a query and its evaluation relative to the specific data model.

Query language structures can range from the rather simple Boolean queries for information retrieval, through relational algebra or calculus forms, up to a high level query with natural language aspects.

Two factors, mainly orthogonal, are responsible for the range of query formulations. The first is the desire for higher level, more nonprocedural queries to provide for a simpler user interface. The second is the requirement to make a sufficient specification in the query, relative to the increasing heterogeneity of the data model, to permit a complete query evaluation. The approach to higher level queries or even natural language is relatively independent of the specification factor in that any higher query must be translated or interpreted into a lower level form. However, in as much as a given data model may be inexact and fuzzy, it can be thought of as being closer to the imprecise representation in a natural language query. Thus, if semantics are required in a data model, such as in the form of linguistic variables to represent fuzziness (Zadeh, 1975), the use of natural language queries may actually be facilitated to a greater degree than in an ordinary data model for which the meaning must be impressed to interpret the query.

In terms of the syntactic structure of retrieval languages, two approaches are generally observed. In the systems whose representations are less strictly relational and more heterogeneous, the query languages vary greatly. These are generally higher level languages and have some natural language aspects and nonprocedural specification of the desired result.

Retrieval of Incomplete Data

The most frequently cited nonfuzzy approaches are those by Codd (1979) and Lipski (1981). Codd proposes a three-value logic using T, F, and $\perp$ (null in the sense of unknown) in conjunction with the following predicates:

$$X \; \theta \; Y \equiv \perp \text{ if } x \text{ or } y \text{ is null and } \theta \text{ is } <, \leq, =, \neq, \geq, >$$

$$\perp \; \varepsilon \; S \equiv \perp \text{ for any set } S$$

$$\{\perp\} \subseteq S \equiv \perp \text{ for any set } S$$

The logic including the null value, $\perp$, is based on the truth tables in Figure 7.

Although Codd embeds these semantics into the relational algebra syntactic form, here Boolean queries will be sufficient to clarify the important issues. One counterintuitive result is that the query, PARTS[COST $\leq$ 10] $\lor$ PARTS[COST $>$ 10], does not yield the entire parts list if there is any part whose cost is null. The operator set is extended to include $\theta - \perp$ (where θ is $<$, $\leq$, and so on) and $\alpha - \perp$ (where α is SELECT, JOIN, and other relational operators). The meaning of these operators is, in brief, "assume actual values for nulls such that the truth value of the expression is T."

Lipski proposes a more general approach. He does not, for instance, assume that null means a value is completely unknown. Given that there may be labeled or restricted value nulls, let $\|Q\|$ denote all real world objects that a query Q could represent. Let T be a database object and

$\land$	F	$\perp$	T
F	F	F	F
$\perp$	F	$\perp$	$\perp$
T	F	$\perp$	T

$\lor$	F	$\perp$	T
F	F	$\perp$	T
$\perp$	$\perp$	$\perp$	T
T	T	T	T

NOT	
F	T
$\perp$	$\perp$
T	F

Figure 7. Three-valued logic truth tables.

$\|T\|$ be all real world objects it could represent. Lipski does not assume a relational database form (or any other), but, for illustration, one will be used here. Assume a relation EMPLOYEE with domains NAME and AGE. The database object

$$T = \langle \text{Bob } 30\text{--}35 \rangle$$

could represent six real world objects (one for each year in the age range). A query, Q, places each database object in one of three categories.

$T \; \varepsilon \; \{\text{surely-set}\}$	if $\|Q\| \subseteq \|T\|$
$T \; \varepsilon \; \{\text{possible-set}\}$	if $\|Q\| \cap \|T\| \neq \Phi$
$T \; \varepsilon \; \{\text{eliminated-set}\}$	if $\|Q\| \cup \|T\| = \Phi$

For instance the query, EMPLOYEE[AGE$>$32], places T in possible-set, while EMPLOYEE[AGE$>$25] $\land$ EMPLOYEE[AGE$<$40] places T in surely set.

Query Evaluation

In systems that are relationally structured and using fuzzy set concepts (Anvari and Rose, 1987; Buckles and Petry, 1982; Umano, 1983; Prade and Testamale, 1984), nearly all research has considered various extensions of the relational algebra. The syntactic structure is modified to the extent that additional specifications are required for query evaluations. Use of the relational calculus with a fuzzy data model has also been studied (Buckles and Petry, 1989). The relational calculus provides a nonprocedural specification for a query and can potentially be extended more easily to a higher level query language.

For more homogeneous data, simpler forms can be used for retrieval formulation. Boolean queries using operators AND, OR, and NOT to combine indexing terms are a typical structure used in information storage and retrieval systems. In the data model, fuzzy indexing can be used. Also possible are combinations of fuzzy term weights in the query and retrieval evaluation using fuzzy subset rules along with the fuzzy indexing.

The process of query evaluation for typical fuzzy data models will now be described. In this discussion, query computation will be considered as having two basic steps: (1) evaluation of matching or comparison predicate(s), and (2) calculation of the result set or relation based on results of the comparison. For systems that are using a relational algebra query language, the JOIN operation will be chosen for illustration, eg, JOIN $R1$ and $R2$ when $D1_i$ is about the same as $D2_j$, where $D1_i$ and $D2_j$ are attribute names in $R1$ and $R2$ that are compatible. In any representation, the fuzzy expression, "is about the same," must be given a concrete interpretation relative to the data representation. In general, this will become more complex as the homogeneity of the data model decreases.

Consider first the data model in which a membership value denotes the degree of belonging to the relation (Fig. 2). Here attributes to be joined are nonfuzzy, and so "about the same" is just equality and thus evaluation is identical with an ordinary JOIN. The second step in this case requires determination of the fuzzy membership and (Giardina, 1979) is simply computed as the minimum of the membership values.

For a representation using similarity relationships, the comparison is specified in the query by the addition of a clause

$$LEVEL(D) = a$$

In the first step of query evaluation, the JOIN of the relations is carried out by the following process: tuples, $t1_i$ in $R1$ and $t2_j$ and $R2$, are joined over the compatible attribute D, if, x,y in D are values in $t1_i$ and $t2_j$, respectively, and SIMILARITY $(x,y) \geq a$. Finally the second step involves merging the redundant tuples that have been formed by the JOIN. The redundancy of tuples is determined, for a given domain of an attribute, by the similarity threshold THRES(D), which is just the minimum similarity over all values in the domain. The ultimate form of the result is obtained by merging as many tuples as possible without violating the constraint THRES(D)$\geq$ LEVEL(D).

With the use of explicit possibility distributions, query evaluation is somewhat more complex. The term "is approximately equal" can be realized (Umano, 1983) by the specification of a fuzzy predicate P($D1_u,D2_j$), where the objects in the domains have possibility distributions. The first step is evaluation of this predicate whose value is itself a possibility distribution. In this specific data model, a membership value is required for each tuple, where the value may be a possibility distribution. Thus, the last step in forming the result is the computation of the membership value possibility distribution. This value is calculated by ANDing the predicate possibility distribution and the two original membership distributions. If $t1_i$ in $R1$ and $t2_j$ in $R2$ are joined over the compatible D, and x,y are values in $t1_i$, $t2_j$, respectively, then

$$\mu = P(x,y) \wedge \mu_{t1_i} \wedge \mu_{t2_j}$$

The above example is similar to that of other heterogeneous representations using possibility distributions, but there are other variations. One difference, for example, is that while allowing tuple membership values, it is possible to not automatically consider them during query interpretation (Prade and Testamale, 1984). Tuple membership values are the truth values of the conditional expression used to construct the result. Such membership values are not permanent attributes of tuples, but measure the degree of compliance to particular query.

Of special interest in such an approach is that the evaluation may be carried out by producing two results based on possibility and necessity. That is, a result set of tuples is developed that possibly satisfy the query, and another set that necessarily satisfy it. This is an interesting approach similar to the distinction of query results made by Lipski in the case of nonfuzzy partial information (Prade, 1984).

OTHER DATABASE MODELS

A variety of databases have been used before the relational model and others have also been recently developed The network model, especially the DBTG model, is a very important early and widely used database system. A DBTG network was studied with respect to introducing imprecision based on fuzzy set theory by various modifications to the basic DBTG set structure (Buckles and co-workers, 1990). However, all attempts were unsatisfactory because of the functionality restrictions on DBTG sets and it was concluded that a less restrictive network was needed. Semantic data models and especially recent developments in object-oriented databases have provided the extended capabilities found wanting in the DBTG database.

Semantic database systems provide more powerful modelling constructs than relational or network models. Fuzzy set theory has been introduced into a semantic data model by identifying levels within the model at which imprecision can be introduced (Rudensteiner and Bic, 1989). Object-oriented approaches are currently being realized with many of the capabilities of semantic models. A typical object oriented data model (OODM) (Kim and Lochovsky, 1989) uses two explicit hierarchies to represent the universe: the class hierarchy and the class composition hierarchy. One approach accommodates impreciseness in data values and in association among data values as well as in modelling of the class hierarchy (Buckles and co-workers, 1991).

A class hierarchy can be represented as $C_i \subset_s C_{i+1} \subset_s$ . . . $\subset_s C_n$ where C_i is an immediate subclass of C_{i+1}. Analysis of class-subclass relations indicates that they can be broadly divided into two different types: (1) specialization subclasses (also referred to as partial subclasses or object-oriented subclasses), where the subclass is a specialization of its immediate class, ie, computer science is a specialization of engineering; and (2) subset subclasses, where the subclass is a subset of its immediate class, eg, the class of employees is a subset subclass of the class of persons.

For the specialization hierarchy, a subclass is given a grade of membership in its immediate class $\mu_{C_{i+1}} (C_i)$ ε [0,1], generalizing the class hierarchy to include the concept of membership. A subclass is represented now by a pair $(C_i,\mu(C_i))$, the second element of which represents the membership of C_i in its immediate class C_{i+1} and the class hierarchy is shown as

$$(C_i,\mu(C_i)) \subset_s (C_{i+1},\mu(C_{i+1})) \subset_s . . . \subset_s (C_n,\mu(C_n))$$

Note $\mu(C_n)$ is for positional convenience only, since the root class does not have membership in any other class. The membership of a class C_i in an arbitrary class C_j

where $C_i \subset_s C_j$ but C_j is not necessarily the immediate superclass of C_i is given by the product rule

$$\mu_{C_j}(C_i) = \mu_{C_{i+1}}(C_i) \times \mu_{C_{i+2}}(C_{i+1}) \times \ldots \times \mu_{C_j}(C_{j-1})$$

For the subset hierarchy, no distinction is made between the subset subclass and the isomorphically embedded subclass (eg, the set of integers is a subclass of the set of reals) in the development of a subset hierarchy theory. In this hierarchy each subclass is a perfect member in its superclass, ie, $\mu_{C_{i+1}}(C_i) = 1$. Notationally the hierarchy may be represented as $(C_i, 1) \subset_s (C_{i+1}, \mu(1)) \subset_s (C_n, 1)$. Since the grade of membership of a class in its immediate superclass is 1, the subset hierarchy behaves similarly to the nonfuzzy OODM. This approach basically assumes that a hierarchy will either be purely a subset hierarchy or a specialization hierarchy. In most real world cases this is incorrect and "mixed" hierarchies are more the rule than the exception.

BIBLIOGRAPHY

ANSI/X3/SPARC, Study Group On Database Management Systems, Interim Report, *Bulletin of ACM SIGFIDET* FDT 7(2) (1975).

M. Anvari and G. Rose, "Fuzzy Relational Databases," in J. Bezdek, ed., *Analysis of Fuzzy Information, Artificial Intelligence and Decision Systems*, Vol. 2, CRC Press, Boca Raton, Fla., 1987, pp. 203–212.

J. Baldwin, "Knowledge Engineering Using A Fuzzy Relational Inference Language," in *Proceedings of the IFAC Conference on Fuzzy Information, Knowledge Representation, and Decision Processes*, Vol. 15, Marseille, France, International Federation for Automatic Control, 1983.

J. Baldwin and S. Zhou, "A Fuzzy Relational Interface Language," *Fuzzy Sets Syst.* **14**, 155–174 (1984).

B. Buckles and F. Petry, "Fuzzy Representation of Data for Relational Databases," *Fuzzy Sets Syst.* **7**, 213–228 (1982).

B. Buckles and F. Petry, "Extending the Fuzzy Database with Fuzzy Numbers," *Inf. Sci.* **34**, 145–155 (1984).

B. Buckles, R. George, and F. Petry, "Towards a Fuzzy Object Oriented Data Model," in *Proceedings of NAFIPS Conference 1991*, University of Missouri, Columbia, Mo., May 1991, pp. 90–93.

B. Buckles, F. Petry, and Y. Cheung, "Attribute Grammars for the Heuristic Translation of Query Languages," *Inf. Syst.* **14**, 507–514 (1989).

B. Buckles, F. Petry, and J. Pillai, "Network Data Models for Representation of Uncertainty," *Fuzzy Sets Syst.* **38**, 171–190 (1990).

B. Buckles, F. Petry, and H. Sachar, "A Domain Calculus for Fuzzy Relational Databases," *Fuzzy Sets Syst.* **29**, 327–340 (1989).

E. Codd, "A Relational Model of Data for Large Shared Data Banks," *CACM* **13**, 377–387 (1970).

E. Codd, "Extending the Database Relational Model to Capture More Meaning," *ACM Trans. Database Syst.* **4**, 397–434 (1979).

D. Dubois and H. Prade, *Possibility Theory: An Approach to Computerized Processing of Uncertainty*, Plenum Press, New York, 1988.

D. Dubois and H. Prade, eds., Special issue: "Fuzzy Sets and Databases," *Inf. Syst.* **14** (1989).

C. Giardina, "Fuzzy Databases (and Fuzzy Relational Associative Processors)," Technical Report, Stevens Institute of Technology, Hoboken, N.J., 1979.

J. Grant, "Null Values in a Relational Database," *Inf. Proc. Lett.* **6**, 156–157 (1977).

J. Kacprzyk, B. Buckles, and F. Petry, eds., Special issue: "Fuzzy Information and Database Systems," *Fuzzy Sets Syst.* **38**, (Nov. 1990).

W. Kim and F. Lochovsky, eds., *Object-Oriented Concepts, Databases and Applications*, Addison-Wesley, New York, 1989.

D. Kraft and D. Buell, "Fuzzy Sets and Generalized Boolean Retrieval Systems," *Int. J. Man-Machine Stud.* **19**, 45–56 (1983).

W. Lipski, "On Semantic Issues Connected with Incomplete Information Databases," *ACM Trans. Database Syst.* **4**, 262–296 (1979).

W. Lipski, "On Databases With Incomplete Information," *J. ACM* **28**, 41–70 (1981).

D. Maier, *The Theory of Relational Databases*, Computer Science Press, Rockville, Md., 1983.

C. Montgomery and E. Ruspini, "The Active Information System: A Data-Driven System For The Analysis of Imprecise Data," in *Proceedings of the International Conference on Very Large Databases*, Cannes, France, 1981, p 376.

A. Motro, ed., "Imprecision in Databases," *Special Issue, Data Eng. Bull.* **12**, (June 1989).

H. Potoczny, "On Similarity Relations In Fuzzy Relational Databases," *Fuzzy Sets Syst.* **12**, 231–237 (1984).

H. Prade, "Lipski's Approach to Incomplete Information Databases Restated and Generalized in the Setting of Zadeh's Possibility Theory," *Inf. Syst.* **9**, 27–42 (1984).

H. Prade and C. Testamale, "Generalized Database Relational Algebra for the Treatment of Incomplete/Uncertain Information and Vague Queries," *Inf. Sci.* **34**, 115–143 (1984).

H. Prade and C. Testamale, "The Possible Approach to the Handling of Imprecision in Database Systems," *Data Eng. Bull.* **12**, 4–11 (June 1989).

K. Raju and A. Majumdar, "Fuzzy Functional Dependencies and Lossless Join Decomposition of Fuzzy Relational Database Systems," *ACM Trans. Database Syst.* **13**, 129–166 (1988).

M. Roth, H. Korth, and D. Batory, "SQL/NF: Query Language for Non-1NF Relational Databases," *Inf. Syst.* **12**, 99–114 (1987).

E. Rudensteiner and L. Bic, "Towards Modeling Imprecision in the Semantic Data Model," in J. Bezdek, ed., *Third IFSA Conference Proceeding*, Aug. 1989, University of Washington, Seattle, Wash., 1989, pp. 153–156.

E. Ruspini, "Possibility Theory Approaches for Advanced Information Systems," *IEEE Computer* **9**, 83 (1982).

H. Schek and M. Scholl, "The Relational Model with Relation-Valued Attributes," *Inf. Syst.* **11**, 137–146 (1986).

S. Shenoi and A. Melton, "Proximity Relations in the Fuzzy Relational Database Model," *Inf. Sci.* **52**, 35–52 (1989).

R. Tong, D. Shapiro, B. McCune, and J. Dean, "A Rule-Based Approach to Information Retrieval," *Proceedings of the Third National Conference on Artificial Intelligence*, Washington, D.C., AAAI, Menlo Park, Calif., 1983, p. 411.

M. Umano, "Retrieval From Fuzzy Database by Fuzzy Relational Algebra," in *Proceedings of IFAC Conference on Fuzzy Information, Knowledge Representation, and Decision Processes*, Vol. 1, Marseille, France, 1983.

L. Zadeh, "Similarity Relations and Fuzzy Orderings," *Inf. Sci.* **3**, 177–195 (1971).

L. Zadeh, "The Concept of a Linguistic Variable and Its Application to Approximate Reasoning," *Inf. Sci.* **8**, 199–249 (1975).

L. Zadeh, "Fuzzy Sets as a Basis for a Theory of Possibility," *Fuzzy Sets Syst.* **1**, 3–28 (1978).

M. Zemankova and A. Kandel, *Fuzzy Relational Databases—A Key to Expert Systems,* Verlag TÜV Rheinland, Köln, FRG, 1984.

M. Zemankova and A. Kandel, "Implementing Imprecision in Information Systems," *Inf. Sci.* **37**, 107–141 (Dec. 1985).

BILL P. BUCKLES
FREDERICK E. PETRY
Tulane University

FUZZY LOGIC: APPLICATIONS TO NATURAL LANGUAGE

Natural language is one of the most complicated structures humans have met with. It plays a fundamental role not only in human communication, but also in human ways of thinking and regarding the world. Therefore, much endeavour has been aimed at developing AI systems that elaborate some parts of natural language. Concerning phonetic and syntactic aspects, the progress has been quite good, though not yet fully satisfactory. A much worse situation prevails in the comprehension of natural language semantics. Linguistic systems, many of them based on set theory and logic, are used in attempts to grasp at least some phenomena of natural language. However, none of them is fully accepted and satisfactory. The tremendous complexity that embraces many intrinsic, not-yet-understood relations among various units is the first serious obstacle to mastering semantics. Another serious obstacle is the vagueness of the meaning of separate lexical units, as well as that of sentences and text. On the other hand, the capability of the human mind to take vagueness into account and to handle vague concepts reflected by the semantics of natural language is the main cause of the extreme power of natural language to convey relevant and succinct information. Vagueness is thus an unavoidable feature of natural language. There is no alternative except to cope with it in the models of natural language semantics, especially if they are to be successfully implemented in AI systems.

Fuzzy set theory is a mathematical theory whose program is to provide methods and tools that make it possible to grasp vague phenomena instrumentally (see FUZZY SETS AND FUZZY LOGIC). Therefore, it seems appropriate for use in modeling natural language semantics and for use in those AI systems where elaborating natural language is important. Fuzzy set theory has also been successfully applied in decision–support systems, cluster analysis, pattern recognition, and many other fields.

How do fuzzy sets reflect the phenomenon of vagueness? In regarding the world, humans encounter various phenomena that can be divided into two principle groups: objects and properties. An *object* is a phenomenon to which we concede its individuality. This individuality maintains its integrity and separates it from the other phenomena. Objects are usually accompanied by other kinds of phenomena called *properties*. However, the same property may accompany more than one object. If all such objects are grouped together, they can be seen as one new object of a special kind. A grouping of objects being seen as one object is called a class. Hence, if φ is a property, then there is a class X of objects x having φ, expressed as:

$$X = \{x;\ \varphi(x)\} \qquad (1)$$

If the property φ is simple and sharp, then the class X forms a set. This means that given an x, it is possible to decide without doubt whether or not $\varphi(x)$ (ie, whether or not x has the property φ). However, most properties encountered in the real world are not of this kind. There is usually no way to name or imagine all the objects x from X without any doubt about the membership of x in X. For example, let $\varphi : =$ *to be a small natural number.* Can we imagine all the small numbers? Clearly, 0 is small, 1 is small as well, etc. But where does this sequence finish? Most people are sure that some big number, eg, 1,000,000,000, is not small. This means that there should exist a small number n, $0 < n < 1,000,000,000$ such that $n + 1$ is not small. However, such a conclusion can hardly be defended. If n is small then $n + 1$ must also be small. Hence, there is no last small number before 1,000,000,000 and no first number $n < 1,000,000,000$ that already is not small. This is the phenomenon of vagueness that leads to the conclusion that the class X may be separated unsharply.

Classical mathematics has no other possibility than to replace the grouping X by a (sharp) set (as discussed above). However, if there are more vague properties in the game, then the result cannot be satisfactory. Unlike classical set theory, fuzzy set theory attempts to find a more suitable model of the class in equation 1. Its main idea is as follows.

The decision about $\varphi(x)$ is tantamount to the question of whether $\varphi(x)$ is true or not. Because there are doubts, it is possible to seek some kind of scale whose elements would express various degrees of the truth of $\varphi(x)$. This leads naturally to many-valued logic, which is not usually called fuzzy logic. The use of a scale for characterization of an unsharp grouping is quite natural for the human mind and is called the *fuzzy approach.* In fact, this solution gives an answer to the question of whether a number, say 500, is small in the same sense as the number 1. All the problems with separation of a vague grouping X probably stem from the inner complexity, still not understood, of the property φ in question.

The objects x are taken from some sufficiently big set U called the universe. Note that this assumption is not restrictive because such a set always exists. In the above example, assume the number $z = 1,000,000,000$ and put $U = \{x \in N;\ x \le z\}$.

Let L be a scale of truth values having the smallest 0 and greatest 1 elements, respectively. $L = \langle 0, 1 \rangle$ is usually stated, though it is not necessary. However, because the use of this interval is quite natural and transparent, it will be considered in all that follows. Thus 1 expresses that $\varphi(x)$ (x has the property φ) with no doubt while 0 means that $\varphi(x)$ does not hold at all. The following function is obtained:

$$A : U \to L \qquad (2)$$

assigning an element

$$Ax \in L$$

from the scale L to each element $x \in U$. The element $Ax \in L$ is a degree of truth that x has the given property φ. Equation 2 is called the membership function of a fuzzy set, and it characterizes (represents) the (unsharp) grouping X in equation 1. In the strict mathematical sense, a fuzzy set is also the function 2, ie, a fuzzy set is identified with its membership function. Thus, the same symbol can be used for both and $A \subseteq U$ if A is a fuzzy set in the universe U. Explicitly, it is written

$$\{Ax/x; x \in U\} \qquad (3)$$

where the couple Ax/x means "the element x belongs to A with the membership degree Ax," $Ax \in L$. Thus the membership degree Ax expresses the degree of truth of $\varphi(x)$ where φ is the property leading to separation of the grouping X in equation 1 and the latter is characterized by the fuzzy set A.

FUNDAMENTALS OF FUZZY SET THEORY

The scale L is assumed to form the structure

$$\mathscr{L} = \langle 0, 1 \rangle, \vee, \wedge, \otimes, \to, 0, 1 \rangle \qquad (4)$$

where $\vee$ and $\wedge$ are the operations of supremum (maximum) and infimum (minimum) respectively, $\otimes$ is the operation of bold product defined by

$$a \otimes b = 0 \vee (a + b - 1)$$

and $\to$ is the operation of residuum defined by

$$a \to b = 1 \wedge (1 - a + b)$$

for all the $a, b \in \langle 0, 1 \rangle$. There are deep reasons for the choice of this structure (Pavelka, 1979a, 1979b, 1979c; Novák, 1989, 1990a). The basic operations on fuzzy sets are defined as follows:

union

$$C = A \cup B \text{ iff } Cx = Ax \vee Bx$$

intersection

$$C = A \cap B \text{ iff } Cx = Ax \wedge Bx$$

bold intersection

$$C = A \boxtimes B \text{ iff } Cx = Ax \otimes Bx$$

and residuum

$$C = A \ominus B \text{ iff } Cx = Ax \to Bx$$

On the basis of residuum, the complement $\bar{A} = A \ominus \emptyset$ can be defined where

$$\emptyset = \{0/x; x \in U\}$$

is the empty fuzzy set. This definition gives $\bar{A}x = 1 - Ax$ for all $x \in U$. This is the usual definition of the complement in fuzzy set theory, introduced by Zadeh (1965) and widely used. This definition allows the law of the excluded middle to be denied because

$$A \cap \bar{A} \neq \emptyset$$

and

$$A \cup \bar{A} \neq U$$

However, this role is taken by the operation of the bold intersection, because

$$A \boxtimes \bar{A} = \emptyset$$

In reasoning that uses fuzzy sets, this operation is more important than ordinary intersection $\cap$.

In modeling of natural language semantics, it is necessary to introduce additional operations:

$$a \leftrightarrow b = (a \to b) \wedge (b \to a)$$

(biresiduation) and

$$a^p = \underbrace{a \otimes \ldots \otimes a}_{p\text{-times}}$$

(power) for all the $a, b \in \langle 0, 1 \rangle$. When introducing a new n-ary operation o on L, the following fitting condition must be fulfilled: there are $p_1, \ldots, p_n$ such that

$$(a_1 \leftrightarrow b_1)^{p_1} \otimes \ldots \otimes (a_n \leftrightarrow b_n)^{p_n}$$
$$\leq o(a_1, \ldots, a_n) \leftrightarrow o(b_1, \ldots, b_n) \qquad (5)$$

holds for every $a_i, b_i \in L$, $i = 1, \ldots, n$. Justification of the fitting condition has been published (Pavelka, 1979a, 1979b, 1979c; Novák and Pedrycz, 1988; Novák, 1989).

All the basic operations fulfill the fitting condition. Moreover, the following holds true:

Theorem 1. All the operations derived from the operations fulfilling the fitting condition fulfill it as well.

For example, the following operations are fitting:

product

$$a \cdot b$$

bounded sum

$$a \oplus b = 1 \wedge (a + b)$$

concentration

$$\mathrm{CON}(a) = a^2$$

dilation

$$\mathrm{DIL}(a) = 2a - a^2$$

and intensification

$$\mathrm{INT}(a) = \begin{cases} 2a^2 & a \in \langle 0, 0.5 \rangle \\ 1 - 2(1 - a)^2 & a \in (0.5, 1 \rangle \end{cases}$$

for all the $a, b \in \langle 0, 1 \rangle$. The widely used operation of dilation $\mathrm{DIL}(a) = a^{0.5}$ is not fitting and thus cannot be used.

The operations in L lead to the operations with fuzzy sets as follows. Let

$$o : L^n \to L$$

and $A_1, \ldots, A_n \subseteq U$ be fuzzy sets. Then o is a basis of the operation O assigning a fuzzy set $C \subseteq U$ to $A_1, \ldots, A_n$ if

$$C = O(A_1, \ldots, A_n) \text{ iff } Cx = o(A_1 x_1, \ldots, A_n x_n) \quad (6)$$

is put for every $x \in U$. For example, the operation of bounded sum of fuzzy sets can be defined as

$$C = A \uplus B \text{ iff } Cx = Ax \oplus Bx$$

for every $x \in U$. This operation is a union counterpart to $\boxtimes$ because

$$A \uplus \bar{A} = U$$

Hence, it may be concluded that the law of the excluded middle is not harmed in fuzzy set theory but different (also fundamental) operations from $\cap$ and $\cup$ must be considered.

Three classical sets play an important role, namely

support

$$\mathrm{Supp}(A) = \{x; Ax > 0\}$$

a-cut

$$A_a = \{x; Ax \geq a\}$$

and kernel

$$\mathrm{Ker}(A) = \{x; Ax = 1\}$$

An important notion is that of a *fuzzy cardinality* of a fuzzy set. There are several kinds (Zadeh, 1983; Novák, 1989); we will use the following, defined for fuzzy sets with finite support.

Absolute fuzzy cardinality of $A \subseteq U$:

$$\mathrm{FCard}(A) = \{\alpha_n/n; n \in N\} \quad (7)$$

where

$$\alpha_n = \bigvee \{\beta; \mathrm{Card}(A_\beta) = n\}$$

and A_β is a β cut of A.
Relative fuzzy cardinality of A with respect to B where $A, B \subseteq U$:

$$\mathrm{FCard}_A(B) = \{\alpha_r/r; r \in Re\} \quad (8)$$

where

$$\alpha_r = \bigvee \left\{ \beta; \frac{\mathrm{Card}(A_\beta \cap B_\beta)}{\mathrm{Card}(A_\beta)} = r \right\}$$

Let $a \subseteq U, B \subseteq V$ be fuzzy sets. Then the Cartesian product of them is a fuzzy set $A \times B \subseteq U \times V$ defined by

$$(A \times B)\langle x, y \rangle = Ax \wedge Bx$$

for all $x \in U$ and $y \in V$.

GRASPING THE SEMANTICS OF NATURAL LANGUAGE

General Representation of the Meaning

A natural language sentence can be viewed several ways. In classical linguistics, it is usual to talk about representation of a sentence on various levels. In the functional generative description of natural language (FGD) (Sgall and co-workers, 1986), five levels are differentiated.

1. Phonetic (PH): how a sentence is composed as a system of sounds
2. Phonemic (PM): how words of a sentence are composed
3. Morphemic (MR): how a sentence is composed of its words
4. Surface syntax (SS): the system of grammatical rules
5. Tectogrammatical (TR): the highest level corresponding to the semantics.

The latter is also called the *deep structure* (qv) of the sentence, and this structure is the objective of possible application of fuzzy set theory. As already stated, words and more complex syntagms of natural language can be understood to be names of properties encountered by a person in the world. In the light of the previous section, fuzzy sets can be used as follows: let $\mathscr{A}$ be a syntagm of natural language. This syntagm corresponds to some property φ encountered in the world. If the class 1 determined by φ is approximated by a fuzzy set $A \subseteq U$ then the meaning $M(\mathscr{A})$ of $\mathscr{A}$ is

$$M(\mathscr{A}) = A \quad (9)$$

Thus the task consists of determining of the membership function A. However, the situation is by no means simple, as not every word of natural language corresponds to such a property, and above all, there are various relations between words. Thus determination of the membership function that corresponds to a complex syntagm may be a complicated task. On the tectogrammatical level, a meaning of a sentence is represented as a complex dependency structure that can be depicted in the form of a labeled graph. For example, the sentence

Daria writes a short letter to her husband.

can be depicted as a graph (Fig. 1). A detailed explanation of Figure 1 has been given (Sgall and co-workers, 1986; Sgall, 1984). The letters t and f mean topic and focus, respectively. A topic is a part of a sentence containing the theme that is spoken about, and a focus contains new information conveyed by the sentence. Of course, one surface structure of a sentence may lead to several deep structures. To date a detailed understanding of all the nuances of the sentence semantics is not known. The present state of the art makes it possible to model the meaning of only few kinds of simple syntagms, ie, certain branches of the tectogrammatical tree as shown in Figure 1. This will be discussed in the subsequent sections.

Fuzzy Semantics of Selected Syntagms

First, the modeling of the semantics of nouns is discussed. In general, if S is a noun, then its meaning is a fuzzy set

$$M(\mathcal{S}) = S, S \subseteq U$$

What is the universe U? The noun $\mathcal{S}$ is a name of a certain property φ_S. The U is a set of objects chosen in such a way that whenever an object x has the property φ_S then $x \in U$. The universe U can be constructed as follows: let K be a set of generic elements called the kernel space. For example, K can be a union of all the objects described in the dictionary, of all objects seen during the last week or of those seen in an apartment. In short, K should contain all the specific objects that have been met or imagined. Let $\mathcal{F}(K)$ be a set of all the fuzzy sets on K and put

$$\mathcal{F}^n(K) = \mathcal{F}(. . . (\mathcal{F}(K) . . .)$$

$$n\text{-times}$$

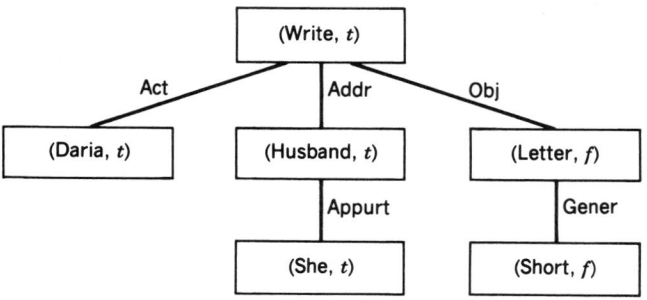

Figure 1. The tectogrammatical tree of the sentence *Daria writes a short letter to her husband.*

Let E_K be the smallest set closed with respect to all the Cartesian powers of K, of $\mathcal{F}^n(K)$, $n = 1, \ldots, n$ and all the Cartesian products of these elements. This set is called the semantic space. Then the universe of S is a sufficiently big subset $U \subseteq E_K$.

A certain problem is the determination of the membership function. There are several methods proposed in the literature (Novák, 1989). The membership function corresponding to the object nouns (eg, *table, car, donkey,* etc) could be constructed on the basis of the outer characteristics of elements. For example, the proportions of some geometric patterns contained in objects may be used. An often used method is statistical analysis of expert (subjective) estimations. Several experiments have been described in the literature. It should be mentioned that fuzzy methods are robust, and thus exact determination of the membership function is not as important as it might seem at first glance. The experience suggests that even individual estimation works well when it is done carefully and seriously.

In practical applications, eg, in artificial intelligence, it is not useful to model the meaning of nouns because it would be necessary to find proper representation of their elements in the computer. In fact, however, the meaning of nouns is often not needed. The most successful applications are based on modeling of the meaning of adjectives and the syntagms of the form

$$(quantifier -) \; adverb - adjective \; (- \; noun)$$

where the syntagm

$$adverb - adjective \tag{10}$$

plays the crucial role. The most important and frequently occurring adjectives are those inducing an ordering $\leq$ in the universe U, for example *young, small, sour, clever*. It is assumed that $\leq$ is linear. According to linguistic considerations as well as experiments (Kuz'min, 1985), there are certain points $m, s, v, \in U$ where $m < s < v$. The point s is called the semantic center. The adjectives inducing an ordering in U usually form antonyms, for example small–big, cold–hot, young–old. In theory, they can be characterized as follows. Let $\mathcal{A}^-$, $\mathcal{A}^+$ be antonyms. Then their meanings are fuzzy sets

$$M(\mathcal{A}^-) = A^-$$
$$M(\mathcal{A}^+) = A^+$$

such that $\text{Supp}(A^-) \subseteq \langle m, s \rangle$ and $\text{Supp}(A^+) \subseteq (s, v)$. $\mathcal{A}^-$ will be called a negative and $\mathcal{A}^+$ a positive adjective, respectively. There are also pairs of antonyms such that a third member $\mathcal{A}^0$ exists. Its meaning is

$$M(\mathcal{A}^0) = A^0$$

where the membership function A^0 has the property

$$s \in \text{Ker}(A^0)$$

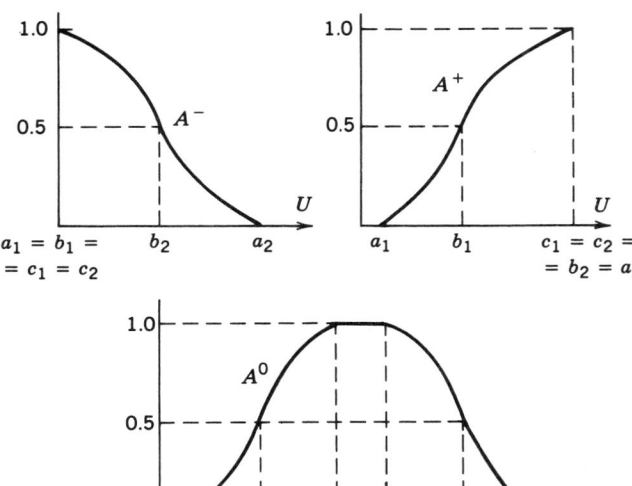

Figure 2. The membership functions corresponding to the meaning of the negative, positive, and zero syntagms.

A typical example of the adjective $\mathscr{A}^0$ is $\mathscr{A}^0 :=$ average. In what follows, $\mathscr{A}^0$ will be called a zero adjective.

The curves corresponding to the fuzzy sets A^-, A^+, A^0 have characteristic shapes depicted in Figure 2. In fuzzy set theory, they are sometimes called the S^-, S^+ and Π fuzzy sets, respectively. A possible general formula for all the three fuzzy sets is the following:

$$F(x, a_1, b_1, c_1, c_2, b_2, a_2) =$$
$$\begin{cases} 0 & \text{if } x < a_1 \text{ or } x > a_2 \\ 1 & \text{if } c_1 \leq x \leq c_2 \\ \frac{1}{2}\left(\frac{x - a_1}{b_1 - a_1}\right)^2 & \text{if } a_1 \leq x < b_1 \\ 1 - \frac{1}{2}\left(\frac{x - c_1}{c_1 - b_1}\right)^2 & \text{if } b_1 \leq x < c_1 \\ 1 - \frac{1}{2}\left(\frac{x - c_2}{b_2 - c_2}\right)^2 & \text{if } c_2 < x \leq b_2 \\ \frac{1}{2}\left(\frac{x - a_2}{a_2 - b_2}\right)^2 & \text{if } b_2 < x \leq a_2 \end{cases} \quad (11)$$

The meaning of the points $a_1, b_1, c_1, a_2, b_2, c_2 \in U$ is clear from Figure 2. The adverb in syntagm 10 is called the intensifying adverb (eg, very, highly, absolutely, slightly) or, as is usual in fuzzy set theory, the linguistic modifier. Let m be a linguistic modifier. Its meaning in general is a pair of functions

$$M(m) = \langle \zeta_m, \nu_m \rangle$$

where $\zeta_m : U \to U$ is a displacement function and $\nu_m : L \to L$ is a unary operation fitting L. Some authors simplify this model by using $\zeta_m = \mathrm{id}_U$ (an identical function on U). Hence, the meaning of syntagm 10 is obtained using the composition of functions

$$M(m\mathscr{A}) = \nu_m \circ A \circ \zeta_m \quad (12)$$

A typical example from fuzzy set theory is the modifier *very* defined as follows:

$$\nu_{very}(a) = \mathrm{CON}(a), \ a \in \langle 0, 1 \rangle$$

and

$$\zeta_{very}(x) = x + (-1)^k \cdot d \cdot \|\mathrm{Ker}(A)\|$$

where $k = 1$ for A^+ or for A^0 if $x \leq s$, and $k = 2$ for A^- or for A^0 if $x \geq s$. $\|\mathrm{Ker}(A)\|$ is the length of the interval $\langle \inf(\mathrm{Ker}(A)), \sup(\mathrm{Ker}(A)) \rangle$. The parameter d was experimentally estimated to be a number $d \in \langle 0.25, 0.40 \rangle$. Examples of some other linguistic modifiers, for example, *more or less* and *roughly* have been published (Lakoff, 1973; Zadeh 1973, 1975a, 1975b, 1975c; Novák, 1989).

The meaning of verbs is a very complicated problem and so far, only the copula *to be* in syntagms as

$$p := \mathscr{P} \text{ is } \mathscr{A} \quad (13)$$

is modeled where $\mathscr{A}$ is usually the syntagm 10. However, Syntagm 13 is interpreted as a simple assignment rather than a verb. The $\mathscr{P}$ in syntagm 13 is a noun but it is not usually treated as such. Thus, there are two ways to model the meaning of syntagm 13. First,

$$M(p) = M(\mathscr{A}) = A$$

ie, the meaning of p is set equal to the meaning of the syntagm $\mathscr{A}$. This is quite reasonable because, as stated above, the meaning of the noun $\mathscr{P}$ is usually not needed in the applications. Secondly, let $M(\mathscr{P}) = P \subseteq V$ and put

$$M(p) \subseteq P \times A \quad (14)$$

where $P \times A$ is the Cartesian product of fuzzy sets.

The inclusion in equation 14 may be proper or improper, depending on the kind of noun $\mathscr{P}$ is. The relation in equation 14 means that each element x from the universe V (a representative of the noun $\mathscr{P}$) is assigned an attribute y from the universe U where $A \subseteq U$, with the degree of membership equal at most to the smaller one of Px and Ay. U is usually the real line. For example, in the syntagms such as *Peter is tall*, the element *Peter* is assigned its height as a real number. It has been suggested that the membership degree $(P \times A)\langle x, y \rangle$ should be interpreted as a possibility degree of the fact that x is A (Zadeh, 1978, 1983). However, the possibility degree concerns uncertainty which does not reflect the vagueness phenomenon contained in the semantics of natural language. Conditional sentences of the form

$$\mathscr{C} := \text{IF } p \text{ THEN } q \quad (15)$$

(where p and q are syntagms of the form of syntagm 13) are important. It is usual in fuzzy set theory to state

$$M(\mathscr{C}) = M(p) \ominus M(q) \quad (16)$$

ie, the implication of condition sentence 15 is interpreted using the residuum operation between fuzzy sets $M(p)$ and $M(q)$. The interpretation of the conditional sentence 15 plays a crucial role in the so called approximate reasoning, which is one of the most successfully applied areas of fuzzy set theory (Gupta and Yamakawa, 1988a, 1988b). It should be noted that many authors interpret conditional sentence 15 as the Cartesian product

$$M(\mathscr{C}) = M(p) \times M(q) \tag{17}$$

In the applications of the approximate reasoning, this may work because all the fuzzy methods are very robust. However, putting the meaning of the implication of conditional sentence 15 equal to the Cartesian product is linguistically as well as logically incorrect, because equation 17 is symmetric and the implication is not. Another reason why equation 17 often works in practical applications may be the fact that the implication of conditional sentence 15 often describes only some kind of a relation between the input and output and it is not, in fact, understood to be the implication. This discrepancy needs more analysis.

The problem of linguistic quantifiers ($\mathscr{Q}$) should also be mentioned. Linguistic qualifiers do not form a uniform group from the linguistic point of view. Among them, numerals are placed, including the indefinite ones (eg, *several*), some adverbs (eg, *many, few, most*), some pronouns (eg, *every*), some nouns (eg, *majority, minority*), and others. From the point of fuzzy set theory, their meaning generally is a fuzzy number, ie, a fuzzy set $M(\mathscr{Q}) = Q \subseteq Re$ in the real line. A method for interpreting the syntagms has been proposed (Zadeh, 1983):

$$\mathscr{Q}\,\mathscr{A} \tag{18}$$

or

$$\mathscr{Q}\,\mathscr{A}'s\ are\ \mathscr{B}'s \tag{19}$$

In equation 18, the quantifier $\mathscr{Q}$ is interpreted as a fuzzy characterization of the absolute fuzzy cardinality 7 of the fuzzy set

$$A = M(\mathscr{A})$$

while in equation 19 it characterizes the relative fuzzy cardinality 8 of $M(\mathscr{A})$ with respect to $B = M(\mathscr{B})$. More exactly, put

$$M(\mathscr{Q}\,\mathscr{A}) = Q \cap \mathrm{FCard}(A) \tag{20}$$

and

$$M(\mathscr{Q}\,\mathscr{A}'s\ are\ \mathscr{B}'s) = Q \cap \mathrm{FCard}_A(B) \tag{21}$$

However, the problem is not finished yet because equations 20 and 21 have sense only for fuzzy sets with finite support.

In the literature on fuzzy set theory (Zadeh, 1973, 1975,

1983; Novák, 1989) the semantics of the compound syntagms of the following form are found:

$$\mathscr{A}\ and\ \mathscr{B} \tag{22}$$

and

$$\mathscr{A}\ or\ \mathscr{B} \tag{23}$$

defined using the operations of intersection and union of fuzzy sets, respectively. However, this is only a tentative solution because the syntagms 22 and 23 are special cases of the very complicated phenomenon known in linguistics as the coordination. The use of the operations of intersection and union of fuzzy sets may work in some special cases of the so called close coordination in syntagms eg, *Peter and Paul,* and *Old and dirty car.*

An even worse situation is encountered with negation. The simple use of the operation of complement of fuzzy sets works only with some kinds of adjectives and nouns. However, negation contained in more complex syntagms is incidental to the phenomenon of the topic–focus articulation when only focus is being negated. Fully comprehensive description of this phenomenon in linguistics, however, is no longer done.

A concept important especially with applications of the above theory in AI is that of a linguistic variable (Zadeh, 1975a, 1975b, 1975c). This concept made it possible to see a certain part of linguistics from a more technical point of view. A linguistic variable is, in general, a quintuple

$$\langle \mathscr{X}, \mathscr{T}(\mathscr{X}), U, G, M \rangle$$

where $\mathscr{X}$ is a name of the variable, $\mathscr{T}(\mathscr{X})$ is its term set, U is the universe, G the syntactic, and M the semantic rules, respectively. For example,

$$\mathscr{X} := age$$
$$U := \langle 0, 120 \rangle$$

G is a certain, usually context-free grammar generating a set $\mathscr{T}(\mathscr{X})$ of terms such as *young, old, very young, rather old, middle aged,* and M is the syntactic rule assigning to each term $\mathscr{A} \in \mathscr{T}(\mathscr{X})$, its meaning being a fuzzy set

$$M(\mathscr{A}) \subseteq U$$

This fuzzy set is constructed according to the rules described above. Linguistic variables play important roles in technical applications. For example, the parameters of a technical system such as *temperature, speed,* and *weight* can be understood to be linguistic variables. Their values can also be crisp, eg, *exactly 165.2*; the concept of a linguistic variable is general enough to capture the classic concept of the variable as well.

In applications, the problem of a linguistic approximation also exists. Let $\mathscr{T}$ be a set of syntagms of natural language eg, the term set of a linguistic variable, given a fuzzy set $A'_0 \subseteq U$. The task is to find a syntagm $\mathscr{A}_0 \in \mathscr{T}$ such that its meaning $M(\mathscr{A}_0) = A_0$ is as close to A'_0 as possible. There are many ways to solve this task. However, no sufficiently efficient and general method is known.

PRACTICAL APPLICATIONS

There are many applications of the above theory. The most successful ones are concerned with the so-called fuzzy controller, which realizes the ideas of the theory of approximate reasoning. Although the controller works very well, its linguistic part is oversimplified. The use of linguistics is confined only to several terms (*negatively big, negatively average, negatively small, zero, positively small, positively average, positively big*), sometimes extended by the linguistic modifiers. The literature on fuzzy controllers is extensive and has been reviewed (Sugeno, 1985).

Another application is automatic generation of verbal comments to the results of mathematical modeling. The main idea behind this is as follows: the user of a mathematical model is provided with a great quantity of numbers representing the situation in a modeled process. The task is to check all the numbers and to form an overall idea about what has happened in the process. In practice, this entails careful inspection of tens, or even hundreds of thousands of numbers. This is difficult, boring, and time-consuming labor, and moreover, some important information may be missed. A computer system can do some of this work. As a result, it can generate verbal comments judging the overall magnitude of the values, find focuses of extreme values, and thus direct the user's attention to interesting places in the modeled system. The method for generating such comments is based on the above model of natural language semantics (Novák, 1987).

A similar application is concerned with querying a database that includes words of natural language. These queries also lead to fuzzy sets constructed on the basis of principles described above. The results (answers) are also presented in the form of fuzzy sets (Kacprzyk and Ziólkowski, 1988; Umano, 1983). Of course, these are not the only possible applications, and their number is still increasing. Their extensive variety is described in the literature.

BIBLIOGRAPHY

M. M. Gupta and T. Yamakawa, eds., *Fuzzy Computing: Theory, Hardware and Applications,* North-Holland, Amsterdam, The Netherlands, 1988a.

M. M. Gupta and T. Yamakawa, eds., *Fuzzy Logic in Knowledge-Based Systems, Decision and Control,* North-Holland, Amsterdam, The Netherlands, 1988b.

J. Kacprzyk and A. Ziólkowski, "New Database Queries with Fuzzy Linguistic Quantifiers via an Alternative Calculus of Linguistically Quantified Propositions," in J. Kacprzyk and A. Straszak, eds., *First Joint IFSA-EC and EURO-WG Workshop on Progress in Fuzzy Sets in Europe,* Instytut Badań Systemowych, Warsaw, Poland, 1988, pp. 139–154.

V. B. Kuz'min, "About Semantical Structure of Linguistic Hedges: An Experimental Hypothesis," *BUSEFAL* **24,** 118–125 (1985).

G. Lakoff, "Hedges: A Study in Meaning Criteria and Logic of Fuzzy Concepts," *J. Philos. Logic* **2,** 485–508 (1973).

V. Novák, "Automatic Generation of Verbal Comments on Results of Mathematical Modelling," in E. Sanchez and L. A. Zadeh, eds., *Approximate Reasoning in Intelligent Systems, Decision and Control,* Pergamon Press, Oxford, UK, 1987.

V. Novák, *Fuzzy Sets and Their Applications,* Adam-Hilger, Bristol, UK, 1989.

V. Novák, "On the Syntactico-Semantical Completeness of First-Order Fuzzy Logic. Part I—Syntactical Aspects," *Kyberentika* **26,** 47–66 (1990).

V. Novák and W. Pedrycz, "Fuzzy Sets and T-Norms in the Light of Fuzzy Logic," *Int. J. Man-Machine Stud.* **29,** 113–127 (1988).

J. Pavelka, "On Fuzzy Logic I," *Zeit. Math. Logic. Grundl. Math.* **25,** 45–52 (1979a).

J. Pavelka, "On Fuzzy Logic II," *Zeit. Math. Logic. Grundl. Math.* **25,** 119–134 (1979b).

J. Pavelka, "On Fuzzy Logic III," *Zeit. Math. Logic. Grundl. Math.* **25,** 447–464 (1979c).

P. Sgall, ed., *Contributions to Functional Syntax, Semantics, and Language Comprehension,* Academia, Prague, 1984.

P. Sgall, E. Hajičová, and J. Panevová, *The Meaning of the Sentence in Its Semantic and Pragmatic Aspects,* D. Reidel, Dordrecht, 1986.

M. Sugeno, ed., *Industrial Applications of Fuzzy Control,* North-Holland, Amsterdam, The Netherlands, 1985.

M. Umano, "Retrieval from Database by Fuzzy Relational Algebra," in E. Sanchez and M. M. Gupta, eds., *Proceedings of the IFAC Symposium on Fuzzy Information, Knowledge Representation, and Decision Analysis,* Pergamon Press, Oxford, UK, 1983.

L. A. Zadeh, "Fuzzy Sets," *Inform. Contr.* **8,** 338–353 (1965).

L. A. Zadeh, "Quantitative Fuzzy Semantics," *Inform. Sci.* **3,** 159–176 (1973).

L. A. Zadeh, "The Concept of a Linguistic Variable and Its Application to Approximate Reasoning I," *Inform. Sci.* **8,** 199–257 (1975a).

L. A. Zadeh, "The Concept of a Linguistic Variable and Its Application to Approximate Reasoning II," *Inform. Sci.* **8,** 301–357 (1975b).

L. A. Zadeh, "The Concept of a Linguistic Variable and Its Application to Approximate Reasoning III," *Inform. Sci.* **9,** 43–80 (1975c).

L. A. Zadeh, "PRUF—A Meaning Representation Language for Natural Languages," *Int. J. Man-Machine Stud.* **10,** 395–460 (1978).

L. A. Zadeh, "A Computational Approach to Fuzzy Quantifiers in Natural Languages," *Compt. Math. Applic.* **9,** 149–184 (1983).

VILÉM NOVÁK
Czechoslovak Academy of
Sciences

FUZZY MATHEMATICAL PROGRAMMING

Despite other uses of the term mathematical programming, it is interpreted here as is normally done in operations research; that is, as an algorithmic approach to solving models of the type

$$\text{maximize} \quad f(x)$$
$$\text{such that} \quad g_i(x) = 0, \qquad i = 1, \ldots, m \qquad (1)$$

Depending on the mathematical character of the objective function, $f(x)$, and the constraints, $g_i(x)$, many types of mathematical programming algorithms exist, such as linear programming, quadratic programming, fractional programming, and convex programming. Exemplarily, this article uses the simplest and most commonly used type, linear programming, which focuses on the model

$$\text{maximize} \quad f(x) = z = c^{\mathrm{T}}x$$
$$\text{such that} \quad Ax \le b$$
$$x \ge 0 \qquad (2)$$
$$\text{with} \quad c, x \in |\mathbb{R}^n, \quad b \in |\mathbb{R}^m, \quad A \in |\mathbb{R}^{m \times n}$$

In this model it is normally assumed that all coefficients of A, b, and c are real (crisp) numbers; that $\le$ is meant in a crisp sense, and that maximize is a strict imperative. This also implies that the violation of any single constraint renders the solution infeasible and that all constraints are of equal importance (weight). Strictly speaking, these are rather unrealistic assumptions, which are partly relaxed in fuzzy linear programming.

If we assume that the LP-decision has to be made in fuzzy environments, quite a number of possible modifications of equation 2 exist. First the decision maker might really not want actually to maximize or minimize the objective function. Rather, he or she might want to reach some aspiration levels that might not even be definable crisply. Thus the decision maker might want to improve the present cost situation considerably or such.

Second, the constraints might be vague in one of the following ways: the $\le$ sign might not be meant in the strictly mathematical sense, but smaller violations might well be acceptable. This can happen if the constraints represent aspiration levels or if, for instance, the constraints represent sensory requirements (taste, color, smell, etc.) that cannot adequately be approximated by a crisp constraint. Of course, the coefficients of the vectors **b** or **c** or of the matrix A itself can have a fuzzy character either because they are fuzzy in nature or because perception of them is fuzzy.

Finally, the role of the constraints can be different from that in classic linear programming where the violation of any single constraint by any amount renders the solution infeasible. The decision maker might accept small violations of different constraints. Fuzzy linear programming offers a number of ways to allow for all those types of vagueness.

Before a specific model of linear programming in a fuzzy environment is developed, it should have become clear that, by contrast to classic linear programming, fuzzy linear programming is not a uniquely defined type of model but that many variations are possible, depending on the assumptions or features of the real situation to be modeled.

Essentially, two families of models can be distinguished: One interprets fuzzy mathematical programming as a specific decision-making environment to which Bellman and Zadeh's definition of a decision in fuzzy environments (1970) can be applied. The other considers components of the model of equation 2 as fuzzy; makes certain assumptions, for instance, about the type of fuzzy sets that as fuzzy numbers replace the crisp coefficients in A, b, or c; and then solves the resulting mathematical problem. The former approach seems to be the more application-oriented one. From experience in applications, a decision maker seems to find it much easier to describe fuzzy constraints or to establish aspiration levels for the objective(s) than to specify a large number of fuzzy numbers for A, b, or c. Therefore, the first approach will be described, and then the other approaches will be elaborated.

SYMMETRIC FUZZY LINEAR PROGRAMMING

As already mentioned, fuzzy LP is considered a special case of a decision in a fuzzy environment. The basis in this case is the definition suggested by Bellman and Zadeh (1970):

Definition 1. Assume that we are given a fuzzy goal $\tilde{G}$ and a fuzzy constraint $\tilde{C}$ in a space of alternatives X. Then $\tilde{G}$ and $\tilde{C}$ combine to form a decision, $\tilde{D}$, which is a fuzzy set resulting from intersection of $\tilde{G}$ and $\tilde{C}$. In symbols, $\tilde{D} = \tilde{G} \cap \tilde{C}$ and correspondingly

$$\mu_{\tilde{D}} = \min \{\mu_{\tilde{G}}, \mu_{\tilde{C}}\}$$

More generally, suppose that we have n goals $\tilde{G}_1$, $\ldots$, $\tilde{G}_n$ and m constraints $\tilde{C}_1$, $\ldots$, $\tilde{C}_m$. Then, the resultant decision is the intersection of the given goals $\tilde{G}_1$, $\ldots$, $\tilde{G}_n$ and the given constraints $\tilde{C}_1$, $\ldots$, $\tilde{C}_m$. That is,

$$\tilde{D} = \tilde{G}_1 \cap \tilde{G}_2 \cap \cdots \cap \tilde{G}_n \cap \tilde{C}_1 \cap \tilde{C}_2 \cap \cdots \cap \tilde{C}_m$$

and correspondingly,

$$\mu_{\tilde{D}} = \min \{\mu_{\tilde{G}_1}, \mu_{\tilde{G}_2}, \ldots, \mu_{\tilde{G}_n}, \mu_{\tilde{C}_1}, \mu_{\tilde{C}_2}, \ldots, \mu_{\tilde{C}_m}\}$$
$$= \min \{\mu_{\tilde{G}_i}, \mu_{\tilde{C}_j}\} = \min \{\mu_i\}$$

This definition implies:

1. The "and" connecting goals and constraints in the model corresponds to the logical "and".
2. The logical "and" corresponds to the set theoretic intersection.
3. The intersection of fuzzy sets is defined in the possibilistic sense by the min-operator.

For the time being, we accept these assumptions. Another important feature of this model is its symmetry, that is, the fact that eventually, it does not distinguish between constraints and objectives. This feature is not considered adequate by all authors (see, for instance, Asai and co-workers, 1975). We feel, however, that this models real behavior of decision makers quite well. If we assume that the decision maker can establish in the model of equation 2 an aspiration level, z, of the objective function which he or she wants to achieve as far as possible, and if the constraints of this model can be slightly violated—without causing infeasibility of the solution—then the model of equation 2 can be written as

Find x
such that $c^T x \gtrsim z$
$Ax \lesssim b$
$x \geq 0$ (3)

Here $\lesssim$ denotes the fuzzified version of $\leq$ and has the linguistic interpretation "essentially smaller than or equal." $\gtrsim$ denotes the fuzzified version of $\geq$ and has the linguistic interpretation "essentially greater than or equal." The objective function in equation 2 might have to be written as a minimizing goal in order to consider z as an upper bound. We see that equation 3 is fully symmetric with respect to objective function and constraints, and we want to make that even more obvious by substituting $\binom{-c}{A} = B$ and $\binom{-z}{b} = d$. Then equation 3 becomes:

Find x
such that $Bx \lesssim d$
$x \geq 0$ (4)

Each of the $(m + 1)$ rows of equation 4 are now represented by a fuzzy set, the membership functions of which are $\mu_i(x)$. The membership function of the fuzzy set "decision" of model 4 is

$$\mu_{\tilde{D}}(x) = \min_i \{\mu_i(x)\}   (5)$$

$\mu_i(x)$ can be interpreted as the degree to which x fulfills (satisfies) the fuzzy inequality $B_i x \lesssim d_i$ (where B_i denotes the ith row of B). Assuming that the decision maker is interested not in a fuzzy set but in a crisp optimal solution, we could suggest the maximizing solution to equation 5, which is the solution to the possibly nonlinear programming problem

$$\max_{x \geq 0} \min_i \{\mu_i(x)\} = \max_{x \geq 0} \mu_{\tilde{D}}(x)   (6)$$

Now we have to specify the membership functions $\mu_i(x)$. $\mu_i(x)$ should be 0 if the constraints (including objective function) are strongly violated, and 1 if they are very well satisfied (ie, satisfied in the crisp sense); and $\mu_i(x)$ should increase monotonously from 0 to 1, that is,

$$\mu_i(x) = \begin{cases} 1 & \text{if } B_i x \leq d_i \\ \in [0, 1] & \text{if } d_i < B_i x \leq d_i + p_i \\ & \quad i = 1, \ldots, m + 1 \\ 0 & \text{if } B_i x > d_i + p_i \end{cases}   (7)$$

Using the simplest type of membership function, we assume them to be linearly increasing over the tolerance interval p_i.

$$\mu_i(x) = \begin{cases} 1 & \text{if } B_i x \leq d_i \\ 1 - \dfrac{B_i x - d_i}{p_i} & \text{if } d_i < B_i x \leq d_i + p_i \\ & \quad i = 1, \ldots, m + 1 \\ 0 & \text{if } B_i x > d_i + p_i \end{cases}   (8)$$

The p_i are subjectively chosen constants of admissible violations of the constraints and the objective function. Substituting equation 8 into equation 6 yields, after some rearrangements (Zimmerman 1976) and with some additional assumptions,

$$\max \min \left(1 - \frac{B_i x - d_i}{p_i}\right)   (9)$$

Introducing one new variable, λ, which corresponds essentially to equation 5, we arrive at

maximize λ
such that $\lambda p_i + B_i x \leq d_i + p_i$ $i = 1, \ldots, m + 1$
$x \geq 0$ (10)

If the optimal solution to equation 10 is the vector (λ, x_0), the x_0 is the maximizing solution (equation 6) of model 2 assuming membership functions as specified in equation 8. It should be realized that this maximizing solution can be found by solving one standard (crisp) LP with only one more variable and one more constraint than in model 4. This makes this approach computationally very efficient.

A slightly modified version of models 9 and 10, respectively, results if the membership functions are defined as follows: A variable t_i, $i = 1, \ldots, m + 1$, $0 \leq t_i \leq p_i$, is defined, which measures the degree of violation of the ith constraint: The membership function of the ith row is then

$$\mu_i(x) = 1 - \frac{t_i}{p_i}   (11)$$

The crisp equivalent model is then

maximize λ
such that $\lambda p_i + t_i \leq p_i$ $i = 1, \ldots, m + 1$
$B_i x - t_i \leq d_i$
$t_i \leq p_i$
$x, t \leq 0$ (12)

This model is larger than model 10, even though the set of constraints $t_i \leq p_i$ is actually redundant. Model 12 has some advantages, however, in particular when performing sensitivity analysis.

LINEAR PROGRAMS WITH FUZZY CONSTRAINTS AND CRISP OBJECTIVE FUNCTIONS

So far, it has been assumed that the objective function could be calibrated by a given z and then reformulated as a fuzzy set, resulting in the symmetric model formulation. It might, however, not be possible to find in a natural way the required z. In this case the symmetry of the model can be gained by applying a specialization of Zadeh's maximizing set to the objective function.

Definition 2 (Werners 1984). Let $f: X \to |R^1$ be the objective function, $\tilde{R}$ = fuzzy feasible region, $S(\tilde{R})$ = support of $\tilde{R}$, and R_1 = α-level cut of $\tilde{R}$ for $\alpha = 1$. The membership function of the goal (objective function) given solution space $\tilde{R}$ is then defined as

$$\mu_{\tilde{G}}(x) = \begin{cases} 0 & \text{if } f(x) \leq \sup_{R_1} f \\ \dfrac{f(x) - \sup_{R_1} f}{\sup_{S(\tilde{R})} f - \sup_{R_1} f} & \text{if } \sup_{R_1} f < f(x) < \sup_{S(\tilde{R})} f \\ 1 & \text{if } \sup_{S(\tilde{R})} f \leq f(x) \end{cases}$$

The corresponding membership function in functional space is then

$$\mu_{\tilde{G}}(r) := \begin{cases} \sup_{X \in f^{-1}(r)} \mu_{\tilde{G}}(x) & \text{if } r \in \mathrm{R}, f^{-1}(r) \neq 0 \\ 0 & \text{else} \end{cases} \qquad (13)$$

Adding this fuzzy set to the fuzzy sets defining the solution space gives again a symmetric model to which equation 10 or equation 12 can be applied. Definition 2 becomes easier to understand if we apply it to a specific given LP-structure.

Let us modify equation 3 by adding a set of crisp constraints, $Dx \leq b$, and changing the objective function to maximize $f(x)$. This yields model

$$\begin{aligned} \text{maximize} \quad & f(x) = c^{\mathrm{T}}x \\ \text{such that} \quad & \left.\begin{array}{l} Ax \lesssim b \\ Dx \leq b' \\ x \leq 0 \end{array}\right\} \tilde{\mathbf{R}} \end{aligned} \qquad (14)$$

Let the membership functions of the fuzzy sets representing the fuzzy constraints be defined in analogy to equation 8 as

$$\mu_i(x) = \begin{cases} 1 & \text{if } A_i x \leq b_i \\ \dfrac{b_i + p_i - A_i x}{p_i} & \text{if } b_i < A_i x \leq b_i + p_i \\ 0 & \text{if } A_i x > b_i + p_i \end{cases} \qquad (15)$$

On the basis of the two LPs following, the membership function of the fuzzy set defined in Definition 2 can then easily be defined:

$$\begin{aligned} \text{maximize} \quad & f(x) = c^{\mathrm{T}}x \\ \text{such that} \quad & Ax \leq b \\ & Dx \leq b' \\ & x \geq 0 \end{aligned} \qquad (16)$$

The optimal solution of this model is $f_1 = \sup_{R^1} f(c^{\mathrm{T}}x)_{\mathrm{opt}}$.

$$\begin{aligned} \text{maximize} \quad & f(x) = c^{\mathrm{T}}x \\ \text{such that} \quad & Ax \leq b + p \\ & Dx \leq b' \\ & x \geq 0 \end{aligned} \qquad (17)$$

The optimal solution of the model is $f_0 = \sup_{S(\tilde{R})} f = (c^{\mathrm{T}}x)_{\mathrm{opt}}$.

The membership function is therefore

$$\mu_{\tilde{G}}(x) = \begin{cases} 1 & \text{if } f_0 \leq c^{\mathrm{T}}x \\ \dfrac{c^{\mathrm{T}}x - f_i}{f_0 - f_1} & \text{if } f_1 < c_{\mathrm{T}}x < f_0 \\ 0 & \text{if } c^{\mathrm{T}}x \leq f_1 \end{cases} \qquad (18)$$

The equivalent model to equation 14 is therefore:

$$\begin{aligned} \text{maximize} \quad & \lambda \\ \text{such that} \quad & \lambda(f_0 - f_1 - c^{\mathrm{T}}x \leq -f_1 \\ & \lambda p + \quad Ax \leq b + p \\ & \qquad\quad Dx \leq b' \\ & \lambda \qquad\qquad \leq 1 \\ & \lambda, x \geq 0 \end{aligned} \qquad (19)$$

EXTENSIONS

So far, two major assumptions have been made in order to arrive at equivalent models that can be solved efficiently by standard LP methods:

1. Linear membership functions were assumed for all fuzzy sets involved.
2. The use of the minimum-operator for the aggregation of fuzzy sets was considered to be adequate.

The relaxation of these two assumptions leads to complications that vary in severity, depending on the type of relaxation.

Nonlinear Membership Functions. The linear membership functions used so far could all be defined by fixing two points, the upper and lower aspiration levels or the two bounds of the tolerance interval. The most obvious way to handle nonlinear membership functions is probably to approximate them piecewise by linear functions. Some authors (Hannan, 1981; Nakamura, 1984) have used this approach and shown that the resulting equivalent crisp problem is still a standard linear programming problem.

This problem, however, can be considerably larger than model 10 because in general one constraint will have to be added for each linear piece of the approximation. Quite often S-shaped membership functions have been suggested, particularly if the membership function is interpreted as a kind of utility function (representing the degree of satisfaction, acceptance, etc). Leberling (1981), for instance, suggests such a function that is also uniquely determined by two parameters. He suggests:

$$\mu_{\mathrm{H}}(x) = \frac{1}{2} \frac{\exp\left[\left(x - \dfrac{a+b}{2}\right)\delta\right] - \exp\left[-\left(x - \dfrac{a+b}{2}\right)\delta\right]}{\exp\left[\left(x - \dfrac{a+b}{2}\right)\delta\right] + \exp\left[-\left(x - \dfrac{a+b}{2}\right)\delta\right]}$$

with $a, b, \delta \geq 0$. This hyperbolic function has the following formal properties:

$\mu_{\mathrm{H}}(x)$ is strictly monotonously increasing.

$$\mu_{\mathrm{H}}(x) = \frac{1}{2}, \quad \text{where } x = \frac{a+b}{2}$$

$\mu_{\mathrm{H}}(x)$ is strictly convex on $[-\infty, (a+b)/2]$ and strictly concave on $[(a+b)/2, +\infty]$.

For all $x \in |\mathrm{R}: = 0 < \mu_{\mathrm{H}}(x) < 1$ and $\mu_{\mathrm{H}}(x)$ approaches asymptotically $f(x) = 0$ and $f(x) = 1$, respectively.

Leberling shows that choosing as lower and upper aspiration levels for the fuzzy objective function $z = cx$ of an LP $a = \underline{c}$ (lower bound of z) and $b = \bar{c}$ (upper limit of the objective function) and representing this (fuzzy) goal by a hyperbolic function one arrives at the following crisp equivalent problem for one fuzzy goal and all crisp constraints:

minimize λ

such that
$$\lambda - \frac{1}{2}\frac{e^{Z'(x)} - e^{-Z'(x)}}{e^{Z'(x)} + e^{-Z'(x)}} \le \frac{1}{2}$$
$$Dx \le b'$$
$$x, \lambda \ge 0 \tag{20}$$

with $Z'(x) = (\Sigma_j c_j x_j - \frac{1}{2}(\bar{c} + \underline{c})\,\delta$. For each additional fuzzy goal or constraint one of these exponential rows has, of course, to be added to equation 20.

$x_{n+1} = \tanh^{-1}(2\lambda - 1)$, model 20 is equivalent to the following linear model:

maximize x_{n+1}

such that
$$\delta \sum_j c_j x_j - x_{n+1} \ge \frac{1}{2}\delta(\bar{c} + \underline{c})$$
$$Dx \le b'$$
$$x_{n+1}, x \ge 0 \tag{21}$$

This is again a standard linear programming model that can be solved, for instance, by any available simplex code.

The above equivalence between models with nonlinear membership functions is not accidental. It has been proved that the following relationship hold (Werners, 1984, p. 143).

Theorem 1. Let $\{f_k\}$, $k = 1, \ldots, K$ be a finite family of functions f_k: $|\mathbb{R}^n \to |\mathbb{R}^1$, $x^0 \in X \subset |\mathbb{R}^n$. g: $|\mathbb{R}^1 \to |\mathbb{R}^1$ strictly monotonously increasing and $\lambda, \lambda' \in |\mathbb{R}$. Consider the two mathematical programming problems

maximize λ

such that $\lambda \le f_k(x)$ $\quad k = 1, \ldots, K$
$$x \in X \tag{22}$$

maximize λ'

such that $\lambda' \le g(f_k(x))$ $\quad k = 1, \ldots, K$
$$x \in X \tag{23}$$

If there exists a $\lambda^0 \in R'$ such that (λ^0, x^0) is the optimal solution of equation 22, then there exists a $\lambda'^0 \in R'$ such that (λ^0, x^0) is the optimal solution of equation 23.

Theorem 1 suggests that quite a number of nonlinear membership functions can be accommodated easily. Unluckily, the same optimism is not justified concerning other aggregation operators.

The computational efficiency of the approach mentioned so far has rested to a large extent on the use of the min-operator as a model for the logical "and" or the intersection of fuzzy sets, respectively. Axiomatic (Hamacher, 1978) as well as empirical (Thole and co-workers, 1979; Zimmermann and Zysno, 1980, 1983) investigations have shed some doubt on the general use of the min-operator in decision models. Quite a number of context free or context dependent operators have been suggested in the mean-

time (see, eg, Zimmermann, 1991, ch. 3). The disadvantage of these operators is, however, that the resulting crisp equivalent models are no longer linear (see, eg, Zimmermann, 1978, p. 45), which reduces the computational efficiency of these approaches considerably or even renders the equivalent models unsolvable within acceptable time limits. There are, however, some exceptions to this rule, and two of them are presented in more detail.

One of the objections against the min-operator (see, for instance, Zimmermann and Zysno, 1988) is the fact that neither the logical "and" nor the min-operator is compensatory in the sense that increases in the degree of membership in the fuzzy sets intersected might not influence at all membership in the resulting fuzzy set (aggregated fuzzy set or intersection). There are two quite natural ways to cure this weakness:

1. Combine the (limitational) min-operator as model for the logical "and" with the fully compensatory max-operator as a model for the inclusive "or". For the former, the product operator might be used alternatively and for the latter the algebraic sum might be used. This approach departs from distinguishing between "and" and "or" aggregation as being somewhere between the "and" and the "or". (Therefore it is often called compensatory and.)

2. Stick with the distinction between "and" and "or" aggregators and introduce a certain degree of compensation into these connectives.

Compensatory "and". For some applications it seems to be important that the aggregator used maps above the max-operator and below the min-operator. The λ-operator (Zimmermann and Zysno, 1980) would be such a connective. For purposes of mathematical programming it has, however, the abovementioned disadvantage of low computational efficiency. An acceptable compromise between empirical fit and computational efficiency seems to be the convex combination of the min-operator and the max-operator:

$$\mu_C(x) = \gamma \min_{i=1}^m \mu_i(x) + (1 - \gamma)\max_{i=1}^m \mu_i(x) \qquad \gamma \in [0, 1] \tag{24}$$

For determining the maximizing decision the following problem has to be solved.

$$\max_{x \in X} \left(\gamma \min_{i=1}^m \{\mu_i(x)\} + (1 - \gamma)\max_{i=1}^m \mu_i\{\mu_i(x)\}\right)$$

or

maximize $\gamma \cdot \lambda_1 + (1 - \gamma)\lambda_2$

such that $\lambda_1 \le \mu_i(x)$ $\quad i = 1, \ldots, m$
$\quad\quad\quad\lambda_2 \le \mu_i(x)$ $\quad$ for at least one $i \in \{1, \ldots, m\}$
$\quad\quad\quad x \in X$

or

maximize $\gamma\lambda_1 + (1 - \gamma)\lambda_2$

such that $\lambda_1 \le \mu_i(x)$ $\quad\quad i = 1, \ldots, m$
$\quad\quad\quad\lambda_2 \le \mu_i(x) + M\gamma_i$ $\quad i = 1, \ldots, m$

$$\sum_{i=1}^{m} \gamma_i \le m - 1$$

$\gamma \in \{0, 1\}$, M is a very large real number

$x \in X$

For linear membership functions of the goals and the constraints, equation 25 is a mixed integer linear program that can be solved by the appropriate available codes.

If one wants to distinguish between an "and" aggregation and an "or" aggregation (for instance, for the sake of easier modeling), one may want to use the following operators.

Definition 3 (Werners 1984). Let $\mu_i(x)$ be the membership functions of fuzzy sets that are to be aggregated in the sense of a fuzzy and (añd). The membership function of the resulting fuzzy set is defined to be

$$\mu_{\widetilde{and}}(x) = \gamma \cdot \min_{i=1}^{m} \mu_i(x) + (1 - \gamma) \frac{1}{m} \Sigma \mu_i(x)$$

with $\gamma \in [0, 1]$.

Definition 4 (Werners 1984). Let $\mu_i(x)$ be membership functions of fuzzy sets to be aggregated in the sense of a fuzzy or (õr). The membership function of the resulting fuzzy set is then defined as

$$\mu_{\widetilde{or}}(x) = \gamma \cdot \max_{i=1}^{m} \mu_i(x) + (1 - \gamma) \frac{1}{m} \sum_{i=1}^{m} \mu_i(x)$$

[with $\gamma \in [0, 1]$.

These two connectives are not inductive and associative, but they are commutative, idempotent, strictly monotonic increasing in each component, continuous, and compensatory (Werners 1984, p. 168). These are certainly very useful and acceptable properties.

If we use the aggregation operator from Definition 2 in model 4, then the equivalent model is:

$$\text{maximize} \quad \lambda + (1 - \gamma) \frac{1}{m} \sum_{i=1}^{m} \lambda_i$$

$$\text{such that} \quad \lambda + \lambda_i \le \mu_i(x) \quad i = 1, \ldots, m$$
$$Dx \le d$$
$$\lambda, \lambda_i, x \ge 0$$
$$0 \le \mu_i(x) \le 1 \quad (26)$$

If $(\lambda^0, \lambda_i^0, x^0)$ is the optimal solution of equation 26, then x^0 is a maximizing solution to equation 3. It is obvious that if $\mu_i(x)$ are linear, equation 26 is again a standard linear programming problem.

So far, the reference model from which we have departed has always been the standard LP. Depending on the type of operator chosen and the operator used, the equivalent model turns out to be either a linear or a nonlinear programming model. Obviously, other reference models can be chosen as reference models. This has already been done, for instance, for integer programming (Zimmermann and Pollatschek, 1984; Ignizio and Daniels, 1983), fractional programming (Luhandjula, 1984), and nonlinear programming (Sakawa and Yano, 1989a,

1989b). The interrelationships between stochastic and fuzzy programming and their possible integration have also been investigated (Buckley, 1990; Dubois and Prade, 1988).

FUZZY MATHEMATICAL PROGRAMMING WITH FUZZY PARAMETERS

Even for the basic approach described above, a unique formulation for the equivalent model, which must eventually be solved, does not exist. The diversity of algorithmic approaches is even larger if other types of fuzzification of elements of mathematical programming models are considered. To demonstrate the basic idea behind most of the approaches, this article will describe an easy-to-understand suggestion. More general models can be found in the literature.

Ramík and Rímánek (1985) consider the problem

$$\text{maximize} \quad f(x)$$

$$\text{such that} \quad \tilde{a}_{i1}x_1 \oplus \tilde{a}_{i2}x_2 \oplus \ldots \oplus \tilde{a}_{in}x_n \le \tilde{b}_i, i = 1, \ldots, m$$
$$x_j \ge 0, j = , \ldots, n \quad (27)$$

The $\tilde{a}_{ij}$ and the $\tilde{b}_i$ are supposed to be fuzzy numbers in L-R-representation. $\oplus$ denotes the extended addition. They show that for two fuzzy L-R numbers $\tilde{a} = (m, n, \alpha, \beta)_{\text{L-R}}$ and $\tilde{b} = (p, q, \gamma, \delta)_{\text{L-R}}$ $\tilde{a} \le \tilde{b}$ holds iff the following four inequalities hold:

$$\varepsilon_L(\gamma - \alpha) \le p - m \qquad \delta_L(\gamma - \alpha) \le p - m$$
$$\varepsilon_R(\beta - \delta) \le q - n \qquad \delta_R(\beta - \delta) \le q - n \quad (28)$$

where $\varepsilon_R = \sup \{u; R(u) = R(0) = 1\}$,

$$\delta_R = \inf \{n; R(n) = \lim_{S \to \infty} R(s)\}$$

and ε_L, δ_L correspondingly for L

For symmetric fuzzy numbers $\tilde{a} = (m, m, \alpha, \alpha)_{\text{L-L}}$. As shown in Figure 1, system 28 reduces to

$$\varepsilon_L|\alpha - \gamma| \le p - m \qquad \delta_2|\alpha - \gamma| \le p - m \quad (29)$$

On the basis of a lemma that they proof in their paper:

$$\tilde{a}_{i1}x_1 \oplus \cdots \oplus \tilde{a}_{in}x_n$$
$$= \left(\sum_j m_{ij}x_j, \sum_j n_{ij}x_j, \sum \alpha_{ij}x_j, \sum B_{ij}x_j \right) \quad (30)$$

Hence, the constraints of equation 27 can be written as

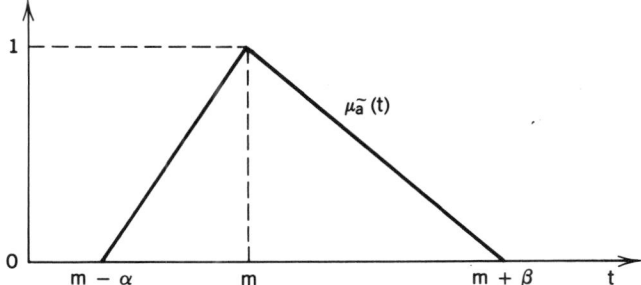

Figure 1. Fuzzy triangular number $\tilde{a} = (m, m, \alpha, \beta)_{\text{L-L}}$.

$$-\varepsilon_L \left(\sum_{j=1}^{n} \alpha_{ij} x_j - \gamma_i \right) \leq p_i - \sum_{j=1}^{n} m_{ij} x_i$$

$$-\delta_L \left(\frac{n}{j=1} \alpha_{ij} x_j - \gamma_i \right) \leq p_i - \sum_{j=1}^{n} m_{ij} x_j$$

$$\varepsilon_R \left(\sum_{j=1}^{n} \beta_{ij} x_j - \delta_i \right) \leq q_i - \sum_{j=1}^{n} n_{ij} x_j$$

$$\delta_R \left(\sum_{j=1}^{n} \beta_{ij} x_j - \delta_i \right) \leq q_i - \sum_{j=1}^{n} n_{ij} x_j \qquad (31)$$

Equation 31 is a system of crisp linear inequalities, which—together with the crisp objective function—can now be solved with any classic LP-method. Not counting the nonnegativity constraints, the number of rows in equation 31 is, however, four times as large as that of equation 27. It should also be noted that equation 28 is a specific interpretation of the fuzzy inequality relation. Two other interpretations are offered by Ramíle and Rímánele (1985), which lead to slightly different results.

Complementary approaches to the one described above are Tanaka and Asai, 1984; Tanaka and co-workers, 1985. There similar assumptions concerning the fuzzy sets are made, but the objective function(s) and the nonnegativity constraints are also fuzzified. Also Rommelfanger (1989) goes into this direction.

More general treatments of this problem can be found in Delgado and co-workers (1989), Dubois (1987), Orlovski (1985), and others.

BIBLIOGRAPHY

K. Asai, H. Tanaka, and T. Okuda, "Decision Making and its Goal in a Fuzzy Environment," in Zadeh and co-workers, 1975, pp. 257–277.

R. E. Bellman and L. A. Zadeh, "Decision-Making in a Fuzzy Environment," *Management Sci.* **17**, B141–164 (1970).

J. J. Buckley, "Solving Possibilistic Linear Programming Problems," *Fuzzy Sets Syst.* **31**, 329–341 (1989).

J. J. Buckley "Stochastic Versus Possibilistic Programming," *Fuzzy Sets Syst.* **34**, 173–177 (1990).

S. Chanas, "Fuzzy Programming in Multiobjective Linear Programming—A Parametric Approach," *Fuzzy Sets Syst.* **29**, 303–313 (1989).

M. Delgado, J. L. Verdegay, and M. A. Vila, "A General Model for Fuzzy Linear Programming," *Fuzzy Sets Syst.* **29**, 21–29 (1989).

D. Dubois, "Linear Programming with Fuzzy Data," in J. C. Bezdek, ed., in *Analysis of Fuzzy Information*, Vol. 3. *Applications in Engineering and Science*, CRC Press, Boca Raton, Fla., 1987.

D. Dubois and H. Prade, "Systems of Linear Fuzzy Constraints," *Fuzzy Sets Syst.* **3**, 37–48 (1980).

D. Dubois and H. Prade, *Possibility Theory*, Plenum, New York, 1988.

L. Fabian and M. Stoica, "Fuzzy Integer Programming" in Zimmermann and co-workers, 1984, 123–132.

H. Hamacher, *Über logische Aggregationen nicht binär expliziter Entscheidungskriterien*, Fischer-Verlag, Frankfurt am Main, Germany, 1978.

H. Hamacher, H. Leberling, and H.-J. Zimmermann, "Sensitivity Analysis in Fuzzy Linear Programming," *Fuzzy Sets Syst.* **1**, 269–281 (1978).

E. L. Hannan, "Linear Programming with Multiple Fuzzy Goals," *Fuzzy Sets Syst.* **6**, 235–248 (1981).

J. P. Ignizio and S. C. Daniels, "Fuzzy Multicriteria Integer Programming via Fuzzy Generalized Networks," *Fuzzy Sets Syst.* **10**, 261–270 (1983).

H. Leberling, "On Finding Compromise Solutions in Multicriteria Problems Using the Fuzzy Min-Operator," *Fuzzy Sets Syst.* **6**, 105–118 (1981).

M. K. Luhandjula, "Fuzzy Approaches for Multiple Objective Linear Fractional Optimization," *Fuzzy Sets Syst.* **13**, 11–24 (1984).

K. Nakamura, "Some Extensions of Fuzzy Linear Programming," *Fuzzy Sets Syst.* **14**, 211–229 (1984).

S. A. Orlovski, "Mathematical Programming Problems with Fuzzy Parameters," in J. Kacprzyk and R. R. Yager, eds., *Management Decision Support Systems Using Fuzzy Sets and Possibility Theory*, TÜV, Cologne, Germany, 1985, 136–145.

J. Ramík and J. Rímánek, "Inequality Relation Between Fuzzy Numbers and Its Use in Fuzzy Optimization," *Fuzzy Sets Syst.* **16**, 123–138 (1985).

W. Rödder and H.-J. Zimmermann, "Duality in Fuzzy Linear Programming," in A. V. Fiacco and K. O. Kortanek, eds., *Extremal Methods and Systems Analyses*, Springer, New York, 1980, 415–429.

H. Rommelfanger, R. Hanuscheck, and J. Wolf, "Linear Programming with Fuzzy Objectives," *Fuzzy Sets Syst.* **29**, 31–48 (1989).

M. Sakawa and H. Yano, "Interactive Decision Making for Multiobjective Nonlinear Programming Problems with Fuzzy Parameters," *Fuzzy Sets Syst.* **29**, 315–326 (1989a).

M. Sakawa and H. Yano, "An Interactive Fuzzy Satisficing Method for Multiobjective Nonlinear Programming Problems with Fuzzy Parameters," *Fuzzy Sets Syst.* **30**, 221–238 (1989b).

H. Tanaka and K. Asai, "Fuzzy Linear Programming Problems with Fuzzy Numbers," *Fuzzy Sets Syst.* **13**, 1–10 (1989).

H. Tanaka, H. Ichihashi, and K. Asai, "Fuzzy Decision in Linear Programming Problems with Trapezoid Fuzzy Parameters," in J. Kacprzyk and R. R. Yager, eds., *Management Decision Support Systems Using Fuzzy Sets and Possibility Theory*, TÜV, Cologne, Germany, 1985, 146–154.

H. Tanaka, T. Okuda, and K. Asai, "On Fuzzy Mathematical Programming," *J. Cybern.* **3**, 37–46 (1974).

U. Thole, H.-J. Zimmermann, and P. Zysno, "On the Suitability of Minimum and Product Operators for the Intersection of Fuzzy Sets," *Fuzzy Sets Syst.* **2**, 167–180 (1979).

B. Werners, "Interaktive Entscheidungsunterstützung durch ein flexibles mathematisches Programmierungssystem," Dissertation, RWTH Aachen, Munich, Germany, 1984.

B. Werners, "Interactive Multiple Objective Programming Subject to Flexible Constraints," *EJOR* **31**, 324–349 (1987).

L. A. Zadeh, K. S. Fu, K. Tanaka, and M. Shimura, eds., *Fuzzy Sets and their Applications to Cognitive and Decision Processes*, Academic Press, New York, 1975.

H.-J. Zimmermann, "Description and Optimization of Fuzzy Systems," *Int. J. Gen. Syst.* **2**, 209–215 (1976).

H.-J. Zimmermann, "Fuzzy Programming and Linear Programming with Several Objective Functions," *Fuzzy Sets Syst.* **1**, 45–55 (1978).

H.-J. Zimmermann, "Fuzzy Set Theory and Mathematical Programming" in A. Jones and co-workers, eds., *Fuzzy Sets Theory and Applications*, Reidel, 1986, 99–114.

H.-J. Zimmermann, "Fuzzy Sets, Decision Making and Expert Systems," Kluwer, Boston, 1987.

H.-J. Zimmermann, *Fuzzy Set Theory—and its Applications*, rev. ed., Kluwer, Boston, 1991.

H.-J. Zimmermann and M. A. Pollatschek, "Fuzzy 0-1 Programs" in Zimmermann and co-workers, 1984, 133–146.

H.-J. Zimmermann, L. A. Zadeh, and B. R. Gaines, eds., *Fuzzy Sets and Decision Analysis*, North Holland, New York, 1984.

H.-J. Zimmermann and P. Zysno, "Latent Connectives in Human Decision Making," *Fuzzy Sets Syst.* **4**, 37–51, 1980.

H.-J. Zimmermann and P. Zysno, "Decisions and Evaluations by Hierarchical Aggregation of Information," *Fuzzy Sets Syst.* **10**, 243–266 (1983).

H.-J. Zimmermann
Rheinisch-Westfällische
Technische Hochschule
Aachen

FUZZY AND PROBABILISTIC UNCERTAINTIES

Classical AI represents knowledge in terms of first-order logic or similar symbolic systems. Symbol manipulation syntactic theorem proving methods with pattern-directed search are used for answering queries about a knowledge base. For many areas of application, such methods are not applicable because information is incomplete. This incompleteness makes probability theory and statistical analysis relevant (Cox, 1961; Smith and Erickson, 1988; Polya, 1954; Jaynes, 1957; Savage, 1954; Garbolino, 1988a, 1988b). This influenced the form of the early expert systems such as Bayesian nets and MYCIN-type systems (Adams, 1976; Shortliffe, 1976). MYCIN (qv) was also influenced by fuzzy set theory (Zadeh, 1965). Both probability and fuzzy set theories play a prominent role in the treatment of uncertainty in knowledge base systems (Nilsson, 1986; Zadeh, 1983). In general terms it can be said that probabilistic uncertainty is concerned with missing data at the time the query is asked whereas fuzzy uncertainty represents the imprecision in the definitions of the various predicates. Such concepts as stable system, fair society, tall person, large house, good student, etc cannot be defined precisely in terms of necessary and sufficient conditions. Some necessary conditions can be given, but examples of the concept in terms of features are used to guide the decision of whether to accept that a given concept is satisfied (Smith and Medin, 1981; Ralescue and Baldwin, 1988; Davey and Priestley, 1990).

Probability and Possibility Distributions

A form of knowledge representation that allows uncertainties to be represented by numbers, and for these to be modified to answer a query, is the frame of discernment. Each variable of the knowledge base is allocated a set of possible values it can be instantiated to, the frame of discernment for that variable. A probability distribution can be associated over the set of possible values for any variable. This would say that one value was more likely than another. A possibility distribution can be associated over the frame of discernment, which describes the degree of possibility that the variable can have such a value (Zadeh, 1978). Possibility distributions are related to fuzzy sets. If a variable V with a frame of discernment X has the fuzzy value x defined by the membership function $X_x(.)$ then the possibility distribution over X is given by $X_x(.)$. Joint probability and possibility distributions can also be defined over label variables where a label variable is a concatenation of variables. This will be the usual form of expressing knowledge statements.

Mass Assignments

A further incompleteness in the knowledge may exist, namely that a complete probability distribution over the frame of discernment cannot be given. In this case a distribution may be given over the power set of the frame of discernment, which will be called a mass assignment (Shafer, 1976). Using a voting model semantics (Baldwin, 1990a) it will be shown that a possibility distribution over the frame of discernment can also be interpreted in terms of a mass assignment over nested subsets. Mass assignments can be combined, corresponding to the conjunction of two knowledge statements, aggregated, corresponding to the combination of alternative knowledge statements and updated, corresponding to forming *a posteriori* mass assignment from an *a priori* mass assignment when given some specific knowledge also expressed as a mass assignment. In the latter case the *a priori* mass assignment corresponds to general knowledge such as relevant to a population as a whole or as given by rules applicable in general. This updating does not cause difficulty with the nonmonotonic logic problem (Ginsberg, 1987). For example, the *a priori* mass assignment would express that most birds can fly but given the specific information that an object is a penguin, the update would indicate that the penguin, although a bird, cannot fly.

Support Logic Programming

Support pairs are associated with mass assignments and represents an interval containing a probability. Knowledge can be represented as rules similar in style to PROLOG clauses but with the addition of support pairs to represent uncertainty. Knowledge systems of this type can be used like PROLOG programs to model applications and are ideal for developing expert systems. This has been called support logic programming (Baldwin, 1986) and implemented in an AI language FRIL (Baldwin and co-workers, 1987). The inference mechanism of support logic programming is based on the philosophy of updating mass assignments. It is, therefore, a form of conditioning and the rules are interpreted in terms of conditional mass assignments rather than implication statements. This brings together inference techniques from logic, probability theory, and fuzzy logic. The language FRIL implements the support logic programming and also ordinary PROLOG. It contains trace packages suitable for ordinary PROLOG programs and a diagnostic shell for testing support logic programs. It contains fuzzy arithmetic predicates and a conceptual graph toolkit (Sowa, 1984), which allows the user to use the conceptual graph alternative form of knowledge representation. Various models of inference can be used in FRIL, depending on the degree of "fill in" of the incomplete information that is desired. Decomposition methods are used to break down the search for the answer to a query into subproblems. One form of decomposition is similar to an ordinary PROLOG control mechanism with support evaluation performed for each possible proof path. These supports are then combined to give the overall support. This cannot always be used and the computational requirements increase for the more complicated cases. A parallel processing machine is suggested that exploits the updating model of the inference used.

SUPPORT PAIRS AND MASS ASSIGNMENTS

Mass Assignments

A mass assignment over a finite frame of discernment X, where X is a set of labels, is a function $m: P(X) \to [0,1]$ where $P(X)$ is the power set of X such that $m(\varnothing) = 0$ and

$$\sum_{A \varepsilon P(X)} m(A) \ 1$$

This corresponds to the basic probability assignment function of the Dempster-Shafer theory (qv) of evidence (Shafer, 1976; Klir and Folger, 1988; Gordon and Shortliffe, 1984). $m(A)$ represents a probability mass assigned exactly to A. It does not include any masses assigned to subsets of A.

The concept of belief and plausibility measures (Shafer, 1976, 1981a, 1981b; Shafer and Tversky, 1985; Shenoy and Shafer, 1990) is used to define necessary support and possible support measures. Names are changed to be consistent with the notation used in support logic programming (Baldwin, 1986, 1987) and the FRIL language (Baldwin and co-workers, 1987) and to avoid confusion with conclusions and derived results based on the use of the Dempster rule of combining evidences (Zadeh, 1986; Smets, 1988, 1990). The methods given here do not use the Dempster rule (Dempster, 1968), and the necessary and possible supports are more in keeping with upper and lower probabilities (Dubois and Prade, 1986). A discussion of belief functions in reasoning has been published (Pearl 1990).

A necessary support measure is a function Sn: $P(X) \to [0,1]$ where X is a set of labels, and $P(X)$ is the power set of X that satisfies the axioms that follow for every collection of subsets of X.

Axiom 1. Boundary Condition.

Sn$(\varnothing) = 0$ and Sn$(X) = 1$ where $\varnothing$ is the empty set

Axiom 2. For every collection of subsets of X,

$$\text{Sn}(A_1 \cup A_2 \cup \ldots \cup A_n) \geq \Sigma_i \, \text{Sn}(A_i) - \Sigma_{i<j} \, \text{Sn}(A_i \cap A_j)$$
$$+ \ldots + (-1)^{n+1} \, \text{Sn}(A_1 \cap A_2 \cap \ldots \cap A_n)$$

For each $A \varepsilon P(X)$, Sn(A) is interpreted as the necessary support, based on available evidence, that a given label of X belongs to the set A of labels. When the sets A_1, $A_2, \ldots, A_n$ in axiom 2 are pairwise disjoint, ie, when $(A_i \cap A_j) = \varnothing$ for all $i, j \varepsilon \{1, 2, \ldots, n\}$ such that $i \neq j$, the axiom requires that the necessary support associated with the union of the sets is not smaller than the sum of the necessary supports pertaining to the individual sets. The basic axiom of necessary support measures is thus a weaker version of the additivity axiom of probability theory.

Possible Support Measure. Associated with each necessary support measure is a possible support measure Sp, defined by the equation

$$\text{Sp}(A) = 1 - \text{Sn}(\overline{A})$$

for all $A \varepsilon P(X)$.
Similarly,

$$\text{Sn}(A) = 1 - \text{Sp}(\overline{A})$$

Given a basic mass assignment m, a necessary support measure and a possible support measure are given by the formulas

$$\text{Sn}(A) = \sum_{B \subseteq A} \text{m}(B)$$

and

$$\text{Sp}(A) = \sum_{A \cap B \neq \varnothing} m(B)$$

which are applicable for all $A \varepsilon P(X)$.

Focal Elements. Every set $A \varepsilon P(X)$ for which $m(A) > 0$ is called a focal element of m. The mass assignment can be represented as (m, F) where F is the set of focal elements. Total ignorance is expressed in terms of the mass assignment by $m(X) = 1$ and $m(A) = 0$ for all $A \neq X$. Using the formula above for Sn in terms of m, total ignorance can also be expressed as Sn$(X) = 1$ and Sn$(A) = 0$ for all $A \neq X$. The total ignorance in terms of the possible support measure is Sp$(\varnothing) = 0$ and Sp$(A) = 1$ for all $A \neq \varnothing$.

A support pair for $A \varepsilon P(X)$ is given by [MIN Sn(A), MAX Sp(A)]. This defines an interval containing the Pr(A) where the MIN and MAX are over the set of values of any possible parameters that Sn(A) and Sp(A) may depend on.

General Assignment Method for Combining Mass Assignments

Let $m1$ and $m2$ be two mass assignments over the power set $P(X)$ where X is a set of labels. Evidence 1 and evidence 2 are denoted by $(m1, F1)$ and $(m2, F2)$, respectively, where $F1$ and $F2$ are the sets of focal elements of $P(X)$ for $m1$ and $m2$, respectively. Suppose $F1 = \{L1k\}$ for $k = 1, \ldots, n1$ and $F2 = \{L2k\}$ for $k = 1, \ldots, n2$ then Lij is a subset of $P(X)$ for which $mi(Li_j) \neq 0$. Let $(m\ F)$ be the evidence resulting from combining evidence 1 with evidence 2 using the general assignment method. This is denoted

$$(m, F) = (m1, F1) \oplus (m2, F2) \text{ where}$$

$$F = \{L1i \cap L2j \mid m(L1i \cap L2j) \neq 0\}$$

$$m(Y) = \sum_{ij:L1i \cap L2j = Y} m'(L1i \cap L2j)$$

for any $Y \, \varepsilon \, F$.
$m'(L1i \cap L2j)$ for $i = 1, \ldots, n1; j = 1, \ldots, n2$ satisfies

$$\sum_j m'(L1i \cap L2j) = m1(L1i)$$

and

$$\sum_i m'(L1i \cap L2j) = m(L2j)$$

for $i = 1, \ldots, n1$ and $j = 1, \ldots, n2$.
$m'(L1i \cap L2j) = 0$ if $L1i \cap L2j = \varnothing$ the empty set; for $i = 1, \ldots, n1; j = 1, \ldots, n2$. If there are more than two evidences to combine, then they are combined two at a time. In general, the solution (m, F) will not be unique and a parameterized family of solutions will be obtained. These possible parameter values must be taken into account when determining support pairs from the necessary and possible support measures. In the case when each member of the family of solutions corresponds to a probability distribution over a partition of X, a unique solution may be obtained by choosing that member of the family of distributions that maximizes the entropy of the system. A more detailed discussion of the general assignment method has been published (Baldwin, 1990b, in press a, in press b, in press c).

Example. Consider the given information $\Pr(a) = 0.9$, corresponding to the mass assignment $m(a) = 0.9$, $m(\neg a) = 0.1$, and $\Pr(b) = [0.8, 1]$, corresponding to the mass assignment $m(b) = 0.8$, $m(\_) = 0.2$, where "_" signifies b or $\neg b$. These can be combined to give $m(ab) = 0.7$, $m(\{a\_\}) = 0.1$, $m(\{\_b\}) = 0.1$, $m(\{\_\_\}) = 0.1$ where "_" in first position stands for a or $\neg a$ and in second position stands for b or $\neg b$ (Fig. 1a). This, the combined mass assignment is the parameterized assignment shown in Figure 1b. For each row in Figure 1a, the addition of the assignments of the row cells equals the given row assignment, and similarly for each of the columns. Any allowed value of x can be added and subtracted around the loop so that a parameterized assignment results. A maximum entropy criterion could be used to obtain a unique mass assignment from this family of assignments.

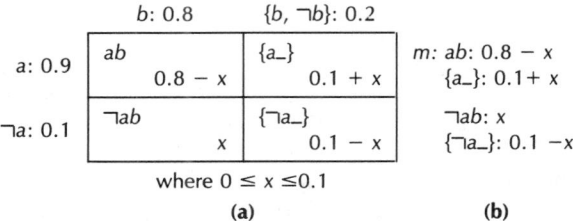

where $0 \le x \le 0.1$

(a)   (b)

Figure 1. Example of the general assignment method: (a) mass assignments for Example 1; (b) the combined mass assignment.

Fuzzy Sets and Mass Assignments

A mass assignment can be associated with any normalized fuzzy set (Klir and Folger, 1988; Baldwin, 1990a). Let $X = \{x1, x2, \ldots, xn\}$ and $A1, A2, \ldots, An$ be nested subsets of X such that

$$A1 \subset A2 \ldots \subset An \text{ where } Ai = \{x1, \ldots, xi\}$$

Let $\mathbf{f} \subset X$ be a normalized fuzzy set with membership function X such that

$$\mathbf{f} = x1/X_1 + x2/X_2 + \ldots + xn/X_n$$

where $X_1 = 1$ and $X_1 \ge X_2 \ge \ldots \ge X_n$.
This induces a possibility distribution p_f over X given by $p_f(xi) = X_i$ with an associated mass assignment over the nested sets $\{Ai\}$ given by

$$m(A1) = 1 - X_2; \ldots,: m(Ai) = X_i - X_{i+1}; \ldots; m(An) = X_n$$

This mass assignment represents the family of possible probability distributions over X induced by the fuzzy set $\mathbf{f}$. This can be generalized to the case of continuous fuzzy sets (Baldwin and Pilsworth, 1990). The continuous case can always be treated by approximating the continuous fuzzy set $\mathbf{f}$ with membership function X_f defined over R by a discrete set of pairs $\{xi/X_i\}$ where $X_f(xi) = X_i$ and the interval R is approximated by the set of points $\{x1, x2, \ldots, xn\}$. Following is an example of a fuzzy set and its associated mass assignment, having a voting model semantics (Baldwin, 1990a).

$$\mathbf{f} = a/1 + b/0.8 + c/0.5 + d/0.1$$

$$m_f:- a: 0.2 \; \{a,b\}: 0.3; \{a,b,c\}: 0.4; \{a,b,c,d\}: 0.1$$

Voting Model Semantics. A voting model with constant thresholds will be used to interpret the meaning of a fuzzy set. Consider the fuzzy set *tall* defined on the height space (4 feet, 8 feet) by means of the membership function X_{tall}. How can X_{tall} (5 feet, 10 inches) be interpreted? Consider a representative population sample of persons S. Each member of S is asked to accept or reject the height 5 feet, 10 inches as satisfying the concept *tall*. Each member must accept or reject; there is no allowed abstention. X_{tall}(5 feet, 10 inches) is put equal to the proportion of S

who accept. The fuzzy set can, therefore, be interpreted as $f1 = a/0.2 + b/0.4 + c/0.8 + d/1$ defined on $\{a, b, c, d, e\}$ as 20% of S accept a as $f1$, 40% of S accept b as $f1$, 80% of S accept c as $f1$, 100% of S accept d as $f1$, 100% of S reject e as $f1$.

One possible voting pattern of acceptances is

1	2	3	4	5	6	7	8	9	10
a	a								
b	b	b	b						
c	c	c	c	c	c	c	c		
d	d	d	d	d	d	d	d	d	d

An alternative pattern is

1	2	3	4	5	6	7	8	9	10
a		a							
b	b		b		b				
c		c		c	c	c	c	c	c
d	d	d	d	d	d	d	d	d	d

The first pattern is more reasonable than the second. In the second pattern, voter 3 accepts a, which has a low membership level but doesn't accept b, which has a higher membership level. It seems that anyone who accepts a member with a certain membership level will accept all members with a higher membership level. This is called the constant threshold assumption. The first pattern satisfies the constant threshold assumption. From the first pattern it can be deduced that 20% of S give acceptance to exactly $\{d\}$, 40% of S give acceptance to exactly $\{c,d\}$, 20% of S accept exactly $\{b, c, d\}$, and 20% of S accept exactly $\{a, b, c, d\}$. This defines a mass assignment over the nested sets $\{d\}$, $\{c, d\}$, $\{b, c, d\}$, and $\{a, b, c, d\}$, namely $\{d\}$: 0.2, $\{c, d\}$: 0.4, $\{b, c, d\}$: 0.2, and $\{a, b, c, d\}$: 0.2. This interpretation is not valid if the fuzzy set is nonnormalized, because the constant threshold model cannot be satisfied.

Nonnormalized fuzzy sets can be treated as an intersection of normalized fuzzy sets. For example, the nonnormalised fuzzy set $g = a/0.9 + b/0.7 + c/0.3$ is the intersection of $g1 = 1/a + 0.7/b + c/0.3$ with m_{g1}: $-a$: 0.3, $\{a, b\}$: 0.4, and $\{a, b, c\}$: 0.3 and $g2 = 0.9/a + b/1 + c/1$ with m_{g2}: $-\{c, b\}$: 0.1 and $\{a, b, c\}$: 0.9. m_{g1} and m_{g2} can be combined using the general assignment method defined above to give $m_{g1} \oplus m_{g1}$: $-a$: 0.3, b: 0.1, $\{a, b\}$: 0.3, and $\{a, b, c\}$: 0.3, where the assignment given to $\{a,b,c\}$ is maximized to give a unique solution. Other solutions of the general assignment method would imply additional assumptions. The solution given is the least restrictive. Consonant approximations of belief functions to aid computation have been discussed (Dubois and Prade, 1990a). It is necessary that the sum of the membership values in g is at least 1 for this method to be valid.

Mass Assignments for Fuzzy Input–Output Pairs

Consider a black box system with possible input A from the set X and output B from the set Y. The behavior of the system is known from a finite number of input–output fuzzy observations as follows

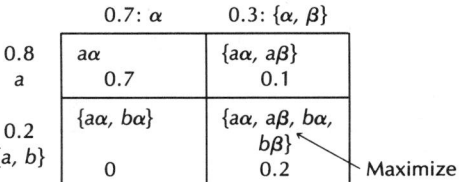

Figure 2. Example of input–output pairs.

A is **f1**, B is **g1** was observed $w1\%$ of the time.
A is **f2**, B is **g2** was observed $w2\%$ of the time.
. . .
A is **fn** if B is **gn** was observed $wn\%$ of the time.

where **fi** $\subset X$ and **gi** $\subset Y$. The mass assignment for the aggregation of these alternatives is defined as

$$m = w1(m_{g1} \oplus^{lr} m_{f1}) + w2(m_{g2} \oplus^{lr} m_{f2}) + \ldots + wn(m_{gn} \oplus^{lr} m_{fn})$$

where $\oplus^{lr}$ means that the least restrictive mass assignment solution is chosen.

Example. let $X = \{a, b, c\}$ and $Y = \{\alpha, \beta, \gamma\}$. Some example input–output pairs are as follows:

A is **f1**, B is **g1** occurs three times where $\mathbf{f1} = a/1 + b/0.2$ and $\mathbf{g1} = \alpha/1 + \beta/0.3$.

A is **f2**, B is **g2** occurs one time where $\mathbf{f2} = a/0.1 + b/1 + c/0.2$ and $\mathbf{g2} = \alpha/0.1 + \beta/1 + \gamma/0.3$.

A is **f3**, B is **g3** occurs two times where $\mathbf{f3} = b/0.2 + c/1$ and $\mathbf{g3} = \beta/0.1 + \gamma/1$

This results in the following (see Figure 2):

$m_{f1} = <a: 0.8, \{a, b\}: 0.2>$ $m_{g1} = <\alpha: 0.7, \{\alpha, \beta\}: 0.3>$

$m_{f2} = <b: 0.8, \{b,c\}: 0.1, \{a, b, c\}: 0.1\}>$
$\qquad m_{g2} = <\beta: 0.7, \{\beta, \gamma\}: 0.2, \{\alpha, \beta, \gamma\}: 0.1>$

$m_{f3} = <c: 0.8, \{b, c\}: 0.2>$ $m_{g3} = <\gamma: 0.9, \{\beta, \gamma\}: 0.1>$

$m_{f1} \oplus m_{g1} = <a\alpha: 0.7, \{a\alpha, a\beta\}: 0.1, \{a\alpha, a\beta, b\alpha, b\beta\}: 0.2>$

Similarly,

$m_{f2} \oplus m_{g2} = <b\beta: 0.7, \{b\beta, b\gamma\}: 0.1,$
$\qquad\qquad\qquad \{b\beta, b\gamma, c\beta, c\gamma\}: 0.1, \{\_\_\}: 0.1>$

and

$m_{f3} \oplus m_{g3} = <c\gamma: 0.8, \{b\gamma, c\gamma\}: 0.1, \{b\beta, b\gamma, c\beta, c\gamma\}: 0.1>$

The weighted combination of these mass assignments, taking into account the frequencies of occurrence of each example input–output pair is given by

m:-	$a\alpha$: 0.35	$b\beta$: 0.1167	$c\gamma$: 0.2667
	$\{a\alpha, a\beta\}$: 0.05	$\{b\beta, b\gamma\}$: 0.0167	$\{b\gamma, c\gamma\}$: 0.0333
	$\{a\alpha, a\beta, b\alpha, b\beta\}$: 0.1	$\{b\beta, b\gamma, c\beta, c\gamma\}$: 0.05	$\{\_\_\}$: 0.0167

It should be noted that the entry of 0.05 in $\{b\beta, b\gamma, c\beta, c\gamma\}$ comes from the addition of 0.0167 associated with $\{b\beta, b\gamma, c\beta, c\gamma\}$ from $(m_{\mathbf{f3}} \oplus m_{\mathbf{g3}})$ and 0.0333 associated with $(m_{\mathbf{f2}} \oplus m_{\mathbf{g2}})$. An alternative viewpoint of treating input–output pairs as implication statements has been discussed along with many related aspects of fuzzy logic (Dubois and Prade, 1990a).

SUPPORT LOGIC PROGRAMMING INFERENCE FROM RULES

The support logic programming system assumes that the probability evaluation of some proposition can be performed as follows

1. Determine a proof path for answering the query as in an ordinary PROLOG program, ignoring any support pairs assigned to rules and facts.
2. Evaluate the probability associated with this proof path to give a support pair.
3. Repeat steps 1 and 2 for all possible proof paths.
4. Combine the results from each of the proof paths into a final probability interval using the intersection rule, which is equivalent to combining the support pairs of the various proof paths with the general assignment method.

A rule in support logic is of the form

$$head \text{ if } body\text{: } [x1, x2] \, [y1, y2]$$

where *head* is a single atom and *body* is a conjunction of literals or disjunction of literals. The support pairs $[x1, x2]$ and $[y1, y2]$ give the intervals containing the probabilities $\Pr(head|body)$ and $\Pr(head|\text{NOT } body)$, respectively. Furthermore, if it is known that

$$body\text{: } [z1, z2]$$

this fact can be used with the rule to infer the fact that *head*: $[w1, w2]$ where the support pairs $[z1, z2]$ and $[w1, w2]$ give intervals containing the probabilities $\text{P}'r(body)$ and $\text{P}'r(head)$, respectively. The support pair $[w1, w2]$ is related to the support pairs $[x1, x2]$, $[y1, y2]$ and $[z1, z2]$ through an inference rule interpreted in terms of intervals rather than point values. The inference rule is Jeffrey's rule if the fact is thought to be specific evidence and the rule, general evidence; it is the theorem of total probabilities if both the rule and fact can be thought of as the same sample space statistics.

$$w1 = \text{MIN}\{\Pr(h|b).\text{P}'r(b) + \Pr(h|\neg b).\text{P}'r(\neg b)\}$$

where $x1 \le \Pr(h|b) \le x2$, $y1 \le \Pr(h|\neg b) \le y2$, and $z1 \le \text{P}'r(b) \le z2$ and the MIN is with respect to $\Pr(h|b)$, $\Pr(h|\neg b)$, and $\text{P}'r(b)$ so that

$$w1 = \text{MIN } \{x1.\text{P}'r(b) + y1.(1 - \text{P}'r(b))\}$$

where $z1 \le \text{P}'r(b) \le z2$ and the MIN is with respect to $\text{P}'r(b)$ so that

$$
\begin{aligned}
w1 &= x1.z2 + y1.(1 - z2) && \text{if } x1 \le y1 \\
&= x1.z1 + y1.(1 - z1) && \text{if } x1 > y1
\end{aligned}
$$

Similarly,

$$
\begin{aligned}
w2 &= x2.z1 + y2.(1 - z1) && \text{if } x2 \le y2 \\
&= x2.z2 + y2.(1 - z2) && \text{if } x2 > y2
\end{aligned}
$$

The support pair for the conjunction of terms in a body of a clause is dependent on the form of conjunction chosen for the program. By default the product rule is used that assumes independence of the terms or a maximum entropy argument. If this assumption cannot be used then an interval version of the following is used. The probability of the conjunction, namely $p1$ AND $p2$, lies in the interval $[\text{MAX}(0, \Pr(p1) + \Pr(p2) - 1), \text{MIN}(\Pr(p1), \Pr(p2))]$. Disjunctions are treated similarly in support logic programming. More details can be found in the FRIL manual (Baldwin, and co-workers, 1987; Martin and Baldwin, 1990).

Fuzzy Sets in FRIL

In FRIL the fuzzy set *tall* would be represented as

(tall [0.0: 0 5.7: 0 6.0: 1 10.0: 1])

The degree of membership is 0 for the height 5.7 feet and all heights below. It is 1 for the height 6.0 feet and all heights above. For any height in between, FRIL uses linear interpolation with respect to the points given to calculate the membership level for this height. Thus the membership level of 5.85 feet would be 0.5.

Semantic Unification. In order to prove a goal, FRIL performs matching of terms making substitutions for variables if necessary. The substitution is the least restrictive possible providing the most general unifier. The unification is purely syntactical. Thus terms like *tall* and *well above average* would not match even though there must be some support for a person being tall if that person is well above average in height. What is required is a semantic match of terms. This would involve comparing meanings in some sense of the two terms, and if they have the same meaning then unification is possible. If they only have similar meanings then the match will not be perfect and can be supported with a support pair. Consider the statements X is $\mathbf{f1}$ and a is $\mathbf{f2}$, where $\mathbf{f1}$ and $\mathbf{f2}$ are fuzzy sets defined on the universe of discourse F. The task is to determine $\Pr\{a \text{ is } \mathbf{f1} \mid a \text{ is } \mathbf{f2}\}$. The mass assignments $(m1, F1)$ and $(m2, F2)$ can be associated with $\mathbf{f1}$ and $\mathbf{f2}$, respectively, where $F1$ and $F2$ are the focal elements and are nested sets. For any member $s1i$ of $F1$ and any member $s2j$ of $F2$ the support pair can be determined for $s1i|s2j$ from the set $\{[0, 0], [1, 1], [0, 1]\}$. Let this be $[\text{Sn}(s1i \mid s2j), \text{Sp}(s1i|s2j)]$ and let $m1 = \{m1i\}$ and $m2 = \{m2j\}$. Therefore, the expected value of $\Pr(a \text{ is } f1|a \text{ is } f2)$ is contained in the support pair $[\text{Sn}(a \text{ is } f1|a \text{ is } f2), \text{Sp}(a \text{ is } f1 \mid a \text{ is } f2)]$ where

$$\text{Sn}(a \text{ is } f1 \mid a \text{ is } f2) = \sum_{i,j} m1i \cdot m2j \cdot \text{Sn}(s1i|s2j)$$

$$\text{Sp}(a \text{ is } f1 \mid a \text{ is } f2) = \sum_{i,j} m1i \cdot m2j \cdot \text{Sp}(s1i|s2j)$$

Example. Consider the fuzzy sets defined on $\{a, b, c, d, e\}$

$$\mathbf{f1} = a/0.2 + b/0.4 + c/0.8 + d/1$$

$$\mathbf{f2} = a/1 + b/0.8 + c/0.1$$

The respective associated mass assignments are:

$$\{d\}: 0.2, \{c,d\}: 0.4, \{b, c, d\}: 0.2, \{a, b, c, d\}: 0.2$$

$$\{a\}: 0.2, \{a, b\}: 0.7,; \{a, b, c\}: 0.1$$

Therefore,

$$\text{S}\{d\}|\{a\}) = [0, 0]$$

$$\text{S}(\{b, c, d\}|\{a\}) = [0, 0]$$

$$\text{S}(\{d\}|\{a, b\}) = [0, 0]$$

$$\text{S}(\{b, c, d\}|\{a, b\}) = [0, 1]$$

$$\text{S}(\{d\} \mid \{a, b, c\}) = [0, 0]$$

$$\text{S}(\{b, c, d\} \mid \{a, b, c\}) = [0, 1]$$

$$\text{S}(\{c, d\}|\{a\}) = [0, 0]$$

$$\text{S}(\{a, b, c, d\}|\{a\}) = [1, 1]$$

$$\text{S}(\{c, d\}|\{a, b\}) = [0, 0]$$

$$\text{S}(\{a, b, c, d\}|\{a, b\}) = [1, 1]$$

$$\text{S}(\{c, d\} \mid \{a, b, c\}) = [0, 1]$$

$$\text{S}(\{a, b, c, d\} \mid \{a, b, c\}) = [1, 1]$$

From this, the following is obtained:

$$\text{Sn}(a \text{ is } \mathbf{f1} \mid a \text{ is } \mathbf{f2}) = 0.2*0.2 + 0.2*0.7 + 0.2*0.1 = 0.2$$

$$\text{Sp}(a \text{ is } \mathbf{f1} \mid a \text{ is } \mathbf{f2}) = 0.2*0.2 + 0.2*0.7 + 0.2*0.7 + 0.4*0.1$$
$$+ 0.2*0.1 + 0.2*0.1 = 0.4$$

The support pair for the unification of **f1** given **f2** is [0.2, 0.4].

Example Program. Consider the following support logic program and accompanying comments.

Program	Comments
((wears_large_shoes X) (is_tall X)): (0.7 1)	

Read as anyone who is tall wears large shoes with a probability that lies in the interval (0.7, 1), the second support pair is missing, so is (0, 1).

Program	Comments
(tall [65:0, 70:0.7, 72:1])	Defines the fuzzy set *tall*
(heavy [160:0, 182:0.8, 200:1, lim:1])	Defines the fuzzy set *heavy.*
((is_tall X)(has_height X tall)): ((1 1)(0 0))	An equivalence statement.
((is_tall X)(is_heavy X) (not is_fat X)): (0.9 1)	Anyone who is heavy and not fat is tall with a probability in interval (0.9, 1).
((is_heavy X)(has_weight X heavy)): ((1 1)(0 0))	An equivalence statement.
((has_weight John [199:0, 200:1, 210:1, 220:0]))	John has weight which is *fairly heavy.*
((has_height John [70:0, 71:1, 72:0]))	John has height that is *well above average.*
((is_fat John)): (0 0.1)	It is very unlikely that John is fat. The following question is now asked, and the solution is obtained.
?((supp_query ((wears_large_shoes John)) (X Y))(pp (X Y)))	Does John wear large shoes?
(0.560769 1)	solution obtained by FRIL.

The support pair for *John is tall* comes from two rules with heads (is tall John) that are supported with (0.739128 0.869565) and (0.801099 1). The first of these comes from the (has height John) body, which is not modified because the first rule is an equivalence rule. The second comes from the support for the body (is heavy John)(not is fat John), which is (0.89011 1) modified by the support associated with the second rule for *is tall*.

MORE GENERAL EVIDENTIAL REASONING UNDER UNCERTAINTY

Iterative Assignment Method

Because a discussion of this method has been published (Baldwin, 1990b, in press a, b, c, d), the method will be summarized here, along with an elaboration of how the method handles incomplete information. Related work with updating distributions has been published (Diaconis and Zabell, 1982; Domotor, 1980, 1985; Domotor and co-workers, 1980; Field, 1978; Williams 1980; Van Fraassen, 1980).

Suppose an *a priori* mass assignment m_a is given over the focal set A whose elements are subsets of the power set $P(X)$ where X is a set of labels. This assignment represents general tendencies and is derived from statistical considerations of some sample space or general rules applicable to such a space. Suppose there is also a set of specific evidences $\{E1, E2, . . ., En\}$ where for each i, Ei is (mi, Fi) where Fi is the set of focal elements of $P(X)$ for Ei and mi is the mass assignment for these focal elements. These evidences are assumed to be relevant to some object and derived by consideration of this object alone and not influenced by the sample space of objects from which the object came. The task is to update the *a priori* assignment m_a with $\{E1, . . .,En\}$ to give the updated mass assignment m. If m_a and the evidences are probability distributions the update should minimize the relative information of m with respect to m_a.

The iterative assignment method updates m_a first with $E1$ to give $m^{(1)}$. This is updated with $E2$ to give $m^{(2)}$ and so

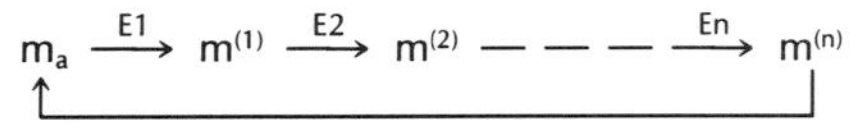

$$m_a \xrightarrow{E1} m^{(1)} \xrightarrow{E2} m^{(2)} ---- \xrightarrow{En} m^{(n)}$$

Figure 3. The iterative assignment process.

on until $m^{(n)}$ is reached. $m^{(i)}$ satisfies Ei but not necessarily $E1, \ldots, E(i-1)$. m_a is then replaced with $m^{(n)}$. The whole process is repeated until the process converges, in which case $m^{(1)} = m^{((2)} = \ldots = m^{(n)} = m'$ say. This process can be depicted as in Figure 3. The one-step algorithm is as follows: consider that it is desirable to update the mass assignment m with E to give the mass assignment m' where $m = (t, T)$ and $t = \{t1, \ldots, tm\}$, $T = \{T1, \ldots, Tm\}$, where Ti is a subset of $P(X)$. That is, $m:- T1:t1, \ldots, Tm: tm$, $E = (t^E, T^E)$, where $t^E = \{t^E1, \ldots, t^Es\}$ and $T^E = \{T^E1, \ldots, T^Es\}$, where T^Ei is a subset of $P(X)$. For example,

$$E:- T^E1: t^E1, \ldots, T^Es: t^Es$$

$$m' = (t', T'), t' = \{t'1, \ldots, t'r\}, T' = \{T'1, \ldots, T'r\},$$
$$T' = \text{Set}\{\text{Bag}\{Ti \cap T^Ej \mid Ti \cap T^Ej \neq \varnothing\}\}$$

$$K_j = \frac{1}{1 - \sum\limits_{q:Tq \cap T^Ej = \varnothing} tq}$$

for $j = 1, \ldots, s$

$$t'k = \sum\limits_{i,j:Ti \cap T^Ej = T'k} K_j \, ti \, t^Ej \quad {}^{i,j:Ti \cap T^Ej = T'k}$$

for $k = 1, \ldots, r$. It should be noted that the label set can change from stage to stage of the complete process.

Example program.

Consider the following program:

a(X): 0.7	The probability that any object satisfies a is 0.7.
a(X):− b(X), c(X): 0.9, 0.1	$\Pr(a(X) \mid b(X)c(X)) = 0.9$, $\Pr(a(X) \mid \neg(b(X)c(X))) = 0.1$ for any X.
b(const): 0.7	The specific object *const* is estimated to satisfy b with probability 0.7.
c(const): [0.8, 1]	The estimated probability for *const* satisfying c is ≥ 0.8.

The first two statements are general statements about a population of objects, while the last two statements are specific to the object *const*. The general statements are used to form an *a priori* mass assignment, and this is updated with the two specific statements expressed as mass assignments.

The *a priori* mass assignment is abc: 0.675, $\neg abc$: 0.075, $\{a\_ \neg c, a \neg bc\}$: 0.025, and $\{\neg a\_ \neg c, \neg a \neg bc\}$: 0.225. This is updated first with b: 0.7, $\neg b$: 0.3 to give a mass assignment on the labels abc; $\neg abc$; $ab \neg c$; $\neg ab \neg c$; $\{a \neg b\_\}$; $\{\neg a \neg b\_\}$, which is further updated with c: 0.8; $\{, \neg c\}$: 0.2.

This gives a mass assignment on labels abc; $\neg abc$; $ab \neg c$; $\neg ab \neg c$; $a \neg bc$; $\neg a \neg bc$; $\{a \neg b\_\}$; $\{\neg a \neg b\_\}$. Further iteration is used to give the final update abc: 0.63; $\neg abc$: 0.7; $a \neg bc$: 0.03; $\neg a \neg bc$: 0.27. This gives a final solution a: 0.66.

Update Interpretation. If the *a priori* mass assignment is a probability distribution p, defined over the set of labels X and the specific evidences $E1, \ldots, En$ are also probability distributions over a partition of X, then the iterative assignment method determines an updated probability distribution over X, p' say, such that

$$\sum_{x \in X} p'(x) \, Ln \, (p'(x)/p(x))$$

is minimized subject to the constraints $E1, \ldots, En$ and is equivalent to using Jeffrey's rule. p' is said to satisfy the minimum information principle (Kullback, 1959), for updating the distribution p over X with specific evidences $E1, \ldots, En$ where each Ei is expressed as a distribution over a partition of X. Convergence of such an iteration has been discussed (Csiszár, 1975). If the evidences are expressed as mass assignments over X with the *a priori* assignment still being a probability distribution over the set of labels X then a more complicated case must be considered. In this case the update solution p' satisfies the following relative information optimisation problem, where

$$\sum_{x \in X} p'(x) \, Ln \, (p'(x)/p(x))$$

is minimized subject to the constraints $Sn(Y) \leq p'(Y) \leq Sp(Y)$ for all subsets Y of $P(X)$ and $m = 1, \ldots, n$, where $Sn(Y)$ and $Sp(Y)$ are determined from the mass assignment (mr, Fr).

For the more general case, in which the *a priori* is a mass assignment and the evidences are mass assignments, the interpretation of the iterative assignment method is much more complicated. This has been discussed in more detail (Baldwin, in press*d*). In the one-stage process the update chosen is that one that is obtained using Jeffrey's rule in which the conditional probabilities are determined such that one has the maximum consistency between the *a priori* mass assignment and the specific evidence of the one-stage update. Alternative criteria can be chosen for estimating the conditional probabilities and this has been discussed further (Baldwin, in press*d*, Ichihashi and Tanaka, 1989).

A Nonmonotonic Example

A familiar example concerning birds and penguins is presented here. Consider the following program, where the "_" signifies *not relevant*.

```
bird (X): 0.7
fly (X):− bird (X): 0.9
fly (X):− bird (X), penguin (X): 0, 0.95, _, 0.1
bird (X):− penguin (X): 1
fly X):− penguin (X): 0
penguin (obj): 0.4
bird(obj): 0.9
```

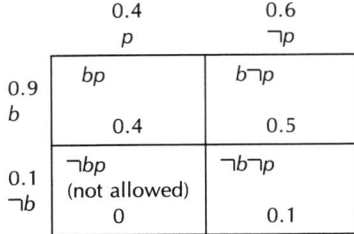

Figure 4. A nonmonotonic example.

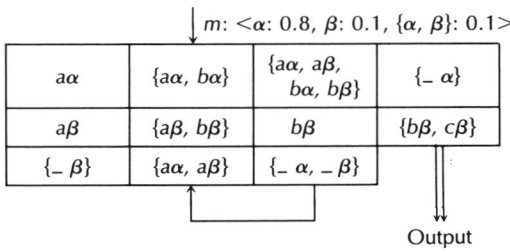

Figure 6. The state of this machine does not change its architecture for the rest of the iteration. When convergence is obtained, the machine outputs the solution to the query.

This program says that the proportion of birds in the relevant population of objects is 70% and 90% of the birds can fly. No object that is a bird and penguin can fly, 95% of birds that are not penguins can fly, and 1% of objects that are not birds can fly. All penguins are birds. No penguin can fly. It also gives specific information about the object *obj*, namely that there is a probability of 0.9 that *obj* is a bird and a probability of 0.4 that *obj* is a penguin.

This information allows the following unique distribution over the relevant labels to be constructed, where *BPF* is the label variable and $B = \{\text{bird}(obj), \neg\text{bird}(obj)\}$ is denoted by $\{b, \neg b\}$, $P = \{\text{penguin}(obj), \neg\text{penguin}(obj)\}$ is denoted by $\{p, \neg p\}$, and $F = \{\text{fly}(obj), \neg\text{fly}(obj), \neg\text{fly}(obj)\}$ is denoted by $\{f, \neg f\}$. *A priori*, $0.27: \neg b\neg p\neg f$, $0.03: \neg b\neg pf$, $0.0332: b\neg p\neg f$, $0.63: b\neg pf$, and $0.0368: bp\neg f$. This problem can be solved by projecting the *a priori* distribution on to the space *BP* to obtain $0.0368: bp$, $0.6632: b\neg p$, $0: \neg bp$, and $0.3: \neg b\neg p$ and updating this using the iterative assignment method with the following specific information: $\Pr'(b) = 0.9$ and $\Pr'(p) = 0.4$ to obtain x1: bp, x2: $b\neg p$, 0: $\neg bp$, and x4: $\neg b\neg p$. This gives $\Pr'\{\text{fly(mary)}\} = \Pr\{f \mid bp\}\Pr'(bp) + \Pr\{f \mid b\neg p\}\Pr'(\neg bp) + \Pr\{f \mid \neg b\neg p\}\Pr'(\neg b\neg p)$ where $\Pr\{f \mid bp\} = 0$, $\Pr\{f \mid b\neg p\} = 0.63/(0.6632) = 0.95$, $\Pr\{f \mid \neg b\neg p\} = 0.03/0.3 = 0.1$, $\Pr'(bp) = x1$, $\Pr'(b\neg p) = x2$, and $\Pr'(\neg b\neg p) = x4$.

In this example the update is very simple to determine because the updated assignment for $\neg bp$ must be zero and there is only one value of $\{\Pr'(bp), \Pr'(b\neg p), \Pr'(\neg b\neg p)\}$ that satisfies this. The specific information constraints as seen using the general assignment method are presented in Figure 4. Hence, $x1 = 0.4$, $x2 = 0.5$, and $x4 = 0.1$ so that $\Pr'\{\text{fly(mary)}\} = 0.95*0.5 + 0.1*0.1 = 0.485$.

m: $<\alpha$: 0.8, β: 0.1, $\{\alpha, \beta\}$: 0.1$>$		
$a\alpha$	$\{a\alpha, a\beta\}$	$\{a\alpha, a\beta, b\alpha, b\beta\}$
$b\beta$	$\{b\beta, b\gamma\}$	$\{b\beta, b\gamma, c\beta, c\gamma\}$
$c\gamma$	$\{b\gamma, c\gamma\}$	$\{\_\_\}$

Figure 5. Initial state of the machine. Each cell contains an assignment. The state of the machine is updated using the input to obtain a new state, given in Figure 5.

Fuzzy Control

Consider the mass assignment for the aggregated input–output pairs given for the fuzzy control example above. This is the *a priori* mass assignment to be used for inference using the iterative assignment method to update with the specific information provided. An approach to approximate reasoning based purely on fuzzy set theory has been published (Baldwin, 1979, 1981; Dubois and Prade, in press*a*, in press*b*; Lopez de Mantaras, 1990; Trillas and Valverde, 1985; Yager, 1985, 1986; Zadeh 1983; Yamakawa, 1989; Sugeno and co-workers, 1989). A treatment of possibilistic logic has also been published (Dubois and Prade, 1990b).

Consider a specific input $\mathbf{g}' = \alpha/0.9 + \beta/0.2$ to the system. This is equivalent to the mass assignment $m_{\mathbf{g}} = m_{\mathbf{g}'1} \oplus m_{\mathbf{g}'2}$ where $\mathbf{g}'1 = \alpha/1 + \beta/0.2$, with associated mass assignment $<\alpha$: 0.8, $\{\alpha,\beta\}$: 0.2$>$, and $\mathbf{g}'2 = \alpha/0.9 + \beta/1$, with associated mass assignment $<\beta$: 0.1, $\{\alpha, \beta\}$: 0.9$>$, which gives $m_{\mathbf{g}} = <\alpha$: 0.8, β: 0.1, $\{\alpha, \beta\}$: 0.1$>$. The output obtained by updating the *a priori* mass assignment with this specific input using the iterative assignment method is a: 0.7047, b: 0.0429, $\{a, b\}$: 0.2023, $\{b, c\}$: 0.0162, and $\{a, b, c\}$: 0.0338.

Parallel Machines. The machine computation for this example is shown below in Figure 5. This is the initial state of the machine. Each cell of the machine has a label, corresponding to one of the *a priori* assignment labels, and a mass assignment corresponding to the corresponding *a priori* assignment. Each cell can be thought to be an elementary processor capable of performing the arithmetic and set intersections required by the iterative assignment method and the maximal amount of parallel computation takes place to compute the update. The input to the machine is used to update the state of the machine according to the iterative assignment method. The parallel computation takes place and the machine state grows into the state given in Figure 6.

BIBLIOGRAPHY

J. B. Adams, "A Probability Model of Medical Reasoning and the MYCIN Model," *Math. Biosci.* **32**, 177–186 (1976).

J. F. Baldwin, "A New Approach to Approximate Reasoning Using Fuzzy Logic," *Fuzzy Sets Syst.* **2**, 309–325 (1979).

J. F. Baldwin, "Fuzzy Logic and Fuzzy Reasoning," in A. Mamdani and B. Gaines, eds., *Fuzzy Reasoning and Its Applications,* Academic Press, Inc., Orlando, Fla., 1979.

J. F. Baldwin, "Support Logic Programming," in A. I. Jones and co-workers, eds., *Fuzzy Sets Theory and Applications,* Reidel, Dordrecht, 1986.

J. F. Baldwin "Evidential Support Logic Programmin," *Fuzzy Sets Sys.* **24,** 1–26 (1987).

J. F. Baldwin, "Computational Models of Uncertainty Reasoning in Expert Systems," *Compt. Math. Applic.* **19**(11), 105–119 (1990a).

J. F. Baldwin, "Towards a General Theory of Intelligent Reasoning," paper presented at the Third International Conference of IPMU, Paris, July 1990b.

J. F. Baldwin, "Combining Evidences for Evidential Reasoning," in press a.

J. F. Baldwin, "Evidential Reasoning under Probabilistic and Fuzzy Uncertainties," in press b.

J. F. Baldwin, "Inference under Uncertainty for Expert System Rules," in press c.

J. F. Baldwin, "Inference for Information Systems Containing Probabilistic and Fuzzy Uncertainties, in press d.

J. F. Baldwin and B. W. Pilsworth, "Semantic Unification of Fuzzy Concepts in FRIL," paper presented at the Third International Conference of IPMU, Paris, July 1990.

J. F. Baldwin, B. W. Pilsworth, and T. Martin, *FRIL Manual,* Fril Systems, Ltd., Bristol, UK, 1987.

I. Csiszår, "I-Divergence Geometry of Probability Distributions and Minimisation Problems," *Annals of Probability* **3**(1), 146–158 (1975).

B. A. Davey and H. A. Priestley, *Introduction to Lattices and Order,* CUP, Cambridge, UK, 1990.

A. P. Dempster, "A Generalisation of Bayesian Inference," *J. R. Stat. Soc. Ser. B* **30,** 205–247 (1968).

P. Diaconis and S. L. Zabell "Updating Subjective Probability," *J. Am. Stat. Assoc.* **77,** 822–830 (1982).

Z. Domotor, "Probability Kinematics and Representation of Belief Change," *Philos. Sci.* **47,** 384–403 (1980).

Z. Domotor, "Probability Kinematics, Conditionals and Entropy Principles," *Synthese* **63,** 75–114 (1985).

Z. Domotor, M. Zannoti, and H. Graves, "Probability Kinematics," *Synthese* **44,** 421–442 (1980).

D. Dubois and H. Prade, "On the Unicity of Dempster Rule of Combination," *Int. J. Intell. Sys.* **1**(2), 133–142 (1986).

D. Dubois and H. Prade, "Resolution Principles in Possibilistic Logic," *Int. J. Approx. Reasoning,* **4**(5/6), 419–445 (1990a).

D. Dubois and H. Prade, "Resolution Principles in Possibilistic Logic," *Int. J. Approx. Reasoning* **4**(1), 1–21 (1990b).

D. Dubois and H. Prade, "Fuzzy Sets in Approximate Reasoning, Part 1, Inferences and Possibility Distributions," in press a.

D. Dubois and H. Prade, "Fuzzy Sets in Approximate Reasoning, Part 2, Logical Approaches," in press b.

H. Field, "A Note on Jeffrey Conditionalisation," *Philos. Sci.* **44,** 361–367 (1978).

P. Garbolino, "Bayesian Theory and Artificial Intelligence: The Quarrelsome Marriage," in E. Hollnagel and co-workers, eds., *Cognitive Engineering in Complex Dynamic Worlds,* Academic Press, Orlando, Fla., 1988a.

P. Garbolino, "A Comparison of Some Rules for Probabilistic Reasoning in Cognitive Engineering in Complex Dynamic Worlds," in E. Hollnagel and co-workers, eds., *Cognitive Engi-*

neering in Complex Dynamic Worlds, Academic Press, Orlando, Fla., 1988b.

M. L. Ginsberg, *Readings in NonMonotonic Reasoning,* Morgan-Kaufmann, San Mateo, Calif., 1987.

H. Ichihashi and H. Tanaka, "Jeffrey-Like Rules of Conditioning for the Dempster-Shafer Theory of Evidence," *Int. J. Approx. Reasoning* **3**(2), 143–156 (1989).

E. T. Jaynes, "How Does the Brain Do Plausible Reasoning?" in Erickson and Smith, eds., *Maximum Entropy and Bayesian Methods in Science and Engineering,* Vol. 1, Kluwer Academic Publishers, Boston, Mass., 1957.

G. J. Klir and T. A. Folger, *Fuzzy Sets, Uncertainty, and Information,* Prentice-Hall, Inc., Englewood Cliffs, N.J., 1988.

S. Kulback, *Information Theory and Statistics,* John Wiley & Sons, Inc., New York, 1959.

R. Lopez de Mantaras, *Approximate Reasoning Models,* Ellis Horwood, Ltd., 1990.

G. Polya, *Patterns of Plausible Inference,* Vol. 2, OUP, Oxford, UK, 1954.

N. Nilsson, "Probabilistic Logic," *Artif. Intell.* **28,** 71–87 (1986).

J. Pearl, "Reasoning with Belief Functions: An Analysis of Compatibility," *Int. J. Approx. Reasoning* **4**(5/6), 363–389 (1990).

A. Ralescue and J. F. Baldwin "Concept Classification from Examples and Counter Examples," *Int. J. Man-Machine Stud.* **30,** 1–26 (1988).

G. Shafer, *A Mathematical Theory of Evidence,* Princeton University Press, Princeton, N.J., 1976.

G. Shafer, "Constructive Probability," *Synthese* **48,** 1–60 (1981a).

G. Shafer, "Jeffrey's Rule of Conditioning," *Philos. Sci.* **48,** 337–362 (1981b).

G. Shafer and Tversky, "Language and Designs for Probability Judgment," *Cogn. Sci.* **9,** 309–339 (1985).

L. Savage, *Foundations of Statistics,* Wiley, New York, 1954.

P. P. Shenoy and G. Shafer, "Axioms for Probability and Belief-Function Propagation," in R. D. Schachter and co-workers, eds., *Uncertainty in Artificial Intelligence,* North-Holland, Amsterdam, 1990.

E. H. Shortliffe, *Computer Based Medical Consultations: MYCIN,* Elsevier Science Publishing Co., Inc., New York, 1976.

J. F. Sowa, *Conceptual Structures,* Addison-Wesley Publishing Co., Inc., Reading, Mass., 1984.

P. Smets, "Belief Functions," in P. Smets and co-workers, eds., *Non-Standard Logics for Automated Reasoning,* Academic Press, Inc., Orlando, Fla., 1988.

P. Smets, "The Combination of Evidences in the Transferable Belief Model," *IEEE Trans. PAMI* **12,** 442–258 (1990).

E. E. Smith and D. L. Medin, *Categories and Concepts,* Harvard University Press, Cambridge, Mass., 1981.

M. Sugeno and co-workers, "Fuzzy Algorithm control of a Model Car by Oral Instruction," *Fuzzy Sets Syst.* **32**(2), 207–221 (1989).

E. Trillas and L. Valverde, "On Mode and Implication in Approximate Reasoning," in M. Gupta and co-workers, eds., *Approximate Reasoning in Expert Systems,* North-Holland, Amsterdam, The Netherlands, 1985, pp. 157–166.

P. M. Williams, "Bayesian Conditionalisation and the Principle of Minimum Information," *Br. J. Philos. Sci.* **31,** 131–144 (1980).

R. R. Yager, "Inference in Multi-Valued Logic System," *Int. J. Man-Machine Stud.* **23,** 27–44 (1985).

R. R. Yager, "Toward General Theory of Reasoning with Uncertainty, 1: Nonspecificity and Fuzziness," *Int. J. Intell. Sys.* **1**(1), 45–67 (1986).

T. Yamakawa, "Stabilisation of an Inverted Pendulum by a High Speed Fuzzy Logic Controller Hardware System," *Fuzzy Sets Syst.* **32**(2), 149–161 (1989).

L. Zadeh, "Fuzzy Sets," *Inform. Contr.* **8**, 338–353 (1965).

L. Zadeh, "Fuzzy Sets as a Basis for a Theory of Possibility," *Fuzzy Sets Syst.* **1**, 3–28 (1978).

L. Zadeh, "The Role of Fuzzy Logic in the Management of Uncertainty in Expert Systems," *Fuzzy Sets Syst.* **11**, 199–227 (1983).

L. Zadeh, "A Simple View of the Dempster-Shafer Theory of Evidence and Its Implications for the Role of Combination," *AI Magazine* **7**(2), 85–90 (1986).

J. F. BALDWIN
University of Bristol

FUZZY SETS AND FUZZY LOGIC

The concepts of a set and set theory are powerful tools in mathematics. Unfortunately, a *sine qua non* condition underlying set theory, ie, that an element can either belong to a set or not, is often inconsistent with many elements in human discourse where vagueness prevails (eg, *large profit, high pressure, moderate temperature*) and cannot be adequately handled by conventional mathematical tools.

If the meaning of such vague terms is to be maintained, a crisp differentiation between elements (eg, pressure values) that are high and those that are not high may be artificial, and some values may be perceived as high to some extent, not fully high, or not fully not high.

An attempt to develop a formal apparatus to involve a partial membership in a set was undertaken by Zadeh in the early 1960s. His works, rooted in systems theory, culminated in a famous paper (Zadeh, 1965) which introduces the concept of a fuzzy set as a collection of objects that might belong to the set to a degree, varying from 1 for full belongingness to 0 for full nonbelongingness, through all intermediate values. This was done by employing the concept of a membership function assigning to each element a number from the unit interval to indicate the intensity of belongingness. This was evidently an extension of the concept of a characteristic function assigning either 0 (nonbelongingness) or 1 (belongingness). Then, basic properties and operations on fuzzy sets were defined as being essentially extensions (in the above spirit) of their conventional counterparts.

Some of the roots of fuzzy sets, mainly in the context of philosophy and logic, are discussed in Gaines (1976). Particularly important here is clearly multiple valued logic, allowing for truth values from, say, [0,1] instead of {0,1},

Zadeh's (1975b) next efforts were to devise a logic to model real-world human-centered reasoning processes in which there are vague predicates (eg, *large, beautiful*), partial truths (very often linguistically defined as *not very true, more or less false*), linguistic quantifiers (eg, *most, almost all, a few*), and linguistic hedges (eg, *very, more or less*), etc. Notice that in the case of a fuzzy set as well as fuzzy logic, linguistic terms play a crucial role. This is not strange, because one of main reasons behind the introduction of fuzzy set theory was an attempt to formalize natural language statements that are commonly used by humans but are incompatible with formal mathematical tools. Crucial here are Zadeh's (1973, 1975a) works on linguistic variables whose values are fuzzy sets.

Since their inception, fuzzy sets theory and fuzzy logic had experienced an unprecedented growth of interest in virtually all scientific fields. The development of a "fuzzy computer" in the mid-1980s, ie, a VLSI chip based on fuzzy logic (instead of on binary Boolean logic) was relevant because it had proven to be useful in subway controllers, video and photographic cameras, car transmissions, domestic appliances, robotics, etc.

The purpose of this article is to provide a brief survey of fuzzy sets and fuzzy logic; the readability and simplicity of exposition will be maintained at the expense of technicalities. The reader interested in a particular topic is referred to the literature; in principle, book references, which may be easier to obtain and may provide a more complete coverage, are given preference and only some of the more important technical articles are cited.

FUNDAMENTALS OF FUZZY SET THEORY

Suppose that $X = \{x\}$ is a universe of discourse, ie, the set of all possible (feasible, relevant) elements with respect to a fuzzy (vague) concept (property). Then a fuzzy subset (or a fuzzy set, for simplicity) A of X, written $A \subseteq X$, is defined as a set of ordered pairs $\{(x, \mu_A(x))\}$, where $x \in X$ and $\mu_A: X \rightarrow [0,1]$ is the membership function of A; $\mu_A(x) \in [0,1]$ is the grade of membership of x in A. Many authors denote $\mu_A(x)$ by $A(x)$. Moreover, a fuzzy set is often equated with its membership function. Notice that if [0,1] is replaced by {0,1}, this definition coincides with the characteristic function based description of an ordinary (nonfuzzy) set. Moreover, the original Zadeh's unit interval is chosen for simplicity, and a similar role may be played by any ordered set as, for example, a lattice (Goguen, 1967).

It is convenient to denote a fuzzy set defined in a finite universe of discourse, say $A \subseteq X = \{x_1, \ldots, x_n\}$ as $A = \mu_A(x_1)/x_1 + \cdots + \mu_A(x_n)/x_n$, where "$\mu_A(x_i)/x_i$" (called a singleton) is a pair "grade of membership-element." For instance, if $X = \{1, 2, \ldots, 10\}$, then a fuzzy set (labeled) *large number* may be given as $A = large\ number = 0.2/6 + 0.5/7 + 0.8/8 + 1/9 + 1/10$ to be meant as: 9 and 10 are surely (to degree 1) "large numbers", 0.8 is a "large number" to degree 0.8, etc and $1, 2, \ldots, 5$ are surely not "large numbers." Notice that the above degrees of membership are subjective (a *large number* is a subjective property!) and context dependent, and, by convention, the singletons with $\mu_A(.) = 0$ are omitted.

It is convenient to depict the membership function of a fuzzy set as in Figure 1. In practice it is usually even more convenient to use a piece-wise linear representation (shown as a dotted line) because only two values, $\underline{x}$ and $\bar{x}$, are needed to specify the fuzzy set.

Basic Properties of Fuzzy Sets

A fuzzy set $A \subseteq X$ is empty, $A = \emptyset$, iff $\mu_A(x) = 0$, $\forall x \in X$. Two fuzzy sets $A, B \subseteq X$ are equal, $A = B$, iff $\mu_A(x) = \mu_B(x)$,

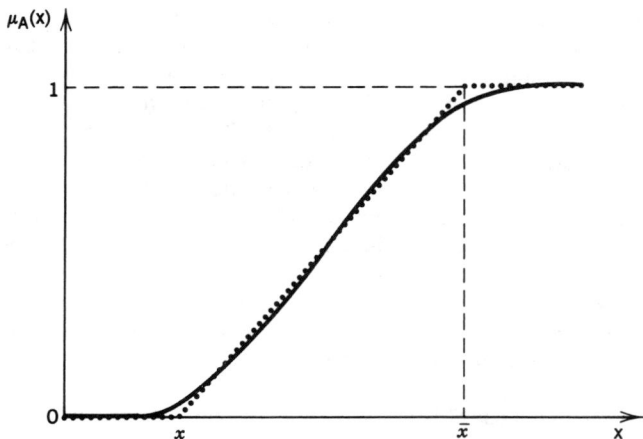

Figure 1. Membership function of a fuzzy set.

$\forall x \in X$. A fuzzy set $A \subseteq X$ is included in (is a subset of) a fuzzy set $B \subseteq X$ if and only if $\mu_A(x) \leq \mu_B(x)$, $\forall x \in X$.

Example 1. Suppose $X = \{1,2,3\}$ and $A = 0.3/1 + 0.5/2 + 1/3$, $B = 0.4/1 + 0.6/2 + 0.8/3$; then $B \subseteq A$. Some "soft" definitions, allowing for a degree of equality and inclusion (between 0 and 1), are described by Bandler and Kohout (1980).

An important concept is the cardinality of a fuzzy set. If $X = \{x_1, \ldots, x_n\}$, and $A = \mu_A(x_1)/x_1 + \cdots + \mu_A(x_n)/x_n$, then the (nonfuzzy) cardinality of A, the so-called ΣCount (sigma-count), is defined as

$$\text{card } A = |A| = \sum_{i=1}^{n} \mu_A(x_i) \qquad (1)$$

Example 2. If $X = \{1,2,3,4\}$ and $A = 0.1/1 + 0.4/2 + 0.7/3 + 1/4$, then card $A = 2.2$. Some other concepts of cardinality, mainly defined as a fuzzy number, are described by Zadeh (1983).

Basic Operations

The basic operations here are naturally the complement, intersection, and union, as in the conventional set theory. The complement of a fuzzy set $A \subseteq X$, $\neg A \subseteq X$, is defined by

$$\mu_{\neg A}(x) = 1 - \mu_A(x), \qquad \forall x \in X \qquad (2)$$

and it corresponds to the negation *not*. The intersection of two fuzzy sets $A, B \subseteq X$, $A \cap B \subseteq X$, is defined by

$$\begin{aligned}\mu_{A \cap B}(x) &= \mu_A(x) \wedge m_B(x) \\ &= \min(\mu_A(x), \mu_B(x)), \qquad \forall x \in X \qquad (3)\end{aligned}$$

and it corresponds to the connective *and*. The union of two fuzzy sets, $A, B \subseteq X$, $A + B \subseteq X$, is defined by

$$\begin{aligned}\mu_{A+B}(x) &= \mu_A(x) \vee \mu_B(x) \\ &= \max(\mu_A(x), \mu_B(x)), \qquad \forall x \in X \qquad (4)\end{aligned}$$

and it corresponds to the connective *or*.

Example 3. If $X = \{1,2, \ldots ,10\}$, $A = small\ number = 1/1 + 1/2 + 0.8/3 + 0.5/4 + 0.3/5 + 0.1/6$, $B = large\ number = 0.1/5 + 0.2/6 + 0.5/7 + 0.8/8 + 1/9 + 1/10$, then

$\neg A = not\ small\ number$
$= 0.2/3 + 0.5/4 + 0.7/5 + 0.9/6 + 1/7 + 1/8 + 1/9 + 1/10$

$A \cap B = small\ number$ and $large\ number$
$= 0.1/5 + 0.1/6$

$A \cup B = small\ number$ or $large\ number$
$= 1/1 + 1/2 + 0.8/3 + 0.5/4 + 0.3/5 + 0.2/6 + 0.5/7 + 0.8/8 + 1/9 + 1/10$

The above definitions are Zadeh's classic and have been commonly employed, although they are evidently by no means the only ones. For instance, the use of a t-norm for the intersection and an s-norm for the union has often been advocated.

A t-norm is a function $t: [0,1] \times [0,1] \to [0,1]$ such that, $\forall a, b, c \in [0,1]$: (1) $a\ t\ 1 = a$, (2) $a\ t\ b = b\ t\ a$, (3) $a\ t\ b \geq c\ t\ d$, if $a \geq b$ and $c \geq d$, and (4) $a\ t\ b\ t\ c = a\ t\ (b\ t\ c) = (a\ t\ b)\ t\ c$. Some examples of t-norms are $a \wedge b = \min(a, b)$, which is the most commonly used; ab; and $1 - (1 \wedge ((1 - a)^p + (1 - b)^p)^{1/p})$, $p \geq 1$.

An s-norm (t-conorm) is a function $s: [0,1] \times [0,1] \to [0,1]$ such that, $\forall a, b, c \in [0,1]$: (1) $a\ s\ 0 = a$, and points 2–4 are the same as for a t-norm. Examples of s-norms are $a \vee b = \max(a, b)$, which is the most commonly used; $a + b - ab$; and $1 \wedge (a^p + b^p)^{1/p}$, $p \geq 1$.

Although "$\wedge$" will be used for the intersection and "$\vee$" for the union, they can usually be replaced by, say, a t-norm or s-norm, respectively. Notice, however, that although the use of t-norms and s-norms has recently gained some popularity, the problem of a proper definition of operations on fuzzy sets is still open (Zimmermann, 1985).

For other operations on fuzzy sets, see, eg, Dubois and Prade, 1980; Kacprzyk, 1983; Zimmermann, 1985).

Further Properties and Related Concepts

An α-cut (α-level set) of a fuzzy set $A \subseteq X$ is defined as the ordinary set $A_\alpha \subseteq X$ such that

$$A_\alpha = \{x \in X: \mu_A(x) \geq \alpha\}, \qquad \forall \alpha \in [0,1] \qquad (5)$$

Example 4. If $A = 1/1 + 0.8/2 + 0.5/3 + 0.1/4$, then $A_{0.1} = \{1,2,3,4\}$, $A_{0.5} = \{1,2,3\}$, $A_{0.8} = \{1,2\}$, and $A_1 = \{1\}$. The concept of an α-cut of a fuzzy set is crucial for the so-called decomposition theorem, which states that any fuzzy set $A \subseteq X$ may be represented as

$$A = \sum_{\alpha \in [0,1]} \alpha A_\alpha \qquad (6)$$

where Σ denotes the union in the sense of equation 4 and $\alpha A_\alpha \subseteq X$ is a fuzzy set whose membership function is

$$\mu_{\alpha A_\alpha}(x) = \begin{cases} \alpha & \text{for } x \in A_\alpha \\ 0 & \text{for } x \notin A_\alpha \end{cases} \qquad (7)$$

An example may be found in Dubois and Prade (1980).

Notice that this theorem provides means for numerical handling of fuzzy quantities that boil down to some (equivalent) operations on conventional sets.

Of fundamental importance here is the so-called extension principle, which gives a formal apparatus to carry over operations (eg, algebraic) from sets to fuzzy sets. Namely, if $f: X \to Y$ is a function (operation) and $A \subseteq X$, then A induces via f a fuzzy set $B \subseteq Y$ given by

$$\mu_B(y) = \begin{cases} \sup_{y=f(x)} \mu_A(x) & \text{if } f^{-1}(x) \neq \emptyset \\ 0 & \text{otherwise} \end{cases} \quad (8)$$

Example 5. Let $X = \{1,2,3,4\}$, $Y = \{1,2, \ldots ,6\}$, and $y = x + 2$. If now $A = 0.1/1 + 0.2/2 + 0.7/3 + 1/4$, then $B = 0.1/3 + 0.2/4 + 0.7/5 + 1/6$.

Fuzzy Numbers

The extension principle is a very powerful tool and can be used, eg, to devise fuzzy arithmetic. A fuzzy number is defined (by many, not all authors) as a fuzzy set in the real line, $A \subseteq R$, which is normalized (ie, $\sup_{r \in R} \mu_A(r) = 1$) and bounded convex (ie, whose α-cuts are all convex and bounded). A fuzzy number may be exemplified by *about five, a little more than 7*, etc.

Notice that function f in equation 8 may be, say, the sum, product, difference, or quotient, and the four main operations: addition, multiplication, subtraction, and division can be extended via equation 6 to fuzzy sets, hence obtaining fuzzy arithmetic. Unfortunately, using the extension principle to define the arithmetic operations on fuzzy numbers is in general numerically inefficient, hence it is usually assumed that a fuzzy number has a triangular or trapezoid membership function (Fig. 2), characterized by three or four points. The arithmetic operations involve only these three or four values, which simplifies the computations (Kaufmann and Gupta, 1985).

Probability of a Fuzzy Event

In everyday discourse randomness and fuzziness are often jointly encountered as, for example, in the question "What is the probability of a good weather tomorrow?" The fuzzy event, *good weather*, cannot be handled by conventional probabilistic tools. Zadeh (1968), therefore, introduced the concept of a fuzzy event defined as a fuzzy set A in the set of elementary events $X = \{x_1, \ldots ,x_n\}$, $A \subseteq X$, with a

Borel measurable membership function. Assuming known probabilities of the elementary events, $p(x_1), \ldots ,p(x_n)$, and $\Sigma_{i=1}^n p(x_i) = 1$, the probability of a fuzzy event A, $P(A)$, was defined as

$$P(A) = \sum_{i=1}^n \mu_A(x_i)p(x_i) \quad (9)$$

which is the expected value of $\mu_A(x)$.

Example 6. If $X = \{1,2, \ldots ,5\}$, $A = 0.1/2 + 0.5/3 + 0.7/4 + 0.9/5$, and $p(x_1) = 0.1$, $p(x_2) = 0.1$, $p(x_3) = 0.1$, $p(x_4) = 0.3$, $p(x_5) = 0.4$, then $P(A) = 0.73$. Notice that although the event here is fuzzy, its probability is not, which may be viewed counterintuitive. Some attempts to define a fuzzy probability of a fuzzy event have been made (Yager, 1979) can be cited. This is, however, still a controversial and difficult issue, but several papers have dealt with this problem (Kacprzyk and Fedrizzi, 1988).

Fuzzy Relations

Fuzzy relations, exemplified by *much larger than, more or less equal*, etc, are clearly omnipresent in human discourse. Formally, if $X = \{x\}$ and $Y = \{y\}$ are two universes of discourse, then a fuzzy relation R is defined as a fuzzy set in the Cartesian product $X \times Y$, $R \subseteq X \times Y$, characterized by its membership function $\mu_R: X \times Y \to [0,1]$; $\mu_R(x,y) \in [0,1]$ reflects the strength of relation between x and y.

Example 7. Suppose that $X = \{$horse, donkey$\}$ and $Y = \{$mule, cow$\}$. The fuzzy relation *similar* may then be defined as

$$R = similar = 0.8/(\text{horse, mule}) + 0.4/(\text{horse, cow}) + 0.9/(\text{donkey, mule}) + 0.5/\text{donkey, cow})$$

to be read that, for example, a horse and a mule are similar to degree 0.8, a horse and a cow to degree 0.4, etc. Notice that for a finite and small enough X and Y, a fuzzy relation may be shown in the matrix form as

$$similar = x \begin{array}{c} \text{horse} \\ \text{donkey} \end{array} \begin{array}{cc} \text{mule} & \text{cow} \\ \left[\begin{array}{cc} 0.8 & 0.4 \\ 0.9 & 0.5 \end{array} \right] \end{array}$$

A fuzzy relation is a fuzzy set, and all properties, operations, etc on fuzzy sets hold here as well. Evidently, a fuzzy relation between more than two quantities can be analogously defined (as a fuzzy set in the Cartesian product of more than two universes of discourse). A crucial concept related to fuzzy relations is their composition. If there are two fuzzy relations $R \subseteq X \times Y$ and $S \subseteq Y \times Z$, then their (max–min) composition is a fuzzy relation $R \circ S \subseteq X \times Z$ defined by

$$\mu_{R \circ S}(x,z) = \sup_{y \in Y}[\mu_R(x,y) \wedge \mu_S(y,z)] \quad (10)$$

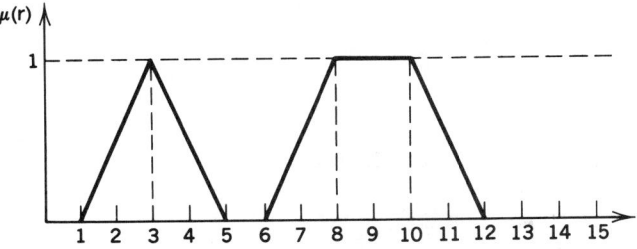

Figure 2. A triangular and a trapezoidal fuzzy number.

Example 8. Let $X = \{1,2\}$, $Y = \{1,2,3\}$ and $Z = \{1,2,3,4\}$. Then, if R and S are as given below, $R \circ S$ is

$$R \circ S = \begin{array}{c} \\ x_1 \\ x_2 \end{array} \overset{\displaystyle \begin{array}{cc} y_1 & y_2 \end{array}}{\begin{bmatrix} 0.3 & 0.8 \\ 0.9 & 0.7 \end{bmatrix}} \circ \begin{array}{c} \\ y_1 \\ y_2 \end{array} \overset{\displaystyle \begin{array}{cc} z_1 & z_2 \end{array}}{\begin{bmatrix} 0.3 & 0.8 \\ 0.9 & 0.7 \end{bmatrix}}$$

$$= \begin{array}{c} \\ x_1 \\ x_2 \end{array} \overset{\displaystyle \begin{array}{cc} z_1 & z_2 \end{array}}{\begin{bmatrix} 0.3 & 0.8 \\ 0.9 & 0.7 \end{bmatrix}}$$

This max–min composition is widely used, although it is by no means the only possible. For instance, we can replace "$\vee$" and "$\wedge$" in equation 10 by other operations, say an s-norm and t-norm, and obtain a different definition of, say, the max-product composition. Fuzzy relations play a crucial role in virtually all applications, notably in decision making and control, and good sources of information have been published (Kacprzyk and Fedrizzi, 1990).

An important area related to fuzzy relations is concerned with fuzzy relational equations of the type $T = R \circ Q$ where T, R, and Q are fuzzy relations, "$\circ$" is a composition, and the problem is to find R or Q knowing T and Q or R. Needless to say, this is a model of many practical problems such as medical or technical diagnosis, control, etc. A good source of information on fuzzy relational equations is available (Di Nola and co-workers, 1989).

Decision Making Under Fuzziness

To finish this short review of basic issues related to fuzzy sets, we will sketch the essence of Bellman and Zadeh's (1970) approach to decision making under fuzziness as a point of departure for virtually all fuzzy approaches to decision making, control, etc. Let $X = \{x_1, \ldots, x_n\}$ be a set of options (alternatives, variants). A fuzzy goal is defined as a fuzzy set $G \subseteq X$, given by $\mu_G(x)$, and a fuzzy constraint as $C \subseteq X$, given by $\mu_C(x)$. A fuzzy decision $D \subseteq X$ is defined as

$$\mu_D(x) = \mu_G(x) \wedge \mu_C(x) \qquad \forall x \in X \tag{11}$$

which reflects the fact that the task is to attain the fuzzy goal *and* satisfy the fuzzy constraint; $\mu_D(x) \in [0,1]$ gives, therefore, the degree to which option $x \in X$ attains the fuzzy goal and satisfies the fuzzy constraint. If it is necessary to single out a best (single) option, an optimal decision is defined as

$$x^* = \arg \sup_{x \in X} \mu_D(x) \tag{12}$$

ie, an option that best attains the fuzzy goal and satisfies the fuzzy goal. The best self-explanatory illustration is shown in Figure 3.

More mathematical treatments of fuzzy set theory are available (Goodman and Nguyen, 1985; Dubois and Prade, 1980; Zimmermann, 1985; Kandel, 1986; Klir and Folger, 1988). More specific information is also available on pattern recognition (Bezdek, 1981), automata (Kandel,

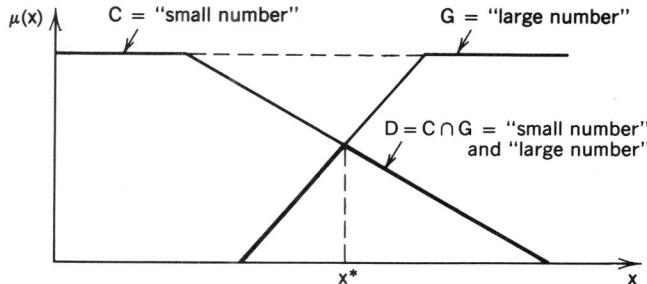

Figure 3. Fuzzy constraint (C), fuzzy goal (G), fuzzy decision (D), and the optimal decision (x^*).

1982), multistage decision making (Kacprzyk, 1983), multiperson decision making (Kacprzyk and Fedrizzi, 1990), optimization (Kacprzyk and Orlovski, 1987), and control (Pedrycz, 1989).

FUNDAMENTALS OF FUZZY LOGIC

The term fuzzy logic is by no means uniquely understood. Basically, for almost 25 yr it has been used to designate a (large) class of models trying to formalize reasoning under imperfect information, mainly of a vague (fuzzy) character. Two basic classes may be distinguished here. In the first, vague or fuzzy, predicates are considered whose vagueness (fuzziness) is implied by the lack of precise boundaries of the set of elements possessing the property represented by the predicate. For instance, if there is a set of balls, and a predicate *large*, a proposition (*ball*) X *is large* may have a degree of truth, $\tau \in [0,1]$, from 0 for full falsity to 1 for full truth. Then, assuming these truth values of fuzzy propositions, a "fuzzy logic" is deviced. For the present purposes, it is basically meant as an apparatus for processing the intersection, union, implication, etc of fuzzy propositions. Needless to say that such a fuzzy logic is in principle a special multivalued logic with some fuzzy interpretations. This approach to fuzzy logic is quite popular and implementable, and recent advances in the synthesis of VLSI fuzzy logic–based chips (fuzzy computers) started in the mid-1980s by Togai and Watanabe in the United States and Yamakawa in Japan have given it an additional impetus.

The second approach consists of a fuzzification of the truth values by introducing fuzzy metalinguistic predicates *true* and *false*. This approach is by far more radical than the former one.

Fuzzy Logic with Nonfuzzy Truth Values

Suppose that we have two propositions: A, "A is a" (eg, ball A is large) and B, "B is b" (eg, car B is expensive) whose truth values are $\tau(A)$, $\tau(B) \in [0,1]$, respectively. Then, in terms of the truth values, the following basic logical connectives can be defined.

- The negation ($\neg A$, ie not A)

$$\tau(\neg A) = 1 - \tau(A) \tag{13}$$

- The intersection $(A \cap B$, ie, A and $B)$

$$\tau(A \cap B) = \tau(A) \wedge \tau(B) = \min [\tau(A), \tau(B)] \quad (14)$$

and, similarly as for the intersection of fuzzy sets in equation 3, "$\wedge$" can be replaced by, eg, a t-norm.

- The union $(A \cup B$, ie, A or $B)$

$$\tau(A \cup B) = \tau(A) \vee \tau(B) = \max [\tau(A), \tau(B)] \quad (15)$$

and, similarly as for the union of fuzzy sets in equation 4, "$\vee$" can be replaced by, eg, an s-norm.

- The implication $(A \Rightarrow B)$

$$\tau(A \Rightarrow B) = 1 \wedge [1 - \tau(A) + \tau(B)] \quad (16)$$

The last definition, although commonly used, may be replaced by, for example, the following:

$$\tau(A \Rightarrow B) = [\tau(A) \wedge \tau(B) \wedge (1 - \tau(A))]$$
$$\tau(A \Rightarrow B) = \tau(A) \wedge \tau(B)$$
$$\tau(A \Rightarrow B) = [1 - \tau(A)] \vee \tau(B)$$
$$\tau(A \Rightarrow B) = 1 - \tau(A) + \tau(A)\tau(B)$$

More information on these and other implication operators and their properties is available (Zadeh and Kacprzyk, in press).

The intersection defined by equation 14 can be extended to "$A_1 \wedge \ldots \wedge A_n$," and $\tau(A_1 \wedge \ldots \wedge A_n) = \min [\tau(A_1), \ldots ,\tau(A_n)]$. On the other hand, the union in equation 15 can be extended to "$A_1, \vee \ldots \vee A_n$," and $\tau(A_1 \vee \ldots \vee A_n) = \max [\tau(A_1), \ldots ,\tau(A_n)]$. The above operations are basic, and some other may also be introduced such as the equivalence $A \Leftrightarrow B$ such that $\tau(A \Leftrightarrow B) = \tau(A \Rightarrow B) \wedge \tau(B \Rightarrow A)$.

An interesting issue related to fuzzy logic is that of linguistically quantified propositions. A linguistically quantified proposition is written "Qy's are F" such as *most experts are convinced*, where Q is a fuzzy linguistic quantifier (eg, *most, almost all*) given by its membership function $\mu_Q: [0,1] \rightarrow [0,1]$, $\mu_Q(r) \in [0,1]$, $Y = \{y\} = \{y_1, \ldots ,y_p\}$ is a set of objects (eg, experts), and $F \subseteq Y$ is a (fuzzy) property (eg, convinced) such that $\tau(y_i$ is $F) = \mu_F(y_i)$, for $i = 1, \ldots ,p$.

The problem is to find the truth of "Qy's are F," $\tau(Qy$'s are $F)$, which is determined in two steps:

$$r = \frac{1}{p} \sum_{i=1}^{p} \mu_F(y_i) \quad (17)$$

$$\tau(Qy\text{'s are } F) = \mu_Q(r) \quad (18)$$

Notice that although linguistically quantified propositions commonly occur in everyday discourse, they cannot be handled by conventional two-valued logic.

Example 9. Suppose that $Y = $ friends $= \{A,B,C\}$, $F = $ *honest* $= 0.1/A + 0.6/B + 0.8/C$, and $Q = $ *most* is given by

$$\mu_Q(r) = \begin{cases} 1 & \text{for } r \geq 0.8 \\ 2x - 0.6 & \text{for } 0.3 < r < 0.8 \\ 0 & \text{for } r \leq 0.3 \end{cases} \quad (19)$$

and truth (most friends are honest) $= $ truth$(Qy$'s are $F) = 0.4$. Importance (B) of the particular objects $y \in Y$ may be added, yielding "QBy's are F" (eg, most of the important experts are convinced), and $\tau(QBy$'s are $F)$ can also be determined (Zadeh, 1983; Kacprzyk, 1985, 1987).

The linguistically quantified propositions sketched above are crucial for the formalization of many real-world reasoning schemes of the type

$$\begin{array}{l} \text{most of expensive cars are big} \\ \underline{\text{almost all big cars are not fuel efficient}} \\ \text{?}Q \text{ expensive cars are fuel inefficient} \end{array} \quad (20)$$

where ?Q is some linguistic quantifier to be determined (Zadeh, 1985). Another approach to the calculation of truth of linguistically quantified proposition is outlined by Yager (1983).

The calculi of linguistically quantified propositions have found applications in a variety of fields, from decision making, optimization, and control to database querying (Kacprzyk, 1985, 1987).

An interesting issue here is the use of some modifiers such as the linguistic hedges *very* and *more or less* (Zadeh, 1973, 1975a).

Fuzzy Logic with Fuzzy Truth Values

The truth value of a (fuzzy) proposition is now a fuzzy set in $[0,1]$, $\Psi \subseteq [0,1]$, whose membership function is $\mu_\Psi: [0,1] \rightarrow [0,1]$. Usually, the set of fuzzy truth values is assumed to contain a number of standard term as, say, $T = \{$true, quite true, very true, not true and not false, rather false, false, $\ldots \}$ each of which is defined as a fuzzy set in $[0,1]$. Notice that the truth values are subjective and local. As discussed above, the truth values (not fuzzy!) of the negation, intersection, union, implication, etc are sought. Because the truth value of a proposition is now a fuzzy number in $[0,1]$, operations 13 through 16 can be extended by using the extension principle of equation 8. Suppose, therefore, that proposition A has a fuzzy truth value $\Psi(A) \subseteq [0,1]$ and proposition B, $\Psi(B) \subseteq [0,1]$, then, the following is obtained $\forall \nu \in [0,1]$:

- For the negation

$$\mu_{\Psi(\neg A)}(\nu) = 1 - \mu_{\Psi(A)}(\nu) \quad (21)$$

and it should be mentioned that $\mu_{\Psi(\neg A)}(\nu) = \mu_{\Psi(A)}(1 - \nu)$ is often employed too.

- For the union

$$\mu_{\Psi(A \cup B)}(\nu) = \sup_{\nu = x \vee y} [\mu_{\Psi(A)}(x) \wedge \mu_{\Psi(B)}(y)] \quad (22)$$

- For the intersection

$$\mu_{\Psi(A \cap B)}(\nu) = \sup_{\nu = x \wedge y} [\mu_{\Psi(A)}(x) \wedge \mu_{\Psi(B)}(y)] \quad (23)$$

• For the implication [assuming the implication given by equation 16]

$$\mu_{\Psi(A \Rightarrow B)}(\nu) = \sup_{\nu = 1 \wedge (1-x+y)} [\mu_{\Psi(A)}(x) \wedge \mu_{\Psi(B)}(y)] \quad (24)$$

The fuzzy truth values resulting from the above negation, union, etc need not be any of the standard truth values. After having obtained a fuzzy truth value via equations 21 through 24, it is usual to approximate it by some (closest) standard truth value. This is called a linguistic approximation and is extensively used in practice.

This concludes the brief exposition of fuzzy logic; for lack of space many crucial issues have remained uncovered here, including approximate reasoning, ie, a reasoning scheme based on imprecise premises, which may be exemplified by equation 20. More information is available (Zadeh and Kacprzyk, in press).

CONCLUSION

This short introduction to fuzzy sets and fuzzy logic underscores their potential as effective and efficient tools of vagueness-related aspects in the management of uncertainty in broadly perceived knowledge-based systems, which are crucial for artificial intelligence.

BIBLIOGRAPHY

W. Bandler and L. J. Kohout, "Fuzzy Power Sets and Fuzzy Implication Operators," *Fuzzy Sets Syst.* **4**, 13–30 (1980).

R. E. Bellman and L. A. Zadeh, "Decision-Making in a Fuzzy Environment," *Management Sci.* **17**, 141–164 (1970).

J. C. Bezdek, *Pattern Recognition with Fuzzy Objective Function Algorithms,* Plenum Press, New York, 1981.

D. Dubois and H. Prade, *Fuzzy Sets and Systems: Theory and Applications,* Academic Press, New York, 1980.

B. R. Gaines, "Foundations of Fuzzy Reasoning," *Int. J. Man-Machine Stud.* **8**, 623–668 (1976).

J. A. Goguen, "L-Fuzzy Sets," *J. Math. Anal. Applic.* **18**, 145–174 (1987).

I. R. Goodman and H. T. Nguyen, *Uncertainty Models for Knowledge-Based Systems,* North-Holland, Amsterdam, 1985.

J. Kacprzyk, *Multistage Decision-Making Under Fuzziness,* Verlag TÜV Rheinland, Cologne, Germany, 1983.

J. Kacprzyk, "Zadeh's Commonsense Knowledge and Its Use in Multicriteria, Multistage and Multiperson Decision Making," in M. M. Gupta and co-workers, eds., *Approximate Reasoning in Expert Systems,* North-Holland, Amsterdam, 1985, pp. 105–122.

J. Kacprzyk, "Towards 'Human-Consistent' Decision Support Systems Through Commonsense Knowledge-Based Decision-Making and Control Models: a Fuzzy Logic Approach," *Computers and Artificial Intelligence* **6**, 97–122 (1987).

J. Kacprzyk and M. Fedrizzi, eds., *Combining Fuzzy Imprecision with Probabilistic Uncertainty in Decision Making,* Springer-Verlag, New York, 1988.

J. Kacprzyk and M. Fedrizzi, eds., *Multiperson Decision Making Models Using Fuzzy Sets and Possibility Theory,* Kluwer, Dordrecht, 1990.

J. Kacprzyk and S. A. Orlovski, eds., *Optimization Models Using Fuzzy Sets and Possibility Theory,* Reidel, Dordrecht, 1987 y.

A. Kandel, *Fuzzy Techniques in Pattern Recognition,* Wiley, New York, 1982.

A. Kandel, *Fuzzy Mathematical Techniques with Applications,* Addison-Wesley, Inc., Reading, Mass., 1986.

A. Kaufmann and M. M. Gupta, *Introduction to Fuzzy Arithmetic,* Van Nostrand Reinhold, New York, 1985.

G. J. Klir and T. A. Folger, *Fuzzy Sets, Uncertainty and Information,* Prentice-Hall, Inc., Englewood Cliffs, N.J., 1988.

A. Di Nola, S. Sessa, W. Pedrycz, and E. Sanchez, *Fuzzy Relation Equations and Their Applications to Knowledge Engineering,* Kluwer, Dordrecht, 1989.

W. Pedrycz, *Fuzzy Control and Fuzzy Systems,* Research Studies Press, Taunton, and Wiley, New York, 1989.

R. R. Yager, "A Note on Probabilities of Fuzzy Events," *Inform. Sci.* **18**, 113–129 (1979).

R. R. Yager, "Quantifiers in the Formulation of Multiple Objective Decision Functions," *Inform. Sci.* **31**, 107–139 (1983).

L. A. Zadeh, "Fuzzy Sets," *Inform. Contr.* **8**, 338–353 (1965).

L. A. Zadeh, "Probability Measures of Fuzzy Events," *J. Math. Anal. Applic.* **23**, 421–427 (1968).

L. A. Zadeh, "Outline of a New Approach to the Analysis of Complex Systems and Decision Processes," *IEEE Trans. Sys. Man Cybernet.* SMC 3, 28–44 (1973).

L. A. Zadeh, "The Concept of a Linguistic Variable and Its Application to Approximate Reasoning," *Inform. Sci.* "Part I," **8**, 199–249; "Part II," **8**, 301–357; "Part III," **9**, 43–80 (1975a).

L. A. Zadeh, "Fuzzy Logic and Approximate Reasoning," *Synthese* **30**, 407–428, (1975b).

L. A. Zadeh, "A Computational Approach to Fuzzy Quantifiers in Natural Languages," *Computers and Mathematics with Applications* **9**, 149–194 (1983).

L. A. Zadeh, "Sylogistic Reasoning in Fuzzy Logic and Its Application to Usuality and Reasoning with Dispositions," *IEEE Trans. Sys. Man Cybernet.* SMC-15, 754–763 (1985).

L. A. Zadeh and J. Kacprzyk, eds., *Fuzzy Logic for the Management of Uncertainty,* in press.

H.-J. Zimmermann, *Fuzzy Sets Theory and Its Applications,* Kluwer-Nijhoff, Dordrecht, 1985.

H.-J. Zimmermann, *Fuzzy Sets, Decision-Making, and Expert Systems,* Kluwer, Dordrecht, 1987.

JANUSZ KACPRZYK
Polish Academy of Sciences

G

GAME PLAYING

An important part of AI research lies in efforts at understanding intelligent behavior as opposed to simulating it for solving a specific problem in an applications domain. For this former area of research games remain an excellent metaphor.

A considerable body of knowledge exists in mathematics about the property of games; there has not been enough interaction between this knowledge and AI research. One reason is that it has been proven (Stockmeyer and Chandra, 1979) for games like chess, checkers, and go that no game-playing strategy can exist that remains efficient over larger and larger boards. As a result, AI research in games has been restricted to two extreme viewpoints. On the one hand, efforts are made to incorporate knowledge of specific games (eg, chess on a standard board) into the program. At the other end of the spectrum, one restricts one's attention to methods of search (qv) reduction.

There are classes of games, however, for which methods of efficient play can be developed and used. Such techniques are often applicable over a wide class of seemingly unrelated games. Study of such classes yields insight into the notion of similarity and analogy, activities of recognized value in automatic learning of problem-solving (qv) and game-playing strategies. Such studies form an important third approach to the study of games.

In what follows all of these aspects of AI research into games are discussed. The second and third approaches are discussed in some detail since a general body of knowledge exists for these. For the first approach the reader is directed to specialized treatises and papers (Frey, 1977; Berliner, 1978; Bramer, 1983). In the next section some formal definitions are made to facilitate the later discussion.

MATHEMATICAL FORMULATION

In the original, most general definition (von Neumann and Morgenstern, 1944) a game is characterized by the set of all sequence of plays possible, as made by N players, and by the payoffs to the N players corresponding to each sequence. Each play reduces the set of sequences to the subset that has that play as the initial one. The moves thus characterize a partition on the set of sequences. However, since all the players do not necessarily know what play was made (eg, in Kriegspiel or bridge), the players' knowledge restricts the set to some superpartition of this partition.

Most of the work on games in the field of AI has been in the case of two-person games with complete information and with alternating moves, although some work on bridge and poker has been reported. As a result, one obtains a considerable simplification on the structure on the partitions over the set of all play sequences. A set of nested subpartitions results as the representation of the plays, and one can analyze the games in terms of trees. Figure 1 indicates the relationship between the game tree and the partitions on the sequences represented by them. It also shows the kind of complications introduced by incomplete information that makes the game tree less useful for general N-person games.

Most of the analyses of games in AI have been in terms of game trees. In these trees each node represents a class of possible continuations of the game. However, one could also consider the node to represent the history of past moves. From the latter point of view, each arc of the tree represents a move by a player. The node also restricts how the rest of the play is allowed to continue.

Of course, two distinct histories of moves do not always restrict the possible continuations in distinct ways. For instance, in chess, the sequence P-K4, Kt-KB3, Kt-KB3 leads to the same situation as Kt-KB3, Kt-KB3, P-K4. Many authors have considered it meaningful to treat the two resulting nodes in the tree as equivalent and represented by the board configuration produced by them. This identifies two nodes of the tree as a single node, and as a result, the structure becomes a graph rather than a tree (see Fig. 2). The nodes of this graph may be considered to be represented by the configuration of pieces on the board together with a specification as to who is on move. The latter specification may or may not be uniquely determined by the node of the graph. Such subtleties need not interest us here. The interested reader will find these discussions in Banerji (1980). For our purposes we shall take the formalization where each node can be considered from the point of view of either player being on the move.

Conway (1976, 1977; Berlekamp, Conway, and Guy, 1982) abstracts the graph away by defining a game (a game node in the above terminology) to be given by two sets of games (ie, game nodes), to wit the ones that one player could reach if he was on move and the ones that the other player could reach if the other player was on move. As Conway would put it, "A game is an ordered pair of two sets of games."

The Conway approach has led to the development of a new area of nonstandard number theory and unified some known theories of impartial games with this extended number theory. However, so far a clear way has not been found to use their results to develop new winning strategies of known interesting games. This theory shall therefore not be discussed any further. However, the interested reader is urged strongly to look into the work of Conway and his colleagues for some extremely exciting and amusing, albeit occasionally strenuous reading.

STRATEGIES

For the rest of this overview the important problem of concern is, given a node in a given game, how does the player on move assure a win if possible? A number of

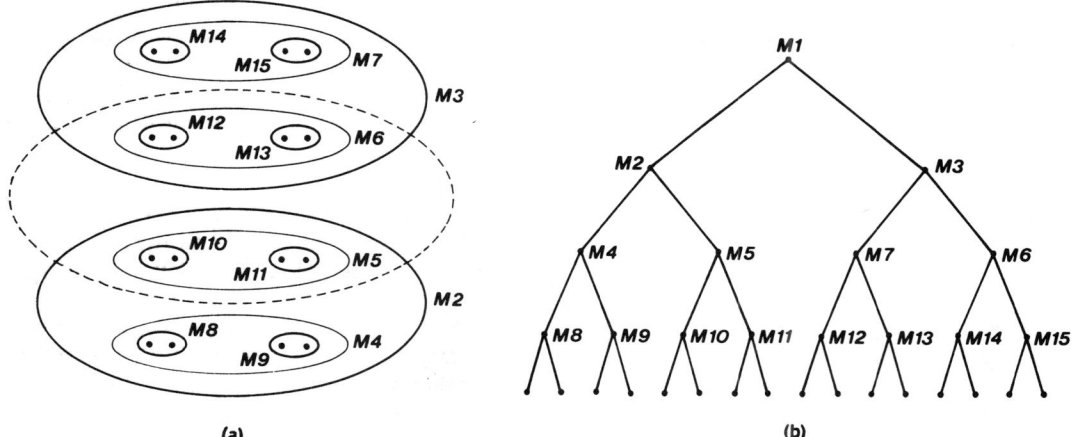

Figure 1. Game with 16 possible plays. (*a*) Partition representation of von Neumann and Morgenstern (1944). The game being with complete information, two persons, and alternate moves, the tree representation (*b*) is also possible. If the second player is not allowed to know the first player's first move, after his move he would not know where the play is and would merely have the play localized in either the set enclosed by the dotted line in (*a*) or its complement. If the player on move is determined by rules other than alternation, more subsets would appear in (*a*) and the simplicity of the tree representation would be lost.

considerations arise in determining how such an assurance can be obtained. First, the only decision available to the player is the choice of a move available at the node. The opponent's move leads the game from the resulting node to a node where the player has to make another choice. This choice cannot be made beforehand: until the opponent has played, the player does not know what the resulting node will be. The player's decision cannot be with respect to a single move or even a sequence of moves. He or she has to decide, not on a move, but on a method by

which, given a node, a move can be chosen. In mathematical parlance, one needs a function mapping nodes to moves. Such a function is called a *strategy*. A winning strategy is one whose repeated application, one at each node where a choice is needed, leads to a win whenever a win is possible.

This concept of strategy in games has a very close relationship with the same concept in game theory as studied in economics (see MINIMAX PROCEDURE). Suffice it to say here that in a two-person game with complete information and

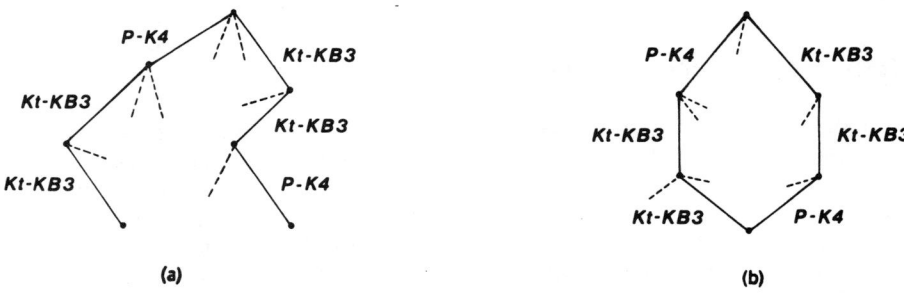

Figure 2. (*a*) Two distinct move sequences can determine the same constraint on possible continuations and are, in that sense, "equivalent." By identifying the equivalent nodes of the game tree, one obtains the game graph (*b*). In the case of most games these equivalent nodes do indeed represent identical "game board configurations" (*c*), giving concrete meaning to the nodes of the graph.

alternating moves the calculation of strategy (albeit still inefficient; see above) becomes much simpler than in the general case. The general method applied to the case of Figure 1 would lead to the calculation of a 32 × 1024 matrix. Only the simple special case is discussed here.

If one unfolds the game graph into a tree, one obtains a method of calculating the winning strategy by a method that, with some modifications (see below), has remained the only error-proof method known. The method can best be described in terms of a recursive definition:

> If the node is a leaf (end of game), the game is already won or lost, and its value is the value of the node. No move needs to be made.
> If the node is the player's move, find the value of each node to which one can move. Make the move that maximizes this value. The value of the node is this maximum value.
> If the node is the opponent's move, the value of the node is the minimum value among the nodes that can be reached by a move.

Figure 3 shows the value of a node. The optimum player's move from a node and for all the nodes reached from it by the optimal move of each player follow the leftmost branch sequence.

This method of evaluation and strategy construction is called the *minimax method*. The trouble with this method of finding the strategy is the amount of calculation involved. Early estimates about chess revealed that such a calculation made from the starting position of chess would involve the generation of about 7^{32} nodes. The most optimistic guess about the speed of calculation and space used by memory still yields the fact that such a calculation would take millenia to calculate on an impossibly large machine.

Thus, playing chess "optimally" is not feasible using such a naive search technique. People do play chess well; nobody knows if anybody has ever played optimal chess. See Frey (1977) and Berliner (1978) for a discussion of how machines can be made to play acceptable chess and how it compares with human play. Some of the principles on which optimal and suboptimal game playing can be based are described below.

SEARCH REDUCTION: KERNELS AND EVALUATIONS

Any method of game playing has to be based on some principle that allows one to reduce the amount of search involved in the calculation of strategy. Such methods have been developed both in AI and in the mathematical theories of games. The latter are described first, since the former are somewhat more difficult to justify in any precise manner.

The set of all nodes in the game graph whose minimax value is 1 are called the winning nodes and the others the losing nodes (for the time being, draws are not considered). The minimax principle can be stated in terms of these sets of nodes: a node is winning if there is at least one node connected to it that is a losing node; a node is losing if all the nodes connected to it are winning nodes; and terminal nodes are winning if their value is 1.

Consider the property of being winning. Of course, every leaf node of the game tree (terminal node of the game graph) has this property if its value is 1. Also, if a node lacks this property, every node connected to it has this property. Again, each node having this property is connected to at least one node lacking this property.

It can be seen that if a property of nodes, which is easy to calculate, is shared by all leaf nodes with value 1 and has the above characteristics, the nodes having the property are precisely the winning nodes. Having minimax

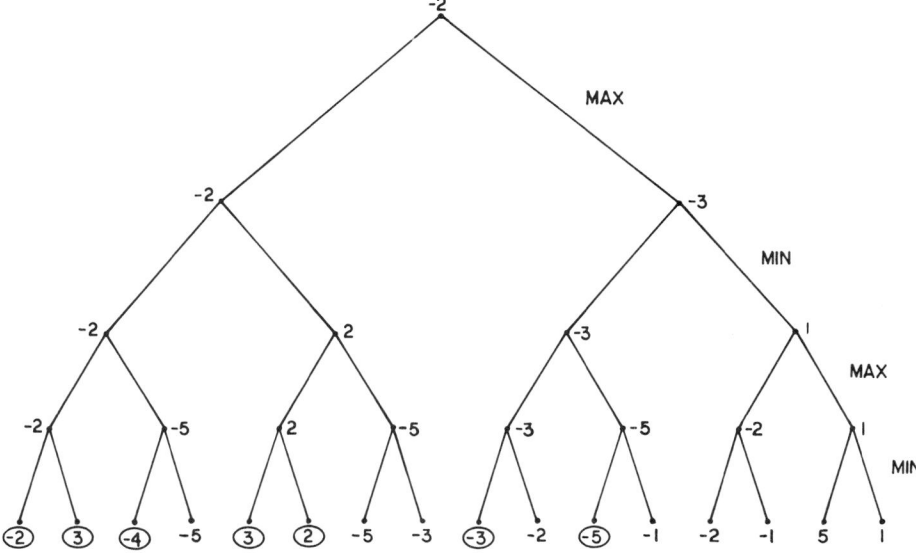

Figure 3. Minimax value of nodes in a game tree. The leaves are evaluated by some intermediate evaluation function. The leaves whose values are enclosed in circles are the only ones that need to be evaluated by an alpha-beta algorithm.

value 1 at a player's move is one such property. However, to check this property, one has to search the whole game tree. In many special games, however, these properties can be calculated in terms of the board configuration in the node itself or just of a few nearby nodes.

A standard example is the following simple take-away game played in elementary school mathematics classes. There is a pile of sticks on the table. Each player in his turn removes at least one and no more than three sticks from the pile. The first player who cannot move (ie, faces an empty table) loses. It is clear that a player can win if he is on move and there are three or less (ie, less than four) sticks on the table. Such positions can be considered leaf nodes with value 1. If there are four sticks on the table, the player on move has to leave less than four and at least one stick. Hence the node with four sticks is a losing node. Induction readily shows that any node with a multiple of four sticks is losing and the rest are winning.

There is thus no need to do a minimax calculation when playing this game: if the player on the move does not have a multiple of four sticks on the table, he or she can reduce the number of sticks to a multiple of four, and the opponent cannot but return him or her to a node where the number of sticks is not a multiple of four.

Kernels

There are games where the winning nodes and winning strategies can be identified without search. The class of such games is not a trivial one: various rather complicated (but efficient) techniques are known for calculation of the values of nodes in such games. See Banerji (1980) and Berlekamp and co-workers, 1982 for many examples. In what follows, the technical term *kernel* calculation means the calculation of winning and losing nodes. (In precise terms, the losing nodes are said to form the kernel of the game graph.)

Such techniques, often called knowledge-based techniques in AI, have also been developed (albeit with lesser success and precision) for chess, yielding methods independent of minimax. See Pitrat (1977) and Bratko (1984) for examples.

The minimax technique "beats" this class of methods in one way, of course. Minimax works for all games. These game-specific methods work only when someone is clever enough to describe the winning nodes. What one needs is some method whereby the computer, given the description of the game, can develop the description of the set of winning nodes by itself. Samuel's checkers-playing program (qv) (1959) succeeded in doing this to an extent, and other programs have achieved similar successes (see below).

There are times when one can approximate the calculation of winning nodes. The method for one such calculation was developed by Koffman (1968) and by Citrenbaum (1972) for another wide class of games which, for want of any better name, is called *positional*. These include such trivial games as tic-tac-toe and more difficult games like Hex and Go-Moku. The game $4 \times 4 \times 4$ tic-tac-toe ("Qubic," as it is often called) is another nontrivial member of this class.

The major strategy for this class of games is the forma-

tion of forks. Indeed, in some sense any winning node in any game is a fork, but in the positional class of games the fork has a clear visual significance that can be very efficiently represented in a computer. The most elementary fork, of course, is when one encounters a board position like that in Figure 4. There are two lines of squares each of which has two empty squares, one of which is common to the two lines. In his turn, X can play at this common intersection and produce two potentially winning lines, and the opponent cannot block both.

The concept of a force can be pushed back much further; 14 or 15 move deep forces of this nature can be recognized on a go-moku board just by the configuration of pieces alone (1967). Without going into the depths of the discussion of the data representation needed to do this (Banerji, 1980), the reader is asked to convince himself that the empty board in $3 \times 3 \times 3$ tic-tac-toe is a forcing configuration: the player on move can assure himself of a win just by playing at the center.

The trouble with the Koffman–Citrenbaum technique (1968, 1972) for recognizing forces was that some deep forces could be upset if one of the defensive moves of the opponent posed a direct threat to the attacking player. The calculation of the winning nodes is thus only approximate in their method. A node recognized to be only three moves away from a win may be further away or even not be a winning move. Thus, the calculation has to be backed up by some search (albeit not a minimax search) of the game tree.

Evaluations

Many approximate measures of the "goodness" of a position (with "goodness" not necessarily defined in terms of kernels as above) have been suggested for various games. In most cases this has been done with the purpose of simplifying the minimax search for games. The arguments that have led to such efforts at simplification are as follows.

Consider the case where there is a method for finding whether a node is winning just by looking at the board configuration. In such a case, if a node is given the value 1 if it is winning and 0 if it is losing, this "static" value will be the same as its minimax value. On the other hand, if nothing is known as to whether a node is winning or los-

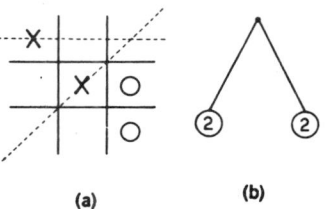

(a)   (b)

Figure 4. *(a)* Simple fork in tic-tac-toe. The two lines shown dotted each have two empty cells, and they intersect in an empty square where the forcing move is to be made. Graph *(b)* expresses the same fact. The two circles stand for the two lines (the numbers indicating the number of empty cells). The empty intersection is the solid node. Graph *(b)* describes not just the figure *(a)* but many other strategically equivalent positions.

ing, a minimax search done to the end of the game also leads to the determination as to whether a node is winning. This seems to indicate that if one has a very good evaluation for a node, very shallow minimax is needed to determine whether a node is winning; conversely, if there is a very bad evaluation available for a node (eg, no evaluation at all), a very deep minimax is needed. One can make a very unsophisticated interpolation from this that seems to indicate that it is possible to get a good idea as to whether a node is winning even if there is an imperfect evaluation function but the minimax on it is deep enough.

This has led to some extensive experimentation with game-playing programs along the following lines. Given a game to play with a computer, the researcher uses his own intuition and the literature on the specific game to decide a method for attaching a value to the nodes in such a way the most winning nodes have a higher value than most losing nodes. One then chooses the "best" move at a node as follows: one considers all the moves one can make and then all the moves an opponent can make from each of the resulting nodes. A part of the game tree is produced this way by alternating these "expansions" of nodes to a certain depth. The leaves of the resulting tree are then evaluated by calculating the static evaluation function. These values are then propagated "up the tree" by minimax to obtain the best move at the node.

Such evaluations have been found useful in constructing game-playing programs in some cases, although there is very little known as to why this is so (see below). However, the general experience has been that the technique is useful only when the depth of the tree is chosen carefully. It may even be that certain parts of the search tree should be explored deeper than some other parts. For a thorough discussion of the strengths and weaknesses of such procedures, see Berliner (1978), Jackson (1974), and Rich (1983). Only one such technique is given here.

This technique deals with the concept of "stability" of a position and is relevant to games like chess and checkers. The basic idea is that one should not evaluate a board position in the middle of a major skirmish, where pieces are being exchanged by a sequence of kills. In a part of the game tree where this is happening, it is better to explore the tree until the end of the skirmish, so the evaluation function does not oscillate violently. At the resulting position, the evaluation can be expected to be stable.

This technique is not foolproof since an apparently stable position can be hiding a threat that can be pushed back due to irrelevant but powerful moves demanding answers, so the threat (on the part of either player) can remain invisible. For a discussion of this so-called *horizon effect*, see Berliner (1978) (see also HORIZON EFFECT).

Many of the game-playing programs augment the minimax evaluation with a static evaluation of moves with respect to their relevance to a position. For instance, one may not want to consider moving a rook's pawn while one is busily engaged building up one's forces at the center of the board. Pruning away the branches of the game tree makes the tree grow at a smaller rate, so that greater depths can be explored.

Three distinct heuristics (qv) are being suggested at this point: one for choosing the intermediate evaluation, one for choosing the depth at which the evaluation is to be made, and one for pruning the search. How the accuracies of the three different heuristics co-operate to increase the accuracy of the final evaluation, indeed what one means by "accuracy" in the case of depth limitation, is not known. All one knows is that if the pruning heuristic is exact, it alone suffices to determine a winning strategy.

Meanwhile, there is always an effort to make the minimax search as deep as resources permit, the conventional wisdom being the argument given a few paragraphs earlier. We shall have occasion for discussing this conventional wisdom again later. However, we should mention another game-independent technique that allows one to increase the depth of search by avoiding the evaluation of every "leaf" at the end of the specified depth of search. This method, known as the alpha-beta search in the literature (Rich, 1983; Knuth and Moore, 1975) was informally suggested by Simon, Newell, and Shaw (1958) and placed on a formal basis by McCarthy (see ALPHA-BETA PRUNING). In Figure 3 the circled leaves of the tree are the only ones that would be evaluated by an alpha-beta procedure. In recent years a number of improvements on the alpha-beta pruning technique have been suggested (Baudet, 1978; Stockman, 1979; Pearl, 1980).

The popular line of attack on games has been on improving intermediate static evaluation of positions and efforts made at deepening the minimax by the use of some ad hoc pruning strategies and by some formal pruning techniques like alpha-beta. It has not been terribly popular to ask questions like, "Why is it better to minimax on static evaluations than to use the evaluation directly in choosing a move?" or "How can one judge the effectiveness of a static evaluation?" Nevertheless, efforts have been made to face these questions.

A DISTURBING RESULT: THE IMPORTANCE OF EVALUATION AND LEARNING

Results obtained by Nau (1983a) seem to confirm (as hinted by all that has gone above) that success at game playing is guaranteed only if one can find automatic methods for calculating kernels (ie, finding good static evaluation). Efforts at finding more efficient methods of minimaxing may be the wrong approach to writing strong game-playing programs.

Nau's result can be paraphrased by saying that if one has an imperfect evaluation function, in a large class of games the quality of the evaluation function deteriorates rather than improves with minimaxing, and its use leads to lower probability of winning than would have if the evaluation function was used directly.

Since the result is counterintuitive and since many game-playing programs (especially in the case of chess) seem to yield greater strength the deeper the minimaxing goes, there is need to understand what Nau's class of games consist of and why chess does not seem to belong to this class. A number of efforts (Nau, 1983b; Pearl, 1980) have shed light on this question.

In those cases where Nau's results apply, however, it seems futile to use approximate evaluation functions and deep search: the only hope seems to be in the use of exact determination of the kernel. Unfortunately, no one knows any general method to find them. The fact that intuitive methods are inadequate is already obvious. The case where mathematically solid methods have succeeded, on the other hand, have not been very general or exciting. Also, the realization has remained that these methods were by themselves the product of hard and sustained human analysis. The automation of such analysis, then, becomes the real challenge. No easy shortcut around this challenge is available, as any consideration of past history would show.

Another difficult question that arises is one on the nature of approximate strategies. After all, human game playing has always been based on such approximations. Nau's results seem to indicate that minimaxing does not guarantee improved approximations. It is not known, given an approximate (in some sense) evaluation, to what extent games played on their basis approximate wins. More precisely, if an evaluation function predicts winning positions with 80% correctness, would a person using a strategy based on it win 80% of the games or would he win 10% of the games?

Pearl (Nau, 1983b) has suggested that perhaps one can skirt the question raised by Nau's results by bypassing minimaxing as a method of move choice. Instead, he suggests that one consider the evaluation as a measure of the probability of a win. So if $p_1, p_2, \ldots$ are the probabilities of win of the nodes reachable from a given node, the probability of win of the node itself, instead of being the maximum of $p_1, p_2, \ldots$ would be

$$1 - (1 - p_1)(1 - p_2), \ldots$$

The consequence of this suggestion on the previous questions apparently has not been analyzed.

Meanwhile, in relation to the search for better evaluation functions, there have been some successful experimentations done with the automatic development of evaluation functions.

Learning

So far as present intuition goes, there are two possible ways one can go about developing kernel descriptions or evaluations on the basis of the description of a game. One can use deduction. One can, if one knows that in go-moku one can win by making five in a row, figure out that two simultaneous four in a rows would be impossible to beat. Such deductive techniques have not been tried in the field so far. Alternatively, one could develop the description of good strategies by making generalization from experience. A technique that was tried in the very early days of AI was for the computer to "remember" the positions that lead to a win for either player. In so far as such a large set can be remembered, this is a perfectly reasonable way of going about the business. Good performance can be obtained if one can develop an encoding method that would enable the storing of a large list of positions. The method becomes inadequate against strong players, however, even in such comparatively simple games like three-dimensional tic-tac-toe.

What is needed here is not a method of encoding individual nodes so that they can be listed and accessed easily, but a method by which one can describe sets of nodes in implicit form, that is, be developing descriptions for them in some language. The importance of language to facilitate description has been discussed at some depth in pattern recognition (qv) literature (occasionally under the presently popular term "learning") (Banerji, 1980; Mitchell, 1983). Learning (qv) techniques of various kinds are also known. Two techniques by which strategies have been learned on the basis of game experience are described below.

It may be significant that in both these techniques the basis for the learning has not been pure experience but a reliance on the formal definition of a kernel. It will be recalled that one of the important properties of a winning position is that its minimax value and its static value are the same. The basis of Samuel's checker-playing program was a learning technique where the description was modified any time the minimax and the static value were not close enough. The description language chosen was one that gained great popularity at the time through the independently described perceptron (qv) (Rosenblatt, 1959; Minsky and Papert, 1969).

Given a node in checkers, certain measurements were made on the board configuration to yield numerical values for such concepts as mobility, center control, material balance, and so on. A linear combination of these numbers was taken as the value of the node. The learning done by Samuel's program consisted of modifying the coefficients of this linear combination so that the static and minimax values of nodes came to be close to one another. The evaluation so obtained would satisfy one property of an evaluation function leading to a kernel. The other property, that is, that the value should be high for winning positions and low for losing positions, was not confirmed. Also, there was no assurance that the technique used for modifying the coefficients would lead to convergence; as a matter of fact, there was a good bit of oscillation in the values found. Also, it was not clear that the kernel would be a linearly separable function of the measurements performed.

The fact remains, however, that the program played checkers very well after a period of learning. Efforts were later made (Samuel, 1985) to improve the learning performance by the use of a technique that had been used previously in the field of pattern recognition under the name of learning logical descriptions (Banerji, 1985). This technique has been discussed quite a bit in the literature in recent times (Valiant, 1984). It seems that the expressive ability of the descriptions learned is somewhat easy to control: one can trade expressive power for efficiency of learning. However, if the basic measurements used in constructing descriptions is well suited, both efficiency and expressive power can be obtained.

The effect of a good choice of language was demonstrated very well in the late sixties in the work of Koffman (1968), whose program learned approximations to the kernels of positional games in stages. Also, the nature of the approximation was clearly understood: any winning node would satisfy the approximate description, but not all nodes satisfying the approximate description would be a winning node. However, the reason for this discrepancy was well understood so that once a node satisfied the approximate description, one could determine with a very limited search of the game tree as to whether the node was winning.

The nature of the descriptions has been indicated above in connection with positional games. The basic measurements of the language consisted of looking at the winning paths on the board (eg, row, columns, and diagonals at every plane of Qubic) and noting which of these were unobstructed by the opponent and among these the number of empty squares on each and which of the paths had empty intersections. Figure 5 indicates a seven deep force in the language and two of its interpretations on a plane of the Qubic board. It will be noticed that the two positions cannot be obtained one from the other by any symmetry of the board. The basic measurements have yielded a language of considerable power.

The design of the language in the sixties could not be automatic. The problem of learning, whether in games or any other activity, lies with discovering the basic measurements. Until very recently, no method was known for the automatic discovery for such measurements. Some recent work on problem solving (qv) (Ernst and Goldstein, 1982; Mitchell, 1983) has thrown some light on learning. The following were developed in the study of problem-solving: a class of nodes exists on problem graphs that has a clear analogy with the winning nodes of game graphs. Languages have been automatically developed for writing easy descriptions for these nodes. A program developed by Ernst and Goldstein (1982) has been effective also in discovering the similarity between a given game and games with known winning strategies. The interested reader is referred to the literature on problem solving and learning for details.

SUMMARY

In this article, a number of concepts that are of importance in research on game-playing programs have been elucidated. Concepts of game graphs and game trees have been introduced as well as the idea of evaluating a position by complete search of game trees. Due to the prohibitive amount of computation involved in such evaluation, one is forced to introduce the idea of shallow search and intermediate evaluations. Precise discussions have been included to explain when such an evaluation can be considered useful. The difficulties in the way of improving a bad evaluation have been indicated. Programs have been described that in the past could develop such evaluations from experience. These learning have been heavily dependent on the quality of the language used in these evaluations. Recent work on automatic modification of languages by definition have been mentioned.

BIBLIOGRAPHY

R. B. Banerji, *Artificial Intelligence: A Theoretical Approach,* North Holland, Amsterdam, 1980.

R. B. Banerji, *The Logic of Learning: A Basis for Pattern Recognition and Improvement of Performance,* Progress in Computers, No. 24, Academic Press, New York, 1985.

G. M. Baudet, "On the Branching Factor of the Alpha-Beta Pruning Algorithm," *Artif. Intell.* **10**, 173 (1978).

H. J. Berliner, A Chronology of Computer Chess and its Literature, *Artif. Intell.* **10**, 201 (1978).

E. R. Berlekamp, J. H. Conway, and R. K. Guy, *Winning Ways,* Academic Press, New York, 1982.

M. A. Bramer, *Computer Game-Playing: Theory and Practice,* Ellis Horwood Series, Wiley, New York, 1983.

I. Bratko, "Advice and Planning in Chess Endgames," in A. Elithorn and R. B. Banerji, eds., *Artificial & Human Intelligence,* North Holland, Amsterdam, 1984.

R. L. Citrenbaum, "Strategic Pattern Generation: A Solution Technique for a Class of Games," *Patt. Recog.* **4**, 317 (1972).

J. H. Conway, *On Numbers and Games,* Academic Press, New York, 1976.

J. H. Conway, "All Games Bright and Beautiful," *Am. Math. Mon.* **84**, 417 (1977).

E. W. Elcock and A. M. Murray, "Experiments With a Learning Component in a Go-Moku Playing Program," in *Machine Intelligence,* Vol. 1, Oliver & Boyd, Edinburgh, UK, 1967.

G. W. Ernst and M. Goldstein, "Mechanical Discovery of Classes of Problem Solving Strategies," *J. Assoc. Comp. Mach.* **29** (1982).

P. Frey, ed., *Chess Skill in Man and Machine,* Springer-Verlag, 1977.

P. C. Jackson, *Introduction to Artificial Intelligence,* Petrocelli, Princeton, N.J., 1974.

D. E. Knuth and R. W. Moore, "An Analysis of Alpha-Beta Pruning," *Artif. Intell.* **6**, 293 (1975).

E. B. Koffman, "Learning Through Pattern Recognition Applied to a Class of Games," *IEEE Trans. Sys. Sci. Cybern.* **SSC-4,** March 1968.

M. Minsky and S. Papert, *Perceptrons: An Introduction to Computational Geometry,* MIT Press, Cambridge, Mass., 1969.

T. M. Mitchell, "Learning and Problem Solving," *Proceedings of the International Joint Conference on Artificial Intelligence,* Karlsruhe, FRG, 1983, p. 1139.

D. S. Nau, "Decision Quality as a Function of Search Depth on Game Trees," *J. Assoc. Comp. Mach.* **30**, 687 (1983).

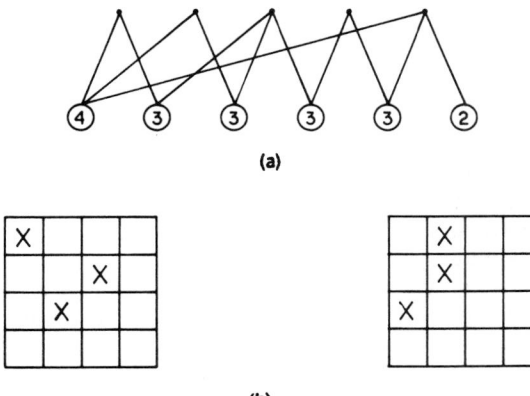

Figure 5. *(a)* Description of a five deep force in positional games; the language is identical to the one used in Figure 4a. *(b)* Two planes on a qubic (three-dimensional tic-tac-toe) board which obey the description. The reader is encouraged to work through the force. Notice that the two positions are not symmetrical with one another.

D. S. Nau, "Pathology on Game Trees Revisited, and an Alternative to Min-Maxing," *Artif. Intell.* **21**, 222 (1983).

A. Newell, J. C. Shaw, and H. A. Simon, "Chess Programs and the Problem of Complexity," *IBM J. Res. Dev.* **2**, 320 (1958).

J. Pearl, "Asymptotic Properties of Minimax Trees and Game Searching Procedures," *Artif. Intell.* **14**, 113 (1980).

J. Pitrat, "A Chess Combination Program which Uses Plans," *Artif. Intell.* **8**, 275 (1977).

E. Rich, *Artificial Intelligence,* McGraw-Hill, New York, 1983.

F. Rosenblatt, "Two Theorems on Statistical Separability in the Perceptron," *Proceedings of the Symposium on the Mechanization of Thought Processes,* Her Majesty's Stationery Office, London, 1959.

A. L. Samuel, "Some Studies in Machine Learning Using the Game of Checkers," *IBM J. Res. Devel.* **3**, 210 (1959).

M. Samuel, "Some Studies in Machine Learning Using the Game of Checkers II," *IBM J. Res. Dev.* **11**, 601 (1985).

G. A. Stockman, "A Minmax Algorithm Better than the Alpha-Beta?" *Artif. Intell.* **12**, 179 (1979).

L. J. Stockmeyer and A. K. Chandra, "Intrinsically Difficult Games," *Scientif. Am.* **240**(5), 140 (1979).

L. G. Valiant, "A Theory of the Learnable," *Proceedings of the Sixteenth Annual Symposium on Theory of Computing,* Washington, D.C., 1984, p. 436.

J. von Neumann and O. Morgenstern, *Theory of Games and Economic Behavior,* Princeton University Press, Princeton, N.J., 1944.

R. BANERJI
St. Joseph's University

GAME TREES

Most games played by computer programs, including chess, checkers, and Go, are two-player, perfect-information games (see CHECKERS-PLAYING PROGRAMS; COMPUTER CHESS AND SEARCH). There are two adversary players who alternate in making moves, each viewing the opponent's failure as his own success. At each turn the rules of the game define both what moves are legal and what effect each possible move will have, leaving no room for chance. In contrast to card games in which the player's hands are hidden or to the game of backgammon, where the outcome of a die determines the available moves, each player has complete information about his opponent's position and about the choices available to him. The game begins from a specified initial state and ends in a position which, using a simple criterion, can be declared a win for one player and a loss for the other, or possibly as a draw.

A game tree is an explicit representation of all possible plays of the game. The root node is the initial position of the game, its successors are the positions the first player can reach in one move, their successors are the positions resulting from the second player's replies, and so on. Terminal or leaf nodes are those representing win, loss, or draw. Each path from the root to a terminal node represents a different complete play of the game.

The correspondence between game trees and AND/OR graphs (qv) is obvious. The moves available to one player from a given position can be represented by OR links, whereas the moves available to his opponent are AND links because a response must be contemplated to each one of them. Another way of obtaining this correspondence is to view each game position J as a problem statement: "Find a winning strategy (for the first player) from J" or, equivalently, "Show that the first player can force a win from J." Clearly, if J admits the first player's moves, this problem is solved if a winning strategy can be found from any one of J's successors, hence the OR links. Similarly, if it is the opponent's turn to move from J, then J is solved if the first player can force a win from each and every one of J's successors, hence the AND links. Thus, in games, the process of problem reduction is completely dictated by the rules of the game; each legal move available to the opponent defines a subproblem or a subgoal, and all these subproblems must be solved before the parent problem is declared solved.

It is common to call the first player max and his opponent min. Correspondingly, game positions where it is max's or min's turn to move are referred to as max or min positions, respectively. The trees representing the games contain two types of node: max nodes, at even levels from the root, and min nodes, at odd levels from the root. Graphically, max and min positions are distinguished by the use of a different node shape; the former is represented by squares and the latter by circles (Fig. 1). The leaf nodes in a game tree are labeled win, loss, or draw, depending on whether they represent a win, loss, or draw position from max's viewpoint (see also MINIMAX PROCEDURE).

Once the leaf nodes are assigned their win–loss–draw status, each node in the game tree can be labeled win, loss, or draw by the following bottom-up process:

Status labeling procedure:

If J is a nonterminal max node, then

$$\text{Status}(J) = \begin{cases} \text{win} & \text{if any of } J\text{'s successors is a win} \\ \text{loss} & \text{if all } J\text{'s successors are loss} \\ \text{draw} & \text{if any of } J\text{'s successors is a draw} \\ & \text{and none is a win} \end{cases} \quad (1)$$

If J is a nonterminal min node, then

$$\text{Status}(J) = \begin{cases} \text{win} & \text{if all } J\text{'s successors are win} \\ \text{loss} & \text{if any of } J\text{'s successors is a loss} \\ \text{draw} & \text{if any of } J\text{'s successors is a draw} \\ & \text{and none is a loss} \end{cases} \quad (2)$$

The function Status(J) should be interpreted as the best terminal status max can achieve from position J if max plays optimally against a perfect opponent. Figure 1 depicts a simple game tree together with the status of all nodes. The status of the leaf nodes are assigned by the rules of the game, whereas those of nonterminal nodes are determined by the preceding procedure.

Solving a game tree T means labeling the root node s as win, loss, or draw. Associated with each root label there is an optimal playing strategy that prescribes how that label can be guaranteed regardless of how min plays. A strategy for max is a subtree T^+ of T called a solution tree, which is rooted at s and contains one successor of every nonterminal max node in T^+ and all successors of every nontermi-

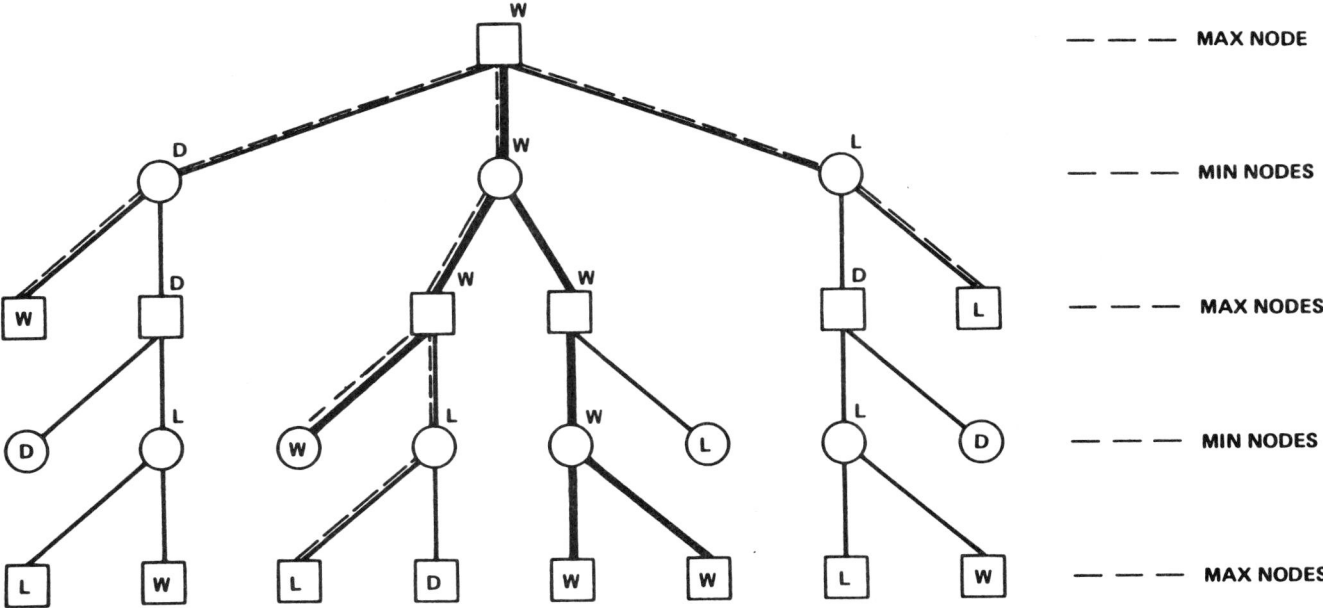

Figure 1. An evaluated win–loss–draw game tree showing a max strategy (boldface tree) and a min strategy (in broken lines).

nal min node in T^+. A game-playing strategy T^- for min will contain, of course, the opposite types of nodes; one successor of every nonterminal min node and all successors of every nonterminal max node included in T^-. Of particular interest are winning strategies, that is, strategies that guarantee a win for max regardless of how min plays. Clearly, a winning strategy for max is a solution tree T^+ whose terminal nodes are all win. Figure 1 shows a winning strategy for max (in heavy lines) and one non-winning strategy for min (following broken lines).

Consider now an arbitrary pair of strategies; one for max, T^+, and one for min, T^-. It is not hard to see that the two sets of terminal nodes associated with the two subtrees have exactly one leaf node in common. Indeed, the intersection of the two strategies defines the unique play path that results if both players adhere to their corresponding strategies, and the one common leaf node is, in fact, the end position that results from this play.

Let (T^+, T^-) denote the leaf node common to strategies T^+ and T^-. Suppose max is forced to choose a strategy T^+ ahead of the play, to show it to the opponent, and then stick to it during the play: what T^+ would be the best choice? Being at such a disadvantage, max should reason as follows: "If I choose T^+, my opponent, knowing all my plans, would definitely respond so as to lead me toward the least favorable leaf in T^+ with label $\min_{T^-}$ Status (T^+, T^-). Now that I have the option of choosing T^+, I can guarantee myself $\max_{T^+} \min_{T^-}$ Status(T^+, T^-)." On the other hand, suppose the roles are reversed and min is put at the disadvantage of adhering to a predisclosed strategy T^-. By a similar argument, min could guarantee that max would not achieve any status better than $\min_{T^-} \max_{T^+}$ Status(T^+, T^-).

An important consequence of the assumption of perfect information games is that these two guarantees are equal to each other, and moreover, they are given by the status of the root node as computed by equations 1 and 2. Thus,

$$\text{Status}(s) = \max_{T^+} \min_{T^-} \text{Status } (T^+, T^-) \qquad (3)$$

or

$$\text{Status}(s) = \min_{T^-} \max_{T^+} \text{Status } (T^+, T^-) \qquad (4)$$

The validity of these two equalities can be easily proven using bottom-up induction on a general game tree. The interpretation of these alternate definitions, however, is rather profound; it implies that in perfect information games it does not matter if a rigid plan is chosen ahead of time or decisions are made as the game goes along. Moreover, rather than conducting an optimization exercise over the enormous space of strategy pairs, an optimal playing strategy can be found using the status labeling procedure of equations 1 and 2.

Although the significance of this result is mainly theoretical, it is sometimes more convenient to view Status(s) as a product of optimization over strategies rather than the value returned by a labeling procedure. An example of such an occasion arises when the answer to the following question is desired: suppose someone claims that the root node of a certain game tree evaluates to a draw, what kind of information must be furnished to substantiate this claim? Had the claim been that s is a win, then clearly all that is needed is to exhibit one winning strategy. Similarly, to defend the assertion "s is a loss," only the existence of one winning strategy for min, that is, a min strategy with all loss leaf nodes must be demonstrated. However, now that the claim is "s is a draw," would a single strategy suffice?

Equations 3 and 4 imply that two strategies are now needed. From equation 3 it is seen that if there exists a max strategy T^+ containing no loss leaves, then no matter what min does, max can guarantee at least a draw. Moreover, if there exists a min strategy T^- with no win nodes, equation 4 implies that, no matter what max does, min can prevent max from obtaining a win. Thus two adversary strategies with compatible values are both necessary and sufficient to verify that the game is a draw.

This result establishes an absolute limit on the number of nodes that must be examined before a game tree can be solved. All the leaf nodes of two compatible strategies, T^+ and T^-, must be examined in case the game is a draw, whereas a single strategy is sufficient in case of a win or a loss. Equivalently, the task of solving a game can be viewed as the task of finding at most one pair of compatible strategies. This statement is true in general, even when the leaf nodes can take on more than three possible values (eg, continuous); a pair of strategies is required to certify the value of any game tree. Because each strategy tree branches out once in every two moves of the game, the number of nodes contained in a typical strategy is about the square root of the number of nodes in the game tree. Therefore, every search strategy that solves or evaluates a game tree must examine at least twice the square root of the number of nodes in the entire game tree.

In practice, this lower bound of twice the square root is rarely achieved because it is not known in advance which of the partially exposed strategies are in fact compatible, and so, many incompatible strategies are partially searched only to be abandoned when more of their leaves are exposed. The knowledge required for guiding the search toward finding two compatible strategies is equivalent to knowing, at each game configuration, what the best next move is for each player. Search strategies (see ALPHA-BETA PRUNING) that use no heuristic information regarding the relative merits of the pending moves will explore, on the average, roughly the four-thirds root of the number of nodes in the game tree (see BRANCHING FACTOR). As the move-rating information becomes more accurate, the number of nodes examined gradually approaches the absolute square-root bound.

BIBLIOGRAPHY

General References

A. Barr and E. A. Feigenbaum, *The Handbook of Artificial Intelligence,* Vol. 1, Kaufmann, Los Altos, Calif., 1981.

N. J. Nilsson, *Principles of Artificial Intelligence,* Tioga, Palo Alto, Calif., 1980.

J. Pearl, "Asymptotic Properties of Minimax Trees and Games-Searching Procedures," *Artif. Intell.* 14(2), 113–128 (1980).

J. Pearl, *Heuristics: Intelligence Search Strategies for Computer Problem Solving,* Addison-Wesley Publishing Co., Inc., Reading, Mass., 1984, Chaps. 8–10.

I. Roizen and J. Pearl, "A Minimax Algorithm Better than Alphabeta? Yes and No," *Artif. Intell.* 21(1–2), 199–220 (1983).

C. E. Shannon, "Programming a Computer for Playing Chess," *Philos. Mag.* 41(7), 256–275 (1950).

J. R. Slagle and J. K. Dixon, "Experiments With Some Programs That Search Game Trees," *JACM* 16(2), 189–207 (1964).

G. Stockman, "A Minimax Algorithm Better Than Alpha-Beta?" *Artif. Intell.* 12(2), 179–196 (1979).

J. PEARL
UCLA

GENERALIZED PHRASE STRUCTURE GRAMMAR. See GRAMMAR, GENERALIZED PHRASE STRUCTURE.

GPS

Developed by Newell, Shaw, and Simon, GPS is an inference system for general problem solving (qv). It solves a problem by finding, through means-ends analysis (qv), a sequence of operators that eliminate the differences between the given initial and goal states (see A. Newell, J. C. Shaw, and H. A. Simon, "Report on a General Problem-Solving Program for a Computer," *Proceedings of the International Conference on Information Processing,* UNESCO, Paris, 1960; A. Newell and H. A. Simon, "GPS, a Program that Simulates Human Thought," in E. A. Feigenbaum and J. Feldman, eds., *Computers and Thought,* McGraw-Hill, New York, 1963, pp. 279–293.)

A. HANYONG YUHAN
AT&T Bell Laboratories

GRAMMAR, AUGMENTED TRANSITION NETWORK

Augmented Transition Network Grammars (ATNs) have been highly successful as a formalism for expressing the syntactic rules of natural languages in a form that can be used efficiently by a computer. They were developed for use in computerized natural language understanding systems (eg, Woods and co-workers, 1972), but have since been used as models of human performance in language understanding (Kaplan, 1972), for linguistic fieldwork in exotic languages (Grimes, 1975), and as models for the development of linguistic theory (Bresnan, 1982). ATNs are routinely taught as a standard technique for constructing computerized grammars for natural language (Tennant, 1981; Winograd, 1981; Allen, 1987; Gazdar and Mellish, 1989) and have been used as the basis for commercial products such as natural language interfaces to database systems and other applications. Generalizations of ATNs have been used for natural language generation (Bates, 1978; Shapiro, 1982), for general-perception problems such as speech and vision (Woods, 1985; Tropf and Walter, 1983), for modeling discourse structure (Reichman, 1985), for dealing with ungrammatical input (Weischedel and Black, 1980), and as parsing automata for unification grammars (Kay, 1982). The classic introduction to ATNs (Woods, 1970) has been reprinted (Pao and Ernest, 1982; Grosz and co-workers, 1986). Further information is also available (Bates, 1978; Winograd, 1981; Bolc, 1983; Allen, 1987, Gazdar and Mellish, 1989).

There are two principal kinds of transition network grammars: recursive transition networks (RTNs) and augmented transition networks (ATNs), the latter being defined as an extension of the former. A recursive transition network is represented by a network of connected states corresponding to partial states of knowledge that arise in the course of parsing a sentence. States are connected by arcs, representing transitions from one state to another caused by constituents (words or phrases) that are recognized in the sentence being analyzed (or dually, by constituents that are produced in the course of generating a sentence). The states in the network can be conceptually divided into levels corresponding to the different kinds of phrase that they recognize. For example, in English there is a level for recognizing sentential clauses, and one for recognizing noun phrases. Each such level has a start state and one or more final states. Each path through the network from a start state to a final state corresponds to a way that a phrase can be recognized (or generated), ie, it expresses a possible sequence of constituents that can make up such a phrase. Each level can be thought of as a recognition (or generation) automaton for one particular kind of phrase. A pictorial example of a simple transition network is illustrated in Figure 1. In this figure, states are represented by small circles and arcs are represented by arrows connecting states. Each arc is labeled with the name of the kind of constituent that will enable that transition if it is found at that point in the input string. This sample grammar has three levels: S for sentence, NP for noun phrase, and PP for prepositional phrase. Each level begins with a state whose name indicates the kind of con-

stituent being sought. In the naming convention used here, a state name consists of the name of the constituent being sought, followed by a slash (/), followed by a brief mnemonic indication of what has been found so far. This naming convention is not an essential part of a transition network grammar, but is a useful device for making grammars readable. Each level ends with one or more final states (indicated by a short arrow labeled POP). These mark the successful completion of a phrase. A sequence of arcs from a start state to a final state defines a sequence of constituents that can make up a phrase of the kind sought by the start state.

The first state in the sample grammar (S/) is the state in which the parser begins, and is the state of knowledge corresponding to the initial assumption that a sentence is to be parsed. The top-most sequence of arcs in Figure 1 shows that a sentence S can consist of a noun phrase NP, followed by a verb V, followed by another noun phrase NP, followed by any number of prepositional phrases PPs. Alternatively, the first noun phrase can be followed by an auxiliary AUX before the verb, or the sentence can begin with an AUX followed by an NP before picking up in state S/NA with the same predicted verb phrase constituents as in the first two cases.

RTNs AND ATNs

The grammar model described above is called a recursive transition network or RTN because the arcs of the grammar can invoke other levels of the network to recognize subordinate constituents, which can in turn invoke other levels (recursively). This process may eventually reinvoke some level "inside itself" (genuine recursion). In the above example, a prepositional phrase PP contains a noun phrase NP, which can contain another PP, which contains another NP, etc, for as many levels as desired. This gives

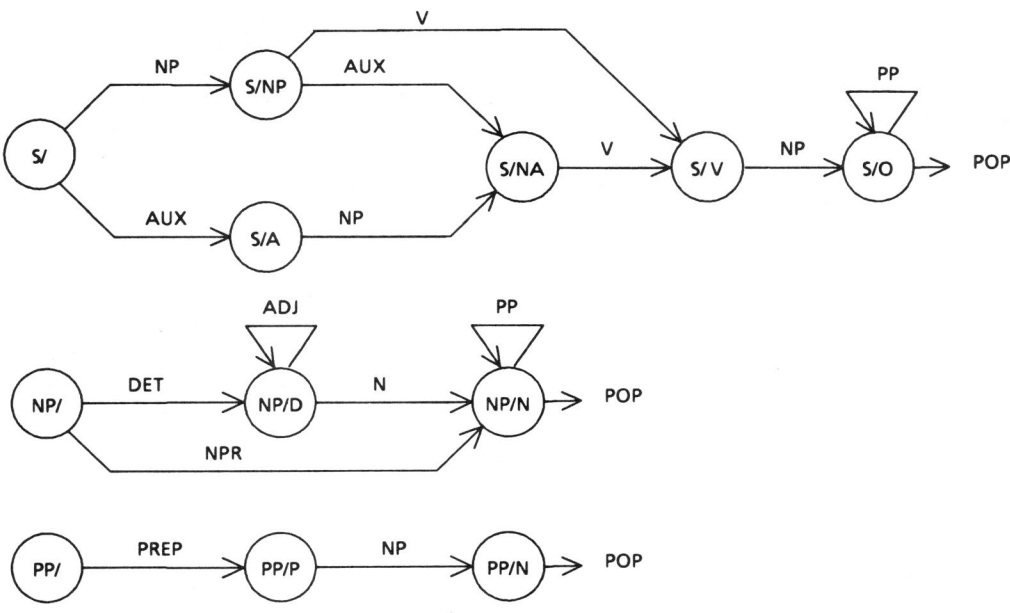

Figure 1. A sample transition network grammar.

rise to sentences such as "John saw the man in the park with a telescope," which can contain as many modifiers as desired.

An augmented transition network grammar (ATN) is a recursive transition network that is augmented with a set of registers that can hold partial parse structures and with conditions and actions on the arcs that can test and set these registers. The registers can be set to record attributes of the phrases being recognized and tested to determine the acceptability of a particular analysis. For example, registers can be used to record the person and number of the subject of a sentence and a condition can be used to check that the subject and the subsequent verb agree in person and number (thus rejecting such sentences as "the boys is tall"). The registers can also be used to record the pieces of structure that will eventually make up the analysis of the phrase being parsed, and actions on the arcs can build a variety of useful structures beyond simply a literal record of the sequence of input phrases consumed. In particular, register-setting actions can be used to build structures corresponding to deep structure analyses as in Chomsky (1965) in which, for example, passive transformations have been undone so that the surface subject of a passive sentence occupies its logical object position in the resulting structure. (Thus the sentence "John was shot" may be parsed into a structure equivalent to "someone shot John.") In the terminology of more current linguistic theories (Chomsky, 1981), such actions can be used to assign surface constituents to underlying conceptual or semantic roles.

Although the above presentation has described ATNs as recognizers that parse sentences, they can also be thought of (dually) as generators that produce sentences. ATNs were the first grammar formalisms that could produce deep structure analyses of the sophistication of a transformational grammar for a substantial range of English and could do so rapidly and efficiently on a digital computer. As Bates (1978) reports, "They have proved to be flexible, easy to write and debug, able to handle a wide variety of syntactic constructions, and easy to interface to other components of a total system. They provide a useful way to give an account of linguistic structures which can be easily communicated to both humans and computers, and they may be partially presented by easily visualized diagrams." This last point has ben referred to as the perspicuity of ATNs relative to transformational grammars (Woods, 1970). Any grammar that covers a substantial portion of a natural language will contain a lot of detail that requires effort to understand, no matter what formalism is used to express it. What ATNs specifically have to offer in this respect is the ability to follow arcs forward and backward through the pictorial representation to determine where registers might be set or tested (ie, where roles are assigned) and to survey what the major constituent sequences are. This is in contrast to a classic transformational grammar, where the only way to tell whether one transformation can apply to the output of another is to imagine the intermediate structures that could be produced by other transformations. In many of the more modern grammatical formalisms (eg, unification grammars and government binding theory) the operations of the grammatical devices are even more difficult to visualize. In many cases, ATNs can be used as abstract automata to explain the operation of these mechanisms, for example, as Kay (1982) with functional unification grammars.

Factoring

ATNs have the advantage of being a class of automata into which ordinary context-free phrase structure grammars (see GRAMMAR, PHRASE STRUCTURE) and augmented phrase structure grammars have a straightforward embedding, but that permit various transformations to be performed to produce grammars that can be more efficient than the original. Such transformations can reduce the number of states or arcs in the grammar or can reduce the number of alternative hypotheses that need to be explicitly considered during parsing. Both kinds of efficiency result from a principle of factoring (Woods, 1977, 1978a, 1978b, 1980). Factoring amounts to merging common parts of alternative paths to reduce the number of alternative combinations explicitly enumerated. Two kinds of factoring can be distinguished: conceptual factoring results from merging common parts of the grammar to make the grammar as compact as possible, whereas hypothesis factoring results from arranging the grammar to merge common parts of hypotheses that will be enumerated at parse time. Conceptual factoring promotes ease of human comprehension of the grammar and should facilitate learning of grammars by machine. Hypothesis factoring promotes efficiency of runtime execution.

The merging of common parts of otherwise separate grammar rules produces a branching decision structure, analogous in some respects to a decision tree, that can compactly represent sequences of alternatives and be used efficiently to guide the analysis (or generation) of sentences. In fact, an ATN can be thought of as a generalization of the notion of a decision tree to permit recursion, looping, register augmentation, and recombination of paths.

History

Augmented transition network grammars, as known today, derive from work conducted in the late 1960s and early 1970s (Woods, 1969, 1970, 1973b). Two less developed similar models appeared independently (Thorn and co-workers, 1968; Bobrow and Fraser, 1969), the latter extending the former. Similar transition diagrams, equivalent to deterministic RTNs, were used by Conway (1963) for programming language compilation. The Woods ATN formalism was developed as a means for efficiently computing syntactic analyses of English sentences for input to a semantic interpretation system. These ATNs were first applied as a front end to a natural language question-answering system for airline flight schedules (Woods, 1968), which was then extended to a system that could interrogate the ATN grammar itself, as if it were a database (Woods, 1979). The first major test of the ATN formalism was in the Lunar Sciences Natural Language Information System (LUNAR), developed at Bolt, Beranek and Newman Inc. for the NASA Manned Spacecraft Center (Woods, 1973a; Woods and co-workers, 1972). The earliest widely available publication describing ATN grammars is Woods (1970). An earlier report (Woods, 1969) contains a more complete description, including some theoretical results on the elimination of left and right recursion, the minimization of branching in an RTN network, and the use of RTNs in a generalization of Earley's (1968) algorithm, none of which have been published elsewhere.

ATN grammars can be motivated by a chain of reasoning that begins with notations commonly used by linguists in the 1960s to abbreviate certain patterns of context-free grammar rules. Specifically, linguists frequently use the following notational devices in the right sides of context-free grammar rules: braces ({}) to indicate alternative choices, the Kleene star operator (*) to indicate arbitrarily repeatable constituents, and parentheses to indicate optional constituents. An example would be $S \rightarrow NP(AUX)V(NP)PP*$, indicating that the auxiliary verb and the object noun phrase are optional and any number (zero or more) of prepositional phrases are permissible. These are notational variants of the Backus Normal Form (BNF) specifications commonly used in computer science to express programming language syntax. Such notations are typically thought of by linguists as abbreviations for sets of ordinary context-free grammar rules, even though the use of the star operator abbreviates what would be an infinite set of equivalent context-free rules.

Prior to the invention of recursive transition networks there was no parsing formalism that could directly handle alternative and arbitrarily repeatable constituents. The insight that led to RTN grammars was to observe that the concise notations used by linguists were equivalent in expressive power to Kleene's formulation of regular sets (Ginsberg, 1966). Regular sets are sets of strings over some vocabulary formed by the closure of the finite strings under the operations of concatenation, set union (+), and arbitrary repeatability (*). (Set union with the empty string as an alternative can be used to indicate optionality of constituents.) Regular sets are equivalent to finite state machines, which in turn can be expressed in the form of finite state transition diagrams (McNaughton and Yamada, 1960). A finite state transition diagram is a labeled, directed graph similar to Figure 1, except that all transitions are labeled with elements from the terminal vocabulary of the language (ie, a transition that invokes a subportion of the network recursively, as in RTNs, cannot be expressed). Finite state transition diagrams were considered as a possible formalism for natural language grammars in the early days of computational linguistics, but they failed to deal practically with self-embedding constructions.

RTNs AND CONTEXT-FREE GRAMMARS

RTNs provide a formalism that can be used by generalizations of ordinary context-free parsing algorithms to deal directly with concepts such as alternative sequences, optional constituents, and arbitrarily repeatable constituents, without having to treat them as abbreviations for (possibly infinite) sets of rules or to reexpress them in terms of rules that introduce fictitious phrase types in order to share common parts of different rules or to express iteration of repeatable constituents.

Any context-free grammar can be transformed into an equivalent recursive transition network by collecting all of the rules that share a given left-hand side (ie, all of the rules for forming a given phrase type) and replacing them with a single rule whose right side is a regular expression corresponding to the union of the right sides of the original rules. The resulting right-side regular expression can then be converted to an equivalent transition diagram by a standard mechanical algorithm (Ott and Feinstein, 1961). Moreover, Woods (1969) shows that the resulting recursive transition network can be further optimized by the elimination of left and right recursion and the application of standard state-minimization techniques (originally developed for finite state machines), whose effect when applied to a recursive transition network yields a transition network grammar with greatly reduced branching (Fig. 2).

A standard theorem of formal language theory (Chomsky, 1963) proves that a language accepted by a context-free grammar can be accepted by a finite state machine unless every context-free grammar for the language contains at least one self-embedding symbol (ie, a phrase type that can contain a proper internal embedding of the same type of phrase, for example, the middle S in the rule: $S \rightarrow$ if S then S). The RTN optimization results show that a given context-free grammar can be converted to an RTN, which can then be optimized until the only remaining PUSH transitions are for self-embedding constituents. Together, these results suggest that a context-free grammar can be thought of as having a finite state part and a recursive part. The RTN optimization constructions show how to extract all of the finite-state part into transition network form, to which conventional finite-state optimization techniques can be applied.

Note that when the standard state minimization transformations are applied to a recursive transition network, they do not quite produce a deterministic parsing network as they do for finite-state grammars, although they do produce a network in which no two transitions leaving a given state will have the same label. This is not sufficient to guarantee determinism for an RTN because two transitions that push for different types of phrase may nevertheless recognize a common sequence of input symbols (ie, the grammar may be ambiguous). Even if the grammar is not ambiguous, two different phrase types may begin with some common initial sequence, and the grammar would not be able to tell which of the two phrase types were present before examining the sequence further. However, the results of such transformations can produce grammars with little nondeterminism that can be parsed quite efficiently. Moreover, an ATN can exploit techniques such as look-ahead conditions and merged subordinate networks to produce grammars whose nondeterminism is reduced still further.

Another result (Woods, 1969) shows that these reduced branching RTNs can be used by a generalization of Earley's (1968) parsing algorithm to minimize the number of state transitions that must be considered in the course of parsing. That is, an optimized RTN is used more effi-

1. $S \rightarrow$ if S then S
2. $S \rightarrow S$ and S
3. $S \rightarrow S$ or S
4. $S \rightarrow P$

(a)

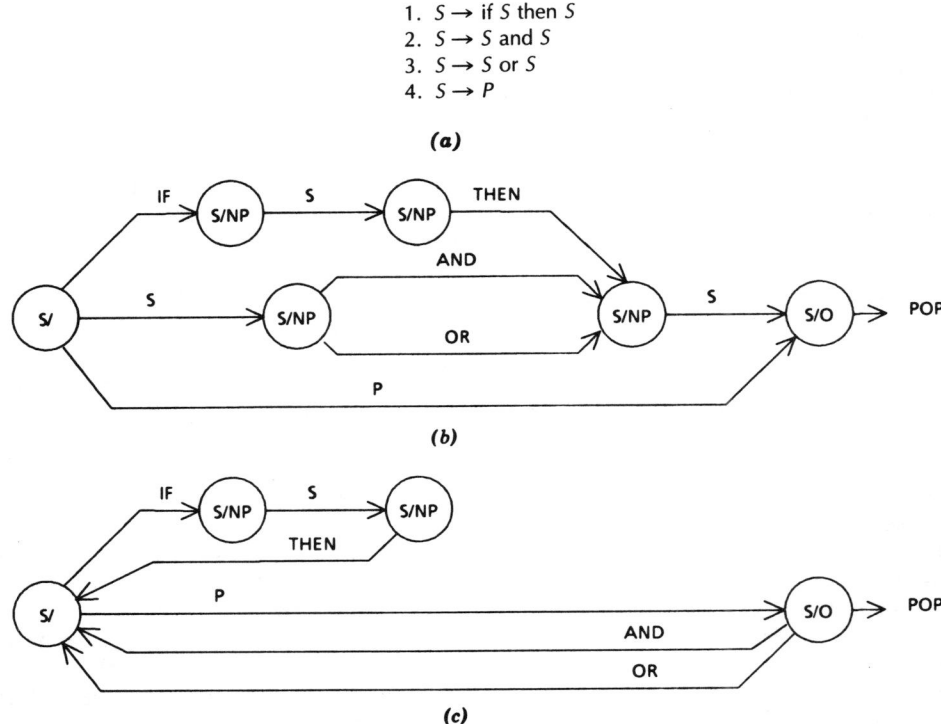

(b)

(c)

Fig. 2. (*a*) A sample context-free grammar. (*b*) An equivalent RTN. (*c*) An Optimized RTN.

ciently by a generalization of Earley's algorithm than an unoptimized RTN or an unaltered context-free grammar. RTNs are equivalent in weak generative power (ie, can characterize the same sets of strings) as context-free grammars or pushdown store automata. RTNs are slightly stronger than context-free grammars in terms of the tree structures they can assign (strong generative power) because they can characterize structures with unbounded branching at a single level (Fig. 3).

AUGMENTED TRANSITION NETWORKS

As mentioned above, an ATN consists of an RTN augmented with a set of registers and with arbitrary conditions and actions associated with the arcs of the grammar. ATNs were developed to obtain a grammar formalism with the linguistic adequacy of a transformational grammar and the efficiency of the various context-free parsing algorithms. As a sentence is parsed with an ATN grammar, the conditions and actions associated with the transitions can put pieces of the input string into registers, use the contents of registers to build larger structures, check

whether two registers are equal, and so on. It turns out that this model can construct the kinds of structural descriptions assigned by a transformational grammar and can do it in a much more economical way. In a similar way, ATNs can be used to assign the kinds of functional role structures used in other modern linguistic formalisms. The merging of common parts of alternative structures, which the network grammar provides, permits a very compact representation of quite large grammars, and this model has served as the basis for several natural language understanding systems. ATNs have also been used in systems for understanding continuous speech, such as the Bolt, Beranek, and Newman HWIM system (Woods and co-workers, 1976; Wolf and Woods, 1980; Woods, 1985). For speech understanding, the transition network grammar is one of the few linguistically adequate grammars for natural English that is efficient in coping with the combinatorial problems that arise from uncertainties in the phonetic identities of the spoken words.

A state in an ATN can be thought of dually as a concise representation of a set of alternative possible sequences of elements leading to it from the left or as a concise prediction of a set of possible sequences of elements to be found on the right. (Alternatively, it can be thought of in a right-to-left mode or even from the middle out.) The reification of these states as concrete entities representing partial states of knowledge or predictions that arise during parsing is one of the major contributions of ATN grammars to the theory and practice of natural language understanding. These states are especially important in

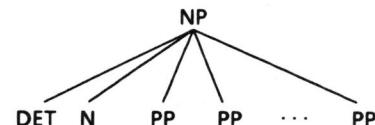

Figure 3. An illustration of unbounded branching.

representing states of partial knowledge in problems involving high degrees of uncertainty or partial information such as speech understanding and discourse understanding.

The ATN formalism suggests a way of viewing a grammar as a map that shows various landmarks encountered in the course of traversing a sentence. Viewed in this way, ATN grammars serve as a conceptual map of possible sentence structures and a framework on which to hang information about constraints that apply between separate constituents and between those constituents and the output structure that the grammar should assign to a phrase. For speech understanding, for example, this perspective allows a grammar to correlate various prosodic characteristics of sentences such as intonation and rhythm with "geographical" landmarks within the structure of a sentence.

Another advantage of the transition network formalism is the ease with which an algorithm can follow the arcs backward and forward to predict the types of constituents or words that could occur to the right or left of a given word or phrase. One of the important roles of a syntactic component in speech understanding is to predict those places where small function words such as *a, an,* and *of* should occur, because such words are almost always unstressed and difficult to distinguish from accidentally similar acoustic patterns in spoken sentences. In the HWIM speech system (Woods, 1985) such words are almost always found as a result of syntactic prediction and are not even looked for during lexical analysis, where more spurious matches would be found than correct ones. Other types of grammar, such as context-free grammars, can be augmented by conditions and actions associated with the grammar rules to achieve benefits similar to those of an ATN. However, such grammars do not gain all of the benefits of recursive transition networks, such as the merging of common parts of different rules and the framework for applying optimizing transformations.

Specifying an ATN

It is important to maintain a distinction between the underlying abstract state transition automaton that constitutes the essence of an ATN and the various surface notations that can be used to specify an ATN grammar. A variety of notations have been developed for specifying ATN grammars. The original ATN parser was written in LISP and used a notation in which the conditions and actions on the arcs were specified in LISP. However, this is not essential. Later ATN implementations have simplified and streamlined the notations for expressing conditions and actions, and a number of other grammar formalisms can be thought of as specialized specification languages whose underlying parsing automaton is an ATN (Paxton, 1977). The advent of widely available graphics interfaces makes possible the graphic presentation of an ATN transition diagram, coupled with an interactive specification of the conditions and actions on the arcs, as a primary specification medium. In such an interactive graphics environment, ATN grammars have additional advantages.

Figure 4 gives a BNF specification for one notation that can be used for specifying ATN grammars. It is similar to most ATN formalisms, except that conditions on arcs are expressed in terms of an action (VERIFY ⟨condition⟩), an infix assignment operator (←) is used in place of the more customary SETR function, and functions (NE and CC) are used to refer to the next input element and the current parsed constituent, respectively, in place of an asterisk, which served both purposes in Woods (1970). In this notation, an ATN specification consists of a list of state specifications, each of which consists of a state-name and a set of arc specifications. Arcs can be one of the five indicated types. A CAT arc accepts a word that is recorded in a dictionary as belonging to the specified syntactic (or semantic) category, a WRD arc accepts the specific word or list of alternative words named on the arc, a PUSH arc

```
⟨ATN⟩          → (⟨state⟩ ⟨state⟩*)
⟨state⟩        → (⟨state-name⟩⟨arc⟩⟨arc⟩*)
⟨arc⟩          → (CAT ⟨category-name⟩ ⟨augmentation⟩* (TO ⟨state-name⟩)) |
                 (WRD ⟨word-list⟩ ⟨augmentation⟩* (TO ⟨state-name⟩)) |
                 (PUSH ⟨state-name⟩ ⟨augmentation⟩* (TO ⟨state-name⟩)) |
                 (POP ⟨expression⟩ ⟨augmentation⟩*) |
                 (JUMP ⟨state-name⟩ ⟨augmentation⟩*)

⟨augmentation⟩ → (VERIFY ⟨condition⟩) |
                 ⟨action⟩

⟨action⟩       → ⟨register-name⟩ ← ⟨expression⟩ |
                 (SENDR ⟨register-name⟩ ⟨expression⟩) |
                 (⟨defined-operator⟩ ⟨expression⟩*)

⟨expression⟩   → (NE) | (CC) |
                 (GETR ⟨register-name⟩) |
                 (BUILDQ ⟨structure schema⟩ ⟨expression⟩*) |
                 (⟨defined-operator⟩ ⟨expression⟩*)
```

Figure 4. A BNF specification of an ATN grammar notation.

invokes a subordinate level of the ATN to recognize a phrase beginning with the specified state, and a POP arc signals the completion of a phrase and specifies an expression for the value that is to be returned as the structure for that phrase. A JUMP arc specifies a transfer of control from one state to another without consuming any input.

Augmentations on an arc indicate further conditions under which the arc may be taken and actions to be performed when the arc is taken. A (VERIFY ⟨condition⟩) operation will block the transition if the condition is not satisfied. An assignment operation (←) will set a register to the value of the specified expression (this operation is known as SETR in most ATN specification languages). A SENDR action specifies an initial value to be used for a register in a subordinate invocation about to be initiated by a PUSH arc (SENDR only makes sense on a PUSH arc and is executed before the subordinate computation is begun). In addition, other operators can be defined that can abbreviate complex manipulations of register contents and complex conditions under which to abort computation paths. In experimental parsing implementations, information can even be sent to the parsing algorithm, and its agendas and tables can be manipulated.

The expressions used in register assignments and as arguments to other actions can access the next element of the input string via the function NE, access the parsed constituent on a push arc via the function CC, access the contents of registers using GETR, and build structures by substituting the values of other expressions into open positions in a specified schematic structure (eg, using BUILDQ, a primitive form of the LISP back-quote operation, a quasi-quoting operator that can specify a literal structure with constituent positions that are to be filled in by the evaluation of subexpressions). Defined structure-building operators can be invoked that encapsulate complex register manipulations or access to other information outside the register context of the ATN (such as records of discourse entities that are candidate antecedents for interpreting pronouns or other aspects of a discourse context such as whether the previous utterance was a question that admits a short answer).

Linguistic Experimentation

ATNs have been used to explore a variety of issues in linguistic theory relating to extending the abilities of grammars to specify difficult linguistic phenomena and to parse them efficiently. A number of experimental explorations are described in Woods (1973b), including

1. VIR (virtual) arcs and HOLD actions for dealing with left-extraposition transformations such as those that move the relativized constituent from its logical place in the structure of a relative clause to the position of the relative pronoun at the beginning of the clause (eg, "the man that I saw," "the man that Mary said ran away.") A HOLD action can make an entry on the stack when the extraposed constituent is found, which then enables a matching VIR arc to use the extraposed constituent from the stack at the position where the grammar would nor-

mally expect it. This stack entry will also block the acceptance of the phrase until some VIR arc has used the held constituent. The HOLD action mechanism in ATN grammars was one of the first parsing devices for dealing with phenomena of displaced constituents in linguistic theory.

2. RESUMETAG and RESUME actions for dealing with right-extraposition transformations that leave dangling modifiers that logically belong with constituents that have been fronted or otherwise moved to the left. For example, in the sentence "What papers has Dan Bobrow written that are about natural language?" the relative clause "that are about natural language" clearly modifies the questioned noun phrase "what papers" but is not adjacent to it. A RESUMETAG action can be executed before popping a constituent that (according to the operating linguistic theory) could have been moved to the left, leaving behind a detached right-extraposed modifier. This enables such a constituent, when recognized in its preposed position, to be reentered by a RESUME action at subsequent points where dangling modifiers that should modify it might occur, thus enabling the resumed constituent to consume any modifiers it can accept at those points.

3. Selective modifier placement for dealing with ambiguous scopings of variable-scope modifiers such as prepositional phrases in sentences such as "I saw the man in the park with a telescope." A special pop arc (SPOP) causes manipulation of the parser's agendas and stacks to determine all of the places where a given such modifier might be attached. These are then evaluated to determine which is the most likely candidate, given a set of semantic preference criteria. The most preferred alternative is then pursued and any others are saved on the agenda to be pursued at a later time if necessary (possibly with a reduced confidence of being correct).

4. A metagrammatical conjunction facility for handling a wide variety of conjunction constructions, including reduced conjunctions that result in apparently conjoined sentence fragments. For example, "Give me the best methods to grow and properties of alkali iodates" involves an apparent conjunction of the fragments "best methods to grow" and "properties of." A special SYSCONJ action, invoked on special active arcs associated with the conjunctions *and* and *or*, trigger a complex manipulation of the agendas and parsing configurations of the ATN so that the parsing of the sentence up to the occurrence of the conjunction is temporarily suspended and some earlier configuration is restarted to parse the string beginning after the conjunction. When the restarted configuration has completed the constituent it was working on, the suspended configuration is resumed in a special mode to complete its corresponding constituent on some tail of the constituent just completed. After this, the two coordinate constituents are conjoined and the two separate configurations merged to continue the parsing. (This produces an analysis of the above example equivalent to "Give me the best methods to grow alkali iodates and the properties of alkali iodates" by conjoining two noun phrase constituents.) A schematic characterization of the phenomenon in question is that a string of the form "r x u and v y t" can be analyzed as equivalent to "r s t" where s is a constitu-

ent whose structure is a conjunction of the form "[x u y] and [x v y]."

Formal Properties of ATN Grammars

In the face of various implementations of ATN parsers and different formulations of the specification language for ATN grammars, it is important to remember that the essence of an ATN is an abstract formal automaton, in a class with finite state machines, pushdown store automata, and Turing machines. Such automata are typically defined by specifying the structure of an abstract instantaneous configuration of a computation and specifying a transition function that expresses the relationship between an instantaneous configuration and those that can result from it in one step of the computation. When the transition function determines a set of possibilities rather than a unique successor configuration, the automaton is called a nondeterministic automaton. From this perspective an ATN can be defined as a nondeterministic automaton whose instantaneous configurations record the position in the input string, the name of the state that is currently active, a set of register contents, and a stack context consisting of a list of stack entries, each of which records the push arc whose actions are to be done when the parse returns to that level and saves a set of register contents to be used by those actions.

As pointed out above, an RTN is equivalent in generative power to a context-free grammar or pushdown store automaton. Adding the augmentations of an ATN produces an automaton that is equivalent in power to an arbitrary Turing machine, unless restrictions are imposed on the conditions and actions on the arcs. Thus an ATN is a universal parsing automaton, capable of implementing any linguistic theory. This is useful in the sense that any linguistic phenomenon that might be discovered can be characterized within the formalism, but it has the disadvantage that it is not guaranteed that the sentences acceptable by such a grammar would be a decidable set. However, there are simple restrictions on an ATN (Woods, 1973b) that guarantee a decidable grammar model. If infinite looping is blocked and the conditions and actions on the arcs are restricted to be totally recursive (ie, decidable), then the resulting automaton will be totally recursive (ie, decidable). The loop-blocking restrictions merely amount to forbidding closed loops of nonconsuming arcs (such as JUMP arcs) and forbidding arbitrary looping of self-embedding singleton recursion (pushing for a single constituent, which in turn pushes for a single constituent, and so on, potentially without limit). These two mechanisms are the only ones that would enable an ATN parser to compute for an arbitrary amount of time without consuming anything.

Perrault (1976) gives a restricted class of ATNs, equivalent to finite-state tree transducers, that are known to lie within the power of a context-sensitive grammar (a decidable class). Finally, although the proof has not been published, it has been shown that restricting the conditions and actions of an ATN to be primitive recursive, coupled with the loop-blocking restrictions described above, results in a parsing automaton that is itself primitive recursive (a powerful subclass of totally recursive functions). The interesting thing about this result is that almost any sensible ATN grammar that could be written would automatically satisfy these restrictions. Thus it is reasonable to think of both ATN grammars and natural English syntax as lying in the realm of primitive recursive computation.

The ATN Perspective

ATNs can be thought of as efficient, abstract parsing automata that can serve as unifying conceptual models for a variety of different high level syntactic specification languages and linguistic formalisms. From this perspective, it is possible to compare, contrast, and understand the capabilities and limitations of various grammar formalisms. For example, Swartout (1978) has shown that Marcus's (1980) PARSIFAL can be viewed as a specialized ATN, and lexical functional grammars (Bresnan, 1982) can be thought of as a high-level specification language, embodying a particular set of linguistic assumptions, which could be parsed by an underlying ATN whose basic arc action is a kind of unification of sets of equations. Similarly, the operational semantics of definite clause grammars (Pereira and Warren, 1980), executed in PROLOG, is almost identical to a standard top-down, left-to-right parser for a restricted class of ATN grammars whose states correspond to the spaces between the subgoals in a rule, and whose registers are the variable bindings of the environment.

Viewed as ATNs, definite clause grammars use a powerful unification operator as a universal condition/action, whose effect is to establish bindings of registers (variables) to structures and may cause a failure (ie, abort the current nondeterministic computation path) if the attempted bindings are not consistent. The structures assigned to registers in this sense may in turn contain variables that point to other structures or will later be bound to other structures. (Alternatively, a definite clause grammar could be modeled using only one register to contain the PROLOG environment as a list of bindings.) The action associated with a final state (ie, the end of the definite clause grammar rule) is to return the variable bindings that it has established to the higher level environment that pushed for the current constituent (ie, that invoked it as a subgoal). This requires PROLOG's facility for automatically renaming variables when pushing for a constituent (ie, invoking a subgoal) to keep the bindings straight, and it uses an open-ended set of register names, but otherwise the mechanism is like a straightforward implementation of an ATN automaton, without some of the factoring capabilities of the ATN. From this point of view, a definite clause grammar (DCG) can be seen as more like an augmented phrase structure grammar than a full ATN because it does not exploit the ability of its states (the "joints" between the subgoals) to support arbitrary repeatability and alternative subsequences of transitions (subgoals). Rather, such phenomena would be handled by creating new kinds of phrases.

From the ATN perspective, a deep similarity between definite clause grammars and lexical functional grammars (LFG) can be seen in the way that the equations of LFGs are used to add constraints to an environment similar to the variable bindings of DCGs. One major difference seems to be the way LFGs use access paths through the functional structure for some of the things that DCGs would do with variables. LFGs thus appear to avoid the need to rename variables. Otherwise, both have a similar emphasis toward specifying syntactic facts in the form of constraints on attributes of phrases that are then realized by some form of unification. The above discussion is one example of the way that the perspective of an abstract ATN automaton can be used to understand different parsing formalisms and syntactic specification notations. Without such a perspective, it would be difficult to see a similarity between two formalisms whose surface presentation is as dramatically different as DCGs and LFGs. Coupled with an understanding of the formal properties of various restrictions on the conditions, actions, and transition structure of an ATN, this perspective can also shed light on the expressive power and computational costs of other formalisms.

ATN Parsers

A variety of different parsing algorithms have been implemented for ATN grammars. The most straightforward is a simple top-down, depth-first, backtracking implementation of the ATN as a parsing automaton. A slightly more powerful implementation for the LUNAR system is described in Woods and co-workers (1972). A standard implementation technique is to create a data structure corresponding to an instantaneous configuration (ic) of an abstract ATN automaton and implement the abstract transition function of the automaton as a procedure that computes the successor ic's of a given ic.

The ic's of the LUNAR parser are extended from the formal definition given above to include a weight, expressing a degree of goodness of the parse (allowing grammars to specify degrees of grammaticality via arc actions that adjust the weight), a hold list (for the HOLD-VIR mechanism), and a historical path (used for the experimental SYSCONJ features). By the setting of various mode flags, this parser is able to pursue parses according to a variety of control strategies including depth-first, breadth-first, best-first, and a variety of combinations of depth-first with priority ordering. There are also some special cases such as pursuing small identified sets of alternatives in parallel (SPLITS). This parser contains the experimental linguistic capabilities described above and a fairly powerful trace facility capable of producing a detailed record of the individual steps of an analysis of a sentence.

The generalization of Earley's algorithm for RTNs can be extended in a natural way to a general ATN parser (although not maintaining Earley's n^3 time bound results if nontrivial use is made of the registers). In general, most of the parsing algorithms for context-free grammars have analogous versions for RTNs and can be extended to algorithms that handle the augmentations of ATNs. Other implementations of ATN parsers include three middle-out parsers for ATNs used in the context of speech-understanding systems (Bates, 1975; Paxton, 1977; Woods,

1985). These are bottom-up, data-directed parsers that can begin in the middle of a sentence and work upward and outward in either direction. The Bates parser is capable of working on several different parts of the utterance as part of a single hypothesis. The Paxton parser provides an especially clean restricted form of ATN grammar specification (although it was not characterized as one). The Woods parser constructs an index that records for any pair of states whether they can be connected by chains of jump, push, and pop transitions used to quickly determine whether a new word can be connected to an existing island and to guide the computation that establishes such a connection.

ATN grammars can also be implemented in languages such as PROLOG, in a style similar to Pereira and Warren (1980), where the unification and backtracking capabilities inherent in the language can be exploited to reduce (or even eliminate) the effort of writing a parsing algorithm. However, when this is done, the algorithmic efficiencies associated with specific parsing algorithms are lost and replaced by PROLOG's default depth-first backtracking algorithm. Finally, ATN grammars can be compiled into an object code that efficiently implements a combination of the parser and the grammar (Burton and Woods, 1976; Christaller, 1983; Finin, 1983; Laubsch and Barth, 1983), a technique that has produced parsing programs roughly 10 times faster than general ATN interpreters.

Misconceptions about ATNs

ATNs are frequently viewed in different ways by different people. A common misconception is the belief that ATNs are strictly top-down, left-to-right parsing algorithms. Another is that an ATN is specified in LISP or contains LISP code or can only be written in LISP. As the preceding discussion makes clear, many of these beliefs are incorrect. ATNs are defined as abstract automata, independent of any programming language, and can be implemented in a variety of programming languages. Similarly, many different parsing algorithms have been implemented for ATN grammars, including top-down, bottom-up, and even middle-out parsing algorithms.

Another common misconception is that ATNs handle unordered constituents (ie, sequences of constituents whose relative order is unspecified) by enumerating all of the possible orderings. This is not usually done. Rather, such phenomena are routinely handled by use of self-looping arcs as shown in Figure 5, in which three arcs accept locative, time, and manner adverbial phrases in arbitrary order at the end of a verb phrase. Conditions on the arcs restrict the parse to not more than one of a kind. (This could be relaxed to permit more than one manner adverbial, for example, by removing the VERIFY condition on that arc.) All three of these adverbials are optional. If one or more such constituents were to be obligatory, a condition could be added to the JUMP arc to block the transition if the appropriate registers are not set. Weak constraints could be expressed on the order in which these modifiers could occur (eg, not allowing manner adverbials to occur after time adverbials) by placing conditions on some of the arcs that would block them if certain registers had already been set or had not been set (eg, adding a condition (NOT (GETR TIME)) to the PUSH MANNER arc). Figure 5 also illustrates how one-shot self-loops can be used to indicate optional constituents by conditioning the arc on the emptiness of the register that the arc sets.

GENERALIZED TRANSITION NETWORKS

ATN grammars are effective for specifying complex grammars of natural language as well as for a variety of other structured entities. They can be thought of as a class of abstract perceptual automata for recognizing structured assemblies of elements. To capture this insight, a generalization of ATN grammars has been formulated, called generalized transition networks (GTNs) (Woods, 1978b, Shapiro, 1982). The idea of a GTN stems from the following observation: in an ATN, the set of transitions leaving a given state of the network does double duty, both specifying the alternative possible next states that can be reached as a result of measuring additional information about the input utterance, and also specifying implicitly that the measurement is to be made immediately to the right of the previous measurement. Thus in following a sequence of arcs through an ATN grammar, a sequence of tests and hypothesis refinements are followed in an abstract search space and the left-to-right sequence of constituents are also followed in the input sentence. This is nice and natural for analyzing sequences of words and phrases in sequences.

For many potential applications, however, the input to recognition is not a linear sequence of symbols. In such cases the above characterization of a sequence of information-gathering activities is still desirable even though the idea of a left-to-right sequence of constituents does not make sense. A GTN provides the appropriate automaton for such applications. It does so by keeping the general state-transition structure of an ATN but removing the implicit assumptions about the kinds and locations of the information-gathering operations that cause transitions.

When following a sequence of transitions through a GTN, a sequence of hypothesis refinement operations will still be followed, but there will no longer be an implicit left-to-right assumption about the successive measurements. Rather, explicit instructions at the state nodes or on the arcs will indicate how successive measurements relate to previous ones, and registers can be used to keep track of the positions of measurements and to reference points in an arbitrary perceptual space. For example, such GTNs could be used to parse two-dimensional mathematical equations, to analyze visual scenes, or to perform knowledge-based perceptual tasks such as medical diagnosis. Tropf and Walter (1983) is an example of such an application to visual perception.

CASCADED ATNS

One of the long-standing problems in natural language understanding has been dealing with the interaction of syntactic and semantic information. Ways of achieving close interaction between syntax and semantics have traditionally involved writing semantic interpretation rules in one-to-one correspondence with phrase structure rules (Thompson, 1963), writing semantic grammars that integrate syntactic and semantic constraints in a single grammar (Burton, 1976), or writing *ad hoc* programs that combine such information in unformalized ways. The first approach requires as many syntactic rules as semantic rules and hence is not really much different from the semantic grammar approach. The third approach, of course, may yield some level of operational system but does not usually shed any light on how such interaction should be organized and the resulting system is usually difficult to extend.

The semantic grammar approach, although effective, tends to miss generalizations, and its results do not extend well to new domains. It misses syntactic generalizations, for example, by having to duplicate the syntactic information necessary to characterize the determiner structures of *NP*s for each of the different semantic kinds of *NP* that can be accepted. Likewise, it tends to miss semantic gen-

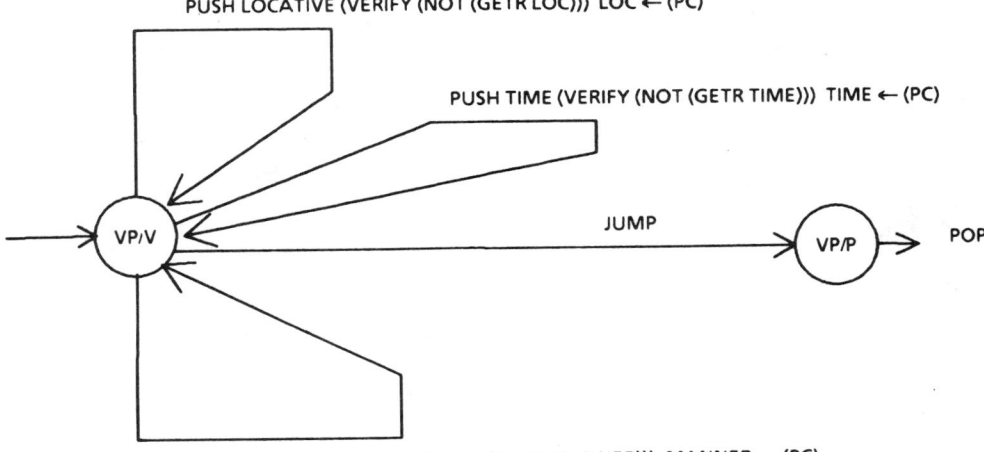

Figure 5. An illustration of unordered constituents.

eralizations by repeating the same semantic tests in various places in the grammar where a given semantic constituent can occur.

An extension of the ATN formalism, called a cascaded ATN (CATN) (Woods, 1980) addresses this problem. A CATN is essentially a sequence of ATN transducers (ie, automata that map an input sequence to an output sequence), with each successive machine taking input from the output of the previous one. Specifically, a CATN is a sequence of ordinary ATNs whose arc actions include operations that transmit elements to the next machine in the sequence. The first machine in the cascade takes its input from the input sequence, and subsequent machines take their input from the transmit operations of the previous ones. The output of the machine as a whole is the output of the final machine in the cascade. Feedback from later stages to earlier ones is provided by an implicit filtering function that causes paths of the nondeterministic computation to die if a later stage cannot accept the output of an earlier one.

A cascade of ATNs provides a way to reduce having to say the same thing multiple times or in multiple places. It provides efficiency comparable to a semantic grammar, while maintaining a clean separation between syntactic and semantic levels of description. It permits the decomposition of an ATN grammar into an assembly of cooperating ATNs, each with its own characteristic domain of responsibility. One instance of a CATN parser is Bobrow's (1978) RUS parser. Another is the interaction between the lexical retrieval component and the linguistic component of the HWIM speech understanding system (Woods and co-workers, 1976; Woods, 1985).

BIBLIOGRAPHY

J. Allen, *Natural Language Understanding*, Benjamin/Cummings, Menlo Park, Calif., 1987.

M. Bates, *Syntactic Analysis in a Speech Understanding System*, Ph.D. dissertation, Harvard University, Cambridge, Mass., 1975.

M. Bates, "The Theory and Practice of Augmented Transition Networks," in L. Bolc, ed., *Natural Language Communication with Computers*, Springer-Verlag, Berlin, pp. 191–259.

D. G. Bobrow and J. B. Fraser, "An Augmented State Transition Network Analysis Procedure," *Proceedings of the First IJCAI*, Washington, D.C., Morgan-Kaufmann, San Mateo, Calif., 1969, pp. 557–567.

R. J. Bobrow, "The RUS System," in B. L. Webber and R. J. Bobrow, eds., *Research in Natural Language Understanding*, Quarterly Technical Progress Report No. **3.**, BBN Report No. 3878, Bolt Beranek and Newman Inc., Cambridge, Mass., 1978.

L. Bolc, ed., *The Design of Interpreters, Compilers, and Editors for Augmented Transition Networks*, Springer-Verlag, Berlin, 1983.

J. W. Bresnan, ed., *The Mental Representation of Grammatical Relations*, MIT Press, Cambridge, Mass., 1982.

R. R. Burton, *Semantic Grammar: An Engineering Technique for Constructing Natural Language Understanding Systems*, BBN Report No. 3453, Bolt Beranek and Newman Inc., Cambridge, Mass., 1976.

R. Burton and W. A. Woods, "A Compiling System for Augmented Transition Networks," *Proceedings of the Sixth International Conference on Computational Linguistics*, Ottawa, Canada, 1976, pp. 65–83.

N. Chomsky, "Formal Properties of Grammars," in R. D. Luce, R. R. Bush, and E. Galanter, eds., *Handbook of Mathematical Psychology*, Vol. 2, John Wiley & Sons, Inc., New York, 1963.

N. Chomsky, *Aspects of the Theory of Syntax*, MIT Press, Cambridge, Mass., 1965.

N. Chomsky, *Lectures on Government and Binding*, Foris Publications, Dordrecht, Holland, 1981.

T. Christaller, "An ATN Programming Environment," in L. Bolc, ed., *The Design of Interpreters, Compilers, and Editors for Augmented Transition Networks*, Springer-Verlag, Berlin, 1983.

M. E. Conway, "Design of a Separable Transition Diagram Compiler," *Comm. ACM* **6**(7), 396–408 (1963).

J. Earley, *An Efficient Context-free Parsing Algorithm*, Ph.D. thesis, Carnegie-Mellon University, Pittsburgh, Pa., 1968.

T. W. Finin, "The Planes Interpreter and Compiler for Augmented Transition Network Grammars," in L. Bolc, ed., *The Design of Interpreters, Compilers, and Editors for Augmented Transition Networks*, Springer-Verlag, Berlin, 1983.

G. Gazdar and C. Mellish, *Natural Language Processing in LISP: An Introduction to Computational Linguistics*, Addison-Wesley Publishing Co., Inc., Reading, Mass., 1989.

S. Ginsberg, *The Mathematical Theory of Context Free Languages*, McGraw-Hill, Inc., New York, 1966.

J. E. Grimes, ed., *Network Grammars*, Summer Institute of Linguistics, University of Oklahoma, Norman, 1975.

B. Grosz, K. Sparck Jones, and B. Webber, eds., *Readings in Natural Language Processing*, Morgan-Kaufmann, San Mateo, Calif., 1986.

R. M. Kaplan, "Augmented Transition Networks as Psychological Models of Sentence Comprehension," *Artif. Intell.* **3**(2), 77–100 (1972).

M. Kay, "Parsing in Functional Unification Grammar," in D. R. Dowty, L. Kartunnen, and A. Zwicky, eds., *Natural Language Parsing*, Cambridge University Press, Cambridge, UK, 1982, pp. 251–278. Reprinted in B. Grosz, K. Sparck Jones and B. Webber, eds., *Readings in Natural Language Processing*, Morgan Kaufmann, San Mateo, Calif., 1986.

J. Laubsch and K. Barth, "Compiling Augmented Transition Networks into MacLisp," in L. Bolc, ed., *The Design of Interpreters, Compilers, and Editors for Augmented Transition Networks*, Springer-Verlag, Berlin, 1983.

R. F. McNaughton and H. Yamada, "Regular Expressions and State Graphs for Automata," *IRE Trans. Elec. Comp.* **EC-9**, 39–47 (1960).

M. P. Marcus, *A Theory of Syntactic Recognition for Natural Language*, MIT Press, Cambridge, Mass., 1980.

G. Ott and N. H. Feinstein, "Design of Sequential Machines from Their Regular Expressions," *J. ACM* **8**(4), 585–600 (1961).

Y. Pao and G. W. Ernest, eds., *Tutorial: Context-Directed Pattern Recognition and Machine Intelligence Techniques for Information Processing*, IEEE Computer Society Press, Silver Springs, Md., 1982.

W. H. Paxton, *A Framework for Speech Understanding*, Technical Note 142, Artificial Intelligence Center, Stanford Research Institute, 1977.

F. Pereira and D. Warren, "Definite Clause Grammars for Language Analysis—A Survey of the Formalism and a Comparison with Augmented Transition Networks," *Artif. Intell.* **13**, 231–278 (1980).

C. R. Perrault, "Augmented Transition Networks and Their Relation to Tree Transducers," *Information Sci.* **11**, 93–119 (1976).

R. Reichman, *Getting Computers to Talk Like You and Me: Discourse Context, Focus, and Semantics (An ATN Model)*, MIT Press, Cambridge, Mass., 1985.

S. C. Shapiro, "Generalized Augmented Transition Network Grammars for Generation from Semantic Networks," *Am. J. Comp. Ling.* **8**(1), 12–25 (Jan.–Mar. 1982).

W. Swartout, *A Comparison of PARSIFAL with Augmented Transition Networks*, A.I. Memo 462, MIT Artificial Intelligence Laboratory, Cambridge, Mass., 1978.

H. Tennant, *Natural Language Processing*, Petrocelli Books, New York, 1981.

F. B. Thompson, *The Semantic Interface in Man-Machine Communication*, Report No. RM 63TMP-35, Tempo, General Electric Co., Santa Barbara, Calif., 1963.

J. Thorn, P. Bratley, and H. Dewar, "The Syntactic Analysis of English by Machine," in D. Michie, ed., *Machine Intelligence 3*, Elsevier Science Publishing Co., Inc., New York, 1968, pp. 281–309.

H. Tropf and I. Walter, "An ATN Model for 3-D Recognition of Solids in Single Images," *Proceedings of the Eighth IJCAI*, Karlsruhe, FRG, Morgan-Kaufmann, San Mateo, Calif., 1983, pp. 1094–1098.

R. M. Weischedel and J. E. Black, "Responding Intelligently to Unparsable Inputs," *Am. J. Comp. Ling.* **6**(2), 97–109 (Apr.–June 1980).

T. Winograd, *Language as a Cognitive Process*, Vol. 1, Addison-Wesley Publishing Co., Inc., Reading, Mass., 1981.

J. J. Wolf and W. A. Woods, "The HWIM Speech Understanding System," in W. A. Lea, ed., *Trends in Speech Recognition*, Prentice-Hall Press, Englewood Cliffs, N.J., 1980, pp. 316–339.

W. A. Woods, "Procedural Semantics for a Question Answering Machine," *AFIPS Conference Proceedings*, 1968, pp. 457–471.

W. A. Woods, *Augmented Transition Networks for Natural Language Analysis*, Report No. CS-1, Aiken Computation Laboratory, Harvard University, Cambridge Mass., 1969. (Available from ERIC as ED-037-733; also from NTIS as Microfiche PB-203-527.)

W. A. Woods, "Progress in Natural Language Understanding: An Application to Lunar Geology," *AFIPS Conference Proceedings*, Vol. 42, 1973a.

W. A. Woods, "An Experimental Parsing System for Transition Network Grammars," in R. Rustin, ed., *Natural Language Processing*, Algorithmics Press, New York, 1973b.

W. A. Woods, "Spinoffs from Speech Understanding Research," in *Proceedings of the Fifth IJCAI*, Cambridge, Mass., Morgan-Kaufmann, San Mateo, Calif., 1977, p. 972.

W. A. Woods, "Taxonomic Lattice Structures for Situation Recognition," *Am. J. Comp. Ling.* **78**, 3 (1978a).

W. A. Woods, "Generalizations of ATN Grammars," in W. Woods and R. Brachman, eds., *Research in Natural Language Understanding*, BBN Report No. 3963, Bolt Beranek and Newman Inc., Cambridge, Mass., 1978b.

W. A. Woods, *Semantics for a Question-Answering System*, Garland Publishing, New York, 1979.

W. A. Woods, "Cascaded ATN Grammars," *Am. J. Comp. Ling.* **6**(1), 1–15 (Jan.–Mar. 1980).

W. A. Woods, "Language Processing for Speech Understanding" in F. Fallside and W. A. Woods, eds., *Computer Speech Processing*, Prentice-Hall Press, Englewood Cliffs, N.J., 1985.

W. A. Woods, "Transition Network Grammars for Natural Language Analysis," *Comm. ACM* **13**(10), 591–606 (1970). Reprinted in Y. Pao and G. W. Ernest, eds., *Tutorial: Context-Directed Pattern Recognition and Machine Intelligence Techniques for Information Processing*, IEEE Computer Society Press, Silver Spring, Maryland, 1982. Also reprinted in B. Grosz, K. Sparck Jones and B. Webber, eds., *Readings in Natural Language Processing*, Morgan Kaufmann, San Mateo, Calif., 1986.

W. A. Woods, M. Bates, G. Brown, B. Bruce, C. Cook, J. Klovstad, J. Makhoul, B. Nash-Webber, R. Schwartz, J. Wolf, and V. Zue, *Speech Understanding Systems—Final Report, 30 October 1974 to 29 October 1976*, BBN Report No. 3438, Vols. I–V, Bolt Beranek and Newman Inc., Cambridge, Mass., 1976.

W. A. Woods, R. M. Kaplan, and B. L. Nash-Webber, *The Lunar Sciences Natural Language Information System: Final Report*, BBN Report No. 2378, Bolt Beranek and Newman Inc., Cambridge, Mass., 1972.

W. A. WOODS
Harvard University

GRAMMAR, CASE

This entry examines the linguistic notion of case as it applies to natural-language processing. Case theory suggests an approach to the representation of sentence meaning and is important in accounting for the way the structure of sentences relates to those meanings. Applications of case theory to intelligent systems have ranged from a medical model of glaucoma (see MEDICINE, AI IN) (Chokhani, 1973; Kulikowski and Weiss, 1971) to speech understanding (qv) (Baranofsky, 1974; Nash-Webber, 1975). Most natural-language systems make use of these ideas in some form. For a survey of implemented systems using case grammar see Bruce (1975).

The problem of meaning representation appears in discussions of deep structures (qv) for natural-language utterances and storage structures for AI programs. General issues of efficiency, flexibility, scope, and grain all need to be considered (Bobrow and Winograd, 1977; Moore and Newell, 1973; Sidner and co-workers, 1981; Winograd, 1975). The focus here is on a particular class of such representations, namely, case structures for natural language.

The notion of "case" has been used to refer to several related concepts. Traditionally, it has meant the classification of nouns according to their syntactic role in a sentence, signaled by various inflected forms. In English, only pronouns have these case inflections. For instance, the first person singular pronoun is "I" (nominative case), "me" (accusative/objective case), or "my" (genitive/possessive case) according to its use as subject, object, or possessive article. In languages such as Greek all nouns are given affixes that indicate their case.

The idea of a direct relationship between inflections and cases is one kind of case, also called "surface" or "syntactic level" case, discussed further below. However, in understanding language, it is not sufficient to recognize the syntactic role of noun phrases (NPs). For example, in the sentence

1. Susan kicked the football with her foot.

each NP has a syntactic role: Subject—Susan, direct object—the football, and object of the preposition "with"—her foot.

Structural features together with lexical and morphological information (see MORPHOLOGY) indicate the semantic role each NP plays in the meaning of the sentence. One can thus determine that sentence 1 describes an event of kicking in which Susan is the kicker, the agent; the football is the kickee, the object; and her foot is used to perform the kicking, the instrument.

Another sense of "case" (also called "deep case," "semantic case," or "theta role") is a categorization of NPs according to their conceptual roles in the action described by a sentence. Conceptual roles are independent of the particular verb or predicate being expressed. The agent case, then, is a generalization of many ideas: kicker, reader, walker, and dancer; one who performs an action. Deep case theory and issues are also described below.

Much of the discussion of deep cases has focused on identifying a small number of these conceptual roles that can be used to describe the meaning of any sentence in any language. Because deep cases describe meanings rather than the words and structure that express those meanings, they are claimed to be language independent. Such a set of cases is called a case system.

SURFACE CASES

The introduction discussed categorizing nouns according to their endings or inflections. For the purposes of natural-language processing, it is more useful to define surface case as a general syntactic categorization of noun phrases. Another way to think of surface case is as a property that is assigned to an NP manifested in the sentence as some syntactic marker or signal, called a case marker.

Various linguistic elements can be case markers. The primary one is the case affix, that is, an ending attached to a noun form. Many would consider that prepositions (or postpositions) serve a similar function. Word order, as in English, can also be viewed as a case marker. In addition, case assignment interacts with such features as gender and definiteness of the NP. This view of case, then, generalizes the notion of surface case from simple noun inflections to a property that all NPs have and that may be expressed with word endings, word order, and so on.

How many distinct surface cases are there? One way to determine this is to consider a language in which cases are expressed by nominal inflections. In Latin, for example, five or six cases are usually distinguished: nominative, accusative, genitive, dative, ablative, and sometimes vocative.

But simply identifying surface cases is not that helpful in processing natural language since surface cases are merely signals in which deep case to assign. In other words, for each conceptual role one needs to account for the case markers that identify it. The degree to which a case-based theory can account for linguistic behavior depends on the way the case mediate between surface forms and conceptual structures.

DEEP CASES AND GRAMMATICAL EXPLANATION

The notion of deep cases is not new. For instance, Sonnencheins's demand that cases "denote categories of meaning" (Jesperson, 1965) is in effect a statement that there are two levels of cases, the surface level indicated by case affixes and a deeper level that may be common to more than one language. Fillmore (1968) presents a good argument for the universality of deep cases in natural language, saying that: "What is needed is a conception of base structure in which case relationships are primitive terms of the theory and in which such concepts as 'subject' and 'direct object' are missing. The latter are regarded as proper only to the surface structure of some (but possibly not all) languages."

Because deep cases focus on (conceptual) events rather than on syntactic constructions, they can help explain the relative "acceptability" of certain sentences. For example, one concept of the event "kicking" is that in sentence 1. This concept encompasses such notions as agent, object, instrument, location, and so on. Knowledge of this concept, along with an understanding of concepts such as "football" and "foot," give an account of how to understand sentence 1. At the same time it leads one to question sentences such as:

2. Susan kicked the new idea.
3. Susan kicked.
4. Susan and her foot kicked the football.

Sentence 2 seems strange because the sense of "kick" used here seems to require a concrete object. Sentence 3 seems strange because the object of the kicking needs to be mentioned explicitly. Strong clues from the discourse as to what was kicked (or a different interpretation of "kick") are needed to make the sentence comprehensible. Sentence 4 is also unacceptable because, although either "Susan" or "her foot" or "Susan and Joe" could be the subject of the sentence, objects that play different roles in the meaning of the sentence cannot be conjoined.

These ideas can be formalized by postulating for each verb a case frame consisting of two elements:

Case structure: What are the case slots or set of cases that play a role in the event denoted by the verb, for example, a "kicking." Which of these slots are optional, which are obligatory?

Selection restrictions: What are the semantic constraints on the objects that fill each slot in the case structure?

Selection restrictions may vary from global constraints on the use of a case with any predicate (eg, "every agent must be animate") to local constraints on the use of a case with a particular predicate (eg, "the object of 'spend' must be a resource"). So, for kicking, one might infer a case frame with the following slots and restrictions:

5. [{agent}: animate object,
object: physical object,
{instrument}: physical object,
{source}: location,
{goal}: location].

The curly brackets are used here to indicate that the slot in the case structure is optional.

As discussed under Surface Cases, the prepositions and word order in a sentence may indicate which case is intended for each NP. If the indicated cases pass the appropriate selection restrictions and if they correspond to the cases allowed by the case structure, the sentence should be easy to understand. Otherwise, it can be considered ungrammatical or at least as grounds to reinterpret the event.

Some language-understanding systems use case frames for semantic checking. A parser must check that the features of nominal constituents in the sentence satisfy the selection restrictions for the verb. The case frame may help to disambiguate among senses of the verb; either the case structure or the selection restrictions will distinguish the two senses. Furthermore, the selection restrictions can help the system identify the referent of a pronoun.

For instance, consider sentence 1. The indicated cases are [agent, object, instrument], each of which are present in case frame 5, and the required object case is present. Susan is animate; the football and her foot are physical. Thus, sentence 1 can be easily mapped into the case structure for "kick."

Sentence 2 also indicates an acceptable case structure, [agent, object], but a new idea is not a physical object. Since the selection restrictions for the object slot are violated, the sentence is less easily mapped into the case frame and is hence less comprehensible. In contrast, sentence 3 obeys the selection restrictions of case frame 5. Susan, the agent, is animate. However, its indicated case structure, [agent], does not contain the object case required by case frame 5. Thus, it too is problematic.

For sentence 4 the case structure seems to be [agent/instrument, object]. Although either the agent or the instrument can be the subject of a kicking sentence, a case cannot be assigned to them when they are conjoined.

Often, discourse information can affect sentence understanding (see DISCOURSE UNDERSTANDING). If sentence 2 follows a discussion of Susan's invention that would not work, the context allows the object case to be interpreted as a physical object. Or, suppose one describes Susan running toward a football and utters sentence 3. In that situation one could infer that the object is the football.

Note that in neither of these situations has the case structure or selection restrictions been violated, but, rather, the context provides information that is missing from the sentence in isolation. Some language-understanding systems allow ellipsis of the obligatory slots in case structures, that is, if there is no filler, the system looks for recent NPs to fill the slot.

DEEP CASES AND MEANING REPRESENTATION

Underlying the discussion thus far is the idea that people have a generic concept of an event such as kicking. A sentence such as 1 serves to describe a particular instance of such an event. That is, events are the primary entities under discussion. Of course, not everything communicated is a description of an event. Objects, states, and perhaps other entities are also described. However, events are of fundamental importance, and it is often useful to see state descriptions and even objects as special types of events. To represent the concept of kicking, imagine a unary predicate, kicking*, which can determine whether an event is a kicking. To express the existence of a kicking event, one can then quantify over the set of all events:

6. (Ex) [kicking* (x)].

Usually, the kind of event is expressed as a verb, for example, "to kick." However, an event description can also be realized as an NP. One could say "they prepared the meal" or "their preparation of the meal." By choosing events as primary entities, the semantic similarities among these phrases is captured naturally.

An event description distinguishes a particular event from other events of the same type by specifying various properties or relationships between objects and the event. Each NP denotes an object, and the relationship is conveyed by the NP's syntactic role in the sentence. By asserting several propositions about the event, sentence 1, for example, indicates which kicking is being discussed. This set of propositions can be expressed as a conjunction of binary relations:

7. (Ex) [kicking* (x) and agent (x, Susan) and object (x, the football) and instrument (x, her foot) and time (x, past)].

Phrases such as "Susan" and "the football" would in general be inadequate representations of the objects participating in the event but are suitable for the purpose here.

These relations suggest a formalism for representing sentence meaning. Some understanding systems, assuming a small number of these fixed relations, parse sentences into their deep case structure rather than the traditional surface structure parse shown in Figure 1.

Because of a class of verbs with related meanings can be used to describe similar events, these verbs share aspects of their case frames. For instance:

8. Fred bought some pickles from Reuben.
9. Reuben sold some pickles to Fred.

A case theory should capture the fact that sentences 8 and 9 describe the same event from a different perspective. The meaning of 8 could be represented as:

10. (Ex) [exchange* (x) and agent (x, Fred) and goal (x, Fred) and object (x, some pickles) and source (x, Reuben)].

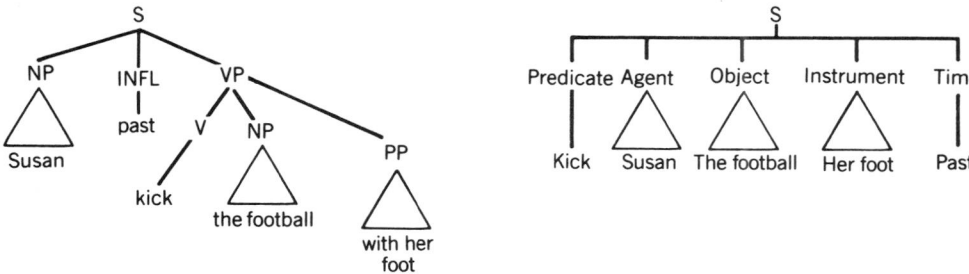

Figure 1. Surface (left) and deep (right) parse for "Susan kicked the football with her foot": S = sentence, INFL = inflection, VP = verb phrase, V = verb, PP = prepositional phrase.

The meaning of 9 differs only in that its agent is Reuben. Note that this account requires that the subject have two deep cases. Jackendoff (1972, pp. 34–35) uses this example to justify his claim that an NP can have multiple deep cases. Systems that make use of these semantic similarities among verbs are described in Hendrix, Thompson, and Slocum (1973); Norman and co-workers (1975); and Schank (1975). Identifying the case generalizations for classes of verbs based on cross-linguistic evidence is the subject on ongoing research (Levin et al., 1985).

One formalism for representing case frames is that of semantic networks (qv). These were originally proposed by Quillian (1966) to capture the objective aspect of word meaning. The associative links between verb concepts (case frames) and real-world knowledge facilitate inferences made from sentence meanings. Semantic network representations with structured inheritance [eg, KL-ONE (Brachman, 1979)] allow information about the syntactic and semantic regularities among verbs to be shared. Discussions of inferencing and case frame representation can be found in Charniak (1975); Sidner and co-workers (1981); Simmons (1972).

One problem is that an indefinite number of properties can be specified for a given event. For example,

11. Because her arm hurt, Susan awkwardly kicked the football to Mary in the park rather than throw it.

could be represented as

12. (Ex) [kicking* (x) and reason $(x$, her arm hurt) and agent $(x$, Susan) and object $(x$, the football) and time $(x$, past) and manner $(x$, awkward) and goal $(x$, Mary) and location $(x$, the park) and preference $(x$, throw it)].

Some of these properties distinguish one event from another, whereas some merely modify or provide additional information. For instance, the thing Susan kicks seems more significant than that she kicks it awkwardly. Unfortunately, the labeling of a property as "distinguishing" or "modifying" is rarely obvious. It is not difficult to imagine a context in which the manner in which an event happens is the distinguishing property, and the object of the event is relatively insignificant. The distinction among properties is sensitive to the purpose of the speaker and the beliefs of both speaker and hearer. Nevertheless, there is often a strong intuition that certain properties belong with certain events. One could say that properties vary in their degree of binding to an event and that those properties that are most tightly bound are the deep cases.

CASE SYSTEMS

Despite the compromises that seem necessary to dichotomize properties of events, there is a strong motivation to do so. By postulating a set of binary relations that represent the distinguishing properties of some generic event, one can define events as structures—known configurations that facilitate parsing (qv) and inference (qv) (Bruce, 1973; Martin, 1973; Norman and co-workers, 1975; Schank, 1971, 1973; Shapiro, 1971; Simmons, 1972). The complete set of deep cases available for describing events is called a case system. This section covers only four of the many proposed case systems.

Fillmore

Fillmore (1968, 1971) has proposed a deep structure based on cases. A sentence (S) in this deep structure consists of a modality plus a proposition:

13. $S \rightarrow M + P$.

The modality constituent (M) includes negation, tense, mood, and aspect. The proposition (P) is a tenseless structure consisting of a verb and cases:

14. $P \rightarrow V + C_1 + C_2 + \cdots + C_n$.

where each C_i is a case name that generates either an NP or an embedded S. There is a global constraint on rules of the form 14: At least one case must be present but no case may appear twice. Rules 13 and 14 are argued to be universal. Case markers are produced by the language-specific Kasus element (K):

15. $C_i \rightarrow K + NP$.

The Kasus element K generates a preposition, postposition, or case affix. One could generalize this notion to a Kasus function, which maps a deep structure proposition

Table 1. Fillmore's Case System[a]

Agent (A)	The instigator of the event
Counter agent (C)	The force or resistance against which the action is carried out
Object (O)	The entity that moves or changes or whose position or existence is in consideration
Result (R)	The entity that comes into existence as a result of the action
Instrument (I)	The stimulus or immediate physical cause of an event
Source (S)	The place from which something moves
Goal (G)	The place to which something moves
Experience (E)	The entity that receives or accepts or experiences or undergoes the effect of an action

[a] From Fillmore, 1971.

into a surface structure clause with possible word order changes.

Fillmore shows by example the deep case markers (Kasus functions) of various languages. He also gives some tentative rules for English. For example (Fillmore, 1968, pp. 32–33):

"The A preposition is *by;* the I preposition is *by* if there is no A, otherwise it is *with;* the O and F [factitive case] prepositions are typically *zero;* the B [benefactive case] preposition is *for;* the D [dative case] preposition is typically *to* . . .

"If there is an A it becomes the subject; otherwise, if there is an I, it becomes the subject; otherwise the subject is the O."

Fillmore makes an argument for deep case relations in analyzing verbs of any language, including English. He has proposed several systems that capture various aspects of the meaning of certain verbs. An example of his case systems appears in Table 1. In addition to these cases there are also other relations "that identify the limits and extents in space and time that are required by verbs of motion, location, duration, etc." (Fillmore, 1971).

Celce

Celce's system (1972) is based on five deep case relations: causal-actant, theme, locus, source, and goal. Verbs are classified into paradigms according to the case sequences they allow. For example, the ergative paradigm consists of the sequences (for the active voice):

(causal-actant 1, theme, causal-actant (2)
(causal-actant 1, theme)
(causal-actant 2, theme)
(theme)

Note that a paradigm consists of both the case structure for the verb and constraints on the order of the case fillers. For example, the ergative paradigm says that the theme can never precede the causal-actant.

"Break" is an example of an ergative verb. Thus,

16. John broke the window with a hammer.
17. John broke the window.
18. The hammer broke the window.
19. The window broke.

are all well formed since in each sentence one of the case sequences is matched (where "John" is the causal-actant 1, "window" is the theme, and "hammer" is the causal-actant 2).

Another example is the reflexive–deletion paradigm, in which the theme is deleted if it matches the causal-actant 1. Thus, "run" may be used in several ways:

20. John ran to school.
21. John ran a machine.
22. The machine ran.
23. The brook ran.

In each of the sentences there is a theme—John, machine, or brook. The paradigm allows the deletion of the theme if it is the same as the causal-actant. Thus the paradigm is

(causal-actant, goal)
(causal-actant, theme)
(theme)

Grimes

Grimes (1972) has developed a case system to serve as a foundation for discourse analysis. The definitions of the cases and their organization reflect his concern with event and episode representations. Grimes distinguishes between two kinds of generic events each with its own set of roles or deep cases. Motion/position events have orientation roles, and changes of state have process roles. In addition, the agent and benefactive roles are common to all events. These cases are shown in Table 2.

The following examples (Grimes, 1972) illustrate the use of these cases:

24. The letter (O) fell to the floor (G)
25. His house (O) is situated on top of a hill (R).
26. The tide (V) floated the oil slick (O) into the harbor (G).
27. This idea (O) came to me (G) from Austin Hale (S).
28. This book (P) costs three dollars (Rf).
29. She (A) makes dresses (P Re) from flour sacks (P M).
30. Fred (A) fixed the engine (P) with this screwdriver (I).
31. Sally (A) handed John (G) the biscuits (O).

Table 2. Grime's Case System[a]

Orientation roles:
Object (O)	The thing whose position or motion is being described
Source (S)	The location of the object at the beginning of a motion
Goal (G)	The location of the object at the end of a motion
Range (R)	The path or area traversed during a motion
Vehicle (V)	The thing that conveys the object and moves along with it

Process roles:
Patient (P)	The thing changed by a process or the thing whose state is being described
Material (M)	The thing changed by a process in its state before the change
Result (Re)	The thing changed by a process in its state after the change
Referent (Rf)	The field or object that defines the limitation of a process (as opposed to the thing affected by the process)

Agentive complex:
Agent (A)	The one who is responsible for an action
Instrument (I)	The tool used in performing an action
Force (F)	The noninstigative cause of an action

Benefactive role:
Benefactive (B)	The someone or something on whom an action has a secondary effect

[a] From Grimes, 1972.

32. He (A) parted the rope (P G) with an axe (O I).

33. The girl (P) died of malaria (F).

34. The milk (P) turned sour on me (B).

35. We (A) talked about politics (Rf).

36. A breeze (O) came to him (G) from the sea (R).

The cases Grimes distinguishes are strongly influenced by linguistic, not conceptual, considerations, for example in sentence 27 the transfer of the idea is not a physical movement. Sentence 27 has the same surface form as sentence 36, which is a description of a physical transfer, so the two have similar case assignments.

Grimes (1972) also suggests the possibility of a more tightly defined role structure based on certain similarities in the roles:

> "The roles set up for orientation all have counterparts on the process side, and vice versa. Both kinds could be considered complementary variants of a single set of roles."

> "For example, object and patient both identify what is affected, the one in terms of motion or position and the other in terms of change of state in a process."

Table 3. Interrelationships among Roles[a]

Orientation	→	Combined	←	Process
		A agent ⎤		
		⎥ Fc force		
		I instrument ⎦		
V vehicle	→	V vehicle		
O object	→	P patient	←	P patient
S source	→	F former	←	M material
G goal	→	L latter	←	Rs result
R Range	→	R range	←	Rf referent
		B benefactive		

[a] From Grimes, 1972.

These observations suggest the combined role structure shown in Table 3.

Schank

Schank's cases (1971, 1973, 1974, 1975) (see CONCEPTUAL DEPENDENCY), unlike those of Fillmore (1968) or Celce (1972), are purely conceptual. Neither the primitive act nor its cases need be explicitly mentioned in an utterance. Instead, the argument for conceptual cases depends on considerations of the pragmatics of human communication. One postulates a conceptual case because it is a relation relevant to the typical kinds of tasks people address via language.

An essential element of most communication is the description of actions. Knowledge of actions implies a conceptual structure built out of actions and their role fillers (Schank, 1974):

Actors perform actions.

Actions have objects.

Actions have instruments.

Actions may have recipients.

Actions may have directions.

One kind of conceptual structure or "conceptualization" comprises an act, with its actor, and the relations object, direction, and either recipient or instrument. Each of these relations must be present (except that only one of direction or recipient is present).

Schank argues that a small number of concepts corresponding to "primitive acts" can be used to construct meaning representations for most descriptions of events. These primitive concepts are simple actions of the kind "move a body part" (MOVE), "build a thought" (MBUILD), "transfer a physical object" (PTRANS), and "transfer mental information" (MTRANS). The primitive ACTS together with the conceptual cases are the components of meaning representation with a "unique representation" feature (Schank, 1974): "We have required of our representation that if two sentences, whether in the same or different language are agreed to have the same meaning, they must have identical representations."

It is questionable whether such a criterion can be met nontrivially. Do distinct utterances (by different speakers using different phrasings, at different times, in different situations) share significant portions of a conceptual network? Furthermore, a nonredundant representation such as Schank's raises serious questions of both psychological validity and efficiency for diverse tasks. Nevertheless, in many cases the mapping of utterances to conceptualizations seems to be exactly the process that humans exhibit. The unique representation also facilitates general inferencing by reducing the number of cases to be considered (Schank, 1974; Schank and co-workers, 1973):

"The use of such primitives severely reduces the inferences problem in AI, since inference rules need only be written once for any ACT rather than many times for each verb that references that ACT. For example, one rule is that if you MTRANS something to your LTM [long-term memory], then it is present there (ie, you know it). This is true whether the verb of MTRANSing was see, hear, inform, remember or whatever. The inference comes from the ACT rather than the verb."

CONCLUSION

In summary, the notion of case has evolved from an account of noun affixes to an account of how syntactic relations between NPs and sentences map into deep relations between objects and events. Application of these ideas to natural-language processing has two basic forms, semantic checking and meaning representation.

In many language systems a case frame is associated with each verb (and sometimes nouns). In recognizing the syntactic role of an NP in a sentence, the parser uses the case frame to verify that the semantic properties of the NP are consistent with some case that can occur in that syntactic position. This process can be used to block a parse path, to reject a sentence as ungrammatical, and to identify constraints for an ellipsed item or the referent of a pronoun.

Deep case systems are an attempt to identify a fixed number of conceptual roles that can be used to describe any event. Representing deep cases as binary relations thus provides a formalization of the meaning of a sentence. This structure for describing knowledge has led to extensive research on semantic networks for knowledge representation. Out of this research, standard techniques for parsing and understanding have evolved to the extent that most current natural-language systems incorporate these techniques in some form.

An important aspect of any case system is an account of how the deep cases are realized in a sentence. Many issues related to this accounting remain unresolved, such as whether an NP can have multiple cases (Jackendoff, 1972), and how to capture the regularities in the way the cases are realized (Levin and co-workers, 1985).

Case grammar per se is no longer an active area of research within AI. However, research on the issues discussed here has continued in the work on relational grammar, lexical functional grammar, generalized phrase structure grammar (qv), and semantic grammar (qv).

BIBLIOGRAPHY

S. Baranofsky, Semantic and Pragmatic Processing in the SRI Speech Understanding System, Technical Report, Stanford Research Institute, Stanford, Calif., 1974.

D. G. Bobrow and T. Winograd, "An Overview of KRL, a Knowledge Representation Language," Cog. Sci. 1, 3–46 (1977).

R. J. Brachman, "On the Epistemological Status of Semantic Networks," in N. V. Findler, ed., Associative Networks, Academic Press, New York, 1979.

B. Bruce, "Case Structure Systems," in Proc. of the Third IJCAI, Stanford, Calif., 1973, pp. 364–371.

B. Bruce, "Case Systems for Natural Language," Artif. Intell. 6, 327–360 (1975).

M. Celce-Murcia, Paradigms for Sentence Recognition, Technical Report HRT-15092/7907, System Development Corporation, Santa Monica, Calif., 1972.

E. Charniak, A Brief on Case, Technical Report 22, Instituto per gli Studi Semantici e Cognitivi, Castagnola, Switzerland, 1975.

S. Chokhani, The Definition and Interpretation of a Causal Network Model for Disease Within the CHRONOS System, Technical Report NIH CBM-TM-17, Computer Science Department, Rutgers University, New Brunswick, N.J., 1973.

C. Fillmore, "The Case for Case," in E. Bach and R. T. Harms, eds., Universals in Linguistic Theory, Holt, Rinehart and Winston, New York, 1968, pp. 1–88.

C. Fillmore, "Types of Lexical Information," in D. D. Steinberg and L. A. Jakobovits, eds., Semantics: An Interdisciplinary Reader, Cambridge University Press, London, 1971, pp. 370–392.

J. Grimes, The Thread of Discourse, Technical Report NSF 1, Cornell University, Ithaca, N.Y., 1972.

G. Hendrix, C. Thompson, and J. Slocum, "Language Processing via Canonical Verbs and Semantic Models," in Proc. of the Third IJCAI, Stanford, Calif., 1973, pp. 262–269.

R. S. Jackendoff, Semantic Interpretation In Generative Grammar, The MIT Press, Cambridge, Mass., 1972.

O. Jespersen, The Philosophy of Grammar, Norton, New York, 1965.

C. Kulikowski and S. Weiss, Computer Based Models for Glaucoma, Technical Report CBM-TR-3, Computer Science Department, Rutgers University, New Brunswick, N.J., 1971.

B. Levin and co-workers, Lexical Semantics in Review, Technical Report 1, Lexicon Project, Center for Cognition Science, MIT, 1985.

W. A. Martin, Translation of English Into MAPL Using Winograd's Syntax, State Transition Networks, and a Semantic Case Grammar, Technical Report Internal Memo 11, Project MAC, Automatic Programming Group, MIT, Cambridge, Mass., 1973.

J. Moore and A. Newell, "How Can MERLIN Understand?" in L. Gregg, ed., Knowledge and Cognition, Lawrence, Los Angeles, Calif., 1973.

B. Nash-Webber, "Semantic Support for a Speech Understanding System," in D. G. Bobrow and A. Collins, eds., Representation and Understanding: Studies in Cognitive Science, Academic Press, New York, 1975, pp. 351–382.

D. A. Norman, D. E. Rumelhart, and the LNR Research Group, *Explorations in Cognition*, Freeman, San Francisco, Calif., 1975.

M. R. Quillian, *Semantic Memory*, Technical Report AFCRL-66-189, Bolt Beranek and Newman, Cambridge, Mass., 1966.

R. Schank, "Finding the Conceptual Content and Intention in an Utterance in Natural Language Conversation," in *Proceedings of the Second IJCAI*, London, 1971, pp. 444–454.

R. Schank, *The Fourteen Primitive Actions and Their Inferences*, Technical Report AIM-183, Stanford University, Stanford, Calif., 1973.

R. Schank, *Causality and Reasoning*, Technical Report 1, Instituto per gli Studi Semantici e Cognitivi, Castagnola, Switzerland, 1974.

R. Schank, *Conceptual Information Processing*, North-Holland, Amsterdam, 1975.

R. Schank, N. Goldman, C. Rieger III, and C. Riesbeck, "MARGIE: Memory Analysis, Response Generation, and Inference on English," in *Proceedings of the Third IJCAI*, Stanford, Calif., 1973, pp. 255–261.

S. Shapiro, "A Net Structure for Semantic Information Storage, Deduction and Retrieval," in *Proc. of the Seventh International Joint Conference on Artificial Intelligence*, London, 1971, pp. 512–523.

C. Sidner, M. Bates, R. Bobrow, R. Brachman, P. Cohen, D. Israel, B. Webber, and W. Woods, *Research in Knowledge Representation for Natural Language Understanding: Annual Report*, Technical Report 4785, Bolt Beranek and Newman, Cambridge, Mass., 1981.

R. F. Simmons, *Semantic Networks: Their Computation and Use for Understanding English Sentences*, Technical Report CAI NL-6, Computer Science Department, University of Texas, Austin, Texas, 1972.

T. Winograd, "Frame Representations and the Declarative/Procedural Controversy," in D. G. Bobrow and A. Collins, eds., *Representation and Understanding: Studies in Cognitive Science*, Academic Press, New York, 1975, pp. 185–210.

B. Bruce and M. G. Moser
Bolt Beranek & Newman

GRAMMAR, GENERALIZED PHRASE STRUCTURE

Generalized phrase structure grammar (GPSG) is a framework for defining the syntax of natural languages (Gazdar and co-workers, 1985; Hukari and Levine, 1986) that was developed within theoretical linguistics in the early 1980s. Since then, GPSG and its siblings and descendants have been widely applied within computational linguistics (qv). Mathematically, GPSG as originally formulated (Gazdar and co-workers, 1985) is simply a version of context-free phrase structure grammar (CF–PSG). Historically, it falls within the family of theories that have developed out of Montague grammar. CF–PSGs attracted renewed interest within linguistics, following two decades of neglect, when it was realized that all of the original arguments that apparently demonstrated their descriptive inadequacy for natural languages were either invalid or dependent on false premises (Pullum and Gazdar, 1982). Despite their presumed linguistic inadequacy,

CF–PSGs had remained of interest within the computational linguistics community, because such grammars are well understood mathematically and known to be computationally tractable. GPSG made this engineering interest theoretically respectable again (*ACL-21*, 1983). In GPSG, the implicit CF–PSG itself is not defined ostensively, but rather it is characterized indirectly by various techniques that have the effect of both allowing the grammar to capture linguistically significant generalizations and making the grammar several orders of magnitude more compact than a simple listing of rules would be.

In the following sections, individual outlines are given of GPSG and a number of closely related grammar formalisms that have been developed and used in computational linguistics during the 1980s. These formalisms, like certain others not considered here, such as lexical functional grammar (LFG) and functional unification grammar (FUG), all adopt (1) a basically CF–PSG rule format (single mother, no application order, no explicit context sensitivity) under (2) a node admissibility rather than a string rewriting interpretation, with (3) a recursively defined attribute-value based category set, and (4) graph unification as the primary operation for combining syntactic information. Finally, (5) these formalisms can, in general, be given a declarative semantics.

GPSG

GPSG defines syntactic categories as sets of syntactic feature specifications. A feature specification is an ordered pair consisting of a feature (eg, CASE) and a feature value. The latter may either be atomic (eg, ACCUSATIVE) or it may be a syntactic category (ie, features are allowed to take categories as their values). A syntactic category is then a partial function from features to their values. The internal makeup of categories is further constrained by feature cooccurrence restrictions (FCR) that are simply Boolean conditions on combinations of feature specifications.

$$\text{FCR: [COMP for]} \supset \text{[VFORM INF]}$$

This example FCR says that if a category is associated with the *for* complementizer then it will also be an infinitive.

Syntactic structures are phrase structure trees of the familiar kind whose nodes are labeled with syntactic categories as characterized above. The well formedness of the local substructures of a tree (and hence, recursively, of the tree as a whole) is determined by (1) immediate dominance (ID) rules, (2) linear precedence (LP) rules, (3) principles of feature instantiation, and (4) feature specification defaults (FSD).

ID rules are like ordinary CF–PSG rules except that they say nothing about the linear order of the items they introduce.

$$S \rightarrow NP, VP$$

$$VP \rightarrow V[\text{SUBCAT } 3], NP, PP[\text{PFORM to}]$$

As such, they simply permit a particular mother category to dominate the given daughter categories. As the second example above illustrates, the subcategorization of lexical items is handled by means of an attribute SUBCAT that takes integer values. These values can be thought of as pointers from lexical items to the syntactic rules responsible for introducing them, thus *give,* for example, would be listed in the lexicon as an instance of the [SUBCAT 3] class of verbs.

Some ID rules are just listed, but others are derived from these and from each other by metarules. A metarule is a clause in the definition of the grammar that enables the definition of one set of rules in terms of another set, antecedently given.

$$VP \rightarrow X, NP \Rightarrow$$

$$VP[VFORM\ PAS] \rightarrow X$$

This example says that for every rule in the grammar that permits an active verb phrase (VP) to dominate a noun phrase (NP) along with other material, there is also another rule that allows a passive VP to dominate the other material, but with the NP omitted. Generalizations that would be lost if the two sets of rules (eg, active VP rules and passive VP rules) were merely listed are captured by the metarule. The technique has also been applied within the categorial grammar paradigm (Morrill, 1987). Metarules do the work done by lexical rules in most other unification-based grammar formalisms. It has been shown that metarules can be eliminated from GPSG by adopting a generalization of the FCR rule-type, which allows Boolean conditions on the featural composition of the categories in an ID rule (Kilbury, 1986).

LP rules state the relevant generalizations about the order of (classes of) sister constituents in the language.

$$V < NP < VP$$

This example says that a VP may not precede an NP or V and that an NP may not precede V. The LP rules define a partial ordering on the set of categories and require this partial ordering to be respected by the linear order of sister categories. In English, for example, they allow one to say that lexical items must always precede their phrasal sisters. It has been shown that ID–LP grammars can be parsed using modified versions of standard CF–PSG parsing techniques (Shieber, 1984a; Kilbury, 1985).

GPSG employs three principles of feature instantiation: the head feature convention (HFC), the control agreement principle (CAP), and the foot feature principle (FFP). The HFC is responsible for equating one class of feature specifications as they appear on the mother category and its head daughter(s). Thus, for example, a verb phrase inherits the tense of its verb. The CAP matches agreement features between locally connected agreeing categories (eg, between a subject noun phrase and its verb phrase sister). And the FFP deals with the matching of category-valued features between mother and daughter categories and is responsible for, for example, unbounded dependencies in questions and relative clauses and for agreement with reflexive pronouns. The formal definitions of these principles crucially depend on notions of extension and unification definable in the partial function theory of categories sketched above.

FSDs are Boolean conditions analogous to FCRs, but employed differently. FCRs are absolute conditions that have to be met, whereas FSDs are conditions that a category must meet if certain other conditions are not met.

$$FSD: [CASE\ ACC]$$

Thus, for example, the default value for CASE might be ACCUSATIVE, but a given noun phrase could appear in some other case if it were required to do so by one of the feature instantiation principles, say. It has been shown that FSDs can be given a semantics in terms of autoepistemic logic (Evans, 1987).

All the mechanisms just described are interpreted in the local tree domain, where a local tree is simply a tree fragment consisting of a mother and its daughters. A tree is satisfied by a grammar if and only if every local tree in the tree is satisfied. A local tree is satisfied by a grammar if and only if (1) it satisfies the HFC, CAP, FFP, one ID rule and every LP rule and (2) each category in the local tree satisfies every FCR and every FSD. In addition, the framework provides a general mapping from local trees and a semantic-type assignment to the component syntactic categories of those local trees to expressions of Montague's higher order logic.

Among the areas of syntax that GPSG work has covered in depth are the subcategorization of verbs, the English auxiliary system, coordination, questions, relative clauses, the passive construction, noun phrases, adjective phrases (including comparatives), prepositional phrases, and infinitival and sentential complements. The earliest GPSG work concentrated on English, but subsequently work was also been done on the grammars of Adyge, Arabic, Basque, Catalan, Chinese, Dutch, French, German, Greek, Hindi, Irish, Japanese, Korean, Latin, Makua, Palauan, Polish, Spanish, Swedish, and Welsh (see Gazdar and co-workers, 1985 for references).

PATR

PATR (not an acronym) is a grammar formalism that was developed by Shieber (1984b) at the same time as GPSG was emerging. It is a much simpler and more elegant framework than GPSG, but is, nonetheless, closely related to it. What GPSG attempts to do by general principles such as the HFC and CAP, PATR does by explicit unification equations associated with CF–PSG–like rules.

Rule {sentence formation}

$$S \rightarrow NP\ VP:$$

$$\langle S\ tense \rangle = \langle VP\ tense \rangle$$

$$\langle NP\ number \rangle = \langle VP\ number \rangle$$

$$\langle NP\ person \rangle = \langle VP\ person \rangle.$$

This example says that an S may dominate an NP followed by a VP provided that the tense of the S and the tense of the VP unify and that the number and person of the NP unify with the number and person of the VP. Verbosity is avoided by means of macrolike notational conventions and a special mechanism known as gap threading is introduced to do the work done by the FFP in GPSG. Likewise, lexical rules take over the role played by metarules in GPSG.

The PATR notation readily permits the GPSG account of subcategorization to be encoded, but, in the absence of metarules, this is not a sensible use of the notation. Instead, PATR grammars standardly treat subcategorization by means of a feature structure that encodes a list of the categories of the objects with which a lexical item combines, a technique that has its conceptual roots in categorial grammar.

> Rule {two-object verbs}
>
> $VP \rightarrow V X Y$:
>
> $\langle V$ subcat first$\rangle = X$
>
> $\langle V$ subcat rest first$\rangle = Y$
>
> $\langle V$ subcat rest rest$\rangle$ = end.

It has been shown that it is possible to give a Scott-Strachey denotational semantics for the PATR formalism (Pereira and Shieber, 1984) and it was subsequently shown that GPSG grammars can be substantially compiled into the PATR formalism in a fairly straightforward way (Shieber, 1986).

HPSG

Head-driven phrase structure grammar (Pollard and Sag, 1987, 1991) is a descendant of GPSG that has been influenced also by both FUG and LFG. The HFC and FFP both reappear, albeit in slightly different guises. Likewise, the ID format for rules also carries over. The expressive potential of LP rules is enlarged, however, to allow them to make reference to the semantic argument status of a constituent in addition to the syntactic category. This enables an HPSG grammar to say, for example, that a direct object must precede other objects, something that cannot be said directly in the more restricted language of GPSG LP rules. Subcategorization follows the model described above in connection with PATR. As with PATR, metarules are replaced by LFG-style lexical rules:

$\langle \alpha, V[VFORM\ BSE, SUBCAT\langle . . . , NP, NP\rangle] \rangle \rightarrow$

$\langle passive(\alpha), V[VFORM\ PAS, SUBCAT\langle\langle PP[PFORM\ by]\rangle,$

$. . . , NP\rangle] \rangle$

This example says that if the lexicon contains an entry for the bare infinitive form of a double object verb, then it should also contain an entry for the passive form of that verb, a form that subcategorizes for only a single object, but that may optionally take a by-phrase. An immediate

consequence of this combination of lexical rules and a categorial grammar-style of ID rule is that the number of ID rules needed by an HPSG grammar is far less than its equivalent GPSG counterpart would need. However, much more syntactic information needs to be encoded in an HPSG lexicon.

HPSG abandons the relatively autonomous Montague semantics of GPSG in favour of a situation theoretic view of meaning that is encoded with the same attribute-value structure as the syntactic information and that various syntactic mechanisms (notably those concerned with agreement) make reference to. A variant of HPSG, KPSG, has recently been proposed as a basis for computational phonology (Chung, 1989).

JPSG

Japanese phrase structure grammar is a formalism developed by Gunji (1987) in connection with the natural language processing work done at ICOT for their "fifth-generation computer." It is the successor to an earlier ICOT grammar formalism known internally as IPSG. JPSG is rather similar to HPSG but takes the latter's view of the lexicon to the limit and postulates only a single phrase structure schema. All differences between syntactic constructions become the consequences of lexical differences, and all the real work of a JPSG grammar is done by the feature system and the feature instantiation principles. Category-valued features take sets of categories as values rather than the single categories of GPSG or the category tuples of HPSG. Like GPSG, JPSG provides a mapping from syntactic structures into Montague-style higher order logic representations.

RGPSG

Revised generalized phrase structure grammar is a by-product of work on the complexity of GPSG (Ristad, 1990). In the interests of reducing one measure of that complexity, RGPSG adopts a stronger constraint on the recursive construction of categories than does GPSG; it requires that all ID rules have nonnull heads and forbids metarules from manipulating those heads; it simplifies the feature instantiation principles so that they are all monotonic; and it eliminates FCRs and FSDs in favor of a set of simple conditional defaults that are applied in a specified order.

IMPLEMENTATION

All of the grammar formalisms described in this article have been implemented in the sense that working parsers have been written for them, and in some cases those parsers have formed part of some larger natural language processing project. For GPSG itself, a great many different implementations exist (see Boguraev, 1988). The largest and most comprehensive is that of the Alvey grammar (Briscoe and co-workers, 1987). Likewise for PATR, a great many implementations exist. The simplest consist of less than a page of PROLOG whereas the most highly developed is probably the D-PATR system (Karttunen, 1986). HPSG has its roots in a major commercial project as the grammar formalism that was developed originally for the Hewlett Packard database front-end project (*ACL-23*, 1985).

BIBLIOGRAPHY

ACL-21, Proceedings of the Twenty-First Annual Meeting of the Association for Computational Linguistics, SRI International, Menlo Park, Calif., 1983. [Papers by A. Joshi; C. R. Perrault; G. K. Pullum; S. M. Shieber; S. M. Shieber and co-workers; H. Thompson; H. Uszkoreit.]

ACL-23, Proceedings of the Twenty-Third Annual Meeting of the Association for Computational Linguistics, Bell Communications Research, Murray Hill, N.J., 1985. [Papers by C. Pollard and L. Creary; D. Flickinger; C. Pollard and T. Wasow; D. Proudian and C. Pollard.]

B. Boguraev, "A Natural Language Toolkit: Reconciling Theory With Practice," in U. Reyle and C. Rohrer, eds., *Natural Language Parsing and Linguistic Theories,* Reidel, Dordrecht, 1988, pp. 95–130.

E. Briscoe, C. Grover, B. Boguraev, and J. Carroll, "A Formalism and Environment for the Development of a Large Grammar of English," in *Proceedings of the Tenth IJCAI,* Milan, Italy, Morgan-Kaufmann, San Mateo, Calif., 1987, pp. 703–708.

H.-S. Chung, "A Phonological Theory Using Unification-Based Grammar Formalism," *Language Res.* **25**(1), 7–17 (1989).

R. Evans, "Towards a Formal Specification for Defaults in GPSG," in *Proceedings of the Stirling Workshop on Natural Language Processing, Unification, and Grammar Formalisms,* Centre for Cognitive Science, Edinburgh, UK, 1987, pp. 3–8.

G. Gazdar, E. H. Klein, G. K. Pullum, and I. A. Sag, *Generalized Phrase Structure Grammar,* Harvard University Press, Cambridge, Mass., 1985. [Contains an extensive bibliography.]

T. Gunji, *Japanese Phrase Structure Grammar,* Reidel, Dordrecht, 1987.

T. Hukari and R. Levine, "Generalized Phrase Structure Grammar: A Review Monograph," *Linguistic Anal.* **16**, 123–245 (1986).

L. Karttunen, "D-PATR: A Development Environment for Unification-Based Grammars," in *Proceedings of the Eleventh International Conference for Computational Linguistics,* 1986, pp. 74–80.

J. Kilbury, "A Modification of the Earley-Shieber Algorithm for Direct Parsing of ID/LP Grammars," in J. Laubsch, ed., *The Eighth German Workshop on Artificial Intelligence,* Springer-Verlag, Heidelberg, 1985, pp. 39–48.

G. Morrill, "Meta-Categorial Grammar," in N. Haddock, E. H. Klein, and G. Morrill, eds., *Working Papers in Cognitive Science, Vol. 1: Categorial Grammar, Unification Grammar and Parsing,* Centre for Cognitive Science, Edinburgh, UK, 1987, pp. 1–29.

F. C. N. Pereira, and S. M. Shieber, "The Semantics of Grammar Formalisms Seen as Computer Languages," in *Proceedings of the Tenth International Conference for Computational Linguistics,* 1984, pp. 123–129.

C. Pollard and I. A. Sag, *Information-Based Syntax and Semantics, Volume 1: Fundamentals,* CSLI/Chicago University Press, Stanford/Chicago, 1987.

C. Pollard and I. A. Sag, *Information-Based Syntax and Semantics, Volume 2: Topics in Binding and Control,* CSLI/Chicago University Press, Stanford/Chicago, 1991.

G. K. Pullum and G. Gazdar, "Natural Languages and Context Free Languages," *Linguistics and Philosophy* **4**, 471–504 (1982).

E. S. Ristad, "Computational Structure of GPSG Models," *Linguistics and Philosophy,* **13**, 521–587 (1990).

S. M. Shieber, "Direct Parsing of ID/LP Grammars," *Linguistics and Philosophy* **7**, 135–154 (1984a).

S. M. Shieber "The Design of a Computer Language for Linguistic Information," in *Proceedings of the Tenth International Conference for Computational Linguistics,* 1984b, pp. 362–366.

GERALD GAZDAR
University of Sussex

GRAMMAR, PHRASE-STRUCTURE

Phrase-structure trees provide structural descriptions for sentences. Phrase structure grammars characterize phrase-structure trees. Both phrase structure trees and grammars, therefore, play a crucial role in natural language processing for computing the structural description of a sentence, which can then be used for further processing in language understanding or generation systems (Winograd, 1983). In this article, phrase-structure trees, phrase-structure grammars, and related grammatical systems are described.

PHRASE-STRUCTURE TREES

A phrase-structure tree encodes a hierarchical structure of a sentence. This information is of two kinds: hierarchical grouping structure (constituent structure) and the syntactic categories of these groupings (Bloomfield, 1933; Wells, 1947; Bach, 1974).

By way of example, we will consider the following example sentence:

John wanted to publish the paper.

which has the (not necessarily unique) grouping structure shown in Figure 1a. This structure can also be represented by a bracketing structure, as in Figure 1b. In both cases, the grouping structure is described without identifying the categories for the constituents. Such structures are called *skeletons*. Skeletons characterize the phrase boundaries without assigning labels to the nodes (Levy and Joshi, 1978).

A skeleton with the category labels is a phrase-structure tree for a sentence. A phrase-structure tree for the sample sentence (Fig. 1c) shows that *John* is a proper noun (NPR) which is also a noun phrase (NP), *wanted* and *publish* are verbs (V), *to* is a preposition (P) [more correctly, *to* should be classified as a particle or tense], *the* is a determiner (DET), *paper* is a noun (N), *the paper* is a noun phrase (NP), *to publish the paper* is a verb phrase (VP), *wanted to publish the paper* is also a verb phrase (VP), and

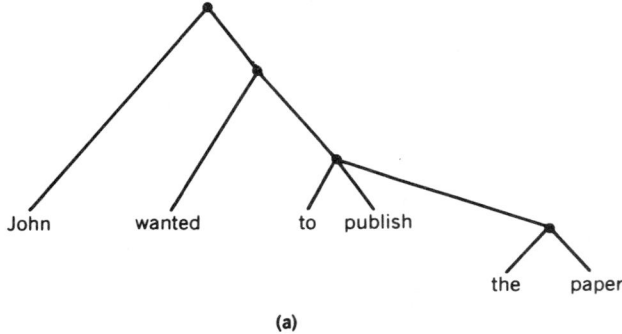

(a)

[[John]][[wanted][[to][publish][[the][paper]]]]]

(b)

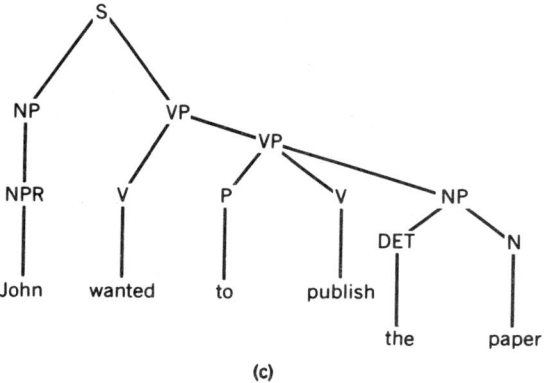

(c)

[S[NP[NPRJohn]][VP[Vwanted][VP[Pto][Vpublish]
[NP[DETthe][Npaper]]]]]]

(d)

Figure 1. A sample sentence represented by (*a*) a grouping structure; (*b*) a bracketing structure; (*c*) a phrase structure tree; (*d*) a
labeled bracketed structure.

finally, *John wanted to publish the paper* is a sentence (S).
(Note that the notion of PSG should not be equated with
the grammar of specific linguistic content: PSG is a type of
grammar in which different linguistic contents can be instantiated.)

Corresponding to the bracketed structure of Figure 1b
is a labeled bracketed structure (Fig. 1d). Phrase-structure trees such as Figure 1c or labeled bracketed structures such as Figure 1d are usually, but not always, the
output of parsers in natural language processing systems.

PHRASE-STRUCTURE GRAMMARS (PSG)

Phrase-structure trees can be characterized by grammatical systems, first by phrase-structure grammars and then
some related systems. Phrase-structure grammars consist
of a set of nonterminal symbols (phrase-structure catego-

ries such as N, V, DET, P, NP, VP, S, etc), a set of terminal
symbols (lexical items such as *buy, John, eaten, in, the,*
etc), and a set of rewriting rules that allow a nonterminal
symbol to be rewritten as a string of terminal or nonterminal symbols. If this rewriting is independent of the context
surrounding the nonterminal, it is a context-free grammar (CFG); otherwise, it is a context-sensitive grammar
(CSG). Thus a CFG has rewriting rules of the form

$$A \rightarrow X \qquad (1)$$

where X is a sequence of terminals or nonterminals and A
is a nonterminal. A CSG has rewriting rules of the form

$$ZAW \rightarrow ZXW \qquad (2)$$

where X, Z, and W are strings of terminals and nonterminals and A is a nonterminal. In rule 2, A is written as X in
the environment Z–W. Rule 2 often takes the form

$$A \rightarrow X|Z—W \qquad (3)$$

The right side of a rule in a CFG can be a null string; such
rules are called null rules. For a CFG with null rules, it is
possible to construct an equivalent CFG (ie, generating
the same set of strings) without null rules. CFGs with null
rules often simplify the grammars for many context-free
languages.

Derivation in a CFG begins with the initial symbol S,
followed by successive applications of the rewriting rules
until no further rules can be applied. It is easy to see how
context-free rules in Figure 2 will help characterize the
phrase-structure tree (Fig. 1c). The order in which the
rewriting rules are applied is irrelevant, because the rewriting depends only on the symbol on the left side of the
rule and not on the context around the occurrence of that
symbol in a string.

Context-sensitive rules are useful in constraining the
rewriting of a nonterminal by specifying a necessary context. For example,

$$V \rightarrow wanted|— VP \qquad (4)$$

constrains the lexical insertion of *wanted* in V only if
there is a VP to the right. Also,

$$V \rightarrow publish|— NP$$

$$V \rightarrow published|— NP$$

$$S \rightarrow NP\ VP$$
$$NP \rightarrow NPR$$
$$NP \rightarrow DET\ N$$
$$VP \rightarrow V\ VP$$
$$VP \rightarrow P\ V\ NP$$

NPR → John, Mary, Bill
N → paper, man, cow
V → wanted, tried, publish, meet, published, want
P → to
DET → the

Figure 2. A context-free grammar.

constrain the lexical insertion of *publish* or *published* in V only if there is a NP to the right. Thus, rule 4 will not permit the insertion of *published* instead of *wanted* in the phrase structure tree of Figure 1c.

Some Formal Properties of PSGs

If all rules of a PSG, G, are context-free, then G is called a context-free PSG, or a context free grammar (CFG). If some rules of a PSG are context sensitive, then G is called a context-sensitive PSG, or a context-sensitive grammar (CSG). A string language of a PSG, G, is defined as the set of all terminal strings, derived in G, and this set is denoted as L(G). A string w is derived in G if w can be obtained by successive rewriting of the initial symbol S using one of the rules in G. A string language L (ie, a set of terminal strings) is called a context-free language (CFL) if there is CFG, G, such that L(G) = L. L is called a strictly context-sensitive language if there is no CFG, G, such that L(G) = L and there is a CSG, G, such that L(G) =L. Note that a grammar G may be context-sensitive, but its string language L(G) need not be a CSL. The class of CSLs properly contains the class of CFLs; in this sense, CSGs are more powerful than CFGs.

There is a sense, however, in which CSGs do not have more power than CFGs. If a CSG, G, is used for analysis, then the language analyzed by G is context-free (Peters and Ritchie, 1969; Joshi and Levy, 1977). In order to explain the use of a context-sensitive grammar G for analysis for a given tree t, let the set of proper analyses of t be defined as follows. Roughly speaking, a proper analysis of a tree is a slice across the tree. More precisely, the recursive definition of the set of proper analyses of a tree t, denoted Pt, set forth in Figure 3 applies. Let G be a context-sensitive grammar, that is, its rules are of the form

$$A \rightarrow \omega/\pi - \phi$$

where $A \in V - \Sigma$ (V is the alphabet and Σ is the set of terminal symbols), $\omega \in V^+$ (set of nonnull strings on V) and $\pi, \phi \in V^*$ (set of all strings on V). If π and ϕ are both null, then the rule is a context-free rule. A tree t is said to be analyzable with respect to G if for each node of t some rule of G holds. It is obvious how to check whether a context-free rule holds of a node. A context-sensitive rule $A \rightarrow \omega/\pi - \phi$ holds of a node labeled A if the string corresponding to the immediate descendants of that node A is ω and there is a proper analysis of t of the form $\rho_1\pi A\phi\rho_2$ that passes through the node ($\rho_1, \rho_2 \in V^*$). The contextual condition $\pi - \phi$ is called a proper analysis predicate.

Similar to these context-sensitive rules, which allow the specification of context on the right and left, rules are often needed to specify context on the top or bottom. Given a node labeled A in a tree t, the DOM(π_ϕ), $\pi, \phi \in V^*$, holds of a node labeled A if there is a path from the root to the frontier of the tree, which passes through the node labeled A, and is of the form

$$\rho_1\pi A\phi\rho_2 \ (\rho_1, \rho_2 \in V^*)$$

The contextual condition associated with such a vertical proper analysis is called a *domination predicate*.

(a) If $t = \phi$ (the empty tree), then Pt = ϕ.

(b) If $t =$

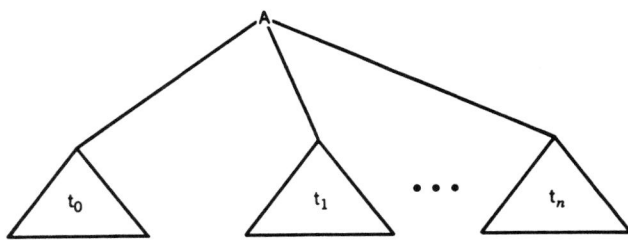

then $Pt = \{A\} \cup P\ (t_0).P(t_1)\ .\ .\ .\ P(t_n)$
where $t_0, t_1, \ .\ .\ .\ t_n$ are trees and ellipsis denotes concatenation (of sets); for example,

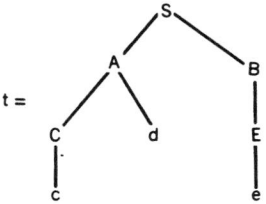

(c) $Pt = \{S, AB, AE, Ae, CdB, CdE, Cde, cdB, cdE, cde\}$

Figure 3. The set of proper analyses of a tree t.

The general form of a local constraint combines the proper analysis and domination predicates as follows: a local constraint rule is a rule of the form

$$A \rightarrow \omega/C_A$$

where C_A is a Boolean combination of proper analysis and domination predicates.

Let G be a finite set of local constraint rules and $\tau(G)$ the set of trees analyzable by G. It is assumed that the trees in $\tau(G)$ are sentential trees, that is, the root node of a tree in $\tau(G)$ is labeled by the start symbol S, and the terminal nodes are labeled by terminal symbols. It can be shown that the string language $L(\tau(G)) = \{x | x$, is the terminal string of t and $t \in \tau(G)\}$ is context free (Joshi and Levy, 1977).

Example

Let V = {S, T, a, b, c, e} and Σ = {a, b, c, e}, and G be a finite set of local constraint rules:

G:

1. S → e
2. S → aT
3. T → aS
4. S → bTc/(a_)) ∧ DOM (T_)
5. T → bSc/(a_)) ∧ DOM (S_)

In rules 1, 2, and 3 above, the context is null, and these rules are context free. In rule 4 (and in rule 5), the constraint requires an a on the left, and the node is dominated (immediately) by a T (by an S in rule 5).

The language generated by G can be derived by G_1:

$$S \rightarrow e \qquad S \rightarrow aT_1$$
$$S \rightarrow aT \qquad T \rightarrow aS_1$$
$$T \rightarrow aS \qquad T_1 \rightarrow bSc$$
$$S_1 \rightarrow bTc$$

In G_1 there are additional nonterminals S_1 and T_1 that enable the context checking of the local constraints grammar, G, in the generation process.

It is easy to see that under the homomorphism that removes subscripts on the nonterminals T_1 and S_1 each tree generable in G_1 is analyzable in G. Also, each tree analyzable in G has a homomorphis preimage in G_1. Consider once again the context-sensitive rule 4:

$$V \rightarrow wanted|\_ VP \qquad (4)$$

When rule 4 is interpreted as a local constraint as described above, the lexical item *wanted* will appear under a V node only if there is a VP node to its right (in the tree in which V appears). The predicate VP to the right of V is defined over the tree in which V and VP nodes appear and not on a string in which V and VP appear. Another way of saying the same thing is to say that to the right of V, there is a string that has an analysis VP in the tree.

Context-sensitive rules in a PSG for describing linguistic grammars are used in this analyzability sense and not string-rewriting rules.

Terminal Symbols in a PSG

So far the terminal symbols in a PSG have been presented as unanalyzed elements. This is done for simplicity. It is necessary to regard the terminal elements as complexes of phonological, syntactic, and semantic features (Bach, 1974; Chomsky, 1965). [In principle, it is possible to eliminate all these features complexes by introducing new nonterminals. However, the number of these new nonterminals will be extremely large (essentially corresponding to all possible combinations of features). Also, there will be enormous redundancy in the grammar.] Each such complex symbol for a terminal symbol is a set of features. For example, when the terminal symbols of Figure 1c are replaced by complex symbols, the result is a structural description (SD), shown in Figure 4. (The possibility of associating complex symbols with intermediate nodes is not discussed in this article.)

PSG is a Transformation Grammar (TG)

TGs are also not discussed in this article. However, it is important to note that PSGs and phrase structure trees play a crucial role in a TG. The basic idea of a TG is that certain SDs are described in a component of a TG, called the base component, and the other SDs are then obtained from these base-derived SDs by certain tree-transforming rules, called transformations. The base component is a phrase-structure grammar and thus defines a set of base phrase-structure trees. The trees obtained by using transformation rules are also phrase-structure trees. This view of TG is a more classic view and also an oversimplified view, but it is adequate for this description. For example, the phrase-structure tree (Fig. 5b) for the sentence in Figure 5a can be base-generated. The phrase structure tree for the sentence 5c is then obtained by applying a transformational rule to Figure 5b, resulting in phrase structure tree (Figure 5d).

REVIVAL OF PHRASE-STRUCTURE GRAMMARS AND PHRASE-STRUCTURE TREES

Although a PSG is used in a TG, it plays a subsidiary role. Beginning around 1975, it was becoming clear that when viewed in a certain way, PSG had more descriptive power than would have been thought without necessarily going beyond the CFG. The results on local constraints are a clear example of this point of view. In the late 1970s a number of grammatical formalisms were proposed that

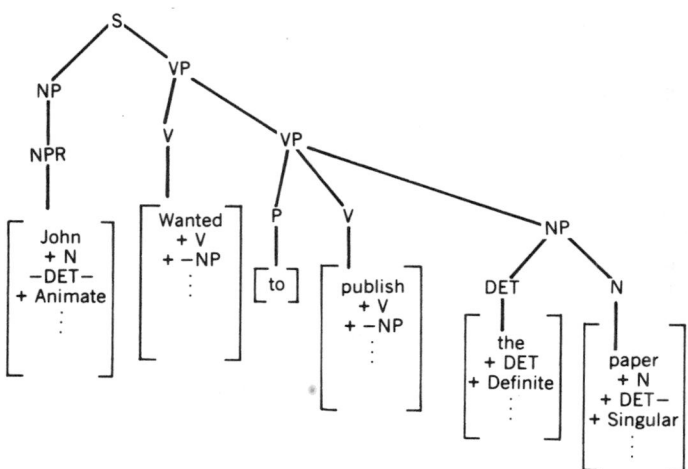

Figure 4. A structural description of the sample sentence.

John saw Mary

(a)

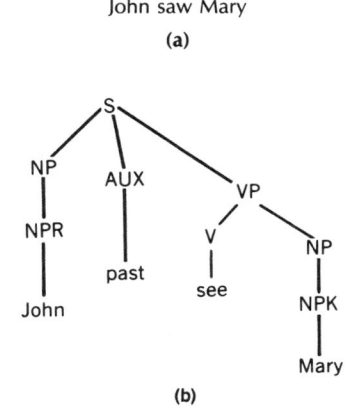

(b)

Mary was seen by John.

(c)

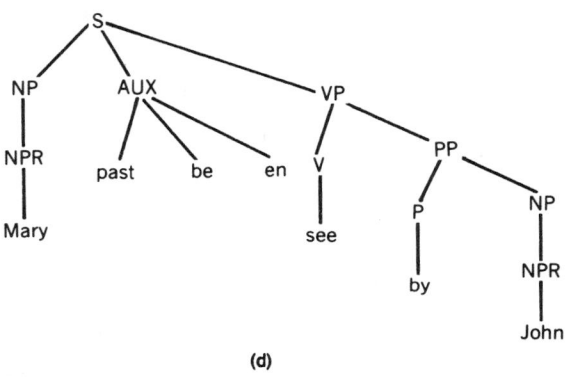

(d)

Figure 5. Phrase structure trees for two sentences (*a*) and (*c*). The tree (*b*) is base-generated and tree (*d*) is obtained using a transformational rule.

were nontransformational in character. Some of these are amendments to PSG without necessarily going beyond CFG [eg, generalized phrase-structure grammars (GPSG) (Gazdar, 1982; Gazdar and co-workers, 1985); others are PSG accompanied by another level of representation to be used for filtering some structures generated by PSG (eg, lexical functional grammar (LFG) (Kaplan and Bresnan, 1979)], and some others are based on tree-building systems for generating phrase-structure trees without the use of rewriting rules [eg, tree-adjoining grammars (TAG) (Joshi and co-workers, 1975; Joshi, 1984)]. Only GPSG and TAG are described here, because they are directly related to phrase-structure grammars.

Generalized Phrase-Structure Grammar (GPSG)

Besides the analyzability (or node admissibility) notion described above, two other notions were introduced in the framework of generalized phrase-structure grammar (GPSG) (Gazdar and co-workers, 1985). These are categories with holes and an associated set of derived rules and linking rules and metarules for deriving rules from one another. The categories with holes and the associated

rules do not increase the weak generative power beyond that of context-free grammars. The metarules, unless constrained in some fashion, will increase the generative power because, for example, a metarule can generate an infinite set of context-free rules that can generate a strictly context-sensitive language. (The language $\{a^n b^n c^n | n \geq 1\}$ can be generated in this way.) The metarules in the actual grammars written in the GPSG framework so far are constrained enough so that they do not increase the generative power.

Gazdar introduced categories with holes and some associated rules in order to allow for the base generation of unbounded dependencies. Let V_N be the set of basic nonterminal symbols. Then a set $D(V_N)$ of derived nonterminal symbols can be defined as follows.

$$D(V_N) = [\alpha/\beta | \alpha, \beta \in V_N]$$

For example, if S and NP are the only two nonterminal symbols, then $D(V_N)$ would consist of S/S, S/NP, NP/NP, and NP/S. The intended interpretation of a derived category (slashed category or a category with a hole) is as follows: a node labeled α/β will dominate subtrees identical to those that can be dominated by α, except that somewhere in every subtree of the α/β type there will occur a node of the form β/β dominating a resumptive pronoun, a trace, or the empty string, and every node linking α/β and β/β will be of the form γ/β. Thus α/β labels a node of type α that dominates material containing a hole of the type β (ie, an extraction site in a movement analysis). For example, S/NP is a sentence that has an NP missing somewhere. The derived rules allow the propagation of a hole, and the linking rules allow the introduction of a category with a hole. For example, from the rule

[S NP VP]

(which is the same as the rule S → NP VP, but written as a node admissibility condition), Two derived rules can be obtained.

[S/NP NP NP/VP]
[S/NP NP VP/NP]

An example of a linking rule is a rule (rule schema) that introduces a category with a hole as needed for topicalization, eg, [S α S/α]. For α = PP, this becomes [S PP S/PP]. This rule will induce a structure like that in Figure 6. The technique of categories with holes and the associated derived and linking rules allows unbounded dependencies to be accounted for in a phrase-structure representation.

The notion of categories with holes is not completely new. Harris (1962) introduces categories such as S-NP or S.NP (like S/NP of Gazdar) to account for moved constituents. He does not, however, seem to provide, at least not explicitly, machinery for carrying the hole downward. He also has rules in his framework for introducing categories with holes. Thus, in his framework, something like the linking rule would be accomplished by allowing for a sentence form (a center string) (not entirely his notation),

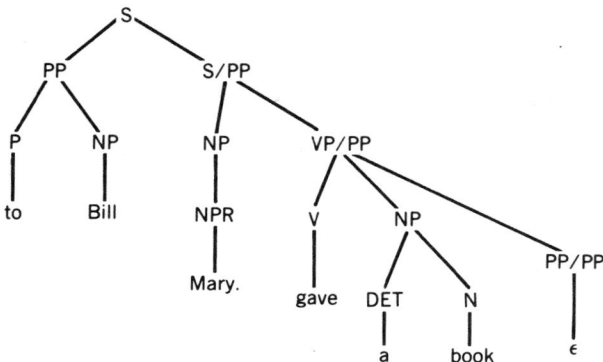

Figure 6. A tree with a linking rule [$_S$PP S/PP].

$$NP\ V\ \Omega\text{-NP}$$

$$\Omega = \text{object or complement of V}$$

This notion also appears in Kuno's context-free grammar (1963), which had node names with associated descriptions that reflected the missing constituent and were expanded as constituents, one of which similarly reflected the missing constituent. This was continued down to the hole.

Sager (1967), who has constructed a substantial parser starting from some of these ideas and extending them significantly, has allowed for the propagation of the hole resulting in structures very similar to those of Gazdar. She has also used the notion of categories with holes in order to carry out some coordinate structure computation. For example, Sager allows for the coordination of S/α and S/α.

Gazdar (1985) is the first, however, to incorporate the notion of categories with holes and the associated rules in a formal framework for his syntactical theory and also to exploit it in a systematic manner for explaining coordinate structure phenomena.

HEAD GRAMMARS AND HEAD-DRIVEN PHRASE-STRUCTURE GRAMMARS

There are two variants of GPSG: head grammars (HGs) and head-driven phrase-structure grammars (HPSGs). HGs were introduced by Pollard (1984) and HPSGs were developed at the Hewlett-Packard Laboratories (Pollard, 1985).

Head Grammars

In HG, the rewriting rules allow not only concatenation of strings, but also the wrapping of one string around another. For example, HG has rules of the form

$$RW\ (uhv, u'gv')$$
$$\uparrow$$

where uhv and u'gv' are two strings with h and g as the designated symbols, called heads and marked by ↑. The result of applying the rule produces the string

$$uhu'gv'v$$
$$\uparrow$$

That is, the string to the right of the head of the first string is wrapped around the second string. The head of the resultant is the head of the first string. It has been shown that HGs are equivalent to the tree-adjoining grammars (TAGs), discussed in the next section (Vijay Shanker and co-workers, (1986). Both HGs and TAGs are more powerful than context-free grammars but less powerful than the context-sensitive grammars. They belong to the class of mildly context-sensitive grammar formalisms (Joshi and co-workers, in press).

Head-Driven Phrase-Structure Grammars (HPSG)

HPSGs use only concatenation rules. HPSG differs from GPSG in various ways, in particular, in the use of lexical rules, which replace the metarules in GPSG, and in the treatment of subcategorization, which uses unification. HPSG uses slots for both the preverbal and postverbal complements. The subcategorization feature is encoded as a stack-valued feature by a feature structure encoding of the list arguments with features *first* and *rest*. The complements appear in the following order: postverbal complements from left or right and then the preverbal subject (Shieber, 1968).

TREE-ADJOINING GRAMMARS AND LEXICALIZED TAG

Both HG and HPSG can be characterized as nonstandard phrase-structure grammars. The space of nonstandard phrase-structure grammars is not limited to just these two formalisms. This section briefly describe TAG, especially lexicalized TAGs. Although TAGs derive phrase-structure–type trees, the derivations are based on tree rewriting rules and not string rewriting rules (HGs and HPSGs are essentially string rewriting rules).

The elementary trees of TAG provide an extended domain of locality (as compared to context-free grammars, GPSG, HPSG, and lexical functional grammars), which allows factoring recursion from the domain of dependencies. Dependencies such as agreement, subcategorization, and even the so-called long distance dependencies, such as topicalization and wh-movement, are all defined on the elementary trees and are thus local. The long distance nature of the dependencies is then a consequence of the adjoining of auxiliary trees to elementary trees or derived trees.

A lexicalized TAG consists of a finite set of structures (trees) associated with each lexical item that is intended to be the anchor of these structures and two operations for composing these structures. (The notion of an *anchor* corresponds here to that of a *functor* in categorial grammars. The elementary tree associated with a lexical item can be regarded as a structured object that is its syntactic type. The anchor of an elementary tree is either a head or a functional head of that tree.) The two operations are substitution and adjoining. The finite set of trees consists of two disjoint sets of trees: initial trees and auxiliary trees. Each elementary tree encapsulates the predicate argument structure. Figure 7 illustrates a lexicalized TAG; some elementary (initial and auxiliary) trees are shown.

The trees in Figure 7a–e are initial trees; Figures 7f and 7g are auxiliary trees. X-type initial trees correspond to the trees that can be substituted for one of the argument positions of elementary trees. Figure 7d is an example of an S-type initial tree. The ↓ near a node indicates that an appropriate substitution must be made at that node. Nodes without ↓, unless they are terminals, are possible sites for adjoining. In particular, note that the foot node of an auxiliary tree (eg, Fig. 7f, 7g) do not have ↓ because these trees are auxiliary trees that can be adjoined at some appropriate node in some tree. The tree in Figure 7f corresponds to an adverbial modifier, and Figure 7g corresponds to a relative clause. The Figure 7f tree has VP as the root node and VP as the foot node; the tree in Figure 7g has NP as the root node and NP as the foot node.

Complex structures are built by substitution and adjoining. If the Figure 7b tree is substituted for DET in the Fig. 7a tree while substituting the Fig. 7a tree at the NP_0 node in the Fig. 7d tree, and the Fig. 7c tree at the NP_1 node of the Fig. 7d tree, the result is:

$$\text{The man likes peanuts.} \qquad (5)$$

Adjoining the tree in Fig. 7f to the derived tree corresponding to the sentence (5) at the VP node produces:

$$\text{The man likes peanuts passionately.} \qquad (6)$$

With appropriate substitutions in the tree in Fig. 7g, adjoining Fig. 7g to the tree corresponding to the sentence (6) at the subject NP node yields:

$$\text{The man who Mary likes likes peanuts.} \qquad (7)$$

Adjoining can be thought of as excising the subtree at a node, inserting an auxiliary tree of the right type, and then attaching the excised subtree at the foot node of the auxiliary tree. Although a TAG provides a phrase structure at the level of elementary trees and at each step of the derivation a new tree is derived, these trees are object language trees and not derivation trees as in a context-free grammar. The derivation structures of TAG are in terms of these elementary trees, ie, they record the history of the derivation of the object language tree in terms of the elementary trees and the nodes where substitution or adjunctions are made.

SUMMARY

Phrase-structure trees provide structural descriptions for sentences. Phrase-structure trees can be generated by phrase-structure grammars. Phrase-structure trees can be shown to be appropriate to characterize structural descriptions for sentences, including those aspects that are usually characterized by transformational grammars, by making certain amendments to CFG, without increasing their power; by adding rules more powerful than concatenation; or by generating them from elementary trees by a

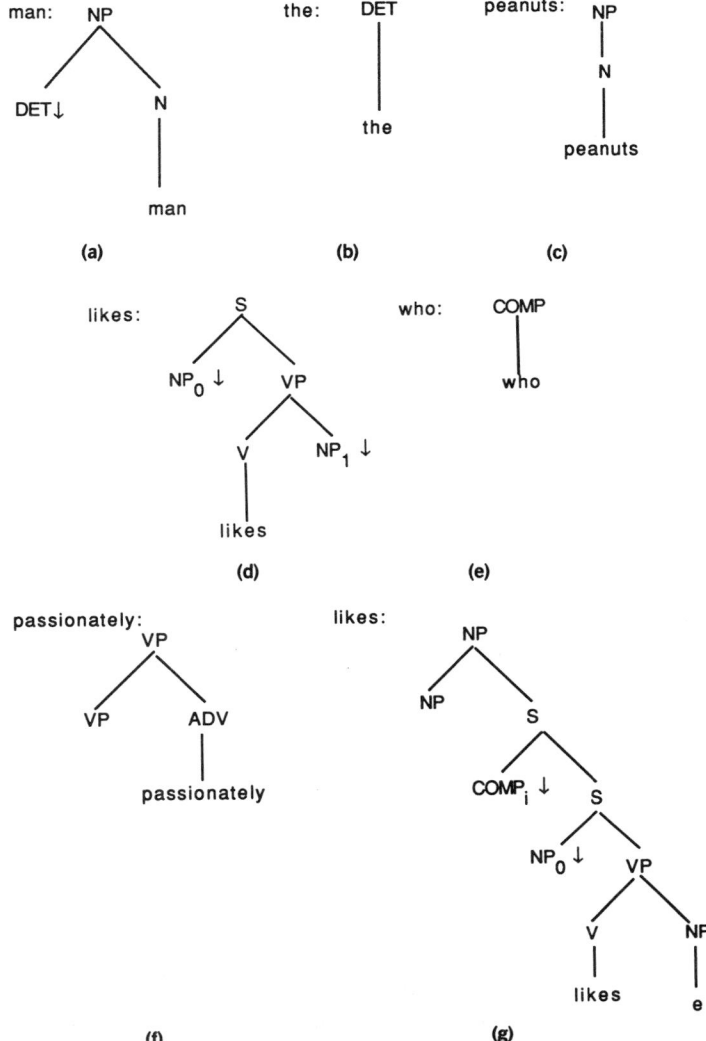

Figure 7. A lexicalized tree-adjoining grammar (TAG).

suitable rule of composition, increasing the power only mildly beyond that of CFG. Structural descriptions provided by phrase-structure trees are used explicitly or implicitly in natural language processing systems (Winograd, 1983). A more recent discussion of alternate conceptions of phrase structure appears in Kroch and Baltin (1990).

BIBLIOGRAPHY

E. Bach, *Syntactic Theory*, Holt, Reinhart, and Winston, New York, 1974.

L. Bloomfield, *Language*, Holt, New York, 1933.

N. Chomsky, *Aspects of the Theory of Syntax*, MIT Press, Cambridge, Mass., 1965, pp. 131–186.

G. J. M. Gazdar, *Phrase Structure Grammar*, in P. Jacobsen and G. K. Pullum, eds., *The Nature of Syntactic Representation*, Reidel, Boston, Mass., 1982.

G. Gazdar, J. M. E. Klein, G. K. Pullum, and I. A. Sag, *Generalized Phrase Structure Grammar*, Blackwell, Oxford, 1985.

Z. S. Harris, *String Analysis of Language Structure*, Mouton and Co., The Hague, 1962.

A. K. Joshi, "How Much Context-Sensitivity is Necessary for Structural Description? Tree Adjoining Grammars," in D. Dowty, L. Karttunen, and A. Zwicky, eds., *Natural Language Parsing*, Cambridge University Press, Cambridge, UK, 1984, pp. 206–250.

A. K. Joshi and L. S. Levy, "Constraints in Structural Descriptions," *SIAM J. Comput.* **6**, 272–284 (1977).

A. K. Joshi, L. S. Levy, and M. Takashaski, "Tree Adjunct Grammars," *J. Comput. Sys. Sci.* **10**, 136–163 (1975).

A. K. Joshi, K. Vijay-Shanker, and D. Weir, "The Convergence of Mildly Context-Sensitive Grammars," in S. M. Shieber and T. Wasow, eds., *The Processing of Natural Language Structure*, MIT Press, in press.

R. Kaplan and J. W. Bresnan, "A Formal System for Grammatical Representation," in J. W. Bresnan, ed., *The Mental Representation of Grammatical Relations*, MIT Press, Cambridge, Mass., 1979, pp. 173–281.

A. Kroch and M. Baltin, eds., *Alternate Conceptions of Phrase Structure*, University of Chicago Press, Chicago, 1990.

S. Kuno, *The Current Grammar for the Multiple Path English Analyzer, Mathematical Linguistics and Automatic Translation*, Report No. NSF 8, Computation Laboratory, Harvard University, Cambridge, Mass., 1963.

L. S. Levy and A. K. Joshi, "Skeletel Structural Descriptions," *Inf. Cont.* **39**, 192–211 (1978).

S. Peters and R. W. Ritchie, "Context-Sensitive Immediate Constituent Analysis," in *Proceedings ACM Symposium on Theory of Computing*, 1969, pp. 150–161.

C. Pollard, *Head Grammars*, Ph.D. dissertation, Stanford University, Stanford, Calif., 1984.

C. Pollard, Lecture notes on head-driven phrase structure grammars, Center for the Study of Language and Information, Stanford University, Stanford, Calif., 1985.

N. Sager, "Syntactic Analysis of Natural Languages," in M. Alt and M. Rubinoff, eds., *Advances of Computers*, Vol. 8, Academic Press, Inc., New York, 1967, pp. 202–240.

S. M. Shieber, Lecture notes on unification-based approaches to grammars, Center for the Study of Language and Information, Stanford University, Stanford, Calif., 1986.

K. Vijay Shanker, D. Weir, and A. K. Joshi, "Adjoining: Wrapping, and Headed Strings," in *Proceedings of the Twenty-fourth Annual Meeting of the Association for Computational Linguistics*, New York, June 1986.

R. S. Wells, "Immediate Constituents," *Language* **23**, 212–226 (1947).

T. Winograd, *Language as a Cognitive Process*, Academic Press, Inc., New York, 1983.

ARAVIND K. JOSHI
University of Pennsylvania

GRAMMAR, SEMANTIC

A semantic grammar is a grammar for language in which the categories refer to semantic as well as syntactic concepts. It was first developed in the early 1970s in the attempt to build practical natural-language interfaces to educational environments, eg, SOPHIE (qv) (Burton, 1976; Burton and Brown, 1979) and databases, eg, LIFER (qv)

(Hendrix, 1977; Hendrix and co-workers, 1978) and PLANES (qv) (Waltz, 1978). It has continued to be used in a variety of commercial and other applications such as ROBOT (also known as INTELLECT) (qv) (Harris, 1977), PHRAN (qv) (Wilensky and co-workers, 1984), XCALIBUR (Carbonell, 1983), and CLOUT. The distinguishing characteristics of a semantic grammar is the type of information it encodes and not the formalism used to represent it. Semantic grammars have been represented in many different formalisms including augmented transition networks (see GRAMMAR, AUGMENTED TRANSITION NETWORK) and augmented phrase structure grammars (see GRAMMAR, PHRASE-STRUCTURE). Unlike natural-language systems generally, the aim of semantic grammars is to characterize a subset of natural language well enough to support casual user interaction. As such, it is primarily a technique from the field of natural-language engineering rather than a scientific theory, [though some researchers have proposed semantic grammars as a psychological theory of language understanding (Wilensky, Yigal, and Chin, 1984)].

To understand semantic grammars, it is helpful to understand a little about theories of natural language. The goal of a theory of language is to explain the regularities of language. Transformational grammars and lexical functional grammars are two good examples of theories of language. The syntax part of the theory explains the structural regularities of a language, for example, things that are true about word order and inflections. The theory does this by providing rules that the words and phrases must obey. This collection of rules is referred to as a grammar. An example of the kind of regularity that the syntactic part of a theory of language seeks to capture can be seen in the relationship between the following two sentences:

1. The boy hit the ball.
2. The ball was hit by the boy.

It is called the passive relationship and exists between an infinite number of other sentences in English as well. A good syntactic grammar will have a small number of rules that account for the passive relationship between all of these sentences. To explain these relationships, the grammar must name and relate broad, abstract concepts. For example, introducing the concept of a noun phrase (NP) as referring, roughly, to the collection of all possible phrases that name things allows a syntactic grammar to contain a rule like:

⟨Noun Phrase1⟩⟨Verb⟩⟨NounPhrase2⟩:=
    ⟨NounPhrase2⟩⟨AuxiliaryVerb⟩⟨Verb⟩ by ⟨NounPhrase1⟩

This gives rise to categories in the grammar that characterize the roles words and phrases play in the structure of language that is in the syntax.

In semantic grammars, the choice of categories is based on the semantics of the world and the intended application domain as well as on the regularities of language. Thus, for example, in a system that was intended to answer questions about electronic circuits (such as SOPHIE), the categories might include measurement, measurable quantity, or part as well as standard categories such as determiner and preposition. For example, the rule

⟨Measurement⟩ :=
    ⟨Determiner⟩⟨Measurable-Quantity⟩⟨Preposition⟩⟨Part⟩

applies in the following phrases:

The voltage across R9.
The current through the voltage reference capacitor.
The power dissipation of the current-limiting transistor.

In Figure 1 are two parse trees of the same sentence that might be generated by typical grammars, the left one with a standard grammar, the right one with a semantic grammar.

ADVANTAGES OF SEMANTIC GRAMMARS

Semantic grammars provide engineering solutions to many problems that are important when building practical natural-language interfaces. These important issues are efficiency, habitability, discourse phenomena, bad inputs, and self-explanation. Efficiency is important because the user is waiting during the time the system spends understanding the input. Semantic grammars are efficient because they allow semantic constraints to be used to reduce the number of alternative parsings that must be considered. They are also efficient because the semantic interpretation (meaning) of the expression follows directly from the grammar rules. When considering a natural-language interface, it is often useful to think of the interpretation of a statement as the command or query the user would have had to type had he or she been talking directly to the system. For example, in a database retrieval system the interpretation of the input is the query or queries in the retrieval language that answer the question (see INFORMATION RETRIEVAL). Typically, in a se-

mantic grammar each rule has an augmentation associated with it that builds its interpretation from the interpretations of the constituents. For example, the interpretation of the rule ⟨Query⟩ := ⟨Question-Intro⟩ ⟨Measurement⟩ is a query to the database that retrieves the measurement specified in the interpretation of ⟨Measurement⟩. The interpretation of ⟨Measurement⟩ specifies the quantity being measured (eg, voltage) and where it should be measured (eg, across R9). The interpretation of ⟨Measurement⟩ can be used differently in, for example, a rule like ⟨Yes-No-Query⟩ := ⟨Be-Verb⟩ ⟨Measurement⟩ ⟨Comparator⟩, as in the question "is the voltage across R9 low?" Having the semantic interpretation associated directly with the grammar is efficient because it avoids a separate process that does semantic interpretation.

The second important issue is habitability. It is unlikely that any natural-language interface written in the foreseeable future will understand all of natural language. What a good interface does is to provide a subset of the language in which users can express themselves naturally without straying over the language boundaries into unallowed sentences. This property is known as habitability (Watt, 1968). Although exactly what makes a system habitable is unknown, certain properties make systems more or less habitable. Habitable systems accept minor or local variations of an accepted input and allow words and concepts that are accepted in one context to be accepted in others. For example, a system that accepts "Is something wrong?" but does not accept "Is there anything wrong?" is not very habitable. Any sublanguage that does not maintain a high degree of habitability is apt to be worse than no natural-language capability because users will continually be faced with the problem of revising their input. Lack of habitability has been found to be a major source of user frustration with natural-language systems.

An important problem in designing habitable natural-language interfaces is the occurrence of discourse phenomena such as pronominal reference and ellipsis. When people interact with a system in natural language, they assume that it is intelligent and can therefore follow a

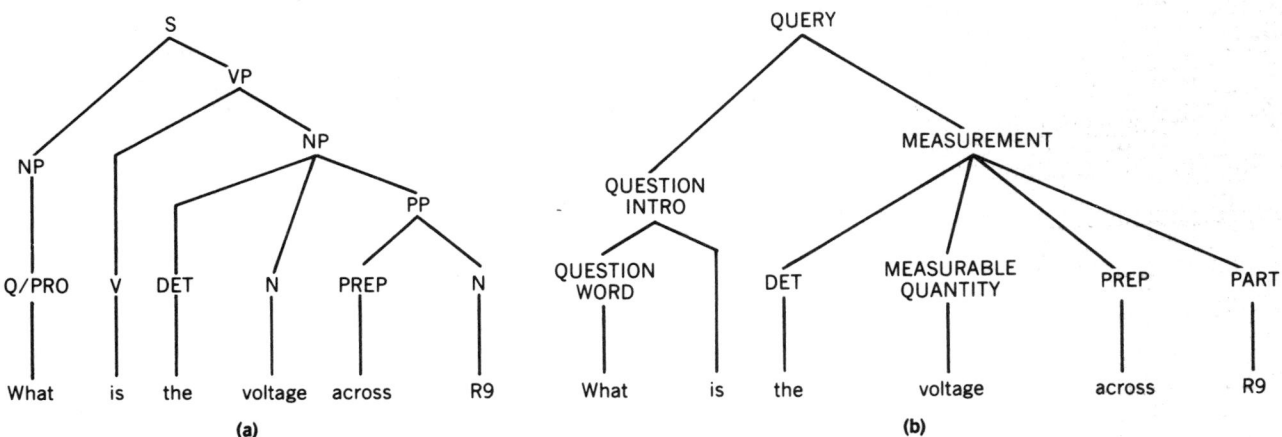

Figure 1. Examples of two parse trees of the same sentence. (a) Standard structure of an English question. (b) Semantic grammar structure of an English question.

dialogue. If it does not, they have trouble adapting. The following sequence of questions exemplifies these problems:

3. What is the population of Los Angeles?
4. What about San Diego?

Input 3 contains all of the information necessary to specify a query. Input 4, however, contains only the information that is different from the previous input. Systems using semantic grammars handle sentence like 4 by recognizing the categories of the phrases that do occur in the ellided input. In this case, "San Diego" might be recognized as being an instance of ⟨City⟩. The most recent occurrence of the same category is located in a previous input, and the new phrase is substituted for the old one. In some systems, such as SOPHIE, PLANES, and XCALIBUR, this is done using the interpretation structure of previous inputs. In some systems, such as PHRAN, the substitution is made in the previous input string, which is then reparsed. Input 4 is an example of the discourse phenomena called ellipsis (qv). Semantic grammars have also been used to handle classes of pronominal and anaphoric reference, as in the sentence "What is it for San Francisco?" Although the techniques used by semantic grammars work on many common cases of discourse constructs, there are many other more complex uses that they do not address (see DISCOURSE UNDERSTANDING and Webber, 1983, for more details).

Another ramification of the fact that the natural-language interface will not understand everything is that it must deal effectively with inputs that lie outside its grammar, that is, sentences that do not parse. The standard solution to this problem is to understand part of the sentence either by ignoring words (sometimes called "fuzzy parsing") or by recognizing phrases that do satisfy some of the grammar. A semantic grammar has the advantage that recognized phrases are meaningful and can be used to provide feedback to the user. For example, if the user's phrase contains the phrase "voltage across R9," the system can display the rules that use ⟨Measurement⟩ to give the user an idea of what sentences the system will accept.

A related difficulty with natural-language interfaces is conveying to the user the capabilities of the system, for example, what the system can do and what concepts it knows about. Semantic grammar systems can use the information in the grammar to provide some help. For example, LIFER allows the user to ask about possible ways of completing a sentence. In the dialogue below, the user requests help in the middle of a sentence. The system responds with the possible ways that the sentence could be completed. Since the grammar is semantic, the terms are meaningful to the user.

USER: What is the voltage ⟨help⟩

SYSTEM RESPONSE: Inputs that would complete the ⟨measurement⟩ rule are

    across ⟨part⟩
    between ⟨node⟩ and ⟨node⟩
    at ⟨node⟩

The NLMENU (Tennant and co-workers, 1983) system attacks this problem by constraining the user's input to a series of menu selections that only produce legal sentences. In addition to obviating the problem of unrecognized sentences, the approach also has the benefit of presenting in the menus an explicit picture of what the system can do.

LIMITATIONS OF SEMANTIC GRAMMARS

Many limitations arise from the merger of semantic and syntactic knowledge that characterizes semantic grammars. The range of linguistic phenomena that have been covered is limited and excludes, for example, complex forms of conjunctions, comparatives, or complex clause-embedding constructs, for example, "Which ships does the admiral think the fourth fleet can spare?" (Winograd, 1983). Moreover, although work in constructing semantic grammars is creating some generalizable principles of design, the grammar itself must be redone for each new domain. Categories that are appropriate to electronics are not applicable to the domain of census data. Even within a single domain, certain syntactic regularities, such as the passive transformation must be encoded for each semantic class that allows active sentences. This not only increases the size of the grammar but, more importantly, results in a great deal of redundancy in the grammar, making it difficult to write or extend. Attempts have been made to overcome this limitation by separating the syntactic knowledge. The simplest approach is to reformulate the categories in the grammar to make them more syntactic. In this case the semantic distinctions that had previously been made by having distinct categories are made in the augmentations associated with each grammar rule that produce the interpretation. Another approach is to capture the syntactic knowledge in the program that applies the grammar rather than in the grammar itself. In PHRAN, for example, aspects of adverbs and relative clauses are handled by the matching process that applies the grammar rules to the input. In a return to the more classical breakdown of linguistic information, some systems seek to maintain the advantages of semantic grammar by closely coupling separate syntactic and semantic components (Bobrow and Webber, 1980). This points to one contribution of semantic grammars to the theory of language (as contrasted to their contributions to the production of usable systems), the identification of phenomena that succumb to simple methods.

BIBLIOGRAPHY

R. J. Bobrow and B. L. Webber, "Knowledge Representation for Syntactic/Semantic Processing," *Proceedings of the First National Conference on AI*, Stanford, Calif., AAAI, Menlo Park, Calif., 1980, pp. 316–323. [Describes the RUS system that arose from attempts to extract knowledge common to semantic grammars in several domains.]

R. R. Burton, *Semantic Grammar: An Engineering Technique for Constructing Natural Language Understanding Systems*, BBN Report 4274, Bolt, Beranek and Newman, Cambridge, Mass., 1976. Burton's Ph.D. dissertation, University of California, Irvine, 1976, which introduced the term "semantic grammar" and described its use and advantages in building the SOPHIE natural-language front-end. Good introduction to the issues surrounding natural-language engineering.

R. R. Burton and J. S. Brown, "Toward a Natural Language Capability for Computer-Assisted Instruction," in H. O'Neill, ed., *Procedures for Instructional Systems Development*, Academic Press, New York, 1979, pp. 273–313. A more accessible paper largely based on "Semantic Grammar: An Engineering Technique for Constructing Natural Language Understanding Systems."

J. G. Carbonell, "Discourse Pragmatics in Task-Oriented Natural Language Interfaces," *Proceeding of the 21st Annual Meeting of the Association for Computational Linguistics*, Cambridge, Mass., 1983, pp. 164–168. Describes XCALIBUR, a general system for interfacing to expert systems.

L. R. Harris, "User-Oriented Data Base Query With the Robot Natural Language Query System," *Int. J. Man-Mach. Stud.* **9**, 697–713 (1977). Describes the system ROBOT that is marketed as INTELLECT.

G. G. Hendrix, *The LIFER Manual: A Guide to Building Practical Natural Language Interfaces*, Technical Note 138, SRI Artificial Intelligence Center, Menlo Park, Calif., Feb. 1977. Complete description of the LIFER system, which includes many elegant user interface features including the ability to change the grammar during the interaction.

G. G. Hendrix, E. D. Sacerdoti, D. Sagalowicz, and J. Slocum, "Developing a Natural Language Interface to Complex Data," *ACM Trans. Database Sys.* **3**(2), 105–147 (June 1978). Provides an overview of the LIFER system.

H. R. Tennant, K. M. Ross, R. M. Saenz, C. W. Thompson, and J. R. Miller, "Menu-Based Natural Language Understanding," *Proceeding of the Twenty-First Annual Meeting of the Association for Computational Linguistics*, Cambridge, Mass., 1983, pp. 151–158. Describes NLMENU, a menu driven natural language input system.

D. L. Waltz, "An English Language Question-Answering System for a Large Data Base," *ACM* **21**, 526–539 (July 1978). Describes the PLANES system that interfaces to relational databases.

W. C. Watt, "Habitability," *Am. Document.* **19**, 338–351 (1968).

B. L. Webber, "So What Can We Talk About Now?" in M. Brady and R. C. Berwick, eds., *Computational Models of Discourse*, MIT Press, Cambridge, Mass., 1983, pp. 331–371. Describes the difficult problems anaphoric reference that arise in natural discourse.

R. Wilensky, A Yigal, and D. Chin, "Talking to UNIX in English: An Overview of UC," *CACM* **27**(6), 574–593 (June 1984). Describes the PHRAN system, which pushes the domain dependence of semantic grammars.

T. Winograd, *Language as a Cognitive Process*, Vol. 1, Syntax, Addison-Wesley, Menlo Park, Calif., 1983, p. 381. Excellent introduction to the area of natural language understanding.

R. Burton
Xerox PARC

GRAMMAR, SYSTEMIC

Systemic grammar [more properly systemic-functional grammar (SFG)] belongs to the family of grammatical frameworks based on statements of the cooccurrence possibilities of grammatical features. In this respect, it is analogous to more recently developed grammar frameworks such as generalized phrase structure grammar (qv) (GPSG) and head-driven phrase structure grammar (HPSG) (Pollard and Sag, 1987), and general formalisms for natural language processing such as Functional Unification Grammar (FUG) (Kay, 1979). However, SFG places central focus on grammar as a complex resource for achieving communicative and social goals. This is in sharp contrast both to other feature-based accounts and to accounts of grammar in the structural tradition descended from, for example, transformational grammar and the work of Chomsky. Within SFG the entire grammatical description of a language is organized around a factorization of the task of finding grammatical structures appropriate for the expression of specified meanings. This is the principal motivation for systemic grammatical features: They provide an account of the functions in context that particular linguistic units may serve. It is then these functions, rather than the structural regularities of syntax, that determine the organization of the grammar. Accordingly, SFG has found ready application in AI and natural language processing (NLP) systems where natural language capabilities are desired: Such systems often need to rely on accounts of how language may be controlled to achieve functional goals. These applications of SFG in computational contexts continue to provide test beds for theoretical claims that can be modified accordingly and passed back into the theory. The developmental cycle of theory, application of theory, and reappraisal of theory is basic to SFL methodology.

The organization of SFG around linguistic function is due to its origins within anthropologically and sociologically oriented schools of thought, mediated primarily through Malinowski and Firth, respectively, and European functional linguistics, particularly the Prague School and its forerunners. The grammar SFG itself grew out of work by Halliday in England throughout the 1960s. A reasonably extensive view of the theoretical assumptions of systemic-functional linguistics (SFL) as a whole and the role of grammar within that can be found in Halliday (1978). A good example of an SFG account of the grammar of English can be found in Halliday (1985), while a more general overview in the context of computational linguistics is given in Winograd (1983). Finally, a detailed overview of SFG, its implementation in the context of text generation, and its position with respect to SFL at large is presented in Matthiessen and Bateman (1991).

LANGUAGE AS CHOICE: THE PARADIGMATIC AXIS

The most important feature of SFG is its organization around the concept of "choice." Within SFG all grammatical variation is captured by abstract choices between minimal grammatical alternatives. This *paradigmatic* orientation contrasts SFG with the *syntagmatic* orientation of most other syntactic accounts. The subordination of the syntagmatic to the paradigmatic guarantees that a grammar can function as a resource for expressing meaning.

All strata of the linguistic system are construed within SFL as paradigmatically organized resources—resources of meaning, wording, and "sounding." This organization captures the possible alternatives that are available given any choices that have already been made; ie, a collection of "paradigms" of the form "a linguistic unit of type *A* is either an *A* of functional subtype *X* or an *A* of functional subtype *Y*, . . . , or an *A* of functional subtype *Z*" is given. At each level these subtypes are disjoint and serve to successively classify linguistic units along ever more finely discriminated dimensions. This formulation of classifications in terms of increasingly fine discrimination is termed the principle of *delicacy* in SFL.

Paradigmatic organization is represented by means of *system networks*. A system network is a directed acyclic graph with labeled arcs whose nodes are choice points called *systems*—the "systems" from which systemic theory takes its name—and whose outward-directed labeled arcs denote the *terms* of the system. Each system has two or more terms, or output features, which at the stratum of grammar represent minimal grammatical alternations. In addition, the inward-directed arcs for each system denote an entry condition that determines the paradigmatic context in which the alternation represented by the system is relevant.

An example of a section of a systemic network for English grammar is shown in Figure 1. This subnetwork consists of eight systems, whose names are capitalized. The grammatical features that form the terms of each system are shown in lowercase. Thus, for example, the grammatical system PROCESS TYPE presents a choice of four possible grammatical features: "material," "mental," "verbal," and "relational." In SFG grammatical features provide an abstract specification not of linguistic structure directly but of the functions that a linguistic structure may realize. Thus, this choice represents the minimal functional alternation of type of process employed in a clause, without yet commiting to a particular structural realization. Similarly, the TAGGING system represents a minimal functional alternation between two distinct discourse functions that an utterance may fulfill (Halliday, 1985, p. 69), realized by the alternation between to tag or not to tag, and the INDICATIVE TYPE system presents the alternation "interrogative"/"declarative," which corresponds to two basic types of speech act that an utterance may fulfill.

Each functional alternation is only relevant in a particular functional, or paradigmatic, context. This is encoded by systems' entry conditions. For example, the PROCESS TYPE system represents a functional alternation that is a finer discrimination of the possible functions of clauses; accordingly the grammatical feature "clauses" is the entry condition for this system. This states that when (and only when) a linguistic unit bearing the grammatical feature "clauses" is being described/generated, is it also necessary to make the selection of feature between "material," "mental," etc. An entry condition can, in general, be an arbitrarily complex logical combination of grammatical features. For example, in the TAGGING system, the alternation between "tagged" and "untagged" is relevant

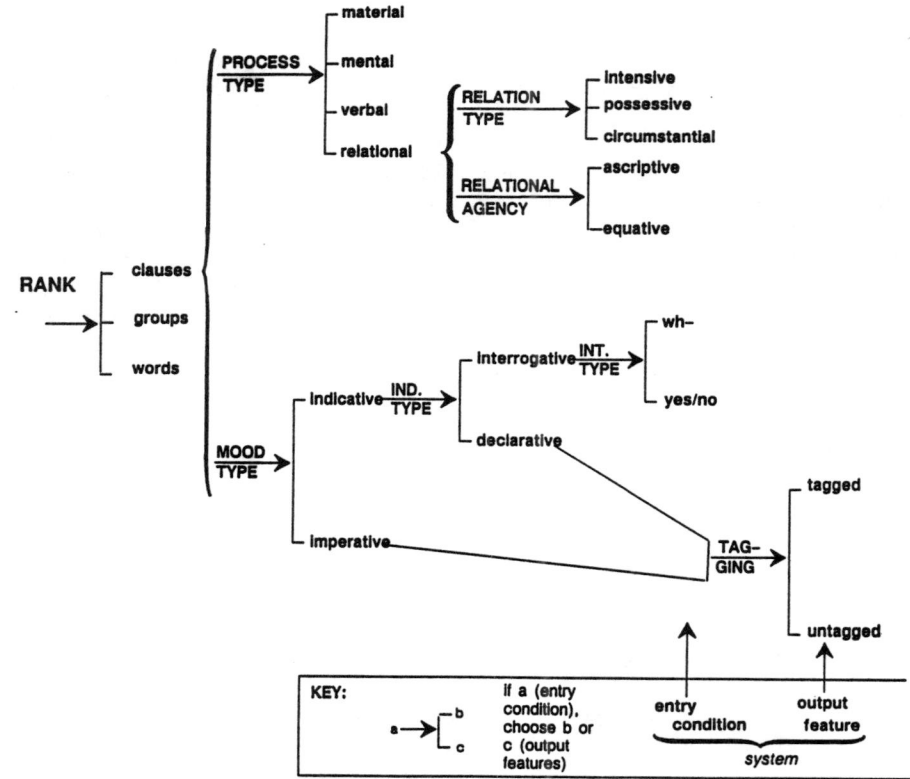

Figure 1. Example portion of an SFG for English.

when either "declarative" or "imperative" are selected but not, for example, when "interrogative" has been chosen. Possible clauses compatible with combinations of these grammatical features as licensed by the network are as follows:

Example Clause	Grammatical Features
(1a) You are going.	{declarative, untagged}
(1b) You are going, aren't you?	{declarative, tagged}
(1c) Go away!	{imperative, untagged}
(1d) Go away, will you?	{imperative, tagged}

Systems can also be *simultaneous*, ie, share common entry conditions. This occurs in the network with the PROCESS TYPE and MOOD TYPE systems: both have the entry condition "clauses" and so both are relevant in the same paradigmatic context. Thus, when we have a linguistic unit bearing the feature "clauses," selections must additionally be made both from MOOD TYPE and from PROCESS TYPE. A further example of simultaneity is that of RELATION TYPE and RELATIONAL AGENCY in the network—the distinctions offered by these systems both occur in the context of the grammatical feature "relational." This connectivity of the network defines a partial ordering of systems from least delicate (most general) to most delicate (most specific). It captures the fact that functional discrimination may proceed along several independent dimensions in parallel.

Generation/analysis proceeds in cycles of actualization: Throughout actualization the grammar is entered at the least level of delicacy and choices are made until the maximally delicate distinctions offered by the network have been drawn. Each such cycle through the grammar is responsible for the construction of a complete paradigmatic description of a linguistic unit of a given "size," or rank. The rank scale for English within SFG is typically given as clause, group/phrase, word, and morpheme. The set of grammatical features accumulated on a cycle through the grammar network is called the *selection expression*. This set contains selections from all of the minimal grammatical alternatives necessary to uniquely determine the function of the linguistic unit described by that cycle; ie, it represents a complete paradigmatic description of a linguistic unit of a given rank. Each linguistic unit has a selection expression that completely describes it and differentiates it from all others that the grammar may generate. The features selected on any cycle must, therefore, together offer an appropriate and complete description for a linguistic unit of a given rank.

Following any particular cycle through the grammar, unresolved possibilities for the fillers of particular structural constituents may remain; eg, we may know that a clause requires a subject but may not yet know what type of subject that might be. Such constituents then need to receive their own paradigmatic descriptions, which motivate further cycles through the grammar. The grammar is then reentered at the least level of delicacy, and choices appropriate for the description of the constituent are made in the same way as they are for the containing linguistic unit as a whole. Cycling through the grammar is repeated until paradigmatic descriptions of the linguistic unit at all structural levels (ranks) have been achieved that are sufficiently detailed as to fully specify a structural product, ie, until constituents have been characterized functionally at a fine enough scale to be realized as words/sounds rather than as constituents requiring further grammatical organization.

BREADTH OF CHOICE: METAFUNCTIONALITY

In addition to the dimension of delicacy in an SFG that provides organization in terms of the depth of a network, SFG also provides organization across the "breadth" of a network. That is, functionality in SFL is further differentiated across three highly generalized and parallel functions, or metafunctions, of language. Metafunctions are generalized functionalities in the sense that any instance of language use is assumed necessarily to be already fulfilling all of these generalized functions in some particular way simply by virtue of the fact that it is an example of language in use. As Halliday writes,

> Whatever we are using language for, we need to make some reference to the categories of our experience; we need to take on some role in the interpersonal situation; and we need to embody these in the form of text. (1974, p. 49)

In SFL these three general types of functionalities are distinguished and explicitly represented. They are termed the *ideational*, the *interpersonal*, and the *textual* metafunctions, respectively (Halliday, 1978, 1985), and may be glossed as follows:

- Ideational: The means we have of representing the world to ourselves; it largely corresponds to what has been termed *propositional content*; it is language "about something." Many accounts of syntax and semantics limit themselves exclusively to the range of variation controlled by this metafunction.
- Interpersonal: The range of meaning concerned with the expression of social relationships and speakers' attitudes and evaluations. This range of meaning represents the participatory function of language; language as doing something, where speakers intrude on the social situation in force and affect and/or create it.
- Textual: The resources responsible for making a use of language appropriate to its particular context of use; the organizational resources that make the difference between connected and cohesive text and unrelated sentences.

Generally an SFG will be organized in terms of the three metafunctions; that is, the metafunctions define distinct functional regions within a grammar. Such regions possess strong intraregion dependencies and weak interregion dependencies. This creates a modularity within grammar design that is beneficial for maintenance and development. Figure 2 gives an overview of the functional regions for English as described in Matthiessen (1990a).

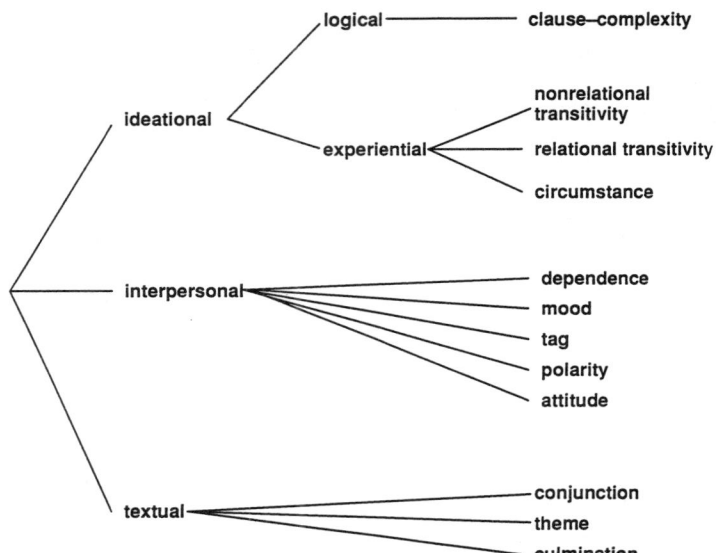

Figure 2. Functional regions of an SFG for English.

Within the system network metafunctional organization is represented simply by simultaneity; ie, systems of the network concerned with functions derived from the ideational metafunction will generally be simultaneous with systems concerned with the interpersonal and textual metafunctions. For example, the MOOD TYPE system and its more delicate dependent systems (eg, INDICATIVE TYPE and TAGGING) form part of the description of the interpersonal component of the grammar of English; they all refer to aspects of discourse interaction. The PROCESS TYPE system and its dependent systems are, however, part of the ideational component; they describe the classification of experience in terms of types of processes and of objects that may participate in those processes. Thus, MOOD TYPE and PROCESS TYPE are simultaneous systems, and the functional discriminations from both metafunctional directions are pursued in parallel.

The selection expression accumulated on a cycle through the grammar network therefore contains features drawn from all three metafunctional components. This demands a rather broad basis of information within the grammar itself: A complete selection expression will already classify a linguistic unit in terms of the functions it achieves with respect to its propositional content, textual organization, and interpersonal force. This represents the theoretical claim that selections from all three metafunctions are necessary for the complete specification of any linguistic entity. Much information that would in other accounts be found, if at all, in a post- or pregrammatical process of interpretation and/or generation are therefore in an SFG already represented as (functional) grammatical phenomena. The difference between sentences (2a) and (2b), for example, is then represented in SFG as a distinctive selection of a *textual* grammatical feature, ie, whether or not the time that is expressed also functions textually as a "theme" or not:

(2a) He went to London in June.   {unmarked-subject-theme}

(2b) In June he went to London.   {marked-theme, temporal-theme}

Representationally, such textual distinctions do not then differ from the ideational distinctions concerned with propositional content that are more traditionally found in grammar descriptions.

The simultaneity of portions of the grammar network according to metafunction also captures the fact that grammatical features motivated by distinct metafunctions can be varied largely independently of one another. Thus, sentence (2b), which itself has the features "declarative" along the interpersonal dimension defined by the INDICATIVE TYPE system and "material" along the ideational dimension defined by the PROCESS TYPE system, can be mutated along both these dimensions independently as shown in (2c)–(2e).

(2c) In June did he go to London?   {marked-theme, temporal-theme, interrogative}

(2d) In June he was in London.   {marked-theme, temporal-theme, relational}

(2e) In June was he in London?   {marked-theme, temporal-theme, interrogative, relational}

The grammar is therefore responsible for taking independent statements of meaning from the different metafunctions and combining these into coherent paradigmatic and syntagmatic linguistic units.

SYNTACTIC STRUCTURE AS A CONSEQUENCE OF CHOICE

The system network does not itself generate grammatical structures; the "bare" system network represents a purely paradigmatic grammar that determines the permissible combinations of grammatical features for each type of linguistic unit handled. In order to create the structural expression of these functional classifications, syntactic structure needs to be created. In SFG this is built up in terms of "syntagmatic specifications," which are derived by means of *realization statements* associated with paradigmatic selections. Syntagmatic realizations are thus always given in particular paradigmatic contexts.

Syntagmatic organization is represented in terms of ordered sequences of constituents composed of grammatical *functions*, such as Subject, Finite, Location, Goal, etc; in this respect, SFG accounts resemble the approach to structure proposed in Lexical-Functional Grammar (LFG) (Bresnan and Kaplan, 1982). The number and range of functions is, however, more finely developed within SFG since structure is specified completely in functional terms: that is, all constituents receive functionally distinctive labels. These functions help perform two main tasks: the correct specification of ordering at each level of structure and an appropriate restriction of possible lower level realizations of constituents. An example of the "functional" description of the clause "In this job, Anne, we're working with silver" [taken from the appendix of Halliday (1985)], which gives a representative example of the kind of information that is specified in an SFG syntagmatic unit, is shown in Figure 3. Here we can see two important features of the SFG representation of structure: first, structure is layered according to metafunction so that functions "codescribe" constituents from the differing perspectives the metafunctions offer and, second, the constituent boundaries do not necessarily match one-to-one across layers.

The first layer shown is the textual layer, consisting of the functions Theme and Rheme. The Theme section of the clause serves to textually situate the interpretation of the Rheme: in Halliday's terms, it marks the "point of departure" of the clause. The second layer is the interpersonal: constituents that realize the functions of the speaker's "intrusion into the speech event" are located here. One of the constituents described interpersonally, the Vocative that explicitly realizes the addressee of the utterance, is also described textually by its colabeling by Theme. The other constituent, labeled the Mood element and consisting of Subject and Finite, realizes the communicative function of the speaker as making a positive statement about something that is currently the case and names the protagonist of the statement as "we." Finally, the third layer represents the structural carriers of ideational functional discriminations, in particular the process (Process), participants (Actor), and circumstances (Locative and Manner) of the event being realized. Here, also, one of the constituents described ideationally, Location, is simultaneously serving a textual function as Theme. Another of the ideational functions, Actor, codescribes the constituent labeled Subject. In general, each column in such a syntagmatic description represents a set of grammatical functions that have been conflated to define a single clause constituent. This provides a means of recombining the distinct contributions to structure made by the different metafunctional components of the system network. In this case, then, the following ordered set of constituents occur:

[Theme/Locative]	In this job
[Theme/Vocative]	Anne
[Rheme/Mood-Subject/Actor]	we
[Rheme/Mood-Finite/Process]	-re
[Rheme/Process	working
[Rheme/Manner]	with silver

The function that each constituent is serving for the clause as a whole, again across all of the metafunctions, is thereby made clear.

Syntagmatic level products such as that of Figure 3 are built up by means of realization statements associated with the paradigmatic level systems of choice. More specifically, grammatical features, as well as being able to lead on to further systems of choice, can also call for various operations to be carried out at the syntagmatic level. Constituency is thus constructed in an SFG by means of the application of a restricted set of realization operators that succesively constrain the structural product that a cycle through the grammar network is defining. Each application of a realization statement is triggered by the selection of a specified grammatical feature from the system network. This defines a "reflex in form" for that par-

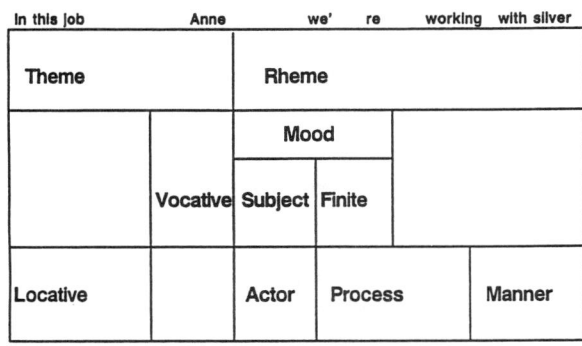

Figure 3. Example of SFG functional description of clause structure.

ticular functional alternation. For example, the reflex in form of the yes-no alternation in the INTERROGATIVE TYPE system is that the constituent of the clause that functions as the Finite element is ordered to the left of the constituent that functions as the Subject [as in (2c) where the Subject is *he* and the Finite is *did*). This rooting of structural constraints paradigmatically rather than syntagmatically is an essential feature of SFG and supports a semantically driven mode of grammar operation.

Three principal types of realization operators are generally employed in SFG. The first type consists of those operators that introduce and build structure; these are: "insert" (for specifying the presence of a functionally labelled constituent), "conflate" (for specifying that two functionally labeled constituents codescribe a single constituent), and "expand" (for constructing internal structure that does not warrant full-rank status). Constraints consistent with the structure shown in Figure 3 are therefore (insert Subject), (conflate Subject Actor), and (expand Mood Subject). The second type consists of those that constrain ordering; the most important of which is simply "order" (for specifying the relative ordering of functions). A constraint again consistent with the example structure is (order Subject Finite). The third type consists of those realization operators that have consequences for subsequent cycles of structure generation; the most important of which is "preselect" (for specifying grammatical features that the selection expression of a function's realization must contain). This constrains the realizations of subconstituents to be linguistic units of particular types; although not shown in the example, relevant constraints here include (preselect Actor nominal-group) and (preselect Manner prepositional-phrase).

Just as the grammatical features of the system network specify minimal points of grammatical contrast, realization statements specify "minimal" aspects of syntagmatic organization. Thus, in an SFG the differentiation of structural constraints now found in, for example, GPSG and HPSG's distinction between immediate dominance and linear precedence rules is already taken further. In particular:

- The presence of a function and its ordering are specified by different realization statements.
- The presence of a function and the nature of its realization are specified by different realization statements.
- The presence of a function and its identification with other functions are specified by different realization statements.

Furthermore, all such constraints are only applied given appropriate paradigmatic feature selections. When it is known that a Manner must be expressed, only then does it become appropriate to insert the necessary functionally labeled constituent; then, subsequently, only when it is known that that Manner has a particular semantic type, does it become necessary to preselect it as having the feature "prepositional-phrase," not before. Similarly, only when it is known that, for example, a Lo-

cation is going to be used as the primary textual contextualization device for the rest of the clause, does it become relevant to conflate Locative with Theme; and so on. In short, structural constraints are only applied in order to realize determinate choices of communicative function that need to be expressed grammatically. A theoretical description of the possibilities for realization statements within an SFG is provided by Matthiessen (1985).

SEMANTICS: METHODS OF CONTROL OF GRAMMAR

The systemic network provides a representational resource for the functional potential of a language—ie, for the types of functions that a language provides for a speaker—and the realization statements provide the means of successively constraining functionally annotated grammatical structures that realize that functional potential. In order to make use of this in a computational context, it is necessary to further motivate the actual choices of grammatical features that are made during traversal of the network. That is, it is not enough to specify that the language offers a minimal functional alternative between, for example, indicative and imperative clauses, which in turn bring specific constraints to bear on structure. It is also necessary to specify the precise conditions under which indicative must be chosen over imperative, or vice versa. This task is handled in current computational implementations of SFGs in two ways: by *chooser and inquiry* semantics (Mann, 1985) and by *register-driven* semantics (Patten, 1988).

Chooser and Inquiry Semantics

The chooser and inquiry framework for SFG arose out of the need to make a text generation system that was modular and reusable across different contexts and across different computational systems, knowledge representation languages, text-planning components, etc. It was necessary to be able to provide semantic control of the grammar component without insisting that a user or other computational system be aware of the grammatical distinctions maintained and organized within the grammar. The chooser and inquiry framework provides such a level of semantic control by associating a chooser with each grammatical system in the system network. A chooser is a semantic procedure that knows how to make a purposeful choice among the grammatical features of the system with which it is associated. It makes the choice by asking one or more questions, called *inquiries*, concerning parameters that typically refer to aspects of the meaning, concepts, etc, that need to be expressed. It is the responsibility of the inquiries to obtain the information relevant for the grammatical decision. As far as the grammar and choosers are concerned, therefore, the inquiries represent oracles that can be relied on to motivate grammatical alternations appropriately for the current communicative goals that need to be accomplished. This is a simpler task than directly requiring a selection of grammatical features, since the choosers and inquiries decompose a single selection among minimal grammatical distinctions into a number of selections among minimal semantic distinc-

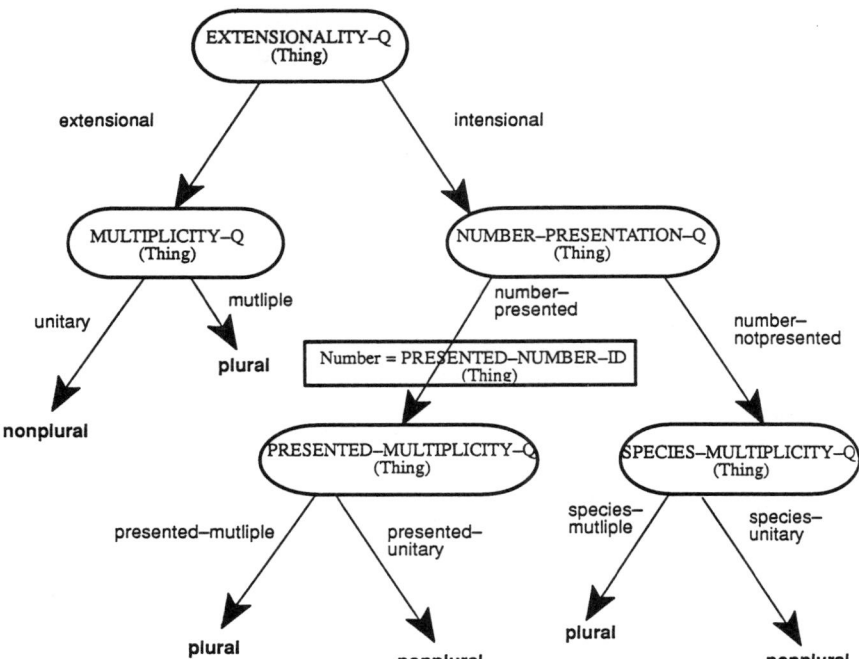

Figure 4. Example of the chooser for number in an SFG.

tions. While the grammatical alternations may not be directly relevant to a component external to the SFG, the semantic distinctions are: This level supplies a situation-independent semantic classification in terms of which a computational system can organize its information for expression in natural language.

An example of a chooser and its component inquiries for a particular grammatical system is shown in Figure 4. This shows the decomposition of a single grammatical opposition, in this case that between "plural" and "nonplural" in the system network for the nominal group, into a number of basic semantic discriminations: In order to motivate selection of either of the grammatical features, the constraints specified in the chooser need to be met. Thus, for the classification of a nominal group as grammatically plural, it needs also to be the case that the concept being realized by means of that nominal group satisfies the semantic conditions shown in Figure 5 (expressed in terms of inquiries and their responses). Inquiries such as those in Figure 5 are termed *branching inquiries*; they decide between a specified set of possible responses that

are then used to navigate through the options of the chooser. For example, the inquiry MULTIPLICITY-Q has two possible responses, MULTIPLE and NONMULTIPLE, and depending on which of these the inquiry offers in a particular context, different lines of reasoning are followed up in the chooser. The three possible paths through the chooser that lead to a selection of the grammatical feature "plural" correspond to the distinct kinds of plurality that can be observed in examples (3a) through (3c), respectively; each can be seen to license a different set of inferences:

(3a) Three *lions* chased me.   [existing individuals]

(3b) *Lions* are almost extinct.   [species consisting of individuals]

(3c) *Lions* have sharp teeth.   [generic statement about individuals]

The meaning of inquiries can be defined in two ways: Either an informal natural language description of the semantic discrimination can be given or an actual process

either			
	EXTENSIONALITY-Q	:	EXTENSIONAL
and	MULTIPLICITY-Q	:	MULTIPLE
or			
	EXTENSIONALITY-Q	:	INTENSIONAL
and	NUMBER-PRESENTATION-Q	:	NUMBERPRESENTED
and	PRESENTED-MULTIPLICITY-Q	:	PRESENTEDMULTIPLE
or			
	EXTENSIONALITY-Q	:	INTENSIONAL
and	NUMBER-PRESENTATION-Q	:	NUMBERNOTPRESENTED
and	SPECIES-MULTIPLICITY-Q	:	SPECIESMULTIPLE

Figure 5. Branching inquiries.

may be implemented that interrogates a knowledge base, text plan, etc, in order to establish the response appropriate for the particular communicative goal being achieved. The inquiry SPECIES-MULTIPLICITY-Q, for example, has the following informal English gloss:

> Is the intensional object (Thing)—species, genus, etc— denoted with respect to some relation or relations among its features, subspecies, or any other aggregation as a multiplicity of structural aspects?

This provides a specification of what needs to be implemented in order to function with respect to any particular computational system that needs to utilize the SFG component. The kinds of distinctions represented within inquiries thus induce organizations of knowledge that a computational system needs to support in order to generate language. Although many inquiries require implementation for a system to interface with an SFG, these implementations are often "natural" with respect to the knowledge of a system and are accordingly simple. For example, a large class of inquiries may be implemented simply as classifications of concepts with respect to inheritance hierarchies, an operation that most knowledge representations already support. The benefit of this style of interfacing is that it achieves very fine *semantic* control of the grammatical possibilities a grammar offers.

Access to knowledge base entities is provided by the parameters specified for the inquiries asked; in the example of Figure 4 the parameter in all of the inquiries is the same, ie, Thing. This parameter is a grammatical function in the sense defined in the previous section. Each grammatical function may be associated with a concept (represented in whatever knowledge representation language is adopted by the system interacting with the SFG) that may then be used by the inquiries as the point of access to information external to the grammar. The fact that choosers are defined entirely in terms of the grammar-internal grammatical functions ensures that they remain application independent and preserve the modularity of the grammar-semantics component. Associations between grammatical functions and external concepts are established by means of *identifying* inquiries that, in contrast to the branching inquiries illustrated before, return pointers to unique concepts. These pointers are then associated with the grammatical functions named in the chooser. An example of this in Figure 4 is the identification of the grammatical function Number by means of the inquiry PRESENTED-NUMBER-ID being put with respect to the grammatical function Thing. An appropriate implementation of this inquiry would examine the knowledge base entity identified by the value of Thing and return a pointer to the information concerning the "numberhood" of that concept.

In general, the inquiries associated with choosers of systems from the different metafunctions in the grammar need to look to different sources for their responses. Ideational inquiries typically examine the knowledge base or domain model of a computational system; interpersonal inquiries examine a user model; and textual inquiries examine the text plan and text history. Matthiessen (1987)

describes the relation between the metafunctions and different kinds of "support knowledge" that are required in some detail.

Register-Driven Semantics

In the chooser and inquiry approach, the impetus for semantic discriminations comes from the grammar; that is, when a grammatical distinction needs to be motivated, the corresponding chooser is activated and its inquiries asked. Another mode of control of the grammar is for the communicative context to directly select features of the grammar. This is typically of use in order to predispose a general grammar to produce sentences of particular styles as appropriate for particular contexts or types of language use. The supporting theoretical construct here from SFL is *register*. Register theory draws attention to the fact that not only do people talk differently in different situations but they also do so predictably. Furthermore, the theory claims that specific types of situations have definable properties, which in turn have determinate consequences on language; that is, given appropriate classifications of situation types, the consequences of these situations on language can be specified, and suitable language can be produced by the "preselection" of the grammatical features that are appropriate for those situations. Patten (1988) provides an implemented example of this approach to semantics within SFG. He defines a number of situation types directly and then specifies these further in terms of the grammatical features that they preselect. This, therefore, reverses the normal "delicacy-increasing" mode of interpreting a systemic network. First arbitrarily delicate features are selected by the situation, and then the consequences of this selection for the less delicate choices that are entailed needs to be computed. It is clear that in the future both directions and modes of control of an SFG will be necessary (Matthiessen, 1990b; Bateman and Paris, 1989).

IMPLEMENTATIONS AND DECLARATIVITY

Two large grammars of English in the SFG tradition have received computational implementations so far: the NIGEL grammar of the PENMAN text generation system (Mann, 1985) and the grammar of the COMMUNAL natural language system (Fawcett and Tucker, 1989). Both of these grammars contain on the order of 900 systems and would, for sentences such as (1) and (2), assign approximately 50 distinctive features for the clause alone. Previous uses of SFGs in computational contexts include the generation component of Davey's text generation system PROTEUS (qv) and the analysis component of Winograd's SHRDLU (qv).

More recently, concern with the nondeclarativity of these implementations has led to a new round of research into possible implementations. In particular, the bias in the directionality of the PENMAN system toward generation motivated Kasper (1988) to consider an implementation of SFG for analysis and parsing using an extension of the formal feature structure formalism adopted within FUG. Although theoretically revealing, the FUG implementation was not able to fully capture the necessary partial ordering of systems within the SFG. This is an essential means for restricting the distinctions that are considered during unification to just those that are licensed by the current paradigmatic or syntagmatic context. In addition, the implementation required the addition of a context-free phrase structure component in order for initial bundles of grammatical features to be gathered for unification to proceed. The FUG implementation was accordingly both slow and theoretically inadequate. New work using the multiple-inheritance hierarchies and classification techniques (Kasper, 1989) and typed-unification feature structures (Zajac, 1989) developed within knowledge representation promises declarativity, bidirectionality, a more complete capturing of the grammatical feature interdependencies represented within an SFG, and more appropriate modeling of SFG syntagmatic organization.

A number of other formalizations of SFG have been attempted, eg, Mellish (1988). However, these generally restrict themselves to capturing the basic logic of a system network when considered as a pure formalism and miss many of the important motivations for particular organizations of SFG that arise from its functional orientation.

SFG IN CONTEXTS OF APPLICATION: THE FUTURE

There are two directions of development that are particularly important at this time for SFG in the context of AI and computational linguistics. The first was described in the previous section; this development remains primarily concerned with the linguistic stratum of grammar and its interaction with semantics. The second direction of development is the extension of computational work to include more from SFL overall; that is, to continue the use of systemic-functional theory in areas other than grammar. As a general theory of language, systemic-functional theory involves considerably more than approaches to grammar, and current computational research is beginning to investigate these possibilities further.

Work here includes the construction of systemic-functional-influenced accounts of user modeling and control of style during text generation using the concept of register, the construction of sophisticated text-planning techniques, the treatment of interaction and conversation, the incorporation of speech and intonation synthesis, the development of conceptual ontologies for knowledge representation, the integration of language with other modalities of information presentation, the development of grammar and semantic components for languages other than English (most notably, German, Japanese and Chinese) enriched accounts of the role of lexical information, and the application of these and other components to machine translation (qv).

BIBLIOGRAPHY

J. A. Bateman and C. L. Paris, "Phrasing a Text in Terms the User Can Understand," in *Proceedings of the Eleventh International Joint Conference on Artificial Intelligence*, Detroit, Michigan, 1989.

J. Bresnan and R. Kaplan, "Lexical-Functional Grammar: A Formal System for Grammatical Representation," in J. Bresnan, ed., *The Mental Representation of Grammatical Relations*, MIT Press, Cambridge, MA, 1982, pp. 173–281.

R. P. Fawcett and G. Tucker, *Prototype Generators 1 and 2*, Communal Technical Report Number 10, Computational Linguistics Unit, University of Wales College of Cardiff, 1989.

M. A. K. Halliday, "The Place of 'Functional Sentence Perspective' in the System of Linguistic Description," in *Papers on Functional Sentence Perspective*, František Daneš, ed., Academia, Prague, 1974, pp. 43–53.

M. A. K. Halliday, *Language as Social Semiotic*, Edward Arnold, London, 1978.

M. A. K. Halliday, *Introduction to Functional Grammar*, Edward Arnold, London, 1985.

R. T. Kasper, "An Experimental Parser for Systemic Grammars," in *Proceedings of the 12th International Conference on Computational Linguistics, August 1988*, Budapest, Hungary, 1988; Association for Computational Linguistics. Also available as Information Sciences Institute Technical Report No. ISI/RS-88-212, Marina del Rey, CA.

R. T. Kasper, "Unification and Classification: An Experiment in Information-Based Parsing," in *Proceedings of the International Workshop on Parsing Technologies*, 1989, 28–31 August, 1989, Carnegie Mellon University, Pittsburgh, Pennsylvania, pp. 1–7.

Martin Kay, "Functional Grammar," in *Proceedings of the Fifth Meeting of the Berkeley Linguistics Society*, Berkeley Linguistics Society, 1979, pp. 142–158.

W. C. Mann, "An Introduction to the Nigel Text Generation Grammar," in *Systemic Perspectives on Discourse: Selected Theoretical Papers from the 9th. International Systemic Workshop*, James D. Benson and William S. Greaves, eds., Ablex Pub. Corp., Norwood, N.J., 1985, pp. 84–95.

C. M. I. M. Matthiessen and John A. Bateman, *Text Generation and Systemic-Functional Linguistics: Experiences from English and Japanese*, Frances Pinter, London, 1991.

C. M. I. M. Matthiessen, "The Systemic Framework in Text Generation: Nigel," in *Systemic Perspectives on Discourse*, James Benson and William Greaves, eds., Ablex, Norwood, NJ, 1985.

C. M. I. M. Matthiessen, "Notes on the Organization of the Environment of a Text Generation Grammar," in *Natural Language Generation: Recent Advances in Artificial Intelligence, Psychology, and Linguistics*, G. Kempen, ed., Kluwer Academic Publishers, Boston/Dordrecht, 1987. Paper presented at the Third International Workshop on Natural Language Generation, August 1986, Nijmegen, The Netherlands.

C. M. I. M. Matthiessen, "Lexicogrammatical Cartography: English Systems. On-going Expanding Draft," Department of Linguistics, University of Sydney, Australia, 1990a.

C. M. I. M. Matthiessen, "Semantic Interfaces in Text Generation," in *13th. International Conference on Computational Linguistics (COLING-90)*, Vol. 2, Helsinki, Finland, 1990b, pp. 322–329.

C. S. Mellish, "Implementing Systemic Classification by Unification," *J. Comput. Ling.* 14(1), 40–51 (1988).

T. Patten, *Systemic Text Generation as Problem Solving*, Cambridge University Press, Cambridge, England, 1988.

Carl Pollard and Ivan A. Sag, *Information-Based Syntax and Semantics*, Center for the Study of Language and Information, Stanford University, Palo Alto, Calif., 1987.

T. Winograd, *Language as a Cognitive Process, Vol. 1: Syntax*, Addison Wesley, New York, 1983, Chap. 6.

R. Zajac, "A Transfer Model Using a Typed Feature Structure Rewriting System with Inheritance," in *Proceedings of the 27th. Annual Meeting of the Association for Computational Linguistics*, University of British Columbia, Vancouver, British Columbia, Canada, 26–29 June 1989, pp. 1–6.

JOHN A. BATEMAN
USC/Information Sciences
Institute

GRAPH-BASED RESOLUTION. See RESOLUTION, GRAPH-BASED.

GRAPHOIDS

Graphoids are models of data dependencies, such as those conveyed by the sentence "X is irrelevant to Y once Z is known." Graphoids are used to characterize dependencies in probabilistic reasoning, relational databases, constraint processing, and Markov fields. The graphoidal properties of a given information model determine what type of graphs would provide a sound representation of its dependencies.

In classic probability theory, conditional independence over finite domains is defined as follows: given a probabilistic distribution over a finite set U of random variables defined over finite domains, let X, Y, and Z be disjoint subsets of U. Let a, b, and c be vectors of possible values of the sets of random variables X, Y, and Z, correspondingly. X is independent from Y given Z if the following functional equation holds true, whenever

$$P_r(Z = c) \neq 0.$$
$$(\forall_a)(\forall_b)(\forall_c)P_r(X = a, Y = b, Z = c)P_r(Z = c)$$
$$= P_r(X = a, Z = c)P_r(Y = b, Z = c)$$

The above definition is inadequate for disciplines devoted to the representation of human reasoning. It is based on complex numerical calculations, which may result in the wrong answer due to rounding or approximations; the database storing the numbers needed for the computation may require exponential space for holding the values $P_r(U = u)$, corresponding to all combinations of values the variables in U may assume. It does not fit the way humans estimate the relevancy or the irrelevancy of some events to other events. The theory of graphoids intends to replace numerical representation of irrelevance relations by graphical and logical representation, and intends to replace numerical derivations of independencies by symbolic and graph–theoretic techniques (Pearl, 1988; Geiger, 1990).

DEFINITIONS

Let U be a finite set of (random) variables such that every variable in U is defined over a finite domain. Let I be a ternary relation over U. If X, Y, and Z are disjoint subsets of $U, I(X,Z,Y)$ is the notation for the statement "the triplet (X,Z,Y) is in I." The relation I is a graphoid if and only if it satisfies the five independent axioms listed below (Dawid, 1979; Pearl and Paz, 1989).

1. *Symmetry.* $I(X,Z,Y) \rightarrow I(Y,Z,X)$.
2. *Decomposition.* $I(X,Z,Y \cup W) \rightarrow I(X,Z,Y)$
3. *Weak union.* $I(X,Z,Y \cup W) \rightarrow I(X,Z \cup Y,W)$
4. *Contraction.* $I(X,Z,Y) \& I(X,Z \cup Y,W) \rightarrow I(X,Z,Y \cup W)$
5. *Intersection.* $I(X,Z \cup Y,W) \& I(X,Z \cup W,Y) \rightarrow I(X,Z,Y \cup W)$

The relation I is a semigraphoid if it satisfies the first four axioms only.

PROPERTIES

Relations as above are studied under the following semantics: the triplet (X,Z,Y) is in the relation I induced by some actual model M (eg, M can be a probabilistic distribution or a relational database) if and only if the values of the variables in Y can add no information on the values of the variables in X, given that the values of the variables in Z are known. It has been shown that graphoids are sound for positive probabilistic distributions (ie, distributions such that every event has a positive probability in the model defined by them) where soundness means that any relation induced by a positive probabilistic distribution satisfies the five graphoid axioms (Pearl, 1988). It has been shown that semigraphoids are sound for general probabilistic distributions (Pearl, 1988). On the other hand, graphoids are not complete for probabilistic distributions, which means that a distribution P, a set of triplets Σ, and a single triplet t can be found such that the triplets Σ and t hold in P but t cannot be derived from Σ by the graphoid axioms (Studeny, 1989). The problem of whether graphoids are polynominally decidable is an open one: given a set of triplets Σ whose size is polynomial in the number of variables in U and given a single triplet t, can t be derived from Σ via the graphoid axioms in polynomial time?

REPRESENTATION OF GRAPHOIDS IN UNDIRECTED GRAPHS

Given a graph $G = (V,E)$, let X, Y, and Z be disjoint subsets of V. Define the ternary relation I_G over V as follows: $(X,Z,Y) \in I_G$ if and only if Z is a cutset between X and Y in G. This relation satisfies all the graphoid axioms and enables the representation of graphoids in graphs under the above semantics with vertices mapped into variables 1–1 and conditional independence represented by cutset separation (Pearl and Paz, 1989).

The graph in Figure 1 can represent a probabilistic distribution, over five variables x_1 to x_5, in which every node represents a variable that, given its neighbors, is independent of all remaining variables. Using the previous notation: $I(x_5, \{x_3,x_4\}, \{x_1,x_2\})$ also $I(x_3, \{x_1,x_4,x_5\}, x_2)$ etc, the relation I defined by the cutset separations satisfies all five graphoid axioms.

The representation of graphoids in graphs has many

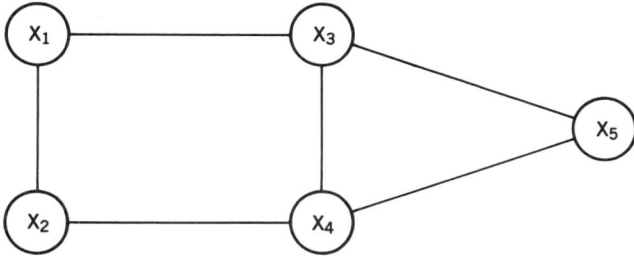

Figure 1. An undirected graph representing a graphoid defined by its cutsets, eg, $I(x_1, \{x_3,x_4\}, x_5)$, $I(x_1, \{x_2,x_3\}, x_4)$ etc.

advantages: there are exponentially many graphs over n vertices thus allowing a multitude of graphoids to be represented; the number of triplets that can be represented in one graph may be exponential, corresponding to the cutsets in the graphs, and graphs are easy to store and manipulate as a database. On the other hand, not every probabilistic distribution can be represented in a graph, because graph relations satisfy additional axioms not satisfied by distributions. Still every distribution can be approximated by a graph (Pearl and Paz, 1989).

REPRESENTATION OF GRAPHOIDS IN DIRECTED GRAPHS

Some graphoids that cannot be represented in undirected graphs can be represented in directed acyclic graphs, or dags, and vice versa. Given a dag D, let X, Y, and Z be the disjoint sets of its vertices. Define the following relation $I_D : (X, Z, Y)$ is in I_D if and only if there is no path between a node in X and a node in Y along which the following conditions hold: (1) every node with converging arrows is in Z or has a descendent in Z and (2) every other node is outside Z. It has been shown that every relation defined as above is a graphoid (Pearl and Verma, 1987; Pearl and co-workers, 1989).

Figure 2 represents the relation induced by a probabilistic distribution in which x_2 is independent from x_3 given x_1, but x_2 may be dependent on x_3 given $\{x_1, x_4\}$. Such relations often occur in causal reasoning, eg, a situation where two symptoms (x_2 and x_3) can be related to the same disease (x_1), but once the disease is apparent, the occurrence of one symptom does not alter the probability of the occurrence of the second symptom. However, once a com-

mon consequence (x_4) of the two symptoms is observed, what is learned about x_2 does not alter the probability of x_3. Representation in dags is more adequate for causal models (Lauritzen and co-workers, 1988).

BIBLIOGRAPHY

A. Dawid, "Conditional Independence in Statistical Theory," *J. Roy. Stat. Soc. Ser. B* **41**(1), 1–31 (1979).

D. Geiger, *Graphoids: A Qualitative Framework for Probabilistic Inference,* Ph.D. dissertation, University of California at Los Angeles, 1990.

S. L. Lauritzen, A. Dawid, B. Larsen and H. Leimer, "Independence Properties of Directed Markov Fields," *Networks* **20** (1990).

J. Pearl, *Probabilistic Reasoning in Intelligent Systems,* Morgan-Kaufmann, San Mateo, Calif., 1988.

J. Pearl, D. Geiger, and T. Verma, "The Logic of Influence Diagrams," in J. Q. Smith and R. M. Oliver, eds., *Influence Diagrams, Belief Nets and Decision Analysis,* John Wiley & Sons, Inc., New York, 1989, Chapt. 3.

J. Pearl and A. Paz, "Graphoids: A Graph-Based Logic for Reasoning about Relevance Relations," in B. Du Boulay and co-workers, eds., *Advances in Artificial Intelligence-II,* North-Holland, Amsterdam, 1989, pp. 357–363.

J. Pearl and T. Verma, "The Logic of Representing Dependencies by Directed Acyclic Graphs," in the *Proceedings of the Sixth National Conference on Artificial Intelligence,* Seattle, Wash., AAAI, Menlo Park, Calif., 1987.

M. Studeny, "Attempts at Axiomatic Description of Conditional Independence," *Kubernetika* **25**, 72–79 (1989).

AZARIA PAZ
Technion IIT

GUIDON

GUIDON is a programming tool for developing instructional programs. The subject material to be taught is expressed as productional rules in the style of MYCIN (qv), that is, in the form of an expert system that models the task to be taught. GUIDON contains approximately 250 teaching rules, organized into 40 procedures, by which it carries out a case-method dialogue with a student, evaluates partial solutions, offers assistance for solving problems, introduces new topics, and opportunistically examines the student's understanding of intermediate results. In effect, the student plays the role of consultant on a particular case; GUIDON compares the student's requests for information and conclusions to those of the embedded expert system and thus develops a differential student model. GUIDON was the first instructional program to be based on this expert systems approach. Because GUIDON is rule-based, it can explain its reasoning, which facilitates development of instructional rules. GUIDON's architecture allows it to discuss with a student any case in the associated expert system's case library, and to teach about any subject material expressed in MYCIN-like rules. GUIDON was demonstrated for use in two medical diagnosis domains as well as for structural engineering

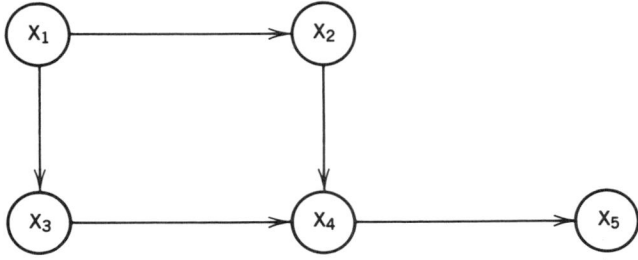

Figure 2. A directed acyclic graph representing a graphoid defined by causal relationships, ie, given its immediate predecessors, every node is independent of its other ancestors.

failure analysis. This flexibility and reuse of software demonstrates the advantages of the AI programming approach of separating knowledge (the subject matter expert system) from procedures for using it (the teaching rules). GUIDON was developed by Clancey at Stanford University in the late 1970s; it is fully described with a historical perspective in W. J. Clancey, *Knowledge-Based Tutoring*, MIT Press, Cambridge, Mass., 1987.

WILLIAM J. CLANCEY
Institute for Research on
Learning

HACKER

A program by Sussman that creates plans for solving problems in the "blocks world" (see G. J. Sussman, *A Computer Model of Skill Acquisition*, Elsevier, New York, 1975). HACKER's creation was guided by introspection of the human problem-solving process. HACKER is viewed as a programmar who first tries to find a solution to a given problem by looking into an "answer library." If no answer is available, the programmer tries to "write" a plan by adapting a known plan with a similar "activation pattern." A "criticizer" then looks for any bugs in the plan and tries to use "patches" to fix them. Skill acquisition is achieved by generalizing and reusing these patches. The implementation of HACKER is based on the CONNIVER (qv) language (see D. V. McDermott and G. J. Sussman, *The CONNIVER Reference Manual*, AI Memo 259, MIT AI Lab, Cambridge, Mass., May 1972).

J. GELLER
New Jersey Institute of
Technology

HADES

Hades is a software development tool that reimplements a large part of the MKRP (qv) system. It is designed as a general framework for implementing deduction systems. The underlying data structure is a clause graph with links representing theory resolution operations. The basic operation is a "link combination" that compiles the clauses successively into the theory and generates links with more information about the theory and the clauses.

The overall aim is to lessen the burden on the resolution part of the system and to have as many simplification and built-in theory transformations performed on a lower level, largely invisible to the user. Hence the resolution steps would correspond more closely to a human proof with details of term transformations and the like omitted.

J. H. SIEKMANN
Universität Kaiserslautern

HAM-ANS

The HAM-ANS project was done between 1981 and 1985 at Hamburg University by von Hahn, W. Wahlster (project leaders), W. Hoeppner, B. Nebel, K. Morik, T. Christaller, and H. Marburger. Complete implementation is in LISP and FUZZY on DEC-10 with parts on a LISP machine.

HAM-ANS is a German-speaking general access system which has been applied and tested in the following areas:

1. Hotel reservations (use of expert systems).
2. Traffic scene descriptions (use of image understanding).
3. Oceanographic information (use of relational databases).

The linguistic processing is accomplished through an explicit morphology—a syntax analysis by a left-right ATN with deep cases, resulting in a semantic representation rather than an explicit syntactic description. Linguistic features include ellipses recognition and generation; anaphorics; user modelling; dialogue memory with syntactic, semantic, and inferential records; and natural language generation. The semantic representation is formulated in a two-level hierarchy of the languages SURF (near the linguistic surface) and DEEP (near to logics and database access). The domain knowledge of the system is represented in a network formalism with three layers:

1. Conceptual network with numerical annotations for nonmonotonic reasoning.
2. Object description.
3. Visual data with spatial coordinates.

The average response time with non-optimized implementation is about one minute. (See W. Hoeppner, K. Morik, H. Marburger, "Talking it Over: The Natural Language Dialogue System HAM-ANS," in L. Bolc and M. Jarke, eds., *Cooperative Interfaces to Information Systems*, Springer Verlag, Berlin, 1986, pp. 189–258.)

WALTHER VON HAHN
University of Hamburg

HARPY

A speech-understanding (qv) system, HARPY was written by Lowerre in 1976 at Carnegie Mellon University under the ARPA Speech-Understanding Research project. Understanding a sentence is realized as a path of transition in a precompiled network of words, where each word is a template of all possible allophones (see B. Lowerre, *The HARPY Speech Recognition System*, Ph.D. dissertation, Carnegie Mellon University, Pittsburgh, Pa., 1976, and B. Lowerre and R. Reddy. "The HARPY Speech Understanding System," in W. Lea, ed., *Trends in Speech Recognition*, Prentice-Hall, Englewood Cliffs, N.J., 1980, pp. 340–360.

A. HANYONG YUHAN
AT&T Bell Laboratories

HEARSAY-II

A speech-understanding (qv) system, HEARSAY-II was written by Lesser and co-workers in 1976 at Carnegie Mellon University under the ARPA Speech-Understanding Research project. Asynchronous activation of different knowledge-source modules communicating through a blackboard allows island parsing (see V. Lesser, R. Fennell, L. Erman, and D. Reddy, "Organization of the HEARSAY-II Speech Understanding System," *IEEE Trans. Acoust. Speech Sig. Proc.* **23,** 11–24, 1975; L. Erman, F. Hayes-Roth, V. Lesser, and D. Reddy, "The HEAR-SAY-II Speech Understanding System: Integrating Knowledge to Resolve Uncertainty," *Comput. Surv.* **12**(2), 213–253, 1980).

A. Hanyong Yuhan
AT&T Bell Laboratories

HERMENEUTICS

Recent debates about the theoretical foundations of AI refer to hermeneutics, the branch of continental philosophy that treats the understanding and interpretation of texts. Applying certain hermeneutic insights, Dreyfus (1979), Winograd (1980), and Winograd and Flores (1986) have questioned the functionalist cognitive-science paradigm that guides most contemporary AI research, particularly in natural language processing (see NATURAL LANGUAGE GENERATION; NATURAL LANGUAGE UNDERSTANDING) and common-sense reasoning (see REASONING, COMMONSENSE). Dreyfus draws on the hermeneutic philosophy of Heidegger (1962) to deny the possibility of formalizing mental processes and, therefore, creating artificial intelligences. [Dreyfus (1986) indicated that he has recently moderated his views and now considers AI very difficult but not necessarily impossible.] Winograd and Flores reach a similar conclusion based on a hermeneutically informed technical argument. Yet, in addition to being a source of doubts, hermeneutics may illuminate problems such as the nature of meaning and understanding and thereby help reconstruct the functionalist paradigm (Winograd, 1980).

To help clarify the relevance of hermeneutics for AI research, this article first reviews the major strains of hermeneutic thought. These positions include the naive hermeneutics of early modern Europe and Dilthey's (1976a) more historically conscious, nineteenth-century methodological hermeneutics, which sought to produce systematic and scientific interpretations by situating a text in the context of its production. In the twentieth century, Heidegger's (1962) and Gadamer's (1975) philosophical hermeneutics shifted the focus from interpretation to existential understanding, which was treated more as a direct, nonmediated, authentic way of being in the world than as a way of knowing. Reacting to the relativism of this position, Apel (1980) and Habermas (1972) introduced critical hermeneutics, a methodologically self-reflective and comprehensive reconstruction of the social foundations of discourse and intersubjective understanding. Finally, Ricoeur (1979) in his phenomenological her-

meneutics, attempted to synthesize the various hermeneutic currents with structuralism and phenomenology.

This background situates AI researchers and critics who draw from the various hermeneutic traditions. In investigations of the affective structure of texts and in a concern with systematic rules for identifying the genres of narrative, a classic hermeneutical program tempered by phenomenological hermeneutics has been pursued (Alker and co-workers, 1985). Other researchers (Winograd, 1980; Bateman, 1983, 1981) draw from philosophical hermeneutics to propose strategies for developing computer systems that understand natural language. A third approach (Winograd and Flores, 1986), aligned with philosophical hermeneutics, argues that computer understanding of natural language is exceedingly difficult and probably intractable. A fourth group (Mallery and Duffy, 1986) has developed an implementation guided in part by ideas from phenomenological hermeneutics but informed by the other variants as well.

Hermeneutic theories differ in several characteristic ways from approaches to meaning and understanding that are better known to AI researchers. Hermeneutics grounds the meaning of texts in the intentions and histories of their authors and in their relevance for readers. In contrast, analytic philosophy usually identifies meaning with the external referents of texts, and structuralism finds meaning in the arrangement of their words. Hermeneutics regards texts as means for transmitting experience, beliefs, and judgments from one subject or community to another. Hence the determination of specific meanings is a matter for practical judgment and common-sense reasoning, not for *a priori* theory and scientific proof. This attitude reflects the origin of hermeneutics in ancient-world efforts to determine systematically the meaning, intent, and applicability of sacred and legal texts. Hermeneutic theories and applications also share the idea of the hermeneutic circle or the notion that understanding or definition of something employs attributes that already presuppose an understanding or a definition of that thing. Circles or spirals of understanding arise in interpreting one's own language, a foreign language or an observed action, in confirming a theory and in distinguishing between background knowledge and facts (Stegmuller, 1977). The existence of these circularities raises questions for hermeneutics regarding the grounding and validity of understanding.

The philosophical concept of the hermeneutic circle resembles the distinctly computational notion of bootstrapping, a process that uses a lower order component (a bootstrap component) to build a higher order component that is used in turn to reconstruct and replace the lower order component. Bootstrapping has been introduced in the design of certain knowledge bases (Lenat, 1982, 1983; Haase, 1986) and in AI-oriented theories of cognitive development (Piaget, 1952, 1970; Drescher, 1986; Minsky, 1986) and should be distinguished from hierarchical layering in systems that do not include the "strange loop" of replacing the bootstrap component. The similarity of the hermeneutic circle and bootstrapping suggests the possibility of an important contribution from hermeneutics to

AI architectures for natural language processing and for commonsense reasoning.

CLASSIC METHODOLOGICAL HERMENEUTICS

Origins

Hermeneutics as a general science of interpretation can be traced back to more domain-specific applications in the ancient Greeks' study of literature and in ancient biblical exegesis. The word *hermeneutics* was coined in the seventeenth century (Palmer, 1969) on the basis of the Greek *hermeneuein*, "to interpret," which signified equally a declamation of a text, an explanation of a situation, or a translation from a foreign tongue. (*Hermeneuein* itself derived from the name of Hermes, the winged messenger god of ancient Greece, who both delivered and explained the messages of the other gods.) Regarding texts as organic or coherent wholes rather than as collections of disjointed parts, the Greeks expected a text to be consistent in grammar, style, and ideas. Accordingly, they codified rules of grammar and style that they used to verify and emend textual passages. By extending the logic of part and whole to a writer's or school's entire output, the Greeks were also able to attribute works with uncertain origin. Although the Jewish rabbis and the early Church fathers deployed similar philological tools, their biblical exegeses were better known for the development of allegorical readings, frequently at the expense of the texts' literal meaning. Their interpretations found within the visible sign a hidden sense in agreement with the intention they beforehand ascribed to the text. Because instances of this method are found for the Vedas, Homer, the Koran, and other sacred writings, it seems a typical strategy for reconciling an enlightened or moral world view with texts whose "outward" earthiness or banality seems beneath the dignity of the gods being celebrated (Bleicher, 1980).

The Middle Ages witnessed the proliferation of nonliteral interpretations of the Bible. Christian commentators could read Old Testament stories simultaneously as precursors of analogous episodes in the New Testament, symbolic lessons about Church institutions, and allegories about spiritual traits (Smalley, 1952). In each case the meaning of the signs was constrained by imputing a particular intention to the Bible, such as teaching morality, but these interpretive bases were posited by the religious tradition rather than suggested by a preliminary reading of the text. Thus when Martin Luther argued that Christians could rediscover their faith by reading the Bible themselves, Catholic Church officials not surprisingly responded that the Bible was too obscure to read without their guidance. The Protestant exegesis, which appeared after Luther's translation of the Bible, tended to view the texts as responses to historical or social situations rather than expressions of theological principles. Assuming that the New Testament documented the Christian faith, one reader's guide proposed that contradictory statements and difficult passages in the New Testament could be clarified by comparing their possible meanings with contempora-

neous Christian practices. The example suggests that interpretation might rely on empathetic understanding, the interpreter's self-projection into the author's space. Indeed, it was just such empathy that Schleiermacher and Dilthey raised to a methodological principle in their attempt to create a general hermeneutics.

Methodological Hermeneutics of Schleiermacher and Dilthey

Schleiermacher (1959) proposed to join classic philology's focus on grammar and style and biblical exegesis' concern for themes, creating a general hermeneutics with principles independent of domain-specific interpretation principles. Schleiermacher compared the reader's approach to a text with the efforts by participants in a dialogue to understand each other, and he depicted the dialogue in terms of a speaker who puts together words to express his thoughts and a listener who understands this speech as part of a shared language and as part of the speaker's thinking (Thompson, 1981). The listener can comprehend the words and sentences because they are drawn from the language's lexicon and follow its grammatical rules, but the listener can also recognize the intentions behind the words by virtue of being in the same situation and sharing a common human nature with the speaker. Because Schleiermacher's concept of understanding includes empathy (projective introspection) as well as intuitive linguistic analysis, it is much richer than the idea in modern communication theories that understanding is merely the decoding of encoded information. Interpretation is built on understanding and has a grammatical, as well as a psychological moment. The grammatical thrust has a bootstrapping flavor: it places the text (or expression) within a particular literature (or language) and reciprocally uses the text to redefine the character of that literature. The psychological thrust is more naive and linear. In it the interpreter reconstructs and explicates the subject's motives and implicit assumptions. Thus Schleiermacher claimed that a successful interpreter could understand the author as well as, or even better than, the author understood himself because the interpretation highlights hidden motives and strategies.

Broadening Schleiermacher's hermeneutics, Dilthey (1976b) developed a philosophy of method for history and the human sciences that he believed could produce objective knowledge but avoid the reductionist, mechanistic, ahistorical explanatory schema of the natural sciences. Dilthey argued that texts, verbal utterances, work of art, and actions were meaningful expressions whose "mental contents" or intentions needed to be comprehended. He claimed that investigating human interactions was more like interpreting a poem or discourse than doing physics or chemistry experiments (Dilthey, 1976a). Dilthey termed the desired comprehension of events and expressions "understanding" (*verstehen*) and attempted to distinguish it from the explanatory knowledge (*erkennen*) generated by the hypotheticodeductive method of the natural sciences.

Dilthey initially followed Schleiermacher in identifying understanding as empathy guaranteed by the notion of a common human nature. Although he recognized that the outlook and values of people varied over different historical periods and cultures, Dilthey argued that because historians themselves thought and acted, they could relive and understand what people in the past were trying to express and accomplish in their writings, speeches, actions, and art. Nevertheless, many of his contemporaries criticized this position because it relied on introspection and an underspecified, noncritical psychology. Stung by this criticism and influenced by the neo-Kantian idea that works of art and literature embodied the formal values of their respective periods, Dilthey revised his position. He began to emphasize that texts and actions were as much products of their times as expressions of individuals, and their meanings were consequently constrained by both an orientation to values of their period and a place in the web of their authors' plans and experiences. In this revision meanings are delineated by the author's *Weltanschauung*, or worldview, reflecting a historical period and social context. Understanding (*verstehen*), the basis for methodological hermeneutics, involves tracing a circle from text to the author's biography and immediate historical circumstances and back again. Interpretation, or the systematic application of understanding to the text, reconstructs the world in which the text was produced and places the text in that world (Dilthey, 1976a; Ermarth, 1978; Plantinga, 1980).

The circular process precludes an interpretation of a text from being unique and scientifically objective, like the explanation of a chemical reaction, inasmuch as knowledge of the author's or agent's world may itself critically depend on the present interpretation (Stegmuller, 1977). Dilthey and his recent followers, Hirsch (1967) and Betti (1980), claim, however, that interpretations become more valid as they assimilate more knowledge about the author and the author's values, instead of reflecting the interpreter's own values or sense of reality. Dilthey's method in effect bootstraps from a whole (a biography, a set of works) whose themes may be repeatedly respecified through the elaboration of one of its parts (the action or work). The process eventually reaches stability because successive interpretations of the work or action serve to constrain subsequent refinements in the background model of the author. The strength and validity of such constraints depends on the currency and robustness of that model. Increases in temporal and cultural distance between the speaker and interpreter decrease the reliability of interpretation, but this neither forecloses the possibility of such a model nor denies the potential for a valid interpretation.

PHILOSOPHICAL HERMENEUTICS

Heidegger's Ontological Hermeneutics

In *Being and Time*, Heidegger (1962) undermines the notion of objectivity in Husserl's (1931) phenomenology and, by extension, in methodological hermeneutics. Concise overviews have been published (Schmitt, 1967; Zaner,

1970), and an extensive analysis of phenomenology (qv) is available (Ricoeur, 1967). Husserl argues that objective interpretation is possible using his transcendental phenomenological method, which requires bracketing the subjectivity inhering in the interpreter's lifeworld (*Lebenswelt*), the world of personal experience and desires. Heidegger denies that this bracketing is possible. He claims instead that the understanding of a situation is directly mediated by a foreknowledge, or sensitivity to situations, that is comprised by the understander's life world. Therefore, suspending that life-world would preclude the possibility of understanding altogether. Heidegger reaches his conclusion by contending that, as a necessary part of human "being-in-the-world" (*Dasein*), things are perceived according to how they are encountered and used in one's everyday routines and tasks. Perception and apprehension thus move from foreknowledge to an existential understanding, a largely unreflective and automatic grasp of a situation that triggers a response. This understanding must be incomplete because *Dasein* is both historical and finite. It is historical in that understanding builds from the foreknowledge accumulated from experience. It is finite due to "throwness," the necessity of acting in situations without the time or ability to grasp the full consequences of actions or plans in advance. Only when actions fail to meet the exigencies of the situation and breakdown occurs do individuals stand back and assume the theoretical attitude of science, which sees things objectively, as discrete objects separate from the self and resistant to one's will.

Heidegger brings hermeneutics from a theory of interpretation to a theory of existential understanding. He depsychologizes hermeneutics by dissociating it from the empathetic perception of other beings. Understanding now appears as a no-longer-conscious component of *Dasein*; it is embedded within the context of specific situations and plans, with, in effect, finite computational resources. Therefore, interpretation (*Auslegung*) that depends on such existential understanding (*Verstehen*) is not the general logical method found in classical philology but refers to a conscious recognition of one's own world. Dilthey's methodological hermeneutic circle is consequently supplanted by the more fundamental ontological hermeneutic circle, which leads from existential understanding situated in a world to a self-conscious interpretive stance. This self-consciousness, however, cannot escape its limitations to achieve a transcendental understanding in the sense of Hegel (1971, 1975), who considered rationality the ability to reflectively accept or reject (transcend) the received sociocultural tradition (Singer, 1983). According to this reading of Heidegger, foreknowledge is accumulated over time and constrains successive exercises of existential understanding. But self-conscious understanding cannot choose which elements in the experience-based foreknowledge are respecified in the bootstrapping process. Green (1967) presents a concise overview of Heidegger's contributions to philosophy. Steiner (1980) and Palmer (1969) provide accessible introductions to Heidegger's thought. Murray (1978) edited an informative collection of essays discussing Heidegger's thought.

Gadamer's Philosophical Hermeneutics

In his philosophical foundation hermeneutics, Gadamer (1975) follows his teacher Heidegger in recognizing that the ties to one's present horizons, one's knowledge and experience, are the productive grounds of understanding. However, Gadamer argues that these limits can be transcended through exposure to others' discourse and linguistically encoded cultural traditions because their horizons convey views and values that place one's own horizons in relief. [This position remedies what Green (1967) contends is Heidegger's failure to show how the historicity of the individual relates to the history of a broader community.] He stresses the role of language in opening the subject to these other subjectivities and their horizons. In forcefully stressing the role of language in opening the subject to other subjectivities in constituting traditions, Gadamer places language at the core of understanding. Gadamer's (1976b) position approximates the hypothesis advanced by the American linguists Sapir (1947) and Whorf (1967), which holds, in its strong version, that the individual's language partially determines his or her conceptual system and world-view. According to the Sapir-Whorf hypothesis, complete translations between languages is impossible, and understanding another language requires complete immersion accompanied by a change in thinking. Consequently, understanding for Gadamer does not scientifically reconstruct a speaker's intention but instead mediates between the interpreter's immediate horizon and his emerging one.

For Gadamer, understanding is bound and embedded in history because understanding deploys the knower's effective history, or personal experience and cultural traditions, to assimilate new experiences. Thus the initial structure of an effective history constrains the range of possible interpretations, excluding some possibilities and calling forth others. As effective history constitutes the prejudices brought to bear in understanding, it simultaneously and dialectically limits any self-conscious attempts to dissolve those prejudices. Gadamer thus explicitly opposes the scientific ideal of prejudiceless objectivity in interpretation. In this respect, he moves beyond Heidegger, who regarded so-called scientific objectivity as a derivative of existential understanding. Gadamer does not deny the importance of either scientific understanding or critical interpretation, a form of interpretation that introspectively questions assumptions unreflectively inherited from cultural traditions. His focus on the human context of knowledge emphasizes the need for repeated attempts at critical understanding, through which people can gain the insight needed to correct their prejudices. But if prejudices may be individually overcome, their fact is inescapable. It imposes a priori limitations on the extent to which a self-reflective methodology can eliminate distortions from scientific inquiry. The critical self-consciousness of a rational agent who introspectively questions received traditions may counter distorting consequences of effective history, but it at best only leads to successive approximations of objectivity. Gadamer's position prompts the philologists Betti (1980) and Hirsch (1967) to complain that its relativism destroys all bases for validating an interpretation and so defeats the purpose of interpretation. Social theorist Habermas (1977) also criticizes Gadamer's relativism.

The resulting theory of meaning differs from the methodological hermeneutics of Schleiermacher and Dilthey, which identifies the meaning of a text with its author's intentions and seeks to decipher the text by uncovering the world view behind it. For Gadamer, understanding recreates the initial intention embodied in the text by elucidating the subject matter that the text addresses (its aboutness). The process moves the text beyond its original psychological and historical contexts and gives it a certain ideality of meaning, which is elaborated in a dialogue between the interpreter and the text. The dialogue is grounded in the concern the interpreter and the author share toward a common question and a common subject matter. In confronting a viewpoint reflecting a different set of horizons, the interpreter can find his or her own horizons' highlighted and reach critical self-consciousness. In seeking the key question, the interpreter repeatedly transcends self horizons while pulling the text beyond its original horizons until a fusion of the two horizons occurs. The interpreter's imagination can also play a role in the dialogue with texts and carry the understanding of the subject matter beyond the finite interpretation realized in methodological hermeneutics. Nevertheless, the interpretations are constrained by the questions posed, because each question calls forth frameworks within which the subject matter must be understood. The meaning of a text then is not fixed but changes over time according to how it is received and read. Thus, for Gadamer, to understand is to understand differently than the author or even one's own earlier interpretations precisely because the process involves creating new horizons by bootstrapping from the old horizons they replace. But the notion of bootstrapping in Gadamer moves beyond the one in Heidegger because Gadamer allows prejudices to come into a conscious focus that may direct their individual supersession.

Gadamer does not merely work through Heidegger's philosophical program. He also redirects philosophical hermeneutics along partly Hegelian lines by appropriating substantial parts of the Hegelian transcendental philosophy that Heidegger eschewed (Gadamer, 1976a). Gadamer's concepts of the openness of language and the ability of people to transcend their interpretive horizons are based on Hegel's dialectic of the limit, in which the recognition of limits constitutes the first step in transcending them. The concept of understanding as a concrete fusing of horizons is derived ultimately from Hegel's idea that every new achievement of knowledge is a mediation, or a refocusing of the past within a new, present situation (Linge, 1976), which attempts to explain mind and logic on the basis of the dialectical resolution of more basic and antithetical concepts (Hegel, 1971). As each opposition is resolved, the resulting synthesis is found to be opposed to yet another concept, and that opposition must also be dialectically resolved. This purely subjective and continual unfolding interacts with and is conditioned by experience, particularly the experience of language, which tends to mold the developing subject in conformity with the traditions encoded in linguistic utterances and in the language itself. However, Gadamer clearly resists Hegel's notion of the self-objectifying, transcendental subject. Instead, he views the logical and ontological categories with which Hegel marks the unfolding of thought as distillations of the logic inherent in language, particularly the German language, whose use as a tool for speculative philosophy Hegel brought to perfection (Gadamer, 1976a). This view affirms the relativist position that thought and reason are always determined by the historical traditions of a linguistic community (Gadamer, 1976a).

CRITICAL HERMENEUTICS

Strategic Orientation

Heidegger's and Gadamer's critique of objectivity was particularly challenging for social theorists because empirical social science and normative social theory depend ultimately on the characterization of events and situations. At a minimum, the practical need to assess truth-claims, and interpretations had to be reconciled with the critique of objectivity. Apel (1980) and Habermas (1972, 1966) sought the means for the reconciliation in conjoining methodological hermeneutics with ordinary language philosophy. Their point of departure was the critique of ideology originated by Marx, which argues that beliefs and ideas reflect the holders' social class interests. (Although implying that an objective social reality might ultimately be described, this view also helps explain conflict in beliefs among members of the same society.) Armed with it, Apel and Habermas could conceive of a hermeneutically inspired analysis of communication in linguistic communities. Thus just as Heidegger's ontological hermeneutic concentrates on the individual's apperception of experience from the inside out, critical hermeneutics concentrates on individuals situated in groups from the outside in.

Apel and Habermas argue that of the three divisions of the study of language (syntax, semantics, and pragmatics) only the first two have been adequately studied by the school of ordinary language philosophy descending from Wittgenstein (1968). They believe that no account of human understanding can be believed if explained as a theory about a single, asocial and ahistorical being. On the contrary, understanding may only be explained by reference to the social and historical setting in which understanding occurs and in the discursive or dialogical situation in which communication takes place. Truth and meaning do not await discovery but are negotiated by actors who come to consensus on issues of truth and meaning through social discourse. This perspective may be contrasted with the first principles of research programs, such as Chomsky's (1957, 1965, 1981), which seek to explicate language use and language learning on the basis of an examination of a monological model of the competence of an ideal speaker–hearer abstracted from his social situation (Apel, 1980). Although studies of syntax and semantics are surely necessary for an adequate grasp of the human linguistic faculty, they are by no means sufficient. Any adequate understanding of language, Habermas (1979, 1976) asserts, must be grounded in the practical purposes for which speakers use language.

Universal Pragmatics

To provide such grounding, Habermas (1979) proposed a universal pragmatics (Thompson, 1982), the primary task of which is the identification and reconstruction of the necessary preconditions for the possibility of understanding in discursive communication. Turning to ordinary language philosophy, he attempts this reconstruction by linking Austin's (1962) and Grice's (1975) notions of felicity conditions underlying discourse to Searle's (1970) theory of speech acts and to a consensus theory of truth, which holds that truth claims are resolved through reasoned discussion culminating in consensus. Habermas does not confine universal pragmatics to the analyses of language and speech. Rather, because he sees language as the medium in which all human action is explicated and justified, he intends universal pragmatics as the groundwork for a general theory of social action.

The resulting critical hermeneutics holds that intersubjective communication is possible despite differences in the participants' preunderstandings, because the participants in effect posit as an ideal the attainment of a consensus (concerning the validity of statements). The desired consensus is free from constraints imposed on them by others and from constraints that they might impose on themselves. That is, a participant posits a situation in which all participants can freely try to convince others (or be convinced by them) and in which all have equal opportunity to take dialogue roles. Participation in dialogue thus admits the possibility of reinterpreting and changing the perceived situation. Habermas and Apel term this idealization the ideal speech situation and consider it the participants' emancipatory interest, the situation of freedom to which they aspire. This ideal might never be attained, but even to approach it, the participants must overcome systematically distorted communication, which suppresses and conceals the speakers' interests. According to Habermas, these distortions are produced by the division of labor and disguise its correlated structure of domination. Habermas turns to a Freudian psychotherapeutic model to prescribe treatment for the pathological consequences of the systematically distorted horizons produced under these conditions. According to him, the task of the social theorist is to act as therapist, encouraging citizens (patients) to reject internalizations of distorted institutional arrangements (class domination). For Habermas, then, understanding involves compensating for these distortions, and interpretation requires an account of how they were generated.

The Habermas-Gadamer Debate

Gadamer (1976c) attacks Habermas's position by pointing out that the psychotherapist or social theorist is not immune from the preunderstandings of tradition and that these preunderstandings are not themselves necessarily free of distortion. Gadamer sees Habermas's effort as part of the traditional social-scientific goal of attaining "objective" knowledge of the social realm. Habermas (1977) appears to believe that the social theorist, like Schleiermacher's interpreter, can understand the social actor better than the social actor understands himself. That is beyond belief for Gadamer, given his notion of ontological preunderstanding. For his part, Habermas sees Gadamer as too ready to submit to the authority of tradition and too reticent to offer any methodological considerations (apart from the exceedingly abstract notion of "interpretive horizons"), thereby giving unwitting support to positivist degradations of hermeneutics.

In reply to Gadamer's claim that prejudices are inescapable, Habermas insists that a self-reflective methodology can overcome prejudices and that an objective social theory can be approached by bootstrapping from an initial understanding of society. Habermas argues that the systematic distortions in communication that bias an initial understanding of society can be analyzed and reduced using generalization from empirical knowledge of society, quasi-causal explanation (deductive verification), and historical critique. To build this comprehensive social theory, Habermas must provide a theory of knowledge grounded in

1. A general theory of communicative action.
2. A general theory of socialization to explain the acquisition of the competence that underpins communicative action.
3. A theory of social systems to show the material constraints on socialization and their reflection in cultural traditions.
4. A theory of social evolution that allows theoretical reconstruction of the historical situations in which communicative action obtains.

But this move apparently fails to counter Gadamer's objection, since the theoretical tools used to forge this theory may themselves be subject to interpretations other than Habermas's vary across the cultural traditions to social interpreters. McCarthy (1982, 1978) reviews the debates, discusses various problems in Habermas's position, and provides a systematic rendition of Habermas's arguments. Ricoeur's proposed resolution of this debate is discussed below.

Theory of Communicative Action

Gadamer's objections notwithstanding, Habermas has embarked on a multivolume statement of a comprehensive social theory centered on communicative action. In the first volume Habermas (1981) concentrates on the connection between the theory of universal pragmatics and the general theory of action descending from Weber (1949) through Parsons (1937) to Schutz (1967) and Garfinkel (1976). His strategy is to align the various types of communication, their inherent truth claims, and their counterparts in rational action. Cognitive communication, in which the correspondence of terms to objects and events is at issue, has its rational action counterparts in instrumental and strategic action. These types of action are oriented toward success and are validated by instrumental reason, which reflects on the efficacy of plans as means to desired ends. Habermas ties interactive communication, in which claims to moral rightness and appropriateness are thematized, to normatively regulated action, in which the norms of a community and the social roles of actors become important constraints on the perceived appropriateness of actions. Finally, Habermas links expressive communication, in which the truthfulness of communicative actions are thematized, to dramaturgical action, which focuses on the fact that actors respectively constitute a public for each other. Dramaturgical action attends to phenomena involving each actor's presentation of the self to others (Goffman, 1959) to those aspects of the actor's subjectivity he chooses to reveal to others and to those he chooses to conceal. These revelations and concealments are, in turn, important factors that rational actors must assess when interpreting the actions of others and when planning their own.

PHENOMENOLOGICAL HERMENEUTICS

Faced with the diversity of hermeneutics, and other continental philosophies including structuralism and phenomenology, Ricoeur (1973c) strives for a grand synthesis in his phenomenological hermeneutics. Ricoeur (1981b) argues that phenomenology and hermeneutics presuppose each other. The connection between hermeneutics and phenomenology traces to Heidegger who took the term hermeneutics from Dilthey to distinguish his own philosophical investigation of everyday being from Husserl's transcendental phenomenology, which tried to achieve objective knowledge by suspending concern for the subject's life world. To capture knowledge of that world, Heidegger retained Hursserl's notion of eidetic phenomenology, which assumes immediate registration of phenomena in a picturelike but uninterpreted manner. Like Heidegger, Ricoeur also follows Husserl to eidetic phenomenology, but like the later Heidegger and, particularly, Gadamer, Ricoeur recognizes the ontological basis of understanding in language. For Ricoeur, then, the subject's being is not identical with immediate experiences. So, instead of attempting a direct description of *Dasein* like Heidegger (1962) and Merleau-Ponty (1962; Olafson, 1967), Ricoeur sees the need for a hermeneutic theory of interpretation to uncover the underlying meaning constituting *Dasein*. Through its emphasis on the prelinguistic, eidetic phenomenology supplies a means of distancing observation from linguistic descriptions and their implicit preconceptions. This distanciation (Ricoeur, 1973b) is precisely what is required for interpretation to proceed. Because the task of uncovering the underlying objectivity cannot be achieved through the suspension of subjectivity, Ricoeur concludes that Husserl's project of transcendental phenomenology can only be realized through the application of a methodological hermeneutics to an eidetic phenomenology.

Ricoeur also argues that structuralism and hermeneutics can be complementary approaches to analyses of language, meaning, and cultural symbolism, for reasons similar to those he advanced for the complementarity of eidetic phenomenology and hermeneutics. Structuralism refers to a mode of inquiry that inventories elements of a system and notes the grammar of possible combinations. It is exemplified by Saussurean linguistics and Levi-Strauss's anthropology (1968). Ricoeur finds that the value of structuralist analysis lies in its ability to catalog phenomena and describe their possible (grammatical) combinations, but its weakness lies in its inability to provide anything more insightful than behavioral descriptions of closed systems. Nevertheless, the ability to generate structural descriptions complements the hermeneutic method, which interprets these descriptions by assigning functional roles to the phenomena.

In his treatment of psychoanalysis, particularly the interpretation of dreams, Ricoeur (1970) shows the complexity involved in the hermeneutic task of assigning functional roles to words and symbols. The analyst must develop an interpretive system to analyze the dream text and uncover the hidden meanings and desires behind its symbols, particularly those that have multiple senses (polysemy). Allowing for the possibility of multiple levels of coherent meaning, hermeneutics aims at ascertaining the deep meaning that may underlie the manifest or surface meaning. Ricoeur distinguishes two approaches for getting at the deeper meaning: a demythologizing one that recovers hidden meanings from symbols without destroying them (in the manner of the theologian Bultmann) and a demystifying one that destroys the symbols by showing that they present a false reality (in the manner of Marx, Nietzsche, and Freud). The demythologizers treat the symbols as a window into a sacred reality they are trying to reach. But the demystifiers treat the same symbols as a false reality whose illusion must be exposed and dispelled so that a transformation of viewpoint may take place, as, for example, in Freud's discovery of infantile illusions in adult thinking. Thus, there are two opposing tendencies, a revolutionary and a conservative hermeneutics. Whereas the critical hermeneutics of Apel and Habermas falls within revolutionary demystification, the phenomenological hermeneutics of Ricoeur and the philosophical hermeneutics of Gadamer fall in the more conservative camp of the demythologizers.

Ricoeur (1981a) attempts a dialectical resolution of the Habermas-Gadamer debate by arguing that the hermeneutics of tradition and the critique of ideology require each other. He denies the alleged antinomy between the ontology of tradition, which limits possible meanings (Gadamer), and the eschatology of freedom, which seeks to transcend that constraints (Habermas). If, as Gadamer believes, understanding should be conceived as the mediation between the interpreter's immediate horizons and his emerging horizon, the interpreter must distance himself to some degree if he hopes to understand the text. That is, when confronted with a text, the interpreter must adopt a stance of critical self-understanding not unlike the stance adopted in the critique of ideology. Hermeneutics thus incorporates a critique of ideology. Likewise, the critique of ideology incorporates tradition. The ideal of undistorted communication and the desire for emancipation do not begin with Habermas. They arise from a tradition, from

the tradition of the Greek conception of *the good life*, from the Exodus, and from the Resurrection. Thus the interests voiced by Gadamer and Habermas are, in Ricoeur's view, not incompatible. One is an interest in the reinterpretation of traditions from the past and the other is the utopian projection of a liberated humanity. Only when they are radically and artificially separated, argues Ricoeur, does each assume the character and tenor of ideology.

The Hermeneutic Arc: Ricoeur's Theory of Interpretation

Ricoeur's (1971) theory of interpretation seeks a dialectical integration for Dilthey's dichotomy of explanation (*erklären*) and existential understanding (*verstehen*). Ricoeur begins by distinguishing the fundamentally different interpretive paradigms for discourse (written text) and dialogue (hearing and speaking). Discourse differs from dialogue in being detached from the original circumstances that produced it, the intentions of the author are distant, the addressee is general rather than specific and ostensive references are absent. In a surprising move, Ricoeur extends his theory of interpretation to action, arguing that action evinces the same characteristics that set discourse apart from dialogue. A key idea in Ricoeur's view is that once objective meaning is released from the subjective intentions of the author, multiple acceptable interpretations become possible. Thus, meaning is construed not just according to the author or agent's world view but also according to its significance in the reader's world view.

Ricoeur's hermeneutic arc combines two distinct hermeneutics: one that moves from existential understanding to explanation and another that moves from explanation to existential understanding. In the first hermeneutic subjective guessing is objectively validated. Here, understanding corresponds to a process of hypothesis formation based on analogy, metaphor, and other mechanisms for "divination." Hypothesis formation must not only propose senses for terms and readings for text but also assign importance to parts and invoke hierarchical classificatory procedures. The wide range of hypothesis formation means that possible interpretations may be reached through many paths. Following Hirsch (1967), explanation becomes a process of validating informed guesses. Validation proceeds through rational argument and debate based on a model of judicial procedures in legal reasoning. It is, therefore, distinguished from verification, which relies on logical proof. As Hirsch notes, this model may lead into a dilemma of self-confirmability when non-validatable hypotheses are proposed. Ricoeur escapes this dilemma by incorporating Popper's (1959) notion of falsifiability into his methods for validation, which he applies to the internal coherence of an interpretation and the relative plausibility of competing interpretations.

In the second hermeneutic that moves from explanation to understanding. Ricoeur distinguishes two stances regarding the referential function of text: a subjective approach and a structuralist alternative. The subjective approach incrementally constructs the world that lies behind the text but must rely on the world view of the interpreter for its preunderstanding. Although the constructed world view may gradually approximate the author's as more text is interpreted, the interpreter's subjectivity cannot be fully overcome. In contrast, Ricoeur sees the structuralist approach as suspending reference to the world behind the text and focusing on a behavioral inventory of the interconnections of parts within the text. As noted earlier, the structural interpretation brings out both a surface and a depth interpretation. The depth semantics is not what the author intended to say but what the text is about, the nonostensive reference of the text. Understanding requires an affinity between the reader and the aboutness of the text, that is, the kind of world opened up the depth semantics of the text. Instead of imposing a fixed interpretation, the depth semantics channels thought in a certain direction. By suspending meaning and focusing on the formal algebra of the genres reflected in the text at various levels, the structural method gives rise to objectivity and captures the subjectivity of both the author and the reader.

Like the other traditions, Ricoeur's hermeneutic arc can be interpreted as a bootstrapping process. Because it grounds the bootstrapping in an eidetic phenomenology, incorporates an internal referential model of the text, and begins interpretation with a structural analysis, Ricoeur's theory of interpretation may be easier to envision in computational terms. But the central bootstrapping engine in his theory is the alternation between forming hypotheses about meanings and validating those hypotheses through argument. This view resonates strongly with computational ideas about commonsense reasoning (qv). Indeed, these ideas lead Ricoeur (1973a, 1977, 1974–1975) to identify metaphor as the main source of semantic innovation, linguistic evolution, and therefore as major question for hermeneutics. An excellent overview and comparison of the treatments of language and cognition found in phenomenological hermeneutics and in other nonhermeneutical traditions of philosophy is provided by Dallmayr (1984).

HERMENEUTICS AS METASCIENCE

The hermeneutic tradition provides a basis for prescribing and criticizing the conduct of inquiry and the development of knowledge in the natural, social, and cognitive sciences (qv). Its representatives have figured prominently in debates concerning how valid knowledge can be acquired and whether there is a need for a separate methodology in the social sciences. Because AI is a new discipline, occupying a middle ground between the natural and social sciences, its researchers can benefit from knowledge of these debates. The choice of the appropriate methodology for inquiry in AI research remains unsettled for such areas as natural language processing, human problem solving, belief systems, and action. On one hand, the substantial contributions to AI from logic, mathematics, engineering, and the natural sciences, like physics, seem to make their strategies for inquiry uncontested. On the other hand, when the subject matter is clearly linked to the human sciences (particularly linguistics, anthropology, and psychology) methods devised for those areas might be more appropriate.

Hermeneutics and the Social Sciences

Dilthey distinguished the cultural and social sciences (*Geistewissenschaften*) from the natural sciences on the basis of their objects and the appropriate means for knowing them. The natural sciences concerned phenomena that, opaque to thought, could only be studied from the outside through observation of uniformities in their behavior and through the construction of causal laws to explain those uniformities. In contrast, the human sciences had objects such as texts, verbal expressions and actions that could be investigated from the inside through an understanding of their authors' experiences and intentions. An interpretive or hermeneutic methodology could more reliably and intelligibly account for these objects by reconstructing the internal cognitive processes that motivated and gave meaning to each of them. The use of hypothetico-deductive methods employed in the natural sciences could only capture the external correlations among these objects at some high level of abstraction. Dilthey's arguments were embraced in the early twentieth century by many social scientists, including the sociologist Weber (1949), whose paradigmatic studies of social institutions interpreted human behavior as intentional action, structured by the agents' goals and beliefs. However, the physics model of the social sciences also persists and is currently manifested in such techniques as Skinnerean stimulus–response modeling of human behaviors and statistical content analysis, which determines the meaning of texts through frequency count of their words.

Contemporary hermeneuticists, such as Apel (1980, 1984), Habermas (1972), and Ricoeur (1979), strengthen Dilthey's distinction by noting that in the human sciences the subject of investigation and the investigator can communicate with each other. The equality suggests that an appropriate methodology will resemble discussions in which members in a community justify their actions. The tools of the natural sciences are simply incapable of representing the key concepts in such discussions, namely motivation, belief, and intention, and the complexity of their interactions. Intentional actions are embedded in groups of varying size and are constrained by (re-)created rules and norms: sociocultural traditions. Because of the complexity of these intertwined and mutually defining webs of relationships, scientific access to them is difficult, and uncertainty principles abound. These involve the difficulties of isolating the object of study from its milieu and preventing changes that communication between the investigator and the subject produces in the subject. These conditions support the notion that cultural and social studies have the role of clarifying the beliefs, plans, motivations, and social roles that led cognitive agents to produce their texts and actions. The inquiry becomes a dialogue through which the inquirer comes to understand the tradition in which the author or agent is embedded, so that the inquirer may either accept or repair the tradition, as Gadamer demands, or even reject it, as Habermas permits. Phases of understanding may be alternated with phases of validating knowledge, as Ricoeur's hermeneutic arc suggests, or of seeking explanations to opaque behaviors, as suggested in Apel's model of psychoanalysis. In any event, hermeneutic studies are inherently interactive and produce self-understanding. In this way they extend the original mission of hermeneutics to mediate cultural traditions by correcting misreadings or distortions.

Logical positivists have nevertheless rejected the claims, for a separate method for social and cultural sciences are groundless challenges to their own program of creating a unified scientific method based on an unambiguous observation language (Radnitzky, 1968). Abel (1976), Hempel, and others argue that empathetic understanding and the attribution of rule following are psychological heuristics, unverifiable hunches, or intuitions based on personal experience. Although Abel concedes that they may be useful in setting up lawlike hypotheses for testing, he concludes that they are neither necessary nor sufficient to constitute a human science.

There are several rebuttals to these claims. First, methodological hermeneutics, which Dilthey initiated and Betti (1980) and Hirsch (1967) continue, holds that an interpretation can be objective and valid, if not verifiable, provided the investigator resists temptations to make the text relevant for his or her own practical affairs. This strategy regards the text as an embodiment of the values of its time and suspends credibility regarding its truth and acceptability, according to present standards. But knowledge of values expressed in other texts and records from the period are allowed to constrain the possible interpretations. Second, the idea of an interpretive or hermeneutic social science has received indirect support from ordinary language philosophy, an analytic that eschews the mentalism to which the logical positivists so strenuously object. The support comes from the sociologist Winch (1958), who generates recommendations for a social science on the basis of the later Wittgenstein's (1968) analysis that particular word use and discourse patterns, language games, reflect and constitute activities in semi-institutionalized, functional areas of life: life forms. Winch contends that the analysis of social actions (both verbal and nonverbal) has a necessarily holistic, situation-oriented, interpretive character rather than a generalizing, explanatory one:

> Understanding . . . is grasping the *point* or *meaning* of what is being done or said. This is a notion far removed from the world of statistics and causal laws: it is closer to the realm of discourse and to the internal relations that link the parts of . . . a discourse (Winch, 1958).

Third, philosophical hermeneutics is not concerned with verifiable accounts, and, as noted above, it denies the possibility of objective knowledge. Instead, it argues that only a person who stands in history, subject to the prejudices of the age, can hope to understand it. A valid understanding of an event, interaction, or text is one that bridges history or sociocultural differences to highlight the inquirer's situation. By this standard, Winch's recommendations are not hermeneutic because they are based on the idea of ahistorical language games. They do not recognize that interpretation includes both translation and application, that is, the mediation between the disintegrating and the emerging language games, on one hand

and the revitalization of the past and its assimilation into the present life form, on the other hand (Apel, 1980).

Hermeneutics and the Natural Sciences

Kuhn's influential *The Structure of Scientific Revolutions* (1962) developed a hermeneutics of the natural sciences by portraying them as historically embedded, linguistically mediated activities organized around paradigms that direct the conceptualization and investigation of the objects of their studies. Scientific revolutions occur when one paradigm replaces another and introduces a new set of theories, heuristics, exemplars, and terms. The notion of a paradigm-centered scientific community consequently seems analogous to Gadamer's notion of a linguistically encoded social tradition. Kuhn (1977) reports that his own development toward this idea began with his distress over Aristotle's theory of motion and the eventual discovery that Aristotle meant by motion something other than what the word signified in Newtonian mechanics. This effort corresponds closely to a programmatic definition of hermeneutics as the study of human actions and texts with the view to discover their meaning in order to understand them, agree with them or even amend them (Radnitzky, 1968).

Debates around Kuhn's thesis have spurred often grudging concessions that data, facts, and lawlike relations are theory dependent, rather than verifiable, coherent, and independent of the scientific theories in which they are embedded (Bernstein, 1983). Noting the inescapable theory dependence of observational sentences and the incommensurabilities across paradigms, Feyerabend (1970, 1978) reaches the radical conclusion that no methodological standards can legitimately be applied. He therefore advocates a methodological anarchism that proceeds from the slogan "in science, anything goes!" Feyerabend's doubts about the possibility of interparadigm communication closely resemble Gadamer's doubts regarding the accessibility of alien traditions.

Putnam (1981), however, argues that Feyerabend conflates concepts with conceptualization. According to Putnam, communication across paradigms does not require that the concepts be the same across paradigms but only that members of one paradigm make their ideas intelligible to members of another paradigm. They can do so provided the fundamental mechanisms conceptualization are the same across paradigms (language communities). According to Putnam, the mechanisms of conceptualization must be universal and *a priori* or empirical experience would not be possible. But making ideas intelligible across paradigms can require rederiving the concepts on which a paradigm's theories rely as well as reconstructing the grounds for those concepts, and so on, recursively. Thus interparadigmatic communication accordingly requires a critique of ideology similar to the one proposed by Apel and Habermas. Apel (1980) clarifies this process of reconstructing paradigms from first principles when he notes that justifications for scientific statements ultimately rely on a common ground in ordinary language statements. This common ground, the communicative *a priori*, provides procedural norms regarding the admissibility of evidence and the validity of argumentation. Thus despite paradigmatic differences, scientific discourse can still reach a consensus and avoid arbitrariness or dogmatism, by falling back on principled argument stated in ordinary language.

Notion of an Emancipatory Science

The hermeneutics tradition also provides the methodological starting point for Marx's critique of ideology, Freud's psychoanalysis, and other studies that seek human emancipation by dissolving obsolete, restrictive, and self-denying traditions and practices. Their initial strategy is to unmask the justifications given for these practices as distortions of the actors' true needs and the conditions of the situation. Yet hermeneutic understanding will not reveal why the actors accept these justifications. In presenting psychoanalysis as the paradigmatic emancipatory science, Apel (1980, 1984) emphasizes that human beings cannot fully acknowledge their own motives or the intentions in their expressions. Consequently, empathy and introspection need to be supplemented by a quasi-naturalistic turn that applies the causal analysis of natural science to the actor's behavior. Any resulting explanations can then be fed back to the actor and appropriated as self-knowledge.

As mentioned earlier, Gadamer and Habermas debated the validity of rejecting past traditions, especially in regard to the critique of Western political and social institutions. Gadamer essentially considers this move incoherent and ungrounded because it rejects the very tradition, including the value of rational, noncoerced consensus, that the investigator must accept to begin the explication. In response, Habermas (1966) and Apel (1980) claim that the preference for reason and understanding, the grounding for hermeneutics, is not just arbitrary or an inherited prejudice in the Western cultural tradition. Instead, they assert that a communicative *a priori* underlies all communication and entails that speech (and speechlike action) must be appropriate, as well as grammatical and sincere, to be meaningful. Because these validity claims imply a process for reaching agreement, the act of speaking itself commits the speakers to prefer reason.

HERMENEUTICS IN AI

Thus far, few AI researchers have incorporated ideas from hermeneutics into their computational models of understanding and interpretation. Hermeneutics, instead, has provided fertile source of arguments for doubting the possibility of the hard AI project, creating true artificial intelligences that can pass the Turing test (qv), which can be thought of as basically the ability to converse in natural language just like a human. Nevertheless, as AI interest in action theory and social interaction deepens, researchers will need to glean the insights of hermeneutics if their programs are to adequately mirror social phenomena and their cognitive foundations. Efforts that fail to consider the variability of meaning according to the intentions and histories of actors as well as the perceptions of observers will not solve the difficult questions of understanding, and may not even perform very well in microworlds. Indeed,

they are more likely to impute the implementor's theory, as embodied in the program, rather than recognize the particular organization in the phenomena under study.

Analyzing the Affective Structure of Text

Alker and co-workers (1985) and Lehnert and co-workers (1983) present a bottom-up model for extracting the affective structure of a text. Their computational hermeneutics builds from Lehnert's (1981, 1982) earlier work on plot units. Plot units provide an unvalidated but nevertheless interesting vocabulary for designating affective relationships and their combinations. In this research they are used to describe many emotional consequences for participants in events and actions. Working within conceptual dependency (qv) theory (Schank and Abelson, 1977), Lehnert identified various combinations of plot units for use in summarizing narrative texts. These story molecules relate changes in actors' affects to successes and failures in the resolutions of problems involving them. In their work Lehnert, Alker, and Schneider manually reduced passages from Toynbee's retelling of events leading up to Christ's crucifixion to a large number of these molecules. The molecules were interrelated through the actors involved and by virtue of some molecules being antecedent conditions for others. After the input of these manual reductions, the central subgraph of the plot structure was computationally extracted, using a program for finding the most strategic and highly connected molecules. This central subgraph was labeled the essential Jesus story.

After studying this affective core, Alker, Lehnert, and Schneider concluded that the Jesus story involves an ironic victory born from adversity and conforms to a well-known genre, the romance of self-transcendence. Their method resembles classical hermeneutics in seeking to uncover the essential structure of text based on systematic linkages between the parts and the whole and in emphasizing the use of explicit rules for objective interpretation. However, their willingness to tolerate multiple interpretations and their structuralist orientation also aligns them with phenomenological hermeneutics. Alker, Lehnert, and Schneider suggest that the Jesus story has been emotively potent because it provides a step-by-step account of affective change in self-transcendence and thus can open its readers to the experience of this process. In its present form, however, this work does not implement a bootstrapping process even though, ironically, the theme of self-transcendence presupposes a mechanism capable of consciously directed bootstrapping.

What Does It Mean to Understand Natural Language?

Winograd (1980) uses insights primarily from philosophical hermeneutics to sketch a new approach to natural language understanding (qv). He intends to overcome the pitfalls of earlier approaches that succumbed to the phenomenological critique advanced by Dreyfus (1979). Focusing on the theory of meaning, Winograd (1972) argues that previous efforts, including his own SHRDLU (qv) fell into the trap of objectivism, or the misplaced belief that the contents of a theory or model correspond directly to reality (the correspondence theory of truth). [Prior (1967) provides a concise overview of the correspondence theory of truth, which holds that the structure of theoretical knowledge corresponds to reality.] Winograd adds that the deductive nature of the formalisms used by AI researchers forced them to adopt an objectivist position but that these formalisms failed to account for the informal, phenomenological knowledge or experience that an understander deploys when interpreting utterances. Hermeneuticists identify this problem as the historicity of understanding or the role of background knowledge in mediating understanding.

Moreover, these deductive formalisms are subject to Heidegger's ontological critique of Husserl. Their failure to address the fundamental ontology of language typified by the conversational situation leads to an inability to account for the role of context in speaker–hearer identification of the intended meanings of utterances (Winograd, 1980). Thus Winograd supports the Heideggerian critique with arguments and examples drawn from ordinary language philosophy (Austin, 1962; Searle, 1970, 1975, 1980). In a vein reminiscent of Gadamer, he argues that making sense of a statement requires knowing how it is intended to answer (implicit or explicit) questions posed by the conversational context. He concludes that deductive logic can account for only a small fraction of human reasoning, and therefore new advances in natural language understanding require a calculus of natural reasoning (Winograd, 1980).

Winograd proposes knowledge–representation language (KRL) (qv) (Bobrow and Winograd, 1977) as a starting point for an alternative approach. KRL's reasoning based on limited computational resources captures Heidegger's thesis of the finititude of *Dasein* and also echoes Simon's (1979) notion of bounded rationality in the theory of decision making. For Winograd, effective reasoning strategies under limited or variable computational resources provide a natural reasoning, which, although formally incomplete, can account for more of everyday natural language usage than can the small fraction that fits the mold of a complete deductive logic (Winograd, 1980). Moreover, this approach must have the ability to deal with partial or imprecise information if it is to work at all. Winograd proposes a control structure that uses matching of the current processing context to trigger actions appropriate for the situation. This view of situated action, in which situational responses are unreflective, resembles the concept of thrownness as developed by Heidegger. The combination of situated action as a control structure and resource-limited reasoning grounded in commonsense, stereotype-based reasoning (Winograd, 1980) resonates with recent work on analogy (Winston, 1980, 1984; Carbonell, 1983), precedential reasoning (Alker and co-workers, 1980), and metaphor (Minsky, 1986; Carbonell, 1982). At its core KRL also incorporates a notion of bootstrapping similar to the one found in the various hermeneutic traditions, particularly in the works of Heidegger and Gadamer.

Winograd argues that spurious reification, or misplaced concreteness, has plagued earlier efforts to develop a formalism for representing natural language. Spurious

reification occurs when a competence is imputed to an understander, not because the understander actually employs the specified competence in performance, but because the observer classifies performances as instances of a particular competence and then mistakenly imputes the competence to the understander. Instead of building from domain-level concepts and structures, Winograd attempts to avoid spurious reification by constructing formal representations based on ontological considerations borrowed from methodological hermeneutics (Winograd, 1980). Because no substantial AI project has been attempted using KRL, the ideas that its designers hoped to capture remain more theoretical than practical.

In discussing hermeneutics, Winograd not only proposes a new research program for AI but also problematizes the philosophical basis of current natural language research. Fundamental assumptions and philosophical orientations underlying research must now be explicitly analyzed and justified. In rejecting objectivism, Winograd advocates a subjectivist hermeneutical position that builds from Maturana's (1977) notion of the nervous system as structure determined, plastic, and closed. According to this model, activities outside the system (stimuli) perturbate the structure of the system, and these perturbations in turn lead to patterns of activity that are different from those that would have happened with different perturbations. Winograd's parallel notion of understanding posits a closed system in which preunderstanding evolves through acts of interpretation. As in Heidegger's hermeneutic circle, the possible horizons that can be understood are constrained by the historically determined structure of preunderstanding or set of stored schemas (Winograd, 1980). Understanding is open to the environment only within this range. Unlike Heidegger, who recognized the importance of the environment but failed to analyze it, Winograd is led to the analysis of the environment by several influences. These include Garfinkel's (1976) ethnomethodology, which emphasizes social context, Searle's focus on speech as social action, and Lakatos's (1976) argument that even in mathematics the meanings of terms are contingent on outside context. Winograd (1980) grounds his theory of meaning in terms of social action, and so takes a position close to critical hermeneutics, between relativism and objectivism.

Stimulated in part by Winograd (1980), Bateman (1983, 1981) examines the consequences of Heidegger's existential phenomenology and agrees with Dreyfus (1979) that this philosophy denies the possibility of modeling thought and action using the specific formalizations proposed by the functionalist paradigm of cognitive science. Bateman says these formalisms are based on the ontological assumption of an interpreter who follows rules in acting upon a mental representation of a situation. Heidegger's notion of being-in-the-world, which includes both situatedness and understanding as ontological modes, precludes the subject–object dichotomy in this assumption. Since one is always in a situation, and its structure and significance are determined by its relevance to one's plans and purposes, no context-free representation is possible.

Bateman, however, does not dismiss the possibility of a

functionalist paradigm for cognitive science. He wants instead to ground it on the later Heidegger's idea of language, which, according to Bateman, seeks to make intelligible the experience of being-in-the-world as it is for anyone, that is, for a generalized subject or member of a language community. As a collective artifact, a language is considered to encode partially the history of the language community through both the admissible and inadmissible combination (association) of words and phrases. The resulting connotational structure captures a kind of collective background knowledge and imposes *a priori* constraints on the actions of individuals who contemplate actions in terms of the language. In Halliday's (1978) systemic grammar there is the notion of a social semiotic that acknowleges that a group's culture can restrict the possible meanings of utterances through constraints on possible ways of acting in situations. Bateman considers this orientation compatible with the hermeneutic view and believes that systemic grammar, with appropriate revisions, can provide an adequate theoretical framework for natural language understanding. Yet despite this openness to social constraints, Bateman does not consider hermeneuticists who came after Heidegger, most notably Gadamer and Habermas.

Foundations of Understanding

In a more recent work Winograd and Flores (1986) draw on philosophical hermeneutics and Maturana's (1980) work on the biology of cognition to deny the possibility of the constructing intelligent computers. They argue that to the extent Heidegger and Gadamer make a persuasive case that certain features of human existence are fundamental, the quest for intelligent machinery is quixotic. These concepts include *throwness, blindness*, and *breakdown*. Throwness denotes that people are thrown into the situations of everyday life and rarely have time to reflect on alternative courses of action. They cannot be impartial, detached observers of the world in which they live, but they must decide and act using heuristics they have as part of their effective histories. Although these heuristics enable some action possibilities, the same heuristics also blind people to other action possibilities that might have predominated had their effective histories been different. When faced with situations where their effective histories fail to provide an adequate guide for action and also blind them to those actions that support their purposes, people experience a kind of breakdown. In breakdown, actions become problematic and tools which had been previously taken for granted are perceived in isolation as objects.

If an expert system is designed to present a user with possible courses of action in particular situations, the concepts of throwness, blindness, and breakdown also come into play. Although expert systems (qv) may operate successfully in well-understood, constrained domains, expert systems in complex domains may be thrown into situations where they cannot evaluate all possible actions and they consequently break down. Systems targeted at complex domains must therefore rely on heuristic rules, but these may blind the program to more propitious courses of action. Winograd and Flores add that the expert-system programmer introduces his own blindness or preconceptions into the program. Because of these difficulties, Winograd and Flores recommend reformulation of the goals of artificial intelligence. Instead of directing efforts toward the putatively impossible goal of creating machines that can understand, programs should be designed to serve as tools for enhancing the quality of life. This could be done by recognizing the role of such programs in the web of conversations (speech acts) that constitute social existence, by attempting to minimize the blindness they engender, and by anticipating the range of their potential breakdowns.

Winograd and Flores present a reasoned critique of two specific categories of AI research. The first comprises AI approaches that incorporate rigidly fixed means of interpretation, such as much work in knowledge-based systems. The second category includes those approaches that proceed from the dualist presumption that truth, meaning, and reference are established by means of a correspondence between entities in the world and entities in the mind (the correspondence theory of truth) rather than in the everyday discourse of intelligent agents. Although they acknowledge that learning approaches might eventually be able to address the criticisms they raise, they do not expect progress in learning during the near term. Thus their work amounts to a critique of the tractability of the hard AI project. As such, it constitutes a continuation of the critique AI begun by Dreyfus (1979) but differs in that it comes from within AI and is argued in more computational terms.

However, Winograd and Flores fail to demonstrate convincingly that computer understanding exceeds the range of the possible. They only demonstrate that the goal is much more difficult than many people, including many AI practitioners, may have thought. Unfortunately, Winograd and Flores unfairly characterize as blind those AI approaches that come closest to overcoming their objections, such as Winston's (1980, 1984, 1982) approach to learning and reasoning by analogy. Winograd and Flores misconstrue Winston's approach as capable of producing results only because it operates in a microworld with primitives fixed in advance by the implementors. Although this criticism may be leveled fairly at many AI programs, Winston's program is in principle not so limited, precisely because it is not based on domain-specific primitives. Indeed, Winston's program is general enough to perform well in any domain because it processes linguistically derived data according to the data's form rather than specific content. Moreover, because it learns rules on the basis of its experience (the effective history over which it can draw analogies), Winston's program represents a first computational approximation of the basic hermeneutic notion of a preunderstanding grounded in effective history.

Grounding Meaning in Eidetic Phenomenology

Mallery and Duffy (1986) present a computational model of semantic perception, the process of mapping from a syntactic representation into a semantic representation.

Some computational and noncomputational linguists (Schank and Abelson, 1977; Katz and Fodor, 1963; Schank, 1972) advocate determining equivalent meanings (paraphrases) through the reduction of different surface forms to a canonicalized semantic form comprised by some combination of semantic universals (eg, conceptual-dependency primitives). Mallery and Duffy reject this view on the grounds that most meaning equivalences must be determined in accordance with the specific linguistic histories of individual language users (or at least linguistic communities based on social groups) and the intentional context of the utterance. Their alternative is lexical-interpretive semantics, an approach to natural language semantics that constructs semantic representation from canonical grammatical relations and the original lexical items (see LEXICAL SEMANTICS). On this view, semantic representations are canonicalized only syntactically, not semantically or pragmatically. Instead of relying on static equivalences determined in advance, lexical-interpretive semantics requires meaning equivalences to be determined at their time of use, reference time. To meet this requirement, Mallery and Duffy introduce the concept of a meaning congruence class, the set of syntactically normalized semantic representations conforming to the linguistic experience of specific language users and satisfying their utterance-specific intentions. Meaning equivalences are then given by the meaning congruence classes to which utterances belong. Lexical-interpretive semantics differs from approaches relying on semantic universals because meaning equivalences are determined dynamically at reference time for specific language users with individual histories rather than statically in advance for an idealized language user with a general but unspecific background knowledge.

The major assumption underlying lexical-interpretive semantics is that meaning equivalences arise because alternative lexical realizations (surface forms) accomplish sufficiently similar speaker goals to allow substitution. Determining meaning congruences in advance, based on static analysis, is hopelessly intractable. This follows from the need to predict in advance all potential utterance situations, intentional contexts, and combinations of language-user effective histories. Although semantic canonicalization on the basis of a general semantic and pragmatic competence renders static analyses of language-user combinations tractable by fiat, it also reduces nuances so dramatically that intentional analysis and individual linguistic histories play a drastically diminished role.

Lexical-interpretive semantics is hermeneutic because it emphasizes interpretation based on the individual effective history of language users and the specific intentional structure of communicative situations. By virtue of its emphasis on innovation in language and polysemy, lexical-interpretive semantics is perhaps most closely aligned with the phenomenological hermeneutics of Ricoeur (1981b). Interpretation builds from an eidetic level of representation, the syntactically normalized semantic representation. The determination of meaning congruence classes becomes an early level of a more general and open-ended hermeneutic interpretation. Stimulated by recent debates about perception (Barsalou and Bower, 1984; Feigenbaum and Simon, 1984), Mallery and Duffy consider semantic perception to be a process of mapping from sense data, in this case natural language sentences, to a semantic representation. But instead of providing an account of perception suited to a theory of meaning based on semantic universals like Feigenbaum and Simon (1984), Mallery and Duffy provide one suited to a hermeneutic theory of meaning.

Duffy and Mallery (1986) have implemented this theory, up to the level of eidetic representation, in the RELATUS natural language system. Although they share some of the hermeneutically oriented views and concerns articulated in Winograd (1980) and Bateman (1983, 1981), their implementation allows more concrete specification and testing of their theory, which currently focuses on earlier processing levels. For example, Mallery and Duffy (1986) have proposed constraint-interpreting reference (Mallery, 1986) as a model that conforms to lexical-interpretive semantics, just as discrimination nets are well suited to approaches relying on semantic primitives (Feigenbaum and Simon, 1984; Feigenbaum, 1959; Kolodner, 1983a, 1983b). They ground this choice both in the available experimental psycholinguistic evidence and in the desirable computational properties of reference based on constraint interpretation. These properties include maximizing monotonicity (minimizing backtracking) in the syntactic processing that precedes reference and optimizing subgraph isomorphism (search) as it arises in reference and in other reasoning operations, particularly commonsense reasoning grounded in analogy.

CONCLUSIONS

This entry has presented hermeneutics primarily as a philosophy of understanding rather than as a set of technologies for interpretation in specific domains. As such, the hermeneutic tradition seems able to speak to AI researchers in two distinct ways. First, hermeneutics provides some basis for arguing against the feasibility of the AI project, at least under its present dispensation. Whether represented by Dilthey's idea of empathetic understanding or Heidegger's idea of situated understanding, hermeneutics seems to have discovered a quality in the human situation that is vital for knowledge of others and oneself but has not yet been simulated mechanically. Because these doubts are generated from an ongoing intellectual tradition and because they refine some fairly common intuitions, they cannot easily be dismissed as irrational technological pessimism. On the other hand, these doubts should stimulate attempts by AI researchers to overcome them, as just some doubts raised by Dreyfus (1979) stimulated earlier research. At the very least, then, the insights of the various hermeneutical camps can be expected to receive increasing attention in the artificial intelligence community.

Second, hermeneutics can suggest constraints, orientations and even criteria in the design of AI systems that are intended either to understand natural language or to represent knowledge of the social world. The lessons of this tradition are, however, equivocal. Dilthey, Heidegger, Gadamer, Habermas, Ricoeur, and others provide very different notions of what constitutes understanding and its grounding. Nevertheless, researchers who are aware of these debates might be more cognizant of the choices they make in their own designs. As a consequence, systems would not merely illustrate isolated and perhaps idiosyncratic theories about linguistic phenomena but would begin to support (or deny) major philosophical positions in ontology, epistemology, and philosophy of mind. But the generally precomputational nature of contemporary hermeneutics calls for specific formulations that can be tested computationally. Computational experimentation, and empirical philosophy, can then feed back into the reformulation and refinement of ideas about both hermeneutics and AI.

BIBLIOGRAPHY

T. Abel, "The Operation Called *Verstehen*," in H. Gadamer, *Hegel's Dialectic: Five Hermeneutical Studies*, Yale University Press, New Haven, Conn., 1976.

H. R. Alker, Jr., J. Bennett, and D. Mefford, "Generalized Precedent Logics for Resolving Insecurity Dilemmas," *Int. Interact.* **7**, 165–206 (1980).

H. R. Alker, Jr., W. G. Lehnert, and D. K. Schneider, "Two Reinterpretations of Toynbee's Jesus: Explorations in Computational Hermeneutics," *Artif. Intell. Text Understand. Quad. Ric. Ling.* **6**, 49–94 (1985).

K. Apel, *Towards a Transformation of Philosophy*, Routledge & Kegan Paul, London, 1980.

K. Apel, *Understanding and Explanation*, MIT Press, Cambridge, Mass., 1984.

J. L. Austin, *How To Do Things with Words*, Harvard University Press, Cambridge, Mass., 1962.

L. W. Barsalou and G. H. Bower, "Discrimination Nets as Psychological Models," *Cogn. Sci.* **8**, 1–26 (1984).

J. A. Bateman, "The Role of Language in the Maintenance of Intersubjectivity: A Computational Investigation," in G. N. Gilbert and C. Heath, eds., *Social Action and Artificial Intelligence*, Grower, Brookfield, Vt., 1981, pp. 40–81.

J. A. Bateman, *Cognitive Science Meets Existential Phenomenology: Collapse or Synthesis?* Working Paper No. 139, University of Edinburgh, Edinburgh, UK, Apr. 1983.

R. J. Bernstein, *Beyond Objectivism and Relativism: Science, Hermeneutics, and Praxis*, University of Pennsylvania Press, Philadelphia, 1983.

E. Betti, "Hermeneutics as the General Methodology of the *Geisteswissenschaften*," in Bleicher, 1980, pp. 51–94.

J. Bleicher, *Contemporary Hermeneutics: Hermeneutics as Method, Philosophy, and Critique*, Routledge & Kegan Paul, London, 1980.

D. G. Bobrow, and T. Winograd, "An Overview of KRL, a Knowledge Representation Language," *Cogn. Sci.* **1**, 3–46 (1977).

J. G. Carbonell, "Metaphor: An Inescapable Phenomenon in Natural Language Comprehension," in W. C. Lehnert and M. H. Ringle, eds., *Strategies for Natural Language Processing*, Lawrence Erlbaum, Hillsdale, N.J., 1982, pp. 415–434.

J. G. Carbonell, "Learning by Analogy: Formulating and Generalizing Plans from Past Experience," in R. S. Michalski, J. G. Carbonell, and T. M. Mitchell, eds., *Machine Learning: An Artificial Intelligence Approach*, Tioga, Palo Alto, Calif., 1983, pp. 137–162.

N. Chomsky, *Syntactic Structures*, Mouton, The Hague, 1957.

N. Chomsky, *Aspects of The Theory of Syntax*, MIT Press, Cambridge, Mass., 1965.

N. Chomsky, *Lectures on Government and Binding*, Foris, Dordrecht, 1981.

F. R. Dallmayr, *Language and Politics: Why Does Language Matter to Political Philosophy?"* University of Notre Dame Press, Notre Dame, Ill., 1984.

W. Dilthey, "The Rise of Hermeneutics," in P. Connerton, ed., *Critical Sociology: Selected Readings*, Penguin, Harmondsworth, UK, 1976a, pp. 104–116.

W. Dilthey in H. P. Rickman, ed., *Selected Writings*, Cambridge University Press, Cambridge, UK, 1976b.

G. L. Drescher, *Genetic AI: Translating Piaget into LISP*, AI Memo No. 890, Artificial Intelligence Laboratory, MIT, Cambridge, Mass., Feb. 1986.

H. Dreyfus, *What Computers Can't Do: A Critique of Artificial Reason*, 2nd ed., W. H. Freeman, San Francisco, 1979.

H. Dreyfus, personal communication, 1986.

G. Duffy and J. C. Mallery, *Relatus: An Artificial Intelligence Tool for Natural Language Modeling*, AI Memo No. 847, Artificial Intelligence Laboratory, MIT, Cambridge, Mass., 1986.

M. Ermarth, *Wilhelm Dilthey: The Critique of Historical Reason*, University of Chicago Press, Chicago, Ill., 1978.

E. A. Feigenbaum, *An Information Processing Theory of Verbal Learning*, Rand, Santa Monica, Calif., 1959.

E. A. Feigenbaum and H. A. Simon, "EPAM-Like Models of Recognition and Learning," *Cogn. Sci.* **8**, 305–336 (1984).

P. Feyerabend, "Consolations for the Specialist," in I. Lakatos and A. Musgrave, eds., *Criticism and the Growth of Knowledge* Cambridge University Press, Cambridge, UK, 1970, pp. 197–230.

P. Feyerabend, *Against Method*, Verso, London, 1978.

H. Gadamer, *Truth and Method*, Continuum, New York, 1975.

H. Gadamer, *Hegel's Dialectic: Five Hermeneutical Studies*, Yale University Press, New Haven, Conn., 1976a.

H. Gadamer, "Man and Language," in D. E. Linge, ed., *Philosophical Hermeneutics*, University of California Press, Berkeley, 1976b, pp. 59–68.

H. Gadamer, "On the Scope and Function of Hermeneutical Reflection," in D. E. Linge, ed., *Philosophical Hermeneutics*, University of California Press, Berkeley, 1976c, pp. 18–43.

H. Garfinkel, What Is Ethnomethodology? in H. Gadamer, *Hegel's Dialectic: Five Hermeneutical Studies*, Yale University Press, New Haven, Conn., 1976,

E. Goffman, *The Presentation of Self in Everyday Life*, Doubleday, New York, 1959.

M. Green, "Martin Heidegger," in P. Edwards, ed., *The Encyclopedia of Philosophy*, Vols. 7 and 8, Macmillan, New York, 1967, pp. 457–465.

P. H. Grice, "Logic and Conversation," in P. Cole and J. L. Morgan, eds., *Studies in Syntax*, Vol. 3, Academic Press, Inc., New York, 1975, pp. 41–58.

K. W. Haase, *ARLO: The Implementation of a Language for Describing Representation Languages*, AI Technical Report No. 901, Artificial Intelligence Laboratory, MIT, Cambridge, Mass., 1986.

J. Habermas, "Knowledge and Human Interest," *Inquiry* **9**, 285–300 (1966).

J. Habermas, *Knowledge and Human Interests*, Heinemann, London, 1972.

J. Habermas, "A Review of Gadamer's *Truth and Method*," in F. R. Dallmayr and T. A. McCarthy, eds., *Understanding and Social Inquiry*, University of Notre Dame, Notre Dame, Ill., 1977, pp. 335–363.

J. Habermas, "Some Distinctions in Universal Pragmatics," *Theor. Soc.* **3**, 155–167 (1976).

J. Habermas, *Communication and the Evolution of Society*, Beacon Press, Boston, 1979, pp. 1–68.

J. Habermas, *The Theory of Communicative Action, Vol. 1, Reason and the Rationalization of Society*, Beacon, Boston, 1981.

M. A. K. Halliday, *Language as Social Semiotic*, Edward Arnold, London, 1978.

G. W. F. Hegel, *The Philosophy of Mind*, Part 3 of *The Encyclopedia of the Philosophical Sciences*, Oxford University Press, Oxford, UK, 1971.

G. W. F. Hegel, *The Science of Logic*, Part 2 of *The Encyclopedia of the Philosophical Sciences*, Oxford University Press, Oxford, UK, 1975.

M. Heidegger, *Being and Time*, Harper & Row, New York, 1962.

E. D. Hirsch, Jr., *Validity in Interpretation*, Yale University Press, New Haven, Conn., 1967.

E. Husserl, *Ideas: General Introduction to Pure Phenomenology*, Allen & Unwin, London, 1931.

J. J. Katz and J. A. Fodor, "The Structure of a Semantic Theory," *Language* **39**(2), 170–210 (1963).

J. L. Kolodner, "Reconstructive Memory: A Computer Model," *Cogn. Sci.* **7**, 280–328 (1983a).

J. L. Kolodner, "Maintaining Organization in a Dynamic Long-Term Memory," *Cogn. Sci.* **7**, 243–280 (1983b).

T. S. Kuhn, *The Structure of Scientific Revolutions*, University of Chicago Press, Chicago, Ill., 1962.

T. S. Kuhn, *The Essential Tension: Selected Studies in Scientific Tradition and Change*, University of Chicago Press, Chicago, Ill., 1977.

I. Lakatos, *Proofs and Refutations*, Cambridge University Press, Cambridge, UK, 1976.

W. C. Lehnert, "Plot Units and Narrative Summarizations," *Cogn. Sci.* **4**, 293–331 (1981).

W. C. Lehnert, "Plot Units: A Narrative Summarization Strategy," in W. C. Lehnert and M. H. Ringle, eds., *Stratgies for Natural Language Processing*, Lawrence Erlbaum, Hillsdale, N.J., 1982, pp. 375–414.

W. C. Lehnert, H. R. Alker, Jr., and D. K. Schneider, "The Heroic Jesus: The Affective Plot Structure of Toynbee's Christus Patiens," in S. K. Burton and D. D. Short, eds., *Proceedings of the Sixth International Conference on Computers and the Humanities*, Computer Science Press, Rockville, Md., 1983, pp. 358–367.

D. B. Lenat, "AM: Discovery in Mathematics as Heuristic Search," in R. Davis and D. B. Lenat, eds., *Knowledge-Based Systems in Artificial Intelligence*, McGraw-Hill Book Co., Inc., New York, 1982, pp. 1–227.

D. B. Lenat, "Eurisko: A Program That Learns New Heuristics and Domain Concepts: The Nature of Heuristics III: Program Design and Results," *Artif. Intell.* **21**, 61–98 (1983).

C. Levi-Strauss, *Structural Anthropology*, Penguin, Harmondsworth, UK, 1968.

D. E. Linge, ed., *Philosophical Hermeneutics*, University of California Press, Berkeley, 1976.

T. McCarthy, *The Critical Theory of Jürgen Habermas*, MIT Press, Cambridge, Mass., 1978.

T. McCarthy, "Rationality and Relativism: Habermas's 'Overcoming' of Hermeneutics," in J. B. Thompson and D. Held, eds., *Habermas: Critical Debates*, MIT Press, Cambridge, Mass., 1982, pp. 57–78.

J. C. Mallery, *Constraint-Interpreting Reference*, AI Memo No. 827, Artificial Intelligence Laboratory, MIT, Cambridge, Mass., 1986.

J. C. Mallery and G. Duffy, *A Computational Model of Semantic Perception*, AI Memo No. 799, Artificial Intelligence Laboratory, MIT, Cambridge, Mass., May 1986.

H. R. Maturana, "Biology of Knowledge," in R. W. Reiber, ed., *The Neurophysiology of Language*, Plenum, New York, 1977.

H. R. Maturana, "Biology of Cognition," in H. R. Maturana and F. Varela, eds., *Autopoeisis and Cognition: The Realization of the Living*, Reidel, Dordrecht, 1980, pp. 2–62.

M. Merleau-Ponty, *Phenomenology of Perception*, Routledge & Kegan Paul, London, 1962.

M. Minsky, *The Society of Mind*, Simon & Schuster, New York, 1986.

M. Murray, *Heidegger and Modern Philosophy: Critical Essays*, Yale University Press, New Haven, Conn., 1978.

F. A. Olafson, "Maurice Merleau-Ponty" in P. Edwards, ed., *The Encyclopedia of Philosophy*, Vols. 5 and 6, Macmillan, New York, 1967, pp. 279–282.

R. Palmer, *Hermeneutics: Interpretation Theory in Schleiermacher, Dilthey, Heidegger, and Gadamer*, Northwestern University Press, Evanston, Ill., 1969.

T. Parsons, *The Structure of Social Action*, McGraw-Hill Book Co., Inc., New York, 1937.

J. Piaget, *The Origins of Intelligence in Children*, W. W. Norton, New York, 1952.

J. Piaget, *Genetic Epistemology*, Columbia University Press, New York, 1970.

T. Plantinga, *Historical Understanding in the Thought of Wilhelm Dilthey*, University of Toronto Press, Toronto, 1980.

K. Popper, *The Logic of Scientific Discovery*, Basic Books, New York, 1959.

A. N. Prior, "Correspondence Theory of Truth," in P. Edwards, ed., *The Encyclopedia of Philosophy*, Vols. 1 and 2, Macmillan, New York, 1967, pp. 223–232.

H. Putnam, *Reason, Truth and History*, Cambridge University Press, Cambridge, UK, 1981.

G. Radnitzky, *Continental Schools of Metasciences: The Metascience of the Human Sciences Based upon the "Hermeneutic-Dialectic" School of Philosophy*, Vol. 2 of *Contemporary Schools of Metascience*, Scandinavian University Books, Goteborg, Sweden, 1968.

P. Ricoeur, *Husserl: An Analysis of His Phenomenology*, Northwestern University Press, Evanston, Ill., 1967.

P. Ricoeur, *Freud and Philosophy: An Essay on Interpretation*, Yale University Press, New Haven, Conn., 1970.

P. Ricoeur, "The Model of Text: Meaningful Action Considered as Text," *Soc. Res.* **38**, 529–562 (1971).

P. Ricoeur, "Creativity in Language," *Philos. Today* **17**, 97–111 (1973a).

P. Ricoeur, "The Hermeneutical Function of Distanciation," *Philos. Today* **17**, 129–143 (1973b).

P. Ricoeur, "The Task of Hermeneutics," *Philos. Today* **17**, (1973c).

P. Ricoeur, "Metaphor and the Main Problem of Hermeneutics," in *New Literary History*, Vol. 6, 1974–1975, pp. 95–110.

P. Ricoeur, *The Rule of Metaphor: Multi-Disciplinary Studies of the Creation of Meaning in Language*, University of Toronto Press, Toronto, 1977.

P. Ricoeur, *Main Trends in Philosophy*, Holmes and Meier, New York, 1979.

P. Ricoeur, "Hermeneutics and the Critique of Ideology," in J. B. Thompson, ed., *Paul Ricoeur: Hermeneutics and the Human Sciences*, Cambridge University Press, Cambridge, UK, 1981a, pp. 63–100.

P. Ricoeur, "Phenomenology and Hermeneutics," in J. B. Thompson, ed., *Paul Ricoeur: Hermeneutics and the Human Sciences*, Cambridge University Press, Cambridge, UK, 1981b, pp. 101–128.

E. Sapir, *Selected Writings of Edward Sapir*, University of California Press, Berkeley, 1947.

R. C. Schank, "Conceptual Dependency: A Theory of Natural Language," *Cogn. Psychol.* **3**, 552–63 (1972).

R. C. Schank and R. Abelson, *Scripts, Plans, Goals, and Understanding*, Lawrence Erlbaum, Hillsdale, N.J., 1977.

F. Schleiermacher in H. Kimmerle, ed., *Hermeneutik*, Carl Winter Universitatsverlag, Heidelberg, FRG, 1959.

R. Schmitt, "Phenomenology," in P. Edwards, ed., *The Encyclopedia of Philosophy*, Vols. 5 and 6, Macmillan, New York, 1967, pp. 135–151.

A. Schutz, *The Phenomenology of a Social World*, Northwestern University Press, Evanston, Ill., 1967.

J. R. Searle, *Speech Acts*, Cambridge University Press, Cambridge, UK, 1970.

J. R. Searle, "A Taxonomy of Illocutionary Acts," in K. Gunderson, ed., *Language and Knowledge: Minnesota Studies in Philosophy of Science*, Vol. 11, University of Minnesota Press, Minneapolis, 1975, pp. 344–369.

J. R. Searle, "The Intentionality of Intention and Action," *Cogn. Sci.* **4**, 47–70 (1980).

H. A. Simon, "Rational Decision Making in Business Organizations," *Am. Econ. Rev.* **69**, 493–513 (1979).

P. Singer, *Hegel*, Oxford University Press, Oxford, UK, 1983.

B. Smalley, *The Study of the Bible in the Middle Ages*, 2d ed., Blackwell, Oxford, UK, 1952.

W. Stegmuller, "The So-called Circle of Understanding," in W. Stegmuller, ed., *Collected Papers on Epistemology, Philosophy of Science and History of Philosophy*, Vol. 3, Reidel, Dordrecht, The Netherlands, 1977.

G. Steiner, *Martin Heidegger*, Penguin, New York, 1980.

J. B. Thompson, *Critical Hermeneutics: A Study in the Thought of Paul Ricoeur and Jurgen Habermas*, Cambridge University Press, Cambridge, UK, 1981.

J. B. Thompson, "Universal Pragmatics," in J. B. Thompson and D. Held, eds., *Habermas: Critical Debates*, MIT Press, Cambridge, Mass., 1982, pp. 116–133.

M. Weber in E. Shils and H. Finch, eds., *The Methodology of the Social Sciences*, Free Press, Glencoe, Ill., 1949.

B. Whorf, *Language, Thought and Reality*, MIT Press, Cambridge, Mass., 1967.

P. Winch, *The Idea of a Social Science and Its Relation to Philosophy*, Routledge & Kegan Paul, London, 1958.

T. Winograd, *Understanding Natural Language*, Academic Press, Inc., New York, 1972.

T. Winograd, "What Does It Mean to Understand Natural Language," *Cogn. Sci.* **4**, 209–241 (1980).

T. Winograd and F. Flores, *Understanding Computers and Cognition: A New Foundation for Design*, Ablex, Norwood, N.J., 1986.

P. H. Winston, "Learning and Reasoning by Analogy," *CACM* **23** (Dec. 1980).

P. H. Winston, "Learning New Principles from Precedents and Exercises," *Artif. Intell.* **19**, 321–350 (1982).

P. H. Winston, *Artificial Intelligence*, Addison-Wesley Publishing Co., Inc., Reading, Mass., 1984.

L. Wittgenstein, *Philosophical Investigations*, 3d ed., Macmillan, New York, 1968.

R. M. Zaner, *The Way of Phenomenology: Criticism as a Philosophical Discipline*, Pegasus, New York, 1970.

J. C. Mallery
R. Hurwitz
MIT

G. Duffy
University of Texas at Austin

HEURISTICS

Heuristics are approximate methods for solving artificial intelligence problems. AI deals primarily with problems for which no practical exact solution algorithms are known. Heuristics provide techniques for solving these problems with limited computational resources, but often at some cost in solution quality. In some cases, however, heuristics reduce computation with no sacrifice in solution quality. The usefulness of heuristics is derived from the fact that a small amount of knowledge often buys a large improvement in solution quality and/or computation time.

Candidate problems for heuristic methods generally fall into two classes: those for which no exact algorithms are known, and those for which exact algorithms are computationally infeasible. An example of the first class is the problem of computer vision. The task is to take the output of a digitizing camera, in the form of a two-dimensional matrix of pixel values representing light intensities, and to transform it into a high level symbolic description of objects and their spatial relationships. Unfortunately, there are no known algorithms for solving this problem that are guaranteed to always yield a "correct" interpretation of the scene.

Computer chess is an example of the second class of problem (see COMPUTER CHESS AND SEARCH). There exists an exact deterministic algorithm for always making an optimal move in a chess game. It requires generating all moves and countermoves in the game until only won, lost, and drawn positions remain, and propagating the outcomes of these positions back to the current position in order to choose an optimal move (see MINIMAX PROCEDURE). Unfortunately, the number of positions that would have to be generated by such an algorithm could be as large as 10^{120}. Thus although an exact solution algorithm for this problem is known, its computational cost makes it infeasible.

In either case, arriving at an exact solution is either impossible or impractical. Thus AI programs resort to heuristic techniques. Their power lies in the nature of the trade-offs between domain knowledge, computation, and solution quality. For example, given no knowledge of chess, it is possible to execute the complete minimax procedure or make random legal moves. The minimax procedure produces perfect play, but at a tremendous cost in computation, whereas the random algorithm is very efficient but generates very poor play.

Introducing some heuristic knowledge improves the trade-off between computation and decision quality. For example, one heuristic for chess is to always make the move that maximizes the relative piece or material advantage. This heuristic provides a relatively efficient means of selecting a next move and results in play that is far superior to random play, but far less than perfect play. Using the same knowledge, but incorporating look-ahead search improves the decision quality at the cost of increased computation.

One of the empirical results of AI research is that for many problems, even a small amount of knowledge greatly reduces the amount of computation necessary for a given level of solution quality. Alternatively, a small amount of knowledge may greatly increase solution quality for the same amount of computation.

In AI, the term heuristic has a general meaning and a more specialized technical meaning. In a general sense, heuristic is used for any advice that is often effective, but is not guaranteed to work in every case. Most of the analytic and experimental work on heuristics per se has occurred in the special case of heuristic evaluation functions. First, heuristic evaluation functions will be considered at some length, and then briefly the more general case of heuristics will be considered.

HEURISTIC EVALUATION FUNCTIONS

A heuristic evaluation function is a function that maps problem situations to numbers. These values are then used to determine which operation to perform next, typically by choosing the operation that leads to the situation with the maximum or minimum evaluation. Heuristic evaluation functions are used in two different contexts: single-agent problems and two-player games.

Single-Agent Problems

A classic AI example of a single-agent problem is the eight puzzle (Figure 1). It consists of a three-by-three square frame containing eight numbered square tiles and one empty position. Any tile horizontally or vertically adjacent to the empty position can be slid into that position. The task is to rearrange the tiles from a given initial configuration into a particular goal configuration by a shortest sequence of legal moves. Other examples include navigating in a network of roads from one location to another, and the traveling salesperson problem (TSP). The TSP task is to find the shortest path connecting a set of cities, visiting each city only once, and returning to the starting city.

The brute-force solutions to these problems involve searching all move sequences up to the length of the optimal solutions (see SEARCH). Although feasible for the eight puzzle with about 10^5 states, this approach is computationally intractable for even the slightly larger four-by-four fifteen puzzle, which has over 10^{13} states. Because the

Figure 1. Eight and fifteen puzzles.

number of TSP tours of N cities is approximately $N!$, brute-force search is practical for only a very small number of cities.

The standard heuristic approach to these problems makes use of an evaluation function to guide the search. A heuristic evaluation function is an estimate of the remaining cost to map the current state to a goal state. For example, the best known heuristic function for the eight puzzle is called Manhattan distance. It is computed by taking each tile individually, measuring its distance from its goal position in grid units, and summing these values for each tile. An obvious heuristic for the road navigation problem is the Euclidean or airline distance to the goal. For TSP, a minimum spanning tree of the remaining cities estimates the cost of completing the current tour.

The important property of all three of these functions is that they can be efficiently computed, compared to determining the exact solutions of the original problems. Manhattan distance can be computed in time proportional to the number of tiles, airline distance can be calculated in constant time, and minimum spanning trees can be determined in time proportional to the square of the number of cities, whereas TSP requires time that is exponential in the number of cities.

Another property that all three functions share is that they are lower bounds on the actual cost being estimated. Because each move of the eight puzzle moves one tile, and each tile must eventually move as many times as its Manhattan distance from its goal position, Manhattan distance is a lower bound on the actual number of moves required to solve a problem instance. Because the shortest path between a pair of points is a straight line, road distance must be at least as great as airline distance. Finally, because a TSP tour minus a single edge is a spanning tree, the cost of the minimum spanning tree is a lower bound on the cost of the minimal TSP tour.

Given such estimates, there are a number of different algorithms that make use of this information to find solutions in much less time than required by brute-force search (see SEARCH). The simplest, pure heuristic search, always selects next a move that leads to a state with the minimum heuristic estimate of distance to the goal. As the accuracy of the heuristic improves, the amount of search required to find a solution and the cost of the resulting solution both decrease.

The A* algorithm (see A* ALGORITHM), adds to the heuristic estimate the actual cost of the path from the initial state to the current state and always selects next the state for which this sum is a minimum. This amounts to selecting states in increasing order of the estimate of the total cost of a solution constrained to pass through that state. If the heuristic function never overestimates the actual cost of a solution, a constraint satisfied by the three heuristics mentioned above, then A^* finds an optimal solution, using much less computation than brute-force search. The actual amount of search depends on the accuracy of the heuristic function (see SEARCH). In this case, the heuristic reduces the computation while still finding optimal solutions.

Heuristics From Simplified Models

Where do heuristic evaluation functions come from, and can their discovery be automated? An answer to the first question, and an approach to the second, is that heuristic evaluation functions are derived from simplified models of the original problem (Pearl, 1984).

For example, one way of describing a legal move in the eight puzzle is that a tile can be moved from one position to another if and only if the two positions are horizontally or vertically adjacent, and the destination position is empty. If either of these constraints is removed, the result is a simpler problem that is easier to solve. The exact number of moves required to solve the simpler problem then serves as an estimate of the number of moves needed to solve the original problem.

For example, if the constraint that the destination position be empty is removed, then the resulting problem allows any tile to move along the grid regardless of where the empty position is. The number of moves required to solve this simplified problem is equal to the Manhattan distance.

If both constraints are removed, the resulting problem allows any tile to move directly to its goal position in one move. The number of moves needed to solve this problem is the number of tiles that are out of place. This heuristic estimator for the original problem is even cheaper to compute than Manhattan distance, but also less accurate.

If only the constraint that the two positions be adjacent is removed, the resulting problem allows one to move any tile into the empty position, adjacent or not. The number of moves required to solve this problem is the number of times the empty position must be swapped with another tile to solve the problem, which is another heuristic estimate for the original problem. Although it is not as obvious how to calculate this value, it can be done in time proportional to the number of tiles.

As another example, the airline distance heuristic for the road navigation problem can be derived by removing the constraint that travel must be along the roads. The exact solution to this simplified problem, which can be thought of as helicopter navigation, is just the airline distance estimator for the original problem. The minimum spanning tree heuristic for the traveling salesman problem is derived by removing the constraint that the graph connecting all the cities be a simple path and allowing free jumps back to previously visited cities.

Because the relaxed problems generated by this approach are strictly easier than the original problems, the optimal solutions to the relaxed problems can be no more expensive than the solution to the original problem. One way of seeing this is that any solution to the original problem is also a solution to the relaxed problem. Thus any heuristics generated by this approach are guaranteed to be lower bounds on the cost of solutions to the original problem. Therefore, algorithms such as A* using these heuristics will find optimal solutions.

One difficulty in completely automating this approach to heuristic generation is in finding efficient algorithms to compute the exact solutions to the simplified problems. If brute-force search is used to solve the simplified problems, then calculating the heuristic values becomes too expensive to be of any use (Valtorta, 1981). Another difficulty is in choosing the right representation of the original problem. The current state of the art in automatic heuristic generation based on this approach is described in Mostow and Prieditis (1989).

Two-Player Games

While a heuristic evaluation function for a single-agent problem is normally an estimate of the distance to the goal, the exact meaning of a heuristic function for a two-player game is not as precise. One approach to providing a precise definition is described in Abramson and Korf (1987). Generally speaking, however, it is a function from a game situation to a number that measures the strength of the position for one player relative to the other. Large positive values reflect good positions for one player, called Max, whereas large negative values indicate strong positions for the opponent, referred to as Min. Max always moves to positions that maximize the heuristic evaluation function, while Min moves to positions that minimize it (see MINIMAX PROCEDURE).

For example, a simple evaluation function for the game of chess is the weighted sum of Max's pieces minus the weighted sum of Min's pieces. The weights reflect the different utilities of the pieces, such as: queen-9, rook-5, bishop-3, knight-3, and pawn-1. Note that the goal of chess, checkmate, is not to maximize material, but material represents only an approximate goal in the game, the status of which can be efficiently computed. Even if the object of the game was to maximize material, as in the game of Othello, it is not necessarily true that maximizing material in the short term is the best way to maximize it over the long run. A more accurate evaluation function for chess would include additional components such as center control, pawn structure, and mobility.

A technique used to increase the accuracy of a heuristic evaluation function, at the cost of increased computation, is called look-ahead search. The basic idea is that instead of directly evaluating the successors of the current position and picking the best, a more accurate evaluation can be obtained by searching forward several moves, evaluating the positions at that level, and then backing up the values to the successors of the current position by the minimax algorithm. The minimax algorithm computes the value of a position where Min is to move as the minimum of the values of its successors, and the value of a position where Max is to move as the maximum of the values of its successors. For most games, minimax look-ahead search improves the accuracy of the evaluation with increasing search depth. Because improved accuracy results in better quality play, look-ahead provides a nearly continuous trade-off between computation cost and quality of play. In practice, programs search as far ahead as possible given the computational resources available and the amount of time allowed between moves. Look-ahead search can also be used to improve the accuracy of single-agent evaluation functions (Korf, 1990) (see SEARCH).

A Unified View of Evaluation Functions

There is a consistent interpretation of heuristic evaluation functions in both single-agent problems and two-player games (Christensen and Korf, 1986). In both cases, an ideal evaluation function returns the outcome of the search when applied to a goal state, and is invariant over an optimal move from any given state. The outcome of a single-agent search is the cost of the solution path, whereas the outcome of a game search is win, lose, or draw, with respect to one player. Taken together, these two properties ensure a function that is a perfect predictor of the outcome of pursuing the best path from any state in the problem space. Therefore, a heuristic search algorithm using such a function will always make optimal moves. Any successful evaluation function should approximate these properties to some extent.

In a single-agent problem, A^* defines the evaluation function to be $f(n) = g(n) + h(n)$, where $g(n)$ is the distance from the initial state to node n and $h(n)$ is an estimate of the distance from node n to a goal. When f is applied to a goal state, the h term is zero, the g term represents the cost of the path from the initial state, and hence f returns the outcome of the search. If h is a perfect estimator, then an optimal move increases g by the cost of the move and decreases h by the same value. Thus the value of f remains invariant along an optimal path. A good evaluation function for a single-agent problem should determine the outcome of the search and be relatively invariant over optimal moves.

In a two-person game, when the heuristic evaluation function is applied to a state where the game is over, the function must return which player won. This is often added as a special case to an evaluation function, returning positive and negative infinity for winning positions for Max and Min, respectively. When applied to a nongoal state, the function should return a value that predicts what the ultimate outcome of the game will be. To the extent that the evaluation is an accurate predictor, its value should not change as the best moves are made. Thus a good evaluation function should be relatively invariant over the actual sequence of moves made in the game.

Learning Evaluation Functions

The idea that heuristic evaluation functions should remain invariant over optimal moves can be used to automatically learn evaluation functions. The idea is to search the space of evaluation functions for one that has this invariance property. This is done by computing the difference between static evaluations of positions and the values returned by look-ahead, and modifying the evaluation function to reduce this difference. This idea was originally used by Samuel (1963) in a pioneering program that automatically learned a very powerful evaluation function for checkers based on a large number of different factors (see CHECKERS-PLAYING PROGRAMS).

A closely related technique used linear regression to automatically learn a set of relative weights for chess pieces in a purely material evaluation function (Christensen and Korf, 1986). Each board position gives rise to an equation where the left-hand side is the static value of the function applied to the given position, and the right-hand side is the backed up value of the function resulting from minimax search. In an ideal evaluation function, these two values would indeed be equal. By generating a large number of such equations, one from each board position, linear regression can be used to find the set of weights that provide the best approximation to an invariant evaluation function. Iterating this entire process over successive approximations of the heuristic function produced a converging sequence of weights for the pieces.

HEURISTICS IN GENERAL

Although most work on heuristics has focused on numerical evaluation functions, Lenat (1982) has studied the nature of heuristics in the more general context of heuristic production rules for determining what action to apply in a given situation. A production rule is composed of a left-hand side that describes the situations in which the rule is applicable and a right-hand side that specifies the action of the rule. Consider the function, Appropriateness(Action, Situation), which returns some measure of the appropriateness of taking a particular action in a particular situation. Lenat's claim is that heuristics derive their power from the fact that this function is usually continuous in both arguments.

Continuity in the situation argument means that if a particular action is appropriate in a particular situation, then the same action is likely to be appropriate in a similar situation. Continuity in the action argument means that if a particular action is appropriate in a particular situation, then a similar action is also likely to be appropriate in the same situation.

Furthermore, this appropriateness function is time invariant, which amounts to continuity in a third variable, time. In other words, if a particular action is appropriate in a particular situation, then that same action will be appropriate in that same situation at a later time.

The notion of continuity of appropriateness over actions and situations was used to automatically learn heuristic production rules. In Eurisko (qv) (Lenat, 1982), both the situation and action sides of a rule are described using a large number of relatively independent features or parameters. Given a useful heuristic, Eurisko generates new heuristics by making small modifications to the individual features or to parameters in the situation or action sides of the given heuristic. The continuity property suggests that a large number of heuristics derived in this way will be useful as well.

BIBLIOGRAPHY

B. Abramson and R. E. Korf, "A Model of Two-Player Evaluation Functions," in *Proceedings of the Sixth National Conference on Artificial Intelligence*, Seattle, Wash., AAAI, Menlo Park, Calif., 1987, pp. 90–94.

J. Christensen and R. E. Korf, "A Unified Theory of Heuristic Evaluation Functions and Its Application to Learning," in *Proceedings of the Fifth National Conference on Artificial Intelligence*, Philadelphia, Pa., AAAI, Menlo Park, Calif., 1986, pp. 148–152.

R. E. Korf, "Real-Time Heuristic Search," *Artif. Intell.* 42(2–3), 189–211 (Mar. 1990).

D. B. Lenat, "The Nature of Heuristics," *Artif. Intell.* 19(2), 189–249 (Oct. 1982).

J. Mostow and A. Prieditis, "Discovering Admissible Heuristics by Abstracting and Optimizing: A Transformational Approach," in *Proceedings of the Eleventh IJCAI*, Detroit, Mich., Morgan-Kaufmann, San Mateo, Calif., 1989, pp. 701–707.

J. Pearl, *Heuristics*, Addison-Wesley Publishing Co., Inc., Reading, Mass., 1984.

A. L. Samuel, "Some Studies in Machine Learning Using the Game of Checkers," in E. Feigenbaum and J. Feldman, eds., *Computers and Thought*, McGraw-Hill Book Co., Inc., N.Y., 1963.

M. Valtorta, "A Result on the Computational Complexity of Heuristic Estimates for the A^* Algorithm," Duke University, Durham, N.C., 1981.

RICHARD E. KORF
University of California,
Los Angeles

This work was supported in part by NSF Grant IRI-8801939, by an NSF Presidential Young Investigator Award, and by a grant from Rockwell International. I would like to thank Judea Pearl for his comments on an earlier draft of this paper.

HIGHER-ORDER LOGIC. See LOGIC, HIGHER-ORDER.

HORIZON EFFECT

Two-person, zero-sum, strictly competitive games such as chess, checkers, and Othello can be played quite skillfully by a computer. The methodology most commonly used today dates back to a seminal paper by Shannon (1950). A state space representation is employed in which specific piece configurations represent discrete states, and the moves that are legal from these positions represent the permissible operators. A look-ahead game tree is developed by generating all of the positions that could be produced by every possible move sequence for the two players. Since it would take literally millions of years to examine all possible lines of play until each reached a terminal state (win, lose, or draw), existing game programs search only a few moves ahead (usually three to six) and then artificially declare the position as "terminal" and make a heuristic evaluation of whether it is good for the player on the move. The values assigned to these end points are then "backed up" to the initial position by using a minimax strategy (Frey, 1983). The backed-up value for each of the potential moves at the initial position determines which is the best.

TERMINAL POSITIONS

Positions that are declared terminal may be, in fact, very turbulent. For example, in chess, a so-called terminal position might be one that is in the middle of a queen exchange. The heuristic evaluation calculated for such a position will be inaccurate because the queen discrepancy will be corrected on the next move. This common problem has been addressed routinely in chess by developing a quiescence function that assesses the relative material threats for each side and adjusts the evaluation function accordingly. Sometimes this is done by direct calculation and sometimes by a minature look-ahead search from each terminal position examining only capturing moves and a subset of checking moves. This approach is usually reasonably accurate with respect to material considerations but is often blind to positional factors, which may be in a turbulent state. An example of positional turbulence is a piece en route to an important location where it will exert a commanding presence. Despite its attractive destination, its current position may appear to be weak or even dangerous. Other dynamic positional factors include a trapped piece, a pawn in a crucial level role, and a pawn aspiring for promotion. Current quiescence functions often misevaluate these positions.

Berliner (1973) provided the name horizon effect to this class of problems because the arbitrary search termination rule caused the program to act as if anything that was not detectable at evaluation time did not exist. Berliner defined two different versions of this phenomena, a negative-horizon effect and a positive-horizon effect. The negative-horizon effect involves a form of self-delusion in which the program discovers a series of forcing moves that push an inevitable unpleasant consequence beyond the search horizon. The program manages to convince itself the impending disaster has gone away when in fact it is still lurking just beyond the search horizon. In essence, the negative-horizon effect is an unsuccessful attempt to avert an unpleasant outcome. The positive-horizon effect is a different form of self-delusion. In this effect the program attempts to accomplish a desired consequence within the search horizon even when the outcome would be much better if postponed a few moves. In Berliner's words the program "prematurely grabs at a consequence that can be imposed on an opponent later in a more effective form." Both of these effects are based on improper quiescence, and usually this has to do with the evaluation of positional factors.

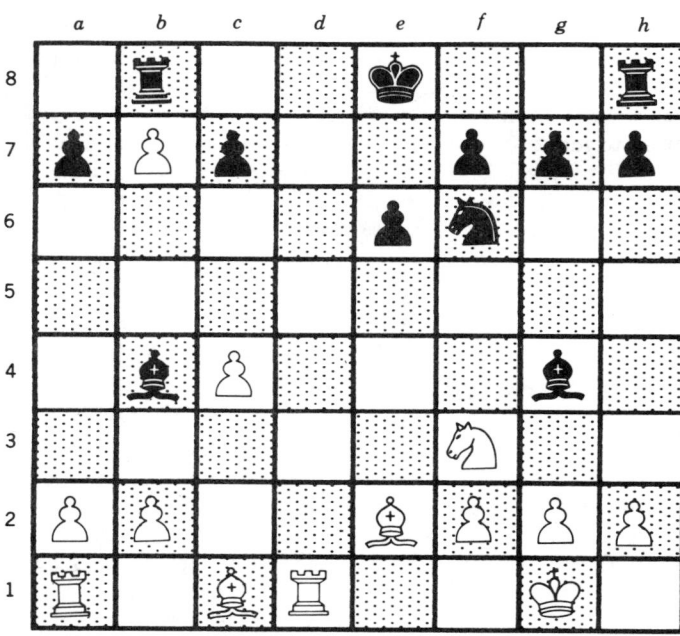

Figure 1.

NEGATIVE-HORIZON EFFECT

An excellent example of the negative-horizon effect occurred in a computer chess match (Mittman, 1983) at the sixth North American computer chess championship (Minneapolis, 1975) between programs from Northwestern University and the University of Waterloo. Figure 1 depicts the game position after black's twelfth move, Ra8 to b8, attacking the advanced white pawn at b7. This position resulted from an early exchange of queens and minor

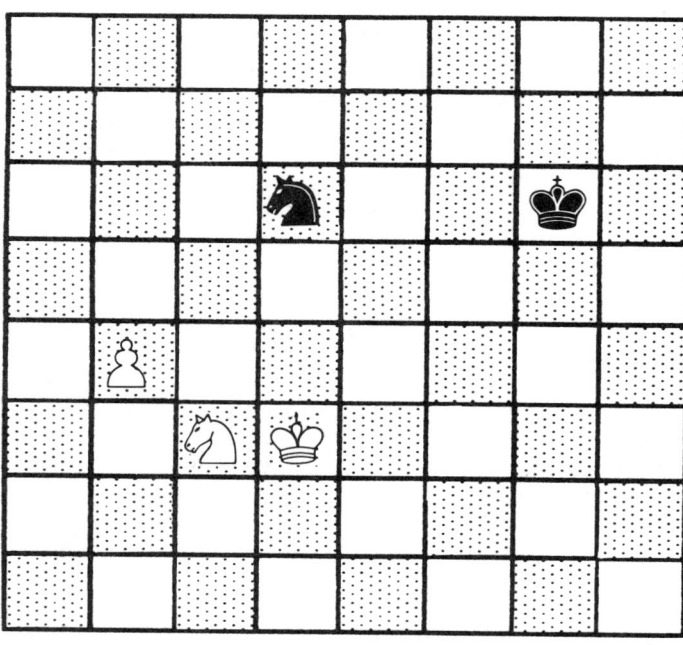

Figure 2.

pieces. At this juncture, white is destined to lose the advanced pawn, which will even up the material but leave white with a slight positional advantage (its king is castled and its rook dominates the queen file). The Northwestern program placed a high value on the passed pawn on the seventh rank. Instead of accepting the inevitable loss of the pawn, white devised a plan to "save" it by making liberal use of the negative-horizon effect. In its look-ahead search white discovered that it could advance pawns on the rook file and knight file, which would force black to retreat the bishops. The tempos used in these pawn thrusts were sufficient to push the eventual capture of the white pawn at b7 over the search horizon. White continued the actual game by playing 13. a3, forcing the black bishop at b4 to retreat. White followed with 14. h3, forcing the black bishop at g4 to retreat. White's next move continued the same theme, 15. g4, forcing the black bishop to move again and substantially weakening white's defensive position. From the computer's perspective these attacking pawn moves were effective because each one saved the pawn at b7. In reality, these moves, especially 15. g4, weakened white's position.

POSITIVE-HORIZON EFFECT

The positive-horizon effect can be demonstrated with the position presented in Figure 2 with white to move. In this situation white's pawn advantage provides excellent winning chances. For most programs the look-ahead search will not be sufficiently deep to "see" the pawn promotion. Therefore, the correct move choice must be based on heuristic factors such as moving the pawn closer to the eighth rank. With a typical shallow search, white is likely to push the pawn immediately, ignoring the black knight's threat to capture because white can recapture. Heuristic evaluation functions usually consider a knight to be worth as much as three pawns, and therefore, the program would assume that black would not initiate such a foolish exchange. In reality, the exchange of the knight for the pawn is good for black since it transforms a losing situation into a draw. This conclusion is based on the knowledge that white can only win by promoting the pawn, and thus the pawn in this situation is much more valuable than the knight. Programs that know about the future only in terms of their immediate look-ahead search underestimate the value of the pawn because its "moment in the sun" lies beyond their search horizon. Most chess programs would throw away the win by giving their opponent the opportunity to exchange the knight for the pawn. This positive-horizon effect differs from the negative-horizon effect in that it results from an inability to understand long-range consequences and is not influenced dramatically by moving the search horizon one or two plies deeper (see also COMPUTER CHESS AND SEARCH).

BIBLIOGRAPHY

H. J. Berliner, "Some Necessary Conditions for a Master Chess Program," *Proceedings of the Third International Joint Con-*

ference on Artificial Intelligence, Stanford, Calif., 1973, pp. 77–85.

P. W. Frey, "An Introduction to Computer Chess," in P. W. Frey, ed., *Chess Skill in Man and Machine*, Springer-Verlag, New York, 1983, pp. 54–81.

B. Mittman, "A Brief History of the Computer Chess Tournaments: 1970–1975," in P. W. Frey, ed., *Chess Skill in Man and Machine*, Springer-Verlag, New York, 1983, pp. 27–28.

C. E. Shannon, "Programming a Computer to Play Chess," *Philos. Mag.* **41**, 256–275 (1950).

P. W. Frey
Northwestern University

HORN CLAUSES. See Logic programming.

HOUGH TRANSFORMS

The Hough transform (HT) denotes any of several parameter estimation strategies based on histogram analysis, in which histogram peaks (modes) in a transform space identify phenomena of interest in an input feature space. The name originates from a 1962 invention for locating lines in bubble chamber photographs (Hough, 1962). Since then, the idea has become widespread and of considerable engineering importance. In computer vision, it was first used to identify parameterized curves (eg, conics) in images (Duda and Hart, 1972). HT has been generalized to detect nonparametric shapes of arbitrary scale and rotation (Ballard, 1981; Ballard and Brown, 1982). The HT process has been postulated to occur in abstract feature spaces during human perception (Barlow, 1981) and is a widely applicable form of evidence combination. A good survey is Illingworth and Kittler (1988).

DESCRIPTION

In the HT, features of phenomena (eg, shape features) in an input space produce votes for phenomena in a parameterized transform space of causes or explanations (eg, shape location) with which the features are compatible. Explanations garnering the most votes are those that account for the most features. For example, points in (x, y) input space may lie on (be explained by) a line described in parameter space by the two parameters m and b in the

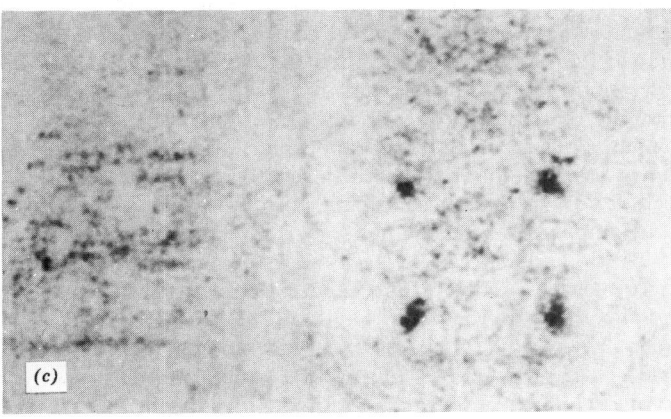

Figure 1. Circle detection. An input grayscale image (*a*) is processed with an edge detector, yielding an orientation at each point. The edge strength, or contrast, is shown in (*b*). For each of several radii R_i there is an accumulator array A_i the same size as the image. Each edge element votes into each A_i for two possible centers R_i away from the edge in both directions orthogonal to it. The accumulator for one of the larger radii is shown in (*c*). Peaks in the three-dimensional (x, y, R) accumulator are interpreted as circles and displayed in (*d*).

equation $y = mx + b$. A point in input (x, y) space presumed to lie on a line produces a locus of votes in parameter space for all lines on which it could lie. (This locus happens to be in a straight line in (m, b) space.) The vote locus of a second point intersects the first (adds to it) only at the (m, b) parameters of the single (infinite) line containing both feature points. All other feature points colinear with the first two contribute votes to this (m, b), and no other points do. If the input space is ideal edge elements—$(x, y,$ orientation) triples describing image brightness discontinuities—each edge element casts a single vote for the one line passing through it at the correct orientation. After voting, peaks (modes) in the parameter space correspond to image lines through the greatest number of lined-up edge elements regardless of their sparseness or other confusing edges in the image. Multiple lines in the input do not interfere but give multimodal results in parameter space. Figure 1 shows circle detection with edge element input. An HT implementation of general shape matching is formally equivalent to template matching (matched filtering). With HT, the computational effort (voting) grows with the number of matchable features in the input, not the size of the input array.

PRACTICAL ISSUES

HT is a form of mode-based parameter estimation that is complementary to mean-based (such as least-squared error) techniques. Least-squared error methods may be preferable if all the data originate from a single phenomenon, there are no "outlier" points, and data are corrupted by zero-mean noise processes. Mode-based estimation is indicated if there are several instances of the phenomenon of interest in the input or if the data are incomplete or immersed in clutter or outliers. Parametric HT finds parameters that may describe infinite objects. Line detection is a good example: Further processing is needed to find end points of line segments. Noise of several varieties can affect HT (Brown, 1983) and can be combated by standard techniques. Uncertainty in any feature parameter (eg, edge orientation) may be accommodated either by using a set of votes spanning the uncertainty range or by smoothing the accumulator array before peak finding.

Votes may be weighted according to the strength of the feature producing them. Votes are usually collected in discrete versions of parameter space implemented as arrays. Parameter spaces involving three-dimensional directions are often represented with more complex data structures, such as spheres or hyperspheres. Combinations of elementary features may be taken to generate votes (eg, consider points pairwise to generate votes for straight lines). High-resolution or high-dimensionality arrays can have large memory requirements. A solution is to implement the accumulator as a hash table. If each feature detector is prewired to its associated parameters, in transform space the "voting" happens in parallel instantaneously and can be considered as excitation in a network (Ballard and co-workers, 1983).

In two-dimensional shape detection the parameter space is usually (x, y, θ, s), for location, orientation, and

scale. A high-dimensional parameter space may sometimes (with ingenuity) be decomposed into a sequence of lower dimensional spaces, making voting less expensive. Parameters in accumulator space must be independent if a mode is to correspond to a unique tuple of parameters. The global nature of the HT, accumulating evidence from the entire input space, can be a drawback for some applications. One remedy is to decompose the input space into a set of regions small enough to enforce the desired locality. The histogram generation and analysis needed for HT admit parallel solutions.

BIBLIOGRAPHY

D. H. Ballard, "Generalizing the Hough Transform to Detect Arbitrary Shapes," *Patt. Recog.* **13**(2), 111–122 (1981).

D. H. Ballard and C. M. Brown, *Computer Vision*, Prentice-Hall, Englewood Cliffs, N.J., 1982.

D. H. Ballard, G. E. Hinton, and T. J. Sejnowski, "Parallel Visual Computation," *Nature* **306**(5938), 21–26 (November 3, 1983).

H. B. Barlow, "Critical Limiting Factors in the Design of the Eye and Visual Cortex," *Proc. R. Soc. London Ser. B* **212**(1), 1–34 (1981).

C. M. Brown, "Inherent Bias and Noise in the Hough Transform," *IEEE Trans. Patt. Anal. Mach. Intell.* **PAMI-5**, 493–505 (September 1983).

R. O. Duda and P. E. Hart, "Use of the Hough Transform to Detect Lines and Curves in Pictures," *CACM* **15**, 11–15 (1972).

P. V. C. Hough, *Method and Means for Recognizing Complex Patterns*, U.S. Pat. 3,069,654 (Dec. 18, 1962).

J. Illingworth and J. Kittler, "A Survey of the Hough Transform," *Comput. Vision, Graphics and Image Proc.* **44**, 87–116 (1988).

C. BROWN
University of Rochester

HUMAN–COMPUTER INTERACTION

The history of advances in the study and techniques of human–computer interaction has been intertwined with that of AI; each has contributed to the other. At times research in AI has developed techniques to improve user–computer communication, and at other times, the unique demands placed on the users and programmers of AI systems have led them to be the first to apply innovative techniques for human–computer communication. Because AI systems are often designed to perform complicated and poorly understood tasks, they must interact with their users more intimately than other systems and in more complex, less stereotyped ways. AI programs are also among the most complicated programs written, least amenable to being specified clearly in advance, and most unpredictable. Hence their programmers have been the first to need such advances as powerful interactive debuggers, editors, programming tools, and environments, and they have developed many of them.

This article examines the reciprocal connections between the study of human–computer interaction or human factors and AI from both directions:

- Developments in the study of the human factors of human–computer interaction that are helpful in designing user interfaces for complex AI systems.
- Specific fields of AI applicable in constructing human–computer interfaces, such as speech recognition (some of these fields are covered in more detail elsewhere and are mentioned only briefly here).

Finally, this article indicates how the two fields of study overlap in their concerns and how insights into cognitive psychology from both fields could help to build more intelligent, natural user interfaces in the future.

DESIGNING HUMAN–COMPUTER INTERFACES

Results from the study of human factors and user psychology are applicable to the design of better user interfaces for AI and other complex systems. AI systems stretch the limits of what has been or can be done with a computer and thus often generate new human–computer communication problems rather than alleviating them. The methods of human factors (task analysis, understanding of interaction techniques and cognitive factors, and empirical testing of alternatives with users) are thus especially applicable to designers of AI systems.

Design of a human–computer interface begins with task analysis, an understanding of the user's underlying tasks and the problem domain. It is desirable that the user–computer interface be designed in terms of the user's terminology and conception of his or her job, rather than the programmer's. A good understanding of the cognitive and behavioral characteristics of people in general as well as the particular user population is thus important, as is knowledge of the nature of the user's work. The task to be performed can then be divided and portions assigned to the user or machine, based on knowledge of the capabilities and limitations of each. AI often expands the capabilities of the computer side but, for all but fully autonomous systems, the user is likely to play some role in performing or guiding the task and hence will have to interact with the machine.

Styles of Human–Computer Interfaces

A style of user interface appropriate to the task should be selected. The principal classes of user interfaces currently in use are command languages, menus, natural language, and direct manipulation. Command language user interfaces use artificial languages, much like programming languages. They are concise and unambiguous, but are often more difficult for a novice to learn and remember. However, because they usually permit a user to combine their constructs in new and complex ways, they can be more powerful for advanced users. They are also most amenable to programming, that is, writing programs or scripts of user input commands.

Menu-based user interfaces explicitly present the options available to a user at each point in a dialogue. Thus they require only that the user be able to recognize the desired entry from a list rather than recall it, placing a smaller load on long-term memory. They are highly suitable for novice users. A principal disadvantage is that they can be annoying for experienced users who already know the choices they want to make and do not need to see them listed. Well-designed menu systems, however, can provide bypasses for expert users. Menus are also difficult to apply to shallow languages, which have large numbers of choices at a few points, because the option display becomes too big.

Natural language user interfaces are considered in more detail below. Their principal benefit is, of course, that the user already knows the language. However, given the state of the art, such an interface must be restricted to some subset of natural language, and the subset must be chosen carefully, both in vocabulary and range of syntactic constructs. Such systems often behave poorly when the user veers even slightly outside the subset. Because they begin by presenting the illusion that the computer really can "speak English," the systems can trap or frustrate novice users. For this reason, the techniques of human factors engineering can help. A human factors study of the task and the terms and constructs people normally use to describe it can be used to restrict the subset of natural language in an appropriate way, based on empirical observation (Michaelis and co-workers, 1982). Human factors study can also identify tasks for which natural language input is good or bad. Although future research in natural language offers the hope of human–computer communication that is so natural it is "just like talking to a person," such conversation may not always be the most effective way of commanding a machine (Small and Weldon, 1983). It is often more verbose and less precise than computer languages. In some settings, people have evolved terse, highly formatted languages, similar to computer languages, for communicating with other people. For a frequent user, the effort of learning such an artificial language is outweighed by its conciseness and precision, and it is often preferable to natural language.

In a graphical or direct manipulation style of user interface, a set of objects is presented on a screen, and the user has a repertoire of manipulations that can be performed on any of them (Shneiderman, 1983). This means that the user has no command language to remember beyond the standard set of manipulations, few cognitive changes of mode, and a reminder of the available objects and their states shown continuously on the display (Hutchins and co-workers, 1986). Some examples of this approach include spreadsheets, the Xerox Star desktop and its descendants (Johnson and co-workers, 1989), STEAMER (Hollan and co-workers, 1984), and, of course, many video games. The key difficulty in designing such interfaces is to find suitable manipulable graphical representations or visual metaphors for the objects in the problem domain. The paper spreadsheet, desk, and filing cabinet (Star) and engine control panel (STEAMER) were fortunate choices. One of the principal drawbacks of direct manipulation is that it is often difficult to create scripts or parameterized programs in such an inherently dynamic and ephemeral language.

Recent work has carried the user's illusion of manipulating real objects still further. By coupling the motion of the user's head to changes in the images presented on a head-mounted display, the illusion of being surrounded by a world of computer-generated images, or a virtual reality, is created. Hand-mounted sensors allow the user to interact with these images as if they were real objects located in the surrounding space (Foley, 1987).

Various modalities of human–computer communication may also be employed as appropriate in designing a user interface. Keyboards, mice, and text displays are common, but some more modern modalities for output include graphics, windows, icons, active value displays, manipulable objects, hypertext and hypermedia, head-coupled displays, speech, and nonspeech audio. Techniques for input include keys that can be dynamically labeled, speech, 3-D pointing, hand gesture, and visual line of gaze. Each must be matched to the tasks for which it is used. Finally, research in the area of computer-supported cooperative work has extended the notion of a single-user–computer interface to an interface that supports the collaboration of a group of users (Malone and co-workers, 1987).

Design Techniques and Guidelines

A variety of tools, techniques, and guidelines from human factors engineering can be brought to bear on the design of the user interface (Shneiderman, 1987; Gaines and Shaw, 1983). One important principle is that of empirical measurement. Decisions about user interface design should be based on observations of users, rather than a designer's or programmer's notions. Careful use of empirical measurement also encourages the establishment of precise performance objectives and metrics early in the development of a system. Alternative designs can then be tested against them empirically as the work progresses (Gould and co-workers, 1983; Landauer and co-workers, 1983; Ledgard, 1986).

In addition to specific usability testing of proposed interfaces, some general principles have been derived from laboratory experiments. For example, a user interface should be consistent; similar rules should apply for interpreting commands when the system is in what appears to the user to be a similar state. Command names, order of arguments, and the like should be as uniform as possible, and commands should generally be available in all states in which they would be plausible. The system should also be predictable; it should not seem erratic. A small difference in an input command should not result in a big difference in the effect (or time delay) of the response. Unpredictability makes the user anxious, continually afraid of making an irrevocable mistake. A general undo capability, which lets the user undo any command after it has been executed is one way to allay this anxiety, although a fully general capability can be difficult to implement. More generally, a system should exhibit causality, the users should be able to perceive that the activity of the system is caused directly by their actions, rather than proceeding seemingly at random. The state of the system should be visible to the user at all times, perhaps by a distinctive prompt or in a reserved portion of the screen (or, in a direct manipulation system, some state information is implicit in the location of the cursor itself).

Systems can be easy to learn or easy to use, but the two are different, sometimes conflicting goals. Designs suitable for novice users may interfere with expert users; features such as help facilities or command menus should be optional for experienced users. A good command language should consist of a few simple primitives (so as not to tax long-term memory) plus the ability to combine them in many ways (to create a wide variety of constructs as needed, without having to commit all of them to long-term memory). The user interface should also exploit nonsymbolic forms of memory. For example, it can attach meaning to the spatial position on a display screen (certain types of message always appear in certain positions) or to icons, typefaces, colors, or formats.

One way to help design a user interface is to consider the dialogue at several distinct levels of abstraction and develop a design for each. This simplifies the designer's task because it can be divided it into several smaller problems. The design of a human–computer dialogue can be divided into the semantic, syntactic, and lexical levels (Foley and co-workers, 1990). The semantic level describes the functions performed by the system. This corresponds to a description of the functional requirements of the system, but does not address how the user will invoke the functions. The syntactic level describes the sequences of inputs and outputs necessary to invoke the functions described. The lexical level determines how the inputs and outputs are actually formed from primitive hardware operations. With appropriate programming techniques, these aspects of the dialogue can be designed and programmed entirely separately (Jacob, 1985).

Another approach that can help the designer and software engineer is the user interface management system (UIMS). A UIMS is a separate software component that conducts all interactions with the user; it is separate from the application program that performs the underlying task. It is analogous to a database management system in that it separates a function used by many applications and moves it to a shared subsystem. It removes the problem of programming the user interface from each individual application and permits some of the effort of designing tools for human–computer interaction to be amortized over many applications and shared by them. It also encourages consistent look and feel in user interfaces to different systems, because they share the user interface component. Conversely, it permits dialogue independence, where changes can be made to the dialogue design without affecting the application code (Hartson and Hix, 1989). It is also useful to have a method for specifying user interfaces precisely, so that the interface designer can describe and study a variety of possible user interfaces before building one (Reisner, 1981; Jacob, 1983).

AI APPLICATIONS TO HUMAN–COMPUTER INTERACTION

Natural Language

Among those areas of AI research useful in improving human–computer interaction, the most obvious is the study of natural language (qv). Research into how natural language is understood can permit human–computer dialogues to be conducted in such language (although this is not an unalloyed benefit, as discussed above). The study of natural language input has its roots in early work in machine translation and, later, in query–answering systems. Systems such as ELIZA (qv), SHRDLU (qv), and BASEBALL (qv) demonstrated that computers could conduct plausible natural language dialogues in restricted domains. But proceeding from that point to a general ability to accept a wide range of natural language has proven exceedingly difficult.

A natural language processing system generally contains three parts: a dictionary or lexicon of the words it accepts, a parser based on a grammar that describes the structures of the sentences it accepts, and a semantic interpreter, which assigns interpretations to or performs actions in response to the input. Syntax is typically represented in the parser by a set of productions or an augmented transition network (qv). Some systems combine the parser and semantic interpreter into a semantic grammar, putting the semantic rules or actions directly into the syntax grammar. They use a specialized grammar designed for a particular domain of discourse and subset of the language (Hendrix and co-workers, 1978). This approach provides an effective way to build systems that accept a relatively constrained subset of natural language in a particular domain, but it is difficult to expand to larger, more general areas of the language. The alternative, use of a purely syntactic grammar and leaving the semantics in a separate component, is helpful for building a system with broad coverage, but the syntactic component will often identify a wide range of possible parses of a sentence, which can only be narrowed by the semantic. Thus such systems tend to perform searches with considerable backtracking. Still other alternative approaches, such as systems driven by semantically based scripts rather than syntax (Schank and Abelson, 1977) and menu-based natural language systems (Tennant and co-workers, 1983), have also been used successfully. Finally, to complete a dialogue in natural language, it is necessary to generate sentences from internally stored information, and approaches that go beyond simply storing canned responses have been studied (Mann, 1983).

Given the present state of the art, it is possible to construct a practical natural language system for a specified subset of a language in some narrow, well-defined domain. Such a system requires that a considerable amount of knowledge about that domain be built into the lexicon, grammar, and semantic interpreter, and thus much effort that cannot be reused in another natural language system. Systems that can handle a broad range of language on many topics remain a research goal.

Speech

Another important area of AI research is the processing of speech: both accepting as input and generating as output. Speech is an attractive input medium because people already know how to use it, they can generally speak faster than they can write or type, and it leaves their hands free for other tasks. Recognition of isolated words is a relatively well-understood problem, and commercial systems are available for this task. Accepting continuous speech

has proven significantly less tractable, largely because normal speakers do not pause between words. It is generally not possible to divide a speech input signal into words simply through signal processing; it requires knowledge of the meaning and context of the utterance. Thus speech understanding (qv) involves both a signal processing or pattern recognition component, which identifies words or other parts of the input signal, and a semantic component, which assigns meanings to the utterance. For systems that go beyond isolated words, there must be feedback between the two, and to function effectively, the latter component requires considerable knowledge about the underlying language and the domain of the discourse. Thus work in continuous speech input is intimately connected to the study of natural language and knowledge representation.

Much work on speech understanding was performed under the aegis of the ARPA Speech Understanding Research Program between 1971 and 1976. The principal projects, which included HEARSAY (qv), HARPY (qv), and HWIM (qv), all emphasized the problems of representation and use of knowledge about the spoken language, and each used different approaches to them. More recent work has attacked the problem on two fronts: some emphasizing better domain knowledge (Young and co-workers, 1989) and others emphasizing improvements to the early processing stages (signal processing and syntactic analysis). Neural network (qv) approaches have also begun to be applied to this problem. Nevertheless, robust, production-quality continuous speech input continues to be an elusive goal.

The area of speech generation is also important, but the basic capability is sufficiently well understood and widely available that it is no longer considered a topic in AI. While straightforward generation of individual words from text is not difficult, current research focuses on obtaining natural-sounding intonation and expression for whole phrases. Another related area of recent interest is the use of sounds other than speech to provide an additional communication channel in a user–computer dialogue (Gaver, 1986).

Pattern Recognition

Computer vision (qv) or pattern recognition, appropriately applied, is also relevant to human–computer interaction, as it can permit computer input in the form of gestures much as people use in communicating with one another. Examples of how this approach might be used have been demonstrated (Schmandt and Hulteen, 1982; Sturman and co-workers, 1989), and human factors studies have investigated its potential usefulness (Gould and Salaun, 1987), but more sophisticated AI-based gesture recognition methods have yet to be applied.

Intelligent User Interfaces and Computer-Aided Instruction

The above has examined some specific techniques or modalities of human–computer interaction derived from AI research. What can be said of a human–computer interface that begins to exhibit more generally intelligent behavior, beyond simply competence in one or more of the specific interaction media discussed? An intelligent human communication partner can

- Accept and compensate for many types of incorrect or incomplete input.
- Realize when the conversational partner has misperceived something and provide explanations to rectify the underlying misconception.
- Infer the underlying goals in a statement or question, even where they are at odds with those stated.
- Follow the changing focus of a conversation.
- Maintain and update an estimate of the partner's interests, knowledge, and understanding.
- Construct replies that take into account that current estimate.

There is research in AI that attempts to understand and duplicate some of these processes, leading to an intelligent interface, that is, a system in which AI is applied to the actual conduct of the dialogue with the user, rather than only to the application domain (Hancock and Chignell, 1989). Much of the research has been conducted in the area of computer-aided instruction (CAI) to build intelligent tutors. Such systems attempt to model a student's (incomplete) understanding of material and present new material or leading questions appropriate to the student's current level of knowledge and ability.

For example, SOPHIE (qv) watches a student troubleshoot electronic equipment, answers questions, and criticizes hypotheses. WEST and WUMPUS both observe students playing computer games and offer suggestions based on inferences about the students' skill made from watching their moves. SCHOLAR (qv) asks its student leading questions when it finds deficiencies in knowledge. MENO-II finds bugs in student programs and identifies the underlying misconception that caused the bug. GUIDON (qv) is built on a rule-based system. By presenting example cases, it attempts to deduce which of the rules in its knowledge base the student already knows and which he or she is ready to learn. It also manages the overall flow of the dialogue with the student, selects topics for study, selects appropriate presentation techniques, maintains context, and allows for unsolicited inputs (Clancey, 1979; Woolf and McDonald, 1984).

Some such work has extended outside traditional CAI. For example, UNIX Consultant (Wilensky and co-workers, 1984) uses these techniques in an intelligent help system. It attempts to infer the user's underlying goals and intentions and provides answers that take this information into account in addition to the specific question asked. Other intelligent help systems volunteer advice when appropriate (Shrager and Finn, 1982; Fischer and co-workers, 1985).

This sort of research into problems, such as modeling a user's information state in a dialogue, inferring user's misconceptions, and constructing appropriate replies, has been concentrated in the area of CAI, but it is applicable to the design of intelligent user interfaces or intelligent dialogues in any area. By combining many of these individual techniques, the notion of an intelligent user interface can be carried somewhat further, to build a user modeling system that can describe and reason about what its user knows and conduct a dialogue with the long-term flow and other desirable properties of dialogues between people. Such a system would maintain and use information about users and their current state of attention and knowledge, the task being performed, and the tools available to perform it (Hayes and co-workers, 1981; Rissland, 1984). For example, when the underlying application program sends information to the user, this user agent can control its presentation based on its model of what the user already knows and is seeking and thereby remove information irrelevant to the current focus.

It is important to remember that such an intelligent user interface is by no means restricted to natural language. Most research on the processes needed to conduct such dialogues has concentrated on natural language, but they apply to any human–computer dialogue conducted in any language. For example, STEAMER (Hollan and co-workers, 1984) demonstrates a dialogue in a rich graphical language, using powerful and natural state-of-the-art input and output modalities. The user's side of the dialogue consists almost entirely of pointing and pressing mouse buttons, and the computer's, of animated pictorial analogues. A dialogue in such a language could also exhibit the intelligent user interface properties discussed here, following focus, inferring goals, and correcting misconceptions.

Adaptation

An intelligent user interface would also exhibit some learning and adaptation to the user. The simplest form such adaptation could take uses explicit input: users enter instructions about the way they want the dialogues to be conducted, and the subsequent dialogues use that information. This is already available in, for example, facilities for defining aliases or command procedures or using profiles. A more sophisticated form of adaptation uses implicit inputs: the computer obtains information about the user without actually asking for it. This can be done in two ways: using information intrinsic to the dialogue or using external information about the user (Rich, 1983). Examples of the former are using information about the user's errors, choice of commands, or use of help features to decide whether the user is an expert or novice; inferring the focus within which a command should be interpreted from the preceding sequence of user commands; and measuring and using the length and distribution of user idle periods. The other possibility is to use implicit measurements obtained from inputs outside the actual dialogue. For example, sensors might try to determine whether the user was actually sitting at the terminal (or had left the room) or what the user was looking at and, from that, the context within which the commands should be interpreted (Bolt, 1982; Jacob, 1990).

Another way to classify adaptation is by time span. Changes such as renaming a command are intended to be long term. Explicit inputs are generally used only for such long-term adaptation, because it is too much trouble to enter them more frequently. Short-term adaptation to changes in the user's state relies on implicit inputs. A system could use the fact that the user is typing faster, making more semantic errors, or positioning a cursor inaccurately to make short-term changes in the pace or nature of the dialogue. Short-term adaptation using implicit inputs is a potentially powerful technique for creating adaptive human–computer dialogues (Edmonds, 1981). However, unless an adaptive interface operates essentially perfectly, it will rapidly begin to confuse and annoy the user, because the result will be a system that seems to change its behavior randomly and inexplicably. Simple-minded systems that try to do what they think the user wants are often annoying when they guess wrong, and experience with them may tarnish the user's view of the potential of more powerful applications of this concept. A far more sophisticated system that nearly always guessed right would be helpful indeed, but remains well beyond the state of the art, at least for nontrivial applications.

Programming Environments

Because of the complexity of AI programs, their programmers have been pioneers in the development and use of innovative human–computer interaction techniques, which are now used in other areas. The development of powerful interactive programming environments was spearheaded by AI programmers developing large LISP programs. They required and developed sophisticated screen-oriented editors, break packages, tracing facilities, and data browsers for LISP programming environments (Weinreb and Moon, 1981; Teitelman, 1978).

Interaction methods, such as overlapping display windows, icons, multiple contexts, use of mice, pop-up menus, and touch screens had their roots in AI programming. Many of these were developed by workers at Xerox PARC in both Interlisp and Smalltalk, in parallel and with considerable interaction between the two. These ideas were spawned and made practical by the availability of powerful graphics-oriented personal workstations in which a considerable fraction of the computing resources in the unit was devoted to the user interface. The combination and effective use of many of these techniques have been demonstrated by a variety of AI systems (Hendler, 1988). Such techniques have moved out of the AI community into all areas of human–computer interaction.

Interface Design

Although interfaces using modern techniques such as direct manipulation are often easier to learn and use than conventional ones, they are considerably more difficult to build, because they are currently typically programmed in a low level, *ad hoc* manner. Appropriate higher level software engineering concepts and abstractions for dealing with these new interaction techniques are needed. Direct-manipulation techniques for the actual design and building of direct-manipulation interfaces are one solution (Cardelli, 1988). Specifying the graphical appearance of the user interface via direct manipulation is relatively straightforward, but describing the dynamic behavior of the dialogue is more difficult. Visual programming languages offer promise in this area (Shu, 1988). A rule-based approach has also been demonstrated for inferring the intended generality of a designer's inputs (Myers, 1988).

AI techniques are now beginning to be applied to the problem of user interface design itself. While a system for automatic generation of good user interfaces is beyond the current state of the art, progress has been made in research into individual aspects of this problem. The most promising area has been in controlling the presentation of graphical information. Given a set of information to be communicated, a knowledge-based program can determine the best graphical representation for communicating the desired content using rules containing knowledge about visual perception and communication as well as information about the user's current knowledge and abilities (MacKinlay, 1986; Seligmann and Feiner, 1989). Automatic generation of a user interface design from a higher level description of the application and its inputs and outputs has been demonstrated (Singh and Green, 1989; Beshers and Feiner, 1989) as have knowledge-based techniques for making transformations between alternative user interface designs for an application (Foley and co-workers, 1988).

ARTIFICIAL INTELLIGENCE AND HUMAN FACTORS: TOWARD NATURAL HUMAN–COMPUTER INTERFACES

The recent histories of research in AI and human factors have been interconnected in many ways. Each has contributed techniques and ideas to the other, and each has found applications in the other. How will these two disciplines cross paths in the future? The answer is in the domain of understanding the user's cognitive processes.

Much work in human factors has been devoted to understanding the mental models and processes by which users learn about, understand, and interact with computer systems. Its purpose is to build systems that are easier to learn and use because they fit these processes more closely. For example, some command languages, text editors, and programming language constructs have been improved by studying and using carefully, but not overloading, the capabilities of human short- and long-term memory in their design (Allen, 1982). Much of AI research, too, is devoted to understanding people's cognitive processes. The results of such study can be a better understanding of how people (specifically, computer system users) process information: perceive data, focus attention, construct knowledge, remember, and make errors. The insights into cognitive psychology developed by research in both fields can be used to make human–computer interfaces more natural, to fit their users better.

The goal of such work is to produce a more intelligent and natural user interface, not specifically natural language, but a naturally flowing dialogue. Such a development will begin with human factors study of good user interface design, using insights from cognitive psychology. Appropriate visual and other metaphors for describing, and proxies for manipulating, the objects and activities of the task at hand must then be chosen. AI techniques can permit the system to obtain, track, and understand information about its user's current conceptions, goals, and mental state well beyond current dialogue systems where most of the context is lost from one query or command to the next. The system will use this information to help interpret users' inputs and permit them to be imprecise, vague, slightly incorrect (eg, typographical errors) or elliptical. This approach, combined with powerful interaction methods such as direct manipulation or virtual reality can produce a highly effective form of human–computer communication.

The research in AI pertinent to human–computer interaction has attempted to discover users' mental models, to build systems that deduce users' goals and misconceptions, and to develop some forms of adaptive or personalizable user interfaces. A collection of powerful interaction modalities has also been developed. The challenge for the future is for research into cognitive psychology in both human factors and AI to combine with new interaction and programming techniques to produce a style of interface between user and computer more closely suited to the human side of the partnership.

BIBLIOGRAPHY

R. B. Allen, "Cognitive Factors in Human Interaction with Computers," in A. Badre and B. Shneiderman, eds., *Directions in Human/Computer Interaction*, Ablex Publishing Co., Norwood, N.J., 1982, pp. 1–26.

C. M. Beshers and S. K. Feiner, "Scope: Automated Generation of Graphical Interfaces," *Proceedings of the ACM SIGGRAPH Symposium on User Interface Software and Technology*, Williamsburg, Va., Addison-Wesley/ACM Press, Reading, Mass., 1989, pp. 76–85.

R. A. Bolt, "Eyes at the Interface," *Proceedings of the ACM Human Factors in Computer Systems Conference*, 1982, pp. 360–362.

L. Cardelli, "Building User Interfaces by Direct Manipulation," *Proceedings of the ACM SIGGRAPH Symposium on User Interface Software*, Banff, Canada, 1988, pp. 152–166.

W. J. Clancey, "Dialogue Management for Rule-Based Tutorials," *Proceedings of the Sixth IJCAI*, Tokyo, Morgan-Kaufmann, San Mateo, Calif., 1979, pp. 155–161.

E. A. Edmonds, "Adaptive Man-Computer Interfaces," in M. J. Coombs and J. L. Alty, eds., *Computing Skills and the User Interface*, Academic Press, Inc., Orlando, Fla., 1981, pp. 389–426.

G. Fischer, A. Lemke, and T. Schwab, "Knowledge-based Help Systems," *Proceedings of the ACM CHI'85 Human Factors in Computing Systems Conference*, 1985, pp. 161–167.

J. D. Foley, "Interfaces for Advanced Computing," *Sci. Am.* **257**(4), 127–135 (1987).

J. D. Foley, C. Gibbs, W. C. Kim, and S. Kovacevic, "A Knowledge Based User Interface Management System," *Proceedings of the ACM CHI'88 Human Factors in Computing Systems Conference*, Addison-Wesley/ACM Press, Reading, Mass., 1988, pp. 67–72.

J. D. Foley, A. van Dam, S. Feiner, and J. Hughes, *Computer Graphics: Principles and Practice*, Addison-Wesley Publishing Co., Inc., Reading, Mass., 1990.

B. R. Gaines and M. L. G. Shaw, "Dialog Engineering," in M. E. Sime and M. J. Coombs, eds., *Designing for Human-Computer Communication*, Academic Press, Inc., Orlando, Fla., 1983, pp. 23–53.

W. W. Gaver, "Auditory Icons: Using Sound in Computer Interfaces," *Human-Computer Interaction* **2**, 167–177 (1986).

J. D. Gould, J. Conte, and T. Hovanyecz, "Composing Letters with a Simulated Listening Typewriter," *Comm. ACM* **26**, 295–308 (1983).

J. D. Gould and J. Salaun, "Behavioral Experiments on Hand-markings," *Proceedings of the ACM CHI+GI'87 Human Factors in Computing Systems Conference*, 1987, pp. 175–181.

P. A. Hancock and M. H. Chignell, *Intelligent Interfaces: Theory, Research, and Design*, North-Holland, Amsterdam, 1989.

H. R. Hartson and D. Hix, "Human-computer Interface Development: Concepts and Systems for its Management," *Comp. Surveys* **21**, 5–92 (1989).

P. Hayes, E. Ball, and R. Reddy, "Breaking the Man-Machine Communication Barrier," *IEEE Comp.* **14**(3), 19–30 (1981).

J. A. Hendler, *Expert Systems: The User Interface*, Ablex Publishing Co., Norwood, N.J., 1988.

G. G. Hendrix, E. Sacerdoti, D. Sagalowicz, and J. Slocum, "Developing a Natural Language Interface to Complex Data," *ACM Trans. Database Syst.* **3**, 105–147 (1978).

J. D. Hollan, E. L. Hutchins, and L. Weitzman, "STEAMER: An Interactive Inspectable Simulation-Based Training System," *AI Magazine* **5**(2), 15–27 (1984).

E. L. Hutchins, J. D. Hollan, and D. A. Norman, "Direct Manipulation Interfaces," in D. A. Norman and S. W. Draper, eds., *User Centered System Design: New Perspectives in Human-Computer Interaction*, Lawrence Erlbaum, Hillsdale, N.J., 1986, pp. 87–124.

R. J. K. Jacob, "Using Formal Specifications in the Design of a Human-Computer Interface," *Comm. ACM* **26**, 259–264 (1983).

R. J. K. Jacob, "An Executable Specification Technique for Describing Human-Computer Interaction," in H. R. Hartson, ed., *Advances in Human-Computer Interaction*, Ablex Publishing Co., Norwood, N.J., 1985, pp. 211–242.

R. J. K. Jacob, "What You Look At is What You Get: Eye Movement-Based Interaction in Techniques," *Proceedings of the ACM CHI'90 Human Factors in Computing Systems Conference*, Addison-Wesley/ACM Press, Reading, Mass., 1990, pp. 11–18.

J. Johnson and co-workers, "The Xerox Star: A Retrospective," *IEEE Comp.* **22**(9), 11–29 (1989).

T. K. Landauer, K. M. Galotti, and S. Hartwell, "Natural Command Names and Initial Learning: A Study of Text-editing Terms," *Comm. ACM* **26**, 495–503 (1983).

H. Ledgard, "Special Section on the Human Aspects of Computing," *Comm. ACM* **29**(7), 593–647 (1986).

J. MacKinlay, "Automating the Design of Graphical Presentations of Relational Information," *ACM Trans. Graphics* **5**(2), 110–141 (1986).

T. W. Malone, K. R. Grant, F. A. Turbak, S. A. Brobst, and M. D. Cohen, "Intelligent Information-Sharing Systems," *Comm. ACM* **30**(5), 390–402 (1987).

W. C. Mann, "An Overview of the PENMAN Text Generation System," *Proceedings of the Third National Conference on Artificial Intelligence*, Washington, D.C., AAAI, Menlo Park, Calif., 1983, pp. 261–265.

P. R. Michaelis, M. L. Miller, and J. A. Hendler, "Artificial Intelligence and Human Factors Engineering: A Necessary Synergism in the Interface of the Future," in A. Badre and B.

Shneiderman, eds., *Directions in Human/Computer Interaction,* Ablex Publishing Co., Norwood, N.J., 1982, pp. 79–94.

B. A. Myers, *Creating User Interfaces by Demonstration,* Academic Press, Inc., Orlando, Fla., 1988.

P. Reisner, "Formal Grammar and Human Factors Design of an Interactive Graphics System," *IEEE Trans. Softw. Eng.* **SE-7,** 229–240 (1981).

E. Rich, "Users are Individuals. Individualizing User Models," *Internat. J. Man-Machine Stud.* **18,** 199–214 (1983).

E. L. Rissland, "Ingredients of Intelligent User Interfaces," *Internat. J. Man-Machine Stud.* **21,** 377–388 (1984).

R. C. Schank and R. P. Abelson, *Scripts, Plans, Goals, and Understanding,* Lawrence Erlbaum, Hillsdale, N.J., 1977.

C. Schmandt and E. A. Hulteen, "The Intelligent Voice-Interactive Interface," in *Proceedings of the ACM Human Factors in Computer Systems Conference,* 1982, pp. 363–366.

D. D. Seligmann and S. K. Feiner, "Specifying Composite Illustrations with Communication Goals," in *Proceedings of the ACM SIGGRAPH Symposium on User Interface Software and Technology,* Addison-Wesley/ACM Press, Williamsburg, Va., 1989, pp. 1–9.

B. Shneiderman, "Direct Manipulation: A Step Beyond Programming Languages," *IEEE Comp.* **16**(8), 57–69 (1983).

B. Shneiderman, *Designing the User Interface: Strategies for Effective Human-Computer Interaction,* Addison-Wesley Publishing Co., Inc., Reading, Mass., 1987.

J. Shrager and T. W. Finin, "An Expert System that Volunteers Advice," *Proceedings of the Second National Conference on Artificial Intelligence,* Pittsburgh, Pa., AAAI, Menlo Park, Calif., 1982.

N. C. Shu, *Visual Programming,* Van Nostrand Reinhold, New York, 1988.

G. Singh and M. Green, "Chisel: A System for Creating Highly Interactive Screen Layouts," in *Proceedings of the ACM SIGGRAPH Symposium on User Interface Software and Technology,* Addison-Wesley/ACM Press, Williamsburg, Va., 1989, pp. 86–94.

D. W. Small and L. J. Weldon, "An Experimental Comparison of Natural and Structured Query Languages," *Human Factors* **25,** 253–263 (1983).

D. J. Sturman, D. Zeltzer, and S. Pieper, "Hands-on Interaction with Virtual Environments," in *Proceedings of the ACM SIGGRAPH Symposium on User Interface Software and Technology,* Addison-Wesley/ACM Press, Williamsburg, Va., 1989, pp. 19–24.

W. Teitelman, *Interlisp Reference Manual,* Technical Report, Xerox PARC, Palo Alto, Calif., 1978.

H. Tennant, K. Ross, R. Saenz, C. Thompson, and J. Miller, "Menu-based Natural Language Understanding," *Proceedings of the Association for Computational Linguistics Conference,* Cambridge, Mass., 1983, pp. 151–157.

D. Weinreb and D. Moon, *Lisp Machine Manual,* MIT Artificial Intelligence Laboratory, Cambridge, Mass., 1981.

R. Wilensky, Y. Arens, and D. Chin, "Talking to UNIX in English: An Overview of UC," *Comm. ACM* **27,** 574–593 (1984).

B. Woolf and D. D. McDonald, "Building a Computer Tutor: Design Issues," *IEEE Comp.* **17**(9), 61–73 (1984).

A. R. Young, A. G. Hauptmann, W. H. Ward, E. T. Smith, and P. Werner, "High Level Knowledge Sources in Usable Speech Recognition Systems," *Comm. ACM.* **32**(2), 183–193 (1989).

ROBERT J. K. JACOB
Naval Research Laboratory

HWIM

HWIM is an experimental continuous speech understanding system developed by W. Woods, J. Makhoul, and colleagues at Bolt, Beranek and Newman as part of the first DARPA Speech Understanding Project from 1971 to 1976. It used a middle-out parser for ATN grammars together with signal processing, acoustic-phonetic, lexical retrieval, and word-matching techniques to understand naturally spoken sentences from unknown speakers with a vocabulary of 1000 words. Its grammar covered a substantial range of natural questions, statements, and commands in a resource management application dealing with travel budgets. The system was the first successful speech understanding system to handle sentences from fluent linguistic grammars with large branching ratios (ie, allowing many possible next words), using phonological, linguistic and domain-specific knowledge that could evolve during a dialog. It is also significant for introducing the shortfall density optimal search algorithm (Woods, 1982). The system included a semantic data base and a travel planner and budget manager, and it could produce synthesized speech output. (See W. A. Woods, M. Bates, G. Brown, B. Bruce, C. Cook, J. Klovstad, J. Makhoul, B. Nash-Webber, R. Schwartz, J. Wolf, and V. Zue, *Speech Understanding Systems—Final Report,* Oct. 30, 1974 to Oct. 29, 1976, BBN Report No. 3438, Vols. I–V, Bolt Beranek and Newman Inc., Cambridge, Mass.; see also W. A. Woods and J. Wolf, "The HWIM Speech Understanding System," in Wayne A. Lea, ed., *Trends in Speech Recognition,* Prentice Hall, Inc., Englewood Cliffs, N.J., 1980; F. Fallside and W. A. Woods, eds., *Computer Speech Processing,* Prentice-Hall, Englewood Cliffs, N.J., 1985; and W. A. Woods, "HWIM: A Speech Understanding System on a Computer" in M. A. Arbib, D. Caplan, and J. C. Marshall, eds., *Neural Models of Language Processes,* Academic Press, New York, 1982. For shortfall density algorithm, see W. A. Woods, "Optimal Search Strategies for Speech Understanding Control," *Artificial Intelligence,* **8**(3) (May, 1982), reprinted in B. Webber and N. Nilsson, eds., *Readings in Artificial Intelligence,* Tioga Publishing Co., Palo Alto, Calif., 1981.)

W. A. WOODS
Harvard University

I

ICSI

The International Computer Science Institute is an independent, nonprofit basic research institute affiliated with the University of California campus in Berkeley, Calif. The ICSI (pronounced 'eye c. s. eye') was started in 1986 as a joint project of the Computer Science Division of the University of California at Berkeley and the German Federal Computer Science Laboratory (GMD). German support of the institute is now provided by a government–industry consortium. Switzerland joined the sponsorship of ICSI in 1989, and Italy joined early in 1990; participation by other countries is under way. The institute also receives support from a variety of U.S. sources. After some pilot operations, ICSI is now building to an operating size of some 30 scientists and a number of students and postdoctoral fellows. The institute occupies a newly designed 21,000 square foot research facility at 1947 Center Street, just off the central U.C. campus in downtown Berkeley.

The International Computer Science Institute carries out basic research projects in selected areas of computer science and engineering. All of the research at the institute is open, and its results are made publicly available. Current emphasis is on distributed and parallel computation, with particular attention to massive parallelism. A more detailed description is available as *ICSI Research Plan 1991–1992*.

STUDIES IN PARALLEL AND DISTRIBUTED COMPUTATION

It has been clear for some years that parallel computation is the key to many desirable applications. Distributed and parallel systems of moderate scale are now fairly well understood and widely employed. However, the problems involved with millions or billions of independent computations appear to be different and to require new techniques. ICSI is currently addressing issues in four key areas: applications of massively parallel systems, realization of such systems, very large distributed networks, and theory of parallel computation.

Massive Parallelism: Applications

The primary focus of the applications of massive parallelism group is the field of artificial intelligence. The tasks studied in AI are of enormous practical and scientific importance and have proven to be quite difficult for conventional programming techniques. Human brains evolved to excel at vision, motor control, speech, language understanding, and so on and are much better at these tasks than artificial systems. The ICSI effort, along with many others, is exploring the possibility that computational models and techniques based on natural intelligence will prove useful in AI tasks. The ICSI project differs from most others in its emphasis on structured networks, strong methods that exploit scientific knowledge and extensive interaction with other computer science techniques and theory. ICSI's structured approach to massively parallel computation requires sophisticated tools for building and working with complex networks. The ICSI connectionist simulator (ICSIM) project, being done in collaboration with the realization group, is an attempt to qualitatively improve the state of such tools and to apply them in ICSI's own efforts. Particular applications under study at ICSI are in the areas of vision, geometric structures and algorithms, speech, knowledge representation, and learning.

The ICSI vision work is concerned with efficient and rigorous solutions to central problems in visual recognition. Particular problems currently under investigation include the recognition of known three-dimensional objects from images, invariant feature extraction by statistical and geometrical methods, categorizing the utility of features, and the representation and matching of curved boundaries. The study of connectionist techniques for matching complex structures is being continued. In addition to direct connectionist realization, it is of great interest to apply the techniques of computational geometry and complexity theory to yield efficient sequential versions of key algorithms. In current research, connectionist models and procedures that appear to be promising are explored. These include the development of modules that efficiently implement a wide variety of geometric operations using geometric data structures and a systematic framework within which geometric and symbolic information can be naturally integrated.

In the field of continuous speech recognition, connectionist learning techniques are explored for two aspects of the problem: adaptive methods for selection of optimal feature combinations as well as for the substitution of contextual networks for the tables of hidden Markov model (HMM) techniques. Special-purpose hardware for these applications is being developed as part of the realization effort.

A major emphasis of ICSI's work is on the related issues of knowledge representation and inference in massively parallel systems. The goal is to construct systems that perform certain tasks well and are consistent with the known biological, behavioral, and computational constraints. Recent efforts have involved interpretation of adjective–noun combinations, connectionist unification networks, constraint networks, and applications to higher level vision. Learning in this paradigm is accomplished by recruitment of uncommitted units in addition to simple weight adjustment.

The goal of the new L_0 project on miniature language acquisition is to produce a system that will learn natural language from the presentation of a sequence of picture–sentence pairs. The domain involves simple two-dimensional scenes of geometric figures and requires only 20 words of English.

Massive Parallelism: Realization of Systems

The goals of the second major group, realization of massively parallel systems, are to answer fundamental questions about the use of architectures and technology, to implement massively parallel systems, and to implement connectionist algorithms for machine perception and intelligence in problem areas such as natural language understanding, speech, vision, and biomedical signal processing. In particular, members of this group are collaborating closely with members of the applications group to design systems with a demonstrable capability for some limited problems in speech and vision. By its nature, the realization effort covers a broad spectrum of issues. Major areas of research in this group are

Systems Design. To establish a framework for testing and operation of large systems of heterogeneous or special-purpose processors, elements, and subsystems as they are designed and built.

Integrated Circuit Design. To develop digital and analogue ICs for implementing connectionist approaches to feature extraction and classification for difficult subproblems in such areas as speech and vision, for example, an IC design to implement speech algorithms as part of a high speed speech recognition system.

Applications Work, Speech Recognition. To continue the development of the hybrid multilayer-perceptron (MLP/HMM) continuous speech recognition system to improve the accuracy of word recognition for continuous speech.

Architectural Studies. To evaluate formally current parallel architectures, both commercial and theoretical; some of the architectural issues are data structures, interconnection topology, node processor requirements, dynamic behavior versus static structure of artificial neural networks (ANN), learning in ANN, and node update regimens.

Simulators. To develop network, architectural, and IC design and evaluation tools; the ICSIM (an ANN simulator) incorporates software engineering principles such as reusability and modularity, support for loosely coupled multiprocessors, object-oriented programming paradigms, and bitmap graphic user interfaces.

The realization group maintains close working relationships with several U.C. Berkeley faculty members from the electrical engineering and computer science department. In particular, ICSI is using many of the hardware design tools developed in the electrical engineering department and is collaborating with faculty members to extend prior joint research on speech recognition done in connection with SRI International.

Very Large Distributed Systems

The research program in the field of very large distributed systems is particularly concerned with the operating system requirements of such systems, especially in such areas as remote service accessibility, security, high-speed real-time communication, support for heterogeneity in all aspects of the system, support for massive distributed computations, and efficient exploitation of architectural parallelism.

Theory of Parallel Computation

The theory group is pursuing a program of research emphasizing parallel computation, computational learning theory, randomized computation, analysis of heuristic algorithms, theory of program checking, and foundations of complexity theory for scientific computation. The general goal is to understand the fundamental laws that govern the efficiency with which computational tasks can be performed and, subject to these laws, to devise the most efficient computational methods possible.

ISCI's research on parallel computation is currently focused on four areas: the solution of combinatorial search problems on highly parallel computers (using methods such as backtrack search, game tree search and branch-and-bound computation); the investigation of parallel computation models that are more realistic than traditional models and which, in particular, take into account phenomena related to synchronization, interprocessor communication, and memory contention; the design of efficient algorithms for certain basic problems that occur as subroutines in a wide variety of higher level parallel algorithms; and the development of fundamental algorithmic techniques, such as general methods of converting randomized parallel algorithms to deterministic methods.

In computational learning theory, ICSI researchers have been particularly interested in Valiant's model of PAC (probably approximately correct) learning, in which the learner formulates a hypothesis on the basis of examples randomly drawn from some probability distribution. Results have been obtained in the effect of storage limitations on the convergence rate of PAC learning, algorithms for learning certain classes of Boolean functions using queries, and the computational intractability of certain problems related to the construction and analysis of neural networks. Future work is planned toward understanding which inductive learning tasks can be carried out efficiently by such networks.

The ICSI research program is oriented toward problems for which interaction among institute subdisciplines is likely to be productive. The subgroup boundaries are loose, and most staff members have interests in more than one area. There is also an explicit effort to develop cooperative research programs with both local and international groups. In addition to the major areas of concentration, ICSI maintains smaller efforts on problems of particular interest. ICSI is an experiment in cooperation in a highly competitive field. By maintaining its emphasis on open, basic research and interacting with other centers, the institute hopes to contribute to international understanding as well as to computer science and engineering.

Jerome A. Feldman
International Computer Science
Institute

IMAGE MODELS

Image modeling refers to the development of analytical representations for explaining the intensity distribution in an image. There are different types of models, each being appropriate for one or more families of applications. Thus, for applications where one is interested in compressing the amount of information in images, one needs a model that can synthesize an image, leading to generative or information preserving models. Such models can be of various type depending on whether interaction between pixels is modeled, or interaction between regions is modeled. On the other hand if one is interested in classifying images into one of several classes, generative models, although useful, may not always be necessary. For example, one can use features derived from joint probability density of gray level distribution, often characterized in the form of co-occurrence matrices for classification of textures. It is difficult to generate images from these features. Each such model captures only some important aspects about the intensity distribution, and no single model can capture all the important aspects of the data. Traditionally, the pixel based models have found wide applications in image and texture synthesis (McCormick and Jayaramamurthy, 1974; Woods, 1972; Pratt and co-workers, 1978; Hassner and Sklansky, 1978; Cross and Jain, 1983; Chellappa and Kashyap, 1985; Chellappa and co-workers, 1985; Kashyap and Lapsa, 1984), image compression (Delp and co-workers, 1979; Maragoss and co-workers, 1984), image restoration (Woods and Radewan, 1977; Jain and Jain, 1978; Chellappa and Kashyap, 1982; Geman and Geman, 1984; Derin and co-workers, 1984; Besag, 1986; Jeng and Woods, 1990; Simchory and co-workers, 1990), edge detection (Zhou and co-workers, 1989), texture classification (Kashyap and co-workers, 1982; Chellappa and Chatterjee, 1985; Kashyap and Khotanzad, 1986), image and texture segmentation (Therrien, 1983; Derin and Elliott, 1987; Derin and Cole, 1986; Fan and Cohen, 1988; Cohen and Cooper, 1987; Geman and Graffigne, 1990; Manjunath and co-workers, 1990). The region based models have been found to be useful for image synthesis (Schacter and Ahuja, 1979; Modestino and co-workers, 1980), image compression (Daut and co-workers, 1981; Modestino and Bhaskaran, 1981), and texture discrimination (Schacter and co-workers, 1978; Ahuja and Rosenfield, 1981; Modestino and co-workers, 1981).

Why do we need image models? The most important reason is the abstraction it provides of a large amount of data contained in images. Using the analytical representations for images, one can develop systematic algorithms for accomplishing a particular image related task. As an example, model based optimal estimation theoretic principles can be applied to find edges in textured images or remove blur and noise from degraded images. Another advantage in using image models is that one can develop a number of techniques to validate a given model for the given image. On the basis of such a validation, performance of several algorithms can be compared. It may be pointed out that for image analysis tasks such as edge detection and segmentation, there are many algorithms usually derived on an ad hoc basis. Even here one can

identify a specific implicit model for an image (Rosenfeld and Davis, 1979).

Most statistical models for image processing and analysis treat images as two-dimensional data, ie no attempt is made to relate the three-dimensional world around us and the two-dimensional projection on the retina. There exists a class of models, known as image formation models, which explicitly relate the three-dimensional information to the two-dimensional brightness array through a nonlinear reflectance map by making appropriate assumptions about the surface being imaged. Such models can be customized for the particular sensor at hand and have been useful for inferring shape from shading (Horn, 1989) and other related applications.

Another class of models known as fractals, originally proposed in Mandelbrot (1981), Barnsley (1988), and Pentland (1984) is good for representing images of natural scenes such as mountains, terrains, etc. Successful applications of fractals for image related problems may be found in Keller and co-workers (1987), Pertgen and Saupe (1988), and Kube and Pentland (1988). One of the important advantages of the fractal model is that the fractal dimension, a characteristic number for such a model, is relatively scale invariant; that is, if a $2M \times 2M$ image is reduced to an $M \times M$ image by averaging over a 2×2 window, the corresponding estimates of fractal dimensions of both the images are close.

This article discusses different types of image models that have proved useful in the literature. Selected applications to image related problems such as smoothing, texture synthesis, segmentation, edge detection, and shape from shading are illustrated.

Simple Statistical Models

One of the simplest models that one can think of in this group is the independent and identically distributed (IID) models; that is, pixels are assumed to be independent with a common distribution. Gaussian distribution has often been used. Although these models cannot synthesize any interesting real image, they have been useful in developing edge detection (Yakimovsky, 1976) and segmentation algorithms (Rosenfeld and Kak, 1982). The implicit assumption in simple threshold based segmentation algorithms is the IID assumption for pixels. These models have also been used in analyzing the response of a median filter (Justusson, 1981). One of the major reasons why these models have not been of much use is that they do not account for correlation between pixels.

A slightly more realistic model is the multivariate Gaussian model (Hunt, 1977). Let $\underline{y}$ be the lexicographically ordered $M^2 \times 1$ vector of the image array. The multivariate Gaussian model represents $\underline{y}$ to have the distribution

$$p(\underline{y}) = \frac{1}{(2\pi)^{\frac{M^2}{2}} |det\, R|^{\frac{1}{2}}}\, exp\left\{ -\frac{1}{2}(\underline{y} - \underline{m})^t\, R^{-1}(\underline{y} - \underline{m}) \right\}$$

$$(1)$$

where $\underline{m} = E[\underline{y}]$ and $R = E[(\underline{y} - \underline{m})(\underline{y} - \underline{m})^t]$. One can make $\underline{m}$ to be a space varying vector. This model has been used in image restoration studies (Haralick, 1981) as prior information for the underlying noise free image in maximum a posteriori restoration. Applications to texture segmentation may be found in Chen and Pavlidis (1981).

In the facet model (Haralick and Watson, 1981), the observed intensity function $y(i, j)$ is written as a sum of a deterministic function-polynomial in (i, j) and an additive noise:

$$y(i, j) = \theta_0 + \theta_1 i + \theta_2 j + \theta_3 ij + \theta_4 i^2 + \theta_5 j^2 + \omega(i, j) \tag{2}$$

Higher-order terms such as i_j^2, ij^2, i^3, j^3 etc. can be introduced with appropriate coefficients. The sequence $\{\omega(i, j)\}$ is independent, has mean zero and variance β. The parameters θ_is, can be estimated by fitting the model to a given image $\{y(i, j), (i, j)\varepsilon\Omega\}$ using the least squares approach (Rao, 1973), where Ω is the finite grid $\{0 \leq i, j \leq M - 1\}$. The facet model has been used for edge detection (Haralick, 1986), and segmentation (Haralick, 1981).

The specific form in (2) is one of the possible deterministic functions. Longuet-Higgins (1957) proposed two-dimensional sinusoids for representing the deterministic part:

$$y(i, j) = \theta_1 \cos(\lambda_1 i + \lambda_2 j + \gamma_1) + \omega(i, j) \tag{3}$$

Again the model parameters θ_1, λ_1, λ_2 and γ_1 can be estimated from the given image using the least squares method. Applications of polynomial models for object recognition may be found Bolle and Cooper (1984; 1986), and Cernuschi-Frias and co-workers (1989). Unsupervised learning of polynomial models using Bayesian clustering has been treated in Silverman and Cooper (1988).

Time Series Models

More generally, it can be assumed that the images have some type of neighbor dependence. Motivated by the success of autoregressive (AR) models in synthesis, analysis, and processing speech signals, research work in the early 70s concentrated on representing images by one-dimensional models. Assuming that the two-dimensional image is a stack of one-dimensional images, an AR model

$$y_i(t) = \sum_{j=1}^{m_i} \theta_j y_i(t - j) + \sqrt{\beta_i} \omega_i(t) \tag{4}$$

can be used to represent each row of the image. In (4), $\{y_i(t), t = 1, \ldots N\}$ represents the ith now and $\{\omega_i(t)\}$ is a sequence of mutually uncorrelated noise random variables.

One can generalize (4) as

$$y_i(t) = \sum_{j=1}^{m_i} \theta_j y_i(t - j) + \sqrt{\beta_i} \omega_i(t) + \sum_{j=1}^{n_i} \phi_j \omega_i(t - j)$$

yielding the autoregressive and moving average (ARMA) representation. ARMA models are attractive as they are parsimonious; however, parameter estimation in ARMA models is more complicated than in AR models. Variations of AR and ARMA models known as "seasonal" AR and ARMA have been used for texture synthesis (McCormick and Jayaramamurthy, 1974), image data compression (Delp and co-workers, 1979) the seasonality resulting from the concatenation of rows or columns. Although one-dimensional AR and ARMA models are inadequate to represent two-dimensional images, there are some examples in image processing where they have been found to be useful. One such application of circular AR (CAR) models (Kashyap and Chellappa, 1981) is in representing two-dimensional closed boundaries on the plane for the purposes of feature extraction and classification. Assume for simplicity that $\{r(1), r(2), \ldots, r(N)\}$ represent the lengths successive radiivectors, separated from each other by $2\pi/N$. Since the boundary is closed, the date $\{r(*)\}$ is circular, ie, $r(k + N) = r(k)$. The boundary data is represented by a CAR model as

$$r(i) = \alpha + \sum_{j=1}^{m} \theta_i r(i - j) + \sqrt{\beta} \omega(i), i = 1, \ldots, N$$

In practice, the parameters α, $\underline{\theta} = col.(\theta_1, \ldots, \theta_m)$, and β are estimated from $\{r(.)\}$, by least squares (LS) principles. The vector $[\underline{\theta}^*, \alpha^*/\sqrt{\beta^*}]$ (* denotes LS estimates) has been shown (Kashyap and Chellappa, 1981) to be invariant to scaling, rotation, and starting point and hence is a useful feature vector for classification purposes. In fact, experiments conducted using the above feature vector (Singer and Chellappa, 1983; Dubois and Glanz, 1986) indicate that good classification accuracy can be obtained.

The notion of one-dimensional Markov models has also found application in boundary estimation. In Cooper (1979), the object boundary is modeled as a Markov process and the noise in the image is assumed to be white Gaussian. The joint likelihood of the hypothesized blob boundary and the entire image is maximized to estimate the boundary.

Two-Dimensional Unilateral Models

Assume that the Gaussian observations $\{y(s), s\varepsilon\Omega\}$, obey the difference equation in (5).

$$y(s) = \sum_{r\varepsilon N} \theta_r y(s + r) + \sqrt{\beta} \omega(s), \forall s \tag{5}$$

The set N associated with (5) is a subset of the set $\{(i, j): i \leq 0, j \leq 0, (i, j) \neq (0, 0)\}$ and the noise sequence $\{\omega(s)\}$ is IID. Typically, (5) has a set of initial conditions associated with it. For $N = \{(-1, 0), (0, -1), (-1, -1)\}$, (5) is characterized by a set of initial conditions made of the observations along the first row and first column. The familiar "causal" models are obtained by restricting N to a subset of a quarter plane. The causal models can be generalized to include as many previously scanned points as possible by using the notion of a nonsymmetric half plane S^+ (Goodman and Ekstrom, 1980) recursively defined as

1. $s \varepsilon S^+, r \varepsilon S^+ \rightarrow r + s \varepsilon S^+$
2. $s \varepsilon S^+, \rightarrow -s \notin S^+$
3. $(0, 0) \notin S^+$

The definition of S^+ is not unique. Without loss of generality, one can consider those half planes generated by vectors colinear with the Cartesian axes. With N being a subset of S^+, the corresponding $\{y(s)\}$ is said to be a strict sense unilateral Markov model with respect to a unilateral neighbor set N if

$$p\left(y(s)\middle|\text{all } y(r), r\varepsilon\Omega_{s,N}\right) = p\left(y(s)\middle|\text{all } y(s+r), r\varepsilon N\right)$$

where $\Omega_{s,N}$ is defined in terms of s and N as follows (Hansen and Chellappa, 1990):

1. $s \not\in \Omega_{s,N}$
2. $s + r \varepsilon \Omega_{s,N}$ for all $r\varepsilon N$
3. $r \varepsilon \Omega_{s,N} \rightarrow (r + t) \varepsilon \Omega_{s,N}$ for all $r\varepsilon N$ provided $r + t \neq s$

Parameter estimation for unilateral models can be done using LS principles. The LS estimates are symptotically consistent; they are also asymptotically efficient for Gaussian $\{y(s)\}$. Using the LS estimates $\hat{\theta}, \hat{\beta}$ one can recursively generate the residuals $\hat{\omega}(s)$ using

$$\hat{\omega}(s) = \frac{1}{\sqrt{\hat{\beta}}}\left[y(s) - \sum_{r\varepsilon N}\hat{\theta}_r y(s+r)\right]$$

The residuals so generated can be used for model validation purposes as in one-dimensional time series analysis. If the two-dimensional unilateral model is adequate for the given image, the residuals $\hat{\omega}(s)$ will almost be mutually uncorrelated and hence can be represented by fewer bits compared to the original image. Thus one can design two-dimensional differential pulse mode modulation (DPCM) schemes for the purpose of image data compression. The estimates $\hat{\theta}$ and $\hat{\beta}$ can be used as features for classification of images and textures. Two-dimensional unilateral models have been used for image compression (Delp and co-workers, 1979; Maragoss and co-workers, 1984), image restoration (Woods and Radewan, 1977), texture synthesis (Delp and co-workers, 1979), texture classification, and segmentation (Therrien, 1983).

Two-Dimensional Noncausal Models

Unlike one-dimensional discrete time series, where the existence of a preferred direction is inherently assumed, no such preferred ordering of the discrete lattice is appropriate. In other words, the notion of past and future, as understood in unilateral one-dimensional Markov processes, is restrictive in two dimensions as it implies a particular ordering in which the observations are scanned top to bottom and left to right. It is quite possible that an observation at s may be dependent on neighboring observations in all directions. The simplest noncausal model is obtained when the dependence is on the nearest north, south, east, and west neighbors. One can think of a more general dependence on nearest diagonal neighbors and neighbors farther away. Such a noncausal representation in two dimensions is not only of interest due to its generality, but is significant due to lack of spectral factorization in two dimensions. Thus, if the given observation set $\{y(s)\}$ indeed obeys a noncausal model whose spectrum does not factorize, any finite order unilateral representation for this data will only be approximate.

In contrast to one-dimensional time series AR models, when noncausality is introduced as two-dimensional, two nonequivalent generalizations of unilateral models result. These models are known as the spatial autoregressive (SAR) model and the Markov random field (MRF) model. The representation for $y(s)$ obeying a SAR model is (Whittle, 1954)

$$y(s) = \sum_{r\varepsilon N}\theta_r y(s+r) + \sqrt{\beta}\omega(s) \tag{6}$$

In (6), $(\theta_r, r\varepsilon N)$ and β are unknown parameters, and $\{\omega(s)\}$ is an IID noise sequence with zero mean and unit variance. The neighbor set N does not include $(0, 0)$ and need not be symmetric. However, if N has symmetric neighbors the corresponding coefficients should be equal; ie, if $r\varepsilon N$ and $-r\varepsilon N$, $\theta_r = \theta_{-r}$ otherwise, the parameters are not identifiable. If N is symmetric, a necessary and sufficient condition for $\{y(.)\}$ to be stationary is

$$\left\{1 - \sum_{(i,j)\varepsilon N}\theta_{i,j}z_1^i z_2^j\right\} \neq 0$$

for all z_1 and z_2 such that $|z_2| = |z_2| = 1$.

Since, for SAR models $E\{y(s)\omega(s+r)\} \neq 0$ for those r belonging to the "future" of s, the LS estimate $\hat{\theta}$ of θ given by

$$\underline{\hat{\theta}} = \left[\sum_{s\varepsilon\Omega}\underline{q}(s)\underline{q}^T(s)\right]^{-1}\left(\sum_{s\varepsilon\Omega}\underline{q}(s)y(s)\right)$$

is not consistent (Whittle, 1954). Better estimates can be obtained by using ML principles if $y(s)$ are Gaussian. Details of exact and approximate ML estimation schemes for SAR models may be found in Whittle (1954), Kashyap (1981), Kashyap and Chellappa (1983), Sharma and Chellappa (1986), and Hansen and Chellappa (1990). The SAR models have been used for image restoration (Chellappa and Kashyap, 1982; Geman and Graffigne, 1987), texture synthesis (Chellappa and Kashyap, 1985), texture classification (Kashyap and co-workers, 1982) and two-dimensional spectral estimation (Sharma and Chellappa, 1986; Hansen and Chellappa, 1990). The texture synthesis application will be discussed in more detail, as this application directly addresses the appropriateness of SAR models for textures.

One way of justifying the appropriateness of SAR models for texture is by analysis-synthesis technique. The synthesis of images obeying SAR models is computationally prohibitive; this may be seen by rewriting the interpolative equation (6) in matrix vector format as

$$B(\underline{\theta})\underline{y} = \sqrt{\beta}\underline{\omega} \tag{7}$$

where $B(\underline{\theta})$ is the $M^2 \times M^2$ transformation matrix from $\underline{\omega}$ to $\underline{y}$. Assuming $B^{-1}(\underline{\theta})$ exists,

$$\underline{y} = \sqrt{\beta}B^{-1}(\underline{\theta})\underline{\omega} \tag{8}$$

Thus by using a vector of pseudo-random numbers of general distribution and appropriate values of θ and β one can generate y obeying (8), by inverting a very large matrix (M is typically 32 or 64). One can, however, synthesize a texture with manageable computations by using doubly periodic boundary conditions. Under these conditions, the texture can be generated using two-dimensional FFT. It may be pointed out that as $M \to \infty$, the doubly periodic boundary conditions yield better and better approximations to y obeying (8).

The noncausal spatial dependence of $y(s)$ on its neighbors can also be represented by a related MRF model. The image data $\{y(s)\}$ generated by an MRF model obeys the two-dimensional Markov condition

$$p\,(y(s)|\text{all } y(r), r \neq s) = p\,(y(s)|\text{all } y(s+r), r\varepsilon N) \quad (9)$$

where N is a noncausal neighbor set. In a general case, the MRF models are specified by the conditional densities $p\,(y(s)|\text{all } y(s+r), r\varepsilon N)$. For instance, if $\{y(s)\}$ is a T–level texture, the conditional density $p\,(y(s)|\text{all } y(s+r), r\varepsilon N)$ can be specified as binomial with parameter $\theta(Q)$ and number of tries $T - 1$ where

$$\theta(Q) = \frac{exp(Q)}{1 + exp(Q)}$$

and

$$Q = \alpha + b_1((s+(0,1)+(s+(0,-1)) \\ + b_2((s+(1,0))+(s+(-1,0))$$

where α, b_1, and b_2 are the MRF model parameters. One can also specify the conditional densities using exponential and Poisson distributions (Gidas, 1986). The non-Gaussian MRF models have been used for texture synthesis with good results for microtextures (Hassner and Sklansky, 1978; Cross and Jain, 1983); however, synthesis of regular textures like brick is not satisfactory. One of the disadvantages of using non-Gaussian MRF models is that the synthesis algorithm is computationally expensive (*ibid*); moreover, the known parameter estimation schemes (Besag, 1974; Geman and Graffigne, 1987; Gidas, 1986) for these models are not fully efficient.

When $\{y(s)\}$ Gaussian, the MRF model can be equivalently specified using the interpolative equation (Woods, 1972; Rosanov, 1967)

$$y(s) = \sum_{r\varepsilon N} \theta_r y(s+r) + e(s) \quad (10)$$

where N is a symmetric neighbor set and $\{e(s)\}$ is a correlated noise array with

$$
\begin{aligned}
E[e(s)\,e(r)] &= -\theta_{r-s}\nu, \quad (s-r)\varepsilon N \\
&= \nu, \quad\quad\quad s = r \\
&= 0 \quad\quad\quad\quad \text{otherwise}
\end{aligned}
$$

Under the above conditions it can be shown that $E(e(s)\,y(r)) = \nu\,\delta(s,r)$ where $\delta(s,r)$ is the two-dimensional delta function. The image $\{y(s)\}$ obeying (10) possesses two-dimensional Markov property (9).

The Gaussian MRF (GMRF) model is said to be of first order when $N = \{(0,1), (0,-1), (-1,0), (1,0)\}$, second order when $N = \{(0,1), (0,-1), (-1,0), (-1,1), (1,-1), (-1,-1), (1,1)\}$, and so on. The GMRF model is more general compared to the SAR model, in that for a given SAR model one can always find an equivalent GMRF model while the converse is not always true. Unlike SAR models, the LS estimates are consistent for the GMRF models. If more accurate estimates are required, ML techniques (Kunsch, 1981; Sharma and Chellappa, 1985) can be used.

The synthesis of textures using GMRF models can be done analogous to SAR models (Chellappa and co-workers, 1985). The GMRF models have also been used for the restoration of degraded images (Chellappa and Kashyap, 1982; Simchony and co-workers, 1990; Simchony and co-workers, 1989), classification of textures (Chellappa and Chatterjee, 1985), and in two-dimensional maximum entropy power spectral estimation (Kunsch, 1981; Sharma and Chellappa, 1985; Tewfik and co-workers, 1988).

Fractals and Fractional Models

Mandelbrot (1977) has argued that the frequency behavior of many "real life" stochastic processes behaves near the zero frequency like λ^{-2d}, here λ is the frequency and $d > 0$, and developed a related family of models called fractals (Mandelbrot, 1977; Mandelbrot and Van Ness, 1968). The image models discussed earlier do not have this property. Hosking (1981) argued that the fractal models explain the low frequency behavior in many cases very well, but cannot explain the high frequency behavior. He suggested an approach for time series which accounts for both long- and short-term effects. We give below the two-dimensional version of the Hosking model (Kashyap and Lapsa, 1984):

$$A(z_1, z_2)\,y(i,j) = (1 - z_1^{-1})^{-d_1}(1 - z_2^{-1})^{-d_1}w(i,j)$$

where $d_1, d_2 > 0$ and $(1 - z_1^{-1})^{-d_1}$ should be interpreted as the corresponding infinite series. $A(z_1, z_2)$ is a polynomial in the two log variables z_1 and z_2 and $w(r,c)$ is an independent sequence. Surprisingly, the process $y(i,j)$ is stationary yielding the fractal behavior for small frequencies. The parameters of these models can be estimated as indicated in Kashyap and Eom (1988).

An important advantage of the fractional model is that parameters d_i are relatively scale-invariant, ie, if a $2M \times 2M$ image is reduced to an $M \times M$ image, the corresponding estimates of d of the two images are close.

Fractals and fractional models have been successfully used for texture segmentation (Kashyap and Eom, 1988; Kube and Pentlend, 1988; Kashyap and Eom, 1989). Fractional models have also been used for modelling and synthesizing three-dimensional textures, ie, textures on three-dimensional objects (Choe and Kashyap, 1990). We may note that the models of earlier sections are useful for representing only two-dimensional textures.

Modeling Real Images

The pixel based models discussed thus far assume that the underlying images are wide sense stationary. In reality, most images are not wide sense stationary, due to the presence of edges, regions with different statistical properties, variation due to shading and illumination, and so on. The handling of nonstationarity in images poses difficult theoretical as well as computational problems. An ad hoc technique used very often in image compression and image restoration studies is to break the image into supposedly stationary segments and process the entire image segment by segment.

A better approach is to regard the given image as composed of several stationary patches separated by edges whose locations are not known. The edge locations and their directions can be estimated using rigorous statistical methods. This approach for texture discrimination is in Eom and Kashyap (1990).

A significant contribution to modeling nonstationary images was made in Geman and Geman (1984) by introducing the concept of dual lattice process. In this work and subsequent extensions (Jeng and Woods, 1990), the intensity array is modeled as a multilevel or Gaussian Markov random field either using the interpolative model or the Gibbs representation. The discontinuities are modeled as line processes, which are defined at the dual lattice sites interposed between the regular pixel sites and take values 0 or 1 depending on whether an edge is absent or present. Whenever the line process is on, the interaction between pixels on either side is broken. Line processes themselves are modeled as multilevel MRFs. Using these representations in MAP estimation framework, a nonconvex optimization problem is formulated. An iterative global minimization algorithm known as simulated annealing (Kirkpatrick and co-workers, 1983) or stochastic relaxation is then presented to compute the global optimal estimate. The work in Geman and Geman (1984) has made important inroads into modeling real images as well as in computational aspects of obtaining the optimum solution.

The annealing algorithms suggested in Geman and Geman (1984) and Jeng and Woods (1990) are computationally intensive, although parallel hardware for implementing such an algorithm has been investigated (Murray and co-workers, 1986). Often, one may be content in developing deterministic approximations to the global optimization algorithm. Several such efforts using different representations for discontinuities are discussed in Blake and Zisserman (1987), Geiger and Gerosi (1989), and Rangarajan and Chellappa (1990).

It is well known that the quality of estimation and other inference methods suffers drastically even when a small amount of bad data is present, which is unavoidable in real life due to poor lighting, etc. Several robust modeling approaches have been developed which perform well even in the presence of bad data. Kashyap and Eom (1988) give an image restoration procedure where the contaminating noise is highly non-Gaussian, the so called "salt and pepper" variety. There are other robust modeling approaches for several image analysis (Haralick and co-workers, 1989; Kim and co-workers, 1989; Besl and co-workers, 1989) problems.

IMAGE MODELS AT THE REGION LEVEL

When we regard images as composed of regions, we obtain an even richer class of possible image models. To begin with, the introduction of regions allows us to consider nonstationary pixel-level models whose properties vary with region type, or with position within a region. More importantly, we must now consider models for the regions themselves, both individually and as an ensemble.

There are many ways of representing image regions, and each such representation allows us to define models for classes of regions. A region can be specified simply as a binary array, where the 1s and 0s denote pixels that do and do not belong to the region, respectively; this allows us to model regions as, eg, binary-valued random fields. Regions can also be represented in more compact ways, eg, as unions of pieces, the choice and arrangement of which can be controlled by a model, or in terms of their boundary curves which can in turn be modeled, eg, as sequence of vectors.

In addition to modeling individual regions, it is also important to model the arrangement of regions of which an image is composed. One way of doing this is to regard the image as composed of objects (ie, regions) on a background; arrangements of objects can then be defined in various ways, eg, as a result of "bombing" or packing processes. Another possibility is to regard the image as partitioned into regions; such partitions can be defined in terms of various types of "occupancy" processes, but it is no longer easy to control the shapes of the individual regions.

The decomposition of an image into regions may involve more than just a single level; it may be hierarchical, with the regions grouped into "super-regions," and these in turn into still larger groupings, etc. This type of hierarchical decomposition is basic to the field of syntactic pattern recognition, and one can define hierarchical region models using various types of (stochastic) grammars. More details on image models at the region level may be found in Schacter and Ahuja (1979), Modestino and co-workers (1980), Daut and co-workers (1981), Modestino and Bhaskaran (1981), Schacter and co-workers (1978), Ahuja and Rosenfeld (1981), and Modestino and co-workers (1981).

Examples

In Figure 1, synthesis results of some natural textures scanned from the Brodatz album are given (1966). A 12 parameter GMRF model was used to synthesize grass, straw and wood, and a 24 parameter model was used to synthesize the plastic bubble texture. In all cases, the LS estimates were used. Synthesis was done using the method described in Chellappa and Kashyap (1982). It can be seen that the synthesized textures of grass, tree bark, and wood reproduce the salient features of the original texture, while in the case of the plastic bubble, the synthesized texture is not good. This is understandable, as the plastic bubble texture has gross features which are not usually captured very well by GMRF.

Examples of texture segmentation using GMRF are

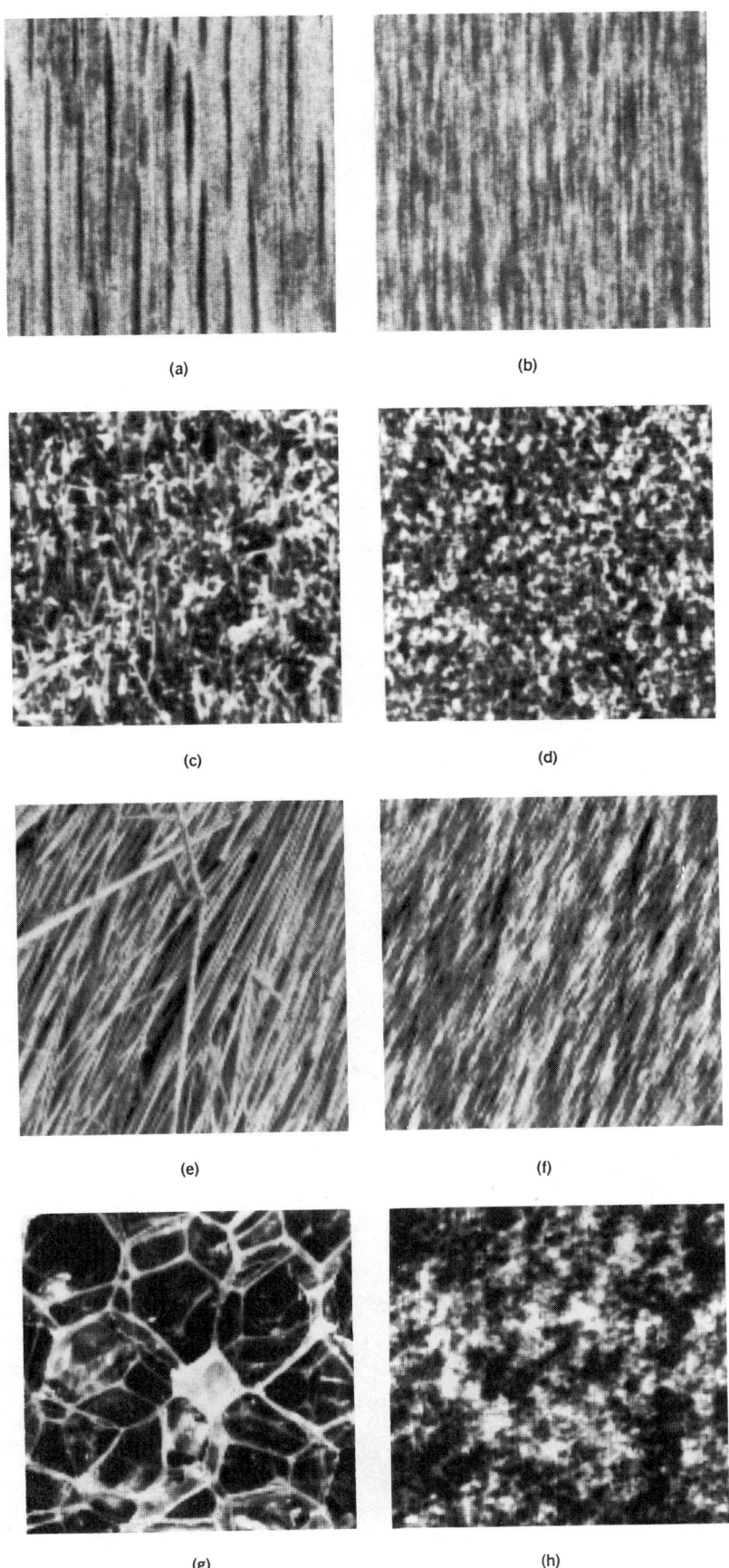

Figure 1. Synthesis of textures using GMRF models. Original pictures of (a) wood, (c) grass, (e) straw, and (g) bubbles; synthesis of textures using a fourth-order GMRF model: (b) wood, (d) grass; (f) straw, and (h) bubbles.

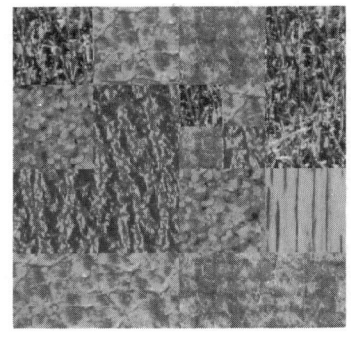
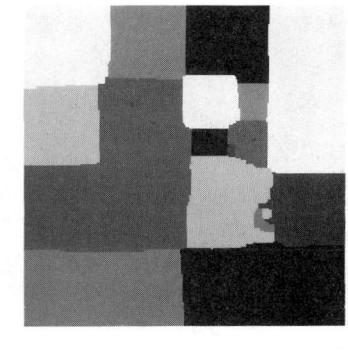

Figure 2. Texture segmentation results using a two-tier MRF model and stochastic relaxation. (*a*) Original, and (*b*) segmented output.

(a)

(b)

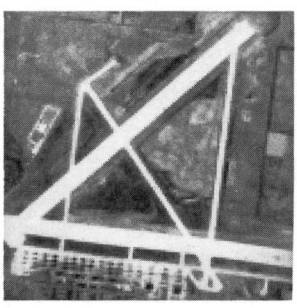
(a)

(b)

(c)

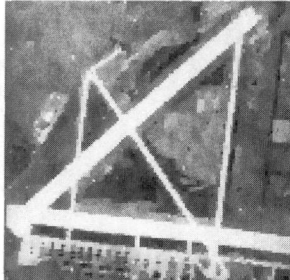
(d)

(e)

Figure 3. Image smoothing using GMRF and line process models. (*a*) Original; (*b*) original image corrupted by Gaussian noise; (*c*) smoothed output using a GMRF model; (*d*) smoothed output using GMRF and line process models; and (*e*) edge output.

(a)

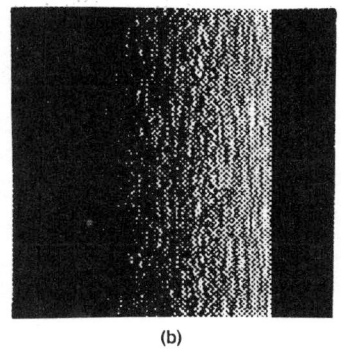
(b)

Figure 4. (*a*) Original tree surface with texture; (*b*) synthesized tree surface image with the composite model (shade and texture).

given in Figure 2. The texture mosaics were originally created in Chatterjee (1987). In this work, the segmentation problem has been formulated as an estimation problem using a two-tier model. The intensity array given the texture label array is modeled as a GMRF and the distribution of different texture labels is modeled as a discrete multilevel Markov model. Decision theoretic methods are then used for finding the texture boundaries.

The application of GMRF and a line process model to image smoothing is illustrated in Figure 3. Here again the intensity array is modeled as a GMRF and the discontinuities using a line process. The smoothing problem is posed as a maximum a posteriori estimation problem leading to a nonconvex optimization problem. Unlike in Geman and Geman (1984) and Jeng and Woods (1990) where stochastic relaxation methods have been employed, the results in Figure 3 were obtained using a deterministic method derived from the GNC algorithm (Simchony and co-workers, 1989). As a by-product one can produce good quality edge maps also.

Figures 4a and 4b show the original of tree texture and its synthesized version using a fractal model and shading. More in-depth survey papers related to image models are those by Kashyap (1981), Chellappa (1985), and Derin and Kelly (1989).

BIBLIOGRAPHY

N. Ahuja and A. Rosenfeld, "Mosaic Models for Textures," *IEEE Trans. Pattern Anal. Mach. Intell.* **PAMI–3,** 1–11 (1981).

M. Barnsley, *Fractals Everywhere,* Academic Press, Boston, Mass., 1988.

J. Besag, "Spatial Interaction and the Statistical Analysis of Lattice Systems," *J. R. Stat. Soc. Ser. B* **36,** 192–236 (1974).

J. Besag, "Statistical Analysis of Dirty Pictures," *J. R. Stat. Soc., Ser. B* **48,** 259–302 (1986).

P. J. Besl, J. B. Birch, and L. T. Watson, "Robust Window Operators," *Mach. Vision Applic.* **2,** 179–1191 (1989).

A. Blake and A. Zisserman, *Visual Reconstruction,* MIT Press, 1987.

R. M. Bolle and D. B. Cooper, "Bayesian Recognition by Approximating Image Intensity Functions with Quadric Polynomials," *IEEE Trans. Pattern Anal. Mach. Intell.* **PAMI–6,** 418–429 (1984).

R. M. Bolle and D. B. Cooper, "On Optimally Combining Pieces of Information, with Application to Estimating 3-D Complex-Object Position from Range Data," *IEEE Trans. Pattern Anal. Mach. Intell.* **PAMI–8,** 619–638 (1986).

P. Brodatz, *Textures: A Photographic Album for Artists and Designers,* Dover, Toronto, Canada, 1966.

B. Cernuschi-Frias and co-workers, "Toward a Model-Based Bayesian Theory for Estimating and Recognizing Parameterized 3-D Objects Using Two or More Images Taken from Different Positions," *IEEE Trans. Pattern Anal. Mach. Intell.* **PAMI–11,** 1028–1052 (1989).

S. Chatterjee, *Synthesis, Analysis and Segmentation of Real Textures,* Ph.D. dissertation, University of Southern California, Los Angeles, Calif., Aug. 1987.

R. Chellappa, "Two-Dimensional Discrete Gaussian Markov Random Field Models for Image Processing," in L. N. Kanal and A. Rosenfeld, eds., Progress in Pattern Recognition, 2, North-Holland Publishing Co., 1985.

R. Chellappa and S. Chatterjee, "Classification of Textures Using Gaussian Markov Random Field Models," *IEEE Trans. Acoust., Speech Signal Process* **33,** 959–963 (1985).

R. Chellappa and R. L. Kashyap, "Digital Image Restoration Using Spatial Interaction Models," *IEEE Trans. Acoust., Speech Signal Process* **30,** 461–472 (1982).

R. Chellappa and R. L. Kashyap, "Texture Synthesis Using Spatial Interaction Models," *IEEE Trans. Acoust., Speech Signal Process* **33,** 194–203 (1985).

R. Chellappa, S. Chatterjee, and R. Bagdazian, "Texture Synthesis and Coding Using Gaussian Markov Random Field Models," *IEEE Trans. System Man Cybernetics* **15,** 298–303 (1985).

P. C. Chen and T. Pavlidis, "Image Segmentation as an Estimation Problem," in A. Rosenfeld, ed., *Image Models,* Academic Press, 1981.

Y. Choe and R. L. Kashyap, "Shape from Textured and Shaded Surface," *Proceedings of the Tenth International Conference on Pattern Recognition,* Atlantic City, N.J., June 1990.

F. S. Cohen and D. B. Cooper, "Simple Parallel Hierarchical and Relaxation Algorithms for Segmenting Noncausal Markovian Fields," *IEEE Trans. Pattern Anal. Mach. Intell.* **PAMI–9,** 195–219 (1987).

D. B. Cooper, "Maximum Likelihood of Markov Process Blob Boundaries in Noisy Images," *IEEE Trans. Pattern Anal. Mach. Intell.* **PAMI–1,** 372–383 (1979).

G. R. Cross and A. K. Jain, "Markov Random Field Texture Models," *IEEE Trans. Pattern Anal. Mach. Intell.* **PAMI–5,** 25–39 (1983).

D. G. Daut, R. W. Fries, and J. W. Modestino, "Two-Dimensional DPCM Image Coding Based on An Assumed Stochastic Image Model," *IEEE Trans. Commun.* **29,** 1365–1374 (1981).

E. J. Delp, R. L. Kashyap, and O. R. Mitchell, "Image Data Compression Using Autoregressive Time Series Models," *Pattern Recognition* **11**, 313–323 (1979).

H. Derin and W. S. Cole, "Segmentation of Textured Images Using Gibbs Random Fields," *Comput. Graph. Image Proc.* **35**, 72–98 (1986).

H. Derin and H. Elliott, "Modeling and Segmentation of Noisy and Textured Images Using Gibbs Random Fields," *IEEE Trans. Pattern Anal. Mach. Intell.* **PAMI–9**, 39–55 (1987).

H. Derin and P. A. Kelly, "Discrete-Index Markov Type Random Processes," *Proc. IEEE* **77**, 1485–1510 (1989).

H. Derin and co-workers, "Bayes Smoothing Algorithms for Segmentation of Binary Images Modeled by Markov Random Fields," *IEEE Trans. Pattern Anal. Mach. Intell.* **PAMI–6**, 707–720 (1984).

S. R. Dubois and F. H. Glanz, "An Autoregressive Model Approach to Two-Dimensional Shape Classification," *IEEE Trans. Pattern Anal. Mach. Intell.* **PAMI–7**, 55–66 (1986).

K. B. Eom and R. L. Kahyap, "Composite Edge Detection with Random Field Models," *IEEE Trans. System Man Cybernetics* **20**, 81–93 (1990).

Z. Fan and F. Cohen, "Textured Image Segmentation as a Multi-Hypothesis Test," *IEEE Trans. Circuits Syst.* **CAS-35**, 691–702 (1988).

D. Geiger and F. Gerosi, "Parallel and Deterministic Algorithms for MRFs Surface Reconstruction and Integration," *AI Memo 1114,* Artificial Intelligence Lab, MIT, June 1989.

S. Geman and D. Geman, "Stochastic Relaxation, Gibbs Distributions and Bayesian Restoration of Images," *IEEE Trans. Pattern Anal. Mach. Intell.* **PAMI–6**, 721–741 (1984).

S. Geman and C. Graffigne, "Markov Random Field Image Models and Their Applications to Computer Vision," *Proceedings of the International Congress of Mathematics,* 1986, A. M. Gleason, ed., American Mathematical Society, 1987.

S. Geman and C. Graffigne, "Boundary Detection by Constrained Optimization," *IEEE Trans. Pattern Anal. Mach. Intell.* **PAMI–12**, 609–628 (1990).

B. Gidas, "Consistency of Maximum Likelihood and Pseudo-Likelihood Estimators for Gibbs Distributions," *Proceedings of the Workshop on Stochastic Differential Systems with Applications in Electrical/Computer Engineering, Control Theory, and Operations Research,* IMA, University of Minnesota, 1986.

D. M. Goodman and M. P. Ekstrom, "Multidimensional Spectral Factorization and Univariate AR Models," *IEEE Trans. Autom. Control* **25**, 258–262, 1980.

R. R. Hansen, Jr. and R. Chellappa, "Noncausal 2–D Spectrum Estimation for Direction Finding," *IEEE Trans. Inf. Theory* **36**, 108–125 (1990).

R. M. Haralick, "Edge and Region Analysis for Digital Image Data," in A. Rosenfeld, ed., *Image Models,* Academic Press, 1981.

R. M. Haralick, "Digital Step Edges from Zero Crossings of Second Directional Derivatives," *IEEE Trans. Pattern Anal. Mach. Intell.* **PAMI–6**, 58–68 (1986).

R. M. Haralick and L. Watson, "A Facet Model for Model Image Data," *Comput. Graph. Image Proc.* **15**, 113–129 (1981).

R. M. Haralick and co-workers, "Pose Estimation from Corresponding Point Data," *IEEE Trans. System Man Cybernetics* **19**, 1426–1446 (1989).

M. Hassner and J. Sklansky, "Markov Random Field Models of Digitized Image Texture," *Pattern Recognition* 538–540 (1978).

B. K. P. Horn, *Shape from Shading,* MIT Press, Boston, Mass., 1989.

J. R. M. Hosking, "Fractional Differencing," *Biometrika* **68**, 165–176, 1981.

B. R. Hunt, "Bayesian Methods in Nonlinear Digital Image Restoration," *IEEE Trans. Comput.* **26**, 219–229 (1977).

A. K. Jain and J. R. Jain, "Partial Differential Equations and Finite Difference Methods in Image Processing—Part II: Image Restoration," *IEEE Trans. Autom. Control* **23**, 817–834 (1978).

F. C. Jeng and J. W. Woods, "Simulated Annealing in Compound Gaussian Random Fields," *IEEE Trans. Inf. Theory* **36**, 94–107 (1990).

B. I. Justusson, "Median Filtering: Statistical Properties," *Two-dimensional Digital Signal Processing* **43**, Springer-Verlag, 1981.

R. L. Kashyap, "Analysis and Synthesis of Image Patterns by Spatial Interaction Models," in L. N. Kanal and A. Rosenfeld, eds., *Progress in Pattern Recognition* **1**, North-Holland Publishing Co., 1981.

R. L. Kashyap and R. Chellappa, "Stochastic Models for Closed Boundary Analysis: Representation and Reconstruction," *IEEE Trans. Inf. Theory* **27**, 627–637 (1981).

R. L. Kashyap and R. Chellappa, "Estimation and Choice Neighbors in Spatial Interaction Models of Images," *IEEE Trans. Inf. Theory* **29**, 60–72 (1983).

R. L. Kashyap and K. B. Eom, "Estimation in Long Memory Time Series Models," *J. Time Series Analysis* **9**, 35–41 (1988).

R. L. Kashyap and K. B. Eom, "Robust Image Modelling Techniques with an Image Restoration Application," *IEEE Trans. ASSP* **36**, 1313–1325 (1988).

R. L. Kashyap and K. B. Eom, "Texture Boundary Detection Using Long Correlation Model," *IEEE Trans. Pattern Anal. Mach. Intell.* **PAMI–11**, 58–67 (1989).

R. L. Kashyap and A. Khotanzad, "A Model-based Method for Rotation Invariant Texture Classification," *IEEE Trans. Pattern Anal. Mach. Intell.* **PAMI–8**, 472–481 (1986).

R. L. Kashyap and P. M. Lapsa, "Synthesis and Estimation of Random Fields Using Long Correlation Models," *IEEE Trans. Pattern Anal. Mach. Intell.* **PAMI–6**, 800–808 (1984).

R. L. Kashyap, R. Chellappa, and A. Khotanzad, "Texture Classification Using Features Derived from Random Field Models," *Pattern Recognition Letters* **1**, 43–50 (1982).

J. M. Keller, R. M. Crownover, and R. Y. Chen, "Characteristics of Natural Scenes Related to the Fractal Dimension," *IEEE Trans. Pattern Anal. Mach. Intell.* **PAMI–9**, 621–627 (1987).

D. Y. Kim, J. J. Kim, P. Meer, D. Mintz, and A. Rosenfeld, "Robust Computer Vision: A Least Median of Squares Based Approach," *Proceedings of Image Understanding Workshop,* Palo Alto, Calif., May 1989, pp. 1117–1134.

S. Kirkpatrick, C. D. Gelatt, and M. P. Vecchi, "Optimization by Simulated Annealing," *Science* **220**, 671–680 (1983).

P. Kube and A. Pentland, "On the Imaging of Fractal Surfaces," *IEEE Trans. Pattern Anal. Mach. Intell.* **PAMI–10**, 704–707 (1988).

H. Kunsch, "Thermodynamics and Statistical Analysis of Gaussian Random Fields," *Z. W. ver GeBrete,* **58**, 407–421 (1981).

M. S. Longuet-Higgins, "Statistical Properties of an Isotropic Random Surface," *Philos. Trans. R. Soc., London, Ser. A* **250**, 151–171 (1957).

B. H. McCormick and S. N. Jayaramamurthy, "Time Series Model for Texture Synthesis," *Intl. J. Comput. Inf. Sci.* **3**, 329–343 (1974).

B. Mandelbrot, *Fractals-form, Chance and Dimension,* Freeman, San Francisco, Calif., 1977.

B. Mandelbrot, *Fractals and a New Geometry of Nature,* Freeman, San Francisco, Calif., 1981.

B. Mandelbrot and J. W. Van Ness, "Fractional Brownian Motions, Fractional Noises and Applications," *SIAM Rev.* **10** (1968).

B. S. Manjunath, T. Simchony, and R. Chellappa, "Stochastic and Deterministic Networks for Texture Segmentation," *IEEE Trans. Acoust., Speech Signal Process* **38**, 1039–1049 (1990).

P. A. Maragoss, R. W. Schafer, and R. M. Mersereau, "Two-Dimensional Linear Prediction and Its Application to Adaptive Predictive Coding of Images," *IEEE Trans. Acoust., Speech Signal Process* **32**, 1213–1229 (1984).

J. W. Modestino and V. Bhaskaran, "Robust Two-Dimensional Tree Encoding of Images," *IEEE Trans. on Commun.* **29**, 1786–1798 (1981).

J. W. Modestino, R. W. Fries, and A. L. Vickers, "Stochastic Models Generated by Random Tessellations of the Plane," *Comput. Graph Image Proc.* **12**, 74–989 (1980).

J. W. Modestino, R. W. Fries, and A. L. Vickers, "Texture Discrimination Based Upon an Assumed Stochastic Texture Model," *IEEE Trans. Pattern Anal. Mach. Intell.* **PAMI-3**, 557–580 (1981).

D. W. Murray, A. Kashko, and H. Buxton, "A Parallel Approach to the Picture Restoration Algorithm of Geman and Geman on an SIMD Machine," *Image Vision Comput.* **4**, 133–142 (1986).

H. O. Peitgen and D. Saupe, *The Science of Fractal Images,* Springer, Berlin, 1988.

A. P. Pentland, "Fractal-based Description of Natural Scenes," *IEEE Trans. Pattern Anal. Mach. Intell.* **PAMI-6**, 661–674 (1984).

W. K. Pratt, O. Faugeras, and A. Gagalowicz, "Visual Discrimination of Stochastic Texture Fields," *IEEE Trans. System Man Cybernetics* **8**, 796–804 (1978).

A. Rangarajan and R. Chellappa, "Generalized Graduated Nonconvexity Algorithm for Maximum A Posteriori Image Estimation," *International Conference on Pattern Recognition, Image and Signal Processing Track,* Atlantic City, N.J., 1990.

C. R. Rao, *Linear Statistical Inference and It's Applications,* John Wiley and Sons, Inc., 1973.

Y. A. Rosanov, "On Gaussian Fields with Given Conditional Distributions," *Theory Probab. Its Appl.* **11**, 381–391 (1967).

A. Rosenfeld and L. S. Davis, "Image Segmentation and Image Models," *Proc. IEEE* **67**, 762–772 (1979).

A. Rosenfeld and A. C. Kak, *Digital Picture Processing* 2, Academic Press, 1982.

B. J. Schacter and N. Ahuja, "Random Pattern Generation Process," *Comput. Graph Image Proc.* **10**, 95–114 (1979).

B. J. Schacter, A. Rosenfeld, and L. S. Davis, "Random Mosaic Models for Textures," *IEEE Trans. on System Man Cybernetics* **8**, 694–702 (1978).

J. F. Silverman and D. B. Cooper, "Bayesian Clustering for Unsupervised Estimation of Surface and Texture Models," *IEEE Trans. Pattern Anal. Mach. Intell.* **PAMI-10**, 482–495 (1988).

G. Sharma and R. Chellappa, "A Model Based Approach for the Estimation of 2-D Maximum Entropy Power Spectra," *IEEE Trans. on Inf. Theory* **31**, 90–99 (1985).

G. Sharma and R. Chellappa, "Two-Dimensional Spectral Estimation Using Noncausal Autoregressive Models," *IEEE Trans. on Inf. Theory* **32**, 268–275 (1986).

T. Simchony, R. Chellappa, and Z. Lichtenstein, "Pyramid Implementation of Optimal Step Conjugate Gradient Algorithms for Some Computer Vision Problems," *IEEE Trans. System Man Cybernetics* **19**, 1408–1425 (1989).

T. Simchony, R. Chellappa, and Z. Lichtenstein, "A Relaxation Algorithms for the MAP Estimation of Gray Level Images Corrupted by Multiplicative Noise," *IEEE Trans. Inf. Theory* **36**, 608–613 (1990).

P. F. Singer and R. Chellappa, "Classification of 2-D Closed Boundaries Using Stochastic Models," *Proceedings of the IEEE Computer Society Conference on Computer Vision and Pattern Recognition,* Washington, D.C., June 1983.

A. H. Tewfik, B. C. Levy, and A. S. Willsky, "An Efficient Maximum Entropy Technique for 2-D Isotropic Random Fields," *IEEE Trans. Acoust. Speech Signal Process.* **36**, 797–812 (1988).

C. W. Therrien, "An Estimation Theoretic Approach to Terrain Image Segmentation," *Comput. Vision, Gr. Image Process.* **22**, 313–326 (1983).

P. Whittle, "On Stationary Processes in the Plane," *Biometrika* **41**, 434–449 (1954).

J. W. Woods, "Two-Dimensional Discrete Markovian Fields," *IEEE Trans. on Inf. Theory* **18**, 232–240 (1972).

J. W. Woods and C. H. Radewan, "Kalman Filtering in Two Dimensions," *IEEE Trans. Inf. Theory* **23**, 473–482 (1977).

Y. Yakimovsky, "Boundary and Object Detection in Real World Images," *J. Assoc. Comput. Mach.* **23**, 599–618 (1976).

Y. T. Zhou, V. Venkateswar, and R. Chellappa, "Edge Detection and Linear Feature Extraction Using the Directional Derivatives of a 2-D Random Field Model," *IEEE Trans. Pattern Anal. Mach. Intell.* **PAMI-11**, 84–95 (1989).

R. CHELLAPPA
University of Maryland

R. L. KASHYAP
Purdue University

IMAGE PROPERTIES

Image descriptions usually regard the image as composed of parts that have various properties and are related in various ways. This article discusses properties of images or image parts and relations among image parts. (On methods of defining image parts, see SEGMENTATION). It also briefly discusses the relevance of image (part) properties to the description of the scene that the image depicts.

This article deals only with digital images, ie, rectangular arrays of given size consisting of elements (pixels) whose values (gray levels) are integers or real numbers that lie in a given bounded range. (Note that we have not required the values to be nonnegative.)

In general, an *image property* is any function that maps images into numbers; the numbers may be integer, real, or complex. A proposition that is either true or false about a given image can be regarded as a two-valued property, where (say) "true" corresponds to the value 1 and "false" to the value 0.

The value of a property may depend only on a given subset of the image. If the subset is small, the property is called a *local property*. If the value depends only on which pixels belong to the subset, but not on the gray levels of these pixels, it is called a *geometric property* of the subset.

LINEAR PROPERTIES

An image property $\mathcal{P}$ is called *linear* if $\mathcal{P}(af + bg) = a\mathcal{P}(f) + b\mathcal{P}(g)$ for all images f, g and all constants a, b. It can be shown (Rosenfeld, 1969; Rosenfeld and Kak, 1982) that for any real-valued linear property $\mathcal{P}$ there exists an image h such that $\mathcal{P}(f) = \Sigma\Sigma hf$ (the pixelwise product of h and f, summed over the rectangular array). In other words, any linear property is a linear combination of the gray levels of the image; h is the array of coefficients of the linear combination.

An important class of linear properties makes use of hs that are digitized versions of standard mathematical functions. For example, if h is a sinusoid, $\Sigma\Sigma hf$ is a Fourier coefficient of f; and similarly for the coefficients in other expansions of f. Note that the coefficients obtained from a set of mutually orthogonal hs constitute a set of uncorrelated properties of f.

The *moments* of f are obtained using hs of the form $x^i y^i$; the (i, j) moment of f is defined by

$$m_{ij} \equiv \Sigma\Sigma x^i y^j f(x, y)$$

Moments can be given a physical interpretation by regarding gray level as mass, ie, regarding f as composed of a set of point masses located at the points (x, y). Thus m_{00} is the total mass of f, and m_{02}, m_{20} are the moments of inertia of f around the x and y axes, respectively. Moments for which i, j, or $i + j$ is odd can be regarded as measures of asymmetry about the y-axis, x-axis, and origin, respectively, since they are zero when f is symmetric around these axes (respectively).

The *centroid* of f is the point $(\bar{x}, \bar{y})$ defined by

$$\bar{x} = m_{10}/m_{00}, \qquad \bar{y} = m_{01}/m_{00}$$

When we take the origin at the centroid, moments computed with respect to this origin are called *central moments*, and denoted by $\bar{m}_{ij}$. Evidently $\bar{m}_{00} = m_{00}$, and it can be verified that $\bar{m}_{10} = \bar{m}_{01} = 0$.

The line about which f has minimum moment of inertia is called the *principal axis* of f; it turns out to be the line through the centroid whose slope $\tan\theta$ satisfies the equation

$$\tan^2\theta + \frac{\bar{m}_{20} - \bar{m}_{02}}{\bar{m}_{11}}\tan\theta - 1 = 0.$$

STATISTICAL AND TEXTURAL PROPERTIES

Statistical properties of the image's gray levels are another useful class of descriptors; for example, the mean gray level is a measure of the overall lightness/darkness of the image, and the gray level standard deviation is a measure of contrast. Higher-order statistics, computed from the gray levels of pairs of pixels in given relative positions, provide measures of image texture. Many other types of properties have been used to characterize textures—for example, properties derived from Fourier coefficients, or first-order statistics of the values of local proper-

ties computed in a neighborhood of every pixel. (See TEXTURE).

GEOMETRICAL PROPERTIES

In this section we define many of the standard geometric properties of subsets of a digital image. A general discussion of image subsets and their properties can be found in Rosenfeld and Kak (1982).

Neighbors

A pixel $P = (x, y)$ of a digital image has four horizontal and vertical neighbors, namely the pixels

$$(x - 1, y), \quad (x, y - 1), \quad (x, y + 1), \quad (x + 1, y)$$

We call these pixels the 4-*neighbors* of P, and say that they are 4-*adjacent* to P. In addition, P has four diagonal neighbors, namely

$$(x - 1, y - 1), \quad (x - 1, y + 1),$$
$$(x + 1, y - 1), \quad (x + 1, y + 1)$$

These, together with the 4-neighbors, are called 8-*neighbors* of P (8-*adjacent* to P). Note that if P is on the border of the image, some of its neighbors may not exist.

Paths and Connectedness

A path Π of length n from P to Q is a sequence of pixels $P = P_0, P_1, \ldots, P_n = Q$ such that P_i is a neighbor of $P_{i-1}, 1 \le i \le n$. Note that there are two versions of this and the following definitions, depending on whether "neighbor" means "4-neighbor" or "8-neighbor." Thus we can speak of Π being a 4-*path* or an 8-*path*.

Let S be a subset of the image, and let P, Q be pixels of S. We say that P is (4- or 8-) *connected* to Q in S if there exists a (4- or 8-) path from P to Q consisting entirely of pixels of S. For any P in S, the set of pixels that are connected to P in S is called a connected *component* of S. If S has only one component, it is called a connected set.

Holes and Surroundedness

Let $\bar{S}$ be the complement of S. It is usually assumed, for simplicity, that the border of the image (ie, its top and bottom rows and its left and right columns) is in $\bar{S}$. The component of $\bar{S}$ that contains the image border is called the *background* of S. All other components of $\bar{S}$, if any, are called *holes* in S. If S is connected and has no holes, it is said to be *simply connected;* if it is connected but has holes, it is said to be *multiply connected*.

Let S and T be any subsets of the image. We say that T *surrounds* S if any path from any pixel of S to the border of the image must meet T, ie, if for any path $P_0, P_1, \ldots, P_n$ such that P_0 is in S and P_n is on the image border, some P_i must be in T. Evidently the background of S surrounds S, and S surrounds any hole in S.

Borders

The border of a set S is the set of pixels of S that are adjacent to $\tilde{S}$. We will assume, for simplicity, that "adjacent" here means "4-adjacent." The set of nonborder pixels of S is called the *interior* of S.

Let C be a component of S, and let D be a component of $\tilde{S}$ that is adjacent to C. The set C_D of pixels of C that are adjacent to D is called the *D-border* of C. It can be shown that if C is adjacent to several components of $\tilde{S}$, then exactly one of those components, say D_0, surrounds C, and the others are surrounded by C. The D_0-border of C is called its *outer border*, and the other D-borders of C, if any, are called *hole borders*.

Distance

The *Euclidean distance* between two pixels $P = (x, y)$ and $Q = (u, v)$ is

$$d_e(P, Q) = \sqrt{(x - u)^2 + (y - v)^2}$$

It is sometimes convenient to work with simpler distance measures on digital images. In particular, the *city block distance* between P and Q is defined as

$$d_4(P, Q) = |x - u| + |y - v|$$

and the *chessboard distance* between them is

$$d_8(P, Q) = \max(|x - u|, |y - v|)$$

It can be verified that all three of these measures, d_e, d_4, and d_8, are *metrics*.

The pixels that lie within a given city block distance from P form a diamond (ie, a diagonally oriented square) centered at P. In particular, the pixels at distance 1 are just the 4-neighbors of P. Analogously, the pixels that lie within a given chessboard distance from P form an upright square centered at P; those at distance 1 are the 8-neighbors of P.

The distance between a pixel P and a set S is defined to be the shortest distance between P and any pixel of S. The *diameter* of a set is the greatest distance between any two of its pixels.

Area and Perimeter

The *area* of S is simply the number of pixels of S. The *perimeter* of S can be defined as the area of its border. A more accurate definition can be formulated in terms of the numbers of steps (from neighbor to neighbor) required to "follow" each border completely around, where steps to horizontal or vertical neighbors count as 1, and steps to diagonal neighbors count as $\sqrt{2}$. On border following see Rosenfeld and Kak (1982). The quantity p^2/A (the square of the perimeter divided by the area) is sometimes called the "shape factor"; in Euclidean geometry, this quantity is smallest if S is a disk.

Extent

The *height* of S is the vertical distance between its highest and lowest pixels, and similarly its *width* is the horizontal distance between its leftmost and rightmost pixels. More generally, the *extent* of S in a given direction θ is the distance between its extreme pixels as measured parallel to θ. The greatest extent of S in any direction is equal to the *diameter* of S.

Elongatedness

The (maximum) thickness of S is twice the greatest distance from any pixel of S to its complement $\tilde{S}$. S is described as *elongated* if its area is large compared to the square of its thickness, or *compact* if the inverse is true. Note that a given S may be partly compact, and its elongated parts may have different thicknesses; on a method of identifying these parts see Rosenfeld and Kak (1982).

Convexity

S is called *convex* if the straight line joining any two of its pixels always lies within unit distance of it. The smallest convex set $H(S)$ containing a set S is called the *convex hull* of S. The *concavities* of S are the connected components of the difference set $H(S) - S$.

Slope and Curvature

The left and right *k-slopes* of a border at a given pixel P are the slopes of the straight lines joining P to the pixels k steps away from it along the border in each direction. The *k-curvature* of the border at P is the difference between the left and right *k-slopes*. Evidently, k should be chosen large enough to smooth out the effects of the digital nature of the image, but it must be small relative to the perimeter of the border. A piece of border is *straight* if it could be the digitization of a straight edge, eg, if the straight line joining its first and last pixels always lies within unit distance of it.

Geometry-based Decomposition of Image Subsets

There are many ways of decomposing an image subset into parts based on geometric criteria. Examples of such parts are connected components; background and holes; borders and interiors; elongated parts; and concavities. A border can be segmented into connected arcs whose slopes (or curvatures) lie in given ranges, or it can be segmented at points where the slope changes abruptly (corners) or where the curvature changes sign (inflections).

Representation of Image Subsets

Any subset of S of a digital image can be represented by a "binary" digital image $B(S)$ (ie, an array whose elements are all 0 or 1), the same size as the given image, having 1's at the pixels of S and 0's elsewhere. This representation requires the same amount of storage space no matter how simple S is. There are various methods of representing simple S's more compactly:

1. *Contour code*. S is determined by specifying the location of a pixel on each of its borders, together with the series of steps (from neighbor to neighbor) required to "follow" the border completely around.

2. *Run length code.* On each row of the image, $B(S)$ consists of a sequence of strings ("runs") of 0s alternating with strings of 1s. Thus S is determined by specifying, on each row, the lengths of the strings and whether the row begins with 0 or 1.

3. *The medial axis transformation.* For any pixel P of S, let $S(P)$ be the largest upright square block of 1s in $B(S)$ centered at P; then $B(S)$ is the union of the $S(P)$s, and so is determined by specifying their sizes and the coordinates of their centers.

4. *The quadtree.* Let the image be of size 2^n by 2^n. We recursively subdivide $B(S)$ into quadrants until we obtain "solid" blocks that consist entirely of 0s or entirely of 1s. The subdivision process is determined by specifying a tree of degree 4 whose root corresponds to $B(S)$ and whose leaves correspond to the solid blocks.

A general discussion of these subset representations, including methods of converting between one representation and another, of computing representations of derived sets (unions, intersections, etc) directly from the representations of the original sets, and of computing geometric properties of a subset directly from a representation, can be found in Rosenfeld and Kak (1982).

Fuzzy Image Subsets and their Geometrical Properties

A fuzzy subset of an image is a function μ that maps each pixel into a real number in the interval [0,1]. We can think of μ as the "degree of membership" of the pixel in the subset. An ordinary subset can be regarded as a special case of a fuzzy subset in which μ can only take on the values 0 and 1; pixel P is in the subset if and only if $\mu(P) = 1$.

Most of the standard geometrical properties of image subsets can be generalized to fuzzy subsets. For example, $\Sigma\Sigma\mu$ is a natural generalization of area. For an introduction to this subject, see Rosenfeld (1984).

INVARIANT PROPERTIES

We often are interested in image properties that remain the same when certain types of operations are performed on the image. For example, we may want the properties to be invariant under gray scale operations such as overall changes in lightness or contrast, or under geometric operations such as translation, rotation, or magnification.

For real images or image subsets, it is easy to define properties that are invariant under such operations. For digital images, however, the invariance is only approximate, since the result of performing the operation is in general not a digital image, and it must be redigitized before the property can be computed.

An important way of defining properties that are invariant under a given set of operations is to *normalize* the given image f with respect to the operations; in other words, to construct an image $N(f)$ such that $N(O(f)) = N(f)$ for all the operations O. Evidently, any property of $N(f)$ is an invariant property of f. Many examples of nor-

malization techniques are described in Rosenfeld and Kak (1982).

RELATIONS

Most of the (binary) relations between image subsets used in describing images are defined in terms of relative values of properties, eg, brighter than, larger than. Ternary (and higher-order) relations can also be defined in this way; for example, the direction from P to Q is defined in terms of the relative values of their coordinates, and Q is between P and R if P and R lie in opposite directions from Q. It should be pointed out that topological relations such as adjacency and surroundedness are not readily definable in terms of relative property values. Most relations (eg, larger than, near) should be regarded as "fuzzy," ie, as numerical-valued rather than propositional; and they are often not easy to define, eg, it is not obvious how to define relations of relative position for image subsets that have noncompact shapes.

THE VIEWPOINT-DEPENDENCE OF PROPERTIES

The image properties treated in this article may provide useful information about the scene depicted in the image, provided the image was obtained from a known viewpoint; but if the viewpoint is not known, the information may be ambiguous. For example, in an image of a uniformly textured surface, the values of textural properties vary with the scale (ie, range) and slant of the surface; if we do not know that the surface texture is uniform, variations in the image texture due to scale and slant cannot be distinguished from variations in the surface texture. (See TEXTURE). Similarly, most of the standard geometric properties that involve metric concepts (distance, area, extent, slope, etc) are sensitive to viewpoint. On the other hand, topological properties and relations (adjacency, connectedness, surroundedness) should in principle be viewpoint-invariant (unless the change in scale is so large that digitization effects become significant), and similar remarks apply to properties based on convexity. It is possible to define metric-based properties (involving ratios) that are in principle viewpoint-invariant; but the accuracy with which such properties can be measured is usually limited by digitization effects. We have assumed here that the image is an intensity image and is obtained from the scene by perspective projection; different considerations apply to properties derived from range images (see RANGE DATA ANALYSIS). It should also be noted that image parts do not always correspond in a natural way to scene parts (see SEGMENTATION).

BIBLIOGRAPHY

A. Rosenfeld, *Picture Processing by Computer*, Academic Press, New York, 1969, Section 7.3.

A. Rosenfeld, "The Fuzzy Geometry of Image Subsets," *Pattern Recognition Letters* **2**, 311–317 (Sept. 1984).

A. Rosenfeld and A. C. Kak, *Digital Picture Processing* (second edition), Academic Press, New York, 1982, Chapter 11 and Section 12.1.

AZRIEL ROSENFELD
University of Maryland

IMAGE UNDERSTANDING

Think about the process by which you understand what you see. Can you determine what is happening and how it is happening when you look out the window and notice that your best friend is walking toward your door? As you may guess, the process by which you arrived at this conclusion, and which caused you to go and open the door before your friend knocked, is not a simple one. Ancient philosophers worried about this problem. Biological scientists have been studying the problem in earnest since Hermann von Helmholtz (1821–1894), commonly credited as the father of modern perceptual science. Computer scientists began looking at this problem only recently in these terms, and the discipline of computer vision is a very young one. The miracle of vision is not restricted to the eye; it also involves the cortex and brain stem and requires interactions with many other specific brain areas. In this sense, vision may be considered an important aspect of AI. It is the major source of input for man's other cognitive faculties.

This article discusses the aspects of vision that deal with the understanding of visual information. Understanding in this context means the transformation of visual images (the input to the retina) into descriptions of the world that can interface with other thought processes and elicit appropriate action. The representation of these descriptions and the process of their transformation are not currently understood by the biological sciences. In AI, researchers are concerned with the discovery of computational models that behave in the same ways that humans do, and thus, representations and processes are defined using the available computational tools.

Image understanding (IU) is the research area concerned with the design and experimentation of computer systems that integrate explicit models of a visual problem domain with one or more methods for extracting features from images and one or more methods for matching features with domain models using a control structure. Given a goal, or a reason for looking at a particular scene, these systems produce descriptions of both the images and the world scenes that the images represent.

The goal of an image-understanding system (IUS) is to transform two-dimensional spatial (and, if appropriate to the problem domain, time-varying) data into a description of the three-dimensional spatio-temporal world. The description can take many forms, and the particular form associated with a given implementation depends strongly on the problem domain and task involved; it may range from simple "yes-no" answers to full surface reconstructions of objects and anything in between. In the early to mid-seventies, this activity was termed *scene analysis*. Other terms for this are *knowledge-based vision* or *high-level vision*. IU is distinguished from *model-based vision*, whose main goal is to locate specific models and derive their transformation parameters in images (see OBJECT RECOGNITION). The descriptions sought in IUSs are more general. Several survey papers have appeared on this topic. The interested reader is particularly referred to papers by Binford (1982), Kanade (1977), Matsuyama (1984), and Tsotsos (1984) as well as the excellent collection of papers in *Computer Vision Systems* (Hansen and Risemon, 1978) and *Readings in Computer Vision* (Fischler and Firschein, 1987). Those readers interested in the biological side of image understanding are referred to an excellent book by Uttal (1981), *A Taxonomy of Visual Processes*.

Integration is the key phrase when describing an IUS. Research on IUSs has experimented with ways of integrating existing techniques into systems and, in doing so, has discovered problems and solutions that would not otherwise have been uncovered. Integrated within a single framework, an IUS must:

Extract Meaningful Two-Dimensional (2–D) Grouping of Intensity-Location-Time Values. Images or image sequences contain a tremendous amount of information in their raw form. The process of transformation thus begins with the identification of groups of image entities, pixels. These pixels are grouped by means of similarity of intensity value, for example, over a particular spatial location. They can also be grouped on the basis of intensity discontinuity or similarity of change or constancy over time. The assumption is that groups of pixels that exhibit some similarity in their characteristics probably belong to specific objects or events. Typical groupings are edges, regions, and flow vectors.

Infer 3–D Surfaces, Volumes, Boundaries, Shadows, Occlusion, Depth, Color, Motion. Using the groupings of pixels and their characteristics, the next major transformational step is to infer larger groupings that correspond, for example, to surfaces of objects or motion events. The result of the inference may be quantitative or qualitative depending on the problem task. The reason for the need for inference is that the pixels by themselves do not contain sufficient information for the unique determination of the events or objects; other constraints or knowledge must be applied. This knowledge can be of a variety of forms, ranging from knowledge of the imaging process including viewpoint, knowledge of the image formation process including camera or sensor motion, and knowledge of physical constraints on the world, to knowledge of specific objects being viewed. Typically, the most appropriate knowledge to use is an open question, but the simplest and least application-specific knowledge is preferred.

Group Information Into Unique Physical Entities. Surfaces can be connected to form 3–D objects, and changes in trajectories can be joined to describe motions of specific types. Again, the original pixel values do not contain sufficient information for this process, and additional knowledge must be applied. This knowledge is perhaps in the form of connectivity and continuity constraints, and in many cases these are embedded in explicit models of objects of the domain.

Transform Image-Centered Representations Into World-Centered Representations. To this point the descriptions created have all been in terms of a coordinate system that is "image centered" (also called "viewer centered" or "retinotopic"). A key transformation is to convert this coordinate system to one that is "world centered" (also called "object centered"), that is, the description is no longer dependent on specific locations in images. This is a crucial step—otherwise, the stored models must be replicated for each possible location and orientation in space.

Label Entities Depending on System Goals and World Models. It almost never occurs that humans are given a picture or told to look out the window and asked to describe everything that is seen in a high and uniform degree of detail. Typically a scene is viewed for a reason. What exactly this goal is has direct impact on how the scene is described, which objects and events are described in detail; and which are not. Second, scenes are always described based on what is known about the world; they are described in terms of the domain that is being viewed. A factory scene, for example, is almost never described in terms of a hospital environment—that would not be a useful description (unless metaphoric use is the goal!). This knowledge base permits the choice of the most appropriate "labels" to associate with objects and events of the scene. Labels are typically the natural-language words or phrases that are used in the applications domain. The process of finding labels and their associated models that are relevant is called "search." Models that are deemed relevant may be termed "hypotheses." Each hypothesis must be "matched" against the data extracted from the images. In the case where the data is insufficient to verify a model, "expectations" may be generated that guide further analysis of the images. Labels are necessary for communication to other components of a complete intelligent system that must use interpreted visual information. The label set forms the language of communication between vision and the remainder of the intelligent system.

Infer Relationships Among Entities. In viewing a scene, not only are individual objects and events recognized but they are also interrelated. Looking out the window, for example, one may see a tree in a lawn, a car on a driveway, a boy walking along the street, or a girl playing on a swing set. The relationships may play an important role in assisting the labeling process as well. These relationships form a spatio-temporal context for objects and events.

Construct a Consistent Internal Description. This really applies to all levels of the transformation process that is being described here. The output of an image-understanding system is a representation of the image contents, usually called an "interpretation." Care is required, however, in defining what an interpretation actually involves. Little attention has been given to this, and current systems employ whatever representation for an interpretation is convenient and appropriate to the problem domain. Basically, an interpretation consists of inferred facts, relationships among facts, and representations of

physical form. Issues of consistency and foundations of the underlying representational formalism are important, yet they have not received much attention with the IUS community. The output of an IUS usually takes one of two forms: a graphic rendition of the objects recognized is displayed, perhaps with natural-language labels identifying various parts, or textual output describing the characteristics of the objects observed and recognized is generated. Some systems employ both methods, and the choice depends on the particular problem domain being addressed.

Two basic questions arise when describing an IUS to the uninitiated. The first question is "Why did this field arise as distinct from so-called low-level vision or early vision?" There are two main reasons for the distinction: the bottom-up approach (see PROCESSING, BOTTOM-UP AND TOP-DOWN) embodied in early vision schemes is inadequate for the generation of complete symbolic descriptions of visual input, and there is a need to describe visual input using the same terminology as the problem domain. There are several basic realities that impact the design of image-understanding systems. The first is that images underconstrain the scenes that they represent. The reason is straightforward: in human vision, a 3-D scene undergoes a perspective projection onto a 2-D retina in order to become an image. Thus, much information is lost, particularly depth information. The image is just a snapshot in time of the scene, and both spatial as well as temporal continuity information is lost. Further, the image created is a distorted view of the scene that it represents. The distortion is not only due to the perspective transformation, but, also, there is noise involved in the image creation process. Finally, a purely bottom-up (or data-directed) approach does not lead to unambiguous results in all cases. A data-directed scheme considers all the data and tries to follow through on every hypothesis generated. Consideration of all data and all possible models in a system of size and scope comparable to the human visual system leads to combinatorial explosion and is thus an intractable approach. Moreover, it can be nonconvergent, can only produce conclusions that are derivable directly or indirectly from the input data, and cannot focus or direct the search toward a desired solution.

A vision system must be able to represent and use a very large number of object and event models. If the input is naturally ambiguous, a purely bottom-up activation of models will lead to a much larger set of models to consider than is necessary or salient. The working hypothesis of IUSs is that domain knowledge (qv), in addition to the bottom-up processes, can assist in the disambiguation process as well as reduce the combinatorial problem. How that knowledge is to be used is a key problem.

The second question that often arises is "Is image understanding computationally the same as speech understanding?" On the surface, it may seem that the techniques applicable to the speech understanding (qv) problem are directly applicable to the image-understanding problem. A simplified view of the speech understanding process leads to this conclusion. The differences arise if content is considered, rather than form alone. Speech understanding (qv) may be regarded as the recognition of phonemes, the grouping of phonemes into words, the grouping of words into sequences, the parsing of word sequences into sentences, and the interpretation of the meaning of the sentences. Indeed, in a paper by Woods (1978), the similarity is presented in some detail. Woods speculates on the applicability of the HWIM architecture for the image-understanding problem and concludes that it may be worth the attempt. However, a closer examination of the differences between speech and image interpretation tasks reveals that the image-understanding task is significantly different and more difficult.

The similarities between the speech and image tasks are many. Both domains exhibit inherent ambiguity in the signal, and thus signal characteristics alone are insufficient for interpretation. Reliability of interpretation can be increased by the use of redundancy provided by knowledge of vocabulary, syntax, semantics, and pragmatic considerations; and both domains seem to involve a hierarchical abstraction mechanism. The differences include the facts that: (a) speech exhibits a single spatial dimension (amplitude) with a necessary temporal dimension, whereas images display two spatial dimensions as well as the temporal dimension; (b) a speech segment has two boundary points, whereas an image segment, as a spatial region, has a large number of boundary points; (c) speech has a relatively small vocabulary that is well documented (eg, in dictionaries) and images have much larger, undocumented vocabularies; (d) grammars have been devised for languages, but no such grammars exist for visual data; (e) although speech differs depending on the speaker, images vary much more because of viewpoint, illumination, spatial position, and orientation of objects, and occlusion; (f) speech has a convenient and well-accepted abstract description, namely, letters and words, whereas images do not; and (g) the speech signal is spatially one-dimensional, and when sampled by the ear, there is no equivalent of the projection of a 3-D scene onto a 2-D retina. Thus, it seems that the image-understanding situation is radically different, particularly in combinatorial terms, and it is for this reason that very different solutions have appeared.

REPRESENTATIONAL AND CONTROL REQUIREMENTS

This section attempts to summarize the experience of the IU community in the design and implementation of IUSs with a statement of components currently believed to be necessary for vision systems. It should be clear that this is not a formal definition of an IUS in a strict sense; many of the requirements are really topics for further research. The section does not contain specific references; instead, it refers to other entries in this encyclopedia. Specific solutions and vision systems and how they deal with each of these requirements appear in a subsequent section.

Representational Requirements

Many IUSs distinguish three levels of representations: a low level, an intermediate level, and a high level. These levels do not necessarily refer to particular types of formalisms but rather simply point out that in the interpretation process, a transformation of representations into more abstract ones is required and that typically three levels of abstraction are considered. These levels can usually be characterized as follows: Low level includes image primitives such as edges, texture elements, or regions; intermediate level includes boundaries, surfaces and volumes; and high level includes objects, scenes, or events. There is no reason why there should be only three levels, and in fact, the task of transforming representations may be made easier by considering smaller jumps between representations. It should be clear in the descriptions that follow which level or levels are being addressed.

Representation of Prototypical Concepts. A prototype provides a generalized definition of the components, attributes, and relationships that must be confirmed of a particular concept under consideration in order to be able to make the deduction that the particular concept is an instance of the prototypical concept. A prototype would be a complex structure spanning many levels of description in order to adequately capture surfaces, volumes, and other events, to construct discrete objects into more complex ones, to define spatial, temporal, and functional relationships for each object, and to assert constraints that must be satisfied in order for a particular object in a scene to be identified.

Concept Organization. Three kinds of abstraction are commonly used, namely, feature aggregation, called "PART-OF", concept specialization, called "IS-A", and instantiation, called "INSTANCE-OF". The PART-OF hierarchy can be considered as an organization for the aggregation of concepts into more abstract ones or as an organization for the decomposition of concepts into more primitive ones, depending on which direction it is traversed. The leaves of the PART-OF hierarchy are discrete concepts and may represent image features. It should be pointed out that concept structure does not necessarily mean physical structure only, but similar mechanisms with different semantics may be used to also represent logical components of concepts. IS-A is a relationship between two concepts, one of which is a specialization of the other. An important property of the IS-A relationship is inheritance of properties from parent to child concept, thus eliminating the need for repetition of properties in each concept. Finally, the relationship between prototypical knowledge and observed tokens is the INSTANCE-OF relationship. These three relationships are typically used in conjunction with one another. Consideration of the semantics of these relationships is important, and such issues are discussed elsewhere (see INHERITANCE HIERARCHY).

Spatial Knowledge. This is perhaps the main type of knowledge that most vision systems employ. This includes spatial relationships (such as "above," "between," "left of"), form information (points, curves, regions, surfaces, and volumes), location in space, geometry, and continuity constraints (see REASONING, SPATIAL). Spatial constraints for grouping have appeared in the Gestalt literature in psychology and include the tendencies to group using smoothness of form, continuity of form, spatial proximity, and symmetry. The PART-OF relationship is used to represent aggregates of simple forms into more complex ones. Properties or attributes of spatial forms are also required, namely, size, orientation, contrast, reflectance, curvature, texture, and color. Maps are common forms of spatial knowledge representation, particularly for vision systems dealing with domains such as aerial photographs or navigation tasks.

Temporal Knowledge. Information about temporal constraints and time is not only necessary for the interpretation of spatio-temporal images but can also provide a context in which spatial information can be interpreted. Time can provide another source of constraints on image objects and events. Temporal constraints for motion groupings, in the Gestalt sense, include the tendencies to group using similarity of motion. The basic types of temporal information include time instants; durations and time intervals; rates, such as speed or acceleration; and temporal relations such as "before," "during," or "start." Each of these has meaning only if associated with some spatial event as well. PART-OF and IS-A relationships can be used for grouping and organizing spatio-temporal concepts in much the same fashion as for purely spatial concepts. A difficulty with the inclusion of temporal information into an IUS is that an implicit claim is made of existential dependency. That is, if a relationship such as "object A appears before object B" is included in a knowledge base, and object B is observed, then according to the knowledge base, it must be true that object A must have appeared previously (see REASONING, TEMPORAL).

The Scale Problem. It has been well understood since the early days of computer vision that spatial and spatio-temporal events in images exhibit a natural "scale." They are large or small in spatial extent and/or temporal duration with respect to scale, for example. This problem is different than the image resolution or coarseness problem, and there is no relationship between the two. It is important that an IUS deal with this as well. There are implications not only for the design of the image-specific operations that extract image events (a given operator cannot be optimal for all scales and thus is limited for a particular range of events that it detects well) but also for the choice of representational and control scheme. If spatio-temporal events require representation at multiple scales, the matching and reasoning processes must also be able to deal with the multiple scales. The unification of information from multiple scales into a single representation is important (see SCALE SPACE).

Description by Comparison and Differentiation. Similarity measures can be used to assist in the determination of other relevant hypotheses when matching of a hypothesis fails. This is useful in the control of growth of the hypothesis space as well as for displaying a more intelligent guidance scheme than random choice of alternates. The similarity relation usually relates mutually exclusive hypotheses. The relation involves the explicit representation of possible matching failures, the context within which the match failure occurred, binding information relevant to the alternative hypothesis, as well as the alternate hypothesis. Thus, the selection of alternatives is guided by the reasons for the failure.

Inference and Control Requirements

A brief note is in order before continuing this section on the difference between inference and control, particularly since in some works they are used as synonyms. Inference refers to the process of deriving new, not explicitly represented facts from currently known facts. There are many methods available for this task, and they are discussed in detail in other entries (see INDUCTVE INFERENCE; INFERENCE; REASONING). Control refers to the process that selects which of the many inference, search, and matching techniques should be applied at a particular stage of processing. The remainder of this section briefly discusses these issues and others in roughly the order that a designer of a typical image-understanding system would confront them.

Search and Hypothesis Activation. The basic interpretation paradigm used in IUSs, as is developed later in the Historical Perspective and Techniques section, is "hypothesize and test." There are several aspects to this, and these are described in turn beginning with search and hypothesis activation. A general vision system must contain a very large number of models that represent prototypical objects, events, and scenes. It is computationally prohibitive to match image features with all of them, and therefore, search schemes are employed to reduce the number of models that are considered. Only the salient models need be considered, and the determination of which are salient is termed the "indexing" problem. The catalog of search methods includes breadth-first, depth-first, hill climbing, best-first, dynamic programming, branch-and-bound, A*, beam search, information gathering or constraint satisfaction, relaxation labeling processes, and production systems. These are all described elsewhere (see A* ALGORITHM; SEARCH, BEAM; CONSTRAINT SATISFACTION; RULE-BASED SYSTEMS; SEARCH, BEST-FIRST; SEARCH, BRANCH-AND-BOUND; SEARCH, DEPTH-FIRST). A different categorization of search types, and one that is more frequently found in the IUS literature, is in terms of knowledge interactions. The following schemes are described below: model-directed search, goal-directed search, data-directed search, failure-directed search, temporally-directed search, hierarchical models, heterarchical models, blackboard models, and beam search. The choice of search method employed depends on a number of factors, including the form of the representation over which the search is to be performed, the potential complexity problems, and the goals of the search process.

Saliency of a model depends on the statement of goals for the search process. The search can be guided by a number of trigger features, for example, and any models that are encountered that embody those features are selected. The selection of a model for further consideration is termed "hypothesis activation." A search process that leads to a very large set of active hypotheses is not desired since the object of search is to reduce the space of models.

Matching and Hypothesis Testing. Once a set of active hypotheses has been determined, further consideration of each hypothesis takes place. The first task to be carried out is to match the active hypothesis to the data. It is important to note that data here do not necessarily only mean image-specific information. Matching is defined as the comparison of two representations in order to discover their similarities and differences. Usually, a matching process in vision compares representations at different levels of abstraction and thus is one of the mechanisms for transforming a given representation into a more abstract one. The result of a match is a representation of the similarities and differences between the given representations and may include an associated certainty or strength of belief in the degree of match.

The specific matching methods used depend largely on the representational formalisms that are used to code the data being compared. They can range from image–image matching, subgraph isomorphisms, or shape matching, to matching only selected features with a model, such as identifying structural components. Matching processes, particularly ones that involve matching images directly, are usually very sensitive to variations in illumination, shading, viewpoint, and 3-D orientation. It is preferred, therefore, to match abstract descriptions such as image features against models in order to overcome some of these problems. However, for 3-D models it is not always the case that image features can trigger proper models for consideration. Rather, the process must also involve the determination of the projection of the model that can be matched (see TEMPLATE MATCHING).

Generation and Use of Expectations. Expectations are beliefs as to what exists in the spatio-temporal context of the scene. The concept of expectation-directed vision is a common one that appears in most systems. Expectations must bridge representations in a downward direction, going from models to image appearance. *Projection* is a term commonly used to denote the connection between representations of the same concept but in differing domains. It is, for example, the relationship between a prototypical object and its actual appearance in an image. Thus, a mechanism is required that takes object position, lighting, observer motion, temporal continuity, and viewpoint into account to create an internal representation of an object's appearance in an image. Complete projections may not always be necessary, and in most cases it seems that expectations of important distinguishing features or structures are sufficient. The most common use of expectations is in directing image-specific processes in the extraction of image features not previously found (see also PARSING).

Change and Focus of Attention. Even the best of search and hypothesis activation schemes will often lead to very large hypothesis sets. Computing resources are always limited, and thus the allocation of resources must be made to those hypotheses that are most likely to lead to progress in the interpretation task. This can be done in a number of ways, including the use of standard operating system measures for resource allocation, as were used in an augmented fashion in HEARSAY (Erman and co-workers, 1980), ranking hypotheses by means of certainty or goodness-of-fit estimates, or by considering the potential of a

hypothesis in conjunction with the expense that would be incurred in its evaluation. These best hypotheses, which are usually those that are confirmed or virtually confirmed, are also termed "islands of reliability."

Not only is it important to determine a focus of attention but it is also important to determine when to abandon a current focus as unproductive. The change of focus can be determined in one of two ways: the focus could be recomputed each time it was required or it could remain fixed and only change when circumstances necessitated the change. The latter is clearly more desirable; yet mechanisms for its implementation are few. It should be pointed out that a focus of attention does not necessarily refer only to a hypothesis set but may also refer to a region on an image or a subset of some representation.

One important type of perceptual attention is that referred to by the term "active vision" (see EARLY VISION; VISUAL RECOVERY). Active perceptual strategies, which provide for dynamic changes in the image acquisition process, are useful in at least the following ways: to see a portion of the visual field otherwise hidden; to compensate for spatial non-uniformity of a processing mechanism; to increase spatial resolution; to disambiguate aspects of the visual world (through induced motion, or lighting changes for example); to enhance the efficiency of processing by restricting the search space; and to provide for a better mathematical problem formulation. All of the above tacitly assume that some hypothesize-and-test mechanism is at work. Only if hypotheses are available, can a particular action due to an active perception mechanism actually yield benefits. Otherwise the search space is simply too large.

Certainty and Strength of Belief. The use of certainty measures in computer vision arose due to two main reasons: biological visual systems employ firing rate (which may be thought of as a strength of response), as the almost exclusive means of neural communication, and computational processes available currently are quite unreliable. This strength of response may be thought of as brightness for simplicity. Lateral inhibition (one of the processes of neural communication), whereby neurons can inhibit the response of neighboring ones based mainly on magnitude of the firing rate, is a common process, if not ubiquitous. It motivated the use of relaxation labeling processes in vision. In relaxation, the strength of response is termed "certainty," and is often used as a measure of reliability of a corresponding decision process, for example, the goodness of fit of a line to the data. Since visual data are inherently noisy due to their signal nature, measures of reliability are important in the subsequent use of information derived using unreliable processes.

Yet another use of certainty is in hypothesis ranking. The ranking of hypotheses is useful not only for the determination of a focus of attention but also for determining the best interpretation. Most schemes introduce some amount of domain dependence into the control structure, and this seems to lead to problems with respect to generality. An important problem is the combination of certainties or evidence from many sources.

Inference and Goal Satisfaction. Inference is the process by which a set of facts or models is used in conjunction with a set of data items to derive new facts that are not explicitly present in either. It is also called reasoning. The many forms of reasoning include logical deduction, inheritance, default reasoning, and instantiation. (See INHERITANCE HIERARCHY; REASONING, DEFAULT.)

However, it should be pointed out that the vision problem adds a few different wrinkles to this task that may not appear in many other reasoning processes. It is not true in general that the data set is complete or correct, and processses that can reliably draw inferences from incomplete data are required. Second, since vision is inherently noisy and as described above requires reliability measures, inference schemes should also permit reliability measures to be attached to derived conclusions. Finally, since the process of vision involves a transformation from images to a final description through many intermediate representations, a reasoning scheme must be able to cross between several representations.

Most IUSs are not explicitly driven by a goal when interpreting images. They typically have implicit goals, such as to describe the scene in terms of volumetric primitives, to describe everything in as much detail as possible, or to describe the scene in the most specific terms possible. Human vision usually does involve a goal of some kind, and the area of AI that is concerned with how to achieve goals given a problem is called "planning." Systems that can plan an attack on a problem must contain metaknowledge, that is, knowledge about the knowledge that the system has about the problem domain (see META-KNOWLEDGE, META-RULES, AND META-REASONING). The metaknowledge allows the system to reason about its capabilities and limitations explicitly. Such systems have a set of operations that they can perform, and they know under which circumstances the operations can be applied as well as what the effects may be. In order to satisfy a goal, a sequence of operations must be determined that, in a stepwise fashion, will eventually lead to the goal. Attempts to find optimal plans usually are included in terms of minimization of cost estimates or maximization of potential for success. In vision the sequence of operators may involve image feature extraction, model matching, and so on (see PLANNING).

HISTORICAL PERSPECTIVE AND TECHNIQUES

The historical development of the techniques of image understanding provides an interesting reflection of the major influences in the entire field of AI. The emphasis in the IU community has been primarily in the control structure, and this discussion begins with the sequence of contributions that led to the current types of control mechanisms. Rather, little emphasis has been placed on integrating the best of the early vision schemes into IUSs, and one notices the range of weak solutions to the extraction of features. Little discussion is thus provided; however, in the description of control structures for specific systems, appropriate notes are made.

Control Structures

The heart of virtually all IU systems is the control structure (qv). Features universal to all working IUSs are cyclic control involving feedback (see CYBERNETICS) and the requirement of specific solutions to the problem of uncertainty. This survey of the development of control structure highlights only those systems that require and use explicit models of objects or events of the domain. Other important contributions that impact IUSs are allocated their appropriate historical due but are not considered part of the direct line of development. Finally, with two exceptions, the hypothesis of Marr and Nishihara (1978) and the intrinsic image concept of Tenenbaum and Barrow (1977), only implemented and tested systems are described in this section.

Developing the Cycle of Perception. Roberts was the first (1965) to lay out a control scheme for organizing the various components of a vision system. They are shown pictorially in Figure 1. He defined several of the major processing steps now found in all vision systems: extract features from the image, in his case, lines; activate the relevant models using those features; project the model's expectations into image space; and finally, choose the best model depending on its match with the data. This is not a true cycle, and because of the lack of feedback, it was very sensitive to noisy input. Falk (1972) realized that Roberts' work involved an assumption that would rarely be satisfied in real application domains, namely, that of noise-free data. If noisy data were to be correctly handled, enhancements to Roberts' processing sequence were required (1972). In Figure 2 Falk adds a new component, the fill in incompleteness step, and closed the loop, allowing partly interpreted data to assist in the further interpretation of the scene. His program was called INTERPRET.

Shirai (1973) defined a system for finding lines in blocks world scenes and interpreting the lines using models of line junctions and vertices for polyhedral objects. Thus, he was able to use interpreted lines as guidance in subsequent line finding. He first extracted features from a reduced image, thus smoothing out some of the noise and smaller detail features, and then used these gross features in subsequent guidance. Shirai's cycle is shown in Figure 3. Shirai, however, was not the first to employ reduced images in a preprocessing stage. Kelly

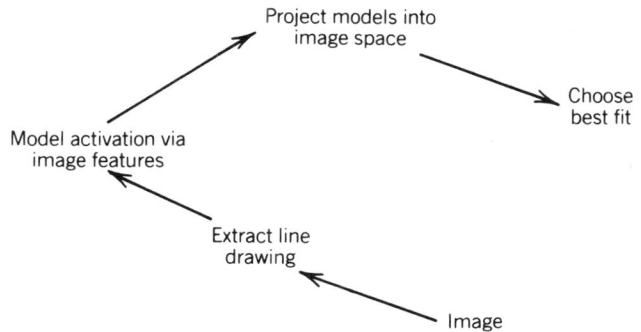

Figure 1. The control structure of Roberts (1965).

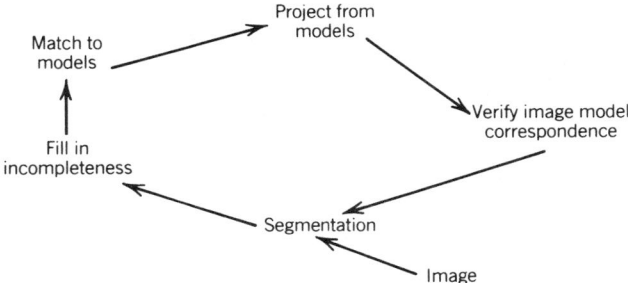

Figure 2. The control structure of Falk (1972).

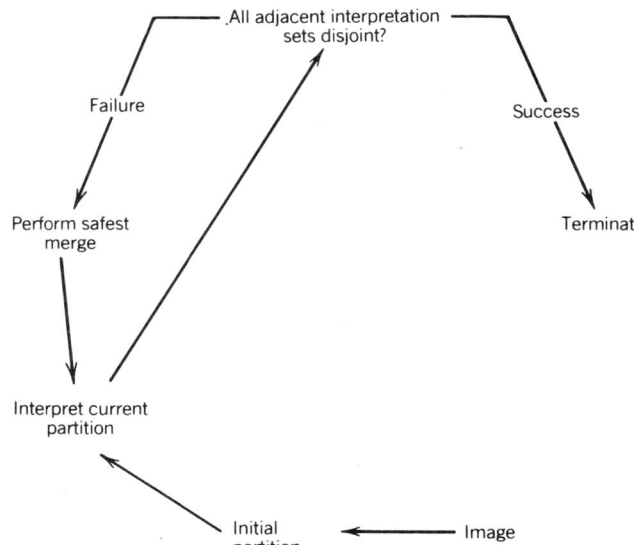

Figure 4. The interpretation-guided segmentation control structure of Tenenbaum and Barrow (1977).

(1971) had the intuition that if an image that was reduced in size was processed initially, instead of the full-size image, much of the noise could be reduced, and the resulting edges of lines could be used as a plan for where to find edges and lines in the full image. This was applied to the domain of face recognition. Kelly reduced an image to 64 × 64 pixel size, thus minimizing noise effects, and then located the outlines of the faces. Those outlines then formed a plan for the full-size image, limiting the search space for the detailed facial outlines. However, Kelly's system contained no models and was a sequential two-step process.

Several incarnations of the cycle appeared subsequently, and one example of note is presented here, namely, the work of Tenenbaum and Barrow (1977) in their interpretation-guided segmentation (IGS) program. Their version of the cycle is shown in Figure 4. IGS experimented with several types of knowledge sources for guidance of the segmentation process: unguided knowledge, interactive knowledge, both user driven and system driven; models; and relational constraints. They concluded that segmentation is improved with the application of knowledge when compared to the unguided case, and with little computational overhead—the more knowledge, the faster the filtering process. Perhaps the most elegant portrayal of the cycle of perception, and also the coining of the term itself, is due to a contribution by Mackworth (1978) and is shown in Figure 5. This basic cycle appears, in a variety of forms, in virtually all IUSs that have appeared since. Kanade's modification of the cycle (1980) explicitly included the separation of scene domain

and image domain considerations, a requirement that was first pointed out by Huffman (1971) and also independently by Clowes (1971). This refers to the difference between an object's 2-D appearance in an image versus an object's 3-D representation in the world. Figure 6 portrays Kanade's cycle.

Tsotsos and co-workers (1985) further elaborated the model for the ALVEN system by specifying exactly at which points of the cycle the different hypothesis activation (or indexing) methods are applied. In addition, since his task was to understand visual motion, the element of time was also added. To this point in the development of the cycle of perception, although use had been made of different representational tools for organizing models, no explicit consideration had been given to how to best take advantage of the organization. Tsotsos used the common organizational tools of specialization (IS-A), decomposition (PART-OF), and SIMILARITY (mutual exclusion of models, or winner take all) and add temporal precedence in order to organize a large set of models. His cycle is

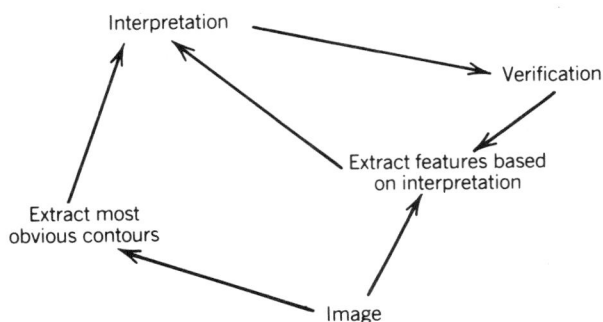

Figure 3. The control structure of Shirai (1973).

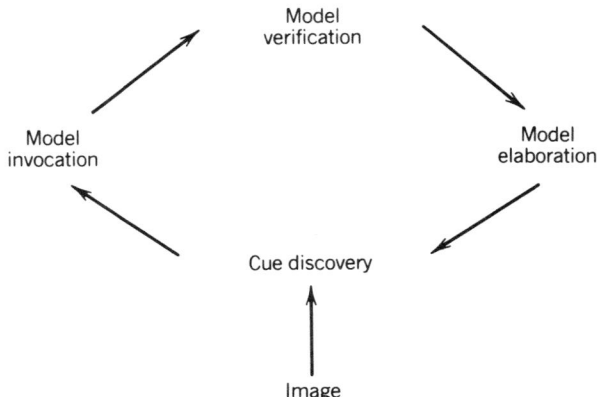

Figure 5. The cycle of perception of Mackworth (1978).

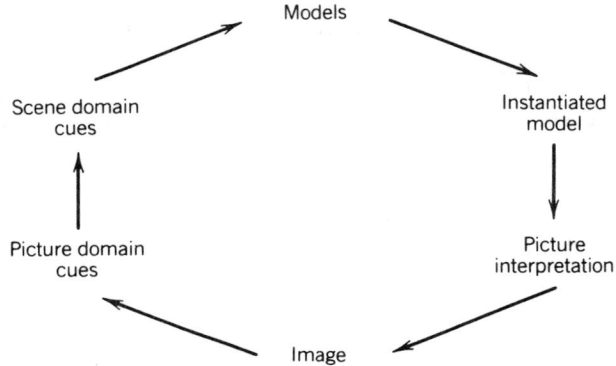

Figure 6. The control structure for Kanade (1980).

Model-Directed Activation. The elaboration of models involves top-down traversal of the PART-OF hierarchy. This too implies a constrained form of hypothesize and test for components of classes that reflect greater resolution of detail. Movement down the PART-OF hierarchy forces activation of hypotheses corresponding to each of the components of the PART-OF parent hypothesis.

Data-Directed Activation. The PART-OF hierarchy can also be traversed bottom up in aggregation mode. Bottom-up traversal implies a form of hypothesize and test, where hypotheses activate other hypotheses that may have them as components.

Failure-Directed Activation. Failure-directed search is along the SIMILARITY dimension. Typically, several SIMILARITY links will be activated for a given hypothesis, and the resultant set of hypotheses is considered as a discriminatory set, that is, at most, one of them may be the correct one. SIMILARITY interacts with the PART-OF relationship in that exceptions raised that specify missing components are handled by the hypothesis' PART-OF parent, the hypothesis that contains the context within which the exception occurred.

Temporally Directed Activation. Temporal search is a special case of model-directed search along the PART-OF dimension. Concepts may represent compound temporal events, such as sequences, simultaneous events, or overlapping events. In a sequence each element of the sequence has a PART-OF relationship with the event. Thus, on activation of the class, it is meaningless to activate all parts, as stated above, at the same time. Activation of the parts only occurs when their particular temporal specifications are satisfied. Temporally-activated hypothesis invocation and prediction is an instance of an active vision

shown in Figure 7. Definitions of the different hypothesis activation methods driven by knowledge organization relationships were also provided by Tsotsos. The methods are briefly summarized below.

Goal-Directed Activation. The goal of the vision system is to find the most specific, or specialized, description in the system's repertoire for the image contents. The specialization of hypotheses involves top-down traversal, from general to specific, on an IS-A hierarchy, moving downward when concepts are verified. Verification of an IS-A parent concept implies that perhaps one of its IS-A children applies, although the confirmation of a concept implies that its IS-A parents must also be true. Multiple IS-A children can be activated, but a more efficient scheme would be to activate one of the children if all children form a mutually exclusive set, or one from several such sets, and then allow failure-directed search to take over.

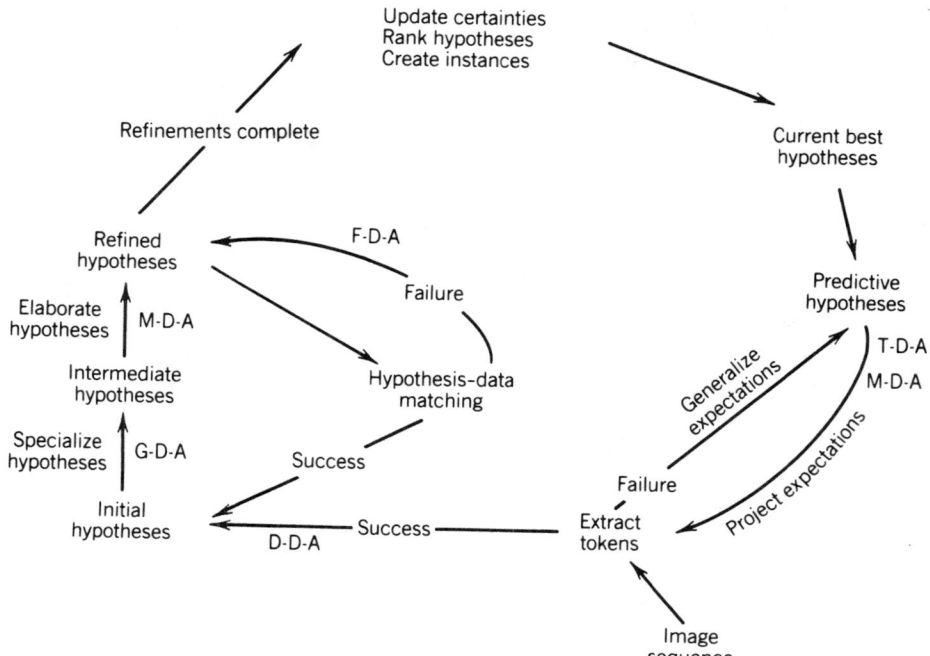

Figure 7. The control cycle for motion understanding of Tsotsos (1985). Hypothesis activation types: DDA, data-directed activation; GDA, goal-directed activation; FDA, failure-directed activation; TDA, temporally directed activation; MDA, model-directed activation.

strategy. This necessarily requires time and image samples acquired over time.

Marr, usually credited with contributions only in early vision, also had specific processes in mind for the high levels of vision presented in his book *Vision* (1982). It would indeed have been interesting to have seen an attempt at implementation and testing of his ideas. Marr, in his own words, viewed "recognition as a gradual process that proceeds from the general to the specific and that overlaps with, guides, and constrains the derivation of a description from the image." He proposed that a catalog of models be constructed using volumetric primitives and organized using a specialization hierarchy (IS-A) as well as a decomposition hierarchy (PART-OF). Models were selected based on the distribution of components along principal axes of the derived volumetric primitives represented in the 3-D sketch. He proposed three indexing schemes: The primary one was the "specificity index," traversal from general to specific models (goal-directed); the secondary ones, used in support of the first, were the "adjunct index," traversal from models to model components (model-directed), and "parent index," traversal from model components to parent models (data-directed). The model provided relative orientation constraints used to determine absolute orientation. An image space processor then related image-centered and object-centered descriptions and computed relative lengths of component axes. This new information can be used to disambiguate shapes at the next level of specificity. It is interesting to note that Marr did not propose a cycle of processing and that the 3-D sketch represented all possible information derivable directly from the image. In general, this is not realizable, and a scheme without feedback is insufficient.

In several models the issue of feedback and the relationship between explicit models and their appearance in an image was mentioned. The projection of hypotheses into image space is a difficult problem for which few solutions exist. As pointed out previously, expectations have been used in most IUSs since Kelly's and Shirai's work. Expectations were used in the SEER system of Freuder (1977) to guide region growing and identification of specific portions of a hammer. A thorough understanding of human body motions and a model of the allowed joint configuration enabled the design of a constraint propagation network that integrated current motions and known body positions with hypothesized ones, producing expected locations in 3-D for given body joints (O'Rourke and Badler, 1980). An interesting conclusion from the ALVEN system's use of expectations is that the information contained in an IS-A hierarchy of concepts can be exploited for the generation, verification, and modification of expectations of actual object appearance in a sequence of images. If expectations fail, movement up the hierarchy to a more general concept provides the next best alternative consistent with the semantics of the interpretation. However, the key problem of relating 3-D object viewpoint-independent models to image-specific ones is still an outstanding one. A good example of work on this topic is the ACRONYM system (Brooks, 1981). Given a geometric object model and viewpoint and illumination, ACRONYM predicts partial object appearance in the image. That is,

only the important features required for identification are predicted since the whole problem is so computationally expensive. Recently, an additional dimension to this problem has been added through active strategies. Califano, Kjeldsen, and Bolle (1990) provide an interesting approach which uses models combined with foveation strategies in order to deal with feedback, tractability, and integration of successive sensor fixations.

Heterarchical Models. A heterarchical model of vision is one made up of a collection of separate modules, each module performing some specialized task and each communicating with all others as appropriate. Freuder was perhaps the first within the vision community to apply such an idea in his system for recognizing tools called SEER (1977). "Active knowledge" was his term for the use of procedural knowledge in directing the control; Freuder's work is thus an early precursor to the recent wave of interest in active perception strategies. Knowledge was represented as semantic networks (qv). Nodes represented objects and links represented how objects help establish one another. Each object encoded procedural knowledge, and together the objects formed the set of modules, each communicating with other relevant modules.

Another form of heterarchy is the "demon" scheme, where each knowledge source continuously monitors a database of assertions about the images and of models to see if its prerequisites are present. If found, the demon then carries out some actions that may involve changes to the database. Badler (1975) used a demon model for event analysis, and each demon represented the knowledge required to recognize a particular event type. Two other specific versions of heterarchy are presented by Nevatia (1978) and Levine (1978). They provide two other views for the composition of the collection of modules. They are presented in Figures 8 and 9. Perhaps the main conclusion that can be drawn from the heterarchical models is that as the number of interacting modules grows, the communication and organization problems increase dramatically.

Hierarchical Models. Hierarchical models are comprised of a specialized collection of modules, but the communication pathways are restricted, reflecting an ordering of both processing steps and levels of abstraction in

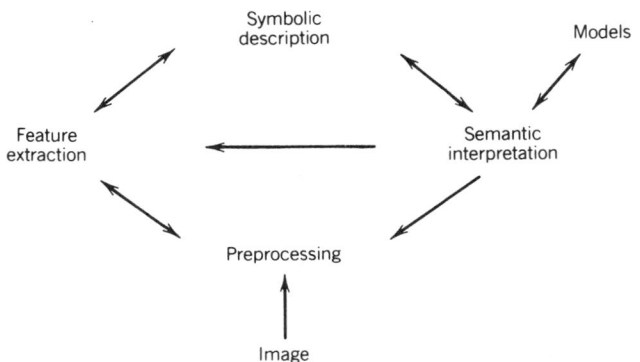

Figure 8. The control structure of Nevatia (1978).

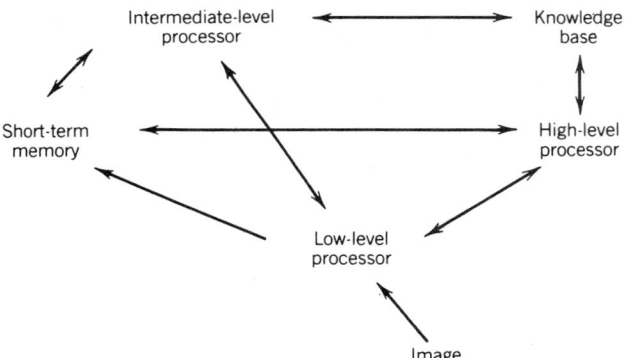

Figure 9. The control structure of Levine (1978).

the computation. One of the best known is due to Barrow and Tenenbaum (1978) and is diagrammed in Figure 10. This model reflects a major contribution in representation, namely the idea of "intrinsic images." This is described in Spatial Relationships, below.

Another important hierarchical model that elaborates on Barrow and Tenenbaum's model is that of the VISIONS system (Hanson and Riseman, 1978). This fills

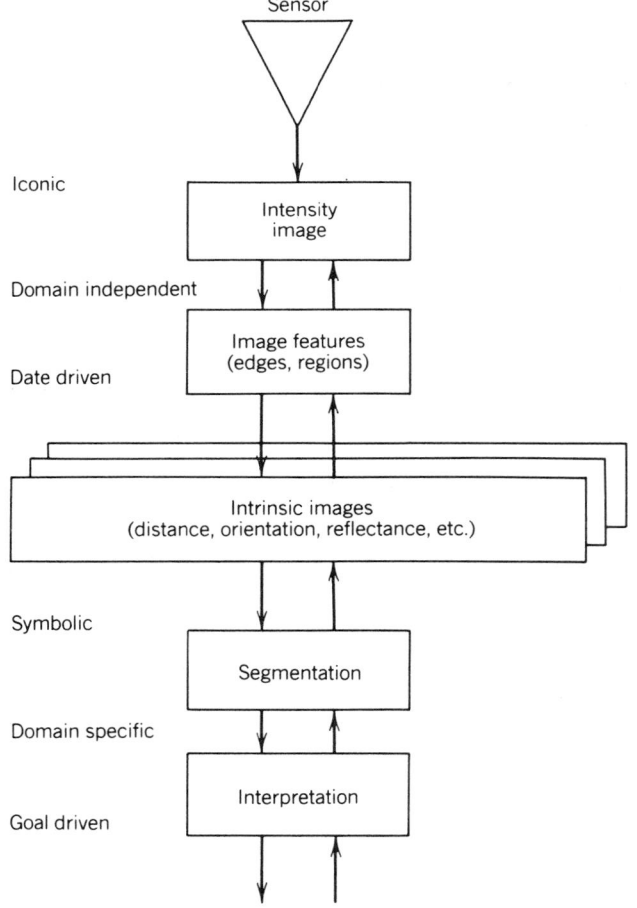

Figure 10. The control structure of Barrow and Tenenbaum (1978).

in several details regarding communication and control across the multiple levels of representation that are present in all image-understanding systems. Yet another specific type of hierarchical model emerged, conforming with the basic definition and philosophy but also attempting to provide a solution to the spatial scale problem. Uhr called these models "recognition cones" in his contribution (1972), and they have also been termed "pyramid models" (Tanimoto and Klinger, 1980). The major distinctions come from the facts that each layer of the cone computes image properties at successively coarser resolutions and each computation communicates only with computations occurring in layers immediately above or below or with computations within the layer. An unfortunate result of this idea is the linking of spatial scale with resolution; as noted earlier, the optimal scale for the detection of specific spatial forms has little relationship to image resolution.

Blackboard Models. Blackboard models (see BLACK-BOARD SYSTEMS) were borrowed for use in vision from the HEARSAY work in speech understanding. In fact, they are a specific form of heterarchy in that each knowledge source (module) can communicate with any other. Knowledge sources are organized hierarchically. The major difference and improvement over the versions of heterarchy that were presented earlier is that the communication occurred through a global data structure called a blackboard rather than the communication pathways being fixed. The VISIONS system (Hanson and Riseman, 1978) incorporates this idea as well as pyramid processes. The knowledge sources defined are inference net, 2-D curve fitting; 2-D shape; occlusion; special attribute matcher; 3-D shape; perspective; horizon; and object size. The VISIONS structure is shown in Figure 11. The advantages of blackboard models include their modularity; however, their utility in speech has not been repeated in vision, primarily because of the important differences between speech and vision.

Beam Models. Once again, speech understanding influenced the design of a vision system. In this case the HARPY system (Lowerre and Reddy, 1980) influenced the 1980 design of the ARGOS system of Rubin (1980). Rubin's work is interesting because it was the only attempt to use beam search (qv) (also called locus search) in vision. Beam search produces a "beam," a pruned search tree that contains a list of near-miss alternatives around the best path. Both signal and model characteristics are included in this consideration. The scheme as realized in ARGOS is not one that has promise for general-purpose vision systems. ARGOS looked at images of downtown Pittsburgh, attempting to classify regions as sky, buildings, or mountains, for example. The network over which the beam search was performed was a large one whose nodes were pixels or image regions and whose arcs were spatial relations.

Rule-Based Approaches. Rules (of the if <premise> then <action> form) were introduced into vision at about the same time that they appeared in production systems. The introduction is due to Baird and Kelly (1974), who

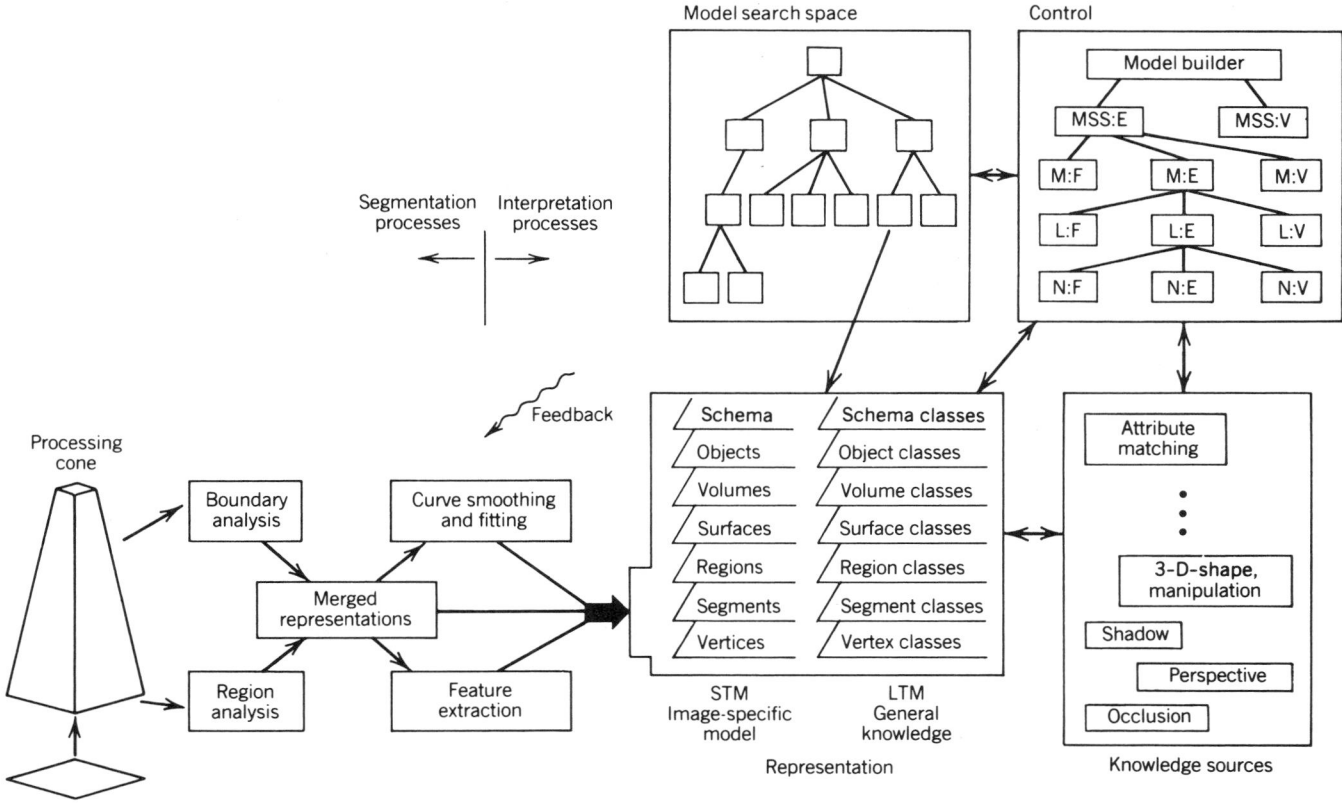

Figure 11. The Blackboard structure of VISIONS (Hanson and Riseman, 1978).

claimed that context is a necessary consideration in the development of their paradigm for semantic picture recognition. They used inference rules to incorporate contextual considerations, and premises were features extracted from images. More recently, perhaps due to the success of the expert systems approach, several other vision systems have appeared that utilize rule-based knowledge and reasoning (see RULE-BASED SYSTEMS).

Typically, pure data-directed reasoning is insufficient as described above, and rules are fired in both goal-directed (backward-chaining) and data-directed (forward-chaining) modes (see PROCESSING, BOTTOM-UP AND TOP-DOWN). Rules are used to represent various facts about images. For example, in SPAM, the system of McKeown and co-workers (1984), rules are used to encode spatial relationships among entities in the scene as well as to encode constraints on sizes and shapes of visual entities. Rule-based reasoning is used to provide the system with the best next task based on the strength of expectations as well as for the generation of expectations. Other IUSs that employ rule-based reasoning are the systems of Nagao and Matsuyama (1980); Ohta (1980); Ferrie, Levine, and Zucker (1982); and Riseman and Hanson (1984).

Representation Formalisms

The development of representational tools used in the IUS community mirrors quite closely developments in other subdisciplines of AI. The use of heuristics (qv) reflects the power-based era of AI. The appearance of semantic networks (qv) in the memory-modeling community and their use by the knowledge representation (qv) and language-understanding communities (see NATURAL LANGUAGE UNDERSTANDING) influenced their use in IUSs. Blackboards and beam searches were developed for the major speech-understanding systems (HEARSAY and HARPY, respectively) and subsequently appeared in vision systems. Minsky's (1975) frame theory (see FRAMES), developed with a specific eye toward vision, was used in several vision systems. The success of expert systems prompted the use of rule-based approaches in IUSs as well.

Spatial Representations. Vision systems require the explicit representation of points, curves, surfaces, and volumes. There are a number of schemes that are employed, namely, points, line segments, splines, fractals, and generalized cylinders, among others. As an example, the VISIONS system employs a representation of 3-D complex surfaces and 2-D curves based on B-splines and surface patches and also makes use of the PART-OF and INSTANCE-OF relationships in building complex structures. ACRONYM uses a generalized cylinder representation in conjunction with PART-OF and IS-A organizations. There is no real consensus yet on what constitutes an adequate set of primitives for spatial representations. Discussions and examples can be found for several representational points of view: Marr and Nishihara (1978) for generalized cylinders; Pentland (1985) for the super-quadric approach; Kass, Witkin and Terzopoulos for snakes (1988); Terzopoulos, Kass and Witkin for deformable, symmetry-seeking 3-D models (1988); and Biederman (1988) for geons, etc (see SHAPE).

Much work in representation and reasoning about space has appeared outside the vision community. Comparison of object location and the representation of the corresponding relations is considered in Freeman (1975). Kuipers (1978) describes his TOUR model for route-solving problems and discusses the spatial knowledge relevant to that task. McDermott and Davis (1984) also include a representation for spatial knowledge and a scheme for reasoning about it. However, both Kuipers and McDermott and Davis were concerned with spatial route-finding tasks, and this is not directly comparable to the reasoning required for vision systems. Spatial representations are covered in other entries (see REASONING, SPATIAL). The representation of maps is quite straightforward and does not require further elaboration. The interested reader should consult articles on the MAPSEE (Mackworth and Havens, 1983) or HAWKEYE (Barrow and co-workers, 1977) systems.

Two specific representations can be considered major contributions, namely, the schemes of Marr (1982) and Barrow and Tenenbaum (1978). Marr proposed a progression of representations that he termed the "primal sketch," the 2½-D sketch, and the 3-D sketch. The primal sketch represented information about the 2-D image, primarily intensity changes and their organization. The 2½-D sketch represented the orientation and depth of surfaces and discontinuity contours. Finally, the 3-D sketch represented shapes and their spatial organization in an object-centered manner. In contrast, Barrow and Tenenbaum claimed that the appropriate intermediate-level representation consisted of a number of separate feature maps, all image centered, that perhaps interact in order to be computed unambiguously. These features include surface discontinuities, range, surface orientation, velocity, and color.

Heuristics. The use of heuristics (qv) appears in most vision systems in one form or another. Systems that used only heuristics, however, appeared only during the power-based era of AI and do not really qualify as IUSs using the definition requiring explicit object or event models. Those systems typically deal with blocks-world scenes.

Semantic Networks. Semantic networks (qv), that is, graph structures whose nodes represent objects or events and whose arcs represent relationships between the objects and events, have made an important impact on IUSs. Two examples are the work of Levine (1978) and that of Badler (1975). Levine's system deals with the interpretation of natural scenes, and he constructs a knowledge base with nodes representing entities such as sky, road, and house. Arcs represent spatial relations, such as left of, above, or behind. Badler used the same idea but represents events as well as objects with nodes, whereas arcs represent spatial as well as temporal relations.

Frames. Minsky's frame theory (1975) was one of the most influential works within the representation community, and since it was designed as a representation for vision, it left a mark on the IUS community as well. Frames are data structures representing a prototypical object or event. The components of the structure are slots that are filled with specific instances of visual entities. Slots may specify a type of instance, may specify a default value that can be used if the instance is not found, and may have associated constraints that relate one slot to others. Frames, sometimes also called "schemata," are used in the SIGMA (Matsuyama and Hwang, 1985), ALVEN (Tsotsos, 1985), ACRONYM (Brooks, 1981), MAPSEE (Mackworth and Havens, 1983), and VISIONS (Hanson and Riseman, 1978) systems among others.

The concept of a "representation space" was described by Bobick and Bolles (1989) in an attempt to deal with the integration of visual information over time as it was acquired. This space is a lattice of evolving representations as the certainty in an object's description increases as more data is acquired. This represents early work on an important issue.

A large collection of frames poses a serious indexing problem, and one solution for this is to organize the frames into a semantic network. In such a representation nodes are frames that represent objects or events, and arcs are network organizational primitives, such as generalization, specialization and aggregation, decomposition. The similarity relationship, motivated by Minsky, is added to the ALVEN scheme, as well as a temporal precedence dimension, as further organizational relations among frames.

Rules. Rules may be used to encode object characteristics, spatial relationships among objects, constraints on shape and sizes, and so on, for use in an IUS. The use of rules in the SPAM system (McKeown and co-workers, 1984) has already been mentioned. In the VISIONS system (Parma and co-workers, 1980) rules are applied to the attributes of the lines and regions in an intermediate representation. Simple rules define ranges over a feature value and, if fired, are considered as a vote for an object label. Here image features include color, texture, shape, size, and location, and feature values include length, location, orientation, contrast, and width. They allow complex combinations of simple rules. For example, they have a rule that measures excess green present in grass by computing the appropriate mean of color values in the R-G-B ranges for pixels in the region in question. This approach can also be found in the work of Nagao and Matsuyama (1980), and Ohta (1980).

Reasoning and Uncertainty

Relaxation-Labelling Processes. Relaxation-labeling processes appeared first as discrete constraint propagation schemes and then as probabilistic ones (see REASONING, PLAUSIBLE). The primary difference between the discrete and continuous schemes is that decisions in the discrete case are binary—a label is either true or it is removed from consideration—and in the continuous case, labels have an associated strength that is increased or decreased depending on the constraints imposed on it by its neighboring context. One may think of strength in this context as a measure of goodness of fit—it is not a probability in the formal sense (see Hummel and Zucker, 1980, on continuous relaxation). Relaxation labeling is commonly used in recognition cone approaches, within layers of the cone, and hierarchically between layers. Also, the excursion into a time-varying continuous relaxation scheme called "temporal cooperative computation" is presented by Tsotsos (1987).

Evidential Reasoning. One method for making decisions based on uncertain information is the use of Bayesian probabilities. This method is described elsewhere (see BAYESIAN INFERENCE METHODS). Another method for combining evidence in order to draw conclusions that has been applied in vision is the Dempster-Shafer Theory (qv). The major difference between Dempster-Shafer and Bayesian probabilities is that an explicit representation of partial ignorance is provided. Belief is represented in the range [0,1], and lower bounds within this interval are moved higher and upper bounds are moved lower, reflecting the addition of supporting or conflicting evidence, respectively. The width of the remaining interval is regarded as ignorance. This scheme is being applied in the VISIONS work (Parma and co-workers, 1980).

Jepson and Richards (1990) have considered perceptual reasoning given beliefs of the world. They have proposed a "lattice theory" where a lattice of belief states reflects the possible interpretations of a scene. A local maximum in the lattice partial ordering is the requirement for an acceptable percept.

Spatiotemporal Reasoning. Reasoning systems that deal primarily with axioms whose propositions are spatial relations or facts can be termed "spatial reasoners." Similarly, those dealing with temporal relations are "temporal reasoners" (see REASONING, TEMPORAL), and those that deal with geometric information are "geometric reasoners." Grouping processes, such as those reflected by inferences along the PART-OF representation dimension, are also included here. It is clear that the inclusion of such reasoning processes is important in IUSs. ACRONYM (Brooks, 1981) uses 3-D object models and can reason about complex coordinate transforms of them. It also includes an algebraic reasoner that reasons about sets of non-linear algebraic symbolic inequalities and bounds and determines satisfying sets for those inequalities. Other systems that explicitly address the problem of spatial reasoning are SIGMA (Matsuyama and Hwang, 1985) and SPAM (McKeown and co-workers, 1984). In both cases, the reasoning is 2-D and is based on image-centered representations. A specific type of spatial reasoning uses maps. The premise behind the use of maps is that explicit map-to-image correspondence can be derived using models of the imaging process and models of the terrain in the maps. The correspondence can be used to guide the interpretation of detailed features of the image (See REASONING, SPATIAL.)

An example of an IUS that deals with temporal reasoning is the ALVEN system (Tsotsos, 1985). The form of reasoning is very different than the temporal calculus of Allen (1984), which is an example of the pure temporal reasoning methods. Allen's scheme was not intended for vision, and it therefore displays several deficiencies that are important for vision: it does not allow for strength of belief in a temporal relation; it does not provide a recognition structure for detecting and labeling temporal relations; and it does not account for the fact that in a real-time recognition situation, all data in time are not available to the system. The ALVEN framework incorporates all of these points, in addition to the fact that all temporal relations in ALVEN are really spatiotemporal.

Planning. As mentioned previously, planning (qv) has played a role in vision since Kelly first used plans in his program for face recognition (1971). Kelly applied edge operators to a reduced image in order to extract the face outline and then expanded the outline to the original image size and searched for details only within this prediction window. This type of planning, using explicit prediction windows, has been used in many systems.

An example of an IUS that uses planning with goal satisfaction is Garvey's system (1976). In the domain of indoor office scenes, Garvey defined operators such as "find seat" (of a chair), "validate seat," "grow seat," and similarly for all objects that were known. Sequences of operators were planned and represented in an AND/OR tree (see AND/OR GRAPHS). Plans were scored depending on cost and confidence. On execution, the outcome of particular steps can be used to modify other parts of the plan. The system of Ballard, Brown, and Feldman (1978) also has a limited planning capability. It is limited in that only a very small number of operators are available, and no plan hierarchy is constructed. In the domain of locating ribs in chest radiographs, for example, Ballard and co-workers included three independent rib-finding procedures that were managed by an executive procedure.

EXAMPLE SYSTEMS FOR SPECIFIC PROBLEM DOMAINS

The description of systems provided in Table 1 is necessarily abbreviated and incomplete. It does not include all systems, nor all details for each system included. The table presents information for each system, along with relevant pointers to the literature. All systems employ the basic cycle of perception in some form, perhaps with important enhancements that have been described previously, unless otherwise noted. Thus, they all involve the interaction of both top-down and bottom-up methods. All systems make the assumption that knowledge can compensate for poor quality input and weak image-specific segmentation processes. All systems have demonstrated some reasonable level of performance, usually on a small set of carefully chosen example images. The systems are grouped according to application domain and are listed alphabetically by the system name or the principal author's name. Within each category, at least one example of

Table 1. Example Systems for Specific Problem Domains

Name	Authors	Institution	References	Domain	Representation	Control
Aerial Photographs						
ACRONYM (see Figure 12)	T. Binford R. Brooks R. Greiner	Stanford University	Brooks, 1981; 1983; Brooks and co-workers, 1979	Airport scenes	3-D geometric models; generalized cones; ellipses, ribbons; frames; PART-OF; IS-A; object graphs for geometric constraints; restriction graphs for algebraic constraints; context graph; coarse-to-fine detail; models independent of view-point; user interface for model definition using volumetric primitives	Line finding; rule-based problem solving; graph matching between prediction, graph, and picture; graph of image features; prediction of object appearance based on viewpoint and illumination, but only of important features; geometric reasoning; algebraic reasoning
Not available	D. Ballard C. Brown J. Feldman	University of Rochester	Ballard and co-workers, 1978	Ship dock scenes in satellite photos	2-D spatial knowledge; semantic network; meta-knowledge for planning; sketch map as intermediate image representation; procedural knowledge	Distributed control; model-image mapping via procedural knowledge of objects; executive chooses most likely mapping procedure
HAWKEYE	H. Barrow R. Bolles T. Garvey T. Kremers J. Tenenbaum H. Wolf	SRI International	Barrow and co-workers, 1977	Aerial photographs	2-D topographic maps as symbolic scene model; geometric camera model	Parametric correspondence for map matching; camera model calibrated on landmarks, then used to predict precise locations of other features
Not available	W. Cole A. Huertas R. Nevatia	University of Southern California	Huertas and co-workers, 1989	Airport scenes	2-D spatial knowledge; generic knowledge about airport and associated structures; structures represented by their parts and boundaries	Hierarchical hypothesize-and-test; perceptual grouping for initial hypotheses; objects decomposed into parts for image search directed by hypotheses
MAPSEE-1, MAPSEE-2, MAPSEE-3	W. Havens A. Mackworth J. Mulder	University of British Columbia	Mackworth, 1977; Mackworth and Havens, 1983; Mulder and co-workers, 1988	Freehand drawings of maps on satellite images	2-D spatial knowledge; cartographic elements; schemata; IS-A; PART-OF; Waltz-like primary cues in drawings such as TEE, OBTUSE L, MULTI; composition and specialization hierarchies; discrimination graphs	Extended Waltz filtering to *n*-ary relations and hierarchies (hierarchical arc consistency); region growing
Not available	T. Matsuyama M. Nagao	Kyoto University	Nagao and Matsuyama, 1980	Aerial photographs of roads, houses, forests, fields, and rivers	2-D spatial knowledge; regions with attributes including spectral information; objects defined using 2-D heuristics	Blackboard-style specialized subsystems for specialized features; interpretation is image centered
SIGMA	V. Hwang T. Matsuyama	Kyoto University, University of Maryland	Matsuyama and Hwang, 1985	Aerial photographs of roads, houses, forests, fields, and rivers	Frames; PART-OF; IS-A; rules attached to slots for constraint and instantiation information; 2-D spatial knowledge; spectral knowledge	Three communicating experts, geometric reasoner, model selector, and low level; intersection of prediction areas in image-centered representation; evidence accumulation in image-centered representation
SPAM (see Figure 13)	W. Harvey J. McDermott D. McKeown	Carnegie Mellon University	McKeown, Harvey, and McDermott, 1984	Airport scenes	2-D spatial knowledge; pyramids for image features; viewpoint dependent; short- and long-term memory; relational database	Short-term memory acts as blackboard; dynamic programming for segmentation; local graph matching for intermediate-level representation; relational database operations; production system for high-level representation; confidence measures for region-object
Outdoor Scenes						
NAOS	B. Neumann H. Novak	University of Hamburg	Neumann and Novak, 1983	Street and traffic scenes	Case frames based on verbs of locomotion hierarchically organized; 3-D shape; temporal knowledge; IS-A; PART-OF	Linear programming for matching; expectations in time; question answering (qv) and connection with a natural-language system
Not available (see Figure 14)	Y. Ohta	Kyoto University	Ohta, 1980	Outdoor color scenes of sky, trees, buildings, and roads	2-D spatial knowledge; color parameter representation; regions and attributes; rules for object properties and relations	Rule-based reasoning; coarse-to-fine region growing; rule applicability ranked on correctness value; focus on best rules for execution

Table 1. (*continued*)

Name	Authors	Institution	References	Domain	Representation	Control
SCHEMA	J. Brolio R. Collins B. Draper A. Hanson E. Riseman	University of Massachusetts at Amherst	Draper, Collins, Brolio, Hanson, and Riseman, 1989	Outdoor scenes of roads and houses	Object schemas; PART-OF; contexts and scenes; 5-point certainty scale; rules; strategies associated with schemas	Blackboard; hierarchical knowledge source organization; expectation; generation; data and goal-driven processing; distributed processing architecture; large number of specialized knowledge sources for computing wide variety of scene physical parameters
VISIONS (see Figure 15)	A. Hanson E. Riseman and many others	University of Massachusetts at Amherst	Hanson and Riseman, 1978; 1984; Parma, Hanson, and Riseman, 1980; York, Hanson, and Riseman, 1981	Outdoor color scenes of houses and trees	Initial development: 2-D spatial knowledge; 3-D spatial knowledge; schemata organized along PART-OF and IS-A; more recent development; rules for object hypothesis and focus of attention	Initial development: blackboard communication; processing cones and relaxation for edge and region extraction; procedural knowledge representation; more recent development: rule-based focus of attention; region and line algorithms without relaxation; intermediate grouping and organizational processes; sensor and representation fusion during interpretation; knowledge-directed feedback to low level processing; some effort to integrate evidential reasoning

Indoor Scenes

Name	Authors	Institution	References	Domain	Representation	Control
ABLS (Address Block Location System)	S. Srihari C. Wang	State University of New York at Buffalo	Wang and Srihari, 1988	Localization of mail labels	Dependency graph organization for knowledge sources; rules with confidence values; Dempster-Shafer evidence combination; statistical mail database; hypothesis, block and context frames	Three-level hierarchical blackboard; top-down and bottom-up control
Not available	T. Garvey	SRI International	Garvey, 1976	Office scenes of known objects, telephones, desks, and chairs	3-D spatial knowledge; relations; objects as conjunctions of histograms of local features; regions are lists of image samples or bounding polygons in space	Based on planning of operator sequences; plans represented as AND/OR tree; involved three stages, acquire samples, validate and bound to object model; operators are object specific; cost/confidence scoring measures
IGS (see Figure 16)	H. Barrow J. Tenenbaum	SRI International	Tenenbaum and Barrow, 1977	Rooms, mechanical equipment, and landscapes	2-D spatial knowledge; region based; relational constraints; object models as 3-D polyhedral representations	Generalized Waltz filtering; semantic region growing; visibility matrix for 3-D models computed using camera model
PSEIKI	K. Andress A. Kak	Purdue University	Andress and Kak, 1988	Hallway-following and sidewalk-following mobile robot	Maps; production system in OPS3; hierarchy of scenes, objects, faces, edges, vertices; geometric constraints	Blackboard control; OPS3 demons; Dempster-Shafer evidential reasoning in hierarchical space; expectation generation based on current scene beliefs

Medical Images

Name	Authors	Institution	References	Domain	Representation	Control
ALVEN (see Figure 17)	H. Covvey J. Mylopoulos J. Tsotsos S. Zucker	University of Toronto	Tsotsos and co-workers, 1980; Tsotsos, 1985; 1987	Evaluation of human left ventricular performance from X-ray movie	2-D spatial knowledge; spatiotemporal representation; frames organized with IS-A, PART-OF, similarity temporal precedence; slots have attached interslots constraints for verification and instantiation	Combination of model, goal, data, failure, and temporally directed hypothesis activation; temporal cooperative computation for hypothesis certainty driven by knowledge organization semantics; temporal expectation generation; expectation failure handled by prediction generalization (see Figure 17)
Not available	D. Ballard C. Brown J. Feldman	University of Rochester	Ballard, Brown, and Feldman, 1978	Identification of ribs in chest radiograph	See entry under Aerial Photographs	See entry under Aerial Photographs

Table 1. (*continued*)

Name	Authors	Institution	References	Domain	Representation	Control
Not available	F. Ferrie M. Levine S. Zucker	McGill University	Ferrie, Levine, and Zucker, 1982	Tracking cell motion and morphology in microphotograph image sequences	2-D spatial knowledge; motion knowledge, including shape changes; region based; cell state changes encoded as rules	Views next state prediction and best-match selection as minimization problems; solution similar in form to a Newton-Raphson method; rule interpreter for cell identification and state changes

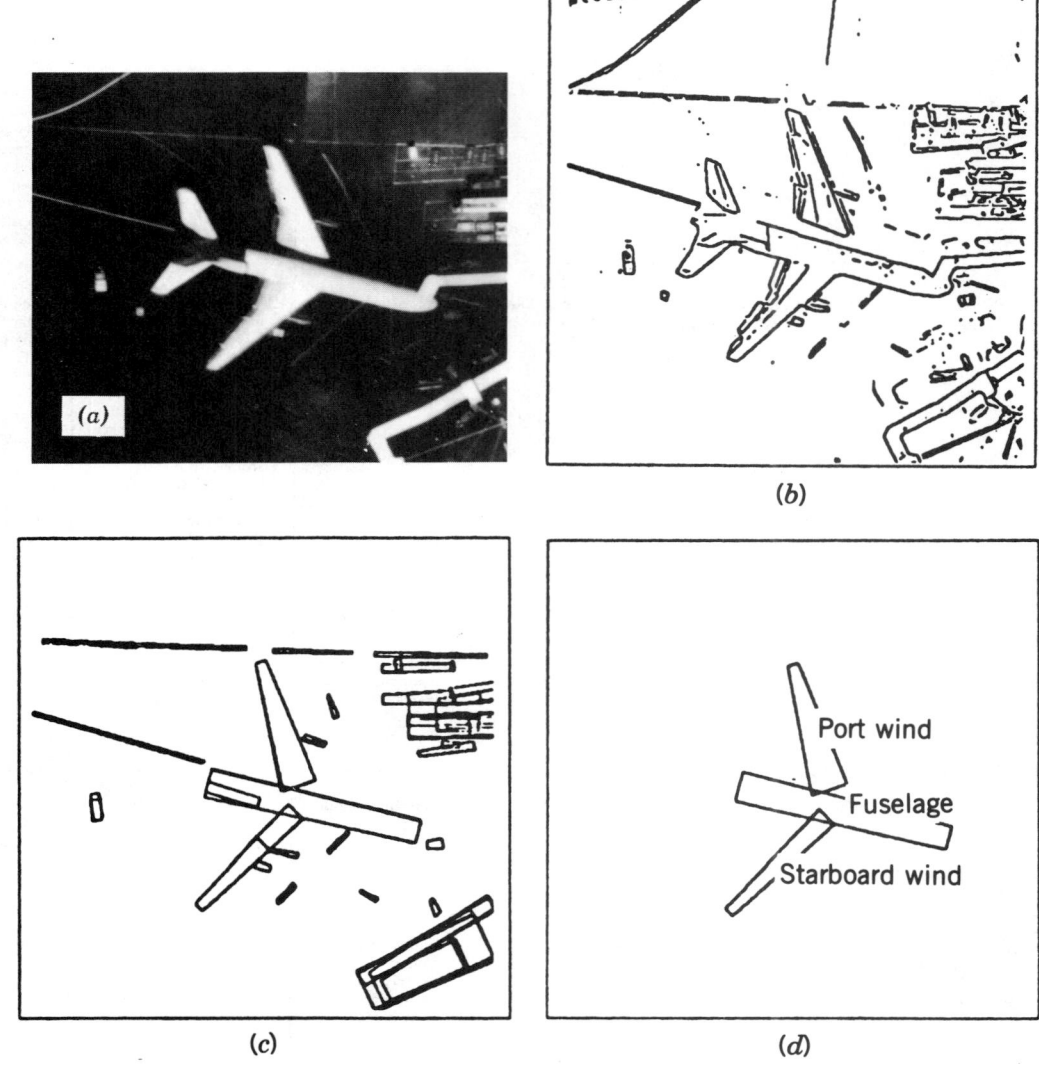

Figure 12. Example of the input and output from the ACRONYM system (Brooks, 1983). An original image is shown, with three steps toward the labeling of the fuselage and wings (*a–d*).

Figure 13. (p. 657) Example of the input and output from the SPAM system (McKeown and co-workers, 1984). (*a*) Original image of an airport scene; (*b*) region-based segmentation produced by SPAM; (*c*) the functional areas extracted by the system.

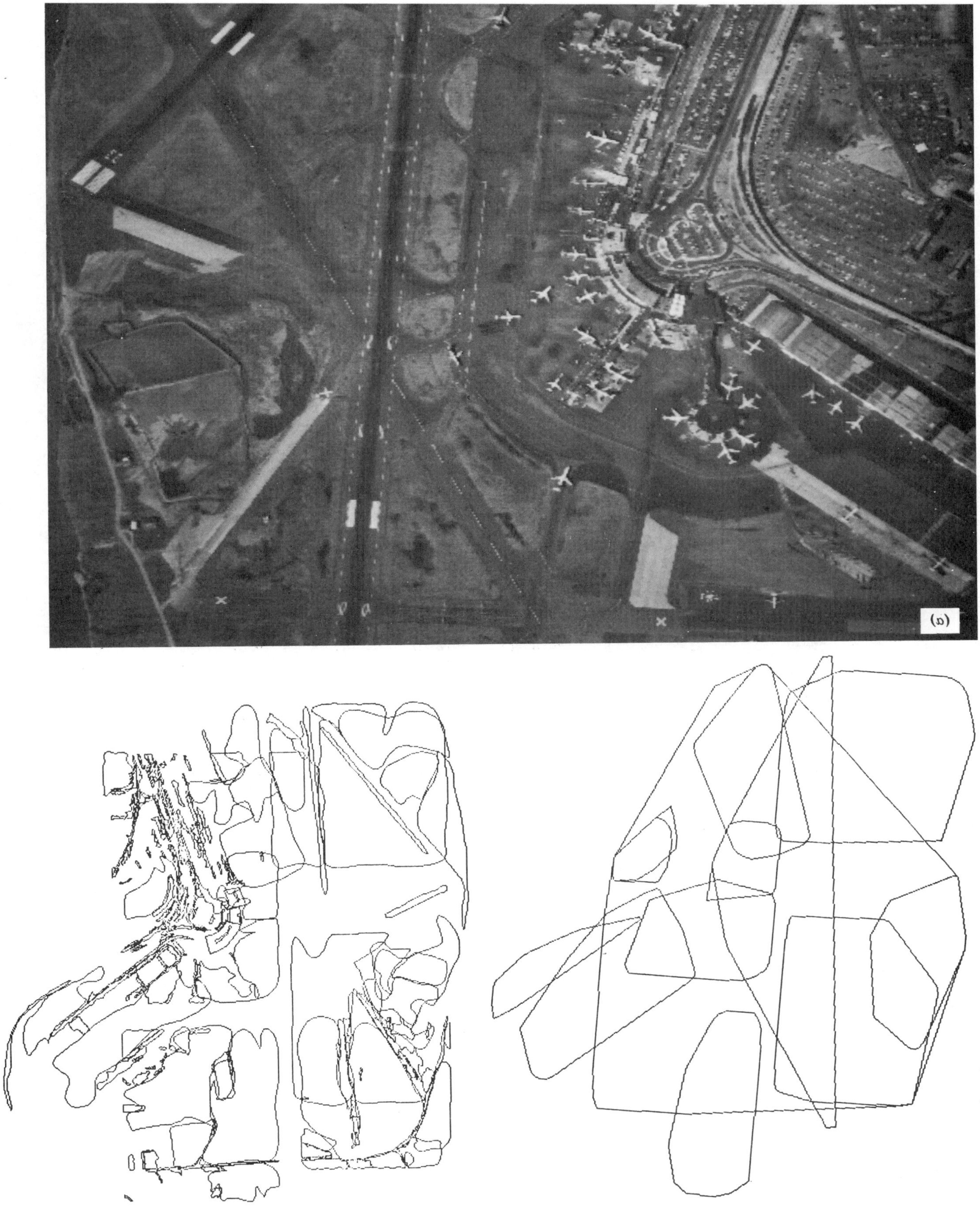

(a)

(b)

(c)

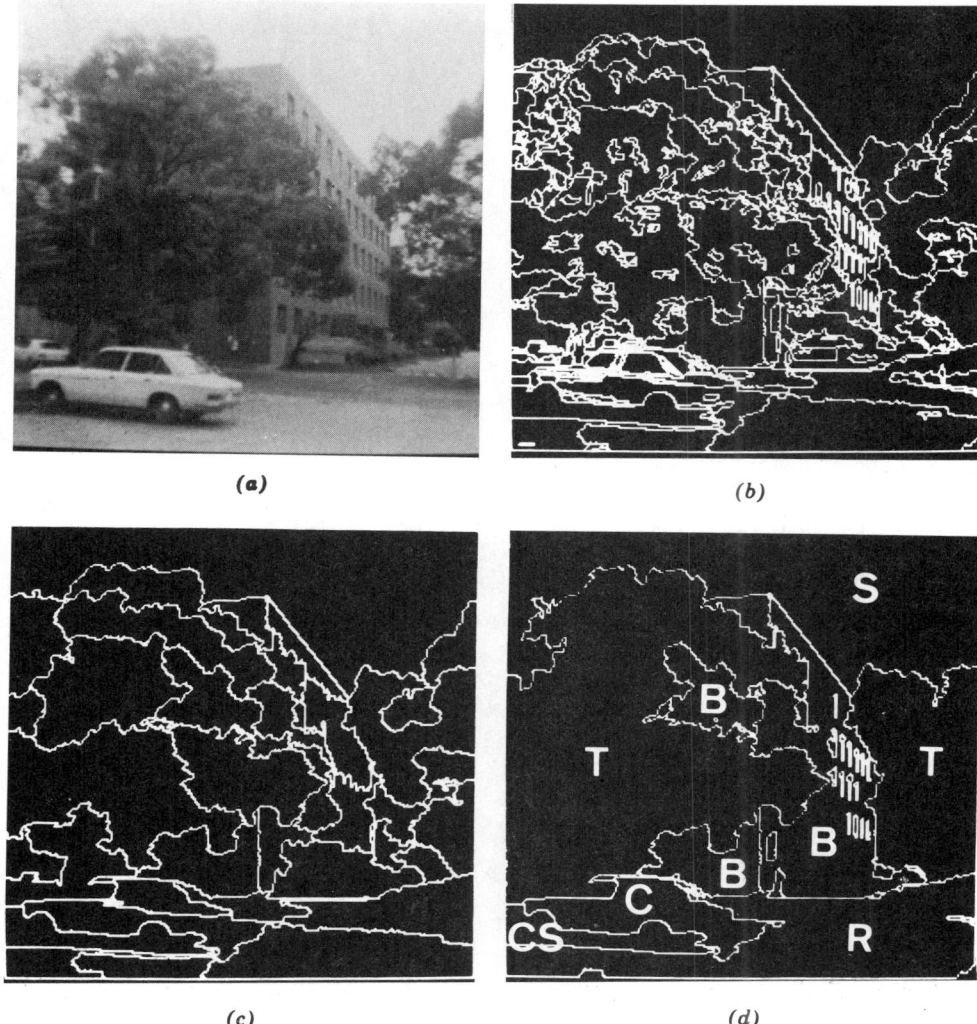

Figure 14. Example of input and output from Ohta's system (1980). (*a*) digitized input scene; (*b*) result of preliminary segmentation; (*c*) plan image; (*d*) result of meaningful segmentation (S = sky, T = tree, B = building, R = road, C = car, CS = car shadow).

sample input and output of a system is provided. Where more than one example is given, it will be for the purpose of illustrating performance of different control structures. The reader should not assume that the omission of examples for a particular system is a statement on the system's quality.

RESEARCH ISSUES

There are a great many issues outstanding in the field. Perhaps the most important one, and one that is not unique to IU, is the need for a scientific framework within which to design, describe, experiment, and document experiences in IUS building. Few if any attempts at independent verification of claims made are carried out. In other scientific fields, independent duplication of results is

a crucial component of the acceptance of a result as a contribution to the field. The lack of much activity in this area may be due to the lack of an overall framework for vision research; the "big picture" within which individual contributions can be placed and interrelated is missing.

Most of the topics covered in this entry require further research, and many issues have already been mentioned. Additional topics specifically addressing the open problems of the IU field are given below.

What Is the Role of Domain Knowledge? Is its application always necessary or does its application depend, perhaps, on the complexity of the scenes being interpreted? Many researchers in the vision community contend that most, if not all, visual interpretation tasks can be carried

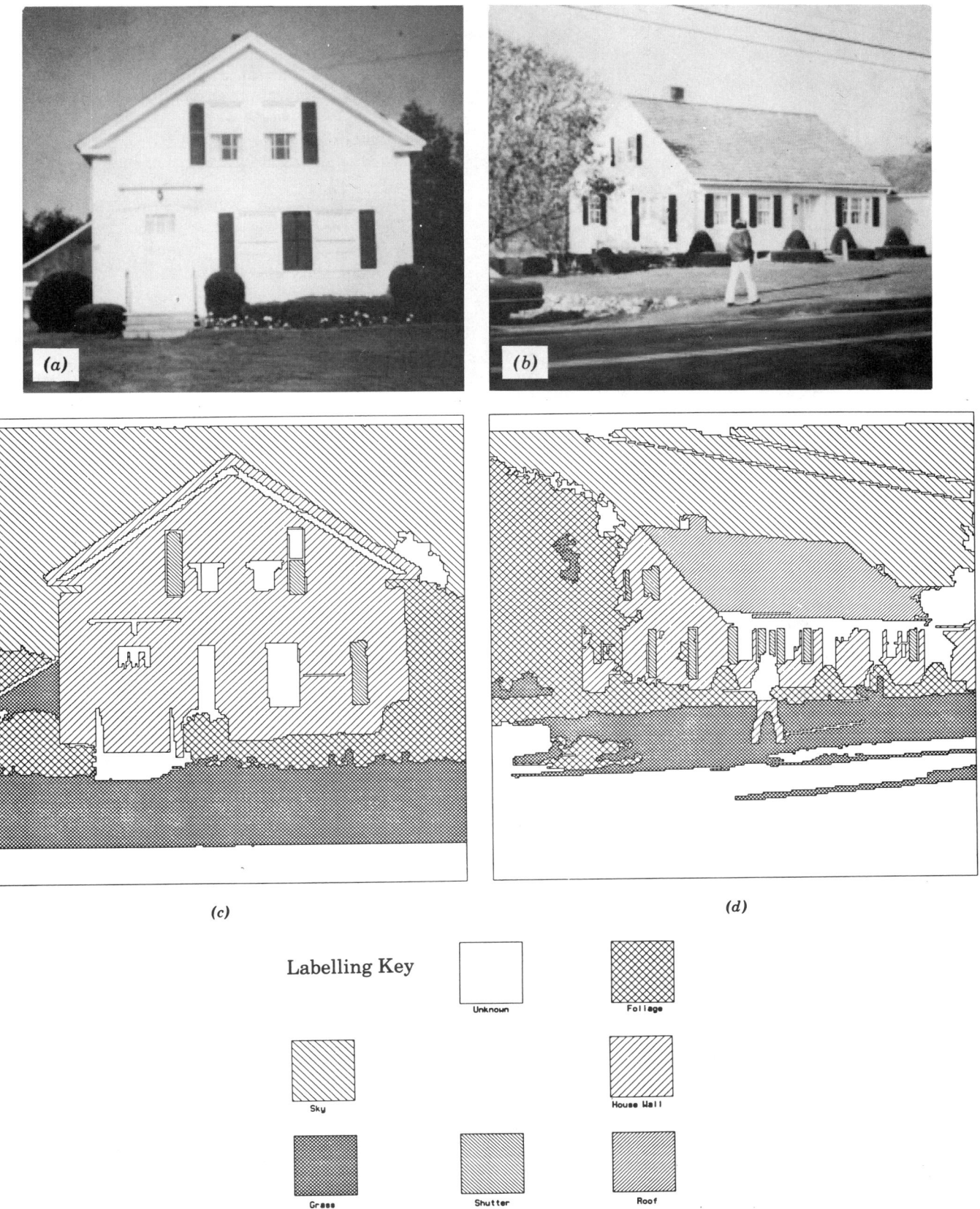

Figure 15. Example of input and output from the VISIONS system (Riseman and Hanson, 1984). (a, b) Original images; (c, d) final segmentation and labeling.

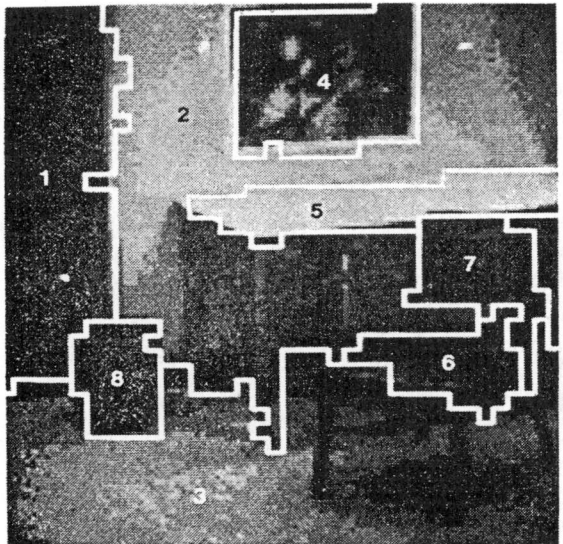

Final Region Interpretations

Interpretations	Regions
Door	1
Wall	2
Floor	3
Picture	4
Tabletop	5
Chairseat	6
Chairback	7
Waste Basket	8

Figure 16. Example of input and output from the IGS system (Tenenbaum and Barrow, 1977).

out without domain knowledge (qv), and this issue needs to be explored more fully. A growing segment of the psychology community raises the distinction between attentive and preattentive vision. These are fundamentally different from the high-level/low-level distinctions that computer vision draws and explicitly address the goals of a system in viewing a particular scene as well as scene complexity. The two visual processes are distinguished by their parallel or serial nature, and domain knowledge may play a role in each.

How Can the Best of the Early-Vision Schemes Be Integrated with High-Level Schemes in a Coherent Manner? There currently seems to be no real relationship between the techniques used to extract image features and those used to interpret them. Yet there must be an effective interface, if not also efficient representation transformations, in biological systems.

What Is the Nature of Top-Down Feedback? Does this only impact search schemes, or could it also play a role in expectation generation, in fine tuning of image operators,

in priming of semantic concepts, or in bridging the gap between image-centered and world-centered representations, and if so, how? Tsotsos has proven that visual tasks (specifically those that can be cast as visual search problems) become significantly easier if task information is provided (1989) in the same way as model-based vision uses models (see OBJECT RECOGNITION).

Does There Exist a Sufficient Set of Image Features for Image Interpretation?

What Should be Done in Parallel and What Serially; Why and How? How can computations be coordinated and organized?

What is the Nature of the Mechanism That Allows for the Combination of Evidence or Response Strengths?

How Can the Biological Sciences Motivate the Design of Image-Understanding Systems? What goes on between the input and the output is a totally unconstrained process, and this points to the major objective in this field: the discovery of computational models that can transform images plus world knowledge into scene interpretations. Guidance from biological research on vision can assist in providing some constraints on the characteristics of the interpretation process. In Tsotsos (1988; 1990), an argument is presented which ties together a great deal of neuroanatomy, neurophysiology, and psychophysics with the thread of complexity satisfaction. An architecture for vision systems, both biological and machine, is derived that satisfies the constraints for human-like visual perception. Much more research along this line is needed however.

Does a Representational Formalism Exist That Spans the Many Required for Vision? Biological vision seems to be nonlinear, time varying, hierarchical, and parallel with a superimposed serial component. Do formalisms exist that can deal with this?

How Can Vision Systems be Integrated into Purposeful, Intelligent Agents Such As Mobile Robots? This research issue incorporates not only topics of vision, sensor and robot control, but also most of AI, specifically knowledge representation, planning, problem-solving, and human-machine communication interfaces.

What Exactly Can Be Learned From System Building? The bottom line is that although image-understanding systems can be engineered to perform reasonably for a tightly constrained domain, the engineering is not yet completely based on sound scientific principles. There is still a long way to go.

Figure 17. Example of input and output from the ALVEN system (Tsotsos, 1985). (a) Example of marker finding using motion hypothesis predictions; (b) highlighted extracted markers for one image of the image sequence; (c, d) inward and outward patterns of motion, respectively, for a complete heart cycle; (e) textual output describing the performance characteristics and anomalies detected by ALVEN.

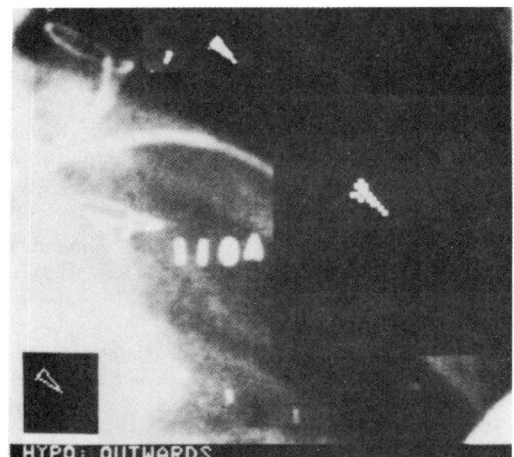

(a) HYPO: OUTWARDS

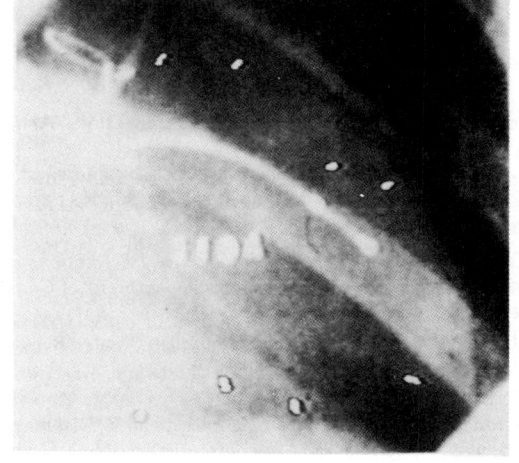

(b)

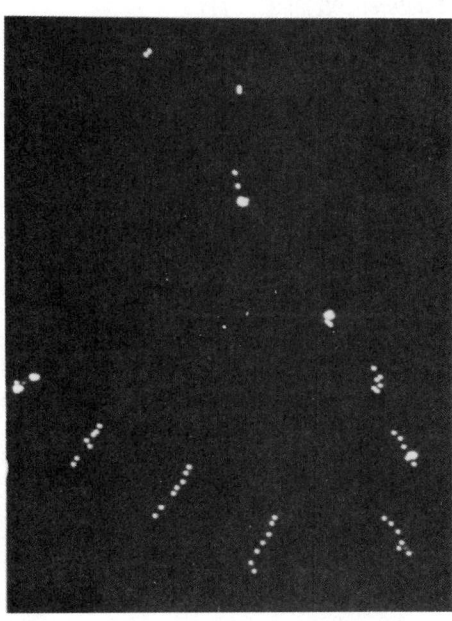

(c)

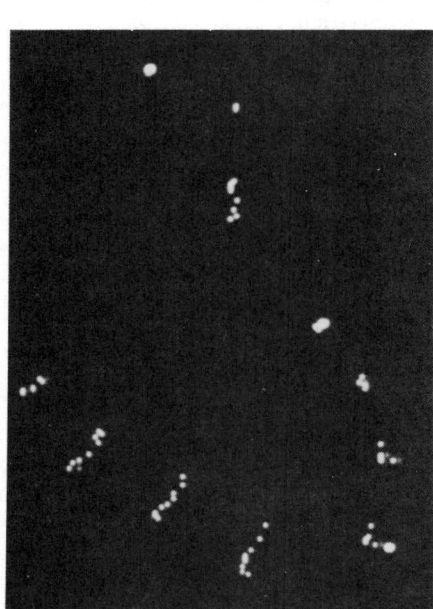

(d)

(e)

LEFT VENTRICLE exhibits:
TRANSLATING—time interval (0, 6)
rate (mm/s) → 15, 33, 15, 33, 1, 21
trajectory (rad) → 4.71, 1.05, 1.24, 1.05, 1.24, 2.36

TRANSLATING—time interval (7, 15)
rate (mm/s) → 15, 15, 15, 15, 15, 15, 15, 15
trajectory (rad) → 4.71, 4.71, 4.71, 3.14, 4.71, 3.14, 0.00, 4.71

VOLUME CHANGE—time interval (0, 16)
rate (ml/s) → −57, −216, −75, −168, −186, −138, 2, 120, 57, 54, 120, 162, 90, 27, 45, 90, 90
specializations:
   UNIFORMLY CONTRACTING during (0, 1)
   SYSTOLE during (1, 6)
   UNIFORMLY CONTRACTING during (2, 6)
   UNIFORMLY EXPANDING during (7, 11)
   DIASTOLE during (7, 16)
   UNIFORMLY EXPANDING during (12, 14)
   UNIFORMLY EXPANDING during (15, 16)

PERIMETER CHANGE—time interval (0, 6)
rate (mm/s) → 15, −150, 15, −165, −165, −105
specializations:
   LENGTHENING during (0, 1)
   SHORTENING during (1, 2)
   LENGTHENING during (2, 3)
   SHORTENING during (3, 6)

PERIMETER CHANGE—time interval (7, 8)
rate (mm/s) → 90
specializations:
   LENGTHENING during (7, 8)

PERIMETER CHANGE—time interval (9, 16)
rate (mm/s) → 30, 75, 150, 60, 15, 60, 60, 60
specializations:
   LENGTHENING during (9, 16)

WIDTH CHANGE—time interval (0, 16)
rate (mm/s) → −15, −15, −60, −15, −60, −60, −60, −60, −60, 60, 75, 45, 45, 45, 45, −15, −15

LENGTH CHANGE—time interval (0, 16)
rate (mm/s) → 30, −45, −15, −60, −60, −30, −30, 45, 15, 15, 15, 45, 45, 45, 45, 45, 45

Others:
   Isometric contraction during (0, 1)
   No translation during (6, 7)
   No perimeter change during (6, 7)
   No perimeter change during (8, 9)
   No translation during (15, 16)
Exceptions to normal detected:
   Mildly dyskinetic—contraction during (3, 4)
   Ischemic anterior isometric relaxation during (6, 7)
   Severely poor systole during (7, 7)
   Moderately dyskinetic—expansion during (9, 15)

BIBLIOGRAPHY

J. Allen, "Towards a General Theory of Action and Time," *Artif. Intell.* **23,** 123–154 (1984).

K. Andress and A. Kak, "Evidence Accumulation and Flow of Control in a Hierarchical Spatial Reasoning System," *AI Magazine* **9**(2), 75–94 (1988).

N. Badler, *Temporal Scene Analysis: Conceptual Descriptions of Object Movements,* Technical Report 80, Department of Computer Science, University of Toronto, 1975.

M. Baird and M. Kelly, "A Paradigm for Semantic Picture Recognition," *Patt. Recog.* **6,** 61–79 (1974).

D. Ballard, C. Brown, and J. Feldman, "An Approach to Knowledge-Directed Image Analysis," in A. Hanson and E. Riseman, eds., *Computer Vision Systems,* Academic Press, New York, 1978, pp. 271–282.

H. Barrow and J. Tenenbaum, "Recovering Intrinsic Scene Characteristics from Images," in A. Hanson and E. Riseman, eds., *Computer Vision Systems,* Academic Press, New York, 1978, pp. 3–26.

H. Barrow, R. Bolles, T. Garvey, T. Kremers, J. Tenenbaum, and H. Wolf, "Experiments in Map-Guided Photo Interpretation," *Proceedings of the Fifth IJCAI,* Cambridge, Mass., 1977, p. 696.

I. Beiderman, "Aspects and Extensions of a Theory of Human Image Understanding," in Z. Pylyshyn, ed., *Computational Processes in Human Vision,* Ablex Press, 1988, pp. 370–428.

T. Binford, "Survey of Model-based Image Analysis Systems," *Int. J. Robot. Res.* **1**(1), 18–64 (Spring 1982).

A. Bobick and R. Bolles, "Representation Space: An Approach to the Integration of Visual Information," *Proceedings of the IEEE Conference on Computer Vision and Pattern Recognition,* San Diego, Calif., 1989, pp. 492–499.

R. Brooks, "Symbolic Reasoning Among Three-Dimensional Models and Two-Dimensional Images," *Artif. Intell.* **17,** 285–348 (1981).

R. Brooks, "Model-based Three-Dimensional Interpretations of Two-dimensional Images," *IEEE Trans. Pattern Anal. Machine Intell.* **PAMI-5**(2), 140–150 (March 1983).

R. Brooks, R. Greiner, and T. Binford, "The ACRONYM Model-Based Vision System," *Proceedings of the Sixth IJCAI,* Tokyo, Japan, 1979, pp. 105–113.

A. Califano, R. Kjeldsen, and R. Bolle, "Data and Model Driven Foveation," *Proceedings of the International Conference on Pattern Recognition,* Atlantic City, N.J., 1990.

M. Clowes, "On Seeing Things," *Artif. Intell.* **2,** 79–116 (1971).

B. Draper, R. Collins, J. Brolio, A. Hanson, and E. Riseman, "The Schema System," *Int. J. Comput. Vision* **2–3,** 209–250 (1989).

L. Erman, F. Hayes-Roth, V. Lesser, and R. Reddy, "The HEARSAY-II Speech Understanding System: Integrating Knowledge to Resolve Uncertainty," *Comput. Surv.* **12,** 213–253 (1980).

G. Falk, "Interpretation of Imperfect Line Data as a Three-Dimensional Scene," *Artif. Intell.* **3**(2), 101–144 (1972).

F. Ferrie, M. Levin, and S. Zucker, "Cell Tracking: A Modeling and Minimization Approach," *IEEE Trans. Pattern Annal. Machine Intell.* **PAMI-4**(3), 277–290 (1982).

M. Fischler and O. Firschein, *Readings in Computer Vision,* Morgan-Kaufmann Press, San Mateo, Calif., 1987.

J. Freeman, "Survey: The Modeling of Spatial Relations," *Comput. Vis. Graph. Img. Proc.* **4,** 156–171 (1975).

E. Freuder, "A Computer System for Visual Recognition Using Active Knowledge," *Proceedings of the Fifth IJCAI,* Cambridge, Mass., 1977, pp. 671–677.

T. Garvey, *Perceptual Strategies for Purposive Vision,* SRI Technical note 117, SRI International, Menlo Park, Calif., 1976.

A. Hanson and E. Riseman, eds., *Computer Vision Systems,* Academic Press, New York, 1978.

A. Hanson and E. Riseman, "VISIONS: A Computer System for Interpreting Scenes," in A. Hanson and E. Riseman, eds., *Computer Vision Systems,* Academic Press, New York, 1978, pp. 303–334.

A. Huertas, W. Cole, and R. Nevatia, "Using Generic Knowledge in Analysis of Aerial Scenes; A Case Study," *Proceedings of the Eleventh IJCAI,* Detroit Mich., Morgan-Kaufmann, San Mateo, Calif., 1989, pp. 1642–1648.

D. Huffman, "Impossible Objects as Nonsense Sentences," *Artif. Intell.* **3,** 295–323 (1971).

R. Hummel and S. Zucker, *On the Foundations of Relaxation Labelling Processes,* Technical Report 80–7, Department of Electrical Engineering, McGill University, Montreal, 1980.

A. Jepson and W. Richards, "What is a Percept?" *Cogn. Sci.* (submitted, 1990).

T. Kanade, "Model Representations and Control Structures in Image Understanding," *Proceedings of the Fifth IJCAI,* Cambridge, Mass., Morgan-Kaufmann, San Mateo, Calif., 1977, pp. 1074–1082.

T. Kanade, "Survey: Region Segmentation: Signal vs Semantics," *Comput. Vis. Graph. Img. Process.* **13,** 279–297 (1980).

M. Kass, A. Witkin, and D. Terzopoulos, "SNAKES: Active Contour Models," *Int. J. Comput. Vision* **1-4,** 321–332 (1988).

M. Kelly, "Edge Detection in Pictures by Computer Using Planning," *Machine Intell.* **6,** 397–409 (1971).

B. Kuipers, "Modelling Spatial Knowledge," *Cogn. Sci.* **2,** 129–154 (1978).

M. Levine, "A Knowledge-Based Computer Vision System," in A. Hanson and E. Riseman, eds., *Computer Vision Systems,* Academic Press, New York, 1978, pp. 335–352.

B. Lowerre and R. Reddy, "The HARPY Speech Understanding System," in W. A. Lea, ed., *Trends in Speech Recognition,* Prentice-Hall, Englewood Cliffs, N.J., 1980, Chapter 15.

D. McDermott and E. Davis, "Planning Routes Through Uncertain Territory," *Artif. Intell.* **22,** 107–156 (1984).

D. McKeown, W. Harvey, and J. McDermott, "Rule-Based Interpretation of Aerial Imagery," *Proceedings of the IEEE Workshop on Principles of Knowledge-Based Systems,* Denver, Colo., 1984, pp. 145–158.

A. Mackworth, "On Reading Sketch Maps," *Proceedings of the Fifth IJCAI,* Cambridge, Mass., Morgan-Kaufmann, San Mateo, Calif., 1977, pp. 598–606.

A. Mackworth, "Vision Research Strategy: Black Magic, Metaphors, Mechanisms, Miniworlds, and Maps," in A. Hanson and E. Riseman, eds., *Computer Vision Systems,* Academic Press, New York, 1978, pp. 53–60.

A. Mackworth and W. Havens, "Representing Knowledge of the Visual World," *IEEE Comput.* **16,** 90–98 (1983).

D. Marr, *Vision,* W. H. Freeman, San Francisco, Calif., 1982.

D. Marr and H. Nishihara, "Representation and Recognition of the Spatial Organization of Three-Dimensional Shapes," *Proc. R. Soc. London Ser. B* **200,** 269–294 (1978).

T. Matsuyama, "Knowledge Organization and Control Structure in Image Understanding," *Proceedings of the ICPR,* Montreal, Quebec, 1984, pp. 1118–1127.

T. Matsuyama and V. Hwang, "SIGMA: A Framework for Image

Understanding: Integration of Bottom-Up and Top-Down Analyses," *Proceedings of the Ninth IJCAI*, Los Angeles, Calif., Morgan-Kaufmann, San Mateo, Calif., 1985, pp. 908–915.

M. Minsky, "A Framework for Representing Knowledge," in P. Winston, ed., *The Psychology of Computer Vision*, McGraw-Hill, New York, 1975, pp. 211–277.

J. Mulder, A. Mackworth, and W. Havens, "Knowledge Structuring and Constraint Satisfaction: The Mapsee Approach," *IEEE Trans. Pattern Anal. Mach. Intell.* **PAMI-10-6**, 866–879 (1988).

M. Nagao and T. Matsuyama, *A Structural Analysis of Complex Aerial Photographs*, Plenum, New York, 1980.

B. Neumann and H. Novak, "Event Models for Recognition and Natural Language Description of Events in Real-World Image Sequences," *Proceedings of the Eighth IJCAI*, Karlsruhe, FRG, Morgan-Kaufmann, San Mateo, Calif., 1983, pp. 724–726.

R. Nevatia, "Characterization and Requirements of Computer Vision Systems," in A. Hanson and E. Riseman, eds., *Computer Vision Systems*, Academic Press, New York, 1978, pp. 81–88.

Y. Ohta, "A Region-Oriented Image Analysis System by Computer," Ph.D. dissertation, Kyoto University, Department of Information Science, 1980.

J. O'Rourke and N. Badler, "Model-based Image Analysis of Human Motion Using Constraint Propagation," *IEEE Trans. Pattern Anal. Mach. Intell.* **PAMI-2**, 522–536 (1980).

C. Parma, A. Hanson, and E. Riseman, "Experiments in Schema-Driven Interpretation of a Natural Scene," *COINS TR* 80–10, University of Massachusetts at Amherst, 1980.

A. Pentland, "Perceptual Organization and the Representation of Natural Form," *SRI Technical Note* 357, SRI International, Menlo Park, Calif., 1985.

E. Riseman and A. Hanson, "A Methodology for the Development of General Knowledge-Based Vision Systems, *Proceedings of the IEEE Workshop on Principles of Knowledge-Based Systems*, Denver, Colo. 1984, pp. 159–172.

L. Roberts, "Machine Perception of Three-Dimensional Solids," in J. Tippett and co-workers, eds., *Optical and Electro-optical Information Processing*, MIT Press, Cambridge, Mass., 1965, pp. 159–197.

S. Rubin, "Natural Scene Recognition Using LOCUS Search," *Comput. Vis. Graph. Img. Process.* **13**, 298–333 (1980).

Y. Shirai, "A Context-sensitive Line Finder for Recognition of Polyhedra," *Artif. Intell.* 4(2), 95–119 (1973).

S. Tanimoto and A. Klinger, eds., *Structured Computer Vision*, Academic Press, New York, 1980.

J. Tenenbaum and H. Barrow, "Experiments in Interpretation Guided Segmentation," *Artif. Intell.* 8(3), 241–274 (1977).

D. Terzopoulos, A. Witkin, and M. Kass, "Constraints on Deformable Models: Recovering 3-D Shape and Nonrigid Motion," *Artif. Intell.* **36**(1), 91–123 (1988).

J. Tsotsos, "Knowledge of the Visual Process: Content, Form and Use," *Patt. Recog.* **17**, 13–28 (1984).

J. Tsotsos, "Knowledge Organization and Its Role in the Interpretation of Time-varying Data: The ALVEN System," *Computat. Intell.* 1(1), 16–32 (1985).

J. Tsotsos, "Representational Axes and Temporal Cooperative Computation," in M. Arbib and A. Hanson, eds., *Vision, Brain and Cooperative Computation*, MIT Press, Bradford Books, Cambridge, Mass., 1987, pp. 361–418.

J. Tsotsos, "A Complexity Level Analysis of Immediate Vision," *Int. J. Comput. Vision* 1-4, 303–320 (1988).

J. Tsotsos, "The Complexity of Perceptual Search Tasks," Proceedings of the Eleventh IJCAI, Detroit, Mich., Morgan-Kaufmann, San Mateo, Calif., 1989.

J. Tsotsos, "A Complexity Level Analysis of Vision," *Behavioral and Brain Sciences,* **12**(3) (1990).

J. Tsotsos, J. Mylopoulos, H. Covvey, and S. Zucker, "A Framework for Visual Motion Understanding," *IEEE Trans. Pattern Anal. Mach. Intell.* **PAMI-2**, 563–573 (1980).

L. Uhr, "Layered 'Recognition Cone' Networks that Preprocess, Classify, and Describe," *IEEE Trans. Comput.* **21**, 758–768 (1972).

W. Uttal, *A Taxonomy of Visual Processes*, Lawrence Erlbaum, Hillsdale, N.J., 1981.

C. Wang and S. Srihari, "A Framework for Object Recognition in a Visually Complex Environment and its Application to Locating Address Blocks on Mail Pieces," *Int. J. Comput. Vision* **2-2**, 125–152 (1988).

W. Woods, "Theory Formation and Control in a Speech Understanding System with Extrapolations towards Vision," in A. Hanson and E. Riseman, eds., *Computer Vision Systems*, Academic Press, New York, 1978, pp. 379–380.

B. York, A. Hanson, and E. Riseman, "3-D Object Representations and Matching with B-Splines and Surface Patches," *Proceedings of the Seventh IJCAI*, Vancouver, B.C., Canada, Morgan-Kaufmann, San Mateo, Calif., 1981, pp. 648–651.

R. Chellappa
University of Southern California

R. L. Kashyap
Purdue University

IMAGERY REPRESENTATION. See Mental imagery representation.

INCIDENCE CALCULUS

The incidence calculus is a logic for probabilistic reasoning. Given upper and lower bounds on the probabilities of the axioms of a logical theory it formalizes the derivation of upper and lower bounds on the remaining formulas of the theory. It differs from other logics for reasoning under uncertainty in two respects:

- Probabilities are not directly associated with any formulas. Rather incidences are directly associated with some formulas and probabilities are calculated from these incidences. An incidence is a set of possible worlds, each with an associated probability. The intended meaning of the incidence of a formula is the set of possible worlds in which the formula is true.

- This indirect encoding enables the incidence calculus to be truth functional, that is, the incidence of a compound formula can be calculated directly from its parts. Any logic in which probabilities, or any numeric uncertainty values, are associated directly with formulas cannot be truth functional (Bundy, 1985). Truth functionality is an important property of any logic because it enables the calculation of tight upper and lower bounds on the uncertainty values of formulas.

A SIMPLE EXAMPLE

To see how this works in practice, consider the following simple example. Let there be two propositions, *rainy* and *windy*, and seven possible worlds, *sun, mon, tues, wed, thurs, fri, sat*. Let each possible world be equally probable, ie, occur $\frac{1}{7}$ of the time.

Let $i(\phi)$ denote the incidence of the formula ϕ and let the incidences of the two propositions be

$$i(rainy) = \{fri,sat,sun,mon\}$$

$$i(windy) = \{mon,wed,fri\}$$

From this, the incidences of $\neg rainy$, $rainy \wedge \neg rainy$ and $rainy \wedge windy$ can be calculated as:

$$i(\neg rainy) = \{mon,tues,wed,thurs,fri,sat,sun\}\backslash$$
$$\{fri,sat,sun,mon\}$$
$$= \{tues,wed,thurs\}$$
$$i(rainy \wedge \neg rainy) = \{fri,sat,sun,mon\}$$
$$\cap \{tues,wed,thurs\}$$
$$= \{\}$$
$$i(rainy \wedge windy) = \{fri,sat,sun,mon\}$$
$$\cap \{mon,wed,fri\}$$
$$= \{fri,mon\}$$

Let $p(\phi)$ denote the probability of the formula ϕ. The probability of each the above formulas can be calculated by adding up the number of possible worlds in its incidence.

$$p(rainy) = \tfrac{4}{7} \quad p(rainy \wedge \neg rainy) = 0$$
$$p(windy) = \tfrac{3}{7} \quad p(rainy \wedge windy) = \tfrac{2}{7}$$
$$p(\neg rainy) = \tfrac{3}{7}$$

Note that although *windy* and $\neg rainy$ have the same probability, three-sevenths, their conjunctions with *rainy* have different probabilities, two-sevenths and zero, respectively. If the probabilities of compound formulas were calculated solely from the probabilities of their parts then the probabilities of these two conjunctions must be the same. This shows that a probabilistic calculus cannot be truth functional. This is because the correlation between two formulas cannot be encoded in their two probabilities, whereas it is encoded in their two incidences.

FORMAL DEFINITIONS

The incidence calculus is defined formally as follows.

Definition 1: Propositional Language. $\mathscr{L}(P)$ is the propositional language formed from P, where P is a finite set of propositions. $\mathscr{L}(P)$ is the smallest set containing the truth values and the members of P and is closed under the operations of negation, disjunction, conjunction, and implication:

$$true, false \in \mathscr{L}(P)$$

if $p \in P$ then $p \in \mathscr{L}(P)$

if $\phi, \psi \in \mathscr{L}(P)$ then $\neg\phi \in \mathscr{L}(P)$, $\phi \vee \psi \in \mathscr{L}(P)$,
$$\phi \wedge \psi \in \mathscr{L}(P) \text{ and } \phi \to \psi \in \mathscr{L}(P)$$

Definition 2: Possible Worlds. A possible world is a primitive, ie, undefined, object of incidence calculus, but can be thought of as a partial interpretation of some logical formulas. The probability that a possible world w is the real world is represented by a function ρ from possible worlds to real numbers between 0 and 1. If I is a set of possible worlds then $wp(I)$ is called the weighted probability of I, and is defined to be

$$wp(I) = \sum_{w\in I} \rho(w) \tag{1}$$

Definition 3: Incidence Calculus. An incidence calculus theory is a quintuple $\langle \mathscr{W}, \rho, \mathscr{P}, \mathscr{A}, i \rangle$, where $\mathscr{W}$ is a finite set of possible worlds. For all $w \in \mathscr{W}$, $\rho(w)$ is the probability of w and $wp(\mathscr{W}) = 1$. $\mathscr{P}$ is a set of propositions. $\mathscr{L}(\mathscr{P})$ is the language of the theory. $\mathscr{A}$ is a distinguished set of formulas in $\mathscr{L}(\mathscr{P})$ called the axioms of the theory; i is a function from the axioms $\mathscr{A}$ to $2^{\mathscr{W}}$, the set of subsets of $\mathscr{W}$; and $i(\phi)$ is called the incidence of ϕ; $i(\phi)$ is to be thought of as the set of possible worlds in $\mathscr{W}$ in which ϕ is true, ie, $i(\phi) = \{w \in \mathscr{W} | w \models \phi\}$. i is extended to a function from $\mathscr{L}(\mathscr{A})$ to $2^{\mathscr{W}}$ by the following defining equations of incidence.

$$i(true) = \mathscr{W} \tag{2}$$
$$i(false) = \{\} \tag{3}$$
$$i(\neg\phi) = \mathscr{W} \setminus i(\phi) \tag{4}$$
$$i(\phi \wedge \psi) = i(\phi) \cap i(\psi) \tag{5}$$
$$i(\phi \vee \psi) = i(\phi) \cup i(\psi) \tag{6}$$
$$i(\phi \to \psi) = (\mathscr{W} \setminus i(\phi)) \cup i(\psi) \tag{7}$$

Note that equations 2 to 7 define i truth functionally, that is, the incidence of a compound formula can be calculated solely from the incidences of its constituent subformulas. In particular, it is easy to calculate that the incidence of any propositional tautology is $\mathscr{W}$ and that of any propositional contradiction is $\{\}$. It is not usually possible to infer the incidence of formulas in $\mathscr{L}(\mathscr{P}) \setminus \mathscr{L}(\mathscr{A})$. What can be done is to define upper and lower bounds on the incidence using the functions i^* and i_*, respectively. For all $\phi \in \mathscr{L}(\mathscr{P})$ these are defined as follows.

$$i^*(\phi) = \bigcap_{\psi\in\mathscr{L}(\mathscr{A})} \{i(\psi) | i(\phi \to \psi) = \mathscr{W}\} \tag{8}$$

$$i_*(\phi) = \bigcup_{\psi\in\mathscr{L}(\mathscr{A})} \{i(\psi) | i(\psi \to \phi) = \mathscr{W}\} \tag{9}$$

It is easy to see that $i_*(\phi) = i(\phi) = i^*(\phi)$ for all $\phi \in \mathscr{L}(\mathscr{A})$ and $i_*(\phi) \subseteq i^*(\phi)$ for all $\phi \in \mathscr{L}(\mathscr{P})$.

Definition 4: Probability. The probability that a formula ϕ is true is represented using the partial function p from formulas to real numbers in the interval 0 to 1. When $i(\phi)$ is defined, $p(\phi)$ is defined as:

$$p(\phi) = wp(i(\phi)) \qquad (10)$$

For all $\phi \in \mathscr{L}(\mathscr{P})$ upper and lower bounds are defined on the probability of ϕ using the functions p^* and p_*, respectively, as follows.

$$p^*(\phi) = wp(i^*(\phi))$$
$$p_*(\phi) = wp(i_*(\phi))$$

The conditional probability that a formula ϕ is true given that another formula ψ is true is represented using the partial binary function p from pairs of formulas to real numbers in the interval 0 to 1. For all $\phi, \psi \in \mathscr{L}(\mathscr{P})$ it is defined as:

$$p(\phi|\psi) = \frac{p(\phi \wedge \psi)}{p(\psi)} \qquad (11)$$

The correlation between two formulas ϕ and ψ is represented using the partial binary function c from pairs of formulas to real numbers in the interval -1 to 1. For all $\phi, \psi \in \mathscr{L}(\mathscr{P})$ it is defined as:

$$c(\phi, \psi) = \frac{p(\phi \vee \psi) - p(\phi).p(\psi)}{\sqrt{p(\phi).p(\neg\phi).p(\psi).p(\neg\psi)}} \qquad (12)$$

The correlation between two formulas is a measure of their degree of dependence: $c(\phi, \psi) = 1$ means ϕ and ψ always co-occur, $c(\phi, \neg\psi) = -1$ means they never co-occur, and $c(\phi, \psi) = 0$ means they are independent, co-occurring in a random way. Note that $p(\neg\phi)$ and $p(\neg\psi)$ are needed to define $c(\phi, \psi)$; it cannot be defined in terms of $p(\phi)$ and $p(\psi)$ alone.

From the definitions of i (eq. 2–7), wp (eq. 1), p (eq. 10), and c (eq. 12), the following rules of probability can be derived.

$$p(true) = 1$$
$$p(false) = 0$$
$$p(\neg\phi) = 1 - p(\phi)$$
$$p(\phi \vee \psi) = p(\phi) + p(\psi) - p(\phi \wedge \psi)$$
$$p(\phi \rightarrow \psi) = p(\neg\phi) + p(\psi) - p(\neg\phi \wedge \psi)$$
$$p(\phi \wedge \psi) = p(\phi).p(\psi) + c(\phi, \psi).\sqrt{p(\phi).p(\neg\phi).p(\psi).p(\neg\psi)}$$
$$(13)$$

Note that these equations do not define p truth functionally. In particular, the probability of $\phi \wedge \psi$ is given not just in terms of the probability of ϕ and ψ but also in terms of $c(\phi, \psi)$. This deficiency is not just an artifact of these equations, but is an endemic property of a probabilistic logic, indeed of any purely arithmetic uncertainty calculus. Similar properties hold for conditional probability,

correlation, and any combination. That is, it is not possible to calculate the conditional probability or correlation of a compound formula solely from the conditional probabilities, correlations, and probabilities of its parts (Bundy, 1985).

INFERRING NEW INCIDENCES FROM OLD

Given an assignment of incidences to a set of axioms of a theory $\mathscr{A}$, it is desirable to derive the incidences of the remaining formulas of the language $\mathscr{L}(\mathscr{P})$. Unfortunately, it is generally only possible to derive upper and lower bounds for the incidences of these formulas. For instance, consider the *modus ponens* rule of inference:

$$\frac{\phi \rightarrow \psi, \phi}{\psi}$$

It is not possible to calculate $i(\psi)$ from $i(\phi \rightarrow \psi)$ and $i(\phi)$ alone. Suppose $\mathscr{W} = \{a, b\}$, $i(\phi \rightarrow \psi) = \{a, b\}$ and $i(\phi) = \{a\}$ then all that can be said about $i(\psi)$ is that it lies between $\{a\}$ and $\{a, b\}$. In fact, $i_*(\psi) = \{a\}$ and $i^*(\psi) = \{a, b\}$.

In general, therefore, the best that can be hoped for is an inference mechanism that, given the upper and lower bounds on the incidences of the hypotheses of an inference step, calculates the tightest upper and lower bounds of the incidence of the conclusion. This has been realized as a process of constraint propagation. Given a finite set of formulas and some initial assignment of upper and lower bounds, new assignments are calculated from old assignments and the process iterates until it terminates. At termination the tightest bounds have been calculated.

The set of formulas on which this constraint propagation is performed (the constraint set) must be defined with some care. For completeness it must be the language of the axioms, the formulas whose incidences are to be calculated, and all subformulas of all these formulas. Unfortunately, this is an infinite set, but constraint propagation must be performed on a finite set if it is to terminate. The solution is to let each formula of the language be represented by a canonical form, where there are only a finite number of these canonical forms.

Definition 5: Canonical Form. A formula in $\mathscr{L}(\mathscr{P})$ is in canonical form if it has the form $\bigwedge_{i=1}^{m}(\neg\bigwedge_{j=1}^{n}l_i^j)$ where $l_i^j = p$ or $l_i^j = \neg p$ for some $p \in P$. Note that for each $\phi \in \mathscr{L}(P)$ there is an equivalent formula in canonical form. First ϕ must be transformed into conjunctive normal form and then de Morgan's law must be used to turn each conjunct $\bigvee_{j=1}^{m} l_i^j$ into $\neg\bigwedge_{j=1}^{m} \neg l_i^j$ and then all double negations must be canceled. Let $\mathscr{L}'(P)$ be the subset of formulas in $\mathscr{L}(P)$ that are in canonical form. For readability a formula in canonical form will sometimes be abbreviated by one of its non-canonical equivalents, eg, $\phi \rightarrow \psi$ stands for $\neg(\phi \wedge \neg\psi)$.

Definition 6: Constraint Set. Let $\mathscr{A}$ be the set of axioms of a theory and $\mathscr{T}$ be the set of formulas whose incidence is to be calculated (the theorems). Let $sf(F)$ be the set of subformulas of the formulas F:

if $\phi \in F$ then $\phi \in sf(F)$

if $\neg\phi \in sf(F)$ then $\phi \in sf(F)$

if $\phi \wedge \psi \in sf(F)$ then $\phi, \psi \in sf(F)$

if $\phi \vee \psi \in sf(F)$ then $\phi, \psi \in sf(F)$

if $\phi \rightarrow \psi \in sf(F)$ then $\phi, \psi \in sf(F)$

The constraint set is $sf(\mathcal{L}'(\mathcal{A} \cup \mathcal{T}))$.

The constraint set is organized as a network in which each formula has pointers to each of its subformulas and superformulas. The initial assignment consists of upper and lower bounds equal to the incidence for the axioms and the default upper and lower bounds $\mathcal{W}$ and {}, respectively, for all other formulas. The idea of the constraint propagation is to improve on these default assignments by replacing them with the values of i^* and i_* for each formula. To describe this constraint propagation process it is necessary to be more precise about the representation of an assignment of upper and lower bounds.

Definition 7: Assignments. Let F be an assignment of upper and lower incidence bounds to a set of formulas and sup_F is a function from formulas to sets of possible worlds that defines the current assignment of upper bounds. inf_F is a function from formulas to sets of possible worlds that defines the current assignment of lower bounds. The rules of inference that propagate the upper and lower bounds around the network of formulas can now be given.

Definition 8: The Rules of Inference. A rule of inference is a mapping from assignments to assignments. Let F be the assignment before the rule fires and G be the assignment afterward. In each case, G is the same as F except for the changes, on some particular formula, defined below for each rule.

Not1: $sup_G(\phi) = (\mathcal{W} \setminus inf_F(\neg\phi)) \cap sup_F(\phi)$

Not2: $inf_G(\phi) = (\mathcal{W} \setminus sup_F(\neg\phi)) \cup inf_F(\phi)$

Not3: $sup_G(\neg\phi) = (\mathcal{W} \setminus inf_F(\phi)) \cap sup_F(\neg\phi)$

Not4: $inf_G(\neg\phi) = (\mathcal{W} \setminus sup_F(\phi)) \cup inf_F(\neg\phi)$

And1: $sup_G(\phi) = (sup_F(\phi \wedge \psi) \cup (\mathcal{W} \setminus inf_F(\psi)))$
$\cap sup_F(\phi)$

And2: $inf_G(\phi) = inf_F(\phi \wedge \psi) \cup inf_F(\phi)$

And3: $sup_G(\psi) = (sup_F(\phi \wedge \psi) \cup (\mathcal{W} \setminus inf_F(\phi)))$
$\cap sup_F(\psi)$

And4: $inf_G(\psi) = inf_F(\phi \wedge \psi) \cup inf_F(\psi)$

And5: $sup_G(\phi \wedge \psi) = sup_F(\phi) \cap sup_F(\psi) \cap sup_F(\phi \wedge \psi)$

And6: $inf_G(\phi \wedge \psi) = (inf_F(\phi) \cap inf_F(\psi)) \cup inf_F(\phi \wedge \psi)$

Note that it is only necessary to give rules for negation and conjunction because these rules only operate on formulas in canonical form. The exhaustive application of these rules of inference will terminate (Bundy, 1986). Suppose the final assignment is F, then $sup_F(\phi) = i^*(\phi)$ and $inf_F(\phi) = i_*(\phi)$ (Correa da Silva and Bundy, 1990).

This inference mechanism can be quite efficiently implemented if sets of possible worlds are represented by bit vectors, with one bit for each possible world in $\mathcal{W}$; $\cap$, $\cup$, and $\setminus$ are then represented by logical *and, or,* and *not,* respectively.

AN EXAMPLE OF INFERENCE

The constraint propagation process can be illustrated with the *modus ponens* example mentioned earlier: $\mathcal{A} = \{\phi \rightarrow \psi, \phi\}$, $\mathcal{T} = \{\psi\}$, $\mathcal{W} = \{a, b\}$, $i(\phi \rightarrow \psi) = \{a, b\}$, and $i(\phi) = \{a\}$. The upper and lower bounds on $i(\psi)$. First, $\phi \rightarrow \psi$ must be translated into its logically equivalent, canonical form: $\neg(\phi \wedge \neg\psi)$. The initial assignment of upper and lower bounds is given and explained in Table 1. Irrelevant members of $sf(\mathcal{L}'(\mathcal{A} \cup \mathcal{T}))$ have been omitted from the table. Ignoring rule applications that have no effect on the assignment, the inference process proceeds as follows.

By rule Not1:

$$sup_2(\phi \wedge \neg\psi) = (\mathcal{W} \setminus inf_1(\neg(\phi \wedge \neg\psi))) \cap sup_1(\phi \wedge \neg\psi)$$
$$= (\{a, b\} \setminus \{a, b\}) \cap \{a, b\}$$
$$= \{\}$$

By rule And3:

$$sup_3(\neg\psi) = (sup_2(\phi \wedge \neg\psi) \cup (\mathcal{W} \setminus inf_2(\phi))) \cap sup_2(\neg\psi)$$
$$= (\{\} \cup (\{a, b\} \setminus \{a\})) \cap \{a, b\}$$
$$= \{b\}$$

By rule Not2:

$$inf_4(\psi) = (\mathcal{W} \setminus sup_3(\neg\psi)) \cup inf_3(\psi)$$
$$= (\{a, b\} \setminus \{b\}) \cup \{\}$$
$$= \{a\}$$

After this none of the rules can change the assignment of these formulas and the process terminates. The final assignment is given in Table 2. As required, this gives $i_*(\psi) = \{a\}$ and $i^*(\psi) = \{a, b\}$.

Table 1. Initial Assignment of Upper and Lower Bounds[a]

Formula	inf_1	sup_1
ϕ	$\{a\}$	$\{a\}$
ψ	$\{\}$	$\{a, b\}$
$\neg\psi$	$\{\}$	$\{a, b\}$
$\phi \wedge \neg\psi$	$\{\}$	$\{a, b\}$
$\neg(\phi \wedge \neg\psi)$	$\{a, b\}$	$\{a, b\}$

[a] The consecutive assignments will be numbered 1, 2, etc. The two axioms ϕ and $\neg(\phi \wedge \neg\psi)$ are assigned upper and lower bounds equal to their incidences. The other formulas are all the proper subformulas of $\neg(\phi \wedge \neg\psi)$. All nonaxioms are assigned the default upper and lower bounds of $\{a, b\}$ and $\{\}$, respectively.

Table 2. Final Assignment of Upper and Lower Bounds[a]

Formula	inf_4	sup_4
ϕ	$\{a\}$	$\{a\}$
ψ	$\{a\}$ (Not2)	$\{a, b\}$
$\neg\psi$	$\{\}$	$\{b\}$ (And3)
$\phi \wedge \neg\psi$	$\{\}$	$\{\}$ (Not1)
$\neg(\phi \wedge \neg\psi)$	$\{a, b\}$	$\{a, b\}$

[a] Those assignments that have been changed from Table 1 have been labeled with the rule of inference that made the change.

ASSIGNING INCIDENCES TO FORMULAS

The incidence calculus inference mechanism assumes that incidences have been assigned to the axioms. Unfortunately, an uncertainty inference problem may not always be presented in this form. Often the uncertainty of formulas will be presented initially as an assignment of probabilities to the axioms, with or without some record of the correlations between them. It is then necessary to assign incidences to the axioms that respect the assignment of probabilities and correlations.

In making this assignment there are several variables: the size of $\mathcal{W}$, the definition of ρ and the definition of i. Only one simple scheme will be considered: $\mathcal{W}$ will be taken to be fixed, eg, 100 possible worlds. The greater this size the greater the sensitivity of the calculations, but the greater their computational expense. Low sensitivity is often enough in artificial intelligence applications. Furthermore, ρ will be taken to give the same value for each possible world, eg, $\frac{1}{100}$. The probability assignment must now be realized solely by the assignment of equiprobable possible worlds to axioms using the function i.

One example of how this can be done is the Monte Carlo method of Corlett and Todd (1985), interleaved with the inference mechanism to take account of the logical structure of the axioms. In this method formulas are assumed to be assigned probabilities and incidences are assigned that respect these probabilities. Correlations are assumed not to be available. Some correlations are forced by the logical structure, but otherwise axioms are assumed to be pairwise independent.

Definition 9: Monte Carlo Incidence Assignment Method. It is assumed that $p(\phi)$ is known for all $\phi \in \mathcal{A}$. Recall that

$$p^*(\phi) = wp(i^*(\phi))$$

and

$$p_*(\phi) = wp(i_*(\phi))$$

Define p' as:

$$p'(\phi) = \frac{p(\phi) - p_*(\phi)}{wp(i^*(\phi) \setminus i_*(\phi))} \left(= 1 - \frac{p^*(\phi) - p(\phi)}{wp(i^*(\phi) \setminus i_*(\phi))} \right)$$

Initialize $i_*(\phi) = \{\}$ and $i^*(\phi) = \mathcal{W}$ for all $\phi \in sf(\mathcal{L}'(\mathcal{A}))$. For each $\phi \in \mathcal{A}$:

1. If $p(\phi) < p_*(\phi)$ or $p(\phi) > p^*(\phi)$ then stop with failure.
2. Else randomly assign each of the possible worlds in $i^*(\phi) \setminus i_*(\phi)$ to $i(\phi)$ with a probability of $p'(\phi)$; let $i^*(\phi) = i_*(\phi) = i(\phi)$.
3. Run the inference mechanism on the formulas in $sf(\mathcal{L}'(\mathcal{A}))$ with initial assignment $inf_1(\psi) = i_*(\psi)$ and $sup_1(\psi) = i^*(\psi)$ for all $\psi \in sf(\mathcal{L}'(\mathcal{A}))$. Suppose F is the assignment on termination; let $i_*(\psi) = inf_F(\psi)$ and $i^*(\psi) = sup_F(\psi)$ for all $\psi \in sf(\mathcal{L}'(\mathcal{A}))$.

For instance, let there be two propositions, *sunny* and *dry*, and 10 equiprobable possible worlds named 1 to 10, ie, $\mathcal{W} = \{1, \ldots, 10\}$, $\rho(w) = 0.1$ for all $w \in \mathcal{W}$. Let the given assignment of probabilities be $p(sunny) = 0.4$, $p(sunny \rightarrow dry) = 0.8$. Suppose an incidence is assigned to *sunny* first: $i_*(sunny) = \{\}$ and $i^*(sunny) = \{1, \ldots, 10\}$, so $p'(sunny) = 0.4$. Suppose the random assignment of possible worlds to $i(sunny)$ yields $\{1, 2, 4, 7\}$. When the inference mechanism is run it will reassign $\{3, 5, 6, 8, 9, 10\}$ to $i_*(sunny \rightarrow dry)$.

Now an incidence must be assigned to *sunny* $\rightarrow$ *dry*: $i_*(sunny \rightarrow dry) = \{3, 5, 6, 8, 9, 10\}$ and $i^*(sunny \rightarrow dry) = \{1, \ldots, 10\}$, so $p'(sunny \rightarrow dry) = 0.5$. The random assignment of possible worlds to $i(sunny \rightarrow dry)$ might then yield $\{1, 2, 3, 5, 6, 8, 9, 10\}$. As a side effect this process gives the following bounds on the probability of *dry*: $0 \cdot 2 \leq p(dry) \leq 1$. Note that the correlation between the two axioms is $c(sunny, sunny \rightarrow dry) \approx 0.61$, so they are not independent. With such a small $\mathcal{W}$ this assignment is necessarily crude, but greater sensitivity can be gained by using larger $\mathcal{W}$.

COMPARISONS WITH OTHER LOGICS

Incidence calculus is similar to Nilsson's (1984) probabilistic logic. The main difference is that instead of taking the concept of possible world as a primitive, probabilistic logic uses Herbrand models of $\mathcal{L}(\mathcal{P})$. A Herbrand model is a model of a logical theory, in the sense of Tarski, which is formed using the symbols of the logic. In this way it is possible to form an exhaustive and disjoint set of models. The number of Herbrand models and which formulas are true in each one is fixed by this process. Thus the incidence of each formula is also known, in contrast with incidence calculus in which only upper and lower incidence bounds may be known for some formulas.

Given some desired assignment of probabilities to the formulae of $\mathcal{A}$, probabilistic logic calculates an assignment of probabilities to the Herbrand models that will yield the desired assignment to the formulas. In general, this is a prohibitively expensive process. Nilsson suggests various ways to circumvent it in special cases. Incidence calculus avoids this problem by using uninterpreted possible worlds rather than Herbrand models. This permits the cruder, but much less expensive probability assignment mechanism described above.

Incidence calculus is also similar to the Dempster-Shafer theory (Shafer, 1976), especially as formalized in Fagin and Halpern (1989). Both systems permit only partial definition of the probabilities of some formulas. The Dempster-Shafer theory achieves this by defining the incidence of all formulas, but not defining the probabilities of all the possible worlds, ie, i is a total function, but ρ is a partial function. Because p, the probability of a formula, is defined using both i and ρ (eq. 1–10), it too is only partially defined. Incidence calculus achieves a similar effect the other way round, ie, ρ is a total but i is partial. In most cases these two alternative solutions are equivalent (Correa da Silva and Bundy, 1990).

However, most implementations of the Dempster-Shafer theory work directly with the upper and lower probability bounds on formulas and not via incidences. This means that their inference mechanism inevitably calculates looser bounds than the incidence calculus mechanism described above. This is because a probability calculus is not truth functional, whereas an incidence calculus is. The following example illustrates this.

Let $p(rainy) = \frac{4}{7}$ and $p(windy) = \frac{3}{7}$. If the attempt to calculate $p(rainy \wedge windy)$ is done solely from the probabilities of its subformulas, then the best that can be done is to place it in a rather wide interval. If it is never both windy and rainy then $p(rainy \wedge windy) = 0$, and if it is always windy when it is rainy then $p(rainy \wedge windy) = \frac{3}{7}$. Every probability between these extremes is possible, thus

$$0 \leq p(rainy \wedge windy) \leq \frac{3}{7}$$

Note that using equation 13 gives an even wider interval with upper bound $\frac{24}{49}$. On the other hand, if the incidences of *rainy* and *windy* are known then it is possible to calculate an exact value for the incidence of *rainy* $\wedge$ *windy* and hence of $p(rainy \wedge windy)$. This is because incidence calculus is truth functional, which no purely probabilistic calculus could be.

CONCLUSION

The incidence calculus is a logic for uncertain reasoning in which the uncertainty value is represented by the set of possible worlds in which it is true rather than by a numeric value. A numeric value, namely the probability, is readily recovered from this set. The advantage of this arrangement is that the incidence calculus is truth functional—leading to the calculation of tighter bounds on the probability of a formula than is possible with a calculus working with probabilities alone. Incidence bounds on new formulas can be inferred from bounds on old formulas by a process of constraint propagation using rules of inference.

BIBLIOGRAPHY

A. Bundy, "Incidence Calculus: A Mechanism for Probabilistic Reasoning," *J. Automated Reasoning* **1**(3), 263–284 (1985). [Earlier versions in *Proceedings of FGCS-84; Proceedings of the Workshop on Uncertainty and Probability.* Available from Edinburgh University as Research Paper No 216.]

A. Bundy, "Correctness Criteria of Some Algorithms for Uncertain Reasoning Using Incidence Calculus," *J. Automated Reasoning* **2**(2), 109–126 (1986). [Available from Edinburgh University as Research Paper No. 259.]

R. A. Corlett and S. J. Todd, "A Monte-Carlo Approach to Uncertain Inference," in P. Ross, ed., *Proceedings of the Conference on Artificial Intelligence and Simulation of Behavior*, 1985, pp. 28–34.

F. S. Correa da Silva and A. Bundy, "On Some Equivalence Relations Between Incidence Calculus and Dempster-Shafer Theory of Evidence," in *Proceedings of the Sixth Conference on Uncertainty in Artificial Intelligence*, GE Corp., 1990, pp. 378–383. [Available from Edinburgh University as Research Paper 470.]

F. S. Correa da Silva and A. Bundy, *A Rational Reconstruction of Incidence Calculus*; Research Paper, Edinburgh University, Edinburgh, UK, in press.

R. Fagin and J. Y. Halpern, "Uncertainty, Belief, and Probability," in *Proceedings of the Eleventh IJCAI*, Morgan-Kaufmann, San Mateo, Calif., 1989, pp. 1161–1167.

N. Nilsson, *Probabilistic Logic*, Technical Note 321, SRI International, Menlo Park, Calif., 1984.

G. Shafer, *A Mathematical Theory of Evidence*, Princeton University Press, Princeton, N.J., 1976.

ALAN BUNDY
University of Edinburgh

INDUCTION, MATHEMATICAL

Mathematical induction is the essential proof technique to verify statements about recursively defined objects. Consequently, induction plays a central role in several subfields of mathematics, such as formal logic, algebra, arithmetic, etc. In computer science induction proofs are indispensable when properties of loops and recursive algorithms must be verified. An induction theorem proving system (ITPS) supports an automated verification. Like a conventional theorem prover, an ITPS is concerned with the problem of how to prove a given statement, but in addition it sometimes also must find out what else to prove: as it turns out, the degree of automatization depends to a great extent on an ITPS's performance to discover new conjectures supporting the proof of a given statement. This makes research in automated induction an exciting enterprise. Several difficult problems have been solved by implemented theorem provers, ranging from pure mathematics, such as proving the prime factorization theorem, to program verification, such as correctness proofs for an encryption algorithm, microprocessor design, and programming language implementation, thereby demonstrating the success as well as the great practical relevance of automated theorem proving by induction.

THEORETICAL FOUNDATIONS

One form of mathematical induction that is familiar to most people is Peano's (first-order) induction principle for natural numbers: $[\varphi(0) \wedge [\forall n \in \mathbb{N}.\ \varphi(n) \rightarrow \varphi(n + 1)]] \rightarrow$

$\forall n \in \mathbb{N}.\ \varphi(n)$. This principle is used as a rule when proving a statement φ of arithmetic: the statement for 0, the induction base, is verified and then the induction step is proved, ie, the induction conclusion $\varphi(n + 1)$ is verified, where it is assumed that the induction hypothesis $\varphi(n)$ holds true. If both proofs are successful, then by the induction principle $\varphi(n)$ holds for all numbers n. However, there is an inherent limitation with this approach: as the result of *Gödel's Incompleteness Theorem*, for each consistent proof system of arithmetic, there is a true arithmetic statement (given as a first-order sentence) unprovable by the system. Consequently, a sound ITPS cannot be designed that verifies each true statement of arithmetic. Viewed from this perspective, automated theorem proving by induction is a hopeless enterprise but as experiments with theorem provers indicate, the systems, albeit incomplete, are powerful enough to live with.

Peano's induction principle for natural numbers can be generalized in the following way. Let M be a set and $<_M$ be an order relation on M, such that there is no infinitely decreasing sequence $m_0 >_M m_1 >_M m_2 >_M \ldots$ of elements in M. Then $<_M$ is called a well-founded order of M and M is a well-founded set *wrt.* $<_M$. For well-founded sets there is the *Generalized Principle of Noetherian Induction:* $[\forall m \in M.\ [\forall k \in M.\ k <_M m \rightarrow \varphi(k)] \rightarrow \varphi(m)] \rightarrow \forall m \in M.\ \varphi(m)$. Defining $M := \mathbb{N}$ and $n <_M n + 1$ Peano's induction principle is obtained as an instance of the generalized induction principle. By the generalized induction principle, one is neither restricted to inferences from n to $n + 1$, nor is one restricted to the set of natural numbers at all when proving statements by induction. For instance, it is now possible to induce also on trees, comparing them with $<_M$ by the subtree relation or by comparing their number of nodes. However, the incompleteness of arithmetic carries over, eg, there are true statements about trees, which cannot be proved by a sound ITPS.

The crucial point in proving theorems by induction is to find an induction axiom as the right instance of the (generalized) induction principle. The invention of a successful well-founded order $<_M$ for a statement constitutes the creativity of a human (and also of an automated) expert in induction theorem proving. Consider, for instance, the statement $[\forall n \in \mathbb{N}.\ GE(n, \mathrm{div2}(n))]$, expressing that each number n is greater than or equal to its truncated quotient by two. The truncated quotient is defined by $\mathrm{div2}(0) = \mathrm{div2}(1) = 0$ and $\mathrm{div2}(n + 2) = \mathrm{div2}(n) + 1$ and it is also known that $GE(n, 0)$ is true, $GE(0, m + 1)$ is false and $GE(n + 1, m + 1) = GE(n, m)$ for all numbers n and m. Using Peano's induction principle, the statement cannot be verified because the induction step $[\forall n \in \mathbb{N}.\ GE(n, \mathrm{div2}(n)) \rightarrow GE(n + 1, \mathrm{div2}(n + 1))]$ cannot be proven. The reason is that the well-founded order $n <_M n + 1$ is not successful here to carry the induction. Using $n <_M n + 2$ instead, it is necessary to verify $[\forall n \in \mathbb{N}.\ GE(n, \mathrm{div2}(n)) \rightarrow GE(n + 2, \mathrm{div2}(n + 2))]$, and now the induction step can be proved. To complete the proof, it remains to verify the induction base: here there are two minimal elements in $\mathbb{N}$ (*wrt,* the well-founded order used), *viz* 0 and 1, and $GE(0, \mathrm{div2}(0))$ and $GE(1, \mathrm{div2}(1))$ are easily verified. Summing up, to verify the given statement first a successful induction axiom was invented and then the induction bases and the induction step were proved by first-order means. These are two of the main problems, which need to be mechanized, when building an automated induction theorem proving system.

AUTOMATED INDUCTION

An induction theorem proving system can be sketched in the following way: the user of the system defines the functions he is concerned with and the domains the functions are operating on. These definitions are formulated in terms of the system's input language, which can be viewed as a kind of functional toy programming language (such as PURE LISP) to define functions by recursive algorithms, as it was indicated for div2 and *GE* above. Also the input language offers a facility to define the domains recursively as data structures, for example, in the spirit of abstract data types, where $\mathbb{N}$ may be stipulated to be the set built only from 0 and the successor function $+1$. The system checks each user input for admissibility, ie, checks syntactical requirements and whether an algorithm given as input terminates. Each admissible input is entered into the system's database and may be referred to on subsequent inputs, eg, when a new algorithm is defined. The input language additionally contains some dialect of a first-order language to formulate statements about the data structures and the algorithms contained in the database. If a statement is given as input, the system attempts to verify it using the facts already in the database. If successful, the statement is admissible and entered into the database, where it may be used as a lemma in subsequent deductions. In this way, a user of an ITPS defines a mathematical theory by formulating definitions and lemmata step by step, as a human does when writing a textbook of mathematics. The theory obtained is consistent, because the system checks each input for admissibility before it is entered into the database. To implement such a system three main problems must be solved: some deduction support is required to verify a statement, ie, (1) to invent a successful induction axiom and then (2) to prove the induction bases and steps, and also some support is needed (3) to recognize the termination of algorithms.

Computing Induction Axioms

To verify a statement, induction is usually required. The problem of finding a successful induction axiom as an instance of the generalized induction principle constitutes one of the main creativities to be mechanized. But how to invent a well-founded set, which carries the induction? As a starting point, the *induction module* of an ITPS inspects the algorithms that are called in the statement. Each terminating algorithm defines a well-founded order $<_M$, where it is stipulated that the argument of each recursive call is $<_M$-smaller than the initial input. This computation order is well founded, because otherwise the algorithm would not terminate. Consequently, each terminating algorithm suggests an induction axiom, and this is a key principle automated induction is based on. In simple cases, such as for $[\forall n \in \mathbb{N}.\ GE(n + 1, n)]$, a successful induction axiom is found.

But usually a statement contains more than one call of an algorithm or different algorithms are called, where each call proposes its own induction axiom. Considering $[\forall n \in \mathbb{N}.\ GE(n, \mathrm{div2}(n))]$, GE proposes an induction of form $(0, n \to n + 1)$ but div2 proposes to induce according to $(0, 1, n \to n + 2)$. To resolve these conflicts, the different induction proposals are rated. There are several heuristics to rate all the proposals. One of them is the *most nested function* heuristic, which suggests to induce according to the innermost call of an algorithm in a statement. Another example is the *subsumption* heuristic, which compares well-founded orders by set theoretic inclusion, disregarding each superset. For the example statement both heuristics will disregard an induction of form $(0, n \to n + 1)$, because GE is not most nested here and also $n <_M n + 1$ is a superset of $n <_M n + 2$. When only one induction axiom survives the rating, as for the example, a solution is found. Otherwise the system attempts to compute a combined induction axiom from all the proposals surviving the rating. There are several heuristics to merge the proposals, where merging generally means to use the set theoretic intersection of all the well-founded orders represented by the proposals.

But sometimes a successful induction axiom cannot be computed this way. Consider, for instance, the factorial function $0! = 1$, $(n + 1)! = (n + 1) \times n!$ and the recursive version of factorial's iterative definition $\mathrm{fac}(0, m) = m$, $\mathrm{fac}(n + 1, m) = \mathrm{fac}(n, (n + 1) \times m)$. Both calls in the statement $[\forall n \in \mathbb{N}.\ \mathrm{fac}(n, 1) = n!]$ suggest to induce according $(0, n \to n + 1)$, but a proof cannot be found this way. This is because the statement is an instance of a more general fact, *viz.* $[\forall n, m \in \mathbb{N}.\ \mathrm{fac}(n, m) = n! \times m]$, such that the specialization prohibits an induction proof. In such cases, an ITPS tries to compute a generalization of the given statement (ie, a statement that entails the original one) and then attempts to verify the generalized statement by induction, as it will work for this example. There are several types of heuristically controlled generalization techniques in an ITPS, ranging from simple replacements of terms by variables to more complicated forms, as for the example above, where the properties of $\times$ have to be recognized as essential for the generalization process.

The Basic Prover

Having computed an induction axiom for a given statement, the ITPS hands over control to the basic prover to verify the antecedent of the induction axiom by first-order techniques. The basic prover is a collection of specialized proof procedures for equality reasoning, symbolic evaluation, the treatment of induction hypotheses as well as certain lemmata, etc. If successful, the basic prover returns TRUE and otherwise returns a simplified but sufficient version of its input. The symbolic evaluator is the most important specialist. It takes a statement and applies the algorithms of the database to the terms of the statement. Given the statement $GE(1, \mathrm{div2}(1))$, the symbolic evaluator applies div2 yielding $GE(1, 0)$ and then applies GE yielding TRUE. The symbolic evaluator does more than a conventional interpreter, because the terms to be evaluated may contain variables (that is why it is called symbolic). Given the statement $GE(n + 2, \mathrm{div2}(n + 2))$, the symbolic evaluator applies div2 yielding $GE(n + 2, \mathrm{div2}(n) + 1)$ and then applies GE yielding $GE(n + 1, \mathrm{div2}(n))$ as the final result.

The basic prover (and its specialists) are controlled by several heuristics. Some of them look for a direct application of an induction hypothesis after symbolic evaluation and, if impossible, for lemmata already in the database, which may help to complete the induction step. Here two lemmata are needed. The simplified induction conclusion $GE(n + 1, \mathrm{div2}(n))$ is inferred from lemma 1: $[\forall n \in \mathbb{N}.\ GE(n + 1, n)]$ and the induction hypothesis $GE(n, \mathrm{div2}(n))$ using the transitivity law for GE. The recognition of useful lemmata in the database is also one of the ambitious research problems in automated induction theorem proving. An even more ambitious problem is the decomposition of a statement into a collection of statements, such that the truth of all members of the collection entails the truth of the given statement and each statement in the collection is provable by the system. Of course, this task involves hypothesis or lemma generation and, therefore, can be arbitrarily difficult. In some cases a useful lemma can be found by machine thus providing an automated decomposition. Given the transitivity of GE, it should be no challenge for an ITPS to synthesize lemma 1 above by recognizing that this lemma would close the gap between the induction hypothesis and the simplified induction conclusion. If the right lemmata neither are members of the database nor can be synthesized, they must be provided by the user. Of course, the system must verify the admissibility of a lemma before it can be used, no matter whether it is system generated or user provided. Human expertise in problem decomposition is necessary at least, when the missing lemma represents deep mathematical knowledge. The induction proof of the *Lifting Theorem* for resolution logics is an example, which is trivial once the *Lifting Lemma* is given. If the basic prover returns a statement different from TRUE, the induction module is called again, but now with the output of the basic prover as the actual input. This handshaking between both subsystems is controlled by certain heuristics to avoid an infinite proof attempt.

Termination of Algorithms and Recursion Analysis

To verify termination, the ITPS synthesizes a termination hypothesis for an algorithm, ie, a statement the truth of which entails the algorithm's termination. For instance, $[\forall n \in \mathbb{N}.\ LT(n, n + 2)]$ would be synthesized as the termination hypothesis for div2, where the definition of LT (denoting the usual order for $\mathbb{N}$) is directly obtained from the user provided definition of the data structure for $\mathbb{N}$. Each data structure defines its structural order, like the subtree relation for trees or here the LT relation for $\mathbb{N}$. The system assumes all structural orders to be well-founded. Based on structural orders, a user may define further well-founded orders, for example, $smaller(q, r) = LT(count(q), count(r))$ compares a pair q, r of trees, where *count* is a user-defined algorithm computing the number of nodes in a tree. This order is different from the structural subtree order but is well-founded (no matter how *count* is defined), because LT

is, and consequently *smaller* may also be used to formulate a termination hypothesis. There are further construction principles, which given well-founded orders yield new well-founded orders, eg, lexicographic combinations or the intersection of orders. These orders are assumed to be well-founded by construction, because well-foundedness cannot be formulated by a first-order statement.

Once a termination hypothesis is generated, the system tries to verify it like a user-provided statement and, if successful, termination is proved for the algorithm. However, to synthesize a termination hypothesis, the ITPS must have some further knowledge about algorithms. This knowledge can be represented in form of so-called induction lemmata, which express the relation between algorithms and orders, which are assumed to be well-founded. For instance, $[\forall k \in \mathbb{N}. \; k \neq 0 \rightarrow LT(\text{div2}(k),k)]$ is an induction lemma for div2. This lemma represents specific knowledge about div2, which is utilized for subsequent generations of termination hypotheses for those algorithms, which call div2 in their recursion. For example, for a user-input $\log(0) = \log(1) = 0$ and $\log(n + 2) = 1 + \log(\text{div2}(n + 2))$ an ITPS would recognize the call of div2 in the recursion, then recall the above induction lemma and instantiate it with the arguments of the actual call yielding $[\forall n \in \mathbb{N}. \; n + 2 \neq 0 \rightarrow LT(\text{div2}(n + 2),n + 2)]$. Consequently $[\forall n \in \mathbb{N}. \; n + 2 \neq 0]$ is a termination hypothesis for log. An induction lemma either is system generated or user provided else, where in the latter case it must be verified by the system before used.

Having verified termination, recursion analysis is performed to find well-founded orders, which are supersets of the algorithm's computation order. These orders, called termination orders here, are used instead of the computation order, when induction axioms are computed. Termination orders support subsumption and merging of induction proposals, because algorithms may differ in their computation order, but agree in some of their termination orders. For instance, $(n,m) <_M (n + 1,m + 1)$ is the computation order of GE and $(n,m) <_M (n + 1,k)$ as well as $(n,m) <_M (k,m + 1)$ are termination orders for GE, because $GE(n + 1,m) = GE(n, \ldots)$ and $GE(n,m + 1) = GE(\ldots,m)$ would also terminate.

IMPLEMENTATIONS

One of the early developments in induction theorem proving was by Aubin (1979) at Edinburgh, who intensively studied the computation of induction axioms and proposed several techniques for statement generalization. The system developed by Boyer and Moore (1979, 1988) at Austin can be viewed as the most successful enterprise in induction theorem proving at present. It incorporates powerful techniques for the basic prover, generation of induction axioms and statement generalization. The Boyer-Moore system is semiautomated, ie, a user may help interactively by providing helpful lemmata together with their intended use, as for example, rewrite lemmata guide the basic prover, generalization lemmata support successful statement generalization, and induction lemmata give hints to recognize an algorithm's termination. Several dif-

ficult theorems have been verified, and the performance of the system is impressive (Moore, 1989).

The architecture of the OYSTER-CLAM system developed by Bundy and colleagues (1990a) at Edinburgh separates object-level reasoning, ie, the construction of a proof, from strategic reasoning, ie, how and when to apply certain inference steps. The system consists of a theorem prover for intuitionist type theory with a plan formation program built on top of it. The planner has access to a number of so called tactics and methods for the construction of induction proofs, many of them modeled from the heuristics of the Boyer-Moore system. To guide the proof of an induction step, the rippling tactic has been developed and proved successful on several example runs (Bundy and co-workers, 1990b).

The INKA system started in Karlsruhe and now developed at Darmstadt by Walther and co-workers attempts to increase the degree of automatization. It integrates several techniques for statement generalization (Hummel, 1990) and has a powerful automated facility to guide symbolic evaluation and lemma recognition when proving the induction step (Hutter, 1990). It also recognizes the termination of many algorithms by machine (Walther, 1988), for example, almost all induction lemmata in Boyer and Moore (1979) are synthesized by the system without any user guidance. As a further facility, the INKA system also processes statements containing existential quantifiers. For instance, asking whether div2 is surjective, ie, $[\forall n \in \mathbb{N}. \; \exists m \in \mathbb{N}. \; \text{div2}(m) = n]$, the system automatically synthesizes an algorithm double such that $[\forall n \in \mathbb{N}. \; \text{div2}(\text{double}(n)) = n]$ is satisfied (Biundo, 1988).

INDUCTIVE COMPLETION

Another approach to automated induction, quite different from the one presented above, has been termed inductionless induction or, less confusingly, proof by consistency (Kapur and Musser, 1987). To illustrate this approach, some formal background is required: the database of an ITPS implicitly defines a theory Th which is the set of all true statements about the data structures and functions contained in the data base. To prove a statement φ then only means to verify, whether $\varphi \in Th$. Because all induction axioms are contained in Th, a deduction of φ in a sound first-order calculus using the facts of the database and any induction axioms as hypotheses is a sufficient requirement for $\varphi \in Th$ to hold. This is the fundamental principle that conventional induction theorem proving (as illustrated above) is based on.

The theory Th implicitly defined by the database is consistent, because all user inputs are required to be admissible. If in addition the theory Th is complete (in the sense of formal logic), then verifying the consistency of $Th \cup \{\varphi\}$ for a user input φ is an equivalent requirement for $\varphi \in Th$ to hold, and this is the fundamental principle inductive completion is based on.

If the input language of an ITPS is restricted to consist only of universally quantified equations, the *Knuth-Bendix Completion Procedure* can be used to verify consistency: given a user statement φ, the completion procedure is applied to the set of rewrite rules obtained from the equations of the database with φ inserted in addition. If completion terminates, it is checked whether some equation relating different elements of a data structure, for example, $0 = 1$, was generated. If so, the input φ is rejected. Otherwise the extended database remains consistent, and consequently $\varphi \in Th$ is proved. The main calculations of Knuth-Bendix completion are the superpositions of terms yielding critical pairs. A superposition with a user input implicitly defines an induction axiom, and this coined the phrase inductionless for this technique. Also generalized statements and lemmata may be computed as results of superpositions. The reduction of critical pairs with the equations of the database used as rewrite rules corresponds to the role of the basic prover in the conventional approach. However, inductive completion presupposes that the database consists only of equations, that this set can be transformed into a canonical term rewriting system, and that the theory Th implicitly defined is complete, which all are restrictive prerequisites that are not required for the conventional method. But if satisfied, this technique can behave very efficiently. See Reddy (1990) for recent results and a bibliography on inductive completion, and see Walther (1991) for a more detailed account on automated induction theorem proving.

BIBLIOGRAPHY

R. Aubin, "Mechanizing Structural Induction," *Theor. Comput. Sci.* **9**, 329–362 (1979).

S. Biundo, "Automated Synthesis of Recursive Algorithms as a Theorem Proving Tool," in *Proceedings of the Eighth European Conference on Artificial Intelligence*, Munich, 1988.

R. S. Boyer and J. S. Moore, *A Computational Logic*, Academic Press, Inc., New York, 1979.

R. S. Boyer and J. S. Moore, *A Computational Logic Handbook*, Academic Press, Inc., New York, 1988.

A. Bundy and co-workers, "The OYSTER-CLAM System," in *Proceedings of the Tenth International Conference on Automated Deduction*, Kaiserslautern, Germany, 1990a.

A. Bundy and co-workers, "Extensions to the Rippling-Out Tactic for Guiding Inductive Proofs," in *Proceedings of the Tenth International Conference on Automated Deduction*, Kaiserslautern, Germany, 1990b.

B. Hummel, *Generation of Induction Axioms and Generalisation*, Ph.D. dissertation, Universität Karlsruhe, Germany, 1990.

D. Hutter, "Guiding Induction Proofs," in *Proceedings of the Tenth International Conference on Automated Deduction*, Kaiserslautern, Germany, 1990.

D. Kapur and D. R. Musser, "Proof by Consistency," *Artif. Intell.* **31**(2), 125–158 (1987).

J. S. Moore, ed., "System Verification," *J. Autom. Reasoning* **5**, 409–530 (1989).

U. S. Reddy, "Term Rewriting Induction," in *Proceedings of the Tenth International Conference on Automated Deduction*, Kaiserslautern, Germany, 1990.

C. Walther, "Argument-Bounded Algorithms as a Basis for Automated Termination Proofs," in *Proceedings of the Ninth International Conference on Automated Deduction*, Argonne, 1988. [Revised version to appear in *Artif. Intell.*]

C. Walther "Mechanizing Mathematical Induction," in B. M. Gabbay, C. J. Hogger, and J. A. Robinson, eds., *Handbook of Logic in Artificial Intelligence and Logic Programming*, Oxford University Press, Oxford, 1991 (in press).

CHRISTOPH WALTHER
Technische Hochschule
Darmstadt

INDUCTIVE INFERENCE

Inductive inference is the process of hypothesizing a general rule from examples. It plays a part in learning as well as in activities that are not generally described as learning, for example, pattern recognition, program synthesis, and the construction of scientific theories.

The primary paradigm in mathematical studies of inductive inference has been the notion of identification in the limit, defined by Gold (1967). A mathematically equivalent notion was used by Putnam (1975), in a 1963 lecture, to point out some of the difficulties with the mechanization of science. In rough terms the idea is to look at the limiting behavior of an inference method as it is given more and more examples of some general rule. The inference method is permitted to make a finite number of mistakes as long as its guesses eventually converge to being correct. A formal definition must specify what is meant by an inference method, rules, examples, guesses, correctness, and convergence, which have been specified in many different ways, and the resulting inductive inference problems compared. Some of the more important ideas and results of inductive inference are described below. Other general treatments of this area may be found in the survey articles of Angluin and Smith (1983) and Klette and Wiehagen (1980) and the comprehensive paper of Case and Smith (1983).

AN EXAMPLE

A simple example is given to motivate later definitions. Consider the problem of attempting to identify polynomials of one variable x from their values on $x = 0, 1, 2, \ldots$. For example, the polynomial $x^2 + 3$ generates the values, 3, 4, 7, 12, 19, $\ldots$.

Imagine that there is an unknown polynomial $p(x)$ in a black box with a button. The first time the button is pressed, the value $p(0)$ comes out of the box. Subsequent button pushes cause the box to produce the values of $p(n)$ for successive numbers n. The button may be pressed arbitrarily often. There is no restriction as to when a guess can be made of what the polynomial $p(x)$ is. The identification will be successful if after some finite time no more guesses are made, and the last guess made is equivalent to $p(x)$, that is, represents the same function as $p(x)$.

There are a variety of methods that will successfully identify all polynomials with integer coefficients. One such method relies on the existence of fast algorithms for interpolating a polynomial of degree d through any $d + 1$

points. This method initializes by pressing the button, receiving a value v_0, and guessing the constant polynomial v_0. Then iterate the following step. Assume that after d stages d values $v_0, v_1, \ldots, v_{d-1}$ have been received. Press the botton to request another value, v_d. Next interpolate a polynomial $p_d(x)$ of degree d through the points (i, v_i) for $i = 0, 1, \ldots, d$. If this polynomial is different from the most recent previous guess, then produce a new guess for $p_d(x)$; otherwise, do nothing. In either case the method then goes on to the next stage.

If the polynomial $p(x)$ in the black box is of degree d, then after $d + 1$ stages this method will converge to a polynomial equivalent to $p(x)$. However, it is not assumed that the method is informed of any bound on the degree of $p(x)$, so it must go on requesting values and interpolating polynomials indefinitely to be assured of correct convergence on all polynomials with integer coefficients. As an illustration, if the sequence of values starts out 1, 1, 1, 1, 1, the constant polynomial 1 might be strongly suspected, but this is also the first five values generated by the polynomial

$$1 + x(x - 1)(x - 2)(x - 3)(x - 4)$$

whose next value is 121.

IDENTIFYING CLASSES OF FUNCTIONS

The above example is a special case of the problem of identifying classes of functions. An identification problem for functions specifies a domain, a range, a set of functions from the domain to the range, a method of representing the functions in the set, and a method of presenting examples of the functions. In the example above the domain and range are the integers, the set is those functions that can be represented by polynomials in one variable with integer coefficients, the method of representation is to give a polynomial expression for computing the function, and examples are pairs $(n, f(n))$ given in increasing domain order.

For a formal theory of inductive inference the general plan is to consider sets of computable functions and choose computational representations for them. For a specific application, consider those functions from lists to lists that can be represented by LISP programs that are instances of some particular recursive scheme. However, to study the power and limitations of inductive inference methods abstractly, it is convenient to restrict attention to functions whose domain and range are the natural numbers and to choose a standard representation of computable functions by a general-purpose programming system, for example, Turing machines (qv) or arbitrary LISP programs. This involves some computable encoding and decoding between the real inputs and outputs (lists, strings, terms, graphs, programs, or whatever) and the natural numbers. The encoding and decoding may affect the efficiency, but not the ultimate power, of an inference method.

Often interest focuses on functions that are total, that is, defined on every possible argument value. Assuming every function in the class of interest is total, it might be

attractive to restrict all the guesses of the inference method to be programs for total computable functions because any other guesses cannot possibly be correct. Inductive inference methods restricted in this way are called Popperian because they in some sense reflect Popper's (1968) requirement that a scientific theory always be falsifiable. A conjectured program, computing a nontotal function, cannot be shown incorrect by using a value for which the program is not defined as a counterexample. To do so would require a solution to the halting problem. For the same reason it is not always possible to convert a non-Popperian inference method into a Popperian one. There is no easy way to weed out the nontotal guesses. In fact, even for the case of identifying sets of total functions, Popperian methods identify a strict subset of the classes identified by non-Popperian methods (Case and Ngo-Manguelle, 1979).

Hence, allowing nontotal intermediate hypotheses increases the potential power of a method, although it may be less convenient in other ways. The remainder of this article is based on the assumption that the classes of functions to be inferred are all total functions but that the methods are not necessarily Popperian. This issue is considered further in the section on search.

Any specification of an inductive inference problem must include a definition of what constitutes examples and how they are presented. In the case of functions, examples are pairs of the form $(n, f(n))$. There are various ways that examples might be presented to an inference method. They might be supplied by some external agency in some arbitrary or predetermined order or they might be supplied in response to queries from the inference method of the form "Tell me the value of f on argument n." If a teacher, or helpful source of examples, is in mind, an order of presentation that depends on the function being presented in a useful way might be considered. In formulating this kind of setting, it is important to avoid trivial solutions that directly encode the answer in the order of presentation. In any case, it is essential to assume that every argument–value pair is available (eventually) to the inference method.

Often, interest will focus on what classes of functions are identifiable and not on the efficiency of the inference method, in which case it is permissible to assume without any loss of generality that all data are always presented as $f(0), f(1), f(2), \ldots$. A method with access to queries can be simulated on data presented in increasing domain order by reading and storing the values of f until the one corresponding to the queried argument appears.

So, to summarize, most results concerning the abstract identifiability of classes of functions are stated in terms of classes of total computable functions from the natural numbers to the natural numbers using examples presented in increasing domain order. The next object to be specified is the actual inductive inference method.

An inductive inference method is a program with special instructions to request the next input value and output its next guess. To run the inference method on a particular function f, start the program; whenever it requests the next input value, it receives the next value $f(n)$ from the sequence $f(0), f(1), f(2), \ldots$, and whenever it outputs a guess, that guess is appended to the end of an initially null guess sequence. The inference method may run forever (as in the example), eventually reading in every input value and outputting an infinite sequence of guesses, or it may stop reading inputs or stop producing guesses, or both. There may be no correlation between when it reads inputs and when it produces guesses. In any case, the inference method produces in the limit a finite or infinite sequence of guesses including every guess the method makes with the function f as input. Each guess is a string of symbols that may be interpreted as a program in the general programming system that has been chosen (LISP programs, Turing machines, etc). It is this sequence of guesses that is used to define the correct convergence of the inductive inference method. There are two basic criteria of correct convergence, called EX and BC.

EX stands for explanatory. An inductive inference method M is said to EX-identify (or explain) a function f if, when M is run with the function f as input, either the sequence of guesses of M is finite and the last guess in the sequence is a program that correctly computes f or the sequence of guesses is infinite and after some finite point all the programs are syntactically equal and correctly compute f. The idea is that the inference method eventually stops changing its guess and settles on a correct guess of a program to compute the function.

In the example above, the method described correctly EX-identifies any function specified by a one-variable polynomial with integer coefficients. EX is defined to be the class of all sets U of functions such that there is an inductive inference method that EX-identifies every function in U. If $Poly$ stands for the set of functions specified by a one-variable polynomial with integer coefficients then $Poly \in$ EX.

BC stands for behaviorally correct. BC is a weaker criterion of success than EX in that the inductive inference method may continue changing its guess indefinitely as long as after some finite time all the guesses are correct programs for the function being presented. That is, an inductive inference method M BC-identifies a function f if, when presented with the function f as input, either the sequence of guesses produced by M is finite and the last guess is a program that correctly computes f or the sequence of guesses is infinite and there is some finite point in the sequence after which all the guesses are programs that correctly compute f. BC is the class of all sets U of functions such that there is an inductive inference method that BC-identifies every function in U. One intuition behind BC is that an inference method might be continuing to tinker with its guess, patching it, making it faster, making it smaller, without quite knowing whether program equivalence was being preserved. If most recent conjecture of an inference method that is correctly BC-identifying some function is always used, then eventually this tactic will only produce correct behavior (outputs).

Clearly if a method M EX-identifies a set U of functions, it also BC-identifies U, so every set in EX is also in BC, that is, EX is a subclass of BC. It has been shown that EX is a proper subclass of BC (Chase and Smith, 1983; Barzdin, 1974). Hence, methods that are allowed to continue tinkering with their guesses are strictly more pow-

erful than methods that must eventually stop tinkering. In fact, if a method could tell for sure whether its changes to its current guess preserved program equivalence, it could be modified to one that stopped tinkering. Thus, to achieve the increased power, methods that make changes without knowing whether equivalence is preserved must be tolerated.

It has been shown that there is no single inductive inference method that BC-identifies every total computable function. If Tot stands for the set of all total computable functions, then $Tot \notin$ BC. The proof is a kind of diagonalization in which a specific total computable function f_M is defined in such a way as to foil any particular inductive inference method M. Consequently, there is no universal method to BC-identify or EX-identify every total computable function. Specific methods identify particular subsets of Tot.

IDENTIFYING CLASSES OF LANGUAGES

Gold's motivation in his foundational paper on inductive inference was to study an abstract model of the process of learning the grammar of a natural language (Harrison, 1978). Using Chomsky's (1956, 1959) formalism of grammar allowed Gold to concentrate on the syntax of language without the complication of a semantic component. Grammatical inference is the name given to the resultant subarea of inductive inference.

A formal language in this sense is any set of strings using symbols from some fixed alphabet. Roughly speaking, a formal grammar for a language L is a program for generating all of the elements contained only in L. For example, the set of all strings of 0s and 1s that contain an even number of 1s is a language, as is the set of all the words in a particular dictionary that are palindromes (read the same backward as forward). The first of these can be listed by a program that systematically goes through all the strings of 0s and 1s and outputs them if the number of 1s is even. The second language can be listed by a program that simply has all of the finitely many palindromes in the dictionary stored in a big table.

A language L could be represented as a function f_L from the set of all strings over the fixed alphabet to the values 0 and 1, with $f_L(w) = 1$ if and only if w is a string in L. This might suggest that grammatical inference is simply a special case of the inference of functions, but the concerns and results are somewhat different. For example, not all the explanatory classes (for language identification) are included in the smallest BC language identification class (Case and Lynes, 1982; Osherson and Weinstein, 1982). One difference between grammatical and functional inference is that a language may be recursively enumerable but not recursive, that is, there are languages L such that there is a program to list all of the elements contained only in L but such that the function f_L defined above is not computable. Another difference is that for a language L it is natural to distinguish between positive examples (elements of L) and negative examples (strings that are not elements of L) and to consider presentations that consist of positive examples only.

An inductive inference problem for formal languages is given by specifying a fixed alphabet of symbols, a class of languages over that alphabet, the set of legal sequences of examples of a given language, the types of inference method allowed, and a criterion of successful identification. Most of the issues of function identification are applicable to the case of language identification, so only some of the considerations unique to language identification are sketched below.

If L is a language, then a positive example of L is an ordered pair $\langle w,1\rangle$ such that w is a string in L, and a negative example is a pair $\langle w,0\rangle$ such that w is a string not in L. A complete presentation of L is an infinite sequence of positive and negative examples of L such that every string eventually appears as the first member of a pair in the sequence. Thus a complete presentation eventually classifies every string as to its membership in L. If L is not the empty language, then a positive presentation of L is an infinite sequence consisting of all and only the positive examples of L. Thus a positive presentation eventually enumerates every element of L but does not give explicit information about strings not in L. In the case of a positive presentation, it is natural to drop the redundant 1s in the pairs. If L is the language consisting of strings of 0s and 1s with an even number of 1s, a complete presentation of L might begin

$$\langle 11,1\rangle, \langle 0100,0\rangle, \langle 000,1\rangle, \langle 110110,1\rangle, \ldots$$

and a positive presentation might begin

$$1111,0,0010010,000,101,1001,000011,11,01010101, \ldots$$

As in the case of functions, methods with access to an oracle or informant to answer questions of the form "Is the string w in the unknown language?" could also be considered. Ignoring efficiency considerations, presentation by informant is equivalent to complete presentation. Another form of presentation that has been considered is stochastic presentation. Assume that each language has an associated probability distribution defined on its elements. Then a sequence of examples is obtained by repeatedly drawing strings from the language in independent experiments according to the probability distribution. The sequences of examples are the same as in the case of positive presentations, but there are now probabilities associated with them.

Gold (1967) investigated the difference between positive and complete presentations of languages and found that positive presentations apparently constitute a severe limitation. For the basic criterion of identification, large classes of languages can be identified from complete presentations, including the regular languages, the context-free languages, and the context-sensitive languages. However, there is no machine to correctly identify in the limit even all the regular languages from positive presentations. If it is believed that children learn language from what is essentially positive presentations, this suggests that it is inappropriate to model their learning as the identification of context-free grammars in the limit. [Wexler and Culicover (1980) have addressed the question of a

more reasonable formal model of language acquisition, as have Osherson and co-workers (1986).]

However, Gold's results concerning positive presentations must be qualified in various ways. Gold also considered limiting the computational resources of the presentation of examples and showed that, under the assumption that the sequence of examples was being generated by a primitive recursive program (Machtey and Young, 1978), all recursively enumerable languages could be identified in the limit from positive presentations. In this case the problem is one of function identification, where the function to be identified is the enumerator of examples. (Roughly speaking, the technique used by Gold was to concentrate on how the source of examples works rather than on what language it is enumerating.) Horning (1969) has shown that if the criterion of identification is relaxed to permit failure with probability zero in the limit, the stochastic context-free grammars can be successfully identified from stochastic presentations. Thus complexity-bounded or stochastic presentations can be used to overcome some of the limitations of positive presentations.

Angluin (1980a, 1980b, 1982) has shown that there are several interesting nontraditional classes of formal languages that are identifiable in the limit from positive data. The limitations of positive data discovered by Gold may partly reflect the inappropriateness of the classes of the Chomsky hierarchy for studying inductive inference (Harrison, 1978).

Another issue in the identification of languages is how to interpret the guesses of the inductive inference method. They might be interpreted as grammars (enumerators) or decision procedures. For context-free languages the inference method might output grammars or parsers. In the case of context-free languages there is an effective and efficient translation between grammars and parsers, but for more general classes of languages there is no effective way to convert grammars (enumerators) into decision procedures, even when they exist. It has been shown that even for the case of identifying classes containing recursive languages (for which decision procedures exist), strictly more classes of languages can be identified when enumerators are allowed as guesses than if only decision procedures are allowed (Case and Lynes, 1982; Wiehagen, 1977).

SEARCH AND ITS VARIANTS

A fundamental method of inductive inference is to search (qv) in some systematic way through the space of possible rules to find the first rule that is consistent with all the examples seen so far and to make that the current guess. In order for this method to be computable, there must be a program to enumerate all possible rules and an algorithm for determining whether a given rule is consistent with a finite set of examples. For correct identification in the limit every incorrect rule must be inconsistent with some finite initial segment of every legal presentation of examples of the correct rule.

Search is applicable to the problem of inferring the context-free languages over some fixed alphabet from complete presentations. It is not difficult to think of a program that will list a context-free grammar for every context-free language over some fixed alphabet. To determine whether a context-free grammar is consistent with some initial segment of a complete presentation, just check that it generates each of the positive examples and none of the negative examples. (There are relatively efficient algorithms for determining whether a given string is generated by a given context-free grammar.) It is clear that if the current guess is a correct grammar for the language, it will never be found to be inconsistent. Also, if the current guess is incorrect, either it generates some negative example or it fails to generate some positive example in any complete presentation, so it is eventually discarded and never later reappears. Because a correct grammar occurs at some first location in the enumeration of grammars, and eventually all the preceding incorrect grammars are discarded, the search does correct identification in the limit of all the context-free languages over the given alphabet.

Search also gives an alternative method of identifying the one-variable polynomials with integer coefficients from their values on $0, 1, 2, \ldots$, the problem described in the first example. There are a finite number of such polynomials of degree d whose coefficients are all bounded in absolute value by d, and it is easy to list them, increment d, and continue. To test whether a given polynomial is consistent with an initial segment of values, just calculate its values on $0, 1, 2, \ldots, n$. However, this search will in general take exponentially longer than the interpolation method first described because the number of polynomials preceding the first polynomial of degree d grows exponentially in d.

Exponential growth of the rule space as a function of the size of the rule being identified is quite typical and is a severe limitation on the practicality of methods based on search. A section below describes some improvements that can be made in the efficiency of methods based on search, but in general the best that can be done is to make it less exponential.

One of the advantages of search is that it is a general method and does not depend on much domain-specific knowledge. For example, it is obvious how to modify the search method described above to allow for functions that are sums of polynomials and exponentials, but it is not at all clear how to modify the more efficient interpolation method for this case. Another advantage of search is that if the hypothesis space is searched in increasing order of size or complexity, the method converges to the smallest or least complex hypothesis consistent with the data.

More Powerful Search

Applying the search method to the problem of identifying all the total computable functions from values $f(0), f(1), f(2), \ldots$ does not yield an effective strategy. This is because there is no effective enumeration of all of the total computable functions. In particular, any program that lists programs must either include programs for nontotal functions (ie, programs that do not halt on some inputs) or must fail to output any program for some total functions.

Given an enumeration that is guaranteed to contain only programs for total functions, it would be possible to check whether each program is consistent with any initial segment of examples, but some total computable functions would not be on the list. On the other hand, if an enumeration that contains programs that may not halt on some inputs is used, there is no effective way of checking whether such an arbitrary program is consistent with the data.

One approximate solution is to set some kind of bound, for example, n^3, and, when checking whether a program is consistent with some finite initial segment of examples, to discard the program if it is found to run for more than n^3 steps on any input of length n. Thus the consistency condition is that the program generate all the examples in the initial segment and do so quickly (ie, within the given bound). This consistency condition is effectively decidable for any program, so the list of programs can be all syntactically legal programs.

The general form of this condition is to set some a priori bound, which is a total computable function $h(x)$, and to consider programs that have execution complexity at most $h(x)$ on all but finitely many inputs x. [Execution complexity might be a measure of running time, space required, or any measure satisfying Blum's (1967) axioms for a complexity measure.] Any function for which there is such a program is called h-easy. A slight refinement is required to deal with the possibility that there may be finitely many exceptions to the complexity bound, but essentially the method described above, with $h(x)$ instead of n^3, successfully identifies in the limit all the h-easy functions. It has been shown that any search method that uses an effectively enumerable list of programs for total computable functions identifies a subset of h-easy functions for some h, so this method is as powerful as any based on enumerating programs for total functions.

One way to make a search method more powerful is to permit the execution complexity to depend not only on the input (as in the h-easy case) but also on the output. In general, a complexity bound that depends on the size of the output is not useful in estimating the resource requirements of a program if only the input is known. However, when checking whether a program is consistent with an initial segment $f(0), f(1), \ldots, f(n)$, not only is the input x known but also the correct value of the output $f(x)$. If $h(x, y)$ is a total computable function of two arguments, a function $f(x)$ is called h-honest if there exists a program to compute $f(x)$ such that for all but finitely many values of x, the execution complexity of the program on input x is at most $h(x, f(x))$. A modification of the h-easy method that discards a program if it runs for more than $h(x, y)$ steps when checking consistency with the example $\langle x, y \rangle$ successfully identifies in the limit all the h-honest functions. Because there are classes of functions that are h-honest but not g-easy for any g, these methods are strictly more powerful than the h-easy methods.

In fact, Blum and Blum (1975) have shown that any class of functions identified by an inference method that is reliable on all the partial computable functions is contained in an h-honest class of functions for some h. (Reliable methods are discussed below.) Thus h-honest methods are as powerful as any method that is reliable in this sense. However, the *h*-honest methods do not identify all the sets of functions that are identifiable; that is, there are sets of functions in EX that are not identified by any *h*-honest method.

A still more powerful class of methods devised by Blum and Blum is based not on an *a priori* estimate of the execution complexity of the programs under consideration but on an a posteriori comparison with competing hypotheses. Roughly, the idea is to discard a program while trying to check its consistency with the data if there is some other program that seems to be getting the correct answers much more quickly and for many more values. "Much more quickly" and "many more values" are quantified in a specific way for each method of this class. Blum and Blum have shown that these methods are as powerful as any that are reliable on all the total computable functions. However, even these methods do not get all identifiable sets of functions; there are sets of functions in EX that are not identified by any method in this class.

More Efficient Search

There are some general techniques to reduce the high cost of search for inductive inference.

Consider the case of identification of languages. When the current hypothesis incorrectly generates some negative example, it is safe to ignore any hypothesis that generates a superset of the language of the current hypothesis, and, dually, if the current hypothesis incorrectly fails to generate some positive example, it is safe to ignore all hypotheses that represent subsets of the current language. To make use of this, there must be useful relationships between the syntax of hypotheses and the languages they generate.

In the case of deterministic finite state machines used as language recognizers, there is a natural generalization operation: merge two states of M and propagate the consequences of the merge to get a new finite state recognizer M'. The language recognized by M' is a superset of the language recognized by M, so this operation can be used in the bottom-up direction; that is, if the current hypothesis fails to generate some positive example, it may be replaced by a more general one by merging two of its states.

Another domain in which useful relationships between syntax and semantics exist is first-order logic. If A and B are atomic formulas, define $A \geq B$ provided that there is a substitution σ such that $B = \sigma(A)$. For example, if $A = P(x, f(y, g(x)))$ and $B = P(a, f(g(x), g(a)))$, the substitution $\sigma = [a/x, g(x)/y]$ shows that $A \geq B$. This syntactic relation is reflected in the semantics: the universal closure of A implies the universal closure of B if and only if $A \geq B$, that is, A is more general than B. Consequently, if B is found to be too general, all the atomic formulas $A \geq B$ may be discarded as well.

Reynolds (1970) has investigated this structure and shown that the atomic formulas (up to alphabetic variation) form a lattice under this ordering. Thus for any set S of atomic formulas there is a least upper bound, called the least common generalization of S, and a greatest lower bound, called the greatest common instance of S. The usual unification (qv) algorithm computes the greatest common instance of two atomic formulas, and the antiunification algorithm discovered by Reynolds and independently by Plotkin (1970) computes the least common generalization of two atomic formulas. Plotkin has extended the notion of a least common generalization.

Reynolds has also shown that the covering relation of the lattice of atomic formulas has a simple, easily computable form. This implies that all the immediate instances (or generalizations) of an atomic formula are easily computed. Shapiro (1981a, 1981b, 1982, 1983) terms this relation a refinement and extends it to a most general refinement for first-order Horn clauses, or PROLOG statements.

Shapiro's refinement consists of three operations: unifying two variables, substituting a most general term for a variable, and adding the negation of a most general atom to the clause. He shows that any Horn clause over a fixed language can be generated by an appropriate sequence of these operations starting from some most general atom. Moreover, if a clause C' is obtained from a clause C by any of these operations, then C logically implies C'.

Shapiro uses this refinement operator in his PROLOG program synthesis system to direct a search for correct candidate axioms from the most general toward the more specific. If a current clause is found to be false by comparison with the examples, its one-step refinements become new candidate axioms. Shapiro has also used a variety of specialized refinement operators to synthesize particular syntactic classes of PROLOG programs.

Laird (1985) has abstracted the notion of refinement and shown that it applies in a variety of domains. He describes very general algorithms applicable to domains that possess (upward or downward) refinements and shows that they converge to a correct hypothesis. One of his examples is a most general refinement for general (not just Horn) clauses, making Shapiro's approach applicable in a wider domain.

Mitchell (1982) has given a different abstract treatment of certain methods of using generalization and specialization operators. He assumes a general-to-specific ordering on the space of all possible hypotheses with certain properties and describes an algorithm that maintains two sets of hypotheses: one set of most general hypotheses that have not been contradicted by any negative example and another set of most specific hypotheses that generate all the positive examples seen so far. The true hypothesis lies somewhere between these two sets; the two sets can be used to give partial information about the true hypothesis and also to choose informative examples for test. Mitchell gives conditions under which his algorithm will eventually converge to the correct hypothesis.

DIRECT METHODS

Sometimes, as in the case of polynomial interpolation, more direct and efficient methods than search have been found that yield good hypotheses from given data or a query-oracle for specific domains. In some cases the methods are simple enough to analyze precisely; in many cases they are heuristics whose performance is difficult to analyze.

Biermann and Feldman (1972) describe a heuristic method they term k-tails for identifying nondeterministic finite state transducers from I/O behavior. The method has a user-controlled parameter k and builds a nondeterministic acceptor by merging all points in the sample strings that exhibit the same (observable) I/O behavior on strings of length k or less. The user's control of k allows some tuning of the method. It is shown that if k is large enough, this method correctly converges in the limit. Brayer and Fu (1977) and Levine (1981, 1982) have generalized the method of k-tails to the problem of inferring tree grammars. Miclet (1980) proposes another heuristic based on state merging, with a more flexible criterion of similarity than k-tails.

Angluin (1982) has also used the generalization structure for finite automata, described above, to give a method that provably finds the smallest k-reversible regular language that includes a given set of positive example strings. The method runs in polynomial time for every fixed k and nearly linear time when $k = 0$.

Crespi-Reghizzi and co-workers have found a class of algorithms for inferring context-free grammars from bracketed samples (Crespi-Reghizzi, 1972; Crespi-Reghizzi and co-workers, 1978; Crespi-Reghizzi and Mandrioli, 1980a, 198b). That is, the examples are equivalent to parse trees for sentences from the unknown language, in which all the labels of internal nodes have been erased. Equivalently, the example sentences are phrase marked, but no grammatical categories are assigned to the phrases. The algorithms they consider assign internal labels (grammatical categories) according to the context of the node in the parse tree and use the labels to construct grammatical productions. Depending on how the context is defined, different algorithms are specified. This general approach is investigated by Crespi-Reghizzi and Mandrioli (1980a), who term it abstract profiles. Particular instances of this class of algorithms yield efficient polynomial time methods for the free operator precedence grammars and the free homogeneous k-profile grammars. These methods find a grammar for the smallest free operator precedence (respectively, free homogeneous k-profile) language that generates all of the given samples.

Angluin (1980a) has given a method that efficiently infers a smallest one-variable pattern language that includes a given positive sample. A one-variable pattern is a pattern such as $34xx9x12$, which generates all strings obtainable from the pattern by substitution of a non-null string for x everywhere. The strings 34119112, 34776776977612 are generated by the example pattern. Shinohara (1982a, 1982b, 1983) has given efficient methods for inferring other classes of pattern languages and has applied them to inferring patterns in a data entry system.

A number of researchers have investigated the structure of LISP programs, data, and computations. They have found a rich source of information to use in the task of identifying LISP programs from samples of their I/O behavior. D. Smith (1982) gives an excellent survey of this work.

Summers (1976, 1977) describes a general approach to synthesizing LISP programs based on a recursive scheme and a pattern-matching procedure. For each pair consisting of an input list and an output list, the output is expressed as a composition of the base functions *car, cdr,* and *cons* and the input list in a unique way. (Certain restrictions are placed on the programs to ensure uniqueness.) A matching procedure is invoked to find a recurrence relation among the expressions from the different pairs. The relation is then synthesized into a recursive program using the given scheme. Summers has shown that if a correct recurrence is found, a correct program is synthesized. The implementation of his matching procedure used a heuristic. Subsequent work (Jouannaud and Guiho, 1979; Jouannaud and Kodratoff, 1979, 1980) has generalized and refined this approach, characterizing the class of programs that are correctly synthesized and the I/O examples that are sufficient and proposing more powerful and more efficient matching algorithms.

COMPLEXITY QUESTIONS

Some identification methods are exhaustive searches and run in time that grows exponentially with the size of the hypothesis to be identified, and others are more efficient, direct methods that run in polynomial time. There are some partial results from the theory of computational complexity that shed light on which problems should not be expected to have efficient solutions.

In the case of finite-state machines used as recognizers of languages, Gold (1978) has shown that the problem of finding a finite-state machine with a minimum number of states compatible with given positive and negative examples is NP-hard. This implies that no algorithm is known that runs in polynomial time to solve this problem. Moreover, it implies that a polynomial time algorithm for this problem could be used to construct polynomial time algorithms for a large collection of other difficult optimization problems, for example, finding a minimum traveling salesman tour in a weighted graph.

Thus it seems unlikely that even a heavily modified search method for this problem will run in polynomial time on all cases as long as it is guaranteed to find a machine with the minimum possible number of states. Realistically, the best that can be hoped for is efficient approximations or methods good on average for this problem. Gold's results have been extended by Angluin (1978) to show that the problem remains NP-hard even if the example set is quite dense and that the related problem of finding a regular expression of minimum length compatible with given positive and negative data is also NP-hard.

These results indicate that finding a hypothesis of minimum size compatible with given data is computationally difficult even for very restricted domains. In the case of general programs the problem is extremely difficult: any algorithm that lists a set of programs all guaranteed to be of minimum size for the functions they compute can only list a finite number of such programs. [Chaitin (1974) gives a quantitative treatment of the relation between the size of a program and how many such programs it can list.]

A somewhat different approach to quantifying the computational complexity of inductive inference problems has been taken by Daley and Smith (1986). They have defined axioms for complexity measures for inductive inference machines in the spirit of Blum's (1967) treatment of the computational complexity of functions. An inference complexity measure prescribes a functional for each inductive inference machine that can be used to determine in the limit the complexity of the machine on a given sequence of inputs. The axioms cover existing measures, such as the number of mind changes made by a machine enroute to a successful identification, and also the number of steps until correct convergence. From the axioms Daley and Smith are able to prove the existence of sets of functions that are arbitrarily difficult to infer and sets for which there is no most efficient inference machine.

OTHER CRITERIA OF IDENTIFICATION

Identification in the limit is only one interpretation of the idea of successful identification. A number of restrictions and extensions of the basic criteria EX and BC have been studied, and some of them are described in the first part of this section. The second part of this section covers some of the definitions of nonlimiting criteria of identification.

Variations of Identification in the Limit

A number of modifications of the basic criteria, EX and BC, of successful identification have been studied. The restriction that all the guesses be programs for total functions is termed Popperian and is discussed above. Popperian inference has been studied by Case and Ngo-Manguelle (1979). In addition to further restrictions on the behavior of machines, some modifications take the form of relaxations of restrictions. Generally, both types of modification are considered to more accurately model particular situations or to render certain technical problems more tractable.

Reliability is an additional restriction on EX-identification that requires that whenever an inductive inference method converges, it does so correctly. Thus failure of identification will be signaled (in the limit) by an infinite number of changes of hypothesis. [Reliability has been studied by Minicozzi (1976), who used the term strong identification.] Different types of reliability may be distinguished, depending on what class of inputs, the total recursive functions, or the partial recursive functions [the requirement applies to Blum and Blum (1975)]. Methods based on search are generally reliable, at least over the total recursive functions. Reliability makes it possible to combine two inference methods (into one that identifies the union of the classes they identify) by switching back and forth between them when there is a change of hypothesis. Although reliability makes certain problems easier, there are classes of functions that are EX-identifiable, but not reliably so.

The class of sets of functions reliably identifiable is closed under union; this is not true of the classes EX or BC. A set of functions is said to be EX-identified by a finite team of machines $M_1, M_2, \ldots, M_k$ provided that every function in the set is EX-identified by at least one of the machines M_i. C. Smith (1982) has shown that there are sets of functions EX-identifiable by a team of $k + 1$ machines, but not by any team of k machines, even with respect to BC-identification. This particularly strong critical mass phenomenon indicates that diversity of approach, more than any other factor, can enhance the likelihood of a successful inference.

Another way to relax the definition of identification is to consider probabilistic methods, that is, methods that have access to a random number generator and may identify a given function for some but not all the possible random sequences. Such an inductive inference method EX-identifies a set of functions with probability p if, for every function in the set, the measure of random sequences that cause the machine to do a successful EX-identification is at least p. Pitt (1984, 1985) has shown that any set of functions EX-identifiable by a team of k machines is EX-identifiable with probability $1/k$, that any set of functions EX-identifiable with probability exceeding $1/(k + 1)$ is EX-identifiable by a team of k machines; and analogously for BC-identification. In particular, a set of functions identifiable with probability exceeding 0.5 is identifiable with certainty. Thus the notions of teams and probability coincide. There is an additional notion of uncertainty, termed frequency identification, that Pitt has also shown to coincide with teams and probabilistic identification.

A different type of relaxation of restrictions is to allow bugs in the final guess, modeling the fact that complex programs and complex scientific hypotheses alike are almost certainly never bug free. Case and Smith (1983) have defined anomalies, that is, argument values where the final guess and the correct function disagree, and proved that for all k there are sets of functions EX-identifiable allowing $k + 1$ anomalies that are not EX-identifiable allowing only k anomalies, and analogously for BC-identification. BC-identification with any finite number of anomalies in the final guess is a relaxed enough identification criterion to admit the existence of an inductive inference method to identify all the total recursive functions. The inference of programs that are correct a certain percentage of the time (perhaps with infinitely many anomalies) has been investigated (Royer, 1984; Smith and Velauthapillai, 1985).

For EX-identification the number of times an inductive inference method changes its hypothesis before converging is one measure of the complexity of the inference process. One may fix a bound of k and consider inductive inference machines that make no more than k changes of hypothesis. In the case $k = 0$, the machine makes at most one guess; this is also termed finite identification. For every k there is a class of functions EX-identifiable with $k + 1$ changes of hypothesis that is not EX-identifiable with k changes of hypothesis by any machine.

Trade-offs have been considered between numbers of machines in a team, changes of hypothesis, probability, and anomalies. C. Smith (1982) has shown an exact trade-off between the number of anomalies and the number of team members for EX-identification. Daley (1983) has shown that the same trade-off also holds for BC-identification. Wiehagen and co-workers (1984) have investigated the relationship between the probability of identification and the number of changes of hypothesis for EX-identification by probabilistic methods.

Another modification of the criterion of EX-identification is to consider that a machine has successfully identified a function only when it converges to a smallest program for the function. The sets of functions identifiable under this criterion are dependent on the particular system chosen for expressing programs, unlike the other general results described herein. However, Chen (1981, 1982) has shown that by interpreting smallest to be "no more than a recursive factor larger than the smallest program," the class is invariant under change of programming system. Chen has shown that not all the sets of functions in EX are identifiable if a nearly minimal program is required unless a finite but unbounded number of anomalies is also permitted.

Identification, Not Necessarily in the Limit

Identification in the limit places no constraint on the rate of convergence or on the quality of the intermediate hypotheses. Attempts to measure the quality of hypotheses with respect to a finite amount of data generally focus on the size, simplicity, or probability of the hypothesis and how well it fits or explains the data.

As a specific example, consider the identification of regular languages. If hypotheses are finite state acceptors, one measure of the size of a hypothesis might be the number of states of the acceptor. One strategy would be to ask for a smallest hypothesis compatible with given data. When the data are positive only, a smallest acceptor will be the one-state machine that accepts every string, so the criterion is trivial in this case. Because the regular sets cannot be identified in the limit from positive data, it is not surprising that this criterion is trivial. When the data include both positive and negative strings, the smallest compatible acceptor is a nontrivial answer (and would lead to identification in the limit), but the difficulty of finding it is NP-hard (Gold, 1978).

An alternative strategy would be to ask for a good fit to the data, that is, the acceptor that generates a minimal set containing the positive part of the sample. This will always be an acceptor for exactly the finite set of strings in the positive part of the sample, another trivial answer. However, restricting the domain to the k-reversible regular sets yields a nontrivial criterion that leads to correct identification in the limit. Moreover, there is a polynomial time algorithm to find a hypothesis satisfying this criterion (Angluin, 1982).

One method of combining the notions of a good hypothesis and a good fit to the data is to use a Bayesian (qv) analysis. Consider the context-free languages. A stochastic context-free grammar has probabilities associated with alternative ways to rewrite each nonterminal and defines a probability distribution on the language that it generates. Given a stochastic context-free grammar G and a finite sequence of strings S, it is possible to calculate the probability that G would generate S in a sequence of independent trials, represented by $\Pr(S \mid G)$. If there is also a probability distribution defined on the space of all stochastic context-free grammars G, denoted $\Pr(G)$, then it is natural to ask for the most probable grammar given a finite sample S. That is, ask for a grammar G that maximizes $\Pr(G \mid S)$, which, by Bayes's theorem is equivalent to finding G to maximize $\Pr(G)\Pr(S \mid G)$. Horning (1969) has formalized this setting, given a particular kind of probability distribution on grammars, and proved that a search algorithm to maximize $\Pr(G)\Pr(S \mid G)$ converges in the limit with probability 1 to the correct grammar, assuming that the strings in the sample are generated by independent trials.

Solomonoff (1964, 1975, 1978) has advocated the use of this kind of Bayesian approach, in which the *a priori* probabilities of the hypotheses are based on the theory of program size complexity. Cook and co-workers (1976) have investigated a hill-climbing approach to the inference of stochastic context-free grammars, in a setting similar to Horning's. The hill climbing avoids the exhaustive search of Horning's approach, but its effectiveness is difficult to analyze. Van der Mude and Walker (1978) have considered the Bayesian approach for inferring stochastic regular grammars. Other mixed measures have been considered by Maryanski and Booth (1977) and Gaines (1976, 1978).

Feldman (1972) and Feldman and Shields (1977) have investigated an axiomatic approach to combinations of grammar or program complexity and derivational or computational complexity. The measure and algorithm of Horning, described above, are an instance of the general theory.

Valiant (1984) has proposed another criterion of successful identification for stochastic languages, which might be termed probably approximately correct identification. The idea is that there is a parameter n related to the size of the unknown hypothesis, and after sampling the unknown hypothesis a polynomial (in n) number of times, the identification algorithm should conjecture a hypothesis that with high probability is not too different from the true hypothesis. High probability and the difference between the conjectured hypothesis and the true one are quantified using n. Valiant gives identification algorithms that succeed in this sense for three classes of propositional formulas using different information oracles.

TWO APPLICATIONS

Shinohara (1982a) has applied his algorithms for the efficient identification of the regular pattern languages to detecting patterns in a data entry system. For example, if in entering a bibliography there is a fixed pattern to the keywords AUTHOR, TITLE, and so on, then his system can detect the pattern and automatically generate the fixed portions of the pattern, prompting the user to supply the variable portions.

Nix (1983, 1984) has designed and implemented an editing-by-example facility in a general-purpose screen editor. It is based on detecting regularities in a sequence of I/O examples of a text transformation. The user confronted with the task of making a sequence of similar transformations to a series of text items may invoke the editing by example system and make two or more of the desired transformations. The system attempts to synthesize a program to make the intended transformations. The user may then run this program, optionally under the user's close control, or may alter the program directly or by giving additional examples of the desired transformations. Nix gives a careful analysis of the class of transformations (which he terms gap programs) that may be synthesized and algorithms and heuristics for synthesizing them.

Other systems that could be viewed as applications of the techniques of inductive inference, for example, META-DENDRAL (1978) are treated fully in other articles.

BIBLIOGRAPHY

D. Angluin, "On the Complexity of Minimum Inference of Regular Sets," *Inform. Contr.* **39**, 337–350 (1978).

D. Angluin, "Finding Patterns Common to a Set of Strings," *J. Comput. Sys. Sci.* **21**, 46–62 (1980a).

D. Angluin, "Inductive Inference of Formal Languages from Positive Data," *Inform. Contr.* **45**, 117–135 (1980b).

D. Angluin, "Inference of Reversible Languages," *JACM* **29**, 741–765 (1982).

D. Angluin and C. Smith, "Inductive Inference: Theory and Methods," *Comput. Surv.* **15**, 237–269 (1983).

J. M. Barzdin, "Two Theorems on the Limiting Synthesis of Functions," *Latvii Gosudarst. Univ. Ucenye Zapiski* **210**, 82–88 (1974) (in Russian).

A. W. Biermann and J. A. Feldman, "On the Synthesis of Finite-State Machines from Samples of Their Behavior," *IEEE Trans. Comput.* **C-21**, 592–597 (1972).

M. Blum, "A Machine-Independent Theory of the Complexity of Recursive Functions," *JACM* **14**, 322–336 (1967).

L. Blum and M. Blum, "Toward a Mathematical Theory of Inductive Inference," *Inform. Contr.* **28**, 125–155 (1975).

J. M. Brayer and K. S. Fu, "A Note on the *k*-Tail Method of Tree Grammar Inference," *IEEE Trans. Sys. Man Cybernet.* **SMC-7**, 293–300 (1977).

B. G. Buchanan and E. A. Feigenbaum, "Dendral and Meta-Dendral: Their Applications Dimension," *Artif. Intell.* **11**, 5–24 (1978).

J. Case and C. Lynes, "Inductive Inference and Language Identification," in *Proceedings of the ICALP 82*, Springer-Verlag, Berlin, 1982, pp. 107–115.

J. Case and S. Ngo-Manguelle, *Refinements of Inductive Inference by Popperian Machines*, Technical Report, SUNY, Buffalo, N.Y., 1979.

J. Case and C. Smith, "Comparison of Identification Criteria for Machine Inductive Inference," *Theor. Comput. Sci.* **25**, 193–220 (1983).

G. J. Chaitin, "Information-Theoretic Limitations of Formal Systems," *JACM* **21**, 403–424 (1974).

K. J. Chen, *Tradeoffs in Machine Inductive Inference*, Technical Report no. 178, SUNY, Buffalo, N.Y., 1981.

K. J. Chen, "Tradeoffs in the Inductive Inference of Nearly Minimal Size Programs," *Inform. Contr.* **52**, 68–86 (1982).

N. Chomsky, "Three Models for the Description of Languages," *IRE Trans. Inform. Theor.* **2**, 113–124 (1956).

N. Chomsky, "On Certain Formal Properties of Grammars," *Inform. Contr.* **2**, 137–167 (1959).

C. M. Cook, A. Rosenfeld, and A. R. Aronson, "Grammatical Inference by Hill-Climbing," *Inform. Sci.* **10**, 59–80 (1976).

S. Crespi-Reghizzi, "An Effective Model for Grammar Inference," *Inf. Proc.* **71**, 524–529 (1972).

S. Crespi-Reghizzi and D. Mandrioli, *Abstract Profiles for Context-Free Languages*, Technical Report no. 80-6, Istituto di Elettrotechnica ed Elettronica del Politechnico di Milano, Milano, Italy, 1980a.

S. Crespi-Reghizzi and D. Mandrioli, *Inferring Grammars by Means of Profiles: A Unifying View*, Internal Report, Istituto di Elettrotechnica ed Elettronica del Politechnico di Milano, Milano, Italy, 1980b.

S. Crespi-Reghizzi, G. Guida, and D. Mandrioli, "Noncounting Context-Free Languages," *JACM* **25**, 571–580 (1978).

R. Daley, "On the Error Correcting Power of Pluralism in Inductive Inference," *Theor. Comput. Sci.* **24**, 95–104 (1983).

R. Daley and C. Smith, "On the Complexity of Inductive Inference," *Inform. Contr.* **69**, 12–40 (1986).

J. A. Feldman, "Some Decidability Results in Grammatical Inference," *Inform. Contr.* **20**, 244–262 (1972).

J. A. Feldman and P. Shields, "Total Complexity and the Inference of Best Programs," *Math. Sys. Theor.* **10**, 181–191 (1977).

B. R. Gaines, "Behavior/Structure Transformations under Uncertainty," *Int. J. Man-Machine Stud.* **8**, 337–365 (1976).

B. R. Gaines, "Maryanski's Grammatical Inferencer," *IEEE Trans. Comput.* **C-28**, 62–64 (1978).

E. M. Gold, "Language Identification in the Limit," *Inform. Contr.* **10**, 447–474 (1967).

E. M. Gold, "Complexity of Automaton Identification from Given Data," *Inform. Contr.* **37**, 302–320 (1978).

M. Harrison, *Introduction to Formal Language Theory*, Addison-Wesley Publishing Co., Inc., Reading, Mass., 1978.

J. J. Horning, *A Study of Grammatical Inference*, Ph.D. dissertation, Stanford University, Stanford, Calif., 1969.

J. P. Jouannaud and G. Guiho, "Inference of Functions with an Interactive System," *Machine Intell.* **9**, 227–250 (1979).

J. P. Jouannaud and Y. Kodratoff, "Characterization of a Class of Functions Synthesized by a Summers-Like Method Using a B.M.W. Matching Technique," *Proceedings of the Sixth IJCAI*, Tokyo, Japan, Morgan-Kaufmann, San Mateo, Calif., 1979, pp. 440–447.

J. P. Jouannaud and Y. Kodratoff, "An Automatic Construction of LISP Programs by Transformations of Functions Synthesized from Their Input–Output Behavior," *Int. J. Pol. Anal. Inform. Sys.* **4**, 331–358 (1980).

R. Klette and R. Wiehagen, "Research in the Theory of Inductive Inference by GDR Mathematicians: A Survey," *Inform. Sci.* **22**, 149–169 (1980).

P. D. Laird, *Inductive Inference by Refinement*, Technical Report RR-376, Yale University, New Haven, Conn., 1985.

B. Levine, "Derivatives of Tree Sets with Applications to Grammatical Inference," *IEEE Trans. Patt. Anal. Machine Intell.* **PAMI-3**, 285–293 (1981).

B. Levine, "The Use of Tree Derivatives and a Sample Support Parameter for Inferring Tree Systems," *IEEE Trans. Patt. Anal. Machine Intell.* **PAMI-4**, 25–34 (1982).

M. Machtey and P. Young, *An Introduction to the General Theory of Algorithms*, North-Holland, Amsterdam, 1978.

F. J. Maryanski and T. L. Booth, "Inference of Finite-State Probabilistic Grammars," *IEEE Trans. Comput.* **C-26,** 521–536 (1977).

L. Miclet, "Regular Inference with a Tail-Clustering Method," *IEEE Trans. Sys. Man Cybernet.* **SMC-10,** 737–743 (1980).

E. Minicozzi, "Some Natural Properties of Strong Identification in Inductive Inference," *Theor. Comput. Sci.* **2,** 345–360 (1976).

T. M. Mitchell, "Generalization as Search," *Artif. Intell.* **18,** 203–226 (1982).

R. Nix, *Editing by Example*, Ph.D. dissertation. Yale University, New Haven, Conn., 1983.

R. Nix, "Editing by Example," in *Proceedings of the Eleventh ACM Symposium on Principles of Programming Languages*, Association for Computing Machinery, New York, 1984, pp. 186–195.

D. Osherson, M. Stob, and S. Weinstein, *Systems that Learn*, MIT Press, Cambridge, Mass., 1986.

D. N. Osherson and S. Weinstein, "Criteria of Language Learning," *Inform. Contr.* **52,** 123–138 (1982).

L. Pitt, "A Characterization of Probabilistic Inference," in *Proceedings of the Twenty-fifth Annual IEEE Symposium on Foundations of Computer Science*, IEEE, New York, 1984, pp. 485–494.

L. Pitt, *Probabilistic Inductive Inference*, Ph.D. dissertation, Yale University, New Haven, Conn., 1985.

G. D. Plotkin, "A Note on Inductive Generalization," *Machine Intell.* **5,** 153–163 (1970).

K. Popper, *The Logic of Scientific Discovery*, Harper Torch Books, New York, 1968.

H. Putnam, *Probability and Confirmation*, Cambridge University Press, New Rochelle, N.Y., 1975.

J. C. Reynolds, "Transformational Systems and the Algebraic Structure of Atomic Formulas," *Machine Intell.* **5,** 135–151 (1970).

J. Royer, *A Note on Asymptotic Explanatory Inductive Inference*, University of Chicago, Chicago, 1984.

E. Shapiro, "A General Incremental Algorithm That Infers Theories from Facts," in *Proceedings of the Seventh IJCAI*, Vancouver, B.C., Morgan-Kaufmann, San Mateo, Calif., 1981a, pp. 446–451.

E. Shapiro, *Inductive Inference of Theories from Facts*, Technical Report 192, Yale University, New Haven, Conn., 1981b.

E. Shapiro, "Algorithmic Program Diagnosis," in *Proceedings of the Ninth ACM Symposium on Principles of Programming Languages*, Albuquerque, N. Mex., 1982, pp. 299–308.

E. Shapiro, *Algorithmic Program Debugging*, MIT Press, Cambridge, Mass., 1983.

T. Shinohara, "Polynomial Time Inference of Pattern Languages and Its Applications," in *Proceedings of the Seventh IBM Symposium on Mathematical Foundations of Computer Science*, Hakone, Japan, 1982a, pp. 191–209.

T. Shinohara, "Polynomial Time Inference of Extended Regular Pattern Languages," in *Proceedings of the RIMS Symposium on Software Science and Engineering*, Kyoto, 1982b.

T. Shinohara, *Lect. Notes Comput. Sci.* **41,** 115–127 (1983).

C. H. Smith, "The Power of Pluralism for Automatic Program Synthesis," *JACM* **29,** 1144–1165 (1982).

C. Smith and M. Velauthapillai, *On the Inference of Approximate Programs*, Technical Report 1427, University of Maryland, 1985.

D. R. Smith, "A Survey of the Synthesis of LISP Programs from Examples," in A. W. Biermann, G. Guiho, and Y. Kodratoff, eds., *Automatic Program Construction Techniques*, Macmillan, New York, 1982.

R. J. Solomonoff, "A Formal Theory of Inductive Inference," *Inform. Contr.* **7,** 1–22, 224–254 (1964).

R. J. Solomonoff, "Inductive Inference Theory: A Unified Approach to Problems in Pattern Recognition and Artificial Intelligence," in *Proceedings of the Fourth IJCAI*, Tbilisi, USSR, Morgan-Kaufmann, San Mateo, Calif., 1975, pp. 274–280.

R. J. Solomonoff, "Complexity-Based Induction Systems: Comparisons and Convergence Theorems," *IEEE Trans. Inform. Theor.* **IT-24,** 422–432 (1978).

P. D. Summers, *Program Construction from Examples*, Ph.D. dissertation, Yale University, New Haven, Conn., 1976.

P. D. Summers, "A Methodology for LISP Program Construction from Examples," *JACM* **24,** 161–175 (1977).

L. G. Valiant, "A Theory of the Learnable," *CACM* **27,** 1134–1142 (1984).

A. Van der Mude and A. Walker, "On the Inference of Stochastic Regular Grammars," *Inform. Contr.* **38,** 310–329 (1978).

R. Wiehagen, "Identification of Formal Languages," *Lect. Notes Comput. Sci.* **53,** 571–579 (1977).

R. Wiehagen, R. Freivalds, and E. B. Kinber, "On the Power of Probabilistic Strategies in Inductive Inference," *Theor. Comput. Sci.* **28,** 111–133 (1984).

K. Wexler and P. Culicover, *Formal Principles of Language Acquisition*, MIT Press, Cambridge, Mass., 1980.

D. ANGLUIN
Yale University

C. H. SMITH
University of Maryland

This work was partially funded by the National Science Foundation under grants numbered MCS-8404226 and MCS-8301536 and by the National Security Agency under grant number MDA-904-85-H-0002.

INFERENCE

Inference in AI refers to various processes by which programs, as opposed to people, draw conclusions from facts and suppositions. It is usually a subactivity of the more general activity of reasoning. Programs that perform in this way are often called inference engines and range from interactive, with the user guiding the generation of inferred statements, to fully autonomous. There are various kinds of inference depending on the methodology used and the requirements of the application.

The most common types of inference methodologies in AI are logical inferences, to conclude B from $A_1, \ldots, A_n$ such that any interpretation that makes all of the A_i true also makes B true. Examples are simple syllogism, modus ponens, and substitution for universally quantified variables (see LOGIC, PROPOSITIONAL; LOGIC, PREDICATE). An important subclass of logical inference is based on the resolution (qv) rule. Resolution works on disjunctions, called clauses, of simple formulas, called literals. In its simple Boolean form the rule allows a program to conclude $C \vee D$ from the two disjunctions $-p \vee C$ and $p \vee D$. (In implicative form this is equivalent to concluding $-D \to C$ from $-D \to p$ and $p \to C$.) In the first-order logic case the program first renames the variables in the two clauses and then finds a most general substitution that produces a pair of opposite-signed literals. For example, $P(a, x) \lor Q(x)$ and $-P(y, b) \lor R(y)$ lead to $Q(b) \lor R(a)$ (see RESOLUTION, BINARY). A similar inference rule, paramodulation, exists for reasoning about equality. As with resolution, two clauses are used. One clause must contain a literal of the form $s = t$, say $s = t \lor C$. A term in the other clause, say s' in $D(s')$, is matched with s after renaming of variables, and the corresponding instance of $C \lor D (t)$ is inferred (see THEOREM PROVING for a more complete description of paramodulation). Other inference rules have been proposed for special applications like set theory and higher-order logic (see LOGIC, HIGHER ORDER) as well as other general-purpose methodologies like matrix reduction.

INFERENCE SYSTEMS

In addition to a set of inference rules, inference systems based on logic require a control system or set of strategies and heuristics (qv) to direct the choice of formulas to use for inferring new information. In most problems the number of possible inferences is vastly larger than the number of inferences actually used in the problem's solution.

Logical Inference

Logical inference systems have been used as the reasoning component for a variety of applications including proving theorems, proving the correctness of programs, generating programs, designing electronic circuits, and many others. Resolution forms a basis for logic programming (qv), of which PROLOG is an example. Most expert systems (qv) and production systems use a type of inference that is very much like (and in some cases identical to) resolution (see LOGIC PROGRAMMING; THEOREM PROVING; EXPERT SYSTEMS).

Nonclassical Logical Inference

Although the majority of inference systems used in AI are based on classical logical inferences as above, these may not be adequate for many situations. Many researchers feel that classical logic inference, for example, does not address the issue of cause and effect in any reasonable way. For example $p \& -p \rightarrow q$ is true because the hypothesis is always false and not because q necessarily has anything to do with p. Various different logics, each with its own special rules of inference, have been proposed (see LOGIC, MODAL). In addition, some more *ad hoc* systems have been proposed (see REASONING, CAUSAL).

Negative Information

An important recent type of inference rule is based on the handling of negative information. Using such a rule, a program can infer a negative statement if that negative statement is normally true and there is no evidence to indicate an unusual situation. An example is "In the desert one can assume (ie, can infer) that it is not raining unless there is some evidence to the contrary." A special application of this kind of inference occurs in database settings where it can often be assumed that data not in the database are not related. For example, if the tuple (100, CS102) is not in the enrolled-in relation in a university database, then it is to be expected that student number 100 is not in the class. In deductive databases this is called the closed-world assumption (CWA). By making such inferences, a system can avoid storing the myriad of negative facts and rules, an important consideration in applications like commonsense reasoning and databases where normally the volume of negative information is orders of magnitude larger than the positive information. Care must be taken when assuming negative information that contradictory results are not obtained. For example, a system might know $p \lor q$ but not have enough evidence to conclude p nor enough evidence to conclude q. However, assuming the negation of both, that is, both $-p$ and $-q$, leads to a contradiction (see CIRCUMSCRIPTION; REASONING, NONMONOTONIC; REASONING, DEFAULT).

Exemplary Generalization

A quite different kind of inference is inductive inference in which a program attempts to abstract from examples. These inference mechanisms are often used in learning situations. For example, a program may attempt to learn to distinguish different shapes by being shown examples of the shapes and attempting to induce abstract properties of the different types.

Probabilistic and/or Statistical Inference

Yet another kind of reasoning involves probabilistic inference and/or statistical inference. Examples of one such kind of inference are described in the entry on Bayesian decision methods. Mathematical theories based on probability and statistics are used to accept or reject proposed hypotheses and to draw other kinds of conclusions. These theories are quite well developed and computable in a straightforward numerical way. Thus, it is the design of the hypotheses and the use to which the conclusions are put that has more to do with AI than the actual method of reaching the conclusion.

The articles in this work cited above and the general references contain more detailed studies of logical inference in AI and its applications.

General References

C.-L. Chang and R. C.-T. Lee, *Symbolic Logic and Mechanical Theorem Proving,* Academic Press, Inc., New York, 1971.

D. Loveland, *Automated Theorem Proving,* North-Holland, Amsterdam, The Netherlands, 1978.

L. Wos, R. Overbeek, E. Lusk, and J. Boyle, *Automated Reasoning: Introduction and Applications,* Prentice-Hall, Englewood Cliffs, N.J., 1984.

L. HENSCHEN
Northwestern University

INFERENCE, GRAMMATICAL. See INDUCTIVE INFERENCE; PATTERN RECOGNITION.

INFORMATION RETRIEVAL

Information retrieval (IR) has not generally attracted the attention of workers in AI. However, there has recently been a growth of interest in IR, and AI may be able to make some specific contributions, although the general problem is highly intractable and the automated intelligent information assistant is a distant goal.

BASIC ELEMENTS

Information retrieval has conventionally been taken to refer to the retrieval of documents, such as scientific papers as opposed to books, from large but specialized bodies of material, through the specification of document content rather than via keys like author names, with the help of automation. It has been distinguished from library retrieval based on traditional, limited, book catalogue information through differences in the nature of the file items, which call for detailed and specialized descriptions and correspondingly refined search procedures.

Thus, as a simple model, an IR system consists of a file of documents with brief content characterizations in the form of index descriptions in an indexing language; a procedure for searching the file given the index description of a user's request for documents derived from his need for information about something; and a matching criterion for evaluating comparisons between request and document descriptions. The system also includes procedures for deriving the index descriptions of documents and requests. It is driven by the user's need and the consequent assessment of retrieved documents for their relevance to this need.

In an automated system, the basic search and match operations on descriptions will be carried out automatically, though modifications of the request description, ie, the search specification, may be done manually. The construction of descriptions may or may not be automatic. The determination of the user's need and its expression as a request may be automatically assisted but is essentially manual; the assessment of relevance is also a human, and specifically end-user, operation.

In practice this simple model is most often modified to take account of the fact that the machine files do not contain the actual document texts themselves but only *surrogate*, notably abstract, texts, so indexing and even relevance assessment are based on these surrogates.

Database Context

Modern IR techniques emerged to meet the challenge of the vast growth of literature in the last forty years by taking advantage of the storage and processing resources of computers. The subsequent development of communications and networking has allowed an enormous development of on-line search services handling thousands of bibliographic and related databases, with individual bases containing millions of items (Gerrie, 1983). Full end-document text bases, first established for legal and news material, are becoming more common, and there are more and more varied quasi-text or "factographic" bases verging on

conventional nonbibliographic databases in form and content. The range of resources also includes traditional book catalogues with many millions of entries. Improvements in terminal technology as well as networking have encouraged end-user searching without the help of professional information officers or intermediaries.

User Need and Document Relevance

The core operations in a retrieval system are clearly document and request description, or *indexing*, on the one hand, and searching and matching, or *retrieving*, on the other. The performance of a retrieval system also depends heavily on the extent to which the user's information need has been identified, and an appropriate request for documents to meet it has been expressed. Need and request have to be distinguished as retrieved documents are eventually and properly assessed for relevance to the user's need, not for relevance to the request, which can only be a substitute predictor of relevance to need. In identifying the user's need it is also necessary to take account of the wider problem context supplied by background components of the user's situation like educational status, work goals, and so forth, which explain the need and may influence, but do not constitute, the request.

Relevance refers to the user's perception of the value of document content in relation to his information need. This judgment is strictly *ad occasionem*, and as need and fulfilment are mutually determining, relevance has to be taken as an undefined primitive notion, with important consequences for system evaluation (see below). It is a fundamental fact of IR life that what makes a document relevant is not obvious. This places one set of constraints, emphasizing hospitality, on system design. It is also a fundamental fact of IR life that the absolute number of documents and, even more, the proportion of the collection that is relevant to a request will be very small. This places a second conflicting set of constraints, emphasizing selectivity, on system design.

Performance Measurement

System performance is therefore normally measured primarily in terms of the system's ability to retrieve all and only relevant documents. If a search partitions a collection of size N into four sets, r = relevant retrieved, $M - r$ = matching but not relevant, $R - r$ = relevant but not retrieved, and $N - M - R + r$ = nonrelevant and not retrieved, then *precision* is defined as r/M and *recall* as r/R, and performance can be defined as some combined function of precision and recall. With an all-or-nothing matching function of the kind commonly used in commercial services, where search specifications are Boolean functions of terms, performance can be simply indicated as a precision-recall pair, and performance for many requests can be derived by straightforward averaging. With functions ranking output, performance can be obtained by computing precision for standard recall values (say .1, .2 . . .), with averaging. Empirical observation has consistently shown that there is an inverse relationship between precision and recall, and also that it is in general very hard to attain, let alone improve on, values of .5 for both at the same time, especially for average performance (Lancaster, 1979; van Rijsbergen 1979; Sparck Jones, 1981; Salton and McGill, 1983).

Document Description

Descriptions or representations of documents are needed for retrieval. They are not simply regrettable substitutes for full texts associated with a lack of the space to store and time to search the texts themselves. Document index descriptions are necessary filters for the end-user who cannot be expected to read many whole documents directly. This information reduction, which titles typically offer, is essential in human searching; it meets a human need even when searching is done automatically and the end user has only to assess a relatively or even absolutely small output document set. Document descriptions have a much more important role as a means of optimizing document-request matches. Document descriptions, like summaries, pick out the key information in a document and make it explicit, so if the user's request is for documents about X, matching the description "X" should indeed return documents that are about X.

Document descriptions are normally provided when documents enter the collection, though in practice they may be constructed at run time only for those documents extracted from the file using some first-pass coarse filter. As descriptions are logical objects, they can be constructed *a posteriori*, at search time, rather than *a priori*, since a request can be taken as an index description for the documents it matches. Thus if the index description for a request consists of a set of three words, any document (or surrogate) texts which also contain these three have this set as an index description. The advantage of independent, as opposed to request-dependent, document descriptions is that it is easier to ensure the description reflects key document content. The disadvantage is that other content is lost. With request-dependent descriptions access to documents is open, but is difficult to control so as to ensure matches on significant rather than incidental document content.

Request-dependent description has been a natural consequence of the ability to store and search masses of running text, most often in the form of abstracts, but also, and increasingly, as full document texts. With abstracts, as these are deliberately designed to be condensed representations of full documents, request-based text searching can be very effective. It may also be useful, as with legal, news, or intelligence material, where any occurrence of the specified words may be valuable regardless of overall document topic, but in general, the flexibility and sensitivity to the user's perspective given by request-dependent indexing has a cost in mismatches. Flexibility can be achieved with independent document descriptions by the way matching is defined, and by procedures for modifying given descriptions, say by substituting more general for specific terms, which are allowed in searching. There is still the problem of failure to capture document content in the initial description; this can be particularly unfortunate when there are topic and perspective shifts in a subject field, because older documents may become inaccessible.

Key Problems

The key problems of IR, bearing directly on indexing and indirectly on retrieving, are of normalization and discrimination, given a context dominated by uncertainty. There is uncertainty in working with descriptions of documents rather than documents themselves, with topic characterizations stemming from different perceptions, and with the linguistic expressions reflecting these; with requests from users who are not yet informed, and with relevance as an idiosyncratic relationship. A balance has to be struck between descriptive normalization and descriptive discrimination. Normalization is intended to reduce uncertainty by limiting variety, and is therefore determined by the units and relations of the indexing language and also by indexing policies affecting eg, description detail. Discrimination is designed to separate the few documents relevant to a request from the many nonrelevant ones, and is equally determined by indexing resources and policies. Indexing a document with a few general terms will blur differences, promoting recall at the expense of precision; indexing a document with a complex, nonmodifiable and specific description will advance precision if any matches occur.

AUTOMATED SYSTEMS

The essential processes of IR as defined earlier are those of information retrieval in a much broader sense, and hence are also those found in libraries. Their particular properties stem from the distinctive features of the task context. Thus the nature of the documents and requests involved, and power of the machine, have led to real and important differences in indexing and retrieving, seen in their simplest form in the ease with which permutation and selection can be done on a set of *keys* constituting an index description (van Rijsbergen, 1979; Salton and McGill, 1983; Willett, 1988).

Distinguishing items in, and selecting them from, a large mass of similar ones, typically without any leverage from relatively unequivocal keys like author names, calls for refined and variable document descriptions. These descriptions also often have to be provided within the context of rapidly developing and changing subjects and disciplines, as in many areas of science and technology. At the same time, there is no practical limit to the number of access routes to a single document topic description, as there used to be with hand-generated catalogues, let alone any need to choose the best single subject location for the physical documents, as there often is with books on library shelves. There is therefore no good basis, or real need, for global description schemes intended to characterize entire or large areas of knowledge in a systematic way, and, to place all the documents in a collection within a single analytic framework, like those of traditional library classifications.

Indexing Forms

In IR therefore, it is customary to provide document descriptions consisting of one or more concept labels drawn from an indexing vocabulary which is not in itself systematically organized into a single whole depending, for example, on hierarchical inclusion. But within this general framework for indexing, covering both the language used and descriptions produced, there are many different possibilities under the major headings of language type, description form, and processing mode. Broadly speaking, the indexing language may be natural language or an artificial controlled language (normally using ordinary words in restricted or nonstandard ways). The description form may be *precoordinate,* where individual words are combined to give fixed complex wholes, or *postcoordinate,* where individual words can be freely combined to give *ad hoc* topic characterizations. The processing mode may be by *derivation,* with description material extracted from the source document text, or by *assignment,* with document elements motivating the assignment of items from an independent indexing language.

It is customary to refer to the basic units of document and request description as *terms.* These are normally wordlike, and if extracted, may be called *keywords.* While (fixed) compounds may be allowed, it is more usual to refer to complex multi-word descriptive units as *subject headings.* The indexing vocabulary may then consist of the basic terms, which if controlled may be called *descriptors,* or of whole subject headings. The vocabulary itself may be given an organized relational structure, such as a thesaurus, a list of subject headings, or a classification.

In practice, many different specific choices and combinations of language, description and mode are to be found, with many variants in particular in the treatment of terms, especially in relation to vocabulary control; of relations between terms, which may be implicit or explicit and natural or artificial; and of description integrity, because this interacts with the use of simple or complex descriptive units (Foskett, 1977; Lancaster, 1979; Chan, Richmond and Svenonius, 1985).

Retrieval Operations

Retrieving covers searching and matching. Searching in the broadest sense can cover the identification of the user's need and the expression of the user's document request as, for example, during browsing of a subject heading list; at this point, it overlaps with request indexing. It is often interpreted more narrowly to refer to the modification of a given request index description, ie, search specification, to change the volume or nature of the matching document set. This may be done manually or automatically. With automated systems, it can also cover filtering operations designed to limit detailed matching to part files, analogous to a human search downwards in a conventional library classification like the UDC. In the narrowest sense, searching refers to the operations required to access items in the database file; with large databases these may be very complex and may depend on sophisticated file structures, or exploit novel architectures (Stanfill, Thau, and Waltz, 1989). Matching refers to the individual comparison between request and document descriptions. Matching can range from simple exact matching, as with Boolean expressions, to elaborate calculation to compute complex scoring functions (Salton and

McGill, 1983). In general, it is important to recognize that retrieval is usually an interactive process, and that searching is iterative (Belkin and Vickery, 1985).

Manual Indexing

With automated systems, the main distinction between systems hitherto has been whether indexing is essentially manual or automatic. Initial request formulation is a primarily human process, though it may be indirect (as in the use of a reference document example) and machine-aided. Subsequent reformulation, normally directly of the search specification, may be manual, automatic, or some mix of the two. In manual indexing, concept labels may be extracted from the document or surrogate (or request) text, or assigned, either freely or from a prespecified vocabulary; and the relations within or between labels may be similarly reflective, free, or constrained. Manual indexing has been particularly associated with the use of a controlled artificial indexing vocabulary and precoordinate subjects, since these normally require some understanding of the document, though with simple controlled terms automatic assignment from text clues is feasible. Controlled vocabularies have also to be constructed and maintained manually, implying substantial effort for large subject areas. Automatic indexing is normally associated with the use of natural language, applying criteria for the selection of key text elements for use in their own right or as leads to other or additional labels (Lancaster, 1979; Willett, 1988).

AUTOMATIC INDEXING

The automatic indexing and retrieval techniques established by IR research have been in part a response to the fundamental constraints stemming from uncertainty, and in part determined by the lack of natural language understanding (qv) (NLU) or even natural language processing (NLP) resources. But they have at the same time been influenced by experiments suggesting that the elaborate approaches, involving deep analysis and complex description, of manual indexing do not pay off in retrieval performance, perhaps because uncertainty implies a corresponding simplicity rather than a complementary refinement. These automatic techniques have also been motivated by a belief that the actual words used in natural language text are of crucial importance as direct content indicators. In addition, the statistical approaches adopted have reflected the importance of scale in IR as opposed to many other NLP applications: for example, if a term occurs in many documents it will be a poor selector even if it is an accurate indicator of individual document content.

Basic Model

The basic model on which automatic indexing and retrieval has been built exploits natural language by using simple extracted terms which are linked by coordination, ie, simple conjunctions, and are weighted by their distribution in and across documents (or their surrogates). The terms will normally be *stems* or fragments, possibly crudely defined from a linguistic point of view. All the terms occurring in a document are candidate description terms. The candidate indexing vocabulary for a collection is the union of these document terms. The actual vocabulary can in principle be manipulated purely statistically to eliminate non-discriminating terms, but common function words are in practice removed via a *stop list*. The operational vocabulary is therefore confined to content words and function words are not retained for their relational utility.

Some content words may also appear unhelpful, but it is better to retain the entire content vocabulary and indicate the status of terms by explicit weights, because these can vary for different documents and can also be manipulated to reflect the properties of requests and relevance assessments, and the behaviour of term cooccurrences. A simple, demonstrably useful weighting formula balances term frequency within documents against frequency across documents: good terms are those with a high within-document frequency but a low across-document frequency, where a term's across-document frequency is just the number of documents in which it occurs. Specifically, if D_k is the number of documents in which term k occurs and N is the size of the collection, the germane properties of across-document frequency can be captured by defining k's inverse document frequency $I_k = \log_2 N - \log_2 D_k$. Then if F_{ik} is k's frequency within document i, both aspects of term behaviour are covered by defining k's weight for i as $w_{ik} = F_k . I_k$.

Requests are indexed in the same way, and request document matching is then determined by some suitable formula. In the simplest case, where there is little within-document variation (as with abstracts), weighting can simply be by inverse document frequency, and for the request terms alone. So for term k in request j, $w_{jk} = I_k$. Matching a request against the collection will give a set of scores, each summing the weights of terms occurring in a document, which can be used to rank documents for presentation to the user. Matching is thus more flexible, and more complex in its effects, than with the Boolean formulas found in most operational services, where the complete search specification has to match for a document to be retrieved.

Model Extensions. The basic model may be elaborated, still on a statistical basis, in various directions. One is to group terms to provide alternative or additional matching terms, either directly, or indirectly via the use of class names as derived descriptors; statistical constraints may also be applied to the formation of compound terms, or term phrases. A second direction is to seek document groups based on shared terms, both to reduce search effort by limiting the initial steps of search matching to group descriptions, and also to concentrate like (and hence hopefully corelevant) documents. A third is to apply relevance feedback, exploiting relevance assessments for initially retrieved documents to modify requests, say by adding new terms from relevant documents and/or reweighting the given terms to reflect their relevant document incidence. Thus using r, R, $n = D_k$ and N to construct a four-way collection partition like that given earlier for searching but now defining the way an individual term occurs in relevant or retrieved documents, for each term k in request j we can obtain a weight

$$w_{jk} = \log_2[(r/(R - r)) / ((n - r) / (N - n - R + r))]$$

with some appropriate adjustment, say adding .5 to the value for each set, to reflect the fact that the term's future relevance utility is being estimated (van Rijsbergen, 1979; Salton and McGill, 1983; Willett, 1988).

Model Performance. The basic model has been shown to compete effectively with conventional "higher quality" manual indexing in many, very different tests; and while grouping strategies have generally not proved helpful, relevance weighting is particularly valuable, especially in the first iteration in searching. However, operational systems using natural language have until recently normally been very crude, without ranking or weighting, and while the necessary conclusive experiments on a really large scale have not been done, there is little doubt that respectable natural language systems could be provided (Sparck Jones, 1981).

Operational systems rely heavily on sensible request formulation by the user. This is always important, and while there may be no real substitute for the user's initiative, the basic model can be developed to support automatic request modification as just indicated, or applied in conjunction with the user's own changes. This has, however, to be done with care, as the user's perceptions of what is useful may not fit the statistical realities. Automation also makes it easy to use other types of search key, like citations, to which statistical techniques may equally apply, and developments in computing and especially in interactive and display technology have encouraged a more varied and cheerful use of all the available information, eg, searching on controlled language terms as if they were ordinary natural language ones, and have assisted search formulation through, eg, related term displays.

On the theoretical side, considerable effort has been put into, and some progress has been made in, developing a coherent formal model to which both the strategies adopted for the different components of an IR system and the alternative approaches to a particular operation, like term weighting, can be related. Much of the research done in IR has been in terms either of the vector model associated with Salton and Yu or of van Rijsbergen and Robertson's Bayesian model (Salton and McGill, 1983; van Rijsbergen, 1979). For some it is evident that the required overall model has to be a probabilistic one, but alternative claims can be made for eg, a fuzzy logic model. One major problem with general theories proposed so far is that they have usually been so abstract it is difficult to know how to apply them practically in system design and operation. At a lower level, a good deal of attention has been paid to combining weighting with Boolean requests as a way of applying research results within the conceptual and data management framework of operational systems. However, there are problems with this, because the two approaches impose very different constraints on search specifications.

SYSTEM TESTING AND EVALUATION

IR systems are very complex with many data variables and system parameters. Their behaviour is not well understood, which leads to conceptual problems that make it difficult to design proper tests. (These also tend to be expensive.) To determine performance for any particular combination of indexing and retrieving methods, or to compare alternative combinations, it is necessary to average across requests, and it may be difficult to find a sound way of doing this (is a match on only two terms out of three better than a match on four out of seven?). It is also generally necessary to determine what relevant documents there are to be retrieved, but it is clearly impossible to assess every document in a large collection for relevance to a user need. Sampling for assessment is, however, problematic when there are only a few relevant documents, as is usually the case. The normal strategy is therefore to search for a request using many different methods and to pool the outputs for assessment. This allows a measure of relative recall for any individual method, but the relevance set is biased towards those documents that are easy to retrieve. It may be helpful to use a measure which can be oriented towards recall or precision, to reflect user preferences. Many specific measures have been proposed, and it is important with operational systems to take account of factors like search effort as well as eg, money costs; but user satisfaction, though important, has to be treated with caution as perceived and real performance, say for recall, can be very different. There is a further difficulty in establishing whether performance differences are significant, given the lack of suitable nonparametric significance tests. The sign test is of some limited use (Lancaster, 1979; Sparck Jones, 1981).

With modern interactive technology testing becomes much more difficult, because searching is determined by assessment. The user cannot be asked to apply alternative devices to the same starting request, for parallel searches before any output assessment, so larger request samples are needed. Testing to allow general claims for particular methods, as opposed to collection-specific claims, is very costly because evaluation across different collections representing different data contexts is needed. In this case, the notion of *test collection* may be taken to refer not only to the document file, but to a particular request and relevance assessment file representing some particular user community.

ARTIFICIAL INTELLIGENCE

AI, defined here as computational reasoning over world knowledge, has not figured significantly in IR so far, but has several possible roles which are beginning to be explored (Croft, 1987; Jacobs, 1990). The most important potential roles are in the central processes of indexing and retrieving referring explicitly to subject or topic information. There are also other tasks for which expert system technology might be useful. Finally, AI may have a part to play in integrating the increasingly varied information bases and information management tasks that technology is offering the user at his desk.

Intelligent Indexing

The claim for AI in relation to indexing can be made in a strong form: because the user is really interested in the information supplied by documents, this information should be extracted to form a single knowledge base replacing the documents themselves, and, of course, their index descriptions. Authority data could be preserved as appropriate in the base, but information is no longer scattered and remote. Searching in consequence becomes reasoning over the knowledge base, and IR is thus assimilated to question answering.

The main problems with this proposal (apart from its practical feasibility) are that the actual expression of information in a natural language document text itself conveys information, and that IR is not necessarily, or even mostly, question answering (Sparck Jones, 1990). Even if it is formally question answering, it is not substantively question answering under the tacitly assumed fact retrieval paradigm, involving knowledge representation in some logical formalism.

A more moderate version of the claim is for a knowledge base superstructure which embodies only the essential collection content, but which allows initial inferential searching of a well-organized kind on this, bottoming out in pointers to documents supplying more detail. The assumption here is that AI techniques would provide a more effective, because more powerful, means of access to the documents than that represented by devices like conventional library classification schemes. There is now a problem in the precise nature of the links between knowledge base and documents, which does not arise with the less exigent classification case, and with the relation between question-answering operations on the knowledge base and any further topic searching operations on the document base.

A yet weaker proposal is for AI-type individual document descriptions eg, in some frame form, as providing a more organized characterization of the documents that allows inferential description searching, both on individual descriptions and through systematic links between multiple descriptions (Lewis, Croft, and Bhandaru, 1989). With this approach, there would be a knowledge base only in an emergent and weak sense, It is, however, a fact that both arguments and examples here are often unwitting reruns of the familiar case for elaborate indexing of the kind hitherto provided manually, which has not been proven significantly better than much simpler automatic procedures. The specific issue is whether descriptions of this type are too constraining, even allowing for some modulation and relaxation.

The final approach is to operate within the generic natural language term model, but to seek to use AI rather than statistics to extract key terms for documents, and more importantly, to identify well-founded compound terms, eg, embodying case relations. Full NLU is beyond the present state of the art, but current NLP techniques might be useful (Lewis, Croft, and Bhandaru, 1989). The particular issues here are first, whether purely syntactic processing (local or global) gives sufficiently better compounds than pure proximity or association methods to be worth the effort; and secondly and more materially, whether term identification can be improved if analysis is semantic as well as syntactic, assuming the necessary semantic resources (lexicon, patterns) can be supplied without too much effort for the wide-ranging material encountered in ordinary document collections. Some operational systems already use syntactic processing. But whether this or semantic analysis, on which only some limited research has yet been done, significantly improves performance has still to be experimentally established (Sparck Jones and Tait, 1984). The plausible argument that sophisticated analysis is needed to identify real as opposed to false coordinations is unfortunately irrelevant if false coordinations do not actually match documents.

The view that strong claims for AI approaches to indexing may be misconceived refers to the general case. The situation may be quite different in specialized contexts, with particular types of material or use, where question answering on a knowledge base has a part to play (Jacobs and Rau, 1988).

Intelligent Searching

In searching, AI would be exploited to automate the intermediary ie, to replace the expert who currently helps users to formulate their requests, indexes these, and conducts searches, frequently through on-line services, on the user's behalf. This requires extensive knowledge of generic user properties, available information resources, indexing languages and practices, search strategies and so forth, as well as considerable general and domain knowledge (Belkin and co-workers, 1987). An analysis of the intermediary's or reference librarian's practical knowledge and skills suggests that automating them is a task well beyond the state of the art. Whether less ambitious support, requiring more complementary initiative from the end user, would be useful, and could be provided, needs and deserves investigation. Expert system techniques have already been applied to request formulation and search specification (Vickery and co-workers, 1987), and more limited facilities eg, for translating requests into controlled languages, have been studied and can work (Pollitt, 1987). At the same time, AI inference methods have been applied to searching and matching using (manually constructed) search concept specifications (Tong and Applebaum, 1988). It has also been suggested that AI techniques could be used not for individual searches, but to allow longer-term system tailoring to the individual. Whether this could be more effectively done than with the non-AI techniques currently available for modifying individual searches or standing interest profiles also needs investigation.

Intelligent Service

It is possible that expert system technology could be used for other less exigent information management tasks still referring to subjects or topics, like categorization, routing, or database selection, though again much simpler term-based techniques might suffice, and also for other support functions like cataloguing. Some work has already been successfully done which combines term extraction without any NLP with rule-based exploitation of the extracted term data for categorization (Hayes and Weinstein, 1990).

Intelligent Systems

The most ambitious proposed role for AI is in sustaining the integrated information system of the future. The aim is not just integration so that the user does not have to work explicitly within different subsystems, say for text preparation and document retrieval, as he typically does now. The goal is a system providing a positive response exploiting different information resources, shifting initiative from the user to the system in the way adaptation also does. This integration presupposes an infrastructure, in the form of a common knowledge base and reasoning apparatus, to make content links between different types of information and function bearing on the user's inferred need. However, a cool look at the range of information types and management functions, both private and public, involving not only a single user but many users, that any serious system would have to support, suggests that this is a remote dream (Sparck Jones, 1990). Much weaker mechanisms relying on associations between the words used in different subsystems may, on the other hand, be not only attainable but also the conceptually correct ones, given the real heterogeneity of these systems.

However this does not imply that AI may not contribute to the individual subsystems within a multi-purpose system, say to create a specialized information base (Young and Hayes, 1985). Linking with other systems would still rely on the language of the subsystem.

CONCLUSION

Conventional operational retrieval systems are well-established and useful, but they are institutionalized and their size makes them difficult to modify, so change stimulated by research findings has been very slow, particularly since helpful mundane improvements, like better document delivery, appear of more value to the consumer. Developments in information technology are having an obvious impact on information retrieval, especially for the end user, but it is not yet clear how these will interact with the approaches suggested by IR or AI research. AI research in the area is itself only beginning and, while promising particularly for some specialized cases like message interpretation, has not yet demonstrated solid, generally applicable results. AI techniques may be relevant for some purposes, like request formulation, which are outside the scope of IR theories. There is a more interesting intellectual challenge in whether knowledge-based AI and statistically-based IR can be legitimately or effectively combined (Salton and McGill, 1983; Lewis, Croft, and Bhandaru, 1989). Modest operations like weighting terms delivered by NLP are clearly feasible, but the issue is what more there may be to do.

BIBLIOGRAPHY

N. J. Belkin and A. Vickery, *Interaction in Information Systems,* Library and Information Research Report 35, The British Library, London, 1985.

N. J. Belkin and co-workers, "Distributed Expert-Based Information Systems: An Interdisciplinary Approach," *Inf. Proc. Man.* **23**, 395–409 (1987).

L. M. Chan, P. A. Richmond, and E. Svenonius, eds., *Theory of Subject Analysis: A Sourcebook,* Libraries Unlimited, Littleton, Colo., 1985.

W. B. Croft, ed., "Artificial Intelligence and Information Retrieval," *Inf. Pro. Man.* **23**(4), 249–366 (1987).

A. C. Foskett, *The Subject Approach to Information,* Bingley, London, 1977.

B. Gerrie, *Online Information Systems—Use and Operating Characteristics, Limitations, and Design Alternatives,* Information Resources Press, Washington D.C., 1983.

P. J. Hayes and S. P. Weinstein, "CONSTRUE/TIS: A System for Content-Based Indexing of a Database of News Stories," *Proceedings of the Second Annual Conference on Innovative Applications of Artificial Intelligence,* Washington, D.C., American Association for Artificial Intelligence, 1990.

P. S. Jacobs, ed., *Text-Based Intelligent Systems: Current Research in Text Analysis, Information Extraction, and Retrieval,* Report 90 CRD 198, General Electric, Schenectady, N.Y., 1990.

P. S. Jacobs and L. F. Rau, "Natural Language Techniques for Intelligent Information Retrieval," *Proceedings of the Eleventh International Conference on Research and Development in Information Retrieval,* Grenoble, France, Association for Computing Machinery Special Interest Group on Information Retrieval, 1988, pp. 85–99.

F. W. Lancaster, *Information Retrieval Systems: Characteristics, Testing and Evaluation,* 2nd ed., John Wiley & Sons, Inc., New York, 1979.

D. D. Lewis, W. B. Croft, and N. Bhandaru, "Language-Oriented Information Retrieval," *Int. J. Intell. Syst.* **4**, 285–318 (1989).

A. S. Pollitt, "CANSEARCH: An Expert Systems Approach to Document Retrieval," *Inf. Proc. Man.* **23**, 119–138 (1987).

C. J. van Rijsbergen, *Information Retrieval,* 2nd ed., Butterworths, London, 1979.

G. Salton and M. J. McGill, *Introduction to Modern Information Retrieval,* McGraw-Hill, New York, 1983.

K. Sparck Jones, ed., *Information Retrieval Experiment,* Butterworths, London, 1981.

K. Sparck Jones, *Retrieving Information or Answering Questions?* The British Library Annual Research Lecture, The British Library, London, 1990.

K. Sparck Jones and J. I. Tait, "Automatic Search Term Variant Generation," *J. Doc.* **40**, 50–66 (1984).

C. Stanfill, R. Thau, and D. Waltz, "A Parallel Indexed Algorithm for Information Retrieval," *Proceedings of the Twelfth Annual International ACMSIGIR Conference on Research and Development in Information Retrieval,* Cambridge, Mass., Association for Computing Machinery Special Interest Group on Information Retrieval, 1989, pp. 88–97.

R. M. Tong and L. Applebaum, "Conceptual Information Retrieval from Full Text," *RIAO 88, Proceedings of the Conference on User-Oriented, Content-Based Text and Image Handling,* Cambridge, Mass., 1988, pp. 899–909.

A. Vickery, H. Brooks, B. Robinson, and B. Vickery, "A Reference and Referral System Using Expert System Techniques," *J. Doc.* **43**, 1–23 (1987).

P. Willett, ed., *Document Retrieval Systems,* Taylor Graham, London, 1988.

S. R. Young and P. J. Hayes, "Automatic Classification of Banking Telexes," *Proceedings of the Second Conference on Artificial Intelligence Applications,* IEEE Computer Society, 1985, pp. 402–408.

General Reference

Annual Review of Information Science and Technology, Vols 1–25, 1966–1989 [various editors and publishers] [latest M. E. Williams, ed., Vol. 25 (1990), Elsevier, Amsterdam].

KAREN SPARCK JONES
University of Cambridge

INHERITANCE HIERARCHY

Inheritance hierarchies are an outgrowth of the classical notion of taxonomic hierarchy as an organization for knowledge. Figure 1 shows a small hierarchy consisting of the class mammal, the superclass vertebrate, and the subclasses elephant, sheep, and dog. In such a representation it is not necessary to state that elephants, sheep, and dogs are vertebrates because that can be derived from the fact that all mammals are vertebrates. Such deductions, which are a form of syllogistic reasoning, are accomplished in AI programs using a specialized inference technique called inheritance.

Taxonomy is only the beginning of inheritance reasoning. AI researchers have added machinery for representing properties of classes, exceptions to inherited properties, multiple superclasses, and structured concepts with specific relations among the structural elements. In addition, inheritance reasoning naturally leads to simple forms of default and nonmonotonic reasoning (see REASONING, DEFAULT; REASONING, NONMONOTONIC), and can be used to reason about prototypes and typical instances of classes (Winograd, 1980).

Today, inheritance hierarchies are the backbone of most LISP-based AI languages, such as FRL (qv) (Roberts and Goldstein, 1977), KRL (qv) (Bobrow and Winograd, 1977; Bobrow and co-workers, 1977), KL-ONE (qv) (Brachman, 1987; Brachman and Schmolze, 1985), SRL

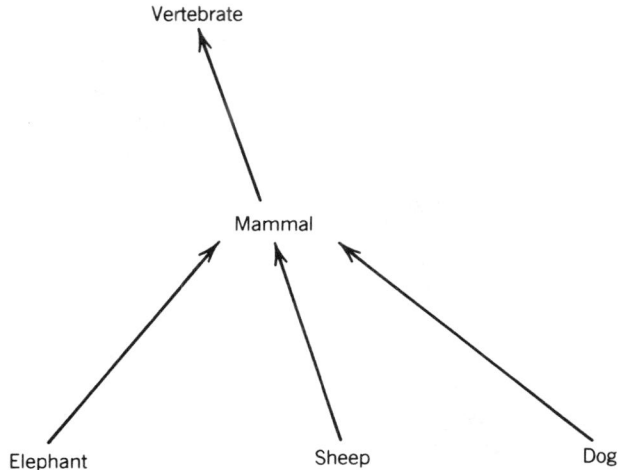

Figure 1. A simple taxonomic hierarchy.

(Wright and Fox, 1983) and Omega (Attardi and Simi, 1982; Hewitt and co-workers, 1980). They are also found in most semantic networks (qv) (Finder, 1979), including parallel ones such as NETL (Fahlman, 1979). Inheritance hierarchies have found their way into programming language design as well: in object-oriented programming languages such as SIMULA (qv) (Dahl, 1968), SMALLTALK (qv) (Borning and Ingalls, 1982), and LOOPS (qv) (Bobrow and Stefik, 1981), in the LISP Machine (qv) flavors system (Weinreb and Moon, 1981), and in the Ada-derived type facility (Department of Defense, 1982). A discussion of the role of inheritance in contemporary programming languages has been published (Carnese, 1984).

SIMPLE TAXONOMIC HIERARCHIES

The simplest inheritance system, a pure taxonomic hierarchy, consists of classes linked by subclass–superclass relationships. Each class has at most one immediate superclass so that the hierarchy is a rooted tree. The links between classes are normally called IS-A links, as in "an elephant IS-A mammal," but there is no standard terminology for the components of an inheritance network, nor is there any standard semantics for the IS-A link (Brachman, 1983). Other names for the IS-A relation are AKO (A Kind Of, used in FRL), SUPERC (Super Concept, used in KL-ONE), and VC (Virtual Copy, used in NETL). The most basic taxonomy question, "is an x a y," can be answered by any inheritance system by taking the transitive closure over the IS-A relation or its equivalent. Other types of query are possible, some of which require that IS-A links be traversed in the opposite direction. One example is "list all the mammals."

Some systems distinguish between classes (such as mammal) and individuals (such as particular mammals, like "Clyde the elephant"), although both types of object can inherit properties. FRL does not make this distinction, but NETL and KL-ONE provide different node types for classes and individuals. NETL uses the same link type for two types of inheritance; a VC link is used to express both "Clyde is a mammal" and "elephants are mammals." KL-ONE prescribes a different link, the INSTANCE-OF link, for individuals to inherit from classes; the SUPERC link is used only from subclasses to superclasses. Few AI systems stop at simple hierarchies of classes and individuals; they usually include additional machinery such as slots, defaults, exceptions, and demons, with which they can perform rather sophisticated sorts of reasoning. But some recent systems, such as Krypton (Brachman and co-workers, 1983), use inheritance purely for efficient taxonomic discrimination and employ a theorem prover for the rest of their reasoning.

INHERITANCE OF PROPERTIES AND SLOTS

Most inheritance systems provide a way to associate properties with each class; the properties may then be inherited by the class's instances and subclasses. In frame-based inheritance systems these properties are called "slots" (Minsky, 1975) (see FRAMES). To indicate that mammals are warm-blooded in a frame system, the mammal frame would be given a blood temperature slot with the value "warm" as its filler. If the value of elephant's blood temperature slot is sought, and this slot is empty, the frame interpreter will proceed up the IS-A chain from elephant to mammal and look in mammal's blood temperature slot. When it finds the value "warm" in that slot, it will conclude that elephants are warm-blooded. Queries about slot values could of course be answered by a conventional database system if all slot values were stored in the database explicitly. But unlike databases, AI knowledge bases use inference mechanisms (of which inheritance is the most important) so that they can avoid storing most of their knowledge explicitly. Inheritance obviates the need for an explicit blood temperature value for elephants, sheep, dogs, or any other subclass of mammal, thus saving a considerable amount of space. Another advantage of inheritance is that it can be used to generate reasonable assumptions in the case of incomplete information.

MULTIPLE INHERITANCE

A natural extension to tree-structured inheritance hierarchies allows objects to inherit from multiple superclasses, as shown in Figure 2. This is called multiple inheritance. In such a system Clyde might inherit properties from three classes called "elephant," "circus star," and "veteran of the Punic wars." Multiple inheritance results in an inheritance graph that is a DAG (directed acyclic graph) rather than a tree. Such graphs are also called tangled hierarchies, a term popularized by Fahlman (1979) in the NETL system. Sometimes inheritance graphs are referred to as lattices, but they are rarely true lattices, because in a lattice every pair of nodes has a unique meet (lowest common superior) and joint (highest common inferior), unless the meet or join is undefined for those two points. This uniqueness constraint does not apply to tangled hierarchies. For example, elephant and giraffe might have several lowest common superiors, such as mammal, herbivore, and jungle dweller.

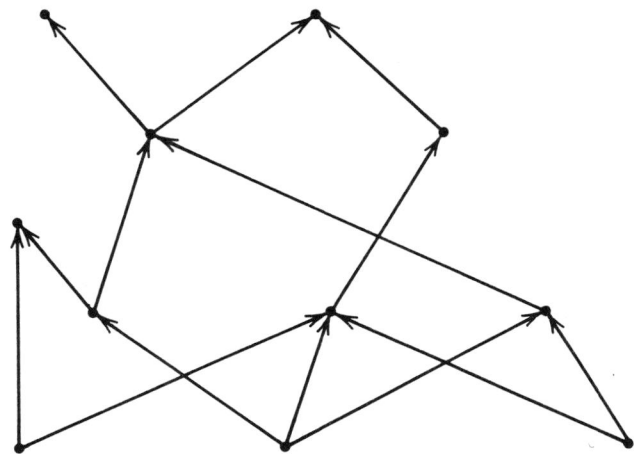

Figure 2. A tangled hierarchy.

The search (qv) algorithm for multiple inheritance systems is more complex than for simple, tree-structured hierarchies. In a tree-structured hierarchy, to test whether x is a subclass of y, it suffices to start at x and follow IS-A links upward until reaching either y or the root of the tree. Multiple inheritance requires a more complex search strategy because at each node there may be several upward paths to consider. One may use depth first, breadth first, or some other search method on the inheritance graph.

Search time grows at worst linearly with the number of nodes in a tree-structured hierarchy, but in a tangled hierarchy it can grow exponentially because the profusion of paths may result in nodes being searched more than once. For example, if *elephant* has IS-A links to both *mammal* and *herbivore,* and both those classes have IS-A links to *animal,* then *elephant* will have two paths to *animal.* An inheritance algorithm based on depth-first search may search the animal node twice in looking for the value of some property of elephants. In practical applications one would not expect redundant searches to be a significant problem, unless the search includes invocation of demons (described below). One technique for avoiding redundant searches altogether is parallel marker propagation (see below).

INHERITANCE AND FIRST-ORDER LOGIC

There is an ongoing rivalry between advocates of frame-based and semantic network representations and advocates of formal logic (qv) as a representation language (Israel, 1983). At one time it was argued that frame-based systems could express concepts outside the domain of logic and, also, that they were a more elegant and natural formalism than logic for organizing knowledge. These arguments have less force today. Inheritance reasoners are easier to implement than theorem provers and are more efficient because of their highly specialized nature. But most inheritance reasoners suffer from a murky semantics: their true meaning can be determined only by examining the code that implements their inference algorithms because there is no independent formal specification to refer to (Brachman, 1979). Logic-based systems offer the twin advantages of a well-understood formal semantics and a universally accepted notation.

Hayes (1977, 1979) and Nilsson (1980) argue that inheritance systems are merely notational variants of logic (qv) because their nodes and links can be translated in a straightforward, mechanical way into sentences in first-order logic. In their translations, classes are one-place predicates, inheritance links from individuals to classes are logical terms, and links from subclasses to super-classes are universally quantified implications. Properties (slot values) can be expressed either using two-place predicates or unary functions plus equality. To illustrate, below are three sentences in first-order logic that together encode the knowledge that Clyde is an elephant, elephants are mammals, and mammals have a blood temperature of "warm."

$$\text{Elephant(Clyde)}$$

$$\text{Elephant}(x) \Rightarrow \text{Mammal}(x)$$

$$\text{Mammal}(x) \Rightarrow \text{Blood Temp}(x, \text{warm})$$

For real inheritance systems, especially frame systems, the situation is more complex than this straightforward logical translation suggests. Real systems include default values and permit exceptions to inherited defaults, but default reasoning cannot be done in first-order logic. Hayes and Nilsson express the belief that this aspect of inheritance is not beyond the reach of logic, it is necessary simply to switch to a nonstandard language, such as non-monotonic logic (McDermott and Doyle, 1980) or default logic (Reiter, 1980) (see REASONING, NONMONOTONIC; REASONING, DEFAULT). But they do not attempt such a translation. None appeared until 1983, when Etherington and Reiter (1983) gave a translation for a small fragment of NETL in nonmonotonic logic. Another reason why real frame systems are difficult to formalize is that the procedural knowledge (demons) found therein can be arbitrary pieces of LISP code capable of all sorts of reasoning strategies, some of which might not be formalizable in any presently understood form of logic, just as default reasoning was once unformalized.

Although logical language is concise and has a well-defined meaning, standard logical notation may not be the best formalism for expressing even simple forms of knowledge. Knowledge in logic is expressed as a set of unordered, unconnected sentences. AI researchers have found it advantageous to group related facts into structures, such as frames. In addition, the organization of knowledge as a graph structure can lead to efficient inference algorithms. The proponents of logical representations point out, though, that the graph-structured organization found in semantic nets can be viewed as merely an efficient indexing scheme for retrieval of logical formulas, with no semantic significance. Inheritance systems of the future might be implemented as theorem provers but continue to use network notation and the network metaphor for knowledge as syntactic sugar for their user interface.

SIMPLE INHERITANCE EXCEPTIONS

Knowledge about the real world is seldom expressed in absolutes; normally it consists of useful generalizations accompanied by exceptions. Mammals generally bear live young, but platypuses, which are mammals, do not; they lay eggs. Of course platypuses are rare. The necessity of reasoning in situations where knowledge is incomplete means programs must be able to make reasonable assumptions based on what they know is typically true. If it is known that x is a mammal but it cannot be proven it is not a platypus, it may be profitable to assume that it is a typical mammal that bears live young unless told otherwise. This sort of reasoning cannot be expressed in first-order logic. Consider the following attempt at formalizing this knowledge about mammals and platypuses:

Mammal(x) $\Rightarrow$ Reproduces(x, live birth)

Platypus(x) $\Rightarrow$ Reproduces(x, egg laying)

Platypus(x) $\Rightarrow$ Mammal(x)

Reproduces(x,y) and Reproduces(x,z) $\Rightarrow$ $y = z$

The last line above expresses the fact that an animal can only have a single method of reproduction. Unfortunately, the above axioms are inconsistent, because from Platypus(Penny) both Reproduces(Penny, egg laying) and Reproduces(Penny, live birth) can be derived. This leads to the false conclusion that egg laying equals live birth. Suppose the rule that mammals normally bear live young is reformulated in order to take platypuses into account:

Mammal(x) and ~Platypus(x) $\Rightarrow$ Reproduces(x, live birth)

Now the only conclusion that can be drawn from Platypus-(Penny) is

Reproduces(Penny, egg laying)

which is correct. But what can be inferred from, say, Mammal(Bertha)? Nothing, because Bertha must be proved a nonplatypus before it can be concluded that she reproduces by live birth. There is no way in classic first-order logic simply to assume, in the absence of contrary evidence, that a particular mammal is not a platypus.

Due to this limitation, default reasoning cannot be done in first-order logic, but it can easily be demonstrated in inheritance systems. The trick of implementing defaults in inheritance systems is in the search algorithm. Suppose a mammal frame is created and given a reproduction slot with value live birth, and a platypus frame is also created whose reproduction slot has the value egg laying. Platypus has an IS-A link to mammal. Let Bertha be an instance of mammal, and Penny an instance of platypus. If the value of Bertha's reproduction slot is asked for, the search algorithm will travel from Bertha to mammal, where it finds the value live birth in the slot, and so it will return live birth. In Penny's case the search would stop at platypus where it finds the value egg laying; therefore, it never reaches the mammal frame and never looks in mammal's reproduction slot.

As long as the search algorithm works by ascending the IS-A hierarchy and stopping at the first slot value it finds, subclasses such as platypus can override the default values they inherit from superclasses, such as mammal, simply by specifying new values. Unfortunately, this simple search technique leads to counterintuitive results in multiple-inheritance systems.

EXCEPTIONS AND MULTIPLE INHERITANCE

The way exceptions are handled in multiple-inheritance systems depends on the multiple-inheritance algorithm. Some systems, when searching for a slot value for a frame, search upward from each of the frame's immediate superiors and return a list of the values they find. In FRL, for

example, if the mammal and herbivore frames both have information in their metabolism slot, as shown in Figure 3, and elephant inherits from both frames, a request for the value of elephant's metabolism slot will return a list containing both values. But if a value is placed directly into elephant's metabolism slot, this value will be the only one returned because the search does not proceed any further. FRL's ability to handle exceptions comes from its policy of not searching a frame's superiors when any information is available locally.

Other choices of search algorithm are possible. A depth-first search could be used to look for slot values and stop as soon as a single value is found. Or it would be possible to search all the frame's superiors in parallel, using breadth-first search, stopping when a single value is found. The latter technique is called shortest-path inheritance since the slot value with the shortest path from the start of the search is the one that will be found first. Shortest-path inheritance is the technique NETL originally used to implement exceptions. In a tree-structured inheritance hierarchy all these search strategies are equivalent, but under multiple inheritance they give different results.

Touretzky (1986, 1984) showed that none of these simple search techniques is guaranteed to give intuitively correct results under multiple inheritance. Consider the hierarchy in Figure 4. Nixon inherits from two frames, Quaker and Republican, and Republican in turn inherits from Hawk. Quakers are typically pacifists, while Hawks are of course nonpacifists. Is Nixon a pacifist or not? The algorithm that searches all a frame's superiors would return both yes and no, which clearly is inconsistent. Depth-first search would arbitrarily return one value or the other, but it cannot be predicted which, because it depends on the order in which the algorithm examines the Nixon frame's superiors. Thus whichever answer is received can-

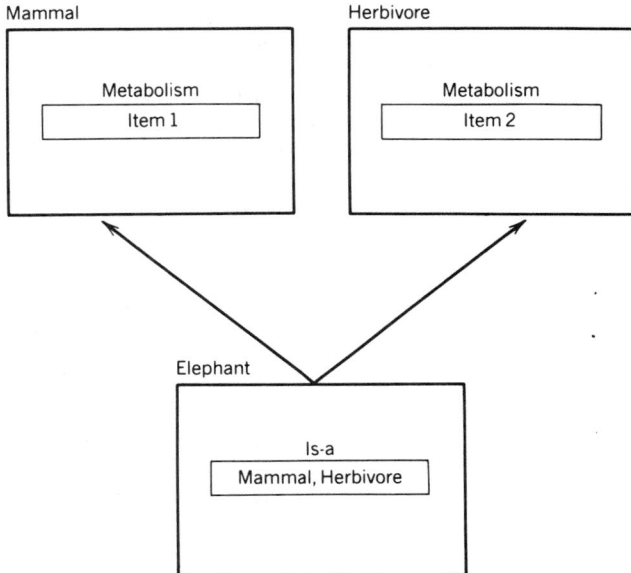

Figure 3. Two sources of metabolism information.

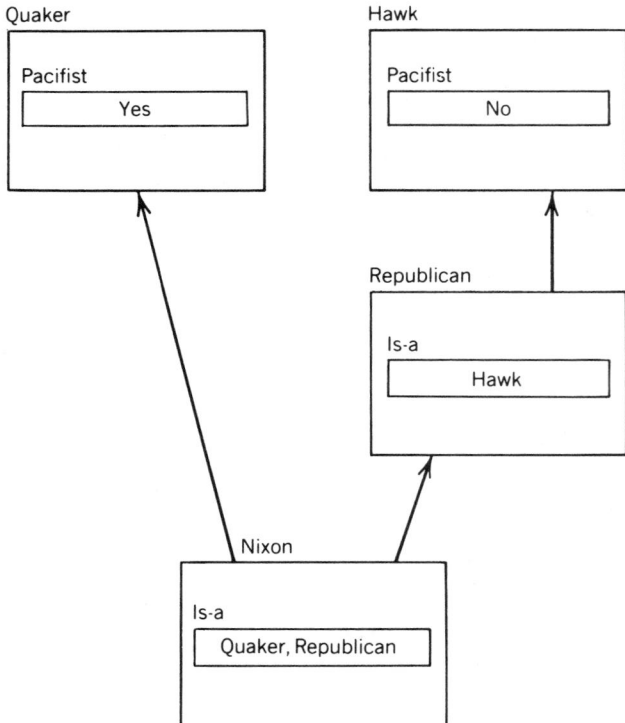

Figure 4. An ambiguous network.

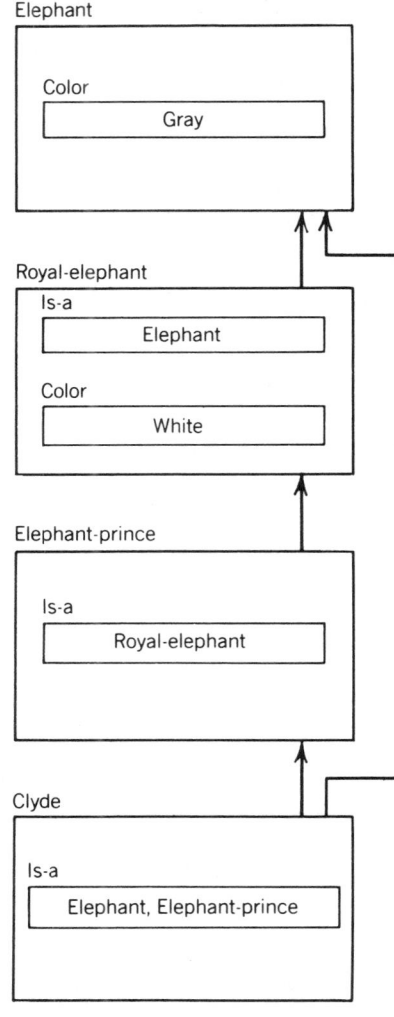

Figure 5. A network with a redundant IS-A link.

not be determined from the knowledge expressed in the network. Shortest-path search would decide that Nixon was a pacifist because the path to Quaker is shorter than the path to Hawk. But this distinction is not really pertinent; the opposite result can be obtained without changing the intuitive meaning of the network by inserting a few extra frames along the path from Nixon to Quaker so that the path to Hawk becomes the shorter of the two. Path length is simply the wrong criterion for choosing between possible inferences under multiple inheritance.

One solution to the dilemma posed by Figure 4 is to write off such networks as inconsistent. But there is a better solution: Figure 4 can be viewed as ambiguous rather than inconsistent. It simply has two interpretations that are both individually consistent, although mutually inconsistent. In one, Nixon is proved to be a pacifist because he is a Quaker. In the other, Nixon is proved to be a nonpacifist because he is a Hawk. But in first-order logic, sets of axioms always have unique theories; they simply cannot have more than one interpretation. Thus, in order to view Figure 4 as an ambiguous set of axioms, it is necessary to go outside first-order logic.

In a second class of examples Touretzky (1986, 1984) introduced redundant IS-A links, as illustrated in Figure 5. Clyde is an elephant prince, hence a royal elephant, and hence an elephant. Royal elephants are not gray. The explicit statement that Clyde is an elephant, although redundant, is certainly true. But conventional inheritance search algorithms depend on a strict hierarchical ordering of classes in order to draw reasonable conclusions about exceptions. Redundant links interfere with this ordering

by allowing the search algorithm to skip levels, for example, to go from Clyde to elephant directly without searching the intervening nodes. A depth-first inheritance reasoner operating in Figure 5 could return either gray or white as the value of Clyde's color, depending on which of his two superiors it examined first. A shortest-path algorithm, on the other hand, would always conclude that Clyde was gray, clearly an error. In FRL, where values from both Clyde's superiors would be returned, the result would be that Clyde was both white and gray, which is also unsatisfactory.

The obvious solution to his dilemma is to ban all redundant statements from inheritance systems. But because such statements are necessarily true, being among the system's own inferences, this would leave one in an awkward position in which it is very difficult to assign meaning to inheritance networks. Touretzky's view is that there is nothing wrong with redundant links; the problem lies with naive search algorithms. He proposes an inferential distance ordering as the proper approach to multiple-inheritance reasoning; this is an ordering on possible proof sequences (and hence inferences) rather than on classes and instances directly. The ordering can be shown to handle exceptions correctly even when redundant links are present, and it admits multiple consistent theories for networks such as Figure 4. Unfortunately, it appears that inference algorithms that operate according to inferential distance are more expensive to implement than simpler strategies such as shortest-path reasoning.

EXPRESSIVENESS OF INHERITANCE SYSTEMS

Inheritance systems are not nearly as expressive as first-order logic even though they can do some things that first-order logic cannot. Most inheritance systems provide no way to make explicit negative statements. It can be said that Clyde is an elephant but can not be said that he is not a giraffe. Instead of admitting negation explicitly, most inheritance systems rely on an idea called negation as failure: if the system fails in an attempt to prove an assertion, it assumes the assertion is false. Negation as failure is useful for default reasoning (as when one assumes a particular instance of a mammal is not a platypus), but it is no substitute for an adequate representation for negation.

Inheritance systems also lack a representation for disjunctions. There is no way to say things like "Clyde is either an elephant or a giraffe" or "Clyde's color is either gray or pink." And inheritance systems permit only a few forms of quantified statements; one cannot arbitrarily nest quantifiers as is possible in logic.

These limitations on expressiveness are not without compensation. The simplicity and efficiency of inheritance reasoners are a direct result of them. As the representation language becomes more flexible, inheritance reasoners become more like theorem provers; the rise in computational complexity can be dramatic (Brachman and Levesque, 1984).

INHERITING SLOT CONSTRAINTS

Slots in a frame system can normally have any type of filler, but sometimes it is desirable to constrain either the type or number of fillers. Suppose a frame describing instances of an action, such as ingestion, has agent and object slots. It may be desirable to restrict the agent slot to contain only animate beings and the object slot to contain only edible objects. Information about the potential fillers of a slot is a constraint on the slot that can be inherited and used in several ways. First, if a slot is filled with something that violates the constraints placed on it, the frame interpreter can generate an error message or invoke procedures called demons to handle the inconsistency. Second, if constraints are accessible, they can be referred to directly by any procedure that operates on the knowledge base. A story-understanding system (see STORY ANALYSIS), for example, could use the known constraints on an ingestion frame's object slot to recognize that the sentence "John ate the cost of the inspection" does not refer to an instance of ingestion; costs are not edible objects. Because constraints are inherited along with the slot, frames

for eating and drinking, being instances of ingestion, inherit the same slots and slot restrictions. But it is often useful to modify inherited constraints. The Object slot of the drinking frame, for example, might be further restricted so that it could be filled only by an instance of a fluid.

The number of fillers a slot may have may also be constrained. A frame describing a bicycle as a type of wheeled vehicle would necessarily constrain the wheels slot to have exactly two fillers. In a recognition-through-matching application, if an object has just one wheel, or three, the bicycle frame cannot match it because a number of constraint would be violated.

In KL-ONE, there are deliberate restrictions on how inherited constraints may be modified. A concept may replace an inherited number constraint only with one that is more restrictive, ie, a subrange of the original range. Inherited value restrictions may not be overridden, but they too may be made more restrictive, for example, replacing "edible thing" with "edible liquid." These restrictions ensure that there are no inheritance exceptions in KL-ONE. Its designers believe that an AI reasoner should treat exceptional cases elsewhere than in the taxonomic component (Brachman and Schmolze, 1985).

STRUCTURED CONCEPTS

Certain semantic network systems, notably KL-ONE and NETL, treat concepts as objects with important internal structure, such as the objects' parts and attributes. Each element of the structure is represented by a node called a "role"; the role names, constraints, and the relationships among roles define the essence of the concept. For example, the KL-ONE concept of an Arch might include three roles called Post1, Post2, and Lintel, whose values are constrained to be blocks. Intrinsic to the definition of an arch are the constraints that each role must be filled by a different block, the posts must both support the lintel, and the post must not touch each other. Figure 6a shows an instance of a blocks-world arch, and Figure 6b shows the concept of an arch in one version of KL-ONE. The RoleD links are role definitions, and the V/R (value restriction) links place value restrictions on the roles. The required relationships between the various roles are described in the portion of the diagram labeled Structural description.

Figure 7 shows an instance of an arch in KL-ONE. The arch is called ARCH-31, and its Post1, Post2, and Lintel roles are filled by BLOCK-18, BLOCK-21, and BLOCK-25, respectively. The Individuates link between ARCH-31 and ARCH shows that ARCH-31 denotes an instance of the ARCH concept and therefore inherits its roles and structural description. The RoleF links connect ARCH-31 with its role fillers, and the Satisfies links show which ARCH role each ARCH-31 role satisfies. The links from ARCH-31 to its superior concept, namely the Individuates link and the various satisfies links, form what in KL-ONE terminology is known as an "inheritance cable." This term calls attention to the fact that inheritance in KL-ONE is a multifaceted relationship, involving inheritance from con-

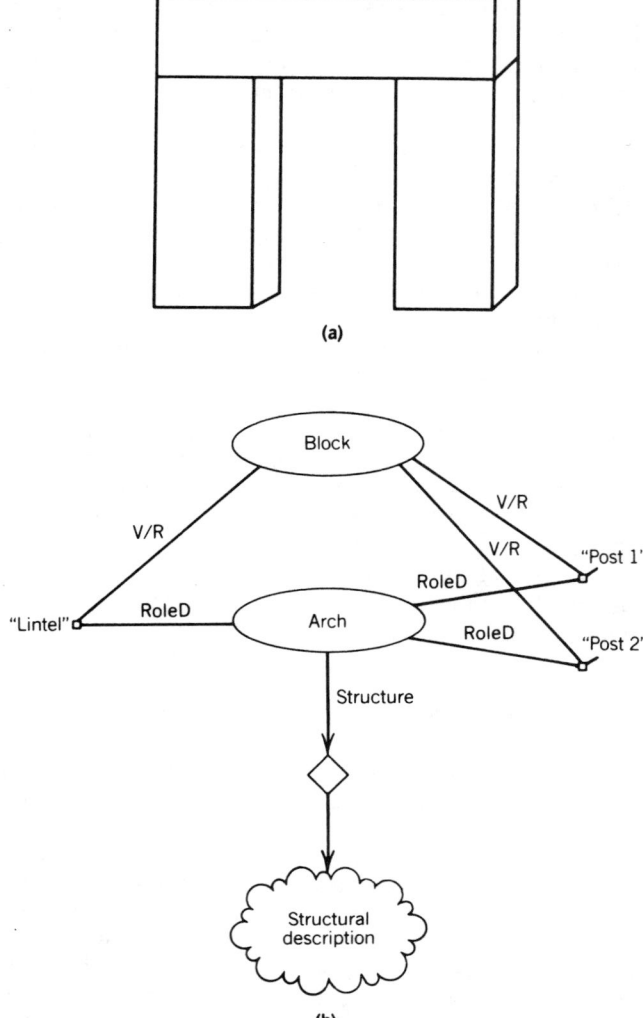

Figure 6. (*a*) A blocks-world arch; (*b*) an arch in KL-ONE.

cept to concept, role to role, and structural description to structural description.

Although roles are similar to the slots of a frame system, they are a more complex and more refined idea than slots. In addition to being inherited, roles can be differentiated into subroles, and subroles can be further constrained and placed in certain relationships. Figure 8 shows how, for the game hide-and-seek, the Players role for games can be differentiated into two subroles, Hiders and Seekers. Any assertions made about the players of games would be inherited by both hiders and seekers in games of hide-and-seek. Thus there is an inherited value restriction on both hiders and seekers that they be animate.

Roles can act as pseudoindividuals in a way that slots do not because assertions can be made about the object that fills a role without saying what the object is. This is illustrated in Figure 9 using NETL notation. Working animals have an owner role, and circus animals, who are working animals, also have a trainer role. Clyde's trainer is also his owner. The nodes for owner and trainer in Figure 9 are called ROLE nodes in NETL because they define new roles. The nodes for circus animal's owner, Clyde's owner, and Clyde's trainer are called MAP nodes because they denote instances of inherited roles. Clyde is represented by an INDV node, indicating that he is an individual who exists in the world. Although ROLE, MAP, and INDV nodes are all drawn as open circles, they are distinct node types; of these, only INDV nodes assert the existence of real-world objects. The IS-A link from trainer to animal lover indicates that any individual who fills the trainer role of some animal may be inferred to be an animal lover. The double-headed arrow between Clyde's owner and Clyde's trainer, called an EQ link, indicates that the two nodes refer to the same object. Thus, although it may not be known who Clyde's owner is, it can be said that his owner is the same as his trainer, and so by

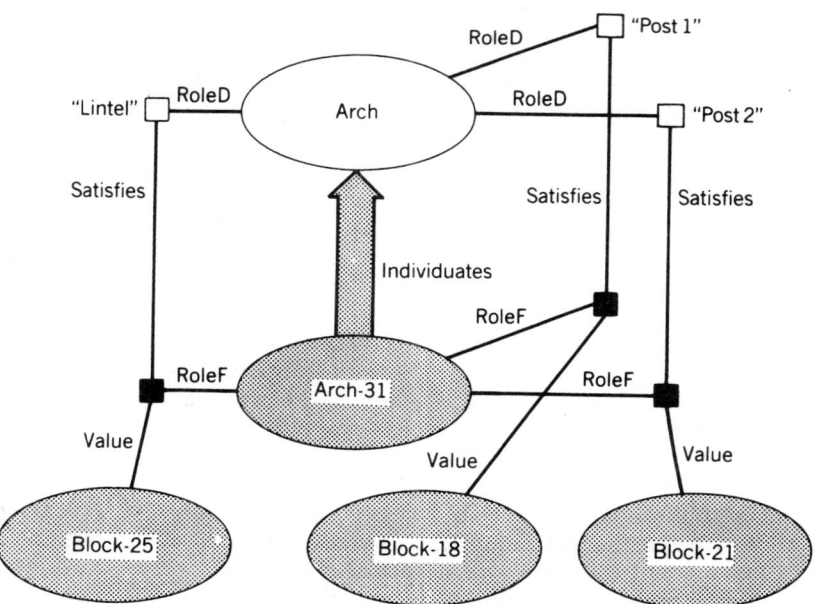

Figure 7. An instance of an arch.

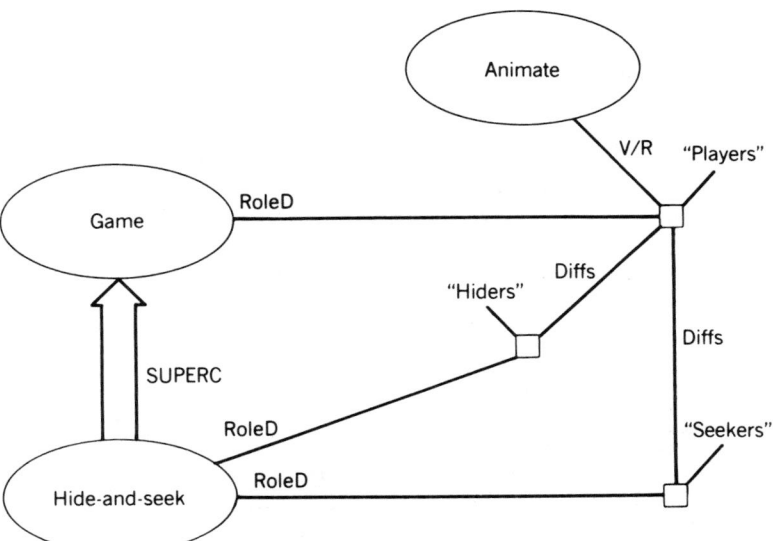

Figure 8. Differentiating a role in KL-ONE.

inheritance it can be deduced that Clyde's owner is an animal lover.

The notion that concepts contain internal structure intrinsic to their definition leads to a different type of inheritance reasoning, one based on matching. Given a hierarchy of concepts, each with its own set of roles and structural descriptions, the goal of a classifier algorithm is to take the description of an object as input and find the most specific concept that describes that object. Thus if there is an object that is a vehicle, has two wheels, and is without a motor, the classifier algorithm will decide that it is not just an instance of a wheeled vehicle, but more specifically, it fits the description of a bicycle. Classifiers are a major use of inheritance in KL-ONE (Schmolze and Lipkis, 1983). Because roles, constraints, and structural descriptions are all inherited, this type of classifier is a form of inheritance reasoner.

SPLITS AND PARTITIONING

It is sometimes useful to split a class into disjoint subclasses, such as splitting living things into animals and plants. Then, if it is known that Clyde is an elephant and an attempt is made to assert that Clyde is a cabbage, the SPLIT node in Figure 10 (NETL notation) will complain. Disjointness constraints can easily be implemented as extensions to a basic inheritance reasoner. Another way to use this information is to figure out, by inheritance, which classes Clyde cannot be a member of: because he is an elephant, he cannot be a plant or any subtype of plant. Parallel marker propagation (described below) is useful for making these types of inferences rapidly.

A split is called a partitioning if all the subclasses are disjoint and their union covers the entire superclass. If cars are partitioned into front-wheel drive, rear-wheel drive, and four-wheel drive models, and one knows that

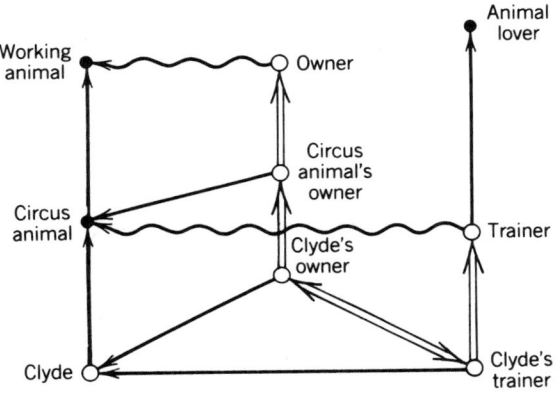

Figure 9. Example of roles in NETL.

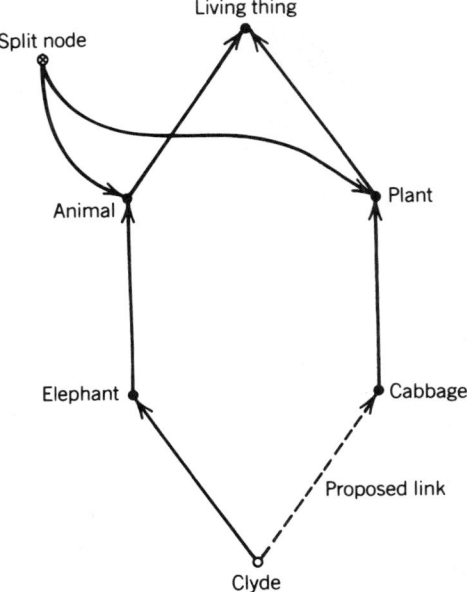

Figure 10. Splitting a class into disjoint subclasses in NETL.

Clyde's car is neither a front-wheel drive car nor a four-wheel drive car, one may conclude that it is a rear-wheel drive car. Although partitioning depends on the inheritance hierarchy to determine class memberships, reasoning about partitionings is more complex than simply taking transitive closures. Given an object lying somewhere in a partition, only when all but one of the subclasses making up the partition have been ruled out can the object be assigned to the remaining one. Partitionings illustrate how, as inheritance languages become richer in expressive power, they become more like logic.

INHERITABLE RELATIONS

Another extension to the inheritance idea allows one to define relations, such as "bigger than," between the members of two classes, and let them be inherited by the respective subclasses and instances (Touretzky, 1986). Thus, when it is asserted that elephants are bigger than rabbits, if it is known that Clyde is an elephant and Joe is a rabbit, it may be inferred that Clyde is bigger than Joe.

Inheritable relations, like inheritable properties, are subject to exceptions. For example, if citizens dislike crooks, but gullible citizens do not dislike elected crooks, then this must be taken into account when reasoning about citizens and crooks. Touretzky (1985) argues that in order to represent relations and their exceptions properly, an explicit representation for negation must first be obtained.

INHERITANCE OF DEMONS

In frame systems the most general form of slot constraint is the demon, or procedural attachment, which is usually just a piece of LISP code. Like other slot information, demons are inherited. The two most common types are IF-NEEDED and IF-ADDED demons. An IF-NEEDED demon will compute slot values as they are needed; this is useful when the values are expensive to compute because values that are not needed will not be computed. Once the demon computes a slot value, it might store it in the slot so that next time the value can be found without invoking the demon. But if the value is expected to change often, the demon might refrain from storing it, so that the demon will be reinvoked every time a request is made for the slot's value.

If one is looking for a value of one of the elephant frame's slots and there is nothing at elephant, mammal, vertebrate, or any higher frame, then one may begin invoking IF-NEEDED demons, starting with those stored at elephant, until one of them returns a value. The order in which demons at various levels of the hierarchy are invoked normally follows the same rules as the algorithm for locating slot values: Start at the bottom and work up the IS-A tree.

IF-ADDED demons are useful for checking for constraint violations by slot fillers and for triggering inference or advisory procedures associated with a frame. For example, the bicycle frame might have an IF-ADDED demon attached to the wheels slot to check the number of fillers; if there are not exactly two wheels, the demon could propose a switch to another frame such as unicycle or tricycle.

Often there is a choice between expressing knowledge procedurally, through demons, or expressing it in a declarative fashion. Consider the number constraint on the bicycle frame's wheels slot. In KL-ONE and SRL, where number constraints are expressed by lists of form (*min max*), the constraint on the wheels slot would be encoded as the list (2 2). Because number constraints are handled directly by the interpreter, it is a trivial operation to add a number constraint to a slot. Furthermore, the declarative representation of number constraints makes them an accessible part of the knowledge base, available for inspection and modification by user-written procedures. If number constraints were implemented as IF-ADDED demons, two penalties would be incurred. It would be necessary to create a separate number constraint demon for every slot to be constrained, which is wasteful of space and fails to capture a significant generalization about number constraints. And, because the *min* and *max* values of each number constraint would be embedded in a piece of LISP code, the constraint information itself would not be directly accessible; it could only be used by the demon in which it was embedded.

In other situations procedural representations are to be preferred. Consider a frame for representing right triangles. The lengths of the three sides of such a triangle are constrained to obey the Pythagorean theorem: the square of the hypotenuse must equal the sum of the squares of the other two sides. Such a constraint would be impossible to express in declarative fashion without extending the slot-restriction language to handle algebraic expressions involving the values of several slots and adding some notation for expressing equality; this would bring with it a corresponding increase in the complexity of the interpreter. In some systems, such as KL-ONE, machinery can be added for expressing almost any sort of restriction in a declarative style, although the interpreter may then become quite complex. In other systems the procedural approach must be used for all but the simplest constraints; yet this is no hindrance because such procedures are easily written (in LISP) and inexpensive to execute. In the late 1970s there was considerable debate over the advantages of each approach to knowledge representation. Winograd (1975) offers a good discussion of what was then called "the procedural/declarative controversy."

PARALLEL-MARKER PROPAGATION

Parallel-marker propagation is an inference technique especially effective in inheritance applications. Historically, it is a refinement of the spreading activation idea introduced by Quillian (1968) in his semantic memory system, one of the earliest semantic networks. Although there has been some discussion of building special-purpose hardware for parallel-marker propagation (Fahlman, 1980), at this point the main attractions of the technique are simplicity and conciseness in expressing inference algorithms.

A parallel-marker propagation machine (PMPM) consists of a collection of simple processors that play the roles of nodes and links in a semantic network. Each processor is provided with a small amount of local memory called marker bits. Processors can set or clear these bits in response to commands received over a broadcast bus. In addition, a processor that acts as a link can copy the state of one of its tail nodes's marker bits to the corresponding bit in its head node, or vice versa. Thus links serve to propagate markers through the network. One of the strengths of the PMPM is that it can compute very fast transitive closures over a given link type, such as IS-A links, because all the processors execute the same commands in parallel.

Figure 11 illustrates how a particular type of market propagation algorithm, called an activation scan, works. Suppose the task is to find out whether Clyde is a mammal. First all the processors are told to clear their marker 1 bit. Then the Clyde node is told to set its market 1 bit, and the result is shown in Figure 11a. Marker 1 is called Clyde's activation mark because it will be used to activate his description in the network. Now a command is broadcast to propagate marker 1 upward across IS-A links, and the result is Figure 11b. When the command is repeated, the result is Figure 11c. Repeating the command one more time does not mark any new nodes, so the transitive closure is complete. Note that the mammal node now bears Clyde's activation mark. This indicates that Clyde is indeed a mammal.

The important thing about marker propagation scans such as the activation scan is that they run in time proportional to the depth of the inheritance graph, independent of the number of nodes in the graph or the fan-out of any particular node. No matter how many facts are learned about Clyde and about elephants, or how many elephants there are in the knowledge base, as long as the depth of the graph does not increase, the knowledge base can be searched in constant time.

INHERITANCE IN PROGRAMMING LANGUAGES

Object-oriented programming languages (qv) such as Simula (Dahl, 1968), SMALLTALK (Borning and Ingalls, 1982), LOOPS (Bobrow and Stefik, 1981), and the LISP Machine flavor system (Weinreb and Moon, 1981) normally organize their object types into a hierarchy. An object type, or class, is essentially a record structure with a set of attached procedures known as methods. Two forms of inheritance take place in these systems. First, a subtype inherits all the components of its parent type's record structure, just as frames inherit all the slots of their parent frame. Second, a subtype inherits all the methods of its parent type, but it can override these methods by supplying methods of its own.

Inheritance in object-oriented programming languages is quite similar to inheritance in frame systems. There is multiple inheritance and a need to represent exceptions, as when a subtype replaces a method of its parent type with one of its own methods. Carnese (1984) gives a detailed account of how these issues are handled in four

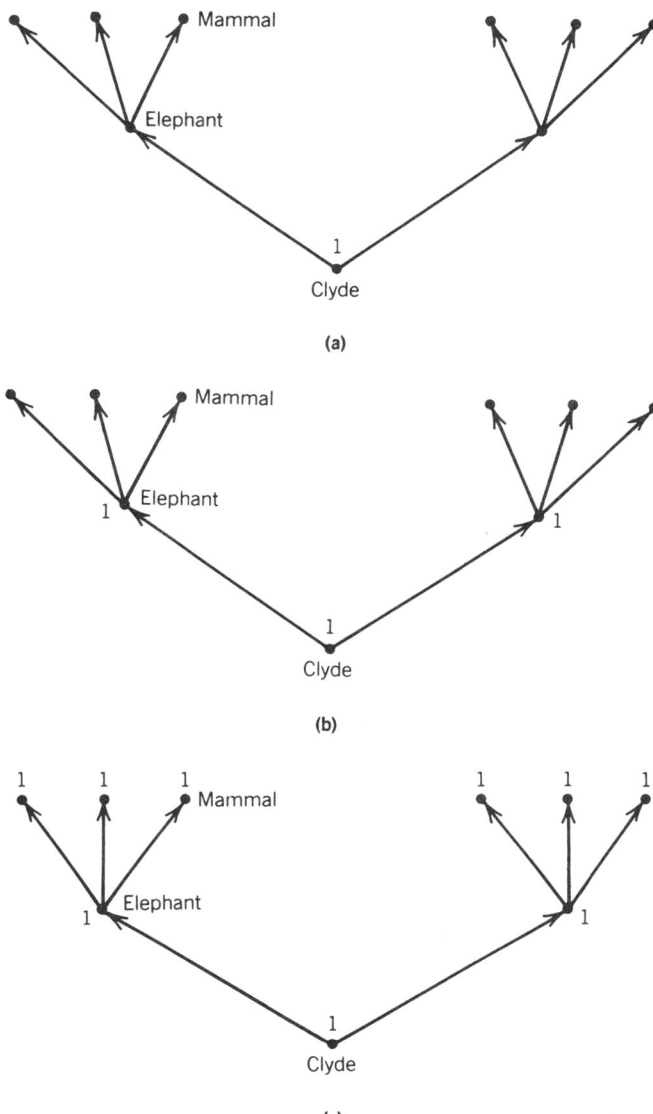

Figure 11. Three steps in the activation scan of Clyde.

contemporary programming languages, and Cardelli (1984) gives a more theoretical account of multiple inheritance in type systems. There are two aspects, though, in which programming language type systems differ from AI inheritance systems. In the latter, although there may be a distinction between classes and individuals, the data structures for the two are similar, as are the primitives for manipulating them. But in object-oriented programming languages there is a sharp distinction between classes and instances. Classes describe things, instances are the things, and the internal representations of the two are entirely different. In AI systems classes are valid objects of discourse, eg, a system can be asked how many legs an elephant has without creating any elephants. In programming languages class definitions have no use except for creating instances. Some languages, such as Simula, do not even provide a way to create or manipulate classes dynamically; the class hierarchy is established by declarations at compile time and remains fixed during the life of the program.

The second aspect in which AI inheritance systems differ from programming language type systems is that only the former are used for default reasoning (qv). The inheritance system is part of the specification of the AI system in which it resides; the behavior of an AI system that does default reasoning depends on the multiple-inheritance algorithm provided and the way exceptions are treated. In contrast, the characteristics of a programming language's type system have no influence on the specifications or behavior of programs written in that language; they are of concern only to the programmer. The inferences made by a programming language's type system merely relieve the programmer from some redundant coding.

BIBLIOGRAPHY

G. Attardi and M. Simi, *Semantics of Inheritance and Attributions in the Description System Omega*, Technical Report AI Memo 642, MIT Artificial Intelligence Laboratory, Cambridge, Mass., 1982.

D. G. Bobrow and M. Stefik, *The LOOPS Manual (preliminary version)*, working paper KB-VLSI-81-13, Xerox Palo Alto Research Center, Aug. 1981.

D. G. Bobrow and T. Winograd, "An Overview of KRL, a Knowledge Representation Language," *Cogn. Sci.* **1**(1), 3–46 (Jan. 1977).

D. G. Bobrow, T. Winograd, and the KRL research group, "Experience with KRL-0: One Cycle of a Knowledge Representation Language," in *Proceedings of the Fifth IJCAI*, Cambridge, Mass., Morgan-Kaufmann, San Mateo, Calif., 1977, pp. 213–222.

A. H. Borning and D. H. H. Ingalls, "Multiple Inheritance in Smalltalk-80," in *Proceedings of the Second National Conference on Artificial Intelligence*, Pittsburgh, Pa., AAAI, Menlo Park, Calif., 1982, pp. 234–237.

R. J. Brachman, "On the Epistemological Status of Semantic Networks," in Findler, 1979, pp. 3–50.

R. J. Brachman, "What IS-A Is and Isn't: An Analysis of Taxonomic Links in Semantic Networks," *IEEE Comput.* **16**(10), 30–36 (Oct. 1983).

R. J. Brachman, *A Structural Paradigm for Representing Knowledge*, Ablex, Norwood, N.J., 1987.

R. J. Brachman, R. E. Fikes, and H. Levesque, "KRYPTON: A Functional Approach to Knowledge Representation," *IEEE Comput.* **16**(10), 67–73 (Oct. 1983).

R. J. Brachman and H. J. Levesque, "The Tractability of Subsumption in Frame-Based Description Languages," in *Proceedings of the Fourth National Conference on Artificial Intelligence*, Austin, Tex., AAAI, Menlo Park, Calif., 1984, pp. 34–37.

R. J. Brachman and J. G. Schmolze, "An Overview of the KL-ONE Knowledge Representation System," *Cogn. Sci.* **9**(2), 171–216 (Apr. 1985).

L. Cardelli, "A Semantics of Multiple Inheritance," in G. Kahn, D. B. MacQueen, and G. Plotkin, eds., *Semantics of Data Types, Lecture Notes in Computer Science*, Vol. 173, Springer-Verlag, New York, 1984, pp. 51–67.

D. J. Carnese, *Multiple Inheritance in Contemporary Programming Languages*, Ph.D. dissertation, MIT, Cambridge, Mass., 1984.

O. Dahl, *Simula 67 Common Base Language*, Technical report, Norwegian Computing Center, Oslo, 1968.

Department of Defense, *Reference Manual for the Ada Programming Language*, Ada Joint Program Office, Washington, D.C., 1982.

D. Etherington and R. Reiter, "On Inheritance Hierarchies with Exceptions," in *Proceedings of the Third National Conference on Artificial Intelligence*, Washington, D.C., AAAI, Menlo Park, Calif., 1983, 104–108.

S. E. Fahlman, *NETL: A System for Representing and Using Real-World Knowledge*, MIT Press, Cambridge, Mass., 1979.

S. E. Fahlman, "Design Sketch for a Million-Element NETL machine," in *Proceedings of the First National Conference on Artificial Intelligence*, Stanford, Calif., AAAI, Menlo Park, Calif., 1980, pp. 249–252.

N. V. Findler, ed., *Associative Networks: Representation and Use of Knowledge by Computers*, Academic Press, Inc., New York, 1979.

P. J. Hayes, "In Defence of Logic," in *Proceedings of the Fifth IJCAI*, Cambridge, Mass., Morgan-Kaufmann, San Mateo, Calif., 1977, pp. 559–565.

P. J. Hayes, "The Logic of Frames," in B. L. Webber and N. J. Nilsson, eds., *Readings in Artificial Intelligence*, Tioga, Palo Alto, Calif., 1979, pp. 451–458.

C. Hewitt, G. Attardi, and M. Simi, "Knowledge Embedding in the Description System OMEGA," in Fahlman, 1980, pp. 157–164.

D. Israel, "The Role of Logic in Knowledge Representation," *IEEE Comput.* **16**(10), 37–41 (Oct. 1983).

D. V. McDermott and J. Doyle, "Non-Monotonic Logic," *Artif. Intell.* **13**(1–2), 41–72 (Apr. 1980).

M. L. Minsky, "A Framework for Representing Knowledge," in P. H. Winston, ed., *The Psychology of Computer Vision*, McGraw-Hill Book Co., Inc., New York, 1975, Chap. 6.

N. J. Nilsson, *Principles of Artificial Intelligence*, Tioga, Palo Alto, Calif., 1980.

M. R. Quillian, "Semantic Memory," in M. L. Minsky, ed., *Semantic Information Processing*, MIT Press, Cambridge,, Mass., 1968, pp. 227–270.

R. Reiter, "A Logic for Default Reasoning," *Artif. Intell.* **13**(1–2), 81–132 (Apr. 1980).

R. B. Roberts and I. P. Goldstein, *The FRL Manual*, Technical report AI memo 409, MIT Artificial Intelligence Laboratory, Cambridge, Mass., June 1977.

J. F. Schmolze and T. A. Lipkis, "Classification in the KL-ONE Knowledge Representation System," in *Proceedings of the Eighth IJCAI*, Karlsruhe, FRG, Morgan-Kaufmann, San Mateo, Calif., 1983, pp. 330–332.

D. S. Touretzky, "Implicit Ordering of Defaults in Inheritance Systems," in Brachman and Levesque, 1984, pp. 322–325.

D. S. Touretzky, "Inheritable Relations: A Natural Extension to Inheritance Hierarchies," in *Proceedings of the CSCSI/SCEIO Workshop on Theoretical Approaches to Natural Language Understanding*, Halifax, N.S., May 1985, pp. 55–60.

D. S. Touretzky, *The Mathematics of Inheritance Systems*, Morgan-Kaufmann, San Mateo, Calif., 1986.

D. Weinreb and D. Moon, *Lisp Machine Manual*, MIT Artificial Intelligence Laboratory, Cambridge, Mass., 1981.

T. Winograd, "Frame Representations and the Declarative-Procedural Controversy," in D. G. Bobrow and A. Collins, eds., *Rep-*

resentation and Understanding, Academic Press, Inc., New York, 1975, pp. 185–210.

T. Winograd, "Extended Inference Modes in Reasoning by Computer Systems," *Artif. Intell.* 3(1–2), 5–26 (Apr. 1980).

J. M. Wright and M. S. Fox, SRL/1.5 User Manual, Technical report, Robotics Institute, Carnegie Mellon University, Pittsburgh, Pa., 1983.

General References

R. J. Brachman, "On the Epistemological Status of Semantic Networks," in R. J. Brachman and H. J. Levesque, eds., *Readings in Knowledge Representation,* Morgan-Kaufmann, San Mateo, Calif., 1985, pp. 191–215.

J. G. Carbonell, "Default Reasoning and Inheritance Mechanisms on Type Hierarchies," in *Proceedings of the Workshop on Data Abstraction, Databases and Conceptual Modelling,* Pingree Park, Colo., June 1980, pp. 107–109.

Minsky, 1975.

D. S. TOURETZKY
Carnegie Mellon University

INSPECTION

While touring a manufacturing plant, we met the three women inspecting the O-rings produced there. Each would grab a handful, spread them in their hands under a magnifier, and pick a few for the trash drum. When asked about training, the manager said, "No training. The ladies are just asked to pick out the bad ones." Visual inspection is like that. Almost everything subject to being sold, man-made or natural, is subject to visual inspection. There could be nothing neater for AI. The domain is usually well restricted, system performance is easy to score, and the best electromechanical engineering fails to accomplish what humans accomplish on pure heuristic grounds.

In contrast to the usual paucity of interesting AI problems, there are tens of thousands of interesting and important domains in industrial and commercial machine vision. There have already been thousands of attempts to have cameras see (Bachelor and co-workers, 1988; Cielo, 1988). The earliest visual inspection systems were developed for glass packaging in the 1950s to detect foreign material in returnable bottles after cleaning (Cielo, 1988). The success of this simple application led to a desire to detect glass cracking in the manufacture of baby food jars (Cielo, 1988; Wilder, 1989). In glass bottle manufacture, physicists concluded that no amount of process engineering could entirely eliminate cracking glass. Bad jars had to be culled out. This is still one of the most challenging areas, because humans are still employed to inspect for cracks as the bottles move relative to a light. Cracks too tiny to measure quickly are easy to see in specular (mirrorlike) reflection, yet no machine vision system to date has been able to see cracks in precisely this way. The problem is not so much seeing the cracks as missing those things that have specular ridges but are not cracks. Most bottles are molded, and the parting lines look like cracks.

There are two principal definitions of inspection which have entirely different consequences for AI (Thibadeau, 1990). One can define inspection as the problem of detecting and classifying defects, ie, seeing a crack, chip, or fisheye distortion. Or, one can decide that the problem is that of seeing the jar, and subtracting anything that is not a quality of good "jar-ness." The first approach is called defect description, and the second is product description. The best inspection systems, on economic grounds, are those that find defects, because they, explicitly or implicitly, have good models of the product.

The role for model-based computer vision is thus clearly laid out but, unfortunately, difficult to fund. The fault lies at least in part in how inspection problems are presented to scientists. The basic quality-control (QC) regimen is to list classes of defect along with severity. This has put pressure on machine vision suppliers to respond with devices that only detect the described defects. A natural consequence of such misdirection is that an inspection system, once installed and accepted as meeting the QC specification, may later be rejected on the grounds that it does not detect some defects that are obvious to the human evaluator. On one occasion, this author voiced such reservations about defect detectors to a group of 18 engineers working on a large-scale inspection project, only to receive a phone call from one of them two years later stating, "It is finally installed, and now that they see what it is doing, they want to change the spec! It isn't the size of the 'mouse bite;' it's the density of them, they think."

One of the most common types of inspection is pattern-free, where the model of the product is perfect uniformity. Pinhole detectors in sheet metal fall into this class. This is also a class where the model is implicit in the design of the device. The model is not explicitly described and compared with the input data. Inspection systems with implicit models are not interesting from an AI perspective, because they cannot adapt qualitatively. But, aspects of an otherwise uninteresting inspection system can be explicit: the pinhole detection systems that classify defects can be interesting because the systems have active models for the defect classes grounded in pattern and context.

PROBLEM SOLVING

The prototypical method for investigating artificial intelligence with respect to a domain of activities is to identify the areas where problem solving, particularly heuristic problem solving, becomes important. Problem-solving activities most significantly exist in the problem of developing the manufacturing process. The QC specifications exist not only for the purpose of culling bad product but also for process engineering. For inspection to be adaptive, it must address problem solving about process problems. Current conditions for manufacture, including perhaps supplier information, voltage levels, time of year, and materials variability, all enter the equation. In the case of the question of "mouse bites" in printed circuit boards, the problem solving that needs to be addressed is one of selecting which quality of mouse bites causes electrical failure in the finished boards. Because these circuits are buried inside the Fiberglas, if mouse bites had no effect, neither QC nor management would care. If inspection devices are not connected to information about the final success or failure of the product there is little opportunity to design artificial intelligence into them.

Problem-solving activity enters in a number of places in inspection. To see how, consider the canonical broad meaning of inspection to include all the applications of industrial machine vision. Industrial machine vision is employed for four major purposes:

- Identification.
- Flaw detection.
- Measurement.
- Causal assignment.

Identification includes classification and the problem of deciding what something is, where it is, or both. Flaw detection involves deciding whether something is wrong with the product. Measurement involves assigning calibrated (referenced) spatial extents, sometimes for the purposes of identification or flaw detection and sometimes for other purposes such as feed forward information flow to control process parameters (correcting for potential flaws). Causal assignment is rarely practiced but involves a visual decision to assign blame for an identified flaw, a detected flaw, or a measurement.

Printed circuit board inspection is a good area for study (Thibadeau, 1985a). Figure 1 shows some of the basic objects, called pads and lines, and their attributes, which define the identification problem. Pads and lines are not always easy to see because they can overlap in different ways. The fill areas are made by painting lines, for exam-

ple. In printed wiring board inspection, systems that inspect for the forms irrespective of position are called *design rule systems,* whereas those that inspect for the position of every object are called *reference systems* (Danielsson and Kruse, 1979; West and co-workers, 1982; Thibadeau, 1985b; Mitchell and co-workers, 1986).

Flaw detection involves finding defects that are considered bad by process engineering. All manufactured products have defects. From year to year the defects that can be eliminated by improved process engineering will change. Only defects that should not appear or that will cause functional failure of the product are considered worth inspecting. Lines in printed circuits can also form alphabet characters. Alphabetic characters have no electrical consequences, but they must be readable.

Recognizing the good parts of a circuit board is not always easy even if the positions of all the entities are known. This is particularly the case in the presence of defects. The defects may not be bad enough to cause rejection but may substantially impact the ease of recognition. The first objective of the inspection system is to label the objects in view. Often problem-solving strategies can be constructed around this labeling objective, but usually labeling is left to constraint satisfaction strategies.

For printed circuit boards, measurements must be made to evaluate whether a defect exists. Most lines are permitted to be 10% wider or thinner than designed, because this cannot be controlled well and does not appreciably affect performance. Measurement can be employed for labeling. A pad can be oblong only to a certain extent before it must be regarded as a line. It is important to properly distinguish such labels because these have functional consequences. Lines that are too thin and do not end in pads may signal alphabetic characters, not circuit components. Measurement is also used to advantage in closing feedback loops, such as the temperature of an acid bath or the duration of the applied treatment. In a significant study it was demonstrated that there is a need for a great deal of top-down knowledge in order to refine measurement (Mitchell and co-workers, 1986). There are also qualitative defects that are defects because the shapes, not just the attributes, are different. Figure 2 shows some typical qualitative defects.

The importance of causal assignment and the many interesting ways to achieve it are well illustrated in printed wiring board inspection. Figure 3 provides a simplified process diagram. More details are available from the Institute for Interconnecting and Packaging Electronic Circuits (Lincolnwood, Ill.). Each rectangle corresponds to one or more machines. Each machine can, by functioning improperly, create defects. The defects are either process defects (the products are defective) or product defects (the wrong products come out). Visual inspection devices can be inserted into a number of places in the fabrication path. This helps to reduce considerably the inference problem in determining where the process failed and may have direct economic consequences in trapping bad product while rework is still possible. However, a failure in a visual inspection device can cause process or product defects too. Thus, it is important to minimize the num-

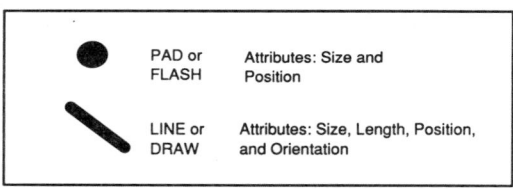

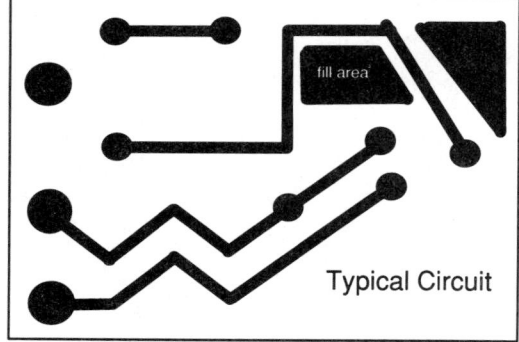

Figure 1. Simplified components of a circuit board and a typical circuit made of those components. Drill holes are made in pads, component leads are soldered into pads, and lines are the wires that connect the components.

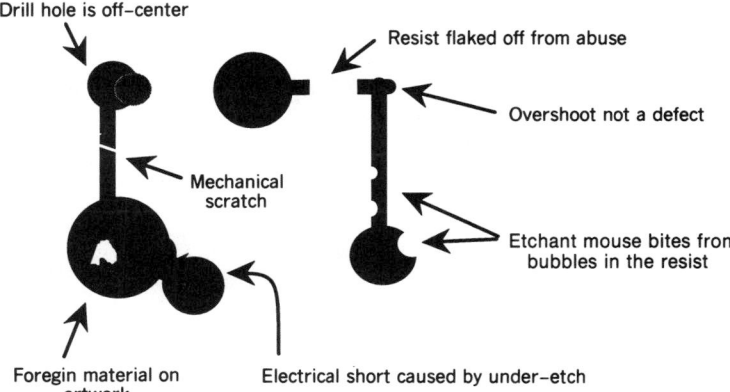

Figure 2. Some types of flaws common to printed circuit boards.

ber of inspections while maximizing effective causal inference.

Among the many thousands of inspection systems in manufacturing today, none can be classified as embodying AI methodologies: the problem solving is largely implicit. In most inspection devices, all the problem solving was done by the engineer who designed the device. For example, a classic demonstration reads speedometers to confirm that they are reading speed within tolerance. The inspection device uses precise mechanical fixturing and a digi-

tizing camera with electronics and programming to read the position of the dial arm. For rotary dial arms, a conversion from image pixel coordinates to polar coordinates is commonly used in order to make the algorithm for reading speed transparent; ie, the rotation of the dial becomes a translation in a rectangular coordinate image (details available from ITRAN Corp., Manchester, N.H.). Similar polar coordinate transformation hardware is employed in inspecting bottle caps for radial symmetry. Note that the engineers, not the machines, determined that radial com-

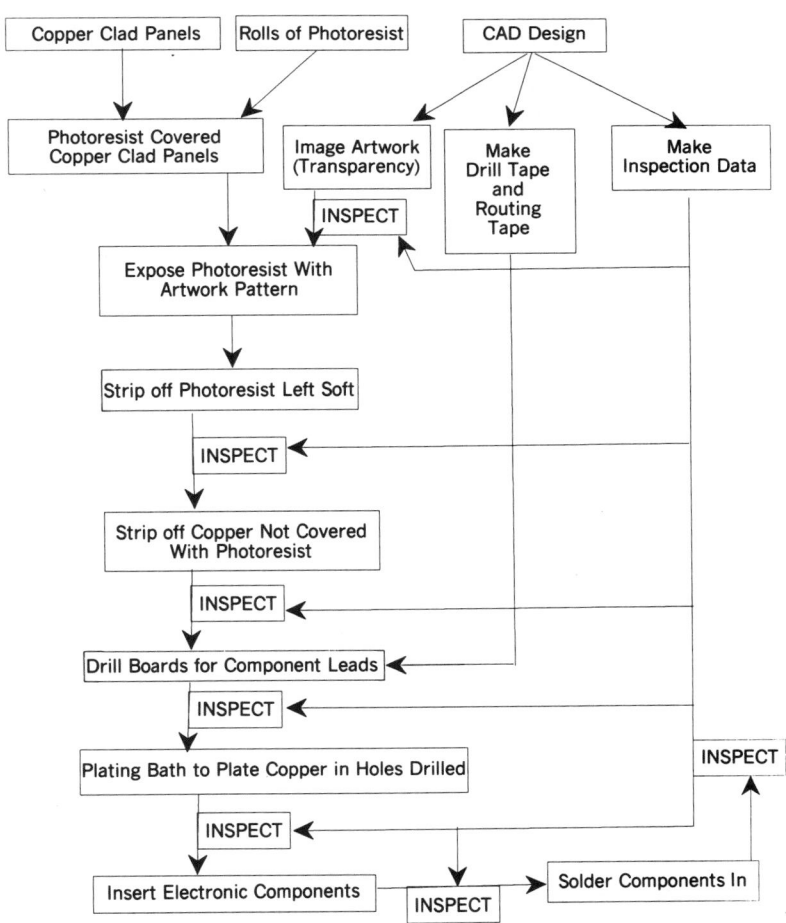

Figure 3. Highly simplified printed wiring board fabrication cycle. Each rectangle is a machine (possibly manned) that can be the cause for a production defect. Transportation between machines can also cause production defects.

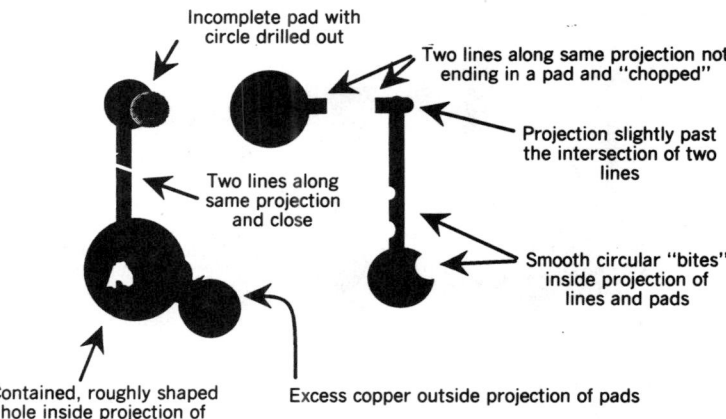

Incomplete pad with circle drilled out

Two lines along same projection not ending in a pad and "chopped"

Projection slightly past the intersection of two lines

Two lines along same projection and close

Smooth circular "bites" inside projection of lines and pads

Figure 4. Examples of production rules that detect causes of defects.

Contained, roughly shaped hole inside projection of pad

Excess copper outside projection of pads

putations were useful and appropriate. More importantly, the process engineers specified the inspection task to such great detail that it became an exercise in engineering to construct the inspection equipment. In effect, the richness of the pictorial information available to the computer is ignored by the algorithms that operate on that information. This is a great loss of potential manufacturing input that is well recongized.

Although it is obvious that this is probably the case for measurement, flaw detection, and perhaps identification, it is somewhat surprising to find that causal assignment can be engineered as well. In one study (Thibadeau, 1985b; Thibadeau and Gabrick, 1986), a simple set of 15 production rules was found effective in assigning causes of defects in printed circuit boards. The production rules are easy to construct: a detected defect shows up as a region of ill-formed copper (Figure 4). The adjacencies of that region to other regions (either good copper regions (lines or pads) or pinhole regions) can easily be computed.

Process engineers cite the cause for a defect by visual inspection alone most of the time. These 15 production rules perform about as well. Once the visual appearance of a cause is learned, problem solving ceases. This finding concurs with other literature which has shown that causation can be directly perceived on visual attributes alone (Leyton, 1989). Leyton's study is sound, although it contains an erroneous assumption that only living objects can cause defects, and that man-made objects are "dead" and do not "grow" and "evolve." Just as the letter "a" can be recognized by its shape, the causation of an acid bath defect in printed circuit manufacture can be recognized by malformations in the shape of the circuits (Thibadeau, 1985b).

This common observation can help in building interesting machine vision devices, and it also has a profound implication for AI: that a device can look to learn visual appearances of causation. Problem solving about appearance can be done in the presence of knowledge about the conditions and consequences of manufacture. It is important, then, that a device to involve AI requires information about manufacturing conditions and consequences as well as product performance. Thus, with the help of

information about product success and manufacturing conditions and consequences, heuristic problem-solving activities can be identified in product identification, measurement, defect description, and causal assignment.

EXPLICIT MODELS OF PROCESS

The topic becomes more interesting as inspection devices are pushed further into the domain of process engineering. Intelligent inspection devices must then incorporate models of the machines that produce the products, and, in order to aid in refining the manufacturing processes, they must also incorporate explicit models of their own behavior. An incomplete but suggestive list of the knowledge and adaptability required of such devices is provided below. For a detailed treatment of the learning-by-watching paradigm, see Constant and co-workers, (1990).

Problem Solving in Model of Machine

Purpose of machine. Did machine achieve purpose?

Actions, Consequences, Side effects. Did action have a consequence? Did action have an undesirable side effect?

Problem Solving in Model of Inspection Device

Repeatable measurements.

Significant feature selection.

Simple and complex class formation.

Class discriminability judgments.

Discovery of class-defect category relationships.

Discovery of reasons for measurement failures.

Discovery of class-cause relationships.

BIBLIOGRAPHY

B. C. Bachelor, D. A. Will, and D. C. Hodgson, *Automated Visual Inspection,* IFS, Ltd., Bedford, UK, 1988.

R. Cielo, *Optical Techniques for Industrial Inspection,* Academic Press, Inc., San Diego, Calif., 1988.

P. Constant, S. Matwin, and F. Oppacher, "LEW: Learning by Watching," *IEEE Trans. Patt. Anal. Mach. Intell. PAMI* **12**(3), 294–308 (1990).

P. Danielsson and B. Kruse, "Distance-checking algorithms," *Compute Graph. Image Proc.* **9**(12), (1979).

M. Leyton, "Inferring Causal History from Shape," *Cogn. Sci.* **13**(3), 357–388 (1989).

R. O. Mitchell, E. P. Lyvers, K. A. Dunkelherger, and M. L. Akey, "Recent Results in Precision Measurements of Edges, Angles, Areas, and Perimeters," in *Proceedings of SPIE Conference 730, Automated Inspection and Measurement*, Cambridge, Mass., Oct. 1986.

R. Thibadeau, "The State of the Art in Printed Wiring Board Inspection," in *Proceedings of the SPIE Conference on Applications of Digital Image Processing VII*, Vol. 504, 1985a, pp. 85–90.

R. Thibadeau, "Automated Visual Inspection as Skilled Perception," in *Proceedings of the SME Vision Conference*, 1985b, pp. 5:1–5:19.

R. Thibadeau, "Commerce and Research in Machine Vision for Print/Packaging," *J. Packaging Tech.* **4**(1), 21–24 (1990).

R. Thibadeau and J. Gabrick, "Intelligent Visual Inspection Machines," in *Proceedings of the SPIE International Conference on Automatic Inspection Measurement*, 1986.

G. A. W. West, L. Norton-Wayne, and W. J. Hill, "The Automatic Visual Inspection of Printed Wiring Boards," *Circuit World* **8**(2), 50–56 (1982).

J. Wilder, "Finding and Evaluating Defects in Glass," in H. Freeman, ed., *Machine Vision for Inspection and Measurement*, Academic Press, Inc., San Francisco, 1989.

ROBERT H. THIBADEAU
Carnegie Mellon University

INTELLECT

A commercial natural language database interface program by AICorp. INTELLECT, formally introduced in 1981, was based on the ROBOT research system. INTELLECT extended the linguistic approach taken in ROBOT by dealing with hierarchical, network, and relational database management systems simultaneously. INTELLECT also interfaced to teleprocessing monitors and graphics systems. INTELLECT was one of the first commercially deployed AI systems and is still one of the most widely used. (See *INTELLECT Reference Manual*, AICorp, Waltham, Mass.)

LARRY R. HARRIS
AICorp, Inc.

INTELLECTICS

The term artificial intelligence first appeared in a project proposal submitted by J. McCarthy, M. Minsky, and C. Shannon to the Rockefeller Foundation in 1956, proposing to hold the (now famous) Dartmouth Conference (McCorduck, 1979). McCarthy had in mind to denote the object of study with this term. As the name of the scientific field concerned with these studies, he later proposed the term *cognology*. This name appears in the title of a talk McCarthy gave at a conference held in Repino (near Leningrad) in 1977. Earlier, it was used by A. Bundy in the title of a trip report in 1976 (according to a private communication). Whatever the reasons, the term *artificial intelligence* came into use for the object of study as well as the name of the field. The term has since been the cause of controversy.

Part of this debate is concerned with the apparent anthropomorphism that attributes to machines a capacity, namely intelligence, thought to be genuinely human. This concern is not well justified because a proper distinction is made in the term by the adjective *artificial* (but there remains an irrational component in the argument).

People with a good sense for language are more concerned with the confusion made by the term of the studied object with the field itself. Imagine if botany, the field studying plants, was just called plants or man was used instead of anthropology. It is for exactly this reason that McCarthy chose different names for the field and the object. He may not have made the best choice of a good name for the field.

The community is aware of these problems and, therefore, tends to substitute artificial intelligence with AI. Many people, especially those with some sense left for a good use of natural language, agree that this exciting area deserves a better name than AI.

For these reasons, in 1980, *intellectics* was suggested as a new name for the field that studies artificial and natural intelligence (Bibel, 1980). This name seems like a perfect construction. In contains the object of studies, intelligence, in the root of the word. It is reminiscent of the intellect, which may be thought of as the machinery in man that produces intelligence, and thus quite appropriately covers what is done in the field. Finally, it implicitly emphasizes both aspects, artificial and human.

For the latter reason, intellectics suggests the union of the fields of artificial intelligence and cognitive science, which recently have experienced a friction that is unfortunate for both communities (and may even to some extent be caused by the lack of an appropriate name for the entire field).

A major problem with the current situation is the fact that the researchers working in intellectics have no name (other than terrible constructs such as AI-ticians). Intellecticians follows common usage in other fields such as mathematics.

There are few things in the world that are absolutely perfect, a rule that also applies to the name *intellectics*. For one, the word's radical is of Latin origin whereas the suffix derives from Greek. Such a combination has precedences and should not be the cause of much worry, however. Intellectics also does not explicitly include a connotation that accounts for the importance of the senses for intelligence. But this is only because the original meaning of the Latin word *intellegere* has shifted somewhat over time. It certainly does not exclude a role for the senses in this context.

In any case, no term, however good, will ever become perfect unless it is used by the community, and a bad term like AI will not become better through continuous use. At the point of writing there are a number of institutions in Europe that have adopted the term intellectics, among them the French Association pour la Recherche Cognitive, which carries the term in its statutes and the universities Technische Universität München and Technische Hochschule Darmstadt, which use it officially for naming the field.

BIBLIOGRAPHY

W. Bibel, "'Intellektik' statt 'KI'—Ein Ernstgemeinter Vorschlag," *Rundbrief der Fachgruppe Künstliche Intelligenz in der Gesellschaft für Informatik* **22,** 15–16 (Dec. 1980).

P. McCorduck, *Machines Who Think*, W. H. Freeman, San Francisco, 1979.

WOLFGANG BIBEL
Technical University of
Darmstadt

INTELLIGENCE, HUMAN

Modern, systematic study of human intelligence began in the mid-1800s. The first such work was conducted by Sir Francis Galton. Galton's view of intelligence was that it distinguished those individuals who had genius (eg, demonstrated by making contributions to science, literature, and art) from normal individuals. His thesis was that men of genius had sense of insight, a better command of knowledge, and so on. Given an assumption that all knowledge must be processed by the senses (such as by sight or hearing), those individuals demonstrating genius must have more refined sensory and motor faculties. Thus, Galton argued, intelligence could be measured by assessing constructs such as visual acuity, reaction time, pitch discrimination, and the like. However, even though a great volume of data was collected on the psychophysical abilities of individuals, no evidence for a general association of genius with those abilities was found.

A great amount of attention, something on the order of 7,000 articles and books were published on intelligence as of 1968 (U.S. Department of Health, Education, and Welfare, 1968), has been given to defining, describing, predicting, and understanding human intelligence in the 100 yr since Galton's investigation of the concept. Early research in this century was primarily devoted to examining intelligence as a single broad construct. More recent study has focused on particular facets and components of intelligence. Several threads of thought have consistently remained central to these investigations. These fundamental issues and findings are discussed in detail below.

DEFINING INTELLIGENCE

Intelligence can be viewed as composed of many facets, or can be defined as a global concept. For example, one theorist (Buckingham, 1921) suggested simply that intelligence "is the ability to learn." On the other hand, other theorists have claimed that intelligence is more complex than such a restricted definition. Binet and Simon (1961) the developers of the first modern test of intelligence, suggested that intelligence represented "judgement, otherwise called good sense, practical sense, initiative, the faculty of adapting one's self to circumstances." The key concept for these and most other definitions regards adaptation of the individual to the demands of the environment. From a broad perspective, approaches to defining and measuring intelligence are concerned with assessing the mechanisms for learning and the results of learning (whether in terms of declarative knowledge, ie, knowledge about things, or procedural knowledge, ie, knowledge of how to do things). A few general approaches to defining intelligence are reviewed.

Global Theories of Intelligence

Humphreys (1979) has given a broad definition of intelligence that adequately summarizes the character of the construct. He states that "intelligence is the resultant of the processes of acquiring, storing in memory, retrieving, combining, comparing, and using in new contexts information and conceptual skills; it is an abstraction." In this framework, intelligence is seen as a product of, rather than the mechanisms for, the processes of learning. In a sense Humphreys has described the individual's repertoire for reasoned, purposeful thought and action. Intelligence from this perspective is the foundation on which all new information is sensed, perceived, integrated, and ultimately acted on.

However, it is important to keep in mind a perspective of intelligence that is somewhat relativistic. As Jensen (1976) points out (at least in regard to the measurement of intelligence), cultural and historical influences put constraints on the view of what intelligence is. Jensen states that in a hunting-based society, intelligence might be defined as involving visual acuity and "running speed, rather than vocabulary and symbol manipulation." Societal influences help focus the concept of what represents intelligence and intelligent behavior. For example, current views of intelligence in Western civilization tend to emphasize structured reasoning over more flexible, and less accessible, concepts of creativity and innovation. Perhaps 50 or 100 yr from now, the emphasis may change. From this perspective the definition of intelligence represents a cultural consensus. Certainly, in everyday life, attributions that people make about the intelligence of others reflect such generalizations (Sternberg, 1985b).

More specificity regarding a definition of intelligence follows from the pragmatic outlook provided by Boring (1961) some 70 yr ago. Boring stated that "intelligence as a measurable capacity must at the start be defined as the capacity to do well on an intelligence test." On the surface, this definition may sound entirely circular; however, this is not the case. In fact, Boring's definition may be a nearly optimal way of demonstrating just what intelligence involves. That is, this view gives impetus to discussing the pragmatics of what intelligence does consist of.

Omnibus intelligence tests have changed little (at least in terms of the general form of contents) in the 80 or so years since the original measures were developed by Binet and Simon (1961). For example, the Wechsler Adult Intelligence Scale (Wechsler, 1955) contains the following components:

1. *Information*. For this component, the examinees must answer questions regarding the environment they live in, including questions about history, geography, and well-known pieces of literature.

2. *Picture Completion*. In this subtest, examinees must examine a series of figures and determine what component must be added to each figure to make the figure complete (a veridical representation of some object).

3. *Digit Span*. For this test of memory facility examinees are given series of numbers (of different lengths) that they are required to repeat back to the examiner; two methods are used in determining the span of memory: the first requires examinees to repeat back the numbers in the order in which they are given and the second requires examinees to repeat back the numbers in a reverse-order sequence.

4. *Picture Arrangement*. This subtest requires examinees to infer, from a set of separate animated panels, what the correct (ie, logical and consistent) temporal order of the panels should be.

5. *Vocabulary*. This is a free-form test of the examinees' command of word meanings; the examiner calls out words, and the examinees give definitions of the words.

6. *Block Design*. In this subtest, examinees must manipulate a set of patterned blocks into configurations designated by given figures; the test taps both spatial visualization and spatial manipulation.

7. *Arithmetic*. This subtest contains word problems involving mental addition, subtraction, multiplication, and division calculations.

8. *Object Assembly*. In this subtest, several puzzle pieces must be put together to complete a figure.

9. *Comprehension*. Here, questions regarding relatively universal concepts must be answered; some of these questions require the interpretation of common sayings.

10. *Digit-Symbol*. In this subtest, examinees must remember (or look up) an arbitrary set of associations between a series of digits and novel symbols; examinees fill in a table of digits with the associated symbols as fast as possible.

11. *Similarities*. In this test, examinees are required to determine the underlying constructs that are common to two objects or concepts.

Without attending to the actual structure of intelligence (ie, the variety of broad and specific intellectual abilities, which will be discussed in detail below), this set of subtests should illustrate the dependence on assessing information retrieval, reasoning, word meanings, concept understanding, facility with memory, spatial visualization, and so on that takes place in most intelligence tests. In this respect, the positions of many researchers are in agreement regarding a definition of intelligence, from both theoretical and pragmatic perspectives.

STRUCTURE OF INTELLIGENCE

While most theorists agree on the defining characteristics of the global construct of intelligence, historically there has been a great deal of conceptual dispute regarding the structure of intelligence. At one end of the continuum some theorists claim that intelligence is a single amorphous construct. At the other end of the continuum of thought are theorists that maintain that there are as many as 180 different, and relatively independent sources of intellectual abilities (Guilford, 1988). Any general depiction of intelligence requires a discussion of these schools of thought, along with a comparison of the various divergent theories.

General Intelligence and Primary Mental Abilities

The first comprehensive theory of intelligence was put forth by Spearman (1904) who maintained, on the basis of patterns of individual differences on a variety of intellectual ability tests (such as those described above), two underlying aspects of intelligence could be found. The first aspect was general intelligence (or *g*). General intelligence was implied from examination of universally positive correlations (ie, similar rank orderings of individuals across tests) among tests requiring mental processing. That is, the factor (or construct) of general intelligence represented the common variance shared by different mental tests. The amount of common variance shared by two measures is described by the magnitude of Pearson Product-Moment Correlations (McNemar, 1969). When it is possible to predict, to some degree, a person's relative standing on one test from knowledge about the person's relative standing on another test, the two tests will have a nonzero correlation, and the tests will be said to have common variance. The fact that all such mental tests revealed positive intercorrelations provided the justification for the construct of general intelligence. For Spearman, the direct inference from these intercorrelations is that the concept of intelligence represents some type of mental energy that determines performance across a wide variety of tasks that are ostensibly dependent on mental operations (to one degree or another).

The positive correlations among tests, though, was not perfect (ie, proportion of shared variance of less than 1.0). This feature of the data led Spearman to maintain that there are specific abilities in addition to general intelligence that are identified with the unique variance of individual tests. Spearman thus posited that any mental test could be decomposed into variance associated with general intelligence and variance associated with that test's specific ability.

While this description of the structure of intelligence was elegant, there were problems in terms of agreement with the data, especially with respect to tests (of similar content or format) that correlated with each other more than would be predicted on the basis of each test's correlation with general intelligence. Thurstone (1938) found that different common intellectual abilities could be found to coalesce from a wide sampling of mental tests. That is, rather than a single mental engine as the sole nonunique determining factor of mental test scores, there appeared to be a small set of primary mental abilities. Through many empirical investigations of human intelligence, Thurstone identified several primary abilities (or factors) that were revealed by common variance shared by mental tests. These abilities were identified as number, visualizing, memory, word fluency, verbal relations, perceptual speed, induction, and deduction.

The initial thrust of this work by Thurstone and his colleagues was on the relatively independent nature of these primary abilities. That is, rather than inferring that individuals either had more or less general intelligence, Thurstone inferred that a profile (or complete view of the relative strengths and weaknesses) of individuals revealed a more precise picture of intelligence. In this view, intelligence was not a single entity, but could be manifest with different capabilities in various domains. For example, a person could be relatively gifted in the number facility but at the same time have an average ability level in terms of verbal relations or perceptual speed.

Further research by Thurstone (1948) demonstrated that general intelligence could be ultimately revealed by examination of the correlations among the primary mental abilities. That is, there is common variance shared by the abilities that implies a general intellectual ability at a higher level of abstraction. This finding, then, indicated that there is some aspect of intelligence that shows that individuals high or low on any particular ability should show relative levels on other abilities that are also high or low, respectively. However, the fact that the correlations between these primary mental abilities are moderate in magnitude leads to a conclusion that intelligence is not uniquely an amorphous mental engine, but may be thought of as a capability that may be expressed in specific ways that do not directly imply superiority on all things intellectual.

Facet and Hierarchical Theories

The discovery of several common intellectual abilities (ie, common to several test measures) led to other developments regarding the mapping out the structure of intelligence. On the one hand, efforts by Guilford (1967, 1988) and his colleagues brought about a fragmented model of intelligence that contains 180 different abilities. On the other hand efforts by a variety of researchers (Burt, 1949; Vernon, 1961; Horn and Cattell, 1966; Cattell, 1963; Horn, 1968; Humphreys, 1979) have focused on describing the interrelations between abilities of varying levels of generality and specificity. Each line of though is important to understanding what the structure of intelligence is, and each will be discussed in turn.

The descriptive framework of intelligence put forth by Guilford has been called the structure of intellect model. Guilford (1982) has maintained that the basic nature of

any specific intellectual ability can be represented by placement in a three-dimensional array of facets. The dimensions considered fundamental (along with the categories in each dimension) are as follows (Guilford, 1988):

Operations—what the respondent does. These include cognition, memory (recording and retention), divergent production (prominent in creative activity), convergent production, and evaluation.
Contents—the nature of the materials or information on which operations are performed. These include visual, auditory, symbolic (eg, letters, numbers), semantic (eg, words), and behavioral (information about other person's behavior, attitudes, needs, etc.)
Products—the form in which information is processed by the respondent. Products are classified into units, classes, relations, systems, transformations, and implications.

A spatial illustration of the structure of intellect model is presented in Figure 1. Illustrations of the products of intellectual processes are presented in Figure 2. Given the array defined by the six operations, five contents, and six products, there are a full 180 facets of intelligence, according to Guilford's (1985, 1988) model. However, even this model cannot be said to be a complete representation of all of the important aspects of intelligence.

Humphreys has proposed that other dimensions should be added to the model, such as speed (ie, requirements for speed of mental processing), sensory modality (eg, kinaesthetic and olfactory), and others. Each addition of a dimension multiplicitively increases the total number of intellectual abilities specified by the model. It should be obvious that a taxonomy of intelligence (a periodic table of intellectual abilities) becomes quite unworkable very rapidly. Also, at least at a basic level, the implied orthogonal-

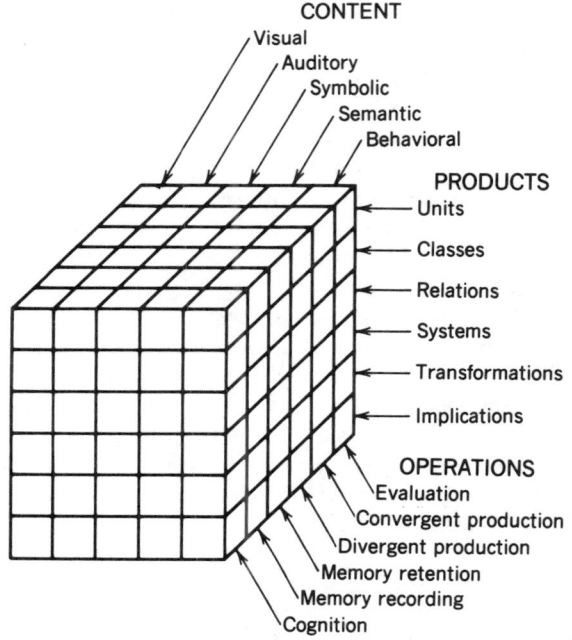

Figure 1. Guilford's structure-of-intellect model (Guilford, 1988). Courtesy of *Educational and Psychological Measurement.*

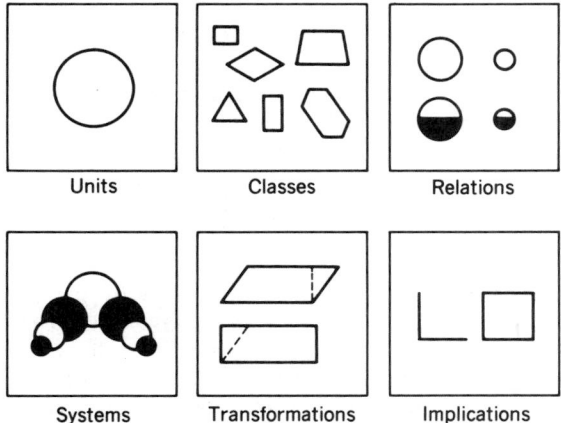

Figure 2. Examples of six different products from Guilford's structure-of-intellect model with figural content. (Guilford, 1967). Reproduced with permission.

ity (ie, independence) of these structure dimensions is at odds with the data that imply the existence of general intelligence. Guilford has acknowledged that, indeed, these dimensions are intercorrelated. No longer can this model be tightly defined as independent dimensions. The problems related to the nonexhaustive nature of the model suggest that this perspective is not plausible as a genuine all-inclusive representation of intelligence. The ultimate utility of the structure of intellect model, though, comes from the specification of what the important dimensions and categories of intellectual operations may be, rather than through provision of a method for determining each and every facet of intelligence.

Two other sets of representations offer greater agreement with the corpus of data on intellectual abilities, as well as provide the open structure necessary to the domain. The first such representations of the structure of intelligence are hierarchical organizations (Fig. 3). Explicit in these theories is a general intellectual ability factor (g). Although the terminology for this general ability is the same as that of Spearman, the construct here is quite different. These theories agree that other ability factors are important components of intelligence. The g ability factor represents the highest node in a hierarchy of

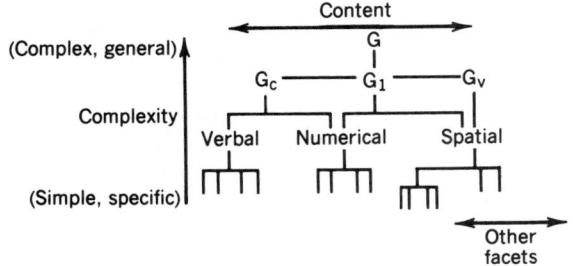

Figure 3. Hierarchical structure of intellectual abilities as designated by Snow and co-workers G = general intelligence, G_c = crystallized intelligence, G_f = fluid intelligence, and G_v = visualization (Marshalek and co-workers, 1983). Reproduced with permission.

ability factors. The influence of such a factor has been estimated by Vernon as reflecting anywhere from roughly 20 to 40% of the variance in a population of all human abilities.

The different theories in this class diverge when it comes to identification of factors that constitute the nodes below g. However, all theories appear to be in agreement about the nature of the hierarchy. That is, the general factor represents the broadest ability, and factors at the next level represent broad, or major group factors (eg, verbal : educational, practical : mechanical, as in Vernon's theory). Each of the abilities at this broad group factor node may be fragmented to reveal their constituent abilities. For example, at the next node, the verbal ability factor might fragment into vocabulary, reading comprehension, associational fluency, and so forth. These lower ability nodes may, in turn, be further subdivided to allow representation of the different test formats for assessing the specific abilities, and so on.

A project in this domain was conducted by Lohman (1979), who reviewed substantial data and found the following structure underlying spatial ability. Three major factors are subsumed under the class denoted as spatial ability. These are (1) spatial relations, (2) spatial orientation, and (3) visualization. At lower nodes, factors such as closure speed, perceptual speed, visual memory, and kinesthetic speed were found that implicate the basic processes of encoding, remembering, transforming, and matching spatial stimuli.

These theories maintain generality by allowing flexibility in the determination of specific abilities. In addition, the actual level of description (or degree of fragmentation) of the ability nodes in the hierarchy is often left indeterminate. Thus researchers may differentially define the broadness of specific nodes to reflect the level of test content analysis of concern. The key to these hierarchical theories is that they purport to describe general intelligence and broad content domains as representing the communality that exists (to varying degrees) at all levels of intellectual tests and tasks (Humphreys, 1979).

The theory put forth by Horn and Cattell (1966), Cattell (1963), and Horn (1968) has elements common to the other hierarchical theories, but also contains additions and deviations. The deviations of particular interest regard the major ability groups and the role of learning in the structure of intellectual abilities. The unique feature of this theory is the exposition of fluid and crystallized classes of ability groups. The distinction is that these are "two major factors, one associated primarily with *physiologically-based* influences [fluid intelligence] and the one associated with *educational*, experiential influences [crystallized intelligence]" (Horn, 1965).

Regarding the fluid intelligence–crystallized intelligence distinction, Horn states that individual differences on fluid intelligence are implied as influential when subjects are confronted with tasks that require the rapid learning and unlearning of information, or require other processes such as educing relations, logical reasoning, and so on. Crystallized intelligence is associated with processing speed and efficiency when tasks contain familiar formats, require use or minor restructuring of previously

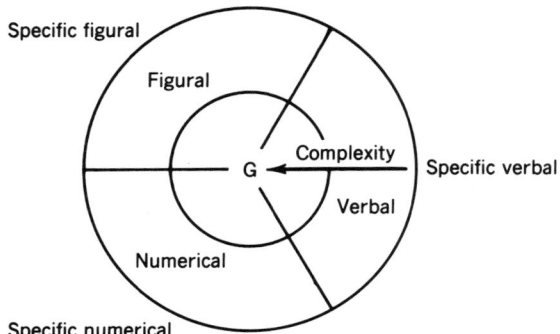

Figure 4. Alternate structure of intelligence map (Marshalek and co-workers, 1983). Reproduced with permission.

formed production systems, or retrieval of information that is stored in long-term memory. As will be discussed further below, the fluid and crystallized types of intelligence in the Cattell and Horn theory are posited to have differential associations with learning on a broad developmental scale.

A different view of the structure of intelligence has been provided (Snow and co-workers, 1984; Marshalek and co-workers, 1983). Although mathematically equivalent to the hierarchical representations discussed above, this approach provides a conceptually divergent portrayal of intelligence. In this theory, depicted in Figure 4, Snow and co-workers describe the structure of intelligence in terms of a circle (ie, two dimensions). General intelligence is defined as the center of the circle, with complexity (which is not distinguished from generality and specificity, per se) defined in terms of distance from the center of the circle. Different regions of the circle correspond to the major content abilities (eg, verbal, numerical, and spatial). The importance of this representation of intelligence is that attention is focused on the degree of similarity and dissimilarity of various types of intellectual process, in terms of content and complexity. From this perspective, the integrated nature of intelligence should be more apparent than from the hierarchical structures or Guilford's structure of intellect.

Information Processing and Intelligence

In the last 15 yr an explosion of research has converged on determining more basic information processing elements of intelligence. In terms of the hierarchical representations presented above, these research programs seek to provide explicit description of intelligence at nodes far removed from general intelligence and major content abilities. The desire is to find the general building blocks for intelligence, whether they be revealed by evoked brain potentials, positive emission tomography (pet) scanning (Haier and co-workers, 1988) or speed and accuracy of stimulus recognition or discrimination. In this sense, the classic psychometric approach has been top-down, from general intelligence to specific abilities. The information-processing approach in experimental psychology has been essentially bottom-up, or moving up from the most basic

processes to more complex levels of thought. Of course, as with any reductionist scientific enterprise, distinctions can be made in terms of the level of analysis in this area as well. A few illustrative paradigms and findings will be described.

Sternberg (1985a) identifies the following four major sources of research in the application of information processing to the study of intelligence (for in-depth treatment, see Sternberg, 1985b):

1. *The Cognitive-Correlates Method.* In this paradigm, basic information-processing tasks are given to subjects of high and low intellectual abilities (tasks such as lexical access, short-term memory, and choice reaction time). The associations between task performance differences and intelligence differences are used to develop theories relating information processing to intelligence. The work by Hunt (1985) and his colleagues falls into this category.

2. *The Cognitive-Components Method.* This is essentially a top-down approach to link intelligence with information processing. In this paradigm, the information-processing components of specific intelligence tests are isolated and measured separately. Research results using this method often have a clearer connection to global intelligence than with a bottom-up approach. For a landmark example of this type of study see Sternberg (1977).

3. *The Cognitive-Training Method.* Within this paradigm, the malleability of cognitive-intellectual processes is studied via specific training programs. Research from this approach has been quite promising in the delineation of cognitive skills from intellectual abilities. Research (Frederiksen and co-workers, 1983; Pellegrino, 1983) is restructuring traditional conceptions of adult intelligence as fixed, by creating training programs that can remediate deficits often viewed as intellectual.

4. *The Cognitive-Content Method.* This is one of the approaches traditionally used in AI research as applied to the study of intelligence. That is, expert–novice differences are evaluated for establishing how intellectual abilities are implicated in the acquisition of expertise. Factors such as knowledge structures and selection and use of strategies fall into this domain. Prototypical work in this area has been done by Chi and co-workers (1982).

Cognitive-correlates research by Hunt and co-workers (1973) has led to identification of several sources of information-processing speed and efficiency that are associated with verbal aspects of intelligence. At a more basic level, work by Lunneborg (1978) and Jensen and Munro (1979) have assessed the degree of association between the most elementary types of information processing, simple reaction time and choice reaction time. Simple reaction time is a measure of the speed that a person can encode and make a response to the onset of some stimulus (usually a single light stimulus and a response of a key depression). Choice reaction time is the next higher level of information processing; it involves a discrimination of two or more stimuli (eg, two different lights), and usually unique key responses to each stimulus. Even at this elemental level of operation, positive correlations are found between speed and accuracy of reactions and global measures of intelligence (Jensen and Munro, 1979; Longstreth, 1984).

Kyllonen (1985) has demonstrated further how a more comprehensive approach may be used to determine the relations between basic information-processing mechanisms and intelligence. In a series of studies, Kyllonen examined information processes with three different methods: a whole-task analysis (where underlying factors of cognitive tasks were determined), a stage analysis (where intelligence and information-processing relations were examined for various stages of processing within tasks), and a coding-analysis procedure (in which relations between intelligence and information processing were examined where the type of information in memory was manipulated). Findings from this series of studies were as follows:

1. *Whole-Task Approach.* Abilities were found to be associated with task difficulty level (consistent with earlier theories of intelligence), and also with speed of mental operations (a construct not separately dealt with in previous theories of intelligence). There appears to be a complex relationship between these two types of ability within a general conception of intelligence.

2. *Stage-Analysis Approach.* Abilities found at these low levels of cognitive operation were consistently found to be associated with both process and content of information. Thus this particular approach gives more validity to the claim that hierarchical theories of intelligence can proceed consistently to the lower nodes of increased specificity.

3. *Code-Analysis Approach.* Additional ability infrastructure was put forth through this study. Low level abilities were found that relate to amount of perceptual processing required and level of processing (eg, from physical feature analysis, to identity of stimulus name, to semantic meaning).

Another major compendium of information processing abilities and some associated intellectual abilities from both task-analysis and ability factor perspectives has been put forth by Carroll (1980, 1989).

LEARNING AND INTELLIGENCE

Given that learning is a major aspect of any theoretical conception of intelligence, it is no surprise that substantial attention has been devoted over the years to establishing empirical connections between the two constructs. Three questions are central to providing an understanding of learning and intelligence. These are (1) How does intelligence come about? (2) How does intelligence influence learning? (3) How is intelligence related to efficacy of information processing subsequent to learning? Much research has been devoted to the developmental aspects of intelligence acquisition. An overview of some important theories and findings of this approach is provided below.

Development of Intelligence

How does acquisition of intelligence come about? Historically, psychologists have argued about the relative importance of genetic endowment (ie, a predisposition to acquiring intelligence) or environmental influences (eg, child-rearing practices and educational opportunities). In brief, this controversy covers the questions that concern relative standing of individuals with respect to measures of intelligence, not specifically how individuals develop intelligence. Detailed discussion of this controversy is beyond the scope of this article but more information is available (Anastasi, 1982; Block and Dworkin, 1976). Rather, the concern here is exactly what role the environment has on the development of intelligence (regardless of which individuals are predestined to be more or less well endowed).

Intelligence, in terms of thinking abstractly, learning complex concepts, reasoning, and developing language skills is certainly not innate, that is, present at birth. Case studies of feral or severely deprived children most strikingly demonstrate that such intellectual faculties as language are not present in the individual, in the absence of particular types of environmental experience. Certainly, environmental influences are crucial to any expression of intellectual development. Many research programs specifically explore the various factors that appear to strongly impact development of intelligence (Bloom, 1964; Bouchard and Segal, 1985). For present purposes, two avenues of theory and research seem especially relevant. First and foremost is the pattern of accretion (and plasticity) of intelligence. The second issue pertains to the possibility of differentiation of intellectual abilities with maturation. Each is discussed in turn.

Two tracks of research have provided notable information about how intelligence is acquired. One track is strictly psychological; it involves analysis of changing patterns of intelligence measures for individuals from infancy to adulthood. The other track includes combined work in neuropsychology and developmental psychology; it involves examination of concurrent changes in brain physiology with development of intellectual abilities. It is important to note first that evidence from the study of intelligence measures can be somewhat problematic when the concerned is infants and young children. This state of affairs comes about because language development appears to be a critical ingredient for reliable measurement of intelligence. Assessments of intelligence in prelanguage infants must, by definition, involve criteria other than vocabulary, verbal reasoning, and so forth. As a result, such measures tend to capitalize on perceptual–motor related intellectual abilities, although work also has been done examining the infant's preference for novelty (Fagan and Singer, 1983). However, when performance on similar types of test items are examined in detail in longitudinal studies, some understanding of the accretion of intelligence is afforded. In early psychometric research, Thurstone (1928) and others have shown that intellectual development can be represented by a function that has positive acceleration at birth, but the function shows rapid deceleration with maturity (eg, children at the age of four appear to have developed roughly 50% of measured adult intelligence). Such findings illustrate how important early experience and stimulation may be toward development of intelligence. By approximately age six, children have developed the necessary intellectual ability foundation for reasoning, reading, talking, and so on that allow them to build declarative knowledge and procedural production systems in memory that ultimately provide for adult operations of thought and action.

Formalized structures of the development of intelligence in stages have been put forth by Piaget (1952) and Uzgiris and Hunt (1975). Piaget's theory of intellectual development states that children proceed through several stages of thought processes, denoted as sensorimotor, preoperational, concrete operational, and formal operational. Each of these stages of development is characterized by certain styles of thinking that imply whether or not a child can understand various concepts (such as object permanence, causality, and object relations in space). In a sense, these stages parallel development of more traditional conceptions of the development of intellectual abilities. In fact, instruments measuring the stages of intellectual development from this framework have shown high levels of agreement with more global measures of intelligence (Humphreys and Parsons, 1979).

The track of research dependent on neuropsychological investigation has shown marked correspondence between intellectual plasticity and neurological development. In one line of work, the process of canalization of the brain is seen to parallel the initial development and negative acceleration of intelligence accretion. Other studies (focusing on language development—a clearly important aspect of intellectual abilities) have demonstrated that there may be similar critical periods for language acquisition. If specific brain damage occurs prior to age 12 individuals may still show development of language, attributable to the fact that connections between neurons are still being established (Lenneberg and Lenneberg, 1975). Subsequent to this age, similar types of brain damage will vastly limit the degree of recovery (and further acquisition) of verbal skills shown at earlier ages. Entirely analogous findings have been reported that demonstrate limitations of even extreme changes in environment that effect changes in relative levels of intelligence (Bloom, 1964). That is, environmental influences on the development of intelligence are maximally effective immediately after birth, and up to age three or four. When environmental changes occur after this point, substantially less change in intelligence (ie, relative to the age norm) is found. The nation's Head Start programs are generally predicated on the belief that the fundamental mechanisms for intelligence are formed quite early in life.

One other line of thought may have ramifications on the development of intelligence. Researchers (Garrett, 1946) have proposed that intelligence for infants and young children is essentially undifferentiated. However, as the individual matures, receives varied educational instruction, and other experiences in the environment, intelligence becomes differentiated or specialized. Adults thus are expected to show much wider varieties of intellectual abilities (from verbal abilities of vocabulary, to spatial abilities of visualization, to perceptual–motor abilities such as scanning speed and accuracy, etc).

Such theorizing is consistent in many ways with the previously discussed structure of intelligence (Horn and Cattell, 1966). That is, in early infancy, fluid abilities essentially constitute intelligence. As the individual matures, fluid intelligence is used for building crystallized intelligence. In a sense, the more specialized abilities are thought to break out from the higher node, more general intellectual abilities. Whether this phenomenon may be primarily determined by the educational system (where specialization often is associated with high school, trade school, and college curricula) or if it may be a result of interests and extramural experiences is not directly specified by the theorists. The data regarding the veridicality of the differentiation hypothesis (as it is known in the psychology literature), however, have been equivocal (Vernon, 1961; Akin and co-workers, 1977). While several studies have tentatively shown that general intelligence declines in its dominance as age increases, other studies have failed to find such changes (Pellegrino and Kail, 1985). The problems in evaluating this hypothesis seem to be encountered in choosing assessment instruments that tap the same abilities (and that are equally appropriate) for individuals in different age groups. For the present purposes, though, the lack of resolution of this hypothesis is less important than the possibilities it raises for those interested in the patterns of intelligence acquisition.

Intelligence and Learning

For adults intelligence (whether general or specific) is seen as the foundation on which all new information is processed by any given individual. As Ferguson (1956) pointed out, the key to understanding learning is that the process is accumulative, where each new fact or procedure incorporated is partly a result of prior and present knowledge. In fact, Ferguson maintained (quite reasonbly) that transfer is implied in nearly all learning. (Transfer, whether of knowledge, skills, prior training, or processing mechanisms, is the concept of building on a structure provided by earlier learning experiences.) That is, learning in the absence of some aspect of transfer is an extremely rare occurrence (such as only with the neonate). Given this fundamental implication of intelligence influencing future learning, it is sensible to ask specifically how intelligence interacts with learning.

There are many cases where demonstrative associations between intelligence and learning are found in the literature (Estes, 1982; Zeaman and House, 1967). Unfortunately, in many situations, measurement (ie, statistical) problems are associated with assessing the amount of learning, independent of initial level of performance (Cronbach and Furby, 1970). What has been determined to date is that intelligence is strongly associated with initial performance on most skilled acquisition tasks (Fleishman, 1972). However, more striking is the fact that on many learning tasks, the influence of intelligence on task performance seems to markedly attenuate as time-on-task increases. Ackerman (1986, 1988) and Ackerman and Schneider (1985) have theorized that a complex, but tractable, relationship is found between intelligence and performance under learning conditions. This theory states that intelligence is crucial in situations of learning, especially when the task is novel, that is, less potential for transfer is present when novel conditions are encountered. The importance of intelligence in learning, though, is predominantly with respect to (1) selection of appropriate task strategies, (2) enabling of previously learned information processing structures, (3) memory capacity, and (4) establishing new production systems.

However, once the appropriate strategies are selected, production systems established, and so on, the influence of intelligence on future learning is vastly diminished when the task is one with consistent information processing requirements. Essentially, when the consistent rules and procedures are internalized by the individual, further learning (to levels of asymptotic performance) is associated with specific abilities. In terms of the structure of intelligence discussed earlier, a predominantly novel task will involve general intelligence (the top node in the hierarchical theories, the central location in Snow's theory). As individuals get more experience on the learning task, specific perceptual speed and psychomotor abilities (the lower nodes of the hierarchies, the peripheral areas of Snow's theory) determine ultimate performance. In fact, when a task becomes automatic (Schneider and Shiffrin, 1977; Ackerman, 1988), such as in aspects of driving a car, moving chess pieces, solving geometry proofs, and so on, the influence of general intelligence on performance is expected to be substantially attenuated.

On the other hand, should a task contain inconsistent information processing components (such that productions to perform the task must constantly be altered or reversed), learning per se fails to occur. In such cases, transfer is also excluded, and intelligence is expected to determine performance from initially novel situations to ones in which individuals are given substantial opportunity for practice and learning. Recent empirical demonstrations of these phenomena support this hypothesized role of intelligence in learning. Figure 5 illustrates how consistency (or lack thereof) of a simple task of memory and verbal categorization moderates the association between general intelligence and performance during learning. The task with inconsistent information-processing requirements shows stable dependence on intelligence for performance. The consistent task, which is also initially novel, shows reduced dependence on intelligence as learning progresses with practice. Findings such as these indicate how intelligence is used during learning, but also show that intelligence is not directly involved in many previously learned information processing operations.

Although it is perhaps not immediately obvious, intelligence is required when new tasks are incompatible with previously learned production systems. For example, when controls are reversed (as is common when adjusting between the right-hand controls on U.S. autos and left-hand controls on European autos; or when a programmer changes from one computer keyboard layout to a different layout), old production systems must be undone, while new productions are established. For both situations, extinguishing the old and putting together the new, intelli-

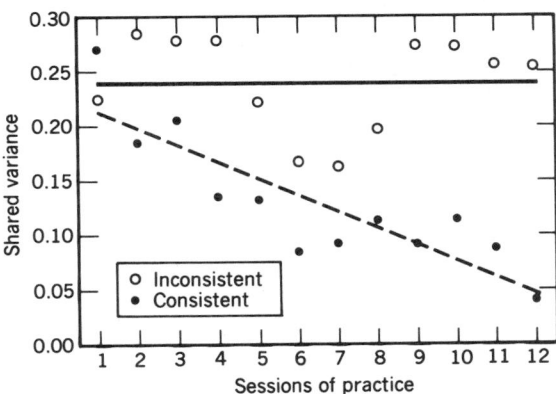

Figure 5. Shared variance between intelligence and performance on information-processing tasks, one with consistent components, the other with inconsistent information processing components. Data collected over 2.5 h of task practice (from Ackerman, 1988).

gence is demanded. The key concept is that intelligence determines the efficiency and accuracy of both novel and inconsistent (or incompatible) types of information processing.

Intelligence and Information Processing after Learning

That intelligence is implicated during learning is not surprising. However, the fact that intelligence is seen as the foundation for building production systems, but not in the postlearning phases of operation is an important aspect of the human information-processing system. As James (1890), Whitehead (1934), and many others have pointed out, normal human functioning involves very little that may be described as intellectual, requiring thinking, and so forth. Instead, much of normal human mental activity is more like a series of flywheels (James, 1890; Reason and Mycielska, 1982). Series of production systems are established, tuned, and ultimately unitized, so that a long series of productions may be triggered by a single stimulus or internally generated intention (such as reaching for a fork at the dinner table, or putting on one's socks). Intelligence is the stuff of which these production systems are created (or modified from previous uses).

Subsequent to the lengthy process of learning, intelligence (or attention) is only needed when series of production systems must be modified (such as driving an unfamiliar car) or added to (as when an electronics troubleshooter encounters a more complex system) or when greater than normal accuracy is needed (eg, taking apart a clock vs taking apart the same clock, when it is connected to a time bomb). In such cases, intelligence is used to provide additional checking on the information-processing system to preserve stricter tolerances.

SUMMARY

Intelligence has been described in many ways, although almost all definitions involve learning as a major component of the construct (ie, adapting to the surroundings).

Ultimately, the domain of knowledge, thought, and action are implicated as making up the framework for intelligence. The concept is consensual, but overlap among different theories is the prominent characteristic of varied definitions.

Regarding structure and the purpose of the inquiry, the construct of intelligence can be segmented into a hierarchy, with general intelligence at the top node and more specific abilities at lower nodes. Similarly, the structure can be described as a circle, with general intelligence at the center and less complex abilities (and components of abilities) moving away from the center of the circle, like spokes of a wheel. Other views provide interesting causal implications about the development and structure of intelligence. Last, for taxonomic purposes, intellectual abilities may be described categorically in three or more dimensions (Guilford, 1985). While somewhat at odds with empirical data, this latter model serves a valuable heuristic purpose in seeking out different types of intellectual process.

Information-processing research and theory developed during the 1970s have allowed for the examination of basic building blocks for intelligence. Experiments have been described that concern aspects of speed of mental operations, accuracy of information processing, contents of processing, and codes of processing (including low level pattern detection of stimulus features to higher level semantic codes present in long-term memory); all of which appear to represent fundamental facets of broader, more general conceptualizations of intelligence.

Acquisition of intelligence appears to parallel neurophysiological development. At early ages, intelligence is plastic and can be influenced in many ways. As the individual ages, though, intelligence (or at least the foundation for intelligence) seems to be less malleable, such that by the time a child enters the school system, the basis for that individual's intelligence is relatively stable. Whether intelligence becomes more specialized (ie, differentiated) with age is not yet established, however, the possibility exists that infant intelligence is more like a general problem-solving system and less similar to adultlike expert systems. Current research is focused on these issues, and answers seem forthcoming in the near future. Such findings about the development of intelligence will have major implications for discussions of mental architecture.

In the domain of human information processing and learning, not all operations require intelligence. Rather, intelligence is required when tasks involve processing of novel or inconsistent information. From a perspective of production systems, intelligence seems to be necessary for establishing production systems, selecting optimal arrangements of productions, modifying previously built production systems for related uses, and undoing established production systems.

Although there are many unanswered questions about the structural characteristics of intelligence, the casual factors determining the development of intelligence, and the specific relations between learning and intelligence, the scientific discipline studying intelligence has shown great progress in the last 100 yr of investigation. Future developments are especially likely to be found in applications of neuropsychological and cognitive, information processing paradigms to the study of intelligence.

BIBLIOGRAPHY

P. L. Ackerman, "Individual Differences in Information Processing: An Investigation of Intellectual Abilities and Task Performance During Practice," *Intelligence* **10**, 101–139 (1986).

P. L. Ackerman, "Determinants of Individual Differences During Skill Acquisition: Cognitive Abilities and Information Processing," *J. Exper. Psychol. Gen.* **117**, 288–318 (1988).

P. L. Ackerman and W. Schneider, "Individual Differences in Automatic and Controlled Information Processing," in R. F. Dillon, ed., *Individual Differences in Cognition*, Vol. 2, Academic Press, Inc., Orlando, Fla., 1985, pp. 35–66.

A. Anastasi, *Psychological Testing*, 5th ed., Macmillan, New York, 1982, pp. 269–370.

R. Atkin, R. Bray, M. Davison, S. Herzberger, L. G. Humphreys, and U. Selzer, "Ability Factor Differentiation, Grades 5 Through 11," *Appl. Psychol. Meas.* **1**, 65–76 (1977).

A. Binet and T. Simon, "The Development of Intelligence in Children," "New Methods for the Diagnosis of the Intellectual Level of Subnormals," and "The Development of Intelligence in the Child," in J. J. Jenkins and D. G. Paterson, eds., *Studies of Individual Differences: The Search for Intelligence*, Appleton-Century-Crofts, East Norwalk, Conn., 1961, pp. 81–111.

N. J. Block and G. Dworkin, eds., *The IQ Controversy: Critical Readings*, Pantheon, New York, 1976.

B. S. Bloom, *Stability and Change in Human Characteristics*, John Wiley & Sons, Inc., New York, 1964.

E. G. Boring, "Intelligence as the Tests Measure It," in J. J. Jenkins and D. G. Paterson, eds., *Studies of Individual Differences: The Search for Intelligence*, Appleton-Century-Crofts, East Norwalk, Conn., 1961, pp. 210–214.

T. J. Bouchard, Jr. and N. Segal, "Environment and IQ," in B. B. Wolman, ed., *Handbook of Intelligence*, John Wiley & Sons, Inc., New York, 1985, pp. 391–464.

B. R. Buckingham, "Intelligence and Its Measurement: A Symposium," *J. Ed. Psychol.* **12**, 271–275 (1921).

C. Burt, "The Structure of the Mind, a Review of the Results of Factor Analysis," *Br. J. Ed. Psychol.* **19**, 110–111, 176–199 (1949).

J. B. Carroll, *Individual Difference Relations in Psychometric and Experimental Cognitive Tasks*, Technical Report No. **163**, University of North Carolina, Chapel Hill, N.C., 1980.

J. B. Carroll, "Factor Analysis Since Spearman: Where Do We Stand? What Do We Know?" in R. Kanfer, P. L. Ackerman, and R. Cudeck, eds., *Abilities, Motivation, and Methodology*, Erlbaum, Hillsdale, N.J., 1989, pp. 43–67.

R. B. Cattell, "Theory of Fluid and Crystallized Intelligence: A Critical Experiment," *J. Ed. Psychol.* **54**, 1–22 (1963).

M. T. H. Chi, R. Glaser, and E. Rees, "Expertise in Problem Solving," in R. J. Sternberg, ed., *Advances in the Psychology of Human Intelligence*, Vol. 1, Erlbaum, Hillsdale, N.J., 1982, pp. 7–76.

W. K. Estes, "Learning, Memory, and Intelligence," in R. J. Sternberg, ed., *Handbook of Human Intelligence*, Cambridge University Press, New York, 1982, pp. 170–224.

J. F. Fagan and L. T. Singer, "Infant Recognition Memory as a Measure of Intelligence," in L. P. Lipsitt, ed., *Advances in Infancy Research*, Vol. 2, Ablex, Norwood, N. J., 1983.

G. A. Ferguson, "On Transfer and the Abilities of Man," *Can. J. Psychol.* **10**, 121–131 (1956).

E. A. Fleishman, "On the Relation Between Abilities, Learning, and Human Performance," *Am. Psychol.* **27**, 1017–1032 (1972).

J. R. Frederiksen, P. A. Weaver, B. M. Warren, H. P. Gillotte, A. S. Rosebery, B. Freeman, and L. Goodman, *A Componential Approach to Training Reading Skills*, Report No. **5295**, Bolt, Beranek, and Newman, Cambridge, Mass., 1983.

H. E. Garrett, "A Developmental Theory of Intelligence," *Am. Psychol.* **1**, 372–378 (1946).

J. P. Guilford, *The Nature of Human Intelligence*, McGraw-Hill, Inc., New York, 1967.

J. P. Guilford, "Cognitive Psychology's Ambiguities: Some Suggested Remedies," *Psychol. Rev.* **89**, 48–59 (1982).

J. P. Guilford, "The Structure-of-Intellect Model," in B. B. Wolman, ed., *Handbook of Intelligence,* Wiley, New York, 1985, pp. 225–266.

J. P. Guilford, "Some Changes in the Structure-of-Intellect Model," *Ed. Psychol. Meas.* **48**, 1–4 (1988).

R. J. Haier and co-workers, "Cortical Glucose Metabolic Rate Correlates of Abstract Reasoning and Attention Studied with Positron Emission Tomography," *Intelligence* **12**, 199–217 (1988).

J. L. Horn, *Fluid and Crystallized Intelligence: A Factor Analytic Study of the Structure among Primary Mental Abilities*, University Microfilms, Ann Arbor, Mich., 1965.

J. L. Horn, "Organization of Abilities and the Development of Intelligence," *Psychol. Rev.* **75**, 242–259 (1968).

J. L. Horn, and R. B. Cattell, "Refinement and Test of the Theory of Fluid and Crystallized General Intelligences," *J. Ed. Psychol.* **57**, 253–270 (1966).

L. G. Humphreys, "The Construct of General Intelligence," *Intelligence* **3**, 105–120 (1979).

L. G. Humphreys and C. Parsons, "Piagetian Tasks Measure Intelligence and Intelligence Tests Assess Cognitive Development," *Intelligence* **3**, 369–382 (1979).

E. Hunt, "Verbal Ability," in Sternberg, 1985a, pp. 31–58.

E. Hunt, N. Frost, and C. Lunneborg, "Individual Differences in Cognition: A New Approach to Intelligence," in G. Bower, ed., *Psychology of Learning and Motivation*, Vol. 7, Academic Press, Inc., Orlando, Fla., 1973, 87–122.

W. James, *Principles of Psychology*, Holt, New York, 1890.

A. R. Jensen, "Race and the Genetics of Intelligence: A Reply to Lewontin," in Block and Dworkin, 1976, pp. 93–106.

A. R. Jensen, and E. Munro, "Reaction Time, Movement Time, and Intelligence," *Intelligence* **3**, 121–126 (1979).

P. C. Kyllonen, *Dimensions of Information Processing Speed*, Air Force Human Resources Laboratory Technical Report, Air Force Systems Command, Brooks AFB, Tex., 1985.

E. H. Lenneberg, and E. Lenneberg, *Foundations of Language Development: A Multidisciplinary Approach*, Vol. 2, Academic Press, Inc., Orlando, Fla., 1975.

D. Lohman, *Spatial Ability: A Review and Reanalysis of the Correlational Literature*, Technical Report No. **8**, Stanford University, Stanford, Calif., 1979.

L. E. Longstreth, "Jensen's Reaction-Time Investigations of Intelligence: A Critique," *Intelligence* **8**, 139–160 (1984).

C. E. Lunneborg, "Some Information-Processing Correlates of Measures of Intelligence," *Multivar. Behav. Res.* **13**, 153–161 (1978).

Q. McNemar, *Psychological Statistics*, 4th ed., John Wiley & Sons, Inc., New York, 1969.

B. Marshalek, D. F. Lohman, and R. E. Snow, "The Complexity Continuum in the Radex and Hierarchical Models of Intelligence," *Intelligence* **7**, 107–127 (1983).

J. W. Pellegrino, *Individual Differences in Spatial Ability: The Effects of Practice on Components of Processing and Reference Test Scores*, paper presented at American Educational Research Association Meetings, Montreal, Canada, 1983.

J. W. Pellegrino, and R. Kail, *Human Intelligence: Perspectives and Prospects*, W. H. Freeman, New York, 1985.

J. Piaget, *The Origins of Intelligence in Children*, International Universities Press, New York, 1952.

J. Reason, and K. Mycielska, *Absent-Minded? The Psychology of Mental Lapses and Everyday Errors*, Prentice-Hall, Englewood Cliffs, N.J., 1982.

W. Schneider, and R. M. Shiffrin, "Controlled and Automatic Human Information Processing: I. Detection, Search, and Attention," *Psychol. Rev.* **84**, 1–66 (1977).

R. E. Snow, P. C. Kyllonen, and B. Marshalek, "The Topography of Ability and Learning Correlations," in R. J. Sternberg, ed., *Advances in the Psychology of Human Intelligence*, Vol. 2, Erlbaum, Hillsdale, N.J., 1984, pp. 47–103.

C. Spearman, "General Intelligence Objectively Determined and Measured," *Am. J. Psychol.* **15**, 201–293 (1904).

R. J. Sternberg, *Intelligence, Information Processing, and Analogical Reasoning: The Componential Analysis of Human Abilities*, Erlbaum, Hillsdale, N.J., 1977.

R. J. Sternberg, ed., *Human Abilities: An Information-Processing Approach*, W. H. Freeman, New York, 1985a.

R. J. Sternberg, *Beyond IQ: A Triarchic Theory of Human Intelligence*, Cambridge University Press, New York, 1985b.

L. L. Thurstone, "The Absolute Zero in Intelligence Measurement," *Psychol. Rev.* **35**, 175–197 (1928).

L. L. Thurstone, *Primary Mental Abilities*, University of Chicago Press, Chicago, 1938.

L. L. Thurstone, "Psychological Implications of Factor Analysis," *Am. Psychol.* **3**, 402–408 (1948).

U.S. Department of Health, Education, and Welfare, *Bibliography of Human Intelligence*, U.S. Government Printing Office, Washington, D.C., 1968.

I. C. Uzgiris, and J. McV. Hunt, *Assessment in Infancy: Ordinal Scales of Psychological Development*, University of Illinois Press, Urbana, 1975.

P. E. Vernon, *The Structure of Human Abilities*, John Wiley & Sons, Inc., New York, 1961.

D. Wechsler, *Manual for the Wechsler Adult Intelligence Scale*, Psychological Corp., New York, 1955.

A. N. Whitehead as cited in M. R. Cohen and E. Nagel, *An Introduction to Logic and Scientific Method*, Harcourt, Brace, New York, 1934, pp. 431–432.

D. Zeaman, and B. J. House, "The Relation of IQ and Learning," in R. M. Gagné, ed., *Learning and Individual Differences*, Charles Merrill, Columbus, Ohio, 1967, pp. 192–212.

PHILLIP L. ACKERMAN
University of Minnesota

INTERLISP. See LISP.

INTERNIST

A mdeical consultation system for diagnosis of internal medicine, INTERNIST was written in 1975 by H. E. Pople and J. Myers at Carnegie Mellon University and is now called CADUCEUS (see H. E. Pople, "Heuristic Methods for Imposing Structure on Ill-Structured Problems: The Structuring of Medical Diagnostics," in P. Szolovitz ed., *Artificial Intelligence in Medicine*, Westview Press, Boulder, Co., 1981, pp. 119–185).

M. TAIE
AT&T Bell Laboratories

J

JUDIS

A system for organizing conversation in distributed artificial intelligence systems, JUDIS was written by Turner at Georgia Institute of Technology. JUDIS merges the communication goals of its associated problem solving systems into a template for conversation via conventional discourse structures. The template is expanded while the conversation progresses and represents a conventional, partially ordered plan for meeting all active communication goals. In creating the template JUDIS relies on conventional structures of conversation, not the order in which goals arrive from the problem solver, to organize the conversation. This makes JUDIS particularly well-suited as an interface for distributed artificial intelligence systems. When choosing the action in the template to execute next, JUDIS considers the priority of the goal an action will achieve. This allows JUDIS to make intention-based decisions within the constraints of convention, as when deciding which possible action in a partial ordering to select next, and to ignore the template to respond quickly to urgent goals. [see Elise H. Turner, "Integrating Intention and Convention to Organize Problem Solving Dialogues," Georgia Institute of Technology, Ph.D. dissertation and Tech. Rep. No. GIT–ICS–90/02 (1990); Elise H. Turner and Richard E. Cullingford, "Using Conversation MOPs in Natural Language Interfaces," *Discourse Processes* **12**(1), 63–90 (1989).]

ELISE H. TURNER
University of New Hampshire

JULIA

JULIA is a case-based reasoning program that solves design problems in the domain of meal planning. It works by using previous cases to propose plausible solutions, decomposing the problem as necessary and posting constraints to guide synthesis. JULIA exploits a repertoire of adaptation methods to transform previous meals and dishes in order to meet constraints on the current problem. These adaptation methods are used both to modify previous cases and to repair previous decisions that have been invalidated by constraints that arrive late. [See T. R. Hinrichs, "Towards an Architecture for Open World Problem Solving," in J. L. Kolodner, ed., *Proceedings: Case-Based Reasoning Workshop (DARPA)*, Morgan-Kaufmann Publishers, Inc., San Mateo, Calif., 1988; T. R. Hinrichs, "Strategies for Adaptation and Recovery in a Design Problem Solver," in K. Hammond, ed., *Proceedings: Case-Based Reasoning Workshop (DARPA), II*, Morgan-Kaufmann Publishers, Inc., San Mateo, Calif., 1989.]

THOMAS R. HINRICHS
Georgia Institute of Technology

K

KAISSA

Based on an older program, KAISSA was rewritten by Mikhail Donskoy along with nine other Soviet scientists. KAISSA won the World Computer Championships (chess) in 1974 at Stockholm by winning all four of its matches (see COMPUTER CHESS AND SEARCH). It uses the alpha-beta algorithm and searches all moves to a specified depth. It also keeps a classification of moves and uses a method called "best-move service" to search optimal moves first [see G. M. Adelson-Velsky, V. L. Arlazarov, and M. V. Donskoy, "On Some Methods of Chess Play Programming," *Artif. Intell.* **6**, 361–371 (1975)].

J. ROSENBERG
Kilchberg, Switzerland

KBMS

A commercial expert-system shell called the Knowledge Base Management System, introduced in 1988 by AICorp. KBMS provides the full range of inference-based reasoning including RETE-based forward chaining, MYCIN and PROLOG style backward chaining and hypothetical reasoning. A unique aspect of KBMS is its extended object system that treats external and remote data bases as object classes. KBMS also supports a full range of object oriented graphics manipulation. (See *KBMS Reference Manual*, AICorp, Waltham, MA 02254.)

LARRY HARRIS
AICorp, Inc.

KEE

The KEE system is a commercial tool for developing knowledge-based systems. The fundamental representational building blocks in KEE are frames. These exist in multiparent hierarchies, with several varieties of inheritance for transferring frame attributes through the hierarchies. Around this object core, KEE integrates various modeling mechanisms, including rules (usable for forward, backward, and mixed chaining), object-oriented programming (by treating the frames of the representation system as the objects), access-oriented programming (allowing demons on frame value retrieval or modification), truth maintenance (using an extension of de Kleer's (1986) ATMS), and multiple contexts (frame values can vary between "worlds," governed by the semantics of the ATMS). KEE also provides a graphic developer interface and an extensive collection of graphic user-interface development tools. Additional products that run in the KEE environment include facilities for knowledge base/database connectivity (Abarbanel, Tou, and Gilbert, 1989) dis-

crete event simulation (Drummond and Stelzner, 1989), database search, scheduling, configuration, and various advanced representation and presentation mechanisms. KEE is a product of IntelliCorp Inc. of Mountain View, California, is implemented within Common Lisp, and is available on many different hardware platforms, including work stations, LISP machines, personal computers, and mainframes. Fikes and Kehler's article (1985) provides more information on the philosophical foundation of KEE's frame system; Filman's (1988) and Morris and Nado's (1980) articles discuss the implementation and import of the interconnection of the frame, ATMS, and worlds mechanisms.

KEE is a registered trademark of IntelliCorp, Inc.

BIBLIOGRAPHY

R. Abarbanel, F. Tou, and V. Gilbert, "KEEConnection: A Bridge Between Databases and Knowledge Bases," in M. Richer, ed., *AI Tools and Techniques*, Ablex, Norwood, New Jersey, 1989, pp. 289–322.

J. De Kleer, "An Assumption-Based Truth Maintenance System," *Artif. Intell.* **28**(2), 127–162 (Jan. 1986).

B. Drummond and M. Stelzner, "SimKit: A Tool for Building Knowledge-Based Simulation Toolkits," in M. Richer, ed., *AI Tools and Techniques*, Ablex, Norwood, New Jersey, 1989, pp. 241–259.

R. E. Fikes and T. Kehler, "The Role of Frame-Based Representation in Reasoning," *CACM* **28**(9), 904–920 (Sept. 1985).

R. E. Filman, "Reasoning with Worlds and Truth Maintenance in a Knowledge-Based Programming Environment," *CACM* **31**(4), 382–401 (April 1988).

P. H. Morris and R. A. Nado, "Representing Actions with an Assumption-Based Truth Maintenance System," in *The Proceedings of AAAI-86: The Fifth National Conference on Artificial Intelligence*, Philadelphia, pp. 13–17, Aug. 1986.

ROBERT FILMAN
PAUL MORRIS
Intellicorp, Inc.

KL-ONE

A frame-based language for knowledge representation (qv) in procedural semantic (qv) approach, KL-ONE was developed by Brachman in 1978 at BBN (see R. Brachman, *A Structural Paradigm for Representing Knowledge*, Report No. 3605, Bolt Beranek and Newman, Inc. Cambridge, Mass., 1978, and R. Brachman, "What's in a Concept: Structural Foundations for Semantic Networks," in N. Findler, ed., *Associative Networks: The Representation and Use of Knowledge by Computers*, Academic Press, New York, 1979, pp. 3–50).

A. HANYONG YUHAN
AT&T Bell Laboratories

KNOWLEDGE ACQUISITION

Acquiring and modeling knowledge effectively can be the most time-consuming portion of the knowledge engineering process. Little methodology is practiced beyond unstructured interviewing. Automated methods are, for the most part, still in the research stage. Several well-known factors contribute to interviewing problems:

- Plausible lines of reasoning can have little to do with actual problem solving.
- Academic (novice) knowledge is often obtained in place of compiled (expert) knowledge.
- Experts may be insecure: they could be afraid of losing their jobs; they may not want computers encroaching on their private domain; they may not want to expose their problem-solving methods to the scrutiny of colleagues or of the general public.
- Interpersonal interviewing problems can result when knowledge engineers are not trained in interviewing techniques.
- There are inherent problems in introspection.
- Protocol analysis (discussed below) is labor intensive, error prone, and results in a series of random behavior samples that must be synthesized by the knowledge engineer.

Clancey (1986b) summarized the problem as follows: "Knowledge acquisition is not just a problem of accessing and translating what is already known, but the familiar scientific and engineering problem of formalizing models for the first time." This article discusses the role of modeling languages, and manual, semiautomated (interactive), and automated (machine learning) knowledge acquisition techniques.

MODELING EXPERTISE: MEDIATING REPRESENTATIONS

Many knowledge acquisition research ideas and experiments for semiautomated techniques have been tested in the last several years. Successful approaches seem to rely on effective mediating representations: problem modeling languages that help bridge the gap between experts and computer implementations (Fig. 1). These representations may be implemented with paper and pencil or in computer systems. Effective mediating representations obviate the need to build and maintain systems in lower level programming languages. They empower effective communication between experts, knowledge engineers, and efficient implementation. The mediating representation should closely match the representation language the expert normally uses to describe and solve problems or should be easily learned and intuitive to use, so that the expert has little difficulty transforming normal language into the new representation.

Some of these representations are at higher levels of abstraction than others (Fig. 2). Lower level representations are often used as building blocks for higher level representations. Higher level representations are often

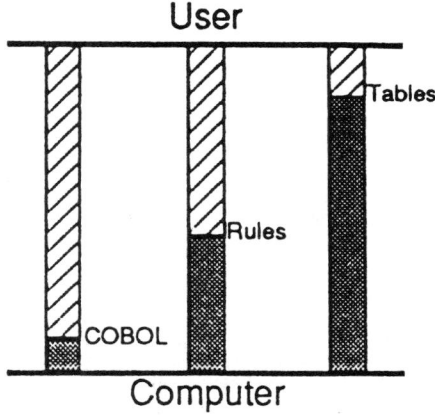

Figure 1. Mediating representations (such as tables) help bridge the gap between the expert (or knowledge engineer) and the computer.

transformed into lower level representations by a computer to perform inference (for instance, decision trees might be transformed into rules). Some representation systems provide a loose framework for collections of other representations (for example, hypertext). Different types of knowledge may be more easily used in one form of representation than another. For instance, tables may emphasize entity-attribute information whereas semantic networks emphasize the relationships between objects.

The use of a spreadsheet is analogous to the use of mediating representations in knowledge acquisition tools. In fact, a spreadsheet could be classified as an effective mediating representation. A spreadsheet provides users

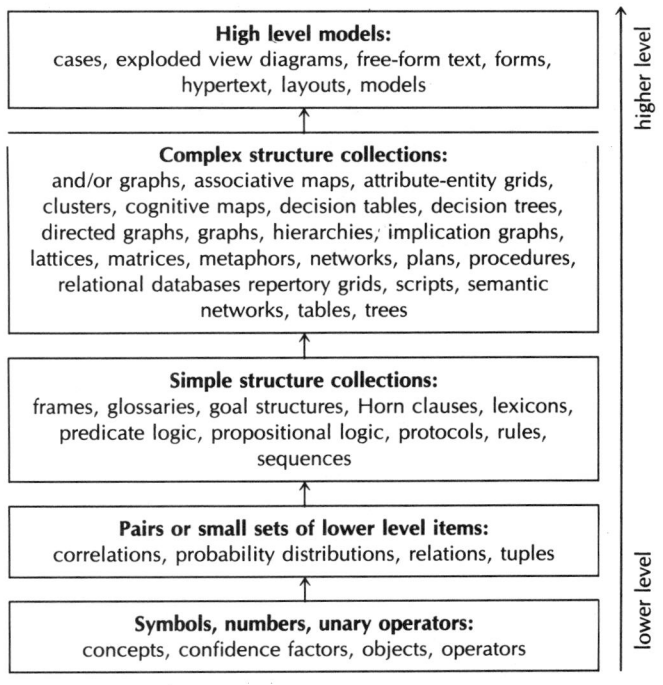

Figure 2. Example mediating representations for knowledge-based systems.

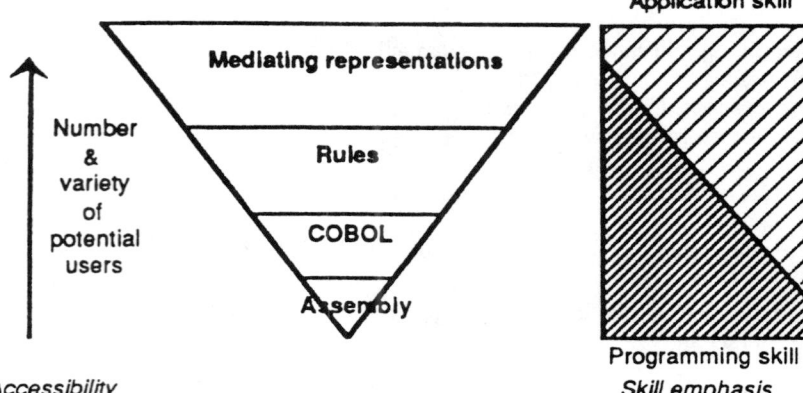

Figure 3. Higher level mediating representations enable access.

with an efficient representation language for building business models. Previously such models were programmed directly in languages such as Basic or COBOL. Many more users can build business models on computers because spreadsheets are available. The emphasis is on business modeling skill, not programming skill (Fig. 3). It can be argued that spreadsheets help improve the quality of business models because users (1) are not burdened with computer programming, (2) concentrate on important aspects of the model directly, (3) can easily change the model, and (4) can more easily maintain the model. Effective mediating representations allow experts and knowledge engineers to concentrate on important aspects of problem-solving. Rules and other lower level knowledge representations were a step forward from LISP or FORTRAN, and higher level representations are a step forward from rules.

There seems to be a basic trade-off in a representation language between acquirability and expressive power (Gruber, 1989a). Programming languages are powerful methods for implementing ideas on computers, but are probably the most difficult to use, especially for nonspecialists. High level representations such as forms may be intuitive to use but are rigid and this limits their applicability. Some representations make it easier to acquire knowledge for specialized applications, some representations have more expressive power. The dotted arrows in the first part of Figure 4 show the dilemma of the knowledge elicitation tool implementor trying to design an ideal representation that combines the naturalness of form-filling interfaces with the power and flexibility of a Turing machine: the more powerful the representation, the more difficult it is to maintain a high level of acquirability. Likewise, developers of programming environments try to represent programming constructs through higher level languages and development environments such as CASE tools. But, inevitably, as representations become more powerful, expressiveness and flexibility are lost. Mediating knowledge representations in knowledge elicitation tools can act to pull the trade-off curve upward to reduce the effects of the trade-off (Bradshaw and co-workers, 1989). References for the tools appear later in this section.

KNOWLEDGE ACQUISITION TOOLS AND TECHNIQUES

Both manual and computer-based knowledge acquisition techniques and tools are described below (Fig. 5). First, a short catalog of manual techniques is listed. Next, computer-based knowledge acquisition tools and techniques are classified and briefly described. Computer-based techniques are divided into interactive (semiautomated) and automated (machine learning) techniques.

Manual Methods

Representative manual knowledge elicitation techniques are described below.

Brainstorming.
   Crawford Slip Method: rapidly generate a large number of ideas (Rusk and Krone, 1984)
Interviewing.
   Unstructured interview: ask general questions and hope for the best, recording as much as possible (B. Brown, 1989; Kidd and Cooper, 1985; Freeman, 1985; von Martial and Victor, 1988; Trimble and Cooper, 1987; Waldron, 1989; Welbank, 1987a).
   Semistructured interview: interview with open questions and a list of topics to cover (Bradshaw, n.d.; Crandall, 1989; Forsythe and Buchanan, 1988, 1989; LaFrance, 1987; Welbank, 1987b).
   Structured interview: interview with strict agenda and list of specific questions relating to features of system (Becker and Balasubramanian, 1989; Bradshaw, n.d.; Clarke, 1987; De La Garza and Ibbs, 1989; Freiling and coworkers, 1985; Haers and d'Y dewalle, 1989; Klein and co-workers, 1989; Shah, 1989; Slocombe and co-workers, 1986; Tournat, 1989).
   Teachback interview: knowledge engineer demonstrates understanding of expertise by paraphrasing or solving a problem (Johnson and Johnson, 1987; Johnson and Tomlinson, 1988).

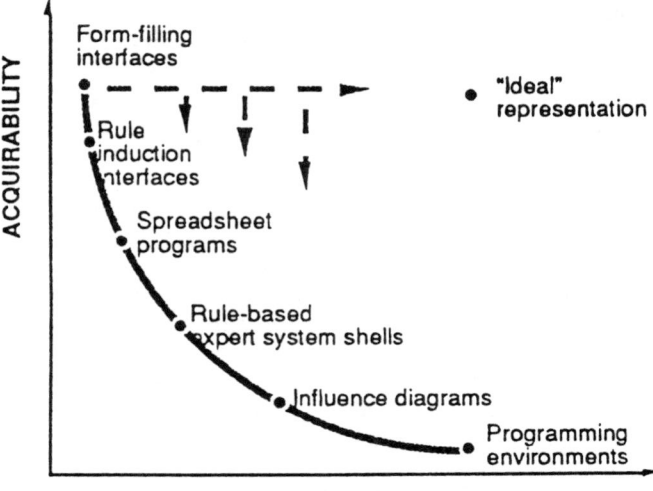

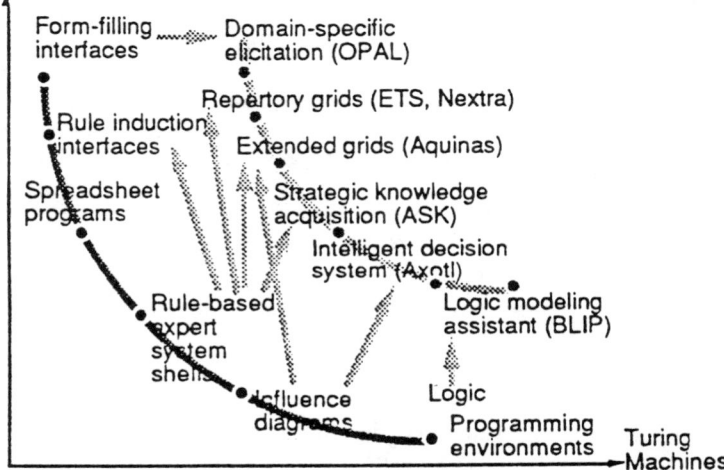

Figure 4. There is a trade-off between knowledge acquirability and expressive power (Gruber, 1989a). The more powerful the representation, the more difficult it is to maintain a high level of acquirability. Mediating knowledge representations in knowledge elicitation tools can act to pull the curve upward to reduce the effects of the trade-off (Bradshaw and co-workers, 1989).

Neurolinguistic programming: observe physical cues (eye movement and body language) to enhance communication with expert (Micciche and Lancaster, 1989).

Tutorial interview: expert delivers a lecture (Welbank, 1987b).

Interviewing process issues: (Fredman, 1987).

Knowledge organization techniques.

Card sorting: sort objects on cards to help structure knowledge (Burton and co-workers, 1987; Gammack and Young, 1984).

Ethnoscience techniques: use anthropological techniques to elicit names of items and categories in a semantic domain (Benfer and Furbee, 1989).

Knowledge analysis: systematically analyze and document knowledge during early phases of knowledge engineering based on mediating representations (Johnson and co-workers, 1988; Regoczei and Hirst, 1988).

Mediating representations: work with representations that mediate between the expert and the implementation (Johnson, 1987; Johnson and co-workers, 1988; Young and Gammack, 1987).

Overcoming bias: recognize and correct bias from knowledge sources (Cleaves, 1987; Meyer and Booker, 1989; Meyer and co-workers, 1989; Moray, 1985; Stephanou, 1987; Tolcott and co-workers, 1989).

Psychological scaling (including multidimensional scaling): use scaling techniques to help structure knowledge (Burton and co-workers, 1987; Saaty, 1981; Golden and co-workers, 1989; Williams and Thomas, 1987; Young and Gammack, 1987).

Uncertain information elicitation and representation: expert encodes uncertainty about the problem (Beyth-Marom and Dekel, 1985; Dean and Kanazawa, 1989; Fischhoff, 1989; Hink and Woods, 1987; Kahneman and co-workers, 1982; Levi, 1989; Mullin, 1989; Pearl, 1986; Shafer and Tversky, 1985; Spetzler and Stael von Holstein, 1983; Stael von Holstein and Matheson, 1978; Tversky and Kahneman, 1974, 1981; Tversky and co-workers, 1987; Wallsten and Budescu, 1983; Yang and Okrent, 1989).

Protocol analysis techniques.

Participant observation: knowledge engineer becomes an apprentice or otherwise participates in the expert's problem-solving process (Welbank, 1987b).

Protocol analysis (case walk-through–eidetic reduction–observation–processstracing): record and analyze transcripts (from experts thinking aloud during tasks or other sources) (Belkin and co-workers, 1987; Breuker and Wielinga, 1987a, 1987b; Burton and co-workers, 1987; Clarke, 1987; Cordingley, 1987; Crandall, 1989; De La Garza and Ibbs, 1989; Ericsson and Simon, 1984; Eskenazi and co-workers, 1989; Gammack and Young, 1984; Grover, 1983; Haers and d'Ydewalle, 1989; Hausen and Neusser, 1987; Johnson and co-workers, 1987; Killin and Hickman, 1986; Kwasnik, 1989; Laske, 1987; Laskey and co-workers, 1989; Littman, 1987; Waldron, 1985; Wetter and Schmalhofer, 1988).

User interface techniques.

Wizard of Oz technique: an expert simulates the behavior of a future system (Sandberg and co-workers, 1988).

Several taxonomies exist that classify manual knowledge elicitation methods. Alternate classification schemes include Hoffman's breakdown including the analysis of familiar tasks, interviewing, special tasks, and constrained processing tasks (Hoffman, 1989); interviewing breakdowns by Shaw and Woodward (1989); and approaches classified by knowledge elicitation task (Morik, 1989). Bradshaw (1991) presents a detailed interviewing methodology for classification problems, emphasizing debiasing techniques. These schemes and others are described in more detail in Boose and Gaines (1990).

Interactive (Semiautomated) Methods

Classification Framework. Interactive knowledge elicitation tools can be associated with knowledge-based appli-

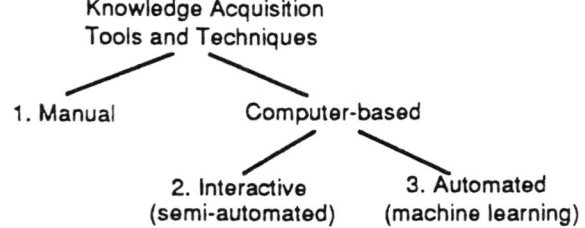

Figure 5. Elicitation tools and techniques are classified by manual, interactive, and automated methods.

cation problems and problem-solving methods. This descriptive approach provides a framework for analyzing and comparing elicitation tools, and focuses the task of building knowledge-based systems on the knowledge elicitation process and accompanying knowledge representations.

Several taxonomies exist for categorizing knowledge-based application problems. One common scheme, illustrated below, divides them into analysis (interpretation) problems and synthesis (construction) problems (Clancey, 1986a). Generally, analysis problems involve identifying sets of objects based on their features. One characteristic of analysis problems is that a complete set of solutions can be enumerated and included in the system. Synthesis (generative or constructive) problems require that a solution be built up from component pieces or subproblem solutions. In synthesis problems there are too many potential solutions to enumerate and include explicitly in the system.

Analysis and synthesis problems can be broken down into subproblem areas. The following classification is used in the remainder of this section, although the same knowledge elicitation tool mapping idea can be applied to other problem taxonomies (Hayes-Roth and co-workers, 1983). Alternate taxonomies have been described (Boose and Gaines, 1990).

Analysis problems.

Classification: categorizing based on observables.

Debugging: prescribing remedies for malfunctions.

Diagnosis: inferring system malfunctions from observables.

Interpretation: inferring situation descriptions from sensor data.

Synthesis (construction) problems.

Configuration: configuring collections of objects under constraints in relatively small search spaces.

Design: configuring collections of objects under constraints in relatively large search spaces.

Planning: designing actions.

Scheduling: planning with strong time or spatial constraints.

Analysis and synthesis problems.

Command and control: ordering and governing overall system control.

Instruction: diagnosing, debugging and repairing student behavior.

Monitoring: comparing observations to expected outcomes.

Prediction: inferring likely consequences of given situations.

Repair: executing plans to administer prescribed remedies.

Relationships exist between problems and problem-solving methods. For instance, the heuristic classification problem-solving method has been used for many knowledge-based systems that solve analysis problems (Clancey, 1986a) and is employed in a variety of knowledge-based system development tools, or "shells" (S.1, M.1, EMYCIN, TI-PC, and so on). In heuristic classification, data are abstracted up through a problem hierarchy, problem abstractions are mapped onto solution abstractions, and solution abstractions are refined down through the solution hierarchy into specific solutions.

General methods for solving synthesis problems are sparse; Clancey classified these methods under heuristic construction. Usually, a specific method is developed to solve a particular problem (such as SALT's propose-and-revise method or OPAL's skeletal-plan-refinement method), but it may be difficult to generalize the method. Some form of directed backtracking or cyclic constraint exploration is often used to explore the problem space.

Many problems require a combination of analysis and synthesis problem-solving methods. For instance, Clancey outlines a maintenance cycle requiring monitoring, prediction, diagnosis, and modification. This combines aspects of heuristic classification and heuristic construction.

Musen and co-workers (1987) proposed that knowledge elicitation tools could be associated with specific problems or specific problem-solving methods. In a related manner, it is proposed that tools be classified with problems and problem-solving methods, because most problems are strongly linked to certain types of problem-solving method. Consequently, certain types of domain knowledge and possibly control knowledge should be acquired to build the corresponding knowledge-based system. This

idea has been discussed in Gaines and Boose (1990). Builders of interactive knowledge elicitation tools were asked to try to classify their research and the research of others in terms of these relationships. Figure 6 shows a possible mapping of such relationships at a high level in the problem classification hierarchy and a problem-solving method classification hierarchy. Lower levels in the problem hierarchy would be subproblems (ie, troubleshooting and symptom analysis would be found under diagnosis), and the leaves of the problem hierarchy would be specific application problems to be solved.

Knowledge elicitation tool research falls into several categories. Descriptions and references for the tools mentioned here are given below.

Research Strategies.
Problem–Method Relationships. (1) Find and clarify knowledge elicitation strategies for a problem-to-method relationship (usually a domain-specific problem employing a highly specialized method using much domain knowledge, or a general problem employing a general method with little domain knowledge). Examples for specific problem domains (bottom up) include ASKE, FIS, MOLTKE, MUM, OPAL, PROTOGÉ, SMAC, and STUDENT. Examples for general analysis problems (top down) include AQUINAS, CLASSIKA, DART, EAR*, ETS, FLEXIGRID, IRA-GRID, KITTEN, KRITON, NEXTRA, KSS0, and SMEE. (2) Pick a problem, find and develop knowledge elicitation strategies for an applicable method, and then see if the method and strategies will generalize to another problem. Examples (middle out) in-

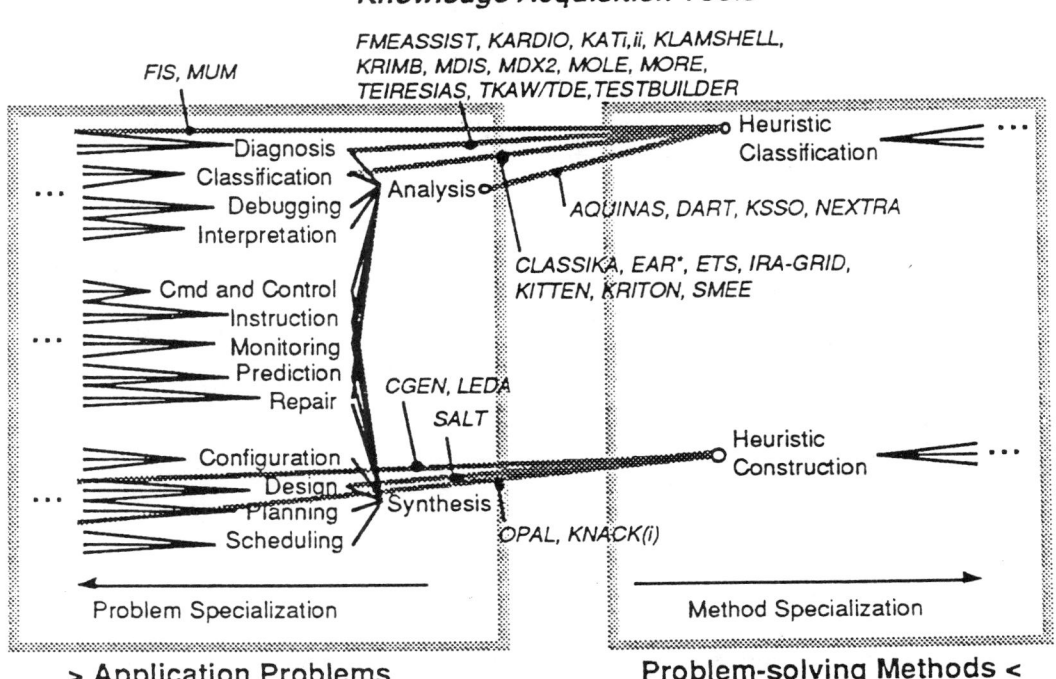

Figure 6. Knowledge elicitation tools may be associated with relationships between application problems and problem-solving methods. Representative tools are shown.

clude 3DKAT, ASKE, BLIP, CANARD, CGEN, DA-CRON, FMEASSIST, GEN-X, INFORM, KARDIO, KAT (i), KAT (ii), KLAMSHELL, KNACK (i), KNACK (ii), KRIMB, LEDA, MDIS, MDX2, MOLE, MORE, ONTOS, ROGET, QUIZ, SALT, SMAC, TEIRESIAS, TEST-BENCH, TESTBUILDER, TKAW/TDE, and VIEW-POINT.

Task and Problem Languages. Develop representation languages for defining and describing problems and methods. To some extent, all successful knowledge elicitation tools and methods must employ representations that knowledge engineers or experts can understand. Examples that place particular emphasis on these languages include ASTEK, CODE, KADS, MAC, concept language (Addis and Bull, 1988), ontology (Alexander and co-workers, 1987; Freiling, 1988; Freiling and Jacobson, 1989; Jacobson and Freiling, 1989), task primitives (Bylander and Mittal, 1986; Bylander and Chandrasekaran, 1987; Chandrasekaran, 1988), knowledge dictionary (Davis and Bonnell, 1989; Rochowiak and Mosley, 1989), task language (Gruber and Cohen, 1987), domain ontology (Hayward and co-workers, 1987; Schreiber and co-workers, 1988), knowledge dictionary integration (Jansen and Compton, 1988, 1989), mediating representations (Johnson and co-workers, 1988), and intermediate representations (Young and Gammack, 1987).

Intelligent Editors, Hypermedia. Build intelligent editors to help AI programmers construct large knowledge bases. Examples include editors such as APPRENTICE, CYC, GKE, KET, KREME, PRED, and SEEGRAPH and hypermedia such as ACQUIST, CAMEO, COGNOSYS, KSS0, ONTOS, and SMAC.

Patterns in Semiautomated Tools. Figure 7 plots elicitation tools on domain and problem axes. There is a strong concentration of knowledge elicitation tools for diagnostic problems, but few knowledge elicitation tools exist for synthesis problems. Other patterns in the tools are apparent. For instance, some tools try to draw power using strong specific domain knowledge (ASKE, FIS, GKE, LAS, LEAP, MOLTKE, MUM, OPAL, PROTOGÉ, SMAC, and STUDENT); other tools try to address a broader range of problems at the expense of built-in domain-specific problem solving power (AQUINAS, CLASSIKA, DART, EAR*, ETS, FLEXIGRID, IRA-GRID, KITTEN, KRITON, NEXTRA, KSS0, and SMEE). The few tools that address synthesis problems are domain dependent (CGEN, LEDA, and SALT). Few strong commercial tools are available (commercial tools include AutoIntelligence, GeneR, KAT (iii), NEXTRA, TestBuilder/Testbench). Most researchers seem to be interested in applying their tools to more domain independent and harder tasks.

Semiautomated Tool Methods. Computer-based tools are described below, indexed by type of method. When specific tools implement these methods, the name of the tool is listed. Work describing methods not implemented as computer-based tools, and tools without names, are referenced as methods. Many tools employ multiple methods and are indexed in several categories.

A. Psychology-based and interviewing methods.
   1. Automated or mixed-initiative interviewing: the tool interviews the expert.
      AQUINAS, ARK, ASK, COGNOSYS, DART, EAR*, ELI, ETS, IRA-GRID, KAT (i), KIT-TEN, KNACK (i), KRIMB, KRITON, KSS0, MDIS, MOLE, MORE, NEXTRA, ODYSSEUS, PLANET, PROTOKI, PROTOS, ROGET, SALT, TEIRESIAS, TKAW/TDE.
      Methods: Furuya and Hattori (1989)
   2. Protocol analysis (case walk through, eidetic reduc-

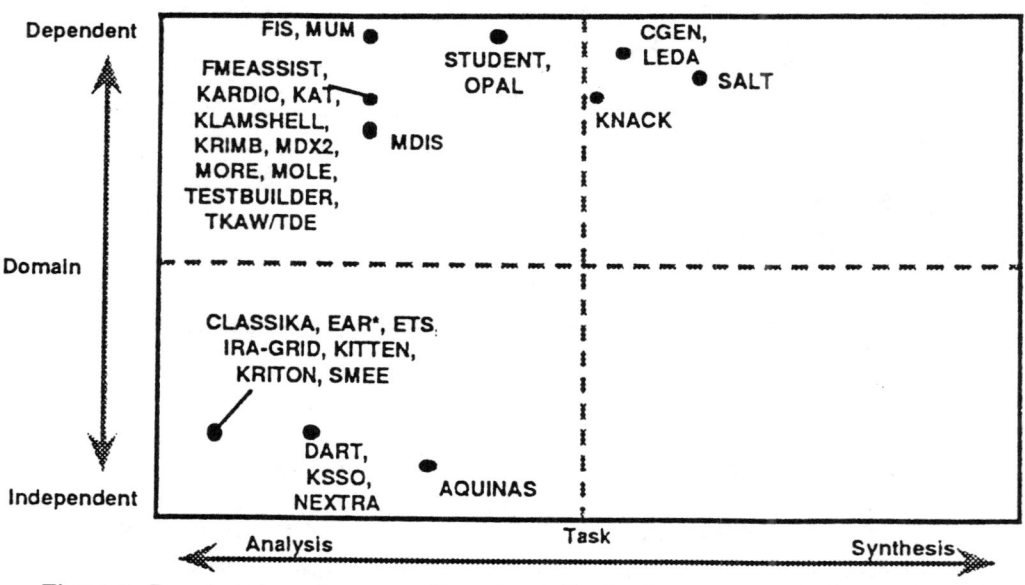

Figure 7. Domain independence vs problem class table showing representative interactive tools.

tion, observation, process tracing): record and analyze transcripts from experts thinking aloud about tasks.

> CODE, COGNOSYS, KRITON, LAPS, MACAO, MEDKAT.

3. Psychological scaling (including multidimensional scaling): use scaling techniques to help structure knowledge.

> AQUINAS, DART, EAR*, IRA-GRID, FLEXI-GRID, KITTEN, KRITON, KSS0, NEXTRA, PATHFINDER, PLANET, SMEE.
>
> Methods: Adelman (1989), Butler and Corter (1986), Furuya and Hattori (1989), and Gaines and Shaw (1981).

4. Repertory grids and PCP: use personal construct psychology and related methods to elicit and analyze knowledge.

> AQUINAS, AUTOINTELLIGENCE, CANARD, DART, EAR*, ETS, FLEXIGRID, IRA-GRID, KITTEN, KRITON, KSS0, NEXTRA, PLANET, SMEE.
>
> Methods: Ford and co-workers (1989), Ford and Petry (1989), Furuya and Hattori (1989), and Kelly (1955).

B. Problem, method, and performance exploitation.

1. Domain problem exploitation (single application): rely heavily on the domain for knowledge acquisition guidance.

> ASKE, FIS, LEAP, MOLTKE, OPAL, PRO-TOGÉ, SMAC, STUDENT.
>
> Methods: Boy and Caminel (1989) and Lee (1989).

2. Problem-solving method exploitation: use information about the problem-solving method to guide knowledge acquisition.

> AQUINAS, ASKE, CANARD, CGEN, CLAS-SIKA, DACRON, DART, FMEASSIST, GEN-X, KARDIO, KAT (i), KAT (ii), KLAM-SHELL, KNACK (i), KNACK (ii), LEDA, MDIS, MDX2, MOLE, MORE, SALT, SMAC, SMEE, TEIRESIAS, TKAW, VIEWPOINT.
>
> Methods: Chu (1989), and Furuya and Hattori (1989).

3. Performance system (direct link or embedded): generate knowledge that may be directly tested by an embedded inference engine or by a separate shell.

> APPRENTICE, AQUINAS, ASK, ASKE, BLIP, CGEN, DART, ETS, GEN-X, IVY, IRA-GRID, KAE, KAT (ii), KLAMSHELL, KNACK (i), KNACK (ii), KRITON, KSS0, LAPS, LEAP, MDIS, MOLE, MOLTKE, MORE, MUM, NEX-TRA, ODYSSEUS, OPAL, PROTOGÉ, RO-GET, TEIRESIAS, TESTBENCH, TEST-BUILDER, TKAW, SALT.
>
> Methods: Boy and Caminel (1989), Boy and Delail (1988), Brown (1989), and Loftin and co-workers (1989)

4. Verification, validation, and maintenance: verify and validate knowledge acquisition techniques; support testing, delivery, and maintenance of KBSs; help with necessity and sufficiency measur-

ing for the knowledge-based system life cycle.

> AQUINAS, TESTBED
>
> Methods: Baum and co-workers (1989), Benbaset and Dhaliwal (1988, 1989a, 1989b), Chadha and co-workers (1989), Dhaliwal and Benbaset (1989), Enand and co-workers (1988), Gale (1988), Kellogg and co-workers (1989), Lehner (1989), Levi (1989), Shadbolt and Burton (1989), Shaw (1988), and Shaw and Woodward (1987).

C. Modeling.

1. Causal modeling: build cause-and-effect models of domain entities and relationships.

> CMET, FIS, MOLE.
>
> Methods: Bradshaw and Young (1988)

2. Cognitive modelng: model thought process and human problem solving.

> BDM-KAT, COGNOSYS, ONTOS
>
> Methods: situation recognition and reasoning patterns (Boy, 1989; Boy and Caminel, 1989; Boy and Delail, 1988; Boy and Nuss, 1988), cognitive modeling (LaFrance, 1989; Nobel, 1989; Shalin and co-workers, 1989; Woods and Hollnagel, 1987), cognitive primitives (Rappaport, 1988), signal and symbol processing (Rouse and co-workers, 1989), and mental models (Shaw and Woodward, 1989).

3. Conceptual modeling: build graphical or other multiple level models.

> APPRENTICE (graphical planning models), BLIP (top-down, bottom-up modeling), GEKA-TOO (syntactic conceptual models), KET (graphical models), METAMATH (multiple level knowledge modeling), PROTOGÉ (conceptual models of knowledge acquisition tools), ROGET (conceptual domain structures), SEE-GRAPH (graphic query), SORTAL (conceptual modeling).
>
> Methods: theories, models and representations (Addis, 1987, 1989); conceptual graphs (Berg-Cross and Price, 1989; Eklund and Kellett, 1989; Pau and Nielsen, 1989); knowledge templates (Brulé, 1989); semantic modeling (Jansson and Rudström, 1989); top-down, bottom-up modeling (Morik, 1987b); conceptual modeling (Regoczei and Hirst, 1988, 1989a, 1989b; Regoczei and Plantinga, 1987); fraphical interface for decision trees (Ribar, 1989); knowledge analysis model (Twine, 1988, 1989); and rule editor (Yoshi, 1989).

4. Consistency analysis, completeness checking: analyze knowledge for consistency or completeness.

> ANALYZER, BLIP, FIS, KAT (ii), KNAC, KNACK (ii), LAPS, LÉZARD, MUM, QMOD, TEIRESIAS, VIEWPOINT.
>
> Methods: Chen (1989) and Polat and Güvenir (1989)

5. Decision analysis: perform probabilistic inference and planning using influence diagrams and related techniques.

> AXOTL, CANARD, INFORM

Methods: Adelman (1989), Bradshaw and Boose (1990), and von Winterfeldt and Edwards (1986).

6. Domain modeling: build rich domain models.

3DKAT (design models), ASKE (domain exemplars), BLIP (domain modeling), CANARD (design alternatives and constraints), CGEN (specification models), FMEASSIST (failure modes and effects), INDE (deep modeling), KARDIO (diagnostic models), KAT (diagnostic models), KRIMB (diagnostic models), LÉZARD (deep modeling), ONTOS (domain and cognitive models), ROGET (conceptual domain structures), QUIZ (domain models from text), TESTBENCH (failure modes models), TESTBUILDER (failure modes models).

Methods: diagnostic models (Araya, 1988; Krishanamurthi and Underbrink, 1989; Linster, 1987), and design knowledge (Boose and co-workers, 1989a; Friel and co-workers, 1989).

7. Ontological modeling, linguistic modeling: build language-based models.

ASTEK (ontology), CODE (concepts and terms), KADS (domain ontology), MAC (domain ontology).

Methods: concept language (Addis and Bull, 1988), ontology (Alexander and co-workers, 1987; Freiling and Jacobson, 1989; Jacobson and Freiling, 1989), text models (Berry-Rogghe and Kaplan, 1986), knowledge dictionary (Davis and Bonnell, 1989; Rochowiak and Mosley, 1989), domain ontology (Hayward and co-workers, 1987; Schreiber and co-workers, 1988), and knowledge dictionary integration (Jansen and Compton, 1988, 1989).

8. Simulation: run simulations to verify knowledge bases or produce rules.

3DKAT, MDIS, QUMAS, SIMULA.

Methods: generate diagnostic rules from simulations (Becker and co-workers, 1989).

D. Knowledge browsers.

1. Graphical browsers: provide knowledge browsers and editors as a primary elicitation tool.

APPRENTICE, CYC, GKE, KET, KREME, NEXPERT, PRED, SEEGRAPH.

2. Hypermedia: use hypermedia to capture and document knowledge.

ACQUIST, CAMEO, COGNOSYS, KAT (iii), KSS0, ONTOS, SMAC.

Methods: Boy (1989), Gaines and Sharp (1987), Kellogg and co-workers (1989), Lee (1989), Lindsay and co-workers (1988), Rantanen (1989), and Wells (1989).

E. Multiple experts.

1. Delphi: gather information from people independently

MEDKAT.

2. Multiple source: elicit and analyze knowledge from multiple sources separately and combine for use and further analysis.

ANALYZER, AQUINAS, CARTER, DART, ETS, GKE, MEDKAT, KITTEN, KSS0, NEXTRA

Methods: Gaines (1987a, 1987b), LeClair (1989), Liou and co-workers (1989), Loftin and co-workers (1989), Mittal and Dym (1985), and Wolf (1989).

F. Other sources of knowledge.

1. CAD database, database management systems: acquire knowledge directly from computer-aided design data or other databases.

CMET.

Methods: Myler and Gonzalez (1989).

2. Textual analysis, natural language analysis: generate knowledge directly by analyzing text.

ACQUIST, KADS, KALEX, KRITON, KSS0, KBAM, LUKES, PETRARCA, PROPOS/EPISTOS, QUIZ, SORTAL, WASTL

Methods: Allgayer and co-workers (1989), Arinze (1989), Berry-Rogghe and Kaplan (1986), Cordingley (1987), De La Garza and Ibbs (1989), Fass (1989), Gomez (1989), Kornecki, (1989), Kwasnik (1989), McHugh (1987), Slator (1988, 1989), Tsui (1988), and Velardi (1989).

Automated (Machine Learning) Tools and Techniques

Interactions Between Automated and Semiautomated Methods. Automated (machine learning) methods typically apply algorithms to make generalizations or induce knowledge from examples. The interaction between interactive and machine learning methods has been discussed (Boose and co-workers, 1989c; Gaines, 1989b; Kodratoff, 1989). Several tools have combined interactive methods with machine learning methods (for example, AQUINAS, BLIP, DISCIPLE, ELI, IVY, KARDIO, KRITON, KSS0, LEDA, NEXTRA, ODYSSEUS, and TEIRESIAS). Typically in such a combined system, information is elicited from the expert and analyzed. Then the tool generates information using a machine learning technique. The expert may use this information to further refine and debug the knowledge base, or the information might be used directly by an expert system "shell."

Gaines (1989a) has studied how the amount of knowledge available from the expert affects the amount of data required for effective empirical induction. He took a set of cases originally defined by Cendrowska (1987) as a test of empirical induction and generated a range of data sets from it by making incorrect decisions with known probability and adding a prescribed number of irrelevant attributes with random values. He then applied an empirical induction algorithm, INDUCT, to the data sets to determine the average amount of data required to obtain a correctly performing set of rules. The original dataset can be correctly modeled with six rules involving four attributes.

Figure 8 shows some of Gaines's results as a plot of the data required on average for empirical induction against the type of knowledge available from the simulated expert. The trade-off between data and expertise is clearly shown, and what is also apparent is the continuum between dependence on empirical induction from cases on the left and dependence on elicitation of expert knowledge on the right. The results validate the claims of those with tools aimed primarily at eliciting relevant attributes and

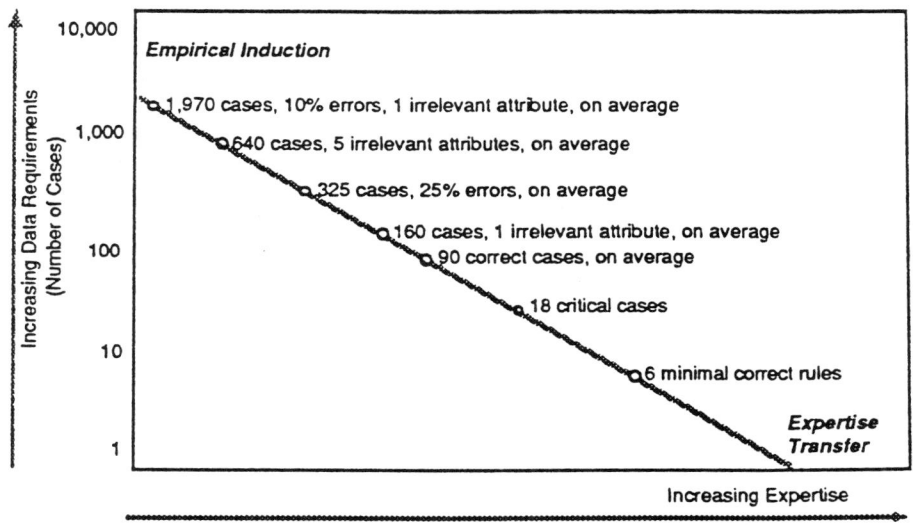

Figure 8. Knowledge–data trade-off in expertise transfer and empirical induction (Gaines, 1989b).

critical cases from experts that this is an efficient approach. They also show that empirical induction and expertise elicitation can be combined to produce a more powerful and versatile acquisition tool than either alone. In the future methodologies and tools will increasingly support a combination of techniques.

Automated Tools and Techniques. Representative machine learning tools appear below, indexed by technique. Alternate classification schemes include Kodratoff's (1989) breakdown into specification-guided and example-guided deductive processes, and inductive learning from examples and observations (adapted from Michalski and co-workers, 1983, 1986; Kodratoff and Michalski, 1989); a division into logical, functional, and procedural methods (MacDonald and Witten, 1989); Michalski and co-workers' (1986) traditional classification of role learning, learning from instruction, by deduction, analogy, example, and discovery; and a classification by representation generation agent, experience generation agent, and representation evaluator (Shalin and co-workers, 1988). These schemes and others have been detailed (Boose and Gaines, 1990).

Analogy: apply knowledge from old situations in similar new situations.
CYC, TEIRESIAS.
Methods: Adelson (1989) and Leishman (1989).
Apprenticeship learning: learn by watching experts solve problems.
CLINT, DISCIPLE, ISG, LEAP, LEDA, MALEFIZ, METAMOUSE, ODYSSEUS, PROTOS.
Methods: Yamada and Tsuji (1989).
Case-based learning: reason directly from a set of stored cases.
AQUINAS, CREEK, ELI, IVY, MOLTKE, PETRARCA.
Methods: Becker (1988), Chadha and co-workers (1989), and Hardt (1988).
Decision tree induction–analysis; question scheduling: generate, analyze decision trees.
CART, ID3, KATE.
Methods: Bramer (1987), Cox (1988), González and Al-

caraz (1989), Goodman and Smyth (1987a, 1987b), Mellis (1989), Merrem (1989), Pettit and Pettit (1987), and Ruberg and co-workers (1988).
Discovery: learn by experimentation and observation.
EURISKO, LEX.
Methods: Thanassas (1989).
Example selection: select an appropriate set of examples for various learning techniques.
Methods: Blythe and co-workers (1987) and Rissland (1987).
Explanation-based learning: deduce a general rule from a single example by relating it to an existing theory.
ACES, EPSILON, INDE, IVY, LAS, LBUE, LEAP, OCCAM, ODYSSEUS, SRAR.
Methods: Kodratoff (1987), Levi and co-workers (1988), Zinßmeister and Hoppe (1989).
Function induction: learn functions from input data.
BACON, MARVIN, NODDY.
Genetic algorithm: genetic operators (crossing-over, mutation, and inversion) are used to adapt a system's behavior.
Methods: Pettit and Pettit (1987).
Induction of models from experience
AM, ATOM.
Neural networks.
Methods: Daley (1989), Hayslip and Eilbert (1989), Oosthuizen (1987) and Tani and co-workers (1989).
Performance feedback: performance feedback is used to reinforce behavior.
ACM, AQUINAS, CHECKERS, MOLE, PROTOS, STELLA.
Rule–knowledge induction and modification: generate rules and other forms of knowledge.
AQ, AQUINAS, BLIP, CHARADE, EPSILON, ETS, KSS0, INDUCE, INDUCT, INSTIL, ISOLDE, ITRULE, KARDIO, KSS0, LEW, NEXTRA, PRISM, TLTS, VERSION SPACES.
Methods: Bergandano and co-workers (1989), Buntine (1987), Cleary (1987), Delgrande (1987), Furuya and Hattori (1989), González and Alcaraz (1989), Goodman and Smyth (1987b), Handa and Ishizaki (1988,

1989), Liang (1989), MacDonald and Witten (1989), Maler (1987), Rissland (1987), Ruberg and co-workers (1988), Sebag and Schoenauer (1988), Subramanian and Freuder (1989), Suwa and Motodd (1989a, 1989b), and Witten and MacDonald (1988).

Similarity-based learning: learn similarities from sets of positive examples and differences from sets of negative examples.

BLIP, GINESYS, ID3, ILROD, INC2, INDE, INSTIL. Methods: Becker and Balasubramanian (1989), Matheus (1989), and Schröder and co-workers (1988).

Systemic principles derivation: use general principles to derive specific laws.

OBJ.

COMPUTER-BASED TOOLS CATALOG

The tools mentioned above are briefly described and referenced here.

3DKAT. Acquire models for design-oriented applications (Dieng and Trousse, 1988).

ACES. Learn heuristics for fault diagnosis from device descriptions using explanation-based learning (Pazzani, 1987).

ACQUIST. Use a hypertext-based tool to acquire knowledge for KEATS (Motta and co-workers, 1988a, 1988b, 1989).

AM. Induce models from experience (Davis and Lenat, 1982).

ANALYZER. Elicit software requirements through a system of distributed cooperating agents (Easterbrook, 1989).

APPRENTICE. Use a graphical language to acquire knowledge about object manipulation for planning domains (Joseph, 1989).

AQ. Induce rules from sets of positive and negative training examples (Michalski, 1983).

AQUINAS. Elicit and model information using a knowledge acquisition workbench including hierarchically structured repertory grid-based interviewing and testing and other methods (Baum and co-workers, 1989; Boose, 1988, 1989; Boose and Bradshaw, 1987a, 1987b; Boose and co-workers, 1988, 1989a, 1989c; Bradshaw and Boose, 1990; Bradshaw and co-workers, 1988; Kitto, 1988; Kitto and Boose, 1987, 1989; Schuler and co-workers, 1988; Shema and Boose, 1988; Shema and co-workers, 1988, 1989).

ARK. Ask experts about the consequences of events (Tonn and co-workers, 1989).

ASK. Acquire strategic knowledge from experts using a justification language (Gruber, 1988a, 1988b, 1989a, 1989b, 1989c; Gruber and Cohen, 1989).

ASKE. Use exemplars from similar domains and task models to elicit problem solving expertise from the expert (Patel, 1988, 1989).

ASTEK. Combine multiple paradigms for knowledge editing in a natural language discourse framework (Jacobson and Freiling, 1988, 1989).

ATOM. Induce models from experience (Gaines, 1977).

AXOTL. Use influence diagrams and other decision analysis techniques to represent process and probabilistic knowledge for problems with large amounts of uncertainty and complex trade-offs (Bradshaw and co-workers, 1988, 1989).

AUTOINTELLIGENCE. Elicit knowledge using repertory grid techniques, commercial tool (Intelligence-Ware).

BACON. Discover empirical scientific laws by inducing functions that account for observed behavior (Langley and co-workers, 1983, 1986).

BDM-KAT. Provide an environment for knowledge engineers and experts to discuss, manipulate, and record objects and relationships (Lancaster and co-workers, 1989; McGraw, 1989; McGraw and Lancaster, 1989).

BLIP. Construct organized domain models automatically by learning from sloppy models (Kietz, 1988; Morik, 1987a, 1989; Wrobel, 1988).

CAMEO. Use hypertext to model and view expertise from multiple perspectives (Jones, 1989).

CARTER. Recognize and repair discrepancies in knowledge bases from multiple experts (Trice and Davis, 1989).

CANARD. Provide an exploratory environment for acquiring and narrowing design alternatives and constraints (Shema and co-workers, 1989).

CART. Employ cross-validation to produce appropriately sized decision trees (Crawford, 1989).

CGEN. Use specifications and generalization to design computers (Birmingham, 1989; Birmingham and Siewiorek, 1988).

CHARADE. Use inductive learning and empirical generalization for preventive maintenance (Dupas and Millot, 1989).

CHECKERS. Learn variable weights by trial and error for playing checkers (Samuel, 1963).

CLASSIKA. Use expert-directed techniques to capture aspects of classification problem-solving (Gappa, 1988, 1989a, 1989b; Gappa and Puppe, 1989).

CLINT. Learn concepts from incomplete, weak examples (De Raedt and Bruynooghe, 1989).

CMET. Acquire causal models from test and display databases (Schaefer, 1989).

CODE. Perform conceptual and terminological analysis (Skuce, 1989; Skuce and co-workers, 1989).

COGNOSYS. Using a hypertext-based system acquire domain definition knowledge (Woodward, 1988).

CREEK. Continuously update diagnostic knowledge bases using case-based learning (Aamodt, 1989).

CYC. Acquire and use knowledge through the use of analogy and a large existing knowledge base (Lenat and co-workers, 1986).

DACRON. Acquire knowledge for situation based calculus planners (Mahling and Croft, 1988).

DART. NASA tool roughly based on AQUINAS, tailored for engineering trade studies (Boose and co-workers, 1990).

DISCIPLE. Integrate various machine learning techniques to adopt to available theories (Kodratoff and Tecuci, 1988).

EAR*. Build knowledge-level structures for heuristic classification using repertory grids and interviewing methods (Plaza and Màntaras, 1989).

ELI. Interview experts and store knowledge in rule-oriented AND/OR graphs (Silverman and co-workers, 1989).

EPSILON. Perform knowledge acquisition by abductive and inductive explanation-based generalization (Taki, 1989; Taki and Fujii, 1989).

ETS. Interview experts using repertory grid-based methods and test the knowledge (Boose, 1984, 1985, 1986a, 1986b; Boose and co-workers, 1989a).

EURISKO. Learn heuristics and concepts by discovery (Lenat, 1983).

FIS. Tie knowledge acquisition closely to the fault diagnosis domain (De Jong, 1987).

FLEXIGRID. Use repertory grid techniques to elicit and analyze knowledge (Tschudi, 1988).

FMEASSIST. Acquire failure characteristics for failure modes and effects analysis (Carnes, 1989).

GEKATOO. Acquire conceptual models, checking for syntactic completeness (Bonarini and co-workers, 1989).

GENER. Acquire object hierarchies from experts and help generate if/then rules, commercial tools from Cognisys (Mychaltchouk and co-workers, 1989).

GEN-X. Acquire decision trees, AND/OR graphs, and if/then rule tables for diagnosis (Crapo and Shah, 1989).

GINESYS. Use confirmation rules, a form of redundant knowledge, to learn in noisy domains (Gams, 1988).

GKE. Decrease representational complexity by supporting multiple viewpoints and structured system design in a graphical framework (Kontio and Lounamaa, 1989).

ID3. Learn similarities and differences from training sets by optimizing global parameters (Quinlan, 1983, 1987).

ILROD. Perform logic-based induction on Horn clauses to learn knowledge of relevance (Dutta, 1988).

INC2. Perform learning by observation using hill climbing through a space of hierarchical classification schemes (Hadzikadic, 1988).

INDE. Generate rules on the basis of counterexamples combining explanation-based learning and similarity-based learning (Terpstra and van Someren, 1988).

INDUCE. Induce knowledge that mimics an expert's behavior (Michalski and Chilausky, 1980).

INDUCT. Induce rules from a training set (Gaines, 1989a, 1989b; Gaines and Rappaport, 1989).

INFORM. Elicit knowledge using decision analysis techniques (Moore and Agogino, 1987).

INSTIL. Acquire knowledge using similarity-based learning combining aspects of both numeric and symbolic approaches (Kodratoff and Manago, 1987).

IRA-GRID. Use repertory grids to acquire knowledge for general classification problems (Linster, 1989a).

ISG. Link evidence to situations by synthesizing rules from interesting situations using an apprenticeship learning approach (Wisniewski and co-workers, 1987).

ISOLDE. Learn organic chemistry through induction (Rose and Gelernter, 1989).

ITRULE. Induce rules using an information–theoretic metric (Goodman and Smyth, 1987a).

IVY. Find gaps in a current knowledge base and formulate plans to fill the gaps (Hunter, 1988).

KADS. Elicit and model knowledge decoupled from the design and implementaton of the system (Anjewierden, 1987; Breuker and Wielinga, 1987a, 1987b; de Greef and Breuker, 1989; Jansen-Winkeln, 1988; Konrad and Tong, 1989; Karbach and co-workers, 1988; Schreiber and co-workers, 1988; Tong, 1989; Tong and Karbach, 1988; Valtorta, 1989; Wielinga and co-workers, 1989).

KAE. Capture scene analysis expertise (Tranowski and co-workers, 1988).

KALEX. Translate sentences from experts into an internal representation (Schmidt and Wetter, 1989).

KARDIO. Generate diagnostic rules from models (Lavrac and Mozetic, 1989).

KAT (i). Acquire knowledge category information for diagnosis (D'Ambrosio, 1989).

KAT (ii). Acquire diagnostic information for a diagnostic refinement language (Bansal and Posco, 1989).

KAT (iii). Acquire knowledge for LEVELS using a hypertext editor, commercial tool (Ribar).

KATE. Given examples of an expert's diagnosis and background domain knowledge, generate a decision tree and rules (Rouveirol and Manago, 1988).

KBAM. Use natural language explanations to construct a domain-specific knowledge base (Silvestro, 1988).

KET. Provide a graphical interface and analyze relationships to help experts write rules (Esfahani and Teskey, 1987, 1988).

KITTEN. Interview experts using repertory grid-based methods (Shaw and Gaines, 1987b; Shaw and Woodward, 1988).

KLAMSHELL. Acquire decision trees for maintenance and troubleshooting (Cochran, 1988).

KNAC. Use acquired assimilation knowledge to help enter new knowledge in a knowledge base (Lefkowitz and Lesser, 1988).

KNACK (i). Elicit and use knowledge about evaluation report generation (Kitto, 1988; Klinker, 1989; Klinker and co-workers, 1987, 1988, 1989).

KNACK (ii). Acquire information from knowledge engineers and experts, allow browsing and editing for classification, diagnosis and repair (Hsieh and co-workers, 1988).

KREME. Include multiple representations in a knowledge editing environment (Abrett and Burstein, 1987).

KRIMB. Interview experts and build diagnostic domain models (Cox and Blumenthal, 1987).

KRITON. Combine repertory grid interviewing and protocol analysis to build knowledge at an intermediate level (Diederich and co-workers, 1987a, 1987b; Linster, 1988a, 1988b, 1989a, 1989b).

KSS0. Elicit knowledge with a repertory grid-based interviewing tool, including text analysis, behavior induction, and psychological scaling techniques (Gaines, 1987a, 1987b, 1988a, 1988b; Gaines and Rappaport, 1989; Gaines and co-workers, 1989; Gaines and Sharp, 1987; Shaw, 1988, 1989a, 1989b; Shaw and Gaines, 1987a, 1988, 1989).

LAPS. Interweave protocol analysis with completeness querying (di Piazza, 1988; di Piazza and Helsabeck, 1989).

LAS. Use apprenticeship learning to learn by watching experts solve problems (Smith and co-workers, 1985).

LBUE. Combine explanation-based learning and causal model learning (Martin and Redmond, 1989).

LEAP. Use apprenticeship learning to learn steps in VLSI design by watching experts solve problems (Mitchell and co-workers, 1985; Smith and co-workers, 1985).

LEDA. Acquire knowledge for chip architecture design by interactively generalizing design plans (Hermann, 1989; Hermann and Franzke, 1988).

LEW. Learn inductively from examples of problem–solution or question–answer pairs (Constant and co-workers, 1988; Matwin and Oppacher, 1989).

LEX. Acquire problem solving heuristics for symbolic integration (Mitchell and co-workers, 1982).

LÉZARD. Find ambiguities and incompleteness from deep knowledge and ask the expert about them (Charlet and Gascuel, 1989).

LUKES. Perform natural language understanding and knowledge acquisition based on concept cluster attachment (Regoczei and Hirst, 1989a).

MAC. Use a model-directed approach to acquire inferrence structures and successive refinements processes within the KADS framework (de Greef and Breuker, 1989; Konrad and Tong, 1989; Tong, 1989).

MACAO. Model expert knowledge based on empirical and conceptual schemes (Aussenac and co-workers, 1989, 1988).

MALEFIZ. Use apprenticeship learning to acquire geometric knowledge for a complex design task (Herrmann and Beckmann, 1989).

MARVIN. Learn hierarchical structures of concepts or functions (Sammut and Banerji, 1983, 1986).

MDIS. Interview experts to elicit mechanisms in a top-down structured manner for diagnostic problems (Antonelli, 1983).

MDX2. Exploit diagnostic problem solving for clinical medicine (Sticklen and co-workers, 1989).

MEDKAT. Automate the Delphi technique to gather information from multiple experts (Jagannathan and Elmaghraby, 1985).

METAMATH. Perform multiple level knowledge modeling for knowledge engineering (Nordbø and co-workers, 1989).

METAMOUSE. Learn procedural descriptions of graphical concepts, such as object structures, spatial relations, and transformations (Maulsby and co-workers, 1989; Maulsby and Witten, 1988).

MOLE. Exploit information about how problems are solved to elicit scarce diagnostic knowledge and use feedback to fine-tune the knowledge (Eshelman, 1988; Eshelman and co-workers, 1987; Green and Eshelman, 1989).

MOLTKE. Acquire knowledge from diagnostic cases for computerized numerical control applications (Althoff and co-workers, 1989).

MORE. Exploit information about how problems are solved to elicit extensive diagnostic knowledge (Kahn and co-workers, 1985a, 1985b).

MUM. Evidential combination knowledge and control knowledge are elicited for medical problems (Gruber and Cohen, 1987).

NEXTRA. Commercial version of KSS0 (from Neuron Data) (Rappaport and Gaines, 1988).

NODDY. Induce functions from traces of robot program executions (Andreae, 1984a, 1984b).

OBJ. Use general principles to derive specific laws (Goguen and Meseguer, 1983).

OCCAM. Learn to predict outcomes of economic sanction episodes using explanation-based learning (Pazzani, 1987).

ODDYSSEUS. Refine and debug knowledge using apprenticeship learning techniques (Chachere, 1989; Wilkens and co-workers, 1987).

ONTOS. Build domain models using cognitive and linguistic factors (Monarch and co-workers, 1989; Monarch and Nirenburg, 1987; Nirenburg and co-workers, 1988).

OPAL. Tie knowledge acquisition closely to the cancer treatment domain (Combs and co-workers, 1988; Musen, 1988a, 1988b; Musen and co-workers, 1987).

PATHFINDER. Use psychological scaling techniques to help structure knowledge hierarchically (Cooke and McDonald, 1987).

PETRARCA. Acquire a case-based semantic dictionary from text (Velardi and co-workers, 1989).

PLANET. Use repertory grids for psychological interviewing and analysis (Shaw, 1984; Gaines and Shaw, 1986).

PM. Acquire a library of plans for programming using a metrics-driven approach (Reynolds and co-workers, 1989).

PRED. Help experts create frame-based windowed knowledge acquisition interfaces (Xie and co-workers, 1988).

PRISM. Induce rules from a training set (Cendrowska, 1987).

PROPOS/EPISTOS. Transform text into a meaning representation and then perform epistemological analysis using pragmatic fields (Möller, 1988).

PROTOGÉ. Develop and edit the conceptual model of

another knowledge acquisition tool (such as OPAL) for skeletal plan refinement tasks (Musen, 1988a, 1988b, 1989a, 1989b, 1989c).

PROTOKI. Critique new knowledge and integrate it into an existing knowledge base (Murray, 1989; Murray and Porter, 1988, 1989).

QMOD. Represent hypotheses graphically for consistency checking (Feldman and co-workers, 1989).

QUIZ. Semiautomatically process technical text and incrementally produce a domain conceptual model (Szpakowicz, 1988).

QUMAS. Run simulations on partially supplied models and learn new parts of the model (Lavrac and Mozetic, 1989).

ROGET. Interview experts and produce conceptual structures of the domain (Bennet, 1985).

SALT. Elicit and deliver knowledge for constructive constraint satisfaction tasks (Marcus, 1987, 1988a, 1988b, 1989; Marcus and co-workers, 1985; Stout and co-workers, 1988).

SEEGRAPH. Use a graphic query language to manipulate and store information in a network database (Kopec and Latour, 1989).

SIMULA. Use basic laws to derive physical models through simulation (Nygaard and Dahl, 1981).

SMAC. Use hypercards to allow entry of domain and problem-solving knowledge (objects and links) (Moulin, 1989).

SMEE. Combine repertory grid methods and Newell and Simon's problem space concept for manufacturing problems (Garg-Janardan, 1988; Garg-Janardan and Salvendy, 1987).

SOAR. Learn for planning and problem solving, producing probability distributions, and operator applicability conditions (Laird and co-workers, 1986).

SORTAL. Perform meaning-triangle–based sortal analysis (Regoczei and Hirst, 1989a, 1989b).

SRAR. Use explanation-based learning techniques to develop intelligent tutoring systems (Boy and Nuss, 1988).

STELLA. Performance feedback is used to reinforce behavior (Gaines and Andreae, 1966).

STRIPS. Learn macro functions for planning and problem solving (Fikes and co-workers, 1972).

STUDENT. Tie knowledge acquisition closely to the statistical consulting domain (Gale, 1987).

TEIRESIAS. Model existing knowledge to monitor refinements and help debug consultations (Davis and Lenat, 1982).

TESTBENCH, TESTBUILDER. Acquire knowledge for fault tree diagnosis, commercial tool (Carnegie Group, Inc.) (Enand and co-workers, 1988; Lewis and Kahn, 1988).

TKAW/TDE. Exploit information about how problems are solved to elicit trouble-shooting knowledge (Kahn and co-workers, 1987).

TLTS. Learn new knowledge sources for a blackboard system using redesign knowledge (Simoudis, 1988, 1989).

VERSION SPACES. Find all descriptions that are consistent with a set of positive and negative examples (Mitchell, 1982).

VIEWPOINT. Acquire troubleshooting knowledge (Caviedes and Reed, 1989).

WASTL. Acquire knowledge for a natural language understanding system based on KADS methodology (Jansen-Winkeln, 1988).

BIBLIOGRAPHY

A. Aamodt, "Towards Robust Expert Systems That Learn From Experience—An Architectural Framework," in *Proceedings of the Third European Workshop on Knowledge Acquisition for Knowledge-Based Systems*, Express-Tirages, Boung-la-Reine, France, 1989, pp. 311–326.

G. Abrett and M. H. Burstein, "The KREME Knowledge Editing Environment," *Man-Machine Stud.* **27**(2), 103–126 (1987).

T. R. Addis, "A Framework for Knowledge Elicitation," in *Proceedings of the First European Workshop on Knowledge Acquisition for Knowledge-Based Systems*, Reading University, UK, 1987, pp. A1.1–16.

T. R. Addis, "Knowledge for Design," in *Proceedings of the Fourth Knowledge Acquisition for Knowledge-Based Systems Workshop*, Banff, Canada, 1989, pp. 1.1–12.

T. R. Addis and S. P. Bull, "A Concept Language for Knowledge Elicitation," in *Proceedings of the Second European Workshop on Knowledge Acquisition for Knowledge-Based Systems*, GMD, Bonn, Germany, 1988, pp. A1.1–16.

L. Adelman, "Measurement Issues in Knowledge Engineering," *IEEE Trans. Sys. Man Cybernet.* **19**(3), 483–488 (1989).

B. Adelson, "Learning by Analogy: A Cognitive Theory," in *IJCAI Workshop on Knowledge Acquisition*, Detroit, Mich., Morgan-Kaufmann, San Mateo, Calif., 1989, pp. 23–27.

J. H. Alexander, M. J. Freiling, S. J. Shulman, S. Rehfuss, and S. L. Messick, "Ontological Analysis: An Ongoing Experiment," *Int. J. Man-Machine Stud.* **26**(4), 473–486 (1987).

J. Allgayer, K. Harbusch, A. Kobsa, C. Reddig, N. Reithinger, and D. Schmauks, "XTRA: A Natural-Language Access System to Expert Systems," *Int. J. Man-Machine Stud.* **31**, 161–196 (1989).

K. D. Althoff, S. Kockskamper, R. Traphöner, W. Wernicke, and B. Faupel, "Knowledge Acquisition in the Domain of CNC Machining Centers: the MOLTKE Approach," in Aamodt, 1989, pp. 180–195.

P. M. Andreae, "Constraint Limited Generalization: Acquiring Procedures from Examples," in *Proceedings of the Fourth National Conference on Artificial Intelligence*, Austin, Tex., AAAI, Menlo Park, Calif., 1984a.

P. M. Andreae, *Justified Generalization: Acquiring Procedures from Examples*, Ph.D. dissertation, MIT, Cambridge, Mass.

A. Anjewierden, "The KADS System," in Addis, 1987, pp. E2.1–12.

D. Antonelli, "The Application of Artificial Intelligence to a Maintenance and Diagnostic Information System (MDIS)," in *Proceedings of the Joint Services Workshop on Artificial Intelligence in Maintenance*, Boulder, Colo., 1983.

A. Araya, "Acquisition of Generic Knowledge in the Context of a Performance System," in *Integration of Knowledge Acquisi-*

tion and Performance Systems Workshop, AAAI, Menlo Park, Calif., 1988.

B. Arinze, "A Natural Language Front-End for Knowledge Acquisition," *SIGART Newsletter*, no. 108, 106–114 (Apr. 1989).

N. Aussenac, J. Frontin, M. H. Riviere, and J. L. Soubie, "A Mediating Representation to Assist Knowledge Acquisition with MACAO," in Aamodt, 1989, pp. 516–529.

N. Aussenac, J. Frontin, and J. L. Soubie, "Macao: A Knowledge Acquisition Tool for Expertise Transfer," in Addis and Bull, 1988, pp. 8.1–12.

R. Bansal and P. Posco, "Knowledge Acquisition Tool Promulgating Expert Systems in a Manufacturing Environment," in Adelson, 1989, pp. 129–132.

L. S. Baum, D. B. Shema, J. H. Boose, and J. M. Bradshaw, "Acquiring and Verifying Control Knowledge for a Blackboard System," in Addis, 1989, pp. 3.1–15.

B. Becker, "Towards a Case-Oriented Concept for Knowledge Acquisition," in Addis and Bull, 1988, pp. 9.1–12.

L. A. Becker, R. Bartlett, and F. Soroushian, "Using Simulation to Compile Diagnostic Rules from a Manufacturing Process Representation," *SIGART Newsletter* [Special issue on knowledge acquisition], no. 108 172–173 (Apr. 1989).

I. Benbasat and J. S. Dhaliwal, "A Framework for the Validation of Knowledge Acquisition," in J. H. Boose and B. R. Gaines, eds., *Proceedings of the Third Knowledge-Acquisition for Knowledge-Based Systems Workshop*, University of Calgary, Calgary, Canada, 1988, pp. 1-1–1-18.

I. Benbasat and J. S. Dhaliwal, "A Framework for the Validation of Knowledge Acquisition," *Knowledge Acquisition: An International Journal* 1(2), 215–233 (1989a).

I. Benbasat and J. S. Dhaliwal, "The Validation of Knowledge Acquisition: Methodology and Techniques," in *Proceedings of the Third European Workshop on Knowledge Acquisition for Knowledge-Based Systems*, Express-Tirages, Boung-la-Reine, France, 1989b, pp. 60–74.

J. S. Bennet, "A Knowledge-Based System for Acquiring the Conceptual Structure of a Diagnostic Expert System," *J. Autom. Reas.* 1, 49–74 (1985).

G. Berg-Cross and M. E. Price, "Acquiring and Managing Knowledge Using a Conceptual Structures Approach: Introduction and Framework," *IEEE Trans. Sys. Man Cybernet.* 19(3), 513–527 (1989).

F. Bergadano, S. Matwin, R. S. Michalski, and J. Zhang, "Learning Flexible Concepts through a Search for Simpler but Still Accurate Descriptions," in Addis, 1989, pp. 4.1–10.

G. Berry-Rogghe and R. M. Kaplan, "On the Structure of Expository Text: Preliminaries in Building an Expert System from Manuals," in *Proceedings of the First Knowledge Acquisition for Knowledge-Based System Workshop*, Banff, University of Calgary, 1986, pp. 4.0–7.

R. Beyth-Marom and S. Dekel, *An Elementary Approach to Thinking Under Uncertainty*, Erlbaum, Hillsdale, N.J., 1985.

W. P. Birmingham, "Automated Knowledge Acquisition for Computer-Aided Design Tools," in Adelson, 1989, pp. 101–104.

W. P. Birmingham and D. P. Siewiorek, "Automated Knowledge Acquisition for a Computer Hardware Synthesis System," in Benbasat and Dhaliwal, 1988, pp. 2.1–20.

J. Blythe, P. Corsi, and D. Needham, "An Experimental Protocol for the Acquisition of Examples for Learning," in Addis, 1987, pp. F1.1–13.

A. Bonarini, M. C. Gallo, and M. Guida, "GEKATOO, A General Support Tool for Knowledge Acquisition," in Adelson, 1989, pp. 28–33.

J. H. Boose, "Personal Construct Theory and the Transfer of Human Expertise," in *Proceedings of the Fourth National Conference on Artificial Intelligence*, Austin, Tex., AAAI, Menlo Park, Calif., 1984, pp. 27–33.

J. H. Boose, "A Knowledge Acquisition Program for Expert Systems Based on Personal Construct Psychology," *Int. J. Man-Machine Stud.* 23, 495–525 (1985).

J. H. Boose, *Expertise Transfer for Expert System Design*, Elsevier Science Publishing Co., Inc., New York, 1986a.

J. H. Boose, "Rapid Acquisition and Combination of Knowledge from Multiple Experts in the Same Domain," *Future Comput. Sys. J.* 1(2), 191–216 (1986b).

J. H. Boose, "Uses of Repertory Grid-Centered Knowledge Acquisition Tools for Knowledge-Based Systems," *Int. J. Man-Machine Stud.* 29(3), 287–310 (1988).

J. H. Boose, "Design Knowledge Capture for a Corporate Memory Facility," in Adelson, 1989, pp. 5–6.

J. H. Boose and J. M. Bradshaw, "Expertise Transfer and Complex Problems: Using Aquinas as a Knowledge Acquisition Workbench for Expert Systems," *Int. J. Man-Machine Stud.* 26(1), 3–28 (1987a).

J. H. Boose and J. M. Bradshaw, "AQUINAS: A Knowledge Acquisition Workbench for Building Knowledge-Based Systems," in Addis, 1987, pp. A6.1–6.

J. H. Boose, J. M. Bradshaw, C. M. Kitto, and D. B. Shema, "From ETS to Aquinas: Six Years of Knowledge Acquisition Tool Development," in *Proceedings of the Third European Workshop on Knowledge Acquisition for Knowledge-Based Systems*, Express-Tirages, Boung-la-Reine, France, 1989a, pp. 502–516.

J. H. Boose, J. M. Bradshaw, and D. B. Shema, "Recent Progress in Aquinas; A Knowledge Acquisition Workbench," in Addis and Bull, 1988, pp. 2.1–15.

J. H. Boose, J. M. Bradshaw, D. B. Shema, and S. P. Covington, "Design Knowledge Capture for a Corporate Memory Facility," in *Proceedings of the Eleventh IJCAI*, Detroit, Mich., Morgan-Kaufmann, San Mateo, Calif., 1989b.

J. H. Boose and B. R. Gaines, "Knowledge Acquisition for Knowledge-Based Systems, Tutorial Notes," in *Proceedings of the Artificial Intelligence Systems in Government*, IEEE, Washington, D.C., 1990.

J. H. Boose, D. B. Shema, and J. M. Bradshaw, "Recent Progress in Aquinas: A Knowledge Acquisition Workbench," *Knowledge Acquisition: An International Journal* 1(2), 185–214 (1989c).

J. H. Boose, D. B. Shema, and J. M. Bradshaw, "Capturing Design Knowledge for Engineering Trade Studies," in B. Wielinga, J. Boose, B. Gaines, G. Schreiber, and M. van Someren, eds., *Current Trends in Knowledge Acquisition*, IOS Press: Amsterdam, Washington, Tokyo, 1989, pp. 78–89.

G. Boy, "The Block Representation in Knowledge Acquisition for Computer Integrated Documentation," in Adelson, 1989.

G. Boy and T. Caminel, "Situations Patterns Acquisition. Improves the Control of Complex Dynamic Systems," in Aamodt, 1989, pp. 160–168.

G. Boy and M. Delail, "Knowledge Acquisition by Specialization/Structuration: A Space Telemanipulation Application," in Araya, 1988.

G. Boy and N. Nuss, "Knowledge Acquisition by Observation: Application to Intelligent Tutoring Systems," in Addis and Bull, 1988, pp. 11.1–14.

J. M. Bradshaw, *Strategies for Selecting and Interviewing Experts*, Boeing Computer Services Technical Report, n.d.

J. M. Bradshaw and J. H. Boose, "Decision Analysis Techniques for Knowledge Acquisition: Combining Situation and Preference Models Using Aquinas and Axotl," *Int. J. Man-Machine Stud.* **32**(2), 121–186 (1990).

J. M. Bradshaw, J. H. Boose, S. P. Covington, and P. J. Russo, "How to Do with Grids What People Say You Can't: The Application of Decision Analysis Methods in Axotl and Personal Construct Methods in Aquinas to Design Problems," in Benbasat and Dhaliwal, 1988, pp. 4.1–15.

J. M. Bradshaw, S. P. Covington, P. J. Russo, and J. H. Boose, "KWACQ'ing with DDUCKS: Knowledge Acquisition Techniques for Decision Analysis, Using Axotl and Aquinas," in Addis, 1989, pp. 7.1–12.

J. Bradshaw and R. Young, "Shared Causal Knowledge as a Basis for Communication Between Expert and Knowledge Acquisition System," in Addis and Bull, 1988, pp. 12.1–6.

M. Bramer, "Automatic Induction of Rules from Examples: A Critical Analysis of the ID3 Family of Rule Induction Systems," in Addis, 1987, pp. F2.1–31.

J. Breuker and B. Wielinga, "Knowledge Acquisition as Modeling Expertise: The KADS Methodology," *Proceedings of the First European Workshop on Knowledge Acquisition for Knowledge-Based Systems*, Reading University, UK, 1987a, pp. B1.1–8.

J. Breuker and B. Wielinga, "Use of Models in the Interpretation of Verbal Data," in A. Kidd, ed., *Knowledge Elicitation for Expert Systems: A Practical Handbook*, Plenum Press, New York, 1987b.

D. Brown, "A Knowledge Acquisition Tool for Decision Support Systems," *SIGART Newsletter*, no. 108, 93–97 (Apr. 1989).

W. Buntine, "Induction of Horn Clauses: Methods and the Plausible Generalization Algorithm," *Int. J. Man-Machine Stud.* **26**(4), 499–520 (1987).

A. M. Burton, N. R. Shadbolt, A. P. Hedgecock, and G. Rugg, "A Formal Evaluation of Knowledge Elicitation Techniques for Expert Systems: Domain 1," in Addis, 1987, pp. D3.1–21.

K. A. Butler and J. E. Corter, "Use of Psychometric Tools for Knowledge Acquisition: A Case Study," in W. A. Gale, ed., *Artificial Intelligence and Statistics*, Addison-Wesley Publishing Co., Inc., New York, 1986, pp. 295–320.

T. Bylander and B. Chandrasekaran, "Generic Tasks in Knowledge-Based Reasoning: The 'Right' Level of Abstraction for Knowledge Acquisition," *J. Man-Machine Stud.* **26**(2), 231–244 (1986).

T. Bylander and S. Mittal, "CSRL: A Language for Classificatory Problem-Solving and Uncertainty Handling," *AI Magazine* (Aug. 1986).

J. R. Carnes, "FMEAssist: A Tool for Acquisition, Engineering, and Operations Using Failure Knowledge," in Adelson, 1989, pp. 151–153.

J. E. Caviedes and M. K. Reed, "ViewPoint: A Troubleshooting-Specific Knowledge Acquisition Tool," *SIGART Newsletter*, no. 108, 155 (Apr. 1989).

J. Cendrowska, "An Algorithm for Inducing Modular Rules," *Int. J. Man-Machine Stud.* **27**(4), 349–370 (1987).

L. F. Chachere, "A Knowledge-Based System That Supports Explanation-Based Learning Applications," in Aamodt, 1989, pp. 327–337.

S. R. Chadha, L. J. Mazlack, and R. A. Pick, "Acquiring and Validating Knowledge for an Expert System Using a Case-Based Approach," in Adelson, 1989.

B. Chandrasekaran, "Generic Tasks as Building Blocks for Knowledge-Based Systems: The Diagnosis and Routine Design Examples," *Knowl. Eng. Rev.* **3**(3), 183–211 (1988).

J. Charlet and O. Gascuel, "Knowledge Acquisition by Causal Model and Meta-Knowledge," in Aamodt, 1989, pp. 212–226.

W. H. Chu, "Knowledge Acquisition for Diagnostic Reasoning," in Adelson, 1989.

W. Clancey, "Heuristic Classification," in J. Kowalik, ed., *Knowledge-Based Problem-Solving*, Prentice Hall Press, New York, 1986a.

W. Clancey, "Knowledge Acquisition," paper presented at the First Knowledge Acquisition for Knowledge-Based Systems Workshop, Banff, Canada, 1986b.

B. Clarke, "Knowledge Acquisition for Real-Time Knowledge-Based Systems," in Addis, 1987, pp. C2.1–7.

J. G. Cleary, "Acquisition of Uncertain Rules in a Probabilistic Logic," *Int. J. Man-Machine Stud.* **27**(2), 145–154 (1987).

E. L. Cochran, "KLAMShell: A Domain-Specific Knowledge Acquisition Shell," in Araya, 1988.

D. M. Combs, S. W. Tu, M. A. Musen, and L. M. Fagan, "From Expert Models To Expert Systems: Translation of an Intermediate Knowledge Representation," in Araya, 1988.

P. Constant, S. Matwin, and F. Oppacher, *LEW: Learning by Watching*, Technical Report, George Mason University, Washington, D.C., 1988.

N. M. Cooke and J. E. McDonald, "The Application of Psychological Scaling Techniques to Knowledge Elicitation for Knowledge-Based Systems," *Int. J. Man-Machine Stud.* **26**(4), 533–549 (1987).

E. S. Cordingley, "Knowledge Acquisition for the Advice System," in Addis, 1987, pp. C3.1–21.

L. A. Cox, "Designing Interactive Expert Classification System That Acquires Knowledge 'Optimally,'" in Addis and Bull, 1988, pp. 13.1–16.

L. A. Cox and R. Blumenthal, "KRIMB: An Intelligent Knowledge Acquisition and Representation Program for Interactive Model Building," in Addis, 1987, pp. E3.1–17.

B. W. Crandall, "A Comparative Study of Think-Aloud and Critical Decision Knowledge Elicitation Methods," *SIGART Newsletter*, no. 108, 144–146 (Apr. 1989).

A. Crapo and R. Shah, "GEN-X: A Graphical Tool for Knowledge Acquisition," in Adelson, 1989.

S. L. Crawford, "Extensions to the CART Algorithm," *Int. J. Man-Machine Stud.* **31**, 197–218 (1989).

A. D'Ambrosio, "Acquiring Knowledge of Real-World Domains: Is the Paradigm the Key," in Adelson, 1989, pp. 120–125.

P. C. Daley, "Using Neural Nets to Automate Knowledge Engineering," in Adelson, 1989, pp. 1–4.

J. P. Davis and R. D. Bonnell, "Concept Abstraction and the Knowledge Dictionary: A Framework for Acquisition and Maintenance of Knowledge Schemata," in Adelson, 1989.

R. Davis and D. B. Lenat, *Knowledge-Based Systems in Artificial Intelligence*, McGraw-Hill Inc., New York, 1982.

T. Dean and K. Kanazawa, "Persistence and Probabilistic Projection," *IEEE Trans. Sys. Man Cybernet.* **19**(3), 574–585 (1989).

P. De Greef and J. Breuker, "A Methodology for Analysing Modalities of System/User Cooperation for KBS," in Aamodt, 1989, pp. 462–473.

K. De Jong, "Knowledge Acquisition for Fault Isolation Expert Systems," *Proceedings of the First Knowledge Acquisition for Knowledge-Based Systems Workshop*, University of Calgary, Calgary, Canada, 1987, pp. 20.0–20.8.

J. De la Garza and C. W. Ibbs, "A Limited Information Knowledge Elicitation Experiment," in Adelman, 1989.

J. P. Delgrande, "A Formal Approach to Learning from Examples," *Int. J. Man-Machine Stud.* **26**(2), 123–142 (1987).

L. De Raedt and M. Bruynooghe, "On Explanation and Bias in Inductive Concept-Learning," in Aamodt, 1989, pp. 338–353.

J. S. Dhaliwal and I. Benbasat, "A Framework for the Comparative Evaluation of Knowledge Acquisition Tools and Techniques," *Proceedings of the Fourth Knowledge Acquisition for Knowledge-Based Systems Workshop*, Banff, Canada, October, 1989, pp. 9.1–23.

J. Diederich, L. Linster, I. Ruhmann, and T. Uthmann, "A Methodology for Integrating Knowledge Acquisition Techniques," in *Proceedings of the First European Workshop on Knowledge Acquisition for Knowledge-Based Systems*, University of Reading, UK, 1987a, pp. E4.1–11.

J. Diederich, I. Ruhmann, and M. May, "KRITON: A Knowledge Acquisition Tool for Expert Systems," *Int. J. Man-Machine Stud.* **26**(1), 29–40 (1987b).

R. Dieng and B. Trousse, "3DKAT, A Dependency-Driven Dynamic Knowledge Acquisition Tool," in Adelson, 1988.

J. S. di Piazza, "Laps: An Assistant for Debriefing Experts," in Addis and Bull, 1988, pp. 14.1–17.

J. S. di Piazza and F. A. Helsabeck, "LAPS: From Cases to Models to Complete Expert Systems," in Adelson, 1989, pp. 126–128.

R. Dupas and P. Millot, "A Learning Expert System for Preventive Maintenance," in Aamodt, 1989, pp. 354–364.

S. Dutta, "Domain Independent Inductive Learning of Relevance," in Addis and Bull, 1988, pp. 15.1–13.

S. M. Easterbrook, "Distributed Knowledge Acquisition as a Model for Requirements Elicitation," in Aamodt, 1989, pp. 530–543.

P. Eklund and J. Kellett, "Prospects for Conceptual Graphs in Acquisition Interfaces," in Aamodt, 1989, pp. 169–179.

R. Enand, G. S. Kahn, and R. A. Mills, "A Methodology for Validating Large Knowledge Bases," in Benbasat and Dhaliwal, 1988, pp. 5.1–11.

L. Esfahani and F. N. Teskey, "KET, A Knowledge Encoding Tool," in Addis, 1987, pp. E5.1–11.

L. Esfahani and F. N. Teskey, "A Self-Modifying Rule-Eliciter," in Addis and Bull, 1988, pp. 16.1–16.

L. Eshelman, "MOLE: A Knowledge Acquisition Tool That Buries Certainty Factors," *Int. J. Man-Machine Stud.* **29**(5), 563–578 (1988).

L. Eshelman, D. Ehret, J. McDermott, and M. Tan, "MOLE: A Tenacious Knowledge Acquisition Tool," *Int. J. Man-Machine Stud.* **26**(1), 41–54 (1987).

B. Z. Feldman, P. J. Compton, and G. A. Smythe, "Hypothesis Testing: An Appropriate Task for Knowledge-Based Systems," in Addis, 1989, pp. 10.1–20.

R. E. Fikes, P. E. Hart, and N. J. Nilsson, "Learning and Executing Generalized Robot Plans," *Artif. Intell.* **3**, 251–288 (1972).

B. Fischoff, "Eliciting Knowledge for Analytical Representation," *IEEE Trans. Sys. Man Cybernet.* **19**(3), 448–461 (1989).

K. M. Ford, J. R. Adams-Webber, F. E. Petry, and P. J. Chang, "An Approach to Knowledge Acquisition Based on the Structure of Personal Construct Systems," in Addis, 1989, pp. 11.1–20.

K. M. Ford and F. E. Petry, "Knowledge Acquisition from Repertory Grids Using a Logic of Conformation," *SIGART Newsletter* no. 108, 146–147 (Apr. 1989).

D. E. Forsythe and B. G. Buchanan, "Knowledge Elicitation in Theory and Practice: An Integrated Program of Research and Training," in Benbasat and Dhaliwal, 1988, pp. 6.1–7.

D. E. Forsythe and B. G. Buchanan, "Knowledge Acquisition for Expert Systems: Some Pitfalls and Suggestions," *IEEE Trans. Sys. Man Cybernet.* **19**(3), 435–442 (1989).

N. E. Fredman, "Knowledge Acquisition in a Secure Environment," in *Proceedings of the Second Knowledge Acquisition for Knowledge-Based System Workshop*, Banff, Canada, 1987, pp. 7.0–8.

P. Freeman, "Knowledge Elicitation—A Commercial Perspective," in *Proceedings of the First International Expert System Conference*, London, University of Reading, Reading, U.K., 1985.

M. J. Freiling, "Synthesizing an Effective Control Strategy from Acquired Domain Knowledge," in Benbasat and Dhaliwal, 1988, pp. 7.1–20.

M. J. Freiling and C. E. Jacobson, "A New Look at Inference Engine Synthesis," *Knowl. Acquisition: An International Journal*, 1(3), 235–254 (1989).

P. G. Friel, J. C. Lockledge, P. Hart, R. J. Mayer, L. Sanders, and J. Shashank, "An Integrated Knowledge Capture/Design Analysis Assistant for Engineering," in Adelson, 1989.

H. Furuya and F. Hattori, "Knowledge Acquisition System for Hierarchical Classification Problems," in *Proceedings of COMPCON*, IEEE, Los Angeles, 1989.

B. R. Gaines, "System Identification Approximation and Complexity," *Int. J. Gen. Sys.* **3**, 145–174 (1977).

B. R. Gaines, "An Overview of Knowledge Acquisition and Transfer," *Int. J. Man-Machine Stud.* **26**(4), 453–472 (1987a).

B. R. Gaines, "Knowledge Acquisition for Expert Systems," in *Proceedings of the First European Workshop on Knowledge Acquisition for Knowledge-Based Systems*, Reading University, UK, 1987b, pp. A3.1–4.

B. R. Gaines, "Advanced Expert System Support Environments," in *Proceedings of the Second Knowledge Acquisition for Knowledge-Based Systems Workshop*, 1988a, pp. 8.0–14.

B. R. Gaines, "Second Generation Knowledge Acquisition Systems," in *Proceedings of the Second European Knowledge Acquisition Workshop*, 1988b, pp. 17.1–14.

B. R. Gaines, *An Ounce of Knowledge Is Worth a Ton of Data: Quantitative Studies of the Trade-Off Between Expertise and Data based on Statistically Well-Founded Empirical Induction*, KSI-89-2, University of Calgary, Calgary, Canada, 1989a.

B. R. Gaines, "Knowledge Acquisition: The Continuum Linking Machine Learning and Expertise Transfer," in *Proceedings of the Third European Workshop on Knowledge Acquisition for Knowledge-Based Systems*, 1989, pp. 90–101.

B. R. Gaines and J. H. Andreae, "A Learning Machine in the Context of the General Control Problem," in *Proceedings of the Third Congress of the International Federation for Automatic Control*, Butterworth & Co. (Publishers) Ltd., Kent, UK, 1966.

B. R. Gaines and J. H. Boose, "A Summary of the AAAI-Sponsored Knowledge Acquisition for Knowledge-Based System Workshops," *AI Magazine*, 1991.

B. R. Gaines and A. T. Rappaport, "The Automatic Generation of Classes, Objects, and Rules at the Interface Between Knowledge Acquisition Tools and Expert System Shells," in Adelson, 1988.

B. R. Gaines, A. T. Rappaport, and M. L. G. Shaw, "A Heterogeneous Knowledge Support System," in Addis, 1989.

B. R. Gaines and M. Sharp, "A Knowledge Acquisition Extension to Notecards," in Addis, 1987, pp. C1.1.–7.

B. R. Gaines and M. L. G. Shaw, "Interactive Elicitation of Knowledge from Experts," *Future Comput. Sys.* 1(2), 151–190 (1986).

W. A. Gale, "Knowledge-Based Knowledge Acquisition for a Statistical Consulting System," *Int. J. Man-Machine Stud.* 26(1), 55–64 (1987).

W. A. Gale, "An Interactive Performance Based Knowledge Acquisition Methodology," in Benbasat and Dhaliwal, 1988, pp. 9.1–17.

J. G. Gammack and R. M. Young, "Psychological Techniques for Eliciting Expert Knowledge," in M. Bramer, ed., *R&D in Expert Systems, Proceedings of the 4th Expert System Conference,* CUP, London, 1984.

M. Gams, "A New Breed of Knowledge Acquisition Systems Uses Redundant Knowledge?!," in Addis and Bull, 1988, pp. 18.1–7.

U. Gappa, "Classika: A Knowledge Acquisition System Facilitating the Formalization of Advanced Aspects in Heuristic Classification," in Addis and Bull, 1988, pp. 19.1–16.

U. Gappa, "CLASSIKA: A Knowledge Acquisition Tool for Use by Experts," in *Proceedings of the Fourth Knowledge Acquisition for Knowledge-Based Systems Workshop,* University of Calgary, Calgary, Canada, 1989a, pp. 14.1–15.

U. Gappa, "The Knowledge Acquisition Tool CLASSIKA," in Adelson, 1989b, pp. 65–67.

U. Gappa and F. Puppe, "The Knowledge Acquisition Tool CLASSIKA," in Adelson, 1989.

C. Garg-Janardan, "Integration Issues in Knowledge Acquisition for Building Expert Systems," in Araya, 1988.

C. Garg-Janardan and G. Salvendy, "A Conceptual Framework for Knowledge Elicitation," *Int. J. Man-Machine Stud.* 26(4), 521–523 (1987).

J. A. Goguen and J. Meseguer, "Programming with Parametrized Abstract Objects" in *OBJ, Theory and Practice of Programming Technology,* North-Holland, Amsterdam, The Netherlands, 1983.

B. Golden, E. Wasil, and P. Harker, eds., *The Analytic Hierarchy Process: Applications and Studies,* Springer-Verlag, New York, 1989.

J. C. González and F. Alcaraz, "A Learning System for INFERNO Inference Networks," in Aamodt, 1989, pp. 365–379.

R. M. F. Goodman and P. Smyth, "ITRULE: An Information Theoretic Rule-Induction Algorithm," in *Proceedings of the First European Workshop on Knowledge Acquisition for Knowledge-Based Systems,* Reading University, UK 1987a, pp. F3.1–8.

R. M. F. Goodman and P. Smyth, "Learning from Examples Using Information Theory," in *Proceedings of the Second Knowledge Acquisition for Knowledge-Based Systems Workshop,* Univeristy of Calgary, Calgary, Canada, 1988, 1987b, pp. 9.0–18.

M. Green and L. Eshelman, "Knowledge Acquisition for Causal Reasoning," in Adelson, 1989, pp. 68–70.

M. D. Grover, "A Pragmatic Knowledge Acquisition Methodology," in *Proceedings of the Eighth IJCAI,* Karlsruhe, FRG, Morgan-Kaufmann, San Mateo, Calif., 1983, pp. 436–438.

T. R. Gruber, "Acquiring Strategic Knowledge from Experts," *Int. J. Man-Machine Stud.* 29(5), 579–598 (1988a).

T. R. Gruber, "A Method for Acquiring Strategic Knowledge," in *Proceedings of the Third Knowledge Acquisition for Knowledge-Based Systems Workshop,* University of Calgary, Calgary, Canada, 1988b, pp. 10.1–21.

T. R. Gruber, *The Acquisition of Strategic Knowledge,* Ph.D. dissertation, University of Massachusetts, Amherst, 1989a.

T. R. Gruber, *The Acquisition of Strategic Knowledge,* Academic Press, Inc., Orlando, Fla., 1989b.

T. R. Gruber, "A Method for Acquiring Strategic Knowledge," *Knowledge Acquisition: An International Journal* 1(3), 255–278 (1989c).

T. R. Gruber and P. R. Cohen, "Design for Acquisition: Principles of Knowledge System Design to Facilitate Knowledge Acquisition," *Int. J. Man-Machine Stud.* 26(2), 143–160 (1987).

M. Hadzikadic, "Inc2: A Prototype-Based Incremental Conceptual Clustering System," in Addis and Bull, 1988, pp. 20.1–13.

M. Haers and G. d'Ydewalle, "The Problem of Knowledge Extraction with Human Experts: A Case of Expert Verbalizations," in Aamodt, 1989, pp. 19–33.

K. Handa and S. Ishizaki, "Learning Importance of Concepts: Construction of Representative Network," in Benbasat and Dhaliwal, pp. 11.1–15.

K. Handa and S. Ishizaki, "Acquiring Knowledge about a Relation between Concepts," in Aamodt, 1989, pp. 380–390.

S. L. Hardt, "The Roles of Core Knowledge and Case History in the Integration of Knowledge Acquisition and Performance in the PACKS Project," in Araya, 1988.

H. L. Hausen and H. J. Neusser, "Knowledge Acquisition for Method and Tool Selection," in Addis, 1987, pp. D5.1–12.

F. Hayes-Roth, D. B. Lenat, and D. A. Waterman, eds., *Building Expert Systems,* Addison-Wesley Publishing Co., Inc., Reading, Mass., 1983.

I. C. Hayslip and J. L. Eilbert, "Capturing Air Combat Maneuvering Knowledge in a Mixed Representation Containing Neural Networks," in Adelson, 1989, pp. 87–90.

S. A. Hayward, B. J. Wielinga, and J. A. Breuker, "Structured Analysis of Knowledge," *Int. J. Man-Machine Stud.* 26(4), 487–499 (1987).

J. Herrmann, "Computer Aided Acquisition of Procedural Knowledge About VLSI-Design," Adelson, 1989, pp. 56–59.

J. Herrmann and R. Beckmann, "Malefiz—A Learning Apprentice System That Acquires Geometrical Knowledge about a Complex Design Task," in Adelson, 1989, pp. 391–405.

J. Hermann and H. Franzke, "Requirements for Computer-Aided Knowledge Acquisition in an Ill-Structured Domain: A Case Study," in Addis and Bull, 1988, pp. 21.1–13.

R. F. Hink and D. L. Woods, "How Humans Process Uncertain Knowledge: An Introduction for Knowledge Engineers," *AI Magazine* 8(3), 41–53 (1987).

R. Hoffman, "A Brief Survey of Methods for Extracting the Knowledge of Experts," *SIGART Newsletter* no. 108, 19–27 (1989).

L. Hsieh, R. Hayes, M. Hofmann, A. Patrick, and J. Mallory, *A Knowledge Acquisition Kit (KNACK),* Technical Report, IBM Scientific Center, Palo Alto, Calif., 1988.

L. Hunter, "Knowledge Acquisition Planning," in Benbasat and Dhaliwal, 1988, pp. 12.1–18.

C. Jacobson and M. J. Freiling, "ASTEK: A Multi-Paradigm Knowledge Acquisition Tool for Complex Structured Knowledge," *Int. J. Man-Machine Stud.* 29(3), 311–328 (1988).

C. Jacobson and M. J. Freiling, "Knowledge Dependencies," in Addis, 1989, pp. 16.1–19.

V. Jagannathan and A. S. Elmaghraby, "MEDKAT: Multiple Expert Delphi-Based Knowledge Acquisition Tool," in *Proceedings of the ACM Northeast Regional Conference,* ACM, Boston, 1985, pp. 103–110.

B. Jansen and P. Compton, "The Knowledge Dictionary: An Application of Software Engineering Techniques to the Design and Maintenance of Expert Systems," in Araya, 1988.

B. Jansen and P. Compton, "The Knowledge Dictionary: Storing Different Knowledge Representations," in Aamodt, 1989, pp. 448–461.

R. M. Jansen-Winkleln, "WASTL: An Approach to Knowledge Acquisition in the Natural Language Domain," in Addis and Bull, 1988, pp. 22.1–15.

C. Jansson and Å. Rudström, "Re-Use of Problem-Solving Experience for the Weekly Planning of School Meals," in Adelson, 1989, pp. 145–148.

N. E. Johnson, "Mediating Representations in Knowledge Elicitation," in Addis, 1987, pp. A2.1–10.

N. E. Johnson and C. M. Tomlinson, "Knowledge Elicitation for Second Generation Expert Systems," in Addis and Bull, 1988, pp. 23.1–10.

N. E. Johnson, C. M. Tomlinson, and L. Johnson, "Knowledge Representation for Knowledge Elicitation," in Benbasat and Dhaliwal, 1988, pp. 13.1–9.

P. E. Johnson, I. Zaulkernan, and S. Garber, "Specification of Expertise: Knowledge Acquisition for Expert Systems," Int. J. Man-Machine Stud. 26(2), 161–182 (1987).

W. P. Jones, "Bringing Corporate Knowledge into Focus with CAMEO," in Addis, 1989, pp. 17.1–23.

R. L. Joseph, "Graphical Knowledge Acquisition," in Addis, 1989, pp. 18.1–16.

G. S. Kahn, E. H. Breaux, R. L. Joeseph, and P. DeKlerk, "An Intelligent Mixed-Initiative Workbench for Knowledge Acquisition," Int. J. Man-Machine Stud. 27(2), 167–180 (1987).

G. Kahn, S. Nowlan, and J. McDermott, "Strategies for Knowledge Acquisition," IEEE Trans. Pattern Anal. Machine Intell. 7(3), 511–522 (1985a).

G. Kahn, S. Nowlan, and J. McDermott, "MORE: An Intelligent Knowledge Acquisition Tool," in Proceedings of the Ninth IJCAI, Los Angeles, Calif., Morgan-Kaufmann, San Mateo, Calif., 1985b, pp. 581–584.

D. Kahneman, P. Slovic, and A. Tversky, eds., Judgment under Uncertainty: Heuristics and Biases, Cambridge University Press, Cambridge, UK, 1982.

W. Karbach, A. Voß, and X. Tong, "Filling in the Knowledge Acquisition Gap: via KADS' Models of Expertise to ZDEST-2's Expert Systems," in Addis and Bull, 1988, pp. 31.1–17.

C. Kellogg, R. A. Gargan, Jr., W. Mark, J. G. McGuire, M. Pontecorvo, J. L. Schlossberg, J. W. Sullivan, M. R. Genesereth, and N. Singh, "The Acquisition, Verification, and Explanation of Design Knowledge," SIGART Newsletter, no. 108, 163–165 (Apr. 1989).

G. A. Kelly, The Psychology of Personal Constructs, W. W. Norton, New York, 1955.

A. L. Kidd and M. B. Cooper, "Man-Machine Interface Issues in the Construction and Use of an Expert System, Int. J. Man-Machine Stud. 22 (1985).

J. U. Kietz, "Incremental and Reversible Acquisition of Taxonomies," in Addis and Bull, 1988, pp. 24.1–11.

J. L. Killin and F. R. Hickman, "The Role of Phenomenological Techniques of Knowledge Elicitation in Complex Domains," Proceedings of Expert Systems '86, Brighton, British Computing Society, Brighton, London, 1986.

C. M. Kitto, "Progress in Automated Knowledge Acquisition Tools: How Close Are We to Replacing the Knowledge Engineer?" in Benbasat and Dhaliwal, 1988, pp. 14.1–13.

C. M. Kitto and J. H. Boose, "Heuristics for Expertise Transfer: The Automatic Management of Complex Knowledge Acquisition Dialogs," Int. J. Man-Machine Stud. 26(2), 183–202 (1987).

C. M. Kitto and J. H. Boose, "Selecting Knowledge Acquisition Tools and Strategies Based on Application Characteristics," Int. J. Man-Machine Stud. 31(2), 149–160 (1989).

G. Klinker, "A Framework for Knowledge Acquisition," in Aamodt, 1989, pp. 102–116.

G. Klinker, J. Bentolila, S. Genetet, M. Grimes, and J. McDermott, "KNACK: Report-Driven Knowledge Acquisition," Int. J. Man-Machine Stud. 26(1), 65–80 (1987).

G. Klinker, C. Boyd, D. Dong, J. Maiman, J. McDermott, and R. Schnelbach, "Building Expert Systems with KNACK," Knowledge Acquisition: An International Journal, 1(3), 299–320 (1989).

G. Klinker, S. Genetet, and J. McDermott, "Knowledge Acquisition for Evaluation Systems," Int. J. Man-Machine Stud. 29(6), 715–732 (1988).

T. Kodratoff, "Characterizing Machine Learning Programs: A European Compilation," CNRS & Université Paris Sud, 1989.

Y. Kodratoff, "Machine Learning and Explanations," in Addis, 1987, pp. A5.1–9.

Y. Kodratoff and M. Manago, "Generalization in a Noisy Environment: The Need to Integrate Symbolic and Numeric Techniques in Learning," Int. J. Man-Machine Stud. 27(2), 181–204 (1987).

Y. Kodratoff and R. S. Michalski, eds., Machine Learning: An Artificial Intelligence Approach, Vol. 3, Morgan-Kaufmann, San Mateo, Calif., 1989.

Y. Kodratoff and G. Tecuci, "Learning at Different Levels of Knowledge," in Addis and Bull, 1988, pp. 3.1–17.

E. Konrad and X. Tong, "Model Directed Inference Structure Acquisition," in Aamodt, 1989, pp. 128–138.

J. Kontio and P. Lounamaa, "A Graphical Framework for Knowledge Acquisition and Representation," in Aamodt, 1989, pp. 490–501.

D. Kopec and L. Latour, "Towards an Expert/Novice Learning System with Application to Infectious Disease," SIGART Newsletter no. 108, 140–143 (Apr. 1989).

M. Krishnamurthi and A. J. Underbrink, "Knowledge Acquisition in a Machine Fault Diagnosis Shell," SIGART Newsletter, no. 108, 84–92 (Apr. 1989).

B. H. Kwasnik, "Extraction of Knowledge about the Cognitive Process of Browsing from Discourse and Thinking-Out-Loud Protocols," in Adelson, 1989, pp. 75–77.

M. La France, "The Knowledge Acquisition Grid: A Method for Training Knowledge Engineers," Intl. J. Man-Machine Studies 26, 2, 245–256 (1987).

M. La France, "The Quality of Expertise: Understanding the Differences Between Experts and Novices," SIGART Newsletter, Special Issue on Knowledge Acquisition, No. 108, 6–14 (April 1989).

J. E. Laird, P. S. Rosenbloom, and A. Newell, "Chunking in SOAR: The Anatomy of a General Learning Mechanism," Machine Learning 1, 11–46 (1986).

J. Lancaster, C. R. Westphal, and K. L. McGraw, "A Cognitively Valid Knowledge Acquisition Tool," SIGART Newsletter, no. 108, 152–154 (Apr. 1989).

P. Langley, G. L. Bradshaw, and H. A. Simon, "Rediscovering Chemistry with the BACON System," in R. S. Michalski, J. G. Carbonell, and T. M. Mitchell, eds., Machine Learning, Vol 2, Morgan-Kaufmann, San Mateo, Calif., 1983, pp. 425–469.

P. Langley, J. M. Zytkow, H. A. Simon, and G. L. Bradshaw, "Rediscovering Chemistry with the BACON System," in R. S. Michalski, J. G. Carbonell, and T. M. Mitchell, eds., *Machine Learning: An Artificial Intelligence Approach*, Vol. 3, Tioga, Palo Alto, Calif., 1986, pp. 307–329.

O. E. Laske, A" Decompilation Approach to Knowledge Acquisition: Using Concurrent Expert Reports as the Basis for Automated Knowledge Modeling," in Addis, 1987, pp. D8.1–13.

K. B. Laskey, M. S. Cohen, and A. W. Martin, "Representing and Eliciting Knowledge for Uncertain Evidence and Its Implications," *IEEE Trans. Sys. Man Cybernet.* **19**(3), 536–545 (1989).

N. Lavrac and I. Mozetic, "Methods for Knowledge Acquisition and Refinement in Second Generation Expert Systems," in Aamodt, 1989, pp. 554–564.

S. R. LeClair, "Interactive Learning: A Multiexpert Paradigm for Acquiring New Knowledge, *SIGART Newsletter*, no. 108, 34–44 (Apr. 1989).

J. Lee, "Task-Embedded Knowledge Acquisition Through a Task-Specific Language," in Adelson, 1989.

L. S. Lefkowitz and V. R. Lesser, "Knowledge Acquisition as Knowledge Assimilation," *Int. J. Man-Machine Stud.* **29**(2), 215–226 (1988).

P. E. Lehner, "Toward an Empirical Approach to Evaluating the Knowledge Base of an Expert System," *IEEE Trans. Sys. Man Cybernet.* **19**(3), 658–662 (1989).

D. Leishman, "Analogy in Knowledge Acquisition: Description of an Analogical Tool," in Addis, 1989, pp. 19.1–13.

D. B. Lenat, "EURISKO: A Program That Learns New Heuristics and Domain Concepts, *Artif. Intell.* **21**, 61–98 (1983).

D. B. Lenat, M. Prakish, and M. Shepard, "CYC: Using Common Sense Knowledge to Overcome Brittleness and Knowledge Acquisition Bottlenecks," *AI Magazine* **6**(4), 65–85 (1986).

K. Levi, "Expert Systems Should be More Accurate Than Human Experts: Evaluation Procedures from Human Judgment and Decision Making," *IEEE Trans. Sys. Man Cybernet.* **19**(3), 647–657 (1989).

K. Levi, D. Perschbacner, and V. Shalin, "Learning Plans and Information Requirements for Pilot Aiding," in Benbasat and Dhaliwal, 1988, pp. 16.1–13.

K. A. Lewis and G. S. Kahn, "TestBuilder: An Integrated Expert System Development Environment," in Araya, 1988.

T.-P. Liang, "Empirical Knowledge Refinement in Noisy Domains," in Addis, 1989, pp. 20.1–15.

E. Lindsay, R. Cameron, J. Fugure, and L. Niem, "Knowledge Acquisition for Canadian Armed Forces Army Battlefield Decision Support System," in Araya, 1988.

M. Linster, "On Structuring Knowledge for Incremental Knowledge Acquisition," in Addis, 1987, pp. D1.1–8.

M. Linster, "Kriton: A Knowledge Elicitation Tool for Expert Systems," in *Proceedings of the Second European Knowledge Acquisition Workshop*, GMD, Bonn, Germany, 1988a, pp. 4.1–9.

M. Linster, "A Critical Look at KRITON," in J. H. Boose, and B. R. Gaines, eds., *Proceedings of the Third Knowledge Acquisition for Knowledge-Based Systems Workshop*, 1988b, pp. 17-1–19.

M. Linster, "Integrating Acquisition, Representation and Interpretation," in *Proceedings of the Third European Workshop on Knowledge Acquisition for Knowledge-Based Systems*, Paris, 1989a, pp. 565–577.

M. Linster, "Towards a Second Generation Knowledge Acquisition Tool, *Knowledge Acquisition: An International Journal*, **1**(2), 163–184 (1989b).

Y. I. Liou, E. S. Weber, and J. F. Nunamaker, "A Methodology for Knowledge Acquisition in a Group Decision Support System Environment," in Addis, 1989, pp. 21.1–19.

D. C. Littman, "Modeling Human Expertise in Knowledge Engineering: Some Preliminary Observations," *Int. J. Man-Machine Stud.* **26**(1), 81–92 (1987).

B. R. Loftin, T. Saito, L. Wang, and P. Baffes, "Automating Knowledge Acquisition for Intelligent Training Systems," in Adelson, 1989, pp. 80–82.

B. A. MacDonald and I. H. Witten, A Framework for Knowledge Acquisition Through Techniques of Concept Learning," *IEEE Trans. Sys. Man Cybernet.* **19**(3), 499–512 (1989).

K. L. McGraw, "Developing a Cognitively-Based Toolkit for Knowledge Acquisition," in Adelson, 1989, pp. 7–9.

K. L. McGraw and J. S. Lancaster, "An Integrated Toolkit for Cognitively-Based Knowledge Acquisition," in Addis, 1989, pp. 22.1–10.

D. E. Mahling and W. B. Croft, "Knowledge Acquisition for Planners," in Benbasat and Dhaliwal, 1988, pp. 18.1–18.

O. Maler, "Student Modeling: Learning a Function from Examples While Knowing a Close Function," in Addis, 1987, pp. F4.1–14.

S. Marcus, "Taking Backtracking with a Grain of SALT," *Int. J. Man-Machine Stud.* **26**(4), 383–398 (1987).

S. Marcus, "Understanding Subtasks from a Piecemeal Collection of Knowledge," in *Proceedings of the Third Knowledge Acquisition for Knowledge-Based Systems Workshop*, Banff, Canada, 1988a, pp. 19.1–22.

S. Marcus, *Automating Knowledge Acquisition for Expert Systems*, Kluwer, Boston, 1988b.

S. Marcus, "Understanding Decision Ordering from a Piece-Meal Collection of Knowledge," *Knowledge Acquisition: An International Journal*, **1**(3), 279–298 (1989).

S. Marcus, J. McDermott, and T. Wang, "Knowledge Acquisition for Constructive Systems," in *Proceedings of the Ninth IJCAI*, Los Angeles, Calif., Morgan-Kaufmann, San Mateo, Calif., 1985, pp. 637–639.

J. D. Martin and M. Redmond, "Acquiring Knowledge by Explaining Observed Problem Solving," *SIGART Newsletter* no. 108, 77–82 (Apr. 1989).

S. Matwin and F. Oppacher, "Knowledge Acquisition Using a Machine Learning System with User-Limited Autonomy," in Adelson, 1989, pp. 133–136.

D. L. Maulsby, G. A. James, and I. H. Witten, "Evaluating Interaction in Knowledge Acquisition: A Case Study," in Aamodt, 1989, pp. 406–419.

D. L. Maulsby and I. H. Witten, "Acquiring Graphical Know-How: An Apprenticeship Model," in Addis and Bull, 1988, pp. 34.1–16.

W. Mellis, "A General Approach to the Use of Background Knowledge in a Numerical Induction Algorithm," in Aamodt, 1989, pp. 420–434.

F. H. Merrem, "Automatic Generation of Knowledge Structures," *SIGART Newsletter*, no. 108, 160–162 (Apr. 1989).

M. A. Meyer and J. M. Booker, "A Practical Program for Handling Bias in Knowledge Acquisition," in Addis, 1989, pp. 23.1–19.

M. A. Meyer, S. M. Mniszewski, and A. T. Peaslee, Jr., "Using Three Minimally Biasing Elicitation Techniques for Knowledge Acquisition," *Knowledge Acquisition: An International Journal of Knowledge Acquisition for Knowledge-Based Systems*, **1**(1), 59–72 (1989).

P. F. Micciche and J. S. Lancaster, "Applications of Neurolinguistic Techniques to Knowledge Acquisition," *SIGART Newsletter*, no. 108, 28–33 (Apr. 1989).

R. S. Michalski, "Theory and Methodology of Inductive Learning," in Michalski and co-workers, eds., 1983.

R. S. Michalski, J. G. Carbonell, and T. M. Mitchell, eds., *Machine Learning: An Artificial Intelligence Approach*, Tioga Publishing Co., Palo Alto, Calif., 1983.

R. S. Michalski, J. G. Carbonell, and T. M. Mitchell, eds., *Machine Learning: An Artificial Intelligence Approach*, Vol. 2, Morgan-Kaufmann, San Mateo, Calif., 1986.

R. S. Michalski and R. L. Chilausky, "Knowledge Acquisition by Encoding Expert Rules versus Computer Induction from Examples—A Case Study Involving Soybean Pathology," *Int. J. Man-Machine Stud.* **12**, 63–87 (1980).

T. M. Mitchell, "Generalization as Search," *Artif. Intell.* **18**, 203–226 (1982).

T. M. Mitchell, S. Mahadevan, and L. I. Steinberg, "LEAP: A Learning Apprentice for VLSI Design," in Marcus and co-workers, 1985.

T. M. Mitchell, P. E. Utgoff, and R. Banerji, *Learning by Experimentation: Acquiring and Modifying Problem-Solving Heuristics*, Technical Report LCSR-TR-31, Rutgers University, Rutgers, N.J., 1982.

S. Mittal and C. Dym, "Knowledge Acquisition from Multiple Experts," *AI Magazine*, 32–36 (Summer 1985).

J. U. Möller, "Knowledge Acquisition from Texts," in Addis and Bull, 1988, pp. 25.1–16.

I. Monarch, T. Kaufmann, and E. Subramanian, "Knowledge-Based Dynamic Hypertext to Guide Decision-Making and Rule Modification in Public Policy Law and Administration," in Adelson, 1989.

I. Monarch and S. Nirenburg, "The Role of Ontology in Concept Acquisition for Knowledge-Based Systems," in Addis, 1987, pp. E1.1–14.

E. A. Moore and A. M. Agogino, "INFORM: An Architecture for Expert-Directed Knowledge Acquisition," *Int. J. Man-Machine Stud.* **26**(2), 213–230 (1987).

N. Moray, "Sources of Bias and Fallibility in Humans," paper presented at *Workshop on Knowledge Engineering in Industry*, University of Toronto, 1985.

K. Morik, "Acquiring Domain Models," *Int. J. Man-Machine Stud.* **26**(1), 93–104 (1987a).

K. Morik, "Knowledge Acquisition and Machine Learning—The Issue of Modeling," in *Proceedings of the First European Workshop on Knowledge Acquisition for Knowledge-Based Systems*, Reading University, UK, 1987b, pp. A4.1–4.

K. Morik, "Integration Issues in Knowledge Acquisition Systems," *SIGART Newsletter*, no. 108, 124–131 (Apr. 1989).

E. Motta, M. Eisenstadt, K. Pitman, and M. West, "Support for Knowledge Acquisition in the Knowledge Engineer's Assistant (KEATS)." *Expert Sys.* **5**(1), 6–28 (1988b).

E. Motta, T. Rajan, and M. Eisenstadt, "A Methodology and Tool for Knowledge Acquisition in KEATS-2," in *Proceedings of the Third Knowledge Acquisition for Knowledge-Based Systems Workshop*, Banff, Canada, 1988b, pp. 21.1–20.

E. Motta, T. Rajan, and M. Eisenstadt, *Knowledge Acquisition as a Process of Model Refinement*, HCRL Technical Report No. 40, Milton Keynes, UK, 1989.

S. Moulin, "SMAC: A Prototype of a Knowledge Modeling and Acquisition Tool for the Expert," in Aamodt, 1989, pp. 579–591.

T. Mullin, "Experts' Estimation of Uncertain Quantities and Its Implications for Knowledge Acquisition," *IEEE Trans. Sys. Man Cybernet.* **19**(3), 616–625 (1989).

K. S. Murray, "A Reactive Approach to Knowledge Integration," in Adelson, 1989, pp. 41–43.

K. S. Murray and B. W. Porter, "Developing a Tool for Knowledge Integration: Initial Results," in Benbasat and Dhaliwal, 1988, pp. 22.1–12.

K. S. Murray and B. W. Porter, "Controlling Search for the Consequences of New Information During Knowledge Integration," in Adelson, 1989.

M. A. Musen, "Conceptual Concepts of Interactive Knowledge Acquisition Tools," in *Proceedings of the Second European Knowledge Acquisition Workshop*, GMD, Bonn, 1988a, pp. 26.1–15.

M. A. Musen, "An Editor for the Conceptual Models of Interactive Knowledge-Acquisition Tools," in *Proceedings of the Third Knowledge Acquisition for Knowledge-Based Systems Workshop*, Banff, Canada, 1988b, pp. 23.1–20.

M. A. Musen, *Automated Generation of Model-based Knowledge-acquisition Tools*, Pitman, New York, 1989a.

M. A. Musen, "Knowledge Acquisition at the Metalevel: Creation of Custom-Tailored Knowledge Acquisition Tools," *SIGART Newsletter*, no. 108, 45–55 (Apr. 1989b).

M. A. Musen, "Conceptual Models of Interactive Knowledge Acquisition Tools," *Knowledge Acquisition: An International Journal of Knowledge Acquisition for Knowledge-Based Systems*, **1**(1), 73–88 (1989c).

M. A. Musen, L. M. Fagan, D. M. Combs, and E. H. Shortliffe, "Use of a Domain Model to Drive an Interactive Knowledge-Editing Tool," *Int. J. Man-Machine Stud.* **26**(1), 105–121 (1987).

P. Mychaltchouk, F. Fayad, and A. Talaslian, "Towards Automating Knowledge Engineering: A Rule Generator: GeneR," in Adelson, 1989, pp. 112–114.

S. Nirenburg, I. Monarch, T. Kaufmann, I. Nirenburg, and J. Carbonell, "Acquisition of Very Large Knowledge Bases: Methodology, Tools and Applications," in Benbasat and Dhaliwal, 1988, pp. 24.1–26.

D. Nobel, "Schema-Based Knowledge Elicitation for Planning and Situation Assessment Aids," *IEEE Trans. Sys. Man Cybernet.* **19**(3), 473–482 (1989).

I. Nordbø, M. Vestli, I. Sølvberg, "METAMETH. Methodology for Knowledge Engineering," in Aamodt, 1989, pp. 226–238.

K. Nygaard and O. J. Dahl, "The Development of the SIMULA Languages," in R. L. Wexelblat, ed., *History of Programming Languages*, Academic Press, Inc., Orlando, Fla., 1981, pp. 439–480.

G. D. Oosthuizen, "Graph Induction," in Addis, 1987, pp. F5.1–13.

J. Patel, *ASKE: Towards an Automated Knowledge Acquisition System*, HCRL Technical Report no. 36, Milton Keynes, UK, 1988.

J. Patel, "ASKE: Towards Automatic Knowledge Acquisition," in Aamodt, 1989, pp. 474–489.

L. F. Pau and S. S. Nielsen, "Conceptual Graphs as a Visual Language for Knowledge Acquisition in Architectural Expert Systems," *SIGART Newsletter*, no. 108, 151 (Apr. 1989).

M. J. Pazzani, "Explanation-Based Learning for Knowledge-Based Systems," *Int. J. Man-Machine Stud.* **26**(4), 413–434 (1987).

J. Pearl, *Fusion, Propagation and Structuring in Belief Networks*, Technical Report CSD-850022, R-42-VI-12, University of California, Los Angeles, 1986.

E. J. Pettit and M. J. Pettit, "Analysis of the Performance of a Genetic Algorithm-Based System for Message Classification in Noisy Environments," *Int. J. Man-Machine Stud.* **27**(2), 205–220 (1987).

E. Plaza and R. L. Mantàras, "Model-Based Knowledge Acquisition for Heuristic Classification Systems," *SIGART Newsletter*, no. 108, 98–105 (Apr. 1989).

J. R. Quinlan, "Learning Efficient Classification Procedures and Their Application to Chess End Games," in Michalski and co-workers, eds., 1983.

J. R. Quinlan, "Simplifying Decision Trees," *Int. J. Man-Machine Stud.* **27**(3), 221–234 (1987).

J. Rantanen, "Hypermedia in Knowledge Acquisition and Specification of User Interface for KBS: An Approach and a Case Study," in Addis, 1989, pp. 24.1–20.

A. Rappaport, "Cognitive Primitives," *Int. J. Man-Machine Stud.* **29**(6), 733–747 (1988).

A. Rappaport and B. R. Gaines, "Integration of Acquisition and Performance Systems," in Benbasat and Dhaliwal, 1988, pp. 25.1–12.

S. Regoczei and G. Hirst, "The Meaning Triangle as a Tool for the Acquisition of Abstract, Conceptual Knowledge," in Benbasat and Dhaliwal, 1988, pp. 26.1–19.

S. Regoczei and G. Hirst, "On 'Extracting Knowledge From Text': Modelling the Architecture of Language Users," in *Proceedings of the Third European Workshop on Knowledge Acquisition for Knowledge-Based Systems*, Paris, 1989a, pp. 196–211.

S. Regoczei and G. Hirst, "Sortal Analysis with SORTAL, a Software Assistant for Knowledge Acquisition," in *Proceedings of the Fourth Knowledge Acquisition for Knowledge-Based Systems Workshop*, Banff, Canada, 1989b, pp. 25.1–18.

S. Regoczei and E. P. O. Plantinga, "Ontology and Inventory: A Foundation for a Knowledge Acquisition Methodology," *Int. J. Man-Machine Stud.* **27**(3), 235–250 (1987).

R. G. Reynolds, J. I. Maletic and S. E. Porvin, "PM: A Metrics Driven Plan Compiler," in Addis, 1989, pp. 26.1–10.

G. S. Ribar, "Graphical Knowledge Acquisition," in Adelson, 1989, pp. 44–48.

E. L. Rissland, "The Problem of Intelligent Example Selection," in Fredman, 1987, pp. 16.0–25.

D. Rochowiak and W. Mosley, "Documentation and Knowledge Acquisition Tools and Techniques," *Proceedings of the Fourth Knowledge Acquisition for Knowledge-Based Systems Workshop*, Detroit, August 1989, pp. 83–86.

J. R. Rose and H. Gelernter, "ISOLDE: A System for Learning Organic Chemistry Through Induction," in Aamodt, 1989, pp. 297–310.

W. B. Rouse, J. M. Hammer, and C. M. Lewis, "On Capturing Humans Skulls and Knowledge: Algorithmic Approaches to Model Identification," *IEEE Trans. Sys. Man Cybernet.* **19**(3), 558–573 (1989).

C. Rouveirol and M. Manago, "Widening the Knowledge Acquisition Bottleneck," in Benbasat and Dhaliwal, 1988, pp. 27.1–18.

K. Ruberg, S. M. Cornick, and K. A. James, "House Calls: Building and Maintaining a Diagnostic Rule-Base," in Benbasat and Dhaliwal, 1988, pp. 28.1–20.

R. A. Rusk and R. M. Krone, "The Crawford Slip Method (CSM) as a Tool for Extraction of Expert Knowledge," in G. Salvendy, ed., *Human-Computer Interaction*, Elsevier Science Publishing Co., Inc., New York, 1984, pp. 279–282.

T. L. Saaty, *The Analytic Hierarchy Process*, McGraw-Hill Inc., New York, 1981.

C. Sammut and R. Banerjii, "Hierarchical Memories: An Aid to Concept Learning, *Proceedings of the International Machine Learning Workshop*, University of Illinois, Urbana, Monticello, Ill., 1983, pp. 22–24.

C. Sammut and R. Banerjii, "Learning Concepts by Asking Questions," in Michalski and co-workers, eds., 1986.

A. L. Samuel, "Some Studies in Machine Learning Using the Game of Checkers," in E. A. Feigenbaum and J. Feldman, eds., *Computers and Thought*, McGraw-Hill Inc., New York, 1963.

J. Sandberg, R. Winkels, and J. Breuker, "Knowledge Acquisition for Intelligent Tutoring System," in Addis and Bull, 1988, pp. 27.1–12.

P. Schaefer, "Automated Knowledge Acquisition of Higher-Level Causal Models," in Adelson, 1989.

G. Schmidt and T. Wetter, "Towards Knowledge Acquisition in Natural Language Dialogue," in Aamodt, 1989, pp. 239–252.

G. Schreiber, J. Breuker, B. Bredeweg, and B. Wielinga, "Modeling in KBS Development," in Addis and Bull, 1988, pp. 7.1–15.

S. Schröder, H. Niemann, and G. Sagerer, "Knowledge Acquisition for a Knowledge Based Image Analysis System," in Addis and Bull, 1988, pp. 29.1–15.

D. C. Schuler, P. J. Russo, J. H. Boose, and J. M. Bradshaw, "Using Personal Construct Techniques for Collaborative Evaluation," in Benbasat and Dhaliwal, 1988, pp. 29.1–15.

M. Sebag and M. Schoenauer, "Generation of Rules with Certainty and Confidence Factors from Incomplete and Incoherent Learning Bases," in Addis and Bull, 1988, pp. 28.1–20.

N. Shadbolt and M. Burton, "The Empirical Study of Knowledge Elicitation Techniques," *SIGART Newsletter*, no. 108, 15–18 (Apr. 1989).

G. Shafer and A. Tversky, "Languages and Designs for Probability Judgment," *Cog. Sci.* **9**, 309–339 (1985).

V. L. Shalin, J. R. Bloomfield, and P. T. Bullemer, "Knowledge Acquisition as Cognitive Modeling," in Addis, 1989, pp. 27.1–15.

V. L. Shalin, E. J. Wisniewski, K. R. Levi, and P. D. Scott, "A Formal Analysis of Machine Learning Systems for Knowledge Acquisition," *Int. J. Man-Machine Stud.* **29**(4), 429–446 (1988).

M. L. G. Shaw, "Interaction Knowledge Elicitation," *Proceedings of the Canadian Information Processing Society Annual Conference*, CIPS, Calgary, Canada, 1984.

M. L. G. Shaw, "Problems of Validation in a Knowledge Acquisition System Using Multiple Experts," in Addis and Bull, 1988, pp. 5.1–15.

M. L. G. Shaw, "A Grid-Based Tool for Knowledge Acquisition: Validation with Multiple Experts," *SIGART Newsletter*, no. 108, 168–169 (Apr. 1989a).

M. L. G. Shaw, "A Grid-Based Tool for Knowledge Acquisition," in *IJCAI Workshop on Knowledge Acquisition*, Detroit, Mich., Morgan-Kaufmann, San Mateo, Calif., 1989b, pp. 19–22.

M. L. G. Shaw and B. R. Gaines, "Techniques for Knowledge Acquisition and Transfer," *Int. J. Man-Machine Stud.* **27**(3), 251–280 (1987a).

M. L. G. Shaw and B. R. Gaines, "KITTEN: Knowledge Initiation & Transfer Tools for Experts & Novices," *Int. J. Man-Machine Stud.* **27**(3), 251–280 (1987b).

M. L. G. Shaw and B. R. Gaines, "A Methodology for Recognizing Conflict, Correspondence, Consensus and Contrast in a Knowledge Acquisition System," in Benbasat and Dhaliwal, 1988, pp. 30.1–19.

M. L. G. Shaw and B. R. Gaines, "Knowledge Acquisition: Some Foundations, Manual Methods and Future Trends," in Aamodt, 1989, pp. 3–18.

M. L. G. Shaw and J. B. Woodward, "Validation of a Knowledge Support System," in J. H. Boose and B. R. Gaines, eds., *Proceedings of the Second Knowledge Acquisition for Knowledge-Based Systems Workshop*, University of Calgary, Calgary, Canada, 1987, pp. 18.0–15.

M. L. G. Shaw and J. B. Woodward, "Validation in a Knowledge Support System: Construing Consistency with Multiple Experts," *Int. J. Man-Machine Stud.* **29**(3), 329–350 (1988).

M. L. G. Shaw and J. B. Woodward, "Mental Models in the Knowledge Acquisition Process," in Addis, 1989, pp. 29.1–24.

D. B. Shema and J. H. Boose, "Refining Problem-Solving Knowledge in Repertory Grids Using a Consultation Mechanism," *Int. J. Man-Machine Stud.* **29**, 447–460 (1988).

D. B. Shema, J. H. Boose, and J. M. Bradshaw, "Recent Progress in AQUINAS: A Knowledge Acquisition Workbench," in Benbasat and Dhaliwal, 1988, pp. 31.1–21.

D. B. Shema, J. M. Bradshaw, S. P. Covington, and J. H. Boose, "Design Knowledge Capture and Alternative Generation Using Possibility Tables in CANARD," in Addis, 1989, pp. 30.1–19.

B. G. Silverman R. G. Wenig, and T. Wu, "COPEing with Ongoing Knowledge Acquisition from Collaborating Hierarchies of Experts," *SIGART Newsletter*, no. 108, 170–171 (Apr. 1989).

K. Silvestro, "Using Explanations for Knowledge Base Acquisition," *Int. J. Man-Machine Stud.* **29**(2), 159–170 (1988).

E. Simoudis, "Learning Redesign Knowledge," in Benbasat and Dhaliwal, 1988, pp. 32.1–20.

E. Simoudis, "Learning Redesign Knowledge," in Adelson, 1989, pp. 52–55.

D. Skuce, "A Generic Knowledge Acquisition Environment Integrating Natural Language and Logic," in Adelson, 1989, pp. 165–169.

D. Skuce, W. Shenkang, and Y. Beauvillé, "A Generic Knowledge Acquisition Environment for Conceptual and Ontological Analysis," in Addis, 1989, pp. 31.1–20.

B. M. Slator, "Extracting Lexical Knowledge From Dictionary Text," in Benbasat and Dhaliwal, 1988.

B. M. Slator, "Extracting Lexical Knowledge from Dictionary Text," *SIGART Newsletter*, no. 108, 173–174 (Apr. 1988).

R. G. Smith, H. A. Winston, T. M. Mitchell, and B. G. Buchanan, "Representation and Use of Explicit Justifications for Knowledge Base Refinements," in Marcus and co-workers, 1985.

C. Spetzler and C. Stael von Holstein, "Probabiliy Encoding in Decision Analysis," in R. Howard and J. Matheson, eds., *Readings on the Principles and Applications of Decision Analysis*, Vol. 2, Strategic Decisions Group, Palo Alto, Calif., 1983, pp. 601–626.

C. Stael von Holstein and J. E. Matheson, *A Manual for Encoding Probability Distributions*, SRI International, Menlo Park, Calif., 1978.

H. Stephanou, "Perspectives on Imperfect Information Processing," *IEEE Trans. Sys. Man Cybernet.* **17**, 780–798 (1987).

J. Sticklen, B. Chandrasekaran, and W. E. Bond, "Distributed Causal Reasoning," *Knowledge Acquisition: An International Journal* **1**(2), 139–162 (1989).

J. Stout, G. Caplain, S. Marcus, and J. McDermott, "Toward Automating Recognition of Differing Problem-Solving Demands," *Int. J. Man-Machine Stud.* **29**(5), 599–611 (1988).

S. Subramanian and E. C. Freuder, "Compiling Rules from Constraint Satisfaction Problem Solving," *SIGART Newsletter*, no. 108, 177–178 (Apr. 1989).

M. Suwa and H. Motoda, "Understanding Metaphors by Frustration-Based Learning Method," in *Proceedings of the Fourth Knowledge Acquisition for Knowledge-Based Systems Workshop*, University of Calgary, Calgary, Canada, 1989a, pp. 33.1–17.

M. Suwa and H. Motoda, "Acquisition of Associative Knowledge by the Frustration-Based Learning Method in an Auxiliary-Line Problem," *Knowledge Acquisition: An International Journal of Knowledge Acquisition for Knowledge-Based Systems* **1**(1), 113–137 (1989b).

S. Szpakowicz, "Semi-Automatic Acquisition of Conceptual Structure from Technical Texts," in Benbasat and Dhaliwal, 1988, pp. 35.1–16.

H. Taki, "Knowledge Acquisition By Abductive and Inductive Explanation," in Addis, 1989, pp. 34.1–19.

H. Taki and Y. Fujii, "Operation Presumption: Knowledge Acquisition by Induction," in Aamodt, 1989, pp. 34–48.

J. Tani, T. Hirobe, K. Niida, L. Koshijima, and H. Murakami, "New Learning Algorithm for Rule Extraction by Neural Network and Its Application," in Addis, 1989, pp. 35.1–16.

P. P. Terpstra and M. W. van Someren, "Inde: A System for Knowledge Refinement and Machine Learning," in Addis and Bull, 1988, pp. 30.1–8.

D. Thanassas, "Knowledge Acquisition for Knowledge Discovery: A Theoretical Perspective," in Adelson, 1989, pp. 176–178.

M. A. Tolcott, F. F. Marvin, and P. E. Lehner, "Expert Decision Making in Evolving Situations," *IEEE Trans. Sys. Man Cybernet.* **19**(3), 606–615 (1989).

X. Tong, "MAC: Acquiring Abstract Knowledge," in Adelson, 1989, pp. 38–40.

X. Tong and W. Karbach, "Filling in the Knowledge Acquisition Gap: via Kads' Models of Expertise to Zdest-2's Expert Systems," in Addis and Bull, 1988, pp. 31.1–17.

B. E. Tonn, L. Arrowood, R. Goeltz, and K. Hake, "Automated Knowledge Acquisition for Contingency Analysis Applications," *IJCAI-89 Workshop on Knowledge Acquisition*, Detroit, August 1989, pp. 183–185.

D. Tranowski, T. Levitt, and K. Riley, "Performance-Based Knowledge Acquisition: A Structural Foundation for Traditional Introspective Knowledge Acquisition," in Benbasat and Dhaliwal, 1988, pp. 36.1–3.

A. Trice and R. Davis, *Consensus Knowledge Acquisition*, Technical Report, MIT, Cambridge, Mass., 1989.

G. Trimble and C. N. Cooper, "Experience of Knowledge Acquisition for Expert Systems in Construction," in Addis, 1987, pp. C5.1–14.

F. Tschudi, "Matrix Representation of Expert Systems," *AI Expert*, 44–53 (Oct. 1988).

C. Tsui, *A Tool for Assisting Booklore Acquisition*, Technical Report, Chinese Academy of Sciences, 1988.

A. Tversky and D. Kahneman, "Judgement Under Uncertainty," in D. Kahneman, eds., *Judgement Under Uncertainty: Heuristics and Biases*, Cambridge University Press, Cambridge, UK, 1974.

A. Tversky and D. Kahneman, "The Framing of Decisions in the Psychology of Choice," *Science* **211**, 453–458 (1974).

A. Tversky, S. Sattah, and P. Slovic, *Contingent Weighting in Judgment and Choice*, Stanford University, Menlo Park, Calif., 1987.

S. Twine, "From Information Analysis Toward Knowledge Acquisition," in Addis and Bull, 1988, pp. 6.1–15.

S. Twine, "A Model for the Knowledge Analysis Process," in Aamodt, 1989, pp. 253–268.

M. Valtorta, "KADS vs. KEATS," in Adelson, 1989.

P. Velardi, M. T. Pazienza, S. Magrini, "Acquisition of Semantic Patterns from a Natural Corpus of Texts," *SIGART Newsletter*, no. 108, 115–123 (Apr. 1989).

F. von Martial and F. Victor, "Collaborative Construction of an Office Knowledge Base: Experiences and Suggestions," in Addis and Bull, 1988, pp. 32.1–14.

V. R. Waldron, "Process Tracing as a Method for Initial Knowledge Acquisition," in *Proceedings of the Second IEEE Conference on AI Applications*, 1985.

V. R. Waldron, "Investigating the Communication Problems Encountered in Knowledge Acquisition," *SIGART Newsletter*, no. 108, 143–144 (Apr. 1989).

T. Wallsten and D. Budescu, "Encoding Subject Probabilities: A Psychological and Psychometric Review," *Management Sci.* **29**(2), 151–173 (1983).

M. Welbank, "Knowledge Acquisition: A Survey and British Telecom Experience," in *Proceedings of the First European Workshop on Knowledge Acquisition for Knowledge-Based Systems*, Reading University, UK, 1987a, pp. C6.1–9.

M. Welbank, *Knowledge Acquisition Update*, Insight Study no. 5, Systems Designers, London, UK, 1987b.

T. T. Wells, "Hypertext as a Means for Knowledge Acquisition," *SIGART Newsletter*, no. 108, 136–138 (Apr. 1989).

T. Wetter and F. Schmalhofer, "Knowledge Acquisition from Text-Based Think-Aloud Protocols: Situational Specification for a Legal Expert System," in Addis and Bull, 1988, pp. 33.1–15.

B. Wielinga, H. Akkermans, G. Schreiber, and J. Balder, "A Knowledge Acquisition Perspective on Knowledge-Level Models," in Addis, 1989, pp. 36.1–22.

D. C. Wilkens, W. J. Clancey, and G. G. Buchanan, "Knowledge Base Refinement by Editing Abstract Control Knowledge," *Int. J. Man-Machine Stud.* **27**(4), 281–294 (1987).

R. V. Williams and J. R. Thomas, "An Interactive Strategic Planning Expert System," in Addis, 1987, pp. E7.1–19.

E. Wisniewski, H. Winston, R. Smith, and M. Kleyn, "Case Generation for Rule Synthesis," *Int. J. Man-Machine Stud.* **27**(3), 295–313 (1987).

I. H. Witten and B. MacDonald, "Using Concept Learning for Knowledge Acquisition," *Int. J. Man-Machine Stud.* **29**(2), 171–196 (1988).

W. A. Wolf, "Knowledge Acquisition from Multiple Experts," *SIGART Newsletter*, no. 108, 138–140 (Apr. 1989).

D. D. Woods and E. Hollnagel, "Mapping Cognitive Demands and Activities in Complex Problems Solving Worlds," *Int. J. Man-Machine Stud.* **26**(2), 257–275 (1987).

B. Woodward, "Knowledge Engineering at the Front-End: Defining the Domain," in Benbasat and Dhaliwal, 1988.

S. Wrobel, "Design Goals for Sloppy Modeling Systems," *Int. J. Man-Machine Stud.* **29**(4), 461–477 (1988).

S. Xie, D. F. Dumaresq, and P. H. Winne, "PRED: An Interface Development Tool for Editing Primitives in Knowledge Representation Languages," in Benbasat and Dhaliwal, 1988, pp. 38.1–17.

S. Yamada and S. Tsuji, "Acquisition of Macro-Operators from Worked Examples in Problem Solving," *SIGART Newsletter*, no. 108, 171–172 (Apr. 1989).

X. P. Yang and D. Okrent, "Knowledge Representation under Uncertainty by Using Bayesian Networks and Stochastic Models," in Adelson, 1989, pp. 91–95.

R. Yoshii, "Portable Rule Acquisition Interface for Maintaining Expert Systems," in Adelson, 1989, pp. 115–119.

R. M. Young and J. Gammack, "Role of Psychological Techniques and Intermediate Representations in Knowledge Elicitation," in Addis, 1987, pp. D7.1–5.

G. Zinßmeister and H. U. Hoppe, "Acquisition of Task-Knowledge for an Adaptive User Interface," in Aamodt, 1989, pp. 269–284.

General References

T. R. Addis, "The Science of Knowledge: A Research Program for Knowledge Engineering," *Proceedings of the Third European Workshop on Knowledge Acquisition for Knowledge-Based Systems*, Paris, July, 1989, pp. 49–59.

E. R. Bareiss, *Protos: A Unified Approach to Concept Representation, Classification, and Learning*, Technical Report AI88-83, AI Laboratory, University of Texas, Austin, Tex., Aug. 1988.

E. R. Bareiss, B. W. Porter, and C. C. Wier, "Protos: An Exemplar-Based Learning Apprentice, Special Issue on the 2nd Knowledge Acquisition for Knowledge-Based Systems Workshop, 1987," *Int. J. Man-Mach. Stud.* **29**(5), 549–562 (1988).

N. J. Belkin, H. M. Brooks, and P. J. Daniels, "Knowledge Elicitation Using Discourse Analysis, *Int. J. Man-Mach. Stud.* **27**(2), 127–144; also in B. R. Gaines, and J. H. Boose, eds., *Knowledge-Based Systems Vol. 1: Knowledge Acquisition for Knowledge-Based Systems*, New York, Academic Press, 1988, pp. 107–124.

R. A. Benfer and L. Furbee, "Knowledge Acquisition in the Peruvian Andes," *AI Expert*, Nov. 1989, pp. 22–29.

J. H. Boose, D. B. Shema, and J. M. Bradshaw, "Design Knowledge Capture for a Corporate Memory Facility," *5th Annual AI in Space Conference*, Huntsville, May 1990.

J. M. Bradshaw, P. J. Russo, S. P. Covington, and J. H. Boose, "Knowledge Acquisition and Decision Analysis; La Folie a Deux," *Proceedings of the AAAI Uncertainty Workshop*, Detroit, Mich., Aug. 1989.

D. A. Cleaves, "Cognitive Biases and Corrective Techniques; Proposals for Improving Elicitation Procedures for Knowledge-Based Systems," *Int. J. Man-Mach. Stud.* **27**(2), 155–156 (1987).

D. Diaper, "POMESS: A People Orientated Methodology for Expert System Specification," *Proceedings of the First European Workshop on Knowledge Acquisition for Knowledge-Based Systems*, Reading University, UK, Sept. 1987, pp. D4.1–14.

D. L. Dvorak, *Guide to CL-PROTOS: An Exemplar-Based Learning Apprentice*, Technical Report AI88-87, AI Laboratory, University of Texas at Austin, Sept. 1987.

K. A. Ericsson and H. A. Simon, *Protocol Analysis: Verbal Reports as Data*, Cambridge, Mass., The MIT Press, 1984.

M. Freiling and co-workers, "Starting a Knowledge Engineering Project: A Step-by-step Approach," *AI Magazine*, Fall, 150–164 (1985).

B. R. Gaines and M. L. G. Shaw, "New Directions in the Analysis and Interactive Elicitation of Personal Construct Systems," in M. L. G. Shaw, ed., *Recent Advances in Personal Construct Technology*, New York, Academic Press, 1981.

L. Johnson and N. E. Johnson, "Knowledge Elicitation Involving Teachback Interviewing," in A. Kidd, ed., *Knowledge Elicitation for Expert Systems: A Practical Handbook*, New York, Plenum Press, 1987.

G. A. Klein, R. Calderwood, and D. MacGregor, "Critical Decision Method for Eliciting Knowledge," special issue of *IEEE Trans. Sys. Man Cybern.* **19**(3), 462–472 (1989).

M. LaFrance, "The Knowledge Acquisition Grid: A Method for Training Knowledge Engineers," *Proceedings of the First*

Knowledge Acquisition for Knowledge-Based System Workshop, Banff, UK, Nov. 1986, pp. 26.0–14.

B. McHugh, "Knowledge Acquisition and Nuclear Safety Advisors," *Proceedings of the First European Workshop on Knowledge Acquisition for Knowledge-Based Systems*, Reading University, UK, Sept. 1987, pp. C4.1–10.

Proceedings of the IJCAI Workshop on Knowledge Acquisition, Detroit, Mich., Morgan-Kaufmann, San Mateo, Calif., Aug. 1989.

M. Sharp, "Knowledge Acquisition for Advice Systems: FUSION, A Network Cognitive Support System," *Proceedings of the Fourth Knowledge Acquisition for Knowledge-Based Systems Workshop*, Banff, Oct. 1989, pp. 28.1–19.

SIGART Newsletter, No. 108 [Special Issue on knowledge acquisition], (Apr. 1989).

S. Tanimoto, *The Elements of Artificial Intelligence*, Computer Science Press, Rockville, Md., 1987.

JOHN H. BOOSE
Boeing Computer Services

KNOWLEDGE LEVEL

The knowledge level is a level of description for a complex system, such as a computer program. A knowledge-level description characterizes the system in terms of goals, beliefs, and reasoning capabilities, without regard for the actual physical mechanisms that cause behavior. Perhaps the most familiar knowledge-level description is a natural language grammar, which is used to describe patterns in speech. Saying that speakers know the grammar is a knowledge-level description. Knowledge-level descriptions are useful for explaining and predicting behavior. As abstractions, they are necessarily incomplete descriptions, but have proven useful for specifying what a computer program should do (Alexander and co-workers, 1986), comparing representation languages (Clancey, 1985), and predicting the learning capabilities of programs (Dieterich, 1986).

A knowledge-level description is to be distinguished from a symbol-level description, that is, the implementation or encoding of knowledge and reasoning procedures. A knowledge-level description is idealized. It is not concerned with the details of how computations are performed, just with what an agent (program or person) can do. In contrast, a symbol-level description is in terms of a representation language: stored structures and the matching and search algorithms that perform computations. This distinction is particularly useful for abstracting problem-solving architectures so they can be compared and reused, avoiding pragmatic issues of efficiency and storage that disguise computational equivalence.

Newell (1982) introduced the term knowledge-level. His intent was to resolve "mystification of the role of representation, the residue of the theorem-proving controversy, and the conflicting webwork of opinions on knowledge representation." First, encoding tricks (alternative representations) suggested that intelligence is not a matter of what is known, but the structures used to store it, which seems counterintuitive when considering that humans can effectively teach people without knowing how

the brain stores knowledge. Second, arguments about the inadequacy of logic as an implementation language obscured its value as a specification language (Hayes, 1977). Third, the proliferating jargon of knowledge representation languages inhibited progress of the community. By highlighting the distinction between the knowledge level and symbol level, Newell sought to bring the question "What is knowledge?" to the forefront, making issues of representation and logic secondary. "Knowledge serves as a specification of what the symbol structure should be able to do" (Newell, 1982).

Newell uses a systems approach, characterizing the whole system (an agent) according to different levels of abstraction. Specifically, a computer system has these levels, viewed from the top down: knowledge, symbol, register–transfer, logic–circuit, circuit, and device. Crucially, knowledge is attributed by an observer to explain why the agent's behavior is rational. That is, the observer assumes that an agent, if it has certain knowledge, will use its knowledge to achieve its goals (the principle of rationality). Observing a pattern of behavior, the pattern is explained in terms of consistent goals and beliefs. For example, if an agent knows where a restaurant is located and the agreed meeting time, then the principle of rationality suggests that the agent will take actions to be at the restaurant at that time. Failures to accomplish goals are thus stated in terms of lack of knowledge or inability to take some action, not in terms of how the knowledge is represented.

Dieterich (1986) effectively applied Newell's levels of analysis to compare machine learning programs. He found that some existing programs are not capable of knowledge-level learning. Instead, the programs modify their symbol structures to access stored representations more efficiently. He called this symbol-level learning. Dieterich found that other programs are capable of learning knowledge, but their behavior cannot be predicted or described at the knowledge level. He called this nondeductive knowledge-level learning. Dieterich's analysis clearly demonstrates the advantage of subtracting away issues of implementation, to describe what a program can do. Levesque's (1984) analysis is similar, characterizing knowledge representations in terms of memory and inference functions.

Knowledge-level descriptions have been especially useful in the area of knowledge engineering (Stefik, in press). A special concern is the development of general-programming tools (generic shells) that can be used to develop expert systems in many domains. By early 1980s, attention turned to formalizing representation languages and problem-solving methods that were specialized for different tasks, such as diagnosis and design. A knowledge-level analysis permits the development of abstract methods in particular programs so they can be reused. Specifically, a knowledge-level description of an expert system indicates what knowledge is necessary for a task and what kinds of inferences can be made, without regard for the particular encoding (eg, rules and frames) or the methods of pattern matching and search control (eg, blackboard and constraint optimization).

Clancey (1985) showed that a wide variety of expert systems can be described at the knowledge-level by a problem-solving method called heuristic classification. These programs relate data (observable information) to hypotheses (conjectured problem solutions) in systematic ways: abstracting data, relating data categories heuristically to hypothesis categories, and refining hypotheses. A key feature of heuristic classification is the selection of a solution from a preenumerated list or hierarchy. Such a description shows how concepts are typically related by the program, without regard for how they are encoded. As Newell intended, this allows researchers to compare their work and separate out symbol-level issues of efficiency and storage.

Clancey argued further that expert systems could be related to traditional systems analysis in this way. Knowledge bases are characterized in terms of the system being modeled, the purpose for constructing a model (the task), the way in which processes are modeled (eg, chronological stage classifications, state-transitions, and functional composition), the modeling method (heuristic classification selecting a process model vs configuration of new process descriptions), encoding in a representation language (eg, production rules), and finally the encoding in a programming language (eg, C and LISP) (Clancey, 1985; in press *a*). These ideas have been applied for developing expert system shells and specialized knowledge acquisition tools (Alexander and co-workers, 1986; McDermott, 1988). Chandrasekaran (1985) and Sticklen (1989) have extended Newell's analysis to describe a problem-solving agent in terms of a cooperating society of more primitive agents. This decomposition deals with complexity by exploiting and formalizing the different roles knowledge plays.

More recently, Clancey (1991) argues that the knowledge level has relativistic properties. A knowledge-level description is of an agent in its environment. It is an observer's theory, not representations possessed by the agent being studied.

Knowledge-level descriptions concern emergent patterns that develop over time, not plans (eg, schemas and grammars) that are represented inside the agent before its history of interaction begins. Knowledge-level descriptions are useful and necessary to describe, predict, explain, etc patterns of interaction that develop between the agent and its environment. Crucially, knowledge-level descriptions cannot be reduced to (replaced by) symbol-level descriptions. That is, they are a level above individual agents. Unlike the relation between register–transfer and logic–circuit levels, for example, the knowledge level cannot be realized as physical structures in an agent in isolation. Extending this idea, Clancey argues that classification models of any system interacting with its environment (eg, disease models) in principle cannot be replaced by structure–function models that describe how the system is constructed (ie, deep models). The identification of such frame of reference issues is currently having a major effect on the design of robots and models of human behavior in what is called situated cognition.

BIBLIOGRAPHY

J. H. Alexander, M. J. Freiling, S. J. Shulman, J. L. Staley, S. Rehfuss, and M. Messick, "Knowledge Level Engineering: On-

tological Analysis," *Proceedings of the Fifth National Conference on Artificial Intelligence*, Philadelphia, Pa., 1986, AAAI, Menlo Park, Calif.

B. Chandrasekaran, "Generic Tasks in Knowledge-Based Reasoning: Characterizing Systems at the 'Right' Level of Complexity," *Proceedings of the IEEE Second Annual Conference on Artificial Intelligence Applications*, 1985.

W. J. Clancey, "Heuristic Classification," *Artif. Intell.* **27**, 289–350 (1985).

W. J. Clancey, "Model Construction Operators," *Artif. Intell.*, in press.

W. J. Clancey, "The Frame of Reference Problem in the Design of Intelligent Machines," in K. vanLehn, ed., *Architectures for Intelligence: The Twenty-Second Carnegie Symposium on Cognition*, Erlbaum, Hillsdale, N.J., 357–422 (1991).

T. Dietterich, "Learning at the Knowledge Level," *Machine Learning* 1(3), 287–315 (1986).

P. Hayes, "In Defence of Logic," in *Proceedings of the Fifth IJCAI*, Cambridge, Mass., Morgan-Kaufmann, San Mateo, Calif., 1977.

H. J. Levesque, "Foundations of a Functional Approach to Knowledge Representation," *Artif. Intell.* **23**(2), 155–212 (1984).

J. McDermott, "Preliminary Steps Toward a Taxonomy of Problem-Solving Methods," in S. Marcus, ed., *Automating Knowledge Acquisition for Expert Systems*, Kluwer Academic Publishers, Boston, 1988.

A. Newell, "The Knowledge Level," *Artif. Intell.* **18**(1), 87–127 (1984).

M. Stefik, *Introduction to Knowledge Systems*, in preparation, Morgan-Kaufmann, Publishers.

J. Sticklen, "Problem-Solving Architecture at the Knowledge Level," *J. Exper. Theor. Artif. Intell.* 1(4), 233–248 (1989).

WILLIAM J. CLANCEY
Institute for Research on
Learning

KNOWLEDGE REPRESENTATION

The dominant paradigm for building intelligent systems since the early 1970s has been based on the premise that intelligence presupposes knowledge. Thus to build a program that performs, say, diagnosis for an infectious disease, it is necessary to identify the units of knowledge used by human experts as they perform the diagnostic task and to make them available to the system under development. Moreover, it is necessary to characterize the patterns of reasoning used by the human expert (deductive, hypothetical, or heuristic) and endow the intelligent system with analogous reasoning capabilities. This methodology is applicable for systems intended to perform any task requiring intelligence, be it diagnosis, planning, design or interpretation. Generally, knowledge is represented in the system's *knowledge base,* which consists of data structures and programs. In addition, the intelligent system is expected to have a program called an *inference engine* that implements the reasoning patterns necessary for the task at hand. Thus current AI theory and practice dictate that intelligent systems be knowledge based, consistent with this simple knowledge base plus inference engine architecture. This emphasis on knowledge has led to suggestions that AI can be arguably called applied epistemology. More important, it has placed knowledge representation and reasoning at center stage in AI research activity. Although the notion of knowledge representation may seem straightforward, its task and methods have stirred considerable controversy. Indeed, it has been repeatedly documented in questionnaires, panel discussions, workshops, surveys and reviews of the field that there is little agreement on how the problem is to be solved or even what constitutes a solution (Brachman and Levesque, 1985; Levesque, 1986; Cercone and McCalla, 1987).

This article begins with a short discussion of terms used to describe the contents of a knowledge base and the enterprise of knowledge representation, followed by a brief history of the field. The main body of the article discusses the basic functionality of a knowledge representation system and the trade-offs between different paradigms for representing knowledge. A number of important issues is also discussed, ranging from the expressiveness and the semantics of a notation for representing knowledge to structuring facilities for knowledge bases and different categories of reasoning. Examples of knowledge representation systems are included and some areas of active research are mentioned. It must be noted that the discussion does not cover nonsymbolic representations, such as ones based on neural networks (qv), or analogical ones (Funt, 1980).

Vocabulary

A knowledge base is a symbol structure representing a collection of facts about some domain of discourse. The term *object* is used to refer to elements in the knowledge base that are intended to denote entities in this domain. For example, a knowledge base having ancient Greece as its domain of discourse might contain an object representing the person Socrates. Objects are also used to represent abstract concepts such as the concept of person and sets of entities such as the set of philosophers. Terms such as *concept, constant symbol,* and *frame* are commonly used synonymously.

A *fact* is a statement that certain relationships hold between entities denoted by some objects. For example, it might be stated that Socrates's birthplace was Athens. Such statements about the world are variously called *propositions, assertions, formulas, sentences, clauses,* or *properties of objects* in different knowledge representation schemes. Notations for representing knowledge will be referred to as knowledge representation schemes. Examples of schemes include logical calculi, graph-theoretic notations, and even some programming languages. A knowledge representation system offers facilities for constructing and querying a knowledge base.

History

Philosophy has concerned itself with the nature of knowledge since Aristotle and the formalization of reasoning since Leibniz. Mathematical logic (see INDUCTION, MATHEMATICAL) developed at the turn of the century placed mathematics and mathematical reasoning on a formal foundation and has served as a linguistic basis and methodological paradigm for much of the work on the field of knowledge representation (McCarthy, 1968; Hayes, 1977).

An edited volume (Minsky, 1968) contains one of the first strong arguments for the advantages of knowledge-based accounts of intelligence. It includes a collection of papers describing a first generation of knowledge-based programs, many of which argue that access to an organized body of knowledge is necessary for programs to find solutions to commonsense problems in a reasonable amount of time. The collection includes a paper by McCarthy, originally published in 1958, which offers an account of how the program Advice Taker could use knowledge about a task, represented in terms of logical formulas, and could even improve its performance through external advice. This work prescribes much of the research on knowledge representation and reasoning that has unfolded since, although McCarthy's original conception of the Advice Taker remains ambitious even by today's standards. Another important paper in this collection, authored by Quillian, introduces the notion of semantic network (qv), a graph-theoretic data structure whose nodes represent word senses and whose arcs express binary semantic relationships between these word senses. This approach to representing knowledge has been adopted by many subsequent knowledge representation systems. Moreover, Quillian's work constitutes an early attempt to offer a computational account of the associative features of human memory, including a spreading activation model of computation that has served as basis for more recent work on massively parallel machine architectures.

The straightforward application of mathematical logic to knowledge representation, originally attempted in the late 1960s, encountered severe difficulties due to a number of factors. First, general-purpose theorem proving (qv) is computationally intractable, even with the advances in efficiency due to the introduction of the resolution principle. Second, logic, because of its initial focus on mathematics and mathematical reasoning, offered little for the type of commonsense, nondeductive reasoning required of many tasks. An early expression of this difficulty is the so-called frame problem: to reason about actions, such as picking up a book from a table, logical representations require explicit representation of the myriad facts that do not change by the action, eg, the location of the table or the agent's car, in addition to those that do. As a reaction to these difficulties, a number of procedural representation schemes were introduced in the early 1970s. These combined the features of programming languages such as LISP (qv) with new associative data structures and event-driven procedure invocations. Notable among these were PLANNER (qv) (Hewitt, 1971) and its successor, CONNIVER (qv) (Sussman and McDermott, 1972).

Production systems constitute another proposal for representing knowledge procedurally, offered during the same period (Newell and Simon, 1972). In a production system, knowledge is expressed in terms of if–then rules, which specify condition–action or premise–conclusion pairs (see RULE-BASED SYSTEMS). For example, a rule might state "*if* the top of a block to be moved is not clear, *then* clear it!" This scheme is the basic representation of knowledge used by most early expert systems (qv) (Hayes-Roth and co-workers, 1983). An early and authoritative collection of papers on production systems has been published (Waterman and Hayes-Roth, 1978).

As semantic network representation schemes proliferated in the 1970s, it became clear that there was no consensus on their form or their semantics (see SEMANTIC NETWORKS). A paper by Woods (1975) notes this difficulty and suggests possible solutions toward a well-founded semantics. This influential paper spawned a new generation of semantic network schemes (Findler, 1979), including schemes that treat semantic networks as a graph-theoretic notation for logical formulas.

Also during the mid-1970s, Minsky (1975) introduced the notion of *frames* (qv) as a means for representing commonsense knowledge, such as the concept of a room or an elephant. A frame is a complex data structure containing information about the components of the concept being described, links to similar concepts, as well as procedural information on how the frame can change over time. Examples of early frame-based representations are KRL (qv) (Bobrow and Windograd, 1977), FRL (qv) (Goldstein and Roberts, 1977), and PSN (Levesque and Mylopoulos, 1979).

Since the early 1980s there have been attempts to offer knowledge representation schemes that adopt and integrate ingredients from logic, semantic networks, and procedural representations. An example of this new trend is KRYPTON (Brachman and co-workers, 1983). A KRYPTON knowledge base consists of two components: a semantic network-based component where terms are described and a logic-based one, including assertions about the domain of discourse. For example, a KRYPTON knowledge base may include a description for the term "bachelor", defined as an unmarried male person, along with an assertion involving "bachelor", for example, "John is a bachelor."

KNOWLEDGE REPRESENTATION SYSTEMS

At the very least, it would be expected that a knowledge representation system would provide functions for incrementally constructing and for querying a knowledge base. These might be defined as follows:

$$\text{Tell } [KB, \alpha] = KB'$$

where KB' is the result of adding fact α to KB,

$$\text{Ask } [KB, \alpha] = \text{yes} \mid \text{no} \mid \text{unknown}$$

depending on question α and the contents of KB. Underlying these operations is a notation for representing facts and queries. Proposed notations will be classified into three basic paradigms: logic-based, procedural, and semantic network.

Logic-Based Representations

Adopting the notation of mathematical logic, one might express facts such as

Socrates is human.
If someone is human, then she is mortal.

with formulas such as

$$\text{human (socrates)}$$

$$(\forall X) [\text{human } (X) \Rightarrow \text{mortal } (X)]$$

A knowledge base can then be viewed as a collection of such formulas and addition of a new fact amounts to an extension of the knowledge base to include another formula:

$$\text{Tell } [KB, \alpha] = KB \cup \alpha$$

From this perspective, querying the knowledge base could be defined semantically or syntactically, using the notions of (logical) consequence and provability from mathematical logic. In particular, if α is a closed formula, representing a yes–no question, then a semantic account of the query operation would be

$$\text{Ask } [KB, \alpha] = \begin{array}{ll} \text{yes} & \text{if } KB \models \alpha \\ \text{no} & \text{if } KB \models \neg\alpha \\ \text{unknown} & \text{otherwise} \end{array}$$

In other words, the answer to α is yes (respectively no) if α is true (respectively false) in all interpretations (or worlds) where all formulas in the KB are true. A syntactic account of the query operation, on the other hand, is

$$\text{Ask } [KB, \alpha] = \begin{array}{ll} \text{yes} & \text{if } KB \vdash \alpha \\ \text{no} & \text{if } KB \vdash \neg\alpha \\ \text{unknown} & \text{otherwise} \end{array}$$

In this case, the answer to α is yes if α can be proved from the facts in the knowledge base using the provability relation associated with the underlying logic. A major advantage of many logics adopted for knowledge representation is that they are sound and complete, which means that derivability and provability lead to the same set of consequences, given a knowledge base.

Choosing a logic that is both expressively adequate for knowledge representation and computationally tractable has turned out to be an elusive goal. Propositional logic is generally considered expressively inadequate, whereas first-order logic is generally conceded to be computationally intractable. Attempts to find an acceptable compromise to the expressiveness versus tractability trade-off generally use variations of first-order logic, following one of two approaches. The first approach limits the expressiveness of the language of representation by restricting the form of the formulas that can be admitted in the knowledge base. The second approach redefines the provability relation of first-order logic to make it computationally tractable.

Relational databases (Date, 1975), widely used to represent "simple" facts, such as people's addresses or salaries, constitute a good example of the first approach. A relational database can be viewed as a collection of ground formulas of the form $P(a_1, a_2, \ldots, a_n)$, where P is a predicate symbol and $a_1 a_2, \ldots, a_n$ are constant symbols. Accordingly, the language of representation (determined by *Tell*) disallows logical variables, connectives, and quantifiers. This restriction makes it impossible to explicitly represent negative knowledge and implications. The query language (determined by *Ask*) does, however, maintain the full power of first-order logic. It should be mentioned that relational databases have a number of built-in axioms, including the so-called closed world assumption (Reiter, 1984), which states that ground facts not present in the database may be assumed to be false. Thanks to the closed world assumption, negative information is represented in the database, albeit implicitly. Computationally, it can be easily established that the complexity of *Ask* and *Tell* depends polynomially on the size of the knowledge base.

Logic programming (qv) constitutes a second popular approach to harnessing the expressiveness of first-order logic. Logic programs admit only two types of formulas: *atomic clauses,* having the form of positive literals, ie, formulas $P(t_1, t_2, \ldots, t_n)$ where $t_1, t_2, \ldots, t_n$ are terms involving function symbols, constants, and (universally quantified) variables, and *horn clauses,* having the form $A_1 \wedge A_2 \wedge \ldots \wedge A_m \Rightarrow B$, where $A_1, A_2, \ldots, A_m$ and B are positive literals. Here queries are restricted to conjunctions of positive literals known as goals. Evaluation of a query is equivalent to proving the conjunction with respect to the clauses in the logic program. The restrictions to the assertion and query languages allow the use of specialized theorem provers. For example, PROLOG (Kowalski, 1979) uses a particular form of resolution called SL resolution, which always starts from the goal to be proved and reduces it, using Horn clauses, to a set of atomic clauses.

Logic programming supports a declarative reading of the clauses constituting a logic program, ie, a reading where each clause is treated as a true statement about the intended domain of discourse. However, it also supports a procedural reading, treating a Horn clause such as

$$A_1 \wedge A_2 \wedge \ldots \wedge A_m \Rightarrow B$$

as the statement "to establish B, establish $A_1, A_2, \ldots, A_m$." Indeed, in programming languages such as PROLOG that support the logic programming paradigm explicit facilities promoting this procedural interpretation of clauses are provided. For instance, the cut operator limits the search that will be undertaken by a PROLOG interpreter for a particular goal.

Like logic programming, deductive databases attempt to establish a computationally tractable class of knowledge-representation systems grounded in logic. Deductive databases impose different types of restriction on the form of allowable formulas. For example, definite deductive da-

tabases allow Horn and atomic clauses, analogous to those of logic programs. Hierarchic databases, on the other hand, restrict Horn clauses to be nonrecursive, thereby simplifying goal evaluation. Efficient algorithms have been developed for goal evaluation and consistency checking of definite deductive databases (Hulin and co-workers, 1989). Deductive databases differ from logic programming in that they assume that the number of atomic clauses in a knowledge base will be much greater than that for nonatomic ones. Moreover, deductive databases emphasize the declarative reading of clauses and rely completely on the efficiency of the adopted goal evaluation and consistency checking algorithms.

Turning to approaches that redefine the provability relation in order to render a logical representation computationally tractable, a logic has been offered that uses the full expressive power of first-order logic but interprets $(\exists X) P (X)$ to mean something like "there exists a known X such that $P (X)$" (Frisch and Allen, 1982; Patel-Schneider, 1985). This apparently slight change in the semantics of existential quantification has a remarkable impact on the provability relation. In particular, *modus ponens* no longer applies as inference rule, and from $P (a) \vee P (b)$ it cannot be inferred that $(\exists X) P (X)$.

Procedural Representations

Declarative representations treat the intended meaning of a knowledge base as a foundation that imposes constraints on knowledge base operations. Procedural representations, on the other hand, reverse this dependence by identifying the meaning of a knowledge base with its use.

Consider a knowledge base consisting of logical formulas:

$$(\forall X) \, \text{person} \, (X) \Rightarrow \text{mortal} \, (X)$$
$$(\forall X) \, \text{dog} \, (X) \Rightarrow \text{mortal} \, (X)$$
$$\text{person (socrates)}$$
$$\text{person (helen)}$$

which states that "all persons are mortal," "all dogs are mortal," "Socrates is a person," and "Helen is a person." Given an inference procedure for first-order logic, it is possible to find out whether Socrates is mortal by attempting to prove the formula *mortal (socrates)* from the facts in the knowledge base. If the inference procedure is sound, inferred facts are true in every interpretation where the facts in the knowledge base are true. A great strength of declarative representations is that the same inference procedure can be used for any knowledge base and any knowledge based system, independently of the domain of discourse and the task to be performed by the system.

A procedural representation, in its purest form, treats the knowledge base creator as a programmer who must decide on a set of data structures and programs that represent the intended facts and generate appropriate inferences. The meaning of the knowledge base is now determined by the data structures and programs that implement it. For example, the same knowledge base above might be represented in terms of a collection of procedures, such as the procedure *person:*

procedure person (X)

if $(X = $ 'socrates') **or** $(X = $ 'helen') **then** return (**true**)

else return (**false**)

which returns true or false, depending on whether its argument is a person or not, or the procedure *mortal,* which answers the corresponding question for the predicate mortal:

procedure mortal (X)

if person (X) **then** return (**true**)

else if dog (X) **then** return (**true**)

else return (**false**)

Here it could be asked whether Socrates is a person by executing *person* ('socrates') and whether Socrates is mortal by executing *mortal* ('socrates'). In this case, the facts constituting the knowledge have been hard coded into the procedures that define the inference engine of the knowledge base.

Clearly, the declarative approach has advantages of flexibility and modularity. First, declarative representations, including logic programming, allow queries such as *mortal* (X), where X is a variable. The variable X is interpreted in this query existentially and the inference procedure can return all bindings of X that make the clause true with respect to a knowledge base. This facility is possible in the procedural representation but requires foresight on the part of the knowledge base creator who much define a separate procedure, say *AllMortals* (), that returns a list of all mortals. Note that the list returned by the new procedure may not be consistent with the rest of the procedures that define the knowledge base.

The advantages of declarative representations are also obvious when a fact is inserted or removed. For example, adding the fact that horses are mortal,

$$(\forall X) \text{ horse } (X) \Rightarrow \text{ mortal } (X)$$

to the declarative knowledge base is quite simple. In the procedural case it would be necessary to modify several existing procedures to effect this change.

The main advantage of the procedural representation lies in the control of search that can be exercised by the knowledge base creator, given that the inference engine is defined for each particular knowledge base and each usage of that knowledge base. In the above simple example, the procedure *mortal* (X) first checks whether X is a person and then whether X is a dog. This choice of alternatives may be based on the programmer's knowledge that the argument of this procedure is more often a person than a dog. In a knowledge base using a declarative representation, on the other hand, there is no room for such pragmatic consideration in the conduct of search by the inference procedure. Note, however, that meta-level control (discussed below) is an attempt to exercise precisely this kind of control within a declarative setting.

Some of the drawbacks of procedural representations can be overcome by generalizing procedural mechanisms such as those found in conventional programming languages. One such proposal concerns the generalization of the mechanism for invoking procedures so that neither the procedure's name nor its arguments need be provided explicitly in a procedure call. Thus instead of writing *mortal* ('socrates') to invoke the procedure called *mortal* with the string 'socrates' as its argument, *goal* (*mortal* ('socrates')) could be written to specify "run any procedure whose description states that it might be able to find out if Socrates is mortal." For this invocation mechanism to work, procedures must have an associated pattern that specifies what the procedure can accomplish and that is matched against the argument of a goal statement to determine whether the procedure can help. This kind of procedure invocation is known as pattern-directed invocation and is clearly akin to the procedural interpretation of Horn clauses.

Procedural representations that support pattern-directed invocation generally allow more than one procedure to be called during the evaluation of a goal expression. If a procedure is unable to provide an answer (because it fails during its execution) others are tried, with the knowledge base restored to its original state. This search regime is called backtracking (qv) and is also used by PROLOG interpreters. However, by incorporating pattern-directed invocation and backtracking into a system, some control of search has been given up.

Another approach to overcoming some of the drawbacks of procedural representations is to combine them with declarative ones. For instance, some authors have proposed knowledge representation schemes that contain both a declarative and a procedural component. In knowledge bases using this representation scheme, some inferences are done by using the inference procedure that comes with the declarative representation. However, under certain conditions, inference is performed by externally defined procedures contained within the knowledge base. For example, it might be specified that the successor property of numbers should be computed by the LISP function ADD1 rather than through inference. Likewise, procedural representations have been combined with semantic network ones leading to frame-based and object-oriented representations (see below). The language PLANNER (qv) and production systems are generally viewed as pioneering proposals for procedural representations.

Semantic Networks

As indicated earlier, semantic networks (qv) (Sowa, 1991) were originally motivated by cognitive models of human memory. However, their popularity and success can best be understood when they are viewed as a convenient compromise between the declarative and procedural extremes. Self-styled semantic network proposals for knowledge representation abound in the literature. One striking feature of this collection is the small number of common themes and the great number of variations that can be found among them. One such theme is that knowledge is represented on a labeled, directed graph whose nodes represent concepts and entities in the domain of discourse, while its arcs represent relationships between these entities and concepts. For example, a knowledge base might be viewed as in Figure 1. In Figure 1a, the nodes represent generic concepts such as *Person, Student, Professor,* and *Number,* or particular entities such as *23, Maria,* and *Harry;* the arcs represent binary relationships, such as *supervisor, age, instance-of,* and *is-a.* This depiction can be thought of as a convenient data structure for representing the knowledge base displayed in Figure 1b.

In general, it has been argued (Shapiro, 1971; Schubert, 1976) that semantic networks simply offer a graphical notation for logical formulas restricted to unary and binary predicates and the two types of quantification illustrated in the example (declaring, respectively, that some concept "is-a" other and that some concept is "part-of" another). Others have argued that semantic networks offer a fundamentally different representational paradigm that is object centered in the sense that it is based on object descriptions rather than arbitrary propositions, and focuses on knowledge organization. Advantages claimed for this paradigm include efficient retrieval, because all facts about Maria, for instance, are directly accessible from the node named *Maria,* as well as the obvious perspicuity of graphic representations.

An interpreter for such a semantic network would be expected to support some inferences, for example, the transitivity of is-a and the typing constraints of part-of ("ages must be numbers and supervisors professors"). However, beyond these, opinions differ on how to represent other kinds of facts involving disjunction, negation,

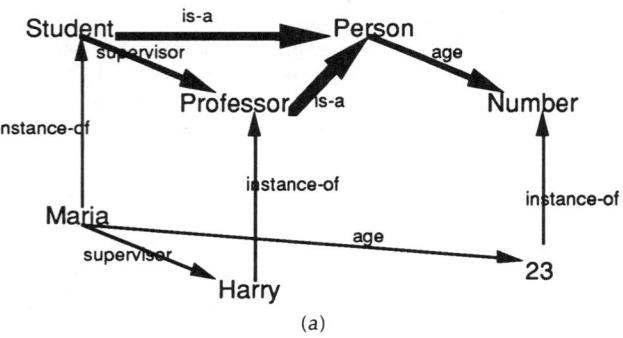

(∀X) student (X) ⇒ person (X)
(∀X) professor (X) ⇒ person (X)
(∀X) person (X) ⇒ (∃Y) [number (Y) ∧ age (X,Y)]
(∀X) student (X) ⇒ (∃Y) [professor (Y) ∧ supervisor (X,Y)]
student (maria)
professor (harry)
number (23)

(b)

Figure 1. A semantic network proposal for knowledge representation. A labeled, directed graph (a) is used to represent a knowledge base (b).

and unconstrained quantification. One approach to this dilemma involves offering a graph-theoretic representation of general logical formulas. This allows the inference procedure to perform retrieval and certain inferences (eg, ones involving *is-a* and *part-of*) efficiently, whereas others are handled using general theorem proving techniques. A second approach allows the attachment of procedures to each node that specify operations on instances of that node and support "local" inferences with respect to the concept being represented by the node. The first approach overcomes some of the drawbacks of logical representations because special-purpose inference procedures can be used for the "built-in" features of semantic network representation. The second approach removes some of the *ad hoc* nature of procedural representation because the representation fixes the data structure and offers a method for defining the procedures that constitute the knowledge base. There are interesting similarities between the second approach and object-oriented programming systems (Keene, 1989).

A major feature of semantic networks since Quillian's proposal was the idea of default inheritance, according to which attributes associated with a node, say *Person,* are only inherited by its *is-a* descendents, such as *Student* and *Professor,* provided they are not redefined explicitly (think of ageless mythical persons or gifted students supervised by committee or by no one at all!). Default inheritance simply acknowledges the fact that descriptions of concepts are not absolute and that they may be contradicted by their specializations or their instances. This aspect of semantic networks is not captured in the simple logical reformulation of semantic networks suggested above. Indeed, default inheritance constitutes an important example of commonsense reasoning that cannot be addressed adequately within the framework of traditional mathematical logic. Minsky's proposal of a frame theory (qv) can be seen as an attempt to extend and refine the semantic network paradigm by adopting a particular stand on what is represented by a node (a frame in Minsky's terminology). A frame is a complex data structure representing a prototypical concept or situation. For example,

Frame	Myrto		
	AKO	**$value**	Person
	name	**$value**	|Myrto Wong|
	address	**$value**	|65 Elm Street|
	interests	**$value**	'AI

defines the frame identified as *Myrto* and declares it to be a *k*ind of (hence AKO) *Person,* with particular name, address, and interests. A frame consists of slots that define its constituent parts. Each slot has a number of facets that specify local information such as the slot's value, as well as inferences and consistency checks that should be performed when the slot value is retrieved or updated. Adopting the principles of default inheritance, all slots are inherited along *AKO* links by default. For example, if the frame *Person* includes the following in its definition,

frame Person

. . .

| state | **$require** | [member (:value, States) **or** |
| | | (member (:value, StateAbbr)] |

. . .

| age | **$type** | Number |
| yearOfBirth | **$value** | !calcYearOfBirth (:age) |

. . .

| salary | **$ifAdded** | [**if** (:value > $100,000) |
| | | **then** add (:frame, VIPList)] |

Myrto inherits a *state* slot with a constraint that its value facet be a member of the list *States,* a *yearOfBirth* slot whose value is computed by the expression *calcYearOf-Birth* (:*age*) where :*age* refers to the *age* slot of *Person,* and a *salary* slot that, when updated, will cause *Myrto* to be added to the list *VIPList* if the person's *salary* value is greater than $100,000.

Frame representations focus on the problem of representing prototypical concepts. Terminological languages, on the other hand, offer facilities for the definition of terms that might be used as vocabulary in expressing facts about a given application. To build a knowledge base about persons, for example, it is possible to start with primitive terms such as *Person, MaritalStatus,* and *Sex* (which are predicates of one, two, and two arguments, respectively) and then proceed to define other terms such as *Unmarried, Man,* and *Bachelor* as follows:

Unmarried ← (VRgeneric Person MaritalStatus single)

Man ← (VRgeneric Person Sex male)

Bachelor ← (Congeneric Man Unmarried)

VRgeneric and *Congeneric* are term-forming operators; *VRgeneric* defines a term from another by restricting a slot value and *Congeneric* defines a term as a conjunction of two terms. Thus *Unmarried* is defined as a person whose marital status is single, *Man* as a person whose sex is male, and *Bachelor* as someone who is both a man and unmarried. Subsumption is another important operation on terms, intended to compare two terms and determine whether one is more specialized than another. For instance, the term *Man* subsumes the term (*Congeneric* (*VRgeneric Person Sex male*) *Unmarried*) in the sense that every instance of the latter is also an instance of the former. Much recent research has focused on the trade-offs between the set of term-forming operators provided by a terminological notation and the tractability of subsumption for that notation (Brachman and Levesque, 1985). KL-ONE (Brachman, 1979) has played a key role in shaping terminological languages and raising a host of research issues related to their design.

Knowledge Organization

Both the semantic network and the frame examples given above adopt primitives for organizing knowledge. In the case of the semantic network example, these primitives are *is-a* and *instance-of* links. In the case of the frame example, they include *AKO* links as well as the slot mech-

anism. This is not an accident. Knowledge organization constitutes a major strength of semantic network and frame-based representations.

Organizing the knowledge included in a knowledge base is important from a cognitive science viewpoint [after all, human memory seems to be highly structured (Anderson, 1990)] as well as for reasons of computational tractability. Human factors considerations also contribute to the importance of knowledge organization. Both developers and users of a large knowledge base will find it easier to understand its contents if it can be visualized as a structured artifact. In this respect, an analogy can be drawn between knowledge bases and programs. Abstraction mechanisms and other means for structuring programs have been accepted for some time as essential tools for addressing the complexities of understanding, using and maintaining large programs.

A review of structuring mechanisms that have been adopted for knowledge organization finds remarkable consensus based on a few themes, but there is also a large number of variations.

Instance-of (or Classification). This structuring mechanism classifies an object into one or more generic classes (makes the object an instance-of these classes), thereby endowing it with properties shared by similar objects. For example, some objects in a knowledge base might be classified under *Person* and can, therefore, have an address and an age, whereas others are classified under *Dog* and, therefore, possess four legs.

Classification has been used in a variety of notations to support syntactic and semantic consistency. For example, sorts in mathematical logic (Cohn, 1989) and types in programming languages are used mostly for syntactic checking. In semantic networks, classification distinguishes between tokens, which represent particular individuals in the domain of discourse, and types or classes, which represent generic concepts. Besides syntactic and semantic consistency, classification can also lead to more efficient search algorithms for a knowledge base. If, for instance, the system is looking for an object whose student number is 98765432 and it is known that only students have student numbers, then only the set of instances of *Student* must be searched.

Some representation schemes (eg, PSN) allow classification to be recursive, ie, classes may (or must) themselves be instances of other classes. In this case the class *Person* might be an instance of the (meta)class *Animate-Class,* which has as instances all classes describing animate objects. In such situations classification may be unconstrained, allowing both a token and a class that it is an instance-of to be instances of some common class, or constrained in the sense that there is a linear order of strata (or levels) and that every object in the knowledge base belongs to a unique stratum and that an object at stratum τ can only be an instance of classes at stratum $\tau + 1$.

Is-a (or Generalization). Generic objects in a knowledge base have been traditionally organized into taxonomies, referred to as is-a, or generalization, hierarchies, which organize all classes in terms of a partial order relation determined by their generality or specificity. For example, *GradStudent* may be declared as a specialization of *Student* ("Every graduate student is a student"), which is in turn a specialization of *Person* ("Every student is a person").

Inheritance is a fundamental ingredient of is-a hierarchies. Inheritance is an inference rule that states that attributes and properties of a class are also attributes and properties of its is-a descendants. Thus the *address* and *age* attributes of *Person,* are inherited by *Student* and, transitively, by *GradStudent*. This inheritance may be strict in the sense that constraints on attributes and properties can be strengthened but cannot be overridden or defaulted, in which case overriding is allowed. For example, if the age of persons has been declared to range from 0 to 100 years, with strict inheritance the age of students can be declared to range from 5 to 80 but not from 5 to 120. Default inheritance, on the other hand, allows students to be 120 years old, although persons were declared to live only up to 100 years, or penguins to not fly although birds were declared to do so.

Another source of variation among generalization mechanisms is their form. In single inheritance, every class has at most one immediate is-a ancestor, hence the graph formed by classes and is-a relationships is a tree. In multiple inheritance, a class is allowed to have multiple immediate is-a ancestors. Single inheritance is computationally and conceptually preferrable but expressively inadequate for sophisticated applications. Multiple inheritance, on the other hand, is expressively more powerful but also computationally expensive and semantically troublesome, particularly when combined with default inheritance.

Part-of (or Aggregation). This mechanism views objects as aggregates of their components or parts. Thus a person can be viewed as a (physical) aggregate of a set of body parts (arms, legs, head and the like) or as a (social) aggregate of a name, address, social security number, etc. Components of an object might themselves be aggregates of yet other simpler components. For example, the address of a person might be declared as the aggregation of a street number, street name, city, etc. Aggregation may be strictly hierarchical or recursive. For instance, *Employee* may be defined as the aggregation of a department, a salary, and an employee, where the latter defines the role of the employee's manager.

A fourth way of organizing objects in a knowledge base is through partitions (Hendrix, 1979) or contexts. A partition is simply a subset of the objects and facts in the knowledge base. One use of a partition is to group together all of the facts about a given situation, eg, the case history of a particular patient. Here partitioning is a useful mechanism for limiting search for relevant facts. A second use of partitions involves the representation of different possible worlds (say, this world versus the world that would have resulted if Napoleon had won the battle of Waterloo) or the representation of facts believed by different agents known to the system. Partitions are usually organized into a hierarchy by a relationship that might be called "obtained from." How a partition B is formed from a partition A is specified by stating what objects and facts have been added to or deleted from A to obtain B. An object that belongs to a partition is said to be visible in that partition. In particular, all objects in A that were not removed in forming B will be visible in B.

Inference. For *Ask* to return a correct answer with respect to a given query and a knowledge base, it must go beyond the facts contained in the knowledge base and draw conclusions from these facts. Inference procedures provide knowledge representation systems with this capability. In general, an inference procedure is a multistep process. Each step of the process involves an inference rule, a set of premises and, if the premises match the rule, a set of conclusions. Returning to an earlier example, if a knowledge base contains

Socrates is human.
If someone is human then he is mortal.

then an inference rule can be applied to these premises to conclude that Socrates is mortal:

Socrates is human.
~~If someone is human then he is mortal.~~
Socrates is mortal.

This inference makes use of *modus ponens,* an inference rule that is sound in the sense that in any situation where its premises are true, its conclusions will also be true. Inference based on sound inference rules is known as deductive inference. Frequently, however, conclusions must be drawn on the basis of their plausibility because information in the knowledge base is incomplete. For example, concluding that all ravens are black from the fact that all ravens observed so far are black involves inductive inference, an important form of learning. Likewise, hypothesizing that a patient has a cold after observing that he or she has a running nose involves a form of abductive inference, which uses as premise a fact such as "If someone has a cold then he has a running nose" and an inference rule that drives the implication backward, unlike the deductive inference rule (*modus ponens*) illustrated above. Analogical inference is a form of reasoning where similarities between situations is used as a basis for drawing conclusions. For example, on the basis of the fact that Charles De Gaul was president of France and was more than six feet tall, and the fact that Francois Mitterand is also president of France, it might be concluded, (erroneously) that Francois Mitterand is more than six feet tall. Probabilistic inference involves reasoning on the basis of probabilistic information, in quantitative or qualitative terms. Default inference involves drawing conclusions in the absence of information. These and other forms of inference have been found useful in endowing a knowledge representation system with a reasoning capability and have been formally studied.

Inference procedures are needed independently of the knowledge representation paradigm adopted for a particular knowledge representation scheme. However, these procedures are quite different, depending on the underlying paradigm. Inference procedures for logic-based paradigms are founded on few inference rules (often some variation of the resolution principle) that are independent of the knowledge base and the task being performed by the system using the knowledge base. Procedural representations offer tools for defining both the inference rules and the search strategy used by an inference procedure. This means that both can be tailored to a particular knowledge base and a particular task, say diagnosis or design, if the designer of the knowledge base so desires. For semantic network representations, on the other hand, a limited inference procedure is required for the axioms that underlie is-a or part-of links. Beyond this, however, *Ask* behaves like a retrieval procedure defined for a graph data structure.

The canonical example of an (deductive) inference procedure is a theorem prover for predicate logic (Stickel, 1982). A second, very different, example is an inference mechanism that might be called spreading activation introduced by Quillian. The idea here is that certain problems, such as interpreting the phrase *dog food,* can be solved by searching for paths connecting particular nodes in a semantic network, say

$$dog \rightarrow (eats) \rightarrow food$$

In general there are several paths, for example

$$dog \rightarrow (made\text{-}of) \rightarrow meat \rightarrow (a\text{-}kind\text{-}of) \rightarrow food$$

In these examples parentheses are used to indicate edge labels. Moreover, these paths can be discovered by an algorithm that starts from the nodes that define the path endpoints and proceeds by iteratively propagating markers to neighbouring nodes. Such marker passing mechanisms have been adopted in Fahlman's (1979) NETL system. A third example of an inference procedure involves the subsumption operation supported by terminological languages. At the heart of any inference procedure is found some form of matching, used to select facts that will be used as premises in an inference step, and a control structure, which determines the sequence of inference steps that will be used to evaluate a query.

Matching. Matching involves the comparison of a pattern with an object in the knowledge base. The match succeeds if the object is unstructured and the pattern primitively matches the object or if the object is structured and each part of the pattern successfully matches one or more parts of the object. For example, if objects are either letters or lists of letters, the pattern $(A\ B\ C)$ would match the object $(A\ B\ C)$.

Pattern matching would be uninteresting if a pattern only matched itself. What makes it powerful are the various ways of specifying a range of objects that can match the pattern. In the above example a pattern element that matches any letter might be allowed. For example, $(A\ ?\ C)$ could be a pattern that matches any list of three letters of which the first is in A and the last a C. Another common mechanism is a notation that matches more than one element. The pattern $(A\ *\ C)$, for example, might match a list

starting with an A, ending with a C, and having any number of intermediate elements. A large variety of mechanisms are possible, and the choice depends on the representation language. There is also a trade-off between the complexity of the pattern and the computational efficiency of the pattern matcher.

A third important ingredient of pattern matching is the ability to associate variables with pattern elements. When a match succeeds, the values of these variables are the parts of the object that matched the corresponding pattern elements. For example, the pattern $(A\ *x\ C)$ might match any list beginning with A, ending with C, and having any number of elements in between, and that when the match succeeds, the value of x will be the list of elements in between. Thus after matching $(A\ W\ X\ Y\ C)$, the value of x would be $(W\ X\ Y)$.

When both the pattern and the object may contain variables corresponding to pattern elements that can match any object element, the resulting operation is a form of unification. In effect, there is no distinction between pattern and object. This was introduced as part of the resolution methods for proving theorems in logic (Robinson, 1979) (see THEOREM PROVING). In this case, both the pattern and object can be viewed as general expressions including variables. The result of unification is the most general substitution of variables that makes the pattern and object identical. Unification has in the past been used in matching linear expressions: recent work has extended unification to frame-based structures (Ait-Kaci, 1983).

The above discussion focused on a kind of matching where the parts of a structured pattern are put into correspondence with the parts of an object having the same structure. This is known as syntactic matching. Semantic matching, on the other hand, involves finding a correspondence between the pattern and object based on some description of the function or role of the parts in an object. For example, a pattern might specify that a successful match would be a set of two people, one of whom is the husband in a marriage and the other the wife in the same marriage; this might be written as x: (*a husband*), y: (*the wife of x*).

Various knowledge representation notations make different uses of matching. First, in pattern-directed procedure invocation, such as that found in PLANNER (qv), the pattern associated with a procedure is matched with the current object of interest to see whether that procedure is relevant. Matching is similarly used in production systems to determine whether a rule is eligible for firing. Second, unification plays a fundamental role in resolution-based inference procedures. A third use of matching involves determining the type of an unknown input by treating the input as object and the types under which it could be classified as patterns. The KL-ONE (qv) classifier is an example of this kind of matching.

Control Structures. When a procedural representation makes use of pattern-directed invocation, it is often the case that more than one procedure matches the pattern. One aspect of the control structure determines how such conflicts are resolved. A second aspect of the control structure involves the direction of inference, ie, the mechanism that chooses the patterns used to select procedures. In the past, the mechanism for conflict resolution has usually been wired into the inference engine. Examples of strategies that have been used include choosing the procedure appearing first in the knowledge base or choosing the procedure with the most complicated pattern. More recently, there has been research into the use of an inference engine using control knowledge to resolve conflicts (Davis, 1980; Genesereth, 1983; Kramer, 1986). This has the advantage that new knowledge about resolving conflicts can be added without the need to recode the inference engine.

An inference engine may use two possible directions to generate inferences. Forward-chaining inference arises when procedures are invoked if their patterns match facts about to be added to or removed from the knowledge base. Generally, such procedures will add and remove facts of their own thus triggering yet other forwardly chained inferences. In contrast, backward-chaining inference works by matching rule patterns to goals. Trying to match a given pattern against the knowledge base may trigger procedures that set other pattern-matching goals in an attempt to achieve the original goal (see PROCESSING, BOTTOM-UP AND TOP-DOWN).

EXAMPLES OF KNOWLEDGE REPRESENTATION SYSTEMS

Planner. PLANNER (qv) is a procedural language extending LISP with a number of mechanisms, including pattern-directed invocation of procedures, an associative database and a backtracking control regime. A system written in PLANNER consists of a database of assertions; these are simply LISP data structures. For example, the fact that Socrates is a man might be represented with the assertion (*MAN SOCRATES*). In addition to the database of assertions a set of procedures can be defined, called theorems, or demons. A theorem is executed when its pattern matches the argument of a database operation. There are two basic kinds of theorems. Antecedent theorems are invoked when their patterns match structures that are being added to the database and correspond to a forward-chaining control structure. Consequent theorems, on the other hand, are invoked in response to a goal statement and, therefore, correspond to backward chaining. A goal statement is used to retrieve information from the database; when the pattern of a goal matches the pattern of a consequent theorem, the theorem is used to derive implicit knowledge matching the goal pattern. The body of the theorem can assert or remove facts or try to prove other goals. For example, a consequent theorem for solving the goal (*MORTAL ?x*) might try to prove the goal (*MAN ?x*). This theorem will fail if it cannot establish this goal. Because more than one theorem might match a goal pattern, if one fails, the system automatically tries another. Note that when this backtracking occurs, it is necessary to undo the effect of all changes to the database resulting from the body of a theorem to the point of its failure. There are obvious analogies between PLANNER theorems and PROLOG Horn clauses, pattern-directed procedure invocation and clause invocation, and even the backtracking control structure used by both PLANNER

and PROLOG. At the same time there are important differences between the two representation schemes. PROLOG offers both a procedural and a declarative semantics and its matching operation, unification, is cleaner and more general than that of PLANNER. PROLOG originated from logic whereas PLANNER was an outgrowth of LISP.

Production Systems. Production systems constitute another class of procedural schemes using pattern-directed invocation. Most commercial expert system shells are based on some form of production system. The basic features of such systems include a global database containing data structures relevant to a computation and a set of production rules that operate on the database. A production rule consists of a procedure called the body of the rule and an associated pattern. Inference is a cycle where the pattern of each rule is matched against the database, a choice is made from the rules whose patterns matched, and the body of the chosen rule(s) is executed. Executing the body of a rule will generally result in changes to the database caused by the addition or deletion of structures. Because rules cannot invoke other rules directly, all communication between rules is done through the database.

There are many sources of variety in production systems. First, the size and complexity of the global database can vary. The early production system proposed by Newell (1973) restricted the contents of the database to a small number of lists. In this work the database was viewed as a model of human short-term memory, and all knowledge stored in long-term memory was to be represented as rules. HEARSAY-II (qv) (Erman and co-workers, 1980), on the other hand, uses a global database called a blackboard, which stores a large number of frames partitioned into layers. Second, production systems can vary in the complexity of the pattern allowed: sometimes the pattern may contain calls to arbitrary functions that decide whether, and how, the pattern matches. Third, the set of actions in the body of rules can vary. Actions can include adding and removing elements from the database, adding and removing rules, and interacting with the user. Fourth, production systems vary in the control structures that are available. When a rule body must always remove the database elements that triggered its evaluation and otherwise may only add elements to the database, the production system can be run using backward-chaining. This control regime has been used by many expert systems.

The final source of variation among production systems is the conflict-resolution mechanism that is used to deal with situations in which more than one rule matches the database. MYCIN (qv) (Shortliffe, 1976), eg, simply executes all of the matching rules. A strict Markovian system, on the other hand, would simply choose the first rule according to some ordering of the rules. Systems such as OPS-5 (qv) (McDermott and Forgy, 1978) have an extensive set of heuristics that use such factors as the complexity of the patterns and the relative ages of competing rules to choose in the case of conflicts. The systems described in Waterman and Hayes-Roth (1978) include a number of additional conflict-resolution schemes. Production systems share features with both PLANNER and PROLOG. Unlike PLANNER and PROLOG, however, production systems offer a lean representational and control structure framework which can be tailored to particular applications.

SNePS. This is a semantic network-based system that represents a subset of logic in terms of a network structure (Shapiro, 1979). A SNePS network consists of nodes of several kinds: nodes corresponding to constant symbols in logic, nodes corresponding to variables, and rule nodes that correspond to propositions. Links are either representations of binary relations or are auxiliary links that are used to represent the properties of nonconstant nodes. The logical foundations of the representation have been exploited in defining a semantics and an inference mechanism.

KRL. KRL (qv) is perhaps the most ambitious frame-based system among early efforts (Bobrow and Winograd, 1977). The basic representational structure is called a unit. A unit consists of several descriptions, each giving a different perspective on the entity. As prescribed by Minsky, a primary form of description is via further specification of a prototype where the prototype is a typical member of a category. Other kinds of description include description of the role played by an object, a logical formula that is true of the entity, membership in a set, and relationships to other objects. Inference in KRL is called matching and is set up as a match between a pattern and an object. However, through information attached to slots, the matcher can do complex inferencing, such as following chains of implications. For example, a slot might specify a subtask that should be done in place of a direct match. The matcher makes use of an agenda (see AGENDA-BASED SYSTEMS) that can be controlled by the application to schedule these subtasks.

KL-ONE. KL-ONE (qv) is by far the most influential semantic network proposal, having spawned a number of terminological and hybrid systems (Brachman, 1979). KL-ONE frames are called concepts and the slots are called roles. Roles can have the usual attached procedures, defaults, constraints, etc. One interesting contribution is the concept of structural descriptions as a mechanism for constraining the value of more than one role in a concept. For example, one could specify that the enrollment date of a student in school precedes the graduation date with a structural description that is linked to the roles for enrollment date and graduation date and to the concept describing the precedence relationship.

KL-ONE concepts are purely descriptive. Therefore, although there is a subconcept link, there is no instance-of link. However, to distinguish concepts describing individuals rather than classes, there is an individuation link that connects individual concepts to their subsuming class concepts. For example, the individual concept (*a student whose name is John*) would be linked by an individuation link to the generic concept *Student*, which might be defined as (*persons who go to school*). Also, in order to be able to assert the existence of objects, an assertional component consisting of nexi was introduced. A nexus would be linked to all descriptions that are true of that object in the world. Nexi could be placed into various contexts, allowing several different models of the world to be explored. Finally, concepts that supply necessary and sufficient conditions on the entities described can be placed automatically into the specialization hierarchy. This was done by the KL-ONE classifier, the primary inference mechanism of the system.

KRYPTON. Krypton (Brachman and co-workers, 1983), a direct successor of KL-ONE, was one of the earliest hybrid knowledge representation systems. KRYPTON offers a clear distinction between the descriptive terminological component, called the TBox, and the assertional component, called the ABox. KL-ONE's nexi are replaced in KRYPTON by sentences in first order logic which use unary and predicates corresponding to concepts and roles defined in the TBox. The prototype implementation used a modified version of Stickel's (1982) nonclausal resolution theorem prover to implement the ABox. The KL-ONE classifier became the TBox term subsumption operation, which tests whether one concept subsumes another. Analysis of this operation has since resulted in a great deal of research on tractability vs expressiveness in the context of subsumption (see below). In addition, the KRYPTON work motivated the development of a host of hybrid knowledge representation schemes.

BACK. BACK is another hybrid representation based on KL-ONE (Nebel, 1977; Nebel and von Luck, 1988; Petalson and co-workers, 1989). As in KRYPTON, the designers of BACK emphasize the tractability of the terminological language. But in contrast to KRYPTON, BACK offers an ABox reasoner that is designed to answer queries in polynomial time. Assertions in the ABox are nondisjunctive, variable-free, and negation is not allowed. The assertional language of BACK is in fact two languages, a *Tell* language for asserting facts and an *Ask* language for querying the knowledge base. The *Tell* language allows the user to define objects using descriptions and to assert relations between them. The *Ask* language, on the other hand, is designed to correspond to the relational database query language SQL: the answers to queries are sets of tuples and set operations corresponding to the relational operators of SQL are provided. In addition, there is a formal semantics for BACK, although TBox and ABox operations are implemented with algorithms that are incomplete with respect to this semantics.

OMEGA. The OMEGA system also combines a language for forming descriptions with a logical language (Hewitt and co-workers, 1980; Attardi and Simi, 1981). This combination is done in a uniform framework that combines a calculus of descriptions with operations for forming logical statements. For example, the descriptions *charles* and ((*a man*) (*with son = harry*)) and the operator *is* can be related to make the assertion *charles is* ((*a man*) (*with son = harry*)). An interesting innovation was that logical variables could appear inside descriptions. Inference is based on a form of subsumption that takes into account the logical statements (also called rules). There is a complete semantics for OMEGA and a complete provability relation that is known to be undecidable, so incomplete but sound inference procedures are used in the implementation. OMEGA was also interesting in that it was reflexive: it allowed statements containing descriptions of OMEGA objects to be made within the language, and a complete axiomitization of the language written in the language itself has been presented. The reflexivity also is used to specify the behavior of the inference engine in a domain-specific fashion.

CycL. A different approach to hybrid knowledge-representation is illustrated by CycL (Lenat and co-workers, 1990). CycL contains an epistemological component that uses a logic-based representation language offering the ability to refer to propositions as objects and a predicate called *ab* for representing defaults. CycL also has a heuristic level where special-purpose representations are used to support the epistemological component and where special-purpose reasoners are defined using these representations. For example, special-purpose reasoners are defined to handle transitive relations. Moreover, CycL provides a facility for automatically translating expressions (in both directions) between these two levels.

RESEARCH ISSUES

Nonmonotonicity and Defaults

When a knowledge base is incomplete, it is often necessary to make assumptions or jump to conclusions to arrive at an answer. For example, there might be an instance of the class *Bird* but what kind of bird it is might not be known. Under such circumstances, it is often reasonable to assume that because the system has not been told otherwise, this bird flies. Such assumptions have traditionally be represented in semantic networks through attributes and properties that are inherited by default and in frame-based representations through default values for slots (Fahlman, 1979). Inferences based on defaults raise some difficult problems. First, suppose that the knowledge base has been used to make inferences about some bird. If it is later discovered that this bird is in fact a penguin, any inferences arising from the assumption that it flies become invalid. This differs from knowledge bases using conventional logics where new knowledge never causes the retraction of inferences based on previously available knowledge. Schemes that have the latter property are called monotonic, whereas schemes that support any form of default reasoning are nonmonotonic (see REASONING, DEFAULT; REASONING, NONMONOTONIC). A second problem that arises is that different defaults may lead to contradictory inferences. If Nixon, for instance, has been declared to be both a Republican and a Quaker, and there are defaults that state that "unless otherwise told, a Quaker is a pacifist" but also "unless otherwise told a Republican is not a pacifist" there is clearly a problem in having the system determine Nixon's attitude toward pacifism. The closed-world assumption and frame axioms are other examples of

default rules. These have been extensively used both within and outside AI, often as unstated assumptions.

There have been numerous formal proposals that attempt to deal rigorously with nonmonotonic reasoning. A pioneering proposal is Reiter's (1978) default logic, which allows inference rules of the form "if α is true and it is consistent to assume β then conclude γ." Using such rules, the default nature of the flying property of birds can be expressed with "If X is a bird and it is consistent to assume that X flies, conclude that X flies." Another pioneering approach to defaults, and perhaps the one most studied, is McCarthy's circumscription (qv) (McCarthy, 1980), which provides a mechanism for specifying schemata that state "all that is true about property P is all that is known about P." Circumscription can be used, for example, over the property of nonflying birds leading to a schema of the form "the only nonflying birds are those objects that are known to be nonflying birds." More recently, attempts have been made to formulate default reasoning in probabilistic terms (Pearl, 1989). Here "Birds fly" is interpreted as "If X is a bird, there is high probability that it flies." Such probabilistic accounts attempt to justify default inferences in terms of the (probabilistic) nature of the domain of discourse, rather than as conversational conventions.

Inconsistency

A knowledge base is inconsistent if it is possible to derive contradictory conclusions from it. As discussed above, if making default inferences, the resulting knowledge base will become inconsistent if a default is later found to be wrong. Inconsistency may also result when new knowledge simply contradicts facts already in the knowledge base. In conventional logics, inconsistency has catastrophic consequences because of so-called paradoxes of implication, which state that "anything implies a true proposition" [formally, $A \Rightarrow (B \Rightarrow A)$] and "a contradiction implies anything" (formally $A \wedge \neg A \Rightarrow B$). One approach to dealing with inconsistency is to support truth maintenance (qv) mechanisms (Doyle and London, 1980). Such mechanisms maintain a network of links representing logical relations among facts. These can be used when inconsistencies are discovered, to identify the source of these inconsistencies and to determine what facts in the knowledge base need to be revised. A second approach to inconsistency involves using logics that explicitly exclude the above paradoxes of implication. Relevance logics (Anderson and Belnap, 1975) achieve this by narrowing the notion of proof: A entails B in relevance logics if there is a proof of B that actually uses A during one of its steps. Relevance logics have turned out to be interesting both from a computational point of view (Patel-Schneider, 1985) and as a useful vehicle for formal models of knowledge and belief (Levesque, 1984).

Incompleteness

Except for toy situations, knowledge bases have incomplete information about their universe of discourse. This incompleteness may arise due to insufficient information about that universe (consider a knowledge base that has not yet been told anything, for instance). It may also come about because of a weak provability relation. For instance, a logic-based knowledge representation system with no inference rules will not be able to infer $\alpha \vee \beta$ from a knowledge base containing both α and β. Alternatively, incompleteness may arise because the inference procedure (implementation of the provability relation) is incomplete, for computational economy, say, or even because the logic is powerful enough so that Godel's incompleteness theorem holds.

From an expressiveness point of view, incompleteness poses serious problems. The facts below, for instance, contain incomplete information.

1. "George or Mary graduated from the University of Toronto."
2. "There are 40,000 registered students at the university."
3. "The morning star is the same as the evening star."

For example, sentence 1 does not specifically relate the state of affairs, sentence 2 declares that all members of a class have a property without specifying who the members are, and sentence 3 declares that two nonidentical expressions refer to the same individual. Moreover, there may be a need to express facts about the completeness or incompleteness of the knowledge base itself, such as the closed-world assumption, used by databases (see above), or

4. "There is an unknown student."

Logic-based schemes that subsume first-order logic can handle sentences 1–3 in a satisfactory way using logical connectives and quantifiers. Expressing these facts in procedural and semantic network schemes is more problematic. Sentence 4, however, is a problem even in first-order logic and has been studied at length in the literature. For example, Levesque (1984) introduces a new operator K that when placed in front of a fact is read as "it is known that . . ." It is then possible to state that there is an unknown student with

$$(\exists X)[\text{student }(X) \wedge \neg K\text{student }(X)]$$

that is, there is a student who is not known to be so. On the other hand, there have been attempts to deal with incompleteness within the framework of first-order logic (Moore, 1980) by introducing a predicate *Know*, which takes as arguments an agent (the "knower") and an encoded formula (the known fact). In both proposals possible world semantics serve as a basis for a semantic theory.

Expressiveness vs Tractability

Expressiveness vs. tractability trade-offs are a fact of life in computer science and have been known at least since the development of formal language and automata theory (Hopcroft and Ullman, 1969). In the context of knowledge representation, Brachman and Levesque (1985) are credited with the introduction of this issue as well as first results focusing on the terminological language FL, a

cleaned-up subset of KL-ONE. FL includes, among others, a term-forming operator *RESTR* that allows type constraints on attributes, as in

(AND person (ALL (RESTR friend male)))

which designates the class "persons all of whose friends are male." Brachman and Levesque show that subsumption in a language without *RESTR* can be determined by an algorithm of complexity $O(n^2)$, where n is the size of the operands, while the same operation in FL is as hard as satisfiability for propositional calculus and, therefore, intractable. This surprising result has led to a broad study of trade-off issues for terminological languages, with more noteworthy results. For example Schmidt-Schauss (1989) proves that subsumption in KL-ONE is, in fact, undecidable, while (Patel-Schneider, 1986) establishes that subsumption can be made tractable even for expressively rich terminological languages if the semantics of the language is weakened.

More recently, complexity results have been reported for many knowledge representation problems. (Borgida and Etherington, 1989) proves, for example, that fast approximate algorithms exist for query evaluations in knowledge bases that include ground clauses, generalization hierarchies, and disjunctive formulas, whereas exact query evaluation algorithms are expensive due to the presence of disjunctive information. Kautz and Selman (1989) studied the complexity of problems such as finding a maximal consistent set of conclusions given a propositional default theory and showed that this problem is tractable only in special cases. Their results suggest that it is easier to fill-out (vivify) an incomplete knowledge base using default rules than to use these rules as extension to normal resolution-type theorem proving. Villain and Kautz (1986) and Villain, Kautz, and van Beek (1989) summarize complexity results on inference with respect to a temporal logic based on intervals, originally proposed by Allen (1981). The decision problem with respect to the original temporal logic is shown to be intractable, but several examples of weaker logics are proven to have tractable decision problems.

Ontologies

The nature of the domain of discourse plays an important role in determining the features of a knowledge representation scheme. For example, if the domain involves time, the knowledge representation scheme may offer appropriate constructs, such as time points or intervals along with temporal relations, for representing temporal facts such as "Mary married before graduating from university." In addition, a specialized inference engine may be used for reasoning with respect to temporal knowledge, using results such as those reported by Allen (1981).

Work on ontologies involves formalizing the properties of a particular class of objects that are supposed to populate the universe of discourse, be they time points or spatial segments, agents performing actions and having goals or knowledge items. Here is a quick overview of some ontologies studied in the literature.

Entities and Relationships. Most representation schemes assume that the world is populated by entities that are endowed with a unique and immutable identity, a lifetime, and relationships to other entities. Basic as this ontology may seem, it is by no means universal. For instance, Hayes (1985) offers an ontology for material substances where entities (say, a liter of water and a pound of sugar) can be merged resulting in a different entity.

Causality and Time. As indicated earlier, time can be modeled in terms of points or intervals, ordered linearly or partially (Allen, 1984). Causality imposes existence constraints on events. If event A causes event B and A has been observed, B can be expected as well, possibly with some time delay. Formal models of causality have been published (McCarthy, 1968; Rieger, 1976).

Space. Space is thought of in terms of two- or three-dimensional points or larger units, including spheres, cubes, pyramids, etc (eg, Davis, 1986).

Agents and Actions. The domain of discourse includes here agents having beliefs and goals and being capable of carrying out actions (Allen, 1981). Maida and Shapiro (1982), among others, address the problem of representing propositional attitudes, such as beliefs, desires, and intentions for agents.

Existence. A distinction is made here between different modes of existence, including physical existence, such as that of the editor of this volume; abstract existence, such as that of the number 7; nonexistence, characteristic of Santa Claus or a canceled trip to Japan; and impossible existence, such as that of the square root of -1 or the proverbial square circle (Hirst, 1989). General ontologies have been studied in philosophy (Carnap, 1967; Bunge, 1977) and may prove useful starting points for future work on ontologies.

Knowledge Base Management

The practice of building and using large knowledge bases imposes a number of requirements on knowledge representation systems. In particular, experience in developing, deploying, and maintaining knowledge bases suggests a number of management facilities that may be supported to a greater or lesser extent by a knowledge representation system. Explanation facilities, available since the very first expert systems (Shortliffe, 1976), allow the system to explain its line of reasoning through *why* and *how* questions, thereby helping the user accept it or determine where it is faulty. Knowledge acquisition has been recognized as a bottleneck in building knowledge bases. State-of-the-art acquisition facilities support a number of mechanisms for acquiring knowledge, including learning of rules from raw data (Boose, 1989) and extraction of knowledge from linguistic expressions. Truth maintenance facilities allow the system to maintain information on logical interdependencies among facts (such as fact α was derived from facts β and γ), which can

then be used to restore a knowledge base (that contains nonmonotonic inferences) to consistency after updates (Doyle, 1979). Validation facilities help the user validate the contents of the knowledge base in a systematic fashion (Ginsberg, 1988). Documentation facilities document the contents of the knowledge base, using natural language and recent technologies such as hypertext (Jansen and Compton, 1988). Maintenance facilities include ones for knowledge base evolution, forgetting, summarizing, and related functions humans find useful in managing a body of knowledge.

In addition, effective management of large knowledge bases presupposes some of the functionality of data-base management systems, including the following. *Persistence* is the ability of a knowledge base to persist beyond the execution of the processes that create and access it. Persistence mechanisms for databases are supposed to be both local (ie, can be associated with a particular datum independently of its type) and implicit (in the sense that the user does not need to specify explicitly that data are to persist). *Secondary storage management* is another standard management feature for databases. Database management systems offer a variety of techniques, such as index management, data clustering, data buffering, access path selection, and query optimization to support the efficient use of secondary storage. *Concurrency and recovery* are taken for granted for database management systems and allow multiple users to efficiently share a database. Mylopoulos and Brodie (1986) and Schmidt and Thanos (1989) present collections of ideas about knowledge base management and the research issues it raises.

CONCLUSIONS

Controversies about what knowledge representation is or does notwithstanding, many schemes have been proposed as general frameworks for knowledge representation and reasoning. These have, in turn, led to hundreds of commercial products and thousands of industrially deployed knowledge bases, mostly as components of expert systems. Despite these successes, many research issues remain unresolved, including ontological and semantic ones for knowledge representation schemes as well as implementation-oriented ones for knowledge representation systems. Apart from expert system applications, knowledge representation is increasingly influential in other areas of computer science, such as databases (Mylopoulos and Brodie, 1988) and software engineering (Rich and Waters, 1986), where "capturing knowledge about the world" is becoming an integral part of the process of building software systems.

BIBLIOGRAPHY

H. Ait-Kaci, *A New Model of Computation Based on a Calculus of Type Subsumption,* MS-CIS-83-40, Department of Computer and Information Science, The Moore School of Electrical Engineering, University of Pennsylvania, Philadelphia, 1983.

J. F. Allen, *A General Model of Action and Time,* Technical Report, Department of Computer Science, University of Rochester, N.Y., 1981.

J. F. Allen, "Towards a General Theory of Action and Time," *Artif. Intell.* **23**, 123–154 (1984).

J. Anderson, *Cognitive Psychology and its Implications*, W. H. Freeman, New York, 1990.

A. R. Anderson and N. D. Belnap, *Entailment: The Logic of Relevance and Necessity*, Vol. I, Princeton University Press, Princeton, N.J., 1975.

G. Attardi and M. Simi, *Semantics of Inheritance and Attributions in the Description System Omega*. Technical Report **S-81-16**, Universita di Pisa, Pisa, Italy, 1981.

D. G. Bobrow and T. Winograd, "An Overview of KRL, a Knowledge Representation Language," *Cogn. Sci.* **1**, 3–46 (1977).

J. Boose and B. Gaines, eds., *Knowledge Acquisition Tools for Expert Systems*, Academic Press, Inc., Orlando, Fla., 1989.

A. Borgida and D. W. Etherington, "Hierarchical Knowledge Bases and Efficient Disjunctive Reasoning," in *Proceedings of the First International Conference on Principles of Knowledge Representation and Reasoning*, Toronto, 1989, pp. 33–43.

R. J. Brachman, "On the Epistemological Status of Semantic Networks," in Findler, 1979.

R. J. Brachman, R. E. Fikes, and H. J. Levesque, "Krypton: A Functional Approach to Knowledge Representation," *IEEE Comp.* **16**(10), 67–74 (Oct. 1983).

R. J. Brachman and H. J. Levesque, "A Fundamental Tradeoff in Knowledge Representation and Reasoning" in R. J. Brachman and H. J. Levesque, eds., *Readings in Knowledge Representation*, Morgan-Kaufmann, San Mateo, Calif., 1985, pp. 41–70.

M. Bunge, *Treatise on Basic Philosophy: Ontology I—The Furniture of the World*, Reidel, 1977.

R. Carnap, *The Logical Structure of the World: Pseudoproblems in Philosophy*, University of California Press, 1967.

N. Cercone and G. McCalla, eds., *The Knowledge Frontier*, Springer-Verlag, New York, 1987.

A. G. Cohn, "On the Appearance of Sortal Literals: a Non Substitutional Framework for Hybrid Reasoning," in Borgida and Etherington, pp. 55–66.

C. Date, *An Introduction to Database Systems*, Vols I–II, Addison-Wesley Publishing Co., Inc., Reading, Mass., 1975.

E. Davis, *Representing and Acquiring Geographic Knowledge*, Pitman, New York, 1986.

R. Davis, "Meta-rules: Reasoning about Control," *Artif. Intell* **15**(3), 179–222 (1980).

J. Doyle, "A Glimpse of Truth Maintenance," in P. Winston and R. Brown, eds., *Artificial Intelligence: An MIT Perspective*, MIT Press, Cambridge, Mass., 1979, pp. 119–136.

J. Doyle and P. London, "A Selected Descriptor-Indexed Bibliography to the Literature of Belief Revision," *SIGART Newslett.* **71**, 7–23 (Apr. 1980).

L. D. Erman, F. Hayes-Roth, V. R. Lesser, and D. R. Reddy, "The HEARSAY-II Speech-Understanding System: Integrating Knowledge to Resolve Uncertainty," *ACM Comput. Surv.* **12**(2), 213–253 (June 1980).

S. E. Fahlman, *NETL: A System For Representing and Using Real World Knowledge*, MIT Press, Cambridge, Mass., 1979.

N. V. Findler, ed., *Associative Networks: Representation and Use of Knowledge by Computers*, Academic Press, Inc., New York, 1979.

A. M. Frisch and J. F. Allen, "Knowledge Retrieval as Limited Inference," in *Proceedings, Sixth Annual international Conference on Automated Deduction*, D. W. Loveland, ed., Springer-Verlag, New York, 1982.

B. V. Funt, "Problem-Solving with Diagrammatic Representations" *Artif. Intell.* **13**(3), 201–230 (1980).

M. R. Genesereth, "An Overview of Metalevel Architecture," in *Proceedings of the Third National Conference on Artificial Intelligence*, Washington, D.C., AAAI, Menlo Park, Calif., 1983.

A. Ginsberg, "Knowledge Base Reduction: A New Approach to Checking Knowledge Bases for Inconsistency and Redundancy," in *Proceedings of the Seventh National Conference on Artificial Intelligence*, St. Paul, Minn., AAAI, Menlo Park, Calif., 1988, pp. 585–589.

I. P. Goldstein and R. B. Roberts, "Nudge: a Knowledge-Based Scheduling Program," in *Proceedings of the Fifth IJCAI*, Cambridge, Mass., Morgan-Kaufmann, San Mateo, Calif., 1977, pp. 257–263.

P. J. Hayes, "In Defense of Logic," in Goldstein and Roberts, 1977, pp. 559–65.

P. J. Hayes, "The Second Naive Physics Manifesto," in J. R. Hobbs and R. C. Moore, eds., *Formal Theories of the Commonsense World*, Ablex Publishing Corp., Norwood, N.J., 1985, pp. 1–36.

F. Hayes-Roth, D. A. Waterman, and D. B. Lenat, eds., *Building Expert Systems*, Addison-Wesley Publishing Co., Inc., Reading, Mass., 1983.

G. G. Hendrix, "Encoding Knowledge in Partitioned Networks," in N. V. Findler, ed., *Associative Networks: Representation and Use of Knowledge by Computers*, Academic Press, Inc., New York, 1979, pp. 51–92.

C. Hewitt, "PLANNER: A Language for Proving Theorems in Robots," in *Proceedings of the Second IJCAI*, London, Morgan-Kaufmann, San Mateo, Calif., 1971.

C. Hewitt, G. Attardi, and M. Simi, "Knowledge Embedding in the Description System Omega," in *Proceedings of the First National Conference on Artificial Intelligence*, Stanford, Calif., 1980, pp. 157–164.

G. Hirst, "Ontological Assumptions in Knowledge Representation," in Borgida and Etherington, 1989, pp. 157–169.

J. E. Hopcroft and J. D. Ullman, *Formal Languages and their Relation to Automata*, Addison-Wesley Publishing Co., Inc., Reading, Mass., 1969.

G. Hulin, A. Pirotte, D. Roelants, and M. Vauclair, "Logic and Databases," in A. Thayse, ed., *From Modal Logic to Deductive Databases—Introducing a Logic-Based Approach to Artificial Intelligence*, John Wiley & Sons, Inc., 1989.

R. Jansen and P. Compton, "The Knowledge Dictionary: An Application of Software Engineering Techniques to the Design and Maintenance of Expert Systems," in *Proceedings of the Seventh National Conference on Artificial Intelligence*, St. Paul, Minn., AAAI, Menlo Park, Calif., 1988.

H. A. Kautz and B. Selman, "Hard Problems for Simple Default Logics," in Borgida and Etherington, 1989, pp. 189–197.

S. E. Keene, *Object-Oriented Programming in COMMON LISP: A Programmer's Guide to CLOS*, Addison-Wesley, 1989.

R. Kowalski, *Logic for Problem Solving*, Elsevier North Holland, New York, 1979.

B. M. Kramer, "Control of Reasoning in Knowledge-Based Systems," Ph.D. Thesis, University of Toronto, Toronto, Ontario, 1986.

D. B. Lenat, R. V. Guha, K. Pittman, D. Pratt, and M. Shepherd, "CYC: Towards Programs with Common Sense," *Communications of the ACM*, **33**, pp. 30–49, 1990.

H. J. Levesque, "A Fundamental Tradeoff in Knowledge Representation and Reasoning," in *Canadian Society for Computational Studies of Intelligence/Société Canadienne pour l'Étude de l'Intelligence par Ordinateur, Proceedings of the Fifth Biennial Conference,* London, Ont., Canada, 1984, pp. 141–152.

H. J. Levesque, "A Logic of Implicit and Explicit Belief," in *Proceedings of the Fourth National Conference on Artificial Intelligence,* Austin, Tex., AAAI, Menlo Park, Calif., 1984, pp. 198–202.

H. J. Levesque, "Knowledge Representation and Reasoning, *Ann. Rev. Comput. Sci.,* no. 1, 255–287 (1986).

H. J. Levesque and J. Mylopoulos, "A Procedural Semantics for Semantic Networks," in Findler, 1979, pp. 93–120.

J. McCarthy, "Programs with Common Sense," in Minsky, 1968, pp. 403–418.

J. McCarthy, "Circumscription—A Form of Non-monotonic Reasoning," *Artif. Intell.* **13**, 27–39 (1980).

J. McDermott and C. Forgy, "Production System Conflict Resolution Strategies," in Waterman and Hayes-Roth, eds., 1978, pp. 177–199.

A. Maida and S. C. Shapiro, "Intensional Concepts in Propositional Semantic Networks," *Cogn. Sci.* **6**, 291–330 (1982).

M. Minsky, ed., *Semantic Information Processing,* MIT Press, Cambridge, Mass., 1968.

M. Minsky, "A Framework for Representing Knowledge," in P. H. Winston, ed., *The Psychology of Computer Vision,* McGraw-Hill Book Co., Inc., New York, 1975, pp. 211–277.

R. C. Moore, *Reasoning about Knowledge and Action,* Technical Note **284**, AI Centre, SRI International, Palo Alto, Calif., 1980.

J. Mylopoulos and M. Brodie, eds., *On Knowledge Base Management Systems: Integrating AI and Database Technologies,* Springer-Verlag, New York, 1986.

J. Mylopoulos and M. Brodie, eds., *Readings in AI and Databases,* Morgan-Kaufmann, San Mateo, Calif., 1988.

B. Nebel, "Computational Complexity of Terminological Reasoning in BACK," *Artif. Intell.* **34**, 371–383 (1988).

B. Nebel and K. von Luck, "Hybrid Reasoning in BACK," in Z. W. Ras and L. Saitta, eds., *Methodologies for Intelligent Systems,* Vol. 3, North-Holland, Amsterdam, The Netherlands, 1988.

A. Newell, "Production Systems: Models of Control Structure," in W. Chase, ed., *Visual Information Processing,* Academic Press, Inc., New York, 1973.

A. Newell and H. A. Simon, *Human Problem Solving,* Prentice-Hall, Inc., Englewood Cliffs, N.J., 1972.

P. F. Patel-Schneider, "A Decidable First Order Logic for Knowledge Representation," in *Proceedings of the Ninth IJCAI,* Los Angeles, Calif., Morgan-Kaufmann, San Mateo, Calif., 1985, pp. 455–458.

P. F. Patel-Schneider, "A Four-Valued Semantics for Frame-Based Description Languages," in *Proceedings of the Fifth National Conference on Artificial Intelligence,* Philadelphia, AAAI, Menlo Park, Calif., 1986, pp. 344–348.

J. Pearl, "Probabilistic Semantics for Nonmonotonic Reasoning: A Survey," in Borgida and Etherington, 1989, pp. 505–526.

C. Peltason, A. Schmiedel, C. Kindermann, and J. Quantz, *The BACK System Revisited,* KIT Report **75**, Technical University of Berlin, 1989.

R. Reiter, "On Closed World Data Bases," in H. Gallaire and J. Minker, eds., *Logic and Databases,* Plenum, New York, 1978, pp. 55–76.

R. Reiter, "A Logical Reconstruction of Relational Theory," in M.

Brodie, J. Mylopoulos, and J. Schmidt, eds., *On Conceptual Modelling: Perspectives from AI, Databases and Programming Languages,* Springer-Verlag, New York, 1984.

C. Rich and R. C. Waters, eds., *Readings in Artificial Intelligence and Software Engineering,* Morgan-Kaufmann, San Mateo, Calif. 1986.

C. Rieger, "An Organization of Knowledge for Problem-Solving and Language Comprehension," *Artif. Intell.* **7**(2), 89–127 (1976).

J. A. Robinson, *Logic: Form and Function,* Edinburgh University Press, Edinburgh, UK, 1979.

J. Schmidt and C. Thanos, eds., *Foundations of Knowledge Base Management,* Springer-Verlag, New York, 1989.

M. Schmidt-Schauss, "Subsumption in KL-ONE is Undecidable," in Brogida and Etherington, 1989, pp. 505–526.

L. K. Schubert, "Extending the Expressive Power of Semantic Networks," *Artif. Intell.* **7**, 163–198 (1976).

S. C. Shapiro, "A Net Structure for Semantic Storage, Deduction, and Retrieval," in Hewitt, 1971.

S. C. Shapiro, "The SNePS Semantic Network Processing System," in Findler, 1979.

E. H. Shortliffe, *Computer-Based Medical Consultations: MYCIN,* Elsevier Science Publishing Co., Inc., New York, 1976.

J. Sowa, ed., *Principles of Semantic Networks,* Morgan-Kaufmann, San Mateo, Calif., 1991.

M. E. Stickel, "A Non-Clausal Connection Graph Resolution Theorem Proving System," in *Proceedings of the Second National Conference on Artificial Intelligence,* Pittsburgh, Pa., AAAI, Menlo Park, Calif., 1982, pp. 229–233.

G. J. Sussman and D. V. McDermott, *Why Conniving Is Better Than Planning,* Technical Report MIT-AI-225A, Cambridge, Mass., 1972.

M. Vilain and H. Kautz, "Constraint Propagation Algorithms for Temporal Reasoning," in Patel-Schneider, 1986, pp. 377–382.

D. A. Waterman and F. Hayes-Roth, eds., *Pattern-Directed Inference Systems,* Academic Press., Inc., New York, 1978.

W. A. Woods, "What's in a Link: Foundations for Semantic Networks," in D. G. Bobrow and A. Collins, eds., *Representation and Understanding,* Academic Press, Inc., New York, 1975, pp. 35–82.

General References

J. Allen and P. Hayes, "A Common Sense Theory of Time," in *Proceedings of the Ninth IJCAI,* Los Angeles, Calif., Morgan-Kaufmann, San Mateo, Calif., 1985.

A. Barr and J. Davidson, "Representation of Knowledge," in A. Barr and E. A. Feigenbaum, eds., *The Handbook of Artificial Intelligence,* Vol. 1, W. Kaufmann, Los Altos, Calif., 1981, pp. 140–121.

R. J. Brachman and H. J. Levesque, eds., *Readings in Knowledge Representation,* Morgan-Kaufmann, San Mateo, Calif., 1985.

R. J. Brachman and B. C. Smith, eds., *Special Issue on Knowledge Representation, SIGART Not.* 70 (1980).

A. M. Frisch and J. F. Allen, "Knowledge Retrieval as Limited Inference," in D. W. Loveland, ed., *Proceedings of the Sixth International Conference on Automated Deduction,* Springer-Verlag, New York, 1982.

G. Hulin, A. Pirotte, D. Roelants, M. Vauclair, "Logic and Databases," in A. Thayse, ed., *From Modal Logic to Deductive Databases—Introducing a Logic-Based Approach to Artificial Intelligence,* John Wiley & Sons, Inc., New York, 1989.

G. McCalla and N. Cercone, eds., *Special Issue on Knowledge Representation, IEEE Comput.* **16**(10) (Oct. 1983).

W. A. Martin, "Descriptions and the Specializations of a Concept," in P. Winston and R. Brown, eds., *Artificial Intelligence: An MIT Perspective,* MIT Press, Cambridge, Mass., 1979, pp. 379–419.

J. Mylopoulos and H. J. Levesque, "An Overview of Knowledge Representations," in M. L. Brodie, J. Mylopoulos, and J. W. Schmidt, eds., *On Conceptual Modelling,* Springer-Verlag, New York, 1984, pp. 3–18.

M. R. Quillian, "Semantic Memory," in M. Minsky, ed., *Semantic Information Processing,* MIT Press, Cambridge, Mass., 1968, pp. 227–270.

M. Vilain, H. Kautz, and P. van Beek, "Constraint Propagation Algorithms for Temporal Reasoning: A Revised Report," in D. S. Weld and J. de Kleer, eds., *Readings in Qualitative Reasoning about Physical Systems,* Morgan-Kaufmann, San Mateo, Calif., 1989.

BRYAN KRAMER
JOHN MYLOPOULOS
University of Toronto

KOKON

KOKON is a system that generates contracts for selling real estate. It was developed in 1988 in collaboration at Technical University Munich and Systemtechnik Berner & Mattner GmbH under the sponsorship of the German government. KOKON integrates techniques of legal reasoning and belief revision (qv). (See D. Kowalewski, J. Schneeberger, and S. Wiefel, "KOKON-3: Ein prototypisches System zur wissensbasierten Vertragskonfigurierung," in M. Paul, ed., *GI-19. Jahrestagung,* Springer, 1989, pp. 79–92.)

J. SCHNEEBERGER
TH Darmstadt

KRL

A frame-based language for knowledge representation (qv), KRL was developed by Bobrow and Winograd in 1977 (see D. Bobrow and T. Winograd, "An Overview of KRL, a Knowledge Representation Language," *Cog. Sci.* **1**, 3–46 (1977); T. Winograd, "Frame Representations and the Declarative/Procedural Controversy," in D. Bobrow and A. Collins, eds., *Representation and Understanding: Studies in Cognitive Science,* Academic Press, New York).

T. WINOGRAD
Stanford University

LAMBDA CALCULUS

HISTORY

The lambda calculus grew out of efforts by logicians in the 1920s and 1930s to understand the notion of a mathematical function. The traditional view of a function as a set of ordered pairs with a fixed domain and range did not adequately describe the behavior of functions like the identity function, which works on any input whatsoever.

The first key discovery, made by Frege in 1893 and rediscovered by Schönfinkel in 1924, was that it sufficed to study functions of a single argument: any function of the form $f: A \times B \to C$ could be replaced by a function $f': A \to (B \to C)$, which, given its first argument, produced another function willing to accept a second argument. The name lambda calculus is derived from Church's (1932) notation for such functions. Let x be a variable, and let M be an expression. A function F may be defined such that for any value of x, $F(x) = M$. Church (1932) proposed that this function be denoted $\lambda x.M$.

Church, Curry, Kleene, and Rosser established the basic theoretical properties of this formalism in the 1930s. In the late 1950s, McCarthy (1960) used the lambda calculus as the basis for the notation of procedures in LISP. This gave it a wide exposure among computer scientists. In the late 1960s and early 1970s, Strachey used the lambda calculus as a tool for specifying programming languages and, motivated by Strachey's work, Scott further developed the foundations of the lambda calculus, leading to a renewed research interest that continues to this day. A lively history of the lambda calculus may be found in Rosser (1984) and an excellent survey of the work of Strachey and Scott may be found in Stoy (1977).

FOUNDATIONS

Notation

Because the lambda calculus involves functions whose result is a function, expressions such as $((f(a))(b))(c)$ are often needed. To avoid excessive parenthesization, it is standard to write fa for the application of f to a, and to assume that application associates to the left. Thus the complicated expression above would be written $fabc$. Parentheses may still be used for grouping.

Basics. If $\lambda x.M$ denotes the function F such that for any value of x, $F(x) = M$, then the value of F on an argument N can be computed by substituting N into the defining equation. This leads to the basic axiom of the lambda calculus, the β-rule:

$$(\lambda x.M)N = M[N/x]$$

where $M[N/x]$ denotes the term M with N substituted for each free occurrence of x, and with bound variables re-

named to avoid capture of free variables (Church, 1932; Barendregt, 1984, 1987; Curry and Feys, 1958; McCarthy, 1960; Rosser, 1984; Stoy, 1977). This axiom can be regarded as a rewriting rule that can be used to reduce any λ term to a term in which the rule no longer applies. Such a term is said to be in normal form. In general, there may be many ways to reduce a term. However, the Church-Rosser Theorem (Barendregt, 1977; Curry and Feys, 1958) states that if a term M reduces, by different paths, to two terms N_1 and N_2, then N_1 and N_2 may be reduced to a common term P. This implies that if a term has a normal form, then that normal form is unique (up to renaming of bound variables). This also implies that the formal system of β-reduction is not degenerate: that is, it is false that all terms are provably equal under the β-rule. For example, the two terms

$$S = \lambda x(\lambda y(\lambda z.xz(yz)))$$
$$K = \lambda x(\lambda y.x)$$

are distinct terms in normal form and, therefore, cannot be proven equal.

Definability. An extremely useful λ term is the fixed-point combinator

$$Y = \lambda f(x.f(xx))(\lambda x.f(xx))$$

It can be shown that for any term M, $M(YM) = YM$. This property of Y can be used to write recursive definitions. Boolean values can be defined by

$$T = \lambda x(\lambda y.x)$$
$$F = \lambda x(\lambda y.y)$$

With these truth values, a conditional operator can be defined by $(M \to N, P) = MNP$. Another useful term is Church's pairing operator:

$$[M, N] = \lambda x.xMN$$

With this operator, the first element of a pair p can be retrieved by the term pT, and the second element by the term pF.

For discussing the expressive power of the lambda calculus, it is useful to have a copy of the integers. The nth numeral $\bar{n}$ can be defined by:

$$\bar{0} = [T, T]$$
$$\overline{n + 1} = [F, \bar{n}]$$

With this representation, the successor function on numerals can be defined as $\lambda x[F, x]$, the predecessor function as $\lambda x.xF$ (taking the second component), and the zero test as $\lambda x.xT$. With these operations and the fixed-point operation, functions can be defined on the numerals. It can be shown that the lambda-definable operations on the numerals are precisely the partial recursive functions (Barendregt, 1984, 1977; Curry and Feys, 1958).

Another useful set of operations concerns combinatory terms. Define a combinatory term to be a term built up from variables S and K by application alone, without any additional use of lambda. Then any lambda term is equal to some combinatory term. To do this, replace each lambda-abstraction $\lambda x \cdot M$ (where M is already a combinatory term) by a term $[x]M$ defined as follows:

$$[x]M = KM$$

if x does not occur free in M

$$[x]x = SKK$$

$$[x](M_1 M_2) = S([x]M_1)([x]M_2)$$

Observing that $SKK = \lambda x.x$, it is easy to show that $[x]M = \lambda x.M$. This algorithm is called bracket abstraction, and has been used as a basis for hardware implementation of reduction.

APPLICATIONS TO ARTIFICIAL INTELLIGENCE

The primary relevance of the lambda calculus to AI is through the medium of LISP. McCarthy used the lambda calculus as the basis of LISP's notation for procedures. Since that time, however, othe programming languages have used the lambda calculus in a more pervasive way. Scheme, for example, uses the lexical scoping rule of the lambda calculus, rather than LISP's dynamic scoping, and fully integrates the concept of functions as first-class values in the language.

Church's pairing combinator serves as the basis for procedural data types like Hewitt's actors or SMALL TALK's objects, which respond to messages in order to communicate. In combination with the concept of functions as first-class citizens, this leads to the paradigm of object-oriented programming, in which all data are encapsulated in functional capabilities.

Because the lambda calculus is a convenient formalism for describing complex functions that take functions as arguments and return functions as results, it has been used to model domains in which such functions arise. One such application is the semantics of Montague grammars for natural language (Warren, 1983). Another such application is as a basis for the description of the semantics of programming languages (Rosser, 1984). These semantic definitions can be used for description, for building interpreters, and for building compilers.

BIBLIOGRAPHY

A. Church, "A Set of Postulates for the Foundations of Logic," *Ann. Math.* 33(2nd series), 346–366 (1932).

H. P. Barendregt, "The Type Free Lambda Calculus," in J. Barwise, ed., *Handbook of Mathematical Logic*, North-Holland, Amsterdam, 1977, pp. 1091–1132.

H. P. Barendregt, *The Lambda Calculus: Its Syntax and Semantics*, rev. ed., North-Holland, Amsterdam, 1984.

H. B. Curry and R. Feys, *Combinatory Logic*, Vol. 1. North-Holland, Amsterdam, 1958.

J. McCarthy, "Recursive Functions of Symbolic Expressions and Their Computation by Machine, Part I," *Comm. ACM* **3**, 184–195 (1960).

J. B. Rosser, "Highlights of the History of the Lambda-Calculus" *Ann. Hist. Comput.* **6**, 337–349 (1984).

J. E. Stoy, *Denotational Semantics: The Scott-Strachey Approach to Programming Language Theory*, MIT Press, Cambridge, Mass., 1977.

D. S. Warren, "Using Lambda-Calculus to Represent Meanings in Logic Grammars," in *Proceedings of the Twenty-first Annual Meeting of the Association for Computational Linguistics*, 1983, pp. 51–56.

MITCHELL WAND
Northeastern University

LANGUAGE ACQUISITION

A TAXONOMY OF AI MODELS OF LANGUAGE ACQUISITION

Artificial intelligence models of language acquisition are a proper subset of AI learning systems and rely heavily on work in computational linguistics (see LEARNING, MACHINE; COMPUTATIONAL LINGUISTICS). AI models of language acquisition fall naturally into two main subdivisions: theoretical models that learn formal languages and cognitive models that embody theories about the way in which children learn a language. Formal models have been influential in defining the complexity of the task of learning language. Cognitive models by contrast are used as tools for linguists and psychologists in the task of exploring and contrasting alternative theories about the way in which children learn their native languages. Cognitive scientists who build computational models to embody psychological theories do so because they believe that such models enable them to achieve a degree of explicitness that is virtually impossible to attain when working only with pencil and paper. Such models encourage a comparison of the results of the theory to actual data that aids in refining hypotheses and evaluating them. The discipline of building theoretical models that embody psychological theories should not be confused with crude comparisons between brain and computer. The development and use of models of language acquisition is becoming more prevalent and as more and more powerful models are developed it is generally expected that they will make a major contribution to our understanding of the fascinating question of how children learn language.

Historical Notes

Models of language acquisition are a relatively new development in artificial intelligence. One early precursor was the Teachable Language Comprehender developed by Quillian (1969). This model learned to understand English text but was developed as a theory of language understanding rather than as a model of the processes of language acquisition. Harris (1974, 1977), a computer scientist, developed a language-learning program for a simulated robot. His rationale was that because it would be an almost impossible task to predict in advance all the language capacity that might be desirable in a robotics system, it would be useful to provide the system the ability to learn language from a teacher. Harris made no claims about the cognitive validity of his system, and it does not fall easily into either of the two classes of language acquisition systems that are defined above; nevertheless, Harris's simulated robot did acquire a subset of English from examples and was one of the earliest systems to acquire language.

Anderson (1977), a psychologist, built a language acquisition system (LAS) that was a psychological model of human language processing. LAS learned both to generate sentences and to understand them. Input to the model consisted of strings of words that were treated as sentences and scene descriptions that were encoded in associative networks. The associative network structure may be thought of as an encoding of a picture so the learning process is meant to represent language learning from sentence-picture pairs. LAS obeyed commands to speak, understand, and learn. LAS understood by encoding the meaning of an input sentence in the associative network, LAS spoke by receiving such a network and encoding it in a sentence, and LAS learned by using a sentence and an encoding of the sentence meaning to derive changes in the current grammar. Although Anderson built LAS as a cognitive model, he pointed out that LAS did not learn language as a child does. Its learning paradigm was more similar to that of an adult learning a second language. LAS was not based on developmental data on the way that children learn language. One large difference between the child and LAS is that all the concepts must exist in the model before the mapping between words and concepts can occur. This was true of Harris's system as well, and it will be seen that the same problem can be observed in many current language acquisition models. Neither Anderson's nor Harris's system proceeds in such a way as to make the same errors children make and to correct them in the manner that children come to correct their errors. This is an important criterion for judging systems that purport to acquire language as the child acquires a first language.

Even earlier than these two models is that of Kelley (1967), who wrote the first computer simulation of language acquisition. Kelley approached his model from the linguist's point of view. His model was a stage model and proceeded through the stages of one-word, two-word, and three-word utterances. Kelley's model focused on attaining a hierarchical representation of the three-word stage. The basic syntactic categories were not learned by the system, but were given. The system relied on a comparator module that indicated whether guessed sentence structure was correct or incorrect. This is a problematic strategy as will be discussed below. One important aspect of this model was a weighting system that allowed guesses that were not confirmed to die out through absence of confirmation. This model succeeded in learning a simple grammar through experience, even if noisy data were given, and it was intelligent enough to ignore sentences that it did not understand and to select those sentences to which it could respond.

Innatists vs. Empiricists

Since Chomsky (1965) published *Aspects of the Theory of Syntax*, the dialogue between innatists and empiricists has fundamentally influenced the course of research in language acquisition. The bias of an individual or research group toward the innatist or empiricist position profoundly influences the questions that are asked and the manner in which they are posed. Chomsky's innatist position is based on the fact that language is simply too complex to be learned in the sense that mathematics, for example, or chess is learned. Yet all normal children the world over succeed in acquiring a native language by the time that they are around five years old. Language, moreover, is productive. The child is creative in the use of language. Every child produces countless original sentences. By what processes can these astonishing facts be explained? Chomsky enumerated five requirements for a child to learn language: (1) a technique for representing signals, (2) a way of representing structural information about these signals, (3) some initial delimitation of a class of possible hypotheses about language structure, (4) a method for determining what each such hypothesis implies with respect to each sentence, and (5) a method for selecting one of the (presumably infinitely many) hypotheses that are allowed by the third requirement and are compatible with the given linguistic data.

Since 1965 Chomsky has modified these criteria somewhat. The need for the fifth requirement is deemphasized by assuming language universals and a set of parameters that narrow the hypothesis space. A universal grammar is defined to be a system of principles that characterize the class of biologically possible grammars. Emphasizing the biological foundations of language, Chomsky likens the growing of language to the growing of any other organ of the body. Children will hear the language of their environment and discover, for example, that their language uses a subject–verb–object word order; this fact might act as a trigger for a set of related assumptions, such as the language is not an inflected one. Universal grammar then has highly restricted options and a few parametric variations. A given language would be acquired by adding rules to this universal grammar (Chomsky, 1977; Chomsky and Lasnik, 1977; Lightfoot, 1987; Hyams, 1986; Roeper and Williams, 1987; Wexler and Culicover, 1980). An important aspect of this innatist theory for language acquisition is that Chomsky continues to define his approach as one in which only the moment of acquisition of the correct grammar is considered. In the discussion of Berwick's (1985) system, it will be seen that he has developed a working model of language acquisition based on this theory. Another way of characterizing the innatist approach to language acquisition is that it proceeds from a characterization of adult grammar and works backward to see how the child might arrive at this characterization.

The alternative approach, that of the empiricists, is to work forward from the evidence that the child provides toward some characterization of the adult language. The empiricist's approach is sometimes confused with the stimulus–response work of Skinner. Skinner (1957) suggested that language might be viewed as behavior taught in the stimulus–response paradigm. No student of language accepts this suggestion today and it is a mistake to confound empiricism with Skinner and the stimulus–response paradigm. Many empiricists view language development from Piaget's (1963) point of view. They emphasize the diversity of the world's languages and view this diversity as weakening of the arguments for a universal grammar. They regard language as only one aspect of the developing cognition of the child and so empiricists tend to view the acquisition of language in a larger cognitive sense than do the innaticists (Arbib and Hill, 1988). The Piagetian approach is to view the child, motivated by an innate desire to communicate, as actively constructing language, aided by innate cognitive schemas and mediated by the perceptive apparatus through which all humans perceive the world. Piatelli-Palmerini (1980) offers a clear exposition of these two contrasting approaches to language acquisition.

Of course, the innatist and empiricist positions are not necessarily antithetical. Most scientists believe that the truth about language acquisition will be shown to contain both empiricist and innatist aspects. Ultimately everyone, innatists and empiricists alike, believe that language acquisition requires some innate schemas. The as yet unresolved question is to determine exactly what is innate. Models of language acquisition are very well suited to contribute to the search for some answers to this question.

LEARNABILITY MODELS

Learnability theory addresses the formal problem of determining the conditions under which certain types of language can be learned. Pinker (1979) offers an overview of work in this framework. The importance of learnability models lies in their clear demonstration of the need for constraints on the possible grammatical systems that can be learned. Gold (1967), a mathematician, posed the formal problem of learnability and demonstrated that the defining set of rules for a grammar for any nontrivial language cannot be learned from positive examples alone. Because children are given no explicit examples of sentences that are not in their language, learnability theory seeks constraints that may be assumed to be innate in humans that would rule out most of the otherwise computationally intractable sets of languages to be learned. Wexler and Culicover (1980) took up the challenge of the learnability question posed by Gold. They have assumed a formulation of language in a traditional transformational framework and have formally demonstrated the need for a set of learnability restrictions or constraints on the operation of transformational rules. They assumed (1) that the child can derive the meaning of adult utterances from extralinguistic information and (2) that the child can derive the deep structures of a transformational grammar

from these meanings. Then, given a pairing of word strings and deep structures, the learning device tries to find a set of transformations in its current hypothesized grammar that will map from the deep string to the word string. Failure to find such a set results in a revision of the grammar. The work of Wexler and Culicover is doubly interesting because restrictions derived from a mathematical approach to learnability theory coincide in many instances with constraints noticed quite separately by linguists working in a traditional framework. Note that no one, certainly not Wexler and Culicover themselves, would claim that their model learns language in the way that children do.

The work of Wexler and Culicover falls in the area of mathematical inquiry because their theories for the most part have not been implemented on a computer. These are models that could in theory be implemented, and some theoretic work by scientists in artificial intelligence is closely related to their work.

Berwick (1985) has developed a model that acquires a syntactic system. Berwick incorporated a theory of generative grammar into his working model of language acquisition. He shows that the acquisition of syntax can be simple if given sufficient constraints. His model learns to parse in a fashion based on Marcus's (1980) deterministic parser. Marcus's parser consists of a structured working memory and a set of productions that add items at specified points in the memory, move the items around within the memory, and add descriptive labels to them. Berwick's learning system assumes that a limited set of productions are innate and proceeds to learn a more complete set of phrase structure rules and transformations on them, ie, the rules for moving items and adding descriptive labels. Given an initial set of abilities, an interpreter, a lexicon, a limited set of phrase structure rules and selectional restrictions, Berwick's model is able to glean a large set of complex rules from simple example sentences. The success of this program is based on constraints. Given a rich set of features and the ability to categorize lexical items as nouns, verbs, or other, the model discovers a variety of word classes within the other category. Learning takes place whenever the parser is unable to build a parse tree for a sentence. If in the midst of a parse no known grammar rules can trigger, then the system tries to build a new grammar rule. Thus a series of parsers are built, each more powerful than its predecessor. A parser has four possible actions and tries each in turn. These involve attaching an item in a parse tree, switching items and inserting items. For example if the system has rules to parse the sentence "Daddy gave the boy the toy," then if the model encounters the sentence, "Did Daddy give the boy the toy?" it is at a loss, because *did* cannot be a noun phrase. However, by means of the switch rule *did* and *Daddy* can be switched and the rest of the parse is successful. Then this new grammar rule is added to the model's repertoire. It is important to note that this model starts with a large body of assumptions about the nature of language and of parsing, including both the assumption of an innate universal grammar and Chomsky's theory of generative grammar. Given these assumptions and the computational constraints, the system is able to infer many complex and high level rules. Berwick's model does not use negative information, but learns as the child does from language experience. Unlike the child, the model is given only grammatical sentences as input. (Transcripts of child–adult conversations show that a large percentage of utterances addressed to a child are not complete grammatical sentences.) There is no provision for the system to make and correct errors. The model learns word order rules, lexical insertion rules, movement rules, and lexical categories. It uses both syntactic and semantic information in the process of lexical categorization. Although included here because of its formal antecedents, the Berwick model may also be viewed as a cognitive model in that the model does reproduce certain child language developmental data. An important hypothesis that this model suggests is that the constraints necessary for efficient parsing may turn out to be the very same constraints that are necessary for learnability.

Wolff (1982) has developed an algorithm that finds the distinct words in pieces of text from which all the spaces have been removed. This algorithm for segmenting input to the model scans for commonly occurring adjacent strings. This work provides concrete illustrations of how at least part of the task of segmenting sound into word units might be dealt with. This work has been expanded by Wolff (1980) into a model that shows how a similar approach can be implemented to segment text into phrasal segments. Wolff makes no claim that his models learn as the child does, but as he points out, valuable insights can be gained by developing and testing computer models of theoretical proposals and observing their strengths and weaknesses.

CHARACTERIZING COGNITIVE MODELS OF LANGUAGE ACQUISITION

Cognitive models of language acquisition not only ask under what conditions a language can be learned by a computer model but also whether the model learns the language in the same way that the child does. As a consequence these models may be distinguished by their attention to the psycholinguistic data on the manner in which children learn their native tongues. The first group of models described below concern themselves with the acquisition of the lexicon. The second group concern themselves with the acquisition of syntax. Even putting both groups of models together it is clear that acquisition of only a small part of the language acquisition task has been addressed by AI modeling.

Psycholinguistic Studies

There exists a wealth of psycholinguistic studies concerning the acquisition of language of children from all over the world. Although the literature abounds with collections of language acquisition data, there are a great variety of ways of explaining and interpreting the data (Brown, 1973; de Villiers and de Villiers, 1978; Braine; Nelson, 1973; Slobin, 1984; Bowerman, 1973; Peters, 1983). There are many methods that psychologists and linguists have used to collect data including diary records

(Bowerman, 1974), elicited production tasks (Tager-Flusberg and co-workers, 1982) in which the child may be asked to describe a picture or a situation, or tests of understanding in which the child is asked to act out with toys sentences presented by the researcher (Matthei, 1979; Solan and Roeper, 1978). Explanations are sought to account for the progress from one-word utterances (Bloom, 1973) to short utterances that include only content words to the acquisition of morphemes that have been shown to appear in all children (Bybee and Slobin, 1982). The stage in which children make use of short utterances containing only content words has been called telegraphic speech because of its resemblance to the cryptic kinds of messages used in telegrams. These brief utterances encode a set of relations that are found in early child speech in all languages.

Particular attention has been paid to the errors that children make, because child speech that differs from adult speech yields clues concerning the processes that the child is using to understand and produce speech. An equally important clue to the child's processes are those errors that the child typically does not make. One frequently noted phenomenon is the overgeneralization of the plural of nouns and of the past tense of verbs in English. Such phenomena need to be explained. A cognitive model of language acquisition, therefore, must not only learn to understand and generate sentences of ever greater complexity, as does the child, but to provide a satisfying explanation of the course of language acquisition the model must also make the same kinds of errors that the child makes and eventually correct the errors after further learning has occurred.

Connectionist Models

A connectionist model is an entirely different kind of model from those previously discussed. Connectionist models (also known as parallel distributed network models) are currently the subject of intense investigation. These models may be characterized by the fact that they do not encode explicit rules in the sense of more traditional AI models that are symbolically encoded. Connectionist models and their applications have been reviewed (Waltz, 1985). Inspired by the parallelism of the brain, these models function by connecting a large number of very small processing units. These units are embodied in networks. A connectionist model embodies the idea of interactively activating subsections of the network. Each of the small units in the network is connected to a large number of others. Each unit samples its input connections from other processing units and modifies its outputs, which are also connections to other processing units. The sum total of these excitatory and inhibitory effects causes the network to converge on a decision about a hypothesis. Thus conspiracies of mental agents permit generalization about lawful behavior.

Rumelhart and McClelland have developed a model of the way that children learn the past tense of verbs in English. This aspect of language acquisition has captured the attention of many researchers because it is an area in which children make some interesting errors. Consider the verb, *go*. It is an empirical fact that children at the earliest stage of language acquisition typically learn the word *went* and use it correctly. One may assume that forms such as this have been learned by rote. Then at a subsequent stage of development the child will start to use the word *goed*. Presumably this is because the child has formed a general schema for forming the past tense of verbs. Eventually, of course, children learn that *go* is an irregular verb and does not obey the general rule in the form of its past tense. But the puzzle is that for a period of time, sometimes for years, both forms exist in the child's vocabulary. How can this period of imbalance between the erroneous and the correct forms be explained? Selfridge (1981) proposed an explanation for this phenomenon. His computer model is described below in more detail. Although the Selfridge model exhibited the three-stage learning progression from a correct form to an overgeneralized form to a correct form, his model was unable to explain the period of time in which both correct and incorrect past tense forms of a particular verb are heard in a child's speech. Hill (1986) proposed an explanation of this phenomenon in her model of language acquisition, which is also described below in more detail. Clearly the phenomenon cannot be explained if the child's lexicon is envisioned as simply containing a rule for forming the past tense of each verb, because the rule would have to be learned and unlearned many times.

Rumelhart and McClelland (1986, 1987) have developed a connectionist model that learns the past tense of some 420 verbs in English, some regular and some irregular. Figure 1 illustrates the basic structure of the model. Input to the model is phonologically encoded. An explicit teaching phase is followed by a testing phase. To achieve the desired results, 10 high frequency verbs were presented first in the teaching phase. Rumelhart and McClelland's model reproduces the three-stage path of learning including the period of instability. They find a rough correlation between the difficulty of learning in their model and in Bybee and Slobin's (1982) observations on the course of learning in the child. Rumelhart and McClelland

claim that the model captures most aspects of the differences in performance of children on different types of verbs. The detail of the analysis of connectionist models such as this is typically finer than that of more symbolic models as is described below.

Rumelhart and McClelland's claims have not gone unchallenged. Pinker and Prince (1988) have written a detailed critique of the system in which they question the means of encoding the phonological input and the interpretation of the results. They also question the validity of teaching the 10 high frequency verbs prior to teaching the remaining verbs. Whether or not the claims for this particular model can be substantiated, Rumelhart and McClelland have provided evidence that rulelike behavior can be exhibited by systems that contain no rules.

The importance of the connectionist models for language acquisition lies in the paradigm for learning. They are an excellent example of the way in which a different kind of AI formalism may modify something so basic as the idea of what a grammar is. Many aspects of computational linguistics have been modeled using the connectionist formalism (McClelland and Rumelhart, 1986). It will be exciting to explore further the strengths and weaknesses of such models for language acquisition.

Models That Acquire a Lexicon

One important aspect of language acquisition is the acquiring of the lexicon. Siskind (1990) has developed a system that can acquire core meanings of words. Although his model is not based on a specific corpus of psycholinguistic data, it is motivated by ideas concerning the manner in which a child may acquire word meanings in the early stages of language acquisition. In this model the words are represented as concept structures. Input to the model consists of sequences of scenes that are described both linguistically and pictorially. The linguistic input consists of a set of simple sentences.

The pictorial information consists of conceptual structure descriptions represented as a set of visual scenes (Fig.

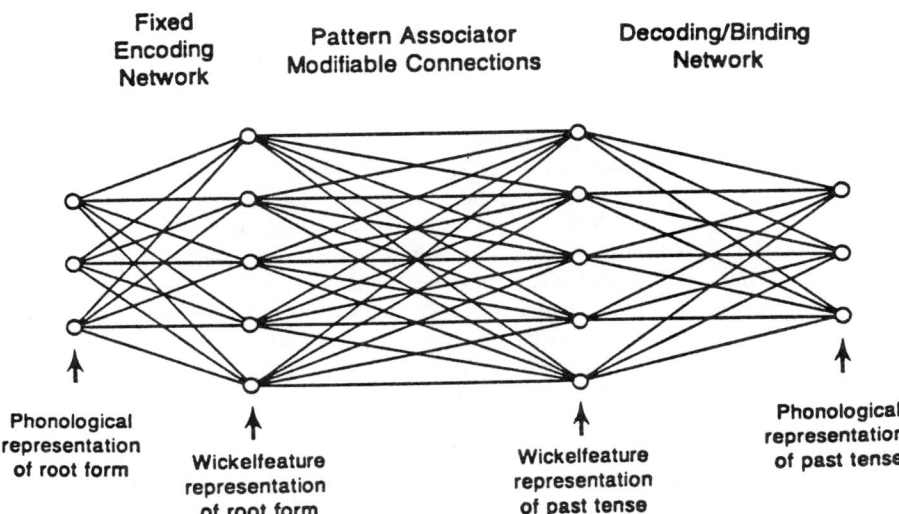

Fixed Encoding Network   Pattern Associator Modifiable Connections   Decoding/Binding Network

Phonological representation of root form

Wickelfeature representation of root form

Wickelfeature representation of past tense

Phonological representation of past tense

Figure 1. The basic structure of the Rumelhart and McClelland (1986) model of past tense acquisition. Courtesy of Bradford Books/MIT Press.

Input:

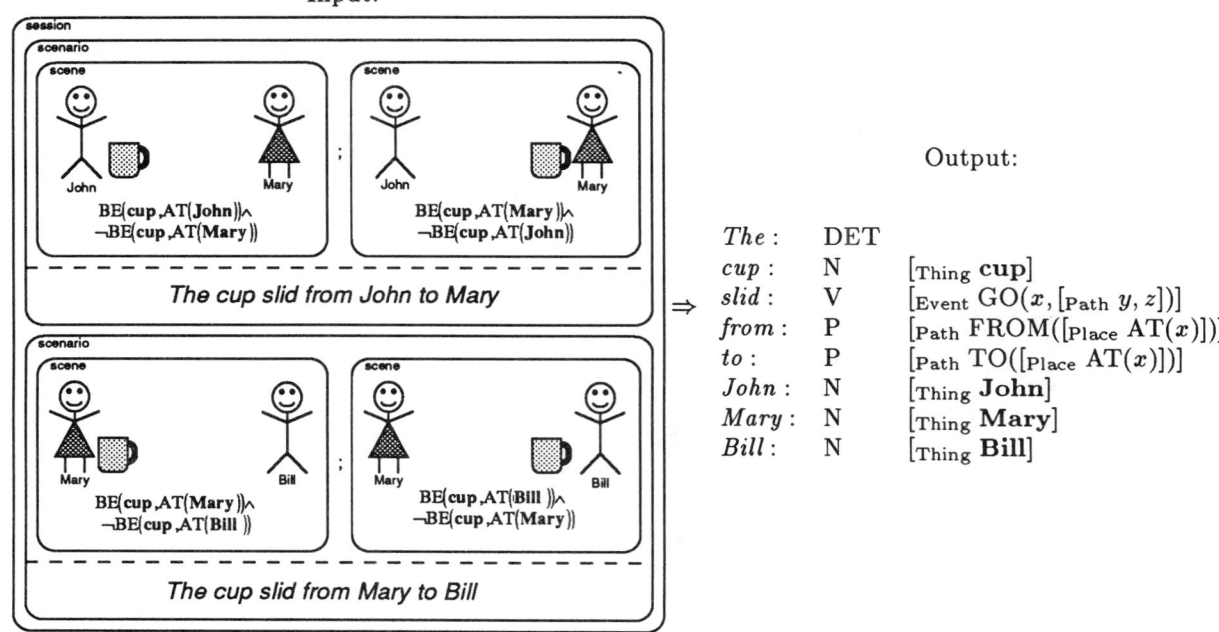

Figure 2. A sample learning session with Siskind's (1990) model. The model is given the two scenarios as input. Each scenario comprises linguistic and nonlinguistic information. The linguistic information is a sequence of sentences; the nonlinguistic information is a sequence of conceptual structure descriptions to describe a sequence of visual scenes. The model produces as output a lexicon that allows the linguistic input to explain the nonlinguistic input. Courtesy of the Association for Computational Linguistics.

2). In a training session the system uses semantic constraint satisfaction and a set of heuristics to match the linguistic and the nonlinguistic inputs in such a way as to infer lexical information. The system is composed of a parser, a linker, and an inference machine. The parser uses a fixed context-free grammar that is assumed to be innate and produces a parse tree. The inference component acts on the nonlinguistic input to produce a semantic structure. In order for the inference component to function correctly, the linguistic input supplied by the teacher must describe the nonlinguistic input in a correct and somewhat constrained fashion. The task of the linker is to associate the syntactic structure and the semantic structure in such a way as to produce a lexicon. One hypothesis suggested by Siskind is that many of the constraints normally assumed to be imposed by syntax actually result from the interplay of multiple modules in a broad cognitive system.

Whereas Siskind's attempts to simulate the kind of word learning that might be performed by children, Zernik (1987) has developed a system that models the acquisition of new words by an adult learning a second language. Related work using a connectionist paradigm is that of Wermter (1989) who built a model that could learn to understand compound nouns. The compound nouns are taken from a scientific technical domain and thus model the acquisition of new technical terms by an adult. Wermter's learning paradigm for differentiating semantic relationships between nouns would seem to be applicable to the kind of learning that children do.

Symbolic Models That Acquire a Grammar

Four different exemplars of cognitive models of language acquisition will be described in this section. The CHILD model of Selfridge (1982) focuses mainly on the use of semantics in the acquisition of language. The first version of Selfridge's model learned to understand commands. A later version (Selfridge, 1981) learned to generate language as well. Some models focus mainly on the acquisition of syntax (Langley, 1982; Hill, 1983, 1985; Arbib and co-workers, 1987; MacWhinney, 1987). Langley's AMBER and MacWhinney's competition model learn to generate language whereas Hill's model learns both to understand and to generate language at the level of the two year old. It is a characteristic of cognitive models of language acquisition that the learning that takes place is more important than the output of the system, so the models must be described in terms of the knowledge structures that are built as the models acquire language.

Selfridge's model has as its input adult sentences together with simulated visual input. The output of the model is the child's response. In the first version of CHILD this response is a description of an action; in the subsequent version (in which a language generator was added) the response may be verbal. Figure 3 is a diagrammatic representation of the model. In Figures 3, 4, 5, and 6 data structures are represented in a large box and the inherent processes that act on these data structures are represented in a smaller box. The series of diagrams highlights certain similarities of structure between the various

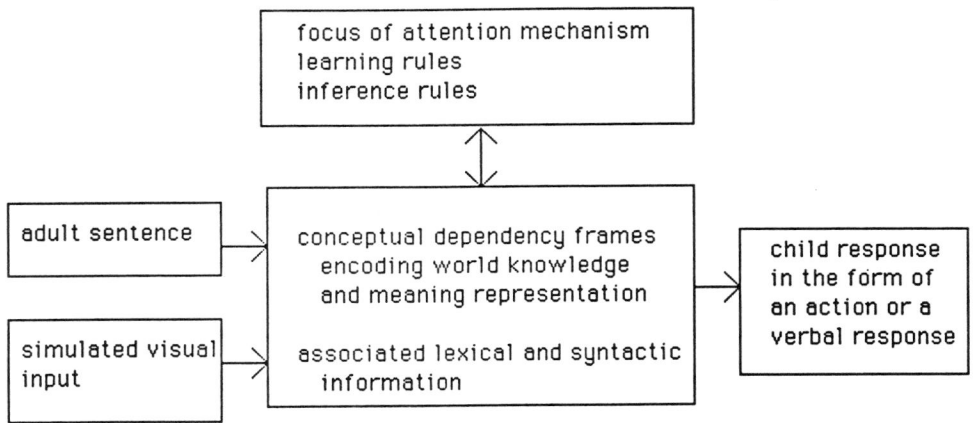

Figure 3. Components of Selfridge's CHILD model.

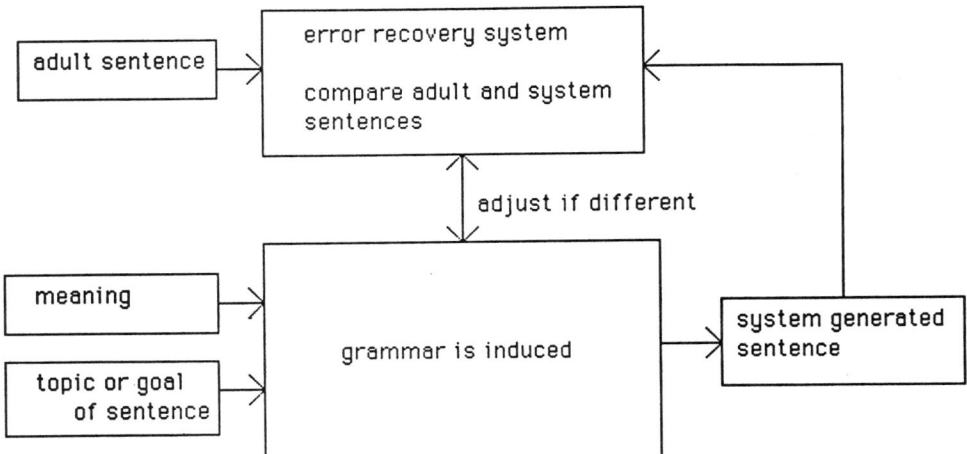

Figure 4. Components of Langley's AMBER model.

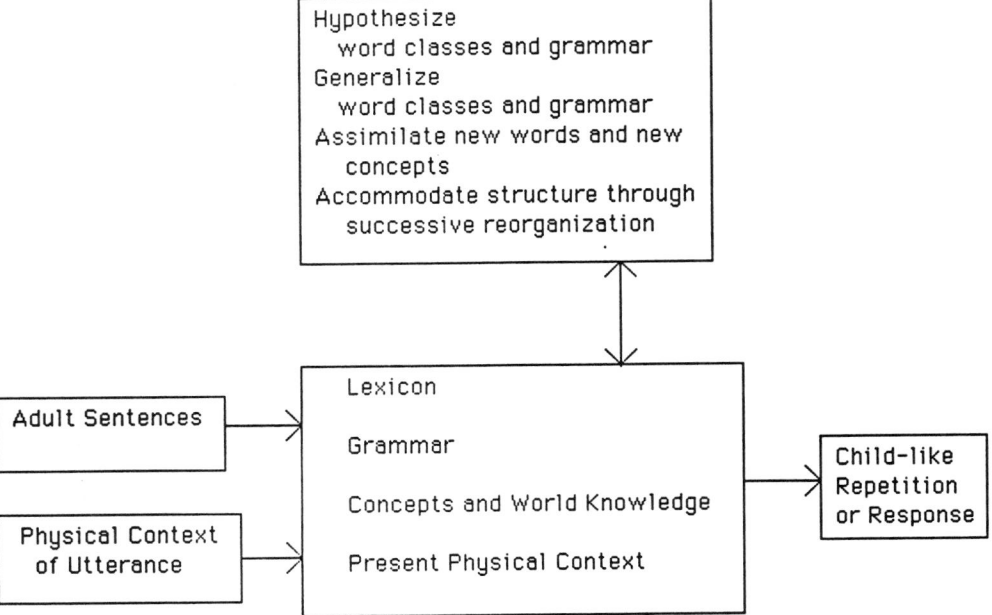

Figure 5. Components of Hill's model of language acquisition in the two year old.

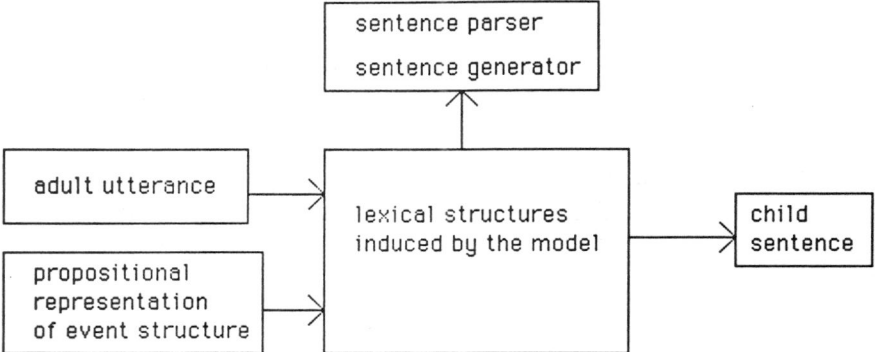

Figure 6. Components of MacWhinney's competition model for the acquisition of syntax.

models. It should be emphasized that the grammars and processes employed by each of these models are quite dissimilar. Selfridge assumes that concepts exist before language is learned. The knowledge structures that are built up consist of attaching lexical knowledge to the concepts that are represented in the conceptual dependency formalism of Schank (1973). Selfridge's (1982) conceptual dependency frame representation embodies a representation based on meaning, which associates slots to be filled with each concept. In this paradigm learning language is essentially learning to fill slots and learning positional information about where slot fillers go in a sentence in relation to other words in the sentence. Using a set of inference and learning rules, Selfridge's model takes words from the input sentences, retrieves appropriate conceptual dependence frames, and matches the words against the conceptual dependency requirements for filling slots. The matching is based on word meaning and word categories. Ultimately CHILD learns to understand simple commands and to produce simple declarative sentences. In the process the model makes overgeneralizations similar to those that children make (Selfridge, 1981). The model makes use of mechanisms for focusing attention and a set of learning rules and rules of inference. Initially the model has no language, and eventually it learns to understand commands and to respond to them. The system was based on psycholinguistic data collected from a child named Joshua and models the way that Joshua proceeded from very little language knowledge to the point where he could understand even unlikely commands such as to "get on the tape recorder." The adult sentences given the model are taken from the recorded interaction between adults and Joshua. The model has successfully learned subsets of both English and Japanese.

Langley's (1982) AMBER is a model of language acquisition through error recovery. Langley's system accounts for the gradual learning of language over time, and also for the order in which morphemes are mastered.

Figure 4 illustrates the components of the model. Input to the model consists of randomly generated adult sentences paired with meaning representations and a representation of the main topic of the sentence. Output of the model is a sentence that the system generates. AMBER gets a proposition, predicts a sentence, then compares the system-generated sentence to the adult sentence it re-

ceived and adjusts the system to account for a discrepancy between the two. The goal of AMBER's generated sentence is to describe the main topic of the sentence. Langley's model employs a process grammar in which the grammar is actually encoded as a set of actions. The model is implemented in the computer language PRISM (Langley and Neches, 1981), which accounts for the gradual learning process. Langley's AMBER starts with one-word utterances and ultimately learns to include appropriate morphemes, suffixes, and prefixes in the utterances produced. Because it is an adaptive production system that attaches weights to rules to indicate the relative strength or weakness of the rule, AMBER learns very slowly. The same rule must be learned many times before the rule is strong enough to mask a previously learned rule. In this respect AMBER's learning paradigm is more cognitively valid than CHILD's. The more complex the conditions on the morpheme use the longer it will take AMBER to master the correct use of the morpheme. AMBER offers an explanation through its learning paradigm of the fact observed by Brown (1973) that it takes the child longer to master certain morphemes than others. One powerful aspect of the system is that the same rules that are learned for producing word combinations can be used at a more advanced level to learn to produce embedded constructions. Meaning is represented in a tree structure employing a small set of relations such as agent, action, object, size, and color. In addition features such as singular, plural, present, past, etc are defined. The system is given the capacity to understand via the meaning representation; it learns to produce language.

Hill's (1983) model of language acquisition is based on data collected from a two-year-old child named Claire. The structure of the model is depicted in Figure 5.

Input to the model consists of adult sentences taken from the transcribed sessions. Output of the model consists of a childlike sentence repeating or responding to the adult input in accordance with the current state of the model's grammar. The internal representation of the model consists of dynamic data structures encoding the child's grammar, the conceptual knowledge of the child, and the physical context of the dialogue. The model is given a basic lexicon and a set of concepts with a mapping between the two. No assumptions are made about the ultimate form of the adult grammar or about what must be built into the model, but the model is developed step by step to represent the progress of the child over very fine time slices. Processes attend to the adult input and use rules of salience to focus on examples within the adult data to form word classes and build a grammar. In Hill's model a template grammar is used, which consists initially of specific examples drawn from the input data. What is learned in each presentation of the sentence depends on the language experience of the model and what has been learned so far. The learning processes in Hill's model emphasize the interaction of cognition and language learning. The learning is highly dynamic in that the same body of input presented to the model a second time causes a different set of grammar schemata and additional lexical class information to be learned. Like Selfridge, Hill's model relies on word order and on encoding relations. The model is a schema-theoretic model (see SCHEMA THEORY) written in LISP using semantic nets (Woods, 1975) whose edges carry weights that are adjusted as the model learns. World knowledge, grammar templates, and the lexicon are all encoded in weighted semantic nets. Eventually with the addition of the concept of coordination this process of generalization causes the initially flat template grammar to evolve into a recursive hierarchical context-free grammar.

MacWhinney's (1987) competition model for the acquisition of syntax builds on his (1978) earlier model of the acquisition of morphophonology. In this earlier work MacWhinney separated out three processes (rote, analogy, and combination) that are joined into a single model in the newer work. The acquisition of syntax model employs a strength-based conflict resolution paradigm to induce a set of lexical structures. Input data are in the form of adult utterances and are taken from the mother–child interactions that appear in Sachs and Truswell's (1978) detailed study of the child Naomi. These data are available through the child language data exchange system (CHILDES) (MacWhinney and Snow, 1985).

A diagram of the model appears in Figure 6. Although the model was built to account specifically for the Sachs data, linguistic data from many languages were taken into account. Each adult utterance is paired with a propositional representation of the event structure that it represents. Output from the model is a childlike sentence. The model is implemented in Franz LISP. Meaning representation in the model takes the form of complex mappings between meaning and utterances. It is assumed that the child attempts to learn words for meanings that the child wants to express. The child, therefore, is granted a form of mental representation that includes the propositional structure that is the basis for semantic interpretation. MacWhinney and Anderson (1986) spell out nine learning strategies: amalgamation acquisition, component analysis, learning syntactic rules, strengthening, generalization, discrimination, proceduralization, composition, and inference. This model relies on attention to word order and characterizing relative word positions as preverbal or postverbal. The model learns strategies for parsing in the sense that learning a new verb leads to opening up new slots to be filled. In this model all learning is targeted toward the acquisition of lexical entries. MacWhinney's model learns a lexicalist grammar that is

much like that of the lexical functional grammar of Bresnan (1982). In the MacWhinney model the lexicon is the sole repository of grammatical knowledge.

Learning, Making Errors, and Correcting Them

To summarize, cognitive models learn from language experience. They generally assume that the child has previously acquired some concepts and world knowledge before language learning begins, and they assume that certain learning abilities are innate. Both the connectionist and symbolic models make errors of overgeneralization just as the child does, but none rely on overt correction of errors because it is generally agreed that explicit overt correction of syntax plays no role in language learning in the child. It is in the area of correcting errors that the models described differ.

The connectionist model learns, makes errors, and corrects them without recourse to manipulation of specific rules. The connectionist paradigm itself takes care of the modeled phenomena. Connectionist models are typically computationally expensive, and the choice of phenomena to model is typically small. These are fine-grained models. In the more symbolic models, Langley, Hill, and MacWhinney all employ some system of weighting factors to differentiate between strong and weak hypotheses. In these models the scope or grain size is much larger and so a phenonemon such as learning the past tense of verbs takes place within a larger framework. Selfridge's CHILD lacks a system of weights or confidence factors and so learns immediately rather than gradually. The unstable period in which both erroneous and correct forms exist simultaneously is not represented in the Selfridge model. The strength-based learning paradigms of Langley's, Hill's and MacWhinney's are close to a connectionist model in spirit. Their learning paradigms focus on schemata that are reinforced or strengthened through use and give greater attention to newly learned schemata than to older ones. The connectionist models require a specific teaching phase, while in the more symbolic models teaching and learning may occur in parallel.

While Selfridge's and Hill's models rely on generalization, Langley's model employs discrimination and MacWhinney's model both generalizes and discriminates. Generalizing is characterized as the process of going from specific schemata to a more general schema. The specific schema is still available but if it is not used it will fail to be reinforced and will eventually decay. Discrimination is the opposite process of starting with overly general schemas and finding and adding missing conditions. It makes little sense to speak of such processes as generalizing or discriminating in the connectionist framework, although the results can be observed in terms of generalizing or discriminating.

EVALUATING THE PRESENT MODELS AND LOOKING TOWARD THE FUTURE

There is clearly much work still to be done in the modeling of language acquisition. These models focus mainly on low level morphosyntactic effects. Much of the rich and detailed patterns of actual language development is as yet virtually untouched. There is a vast amount of data collected on the child's learning of anaphora, pronouns, question forms, and the like that have not been addressed by any cognitive model.

Realizing the broad scope of the task, and that at this time too little is understood about the child's acquisition of language to build a full-blown model, workers at the University of the New South Wales/Macquarie research group have taken the interesting approach of devising sets of small computational learning experiments, each of which yields new insights into some aspect of the larger problem (Powers and Turk, 1989). To explore machine learning within an intermodal context they have situated some of their experiments in a simulated robot world environment. This is a creative approach and one that may ultimately prove most fruitful.

It is hoped that in the future models will be built that will provide ease of experimentation for linguists and psycholinguists. Today's models unfortunately must be built by skilled practitioners of artificial intelligence techniques and are not easily modified or embellished by any others than the authors and their students. The models are important in that they are prototypes for more extensive models of the future.

Berwick's and Wolff's models deal with questions of learnability and future models of this ilk will continue to yield important results in learnability theory concerning the kinds of languages that can be learned and the constraints necessary to make learning possible.

Siskind's and Zernik's models concentrate on acquiring a lexicon. Current research tends toward placing more linguistic knowledge in the lexicon, so this area will be seen to be of increasing importance.

Selfridge's model starts where the child starts with some concepts in place but no language skills. The model starts as a poor language user, gains experience, makes appropriate errors and learns to correct them, and gets progressively better at understanding. Having learned to understand first just words it eventually learns to understand syntactic information and to associate syntactic information with words. The model's ability to learn to talk is driven by the ability to learn to understand, which is inherently satisfying. The model can learn languages other than English, and Selfridge predicts that the processes employed can be extended to learn language up to the adult level.

Langley's model begins with single-word utterances and gradually learns to utter sentences of the complexity of the adult. Unlike Hill's model, Langley's model learns suffixes, prefixes, and morphemes. It does not learn to understand, but is given a meaning representation for adult utterances, which it eventually learns to mimic in all their complexity. The system has little need of complex world knowledge because it does not try to answer questions. The idea of a grammar as embodied in a system of processes for understanding or producing language is cognitively appealing.

Hill's model starts with little information, and learns to understand and produce language at the level of a two year old. The model progressively acquires more and better language skills. It can repeat adult sentences in a childlike manner and answer questions as well. The paradigm suggests a manner in which language, based initially on cognitive knowledge, may grow into a syntactic system that will be increasingly independent of its semantic and cognitive origins, thus suggesting a way that child language may evolve into that of the adult. The model, however, never progresses beyond the level of the two year old. This model more than the others is offered as a theoretical tool for linguistic experimentation and contains a great deal of flexibility including a variety of parameters, and alternative modules that can be added or omitted in order that the differing results may be observed.

MacWhinney's model like the others begins with single-word utterances and proceeds to acquire more and more complex language skills. The model is given a careful and extensive meaning representation to accompany the input sentences. As a consequence of the detailed information given, it is anticipated that the model could in principle acquire the capacity to deal even with such tough problems as center embedding and relative clauses.

Although none of the cognitive models assume a specific set of linguistic universals, as Berwick's does, none are inconsistent with a theory of linguistic universals and all may be seen to embody certain innate processes. Because it is incumbent on a computational model to be precisely explicit about what is built in and what is learned, it will be possible in the future as more and better models are constructed to clarify in a fashion that was heretofore impossible exactly what may be learned, given a set of innate schemata and a set of processes for acting on those schemata.

A great deal of interest is centered on the connectionist paradigm for learning. Rumelhart and McClelland have pointed the way toward adapting this paradigm to language acquisition. Wermter and Lehnert (1989) have developed a hybrid symbolic–connectionist model to understand noun phrases. They observe that increased attention has been directed toward connectionist techniques because of their learning behavior and neural plausibility, yet symbolic models have advantages in representing schemata, inheritance hierarchies, and sequential control. Hence the models of the future will be hybrid models that combine both connectionist and symbolic processing techniques.

BIBLIOGRAPHY

J. R. Anderson, "Induction of Augmented Transition Networks," *Cog. Sci.* 1, 125–157 (1977).

M. A. Arbib and J. C. Hill, "Language Acquisition: Schemas Replace Universal Grammar," in J. H. Hawkins, ed., *Explaining Language Universals*, Basil Blackwell, New York, 1988, pp. 56–101.

M. A. Arbib, E. J. Conklin, and J. C. Hill, *From Schema Theory to Language*, Oxford University Press, New York, 1987.

R. Berwick, *The Acquisition of Syntactic Knowledge*, MIT Press, Cambridge, Mass., 1985.

L. Bloom, *One Word at a Time: The Use of Single Word Utterances before Syntax*, Mouton, The Hague, 1973.

M. Bowerman, "Early Syntactic Development, A Cross-Linguistic Study with Special Reference to Finnish," in *Cambridge Studies in Linguistics*, No. 11, Cambridge University Press, London, 1973.

M. Bowerman, "Learning the Structure of Causative Verbs: A Study in the Relationship of Cognitive, Semantic, and Syntactic Development," in E. Clark, ed., *Papers and Reports on Child Language Development*, No. 8, Stanford University Committee on Linguistics, Stanford, Calif., 1974, pp. 142–178.

M. D. S. Braine, "Children's First Word Combinations," in *Monographs of the Society for Research in Child Development*, University of Chicago Press, Chicago.

J. Bresnan, ed., *The Mental Representation of Grammatical Relations*, MIT Press, Cambridge, Mass., 1982.

R. A. Brown, *A First Language: The Early Stages*, Harvard University Press, Cambridge, Mass., 1973.

J. L. Bybee and D. I. Slobin, "Rules and Schemas in the Development and Use of the English Past Tense," *Language* **58**, 265–289 (1982).

N. Chomsky, *Aspects of the Theory of Syntax*, MIT Press, Cambridge, Mass., 1965.

N. Chomsky, *Language and Responsibility*, Pantheon Books, New York, 1977.

N. Chomsky and H. Lasnik, "Filters and Control," *Linguistic Inquiry* **8**, 425–504 (1977).

J. G. deVilliers and P. A. deVilliers, *Language Acquisition*, Harvard University Press, Cambridge, Mass., 1978.

M. E. Gold, "Language Identification in the Limit," *Information and Control* **10**, 447–474 (1967).

L. R. Harris, *Natural Language Acquisition by Robot*, Technical Report TR74-1, Dartmouth College, Dartmouth, New Hampshire, Oct. 1974.

L. R. Harris, "A System for Primitive Natural Language Acquisition," *Int. J. Man-Machine Stud.* **9**, 153–206 (1977).

J. C. Hill, "A Computational Model of Language Acquisition in the Two-Year-Old," *Cog. Brain Theory* **6**(3), 287–317 (1983).

J. C. Hill, "Using a Computational Model of Language Acquisition to Address Questions in Linguistic Inquiry," in *Proceedings of the Seventh Annual Conference of the Cognitive Science Society*, University of California, Irvine, Aug. 1985.

J. C. Hill, "Using a Computational Model of Language Acquisition to Address Questions in Linguistic Inquiry," in *Proceedings of the Eighth Annual Conference of the Cognitive Science Society*, University of Massachusetts, Amherst, Aug. 1986, pp. 407–419.

N. M. Hyams, *Language Acquisition and the Theory of Parameters*, Reidel, Dordrecht, 1986.

K. L. Kelley, *Early Syntactic Acquisition*, Ph.D. dissertation, University of California, Los Angeles, 1967.

P. Langley, "Language Acquisition Through Error Recovery," *Cog. Brain Theory* **5**, 211–255 (1982).

P. Langley and R. T. Neches, *PRISM User's Manual*, Technical Report, Carnegie-Mellon University, Pittsburgh, Pa., 1981.

D. Lightfoot, *The Language Lottery: Toward a Biology of Grammars*, MIT Press, Cambridge, Mass., 1987.

J. L. McClelland and D. E. Rumelhart, *Parallel Distributed Processing*, Bradford/MIT Press, Cambridge, Mass., 1986.

B. MacWhinney, "The Acquisition of Morphophonology," *Monographs of the Society for Research in Child Development* **43**(1½) (1978).

B. MacWhinney, "The Competition Model," in B. MacWhinney, ed., *Mechanisms of Language Acquisition*, Erlbaum, Hillsdale, N.J., 1987, pp. 249–308.

B. MacWhinney and J. Anderson, "The Acquisition of Grammar," in I. Gopnik and M. Gopnik, eds., *From Models to Modules: Studies in Cognitive Science*, Ablex, Norwood, N.J., 1986.

B. MacWhinney and C. Snow, "The Child Data Exchange System," *J. Child Lang.* **12**, 271–296 (1985).

M. Marcus, *A Theory of Syntactic Recognition for Natural Language*, MIT Press, Cambridge, Mass., 1980.

E. Matthei, *The Acquisition of Prenominal Modifier Sequences: Stalking the Second Green Ball*, Ph.D. dissertation, University of Massachusetts, Amherst, Mass., 1979.

K. Nelson, "Structure and Strategy in Learning to Talk," *Monographs of the Society for Research in Child Development* **38**(1–2), ser. 149 (1973).

A. M. Peters, *The Units of Language Acquisition*, Cambridge University Press, Cambridge, UK, 1983.

J. Piaget, *Child's Conception of the World*, J. Tomlinson and A. Tomlinson, trans., Littlefield Adams & Co., Totowa, N.J., 1979.

M. Piatelli-Palmarini, ed., *Language and Learning: The Debate Between Jean Piaget and Noam Chomsky*, Harvard University Press, Cambridge, Mass., 1980.

S. Pinker, "Formal Models of Language Learning," *Cognition* **7**, 217–283 (1979).

S. Pinker and A. Prince, "On Language and Connectionism: Analysis of a Parallel Distributed Processing Model of Language Acquisition," in S. Pinker and J. Mehler, eds., *Cognition: Special Issue on Connections and Symbols*, Bradford/MIT Press, Cambridge, Mass., 1988.

D. M. W. Powers and C. C. R. Turk, *Machine Learning of Natural Language*, Springer-Verlag, New York, 1989.

M. R. Quillian, "The Teachable Language Comprehender: A Simulation Program and Theory of Language," *Commun. ACM* **12**, 459–476 (1969).

T. Roeper and E. Williams, eds., *Parameter Setting*, Reidel, Dordrecht, 1987.

D. E. Rumelhart and J. L. McClelland, "On Learning the Past Tenses of English Verbs," in *Parallel Distributed Processing*, Vol. 2, Bradford/MIT Press, Cambridge, Mass., 1986, pp. 216–271.

D. E. Rumelhart and J. L. McClelland, "Learning the Past Tenses of English Verbs: Implicit Rules or Parallel Distributed Processing," in B. MacWhinney, 1987, pp. 195–248.

J. Sachs and L. Truswell, "Comprehension of Two-Word Instruction by Children in the One-Word Stage," *J. Child Lang.* **5**, 17–24 (1978).

R. C. Schank, "Identification of Conceptionalizations Underlying Natural Language," in R. C. Schank and K. M. Colby, eds., *Computer Models of Thought and Language*, Freeman, San Francisco, 1973, pp. 187–248.

M. Selfridge, "Why Do Children Say 'Goed'?: A Computer Model of Child Generation," in *Proceedings of the Third Annual Conference of the Cognitive Science Society*, Berkeley, Calif., 1981, pp. 131–132.

M. Selfridge, "Inference and Learning in a Computer Model of the Development of Language Comprehension in a Young Child," in W. Lehnert and M. H. Ringle, eds., *Strategies for Natural Language Processing*, Hillsdale, N.J., 1982, pp. 299–326.

J. M. Siskind, "Acquiring Core Meanings of Words, Represented as Jackendoff-Style Conceptual Structures, from Correlated Streams of Linguistic and Non-Linguistic Input," in *Proceed-*

ings of the Twenty-eighth Annual Meeting of the Association for Computational Linguistics, University of Pittsburgh, Pittsburgh, Penn., 1990.

B. F. Skinner, Verbal Behavior, Appleton-Century-Crofts, New York, 1957.

D. Slobin, "Crosslinguistic Evidence for the Language-Making Capacity," in D. Slobin, ed., The Crosslinguistic Study of Language Acquisition, Erlbaum, Hillsdale, N.J., 1984.

L. Solan and T. Roeper, "Children's Use of Syntactic Structure in Interpreting Relative Clauses," in H. Goodluck and L. Solan, eds., Papers in the Structure and Development of Child Language, University of Massachusetts Occasional Papers in Linguistics, Vol. 4, 1978, pp. 105–126.

H. Tager-Flusberg, J. deVilliers, and K. Hakuta, "The Development of Sentence Coordination," in S. Kuczaj II, ed., Language Development: Problems, Theories and Controversies, Vol. 1: Syntax and Semantics, Erlbaum, Hillsdale, N.J., 1982.

D. Waltz, ed., "Special Issue: Connectionist Models and Their Applications," Cog. Sci. 9(1) (1985).

S. Wermter, "Learning Semantic Relationships in Compound Nouns with Connectionist Networks," in Proceedings of the Eleventh Annual Conference of the Cognitive Science Society, 1989.

S. Wermter and W. G. Lenhert, "A Hybrid Symbolic/Connectionist Model for Noun Phrase Understanding," Connection Sci. 1(3) (1989).

K. Wexler and P. Culicover, Formal Principles of Language Acquisition, MIT Press, Cambridge, Mass., 1980.

J. G. Wolff, "Language Acquisition and the Discovery of Phrase Structure," Lang. Speech 23, 255–269 (1980).

J. G. Wolff, "Language Acquisition, Data Compression and Generalization," Lang. Commun. 2(1), 57–89 (1982).

W. Woods, "What's in a Link: Foundations of Semantic Networks," in D. Bobrow and A. Collins, eds., Representation and Understanding: Studies in Cognitive Science, Academic Press, Orlando, Fla., 1975.

U. Zernik, Strategies in Language Acquisitions: Learning Phrases from Example in Context, Ph.D. dissertation, University of California, Los Angeles, 1987.

General References

Berwick (1985) and McClelland and Rumelhart (1986) are good general references.

J. R. Anderson, "A Theory of Language Acquisition Based on General Learning Principles," Proceedings of the Seventh International Conference on Artificial Intelligence, 1981, pp. 97–103.

E. Bates and B. MacWhinney, "Functionalist Approaches to Grammar," in E. Wanner and L. Gleitman, eds., 1982.

M. D. S. Braine, "The Acquisition of Language in Infant and Child," in C. Reed, ed., The Learning of Language, Appleton-Century-Crofts, New York, 1971.

J. Bresnan, "A Realistic Transformational Grammar," in G. Miller, J. Bresnan, and M. Halle, eds., Linguistic Theory and Psychological Reality, MIT Press, Cambridge, Mass., 1978.

N. Chomsky, "A Review of B. F. Skinner's Verbal Behavior," Language 35(1), 26–58 (1959).

E. V. Clark, "What's in a Word? On the Child's Acquisition of Semantics in His First Language," in T. E. Moore, ed., Cognitive Development and the Acquisition of Language, Academic Press, Orlando, Fla., 1973.

J. C. Hill and M. A. Arbib, "Schemas, Computation, and Language Acquisition," Hum. Dev. 27, 282–296 (1984).

J. Moulton and G. Robinson, The Organization of Language, Cambridge University Press, London, 1981.

A. M. Peters, "Language Segmentation: Operating Principles for the Perception and Analysis of Language," in D. Slobin, ed., The Crosslinguistic Study of Language Acquisition, Erlbaum, Hillsdale, N.J., 1984.

S. A. Pinker, "A Theory of the Acquisition of Lexical-Interpretive Grammars," in J. Bresnan, ed., The Mental Representation of Grammatical Relations, MIT Press, Cambridge, Mass., 1982.

S. Pinker, Learnability and Cognition, Bradford/MIT Press, Cambridge, Mass., 1989.

E. L. Rissland, "Examples and Learning Systems," in O. Selfridge, E. Rissland, and M. A. Arbib, eds., Adaptive Control of Ill-Defined Systems, Plenum Press, New York, 1984.

S. L. Tavakolian, ed., Language Acquisition and Linguistic Theory, MIT Press, Cambridge, Mass., 1981.

E. Wanner and L. Gleitman, eds., Language Acquisition: The State of the Art, Cambridge University Press, London, 1982.

J. C. HILL
Dickinson College

LANGUAGES, OBJECT ORIENTED

Object. *Noun.*
1. *Something physical or mental of which a subject is cognitively aware.*
2. *Something which arouses emotion in an observer.*
Webster's New Collegiate Dictionary

Object-oriented programming is a style of programming that is based on directly representing physical objects and mental concepts in the machine. The goal is to make the machine cognitively aware of the physical world and able to reason about it using mental representations. Because this goal is at the heart of AI, object-oriented programming is recognized among many researchers as the most appropriate vehicle for intelligent computation. But the second dictionary definition applies to object-oriented programming as well. The debate between adherents of object-oriented programming and advocates of alternative styles often arouses strong emotions.

OBJECT-ORIENTED LANGUAGES PROVIDE BUILDING BLOCKS FOR CONSTRUCTING INTELLIGENT PROGRAMS

It is the task of AI programmers to bridge the seemingly unfathomable gap between the flexible, creative, unpredictable performance of humans in problem solving and the rigid, mechanical, step-by-step nature of contemporary computers. Obviously, it is too difficult to try to impart intelligence to the machine all at once. Instead, an intelligent program is built out of parts, each of which is slightly less intelligent. Each of these parts is further broken down into smaller fragments, each of which relies on less knowledge and expertise. Finally, there are the least intelligent parts, which behave mechanistically, blindly following rules just like the robots portrayed in cartoons.

A good programming language for AI must support this kind of program construction, building a problem solver out of parts, each of which can act like a little problem solver itself. That's how object-oriented programming works. An AI program is implemented as a collection of active objects, or actors. Each object represents a specialized part of a problem solver and has its own local knowledge and expertise. Each object is defined in terms of other objects to which it can send messages to solve problems for it. Each object is defined by its behavior in response to messages received from other objects. What kinds of problem-solving (qv) capabilities should intelligent building blocks for AI programs have?

Each Object Has the Ability to Store Information. A problem solver must have memory to remember information it learns, which may be of use in the future. In an object-oriented language each object has a set of private data, called its acquaintances, or instance variables. Giving each object the ability to store information means that any object in the system can be made to learn over time.

Each Object Has the Ability to Process Information. Thinking requires processing power. Rather than concentrating processing power in a centralized interpreter, object-oriented programming distributes the ability to process information among the collection of objects that make up a system (see LOGIC; INFERENCE). Each object is defined by its behavior, expressed in a program called a script, which says what action an object takes when it receives a message. Procedures specific to a particular subset of messages are called methods. In conventional languages procedures are active, but data like numbers and arrays are passive. In object-oriented languages even numbers and arrays can potentially be active, taking actions in response to messages. A simple array object could respond to a message, asking it to look up an element by indexing into a table, but a more complex object could perhaps perform logical deduction or apply heuristics to respond to a similar message.

Each Object Has the Ability to Communicate. A problem solver may need to ask other problem solvers for information necessary for its work and help out other problem solvers with the results of its efforts. Object-oriented languages perform computation by sending messages between objects. Giving each object the ability to communicate means that knowledge can be partitioned into independent areas of expertise. They can interact with each other to solve problems the way different people in a society cooperate to accomplish goals (Kornfeld and Hewitt, 1981; Minsky, 1987).

Each Object Has the Ability to Create New Information. Problem solving may generate new information or new solution methods in the course of processing. The amount and kind of information generated often cannot be predicted in advance. With object-oriented programming, an object may create new objects dynamically as the problem-solving process proceeds. This may mean just creating new instances or copies of previously introduced objects. It may also imply the creation of completely new kinds of objects, with behavior that abstracts, generalizes, specializes, or combines that of others.

Object-oriented programming endows each object with all of the fundamental capabilities mentioned above: storage, processing power, and communication. In conventional languages these capabilities are fragmented. Each basic data type has only a fixed and very limited repertoire of behavior, only allowing some of the fundamental problem-solving capabilities outlined above. Only procedures have the ability to compute; data structures like numbers, strings, and lists cannot be programmed to take action like procedures can. Only mutable variables, arrays, and list cells have the ability to store information. Only I–O primitives have the ability to communicate. Integrating all of these capabilities is what gives object-oriented programming its power.

Because software for AI evolves rapidly, it is difficult to foresee what capabilities will be needed in representing a concept. It is possible to start by representing a block in a blocks-world program with the use of a list of position and color. A later decision to change the format of the list or reimplement the block as a procedure would normally require changing all the programs that access the block. Implementing the block as an active object means that the representation of the block concept can always be made smarter without altering programs that use it.

A MEDICAL EXAMPLE ILLUSTRATES OBJECT-ORIENTED PROGRAMMING IN AI APPLICATIONS

The best way to write an object-oriented program is to anthropomorphize the concepts that make up the program. For each important concept the programmer can imagine an intelligent expert whose job it is to deal with that concept. The expert stores knowledge about that particular concept, can solve problems regarding it, and can answer questions about it. Each such expert is implemented as an object.

The process of writing an object-oriented program consists of deciding what kinds of objects are needed, what kinds of messages they will respond to, and what kinds of actions the objects will take in response to the messages. Describing the program using a procedural English notation will avoid the distraction of discussing the syntax of particular object-oriented languages. Names of particular objects and messages are capitalized, and the descriptions are indented to show the structure of the program.

How would object-oriented programming apply in an example AI application? An example from the domain of medical diagnosis serves to illustrate how the programming techniques are used (see MEDICINE, AI IN). An apology to medical experts: the examples here have been drastically simplified for expository purposes. They are meant to be suggestive rather than accurate.

First an object is introduced that serves as the computer's representation of the patient. The messages to this object represent the interactions between the medical system and the human patient. The patient object can receive a message asking for symptoms, and, of course, each symptom, such as fever, is itself an object. Each fever object may carry with it particular information such as its temperature and duration. A simple model of diagnosis is to associate with each symptom a set of possible causes and investigate each hypothesized cause in order of its likelihood. The fragment of the program dealing with fevers might read as follows (again, keep in mind that these examples are oversimplified):

Define a Fever object as a kind of Symptom object
    Each Fever object has
        A Temperature, by default 100°F.
        A Duration, for example, 2 days.

If I'm a Fever object, and I get a message asking for my Most Likely Cause,
    I ask my Temperature whether it is greater than 100, and ask my Duration whether it is greater than 3 days.
    If so, I reply with a Serious-Infection.
    Otherwise I reply with the Flu.

Diseases like the flu, of course, are represented by objects in the same way. A disease might, in turn, store a list enumerating its most probable symptoms. Thus a simple top-level control structure for a diagnosis program might read as follows:

Send a message to the Patient object asking for Symptoms.
Pick a Symptom object, and ask the Symptom for its Likely Cause, returning a Disease object.
Ask the Disease object for its typical Symptoms, and see if the Patient has any of these other Symptoms as well.
If the Symptoms of the Disease are all the same as the Symptoms the Patient has
    Send a message to the Disease object asking for its Treatment.
    Suggest the Treatment for the Patient.

A treatment is another kind of object. Specific kinds of treatments can be built out of the object for treatment by the technique of inheritance or delegation, discussed below. Other kinds of treatments might include physical therapy or surgery. Drug treatment objects may respond to messages asking for their recommended dosage or contraindications by accessing an on-line version of the *Physician's Desk Reference*.

By defining an object to represent a category of drugs, such as Antibiotics, general information about antibiotics need not be repeated in the objects representing particular drugs, such as Penicillin. When an object like Penicillin receives a message, it first tries to reply based on its own local knowledge and expertise. If the knowledge specific to penicillin is not sufficient, the message is delegated to the object for its drug family, such as antibiotics. If this does not suffice, the object for all drugs is called on, and so on.

This inventory of objects for medical diagnosis programs illustrates a fundamental principle of organization for object-oriented programs. Knowledge about how to use each individual concept in a domain resides in the object

for that concept. A large part of becoming an expert in a domain is assimilating technical concepts. These are useful because the knowledge for each one is relatively independent of the others, and they can interact with each other in predictable ways. Objects provide a means for directly representing the kinds of technical concepts that give human experts their problem-solving power.

Contrast this with the alternative rule-based style of AI programming (see RULE-BASED SYSTEMS). A rule-based program consists of a large number of independent rules, in an if–then form, of which the following might be typical:

If the patient has a fever,
    and the fever is above 100°F,
    and the fever lasts for more than 3 days,
Then the patient probably has a serious infection (with probability 75%).

Instead of being organized around objects that represent the important concepts of the problem domain, a rule-based program is a uniform collection of rules, each of which describes a certain situation that can occur. The chief advantage of rules is that it is easy to add a new rule to the collection. The corresponding disadvantage is that knowledge about particular concepts such as fevers or penicillin is scattered throughout the program. Adding a new rule regarding fevers to a large set of rules may cause surprising interactions that can be difficult to debug. If one wants to state what to do if the fever is above 100°F but less than three days in duration, the conditions in the rule must be repeated, making it harder to share knowledge about similar situations. Object-oriented programs keep knowledge associated with a particular concept more localized.

In addition to an association-oriented approach to diagnosis, which simply tries to match diseases and symptoms that are commonly found together, a more advanced approach might try to reason about the functionality of parts of the body to trace causes. Object-oriented programming becomes useful here in modeling organs, blood vessels, and other body parts as objects. Each part keeps track of other parts to which it is connected. Messages sent from one part to another model the actions that each part performs.

Define a Lung object to be a kind of Organ object.
    With entering Blood Vessels and Leaving Blood Vessels.

If I'm a Lung and I get a Breathe message, with a Blood-Flow,
    I send the Entering Blood Vessels a message to Decrease the Carbon Dioxide content of the Blood Flow.
    I send the Leaving Blood Vessels a message to Increase the Oxygen content of the Blood Flow.

Thus an important component of a medical program can be a functional simulation of the body's various systems. Knowing that a disease affects the lungs might lead to the hypothesis that there will be an adverse effect on the oxygen content of the blood.

The top-level control in such a simulation consists of sending messages to objects representing all the body systems in parallel, telling each one to begin performing its specific function. Object-oriented programming is especially well suited to this kind of simulation. Because object-oriented programs can have many objects active simultaneously, sending and receiving messages, the kind of parallelism that takes place in the body, where all the various systems are active simultaneously, can be naturally modeled.

DEFINING OBJECTS BY THEIR MESSAGE-PASSING BEHAVIOR YIELDS MODULARITY AND EXTENSIBILITY

Why is it so important for AI to represent concepts as active objects and computation by message-passing behavior? Although simple scientific and business applications can get away with representing concepts in only a single way, complex AI programs may need more than one representation for a concept. Conventional programming usually requires choosing specific storage formats for data, and users of that data are dependent on knowledge of the storage format. Having multiple representations of a concept in a traditional program usually means that the users must know which particular representation is being used at any given time. Because objects are defined solely by their message-passing behavior, each object is free to implement its response in a unique way. A program can make use of a concept without knowing the exact details of its internal representation. Thus object-oriented programming provides better support for programs that make frequent use of multiple representations.

Computation in AI is so diverse that the flexibility of changing implementation details of a component of a program without affecting users of that component is essential. In the medical example, symptom objects might have many different ways of responding to a message asking for their possible causes. A symptom might merely store a list of possibilities and deliver that list whenever it is asked the question. In this case it would be playing the role of a data structure in conventional languages. In another case determining the possible causes of a symptom might require running a functional simulation so that the symptoms's role would be more akin to that of a procedure in conventional languages. If users of the symptom object interact with it only via messages, the resulting program is insensitive to the details of the implementation of the symptom.

OBJECT-ORIENTED PROGRAMMING PERMITS SHARING KNOWLEDGE BETWEEN RELATED GROUPS OF OBJECTS

All knowledge pertaining to drugs in general should be grouped in a single object, and this knowledge extended to particular drugs, such as penicillin and digitalis, by simply defining the unique characteristics of each drug without repeating common information. There are two major

mechanisms for this, and different object-oriented languages take different positions on this issue.

One is inheritance (see IHERITANCE HIERARCHY), which involves defining a class to represent a set of objects and to be used as a blueprint for making instance objects representing particular members of that set. The class is given a list of names for instance variables, and each instance can supply its own values for these variables. The class defines methods, procedures for responding to particular kinds of messages. Every instance uses its class's methods to decide how to respond to messages.

Subclasses can build on the knowledge of previous classes, adding more instance variables and methods, so that antibiotic is defined as a subclass of drug. Each instance object gets a new copy of each of the variables of its class, the superclass of that class, and so on. When a message is sent to an instance, first the methods of the class are tried, then the message of its superclass, and so on, going up the class chain.

An alternative strategy is delegation. Rather than divide the world into classes and instances, each object serves as a prototype. A prototypical object can form new objects by making copies of itself (perhaps with modifications) or by creating new objects that have additional behavior and forward the message to the prototype in the event that the additional behavior is not appropriate. This kind of forwarding messages is called delegation, analogous to the way a specialist physician might delegate responsibility for a patient to a physician in another specialty if the patient's malady proves outside the original physician's area of expertise. A penicillin object can be made by copying a prototypical antibiotic object and adding additional information. When a message is sent to the penicillin object, it can either respond based on its own local information and expertise or delegate the message to the more general antibiotic object.

OBJECT-ORIENTED LANGUAGES ARE WELL SUITED FOR PARALLELISM

AI programs have traditionally had a voracious appetite for computation power. The changing technology and economics of computer systems in the near future indicate that the primary route to increased performance will lie in the exploitation of parallelism in multiprocessor computer networks. Thus AI applications must move increasingly toward parallel programming techniques. Because neurons in the brain are slow compared to computer hardware, it is clear that the brain must rely on parallelism for its tremendous computation power. Modeling the parallelism of the mind requires computer languages that can exploit parallelism effectively.

One of the primary reasons AI researchers should be interested in object-oriented programming is that these languages are among the best for exploiting parallelism. Because knowledge in object-oriented programs is localized, each object containing its own local knowledge and expertise, different processors can work on different objects at the same time. Object-oriented programs do not rely on having global state, which can become a bottleneck in parallel systems. For example, the blackboard architecture (see BLACKBOARD SYSTEMS) adopted by some AI programs can clog up if many processors attempt to access the single blackboard simultaneously unless special care is taken to prevent this situation.

Parallelism brings with it the problem of synchronization, and object-oriented languages can contribute by providing objects that manage access to shared resources. Objects such as the serializers in Actor languages (Hewitt and co-workers, 1979), which protect actors with changeable internal state, can receive messages from many processes simultaneously but queue up requests so that changes to the internal state happen serially, avoiding inconsistencies. In languages that are wholly object oriented, where all computation happens by message passing, objects can be implemented that provide parallel computation and synchronization transparently. Uses of parallel resources need not be concerned with the prevention of low level timing errors, allowing parallel problem solvers to be programmed as easily as their serial counterparts.

Because objects are created dynamically, recovered by garbage collection, and dependent only on their message-passing behavior, objects can move from processor to processor in a parallel system in a flexible way. The number of processes need not be fixed in advance, and the allocation of problem-solving processes to physical processors can be made dynamically (Lieberman, 1986).

OBJECT-ORIENTED LANGUAGES HAVE A LONG HISTORY

It is nearly impossible to say who invented object-oriented programming; the ideas have developed out of a diverse group of programming cultures to which many have contributed.

The roots of object-oriented programming come from two strands: from the community of LISP programmers in AI and the community of Simula programmers working on simulation. Even early programs written in LISP, the second oldest programming language, made use of LISP's symbols to represent concepts in a manner reminiscent of today's object-oriented languages. Each symbol has a property list that can store information retrieved using another symbol as a key. The key acts like a message sent to the symbol representing an object. Because programs can be used as data in LISP, programs could be stored on property lists. Running programs retrieved from property lists was a popular technique for doing object-oriented programming. LISP's CONS primitive and garbage collection permitted creation of lists dynamically, so the essential ability to have dynamic objects was present. Papert's (1981) similar Logo language was taught to children with a model that explicitly talked about programming in terms of objects.

Simula (Britwistle and co-workers, 1973) pioneered the idea of classes, used to implement general objects that have knowledge to be shared by several instances. Subclasses could build on the behavior of previously defined classes, introducing the idea of inheritance among objects.

The simulation applications for which Simula was used required conceptual parallelism, having many objects active at the same time, but Simula provided only the pseudoparallelism of coroutines and a global scheduler.

At roughly the same time, Kay and Goldberg (1977) at Xerox and Hewitt (1979) at MIT realized that these techniques found in LISP and Simula could form the basis of a fundamentally different way of looking at computation and created the first object-oriented programming languages. Kay's SMALLTALK was designed as a language for people other than computer scientists to use for general information-handling needs (Goldberg and Robinson, 1983; Goldberg, 1984; Krasner, 1984). Hewitt's Actors were developed for AI applications (Hewitt and co-workers, 1980) and for understanding the theoretical nature of computation (Hewitt and Baker, 1977).

OBJECT-ORIENTED LANGUAGES HAVE GREAT DIVERSITY

It is difficult to say which current languages are truly object oriented because the ideas appear in different forms in different languages and supported to varying extents. Object-oriented programming is more a frame of mind than a particular language. It is possible to write object-oriented programs in nearly any language, even machine languages. Nevertheless, having explicit representations for objects, messages, and responses to messages can make a big difference in the convenience with which object-oriented programming can be used.

Object-oriented languages fall into two major categories: the uniform object-oriented languages and extensions to traditional languages. The uniform languages represent all computation in terms of objects and message passing. In these systems there are no passive data; every object can be active and receive messages. This is the most radical approach. To date, only SMALLTALK and the Actor languages are really uniform object-oriented languages in this sense.

The language extensions take an existing language with passive data and active procedures add a new data type to represent objects that can respond to messages. Traditional data types in the language, like numbers and arrays, are not themselves objects. LISP has been extended in this way in several different implementations, as have Algol-derived languages such as Pascal, C, and Ada, though the Algol family of languages are hampered by the lack of truly dynamic storage allocation with garbage collection. Examples of these are Flavors (Moon and co-workers, 1984), Loops (Bobrow and Stefik, 1983), and Director (Kahn, 1978) on the LISP side and Intermission (Kahn, 1982) in PROLOG, Traits (Curry and co-workers, 1982) and Clu (Liskov and co-workers, 1977) based on Algol-like languages, and Objective C and Apple's Object Pascal.

The advantage of a uniform representation is greater modularity and extensibility. Uniformity allows building new kinds of numbers and lists or other system data types as easily as any other sort of object. It obviates the need to determine that an expression yields a user-defined object before attempting to send it a message. The disadvantage is that uniform implementations can be less efficient on conventional machines because conventional optimizations may involve knowledge of specific storage formats in violation of the message-passing protocol.

The emergence of new machine architectures that specifically support object-oriented programming holds out the promise that object-oriented languages will be no less efficient than procedural languages. Parallelism holds out the promise that object-oriented languages will be a more effective way to harness increased processing power for AI applications. Object-oriented languages will no doubt win an increasingly prominent place in the tool kit of the AI programmer.

BIBLIOGRAPHY

G. M. Birtwistle, O-J. Dahl, B. Myhrhaug, and K. Nygaard, *Simula Begin*, Van Nostrand Reinhold, New York, 1973.

D. Bobrow and M. Stefik, "Knowledge Programming in Loops," *AI Mag.* 4(3), 3–13 (1983).

G. Curry, L. Baer, D. Lipkie, and B. Lee, "Traits: An Approach to Multiple-Inheritance Subclassing," *Conference on Office Information Systems*, Philadelphia, Pa., ACM SIGOA, 1982, pp. 1–9.

A. Goldberg, *Smalltalk-80: The Interactive Programming Environment*, Addison-Wesley Publishing Co., Inc., Reading, Mass., 1984.

A. Goldberg and D. Robson, *Smalltalk-80: The Language and its Implementation*, Addison-Wesley Publishing Co., Inc., Reading, Mass., 1983.

C. Hewitt, "Viewing Control Structures as Patterns of Passing Messages," in P. Winston and R. Brown, eds., *Artificial Intelligence, an MIT Perspective*, MIT Press, Cambridge, Mass., 1979, pp. 433–465.

C. Hewitt and H. Baker, "Laws for Communicating Parallel Processes," in *1977 IFIP Congress Proceedings*, Toronto, Ont., 1977, pp. 987–992.

C. Hewitt, G. Attardi, and H. Lieberman, "Specifying and Proving Properties of Guardians for Distributed Systems," in *Conference on Semantics of Concurrent Computing*, Evian, France, Springer-Verlag, New York, 1979, pp. 316–336.

C. Hewitt, G. Attardi, and M. Simi, "Knowledge Embedding with a Description System," in *Proceedings of the First National Annual Conference on Artificial Intelligence*, Stanford, Calif., AAAI, Menlo Park, Calif., 1980, pp. 157–164.

K. Kahn, "Dynamic Graphics Using Quasi-Parallelism," in *ACM SigGraph Conference*, Atlanta, Ga., 1978, pp. 357–362.

K. Kahn, "Intermission—Actors in Prolog," in *Logic Programming*, Academic Press, Inc.., Orlando, Fla., 1982, pp. 213–230.

A. Kay and A. Goldberg, "Personal Dynamic Media," *IEEE* 10(3), 31–39 (1977).

W. A. Kornfield and C. Hewitt, "The Scientific Community Metaphor," *IEEE Trans. Sys. Man Cybernet.* SMC-11(1), 24–33 (1981).

G. Krasner, ed., *Smalltalk-80: Bits of History and Words of Advice*, Addison-Wesley Publishing Co., Inc., Reading, Mass., 1984.

H. Lieberman, "Expecting the Unpredictable: When Computers Can Think in Parallel," in L. Vaina, ed., *Matters of Intelligence*, D. Reidel, Amsterdam, 1986.

B. Liskov, A. Snyder, R. Atkinson, and C. Schaffert, "Abstraction Mechanisms in Clu," *CACM* 20(8), 564–576 (1977).

M. Minsky, *The Society of Mind*, Simon & Shuster, New York, 1987.

D. Moon and co-workers, *Lisp Machine Manual*, Symbolics and MIT Press, Cambridge, Mass., 1984.

S. Papert, *Mindstorms*, Basic Books, New York, 1981.

General References

H. Baker and C. Hewitt, "The Incremental Garbage Collection of Processes," in *Conference on Artificial Intelligence and Programming Languages*, ACM, Rochester, N.Y., 1977, pp. 55–60.

A. Borning, "ThingLab—An Object-Oriented System for Building Simulations Using Constraints," in *Proceedings of the Fifth IJCAI*, Cambridge, Mass., Morgan-Kaufmann, San Mateo, Calif., 1977, pp. 497–498.

R. J. Byrd, S. E. Smith, and S. P. deJong, "An Actor-Based Programming System," in *Conference on Office Information Systems*, Philadelphia, 1982, Association for Computing Machinery, New York, pp. 67–78.

C. Hewitt and H. Lieberman, "Design Issues in Parallel Systems for Artificial Intelligence," in *Proceedings of the CompCon-84 Conference*, IEEE, San Francisco, 1984, pp. 418–423.

K. Kahn, *Uniform—A Language Based upon Unification which Unifies (much of) Lisp, Prolog, and Act 1*, Technical Report, University of Uppsala, Uppsala, Sweden, 1981.

H. Lieberman, *A Preview of Act 1*, AI Memo **625**, MIT, Cambridge, Mass., 1981.

H. Lieberman, "Machine Tongues: Object Oriented Programming," *Comput. Mus. J.* 6(3), 8–21 (1982).

H. Lieberman, "An Object Oriented Simulator for the Apiary," in *Proceedings of the Third Conference on Artificial Intelligence*, Washington, D.C., AAAI, Menlo Park, Calif., 1983, pp. 241–246.

H. LIEBERMAN
MIT

LAW, AI IN

Since the earliest days of computing, there have been lawyers who were excited by the prospect of intelligent machines. Well before the term artificial intelligence was invented, there had been proposals to use computers for retrieving legal source materials (Kelso, 1946) and for analyzing the leeways available to a judge in deciding a new case (Frank, 1949). There were also, of course, many ideas about less ambitious uses of computers in the law (Tapper, 1973; Bigelow, 1981).

There were good reasons for lawyers to envision more than routine data-processing applications of computers. The reasons stem from the philosophy of law, or jurisprudence, which in the United States has dealt mainly with the problem of judicial decision making (Hart, 1977). The underlying concern is a practical one. Given that judicial decisions may be highly controversial and may affect everyone, what is it for a decision to be rationally justified? From this question, it is only a short step to the questions of how far legal reasoning is mechanizable and how far legal decisions are, or ought to be, computable. The relevant writers include Holmes (1897), Cardozo (1921), Levi

(1949), Llewellyn (1960a, 1960b), Hart (1961), and Dworkin (1977). A concise survey of the issues appears in Hart (1967). Gilmore (1977) provides a salutary historical perspective.

Early thinking about intelligent programs in law (Jones, 1962; Baade, 1963; Allen and Caldwell, 1965) was concurrent with the early development of AI; there was not much interaction. The actual programs were of two main types. One group of programs was described as concerned with the prediction of judicial decisions or, more generally, with the analysis of judicial behavior. In these programs the data represented the fact patterns in a large number of somewhat similar cases. The universe of possible fact patterns was defined by a predetermined set of propositions, some subset of which (or their negations) was taken to represent the facts of any particular case. The outcome of each case was viewed as a mathematical function of its facts. The general problem was to determine a good function, which could then be used to predict the results in other cases. Surveys of this work (Tapper, 1973; Mackaay and Robillard, 1974) and some related recent projects (Harr and co-workers, 1977; Bing, 1980; Borchgrevink and Hansen, 1980) have been published.

Second, there was the problem of information retrieval or, more accurately, document retrieval. After many experiments and much debate (Fraenkel, 1968; Bing and Harvold, 1977) the approach to this task generally settled down to a common one. It involved storing essentially the full text of the statutes, court decisions, and other documents to be retrieved; the user queried the database by giving a Boolean combination of keywords that were expected to appear in the relevant documents. This approach has been refined and made the basis of the major commercial retrieval systems (Bing and Harvold, 1977; Sprowl, 1976).

A third area of early work, not so immediately focused on computer implementation, was the application of formal logic (qv) to the law. This topic is associated primarily with the work of Allen (eg, 1957, 1963, 1980). The aim was to represent statutes and other legal documents in a way that avoided syntactic ambiguity, in particular, ambiguity about the scope of logical connectives and about the mapping from English words like *if* and *unless* to these connectives. There was also interest in deontic logic, the logic of statements about what is required, permitted, or prohibited (Anderson, 1958).

By the early 1970s, the initial efforts in all these areas had lost much of their intellectual momentum. In the area of predicting judicial decisions the premises and the significance of the research had been criticized as, at best, unclear (Stone, 1966, 1964a; Fuller, 1966). In information retrieval a number of observers felt that the keyword approach had reached its limits (Boyd, 1972; Leininger and Gilchrist, 1973), and in Canada a report prepared for the government recommended against continued public funding (Slayton, 1974). In addition, the translation of law into formulas of logic was subject to two difficulties. First, the work was limited to the propositional level; problems of intrapropositional structure and the meaning of the non-logical vocabulary remained untouched. Second, when real ambiguities were found, the formalism pressed the translator to make a choice among readings, even if it was an open question what reading the courts would eventually adopt. For this reason, the development of a normal form for statutes seemed much better adapted for use in the initial drafting of statutes than for representation of existing ones.

EARLY AI WORK IN LAW

The beginning of AI work proper in law can be dated to 1970, with a paper by Buchanan and Headrick (1970) and also Mehl (1958). The lawyer's task, as Buchanan and Headrick saw it, was always goal directed, on behalf of a client. Two general situations were envisioned. In one the relevant events had already occurred; the lawyer's task was to advise the client about rights and liabilities and to construct an argument why the client should win the case. Suggesting that clear yes or no answers are rare in the law, the authors emphasized the problem of argument construction. In the second situation the client sought advice about future actions to achieve the goals, including business and other goals as well as legal ones. Here, the ideal was to find a plan in which the client's actions closely matched some favorable, prototypical legal situation and which also minimized the risks to the client's other goals.

In the remainder of their paper Buchanan and Headrick tried to identify some of the lawyer's thought processes and to map these onto some of the then-current work in AI. The thought processes mentioned are finding conceptual linkages in pursuing goals; recognizing and characterizing relevant facts; resolving rule conflicts, by finding or constructing other rules; and finding and using analogies. The AI work discussed includes Heuristic DENDRAL (Lindsay and co-workers, 1980), the General Problem Solver Newell and Simon, 1963), and Evans's (1968) analogy program. From the perspective of 15 years later, the paper shows an interesting tension between the complexities of legal reasoning (then and now, far from fully analyzed) and the relative simplicity of the early AI techniques and the well-formed problems to which they had been applied. The importance of DENDRAL was that it succeeded in reducing a significant real-world problem to a well-formed one within the grasp of AI and yet produced results of interest to chemists who were concerned with the original problem, not with the AI version. The question raised by Buchanan and Headrick was whether the same could be done for law. AI researchers are still exploring that question.

The first implemented AI programs in law were, of necessity, much narrower in scope than the one Buchanan and Headrick envisioned. Maggs and deBessonet (1972) looked toward developing "a generalized formal language approach to the analysis of systems of legal rules" that would permit "questions of an extremely specific nature" to be answered. These authors used a set of rules based on statutes and expressed in a normalized propositional calculus (see LOGIC, PROPOSITIONAL). The main element of their program was a theorem prover (see THEOREM PROVING) implemented in LISP and using a British Museum algorithm (Newell and Simon, 1972). Suggested applications of the program included determining whether the rules were consistent and nonredundant, answering questions about liability, and generating questions to be asked in a client interview.

Popp and Schlink's (1975) program, JUDITH, was an interactive consultation system patterned on MYCIN (Shortliffe, 1976). Its rule base, which apparently dealt mostly with the law of negligence, was drawn from the German Civil Code. The program's dialogue with the user proceeded top down, asking yes–no questions in an attempt to establish a basis for liability. A user response meaning "I don't know" was permitted; its effect was to invoke the next lower level of rules. The authors suggested that if the rules bottomed out and the user still did not know, the program should refer him to an information retrieval system.

Both JUDITH and the Maggs and deBessonet program represented legal rules at the propositional level. There was no separate representation for the facts of a case; the situation to which the rules were being applied could be described only in terms of whether these legal propositions were true. This left a heavy burden of legal expertise on the system user. From another viewpoint, it meant that the approach captured only one small aspect of legal knowledge.

The next steps were taken by McCarty (1977), in the program TAXMAN I, and Meldman (1977). In each of these projects the input was a statement of the facts of a case; the output, some conclusions about their legal import. Both the facts and the law were now represented with predicate—argument structures, not unanalyzed propositions. In McCarty's case the language used was a modified version of Microplanner (Sussman and co-workers, 1971); in Meldman's, a notation meant to be converted to the not-yet-implemented language OWL (Szolovits and co-workers, 1977).

In TAXMAN I, the subject matter was the taxation of corporate reorganizations under the Internal Revenue Code. The relevant code provisions define several types of tax-free reorganization. Given a representation of facts such as "Phellis owns 250 shares of the common stock of the Delaware corporation" and "the Delaware corporation transferred its assets to the New Jersey corporation," TAXMAN I determined whether, according to its definitions, any of three different types of tax-free corporate reorganization had taken place.

As McCarty pointed out, TAXMAN I embodied much too narrow a picture of legal reasoning to be accurate. The program reached its conclusions deductively, leaving no space within which opposing lawyers might argue about whether a given reorganization qualified as tax free. Furthermore, although the axioms defining a tax-free reorganization were based on the definitions in the Internal Revenue Code, there had been three Supreme Court cases in which the literal definition was satisfied but in which, the Court held, the reorganization was taxable because some other element was missing. How could such a move

be legitimate, and how could a program have found the move? These questions were the impetus for the TAXMAN II project described below.

In Meldman (1977), the subject matter was the tort law of assault and battery. Unlike the statute law of the projects mentioned above, assault and battery is primarily a case law area—that is, an area in which the rules have developed out of judicial decisions over the years, not by discrete legislative enactment. In this respect the law of torts is typical of the subjects traditionally stressed in U.S. legal education and jurisprudence. But given the primacy of judicial decisions and, at the same time, the practice of describing the law in terms of general rules, Meldman had to treat the relationship between the rules and the precedents as well as the bearing of both on the analysis of a new case. Thus his was the first AI project to represent more than one source of legal knowledge.

For Meldman, the dichotomy between specific cases and general rules was in part a distinction between primary and secondary authority. The most general rules in the knowledge base were attributed to secondary authority, namely, to a fictitious encyclopedia called *Corpus Juris Mechanicum*. With the cases as primary legal authority, the question arose, as it always does in studies of legal reasoning, of how a case can be authority for anything beyond its own particular facts. Meldman (1977) managed the answer in a very simple way: the case was itself represented as a rule. The content of the rule differed from the rules of secondary authority only in that it was "often more specific"; the form differed in that it was attributed to a particular decision, whose specific facts were also stored but not used in the reasoning process.

The input to Meldman's (1977) system was a representation of a simple hypothetical case, such as the following: "With the purpose of frightening Gordon Good, Howard Hood visibly points a saturday-night special at him and grabs the umbrella that he is holding. The Saturday-night special is not loaded." The top-level goal of the system was to find an instance of assault, or battery, or both. Subgoals could succeed by the application of rules based on secondary authority, by matching to the rules of the cases, and if all else failed, by asking the user. The use of cases differed from the use of other rules in that a case could match either exactly, with the help of an abstraction hierarchy; or by analogy. The version of analogy used was too simple, as Meldman recognized. In effect, it simply permitted the rule of a case to be temporarily generalized by replacing all its predicates by their parents in the abstraction hierarchy. A more basic problem, however, was the way cases were used even for exact (nonanalogical) matching. Meldman assumed a functional correspondence between cases and the rules they stood for; in doing so, he relied centrally on the concept of the holding or *ratio decidendi* of a case. This concept is a standard one in the law, but it quickly breaks down under examination: a finite amount of data, which can be described in many different ways, does not determine a unique general rule (Stone, 1964b). The question of how best to represent and use cases in a legal reasoning program is still a research problem.

RECENT DEVELOPMENT OF LEGAL ANALYSIS PROGRAMS

TAXMAN II

A question that runs throughout legal analysis programs is how should the connection between the general words or concepts employed in legal rules and the situations to which the rules may be applied be thought of. Clearly, there is always a description of the situation to work with, not the situation itself. It is assumed, in most research, that this description is fixed and undisputed. But the situation description itself must use general language. The question becomes how that language connects with the general language of the rule.

In TAXMAN I, the connections were treated as definitional. For instance, one kind of corporate reorganization, a B-REORGANIZATION, was defined in terms of ACQUISITION and CONTROL; ACQUISITION, in terms of a list of EXCHANGES: EXCHANGE, in terms of a pair of TRANSFERS. Furthermore, the definitions were thought of as creating a conceptual hierarchy whose elements were connected by relations of abstraction and expansion. Thus a legal concept like B-REORGANIZATION was seen as a straightforward abstraction from more concrete descriptions of situations.

Some legal concepts, McCarty observed, do not have this tidy structure. The initial examples were the extra requirements for a tax-free reorganization, which had been imposed by the Supreme Court although they were not mentioned in the statute. The concepts the Court used, which go under the names *continuity of interest, business purpose,* and *step transactions,* were seen as amorphous concepts, which TAXMAN I was unable to represent.

Understanding the nature and use of amorphous concepts is the major goal of TAXMAN II (McCarty and co-workers, 1979; McCarty and Sridharan, 1980, 1981). In this work, now using the representation language AIMDS (Sridharan, 1978), two styles of conceptual representation are provided. The simpler, which provides the capabilities of TAXMAN I, is called a logical template representation. For concepts treated as amorphous, the representation is in terms of prototypes, an idea whose background in the literature includes Wittgenstein's (1958) family resemblances, Hart's (1960) open texture, Putnam's (1975) stereotypes, and Minsky's (1975) similarity networks of frames. The representation proposed, called a *prototype-and-deformation* model of conceptual structure, is described as having three elements: (*1*) optionally, an invariant that states necessary, but not sufficient, conditions for an instance of the concept; (*2*) a set of exemplars of the concept; and, to make the exemplars into more than a disjunctive definition, (*3*) a set of transformations stating how one exemplar can be mapped into another (McCarty and Sridharan, 1981). Algorithms for using the prototype-and-deformation structures are still under development (Nagel, 1983); there is also related work on analogy using the assumed purposes of legal rules (Kedar-Cabelli, 1984).

So far, the TAXMAN II work has focused on a different tax problem, namely, on the meaning of income in the 1913 constitutional amendment authorizing a federal income tax. In particular, McCarty and Sridharan (1981) consider a 1920 case in which the Supreme Court had to decide whether a stock dividend is income. Use of the representation is directed not to computing an answer to this question but to modeling the arguments made in the majority and dissenting opinions. One important aspect of the argument involved being able to say what it is to own common stock or other securities in terms of the rights and obligations that ownership entails. Largely for this reason, McCarty (1983a) has recently turned his attention to the logic of these concepts, deontic logic.

Gardner's Dissertation

In the work described above, two very different approaches to legal reasoning have been taken. One side, including the propositional logic programs and TAXMAN I, represents the law as a set of rules that can be applied deductively to reach a conclusion about liability in a given case. The other side, including the early prediction programs and the prototype structures of TAXMAN II, treats legal knowledge as knowledge of cases, from which it is possible to reason by comparison to other cases. Meldman's thesis encompassed both sides, but only by making drastic oversimplifications. TAXMAN II allows the two sides to coexist but says nothing about how they fit together. A starting point for Gardner's (1987, 1985) project is the need for a unified framework that can account for both these aspects of legal reasoning.

A second focus of Gardner's work concerns the problem of validation for a legal reasoning program or, viewed another way, the allocation of responsibility between the providers of such programs and their hypothetical users. To the extent that a program reaches definite conclusions (as opposed to finding analogies, for instance), there is an implicit claim that a user can rely on them. On some legal issues no such claim can be made, as in McCarty's stock dividend case, on which the justices of the Supreme Court disagreed. The question then arises, on what kinds of issues (if any) is it appropriate for a program to produce an answer? A program's conclusion about a legal issue must always be understood as only a default conclusion; any case may present special circumstances that were not anticipated in the knowledge base but that, once they occur, can be argued to override the computed result. Nevertheless, there are many points in each case that a legal reasoning program must determine but that lawyers would not even call issues, because it is somehow obvious to the parties on both sides that, with respect to these points, the case does not present any special circumstances. A framework for legal reasoning programs is proposed that has two main phases: first, heuristically settling the obvious points and identifying the serious issues, the hard questions in the case; and second, finding arguments on both sides of the hard questions. Reasoning from precedent cases, as providing analogies, prototypes, and the like, is viewed as part of the argument of hard questions, to be undertaken only on selected points in a case in a context of other findings that seem not to be problematical.

In the dissertation Gardner applies this framework to problems involving the formation of contracts by offer and acceptance. The program, written in LISP and using the representation language MRS (Genesereth, 1984), takes as input a representation of a problem from a law school or bar examination. The output is a data structure similar to a decision tree, in which the decision points correspond to the hard questions that must be resolved to decide the case. Two kinds of legal questions can be recognized. One kind asks what rule of law is to be applied; such questions reflect disagreement among courts or commentators about what the rules are or ought to be. The other, more common kind asks about the meaning of some word or phrase within a legal rule, that is, whether the case at hand presents an instance of some legal predicate. The need to raise such questions arises from a crucial feature of legal language: its meaning is not fully fixed in advance of its use in application to particular cases. This feature, often referred to as *open texture*, must be allowed for in any realistic legal reasoning program. In McCarty's terminology, all concepts are potentially amorphous concepts.

The problem then arises on how legal words can ever be applied confidently to situations described in nontechnical language. In other words, how can legal questions ever have clear answers, and how can a program recognize those that do? Gardner uses some initial heuristics based on the cases, in particular, on knowledge of situations that legal predicates have standardly been used to cover. For the further development of these heuristics, a novel kind of study of precedent cases is proposed. In the context of a dispute involving a described fact situation and some applicable legal rules, what points did all sides find so obvious as not to be worth discussing? How do these situations presenting clear cases on certain points, compare with cases in which those points were the important issues? Such a study may prove illuminating with respect to the general problem of commonsense knowledge (see REASONING, COMMONSENSE), which is a central problem for current AI (McCarthy, 1984a, 1984b).

Other Current Projects

Two other representative projects are those of Rissland at the University of Massachusetts and Waterman and Peterson at the Rand Corp. This pair of projects continues the contrast, introduced above, between case-based and rule-based approaches to legal reasoning.

Rissland's special interest is the use of examples in reasoning. Originally concerned with the elements of mathematical knowledge, in which examples figured prominently (Michener, 1978), she has turned to law as another domain where cases have an important role. The current work (Rissland, 1983, 1985; Rissland and co-workers, 1984; Ashley, 1985) deals largely with hypothetical cases, especially as they may be used in law teaching and in developing arguments in preparation for litigation. The principal domain is the law of trade secrets as applied to the protection of software. Each case, hypothetical or actual, is represented in a frame-based format (see FRAMES), where the slots are chosen to correspond to classes of facts, called dimensions, that have been identified as legally significant in the secondary literature. Unlike most projects, which take as fixed the description of the case at hand, Rissland's HYPO program treats the description as a hypothetical situation that is to be modified, along specified dimensions, to produce a new hypothetical case that is stronger for a specified party. The modifications are guided by comparison with cases stored in the knowledge base; they are to be used for purposes such as developing an argument from the precedents, assessing the strength of one's case, and coping with uncertainty about what will be proved at trial. Another aspect of the project involves the classification of detailed moves in argumentation, particularly the various purposes that can be served by introducing new facts or deleting facts from one's description of a situation.

Waterman and Peterson's project, (1981, 1984) unlike Rissland's, follows the paradigm of a rule-based system (qv). Noteworthy in this project is the kind of expert behavior to be modeled. Given a description of a personal injury claim, the question for the system is not how the case should be argued or decided but what dollar amount represents the worth, or settlement value, of the case. Among experienced lawyers and insurance claims adjusters, Waterman and Peterson find that this amount depends not just on the law but also on matters such as conventions for assigning a dollar value to pain and suffering, the nearness of the trial date, and the skill of the attorneys on both sides. Originally, the knowledge engineering approach to determining case worth was described as a way of doing empirical research into out-of-court-settlement practices (Waterman and Peterson, 1981). Currently, however, the authors are developing a system to estimate settlement values for asbestos personal injury claims, and this system is reportedly to be used in litigation pending in the U.S. District Court (Peterson, 1985).

Finally, there are several other projects for legal analysis that have narrower goals, different methods, or both. Welch (1982) and Finan (1982) report a program, LAWGICAL, which is similar to JUDITH (Popp and Schlink, 1975) but with a different user interface. Hellawell (1980, 1982) has written BASIC programs for applying particularly complicated provisions of the tax law; the most recent (Hellawell, 1982) makes some use of AI search methods. Several writers (Hustler, 1982; Sergot, 1982; Sergot and co-workers, 1986, Gordon, 1985; Schlobotim, 1985; Mackae, 1986) have looked at PROLOG as a language for legal analysis programs. A serious question here, only beginning to be addressed, is PROLOG's treatment of failure as negation, given that legal rules may or may not be given this interpretation and that statements of legal problems may or may not satisfy the closed-world assumption (Reiter, 1978). Most ambitious is the LEGOL project (Stamper, 1976, 1977, 1980; Jones and co-workers, 1979), whose goals include creating a language in which all legal rules can be stated and automating the application of the rules in routine situations. However, the author explicitly dissociates himself from AI, favoring instead an "information systems approach" (Stamper, 1976). The result is described as a high level system specification language intended for database applications (Jones and co-workers, 1979).

TASKS FOR LAW APPLICATIONS OF AI

In the application of AI to law, the projects described above represent the most extensive line of work so far. Although there is considerable variation among them, each assumes that there is a present situation, often a dispute, with respect to which the program is to suggest issues, arguments, or an outcome. Other legal tasks are possible; some AI work has been done on planning, drafting, and text retrieval. In addition, a few projects have been concerned not so much with a generic task as with providing assistance to government officials in administering particular provisions of the law (Buchanan and Fennell, 1977; Feinstein, 1985). McCarty (1983b) has surveyed some of this work in terms of Hart's (1982) distinction between deep and surface systems.

In the planning (qv) area, Michaelson (1982, 1984) has developed a program called Taxadvisor, which consults on income tax and transfer tax planning for individuals. Its recommendations cover topics such as retirement income, tax-sheltered investments, gifts, and will provisions. Written in EMYCIN (Van Melle and co-workers, 1981), the program is described as a rather straightforward application of current expert system technology.

The task of drafting legal documents has been addressed by several writers, including Sprowl (1979), Sprowl and Staudt (1981), Saxon (1982), and Boyd and Saxon (1981). The documents considered include wills, divorce complaints, and security agreements; in general, they are those that can be composed largely of standardized passages, or boilerplate, with some tailoring for the particular client. Both the selection of passages and the tailoring (as by filling in blanks) are computed on the basis of the program's representation of the law and on user-supplied information, some of which requires legal judgment. Boyd and Saxon conclude that to aid the attorney in exercising this judgment, the system should provide help messages and warnings from an extensive database, including statutory provisions, decisions, and related commentary, and amounting, for the domain of secured transactions, to "an informational filing system that is arranged around the transaction it governs" (Boyd and Saxon, 1981).

With this proposal Boyd and Saxon touch on the traditional problem area of document retrieval. Here AI researchers have dealt primarily with the question of how to represent the content of statutes, decisions, and other source materials. Hafner (1981) has produced a semantic network (qv) representation for part of the law of negotiable instruments; Karlgren and Walker (1983) and Walker (1981), in a project called Polytext, have experimented with three different representations for a small set of rules regarding arbitration, and deBessonet and Cross (1985) are working on a representation to support conceptual retrieval of the provisions of the Civil Code of Louisiana. Blair and Maron (1985) have recently shown the need for improved representations to be even greater than is generally supposed. Studying standard full-text retrieval from a large database of documents to be used in the defense of a single lawsuit (a litigation support system), they found that queries retrieved only about 20% of the relevant documents even though the lawyers and paralegals using the system believed the rate was over 75%. Karlgren and Walker (1983), who also discuss problems with current retrieval systems, propose desiderata for a better design, most significantly, that the system should be "a computer conference system that is endowed with more intelligence," not an oracle.

LAW AND COGNITIVE PROCESSES

Newell and Simon (1972), in their discussion of human problem solving, make a distinction useful for AI and law: between the demands of the task environment and the psychology of the problem-solving subject. Most of the projects described above are concerned primarily with the task environment. States differently, most are concerned with what moves are legitimate in legal reasoning, not with how any particular individual comes to find them. In a more psychological mode, protocol analysis has been proposed by Johnson and co-workers (1984) for comparing expert and novice legal performance and by Stratman (1984, 1985) for studying lawyers' composition of arguments to an appellate court as well as judges' deliberation and opinion writing.

Another line of work is concerned not so much with the professional's thinking as with aspects of the law that are familiar to everyone. Schank and Carbonell (1979), looking at newspaper headlines such as "Catawba Indians land claim supported" and "Burma appeals to UN to settle border dispute with Thailand," propose a vocabulary of basic social acts that includes notions such as disputes, petitions to an authority, governmental decisions, and resolution of disputes through other means (see SCRIPTS). Using this vocabulary, Schank and Carbonell suggest representations for sentences, including "the Supreme Court decided segregation is illegal," "the cop gave the speeder a ticket," and "Nader brought suit against GM, but the matter was settled out of court." Dyer (1983), in an ambitious project for natural language story understanding (see NATURAL LANGUAGE UNDERSTANDING; STORY ANALYSIS), concentrated on stories about divorce. Understanding them required some knowledge, in the form of memory organization packets (qv) (MOPs), of things such as marital contracts and legal disputes, as well as an ability to represent and recognize the characters' chains of reasoning, sometimes faulty, about the outcome of a divorce case.

Finally, law may be used as a source of illustrations of various kinds of cognitive processing. Rissland's work on examples in law and mathematics could well be placed in this category (Rissland, 1983, 1985; Michener, 1978; Rissland and co-workers, 1984). In work at UCLA Dyer and Flowers (1985) emphasize the richness of law as a domain for studying cognitive processes, including natural language use, memory organization and retrieval, learning, analogy, argumentation, and the commonsense background of legal expertise. Another such project is that of Bain (1984) at Yale, whose theme is the importance of a reasoner's own goals in interpreting the actions of others. Bain uses the context of a mock plea-bargaining session, with a prosecutor, a defense attorney, and a judge as participants, to examine reasoning about whether a criminal defendant's actions were justified, for instance by self-defense.

FURTHER READING

Interest in law and AI has increased rapidly in the past few years, and several new collections of papers can be expected to appear soon. At the University of Houston Law Center, conferences on law and technology were held in 1984 (Walter, 1985) and 1985 and are expected to become an annual event. A panel on legal reasoning was conducted at the Ninth International Joint Conference on Artificial Intelligence. In Europe a 1981 conference on logic, informatics, and law produced a large collection of papers (Ciampi, 1982; Martino, 1982); a second such conference took place in Florence in September 1985. Readers of the European work should be aware that continental law and Anglo-American law stem from distinct traditions. Merryman (1969) provides a readable introduction to their differences.

BIBLIOGRAPHY

L. E. Allen, "Symbolic Logic: A Razor-Edged Tool for Drafting and Interpreting Legal Documents," *Yale Law J.* **66**, 833–879 (1957).

L. E. Allen, "Beyond Document Retrieval Toward Information Retrieval," *Minn. Law Rev.* **47**, 713–767 (1963).

L. E. Allen, "Language, Law and Logic: Plain Drafting for the Electronic Age," in B. Niblett, ed., *Computer Science and Law*, Cambridge University Press, Cambridge, UK, 1980, pp. 75–100.

L. E. Allen and M. E. Caldwell eds., *Communication Sciences and Law: Reflections from the Jurimetrics Conference*, Bobbs-Merrill, Indianapolis, Ind., 1965.

A. R. Anderson, "The Logic of Norms," *Log. et Anal.* **1**, 84–91 (1958).

K. D. Ashley, "Reasoning by Analogy: A Survey of Selected A.I. Research with Implications for Legal Expert Systems," in C. Walter, 1985, pp. 105–127.

H. W. Baade, ed., *Jurimetrics*, Basic Books, New York, 1963.

W. M. Bain, *Toward a Model of Subjective Interpretation*, YALEU/CSD/RR No. 324, Department of Computer Science, Yale University, New Haven, Conn., 1984.

R. P. Bigelow, ed., *Computers and the Law: An Introductory Handbook*, 3rd ed., Commerce Clearing House, Chicago, Ill., 1981

J. Bing, "Legal Norms, Discretionary Rules and Computer Programs," in B. Niblett, ed., *Computer Science and Law*, Cambridge University Press, Cambridge, UK, 1980, pp. 119–136.

J. Bing and T. Harvold, *Legal Decisions and Information Systems*, Universitetsforlaget, Oslo, 1977.

D. C. Blair and M. E. Maron, "An Evaluation of Retrieval Effectiveness for a Full-Text-Document-Retrieval System," *CACM* **28**, 289–299 (1985).

M. Borchgrevink and J. Hansen, "SARA: A System for the Analysis of Legal Decisions," in J. Bing and K. S. Selmer, eds., *A Decade of Computers and Law*, Universitetsforlaget, Oslo, 1980, pp. 342–375.

W. E. Boyd, "Law in Computers and Computers in Law: A Lawyer's View of the State of the Art," *Ariz. Law Rev.* **14**, 267–311 (1972).

W. E. Boyd and C. S. Saxon, "The A-9: A Program for Drafting Security Agreements under Article 9 of the Uniform Commercial Code," *Am. Bar Found. Res. J.* **1981**, 637–669 (1981).

J. R. Buchanan and R. D. Fennell, "An Intelligent Information System for Criminal Case Management in the Federal Courts," in *Proceedings of the Fifth IJCAI*, Cambridge, Mass., Morgan-Kaufmann, San Mateo, Calif., 1977, pp. 901–902.

B. G. Buchanan and T. E. Headrick, "Some Speculation About Artificial Intelligence and Legal Reasoning," *Stanford Law Rev.* **23**, 40–62 (1970).

B. N. Cardozo, *The Nature of the Judicial Process*, Yale University Press, New Haven, Conn., 1921.

C. Ciampi, ed., *Artificial Intelligence and Legal Information Systems*, Vol. 1, North-Holland, Amsterdam, The Netherlands, 1982.

C. G. deBessonet and G. R. Cross, "Representation of Some Aspects of Legal Causality," in Walter, 1985, pp. 205–214.

M. G. Dyer, *In-Depth Understanding: A computer Model of Integrated Processing for Narrative Comprehension*, MIT Press, Cambridge, Mass., 1983.

M. G. Dyer and M. Flowers, "Toward Automating Legal Expertise," in Walter, 1985, pp. 49–68.

R. Dworkin, *Taking Rights Seriously*, Harvard University Press, Cambridge, Mass., 1977.

T. G. Evans, "A Heuristic Program to Solve Geometric Analogy Problems," in M. Minsky, ed., *Semantic Information Processing*, MIT Press, Cambridge, Mass., 1968.

J. L. Feinstein, "A Knowledge-Based Expert System Used to Prevent the Disclosure of Sensitive Information at the United States Environmental Protection Agency," in Walter, 1985, pp. 661–697.

J. P. Finan, "LAWGICAL: Jurisprudential and Logical Considerations," *Akron Law Rev.* **15**, 675–711 (1982).

A. S. Fraenkel, "Legal Information Retrieval," in F. L. Alt and M. Rubinoff, eds., *Advances in Computers*, Vol. 9, Academic Press, Inc., New York, 1968, pp. 113–178.

J. Frank, *Courts on Trial*, Princeton University Press, Princeton, N.J., 1949, pp. 206–208.

L. L. Fuller, "Science and the Judicial Process," *Harvard Law Rev.* **79**, 1604–1628 (1966).

A. v. d. L. Gardner, "Overview of an Artificial Intelligence Approach to Legal Reasoning," in Walter, 1985, pp. 247–274.

A. v. d. L. Gardner, *An Artificial Intelligence Approach to Legal Reasoning*, MIT Press, Cambridge, Mass., 1987.

M. R. Genesereth, R. Greiner, M. R. Grinberg, and D. E. Smith, *The MRS Dictionary*, Memo HPP-80-24, Stanford Heuristic Programming Project, Stanford University, Jan. 1984.

G. Gilmore, *The Ages of American Law*, Yale University Press, New Haven, Conn., 1977.

T. F. Gordon, "Object-Oriented Predicate Logic and Its Role in Representing Legal Knowledge," in Walter, 1985, pp. 163–203.

C. M. Haar, J. P. Sawyer, Jr., and S. J. Cummings, "Computer Power and Legal Reasoning: A Case Study of Judicial Decision Prediction in Zoning Amendment Cases," *Am. Bar Found. Res. J.* **1977**, 651–768 (1977).

C. D. Hafner, *An Information Retrieval System based on a Computer Model of Legal Knowledge*, UMI Research, Ann Arbor, Mich., 1981.

H. L. A. Hart, *The Concept of Law,* Clarendon Press, Oxford, UK, 1961.

H. L. A. Hart, "American Jurisprudence Through English Eyes: The Nightmare and the Noble Dream," *Ga. Law Rev.* **11,** 969–988 (1977).

H. L. A. Hart, "Problems of Philosphy of Law," in P. Edwards (ed.), *The Encyclopedia of Philosphy,* Vol. 6, Macmillan New York, 1967, pp. 264–276.

P. E. Hart, "Directions for AI in the Eighties," *SIGART Newslett.,* (79), 11–16 (1982).

R. Hellawell, "A Computer Program for Legal Planning and Analysis: Taxation of Stock Redemptions," *Columbia Law Rev.* **80,** 1363–1398 (1980).

R. Hellawell, "SEARCH: A Computer Program for Legal Problem Solving," *Akron Law Rev.* **15,** 635–653 (1982).

O. W. Holmes, "The Path of the Law," *Harvard Law Rev.* **10,** 457–478 (1897).

A. Hustler, *Programming Law in Logic,* Research Report CS-82-13, Department of Computer Science, University of Waterloo, Ont., 1982.

P. E. Johnson, M. G. Johnson, and R. K. Little, "Expertise in Trial Advocacy: Some Considerations for Inquiry into Its Nature and Development," *Campbell Law Rev.* **7,** 119–143 (1984).

E. A. Jones, Jr., ed., *Law and Electronics: The Challenge of a New Era, Proceedings of the First National Law and Electronics Conference,* Lake Arrowhead, Oct. 21–23, 1960, Matthew Bender, New York, 1962.

S. Jones, P. Mason, and R. Stamper, "LEGOL 2.0: A Relational Specification Language for Complex Rules," *Inf. Sys.* **4,** 293–305 (1979).

H. Karlgren and D. E. Walker, "The Polytext System: A New Design for a Text Retrieval System," in F. Kiefer, ed., *Questions and Answers,* D. Reidel, Dordrecht, The Netherlands, 1983, pp. 273–294.

S. Kedar-Cabelli, *Analogy with Purpose in Legal Reasoning from Precedents: A Dissertation Proposal,* LRP-TR-17, Laboratory for Computer Science Research, Rutgers University, New Brunswick, N.J., 1984.

L. O. Kelso, "Does the Law Need a Technological Revolution?" *Rocky Mt. Law Rev.* **18,** 378–392 (1946).

J. E. Leininger and B. Gilchrist, eds., *Proceedings of the AFIPS/ Standford Conference on Computers, Society and Law: The Role of Legal Education,* Montvale, N.J., June 25–27, 1973.

E. H. Levi, *An Introduction to Legal Reasoning,* University of Chicago Press, Chicago, Ill., 1949.

R. K. Lindsay, B. G. Buchanan, E. A. Feigenbaum, and J. Lederberg, *Applications of Artificial Intelligence for Chemistry: The DENDRAL Project,* McGraw-Hill Book Co., Inc., New York, 1980.

K.N. Llewellyn, *The Bramble Bush: On Our Law and Its Study,* Oceana Publications, Dobbs Ferry, N. Y., 1960a.

K. N. Llewellyn, *The Common Law Tradition: Deciding Appeals,* Little, Brown, Boston, 1960b.

J. McCarthy, "Some Expert Systems Need Common Sense," in H. R. Pagels, eds., *Computer Culture: The Scientific, Intellectual, and Social Impact of the Computer,* New York Academy of Sciences, New York, 1984a, pp. 129–137.

J. McCarthy, "What Is Common Sense?" paper presented at the Fourth National Conference on Artificial Intelligence, Austin, Tex., 1984b.

L. T. McCarty, "Reflections on TAXMAN: An Experiment in Artificial Intelligence and Legal Reasoning," *Harvard Law Rev.* **90,** 837–893 (1977).

L. T. McCarty, "Permissions and Obligations," in *Proceedings of the Eighth IJCAI,* Karlsruhe, FRG, Morgan-Kaufmann, San Mateo, Calif., 1983a, pp. 287–294.

L. T. McCarty, "Intelligent Legal Information Systems: Problems and Prospects," *Rutgers Comput. Technol. Law J.* **9,** 265–294 (1983b).

L. T. McCarty and N. S. Sridharan, *The Representation of Conceptual Structures in TAXMAN II: Part One: Logical Templates,* LRP-TR-4, Laboratory for Computer Science Research, Rutgers University, 1980.

L. T. McCarty and N. S. Sridharan, *A Computational Theory of Legal Argument,* LRP-TR-13, Laboratory for Computer Science Research, Rutgers University, 1981.

L. T. McCarty, N. S. Sridharan, and B. C. Sangster, *The Implementation of TAXMAN II: An Experiment in Artificial Intelligence and Legal Reasoning,* LRP-TR-2, Laboratory for Computer Science Research, Rutgers University, New Brunswick, N.J., 1979.

E. Mackaay and P. Robillard, "Predicting Judicial Decisions: The Nearest Neighbor Rule and Visual Representation of Case Patterns," *Datenverarbeitung im Recht* **3,** 302–331 (1974).

C. D. MacRae, "User Control Knowledge in a Tax Consulting System," in L. F. Pau, ed., *Artificial Intelligence in Economics and Management,* North-Holland, Amsterdam, The Netherlands, 1986.

P. B. Maggs and C. G. deBessonet, "Automated Logical Analysis of Systems of Legal Rules," *Jurimetr. J.* **12,** 158–169 (1972).

A. A. Martino, ed., *Deontic Logic, Computational Linguistics, and Legal Information Systems,* Vol. 2, North-Holland, Amsterdam, The Netherlands, 1982.

L. Mehl, "Automation in the Legal World: From the Machine Processing of Legal Information to the 'Law Machine,' " in *Mechanisation of Thought Processes,* National Physical Laboratory Symposium No. **10,** Nov. 1958.

J. A. Meldman, "A Structural Model for Computer-Aided Legal Analysis," *Rutgers J. Comput. Law* **6,** 27–71 (1977).

J. H. Merryman, *The Civil Law Tradition: An Introduction to the Legal Systems of Western Europe and Latin America,* Stanford University Press, Stanford, Calif., 1969.

R. H. Michaelson, *A Knowledge-Based System for Individual Income and Transfer Tax Planning,* Ph.D. dissertation, University of Illinois at Urbana-Champaign, 1982.

R. H. Michaelson, "An Expert System for Federal Tax Planning," *Expert Sys.* **1,** 149–167 (1984).

E. R. Michener, "Understanding Understanding Mathematics," *Cogn. Sci.* **2,** 361–383 (1978).

M. Minsky, "A Framework for Representing Knowledge," in P. H. Winston, ed., *The Psychology of Computer Vision,* McGraw-Hill Book Co., Inc., New York, 1975; pp. 211–277.

D. Nagel, *Concept Learning by Building and Applying Transformations between Object Descriptions,* LRP-TR-15 Laboratory for Computer Science Research, Rutgers University, New Brunswick, N.J., 1983.

A. Newell and H. A. Simon, "GPS, a Program That Simulates Human Thought," in E. A. Feigenbaum and J. Feldman, eds., *Computers and Thought,* McGraw-Hill Book Co., Inc., New York, 1963, pp. 279–293.

A. Newell and H. A. Simon, *Human Problem Solving,* Prentice-Hall, Inc., Englewood Cliffs, N.J., 1972, p. 108.

M. A. Peterson, "New Research Tools to Watch for," *Calif. Law.* **5**(3), 19–21 (1985).

W. G. Popp and B. Schlink, "JUDITH, a Computer Program to Advise Lawyers in Reasoning a Case," *Jurimetr. J.* **15,** 303–314 (1975).

H. Putnam, "The Meaning of 'Meaning,' " in K. Gunderson, ed., *Language, Mind, and Knowledge, Minnesota Studies in the Philosophy of Science,* Vol. 7, University of Minnesota Press, Minneapolis, 1975, pp. 131–193.

R. Reiter, "On Reasoning by Default," in *TINLAP-2: Theoretical Issues in Natural Language Processing-2,* Urbana, Ill., 1978, pp. 210–218.

E. L. Rissland, "Examples in Legal Reasoning: Legal Hypotheticals," in *Proceedings of the Eighth International Joint Conference on Artificial Intelligence,* Karlsruhe, FRG, Morgan-Kaufmann, San Mateo, Calif., 1983, pp. 90–93.

E. L. Rissland, "Argument Moves and Hypotheticals," in Walter 1985, pp. 129–143.

E. L. Rissland, E. M. Valcarce, and K. D. Ashley, "Explaining and Arguing with Examples," in *Proceedings of the Fourth National Conference on Artificial Intelligence,* Austin, Tex., AAAI, Menlo Park, Calif., 1984, pp. 288–294.

C. S. Saxon, "Computer-Aided Drafting of Legal Documents," *Am. Bar Found. Res. J.* **1982,** 685–754 (1982).

R. C. Schank and J. G. Carbonell, Jr., "Re: the Gettysburg Address—Representing Social and Political Acts," in N. V. Findler (ed.), *Associative Networks: Representation and Use of Knowledge in Computers,* Academic Press, Inc., New York, 1979, pp. 327–362.

M. Sergot, "Prospects for Representing the Law as Logic Programs," in K. L. Clark and S.-A. Tarnlund eds., *Logic Programming,* Academic Press, Inc., New York, 1982, pp. 33–42.

D. A. Schlobohm, "TA: A Prolog Program which Analyzes Income Tax Issues under Section 318(a) of the Internal Revenue Code," in Walter, 1985, pp. 765–815.

M. J. Sergot, F. Sadri, R. A. Kowalski, F. Kriwaczek, P. Hammond, and H. T. Cory, "The British Nationality Act as a logic program," *CACM* **29,** 370–386 (1986).

E. H. Shortliffe, *Computer-Based Medical Consultations: MYCIN,* Elsevier, New York, 1976.

P. Slayton, *Electronic Legal Retrieval: A Report Prepared for the Department of Communications of the Government of Canada,* Information Canada, Ottawa, 1974.

J. A. Sprowl, *A Manual for Computer-Assisted Legal Research,* American Bar Foundation, Chicago, Ill., 1976.

J. A. Sprowl, "Automating the Legal Reasoning Process: A Computer That Uses Regulations and Statutes to Draft Legal Documents," *Am. Bar Found. Res. J.* **1979,** 1–81 (1979).

J. A. Sprowl and R. W. Staudt, "Computerizing Client Services in the Law School Teaching Clinic: An Experiment in Law Office Automation," *Am. Bar Found. Res. J.* **1981,** 699–751 (1981).

N. S. Sridharan, *AIMDS User Manual, Version 2,* CBM-TR-89, Department of Computer Science, Rutgers University, New Brunswick, N.J., 1978.

R. K. Stamper, "The Automation of Legal Reasoning: Problems and Prospects," in J. Madey, ed., *Selected Topics in Information Processing: IFIP-INFOPOL-76,* North-Holland, Amsterdam, The Netherlands, 1976, pp. 433–447.

R. K. Stamper, "The LEGOL 1 Prototype System and Language," *Comput. J.* **20,** 102–108 (1977).

R. Stamper, "LEGOL: Modelling Legal Rules by Computer," in Allen, 1980, pp. 45–71.

J. Stone, "Man and Machine in Search for Justice," *Stanford Law Rev.* **16,** 515–560 (1964).

J. Stone, *Law and the Social Sciences in the Second Half Century,* Lecture 3, University of Minnesota Press, Minneapolis, 1966.

J. Stone, *Legal System and Lawyers' Reasonings,* Stanford University Press, Stanford, Calif., 1964.

J. F. Stratman, "Studying the Appellate Brief and Opinion Composing Process: A Window on Legal Thinking," *Juris* **19**(1), 9–14 (Fall 1984);

J. F. Stratman, *Juris* **19**(2) 12–19 (Winter 1985).

G. Sussman, T. Winograd, and E. Charniak, *Micro-Planner Reference Manual,* rev., A.I. Memo 203A, Artificial Intelligence Laboratory, MIT, Cambridge, Mass., 1971.

P. Szolovits, L. B. Hawkinson, and W. A. Martin, *An Overview of OWL, a Language for Knowledge Representation,* MIT/LC/TM-86, Laboratory for Computer Science, MIT, Cambridge, Mass., 1977.

C. Tapper, *Computers and the Law,* Weidenfeld and Nicolson, London, 1973.

W. Van Melle, A. C. Scott, J. S. Bennett, and M. A. S. Peairs, *The EMYCIN Manual,* Report No. STAN-CS-81-885, Department of Computer Science, Stanford University, Stanford, Calif., 1981.

D. E. Walker, "The Organization and Use of Information: Contributions of Information Science, Computational Linguistics and Artificial Intelligence," *J. Am. Soc. Inf. Sci.* **32,** 347–363 (1981).

C. Walter, ed., *Computing Power and Legal Reasoning,* West Publishing, St. Paul, Minn., 1985.

D. A. Waterman and M. A. Peterson, *Models of Legal Decision-Making,* Report R-2717-ICJ, Institute for Civil Justice, Rand Corp., 1981.

D. A. Waterman and M. A. Peterson, "Evaluating Civil Claims: An Expert Systems Approach," *Expert Sys.* **1,** 65–76 (1984).

J. T. Welch, "LAWGICAL: An Approach to Computer-Aided-Legal Analysis," *Akron Law Rev.* **15,** 655–673 (1982).

L. Wittgenstein, *Philosophical Investigations,* 3rd ed., G. E. M. Anscombe, trans., Macmillan, New York, 1958.

A. v. d. L. Gardner
Stanford University

LEARNING, MACHINE

One central insight of artificial intelligence is that expert performance requires domain-specific knowledge. Machine learning is the subfield of AI that studies the automated acquisition of such knowledge. The aim is intelligent systems that learn—that is, that improve their performance as the result of experience (see EXPERT SYSTEMS). Researchers study learning for a variety of reasons: to discover general principles of intelligence, to better understand human learning, and to automate the process of knowledge acquisition. However, the discipline is united in its concern with mechanisms for learning, and methods proposed with one goal in mind often serve other purposes equally well.

Despite its separate identity, there are two important senses in which machine learning is an integral part of the larger AI field. First, learning researchers must consider central AI issues of knowledge representation (qv), memory organization, and performance. Second, learning can occur in any domain requiring intelligence, whether the basic task involves classification, problem solving, reasoning, natural language processing, or vision. Thus, one can view machine learning as more a framework for AI research and development than as a subfield of AI.

This article reviews the current state of machine learning. It begins by identifying relevant dimensions along which learning systems differ. Next, it describes five of the different paradigms for machine learning that have emerged over the past two decades:

- Connectionist (neural network) learning methods
- Genetic algorithms and classifier systems
- Empirical methods for inducing rules and decision trees
- Analytic learning methods
- Case-based approaches to learning

Despite differences in the representations and algorithms used by these approaches, all aim to improve performance through the acquisition of knowledge from experience. Moreover, they must address many similar issues, and they share many open problems. After examining each of these paradigms, this article will consider some recent developments in the field as a whole and their potential impact on future research and applications.

One related area that will not be examined is knowledge acquisition (qv) (eg, Marcus, 1988). Like machine learning, this subfield of AI is concerned with improving performance through the storage of domain-specific knowledge. However, research on knowledge acquisition focuses primarily on direct interaction with an expert by asking questions, taking advice, and the like. In contrast, most work on machine learning emphasizes the acquisition of knowledge through experience with an external environment or experience with internal problem-solving traces.

DIMENSIONS OF MACHINE-LEARNING RESEARCH

Before delving into recent research on machine learning, let us identify some dimensions along which alternative learning paradigms vary. Six issues are discussed below: the representation of experience, the representation of acquired knowledge, the performance task, the difference between supervised and unsupervised learning, the distinction between incremental and nonincremental learning, and the complementary notions of induction and explanation.

Representation of Experience

Most learning is based on experience, and this requires a representation for the experiential input given to the learning system. Researchers have employed three broad classes of data structures, each with different representational power. The simplest describes each individual experience as a list of binary *features,* each corresponding to the presence or absence of some aspect of the environment. For example, a particular symptom (eg, jaundice) may be present or absent for a given patient. Connectionist and genetic algorithms typically employ feature-based input.

A second scheme assumes a known set of *attributes,* each having a set of mutually exclusive values. Thus, one might describe an object as blue or red, but not both at the same time. Some attributes take on numeric values (eg, length, weight). Attribute-value representations are typically used by empirical methods, such as those for rule induction and decision-tree construction.

A final approach employs relational or structural representations. These describe relations between two or more objects, such as the fact that object *A* is above object *B* (ie, arbitrary predicates). Such structural information can be stated in many formalisms, including predicate logic (see Logic, predicate) and semantic networks (qv). Although relational schemes have significantly more expressive power than the other representations, they also introduce significant complexity into the matching process, and this affects learning methods that use them. Research on analytic learning typically deals with relational data structures, as does some work on empirical rule learning and case-based reasoning.

Representation of Acquired Knowledge

All learning systems acquire new knowledge, and they must represent that knowledge in some fashion. The choice of knowledge representation is central in that it strongly influences choices of performance and learning components. In fact, the five learning paradigms to be discussed in the next main section are distinguished largely in terms of representational issues.

One choice is whether to store individual, concrete experiences or only abstractions based on these data. Most work on machine learning has taken the latter path and attempts to move beyond the data to build more general knowledge structures that summarize previous experience. Of course, hybrid approaches are possible; these are often called *case-based* approaches and are discussed in a latter section (see also Reasoning, case-based). Note that methods that attempt to store only concrete experiences must at some point generalize beyond the data if they hope to apply to new experiences. Thus, the real issue is whether such abstraction occurs aggressively as new experiences are stored (as in most approaches) or lazily as needed during knowledge access (as with case-based approaches).

For abstract knowledge structures, another choice is whether to use a logical, discrete formalism or one that involves numeric, continuous information. This is primarily a choice between using logical connectives or numeric ones, respectively. Empirical rule learning and analytic learning methods have predominantly used the first path, whereas connectionist systems have relied on the second. Genetic algorithms can be profitably viewed as combining these two formalisms, as can recent work on probabilistic learning. A related choice is whether to use an aggregated, coarse-grained representation or a finer-grained one. These options are sometimes referred to as symbolic and subsymbolic representations, respectively. Conventional wisdom associates the former scheme with empirical and analytic methods, and the latter with connectionist and genetic approaches. However, as we will argue in the subsection on Relationships Among the Paradigms, these associations are more myth than fact.

The Performance Task

Learning involves improvement in performance, and thus learning cannot occur in the absence of some performance task. The vast majority of machine-learning research has focused on two broad classes of domains: classification and problem-solving (qv). Each has led to different concerns, distinct insights, and unique applications.

Intelligent agents are repeatedly confronted with the need to classify or label their experience. For example, on encountering certain symptoms, a doctor diagnoses a specific disease. The generic task can be easily stated: given some description of an experience, along with a set of known classes and their descriptions, assign that experience to one or more classes. The most frequent successes in expert systems have involved just such classification or diagnostic tasks (Davis and Lenat, 1982). Much of the work on machine learning has focused on learning descriptions for classification.

However, an intelligent agent must also be able to solve novel problems and formulate plans. For example, when going to a meeting, an agent devises a path from its current location to the target site. The generic task can be stated as: given some desired state or goal, find some sequence of actions that takes you from the current state to the desired one. Navigation and robot manipulation (see ROBOT MANIPULATORS) are the most obvious applications of problem-solving techniques, but there are many others, including scheduling. This area has been less popular within machine learning, but much of the recent work has focused on acquiring knowledge to improve the speed and quality of methods for planning and reasoning.

Finally, intelligent agents also participate in other high-level behaviors that may not fit neatly into either the classification or problem-solving paradigms. Such behaviors include the design of new artifacts, communication with other agents, and the control of motor effectors. To date, the machine learning community has placed little emphasis on these areas, but because of their potential, this will undoubtedly change in the future.

Supervised and Unsupervised Learning

Another dimension that influences learning is the degree of supervision. In some cases, a tutor or domain expert may be present to give the learner immediate feedback about the appropriateness of its behavior. This situation is typically called *supervised* learning. In other cases, an *unsupervised* learner may have to fend for itself. Here the learner has little or no external guidance in building knowledge structures or composing solutions to problems; at most, the environment provides coarse-grained feedback about the learner's overall effectiveness on the task at hand.

Early work in machine learning focused on the simpler supervised task, and it continues to receive considerable attention. There are good practical reasons for this interest. Although experts generally have poor ability to introspect about their domain knowledge, they are much better at providing examples of correct and incorrect behavior.

Both forms of learning can occur in many contexts, though they take on different forms in different domains.

In classification domains, the supervised task is usually called *learning from examples,* and the individual training experiences are called *instances.* This task can be stated as:

- Given: A set of instances (eg, patient symptoms) and their associated classes (eg, diseases).
- Find: A general description for each class that matches only its instances.

This basic task has been examined within all the major paradigms of machine learning and, until recently, the vast majority of research papers have dealt with this topic. However, there is now also considerable interest in unsupervised concept learning (qv), in which the learner must decide for itself not only the class in which it should place each experience, but also the number of such classes. This has been called clustering (qv) (Fisher and Langley, 1985).

In problem-solving domains, supervised learning occurs when a tutor is available to suggest the correct operator or subgoal at each point in the search for a solution. Methods that operate in this context are sometimes called *learning apprentices,* and they show promise as a way of extracting knowledge from an expert (Mitchell and co-workers, 1985) in problem-solving and design domains. However, more research in this area has focused on unsupervised learning, in which the agent must distinguish desirable actions from undesirable ones for itself. This has been called the credit assignment problem (Sleeman and co-workers, 1982), and researchers have explored a variety of responses across a number of paradigms.

Incremental and Nonincremental Learning

Some learning algorithms process experiences one at a time, whereas others process a large set of experiences at once. The former class is often called *incremental* and the latter, *nonincremental.* However, examining only the surface behavior of a system can be misleading, as an inherently nonincremental system can always be run in incremental mode and vice versa. For example, if one lets a nonincremental technique retain exact copies of previous experience in memory, it can process the first experience, then process the first two experiences, then process the first three experiences, and so forth. Similarly, one can take an incremental method and iteratively run it through the same set of experiences again and again. A better definition of incremental involves the number of previously seen experiences the method must reprocess during learning (Schlimmer and Fisher, 1986).

Both nonincremental and incremental approaches have advantages. The former can collect statistics about all the data, giving a learning method more information on which to base its decisions. On the other hand, incremental methods tend to be more efficient and, in principle, can deal with much larger data sets. Much of recent machine-learning research has focused on incremental approaches, though there are some notable exceptions in the literature on connectionist methods and on the induction of rules and decision trees.

Inductive and Analytic Learning

A sixth important dimension relates to the type of learning used to acquire knowledge. In one class of approaches, inductive learning methods formulate knowledge based mainly on observed data. Empirical, genetic, and connectionist techniques are instances of this general strategy. These methods are inductive in the sense that they move beyond their input and generalize it to create knowledge that was not previously in memory. In contrast, analytic learning methods formulate knowledge based mainly on other knowledge already in memory. Explanation-based learning is a clear example of this type of approach; it uses prior knowledge to explain new experiences, then simplifies the explanation and stores it in memory.

Inductive methods have also been called *knowledge-level* learners, as their acquired knowledge structures change the deductive closure of the system (Dietterich, 1987) (see KNOWLEDGE LEVEL). In contrast, analytic methods are *symbol-level* learners; their compiled knowledge may increase efficiency but leave the deductive closure unchanged. However, later some applications in which inductive techniques produce symbol-level learning and some conditions under which analytic methods can produce knowledge-level shifts will be considered.

Of course, more unified approaches are possible. A learner could use prior knowledge from the domain to constrain induction, producing partial explanations that still require inductive leaps to form general structures. Alternatively, instead of using deductive rules to construct explanations, a learner could use plausible inference rules; the resulting explanations may be plausible, but they are not guaranteed to hold, and thus involve a sophisticated form of induction. Some researchers have argued that the unification of inductive and analytic approaches should be given high priority (Langley, 1989).

FIVE PARADIGMS

This section will examine some recent research on machine learning. The field has been divided into five paradigms based on the basic representations and learning methods employed: connectionist approaches, genetic algorithms, empirical rule learning, analytic learning, and case-based methods. In each case, the basic approach is reviewed, recent advances are examined, and some open research issues are considered.

Each paradigm is loosely defined not only by a shared set of assumptions, concerns, and methods, but also by the amount of interaction among researchers. Generally, people within a given paradigm read and reference each other's papers, attend the same meetings and presentations, and all too often ignore work in other paradigms. Some important relations among these paradigms that reveal more similarities than appear at first glance are identified after discussing the five paradigms.

Connectionist (Neural Network) Learning

Some of the earliest research on machine learning focused on connectionist methods (Nilsson, 1965). Recently there has been a resurgence of interest in this approach. The name derives from the basic representation for learned knowledge: a network composed of nodes connected by directed, weighted links (sometimes called neural networks (qv) because of the suggestive similarity between the computational style of network nodes and neurons). Such systems typically assume that inputs are represented as a set of binary features, with each feature being present or absent. In operation, features that are present activate the network's initial nodes. Then, the weights on links from these nodes to others determine whether subsequent nodes will be activated. The process iterates until activation has a chance to reach the network's final nodes, with the output of the network being the activation of the final nodes.

Let us examine the connectionist framework's position on the dimensions discussed in the previous section. Learning consists of modifying link weights to better mimic the desired relations among the inputs and outputs. Thus connectionist approaches lend themselves naturally to performance tasks that involve classification, but they can be adapted to more complex domains. Although not logical in form, the connections encode the acquired knowledge and summarize the data encountered. Researchers have focused predominantly on methods for supervised learning situations, but there are some exceptions. Connectionist researchers have also examined many alternative strategies for adjusting link weights; many are incremental, and all are inductive in nature.

Perceptrons and Linear Threshold Units. The simplest form of connectionist network is the perceptron or linear threshold unit (Rosenblatt, 1962). In this framework, there is a single output node to which each input node is connected by a single weighted link. The output node also has an associated threshold. Given a datum, the output node sums the weights of the links from active input nodes (those whose features are present). If this sum exceeds the threshold, the output node is activated; otherwise it remains inactive. Figure 1 presents an example of a simple perceptron.

Despite their simplicity, perceptrons can represent a variety of functions. For example, consider a network in which N links have a weight of one and all others are zero. If the threshold is set to N, the network encodes a rule that matches only when the conjunction of the nonzero features are present. Similarly, if the threshold is set to one, the same network encodes a disjunctive rule. Using a threshold of K (where $N > K > 1$) lets the network concisely express the K of N function. Unlike the former two, this latter function is difficult to represent using logical notation. Moreover, allowing weights other than one supports an even broader class of functions. In fact, given the appropriate weights, a perceptron can represent any linearly separable class. In other words, if we view the F features as defining an F-dimensional space, the network can describe any class that involves placing a single hyperplane between the instances of two classes.

There are a number of straightforward methods for learning appropriate link weights given example input-output pairs. One of these, the perceptron learning rule,

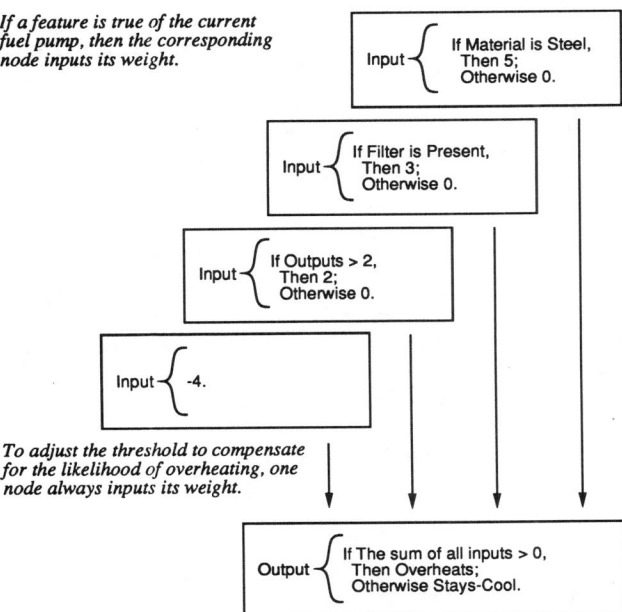

If a feature is true of the current fuel pump, then the corresponding node inputs its weight.

Input { If Material is Steel, Then 5; Otherwise 0.

Input { If Filter is Present, Then 3; Otherwise 0.

Input { If Outputs > 2, Then 2; Otherwise 0.

Input { -4.

To adjust the threshold to compensate for the likelihood of overheating, one node always inputs its weight.

Output { If The sum of all inputs > 0, Then Overheats; Otherwise Stays-Cool.

Figure 1. Schematic of the organization of a linear threshold unit. Inputs correspond to instance features (shown at top). If these features are present, their weights are summed by the output unit (at bottom). Learning modifies the weights associated with inputs and thereby alters the summed output. An additional constant input (lowest and leftmost input) allows the linear threshold unit to adjust its threshold.

learns only when it makes a prediction error. If the output unit is not active when it should be, then its incoming weights are too low; accordingly, they are incremented by a small constant. By the same reasoning, if the output unit is active when it should not be, the weights are too high and are decremented by the same small constant. Part of the appeal of this incremental method is that it is guaranteed to converge on any linearly separable class given a finite number of instances (Minsky and Papert, 1969).

Other learning methods, such as the LMS procedure (Widrow and Hoff, 1960), modify each weight differentially in an attempt to reduce the mean-squared error between the desired and generated output. This approach can be run incrementally or nonincrementally (using all available instances), and it can be generalized to handle networks with continuous rather than binary inputs. Linear threshold units have been used to learn regular and irregular endings for the past tense of English verbs (Rumelhart and McClelland, 1986), and a perceptron-like learning method has demonstrated its ability to acquire expert-level performance in the game of checkers (Samuel, 1959).

Backpropagation in Multilayer Networks. Despite their attractiveness, single linear threshold units cannot represent or learn class descriptions that are not linearly separable. Although higher-order components such as quadratic threshold nodes might be feasible, a more common approach uses a network with multiple layers. These

structures include intermediate, or hidden, nodes that are indirectly connected to the inputs and outputs of the network. Given sufficient breadth in this structure, the network can express an arbitrary function of the input features. Moreover, if the structure is relatively shallow (ie, only short paths from inputs to outputs), large networks of this sort are computationally efficient to use. However, learning the weights for such networks is another matter entirely, and much of the recent research on connectionist learning has focused on this issue.

One of the most intuitive approaches to learning appropriate link weights in a multiple layer network applies the LMS procedure recursively. Known as *backpropagation,* this procedure first propagates activation through the network in the normal, forward direction. Based on the differences between observed and desired outputs, backpropagation uses LMS to compute the desired activation levels on the hidden nodes one level back. Not only does this indicate the appropriate weight change in the final links, it also allows backpropagation to treat the hidden nodes as if they were output nodes. Using the difference between the observed and desired activation for hidden nodes, backpropagation applies LMS recursively until it reaches the input nodes.

Like the perceptron learning rule, backpropagation is conducting a search in the space of link weights. Effectively, both carry out a hill-climbing search in which the gradient is defined by error reduction. Unlike the convergence result for the simpler learning rule, backpropagation may become stuck in local optima. This has not emerged as a significant problem in studies to date, but it remains an open issue. More pressing problems include a very slow rate of learning and some dependence on the number of hidden nodes. One noteworthy application demonstrates that backpropagation can acquire pronunciation knowledge that accurately predicts phenomes from English text (Sejnowski and Rosenberg, 1987).

Alternative Approaches to Connectionist Learning. Researchers have explored a number of other approaches to learning in multilayer networks. For example, Boltzmann machines (qv) are a probabilistic technique based on an analogy with thermodynamics in which nodes settle into stable configurations as the "temperature" of the system decreases (Ackley and co-workers, 1987). Such methods must be run many times, in order to reach equilibrium and to collect statistics about the probability of connected nodes being active simultaneously. As a consequence, they are typically even slower than backpropagation. Nevertheless, Boltzmann machines also have advantages, and active research continues in the area, including applications to speech recognition (Prager and co-workers, 1986).

Other researchers have taken a reinforcement-learning approach. In this framework, instead of fine-grained feedback about each of the network's outputs, the only information available is a single evaluation score for the network's overall behavior on each instance. For example, the AR-P algorithm rewards or penalizes each weight in the network equally as a function of the reinforcement evoked by the network's overall behavior (Barto and co-workers, 1983). This learning scheme has been successfully applied to a number of domains, including a pole-balancing task involving the dynamic control of forces over time. Like the other methods, this approach extends to domains in which the inputs are real-valued rather than binary.

In other studies, researchers have explored the behavior and capabilities of cyclic and deeply nested network structures. For example, a cyclic network has its input nodes connected to its output nodes and vice-versa. This design allows networks to memorize patterns, and given a partial or noisy pattern to recall, the net can reconstruct the complete, noise-free original (Kohonen and co-workers, 1981). In a deeply nested network, hidden nodes are ordered, and each successive hidden node receives input from all prior hidden nodes. Nesting the hidden nodes capitalizes on the representations they have learned, and the resulting structure tends to generalize better (Fahlman and Lebiere, 1990).

Open Issues in Connectionist Learning. Research on learning in the connectionist framework has made significant strides since the early results with perceptrons, and initial applications have started to emerge. Still, a number of serious issues remain to be addressed.

- *Increasing the Rate of Learning.* Existing methods learn very slowly, often requiring many iterations through the training instances. Future research should examine the factors that affect the learning rate and develop connectionist methods that learn more rapidly (Fahlman, 1988; Hampson and Volper, 1987).
- *Generalization.* Current methods converge on weight settings that summarize training instances, but sometimes this is at the expense of accurate generalization over unseen instances. This issue becomes especially important when the training data are noisy (Fisher and McKusick, 1989; Knight, 1989; Weiss and Kapouleas, 1989).
- *Structural Knowledge.* Some domains seem inherently relational, but connectionist methods rely on feature-based representations. The framework must be adapted to represent and learn from relational and structural input (Hinton, 1986).
- *Sequential Behavior.* Connectionist techniques lend themselves to parallel implementations, but they have difficulty carrying out ordered actions like those required for problem solving. Extended architectures are needed that can handle sequential behavior, along with learning methods that can support them (Elman, 1990; Mozer and Bachrach, in press).
- *Incorporating Domain-Specific Bias.* Perceptrons have a strong bias toward learning linearly separable classes, but multilayer networks search a much larger space. Future research should examine methods for incorporating biases into multilayer networks that constrain the learning methods' search and improve their learning rates (Towell and co-workers, 1990).

Growing numbers of researchers are examining the connectionist paradigm seriously and many are concerned with issues of learning. Theoretical analyses and experimental studies have begun to reveal a deeper understanding of these methods' advantages and drawbacks, pointing the way to the extensions and improvements outlined above.

Genetic Algorithms and Classifier Systems

Genetic algorithms are a family of adaptive search methods that derive their name from a loose analogy with genetic change in a population of individuals. Like connectionist methods, most genetic algorithms assume a feature-based representation of instances and events. However, rather than using a weighted network to represent acquired knowledge, they employ a disjunctive set of knowledge structures or patterns. Each pattern is conjunctive and specifies the presence (or absence) of some features. Patterns also have an associated weight, sometimes called the pattern's fitness, that summarizes its performance on past experiences. Given a new instance, a stochastic scheme follows the recommendations of strong matching patterns to reach a decision (Wilson, 1987).

In terms of the dimensions of the preceding section, this paradigm lends itself naturally to performance tasks that involve both classification and problem solving, as is discussed below. Research on genetic algorithms has focused on supervised learning situations, although often the feedback is some overall score, as in the reinforcement learning framework discussed above. Researchers have explored a number of inductive approaches to incrementally modifying the content of individual patterns and their weights, and they have successfully applied genetic algorithms and classifier systems to a variety of tasks (Goldberg, 1990).

Learning with Genetic Algorithms. In addition to using a different learned representation, genetic algorithms and connectionist techniques also carry out a different type of search during learning. Whereas connectionist methods apply a hill-climbing operator to a single state (one set of weights), genetic algorithms apply several heuristic operators to a set of states (patterns). As shown in Figure 2, genetic algorithms follow three steps in processing new experiences: updating pattern strengths, applying search operators, and pruning ineffective patterns. Methods for updating weights vary widely among specific genetic algorithms; several are discussed below. For the second step, genetic algorithms typically use two operators, crossover and mutation, that apply to strongly weighted patterns to produce syntactically similar new patterns; crossover is analogous to gene splicing, whereas mutation introduces random, minor variations. To maintain the size of the pattern set, the third step replaces prior, weakly weighted patterns with new patterns. In a sense, patterns compete with each other to produce offspring in the next cycle or generation. There is a large body of both theoretical and empirical evidence showing that, even for very large and complex search spaces, genetic algorithms can rapidly lo-

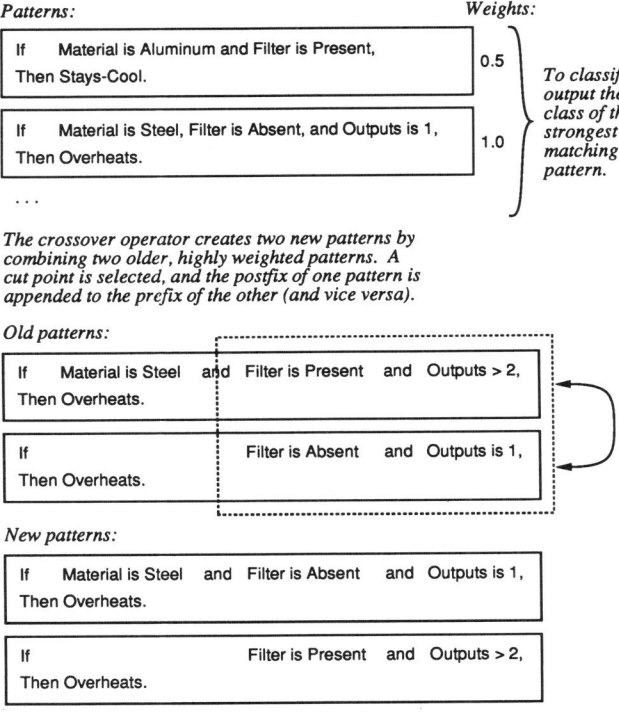

Patterns: Weights:

| If   Material is Aluminum and Filter is Present, Then Stays-Cool. | 0.5 |

| If   Material is Steel, Filter is Absent, and Outputs is 1, Then Overheats. | 1.0 |

To classify, output the class of the strongest matching pattern.

The crossover operator creates two new patterns by combining two older, highly weighted patterns. A cut point is selected, and the postfix of one pattern is appended to the prefix of the other (and vice versa).

Old patterns:

| If   Material is Steel   and   Filter is Present   and   Outputs > 2, Then Overheats. |

| If   Then Overheats.   Filter is Absent   and   Outputs is 1, |

New patterns:

| If   Material is Steel   and   Filter is Absent   and   Outputs is 1, Then Overheats. |

| If   Then Overheats.   Filter is Present   and   Outputs > 2, |

Figure 2. Schematic of the representations and operators used in the genetic algorithm. The weights of conjunctive patterns (shown at top) are used to classify instances. Learning modifies both the weights of patterns and their conditions. The simplest operator generates new patterns that are minor random variations of old ones (not shown). The crossover operator (shown at bottom) splices together an arbitrary prefix of one pattern with an arbitrary suffix of another (and vice versa).

cate effective knowledge structures using about 50 to 100 patterns.

Applying genetic algorithms to classification tasks is straightforward when instances can be represented as features. The set of knowledge structures is initialized to N random patterns, some of which will be very specific and others of which will be quite general. Each pattern is assigned a class. To adjust the weights, each time a pattern is successful (ie, it matches an instance from its own class or it fails to match an instance from another class), its weight is incremented; each time a pattern is unsuccessful (ie, it fails to match its class or matches another class), its weight is decremented. Because pattern weights are decremented when they fail to match instances in their class, if the concept to be learned is disjunctive, the weight of every pattern will be decremented at one time or another. Nevertheless, pattern strength is still a useful heuristic for directing search through the space of descriptions, and genetic algorithms can learn complex disjunctive concepts, even in noisy domains (Wilson, 1987). This ability results in part from the inclusion of many patterns in each generation, some of which compete and others of which complement each other, in that they come to occupy different niches.

Classifier Systems and Problem Solving. Classifier systems are an architecture for problem solving that incorporates a genetic algorithm as a component. Most work along these lines assumes a simple, forward-chaining production system, consisting of a set of condition-action rules and a dynamic working memory. Each rule is weighted and has one or more feature patterns as its condition and a single pattern as its action. Memory contains a set of fully specified patterns, or messages, that have a value for all features. Through encoding conventions, some messages originate as inputs to the system and others trigger outputs.

The classifier system framework extends the standard forward-chaining recognize-act cycle. On every cycle, each rule whose conditions match messages in memory makes a bid proportional to its weight. One or more rules are then selected for application, with probabilities proportional to their bids. The selected rules are applied by adding the patterns in their actions to working memory. These new messages may allow other rules to match, and the cycle continues.

There are two main aspects to learning in classifier systems. First, a genetic algorithm is used to generate new candidate rules from existing, strongly weighted rules (similar to the process described above). Second, the classifier system adjusts the weights of rules based on their contribution to desirable behavior. This involves assigning credit to useful rules and blame to faulty ones. An effective approach to this latter learning problem is called the *bucket brigade* (Holland, 1985). As rules apply, they pass along a portion of their weight to the rules that applied in the cycle before them. Some rule ultimately is rewarded directly by the environment, and this reward is iteratively passed back through the rules in the application chain, increasing their weights. In the simplest case, the weight of any rule that participates in the chain eventually converges on the amount received by the last rule in the chain. As a consequence, rules that apply but do not lead to external reward are consistently paying out their weight without receiving any reinforcement, and their weight diminishes. Classifier systems have been successfully applied to a variety of domains, including regulation of gas flow through pipelines (Goldberg, 1985) and survival in a resource-scarce environment (Booker, 1988).

Alternative Uses of Genetic Algorithms. Unlike classifier systems, which apply operators to propose individual new rules, another approach to using genetic algorithms for problem solving applies genetic operators to entire rule sets. Rather than exploring variations of rule conditions, the operators primarily explore variations on rule combinations. Because of this, the knowledge structure is composed of multiple rule sets, each of which constitutes a forward-chaining production system that has an associated weight.

In this framework, the weight of each rule set is evaluated by running the rules on a set of training problems. Because rule sets with strong weights tend to be selected by the search operators, useful combinations of rules are propagated through the knowledge structure, and less useful rule combinations are gradually eliminated. The operators occasionally introduce new rules, but these are always evaluated in the context of their rule set. The power of these ideas has been demonstrated by a state-of-the-art poker-playing system (Smith, 1983) and by an effective system for multiple class discrimination in the domain of human gait analysis (Schaffer and Grefenstette, 1985). Recent research also shows that a combination of this approach and classifier systems performs better in some domains than either in isolation (Grefenstette and co-workers, 1990).

Open Issues in Genetic Algorithms. Although considerable progress has occurred in the understanding of genetic algorithms since their inception, many open research issues remain. These include:

- *Alternative Representations.* Genetic algorithms typically assume a feature-based representation of knowledge. Future work should explore the application of these methods to more sophisticated representations (Gordon and Grefenstette, 1990; Koza, 1989), adding new genetic operators if necessary.

- *Acquired Representations.* Classifier systems can represent complex class descriptions by the organization, variability, and distribution of weights in clusters of rules. However, we need to better understand the underlying nature of such learned representations and how are they acquired (Belew and Forrest, 1988).

- *Emergence of Useful Symbols.* Classifier systems can use tags to build associations between rules, producing behavioral sequences. Recent work has explored the development of such internal symbols and the conditions under which they emerge (Shaefer, 1987).

- *Credit Assignment.* The issue of credit assignment is central to applying genetic algorithms to problem solving, and a variety of methods have been proposed, including weight update, conflict resolution, and the use of "taxes." Research is needed to determine the conditions under which each approach behaves well and to explore hybrids that might do better than any method in isolation (Grefenstette and co-workers, 1990).

- *Incorporating Domain Knowledge.* Genetic algorithms seem especially well suited for knowledge-lean domains in which extensive search is necessary, but they may also be able to use and refine existing domain knowledge (qv).

- *Population Size.* In some domains, genetic algorithms should behave significantly better than hill-climbing techniques (eg, connectionist methods). Some research has studied the effect of the number of patterns in a knowledge structure (Robertson, 1988), but future work should identify the broader conditions under which maintaining a redundant knowledge structure is worth the cost.

Researchers in the genetic algorithm community are already attacking these problems, but more work remains before this promising approach achieves its full potential.

Empirical Learning Methods

Another community of machine-learning researchers have studied empirical methods for the acquisition of more explicit knowledge structures. Let us consider the dimensions of machine-learning research for this approach. Like connectionist and genetic methods, these techniques are inductive, in that they move beyond training instances to make predictions about novel cases. Unlike them, empirical learning methods have employed relational and structural representations for both experiences and acquired knowledge, though the majority of research has thus far focused on propositional representations. Much of the early work on empirical learning dealt with classification domains, but there has also been progress on problem solving and natural language acquisition.

Currently there are a variety of well-understood methods that learn production rules, decision trees, and concept hierarchies (to name a few of the many learned representations). Some methods require the close supervision of a tutor, as described in the above section on Supervised and Unsupervised Learning, whereas others learn in an unsupervised fashion. Some techniques require all instances at the outset, whereas others learn incrementally and can process new instances with little additional effort. This section reviews three main approaches to empirical learning, along with some open research problems.

Empirically Learning Production Rules. One common scheme for representing domain expertise uses production rules whose conditions test properties of experiences and whose actions specify classifications. Researchers have explored a variety of empirical methods for learning such rules from a set of preclassified training instances, and most approaches rely on the fact that the space of rule conditions are partially ordered according to generality. Thus, one can start with the most specific possible description, using a generalization operator to remove or relax conditions. Alternatively, one can start with the most general possible description, using a specialization operator to add or constrain conditions. The candidate-elimination algorithm (Mitchell, 1977) employs both these ideas to carry out a bidirectional exhaustive search to identify conditions for classification rules. For each possible class, the algorithm maintains a version space that summarizes the space of hypothesized conditions in terms of a most-specific boundary set and a most-general boundary set. New positive instance may indicate the need for more general descriptions, forcing revision of the specific boundary, whereas negative instances may suggest more specific descriptions, leading to revision of the general boundary. This continues until the algorithm converges on a single conjunctive description in both sets, or until one of the boundary sets becomes empty, indicating an inconsistency.

The candidate-elimination algorithm assumes that a single, conjunctive rule can describe each class, and that training instances are free of noise. However, disjuncts and noise are common in applied settings. Another appealing family of learning methods relaxes these assumptions and uses heuristic search to limit computational expense. These methods employ beam search (see SEARCH, BEAM) or related methods to find individual rules that discriminate between positive and negative instances of a class. Search may occur from general to specific rules or in the opposite direction. During each search, candidate rule conditions are minimally specialized (or generalized) in all possible ways, each specialization (or generalization) is heuristically evaluated for predictive accuracy on the training instances, and the best are further modified. Search terminates when none of the new specializations (or generalizations) are statistically better predictors than their predecessors, at which point the best candidate is used to construct a classification rule. To handle disjunctive domains, some methods then remove all positive instances from the training set that are covered by this rule and repeat the search process over the remaining instances, continuing until all positive instances are covered by some rule (Michalski, 1983; Clark and Niblett, 1989). Figure 3 depicts this approach graphically.

Methods of this sort have been successfully applied to moderately realistic tasks. For example, in the domain of lymphography, some rule-learning systems (Michalski, 1987; Clark and Niblett, 1989) have equaled the classification accuracy of human experts (82% correct). Another rule-learning system (Schlimmer, 1987) has demon-

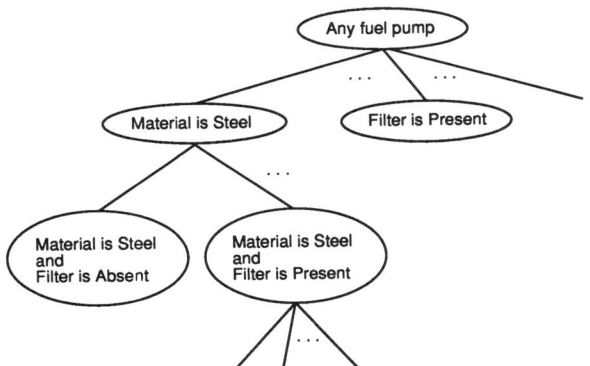

Search moves from general rule conditions to specific ones until the matching pumps are not statistically distinguishable.

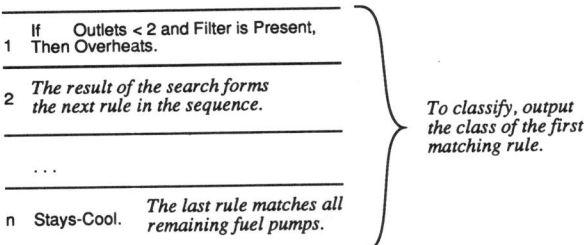

Figure 3. Schematic of the representation and search used in CN2, a recent rule learning method. Learned rules (shown at bottom) are ordered, with the last rule identifying the class of any remaining instances. Search maintains a limited size boundary as it looks for rule conditions that are both predictive and reliable. Initially, it looks for a consistent description of a single class given all the instances, and subsequently it searches for a consistent description of those examples not covered by any rules found thus far. Search terminates when all instances are covered by some rule.

strated similar results for recognizing poisonous mushrooms (95%) and predicting the political party of Congressmen based on their voting records (90%).

In spirit, methods for learning production rules are similar to connectionist and genetic methods. However, there are some significant differences. As we have seen, most of these methods take advantage of the fact that the space of class descriptions can be partially ordered by generality. Thus, most rule-learning schemes search using specialization operators, generalization operators, or both. Second, the search in most rule-learning methods is biased toward finding simple descriptions. If this is appropriate in a given domain, then these methods tend to learn much more quickly than connectionist or genetic methods. Finally, some rule-learning methods represent experience and learned knowledge using relational and structural representations, giving them more expressive power than other approaches.

Although methods for empirical rule learning were originally designed with classification domains in mind, they can also be applied to problem-solving tasks. For example, given a set of legal operators for carrying out state-space search, the same methods can acquire the heuristic conditions under which each operator should be applied. However, this approach requires first identifying appropriate and inappropriate applications of each operator, and this is equivalent to assigning credit and blame to steps along a search path. One response to this latter issue involves waiting until a complete solution has been found. Then, steps along the solution are labeled as appropriate operator applications, whereas all steps leading off the solution are labeled as inappropriate (Langley, 1985; Mitchell and co-workers, 1983). Another response to the credit/blame assignment issue involves interacting directly with a domain expert who provides immediate feedback about the desirability of each action. In either case, one can then apply empirical learning methods to the appropriate and inappropriate applications (as positive and negative instances of the class, respectively), producing heuristic rules as output.

Constructing Decision Trees. Other work on empirical learning takes quite a different approach to the supervised learning task. This framework assumes the same input as systems that learn production rules (ie, a set of instances assigned to classes), but the learned knowledge is represented as a decision tree (Brieman and co-workers, 1984; Quinlan, 1983). Each nonterminal node of this tree specifies some attribute to test, each branch specifies an alternative value, and each terminal node specifies a class. To classify a new instance, a decision tree iteratively tests nonterminal node attributes of that instance and follows matching branches until it reaches a terminal leaf that classifies the instance.

The most common decision-tree learning method uses a divide-and-conquer algorithm, selecting domain attributes to partition the instances and recursively building subdecision trees to describe partitions. An evaluation function selects the most discriminating attribute for each nonterminal node's test. Instances are partitioned based on their value for the test attribute, and subtrees are con-

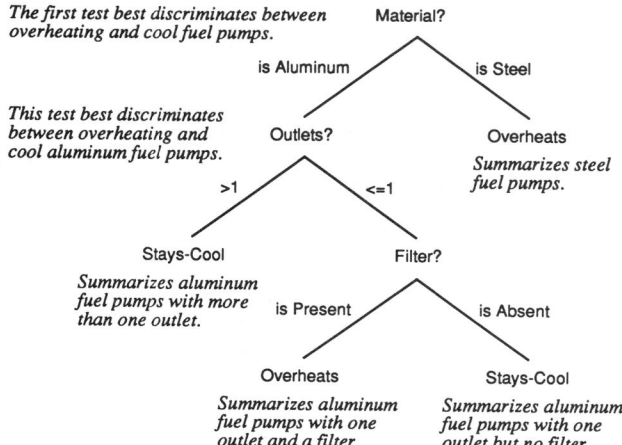

The first test best discriminates between overheating and cool fuel pumps.

This test best discriminates between overheating and cool aluminum fuel pumps.

Material?

is Aluminum   is Steel

Outlets?   Overheats

Summarizes steel fuel pumps.

>1   <=1

Stays-Cool   Filter?

Summarizes aluminum fuel pumps with more than one outlet.

is Present   is Absent

Overheats   Stays-Cool

Summarizes aluminum fuel pumps with one outlet and a filter.   *Summarizes aluminum fuel pumps with one outlet but no filter.*

Figure 4. Schematic of the representation and search used in decision tree learning. To classify an instance, the test at the root of the tree (shown at top) is applied first, and based on the outcome, classification proceeds with the appropriate subtree. The search begins by determining the single most discriminating test. Instances are then partitioned by their outcome for this test. The standard method terminates search when all instances in a partition are of the same class (or there are no more tests), but some variants use statistical tests to halt earlier as an effort to avoid overfitting.

structed to describe each partition. As the process iterates, subtrees are complete when all instances in their partition have the same class (or when there are no more attributes to test). This process can be viewed as a greedy, general-to-specific search through the space of decision trees. Figure 4 shows an example of this approach.

Decision-tree methods have been applied to a variety of classification tasks, representing a mix of synthetic and natural domains. For example, induced decision trees can successfully recognize lost chess endgames (100% for losses in three-ply) (Quinlan, 1983), and they can accurately classify thyroid diseases (99%) (Quinlan and co-workers, 1986). The latter application resulted in a decision tree that outperformed a handcrafted expert system that took years to construct.

Methods for inducing decision trees constitute some of the most widely studied algorithms within the machine learning community. Extensions include techniques for pruning trees in response to noisy training data (Brieman and co-workers, 1984; Kononenko and co-workers, 1984; Quinlan, 1986b), methods for detecting useful thresholds on numeric attributes (Quinlan, 1986a), and algorithms for incrementally revising a tree in response to new data (Schlimmer and Fisher, 1986; Utgoff, 1989). Decision-tree methods have received significant attention within applied AI circles, and some industrial groups have used them to construct expert-level diagnostic systems automatically.

Forming Concept Hierarchies. In unsupervised concept learning tasks, no expert is available to classify instances for the learner. Instead, the learner is given a set of unlabeled instances and is asked to form "useful" concept de-

scriptions. A common approach to this problem, called *conceptual clustering* (see CLUSTERING) (Michalski and Stepp, 1983), involves (1) determining how to cluster the instances and (2) building descriptions for those clusters. Typically, conceptual clustering methods form a hierarchy or taxonomy of concepts. Although they are superficially similar to decision trees, each node in a concept hierarchy has an associated concept description that is used during classification. Also, although both paradigms typically involve a top-down search from simple to more complex representations, conceptual clustering methods use different search operators and evaluation functions than those used for building decision trees. For example, some techniques measure the simplicity of the potential clusters' descriptions; others aim to maximize predictive accuracy over all attributes, since no class information is available.

Conceptual clustering is an active area of research within the empirical learning paradigm. Recent work has focused on using goals to direct the clustering process (Stepp and Michalski, 1986), on devising incremental methods for hierarchy formation (Fisher, 1987; Lebowitz, 1987), and on the role of probabilistic descriptions in clustering (Cheeseman and co-workers, 1988; Fisher, 1987). These methods hold considerable promise because they address the issue of organizing concepts into integrated memory structures.

Methods for conceptual clustering appear to be appropriate for classification domains where no expert is readily available. For example, musicologists viewed the taxonomy formed by one conceptual clustering algorithm as a significant scientific contribution (Michalski and Stepp, 1983). Similarly, a learned set of classes of infrared stellar bodies were judged significant by astronomers (Cheeseman and co-workers, 1988). Finally, conceptual clustering methods have led to improved performance on prediction tasks for other domains, including soybean diagnosis and congressional voting records (Fisher, 1987).

Open Issues in Empirical Learning. Although our understanding of empirical learning methods has reached the stage where initial applications are feasible, basic research is still in progress. Active areas of research include:

- *Incremental Learning.* Many existing empirical methods are nonincremental: They must reprocess many instances to incorporate new information. Incremental methods can be more efficient, but most are not yet as robust as their nonincremental counterparts (Fisher, 1989; Utgoff, 1989).

- *Search-Limited Methods.* Many existing empirical techniques carry out a significant search through their space of descriptions. Search-limited methods, such as hill climbing and greedy algorithms, are much more efficient, but they should be modified to increase their chances of finding satisfactory solutions (Quinlan, 1986a; Langley and co-workers, 1987).

- *Incorporating Domain Knowledge.* Most empirical learning systems use domain knowledge in minimal ways. These methods should be extended to use available knowledge to constrain search and produce clearer knowledge structures (Drastal and co-workers, 1989; Elio and Watanabe, in press; Hirsh, 1989).

- *Representation Change.* Most learning systems are unable to extend their initial representation language. Empirical methods for defining new terms hold great promise, but they must constrain their search for such terms and generate effective candidates (Muggleton and Buntine, 1988; Pagallo, 1989; Matheus and Rendell, 1989).

- *Noise and Concept Drift.* Some methods are robust with respect to noise and changing environments (Schlimmer and Granger, 1986), but researchers should explore the general principles underlying these issues and identify the class of techniques that can handle them.

- *Uncertainty and Probability.* Many expert systems for classification employ probability or other techniques for handling uncertainty, but few learning methods incorporate these ideas. Researchers need to extend existing representations and methods so as to handle uncertainty (Fisher, 1987; Geiger and co-workers, 1990).

Research on empirical techniques is leading to continual progress on the foregoing problems, but much remains to be done in this promising area of machine learning.

Analytic Learning

In contrast to the inductive learning methods discussed so far, another major paradigm in machine learning focuses on analytic learning. This approach emphasizes the transformation of existing domain knowledge into a more useful form, using data only to guide the application of deductive processes to this knowledge. These methods are sometimes called *symbol-level* learners (Dietterich, 1987) because the learned knowledge increases efficiency. [However, in some applications, inductive methods can also improve efficiency (Langley, 1985; Mitchell and co-workers, 1983).] If the performance system must operate under limited resources, such as time or memory, then such learning can indirectly lead to improvements in accuracy as well.

In terms of the dimensions of machine-learning research, learning methods in this paradigm typically encode experiences, domain knowledge, and learned knowledge with relational representations. Because efficiency is the most obvious benefit of analytic learning, these methods have typically been applied to problem-solving performance tasks. They have also been studied in both supervised and unsupervised learning situations; in addition to constructing new operators, these methods have also been applied to the task of improving operator selection. As many have observed, methods of this type could be applied to existing knowledge without the aid of data to guide learning. This nonincremental approach has been predominantly shunned in favor of more computationally efficient, incremental approaches, though there are recent exceptions (Etzioni, 1990).

Explanation-based learning is one common approach that can be viewed as compiling knowledge into an efficient form rather than creating or extending knowledge. This class of learning methods can simplify a problem solver's reasoning process by composing rules into useful combinations. Explanation-based learning can also acquire control knowledge that limits alternatives, thus reducing the amount of search problem solving incurs. There currently exists a number of well-specified algorithms for explanation-based learning, and recently there have been some successful applications to significant problem-solving tasks. This section reviews the basic approach, its adaptation to problem solving, and open research questions.

Compiling Explanations into Rules. Much of AI research on reasoning and theorem proving takes a problem-reduction approach. This framework assumes that domain knowledge is specified as a set of inference rules or goal decompositions. For example, to get from Washington to New York, an agent can drive to National airport, fly to LaGuardia, and take a taxi into the city. Given a top-level goal, an agent can use AND-OR search to find some set of primitive actions, states, or beliefs that will achieve that goal. Some programming languages, such as PROLOG, support this form of reasoning directly.

The result of a problem-reduction search is a proof tree or explanation for how to achieve the initial goal. Methods for explanation-based learning use this information during the learning process to create summarizations of search that can simplify future search for similar goals (DeJong and Mooney, 1986; Mitchell and co-workers, 1986). More precisely, given a problem and its solution, explanation-based learning uses a proof tree for the solution of a problem to: (1) focus attention on relevant problem features, and (2) summarize the problem-solution pair as a general rule. The resulting rule states the conditions under which the proof will hold, and, in the future, similar problems can be solved in fewer search steps.

Figure 5 summarizes the basic ideas that underlie explanation-based learning. This approach proves an important demonstration of the use of knowledge in learning, and the basic method can be applied to any domain in which knowledge can be stated as monotonic production rules (ie, rules that only add knowledge). This includes problem-solving domains for which useful goal decompositions are already known, as well as many reasoning tasks and design problems.

Learning Macro-Operators. Not all research on problem solving views this process in terms of AND-OR search. In contrast, some work focuses on state-space search, in which one applies a sequence of operators to problem states in order to achieve some desired state or goal. For example, in the blocks-world domain, states and goals involve specific configurations of objects, whereas operators specify the preconditions and results of actions that manipulate objects. Explanation-based methods can use knowledge of such legal operators to construct general rules that increase problem-solving efficiency (Fikes and co-workers, 1972).

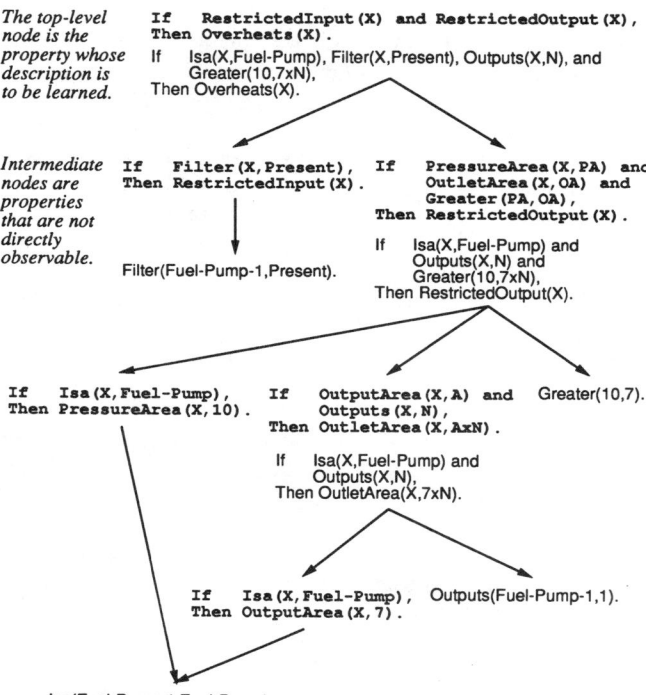

The top-level node is the property whose description is to be learned.

```
If  RestrictedInput(X) and RestrictedOutput(X),
Then Overheats(X).
If  Isa(X,Fuel-Pump), Filter(X,Present), Outputs(X,N), and
    Greater(10,7xN),
Then Overheats(X).
```

Intermediate nodes are properties that are not directly observable.

```
If  Filter(X,Present),        If  PressureArea(X,PA) and
Then RestrictedInput(X).          OutletArea(X,OA) and
                                  Greater(PA,OA),
                              Then RestrictedOutput(X).

Filter(Fuel-Pump-1,Present).  If  Isa(X,Fuel-Pump) and
                                  Outputs(X,N) and
                                  Greater(10,7xN),
                              Then RestrictedOutput(X).
```

```
If  Isa(X,Fuel-Pump),      If  OutputArea(X,A) and     Greater(10,7).
Then PressureArea(X,10).       Outputs(X,N),
                           Then OutletArea(X,AxN).

                           If  Isa(X,Fuel-Pump) and
                               Outputs(X,N),
                           Then OutletArea(X,7xN).
```

```
If  Isa(X,Fuel-Pump),      Outputs(Fuel-Pump-1,1).
Then OutputArea(X,7).
```

```
Isa(Fuel-Pump-1,Fuel-Pump).
```

Leaf nodes are immediately observable properties.

Figure 5. Schematic of the representation used by explanation-based generalization. Properties of an instance (depicted as leaves) and domain knowledge encoded as rules (depicted in teletype font) justify or *explain* other properties of the instance that may not be immediately observable. By extracting the weakest preconditions under which this justification holds, one can construct rules that are more general than the specific instance but more special than the general domain knowledge rules (depicted below each domain knowledge rule in sans-serif font). These rules allow inferring a non-observable property by testing only immediately observable properties of an instance.

The most basic application of explanation-based learning to state-space search is straightforward. Once a problem-solving system has found a sequence of operators that transform an initial state to a goal, one composes this solution path into a single rule or macro-operator (Fikes and co-workers, 1972; Iba, 1989). The conditions of this rule include all aspects of the initial problem state that were required for the solution to hold, and the results include all those actions not undone by others along the way. This composition process is more complex than the one just described because operators can be nonmonotonic (ie, they add and delete facts). However, it is simpler in other ways because solution paths are sequential rather than tree structured.

The construction of macro-operators lets a problem solver take larger steps through a problem space and thus shorten the effective length of solution paths. In contrast to inductive learning methods, macro construction is a purely deductive process: the form of the new rule is completely determined by the primitive operators and their instantiations. Most work on discovering macro-operators has focused on abstract tasks such as the eight puzzle and

the blocks world, but it should apply to any task that can be cast in terms of state-space search. The same basic method also applies to planning approaches, in which subgoals are created during the problem-solving process (Minton, 1985).

Learning Preference Rules for Problem Solving. Another approach to explanation-based learning generates heuristics for problem solving. Although early work on rule-based problem solving used domain-independent heuristics to select which state to expand and which operator to apply during search, some recent learning research has focused on the acquisition of domain-specific search control rules that conditionally prefer one state or operator to another. In the section on Empirically Learning Production Rules, it was shown that one could use empirical methods to learn such heuristics, but this task also fits the requirements of explanation-based methods. [In particular, preference rules are monotonic (ie, they only add facts), so they may be acquired using explanation-based methods.] More work on learning search control has occurred within this paradigm.

In one version of this approach, a mean–ends planning system uses control rules to select a state to expand, an operator to apply, and a binding for the variables in the operator (Minton and co-workers, 1989). When no control rules are available, the problem solver defaults to performing a depth-first search (see SEARCH, DEPTH-FIRST). When search leads to failure or success, the system tries to explain that failure or success using general knowledge of problem solving. In both cases, explanation-based learning compiles the AND-OR explanation into a control rule that the system stores away for future use. This approach has been tested on a number of planning domains, including moderately complex scheduling tasks.

In a related but somewhat different approach, new control rules are learned only when existing control rules result in an ambiguous decision or impasse (Laird and co-workers, 1986). In such cases, the problem-solving system searches to determine the correct answer and compiles the result into a new control rule. Instead of using explicit knowledge about the operators themselves, the conditions of the new control rule incorporate those facts that were used in determining the correct decision, while its actions contain the results of the search. This approach has been tested on a wide range of domains, including design, puzzle-solving, and a computer configuration task (Rosenbloom and co-workers, 1985).

Open Issues in Analytic Learning. Although there have been rapid advances in our understanding of analytic approaches to learning, there remain many significant research issues. The current open problems include:

- *Incorrect and Incomplete Knowledge.* Most existing analytic methods rely on a complete and correct knowledge, but this is seldom a realistic assumption. Researchers should develop methods that behave robustly when some knowledge is missing or faulty (Laird, 1988; Smith and co-workers, 1985).

- *Extending and Revising Knowledge.* Another response to incomplete and incorrect domain knowledge is to extend and revise the knowledge base (Carbonell and Gil, 1987; Muggleton and Buntine, 1988; Ourston and Mooney, 1990). We need methods to detect such problems and alter the knowledge base; note that this requires some form of inductive learning, though deduction may also play a role.

- *Intractable Knowledge.* For useful learning to occur in this framework, the system must already be able to perform search tractably, at least until sufficient knowledge is acquired to control this search. Knowledge bases for some domains, such as chess, are complete but intractable. What types of methods can handle approximate knowledge bases (Tadepalli, 1989), and how can this knowledge be used effectively? Some promising approaches include the use of abstraction (Ellman, 1988; Knoblock, 1990).

- *Nonlogical Knowledge.* Not all domain knowledge is logical in content; in some domains one must rely on heuristic rules or probabilistic relations. Researchers should extend explanation-based methods to use such knowledge to construct explanations and to generate useful rules.

- *Evaluating Alternative Explanations.* Given multiple proofs, a learning method must decide which to compile into the knowledge base for future use. Researchers need to identify the basis for judging an explanation's quality, and they need to devise efficient implementation techniques for this (Ng and Mooney, 1990).

- *The Utility Problem.* Having selected an explanation, a learning method must still determine whether the resulting compiled rule is worth retaining. Additional knowledge can increase retrieval costs and branching factors (qv) on future problems, and learning methods must decide if the cost outweighs the benefit. Recent advances have focused on simplifying compiled rules (Keller, 1987; Minton, 1990), limiting the expressiveness of acquired knowledge (Tambe and Rosenbloom, 1989), and collecting statistics on rule utility (Markovitch and Scott, 1989; Minton, 1990).

As with the other approaches to learning that have been examined, research on explanation-based methods continues to make steady progress, but much more remains to be done.

Case-Based Methods and Analogy

There is mounting evidence that human experts rely at least partly on memory for individual cases, particularly in domains such as law (qv), mathematics (see INDUCTION, MATHEMATICAL), design (qv), and planning (qv). Thus, it seems natural to exploit this idea in constructing AI systems, using memory of specific cases to classify new cases and to formulate plans. This is commonly called the case-based approach, and it constitutes a fifth major paradigm of machine-learning research (see REASONING, CASE-BASED).

Work on reasoning by analogy also falls within this general framework.

Unlike many other machine-learning methods, a general theme of case-based methods is that abstraction of prior experience primarily occurs in a lazy fashion. Rather than aggressively abstracting or compiling experience in anticipation of future use, case-based methods typically save the bulk of their processing until an actual use occurs for this experience. With this deferred processing scheme, three fundamental issues arise: (1) retrieving case(s) that may help with a new case, (2) matching and applying the retrieved case(s) to the new case, and (3) storing the outcome of the new case for future use. Rather than discuss each of these issues separately, this section reviews three subparadigms within the case-based paradigm and discusses the issues as they arise.

Consider the placement of case-based methods on the dimensions of machine-learning research. This framework represents individual experience either propositionally or with relational languages, although the latter are not as widespread because of the undesirable matching complexity that may result. Like empirical learning methods, case-based methods have been applied to both classification and problem-solving tasks; they have been applied in both supervised and unsupervised learning situations; and they are predominantly incremental. Current case-based methods always perform induction (usually at retrieval time), but many include an analytic learning component as well.

Nearest-Neighbor Techniques. In the simplest variant on the case-based framework, one simply stores past instances verbatim. When a new case is encountered, one finds the best match from among the stored instances, and then uses that case to supply the missing information directly. For example, in a medical diagnosis domain, each case would consist of a patient's symptoms along with his disease. Given a new patient's symptoms, this simple variant enumerates stored cases to find the "nearest neighbor" and uses its associated disease to predict the patient's malady. Figure 6 illustrates the basic technique. Nearest-neighbor algorithms are not limited to classification domains, as shown in recent work using case-based techniques for state-space problem solving (Bradtke and Lehnert, 1988).

Variants on this method are possible, such as expanding retrieval to making predictions based on a weighted average using the K nearest neighbors. Applying this technique to the task of mapping letters to phonemes achieves an 88% predictive accuracy on a test set of 1024 instances (Stanfill, 1987). The same research also demonstrates that this method degrades gracefully as one adds noise and as one decreases the size of the case base.

Uncontrolled growth of the case base is a natural concern in this paradigm. Thus, one may want to store cases selectively and delete others on occasion. In one instance of this approach, new cases are stored only when the existing knowledge base leads to a classification error (Aha and co-workers, in press). Although relatively unsophisticated, the predictive accuracy of this approach compares favorably to methods for inducing decision trees, and a

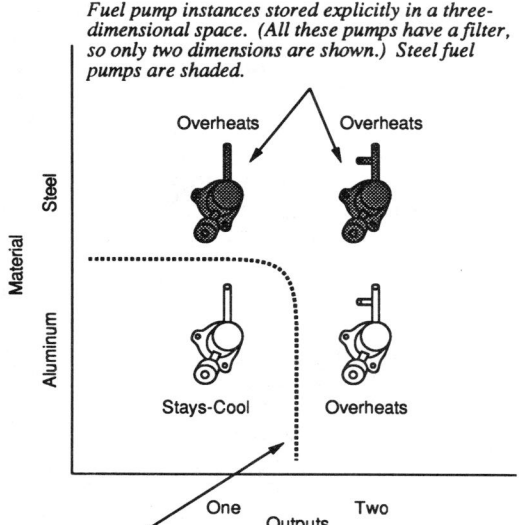

Fuel pump instances stored explicitly in a three-dimensional space. (All these pumps have a filter, so only two dimensions are shown.) Steel fuel pumps are shaded.

Virtual boundary that separates cool from overheating fuel pumps, defined by nearest neighbors. Shown for clarity.

Figure 6. Schematic of the representation used in nearest neighbor learning methods. Instances are stored explicitly in a space of N dimensions, where each dimension describes one feature of the instance. The figure depicts the two-dimensional case. To classify an instance, one finds the nearest stored instance and predicts its class. It is possible to define a decision boundary representing equal distance from stored instances of different classes (shown as a curved line in the middle of the figure). Typically these decision boundaries are not stored explicitly.

similar approach has been successfully applied to the challenging domain of speech recognition (Bradshaw, 1987).

Analogical Matching. Given feature-based or attribute-based representations, the process of matching two cases is simple and inexpensive. However, domains like planning and design require structural or relational representations, and these introduce serious complexities into the match process. Because the new case and the stored case are unlikely to match exactly, one must perform some form of partial matching, and this problem is exponential (Watanabe and Rendell, 1990).

Researchers concerned with the process of analogy have devoted considerable attention to this issue, with most approaches involving some form of heuristic search through the space of partial matches. In this framework, the main issue becomes findings ways to constrain and direct the search for a useful match. For instance, one approach finds mappings that preserve higher-order relations between two cases in preference to ones that preserve simple features shared by the cases (Falkenhainer and co-workers, 1989). Other researchers (eg, Winston, 1984) have proposed different but related methods. In a complementary vein, knowledge about the domain can help evaluate potential matches and identify meaningful partial matches (Koton, 1988b).

Indexing and Memory Organization. Even with selective storage of cases, complex real-world domains might require thousands of instances, some having considerable structure that requires complex analogical matching. In such situations, one cannot afford to match against all cases stored in memory exhaustively, and the initial storage and subsequent retrieval of relevant cases become central issues. The natural response is to index cases by appropriate features, thus making the retrieval process more selective and reducing the effect of memory size. Early work on analogy focused on matching to the exclusion of indexing issues, but this has changed in recent years.

The first step in indexing cases involves selecting an appropriate set of indexes. The programmer can fix the indexes at the outset, but this produces an inflexible system that cannot adapt to new domains. Some researchers (eg, Lebowitz, 1987) have invoked inductive learning methods to identify predictive features, which are then used as indexes. Others have used explanation-based techniques to determine relevant features for each case and index on these instead. Problem-solving domains are especially well-suited to the latter approach, as the trace of problem-solving behavior (ie, goal trees) provides ready-made information for explaining success or failure (Carbonell, 1986; Hammond, 1986), which can then be used to index complex cases. The notion of derivational replay (Mostow, 1989) based on such problem-solving traces has received attention in many circles, including software engineering and automated VLSI design.

However, indexing by itself is not sufficient to allow efficient retrieval of relevant cases. For large knowledge bases, one must also organize memory into some manageable structure. Discrimination networks (Feigenbaum, 1963) are one approach to memory organization, but retrieval of a case often depends on a conjunction of features being present. This leads to fragility in domains where features can be missing, but the basic approach can be extended to support redundant indexing (Kolodner, 1983; Lebowitz, 1987; Fisher, 1987). In addition, one can store abstract summary descriptions at internal nodes in the network, giving generalization beyond individual cases. The construction of prototypes in this manner reveals an underlying similarity between case-based learning and conceptual clustering, which was discussed under Forming Concept Hierarchies.

Open Issues in Case-Based Learning. Research on case-based approaches has led to a number of promising methods, some of which have been tested on challenging domains. However, a number of open issues remain to be addressed:

- *Selecting Indexes.* A number of methods exist for selecting indexes. However, we need to identify common processes that underlie these approaches and the common information they exploit (Bareiss and co-workers, 1987; Hammond, 1986). We also need to better understand methods that generate indexes dynamically (Barletta and Mark, 1988; Kolodner, 1989; Owens, 1989).

- *Memory Organization*. Some initial work has addressed the organization of memory, but we need to identify the general properties that a memory should exhibit and to improve methods for dynamically reorganizing memory as new cases are encountered (Kolodner, 1983).

- *Matching Metrics*. Many existing techniques employ ad hoc schemes for matching against cases in memory. Researchers need to search for underlying principles involved in determining a good match and to develop methods for predicting good matches (Kolodner, 1989; Koton, 1988a; Salzberg, 1990).

- *Multiple Cases*. Analogy has predominantly focused on using sophisticated information from a single case, whereas *K* nearest-neighbor methods illustrate how to use simple information from multiple cases. Some early work has focused on combining highly relevant but contrasting cases (Ashley and Rissland, 1988), but we need to identify other types of information that multiple cases can provide (Aha and Kibler, 1990; Redmond, 1990).

- *Connections Among Cases*. In some domains, each case may have a complex, internal structure, effectively consisting of many component cases. Researchers should devise principled representational schemes that can capture connections between component cases and find methods for efficiently storing and retrieving such structures (Jones, 1989; Redmond, 1990; Sycara, 1988).

- *Forgetting*. Although most cases are useful, storage of all cases can lead to overfitting effects in noisy domains. We need techniques that can efficiently determine when to forget cases (Aha and co-workers, in press). An alternative is to develop methods that selectively acquire knowledge, thereby limiting the discovery of useless cases and unnecessary processing (Hunter, 1990).

Work on case-based reasoning has produced some promising techniques, but researchers need to explore the space of such methods more fully and to evaluate alternative approaches carefully in terms of their performance on real-world domains.

Relationships Among the Paradigms

Historically, machine-learning researchers have emphasized differences among the five paradigms we have discussed, rather than their similarities. This trend has been encouraged by differences in terminology, notation, test cases, and methods of evaluation. For instance, researchers studying connectionist techniques, genetic algorithms, and rule induction often run experiments with their inductive methods, but they typically use different data sets and measure different aspects of learning behavior. The same problem occurs between workers in the explanation-based and case-based paradigms. Our discussion so far has reflected this trend, focusing on the differences between the five learning frameworks.

However, understanding the similarities among these paradigms is equally important to the science of machine learning. To this end, let us briefly consider some possible connections.

- *Symbolic and Subsymbolic Induction*. Many distinguish the subsymbolic approach of connectionist and genetic algorithms from the symbolic approach taken by empirical methods for rule induction and decision-tree construction. But despite differences in the representation of acquired knowledge, the spaces searched, and the learning operators employed, all three approaches are inductive in nature, and one can generally apply them to the same learning tasks. Recent comparative studies have clarified this fact (Mooney and co-workers, 1989; Dietterich and co-workers, 1990), producing comparable results for a variety of methods.

- *Induction and Explanation*. Researchers often make a dichotomy between inductive (eg, empirical) methods and analytic (eg, explanation-based) ones, characterizing the former as knowledge lean and the latter as knowledge intensive. Yet there is nothing mutually exclusive about these approaches, and hybrid methods should prove better than either in isolation. For instance, recent work on empirical methods has shown that domain knowledge and deduction can improve learning (Drastal and co-workers, 1989; Elio and Watanabe, in press). Similarly, one can use empirical methods to extend incomplete domain knowledge and to revise incorrect rules (Carbonell and Gil, 1987; Ourston and Mooney, 1990).

- *Explanations and Cases*. Explanation-based methods use domain knowledge to construct explanations and compile rules, but some case-based techniques rely just as heavily on domain expertise (Braverman and Wilensky, 1990; Redmond, 1989). Although one approach stores general rules and the other stores specific cases, the reasoning processes can be remarkably similar.

- *Cases and Abstractions*. Researchers often emphasize the distinction between storing specific cases and forming abstractions. Yet many case-based systems create abstractions as indexes for cases (Kolodner, 1983; Fisher, 1987), making them more accurately described as hybrids. Nor must a system that stores cases always use them during performance; in some situations, a hybrid system may prefer to use an abstraction. (Fisher, 1989). Moreover, work on conceptual clustering and on case-based learning shares a concern with the organization of memory, relying on similar structures and mechanisms.

In summary, there is considerable overlap between the paradigms in both their concerns and their approaches, although this is seldom apparent from research papers. Machine learning has just begun to converge on a set of standard terms and notations for describing systems and on a set of standard test beds and experimental methodologies for evaluating systems.

As researchers start to communicate across paradigm

boundaries, they can begin exploring the relationships more seriously. For instance, one can imagine a unified theory of induction that explains the behavior of decision-tree methods, genetic algorithms, and connectionist networks and that predicts the conditions under which each method would be most appropriate. One can also expect the development of hybrid algorithms that cut across paradigms to achieve better results than either in isolation. Some research along these lines has already begun, such as recent work on combining decision trees with perceptrons (Utgoff, 1988). We hope that some researchers will concentrate their efforts on such cross-paradigm research, as this may lead to new techniques that otherwise might never come to light. If such systems were successful, this would further strengthen the ties between areas, ultimately transforming machine learning into a unified field rather than many subdisciplines.

METHODOLOGICAL DEVELOPMENTS

Machine learning is a scientific discipline; thus careful methodological foundations are essential to its success. Over the past few years, some significant methodological advances have occurred in the field, paving the way for more careful work in the future. These include new techniques for the formal analysis of learning algorithms, new experimental approaches to studying learning, successful applications to real-world domains, and the development of integrated cognitive architectures. These changes bode well for this emerging subfield of artificial intelligence. Each of them is discussed briefly in this section.

Theoretical Analyses of Learning Algorithms

Although formal studies of inductive inference have a long history in computer science (Angluin and Smith, 1983), only recently have theorists started to address issues of concern to researchers who actually build machine-learning systems. Initial ideas focused on the notion of convergence: would the learning method eventually construct the exact knowledge desired (Gold, 1967)? This approach constituted an important first step, but it did not afford much insight into realistic learning problems.

A major breakthrough came when researchers turned their focus to the question of evaluating the quality of inductively learned knowledge. The notion of probably approximately correct (PAC) learning forwarded the idea that learned knowledge should usually be relatively accurate when applied in novel situations. Coupling this idea with computational feasibility yields a definition for problems that are polynomially learnable: (1) it must not require too many instances to learn; (2) there must exist an efficient learning method that can produce PAC knowledge; and (3) it must be possible to efficiently determine whether knowledge is consistent with any given instance (Blumer and co-workers, 1987).

When studying the learnability of a particular problem, one common research tactic is to show that one of the three criteria cannot be met. However, because each of these three criteria depends on how acquired knowledge is

represented, results of negative learnability can be brittle. For instance, learning K of N functions using a linear threshold unit with only zero or one weights is not polynomially learnable, but the same class of functions are learnable if the linear threshold unit can use integer weights (Haussler, 1990).

The initial theoretical frameworks focused on learning logical, feature-based concepts in a supervised setting (Kearns and co-workers, 1987), but researchers have since extended the basic framework to other paradigms, including structural concepts (Haussler, 1987), decision lists (Rivest, 1987), conceptual clustering (Pitt and Reinke, 1988), and connectionist networks (Valiant, 1988). They have also addressed learning in the presence of noise (Angluin and Laird, 1988), and they have moved beyond inductive methods to deal with explanation-based methods (Natarajan and Tadepalli, 1988). Even many nontheorists follow this work closely, and many theorists actively read the empirical literature in search of challenging problems.

Experimental Studies of Learning Algorithms

Despite progress on the theoretical front, many learning algorithms remain too complex for formal analysis, and recent progress has also been made in the experimental study of learning methods (Kibler and Langley, 1988). Much of the experimental work has focused on inductive methods (Fahlman, 1988; Fisher, 1987; Quinlan, 1986b; Schlimmer, 1987), but there are also a growing number of experimental studies of explanation-based techniques (Minton and co-workers, 1989; Shavlik, 1990).

One important insight is that performance is the natural dependent measure for such empirical studies, because one can define learning as improvement in performance. There are many measures of performance, including classification accuracy, quality of solution paths, and even CPU time. Different measures are appropriate for different domains and different learning methods, as they may have different goals. However, having at least some measure of performance is essential to evaluating a learning system's behavior. In some cases, intuitively plausible learning methods actually lead to worse performance (Minton, 1985). In other cases, one can use performance measures to determine which components significantly aid the learning process (Schlimmer, 1987).

Researchers have also started to carefully examine the aspects of domains that affect learning behavior. Some experimental studies have focused on naturalistic data in order to show real-world relevance, but others have constructed synthetic domains to allow control of domain characteristics. Two obvious features include complexity of the knowledge to be learned and amount of noise in the data, but others certainly exist. The important point is that many researchers now realize that, in order to make progress, the field requires some explicit methods for evaluating alternative methods and for identifying the conditions under which they work well. Theoretical analyses provide one route to such understanding, but systematic experimentation is another important path.

Common Testbeds and Applications

Early research in machine learning focused on idealized, handcrafted examples, and researchers often tested their systems on only a handful of cases. This has changed drastically in recent years, and papers in the literature now commonly report results on realistic learning tasks that involve many test cases. Moreover, researchers typically report results on a number of different data sets, to show the robustness and generality of their algorithms. The average number of test domains should increase as the standards of the field become higher.

Another encouraging sign is that researchers are starting to test their algorithms on the same task domains, allowing comparisons to be made. This trend has been aided by the collection and distribution of standard data sets. For instance, data on soybean diseases (Michalski and Chilausky, 1980), thyroid diseases (Quinlan, 1987), edibility of mushrooms (Schlimmer, 1987), and Congressional voting records (Fisher, 1987) have been widely distributed and used in testing a number of learning algorithms. Major repositories have emerged, with researchers collecting, documenting, and distributing benchmark data sets. Many of these deal with classification and diagnosis, but standard problem-solving and reasoning tasks are also beginning to emerge.

Despite these encouraging developments, most of these real-world domains remain relatively simple and straightforward. Hopefully, future application efforts will tackle more difficult testbeds that provide greater challenges for machine-learning methods. It is also hoped that the trend will expand to include the documentation and distribution of published algorithms, so that researchers can employ each others' software. This has started to occur within some machine-learning paradigms, but more remains to be done.

Integrated Cognitive Architectures

Another methodological advance relates to the development of integrated architectures for cognition. Early AI researchers commonly implemented a separate system for each new task they encountered. As the field gained experience, high-level languages (eg, production systems) were developed and used to implement new systems, with considerable savings in time and effort. However, these languages incorporated only minor theoretical commitments about the nature of intelligent behavior, and thus provided few constraints on the resulting AI systems. For instance, few formalisms included any automated learning mechanisms.

This trend has changed in recent years, with many researchers now turning to integrated architectures that make strong assumptions about the control structures needed to support intelligence. SOAR (qv) is a prime example of this approach (Laird and co-workers, 1986), and the classifier systems of the genetic algorithm community constitute another instance. Most work in this growing movement includes some automated learning mechanism as an integral part of the architecture, and generality is a central concern, with researchers testing their frameworks on a variety of domains. For instance, the PROD-

IGY (Minton and co-workers, 1989) and THEO (Mitchell and co-workers, in press) architectures incorporate explanation-based methods into their problem-solving engines, whereas ICARUS (Langley and co-workers, in press) relies on case-based concept formation as its main learning mechanism, and DYNA (Sutton, 1990) uses connectionist learning methods. Such integrated frameworks will be necessary if we ever hope to construct intelligent artifacts that can interact with the physical world. We predict that learning will occupy a central role in successful cognitive architectures.

SUMMARY

Over the last decade, the theoretical and methodological advances described in the previous sections have transported machine learning from the sidelines of AI into one of its central foci. Along with this shift has come increased contact with other subcommunities, and as methods for machine learning become more robust, they are gaining increased attention from researchers concerned with planning, diagnosis, natural language, and other problem-oriented areas of artificial intelligence. In turn, these domains provide significant real-world challenges for scientists who have traditionally been concerned with abstract issues in machine learning.

Without doubt, the growing concern with applications will reveal limitations of the existing paradigms and suggest novel directions for automating the acquisition of knowledge. Thus, researchers will be forced to devise new representations, search frameworks, and control schemes to support the learning process. The resulting approaches may initially be domain specific, inefficient, and inelegant, but they will respond to issues that have been previously ignored. Such learning methods may not fit nicely into the organization we have presented, but that is often the nature of scientific progress.

At the same time, others will continue to pursue basic research on learning mechanisms, driven by recognized open issues such as those listed above. These scientists will explore variations and hybrids of existing methods, propose frameworks that unify apparently different techniques, and carry out experimental and theoretical studies to identify the behavior of alternative methods under varying conditions. They should also begin to relate experimental results to those predicted by theory, revising the theory when necessary. Finally, they will attempt to identify new dimensions and new themes that have emerged from the applied work, idealizing them in ways that lets them be studied in the same manner as existing paradigms.

Taken together, basic and applied research in this area should continue to improve the range and capabilities of learning algorithms and to increase our understanding of mechanisms for improving performance with experience. These advances in turn will have far-ranging implications for the rest of artificial intelligence, letting the field move beyond static systems to ones that change their behavior over time as they acquire and refine knowledge.

BIBLIOGRAPHY

D. H. Ackley, G. E. Hinton, and T. J. Sejnowski, "A Learning Algorithm for Boltzmann Machines," *Cog. Sci.* **9**, 147–169 (1987).

D. W. Aha and D. Kibler, "Noise-Tolerant Instance-Based Learning Algorithms," *Proceedings of the Eleventh International Joint Conference on Artificial Intelligence,* Detroit, Morgan-Kaufmann, San Mateo, Calif., 1990, 794–799.

D. W. Aha, D. Kibler, and M. K. Albert, "Instance-Based Learning Algorithms," *Machine Learning* (in press).

D. Angluin and P. Laird, "Learning from Noisy Examples," *Machine Learning,* **2**, 343–370 (1988).

D. Angluin and C. Smith, "Inductive Inference: Theory and Methods," *Comput. Surv.* **15**, 237–269 (1983).

K. D. Ashley and E. L. Rissland, "Waiting on Weighting: A Symbolic Least Commitment Approach," *Proceedings of the Seventh National Conference on Artificial Intelligence,* St. Paul, Minn., AAAI Press, Menlo Park, Calif., 1988, 239–244.

É. R. Bareiss, B. W. Porter, and C. C. Wier, "PROTOS: An Exemplar-Based Learning Apprentice," *Proceedings of the Fourth International Workshop on Machine Learning,* Irvine, Calif., Morgan-Kaufmann, San Mateo, Calif., 1987, 12–23.

R. Barletta and W. Mark, "Explanation-Based Indexing of Cases," *Proceedings of the Seventh National Conference on Artificial Intelligence,* St. Paul, Minn., AAAI Press, Menlo Park, Calif., 1988, 541–546.

A. G. Barto, R. S. Sutton, and C. W. Anderson, "Neuronlike Elements That Can Solve Difficult Learning Control Problems," *IEEE Trans. System Man Cybernetics,* **13**, 835–846 (1983).

R. K. Belew and S. Forrest, "Learning and Programming in Classifier Systems," *Machine Learning* **3**, 193–223 (1988).

A. Blumer, A. Ehrenfeucht, D. Haussler, and M. K. Warmuth, "Occam's Razor," *Info. Proc. Lett.* **24**, 377–380 (1987).

L. B. Booker, "Classifier Systems That Learn Internal World Models," *Machine Learning* **3**, 161–192 (1988).

G. Bradshaw, "Learning About Speech Sounds: The NEXUS project," *Proceedings of the Fourth International Workshop on Machine Learning,* Irvine, Calif. Morgan-Kaufmann, 1987, 1–11.

S. Bradtke and W. G. Lehnert, "Some Experiments with Case-based Search," *Proceedings of the Seventh National Conference on Artificial Intelligence,* St. Paul, Minn., AAAI Press, Menlo Park, Calif. 1988, 133–138.

M. S. Braverman and R. Wilensky, "Toward a Unification of Case-Based Reasoning and Explanation-Based Learning," *Proceedings of the 1990 AAAI Spring Symposium on Case-Based Reasoning,* Stanford, Calif., 1990.

L. Brieman, J. H. Friedman, R. A. Olshen, and C. J. Stone, *Classification and Regression Trees,* Wadsworth, Belmont, Calif., 1984.

J. G. Carbonell, "Derivational Analogy: A Theory of Reconstructive Problem Solving and Expertise Acquisition" in R. S. Michalski, J. G. Carbonell, and T. M. Mitchell, eds., *Machine Learning: An Artificial Intelligence Approach,* vol. 2, Morgan-Kaufmann, San Mateo, Calif., 1986.

J. G. Carbonell and Y. Gil, "Learning by Experimentation," *Proceedings of the Fourth International Workshop on Machine Learning,* Irvine, Calif., Morgan-Kaufmann, San Mateo, Calif., 1987, 256–266.

P. Cheeseman, J. Kelly, M. Self, J. Stutz, W. Taylor, and D. Freeman, "AUTOCLASS: A Bayesian Classification System," *Proceedings of the Fifth International Conference on Machine Learning,* Ann Arbor, Mich., Morgan-Kaufman, San Mateo, Calif., 1988, 54–64.

P. Clark and T. Niblett, "The CN2 Induction Algorithm," *Machine Learning 3,* 261–284 (1989).

T. R. Cover and P. E. Hart, "Nearest Neighbor Pattern Classification," *IEEE Trans. Inf. Theory* **13**, 21–27 (1967).

R. Davis and D. B. Lenat, *Knowledge-Based Systems in Artificial Intelligence,* McGraw-Hill, New York, 1982.

G. DeJong and R. J. Mooney, "Explanation-based Learning: An Alternative View," *Machine Learning* **1**, 145–176 (1986)

T. G. Dietterich, "Learning at the Knowledge Level," *Machine Learning* **1**, 287–316 (1987).

T. G. Dietterich, H. Hild, and G. Bakiri, "A Comparative Study of ID3 and Backpropagation for English Text-to-Speech Mapping," *Proceedings of the Seventh International Conference on Machine Learning,* Austin, Tex., Morgan-Kaufmann, San Mateo, Calif., 1990, 24–31.

G. Drastal, G. Czako, and S. Raatz, "Induction in an Abstraction Space: A Form of Constructive Induction," *Proceedings of the Eleventh International Joint Conference on Artificial Intelligence,* Detroit, Mich., Morgan-Kaufmann, San Mateo, Calif., 1989, 708–712.

R. Elio and L. Watanabe, "An Incremental Deductive Strategy for Controlling Constructive Induction in Learning from Examples," *Machine Learning* (in press).

T. Ellman "Approximate Theory Formation: An Explanation-Based Approach," *Proceedings of the Seventh National Conference on Artificial Intelligence,* St. Paul, Minn., AAAI Press, Menlo Park, Calif., 1988, 570–574.

J. L. Elman, "Finding Structure in Time," *Cog. Sci.* **14**, 179–211 (1990).

O. Etzioni, "Why PRODIGY/EBL Works," *Proceedings of the Eighth National Conference on Artificial Intelligence,* Boston, AAAI Press, Menlo Park, Calif., 1990, 916–922.

S. E. Fahlman, "Faster-Learning Variations on Back-Propagation: An Empirical Study," *Proceedings of the 1988 Connectionist Models Summer School,* Pittsburgh, Morgan-Kaufmann, San Mateo, Calif., 1988, 38–51.

S. E. Fahlman and C. Lebiere, *The Cascade-Correlation Learning Architecture.* Technical Report CMU-CS-90-100, Carnegie Mellon University, School of Computer Science, Pittsburgh, 1990.

B. Falkenhainer, K. D. Forbus, and D. Gentner, "The Structure-Mapping Engine: Algorithm and Examples," *Artif. Intell.* **41**, 1–63 (1989).

E. A. Feigenbaum, "The Simulation of Verbal Learning Behavior," in E. A. Feigenbaum and J. Feldman, eds., *Computers and Thought,* McGraw-Hill, New York, 1963.

R. E. Fikes, P. E. Hart, and N. J. Nilsson, "Learning and Executing Generalized Robot Plans," *Artif. Intell.* **3**, 251–288 (1972).

D. H. Fisher, "Knowledge Acquisition via Incremental Conceptual Clustering," *Machine Learning* **2**, 139–172 (1987).

D. H. Fisher, "Noise-Tolerant Conceptual Clustering," *Proceedings of the Eleventh International Joint Conference on Artificial Intelligence,* Detroit, Morgan-Kaufmann, 1989, 825–830.

D. H. Fisher and P. Langley, "Approaches to Conceptual Clustering," *Proceedings of the Ninth International Joint Conference on Artificial Intelligence,* Los Angeles, Morgan-Kaufmann, San Mateo, Calif., 1985, 691–697).

D. Fisher and K. B. McKusick, "An Empirical Comparison of ID3 and Back-Propagation," *Proceedings of the Eleventh International Joint Conference on Artificial Intelligence,* Detroit, Morgan-Kaufmann, San Mateo, Calif., 1989, 788–793.

D. Geiger, A. Paz, and J. Pearl, "Learning Causal Trees from Dependency Information," *Proceedings of the Eighth National Conference on Artificial Intelligence,* Boston, AAAI Press, Menlo Park, Calif., 1990, 770–776.

E. Gold, "Language Identification in the Limit," *Inf. Control* **16,** 447–474 (1967)

D. E. Goldberg, "Genetic Algorithms and Rule Learning in Dynamic System Control," *Proceedings of the First International Conference on Genetic Algorithms and Their Applications,* Pittsburgh, Lawrence Erlbaum, Hillsdale, N.J., 1985, 8–15.

D. E. Goldberg, *Genetic Algorithms in Search, Optimization, and Machine Learning,* Addison-Wesley, Reading, Mass., 1990.

D. F. Gordon and J. J. Grefenstette, "Explanations of Empirically Derived Reactive Plans," *Proceedings of the Seventh International Conference on Machine Learning,* Austin, Tex., Morgan-Kaufmann, San Mateo, Calif., 1990, 198–203.

J. J. Grefenstette, C. L. Ramsey, and A. C. Schultz, "Learning Sequential Decision Rules Using Simulation Models and Competition," *Machine Learning* **5,** 355–381 (1990).

K. Hammond, "Learning to Anticipate and Avoid Planning Problems Through the Explanation of Failures," *Proceedings of the Fifth National Conference on Artificial Intelligence,* Philadelphia, AAAI Press, Menlo Park, Calif., 1986, 556–560.

S. E. Hampson and D. J. Volper, "Disjunctive Models of Boolean Category Learning," *Biol. Cybern.* **56,** 121–137 (1987).

D. Haussler, "Bias, Version Spaces, and Valiant's Learning Framework," *Proceedings of the Fourth International Workshop on Machine Learning,* Irvine, Calif., Morgan-Kaufmann, San Mateo, Calif., 1987, 324–336.

D. Haussler, "Probably Approximately Correct Learning," *Proceedings of the Eighth National Conference on Artificial Intelligence,* Boston, AAAI Press, Menlo Park, Calif., 1990, 1101–1108.

G. E. Hinton, "Learning Distributed Representations of Concepts," *Proceedings of the Eighth Annual Conference of the Cognitive Science Society,* Amherst, Mass., Lawrence Erlbaum, Hillsdale, N.J., 1986, 1–12.

G. E. Hinton, "Connectionist Learning Procedures," *Artif. Intel.* **40,** 185–234 (1989).

H. Hirsh, "Combining Empirical and Analytical Learning with Version Spaces," *Proceedings of the Sixth International Workshop on Machine Learning,* Ithaca, N.Y., Morgan-Kaufmann, Publishers, San Mateo, Calif., 1989.

J. H. Holland, "Properties of the Bucket Brigade Algorithm," *Proceedings of the First International Conference on Genetic Algorithms and Their Applications,* Pittsburgh, Lawrence Erlbaum, Hillsdale, N.J., 1985, 1–7.

L. Hunter, "Planning to Learn," *Proceedings of the Twelfth Annual Conference of the Cognitive Science Society* Cambridge, Mass., Lawrence Erlbaum, Hillsdale, N.J., 1990, 261–268.

G. A. Iba, "A Heuristic Approach to the Discovery of Macro-Operators," *Machine Learning* **3,** 285–317 (1989).

R. Jones, *A Model of Retrieval in Problem Solving,* Technical Report 89-27, Ph.D. dissertation, University of California, Irvine, Department of Information and Computer Science, 1989.

M. Kearns, M. Li, L. Pitt, and L. G. Valiant, "Recent Results on Boolean Concept Learning," *Proceedings of the Fourth International Workshop on Machine Learning,* Irvine, Calif., Morgan-Kaufmann, San Mateo, Calif., 1987, 337–352.

R. M. Keller, "Concept Learning in Context," *Proceedings of the Fourth International Workshop on Machine Learning,* Irvine, Calif., Morgan-Kaufmann, San Mateo, Calif., 1987, 91–102.

D. Kibler and P. Langley, "Machine Learning as an Experimental Science," *Proceedings of the Third European Working Session on Learning,* Pittman, London, 1988.

K. Knight, *A Gentle Introduction to Subsymbolic Computation: Connectionist for the A.I. Researcher,* Technical Report CMU-CS-89-150, Carnegie Mellon University, School of Computer Science, Pittsburgh, 1989.

C. Knoblock, "Learning Abstraction Hierarchies for Problem Solving," *Proceedings of the Eighth National Conference on Artificial Intelligence,* Boston, AAAI Press, Menlo Park, Calif., 1990, 923–928.

T. Kohonen, E. Oja, and P. Lehtiö, "Storage and Processing of Information in Distributed Associative Memory Systems," in G. E. Hinton and J. A. Anderson, eds., *Parallel Models of Associative Memory,* Lawrence Erlbaum, Hillsdale, N.J., 1981.

J. L. Kolodner, "Maintaining Organization in a Dynamic Long-term Memory," *Cog. Sci.* **7,** 243–280 (1983).

J. L. Kolodner, "Selecting the Best Case for a Case-Based Reasoner," *Proceedings of the Eleventh Annual Conference of the Cognitive Science Society,* Ann Arbor, Mich., Lawrence Erlbaum, Hillsdale, N.J., 1989, 155–162.

I. Kononenko, I. Bratko, and E. Roskar, *Experiments in Automatic Learning of Medical Diagnostic Rules,* Josef Stefan Institute, Ljubljana, Yugoslavia, 1984.

P. Koton, "Integrating Case-based and Causal Reasoning," *Proceedings of the Tenth Annual Conference of the Cognitive Science Society,* Montreal, Quebec, Canada, Lawrence Erlbaum, Hillsdale, N.J., 1988a, 167–173.

P. Koton, "Reasoning About Evidence in Causal Explanation," *Proceedings of the Seventh National Conference on Artificial Intelligence,* St. Paul, Minn., AAAI Press, Menlo Park, Calif., 1988b, 256–261.

J. R. Koza, "Hierarchical Genetic Algorithms Operating on Populations of Computer Programs," *Proceedings of the Eleventh International Joint Conference on Artificial Intelligence,* Detroit, Morgan-Kaufmann, San Mateo, Calif., 1989, 768–774.

J. E. Laird, "Recovery from Incorrect Knowledge in SOAR," *Proceedings of the Seventh National Conference on Artificial Intelligence,* St. Paul, Minn., AAAI Press, Menlo Park, Calif., 1988, 618–623.

J. E. Laird, P. S. Rosenbloom, and A. Newell, "Chunking in SOAR: The Anatomy of a General Learning Mechanism," *Machine Learning* **1,** 11–46 (1986).

P. Langley, "Learning to Search: From Weak Methods to Domain-Specific Heuristics," *Cog. Sci.* **9,** 217–260 (1985).

P. Langley, "Unifying Themes in Empirical and Explanation-based Learning," *Proceedings of the Sixth International Workshop on Machine Learning,* Ithaca, N.Y., Morgan-Kaufmann, San Mateo, Calif., 1989.

P. Langley, J. H. Gennari, and W. Iba, "Hill-Climbing Theories of Learning," *Proceedings of the Fourth International Workshop on Machine Learning,* Irvine, Calif., Morgan-Kaufmann, San Mateo, Calif., 1987, 312–323.

P. Langley, K. Thompson, W. Iba, J. H. Gennari, and J. A. Allen, "An Integrated Cognitive Architecture for Autonomous Agents," in W. Van De Velde, ed., *Representation and Learning in Autonomous Agents,* North Holland, Amsterdam (in press).

M. Lebowitz, "Experiments with Incremental Concept Formation: UNIMEM," *Machine Learning* **2,** 103–138 (1987).

S. Marcus, ed., *Automating Knowledge Acquisition for Expert Systems,* Kluwer, Boston, 1988.

S. Markovitch and P. D. Scott, "Utilization Filtering: A Method for Reducing the Inherent Harmfulness of Deductively Learned Knowledge," *Proceedings of the Eleventh International Joint Conference on Artificial Intelligence,* Detroit, Morgan-Kaufmann, San Mateo, Calif., 1989, 738–743.

C. J. Matheus and L. A. Rendell, "Constructive Induction on Decision Trees," *Proceedings of the Eleventh International Joint Conference on Artificial Intelligence,* Detroit, Morgan-Kaufmann, San Mateo, Calif., 1989, 645–650.

R. S. Michalski, "A Theory and Methodology of Learning from Examples," in R. S. Michalski, J. G. Carbonell, and T. M. Mitchell, eds., *Machine Learning: An Artificial Intelligence Approach,* vol. 1, Morgan-Kaufmann, San Mateo, Calif., 1983.

R. S. Michalski, "How to Learn Imprecise Concepts: A Method for Employing a Two-Tiered Knowledge Representation in Learning," *Proceedings of the Fourth International Workshop on Machine Learning,* Irvine, Calif., Morgan-Kaufmann, San Mateo, Calif., 1987, 50–58.

R. S. Michalski and R. L. Chilausky, "Learning by Being Told and Learning from Examples: An Experimental Comparison of Two Methods of Knowledge Acquisition in the Context of Developing an Expert System for Soybean Disease Diagnosis," *Int. J. Policy Anal. Infor. Syst.* **4** (1980).

R. S. Michalski and R. Stepp, "Learning from Observation: Conceptual Clustering," in R. S. Michalski, J. G. Carbonell, and T. M. Mitchell, eds., *Machine Learning: An Artificial Intelligence Approach,* vol. 1, Morgan-Kaufmann, San Mateo, Calif., 1983.

M. Minsky and S. Papert, *Perceptrons: An Introduction to Computational Geometry,* MIT Press, Cambridge, Mass., 1969.

S. N. Minton, "Selectively Generalizing Plans for Problem Solving," *Proceedings of the Ninth International Joint Conference on Artificial Intelligence,* Morgan-Kaufmann, San Mateo, Calif., 1985, 596–599.

S. N. Minton, "Quantitative Results Concerning the Utility of Explanation-Based Learning," *Artif. Intell.* **42**, 363–391 (1990).

S. N. Minton, J. G. Carbonell, C. A. Knoblock, D. R. Kuokka, O. Etzioni, and Y. Gil, "Explanation-Based Learning: A Problem Solving Perspective," *Artif. Intell.* **40**, 63–118 (1989).

T. M. Mitchell, "Version Spaces: A Candidate Elimination Approach to Rule Learning," *Proceedings of the Fifth International Joint Conference on Artificial Intelligence,* Cambridge, Mass., Morgan-Kaufmann, San Mateo, Calif., 1977, 305–310.

T. M. Mitchell, J. Allen, P. Chalasani, J. Cheng, O. Etzioni, M. Ringuette, and J. C. Schlimmer, "THEO: A Framework for Self-Improving Systems," in K. VanLehn, ed., *Architectures for Intelligence,* Lawrence Erlbaum, Hillsdale, N.J., (in press).

T. M. Mitchell, R. M. Keller, and S. T. Kedar-Cabelli, "Explanation-Based Generalization: A Unifying View," *Machine Learning* **1**, 47–80 (1986).

T. M. Mitchell, S. Mahadevan, and L. Steinberg, "LEAP: A Learning Apprentice for VLSI Design," *Proceedings of the Ninth International Joint Conference on Artificial Intelligence,* Los Angeles, Morgan-Kaufmann, San Mateo, Calif., 1985, 573–580.

T. M. Mitchell, P. E. Utgoff, and R. B. Banerji, "Learning Problem Solving Heuristics by Experimentation," in R. S. Michalski, J. G. Carbonell, and T. M. Mitchell, eds., *Machine Learning: An Artificial Intelligence Approach,* vol. 1, Morgan-Kaufmann, San Mateo, Calif., 1983.

R. J. Mooney, J. W. Shavlik, G. G. Towell, and A. Gove, "An Experimental Comparison of Symbolic and Connectionist Learning Algorithms," *Proceedings of the Eleventh International Joint Conference on Artificial Intelligence,* Detroit, Morgan-Kaufmann, San Mateo, Calif., 1990.

J. Mostow, "Design by Derivational Analogy: Issues in the Automated Replay of Design Plans," *Artif. Intell.* **40**, 119–184 (1989).

M. Mozer and J. Bachrach, "SLUG: A Connectionist Architecture for Inferring the Structure of Finite-State Environments," *Machine Learning* (in press).

S. Muggleton, and W. Buntine, "Machine Invention of First-Order Predictates by Inverting Resolution," *Proceedings of the Fifth International Conference on Machine Learning,* Ann Arbor, Mich., Morgan-Kaufmann, San Mateo, Calif., 1988, 339–352.

B. K. Natarajan and P. Tadepalli, "Two New Frameworks for Learning," *Proceedings of the Fifth International Conference on Machine Learning,* Ann Arbor, Mich., Morgan-Kaufmann, San Mateo, Calif., 1988, 402–415.

H. T. Ng and R. J. Mooney, "On the Role of Coherence in Abductive Explanation," *Proceedings of the Eighth National Conference on Artificial Intelligence,* Boston, 1990, 337–342.

N. Nilsson, *Learning Machines.* McGraw-Hill, New York, 1965.

D. Ourston and R. J. Mooney, "Changing the Rules: A Comprehensive Approach to Theory Refinement," *Proceedings of the Eighth National Conference on Artificial Intelligence,* Boston, AAAI Press, Menlo Park, Calif., 1990, 815–820.

C. Owens, "Integrating Feature Extraction and Memory Search," *Proceedings of the Eleventh Annual Conference of the Cognitive Science Society,* Ann Arbor, Mich., Lawrence Erlbaum, Hillsdale, N.J., 1989, 163–170.

G. Pagallo, "Learning DNF by Decision Trees," *Proceedings of the Eleventh International Joint Conference on Artificial Intelligence,* Detroit, Morgan Kaufmann, San Mateo, Calif., 1989, 639–644.

L. Pitt and R. E. Reinke, "Criteria for Polynomial-Time (Conceptual) Clustering," *Machine Learning* **2**, 371–396 (1988).

R. Prager, T. D. Harrison, and F. Fallside, "Boltzmann Machines for Speech Recognition," *Comput. Speech Lang.* **1**, 1–20 (1986).

J. R. Quinlan, "Learning Efficient Classification Procedures and Their Application to Chess Endgames," in R. S. Michalski, J. G. Carbonell, and T. M. Mitchell, eds., *Machine Learning: An Artificial Intelligence Approach,* vol. 1, Morgan-Kaufmann, San Mateo, Calif., 1983.

J. R. Quinlan, "Induction of Decision Trees," *Machine Learning* **1**, 81–106 (1986a).

J. R. Quinlan, "The Effect of Noise on Concept Learning," in R. S. Michalski, J. G. Carbonell, and T. M. Mitchell, eds., *Machine Learning: An Artificial Intelligence Approach,* vol. 2, Morgan-Kaufmann, San Mateo, Calif., 1986b.

J. R. Quinlan, "Generating Production Rules from Decision Trees," *Proceedings of the Tenth International Joint Conference on Artificial Intelligence,* Milan, Italy, Morgan-Kaufmann, 1987, 304–307.

J. R. Quinlan, P. J. Compton, K. A. Horn, and L. Lazarus, "Inductive Knowledge Acquisition: A Case study," *Proceedings of the Second Australian Conference on Applications of Expert Systems,* Sydney, Australia, 1986.

M. Redmond, "Combining Case-based Reasoning, Explanation-based Learning, and Learning from Instruction," *Proceedings of the Sixth International Workshop on Machine Learning,* Ithaca, N.Y., Morgan-Kaufmann, San Mateo, Calif., 1989, 20–22.

M. Redmond, "Distributed Cases for Case-based Reasoning: Facilitating Use of Multiple Cases," *Proceedings of the Eighth National Conference on Artificial Intelligence,* Boston, AAAI Press, Menlo Park, Calif., 1990, 304–309.

R. L. Rivest, "Learning Decision Lists," *Machine Learning* **2**, 229–246 (1987).

G. G. Robertson, "Population Size in Classifier Systems," *Proceedings of the Fifth International Conference on Machine Learning,* Ann Arbor, Mich., Morgan-Kaufmann, San Mateo, Calif., 1988, 142–152.

F. Rosenblatt, *Principles of Neurodynamics,* Spartan Books, New York, 1962.

P. S. Rosenbloom, J. E. Laird, J. McDermott, A. Newell, and E. Orciuch, "R1-SOAR: An Experiment in Knowledge-Intensive Programming in a Problem-Solving Architecture," *IEEE Trans. Pattern Anal. Mach. Intell.* **7**, 561–569 (1985).

D. E. Rumelhart and J. L. McClelland, "On Learning the Past Tenses of English Verbs," in J. L. McClelland and D. E. Rumelhart, eds., *Parallel Distributed Processing: Explorations in the Microstructure of Cognition,* vol. 2, MIT Press, Cambridge, Mass., 1986.

S. Salzberg, *Learning with Nested Generalized Exemplars,* Kluwer, Boston, 1990.

A. L. Samuel, "Some Studies in Machine Learning Using the Game of Checkers," *IBM J. Res. Dev.* **3**, 210–229 (1959).

J. D. Schaffer and J. J. Grefenstette, "Multi-Objective Learning via Genetic Algorithms," *Proceedings of the Ninth International Joint Conference on Artificial Intelligence,* Los Angeles, Morgan-Kaufmann, San Mateo, Calif., 1985, 593–595.

J. C. Schlimmer, "Incremental Adjustment of Representations for Learning," *Proceedings of the Fourth International Workshop on Machine Learning,* Irvine, Calif., Morgan-Kaufmann, San Mateo, Calif., 1987, 79–90.

J. C. Schlimmer and D. H. Fisher, "A Case Study of Incremental Concept Induction," *Proceedings of the Fifth National Conference on Artificial Intelligence,* Philadelphia, 1986, 496–501.

J. C. Schlimmer and R. H. Granger, Jr., "Beyond Incremental Processing: Tracking Concept Drift," *Proceedings of the Fifth National Conference on Artificial Intelligence,* Philadelphia, 1986, 502–507.

T. J. Sejnowski and C. R. Rosenberg, "Parallel Networks that Learn to Pronounce English Text," *Complex Systems* **1**, 145–168 (1987).

C. G. Shaefer, "The ARGOT Strategy: Adaptive Representation Genetic Optimizer Technique," *Proceedings of the Second International Conference on Genetic Algorithms,* 1987.

J. W. Shavlik, (1990). "Acquiring Recursive and Iterative Concepts with Explanation-based Learning," *Machine Learning,* **5**, 39–70 (1990).

D. Sleeman, P. Langley, and T. Mitchell, "Learning from Solution Paths: An Approach to the Credit Assignment Problem," *AI Mag.* **3**, 48–52 (1982).

R. G. Smith, H. A. Winston, T. M. Mitchell, and B. G. Buchanan, "Representation and Use of Explicit Justifications for Knowledge Base Refinement," *Proceedings of the Ninth International Joint Conference on Artificial Intelligence,* Los Angeles, Morgan-Kaufmann, Publishers, San Mateo, Calif., 1985, 673–680.

S. F. Smith, "Flexible Learning of Problem Solving Heuristics Through Adaptive Search," *Proceedings of the Eighth International Joint Conference on Artificial Intelligence,* Karlsruhe, Germany, Morgan-Kaufmann, Publishers, San Mateo, Calif., 1983, 422–425.

C. W. Stanfill, "Memory-Based Reasoning Applied to English Pronunciation," *Proceedings of the Sixth National Conference on Artificial Intelligence,* Seattle, AAAI Press, Menlo Park, Calif., 1987, 577–581.

R. E. Stepp and R. S. Michalski, "Conceptual Clustering: Inventing Goal-Oriented Classifications of Structured Objects," in

R. S. Michalski, J. G. Carbonell, and T. M. Mitchell, eds., *Machine Learning: An Artificial Intelligence Approach,* vol. 2, Morgan-Kaufmann, San Mateo, Calif., 1986.

R. S. Sutton, "Integrated Architectures for Learning, Planning, and Reacting based on Approximating Dynamic Programming," *Proceedings of the Seventh International Conference on Machine Learning,* Austin, Tex., Morgan-Kaufmann, San Mateo, Calif., 1990, 216–224.

K. Sycara, "Patching Up Old Plans," *Proceedings of the Tenth Annual Conference of the Cognitive Science Society,* Montreal, Quebec, Canada, Lawrence Erlbaum, Hillsdale, N.J., 1988, 405–411.

P. Tadepalli, "Planning in Games Using Approximately Learned Macros," *Proceedings of the Sixth International Workshop on Machine Learning,* Ithaca, N.Y., Morgan-Kaufmann, San Mateo, Calif., 1989, 221–223.

M. Tambe and P. Rosenbloom, "Eliminating Expensive Chunks by Restricting Expressiveness," *Proceedings of the Eleventh International Joint Conference on Artificial Intelligence,* Detroit, Morgan-Kaufmann, San Mateo, Calif., 1989 731–737.

G. G. Towell, J. W. Shavlik, and M. O. Noordewier, "Refinement of Approximate Domain Theories by Knowledge-based Neural Networks," *Proceedings of the Eighth National Conference on Artificial Intelligence,* Boston, AAAI Press, Menlo Park, Calif., 1990, 861–866.

P. E. Utgoff, "Perceptron Trees: A Case Study in Hybrid Concept Representations," *Proceedings of the Seventh National Conference on Artificial Intelligence,* St. Paul, Minn., AAAI Press, Menlo Park, Calif., 1988, 601–606.

P. E. Utgoff, "Incremental Induction of Decision Trees," *Machine Learning* **4**, 161–186 (1989).

L. G. Valiant, "Functionality in Neural Networks," *Proceedings of the Seventh National Conference on Artificial Intelligence,* St. Paul, Minn., AAAI Press, Menlo Park, Calif., 1988, 629–640.

L. Watanabe and L. Rendell, "Effective Generalization of Relational Description," *Proceedings of the Eighth National Conference on Artificial Intelligence,* Boston, AAAI Press, Menlo Park, Calif., 1990, 875–881.

S. M. Weiss and I. Kapouleas, "An Empirical Comparison of Pattern Recognition, Neural Nets, and Machine Learning Classification Methods," *Proceedings of the Eleventh International Joint Conference on Artificial Intelligence,* Detroit, Morgan-Kaufmann, 1989, 781–787.

B. Widrow and M. E. Hoff, "Adaptive Switching Circuits. IRE WESCON," *Convention Record* **4** (1960).

S. W. Wilson, "Classifier Systems and the Animat Problem," *Machine Learning* **2**, 199–228 (1987).

P. H. Winston, "Learning New Principles from Precedents and Exercises," *Artif. Intell.* **19**, 321–350 (1984).

JEFFREY C. SCHLIMMER
Carnegie Mellon University

PAT LANGLEY
NASA Ames Research Center

The authors appreciate the thoughtful comments and suggestions of Andrew Barto, Gerald DeJong, John Grefenstette, Janet Kolodner, Amy Lansky, and Edwina Rissland. Any errors or ambiguities are the sole responsibility of the authors.

LEGGED LOCOMOTION. See ROBOTS, LEGGED.

LEXICAL DECOMPOSITION

Lexical decomposition is that branch of lexical semantics (qv) concerned with the internal semantic structure of lexical and conceptual items within a lexicon (see DICTIONARY/LEXICON). A lexicon can be thought of as the collection of all lexical items spoken by an individual speaker or group of speakers, or alternatively as those items contained in a particular subject domain or language. The focus of lexical decomposition is on how the lexical items are semantically similar and distinct by virtue of shared knowledge structures containing semantic primitives. Numerous sorts of structures (eg, frames and prototypes) and primitives (eg, semantic features and semantic markers) have been proposed.

Lexical decomposition is not centrally concerned with morphology (qv), phonology, or syntax and hence must be distinguished from decompositional work on parts of speech and feature-based techniques and the general ideas of syntactic decomposition (Chomsky, 1970) and a host of other approaches. Currently, lexical decomposition is also not centrally concerned with linguistic expressions larger that lexical items, such as sentences (the domain of compositional semantics) and paragraphs (the domain of text structure and coherence theory), although it has been in the past (see below).

The goal of lexical decomposition is to provide the necessary and sufficient conditions for the meaning of every lexical item in a subject domain or language. In many ways, this goal is similar to that of syntactic analysis of sentences in a language. If primitives and structures are taken as an exhaustive set on top of which all expressions in the language are expressed, then the meaning of any lexical item in the language must be derived from these terms.

THE NATURE OF LEXICAL ITEMS

The question of what constitutes a lexical item has long been a puzzle and presents problems for those concerned with lexical decomposition. One problem is that a lexical item may have morphological variants all sharing the same basic meaning, eg, *walk* has the variant forms *walks* and *walking*.

A second, more serious problem is lexical ambiguity: most lexical items have several meanings or senses. Moreover, many of the senses of an individual item may be either polysemous (ie, have related meanings), for example, the senses of *mouth* meaning "animal aperture" and "entrance to a river," or homonymous (ie, unrelated meanings), for example, *bark* means both "noise made by a dog" and "material on exterior of a tree"). Polysemous meanings may furthermore be related metaphorically or metonymically (Stern, 1965; Waldron, 1967; Nunberg, 1979). The problem for lexical decomposition is how to represent lexical ambiguity, that is, how to represent

senses and the relationships between those senses. Much of the recent artificial intelligence (AI) work on lexical ambiguity can be found in Small and co-workers (1988). Within AI, there has been recent work on the extension of senses by metaphorical means (Martin, 1990) and metonymic means (Pustejovsky, 1991).

A third problem is idiomatic expressions (eg, "like a bat out of hell" and "kick the bucket") and fixed phrases (eg, "to post a score"). It seems that these phrases should be assigned single meanings. The problem for lexical semantics, and lexical decomposition in particular, is that the meanings of these phrases is not a simple function of their component parts. For example, putting together the meanings of *kick* and *bucket* does not give "kick the bucket." A good treatment of the problem of idioms within linguistics and lexicography is available (Cowie, 1981). Idioms are a major problem in machine translation (Schenk, 1986) and have been studied within AI (Zernik and Dyer, 1987; Stock, 1989).

A fourth problem related to idioms and fixed phrases is that of collocation, where two or more individual lexical items are used in habitual association with one another in a language (Hartmann and Stork, 1972), eg, "rancid butter." Collocational patterns were extensively studied by structuralists in the 1950s (Firth, 1957) and have figured prominently in some theories of lexical meaning (Mel'čuk and Poguère, 1987). As has been pointed out (Lyons, 1977), the restrictiveness of collocations varies. The adjective *rancid*, for example, applies to *butter* but to little else (as with *addled* to *eggs* or *brains*) whereas *good* or *bad* apply to almost any noun. The more fixed a collocation becomes, the more people view it as an idiom or phrase. Recent computationally based research on collocation has been published (Church and Hanks, 1990; Church and Hindle, 1990).

LINGUISTIC APPROACHES TO LEXICAL DECOMPOSITION

Although psychology (Marslen-Wilson, 1989), philosophy, and artificial intelligence have all made recent contributions to lexical decomposition, the classic studies have come from linguistics. These contributions will be examined and their impact on AI will be described. The basic approaches examined are sense relations, dictionaries and thesauri, field theory, componential analysis, interpretive semantics, generative semantics, case grammar, and frame-based semantics. Most of these approaches are linguistically motivated, starting from the assumption that the lexical items of the language are what is being modeled and that the primitives and structures used in the approaches are to provide a compositional analysis of all expressions in the language. Thus, although some theories in this tradition do claim strong cognitive groundings for the primitives chosen and used (Talmy, 1978, 1988; Jackendoff, 1983), there is in general no claim to cognitive universality or utility for the primitives used.

Some other approaches are more cognitively motivated. Their primary goal is to generalize about the cognitive underpinnings of the lexical items in the language, without necessarily providing an analytic treatment of the language itself. Most often, these analyses use methodologies and knowledge structures from psychology or AI, such as frames, prototypes, and exemplars. Included in this approach is later frame-based semantics work (Fillmore, 1977a), cognitive semantics (Langacker, 1986), and other work (Rosch, 1973; Miller and Johnson-Laird, 1976).

Sense Relations

Sense relations are a means of categorizing relationships between word senses (see LEXICAL SEMANTICS). The main sense relations are synonymy, antonymy, and hyponymy. Synonymy refers to sameness of meaning, eg, *gorse* and *furze*. Antonymy refers to opposition of meaning, eg, *hot* and *cold, female* and *male*. Hyponymy refers to inclusion of meaning, eg, *plant* and *tulip*. Other sense relations include hypernymy (the inverse of hyponymy), partonomy (eg, *wheel* and *bicycle, second* and *minute* and *hour*), collectives, converses, ranks, and scales (Lyons, 1977; Evens and co-workers, 1980; Cruse, 1986).

Dictionaries and Thesauri

Dictionaries and thesauri are perhaps the most familiar method of organizing lexical knowledge. Dictionaries contain a list of lexical items, usually ordered alphabetically, together with information about their pronunciation, etymology, syntax, and definitions of their senses and idiomatic uses. Hyponymy and synonymy are heavily used in word sense definitions. A typical definition contains a superordinate or genus term and a set of differentia that distinguish the item being defined from other sister items. Consider, for example, "car: a motor vehicle with four wheels that carries a driver and from one to five passengers." The genus term here is *motor vehicle* and the differentia are *with four wheels* . . . . (see DICTIONARY/LEXICON).

A thesaurus (qv) is a book of lexical items or of information about a particular subject domain or set of concepts. A thesaurus provides a comprehensive classification of heads and subheads that supply any lexical item with a context. The lexical items that act as heads are labels for general ideas or categories. Roget's classification has six main categories (abstract relations, space, matter, intellect, volition, and affections) which cover the abstract, physical, and mental.

A thesaurus groups together lexical items of synonymous meaning, the opposite of a dictionary, which seeks to define all the meanings of a lexical item in a single place. Lexical ambiguity is acknowledged in a thesaurus, although senses are not explicitly labeled, but instead are listed in their appropriate contexts (that is, under suitable genus terms). Hence, for example, the sense of *lion* meaning "an animal" is set in the context of cats, whereas the sense meaning "courageous person" is listed under brave persons.

The Wordtree (Burger, 1984) is a hybrid thesaurus–dictionary. It resembles a thesaurus because it hierarchically organizes lexical items into near synonyms. There are 42 basic categories, mainly pairs (eg, *to order* and *to disorder*), which head a hierarchy of 20,500 categories.

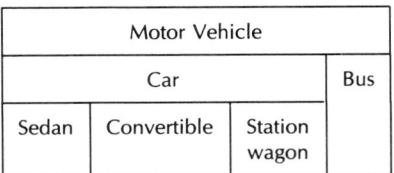

Motor Vehicle			
Car			Bus
Sedan	Convertible	Station wagon	

Figure 1. Field theory.

However, like a dictionary, lexical items are given definitions, although the definitions consist of only two other lexical items, for example,

$$\text{TO SUN} = \text{TO LIGHT} + \text{TO WARM}$$
$$\text{JOCKEY} = \text{RIDE} + \text{MANEUVER}$$

For a review from an artificial intelligence perspective, see Lesk (1987).

Field Theory

The notion of a semantic field was first advanced by Trier (1931) and has since been promoted (Lehrer, 1974; Lyons, 1977). The basic idea is that the spatial analogy of a two-dimensional mosaic in which related meanings of lexical items are arranged into fields. If two lexical items A and B occupy the same field then A and B have the same meaning (synonymy). If field A is above field B then the meaning of A includes the meaning of B (hyponymy). If field A is side by side with field B then the meaning of A contrasts with the meaning of B (antonymy) (Fig. 1).

Componential Analysis

Componential analysis, used by anthropologists to study kinship terminology, is a method for breaking down the meanings of lexical items into a set of features, thereby illustrating similarities and differences of meaning between the items. The goal of such analysis was simply to classify the lexical items in the language with some finite set of features, and in general they had no pretensions to investigating how this structure relates to cognitive generalizations. Hjelmslev (1953), for example, decomposed lexical items into paradigms that pattern the same way distributionally in the language. For example, in Figure 2, the members of each row form a semantic class, distinguishable by features defined over each column.

Jakobson (1936, 1957), Trubetzkoy (1969), and members of the Prague school of linguistics adapted the feature-based analysis of linguistic expressions, developing the notion of markedness, for example, *lion* is unmarked for the features [female] and [male], but the suffix *-ess* in *lioness* marks the word as [+female].

	+Female	+Male	−Adult
+Human	Woman	Man	Child
+Bovine	Cow	Bull	Calf
+Equine	Mare	Stallion	Foal
+Poultry	Hen	Rooster	Chick

Figure 2. Componential analysis.

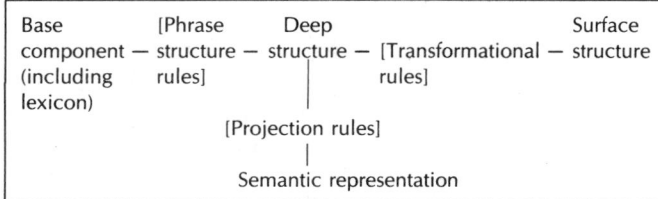

Figure 3. Interpretive semantics (after Lyons, 1977).

Interpretive Semantics

Interpretive semantics and generative semantics were both put forward within the framework of Chomsky's standard theory of transformational grammar (Fodor, 1977). Chomsky assigned semantics a limited role, arguing that in a model of linguistic description, it should generate only semantically well-formed sentences. The first semantic theory was developed by Katz and Fodor (1963) and Katz and Postal (1964). In line with Chomsky, the role of the semantics was limited: to detect semantic anomalies and determine the number of readings associated with a sentence. The theory offered proposals for the decomposition of sentences and lexical items, with explicit rules for linking items to syntactic structures, outlined in Figure 3.

The difference between the surface and deep structure (qv) of a sentence is that the former concerns the structure of a sentence as it is actually produced (ie, pronounced or written) whereas the latter contains the components and relationships necessary for interpreting the meaning of the sentence (Chomsky, 1965). The base component contains a lexicon of entries for lexical items. The entries contain syntactic information about form and subcategorization, and semantic information including selection restrictions. Deep structures are generated by applying phrase structure rules to the syntactic information in the entries. Semantic representations, which represent the meaning of sentences, are constructed by applying projection rules to the semantic information in the entries.

The semantic description in the lexical entries use two types of entity: semantic markers and distinguishers. The semantic markers are the principal component for decomposition purposes. For a lexical item that is ambiguous, there are branching paths, with each path representing a separate sense and having a distinct marker. The distinguishers contain all the remaining information.

Selection restrictions prescribe what lexical items may occur together and consist of pairings of grammatical constructions and semantic features, hence for a verb there are selection restrictions for subject, direct object, etc, restricting which constructions it can appear in. For example, *sleep* requires a subject with the feature [+animate], *hit* (in the general sense) requires a direct object with the feature [+physical object], and so on.

Although many ideas from the Katz-Fodor model still have some currency, it has been all but abandoned as an adequate theory of meaning. There is no simple way of maintaining the distinction between markers and distin-

guishers and the Boolean nature of selection restrictions (either satisfied or violated) is a step back from the calculus of relations and more sophisticated logical systems (Weinreich, 1972).

Generative Semantics

Generative semanticists thought that the interpretive theory of semantics contained needless redundancy, regarding it as unnecessary to have both deep structures and semantic representations, on the one hand, and transformational rules and projection rules, on the other. Generative semanticists argued that deep structure be the semantic structure and that only transformational rules need operate on that structure. In generative semantics, lexical items are decomposed into a set of abstract components and transformations are done on those components (Lakoff, 1970; Ross, 1970). For example, the lexical item *kill* is decomposed into the predicate *dead* and two higher level predicates *cause* and *become*. The terminal nodes of deep semantic structure are these semantic components, as shown in Figure 4.

While the framework of generative semantics is no longer generally adopted, some significant generalizations about semantic structure were made. For example, the sentences below form a sort of paradigm for the concept *cool*, related by the application of abstract predicates that systematically change the meaning of the word.

1. The soup was cool.
2. The soup cooled.
3. Mary cooled the soup.

To derive the word in sentence 2, the predicate *cool* from sentence 1 has been embedded within an abstract predicate [+inchoative], giving the intransitive sense. The sense in sentence 3 is derived by embedding this expression within an abstract causative predicate, [+cause], giving the transitive form.

Jackendoff's Theory of Decomposition

Pursuing a similar line of reasoning to the generative semanticists concerning lexical decomposition, Jackendoff (1972) built on Gruber (1965) to argue that predicates such as [+cause] and [+inchoative] are encoded in the meaning of the word itself. Jackendoff's (1983, 1987) more recent approach to lexical decomposition makes claims for cognitive relevance that are not important motivations for many researchers. However, Jackendoff believes in the cognitive primacy of the primitives used within his system, and the role of these primitives in performing inferences. Jackendoff's semantic representation as it pertains to lexical decomposition will be examined.

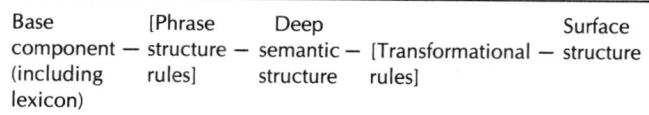

Figure 4. Generative semantics (after Lyons, 1977).

First it is important to realize that Jackendoff sees semantic representation in general as a subset of conceptual structure. The conceptual structure is a term for the language of mental representation. Much of Jackendoff's approach begins with an analysis of spatial relations and how they are realized in language. Jackendoff (1975) isolated three primitive predicates, GO, STAY, and BE, all of which pertain to the representation of events. As an example of how the primitive predicate GO is employed to represent the semantics of a sentence, consider the sentence below:

4a. The plane flew from New York to Boston.

4b. GO(plane, New York, Boston)

The spatial predicates which Jackendoff employs can be seen as one dimension of decompositional analysis. Another dimension Jackendoff employs could be called the causal dimension. These include two predicates, CAUSE and LET, each of which takes an agent and event as arguments. To illustrate, take the sentence from above and embed it within a causative construction.

5a. John flew the plane from New York to Boston.

5b. CAUSE(John, GO(plane, New York, Boston))

Although these predicates are spatial in origin, Jackendoff, like many others interested in the nature of semantic extension, explores the idea that the predicates within the spatial domain may be used to analyze concepts within other semantic domains. The basic idea here is that for different semantic fields such as possession, identification, circumstantial, and temporal, a verb from the spatial field can acquire a new meaning using the same primitives because it is being evaluated relative to a new field. Examples of this include:

Possessional. John will take the house and Mary the kids.

Identificational. John turned into a great father.

Circumstantial. Mary led me to believe she was younger than I.

Temporal. The seminar has been moved to Wednesdays.

The following questions might be asked about this decompositional system: Do its primitives provide a complete and exhaustive description of the concepts of natural language? How open-ended is the system? What is the additional information which distinguishes the meaning of one lexical item from another? That is, the primitives do allow for generalizations, but what allows for the discrimination of concepts (the function filled by distinguishers in Katz and Fodor's theory), and how many features are necessary to that end?

Case Grammar

Case grammar is a semantically oriented grammar developed by Fillmore (1968) and others (Anderson, 1971, 1977; Starosta, 1988) (see GRAMMAR, CASE). Case was first used for the morphological analysis of noun endings in, eg, German and Russian. Fillmore showed that these noun endings serve the same purpose as the positioning of nouns and prepositions in lexical surface structures.

Fillmore introduced the notion of a case frame, a predicate containing arguments that are a set of obligatory and optional cases. Implicit in the theory is that each noun phrase in a sentence can be assigned only one case and that the cases assigned by a verb can be realized only once in a sentence. Fillmore (1968) defined a number of cases, including

Agentive (A). An animate perceived instigator of the action identified by the verb.

Instrumental (I). An inanimate force or object causally involved in the action or state identified by the verb.

Dative (D). An animate being affected by the action identified by the verb.

Objective (O). The semantically most neutral case.

The verb *open* requires that its objective role be filled: something must open or be opened. In sentence 6, only the objective role is filled. In sentences 7 and 8, agentive and objective roles are filled. In sentence 9, the instrumental and objective roles are filled. In sentence 10, the agentive, objective, and instrumental roles are filled.

6. The door opened.

7. Mary opened the door.

8. The door was opened by Mary.

9. The key opened the door.

10. Mary opened the door with the key.

Fillmore noted that different case roles can occupy the same grammatical function, eg, the grammatical subject is *door* in sentences 6 and 8 and occupies the objective role; *Mary,* in sentences 7 and 10 and has the agentive role; and *key;* in sentence 8 and has an instrumental role.

Fillmore's theory attempts to explain how the arguments of a predicate are assigned to particular syntactic structures and is not concerned with establishing an independent level of semantic representation. To handle assignment, Fillmore assumed a principle of a case hierarchy, which allowed the selection of grammatical subject and object in default configurations. As an example of case assignment, consider the verb *break*, which assigns both obligatory and optional cases. Obligatory cases include the objective, whereas optional cases include both the agentive and instrumental cases.

11. John broke the window with a rock.

In sentence 11 by a default assignment, agentive is assigned to the subject, objective to the object, and instrumental to the phrase within the prepositional phrase. This is a type of default selection that can be violated if the verbal morphology indicates a structure such as a passive as in sentence 8.

Fillmore's case theory will be briefly examined in terms of an adequate representation of semantic knowledge. Fillmore (1971, 1977b) noted some deficiencies and limitations of case grammar. Although case grammar is useful as a guide to the decomposition of verb meaning, the theory does nothing to clarify the nature of sense relations such as antonymy and hyponymy. Case grammar allows the recognition of sentences as partially synonymous by matching case structures. Because it does not claim to be a complete model for meaning, case grammar avoids the pitfalls of the decomposition model of Katz-Fodor; on the other hand, because of its incompleteness, it is unclear what role such a system of cases might play in a comprehensive semantic theory.

Thematic Roles

One influential development from Jackendoff's initial formalization of Gruber's thesis is a more limited notion of thematic role. In this view, which is quite similar to Fillmore's conception of cases, Jackendoff (1972) classified verbs according to which thematic (theta) roles they assign to their arguments. Thus theta theory, as this view has come to be known, is a minimal decomposition of verb meaning, where features and abstract predicates have been replaced by named functional roles, as in case grammar. The success of theta theory has come not from how well it characterizes verb denotations, but in how functional roles interact with other principles of syntax to determine the well formedness of a sentence. Within the last five years, there has been some criticism of the adequacy of theta theory (Levin and Rappaport, 1986, Jackendoff, 1987) (see LEXICAL SEMANTICS).

FRAME-BASED SEMANTICS

In the 1970s, work in linguistic semantics was influenced by the idea of frames coming from AI, notably scenes-and-frames semantics (Fillmore, 1977a, 1977c) and the notion of linguistic gestalts (Lakoff, 1977). Fillmore began to rethink his views of semantics in the early 1970s and developed a scenes-and-frames semantics to overcome the deficiencies and limitations he had noted with case grammar. The basic ideas of the new semantics, heavily influenced by Minsky (1975), were that "people associate certain scenes with certain linguistic frames" and that "meanings are relativized to scenes," ie, lexical items or expressions are understood by placing them within scenes or images in which they have some linguistic functions, eg, naming.

In the theory, frames are linguistic entities that represent the meanings of lexical items. Scenes can be visual and also refer to "interpersonal transactions, standard scenarios, familiar layouts" (Fillmore, 1977a) and "body image" (the way linguistic frames are oriented and classified, such as *up–down* and *left–right*). Fillmore believes that scenes-and-frames offers an alternative to traditional accounts of lexical decomposition issues such as lexical ambiguity, synonymy, semantic fields, and selection restrictions (Fillmore, 1975). Synonymy can be understood as "indistinguishable scenes for which the frame offers lexical options" (eg, *gorse* and *furze*); "the same object is labeled in one way for one scene and in another way for another scene") or that "the same cognitive scene is associated with two different linguistic frames, but the interaction scenes are different" (eg, *wee wee* and *urinate*) (Fillmore, 1977a). A selection restriction is viewed as the relation between a frame and a scene: the "selection restriction information about the use of a word can be stated as a specification of the nature of the appropriate scene" (Fillmore, 1977a).

Fillmore (1975) also argued that the denotations of lexical items are better characterized by a sort of prototype theory, that is, "instead of the meaning of a linguistic form being represented in terms of a checklist of conditions that have to be satisfied in order for the form to be appropriately or truthfully used, it is held that the understanding of meaning requires, at least for a great many cases, an appeal to an exemplar or prototype." A prototype is an ideal example of some concept to which other instances of the same concept bear a strong (but not necessarily total) resemblance. For example, a prototypical bird might have a beak, wings, feathers, and be able to fly, but an ostrich would still be recognized as a bird. The prototype idea can be seen in studies of color terms (Berlin and Kay, 1969), in work on the boundary criteria between cups and bowls (Labov, 1973), and in the work of the psychologist Rosch.

IMPACT ON ARTIFICIAL INTELLIGENCE

Sense Relations. Many of the articles in Evens (1988) concern sense relations. More specific computational work includes work on synonymy (Sparck Jones, 1986) and partonomy (Hayes, 1977; Schubert and co-workers, 1979).

Dictionaries. There have been many recent studies of machine-readable dictionaries (Walker and co-workers, 1987) especially on defining vocabularies, which are the terms used to define lexical items and their senses. Much of this work has focused on constructing hierarchies of genus terms (Chodorow and co-workers, 1985). Particular attention has been paid to *The Longman Dictionary of Contemporary English,* which has a controlled vocabulary of about 2,000 words (Boguraev and Briscoe, 1989).

Thesauri. There has been work on automatic thesaurus production (Michiels and Noël, 1982; McNaught, 1983; Fox and co-workers, 1988) and on sets of semantic primitives that provide extensive conceptual coverage like Roget's six main categories, eg, the 11–14 primitives of conceptual dependency theory (qv) and the primitives of the LNR group (Norman and co-workers, 1975).

Componential Analysis. Feature-based representations of lexical items are prominent in recent connectionist approaches to language analysis (Waltz and Pollack, 1985).

Interpretive Semantics. Katz's semantic theory has strongly influenced AI approaches to representing and resolving word sense ambiguity (eg, Hayes, 1976; Fass and Wilks, 1983).

Generative Semantics. The generative semantics idea of deep semantic structure is seen in preference semantics (qv) and in conceptual dependency theory, developed by Schank and others. Schank, like Jackendoff, believes in the cognitive primacy of the primitives used within his system, and the role of these primitives in performing inferences. The legacy of generative semantics is present in many current lines of research in linguistics and AI, eg, Dowty (1979) and others. A related approach to decomposition is found in Hobbs and co-workers (1987) (see LEXICAL SEMANTICS).

Jackendoff's Theory of Decomposition. Dorr (1990) uses Jackendoff's (1983) semantic theory in a machine translation (qv) system.

Case Grammar. This has been a major influence on AI (Bruce, 1975; Wilks, 1976; Somers, 1985).

Frame-Based Semantics. This is part of an ongoing interaction between linguistics and AI although no one, to our knowledge, has incorporated Lakoff's or Fillmore's ideas on frames (qv) into an AI-based theory of lexical decomposition.

BIBLIOGRAPHY

J. Anderson, *The Grammar of Case: Towards a Localistic Theory,* Cambridge University Press, Cambridge, UK, 1971.

J. Anderson, *On Case Grammar: Prolegomena to a Theory of Grammatical Relations,* Croom Helm, London, UK, 1977.

B. Berlin and P. Kay, *Basic Color Terms: Their Universality and Evolution,* University of California Press, Berkeley, Calif., 1969.

B. Boguraev and E. Briscoe, eds., *Computational Lexicography for Natural Language Processing,* Longman, Harlow, UK, 1989.

B. Bruce, "Case Systems for Natural Language," *Artif. Intell.* **6,** 327–360 (1975).

H. Burger, *The Wordtree,* Merriam, Kans., 1984.

M. S. Chodorow and co-workers, "Extracting Semantic Hierarchies from a Large On-Line Dictionary," *Proceedings of the Twenty-Third Annual Meeting of the ACL,* Chicago, Ill., 1985, pp. 299–304.

N. Chomsky, *Aspects of the Theory of Syntax,* MIT Press, Cambridge, Mass., 1965.

N. Chomsky, "Remarks on Nominalization," in R. A. Jacobs and P. S. Rosenbaum, eds., *Readings in English Transformational Grammar,* Ginn, Waltham, Mass., 1970.

K. Church and P. Hanks, "Word Association Norms, Mutual Information and Lexicography," *Computat. Ling.* **16**(1), 22–29 (1990).

K. Church and D. Hindle, "Collocational Constraints and Corpus-Based Linguistics," in *Working Notes of the AAAI Symposium: Text-Based Intelligent Systems,* Stanford, Calif., Mar. 1990.

A. P. Cowie, "The Treatment of Collocations and Idioms in Learners' Dictionaries," *Appl. Ling.* **2,** 223–35 (1981).

D. A. Cruse, *Lexical Semantics,* Cambridge University Press, Cambridge, UK, 1986.

B. Dorr, "Solving Thematic Divergences in Machine Translation," in *Proceedings of the Twenty-eighth Annual Meeting of the Association for Computational Linguistics,* Pittsburgh, Pa., 1990, pp. 127–134.

D. R. Dowty, *Word Meaning and Montague Grammar,* Reidel, Dordrecht, The Netherlands, 1979.

M. W. Evens, ed., *Relational Models of the Lexicon: Representing Knowledge in Semantic Networks,* Cambridge University Press, Cambridge, UK, 1988.

M. W. Evens and co-workers, *Lexical-Semantic Relations: A Comparative Survey,* Linguistic Research, Inc., Edmonton, Canada, 1980.

D. C. Fass and Y. A. Wilks, "Preference Semantics, Ill-Formedness and Metaphor," *Am. J. Comput. Ling.* **9**(3–4), 178–187 (1983).

C. J. Fillmore, "The Case for Case," in E. Bach and R. T. Harms, eds., *Universals in Linguistic Theory,* Holt, Rinehart, and Winston, New York, 1968, pp. 1–88.

C. J. Fillmore, "Some Problems for Case Grammar," in R. J. O'Brien, ed., *Report of the Twenty-second Annual Roundtable Meeting on Linguistics and Language Studies,* Georgetown University Press, Washington, D.C., 1971.

C. J. Fillmore, "An Alternative to Checklist Theories of Meaning," in C. Cogen, ed., *Proceedings of the 1st Annual Meeting of the Berkeley Linguistics Society,* Berkeley, Calif., 1975, pp. 123–131.

C. J. Fillmore, "Scenes and Frames Semantics," in A. Zampolli, ed., *Linguistic Structures Processing,* North-Holland, Amsterdam, The Netherlands, 1977a, pp. 55–81.

C. J. Fillmore, "The Case for Case Reopened," in P. Cole and J. M. Sadock, eds., *Syntax and Semantics 8: Grammatical Relations,* Academic Press, Inc., New York, 1977b, pp. 59–81.

C. J. Fillmore, "Topics in Lexical Semantics," in R. W. Cole, ed., *Current Issues in Linguistic Theory,* Indiana University Press, Bloomington, Ind., 1977c, pp. 76–138.

J. R. Firth, "Modes of Meaning," in J. R. Firth, ed., *Papers in Linguistics 1934–1951,* Oxford University Press, London, UK, 1957.

J. D. Fodor, *Semantics: Theories of Meaning in Generative Grammar,* Thomas Y. Crowell Co., New York, 1977.

E. A. Fox and co-workers, "Building a Large Thesaurus for Information Retrieval," in *Proceedings of the Second Conference on Applied Natural Language Processing,* Austin, Tex., 1988, pp. 101–108.

J. Gruber, *Lexical Structures in Syntax and Semantics,* Ph.D. dissertation, MIT, Cambridge, Mass., 1965.

R. R. K. Hartmann and F. C. Stork, *Dictionary of Language and Linguistics,* John Wiley & Sons, Inc., New York, 1972.

P. J. Hayes, "Semantic Markers and Selectional Restrictions," in E. Charniak and Y. A. Wilks, eds., *Computational Semantics,* North-Holland, Amsterdam, The Netherlands, 1976, pp. 41–54.

P. J. Hayes, "On Semantic Nets, Frames and Associations," in *Proceedings of the Fifth IJCAI,* Cambridge, Mass., Morgan-Kaufmann, San Mateo, Calif., 1977, pp. 99–107.

L. Hjelmslev, *Prolegomena to a Theory of Language,* Indiana University Press, Bloomington, Ind., 1953.

J. R. Hobbs and co-workers, "Commonsense Metaphysics and Lexical Semantics," *Computat. Ling.* **13**(3–4), 241–250 (1987).

R. S. Jackendoff, *Semantic Interpretation in Generative Grammar,* MIT Press, Cambridge, Mass., 1972.

R. S. Jackendoff, "A System of Semantic Primitives," in *Proceedings of the First Workshop on Theoretical Issues in Natural Language Processing (TINLAP-1),* Cambridge, Mass., 1975, pp. 24–29.

R. S. Jackendoff, "Towards an Explanatory Semantic Representation," *Ling. Inquiry* **28,** 89–150 (1976).

R. S. Jackendoff, *Semantics and Cognition,* MIT Press, Cambridge, Mass., 1983.

R. S. Jackendoff, "The Status of Thematic Relations in Linguistic Theory," *Ling. Inquiry,* **28,** 369–412 (1987).

R. Jakobson, "Beitrag zur allgemeinen Kasuslehre," *Travaux du Cercle Linguistique de Prague,* **6,** 240–87 (1936).

R. Jakobson, *Shifters, Verbal Categories, and the Russian Verb,* Harvard University, Cambridge, Mass., 1957.

J. J. Katz and J. A. Fodor, "The Structure of a Semantic Theory," *Language* **39,** 170–210 (1963).

J. J. Katz and P. Postal, *An Integrated Theory of Linguistic Description,* MIT Press, Cambridge, Mass., 1964.

W. Labov, "The Boundaries of Words and Their Meanings," in C-J. N. Bailey and R. Shuy, eds., *New Ways of Analyzing Variation in English,* Georgetown University Press, 1973.

G. Lakoff, *Irregularity in Syntax,* Holt, Rinehart and Winston, New York, 1970.

G. Lakoff, "Linguistic Gestalts," in *Proceedings of the Thirteenth Annual Meeting of the Chicago Linguistics Society,* Chicago Linguistics Society, University of Chicago, Chicago, Ill., 1977.

R. Langacker, *Foundations of Cognitive Grammar,* Vol. 1, Stanford University Press, Stanford, Calif., 1986.

A. Lehrer, *Semantic Fields and Lexical Structure,* North-Holland, Amsterdam, The Netherlands, 1974.

B. Levin and M. Rappaport, "The Formation of Adjectival Passives," *Ling. Inquiry* **17**(4) (1986).

J. Lyons, *Semantics,* Vols. 1–2, Cambridge University Press, Cambridge, UK, 1977.

J. McNaught, "The Generation of Term Definitions from an On-Line Terminological Thesaurus," in *Proceedings of the First Conference of the European Chapter of the ACL,* Pisa, Italy, 1983, pp. 90–95.

W. Marlsen-Wilson, ed., *Lexical Representation and Process,* MIT Press, Cambridge, Mass., 1989.

J. H. Martin, *A Computational Model of Metaphor Interpretation,* Academic Press, Inc., New York, 1990.

I. Mel'čuk and A. Poguère, "A Formal Lexicon in Meaning-Text Theory (Or How to Do Lexica with Words)," *Computat. Ling.* **13**(3–4), 261–275 (1987).

A. Michiels and J. Noël, "Approaches to Thesaurus Production," in *Proceedings of the Ninth International Conference on Computational Linguistics (COLING-82),* Prague, Czechoslovakia, 1982, pp. 227–232.

G. A. Miller and P. N. Johnson-Laird, *Language and Perception,* Cambridge University Press, Cambridge, UK, 1976.

M. Minsky, "A Framework for Representing Knowledge," in P. H. Winston, ed., *The Psychology of Computer Vision,* McGraw-Hill Book Co., Inc., New York, 1975, pp. 211–277.

D. A. Norman and co-workers, *Explorations in Cognition,* W. H. Freeman, San Francisco, Calif., 1975.

J. Nunberg, "The Non-Uniqueness of Semantic Solutions: Polysemy," *Ling. Philos.* **3**(2), 143–184 (1979).

J. Pustejovsky, "Towards a Generative Lexicon," *Comput. Ling.* **17**(3) (1991).

E. Rosch, "Natural Categories," *Cogn. Psych.* **4,** 328–350 (1973).

J. R. Ross, "On Declarative Sentences," in R. A. Jacobs and P. S. Rosenbaum, eds., *Readings in English Transformational Grammar,* Ginn, Waltham, Mass., 1970.

A. Schenk, "Idioms in the Rosetta Machine Translation System," in *Proceedings of the Eleventh International Conference on Computational Linguistics (COLING-86),* Bonn, FRG, 1986, pp. 319–324.

L. K. Schubert, M. Papalaskaris, and J. Taugher, "Determining Type, Part, Color, and Time Relationships," *IEEE Comput.* **16,** 53–60 (1979).

S. L. Small, G. W. Cottrell, and M. K. Tanenhaus, eds., *Lexical Ambiguity Resolution: Perspectives from Psycholinguistics, Neuropsychology, and Artificial Intelligence,* Morgan-Kaufmann, San Mateo, Calif., 1988.

H. L. Somers, *Valency and Case in Computational Linguistics,* Edinburgh University Press, Edinburgh, UK, 1985.

K. Sparck Jones, *Synonymy and Semantic Classification,* Edinburgh University Press, Edinburgh, UK, 1986.

S. Starosta, *The Case for Case: An Outline of Lexicase Grammatical Theory,* Pinter Publishers, London, UK, 1988.

G. Stern, *Meaning and Change of Meaning,* Indiana University Press, Bloomington, Ind., 1965.

O. Stock, "Parsing with Flexibility, Dynamic Strategies, and Idioms in Mind," *Computat. Ling.* **15**(1), 1–18 (1989).

L. Talmy, "The Relation of Grammar to Cognition—A Synopsis," in *Proceedings of the Second Workshop on Theoretical Issues in Natural Language Processing (TINLAP-2),* University of Illinois at Urbana-Champaign, 1978, pp. 14–24.

L. Talmy, "Force Dynamics in Language and Cognition," *Cogn. Sci.* **12**(1), 49–100 (1988).

J. Trier, *Der Deutsche Wortschatz im Sinnbezirk des Verstandes,* Winter, Heidelberg, FRG, 1931.

N. S. Trubetzkoy, *Principles of Phonology,* University of California Press, Los Angeles, 1969.

R. Waldron, *Sense and Sense Development,* Deutsch, London, UK, 1967.

D. E. Walker and co-editors, "Special Issue of the Lexicon," *Computat. Ling.* **13**(3–4) (1987).

D. L. Waltz and J. B. Pollack, "Massively Parallel Parsing: A Strongly Interactive Model of Natural Language Interpretation," *Cogn. Sci.* **9,** 51–74 (1985).

U. Weinreich, *Explorations in Semantic Theory,* Mouton & Co., The Hague, The Netherlands, 1972.

Y. A. Wilks, "Processing Case," *Am. J. Computat. Ling.* **56** (1976).

U. Zernik and M. Dyer, "The Self-Extending Phrasal Lexicon," *Computat. Ling.* **13**(3–4), 308–327 (1987).

D. Fass
Simon Fraser University

J. Pustejovsky
Brandeis University

LEXICAL SEMANTICS

THE NATURE OF LEXICAL KNOWLEDGE

The study of natural language semantics is the investigation of how and what linguistic utterances denote. The subdiscipline of lexical semantics, then, can be seen as the study of how and what the words in a language denote. We can partition the concerns of lexical semantics into the two issues of *meaning* (the how) and *reference* (the what). Some lexical semantic theories actually have little if anything to say about the problem of reference, and concentrate on the *structural* properties of word meaning (Jackendoff, 1983; Lakoff, 1987), while those providing for modes of reference often have nothing to contribute to the structural aspects of word meaning (Montague, 1973).

Broadly, we can divide the study of word meaning into four approaches, each motivated by different concerns:

A. Linguistic approaches to lexical structures
B. Knowledge representation approaches to word-concept pairs
C. Psychological theories of the mental lexicon
D. Lexicographic approaches to word sense distinctions

These approaches are distinguishable on the basis of one issue: *What kind of data are being accounted for by the theory?* That is, what is the approach a theory *of*, if anything? With this question in mind, there are basically four major data sets that have been studied:

1. Linguistic tokens which have internal structure with well-formedness conditions. The data in this view are the words in the language, and are evaluated with respect to how they are mapped to syntax (Approach A).
2. Linguistic tokens which have no internal structure but are merely literals within a larger theory of logic as used for deduction. Words have for the most part a direct translation to a logical vocabulary, where they are interpreted with respect to a model. On this view, there are no data independent of the truth-conditional semantics (Approaches A and B).
3. Conceptual structures that reflect our basic cognitive processes when words are used. The data are not linguistic tokens, but are rather cognitive structures abstracted away from a surface form of any kind (Approaches B and C).
4. Items in a dictionary which carry multiple word senses depending on the contexts of usage. The data are the usages themselves from which senses are extracted (Approach D).

Because these types of data are so distinct, researchers in these four approaches appear to be studying radically different objects. However, there are some points of convergence, having to do primarily with how words behave in different syntactic contexts. This article, therefore, will concern itself with issues in the general semantic behavior of words, and not with specific solutions to these problems. Where appropriate, reference to other entries and the literature will be made.

VARIETIES OF LEXICAL MEANING

Semantic Classes

The most fundamental aspect of a word's meaning is perhaps its category or type. Categorial or type information determines not only how a word behaves syntactically, but also what the elements of the category refer to. For

example, the verbs *love* and *hate* can be viewed as relations between individuals in the world, whereas the noun *woman* picks out the set of all individuals in the world who are women. Logical words such as *the* and *or* might be viewed as set-theoretic operations over sets of individuals in the world (cf Montague, 1974, for example).

Because type distinctions are generally so broad, lexical semantics further distinguishes selectional subsets of members of these categories. Conventionally, this is accomplished by applying standard distributional analysis on the basis of collocation and cooccurrence tests (Chomsky, 1955). For example, the nouns *dog* and *book* partition into different selectional classes due to contexts involving *animacy*, while the nouns *book* and *literature* partition into different selectional classes due to a mass/count distinction (Pelletier and Schubert, 1989).

Another useful linguistic methodology for grouping the meanings of words into semantic classes is to discover the syntactic patterns that words participate in (eg, common grammatical alternations). For example, the verbs *break, drop,* and *spill* are ambiguous between intransitive and transitive forms, while *die* and *arrive* are not. Although this is a simple example, it illustrates how grammatical alternations help to distinguish semantic classes, in this case, revealing that the former verbs have both causative and inchoative meanings, while the latter do not (Fillmore, 1968; Lakoff, 1970; Hale and Keyser, 1986):

1. a. The glass broke.
   b. John broke the glass.
2. a. The plate dropped to the floor.
   b. Bill dropped the plate to the floor.
3. a. The beer spilled on the table.
   b. Mary spilled the beer on the table.
4. a. Mary died.
   b. *John died Mary.
5. a. John arrived.
   b. *Bill arrived John.

Such grammatical alternations can be used throughout the grammar of a language to make semantic distinctions on the basis of syntactic behavior. Using category and selectional information as well as grammatical alternation data, words can be grouped into semantic classes with more or less predictable syntactic behaviors.

One very influential tradition of semantic classification for verbs, dating back to Aristotle (McKeon, 1941; Lloyd, 1968), is based on the notion of aspectual classes. The basic idea behind this classification is that verbs and verb phrases differ in the kinds of events in the world they denote. It is normally assumed that there are at least three aspectual types: *state, activity,* and *event,* sometimes broken down into *accomplishment,* and *achievement* events. For example, the verb *walk* in sentence (1a) denotes an activity of unspecified length. That is, the sentence itself does not convey information regarding the temporal extent of the activity.

6. a. Harry walked yesterday.
   b. Harry walked to the store yesterday.

Such a sentence is said to denote an *activity* (cf Kenny, 1963; Vendler, 1967; Ryle, 1949; Mourelatos, 1978; Verkuyl, 1989; Dowty, 1979). Other examples of activity verbs are *swim, run, work,* and *drink.* Sentence (6b) conveys the same information as (6a), with the additional constraint, however, that Harry terminated his activity of walking at the store. Although not making explicit reference to the temporal duration of the activity, (6b) does assert that the process has a logical culmination, whereby the activity is over when Harry is at the store. This type of sentence is said to denote an event, or *accomplishment.*

Just as the verb *walk* seems to lexically default to an activity, there are verbs which seem to lexically denote accomplishments. For example, the verbs *build* and *destroy,* in their typical transitive use, denote accomplishment events because there is a logical culmination to the activity performed.

> 7. a. Mary built a house.
>   b. Mary destroyed the table.

In (7a) the existence of the house is the culmination of Mary's act, while in (7b), the nonexistence of something denotable as a table is the direct culmination of her act.

One useful diagnostic for testing whether a verb or verb phrase denotes an accomplishment is modification by temporal adverbials such as *in an hour,* ie, the so-called frame adverbials. Notice in (8) that both derived and lexical accomplishments license such modification, while activities (9) do not.

> 8. a. Mary walked to the store in an hour.
>   b. Mary built a house in a year.
> 9. a. *John drank in 20 minutes.
>   b. *Mary worked in an hour.

The frame adverbial seems to require that the verb or verb phrase make reference to an explicit change of state, a precondition missing in (9a) and (9b).

Another aspectual class is that of achievement. An achievement is an event that results in a change of state, just as an accomplishment does, but where the change is thought of as occurring instantaneously. For example, in sentences (10a), (10b), and (10c) the change is not a gradual one, but something that has a "point-like" quality to it. In fact, modification by *point adverbials* such as *at noon* is a diagnostic that a sentence denotes an achievement (cf Dowty, 1979).

> 10. a. John died at 3 pm.
>   b. John found his wallet at 3 pm.
>   c. Mary arrived at noon.

What are apparently lexical properties of the verb can be affected by factors that could not possibly be lexical. For instance, consider the sentences in (11), where one sees a shift in the meaning of *eat* from an accomplishment as in (11a) to an activity as in (11b).

> 11. a. Mary ate a cookie.
>   b. Mary ate cookies.

The presence of a bare plural object shifts the interpretation of a logically culminating event to an unbounded process (cf Bach, 1986; Pelletier and Schubert, 1989; and Krifka, 1987, for details).

Finally, let us consider the behavior of *states,* such as those sentences in (12).

> 12. a. Cathie is in Boston.
>   b. Peter is late.
>   c. John thinks he is intelligent.

The verb *think,* for example, denotes a relation between an individual and a proposition, but also a state in the world which has no logical culmination or beginning. Unlike activities, we do not think of change as occurring during a state. States are identified by several diagnostics. First, they allow modification by durative adverbials (13a), and secondly, they do not appear as imperatives (13b) (cf Dowty, 1979).

> 13. a. Mary was sick for two months.
>   b. *Be sick!

One final test for distinguishing activities from accomplishments, known as the "imperfect paradox" (cf Bach, 1986; Dowty, 1979), involves the possible entailments from the progressive aspect. To illustrate the nature of this paradox, consider the sentences in (14).

> 14. a. John is running. *entails* John has run.
>   b. John is building a house. *does not entail* John has built a house.

What this difference in entailment indicates is whether an action is homogeneous in nature or has a culmination of some sort. Sentence (14a) is an activity and entails the statement *John has run.* That is, John has already engaged in some running. Sentence (14b), on the other hand, does not allow the entailment *John has built a house* because building is not a homogeneous process, but rather culminates in a changed state, ie, it is an accomplishment. Thus, if x *is* ϕ*ing* entails x *has* ϕ*ed,* then either the verb or the predicate is an activity. A theory of lexical semantics should be able to account for this behavior, and not just use it to classify propositions into aspectual types.

Summarizing, we have considered the following categorization of aspectual types for verbs and verb phrases:

> 15. a. *Activities:* walk, run, swim, drink
>   b. *Accomplishments:* build, destroy, break
>   c. *Achievements:* die, find, arrive
>   d. *States:* sick, know, love, resemble, think, be

Membership in an aspectual class determines much of the semantic behavior of a lexical item, but it should be noted that the aspectual properties of a sentence may change as the result of other factors, such as adverbials (both durative and frame), the structure of the NP in an argument position (eg, definite vs bare plural), or the presence of a prepositional phrase. Such non-lexical issues are problems in compositional semantics and are discussed in the context of "type-shifting" phenomena in Bach (1986), Link (1983), and Krifka (1987).

Semantic Relations between Words

Besides grouping words into distinct semantic classes, lexical semantics is the study of how words are semantically related to one another. In this section, we will examine five classes of lexical relations:

1. Synonymy
2. Antonymy
3. Hyponymy and Lexical Inheritance
4. Meronymy
5. Entailment and Presupposition

Perhaps the most familiar of these relations are synonymy and antonymy. Synonymy is generally taken to be a relation between words rather than concepts. One fairly standard definition states that two expressions are synonymous if substituting one for the other in all contexts does not change the truth value of the sentence where the substitution is made (cf Lyons, 1977; Cruse, 1986). A somewhat weaker definition makes the substitution relative to a linguistic context. For example in the context of carpentry, *plank* and *board* might be considered synonyms, but not necessarily in other domains (cf Miller and co-workers, 1990). It should be noted that if synonymy is defined by substitutability of expressions, then it is an intra-category relation, eg, nouns for nouns, verbs for verbs, etc.

Antonymy is a relation characterized in terms of semantic opposition, and, like synonymy is properly defined over pairs of lexical items rather than concepts. Examples of antonymy are *rise/fall, heavy/light, fast/slow, long/short* (cf Cruse, 1986; Miller, 1991). It is interesting to observe that synonyms do not necessarily share the same antonyms. For example, *rise* and *ascend* as well as *fall* and *descend* are similar in meaning, yet neither *fall/ascend* nor *rise/descend* are antonym pairs. (For further details, see Miller and co-workers, 1990.)

Perhaps the most familiar lexical relation to the AI community is hyponymy, essentially the taxonomic relation defined in inheritance networks. For example, saying *car* is a hyponym of *vehicle* is equivalent to saying that *vehicle* is a superconcept of the concept *car* (cf. KNOWLEDGE REPRESENTATION; INHERITANCE HIERARCHY).

One of the most difficult lexical relations to define and treat formally is that of meronymy, the relation of parts to the whole. The relation is familiar from knowledge representation languages with predicates or slot-names such as part-of and made-of (cf Brachman and Schmolze, 1985; Hobbs and co-workers, 1987). Similarly in the domain of planning, the issue of meronymy arises when defining the necessary or optional subparts of a plan or event. For treatments of this relation in lexical semantics, see Miller and co-workers (1990); Cruse (1986); Pustejovsky (1991).

Another important respect in which words can be related is through entailment and presupposition. Although there is no complete agreement on how to define these

relations, one fairly uncontroversial distinction is the following. An expression A *semantically entails* an expression B if and only if every situation that makes A true, makes B true. On the other hand, A *semantically presupposes* B if and only if both (a) in all situations where A is true, B is true, and (b) in all situations where A is false, B is true (cf Strawson, 1950; Keenan, 1972).

To see how important these concepts are for determining lexical meanings, observe how (1a) entails the proposition denoted by sentence (1b).

1. a. John killed Bill.
   b. Bill died.

That is, if there is a *killing* event, then there is also a *dying* event. Capturing such entailment relations was one of the motivations for lexical decomposition (qv) in linguistics in the 1960s, and still motivates much research (eg, Jackendoff, 1983; Dowty, 1979). That *kill* entails rather than presupposes an event associated with *dying*, becomes clear when examining the negation of (1a), where no dying event occurs.

This is not the behavior of presupposition, however. Notice in (2) that the verb *manage* presupposes an *attempt* (3), whether it succeeds or not.

2. a. Mary managed to finish the exam.
   b. Mary didn't manage to finish the exam.
3. Mary *attempted* to finish the exam.

Thus, the lexical semantics of a verb like *manage* must presuppose that the agent of the managing event also *attempts* to bring this event about (cf Katz and Fodor, 1963; Karttunen, 1971, 1974; Seuren, 1985).

For some lexical items, determining what the presuppositions are is not so straightforward. For example, the verb *forget* in (4a) and (4b) appears to presuppose the truth of the complement (hence, it is called a *factive* verb; cf Kiparsky and Kiparsky, 1971).

4. a. John forgot that he locked the door.
   b. John didn't forget that he locked the door.

That is, regardless of John's memory, there is a fact in the world that John locked the door. It would furthermore appear that this factivity is associated with the verb *forget*. Notice, however, that in (5) there is no factive interpretation associated with the complement.

5. John forgot to lock the door.

In fact, in some ways it appears to be counterfactive, in that the process of forgetting prevents the event from even occurring. For explanation of such phenomena, see Pustejovsky (1991).

LEXICAL AMBIGUITY AND POLYSEMY

One of the most difficult problems in lexical semantics is that of lexical ambiguity. In this section, we discuss the theoretical aspects of this problem. The computational issues associated with disambiguation are discussed in DICTIONARY/LEXICON.

It is certainly true that most words in a language have more than one meaning, a property we will call polysemy. But the ways in which words carry multiple meanings can vary. For example, Weinreich (1964) distinguishes between *contrastive polysemy* and *complementary polysemy*. The former is basic homonymy, where a lexical item accidently carries two distinct and unrelated meanings. Examples of this are given in (1) and (2) below.

1. a. the **bank** of the river
   b. the richest **bank** in the city
2. a. Drop me a **line** when you are in Boston.
   b. We built a fence along the property **line**.

In contrast to this, the senses in (3) through (5) exhibit a complementary polysemy, where the senses are manifestations of the same basic sense as it occurs in different contexts.

3. a. The **bank** raised its interest rates yesterday. (ie, the institution)
   b. The store is next to the new **bank**. (ie, the building)
4. a. John crawled through **the window**.
   b. **The window** is closed.
5. a. Mary painted **the door**.
   b. Mary walked through **the door**.

The semantics must somehow account for how a bank can be both an institution and a building, and how a window or door can be both an aperture and a physical object (cf Pustejovsky, 1991).

Then there are cases of verbal polysemy which pose some difficult problems for lexical semantics as well. These involve verbs which appear to behave polymorphically, taking several different complement types, eg (6).

6. a. Mary **began** to read the novel.
   b. Mary **began** reading the novel.
   c. Mary **began** the novel.

Verbs such as *begin* are polysemous in that they must be able to select for a multiple number of syntactic and semantic contexts, such as verb phrase, gerundive phrase, or noun phrase. How this is accomplished without proliferating word senses is a difficult task and requires major rethinking of how a verb's arguments are in fact selected (see Pustejovsky, 1991; Dixon, 1991; Briscoe and coworkers, 1990).

Another example of contextually determined polysemy comes from the semantic behavior of adjectival modification. Here we consider only evaluative predicates such as *fast* in (7) below.

7. a. a **fast** typist: one who types quickly
   b. a **fast** car: one which can move quickly
   c. a **fast** waltz: one with a fast tempo

The interpretation being selected for depends on the noun that the adjective is modifying. The difficulty here for semantics and computational lexicons is that word sense enumeration cannot characterize all the possible meanings of the adjective in the lexicon. Somehow, lexical semantics must be able to account for the creative use of words in different contexts, without allowing for unrestricted interpretations (cf Pustejovsky and Boguraev, 1991).

This article just briefly characterizes some of the techniques that have been useful for arriving at pre-theoretic notions of word meaning, and some of the major problems that face the lexical semantics community.

RELATED WORK

Perhaps the longest tradition of research on lexical semantics comes from the linguistics and philosophical community (see LEXICAL DECOMPOSITION; SEMANTIC NETWORKS). Much of this work has been influential in both cognitive psychology and AI. In particular, the works of Fillmore (1968, 1977), Gruber (1965), Lakoff (1971), and Jackendoff (1972, 1983) have influenced knowledge representation design as it pertains to representing natural language input. These approaches assume a vocabulary of semantic primitives and account for semantic generalizations on the basis of underlying primitives (cf Wilks, 1975a, 1975b; Schank, 1972, 1975). The major difference between linguistic approaches to the study of word meaning and those concerned with non-linguistic data is a methodological one. Wilks, Schank, and others were interested in how to express conceptual knowledge. Similarly, work in semantic networks (qv) and commonsense reasoning (see REASONING, COMMONSENSE) is primarily concerned with human reasoning rather than the sentences or words of any particular language. Thus, when used for representing the meanings of sentences in language, some of these representation languages sometimes appear ill-equipped to handle the subtleties and nuances of natural language. They do, however, provide a direct mechanism for reasoning about the world as expressed through language, a task not addressed by lexical semantics per se. (See also CONCEPTUAL DEPENDENCY; PREFERENCE SEMANTICS; KNOWLEDGE REPRESENTATION; LEXICAL DECOMPOSITION.)

BIBLIOGRAPHY

B. T. Atkins, "Semantic ID Tags: Corpus Evidence for Dictionary Senses," in *Proceedings of the Third Annual Conference at University of Waterloo*, Center for the New OED, 1987, pp. 17–36.

B. T. Atkins, J. Kegl, and B. Levin, "Anatomy of a Verb Entry," *J. Lexicographic Res.* **1** (1988).

E. Bach, "The Algebra of Events," *Linguistics and Philosophy* **9**, 5–16, 1986.

L. Barselou, "Ad Hoc Categories," *Memory and Cognition* **11**(3) (1983).

R. Beckwith, C. Fellbaum, D. Gross, and G. Miller, "WordNet: A Lexical Database Organized on Psycholinguistic Principles," in U. Zernik, ed., *Proceedings of the First International Workshop on Lexical Acquisition*, at IJCAI 1989, Detroit, 1989.

M. Bierwisch, "On Certain Problems of Semantic Representation," *Foundations of Language* **5**, 153–184 (1969).

D. G. Bobrow and T. Winograd, "An Overview of KRL, a Knowledge Representation Language," *Cogn. Sci.* 1(1) (1977).

B. Boguraev and T. Briscoe, eds., *Computational Lexicography for Natural Language Processing*, Harlow, Essex, Longman, 1988.

B. Boguraev and J. Pustejovsky, "A Richer Characterization of Dictionary Entries," in B. Atkins and A. Zampolli, eds., *Automating the Lexicon*, Oxford University Press, in press.

R. J. Brachman, "On the Epistemelogical Status of Semantic Networks," in N. Findler, ed., *Associative Networks: Representation and Use of Knowledge by Computers*, Academic Press, New York, 1979.

R. J. Brachman and J. Schmolze, "An Overview of the KL-ONE Knowledge Representation System," *Cogn. Sci.* **9**(2) (1985).

J. Bresnan, ed., *The Mental Representation of Grammatical Relations*, MIT Press, Cambridge, Mass., 1982.

T. Briscoe, A. Copestake, and B. Boguraev, "Enjoy the Paper: Lexical Semantics via Lexicology," *Proceedings of the Thirteenth International Conference on Computational Linguistics*, Helsinki, Finland, pp. 42–47.

L. Cardelli and P. Wegner, "On Understanding Types, Data Abstraction, and Polymorphism," *ACM Computing Surveys* **17**(4), 471–522, 1985.

G. Carlson, *Reference to Kinds in English*, Ph.D. dissertation, University of Massachusetts, 1977.

R. Carnap, *Meaning and Necessity*, University of Chicago Press, 1956.

E. Charniak and R. Goldman, "A Logic for Semantic Interpretation," in *Proceedings of the Twenty-Sixth Annual Meeting of the Association for Computational Linguistics*, Buffalo, N.Y., ACL, Morristown, N.J., 1988.

G. Chierchia, "Structured Meanings, Thematic Roles, and Control," in G. Chierchia, B. Partee, and R. Turner, eds., *Properties, Types, and Meaning*, Vol. 2, Kluwer, Boston.

N. Chomsky, *The Logical Structure of Linguistic Theory*, University of Chicago Press, 1st ed., 1975.

N. Chomsky, *Aspects of the Theory of Syntax*, MIT Press, Cambridge, Mass., 1965.

N. Chomsky, *Lectures on Government and Binding*, Foris Publications, Dordrecht, Holland, 1981.

A. Collins and M. Quillian, "Retrieval Time from Semantic Memory," *J. Verbal Learning and Verbal Behavior* **9**, 240–247 (1969).

A. Copestake and T. Briscoe, "Lexical Operations in a Unification-Based Framework," in J. Pustejovsky J. and S. Bergler, eds., *Proceedings of the SIGLEX Workshop on Lexical Semantics and Knowledge Representation*, Berkeley, Calif., 1991.

W. Croft, *Categories and Relations in Syntax: The Clause-Level Organization of Information*, University of Chicago Press, 1991.

D. A. Cruse, *Lexical Semantics*, Cambridge University Press, 1986.

R. M. W. Dixon, *A New Approach to English Grammar, on Semantic Principles*, Oxford University Press, 1991.

D. R. Dowty, *Word Meaning and Montague Grammar*, D. Reidel, Dordrecht, Holland, 1979.

D. R. Dowty, "On Some Recent Analyses of Control," *Linguistics and Philosophy* **8**, 1–41 (1985).

D. R. Dowty, "On the Semantic Content of the Notion 'Thematic Role'," in G. Chierchia, Barbara Partee, and R. Turner, eds., *Properties, Types, and Meaning*, Vol. 2, Kluwer, Dordrecht, Holland, 1989.

D. E. Elliot, "Towards a Grammar of Exclamations," *Foundations of Language*, Vol. 11, 1974.

R. Evans and G. Gazdar, "Inference in DATR," in *Proceedings of the Fourth European ACL Conference*, Manchester, UK, Apr. 1989.

R. Evans and G. Gazdar, *The DATR Papers: February 1990*, Cognitive Science Research Paper CSRP 139, School of Cognitive and Computing Science, University of Sussex, Brighton, UK, 1990.

D. Fass, *Collative Semantics: A Semantics for Natural Language Processing*, MCCS-99-118, Computing Research Laboratory, New Mexico State University, Las Cruces, New Mexico, 1988.

D. Fass, "Lexical Semantic Constraints," J. Pustejovsky, ed., *Semantics and the Lexicon*, Kluwer, Dordrecht, Holland, 1992.

G. Fauconnier, *Mental Spaces*, MIT Press, Cambridge, Mass., 1985.

C. Fillmore, "The Case for Case," in E. Bach and R. Harms, eds., *Universals in Linguistic Theory*, Holt, Rinehart, and Winston, New York, 1968.

C. Fillmore, "Construction Grammar," 1985 [unpublished].

D. Flickinger, C. Pollard, and T. Wasow, "Structure-Sharing in Lexical Representation," *Proceedings of the Twenty-Third Annual Meeting of the ACL*, Chicago, 1985, pp. 262–267.

J. Fodor, *The Language of Thought*, Harvard University Press, Cambridge, Mass., 1975.

A. F. Freed, *The Semantics of English Aspectual Complementation*, Reidel, Dordrecht, Holland, 1979.

G. Gazdar, E. Klein, G. Pullum, and I. Sag, *Generalized Phrase Structure Grammar*, Harvard University Press, Cambridge, Mass., 1985.

N. Goodman, *The Structure of Appearance*, Reidel, Dordrecht, Holland, 1951.

H. P. Grice, "Meaning," in D. Steinberg and L. Jacobovits, eds., *Semantics: An Interdisciplinary Reader in Philosophy, Linguistics, and Psychology*, Cambridge University Press, Cambridge, UK, 1971.

J. Grimshaw, "Complement Selection and the Lexicon," *Linguistic Inquiry* (1979).

J. Grimshaw, *Argument Structure*, MIT Press, Cambridge, Mass. (in press).

J. Gruber, *Studies in Lexical Relations*, Ph.D. dissertation, MIT, Cambridge, Mass., 1965.

K. Hale and S. J. Keyser, "Some Transitivity Alternations in English," *Lexicon Project Working Papers 7*, Center for Cognitive Science, MIT, Cambridge, Mass., 1986.

K. Hale and S. J. Keyser, "A View from the Middle," *Lexicon Project Working Papers 10*, Center for Cognitive Science, MIT, Cambridge, Mass., 1987.

P. Hayes, "Naive Physics Manifesto," in D. Mitchie, ed., *Expert Systems in the Micro-electronic Age*, Edinburgh University Press, Edinburgh, UK, 1979.

J. Higginbotham, "On Semantics," *Linguistic Inquiry* (1985).

E. W. Hinrichs, *A Compositional Semantics for Aktionarten and NP Reference in English*, Ph.D. dissertation, Ohio State University, 1985.

G. Hirst, *Semantic Interpretation and the Resolution of Ambiguity*, Cambridge University Press, Cambridge, UK, 1987.

J. Hobbs, "Towards an Understanding of Coherence in Discourse," in W. Lehnert and M. Ringle, eds., *Strategies for Natural Language Processing*, Lawrence Erlbaum Associates, Hillsdale, N.J., 1982.

J. Hobbs, "World Knowledge and Word Meaning," in *Proceedings of TINLAP-3*, Las Cruces, New Mexico, 1987.

J. Hobbs, W. Croft, T. Davies, D. Edwards, and K. Laws, "Commonsense Metaphysics and Lexical Semantics," *Comput. Ling.* **13**(3–4) (1987).

J. Hobbs, M. Stickel, P. Martin, D. Edwards, "Interpretation as Abduction," in *Proceedings of the Twenty-Sixth Annual Meeting of the Association for Computational Linguistics*, Buffalo, N.Y., ACL, Morristown, N.J., 1988.

R. Ingria and J. Pustejovsky, "Active Objects in Syntax, Semantics, and Parsing," in C. Tenny, ed., *The MIT Parsing Volume, 1988–1989*, Center for Cognitive Science, MIT, Cambridge, Mass., 1990.

R. Jackendoff, *Semantic Interpretation in Generative Grammar*, MIT Press, Cambridge, Mass., 1972.

R. Jackendoff, *Semantics and Cognition*, MIT Press, Cambridge, Mass., 1983.

J. J. Katz, *Semantic Theory*, Harper and Row, New York, 1972.

J. J. Katz and J. Fodor, "The Structure of a Semantic Theory," Language **39**(2), 170–210.

L. Karttunen, "Implicative Verbs," *Language* **47**, 340–358 (1971).

L. Karttunen, "Presupposition and Linguistic Context," *Theoretical Linguistics* **1**, 181–193 (1974).

E. Keenan, "On Semantically Based Grammar," *Linguistic Inquiry*, **3**, 413–461 (1972).

E. Keenan and L. Faltz, *Boolean Semantics for Natural Language*, Reidel, Dordrecht, Holland, 1985.

R. Kempson, *Semantic Theory*, Cambridge University Press, New York, 1972.

P. Kiparsky and C. Kiparsky, "Fact," in Steinberg and Jackobovits, eds., *Semantics: An Interdisciplinary Reader in Philosophy, Linguistics, and Psychology*, Cambridge University Press, Cambridge, UK, 1971.

E. Klein and I. Sag, "Type-Driven Translation," *Linguistics and Philosophy* **8**, 163–202 (1985).

M. Krifka, "Nominal Reference and Temporal Constitution: Towards a Semantics of Quantity," FNS-Bericht 17, Forschungsstelle für Natürlich-Sprachliche Systeme, Universität Tübingen, Tübingen, FRG.

G. Lakoff, *Irregularity in Syntax*, Holt, Rinehart, and Winston, New York, 1970.

G. Lakoff, "On Generative Semantics," in D. Steinberg and L. Jakobovits, eds., *Semantics: An Interdisciplinary Reader*, Cambridge University Press, 1971.

G. Lakoff, *Women, Fire, and Dangerous Objects*, University of Chicago Press, Chicago, 1987.

A. Lehrer, *Semantic Fields and Lexical Structures*, North Holland, Amsterdam, 1974.

B. Levin, ed., "Lexical Semantics in Review," *Lexicon Project Working Papers Number 1*, MIT, Cambridge, Mass., 1985.

B. Levin, *Towards a Lexical Organization of English Verbs*, University of Chicago Press, Chicago, in press.

B. Levin and T. R. Rapoport, "Lexical Subordination," *Proceedings of CLS 24*, 1988, pp. 275–289.

B. Levin and M. Rappaport, "The Formation of Adjectival Passives," *Linguistic Inquiry* **17**(4) (1986).

B. Levin and M. Rappaport, "On the Nature of Unaccusativity," in *Proceedings of NELS 1988*, 1988.

G. E. R. Lloyd, *Aristotle: The Growth and Structure of his Thought*, Cambridge University Press, 1968.

R. McKeon, *The Basic Works of Aristotle*, Random House, New York, 1941.

I. Mel'čuk, *Dependency Syntax*, SUNY Press, Albany, New York, 1988.

G. Miller, "Dictionaries of the Mind," in *Proceedings of the Twenty-Third Annual Meeting of the Association for Computational Linguistics*, Chicago, 1985.

G. Miller and C. Fellbaum, "Semantic Networks of English," *Cognition* (October 1991, in press).

G. Miller and P. Johnson-Laird, *Language and Perception*, Belknap, Harvard University Press, Cambridge, 1976.

M. Moens and M. Steedman, "Temporal Ontology and Temporal Reference," *Comput. Ling.* **14**(2), 15–28.

R. Montague, R. Thomason, ed., *Formal Philosophy: The Collected Papers of Richard Montague*, Yale University Press, New Haven, Conn., 1974.

J. M. Moravcsik, "Aitia as Generative Factor in Aristotle's Philosophy," *Dialogue* (1975).

A. Mourelatos, "Events, Processes, and States," in P. Tedeschi and A. Zaenen, eds., *Syntax and Semantics: Tense and Aspect*, Academic Press, New York, 1981.

G. Nunberg, *The Pragmatics of Reference*, Indiana University Linguistics Club, Bloomington, Indiana, 1978.

M. R. Quillian, "Semantic Memory," in M. Minsky, ed., *Semantic Information Processing*, MIT Press, Cambridge, Mass., 1968.

B. Partee and M. Rooth, "Generalized Conjunction and Type Ambiguity," in Bäuerle, Schwarze, and von Stechow, eds., *Meaning, Use, and Interpretation of Language*, Walter de Gruyter.

R. J. Passonneau, "A Computational Model of the Semantics of Tense and Aspect," *Comput. Ling.* **14**(2) (1988).

J. Pustejovsky, "Issues in Computational Lexical Semantics," in the *Proceedings of the Fourth European ACL Conference*, Manchester, UK, April 1989.

J. Pustejovsky, "The Generative Lexicon," *Comput. Ling.* **17**(4) (1991).

R. B. Roberts and Goldstein, *The FRL Manual*, Technical Report AI Memo 409, MIT Artificial Intelligence Laboratory, Cambridge, Mass., 1977.

R. Scha, *Logical Foundations for Question Answering*, MS 12.331, Philips Research Laboratories, Eindhoven, Holland, 1983.

R. Schank, *Conceptual Information Processing*, North-Holland, Amsterdam, 1975.

P. Strawson, "On Referring," *Mind* **59**, 320–44 (1950).

P. Sueren, *Discourse Semantics*, Blackwell Publishers, Oxford, UK, 1985.

G. Smolka, *A Feature Logic with Subsorts*, LILOG-Report 33, Wissenschaftliches Zentrum der IBM Deutschland, 1988.

G. Stump, "Frequency Adjectives," *Linguistics and Philosophy* (1982).

L. Talmy, "Semantics and Syntax of Motion," in J. P. Kimball, ed., *Syntax and Semantics 4*, Academic Press, New York, 1975.

L. Talmy, "Lexicalization Patterns," in T. Shopen, ed., *Language Typology and Syntactic Description*, Cambridge, 1985.

C. Tenny, *Grammaticalizing Aspect and Affectedness*, Ph.D. dissertation, MIT, Cambridge, Mass., 1987.

D. Touretzky, *The Mathematics of Inheritance Systems*, Morgan Kaufmann, Los Altos, Calif., 1986.

Z. Vendler, *Linguistics and Philosophy*, Cornell University Press, Ithaca, N.Y., 1967.

D. Walker, A Zampolli, and N. Calzolari, eds., *Automating the Lexicon*, Oxford University Press, in press.

U. Weinreich, "*Webster's Third*: A Critique of its Semantics," *Int. J. American Ling.* **30**, 405–9 (1964).

U. Weinreich, *Explorations in Semantic Theory*, Mouton, The Hague, 1972.

A. Wierzbicka, *The Semantics of Grammar*, John Benjamins, Amsterdam, 1988.

Y. Wilks, "A Preferential Pattern Seeking Semantics for Natural Language Inference," *Artif. Intell.* **6**, 53–74 (1975).

Y. Wilks, "An Intelligent Analyser and Understander for English," *CACM* **18**, 264–274 (1975).

Y. Wilks, D. Fass, C-M. Guo, J. McDonald, T. Plate, and B. Slator, "A Tractable Machine Dictionary as a Resource for Computational Semantics," in B. Boguraev and T. Briscoe, eds., *Computational Lexicography for Natural Language Processing*, Harlow, Essex, Longman.

E. Williams, "Argument Structure and Morphology," *Linguistic Review* (1981).

G. H. von Wright, *Norm and Action: A Logical Inquiry*, Routledge and Kegan Paul, London, 1963.

JAMES PUSTEJOVSKY
Brandeis University

LEXICON. See DICTIONARY/LEXICON.

LIFER

A top-down, left-to-right-driven, natural-language parser (see PARSING), controlled by a transition tree grammar, LIFER was designed by Hendrix in 1977 to interface a natural-language front-end with LADDER, a distributed database system developed at SRI [see G. Hendrix, "LIFER: A Natural Language Interface Facility," *SIGART Newslett.* **61**, 25–26 (1977); G. Hendrix, E. Sacerdoti, D. Sagalowicz, and J. Slocum, "Developing a Natural Language Interface to Complex Data," *ACM Trans. Database Sys.* **3**, 105–147 (1978)].

A. HANYONG YUHAN
AT&T Bell Labs

LINGUISTICS. See COMPUTATIONAL LINGUISTICS.

LISP

LISP was invented in 1956 by John McCarthy. Since then it has been in constant use as the language of choice for AI programming. Even now it is the premier language for AI, and its acceptance by the larger programming community is growing.

Unlike many other programming languages, LISP was designed primarily for symbolic processing. Since LISP's early days it has moved from being an exclusively symbolic processing language toward being a truly general-purpose programming language. For example, Common LISP supports many floating-point data types, several types of vectors and arrays, strings, and abstract data-structuring constructs.

This entry discusses three main topics: a description of

LISP constructs using Common LISP, the history of LISP, and a comparison of the major dialects in use over the history of LISP.

SIMPLE EXAMPLE OF LISP

The following is an example of a LISP program. This example is intended to give the reader an idea of what LISP is like so that the remaining discussion is not entirely abstract:

```
;;; This function computes factorial of n
(defun factorial (n)
  (cond ((= n 0) 1)                      ;base case
        (t (* n (factorial (- n 1))))))  ;simple recursion
```

The mathematical definition of factorial is

$$0! = 1 \qquad n! = n(n - 1)!$$

The correspondence between the LISP definition and the mathematical definition of factorial is quite striking.

To apply the LISP factorial function to 3, one writes

$$(factorial\ 3)$$

Syntactically this differs only slightly from the usual mathematical expression for function invocation, which is

$$factorial(3)$$

When factorial is called with 3 as the argument, the variable, n is bound to the value 3. In this particular case, wherever the identifier n is mentioned in the program text, the variable n is referenced, and the value 3 will be obtained.

The first line of the function is the beginning of a conditional statement; COND is a generalization of an if–then–else special form. The line

```
(cond ((= n 0) 1)              ;base case
```

is the beginning of the conditional clause; the value of n is fetched and compared with 0. If the value of n is numerically equal to 0, 1 is returned. This corresponds to the case of $0! = 1$.

Next the line

```
(t (* n (factorial (-n 1))))))   ;simple recursion
```

is the else clause in the conditional; T is a symbol whose value is itself, and the symbol T is taken to be the canonical truth value in LISP. If the value of n is not equal to 0, the current value of n will be multiplied by the value of $(n - 1)!$. The expression

$$(-\ n\ 1)$$

takes the current value of n, decrements it by 1, and returns that as its value. The expression (factorial (− n 1))

calls the function factorial recursively on the value $n - 1$. When this expression returns its value, $(n - 1)!$ that value is multiplied by the original value of n to produce the final value $n! = n(n - 1)!$

LISP BASICS

LISP (*list* processing) is a symbolic manipulation language. Although LISP can manipulate numbers in various formats, its strength lies in being able to manipulate pointers to objects, such as complex data structures. Processing pointers to objects and altering data structures comprising other such pointers is the essence of symbolic processing. Typical data structures in LISP are symbols, lists, trees, vectors, records, arrays, and strings. out of these data structures can be built representations for formulas, real-world objects, natural-language sentences, visual scenes, stories, medical concepts, geological concepts, and other symbolic data. These objects can be manipulated in ways that correspond to actions in the real world or in ways that correspond to thinking about those objects—or so the AI community hopes.

Among the objects that can be represented easily in LISP are LISP programs themselves. Therefore, programs, such as compilers and program verifiers, that reason about other programs can be easily written in LISP—at least the mechanics of manipulating the programs can be easily written. In fact, some of the first programs written in LISP were LISP interpreters (see below). Interpreters execute programs written in LISP by tracing through their structures and performing appropriate actions.

Most LISP programs are in the form of functions, which return values, and programming in LISP is very much like functional composition: the values of expressions are computed, and those values are passed on to other functions, which use those values to compute further values. In other languages one refers to procedures, subroutines, and programs; in LISP all of these concepts are described using the term *function*.

When a programmer is working with LISP, there is an extensive LISP programming environment in which that work takes place. A programmer will type interactively to the LISP interpreter in order to run programs. The LISP interpreter reads LISP expressions and evaluates them, printing out their values. This part of LISP is called the LISP toplevel. The programming environment also maintains a dynamic heap or area of storage. User programs can allocate objects in the heap, and a garbage collector is responsible for freeing storage that is no longer in use.

The concept of evaluation is important to understanding the nature of LISP. Given an expression, LISP will evaluate that expression, yielding a value. Simple expressions, representing constants, variables, and literals, are evaluated directly; composite expressions, representing functional application or date structure access, are evaluated by first evaluating all of the subexpressions in the original expression and then applying the function speci-

fied in the expression or then performing the actions required by the special form designated in the expression. This process is discussed more precisely below, but for now it suffices to appreciate that the process of evaluation is the key to understanding LISP.

LISP SYNTAX

LISP uses a minimal syntax in which parentheses are significant. The name for a LISP object written in this syntax is *S-expression*.

LISP has a facility, called the reader, that parses the forms that LISP can manipulate. The reader is responsible for building data structures in the LISP environment that correspond to an external representation of these structures.

The LISP reader can recognize and construct a relatively small number of objects; among them are symbols, arrays, floating-point numbers, strings, quoted objects, CONSes, lists, vectors, and *fixnums*. Fixnums are integers that can be represented compactly. Usually a fixnum corresponds to a number such that the bits that represent the number plus the bits that represent the tag for the fixnum fit in a machine word.

Symbols and Atoms

The LISP reader reads characters presented to it by some input stream—usually a keyboard or a disk file—and interprets the sequence of characters as a LISP object. The most basic LISP object is a symbol or an atom; its printed representation is as a sequence of alphabetic, numeric, pseudoalphabetic, and special characters. Different LISP systems define symbols differently, but the essential features are usually very much along these lines.

Here are several examples of the printed representation of symbols:

```
foo     ;a symbol with 3 letters
foo3    ;a symbol with a digit as a character
foo-bar ;a symbol can have special characters in it
 +$     ;a symbol with only pseudoalphabetic characters
/usr/r  ;a symbol with slashes in it
```

Symbols and their roles will be described in detail later. Their main use is as a way of describing programs and data for programs. Some LISP dialects use the term *atom* in place of the term *symbol*. Here *symbol* is used uniformly.

CONS Cells and Lists. The CONS cell is the original basic building block for data structures. With the CONS cell lists and binary trees can be constructed. A CONS cell is a data structure that holds two pointers. The CONS cell that holds the numbers 1 and 2 is written as:

$$(1 . 2)$$

This data structure is not the same as the one written

$$(2 . 1)$$

The order of the two elements is important. A CONS cell written as above is said to be written in dot notation; sometimes it is referred to as a *dotted list* or a *dotted pair*.

A list is written as

$$(e_1 \, e_2 \, . \, . \, . \, e_n)$$

This form is a shorthand for the following tree structure:

$$(e_1 \, . \, (e_2 \, . \, . \, . \, (e_n \, . \, \text{NIL}) \, . \, . \,))$$

The symbol NIL is special in that it represents the empty list. NIL is described below in more detail.

Lists are represented as binary trees whose left branches point to elements in the list and whose right branches point to the remainder of the list.

The list

$$(1 \; 2 \; 3 \; 4)$$

is synonymous with

$$(1 \, . \, (2 \, . \, (3 \, . \, (4 \, . \, \text{NIL}))))$$

(The use of CONS cells to represent lists has been pervasive from the earliest LISP dialects. (The LISP printer—a function that produces a character or typed representation of LISP data structures—produces lists from CONS cells wherever possible.)

The LISP reader and system will produce a CONS cell with a 1 in its left branch and a 2 in its right branch when presented with

$$(\text{quote} \; (1 \, . \, 2))$$

The "QUOTE" informs the LISP system that the form

$$(1 \, . \, 2)$$

is to be interpreted as a LISP object rather than as some other sort of command or statement. A LISP reader normally supplies a number of shorthand notations, and the most prevalent over many dialects of LISP is the single quote, which is used as a shorthand for QUOTE.

$$(\text{quote} \; (1 \, . \, 2))$$

is equivalent to

$$'(1 \, . \, 2)$$

LISP programs can construct CONS cells with the function CONS.

The code

$$(\text{cons} \; 1 \; 2)$$

builds the dotted pair

$$(1 \, . \, 2)$$

The code

$$(\text{cons e1 (cons e2 . . . (cons en NIL) . . .)})$$

constructs the list

$$(e_1 \, e_2 \, . \, . \, . \, e_n)$$

To access the first element of a CONS cell, one writes

$$(\text{car} \; \langle \text{cell} \rangle)$$

And the second element of a CONS cell is accessed by writing

$$(\text{cdr} \; \langle \text{cell} \rangle)$$

The left branch of a CONS cell is called the CAR of the cell, and the right branch of a CONS cell is called the CDR.

To alter the CAR of a CONS cell destructively, one writes

$$(\text{rplaca} \; \langle a \rangle \; \langle c \rangle)$$

which alters the CAR of the CONS cell $\langle a \rangle$ to be $\langle c \rangle$. And to alter the CDR of a CONS cell destructively, one writes

$$(\text{rplacd} \; \langle a \rangle \; \langle d \rangle)$$

which alters the CDR of the CONS cell $\langle a \rangle$ to be $\langle d \rangle$.

Manipulating List Structure

Lists are quite easily manipulated; it is natural to use structural recursion on binary trees. Here is the definition of a function that counts the number of atoms in a tree:

```
(defun count-atoms (LST)
  (cond ((null LST) 0)
        ((atom LST) 1)
        (t (+ (count-atoms (car LST))
              (count-atoms (cdr LST))))))
```

NULL tests whether the end of a list has been reached; ATOM tests whether an object is an atom. This function can be applied to the definition of count-atoms itself, in which case it returns 18 (0 and 1 are regarded as atoms).

Programs and Data. That LISP programs and LISP data structures so closely correspond is of major significance to the success of LISP in the research community. Using this feature, researchers have been able to implement other programming languages on top of LISP easily. In addition, LISP structure editors and compilers have proven to be easily written in LISP.

Recall the definition of factorial given above. It is a list whose first element is "defun," whose second element is factorial, whose third element is a list whose first element is *n*, and so on.

Algebraic Syntax

Some LISP dialects have chosen to provide an algebraic or algorithmic syntax in addition to the standard LISP syntax. InterLisp (W. Teitelman and co-workers, 1978) supports CLISP (conversational LISP); PSL (The Utah Symbolic Computation Group, 1982; M. L. Griss and E. Benson, 1982) supports RLISP (REDUCE LISP syntax); and MacLisp (D. Moon, 1974) supports CGOL. Although these syntaxes have their advocates, the bulk of the LISP programming community uses standard LISP syntax.

To demonstrate the differences in the various syntaxes for these dialects, the iterative definitions for the factorial function are shown.

Common LISP

```
(defun fact (n)
  ;; Iterative factorial
  (do ((i 2 (1+ i))
       (result 1 (* result i)))
      ((< n i) result)))
```

InterLisp

```
(DEFINEQ
 (FACT
  (LAMBDA (N)
   (* Iterative factorial)
   (bind (RESULT 1) for I from 1 to N do
    (SETQ RESULT (TIMES RESULT I))
    finally (RETURN RESULT)))))
```

RLISP

```
symbolic procedure fact n;
  % Iterative factorial
  for i := 1:n product i;
```

CGOL

```
define factorial (n);
  % Iterative factorial
  prog result;
  result := 1;
  for i in 1 to n do
   result := result * i;
  return(result)$
```

SYMBOLS, IDENTIFIERS, LOCATIONS, AND BINDINGS

In this article, a distinction is made between symbols, identifiers, locations, and bindings. A location is a temporarily allocated piece of storage—as in other programming languages. An identifier is a name for a location or for a symbol. An identifier is usually written as a string of characters and is recognized by a reader (parser) as an identifier. The place in a symbol where the value is stored is called the *value cell*.

The pair of an identifier and a storage location is called a *variable*. In LISP variables are introduced by lambda expressions, let expressions, function definitions, and a few other basic constructs. In Common LISP variables are

treated as lexical variables unless they are declared special. A lexical variable is a variable whose scope is lexical or textual. The value of a lexical variable can only be accessed or altered by expressions that appear within the same expression that introduces the variable.

A symbol is a LISP object. It has a name associated with it, and it also has a number of aspects or uses. First it has a value, which can be accessed or altered using exactly the same forms that access or alter the value of a lexical variable. In fact, the methods of naming symbols are the same as those used for naming a lexical variable. When a programmer declares that a variable is special, the LISP system will generate a symbol instead of a lexical variable. When an identifier is created at the toplevel of LISP, the LISP system will also generate a symbol.

In addition to a value, a symbol can have a property list, a package, a print name, and possibly a function definition associated with it. A property list is simply a list of indicators and values; a property list can be used to store properties associated with the symbol or perhaps associated with some object that the symbol is defined by the programmer to represent. A print name is usually the string of characters that constitutes the identifier.

A package is a structure that establishes a mapping between an identifier and a symbol. A package is usually a hash table containing symbols. There is always a current package, and when the LISP reader finds an identifier, it examines the current package to determine whether there is a symbol with that name in the current package. If there is such a symbol, the reader returns that symbol; otherwise it creates a symbol in the current package with the identifier string as its print name and returns that new symbol. It is in this manner that the mapping is established.

A function is normally associated with a lexical variable or a symbol. Associating a function definition with a symbol is much more commonly done than associating a function definition with a lexical variable. When a function is applied, the application mentions the name of a symbol or a variable. The associated function is then invoked.

The example

$$(foo\ x\ y)$$

is a function application, and the identifier, foo, is associated with a function definition. From the context shown one cannot tell whether foo is a symbol or a lexical variable. Later there are examples of both sorts of references to functions.

Binding

A related concept is binding. A binding is an association of an identifier with a location or a symbol. A binding is often temporarily made, and after some context is exited, the binding reverts back to the previous one. Above, a variable is defined to be a binding of an identifier with a location. A location is a place to store a value, and thus a binding may associate a name with a value.

Many LISP systems implement a location as a memory location, a stack location, or a register, and the compiler is free to choose the most appropriate location or locations to store the value of the variable during the computation involving them. Likewise, the interpreter will manage bindings and locations, and sometimes the interpreter's management will be identical to the compiled code's management of bindings and locations, though it need not be.

A symbol's value cell is a location in which a value can be stored, and bindings of these cells can be made. Such bindings are called *special bindings*.

Here are some examples of these concepts in use.

x

This expression—the identifier x—refers to the location containing the value of the lexical variable named x or it refers to the symbol named x. In either case, it is said to refer to the value of x—in particular, it refers to the value part of the binding.

(setq x ⟨expression⟩)

This expression alters the value part of the binding of the x. If x is a symbol, its value is altered; if it is a lexical variable, the location to which x refers is altered.

(let ((x ⟨expression⟩))
  ⟨form⟩)

This is the most common method of establishing a binding. This form causes a new binding of x to be established with an initial value corresponding to the value of the expression. The form, ⟨form⟩, is evaluated in the context of the binding; any references to x, either to access or to alter its value, will access or alter this binding. This binding of x will exist from the time that the form is entered until it is exited. Here the distinction between a symbol and a lexical variable is important. The lexical scope of the variable x above is defined to be the textual extent of the LET expression. References to a lexical variable are allowed only within the lexical scope. If x were special—x refers to a symbol—references to x could be made anywhere during the execution of the form, ⟨form⟩, even outside the lexical scope of the binding of x.

Free and Bound References

Important notions to understanding LISP are free references and bound references to variables. In the LET expression above, any references to x that are lexically or textually apparent in ⟨form⟩ are called *bound* references to x. Suppose the entire LET expression were

(let ((x (foo)))
  (+ x x))

The references to x are bound: Each refers to the binding of x that is lexically apparent. It can be seen that the value of x will be precisely the value of the expression (foo). Suppose, on the other hand, the entire LET expression were

(let ((x (foo)))
  (+ y y))

The references to y are free references to the value of y. In this case the reference is to the value of the symbol, y; the binding of y to which this reference refers is neither lexically nor textually apparent. By examining the program text, one cannot see the intended value for y; the value must be that obtained from an earlier binding for the symbol y.

Declaring Variables Special

The binding of an identifier that refers to a symbol is called a *special binding*. Whenever a binding is made, unless the identifier is declared special, the binding is of an identifier to a location that is not the value cell of a symbol.

(let ((x (foo)))
  (declare (special y))
  (+ y y))

This states that y is special. A special variable is a binding whose value part is the value cell of a symbol, and the binding alters the value of the symbol temporarily. Recall that to get the value of a symbol, the value cell of the symbol is examined.

When a binding is established by the action of a let or some other similar constructs (eg, PROG, DEFUN, FLET, MACROLET, LABELS, and MULTIPLE-VALUE-BIND), the establishing process is called *let binding* or *lambda binding*.

Consider this example:

(let ((x ⟨expression⟩))
  (declare (special x))
  ⟨form⟩)

This code let-binds a symbol. Let-binding the symbol x temporarily changes the value of x for the duration of the LET. (The implementation of a LISP system may not actually perform exactly the operations described here. The operations presented are intended to present an informal operational semantics for LISP. Some LISPs might alter the value of the symbol, and others might put the value of a special variable on the control stack; in order to find the value of this special variable, the control stack is searched. LISPs that change value cells are called *shallow-binding* LISPs, and LISPs that put bindings on the stack are called *deep-binding* LISPs. The implications of these implementation choices are in terms of performance: Certain operations are performed faster in one type of implementation than in another. The implementors make decisions regarding the frequency or importance of certain operations and optimize their implementations according to those decisions.)

In the code above, the symbol x is a global LISP object. Changing its value temporarily alters the value of x throughout the evaluation of the form, ⟨form⟩. For example, suppose that the above piece of code is expanded to

(let ((x 3))
  (declare (special x))
  (foo))

The function foo is being applied to no arguments. The declaration tells LISP that x is to be treated as a symbol. The binding of x is visible to any free occurrences of x in the function foo.

Suppose foo were defined as

```
(defun foo ()
  (+ x x))
```

The reference to x is a free reference, and the value of x is the last binding of the special variable. In the code fragment above, x would be specially bound to 3, foo would be called and see that binding. Adding 3 + 3 yields 6, which is the value of the LET.

The scope of the special binding of x in the code fragment extends through the duration of time that control is within or underneath the forms in the let. This is often termed *dynamic* scope.

Different dialects of LISP use different terms to refer to the concept that is here termed *special*. They are dynamic, fluid, and specvar.

Symbols

Recall that LISP has an interactive environment in which the user can type expressions; LISP evaluates the expressions and prints out the value of the expressions. This toplevel is often called the *read–eval–print* loop—the three words *read, eval,* and *print* indicate the three actions that the toplevel performs.

At the toplevel of LISP, if the user types x, this is taken as a request to evaluate the symbol whose name is x. To evaluate x, LISP will find its value and return that value. If the symbol does not exist, it is created, as discussed earlier.

Generally, a freshly created symbol has no value, so the evaluator will report this fact. LISP 370 and LISP/VM return the symbol itself as the value of a symbol that has never been assigned a value. A value can be assigned to a symbol using SETQ:

```
(setq x 3)
```

This assigns the value 3 to the symbol x. Had x not existed earlier, the reader would have created it when it read the identifier, x, in this expression.

There is a convention concerning what values are regarded as representing true and false. NIL represents falsehood and anything else represents truth. The symbol T is conventionally used to mean true if there is no particular reason to use any other value. Recall that NIL is a symbol and also is the empty list—the empty list is also written ( ).

In Common LISP the symbol NIL has the property that it is synonymous with the empty list. One of the ongoing controversies in the LISP implementation community is whether NIL ought be the same as ( ). NIL is a symbol, and ( ) is a list.

Some writers discussing LISP programming style maintain that ( ) should be written when the programmer intends the empty list, NIL when the programmer intends

falsehood, and 'NIL when the programmer intends the symbol named NIL.

Suppose one types at LISP

```
(setq x 3)
```

and one has the compiled function,

```
(defun square-x ()
  (declare (special x))
  (* x x))
```

If square-x is invoked immediately after the SETQ, the result will be 9. In other words, the interpreter environment is accessible to compiled code.

In the LISP literature the concepts of identifier and symbol are often collapsed into a single concept. Sometimes the concepts of print name and identifier—identifier, as used here—are collapsed. All concepts of variables and bindings can be explained without recourse to the definition of the symbol, but, as with CONS cells, it is often easier to understand special binding using the concrete implementation concept of the symbol rather than a formal definition of the semantics for special binding. As a further motivation for this approach, it is often easier to understand the implementation history of LISP with this treatment in mind than it would be with any other explanatory approach.

FUNCTIONS

All programs in LISP are functions or collections of functions. A function takes some number of arguments, binds those arguments to some variables, and then evaluates some forms in the context of those bindings. After the evaluation takes place, a value or values are returned.

The argument-passing convention is call-by-value: Every argument to a function is first evaluated; and then LISP pointers to those values are passed to the function. This last point is important. Although LISP is call-by-value, the values that are passed are in fact pointers to values, so that if the value is a complex data structure, that data structure is not copied but a pointer to it is passed. If the function alters that data structure—suppose it is a vector, and an element of that vector is altered—then the data structure is altered by side-effect. An exception to this is the case of immediate objects, like fixnums and characters, which are stored in the pointer itself.

Here is a simple function:

```
;;; This computes v*(n!)
;;;
(defun cfact (n v)
  (if (zerop n)
      v
      (cfact (1 - n) (* n v))))
```

This function computes a variant on the factorial function—$v(n!)$; but it does it in a manner that allows a compiler to do a transformation from recursion to iteration.

That is, this function is inherently iterative, although, syntactically, the body of the function calls itself recursively.

The function takes two arguments: n and v. The function is called like this:

$$\text{(cfact 10 1)}$$

which will compute 10!. The value 10 is bound to the variable n and 1 to v. The body of the function is then evaluated within the context of these bindings. The body is

```
(if (zerop n)
    v
    (cfact (1− n) (* n v))))
```

When n is tested, it is not 0, and so the recursive call is made to cfact. Because there is no reason to return to the context in which n is bound to 10 and v to 1, the evaluator can choose not to save this environment: it can, instead, change the bindings of n and v and simply jump to the beginning of the body of cfact. When the evaluator can do this, the function to which it can be done is called *tail recursive,* and this type of optimization is called *tail recursion removal* or *tail merging.*

The first version of factorial shown at the beginning is not tail recursive.

One dialect of LISP, Scheme, depends critically on tail recursion removal to do iteration because Scheme does not provide any iteration constructions such as DO or PROG and GO.

Anonymous Functions

Consider the simple function add7:

```
(defun add7 (x)
    (+ x 7))
```

This simple function adds 7 to its single argument. Suppose this function is needed as part of a larger expression:

$$\text{(setq y (* z (add7 q)))}$$

To evaluate this expression requires doing a function call to the function add7, which can, in certain implementations, be a time-consuming action. The following code fragment achieves the same purpose:

```
(setq y (* z
        ((lambda (x) (+ x 7))
         q)))
```

The expression

$$\text{(lambda (x) (+ x 7))}$$

is an anonymous function. That is, it acts just like a function, but it is not associated with any symbol (function name). Moreover, to call this function does not require a function call. A compiler, seeing both the function definition and its use, can open code or inline code the function invocation. Open coding is creating assembly language code to perform a function rather than creating assembly language code that performs a call to that function.

MACROS

LISP supports a powerful macro facility. When the evaluator finds what appears syntactically to be a function application (sometimes called a combination in the literature), it first checks whether it has found a macro instead. If it is a macro call, then the macro code is evaluated, the result of the macro evaluation is substituted for the original form, and the evaluator attempts the evaluation again. Here is an example:

```
(defmacro add7 (x) (list '+ x 7))
(setq z (* y (add7 q)))
```

When the evaluator is evaluating (add7 q), it notices that (add7 q) is a macro call. It binds the variable x in the macro definition of add7 to the symbol q and then evaluates the body of the macro. The body creates a list whose first element is + and whose second element is the value of the variable x. Here x is bound to the symbol q, so the result of the macro evaluation is

$$\text{(+ q 7)}$$

This expression is then substituted for (add7 q) in the original expression, and the evaluator goes on. With add7 defined as a macro, the original expression is treated exactly as if it had been

$$\text{(setq z (* y (+ q 7)))}$$

BACKQUOTE

Recall the definition of the macro add7:

$$\text{(defmacro add7 (x) (list '+ x 7))}$$

The use of the function LIST was necessary in order to produce a list that had some constant elements intermixed with elements that were the values of other LISP objects. Because writing macros in this style is pervasive in Common LISP, a special construct—backquote—was invented to make writing such macros simpler.

The basic idea is to provide a template for a piece of list structure. The template contains constant as well as variable components. In backquote syntax the list constructor,

$$\text{(list '+ x 7)}$$

is written

$$\text{`(+ ,x ,7)}$$

The expression is preceded by a backquote (`); wherever a common (,) appears, the expression to its right is evaluated, and the resulting value is placed at that point in the list structure. Because the value of 7 is 7, the above expression can be written

'(+ ,x 7)

In Common LISP programs the backquote syntax is entensively used.

DATA ABSTRACTION

The powerful macro facility in LISP has enabled programmers to develop a sophisticated programming style in which data abstractions play a significant role. All representation commitments can be delayed until the program is developed, and these commitments can be hidden within macro definitions in a separate area of the program. In Common LISP a data structure definition facility is defined that is an extension of the fundamental macro facility just described.

Common LISP Defstruct

The Common LISP defstruct capability is similar to capabilities available in other LISP implementations for defining record structures. The user can define new data types and data structures using defstruct:

(defstruct person name age)

This expression defines a record structure named person.
    Consider the example

(setq ralph (make-person :name "Ralph" :age 53))

This expression creates an instance of this data structure. The symbol ralph is given this structure as its value. The person defined has the string "Ralph" as the filler of the name slot and the integer 53 as the filler of the age slot.
    To access the name slot, one writes

(person-name ralph)

Moreover, the type of the structure returned by make-person is person. This enables the programmer to extend the type system defined by the LISP system. The expression

(typep ralph 'person)

returns T. To change the age of ralph (this should be done once a year), one writes

(setf (person-age ralph) (+ 1 (person-age ralph)))

SETF is a generalized value-setting macro: given any LISP location that can be altered, SETF can be used to set the value in that location. For example, to change the CAR of a CONS cell, one can write

(setf (car cell) new-car)

One can define new structures that can be taken as subtypes of existing structures:

(defstruct (astronaut (:include person))
    helmet-size
    (favorite-beverage 'scotch))

This expression defines a new data type, astronaut, which is a subtype of person. If one writes

(setq typical-astronaut
    (make-astronaut
    :name "Buzz"
    :age 45
    :helmet-size 17.5))

This creates a new instance of an astronaut. In a DEFSTRUCT, slots can specify default values, which are used in the event that not all slot values are supplied during instance creation. In this example the favorite-beverage slot has scotch as its default value. The slots of astronaut includes the slots of person, and the instance so created is both of type person and astronaut. In the following example the notation 'expression ⇒ value' is used to indicate the LISP result of evaluating an expression. The LISP expression is to the left of the ⇒, and the value of that expression is to the right.

(person-name typical-astronaut) ⇒ "Buzz"
(astronaut-name typical-astronaut) ⇒ "Buzz"
(astronaut-favorite-beverage typical-astronaut) ⇒ scotch
(typep typical-astronaut 'person) ⇒ t
(typep typical-astronaut 'astronaut) ⇒ t

CLOSURES

In some dialects of LISP—Common LISP, for example—anonymous functions are generalized one step further: Functions are treated as first-class objects, just like any other LISP object. Consider the expression

#'(lambda (x) (+ x 7))

This expression, as any other in LISP, should have a value. In LISPs that support expressions like this having values, the value is called a *closure*. A closure is a function that retains the binding context current when the closure was created, so that that context may be used for references to free variables from within the function's body.
    The #' syntax signifies that the expression following it is a function or a closure. Some LISP dialects, such as Scheme, denote closures exactly as above but without the #'.
    A more complex example is

(let ((x 7))
    #'(lambda (y)(+ x y)))

A function is created within a context of bindings that, when applied to a single argument, will add 7 to it. The function itself will refer freely to x when the function is called. Creating this closure requires retaining the lexical environment of bindings throughout the lifetime of the closure.

A simple example of the use of closures is

```
(labels ((factorial (n)
          (if (= n 0)
              1
              (* n (factorial (- n 1))))))
  (+ (factorial x) (factorial y)))
```

In this piece of code the function factorial is locally defined and then locally applied to the apparently free variables x and y.

The construct LABELS is like LET in that it establishes bindings, but it is used to define recursive functions locally. Note that the definition of factorial refers to itself; the LABELS construct is used to establish this self-reference.

With closures it is possible to create several objects that retain a shared context that can be manipulated. Using this mechanism, it is possible to write modules and other sorts of structuring constructs. However, not all LISP dialects support closures.

Recall that CONS, CAR, and CDR are defined above. Here is a way to implement these constructs using closures; the functional correspondents to these functions are called fcons, fcar, and fcdr, respectively.

```
;;; A functional definition of cons
(defun fcons (a b)
  #'(lambda (message &optional value)
      ;;; There are 4 message types:
      ;;; fcar: returns the car of the cons cell
      ;;; fcdr: returns the cdr of the cons cell
      ;;; frplaca: takes another argument and changes the
      ;;;   car of the cons cell to that argument
      ;;; frplacd: takes another argument and changes the
      ;;;   cdr of the cons cell to that argument
      (case message
        (fcar a)                    ;fetch the car
        (fcdr b)                    ;fetch the cdr
        (frplaca (setq a value))    ;change the car
        (frplacd (setq b value))    ;change the cdr
        (t (error "Invalid message to a cons cell: S."
                  message)))))
```

This function takes two arguments and produces a closure that will act as a CONS cell would. The function that is returned by fcons takes one or two arguments. The first argument should be one of four different messages. The message fcar will return the CAR of the CONS cell, the message fcdr will return the cdr of the CONS cell, and the other two messages will change the CAR and the CDR parts of the CONS cell. If the first argument is either fcar or fcdr, the second argument, if supplied, is ignored.

The messages frplaca and frplacd correspond to RPLACA and RPLACD. If the first argument is frplaca, the second argument is the new value for the CAR, and if the first argument is frplacd, the second argument is the

new value for the CDR. A second argument only makes sense if the first argument is either frplaca or frplacd. There is a way to detect that the optional argument value was supplied erroneously and to signal an error if it was.

Here is an example of the use of these constructs.

```
(setq cell (fcons 'a 'b))
```

This expression sets the value of the symbol cell to the closure created by fcons. To obtain the CAR of cell, one writes

```
(funcall cell 'fcar)
```

This expression calls the function that is the value of cell with the single argument fcar. To obtain the CDR of cell, one writes

```
(funcall cell 'fcdr)
```

To change the CAR of cell to be c, one writes

```
(funcall cell 'frplaca 'c)
```

and to change the CDR of cell to be d, one writes

```
(funcall cell 'frplacd 'd)
```

To illustrate a simple use of macros, suppose one wishes to write

```
(fcar cell)
```

to obtain the CAR cell, where cell is as it is defined above. Then the macro fcar can be defined as

```
(defmacro fcar (cell)
  '(funcall ,cell 'fcar))
```

Lambda Lists

The explanation of closures has introduced the notion of &optional arguments to a function. The closure returned by fcons can take one or two arguments. The notation

```
(message &optional value)
```

in the lambda list for that closure has the marker &optional in it. The arguments to the left of this marker are required to be passed to this function, and the arguments to the right may be passed. In fact, there is a wide variety of special markers that can appear in a lambda list. These markers can enable functions to take keyword arguments, in which the order of arguments to the function may not be known to the programmer, and special keywords are used to cause arguments passed to be matched to the proper variables by matching the keywords. Also, some of the arguments passed to a function can be turned into a LISP list in the event that the function can take a widely varying number of arguments.

THE SIMPLE EVALUATION MODEL

Earlier the concept of evaluation was introduced as the key to understanding LISP. LISP can be defined by an informal operational semantics in which the method of evaluating forms and expressions is given. The simple rule of evaluation starts with an expression and specifies a method for determining its value. An expression is either a constant, a variable, a symbol, a combination, or a special form. Special forms look like combinations.

A constant is a number, a string, or a quoted object. As noted above, a quoted object is written

$$(\text{quote } \langle \text{object} \rangle)$$

And the value of the quoted object above is $\langle \text{object} \rangle$. A quoted object can be abbreviated

$$'\langle \text{object} \rangle$$

using a special feature of the reader.

The value of a constant is the constant itself. The value of a symbol is the contents of the value cell of the symbol, and the value of a variable is obtained from its associated location. Both T and NIL evaluate to themselves.

A combination is a list whose first element is not quote. Normally a combination is a function invocation, a macro invocation, or a special form. For example, a combination would look like

$$(\text{cfact } 13 \ 1)$$

This combination is a function invocation that calls the function cfact, which is defined above. The first element of the list is the function to apply, and the remaining elements are the arguments to which the function is to be applied. To evaluate a combination, the evaluator evaluates the arguments recursively and then passes those arguments to the function, where the arguments will be bound to the variables specified in the function definition. At this point the body of the function is evaluated within the context of the bindings thus established, and the value of the body is the value of the original combination.

A combination can be a macro invocation, in which case the first element of the list is the name of a macro. To evaluate a macro invocation, the combination is passed as an argument to the macro function, and the body of the macro is evaluated to produce a form that is evaluated in place of the original combination. Defmacro allows the programmer to name the parts of the combination, as in the definition of the macro version of add7. However, this practical facility is built upon the basic LISP macro facility—which is uniform over almost all LISP dialects—in which the entire combination is passed as the single argument to the macro function.

A special form is one in which the simple evaluation method is different—or special—from the normal method. For example, the form

$$(\text{quote foo})$$

is special because the value of the form is the symbol whose name is foo, not the value of the symbol whose name is foo. If this form were evaluated according to the rules above, the evaluator would first recursively evaluate its subform before passing that subform's value to the function quote.

In order to achieve the intent of quote, the basic evaluation rules must be broken. Hence the concept of a special form.

Another special form is if, the conditional expression:

$$(\text{if } \langle \text{pred} \rangle \ \langle \text{then} \rangle \ \langle \text{else} \rangle)$$

The expression $\langle \text{pred} \rangle$ is evaluated; if it returns something regarded as true, then the value of the if is the value of the expression $\langle \text{then} \rangle$, and the expression $\langle \text{else} \rangle$ is not evaluated; otherwise, the value of the if is the value of the expression $\langle \text{else} \rangle$, and the expression $\langle \text{then} \rangle$ is not evaluated. In the history section a possible definition of it is presented.

Some other special forms are COND, AND, OR, PROG, and GO.

COND is a special form that enables the programmer to write a conditional with more than one predicate.

$$(\text{if } \langle \text{pred} \rangle \ \langle \text{then} \rangle \ \langle \text{else} \rangle)$$

is equivalent to

$$(\text{cond } (\langle \text{pred} \rangle \ \langle \text{then} \rangle)$$
$$(\text{t } \langle \text{else} \rangle))$$

And the general form of the conditional is

$$(\text{cond } (\text{pred}_1 \ \text{form}_{1,1} \ . \ . \ . \ \text{form}_{1,n_1})$$
$$(\text{pred}_2 \ \text{form}_{2,1} \ . \ . \ . \ \text{form}_{2,n_2})$$
$$.$$
$$.$$
$$.$$
$$(\text{pred}_n \ \text{form}_{m,1} \ . \ . \ . \ \text{form}_{m,n_m})$$

In this expression, pred_i are predicates. They are evaluated in order until all have been evaluated or until one produces a non-NIL result. In the latter case the corresponding forms are evaluated, and no more predicates are evaluated. Frequently T is written for the last predicate to mean otherwise. Here T is guaranteed to evaluate to something non-NIL, and so if no pred_i evaluates to non-NIL, this clause will be executed. To execute a clause, the individual forms $\text{form}_{i,j}$ are evaluated, and the value of the last form form_{i,n_i} in the clause is returned as the value of the cond.

The form cond is one of three major propositional forms; the other two propositional forms are AND and OR; and has the form

$$(\text{and } \text{pred}_1 \ . \ . \ . \ \text{pred}_n)$$

The pred_i are evaluated in left-to-right order; if all of them evaluate to a non-NIL value, then the value of the AND is the value of pred_n, the last form in the and. If, in evaluating the forms left to right, one of the forms evaluates to NIL, then the value of the and is NIL, and evaluation of the remaining pred, is terminated. Sometimes this sort of and is referred to as a conditional AND. In most other programming languages Boolean expressions always evaluate each of their clauses before the propositional result is computed; in LISP evaluation stops as soon as the result can be determined.

The special form OR is defined similarly:

$$(\text{or pred}_1 \ . \ . \ . \ \text{pred}_n)$$

The pred_i are evaluated in left-to-right order; if all of them evaluate to NIL, then the value of the or is NIL; if one of them evaluates to a non-NIL value, then the value of the OR is that non-NIL value, and evaluation of the remaining pred_i is terminated.

PROG and GO are a means for writing simple sequential programs. PROG is often called "the program feature." The form of a PROG is

$$(\text{prog } (\langle\text{variables}\rangle) \ e_1 \ . \ . \ . \ e_n)$$

where $\langle\text{variables}\rangle$ are local variables whose values may be assigned using SETQ, and each e_i is either a LISP expression or a symbol. If e_i is a LISP expression, it is evaluated; if it is a symbol, it is taken as a tag or a label. The special form

$$(\text{go } \langle\text{tag}\rangle)$$

causes control to transfer to the tag named $\langle\text{tag}\rangle$, if it exists; an error is signaled otherwise. The expression

$$(\text{return } \langle\text{expression}\rangle)$$

returns the value of $\langle\text{expression}\rangle$ from the PROG. If the last expression, e_n, is not a transfer of control using GO or RETURN, the PROG is exited, and the its value is NIL.

Here is a simple example of the definition of a factorial function using PROG:

```
(defun factorial (n)
  (prog (answer)
        (setq answer 1)
   loop (when (zerop n) (return answer))
        (setq answer (* n answer))
           n (1- n))
        (go loop)))
```

RUN TIME TYPING

One of the most interesting aspects of LISP is that it supports run time typing, the ability to determine what type an object is at run time. In many other programming languages variables, not objects, are typed, so that a compiler is able to generate very specific and efficient code for operations on variables. In LISP, though it is possible for the compiler to understand type declarations that refer to variables, it must always be possible at run time to determine the type of an object.

LISP manipulates objects by passing around pointers to those objects rather than passing the objects themselves. LISP is call-by-value, so that all of the arguments to a function are evaluated, and pointers to the values are passed to the function. The pointers are usually considered to contain the type information, but in an actual implementation the type information may be contained in the address or stored with the object.

To be more specific, there are three primary methods for encoding type information. The first is for pointers to contain type information directly. For example, in a computer addresses might take up only part of a machine word. In this case it might be possible to use the remaining extra bits to store the type. A combination of an address and type information is called a *pointer*. In fact, the term as used in the LISP literature is usually taken to mean such a combination. When the type information is stored in the pointer itself, that type information is called a *tag*.

The second type of mechanism for encoding the type of a pointer is to partition memory into blocks of storage. Objects that reside in a particular block are defined to hold some specific type, and whenever an object of that specific type is created, the storage allocated to contain the object will be allocated within that block. The type can be identified by looking in a table of block descriptors that outline the block of memory and store the type of the objects contained therein. This method also stores the type as part of the pointer, but indirectly through a table-lookup operation. That is, given a pointer—which is simply a machine address—it is possible to determine the type of the object to which the pointer points without examining the object.

The third basic method for storing type information is to store that information with the object itself. In order to determine the type of a pointer, the object itself (the memory indicated by the pointer address) must be examined to find the type information.

In practice, most LISP implementations use a hybrid of these methods. In these hybrids there are three major types of objects: immediate pointers, CONS cells, and objects with headers. The general strategy of implementation of the storage management for these objects in the most common hybrid system of LISP implementation on stock hardware (not LISP machines) will be presented. Some of the differences between this style of implementation and that used on LISP machines are described below.

In the most common hybrid, short objects, such as fixnums, are passed as immediate pointers: The tag for the object indicates that the object is contained in the remainder of the word that represents the pointer. A short floating-point number might be represented by 29 bits of storage, and the tag might be 3 bits; in this situation the tag and the data could be represented by a single 32-bit word. There is a trade-off regarding whether it is expedient to pack a short floating-point number into a word like this; it might be better to pass a pointer, which contains the tag and an address, where the pointer points to a floating-point number in the normal machine format for that number. In the first implementation there is an advantage that to create a short floating-point number does not require a memory location to be allocated for the number, and the second technique does not require the bits in the number to be extracted from the pointer when a short floating-point number is numerically manipulated.

Normally short floating-point numbers, fixnums, and characters are represented as immediate objects.

CONS cells are stored as two words of storage. The two words represent the CAR and the CDR of the CONS cell, and using CONS cells, binary trees and lists can be represented. A pointer to a CONS cell is created and passed around. The tag of the pointer indicates that the object at the address indicated by the pointer is a CONS cell. Each of the two words of storage beginning at that address are LISP pointers and can point to anything—immediate pointers can be stored in a CONS cell as well as any other sort of pointer.

The third type of object is an object with a header; this includes vectors, arrays, strings, blocks of code, functions, and user-defined record structures. The first part of the header is a tag that indicates that some specified amount of storage following this header represents the object. The data part of the immediate pointer contains the size of the block of storage and, usually, a subtype or a secondary tag, which states what type of object is stored in this storage—vector, array, string, and so on. Depending on this subtype, the subsequent storage is used in various ways. A vector typically contains sequential units of storage (bits, bytes, words, etc) that represent the elements of the vector; a user-defined record structure contains one or more words specifying the user-defined type for the object; a string contains a sequence of characters, probably in the format for strings that the underlying hardware provides.

The pointer to such an object contains a tag that states that the object stored at the address indicated by the pointer contains a header with a secondary tag. In order to determine the type of such an object, the header of the object is fetched or otherwise examined.

This hybrid scheme has certain aspects important to the overall implementation of the LISP system. For example, a stop-and-copy garbage collector, which does a linear scan of parts of memory, must be able to recognize enough about the objects it finds to be able to decide whether the garbage collector should trace the parts of the object as pointers. The garbage collector must do different things for vectors containing pointers from what it must do for vectors containing non-LISP objects.

Data Structures

Some of the other LISP data structures not mentioned above are presented here.

Numbers. Modern LISPs have a variety of numeric data types. The following are the numeric data types defined in Common LISP: integers, ratios, floating-point numbers, and complex numbers.

For integers a distinction is made between integers that can be efficiently represented by the underlying computer and integers that cannot be efficiently represented. A *fixnum* is an integer that roughly corresponds to the machine-representable fixed-point number. These num-

bers typically fall into some range -2^n through $2^n - 1$ for suitable values of n. An integer that is not a fixnum is called a *bignum* (big number). These integers are sometimes represented in computers as a vector of bits or as a list of fixnums.

Bignums are especially useful for doing symbolic algebra and symbolic mathematics. For example, it is often necessary to compute the factorial of a number exactly as an integer rather than approximately as a floating-point number. The number 1000! has 2568 decimal digits; this number can be computed exactly in Common LISP using bignums.

A ratio is a number that represents the mathematical ratio of two integers. These are denoted by the form

$$\langle numerator \rangle / \langle denominator \rangle.$$

Common LISP defines four different precisions of floating-point numbers: short floating point, single floating point, double floating point, and long floating point. These four precisions are defined in order to cover the case where a particular implementation of LISP might be able to provide some hardware support for some or all of them.

Complex numbers are pairs of noncomplex numbers. The two parts of a complex number must be of the same numeric type.

Characters and Strings. Common LISP supports both ASCII and EBCDIC character sets. Strings are vectors of characters. A variety of string operations is provided.

Vectors and Arrays. Vectors, both with and without fill pointers, are supported. Multidimensional arrays, with general as well as specialized elements, are also defined.

INTERPRETATION

LISP has been presented by specifying an informal operational semantics—a semantics based on a model of evaluation. Often this model is directly implemented by a LISP interpreter.

A LISP interpreter examines a representation of a LISP program and performs the operations expressed therein. For example, when a LISP system reads the following expression,

$$(+ \ 1 \ 2)$$

the LISP interpreter sees that it has a combination that is not a special form; in fact, the combination is a request to call the function + on two arguments. The arguments are evaluated and found to be the integers 1 and 2. These arguments are passed to the function +, which has already been defined.

Functions like + are defined by writing programs in some language that manipulates the internal data structures used to implement the LISP data structures. In the early days of serious LISP implementation efforts—the mid-1960s through the early 1970s—the language chosen to implement the LISP interpreter was assembly language, though occasionally FORTRAN or C was used. In this example + would be implemented as an assembly language program that would receive its arguments in some standard locations, such as on a stack or in some registers.

More recently, production LISPs are being implemented in LISP, and compilers are used to translate the LISP code into machine language.

When the interpreter recognizes a function call, such as a call to +, the interpreter places the evaluated arguments on the stack and jumps to the function definition. The interpreter is recursive in the sense that to evaluate the arguments to a function, the interpreter is called recursively.

The interpreter causes the special forms to be evaluated by taking special actions. For example, in one possible implementation of a LISP interpreter, to evaluate an IF expression, the then and the else clauses are placed on the stack. The predicate is evaluated, and if non-NIL, the then clause is pulled off of the stack, the else clause is removed, and the then clause is handed to the evaluator. If the predicate returns NIL, then the then clause is discarded, and the else clause evaluated. Similar sorts of actions are taken for the other special forms.

Constants are immediately evaluated, and lexical variables are evaluated by finding their values in the environment. Symbol values are located by looking in the value cell for the symbol.

COMPILATION

Although LISP has been presented by specifying an informal operational semantics, and though this semantics can be easily implemented with an interpreter, LISP is also a compiled language. Every major dialect of LISP has a compiler. Compiling LISP programs is very easy to do when only a low level of sophistication is required of the compiled code, but such compilation is relatively difficult when a high degree of optimization in the compiled code is required.

A LISP interpreter examines a representation of a LISP program and performs the operations that the code indicates. A LISP compiler examines a representation of a LISP program and produces machine language code that implements the operations that the LISP code expresses.

Each special form is compiled according to its own specific stylized technique. For example, a conditional expression is compiled as blocks of code that expresses the evaluation of the various predicates and forms, with conditional branches among the blocks at the machine language level corresponding to the logic of the conditional expression.

Let-binding is compiled by producing machine language that stores values in the locations determined to hold them. Consider the expression

$$(let ((x (foo)))$$
$$\langle body \rangle)$$

The compiler produces code to evaluate (foo); then it decides which location to use to store the value that (foo)

produces. A typical LISP compiler will select a location on the control stack to hold the value, though registers and memory locations are possible candidates. Code is produced that stores the value that foo returns in the location selected to hold it. Finally the compiler produces code to evaluate ⟨body⟩. If ⟨body⟩ refers to x, then the compiled code will fetch the value from the selected location.

Function calls are compiled in a stylized manner. In some LISP systems there are a variety of styles of compiled function calls. Typical compilers use the control stack to store function return information and to pass arguments.

A typical LISP compiler is structured as a series of phases, each phase having, perhaps, a number of passes. The phases are partitioned into two parts: The first part builds a computation graph that represents the computation that the LISP program expresses, and the second part uses the computation graph to generate machine language code.

Each node in the computation graph is a block of computations, and arcs represent relationships between the blocks. For example, if the value of one expression is required to evaluate another expression, the arc between the nodes representing the two expressions indicates this relationship.

At each node in the computation graph a set of properties is computed, such as the nature the side effects produced. Usually a separate phase is performed to complete or refine some aspect of the computation graph structure.

During an early phase all identifiers are made distinct from one another, macros are expanded, declarations are noted, and syntax checking is performed. Arcs are placed between the places where variables are referenced and the place where they are bound.

Optimizations are generally expressed as transformations on this computation graph. Often the transformations have a clean representation as source-to-source transformations on the LISP code—although the transformations are not implemented that way. Optimizations include removing unnecessary bindings, constant folding, strength reduction, dead-code elimination, and tail recursion removal. One or more phases are dedicated to performing these optimizations.

One or more phases allocate registers and temporary memory. There is generally a stylized manner in which the stack is used, and the stack is typically organized as a stack of frames, in which every frame has the same format.

Finally code generation takes place.

An important compiler optimization is to remove as many run type checks as possible. Common LISP supports a set of type declarations, and the user may supply declarations to help the compiler deduce the types of variables. When the types of variables are known, the compiler can specialize the LISP operations expressed in the code to take advantage of this additional knowledge. For example, suppose that the user writes

$$(+ x y)$$

If the compiler has no information about what types of

numbers x and y are, it must produce code that will work for all possible types of numbers. But if the compiler can determine that x, y, and the result of the + are all fixnums, then the machine instruction for addition can be used to add the numbers—assuming that the representation of fixnums is preserved by the machine addition instruction.

Typically, compiled LISP code runs 10–100 times faster than interpreted LISP code.

COMPARATIVE HISTORY OF LISP: 1956–1960

Some of the key ideas in LISP were developed by John McCarthy during the Dartmouth Summer Research Project on Artificial Intelligence, which was the first organized study of Artificial Intelligence (McCarthy, 1985). This meeting was held during the summer of 1956. McCarthy's motivation was to develop an algebraic list-processing language for AI work on the IBM 704 computer.

During the Dartmouth meeting Newell, Shaw, and Simon (researchers at Carnegie-Mellon University) described IPL 2 (Newell, 1963), a list-processing language for the Rand Corporation JOHNNIAC computer (Rand Corp., 1968) in which they implemented their Logic Theorist program.

McCarthy decided against creating a language similar to IPL 2 because its form was based on a JOHNNIAC loader that happened to be available to them and because the FORTRAN idea of writing programs algebraically was attractive. A primary motivation was that arbitrary subexpressions of symbolic expressions could be obtained by composing the functions that extract immediate subexpressions.

During the period from the summer of 1956 through the summer of 1958, McCarthy worked concurrently on the form of LISP and on his research in AI. The AI research centered around ideas that led to his Advice Taker proposal (McCarthy, 1968).

The Advice Taker is a reasoning program that decides what to do in specific situations by making logical inferences. In the Advice Taker information about the world is represented by sentences in a suitable formal language. Representing sentences by list structure seemed appropriate to McCarthy, and a list-processing language also seemed appropriate for programming the operations involved in deduction.

At that time the key ides in LISP were computing with symbolic expressions rather than numbers, representation of symbolic expressions and other information by list structure in the memory of a computer, representation of information in external media mostly by multilevel lists and sometimes by S-expressions, a small set of selector and constructor operations expressed as functions, composition of functions as a tool for forming more complex functions, use of conditional expressions for introducing branching into function definitions, the recursive use of conditional expressions as a sufficient tool for building computable functions, the use of lambda expressions for naming functions, the storage of information on the property lists of symbols, the representation of LISP programs

as LISP data, the conditional expression interpretation of Boolean connectives, the LISP function EVAL that serves both as a formal definition of the language and as an interpreter, and garbage collection as a means of handling the erasure problem. The erasure problem is that of how to free storage that is no longer in use.

Until 1958 there was no such thing as a conditional expression that returned a value. At that time all conditional expressions resulted in a branch to different code depending on the condition.

Some of the above ideas were taken from other languages, but most were new. Toward the end of the initial period, it became clear that this combination of ideas made an elegant mathematical system as well as a practical programming language. Then mathematical neatness became a goal and led to pruning some features from the core of the language. This was partly motivated by aesthetic reasons and partly by the belief that it would be easier to devise techniques for proving programs to be correct if the semantics were compact and without exceptions.

Early Implementation Considerations

The first LISP, LISP 1, was implemented for the IBM 704 computer. This computer has a 36-bit word; this word is broken up into four parts: two 15-bit parts (called the address and decrement), a 3-bit tag, and a 3-bit prefix. There are special instructions for moving the contents of the address and decrement parts of a word to and from the 15-bit index registers. Addresses in the machine were 15 bits, so it was decided that list structure should use 15-bit pointers. A CONS cell, then, was a single word with two 15-bit addresses in it.

Four functions were proposed for dealing with CONS cells, one to extract each of the four parts mentioned above. Additionally, a function was provided to fetch a word from memory; this instruction was called CWR, standing for *c*ontents of the *w*ord in *r*egister number. It was soon noted that to chain down a list, the CWR function was being composed with the instruction to extract the decrement part of the word. A function was defined to achieve this composition, and it was called CDR, standing for *c*ontents of the *d*ecrement part of *r*egister number. Similarly, CAR was defined, and its name stands for *c*ontents of the *a*ddress part of *r*egister number. CONS was defined as a subroutine rather than as a function.

This work was done with paper and pencil at Dartmouth because there was no IBM 704 computer there.

The first real LISP implementation was FLPL—*F*ortran *l*ist *p*rocessing *l*anguage. This was a set of subroutines that were added to FORTRAN on the IBM 704 computer. This work was undertaken by Herbert Gelenter and Carl Gerberich (McCarthy and co-workers, 1962) under the direction of Nathaniel Rochester; FLPL did not have conditional expressions, it did not support recursion (because FORTRAN did not), and erasure was handled explicitly by the user program. One of the key ideas added to LISP by Gerlenter and Gerberich was to make CONS a function rather than a subroutine. The value of the function is the word allocated by the cons, and with this mechanism new expressions can be constructed out of subexpressions by composing occurrences of cons.

In the summer of 1958, while McCarthy was at IBM working on symbolic differentiation at the invitation of Nathaniel Rochester, conditional expressions and MAPCAR were added to the definition of LISP. In addition, lambda notation for anonymous functions was developed.

In the fall of 1958 the first real implementation of LISP was started at MIT. The initial plan was to implement a compiler, but this was believed to require man-years of effort, so various LISP functions were hand-compiled into assembly language to experiment with subroutine linkage, stack handling, and erasure. Subroutines were written to create a LISP environment in which one could read and print list structure using the parenthesized notation.

On paper, LISP functions were written in an informal notation called M-expressions—for Meta expressions—intended to resemble FORTRAN as much as possible. Besides FORTRAN-like assignment statements and GO-TO, the language allowed conditional expressions and the basic functions of LISP. The M-notation also used brackets instead of parentheses to enclose the arguments of functions in order to reserve parentheses for list structure constants.

The READ and PRINT programs induced a de facto standard external notation for symbolic information. For example, $x + y$ was written as $(+ x y)$. Any other notation necessarily requires special programming because standard mathematical notations treat different operators in syntactically different ways. This notation later came to be called "Cambridge Polish" because it resembled the prefix notation of Lukasiewicz (1934) and because the Harvard philosopher Quine (1961) had also used a parenthesized prefix notation.

Explicit erasure of list structure, as was done in IPL, was regarded as unaesthetic; implicit erasure using reference counts was the first idea considered, but the 6 bits in the IBM 704 word not used by addresses in a CONS cell were in separated parts of the word. The chosen alternative was garbage collection, in which data still in use was marked by tracing from known roots; the storage no longer in use was returned to a free pool.

A single contiguous stack was used to store local variables, CONS was made a function, and the prefix and tag parts of the CONS cell were abandoned. This resulted in a single type of object, the 15-bit address, and the language therefore required no type declarations.

McCarthy wrote a paper about recursive function theory, based on LISP, called "Recursive Functions of Symbolic Expressions and Their Computation by Machine, Part I" (1960). Part II was never written but was intended to contain applications to computing with algebraic expressions. The recursive function theorists tended to prefer the Turing machine as the paradigmatic computing engine.

McCarthy felt that one way to show that LISP was neater than Turing machines was to write a universal LISP function and show that it is briefer and more comprehensible than the description of a universal Turing machine. This was the Lisp function EVAL, where (eval e a) computes the value of a LISP expression e, the second argument a being a list of assignments of values to variables.

Writing EVAL required inventing a notation representing LISP functions as LISP data. Logical completeness required that the notation used to express functions used as functional arguments be extended to provide for recursive functions, and the LABEL notation was invented by Nathaniel Rochester for that purpose (McCarthy and co-workers, 1962).

Stephen Russell noticed that EVAL could serve as an interpreter for LISP and hand-coded it, producing an interpreter-based programming language (McCarthy and co-workers, 1962).

The appearance of an interpreter tended to freeze the form of the language to use S-expressions. Moreover, the early implementors expected to switch to writing programs as M-expressions. The project of defining M-expressions precisely and compiling them or at least translating them into S-expressions was neither finalized nor explicitly abandoned. It just receded into the indefinite future, and a new generation of programmers appeared who preferred internal notation to any FORTRAN-like or ALGOL-like notation that could be devised. Moreover, a machine-readable M-notation would have required redefinition because the pencil-and-paper M-notation used characters unavailable on the IBM 026 keypunch.

LISP 1.5

LISP 1.5 was an extension of LISP 1, which was implemented by McCarthy and Russell (McCarthy and co-workers, 1962). The additions to LISP 1 to create LISP 1.5 are summarized below.

Property Lists. This concept is necessary for the implementation of the Advice Taker.

Destructive List Operations. RPLACA, RPLACD, and NCONC enabled the user to alter, destructively, existing list structure. This feature is used to implement efficient list structure editing functions. Given that LISP source code is represented by lists, this enables structure editors for LISP code to be written. The InterLisp structure editor is the best example of this type of editor.

Numbers. Numbers in LISP 1 were represented as lists of atoms. LISP 1.5 used a more efficient representation; but even this new representation was still insufficiently efficient to compete with FORTRAN. It was not until 1971 when the MIT LISCOM and NCOMPLR compilers for MacLisp were available that numeric code written in LISP was fast enough for serious numeric applications.

FUNARGS. The ability to capture a binding environment at the point of a function definition was added, although the functionality of the construct is considerably below what would be ideal. Later LISPs extended this to the notion of closures, discussed earlier.

Special Forms. The existence of EVAL made special forms possible. This enabled experimenters to try out new constructs easily.

Functions of a Variable Number of Arguments. Functions like LIST take a variable number of arguments. This facility enabled programmers to experiment further with the function-calling mechanisms, such as the sophisticated Common LISP lambda lists.

Program Feature. The idea of executing sequential programs, much as FORTRAN does, was not an afterthought: It preceded the concept of functional composition. The syntax of PROG's and GO's, however, was an inelegant afterthought.

Compiler. The first LISP compiler was written by Timothy Hart and Michael Levin (McCarthy and co-workers, 1962). It was written in LISP and may have been the first compiler written in the language to be compiled.

LISP 1.5 is the real takeoff point for LISP implementations and experiments. At the same time as the first implementation, on the IBM 7090, *Lisp 1.5 Programmer's Manual* was published (McCarthy and co-workers, 1962). This book has been used by generations of LISP programmers to learn LISP.

LISP 1.5 was implemented by Levin, Russell, Edwards, Hart, and Brayton (McCarthy and co-workers, 1962).

The following is an example of the definition of the function member in LISP 1.5. It is reproduced exactly as it appeared in *Lisp 1.5 Programmer's Manual:*

```
DEFINE((
(MEMBER (LAMBDA (A X) (COND ((NULL X) F)
    ((EQ A (CAR X) ) T) (T (MEMBER A (CDR X))) )))
))
```

Note that the S-expressions are not indented in the style used in this entry. The indentation of LISP code to indicate which parts were subordinate to others was in common use by the mid-1960s, but some programmers continued to not indent LISP code.

However, the style of indentation has changed over the years; here is an example of MEMBER written in a LISP style in use in 1966:

```
DEFINE((
    (MEMBER (LAMBDA (A X) (COND
    ((NULL X) F)
    ((EQ A (CAR X) ) T)
    (T (MEMBER A (CDR X))) )))
))
```

The following is the definition of member as an M-expression, indented in modern style:

$$member[a;x] = [null[x]=>F;$$
$$eq[a;car[x]]=>T;$$
$$T=>member[a;cdr[x]]]$$

Special and Common Variables. In LISP 1.5 a special variable is a binding of an identifier to a location, a pointer to which is placed on the property list of the symbol whose name is the identifier. When a programmer declares x to be special, the compiler and loader combine to create a symbol named x. The property list for x has a property with the indicator special, and its value is a cell. That cell is the location to which x refers and where assignments to x place values. When x is let bound, the old value stored in this cell is placed on the control stack along with enough information to restore the old value to this cell when control returns past the let-binding point.

A common variable is one in which the value cell is used to hold the value, and binding a common variable requires the use of an explicit a-list. Evaluating a common variable at run time requires a call to EVAL.

Special variables can be shared among different compiled functions but cannot be shared with interpreted functions; common variables can be shared by compiled functions and interpreted functions but are much slower than special variables.

In terms of implementation, special variables are the precursors of what is now known as shallow binding, whereas common variables are the precursors of deep binding.

In shallow binding, the value of a special variable is always kept in the value cell of a symbol. LET binding the symbol causes the old value to be placed on the control stack and the new value to be placed in the value cell. References to the value of the symbol within the dynamic scope of the LET will see this new value. When control exits the LET, the old value is restored.

In deep binding, the identifier–value pair is placed on the control stack when LET binding occurs. Reference to the value of a symbol first looks at the stack for any bindings there, and if none are found, the value cell is referenced. Searching the stack can be done relatively efficiently by linking together special-binding blocks (the places where identifier–value pairs are stored on the stack) by putting a flag in the symbol stating whether the symbol has been bound (and therefore should be looked up on the stack) or by caching special variables in stack frames in which they will be frequently referenced. These techniques can be used alone or in combinations.

COMPARATIVE HISTORY OF LISP: 1960–1970

In the early 1960s Timothy Hart and Thomas Evans implemented LISP 1.5 on the Univac M 460, a military version of the Univac 490 (Berkeley and Bobrow, 1964). It was bootstrapped off of LISP 1.5 on the IBM 7090: A cross-compiler that ran on the IBM 7090 and compiled code for the Univac machine was used to compile the bulk of the LISP code. A small amount of machine language code was written for the lowest levels of the LISP implementation (Berkeley and Bobrow, 1964).

Robert Saunders and his colleagues at System Development Corporation implemented LISP 1.5 on the IBM-built AN/FSQ-32/V computer, often called the Q-32 (Berkeley and Bobrow, 1964). The implementation was bootstrapped from the IBM 7090 and PDP-1 computers at Stanford University. This project was a joint effort between System Development Corporation and Information International.

The PDP-1 LISP at Stanford was implemented by McCarthy and Russell (Berkeley and Bobrow, 1964).

In 1963 L. Peter Deutsch, then a high school student, implemented a LISP similar to LISP 1.5 on the PDP-1 at Bolt, Beranek, & Newman (BBN) (Berkeley and Bobrow, 1964). This LISP was called Basic PDP-1 LISP. BBN also implemented one of the first time-sharing operating systems for the PDP-1.

By 1964 a version of LISP 1.5 was running at MIT, in the Electrical Engineering Department, on an IBM 7094 computer, under the Compatible Time Sharing System (CTSS) (F. J. Corbato and co-workers, 1962). This LISP and Basic PDP-1 LISP were the main influences on the PDP-6 LISP implemented by DEC and some members of the MIT Model Railroad Club in the spring of 1964. This LISP was the first program written on the PDP-6. Also, this LISP was the ancestor of MacLisp, the LISP written to run under the Incompatible Time Sharing System (ITS) (Eastlake and coworkers, 1969) at MIT on the PDP-6 and later on the PDP-10.

At BBN a successor to Basic PDP-1 LISP was implemented on the PDP-1 and an upward-compatible version, patterned after LISP 1.5 on the MIT CTSS system, was implemented on the Scientific Data Systems 940 (SDS 940), by Daniel Bobrow and D. L. Murphy (Berkeley and Bobrow, 1964). A further upward-compatible version was written for the PDP-10 by Alice Hartley and Murphy, and this LISP was called BBN LISP (Berkeley and Bobrow, 1964). In 1973, around the time that SDS was acquired by Xerox and named Xerox Data systems, the maintenance of BBN LISP was shared by BBN and Xerox Palo Alto Research Center, and the name of the LISP was changed to InterLisp.

The PDP-6 and PDP-10 computers were, by design, especially suited for LISP because they had 36-bit words and 18-bit addresses. This allowed a CONS cell, a pair of pointers or addresses, to be stored efficiently in a single word. The PDP-6 and PDP-10 had fast, powerful stack instructions, which enables fast function calling for LISP.

Almost all of these implementations had a small hand-coded core and a compiler; the rest of the LISP was written in LISP and compiled.

In 1965 virtually all of the LISPs in existence were identical to each other or differed only in trivial ways. After 1965, or more precisely, after MacLisp and BBN LISP diverged from each other, there came a plethora of LISP dialects.

COMPARATIVE HISTORY OF LISP: 1970–1980

Early MacLisp

In the early MIT PDP-6 MacLisp (White, 1970) Greenblatt (1974) decided that having both common and special variables, as in LISP 1.5, was inelegant and removed common variables from the language but made special variables work using the value cell. This was the first implementation of LISP to use what is called *shallow binding*.

The toplevel of LISP 1.5 was EVALQUOTE. The toplevel of MacLisp is EVAL and not EVALQUOTE. In Lisp 1.5 one could type expressions like this to EVALQUOTE:

cons(a b)

to create the pair of *a* and *b*. In MacLisp one could type this expression, instead, to EVAL:

(cons 'a 'b)

The "quote" in EVALQUOTE signifies the implicit quoting of the arguments to the function applied. InterLisp retained EVALQUOTE as a toplevel evaluation form while MacLisp forked off and used EVAL.

In LISP 1.5 and MacLisp special forms are implemented by placing a function on the property list of the symbol whose print name corresponds to the special form's name. For example, in MacLisp, COND has an fsubr property, where the "f" in fsubr signifies a special form, and the "subr" signifies a compiled subroutine. The evaluation process for arguments is then left up to the programmer. Here is how IF could be defined as a special form in MacLisp:

```
(defun if fexpr (form)
  (let ((predicate (car form))
        (then (cadr form))
        (else (caddr form)))
    (cond ((eval predicate) (eval then))
          (t (eval else)))))
```

This code is not as efficient as it could be, but it illustrates that special forms can be extended by user-written code.

MacLisp introduced the lexpr, which is a function that can take any number of arguments and puts them on the stack: the single argument to the function is bound to the number of arguments passed. The form of the lambda list for this argument, a symbol and not a list, signals the lexpr case. Here is an example of how to define LIST, a function of a variable number of arguments that returns the list of those arguments:

```
(defun list n
  (do ((i n (1- i))
       (answer () (cons (arg i) answer)))
      ((zerop i) answer )))
```

The single argument, n, is bound to the number of arguments passed. The expression, (arg i), refers to the *i*th argument passed.

Other major additions to LISP 1.5 were arrays, the modification of simple predicates, such as MEMBER, to be functions that return useful values, PROG2, and the introduction of the pair of functions ERR and ERRSET.

ERRSET was useful when one wanted to execute a piece of code that might cause an error. One wrote

(errset ⟨form⟩)

which would evaluate ⟨form⟩ in a context in which errors would not cause a breakpoint to occur. If ⟨form⟩ did not cause an error, ERRSET would return a pair of the value and NIL. If ⟨form⟩ caused an error, no error would be signaled, and the ERRSET would return NIL.

If, in evaluating ⟨form⟩, the expression

$$(err \ ⟨expression⟩)$$

is evaluated, the value of ⟨expression⟩ would be returned as the value of the ERRSET. ERRSET was later generalized to CATCH and ERR to THROW.

The simple but powerful macro facility on which DEFMACRO is based was introduced in MacLisp in the mid-1960s.

Later MacLisp

The most significant development for MacLisp occurred in the early 1970s when the techniques in the "fast arithmetic compiler," LISCOM, were incorporated into the MacLisp compiler. This new compiler, NCOMPLR, would become a standard against which all other Lisp compilers were measured in terms of the speed of running code. Inspired by the needs of the MIT Artificial Intelligence Laboratory (AI Lab), whose needs covered the numeric computations done in vision and robotics, several new ways of representing and compiling numeric code resulted in numeric performance of compiled MacLisp on a near par with FORTRAN compilers.

LISCOM was largely the work of Jeff Golden and John L. White at MIT (1970). The relative performances of compiled numeric LISP code and FORTRAN numeric code on the PDP-10 stirred the Digital compiler writers to improve the DEC FORTRAN compiler to the point where it was difficult for the LISP compilers to compete. The relative performance of subsequent LISP compilers on numeric code has never reached the high water mark achieved in 1972, but some LISP compilers have done very well.

During the mid-1970s, in conjunction with work on LISP machines by Richard Greenblatt, David Moon, and others, MacLisp began to expand toward a much fuller language. The sophisticated lambda lists seen in Common LISP are the results of early experimentation with programming styles by the LISP machine group; these styles found their way into MacLisp.

MacLisp was implemented on related operating systems to ITS for PDP-10s. By 1978 MacLisp ran on ITS, TOPS-10, TOPS-20, TENEX, and WAITS (Harvey, 1982). The last operating system is the Stanford Artificial Intelligence Laboratory PDP-10 operating system. MacLisp and InterLisp were the dominant LISP dialects from 1970 through approximately 1978.

InterLisp

InterLisp introduced many radical ideas into LISP programming style and methodology. The most visible of these ideas are embodied in programming tools, like the spelling corrector, DWIM, the file package, CLISP, the structure editor, and MASTERSCOPE.

The spelling corrector is a program that compares a possibly misspelled word, usually a symbol, with a list of known words. The spelling corrector is invoked when a symbol is unknown. The user has options for controlling the behavior of the system with respect to spelling correc-

tion. The system can correct automatically, it can pause and ask whether the correction is acceptable, or it can simply signal an error.

The spelling corrector is under the general control of a much larger program, called DWIM, standing for *do what I mean*. Whenever an error of any sort is detected by the LISP system, DWIM is invoked to determine the appropriate action. Among other things, the spelling corrector might be invoked.

DWIM is able to correct some forms of parenthesis errors, and this, along with the spelling correction of identifiers, comprise the most common user typographical errors.

DWIM would not be especially useful unless correcting errors were done permanently. InterLisp does not maintain a file of function definitions in the same way that, say, MacLisp does. In MacLisp files of LISP code are simply text files, which are read into MacLisp or compiled for MacLisp. In InterLisp a file is used as an external storage medium for user source code, but the fact that it is a file is unimportant. What is important is that the file is a permanent repository for user source code, and all modifications to the user code is done within the InterLisp programming environment. What is unimportant is the representation used in those files because the user never uses a text editor to edit the sources but a resident LISP structure editor.

The ideal situation that is approximated by using files is that the user is interacting with a LISP system that never terminates, and the programs as they are in use are important, not their representation as text in a file.

When errors are corrected by DWIM, the source in the user's system and, as an incidental side effect, in the file in which the source is located is altered to reflect the correction. Therefore, once a bug is corrected, it is permanently corrected.

CLISP, standing for *conversational LISP*, is an ALGOL-like syntax used along with a normal LISP syntax. For example, here is a valid definition of FACTORIAL written in InterLisp CLISP syntax:

```
(DEFINEQ
(FACTORIAL
(LAMBDA (N) (if N=0 then 1 else
                N*(FACTORIAL N−1)))))
```

A number of infix operators are defined in CLISP, list construction syntax is defined, and a useful set of iteration constructs is defined. Here is a simple program to print all of the prime numbers in the range $m \leq p \leq n$:

```
(for X from M to N do (PRINT X) while (PRIMEP X))
```

CLISP, DWIM, and the spelling corrector can work together to recognize the following as a valid definition of FACTORIAL:

```
(DEFINEQ
(FACTORIAL
LAMBDA (N) (iff N=0 thenn1 else
                N*8FACTORIALNN−1))))
```

The editor used in InterLisp is a structure editor. With this editor LISP code is displayed and altered within the LISP system. Operations in the editor apply to the current S-expression, as selected by the user, or to a small surrounding context of the current expression. This editor was developed when teletypes and other slow printing terminals were standard; the InterLisp structure editor enables a programmer to edit LISP source code very efficiently on such terminals. This style of editing is natural to people who are almost exclusively programming in LISP, though some people prefer to edit text.

Other programming tools, such as MASTERSCOPE, help the programmer to develop large systems. MASTERSCOPE is a facility for finding out information about the functions in a large system. The user asks questions about the system, and MASTERSCOPE analyzes the code, building up a database, to answer the question. Questions include which functions call which others (directly or indirectly), which variables are bound where, which functions destructively alter structures, and several others.

InterLisp does not implement a macro facility that is as easily used as MacLisp's. InterLisp introduced the concept of block compilation, in which multiple functions are compiled as a single block; this results in faster function calling than would otherwise be possible in InterLisp.

InterLisp runs on PDP-10s, Vaxes, and a variety of special-purpose LISP machines developed by Xerox and BBN. The most commonly available InterLisp machines are the Dolphin, the Dorado, and the Dandelion. The Dorado is the fastest of the three, and the Dandelion is the most commonly used. InterLisp-10, the PDP-10 version of InterLisp, is a shallow-bound LISP, and InterLisp-D, the special-purpose LISP machine version, is a deep-bound LISP.

Like MacLisp, InterLisp extended the function-calling mechanisms in LISP 1.5 with respect to how arguments can be passed to a function. InterLisp function definitions specify arguments as the cross-product of two attributes: lambda versus nlambda, and spread versus nospread.

Lambda functions evaluate each of their arguments; nlambda evaluates none of their arguments. Spread functions required a fixed number of arguments; nospread functions accept a variable number. Nospread functions treat their arguments very much as MacLisp does in the lexpr case.

One of the most innovative of the language extensions introduced by InterLisp was the spaghetti stack (Bobrow and Wegbreit, 1973). The problem of retention of the dynamic function-definition environment in the presence of special variables was never completely solved until spaghetti stacks were invented.

The idea behind spaghetti stacks is to generalize the structure of stacks to be more like a tree, with various branches of the tree subject to retention whenever a pointer to that branch is retained. That is, parts of the stack are subject to the same garbage collection policies as are other LISP objects. Unlike closures, the retained environment captures both the control environment and the binding environment.

Spaghetti stacks per se are an efficient implementation of tree-structured stacks using a linear stack; in the situation where parts of the stack are not retained, there is almost no performance penalty incurred.

InterLisp retained the LISP 1.5 flavor to a greater extent than did MacLisp. MacLisp changed the order of some arguments to some functions (such as MAPCAR and the other map functions) while InterLisp retained the original order. InterLisp programming style is heavily influenced by the programming environment, CLISP, and DWIM; therefore, the LISP portion of InterLisp remains very similar to early LISPs, the effort in improving programming style focusing on CLISP and DWIM. In dialects like MacLisp, in which a "Lispy" style was retained, the LISP part of the language itself was advanced.

One of the minor, but interesting, modifications to LISP 1.5 that InterLisp made was the introduction of the superparenthesis. If a right square bracket (]) is encountered during a read operation, it balances all outstanding open left parentheses or it matches the last outstanding left square bracket ([). Here is a simple example of this syntax:

```
(DEFINEQ
(FACTORIAL
(LAMBDA (N)
(cond [(zerop n 0) 1]
(t (times n (FACTORIAL (sub1 n]
```

Other Lisp Dialects

There are several other major LISP dialects from this era. Most are more similar to MacLisp than to InterLisp. The two primary dialects are Standard LISP (Marti and co-workers, 1978) and Portable Standard LISP (Utah Symbolic Computation Group, 1982).

Standard LISP was first defined in 1969 by Anthony Hearn and Martin Griss, along with their students and colleagues (Marti and co-workers, 1978). The motivation was to define a subset of LISP 1.5 and the other prevailing LISP dialects that could serve as a common transportation mechanism for programs. The intended use of Standard LISP was to transport REDUCE, a symbolic-algebra system, that was written by Hearn and his colleagues and which was of interest in the scientific and engineering community.

Standard LISP was designed so that if an existing LISP implementation (called the target LISP) could implement the Standard LISP constructs, then Standard LISP and REDUCE could run on top of that existing dialect.

Later Hearn and his colleagues discovered that they would need more control over the environment and the compiler, and Portable Standard LISP (PSL) was born (Griss and Benson, 1982). This dialect shared the simplicity of Standard LISP, but it was a full implementation with a portable compiler. At the end of the 1970s PSL ran on about a dozen different computers.

At Stanford an early version of MacLisp was adapted to the PDP-6; this LISP was called LISP 1.6. The early adaptation was rewritten by John Allen and Lynn Quam, and later compiler improvements were made by Whit Diffie (Quam and Diffie, 1972). UCI LISP (Bobrow, Burton, and Lewis, 1972) is an extended version of LISP 1.6 in which an InterLisp style editor and other programming environment improvements were made.

The Demise of the PDP-10

By the middle of the 1970s it became apparent that the 18-bit address space of the PDP-10 would not provide enough working space for what were becoming average-sized AI programs. The PDP-10 line of computers (KL-10s and DEC-20s) were being altered to use an extended addressing scheme in which multiple 18-bit address spaces could be addressed using a base register. However, this addition was not a smooth expansion to the existing addressing modes as far as the LISP implementor was concerned; moreover, the PDP-10 line was abandoned by DEC.

One response to the address space problem was the LISP machine, a special-purpose computer that specializes in running LISP programs. This is the topic described below. The other response was to use computers with larger address spaces than 18 bits. Digital Equipment Corporation introduced such computers, the Vax line of computers.

Vaxes presented both an opportunity and a problem for LISP implementors. The Vax instruction set provided some good opportunities for implementing the low-level LISP primitive efficiently; the exception to this was LISP function calling, which could not be accurately modeled with the Vax function-calling instructions. The problem with the Vax was two-fold. First, several major LISP implementations at the time had a large assembly language base—foremost among them was MacLisp. This style enabled the implementor to provide a fast, compact LISP but not one that was easily portable. Second, the Vax, although it had a large address space, was intended for use by many small programs, not several large ones. Thus, paging overhead for large LISP programs would remain a problem not fully solved on the Vaxes.

The primary Vax LISP dialects developed in the 1970s were Franz LISP, NIL, and PSL. (new implementation of LISP) (Burke, Currette, and Eliot, 1983) was the successor to MacLisp and was designed by John L. White; Guy L. Steele Jr., and others at MIT, under the influence of LISP Machine LISP, also developed at MIT. NIL was a large LISP, and soon its implementation was centered around a large assembly language base.

Franz LISP was written to enable research on symbolic algebra to continue at the University of California at Berkeley, under the supervision of Richard J. Fateman, who was one of the principal implementors of Macsyma at MIT (Blair, 1975). Fateman and his students started with a PDP-11 version of LISP written at Harvard and extended it into a MacLisp-like LISP that can run on virtually all Unix-based computers. This is a result of the fact that Franz is almost entirely written in C.

Because Franz was intended to be a vehicle for research in symbolic algebra, it never became a solid LISP in the same sense that MacLisp did. On the other hand, it was a widely available LISP dialect on one of the most widely available computers in the AI community.

In 1978 a LISP project was begun at Lawrence Livermore National Laboratories by Richard P. Gabriel and Guy L. Steele Jr. to implement NIL on the S-1 Mark IIA supercomputer (Brooks, Gabriel, and Steele, 1982a,b). This LISP, never completely functional, would be the testbed for adapting advanced compiler techniques to LISP implementation. With the development of the S-1 LISP compiler, it once again became feasible to implement LISP in LISP and to expect similar performance to the best hand-tuned, assembly-language-based LISP systems.

Scheme

One of the most important developments in LISP occurred during the second half of the 1970s: Scheme. Scheme is a simple dialect of LISP that brought together some of the programming language semantics ideas developed in the 1960s with the LISP culture that had largely developed by seat-of-the-pants efforts.

The major contributions of Scheme were lexical scoping, first-class functions (closures), and a pure programming style.

IBM

Although the first LISPs were implemented on IBM computers, IBM faded from the LISP scene during the latter half of the 1960s. The original LISP 1.5 continued in the form of LISP 360, which was improved and developed until the early 1970's, when the LISP 370 implementation began. LISP 370 is now called LISP/VM.

The LISP 370 project was under the direction of Fred Blair (1975) at the Thomas J. Watson Research Center in Yorktown Heights, New York. LISP 370 is an elegant variant of LISP that highlighted both special and lexical binding, closures over both special and lexical variables (using a technique like spaghetti stacks), and a programming environment strongly influenced by InterLisp.

COMPARATIVE HISTORY OF LISP: LISP MACHINES, 1970–1985

The discussion of LISP implementation thus far has concentrated on implementations of LISP on stock hardware. A stock hardware computer is a computer that is not designed specifically to support LISP. For example, a Digital Equipment Corporation Vax 11/780 is stock hardware, and a Symbolics 3600 is an example of a computer designed specifically to support LISP.

Several of the operations frequently performed while executing LISP programs can be better performed or significantly sped up by special hardware. The hardware-assisted operations most frequently performed by special hardware on LISP machines are tagging, function calling, and garbage collection.

The words of storage in a LISP machine can be designed to have enough bits to support pointers directly; the address and the tag bits can both fit in a word of storage without losing any addressing bits. Instructions to check the tag of a pointer can be made fast with special data paths in the computer. Operations, such as addition, can check the types of their operands in parallel with the operation itself, and if the types are not suitable, an exceptional condition can be flagged, and a more general course of action can then be taken.

Function calling is one of the most frequent operations in LISP programs. The construction of stack frames can be performed by hardware. Caching parts of the stack can make a major performance difference to a LISP implementation.

Garbage collection is often performed by need—when the dynamic heap runs out of free space, a garbage collection can be initiated to gain some free space. Garbage collection can take a relatively long time; performing it concurrently with other LISP operations can eliminate the long pause associated with garbage collection. Most of the known techniques for incremental garbage collection are best implemented with special hardware.

Many LISP machines are essentially general-purpose computers that have been specially microcoded for LISP.

Commercial LISP Machines

In the early 1970s, at MIT, the LISP Machine project began. The machine constructed, called the CADR, was a specially microcoded, 32-bit processor, with some data paths of particular usefulness to LISP. LISP Machine, Incorporated (LMI) was the first to commercialize this machine in the late 1970s.

Also in the late 1970s a second LISP machine company emerged, Symbolics, which also sold a CADR copy. In the early 1980s Symbolics introduced a new LISP machine, the 3600, which would become the industry leader in LISP machine performance for the next 5 years.

The dialect of LISP on the LISP machines is called LISP Machine LISP or ZetaLisp (Weinreb and Moon, 1981).

In the late 1970s BBN built an InterLisp LISP machine, called the Jericho. It remained a BBN internal machine.

About the same time, Xerox microcoded the Dorado, also known as the Xerox 1132, to execute an InterLisp instruction set. This work was based on the earlier attempt to microcode the Xerox Alto computer to implement the InterLisp virtual machine specification (Moore, 1976). A second machine, the Dolphin, was similarly microcoded, resulting in a second Xerox LISP machine. The Dorado, a high-speed computer, was originally a Mesa machine, Mesa being an ALGOL-like programming language.

LISP Machine Software

An important contribution of the LISP machines was to programming languages and the programming environment. All of the LISP machine companies added graphics, windowing capabilities, and mouse interaction capabilities to their programming environments. LISP, particularly on the MIT-style LISP machines, grew in complexity and completeness. SETF, DEFSTRUCT, multiple values, and a better style for arrays were important additions to LISP based on the MIT LISP machine work.

At MIT, Flavors, an object-oriented programming system, was developed and integrated into the LISP ma-

chines. The window system, in particular, is written in flavors (Weinreb and Moon, 1981).

At Xerox the experience with Smalltalk (Goldberg and Robeson, 1983) led to the development of LOOPS (Bobrow and Stefik, 1983), an object-oriented programming system.

HISTORY OF LISP: 1980–PRESENT

In 1980 the LISP situation was that Symbolics and LMI were developing ZetaLisp, stock-hardware implementation groups were developing NIL, Franz LISP, and PSL, Xerox was developing InterLisp, and the Scientific Personal Integrated Computing Environment project (SPICE) at CMU was developing a MacLisp-like dialect of LISP called SpiceLisp.

Several of these groups got together and began to define Common LISP. Of the above LISPS, most are MacLisp derivatives. Symbolics, the SPICE project, the NIL project at MIT, and the S-1 LISP Project joined together in this effort, which was led by Scott Fahlman, Daniel Weinreb, David Moon, Guy L. Steele Jr., and Richard P. Gabriel (Steele and co-workers, 1984).

The definition of Common LISP was as a description of a family of languages; if certain specifications were met, a particular LISP dialect could be a member of the Common LISP family. The main goals, stated in the book *Common Lisp: the Language,* (Steele and co-workers, 1984) were to be portable, common, stable, powerful, expressive, and efficient.

The bulk of the design work was carried on in the form of network mail over the ARPANET. In addition, there were two face-to-face meetings before the Common LISP book was published.

The primary influences on Common LISP were ZetaLisp, MacLisp, NIL, S-1 LISP, Spice LISP, and Scheme.

Since then, Common LISP has become a de facto standard, with virtually every commercial LISP vendor and many hardware vendors offering a Common LISP. However, Common LISP is not an ideal LISP (as was pointed out by Brooks and Gabriel, 1984), being a compromise among many similar and large dialects of LISP.

EXTENDING LISP

A primary strength of LISP is the ability to extend the language; with such a facility researchers are free to define their own languages and to then program in them. As long as the language designer is willing either to live with LISP syntax or to live with a syntax that can be easily translated into LISP, there is no better language design language than LISP.

In earlier examples of LISP code it could be seen that the syntax of the special forms was the same as the syntax of user-defined functions. Moreover, macro invocations are also in the same syntax as the rest of LISP. If a LISP programmer adds a new function to LISP, loading that new function into LISP and possibly informing the compiler of its existence in one of several ways is sufficient to add that function to LISP exactly as if it had been designed into the LISP originally.

Consider the example

(defun cube (x) (* x x x))

When this function is loaded into the LISP system, the programmer can write

(+ (cube x) (* x y))

and the reference to the function cube is syntactically indistinguishable from the reference to *.

If the user writes

(defmacro cube (x)
(let ((var (gensym)))
'(let ((,var ,x))
(*,var ,var ,var))))

then the compiler will also be able to compile code involving CUBE correctly, and the compiler will also be able to use the optimization techniques it uses for * to optimize uses of CUBE, if possible. GENSYM returns a symbol that has never appeared in the currently running LISP system. In this macro definition it is used to create an identifier that is guaranteed not to conflict with any other identifier that has been declared special. The expression that is to be cubed should be bound to some variable because that expression might perform side effects that cannot be done three times, which is what would happen had the macro been written as

(defmacro cube (x)
'(* ,x ,x ,x))

PROGRAM DEVELOPMENT STRENGTHS OF LISP

LISP, being uniform in its own syntax and also in its syntax as extended to the user, is a friendly system in which to develop large systems. There are three other important features of LISP for developing systems: separate compilation, typelessness, and the debugging environment.

Separate Compilation

Separate compilation is the ability of the compiler to produce code that calls functions even though the compiler has never seen the functions being called. That is, if a LISP program comprises a number of functions, each function can be compiled in complete isolation from the others, and loading all of the functions into a single LISP system will produce a working program. Moreover, the LISP program can contain a mixture of compiled and interpreted code, which can help the programmer both develop and debug large systems.

A typical use of this feature is to write and debug a portion of a large program before the entire program has been written. Several people can divide the work among themselves and only have to agree on the interfaces among the parts and on the macro files to use.

It might be the case that better code can be produced when the compiler can analyze all of the functions together, but for development and debugging the modularity is useful. With facilities such as InterLisp block compilation, the advantages of modularity at development time and speed at delivery time can be realized in the same system.

Typelessness

A LISP program need not have the types of all, or of any, variables declared in order to produce a working program. This speeds up the debugging cycle in some cases by enabling the programmer to write a simple version of a larger function quickly, to test it out, and to refine the algorithm and data structures without having to make a commitment to the types of all variables before the program can be tested.

Of course, in many situations the need to declare the types of variables can lead the programmer to more carefully consider the program, the algorithm, and the data structures before too much time is wasted "hacking" the program together. But in many other situations, particularly in those where there is no good understanding of the nature of the algorithm, time can be saved if a prototype program can be tested early in the programming cycle. LISP enables the programmer to pursue either one of these program development methodologies.

Debugging Environment

LISP provides an extensive debugging environment. Because LISP can treat interpreted LISP programs exactly like data, debugging tools can be written to examine and modify programs while they are being debugged.

Examples of LISP debugging tools are single steppers, tracers, inspectors, and breakpoints.

A single stepper is an addition to the interpreter that enables the programmer to execute "one line" of LISP code at a time, stopping after each expression, allowing the programmer to examine the LISP environment. This examination is performed by invoking the interpreter in a reentrant manner. Variations on the single stepper include the ability to save state during the stepping process so that the code can be, in effect, stepped through backward.

A tracer is a function that is invoked on function entry and/or exit. Statements can be printed at these points, conditions can be tested, additions to a database can be made for later analysis, and any LISP action can be taken.

An inspector is a program that helps a programmer examine an instance of a data structure. For example, the programmer might have defined a complex graph structure using data abstractions. An inspector will help the programmer browse through the instance of the data structure, printing its parts as appropriate for the data structure definitions.

Finally, breakpoints can be inserted anywhere in a LISP function so that execution can be stopped and the LISP environment examined. Code can be a mixture of compiled and interpreted code.

REAL LISP IMPLEMENTATIONS

Modern LISP implementations are almostly entirely written in LISP. Bootstrapping the LISP involves writing a cross-compiler that runs in some other dialect of LISP, perhaps on some other machine. All of the code that makes up the interpreter and the function definitions of LISP can be written in LISP and compiled.

Such implementations might be slower than implementations that depend on a hand-coded assembly language interpreter, but LISP-in-LISP implementations are easier to understand, to write, to debug, and to port to other machines than implementations based on other techniques.

CONCLUSIONS

LISP is a powerful programming language and environment for developing large programs. Artificial intelligence programming requires the flexibility, the extensibility, the modularity, and the underlying data structures and data abstraction facilities that LISP provides.

Although LISP is one of the older programming languages in use, it has remained the most widely used language in AI programming.

BIBLIOGRAPHY

E. C. Berkeley and D. G. Bobrow, *The Programming Language Lisp: Its Operation and Applications,* MIT Press, Cambridge, Mass., 1964.

F. U. Blair, The Definition of Lisp 1.8+0.3i, Unpublished Memo, IBM Thomas J. Watson Research Center, Yorktown Heights, N.Y., 1975.

D. G. Bobrow and M. J. Stefik, *The Loops Manual,* Intelligent Systems Laboratory, Xerox Corporation, 1983.

D. Bobrow and B. Wegbreit, "A Model and Stack Implementation of Multiple Environments," *CACM* **16**(10), 591–603 (Oct. 1973).

R. J. Bobrow, R. R. Burton, and D. Lewis, *UCI Lisp Manual (An Extended Stanford Lisp 1.6 System),* University of California at Irvine, Information and Computer Science Technical Report No. 21, 1972.

R. A. Brooks and R. P. Gabriel, "A Critique of Common Lisp," *Proceedings of the 1984 ACM Symposium on Lisp and Functional Programming,* Aug. 1984, pp. 1–8.

R. A. Brooks, R. P. Gabriel, and G. L. Steele, "An Optimizing Compiler For Lexically Scoped Lisp," *Proceedings of the 1982 ACM Compiler Construction Conference,* June 1982a, pp. 261–275.

R. A. Brooks, R. P. Gabriel, and G. L. Steele, "S-1 Common Lisp Implementation," *Proceedings of the 1982 ACM Symposium on Lisp and Functional Programming,* August 1982b, pp. 108–113.

G. S. Burke, G. J. Carrette, and C. R. Eliot, *NIL Reference Manual,* Massachusetts Institute of Technology, MIT/LCS/TR-311, 1983.

F. J. Corbato and co-workers, "An Experimental Time-Sharing System," *AFIPS Conference Proceedings,* Spring Joint Computer Conference, Vol. 21, pp. 335–344, 1962.

D. Eastlake, R. Greenblatt, J. Holloway, T. Knight, and S. Nelson, *ITS 1.5 Reference Manual,* MIT Artificial Intelligence Memo No. 161A, 1969.

A. Goldberg and D. Robson, *Smalltalk-80: The Language and its Implementation,* Addison-Wesley, Reading, Mass., 1983.

J. P. Golden and J. L. White, "A User's Guide to the A. I. Group LISCOM Compiler: Interim Report," MIT Artificial Intelligence Memo No. 210, Dec. 1970.

R. Greenblatt, *The Lisp Machine,* Working Paper 79, MIT Artificial Intelligence Laboratory, Cambridge, Mass., 1974.

M. L. Griss and E. Benson, PSL: A Portable Lisp System, *Proceedings of the 1982 ACM Symposium on Lisp and Functional Programming,* Aug. 1982, pp. 88–97.

B. Harvey, *Monitor Command Manual,* Stanford University, SAILON 54.7, Stanford, Calif., 1982.

J. Lukasiewicz, "Philosophiche Bemerkungen zu Mehrwertigen Systemen des Aussagenkalküls," *Comptes Rendus des Seances de la Société Sciences et de la Lettres des Varsovie* **23**(Classe III), 51–77 (1930); see also same author in "Zur Geschichte der Aussagenlogik," *Erkenntnis* **5**, 111–131 (1934) Berlin (original in Polish).

J. B. Marti, A. C. Hearn, M. L. Griss, and C. Griss, *Standard Lisp Report,* University of Utah, Salt Lake City, UUCS-78-101, 1978.

J. McCarthy, "Recursive Functions of Symbolic Expressions and their Computation by Machine, Part I," *CACM* **3**(4), 184–195 (1960).

J. McCarthy, Programs with Common Sense, *Proceedings of the Symposium on the Mechanization of Thought Processes,* National Physical Laboratory, I, pp. 77–84, (1958) [reprinted in M. L. Minsky, ed., *Semantic Information Processing,* MIT Press, Cambridge, Mass., 1968].

J. McCarthy, Stanford University, private communication, 1985.

J. McCarthy, P. W. Abrahams, D. J. Edwards, P. A. Fox, T. P. Hart, and M. J. Levin, *Lisp 1.5 Programmer's Manual,* MIT Press, Cambridge, Mass., 1962.

D. Moon, *MacLisp Reference Manual, Revision 0,* MIT Project MAC, Cambridge, Mass., April 1974.

S. J. Moore, *The InterLisp Virtual Machine Specification,* Xerox PARC CSL-76-5, 1976.

A. Newell, *IPL-V Programmers' Reference Manual, RM-3739-RC,* Rand Corporation Technical Report, 1963.

L. Quam and W. Diffie, *Stanford Lisp 1.6 Manual,* Stanford University, SAILON 28.7, Stanford, Calif., 1972.

W. V. Quine, *Mathematical Logic,* Harvard University Press, Cambridge, Mass., 1961.

Rand Corporation, *The History of the Johnniac,* Rand Corporation Technical Report AD-679-152, Santa Monica, Calif., 1968.

G. L. Steele, Jr. and co-workers, *Common Lisp: The Language,* Digital, Burlington, Mass., 1984.

W. Teitelman and co-workers, *InterLisp Reference Manual,* Xerox Palo Alto Research Center, Palo Alto, Calif., 1978.

The Utah Symbolic Computation Group, *The Portable Standard Lisp Users' Manual,* Department of Computer Science, University of Utah, Salt Lake City, TR-10, 1982.

D. Weinreb and D. Moon, *Lisp Machine Manual,* 4th ed., Massachusetts Institute of Technology Artificial Intelligence Laboratory, Cambridge, Mass., July 1981.

J. L. White, *An Interim Lisp User's Guide,* MIT Artificial Intelligence Memo No. 190, 1970.

General References

H. Abelson and G. Sussman, *Structure and Interpretation of Computer Programs,* MIT Press, Cambridge, Mass., 1984.

J. Allen, *Anatomy of Lisp,* McGraw-Hill, New York, 1978.

H. B. Baker, "List Processing in Real Time on a Serial Computer," *CACM* **21**(4), 280–294 (April 1978).

H. B. Baker, "Shallow Binding in Lisp 1.5," *CACM* **21**(7), 565–569 (July 1978).

R. Bates, D. Dyer, and H. Koomen, "Implementation of InterLisp on a Vax," *Proceedings of the 1982 ACM Symposium on Lisp and Functional Programming,* Aug. 1982.

D. Bobrow and D. Clark, "Compact Encodings of List Structure," *ACM Trans. Prog. Lang. Sys.* **1**(2), 266 (Oct. 1979).

D. Bobrow and B. Raphael, "New Programming Languages for Artificial Intelligence," *ACM Comput. Surv.* **6**(3), 153–174 (1974).

R. R. Burton and co-workers, InterLisp-D Overview, *Papers on InterLisp-D,* Xerox Palo Alto Research Center, CIS-5 (SSL-80-4), 1981.

E. Charniak, C. Riesbeck, and D. McDermott, *Artificial Intelligence Programming,* Lawrence Erlbaum, Hillsdale, N.J., 1980.

J. Cohen, "Garbage Collection of Linked Data Structures," *ACM Comput. Surv.* **13**(3), 341–367 (Sept. 1981).

L. P. Deutsch and D. Bobrow, "An Efficient Incremental, Automatic Garbage Collector," *CACM* **19**(9), 522–526 (Sept. 1976).

J. K. Foderaro and K. L. Sklower, *The FRANZ Lisp Manual,* University of California, Berkeley, Calif., April 1982.

R. P. Gabriel, *Performance and Evaluation of Lisp Systems,* MIT Press, Cambridge, Mass., 1985.

J. Marti, A. C. Hearn, and M. L. Griss, "Standard Lisp Report," *SIGPLAN Notices* **14,** Oct. 10, 1979.

L. Masinter, *InterLisp-VAX: A Report,* Department of Computer Science, Stanford University, STAN-CS-81-879, Aug. 1981.

L. M. Masinter and L. P. Deutsch, "Local Optimization For a Compiler for Stack-based Lisp Machines," *Papers on InterLisp-D,* Xerox Palo Alto Research Center, CIS-5 (SSL-80-4), 1981.

J. McCarthy, "History of Lisp," in D. Wexelblat, ed., *History of Programming Languages,* Academic Press, New York, 1978.

J. Moses, "The Function of FUNCTION in Lisp," *ACM SIGSAM Bull.* **13,** 27 (1970).

G. L. Steele, Jr. and G. Sussman, *LAMBDA—The Ultimate Imperative,* Memo No. 353, Artificial Intelligence Laboratory, MIT, Cambridge, Mass., 1976.

G. L. Steele, Jr., "Data Representations in PDP-10 MacLisp," *Proceedings of the 1977 MACSYMA Users' Conference,* NASA Scientific and Technical Information Office, Washington, D.C., July 1977.

G. L. Steele, Jr., "Fast Arithmetic in MacLisp," *Proceedings of the 1977 MACSYMA Users' Conference,* NASA Scientific and Technical Information Office, Washington, D.C., July 1977.

G. L. Steele, Jr. and G. Sussman, *The Revised Report on Scheme: A Dialect of Lisp,* Memo No. 452, Artificial Intelligence Laboratory, MIT, Cambridge, Mass., 1978.

G. L. Steele, Jr. and co-workers, "An Overview of Common Lisp," *Proceedings of the 1982 ACM Symposium on Lisp and Functional Programming,* Aug. 1982, pp. 98–107.

D. Touretzky, *Lisp—A Gentle Introduction to Symbolic Computation,* Harper & Row, New York, 1984.

J. L. White, NIL: A Perspective, *Proceedings of the 1979 MACSYMA Users' Conference,* July 1979, pp. 190–199.

P. H. Winston and K. P. H. Horn, *Lisp,* 2nd ed., Addison-Wesley, Reading, Mass., 1984.

R. Gabriel
Lucid, Inc.

LISP MACHINES

The development of commercially available LISP (qv) processors has made a dramatic impact on the use of AI and LISP-based technology. Once oriented almost exclusively toward research, LISP machines have catalyzed widespread interest in the commercial application of this technology.

The genesis of today's commercial LISP machines began in 1973 at the MIT AI Laboratory. The key to achieving high throughput for LISP programs was to integrate the run-time Typed nature of the language with a tagged hardware architecture. A thorough review of past evolution was done, and a LISP-oriented macrocode was defined. In addition, two new LISP extension resulted: the AREA feature for storage management and the PACKAGE system allowing multiple LISP programs to coexist.

In 1974, after completing this initial software, work began on hardware. Called the CONS machine (named after the CONStructor operator of LISP), it had a tagged architecture, a bit-mapped display (inspired from work done at both Xerox and MIT), and a writable control store. The CONS was completed in 1976.

In late 1976 a second generation, the CADR, was started (CADR is the LISP function for selecting the second element of a LISP). Operational in 1977, the CADR exhibits many of the features that are seen on today's LISP machines. These are described below.

Large Virtual-Address Space

The CADR had a 16-megaword (32-bit-word) virtual-address space. In comparison, the DEC PDP-10, the standard research tool of the day, had 0.25 megawords (36-bit word).

Graphical Display Console

The display on the CADR was 800×1024 monochrome, which provided a high-resolution display to the user. Along with the keyboard (providing a superset of ASCII character set), the CADR also provided a mouse pointing device promoting the utilization of menus and other point-sensitive graphical objects in lieu of keyboard commands.

Garbage Collection

The tagged architecture of the CADR combined with some hardware assist allowed for the first real-time or incremental garbage collector for LISP systems. Earlier LISP garbage collectors were characterized by occasional pauses in LISP computation while the garbage collector executed. The CADR approach allowed interleaved execution.

LISP Software Environment

The MIT ZETALISP system (originally called LISP Machine LISP) was, and is, a single, fully integrated, runtime system consisting of only LISP and microcode, providing a uniform program development and execution environment. ZETALISP served as a testbed for object-oriented programming languages (qv), receiving inspiration from the Smalltalk system developed at XEROX. This effort culminated in the FLAVORS system, a second-generation extension of Smalltalk, with control fully integrated into LISP.

One of the utilities developed for the CADR was the ZMACS editor, a superset of the EMACS editor originally developed on the PDP-10. ZMACS provides the user with over 400 commands, many of which are LISP-specific, and also allows users to write their own commands. The CADR software also includes the Window System, the basic user interface managing the high-resolution display (written in FLAVORS), and the INSPECTOR, a data-structure-examination facility that makes heavy use of the graphic capabilities of the display.

MIT built 35 CADRs to be used internally. In 1980 both LISP Machine (LMI) and Symbolics were granted licenses from MIT for utilization of LISP machine technology. LMI started producing CADR systems in May 1981. Symbolics repackaged the CADR to be more production compatible and produced the LM-2 in September 1981. The LMI CADR and the Symbolics LM-2 were functionally identical.

Both companies realized that new-generation machines were required. Symbolics developed their second-generation LISP machine, the 3600, and delivered the first unit in December 1982. LMI introduced the Lambda in August 1983.

Although the 3600 and the Lambda both execute variants of the ZETALISP software environment, and as a result are quite similar, the hardware architectures of the machines are extremely different. The 3600, which takes a totally different approach than the Lambda to the CADR architecture, is a unit processor with an instruction-fetch unit to increase macrocode performance. The 3600 has 8,000 words of control memory, a 36-bit word and a variable-length tag field. The system provides a 68,000 I/O front end and has a 256-megaword virtual-address space.

The Lambda provides the user with a bus-centered architecture based on the NuBus, a processor-independent bus originally developed at MIT's Laboratory of Computer Science. There is also an integral MULTIBUS for access to third-party peripherals. The LISP processor maintains the architectural philosophy of the CADR with extensive modifications and improvements. It provides users with a 32-megaword virtual-address space and supports a 64,000-word user-programmable control memory. An optional microcompiler is also supported providing direct translation of LISP source to system microcode.

Since their initial introduction, both Symbolics and LMI have introduced additional production options all based on the same processor architecture.

With technology licensed from LMI, Texas Instruments (TI) has also introduced a LISP machine in the spring of 1985, called the Explorer. Distributed by both TI and LMI, the Explorer is a compact unit-processor machine utilizing an architectural philosophy similar to the Lambda and the CADR. The Explorer is based on the NuBus and provides the user with a 32-megaword virtual-address space. Its processor resides on one printed circuit (PC) board.

Near-term commercial offerings of LISP machines will obey certain guidelines. First, the cost per user must become more competitive with non-LISP machine work-station technology. Second, LISP machines must be able to be more readily interfaced to generic-mainframe computing environments through networks, system-level bus links, low-speed peripheral buses, and optional processors. Finally, performance will continue to increase as processor architectures are refined.

In the next 5–10 years the goal of most AI systems is to search a large state space as efficiently as possible. With current LISP machine technology, that search procedure is carried out by a single processor. Research is currently underway to allow a large number of processors to participate in the search simultaneously, thus decreasing the time required to complete the search by many orders of magnitude. These machines, when commercially available, will catalyze a major leap in the applicability of AI. This advance, although similar to the effect that commercial LISP Machines had on AI, will, by nature of the problems that it will allow to be solved, be much larger.

BIBLIOGRAPHY

General References

R. Brooks and R. Gabriel, "A Critique of Common Lisp," *Proceedings of the 1984 ACM Symposium on Lisp and Functional Programming*, pp. 1–8.

R. Gabriel, *Performance Evaluation of LISP Systems*, MIT Press, Cambridge, Mass., 1985.

R. Greenblatt, T. Knight, J. Holloway, D. Moon, and D. Weinreb, "The Lisp Machine," in D. Barstow, H. Shrobe, and E. Sandewall, eds., *Interactive Programming Environments*, McGraw-Hill, New York, 1984, pp. 326–352.

K. Kahn and M. Carlsson, "How to Implement Prolog on a Lisp Machine," in J. A. Campbell, ed., *Implementations of Prolog*, Ellis Horwood, 1984.

E. Sandewall, "Programming in an Interactive Environment: The Lisp Experience," ACM Computing Surveys, March, 1978, in *Interactive Programming Environments*, McGraw-Hill, New York, 1984, pp. 31–80.

B. Shiel, "Power Tools for Programmers," in *Interactive Programming Environments*, McGraw-Hill, New York, 1984, pp. 19–30.

D. Weinreb and D. Moon, *The Lisp Machine Manual*, MIT Technical Report.

S. Wholey and S. Fahlman, "The Design of an Instruction Set for Common Lisp," *Proceedings of the 1984 ACM Symposium on Lisp and Functional Programming*, pp. 150–158.

R. Greenblatt
G. Curet
M. Kreeger
LISP Machines Company

LIST PROCESSING. See LISP.

LITERATURE, AI

Artificial intelligence has undergone considerable changes in its history, and each change has been accompanied by a change in the nature of the AI literature. Four historic periods may be identified: pre-AI, beginnings of AI, preexpert systems AI, and commercial AI. Only in the last period has an awareness of AI on the part of the general public begun to emerge, and with it, a recognition by the scientific and reference-publishing community of a need to package the literature of AI for easier access. Being a field with multidisciplinary origins, AI has until now been very difficult to track through the labyrinth of indexing and bibliographic tools designed to serve more traditional fields such as psychology, mathematics, engineering, and computing. To this date there is no one of these disciplines within which AI can be said to wholly reside—and hence no traditional tools to help librarians in these disciplines completely cover the AI literature.

AI has also been among the first fields to exploit additional forms of information not associated with traditional library science. These have included extensive use of technical reports, on-line machine-readable text files, and electronic-mail digests.

PRE-AI LITERATURE: 1940s

Cybernetics. Weiner ([1948] 1961) and Bigelow coined the term cybernetics (qv) to describe what they saw as "the essential unity of the problems centering about communication, control, and statistical mechanics, whether in the machine or in living tissue." In 1943 two papers were published that Papert described as the birth of cybernetics (McCorduck, 1979): "Behavior, Purpose, and Teleology," by Rosenblueth and co-workers (1943), and "A Logical Calculus of the Ideas Immanent in Nervous Activity," by McCulloch and Pitts (1943).

The more famous work, by Wiener, was, of course, *Cybernetics* ([1948] 1961). However, although cybernetics persists to this day, it was not to be the true origin of AI. The distinction seems to have been between basing the new field on modeling human cognition vs extending earlier concepts of regulating machinery. In some sense, AI was true heresy, whereas cybernetics was a logical extension of the capabilities of existing mechanisms.

The true inspirational origins of AI seem clearly related to the work of computing pioneer Turing. Turing's early papers, such as "Intelligent Machinery" ([1947] 1970) and "Computing Machinery and Intelligence" ([1950] 1963), are seen even today as remarkably endowed with the philosophical emphasis of much more modern AI research.

BEGINNINGS OF AI: THE 1950s

The AI literature of the 1950s consists largely of scattered journal articles published in the literatures of other disci-

plines in which its early pioneers began: computing, psychology, engineering, and mathematics.

Game-Playing Programs. Of particular interest at this time is early work on game-playing (qv) programs, which has been an enduring subdivision of AI since its beginnings. Game-playing behavior bridges the boundary between automata and human behavior in a nearly unique manner. Thus the earliest work on chess is by Shannon (1950a, 1950b) as in "A Chess-Playing Machine" and "Programming a Computer for Playing Chess." Work with a more cleanly AI character followed later, as in "Chess Playing Programs and the Problem of Complexity" (Newell and co-workers, 1958) (see also COMPUTER CHESS AND SEARCH).

Automata Theory. A field parallel to AI at the time was automata theory. *Automata Studies* (Shannon and McCarthy, 1956) summarized the work in automata theory, but this work also represented an uneasy bond between these pioneers and one that led to the dramatic naming of AI as a separate field shortly thereafter.

Dartmouth Conference. Artificial intelligence as a term was coined by McCarthy in proposing a now-historic conference held at Dartmouth College in the summer of 1956. The name was chosen deliberately to set the field apart from the existing domains of cybernetics and automata.

Technical Reports. In the aftermath of the Dartmouth Conference of 1956, the established centers of AI were formed. MIT, BBN, CMU, Stanford University, and the then Stanford Research Institute (now SRI International) became pioneering centers of AI research. Their impact on the early literature, however, was largely available only in technical reports and published articles. The book as a factor in AI had yet to become commonplace. Fortunately for the contemporary follower of AI, the recognition of the importance of these original technical reports has led to their being reprinted on microfiche for general dissemination. Scientific Datalink, a division of Comtex Scientific Corp., has brought to the market packaged sets of microfiche containing the 525 CMU AI Research Reports since 1956, the 451 MIT AI Laboratory Reports since 1958, the 279 BBN Artificial Intelligence Reports since 1960, the 350 Stanford AI Memoranda since 1963, and the 318 SRI AI Technical reports since 1968. Other research centers and universities continue to be added.

AI: THE 1960s

Journals. The use of technical reports may have been forced on the fledgling field as early works in AI did not fall within the traditional characterizations of existing periodicals. Early AI was published in journals belonging to the fields in which its practitioners had obtained their degrees, but only in limited quantities. AI articles were published within *Communications of the Association for Computing Machinery* (*CACM*) and *Journal of the Association for Computing Machinery* (*JACM*) throughout the

1960s. Such classics as Simmons's (1965, 1970) question–answering system surveys, Weizenbaum's (1966) ELIZA, Quillian's (1969) Teachable Language Comprehender, Woods's (1970) Transition Networks, and Simmons and Slocum's (1972) natural-language-generation paper all appeared in *CACM*, whereas *JACM* published early heuristic search and theorem-proving papers (Slagle and Dixon, 1969; Slagle, 1963). With such a shortage of journals in which to publish AI work, it became accepted practice at major universities at which AI developed to publish theses and dissertations as technical reports. Only considerably later did these works begin to appear in edited collections as books.

One exception to this immersion of AI in other discipline's literatures is the literature of computational linguistics (qv). Perhaps because it could easily be seen as relevant to one major discipline, linguistics, computational linguistics has a solid and early (ancient) journal-level heritage. *The Finite String* began publication in 1964 and was edited by Roberts until 1973. The much earlier, *MT: Mechanical Translation,* founded by Yngve in 1954, was adopted by the Association for Computational Linguistics (ACL) as *Mechanical Translation and Computational Linguistics* in 1965, but would only survive until 1968. In 1974 the ACL began publishing the *American Journal of Computational Linguistics,* shortening its name in 1984 to *Computational Linguistics. The Finite String* continues to be published as a part of *Computational Linguistics.* Supplementing the computational-linguistics literature, *Computers and the Humanities* appeared in 1966.

Conference Literature. Just as in the journal literature, AI at conferences first emerged within the context of AI sessions at other established meetings. The Spring and Fall Joint Computer Conferences of the late 1960s contained major early papers in AI before the IJCAI conference series started in 1969. Also as in journal literature, computational linguistics appeared earlier than AI itself. The ACL first met in conjunction with the 1963 ACM National Conference. The first International Conference on Computational Linguistics (now termed COLING) occurred in 1965.

Books. Much of the earliest AI work appeared in a classic volume edited by Feigenbaum and Feldman (1963) titled *Computers and Thought.* This work, featured in early courses in AI throughout the United States, included the first comprehensive bibliography of the earliest AI literature. It organized the literature with an elaborate system of cross-references by subject areas, clearly declaring the highly interdisciplinary nature of AI research. The remarkable thing about this book is that it remained for so long virtually the only AI book at the top of everyone's list of recommended reading. Its royalties were used to establish the "Computers and Thought" lectures, which are given biennially at the IJCAI conferences.

The British AI effort began publishing the classic *Machine Intelligence Series* (Michie and co-workers, 1967; Dale and Michie, 1967; Michie, 1968; Meltzer and Michie, 1969, 1970, 1971, 1977; Elcock and Michie, 1977; Hayes

and co-workers, 1979, 1982, 1986). However, it was nearly five years after *Computers and Thought* until Minsky (1968) brought together a set of papers and dissertations from MIT to produce another classic anthology, *Semantic Information Processing.* That year also marked the beginning of an essentially steady stream of new AI books: Minsky and Papert's (1968) *Perceptrons* (qv), Simon's (1969) *Sciences of the Artificial,* and Ernst and Newell's (1969) *GPS: A Case Study in Generality and Problem Solving* (qv).

AI: THE 1970s

Journals. The 1970s began auspiciously with AI's first journal, appropriately named *Artificial Intelligence.* The *International Journal of Man–Machine Studies,* which also publishes AI articles, began the year before, in 1969. The Association for Literary and Linguistic Computing began publishing the *ALLC Bulletin* in 1973 and the *ALLC Journal* in 1980, which again supplemented the computational linguistics literature.

Books. The year 1972 marks the date of the appearance of a significant AI dissertation as a separate book, Winograd's (1972) *Understanding Natural Language.* Winograd also represents the boundary between what might be termed the first-generation AI authors and the second generation. Winograd was a student of Minsky. There would be new pioneers after Winograd, to be sure, but the groundwork of AI had been established. Winograd's work was not only a landmark in this way but was also a significant advance for computational linguistics. It was soon followed by further significant computational linguistics books such as Schank and Colby's (1973) *Computer Models of Thought and Language,* Rustin's (1973) *Natural Language Processing,* Schank's (1975) *Conceptual Information Processing,* Charniak and Wilks's (1976) *Computational Semantics: An Introduction to Artificial Intelligence and Natural Language Comprehension,* Schank and Abelson's (1977) *Scripts, Plans, Goals and Understanding,* Walker's (1978) *Understanding Spoken Language,* Fahlman's (1979) *NETL: A System for Representing and Using Real-World Knowledge,* and Findler's (1979) semantic networks survey collection, *Associative Networks: Representation and Use of Knowledge by Computer.*

Cognitive Science. Also during the 1970s several works were published that clearly marked the creation of cognitive science (qv) and its eventual semiseparation from AI as that portion of AI research concerned primarily with emulating human performance, whether correct or abnormal (Colby, 1974) rather than merely performing tasks at a human level of proficiency. Anderson and Bower's (1973, 1980) *Human Associative Memory* clearly represented the cognitive psychologist's perspective. Bobrow and Collins's (1975) *Representation and Understanding* may have been the first book to introduce the term *cognitive science.* Winston's (1975) *The Psychology of Computer Vision* (1975) [contrasting with the totally engineering view of Duda and Hart's (1973) *Pattern Classification and Scene Analysis* only two years before], Norman and Rumelhart's (1975) *Explorations in Cognition,* and Lindsay and Norman's (1977) *Human Information Processing* added to the concept of AI as a new paradigm for psychology. Psychologists such as Miller and Johnson-Laird (1976) also began contributing literature to this parallel channel of development with their *Language and Perception.* In 1977 the first issue of the journal *Cognitive Science* (Cognitive Science Society, 1981) appeared, firmly establishing the field as desiring its own publication apart from whatever avenue existed for AI articles.

Overviews. Another new trend in AI books at this stage is the generation of a new set of general overviews of AI. Jackson (1974), a student at MIT, produced a comprehensive survey of AI in his *Introduction to Artificial Intelligence,* which startled many in that it was a book about AI written not by one of its primary practitioners but by someone from the outside looking in. The professionals had been too busy doing AI to describe it in overview. This soon changed with Winston's ([1977] 1984) *Artificial Intelligence.* Prior to this the term AI had been used more in the sense of "This book is about my view of something called AI" [such as in Fogel's (1967) *Artificial Intelligence Through Simulated Evolution,* Banerji's (1969) *Theory of Problem Solving: An Approach to Artificial Intelligence,* Nilsson's (1971) *Problem Solving Methods in Artificial Intelligence,* Slagle's (1971) *Artificial Intelligence: The Heuristic Programming Approach,* and Arbib's (1971) *The Metaphorical Brain: An Introduction to Cybernetics as Artificial Intelligence and Brain Theory.*] The field had reached its first self-conscious stage.

Anti-AI Literature. Speaking of self-consciousness, the 1970s also marked the beginnings of the first disharmonious chords to the technological symphony of AI authors. Dreyfus's (1972) first book, *What Computers Can't Do: A Critique of Artificial Reason* and Weizenbaum's (1976) *Computer Power and Human Reason: From Judgement to Calculation* sounded two notes of concern. AI was not going to be able to claim successes without being challenged that its results were misleading. A recent study of the philosophical aspects of AI and the limits of AI is Torrance's (1984) *The Mind and the Machine.*

LISP, the Programming Language of AI. The AI programming language LISP (qv) saw a number of new books appear. Whereas McCarthy's (1965) "Blue Book" *LISP 1.5 Programming's Manual* and Weissman's (1967) *LISP 1.5 Primer* were virtually the only LISP manuals available for the 1960s; Friedman's (1974) *The Little LISPer* (1976) Siklossy's (1976) *Let's Talk LISP,* Allen's (1978) *Anatomy of LISP,* and Meehan's (1979) *New UCI Lisp Manual* appeared in the 1970s as well as the Interlisp manual from XEROX, which appeared in several versions.

AI History Literature. In 1979 McCorduck's (1979) *Machines Who Think: A Personal Inquiry into the History and Prospects of Artificial Intelligence* became the field's first true history book. McCorduck effectively captured

the spirit and goals of AI up to that year. However, the field was evolving rapidly. The next few years would see a virtual explosion of work in AI as the new hardware and software displayed its potential for an ever larger audience of observers.

AI: THE 1980s

Books. The 1980s saw a number of substantial books on AI being released every year. During 1981–1982 the first truly comprehensive survey of AI, *The Handbook of Artificial Intelligence,* was compiled in three volumes (Barr and Feigenbaum, 1981; Cohen and Feigenbaum, 1982). This book, although now beginning to age slightly, is an unparalleled introductory exposition of the field and the single best starting source for someone trying to understand AI. AI also began to expand its horizons to include a growing applied and lay audience. *AI Magazine* published its first issue in 1980 as if to symbolize the beginning of this new view of AI.

Other significant books issued in the 1980s include a number in computational linguistics, such as: Marcus's (1980) *A Theory of Syntactic Recognition for Natural Language,* de Beaugrande's (1980) *Text, Discourse, and Process: Toward a Multidisciplinary Science of Texts,* Joshi and co-workers' (1981) *Elements of Discourse Understanding,* Sager's (1981) *Natural Language Information Processing: A Computer Grammar of English and its Applications,* Schank and Riesbeck's (1981) *Inside Computer Understanding: Five Programs Plus Miniatures,* Harris's (1982) *A Grammar of English on Mathematical Principles,* King's (1983) *Parsing Natural Language,* Winograd's (1983) *Language as a Cognitive Process,* Simmons's (1984) *Computations from the English,* Sowa's (1984) *Conceptual Structures: Information Processing in Mind and Machine,* and Sparck Jones's (1985) *Automatic Natural Language Parsing.*

In addition, general AI continued to see new books appearing every year, such as: Banerji's (1980) *Artificial Intelligence: A Theoretical Approach,* Nilsson's (1980) *Principles of Artificial Intelligence,* Rich's (1983) *Artificial Intelligence,* the second edition of Winston's ([1977] 1984) *Artificial Intelligence,* and Charniak and McDermott's (1985) *Introduction to Artificial Intelligence.*

LISP. The 1980s saw the introduction of many new LISP books, featuring more integrated approaches to using LISP for AI applications as in Charniak's (1980) *Artificial Intelligence Programming* and Winston and Horn's ([1981] 1984) *LISP,* rather than just describing the syntax of a particular dialect or tutoring beginners on how to write syntactically valid LISP code. LISP also became the subject of its own series of conferences, with the first being held at Stanford in 1980, *Conference Record of the 1980 LISP Conference* (The LISP Co., 1980). LISP underwent a dramatic increase in dialects as new versions for minicomputers [Franz LISP (Willensky, 1984)] and workstations [eg, Apollo's Portable Standard Lisp (PSL)] and even personal computers (eg, IQ LISP for the IBM PC) began to appear. DARPA exercised its influence to attempt to bring together the several dialects to LISP that existed, and *common Lisp* was coined as a term for this approved dialect. Steele's (1984) *Common LISP: The Language* describes this version, and the implementation called *golden common LISP* provides the PC counterpart.

Logic Programming and PROLOG. PROLOG (qv) first appeared as a book in Clocksin and Mellish's (1981) *Programming in Prolog* (see LOGIC PROGRAMMING). Unlike LISP, which appeared at a time when AI was not rapidly churning out books, PROLOG appeared at a time when AI's major form of publication was the book. Hence several new PROLOG books now appear every year. For example, Clark and Tarnlund's (1982) *Logic Programming,* Campbell's (1984) *Implementations of Prolog,* and Li's (1984) *A PROLOG Database System.*

The Fifth Generation. Since Feigenbaum and McCorduck (1983) published *The Fifth Generation: Artificial Intelligence and Japan's Computer Challenge to the World* the field of AI has not been the same (see COMPUTER SYSTEMS). This book, intended for a mass audience, sounded an alarm similar to the one sounded by the launching of *Sputnik* by the USSR in the 1950s. It was a call to U.S. industry and government to accept the fact that the Japanese had mastered computer technology to such a degree that without major commitments to research and development by the United States, they would become the dominant technological nation of the world. The very fact that the *Encyclopedia of AI* exists may be due to the response occasioned by this realization. A bibliography by Bramer and Bramer (1984), *The Fifth Generation: An Annotated Bibliography,* and an introduction by Shirai and Tsujii (1985), *Artificial Intelligence—Concepts, Techniques, and Applications,* drawn from the Japanese fifth-generation computer program appeared.

Expert Systems. Professionally, AI changed gears. An entire new audience tens or hundreds of times larger than the previous group of researchers focused attention on the new field of AI. Some shifts in the semantics of AI terminology occurred with expert systems, heretofore but one small methodology for AI research, becoming a more generic label apt to be applied to nearly any AI approach. A vast new crop of books designed to tutor newcomers to AI appeared. The book, in fact, became the standard means of publishing AI, with dozens of dissertations appearing as books rather than just as technical reports.

Among the books to have recently appeared dealing with expert systems are Hayes-Roth's (1983) *Building Expert Systems,* Bigger and Coupland's (1984) *Expert Systems: A Bibliography,* Forsyth's (1984) *Expert Systems: Principles and Case Studies,* Weiss and Kulikowski's (1984) *A Practical Guide to Designing Expert Systems,* and Naylor's (1985) *Build Your Own Expert System.*

AI in Business. Perhaps one of the most startling developments to have occurred in the AI field is the effort by businesspeople to understand the new technology. AI became a cover story in publications such as *Fortune* and *Time,* which even featured a computer as the "Man of the Year." Today, nearly every discipline's journals may contain articles on AI in an effort to explain how it will impact on fields from aviation through zoology. The NYU Symposium on Artificial Intelligence Applications for Business (Reitman, 1984) Johnson's (1984) *The Commercial Application of Expert Systems Technology,* Winston and Prendergast's (1984) *The AI Business: The Commercial Uses of Artificial Intelligence,* and Harmon's (1985) *Expert Systems—Artificial Intelligence in Business* all evidence this commercial trend.

Journals. A number of new journals started in 1983 to 1985. They include *Computational Intelligence/Intelligence Informatique, Expert Systems, Data and Knowledge Engineering, Future Generations Computer Systems (FGCS), Journal of Automated Reasoning, The International Journal of Intelligent Systems, The Journal of Logic Programming,* and *New Generation Computing.*

Newsletters. Several business-oriented newsletters, the sure earmark of an era of economic concern, appeared, including: *Applied Artificial Intelligence Reporter,* the *Spang Robinson Report,* and *Knowledge Engineering.*

Conferences. In 1980 the AAAI created its own conference series. Today, several new conference series have been started by local institutions and national AI conferences such as the Canadian AI conferences and European AI conferences have begun to proliferate. *The Proceedings of the First Conference of the European Chapter of the Association for Computational Linguistics* appeared in 1983 (Assoc. for Computational Linguistics, 1983). Morgan-Kaufmann Publishers have provided a single source for all of the IJCAI and AAAI proceedings, greatly simplifying access to these originally separately issued AI books.

However, AI has moved so rapidly into applications that new subsets of AI literature are separating from the mainstream and forming their own conferences and literatures. Robotics is certainly one such discipline. Medical AI is another. Computer vision, factory automation, military and space applications of AI, speech processing, educational uses of AI, and of course the businessman's interest in expert systems also seem to be evolving into separate AI spinoff literatures (see MANUFACTURING, AI IN; EARLY VISION; EDUCATION, AI IN; EXPERT SYSTEMS; MEDICINE, AI IN; MILITARY APPLICATIONS OF AI; ROBOTICS; SPEECH UNDERSTANDING).

Electronic Text. The development of the ARPANET as a mechanism for the communication within the AI community and early access to computer text-formatting facilities at many ARPANET sites led to the creation of online technical reports at a few major institutions such as MIT, Stanford, and CMU. The evolution of electronic-mail messages into electronic-mail digests has led to the creation of an AI electronic-news digest AILIST, by Laws at SRI-AI.ARPA and a separate mailing list for AI in Education AI-ED, by Richer at Stanford's SUMEX-AIM.ARPA. Other mailing lists such as the IRLIST, for information-retrieval news and the PHILOSOPHY-OF-SCIENCE mailing list further emphasize AI-related themes in their texts. In addition, there are numerous mailing lists for AI-related hardware and its accompanying software, such as the Symbolics LISP Users Group mailing list, SLUG, and other lists for other advanced work stations. A full list of the ARPANET mailing lists is available on the ARPANET at the Network Information Center.

THE FUTURE

What of the future of AI literature? Clearly the publication of standard reference works such as handbooks, encyclopedias, and even dictionaries seems likely. The periodical literature still lacks a coherent AI literature survey, but much progress has been made in volumes such as the *Bibliography of the AI Literature* (Rylko, 1984–1985).

Will AI develop new media any further than other disciplines have? The creation of a full-text AI literature database would seem reasonable, but this goal has eluded many other disciplines before AI. Microfiche seems an uncomfortable solution to the newer literature of AI, which is all created on electronic text-formatting machinery, yet only sees publication as printed paper disseminated via traditional methods.

The number of articles on AI published in magazines and journals seems to be growing rapidly with a count of AI articles in *The Business Periodicals Index* showing 15 articles in 1981–1982, only 6 in 1982–1983, but then jumping to 49 in 1983–1984 and 88 in 1984–1985.

It remains to be seen whether the AI literature will be as enduring as the literatures of the sciences or rather fall into a pattern more like that of engineering with rapid technological obsolescence. Most AIers would describe the AI literature of little more than a decade ago as largely only of historic interest today, yet more and more AI literature from this period is being made available every year as it is retroactively reissued by new publishers. Clearly the AI literature will continue to evolve as the field grows larger.

BIBLIOGRAPHY

J. Allen, *Anatomy of LISP*, McGraw-Hill Book Co., Inc., New York, 1978.

J. Anderson, and G. Bower, *Human Associative Memory*, Winston, Washington, D.C., 1973.

J. Anderson and G. Bower, *Human Associative Memory: A Brief Edition*, rev. ed., Erlbaum, Hillsdale, N.J., 1980.

M. A. Arbib, *The Metaphorical Brain: An Introduction to Cybernetics as Artificial Intelligence and Brain Theory*, John Wiley & Sons, Inc., New York, 1972.

Association for Computational Linguistics, *Proceedings of the First Conference of the European Chapter of the Association for Computational Linguistics*, 1983.

R. B. Banerji, *Theory of Problem Solving: An Approach to Artifical Intelligence*, Elsevier Science Publishing Co., Inc., New York, 1969.

R. B. Banerji, *Artificial Intelligence: A Theoretical Approach*, North-Holland, Amsterdam, The Netherlands, 1980.

A. Barr and E. Feigenbaum, *The Handbook of Artificial Intelligence*, Vols. 1–2, Morgan-Kaufmann, San Mateo, Calif., 1981.

C. J. Bigger and J. W. Coupland, *Expert Systems: A Bibliography*, Institution of Electrical Engineers, 1984.

D. G. Bobrow and A. Collins, eds., *Representation and Understanding*, Academic Press, Inc., New York, 1975.

M. A. Bramer, and D. Bramer, *The Fifth Generation: An Annotated Bibliography*, Addison-Wesley Publishing Co., Inc., Reading, Mass., 1984.

J. A. Campbell, ed., *Implementations of Prolog*, Ellis Horwood, 1984.

E. Charniak, *Artificial Intelligence Programming*, Lawrence Erlbaum, Hillsdale, N.J., 1980.

E. Charniak and D. V. McDermott, *Introduction to Artificial Intelligence*, Addison-Wesley Publishing Co., Inc., Reading, Mass., 1985.

E. Charniak and Y. Wilks, eds., *Computational Semantics: An Introduction to Artificial Intelligence and Natural Language Comprehension*, North-Holland, Amsterdam, The Netherlands, 1976.

K. L. Clark and S.-A. Tarnlund, eds., *Logic Programming*, Academic Press, Inc., New York, 1982.

W. F. Clocksin and C. S. Mellish, *Programming in Prolog*, Springer-Verlag, New York, 1981.

Cognitive Science Society, *Perspectives on Cognitive Science: Papers Presented at the First Annual Meeting of the Cognitive Science Society*, La Jolla, Calif., 1981.

P. R. Cohen and E. Feigenbaum, *The Handbook of Artificial Intelligence*, Vol. 3, Morgan-Kaufmann, San Mateo, Calif., 1982.

K. M. Colby, *Artificial Paranoia: A Computer Simulation of Paranoid Processes*, Pergamon, New York, 1974.

N. L. Collins and D. Michie, eds., *Machine Intelligence*, Vol. 1, Oliver and Boyd, London, 1967.

E. Dale and D. Michie, eds., *Machine Intelligence*, Vol. 2, Elsevier Science Publishing Co., Inc., New York, 1967.

R. de Beaugrande, *Text, Discourse, and Process: Toward A Multidisciplinary Science of Texts*, Ablex, Norwood, N.J., 1980.

H. L. Dreyfus, *What Computers Can't Do: A Critique of Artificial Reason*, Harper & Row, New York, 1972.

R. O. Duda and P. E. Hart, *Pattern Classification and Scene Analysis*, John Wiley & Sons, Inc., New York, 1973.

E. W. Elcock and D. Michie, eds., *Machine Intelligence*, Vol. 8, Halsted Press, a division of John Wiley & Sons, Inc., New York, 1977.

G. E. Ernst and A. Newell, *GPS: A Case Study in Generality and Problem Solving*, Academic Press, Inc., New York, 1969.

S. E. Fahlman, *NETL, A System for Representing and Using Real-World Knowledge*, MIT Press, Cambridge, Mass., 1979.

E. A. Feigenbaum and J. Feldman, eds., *Computers and Thought*, McGraw-Hill Book Co., Inc., New York, 1963.

E. A. Feigenbaum and P. McCorduck, *The Fifth Generation: Artificial Intelligence and Japan's Computer Challenge to the World*, Addison-Wesley Publishing Co., Inc., Reading, Mass., 1983.

N. V. Findler, ed., *Associative Networks: Representation and Use of Knowledge by Computers*, Academic Press, Inc., New York, 1979.

L. J. Fogel, *Artificial Intelligence through Simulated Evolution*, John Wiley & Sons, Inc., New York, 1967.

R. Forsyth, ed., *Expert Systems: Principles and Case Studies*, Chapman & Hall, London, 1984.

D. Friedman, *The Little LISPer*, Science Research Associates, Chicago, Ill., 1974.

P. Harman, *Expert Systems—Artificial Intelligence in Business,* John Wiley & Sons, Inc., New York, 1985.

Z. S. Harris, *A Grammar of English on Mathematical Principles,* John Wiley & Sons, Inc., New York, 1982.

J. E. Hayes, D. Michie, and L. I. Mikulich, eds., *Machine Intelligence,* Vol. 9, Halsted Press, a division of John Wiley & Sons, Inc., New York, 1979.

J. E. Hayes, D. Michie, and Y. H. Pao, eds., *Machine Intelligence,* Vol. 10, Halsted Press, a division of John Wiley & Sons, Inc., New York, 1982.

J. E. Hayes, D. Michie, and J. Richards, eds., *Machine Intelligence,* Vol. 11, Oxford University Press, Oxford, UK, 1986.

F. Hayes-Roth, D. A. Waterman, and D. B. Lenat (eds.), *Building Expert Systems,* Addison-Wesley Publishing Co., Inc., Reading, Mass., 1983.

P. C. Jackson, *Introduction to Artificial Intelligence,* Masor./Charter, 1974.

T. Johnson, *The Commercial Application of Expert Systems Technology,* Ovum, London, 1984.

A. Joshi, B. Webber, and I. Sag, eds., *Elements of Discourse Understanding,* Cambridge University Press, Cambridge, UK, 1981.

M. King, ed., *Parsing Natural Language,* Academic Press, Inc., New York, 1983.

D. Li, *A PROLOG Database System,* Research Studies, Addison-Wesley Publishing Co., Inc., Reading, Mass., 1984.

P. H. Lindsay and D. A. Norman, *Human Information Processing: An Introduction to Psychology,* 2nd ed., Academic Press, Inc., New York, 1977.

The LISP Company, *Conference Record of the 1980 Stanford LISP Conference,* Santa Clara, Calif., 1980.

J. McCarthy, *Lisp 1.5 Programmer's Manual.* MIT Press, Cambridge, Mass., 1965.

P. McCorduck, *Machines Who Think, A Personal Inquiry into the History and Prospects of Artificial Intelligence,* W. H. Freeman, San Francisco, Calif., 1979.

W. McCulloch and W. Pitts, "A Logical Calculus of the Ideas Immanent in Nervous Activity," *Bull. Math. Biophys.* (1943).

M. P. Marcus, *A Theory of Syntactic Recognition for Natural Language,* MIT Press, Cambridge, Mass., 1980.

J. R. Meehan, *New UCI LISP Manual,* Lawrence Erlbaum, Hillsdale, N.J., 1979.

B. Meltzer and D. Michie, eds., *Machine Intelligence,* Vol. 4, Elsevier Science Publishing Co., Inc., New York, 1969.

B. Meltzer and D. Michie, eds., *Machine Intelligence,* Vol. 5, Elsevier Science Publishing Co., Inc., New York, 1970.

B. Meltzer and D. Michie, eds., *Machine Intelligence,* Vol. 6, Elsevier Science Publishing Co., Inc., New York, 1971.

B. Meltzer and D. Michie, eds., *Machine Intelligence,* Vol. 7, John Wiley & Sons, Inc., New York, 1977.

D. Michie, ed., *Machine Intelligence,* Vol. 3, Elsevier Science Publishing Co., Inc., New York, 1968.

G. A. Miller and P. N. Johnson-Laird, *Language and Perception,* Harvard University Press, Belknap, Cambridge, Mass., 1976.

M. L. Minsky, ed., *Semantic Information Processing,* MIT Press, Cambridge, Mass., 1968.

M. L. Minsky and S. Papert, *Perceptrons,* MIT Press, Cambridge, Mass., 1968.

C. Naylor, *Build Your Own Expert System,* John Wiley & Sons, Inc., New York, 1985.

A. Newell, J. C. Shaw, and H. A. Simon, "Chess Playing Programs and the Problem of Complexity," in E. A. Feigenbaum and J. Feldman, eds., *Computers and Thought,* McGraw-Hill Book Co., Inc., New York, 1958.

N. J. Nilsson, *Problem Solving Methods in Artificial Intelligence,* McGraw-Hill Book Co., Inc., New York, 1971.

N. J. Nilsson, *Principles of Artificial Intelligence,* Tioga, Palo Alto, Calif., 1980.

D. A. Norman and D. E. Rumelhart, *Explorations in Cognition,* W. H. Freeman, San Francisco, Calif., 1975.

M. R. Quillian, "The Teachable Language Comprehender: A Simulation Program and the Theory of Language," *CACM* **12,** 459–476 (1969).

W. Reitman, ed., *Artificial Intelligence Applications for Business: Proceedings of the NYU Symposium, May, 1983,* Ablex, Norwood, N.J., 1984.

A. Rosenblueth, N. Wiener, and J. Bigelow, "Behavior, Purpose, and Teleology," *Philos. Sci.* **10**(1), 18–24 (1943).

R. Rustin, ed., *Natural Language Processing,* Algorithmics, New York, 1973.

H. M. Rylko, ed., *Artificial Intelligence: Bibliographic Summaries of the Select Literature,* Vols. 1–2, The Report Store, Lawrence, Kans., 1984–1985.

N. Sager, *Natural Language Information Processing: A Computer Grammar of English and Its Applications,* Addison-Wesley Publishing Co., Inc., Reading, Mass., 1981.

R. C. Schank, *Conceptual Information Processing,* Elsevier Science Publishing Co., Inc., New York, 1975.

R. C. Schank and R. P. Abelson, *Scripts, Plans, Goals, and Understanding,* Lawrence Erlbaum, Hillsdale, N.J., 1977.

R. C. Schank and K. M. Colby, eds., *Computer Models of Thought and Language,* W. H. Freeman, San Francisco, Calif., 1973.

R. C. Schank and C. K. Riesbeck, eds., *Inside Computer Understanding: Five Programs Plus Miniatures,* Lawrence Erlbaum, Hillsdale, N.J., 1981.

C. Shannon, "A Chess-Playing Machine," *Sci. Am.* **182,** 48–51 (Feb. 1950a).

C. Shannon, "Programming a Computer for Playing Chess," *Philos. Mag., Ser. 7* **41,** 265–275 (1950b).

C. Shannon and J. McCarthy, *Annals of Mathematical Studies,* Vol. 34, *Automata Studies,* Princeton University Press, Princeton, N.J., 1956.

Y. Shirai and J. Tsujii, and F. R. D. Apps, *Artifical Intelligence: Concepts, Techniques, and Applications,* John Wiley & Sons, Inc., New York, 1985.

L. Siklossy, *Let's Talk LISP,* Prentice-Hall, Inc., Englewood Cliffs, N.J., 1976.

R. F. Simmons, "Answering English Questions by Computer: A Survey," *CACM* **8,** 53–70 (Jan. 1965).

R. F. Simmons, "Natural Language Question Answering Systems: 1969," *CACM* **13,** 15–30 (Jan. 1970).

R. F. Simmons, *Computations from the English,* Prentice-Hall, Inc., Englewood Cliffs, N.J., 1984.

R. F. Simmons and J. Slocum, "Generating English Discourse from Semantic Networks," *CACM* **15,** 891–905 (1972).

H. A. Simon, *Sciences of the Artificial,* MIT Press, Cambridge, Mass., 1969.

J. R. Slagle, "A Heuristic Program That Solves Symbolic Integration Problems in Freshman Calculus," *J. Assoc. Comput. Mach.* **10,** 507–520 (1963).

J. R. Slagle, *Artificial Intelligence: The Heuristic Programming Approach,* McGraw-Hill Book Co., Inc., New York, 1971.

J. R. Slagle and J. K. Dixon, "Experiments with Some Programs That Search Game Trees," *J. Assoc. Comput. Mach.* **16**, 189–207 (1969).

J. F. Sowa, *Conceptual Structures: Information Processing in Mind and Machine,* Addison-Wesley Publishing Co., Inc., Reading, Mass., 1984.

K. Sparck Jones and Y. Wilks, eds., *Automatic Natural Language Parsing,* John Wiley & Sons, Inc., New York, 1985.

G. L. Steele Jr., *Common Lisp: The Language,* Digital, Burlington, Mass., 1984.

S. Torrance, *The Mind and The Machine,* John Wiley & Sons, Inc., New York, 1984.

A. Turing, "Intelligent Machinery," in B. Meltzer and D. Michie, eds., *Machine Intelligence,* Vol. 5, Elsevier Science Publishing Co., Inc., New York, [1947] 1970.

A. Turing, "Computing Machinery and Intelligence," in E. A. Feigenbaum and J. Feldman, eds., *Computers and Thought,* McGraw-Hill Book Co., Inc., New York, [1950] 1963.

D. E. Walker, ed., *Understanding Spoken Language,* North-Holland, New York, 1978.

S. M. Weiss and C. A. Kulikowski, *A Practical Guide to Designing Expert Systems,* Rowman and Allanheld, Totowa, N.J., 1984.

C. Weissman, *LISP 1.5 Primer,* Dickensen, Belmont, Calif., 1967.

J. Weizenbaum, "ELIZA—A Computer Program for the Study of Natural Language Communication between Man and Machine," *CACM* **9**, 36–45 (1966).

J. Weizenbaum, *Computer Power and Human Reason: From Judgement to Calculation,* W. H. Freeman, San Francisco, Calif., 1976.

N. Wiener, *Cybernetics: Or Control and Communication in the Animal and the Machine,* MIT Press, Cambridge, Mass., [1948] 1961.

R. Wilensky, *LISPCraft,* W. W. Norton & Co., New York, 1984.

T. Winograd, *Understanding Natural Language,* Academic Press, Inc., New York, 1972.

T. Winograd, *Language as a Cognitive Process, Vol. 1, Syntax.* Addison-Wesley Publishing Co., Inc., Reading, Mass., 1983.

P. H. Winston, ed., *The Psychology of Computer Vision,* McGraw-Hill Book Co., Inc., New York, 1975.

P. H. Winston, *Artificial Intelligence,* Addison-Wesley Publishing Co., Inc., Reading, Mass., [1977] 1984.

P. H. Winston and B. K. P. Horn, *Lisp,* Addison-Wesley Publishing Co., Inc., Reading, Mass., [1981] 1984.

P. Winston and K. A. Prendergast, eds., *The AI Business: The Commercial Uses of Artificial Intelligence,* MIT Press, Cambridge, Mass., 1984.

W. A. Woods, "Transition Network Grammars for Natural Language Analysis," *CACM* **13**, 591–606 (1970).

General References

Microfiche Collections

SDL. AI Microfiche Collections, Scientific Datalink, New York. Collections are from The AI Laboratory (MIT), Stanford University, University of Illinois, Edinburgh University, University of Rochester, Yale University, Carnegie-Mellon University, SRI International, Purdue University, University of Maryland, Rutgers University, Bold Bernaek & Newman, ISI, and Stanford KSL.

Journals

AI Magazine, American Association for Artificial Intelligence, Menlo Park, Calif.

The American Journal of Computational Linguistics.

Artificial Intelligence: An International Journal, North-Holland, Amsterdam, The Netherlands.

Communications of the Association for Computing Machinery (CACM), Association for Computing Machinery, New York.

Computational Intelligence/Intelligence of Informatique, National Research Council of Canada, Ottawa, Canada.

Computational Linguistics, Association for Computational Linguistics, Bell Communications Research, Morristown, N.J.

Computers and the Humanities, North-Holland, Amsterdam, The Netherlands.

Data and Knowledge Engineering, Elsevier Science Publishing Co., Inc., New York.

Expert Systems, Learned Information, Medford, N.J.

Future Generations Computer Systems (FGCS), Elsevier Science Publishing Co., Inc., New York.

International Journal of Intelligence Systems, John Wiley & Sons, Inc., New York.

International Journal of Man-Machine Studies, Academic Press, Inc., New York.

Journal of the Association for Computing Machinery, Association for Computing Machinery, New York.

Journal of Automated Reasoning, Kluwer Academic, Hingham, Mass.

Journal of Logic Programming, Elsevier Science Publishing Co., Inc., New York.

Mechanical Translation and Computational Linguistics (1965–1968).

MT: Mechanical Translation (1954–1964).

New Generation Computing, Springer-Verlag, New York.

Newsletters

Applied Artificial Intelligence Reporter, Intelligent Computer Systems Research Institute, Fort Lee, N.J.

Finite String (1964–1973) (now included in the *Journal Computational Linguistics*).

Knowledge Engineering, Richmond Publishing Corp., New York.

The Spang Robinson Report, Spang Robinson Report, Palo Alto, Calif.

Conference Proceedings Series

American Association for Artificial Intelligence, *National Conferences on Artificial Intelligence,* AAAI, Menlo Park, Calif.

Association of Computational Linguistics, *Proceedings of the International Conferences on Computational Linguistics,* ACL, Morristown, N.J.

Canadian Society for Computational Studies of Intelligence, *Proceedings of the CSCSI/SCEIO National Conference: Computational Studies in Intelligence.*

International Joint Conferences on Artificial Intelligence, *Proceedings of the IJCAI,* Morgan-Kaufmann, San Mateo, Calif.

R. A. AMSLER
Bell Communications Research

LOCAL FEATURE DETECTION. See EDGE AND LOCAL FEATURE DETECTION.

LOCOMOTION. See Robots, legged; Robots, mobile.

LOGIC

THE NATURE OF LOGIC

A central concern of logic is to take a situation described by a particular set of statements that are assumed, supposed, or otherwise accepted as true and then to determine what other statements must also be true in that situation. These other true statements are implicit in that situation and are, thus, said to be implied by the original ones. Thus, logic can be used to make implicitly true statements explicit. The original statements are called premises, the "new" statements are called conclusions, and the process of making conclusions explicit is called inference.

One natural criterion for such inference is to be truth preserving. Deductive logic employs inferential methods that achieve this goal: A deductive argument—a set of premises and a conclusion inferred from them—is said to be valid iff any situation in which the premises are (assumed to be) true is thereby also a situation in which the conclusion is (assumed to be) true.

The rules for determining when a statement is true in a situation are among the concerns of semantics. A valid argument whose premises are in fact true is said to be sound. However, the determination of the actual truth value of a given statement is beyond the scope of both logic and semantics; it is either subject-matter specific or else depends on observation (empirical investigation). It should be noted that "actual truth," or correspondence to "facts" in the actual world, is not required. Statements can merely be assumed to be true, or taken as if true, and deduction proceed from there.

The rules for inferring a statement from other statements can be arbitrary relations among statements serving as premises and conclusions. The study of such rules is among the concerns of syntax. It is a not always reachable ideal of logic that syntactic and semantic methods should "overlap":

1. that all statements syntactically inferrable from others (ie, those conclusions that follow from premises according to rules of inference) also be validly inferrable from them, that is, that the conclusions be true if the premises are;
2. that all statements semantically inferrable from others (including those that are tautologies—true in all situations) be syntactically inferrable from them (or be theorems).

A perfect overlap, in which both 1 and 2 hold, is referred to as completeness (qv) of the logic in question.

SYSTEMS OF LOGIC

Traditionally, systems of logic have been classified as either inductive or deductive. Inductive logics employ inferential methods that can fall short of truth preservation. They are used for reasoning in situations where there is incomplete information, such that only statistical or provisional conclusions can be drawn. For example, inductive inference (qv) might only guarantee that a conclusion is highly likely to follow from given premises. Nonmonotonic logics can be considered to fall under this category.

Besides the standard propositional and predicate logics, there are several varieties of deductive logics: Modal logics deal with the concepts of necessity and possibility; epistemic and doxastic logics deal with the concepts of knowledge and belief, respectively; deontic logics deal with moral notions such as obligation and permission; erotetic logics are the logics of questions; and there are also several logics of commands. Relevance logics and logics of counterfactual conditionals deal with more subtle analyses of the if–then connective. (Relevance logic is historically related to the development of modal logic.) Deductive logics need not be limited to the two truth values of truth and falsity: There are many-valued logics and logics with truth value "gaps" (for dealing with statements whose truth values are not determinable). Nor need deductive logics be limited to what actually exists or whether anything exists: There are logics of nonexistent objects (including fictional objects), logics for dealing with inconsistent situations (Rescher and Brandom, 1979), and free logics (logics that are free of existence presuppositions).

Discussions of many of these logics and references to the literature may be found in the articles on logic in this encyclopedia. An especially good survey is Gabbay and Guenthner (1983), and issues of the *Journal of Philosophical Logic* frequently contain articles of relevance to AI.

LOGIC AND ARTIFICIAL INTELLIGENCE

The relevance of logic to AI should be clear. First, logic is at the heart of reasoning, and reasoning is at the heart of intelligence. Since so much is known about the nature of logical reasoning, and since its algorithmic nature has been well-studied, it was one of the earliest and most successful targets of AI researchers [eg, the Logic Theorist (Newell and co-workers, 1963) and the method of resolution (qv) (Robinson, 1979)]. Second, the wide variety of systems of logic offers an equally wide variety of formats for representing information (together with built-in inference mechanisms). Thus, the expressive power of various logics has become one of the central aspects of the field of knowledge representation (qv).

Because actual human reasoning is often not logical (Kahneman, Slovic, and Tversky, 1982) and because some researchers have perceived or misperceived standard logic to be overly formal or limiting, several AI researchers have disdained the use of logic. This has given rise to what has been called the "neat–scruffy debate." In a survey article, Kolata (1982) characterized these two positions as follows: The so-called neat approach to AI "is to design computer programs to reason according to well worked out languages of mathematical logic, whether or not that is actually the way people think"; John McCarthy and Patrick Hayes are among the leading proponents of this approach. The so-called scruffy "approach is to try to get computers to imitate the way the human mind works which . . . is almost certainly not with mathematical logic;" Marvin Minsky and Roger Schank are among the leading proponents of this approach. Thus, neatness is associated with formality, mathematics, and logic, and scruffiness is associated with psychological validity. Scruffy methods are attacked as being not well-defined, whereas neat methods are attacked as being overly defined, hence not flexible enough. Neat methods are seen as artificial and unable to handle certain phenomena, such as default reasoning or nonmonotonicity; yet surely any realm that is amenable to algorithmic treatment is thereby formalizable. On the scruffy side, automatic theorem provers (see THEOREM PROVING) and general problem solvers (see PROBLEM SOLVING) are objected to on the grounds that they are not intelligent or that they are too general; as one neat-sympathizer paraphrases the scruffy position, "classical theorem-provers know very little about what to do, and are incapable of being told it" (Hayes, 1977). On the neat side, logic, because of its semantics, is considered to be "the most successful precise language ever developed to express human thought and inference" (Hayes, 1977). Logic "*justifies* inferences," whereas a processor "*performs* inferences" (Hayes, 1977). The two are independent, and the way in which the processor infers need not be an automated theorem prover. The neat–scruffy dispute overlaps another dispute about the goals of AI: so-called weak AI tries to "simulate" human intelligent behavior without attempting to do it in precisely the way humans do, without attempting to be psychologically accurate; so-called strong AI tries to "emulate" human intelligent behavior, to be psychologically accurate (Searle, 1980). Thus, perhaps, the real issue in the neat–scruffy debate is a dispute over the level at which logic or psychology enters into the analysis and solution of problems in AI. [But see Cherniak (1984) for a recent argument concerning computational limitations on neatness, and see Levesque (1987), Nilsson (1991), and Birnbaum (1991) for recent neat–scruffy debates.]

GUIDE TO LOGIC ARTICLES IN THIS ENCYCLOPEDIA

The following articles provide more references and more detailed discussions of logic, reasoning, and inference, and their relations to AI:

BIBLIOGRAPHY

L. Birnbaum, "Rigor Mortis: A Response to Nilsson's 'Logic and Artificial Intelligence'," *Artifi. Intell.* **47**, 57–177 (1991).

C. Cherniak, "Computational Complexity and the Universal Acceptance of Logic," *J. Philos.* **81**, 739–758 (1984).

D. Gabbay and F. Guenthner, *Handbook of Philosophical Logic*, 4 vols., D. Reidel, Dordrecht, 1983.

P. J. Hayes, "In Defence of Logic," *Proceedings of the Fifth International Joint Conference on Artificial Intelligence*, Cambridge, Mass., Morgan-Kaufmann, San Mateo, Calif., 1977, pp. 559–565.

D. Kahneman, P. Slovic, and A. Tversky, *Judgment under Uncertainty: Heuristics and Biases*, Cambridge University Press, Cambridge, U.K., 1982.

G. Kolata, "How Can Computers Get Common Sense?" *Science* **217**, 1237–1238 (1982).

H. Levesque, ed., "Taking Issue/Forum: A Critique of Pure Reason," *Comput. Intell.* **3**, 147–237 (1987).

A. Newell, J. C. Shaw, and H. A. Simon, "Empirical Explorations with the Logic Theory Machine: A Case Study in Heuristics," in E. A. Feigenbaum and J. Feldman, eds., *Computers and Thought*, McGraw-Hill, New York, 1963.

N. J. Nilsson, "Logic and Artificial Intelligence," *Artif. Intell.* **47**, 31–56 (1991).

N. Rescher and R. Brandom, *The Logic of Inconsistency: A Study in Non-Standard Possible-World Semantics and Ontology*, Rowman and Littlefield, Totawa, N.J., 1979.

J. A. Robinson, *Logic: Form and Function; The Mechanization of Deductive Reasoning*, Elsevier North-Holland, New York, 1979.

J. R. Searle, "Minds, Brains, and Programs," *Behav. Brain Sci.* **3**, 417–457 (1980).

General References

J. McCarthy, "Epistemological Problems of Artificial Intelligence," *Proceedings of the Fifth International Joint Conference on Artificial Intelligence*, Cambridge, Mass., Morgan-Kaufmann, San Mateo, Calif., 1977, pp. 1038–1044.

R. C. Moore, "Problems in Logical Form," *Proc. ACL* **19**, 117–124 (1981).

P. Wallich, "AI Specialists Debate Logic at Conference," *IEEE The Institute* **7**, 2 (Nov. 1983).

W. J. RAPAPORT
SUNY at Buffalo

LOGIC AND DEPICTION

Logic-based tools have been widely used in artificial intelligence. Many cognitive areas, for example, language understanding, robot planning, commonsense reasoning, and problem solving (qv) have benefited from various uses of logic. However, the perceptual areas, such as computational vision have not generally been seen as amenable to logic-based approaches. In this article, a theory of depiction is outlined within a framework for image interpretation tasks (Reiter and Mackworth, 1989). The theory has two sets of goals: scientific and engineering. The scientific goals include understanding the concept of an interpretation of an image and understanding the role constraint satisfaction (qv) plays in image interpretation. The engineering goals include the provision of tools for specifying the behavior of image interpretation systems and tools for verifying that a system meets its specification. Potential benefits include the advantages of a common framework for vision and graphics systems and the provision of more modular and portable systems.

The methods proposed are based on a two-domain theory of perception. For any perceptual task at least two domains must be distinguished: the signal domain and the referent domain (or, for deconstructionists, the signifier and the signified). For vision the image domain and the scene domain are initially distinguished. All objects are either image objects or scene objects. Given those domains axioms can be written down in, say, first-order logic, constraining the image and scene objects. For a given application there are three classes of general axioms: image axioms I, scene axioms S, and mapping axioms M. Axioms in I mention only image domain objects and their attributes and relations. Similarly, axioms in S are confined to describing legitimate scenes. Each axiom in M mentions objects in both domains; it may use a reserved predicate $\Delta(i,s)$ signifying that image object i depicts scene object s. If the theory is to be used for image interpretation axioms that describe the particular image to be interpreted, I_0 are also required. The theory states that an interpretation of an image corresponds to a logical model of the set of axioms $I_o \cup I \cup S \cup M$. This provides a formal task specification for image interpretation. This specification is then refined by model-preserving transformations to a provably correct implementation that computes all or some of the interpretations of the image.

The theory is illustrated with a specification in first-order logic of a simple sketch map interpretation task.

Consider the sketch maps shown in Figure 1. For this task each region must depict a land area or water area and each chain of line segments must depict a road, a river, or a shore. Roads and rivers appear only on land; shores separate land and water. Rivers must flow into other rivers or shores. Given that background knowledge the image in Figure 1a depicts one of three possible scenes. Either regions r_1 and r_2 both depict land while chain c_1 depicts a road; r_1 depicts land (an island), r_2 depicts water, and c_1 depicts a shore; or finally, r_1 depicts water (a lake), r_2 depicts land, and c_1 depicts a shore. For this application I consists of taxonomy axioms (eg, "each image object is a chain or a region"). I_o consists of a description of the image in terms of primitive predicates ("chain c_1 bounds region r_1") and closure axioms (eg, "c_1 is the only chain"). S consists of taxonomy axioms ("each linear-scene-object is a road, a river, or a shore"), and general scene knowledge ("the inside area of a shoreline is land if and only if its outside is water" and "rivers lead to other rivers or shores"). The mapping knowledge M includes axioms such as "each image object i depicts a unique scene object $\sigma(i)$," "depiction holds only between image and scene objects," "a chain depicts a linear-scene-object," and the like. Given that specification it is possible to refine it to an equivalent formula in propositional logic by eliminating the quantifiers over finite domains and various other database-oriented transformations. To find all the visual interpretations it is necessary only to find all the logical models of that formula using standard SAT or CSP techniques (see CONSTRAINT SATISFACTION).

For the map domain these models all share in common fixed extensions of all the image, scene, and mapping predicates except $ROAD(.)$, $RIVER(.)$, $SHORE(.)$, $LAND(.)$ and $WATER(.)$. For the example in Figure 1a the three models correspond to the descriptions:

$$LAND(\sigma(r_1)) \wedge LAND(\sigma(r_2)) \wedge ROAD(\sigma(c_1))$$

$$WATER(\sigma(r_1)) \wedge LAND(\sigma(r_2)) \wedge SHORE(\sigma(c_1))$$

$$LAND(\sigma(r_1)) \wedge WATER(\sigma(r_2)) \wedge SHORE(\sigma(c_1))$$

For the map shown in Figure 1b there are four possible interpretations corresponding to:

$$LAND(\sigma(r_1)) \wedge LAND(\sigma(r_2)) \wedge ROAD(\sigma(c_1))$$
$$\wedge ROAD(\sigma(c_2)) \wedge ROAD(\sigma(c_3))$$

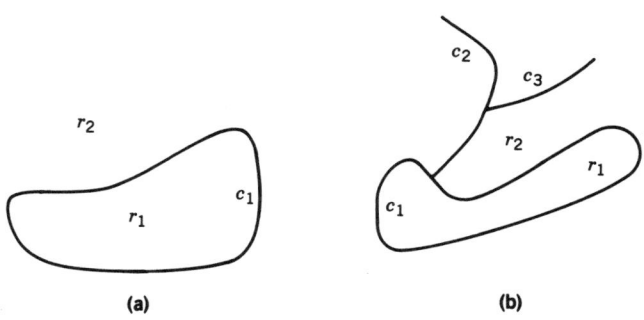

Figure 1. Two simple maps.

$$WATER(\sigma(r_1)) \wedge LAND(\sigma(r_2)) \wedge SHORE(\sigma(c_1))$$
$$\wedge ROAD(\sigma(c_2)) \wedge ROAD(\sigma(c_3))$$

$$WATER(\sigma(r_1)) \wedge LAND(\sigma(r_2)) \wedge SHORE(\sigma(c_1))$$
$$\wedge RIVER(\sigma(c_2)) \wedge ROAD(\sigma(c_3))$$

$$WATER(\sigma(r_1)) \wedge LAND(\sigma(r_2)) \wedge SHORE(\sigma(c_1))$$
$$\wedge RIVER(\sigma(c_2)) \wedge RIVER(\sigma(c_3))$$

Image interpretation is just an instance of the task of evidential reasoning. In general, suppose there is a system S whose system description is available as a set of first-order sentences SD. Given a set of observations of the system Obs the task is to determine a description of the system's internal state $State$ chosen from a set of possible internal states $States$. This characterization of evidential reasoning tasks covers, for example, both image interpretation and diagnosis.

There are essentially two competing logical frameworks for solving such tasks: consistency based and abductive (Poole, 1989a). The consistency-based approach allows any $State \in States$ such that $SD \cup Obs \cup \{State\}$ is consistent (Reiter, 1987; de Kleer and co-workers, 1990). The abductive approach imposes the stronger requirements that $SD \cup \{State\}$ be consistent and $SD \cup \{State\} \models Obs$. The logical framework for depiction and image interpretation described above is a consistency-based theory. The abductive approach is typified by Theorist (Poole and co-workers, 1987). Poole (1989b) describes how to implement in Theorist a system for map interpretation using essentially the same image domain, scene domain, and mapping knowledge.

BIBLIOGRAPHY

J. de Kleer, A. K. Mackworth, and R. Reiter, "Characterizing Diagnoses," in *Proceedings of the Ninth National Conference on Artificial Intelligence*, Boston, AAAI, Menlo Park, Calif., 1990, pp. 324–330.

D. L. Poole, "Normality and Faults in Logic-Based Diagnosis," in *Proceedings of the Eleventh IJCAI*, Detroit, Mich., Morgan-Kaufmann, San Mateo, Calif., 1989a, pp. 1304–1310.

D. L. Poole, "A Methodology for Using a Default and Abductive Reasoning System," TR89-20, Department of Computer Science, University of British Columbia, Vancouver, B.C., 1989b.

D. L. Poole, R. G. Goebel, and R. Aleliunas, "Theorist: A Logical Reasoning System for Defaults and Diagnosis," in N. Cercone and G. McCalla, eds., *The Knowledge Frontier: Essays in the Representation of Knowledge*, Springer-Verlag, New York, 1987, pp. 331–352.

R. Reiter, "A Theory of Diagnosis from First Principles," *Artif. Intell.* **32**, 57–95 (1987).

R. Reiter and A. K. Mackworth, "A Logical Framework for Depiction and Image Interpretation," *Artif. Intell.* **41**, 125–155 (1989).

ALAN K. MACKWORTH
University of British Columbia
at Vancouver

LOGIC, CONDITIONAL

Conditional logic examines the proof theory and semantics for ordinary conditionals in natural language. Contemporary work in this area is motivated by the so-called paradoxes of material implication and by the apparent non truth-functionality of many ordinary conditionals. A standard formal language for representing the logical structure of conditionals has been developed, and several conditional logics have gained widespread attention. Both possible worlds and probabilistic semantics have been proposed as alternatives to the classic truth functional account of conditionals. Within the artificial intelligence community there have been several efforts to develop nonmonotonic reasoning systems based on conditional logic (see REASONING, NONMONOTONIC).

PROBLEMS WITH MATERIAL IMPLICATION

The typical conditional has the structure "If A, then C" where A is called the antecedent and C the consequent of the conditional. The classic treatment of conditionals translates ordinary language conditionals into *material conditionals*. A material conditional, represented $A \supset C$, is a compound expression of which the truth value is a function of the truth values of its antecedent and consequent as defined by Table 1. $A \supset C$ is true whenever A is false or C is true, and this is the source of the so-called paradoxes of implication. Where A is the false sentence "Shakespeare didn't write *Hamlet*" and C is the sentence "Someone other than Shakespeare wrote *Hamlet*," both the material conditional $A \supset C$ and the corresponding English conditional

1. If Shakespeare didn't write *Hamlet,* then someone else wrote *Hamlet*

are true. But if the mood of sentence 1 is changed from indicative to subjunctive, the resulting English conditional

2. If Shakespeare had not written *Hamlet,* then someone else would have written *Hamlet*.

is at least improbable. Perhaps indicative conditionals can be represented as material conditionals, but most conditionals in the subjunctive mood cannot. The problem is not that the material conditional is the wrong truth function for representing English subjunctive conditionals; these conditionals cannot be represented by any truth function. Consider the following four conditionals:

Table 1.

A	C	$A \supset C$
t	t	t
t	f	f
f	t	t
f	f	t

3. If the polar ice caps had recently melted, Venice would be under water.

4. If the polar ice caps had recently melted, Venice would be in the southern hemisphere.

5. If the polar ice caps had recently melted, Venice would be in the northern hemisphere.

6. If the polar ice caps had recently melted, Venice would have a large population.

All of these conditionals have the same false antecedent. Sentences 3 and 4 have a false consequent and sentences 5 and 6 have a true consequent, but sentences 3 and 5 are true whereas sentences 4 and 6 are false. Thus the truth value of a subjunctive conditional is not in general a function of the truth values of its antecedent and consequent, at least when the antecedent is false.

Because the difficulty with a truth functional account of conditionals in ordinary language is so vividly portrayed by examples like those in the previous paragraph, examples all having false antecedents, conditional logic was early identified with the logic of counterfactual conditionals. The situation is not so simple. Some theorists argue that conditionals in the indicative mood are truth functional and others argue that some conditionals in the subjunctive mood or in the future tense are not truth functional even in those cases where the antecedent is true. This suggests that conditional logic rather than counterfactual logic is the more appropriate term for the field.

PROOF THEORY

Most work in conditional logic assumes a formal language that is sentential or propositional. The primitive symbols of this language consist of a countably infinite set of sentence letters $P_1, P_2, P_3, \ldots$; truth functional operators $\neg, \wedge, \vee, \supset, \equiv$; and a special binary conditional operator $>$. All the sentence letters are sentences of this language, and if A and B are sentences, then so are $\neg A, A \wedge B, A \vee B, A \supset B, A \equiv B$, and $A > B$. Nothing is a sentence unless it can be constructed by some finite number of applications of these principles. A conditional logic Σ is a set of sentences that contains all tautologies and is closed under *modus ponens*: from $A \supset B$ and A, to infer B. Conditional logics are typically characterized by some additional set of inference rules and axioms. Among the rules and axioms proposed for conditional logic are the following.

RCEC: From $A \equiv B$, to infer $(C > A) \equiv (C > B)$

RCK: From $(A_1 \wedge \ldots \wedge A_n) \supset B$, to infer $[(C > A_1) \wedge \ldots \wedge (C > A_n)] \supset (C > B), n \geq 0$

ID: $A > A$

MP: $(A > B) \supset (A \supset B)$

MOD: $(\neg A > A) \supset (B > A)$

CSO: $[(A > B) \wedge (B > A)] \supset [(A > C) \equiv (B > C)]$

CV: $[(A > B) \wedge \neg(A > \neg C)] \supset [(A \wedge C) > B]$

CS: $(A \wedge B) \supset (A > B)$

CA: $[(A > B) \wedge (C > B)] \supset [(A \vee C) > B]$

CEM: $(A > B) \vee (A > \neg B)$

RCEC says that one of two provably equivalent sentences can be substituted for the other in the consequent of a conditional, and RCK supports a kind of conditional detachment. MP is so named because it supports a detachment rule for conditionals as a derived inference rule that is similar to *modus ponens*. A model sentence $\Box A$, which is read as "A is necessarily true," is often defined by the equivalence $\Box A \equiv (\neg A > A)$. Using this defined operator, MOD becomes $\Box A \supset (B > A)$. Thus if A is necessary, then A would be true if B were true no matter what B might be. CSO ensures that conditionally (counterfactually) equivalent sentences have the same (counterfactual) consequences. CEM is an acronym for conditional excluded middle.

The following five conditional logics are representative of the kinds of systems that have been defined in the literature.

$$\mathbf{V} = <\text{RCEC,RCK;ID,MOD,CSO,CV}>$$
$$\mathbf{VW} = <\text{RCEC,RCK;ID,MP,MOD,CSO,CV}>$$
$$\mathbf{VC} = <\text{RCEC,RCK;ID,MP,MOD,CSO,CV,CS}>$$
$$\mathbf{SS} = <\text{RCEC,RCK;ID,MP,MOD,CSO,CA,CS}>$$
$$\mathbf{C2} = <\text{RCEC,RCK;ID,MP,MOD,CSO,CV,CEM}>$$

Where Σ is any one of these five systems and Γ is any set of sentences, a "proof from Γ in Σ" is defined as a sequence of sentences satisfying the condition that each sentence in the proof is either a member of Γ, a tautology, a substitution instance of one of the axioms of Σ, or follows from earlier members of the proof by *modus ponens* or by one of the other inference rules for Σ. A is derivable from Γ in Σ (in symbols, $\Gamma \vdash_\Sigma A$) if and only if there is a proof from Γ in Σ of which the last member is A. A is a theorem of Σ (in symbols, $\vdash_\Sigma A$) if and only if there is a proof of A from $\emptyset$ in Σ. Thus $\vdash_\Sigma$ represents a relation between sets of sentences and individual sentences that is called the derivability relation for Σ. Axiomatizations of **V**, **VW**, and **VC** appeared in Lewis (1973), **SS** was discussed in Pollock (1975), and **C2** was discussed in Stalnaker (1968). The particular axiomatizations given here are from Nute (1980). **C2** is the strongest of the five systems, because every theorem of **V**, **VW**, **VC**, or **SS** is a theorem of **C2**. The axiom CEM is not a theorem of any of these weaker systems. **VC** is the next strongest system, containing all theorems of **VW** and **SS**. CS is not a theorem of **VW** and CV is not a theorem of **SS**; thus neither **VW** nor **SS** is stronger than the other. **V** is weaker than **VW**. MP is generally considered a necessary feature of any logic of ordinary language conditionals, which means that **V** is too weak for this purpose. Lewis (1973) proposes **V** as a possible logic for conditional obligation. Reading $A > B$ as "If A were the case, B ought to be the case," MP is inappropriate because what ought to be the case too often is not. Two derived inference rules valid for all five systems are of interest:

RCEA: From $A \equiv B$, to infer $(A > C) \equiv (B > C)$

RCE: From $A \supset B$, to infer $A > B$

RCEA and RCEC taken together extend substitution of

provable equivalents to all contexts in sentences of conditional logic. This is usually assumed and neither rule is explicitly mentioned in most axiomatizations.

Taking **VW, VC, SS,** and **C2** together as establishing a kind of middle ground suggests that RCEC, RCK, ID, MP, MOD, CV, and CA are generally accepted whereas CSO, CS, and CEM are more controversial. The controversies are best illustrated by some examples. Consider the following claims about an ordinary flashlight.

7. If the switch were on, the bulb would be lit.
8. If the bulb were lit, the switch would be on.
9. If the bulb were lit, the battery would be good.
10. If the switch were on, the battery would be good.

Sentences 7, 8, and 9 are intuitively acceptable, but sentence 10 is questionable. Sentences 7 and 8 together say that "the switch is on" and "the bulb is lit" are conditionally equivalent. This being the case, CSO implies that sentences 9 and 10 should be both true or both be false. From CS two theorems follow:

$$A \supset [(A > B) \equiv (A \supset B)]$$
$$A \supset [(A > B) \equiv B]$$

CS says that a conditional $A > B$ can be accidentally true, without any connection between A and B. In fact, $A > B$ can be true even when A is the kind of situation that would tend to make B false. Consider the conditional

11. If Nixon had been elected president and Agnew had been elected vice-president in 1972, then Betty Ford would have lived in the White House in 1974.

Both the antecedent and the consequent of this conditional are true, but not all theorists agree that the conditional itself is true. CEM should not be confused with the unproblematic $A > (B \lor \neg B)$, which is a theorem of all five systems. What CEM claims is that for any A and B, either $A > B$ is true or $A > \neg B$ is true. Suppose George frequently drives to Atlanta on the weekend to see a musical when one is playing there. Last weekend, no musical was playing in Atlanta and George did not travel to Atlanta. Consider the following two sentences:

12. If a musical had been playing in Atlanta last weekend, then George would have traveled to Atlanta.
13. If a musical had been playing in Atlanta last weekend, then George would not have traveled to Atlanta.

Neither of these is clearly true. Certainly if a musical had been playing there, this would have made it more likely that George would have gone to Atlanta, but it would not have guaranteed his going. Because neither claim is clearly true, neither is their disjunction.

The next three important theses are theorems of none of these five systems.

HS: $[(A > B) \land (B > C)] \supset (A > C)$

CONTRA: $(A > B) \supset (\neg B > \neg A)$
MON: $(A > B) \supset [(A \land C) > B]$

These three theses do not appear to be related to each other at all closely, yet from the point of view of our five conditional logics they are equivalent. If any one of the three is added to **V, VW, VC, SS,** or **C2** as an axiom, then the other two are derivable as theorems.

It is not difficult to find intuitive counterexamples to the familiar hypothetical syllogism. Perhaps George's health would improve if he stopped smoking, and perhaps George would stop smoking if he contracted emphysema; but surely George's health would not improve if he contracted emphysema. In **V, VC, VW, SS,** and **C2,** HS is replaced by a restricted hypothetical syllogism, which is a theorem of all five systems.

RHS $\{(A > B) \land [(A \land B) > C]\} \supset (A > C)$

MON is a left-downward monotonicity principle. A corresponding right-upward monotonicity principle,

$$(A > B) \supset [A > (B \lor C)]$$

is a theorem common to the five conditional logics. Again, counterexamples to MON are easy to construct. If George turned his flashlight on it would light; but if he removed its batteries and turned it on, it would not light. It is sometimes said that the conditional operator in conditional logic is not monotonic because MON is not a theorem of these systems. An example that casts doubt on CONTRA is

14. If Dukakis does not live in Boston, he certainly lives in Massachusetts.
15. If Dukakis does not live in Massachusetts, then he lives in Boston.

There is nothing very unusual about sentence 14, but sentence 15 is patently absurd. Another example, perhaps less clear, is

16. If the patient has pneumonia, penicillin will make her better.
17. If penicillin does not make her better, the patient does not have pneumonia.

A reason for rejecting sentence 17, even though sentence 16 is accepted, is that the patient might be suffering from some other serious disease in addition to pneumonia if penicillin is not effective. For the same reason, the following is rejected.

18. If the patient has pneumonia and some other serious disease, penicillin will make her better.

These are *ceteris paribus,* or "other things being equal," conditionals. If a condition is added to the antecedent that says other things are not equal, the modified conditional may not be true. By the same token, if the consequent of the conditional is false, this may suggest either that the antecedent is also false or that other things are not equal after all. The counterexamples for CONTRA may seem more contrived, more limited, or otherwise less persuasive than the counterexamples to HS and MON. This is one reason it is somewhat surprising that the three are equivalent from the perspective of the five conditional logics defined above.

SEMANTICS

There are two familiar versions of possible world semantics for conditionals logics, one involving selection functions and the other based on systems of spheres. A possible world is usually described as a way the world is or could have been. It might be thought of as a complete specification of a real or only possible past, present, and future. A probabilistic semantics has been proposed as an alternative to possible worlds semantics for conditional logic.

A selection function f assigns to a proposition A and a world w either a world or a set of worlds $f(A,w)$, which is intended to be the world most like w in which A is true or the set of worlds most like w or sufficiently like w in which A is true. A conditional $A > B$ is true at a world w just in case B is true in every world in $f(A,w)$, ie, if B is true in the A world or A worlds most like or sufficiently like w. Representing the set of B worlds (the set of worlds at which B is true) as $[B]$, this condition can be rephrased as

$$w \in [A > B] \text{ iff } f(A,w) \subseteq [B]. \qquad \text{(SEL)}$$

If $f(A,w)$ is interpreted as an individual A world closest to w, some value is needed for impossible propositions, eg, $f(A \wedge \neg A, w)$. Stalnaker (1968) suggested positing an absurd world at which every proposition is true. Alternatively, a selection function that picks a unique closest world is equivalent to a function that picks a set of worlds with at most one member. Then the empty set plays the same role as the absurd world. The assumption that there is a unique A world closest to w was also suggested by Stalnaker, and this assumption is enough to guarantee that CEM is true at every world in every model for conditional logic. Making the usual assumptions that possible worlds are consistent, that $[A \wedge B] = [A] \cap [B]$, etc, RCEC and RCK follow immediately from selection function semantics. Other conditions for selection functions are listed below labeled by the theses that they validate.

$f(A,w) \subseteq [A].$ (ID)
If $w \in [A]$, then $w \in f(A,w)$.   (MP)
If $w \in [A]$, then $f(A,w) = \{w\}$.   (CS)
If $f(A,w) = \emptyset$, then $f(B,w) \cap [A] = \emptyset.$ (MOD)
$f(A \vee B,w) \subseteq f(A,w) \cup f(B,w).$ (CA)
If $f(A,w) \cap [B] \neq \emptyset$, then $f(A \wedge B,w) \subseteq f(A,w).$ (CV)
If $f(A,w) \subseteq [B]$ and $f(B,w) \subseteq [A]$, then $f(A,w) = f(B,w).$ (CSO)

By imposing the proper set of restrictions on selection functions, a set of models that characterize any of the five conditional logics **V, VW, VC, SS,** or **C2** can be produced.

Systems of spheres are the invention of Lewis (1971, 1973). A system of spheres is a function $ that assigns to each possible world w a nested set $_w$ of sets of worlds closed under unions and finite intersections. If $S \in \$_w$, then any world in S is considered to be closer or more similar to w than any world not in S. Using a system of spheres, a rather different truth condition for conditionals is obtained.

$$w \in [A > B] \text{ iff } \cap\$_w \cap [A] = \emptyset \text{ or there is } S \in \$_w \text{ such that } S \cap [A] \neq \emptyset \text{ and } S \subseteq [A \supset B]. \qquad \text{(SOS)}$$

In other words, $A > B$ is true at a world w just in case there is no A-permitting sphere around w or there is an A-permitting sphere around w in which every A world is also a B world. Systems of spheres also guarantee RCEC and RCK. No further condition on spheres is needed for ID, MOD, CA, or CSO. MP and CS are characterized by what Lewis calls weak and strong centering.

Weak centering   If $S \in \$_w$, then $w \in S$.   (MP)
Strong centering $\{w\} \in \$_w.$ (CS)

V is characterized by the class of all systems of spheres, **VW** is characterized by the class of weakly centered systems of spheres and **VC** is characterized by the class of strongly centered systems of spheres. The class of systems of spheres satisfying the condition that for each proposition A, there is $S_A \in \$_w$ such that S_A contains exactly one A world, characterizes the conditional logic **C2**. Because CSO is validated by every system of spheres and because CSO is not a theorem of **SS**, there is no class of systems of spheres that characterizes **SS**. So selection function semantics is more general than system of spheres semantics.

Both selection functions and systems of spheres assume that worlds can be compared in terms of some overall similarity to each other. This similarity relation is presumed to be vague and even to vary from one occasion to another as our purposes vary. This vagueness helps explain the perceived vagueness of conditionals. Take for example the two conditionals

19. If pennies were plastic, then some plastic would be legal tender.
20. If pennies were plastic, then pennies would not be legal tender.

Intuitively, either of these conditionals is acceptable by itself although it is unlikely that both would be accepted on the same occasion. The first is true if worlds in which some money is plastic are taken to be closer to the real world than worlds in which pennies are not money; the second is true if the nonmonetary status of plastic is taken as the more important criterion for similarity. If these criteria are understood to be equally important, some worlds would be considered in which the plastic pennies are money and some in which they are not. Then both sentences 19 and 20 would be rejected.

Adams (1975) offered a probabilistic alternative to possible worlds semantics for conditionals. Adams assumed that conditionals have probabilities but do not have truth values. The formal language is restricted so the conditional operator > does not occur within the scope of another conditional operator or within the scope of any truth-functional operator. The probabilistic semantics, then, only applies to first-degree conditionals. The probability of a conditional $A > B$ is just the corresponding standard conditional probability:

$$\mathrm{pr}(A > B) = \mathrm{pr}(A \wedge B)/\mathrm{pr}(A)$$

where $\mathrm{pr}(A) \neq \emptyset$. Adam's proposal is based on a notion of *probabilistic entailment*. A set of propositions and conditionals S p-entails a conclusion C if and only if for any small value $\varepsilon > 0$ there is a value $\delta > 0$ such that if $\mathrm{pr}(A) > 1 - \delta$ for each $A \in S$, then $\mathrm{pr}(C) > 1 - \varepsilon$. An argument is p-sound if its premises p-entail its conclusion. Adams (1977) showed that p-soundness is equivalent to validity in the first-degree fragment of **VC**. Pearl (1988) rediscovered Adams's semantics and called it ε-semantics.

NONMONOTONICITY

In classical logic, whenever there are two sets of sentences K and Γ and an individual sentence A such that $K \subseteq \Gamma$ and $K \vdash A$, then $\Gamma \vdash A$. Or to put it in common language, whatever can be deduced from some body of evidence, can also be deduced from any larger body of evidence. Any logical system whether it is classical modal, or whatever that satisfies this condition on its derivability relation is called *monotonic*. Human reasoning does not appear to be characterizable by any nonmonotonic system. All kinds of diagnoses, for example, proceed by forming tentative conclusions based on available information and then replacing those conclusions with others as additional information becomes available. Planning while acting also depends on drawing tentative conclusions about the consequences of various actions and then modifying these conclusions as events occur. The method of the scientist is to propose explanatory hypotheses on the basis of available data and then to refine or even to replace these hypotheses as additional data become available by observation or by deliberate experiment. These and other ordinary activities involve nonmonotonic reasoning. Familiar conditional logics have several features that an adequate logic of nonmonotonic reasoning would be expected to have. Most obvious is the absence of MON as a theorem of any of these conditional logics, but the failure of HS is also important. Despite these attractive features, all conditional logics that have been discussed are monotonic in the sense defined above. It is possible to have $A > C$ and $(A \& B) > \neg C$ in the same consistent theory in conditional logic, but if both A and B are added to such a theory the result is inconsistent. This applies to all of the logics that have been discussed except **V** because these logics include MP. In the case of **V**, there is no way to detach the consequent of a conditional whose antecedent is derivable.

Glymour and Thomason (1984) investigated the possibilities of developing a nonmonotonic account of belief revision based on conditional logic. Their goal was to pro-

vide a method for representing how a consistent theory T, which might contain subjunctive conditionals, could be transformed into a new consistent theory $T[A]$ to accommodate learning that A is true. The interesting case is where A is inconsistent with T. The procedure is to first generate a set T_A containing A and everything that follows directly from A and subjunctive conditionals in T. Then a subset $T - A$ of T is arbitrarily chosen that is maximally consistent with T_A. Finally, $T[A]$ is the logical closure of $T_A \cup (T - A)$. A problem with this account is that learning the same two facts in different order can result in radically different revisions of a theory. Ignore logical closure for the moment. Suppose $T = \{A > \neg B\}$, ie, T is a theory consisting of a single conditional $A > \neg B$. Then $T[A][B] = \{A, B\}$ and $T[B][A] = \{A > \neg B, A, \neg B\}$. Thus if the initial belief is that if A were true, B would be false, and subsequently A is learned first and then B, it will no longer be believed that B would be false if A were true. This is certainly reasonable. On the other hand, if B is learned first and then A, $A > \neg B$ will be clung to, rejecting B, and instead $\neg B$ will be believed. This is not so reasonable. Another problem concerns situations where there is more than one possible choice of a subset of T that is maximally consistent with T_A for some newly learned A. Some criteria for deciding which of these subsets to choose are needed, but no systematic method suggests itself. Glymour and Thomason seem to have abandoned this research.

Notice that in the Glymour-Thomason account, one theory is replaced by another through some process of belief revision. In the process, bits and pieces of the earlier theory disappear. Thus the actual derivability relation remains monotonic. An appearance of nonmonotonicity is achieved only by deleting beliefs from the earlier theory. Nute (1984, 1985) took another approach to developing a nonmonotonic system based on conditional logic. What was needed was a way to weaken the inference mechanism that allows the consequent of a conditional to be detached when its antecedent is true. Then there would be a consistent theory that contained $A > B$, A, and $\neg B$. This approach shared with Adams the view that conditionals lack truth values. Instead, they are treated as defeasible rules or policies for belief formation and revision. They may have probabilities, but these provide only a justification for accepting and using them. The system is not provided with a probabilistic semantics, and Pearl and Geffner (1988) have shown that the ε-semantics is not appropriate for nonmonotonic reasoning. As in Adam's account, conditionals cannot be iterated or occur as the arguments of truth functional connectives. In fact, the language is restricted even further and only conditionals whose antecedents are conjunctions of literals and whose consequents are simple literals are permitted. The basic idea behind conditionals as defeasible rules was the way that these rules may be defeated. If $A > B$ is in a theory T and A is nonmonotonically derivable from T, then B is also nonmonotonically derivable from T unless $\neg B$ is monotonically derivable from T or there is a competing rule $C > \neg B$ in T and C is also nonmonotonically derivable. Given competing rules $A > B$ and $C > \neg B$, a way to resolve the conflict is needed. The task is simplified by the restriction that A and C are conjunctions of literals. If the set of conjuncts in one antecedent properly contains the set of conjuncts in the other, then the conditional with the larger antecedent is applicable and defeats the other. If neither antecedent properly contains the other, then each conditional defeats the other and neither is applicable. This specificity criterion has evolved greater sophistication in later work (Nute, 1990). A feature of Nute's earliest attempt at a nonmonotonic logic based on conditional logic is a restriction on the chaining of conditionals. If $A > B$ and $B > C$ are in a theory from which A is nonmonotonically derivable and neither conditional is defeated, B will be nonmonotonically derivable but C will not be unless the theory also contains the conditional $(A \& B) > C$. Thus the system rejects HS but implements RHS. An intermediate version of the system allows long chains of reasoning requiring satisfaction of RHS at each step. This inference mechanism is tedious, because long conditionals with complex antecedents are required to sustain long chains of reasoning. A later strategy takes HS itself as defeasible. Chains are allowed unless some link in the chain is defeated. Another feature Nute borrows from conditional logic is the use of might conditionals. Conditionals of the form "Were A true, then it might be that B" are generally taken to be equivalent to $\neg(A > \neg B)$. Nute takes a different approach and introduces a new connective $\rightsquigarrow$ for might conditionals. Such a conditional undercuts a conditional $C > B$ without supporting the contrary conclusion $\neg B$. These serve as simple defeaters and no principle of detachment applies to them. Pollock (1987) gave an account of undercutting defeaters that more closely resembles the original treatment of might conditionals in conditional logic.

Delgrande's (1988) approach to developing a nonmonotonic system based on conditional logic assumed a quantified language in which the conditional operator is never iterated, although it may occur within the scope of truth functional operators. Delgrande provided a class selection function semantics for this language where the selection function is derived from a reflexive and transitive relation $\leq$ on worlds satisfying the following partial conductivity condition:

If $w_1 \leq w$ and $w_2 \leq w$, then $w_1 \leq w_2$ or $w_2 \leq w_1$

Intuitively, $w_1 \leq w_2$ just in case w_1 is "at least as uniform, or at least as unexceptional" as w_2. For a world w and a sentence A,

$f(w,A) = \{w_1 : w_1 \leq w, w_1 \in [A], \text{ and for all } w_2, \text{ if } w_2 \leq w$ and $w_2 \in [A], \text{ then } w_1 \leq w_2\}$

So $f(w,A)$ is the set of least exceptional A worlds that are no more exceptional than w. The conditional logic $\mathbf{N}$ corresponding to Delgrande's semantics is a quantified extension of the sentential logic

$\mathbf{SN}$ = <RCEC,RCK;ID,CSO,CV>

$\mathbf{SN}$ is apparently a proper fragment of $\mathbf{V}$, not only because the language is restricted but also because MOD does not

hold in $\mathbf{SN}$. Delgrande did not make the limit assumption regarding the relation $\leq$; that is, he did not assume that for a w and A, if there is a world $w_1 \leq w$ such that $w_1 \in [A]$, then there is a $w_2 \leq w$ such that $w_2 \in [A]$ and for every w_3, if $w_3 \leq w$ and $w_3 \in [A]$, then $w_2 \leq w_3$. So there can be an infinite string of A worlds, each less exceptional than w and each less exceptional than its predecessor. When this happens, $f(w,A) = \emptyset$ even though there are A worlds no more exceptional than w. It is this possibility that invalidates MOD. Delgrande used $\mathbf{N}$ to develop a notion of default provability in two equivalent ways, the first of which is described here. A conditional $A > B$ is supported in a set Γ if there is a sentence C such that $A \supset C$ is a theorem of first-order logic (FOL), $C > B$ is derivable from Γ in $\mathbf{N}$, and for every sentence D, if $A > D$ is a theorem of FOL and $\neg(D > C)$ is derivable from Γ in $\mathbf{N}$, then $C \supset D$ is a theorem of FOL. Delgrande used the notion of a supported conditional to formulate a recursive definition of a maximal default extension of a theory. Beginning with the conditionals in the initial theory, every conditional is examined in turn and added to the extension if it is supported by what is already in the extension. According to Delgrande, this process yields the same extension no matter in what order the conditionals are examined. A sentence A is default provable from a theory Γ containing the set S of contingent, unconditional facts, if $\wedge S > A$ is derivable from the maximal default extension of Γ, where $\wedge S$ is the conjunction of all the members of S. Default derivability is truly nonmonotonic. Delgrande's work tied a theory of nonmonotonic reasoning more closely to conditional logic than any other approach that has been tried. Nute began by looking at conditional logics that included MP and trying to find a way to restrict the procedure for detaching the consequent of a conditional. Delgrande, on the other hand, began with a conditional logic somewhat weaker than $\mathbf{V}$, a logic that lacks a detachment principle for conditionals. His default provability in effect provides a defeasible detachment principle for conditionals.

BIBLIOGRAPHY

E. Adams, *The Logic of Conditionals*, Reidel, Dordrecht, The Netherlands, 1975.

E. Adams, "A Note on Comparing Probabilistic and Modal Logics of Conditionals," *Theoria* **43**, 186–194 (1977).

J. Delgrande, "An Approach to Default Reasoning Based on a First-order Conditional Logic: Revised Report," *Artif. Intell.* **36**, 63–90 (1988).

C. Glymour and R. Thomason, "Default Reasoning and the Logic of Theory Perturbation," in *Proceedings of the AAAI Workshop on Non-Monotonic Reasoning*, New Paltz, New York, Oct. 17–19, 1984.

D. Lewis, "Completeness and Decidability of Three Logics of Counterfactual Conditionals," *Theoria* **37**, 74–85 (1971).

D. Lewis, *Counterfactuals*, Basil Blackwell, Oxford, UK, 1973.

D. Nute, *Topics in Conditional Logic*, Reidel, Dordrecht, The Netherlands, 1980.

D. Nute, *Non-monotonic Reasoning and Conditionals*, Research Report 01-0002, University of Georgia, 1984.

D. Nute, *A Non-Monotonic Logic Based on Conditional Logic,* Research Report 01-0007, University of Georgia, 1985.

D. Nute, "Defeasible Logic and the Frame Problem," in H. Kyburg, R. Loui, and G. Carlson, eds., *Knowledge Representation and Defeasible Reasoning, Studies in Cognitive Systems,* Kluwer Academic Publishers, Boston, Mass., 1990, pp. 3–21.

J. Pearl, *Probabilistic Reasoning in Intelligent Systems,* Morgan-Kaufmann, San Mateo, Calif., 1988.

J. Pearl and H. Geffner, *Probabilistic Semantics for a Subset of Default Reasoning,* Technical Report TR-93-III, Cognitive Systems Laboratory, UCLA, Mar. 1988.

J. Pollock, *Subjunctive Conditionals,* Reidel, Dordrecht, The Netherlands, 1975.

J. Pollock, "Defeasible Reasoning," *Cogn. Sci.* **11,** 481–518 (1987).

R. Stalnaker, "A Theory of Conditionals," in N. Rescher, ed., *Philosophical Quarterly Monograph Series,* No. 2, Basil Blackwell, Oxford, UK, 1968.

Donald Nute
University of Georgia

LOGIC, DEFAULT. See Reasoning, nonmonotonic.

LOGIC, FUZZY. See Fuzzy sets and fuzzy logic.

LOGIC, HIGHER-ORDER

Although first-order logic has syntactic categories for individuals, functions, and predicates, only quantification over individuals is permitted. Many concepts when translated into logic are, however, naturally expressed using quantifiers over functions and predicates. Leibniz's principle of equality, for example, states that two objects are to be taken as equal if they share the same properties; that is, $a = b$ can be defined as $\forall P[P(a) \equiv P(b)]$. Of course, first-order logic is very strong, and it is possible to encode such a statement into it. For example, let *app* be a first-order predicate symbol of arity two that is used to stand for the application of a predicate to an individual. Semantically, $app(P, x)$ would mean P satisfies x or that the extension of the predicate P contains x. In this case, the quantified expression could be rewritten as the first-order expression $\forall P[app(P, a) \equiv app(P, b)]$ (appropriate axioms for describing *app* are required). Such an encoding is often done in a multi-sorted logic setting, where one sort is for individuals and another sort is for predicates over individuals. Set theory is another first-order language that encodes such higher-order concepts using membership $\in$ as the converse of *app*. Higher-order logics arise from not doing this kind of encoding: instead, more immediate and natural representations of higher-order quantification are considered. Indeed naturalness of higher-order quantification is part of the reason why higher-order logics were initially considered by Frege and Russell as a foundation for mathematics.

SYNTAX OF HIGHER-ORDER LOGIC

A common approach to describing the syntax of a higher-order logic is to introduce some kind of typing scheme. One approach types first-order individuals with ι, sets of individuals with $\langle \iota \rangle$, sets of pairs of individuals with $\langle \iota\iota \rangle$, sets of sets of individuals with $\langle \langle \iota \rangle \rangle$, etc. Such a typing scheme does not provide types for function symbols. Because in some treatments of higher-order logic, functions can be represented by their graphs, ie, certain kinds of sets of ordered pairs, this lack is not a serious restriction. Identifying functions up to their graphs does, of course, treat functions extensionally, something that might be too strong in some applications. (A logic is extensional if whenever two predicates or two functions are equal on all their arguments, they themselves are equal.) A more general approach to typing is that used in the simple theory of types (Church, 1940). Here again, the type ι is used to denote the set of first-order individuals, and the type o is used to denote the sort of Booleans {*true, false*}. In addition to these two types, it is possible to construct functional types: if σ and τ are types, then $\sigma \to \tau$ is the type of functions from objects of type σ to objects of type τ. Thus an expression of type $\iota \to \iota$ represents a function from individuals to individuals. Similarly, an expression of type $\iota \to o$ represents a function from individuals to the Booleans. Using characteristic functions to represent predicates, this latter type is used as the type of predicates whose one argument is an individual. Similarly, an expression that is of the type o is defined to be a formula. Typed expressions are built by application (if M is of type $\sigma \to \tau$ and N is of type σ, then their application $(M\ N)$ is of type τ) and abstraction (if x is a variable of type σ and M is of type τ, then the abstraction $\lambda x\ M$ is of type $\sigma \to \tau$). Equality on such λ-terms is taken to include at least the conversion rules of alphabetic change in bound variables (α-conversion) and the substitution of a λ-bound variable with an argument to which it is applied, (β-conversion, namely, relating $(\lambda x\ M)N$ to $M(x/N)$).

Propositional connectives can be added to these terms by introducing the constants $\wedge$, $\vee$, and $\supset$ of type $o \to o \to o$ and $\neg$ of type $o \to o$. Expressions such as $((\wedge M)N)$ are generally written in the more usual infix notation $M \wedge N$. Quantification arises by adding (for each type σ) constants $\forall_\sigma$ and $\exists_\sigma$ both of type $(\sigma \to o) \to o$. The intended denotation of $\forall_\sigma$ is the set that contains one element, namely, the set of all terms of type σ. Thus, the expression $\forall_\sigma \lambda x\ M$ (where x is a variable of type σ and M is a formula) is intended to be true if $\lambda x\ M$ denotes the set of all members of type σ; that is, if for all x of type σ, M is true. For this reason, the above expression is abbreviated as $\forall_\sigma x\ M$. Similarly, setting the intended meaning of $\exists_\sigma$ to be the collection of all nonempty subsets of type σ yields the existential quantifier. This approach to formulating logic elegantly integrates formulas and terms into a smooth, functional framework.

SEMANTICS OF HIGHER-ORDER LOGIC

There are many ways to interpret higher-order logic, and category theory provides one of the richest possibilities

(Lambek and Scott, 1986). Here an early approach is outlined (Henkin, 1950). Higher order logic can be interpreted over a pair $\langle\{\mathscr{D}_\sigma\}_\sigma, \mathscr{T}\rangle$, where σ ranges over all types. The set $\mathscr{D}_\sigma$ is the collection of all semantic values of type σ and $\mathscr{T}$ maps (logical and nonlogical) constants to particular objects in their respectively typed domain. Thus $\mathscr{D}_\iota$ is the set of all first-order individuals, $\mathscr{D}_o$ is the set {*true, false*}, $\mathscr{D}_{\iota\to o}$ is the set of characteristic functions of subsets of $\mathscr{D}_\iota$, etc. The mapping $\mathscr{T}$ must send the logical constants to their intended meanings, for example, $\mathscr{T}(\wedge)$ is the curried function that returns true when its arguments are both true, and false otherwise. A standard model is one in which the set $\mathscr{D}_{\sigma\to\tau}$ is the set of all functions from $\mathscr{D}_\sigma$ to $\mathscr{D}_\tau$. Such models are completely determined by supplying only $\mathscr{D}_\iota$ and $\mathscr{T}$. If $\mathscr{D}_\iota$ is denumerably infinite, then $\mathscr{D}_{\iota\to o}$ is uncountable: standard models can be very large. In fact, if $\mathscr{D}_\iota$ is infinite, it is possible to build a model of Peano's axioms for the nonnegative integers. As a corollary of Gödel's incompleteness theorem, the set of true formulas in such a standard model are not recursively axiomatizable; that is, there is no theorem proving a procedure that could (even theoretically) uncover all true formulas. This interpretation of higher-order logic as denoting truth in a standard model is often used by those studying the mathematical properties of integers and structures that can be built from them (Shapiro, 1985).

It is possible to interpret higher-order formulas over domains other than the standard one. Henkin (1950) developed a notion of general model that included nonstandard as well as standard models. In the general setting, it is possible for $\mathscr{D}_{\sigma\to\tau}$ to be a proper subset of the set of all functions from $\mathscr{D}_\sigma$ to $\mathscr{D}_\tau$ as long as there are enough functions to properly interpret all expressions of the language of type $\sigma\to\tau$. Henkin's completeness result is that a higher-order formula is valid in all general models if and only if it has a proof (possibly involving the axiom of extensionality). Thus considered from the point of view of general models, higher-order logic with extensionality can be given a completeness result, and this avoids the negative result caused by Gödel's incompleteness results. The cost of this completeness result is giving up the desire to model only the standard model. Because that model is uncountable and includes functions and predicates that are not computable, such a cost is acceptable in many areas of computer science and artificial intelligence.

PROOF THEORY OF HIGHER-ORDER LOGIC

A series of axioms have been presented to describe the higher order logic called the simple theory of types (Church, 1940). The first six axioms (which do not include extensionality) describe a logic that extends first-order logic by permitting quantification at all types and by replacing first-order terms by the simply typed λ-terms modulo β- and η-conversion (if M is of functional type then it is η-convertible to $\lambda x(Mx)$, provided x is not free in M). Many standard proof-theoretic results—such as cut elimination (Girard, 1986), unification (Huet, 1975), resolution (Andrews, 1971), and Skolemization and Herbrand's theorem (Miller, 1987)—have been formulated for this frag-

ment. Using these results as a foundation, it is possible to write theorem provers for this fragment of higher order logic (Andrews and co-workers, 1984). The presence of predicate quantification, however, can make theorem proving very challenging. In first-order logic, the result of substituting into an expression does not change its logical structure. In the higher order setting, however, universal instantiation may increase the number of logical connectives and quantifiers in a formula. For example, if P in the expression $[\ldots \wedge (Pc) \wedge \ldots]$ is substituted with $\lambda x[\exists w(Axw \supset Bww)]$ then the resulting expression (after doing β-conversion) would be $[\ldots \wedge [\exists w(Acw \supset Bww)] \wedge \ldots]$, which has one new occurrence each of a quantifier and logical connective. Theorem provers in first-order logic need to consider only substitutions that are generated by the unification of atomic formulas. Because logical connectives within substitutions are possible in higher-order logic, as this example shows, atomic formula unification does not suggest enough substitution terms.

COMPUTATIONAL APPLICATIONS OF HIGHER-ORDER LOGIC

Computational systems based on higher-order logic have recently been built and applied to subjects such as natural language parsing and theorem proving. In many of these cases, a treatment based on higher-order logic can provide flexible and perspicuous implementations. For example, a theoretical understanding of meaning in natural language is frequently based on higher-order logic: Montague's compositional semantics for natural language is a good example (Dowty and co-workers, 1981). Forcing the implementor to encode the theoretician's meanings into first-order logic can place a great distance between theory and implementation and can detract from the clarity of such implementations. Using a higher-order version of logic programming (Nadathur and Miller, 1990), for example, can remove some of the need for these encodings. Computational higher order logics have also been used as a kind of metalanguage for the implementation of theorem provers. In higher order logics with λ-abstractions within terms (such as the simple theory of types), bound variables are handled by the logic via α-, β-, and η-conversion (in comparison to, say, a first-order system such as PROLOG where bound variables are handled only by programmer-supplied clauses). From the point of view of implementing an object logic using such λ-terms, substitutions and details concerning bound variable names and scopes are all handled by the metalogic's notions of conversion. As a result, the specification of a wide range of theorem provers can be achieved rather elegantly. A couple of computer systems (Nadathur and Miller, 1988; Paulson, 1990) have been developed using fragments of the simple theory of types as their foundation. These systems have been used to specify and implement theorem provers in this metalevel fashion. The logic underlying these computer systems is restricted enough that unification of atomic formulas does, in fact, suggest all substitutions that need to be considered in making deductions.

There are good sources for more information on higher-order logic (Andrews, 1986; van Benthem and Doets, 1983) and intuitistic type theory (Nordstrom and co-workers, 1990), which overlaps higher-order logic in many ways.

BIBLIOGRAPHY

P. Andrews, "Resolution in Type Theory," *J. Symbol. Logic* **36**, 414–432 (1971).

P. Andrews, *An Introduction to Mathematical Logic and Type Theory*, Academic Press, Inc., Orlando, Fla., 1986.

P. Andrews, D. Miller, E. Cohen, and F. Pfenning, "Auatomating Higher-Order Logic," in W. W. Bledsoe and D. W. Loveland, eds., *Automated Theorem Proving: After 25 Years*, AMS Contemporary Mathematics Series 29, AMS, Providence, R.I., pp. 169–192, 1984.

J. van Benthem and K. Doets, "Higher-Order Logic," in D. Gabbay and F. Guenthner, eds., *Handbook of Logic for Computer Science I*, Reidel Publishing Co., Boston, 1983, pp. 275–329.

A. Church, "A Formulation of the Simple Theory of Types," *J. Symbol. Logic* **5**, 56–68 (1940).

D. Dowty, R. Wall, and S. Peters, *Introduction to Montague Semantics*, Reidel Publishing Co., Boston, 1981.

J. -Y. Girard, "The System F of Variable Types: Fifteen Years Later," *Theor. Comput. Sci.* **45**, 159–192 (1986).

L. Henkin, "Completeness in the Theory of Types," *J. Symbol. Logic* **15**, 81–91 (1950).

G. Huet, "A Unification Algorithm for Typed λ-Calculus," *Theoret. Comput. Sci.* **1**, 27–57 (1975).

J. Lambek and P. J. Scott, *Introduction to Higher Order Categorical Logic*, Cambridge University Press, Cambridge, UK, 1986.

D. Miller, "A Compact Representation of Proofs," *Studia Logica* **46**, 347–370 (1987).

G. Nadathur and D. Miller, "An Overview of λ Prolog," in K. A. Bowen and R. A. Kowalski, eds., *Proceedings of the Fifth International Logic Programming Conference*, Seattle, Wash., MIT Press, Cambridge, Mass., 1988, pp. 810–827.

G. Nadathur and D. Miller, "Higher-Order Horn Clauses," *J. ACM* **37**, 777–814 (1990).

B. Nordstrom, K. Petersson, and J. M. Smith, *Programming in Martin-Löf's Type Theory: An Introduction*, Clarendon, Oxford, UK, 1990.

L. Paulson, "Isabelle: The Next 700 Theorem Provers," in P. Odifreddi, ed., *Logic and Computer Science*, Academic Press, Inc., Orlando, Fla., pp. 361–386.

S. Shapiro, "Second-Order Languages and Mathematical Practice," *J. Symbol. Logic* **50**, 714–742 (1985).

DALE MILLER
University of Pennsylvania

LOGIC, MODAL

Modal logic goes back at least to Aristotle, but the current phase of its development begins with the work of the American logician, C. I. Lewis (1883–1964) (Lewis and Langford, 1932) who defined a number of axiomatic systems for it. Modal and related logics like temporal logic, dynamic logic, and the logics of knowledge and belief have recently acquired importance for computer science, largely because of potential applications in AI and program correctness.

Modal logic is concerned principally with the notion of necessity and its companion notion of possibility. A proposition is said to be necessarily true if it could not be the case that it was false. Thus, the propositions "everything that is green is colored" or "two plus two is four" could not possibly have been false (or so it seems) and hence are not just true, but necessarily so. By contrast, the proposition "Ronald Reagan is President of the United States in 1985" is true but might have been false since he might have lost the election to Mondale. In other words, it is not necessarily true but only contingently so. The formula $\Box A$ indicates that A is necessary.

A proposition is possible if it is not necessary that it be false. Then every true proposition is possible, but not vice versa, and every necessary proposition is true but not vice versa. That A is possible is written $\Diamond A$. Note that $\Diamond A$ is equivalent to $\neg\Box\neg A$.

Lewis was interested in the notion of necessity because of his dissatisfaction with material- or truth-functional implication. Using $\to$ to indicate material implication, it is true that (pigs lack wings) $\to$ (you are reading this entry). But there is no connection between the two facts, and Lewis felt that the intuitive notion of implication was not adequately expressed by $\to$. Lewis proposed to remedy this defect by introducing the strict implication $\prec$, where $A \prec B$ is an abbreviation for $\Box(A \to B)$. Thus, A strictly implies B if it is impossible that A be true and B false. However, there are paradoxes of strict implication analogous to those of material implication, and it is not clear that Lewis's attempt was wholly successful.

FORMALISMS FOR MODAL LOGIC

The language of propositional modal logic is obtained from that of the propositional calculus by adding the operator $\Box$ for necessity. Then the set of formulas of propositional modal logic will be obtained from some propositional atoms P, Q, etc, by closure under truth-functional connectives (say $\neg$ and $\vee$) and the operator $\Box$. Note now that under this interpretation, the formula $\Box(P \vee \neg P)$ will be true since P is necessarily true or false, but the formula $\Box P \vee \Box \neg P$, which says that either P is necessarily true or it is necessarily false, may not be true since P might have been contingently true.

Axiomatic Systems

The system T (sometimes called M) is due essentially to Gödel and Feys (1933). It has the language just described above, with axioms consisting of all propositional tautologies (or enough of them) together with the two axiom schemes

$$\Box A \to A \qquad (A1)$$

$$\Box(A \to B) \to \Box A \to \Box B \qquad (A2)$$

These schemes say, in effect, that every necessary proposition is true and that if one proposition A necessarily implies another, B, the necessity of A implies that of B. The rules of inference are modi ponentes (derive B from A and $A \rightarrow B$) and necessitation (derive $\Box A$ from A).

There is a subsystem K of T that lacks axiom scheme (A1) and is used as a basis for deontic logic. In deontic logic the symbol $\Box$ would not represent necessity but desirability. In this case the axiom scheme (A1) would be unsuitable since a proposition that is desired may well be false. Again, in a logic of knowledge, $\Box$ will stand for "is known," and such a logic will tend to have axiom scheme (A1) since a proposition cannot be known unless it is true. However, in a logic of belief, $\Box$ would stand for "is believed," and (A1) would not be wanted since false propositions may be believed. [In practice, these logics tend to use symbols other than $\Box$ and $\Diamond$, but a uniformity of notation makes the comparison easier [see Hintikka (1962); Halpern and Moses (1984); Parikh and Ramanujam (1985) for a discussion of modal logics of knowledge and belief).]

There are two systems stronger than T, namely the systems S4 and S5 of Lewis. S4 is obtained from T by adding the scheme

$$\Box A \rightarrow \Box \Box A \qquad (A3)$$

so that all propositions that are necessary are necessarily necessary. It follows at once that all propositions that are possibly possible are possible, ie,

$$\Diamond \Diamond A \rightarrow \Diamond A \qquad (A3')$$

and indeed, (A3) and (A3') are equivalent. The yet stronger system S5 can then be obtained from S4 by adding the axiom scheme

$$\Diamond A \rightarrow \Box \Diamond A \qquad (A4)$$

There is a semantics for modal logics, due chiefly to Kripke (1963) (Hughes and Creswell, 1968), that brings out the differences between the systems in a striking way.

KRIPKE MODELS

A Kripke model is based on a frame $\langle W, R \rangle$, where W is a set of possible worlds or, more prosaically, a set of state. Individual states are denoted $s, t, \dots$. Here R is a binary relation on W called the accessibility relation and sRt is read "t is accessible from s." Usually, there is a special state r that stands for the real world or the start state. The model M is then obtained from the frame by assigning a truth value to each atom P at each state s. The truth value $v(A, s)$ of an arbitrary formula A at each state s is then defined as

$v(A \lor B, s) =$ true iff either $v(A, s) =$ true or $v(B, s)$
$\qquad\qquad = $ true

$v(\neg A, s) =$ true iff $v(A, s) =$ false

$v(\Box A, s) =$ true iff for all t such that sRt, $v(A, t) =$ true

The models as described above are the K models. In T models the relation R is required to be reflexive. S4

models are obtained by restricting R further, to be also transitive, and for S5 models it must be an equivalence relation, ie, be reflexive, symmetric, and transitive. Then each of the four axiomatic systems is complete for its particular models. That is, a formula A is a theorem of S, where S is any of the systems K, T, S4, and S5, iff it is true in all S models at all states (Parikh and Ramanujam, 1985; Kripke, 1963).

TEMPORAL LOGIC

Temporal logic (with linear time) is a case between S4 and S5. In it W is the set of instants of time, and R is the before–after relation so that sRt holds just in case t either equals or comes after s. Since R is reflexive and transitive in this case, all theorems of S4 will hold. However, there will also be some additional laws that are not theorems of S4. For example, all formulas $\Diamond \Box A \rightarrow \Box \Diamond \Box A$ will be valid, but they are not theorems of S4. See Manna and Pnueli (1982) for a computer-science-oriented introduction to temporal logic.

All the systems K, T, S4, and S5 have the finite-model property. If S is any of the four systems, a formula A has an S model if and only if it has a finite S model. This fact, together with the completeness of the appropriate axioms, yields decidability. However, Ladner (1977) has shown recently that the system S5 is NP complete, whereas the systems K, T, and S4 are PSPACE complete. Thus, any implemented decision procedure can only decide relatively short formulas.

FIRST-ORDER MODAL LOGIC

It is easy enough to obtain a language for first-order (or quantified) modal logic. One simply adds the modalities $\Box$ and $\Diamond$ to the usual language for first-order logic. One can also define a semantics for first-order modal logic as an enrichment of that for propositional modal logic. Frames are as before, but each state s is now a model of ordinary first-order logic, and the semantics of first-order logic can be easily extended to one for first-order modal logic. The new enriched states are now the possible worlds of first-order modal logic.

Unfortunately, there is little agreement on what these possible worlds might be like and hence about the right first-order modal logic. See Ref. 7 for some of the issues that arise. Below is one that has some interest even for nonphilosophers.

The law $a = b \rightarrow (A(a) \rightarrow A(b))$, substitutivity of equals, is a fundamental principle governing identity. However, Quine (1961) has pointed out that this law seems to fail in contexts involving modalities, knowledge, or belief. For example, it is true that the number of planets equals 9. It is also true that 9 is necessarily greater than 7. However, it is not true that the number of planets is necessarily greater than 7. Similar examples exist where "necessarily" is replaced by "John knows that" or "Mary believes that." Contexts in which the law fails are sometimes called referentially opaque, whereas those in which it holds are called referentially transparent.

There is an axiomatization of first-order modal logic in constant-domain models, ie, models in which all worlds have the same individuals, which is due essentially to Ruth Barcan Marcus (Hughes and Cresswell, 1968).

The axiomatization includes axioms for first-order logic and laws inherited from propositional modal logic of the appropriate kind. It also includes the well-known Barcan formula and its converse. These last two say that the universal quantifier commutes with $\Box$, so that $\Box \forall x A(x)$ is equivalent to $\forall x \Box A(x)$ (see Kripke, 1963 for details).

DYNAMIC LOGIC

Consider a world W whose states s are the possible states of some actual or abstract computer. The formulas A of the language express properties of individual states. Now each program a, considered as an I/O relation, is a binary relation on W and generates a modality $[a]$. To be precise, let $sR_a t$ mean that there is an execution of the program a that begins in the state s and terminates in t. Then the state s satisfies the formula $[a]A$ if, for every t such that $sR_a t$, t satisfies A. Since there are infinitely many programs, there are infinitely many accessibility relations and hence infinitely many modalities. These modalities all satisfy the laws of the logic K and other laws that depend on the particular program a.

Intuitively, $[a]A$ is the property that has to hold now so that A must hold if and when the program a terminates. The formula $\langle a \rangle A$, where $\langle a \rangle$ is $\neg [a] \neg$, says that the property A may hold after a terminates. Since programs are allowed to be nondeterministic, [ ] and $\langle \rangle$ are distinct.

However, there are interactions not only between these modalities and the usual logical notions but also among themselves. For example, if a and b are two programs, and they are composed to form a third program $c = a; b$, the formula $[c]A$ is equivalent to the formula $[a][b]A$. A more interesting example expresses a fundamental property of the "while do" construct. If B is a formula, and d is the program "while B do a," then the formula $[d]A$ is equivalent to the formula

$$(\neg B \ \& \ A) \lor (B \ \& [a][d]A).$$

It is now possible to express the partial correction assertion $\{A\}a\{B\}$, where A and B are formulas and a is a program. The assertion $\{A\}a\{B\}$ says that if the formula A holds before the program a begins, then B must hold if and when a terminates. This fact can be expressed by the dynamic logic formula $A \rightarrow [a]B$. Thus, dynamic logic becomes an effective tool for studying the properties of programs. However, it also has a potential for applications in the logic of actions and in formalizing legal reasoning, both of which are areas with relevance to AI. See Pratt (1976) and Harel (1979) for further reading on dynamic logic and McCarty (1983) for an application of dynamic logic to legal reasoning. Fitting (1983); Linsky (1971); and Prior (1967) provide a more detailed treatment of modal logic and various issues connected with it.

BIBLIOGRAPHY

M. Fitting, *Proof Methods for Modal and Intuitionist Logics*, D. Reidel, Boston, Mass., 1983.

K. Gödel, *Collected Works*, M. Feferman and co-workers, eds., Oxford University Press, New York, 1986, pp. 301–302. Originally published as "Eine Interpretation des Intuitionistichen Aussagenkalküls," *Ergebnisse eines Mathematischen Kolloquiums* 4, 34–38 (1933).

J. Halpern and Y. Moses, "Knowledge and Common Knowledge in a Byzantine Environment," *Proceedings of the Third Annual Symposium on the Principles of Distributed Computing*, Association of Computing Machinery, New York, 1984, pp. 50–61.

D. Harel, *First Order Dynamic Logic*, Lecture Notes in Computer Science No. 68, Springer-Verlag, New York, 1979.

J. Hintikka, *Knowledge and Belief*, Cornell University Press, Ithaca, N.Y., 1962.

G. E. Hughes and M. J. Cresswell, *An Introduction to Modal Logic*, Methuen, London, 1968.

S. Kripke, "Semantical Considerations on Modal Logic," *Acta Philos. Fenn.* **16**, 83–94 (1963).

R. Ladner, "The Computational Complexity of Provability in Systems of Modal Propositional Logic," *SIAM J. Comput.* **6**, 467–480 (1977).

C. I. Lewis and C. H. Langford, *Symbolic Logic*, Dover, Mineola, N.Y., 1932.

L. Linsky, *Reference and Modality*, Oxford University Press, New York, 1971.

Z. Manna and A. Pnueli, "Verification of Concurrent Programs: The Temporal Framework," in Boyer and Moore, eds., *The Correctness Problem in Computer Science*, Academic Press, New York, 1982, pp. 215–273.

L. McCarty, Permissions and Obligations, *Proc. of the Eighth IJCAI*, Karlsruhe, FRG, 1983, pp. 287–294.

R. Parikh and R. Ramanujam, "Distributed Processes and the Logic of Knowledge," in *Logics of Programs*, Lecture Notes in Computer Science No. 193, Springer-Verlag, New York, 1985, pp. 156–168.

V. Pratt, "Semantical Considerations on Floyd-Hoare Logic," *Proceedings of the Seventeenth Annual IEEE Symposium on Foundations of Computer Science*, IEEE Computer Society, Piscataway, N.J., 1976, pp. 109–121.

A. Prior, "Logic, Modal," in P. Edwards, ed., *Encyclopedia of Philosophy*, Vol. 5, Collier-MacMillan, New York, 1967.

W. V. Quine, Reference and Modality, in *From a Logical Point of View*, Harper & Row, New York, 1961, pp. 139–157.

R. Parikh
Brooklyn College, City
University of New York

LOGIC NONMONOTONIC. See Belief revision; Circumscription; Reasoning, nonmonotonic; Truth maintenance.

LOGIC, ORDER-SORTED

Order-sorted logic is a generalization of many-sorted logic, which is a variant of predicate calculus obtained by partitioning the universe of discourse into nonempty subsets, called sorts. In order-sorted logic, these sorts may overlap, and an ordering is induced from the set inclusion relationships. A sorted logic has a set of sort symbols S, which denote sorts in any interpretation. There are also mechanisms for attaching sort constraints to variables (restricting their domain of quantification) and describing the sortal behavior of the nonlogical symbols. These declarations comprise the signature of a sorted logic and affect the semantics by restricting the possible interpretations of the nonlogical symbols and allowing function symbols to be interpreted as partial functions. Sorted logics can be seen as a hybrid representation language where special-purpose representations and reasoning are employed for taxonomic knowledge.

AI's main interest in sorted logics has been in their computational efficiency: the search space may be much reduced compared to a corresponding formulation in unsorted logic, because it is easy to detect that certain inferences cannot lead to a successful proof; these inferences are those that produce ill-sorted formulas (ie, where the sorts of terms do not match the sorts of the argument positions they occupy) or those generated by the application of ill-sorted substitutions (ie, where the sort of a term does not fit the sort constraints of the variable it is being substituted for).

It should be noted that the preprocessing steps of the connection method (Letz and co-workers, in press) that can delete literals or entire axioms may make most, or sometimes all, of a sorted representation redundant. However, the technique does not subsume all sorted calculi. Moreover, one advantage claimed for sorted logics is that the ontology of the domain is made explicit and the sortal behavior of the nonlogical symbols explicitly declared. This can be valuable not only for documentation purposes but also for knowledge base verification and integrity checking through well-sortedness checking. These benefits do not arise in Letz and co-workers' representation, although the user is relieved from the perhaps onerous task of specifying all the sort information. There has been some work on automatically transforming unsorted to sorted formulations (Schmidt-Schauss, 1989), but sort information may be deeply hidden in an axiomatization and determining an optimum signature is undecidable in general.

An early computational sorted logic with a sound theoretical footing was that of Walther (1987); the implementation of this logic achieved the first mechanical solution to the well known Schubert's steamroller problem where the Herbrand Universe is finite in the sorted but infinite in the unsorted representation. There are, in fact, many order-sorted logics. The dimensions of variability are (1) the nature of the sort structure, (2) the language used to describe the sortal behavior of the nonlogical symbols, (3) the mechanism used to attach sortal constraints to variables, and (4) the precise definition of what constitutes well sortedness. Each of these aspects will be considered in turn.

The sort structure may simply be described as a poset, ie, a pair $\langle S, \sqsubseteq \rangle$ where $\sqsubseteq$ is the (transitive) partial ordering, which is interpreted as $\subseteq$ in any model. If $\tau_1 \sqsubseteq \tau_2$ then τ_1 is said to be a subsort of τ_2. Some logics allow explicit greatest lower bound, least upper bound, and relative complement information to be given, in such logics it is possible, for example, to specify that $\tau_1 = \tau_2 \sqcap \tau_3$, and thus in any interpretation, σ, $\sigma(\tau_1) = \sigma(\tau_2) \cap \sigma(\tau_2)$. This is stronger than simply declaring that $\tau_1 \sqsubseteq \tau_2$ and $\tau_1 \sqsubseteq \tau_3$. However, such extra information cannot be exploited unless sort literals are allowed (see below). Sort expressions are usually atomic, but by allowing non rank zero sort constructors parametric polymorphism is achieved (Smolka, 1989), which is of particular use in logic programming.

In the simplest case, an $n + 1$ tuple of sort symbols is associated with every rank n function symbol, the $n + 1$st position specifying the result. *Ad hoc* polymorphism (or overloading) allows more than one such $n + 1$ tuple per function symbol. Further increases in expressiveness include term declarations (Schmidt-Schauss, 1989), of the form $\tau(\alpha)$, eg, Even(plus(x,x)). It is also possible to declare the sortal behavior of predicate symbols. In the absence of equality (or unless variables derive their sortal constraints implicitly as described below), then such declarations do not affect the search space dynamically but only the well sortedness of the initial axiomatization. Polymorphic predicates are most useful when treated as functions with a result sort from one of four special Boolean sorts (Cohn, 1987).

Normally, variables are simply declared to be of a particular sort (usually atomic, but possibly a lattice theoretic expression). However, this does not allow overloading to be exploited fully. Alternatively, a set of n-tuples of sorts may be associated with every formula; each n-tuple specifies a conjunction of sort constraints for the n variables in the formula. These constraints may be specified explicitly or derived implicitly from the sorts of the argument positions variables occur in.

Usually, the sort of a nonvariable term is constrained to be a subsort of the sort of the argument position it occurs in; this ensures that in any interpretation every term is guaranteed to denote. However, it is still possible for expressions that are ill-sorted according to this definition to denote in some interpretations. These are those where the sort of the term and the sort of the argument position it occupies or the variable it is being substituted for overlap, ie, they have a glb in the sort hierarchy, which is not $\perp$; expressions where overlapping occurs are best called sort consistent rather than well sorted, because there are interpretations where they denote and others where they do not. Care is required if sort consistent expressions are allowed because, for example, from $\forall x{:}\tau\, P(x)$ $P(c)$ cannot be soundly inferred when the sort of the constant c overlaps with the sort of x,τ; rather it is necessary to infer $\tau(c){\rightarrow}P(c)$. The literal $\tau(c)$ is a sort or characteristic literal, because its predicate is a sort symbol. Allowing sort literals may be regarded as against the spirit of a sorted logic where the idea is to represent and reason with sort information by special-purpose means; however, allowing sort literals increases expressiveness in useful ways (Cohn, 1989b).

Almost all work on computational sorted logics has been done within a resolution framework. Although it is possible to perform all well-sortedness checks in many-sorted logic statically, order-sorted logic requires dynamic well-sortedness checking, which usually occurs during unification. Depending on the expressive power of the signature, sorted unification may be unitary, finitary, or infinitary (Walther, 1988; Schmidt-Schauss, 1989; Meseguer and co-workers, 1989). Allowing sets of sort constraints on variables or embedding a poset with non-unique glbs into a semilattice can turn the finitary into the unitary case. In some situations, sorted unification is not decidable. Schmidt-Schauss (1989) has investigated sorted unification under nonempty theories and presents a sorted paramodulation rule. If sort literals and overlapping are allowed then further inference rules are required to retain completeness (Cohn, 1987), for example, a rule to resolve two characteristic literals that do not have the same predicate symbol is needed; this rule is an instance of theory resolution (see Resolution, theory). Often, a translation to unsorted logic is given (a relativisation) and a sort theorem proved, which shows that the sorted logic is no more expressive (although it may be more efficient). If the logic is substitutional (Frisch, in press), that is, if it obeys certain syntactic restrictions (in particular there are no sort literals), then a sound and complete inference procedure for an arbitrary sorted calculus can be automatically synthesized from an unsorted one. Frisch's approach to sorted deduction is not a sorted logic in the conventional sense because there is no signature, but rather a logical theory, which can be used to specify very general information about sorts and the sortal behavior of the nonlogical symbols. This theory does not affect the semantics as a signature does, and there is no notion of well-sorted formulas (only substitutions).

There are many other representation languages that treat taxonomic knowledge specially, in particular, semantic or associative networks and the KL-ONE family of languages. The TBOX of these latter languages is usually sufficiently expressive to make subsumption computationally intractable, whereas the signature of most sorted logics allows testing whether a term is of a particular sort (performing a subsumption test in KL-ONE terminology) to be cheap. Feature logics (Smolka and Aït-Kaci, 1989) are also closely related to sorted logics.

BIBLIOGRAPHY

K. H. Blasius, U. Hedstueck, C. Rollinger, *Sorts and Types in AI*, Springer Verlag, Berlin, 1990.

A. G. Cohn, "A More Expressive Formulation of Many Sorted Logic," *J. Automated Reasoning* 3(2), 113–200 (1987).

A. G. Cohn, "Taxonomic Reasoning with Many Sorted Logics," *Artif. Intell. Rev.* **3**, 89–128 (1989a).

A. G. Cohn, "On the Appearance of Sortal Literals: A Non Substitutional Framework for Hybrid Reasoning," in R. J. Brachman, H. J. Levesque, and R. Reiter, eds., *Principles of Representation and Reasoning*, Morgan-Kaufmann, San Mateo, Calif., 1989b.

A. G. Cohn, "Completing Sort Hierarchies," *Computers and Mathematics with Applications*, in press.

A. M. Frisch, "The Substitutional Framework for Sorted Deduction: Fundamental Results on Hybrid Reasoning," *Artif. Intell.* (in press).

R. Letz, J. Schumann, S. Bayerl, and W. Bibel, "SETHEO—A High Performance Theorem Prover for First Order Logic," *J. Automated Reasoning* 7 (in press).

J. Meseguer, J. A. Goguen, and G. Smolka, "Order Sorted Unification," *J. Symbol. Comput.* **8**, 383–413 (1989).

M. Schmidt-Schauss, *Computational Aspects of an Order Sorted Logic with Term Declarations*, Springer-Verlag, New York, 1989.

G. Smolka, *Logic Programming over Polymorphically Order-Sorted Types*, Ph.D. dissertation, Universität Kaiserslautern, Germany, 1989.

G. Smolka and H. Aït-Kaci, "Inheritance Hierarchies: Semantics and Unification," *Symbol. Comput.* **8**, 383–413 (1989).

C. Walther, *A Many Sorted Calculus Based on Resolution and Paramodulation*, Pitman, London, 1987.

C. Walther, "Many Sorted Unification," *JACM* **35**(1), 1–17 (1988).

A. G. Cohn
University of Leeds

LOGIC, PREDICATE

Predicate logic—also known as predicate calculus or first-order (predicate) logic—is the study of inferences that can be made on the basis of an analysis of atomic sentences into "terms" (essentially, noun phrases) and "predicates" (essentially, verb phrases). It is an extension of propositional (or sentential) logic and is the modern descendant of Aristotle's logic of subjects and predicates (see Logic, propositional). For discussions of traditional Aristotelian syllogistic logic see Kneale and Kneale (1962), Kneebone (1963), and Prior (1967a,b). For a general discussion of logic and references to other articles on logic in this *Encyclopedia*, see Logic. Secondarily, it is also the study of the representation of information (see Knowledge representation) by predicates and their terms. Because of the relationships of predicates and terms to noun phrases and verb phrases, predicate logic has often served as a foundation for natural-language syntax and semantics (see the Natural-language entries; Parsing).

In this article, the syntactic items that are used in the representation of information are called sentences, and the items in the "world" that sentences mean or express are called propositions. A "predicate" is, as suggested above, usually taken to be a verb phrase or the name of a property, relation, or class of objects. Thus, in the sentence

Roses are red

"(is) red" is the predicate; it can be taken to name the property or attribute of being red or of redness, or the class $\{x: x \text{ is red}\}$ or $\{x: x \text{ has redness}\}$. In addition to this "subatomic" analysis of the atomic sentences treated by propositional logic, predicate logic employs a machinery of variables and quantifiers that allows it to express how many objects fall under a given predicate. The adjective "first-order" indicates that the quantifiers only range over individuals, not properties, relations, or classes (ie, they range over the things represented by terms, not the things represented by predicates). Second-order logic (see below) quantifies over predicates; by extrapolation, propositional logic may be thought of as being of "zero order."

Although predicate logic is usually taken to be a way of analyzing propositions or declarative sentences, there are also predicate logics for other types of sentences (eg, quantified modal logic and quantified epistemic logic). In fact, the logic of some sentences, such as interrogatives (erotetic logic), only becomes interesting in the quantified case. (For discussions of epistemic and other modal logics, see LOGIC, MODAL; BELIEF REPRESENTATION SYSTEMS; Gabbay and Guenthner, 1984; Hintikka, 1962; Hughes and Cresswell, 1968; Nute, 1981; Prior, 1967c. For erotetic logic, see Belnap and Steel, 1976; Harrah, 1984; and Lambert, 1969.)

As is the case with propositional logic, the representational system of predicate logic is its underlying language, consisting essentially of terms, predicates, quantifiers, and truth-functional connectives, with a grammatical syntax and a semantics in terms of individuals and properties (or classes). The syntax is often extended to include functions (or term-producing operators), the identity predicate, and definite and indefinite description operators. The deductive system of predicate logic extends that of propositional logic to include axioms and rules for manipulating quantifiers.

THE LANGUAGE OF PREDICATE LOGIC

Informally, an atomic proposition is analyzed into a single verb phrase (the predicate) and a sequence of noun phrases (grammatically, its subjects and objects) called the *arguments* of the predicate. For example,

Socrates is Greek

consists of the predicate ". . . is Greek" together with its argument "Socrates"; and

Fredonia is between Erie and Buffalo

consists of the predicate ". . . is between . . . and . . ." together with its arguments "Fredonia," "Erie," and "Buffalo" (or the argument sequence, ⟨Fredonia, Erie, Buffalo⟩). In the first case the predicate names the property: being Greek, or the class: $\{x: x$ is Greek$\}$; in the second case the predicate names the relation: being between . . . and . . ., or the class of ordered triples: $\{⟨x, y, z⟩: x$ is between y and $z\}$. Discussed below are important theoretical differences between the full first-order logic of relations and monadic first-order logic, which only has one-place predicates.

To be able to express propositions such as

All humans are mortal.
Some philosophers are computer scientists.
There are no unicorns.

quantifiers and variables are used. Thus, the first of these

Table 1. Alphabet of $\mathscr{L}$

n-place predicate symbols (n an integer)	A, . . . , Z; A_i, B_i, . . . (i an integer); any sequence of words separated by hyphens
n-place function symbols (n an integer)	f, g, h; f_i, g_i, h_i (i an integer); any sequence of words separated by hyphens
Individual variables	u, . . . , z; u_i, . . . , z_i (i an integer)
Individual constants	a, . . . , e; a_i, . . . , e_i (i an integer); any noun phrase (the words separated by hyphens)
Connectives	$\wedge$, $\neg$
Punctuation	",", "[", "]", "(", ")"
Quantifiers	
Universal	$\forall$
Existential	$\exists$

examples might be expressed using the universal quantifier ("for all"):

For all x, if x is human, then x is mortal.

and the second might be expressed using the existential quantifier ("for some" or "there exists"):

For some x, x is a philosopher and x is a computer scientist.
There exists an x such that x is a philosopher and x is a computer scientist.

Syntax

A formal syntax for a language $\mathscr{L}$ of predicate logic can be presented by giving an alphabet, a recursive definition of *term*, and a recursive definition of *well-formed formula* (wff) (given in Tables 1–3). In order to define the notion of a sentence and to give the inference rules, the following definitions are necessary:

(D1) Let φ be a wff prefixed by a quantifier phrase (ie, either $\forall$v or $\exists$v). Then φ is the *scope of* the quantifier phrase. For example, the scope of $\forall x$ in $\forall x\varphi(x)$ is $\varphi(x)$, but the scope of $\exists y$ in $(\exists y\ \varphi(y) \vee \psi)$ is $\varphi(y)$.

Table 2. Terms of $\mathscr{L}$

(T1) All individual variables are terms.
(T2) All individual constants are terms.
(T3) If t_1, . . . , t_n are terms and f is an n-place function symbol, then $f(t_1, . . . , t_n)$ is a term.
(T4) Nothing else is a term.

For example, each of the following is a term:
x
x_1
a
a_{23}
John
Mother-of(Bill)
Son-of(Harriet, Frank)

Table 3. Well-formed Formulas of $\mathcal{L}$

(wff.1) If $t_1, \ldots, t_n$ are terms and $\mathbf{P}$ is an n-place predicate symbol, then $\mathbf{P}(t_1, \ldots, t_n)$ is a(n atomic) well-formed formula.

(wff.2) If φ and ψ are well-formed formulas, $\mathbf{v}$ is an individual variable, and $\varphi(\mathbf{v}^*)$ is a well-formed formula containing zero or more occurrences of $\mathbf{v}$, then

$$\neg\, \varphi$$
$$(\varphi \lor \psi)$$
$$\forall\mathbf{v}[\varphi(\mathbf{v}^*)]$$
$$\exists\mathbf{v}[\varphi(\mathbf{v}^*)]$$

are well-formed formulas.

(wff.3) Nothing else is a well-formed formula.

Parentheses and brackets will sometimes be omitted when no ambiguity results. For example, each of the following is a wff:

$$A(x, y)$$
$$\text{In(Eiffel-tower, France)}$$
$$\neg\ \text{Republican(John-F.Kennedy)}$$
$$(\text{Capital(Albany, New-York)} \lor B)$$
$$\forall x Fx$$
$$\forall x[\neg\ \text{Human}(x) \lor \text{Mortal}(x)]$$
$$\neg\ \exists x\ \text{Unicorn}(x)$$

(Note that a zero-place "predicate," like B, is an atomic wff.)

(D2) Let the variable in a quantified phrase be called its *variable of quantification*. Then:

(a) An occurrence of an individual variable in a wff φ is *bound* means: the variable occurs in the scope of a quantifier phrase in φ that has that variable as its variable of quantification.

(b) An occurrence of an individual variable in a wff φ is *free* means: the occurrence of that variable is not bound.

(c) A variable is *bound* means: there is an occurrence of that variable that is bound.

(d) A variable is *free* means: there is an occurrence of that variable that is free.

For example, in

$$(Fx \lor \forall x Gx)$$

the first occurrence of x is free and the second is bound; the variable x is both free and bound in this wff. Finally,

(D3) A *sentence* is a wff with no free variables.

For further discussion of the grammatical syntax of a first-order language and translations of natural-language sentences into it, see Kalish, Montague, and Mar (1980), Otto (1978), Schagrin (1979).

Semantics

Providing a semantics for such a first-order language is somewhat more problematic than it is in the propositional

case. The main reason for this is that a decision must be made about the domain (or universe) of discourse. It was noted above that a predicate can name a property (or relation) or a class. But classes are extensional ("two" classes are identical if they have the same members), whereas properties are intensional (ie, nonextensional). Moreover, there are important questions about what counts as an individual:

1. Can properties or classes themselves be individuals? This is surely plausible; consider such propositions as:

   > Red is a color.
   > Colors are properties.
   > $\{x: x \text{ is a rational number}\}$ is countable.

   However, care must be taken to avoid paradox, as in Russell's (Whitehead and Russell, 1927) well-known example:

   $$\{x: x \notin x\} \in \{x: x \notin x\}$$
   $$\text{if and only if } \{x: x \notin x\} \notin \{x: x \notin x\}$$

2. Must the individual actually exist? If variables and terms may only range over existents, how does one express such sentences as the following?

   > There are no round squares.
   > Santa Claus does not exist.
   > All unicorns are white.

Thus, a semantics for a first-order language cannot be completely specified independently of an ontology—a precise specification of the domain. Nevertheless, the general form of such a semantics (often called *formal semantics*, see Nute (1981)) does not vary. Metatheoretical results are given here in terms of set-theoretic semantics (ie, in terms of an ontology of sets and their members), which is the way they are given in most of the literature.

Let $\mathbf{M}$ be the structure $\langle \mathbf{D}, \mathbf{R}, \mathbf{F}\rangle$, where $\mathbf{D}$ is a non-empty set, $\mathbf{R}$ is a set of n-place relations on the elements of $\mathbf{D}$, and $\mathbf{F}$ is a set of n-place functions on the elements of $\mathbf{D}$. An interpretation, I, on $\mathbf{M}$ for $\mathcal{L}$ is a function from the symbols of $\mathcal{L}$ to $\mathbf{D} \cup \mathbf{R} \cup \mathbf{F}$ such that:

If t is an individual constant or individual variable, then $I(t) \in \mathbf{D}$.

If f is a function symbol, then $I(f) \in \mathbf{F}$.

If f is an n-place function symbol and $t_1, \ldots, t_n$ are terms, then $I(f(t_1, \ldots, t_n)) = I(f)\langle I(t_1), \ldots, I(t_n)\rangle \in \mathbf{D}$.

If $\mathbf{P}$ is an n-place predicate symbol, then $I(\mathbf{P}) \in \mathbf{R}$.

The notion of "truth on an interpretation" (symbolized as: $\models_I$) can be defined recursively as follows:

1. If $\mathbf{P}$ is an n-place predicate symbol, and $t_1, \ldots, t_n$ are terms, then $\models_I \mathbf{P}(t_1, \ldots, t_n)$ if and only if $\langle I(t_1), \ldots, I(t_n)\rangle \in I(\mathbf{P})$.

2. If φ and ψ are wffs and **v** is an individual variable, then

   (a) $\models_I \neg \varphi$ if and only if not-$\models_I\varphi$;

   (b) $\models_I(\varphi \vee \psi)$ if and only if $\models_I\varphi$ or $\models_I\psi$;

   (c) $\models_I\forall\mathbf{v}\varphi$ if and only if $\models_{I'}\varphi$ for every interpretation I' that differs from I at most on what it assigns to **v**;

   (d) $\models_I\exists\mathbf{v}\varphi$ if and only if $\models_{I'}\varphi$ for some interpretation I' that differs from I at most on what it assigns to **v**.

Finally,

A wff φ is valid in **M** (written: $\mathbf{M} \models \varphi$) if and only if $\models_I\varphi$ for every interpretation I on **M**.

A structure **M** is a model for a set **H** of wffs if and only if $\mathbf{M} \models \mathbf{H}_i$ for every wff $\mathbf{H}_i \in \mathbf{H}$.

Expressibility. As is the case with propositional logic, one can choose to employ either a small number of connectives and quantifiers (for elegance and metatheoretical simplicity) or a wide variety (for expressive power). Thus, on the one hand, the formal system presented above may be extended in a natural way to include the other truth-functional connectives or, on the other hand, restricted to using (say) only $\neg$, $\vee$, and $\forall$. The latter can be accomplished as in propositional logic, together with the following definition:

$$\exists\mathbf{v}\varphi =_{df} \neg \forall\mathbf{v} \neg \varphi$$

Another variation is to employ restricted quantifiers. Instead of translating

All As are Bs.

Some As are Bs.

as, respectively,

$$\forall x[Ax \rightarrow Bx] \text{ and } \exists x[Ax \wedge Bx]$$

with the noticeable change in syntactic structure, a family of restricted quantifiers can be introduced:

$$(\forall x: \varphi(x)) \text{ and } (\exists x: \varphi(x))$$

Using this notation, the translations become the more uniform-looking

$$(\forall x: Ax)Bx \text{ and } (\exists x: Ax)Bx$$

This notation has the additional advantage of being extendible to generalized quantifiers for handling such sentences as

Most As are Bs.

Many As are Bs.

as well as numerical quantifiers:

Exactly 4116 As are Bs.

Greater than 5 As are Bs.

Between 5 and 10 As are Bs.

Generalized and numerical quantifiers are, however, beyond the scope of first-order logic (for discussions of these issues, see Barwise and Cooper (1981), Brown (1984), McCawley (1981), Montague (1970), and Shapiro (1979).

Other alternatives to first-order languages and logics have been motivated by ontological concerns. As is seen below, when deduction is discussed, $\forall x\varphi(x)$ implies $\exists x\varphi(x)$ in a nonempty domain. But what about the empty domain? Why should logic imply that something exists? Shouldn't logic be independent of ontology? Attempts to broaden the scope of first-order logic have included free logics (ie, logics that are free of existence presuppositions) and Meinongian logics that allow [for representing and reasoning about nonexistents. Both of these kinds of logics often choose to represent existence by a special predicate, $E!$, rather than by trying to define existence in purely first-order terms (as, eg, "$\exists x[x = a]$" for "a exists") [for discussions of free logics, see Hintikka (1966), Lambert (1969, 1970, 1981, 1984), Leblanc and Thomason (1968), and Scott (1967) and for discussions of Meinongian logics, see Castañeda (1972), Parsons (1980), Rapaport (1978, 1981, 1984, 1985a,b), Routley (1979), and Zalta (1983)].

DEDUCTIVE SYSTEMS OF PREDICATE LOGIC

As with propositional logic, a deductive system for predicate logic can be presented axiomatically or as a natural deduction system.

Axiomatic Predicate Logic

In this section a set of axioms and rules of inference for predicate logic are presented using the terminology introduced in the article LOGIC, PROPOSITIONAL. As is done there, the wffs are restricted to those whose only connectives are $\neg$ and $\rightarrow$; and the only quantifier is the universal quantifier. All wffs of the following forms will be axiom schemata:

(A1) $(\varphi \rightarrow (\psi \rightarrow \varphi))$.

(A2) $((\varphi \rightarrow (\psi \rightarrow \chi)) \rightarrow ((\varphi \rightarrow \psi) \rightarrow (\varphi \rightarrow \chi)))$.

(A3) $((\neg \varphi \rightarrow \neg \psi) \rightarrow (\psi \rightarrow \varphi))$.

(A4) $(\forall\mathbf{v}[\varphi \rightarrow \psi] \rightarrow (\varphi \rightarrow \forall\mathbf{v}\psi))$, where **v** is not free in φ.

(A5) $(\forall\mathbf{v}\varphi(\mathbf{v}^*) \rightarrow \varphi(\mathbf{t}/\mathbf{v}))$, where $\varphi(\mathbf{t}/\mathbf{v})$ is the result of replacing all free occurrences of **v** in φ by any term **t** and where all variables in **t** are free at all locations in φ where **v** occurs freely.

There are two rules of inference:

Modus ponens: From φ and $(\varphi \rightarrow \psi)$, infer ψ.

Universal generalization: From φ, infer $\forall\mathbf{v}\varphi$.

A Natural-Deduction System for Predicate Logic

The natural-deduction system for propositional logic introduced in LOGIC, PROPOSITIONAL may be extended to predicate logic by providing introduction and elimination rules for the quantifiers. Because these rules involve the substitution of variables by constants, and vice versa, care must be taken not to accidentally bind a previously free variable or free a previously bound one. Consequently, the quantifier rules are not as "natural" as the rules for the connectives.

∀ *Elimination:* From $\forall \mathbf{v}\varphi(\mathbf{v}^*)$, infer $\varphi(\mathbf{c}/\mathbf{v})$, where $\varphi(\mathbf{c}/\mathbf{v})$ is the wff that results from $\varphi(\mathbf{v}^*)$ by replacing all free occurrences of the variable $\mathbf{v}$ by the constant $\mathbf{c}$.

∀ *Introduction:* From $\varphi(\mathbf{c}^*)$, infer $\forall \mathbf{v}\varphi(\mathbf{v}/\mathbf{c})$, where $\varphi(\mathbf{v}/\mathbf{c})$ is the wff that results from $\varphi(\mathbf{c}^*)$ by replacing all occurrences of $\mathbf{c}$ by $\mathbf{v}$, provided: $\mathbf{c}$ does not occur in a premise; if $\varphi(\mathbf{c}^*)$ occurs in a subproof, then no individual constant in $\varphi(\mathbf{c}^*)$ occurs in an assumption that is global to the subproof; and all new occurrences of $\mathbf{v}$ must be free after the replacement.

∃ *Introduction:* From $\varphi(\mathbf{c}^*)$, infer $\exists \mathbf{v}\varphi(\mathbf{v}/\mathbf{c}^*)$, where $\varphi(\mathbf{v}/\mathbf{c}^*)$ is the formula that results from $\varphi(\mathbf{c}^*)$ by replacing zero or more occurrences of $\mathbf{c}$ by $\mathbf{v}$.

∃ *Elimination:* From $\exists \mathbf{v}\varphi(\mathbf{v}^*)$ and a subproof that begins with the assumption $\varphi(\mathbf{c}/\mathbf{v})$ and that ends with

a proposition ψ not containing $\mathbf{c}$, infer ψ, where $\mathbf{c}$ is an individual constant that has not been used before and $\varphi(\mathbf{c}/\mathbf{v})$ is as described above.

[These rules are adapted from Schagrin, Rapaport, and Dipert (1985). For further discussion and other sets of rules, see other standard introductory texts such as Copi (1979), Jeffrey (1981), Kalish, Montague, and Mar (1980), Mendelson (1979), Quine (1951, 1980, 1982).] As with the case of propositional logic, there is a form of the inference rule Resolution that has proved to be of importance in AI contexts (see Chang and Lee, 1973; Manna, 1974; Nilsson, 1971, 1980; Raphael, 1976; Rich, 1983; Winston, 1984 and THEOREM PROVING).

As an example of the use of the introduction and elimination rules, Figure 1 shows a translation and natural-deduction proof of the argument:

Horses are animals.
∴ Every head of a horse is a head of an animal.

The rules of → *Elimination* and → *Introduction* used on lines 7 and 11 can be derived from the rules for the connectives ¬ and ∧ and the logical equivalence "material conditional"; the former rule is, essentially, *modus ponens* (see LOGIC, PROPOSITIONAL and Schagrin, Rapaport, and Dipert (1985) for details of these rules and the derivations).

Translation:

$$\forall x[\text{Horse}(x) \rightarrow \text{Animal}(x)] \vdash \forall y[\exists x[\text{Horse}(x) \wedge \text{Head-of}(y, x)]$$
$$\rightarrow \exists z[\text{Animal}(z) \wedge \text{Head-of}(y, z)]]$$

Proof:

1. $\forall x[\text{Horse}(x) \rightarrow \text{Animal}(x)]$; premise of argument
    ; BEGIN subproof using → *Introduction* to prove
    ;$(\exists x[\text{Horse}(x) \wedge \text{Head-of}(a, x)] \rightarrow \exists z[\text{Animal}(z) \wedge \text{Head-of}(a, z)])$
* 2. $\exists x[\text{Horse}(x) \wedge \text{Head-of}(a, x)]$; assumption for → *Introduction*
    ; BEGIN sub-subproof using ∃ *Elimination* to prove $\exists z[\text{Animal}(z) \wedge \text{Head-of}(a, z)]$
* * 3. $(\text{Horse}(b) \wedge \text{Head-of}(a, b))$; from line 2 (assumption for ∃ *Elimination*)
* * 4. $\forall x[\text{Horse}(x) \rightarrow \text{Animal}(x)]$; sent in from line 1
* * 5. $(\text{Horse}(b) \rightarrow \text{Animal}(b))$; from line 4, by ∀ *Elimination*
* * 6. $\text{Horse}(b)$; from line 3, by ∧ *Elimination*
* * 7. $\text{Animal}(b)$; from lines 5 and 6, by → *Elimination*
* * 8. $\text{Head-of}(a, b)$; from line 3, by ∧ *Elimination*
* * 9. $(\text{Animal}(b) \wedge \text{Head-of}(a, b))$; from lines 7 and 8, by ∧ *Introduction*
* * 10. $\exists z[\text{Animal}(z) \wedge \text{Head-of}(a, z)]$; from line 9, by ∃ *Introduction*
    ;END of sub-subproof that used ∃ *Elimination* to prove $\exists z[\text{Animal}(z) \wedge \text{Head-of}(a, z)]$
* 11. $\exists z[\text{Animal}(z) \wedge \text{Head-of}(a, z)]$; returned to outer subproof from line 10 of innermost sub-subproof
* 12. $(\exists x[\text{Horse}(x) \wedge \text{Head-of}(a, x)] \rightarrow \exists z[\text{Animal}(z) \wedge \text{Head-of}(a, z)])$
    ; from lines 2 and 11, by → *Introduction*
    ; END of subproof that used → *Introduction* to prove
    ; $(\exists x[\text{Horse}(x) \wedge \text{Head-of}(a, x)] \rightarrow \exists z[\text{Animal}(z) \wedge \text{Head-of}(a, z)])$
13. $(\exists x[\text{Horse}(x) \wedge \text{Head-of}(a, x)] \rightarrow \exists z[\text{Animal}(z) \wedge \text{Head-of}(a, z)])$
    ; returned to main proof from line 12 of outer subproof
14. $\forall y[\exists x[\text{Horse}(x) \wedge \text{Head-of}(y, x)] \rightarrow \exists z[\text{Animal}(z) \wedge \text{Head-of}(y, z)]]$
    ; from line 13, by ∀ *Introduction*

Figure 1. An example of *Introduction* and *Elimination* rules to prove the argument that if horses are animals, then every head of a horse is a head of an animal.

EXTENSIONS OF PREDICATE LOGIC

First-order languages are often extended by the addition of two important symbols: the two-place predicate symbol for identity, =, and the definite-description operator ι (in many AI and natural-language contexts, words such as *equal* and *the* are used instead). These additions to the representational power of the language also entail greater deductive power.

Identity

Syntactically, the identity predicate can be defined by adding the following to the definition of wff:

(wff.=) If t_1 and t_2 are terms, then $(t_1 = t_2)$ is a(n atomic) well-formed proposition.

Often, $(t_1 \neq t_2)$ is defined as an abbreviation for $\neg(t_1 = t_2)$. Semantically $\models_I (t_1 = t_2)$ if and only if $I(t_1) = I(t_2)$. The axiomatic formulation of predicate logic can then be extended by the following two axiom schemata:

(A6) $\forall \mathbf{v}[\mathbf{v} = \mathbf{v}]$.

(A7) $\forall \mathbf{v}_1 \forall \mathbf{v}_2[(\mathbf{v}_1 = \mathbf{v}_2) \rightarrow (\varphi(\mathbf{v}_1{}^*) \leftrightarrow \psi(\mathbf{v}_2/\mathbf{v}_1{}^*))]$, where $\psi(\mathbf{v}_2/\mathbf{v}_1{}^*)$ is the result of replacing $\mathbf{v}_2$ for $\mathbf{v}_1$ at zero or more of the free occurrences of $\mathbf{v}_1$ in φ where $\mathbf{v}_2$ would not be bound.

Descriptions

Definite Descriptions. Noun phrases such as

the first human on the Moon
the present King of France
the woman who wrote "The Story of an Hour"

can be treated as having the form

the x such that $\varphi(x)$.

Thus, the expressive capabilities of the first-order language (and hence the deductive capabilities of first-order logic) introduced here can be extended by introducing a new variable-binding operator in addition to the quantifiers. Unlike the quantifiers, which are wff-producing operators, the definite description operator ι is a term-producing operator. The definition of *term* can be augmented as follows:

(T5) If φ is a wff and $\mathbf{v}$ is an individual variable, then $\iota\mathbf{v}[\varphi]$ is a term.

There has been a great deal of controversy over the semantics of such terms. The approach due to B. Russell (1971) has become the standard logical one. According to Russell's analysis, sentences of the form $\psi(\iota x\, \varphi(x))$ should not be treated as subject–predicate sentences; that is, they should not be parsed as consisting of a noun phrase, $\iota x\, \varphi(x)$, and a verb phrase, ψ. Rather, they are to be analyzed as

$$\exists x[\varphi(x) \wedge \forall y[\varphi(y) \rightarrow y = x] \wedge \psi(x)]$$

For instance, to use Russell's famous example,

The present King of France is bald

is to be represented as

$$\exists x[\text{Present-King-of-France}(x) \wedge \forall y[\text{Present-King-of-France}(y) \rightarrow y = x] \wedge \text{Bald}(x)]$$

that is,

One and only one thing is a present King of France and he is bald.

It is a consequence of this analysis that the sentence comes out false, since there is no present King of France. Similarly,

The book that Knuth wrote is interesting

is false, since Knuth has written more than one book; and

The winged horse captured by Bellerophon is named "Pegasus"

is false, since the winged horse captured by Bellerophon does not exist.

The addition to the axiomatic formulation of predicate logic is straightforward: Simply add the axiom schema

(A8) $\psi(\iota\mathbf{v}_1\varphi(\mathbf{v}_1)) \leftrightarrow \exists \mathbf{v}_1[\varphi(\mathbf{v}_1) \wedge \forall \mathbf{v}_2[\varphi(\mathbf{v}_2) \rightarrow \mathbf{v}_2 = \mathbf{v}_1] \wedge \psi(\mathbf{v}_1)]$.

Semantically, $\models_I \psi(\iota\mathbf{v}\varphi))$ if and only if

1. there is a unique element $d \in \mathbf{D}$ such that $d \in I(\varphi)$ and
2. $d \in I(\psi)$.

An alternative analysis, due to Strawson (1985) takes $\psi(\iota x\varphi(x))$ to be of subject–predicate form, but the interpretation I is taken to be a partial function: $\psi(\iota x\varphi(x))$ is neither true nor false on I if $I(\iota x\varphi(x))$ is undefined. That is, if $\iota x\varphi(x)$ does not denote a member of $\mathbf{D}$ (ie, if nothing satisfies the predicate φ), then $\psi(\iota x\varphi(x))$ is truth-valueless (for further discussion on truth-value gaps, see Lambert, 1969, 1970).

A third approach, stemming from work done by Meinong (1960), takes $\psi(\iota x\varphi(x))$ to be of subject–predicate form but chooses a universe of discourse that allows I to be total by providing an object for each definition description. This strategy can be made plausible if the universe of discourse is taken to consist of the objects of thought and, hence, is the most appropriate one for AI applications [for details see Castañeda (1977), Parsons (1980), Rapaport (1978, 1981, 1984, 1985a,b) and Routley (1979)].

Indefinite Descriptions. A noun phrase such as

a person I met today

can be treated as having the form

an x such that $\varphi(x)$.

The indefinite description operator ε, which is also variable binding and term producing, can be added to predicate logic in a manner similar to the addition of $\imath$ (for details, see Kaplan (1972) and Leisenring (1969)).

METATHEORETIC RESULTS

A few major metatheoretic results are worth mentioning briefly. As is the case for propositional logic, predicate logic is sound (all theorems are valid, ie, true on all interpretations—in symbols: if $\vdash\varphi$, then $\models\varphi$) and consistent (no wff φ is such that both $\vdash\varphi$ and $\vdash\neg\varphi$). And Gödel showed that it is complete (all valid wffs are theorems—if $\models\varphi$, then $\vdash\varphi$) (see COMPLETENESS).

Löwenheim (and, later, Skolem) (Kleene, 1950, p. 394) showed that monadic first-order logic (ie, first-order logic without relations) is decidable: for any wff φ, if there is a nonempty universe of discourse **D** and there is an interpretation I whose range is **D** and that is such that $\models_I\varphi$, then there is an interpretation I' whose range is the set of all positive integers and that is such that $\models_{I'}\varphi$. However, Church showed that the full first-order predicate calculus is undecidable (for details, see Blumberg (1967), Church (1956), and Jeffrey (1981)).

SECOND-ORDER LOGIC

If quantifiers are allowed to range over predicate variables, the resulting language allows the expression of such propositions as

There is a relation that holds between Bill and Hector,

which would seem to be a logical consequence of

Bill is a student of Hector.

In symbols,

Student-of(Hector, Bill)

implies

$\exists\mathbf{P}\ \mathbf{P}(\text{Hector, Bill})$

as well as

$\exists x\exists y\exists\mathbf{P}\ \mathbf{P}xy$

In such a language, identity can be defined by

$$\forall x\forall y[x = y \leftrightarrow \forall\varphi[\varphi(x) \leftrightarrow \varphi(y)]]$$

And, if predicates can be quantified over, then they can be the arguments of other, "higher-order" predicates. Thus, for example, that a relation is reflexive can be expressed as

$$\forall\mathbf{R}[\text{Reflexive}(\mathbf{R}) \leftrightarrow \forall x\mathbf{R}xx]$$

with **R** appearing in both subject and predicate position. Such a logic is termed second- or higher-order logic or the extended predicate calculus.

Although second-order logic clearly has greater expressive power than first-order logic, it also has some metatheoretic disadvantages. For one thing, a form of Russell's paradox can be developed:

$$\forall\varphi[\text{Self-referential}(\varphi) \leftrightarrow \varphi(\varphi)]$$

implies, by $\forall$ Elimination,

Self-referential ($\neg$ Self-referential)
$\leftrightarrow \neg$ Self-referential($\neg$ Self-referential)

For another, one version of Gödel's famous incompleteness theorem is that second-order logic is incomplete: There are true second-order wffs that are not theorems (for discussions of second-order logic, see Church (1956), Copi (1979), Jeffrey (1981), Kleene (1950), and Kneebone (1963, p. 110–118)).

BIBLIOGRAPHY

J. Barwise and R. Cooper, "Generalized Quantifiers and Natural Language," *Ling. Philos.* **4,** 159–219 (1981).

N. D. Belnap, Jr. and T. B. Steel, Jr., *The Logic of Questions and Answers,* Yale University Press, New Haven, Conn., 1976.

M. Brown, "Generalized Quantifiers and the Square of Opposition," *Notre Dame J. Form. Logic* **25,** 303–322 (1984).

A. E. Blumberg, "Logic, Modern," in P. Edwards, ed., *Encyclopedia of Philosophy,* Vol. 5, Macmillan and Free Press, New York, pp. 12–34, 1967.

H.-N. Castañeda, "Thinking and the Structure of the World," *Philosophia* **4,** 3–40 (1974); reprinted in *Critica* **6,** 43–86 (1972).

H.-N. Castañeda, "Perception, Belief, and the Structure of Physical Objects and Consciousness," *Synthèse* **35,** 285–351 (1977).

C.-L. Chang, and R. C.-T. Lee, *Symbolic Logic and Mechanical Theorem Proving,* Academic, New York, 1973.

A. Church, *Introduction to Mathematical Logic,* Princeton University Press, Princeton, N.J., 1956.

I. M. Copi, *Symbolic Logic,* 5th ed., Macmillan, New York, 1979.

D. Gabbay and F. Guenthner, eds., *Handbook of Philosophical Logic,* Vol. 2, *Extensions of Classical Logic,* D. Reidel, Dordrecht, 1984.

D. Harrah, in "The Logic of Questions," in Gabbay and Guenthner, 1984, pp. 715–764.

J. Hintikka, *Knowledge and Belief: An Introduction to the Logic of the Two Notions,* Cornell University Press, Ithaca, N.Y., 1962.

J. Hintikka, "Studies in the Logic of Existence and Necessity," *Monist* **50,** 55–76 (1966).

G. E. Hughes and M. J. Cresswell, *An Introduction to Modal Logic,* Methuen, London, 1968.

R. Jeffrey, *Formal Logic: Its Scope and Limits,* 2nd ed., McGraw-Hill, New York, 1981.

D. Kalish, R. Montague, and G. Mar, *Logic: Techniques of Formal Reasoning,* 2nd ed., Harcourt Brace Jovanovich, New York, 1980.

D. Kaplan, "What is Russell's Theory of Descriptions?," in D. F. Pears, ed., *Bertrand Russell: A Collection of Critical Essays,* Doubleday, Garden City, N.Y., pp. 227–244, 1972.

S. C. Kleene, *Introduction to Metamathematics,* Van Nostrand, Princeton, 1950.

W. Kneale and M. Kneale, *The Development of Logic,* Oxford University Press, Oxford, 1962.

G. T. Kneebone, *Mathematical Logic and the Foundations of Mathematics: An Introductory Survey,* Van Nostrand, London, 1963.

K. Lambert, ed., *The Logical Way of Doing Things,* Yale University Press, New Haven, Conn., 1969.

K. Lambert, *Philosophical Problems in Logic: Some Recent Developments,* D. Reidel, Dordrecht, 1970.

K. Lambert, "On the Philosophical Foundations of Free Logic," *Inquiry* **24,** 147–203 (1981).

K. Lambert, *Meinong and the Principle of Independence,* Cambridge University Press, Cambridge, UK, 1984.

H. Leblanc and R. H. Thomason, "Completeness Theorems for Some Presupposition-Free Logics," *Fund. Math.* **62,** 125–164 (1968).

A. C. Leisenring, *Mathematical Logic and Hilbert's ε-Symbol,* Gordon and Breach, New York, 1969.

Z. Manna, *Mathematical Theory of Computation,* McGraw-Hill, New York, 1974.

J. McCawley, *Everything that Linguists Have Always Wanted to Know About Logic but Were Ashamed to Ask,* University of Chicago Press, Chicago, 1981.

A. Meinong, "Über Gegenstandstheorie," in R. Haller, ed., *Alexius Meinong Gesamtausgabe,* Vol. 2, Akademische Druck- u. Verlagsanstalt, Graz, Austria, pp. 481–535, 1971. English translation "The Theory of Objects" by I. Levi and co-workers, in R. M. Chisholm, ed., *Realism and the Background of Phenomenology,* Free Press, New York, pp. 76–117, 1960.

E. Mendelson, *Introduction to Mathematical Logic,* 2nd ed., Van Nostrand, New York, 1979.

R. Montague, "The Proper Treatment of Quantification in Ordinary English," in K. J. J. Hintikka, J. M. E. Moravcsik, and P. Suppes, eds., *Approaches to Natural Language: Proceedings of the 1970 Stanford Workshop on Grammar and Semantics,* D. Reidel, Dordrecht, pp. 221–242, 1970.

N. J. Nilsson, *Problem-Solving Methods in Artificial Intelligence,* McGraw-Hill, New York, 1971.

N. J. Nilsson, *Principles of Artificial Intelligence,* Tioga, Palo Alto, Calif., 1980.

D. Nute, *Essential Formal Semantics,* Rowman and Littlefield, Totowa, N.J., 1981.

H. R. Otto, *The Linguistic Basis of Logic Translation,* University Press of America, Washington, D.C., 1978.

T. Parsons, *Nonexistent Objects,* Yale University Press, New Haven, 1980.

A. N. Prior, "Logic, History of," in P. Edwards, ed., *Encyclopedia of Philosophy,* Vol. 4, Macmillan and Free Press, New York, pp. 513–571, 1967a.

A. N. Prior, "Logic, Traditional," in P. Edwards, ed., *Encyclopedia of Philosophy,* Vol. 5, Macmillan and Free Press, New York, pp. 34–45, 1967b.

A. N. Prior, "Logic, Modal," in P. Edwards, ed., *Encyclopedia of Philosophy,* Vol. 5, Macmillan and Free Press, New York, pp. 5–12, 1967c.

W. V. O. Quine, *Mathematical Logic,* rev. ed., Harper & Row, 1951.

W. V. O. Quine, *Elementary Logic,* rev. ed., Harvard University Press, Cambridge, 1980.

W. V. O. Quine, *Methods of Logic,* 4th ed., Harvard University Press, Cambridge, 1982.

W. J. Rapaport, "Meinongian Theories and a Russellian Paradox," *Noûs* **12,** 153–180 (1978); errata, *Noûs* **13,** 125 (1979).

W. J. Rapaport, "How to Make the World Fit Our Language: An Essay in Meinongian Semantics," *Graz. Philos. Stud.* **14,** 1–21 (1981).

W. J. Rapaport, "Critical Notice of Routley [1979]," *Philos. Phenomenol. Res.,* **44,** 539–552 (1984).

W. J. Rapaport, "Meinongian Semantics for Propositional Semantic Networks," *Proc. Assoc. Computat. Ling.* **23,** 43–48 (1985a).

W. J. Rapaport, "To Be and Not to Be: Critical Study of Parsons [1980]," *Noûs* **19,** 255–271 (1985b).

B. Raphael, *The Thinking Computer: Mind Inside Matter,* W. H. Freeman, San Francisco, 1976.

E. Rich, *Artificial Intelligence,* McGraw-Hill, New York, 1983.

R. Routley, *Exploring Meinong's Jungle and Beyond,* Australian National University, Research School of Social Sciences, Department of Philosophy, Canberra, 1979.

B. Russell, "On Denoting," in R. C. Marsh, ed., *Logic and Knowledge,* G. P. Putnam's Sons, New York, pp. 39–56, 1971.

M. L. Schagrin, *The Language of Logic: A Self-Instruction Text,* 2nd ed., Random House, New York, 1979.

M. L. Schagrin, W. J. Rapaport, and R. R. Dipert, *Logic: A Computer Approach,* McGraw-Hill, New York, 1985.

D. Scott, "Existence and Description in Formal Logic," in R. Schoenman, ed., *Bertrand Russell: Philosopher of the Century,* Allen and Unwin, London, pp. 181–200, 1967.

S. C. Shapiro, "Numerical Quantifiers and Their Use in Reasoning with Negative Information," *Proc. of the Sixth Int. Joint Conf. Artif. Intell.,* Tokyo, Japan, pp. 791–796, 1979.

P. F. Strawson, "On Referring," in A. P. Martinich, ed., *The Philosophy of Language,* Oxford University Press, New York, pp. 220–235, 1985.

A. N. Whitehead and B. Russell, *Principia Mathematica,* 2nd ed., Cambridge University Press, Cambridge, UK, 1927.

P. H. Winston, *Artificial Intelligence,* 2nd ed., Addison-Wesley, Reading, Mass., 1984.

E. Zalta, *Abstract Objects,* D. Reidel, Dordrecht, 1983.

W. J. Rapaport
SUNY at Buffalo

LOGIC PROGRAMMING

Logic programming can be broadly understood as the use of logic to represent problems and problem-solving methods, together with the use of appropriate proof procedures for the effective solution of those problems. For the most part, logic programming today uses Horn-clause logic augmented with negation-as-failure to represent knowledge and employs backward reasoning to solve problems by problem reduction.

THE PROCEDURAL INTERPRETATION OF HORN CLAUSES

Written in the declarative syntax of logic, Horn clauses are of three kinds:

1. Atomic formulas (or facts), such as

    a is_joined_to b

    b is_joined_to a

2. Implications (or rules), such as

    path(X, Y)   if X is_joined_to Z & path(Z, Y)

    path(X, Y)   if X is_joined_to Y

    (Note that the first of these rules is recursive, in that *path* occurs on both sides of the *if*.

3. Negated conjunctions (denials) of atomic formulas, such as

    $\neg(X$ is_joined_to Y & Y is_joined_to $X)$

Atomic formulas (or predicates) may be written in prefix form as in the case of path(X, Y), or in infix form as in the case of X is_joined_to Y; the difference between such forms is wholly presentational. The arguments of predicates are commonly called terms. The simplest kinds of terms are constants and variables; in this article, they are distinguished by the convention that the names of variables begin with upper-case letters. In addition, compound terms can be constructed by applying function symbols to arguments that may themselves be any kind of term. Terms containing no variables are said to be ground.

All variables, such as X, Y, and Z used in clauses 1–3 above, are implicitly universally quantified in front of the clause in which they occur. Thus the first rule in clause 2 stands for

$$(\forall X, Y, Z)(\text{path}(X, Y) \quad \text{if} \quad X \text{ is\_joined\_to } Z \,\&$$
$$\text{path}(Z, Y))$$

The predicate on the left of the *if* is called the head of the rule, whereas those on the right are jointly called the body of the rule.

Horn clauses enjoy a simple procedural interpretation. Clauses of types 1 and 2 are interpreted as procedures, and clauses of type 3 as conjunctions of procedure calls. A logic program is just a set of procedures. Procedure calls are executed by backward reasoning, starting with some clause of type 3, which represents the initial problem to be solved, and consecutively using clauses of types 1 and 2 to derive new clauses of type 3, which represents reductions of the original problem, and pursuing this course until no more subproblems remain to be solved.

Each backward reasoning step begins by unifying some procedure call in a clause of type 3 with the head of some procedure: their unifier is some (possibly empty) set of bindings (of variables to terms) the application of which to the call and the head makes them identical. The step is completed by replacing the call by the procedure's body and applying the unifier to the resulting clause.

Using the clause $\neg$path(X, X) as the initial problem and the clauses in 1 and 2 above as the program, backward reasoning can derive this sequence of clauses:

$\neg$path(X, X)

$\neg(X$ is_joined_to Y & path(Y, X))

$\neg$path(b, a)

$\neg b$ is_joined_to a

$\neg true$

The last clause in this derivation can be regarded as the empty clause in resolution and the entire derivation as a resolution refutation that shows that the assumption

$$\forall X \; \neg\text{path}(X, X)$$

that is,

$$\neg \exists X \; \text{path}(X, X)$$

is inconsistent with the program. Moreover, the unifications performed in the course of constructing this derivation bind X to a value (namely a); this binding is denoted by X/a.

The denial $\neg$path(X, X) representing the initial problem can also be viewed as a query ?path(X, X) and the refutation as a successful computation; this computation returns an answer path(a, a) obtained by substituting for X in the query the value to which it has been bound.

Given an initial problem and a program represented by Horn clauses, there may be several distinct computations that can be generated by backward reasoning. This possibility makes logic programming nondeterministic. For the example just considered there are infinitely many other successful computations that return only the answers path(a, a) and path(b, b). In general, computations need not terminate, and even if they do they need not do so successfully. Nondeterminism will be discussed again later in this article.

Historical Origins

Horn clauses are a special case of the clausal form of logic, whereas the backward reasoning strategy is a special case of resolution (qv). Clausal form was developed within the field of automated theorem proving to facilitate the representation and manipulation of logical statements within a computer. Resolution was developed in the 1960s as a machine-oriented logic using clausal form (Robinson, 1965). Model elimination, a goal-oriented proof procedure using a variation of clausal form, was developed shortly afterward (Loveland, 1968).

Early attempts to use logic as a declarative computer language were made at the end of the 1960s (Green, 1969; Elcock, 1990). However, by that time there was a prevailing view in the AI community that logic was too declarative and too general purpose for useful, practical applications. The AI language PLANNER (qv) was presented as a procedural alternative to the uniform theorem-proving methods based on resolution (Hewitt, 1969). At about the same time, one study showed how to combine resolution with model elimination's backward reasoning in a system called SL resolution (Kowalski and Kuehner, 1971). Related discoveries were also made (Loveland, 1970; Reiter, 1971).

The basic idea of Horn-clause logic programming arose in the early 1970s from collaboration between Kowalski at the University of Edinburgh and Colmerauer at the University of Aix-Marseilles. At the same time, it was being argued in general terms that computation could be regarded as controlled deduction (Hayes, 1973). By the end of the summer of 1972, the design and implementation of the first PROLOG (*Programmation en Logique*) interpreter based on SL-resolution had been completed (Colmerauer and co-workers, 1973), and a substantial French-language question–answering system had already been implemented. More detailed accounts of the early history of logic programming have been published (Kowalski, 1988; Cohen, 1988).

Procedural vs Declarative Representation of Knowledge

Perhaps the distinguishing characteristic of logic programming is that declarative and procedural representations of knowledge can be combined in the same statement. This contrasts with a common view that pure logic programming is nonprocedural. In this common view the programmer uses logic declaratively to represent properties of relations in the problem domain, treating the procedural interpretation as a theorem-proving method for using those properties to solve problems in the domain.

Such a nonprocedural way of using logic programming is appropriate for many applications, for example, for program specification and deductive databases. It is not useful, however, when the knowledge to be represented is explicitly procedural, as in such sentences as

- Press the alarm signal button,
  to alert the driver.
- Use an umbrella, if it is raining,
  to stay dry.
- If you want to be a British citizen, then
  marry a British citizen,
  live in Britain for at least three years,
  apply for naturalization.
- To quick sort a list X into Y,
  partition X into a small list $X1$ and a large list $X2$,
  quick sort $X1$ into $Y1$,
  quick sort $X2$ into $Y2$,
  append $Y2$ onto $Y1$ to obtain Y.

It is a corollary of the procedural interpretation that problem-reduction procedures such as these can be represented as logic programs by representing the purpose of a procedure as the conclusion of an implication and by representing the procedure calls as the conditions of the implication. Thus the procedures written above can be obtained by applying backward reasoning to the Horn clauses

- You alert the driver
  if you press the alarm signal button.

- You stay dry
  if it is raining
  and you use an umbrella.
- You can become a British citizen
  if you marry a British citizen
  and you live in Britain for at least three years
  and you apply for naturalization.
- List X is quick sorted into Y
  if X is partitioned into small $X1$ and large $X2$
  and list $X1$ is quick sorted into $Y1$
  and list $X2$ is quick sorted into $Y2$
  and appending $Y2$ onto $Y1$ gives Y.

For many applications, it is natural to think in terms of procedures. For these applications, the procedural interpretation can be used both to represent the procedures by logic programs and to give them a declarative interpretation.

Viewed procedually, logic programming differs most notably from conventional programming in two respects: nondeterminism and procedure call by unification. The main potential benefits of these features from the programmer's viewpoint are that the mechanisms for seeking all solutions to a query and for handling different input–output query modes are built into the formalism, thereby substantially reducing programming effort.

AND- vs OR-Nondeterminism

Logic programs do not by themselves determine the order in which calls and procedures are selected for execution. In a query such as

?(path(a, b) & path(b, c))
"find a path from a to c through b"

the procedure calls path(a, b) and path(b, c) can be selected for processing either in parallel or in sequence (in any order). Also, if several procedures

path(X, Y) if X is_joined_to Z & path(Z, Y)
path(X, Y) if X is_joined_to Y

apply, say, to the call path(a, b) then any or all of them can be used, either in parallel or in sequence (in any order), to show path(a, b). The freedom of call selection is known as AND-nondeterminism, and the freedom of procedure selection is known as OR-nondeterminism. Ideally, whichever selection rules are imposed in practice, they should influence only execution efficiency and should not affect what the execution achieves logically.

Once call selection rules have been decided on, they determine, in respect of any given query and set of procedures, a search space comprising the derivable computations. In order to explore this search space it is necessary to deploy some sort of search strategy. Such a strategy is said to be fair if it is able eventually to explore all computations exhaustively, but is otherwise unfair. A fair strategy is guaranteed to find, in finite time, any derivable answer present in the search space, even when the latter is infinite; the same may not be true of an unfair strategy.

Unconstrained call selection corresponds to SLD resolution (Apt and van Emden, 1982). It has been proven (Hill, 1974) that SLD resolution is complete in that it is capable of refuting any logically inconsistent denial (ie, solving any logically solvable query); consequently, its use under the control of a fair search strategy is bound to generate some answer to that query. A stronger completeness result, termed the *independence of the computation rule* (Clark, 1979), ensures that all the answers to a query are logically derivable by SLD no matter how calls are selected; these results ensure the completeness of logic programming systems that employ coroutining strategies, wherein calls are selected according to criteria based on the data flow through their variables.

The policy employed for procedure selection affects only the relative order in which different ways of solving a problem are tried, and hence the relative order in which answers, if any, are discovered. OR-nondeterminism enables either the programmer or the executing system to decide these matters in the certainty that the decision cannot affect which answers are logically derivable. However, an unfair procedure selection strategy can render some answers inaccessible in practice.

Recursive Data Structures

The data items manipulated during logic program execution consist of the terms making up the arguments of procedure calls. Such terms are similar to those employed in LISP. For example, the compound term

$$cons(a, cons(b, cons(c, nil)))$$

which represents the list $[a, b, c]$ can be used both in LISP and logic programs. Compound terms of this sort are employed typically for representing trees and lists. For example, the binary tree shown in Figure 1 can be represented by the term $t(t(a, b), t(c, d))$ using the function symbol t.

Trees and lists are examples of recursively definable data structures. The definition of a list, for example, can be expressed recursively by the logic program

> list(nil)
> list(cons(U, X))   if   element(U) & list(X)

The recursive nature of such a definition is inherited typically by procedures designed to access or manipulate the data structure. For example, to compute the length L of the list $[a, b, c]$ the following recursive program might be used.

> 0 is_length_of nil
> L is_length_of cons(U, X)   if $L1$ is_length_of X &
> $\qquad\qquad\qquad\qquad\qquad\qquad L$ is $L1+1$
>
> 1 is 0+1
> 2 is 1+1
> 3 is 2+1

to solve the query

> ?L is_length_of cons(a, cons(b, cons(c, nil)))

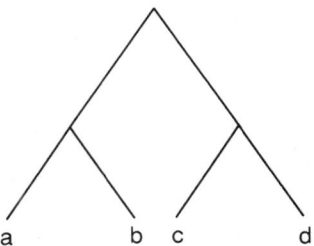

Figure 1. A binary tree.

The procedures that apply to the query's call are just those whose conclusions can be unified with the call, in this case, just the second procedure. The same program could also be used to compute lists of arbitrary lengths by solving the query

> ?L is_length_of List

Of which the first argument conveys output data rather than, as formerly, input data. In this case both procedures apply to the call, because both their conclusions unify with it. In practice this use would need to be constrained, otherwise the execution would proceed indefinitely. Nonetheless, the capability in principle of using a procedure in a variety of input–output modes is a feature of logic programming not shared by functional programming formalisms, such as LISP, and is practical in many cases even with standard logic programming execution strategies.

When computing on domains represented only by finite terms, it is necessary, for sound computation, to include in the unification algorithm a particular test called the *occur check*. This test eliminates the possibility of generating a self-referential binding, such as $X/f(X)$, denoting an infinite term. For the execution of a program that is known not to generate such bindings, the occur check may be profitably omitted from the unification algorithm to improve processing speed. In other contexts, however, omission of the occur check can be combined with special arrangements for processing self-referential bindings to cater for infinite data structures. An example of such a system is PROLOG II (Colmerauer, 1984). The formal semantics of logic programs supporting infinite terms have been investigated (Lloyd, 1987).

Minimal Model Semantics

The semantics of Horn-clause programs can be formulated in the framework of model theory. A model for a clause-set P associates relations in some domain D with P's predicate symbols. The simplest domain to consider, because it depends only on the language L in which P is written, is called the Herbrand universe and comprises just the ground terms of L. The models based on this domain are called Herbrand models and are defined as follows. The Herbrand base (HB) is the set of all ground atoms (variable-free atomic formulas) in L. A Herbrand interpretation is any subset of HB comprising just those atoms assigned true (the remainder are assigned false); it is a

Herbrand model for P if and only if these truth assignments satisfy P.

It is provable that a set of Horn clauses has a model if and only if it has a Herbrand model. Moreover, a Horn-clause program always possesses Herbrand models, and these are partially ordered by the relation of set inclusion so as to determine a unique minimal model. This contains exactly those ground atoms that are logically implied by P and hence, owing to the completeness of SLD, exactly those that are provable by SLD (or computable) from P.

The semantics of Horn-clause programs may also be defined by means of the least fixpoint of a function T_P. The application of T_P to any Herbrand interpretation I yields another Herbrand interpretation $T_P(I)$ comprising every atom A for which P contains a clause having a ground instance which is

either   the fact A
or   a rule with head A and body B such that all the atoms in B are contained in I.

The least fixpoint of T_P is identical to the minimal model of P.

The connections between the model-theoretic, least fixpoint, and operational (proof-theoretic) semantics were first articulated by Maarten van Emden and Kowalski (1976). A detailed account of these semantics and their relationships has been published (Lloyd, 1987).

PROLOG

The best-known and most widely used logic programming formalism is PROLOG, whose language includes pure Horn-clause logic and whose execution strategy relies on built-in policies for call selection and procedure selection.

Sequential Control

For the sake of efficiency and to facilitate the programmer's control over program execution, PROLOG selects calls and procedures in the order in which they are written. These selection policies operate within the particular search strategy employed by PROLOG. This is a depth-first, backtracking strategy (see SEARCH, DEPTH FIRST; BACK-TRACKING), which determines only that each computation shall be fully explored before attention is given to other computations and which is, therefore, inherently unfair.

The significance of the call-selection policy, which is the chief determinant of the execution's overall efficiency, can be seen by considering the PROLOG procedure.

X is_grandparent_of Y if X is_parent_of Z & Z is_parent_of Y

In general, using this will be more efficient for the purpose of finding Y given X than using the logically identical procedure

X is_grandparent_of Y if Z is_parent_of Y & X is_parent_of Z

whose calls are written (and hence executed) in the opposite order. This is because the task of solving the first call in the latter case is unconstrained. Scheduling calls by means of text order is thus a simple but powerful way for the programmer to exploit AND-nondeterminism in order to influence efficiency.

Similarly, scheduling procedures by means of text order is a simple but powerful way of exploiting OR-nondeterminism. Its main use is to control the order in which computations are generated; this can be useful for computing certain answers before others, or to give priority to finite computations. For example, the task may be to compute the grandsons of X before computing the grand-daughters. This can be achieved by appropriately ordering the auxiliary facts about parents, listing all sons before listing all daughters:

        jane is_parent_of john
        john is_parent_of peter
        anne is_parent_of peter
                .
                .
                .
        jane is_parent_of mary
        john is_parent_of susan
        anne is_parent_of susan
                .
                .
                .

The procedure-selection policy does not affect the overall efficiency of executing an exhaustive search for answers; however, it can affect the efficiency with which any individual answer is obtained, because this depends on which particular computations, if any, precede the one yielding that answer. This fact is particularly important in cases where not all the computations are finite, because some logically derivable answers may then be rendered effectively uncomputable.

Pruning Computations Using Cut

The *cut* (denoted here by !) is a control device enabling the programmer to prune unwanted computations during execution. Inserted into any procedure or query as an extra call, its function when executed is to eliminate all untried alternative computations which have become pending either on or since invoking the clause in which it occurs. Returning to the grandparent example, if the task were to find the grandchildren born to just one child of a given X then this procedure

X is_grandparent_of Y if X is_parent_of Z & ! & Z is_parent_of Y

would suffice: the pruned SLD-tree generated in the case where X is given as jane is shown in Figure 2 (in which predicate symbols have been abbreviated). The effect of the cut is thus to make execution more OR-deterministic;

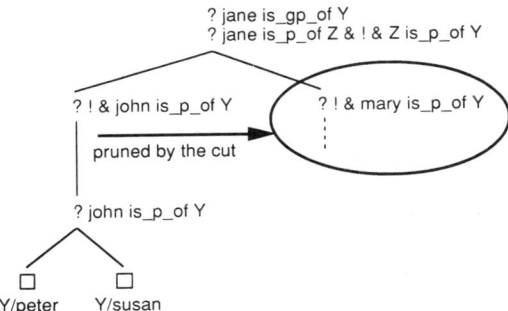

Figure 2. An SLD-tree pruned by a cut.

however, there is a concomitant loss of completeness when, as in the example, the pruned computations determine answers to the initial query that are distinct from those given by the unpruned computations.

The cut is subject to serious misuse. Consider, for instance, the following program that rounds a real number, represented by a whole part X and a fractional part F, to the nearest whole number Y:

round(X, F, X)   if $F \leq 0.5$ & !
round(X, F, Y)   if Y is $X + 1$

This program works correctly whenever *round* is called with its first and second arguments specified and its third argument unspecified, because the second (rounding-up) procedure is applied if and only if the first (rounding-down) procedure fails to find that $F \leq 0.5$. However, the query

?round(2, 0.1, 3)

incorrectly succeeds; this is because the second procedure, which omits to check that F exceeds 0.5, is not a true declaration about the intended *round* relation. This program demonstrates the use of the cut partially to simulate negation, in that it is motivated, for efficiency's sake, by the desire to eliminate the second procedure's obligation to check that F is not less than or equal to 0.5. It is a classic example of the dangers entailed in concentrating only on procedural considerations without paying sufficient regard to the program's declarative interpretation.

The cut's most celebrated use is in representing negation-as-failure by the program

not(Z)   if Z & ! & fail
not(Z)

intended for processing a quasi-negated call such as not($p(a)$). If the call $p(a)$ passed through the metavariable Z can be solved in the first procedure then the cut blocks use of the second procedure and the ensuing fail call (which unifies with the head of no procedure) then forces failure of the original call; otherwise, execution can solve that call using the second procedure instead.

Addition and Deletion of Clauses

Most PROLOG systems permit special calls that add clauses to, or delete clauses from, the program. The use of such devices is generally liable to conflict with the declarative reading of programs. It is nevertheless possible to justify their use in certain cases.

Run-time deletion of a clause not only eliminates possibly unwanted computations dependent on it, but also usefully deallocates the memory assigned to it. Provided subsequent execution never requires the clause, the deletion carries no logical penalties; otherwise the penalty is incompleteness in the solutions computed. Adding a clause during program execution is often used to assert some already-computed result as a lemma, making the result more accessible to future procedure calls than it would be if it had to be recomputed from the original clauses. This use of adding clauses respects the logical semantics while improving efficiency. On the other hand, adding an arbitrary clause may have computational consequences that are impossible to justify logically in terms of the original program.

The combination of addition with deletion promotes a programming style analogous to the use of scratch memory. In particular, it can be used to simulate destructive assignment. For example, suppose it was required to update a sequence by interchanging the members in two given positions. Using element(X, I, U) to express that U is the element occupying position I in sequence X, any sequence X of interest can be represented by a particular set of element facts. The updating of X can then be achieved in PROLOG through the use of assert and retract primitives as follows:

update(X, I, J)   if   element(X, I, U) &
                         element(X, J, V) &
                         retract(element(X, I, U)) &
                         retract(element(X, J, V)) &
                         assert(element(X, I, V)) &
                         assert(element(X, J, U)) &

When queried in such a way as to ensure that assert and retract are called with ground arguments, this clause achieves the desired effect. However, the update conclusions so derived are not logical consequences of the program, owing to the nonlogical nature of the primitives.

EXTENSIONS OF HORN-CLAUSE PROGRAMMING

Negation-as-Failure

Although Horn-clause form is an adequate basis for computation, extensions of its logic can greatly improve its suitability for practical applications. Negation-as-failure is the most important of such extensions. Its uses range from the representation of conditionals to default reasoning.

Negation-as-failure implements the closed world assumption (CWA) that treats failure to prove as proof of negation: a negated procedure call $\neg p$ (in PROLOG, not p) is deemed to hold if and only if the attempt to solve p finitely fails. For example, given

fly(X) if bird(X) & ¬abnormal(X)
abnormal(X) if ostrich(X)
bird(X) if ostrich(X)
bird(tweety)
ostrich(ozzy)

the procedure call fly(tweety) succeeds

    because   ¬abnormal(tweety) succeeds
    because   abnormal(tweety) finitely fails

whereas the call fly(ozzy) finitely fails

    because   ¬abnormal(ozzy) finitely fails
    because   abnormal(ozzy) succeeds

The negation-as-failure principle was a prominent feature of Hewitt's (1969) language PLANNER. The first major theoretical result regarding its use in logic programming was obtained by Clark (1978) who showed that negation as failure is a sound implementation of standard classical negation, provided that the assumption that the program wholly determines the relations mentioned in it is made explicit. For the example above, this assumption can be expressed explicitly by the sentences

fly(X) iff bird(X) & ¬abnormal(X)
abnormal(X) iff ostrich(X)
ostrich(X) iff X = ozzy
bird(X) iff ostrich(X) or X = tweety

together with an appropriate set of axioms for '=', including the inequality

¬ozzy = tweety

This more complete specification, termed the *completion* of the program, then classically implies

fly(tweety)

Negation-as-failure in the context of a sequential call-selection policy requires, for the sake of soundness, that the selection of negated calls be safe. Safety requires that a negated call be selected only if it is ground and that, once it has been selected, it be fully evaluated before selecting any of its sibling calls in the query; the inference system so obtained is commonly called SLDNF-inference. SLDNF is inevitably incomplete owing to the possibility that the query may contain only negated nonground calls, a situation known as floundering; no straightforward way has been found of eliminating this possibility. The support of negation as failure in PROLOG is not only incomplete but is also potentially unsound in that the safety requirement is not enforced.

The negation-as-failure rule has been proved complete for a restricted class of logic programs (Jaffer and co-workers, 1983). More generally, however, it is incomplete and oversensitive to context of use. In particular it cannot bind variables occurring in selected nonground negated calls; it is unable, for instance, to compute the intuitive solution X/tweety for the query ?not ostrich(X). Various modifications of the negation-as-failure principle have been proposed (Chan, 1988) to solve such queries constructively.

Two main approaches have been pursued in investigating the semantics of negation-as-failure. The first approach is based on ordinary logical consequence, seeking a logical construction based on the given program, the completion being a notable example, of which the negative atomic consequences are just those atoms that finitely fail from the program; another example of such a construction is the circumscription of the program's predicates (McCarthy, 1980).

The second approach seeks to identify a particular model or fixpoint as the intended meaning of the program. In the case of a Horn clause program, it is appropriate to choose the unique minimal Herbrand model. By contrast, a program containing one or more non-Horn clauses possesses multiple minimal models besides multiple nonminimal ones, so there may be no immediately obvious reason to prefer one model to another. The aim is to identify a model (or class of models) such that the atoms that are false in that model (or class) are just those that fail from the program. Discussions of both these and other approaches and the relationships between them have been published (Przymusinski, 1989).

The negation-as-failure extension confers on logic programming the capability for nonmonotonic reasoning. In particular it provides a solution to the following problem, which has been much discussed in the artificial intelligence community.

The Yale Shooting Problem

This problem was presented (Hanks and McDermott, 1986) to illustrate the failure of various nonmonotonic logics to formalize satisfactorily the notion of temporal default reasoning. The problem has given rise to a large body of literature. Despite the attention that the problem has received, few investigators have noticed that the problem has the form of a logic program and is solved by using negation-as-failure. The appropriate query is

?t(X, result(shoot, result(wait, result(load, $s0$))))

and the appropriate program is

t(alive, $s0$)
t(loaded, result(load, S))
t(dead, result(shoot, S)) if t(loaded, S)
t(F, result(E, S)) if t(F, S) and ¬ab(F, E, S)
ab(alive, shoot, S) if t(loaded, S)

It was pointed out that using circumscription to minimize the predicate ab one obtains two minimal models (Hanks and McDermott, 1986). In one, the atoms

ab(alive, shoot, result(wait, result(load, $s0$)))
t(dead, result(shoot, result(wait, result(load, $s0$))))

hold, corresponding to one solution X/dead to the query. In the other, the atoms

ab(loaded, wait, result(load, $s0$))

t(alive, result(shoot, result(wait, result(load, $s0$))))

hold, corresponding to a second solution X/alive. Both models are minimal in terms of the abnormalities that are true, but only the first model is the one that is intuitively intended by the axioms.

It is easy to see that negation-as-failure computes only the intuitively correct result and that both the semantics associated with the completion of the program and the various semantics defined in terms of minimal models give only the correct results as well. It is also easy to see that this problem is not inherently associated with temporal reasoning.

Arbitrary Subgoals

Horn clauses can be extended to admit subgoals and queries that are arbitrary formulas of first-order logic, as in the example

$?(\forall X)(p(X)$ if $q(X))$

Such an extension bridges much of the gap between Horn-clause logic and full first-order logic. Programs using it can be converted to Horn clauses augmented by negation-as-failure. For instance, the query above can be rewritten in PROLOG as

?not exception

exception   if $q(X)$ & not $p(X)$

where *exception* is any arbitrary proposition symbol not occurring in the original program. The original query requires that all solutions of $q(X)$ also solve $p(X)$. PROLOG execution of the rewritten form seeks to show that there is no exception to this requirement; it does so by iteratively generating each solution of $q(X)$ and testing whether it also solves $p(X)$.

Any rule or query containing nonatomic subgoals can be translated into Horn-clause logic supplemented with negation-as-failure. The transformation steps needed to accomplish such translations have been articulated (Lloyd and Topor, 1984).

Sets of Solutions

Another useful extension, essentially a metalevel feature, is the ability to collect all solutions to a call into a set represented by a single term. This mechanism is commonly called *aggregation*. For example, to construct and then count the set Y of all persons X liked by john, it could be written

$?Y$ set-of $(X$: john likes $X)$ & N is_length_of Y

The set-of call can be implemented by posing the call "john likes X" and collecting distinct solutions for X into a single list Y until failing to generate any more. The soundness of this principle depends, as do the implementations suggested for negation-as-failure and arbitrary subgoals, on making the closed-world assumption explicit. Also, like both those extensions, it is susceptible to incompleteness, looping, and sensitivity to the input–output status of predicate arguments.

Metalevel Programming

Horn-clause logic and its extensions can be used at the metalevel to enable programs to describe the logical and behavioral properties of themselves and other programs. This use of metalevel logic is exemplified by the metainterpreters typically used for implementing expert system shells. The simplest metainterpreter, commonly termed the "vanilla" metainterpreter, implements pure PROLOG:

solve ([ ])

solve([One|Others])   if   clause([One|Body]) &

    solve(Body) &

    solve(Others)

The argument of 'solve' is a list, where $[X|Y]$ is PROLOG's list notation for cons(X, Y), representing a sequence of procedure calls. The predicate 'clause' holds if its argument, which is a list of terms representing atomic formulas, names a clause in the given object program whose procedure head is the first member of that list and whose procedure calls are the remaining members.

More elaborate metainterpreters may have extra arguments which name, for example, proof trees, time values, or certainty factors. Variations of the vanilla metainterpreter can also be defined to implement richer logics or special strategies for selecting calls and procedures.

More generally, metalevel programming is also useful for implementing program verifiers, synthesizers, and transformers. For these kinds of applications, it is useful to employ a more complicated naming convention, whereby object-level variables are named by ground metalevel terms. Systems for metalevel logic programming that employ such a convention have been devised (Bowen and Kowalski, 1982; Hill and Lloyd, 1989). The first of these allows programs that amalgamate object-level and metalevel expressions and admits the use of reflection rules for linking the two levels, as in the FOL system (Weyhrauch, 1980). The second one is integrated within a comprehensive, pure logic programming language named Gödel (Burt and co-workers, 1990). Current research in metalevel logic programming has been well documented in the proceedings of the Meta88 and Meta90 conferences (Bruynooghe, 1990).

SPECIFICATION VS PROGRAM

Executing Specifications

Independently of logic programming, logic has been used traditionally to express declarative specifications serving program analysis and construction. However, the mechanization of logic through computer-based proof procedures has made such specifications executable in their own right.

As a preliminary problem description, a nonprocedural, logical specification is, or at least ought to be, both simpler to reason about and more flexible to modify than a program containing greater commitment to a particular problem-solving method. Such specifications can be used not only as precursors to program development but also as queries to a database. A declarative style for such queries is essential to users unconcerned with the database's storage and access mechanisms.

Although not as rich as full classical logic, Horn-clause logic and its various extensions can be used both for specifying and for programming. These uses are distinguished only by their intent and by their relative efficiency. For example, the sentence

Y is_sort_of X if Y is_permutation_of X &
Y is_ordered.

is more of a declarative specification of the sorting relation than is the sentence

Y is_sort_of X if X decomposes_into $(X1, X2)$ &
$Y1$ is_sort_of $X1$ &
$Y2$ is_sort_of $X2$ &
Y is_merge_of $(Y1, Y2)$

which, depending on the definitions of 'decomposes_into' and 'is_merge_of', anticipates some kind of bipartitioning algorithm such as merge-sort or quick-sort. Both sentences, however, are directly executable, with greatly different efficiencies, in PROLOG.

Logic can also be used to encode and animate (possibly incomplete) knowledge formulated prior to formal specifications in the early stages of user-requirements definition and systems analysis. For instance, the knowledge content of conventional data-flow diagrams in structured systems analysis can often be transcribed directly into Horn clauses.

While run-time inefficiency may be tolerable when experimenting with specifications, deliberate disregard of the problem solver's behavior raises the hazard of infinite computations (loops). The naive specification

X is_joined-to Y if Y is_joined-to X

of connectivity in a network defined by

a is_joined_to b
b is_joined_to c
.
.
.

when executed by PROLOG to determine the network's connections via the query

?X is_joined_to Y

will loop indefinitely, without computing any solutions and without even accessing the data defining the network, if the general rule for is_joined_to textually precedes the data. Fundamentally this is due to the unfairness of PROLOG's depth-first search strategy. However, if the data precede the rule instead, then all solutions are generated but infinitely many times. In either case there is a penalty for ignoring the procedural consequences of what has been written. One way of overcoming this while preserving declarative freedom of style is to incorporate loop detection into the problem solver. Another is to transform the program into one that computes the same answers but does not give rise to loops.

Deriving Programs

A specification assumed to describe a relation correctly can be used to derive some new specification or some program more suited to computational purposes. In particular, a specification that is itself written in logic serves as an axiom set from which may be derived, by first-order inference, a more efficient logic program.

Consider how the relation between a list and its least member might be specified. The specification

W is_least_of X if W is_member_of X &
$(\forall Y)(W \leq Y$ if Y is_member_of $X)$

presents a clear definition of that relation but has little computational utility for solving a query such as

?W is_least_of $[3, 2, 1, 4]$

However, after rewriting the *if* as *if and only if* and adding known properties of the auxiliary relations it is quite easy to derive, by first-order inference, this Horn-clause program

W is_least_of $[W]$
W is_least_of $[U, V|X]$ if $U \leq V$ & W is_least_ of $[U|X]$
W is_least_of $[U, V|X]$ if $U > V$ & W is_least_of $[V|X]$

which solves the query efficiently. Here, $[U, V|X]$ is just PROLOG's more concise way of writing $[U|[V|X]]$.

Program derivation can also be applied to given logic programs to transform them into equivalent but computationally different ones. For instance, the connectivity program examined previously generated a loop by using the procedure

X is_joined-to Y if Y is_joined-to X

A new, nonlooping program can be derived by first adding to the old program exactly one procedure for a new relation 'connects_to', namely

X connects_to Y if X is_joined_to Y

so that the two relations will be identical. Using the available procedures the query ?X connects_to Y can be partially evaluated as shown in Figure 3. The subtree **T** displayed in dashed lines denotes all those computations that solve the derived query ?X is_joined_to Y using the program's ground facts. It is easy to infer that the values for

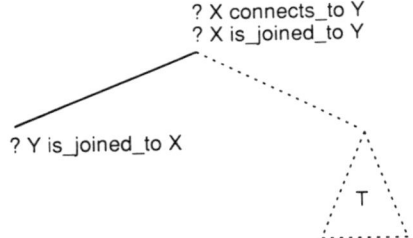

Figure 3. Partial evaluation using the given program.

X and Y computable from the old program in response to the query $?X$ is_joined_to Y may be computed instead, without looping, from this new program in response to the query $?X$ connects_to Y:

X connects_to Y if Y is_joined to X
X connects_to Y if X is_joined to Y

together with the same ground facts. The search tree so obtained (Fig. 4) clearly yields the same answers as the former search tree.

Early studies of logic program verification and derivation were undertaken by Clark and Darlington (1980) and Hogger (1981). More recent work includes the use of partial evaluation and metainterpretation (Takeuchi and Furukawa, 1986).

CONNECTION WITH FUNCTIONAL PROGRAMMING

Functional programming can be regarded as logic programming in the broad sense of computation by deriving consequences from assumptions. Assumptions in functional programs are expressed as equations; for example, the equations

$$\text{length(nil)} = 0 \qquad (1)$$

$$\text{length}(X \cdot Y) = \text{length}(Y) + 1 \qquad (2)$$

recursively define the function that computes the length of a list in terms of the addition function $+$ and the list-constructor function $\cdot$. To compute the length of the list $a \cdot b \cdot c \cdot \text{nil}$ it is necessary to derive a conclusion of the form

$$\text{length}(a \cdot b \cdot c \cdot \text{nil}) = n$$

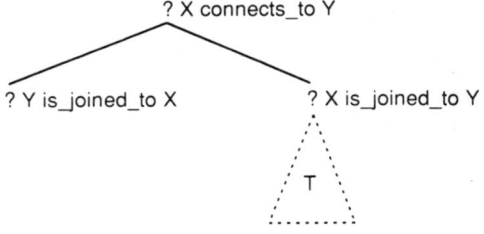

Figure 4. Partial evaluation using the transformed program.

where n is expressed only in terms of undefined symbols such as 1, 2, or 3. The derivation uses the equations as rewrite rules:

$$
\begin{aligned}
&\text{length}(a \cdot b \cdot c \cdot \text{nil}) \\
={}& \text{length}(b \cdot c \cdot \text{nil}) + 1 \\
={}& (\text{length}(c \cdot \text{nil}) + 1) + 1 \\
={}& ((\text{length(nil)} + 1) + 1) + 1 \\
={}& ((0 + 1) + 1) + 1 \\
={}& (1 + 1) + 1 \\
={}& 2 + 1 \\
={}& 3
\end{aligned}
$$

In logic programming understood as backward reasoning applied to Horn clauses and their extensions, defined function symbols such as 'length' are represented by relation symbols, and term rewriting is replaced by problem reduction. Thus equations 1 and 2 are reformulated as the Horn-clause procedures

0 is_length_of nil
N is_length_of $X \cdot Y$ if M is_length_of Y &
                                   N is $M + 1$

and the desired conclusion as the Horn-clause query

$?N$ is_length_of $a \cdot b \cdot c \cdot \text{nil}$

whose answer $N = 3$ can be computed by logic programming's standard backward reasoning strategy.

This example illustrates the general fact that all computation by means of equations used as rewrite rules can be simulated by means of backward reasoning using Horn clauses. Because all computation can be represented by rewrite rules (Kleene, 1952), this suggests a particularly simple and transparent proof that all computable functions can be represented by means of Horn clauses and all computation can be performed by backward reasoning.

The adequacy of Horn clause logic for computation was first proved by Aanderaa (1970) and Boerger (1971) who showed that every computable n-ary function can be computed by some Horn-clause program using only terms constructible from the constant 0, unary function symbol s and $(n + 2)$ variables. Related conclusions were reached by Andreka and Nemeti (1976), who used Horn clauses to simulate partial recursive functions, and by Tarnlund (1977), who used them to simulate Turing machines.

The representation of n-ary functions by means of $(n + 1)$-ary relations as illustrated above is only one of several possible correspondences between functional programming and Horn-clause programming. Another correspondence useful for expressing Horn-clause programs as functional programs employs n-ary Boolean-valued partial functions to represent n-ary relations. For example, the Horn clauses

X is_member_of $X \cdot Y$
X is_member_of $Z \cdot Y$ if X is_member_of Y

can be represented by equations

$$member(X, X \cdot Y) = true$$

$$member(X, Z \cdot Y) = member(X, Y)$$

One of the problems with this correspondence is that, with the normal algorithm for rewriting terms, the equations can be used only to test for membership, whereas the Horn clauses can equally well be used to generate members.

The relationship between Horn-clause programming and functional programming has been explored in detail (Darlington and co-workers, 1985); this work has led to the incorporation of certain logic-programming features, notably unification, in otherwise functional languages such as HOPE. The earliest example of such a hybrid language was LOGLISP (Robinson and Sibert, 1980), which combined Horn-clause programming with LISP. There has also been much interest in extending Horn-clause programming so as to support those features that are held to be of particular significance in functional programming, the most important being data types and higher-order functions; the λ-PROLOG formalism (Miller and Nadathur, 1986) is a notable contribution to the work in this area.

It happens that some higher-order effects can be achieved even in unextended Horn-clause logic. For instance, the solution $X = U \cdot V \cdot nil$ computed from the query

?2 is_length_of X

can be regarded as a binary function: given, as input, values for U and V it returns, as output, a list comprising those two items. This example demonstrates the special power of the logical variable in being able to return partially instantiated answers.

DEDUCTIVE DATABASES

Relational databases, which have emerged from the world of commercial data processing, can be regarded as a special case of logic programs consisting of variable-free and function-free facts. Relational database queries may be arbitrary formulas of first-order logic, augmented with aggregation operators such as set-of. These can be represented by logic program queries extended to include arbitrary subgoals and sets of solutions. Thus, for example, the database in Figure 5 can be represented by the set of facts

supplies(john, nuts, 0.05)
supplies(mary, nuts, 0.06)
supplies(mary, bolts, 0.10)

supplies	supplier	article	price
	john	nuts	.05
	mary	nuts	.06
	mary	bolts	.10

Figure 5. A simple relational database.

The query "find the cheapest suppliers of nuts" can be represented in first-order logic by the formula

?supplies(X, nuts, Y) &
($\forall U, V$)($Y \leq V$ if   supplies(U, nuts, V))

Deductive databases extend relational databases by including function symbols and by containing implications as well as facts. Much attention has been devoted to the function-free case of deductive databases, because in this case the Herbrand base is finite and query processing is, therefore, decidable. The language of such databases is often referred to as Datalog (Maier and Warren, 1988).

Although deductive databases have the same syntactic form as logic programs, their use in practice tends to be entirely declarative, whereas the use of logic programs is generally both procedural and declarative. The declarative nature of deductive databases facilitates the design and implementation of query-optimization procedures. Sophisticated procedures have been developed that combine backward and forward reasoning and that are sensitive to the variation of input and output arguments. Such procedures can automatically adjust for the different execution strategies needed, for example, for the different queries

?john is_grandparent_of W

and

?W is_grandparent_of john

given the definition

X is_grandparent_of Y if X is_parent_of Z &
                                  Z is_parent_of Y

Executed by a simpler processor such as PROLOG, this definition would behave efficiently for the first query but not for the second.

A second respect in which deductive databases differ from logic programs is on the emphasis given both to updates and to integrity constraints. In a database it is generally just as important to be able to make frequent changes and to maintain the integrity of data as it is to process queries efficiently. Thus the problem of representing and efficiently processing integrity constraints has become an increasing object of investigation in the field of deductive databases.

Different views have been expressed about the nature of integrity constraints. The four most popular are that they should be

- Theorems implied by the completion of the database.
- Statements consistent with the completion of the database.
- Metalevel statements about what can be proved from the database.
- Modal, epistemic statements about what the database knows.

Different integrity-checking methods are associated with these different views. Consider, for example, the statement that "the price of nuts must not exceed 0.07." In the first and second views of integrity constraints this can be represented as a statement

$$Z \leq 0.07 \text{ if } supplies(X, Y, Z)$$

to be proved from, or shown to be consistent with, the completion of the database. In the third and fourth views it can be represented as a statement of the form

$$solve(Z \leq 0.07) \quad \text{if} \quad solve(supplies(X, Y, Z))$$

where *solve* is interpreted as, respectively, either a meta-predicate or a modal operator.

It is interesting to consider what role integrity constraints and integrity checking might play in logic programming more generally. First steps toward interpreting program properties as integrity constraints and proving program properties by verifying integrity constraints have already been taken (Hogger and Lever, 1990).

APPLICATION TO EXPERT SYSTEMS

Production Rules

Many expert systems are implemented in the form of production rules. In some systems, these rules have a logical character

    if conditions then conclusion

while in others, they have a more procedural flavor

    if conditions then actions

For a long time, LISP was the traditional formalism in which to implement both these species of rule. In recent years, however, PROLOG has played an increasing role in the implementation of rule-based expert systems. Early work in this area was undertaken by Hammond (1984) who, in particular, compared PROLOG with EMYCIN. EMYCIN rules do not contain explicit variables. Instead, the effect of variables must be obtained by indirect reference to global contexts, reminiscent of object-oriented programming. PROLOG (and logic programming in general) requires that such contexts be represented explicitly as predicate arguments. Hammond showed that the lack of explicit variables in EMYCIN meant that many rules were needed in situations where PROLOG could make do with only a single rule and a set of facts.

Both PROLOG and EMYCIN reason backward, reducing desired conclusions to conditions. By contrast, expert systems relying on the condition-action style of rules must first test the conditions and then perform the actions. If these actions happen to be logical conclusions then the system merely implements forward reasoning and is logically intelligible. But in many traditional systems, the actions exert side effects on some global database, the logical status of which may be far from obvious. Such systems often benefit substantially in clarity when reconstructed as logic programs.

Declarative Input–Output

Owing to their side effects, the use of input and output facilities as provided by typical PROLOG systems may compromise the logicality of expert systems and their interfaces, as in the following PROLOG-like example:

X is_a_citizen   if   write("was") & write(X) &
                        write("born in the USA?") &
                        read("yes") &
                        write("I confirm") & write(X) &
                        write("is a citizen")

The intended meaning here is obscured by the 'read' and 'write' primitives whose implementations entail side effects. A clear representation of the meaning can be obtained by separating the knowledge

X is_a_citizen if X born_in_the_USA

from the input–output mechanism. Using an implicit input–output query-the-user scheme, the evaluation of a query $?X$ is_a_citizen generates a subquery

$?X$ born_in_the_USA

expecting input data such as the facts

john born_in_the_USA
mary born_in_the_USA

This input data might be made available either (*1*) as an integral part of the source program, (*2*) via an external file, or (*3*) by interacting with the user. In the latter two cases, input can be viewed as an integral part of the overall knowledge base, which includes the external file or user.

Analogously, output can be viewed as comprising those consequences of the knowledge base that are answers to the query. Thus the output elicited by the query $?X$ is_a_citizen might be a set of facts such as

john is_a_citizen
mary is_a_citizen

This treatment makes input/output a purely logical concept, free from system-dependent side effects. It was a central feature of the query-the-user system developed by Sergot (1983).

Heuristic Programming vs Algorithmic Programming

Many of the advantages claimed for expert systems are arguably advantages of the manner in which they are usually implemented: using AI languages and knowledge representation schemes that separate knowledge from the inference mechanisms that put that knowledge to use.

Such separation of knowledge from use renders knowledge easier to understand and easier to change. It also facilitates the development of systems that can explain and justify their conclusions. Some commentators on expert systems seem to identify expert systems with the general methodology of separating knowledge from use. If that analysis were correct, then every well-structured PROLOG program would be an expert system. But this fails to recognize the heuristic, as opposed to algorithmic, nature of expert systems. PROLOG and logic programming more generally are equally suited to the representation of both algorithms and heuristics.

A heuristic is a problem-solving method that is useful for solving some class of problems but is not guaranteed to be correct or complete. The use of heuristics to represent domain-specific knowledge and the successive refinement of heuristics by trial and error are characteristic features of expert systems. Such heuristic programming contrasts with traditional software engineering methodology, which favors the development of correct and complete programs from rigorous specifications.

The separation of knowledge from use, which is characteristic of rule-based languages such as PROLOG, is especially well suited for heuristic, trial-and-error programming. It facilitates the assimilation of additional heuristics and the correction of errors. The traditional software engineering methodology aims instead to eliminate errors by the sound derivation of programs from specifications. Logic programming is conducive to both styles of programming; indeed, because of its foundations in formal logic, it has greater potential for rigorous program development than have conventional programming formalisms.

ALTERNATIVE EXECUTION STRATEGIES

The Role of Intelligent Execution

The use of text order for goals and clauses gives the PROLOG programmer a powerful and relatively easy-to-use tool for controlling program execution. More sophisticated tools are comparatively more difficult for the programmer to control. Such tools are likely to be used, therefore, only by relatively sophisticated programmers or autonomously by the system itself.

Dependency-Directed Backtracking

Some of the problems with PROLOG's problem-solving strategy are exemplified by Pereira's formulation of the map-coloring problem. The problem is to show that all of the regions in a map, such as the one in Figure 6, can be assigned one of four colors r, y, b, or g without assigning the same color to any two adjacent regions. The problem can be specified by the goal

?next(X, Y) & next(X, Z) & next(X, V) &
next(Y, Z) & next(Y, U) & next(Y, V) &
next(Z, U) & next(Z, V) & next(U, V)

The relation *next* defines all acceptable pairs of colors that

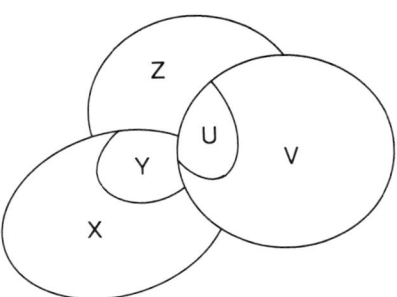

Figure 6. A map with five regions.

can be assigned to adjacent regions, by means of the ground database

next(r, y)	next(y, r)	next(b, r)	next(g, r)
next(r, b)	next(y, b)	next(b, y)	next(g, y)
next(r, g)	next(y, g)	next(b, g)	next(g, b)

Note that this is a typical instance of the way in which a relational database problem may be formulated using logic programming. Suppose PROLOG is used to evaluate the query. In this event the same first fact next(r, y) will be used to solve each of the first three subgoals, leaving the subgoals

?next(y, y) & next(y, U) & next(y, y) &
next(y, U) & next(y, y) & next(U, y)

The first of these remaining subgoals is unsolvable, due to the bindings already made: Y/y and Z/y. PROLOG, therefore, backtracks to the previous subgoal next(r,V) and tries to solve it in the next available way. But no new solution of the subgoal can affect the substitutions for Y and Z, which caused the original failure; the subproblem next(y, y) repeatedly fails as before.

Dependency-directed backtracking strategies have been devised to identify the cause of failure and to direct backtracking to a previous subgoal whose different solution can remove the cause of failure. In this case such a strategy would try a different way of solving the second subgoal next(r, Z). Dependency-directed backtracking can be likened to "learning from one's mistakes."

Subgoal Selection

An alternative to dependency-directed backtracking is often to select the right subgoal in the first place. In the example of the map-coloring problem, having solved the first two subgoals as before, leaving the subgoals

?next(r, V) &
next(y, y) & next(y, U) & next(y, V) &
next(y, U) & next(y, V) & next(U, V)

an intelligent subgoal-selection strategy would focus on the second remaining subgoal next(y, y), recognize its unsolvability, and then backtrack normally to the previous subgoal.

Several useful heuristics can be used to guide the selection of subgoals. For example,

- Select a subgoal containing fewest variables.
- Select a subgoal having fewest expected solutions.

Both of these heuristics are especially suitable for declarative programming, where the user delegates responsibility for efficiency to the program executor. However neither of these heuristics is foolproof. Examples can easily be constructed where they lead to disastrous results. Other subgoal selection strategies are better suited to procedural, user-controlled programming style. The most common of these strategies are probably *eager, lazy*, and *parallel*, or pseudo-parallel, execution.

Eager execution is controlled by working forward from inputs to outputs, executing subgoals eagerly as soon as sufficient data are available. Eager execution is also associated with data-flow evaluation of functional programs. Lazy execution is controlled by working backward from outputs to inputs, executing subgoals lazily only when their outputs are required as inputs for other subgoals. Lazy execution is also called "call by need" in functional programming languages. Subgoals that share no variables can often usefully be executed in parallel or at least in pseudo-parallel on sequential machines. This can be especially useful when one of the subgoals proves to be unsolvable.

Loop Detection

Purely declarative use of PROLOG can often give rise to nonterminating loops. Consider the following program and query:

```
john likes mary
mary likes X  if  X likes mary

?mary likes mary
```

The second clause repeatedly reduces the original goal to itself without end. It is relatively easy to design and implement loop-detection strategies that eliminate this type of loop. In general, however, it is impossible to detect and avoid all possible loops, because the existence of a general loop-detection algorithm would contradict the unsolvability of the halting problem. Moreover, even relatively straightforward types of loop can be prohibitively expensive to detect.

Looping is a greater problem with declarative uses of logic programming than it is with procedural uses. In both cases, however, some improvement can be obtained by performing compile-time program transformations. In general, program transformation can often obtain at compile-time the same effect as improved program execution at run time.

ALTERNATIVE LOGIC PROGRAMMING SCHEMES

During the 1970s, the only practical logic programming language in widespread use was PROLOG. Since then,

new logic programming languages have been developed with the aim of improving expressive power, programming productivity, and execution performance. The most important of these developments have been those concerned with parallelism, concurrency, and constraint processing.

Scope for Parallelism

The lack of commitment of logic programs to particular processing schemes makes them amenable to parallel processing. Procedure calls can be executed in parallel rather than one at a time, multiple procedures responding to any call can also be tried in parallel, backward reasoning can be combined in parallel with forward reasoning, and at the lowest processing level, procedure invocation by unification can be performed in parallel. All such parallel processing schemes can be applied to logic programs while respecting their logical semantics. The work on parallel logic languages has exerted a strong influence on the design of new-generation computer architectures. For example, the guarded Horn clause (GHC) language underlies the AND-parallel implementation language KL1 for the multi-PSI computer (Ueda and Chikayama, in press).

AND Parallelism

The AND nondeterminism of logic programs allows calls to be executed in parallel. However, the AND parallel evaluation of calls may be inhibited in practice by the presence of shared variables; no two calls that are logically interdependent may simultaneously bind a shared variable to two distinct values. Nonetheless much useful parallelism remains feasible for calls that are logically independent.

In the case where calls do share variables it is still possible to achieve some of the effect of parallelism through the use of a coroutining scheme. The best-known way of controlling such a scheme is by using producer–consumer protocols that make the activation and suspension of call evaluations contingent on the data flow through the variables in the calls. Such protocols are useful even for single-processor architectures implementing (quasi-parallel) coroutining, as was originally demonstrated by the IC-PROLOG system (Clark and McCabe, 1979).

The eight-queens problem provides a simple demonstration of such a scheme. The conventional algorithm for the problem can be regarded as a consumer–producer execution of the logic specification

```
X solves-the-8-queens-problem
   if  X is-8-queens-configuration &
       X has-no-takeable-queens
```

in which partially completed configurations, in the form of partially instantiated terms, generated by the first call are rejected immediately whenever they violate the requirements of the second. By contrast, the normal PROLOG execution of the calls in sequence would pointlessly generate many completed configurations from the first call that could not possibly satisfy the second.

OR Parallelism

The OR nondeterminism of logic programs raises the possibility of executing alternative computations in parallel. OR parallelism can be approximated in single-processor machines through the use of breadth-first search, as exemplified by the original LOGLISP system (Robinson and Sibert, 1980). The closest analogue of OR nondeterminism in functional languages is the nondeterminism of the order of evaluation of different branches of conditional expressions. Such branches can also be evaluated in parallel. However, OR nondeterminism is closer to the search nondeterminism associated with database query evaluation.

Unrestrained exploitation of OR parallelism, both by itself and, even more so, in combination with AND parallelism, can overwhelm the resources of even the most powerful architectures. Some logic programming languages, therefore, support only restricted forms of parallelism. For example, each principal cycle of the Andorra scheme (Haridi and Brand, 1988) applies AND parallel evaluation only to deterministic calls until no such calls remain pending, whereupon the textually first remaining call is evaluated, applying all procedures in parallel. Other schemes replace full OR parallelism by nondeterministic, single-choice commitment, giving rise to the so-called committed-choice languages.

Committed-Choice Languages

A committed-choice language allows only one clause to be invoked by any particular call. Given that several clauses may be logically invokable by the call, the choice of which one to commit to is determined only by time-dependent factors outside the control of the program. This scheme corresponds to the don't-care form of nondeterminism, first incorporated in Dijkstra's (1976) guarded commands: at most, one solution to the call may be computed, but the programmer does not care which one it is.

A common feature of these languages is that each clause body may be prefixed by a (possibly empty) set of calls referred to as a guard: typically, some clause whose guard is fully evaluated the soonest is the clause to which the execution thereafter commits in order to evaluate the activating call. Languages in which the guards are restricted to sets of built-in system primitives, whose evaluations do not themselves generate any derived calls, are said to be flat.

The best-known exemplars of committed-choice languages are PARLOG, Concurrent Prolog, and GHC, all of which are associated more with the notion of concurrency than with that of parallelism. PARLOG was developed by Clark and Gregory (1986), Concurrent Prolog by Shapiro (1983), and GHC by Ueda (1985). All of these languages have their origins in the parallel relational language developed by Clark and Gregory (1981). They are distinguished mainly by the different ways in which they achieve synchronization, the role of which is to ensure consistency in the way communication takes place between processes. Communication between processes is conceived as the act of binding (or further instantiating) any variable common to the calls that spawned the processes: consistency in this context means that no such common variable shall be bound differently by more than one process.

The GHC formalism is particularly simple. When any (nonguard) call C is activated, the evaluator first indentifies those clauses whose invocations would not bind any variables in C. The guards of all those clauses are then executed concurrently: any guard call whose evaluation would bind some variable in C is suspended until such time as it could be reactivated so as not to bind such a variable. As soon as some guard succeeds, the evaluation of C then commits to (the main body of) the associated clause, and the former binding restriction is relaxed. This mechanism is the means of synchronization in GHC. By contrast, PARLOG and Concurrent Prolog employ mode declarations and read-only annotations, respectively, in order to synchronize process communication.

The flavor of (flat) GHC is indicated by the following simple program for choosing any member U from a given list L:

$$\text{member}(U, L) :- L = [V|T] / U = V.$$
$$\text{member}(U, L) :- L = [V|T] / \text{member}(U, T).$$

Here the guards comprise those calls preceding the / delimiters. It is indeterminate as to which will succeed first, and hence indeterminate as to which member U will be returned as the solution. All that can be said is that no more than one such solution will be returned and that it is not important which one it is.

Constraint Logic Programming

Not every call need be executed using the standard inference mechanism of logic programming. It is often better to delegate the responsibility for executing a call to a distinct processing scheme specialized for the domain to which the call refers in its intended interpretation. Consider, for example, an ordinary logic program containing the procedure

$$\text{triangle}(X, Y, Z) \quad \text{if} \quad X \text{ exceeds } 0 \ \&$$
$$Y \text{ exceeds } 0 \ \&$$
$$Z \text{ exceeds } 0 \ \&$$
$$\text{plus}(X, Y, XY) \ \& \ XY \text{ exceeds } Z \ \&$$
$$\text{plus}(Y, X, YZ) \ \& \ YZ \text{ exceeds } X \ \&$$
$$\text{plus}(X, Z, XZ) \ \& \ XZ \text{ exceeds } Y$$

Here, $\text{triangle}(X, Y, Z)$ expresses that it is possible to construct a triangle whose sides have lengths X, Y, and Z. The other predicates serve the tasks of adding and comparing numbers. Ordinarily, these would have to be defined by further clauses supplied by the programmer. Several penalties might then arise: first, there is the effort entailed in writing those further clauses; second, evaluating calls to 'plus' and 'exceeds' using resolution inference takes no advantage of the knowledge that their arguments denote numbers; third, it may be difficult to construct definitions that cater to all input/output modes.

The program can be reformulated in the framework of constraint logic programming (CLP) as follows:

$$\text{triangle}(X, Y, Z) \quad \text{if} \quad X > 0 \ \& \ Y > 0 \ \& \ Z > 0 \ \&$$
$$X + Y > Z \ \&$$
$$Y + Z > X \ \&$$
$$X + Z > Y$$

The special symbols $+$ and $>$ are assumed to be recognizable to the system as, respectively, an operator and a predicate symbol specific to the domain $\mathcal{R}$ of (real) numbers. The new calls, such as $X + Y > Z$, are referred to as constraints posed in the theory of $\mathcal{R}$, and are evaluated using algorithms, tightly integrated into the implementation, which are specially tailored to $\mathcal{R}$. The resulting scheme is conventionally denoted by the notation CLP($\mathcal{R}$); clearly, other schemes can be constructed for other domains. The general constraint logic programming framework CLP(**D**) for arbitrary domain **D** has been formally characterized (Jaffar and Lassez, 1987).

The most obvious benefits obtained in the above example are greater concision in the program and the likelihood of faster execution. There are other benefits, however, that are less obvious yet highly significant. For instance, a nonground call such as triangle(3, 4, Z) can now be solved in the sense of returning an answer in the form of a new set of maximally reduced constraints, which in this case might take the form

$$\{7 > Z, Z > 1\}$$

In this way, CLP systems can cater to variations in input–output query modes far better than can ordinary logic programming systems.

Despite originating relatively recently, constraint logic programming is already proving to be of commercial importance. New constraint processors have been developed, as have specialized languages associated with them. For example, the knowledge-crunching machine KCM produced by the European Computer-Industry Research Centre supports the CHIP language (Dincbas and co-workers, 1988), which is capable of solving equational constraints over finite domains, Boolean terms, and rational terms. Another example is the PROLOG III language under development (Colmerauer, 1987).

STRUCTURING METHODS FOR LOGIC PROGRAMS

For large and complex applications it is important to organize and structure programs so as to facilitate their development and maintenance. Logic programs, by their very nature, have an implicit hierarchical structure associated with the hierarchy of procedure calls. The definition of *grandparent*, for example, is higher in the hierarchy than the definition of *parent*. This hierarchical structure, however, is often too weak in practice. Consequently other structuring devices corresponding to those provided by structured types, object-oriented programming and modules have been proposed.

Structured Types

The argument places of predicates can have data types assigned to them. For example, the first and second arguments of

$$\text{length}(X, Y)$$

can be assigned the types list and nonnegative integer respectively. The single argument of

$$\text{sentence}(X)$$

can be assigned the type word-list. The definitions of 'length' and 'sentence' can then be associated with the data types of their arguments. The data types might be thought of as objects that "own" the definitions of the predicates, and the definitions might be regarded as hidden within the objects. Data types such as word-list and list can be structured in hierarchies and types can inherit definitions of predicates from supertypes. For example, the data type word-list can inherit the definition of length from the supertype list.

Such a notion of structured types can provide an abstract. The overall structure within which the individual clauses of logic programs can be organized and maintained. It can be superimposed on logic programs without affecting their underlying logic, or it can be built into the logic and incorporated in the unification algorithm. Perhaps the most influential logic programming language incorporating structured types is the language LOGIN (Ait-Kaci and Nasr, 1986).

Object-Oriented Programming and the Process Interpretation

Object-oriented programming can be viewed as combining the notion of objects as structured types with the idea that objects may have local states and communicate with one another through message passing. This latter idea can be realized in logic programming by the process interpretation developed by Shapiro and Takeuchi (1983).

In the process interpretation, objects are processes represented by predicates, and messages are data items flowing in input–output streams represented by predicate arguments. This can be illustrated by the example of two generators connected to a printer via a merger in a data-flow network (Fig. 7). Items to be merged and printed are sent as messages from one object process to another. The data-flow diagram can be represented by the collection of goals:

$$?\text{generate}(X) \ \& \ \text{generate}(Y) \ \&$$
$$\text{merge}(X, Y, Z) \ \& \ \text{print}(Z)$$

where X, Y, and Z range over possibly nonterminating lists that represent input–output streams. The subgoals can be executed concurrently. The different committed-choice logic programming languages provide different mechanisms for controlling execution, so that, for example, merge(X, Y, Z) will be selected for execution only

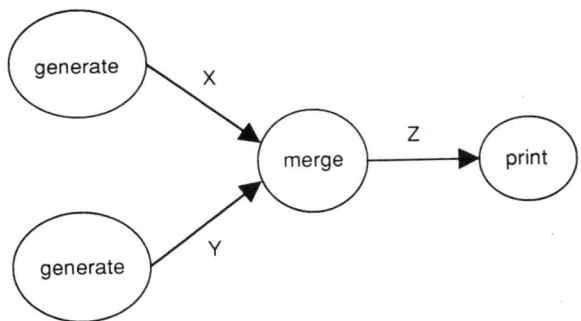

Figure 7. A simple data-flow network.

when X or Y is sufficiently instantiated. An unannotated definition of 'merge' is

merge([ ], [ ], [ ])
merge([$U|X$], Y, [$U|Z$]) if merge(X, Y, Z)
merge(X, [$U|Y$], [$U|Z$]) if merge(X, Y, Z)

When more than one clause applies to a given merge subgoal, a committed choice is made to one of them. This commitment is time dependent, the first stream that has input available transmits its input to the output stream. The merge definition is also nondeterministic in the sense that if both input streams have items to be merged then which item will be transferred first to the output stream depends on whether the second or the third clause is used. The process interpretation is well suited for concurrent programming applications. However, reliance on time dependency and committed choice nondeterminism can sometimes compromise the declarative logic of the resulting programs.

Modules and Metalevel Structures

Several proposals have been made for adding modules to logic programming, and many commercial PROLOG systems incorporate module facilities. O'Keefe (1985), for example, has proposed an algebra for combining modules, while Monteiro and Porto (1989) have developed a form of contextual logic programming that provides many of the features of modules.

Conceptually a module can be interpreted as a logic program that can be combined, by manipulation at the metalevel, with other modules in order to build a larger program. Such a metalevel scheme for combining programs has been developed by Brogi and co-workers (1990).

CONCLUSION

Logic programming attempts to unify different formalisms in different areas of computing. Logic programming is generally regarded as a development of artificial intelligence. However, it also has important links with formal methods of software engineering and with the field of databases. Another important relationship within the area

of computer science, which was not discussed here, is with formal language theory.

Logic programming is often identified with the language PROLOG. Indeed to a large extent the success of logic programming is due to the success of PROLOG. This must not distract attention, however, from other logic programming languages under development, from the development of parallel architectures, or from other longer-term developments. Logic programming is as much a research program for the future as it is a collection of results from the past.

BIBLIOGRAPHY

S. O. Aanderaa, "On the Decision Problem for Formulas in Which all Disjunctions are Binary," *Proceedings of the Second Scandinavian Logic Symposium*, Oslo, Norway, 1970, pp. 1–18.

H. Ait-Kaci and R. Nasr, "LOGIN: A Logic Programming Language with Built-in Inheritance," *J. Logic Program.* **3**, 185–215 (1986).

H. Andreka and I. Nemeti, *The Generalized Completeness of Horn Predicate Logic as a Programming Language*, Research Report **21**, Department of Artificial Intelligence, University of Edinburgh, Edinburgh, UK, 1976.

K. R. Apt and M. H. van Emden, "Contributions to the Theory of Logic Programming," *JACM* **29**, 841–862 (1982).

E. Boerger, *Reduktionstypen in Krom- und Hornformeln*, Doctoral dissertation, University of Münster, FRG, 1971.

K. A. Bowen and R. A. Kowalski, "Amalgamating Language and Metalanguage in Logic Programming," in K. L. Clark and S.-A. Tarnlund, eds., *Logic Programming, APIC Studies in Data Processing, Vol. 16*, Academic Press, Inc., New York, 1982, pp. 153–172.

A. Brogi, P. Mancarella, D. Pedreschi, and F. Turini, "Composition Operators for Logic Theories," *Proceedings of a Symposium on Computational Logic*, Springer-Verlag, New York, 1990.

M. Bruynooghe, ed., *Proceedings of the Meta90 Workshop on Metaprogramming for Logic Programming*, Katholieke Universiteit, Leuven, Belgium, 1990.

A. D. Burt, P. M. Hill, and J. W. Lloyd, *Preliminary Report on the Logic Programming Language Gödel*, Technical Report TR-90-02, Department of Computer Science, University of Bristol, UK, 1990.

D. Chan, "Constructive Negation Based on the Completed Database," in *Proceedings of the Fifth International Conference and Symposium on Logic Programming*, 1988, pp. 111–125.

K. L. Clark, "Negation as Failure," in H. Gallaire and J. Minker, eds., *Logic and Databases*, Plenum Press, New York, 1978, pp. 293–322.

K. L. Clark, *Predicate Logic as a Computational Formalism*, Ph.D. dissertation, Imperial College of Science and Technology, University of London, 1979.

K. L. Clark and J. Darlington, "Algorithm Classification Through Synthesis," *Comput. J.* **23**, 61–65 (1980).

K. L. Clark and S. Gregory, "A Relational Language for Parallel Programming," in *Proceedings of the ACM Conference on Functional Programming Languages and Computer Architecture*, Portsmouth, N.H., 1981, pp. 171–178.

K. L. Clark and S. Gregory, "PARLOG: Parallel Programming in Logic," *ACM Trans. Progr. Lang.* **8**, 1–49 (1986).

K. L. Clark and F. G. McCabe, "The Control Facilities of IC-

PROLOG," in D. Michie, ed., *Expert Systems in the Microelectronic Age*, Edinburgh University Press, Edinburgh, UK, 1979, pp. 122–149.

J. Cohen, "A View of the Origins and Development of PROLOG," *Comm. ACM* **31**, 26–36 (1988).

A. Colmerauer, "Equations and Inequations on Finite and Infinite Trees," *Proceedings of International Conference on Fifth Generation Computer Systems*, Tokyo, Japan, 1984, pp. 85–102.

A. Colmerauer, "Opening the PROLOG III Universe," *BYTE Mag.*, 177–182 (Aug. 1987).

A. Colmerauer and co-workers, *Un Systeme de Communication Homme-Machine en Francais*, Research Report, Groupe Intelligence Artificielle, Université d'Aix Marseille, Luminy, 1973.

J. Darlington, A. J. Field, and H. Pull, *The Unification of Functional and Logic Languages*, Research Report, Department of Computing, Imperial College, London, 1985.

E. W. Dijkstra, *A Discipline of Programming*, Prentice-Hall, Inc., Englewood Cliffs, N.J., 1976.

M. Dincbas and co-workers, "The Constraint Programming Language CHIP," in *Proceedings of the International Conference on Fifth Generation Computer Systems 88*, North Holland, Amsterdam, The Netherlands, 1988, pp. 693–702.

E. W. Elcock, "ABSYS: The First Logic Programming Language," *JACM* **9**, 1–18 (1990).

C. C. Green, "Theorem Proving by Resolution as a Basis for Question-Answering Systems," *Machine Intell.* **4**, 183–205 (1969).

P. Hammond, "Micro-PROLOG for Expert Systems," in K. L. Clark and F. G. McCabe, eds., *Micro-PROLOG: Programming in Logic*, Prentice-Hall, Englewood Cliffs, N.J., 1984, pp. 294–319.

S. Hanks and D. McDermott, "Default Reasoning, Non-Monotonic Logics and the Frame Problem," in *Proceedings of the Fifth National Conference on Artificial Intelligence*, Philadelphia, Pa., AAAI, Menlo Park, Calif., 1986, pp. 328–333.

S. Haridi and P. Brand, "Andorra Prolog—An Integration of Prolog and Committed Choice Languages," in Dincbas and co-workers, 1988, pp. 745–754.

P. J. Hayes, "Computation and Deduction," in *Proceedings of the Second Symposium on the Mathematical Foundations of Computer Science*, Czechoslovak Academy of Sciences, High Tatras, Czechoslovakia, 1973, pp. 105–118.

C. Hewitt, "PLANNER: A Language for Proving Theorems in Robots," in *Proceedings of the First IJCAI*, Washington, D.C., Morgan-Kaufmann, San Mateo, Calif., 1969, pp. 295–301.

R. Hill, *LUSH Resolution and Its Completeness*, DCL Memo No. **78**, Department of Artificial Intelligence, University of Edinburgh, Edinburgh, UK, 1974.

P. M. Hill and J. W. Lloyd, "Analysis of Metaprograms," in H. D. Abramson and M. H. Rogers, eds., *Metaprogramming in Logic Programming*, MIT Press, Cambridge, Mass., 1989, pp. 23–52.

C. J. Hogger, "Derivation of Logic Programs," *JACM* **28**, 372–392 (1981).

C. J. Hogger and J. M. Lever, *Program Equivalence for Locally-Stratified Logic Programs*, Computational Logic Group Research Report, Department of Computing, Imperial College, London, 1990.

J. Jaffar and J.-L. Lassez, "Constraint Logic Programming," in *Proceedings of the Fourteenth ACM Conference on Principles of Programming Languages*, 1987.

J. Jaffar, J.-L. Lassez, and J. W. Lloyd, "Completeness of the Negation as Failure Rule," in *Proceedings of the Eighth IJCAI*, Karlsruhe, FRG, Morgan-Kaufmann, San Mateo, Calif., 1983, pp. 500–506.

S. Kleene, *Introduction to Metamathematics*, Van Nostrand Reinhold Co., Inc., New York, 1952.

R. A. Kowalski, "The Early Years of Logic Programming," *Comm. ACM* **31**, 38–43 (1988).

R. A. Kowalski and D. Kuehner, "Linear Resolution with Selection Function," *Artif. Intell.* **2**, 227–260 (1971).

J. W. Lloyd, *Foundations of Logic Programming*, 2nd ed., Springer-Verlag, New York, 1987.

J. W. Lloyd and R. W. Topor, "Making Prolog More Expressive," *J. Logic Program.* **1**, 225–240 (1984).

D. W. Loveland, "Mechanical Theorem Proving by Model Elimination," *JACM* **15**, 236–251 (1968).

D. W. Loveland, "A Linear Format for Resolution," *Lecture Notes in Mathematics*, Vol. 125, Springer-Verlag, New York, 1970, pp. 147–162.

J. McCarthy, "Circumscription—A Form of Non-Monotonic Reasoning," *Artif. Intell.* **13**, 27–39 (1980).

D. Maier and D. S. Warren, *Computing with Logic*, Benjamin/Cummins Publishing Co., Menlo Park, Calif., 1988.

D. Miller and G. Nadathur, "Higher-Order Logic Programming," in *Proceedings of the Third International Conference on Logic Programming*, London, 1986, pp. 448–462.

L. Monteiro and A. Porto, "Contextual Logic Programming," in *Proceedings of the Sixth International Conference on Logic Programming*, Lisbon, Portugal, 1989, pp. 284–299.

R. O'Keefe, "Towards an Algebra for Constructing Logic Programs," in *Proceedings of the Second Symposium on Logic Programming*, Boston, Mass., 1985, pp. 152–160.

T. C. Przymusinski, "Non-Monotonic Formalisms and Logic Programming," in Monteiro and Porto, 1989, pp. 655–674.

R. Reiter, "Two Results on Ordering for Resolution with Merging and Linear Format," *JACM* **18**, 630–646 (1971).

J. A. Robinson, "A Machine-Oriented Logic Based on the Resolution Principle," *JACM* **12**, 23–42 (1965).

J. A. Robinson and E. E. Sibert, *Logic Programming in LISP*, Research Report, School of Computer and Information Science, Syracuse University, New York, 1980.

M. J. Sergot, "A Query-the-User Facility for Logic Programming," in P. Degano and E. Sandewall, eds., *Integrated Interactive Computer Systems*, North-Holland, Amsterdam, The Netherlands, 1983, pp. 27–41.

E. Y. Shapiro, *A Subset of Concurrent Prolog and Its Interpreter*, ICOT Technical Report TR-003, Institute for New Generation Computing Technology, Tokyo, Japan, 1983.

E. Y. Shapiro and A. Takeuchi, "Object Oriented Programming in Concurrent Prolog," *New Gen. Comput.* **1**, 25–48 (1983).

A. Takeuchi and K. Furukawa, "Partial Evaluation of Prolog Programs and Its Application to Metaprogramming," in *Proceedings of Information Processing 86*, Dublin, Ireland, 1986, pp. 415–420.

S.-A. Tarnlund, "Horn Clause Computability," *BIT* **17**, 215–226 (1977).

K. Ueda, *Guarded Horn Clauses*, ICOT Technical Report TR-103, Institute for New Generation Computing Technology, Tokyo, Japan, 1985.

K. Ueda and T. Chikayama, "Design of the Kernel Language for the Parallel Inference Machine," *Comput. J.*, in press.

M. H. van Emden and R. A. Kowalski, "The Semantics of Predicate Logic as a Programming Language," *JACM* **23**, 733–742 (1976).

R. Weyhrauch, "Prolegomena to a Theory of Mechanized Formal Reasoning," *Artif. Intell.* **13**, 133–170 (1980).

General References

Lloyd (1987) and Maier and Warren (1988) are good general references.

H. Abramson and M. H. Rogers, eds., *Meta-Programming for Logic Programming*, MIT Press, Cambridge, Mass., 1989.

J. A. Campbell, ed., *Implementations of PROLOG*, Ellis Horwood, Chichester, UK, 1984.

K. L. Clark, "Logic Programming Schemes," in *Proceedings of the International Conference on Fifth Generation Computer Systems 88*, North-Holland, Amsterdam, The Netherlands, 1988.

H. Gallaire and J. Minker, eds., *Logic and Databases*, Plenum Press, New York, 1978.

C. J. Hogger, *Introduction to Logic Programming*, Academic Press, Inc., New York, 1984.

C. J. Hogger, *Essentials of Logic Programming*, Oxford University Press, Oxford, UK, 1990.

IEEE Symposia on Logic Programming, IEEE Computer Society Press.

Journal of Logic Programming, published by Elsevier Science Publishing Co., New York.

R. A. Kowalski, "Predicate Logic as a Programming Language," in *Proceedings of IFIP-74*, North-Holland, Amsterdam, The Netherlands, 1974, pp. 569–574.

R. A. Kowalski, *Logic for Problem Solving*, Elsevier, Amsterdam, The Netherlands, 1979.

U. Nilsson and J. Maluszynski, *Logic, Programming and Prolog*, John Wiley & Sons, Inc., New York, 1990.

Proceedings of the International Conferences on Logic Programming, MIT Press, Cambridge, Mass.

Proceedings of the North Atlantic Conferences on Logic Programming, MIT Press, Cambridge, Mass.

L. Sterling and E. Y. Shapiro, *The Art of Prolog*, MIT Press, Cambridge, Mass., 1986.

C. J. HOGGER
R. A. KOWALSKI
University of London

LOGIC, PROPOSITIONAL

Propositional logic is the study of inferences that can be made from propositions. Roughly, propositions are the "meanings" or "thoughts" expressed by declarative sentences (Church, 1956; Gale, 1967). Secondarily, it is also the study of the representation of information by propositions. Other names for it are propositional calculus, sentential logic, and—when its subject matter is taken to be those things that can have truth values (ie, that are either true or false)—it is often called truth-functional logic. The bearers of truth values are sometimes considered to be propositions, (declarative) sentences, or truth functions. Typically, propositional logics are distinguished from first-order logics by their lack of internal analysis of propositions (eg, they do not distinguish between subject and predicate (see LOGIC, PREDICATE). Such logics also exist for other types of sentences (such as imperatives) and for more than two truth values. For details, see the logics of imperatives presented by Castañeda (1975) and Rescher (1966), the many-valued logics discussed by Rescher (1969), and the various *Proceedings of the International Symposium on Multiple-Valued Logic*.

The representational system of propositional logic is its underlying language. This consists of propositions and propositional (or, in the case of truth-functional propositional logic, truth-functional) connectives; a syntax that specifies the grammar of propositions; and a semantics that provides the "meanings" of propositions in terms of their truth conditions. The deductive system of propositional logic consists of rules that only permit inferences that lead from truths to truths (thereby preventing inferences that would lead from truths to falsehoods). Its (deductive) syntax consists of such rules and axioms, and its semantics characterizes these rules in terms of truth values. (This entry is concerned primarily with truth-functional propositional logic, except where indicated.)

LANGUAGE OF PROPOSITIONAL LOGIC

There are two kinds of propositions: atomic and molecular (also called simple and compound). Molecular propositions are formed from (one or more) atomic ones by means of truth-functional connectives (or truth-functional operators). For instance,

Andrea is a philosopher

is atomic;

Andrea is a philosopher and Mike is not French

is molecular, formed from the two atomic propositions

Andrea is a philosopher
Mike is French

by the connective *and* and the connective (or operator) *not*. But

Ruth believes that Marvin is a logician

is not molecular (rather, it is atomic), since the operator *Ruth believes that* is not truth-functional. [A branch of logic that does treat the latter proposition as molecular is modal logic, in particular, doxastic modal logic (see LOGIC, MODAL; BELIEF REPRESENTATION SYSTEMS).] In propositional logic, atomic propositions are considered to be unanalyzable; the branch of nonmodal logic that analyzes atomic propositions is called predicate logic (see LOGIC, PREDICATE).

In truth-functional propositional logic a molecular proposition must be such that its truth value is a function of the truth values of its atomic parts. The particular function is determined by the connectives. In addition to the one-place "connective" or operator, negation (usually expressed in English by *not* or *it is not the case that*), there are 16 two-place truth-functional connectives. Of these, the most common are given in Table 1. For a list of others, see Church (1956) and Schagrin, Rapaport, and Dipert (1985). There are, of course, other n-place connectives (for $n \neq 2$), for example, the three-place connective *if . . . then . . . else* (see Manna, 1974); but these are either trivial (when $n = 1$) or (for $n > 2$) expressible in terms of two-place connectives, as discussed below (Minimal Sets of

Table 1. Common Two-Place Truth-Functional Connectives

Conjunction	and
Inclusive disjunction	or
Material conditional	if . . . then . . .
Material biconditional	if and only if
Exclusive disjunction	xor; ie, either . . . or . . . but not both
Joint denial	nand
Disjoint (or alternative) denial	nor

Connectives). (For interesting generalizations of these connectives as operators on sets of propositions, see Shapiro (1979) for a discussion in an AI context and McCawley (1981) for a discussion in a linguistic context.)

Syntax

A formal syntax for a language of propositional logic can be presented by a recursive definition of well-formed proposition. One such definition, using the most common connectives, follows.

1. The letters $A, . . . , Z$ and these letters subscripted with positive-integer numerals (eg, A_1, B_{27}) are well-formed (atomic) propositions.
2. If **P** and **Q** are well-formed propositions, then so are

¬ **P**	(the negation of **P**)
(**P** ∧ **Q**)	(the conjunction of **P** with **Q**)
(**P** ∨ **Q**)	(the inclusive disjunction of **P** with **Q**)
(**P** → **Q**)	(the material conditional whose antecedent is **P** and whose consequent is **Q**)
(**P** ↔ **Q**)	(the material biconditional of **P** with **Q**)
(**P** + **Q**)	(the exclusive disjunction of **P** with **Q**)
(**P**|**Q**)	(the joint denial of **P** with **Q**)
(**P** ↓ **Q**)	(the disjoint denial of **P** with **Q**)

3. Nothing else is a well-formed proposition.

The boldface letters in the second clause of this recursive definition are metavariables ranging over propositions. The outer parentheses in clause 2 prevent ambiguity. For instance, **P** ∧ **Q** ∨ **R** is ill-formed; instead, one must write either ((**P** ∧ **Q**) ∨ **R**) or (**P** ∧ (**Q** ∨ **R**)), depending on which is wanted. On occasion, parentheses can be dropped for purposes of readability. Other systems can be defined by using different symbols or by using different conventions for disambiguation—such as precedence of connectives.

There are several ways to express the connectives in English, many of which have non-truth-functional connotations; however, propositional logic studies only the truth-functional properties of such phrases. Thus, propositional logic ignores the important distinctions between

Marie is a vice-president *and* Ben is a clerk

and

Marie is a vice-president *but* Ben is a clerk

(the latter suggesting, perhaps, that Ben is *merely* a clerk) as well as the important distinctions between

I got into bed and I fell asleep

and

I fell asleep and I got into bed

(the latter suggesting, perhaps, that I sleepwalk).

There are also several other families of symbols used for the connectives, most notably Polish (or prefix) notation. Polish notation has the advantage of not requiring parentheses for disambiguation. The first five connectives of clause 2 expressed in Polish notation are

N**P**

K**PQ**

A**PQ**

C**PQ**

E**PQ**

As an example, the ambiguous proposition in infix notation discussed earlier cannot be written in Polish notation. Instead, one is forced to write either AK**PQR** or $KP A$**QR**. (It is standard practice in Polish notation to use the letters $N, K, A, C,$ and E instead of the connective symbols ¬, ∧, ∨, →, and ↔, respectively. For a thorough discussion of these notational issues, consult a standard introductory textbook, such as Copi (1979), Schagrin, Rapaport, and Dipert (1985), and especially Schagrin (1979).

It is also important to recall that propositional logic does not provide an analysis of the internal structure of propositions; thus, it does not provide a way to represent or reason about individuals or classes; that is the province of first-order (or predicate) logic.

Semantics

The semantics of molecular propositions can be given by means of the equivalences in Table 2.

The semantics can also be given by means of truth tables. Typically, these have two sets of columns, one for the atomic propositions (the "input") and one for the molecular proposition (the "output"); and 2^n rows, where n is

Table 2. Semantics of Molecular Propositions

¬ **P** is true	if and only if	**P** is false.
(**P** ∧ **Q**) is true	if and only if	both of **P** and **Q** are true.
(**P** ∨ **Q**) is false	if and only if	both of **P** and **Q** are false.
(**P** → **Q**) is true	if and only if	**P** is false or **Q** is true (or both).
(**P** ↔ **Q**) is true	if and only if	**P** and **Q** have the same truth value.
(**P** + **Q**) is true	if and only if	**P** and **Q** have opposite truth values.
(**P**|**Q**) is false	if and only if	both of **P** and **Q** are true.
(**P** ↓ **Q**) is true	if and only if	both of **P** and **Q** are false.

Table 3. Sample Truth Tables

Input	Output	Input		Output	Input		Output	Input		Output
P	**¬ P**	**P**	**Q**	**(P ∧ Q)**	**P**	**Q**	**(P ∨ Q)**	**P**	**Q**	**(P → Q)**
T	F	T	T	T	T	T	T	T	T	T
F	T	T	F	F	T	F	T	T	F	F
		F	T	F	F	T	T	F	T	T
		F	F	F	F	F	F	F	F	T

Table 4. Truth Table with Intermediate Computations

Input		Computations			Output
P	**Q**	**(P ∨ Q)**	**(P ∧ Q)**	**¬ (P ∧ Q)**	**((P ∨ Q) ∧ ¬ (P ∧ Q))**
T	T	T	T	F	F
T	F	T	F	T	T
F	T	T	F	T	T
F	F	F	F	T	F

Table 5. Some Important Logical Equivalences

Double negation	**P**	is logically equivalent to	**¬ ¬ P**
Idempotency	**P**	is logically equivalent to	**(P ∧ P)**
	P	is logically equivalent to	**(P ∨ P)**
Commutative laws	**(P ∧ Q)**	is logically equivalent to	**(Q ∧ P)**
	(P ∨ Q)	is logically equivalent to	**(Q ∨ P)**
Associative laws	**(P ∧ (Q ∧ R))**	is logically equivalent to	**((P ∧ Q) ∧ R)**
	(P ∨ (Q ∨ R))	is logically equivalent to	**((P ∨ Q) ∨ R)**
Distributive laws	**(P ∧ (Q ∨ R))**	is logically equivalent to	**((P ∧ Q) ∨ (P ∧ R))**
	(P ∨ (Q ∧ R))	is logically equivalent to	**((P ∨ Q) ∧ (P ∨ R))**
De Morgan's laws	**¬ (P ∧ Q)**	is logically equivalent to	**(¬ P ∨ ¬ Q)**
	¬ (P ∨ Q)	is logically equivalent to	**(¬ P ∧ ¬ Q)**
Contraposition	**(P → Q)**	is logically equivalent to	**(¬ Q → ¬ P)**
Material conditional	**(P → Q)**	is logically equivalent to	**(¬ P ∨ Q)**
	(P → Q)	is logically equivalent to	**¬ (P ∧ ¬ Q)**
Exportation	**(P → (Q → R))**	is logically equivalent to	**((P ∧ Q) → R)**

the number of distinct atomic propositions, one for each possible combination of truth values of the atomic propositions. Samples are given in Table 3 (T and F stand for true and false, respectively).

Truth tables can also be used to compute the truth values of more complicated molecular propositions. Sometimes this is done using a third set of columns for intermediate computations of "subpropositions," as in Table 4. (Algorithms for computing with truth tables are given in Schagrin, Rapaport, and Dipert, 1985).

Two propositions are logically equivalent if they have the same truth values for all possible combinations of truth values of their atomic parts. Table 5 lists some of the important logical equivalences.

Minimal Sets of Connectives. The choice of which connectives to use depends on one's purposes. Generally, if the language of propositional logic is to be used in a representational system, especially one for natural language, then a large set of connectives is appropriate. This permits distinguishing between distinct but logically equivalent propositions. However, for deductive purposes, a smaller number of connectives is better, both because fewer infer-

ence rules are then needed and because metatheoretic proofs about propositional logic then become easier.

It can be shown that all n-place truth-functional connectives can be expressed using only negation and conjunction, or else negation and disjunction, or else negation and the material conditional. They can also all be expressed using only one connective, either joint denial or disjoint denial. (For further discussion and proofs, see, eg, Copi, 1979 and Mendelson, 1979.) Usually, a compromise is found between the extremes of using all of the connectives (for representational adequacy) and only one or two (for elegance or metatheoretic simplicity): It is common to use negation, disjunction, and conjunction to express a proposition in either conjunctive normal form (CNF) or disjunctive normal form (DNF). In the former a proposition is expressed as a (logically equivalent) conjunction of disjunctions of atomic propositions and negations; in the latter, as a (logically equivalent) disjunction of conjunctions of atomic propositions and negations. For example, the proposition

$$(((P → Q) ∨ Q) → (R ∧ Q))$$

is logically equivalent to the CNF proposition

$(\neg \mathbf{P} \vee \neg \mathbf{Q} \vee \mathbf{R}) \wedge (\mathbf{P} \vee \neg \mathbf{Q} \vee \mathbf{R})$
$$\wedge (\mathbf{P} \vee \mathbf{Q} \vee \neg \mathbf{R}) \wedge (\mathbf{P} \vee \mathbf{Q} \vee \mathbf{R})$$

as well as to the DNF proposition

$(\neg \mathbf{P} \wedge \mathbf{Q} \wedge \mathbf{R}) \vee (\mathbf{P} \wedge \neg \mathbf{Q} \wedge \neg \mathbf{R})$
$$\vee (\mathbf{P} \wedge \neg \mathbf{Q} \wedge \mathbf{R}) \vee (\mathbf{P} \wedge \mathbf{Q} \wedge \mathbf{R})$$

Algorithms for converting a proposition into a logically equivalent proposition in CNF or DNF may be found in Copi (1979) and Schagrin, Rapaport, and Dipert (1985).

Tautologies, Contradictions, and Contingent Propositions. Propositions that are true for all possible combinations of truth values of their atomic parts are called tautologies; those that are false for all possible combinations are called contradictions; and the others are said to be contingent. For example, $((\mathbf{P} \wedge (\mathbf{P} \to \mathbf{Q})) \to \mathbf{Q})$ is a tautology; $(\mathbf{P} \wedge \neg \mathbf{P})$ is a contradiction; and $(\mathbf{P} \to \mathbf{Q})$ is contingent. Because of the semantics of negation, the negation of a tautology is a contradiction, and vice versa. All tautologies are logically equivalent to each other, as are all contradictions. This fact is of some significance for representational issues since all tautologies clearly do not "say" the same thing. For example, $(\mathbf{P} \vee \neg \mathbf{P})$ and $((\mathbf{P} \wedge (\mathbf{P} \to \mathbf{Q})) \to \mathbf{Q})$ are both tautologies and hence logically equivalent; yet, in an important sense, they do not "mean" the same thing.

The Paradox of the Material Conditional. There are other limitations on the use of the language of propositional logic as a representational system for natural-language sentences. Most notably, the semantics of the material conditional do not correspond to the ordinary English use of if–then. For instance, $((\mathbf{P} \wedge \neg \mathbf{P}) \to \mathbf{Q})$ is a tautology simply because its antecedent is a contradiction and, hence, false. But a corresponding English sentence such as "If $1 + 1 = 2$ and $1 + 1 \neq 2$, then Bertrand Russell is the Pope" does not seem to be true even though it is a tautology. For this reason, such phenomena are called "paradoxes of the material conditional." Attempts to overcome these "paradoxes" have generally taken the form of introducing new, non-truth-functional operators and connectives whose semantics are closer to their natural-language counterparts. The two main kinds of logic that have been developed along these lines are modal logic and relevance logic. (For the former, see LOGIC, MODAL, and Hughes and Cresswell, 1968; for the latter, see Anderson and Belnap, 1975.)

DEDUCTIVE SYSTEMS OF PROPOSITIONAL LOGIC

Syntax

A deductive system for any logic can be presented in one of two ways: as an axiomatic system or by means of a natural deduction system.

Axiomatic Propositional Logic. An axiomatic system typically has several axioms (which ought to be tautolo-

gies) and a minimal number of rules of inference (which ought to lead from truths to truths). To present propositional logic axiomatically, the well-formed propositions (WFPs) are restricted here to those whose only connectives are $\neg$ and $\to$. All WFPs of the following three tautological forms, called axiom schemata, may be taken as axioms (others are possible; note, again, that boldface letters are metavariables ranging over propositions):

(A1) $(\mathbf{P} \to (\mathbf{Q} \to \mathbf{P}))$ (confirmation of the consequent)

(A2) $((\mathbf{P} \to (\mathbf{Q} \to \mathbf{R})) \to ((\mathbf{P} \to \mathbf{Q}) \to (\mathbf{P} \to \mathbf{R})))$
(self-distribution)

(A3) $((\neg \mathbf{P} \to \neg \mathbf{Q}) \to (\mathbf{Q} \to \mathbf{P}))$ (contraposition)

There is one rule of inference:

(MP)   From $\mathbf{P}$ and $(\mathbf{P} \to \mathbf{Q})$, infer $\mathbf{Q}$ (modus ponens)

A *proof* of a WFP $\mathbf{P}_n$ is a sequence $\mathbf{P}_1, \ldots, \mathbf{P}_n$ of WFPs such that for each $k (1 \leq k \leq n)$, either $\mathbf{P}_k$ is an axiom or there are $i, j < k$ such that $\mathbf{P}_i = (\mathbf{P}_j \to \mathbf{P}_k)$. (Note: $\mathbf{P}_i$ is not merely logically equivalent to $(\mathbf{P}_j \to \mathbf{P}_k)$; it *is* $(\mathbf{P}_j \to \mathbf{P}_k)$.) A *theorem* of our propositional logic is a WFP $\mathbf{P}$ such that there is a proof of $\mathbf{P}$ (viz, $\mathbf{P}_1, \ldots, \mathbf{P}_{n-1}, \mathbf{P}$). Finally, $\mathbf{P}$ is *provable* means: $\mathbf{P}$ is a theorem—the notation for this is: $\vdash \mathbf{P}$. (Sometimes, the turnstile, $\vdash$, is subscripted by the name of the system of logic of which $\mathbf{P}$ is a theorem.)

As an example, a proof of $(\mathbf{P} \to \mathbf{P})$ is given in Table 6. Comments, preceded by semicolons, are not formally part of the proof. Note, however, that they would be formally part of a proof that the proposition is a theorem of propositional logic, that is, of a proof that $\vdash (\mathbf{P} \to \mathbf{P})$.

The notion of "proof" can be extended to "proof from hypotheses," where the hypotheses are nonlogical principles (or *postulates*) typically belonging to some particular subject matter (eg, laws of physics or "world knowledge"). They would not usually be tautologies. Formally, a sequence of WFPs $\mathbf{P}_1, \ldots, \mathbf{P}_n$ is a *proof of $\mathbf{P}_n$ from a set of hypotheses* $\mathbf{H}$ iff for all k $(1 \leq k \leq n)$, either $\mathbf{P}_k$ is an axiom, or $\mathbf{P}_k \in \mathbf{H}$, or $\mathbf{P}_k$ is inferred by (MP) from previous WFPs in the sequence. The notation for this is: $\mathbf{H} \vdash \mathbf{P}_n$; if $\mathbf{H} = \{\mathbf{H}_1, \ldots, \mathbf{H}_m\}$, then the notation is $\mathbf{H}_1, \ldots, \mathbf{H}_m \vdash \mathbf{P}_n$ [for complete details of an axiomatic propositional logic, see Mendelson (1979) and Kleene (1950)].

A Natural Deduction System for Propositional Logic. A natural deduction system typically has no axioms but has several rules of inference, and it allows for the possibility of introducing *assumptions* in the middle of a proof. These can be viewed as "temporary axioms" that are "discharged" when no longer needed.

To present propositional logic in this fashion, the WFPs are restricted here to those whose only connectives are $\neg$ and $\wedge$. The following may be used as rules of inference:

($\wedge$ Introduction)   (a) From $\mathbf{P}$ and $\mathbf{Q}$, infer $(\mathbf{P} \wedge \mathbf{Q})$.
     (b) From $\mathbf{P}$ and $\mathbf{Q}$, infer $(\mathbf{Q} \wedge \mathbf{P})$.

($\wedge$ Elimination)   (a) From $(\mathbf{P} \wedge \mathbf{Q})$, infer $\mathbf{P}$.
     (b) From $(\mathbf{P} \wedge \mathbf{Q})$, infer $\mathbf{Q}$.

Table 6. A Proof from Axioms

1. $((P \rightarrow ((P \rightarrow P) \rightarrow P)) \rightarrow$ $((P \rightarrow (P \rightarrow P)) \rightarrow$ $(P \rightarrow P)))$	; this is an axiom, since it is a ; WFP with the form of axiom ; schema (A2), with **P** and **R** both ; replaced by **P**, and **Q** replaced ; by '$(P \rightarrow P)$'
2. $(P \rightarrow (P \rightarrow P))$	; (A1), with **Q** replaced by **P**
3. $(P \rightarrow ((P \rightarrow P) \rightarrow P))$	; (A1), with **Q** replaced by ; '$(P \rightarrow P)$'
4. $((P \rightarrow (P \rightarrow P)) \rightarrow (P \rightarrow P))$	; from 3, 1 by (MP)
5. $(P \rightarrow P)$	; from 2, 4 by (MP)

(¬ Introduction)   If both **Q** and ¬ **Q** can be inferred from an assumption **P**, then infer ¬ **P**.

(¬ Elimination)   If both **Q** and ¬ **Q** can be inferred from an assumption ¬ **P**, then infer **P**.

A notion of *subproofs* is needed for the last two rules, along with rules allowing propositions to be "sent" into the subproofs and "returned" from them under certain restrictions. Subproofs can be indicated by prefixing stars to the lines of a subproof, where the number of stars indicates the level of nesting of the subproof [for details, see Schagrin, Rapaport, and Dipert (1985)]. As an example, Table 7 contains a natural deduction proof of the argument

$$\neg (A \wedge B), A \vdash \neg B$$

Each line of the proof has a comment following the semicolon, and subproofs have "begin" and "end" comments; these are not formally part of the proof, but they play the same role that comments do in computer programs. For details and for rules of inference for other connectives, see Copi (1979); Kalish, Montague, and Mar (1980); Schagrin, Rapaport, and Dipert (1985). Natural deduction systems have been extensively investigated (see Szabo, 1969).

AI and Propositional Logic. Newell, Shaw, and Simon's Logic Theorist program (1963), considered by some to be the first AI program, used a breadth-first search procedure to prove theorems of propositional logic. It successfully proved 38 of the first 52 theorems of Whitehead and Russell's *Principia Mathematica* (1927). A successor program, the General Problem Solver (Ernst and Newell, 1969; Newell, Shaw, and Simon, 1960) used means-ends analysis to solve problems in a variety of domains, including propositional logic. Discussions of these programs may be found in Barr and Feigenbaum (1981) and Slagle (1971).

Another important propositional logic program is Wang's algorithm, which is a more efficient method for determining whether a given argument is valid than using truth tables. This algorithm attempts to interpret the premises of the argument as all true and the conclusion as false. If it succeeds in this attempt, the argument is shown to be invalid; if it fails, the argument is shown to be valid. For details, see Schagrin, Rapaport and Dipert, 1985.

A rule of inference that has proved to be of importance in AI and automated theorem proving, in part because most of the introduction and elimination rules can be shown to be instances of it, is

(Resolution)   From $(\neg P \vee Q)$ and $(P \vee R)$, infer $(Q \vee R)$

For a discussion of AI systems that use propositional logic inference techniques based on Resolution, see RESOLUTION; THEOREM PROVING; as well as such AI texts as Manna (1974), Nilsson (1971, 1980), Raphael (1976), Rich (1983), and Winston (1984).

Table 7. A Natural-Deduction Proof

1. ¬ (A ∧ B)	; this is the first premise
2. A	; this is the second premise
	; BEGIN subproof using ¬ Introduction to prove ¬ B
* 3. B	; an assumption for use by ¬ Introduction
* 4. A	; sent in from line 2 of main proof ; (similar to parameter passing in ; procedures)
* 5. (A ∧ B)	; ∧ Introduction using lines 3, 4
* 6. ¬ (A ∧ B)	; sent in from line 1 of the main proof
* 7. ¬ B	; ¬ Introduction, from lines 3, 5, 6
	; END of subproof that proved ¬ B by ¬ Introduction
8. ¬ B	; returned from line 7 of subproof ; (similar to a procedure returning a ; value)

Semantics

An *argument* is any inference from *hypotheses* (or *premises*) to a *conclusion*. Thus, rules of inference are essentially forms of argument. A rule of inference or an argument should never lead from truth to falsehood. To say that a rule of inference or an argument is *valid* means: if the hypotheses are true, then the conclusion must be true. Validity, thus, can be construed as a notion of truth *relative* to the premises. An argument is said to be *sound* (in one sense) iff it is valid and its hypotheses are, in fact, true.

Truth tables can be used for semantic inference—as opposed to the syntactic inference discussed in the previous section. Here, a truth table is constructed whose "input" columns contain the premises and whose "output" column contains the conclusion. The argument is valid iff there is no line of the truth table with T in all premise columns and F in the conclusion column.

Propositional logic is also said to be *sound* in the sense that all of its theorems are tautologies. It is also *complete*: all propositional tautologies are theorems of propositional logic. There is a link between a proposition's being a tautology and an argument's being valid: For any proof $\mathbf{P}_1$, . . . , $\mathbf{P}_{n-1} \vdash \mathbf{P}_n$, there corresponds the material-conditional proposition: $((\mathbf{P}_1 \wedge \cdots \wedge \mathbf{P}_{n-1}) \rightarrow \mathbf{P}_n)$. The former is valid iff the latter is a tautology [for details on these topics, see Mendelson (1979) and Kleene (1950)]. This follows (by soundness and completeness) from the Deduction Theorem, which states that the former is valid iff the latter is a theorem. Finally, propositional logic is also *decidable*: There is an algorithm such that for any WFP, the algorithm decides whether the WFP is a theorem (ie, one can use a truth table to determine whether the WFP is a tautology). However, the decidability of propositional logic is an NP-complete problem and hence computationally "intractable"; this fact has been employed in philosophical arguments to the effect that such logics are not well-suited to computational models of rationality (Cherniak, 1984).

BIBLIOGRAPHY

A. R. Anderson and N. D. Belnap, Jr., *Entailment: The Logic of Relevance and Necessity,* Princeton University Press, Princeton, New Jersey, 1975.

A. Barr and E. A. Feigenbaum, eds., *The Handbook of Artificial Intelligence,* Vol. 1, William Kaufmann, Los Altos, Calif., 1981.

H.-N. Castañeda, *Thinking and Doing,* D. Reidel, Dordrecht, 1975.

C. Cherniak, "Computational Complexity and the Universal Acceptance of Logic," *J. Philos.* **81,** 739–758 (1984).

A. Church, *Introduction to Mathematical Logic,* Princeton University Press, Princeton, New Jersey, 1956, pp. 23–31.

I. M. Copi, *Symbolic Logic,* 5th ed., Macmillan, New York, 1979.

G. W. Ernst and A. Newell, *GPS: A Case Study in Generality and Problem Solving,* Academic Press, New York, 1969.

R. M. Gale, "Propositions, Judgments, Sentences, and Statements," in P. Edwards, ed., *Encyclopedia of Philosophy,* Vol. 6, Macmillan and Free Press, New York, 1967, pp. 494–505.

G. E. Hughes and M. J. Cresswell, *An Introduction to Modal Logic,* Methuen, London, 1968.

D. Kalish, R. Montague, and G. Mar, *Logic: Techniques of Formal Reasoning,* 2nd ed., Harcourt Brace Jovanovich, New York, 1980.

S. C. Kleene, *Introduction to Metamathematics,* Van Nostrand, Princeton, N.J., 1950.

Z. Manna, *Mathematical Theory of Computation,* McGraw-Hill, New York, Chapt. 2, 1974.

J. D. McCawley, *Everything that Linguists Have Always Wanted to Know about Logic but Were Ashamed to Ask,* University of Chicago Press, Chicago, 1981.

E. Mendelson, *Introduction to Mathematical Logic,* 2nd ed., Van Nostrand, New York, 1979.

A. Newell, J. C. Shaw, and H. Simon, "A Variety of Intelligent Learning in a General Problem-Solver," in M. C. Yovits and S. Cameron, eds., *Self-Organizing Systems,* Pergamon, New York, 1960, pp. 153–189.

A. Newell, J. C. Shaw, and H. Simon, "Empirical Explorations of the Logic Theory Machine," in E. Feigenbaum and J. Feldman, eds., *Computers and Thought,* McGraw-Hill, New York, 1963, pp. 109–133.

N. J. Nilsson, *Problem-Solving Methods in Artificial Intelligence,* McGraw-Hill, New York, 1971.

N. J. Nilsson, *Principles of Artificial Intelligence,* Tioga, Palo Alto, Calif., 1980.

B. Raphael, *The Thinking Computer: Mind Inside Matter,* W. H. Freeman, San Francisco, 1976.

N. Rescher, *The Logic of Commands,* Routledge and Kegan Paul, London and Dover, New York, 1966.

N. Rescher, *Many-Valued Logic,* McGraw-Hill, New York, 1969.

E. Rich, *Artificial Intelligence,* McGraw-Hill, New York, 1983.

M. L. Schagrin, *The Language of Logic: A Self-Instruction Text,* 2nd ed., Random House, New York, 1979.

M. L. Schagrin, W. J. Rapaport, and R. R. Dipert, *Logic: A Computer Approach,* McGraw-Hill, New York, 1985.

S. C. Shapiro, "The SNePS Semantic Network Processing System," in N. V. Findler, ed., *Associative Networks,* Academic Press, New York, 1979, pp. 179–203.

J. R. Slagle, *Artificial Intelligence: The Heuristic Programming Approach,* McGraw-Hill, New York, 1971.

M. E. Szabo, ed., *Collected Papers of Gerhard Gentzen,* North-Holland, Amsterdam, 1969.

A. N. Whitehead and B. Russell, *Principia Mathematica,* 2nd ed., Cambridge University Press, Cambridge, UK, 1927.

P. H. Winston, *Artificial Intelligence,* 2nd ed., Addison-Wesley, Reading, Mass., 1984.

General References

A. E. Blumberg, "Logic, Modern," in P. Edwards, ed., *Encyclopedia of Philosophy,* Vol. 5, Macmillian and Free Press, New York, 1967, pp. 12–34.

R. C. Jeffrey, *Formal Logic: Its Scope and Limits,* 2nd ed., McGraw-Hill, New York, 1981.

W. Kneale and M. Kneale, *The Development of Logic,* Oxford University Press, Oxford, 1962.

W. V. O. Quine, *Mathematical Logic,* rev. ed., Harper & Row, New York, 1951.

W. V. O. Quine, *Elementary Logic,* rev. ed., Harvard University Press, Cambridge, Mass., 1980.

W. V. O. Quine, *Methods of Logic,* 4th ed., Harvard University Press, Cambridge, Mass., 1982.

W. J. RAPAPORT
SUNY at Buffalo

LOGO

LOGO is a programming language in the spirit of LISP invented in the MIT AI Lab to teach mathematical concepts to little children [see S. Papert, "Teaching Children to be Mathematicians versus Teaching about Mathematics," *Int. J. Math. Educ. Sci. Technol.* **3,** 249–262 (1972)]. A program in LOGO manipulates a little device called the "turtle." This turtle moves on a large flat surface. With two commands, PENUP and PENDOWN, it is possible to create a trace of the turtle movements. The goal of a program is usually to draw a certain figure; therefore, programming in LOGO is referred to as "turtle geometry." Typically, commands would be FORWARD 100, RIGHT 60, and BACK 100. It is possible to define procedures. In later research, LOGO has been used to help people learn about powerful ideas and to study the acquisition of computational skills by young children (see C. J. Solomon and S. Papert, "A Case Study of a Young Child Doing Turtle Graphics in LOGO," *Proceedings of the National Computer Conference,* AFIPS, pp. 1049–1056, 1976). More information can be found in the MIT AI Lab LOGO Memos.

J. GELLER
New Jersey Institute of
Technology

LOOPS

LOOPS was one of the first multi-paradigm programming environments. Developed at Xerox PARC in Interlisp, it added an object-oriented programming system similar to Smalltalk to the procedure-oriented programming of LISP. It also incorporated access-oriented programming allowing changes in objects to trigger computation (useful for monitoring), rule-oriented programming often used for simple expert systems, and a visual programming interface that supported graphic exploration and modification of program and data structures. The integration of paradigms was designed to support the rapid development of knowledge-based systems. [See M. Stefik, D. G. Bobrow, S. Mittal, and L. Conway, "Knowledge Programming in LOOPS: Report on an Experimental Course," *AI Magazine* 4(3), 3–13 (1983).] Recent versions of Common LISP integrate CLOS (qv), a new standard object-oriented programming substrate that carries over many of the ideas from LOOPS.

DANIEL G. BOBROW
Xerox PARC

LOPS

An approach to program synthesis, based on transformation of logical formulas and guided by powerful fundamental strategies [see W. Bibel, "Syntax-Directed, Semantics-Supported Program Synthesis," *Artif. Intell.* **14,** 243–261 (1980)]. A LISP implementation of this approach is presented in W. Bibel and K. M. Hörnig, "LOPS—A System Based on a Strategical Approach to Program Synthesis," in A. Biermann, G. Guiho, and Y. Kodratoff, eds., *Automatic Program Construction Techniques,* MacMillan, New York, 1984. A more elaborate and logic programming oriented implementation is described in G. Neugebauer, B. Fronhöfer, and C. Kreitz, "XPRTS—An Implementation Tool for Program Synthesis," in D. Metzing, ed., *Proceedings of the Thirteenth German Workshop on Artificial Intelligence,* Geseke, Germany, Sept. 1989, Informatik-Fachberichte 216, Springer, Berlin, 1989, pp. 348–357.

BERTRAM FRONHÖFER
Technical University Munich

LUNAR

LUNAR is a natural language question-answering system developed by W. Woods and his colleagues at BBN in the early 1970s for the NASA Manned Spacecraft Center. The system answered questions about the chemical composition of the Apollo 11 moon rocks. LUNAR was one of the first successful natural language understanding systems and pioneered the concept of natural language front ends to databases. Its linguistic fluency was substantial: it handled relative clauses, passive sentences, verb complement constructions, complex quantification, and pronominal references. It could specify and perform averaging calculations and included capabilities for both document retrieval and fact retrieval. LUNAR was demonstrated to the public at the Second Annual Lunar Sciences Conference in Houston, Texas in 1971. [See W. A. Woods, R. M. Kaplan, and B. Nash-Webber, *The LUNAR Sciences Natural Language Information System: Final Report,* BBN Report No. 2378, Bolt, Beranek and Newman, Cambridge, Mass., 1972 (available from NTIS as N72-28984); see also W. A. Woods, "Progress in Natural Language Understanding: An Application to Lunar Geology," *AFIPS Conference Proceedings,* Vol. 42, National Computer Conference and Exposition, 1973; and W. A. Woods, *Semantics for a Question-Answering System,* Garland Publishing Co., New York, 1979.]

W. A. WOODS
Harvard University

INDEX

neural networks
  optic flow, 1027
  optimization, 1023
  schema theory, 1432
Matching techniques
  frame theory and, 498–499
  image understanding and, 644–645
  knowledge representation and, 751
Material conditional paradox, 854–855
  propositional logic, 894
Material implication, conditional logic, 854–855
Mathematics
  binary resolution, 1351
  game playing and, 543
  induction, 668–672
    algorithm termination and recursion analysis, 670–671
    automated induction, 669–671
    axiom computation, 669–670
    basic prover, 670
    completion, 671–672
    implementation, 671
    theoretical foundations, 668–669
  knowledge representation, 909
  machine learning and, 797–799
  perceptrons, 1130
  programming, fuzzy programming, 521–527
Matrix reduction, connection calculus, 267
Matrix sensors, 1368
Matsuoka, K., 1404–1405
Maximum entropy principle (MEP)
  Hopfield networks optimization, 1021
  epsilon-semantics, 474
  probabilistic reasoning, 1312
Maximum likelihood estimates
  texture analysis, 1593–1594
  visual recovery, shape from contour, 1676
McCarthy, John, 21, 832–834, 851–852
  circumscription, 166
McClelland, J., 765
McCulloch, W. S., 1430
McCulloch-Pitts neuron
  Hopfield networks optimization, 1020–1021
  neural network modeling, 1017–1018
  winner-take-all networks, 1025
McDermott, D. V., 1335–1336
MDX system
  AI in medicine (AIM) and, 918
Meaning
  deep structure, 329–330
  eidetic phenomenology, 607–608
  Gadamer's hermeneutics and, 599–600
  lexical semantics, 812–813
  memory and, 457
  representation, in case grammar, 565–566
Means-ends analysis, 909–915
  ABSTRIPS program, 913
  FDS program, 912
  good difference information, 914–915
  GPS (general problem solver), 909–912
  MPS technique, 913–914
  problem solving reduction schema, 1224
  STRIPS program, 912–913
Mechanical design
  constraint satisfaction, 290
  legged robots, 1407
Mechanized assistant
  automatic programming, 77–81
    automatically generating search programs, 79–81
    programmer's assistant, 78–79
Mediating representations, knowledge acquisition, 719–720
MEDIATOR system, 915–916
  case-based reasoning, 1270, 1273
  dynamic memory, 392
  memory organization packets (MOPs), 927
MEDIC system, 916
  case-based reasoning, 1274
Medicine, AI in, 961–924
  biomedical taxonomy and, 917–918
  case grammar, 563
  causal reasoning and, 1280–1281
  decision theory, 318–319
  evaluation functions, 919
  example systems, 922–924
    human issues, 924
    ONCOCIN, 924
    Pathfinder and Intellipath, 923–924
    Quick Medical Reference, 922–923
  inference and control methods, 918
  knowledge structure, 918
  medical knowledge base, 917
  object-oriented languages, 773–775
  overview, 916–917
  pattern recognition, 1126
  protocol analysis, 917
  research themes, 919–922
    causal reasoning, 920–921
    decision-theoretic expert systems, 919–920

diagnostic strategies, 921
explanation and critiquing, 921–922
knowledge acquisition, 919
temporal reasoning and planning, 921
validation, 922
systems
  CADUCEUS, 131
  CASEY system, 131
  certainty-factor (CF) models, 131–132
  subject headings, (MeSH), 918
  thesaurus development, 1607
  uncertainty management, 918–919
Medium-term memory (MTM), adaptive resonance theory and, 14–16
Meldman, J. A., 779
Memo functions, concept learning, 250
Memory
  associative, 57–58
  case-based reasoning
    organization, 1270
    theory, 1266
    updating and, 1268–1269
  cognitive modeling, 179
  cognitive psychology and, 184
  dynamic, 391–392
  episodic, 454–459
  events as experienced, 456–457
  frame theory and, 497–499
  machine-learning and, 798
  management of, in computer systems, 243, 245–246
  mental imagery representation, 928–931
  neural networks, 1051–1052
  primary, 455–456
  recollection, 458–459
  rule-based systems, 1419–1420
  schema theory, 1433–1434
  secondary, 456–459
  semantic, 454–455
  text summarization, 1583–1584
  see also Long-term and Short-term memory
Memory-based reasoning (MBR), 1300–1301
  data parallelism and, 316–317
  parallel machine architecture, 1097
Memory organization packets (MOPs), 926–927
  case-based reasoning, 1266
  computational linguistics, 216
  conceptual dependency and, 264
  Cyrus system, 312
  dynamic memory, 392
  E-MOPs (episodic MOPs), 1458
  integrated in-depth parsing and, 1452–1453
  law in AI and, 782–783
  S-MOPs (simple MOPs), 1457–1458
  scripts, 1449
    acquisition, 1457–1458
  semantic networks, 1508
  span, primary memory capacity and, 456
  tables, computer chess and, 237–238
MENO-II system, 622
Mental abilities, intelligence and, 707–708
Mental imagery representation, 928–931
  behavioral evidence, 930–931
  computational systems, 931
  epiphenomenality, 929
  historical background, 928
  methodology, 920
  propositional representation, 928–929
  representational debate, 929–931
Mental lexicon, dictionary/lexicon construction, 353–354
Mental models, 932–938
  algorithms for model-based deduction, 935–938
    predicate calculus, 937–938
    propositional reasoning, 935–937
  cognitive science and, 190
  comprehension and discourse models, 933–934
  deduction and, 934–935
  knowledge acquisition, 934
  machine translation, 900–901
  neural networks, 1040
  perception, 932–933
  qualitative physics, 1150
Menu-based user interface, 619
Merchant, M. E., 907–908
Merging algorithms, segmentation and, 1486–1487
Merleau-Ponty, 1132, 1134
MERLIN system, 939
Message passing
  actor formalisms, 4
  control structures, 294
  object-oriented languages, 775
Message refinement, natural language generation, 988–990
Meta-argument units, 46–48
Meta-DENDRAL program
  chemistry in AI and, 158
  concept learning, 255

Metafunctionality, systemic grammar and, 585–586
Meta-interpretation, 939–940
Meta-knowledge, 940–946
  connecting theories, 944–945
  design and, 335
  human cognition, 941–942
  knowledge and, 944
  motivations, 942–943
  rule-based systems, 1421–1422
  systems with, 945–946
Metalevel programming
  Horn-clause logic, 880
  logic programming, 889
Metalinguistic utterances, natural language understanding, 1011
Meta-MOPs, dynamic memory, 392
Metaphorical interpretation, machine translation, 901
Meta-reasoning, 940–946
  knowledge and, 944
  reasoning and, 942–944
  rule-based systems, 1421–1422
Meta-rules, 940–946
  explanation and, 490
  knowledge and, 944
  planning and, 1165–1166
  rule-based systems, 1421–1422
  TEIRESIAS system, 945–946
Metascience, hermeneutics and, 603–605
Meta-theorems
  epsilon-semantics, 470
  predicate logic, 872
Methodological hermeneutics, 604
Methodological solipsism, phenomenology and, 1132–1133
Metropolis method, simulated annealing, 1538–1540
Microfeature, distributed connectionism, 271–272
Micromanipulator, robotics research and, 1379
MICRO-PLANNER, 947
  computational linguistics, 208
  constraint satisfaction, 287
Microrelations, distributed connectionism, 271–272
MIDI program, AI in music and, 977–978
Military applications of AI, 947–958
  autonomous land vehicle (ALV), 949
  background, 947–949
  combat resource allocation, 952–953
  equipment maintenance and troubleshooting, 954–956
    automatic test equipment, 954–955
    built-in testing (BIT), 955
    interactive aids, 955–956
  HASP system, 119
  mission planning, 953–954
  natural language understanding, 956–958
  naval battle management, 949–950
  pilot's associate, 949
  sensor information integration, 959–952
  training programs, 956
MIMD parallel model, data parallelism and, 316
Minimal game tree, computer chess and, 227–228
Minimal model semantics, logic programming, 876–877
Minimal window search, computer chess and, 229
Minimality conditions, situation semantics, 1543
Minimax procedure, 959–962
  computer chess and, 226–227
  game playing and, 544–545, 959
    kernal calculations, 546
  zero-sum two-person games, 960–962
  game trees, 550
  heuristics and, 613–614
  strategies and payoffs, 959–960
Minimum search, 1465–1466
Minimum spanning trees, heuristics and, 612–613
Minsky, Marvin
  frame theory, 493–494
  knowledge representation and, 748–749
  logic, 852
  neural networks, 1037–1038
  nonmonotonic reasoning, 1302–1305
  pattern recognition, 1124–1125
  perceptrons, 1130
  programming paradigms and, 1236–1237
  schema theory, 1430, 1432–1433
MIP Expert System, engineering and KBES, 451–452
Misrecognition, frame theory and, 496
Mission planning, AI military applications, 953–954
MIT CONS machine, control structures, 298–299
Mix system, knowledge system building, 487–488
Mixed-initiative dialogue, education and AI, 435–436
ML system, POPLOG systems and, 1182
Mobile robots, 1409–1415
  architectures for, 1414–1415